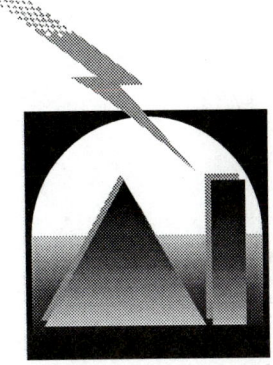

AAAI–98 / IAAI–98

Proceedings

Fifteenth National Conference on
Artificial Intelligence (AAAI-98)

Tenth Conference on Innovative Applications
of Artificial Intelligence (IAAI-98)

AAAI PRESS / THE MIT PRESS
Menlo Park, California • Cambridge, Massachusetts • London, England

Copyright © 1998, American Association for Artificial Intelligence
445 Burgess Drive
Menlo Park, CA 94025
All rights reserved.

No part of this book may be reproduced in any form by any electronic or mechanical means (including photocopying, recording, or information storage and retrieval) without permission in writing from the publisher.

Distributed by The MIT Press,
Massachusetts Institute of Technology,
Cambridge, Massachusetts and London, England.

ISBN 0-262-51098-7

Printed on Acid-Free Paper in the United States of America

Contents

Preface / xix

AAAI-98/IAAI-98 Program Committee / xxi

Sponsoring Organizations and Outstanding Papers / xxiv

AAAI-98 Technical Papers

AAAI-98 Outstanding Papers

Learning Evaluation Functions for Global Optimization and Boolean Satisfiability / 3
Justin A. Boyan and Andrew W. Moore, Carnegie Mellon University

The Interactive Museum Tour-Guide Robot / 11
Wolfram Burgard, Armin B. Cremers, Dieter Fox and Dirk Hähnel, University of Bonn; Gerhard Lakemeyer, Aachen University of Technology; Dirk Schulz and Walter Steiner, University of Bonn; Sebastian Thrun, Carnegie Mellon University

Acceleration Methods for Numeric CSPs / 19
Yahia Lebbah and Olivier Lhomme, Ecole des Mines de Nantes - La Chantrerie

Agents

Agent Interaction

Minimal Social Laws / 26
David Fitoussi and Moshe Tennenholtz, Technion-Israel Institute of Technology

Optimal Auctions Revisited / 32
Dov Monderer and Moshe Tennenholtz, Technion-Israel Institute of Technology

Formal Models of Agents' Commitments

Leveled Commitment Contracts with Myopic and Strategic Agents / 38
Martin R. Andersson and Tuomas W. Sandholm, Washington University

Anytime Coalition Structure Generation with Worst Case Guarantees / 46
Tuomas Sandholm, Kate Larson and Martin Andersson, Washington University; Onn Shehory, Carnegie Mellon University; Fernando Tohmé, Washington University

Motivation and Emotion

A Motivational System for Regulating Human-Robot Interaction / 54
Cynthia Breazeal (Ferrell), Massachusetts Institute of Technology

Emotion Model for Life-Like Agent and Its Evaluation / 62
Hirohide Ushida, Yuji Hirayama and Hiroshi Nakajima, OMRON Corporation

When Robots Weep: Emotional Memories and Decision-Making / 70
Juan D. Velásquez, MIT Artificial Intelligence Laboratory

Parallel AI / Agents and Representation

Natural Language Multiprocessing: A Case Study / 76
Enrico Pontelli, Gopal Gupta, Janyce Wiebe and David Farwell, New Mexico State University

Metacognition in Software Agents Using Classifier Systems / 83
Zhaohua Zhang, Stan Franklin and Dipankar Dasgupta, The University of Memphis

Social Agents

Agents that Work in Harmony by Knowing and Fulfilling their Obligations / 89
Mihai Barbuceanu, University of Toronto

What Is Wrong With Us? Improving Robustness through Social Diagnosis / 97
Gal A. Kaminka and Milind Tambe, University of Southern California

AI and Education

Procedural Help in Andes: Generating Hints Using a Bayesian Network Student Model / 106
Abigail S. Gertner, Cristina Conati and Kurt VanLehn, University of Pittsburgh

Generating Coordinated Natural Language and 3D Animations for Complex Spatial Explanations / 112
Stuart G. Towns, Charles B. Callaway and James C. Lester, North Carolina State University

Automated Reasoning

Belief Revision and Inconsistency

Reasoning under Inconsistency Based on Implicitly-Specified Partial Qualitative Probability Relations:
A Unified Framework / 121
S. Benferhat, D. Dubois, J. Lang and H. Prade, IRIT, Université Paul Sabatier; A. Saffiotti and P. Smets, IRIDIA, Université Libre de Bruxelles

Belief Revision with Unreliable Observations / 127
Craig Boutilier, University of British Columbia; Nir Friedman, University of California, Berkeley; Joseph Y. Halpern, Cornell University

Design and Diagnosis

Toward Design as Collaboration / 135
Susan L. Epstein, Hunter College and The Graduate School of The City University of New York

An Architecture for Exploring Large Design Spaces / 143
John R. Josephson, B. Chandrasekaran, Mark Carroll and Naresh Iyer, The Ohio State University; Bryon Wasacz, The Ohio State University and Motorola SPS; Giorgio Rizzoni and Qingyuam Li, The Ohio State University; David A. Erb, The Ohio State University and ERB Professional Services

Constructing the Correct Diagnosis When Symptoms Disappear / 151
Nancy E. Reed, Linköpings Universitet

Graphical Probabilistic Models

Structured Representation of Complex Stochastic Systems / 157
Nir Friedman, University of California, Berkeley; Daphne Koller and Avi Pfeffer, Stanford University

Solving Very Large Weakly Coupled Markov Decision Processes / 165
Nicolas Meuleau, Milos Hauskrecht, Kee-Eung Kim, Leonid Peshkin, Leslie Pack Kaelbling and Thomas Dean, Brown University; Craig Boutilier, University of British Columbia

Speech Recognition with Dynamic Bayesian Networks / 173
Geoffrey Zweig and Stuart Russell, University of California, Berkeley

Model Construction and Analysis

Multimodal Reasoning for Automatic Model Construction / 181
Reinhard Stolle and Elizabeth Bradley, University of Colorado at Boulder

Discovering Admissible Simultaneous Equations of Large Scale Systems / 189
Takashi Washio and Hiroshi Motoda, Osaka University

Decompositional, Model-Based Learning and its Analogy to Diagnosis / 197
Brian C. Williams, NASA Ames Research Center and William Millar, NASA Ames Research Center/Caelum Research Corporation

Modeling the Web

What Can Knowledge Representation Do for Semi-Structured Data? / 205
Diego Calvanese, Giuseppe De Giacomo and Maurizio Lenzerini, Università di Roma "La Sapienza"

Modeling Web Sources for Information Integration / 211
Craig A. Knoblock, Steven Minton, Jose Luis Ambite, Naveen Ashish, Pragnesh Jay Modi, Ion Muslea, Andrew G. Philpot, and Sheila Tejada, University of Southern California

Qualitative Modeling

An Ontology for Transitions in Physical Dynamic Systems / 219
Pieter J. Mosterman, DLR Oberpfaffenhofen; Feng Zhao, The Ohio State University; Gautam Biswas, Vanderbilt University

A New Architecture for Automated Modelling / 225
Neil Smith, De Montfort University

Qualitative Reasoning Techniques

Qualitative Analysis of Distributed Physical Systems with Applications to Control Synthesis / 232
Christopher Bailey-Kellogg and Feng Zhao, Xerox Palo Alto Research Center

Qualitative Simulation as a Temporally-Extended Constraint Satisfaction Problem / 240
Daniel J. Clancy, Caellum/NASA Ames Research Center and Benjamin J. Kuipers, University of Texas at Austin

Temporal Reasoning

Backtracking Algorithms for Disjunctions of Temporal Constraints / 248
Kostas Stergiou and Manolis Koubarakis, UMIST

Fast Transformation of Temporal Plans for Efficient Execution / 254
Ioannis Tsamardinos, University of Pittsburgh; Nicola Muscettola and Paul Morris, NASA Ames Research Center

Theorem Proving

An Algorithm to Evaluate Quantified Boolean Formulae / 262
Marco Cadoli, Andrea Giovanardi and Marco Schaerf, Università di Roma "La Sapienza"

Two Forms of Dependence in Propositional Logic: Controllability and Definability / 268
Jérôme Lang, IRIT-UPS and Pierre Marquis, CRIL/Université d'Artois

Anytime Approximate Modal Reasoning / 274
Fabio Massacci, Università di Roma "La Sapienza"

Tractable Inference

Algorithms for Propositional KB Approximation / 280
Yacine Boufkhad, CRIL Université d'Artois

A Non-Deterministic Semantics for Tractable Inference / 286
James M. Crawford, i2 Technologies and David W. Etherington, University of Oregon

Computing Intersections of Horn Theories for Reasoning with Models / 292
Thomas Eiter, Universität Gießen; Toshihide Ibaraki, Kyoto University; Kazuhisa Makino, Osaka University

Constraint Satisfaction and Search

Analysis of Search

The Branching Factor of Regular Search Spaces / 299
Stefan Edelkamp, Universität Freiburg and Richard E. Korf, University of California, Los Angeles

Complexity Analysis of Admissible Heuristic Search / 305
Richard E. Korf, University of California, Los Angeles and Michael Reid, Brown University

Constraint Satisfaction Problems

On the Conversion between Non-Binary and Binary Constraint Satisfaction Problems / 311
Fahiem Bacchus, University of Waterloo and Peter van Beek, University of Alberta

Generalizing Partial Order and Dynamic Backtracking / 319
Christian Bliek, Swiss Federal Institute of Technology

On the Computation of Local Interchangeability in Discrete Constraint Satisfaction Problems / 326
Berthe Y. Choueiry, Stanford University and Guevara Noubir, Centre Suisse d'Electronique et de Microtechnique

Supermodels and Robustness / 334
Matthew L. Ginsberg, Andrew J. Parkes and Amitabha Roy, University of Oregon

"Squeaky Wheel" Optimization / 340
David E. Joslin, i2 Technologies and David P. Clements, University of Oregon

Reversible DAC and Other Improvements for Solving Max-CSP / 347
Javier Larrosa, Univ. Pol. de Catalunya; Pedro Meseguer, IIIA-CSIC; Thomas Schiex, INRA; Gérard Verfaillie, ONERA-CERT

Branch and Bound Algorithm Selection by Performance Prediction / 353
Lionel Lobjois and Michel Lemaître, ONERA-CERT

A Fast Algorithm for the Bound Consistency of Alldiff Constraints / 359
Jean-Francois Puget, ILOG

Using Arc Weights to Improve Iterative Repair / 367
John Thornton, Griffith University Gold Coast and Abdul Sattar, Griffith University

An Integer Local Search Method with Application to Capacitated Production Planning / 373
Joachim P. Walser, Universität des Saarlandes; Ramesh Iyer and Narayan Venkatasubramanyan, i2 Technologies

Extending GENET to Solve Fuzzy Constraint Satisfaction Problems / 380
Jason H. Y. Wong and Ho-fung Leung, The Chinese University of Hong Kong

Constraint Satisfaction Problems—Local Search

Local Search for Statistical Counting / 386
Olivier Bailleux, CRIL Université d'Artois

A Tractable Walsh Analysis of SAT and its Implications for Genetic Algorithms / 392
Soraya Rana, Robert B. Heckendorn and Darrell Whitley, Colorado State University

Constraint Satisfaction Problems—Understanding Intractability

Hard Problems for CSP Algorithms / 398
David G. Mitchell, University of Toronto

The Constrainedness Knife-Edge / 406
Toby Walsh, University of Strathclyde

Heuristic Search

Heuristic Search in Cyclic AND / OR Graphs / 412
Eric A. Hansen and Shlomo Zilberstein, University of Massachusetts

Single-Agent Search in the Presence of Deadlocks / 419
Andreas Junghanns and Jonathan Schaeffer, University of Alberta

Complete Anytime Beam Search / 425
Weixiong Zhang, University of Southern California

Random Approaches to Search

Boosting Combinatorial Search through Randomization / 431
Carla P. Gomes and Bart Selman, Cornell University; Henry Kautz, AT&T Labs

Which Search Problems Are Random? / 438
Tad Hogg, Xerox Palo Alto Research Center

Search and Limited Resources

A* with Bounded Costs / 444
Brian Logan and Natasha Alechina, University of Birmingham

Stochastic Node Caching for Memory-Bounded Search / 450
Teruhisa Miura and Toru Ishida, Kyoto University

Search Control in Theorem Proving

A Feature-Based Learning Method for Theorem Proving / 457
Matthias Fuchs, Australian National University

Learning Investment Functions for Controlling the Utility of Control Knowledge / 463
Oleg Ledeniov and Shaul Markovitch, Technion

Uncertainty Search and Optimization

Fast Probabilistic Modeling for Combinatorial Optimization / 469
Shumeet Baluja, Justsystem Pittsburgh Research Center and Carnegie Mellon University and Scott Davies, Carnegie Mellon University

Highest Utility First Search Across Multiple Levels of Stochastic Design / 477
Louis Steinberg, J. Storrs Hall and Brian D. Davison, Rutgers University

Evolvable Hardware

Evolvable Hardware Chip for High Precision Printer Image Compression / 486
Hidenori Sakanashi, Mehrdad Salami and Masaya Iwata, Electrotechnical Laboratory; Shogo Nakaya, Tsukasa Yamauchi, Takeshi Inuo, and Nobuki Kajihara, RWCP Adaptive Device NEC Laboratory; Tetsuya Higuchi, Electrotechnical Laboratory

Game Playing

Opponent Modeling in Poker / 493
Darse Billings, Denis Papp, Jonathan Schaeffer and Duane Szafron, University of Alberta

Finding Optimal Strategies for Imperfect Information Games / 500
Ian Frank, Electrotechnical Laboratory; David Basin, Universität Freiburg; Hitoshi Matsubara, Electrotechnical Laboratory

Information Extraction

Learning to Extract Symbolic Knowledge from the World Wide Web / 509
Mark Craven, Dan DiPasquo and Dayne Freitag, Carnegie Mellon University; Andrew McCallum, Just Research and Carnegie Mellon University; Tom Mitchell, Kamal Nigam and Seán Slattery, Carnegie Mellon University

Information Extraction from HTML: Application of a General Machine Learning Approach / 517
Dayne Freitag, Carnegie Mellon University

Towards Text Knowledge Engineering / 524
Udo Hahn and Klemens Schnattinger, Freiburg University

Answering Questions for an Organization Online / 532
Vladimir A. Kulyukin, Kristian J. Hammond and Robin D. Burke, University of Chicago

Integrated AI Systems

BIG: A Resource-Bounded Information Gathering Agent / 539
Victor Lesser, Bryan Horling, Frank Klassner, Anita Raja, Thomas Wagner and Shelley XQ. Zhang, University of Massachusetts, Amherst

Intelligent Environments

Design Principles for Intelligent Environments / 547
Michael H. Coen, MIT Artificial Intelligence Lab

Cooperating with People: The Intelligent Classroom / 555
David Franklin, University of Chicago

Planning and Problem Solving

Integrating AI Components for a Military Planning Application / 561
Marie A. Bienkowski, SRI International and Louis J. Hoebel, General Electric CRD

TRIPS: An Integrated Intelligent Problem-Solving Assistant / 567
George Ferguson and James F. Allen, University of Rochester

Knowledge Representation

Concepts and Context

Knowledge Intensive Exception Spaces / 574
Sarabjot S. Anand, David W. Patterson and John G. Hughes, University of Ulster at Jordanstown

Probabilistic Frame-Based Systems / 580
Daphne Koller and Avi Pfeffer, Stanford University

Fuzzy Logic

Logical Representation and Computation of Optimal Decisions in a Qualitative Setting / 588
Didier Dubois, Daniel Le Berre, Henri Prade, and Régis Sabbadin, IRIT - Université Paul Sabatier

A Fuzzy Description Logic / 594
Umberto Straccia, I.E.I. - C.N.R.

Knowledge Base Design

OKBC: A Programmatic Foundation for Knowledge Base Interoperability / 600
Vinay K. Chaudhri, SRI International; Adam Farquhar and Richard Fikes, Stanford University; Peter D. Karp, Pangea Systems; James P. Rice, Stanford University

Usability Issues in Knowledge Representation Systems / 608
Deborah L. McGuinness, AT&T Labs—Research and Peter F. Patel-Schneider, Bell Labs Research

Representing Scientific Experiments: Implications for Ontology Design and Knowledge Sharing / 615
Natalya Fridman Noy and Carole D. Hafner, Northeastern University

Representation of Action

An Action Language Based on Causal Explanation: Preliminary Report / 623
Enrico Giunchiglia, DIST - Università di Genova and Vladimir Lifschitz, University of Texas at Austin

Abductive Planning with Sensing / 631
Matthew Stone, University of Pennsylvania

Robotics

A Formal Methodology for Verifying Situated Agents / 637
Phan Minh Dung, Asian Institute of Technology

An Algebra for Cyclic Ordering of 2D Orientations / 643
Amar Isli and Anthony G. Cohn, University of Leeds

Time and Representation

The Temporal Analysis of Chisholm's Paradox / 650
Leendert W. N. van der Torre, Paul Sabatier University and Yao-Hua Tan, Erasmus University

Temporal Reasoning with Qualitative and Quantitative Information about Points and Durations / 656
Rattana Wetprasit and Abdul Sattar, Griffith University

Learning

Iterated Phantom Induction: A Little Knowledge Can Go a Long Way / 665
Mark Brodie and Gerald DeJong, University of Illinois at Urbana-Champaign

SUSTAIN: A Model of Human Category Learning / 671
Bradley C. Love and Douglas L. Medin, Northwestern University

Genetic Algorithm Applications

Optimal 2D Model Matching Using a Messy Genetic Algorithm / 677
J. Ross Beveridge, Colorado State University

Learning Cooperative Lane Selection Strategies for Highways / 684
David E. Moriarty, University of Southern California and Pat Langley, Daimler-Benz Research & Technology Center

Inductive Learning

Boosting in the Limit: Maximizing the Margin of Learned Ensembles / 692
Adam J. Grove and Dale Schuurmans, NEC Research Institute

Boosting Classifiers Regionally / 700
Richard Maclin, University of Minnesota-Duluth

Robust Classification Systems for Imprecise Environments / 706
Foster Provost and Tom Fawcett, Bell Atlantic Science and Technology

Learning about People

Recommendation as Classification: Using Social and Content-Based Information in Recommendation / 714
Chumki Basu, Bell Communications Research and Rutgers University; Haym Hirsh, Rutgers University; William Cohen, AT&T Laboratories

Learning to Predict User Operations for Adaptive Scheduling / 721
Melinda T. Gervasio, Wayne Iba and Pat Langley, Institute for the Study of Learning and Expertise

Adaptive Web Sites: Automatically Synthesizing Web Pages / 727
Mike Perkowitz and Oren Etzioni, University of Washington

Learning from Sequences

Feature Generation for Sequence Categorization / 733
Daniel Kudenko and Haym Hirsh, Rutgers University

Concepts from Time Series / 739
Michael T. Rosenstein and Paul R. Cohen, University of Massachusetts

Reinforcement Learning

The Dynamics of Reinforcement Learning in Cooperative Multiagent Systems / 746
Caroline Claus and Craig Boutilier, University of British Columbia

Applying Online Search Techniques to Continuous-State Reinforcement Learning / 753
Scott Davies, Carnegie Mellon University; Andrew Y. Ng, Massachusetts Institute of Technology; Andrew Moore, Carnegie Mellon University

Bayesian Q-Learning / 761
Richard Dearden, University of British Columbia; Nir Friedman and Stuart Russell, University of California, Berkeley

Tree Based Discretization for Continuous State Space Reinforcement Learning / 769
William R. B. Uther and Manuela M. Veloso, Carnegie Mellon University

Natural Language

Grammar and Language

A Sampling-Based Heuristic for Tree Search Applied to Grammar Induction / 776
Hugues Juillé and Jordan B. Pollack, Brandeis University

Ambiguity and Constraint in Mathematical Expression Recognition / 784
Erik G. Miller and Paul A. Viola, Massachusetts Institute of Technology

Learning in Natural Language

Learning to Classify Text from Labeled and Unlabeled Documents / 792
Kamal Nigam, Carnegie Mellon University; Andrew McCallum, Just Research and Carnegie Mellon University; Sebastian Thrun and Tom Mitchell, Carnegie Mellon University

Knowledge Lean Word—Sense Disambiguation / 800
Ted Pedersen, Southern Methodist University and Rebecca Bruce, University of North Carolina at Asheville

Learning to Resolve Natural Language Ambiguities: A Unified Approach / 806
Dan Roth, University of Illinois at Urbana-Champaign

Natural Language Generation

Generating Inference-Rich Discourse through Revisions of RST-Trees / 814
Helmut Horacek, Universität des Saarlandes

Machine Learning of Generic and User-Focused Summarization / 821
Inderjeet Mani and Eric Bloedorn, The MITRE Corporation

Natural Language Generation—Argumentation

Hermes: Supporting Argumentative Discourse in Multi-Agent Decision Making / 827
Nikos Karacapilidis, Swiss Federal Institute of Technology and Dimitris Papadias, Hong Kong University of Science and Technology

Bayesian Reasoning in an Abductive Mechanism for Argument Generation and Analysis / 833
Ingrid Zukerman, Richard McConachy and Kevin B. Korb, Monash University

Nonmonotonic Reasoning

Fixpoint 3-Valued Semantics for Autoepistemic Logic / 840
Marc Denecker, K. U. Leuven; Victor Marek and Miroslaw Truszczynski, University of Kentucky

Experimenting with Power Default Reasoning / 846
Eric Klavins and William C. Rounds, University of Michigan; Guo-Qiang Zhang, University of Georgia

Reducing Query Answering to Satisfiability in Nonmonotonic Logics / 853
Riccardo Rosati, Università di Roma "La Sapienza"

Planning

Improving Big Plans / 860
Neal Lesh, Nathaniel Martin and James Allen, University of Rochester

Controlling Communication in Distributed Planning Using Irrelevance Reasoning / 868
Michael Wolverton and Marie desJardins, SRI International

Frameworks for Plan Generation

Automatic OBDD-Based Generation of Universal Plans in Non-Deterministic Domains / 875
Alessandro Cimatti, Marco Roveri and Paolo Traverso, IRST

Hybrid Planning for Partially Hierarchical Domains / 882
Subbarao Kambhampati, Amol Mali and Biplav Srivastava, Arizona State University

Graph Plan

Conformant Graphplan / 889
David E. Smith, NASA Ames Research Center and Daniel S. Weld, University of Washington

Extending Graphplan to Handle Uncertainty & Sensing Actions / 897
Daniel S. Weld and Corin R. Anderson, University of Washington; David E. Smith, NASA Ames Research Center

Plan Efficiency

Inferring State Constraints for Domain-Independent Planning / 905
Alfonso Gerevini, Università di Brescia and Lenhart Schubert, University of Rochester

Analyzing External Conditions to Improve the Efficiency of HTN Planning / 913
Reiko Tsuneto, James Hendler and Dana Nau, University of Maryland

Plan Execution

Managing Multiple Tasks in Complex, Dynamic Environments / 921
Michael Freed, NASA Ames Research Center

Maintaining Consistency in Hierarchical Reasoning / 928
Robert E. Wray, III and John Laird, The University of Michigan

Plan Recognition

Acquisition of Abstract Plan Descriptions for Plan Recognition / 936
Mathias Bauer, German Research Center for Artificial Intelligence

Needles in a Haystack: Plan Recognition in Large Spatial Domains Involving Multiple Agents / 942
Mark Devaney and Ashwin Ram, Georgia Institute of Technology

Planning as Satisfiability

Act, and the Rest Will Follow: Exploiting Determinism in Planning as Satisfiability / 948
Enrico Giunchiglia and Alessandro Massarotto, DIST - Università di Genova; Roberto Sebastiani, IRST

Using Caching to Solve Larger Probabilistic Planning Problems / 954
Stephen M. Majercik and Michael L. Littman, Duke University

Robotics

Human-Robot Interaction

Alternative Essences of Intelligence / 961
Rodney A. Brooks, Cynthia Breazeal (Ferrell), Robert Irie, Charles C. Kemp, Matthew Marjanovic, Brian Scassellati and Matthew M. Williamson, MIT Artificial Intelligence Lab

Eye Finding via Face Detection for a Foveated Active Vision System / 969
Brian Scassellati, MIT Artificial Intelligence Laboratory

Template-Based Recognition of Pose and Motion Gestures on a Mobile Robot / 977
Stefan Waldherr, Sebastian Thrun, Roseli Romero and Dimitris Margaritis, Carnegie Mellon University

Robot Navigation

Position Estimation for Mobile Robots in Dynamic Environments / 983
Dieter Fox and Wolfram Burgard, University of Bonn; Sebastian Thrun, Carnegie Mellon University; Armin B. Cremers, University of Bonn

Integrating Topological and Metric Maps for Mobile Robot Navigation: A Statistical Approach / 989
Sebastian Thrun, Carnegie Mellon University; Jens-Steffen Gutmann, Universität Freiburg; Dieter Fox and Wolfram Burgard, University of Bonn; Benjamin J. Kuipers, University of Texas at Austin

Sound Understanding

The Role of Data Reprocessing in Complex Acoustic Environments / 997
Frank Klassner, Villanova University; Victor Lesser, University of Massachusetts, Amherst; Hamid Nawab, Boston University

Sound Ontology for Computational Auditory Scence Analysis / 1004
Tomohiro Nakatani and Hiroshi G. Okuno, NTT Basic Research Laboratories

Innovative Applications of Artificial Intelligence Papers

Deployed Applications

Multi Machine Scheduling: An Agent-Based Approach / 1013
Rama Akkiraju, Pinar Keskinocak, Sesh Murthy and Frederick Wu, IBM T.J. Watson Research Center

Producing BT's Yellow Pages with Formation / 1020
Gail Anderson, Andrew Casson-du Mont, Ann Macintosh and Robert Rae, University of Edinburgh; Barry Gleeson, Pindar Set Ltd.

Using Artificial Intelligence Planning to Automate SAR Image Processing for Scientific Data Analysis / 1027
Forest Fisher and Steve Chien, Jet Propulsion Laboratory/California Institute of Technology; Edisanter Lo and Ronald Greeley, Arizona State University

Turbine Engine Diagnostics (TED): An Expert Diagnostic System for the M1 Abrams Turbine Engine / 1032
Richard Helfman, Ed Baur, John Dumer, Tim Hanratty and Holly Ingham, U.S. Army Research Laboratory

Countrywide Automated Property Evaluation System - CAPES / 1039
Ingemar A. E. Hulthage and Iain Stobie, Countrywide Home Loans

Automated Intelligent Pilots for Combat Flight Simulation / 1047
Randolph M. Jones, John E. Laird and Paul E. Nielsen, University of Michigan

The NASD Regulation Advanced Detection System (ADS) / 1055
J. Dale Kirkland and Ted E. Senator, National Association of Securities Dealers Regulation, Inc.; James J. Hayden, SRA International Inc.; Tom Dybala, Henry G. Goldberg and Ping Shyr, National Association of Securities Dealers Regulation, Inc.

A New Technique Enables Dynamic Replanning and Rescheduling of Aeromedical Evacuation / 1063
Alexander Kott, Victor Saks and Albert Mercer, Carnegie Group, Inc.

Knowledge-Based Avoidance of Drug-Resistant HIV Mutants / 1071
Richard H. Lathrop, Nicholas R. Steffen, Miriam P. Raphael, Sophia Deeds-Rubin and Michael J. Pazzani, University of California, Irvine; Paul J. Cimoch, Center for Special Immunology; Darryl M. See and Jeremiah G. Tilles, University of California, Irvine

Success in Spades: Using AI Planning Techniques to Win the World Championship of Computer Bridge / 1079
Stephen J. J. Smith, Hood College; Dana S. Nau, University of Maryland; Thomas A. Throop, Great Game Products

ANSWER: Network Monitoring Using Object-Oriented Rules / 1087
Gary M. Weiss, AT&T Labs and Rutgers University; Johannes P. Ros and Anoop Singhal, AT&T Labs

Emerging Applications

Warfighter's Information Packager / 1095
Yigal Arens and Weixiong Zhang, USC/Information Sciences Institute; Yongwon Lee and Jon Dukes-Schlossberg, Lockheed Martin; Marc Zev, ISX Corporation

Realtime Constraint-Based Cinematography for Complex Interactive 3D Worlds / 1101
William H. Bares, Joël P. Grégoire and James C. Lester, North Carolina State University

Expert System Technology for Nondestructive Waste Assay / 1107
J. C. Determan and G. K. Becker, Idaho National Engineering and Environmental Laboratory

Bayesian Network Models for Generation of Crisis Management Training Scenarios / 1113
Eugene Grois, William H. Hsu, Mikhail Voloshin and David C. Wilkins, University of Illinois at Urbana-Champaign

Hybrid Knowledge Based System for Automatic Classificaton of B-scan Images from Ultrasonic Rail Inspection / 1121
J. Jarmulak, Delft University of Technology and TNO - Institute of Applied Physics; E. J. H. Kerckhoffs, Delft University of Technology; P. P. van't Veen, TNO - Institute of Applied Physics

Control Strategies in HTN Planning: Theory Versus Practice / 1127
Dana S. Nau, University of Maryland; Stephen J. J. Smith, Hood College; Kutluhan Erol, Intelligent Automation Inc.

A Prototype Application of Fuzzy Logic and Expert Systems in Education Assessment / 1134
James R. Nolan, Siena College

Intelligent Control of Life Support Systems for Space Habitats / 1140
Debra Schreckenghost, Daniel Ryan, Carroll Thronesbery, Peter Bonasso and Daniel Poirot, NASA Johnson Space Center/ER

Split Up: The Use of an Argument Based Knowledge Representation to Meet Expectations of Different Users for Discretionary Decision Making / 1146
Andrew Stranieri, University of Ballarat and John Zeleznikow, La Trobe University

An Expert System for Alarm System Planning / 1152
Akira Tsurushima, Kenji Urushima, Daigo Sakata, Hiroyuki Date, Masatomo Nakata, Yoshinobu Adachi and Kazuhisa Takahashi, SECOM Intelligent Systems Laboratory

Conversation Machines for Transaction Processing / 1160
Wlodek Zadrozny, Catherine Wolf, Nanda Kambhatla and Yiming Ye, IBM T.J. Watson Research Center

SIGART / AAAI Doctoral Consortium Abstracts

Optimizing Information Agents by Selectively Materializing Data / 1168
Naveen Ashish, University of Southern California

Generating Adequate Instructions: Knowing When to Stop / 1169
Juliet C. Bourne, University of Pennsylvania

HR - Automatic Concept Formation in Finite Algebras / 1170
Simon Colton, University of Edinburgh

Optimizing Initial Configurations of Neural Networks for the Task of Natural Language Learning / 1171
Jaime J. Dávila, City University of New York

Pragmatic Multi-Agent Learning / 1172
Andrew Garland, Brandeis University

Perception, Memory, and the Field of View Problem / 1173
William S. Gribble, University of Texas at Austin

Exploiting Diversity for Natural Language Processing / 1174
John C. Henderson, Johns Hopkins University

Multimodal, Multilevel Selective Attention / 1175
Micheal Hewett, University of Texas at Austin

Learning in Markov Games with Incomplete Information / 1176
Junling Hu, University of Michigan

Extending the Classification Paradigm to Temporal Domains / 1177
Mohammed Waleed Kadous, University of New South Wales

Data Mining for Maintenance of Complex Systems / 1178
Sylvain Létourneau, University of Ottawa

Empirical Acquisition of Word-Sense Distinctions / 1179
Tom O'Hara, New Mexico State University

Neural Approaches to Blind Separation and Cumulant Analysis and Its Application to

Diagnostics of Nuclear Power Plants / 1180
Alexei Ourmanov, Institute of Physics and Power Engineering

Bayesian Reasoning for Tropical Cyclone Intensity Forecasting and Risk Analysis / 1181
Grace W. Rumantir, Monash University

Rational Multiagent Organization and Reorganization / 1182
Wayne A. Smith, University of South Carolina

A Script-Based Approach to Modifying Knowledge-Based Systems / 1183
Marcelo Tallis, University of Southern California

Student Abstracts

Learning to Teach with a Reinforcement Learning Agent / 1185
Joseph E. Beck, University of Massachusetts, Amherst

Genetic Search for Accurate Feature Sets / 1186
Brendan Burns, Williams College

A First Analysis of Qualitative Influences and Synergies / 1187
Jesús Cerquides and Ramon López de Màntaras, Spanish Council for Scientific Research

A New Approach to Rule Interest Measures / 1188
Jesús Cerquides and Ramon López de Màntaras, Spanish Council for Scientific Research

Classification Using an Online Genetic Algorithm / 1189
Brian D. Davison, Rutgers, The State University of New Jersey

Plan Recognition in Complex Spatial Domains / 1190
Mark Devaney, Georgia Institute of Technology

Nested Joint Probability Model for Morphological Analysis and its Grid Pruning / 1191
Koji Fujimoto, Nobuo Inui and Yoshiyuki Kotani, Tokyo University of Agriculture and Technology

Generalized A* for Cyclic AND/OR Graphs / 1192
Supriyo Ghose, Price Waterhouse Associates Pvt. Ltd.

Selection of Conflict Resolution Strategies in Dynamically Organized Sensible Agent-Based Systems / 1193
T. H. Liu and K. S. Barber, The University of Texas at Austin

Refinement-Based Planning as Satisfiability / 1194
Amol D. Mali, Arizona State University

Goal and Responsibility Allocation in Sensible Agent-Based Systems / 1195
Ryan McKay and K. S. Barber, The University of Texas at Austin

Tutorial Response Generation in a Writing Tool for Deaf Learners of English / 1196
Lisa N. Michaud, University of Delaware

Dependent Bigram Identification / 1197
Ted Pedersen, Southern Methodist University

Raw Corpus Word Sense Disambiguation / 1198
Ted Pedersen, Southern Methodist University

DISCOURSE LEARNING: Dialogue Act Tagging with Transformation-Based Learning / 1199
Ken Samuel, The University of Delaware

Estimating the Expected Error of Empirical Minimizers for Model Selection / 1200
Tobias Scheffer, Technische Universität Berlin and Thorsten Joachims, Uni Dortmund

PLUTO: Managing Multistrategy Learning through Planning / 1201
Gordon T. Shippey, J. William Murdock and Ashwin Ram, Georgia Institute of Technology

A Framework for Reinforcement Learning on Real Robots / 1202
William D. Smart and Leslie Pack Kaelbling, Brown University

Handling Inconsistency for Multi-Source Integration / 1203
Sheila Tejada, Craig A. Knoblock and Steven Minton, University of Southern California/ISI

Emotion-Based Agents / 1204
Rodrigo M. M. Ventura and Carlos A. Pinto-Ferreira, Instituto Superior Técnico

DL-$elect: A Decision-List-Based Data-Mining System / 1205
Karl Weinmeister, Duke University

Ensuring Reasoning Consistency in Hierarchical Architectures / 1206
Robert E. Wray, III and John Laird, The University of Michigan

Building Agents from Shared Ontologies through Apprenticeship Multistrategy Learning / 1207
Kathryn Wright, Mihai Boicu, Seok Won Lee and Gheorghe Tecuci, George Mason University

Development of Outdoor Navigation for a Robotic Wheelchair System / 1208
Holly A. Yanco, MIT Artificial Intelligence Laboratory

Invited Talk

Structured Probabilistic Models: Bayesian Networks and Beyond / 1210
Daphne Koller, Stanford University

Index / 1212

Preface

The National Conference on Artificial Intelligence is the main yearly occasion for a broad spectrum of AI researchers to gather together, share results, and recharge the enthusiasm needed to spend another year fighting the day-to-day technical battles that are the "99% perspiration" part of AI research —the conference provides some of the "1% inspiration" (which is fortunate, since we don't need any more perspiration in July!).

This volume is the permanent record of the technical program of the conference, which is the backbone of the meeting. The 143 papers reproduced here were selected out of 475 submissions by a rigorous double-blind referee process, which we describe in more detail below.

The reviewing process would not have been possible without the supporting software developed by Ramesh Patil and diligently maintained at the AAAI office by Rick Skalsky. Ramesh has volunteered his time for this task year after year, greatly above and beyond the call of duty.

Like Ramesh, all the members of the Conference Committee are volunteers who have taken time from their own research and other agendas to help make this conference a success. Thank you.

We would also like to thank Carol Hamilton, Executive Director of AAAI, and all of her able staff at the AAAI office for their competent support and unflappable good humor throughout all aspects of organizing the conference.

How the Review Process Works

Careful review is one of AAAI's most important functions in the AI research community and entails a considerable investment of resources to assign, review, and discuss each paper. Including actual expenses, such as meetings and office staff time, and unpaid reviewer time, each paper costs hundreds of dollars to review on average.

Each paper was assigned to a supervising member of the Senior Program Committee and three members of the AAAI-98 Program Committee, all selected for their relevant expertise. To support impartiality, conflicts of interest are checked during paper assignment and reviewers are not told the identity of paper authors.

Selecting qualified reviewers for each paper is obviously key to obtaining high-quality reviews. AAAI has evolved a semi-automated, web-based mechanism for this purpose. Authors submit paper titles and abstracts electronically along with keywords from a predefined list. Reviewers then examine these online entries (without author identification) and "bid" for the papers they are most qualified for and would most like to review. Ramesh Patil's software then performs a global assignment algorithm to assign as many papers as possible to the best qualified reviewers. In cases where a paper has too few bids, the algorithm falls back on a reviewer profile in which each reviewer has rated his/her expertise in each keyword area. Finally, the Program Cochairs meet in January to review all the assignments with special attention to keyword-only matches.

Each of the three members of the Program Committee initially wrote independent reviews of each paper and emailed them to the supervising member of the Senior Program Committee. Once all the reviews for a given paper were completed, the reviewers exchanged and discussed their reviews, in some cases at great length. Based on this discussion (and in some cases after writing his or her own review or obtaining an additional reviewer), the supervising member recommended whether to accept the paper. The entire Senior Program Committee then met in person with the Program Cochairs for a weekend in March to discuss problematic papers and make final decisions. For some papers, additional reviews were written during this meeting by Senior Program Committee members to clarify the reasons for decisions that might not be obvious from the initial reviews.

Generally speaking, an AAAI paper should clearly present an interesting idea with convincing evidence that it significantly advances the field by solving an important new problem or improving over previous approaches. Reviews often include suggestions for how the paper can be improved; we hope authors use them as a guide both in revising their AAAI submissions and for future research and presentation.

We are very proud of the seriousness and dedication of everyone who participated in the reviewing process. On behalf of the whole research community, we thank them for their work.

Conference Events

In addition to continuing the popular regular events and the successful Hall of Champions experiment initiated last year, this year's program included several innovations—the Integrated AI Systems track, the Intelligent Systems Demonstrations, and an invited panel of chairs from the collocated conferences.

Integrated AI Systems. An important force holding our field together is the shared goal of building "artificial intelligences" that perform valued activities in real environments by integrating capabilities from AI's diverse subdisciplines. To encourage and support the development of such systems, the AAAI-98 conference program included a special track for papers about systems that integrate methods from multiple AI subdisciplines. These submissions were reviewed by a specially selected pool of reviewers, headed by Milind Tambe, who were sensitive to the challenges of presenting this kind of work in a conference format. Quality standards for this track were high: out of 20 submitted papers, 6 were accepted for presentation, including one which received an Outstanding Paper award.

Intelligent Systems Demonstrations The purpose of the Intelligent Systems Demonstrations, organized by George Ferguson and Randy Jones, was primarily to encourage the early exhibition of research prototypes. Each demonstration was attended by someone, usually the architect of the system, who could answer in-depth technical questions. Submissions to this program were reviewed on the basis of their innovation, relevance, scientific contribution, and presentation. A special invitation was made to authors of accepted papers.

Collocated Conferences

- Eighth International Conference on Inductive Logic Programming (ILP '98), July 22-24, 1998
- Third Annual Genetic Programming Conference (GP-98), July 22-25, 1998
- Symposium on Genetic Algorithms (SGA-98), July 22-25, 1998
- Eleventh Annual Conference on Computational Learning Theory (COLT '98), July 24-26, 1998
- Fifteenth International Conference on Machine Learning (ICML '98), July 24-26, 1998
- Fourteenth Annual Conference on Uncertainty in Artificial Intelligence (UAI-98), July 24-26, 1998
- Eighth Annual Meeting of the Society for Text and Discourse (ST&D98), July 29-31, 1998
- Twentieth Annual Meeting of the Cognitive Science Society, August 1-4, 1998

The eight organizations above chose to hold their meetings in Madison contiguous with AAAI-98 this year. In honor of this special occasion, we invited a chairperson from each of these conferences to join a panel on the opening morning of AAAI-98 to answer the following question: What is the most important recent result/experiment/discovery in the area of your conference that the general AI audience doesn't know/understand/appreciate, but should (and why)?

We hope this event will stimulate further public discussion about how the relationship between the National Conference on AI and the—now many—subfield conferences might evolve in the future.

Finally, just to let you know that this job can have its lighter moments, we would like to end by sharing with you the most amusing referee comment we received:

This paper generated enough interest in me to spend far more time criticizing it than I should have. Perhaps AAAI attendees should be given the same pleasure.

(We won't tell you whether the paper was accepted or not!)

– Jack Mostow and Charles Rich
AAAI-98 Program Cochairs

IAAI–98

The Tenth Annual Conference on Innovative Applications of Artificial Intelligence (IAAI-98) continues the IAAI tradition of case studies of deployed applications with measurable benefits whose value depends on the use of AI technology. In addition, IAAI-98 augments these case studies with papers and invited talks that address emerging areas of AI technology or applications. IAAI is organized as an independent program within the National Conference, with schedules coordinated to allow attendees to move freely between IAAI and National Conference sessions. IAAI and the National Conference are jointly sponsoring several invited talks that fit the theme of both programs.

AI applications developers will benefit from learning about new AI techniques that will enable the next generation of applications. Basic AI research will benefit by learning about challenges of real-world domains and difficulties and successes in applying AI techniques to real business problems. IAAI-98 will address the full range of AI techniques including knowledge-based systems, natural language, and vision.

IAAI-98 showcases the deployed applications on the first day. The papers are case studies that provide a valuable guide to designing, building, managing, and deploying systems incorporating AI technologies. These applications provide clear evidence of the impact and value that AI technology has in today's world.

Papers in the Emerging Applications and Technologies track describe efforts whose goal is the engineering of AI applications. They inform AI researchers about the utility of specific AI techniques for applications domains and also inform applications developers about tools and techniques that will enable the next generation of new and more powerful applications.

This year's papers address applications in education, the military, networking, spacecraft, medicine, games, the stock market, and more. AI techniques include, among others, planning, natural language processing, diagnostic reasoning, and cognitive simulation.

– Bruce G. Buchanan, Program Chair &
Ramasamy Uthurusamy, Program Cochair

AAAI–98 / IAAI–98 Program Committees

Conference Committee

AAAI-98/IAAI-98 Conference Chairs
Jack Mostow, Carnegie Mellon University
Charles Rich, MERL - Mitsubishi Electric Research Laboratory

IAAI-98 Conference Chair
Bruce Buchanan, University of Pittsburgh

IAAI-98 Conference Cochair
Ramasamy Uthurusamy, General Motors Research

Hall of Champions Cochairs
Jonathan Schaeffer, University of Alberta
Dana Nau, University of Maryland

Intelligent Systems Demonstrations Cochairs
George Ferguson, University of Rochester
Randy Jones, University of Michigan

Mobile Robot Competition Cochairs
Greg Dudek, McGill University
Robin Murphy, Colorado School of Mines
David Kortenkamp, NASA Johnson Space Center

Mobile Robot Exhibition Cochairs
Tucker Balch, Georgia Institute of Technology
Karen Haigh, Carnegie Mellon University

Robot Building Laboratory Chair
David Miller, KISS Institute for Practical Robotics

Student Abstract and Poster Chair
Michael Littman, Duke University

Tutorial Cochairs
Padrahic Smyth, University of California, Irvine
Bart Selman, Cornell University

Workshop Cochairs
David Leake, University of Indiana
Raymond C. Mooney, University of Texas at Austin

SIGART/AAAI-98 Doctoral Consortium Organizer
Janyce M. Wiebe, New Mexico State University

Senior Program Committee Members
Gautam Biswas, Vanderbilt University
Piero P. Bonissone, General Electric
 Corporate Research & Development
Alex Borgida, Rutgers University
Craig Boutilier, University of British Columbia
James Crawford, i2 Technologies
Susan L. Epstein, Hunter College
David W. Etherington, University of Oregon
Tim Finin, University of Maryland, Baltimore County
Ken Forbus, Northwestern University
Eugene C. Freuder, University of New Hampshire
Moises Goldszmidt, SRI International
Jonathan Gratch, University of Southern California
Russell Greiner, University of Alberta
James C. Hendler, University of Maryland
Haym Hirsh, Rutgers University
Eric Horvitz, Microsoft Research
Craig A. Knoblock, University of Southern California
Kurt Konolige, SRI International
Karen Lochbaum, U S WEST Advanced Technologies
Johanna D. Moore, University of Pittsburgh
Leora Morgenstern, IBM TJ Watson Research Center
Karen Myers, SRI International
Fernando C. Pereira, AT&T Laboratories-Research
Bruce Porter, University of Texas at Austin
Reid Simmons, Carnegie Mellon University
Devika Subramanian, Rice University
Rich Sutton, University of Massachusetts, Amherst
Milind Tambe, University of Southern California

Program Committee Members
Chinatsu Aone, SRA International
Ron Arkin, Georgia Institute of Technology
Lars Asker, Stockholm University
Fahiem Bacchus, University of Waterloo
Shumeet Baluja, Justsystem Pittsburgh Research Center
Chitta Baral, University of Texas at El Paso
Andy Barto, University of Massachusetts
Michael Beetz, University of Bonn
Richard K. Belew, University of California, San Diego
Larry Birnbaum, Northwestern University
Jim Blythe, University of Southern California
Pete Bonasso, Texas Robotics & Automation Center

Justin Boyan, Carnegie Mellon University
Jeff Bradshaw, Institute for Human and Machine Cognition
Ronen Brafman, Ben Gurion University
Karl Branting, University of Wyoming
Eric Brill, Johns Hopkins University
Carla E. Brodley, Purdue University
Wolfram Burgard, University of Bonn
Marco Cadoli, Universitá di Roma "La Sapienza"
Claire Cardie, Cornell University
Anthony R. Cassandra, Microelectronics and Computer Technology Corporation
B. Chandrasekaran, Ohio State University
Mike Chantler, Heriot-Watt University
David Maxwell Chickering, Microsoft Research
Steve Chien, Jet Propulsion Laboratory
Luca Chittaro, Universita di Udine
Jennifer Chu-Carroll, Bell Laboratories
Dan Clancy, NASA Ames/Caelum Research
Peter Clark, The Boeing Company
Gary Cottrell, University of California, San Diego
Richard Crouch, University of Nottingham
Ido Dagan, Bar Ilan University
Mukesh Dalal, i2 Technologies
Adnan Darwiche, American University of Beirut
Ernie Davis, New York University
Giuseppe De Giacomo, Universitá di Roma "La Sapienza"
Johan De Kleer, Xerox Palo Alto Research Center
Rina Dechter, University of California, Irvine
James Delgrande, Simon Fraser University
Marie desJardins, SRI International
Tom Dietterich, Oregon State University
Pedro Domingos, Instituto Superior Tecnico
Richard Doyle, Jet Propulsion Laboratory
Brian Drabble, University of Oregon
Denise Draper, Rockwell Palo Alto Laboratory
Didier Dubois, Universite Paul Sabatier
Oliver M. Duschka, Stanford University
Charles Elkan, University of California, San Diego
John Everett, Xerox Palo Alto Research Center
Matthew Evett, Florida Atlantic University
Boi Faltings, Swiss Federal Institute of Technology
Adam Farquhar, Stanford University
Usama Fayyad, Microsoft Research
Ronen Feldman, Bar-Illan University
Dieter Fox, University of Bonn
Nir Friedman, University of California, Berkeley
Hector Geffner, Universidad Simon Bolivar
Dan Geiger, Microsoft Research
Melinda T. Gervasio, Institute for the Study of Learning and Expertise
Yolanda Gil, University of Southern California/Information Sciences Institute
Andy Golding, MERL - A Mitsubishi Electric Research Laboratory
Diana Gordon, Naval Research Laboratory
Georg Gottlob, Technische Universitaet Wien
Lloyd Greenwald, University of Pennsylvania
Adam Grove, NEC Research Institute

Bill Grundy, University of California, San Diego
Peter Haddawy, University of Wisconsin, Milwaukee
Larry Hall, University of South Florida
Steve Hanks, University of Washington
Marti Hearst, University of California, Berkeley
Peter Heeman, Oregon Graduate Institute
Tad Hogg, Xerox Palo Alto Research Center
Ian Horswill, Northwestern University
John Horty, University of Maryland
Adele Howe, Colorado State University
Chun-Nan Hsu, Arizona State University
Jane Yung-jen Hsu, National Taiwan University
Michael Huhns, University of South Carolina
Yumi Iwasaki, Stanford University
Sverker Janson, Swedish Institute of Computer Science
Thorsten Joachims, Universitaet Dormund
Mark Johnson, Brown University
W. Lewis Johnson, University of Southern California/Information Sciences Insitute
Ari K. Jonsson, RIACS/NASA Ames Research Center
Dan Jurafsky, University of Colorado
Leslie Pack Kaelbling, Brown University
Subbarao Kambhampati, Indian Institute of Science
G. Neelakantan Kartha, i2 Technologies
Henry Kautz, AT&T Laboratories
Andy Kehler, SRI International
Hiroaki Kitano, Sony Computer Science Laboratory
Sven Koenig, Georgia Institute of Technology
Daphne Koller, Stanford University
David Kortenkamp, Metrica Inc Robotics and Automation Group
Jana Kosecka, University of California, Berkeley
Sarit Kraus, Bar-Ilan University and University of Maryland
Nicholas Kushmerick, Dublin City University
James Lester, North Carolina State University
Alon Levy, University of Washington
Diane Litman, AT&T Laboratories
Sridhar Mahadevan, Michigan State University
Heikki Mannila, University of Helsinki
Daniel Marcu, University of Southern California/Information Sciences Institute
Shaul Markovitch, Technion
Maja J. Mataric, University of Southern California/Information Sciences Institute
James Mayfield, Johns Hopkins University APL
Andrew McCallum, Justsystem Pittsburgh Research Center
Robert McCartney, University of Connecticut
Sheila McIlraith, Stanford University
Donald P. McKay, Lockheed Martin
Chris Mellish, University of Edinburgh
Robert C. Moore, SRI International
Alice Mulvehill, GTE/BBN Technologies
Robin R. Murphy, Colorado School of Mines
Nicola Muscettola, NASA Ames Research Center
David Musliner, Honeywell Technology Center
John Mylopoulos, University of Toronto
Christine H. Nakatani, AT&T Laboratories
Dana Nau, University of Maryland

Pandurang Nayak, NASA Ames Research Center
Eric Neufeld, University of Saskatchewan
Ann Nicholson, Monash University
Illah Nourbakhsh, Carnegie Mellon University
Werner Nutt, Hebrew University of Jerusalem
Cecile Paris, CSIRO Mathematical and Information Sciences
Ron Parr, University of California, Berkeley
Peter Patel-Schneider, Bell Laboratories
Joseph Pemberton, ISX Corporation
Mark Alan Peot, Stanford University
Enric Plaza i Cervera, IIIA-AI Research Insitute, CSIC
David Poole, University of British Columbia
Malcolm Pradhan, University of Adelaide
Foster Provost, Bell Atlantic Science and Technology
Jean-Francois Puget, ILOG
Ashwin Ram, Georgia Institute of Technology
Owen Rambow, Univesite Paris
R. Bharat Rao, Siemens Corporate Research
Philip Resnik, University of Maryland
Jeff Rickel, University of Southern California/ Information Science Institute
Justinian Rosca, Siemens Corporate Research
Francesca Rossi, Università di Pisa
Dan Roth, University of Illinois, Urbana-Champaign
Nicolas Rouquette, Jet Propulsion Laboratory
Daniela Rus, Dartmouth University
Enrique H. Ruspini, SRI International
Alessandro Saffiotti, Universite Libre de Bruxelles
Mehran Sahami, Stanford University
Tuomas Sandholm, Washington University
Ethan Scarl, Boeing Defense and Space
Jonathan Schaeffer, University of Alberta
Robert Schapire, AT&T Laboratories
Torsten Schaub, University of Potsdam
Thomas Schiex, Institut National de la Recherche Agronomique
Robert C. Schrag, Information Extraction and Transport
Dale Schuurmans, University of Pennsylvania
Bart Selman, Cornell University
Sandip Sen, University of Tulsa
Ross D. Shachter, Stanford University
Yuval Shahar, Stanford University
Wei-Min Shen, University of Southern California/Information Sciences Institute
Yoav Shoham, Stanford University
Moninder Singh, University of Pennsylvania
Satinder Singh, University of Colorado
Wolfgang Slany, Technische Universitaet Wien
David E. Smith, NASA Ames Research Center
Stephen F. Smith, Carnegie Mellon University
Lee Spector, Hampshire College
Peter Spirtes, Carnegie Mellon University
Anthony Stentz, Carnegie Mellon University
Bill Swartout, University of Southern California/Information Sciences Institute
Katia Sycara, Carnegie Mellon University
Prasad Tadepalli, Carnegie Mellon University
Gerald Tesauro, IBM Research TJ Watson Research Center
Daniele Theseider Dupre, Universita di Torino

Richmond H. Thomason, University of Pittsburgh
Sebastian Thrun, Carnegie Mellon University
Geoff Towell, Siemens Corporate Research
David R. Traum, University of Maryland
John K. Tsotsos, University of Toronto
Peter van Beek, University of Alberta
Frank van Harmelen, Vrije Universiteit
Moshe Vardi, Rice University
Manuela Veloso, Carnegie Mellon University
K. Vijay-Shanker, University of Delaware
Marilyn Walker, AT&T Laboratories
Toby Walsh, University of Strathclyde
Rich Washington, NASA Ames Research Center
Takashi Washio, Osaka University
Bonnie Webber, University of Pennsylvania
David E. Wilkins, SRI International
Mary-Anne Williams, University of Newcastle
Michael Wolverton, SRI International
Michael J. Wooldridge, University of London
Qiang Yang, Simon Fraser University
David Yarowsky, Johns Hopkins University
John Yen, Texas A & M University
Makoto Yokoo, NTT Communication Science Labs
R. Michael Young, Carnegie Mellon University
Nevin L. Zhang, Hong Kong University of Science and Technology
Feng Zhao, Xerox Palo Alto Research Center
Shlomo Zilberstein, University of Massachusetts

1998 Auxiliary Reviewers

Yngvi Bjornsson, Charles Callaway, Diego Calvanese, Urszula Chajewska, Johnny Chen, Craig W. Codrington, Dennis DeCoste, Jurgen Dorn, Daniel Dvorak, Uwe Egly, Thomas Eiter, Ariel Felner, Dani Goldberg, Merav Hadad, Karen Haigh, Angreas Junghanns, Ravi Kapadia, Terran Lane, Paolo Liberatore, Silvia Miksch, Steven Minton, Daniele Nardi, Denis Papp, Avi Pfeffer, Dean Pomerleau, Lars Rasmusson, Riccardo Rosati, Kathryn Sanders, Ananth Sankar, Orna Schechter, Dirk Schulz, Rina Schwartz, Onn Shehory, Peter Stone, Hans Tompits, Mitchel Weintraub, Barry Brian Werger

IAAI-98 PC Members

Bruce Buchanan, University of Pittsburgh
Robert S. Engelmore, Stanford University
Philip Klahr
Alain Rappaport, Carnegie Mellon University
Charles Rosenberg, Carnegie Mellon University
Ted Senator, National Association of Securities Dealers
Howard E. Shrobe, Massachusetts Institute of Technology
Reid Smith, Schlumberger Cambridge Research
Ramasamy Uthurusamy, General Motors Corporation
Marilyn Walker, AT&T Laboratories

Sponsoring Organizations

- ACM/SIGART
- Defense Advance Research Projects Agency
- Microsoft Corporation
- Office of Naval Research
- NASA Ames Research Center
- National Science Foundation

AAAI-98 Outstanding Paper Awards

This year, AAAI's National Conference on Artificial Intelligence honors three papers that exemplify high standards in technical contribution and exposition. During the blind review process, members of the Program Committee recommended which papers to consider for the Outstanding Paper Award. A subset of the Senior Program Committee, carefully chosen to avoid conflicts of interest, reviewed all such papers and selected the winning papers:

Learning Evaluation Functions for Global Optimization and Boolean Satisfiability
Justin A. Boyan and Andrew W. Moore, Carnegie Mellon University

The Interactive Museum Tour-Guide Robot
Wolfram Burgard, Armin B. Cremers, Dieter Fox and Dirk Hähnel, University of Bonn; Gerhard Lakemeyer, Aachen University of Technology; Dirk Schulz and Walter Steiner, University of Bonn; Sebastian Thrun, Carnegie Mellon University

Acceleration Methods for Numeric CSPs
Yahia Lebbah and Olivier Lhomme, Ecole des Mines de Nantes - La Chantrerie

AAAI–98 Technical Papers

AAAI–98 Outstanding Papers

Learning Evaluation Functions for Global Optimization and Boolean Satisfiability

Justin A. Boyan and Andrew W. Moore

Computer Science Department
Carnegie Mellon University
Pittsburgh, PA 15213
{jab,awm}@cs.cmu.edu

Abstract

This paper describes STAGE, a learning approach to automatically improving search performance on optimization problems. STAGE learns an evaluation function which predicts the outcome of a local search algorithm, such as hillclimbing or WALKSAT, as a function of state features along its search trajectories. The learned evaluation function is used to bias future search trajectories toward better optima. We present positive results on six large-scale optimization domains.

Introduction

VLSI design, engineering design, Boolean formula satisfaction, bin-packing, medical treatment planning and Bayes net structure finding are all examples of global optimization—the problem of finding the best possible configuration from a large space of possible configurations. Formally, a global optimization problem consists of a *state space* X and an *objective function* Obj : $X \to \Re$. The goal is to find a state $x^* \in X$ which minimizes Obj. If X is large, then finding x^* is generally intractable unless the problem has a very specialized structure (e.g., a linear program). However, many general-purpose *local search* algorithms attempt to exploit Obj's structure to locate good approximate optima; for example, hillclimbing, simulated annealing, and tabu search. All of these work by imposing a neighborhood relation on the states of X and then searching the graph that results, guided by Obj.

Local search has been likened to "trying to find the top of Mount Everest in a thick fog while suffering from amnesia" (Russell & Norvig 1995, p.111). The climber considers each step by consulting an altimeter and deciding whether to take the step based on the change in altitude. But suppose the climber has access to not only an altimeter, but also additional senses and instruments—for example, the current x and y location, the slope of the ground underfoot, and whether or not the current location is on a trail. These additional "features" may enable the climber to make a more informed, more foresightful, evaluation of whether to take a step.

In real optimization domains, such additional state features are generally plentiful. Practitioners of local search algorithms often append additional terms to their objective function, and then spend considerable effort tweaking the coefficients. This excerpt, from a book on VLSI layout by simulated annealing (Wong, Leong, & Liu 1988), is typical:

> Clearly, the objective function to be minimized is the channel width w. However, w is too crude a measure of the quality of intermediate solutions. Instead, for any valid partition, the following cost function is used:
>
> $$C = w^2 + \lambda_p \cdot p^2 + \lambda_U \cdot U \qquad (1)$$

U measures the sparsity of the horizontal tracks, while p measures the longest path length in the current partition. In this application, the authors hand-tuned the coefficients of the extra state features p^2 and U, setting $\lambda_p = 0.5$ and $\lambda_U = 10$. (We will show that our algorithm learned to assign, counterintuitively, a *negative* value to λ_U, and achieved much better performance.) Similar examples of evaluation functions being manually configured and tuned for good performance can be found in, e.g., (Falkenauer & Delchambre 1992; Szykman & Cagan 1995).

The question we address is the following: can extra features of an optimization problem be incorporated automatically into improved evaluation functions, thereby guiding search to better solutions?

The STAGE Algorithm

STAGE analyzes sample trajectories and automatically constructs predictive evaluation functions. It then uses these new evaluation functions to guide further search. A preliminary version of STAGE, described in

Copyright ©1998, American Association for Artificial Intelligence (www.aaai.org). All rights reserved.

(Boyan & Moore 1997), showed promising performance on VLSI layout. This paper describes an improved version of STAGE with superior results on VLSI layout and thorough results for five other global optimization domains. We also overview the theoretical foundations of STAGE, one consequence of which is an extension allowing STAGE to accelerate non-monotonic search procedures such as WALKSAT.

Learning to Predict

The performance of a local search algorithm depends on the state from which the search starts. We can express this dependence in a mapping from starting states x to expected search result:

$$V^\pi(x) \stackrel{\text{def}}{=} \text{expected best Obj value seen on a trajectory that starts from state } x \text{ and follows local search method } \pi \quad (2)$$

Here, π represents a local search method such as hillclimbing or simulated annealing. $V^\pi(x)$ evaluates x's *promise* as a starting state for π.

For example, consider minimizing the one-dimensional function $\text{Obj}(x) = (|x|-10)\cos(2\pi x)$ over the domain $X = [-10, 10]$, as depicted in Figure 1. Assuming a neighborhood structure on this domain where tiny moves to the left or right are allowed, hillclimbing (greedy descent) search clearly leads to a suboptimal local minimum for all but the luckiest of starting points. However, the quality of the local minimum reached does correlate strongly with the starting position: $V^\pi(x) \approx |x| - 10$. Gathering data from only a few suboptimal trajectories, a function approximator can easily learn to predict that starting near $x = 0$ will lead to good performance.

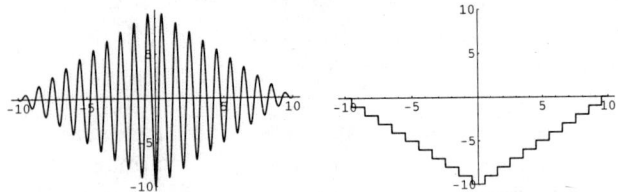

Figure 1: Left: Obj(x) for a one-dimensional minimization domain. Right: the value function $V^\pi(x)$ which predicts hillclimbing's performance on that domain.

We approximate V^π using a function approximation model such as polynomial regression, where states x are encoded as real-valued feature vectors. As discussed above, these input features may encode any relevant properties of the state, including the original objective function Obj(x) itself. We denote the mapping from states to features by $F : X \to \Re^D$, and our approximation of $V^\pi(x)$ by $\tilde{V}^\pi(F(x))$.

Training data for supervised learning of $\tilde{V}^\pi$ may be readily obtained by running π from different starting points. Moreover, if the algorithm π behaves as a Markov chain—i.e., the probability of moving from state x to x' is the same no matter when x is visited and what states were visited previously—then intermediate states of each simulated trajectory may also be considered alternate "starting points" for that search, and thus used as training data for $\tilde{V}^\pi$ as well. This insight enables us to get not one but perhaps hundreds of pieces of training data from each trajectory sampled. For the remainder of this paper, except in the section on WALKSAT, we will set π to be stochastic hillclimbing, rejecting equi-cost moves, terminating as soon as a fixed number (*patience*) of consecutive moves produces no improvement. This choice of π satisfies the Markov property. We will also always use simple linear or quadratic regression to fit $\tilde{V}^\pi$, since training these models incrementally is extremely efficient in time and memory (Boyan 1998).

Using the Predictions

The learned evaluation function $\tilde{V}^\pi(F(x))$ evaluates how promising x is as a starting point for algorithm π. To find the best starting point, we must optimize $\tilde{V}^\pi$ over X. We do this by applying stochastic hillclimbing with $\tilde{V}^\pi$ instead of Obj as the evaluation function.[1]

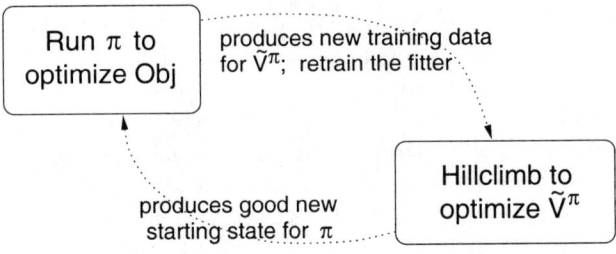

Figure 2: A diagram of the main loop of STAGE

The STAGE algorithm provides a framework for learning and exploiting $\tilde{V}^\pi$ on a single optimization instance. As illustrated in Figure 2, STAGE repeatedly alternates between two different stages of local search: running the original method π on Obj, and running hillclimbing on $\tilde{V}^\pi$ to find a promising new starting state for π. Thus, STAGE can be viewed as a *smart multi-restart* approach to local search.

---

[1] Note that even if $\tilde{V}^\pi$ is smooth with respect to the feature space—as it surely will be if we represent $\tilde{V}^\pi$ with a simple model like quadratic regression—it may still give rise to a complex cost surface with respect to the neighborhood structure on X. The existence of a state with a set of features similar to the current state's does not imply there is a step in state-space that will take us to that state.

STAGE effectively plots a single long trajectory through the state space, periodically switching between the original objective function Obj(x) and the newly-learned evaluation function $\tilde{V}^\pi(x)$. The trajectory is only broken if the $\tilde{V}^\pi$ search phase accepts no moves, indicating that x is a local minimum of *both* evaluation functions. When this occurs, STAGE resets the search to a random starting state.

Illustrative Example

We will now work through a detailed illustrative example of STAGE in operation. Then we will provide results on six large, difficult, global optimization problems.

Our example comes from the practical, NP-complete domain of bin-packing (Coffman, Garey, & Johnson 1996). In bin-packing, we are given a *bin capacity C* and a list $L = (a_1, a_2, ...a_n)$ of *n items*, each having a *size* $s(a_i) > 0$. The goal is to pack the items into as few bins as possible. Figure 3 depicts an example bin-packing instance with thirty items. Packed optimally, these items fill 9 bins exactly to capacity.

Figure 3: A small example bin-packing instance

To apply local search, we define a neighborhood operator which moves a single random item to a random new bin having sufficient spare capacity. STAGE predicts the outcome of stochastic hillclimbing using quadratic regression over two features of the state x:

1. The actual objective function, Obj = # of bins used.
2. Var = the variance in fullness of the non-empty bins. This feature is similar to a cost function term introduced in (Falkenauer & Delchambre 1992).

Figure 4 depicts the first three iterations of a STAGE run on the example instance. On the first iteration (4a), STAGE hillclimbs from the starting state (Obj = 30, Var = 0.011) to a local optimum (Obj = 13, Var = 0.019). Training each of the 18 states of that trajectory to predict the outcome 13 results in the flat $\tilde{V}^\pi$ function shown in 4b. Hillclimbing on this flat $\tilde{V}^\pi$ accepts no moves, so STAGE resets to the initial state.

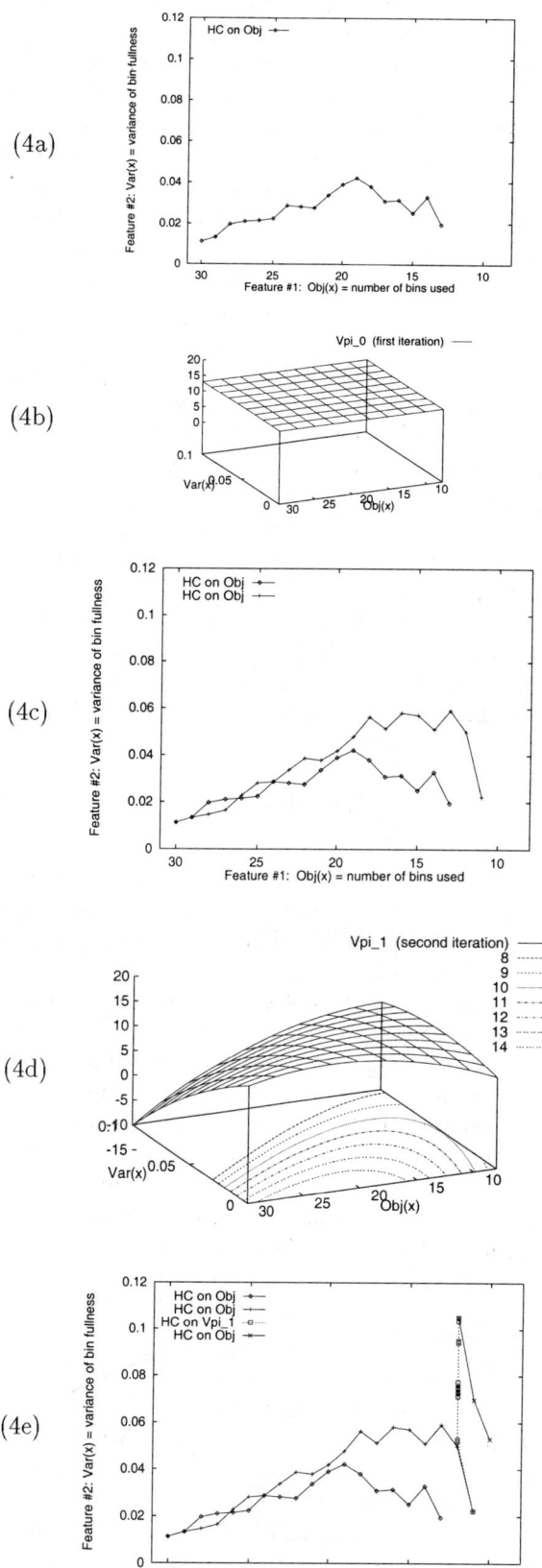

Figure 4: STAGE working on the bin-packing example

On the second iteration of STAGE (4c), the new stochastic hillclimbing trajectory happens to do better than the first, finishing at a local optimum (Obj = 11, Var = 0.022). Our training set is augmented with target values of 11 for all states on the new trajectory. The resulting quadratic $\tilde{V}^\pi$ already has significant structure (4d). Note how the contour lines of $\tilde{V}^\pi$, shown on the base of the surface plot, correspond to smoothed versions of the trajectories in our training set. Extrapolating, $\tilde{V}^\pi$ predicts that the the best starting points for hillclimbing are on arcs with higher Var(x).

STAGE hillclimbs on the learned $\tilde{V}^\pi$ to try to find a good starting point. The trajectory, shown as a dashed line in 4e, goes from (Obj = 11, Var = 0.022) up to (Obj = 12, Var = 0.105). Note that the search was willing to accept some harm to the true objective function during this stage. From the new starting state, hillclimbing on Obj does indeed lead to a yet better local optimum at (Obj = 10, Var = 0.053).

During further iterations, the approximation of $\tilde{V}^\pi$ is further refined. Continuing to alternate between hillclimbing on Obj and hillclimbing on $\tilde{V}^\pi$, STAGE manages to discover the global optimum at (Obj = 9, Var = 0) on iteration seven.

Results

Extensive experimental results are given in Table 1. For six problems with widely varying characteristics, we contrast the performance of STAGE with that of multi-start stochastic hillclimbing, simulated annealing, and domain-specific algorithms where applicable. The hillclimbing runs accepted equi-cost moves and restarted whenever *patience* consecutive moves produced no improvement. The simulated annealing runs made use of the successful "modified Lam" adaptive annealing schedule (Ochotta 1994, §4.5); its parameters were hand-tuned to perform well across the whole range of problems but not exhaustively optimized for each individual problem instance. On each instance, all algorithms were held to the same number M of total search moves considered, and run N times.

Bin-packing

The first set of results is from a 250-item benchmark bin-packing instance (u250_13, from (Falkenauer & Delchambre 1992)). Table 1 compares STAGE's performance with that of hillclimbing, simulated annealing, and *best-fit-randomized* (Coffman, Garey, & Johnson 1996), a bin-packing algorithm with good worst-case performance guarantees. STAGE significantly outperforms all of these. We obtained similar results for all 20 instances in the u250 suite (Boyan 1998).

Channel Routing

The problem of "Manhattan channel routing" is an important subtask of VLSI circuit design. Given two rows of labelled pins across a rectangular channel, we must connect like-labelled pins to one another by placing wire segments into vertical and horizontal tracks. Segments may cross but not otherwise overlap. The objective is to minimize the area of the channel's rectangular bounding box—or equivalently, to minimize the number of different horizontal tracks needed.

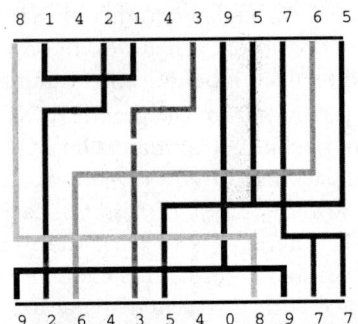

Figure 5: A small channel routing instance

We use the clever local search operators defined by Wong for this problem (Wong, Leong, & Liu 1988), but replace their contrived objective function C (see Equation 1 above) with the natural objective function Obj(x) = the channel width w. Wong's additional objective function terms, p and U, along with w itself, were given as the three input features to STAGE's function approximator.

Results on YK4, an instance with 140 vertical tracks, are given in Table 1. All methods were allowed to consider 500,000 moves per run. Experiment (A) shows that multi-restart hillclimbing finds quite poor solutions. Experiment (B) shows that simulated annealing, as used with the objective function of (Wong, Leong, & Liu 1988), does considerably better. Surprisingly, the annealer of Experiment (C) does better still. It seems that the "crude" evaluation function Obj$(x) = w$ allows a long simulated annealing run to effectively random-walk along the ridge of all solutions of equal cost w, and given enough time it will fortuitously find a hole in the ridge. In fact, increasing hillclimbing's patience to ∞ (disabling restarts) worked nearly as well (D).

STAGE used simple linear and quadratic regression models for learning. The results (E,F) show that STAGE learned to optimize superbly, not only improving on the performance of hillclimbing as it was trained to do, but also finding better solutions on average than the best simulated annealing runs. This seems too good to be true; did STAGE really work according to its design?

We considered and eliminated two hypotheses:

1. *Since STAGE alternates between simple hillclimbing and another policy, perhaps it simply benefits from having more random exploration?* This is not the case: we tried the search policy of alternating hillclimbing with 50 steps of random walk, and its performance (G) was much worse than STAGE's.
2. *The function approximator may simply be smoothing $Obj(x)$, which helps eliminate local minima and plateaus?* No: we tried a variant of STAGE which learned to smooth $Obj(x)$ directly instead of learning $\tilde{V}^\pi(H)$; this also produced much less improvement than STAGE.

Bayes Network Structure-Finding

Given a data set, an important data mining task is to identify the Bayes net structure that best matches the data. We search the space of acyclic graph structures on A nodes, where A is the number of attributes in each data record. Following (Friedman & Yakhini 1996), we evaluate a network structure by a *minimum description length score* which trades off between fit accuracy and low model complexity. STAGE was given the following 7 features:

- mean & standard deviation of the conditional entropy score at each node
- mean & std. dev. of the number of parameters in each node's probability table
- mean & std. dev. of the number of parents of each node
- the number of "orphan nodes"

Results for a large dataset (ADULT2, 30162 records, 15 attributes) are shown in Table 1. All methods found comparably good solutions, although STAGE's performance was slightly better on average.

Radiotherapy Treatment Planning

Radiation therapy is a method of treating tumors. A linear accelerator which produces a radioactive beam is mounted on a rotating gantry, and the patient is placed so that the tumor is at the center of the beam's rotation. Depending on the exact equipment being used, the beam's intensity can be modulated in various ways as it rotates around the patient. A *radiotherapy treatment plan* specifies the beam's intensity at a fixed number of source angles.

A map of the relevant part of the patient's body, with the tumor and all important structures labelled, is available. Also known are good clinical forward models for calculating, from a treatment plan, the distribution of radiation that will be delivered to the patient's tissues. The optimization problem, then, is to produce a treatment plan which meets target radiation doses for the tumor while minimizing damage to sensitive nearby structures. The current practice is to use simulated annealing for this problem (Webb 1991).

Figure 6 illustrates a planar instance of the radiotherapy problem. The instance consists of an irregular-shaped tumor and four sensitive structures (the eyes, the brainstem, and the rest of the head). Given a treatment plan, the objective function is calculated by summing ten terms: an overdose penalty and an underdose penalty for each of the five structures. These ten subcomponents were the features for STAGE's learning.

Objective function evaluations are computationally expensive in this domain, so our experiments considered only 10,000 moves per run. Again, all algorithms performed comparably, but STAGE's solutions were best on average.

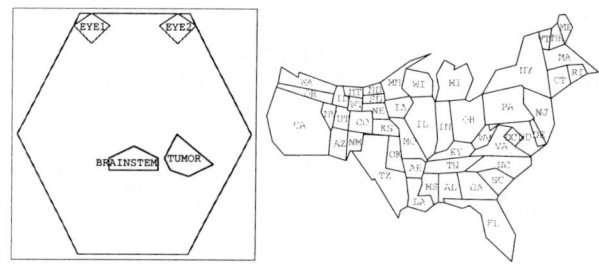

Figure 6: Left: a radiotherapy instance. Right: a cartogram in which each state's area is proportional to its electoral vote for U.S. President.

Cartogram Design

A "cartogram" is a map whose boundaries have been deformed so that population density is uniform over the entire map (Dorling 1994). We considered redrawing the map of the United States such that each state's area is proportional to its electoral vote. The goal is to best meet the new area targets while minimally distorting the states' shapes and borders.

We represented the map as a collection of 162 points in 2-space; each state is a polygon over a subset of those points. The search operator consisted of perturbing a random point slightly; perturbations that would cause two edges to cross were disallowed. The objective function was defined as

$$Obj(x) = \Delta\text{area} + \Delta\text{gape} + \Delta\text{orient} + \Delta\text{segfrac}$$

where Δarea penalizes states for missing their new area targets, and the other three terms penalize states shaped differently than in the true U.S. map. For STAGE, we represented each configuration by the four subcomponents of Obj. Learning a new evaluation

Problem Instance	Algorithm	Performance over N runs		
		mean	best	worst
Bin-packing (u250_13, opt=103) $M = 10^5, N = 100$	Hillclimbing, patience=250	109.38± 0.10	108	110
	Simulated annealing	108.19± 0.09	107	109
	Best-Fit Randomized	106.78± 0.08	106	107
	STAGE, quadratic regression	**104.77± 0.09**	**103**	**105**
Channel routing (YK4, opt=10) $M = 5 \cdot 10^5, N = 100$	(A) Hillclimbing, patience=250	22.35± 0.19	20	24
	(B) Simulated annealing, Obj$(x) = w^2 + 0.5p^2 + 10U$	16.49± 0.16	14	19
	(C) Simulated annealing, Obj$(x) = w$	14.32± 0.10	13	15
	(D) Hillclimbing, patience=∞	14.69± 0.12	13	16
	(E) STAGE, linear regression	**12.42± 0.11**	**11**	**14**
	(F) STAGE, quadratic regression	14.01± 0.77	**11**	31
	(G) Hillclimbing + random walk	17.26± 0.14	15	19
	(H) Modified STAGE—only smooth Obj	16.88± 0.22	14	19
Bayes net (ADULT2) $M = 10^5, N = 100$	Hillclimbing, patience=200	440567± 52	439912	441171
	Simulated annealing	440924± 134	**439551**	444094
	STAGE, quadratic regression	**440432± 57**	439773	**441052**
Radiotherapy (5E) $M = 10^4, N = 200$	Hillclimbing, patience=200	18.822±0.030	**18.003**	19.294
	Simulated annealing	18.817±0.043	18.376	19.395
	STAGE, quadratic regression	**18.721±0.029**	18.294	**19.155**
Cartogram (US49) $M = 10^6, N = 100$	Hillclimbing, patience=200	0.174±0.002	0.152	0.195
	Simulated annealing	**0.037±0.003**	**0.031**	0.170
	STAGE, quadratic regression	0.056±0.003	0.038	**0.132**
Satisfiability (par32-1.cnf, opt=0) $M = 10^8, N = 100$	(J) WALKSAT, noise=0, cutoff=10^6, tries=100	15.22± 0.35	9	19
	(K) WALKSAT + $\delta_w = 0$ (hillclimbing)	690.52± 1.96	661	708
	(L) WALKSAT + $\delta_w = 10$	15.56± 0.33	11	19
	(M) STAGE(WALKSAT), quadratic regression	5.36± 0.33	**1**	9
	(N) STAGE(WALKSAT/Markov), linear regression	**4.43± 0.28**	2	**8**

Table 1: Comparative results on a variety of minimization domains. For each problem, all algorithms were allowed to consider the same fixed number of moves M. Each line reports the mean, 95% confidence interval of the mean, best, and worst solutions found by N independent runs of one algorithm on one problem. Best results are boldfaced.

function with quadratic regression over these features, STAGE produced a significant improvement over hillclimbing, but did not outperform simulated annealing.

Satisfiability

Finding a variable assignment which satisfies a large Boolean expression is a fundamental (indeed, the original) NP-complete problem. In recent years, surprisingly difficult formulas have been solved by WALKSAT (Selman, Kautz, & Cohen 1996), a simple local search method. WALKSAT, given a formula expressed in CNF (a conjunction of disjunctive clauses), conducts a random walk in assignment space which is biased toward minimizing

Obj(x) = # of clauses unsatisfied by assignment x.

When Obj$(x) = 0$, all clauses are satisfied and the formula is solved.

WALKSAT searches as follows. On each step, it first selects an unsatisfied clause at random; it will satisfy that clause by flipping one variable within it. To decide which one, it first evaluates how much overall improvement to Obj would result from flipping each variable. If the best such improvement is positive, it greedily flips a variable that attains that improvement. Otherwise, it flips a variable which worsens Obj: with probability (1-*noise*), a variable which harms Obj the least, and with probability *noise*, a variable at random from the clause. The best setting of *noise* is problem-dependent (McAllester, Kautz, & Selman 1997).

WALKSAT is so effective that it has rendered nearly obsolete an archive of several hundred benchmark problems collected for a DIMACS Challenge on satisfiability (Selman, Kautz, & Cohen 1996). Within that archive, only the largest "parity function learning" instances (nefariously constructed by Kearns, Schapire, Hirsh and Crawford) are known to be solvable in principle, yet not solvable by WALKSAT. We report here results of experiments on the instance par32-1.cnf, a formula consisting of 10277 clauses on 3176 variables. Each experiment was run 100 times and allowed to consider 10^8 bit flips per run.

Experiment J (see Table 1) shows results with the best hand-tuned parameter settings for WALKSAT. The best such run still left 9 clauses unsatisfied. We introduced an additional WALKSAT parameter δ_w, with the following effect: any flip that would worsen Obj by more than δ_w is rejected. Normal WALKSAT has $\delta_w = \infty$. At the other extreme, when $\delta_w = 0$, no harmful moves are accepted, resulting in an ineffective form of hillclimbing (K). However, using intermediate settings of δ_w—thereby prohibiting only the most destructive of WALKSAT's moves—seems not to harm performance (L), and in some cases improves it.

For STAGE's learning, a variety of potentially useful additional state features are available, e.g.:

- % of clauses currently unsatisfied ($= \mathrm{Obj}(x)$)
- % of clauses satisfied by exactly 1 variable
- % of clauses satisfied by exactly 2 variables
- % of variables set to their "naive" setting[2]

Can STAGE, by observing WALKSAT trajectories, learn to combine these features usefully, as it did by observing hillclimbing trajectories in other domains?

Theoretically, STAGE can learn from any procedure π that is proper (guaranteed to terminate) and Markovian. WALKSAT's normal termination mechanism, cutting off after a pre-specified number of steps, is not Markovian: it depends on an extraneous counter variable, not just the current assignment. Despite this technicality, STAGE with quadratic regression (M) very nearly completely solved the problem, satisfying all but 1 or 2 of the 10277 clauses on several runs. With a properly Markovian cutoff criterion for WALKSAT (terminating with probability 1/10000 after each step) and linear instead of quadratic regression (N), STAGE's improvement over plain WALKSAT was about the same. Results on four other 32-bit parity benchmark instances were similar. In these experiments, WALKSAT was run with $noise=25$ and $\delta_w=10$; full details may be found in (Boyan 1998).

Future work will pursue this further. We believe that STAGE shows promise for hard satisfiability problems—perhaps for MAXSAT problems where near-miss solutions are useful.

Transfer

There is a computational cost to training a function approximator on $\tilde{V}^\pi$. Learning from a π-trajectory

---

[2]Given a CNF formula F, the naive setting of variable x_i is defined to be 0 if $\neg x_i$ appears in more clauses of F than x_i, or 1 if x_i appears in more clauses than $\neg x_i$.

of length L, with least-squares linear regression over D features, costs STAGE $O(D^2 L + D^3)$ per iteration; quadratic regression costs $O(D^4 L + D^6)$. In the experiments of the previous section, these costs were minimal—typically, 0–10% of total execution time. However, STAGE's extra overhead would become significant if many more features or more sophisticated function approximators were used.

For some problems such cost is worth it in comparison to a non-learning method, because a better or equally good solution is obtained with overall less computation. But in those cases where we use more computation, the STAGE method may nevertheless be preferable if we are then asked to solve further similar problems (e.g., a new channel routing problem with different pin assignments). Then we can hope that the computation we invested in solving the first problem will pay off in the second, and future, problems because we will already have a $\tilde{V}^\pi$ estimate. We call this effect *transfer*; the extent to which it occurs is largely an empirical question.

To investigate the potential for transfer, we re-ran STAGE on a suite of eight problems from the channel routing literature. Table 2 summarizes the results and gives the coefficients of the linear evaluation function learned independently for each problem. To make the similarities easier to see in the table, we have normalized the coefficients so that their squares sum to one; note that the search behavior of an evaluation function is invariant under linear transformations.

Problem instance	lower bound	best STAGE	learned coefficients $< w, p, U >$
YK4	10	12	$< 0.71, 0.05, -0.70 >$
HYC1	8	8	$< 0.52, 0.83, -0.19 >$
HYC2	9	9	$< 0.71, 0.21, -0.67 >$
HYC3	11	12	$< 0.72, 0.30, -0.62 >$
HYC4	20	23	$< 0.71, 0.03, -0.71 >$
HYC5	35	38	$< 0.69, 0.14, -0.71 >$
HYC6	50	51	$< 0.70, 0.05, -0.71 >$
HYC7	39	42	$< 0.71, 0.13, -0.69 >$
HYC8	21	25	$< 0.71, 0.03, -0.70 >$

Table 2: STAGE results ($M = 10^5, N = 3$) on eight problems from (Chao & Harper 1996).

The similarities among the learned evaluation functions are striking. Like the hand-tuned cost function C of (Wong, Leong, & Liu 1988) (Equation 1), all but one of the STAGE-learned cost functions (HYC1) assigned a relatively large positive weight to feature w and a small positive weight to feature p. Unlike the hand-tuned C, all the STAGE runs assigned a *negative* weight to feature U. The similarity of the learned functions suggests that transfer between problem instances would indeed be fruitful.

The assignment of a negative coefficient to U is surprising, because U measures the sparsity of the horizontal tracks. U correlates strongly positively with the objective function to be minimized; a term of $-U$ in the evaluation function ought to pull the search toward terrible solutions in which each subnet occupies its own track. However, the positive coefficient on w cancels out this bias, and in fact a proper balance between the two terms can be shown to bias search toward solutions with an *uneven* distribution of track sparsity levels. Although this characteristic is not itself the mark of a high-quality solution, it does help lead hillclimbing search to high-quality solutions. STAGE successfully discovered and exploited this predictive combination of features.

Discussion

Under what conditions will STAGE work? Intuitively, STAGE maps out the attracting basins of a domain's local minima. When there is a coherent structure among these attracting basins, STAGE can exploit it. Identifying such a coherent structure depends crucially on the user-selected state features, the domain's move operators, and the regression models considered. What this paper has shown is that for a wide variety of large-scale problems, with very simple choices of features and models, a useful structure can be identified and exploited.

A very relevant investigation by Boese et. al. (Boese, Kahng, & Muddu 1994) gives further reasons for optimism. They studied the set of local minima reached by independent runs of hillclimbing on a traveling salesman problem and a graph bisection problem. They found a "big valley" structure to the set of minima: the better the local minimum, the closer (in terms of a natural distance metric) it tended to be to other local minima. This led them to recommend a two-phase "adaptive multi-start" hillclimbing technique similar to STAGE. A similar heuristic, Chained Local Optimization (Martin & Otto 1994), also works by alternating between greedy search and a user-defined "kick" that moves the search into a nearby but different attracting basin. The main difference is that these authors hand-build a problem-specific routine for finding good new starting states, whereas STAGE uses machine learning to do the same.

Zhang and Dietterich have explored another way to use learning to improve combinatorial optimization: they learn a search strategy from scratch using on-line value iteration (Zhang 1996). By contrast, STAGE begins with an already-given search strategy and uses prediction to learn to improve on it. Zhang reported success in transferring learned search control knowledge from simple job-shop scheduling instances to more complex ones.

STAGE offers many directions for further exploration. Among those currently under investigation are: reinforcement learning methods for building $\tilde{V}^\pi$ more efficiently; algorithms for robust transfer of learned $\tilde{V}^\pi$ functions between instances; and direct meta-optimization methods for feature weighting.

Acknowledgments: The first author acknowledges the support of a NASA GSRP Fellowship.

References

Boese, K. D.; Kahng, A. B.; and Muddu, S. 1994. A new adaptive multi-start technique for combinatorial global optimizations. *Operations Research Letters* 16:101–113.

Boyan, J. A., and Moore, A. W. 1997. Using prediction to improve combinatorial optimization search. In *Proceedings of AISTATS-6*.

Boyan, J. A. 1998. *Learning Evaluation Functions for Global Optimization*. Ph.D. Dissertation, Carnegie Mellon University.

Chao, H.-Y., and Harper, M. P. 1996. An efficient lower bound algorithm for channel routing. *Integration: The VLSI Journal*.

Coffman, E. G.; Garey, M. R.; and Johnson, D. S. 1996. Approximation algorithms for bin packing: a survey. In Hochbaum, D., ed., *Approximation Algorithms for NP-Hard Problems*. PWS Publishing.

Dorling, D. 1994. Cartograms for visualizing human geography. In Hearnshaw, H. M., and Unwin, D. J., eds., *Visualization in Geographical Information Systems*. Wiley. 85–102.

Falkenauer, E., and Delchambre, A. 1992. A genetic algorithm for bin packing and line balancing. In *Proc. of the IEEE 1992 International Conference on Robotics and Automation*, 1186–1192.

Friedman, N., and Yakhini, Z. 1996. On the sample complexity of learning Bayesian networks. In *Proc. 12th Conference on Uncertainty in Artificial Intelligence*.

Martin, O. C., and Otto, S. W. 1994. Combining simulated annealing with local search heuristics. Technical Report CS/E 94-016, Oregon Graduate Institute Department of Computer Science and Engineering.

McAllester, D.; Kautz, H.; and Selman, B. 1997. Evidence for invariants in local search. In *Proceedings of AAAI-97*.

Ochotta, E. 1994. *Synthesis of High-Performance Analog Cells in ASTRX/OBLX*. Ph.D. Dissertation, Carnegie Mellon University Department of Electrical and Computer Engineering.

Russell, S., and Norvig, P. 1995. *Artificial Intelligence: A Modern Approach*. Prentice Hall.

Selman, B.; Kautz, H.; and Cohen, B. 1996. Local search strategies for satisfiability testing. In *Cliques, Coloring, and Satisfiability: Second DIMACS Implementation Challenge*. American Mathematical Society.

Szykman, S., and Cagan, J. 1995. A simulated annealing-based approach to three-dimensional component packing. *ASME Journal of Mechanical Design* 117.

Webb, S. 1991. Optimization by simulated annealing of three-dimensional conformal treatment planning for radiation fields defined by a multileaf collimator. *Phys. Med. Biol.* 36:1201–1226.

Wong, D. F.; Leong, H.; and Liu, C. 1988. *Simulated Annealing for VLSI Design*. Kluwer.

Zhang, W. 1996. *Reinforcement Learning for Job-Shop Scheduling*. Ph.D. Dissertation, Oregon State University.

The Interactive Museum Tour-Guide Robot

**Wolfram Burgard, Armin B. Cremers, Dieter Fox, Dirk Hähnel,
Gerhard Lakemeyer[†], Dirk Schulz, Walter Steiner, and Sebastian Thrun[‡]**

Computer Science Department III
University of Bonn
Bonn, Germany

[†]Computer Science Department
Aachen University of Technology
Aachen, Germany

[‡]School of Computer Science
Carnegie Mellon University
Pittsburgh, PA

Abstract

This paper describes the software architecture of an autonomous tour-guide/tutor robot. This robot was recently deployed in the "Deutsches Museum Bonn," were it guided hundreds of visitors through the museum during a six-day deployment period. The robot's control software integrates low-level probabilistic reasoning with high-level problem solving embedded in first order logic. A collection of software innovations, described in this paper, enabled the robot to navigate at high speeds through dense crowds, while reliably avoiding collisions with obstacles—some of which could not even be perceived. Also described in this paper is a user interface tailored towards non-expert users, which was essential for the robot's success in the museum. Based on these experiences, this paper argues that time is ripe for the development of AI-based commercial service robots that assist people in everyday life.

Introduction

Building autonomous robots that assist people in everyday life has been a long-standing goal of research in artificial intelligence and robotics. This paper describes an autonomous mobile robot, called RHINO, which has recently been deployed at the "Deutsches Museum" in Bonn, Germany. The robot's primary task was to provide interactive tours to visitors of the museum. In addition, the robot enabled people all around the world to establish a "virtual presence" in the museum, using a Web interface through which they could watch the robot operate and send it to specific target locations.

The application domain posed a variety of challenges, which we did not face in our previous research, carried out mostly in office-like buildings. The two primary challenges were (1) navigating safely and reliably through crowds, and (2) interacting with people in an intuitive and appealing way.

1. **Safe and reliable navigation.** It was of ultimate importance that the robot navigated at approximate walking speed, while not colliding with any of the various obstacles (exhibits, people). Three aspects made this problem difficult. First, RHINO often had to navigate through dense crowds of people (c.f. Figures 1 and 2). People often blocked virtually all sensors of the robot for extended durations of time. Second, various exhibits were "invisible" to the robot, that is, the robot could not perceive them with its sensors. This problem existed despite the fact that our robot possessed four state-of-the-art sensor systems (laser, sonar, infrared, and tactile). Invisible obstacles included glass cages put up to protect exhibits, metal bars at various heights, and metal plates on which exhibits were placed (c.f., the glass cage labeled "o1" and the control panel labeled "o2" in Figure 3). Navigating safely was particularly important since many of the exhibits in the museum were rather expensive and easily damaged by the 300 pound machine. Third, the configuration of the environment changed frequently. For example, the museum possessed a large number of stools, and people tended to leave them behind at random places, sometimes blocking entire passages. Museum visitors often tried to "trick" the robot into an area beyond its intended operational range, where unmodeled and invisible hazards existed, such as staircases. For the robot to be successful, it had to have the ability to quickly detect such situations and to find new paths to exhibits if possible.

2. **Intuitive and appealing user interaction.** Tutoring robots, by definition, interact with people. Visitors of the museum were between 2 and 80 years old. The average visitor had no prior exposure to robotics or AI and spent less than 15 minutes with the robot, in which he/she was unable to gain any technical understanding whatsoever. Thus, a key challenge was to design a robot that was "intuitive" and user friendly. This challenge included the design of easy-to-use interfaces (both for real visitors and for the Web), as well as finding mechanisms to communicate intent to people. RHINO's user interfaces were an important component in its practical success.

The specific application domain was chosen for two pri-

Copyright 1998, American Association for Artificial Intelligence (www.aaai.org). All rights reserved.

Fig. 1: RHINO gives a tour

Fig. 2: Interaction with people

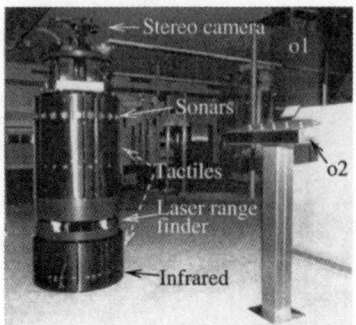
Fig. 3: The Robot and its sensors.

mary reasons. First, we believe that these two challenges, safe navigation and easy-to-use interfaces, are prototypical for a large range of upcoming service robot applications. Second, installing a robot in a museum gave us a unique and exciting opportunity to bridge the gap between academic research and the public.

This paper describes the key components of RHINO's software architecture. The software performs, in real-time, tasks such as collision avoidance, mapping, localization, path planning, mission planning, and user interface control. The overall software architecture consists of approximately 25 independent modules (processes), which were executed in parallel on three on-board PCs and three off-board SUN workstations, connected via a tetherless Ethernet bridge (Thrun *et al.* 1998a). The software modules communicate using TCX (Fedor 1993), a decentralized communication protocol for point-to-point socket communication.

RHINO's control software applies several design principles, the most important of which are:

1. **Probabilistic representations, reasoning, and learning.** Since perception is inherently inaccurate and incomplete, and since environments such as museums change frequently in rather unpredictable ways, RHINO pervasively employs probabilistic mechanisms to represent state and reason about change of state.

2. **Resource adaptability.** Several resource-intensive software components, such as the motion planner or the localization module, can adapt themselves to the available computational resources. The more processing time is available, the better and more accurate are the results.

3. **Distributed, asynchronous processing with decentralized decision making.** RHINO's software is highly distributed. There is no centralized clock to synchronize the different models, and the robot can function even if major parts of its software fail or are temporarily unavailable (e.g., due to radio link failure).

The remainder of this paper will describe those software modules that were most essential to RHINO's success. In particular, it will present the major navigation components and the interactive components of the robots.

Navigation

RHINO's navigation modules performed two basic functions: perception and control. The primary perceptual modules were concerned with localization (estimating a robot's location) and mapping (estimating the locations of the surrounding obstacles). The primary control components performed real-time collision avoidance, path planning, and mission planning.

Localization

Localization is the problem of estimating a robot's coordinates (also called: *pose* or *location*) in x-y-θ space, where x and y are the coordinates of the robot in a 2D Cartesian coordinate system, and θ is its orientation. The problem of localization is generally regarded to be difficult (Cox 1991; Borenstein, Everett, & Feng 1996). It is specifically hard in densely populated domains where people may block the robot's sensors for extended periods of time.

RHINO employs a version of *Markov localization*, a method that has been employed successfully by several teams (Nourbakhsh, Powers, & Birchfield 1995; Simmons & Koenig 1995; Kaelbling, Cassandra, & Kurien 1996). RHINO utilizes a *metric* version of this approach (Burgard *et al.* 1996), in which poses are estimated in x-y-θ space.

Markov localization maintains a probabilistic belief as to where the robot currently is. Let $P(l)$ denote this belief, where l is a pose in x-y-θ space. Initially, when the pose of the robot is unknown, $P(l)$ is initialized by a uniform distribution. To update $P(l)$, Markov location employs two probabilistic models, a perceptual model and a motion model. The perceptual model, denoted $P(s \mid l)$, denotes the probability that the robot observes s when its pose is l. The motion model, denoted $P(l' \mid l, a)$, denotes the probability that the robot's pose is l' if it previously executed action a at location l.

Both models are used to update the robot's belief $P(l)$

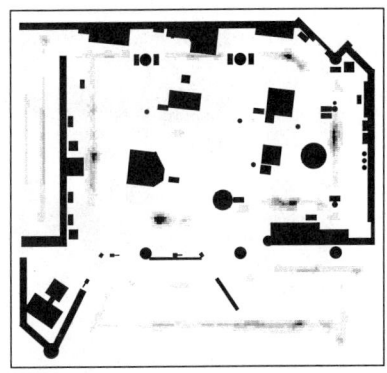
Fig. 4: Global localization. Obstacles are shown in black; probabilities $P(l)$ in gray.

Fig. 5: Typical laser scan in the presence of people. The gray-shaded sensor beams correspond to people and are filtered out.

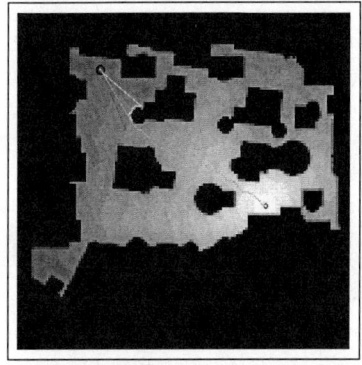
Fig. 6: RHINO's path planner: The grey-scale indicates the proximity of the goal.

when the robot senses, and when it moves, respectively. Suppose the robot just sensed s. Markov localization then updates $P(l)$ according to Bayes rule:

$$P(l \mid s) = \alpha \, P(s \mid l) \, P(l) \quad (1)$$

where α is a normalizer that ensures that the resulting probabilities sum up to one. When the robot moves, Markov localization updates $P(l)$ using the Theorem of total probability:

$$P(l') = \int P(l' \mid a, l) \, P(l) \, dl \quad (2)$$

Here a denotes an action command. These two update equations form the basis of Markov localization. Strictly speaking, they are only applicable if the environment meets a *conditional independence assumption* (Markov assumption), which specifies that the robot's pose is the *only* state therein. Put differently, Markov localization applies only to static environments.

Unfortunately, the standard Markov localization approach is prone to fail in densely populated environments, since those violate the underlying Markov assumption. In the museum, people frequently blocked the robot's sensors, as illustrated in Figure 1. Figuratively speaking, if people line up as a "wall" in front of the robot—which they often did—, the basic Markov localization paradigm makes the robot eventually believe that it is indeed in front of a wall.

To remedy this problem, RHINO employs an "entropy filter" (Fox *et al.* 1998b). This filter, which is applied to all proximity measurements individually, sorts measurements into two buckets: one that is assumed to contain all corrupted sensor readings, and one that is assumed to contain only authentic (non-corrupted) ones. To determine which sensor reading is corrupted and which one is not, the entropy filter measures the relative entropy of the belief state *before* and *after* incorporating a proximity measurement:

$$\Delta H(l, s) := \quad (3)$$

$$-\int_l P(l) \, \log P(l) \, dl + \int_l P(l \mid s) \, \log P(l \mid s) \, dl$$

Sensor readings that increase the robot's certainty ($\Delta H(l, s) > 0$) are assumed to be authentic. All other sensor readings are assumed to be corrupted and are therefore not incorporated into the robot's belief. In the museum, certainty filters reliably identified sensor readings that were corrupted by the presence of people, as long as the robot knew its approximate pose. Unfortunately, the entropy filter can prevent recovery once the robot looses its position entirely. To prevent this problem, our approach also incorporates a small number of randomly chosen sensor readings in addition to those selected by the entropy filter. See (Fox *et al.* 1998b) for an alternative solution to this problem.

In practice, our approach proved to be robust in the museum. RHINO's localization module was able (1) to globally localize the robot in the morning when the robot was switched on (see Figure 4 for a typical belief state during this procedure), and (2) to keep track of the robot's position reliably and accurately (see Figure 5). RHINO's localization error, measured over a set of 118 randomly selected reference locations, was consistently below 15 cm. This accuracy was essential for safe navigation. In the entire six-day deployment period, we are only aware of a single occasion in which the robot suffered a localization error larger than its 30cm safety margin, and this incident was preceded by partial loss of sensing. A comparison between our approach and plain Markov localization (i.e., our approach without the entropy filter) showed that the standard Markov algorithm would have lost track of the robot's position frequently, whenever large crowds surrounded the robot (Fox *et al.* 1998b).

Mapping

Mapping addresses the problem of determining the locations of the obstacles in global world-coordinates. In the museum domain, the problem of mapping was simplified significantly, since an accurate metric map of the museum was provided to the robot beforehand. However, the configuration of the museum changed frequently—people moved stools around and sometimes people blocked entire passages—, making necessary the revision of the map in real-time.

RHINO employed a probabilistic *occupancy grid algorithm* for modifying the initial map, a technique that was originally developed in the mid-eighties and since has been used successfully in many mobile robot applications (Moravec 1988; Elfes 1989). Occupancy grid techniques approximate the environment by a 2D grid, where each grid cell is annotated by a numerical "occupancy value" that represents the probability that this cell contains an obstacle.

In our approach (Thrun 1998), occupancy maps are generated using a Backpropagation-style network, which maps sensor measurements to local occupancy maps. The network is trained off-line, using labeled data obtained in environments where the exact locations of all obstacles are known. After training, the network generates conditional probability estimates for occupancy, denoted $P(o_{x,y} \mid s)$, for grid cells $\langle x, y \rangle$ that lie in the sensors' perceptual range. Figure 7a shows an example sonar scan, taken in a hallway, along with the local map. The shading encodes the likelihood of occupancy: The darker a location, the more likely it is to be occupied. As is easy to be seen, the two walls are detected with high certainty, as is the free space in between. Behind the walls, however, the network outputs 0.5, to indicate maximum uncertainty. Local maps are integrated over time using Bayes rule and likelihood ratios, as described in (Moravec 1988; Thrun 1998):

$$P(o_{x,y} \mid s^1, s^2, \ldots, s^T) = \\ 1 - \left(1 + \frac{P(o)}{1-P(o)} \prod_\tau \frac{P(o_{x,y} \mid s^\tau)}{1-P(o_{x,y} \mid s^\tau)} \frac{1-P(o)}{P(o)} \right)^{-1} \quad (4)$$

Here s^τ denotes the sensor reading at time τ, and $P(o)$ denotes the *prior* probability for occupancy.

Figure 7 shows an example map, in which a narrow passage (upper left) has been blocked, forcing the robot to take a detour. When RHINO reaches a tour item, it reset its map to the original, pre-supplied one. This strategy ensures that passages, once blocked, will not be avoided indefinitely. The ability to modify the map on-the-fly was essential for RHINO's success. In some occasions, lack thereof would have caused the robot to be "stuck" for extended periods of time. RHINO frequently surprised people by successfully carrying out its mission even in the presence of major, permanent obstacles.

Collision Avoidance with "Invisible" Obstacles

RHINO's collision avoidance protects the robot from colliding with obstacles—exhibits and humans alike. It does

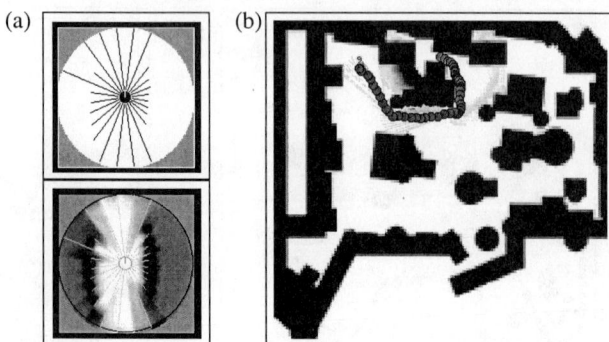

Fig. 7: (a) Sonar scan and local map, generated by the neural network. (b) This map is partially pre-supplied, partially learned. Here the motion planner chooses to take a detour to avoid a blocked passage on the top of this figure.

this by controlling the actual motion direction and the speed of the robot, based on sensor input and based on a "target location" prescribed by the motion planner.

RHINO employed an extension of the dynamic window algorithm (DWA) (Fox, Burgard, & Thrun 1997; Fox *et al.* 1998a). In a nutshell, DWA controls—four times a second—the *translational* and *rotational* velocity of the robot. It does this in accordance with several hard and soft constraints. Hard constraints restrict the space of velocities. They are imposed to avoid velocities that, if chosen, would inevitably lead to a collision, taking into account the robot's inertia and torque limits. Soft constraints, on the other hand, express preferences in the space of control. DWA employs essentially two soft constraints, one which encourages the robot to make progress towards its target location, and one which seeks to maximize the robot's velocity (thereby favoring motion directions towards uncluttered space). Together, these soft constraints lead to a behavior that makes the robot navigate smoothly around obstacles while making progress towards its target whenever possible. In particular, the second constraint ensures that the robot moves at high speeds whenever the situation permits.

The complicating factor in the museum was the presence of the various "invisible" obstacles, as described in the introduction to this article. The basic DWA, just like any other sensor-based collision avoidance approach, does not allow for preventing collisions with such obstacles. To avoid collisions with those, the robot had to consult its map. Of course, obstacles in the map are specified in world coordinates, whereas DWA requires the location of those obstacles in robo-centric coordinates. Thus, we extended the DWA approach to use the maximum likelihood position estimate $l^* = \mathrm{argmax}_l P(l)$ produced by RHINO's localization module. Given the robot's location in the map, the μDWA algorithm (Fox *et al.* 1998a) generates "virtual" proximity measurements and integrates them with the "real" proximity measurements, obtained from the robot's various sensors (tactile, infrared, sonar, laser). This extension of the dynamic window approach proved to be highly effective in the museum. Figure 10 shows a trajectory of the robot travelled during the opening hours of the museum. The length of this trajectory is 1.6km. Apparently, the robot safely avoids "invisible" objects which are marked by the grey-shaded areas. The same mechanism was used to limit the operational range of the robot. With it, the robot successfully withstood all attacks by visitors to force it into unmapped terrain. The collision avoidance routine was also instrumental in quickly finding ways around unanticipated obstacles, such as humans that stepped in the robot's path, or stools left behind by visitors.

In order to deal with situations in which RHINO's localization module assigns high probability to multiple poses, we recently developed a more conservative strategy, which was not ready at the time of the museum installation, but which is now part of μDWA (Fox et al. 1998a). This approach generates "virtual" sensor readings that are with 99% probability *shorter* than the actual distances to the nearest invisible obstacles. Let s be a proximity measurement that one would expect if all invisible obstacles were actually detectable. Then

$$P(s) = \int P(s \mid l) \, P(l) \, dl. \quad (5)$$

is the probability distribution over all s that is induced by the map and the uncertainty in the location l. Suppose the robot's virtual sensor were set to one such value, say s^*. With probability

$$\mu(s^*) := \int_{s > s^*} P(s) \, ds \quad (6)$$

this value s^* will be *smaller* than the real value, that is, with probability μ_{s^*}, the proximity returned by the virtual sensor will be underestimating the true distance to an invisible obstacle, and the robot will be safe. In our implementation of μDWA, s^* is chosen so that $\mu(s^*) \geq .99$, that is, the virtual sensor measurements prevent collisions with invisible obstacles with 99% probability. Empirical results presented elsewhere demonstrate that this extension yields safer control in situations with high uncertainty.

Path Planning

RHINO's path planner generates paths from one exhibit to another. In the museum, such paths could not be pre-determined in advance, since the environment was highly dynamic and the map changed continuously. This made it imperative that the robot adapted its path to the situation on-the-fly.

RHINO's path planner is based on *value iteration*, a popular dynamic programming/reinforcement learning algorithm (Bellman 1957; Howard 1960). Value iteration computes values $V_{x,y}$ for each grid cell $\langle x, y \rangle$. Initially, the grid cell containing the goal is set to 0, and all others are set to ∞. Value iteration then updates the values of all unoccupied grid cells by the value of their best unoccupied neighbor plus by the costs of moving there. After convergence, each value $V_{x,y}$ corresponds to the distance between $\langle x, y \rangle$ and the goal location. Figure 6 shows a value function after convergence. Here the goal is located at the bottom right (white), the robot's location is shown on the top left, and the shading of the space indicates the values $V_{x,y}$. Notice how the values "spread" through the free-space. After convergence, steepest decent in the value function leads to the shortest path to the goal.

As described in more detail in (Thrun 1998), RHINO's path planner employs two additional mechanisms, aimed to increase its run-time efficiency:

1. It uses a bounding box technique to focus computation on regions where it matters.

2. It uses an algorithm similar to value iteration, to identify areas that require re-planning when the map changes. Such changes are often local, leading to a high degree of re-use when planning in dynamic environments.

Paths generated by the path planner are not executed directly; instead, they are passed on to the collision avoidance routine, using visibility considerations to generate intermediate "target locations." When computing these target locations, paths are also post-processed to maximize the robot's side-clearance.

RHINO's path planner is an *any-time* algorithm, i.e., it returns an answer at any time, whenever needed (Dean & Boddy 1988). As a pleasing consequence, the robot never halts to wait for its planner to generate a plan; instead, it moves continuously—unless, of course, it explains an exhibit.

In the museum, running value iteration to completion and finding the *optimal* path usually took less than one second. The path planner proved to be highly effective in adapting to new situations. Figure 7 shows an example, in which a passage is blocked by stools, forcing the robot and the people following it to take a detour. All these decisions are made in real-time, and people usually do not notice the change in venue.

Task Planning

The task planner coordinates the various robot activities related to motion and interaction. It transforms abstract, user-level commands (such as: "give tour number three") into a sequence of actions, which correspond to motion commands (e.g. "move to exhibit number five") or controls for the robot's interface (e.g. "display image four" and "play pre-recorded message number seventeen"). The task planner also monitors the execution of the plan and modifies it if necessary.

 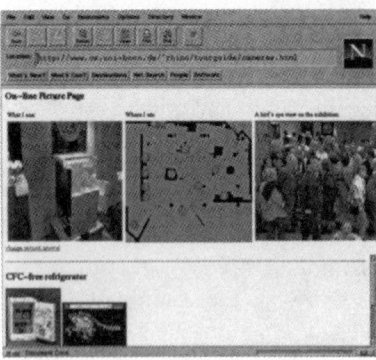 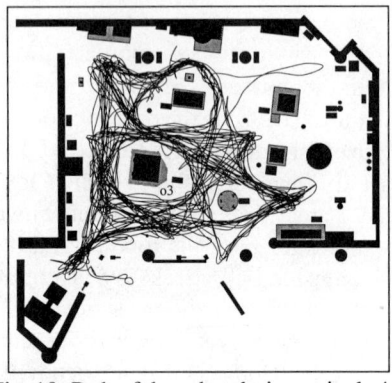

Fig. 8: RHINO's on-board user interface: A screen and four buttons.

Fig. 9: On-line image page for the Web.

Fig. 10: Path of the robot during a single 4.5 hour run (1.6 km).

RHINO's task planner uses GOLOG (Levesque *et al.* 1997), which is an extension of the situation calculus (McCarthy 1968). GOLOG is a language for specifying complex actions using structures like if-then-else or recursive procedures. Based on these specifications, GOLOG generates, in response to a user request, a sequence of elementary (symbolic) actions which provably fulfil this request. To achieve robust and coherent behavior, and to allow the correction of possible errors of the underlying components, we have developed GOLEX. GOLEX complements GOLOG by supplying a run-time component that turns linear plans constructed by GOLOG into (1) hierarchical and (2) conditional plans, and (3) that also monitors their execution. None of these extensions are universal (they are in fact quite limited), but they are all necessary in the context of mobile robot control.

1. **Hierarchical plans.** GOLEX converts each GOLOG action into a pre-specified sequence of elementary commands for RHINO's lower level software. For example, the GOLOG action "move to exhibit number five" is translated into a sequence of robot motion commands ("move to a position next to exhibit number five," "turn towards exhibit number five"), pan/tilt control commands ("track exhibit number five"), and graphical and acoustical display commands ("announce exhibit number five"). The advantage of the hierarchical decomposition is an enormous reduction in the complexity of the task planning problem.

2. **Conditional plans.** Some of GOLOG's actions are translated into pre-specified conditional plans, i.e., plans that are conditioned on the outcome of sensing actions. In GOLEX, conditional plans must always succeed; however, the specific sequence of sub-actions may vary. For example, the action "explain exhibit number five" is translated into a conditional plan that incorporates user feedback (e.g. the user chooses the level of detail in the robot's explanation).

3. **Execution monitor.** GOLEX monitors the execution of its plans. Using time-out mechanisms, it is able to invoke new actions and to plan pro-actively. For example, in the museum, people often pushed no button when they were asked to make a decision. In such situations, GOLEX's execution monitor made a default decision (e.g. it made the robot move to the next tour item) after waiting for a certain amount of time.

GOLEX provided the necessary "glue" between the high-level and the rest of the robot software, thereby bridging the gap between AI-style symbolic reasoning and numerical, sub-symbolic navigation software.

User Interaction

An important aspect of the tour-guide robot is its interactive component. User interfaces are generally of great importance for robots that interact with people. In application domains such as museums, the user interfaces must be intuitive, so that untrained, non-technical users can operate the system without instruction. It must also be appealing, so that people feel attracted to the robot and participate in a tour. While navigation has been studied extensively in the mobile robotics literature, the similarly important issue of human robot interaction has received considerably little attention. RHINO possesses two primary user interfaces, one on-board interface for interacting with people directly, and one on the Web.

On-board Interface

The on-board interface is a mixed-media interface that integrates text, graphics, pre-recorded speech, and sound. When visitors approach the robot, they can choose a tour or, alternatively, listen to a brief, pre-recorded explanation (the "help text"). They indicate their choice by pressing one of four colored buttons shown in Figure 8. When RHINO moves towards an exhibit, it displays an announcement on its screen. It also indicates the direction of its intended destination by continually pointing the camera in the direction of the next exhibit. At each exhibit, the robot plays a brief

hours of operation	47
number of visitors	>2,000
number of Web visitors	2,060
total distance	18.6 km
maximum speed	>80 cm/sec
average speed during motion	36.6 cm/sec
number of collisions	6
number of requests	2,400
success rate	99.75%

Table 1: Survey of key results.

pre-recorded verbal explanation. Users can then request further information about the specific exhibit or, alternatively, make the robot proceed. When a tour is finished, the robot returns to a pre-defined starting position in the entrance area where it awaits new visitors.

An important aspect of RHINO's interactive component is the robot's physical reaction to people. RHINO uses body and head motion and sound to express *intent* and *dissatisfaction*. As mentioned above, RHINO's camera head is used to communicate the intended motion direction. In addition, RHINO uses a modified version of the entropy filter (a probabilistic *novelty filter* (Fox et al. 1998b)) to detect people or other unexpected obstacles. If such obstacles block the robot's path, it uses its horn to indicate its "dissatisfaction." In the museum, people usually cleared the robot's path once they heard the horn. Some even blocked the robot's path intentionally in expectation of an acoustic "reward."

Web Interface

RHINO's Web interface consists of a collection of Web pages, some of which are interactive, others provide background information. In addition to previous Web interfaces (see e.g., (Simmons et al. 1997)), which basically rely on client-pull/server-push mechanisms, RHINO's interface also offers Java applets for instant update of information (both state and intent) as the robot moves. One of the main pages of the Web interface is shown in Figure 9. This page enables Web users to observe the robot's operation on-line. The camera image on the left is obtained with one of RHINO's cameras. The right image is taken with one of two fixed, wall-mounted cameras. The center display shows a map of the robot's environment from a bird's eye perspective, along with the actual location of the robot. The bottom portion of this page contains information about RHINO's current actions. When RHINO is explaining an exhibit, this area displays information about the exhibit, including hyperlinks to more detailed background information. Information may be updated synchronously in user-specified time intervals. Alternatively, certain information (such as the robot's position in its map) can be visualized smoothly, using a Java applet that "simulates" the robot.

Statistics

RHINO was deployed for a period of six days, in which it operated for approximately 47 hours without any significant downtime (see Table 1). Over this period of time, the robot travelled approximately 18.6km. More than 2,000 real visitors and over 600 "virtual" Web-based visitors were guided by RHINO. The robot fulfilled 2,400 tour requests by real and virtual visitors of the museum. Only six requests were not fulfilled, mostly due to scheduled battery changes at the time of the request. Thus, RHINO's overall success-rate was 99.75%. Whenever possible, RHINO chose its maximum speed (80 cm/sec when guiding real people, 50 cm/sec when controlled through the Web). The discrepancy between the top and the average speed (36.6cm/sec), however, was due to the fact that in the presence of obstacles, the collision avoidance module was forced to slow the robot down.

During its 47 hours of operation, RHINO suffered a total of six collisions with obstacles, all of which occurred at low speed and did not cause any damage. Only one of these collisions was caused by a software failure. Here the localization module failed to compute the robot's pose with the necessary accuracy. All other collisions were results of various hardware failures (which were usually caused by neglect on our side to exchange the batteries in time) and by omissions in the manually generated map (which were fixed after the problem was observed).

Overall, RHINO was received with enthusiasm in all age groups. We estimate that more than 90% of the museum's visitors followed the robot for at least a fraction of a tour. Kids often followed the robot for more than an hour. According to the director of the museum, RHINO raised the overall attendance by at least 50%.

Discussion

This paper described the major components of a software architecture of a successfully deployed mobile robot. The robot's task was to provide interactive tours to visitors of a museum. In a six-day deployment period in the Deutsches Museum Bonn, the robot gave tours to a large number of visitors, safely finding its way through dense crowds. RHINO's software integrates a distributed navigation package and modules dedicated to human robot interaction. While the approach is mostly based on existing AI methods of various flavors, it contains several innovations that were specifically developed to cope with environments as complex and as dynamic as the museum. These include a method for localization in dense crowds, an approach for collision avoidance with "invisible" obstacles, a method (GOLEX) that glues together first order logic and numerical robot control, and a new, task-specific user interface. Among the various design principles that came to bear, three stick out as the most important ones. We strongly believe that the use of probabilistic representations for on-line state estimation and learning, the use of resource-adaptive algorithms for state estimation and planning, and the decentralized and distributed nature of the control scheme were all essential to produce the level of robustness and reliability demonstrated here.

What lessons did we learn? From hours of watching the robot operate, we concluded that interaction with people is an essential element in the success of future robots of this and similar kinds. We believe that there is a real need for research in the area of human robot interaction. We are also interested in methods accelerating the installation procedure. For example, one of us spent a week constructing a map of the museum by hand. Based on work by (Lu & Milios 1997; Gutmann & Schlegel 1996; Thrun, Fox, & Burgard 1998), we now have clear evidence that this task can be automated (Thrun et al. 1998b), and the time for acquiring such a map from scratch can be reduced to a few hours.

We see a significant potential to leapfrog much of the technology developed in this and similar projects (e.g., (King & Weiman 1990)) into other service robot applications, such as applications in the areas of health care, cleaning, inspection, surveillance, recreation etc. We conjecture that time is ripe for developing AI-based commercial service robots that assist people in everyday life.

References

Bellman, R. E. 1957. *Dynamic Programming*. Princeton, NJ: Princeton University Press.

Borenstein, J.; Everett, B.; and Feng, L. 1996. *Navigating Mobile Robots: Systems and Techniques*. Wellesley, MA: A. K. Peters, Ltd.

Burgard, W.; Fox, D.; Hennig, D.; and Schmidt, T. 1996. Estimating the absolute position of a mobile robot using position probability grids. In *Proc. of the Fourteenth National Conference on Artificial Intelligence*, 896–901.

Cox, I. 1991. Blanche—an experiment in guidance and navigation of an autonomous robot vehicle. *IEEE Transactions on Robotics and Automation* 7(2):193–204.

Dean, T. L., and Boddy, M. 1988. An analysis of time-dependent planning. In *Proceeding of Seventh National Conference on Artificial Intelligence AAAI-92*, 49–54. Menlo Park, CA: AAAI.

Elfes, A. 1989. *Occupancy Grids: A Probabilistic Framework for Robot Perception and Navigation*. Ph.D. Dissertation, ECE, CMU.

Fedor, C. 1993. *TCX. An interprocess communication system for building robotic architectures. Programmer's guide to version 10.xx.* CMU.

Fox, D.; Burgard, W.; Thrun, S.; and Cremers, A. 1998a. A hybrid collision avoidance method for mobile robots. In *Proceedings of the IEEE International Conference on Robotics and Automation*.

Fox, D.; Burgard, W.; Thrun, S.; and Cremers, A. 1998b. Position estimation for mobile robots in dynamic environments. In *Proceedings of AAAI-98*. AAAI Press/The MIT Press.

Fox, D.; Burgard, W.; and Thrun, S. 1997. The dynamic window approach to collision avoidance. *IEEE Robotics and Automation* 4(1).

Gutmann, J.-S., and Schlegel, C. 1996. Amos: Comparison of scan matching approaches for self-localization in indoor environments. In *Proceedings of the 1st Euromicro Workshop on Advanced Mobile Robots*. IEEE Computer Society Press.

Horswill, I. 1994. Specialization of perceptual processes. Technical Report AI TR-1511, MIT, AI Lab, Cambridge, MA.

Howard, R. A. 1960. *Dynamic Programming and Markov Processes*. MIT Press and Wiley.

Kaelbling, L.; Cassandra, A.; and Kurien, J. 1996. Acting under uncertainty: Discrete bayesian models for mobile-robot navigation. In *Proc. of the IEEE/RSJ International Conference on Intelligent Robots and Systems*.

King, S., and Weiman, C. 1990. Helpmate autonomous mobile robot navigation system. In *Proceedings of the SPIE Conference on Mobile Robots*, 190–198. Volume 2352.

Levesque, H.; Reiter, R.; Lespérance, Y.; Lin, F.; and Scherl, R. 1997. GOLOG: A logic programming language for dynamic domains. *Journal of Logic Programming* 31:59–84.

Lu, F., and Milios, E. 1997. Globally consistent range scan alignment for environment mapping. *Autonomous Robots* 4:333–349.

McCarthy, J. 1968. Situations, actions and causal laws. In *Semantic Information Processing*. MIT Press. 410–417.

Moravec, H. P. 1988. Sensor fusion in certainty grids for mobile robots. *AI Magazine* 61–74.

Nourbakhsh, I.; Powers, R.; and Birchfield, S. 1995. DERVISH an office-navigating robot. *AI Magazine* 16(2):53–60.

Simmons, R., and Koenig, S. 1995. Probabilistic robot navigation in partially observable environments. In *Proc. International Joint Conference on Artificial Intelligence*.

Simmons, R.; Goodwin, R.; Haigh, K.; Koenig, S.; and O'Sullivan, J. 1997. A layered architecture for office delivery robots. In *Proceedings of the First International Conference on Autonomous Agents*.

Thrun, S.; Bücken, A.; Burgard, W.; Fox, D.; Fröhlinghaus, T.; Hennig, D.; Hofmann, T.; Krell, M.; and Schimdt, T. 1998a. Map learning and high-speed navigation in RHINO. In Kortenkamp, D.; Bonasso, R.; and Murphy, R., eds., *AI-based Mobile Robots: Case studies of successful robot systems*. Cambridge, MA: MIT Press.

Thrun, S.; Gutmann, S.; Fox, D.; Burgard, W.; and Kuipers, B. 1998b. Integrating topological and metric maps for mobile robot navigation: A statistical approach. In *Proceedings of AAAI-98*. AAAI Press/The MIT Press.

Thrun, S.; Fox, D.; and Burgard, W. 1998. A probabilistic approach to concurrent mapping and localization for mobile robots. *Machine Learning and Autonomous Robots (joint issue)*. to appear.

Thrun, S. 1998. Learning maps for indoor mobile robot navigation. *Artificial Intelligence*. to appear.

Acceleration methods for numeric CSPs

Yahia LEBBAH, Olivier LHOMME
Ecole des Mines de Nantes - La Chantrerie
4, rue Alfred Kastler - B. P. 20722
44 307 Nantes Cedex 3 - France
{Yahia.Lebbah, Olivier.Lhomme}@emn.fr

Abstract

This paper introduces a new way of accelerating the convergence of numeric CSP filtering algorithms, through the use of extrapolation methods. Extrapolation methods are used in numerical analysis to accelerate the convergence of real number sequences. We will show how to use them for solving numeric CSPs, leading to drastic improvement in efficiency.

Introduction

Many industrial and engineering problems can be seen as constraint satisfaction problems (CSPs). A CSP is defined by a set of variables, each with an associated domain of possible values and a set of constraints on the variables. This paper deals with CSPs where the constraints are numeric relations and where the domains are continuous domains (numeric CSPs). Numeric CSPs can be used to express a large number of problems, in particular physical models involving imprecise data or partially defined parameters.

In general, numeric CSPs cannot be tackled with computer algebra systems, and most numeric algorithms cannot guarantee completeness. The only numeric algorithms that can guarantee completeness – even when floating-point computations are used – are coming either from the interval analysis community or from the AI community (CSP).

Those constraint-solving algorithms are typically a search-tree exploration where a pruning (or filtering) technique is applied at each node. The challenge is to find the best compromise between a filtering technique that achieves a strong pruning at a high computational cost and another one that achieves less pruning at a lower computational cost.

The filtering technique used may be a kind of arc-consistency filtering adapted to numeric CSPs (Davis 1987; Hyvönen 1992; Lhomme 1993). Other works (Lhomme 1993; 1994; Haroud & Faltings 1996) aim at defining concepts of higher order consistencies similar to k-consistency (Freuder 1978). (Faltings 1994; Faltings & Gelle 1997) propose in a sense to merge the constraints concerning the same variables, giving one "total" constraint (thanks to numerical analysis techniques) and to perform arc-consistency on the total constraints. (Benhamou, McAllester, & Van-Hentenryck 1994; Van-Hentenryck, Mc Allester, & Kapur 1997) aim at expressing interval analysis pruning as partial consistencies. All the above works address the issue of finding a new partial consistency property that can be computed by an associated filtering algorithm with a good efficiency (with respect to the domain reductions performed).

Another direction in the search of the best compromise, is to try to optimize the computation of already existing consistency techniques. Optimizing a given consistency technique may itself be of great interest, but providing general methods for optimizing a class of consistency techniques is better. In this category, (Lhomme et al. 1996; Lhomme, Gotlieb, & Rueher 1998) propose a method for dynamically detecting and simplifying cyclic phenomena during the running of a consistency technique. In this paper, we are pursuing the same goal of giving some general methods for accelerating numeric CSPs consistency techniques. Let us outline our approach in very general terms.

1. The computations achieved by numeric CSPs consistency techniques are seen as a sequence.

2. Since numerical analysis provides different mathematical tools for accelerating the convergence of sequences, we study the use of such tools for optimizing our sequences. More specifically, the paper focuses on the use of extrapolation methods.

3. Filtering techniques never lose a solution, they are said to be *complete*. A direct use of extrapolation

methods fails to preserve completeness. We will show how to preserve completeness while using extrapolation methods for accelerating filtering techniques.

The paper is organized as follows. In section 2, some definitions concerning numeric CSPs are summarized. Section 3 presents extrapolation methods. Section 4 shows how to use extrapolation methods to accelerate the convergence of CSP filtering algorithms. Section 5 contains an additional discussion.

Numeric CSPs

This section presents numeric CSPs in a slightly non-standard form, which will be convenient for our purposes.

A numeric CSP is a triplet $<\mathcal{X}, \vec{\mathcal{D}}, \mathcal{C}>$ where:

- X is a set of n variables $x_1, \ldots, x_n$

- $\vec{\mathcal{D}} = (D_1, \ldots, D_n)$ denotes a vector of domains. The ith component of $\vec{\mathcal{D}}$, D_i, is the domain containing all acceptable values for x_i.

- $\mathcal{C} = \{C_1, \ldots C_m\}$ denotes a set of constraints. $var(C)$ denotes the variables appearing in C.

This paper focuses on CSP where the domains are intervals. The following notation is used throughout the paper. The lower bound and the upper bound of an interval D_i are respectively denoted by $\underline{D_i}$ and $\overline{D_i}$. $\vec{\mathcal{D}}' \subset \vec{\mathcal{D}}$ means $D'_i \subset D_i$ for all $i \in 1\ldots n$. $\vec{\mathcal{D}}' \cap \vec{\mathcal{D}}''$ means $(D'_1 \cap D''_1, \ldots, D'_n \cap D''_n)$.

A k-ary constraint $C(x_1, \ldots, x_k)$ is a relation over the reals. The algorithms used over numeric CSPs typically work by narrowing domains and need to compute the projection of a constraint $C(x_1, \ldots, x_k)$ over each variable x_i in the space delimited by $D_1 \times \ldots \times D_k$. Such a projection cannot be computed exactly due to several reasons, such as: (1) the machine numbers are floating point numbers and not real numbers so round-off errors occur; (2) the projection may not be representable as floating point numbers; (3) the computations needed to have a close approximation of the projection of only one given constraint may be very expensive, (4) the projection may be discontinuous whereas it is much more easy to handle only closed intervals for the domains of the variables.

Thus, what is usually done is that the projection of a constraint over a variable is approximated. Let $\pi_i(C, D_1 \times \ldots \times D_k)$ denote such an approximation. All that is needed is that $\pi_i(C, D_1 \times \ldots \times D_k)$ includes the exact projection; this is possible thanks to interval analysis (Moore 1966). $\pi_i(C, D_1 \times \ldots \times D_k)$ hides all the problems seen above. In particular, it allows us

```
proc 2B(inout D⃗)
    while (Op2B(D⃗) ≠ D⃗)
        D⃗ ← Op2B(D⃗)
    endwhile

funct Op2B(D⃗)
    return ∩_{j=1..m} Π_{C_j}(D⃗)
```

Figure 1: 2B–consistency filtering algorithm

not to go into the details of the relationships between floating point and reals numbers (see for example (Alefeld & Hezberger 1983) for those relationships) and to consider only reals numbers.

For notational convenience, the k projections of a k-ary constraint C over $(x_{i_1}, \ldots, x_{i_k})$ are computed by only one operator $\Pi_C(\vec{\mathcal{D}})$. This is a filtering operator over *all* the domains. It performs reductions, if any, over the domains $D_{i_1}, \ldots, D_{i_k}$ and leaves the other domains unchanged. That is: let $\vec{\mathcal{D}}' = \Pi_C(\vec{\mathcal{D}})$
$\forall j \in \{1, \ldots, n\}$

$$D'_j = \begin{cases} D_j & \text{if } x_j \notin var(C) \\ \pi_j(C, D_{i_1} \times \ldots \times D_{i_k}) & \text{if } x_j \in var(C) \end{cases}$$

Most of the numeric CSPs systems (e.g., BNR-prolog (Older & Velino 1990), CLP(BNR) (Benhamou & Older 1997), PrologIV (Colmerauer 1994), UniCalc (Babichev *et al.* 1993), Ilog Solver (Ilog 1997) and Numerica (Van-Hentenryck, Michel, & Deville 1997) compute an approximation of arc-consistency (Mackworth 1977) which will be named 2B–consistency in this paper[1]. 2B-consistency states a local property on a constraint and on the bounds of the domains of its variables (B of 2B-consistency stands for *bound*). Roughly speaking, a constraint C is 2B-consistent if for any variable x_i in C the bounds $\underline{D_i}$ and $\overline{D_i}$ have a support in the domains of all other variables of C (wrt the approximation given by π). 2B-consistency can be defined in our formalism as:

Definition 1 (2B-consistency) *We say that a CSP $<\mathcal{X}, \vec{\mathcal{D}}, \mathcal{C}>$ is 2B-consistent iff $\forall C, \forall i$*
$(C \in \mathcal{C} \wedge x_i \in var(C) \Rightarrow \pi_i(C, D_1 \times \ldots \times D_k) = D_i)$

The fixpoint algorithm in Figure 1 achieves the filtering by 2B–consistency. The operator $Op2B$ applies on the *same* vector $\vec{\mathcal{D}}$ all the Π_C operators. This has the drawback of increasing the upper bound of the complexity, but has the advantage of generating a much

---

[1] We have a lot of freedom to choose $\pi_i(C, D_1, \ldots, D_k)$, so the definition of 2B-consistency here both abstracts 2B-consistency in (Lhomme 1993) and *box*-consistency in (Benhamou, McAllester, & Van-Hentenryck 1994)

more "regular" sequences of domains (see section 5). For the sake of simplicity, AC3-like optimization, which consists in applying only those projection functions that may reduce a domain, does not appear explicitly in this algorithm schema.

We say that a CSP is $2B$-satisfiable if the $2B$ filtering of this CSP does not produce an empty domain.

In the same way that arc-consistency has been generalized to higher consistencies (e.g. path-consistency), $2B$-consistency can be generalized to kB-consistency (e.g. $3B$-consistency (Lhomme 1993)). In the rest of this paper, we focus on $3B$-consistency, but the results can be straightforwardly generalized to kB-consistencies.

$3B$-consistency ensures that when a variable is instantiated to one of its two bounds, then the CSP is $2B$-satisfiable. More generally, $3B(w)$-consistency ensures that when a variable is forced to be close to one of its two bounds (more precisely, at a distance less than w), then the CSP is $2B$-satisfiable.

Definition 2 ($3B(w)$-consistency) *We say that a CSP $< \mathcal{X}, \vec{\mathcal{D}}, \mathcal{C} >$ is $3B(w)$-consistent iff :*

$$\forall i, i \in \{1, \ldots, n\} \Rightarrow$$
$$< \mathcal{X}, \underline{\psi}(\vec{\mathcal{D}}, i, w), \mathcal{C} > \text{ is 2B-satisfiable}$$
$$\text{and}$$
$$< \mathcal{X}, \overline{\psi}(\vec{\mathcal{D}}, i, w), \mathcal{C} > \text{ is 2B-satisfiable}$$

Where $\underline{\psi}(\vec{\mathcal{D}}, i, w)$ (resp. $\overline{\psi}(\vec{\mathcal{D}}, i, w)$) denotes the same domain as $\vec{\mathcal{D}}$ except that D_i is replaced by $D_i \cap [\underline{D_i}, \underline{D_i} + w]$ (resp. D_i is replaced by $D_i \cap [\overline{D_i} - w, \overline{D_i}]$).

$3B$-consistency filtering algorithms, used for example in Interlog (Dassault-Electronique. 1991), Ilog Solver or Numerica, are based on the schema of algorithms given in Figure 2, which uses a kind of proof by contradiction: the algorithm tries to increase the lower bound of D_i by proving that $\underline{\psi}(\vec{\mathcal{D}}, i, w)$ is not $2B$-satisfiable and it tries to decrease the upper bound in a symmetric way.

Implementations using this schema may be optimized considerably, but we do not need to go into details here.

Acceleration by extrapolation methods

This section summarizes the field of extrapolation methods of accelerating the convergence of sequences; for a deeper overview see (Brezinski & Zaglia 1990). Let $\{S_n\} = (S_1, S_2, \ldots)$ be a sequence of real numbers. A sequence $\{S_n\}$ converges if and only if it has a limit S: $\lim_{n \to \infty} S_n = S$.

Accelerating the convergence of a sequence $\{S_n\}$ amounts of applying a transformation $\mathcal{A}$ which produces a new sequence $\{T_n\}$: $\{T_n\} = \mathcal{A}(\{S_n\})$.

```
proc 3B(in w, inout D⃗)
    while (Op3B(D⃗) ≠ D⃗)
        D⃗ ← Op3B(D⃗)
    endwhile

funct Op3B(in D⃗)
    for i := 1 to n do
        if ¬2B-satisfiable(ψ(D⃗, i, w))
            D_i ← D_i + w
        if ¬2B-satisfiable(ψ̄(D⃗, i, w))
            D̄_i ← D̄_i − w
    endfor
    return D⃗
```

Figure 2: $3B(w)$-consistency filtering schema

As given in (Brezinski & Zaglia 1990), in order to present some practical interest the new sequence $\{T_n\}$ must exhibit, at least for some particular classes of convergent sequences $\{S_n\}$, the following properties:

1. $\{T_n\}$ must converge

2. $\{T_n\}$ converges to the same limit as $\{S_n\}$: $\lim_{n \to \infty} T_n = \lim_{n \to \infty} S_n$

3. $\{T_n\}$ converges faster than $\{S_n\}$: $\lim_{n \to \infty} \frac{T_n - S}{S_n - S} = 0$

As explained in (Brezinski & Zaglia 1990), these properties do not hold for all converging sequences. Particularly, a universal transformation $\mathcal{A}$ accelerating all converging sequences cannot exist (Delahaye & Germain-Bonne 1980). Thus any transformation can accelerate a limited class of sequences. This leads us to a so-called *kernel*[2] of the transformation which is the set of convergent sequences $\{S_n\}$ for which $\exists N, \forall n \succeq N, T_n = S$ where $\{T_n\} = \mathcal{A}(\{S_n\})$.

A famous transformation is the iterated Δ^2 process from Aitken (Aitken 1926) $\{T_n\} = \Delta^2(\{S_n\})$, which gives a sequence $\{T_n\}$ of nth term:

$$T_n = \frac{S_n S_{n+2} - S_{n+1}^2}{S_{n+2} - 2S_{n+1} + S_n}$$

The kernel of Δ^2 process is the set of the converging sequences which have the form:

$$S_n = S + \alpha \lambda^n$$

where $\alpha \neq 0$ and $\lambda \neq 1$.

Let us see the behavior of Δ^2 transformation on the following sequence:

$$S_n = \begin{cases} 1 & \text{if } n = 0 \\ S_{n-1}/1.001 & \text{if } n > 0 \end{cases}$$

---

[2]The definition of the kernel given here considers only converging sequences.

Let $\{T_n\} = \Delta^2(\{S_n\})$, we have:

$$S_0 = 1$$
$$S_1 = 0.9990009990009991$$
$$S_2 = 0.9980029960049943 \longmapsto T_0 = 0.0$$
$$S_3 = 0.9970059900149795 \longmapsto T_1 = 0.0$$
$$\ldots$$
$$S_{1000} = 0.36843136759310596 \longmapsto T_{998} = 0.0$$

Δ^2 process enables the limit of that sequence to be found immediately.

Of course we can apply several times the transformation leading to a new transformation. For example, we can apply Δ^2 twice, giving $\Delta^2(\Delta^2(\{S_n\}))$.

Many acceleration transformations (G-algorithm, ϵ-algorithm, θ-algorithm, *overholt*-process,...) are multiple application of transformations (see (Brezinski & Zaglia 1990).

Such accelerating convergence methods have been generalized to sequences of vectors or matrices.

Extrapolation for filtering

Filtering algorithms can be seen as sequences of domains. For example, the sequence $\{\vec{\mathcal{D}}_n\}$ generated by $2B$-filtering is:

$$\vec{\mathcal{D}}_n = \begin{cases} \vec{\mathcal{D}} & \text{if } n = 0 \\ Op2B(\vec{\mathcal{D}}_{n-1}) & \text{if } n > 0 \end{cases}$$

and the sequence $\{\vec{\mathcal{D}}_n\}$ generated by $3B$-filtering is:

$$\vec{\mathcal{D}}_n = \begin{cases} \vec{\mathcal{D}} & \text{if } n = 0 \\ Op3B(\vec{\mathcal{D}}_{n-1}) & \text{if } n > 0 \end{cases}$$

So, in order to optimize a filtering algorithm, it suffices to accelerate the convergence of its associated domains sequence $\{\vec{\mathcal{D}}_n\}$. $\{\vec{\mathcal{D}}_n\}$ is a sequence of interval vectors. There does not exist any method to accelerate interval sequences, but an interval can be seen as two reals and $\vec{\mathcal{D}}$ can be seen as a 2-columns matrix of reals (the first column is the lower bounds, and the second the upper bounds). Thus we can apply the acceleration methods $\{\Delta^2, \epsilon, \theta, \ldots\}$ seen in the previous section.

In our experiments, scalar extrapolations, which consider each element of the matrix — each bound of a domain– independently of the others, appear to be much more robust than vectorial extrapolations. Consequently the results given in the rest of the paper are for scalar extrapolations. For example, the scalar Δ^2 process uses for each bound of domain the last three different values to extrapolate a value.

Two kinds of optimization for filtering algorithms are now given. The first makes a direct use of extrapolation methods while the second is a somewhat tricky one.

First kind of optimization

Let $\{\vec{\mathcal{D}}_n\}$ be a sequence generated by a filtering algorithm. Accelerating the convergence of $\{\vec{\mathcal{D}}_n\}$ can dramatically boost the convergence, as illustrated in the following problem:

$$x*y + t - 2*z = 4, \quad x*\sin(z) + y*\cos(t) = 0,$$
$$x - y + \cos(z)^2 = 0, \quad x*y*z - 2*t = 0$$
$$x \in [0, 1000], y \in [0, 1000], z \in [0, \pi], t \in [0, \pi]$$

The following table shows the domain of the variable t in the $278^{th}, 279^{th}, 280^{th}$ and 281th iterations of $3B$-filtering (after a few seconds). The precision obtained is about 10^{-4}.

it	t
278	[3.14133342842583$\cdots$, 3.14159265358979$\cdots$]
279	[3.14134152921220$\cdots$, 3.14159265358979$\cdots$]
280	[3.14134937684900$\cdots$, 3.14159265358979$\cdots$]
281	[3.14135697924715$\cdots$, 3.14159265358979$\cdots$]

By applying the Δ^2 process on the domains of the iterations $278, 279$ and 280 we obtain the domain below. The precision of this extrapolated domain is 10^{-8}. Such a precision has not been obtained after 5 hours of the $3B$–filtering algorithm without extrapolation.

t
[3.14159265358977$\cdots$, 3.14159265358979$\cdots$]

The extrapolated sequence may or may not converge to the same limit as the initial sequence. This can be explained by the kernel of the transformation: when the initial sequence belongs to the kernel, then we are sure that the extrapolated sequence converges to the same limit. Furthermore, intuition suggests that, if the initial sequence is "close" to the kernel then there are good hopes to get the same limit. However it may be the case that the limits are quite different. This is cumbersome for the filtering algorithms which must ensure that no solution is lost.

We must now address the question of how to apply acceleration methods on filtering algorithms without losing any solution.

Second kind of optimization

We propose below an answer to the question above, for the domain sequences generated by algorithms that are based on the $3B$–algorithm schema of Figure 2.

This answer is built on the proof–by–contradiction mechanism used in $3B$-algorithm: it tries to prove that no solution exists in a subpart of a domain. If such a proof is found, then the subpart is removed from the domain, else the subpart is not removed.

The point is that we may waste a lot of time trying to find a proof that does not exist. If we could predict

```
proc 3B-acc(in w, inout 𝒟⃗)
    while (OpAcc3B(𝒟⃗) ⊂ 𝒟⃗)
        𝒟⃗ ← OpAcc3B(𝒟⃗)
    endwhile

funct OpAcc3B(in 𝒟⃗)
    for i := 1 to n do
      (1).  if ¬2B-sat-predict(ψ(𝒟⃗, i, w))
      (2).    if ¬2B-satisfiable(ψ(𝒟⃗, i, w))
              D_i ← D_i + w
      (3).  if ¬2B-sat-predict(ψ̄(𝒟⃗, i, w))
      (4).    if ¬2B-satisfiable(ψ̄(𝒟⃗, i, w))
              D̄_i ← D̄_i + w
    endfor
    return 𝒟⃗

funct 2B-sat-predict(in 𝒟⃗)
    if it predicts 2B-satisfiability
            by extrapolation methods.
        return true
    else return false
```

Figure 3: Accelerated $3B-acc(w)$ filtering schema

with a good probability that such a proof does not exist, we could save time in not trying to find it. Well, extrapolation methods can do the job !

The idea is simply that if an extrapolated sequence converges to a $2B$-satisfiable CSP (which can be quickly known), then it is probably a good idea not to try to prove the $2B$-unsatisfiability.

Following that idea, the algorithm schema for $3B(w)$-consistency can be modified, as given in Figure 3. The main difference is that before testing for $2B$-satisfiability, it tries to predict $2B$-satisfiability by extrapolation methods.

We artificially separate step (1) from step (2) and step (3) from step (4) in the schema for reasons of clarity only. In an implementation of that algorithm schema, these steps are better taken together: that is $2B$-sat-predict is permanently maintained during the computation of $2B$-satisfiability. The computation may thus be interrupted as soon as the prediction allows it.

The following proposition means that this algorithm schema allows acceleration methods to be applied while keeping the completeness property of filtering algorithms.

proposition 1 (Completeness) *The accelerated $3B-acc(w)$ algorithm does not lose any solution.*

The proof is built on the fact that a domain is reduced only when we have a proof — by $2B$-satisfiability and without extrapolation— that no solution exists for the removed part.

The counterpart of this result is that improvements in efficiency of $3B-acc(w)$ compared with $3B$ may be less satisfactory than improvement provided by the first kind of optimization.

Nevertheless, the improvement in efficiency may also be of several orders of magnitude. For example, let us consider the following example from (Brezinski 1978):

$$-t + 4*x - 1/2 = 0, \quad -x + y^2/2 + t = 0,$$
$$-y + \sin(x) + \sin(y-1) + 1 = 0$$
$$x \in [-3, 3], y \in [-100, 100], t \in [-100, 100]$$

The acceleration method used is Δ^2. To reach a precision of 10^{-8}, we obtained the following results.

algorithm	$3B$	$3B$-acc
CPU-time(sec)	154	0.1
nb-calls-of-$Op2B$	699735	284
nb-calls-of-$Op2B$-$true$	699642	152
nb-calls-of-$Op2B$-$false$	93	132

As we see, the improvement in time is about three orders of magnitude. We gain about 99.95% on successful calls to $Op2B$, thanks to extrapolation methods. However, we have a few more failed calls to $Op2B$ than the standard algorithm.

The first experimentations that have been done over some standard benchmarks of numeric CSPs lead to an average improvement in time of about 3. The overhead in time has always been negligible.

Discussion

Extrapolation methods are worth applying for filtering algorithms when:

- *convergence is slow.* When the convergence of the filtering algorithms is fast, there is little or nothing to gain in applying extrapolation methods. At first sight, one could think that slow convergences do not occur very often in filtering algorithms. This is not true. $2B$-consistency filtering leads relatively often to slow convergence and kB-filtering most of the time leads to slow convergence.

- *sequences to be extrapolated follow a kind of "regularity".* All the work of an extrapolation method is to capture that regularity early in the sequence for predicting the fixpoint of the sequence. Of course, the concept of regularity is only intuitive and may greatly vary depending on the extrapolation method used.

In our experiments, we used a $2B$-filtering as given in Figure 1, which applies the projection functions to the *same* vector of domains. It is in no way mandatory, but its advantage, against a standard AC3-like algorithm that applies the projection functions sequentially, was mainly for studying different extrapolation methods. In fact, the order in which the projection functions are applied in a standard AC3-like algorithm may hide the regularity of the sequence, whereas in our version, this cannot happen. Also, it allows vectorial extrapolation methods to be used much more easily.

The first kind of optimization can be applied over all filtering algorithms. The second kind of optimization for $3B$ consistency algorithms can be straightforwardly generalized to higher consistency algorithms.

Conclusion

A product like Numerica (Van-Hentenryck, Michel, & Deville 1997) has shown that an efficient way of solving numeric CSPs is to put many different algorithmic tools to work together. This paper proposes a new family of tools that can be combined with existing ones easily and at a negligible overhead cost. They consist in applying extrapolation methods over the sequence of domains given by filtering algorithms.

Extrapolation methods can be directly applied, leading to drastic improvements in efficiency, but solutions of the CSP may be lost.

Extrapolation methods can also be used in a more subtle way, allowing solutions of the CSP to be preserved. The idea is that before doing a hard work that may succeed or may fail, we may want to have a strong presumption that it is worth doing. Extrapolation methods are used to give such a presumption.

We are now working on three directions: an efficient AC3-like implementation using only scalar extrapolations; other ways of extrapolating a sequence of domains without loss of solution; the study of the improvement of different extrapolation methods on the different filtering algorithms.

References

Aitken, A. C. 1926. On bernoulli's numerical solution of algebraic equations. In *Proc. R. Soc. Edinb.*, 46:289–305.

Alefeld, G., and Hezberger, J., eds. 1983. *Introduction to Interval Computations*. Academic press.

Babichev, A.; Kadyrova, O. B.; Kashevarova, T. P.; Leshchenko, A. S.; and Semenov, A. 1993. Unicalc, a novel approach to solving systems of algebraic equations. *Interval Computations* 2:29–47.

Benhamou, F., and Older, W. 1997. Applying interval arithmetic to real, integer and boolean constraints. *Journal of Logic Programming* 32(1):1–24.

Benhamou, F.; McAllester, D.; and Van-Hentenryck, P. 1994. Clp(intervals) revisited. In *Proceedings of the 1994 International Symposium*, 109–123.

Brezinski, C., and Zaglia, R., eds. 1990. *Extrapolation methods*. Studies in Computational Mathematics. North-Holland.

Brezinski, C., ed. 1978. *Algorithmes d'accélération de la convergence: étude numériques*. Technip.

Colmerauer, A. 1994. Spécifications de prolog iv. Technical report, GIA, Faculté des Sciences de Luminy,163, Avenue de Luminy 13288 Marseille cedex 9 (France).

Dassault-Electronique. 1991. Interlog 1.0: Guide d'utilisation. Technical report, Dassault Electronique, 55 Quai M. Dassault, 92214 Saint Cloud, France.

Davis, E. 1987. Constraint propagation with interval labels. *Journal of Artificial Intelligence* 32:281–331.

Delahaye, J. P., and Germain-Bonne, B. 1980. Résultats négatifs en accélération de la convergence. *Numer. Math* 35:443–457.

Faltings, B., and Gelle, E. 1997. Local consistency for ternary numeric constraints. In *Proceedings of International Joint Conference on Artificial Intelligence*.

Faltings, B. 1994. Arc consistency for continuous variables. *Journal of Artificial Intelligence* 60(2):363–376.

Freuder, E. C. 1978. Synthesizing constraint expressions. *Communications of the ACM* 21:958–966.

Haroud, D., and Faltings, B. 1996. Consistency techniques for continuous constraints. *Constraints* 1(1–2):85–118.

Hyvönen, E. 1992. Constraint reasoning based on interval arithmetic: the tolerance propagation approach. *Journal of Artificial Intelligence* 58:71–112.

Ilog., ed. 1997. *ILOG Solver 4.0, Reference Manual*. Ilog.

Lhomme, O.; Gotlieb, A.; Rueher, M.; and Taillibert, P. 1996. Boosting the interval narrowing algorithm. In *Proc. of the 1996 Joint International Conference and Symposium on Logic Programming*, 378–392. MIT Press.

Lhomme, O.; Gotlieb, A.; and Rueher, M. 1998. Dynamic optimization of interval narrowing algorithms. *Journal of Logic Programming* Forthcoming.

Lhomme, O. 1993. Consistency techniques for numeric CSPs. In *Proceedings of International Joint Conference on Artificial Intelligence*, 232–238.

Lhomme, O. 1994. *Contribution à la résolution de contraintes sur les réels par propagation d'intervalles*. Ph.D. Dissertation, Université de Nice — Sophia Antipolis BP 145 06903 Sophia.

Mackworth, A. 1977. Consistency in networks of relations. *Journal of Artificial Intelligence* 8(1):99–118.

Moore, R., ed. 1966. *Interval Analysis*. Prentice Hall.

Older, W. J., and Velino, A. 1990. Extending prolog with constraint arithmetic on real intervals. In *Proc. of IEEE Canadian conference on Electrical and Computer Engineering*, 14.1.1–14.1.4. IEEE Computer Society Press.

Van-Hentenryck, P.; Mc Allester, D.; and Kapur, D. 1997. Solving polynomial systems using branch and prune approach. *SIAM Journal on Numerical Analysis* 34(2):797–827.

Van-Hentenryck, P.; Michel, L.; and Deville, Y., eds. 1997. *Numerica, a modeling language for global optimization*. the MIT press.

Agents

Minimal Social Laws

David Fitoussi and Moshe Tennenholtz
Faculty of Industrial Engineering and Management
Technion–Israel Institute of Technology
Haifa 32000, Israel

Abstract

Research on social laws in computational environments has proved the usefulness of the law-based approach for the coordination of multi-agent systems. Though researchers have noted that the imposition of a specification could be attained by a variety of different laws, there has been no attempt to identify a criterion for selection among alternative useful social laws. We propose such a criterion which is based on the notion of *minimality*. A useful social law puts constraints on the agents' actions in such a way that as a result of these constraints, they are able to achieve their goals. A minimal social law is a useful social law that minimizes the amount of constraints the agents shall obey. Minimal social laws give an agent maximal flexibility in choosing a new behavior as a function of various local changes either in his capabilities or in his objectives, without interfering with the other agents. We show that this concept can be usefully applied to a problem in robotics and present a computational study of minimal social laws.

1. Introduction

The design of an agent which is about to operate in a multi-agent environment is quite different from the design of an agent which performs his activities in isolation from other agents. Typically, a plan that would have allowed an agent to obtain his goals had he operated in isolation might yield unexpected results as a consequence of other agents' activities. Various approaches to multi-agent coordination have been considered in the DAI literature (Bond & Gasser 1988; Durfee 1992). We could, for instance, subordinate the agents to a central controller. This approach may be useful in various domains (Stuart 1985; Lansky 1988), but might suffer from well-known limitations (e.g. bottleneck at the central site or sensitivity to failure). Another approach is to design rules of encounter, i.e. rules which determine the agent's behavior (and in particular, the structure of negotiation) when his activities

Copyright ©1998, American Association for Artificial Intelligence (www.aaai.org). All rights reserved.

interfere with those of another agent (Rosenschein & Zlotkin 1994; Kraus & Wilkenfeld 1991). Rules of encounter may be quite useful for conflict resolution, but might sometimes be inefficient, requiring repeated negotiations to solve on-line conflicts.

In this paper we consider an intermediate approach to coordination, referred to as the *artificial social systems* approach (Moses & Tennenholtz 1990; Shoham & Tennenholtz 1995). An artificial social system institutes a *social law* (Shoham & Tennenholtz 1995; Minsky 1991a; Briggs & Cook 1995) that the agents shall obey. Intuitively, a social law restricts, off-line, the actions legally available to the agents, and thus minimizes the chances of an on-line conflict, and the need to negotiate. Similarly to a code of laws in a human society (Rousseau 1762), an artificial social law regulates the individual behavior of the agents and benefits the community as a whole. Yet, the agents should still be able to achieve their goals, or any other specification of the system, and restricting their legal actions to a too wide extent might leave them with no possible way to do so. Consider for instance a domain consisting of roads on which our agents travel. These roads cross one another at junctions where total freedom on the side of the agents makes an accident a likely event. In order to guarantee accident-free traffic we could set a law that allows an agent to enter an intersection only if the crossing road is free. This law certainly prevents accidents. However, it restricts the agents too much. Although we have guaranteed an accident-free environment, we have also introduced a possibility of a deadlock: when two agents reach the intersection via crossing roads, they might find themselves waiting indefinitely for the crossing road to get free before initiating their move. This example illustrates the fact that we must be careful in designing social laws: Only useful social laws, i.e laws which guarantee that each agent achieves his goals, are to be considered. In the example above, the law could oblige the agents to cross the intersection one at a time, in a round-robbin policy. Roughly speaking, a useful law will set constraints on the set of actions available to the agents, but not so much that they cannot achieve their goals anymore.

The previous discussion emphasizes that meeting the system specification is an essential requirement for accepting a candidate social law. This raises the question of whether this condition is the only requirement one may need to consider. Should we be satisfied once the law we designed guarantees the system specification? Clearly, there might still be quite a diversity of laws with such a characteristic. In this paper, we look for a way to further classify social laws, and define the notion of *minimal social laws* on which we found our analysis. The idea behind minimal social laws is to prefer a useful social law to another useful social law if the former imposes less restrictions than the other. Hence, minimal social laws capture the idea of maximal individual flexibility. We wish to enable the agents to behave arbitrarily, as long as the original specification of the system can be guaranteed. There is no need to disallow particular actions if doing so will not prevent other agents from obtaining their goals. We further discuss the implications of choosing minimal social laws in the following sections.

The study of social laws has concerned itself with various semantic and computational issues, as well as with applications (Onn & Tennenholtz 1997; Ben-Yitzhak & Tennenholtz 1997). A problem that we believe to be essential to the understanding of social laws and their role in multi-agent systems is the search for an optimal law according to some measure of optimality. With this purpose in mind, we shall now investigate the notion of minimal social laws. The remainder of this paper is structured as follows. In Section 2 we introduce and define minimal social laws. In Section 3 we present a study of minimal social laws in the context of mobile robots, or Automated Guided Vehicles (Sinreich 1995; Latombe 1991). In Section 4 we present a computational study of minimal social laws. We show that the problem of deciding whether a law can be minimized by dropping constraints on actions is NP-hard. We then show that an efficient algorithm can be obtained in a restricted setting.

2. Minimal Social Laws

A central issue in the design of social laws, which has not been addressed yet is the design of optimal laws, according to some measure of optimality. Given a system of agents and a specification, the job of the designer is to find an implementation consistent with this specification. A possible way to come up with a suitable implementation will be to identify a strategy profile such that if each agent acts according to the strategy assigned to him in this profile, the specification is satisfied. This behavior will then be enforced and serve as the law of the system (Minsky 1991a; 1991b). Clearly, this law will be consistent with the system specification (according to which it has been designed). Most often, a less restrictive law will exist, and we should be able to compare the two laws. How to do so? When could we say that we have found an optimal law, and under which criterion?

Following the literature on mechanism design in Economics (Kreps 1990) a law could be considered as optimal if it brings maximal utility to the designer of the system. Although legitimate, this definition does not capture the fact that the purpose of social laws is to provide a flexible framework for a system to evolve in. This will therefore motivate another notion of optimality, that we call minimality, and which we would like to relate to the impact social laws have on the dynamics of the system (and its components).

Roughly speaking, given two different useful laws l_1 and l_2, we say that l_2 is smaller than l_1 if the set of behaviors induced by strategies consistent with l_1 is included in the set of behaviors induced by strategies consistent with l_2 (i.e., if we regard a law l as a set of restrictions, l_2 imposes *less* restrictions than l_1). Intuitively, a smaller law is a law that rules out less behaviors consistent with the agents' goals. We then relate the size of a law to optimality in the following way: a useful social law l^* is minimal (and optimal) for some system specification, if-f for any other useful social law l, l is not smaller than l^*.

A minimal law will grant the agents maximal freedom in the process of choosing an appropriate behavior for achieving their goals, while ensuring that they conform to the system specification. Systems with smaller social laws are therefore more robust to changes in the environment specification or in the capabilities of the agents. Notice that minimal laws need not be unique, and choosing among them might require some other exogenous criterion (either quantitative or qualitative).

We now define the notions of useful and minimal social laws in the framework of a general strategic model. For ease of exposition, we present the definitions for environments consisting of two agents. Extension to the case of n agents ($n \geq 2$) follows easily.

Definition 1 *An* environment *is a tuple* $\langle N, S_1, S_2 \rangle$, *where* $N = \{1, 2\}$ *is a set of agents, and* S_i *is a set of strategies available to agent* i.

Given an environment, agents are assigned goals which they must fulfil by selecting an appropriate strategy among their possible strategies. In addition, there might be some safety goals that should always be guaranteed.

Definition 2 *Given an environment* $\langle N, S_1, S_2 \rangle$, *a goal g is a subset of the Cartesian product over the agents' strategy spaces, i.e., $g \subseteq S_1 \times S_2$.*

The above definition captures goals in very general terms. Roughly speaking, a goal is associated with the set of joint strategies in which it is indeed obtained.

We distinguish between several sets of goals. Let us denote by G_i the set of *liveness goals for agent i*. These are goals that agent i need to obtain. Naturally, at a given initial state the agent may wish to obtain a particular goal and another goal may be irrelevant.[1] In addition, there is a set G_{safe} of *safety goals*. These are goals that should always be obtained. The formal definition of goal achievement for liveness and safety goals will be given below.

The purpose of (useful) social laws is to set regulations that ensure safety and guarantee that liveness is achievable. When searching for minimal social laws, we seek a minimal set of such regulations. Given an environment and a goal for agent i, it is not certain that the agent has a strategy such that, independently of the strategy profile chosen by his fellow agents, he will achieve his goals. The job of the designer is to devise a social law (if one exists) which makes sure that each agent in the resulting system achieves his goals, regardless of the (legal) behavior chosen by the other agents. Fulfilling this condition will qualify the law as useful.

Definition 3 *Given an environment* $< N, S_1, S_2 >$, *and given the sets of goals G_1, G_2, and G_{safe}, a social law is a set of restrictions $SL = < \overline{S_1}, \overline{S_2} >$ such that $\overline{S_1} \subseteq S_1$ and $\overline{S_2} \subseteq S_2$. SL is useful if:*

1. *for every goal $g_{1_i} \in G_1$ there exists $s_{1_i} \in S_1 \setminus \overline{S_1}$ such that for all $s_2 \in S_2 \setminus \overline{S_2}$ we have $(s_{1_i}, s_2) \in g_{1_i}$.*

2. *for every goal $g_{2_i} \in G_2$ there exists $s_{2_i} \in S_2 \setminus \overline{S_2}$ such that for all $s_1 \in S_1 \setminus \overline{S_1}$ we have $(s_1, s_{2_i}) \in g_{2_i}$.*

3. *for every $g_j \in G_{safe}$ and for all $s_1 \in S_1 \setminus \overline{S_1}$, $s_2 \in S_2 \setminus \overline{S_2}$, we have that $(s_1, s_2) \in g_j$.*

Notice that in general, social laws need not be symmetric and may assign roles to agents.[2] In addition, notice that a social law precisely defines which strategies are allowed and which are not (see the semantics of artificial social systems in (Moses & Tennenholtz 1995)). Hence, a social law is different from a refined specification in which the set of allowed actions for a particular agent is to be determined at a later point (e.g., do not collide will not be a typical social law, but drive in the right lane will be one).

As discussed before, social laws differ in their properties, and some (useful) social laws are more stringent than others. Our approach to selecting among laws is to prefer those that satisfy the safety and liveness conditions with minimal constraints. Formally,

Definition 4 *Consider an environment with a specification of liveness and safety goals. A useful social law $SL = < \overline{S_1}, \overline{S_2} >$ is minimal if there is no other useful social law $SL' = < S'_1, S'_2 >$ that satisfies $S'_i \subseteq \overline{S_i}$ for all i.*

In the sequel we will refer, unless stated otherwise, to minimal useful social laws as *minimal social laws*. It is quite clear that if an agent need to modify his behavior (such a change might be motivated e.g., by changes in his capabilities or in his goals), minimal social laws will grant him maximal freedom to do so.

This will be illustrated in the next section and in part of our computational study. The reader should be careful not to confuse minimality and anarchy: minimality is bounded by the need to satisfy the basic specification (including safety and liveness goals). Needless to say, from time to time, changes in the system and new requirements require a re-design of the social law. The role of minimal social laws is to serve as a basic optimization tool in between these transitions, allowing the agents maximal choice of behaviors (in order to adapt to changes) while enabling them to obtain the original specification. It is this delicate tradeoff between free choice and the need to obtain the original specification that minimality attempts to capture.

3. A case study: AGVs in a circular automated assembly line

In this section we study minimal social laws in the domain of Automated Guided Vehicles (AGVs). We wish to emphasize that although we use this study mainly for purposes of illustration, the simple setting discussed below and variants of it are quite popular in the AGVs literature (Sinreich 1995).

In a single-robot automated assembly line, a robot is programmed to perform some activity which will lead it to a goal state, i.e. a situation where its goal has been fulfilled. When several robots are acting together, interactions between the actions of the robots may tamper with normal operation. To make the ideas more concrete, let us consider a simple automated assembly line, where m robots can move between n stations in

---

[1] The initial state is implicit in the agent's strategy in our general model. It will be treated more specifically in our more concrete applications and computational study.

[2] This point is discussed in a more complete version of this paper, and is omitted due to space constraints.

a circular fashion ($2 \leq m \leq n$). This domain is represented by a connected undirected graph $G = (V, E)$ where $|V| = n, |E| = n$ and for all $v \in V, deg(v) = 2$ (where $deg(v)$ is the degree of the vertex v) i.e. the domain is represented by a graph with n vertices and a ring topology. Each node in the ring represents a station. In our simple model, a robot can move at time t (we will assume that time steps are discrete and that time is infinite) from the station it stands at to one of its two neighbors, or stay immobile. All the robots move at the same speed, and a robot which left a station at time t will reach one of the adjacent stations at time $t+1$. A collision occurs when two robots are at the same station. We will assume knowledge of the immediate environment, in the sense that each robot can observe the state (occupied or free) of the two stations following it (in clockwise order), and the two stations preceding it. Initially the system may be in any configuration where no collision occurs.

The specification of the system consists of liveness and safety goals. A liveness goal specifies a particular station to be reached. We will assume that any of the stations can be the target of such a goal. The safety goal prohibits collisions. We now describe a simple social law which obtains this specification:

Traffic Law 1: Each robot is required to move constantly clockwise, from one station to the other along the ring.

It is easy to show that the following holds:

Proposition 1 *Traffic Law 1 guarantees that no collision will occur and that each robot will reach any location it might want to get to in $O(n)$ steps.*

Although very simple (and certainly as a consequence of its simplicity), Traffic Law 1 is also very constraining. It does not leave any choice to the robot when selecting its actions. Notice that from a design perspective it is not enough to require usefulness (that is, meeting the system requirements) from a law, since a useful law might be too tightly related to the specification. There is no need to put a particular restriction on a robot, if this restriction does not interfere with goal achievement by other robots or might lead to unsafe situations. For example, we may wish to allow a robot to move back and forth as it wishes, in order to obtain some temporary new goals, as long as the basic specification can also be fulfilled. Hence, we need to go further and examine the notion of a minimal law.

Note that our study fits nicely in the general model presented in the previous section. Strategies are built using the three basic actions a robot can take at each station (move left, right, or rest). The state of a robot consists of its recent location/observation and its history, and a strategy for a a robot will be a function from its state to action. Goals involve getting from one station to another station on the ring (a liveness goal) as well as avoiding collisions when moving around (a safety goal). We now present a minimal social law for the related setting.

Traffic Law 2:

1. Staying immobile is forbidden if the station which can be reached by a single anti-clockwise movement is occupied.

2. Moving anti-clockwise is allowed only if the two stations which can be reached by moving anti-clockwise *twice* are free.

Proposition 2 *Traffic Law 2 is a minimal (and useful) social law.*

It is easy to check that when the robots follow Traffic Law 2, they can still choose behaviors which are as efficient as the one induced by Traffic Law 1 (according to the basic specification). Still, Traffic Law 2 is to be prefered as it adds maximal flexibility.

4. A computational study of minimal social laws

In this section we initiate a computational study of minimal social laws. We wish to emphasize that we see the design of social laws, and minimal social laws in particular, as an off-line activity. This implies that the automatic synthesis of minimal social laws, its considerable importance notwithstanding, is not the ultimate way to design them. As we showed in the previous section, minimal social laws are central to the design of specific social systems and address issues not necessarily related to computational problems. Nevertheless, a computational study of minimal social laws can shed light both on their design and on their connection to related concepts and issues.

We model a (two-agent) *system* as a tuple $S = (L_1, L_2, c_0, A, A_1, A_2, \tau)$ where L_i is a finite set of states of agent i, $c_0 \in L_1 \times L_2$ is an initial configuration, A is a finite set of actions, A_i is a function from L_i to 2^A that determines the actions that are physically possible for agent i (as a function of its state), and τ is a transition function $\tau : L_1 \times L_2 \times A_1 \times A_2 \to L_1 \times L_2$.

A plan for agent i is a total function from L_i to A, such that the action prescribed to agent i by the plan at any state $s \in L_i$ is in $A_i(s)$. An execution of a plan $\mathcal{P}$ by agent i is a sequence $s_0, s_1, \ldots, s_k$ of states in L_i, where s_0 is the state of agent i in c_0, and where the s_i's are the states visited by agent i when it follows his plan and the other agent follows one of his possible plans. An execution of a joint plan (consisting of one plan for each agent) is the sequence of configurations reached by following it (by both agents respectively). We assume that each state includes a time stamp, so that an action will lead from a state with time stamp t to a state with time stamp $t+1$.

A liveness goal for agent i is associated with a state $s_{goal} \in L_i$. A *safety* goal is associated with a subset of $L_1 \times L_2$. A plan for agent i is said to *guarantee* a liveness goal s_{goal} if all of its executions include s_{goal}, and the length of the prefix up to the state s_{goal} in each execution is polynomially bounded (in the size of the system, that we take to be $|A| + max_i |L_i|$). A system is said to guarantee a safety goal g_{safe} if there does not exist an execution of a joint plan in the system that includes configurations which are not in g_{safe}.

A social law $\sigma \in \Sigma$ is a set of functions, one for each agent, that restrict the plans available to the agents. Formally, a social law σ consists of functions $\langle A'_1, A'_2 \rangle$, for agents 1 and 2 respectively, where A'_i is a function from L_i to 2^A that defines the subset of actions prohibited for agent i in each state ($A'_i(s) \subseteq A_i(s)$ for every agent i and state $s \in L_i$). A social law σ and a system S induce a *social system* S_σ similar to S, where the A_i functions are altered based on the functions A'_i (i.e., in the state s only actions in $A_i(s) \setminus A'_i(s)$ are allowed). The social law σ is useful if the system guarantees each safety goal (regardless of the law-abiding strategies chosen by the agents), and for every liveness goal s_{goal} of agent i there exists a plan $\mathcal{P}$ in S_σ that guarantees s_{goal}.

Consider the set Σ_S of useful social laws for the system S. We define a partial order $\prec$ on the set Σ_S of useful social laws: given two social laws $\sigma_1 = \langle A_1^{\sigma_1}, A_2^{\sigma_1} \rangle$ and $\sigma_2 = \langle A_1^{\sigma_2}, A_2^{\sigma_2} \rangle$ in Σ_S, we say that $\sigma_1 \prec \sigma_2$ if $A_i^{\sigma_1}(s) \subseteq A_i^{\sigma_2}(s)$ for all i and all $s \in L_i$, with at least one strict inclusion for one s and i. A minimal social law σ_i is a useful social law such that there is no useful social law σ_j in Σ_S, $\sigma_j \neq \sigma_i$, that satisfies $\sigma_j \prec \sigma_i$.

Roughly speaking, the algorithm we have in mind when searching for minimal social laws starts from a useful social law and decrements the set of constraints. We can formulate the decision problem underlying this algorithm as follows: given a system, an appropriate useful social law, and a pair that consists of a state s and an action a prohibited in s for agent i, can we allow i to take action a in s, i.e do we still remain with a useful social law after such an addition? The answer to this question reveals an interesting connection between problems of planning with incomplete information and the design of minimal social laws. We can show:

Theorem 1 *Given a system S, and a useful social law σ that prohibits action a in state s of agent 1, deciding whether by allowing a in s we remain with a useful social law, is NP-hard.*

The above theorem shows that a most basic question in the construction of minimal social laws is NP-hard. The proof of this theorem is not less important than its statement. Although the proof is omitted from this version of the paper, we wish to emphasize that it exposes a connection between the construction of minimal social laws and the problem of Planning while Learning (Safra & Tennenholtz 1994). In Planning while Learning (PWL) we look for a plan which achieves an agent's goal for any environment behavior (while learning on the structure of the environment). As it turns out, by allowing a forbidden action we may move from a situation where goals are guaranteed with simple plans, to a situation where we need to answer the question of whether a goal is achievable regardless of the environment behavior. This situation is captured by a reduction from the PWL-problem (which is known to be NP-complete) to our problem.

The above result leads us to consider a special class of systems. In the sequel, we study the case where an agent's basic goal is to follow a predefined plan $\mathcal{P}_i$. This goal or the agents' capabilities may change over time and therefore, we wish to avoid the much too restricted law which would oblige each agent to follow this and only this plan. We show that an efficient incremental algorithm for the computation of minimal social laws exists for this class of systems.

Given a system, consider a pair of plans $\mathcal{P}_1$ and $\mathcal{P}_2$, where $\mathcal{P}_i$ is a plan for agent i. Let t_i be a bound on the number of steps of $\mathcal{P}_i$. Let $(s_0^i, s_1^i, \ldots, s_{t_i}^i)$ be the execution of the joint plan $(\mathcal{P}_1, \mathcal{P}_2)$ projected on the states of agent i. We will associate this execution with the goal of agent i. In the AGVs example this sequence can be associated with a sequence of stations $l_1, l_2, \ldots, \ldots$ where l_{i+1} and l_i are neighboring stations. Basically, this kind of goals is quite typical in systems where agents must follow given protocols. Such systems also provide an excellent illustration of the role of social systems, namely to allow maximal freedom by relaxing unnecessary constraints.

The Minimal Social Law Algorithm (MSLA)

1. Let s_k^i denote the k-th state to be visited in the execution that corresponds to the achievement of the original goal. Let s_0^i denote the initial state of agent i. Let $(a_0^i, \ldots, a_{t_i}^i)$ be the sequence of actions executed by agent i in the corresponding plan (P_i).

2. Initialization step: $k = 0$ and $A'_i(s) = \emptyset$ for all i and s.

3. Let B_k^j be the set of reachable states at step k for agent j when agent $3-j$ follows his (original/basic) plan. Initially, B_0^1 contains the initial state of agent 1 in c_0, B_0^2 contains the initial state of agent 2 in c_0, and all the other B_k^j's are empty sets.

4. For each state $s \in B_k^1$ and for each action $a \in A_1(s) \setminus$

$A'_1(s)$, if $\tau(s, s^2_k, a, a^2_k) = (s^1, s^2_{k+1})$, $s^1 \in L_1$, then add s^1 to B^1_{k+1}. Otherwise, add a to $A'_1(s)$.

5. Increment k. While $i \leq t_i$, go to 4.

6. Execute steps 4–5 again, switching the indexes for the agents.

7. Output the social law whose components are the functions A'_1, A'_2.

Proposition 3 *Given a system S, and a goal that is a projection of a given joint plan, MSLA outputs a minimal social law for the system S in polynomial time.*

Notice that the algorithm computes a law in which the original plan of each agent remains available. Hence the law maximizes flexibility in the selection of behaviors while leaving the original behavior intact.

The AGVs case study presented in Section 3 can be represented and solved within our model. We now describe a sketch of how this can be done. Each robot has a finite set of states L_i which is a product of two components. Each state of one of the components refers to a station the AGV may be in, and each state of the other component refers to a station it may be in and observations it may have (i.e., in this second component a state refers both to a station and to the local observations made). There is an initial state where the robot selects once and for all whether it will observe only its station or the neighboring coordinates as well (i.e, a decision about the component of states to be visited). There is also a distinguished state that denotes collision. The goal is to follow a particular path along the ring without (the need to) observing the neighborhood, and without colliding. This can be easily defined by a path of states of the first component. The transition function will capture movements in the ring topology and potential collisions. The MSLA algorithm can be used now in order to build a minimal social law that is similar to the one presented in Section 3.

Further work: In the full paper we discuss minimal social laws in the context of a typical consensus problem. In difference to the AGVs case study, this part of our study deals with non-symmetric laws, which allow the assignment of different roles to the agents. The study illustrates subtle points in the inter-relationships between minimality and usefulness. Notice that although our work has been concerned with specifications of liveness and safety conditions, one can discuss a situation where efficiency stated as a cardinal measure over the goal space (not expressible in the above general form) is taken into account. This calls for work on tradeoffs between efficiency and minimality, which we hope to pursue in the future.

References

Ben-Yitzhak, O., and Tennenholtz, M. 1997. On the Synthesis of Social Laws for Mobile Robots: A Study in Artificial Social Systems (Part I). *Computers and Artificial Intelligence* 14.

Bond, A. H., and Gasser, L. 1988. *Readings in Distributed Artificial Intelligence*. Ablex Publishing Corporation.

Briggs, W., and Cook, D. 1995. Flexible Social Laws. In *Proc. 14th International Joint Conference on Artificial Intelligence*, 688–693.

Durfee, E. 1992. What your computer really needs to know, you learned in kindergarten. In *10th National Conference on Artificial Intelligence*, 858–864.

Kraus, S., and Wilkenfeld, J. 1991. The Function of Time in Cooperative Negotiations. In *Proc. of AAAI-91*, 179–184.

Kreps, D. 1990. *A Course in Microeconomic Theory*. Princeton University Press.

Lansky, A. L. 1988. Localized Event-Based Reasoning for Multiagent Domains. Technical Report 423, SRI International.

Latombe, J. 1991. How to move (physically speaking) in a multi-agent world. In *MAAMAW91*.

Minsky, N. 1991a. The imposition of protocols over open distributed systems. *IEEE Transactions on Software Engineering* 17(2):183–195.

Minsky, N. 1991b. Law-governed systems. *Software Engineering Journal* 285–302.

Moses, Y., and Tennenholtz, M. 1990. Artificial Social Systems Part I: Basic Principles. Technical Report CS90-12, Weizmann Institute.

Moses, Y., and Tennenholtz, M. 1995. Artificial Social Systems. *Computers and Artificial Intelligence* 14(6):533–562.

Onn, S., and Tennenholtz, M. 1997. Determination of Social Laws for Agent Mobilization. *Artificial Intelligence*. 95:155–167.

Rosenschein, J. S., and Zlotkin, G. 1994. *Rules of Encounter*. MIT Press.

Rousseau, J. 1762. *Du Contrat Social*. Translated and introduced by Maurice Cranston (1968). First published in 1762. (also published by Dent Everyman along with the Discourses).

Safra, S., and Tennenholtz, M. 1994. On Planning while Learning. *Journal of Artificial Intelligence Research* 2:111–129.

Shoham, Y., and Tennenholtz, M. 1995. Social Laws for Artificial Agent Societies: Off-line Design. *Artificial Intelligence* 73.

Sinreich, D. 1995. Network design models for discrete material flow systems: A literature review. *International Journal of Advanced Manufacturing Technology* 10:277–291.

Stuart, C. 1985. An Implementation of a Multi-Agent Plan Synchronizer. In *Proc. 9th International Joint Conference on Artificial Intelligence*, 1031–1033.

Optimal Auctions Revisited

Dov Monderer and Moshe Tennenholtz
Faculty of Industrial Engineering and Management
Technion–Israel Institute of Technology
Haifa 32000
Israel

Abstract

The Internet offers new challenges to the fields of economics and artificial intelligence. This paper addresses several basic problems inspired by the adaptation of economic mechanisms, and auctions in particular, to the Internet. Computational environments such as the Internet offer a high degree of flexibility in auctions' rules. This makes the study of optimal auctions especially interesting in such environments. Although the problem of optimal auctions has received a lot of attention in economics, only partial solutions are supplied in the existing literature. We present least upper bounds (l.u.b) R_n on the revenue obtained by a seller in any auction with n participants. Our bounds imply that if the number of participants is large then the revenue obtained by standard auctions (e.g., English auctions) approach the theoretical bound. Our results heavily rely on the risk-aversion assumption made in the economics literature. We further show that without this assumption, the seller's revenue (for a fixed number of participants) may significantly exceed the upper bound.

1. Introduction

The Internet exhibits forms of interactions which are not captured by current studies and theories in Economics. The highly distributed nature of the Internet, the relatively easy access to economic trades carried out in remote locations, and the ability of defining various types of Internet trades by individual users, lead to new kind of settings for which new theories should be developed and evaluated.

The Internet is a distributed environment where self-interested parties may interact. The strategic interaction among agents is a major topic of study in Microeconomics (Kreps 1990) and Game Theory (Fudenberg & Tirole 1991). In particular, the design of protocols for strategic interactions is the subject of the field termed *mechanism design* (Fudenberg & Tirole 1991; Myerson 1991). Research on strategic aspects of multi-agent activity in Artificial Intelligence has grown rapidly in the recent years. Work in AI has mostly concentrated on the design of protocols for agents' interaction. Hence, work in AI shares much in common with work on mechanism design in Economics (Bond & Gasser 1988; Demazeau & Muller 1990; Rosenschein & Zlotkin 1994; Durfee 1992). Many basic principles and ideas grew up from the mechanism design literature. Much of the research in mechanism design has been devoted to the study of auctions (McAfee & McMillan 1987; Wolfstetter 1996). There are two reasons for that. One is the popularity of auctions as an economic trade, and the other is the understanding that many of the features studied in the auctions literature shed light on other economic mechanisms (Fudenberg & Tirole 1991). Evidentially, auctions have turned to be a most popular strategic tool in electronic commerce as well, and the number of different auctions carried out in the Internet is huge.

In an auction a good is sold to a single buyer taken from a set of potential buyers (or more generally, several goods are sold to a set of agents), according to some bidding rules and rules for determining the auction's outcome (e.g., the exact price to be paid). There are several auctions that have been found to be representative ones, and which are most widely used in Economic trades. Basic theories regarding these auctions have been developed and few basic results on the seller's revenue in different types of auctions have been obtained (e.g., (Myerson 1982; Milgrom & Weber 1982)). Some preliminaries regarding basic auction theory will be presented in the next section. Given the popularity of auctions in the Internet, and their fundamental role in Economic theories, the adaptation of auction theory to computational settings becomes a task of considerable importance. Naturally, when one considers economic trades in computational settings, he may wish to consider the effects of computational bounds on agents' behavior in auctions.

Copyright ©1998, American Association for Artificial Intelligence (www.aaai.org). All rights reserved.

This is the approach taken for example in (Sandholm 1996). However, as we show, the computational setting also suggests the need for a careful study of basic issues in economics that have (somewhat surprisingly) been neglected.

The Internet is a computational setting, with flexible software which is used by relatively sophisticated users. This makes the study of optimal auctions (e.g., (Myerson 1991; Riley & Samuelson 1981; Maskin & Riley 1984)) highly relevant to this setting. In an optimal auction the seller chooses an auction mechanism that maximizes her revenue in equilibrium. A major claim against optimal (non-standard) auctions is that they are hard to handle, but given the computational environment this task becomes much more reasonable and doable. All that is needed in order to define and manage a new kind of auction is a simple software; typical Internet users will have little problem in participating in such auctions. Indeed, the reader may easily find in the Internet various novel modifications of existing auctions. This leads to the following central questions. What is an upper bound on the revenue one can obtain by an optimal auction, can it be obtained in certain cases, and can it be obtained by classical auctions?

Another basic feature of electronic sales is the lack of commitment power of the seller, and the relatively high-risk for the buyers. This suggests that one may wish to relax the assumption that the buyers are risk-averse (or risk-neutral) agents, that is (always) taken in economics. How does the expected revenue of the seller (from relatively standard auctions) change when we remove the risk-aversion assumption?

We show:

1. The expected highest valuation of an object from the point of view of the participants is a least upper bound on the gain a seller can obtain in any auction for risk-averse (and in particular for risk-neutral) agents. This result is not obvious given that the bids of agents in equilibria (in relatively standard auctions) may be higher than their actual valuation for the good. This result solves a basic problem in the theory of optimal auctions.

2. If the number of participants is large, then the seller's revenue in an English auction approaches the upper bound.

3. We suggest that the modeling of agents as risk-seeking may be appropriate for the Internet setting. We show that in this case a third-price auction enables the seller to obtain a revenue that is higher than the expected highest valuation for the good.

In Section 2 we introduce some preliminaries. In particular, we describe the classical model of auctions. In Section 3 we present a least upper bound on the revenue obtained by the seller in any auction for risk-averse (or risk-neutral) agents. We also show that this upper bound can be almost matched in English auctions when the number of agents is large enough. In Section 4 we discuss the potential need for modeling agents as having a risk-seeking attitude, and show that in this case a third-price auction can lead to a seller's revenue that is higher than the previously mentioned upper bound.

2. Preliminaries

Consider a seller who wishes to sell a particular good, where there are n agents denoted by $1, 2, \ldots, n$ who wish to buy this good. An auction is a procedure in which participants submit messages (typically monetary bids) for the good.[1] The auction's rules specify the type of messages, and as a function of the messages submitted by the participants they determine the winner and the payments to be made by the participants (to the auction organizer). Formally, an auction procedure for n potential participants, $N = \{1, 2, \ldots, n\}$ is characterized by 4 parameters, M, g, c, d, where M is the set of messages, $g = (g_1, \ldots, g_n)$ with $g_i : M^N \to [0, 1]$ for all i and $\sum_{i=1}^n g_i(m) \leq 1$ for all m, and $c = (c_1, \ldots, c_n); d = (d_1, \ldots, d_n)$ with $c_i, d_j : M^n \to R$ for all i, j. Participant i submits a message $m_i \in M$. Let $m = (m_1, m_2, \ldots, m_n)$ be a vector of messages, then the organizer conducts a lottery to determine the winner, in which the probability that i is the winner equals $g_i(m)$. The winner, say j, pays $c_j(m)$ and every other participant i pays $d_i(m)$. It is assumed that M contains the null message e, which is interpreted as non-participation. It is further assumed that if $m_i = e$, then $g_i(m) = c_i(m) = d_i(m) = 0$. Classical auction theory associates a (Bayesian) game with each auction procedure and analyses the behavior of the agents under the equilibrium assumption. To do this we have to define the information structure of the game. Let $(\hat{v}_i)_{i=1}^n$ be mutually independent non-negative random variables. When $\hat{v}_i = v_i$, v_i is interpreted as the maximal willingness to pay of Agent i. v_i is called the type of i.[2] The distribution of $\hat{v}_i$ is denoted by F_i. That

---
[1]These messages can also refer to complete strategies. Hence, the analysis does not refer only to one-shot interactions.

[2]We use the independent-private-value model of information. There exist more complicated information models in which an agent does not know his own type, and the agents' types are correlated (see Milgrom and Weber (1982)). We believe that the independence assumption is the right one in the Internet auctions setup where there are

is, $F_i(v) = Prob(\hat{v}_i \leq v)$. We take F_i to be the uniform distribution on some interval $[a_i, b_i]$[3]. The probability measure induced by F_i on R_+ is denoted by P_i. Let P denote the product probability measure of $(P_i)_{i \in N}$ on R_+^N and let P_{-i} denote the product probability measure defined by $(P_j)_{j \in N \setminus \{i\}}$ on $R^{N \setminus \{i\}}$. Each agent i has a utility function for money $u_i : R \to R$, normalized with $u_i(0) = 0$. It is assumed that Agent i is an expected utility maximizer. It is further assumed that if Agent i with the type v_i receives the item and pays x_i, his utility is $u_i(v_i - x_i)$. Agent i is risk-averse if u_i is a concave function. A risk-averse agent weakly prefers a certain amount to a lottery whose expected payoff equals this amount. Agent i is risk-neutral if u_i is linear. Such an agent is indifferent between a lottery and its expected payoff.[4] A strategy for agent i is a function $b_i : R_+ \to M$, where $b_i(v_i)$ is the message submitted by i when his type is v_i. Let $b = (b_1, b_2, \ldots, b_n)$ be an $n-tuple$ of strategies. b is in equilibrium if for every agent i and for every v_i, the expected utility of agent i given that his type is v_i and given that each agent j, $j \neq i$ uses b_j is maximized over $m_i \in M$ at $m_i = b_i(v_i)$. Before expressing the above verbal description with the appropriate formula we remark that this definition makes sense only if certain technical conditions are imposed on all functions under discussion. For simplicity we do not explicitly present these conditions, which are quite common in the economic literature.[5] For a vector of strategies $b = (b_i)_{i \in N}$ we denote $b_{-i} = (b_j)_{j \neq i}$, for $v \in R_+^N$ we denote $b(v) = (b_1(v_1), b_2(v_2), \ldots, b_n(v_n))$ and for agent i we denote $b_{-i}(v_{-i}) = (b_j(v_j))_{j \neq i}$. Thus, b is in equilibrium if for every agent i and for every type v_i,

$$\max_{m_i \in M_i} E_{P_{-i}}(u_i(v_i - c_i(m_i, b_{-i}))g_i(m_i, b_{-i}) +$$

---

many anonymous participants.

[3]In the economic literature other distributions are discussed as well. We find uniform distributions quite natural for the Internet setting. Nevertheless, some of our results hold for any distribution. In particular, our proof about the upper bound on the expected revenue can be extended to the case of arbitrary (twice continuously differentiable) distributions.

[4]Notice that a risk-neutral agent is a specific instance of a risk-averse agent. A risk-neutral agent has (up to an increasing linear transformation) a specific utility function ($u_i(x) = x$), while the set of concave utility functions that represent risk-averse agents is huge. In fact, the standard assumption in Economics is that agents/buyers are risk-averse, and the assumption of risk-neutral agents is taken only as an approximation to risk-averse agents, for mathematical convenience.

[5]These conditions refer to the structure of the utility and distribution functions. In particular, it is assumed that both are twice continuously differentiable.

$$u_i(-d_i(m_i, b_{-i}))(1 - g_i(m_i, b_{-i}))$$

is attained at $m_i = b_i(v_i)$, where $E_{P_{-i}}$ denotes the expected value operator with respect to P_{-i}.

Under the equilibrium assumption (i.e, the assumption that economic agents use equilibrium strategies), if the auction game $G = G(n, A, \bar{u}, \bar{F})$, where $\bar{u} = (u_i)_{i=1}^n$ and $\bar{F} = (F_i)_{i=1}^n$, has a unique equilibrium profile $b = (b_1, b_2, \ldots, b_n)$, then the seller expected revenue is denoted by R_G. That is,

$$R_G = E_P \left(\sum_{i=1}^n (g_i(b)c_i(b) + (1 - g_i(b))d_i(b) \right).$$

When the auction game has more than one equilibrium profile, we denote by R_G the revenue of the seller in the worst case, that is the greatest lower bound of the revenues obtained in some equilibrium. We do not consider auction procedures A that are over complicated such that the associated game does not have an equilibrium. Consider a fixed information structure $\bar{F}$, a fixed vector of utility functions $\bar{u}$ with $u_i = u$ for all i and $u(x) = x$ for all x, and a fixed number of participants n. Myerson (Myerson 1982) has solved the optimality problem $\max_A R_G$ and proved that an optimal auction procedure is a second-price auction with an appropriate reservation price. Maskin and Riley (Maskin & Riley 1984) have investigated the optimality problem with a fixed symmetric information structure and a fixed symmetric utility structure in which $u_i = u$ for all i, and u is a concave function. Their results indicate, that if an optimal solution exists, it should involve a very sophisticated auction procedure. In the next section we will present a least upper bound $R_n(\bar{F}) = \sup_{A,\bar{U}} R_G$ to the seller's revenue, where $\bar{u}$ ranges over all utility structures of risk averse agents, and A ranges over all auction rules. A seller, whose revenue is close to this upper bound does not have to worry about optimality. Obviously $R_n(\bar{F})$ is an upper bound for every fixed utility structure, but it is not a necessarily a least upper bound for a fixed utility structure.

Classical Auction Mechanisms

In this section we discuss some classical auction mechanisms and show how they can be described in the framework mentioned above.

First Price Auctions One of the most popular auction mechanisms is the first-price auction. In such an auction, each participant submits a bid in a sealed envelop. The agent with the highest bid wins the object and pays his bid, all other participants pay nothing.

Ties are broken with some lottery mechanism. In a first-price auction, $M = R_+ \cup \{e\}$, and for $x \in R_+^N$, $g_i(x) = 0$, if $x_i < w(x) = \max\{x_j : j \in N\}$, and $g_i(x) = \frac{1}{k(x)}$ if $x_i = w(x)$ and $k(x)$ denotes the number of agents j for which $x_j = w(x)$. Also, $c_i(x) = x_i$ and $d_i(x) = 0$.[6] In the next section we will use the standard equilibrium analysis of first-price auctions that we now present: We assume that all agents are symmetric ($u_i = u$) and $F_i = F$ for all i, and that F is supported in the interval $[0, 1]$ in the sense that $F(0) = 0$, $F(1) = 1$, and $F'(x) > 0$ for all $x \in [0, 1]$. It can be shown that if u is twice continuously differentiable, $u'(x) > 0$ for all x, and $\frac{u}{u'}$ is increasing, then there exists a unique equilibrium, $(b_1, b_2, \ldots, b_n) = (b, b \ldots, b)$, where b is the unique solution of the differential equation (see (Riley & Samuelson 1981)):

$$b'(v) = (n-1)\frac{u(v - b(v))F'(v)}{u'(v - b(v))F(v)}; \quad b(0) = 0.$$

In particular, if the agents are risk-neutral and $F(x) = x$ is the uniform distribution on $[0, 1]$, then $b(v) = \frac{n-1}{n}v$ for all $v \in [0, 1]$.

k-price auctions In a k-price auction each participant submits a bid in a sealed envelop, the winner is the one with the highest bid and he pays the k-order statistics of the vector of bids. For example, in a second-price auction if the three highest bids were $10, 9$ and 8, then the winner is the one whose bid was 10, and he pays 9. However, if the first three bids were $10, 10, 9$, then the winner is selected with a probability 0.5 from the two agents with the bid of 10, and he pays 10. It can be easily verified (and it is well-known) that in a second-price auction, the strategies $b_i(v_i) = v_i$ are in equilibrium for every information and utility structures. k-price auctions, $k \geq 3$ have the interesting feature that in equilibrium the agents overbid (see (Wolfstetter 1996)). That is, $b_i(v_i) > v_i$.

English auctions The English auction is the most popular open auction. In such an auction, there is an initial reservation price (which can be zero) and at each time every player can increase the bid publicly. The auction is over if for a certain (fixed in advanced) time period no one increases the bid. The agent with the last bid wins the object and pays the last bid. Such an auction, like all other open auctions, is analyzed in the framework described above by defining the message space M to be the set of strategies (protocols) in the dynamic game induced by the mechanism. Though formally, participants do not actually have to submit a protocol, it is obvious that had they have to do it,

[6] If the seller announces a participation fee of $c > 0$, then $c_i(x) = x_i + c$ and $d_i(x) = c$.

they will submit their true protocol, because this protocol is optimal with respect to their beliefs concerning the behavior of the other participants. It is interesting to note that English auctions are equivalent to second-price auctions in the sense that for every vector of types, both auctions yield the same winner and the same payoffs to the organizer. In particular, the seller's revenue in both auctions is identical.[7]

Dutch Auctions In a Dutch auction, the auctioneer initially calls for a very high price, and then continuously lowers the price until some bidder stops the auction and claims the good for that price. Dutch auctions are strategically equivalent to first-price auctions, and their analysis (and in particular, the expected revenue of the seller) coincide.

3. An Upper Bound on Optimal Auctions

In this section we supply an upper bound on the revenue obtained by the seller in any auction for risk-averse agents. We will be able to show that no matter how sophisticated an auction is, although agents may have bids that are higher than their actual evaluation of a good [8] the seller's revenue can not be higher than the expected highest valuation of the auction's participants for this good.

Theorem 1 *Let $n \geq 2$. Let $\bar{F} = (F_i)_{i=1}^n$ be a fixed information structure. Then for every utility structure of risk-averse agents $\bar{u} = (u_i)_{i=1}^n$, for every auction procedure $A = (M, g, c, d)$, and for every equilibrium strategies $b = (b_i)_{i=1}^n$, the expected revenue of the seller from the auction is bounded by the expected highest type. That is,*

$$R_G \leq E_P(\max(\hat{v}_1, \hat{v}_2, \ldots, \hat{v}_n)),$$

where $G = G(n, A, \bar{u} = (u_i)_{i=1}^n, \bar{F} = (F_i)_{i=1}^n)$ is the auction game.

Moreover, the above-mentioned upper bound is a least upper bound.

Proof: Consider agent i, who participates in the auction, and denote the expected revenue from agent i by $\bar{R}_i$. If agent i is of type v_i, then his expected utility $B_i(v_i)$ when bidding $b(v_i)$, while the bidding strategies of the other agents are $b_j, j \neq i$, is given by:

$$B_i(v_i) = E_{P_{-i}}(u_i(v_i - c_i(b_i(v_i), b_{-i}))g_i(b_i(v_i), b_{-i})+$$

[7] This equivalence principle does not hold if we do not assume the independence of types (see (Milgrom & Weber 1982)).
[8] See the discussion of k-price auctions in the previous section.

$$u_i(-d_i(b_i(v_i), b_{-i}))(1 - g_i(b_i(v_i), b_{-i}))).$$

As i can always choose not to participate we conclude that $B_i(v_i) \geq 0$. Because u_i is concave (i.e., $u_i(\alpha x + (1-\alpha)y) \geq \alpha u_i(x) + (1-\alpha)u_i(y)$), we have that

$$u_i(E_{P_{-i}}((v_i - c_i(b_i(v_i), b_{-i}))g_i(b_i(v_i), b_{-i}) +$$

$$(-d_i(b_i(v_i), b_{-i})(1 - g_i(b_i(v_i), b_{-i}))) \geq 0.$$

Because u_i is increasing, $u_i(0) = 0$, and u is concave, Jensen inequality (i.e., $u_i(E(\cdot)) \geq E(u_i(\cdot))$) implies that:

$$E_{P_{-i}}((v_i - c_i(b_i(v_i), b_{-i}))g_i(b_i(v_i), b_{-i}) +$$

$$(-d_i(b_i(v_i), b_{-i})(1 - g_i(b_i(v_i), b_{-i})))) \geq 0.$$

Let $R_i(v_i)$ be the expected revenue from Agent i given that his type is v_i. The last inequality yields

$$\bar{R}_i = E_{P_i}(R_i) \leq E_P(\hat{v}_i g_i(b)).$$

Therefore

$$R_G = \sum_{i=1}^n \bar{R}_i \leq E_P(\sum_{i=1}^n \hat{v}_i g_i(b)) \leq E_P(\max(\hat{v}_i)_{i=1}^n).$$

We prove that our bound in an l.u.b in the case where each F_i is the uniform distribution over $[0, 1]$. The proof of the general case is similar. Consider a first-price auction, and assume $u_i = u_\alpha$ ($0 < \alpha < 1$) where $u_\alpha(x) = x^\alpha$ for every $x \geq 0$.[9] We will show that when α approaches zero the expected gain in this auction approaches the above-mentioned upper bound.

From the equilibrium equation is Section 2 we can deduce that in equilibrium $b_i = b$ for all i and

$$b'(v) = \frac{n-1}{\alpha} \cdot \frac{(v - b(v))}{v}.$$

This implies that

$$b'(v) \cdot v + \frac{n-1}{\alpha} \cdot b(v) = \frac{n-1}{\alpha} \cdot v.$$

By multiplying both sides of the equality by $v^{\frac{n-1}{\alpha}-1}$ we get that:

---
[9]Notice that u_α is not defined for $x < 0$, and that it can not be extended to a concave function on the whole real line. Therefore, the complete proof makes use of appropriate modifications of the u_α's. For simplicity, we omit these modifications in the proof presented here.

$$b'(v) \cdot v^{\frac{n-1}{\alpha}} + \frac{n-1}{\alpha} \cdot b(v) \cdot v^{\frac{n-1}{\alpha}-1} = \frac{n-1}{\alpha} \cdot v^{\frac{n-1}{\alpha}}.$$

The above is equivalent to:

$$(b(v) \cdot v^{\frac{n-1}{\alpha}})' = \frac{n-1}{\alpha} \cdot v^{\frac{n-1}{\alpha}}.$$

By taking the integral of both sides we get:

$$(b(v) \cdot v^{\frac{n-1}{\alpha}}) = \frac{n-1}{\alpha} \cdot \frac{v^{\frac{n-1}{\alpha}+1}}{\frac{(n-1)}{\alpha}+1}.$$

Hence, we have:

$$b(v) = v \cdot \frac{n-1}{n-1+\alpha}.$$

Therefore, the expected revenue of the seller is

$$E(b(v_{max})) = \frac{n-1}{n-1+\alpha} E(v_{max}).$$

where $v_{max} = \max(\hat{v}_i)_{i=1}^n$. Hence, the seller's revenue approaches our bound when α approaches 0. ∎

Optimality of English Auctions

The above theorem has shown a least upper bound on the expected revenue of the seller in any auction for risk-averse agents. A natural question is whether this least upper bound can be obtained by standard auctions. In the following theorem we use the fact that the revenue of the seller in English auctions does not depend on the utility functions. We can show:

Theorem 2 *Let $(F_i)_{i=1}^\infty$ be a sequence of distribution functions supported in a fixed bounded interval. Let A_n be an English auction for n participants with $\bar{F} = (F_1, \ldots, F_n)$. Let $R(A_n)$ denote the expected revenue for the seller in the auction A_n. Then, R_n approaches $E_P(\max(\hat{v}_1, \hat{v}_2, \ldots, \hat{v}_n))$, when n approaches infinity (in the sense that the limit of the ratio approaches 1, when n approaches ∞).*[10]

Hence, the optimal expected revenue can be almost obtained in English auctions, when the number of agents is large enough (which one may expect in Internet auctions). Our results have also an interpretation which is somewhat complementary to the revenue equivalence principle mentioned before. The famous revenue equivalence theorem implies that we can not improve upon the revenue obtained in classical auctions when the agents are risk-neutral. Our results tell us that, at least in what seem to be a setup which is appropriate for many Internet auctions, this is also true when we have arbitrary risk-averse agents.

---
[10]Proof will appear in the full paper.

4. Risk-Seeking Agents

The number of Internet auctions grow relatively fast, and various modifications for the classical auctions are considered. However, as we have shown, under the classical assumptions made in Economics one can not go far in optimizing the seller's revenue. In this part of the paper we wish to consider a different kind of setting that may explain some of the phenomena that occur in the Internet setting, and which explore the potential of obtaining a revenue that is higher than the highest participants' valuation.

Indeed, most of the Internet auctions are English auctions, which are known to be strategically equivalent to second-price auctions. There used to be some Dutch auctions (which are strategically equivalent to first-price auctions) but they seem to disappear. On the other hand, a central theorem of auction theory is that the expected revenue obtained by the seller in first-price auctions is greater than her expected revenue in second-price auctions, assuming the agents are risk-averse. So, how can one explain this situation? One way of explaining the related phenomena is by considering participants that are risk-seeking rather than risk-averse. Although this assumption does not appear in classical work in Economics, it may make sense in the Internet setting. Indeed, in the Internet setting agents attempt to buy items that they can not really see, and that are sold by an unknown seller, and with no real commitment of the seller. On the other hand, the buyers need to reveal their credit card information. Although we do not formally argue for this point, we believe that the modeling of agents as having a risk-seeking attitude rather than risk-aversion attitude should be treated carefully and seriously. In another paper (Monderer & Tennenholtz 1998) we discuss the risk-seeking assumption and show that if the agents are risk-seeking then second-price auctions lead to higher revenue to the seller than first-price auctions. We wish now to re-consider our upper bound on the seller's revenue in view of this different modeling perspective. Technically, the only difference from the previously mentioned setting, is that in the case of risk-seeking agents the utility function will be convex rather than concave.

It is well-known that a risk-neutral seller can sell lottery tickets with negative expected gain to a risk-seeking agent and obtain as a result very high gains. Our aim here is different. We wish to show that a value that is higher than the upper bound obtained, can be achieved in what can be considered as standard auctions. In particular, we consider the third-price auction, which is another (less studied) instance of k-price auctions.

We will be interested in the following utility function that captures risk-seeking attitude (and is complementary to the one discussed in (Sandholm 1996) with regard to risk-averse agents). We assume that $u(x) = x$ when $x \leq 0$ and that $u(x) = \alpha x$ for some constant $\alpha > 1$ where $x > 0$. We can show:

Theorem 3 *A third-price auction for risk-seeking agents can lead to an expected revenue which is higher than the expected highest participant's valuation for the good.*[11]

References

Bond, A. H., and Gasser, L. 1988. *Readings in Distributed Artificial Intelligence*. Ablex Publishing Corporation.

Demazeau, Y., and Muller, J. 1990. *Decentralized AI*. North Holland/Elsevier.

Durfee, E. 1992. What your computer really needs to know, you learned in kindergarten. In *10th National Conference on Artificial Intelligence*, 858–864.

Fudenberg, D., and Tirole, J. 1991. *Game Theory*. MIT Press.

Kreps, D. 1990. *A Course in Microeconomic Theory*. Princeton University Press.

Maskin, E., and Riley, J. 1984. Optimal auctions with risk-averse buyers. *Econometrica* 52(6):1473–1518.

McAfee, R., and McMillan, J. 1987. Auctions and bidding. *Journal of Economic Literature* 25:699–738.

Milgrom, P., and Weber, R. 1982. A thoery of auctions and competitive bidding. *Econometrica* 50:1089–1122.

Monderer, D., and Tennenholtz, M. 1998. Internet Auctions. Working paper.

Myerson, R. 1982. Optimal auction design. *Mathematics of Operations Research* 6:58–73.

Myerson, R. B. 1991. *Game Theory*. Harvard University Press.

Riley, J., and Samuelson, W. 1981. Optimal auctions. *American Economic Review* 71:381–392.

Rosenschein, J. S., and Zlotkin, G. 1994. *Rules of Encounter*. MIT Press.

Sandholm, T. 1996. Limitations of the vickrey auction in computational multiagent systems. In *2nd International Conference on Multi-Agent Systems*.

Wolfstetter, E. 1996. Auctions: An introduction. *Journal of Economic Surveys* 10(4):367–420.

---

[11]Proof will appear in the full paper.

Leveled Commitment Contracts with Myopic and Strategic Agents

Martin R. Andersson and Tuomas W. Sandholm[1]
{mra, sandholm}@cs.wustl.edu
Department of Computer Science,
Washington University
One Brookings Drive
St. Louis, MO 63130-4899

Abstract

In automated negotiation systems consisting of self-interested agents, contracts have traditionally been binding, *i.e.*, impossible to breach. Such contracts do not allow the agents to efficiently deal with future events. This deficiency can be tackled by using a *leveled commitment contracting protocol* which allows the agents to decommit from contracts by paying a monetary penalty to the contracting partner. The efficiency of such protocols depends heavily on how the penalties are decided. In this paper, different leveled commitment protocols and their parameterizations are empirically compared to each other and to several full commitment protocols. In the different experiments, the agents are of different types: self-interested or cooperative, and they can perform different levels of lookahead.

Surprisingly, self-interested myopic agents reach a higher social welfare quicker than cooperative myopic agents when decommitment penalties are low. The social welfare in settings with agents that performed lookahead did not vary as much with the decommitment penalty as the social welfare in settings that consisted of myopic agents. For a short range of values of the decommitment penalty, myopic agents performed almost as well as agents that performed lookahead. In all of the settings studied, the best way to set the decommitment penalties was to choose low penalties, but ones that were greater than zero. This indicates that leveled commitment contracting protocols outperform both full commitment protocols and commitment free protocols.

Introduction

Systems which include *automated negotiation* are playing an increasingly important role in our society. This is due both to *technology push* and *application pull*. New technology has made global communication possible with the help of standardized protocols, *e.g.*, IP, WWW, Java, HTML, KQML, which have made it possible for independent hardware platforms and software to communicate with each other. With the expansion of the Internet and novel methods for electronic payments, electronic commerce is also becoming widespread (Kalakota & Whinston 1996). Another application of automated contracting systems is automated markets for electric power (Sandholm & Ygge 1997; Ygge & Akkermans 1996) which are a reality in both the United States and in Europe.

Contracts in automated negotiation systems consisting of *self-interested* agents have traditionally been binding, *i.e.*, impossible to breach. Such contracts do not allow the agents to act efficiently upon future events because contracts might become unfavorable to one or both of the agents after the contracting. If the agents were allowed to breach contracts, they could accommodate changes in the environment more efficiently and the social welfare would improve.

In systems with cooperative agents, decommitting from contracts without reprisals can be accepted, even after the other party has partly completed the task of the contract (Sen & Durfee 1994; Smith 1980). On the other hand, in the case of self-interested agents, there is a need to compensate the party who is the victim of a decommitment.

Contingency contracts have been suggested to be used between self-interested agents when they do not have knowledge (or only have probabilistic knowledge) about future events (Raiffa 1982). In these contracts the obligations of the contract are made conditional on future events. Contingency contracts can increase the payoff of both parties, so contracts not possible with full commitment protocols may become beneficial for both parties. However, it may be impossible to anticipate and enumerate all future events. Monitoring all events after the contract is made can also be impractical. If some events are observable by only one of the parties, another problem arises: one party can have an incentive to lie about the events in order to be better off himself.

Recently, a *leveled commitment protocol* has been proposed that allows self-interested agents to decommit from a contract by simply paying a decommitment penalty to the partner of the contract (Sandholm & Lesser 1996). In that protocol, the decommitment penalties are decided at the time of contracting and the penalties do not need to be the same for the two contracting parties. It has been shown through formal game theoretic analysis that this leveled commitment feature increases the Pareto efficiency of contracts and can make contracts individually rational to both parties even in cases where full commitment contracts can-

---

[1] Supported by NSF CAREER award IRI-9703122 and NSF grant IRI-9610122.

Copyright ©1998, American Association for Artificial Intelligence (www.aaai.org). All rights reserved.

not.

The leveled commitment contracts, which only can handle one task, could emulate full commitment contracts that are capable of handling several tasks in one single contract (Andersson 1998; Andersson & Sandholm 1998; Sandholm 1996; 1998).

With leveled commitment protocols there is no need for an agent to conduct a feasibility check before contracting. If the contract cannot be performed, because of lack of resources *etc.*, the agent can decommit from the engagement. Also, the agents do not need to perform a complete computation of the marginal costs before taking on a contract, but can complete the computation after contracting.[2]

The concept of breaching contracts in the real world is analyzed by Posner (Posner 1977). The main ideas are that the party that breaches must compensate the victim for lost profit and that the penalties for breaching contracts should be set so that the social welfare is maximized.

Strategic thinking behind contracting and one-sided decommitment among self-interested agents has been studied (Park, Durfee, & Birmingham 1996), where the decision making mechanism is modeled as a Markov-process. They assume that the agents expect none of their bids to be accepted, which makes the approach unsound from the perspective of game theory.

Diamond and Maskin (Diamond & Maskin 1979) have studied systems in which both agents can decommit from a contract by paying a decommitment penalty to the other party of the contract. Those penalties can be set in different ways: they can be compensatory or privately decided (*i.e.* liquidated; not necessarily decided by the parties of the contract – maybe imposed by a court) in the contract. The compensatory decommitment penalties are favored because of efficiency, *i.e.*, they provide, whenever possible, an increasing mutual welfare between the agents that enter a new contract.[3] Another argument for the compensatory penalties is that they are exactly the penalties that two rational parties would agree on for privately decided penalties.[4]

---

[2]This allows the agent to act faster and with less constraints in the contracting process than if it always had to perform a feasibility check and a thorough marginal cost calculation before contracting. The system also becomes more efficient if one agent (the one that takes on the task) conducts a full marginal cost calculation, than if all the agents would perform such a calculation.

[3]However, the social welfare may decrease because of the inefficiency arising from the contract that is breached.

[4]One reason for having over-compensating penalties is that one agent can make himself more trustworthy and the expected utility of the other agent will increase enough to make the contract possible (Posner 1977). Hence, over-compensating penalties can increase the space of possible contracts. However, it would limit the space of possible decommitments.

The next section discusses leveled commitment protocols. Then, the example problem domain is described, which is followed by a presentation of the types of agents and protocols included in the study. Next, is the notation of the different protocols presented, followed by a description how the data was evaluated. Then the results are presented and discussed.

Leveled Commitment Protocols

The penalties could be chosen freely by the agents, in which case the agents would try to optimize the penalties in its favor (Sandholm & Lesser 1996). The negotiation will be more complex if the agents can decide the penalties themselves compared to when they are set by the protocol because there would be more variables to agree on in order for all parties to accept a contract. If the penalties are set by the protocol, the negotiation becomes easier, but the result may not be optimal (*e.g.* fixed penalties does not guarantee that it is is profitable for the agents to decommit in all situations when a decommitment is mutually profitable for the agents involved in the contract).

Another method is to relate the decommitment penalty to the price of the contract. This could be done by choosing the penalty as a percentage (or a more complex function) of the price. Another way is to make the penalties compensate the victim of the breach for its lost profit. Because the victim would have an incentive to lie about the expected profit, a mechanism for calculating the lost profit would be necessary. The state of both agents might have changed since the contract was made, so the expected lost profit at contracting time and breaching time may differ. In the extreme the lost profit for the victim can be negative at breaching time, that is, also the victim of the breach benefits from being freed from the contract obligations.

A breach close to the execution deadline of the contract or late in a negotiation is likely to be more costly for the victim since it can be hard to find someone else to contract with within a short amount of time. In order to prevent such occurrences, the decommitment penalties can be increased over time.

The leveled commitment protocols were studied in order to conclude which mechanism should be used for setting the decommitment penalties among qualitatively different agents. Several environments were studied, and in each of them, 16 protocols with many parameterizations were tested.

Description of the Problem Domain

To investigate the performance of different mechanisms of setting the decommitment penalty for leveled commitment protocols, the agents are divided into two subsets. One subset consisted of *contractors* which each had one task with a cost associated to it. A contractor considers to contract out its task to a *contractee* which would be able handle the task at a potentially cheaper cost. The other subset consists of the contractees which do not have any tasks initially, but resources to handle a maximum of one task at a cost specific to each combination of contractees and tasks. There is no other differences between a contractor and a contractee other than that the former initially has a task and is willing to give it away, and the latter is willing to take on a task. The fallback position of a contractor is the cost of handling the task it has at the start of the negotiation, while the fallback of the contractees are zero (*i.e.*, they do not have any tasks at the start of negotiation and therefore no pending expenses).

Types of Agents

Four types of agents are included in the study. Each type is designed from two properties: the amount of *lookahead* the agent performs before it accepts or rejects a proposed contract, and how *self-interested* the agent is.

Agents With and Without Lookahead

The agents can either perform full lookahead or none at all. If they perform full lookahead, they compute the payoff of all possible future events and agree to the contract only if the expected payoff of agreeing is greater than rejecting, *i.e.*, they act strategically as game theoretic agents would. The other option of lookahead is to do none at all. If the agents perform no lookahead, they act myopically, and only consider the immediate payoff of the contract under negotiation.

Individual Rational and Cooperative Agents

The agents can be *self-interested* (*SI*) and only agree to contracts which increase their own payoff (expected or immediate, depending on whether they perform lookahead or not). They could also be explicit social welfare maximizers (*SWF-maximizer*), *i.e.* cooperative agents, which consider the summed payoff of all agents in the system when deciding to accept or reject a contract. That is, a SWF-maximizing agent can agree to a contract even if it makes itself worse off, as long as the total social welfare in the system increases.

Types of Leveled Commitment Protocols

The leveled commitment contracts are defined as follows:

Definition. 1 *A leveled commitment contract is a tuple $\langle \mathcal{C}, \Gamma \rangle$, where $\mathcal{C}$ is the underlying full commitment contract and Γ is the set of decommitment penalties. Let $A_\mathcal{C}$ be the set of agents involved in the contract $\mathcal{C}$. Then Γ will consist of one decommitment penalty for each pair of agents in $A_\mathcal{C}$, so that $|\Gamma| = \frac{|A_\mathcal{C}|^2 - |A_\mathcal{C}|}{2}$.*

This definition has the nice feature of separating the leveled commitment framework from the obligations of the contract, called the underlying contract $\mathcal{C}$. This means that the leveled commitment protocol can be applied to any type of full commitment contract. If an agent wants to decommitment from the underlying contract, it has to pay the decommitment penalties stated in Γ to all agents involved in the contract.[5]

Four different mechanisms of deciding the decommitment penalties are studied: *fixed*; *percentage* of contract price; increasing and decided at the time of *contracting*; and increasing and decided at the time of *breaching*. Two more properties (how to compute the price of the contract, and the sequence in which the agents meet each other in the negotiation) are also varied for different protocols in the study. All of these alternatives are now discussed.

Decommitment Penalties as a Fixed Value (FIX-protocol)

In the FIX-protocol, all contracts have the same fixed decommitment penalty decided prior to the start of the negotiation and that penalty is used throughout the negotiation. In the study, experiments with six different values of the fixed decommitment penalty were conducted. A summary of the different values can be found in Table 1.

Decommitment Penalties as a Percentage of Contract Price (PER-protocol)

The percentage decommitment penalties, used in the PER-protocol, consist of a fraction of the price of the contract. It is referred to as percentage since the most efficient parameterizations are fractions less than one. The same percentage is used for all contracts throughout the negotiation. The percentages in the study can be found in Table 1.

FIX-protocol	PER-protocol	CON-protocol BRE-protocol
0	0.1	0.25
5	0.25	0.5
10	0.4	0.75
15	0.5	1.0
30	0.75	2.0
50	1.0	4.0

Table 1: *Parameterizations in the study of leveled commitment protocols in different environments. (Note that 10% is written as 0.1 in the table.)*

Decommitment Penalties Decided at Time of Contracting (CON-protocol)

In the CON-protocol, the decommitment penalty varies during the negotiation. For a certain contract, the decommitment penalty is fixed at the time of contracting. The decommitment penalty is linearly increasing from zero to the highest penalty used. This highest penalty is set by the protocol to be a percentage of the contract price, which is applied to a contract

---

[5]The concept of leveled commitment is not specific to task allocation problems, although the empirical studies of this paper focus on task allocation. All the leveled commitment protocols in this study have a full commitment contract that only can transfer one task from one agent to another as the underlying full commitment contract.

agreed on at the second to last round and then decommitted in the last round. The percentages for setting the highest penalty in the study can be found in Table 1.

Decommitment Penalties Decided at Time of Breaching (BRE-protocol)

In BRE-protocols the decommitment penalty also varies with the time of the negotiation, as in the CON-protocol. The difference is that the decommitment penalties are fixed at the time of breaching instead of the time of contracting. The decommitment penalty is linearly increasing over time and a contract which is decommitted in the last round has the highest penalty. This highest penalty is decided as a percentage of the contract price and Table 1 shows the percentages used in the study.

Methods of Computing the Contract Price

The price of a contract is set such that the profit of the contract is divided equally between the agents involved in the contract. However, the profits are calculated in two different ways: including and not including decommitment penalties:

- The price is set so that the profits from the fallback positions of the agents are divided equally between the agents. The current payoffs are not considered when the price is calculated and neither are the potential decommitment penalties.

- The price is set so that the increase from the current mutual profit of the agents is equally divided between them, including discounts for decommitment penalties that are to be paid.

Sequencing of Contracts

The order in which the agents meet for negotiation is either stochastic or deterministic. In the stochastic model, one contractor and one contractee are randomly picked to negotiate with each other. In the deterministic model, the order is decided prior to negotiation (contractor 1 meets contractee 1, contractor 1 meets contractee 2, ..., contractor 2 meets contractee 1, ...). The negotiation protocol is sequential, that is, only two agents (one contractor and one contractee) negotiate at a time.

If the agents are individually rational, a contract is accepted if the payoffs (immediate or with lookahead) after the contract will be greater for both the contractor and the contractee compared to the payoffs before a potential acceptance of the contract. If one of the agents is indifferent, that is, the contract does not increase its payoff, the other agent decides whether or not to perform the contract. However, if both the agents are indifferent, the contract is rejected.

Studied Parameterizations

The parameterizations of the leveled commitment protocol that were studied can be found in Table 1. The

Notation of a leveled commitment protocol in a certain domain: Cab.Dd. Cab characterizes the protocol and Dd the domain.	
$C \in \{FIX, PER, CON, BRE\}$	The type of penalty.
$a \in \{w, d\}$	The type of price computation: based on fallback positions (w) or current profit (d).
$b \in \{n, r\}$	The contract sequencing: random (r) or not random (n).
$D \in \{SI, SWF\}$	Agent type: willingness to cooperate: self-interested (SI) or cooperative (SWF).
$d \in \{l, m\}$	Agent type: lookahead depth: lookahead (l) or no lookahead (myopic) (m).

Table 2: *Notation of the leveled commitment protocols and the domain.*

percentages for CON- and BRE-protocols are considerably greater than the percentages for the PER-protocol. This is because in the CON- and BRE-protocols these great percentages are only used in the last negotiation round, since the penalty is increased linearly from zero to the specified percentage with time of negotiation.

Conventions in Naming the Protocols and Domains

The notation for the different combinations of features of the leveled commitment protocols is summarized in Table 2. One or more properties may be left out if it is clear from the context which properties are referred to. If there is a star ("*") in place of a property, all possible types of that property are considered.

Evaluation

In our experiments, two contractors negotiated with two contractees over the contractors' initial tasks. Initially, each agent was randomly assigned a cost for handling each task. The contractors' costs were in the interval $[100, 200]$ and the contractees' in the interval $[0, 100]$. Since the contractors never can handle a task cheaper than a contractee, they never have to negotiate with each other. The problem was solved for 100 randomly initiated problem instances with five negotiation rounds in each. The number of negotiation rounds was assumed common knowledge among the agents.

To compare the different protocols, the ratio bound (ratio of the welfare of the obtained local optimum for a given type of contracts to the welfare of the global optimum) was used. The mean ratio bounds (over the 100 problem instances) were calculated for all the different leveled commitment protocols and agents. The 95% confidence intervals were also computed from which

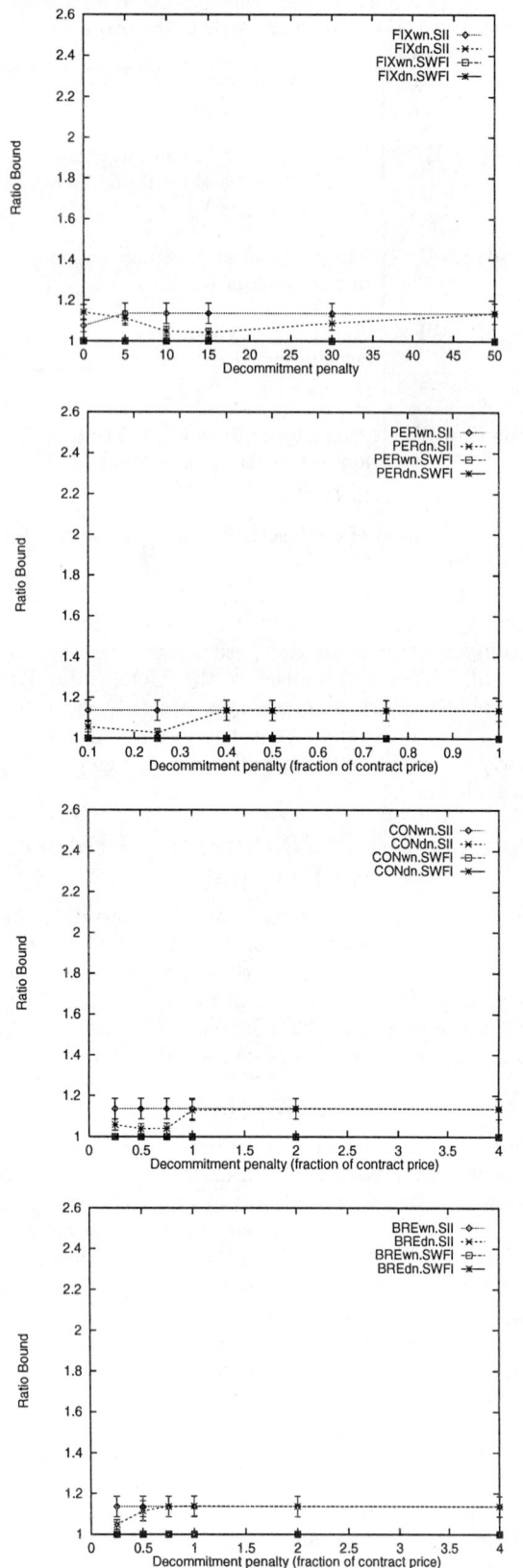

Figure 1: *Agents that perform lookahead using deterministic protocols.*

the results could be statistically analyzed.[6]

Results

The results are presented in the following order: First, the agent types are compared, then the methods of sequencing the contracts, the different ways of deciding on a contract price, and the best protocols for each agent type are discussed.

Comparison of Agent Types

Over all, agents which performed lookahead reached a higher social welfare than myopic agents. By definition the SWFl-agents (SWF-maximators conducting full lookahead) always reach the global optimum that could be reached considering the sequence of the contracts. The impact of the sequencing of the contracts will be discussed later. SWFl-agents contracting with a deterministic protocol always reached the global optimum (Figure 1).

Comparing the SIm- and SWFm-agents using a deterministic protocol, the SIm-agents outperformed the SWFm-agents in the region of low decommitment penalties (Figures 1 and 2). They did that for all the eight deterministic protocols. We can see that the *dn-protocols performs better than the *wn-protocols in the area of decommitment penalties where SIm-agents perform better than SWF-agents. This might be surprising, but without lookahead not even cooperative agents will reach the global optimum for sure, in a limited time. Technically, the reason why this happens is that a decommitment, which is not SWF-maximizing, is conducted by the SIm-agents. For some instances, if the negotiation contained more rounds, the SWFm-agents reached the same social welfare as the SIm-agents.

In several cases the myopic agents performed almost as well as the agents with full lookahead (Figures 1-4). There is a clear trade-off between reaching the globally optimal solution, and computation. In these experiments (with small problem sizes) the agents do not gain much by performing a full lookahead compared to myopic agents with well set decommitment penalties. It is considerably more complex to perform a full lookahead than no lookahead, and for large problem instances a full lookahead is not even possible. On the other hand, the decommitment penalties do not have to be chosen so carefully if the agents perform a full lookahead. That is because the agents can evaluate the future events and acting upon that knowledge up front, reducing the risk in a commitment.

Comparison of Methods of Sequencing the Contracts

Comparing the stochastic and the deterministic sequencing methods, the deterministic method always

---

[6] When using random sequenced leveled commitment protocols, the expected outcome was computed: a randomization device was not used to compute one of the possible outcomes for one instance, but all possible outcomes were computed and the expected value found.

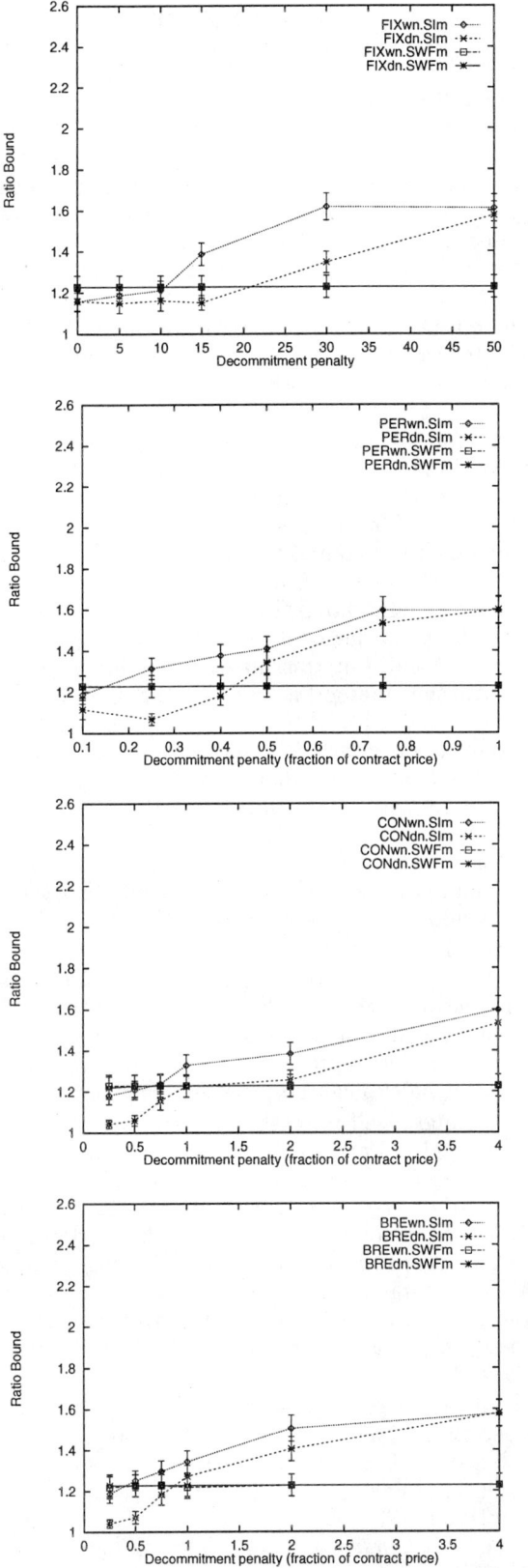

Figure 2: *Myopic agents using deterministic protocols.*

yields a lower ratio bound (Figures 1-4). That can be explained by the fact that the best possible ratio bound which is achievable with a stochastic method is greater than one. That is because the ratio bound is averaged over all possible outcomes, including those that never can reach the global optimum. The extreme example is when the same contractor and contractee meet each other in every round of the negotiation. The best result achievable, with the protocols using the stochastic method, was always reached by the SWFl-agents (SWF-maximators conducting full lookahead). For the sequences where the stochastic protocol could perform well it did (*i.e.*, where all the agents participated in the negotiation).

Comparison of Methods of Computing the Contract Price

Of the two methods of computing the contract price (the method that considered the current profit and not only the original fallback positions) never reached a higher ratio bound than the other method for all protocols, if the optimal parameterization for each protocol was used (Table 3). For other parameterizations, the optimal method of setting the price varied. The method that considers the current profit performs well for low penalties with the deterministic protocols, while the method based on the fallback positions performs well in the case of low penalties and a stochastic protocol.

Comparison of Methods and Parameterizations of Setting the Decommitment Penalty

A summary of the protocol that achieved the lowest ratio bound for each agent is found in Table 3. Two sets of best protocols are extracted, one among the stochastic protocols and one among the deterministic protocols. For all the protocols, the optimal choice of parameters was to use a low decommitment penalty (or a low percentage of contract price) which was greater than zero. Neither zero penalties nor high penalties performed well.

	Stochastic sequencing	
	Lookahead	Myopic
SI	BREd	PERd
SWF	All	CONd

	Deterministic sequencing	
	Lookahead	Myopic
SI	PERd	BREd
SWF	All	CONd/BREd

Table 3: *Summary of the optimal choice of protocols for each agent and each parameterization.*

Conclusions

In automated negotiation systems with self-interested agents it has traditionally not been possible to breach accepted contracts. Because of that, the agents have been lacking the ability to act efficiently in a dynamic environment, since they cannot accommodate future

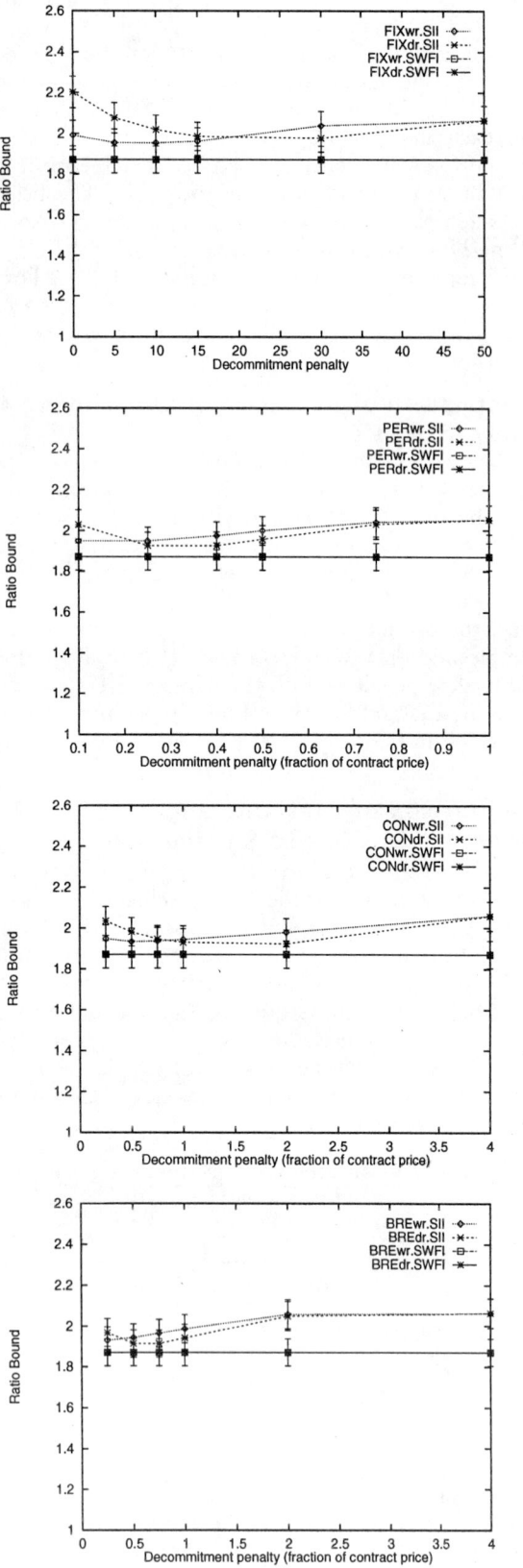

Figure 3: *Agents that perform lookahead using stochastic protocols.*

events efficiently. Contingency contracts have been suggested to solve this problem but they are not practical in all environments. Another alternative is to renegotiate, but that incurs extra negotiation overhead and requires all parties of the contract to accept the new contract. Later, leveled commitment protocols were introduced and it has been shown that they are more efficient than full commitment protocols. In a leveled commitment protocol the agents can decommit from a contract by paying a penalty to the partner(s) of the contract.

The efficiency of leveled commitment protocols depends drastically on how the decommitment penalties are decided. In this work, we have investigated several different methods of setting them. If it would be possible for the agents to choose the penalties freely, they would try to optimize the penalties in their favor. As a result, the negotiation would be more complex: there would be more variables to agree on in order for all parties of the contract to accept. If the penalties are set by the protocol, on the other hand, complexity would be eliminated from the negotiation. For example, the penalties could be fixed at a certain level by the protocol, but this may lead to suboptimal results. Another method is to relate the decommitment penalty to the price of the contract. The penalty can be either a percentage or a more complex function of the contract price. Another approach is to choose the penalties so that they compensate the victim of the breach for its lost profit. In that case, the agent would have an incentive to lie about the expected profit, so a non-manipulable mechanism for calculating the lost profit would be necessary.

A breach close to the execution deadline of the contract, or late in a negotiation, is likely to be more costly to the victim of the breach, since it could be hard to find someone to contract with within a short amount of time. In order to prevent such behavior, the decommitment penalties can be increased over time.

Surprisingly, self-interested myopic agents reach a higher social welfare quicker than cooperative myopic agents when decommitment penalties are low. The social welfare in the settings with agents that performed lookahead did not vary as much with the decommitment penalty as the social welfare in settings that consisted of myopic agents. For a short range of values of the decommitment penalty, the myopic agents performed almost as well as the agents that performed lookahead.

In all of the settings studied, the best way to set the decommitment penalties was to choose low penalties, but ones that were greater than zero. Concerning the solution quality, allowing decommitting for free is not optimal. The best strategy is to have a low decommitment penalty and a low rate of increase of the decommitment penalties.

In future research, we will study longer negotiations for agents with a full lookahead to compare the opti-

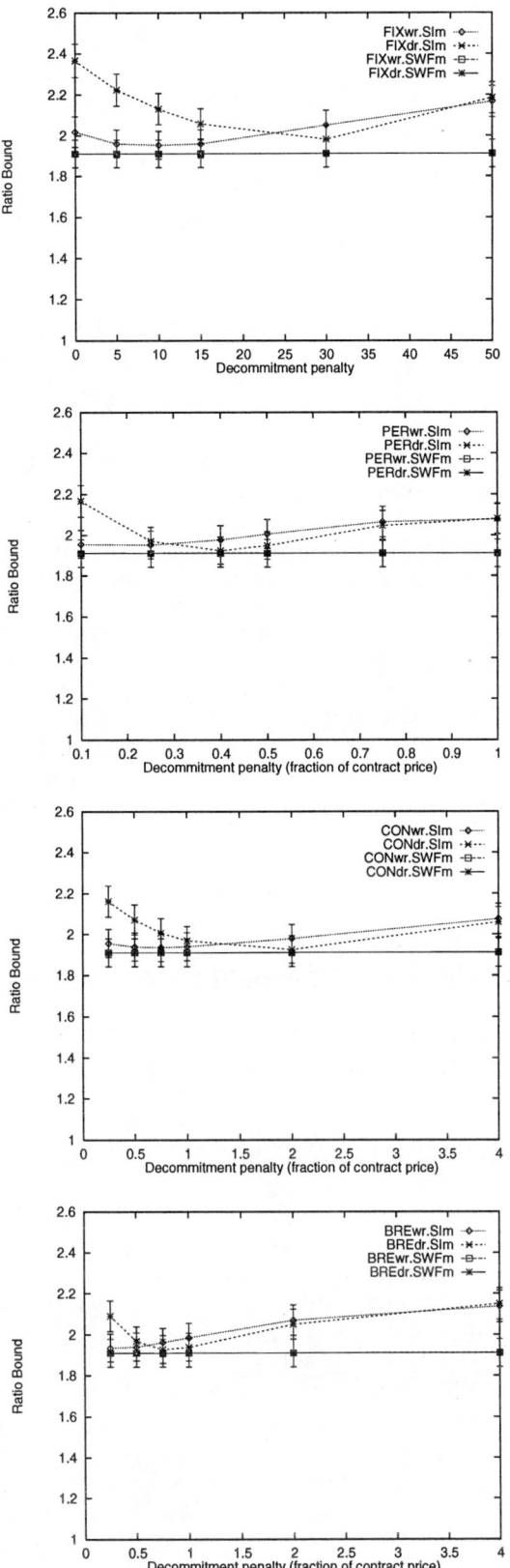

Figure 4: *Myopic agents using stochastic protocols.*

mal protocols for them with the ones for myopic agents. Optimal in the sense that they achieve a optimal social welfare with self-interested agents. Another topic of interest is to study domains with different types of agents, performing different amounts of lookahead.

Yet another important part of our future work will be to come up with better mechanisms for deciding the decommitment penalties. In this work they have been decided by the protocol, but the agents could also be allowed to conduct a negotiation over the decommitment penalties. Effective negotiation protocols for these decommitment penalties must also be developed.

References

Andersson, M. R., and Sandholm, T. W. 1998. Leveled commitment contracting among myopic individually rational agents. In *Proceedings of the Third International Conference on Multi-Agent Systems (ICMAS-98)*.

Andersson, M. R. 1998. Performance of leveled commitment protocols for automated negotiation: An empirical study. Master's thesis, Royal Institute of Technology, Stockholm, Sweden.

Diamond, P. A., and Maskin, E. 1979. An equilibrium analysis of search and breach of contract, I: Steady states. *Bell Journal of Economics* 10:282–316.

Kalakota, R., and Whinston, A. B. 1996. *Frontiers of Electronic Commerce*. Addison-Wesley Publishing Company, Inc.

Park, S.; Durfee, E. H.; and Birmingham, W. P. 1996. Advantages of strategic thinking in multiagent contracts. In *Proceedings of the First International Conference on Multi-Agent Systems (ICMAS-95)*, 259–266.

Posner, R. A. 1977. *Economic Analysis of Law*. Little, Brown and Company, 2nd edition.

Raiffa, H. 1982. *The Art and Science of Negotiation*. Cambridge, Mass.: Harvard Univ. Press.

Sandholm, T. W., and Lesser, V. R. 1996. Advantages of a leveled commitment contracting protocol. In *Proceedings of the National Conference on Artificial Intelligence*, 126–133.

Sandholm, T. W., and Ygge, F. 1997. On the gains and losses of speculation in equilibrium markets. In *Proceedings of the Fifteenth International Joint Conference on Artificial Intelligence*, 632–638.

Sandholm, T. W. 1996. *Negotiation among Self-Interested Computationally Limited Agents*. Ph.D. Dissertation, University of Massachusetts, Amherst.

Sandholm, T. W. 1998. Contract types for satisficing task allocation: I theoretical results. In *AAAI Spring Symposium Series: Satisficing Models*, 68–75.

Sen, S., and Durfee, E. 1994. The role of commitment in cooperative negotiation. *International Journal on Intelligent Cooperative Information Systems* 3(1):67–81.

Smith, R. G. 1980. The contract net protocol: High-level communication and control in a distributed problem solver. *IEEE Transactions on Computers* C-29(12):1104–1113.

Ygge, F., and Akkermans, J. M. 1996. Power load management as a computational market. In *Proceedings of the Second International Conference on Multi-Agent Systems (ICMAS-96)*, 393–400.

Anytime Coalition Structure Generation with Worst Case Guarantees[*]

Tuomas Sandholm[1] Kate Larson[2] Martin Andersson[3] Onn Shehory[4] Fernando Tohmé[5]

[1,2,3,5] Washington University
Department of Computer Science
St. Louis MO 63130-4899
{sandholm,ksl2,mra,tohme}@cs.wustl.edu

[4] Carnegie Mellon University
The Robotics Institute
Pittsburgh PA 15213-3890
onn@cs.cmu.edu

Abstract

Coalition formation is a key topic in multiagent systems. One would prefer a coalition structure that maximizes the sum of the values of the coalitions, but often the number of coalition structures is too large to allow exhaustive search for the optimal one. But then, can the coalition structure found via a partial search be guaranteed to be within a bound from optimum?

We show that none of the previous coalition structure generation algorithms can establish any bound because they search fewer nodes than a threshold that we show necessary for establishing a bound. We present an algorithm that establishes a tight bound within this minimal amount of search, and show that any other algorithm would have to search strictly more. The fraction of nodes needed to be searched approaches zero as the number of agents grows.

If additional time remains, our anytime algorithm searches further, and establishes a progressively lower tight bound. Surprisingly, just searching one more node drops the bound in half. As desired, our algorithm lowers the bound rapidly early on, and exhibits diminishing returns to computation. It also drastically outperforms its obvious contenders. Finally, we show how to distribute the desired search across self-interested manipulative agents.

Introduction

Multiagent systems with self-interested agents are becoming increasingly important. One reason for this is the *technology push* of a growing standardized communication infrastructure—Internet, WWW, NII, EDI, KQML, FIPA, Concordia, Voyager, Odyssey, Telescript, Java, *etc*—over which separately designed agents belonging to different organizations can interact in an open environment in real-time and safely carry out transactions (Sandholm 1997). The second reason is strong *application pull* for computer support for negotiation at the operative decision making level. For example, we are witnessing the advent of small transaction commerce on the Internet for purchasing goods, information, and communication bandwidth. There is also an industrial trend toward virtual enterprises: dynamic alliances of small, agile enterprises which together can take advantage of economies of scale when available (e.g., respond to more diverse orders than individual agents can), but do not suffer from diseconomies of scale.

Multiagent technology facilitates the automated formation of such dynamic coalitions at the operative decision making level. This automation can save labor time of human negotiators, but in addition, other savings are possible because computational agents can be more effective at finding beneficial short-term coalitions than humans are in strategically and combinatorially complex settings.

This paper discusses coalition structure generation in settings where there are too many coalition structures to enumerate and evaluate due to, for example, costly or bounded computation and/or limited time. Instead, agents have to select a subset of coalition structures on which to focus their search. We study which subset the agents should focus on so that they are guaranteed to reach a coalition structure that has quality within a bound from the quality of the optimal coalition structure.

Coalition formation setting

In many domains, self-interested real world parties—e.g., companies or individual people—can save costs by coordinating their activities with other parties. For example, when the planning activities are automated, it can be useful to automate the coordination activities as well. This can be done via a negotiating software agent representing each party. Coalition formation includes three activities:

1. *Coalition structure generation*: formation of coalitions by the agents such that agents within each coalition coordinate their activities, but agents do not coordinate between coalitions. Precisely, this means partitioning the set of agents into exhaustive and disjoint coalitions. This partition is called a *coalition structure* (CS).

2. *Solving the optimization problem* of each coalition. This means pooling the tasks and resources of the agents in the coalition, and solving this joint problem. The coalition's objective is to maximize monetary value: money received from outside the system for accomplishing tasks minus the cost of using resources.

3. *Dividing the value* of the generated solution among agents.

---

[*]Copyright 1998, American Association for Artificial Intelligence (www.aaai.org). All rights reserved. Supported by NSF CAREER award IRI-9703122 and NSF grant IRI-9610122.

These activities interact. For example, the coalition that an agent wants to join depends on the portion of the value that the agent would be allocated in each potential coalition.

This paper focuses on settings were the coalition structure generation activity is resource-bounded: not all coalition structures can be enumerated.

Our model of coalition structure generation

Let A be the set of agents, and $a = |A|$. As is common practice (Kahan & Rapoport 1984; Shehory & Kraus 1995; 1996; Zlotkin & Rosenschein 1994; Ketchpel 1994; Sandholm & Lesser 1997), we study coalition formation in *characteristic function games* (CFGs). In such games, the value of each coalition S is given by a characteristic function v_S.[1,2] We assume that v_S is bounded from below for each coalition S, i.e. no coalition's value is infinitely negative. We normalize the coalition values by subtracting at least $\min_{S \subset A} v_S$ from all coalition values v_S.[3] This rescales the coalition values so that $v_S \geq 0$ for all coalitions S. This rescaled game is strategically equivalent to the original game.

A coalition structure CS is a partition of agents, A, into coalitions. Each agent belongs to exactly one coalition. Some agents may be alone in their coalitions. We will call the set of all coalition structures M. For example, in a game with three agents, there are 7 possible coalitions: $\{1\}, \{2\}, \{3\}, \{1,2\}, \{2,3\}, \{3,1\}, \{1,2,3\}$ and 5 possible coalition structures: $\{\{1\}, \{2\}, \{3\}\}$, $\{\{1\}, \{2,3\}\}, \{\{2\}, \{1,3\}\}, \{\{3\}, \{1,2\}\}, \{\{1,2,3\}\}$.

Usually the goal is to maximize the social welfare of the agents A by finding a coalition structure

$$CS^* = \underset{CS \in M}{\operatorname{argmax}} V(CS), \qquad (1)$$

where

$$V(CS) = \sum_{S \in CS} v_S \qquad (2)$$

The problem is that the number of coalition structures is large ($\Omega(a^{a/2})$), so not all coalition structures can be enumerated—unless the number of agents is extremely small (below 15 or so in practice).[4] Instead, we would like to search through a subset $N \subseteq M$ of coalition structures, pick the best coalition structure we have seen

$$CS_N^* = \underset{CS \in N}{\operatorname{argmax}} V(CS), \qquad (3)$$

and be guaranteed that this coalition structure is within a bound from optimal, i.e. that

$$k \geq \frac{V(CS^*)}{V(CS_N^*)} \qquad (4)$$

is finite, and as small as possible. We define n_{min} to be the smallest size of N that allows us to establish such a bound k.

A	The set of agents.
a	The number of agents, i.e. $|A|$.
S	Symbol for a coalition.
CS	Symbol for a coalition structure.
CS^*	Welfare maximizing coalition structure.
M	The set of all possible coalition structures.
m	$|M|$, total number of coalition structures.
N	Coalition structures searched so far.
n	$|N|$.
n_{min}	Minimum n that guarantees a bound k.
CS_N^*	Welfare maximizing CS among ones seen.
$V(CS)$	Value of coalition structure CS.
k	Worst case bound on value, see Eq. 4.

Table 1: *Important symbols used in this paper.*

Lack of prior attention

Coalition structure generation has not previously received much attention. Research has focused (Kahan & Rapoport 1984; Zlotkin & Rosenschein 1994) on super-additive games, i.e. games where $v_{S \cup T} \geq v_S + v_T$ for all disjoint coalitions $S, T \subseteq A$. In such games, coalition structure generation is trivial because the agents are best off by forming the grand coalition where all agents operate together. In other words, in such games, $\{A\}$ is a social welfare maximizing coalition structure.

---

[1] These coalition values v_S may represent the quality of the optimal solution for each coalition's optimization problem, or they may represent the best bounded-rational value that a coalition can get given limited or costly computational resources for solving the problem (Sandholm & Lesser 1997).

[2] In other words, each coalition's value is independent of nonmembers' actions. However, in general the value of a coalition may depend on nonmembers' actions due to positive and negative externalities (interactions of the agents' solutions). Negative externalities between a coalition and nonmembers are often caused by shared resources. Once nonmembers are using the resource to a certain extent, not enough of that resource is available to agents in the coalition to carry out the planned solution at the minimum cost. Negative externalities can also be caused by conflicting goals. In satisfying their goals, nonmembers may actually move the world further from the coalition's goal state(s) (Rosenschein & Zlotkin 1994). Positive externalities are often caused by partially overlapping goals. In satisfying their goals, nonmembers may actually move the world closer to the coalition's goal state(s). From there the coalition can reach its goals less expensively than it could have without the actions of nonmembers. General settings with possible externalities can be modeled as *normal form games* (NFGs). CFGs are a strict subset of NFGs. However, many real-world multiagent problems happen to be CFGs (Sandholm & Lesser 1997).

[3] All of the claims of the paper are valid as long as $v_S \geq 0$ for the coalitions that the algorithm *sees*: coalitions not seen during the search may be arbitrarily bad.

[4] The exact number of coalition structures is $\sum_{i=1}^{a} S(a, i)$, where $S(a, i) = i S(a-1, i) + S(a-1, i-1)$, and $S(a, a) = S(a, 1) = 1$.

Superadditivity means that any pair of coalitions is best off by merging into one. Classically it is argued that almost all games are superadditive because, at worst, the agents in a composite coalition can use solutions that they had when they were in separate coalitions.

However, many games are not superadditive because there is some cost to the coalition formation process itself. For example, there might be coordination overhead like communication costs, or possible anti-trust penalties. Similarly, solving the optimization problem of a composite coalition may be more complex than solving the optimization problems of component coalitions. Therefore, under costly computation, component coalitions may be better off by not forming the composite coalition (Sandholm & Lesser 1997). Also, if time is limited, the agents may not have time to carry out the communications and computations required to coordinate effectively within a composite coalition, so component coalitions may be more advantageous.

In games that are not superadditive, some coalitions are best off merging while others are not. In such cases, the social welfare maximizing coalition structure varies. This paper focuses on games that are not superadditive (or if they are, this is not known in advance). In such settings, coalition structure generation is highly nontrivial.

Search graph for coalition structure generation

Taking an outsider's view, the coalition structure generation process can be viewed as search in a *coalition structure graph*, Figure 1. Now, how should such a graph be searched if there are too many nodes to search it completely?

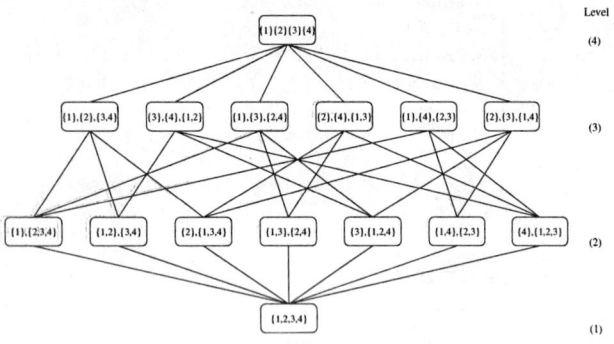

Figure 1: *Coalition structure graph for a 4-agent game. The nodes represent coalition structures. The arcs represent mergers of two coalition when followed downward, and splits of a coalition into two coalitions when followed upward.*

Minimal search to establish a bound

This section discusses how a bound k can be established while searching as little of the graph as possible.

Theorem 1 *To bound k, it suffices to search the lowest two levels of the coalition structure graph (Figure 1). With this search, the bound $k = a$, and the number of nodes searched is $n = 2^{a-1}$.*

Proof. To establish a bound, v_S of each coalition S has to be observed (in some coalition structure). The a-agent coalition can be observed by visiting the bottom node. The second lowest level has coalition structures where exactly one subset of agents has split away from the grand coalition. Therefore, we see all subsets at this level (except the grand coalition). It follows that a search of the lowest two levels sees all coalitions.

In general, CS^* can include at most a coalitions. Therefore,

$$V(CS^*) \leq a \max_S v_S \leq a \max_{CS \in N} V(CS) = aV(CS_N^*).$$

Now we can set $k = a \geq \frac{V(CS^*)}{V(CS_N^*)}$.

The number of coalition structures on the lowest level is 1. The number of coalitions on the second lowest level is $2^a - 2$ (all subsets of A, except the empty set and the grand coalition). There are two coalitions per coalition structure on this level, so there are $\frac{2^a - 2}{2}$ coalition structures at the second to lowest level. So, there are $1 + \frac{2^a - 2}{2} = 2^{a-1}$ coalition structures (nodes) on the lowest two levels. □

Theorem 2 *For the algorithm that searches the two lowest levels of the graph, the bound $k = a$ is tight.*

Proof. We construct a worst case via which the bound is shown to be tight. Choose $v_S = 1$ for all coalitions S of size 1, and $v_S = 0$ for the other coalitions. Now, $CS^* = \{\{1\}, \{2\}, ..., \{a\}\}$, and $V(CS^*) = a$. Then $CS_N^* = \{\{1\}, \{2, ..., a\}\}$.[5] Because $V(CS_N^*) = 1$, $\frac{V(CS^*)}{V(CS_N^*)} = \frac{a}{1} = a$. □

Theorem 3 *No other search algorithm (than the one that searches the bottom two levels) can establish a bound k while searching only $n = 2^{a-1}$ nodes or fewer.*

Proof. In order to establish a bound k, v_S of each coalition S must be observed. The node on the bottom level of the graph must be observed since it is the only node where the grand coalition appears. Assume that the algorithm omits m nodes on the second level. Each of the omitted nodes has $CS = \{P, Q\}$. Since coalitions P and Q are never again in the same coalition structure, two extra nodes in the graph have to be visited to observe v_P and v_Q. Assume m coalition structures $\{P_1, Q_1\}, \{P_2, Q_2\}, ..., \{P_m, Q_m\}$ are omitted. Since for $i, j, i \neq j$, at least one of the following is true, $P_i \cap P_j \neq \emptyset$, $P_i \cap Q_j \neq \emptyset$, or $Q_i \cap Q_j \neq \emptyset$, at least $m + 1$ coalition structures must be visited to replace the

---

[5]This is not unique because all coalition structures where one agent has split off from the grand coalition have the same value.

m coalition structure omitted. Therefore, for the algorithm to establish k, it must search $n > 2^{a-1}$ nodes. □

So, $n_{min} = 2^{a-1}$, and this is uniquely established via a search algorithm that visits the lowest two levels of the graph (order of these visits does not matter).

Positive interpretation

Interpreted positively, our results (Theorem 1) show that—somewhat unintuitively—a worst case bound from optimum can be guaranteed without seeing all CSs. Moreover, as the number of agents grows, the fraction of coalition structures needed to be searched approaches zero, i.e. $\frac{n_{min}}{m} \to 0$ as $a \to \infty$. This is because the algorithm needs to see only 2^{a-1} coalition structures while the total number of coalition structures is $\Omega(a^{a/2})$. See Figure 2.

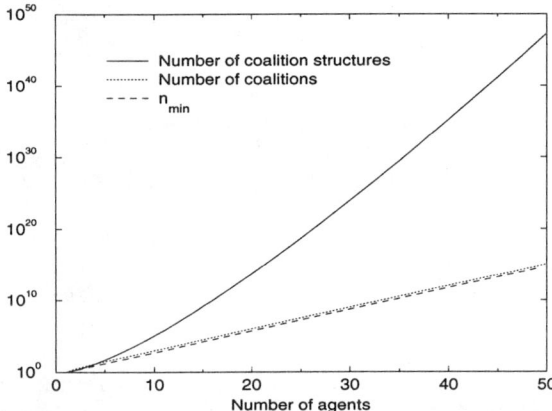

Figure 2: *Number of coalition structures, coalitions, and coalition structures needed to be searched. We use a logarithmic scale on the value axis; otherwise n_{min} and the number of coalitions would be so small compared to the number of coalition structures that their curves would be indistinguishable from the category axis.*

Interpretation as an impossibility result

Interpreted negatively, our results (Theorem 3) show that exponentially many (2^{a-1}) coalition structures have to be searched before a bound can be established. This may be prohibitively complex if the number of agents is large—albeit significantly better than attempting to enumerate all coalition structures.

Viewed as a general impossibility result, Theorem 3 states that no algorithm for coalition structure generation can establish a bound in general characteristic function games without trying at least 2^{a-1} coalition structures. This sheds light on earlier algorithms. Specifically, all prior coalition structure generation algorithms for general characteristic function games (Shehory & Kraus 1996; Ketchpel 1994)—which we know of—fail to establish such a bound. In other words, the coalition structure that they find may be arbitrarily far from optimal.

Lowering the bound with further search

We have devised the following algorithm that will establish a bound in the minimal amount of search, and then rapidly reduce the bound further if there is time for more search.[6]

Algorithm 1
COALITION-STRUCTURE-SEARCH-1

1. *Search the* **bottom** *two levels of the coalition structure graph.*

2. *Continue with a breadth-first search from the* **top** *of the graph as long as there is time left, or until the entire graph has been searched (this occurs when this breadth-first search completes level 3 of the graph, i.e. depth $a-3$).*

3. *Return the coalition structure that has the highest welfare among those seen so far.*

In the rest of this section, we analyze how this algorithm reduces the worst case bound, k, as more of the graph is searched. The analysis is tricky because the elusive worst case (CS^*) moves around in the graph for different searches, N. We introduce the notation $h = \lfloor \frac{a-l}{2} \rfloor + 2$, which is used throughout this section.

Lemma 1 *Assume that Algorithm 1 has just completed searching level l. Then*

1. *If $a \equiv l \pmod 2$ coalitions of size h will have been seen paired together with all coalitions of size $h-2$ or smaller.*

2. *If $a \not\equiv l \pmod 2$ coalitions of size h will have been seen paired together with all coalitions of size $h-1$ and smaller.*

Proof.

1. At level l the largest coalition in any coalition structure has size $a-l+1$. Therefore, one of the coalition structures at level l is of the form $S_1, S_2, \ldots, S_l$ where $|S_i| = 1$ for $i < l$ and $|S_l| = a-l+1$. Since $a \equiv l \pmod 2$, $h = \frac{a-l}{2}+2$. Take coalition S_l and remove h agents from it. Call the new coalition formed by the h agents S'_l. We will distribute the remaining $\frac{a-l}{2}-1$ agents among the coalitions of size 1. By doing this we can enumerate all possible coalitions that can appear pairwise with coalition S'_l on level l. For all $j = 1, 2, \ldots, \frac{a-l}{2}-1$, place $\frac{a-l}{2}-j$ agents in coalition S_1 and call the new coalition S_1^j. Redistribute the remaining $j-1$ agents among coalitions $S_2, \ldots, S_{l-1}$. For each j we have listed a coalition structure containing both S'_l and S_1^j. The largest of these S_1^j has size $\frac{a-l}{2}$, or $h-2$.

2. Since $a \not\equiv l \pmod 2$, $h = \frac{a-1-l}{2}+2$. Follow the same procedure as for the case 1 except that this time there

---

[6]If the domain happens to be superadditive, the algorithm finds the optimal coalition structure immediately.

are $\frac{a-1-l}{2}$ remaining agents to be redistributed once S'_l has been formed. Therefore, when we redistribute all these agents among the coalitions $S_1, \ldots S_{l-1}$, we get all coalitions that were found in part 1, along with coalitions of size $h-1$. □

From Lemma 1, it follows that after searching level l with Algorithm 1, we cannot have seen two coalitions of h members together in the same coalition structure.

Theorem 4 *After searching level l with Algorithm 1, the bound $k(n)$ is $\lceil \frac{a}{h} \rceil$ if $a \equiv h-1 \pmod{h}$ and $a \equiv l \pmod 2$. Otherwise the bound is $\lfloor \frac{a}{h} \rfloor$.*

Proof. Case 1. Assume $a \equiv l \pmod 2$ and $a \equiv h-1 \pmod{h-1}$. Let α be an assignment of coalition values which give the worst case. For any other assignment of coalition values, β, the inequality $k(n) = \frac{V_\alpha(CS^*)}{V_\alpha(CS_l)} \geq \frac{V_\beta(CS^*)}{V_\beta(CS_l)}$ holds. Since CS^* is the best coalition structure under α, we can assume that $V_S = 0$ for all coalitions $S \notin CS^*$ without decreasing the ratio $\frac{V_\alpha(CS^*)}{V_\alpha(CS_l)}$. Also, no two coalitions $S, S' \in CS^*$ can appear together if $v_S + v_{S'} > \max\{v_{S''}\}$ for $S'' \in CS^*$, since otherwise we could decrease the ratio $k(n)$. Therefore $V_\alpha(CS_l) = \max\{v_S\}$ for $S \in CS^*$ Call this value v^*. We can derive an equivalent worst case, α', from α as follows:

1. Find a coalition structure CS' with $\lfloor \frac{a}{h} \rfloor$ coalitions of size h and one coalition of size $h-1$.
2. Define $\bar{v} = \frac{V_\alpha(CS^*)}{\lfloor \frac{a}{h} \rfloor + 1}$.
3. Assign a value $v'_S = \bar{v}$ to each coalition in CS'.

Clearly $V_\alpha(CS^*) = V_{\alpha'}(CS')$. From Lemma 1 we know that no two coalitions in CS' have been seen together. The best value of a coalition structure seen during the search is $V_{\alpha'}(CS_l) = \bar{v}$. Therefore the following inequalities hold;

$$V_{\alpha'}(CS') = (\lfloor \frac{a}{h} \rfloor + 1)\bar{v} = (\lfloor \frac{a}{h} \rfloor + 1)V_{\alpha'}(CS_l)$$

$$(\lfloor \frac{a}{h} \rfloor + 1)V_{\alpha'}(CS_l) \leq (\lfloor \frac{a}{h} \rfloor + 1)v^* \leq (\lfloor \frac{a}{h} \rfloor + 1)V_\alpha(CS_l).$$

Since $V_\alpha(CS^*) = V_{\alpha'}(CS')$ and $V_{\alpha'}(CS_l) \leq V_\alpha(CS_l)$,

$$k(n) = \frac{V_\alpha(CS^*)}{V_\alpha(CS_l)} \leq \frac{V_{\alpha'}(CS')}{V_{\alpha'}(CS_l)} = \lfloor \frac{a}{h} \rfloor + 1 = \lceil \frac{a}{h} \rceil.$$

Therefore the bound is $\lceil \frac{a}{h} \rceil$.

Case 2. This is a similar argument as in Case 1, except that the assignment of values to the coalitions in the equivalent worst case coalition structure is different. Define α as before and let CS^+ be a coalition structure with $\lfloor \frac{a}{h} \rfloor$ coalitions of size h and one possible remainder coalition of size less than h. Define $\bar{v} = \frac{V_\alpha(CS^*)}{\lfloor \frac{a}{h} \rfloor}$ and assign value $v_S^+ = \bar{v}$ if $|S| = h$ and $S \in CS^+$, otherwise let $v_S = 0$ for all other coalitions including the remainder coalition in CS^+. Thus the best coalition seen has value $V_{\alpha^+}(CS_l) = \overline{v_S}$ and we have the following inequalities:

$$V_{\alpha^+}(CS^+) = (\lfloor \frac{a}{h} \rfloor)\bar{v} = (\lfloor \frac{a}{h} \rfloor)V_{\alpha^+}(CS_l)$$

$$(\lfloor \frac{a}{h} \rfloor)V_{\alpha^+}(CS_l) \leq (\lfloor \frac{a}{h} \rfloor)v^* \leq (\lfloor \frac{a}{h} \rfloor)V_\alpha(CS_l).$$

Therefore the bound $k(n) = \lfloor \frac{a}{h} \rfloor$. □

Theorem 5 *The bound in Theorem 4 is tight.*

Proof. Case 1: Assume $a \equiv l \pmod 2$ and $a \equiv h-1 \pmod{h}$. The bound is $\lceil \frac{a}{h} \rceil$. Assume you have the coalition structure CS' from Theorem 4. Assign value 1 to each coalition $S \in CS'$ and assign value 0 to all other coalitions. Then $V(CS') = \lceil \frac{a}{h} \rceil$. Since (Lemma 1) no two of the coalitions in CS' have ever appeared in the same coalition structure, $V(CS_l) = 1$. Therefore $\frac{V(CS')}{V(CS_l)} = \frac{\lceil \frac{a}{h} \rceil}{1} = \lceil \frac{a}{h} \rceil$ and the bound is tight.

Case 2: Assume $a \not\equiv l \pmod 2$ or $a \not\equiv h-1 \pmod h$. The bound is $\lfloor \frac{a}{h} \rfloor$. Assign value 1 to each coalition $S \in CS^+$ from Theorem 4 and assign value 0 to all other coalitions. Then $V(CS^+) = \lfloor \frac{a}{h} \rfloor$ and $V(CS_l) = 1$. Therefore $\frac{V(CS^+)}{V(CS_l)} = \frac{\lfloor \frac{a}{h} \rfloor}{1} = \lfloor \frac{a}{h} \rfloor$ and the bound is tight. □

As we have shown in the previous section, before 2^{a-1} nodes have been searched, no bound can be established, and at $n = 2^{a-1}$ the bound $k = a$. The surprising fact is that by seeing just one additional node ($n = 2^{a-1}+1$), i.e. the top node, the bound drops in half ($k = \frac{a}{2}$). Then, to drop k to about $\frac{a}{3}$, two more levels need to be searched. Roughly speaking, the divisor in the bound increases by one every time two more levels are searched. So, the anytime phase (step 2) of Algorithm 1 has the desirable feature that the bound drops rapidly early on, and there are overall diminishing returns to further search, Figure 3.

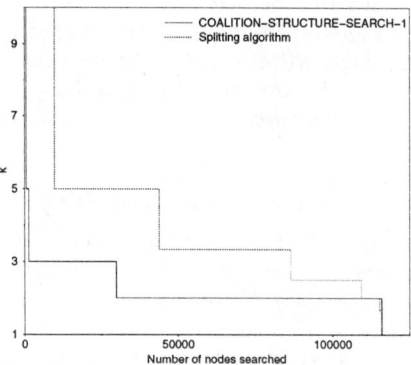

Figure 3: *Ratio bound k as a function of search size in a 10-agent game.*

Comparison to other algorithms

All previous coalition structure generation algorithms for general CFGs (Shehory & Kraus 1996; Ketchpel 1994)—that we know of—fail to establish any worst case bound because they search fewer than 2^{a-1} coalition structures. Therefore, we compare our Algorithm 1 to two other obvious candidates:

- **Merging algorithm**, i.e. breadth first search from the top of the coalition structure graph. This algorithm cannot establish any bound before it has searched the entire graph. This is because, to establish a bound, the algorithm needs to see every coalition, and the grand coalition only occurs in the bottom node. Visiting the grand coalition as a special case would not help much since at least part of level 2 needs to be searched as well: coalitions of size $a - 2$ only occur there.

- **Splitting algorithm**, i.e. breadth first search from the bottom of the graph. This is identical to Algorithm 1 up to the point where 2^{a-1} nodes have been searched, and a bound $k = a$ has been established. After that, the splitting algorithm reduces the bound much slower than Algorithm 1. This can be shown by constructing bad cases for the splitting algorithm: the worst case may be even worse. To construct a bad case, set $v_S = 1$ if $|S| = 1$, and $v_S = 0$ otherwise. Now, $CS^* = \{\{1\},...,\{a\}\}$, $V(CS^*) = a$, and $V(CS_N^*) = l-1$, where l is the level that the algorithm has completed (because the number of unit coalitions in a CS never exceeds $l-1$). So, $\frac{V(CS^*)}{V(CS_N^*)} = \frac{a}{l-1}$,[7] Figure 3. In other words the divisor drops by one every time a level is searched. However, the levels that this algorithm searches first have many more nodes than the levels that Algorithm 1 searches first.

Variants of the problem

In general, one would want to construct an anytime algorithm that establishes a lower k for any amount of search n, compared to any other anytime algorithm. However, such an algorithm might not exist. It is conceivable that the search which establishes the minimal k while searching n' nodes ($n' > n$) does not include all nodes of the search which establishes the minimal k while searching n nodes. This hypothesis is supported by the fact that the curves in Figure 3 cross in the end. However, this is not conclusive because Algorithm 1 might not be the optimal anytime algorithm, and because the bad cases for the splitting algorithm were not shown to be worst cases.

If it turns out that no anytime algorithm is best for all n, one could use information (e.g. exact, probabilistic, or bounds) about the termination time to construct a *design-to-time algorithm* which establishes the lowest possible k for the specified amount of search.

In this paper we have discussed algorithms that have an *off-line search control* policy, i.e. the nodes to be searched have to be selected without using information accrued from the search so far. With *on-line search control*, one could perhaps establish a lower k with less search because the search can be redirected based on the values observed in the nodes so far. With on-line search control, it might make a difference whether the search observes only values of coalition structures, $V(CS)$, or values of individual coalitions, v_S, in those structures. The latter gives more information.

None of these variants (anytime vs. design-to-time, and off-line vs. on-line search control) would affect our results that searching the bottom two levels of the coalition structure graph is the unique minimal way to establish a worst case bound, and that the bound is tight. However, the results on searching further might vary in these different settings. This is a focus of our future research.

Distributing coalition structure search among insincere agents

This section discusses the distribution of coalition structure search across agents (because the search can be done more efficiently in parallel, and the agents will share the burden of computation) and the methods of motivating self-interested agents to actually follow the desired search method. Self-interested agents prefer greater personal payoffs, so they will search for coalition structures that maximize personal payoffs, ignoring k. In order to motivate such agents to follow a particular search that leads to desirable social outcomes (e.g. a search that guarantees a desirable worst case bound k), the interaction protocol has to be carefully designed. It is also necessary to take into account that an agent's preference between CSs depends on the way in which $V(CS)$ is distributed among the agents. Classical game theoretic CS selection and payoff division methods are not viable (unless modified) in our setting since they require knowledge of every $CS \in M$. This is because, according to those solution concepts, an agent can justifiably claim more than others receive from $V(CS)$ by objecting to CS (both to the structure and to the payoff distribution). A justified objection (as defined classically e.g. in (Kahan & Rapoport 1984)) depends on all possible CSs. Thus it uses information beyond the region of the search space that any nonexhaustive algorithm should search. The protocol designer cannot prohibit access to information that may support such objection because the agents can locally decide what to search. However, the protocol designer can forbid objections and make additional search unbeneficial, as we demonstrate below.[8] The distributed search consists of the following stages:

1. **Deciding what part of the coalition structure graph to search:** This decision can be made in advance (outside the distributed search mechanism), or be dictated by a central authority, or by a randomly chosen agent[9], or be decided using some form

---

[7] The only exception comes when the algorithm completes the last (top) level, i.e $l = a$. Then $\frac{V(CS^*)}{V(CS_N^*)} = 1$.

[8] The protocol designer cannot prevent agents from opting out, but such agents receive null excess payoffs since they do not collude with anyone. That is, for $|S| = 1$, the payoff to the agent is equal to its coalition value v_S. This assumes that agents do not recollude outside the protocol, but such considerations are outside of protocol design.

of negotiation. The earlier results in this paper give prescriptions about which part to search. For example, the agents can decide to use Algorithm 1.

2. **Partitioning the search space among agents:** Each agent is assigned some part of the coalition structure graph to search. The enforcement mechanism, presented later, will motivate the agents to search exactly what they are assigned, no matter how unfairly the assignment is done. One way of achieving *ex ante* fairness is to randomly allocate the set search space portions to the agents. In this way, each agent searches equally on an expected value basis, although *ex post*, some may search more than others.[9] The fairest option is to distribute the space so that each agent gets an equal share.

3. **Actual search:** Each agent searches part of the search space. The enforcement mechanism guarantees that each agent is motivated to search exactly the part of the space that was assigned to that agent. Each agent, having completed the search, tells the others which CS maximized $V(CS)$ in its search space.

4. **Enforcement of the protocol:** One agent, i, and one search space of an agent j, $j \neq i$, will be selected randomly.[9] Agent i will re-search the search space of j to verify that j has performed its search as required. Agent j gets caught of mis-searching (or misrepresenting) if i finds a better CS in j's space than j reported (or i sees that the CS that j reported does not belong to j's space at all). If j gets caught, it has to pay a penalty P. To motivate i to conduct this additional search, we make i the claimant of P. There is no pure strategy Nash equilibrium in this protocol.[10] If i searches and the penalty is high enough, then j is motivated to search sincerely. However, i is not motivated to search since it cannot receive P. Instead, there will be a mixed strategy equilibrium where i and j search truthfully with some probabilities. By increasing P, the probability that j searches can be made arbitrarily close to one. The probability that i searches approaches zero, which minimizes enforcement overhead.[11]

5. **Additional search:** The previous steps of this distributed mechanism can be repeated if more time to search remains. For example, the agents could first do step 1 of Algorithm 1. Then, they could repeatedly search more and more as time allows, again using the distributed method.

---

[9]The randomization can be done without a trusted third party by using a distributed nonmanipulable protocol for randomly permuting agents (Zlotkin & Rosenschein 1994). Distributed randomization is also discussed in (Linial 1992).

[10]See (Mas-Colell, Whinston, & Green 1995) for a definition of Nash equilibrium.

[11]Agent j will try to trade off the cost of search against the risk of getting caught, and could decide that the risk is worth taking. This problem can be minimized by choosing a high enough P.

6. **Payoff division:** Many alternative methods for payoff division among agents could be used here. The only concern is that the division of $V(CS)$ may affect what CS an agent wants to report as a result of its search since different CSs may give the agent different payoffs (depending on the payoff division scheme). However, by making P high enough compared to $V(CS)$s, this consideration can be made negligible compared to the risk of getting caught.

Related research on computational coalition formation

Coalition formation has been widely studied in game theory (Kahan & Rapoport 1984; Bernheim, Peleg, & Whinston 1987; Aumann 1959). They address the question of how to divide $V(CS^*)$ among agents so as to achieve stability of the payoff configuration. Some also address coalition structure generation. However, most of that work has not taken into account the computational limitations involved. This section reviews some of the work that has.

(Deb, Weber, & Winter 1996) bound the maximal number of payoff configurations that must be searched to guarantee stability. Unlike our work, they neither address a bound on solution quality nor provide methods for coalition structure generation.

(Ketchpel 1994) presents a coalition formation method which addresses coalition structure generation as well as payoff distribution. These are handled simultaneously. His algorithm uses cubic time in the number of agents, but guarantees neither a bound from optimum nor stability of the coalition structure. There is no mechanism for motivating self-interested agents to follow his algorithm.

(Shehory & Kraus 1996) analyze coalition formation among self-interested agents with perfect information in CFGs. Their protocol guarantees that if agents follow it (nothing necessarily motivates them to do so), a certain stability criterion (K-stability) is met. Their other protocol guarantees a weaker form of stability (polynomial K-stability), but only requires searching a polynomial number of coalition structures. Their algorithm is an anytime algorithm, but does not guarantee a bound from optimum.

(Shehory & Kraus 1995) also present an algorithm for coalition structure generation among cooperative agents. The complexity of the problem is reduced by limiting the number of agents per coalition. The greedy algorithm guarantees that the solution is within a loose ratio bound from the best solution that is possible *given the limit on the number of agents*. However, this benchmark can, itself, be arbitrarily far from optimum. On the other hand, our work computes the bound based on the actual optimum. Our result that no algorithm can establish a bound while searching less than 2^{a-1} nodes does not apply to their setting because they are not solving general CFGs. Instead, they address a more specialized setting where the v_S values have special structure. In such settings it may be possible to establish a worst case bound with less search than in general CFGs.

(Sandholm & Lesser 1997) study coalition formation with a focus on the optimization activity: how do computational limitations affect which coalition structure should form, and whether that structure is stable? That work used a normative model of bounded rationality based on the agents' algorithms' performance profiles and the unit cost of computation. All coalition structures were enumerated because the number of agents was relatively small, but it was not assumed that they could be evaluated exactly because the optimization problems could not be solved exactly due to intractability. The methods of this paper can be combined with their work if the performance profiles are deterministic. In such cases, the v_S values represent the value of each coalition, given that that coalition would strike the optimal tradeoff between quality of the optimization solution and the cost of that computation. Our algorithm can be used to search for a coalition structure, and only afterwards would the coalitions in the chosen coalition structure actually attack their optimization problems. If the performance profiles include uncertainty, this separation of coalition structure generation and optimization does not work e.g. because an agent may want to redecide its membership if its original coalition receives a worse optimization solution than expected.

Conclusions and future research

Coalition formation is a key topic in multiagent systems. One would prefer a coalition structure that maximizes the sum of the values of the coalitions, but often the number of coalition structures is too large to allow exhaustive search for the optimal one. This paper focused on establishing a worst case bound on the quality of the coalition structure while only searching a small portion of the coalition structures.

We showed that none of the prior coalition structure generation algorithms for general CFGs can establish any bound because they search fewer nodes than a threshold that we showed necessary for establishing a bound. We presented an algorithm that establishes a tight bound within this minimal amount of search, and showed that any other algorithm would have to search strictly more. The fraction of nodes needed to be searched approaches zero as the number of agents grows.

If additional time remains, our anytime algorithm searches further, and establishes a progressively lower tight bound. Surprisingly, just searching one more node drops the bound in half. As desired, our algorithm lowers the bound rapidly early on, and exhibits diminishing returns to computation. It also drastically outperforms its obvious contenders: the merging algorithm and the splitting algorithm. Finally, we showed how to distribute the desired search across self-interested manipulative agents.

Our results can also be used as prescriptions for designing negotiation protocols for coalition structure generation. The agents should not start with everyone operating separately—as one would do intuitively. Instead, they should start from the grand coalition, and consider different ways of splitting off exactly one coalition. After that, they should try everyone operating separately, and continue from there by considering mergers of two coalitions at a time.

Future research includes studying design-to-time algorithms and on-line search control policies for coalition structure generation. We are also analyzing the interplay of dynamic coalition formation and belief revision among bounded-rational agents (Tohmé & Sandholm 1997). The long term goal is to construct normative methods that reduce the complexity—in the number of agents and in the size of each coalition's optimization problem—for coalition structure generation, optimization and payoff division.

References

Aumann, R. 1959. Acceptable points in general cooperative n-person games. volume IV of *Contributions to the Theory of Games*. Princeton University Press.

Bernheim, B. D.; Peleg, B.; and Whinston, M. D. 1987. Coalition-proof Nash equilibria: I concepts. *Journal of Economic Theory* 42(1):1–12.

Deb, R.; Weber, S.; and Winter, E. 1996. The Nakamura theorem for coalition structures of quota games. *International Journal of Game Theory* 25(2):189–198.

Kahan, J. P., and Rapoport, A. 1984. *Theories of Coalition Formation*. Lawrence Erlbaum Associates Publishers.

Ketchpel, S. 1994. Forming coalitions in the face of uncertain rewards. In *AAAI*, 414–419.

Linial, N. 1992. Games computers play: Game-theoretic aspects of computing. Technical Report 92-5, Leibniz Center for Computer Science, Hebrew University, Jerusalem.

Mas-Colell, A.; Whinston, M.; and Green, J. R. 1995. *Microeconomic Theory*. Oxford University Press.

Rosenschein, J. S., and Zlotkin, G. 1994. *Rules of Encounter*. MIT Press.

Sandholm, T. W., and Lesser, V. R. 1997. Coalitions among computationally bounded agents. *Artificial Intelligence* 94(1):99–137. Special issue on Economic Principles of Multiagent Systems. Early version at IJCAI-95.

Sandholm, T. W. 1997. Unenforced ecommerce transactions. *IEEE Internet Computing* 1(6):47–54. Special issue on Electronic Commerce.

Shehory, O., and Kraus, S. 1995. Task allocation via coalition formation among autonomous agents. In *IJCAI*, 655–661.

Shehory, O., and Kraus, S. 1996. A kernel-oriented model for coalition-formation in general environments: Implemetation and results. In *AAAI*, 134–140.

Tohmé, F., and Sandholm, T. W. 1997. Coalition formation processes with belief revision among bounded rational self-interested agents. In *IJCAI Workshop on Social Interaction and Communityware*, 43–51.

Zlotkin, G., and Rosenschein, J. S. 1994. Coalition, cryptography and stability: Mechanisms for coalition formation in task oriented domains. In *AAAI*, 432–437.

A Motivational System for Regulating Human-Robot Interaction

Cynthia Breazeal (Ferrell)
Massachusetts Institute of Technology
Artificial Intelligence Laboratory
545 Technology Square, Room 938
Cambridge, MA 02139 USA
email: ferrell@ai.mit.edu

Abstract

This paper presents a motivational system for an autonomous robot which is designed to regulate human-robot interaction. The mode of social interaction is that of a caretaker-infant dyad where a human acts as the caretaker for the robot. An infant's emotions and drives play a very important role in generating meaningful interactions with the caretaker, and regulating these interactions to maintain an environment suitable for the learning process (Bullowa 1979). Similarly, the learning task for the robot is to apply various communication skills acquired during social exchanges to manipulate the caretaker such that its drives are satisfied. Toward this goal, the motivational system implements **drives**, **emotions**, and facial expressions. Although the details of the learning itself are beyond the scope of this paper, this work represents an important step toward realizing robots that can engage in meaningful bi-directional social interactions with humans.

Introduction

We want to build robots that engage in meaningful social exchanges with humans. In contrast to current work in robotics that focus on robot-robot interactions (Billard & Dautenhahn 1997), this work concentrates on human-robot interactions. By doing so, it is possible to have a socially sophisticated human assist the robot in acquiring more sophicticated communication skills and help it learn the meaning these acts have for others. Toward this end, our approach is inspired by the way infants learn how to communicate with adults.

This work represents the first stages of this long term endeavor. We present a motivational system for an autonomous robot specialized for learning in a social context. Specifically, the mode of social interaction is that of a caretaker-infant dyad where a human acts as the caretaker for the robot. The communication skills targeted for learning are those exhibited by infants,

i.e., turn taking, shared attention, vocalizations. The context for learning involves social exchanges where the robot learns how to manipulate the caretaker into satisfying its internal drives.

An infant's emotions and drives play an important role in generating meaningful interactions with the caretaker (Bullowa 1979). These interactions constitute learning episodes for new communication behaviors. In particular, the infant is strongly biased to learn communication skills that result in having the caretaker satisfy the infant's drives (Halliday 1975). The infant's emotional responses provide important cues which the caretaker uses to assess how to satiate the infant's drives, and how to carefully regulate the complexity of the interaction. The former is critical for the infant to learn how its actions affect the caretaker, and the later is critical for establishing and maintaining a suitable learning environment for the infant where he is neither bored nor over-stimulated.

The robot's motivational system is designed to generate an analogous interaction for a robot-human dyad as for an infant-caretaker dyad. As such, the motivational system implements **drives**, **emotions**, and facial expressions. These components interact with one another to maintain a mutually regulated interaction with the human at an appropriate level of intensity. This paper focuses on the details of how the motivational system performs this regulatory function, the details of what is learned and how the learning occurs are left for future papers.

A picture of the robot is shown in figure 1. It consists of two active stereo systems, vision and audio, embellished with facial features for emotive expression. Currently, these facial features include eyebrows, ears, eyeballs, and eyelids (with a mouth soon to follow). The robot is able to show recognizable expressions analogous to anger, fatigue, fear, disgust, excitement, happiness, interest, sadness, and surprise.

This paper is organized as follows: first we discuss the numerous roles motivations play in natural systems—particularly as it applies to behavior selection, regulating the intensity of social interactions, and learning in a social context. Next we present a frame-

Copyright ©1998, American Association for Artificial Intelligence (www.aaai.org). All rights reserved.

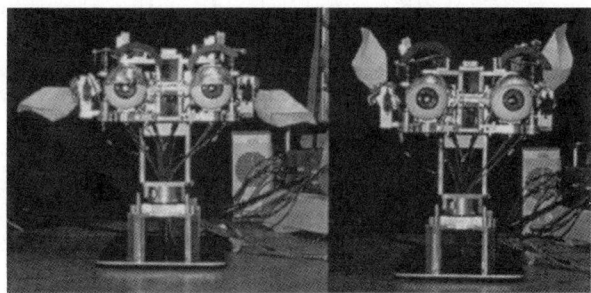

Figure 1: At left, Kismet displays an angry expression. At right, it displays a look of surprise. Kismet has an active stereo vision system with color CCD cameras mounted inside the eyeballs. A small microphones is mounted on each ear providing audio inputs.

work (inspired by ideas from ethology, psychology, and cognitive development) for the design of the motivational system and its integration with behavior and expressive motor acts. After we illustrate these ideas with a particular implementation on a physical robot, we present the results of some early human-robot interaction experiments. Finally, we discuss planned extensions to the existing system.

A Framework for Designing Motivational Systems

A framework for how the motivational system interacts with and is expressed through behavior is shown in figure 2. The system architecture consists of four subsystems: *the motivation system*, the *behavior system*, the *perceptual system*, and the *motor system*. The motivation system consists of **drives** and **emotions**, the behavior system consists of various types of behaviors as conceptualized by Tinbergen (1951) and Lorenz (1973), the perceptual system extracts salient features from the world, and the facial expressions are implemented within the motor system along with other motor skills. The organization and operation of this framework is heavily influenced by concepts from psychology, ethology, and developmental psychology.

Computational Substrate: The overall system is implemented as an agent-based architecture similar to that of (Blumberg 1996) and (Maes 1990). For this implementation, the basic computational process is modeled as a transducer. Its activation energy x is computed by the equation: $x = (\sum_{n}^{j=1} w_j \cdot i_j) + b$ for integer values of inputs i_j, weights w_j, bias b where n is the number of inputs. The weights can be either positive or negative; a positive weight corresponds to an excitatory connection and a negative weight corresponds to an inhibitory connection. The process is *active* when its activation level exceeds an *activation threshold*. When active, the process may perform

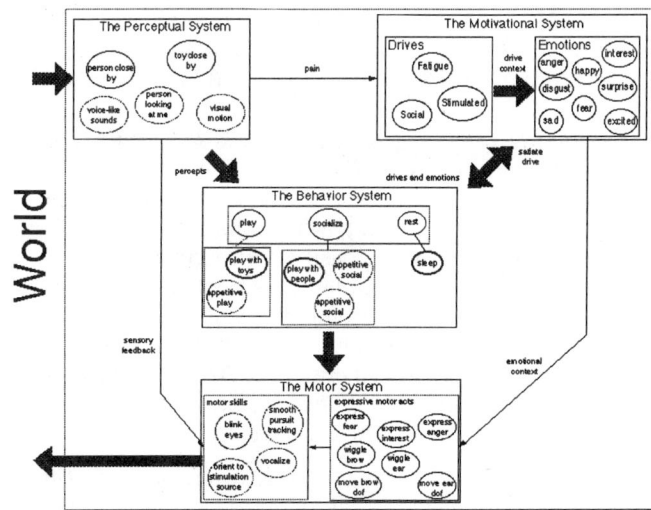

Figure 2: This figure illustrates our framework for building a motivational system and integrating it with behavior in the world. The implementation used in our experiments is shown in figure 3

some special computation, send output messages to connected processes, spread some of its activation energy to connected units (Maes 1990), and/or express itself through behavior. Each **drive**, **emotion**, behavior, percept, and motor skill are modeled as a separate transducer process specifically tailored for its role in the overall system architecture. Details are presented in the following section.

Drives: The robot's drives serve three purposes. First, they influence behavior selection by preferentially passing activation to some behaviors over others. Second, they influence the **emotive** state of the robot by passing activation energy to the **emotive** processes. Since the robot's expressions reflect its **emotive** state, the **drives** indirectly control the expressive cues the robot displays to the caretaker. Third, they provide a learning context – the robot learns skills that serve to satisfy its **drives**.

The design of the robot's drive subsystem is heavily inspired by ethological views (Lorenz 1973), (Tinbergen 1951). One distinguishing feature of **drives** is their temporally cyclic behavior. That is, given no stimulation, a **drive** will tend to increase in intensity unless it is satiated. For instance, an animal's hunger level or need to sleep follows a cyclical pattern.

Another distinguishing feature of **drives** are their homeostatic nature. For animals to survive, they must maintain a variety of critical parameters (such as temperature, energy level, amount of fluids, etc.) within a bounded range. As such, the **drives** keep changing in intensity to reflect the ongoing needs of the robot and the urgency for tending to them. There is a desired operational point for each **drive** and an acceptable

Agents 55

bounds of operation around that point. We call this range the *homeostatic regime*. As long as a `drive` is within the homeostatic regime, the robot's "needs" are being adequately met.

For my robot, each drive is modeled as a separate process with a temporal input to implement its cyclic behavior. The activation energy of each `drive` ranges between $[-max, +max]$, where the magnitude of the `drive` represents its intensity. For a given `drive` level, a large positive magnitude corresponds to being understimulated by the environment, whereas a large negative magnitude corresponds to being overstimulated by the environment. In general, each `drive` is partitioned into three regimes: an *under-whelmed regime*, an *over-whelmed regime*, and the *homeostatic regime*.

Behaviors: `Drives`, however, cannot satiate themselves. They become satiated whenever the robot is able to evoke the corresponding *consummatory behavior*. For instance, with respect to animals, eating satiates the hunger drive; sleeping satiates the fatigue drive, and so on. At any point in time, the robot is motivated to engage in behaviors that maintain the `drives` within their homeostatic regime. Furthermore, whenever a `drive` moves farther from its desired operation point, the robot becomes more predisposed to engage in behaviors that serve to satiate that `drive` — as the `drive` activation level increases, it passes more of its activation energy to the corresponding consummatory behavior. As long as the consummatory behavior is active, the intensity of the `drive` is reduced toward the homeostatic regime. When this occurs, the `drive` becomes satiated, and the amount of activation energy it passes to the consummatory behavior decreases until the consummatory behavior is eventually released.

For each consummatory behavior, there may also be one or more affiliated *appetitive behaviors*. One can view each appetitive behavior as a separate behavioral strategy for bringing the robot to a state where it can directly activate the desired consummatory behavior. For instance, the case may arise where a given `drive` stongly potentiates its consummatory behavior, but environmental circumstances prevent it from becoming active. In this case, the robot may be able to activate an affiliated appetitive behavior instead, which will eventually enable the consummatory behavior to be activated.

In this implementation, every behavior is modeled as a separate goal-directed process. In general, both internal and external factors are used to compute their relevance (whether or not they should be activated). The activation level of each behavior can range between $[0, max]$ where max is an integer value determined empirically. The most significant inputs come from the `drive` they act to satiate and from the environment. When a consummatory behavior is active, its output acts to reduce the activation energy of the `drive` it is associated with. When an appetitive behavior is active, it serves to bring the robot into an environmental state suitable for activating the affiliated consummatory behavior.

Emotions: For the robot, `emotions` of the robot serve two functions. First, they influence the `emotive` expression of the robot by passing activation energy to the face motor processes. Second, they play an important role in regulating face to face exchanges with the caretaker. The `drives` play an important role in establishing the `emotional` state of the robot, which is reflected by its facial expression, hence `emotions` play an important role in communicating the state of the robot's "needs" to the caretaker and the urgency for tending to them. The emotions also play an important role in learning during face to face exchanges with the caretaker, but we leave the details of this to another paper.

The organization and operation of the emotion subsystem is strongly inspired by various theories of emotions in humans (Ekman & Davidson 1994), (Izard 1993), and most closely resembles the framework presented in (Velasquez 1996). The robot has several `emotion` processes. Although they are quite different from emotions in humans, they are designed to be rough analogs — especially with respect to the accompanying facial expressions. As such, each `emotion` is distinct from the others and consists of a family of similar `emotions` which are graded in intensity. For instance, `happiness` can range from being `content` (a baseline activation level) to `ecstatic` (a high activation level). Numerically, the activation level of each `emotion` can range between $[0, max]$ where max is an integer value determined empirically. Although the `emotions` are always active, their intensity must exceed a threshold level before they are expressed externally. When this occurs, the corresponding facial expression reflects the level of activation of the `emotion`. Once an `emotion` rises above its activation threshold, it decays over time back toward the base line level (unless it continues to receive inputs from other processes or events). Hence, unlike `drives`, `emotions` have an intense expression followed by a fleeing nature. Ongoing events that maintain the activation level slightly above threshold correspond to `moods` in this implementation. `Tempermanents` are established by setting the bias term. `Blends` of emotions occur when several compatible emotions are expressed simultaneously. To avoid having conflicting `emotions` active at the same time, mutually inhibitory connections exist between confliting emotions.

Facial Expressions: For each `emotion` there is an accompanying facial expression. These are implemented in the motor system among various motor processes. The robot's facial features move analgously to how humans adjust their facial features to express different emotions, and the robot's ears move analogously to how dogs to move theirs to express motivational state.

Design of the Motivational System

The robot's motivational system is composed of three inter-related subsystems. One subsystem implements the robot's **drives**, another implements its **emotions**, and the last implements its facial expressions. Although the expressive skills are implemented in the motor system, here we consider them as part of the motivational system. We also present relevant aspects of the behavior system. We present the design specification of each subsystem in the remainder of this section.

Motivations establish the nature of a creature by defining its needs and influencing how and when it acts to satisfy them. The "nature" of my robot is to learn in a social environment. All **drives**, **emotions**, and behaviors are organized such that the robot is in a state of homeostatic balance when it is functioning adeptly and is in an environment that affords high learning potential. This entails that the robot be motivated to engage in appropriate interactions with its environment (i.e. the caretaker), and that it is neither under-whelmed or over-whelmed by these interactions.

The Drive Subsystem: For an animal, adequately satisfying its drives is paramount to survival. Similarly, for my robot, maintaining all its **drives** within their homeostatic regime is a never-ending, all important process.

So far, the robot has four basic drives. They are as follows:

- **Social drive**: One **drive** is to be social, i.e. to be in the presence of people and to be stimulated by people. This is important for biasing the robot to learn in a social context. On the under-whelmed extreme the robot is **lonely**, i.e., it is predisposed to act in ways to get into face to face contact with people. If left unsatiated, this **drive** will continue to intensify toward the **lonely** end of the spectrum. On the over-whelmed extreme, the robot is **asocial**, i.e. it is predisposed to act in ways to disengage people from face to face contact. The robot tends toward the **asocial** end of the spectrum when a person is over-stimulating the robot. This may occur when a person is moving to much, is too close to the camera, an so on.

- **Stimulation drive**: Another **drive** is to be stimulated, where the stimulus can either be generated externally by the environment or internally through spontaneous self-play. On the under-whelmed end of this spectrum, the creature is **bored**. This occurs if the creature has been inactive or unstimulated over a period of time. With respect to learning, this **drive** also tends toward the **bored** end of the spectrum if the current interaction becomes very predictable for the robot. This biases the robot to engage in new kinds of activities and encourages the caretaker to challenge the robot with new interactions. On the over-whelmed part of the spectrum, the creature is **confused**. This occurs when the robot receives more stimulation than it can effectively assimilate, and predisposes the robot to reduce its interaction with the enviroment, perhaps by closing its eyes, turning its head away from the stimulus, and so forth.

- **Security Drive**. Much of what the robot learns are anticipatory models of the effects of its actions on the world. If these models hold true, the implication is that the the robot can use these expectations to behave adeptly within the environment. This **drive** plays an important role in regulating the robot's interaction with its environment where many (but not all) of these models are effective in guiding behavior. By doing so, the robot maintains an environment where it is competent yet slightly challenged, i.e. it needs to modify its existing models to better suit its environment or learn new ones. As time passes and if left unsatiated, the **drive** tends toward the **secure** end of the spectrum. This implies that the robot's expectations hold true for its interactions with the environment. If this is not true, its consummatory behavior moves the **drive** toward the **insecure** end.

- **Fatigue drive**. This **drive** is unlike the others in that its purpose is to allow the robot to shut out the external world instead of trying to regulate its interaction with it. While the creature is "awake", it receives repeated stimulation and learns new predictive models for how its actions affect the world. As time passes (and as the number of learned events increases) this **drive** approaches the **exhaused** end of the spectrum. Once the intensity level exceeds a certain threshold, it is time for the robot to "sleep". This is the time for the robot to do "internal housekeeping", i.e. try to consolidate its learned anticipatory models and integrate them with the rest of the internal control structure. While the robot "sleeps", the **drive** returns to the homeostatic regime, the robot awakens and is ready to exercise its newly modified control structure.

The Behavior Subsystem: For each **drive** there is an accompanying consummatory behavior. Ideally, it becomes active when the **drive** enters the under-whelmed regime and remains active until it returns to the homeostatic regime. The consummatory behaviors are as follows:

- **Play with People** acts to move the **social drive** back toward the **asocial** end of the spectrum. It is potentiated more strongly as the **social** drive approaches the **lonely** end of the spectrum. Its activation level increases above threshold when the robot can engage in face to face interaction with a person, and it remains active for as long as this interaction is maintained. Only when active does it act to reduce the intensity of the drive.

- **Play with Toys** acts to move the **stimulation drive** back toward the **confused** end of the spectrum. It is potentiated more strongly as the `stimulation drive` approaches the `bored` end of the spectrum. The activation level increases above threshold when the robot can engage in some sort of stimulating interaction, either with the environment such as visually tracking an object or with itself such as playing with its voice. It remains active for as long as the robot maintains the interaction, and while active it continues to move the `drive` toward the over-whelmed end of the spectrum.

- `Expectation Violation` acts to move the `security drive` toward the `insecure` end of the specturm. It is potentiated more strongly as the `security drive` approaches the `secure` end of the spectrum (implying the robot is becoming "bored" with its interactions). Its activation level increases whenever the robot's current expectations are violated. When the activation level rises above threshold, it moves the `security drive` toward the over-whelmed side of the spectrum.

- `Sleep` acts to satiate the *fatique drive*. When the `fatigue drive` reaches a specified level, the `sleep` consummatory behavior turns on and remains active until the `fatigue drive` is restored to the homeostatic regime. When this occurs, it is released and the robot "wakes up".

`Sleep` also serves a special "motivation reboot" function for the robot. When active, it not only restores the `fatige drive` to the homeostatic regime, but all the other drives as well. If any `drive` moves far from its homeostatic regime, the robot displays stronger and stronger signs of distress, which eventually culminates in extreme `anger` if left uncorrected. This expressive display is a strong sign to the caretaker to intervene and help the robot correct its `drive` imbalance. If the caretaker fails to act appropriately and the drive reaches an extreme, a protective mechanism kicks in where the robot shuts itself down by going to `sleep`. This is a last ditch method for the robot to restore all its `drives` by itself. A similar behavior is observed in infants. When they are in extreme distress, perhaps throwing a tantrum, they may fall into a disturbed sleep. This is a self regulation tactic they use in extreme cases (Bullowa 1979).

Three of the four consummatory behaviors cannot be activated by the intensity of the `drive` alone. Instead, they require a special sort of environmental interaction to become active. For instance, `Play with People` cannot become active without the participation of a person. Analogous cases hold for `Play with Toys` and `Expectation Violation`. Furthermore, it is possible for these behaviors to become active by the environment alone if the interaction is strong enough.

This has an important consequence for regulating the intensity of interaction. For instance, if the nature of the interaction is too intense, the `drive` may move into the over-whelmed regime. In this case, the `drive` is no longer potentiating the consummatory behavior; the enviromental input alone is strong enough to keep it active. When the `drive` enters the overwhelmed regime, the system is strongly motivated to engage in behaviors that act to stop the stimulation. For instance, if the caretaker is interacting with the robot too intensely, the `social drive` may move into the `asocial` regime. When this occurs, the robot displays an expression of displeasure, which is a cue for the caretaker to back off a bit.

The Emotion Subsystem: So far, there are eight `emotions` implemented in this system, each as a separate process. The overall framework of the emotion system shares strong commonality with that of (Velasquez 1996), although its function is specifically targeted for social exchanges and learning. Of the robot's `emotions`, `anger`, `disgust`, `fear`, `happiness`, and `sadness` are analogs of the primary emotions in humans. The last three `emotions` are somewhat controversal in classification, but they play in an important role in learning and social interaction between caretaker and infant so they are included in the system: `suprise`, `interest`, `excitement`. Many experiments in developmental psychology have shown that infants show suprise when witnessing an unexpected or novel outcome to a familiar event (Carey & Gelman 1991). Furthermore, parents use their infant's display of excitement or interest as cues to regulate their interaction with them (Wood, Bruner & Ross 1976).

In humans, four factors serve to elicit emotions, i.e. neurochemical, sensorimotor, motivational, and cognitive (Izard 1993). In this system, emphasis has been placed on how `drives`, other `emotions` and `pain` contribute to a given `emotion`'s level of activation. The active `emotions` and accompanying facial expressions provide the caretaker with cues as to the motivational state of the robot and how the caretaker should act to help satiate the robot's drives.

- Pain: `Pain` information comes from perceptual processing when the intensity of the signal is too strong. Perhaps a bright light is shining in the camera which "blinds" the robot, or perhaps a sound is so loud that the robot cannot hear anything else, etc. In this case, the `pain` signals serve to increase the level of `anger` and `sadness` so the robot exhibits signs of distress. This may be accompanied by other protective responses such as closing its eyes, rotating its ears away from the loud sound source, etc. Nominally, the caretaker would interpret these cues as "discomfort" for the robot and seek out the source.

- Other Emotions: The influence from other `emotions` serve to prevent conflicting `emotions` from becoming active at the same time. To implement this, conflicting `emotions` have mutually inhibitory connections between them. For instance, inhibitory connections exist between `happiness` and `sadness`, between `disgust` and `happines`, and between `happiness` and anger.

- Drives: Recall that each `drive` is partitioned into three regimes: homeostatic, over-whelmed or under-whelmed. This establishes the *drive context* for the system. For a given drive, each region potentiates a different emotion and hence a different facial expression. In this way the facial expressions provide cues as to what drive is out of balance and how the caretaker should respond to correct for it.

In general, when a `drive` is in its homeostatic regime, it potentiates positive emotions such as `happiness` or `interest`. The accompanying expression tells the caretaker that the interaction is going well and the robot is poised to play and learn. When a `drive` is not within the homeostatic regime, negative emotions are potentiated (such as `anger`, `disgust`, or `sadness`) which produces signs of distress on the robot's face. The particular sign of distress provides the caretaker with additional cues as to what is "wrong" and how she might correct for it. With respect to learning, one could easily envision a scenario where a look of suprise appears on the robot's face whenever an unexpected event occurs. This would be a cue to the caretaker that the robot does not have an anticipatory model for this event, in which case the caretaker may choose repeat the event to help the robot learn a suitable expectation.

Note that the same sort of interaction can have a very different "emotional" affect on the robot depending on the drive context. For instance, playing with the robot while all `drives` are within the homeostatic regime elicits `happiness`. This tells the caretaker that playing with the robot is a good interation to be having at this time. However, if the `fatigue` drive is deep into the `exhausted` end of the spectrum, then playing with the robot actually prevents the robot from going to `sleep`. As a result, the `fatigue drive` continues to increase in intensity. When high enough, the `fatigue drive` begins to potentiate `anger`. The caretaker may interpret this as the robot acting "cranky" because it is "tired". In the extreme case, `fatigue` may potentiate `anger` so strongly that the robot displays "fury". The caretaker may construe this as the robot throwing a "tantrum". Nominally, the caretaker would back off before this point and allow the `sleep` behavior to be activated.

The Motor Subsystem: For each `emotion` there is an accompanying facial expression. These are implemented in the motor system where there are various motor processes. The low level face motor primitives are separate processes that control the position and velocity of each degree of freedom. The motor skill processes are one level above the primitives. They implement coordinated control of the facial features such as wiggling the ears or eyebrows independently, arching both brows inward, raising the brows, and so forth. Generally, they are the coordinated motions used in common facial expressions. On top of the motor skills are the face expression processes. These direct all facial features to show a particular expression. For each expression, the facial features move to a characteristic configuration, however the intensity can vary depending on the intensity of the emotion evoking the expression. In general, the more intense the expression, the facial features move more quickly to more extreme positions. Blended expressions are computed by taking a weighted average of the facial configurations corresponding to each evoked emotion.

Experiments and Results

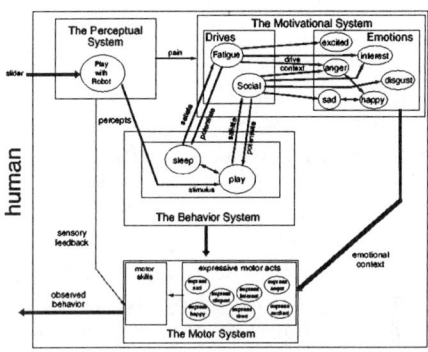

Figure 3: Diagram of the motivational system used in the following experiments. Double headed arrows represent mutually inhibitory connections between nodes.

A series of early experiments were performed with the robot using the motivational system shown in figure 3. The system consists of two drives (`fatigue` and `social`), two consummatory behaviors (`sleep` and `play`), one external input stimulus, and a number of `emotions` and corresponding facial expressions. The external input is provided by a human through a GUI interface and represents the intensity of interaction. The robot's face changes expression over time as the human interacts with it through the slider, reflecting its ongoing motivational state and providing the human with visual cues as to how to modify the interaction to keep the robot's drives within homeostatic ranges.

In general, as long as the robot's drives remain within their homeostatic ranges, the robot displays "interest". If the human interacts with the robot while in the drives are within their homeostatic regime, the robot displays "happiness". However, once a drive leaves its homeostatic range, the robot's "interest" and "happiness" wane as it grows increasingly distressed. As this occurs, the robot's expression reflects its distressed state. This visual cue tells the human that all is not well with the robot, and whether the human should intensify the interaction, diminish it, or maintain it at its current level.

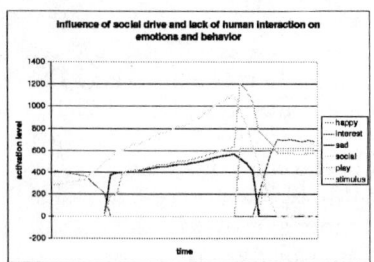
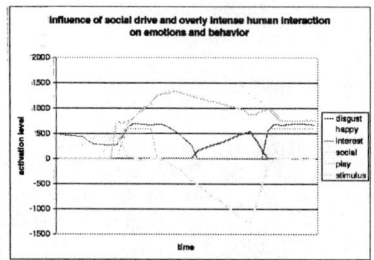
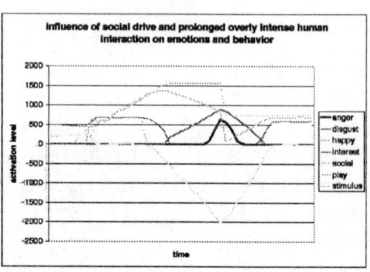

Figure 4: Changes in state of the motivational and behavior systems in response to the `social` drive and various intensities of human interaction. The left figure (a) corresponds to a short period of insufficient human interaction, the middle figure (b) corresponds to a short period of overly intense human interaction, and the right figure (c) corresponds to an extended period of overly intense interaction.

Figures 4(a), (b), and (c) illustrate the influence of the `social` drive on the robot's motivational and behavioral state when interacting with a human. The activation level of the robot's `play` behavior cannot exceed the activation threshold unless the human interacts with the robot with sufficient intensity – low intenisty interaction will not trigger the `play` behavior even if highly potentiated by the `social` drive. If the interaction is intense, even too intense, the robot's `play` behavior remains active until the human either stops the activity, or the robot takes action to end it.

Due to a low intensity of human interaction, figure 4(a) shows the robot becoming increasingly "sad" over time as the `social` drive tends toward the "lonely" end of the spectrum. The robot's expression of sadness continues to increase, until the human finally responds by intensifying the interaction. Consequently, the human sees the robot's "sadness" decaying over time which indicates that the robot's `social` drive is returning to the homeostatic regime. When the robot displays an expression of interest again, its social drive is within homeostatic bounds.

In contrast, figure 4(b) shows the robot acquiring more "asocial" tendencies when the interaction is too intense. If the interaction is over-whelming, the `social` drive tends toward the "asocial" end of the spectrum. As this drive leaves the homeostatic range, the robot becomes increasingly "disgusted" and its expression of disgust intensifies over time. When the `social` drive reaches a fairly large negative value of -1200, the robot displays a fairly intense look of disgust, and the human backs off the interaction. This causes the `social` drive to return to the homeostatic range and the robot re-establishes an "interested", "happy" `emotional` state.

Figure 4(c) illustrates how the robot can terminate the interaction when the human refuses engage the robot appropriately. As discussed in previous sections, infants fall into a disturbed sleep when put into an extremely anxious state for a prolonged time. Analogously for the robot, if the interaction is over-whelming for long period of time, the robot will first show increasing signs of "disgust", eventually blending with increasingly intense signs of anger, as the `social` drive continues to move toward the over-whelmed end of the spectrum. If still no relief is encountered and the drive hits its outer limit, the robot goes into an emergency sleep mode. As discussed previously, sleeping serves as a sort of "motivational reboot" for the robot by restoring all drives to their homeostatic ranges. Hence, upon "awakening", the robot is in a balanced, "interested" state.

Figures 5(a) and (b) illustrate the influence of the `fatigue` drive on the robot's motivational and behavioral state when interacting with a human. Over time, the `fatigue` drive increases toward the "exhaused" end of the spectrum. As the robot's level of "fatigue" increases, the robot displays stronger signs of being "tired".

Figure 5(a) shows that the robot will activate it's `sleep` behavior when its `fatigue` drive moves above the threshold value of 1600, provided no one is engaging the robot. The robot remains "asleep" until all drives are restored to their homeostatic ranges. Once this occurs, the activation level of the "sleep" behavior decays until the behavior is no longer active and the robot "wakes up" in an "interested" state.

Figure 5(b) shows what happens if a human continues to interact with the robot dispite its "fatigued" state. The robot cannot fall asleep as long as a person interacts with it because its `play` behavior remains active (note the mutually inhibitory connections in figure 3). If the `fatigue` drive exceeds threshold and the robot cannot fall "asleep", the robot begins to show signs of "anger". Eventually the robot's level of "anger" reaches an intense level of 1100, and the robot appears rageful – akin to throwing a "tantrum". Still the human persists with the interaction, but even-

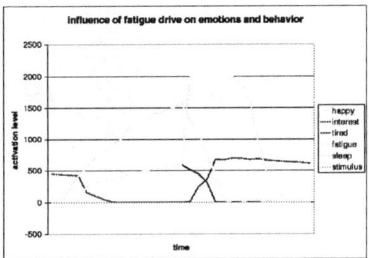 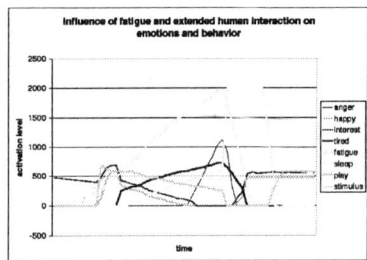

Figure 5: Changes in state of the motivational and behavior systems in response to the `fatigue` drive and various intensities of human interaction. The left figure (a) corresponds to minimal human interaction, and the right figure (b) corresponds to an overly extended period of human interaction.

tually the robot's fatigue level reaches near maximum and emergeny actions are taken by the robot to force an end to the interaction. The robot falls into a distressed sleep to restore its drives.

The experimental results described above characterizes the robot's behavior when interacting with a human. It demonstrates how the robot's "emotive" cues are used to regulate the nature and intensity of the interaction, and how the nature of the interaction influences the robot's behavior. The result is an ongoing "dance" between robot and human aimed at maintaining the robot's drives within homeostatic bounds. If the robot and human are good partners, the robot remains "intersted" and/or "happy" most of the time. These expressions indicate that the interaction is of appropriate intensity for learning and the robot displays a look of readiness to learn.

Summary

We have presented a framework (heavily inspired from work in ethology, psychology, and cognitive development) for designing motivational systems for autonomous robots specifically geared to regulate human-robot interaction. We have shown how the `drives`, `emotions`, behaviors, and facial expressions influence each other to establish and maintain social interactions that can provide suitable learning episodes, i.e., where the robot is proficient yet slightly challenged, and where the robot is neither under-stimulated nor over-stimulated by its interaction with the human. With a specific implementation, we demonstrated how the system engages in a mutually regulatory interaction with a human.

In these early experiments, the human's input is restricted to GUI sliders. The next step is to incorporate visual and auditory inputs. Furthermore, the specifics of learning in a social context (what is learned and how it is learned) was not addressed in this paper. That is the subject of work soon to follow, which will include tuning and adjusting this early motivation system to appropriately regulate the intensity of interaction to benefit the learning process.

Acknowledgments

Support for this research was provided by a MURI grant under the Office of Naval Research contract N00014-95-1-0600 and the Santa Fe Institute.

References

Billard, A. & Dautenhahn, K. (1997), Grounding Communication in Situated, Social Robots, Technical report, University of Manchester.

Blumberg, B. (1996), Old Tricks, New Dogs: Ethology and Interactive Creatures, PhD thesis, MIT.

Bullowa, M. (1979), *Before Speech: The Beginning of Interpersonal Communicaion*, Cambridge University Press, Cambridge, London.

Carey, S. & Gelman, R. (1991), *The Epigenesis of Mind*, Lawrence Erlbaum Associates, Hillsdale, NJ.

Ekman, P. & Davidson, R. (1994), *The Nature of Emotion: Fundamental Questions*, Oxford University Press, New York.

Halliday, M. (1975), *Learning How to Mean: Explorations in the Development of Language*, Elsevier, New York, NY.

Izard, C. (1993), Four Systems for Emotion Activation: Cognitive and Noncognitive Processes, *in* 'Psychological Review', Vol. 100, pp. 68–90.

Lorenz, K. (1973), *Foundations of Ethology*, Springer-Verlag, New York, NY.

Maes, P. (1990), 'Learning Behavior Networks from Experience', *ECAL90*.

Tinbergen, N. (1951), *The Study of Instinct*, Oxford University Press, New York.

Velasquez, J. (1996), Cathexis, A Computational Model for the Generation of Emotions and their Influence in the Behavior of Autonomous Agents, Master's thesis, MIT.

Wood, D., Bruner, J. S. & Ross, G. (1976), 'The role of tutoring in problem-solving', *Journal of Child Psychology and Psychiatry* **17**, 89–100.

Emotion Model for Life-like Agent and Its Evaluation

Hirohide Ushida   Yuji Hirayama   Hiroshi Nakajima

Human Understanding Group
Fuzzy Technology and Business Promotion Division
OMRON Corporation
Shimokaiinji, Nagaokakyo, Kyoto 617-8510, Japan
E-mail: {ushida, hirayama, nak}@zoo.ncl.omron.co.jp

Abstract

This paper proposes an emotion model for life-like agents with emotions and motivations. This model consists of reactive and deliberative mechanisms. The former generates low-level instantaneous responses to external stimuli that come from the real world and virtual worlds. The latter mechanism especially focuses on emotions. A basic idea of the model comes from a psychological theory, called the cognitive appraisal theory. In the model, cognitive and emotional processes interact with each other based on the theory. A multi-module architecture is employed in order to carry out the interactions. The model also has a learning mechanism to diversify behavioral patterns. These features are effective in giving users the illusion of life. We applied the proposed model to characters in a virtual world and show the results obtained from three experiments with users.

Introduction

A goal of the present study is to develop life-like agents which can effectively communicate with humans. People communicate with each other by simulating their partner's mental processes in their mind. This paper argues that an agent communicating with people should have an ability to simulate their mental processes, and proposes an agent with an artificial mind.

What are important features for such artificial minds?

One important feature of the artificial minds is the ability to understand emotions because people communicate with each other via expressing and estimating emotions. William James emphasizes that emotion is the predominant operation, mediating both cognition and action (James 1980). Minsky argues that emotion influences goal constructing in problem solving and that AI should have the ability of processing emotion (Stork 1997). Therefore, a machine should be able to process information about a user's emotions so that it can understand the user's goals as well as other information. To achieve this, it is crucial to build computational models of emotion.

Another important feature of the artificial mind is the ability to understand motivation. Dreyfus says that people interpret the meaning of matters according to their desires and concerns (Dreyfus 1978). People consider others' motivation when they estimate their emotion and intention, explain their action, predict their future action. Therefore, it is necessary for user interface agents to understand user's motivation. Conversely, it will be easy for users to predict agent's behavior which is based on its motivation. Dennett's intentional stance is the strategy of interpreting behavior of an entity (person, animal, artifact, whatever) by treating it as if it were a rational agent that governs its action selection by a consideration of its beliefs and desires (Dennett 1996). Behavior of an intentional system is predictable and explainable if people attribute beliefs and desires to it.

Thirdly, agents should be adaptable to their environment and users' preferences. Agents that lack these abilities have limitations of satisfying their users. An electronic secretary repeats the same error if she cannot learn.

Fourthly, resources for computation, such as the number of processors and the capacity of working memory, are limited. Selective attention is required for the agent to process the most important matter in a given situation.

Finally, not all behaviors are generated under deliberative mechanisms in the case of real life. For instance, reactive mechanisms are required to avoid a sudden obstacle. Brooks has proposed an architecture for such reactive behaviors (Brooks 1986). An agent should have both reactive and deliberate behaviors. Therefore, the integration of the behavior-based AI (i.e. bottom-up approach) and the symbolic-based AI (i.e. top-down approach) is crucial in life-like behavior.

This paper proposes a mind model for life-like agents which have the features described above: i.e., 1) expressing emotion, 2) generating behavior based on motivation, 3) learning, 4) selective attention, and 5) generating reactive behavior. We especially focus on how to express emotions and personalities in this paper because information processing with emotions is not only important but also useful for many applications such as electronic secretaries, tutoring systems, and autonomous characters in entertainment (Maes 1995; Picard 1995). For instance, children tend to be under the impression that characters in Disney animation have minds. A reason for this phenomenon is that the characters express rich emotions and personalities. Character's behaviors with emotions and personalities facilitate anthropomorphic view (Hayes-Roth 1997). Reeves and Nass state that modern media engage old brains which are not evolved to twenty-century

---

Copyright © 1998, American Association for Artificial Intelligence (www.aaai.org). All rights reserved.

technology. There is no switch in the brain that can be thrown to distinguish the real and mediated worlds (Reeves and Nass 1996). These are some of the reasons why people personify behavior of a machine and have illusions that cartoon characters have human-like mind. Artificial agents with emotions give such illusions to the users by utilizing these human characteristics.

Implementation issues concerning the present model are as follows. Firstly, the model uses a multi-module architecture to realize emergence of behaviors by interactions between cognitive and emotional processes. Secondly, fuzzy inference is applied to realize flexibility in the behavior. Thirdly, the agent can learn causal relations between stimuli and their goals. This learning mechanism diversifies the behavior. Finally, a set of tactile sensors to detect stimuli from the real world is integrated with reactive behavior.

The remainder of the paper is organized as follows. Next section presents our model. In the third section, the model is applied to cartoon characters in a virtual world. The fourth section shows the results of evaluations from the point of life-like behavior. The fifth section discusses some related work. The final section describes summary and future work.

Emotion Model

Figure 1 illustrates our conceptual model. It consists of reactive and deliberative mechanisms. The former mechanism covers direct mapping from sensors to effectors. We employ the terms, "sensors" and "effectors", in both the real and virtual worlds. The deliberative mechanism has two processes: the cognitive and emotional processes. The cognitive process executes recognition, decision-making, and planning. The emotional process generates emotions according to the cognitive appraisals which are described in the next paragraph.

The deliberative mechanism is based on the cognitive-based emotion model of the cognitive appraisal theory (Ortony, Collins, and Clore 1988). In the theory, a person's appraisal of an emotion-inducing situation consists of three central variables: *desirability*, *praiseworthiness*, and *appealingness*. These variables are applied to event-based emotions, agent-based emotions, and object-based emotions, respectively. Desirability is evaluated in terms of a complex structure, where there is a focal goal that governs the interpretation of any event. The desirability of the event is appraised in terms of how it facilitates or interferes with this focal goal and the sub-goals that support it. Similarly, the praiseworthiness of the agent's actions is evaluated with respect to a hierarchy of standards, and the appealingness of an object is evaluated with respect to a person's attitudes. Emotions, which are generated according to the cognitive appraisals, influence cognitive processes such as sub-goal constructing and conflict dissolving in problem solving (Minsky 1986; Stork 1997). Damasio argues that emotions are necessary for problem solving because when we plan our lives, rather than examining every opinion, some possibilities are emotionally blocked off (Damasio 1994). Thus, the cognitive and the emotional processes interact with each other.

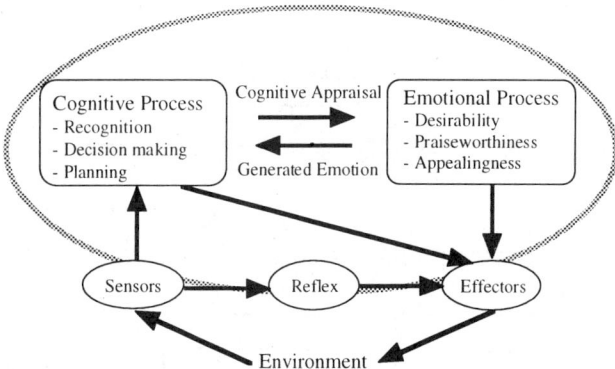

Figure 1: A Conceptual model of the cognitive appraisal theory.

Model Configuration

This section describes the model configuration. Minsky has presented an idea that a mind consists of many small components called agencies. Each component has a very simple function but the interaction among them lead to complex behaviors (Minsky 1986). We adopt this idea for developing our model. The configuration of our model is illustrated in Figure 2. Each rectangle with squared corners represents a functional module, while each rectangle with rounded corners represents a memory module. The modules in our model are executed in parallel. It has no central commander which directly influences all modules. Each module interacts with its neighbors. This local interaction in a multi-module architecture lead to emergence of complex behaviors. The memories and functional modules are described as follows;

There are three kinds of memory components in the model: Innate goals, Empirical goals, and Long Term Memory (LTM). The Innate goals are built-in goals. The Empirical goals are generated depending on the situation and experiences. The LTM keeps captured knowledge to be used for recognizing outer stimuli and generating the empirical goals.

Innate Goals. The Innate goals are built-in goals and assumed to correspond to the instinct of self-preservation in animals. Some examples are thirst, hunger, sleepiness, defense. There is a desire level for each goal. The levels of thirst, hunger, and sleepiness increase according to time series and decrease when the goals are satisfied.

Empirical Goals. The Empirical goals are concrete goals for the innate desires described above and are generated in the Goal-creator. The goal creation depends on the situation and experiences in interactions with the environment. The agents learn causal relations between stimuli and the innate goals. For example, they empirically find objects which contribute to satisfying hunger, and stores the knowledge in the LTM. Learning is executed in the Perceptor described below.

Long Term Memory (LTM). The LTM stores knowledge which is captured via interactions with the environment. Continual changes in the empirical knowledge diversify behavioral patterns. The knowledge includes the following

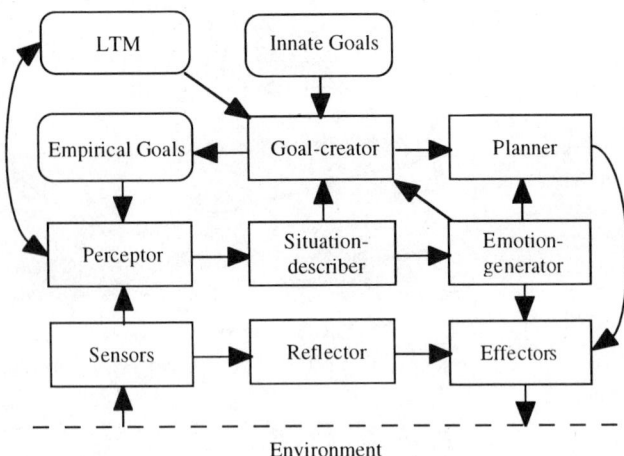

Figure 2: Configuration of the emotion model.

variables for each object:

- *Attribute values* are physical features of objects (e.g. colors, shapes, etc.). They are used to recognize objects and stimuli.
- *Novelty value* is set to the highest value at first and decreases according to the number of contact times.
- *Contribution degree value* represents how much an object contributes to each innate goal. For example, the degree value of hunger is high if an object is food.
- *Preference degree value* represents how much an agent likes an object or another agent. If the agent is threatened by another, the degree value decreases. But it increases if the agent is helped by another. The degree for a user changes depending on his/her contacting manner.
- *Decay coefficient value* is used for deciding whether an object should be memorized or not. It increases when the agent contacts an object, and decreases as time elapses. If it becomes lower than zero, the memory about the object is deleted. This oblivion contributes to saving the memory capacity and diversifying behaviors.

There are eight functional modules as follows;

Sensors. The Sensors detect stimuli from the environment to extract physical features. In our study, an agent deals with information from both the real and virtual worlds. The information from the virtual world consists of the coordinates and attribute values of objects. For the information in the real world, we use tactile sensors to recognize whether the user beats or pets the agent's body.

Reflector. The Reflector has direct mapping functions from the Sensors to the Effectors. For example, the agent blinks its eyes when it is beaten by the user.

Perceptor. The Perceptor consists of three kinds of processes. The first process recognizes objects and their states by comparing sensory data with the knowledge in the LTM. It also recognizes the types of tactile stimuli from the real world. The second one computes concern levels which are utilized for selective attention. The computation takes an account of goal's importance, object's contribution to the goal, novelty, momentum, etc. If an object's concern level exceeds its threshold, the object's information goes to the Situation-describer. The last process is learning. The agent learns whether an object or stimulus contributes to its goals or not. The learned result is memorized in the form of contribution and preference degree values in the LTM.

Situation-describer. The Situation-describer represents the outputs from the Perceptor in two ways. One is symbolic description and the other is numeric. The symbolic description represents structural relationships using case relation. Fillmore's case categories are employed to represent the case relations (Fillmore 1971). The numerical description represents locations and movements of objects, and intensities of stimuli. The Goal-creator, Emotion-generator, Planner, and Effectors refer to the Situation-describer.

Emotion-generator. The Emotion-generator generates emotions using contents of the Situation-describer and the LTM. Figure 3 shows this process. It is divided in two steps. In the first step, cognitive appraisals (i.e. desirability, praiseworthiness, and appealingness) are computed. For example, happiness is generated if an important goal succeeds, while sadness emerges if the goal fails. An agent gets angry if another agent is responsible for the goal failing. In other words, the cognitive appraisals are regarded as emotional factors. Emotional intensities depend on the levels of the emotional factors. The levels of the emotional factors are obtained using the emotion eliciting condition rules, which are implemented by means of fuzzy inference rules. Our model uses seven emotional factors. Examples of the emotion eliciting condition rules are as follows;

- *Goal success level (GSL)*: IF getting an object succeeds AND its contribution degree to a goal is high AND the goal's importance is high, THEN the *GSL* is high.
- *Goal failure level (GFL)*: IF getting an object fails AND its contribution degree to a goal is high AND the goal's importance is high, THEN the *GFL* is high.
- *Blameworthy level (BWL)*: IF getting an object is prevented by another agent AND its contribution degree to a goal is high AND the goal's importance is high, THEN the *BWL* is high.
- *Pleasant feeling level (PFL)*: IF a good tactile stimulus is sensed AND its desire level is high AND its intensity is high, THEN *PFL* is high.
- *Unpleasant feeling level (UFL)*: IF a bad tactile stimulus is sensed AND its intensity is high, THEN *UFL* is high.
- *Unexpected level (UEL)*: IF a new or unexpected stimulus is sensed AND its intensity is high, THEN *UEL* is high.
- *Goal crisis level (GCL)*: IF a goal is threatened by another AND the goal's importance is high, THEN *GCL* is high.

The second step of the Emotion-generator is to compute emotion intensities. There are many kinds of emotion theories in the fields of psychology, physiology, and cognitive science. James denied the existence of explicit emotional components in our minds and argued that an emotion is the feeling of what is going on inside our body (1884 James). This idea

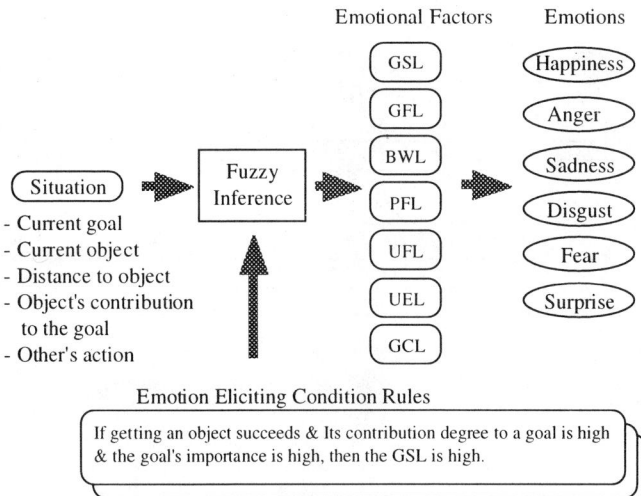

Figure 3: Framework for emotion generation.

that emotions arise as sensations in the body has become known as the peripheral theory. Cannon had argued against the peripheral theory and proposed that bodily changes are produced by the brain (Cannon 1927). Other theorists proposed explicit components for emotion types (Ekman 1992; Johnson-Laird 1988). We employ the following emotion types because they are easy to explain and understand; *happiness, sadness, anger, disgust, surprise*, and *fear*. Emotion intensities are obtained by using emotional factors, time decay, and other emotions. Emotional factors influence the intensities by using production rules as follows;

- IF the *GSL* is higher than its threshold, THEN increase the Happiness intensity in proportion to it.
- IF the *GFL* is higher than its threshold, THEN increase the Sadness intensity in proportion to it.
- IF the *GFL* is higher than its threshold and the *BWL* is higher than its threshold, THEN increase the Anger intensity in proportion to their product.
- IF the *BWL* is higher than its threshold, THEN increase the Disgust intensity in proportion to it.
- IF the *PFL* is higher than its threshold, THEN increase the Happiness intensity in proportion to it.
- IF the *UFL* is higher than its threshold, THEN increase the Disgust intensity in proportion to it.

The emotion intensity is calculated using equation (1).

$$E_i(t) = \frac{1}{1 + \exp\{(-X(t) + 0.5)/0.1\}} \quad (1)$$

$$X(t) = X(t-1) + \delta - \gamma + \sum_j W_{ji} E_j(t-1)$$

where E_i is the intensity for Emotion i at time step t; δ is the input from the rule set described above; γ is a decay coefficient, and W_{ji} is excitatory or inhibitory gain from Emotion j to Emotion i. The nonlinear function constraints the intensity between 0 and its saturation value.

There is a threshold for each Emotion. If E_i is higher than both the threshold and other emotion intensities, then Emotion i become active.

Goal-creator. The Goal-creator creates empirical goals using desire levels of the innate goals, the contribution and preference degrees in the LTM, contents of the Situation-describer, and emotion intensities. The goal creation process uses production rules. For example, when the degree of hunger is higher than other desires and there is an object to eat, the goal to obtain the object and eat it is created. The object's contribution degree for satisfying hunger in the LTM is used to judge whether it can be eaten or not. When the degree of hunger is higher than other desires and there is nothing to eat, the goal to search an object to eat is created. Emotion also influences the goal creation. For example, *Disgust* or *Fear* for an object creates a goal to avoid it. Every empirical goal has importance and holding degrees. Each importance degree value is computed by using the desire level, the contribution degree, and the emotion intensity. The initial value of each holding degree is 1 and it decreases as time elapses. When a goal cannot be achieved and its holding degree becomes lower than 0, then the goal is canceled. This process is useful for preventing an agent from pursuing a hopeless goal.

Planner. The Planner has action selection rules and selects a proper action depending on the situation. For example, if the goal is to eat an object and that isn't within an agent's reach, then the next action is to approach it. If the goal is to eat an object and another agent is approaching it, then the next action is to threaten the agent. Here, emotions also influence the Planner. If the goal is to eat an object and another agent is approaching it and there is fear for the agent, then the next action is not to threaten but rather to run away from the agent.

Effectors. The Effectors integrate the data from the Reflector, the Emotion-generator, and the Planner. Subsumption architecture is employed to integrate the data (Brooks 1986). The system gives priority to the input from the Reflector for the purpose of, for instance, urgent defense. Emotion expressions (e.g. facial and vocal expression) have higher priority than the planned actions. But it is possible for the Planner to suppress the reflexes and the emotion expressions. As the result of these integration, agent performs multiple actions at one time. For instance, the agent can express emotion, while drinking water.

Personality Control Parameters

Personality is an important factor for life-like characters. We apply emotions to representation of various personality. In other words, distinctive personalities are realized by differences in expressing emotion. Tuning the rules and parameters in the modules generates various personalities. Examples of personality control parameters in each module are as follows;

Innate goals. The threshold for the desire level of appetite relates to the degree of being greedy. The threshold for the desire level of user contact relates to the degree of being friendly. The increasing ratio of the desire level also leads to the same effect.

Empirical goals. The decreasing ratio of the holding degrees relates to the degree of being persistent.

Emotion-generator. The threshold for emotion is used to define how much it should be expressed. The threshold for Anger relates to the degree of being irritable. The threshold for Fear relates to the degree of being cowardly.

Planner. For instance, the threshold for the action selection rule of threat relates to the degree of being offensive.

Virtual World Characters

We applied the proposed model to characters in a virtual world, which is represented using computer graphics on a PC. A software program is implemented using the Java language and environment. There are three characters in the world. Their names are Blue, Yellow, and Pink according to their body colors. Figure 4 illustrates a whole image of the virtual world. There is a puddle in the lower center of the field. When a character is thirsty, she goes to the puddle to drink water. The user can interact with the characters in two ways. One is to give them apples. When the user puts an apple on the ground, a hungry character eats it. The other way is touching the characters via tactile sensors. A stuffed puppet illustrated in Figure 5 has built-in tactile sensors. A metaphor of the user's hand is displayed on the screen and it can be manipulated by means of a mouse. If the user selects a character using the mouse and touches the stuffed animal, the sensed information is transmitted to the character and the character reacts. The Perceptor can recognize whether the touch is a good or bad feeling for the character.

The characters express six emotions according to the situations as shown in Table 1. The emotions are represented by facial and vocal expressions. There are two levels for expressing each emotion. The levels are defined using thresholds for emotion intensities. The facial expressions are designed based on the theory proposed by (Ekman and Friesen 1975). The designs of facial and vocal expressions are different among the characters.

Examples of actions by the characters are as follows; approach a <character or object>, leave a <character or object>, look at a <character or object>, search a <character or object>, occupy an <object>, eat an apple, drink water, walk around, sleep, run away, threaten a <character or user hand>, attack a <character>, ask a <character> to give an <object>, refuse a request from a <character>, rub oneself on an <object>, ask the user to give good feeling. Here, <object> is an apple, puddle, or user hand. These actions are represented by facial and voice expressions, and body movements.

Evaluation

We conducted three experiments to evaluate the emotion model and the characters for their life-like behaviors. In the

Table 1: Emotions and their situation examples.

Emotion	Example of Situation
Happiness	- An agent is petted by a user. - An agent eats food when she is hungry.
Anger	- Another agent steals food.
Sadness	- A user's hand goes away when an agent wants to be petted.
Fear	- Another agent theatens of attacks.
Disgust	- Disliked object approaches.
Surpraise	- A loud noise is heard suddenly.

Figure 4: The virtual world.

Figure 5: A stuffed puppet, which connects with a PC, has built-in sensors to detect tactile stimuli.

first experiment, the intended emotions displayed by the model were compared with the users' observations on the characters' expressional states. In the second experiment, the users after interacting with the characters in virtual world, reported their impression about the characters. In the third experiment, the users evaluated the characters' emotions and personalities in eight dimensions. Twenty-three users (13 males and 10 females) participated in each experiments. Prior to the experiments, the participants were only given the information about the virtual world as the following: (1) There are three characters in the world and they behave autonomously. (2) The characters drink water at the puddle if thirsty and eat an apple that the user puts in the environment if hungry. (3) The user can pet or beat the characters with the

Table 2: Personality Parameters Setting.

Factor	Parameter Setting (B: Blue, Y: Yellow, P: Pink)
Innate goal	- Desire level for good tactile stimuli: P < Y < B
Empirical goal	- Decreasing ratio of holding degree: P << B, Y
Emotion threshold	- Happiness: B < Y < P
	- Anger: P < Y < B
	- Sadness: B < Y < P
	- Fear: B < Y < P
	- Disgust: P < Y < B
	- Surprise: B < P < Y
Action threshold	- Threat: P < Y < B
	- Request to give good tactile stimuli: B < Y < P
	- Request to give an object: B < Y < P

simulated hand. (4) The characters express their emotions depending on the situation. (5) Emotions are displayed via facial or vocal expressions. The users, however, were not told of the emotions, motivations, personalities assigned to each character. Table 2 shows the setting scheme for each parameter. For instance, "B<Y" means that a parameter of Blue is set to a smaller value than that of Yellow.

Experiment 1: Comparison between expressed emotion and user estimation.

The procedure for the experiment is as follows: The participant verbally described their observations about each character's emotional states as they viewed a six-minute video segment of the virtual world. The user's protocol was recorded. A total of 522 reports were collected. The protocol data were analyzed and classified into six emotional states. The observed emotions were compared to the intended emotions displayed by the characters. Table 3 shows the results of the comparison analysis. The ratio was obtained using Equation (2).

$$Ratio = \frac{Number\ of\ mached\ emotions}{Number\ of\ user\ utterances} \quad (2)$$

The results in general showed high matching rates between the observed emotions and the intended emotions. *Happiness* and *Anger* showed an especially high matching rate. One reason for that is that their expressions and situation is easy to understand. *Surprise* had the lowest matching rate. Most of the misinterpretations were confusions with *Fear*. This can be explained by similarity of the situations in which these emotions are displayed. If one character is yelled at by another, which tries to receive attention, it feels *Fear*. On the other hand, if one character suddenly hears a loud noise while paying attention to something else, it displays *Surprise* at the noise. In addition, the facial expressions for these emotions are also similar. *Disgust* had the second lowest rate and was often misinterpreted as *Anger* or *Pain*. Thus, these results suggest that the users based their interpretations of the character's emotions on the situations in which they were displayed. This implies that the design of the emotion mechanisms should integrate the context.

Experiment 2: Enumerating emotions, motivations, and personalities.

In this experiment, the users were asked to actually interact with them in the virtual world on the computer. They could, for example, feed and touch the characters with a mouse and a stuffed puppet connected to the virtual world. After a five-minute interactive session, the user was asked to write down their impressions about the character's emotions, motivations, and personalities.

The emotions elicited by the participants were as follows: *Happiness* (19), *Anger* (19), *Fear* (16), *Sadness* (15), *Surprise* (4), *Disgust* (3), *Perplexity* (4), *Sulk* (3), *Threat* (3), *Lonesome* (2), and *Regret* (2). The following have one answer; *Liking, Discouragement, Expectation, Uneasiness, Curiosity, Hunger, Desire, Trouble, Spoilt, Perverseness, Pain, Displeasure, Caution, Satisfaction,* and *Tickle*. Here, each parenthesized number represents the number of users and the total number of the users are 23. These results suggest that *Happiness*, *Anger*, *Fear*, and *Sadness* gave strong impressions to the users. An interesting point to note is that the users drew more variety of emotions from the character's behaviors than the six emotional states that each character displayed. Context seems to play a significant role for this phenomenon. It is feasible to assume that the user interprets a character's emotion by taking into consideration the context of the virtual world.

Motivations pointed out were as follows: *Appetite* (18), *Thirst* (10), *Monopoly* (8), *Playing with a user* (5), *Feeling good tactile stimuli* (6), *Avoiding bad tactile stimuli* (3), *Defending territory* (2), *Communication* (2), and *Fight* (1). This results shows that instinctive motivations were easy to understand for many users. But some users could find social motivations such as *Monopoly, Defending territory,* and *Communication*. Not a few users pointed out *Monopoly* because the decreasing ratio of Pink's holding degree was very small as shown in Table 2. This result shows an effect of the personality parameter.

Personalities pointed out by the users were shown in Table 4. The result shows that there is correlation with the parameters in Table 2. In particular, Pink's personality seemed obvious to the users. Many of them indicated that the character was *Irritable*. The thresholds for *Anger* and *Threat* are considered to have caused this result. Likewise, the threshold for Threat can be attributed to *Offensiveness*. *Egoism* can be explained using the decreasing ratio of the holding degree. Pink, for example, tended to occupy the puddle because of the parameter. Blue gave the impression of *Timidness* because the thresholds for *Sadness, Fear* and *Surprise* are lower than those for the other characters. The threshold for *Anger* and *Threat* seem to affect *Gentleness* of Blue. It is supposed that *Spoilt, Sociable,* and *Curious* of the character were caused

Table 3: The result of comparison between the expressed emotions and the user estimation.

	Happ.	Anger	Sad.	Fear	Disgust	Surprise	Total
Ratio(%)	100.0	100.0	80.2	89.0	67.9	63.8	87.7

by the lowest threshold of two requests in Table 2. *Lonesomeness* may be caused by the lowest threshold of *Sadness*. Yellow was seemed to be *Normal* because most parameters of that character were set to be middle among the characters. Thus, these result shows that parameter control is effective to express the character personalities.

Experiment 3: General impressions.

In this experiment, the users were given a questionnaire, which asked them to evaluate the characters' behaviors in eight dimensions. The users answered to each dimension using seven levels of responses. The results were summarized in Table 5. Each number in this table represents the number of users. These result shows that about 65 % of the users agreed with the life-likeness of the behavior. Especially, motivated and emotional behavior gave remarkable impressions. Personalities were also effective. But the impression of learning ability is relatively weak. This is one of problems to be solved.

Related Work

There have been several researches about agents with emotion. Daydreamer simulated human daydreaming using emotion and episodic memory (Mueller 1989). One of features of Daydreamer is emotional feedback system such as rationalization. For instance, Daydreamer modifies the interpretation of a goal failure in order to reduce the negative emotional state resulting from that failure. The daydreaming inference is triggered by text input, but not used to interact with its outer world.

On the contrary, ALIVE system (Maes et al. 1994) can interact with users. It expresses emotional behavior, but doesn't have internal states of emotion.

The Cathexis model is also computational model of emotion (Velasquez 1997). Emotions, moods, and temperaments are modeled in a network composed of special emotional systems comparable to Minsky's "proto-specialist" agents (Minsky 1986). The model is influenced from Izard's system (Izard 1993). Izard arranged emotion elicitors into four categories: neural, sensorimotor, motivational, and cognitive. The Cathexis model mainly focuses on emotion generation and action selection, but it doesn't have functions for deliberative behavior and learning.

Affective Reasoner (Elliott 1992) is based on the cognitive appraisal theory. A main feature of Affective Reasoner is to express sympathetic emotions by estimating other agent's emotions and concerns. By the nature of a symbolic-based system, however, it has limitation in flexible behavior. Furthermore, it doesn't seem to create empirical goals.

Woggles and Lyotard in the Oz project (Bates, Loyall, and Reilly 1994; Reilly and Bates 1992) uses an emotion model which is also based on the cognitive appraisal theory. The model has the ability of generating flexible behaviors and creating empirical goals, but it has two main differences from ours. Firstly, the Oz model doesn't take account of mutual influence among emotions and moods. Psychologists argue that emotions and moods influence each other (Nowlis 1970; Toda 1992). For instance, an agent rarely gets angry when she is in a good mood. Secondly, the Oz model uses *behavior features* to express personality. Such a character-specific approach is able to create rich personalities, but it requires artists to rebuild program code.

Hayes-Roth, et al. have proposed a *mind model* based on her blackboard architecture and apply it to life-like characters (Hayes-Roth and van Gent 1997). The character features improvisation in interaction with users, and focuses on mood and personality rather than emotion types. Their character possesses a distinct personality which she expresses through actions based on her mood and position. The moods vary along three continuous dimensions: an emotional dimensions ranging from happy to sad, a physiological dimension ranging from peppy to tired and a social dimension ranging from friendly to shy.

Table 4: Personalities pointed out by users.

Character	Personalities pointed out by users
Blue	*Timid* (7), *Obedient* (3), *Gentle* (2), *Spoilt* (2), *Sociable* (2), *Curious* (1), *Lonesome* (1)
Yellow	*Normal* (5), *Own pace* (3), *Timid* (3)
Pink	*Irritable* (15), *Offensive* (3), *Egoistic* (3), *Unkind* (2)

Table 5: General impressions of the character's behavior. Each figure represents the number of users.

	YES			Neither	NO		
	absolutely	almost	slightly		slightly	almost	absolutely
Life-like behavior	1	8	6	4	2	2	0
Autonomous behavior	2	10	1	4	5	1	0
Motivated behavior	1	11	9	0	0	2	0
Learning ability	0	7	3	9	2	2	0
Emotional behavior	2	11	9	0	0	1	0
Personality	9	12	2	0	0	0	0
Interaction with users	2	4	10	4	3	0	0
Interaction with others	4	15	4	0	0	0	0

Summary and Future Work

An emotion model for life-like agents was proposed in this work. The model consists of reactive and deliberative mechanisms. The former generates low-level instantaneous responses to stimuli that come from the real and virtual worlds. The latter mechanism especially focused on emotions and personalities. A basic idea of the model has come from a psychological theory. The concept of the theory is based on interactions between cognitive and emotional process in a mind. The model realized life-like agents with motivations and emotions. The authors applied it to the characters in a virtual world. Evaluation results showed that the proposed method is effective to give users the illusion of life.

One of our future work is adding a function of processing long term contexts. This function is required to smoothly communicate with users. The history of interaction will be memorized to generate more intelligent behavior by means of the function. For example, an agent, who is able to use the conversation history, will not repeat the same utterance. We also have plans to realize mixed emotion, emotion transition and mood. Then, tuning method of personality parameters will be established.

Acknowledgment

We would like to acknowledge the valuable contribution of Dr. Yasunori Morishima and Mr. Masaki Arao. We would also like to thank our anonymous reviewers for their useful comments on this paper.

References

Bates, J., Loyall, A.B., and Reilly, W.S. 1994. An Architecture for Action, Emotion, and Social Behavior, *Fourth European Workshop on Modelling Autonomous Agents in a Multi-Agent World*, 55-68. Berlin: Springer-Verlag.

Brooks, R.A. 1986. A Robust Layered Control System for a Mobile Robot, *IEEE Journal of Robotics and Automation*, RA-2:14-23.

Cannon, W.B. 1927. The James-Lange theory of emotion: A critical examination and an alternative theory. American Journal of Psychology. 39. 106-124.

Damasio, A.R. 1994. *Descartes' error*. New York: Putnam.

Dennett, D.C. 1996. *Kinds of Minds*. Basic Books, Harper Collins Publishers, Inc.

Dreyfus, H.L. 1979. *What Computers Can't Do: The Limits of Artificial Intelligence*. New York: Harper and Row.

Ekman, P. 1992. An Argument for Basic Emotions. In: Stein, N.L. and Oatley, K. eds. *Basic Emotions*, 169-200. Hove, UK: Lawrence Erlbaum.

Ekman, P. and Friesen, W.V. 1975. *Unmasking the Face*. New Jersey: Prentice-Hall, Inc.

Elliott, C. 1992. The Affective Reasoner: A Process Model of Emotions in a Multi-agent System, Ph.D. Dissertation, Technical Report No.32. Northwestern University, The Institute for the Learning Sciences.

Fillmore, C.J. 1971. Some Problems for Case Grammar. In O'Brien, R. ed. *Monograph series on languages and linguistics 24*. : Georgetown University Press.

Heyes-Roth, B. 1997. Improvisational Characters, In *Proceedings of the IJCAI-97 Workshop on Animated Interface Agents*: Making Them Intelligent.

Hayes-Roth, B. and van Gent, R. 1997. Story-Making Improvisational Puppets, In Proceedings of the First International Conference on Autonomous Agents.

Izard, C.E. 1993. Four Systems for Emotion Activation: Cognitive and Noncognitive Processes. Psychological Review 100(1): 68-90.

James, W. 1884. What is an emotion? *Mind*, 9, 188-205.

James, W. 1980. *The Principles of Psychology*. New York: Holt.

Johnson-Laird, P.N. 1988. *The Computer and the Mind: An Introduction to Cognitive Science*. Harvard University Press.

Maes, P. 1995. Artificial Life Meets Entertainment: Lifelike Autonomous Agents, *Communications of the ACM*, 38(11): 108-114.

Maes, P., Darrell, T., Blumberg, B., Pentland, S., Foner, L. Interacting with Animated Autonomous Agents. *Communications of the ACM*, 37(7).

Minsky, M. 1986. *The Society of Mind*. New York: Simon & Schuster.

Mueller, E.T. 1989. *Daydreaming in Humans and Machines: A Computer Model of the Stream of Thought*. :Ablex Publishing Corporation.

Nowlis, V. 1970. Mood: Behavior and Experience. In Arnold, M.B. ed. *Feelings and Emotions: The Loyola Symposium*. New York: Academic Press.

Ortony, A., Clore, G.L., and Collins, A. 1988. *The Cognitive Structure of Emotions*. : Cambridge University Press.

Picard, R.W. 1995. Affective Computing, Technical Report No. 321. MIT Media Laboratory.

Reeves, B. and Nass, C. 1996. *The Media Equation*. Cambridge University Press.

Reilly, W.S. and Bates, J. 1992. Building Emotional Agents, Technical Report CMU-CS-92-142, School of Computer Science, Carnegie Mellon University.

Stork, D.G. 1997. Scientist on the Set: An Interview with Marvin Minsky. In Stork, D.G. ed. *HAL's Legacy: 2001's Computer as Dream and Reality*. 15-31. MIT Press.

Toda, M. 1992. *Emotion: The Innate Adaptive Software System That Drives Human Beings*. Tokyo: University of Tokyo Press.

Velasquez, J.D. 1997. Modeling Emotions and Other Motivations in Synthetic Agents. In *Proceedings of the Fourteenth National Conference on Artificial Intelligence*, 10-15. Menlo Park, Calif.: AAAI Press.

When Robots Weep: Emotional Memories and Decision-Making

Juan D. Velásquez

MIT Artificial Intelligence Laboratory
545 Technology Square, NE43-935
Cambridge, Massachusetts 02139
jvelas@ai.mit.edu

Abstract

We describe an agent architecture that integrates emotions, drives, and behaviors, and that focuses on modeling some of the aspects of emotions as fundamental components within the process of decision-making. We show how the mechanisms of primary emotions can be used as building blocks for the acquisition of emotional memories that serve as biasing mechanisms during the process of making decisions and selecting actions. The architecture has been implemented into an object-oriented framework that has been successfully used to develop and control several synthetic agents and which is currently being used as the control system for an emotional pet robot.

Introduction

The traditional view on the nature of rationality has proposed that emotions and reason do not mix at all. For an agent to act rationally, it should not allow emotions to intrude in its reasoning processes. Research in Neuroscience, however, has provided evidence indicating quite the contrary, showing that emotions play a fundamental role in perception, learning, attention, memory, and other abilities and mechanisms we tend to associate with basic rational and intelligent behavior [Damasio 1994; LeDoux 1966; Adolphs 1966]. In particular, recent studies of patients with lesions of the prefrontal cortex suggest a critical role for emotions in decision-making [Bechara et al. 1997; Churchland 1996; Damasio 1994]. Although the studied patients can perform well on a variety of intelligence and memory tests, when faced with real-life situations they seem to be unable to make "good" decisions. Apparently, these patients lack intuition abilities, which, as many researchers think, may be based on memories of past emotions. These findings indicate that contrary to popular belief, intuition and emotions play significant roles in our abilities to make smart, rational decisions.

To this date, the field of Artificial Intelligence has largely ignored the use of emotions and intuition to guide reasoning and decision making. Several models of emotions have been proposed, but most of the work in this area has focused on specific aspects, such as recognizing emotions [Picard 1997], synthesizing emotions as the primary means to create believable synthetic agents [Bates 1994; Blumberg 1994; Elliot 1992; Maes 1995; Reilly 1996;], or synthesizing emotions and some of their influences in behavior and learning [Frijda 1996; Kitano 1995; Pfeifer 1988; Velásquez 1997].

The work described in this paper derives from, and extends previous research on computational models of emotions [Velásquez 1997]. Our main contribution is to show how drives, emotions, and behaviors can be integrated into a robust agent architecture, that uses some of the mechanisms of emotions to acquire memories from past emotional experiences that serve as biasing mechanisms while making decisions during the action-selection process.

Emotions as Biasing Mechanisms

The studies on patients with lesions in the prefrontal cortex mentioned above, motivated Damasio and colleagues to suggest that human reasoning and decision-making involves several mechanisms at different levels, extending from those that perform basic body regulation, to those that deal with more cognitive control of complex strategies. An interesting and novel component of this view is that reasoning depends also on emotions and the feelings accompanying them, which involve images that relate to the state of the body [Damasio 1994].

According to Damasio, part of this process includes the use of a covert, nonconscious biasing mechanism that directs us towards the "right" decision. This biasing step is known as the *somatic marker hypothesis*. The main idea behind this hypothesis is that decisions that are made in circumstances similar to previous experience, and whose outcome could be potentially harmful, or potentially advantageous, induce a *somatic* response used to *mark* future outcomes that are important to us, and to signal their danger or advantage. Thus, when a negative somatic marker is linked to a particular future outcome it serves as an alarm signal that tell us to avoid that particular course of action. If instead, a positive somatic marker is linked, it becomes an incentive to make that particular choice.

These ideas inspired the model described below.

The Computational Model

This section describes *Cathexis*, a computational model of emotions and action-selection inspired by work in different fields, including Neuropsychology, Artificial Intelligence, and Ethology. In particular, it has a strong influence from neuropsychological theories about the functional organization of the prefrontal lobes and their interaction with other neural systems involved in mediating emotions and sensorimotor responses that guide decision-making [Damasio 1994; Adolphs et al. 1996; Churchland 1996; Altman 1996]. Figure 1 provides a high level view of the model's architecture.

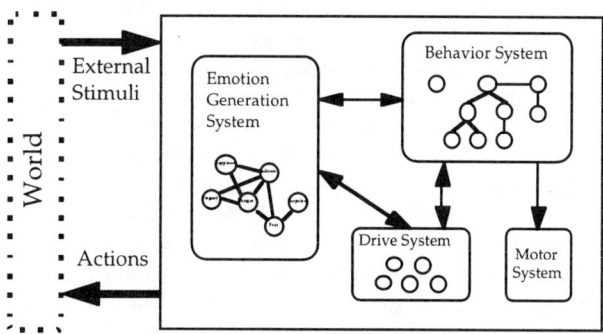

Figure 1 The Model's Architecture.

The Drive System

The Drive System consists of a set of motivational systems, or drives, representing urges that impel the agent into action. For instance, a *Hunger* drive will aid in controlling behaviors that directly affect the level of food intake by the agent.

Each Drive includes a set of Releasers which filter sensory data and identify special conditions which will either increase or decrease the value of the drive they belong to. These releasers represent control systems that maintain a controlled variable within a certain range. Drive control systems measure this variable through some of the agent's sensors and compare it to a desired value or set point. If its value does not match the set point, an error signal is produced. This error signal is fed to the appropriate drive, in which it can be combined with error signals from other relevant control systems. For instance, a *TemperatureRegulation* drive would combine the signals from two different control systems: one controlling peripheral temperature and one controlling brain temperature.

The value of each drive is determined by a linear combination of its control systems as described in Equation (1):

$$D_{it} = \sum_k (C_{ki} \cdot W_{ki}) \qquad (1)$$

Where D_{it} is the value of Drive i at time t; C_{ki} is the value of Control System k, and W_{ki} is the weight associated to control system k, where k ranges over the releasers for Drive i.

The Emotion Generation System

Following a neuropsychological perspective, the Emotion Generation System bears resemblance to some of the aspects in which the interactions between neural systems involving the amygdala, the hippocampus, and the prefrontal cortices have been considered to mediate emotions, such as assigning an emotional valence to different stimuli, activation of emotional behaviors, and emotional learning [Damasio 1994; LeDoux 1993; Panksepp 1995].

This system consists of a distributed network of self-interested emotional systems representing different families of related affective states, such as Fright, Fear, Terror, and Panic. Each member of an emotion family shares certain mechanisms and characteristics, including similarities in antecedent events, expression, likely behavioral response, and physiological patterns. These characteristics differ between emotion families, distinguishing one from another.

Drawing upon ideas from different theorists [Ekman 1992; Izard 1991; Johnson-Laird and Oatley 1992], we have identified and created explicit models for six different emotion families: *Anger, Fear, Distress/Sadness, Enjoyment/Happiness, Disgust,* and *Surprise.* The selection of this core set of emotion types is not arbitrary, but rather it is based upon evidence suggesting their universality, including distinctive universal facial expressions, as well as eight other properties [Ekman 1992].

Emotional Systems have a set of Releasers that constantly check for the appropriate conditions that would elicit the emotion they belong to. Influenced by Izard's multi-system for emotion activation [Izard 1993], we consider both cognitive and noncognitive releasers and divide them into four different groups:

- *Neural*: Includes the effects of neurotransmitters, brain temperature, and other neuroactive agents that can lead to emotion and which can be mediated by hormones, sleep, diet, and environmental conditions. For instance, there is a great deal of evidence that shows that decreased levels of norepinephrine and serotonin are associated with depression [Meltzer et al. 1981]. Similarly, it is clear that several chemical agents, such as carbon dioxide, yohimbine, and amphetamines produce anxiety in humans by activating the noradrenergic system [Charney and Redmon 1983].

- *Sensorimotor*: This system covers sensorimotor processes, such as facial expressions, body posture, muscle action potentials, and central efferent activity, that not only regulate ongoing emotion experiences but can also elicit emotion. Some evidence supporting this type of elicitors comes from neuropsychological studies in which experimenter-directed manipulation of facial muscles, composing a specific emotional expression, produces the subjective feeling corresponding to that emotion, as well as emotion-specific patterns of autonomic nervous system (ANS) activity [Ekman, Levenson, and Friesen 1993].

- *Motivational*: This system includes all motivations that lead to emotion. In this model, motivations include drives (e.g. *Thirst* and *Hunger*), emotions (e.g. *Anger,* and *Happiness*), and pain regulation. Some examples of elicitors in this system include the innate response to foul odors or tastes producing disgust, as measured in neuropsychological studies by [Fox and Davidson 1986], pain or aversive stimulation causing anger, and emotions like sadness eliciting others such as anger.

• *Cognitive*: This system includes all type of cognitions that activate emotion, such as appraisal of events, comparisons, attributions, beliefs and desires, memory, and so on. In previous work, these elicitors were based on a cognitive appraisal theory (See [Velásquez 1997] for details). In an effort to design a more plausible model, we have revised the Emotion Generation System so that it does not include any pre-wired cognitive elicitors, but rather allows for them to be learned through emotional experiences, as the agent interacts with its environment.

Besides its releasers, each Emotional System includes two different thresholds. The first one, α, is used to determine when an emotion episode occurs. That is, once its intensity goes above this threshold, the Emotional System releases its output signal to other Emotional Systems and to the Behavior System which in turn selects and controls an appropriate behavior according to the agent's motivational state. The second threshold, ω, specifies the level of saturation for that emotion. This is consistent with real life emotional systems in which levels of arousal will not exceed certain limits. In addition to these parameters, each Emotional System has a function, $\Psi()$, which controls the temporal decay of its intensity. These kinds of mechanisms contribute to the nonlinear behavior exhibited by the model. Figure 2 illustrates these ideas.

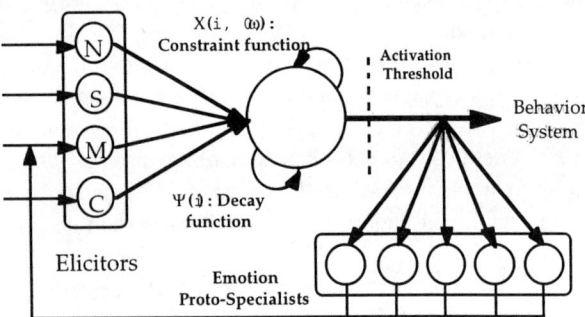

Figure 2 Emotional Systems.

The intensity of an Emotional System depends on all the factors that contribute to it, including its previous level of arousal, the contributions of each of its elicitors, and the interaction (inhibitory and excitatory) with other Emotional Systems. This is summarized in Equation (2):

$$I_{et} = \chi\left(\Psi(I_{et-1}) + \sum_k L_{ke} + \sum_l (G_{le} \cdot I_{lt}) - \sum_m (H_{me} \cdot I_{mt})\right) \quad (2)$$

Where I_{et} is the value of the intensity for Emotion e at time t; I_{et-1} is its value at the previous time step; $\Psi()$ is the function that represents how Emotion e decays; L_{ke} is the value of Emotion Elicitor k, where k ranges over the Emotion Elicitors for Emotion e; G_{le} is the Excitatory Gain that Emotion l applies to Emotion e; I_{lt} is the intensity of Emotion l at time t; H_{me} is the Inhibitory Gain that Emotion m applies to Emotion e; I_{mt} is the intensity of Emotion m at time t; and $X()$ is the function that constrains the intensity of Emotion e between 0 and its saturation value.

This model of Emotional Systems allows for the distinction between different affective phenomena. For instance, primary emotions are modeled as the activation of one particular Emotional System such as *Sadness* or *Disgust*. Emotion blends, such as *Jealousy*, emerge as the co-activation of two or more of these Emotional Systems. Similarly, and following a psychobiological perspective [Panksepp 1995], moods are differentiated from emotions in terms of levels of arousal. While emotions consist of high arousal of specific Emotional Systems, moods may be explained as low tonic levels of arousal within the same systems (i.e. levels below the α threshold). This representation is consistent with the enormous subtleties of human moods and feelings, as well as with the common observation that moods seem to lower the threshold for arousing certain emotions. This occurs because emotional systems that are aroused, as it happens in the representation of moods, are already providing some potential for the activation of an emotion. Finally, it is consistent with the observation that the duration of moods appears to be longer than that of the emotions, since at low levels of arousal, the intensity of the Emotional Systems will decay more slowly.

Finally, temperaments are modeled through the different values that parameters (e.g., thresholds, gains, and decay rates) within each Emotional System can have. Thus, for instance, if we want to model a depressed agent, we might lower the activation threshold and decay rate for the *Sadness* emotion as well as lowering the inhibitory gain between *Happiness* and *Sadness*. The result is a flexible, distributed model that can synthesize a variety of affective phenomena simultaneously.

The Behavior System

Following Damasio's view, reasoning and decision-making define a domain of cognition in which an agent must choose how to respond to a situation. Concepts like *decision*, *reason*, *action-selection*, and *rationality* are fundamentally linked to behavior. When an agent faces a situation, a decision of what to do next must be made. This choice is responsibility of the Behavior System. The action-selection process is mediated by the reasoning engaged. If the outcome of the reasoning and the selected behavior are adaptive (oversimplified in this model as selecting a behavior that avoids negative outcomes), the choice is considered rational.

The Behavior System is a distributed network of self-interested behaviors, such as *"approach human"*, *"play"*, *"request attention"*, and *"avoid obstacle"*.

Like Drives and Emotional Systems, Behaviors have Releasers that obtain and filter sensory data in order to identify special conditions which will either increase or decrease the value of the Behavior. Releasers might represent objects and conditions such as "battery recharger is present", and motivational states such as "battery level is low" and "distress is high", which would most likely increase the value of a *"recharge batteries"* behavior.

Behaviors may mutually inhibit or excite each other. For instance, *"wag the tail"* might inhibit *"running"* and vice-versa. Whereas behaviors such as *"play with human"* might excite lower-level ones like *"find human"*.

In earlier work, the Behavior System followed a winner-take-all strategy in which only one behavior could be active at a time. This made it impossible for non-conflicting Behaviors, such as *"walk"* and *"cry"* to execute at the same time. Given the parallelism of the model, we revised the Behavior System so that active, non-conflicting Behaviors can issue motor commands simultaneously. The value for each Behavior is computed as described in Equation (3):

$$B_{jt} = \sum_n (R_{nj} \cdot W_{nj}) + \sum_l (G_{lj} \cdot B_{lt}) - \sum_m (H_{mj} \cdot B_{mt}) \quad (3)$$

Where B_{jt} is the value of Behavior j at time t; R_{nj} is the value of releaser n and W_{nj} is the weight for releaser n, where n ranges over the releasers for Behavior j; G_{lj} is the Excitatory Gain that Behavior l applies to Behavior j, and B_{lt} is the intensity of Behavior l at time t, where l ranges over the set of behaviors that excite Behavior j; H_{mj} is the Inhibitory Gain that Behavior m applies to Behavior j, and B_{mt} is the intensity of Behavior m at time t, where m ranges over the set of behaviors that inhibit Behavior j.

Integrating Emotional Memories

The mechanisms described above for primary emotions do not describe the whole range of emotions we experience. In fact, most of our emotional experiences can be considered secondary which occur after we begin experiencing feelings and start making orderly associations between objects and situations, and primary emotions. Thus, for instance, whereas a loud noise might activate an innate fear response (primary emotion), thinking about not making a paper deadline might activate a learned one (secondary emotion). This latter kind of emotion requires more complex processing, including in most cases, the retrieval of emotional memories of similar previous experiences. Following the ideas behind both Damasio's somatic-marker hypothesis [Damasio 1994], and LeDoux's work on fast (low-road) and slow (high-road) pathways for emotion activation [LeDoux 1993], we have extended our model to consider not only pre-wired, stimuli-driven emotions, but also, more cognitive, memory-based, learned ones.

These secondary emotions have been modeled with an associative network comparable to Minsky's K-lines [Minsky 1986], in which primary emotions are connected to the specific stimuli (e.g., executed behaviors, objects, or agents) that have elicited them during the agent's interaction with the world. The connections between primary emotions and different stimuli specify the amount (averaged throughout different occurrences) of emotional energy (intensity of the Emotional System) applied to each stimulus when encountered.

For instance, supposing that an agent is about to engage in *Feeding* and the only available food is a bad-tasting soup, it is likely that once the agent eats, the *Disgust* Emotional System will become active at some particular intensity because it has a pre-wired elicitor for foul odors and tastes. Once this happens, an association is made between the primary emotion (*Disgust*) and the stimulus that provoked it (soup), and an emotional memory is created.

The emotional memory by itself is not very useful. Instead, the model described above has been extended so that it uses this information as part of the behavior selection process. Thus, the next time an agent encounters a *marked* stimulus, such as the soup in our example, the memory represented in the associative network will be relived, reproducing the emotional state previously experienced, and influencing the selection of actions to follow.

Thus, although the agent had no pre-wired aversion for soup, its previous negative experience has created a learned one for it. Furthermore, even if the agent is very hungry, it is likely that the *Feeding* behavior will not become active if soup is the only food present. Hence, the purpose of emotional memories is twofold. First, they allow for the learning of secondary emotions as generalizations of primary ones. And second, they serve as markers or biasing mechanisms that influence what decisions are made and how the agent behaves.

Implementation and Results

The model described in the previous sections has been implemented in its totality as part of an object-oriented framework for building autonomous agents. We have used this framework to develop and control various synthetic agents, including *Simón the Toddler* (See [Velásquez 1997] for a description), and *Virtual Yuppy*, a simulated emotional pet robot, shown in Figure 3.

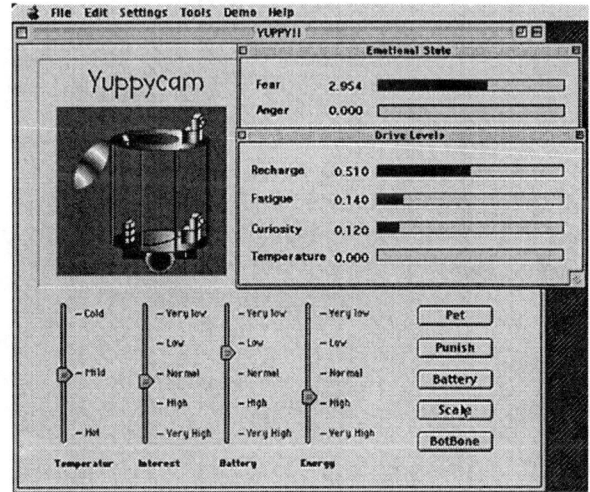

Figure 3 Virtual Yuppy

As part of our ongoing research, the same framework has

been used to control Yuppy, the actual physical robot shown in Figure 4.

The implementation details and results described in this section correspond in most part to the simulated robot, but are also applicable to current observations with the physical robot.

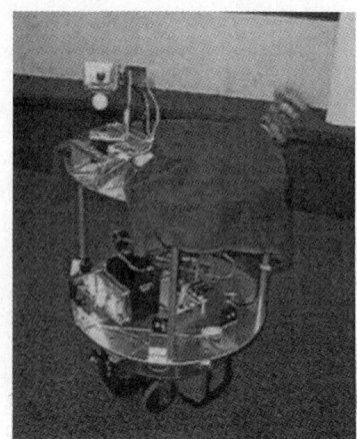

Figure 4 Yuppy, an Emotional Pet Robot

Virtual Yuppy has different sensors, including one for very simple synthetic vision, as well as simulated tactile sensors to model painful and pleasurable stimuli.

Its Drive System is composed of four different drives: *RechargingRegulation, TemperatureRegulation, Fatigue,* and *Curiosity*, each of which controls internal variables representing the agent's *battery, temperature, energy,* and *interest* levels, respectively.

Its Emotion Generation System includes emotional systems with innate releasers for the set of basic emotion families described before. These releasers have been grouped under the Neural, Sensorimotor, and Motivational elicitor categories, modeling the primary emotions for the agent. For instance, via motivational elicitors, unsatisfied drives produce *Distress* and *Anger*, whereas satiation generates *Happiness*. Similarly, "synthetic bones" and "petting" elicit *Happiness, Fear* includes an innate releaser for darkness, and pain produces *Distress* and *Anger*.

The robot's Behavior System is composed of a distributed network of approximately nineteen different self-interested behaviors, directed in most part towards satisfying its needs and interacting with humans. Examples of such behaviors include *"search for bone", "approach bone", "recharge battery", "wander", "startle", "avoid obstacle", "approach human",* and *"express emotion"*.

The user interacts with the robot in two different ways: First, by controlling its affective style, which is done by tweaking the different parameters described above (e.g., thresholds, gains, or inhibitory and excitatory connections) for each Emotional System. And second, by providing stimuli for the agents, whether in the form of internal stimuli, such as modifying the level of synthetic neurotransmitters and internal variables, or external stimuli, such as hitting the robot, showing the bone, and so on.

Using the model described before, Virtual Yuppy produces emotional behaviors under different circumstances. For instance, when its *Curiosity* drive is high, Virtual Yuppy wanders around, looking for the synthetic bone which some humans carry. When it encounters one, its level of *Happiness* increases and specific behaviors, such as *"wag the tail"* and *"approach the bone"* become active. On the other hand, as time passes by without finding any bone, its Distress level rises and sad behaviors, such as "droop the tail", get executed. Similarly, while wandering around, it may encounter dark places which will elicit fearful responses in which it backs up and changes direction.

Besides regulating action-selection and generating emotional behaviors through primary emotions, Virtual Yuppy learns secondary emotions which are stored as new or modified cognitive elicitors based on the associative network model described before. For instance, after locating a bone, the robot may approach it, thus approaching the human who is carrying it. Depending on these interactions (e.g., humans pet or hit the robot), Virtual Yuppy will create positive or negative emotional memories with respect to humans, and future selection of behaviors such as approaching or avoiding them will be influenced.

Related Work

Given the space limitations, a comprehensive review of related work is not possible, and only the most relevant work is discussed in this section. For an overview of various models the reader is referred to [Picard 1997; Pfeifer 1988; Hudlicka and Fellows 1996].

Most of the recent work on this area has focused on modeling emotions for entertainment purposes. Some excellent work in the area of believable agents includes Reilly's *Em* architecture [Reilly 1996] and Elliot's *Affective Reasoner* [Elliot 1992]. Both differ from our work in several important ways. Their approach is mostly concerned with contribution of appraisal to emotion, hence they emphasize on cognitively generated emotions. In contrast, fast, primary emotions, emergent emotions, and other affective phenomena are not explicitly modeled or are otherwise oversimplified. Also, they do not model interactions with other processes, including regulatory mechanisms (i.e. drives), decision-making, and emotional learning.

It should be noted, however, that some of these differences may be due, in part, to the specific purpose for which each model was designed. Their work is mostly aimed at designing tools and models to create believable agents. Therefore, rule-based approaches that emphasize more on cognitive generation of emotion and less on designing a plausible model, may be the most appropriate ones.

Our work also relates to models of action-selection. A number of researchers have proposed successful models of action-selection for agents with multiple goals that operate in unpredictable environments [Brooks 1986; Maes 1990, Blumberg 1994; Tyrell 1993]. However, and in contrast to the work presented here, most of these models do not consider emotions as an integral part of the action-selection process, and when they do, they do not include explicit emotion models, emotional states, or moods, but rather simplified internal variables that represent emotions as well as other motivations such as hunger or thirst.

Conclusions

We have presented a flexible agent architecture that integrates drives, emotions, and behaviors and that focuses on emotions as the main motivational system that influences how behaviors are selected and controlled. We have showed how the mechanisms of primary emotions included in the proposed model, and which have been inspired by work in Neuropsychology and other fields, can be used to create emotional memories, or secondary emotions that act as biasing mechanisms during the process of making decisions and selecting actions.

Acknowledgments

The author would like to thank Professor Rod Brooks for his support of this work. Also, thanks to the entire Yuppy team for their help. In particular, thanks to Charles Kemp for his suggestion on simultaneous activation of non-conflicting behaviors. This research is part of the Yuppy project which is funded by Yamaha.

References

Adolphs, R et al. 1996. Neuropsychological Approaches to Reasoning and Decision-Making. In: Damasio, A., et al. Eds. *Neurobiology of Decision-Making*. Berlin: Springer-Verlag.

Altman, J. 1996. Epilogue: Models of Decision-Making. In: Damasio, A., et al. Eds. *Neurobiology of Decision-Making*. Berlin: Springer-Verlag.

Bates, J. 1994. The Role of Emotion in Believable Agents. *Communications of the ACM* 37(7):122-125.

Bechara, A., et al. 1997. Deciding Advantageously Before Knowing the Advantageous Strategy. In: *Science*, 275, 1293-1295.

Blumberg, B. 1994. Action-Selection in Hamsterdam: Lessons from Ethology. In *Proceedings of SAB94*, 108-117. Brighton, England: MIT Press.

Brooks, R. 1986. A Robust Layered Control System For A Mobile Robot. In: *Robotics and Automation*, RA-2(1).

Charney, D.S., and Redmond, DE. 1983. Neurobiological Mechanisms in Human Anxiety. In: *neuropharmacology*, 22, 1531-1536.

Churchland, P.S. 1996. Feeling Reasons. In: Damasio, A., et al. Eds. *Neurobiology of Decision-Making*. Berlin: Springer-Verlag.

Damasio, A. 1994. *Descartes' Error: Emotion, Reason, and the Human Brain*. New York: Gosset/Putnam.

Ekman, P. 1992. An Argument for Basic Emotions. In: Stein, N. L., and Oatley, K. eds. *Basic Emotions*, 169-200. Hove, UK: Lawrence Erlbaum.

Ekman, P., Levenson, R., and Friesen, W. 1983. Autonomic Nervous System Activity Distinguishes Among Emotions. In: *Science*, 221, 1208-1210.

Elliot, C.D. 1992. The Affective Reasoner: A Process Model of Emotions in a Multi-Agent System. Ph.D. Thesis, Institute for the Learning Sciences, Northwestern University.

Fox, N., and Davidson, R. 1986. Taste-Elicited Changes in facial Signs of Emotion and the Asymmetry of Brain Electrical Activity in Human Newborns. In: *Neuropsychologia*, 24, 417-422.

Frijda, N. 1986. *The Emotions*. Cambridge, UK: Cambridge University Press.

Hudlicka, E., and Fellows, J. 1996. Review of Computational Models of Emotions. Tech. Report 9612, Psychometrix.

Izard, C. 1991. *The Psychology of Emotions*. New York: Plenum Press.

Izard, C. E. 1993. Four Systems for Emotion Activation: Cognitive and Noncognitive Processes. *Psychological Review* 100(1):68-90.

Johnson-Laird, P. and Oatley, K. 1992. Basic Emotions, Rationality, and Folk Theory. In: Stein, N. L., and Oatley, K. eds. *Basic Emotions*, 169-200. Lawrence Erlbaum.

Kitano, H. 1995. A Model for Hormonal Modulation of Learning. In: *Proceedings of IJCAI-95*. Montreal.

LeDoux, J. 1993. Emotional Memory Systems in the brain. *Behavioral and Brain Research*, 58.

LeDoux, J. 1996. *The Emotional Brain*. New York: Simon and Schuster.

Maes P. 1995. Artificial Life meets Entertainment: Lifelike Autonomous Agents. *Communications of the ACM. Special Issue on Novel Applications of AI*.

Maes P. 1990. Situated Agents Can Have Goals. *Robotics and Autonomous Systems*, 6(1&2).

Meltzer, H.Y. et al. 1981. Serotonin Uptake in Blood Platelets of Psychiatric Patients. In: *Archives of General Psychiatry*, 38:1322-1326.

Minsky. M. 1986. *The Society of Mind*. New York: Simon & Schuster.

Panksepp, J. 1995. The Emotional Brain and Biological Psychiatry. *Advances in Biological Psychiatry*, 1, 263-286.

Pfeifer, R. 1988. Artificial Intelligence Models of Emotion. In: Hamilton, V., Bower, G. H., and Frijda, N. eds. *Cognitive Perspectives on Emotion and Motivation*, 287-320. Netherlands: Kluwer.

Picard, R. 1997. *Affective Computing*. MIT Press.

Reilly S. 1996. Believable Social and Emotional Agents. Technical Report, CMU-CS-96-138, School of Computer Science, Carnegie Mellon University.

Tyrell, T. 1993. The Use of Hierarchies for Action Selection. In: *Proceedings of SAB92*.

Velásquez, J. 1997. Modeling Emotions and Other Motivations in Synthetic Agents. In: *Proceedings of AAAI-97*.

Natural Language Multiprocessing: A Case Study

Enrico Pontelli and **Gopal Gupta** and **Janyce Wiebe** and **David Farwell**
Dept. Computer Science and Computing Research Laboratory
New Mexico State University
{epontell,gupta,wiebe}@cs.nmsu.edu, david@crl.nmsu.edu

Abstract

This paper presents two case studies of parallelization of large Natural Language Processing (NLP) applications using a parallel logic programming system (called "ACE") that automatically exploits implicit parallelism. The first system considered is *Artwork*, a system for semantic disambiguation, speech act resolution, and temporal reference resolution. The second system is *ULTRA*, a multilingual translation system. Both applications were originally developed in Prolog without any consideration for parallel processing. The results obtained confirm that NLP is a ripe area for exploitation of parallelism. Most previous work on parallelism in NLP focused primarily on parallelizing the parsing phase of language processing. The case studies presented here show that parallelism is also present in the semantic and discourse processing phases, which are often the most computationally intensive part of the application.

Introduction

Logic programming has been for a long time one of the programming paradigms of choice for the development of NLP systems. Logic programming languages (e.g., Prolog) offer features such as backtracking, unification, and symbolic data representation which greatly facilitate the development of NLP applications (Pereira 1987). In recent years the use of declarative languages, such as Prolog and Lisp, for NLP applications has declined. This is mostly due to the increasing computational requirements of these applications, which were not satisfied by the older slow implementations of declarative languages. Even though implementations of these languages comparable in efficiency to imperative languages are available today (e.g., (Carlson & Gupta 1996)), past experience has discouraged designers of NLP systems from using them.

The computational demands of today's NLP systems have reached the level where they are challenging for even the most efficiently implementable programming paradigms, including imperative languages. Exploitation of parallelism is an important technique, especially given that multiprocessor machines (e.g., dual and quad Pentium-based PCs) are readily and cheaply available in the market today. Logic programming languages have a distinct advantage over imperative languages with regards to parallelism: their mathematical semantics allow for *automatic* or *semi-automatic* exploitation of parallelism, thus relieving the programmer from most of the intricacies of parallel programming and debugging. One of the goals of this paper is to make the NLP community aware of the recent advances made in implementation and parallelization technology for logic programming, and their potential benefits to NLP systems. The current implementations of logic programming systems are comparable in execution efficiency to any other programming paradigm. We hope that all of these attractive features—the ability to automatically or semi-automatically exploit parallelism, realization of non-determinism, support of symbolic data representation, and efficiency comparable to imperative paradigms—will convince NLP system designers to reconsider logic programming as an excellent implementation choice for many NLP applications. Given that parallelism can be exploited automatically, existing Prolog-based NLP applications can also be parallelized, by porting them with little or no effort to parallel systems. Fast parallel implementations of Prolog are currently available (e.g., (Ali & Karlsson 1990)) or about to be released into the public domain, including the ACE system (Gupta *et al.* 1994) used in this work.

In this work we present two case studies in which two large NLP applications, independently developed with no goal of parallelization in mind, have been studied and parallelized using the ACE parallel Prolog system. The parallelization effort was very limited in both cases and lead to excellent performance and speedups for both applications. In the rest of this paper we give a brief description of parallel logic programming and the ACE system followed by an overview of the two NLP applications considered (Artwork and ULTRA). Finally, we analyze the performance results obtained.

Parallelism in Logic Programming

Logic programming is a programming paradigm in which programs are expressed as logical implications.

Copyright ©1998, American Association for Artificial Intelligence (www.aaai.org). All rights reserved.

An important property of logic programming languages is that they are single assignment languages. Unlike conventional programming languages, they disallow destructive assignment and explicit control information. Not only does this allow cleaner (declarative) semantics for programs, and hence a better understanding of them by their users, it also makes it easier for a runtime evaluator of logic programs to employ different control strategies for evaluation. That is, different operations in a logic program can be executed in any order without affecting the (declarative) meaning of the program. In particular, these operations can be performed *implicitly in parallel*. Parallelization can be done directly by the runtime evaluator as suggested above, or, alternatively, it can also be done by a parallelizing compiler. The task of the parallelizing compiler is to unburden the evaluator from making run-time decisions regarding which parts of the program to run in parallel. Note that the program can also be parallelized by the user (through suitable annotations). In all cases, the advantage offered by logic programming is that the process is easier because of the more declarative nature of the language.

Three principal kinds of (implicitly exploitable) control parallelism can be identified in logic programs: *(i) Or-parallelism* arises when more than one clause defines some predicate and a literal unifies with more than one clause head—the corresponding bodies can then be executed in parallel with each other. Or-parallelism is thus a way of efficiently searching for solutions to the query, by exploring alternative solutions in parallel. *(ii) Independent and-parallelism (IAP)* arises when more than one goal is present in the query or in the body of a clause, and at runtime these goals to do not compete for any unbound variable. *(iii) Dependent and-parallelism (DAP)* arises when two or more goals of a clause access common variables and are executed in parallel.

The ACE System

The ACE model (Gupta *et al.* 1994; Pontelli 1997) uses stack-copying (Ali & Karlsson 1990) and recomputation (Gupta *et al.* 1994) to efficiently support combined or- and independent and-parallel execution of logic programs. ACE represents an efficient combination of or- and independent and-parallelism in the sense that penalties for supporting either form of parallelism are paid only when that form of parallelism is actually exploited. This efficiency in execution is accomplished by introducing the concept of *teams of processors* and extending the stack-copying techniques to deal with this new processor organization.

Or-Parallelism in ACE: ACE exploits or–parallelism by using a stack copying approach (Ali & Karlsson 1990). In this approach, a set of processing *agents* (processors in the case of MUSE, teams of processors in the case of ACE—as explained later) working in or-parallel maintain a *separate* but *identical* address space (i.e. they allocate their data structures starting at the same logical addresses). Whenever an *or-agent* (agents working in or-parallel are termed or-agents) $\mathcal{A}$ is idle, it will start looking for unexplored alternatives generated by some other or-agent $\mathcal{B}$. Once a choice point p with unexplored alternatives is detected in the computation tree $\mathcal{T}_\mathcal{B}$ generated by $\mathcal{B}$, then $\mathcal{A}$ creates a local copy of $\mathcal{T}_\mathcal{B}$ and restarts computation by backtracking over p and executing one of the unexplored alternatives. The fact that all the or-agents maintain an identical logical address space reduces the creation of a local copy of $\mathcal{T}_\mathcal{B}$ to a simple block memory copying operation.

In order to reduce the number of copying operations performed (since each copying operation may involve a considerable amount of overhead), unexplored alternatives are always searched starting from the bottommost part of the tree; during the copying operation all the choice points in between are shared between the two agents (i.e., at each copying operation we try to maximize the amount of work shared between the two agents). Furthermore, in order to reduce the amount of information transferred, copying is done *incrementally*, i.e., only the difference between $\mathcal{T}_\mathcal{A}$ and $\mathcal{T}_\mathcal{B}$ is actually copied.

And-Parallelism in ACE: ACE exploits IAP using a recomputation based scheme—no sharing of solutions is performed (at the and-parallel level). This means that for a query like ?- a,b, where a and b are non-deterministic, b is completely recomputed for every solution of a (as in Prolog). The computation tree created in the presence of and-parallel computation has a *parbegin-parend* structure, and the different branches are assigned to different agents. Since we are exploiting only *independent and-parallelism*, only independent subgoals are allowed to be executed concurrently by different *and-agents* (and-agents are processing agents working in and-parallel with each other). Dependencies are detected at run-time by executing some simple tests introduced by the *parallelizing compiler*. ACE adopts the technique originally designed by DeGroot (DeGroot 1984) and refined by Hermenegildo (Hermenegildo *et al.* 1995) of annotating the program at compile time with *Conditional Graph Expressions (CGEs)*:

$$(\langle \textit{conditions} \rangle \Rightarrow B_1 \& \cdots \& B_n)$$

where $\langle \textit{conditions} \rangle$ is a conjunction of simple tests on variables appearing in the clause that verifies whether the arguments share any variables with arguments of other goals, and & denotes *parallel conjunction*. Intuitively, if the tests present in *conditions* succeed, then the subgoals $B_1 \& \cdots \& B_n$ can be executed in and-parallel, else they should be executed sequentially.

Since and-agents are computing just different parts of the same computation (i.e. they are cooperating in building one solution of the initial query) they need to have *different* but *mutually accessible* address spaces.

When a CGE is seen, a new descriptor for the parallel call (named *parcall frame*) is allocated, initialized, and all the subgoals but the leftmost one are loaded in a local work queue (*goal stack*) (the leftmost subgoal is directly executed by the same and-agent that created the parcall frame). The same processor performing the creation of the parallel call will eventually fetch and execute other unexecuted parallel subgoals from this parallel call, if necessary. An idle processor may pick work from the work queue of other processors. This will entail the identification of the subgoal to execute, the allocation of an initial data structure, the actual computation of the subgoal, and finally the allocation of further structures to identify the completion of the subgoal. *Backward execution* denotes the series of steps that are performed following a *failure*—due to unification or lack of matching clauses. In ACE, where both or- and and-parallelism are exploited, backtracking should also avoid taking alternatives already taken by other or-agents. In the presence of CGEs, standard backtracking should be upgraded in order to deal with computations which are spread across processors.

And-Or Parallelism in ACE: In ACE a clear separation is made between exploitation of or-parallelism and exploitation of and-parallelism. Processors in the multiprocessor system are divided into *teams of processors*. At a higher level, these teams of processors *execute in or-parallel* with each other (i.e., a team will take up only or-parallel work). At a lower level, i.e., within each team, processors in the team *execute in and-parallel* with each other (i.e., along an or-branch taken by a team, processors in that team will execute goals arising in that branch in and-parallel). Thus, the the notion of *or-agent* is mapped to the notion of *team of processors* while the notion of *and-agent* is mapped to the notion of processors inside a team (i.e. each processor is an and-agent). Different approaches to incremental copying and heuristics have been developed (Gupta *et al.* 1994).

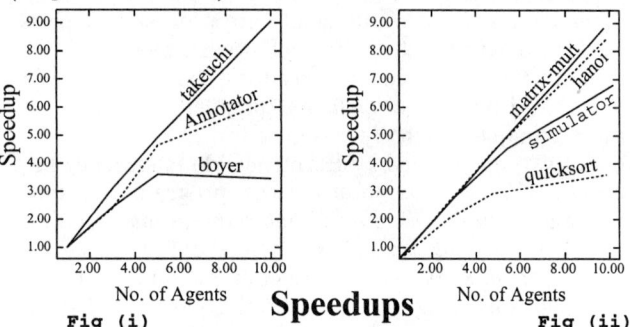

Figure 1: Speedups in ACE

ACE has shown remarkable performance results on a large selection of programs (Figure 1 presents the speedup curves obtained on some benchmarks). Furthermore, the parallelization overhead is extremely low, on average 5 to 10% w.r.t. sequential SICStus Prolog, on which the ACE engine is based.

NLP Applications

The field of NLP has changed dramatically over the last few years. The pressure from the users community has pushed NLP to increase the amount of effort towards the development of specific, practical applications and large-scale language processing systems. This has created an increasing need for efficient implementation schemes for many of the theoretical concepts developed in the past. NLP is probably one of the application fields with the highest computational requirements. Problems tend to generate high levels of nondeterminism and ambiguity, making exhaustive approaches entirely not feasible. This forces researchers to focus on smaller problems or operate under more conservative assumptions. Our thesis in this paper is that by resorting to exploitation of parallelism many of these conservative assumptions can be relaxed, as well as larger problems solved. We take advantage of parallelism implicit in NLP applications to achieve efficient execution as well as improve the precision of the solutions obtained (by exploring a larger portion of the search space). Our experience with parallelizing the Artwork and the ULTRA systems and the results obtained confirm our thesis. The elegance and the semantic clarity of logic programming not only allowed simplification of the software development process, but also permitted automatic exploitation of parallelism; such exploitation of parallelism and execution speedups would not have been possible if the code were written in an imperative programming language, since for such languages automatic parallelization is extremely difficult.

Artwork: When people write or converse, they leave much of what they are communicating implicit, leaving the listener or hearer to fill in the missing information by considering the surrounding context. Consider, for example, understanding the pronouns in the sentence "She was there that day." Who was where on what day depends on what was said previously. The tasks of the discourse processing component of a NLP system involve recovering information that is implicitly communicated in the text or dialog. Such a component performs these tasks by considering information across sentence boundaries, rather than processing each sentence in isolation.

Only recently have major efforts been invested in empirical investigations of computational theories of discourse processing (see, for example, the special issue of *Computational Linguistics* devoted to empirical studies in discourse (23(1) 1997)). The Artwork project is one such NLP project, funded by the Department of Defense. It targets *scheduling dialogs*, dialogs in which the participants schedule a meeting with one another. A fully automatic rule-based system was developed that performs many kinds of natural language disambiguation, including *semantic* disambiguation, and two types of discourse disambiguation: *speech-act* and *temporal reference* resolution.

The input to the system is the output of a semantic parser developed as part of the Enthusiast speech-to-speech machine translation project at CMU (Levin 1995); it determines, among other things, what type of event each utterance is about, and who the participants are. The output of the parser is ambiguous, so must be disambiguated by the Artwork system.

The first of the discourse ambiguities addressed involves a prominent view of language as goal-oriented behavior. Under this view, which is adopted in this project, utterances are produced by actions that are executed with the goal of having some particular effect on the hearer. These actions are called *speech acts*. The task of an understanding system is to recognize which speech acts the speaker is performing with his or her utterances (Reithinger & Maier 1995; Rosé et al. 1995; Wiebe et al. 1996). Consider the utterance "2 to 4" (dos a cuatro), a common type of utterance in the scheduling dialogs. The speaker might be *suggesting* that they meet from 2 to 4; they might be *confirming* that 2 to 4 is the time currently being discussed; they might, with the right intonation, be *accepting* 2 to 4; and so on. The other kind of discourse ambiguity addressed is temporal (Wiebe et al. 1997). The Artwork system tracks the times being talked about, determining implicit contextual information. For example, when a speaker refers to "2 to 4 am", Artwork looks back at the previous utterances, and decides which day, date, and month are being referred to. This involves a search for the best possible candidate which fits the constraints generated by the previous utterances. Temporal reference resolution is the primary focus of the current Artwork system. Wiebe et al. (1997) present the results of the system performing this task on unseen, held-out test data, taking as input the ambiguous output of the semantic parser (which itself takes as input the output of a speech recognition system (Levin 1995)). The system performs well, and comparable results on similar tasks have not been published elsewhere.

The system parallelized in this work is an earlier version which performed speech-act and temporal reference resolution, but not semantic disambiguation. It includes the core architecture and speech-act and temporal-reference resolution rules of the current system. We expect the results obtained in this study to transfer easily to the latest versions of Artwork.

ULTRA: *ULTRA (Universal Language TRAnslator)* is a multilingual, interlingual machine translation system. It can currently translate between five languages (Chinese, English, German, Spanish, and Japanese) with vocabularies in each language based on about 10,000 word senses. The multilingual system is based on a language-independent interlingual representation (IR) (Farwell & Wilks 1991) for representing expressions as elements of linguistic acts of communication (e.g., asking questions, describing the world, promising that things will get done, etc.). Translation can be viewed as the use of the target language to express the same act as the one expressed in the source language. The IR is then used as the basis for analyzing or for generating expressions as elements of such acts in each of the languages (Farwell & Wilks 1991).

Each individual language system is independent and has its own rules to associate the appropriate IRs to each expression of the language. The different language components interact exclusively via IRs—thus allowing, for example, a clear system design and making the addition of new languages very easy without unpredictable effects on the rest of the system. It also gives freedom to the implementor to choose the class of grammars and the parser (s)he prefers. Currently most of the language components are implemented as context-free grammars with complex categories.

The system uses relaxation techniques (grammatical relaxation, semantic relaxation, and structure relaxation) to provide robustness by giving preferred or "near miss" translations (Farwell & Wilks 1991). In addition, the adoption of language-independent semantic and pragmatic procedures allows, given a context, the selection of the best IR from the set of possible IRs for a given expression. The use of Prolog allowed the design of a highly declarative and perfectly bidirectional application.

The current prototype produces word, phrase, or sentence level translations and handles most basic declarative, interrogative, and imperative structures, including conjoined and subjoined constructions, while dealing with various types of sense disambiguation and structurally dependent anaphora and ellipsis.

Experimental Results

Parallelization of Artwork: The parallelization of Artwork was performed semi-automatically. The ACE compiler was used to identify potential sources of parallelism. Additionally, the rich output of the ACE static analyzer (Pontelli et al. 1997) (e.g., sharing information) allowed us to identify features of the program that were limiting the parallelism exploitable. Very few hand-modifications of the original code were needed to considerably improve the speedups achieved, as discussed in the next subsection.

Ambiguity in NLP gives rise to a "combinatorial explosion" of possible interpretations. Consequently, Artwork may take up to a couple of hours to process a dialog (Wiebe et al. 1996). Artwork offers a great deal of inherent parallelism to exploit, including or-parallelism and both DAP and IAP.

To process each utterance, the system applies all rules in its knowledge base. Each rule that matches the utterance fires, producing a partial representation. The rules are not all competitors; some of them target one ambiguity while other rules target others. All possible maximal merging of the results are formed, resulting in the set of interpretations the system chooses among to be the representation of the utterance. The application of the rules is realized through a subgoal of the form:

```
findall(R,int(PrevI,PrevUt,CurI,T_Ut,_,_,R),List)
```
where the `int` predicates is defined as:
```
int(PrevI,PrevUt,CurI,CurUt,CF,Rule,Res):-
    int01(PrevI,PrevUt,CurI,CurUt,CF,Rule,Res).
int(PrevI, PrevUt,CurI,CurUt,CF,Rule,Res):-
    int02(PrevI,PrevUt,CurI,CurUt,CF,Rule,Res).
....
```

The rules are independent of one another, which allows their application to the current utterance in parallel. The `findall` was unfolded giving rise to instances of IAP. The unfolding into and-parallelism was preferred to an or-parallel execution of `findall` to reduce the amount of parallel overhead.

The ACE compiler was capable of detecting a good source of DAP in the merging process, where partial results become known, by performing in parallel the separate merging of two incompatible partial representations with the others. The parallel annotation produced for this phase is:
```
buildComplete(ILTlist,PrevI,Ut,PrevU,Comp,CList):-
  getfirst(ILT,ILTlist,R), normalize(ILT,CurI),
  (dep([PList]) →
    buildPartials(PrevI,CurI,PrevU,Ut,PList) &
    merge(PList,CurI,NewComp)),
  append(Comp,NewComp,NList),
  buildComplete(R,PrevI,Ut,PrevU,NList,CList).
```
The two subgoals separated by '&' can be executed concurrently, and the variable annotated with `dep` represents the communication channel between the two parallel threads. Unfortunately, the presence of the `append` subgoal represents a barrier which does not allow the results to be immediately propagated to the continuation of the computation. This problem was tackled by hand-modifying the code to allow exploitation of parallelism between the processing of the different elements of the input list `ILTlist`. Smaller sources of parallelism are present in various parts of the program, e.g., IAP between different actions in the body of each rule.

From the point of view of or-parallelism, we have identified various components of the systems where a local search is performed, making them suitable for or-parallel execution. For example, table 1 illustrates the improvement in execution of the selection of prediction phase. Globally, or-parallelism did not produce excessive speedups, due to the shallow searches produced by the Artwork benchmarks available. Furthermore, or-parallelism in Artwork was negatively affected by frequent use of various side-effect predicates and cuts.

Query	ACE Agents			
	1	2	3	4
Sentence$_1$	4810	3620	1623	1503

Table 1: Parallel prediction (Sun Sparc, times in ms.)

Speedups of the Artwork system from exploiting and-parallelism was considerably more satisfactory. The initial speedups observed were modest, as illustrated in the first two lines of table 2. These modest speedups, as discussed above, are not due to a lack of parallelism inherent in the application, but to the occasional use of some partially non-declarative constructions. Very few hand-coded modifications (driven by the results obtained from the static analyzer) were performed to make the code more declarative. These modifications should not be regarded as "tinkering" with the program to elicit better speedups; rather, they were simply attempts to replace extra-logical built-ins and features of Prolog with declarative ones. The more declarative and semantically elegant the program the more parallelism there is to exploit. The excellent results obtained from this modified version of the system can be seen in the last two lines of table 2 (speedups in fig. 2). The parallel overhead recorded is less than 10%.

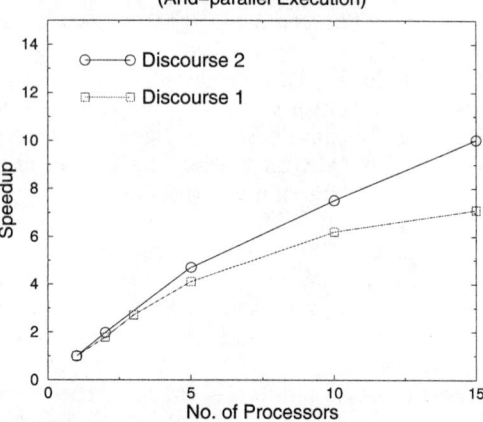

Figure 2: Speedups for and-Parallel Artwork

As part of future work, we plan to explore the use of or-parallelism to relax limitations in the number of input alternatives considered by the current system (recall that the input to the current system is ambiguous). The current limitations may lead to the exclusion of correct interpretations. We expect that processing alternative interpretations in parallel will allow the system to consider additional candidate interpretations, increasing the chance of a correct interpretations.

Parallelization of ULTRA: The parallelization of the ULTRA system was performed completely automatically (note that the ULTRA system was developed long before the development of the ACE system was begun).

The analyzer was quite successful in detecting parallelism in the program. At the highest level, IAP was exploited by allowing concurrent translation of successive phrases belonging to the source text. The translation of each phrase was marked as a potential source of DAP by the dependent and-parallel analyzer (Pontelli et al. 1997), as illustrated below:
```
ctrans(Src_lg,Trg_lg,In,Out) :-
  (dep([I_rep])-> (analyse(Srg_lg,In,I_rep) &
  generate(Trg_lg,I_rep,Out));
  Out_String = "< unable to translate >").
```
where '&' denotes a parallel conjunction and the `dep` annotation identifies the source of dependency (*shared variable*). Similarly, the process of analyzing of each individual sentence to produce the corresponding IR contains considerable amounts of both DAP and IAP, as illustrated in the example below:
```
e_analyse(String,Struc) :-
  dep([List]) -> (prep_list(String,List) &
    e_prdctn(_A,_B,_C,Struc,List,[])).
```

Goals	ACE agents						
executed	1	2	3	5	10	15	18
Discourse 1	78300	62060 (1.26)	51679 (1.52)	50389 (1.55)	50192 (1.56)	50190 (1.56)	50190 (1.56)
Discourse 2	48570	31234 (1.56)	21539 (2.25)	21500 (2.26)	20935 (2.32)	20650 (2.35)	20622 (2.36)
Modified 1	73594	41345 (1.78)	27156 (2.71)	17950 (4.1)	11870 (6.2)	10365 (7.1)	10301 (7.14)
Modified 2	46529	23639 (1.97)	15919 (2.92)	9889 (4.71)	6200 (7.5)	4640 (10.03)	4409 (10.55)

Table 2: Execution Times for Artwork (Sequent Symmetry, times in ms.)

All the lower level rules which identify the various sentence structures provide additional IAP:

```
e_prdctn(indpnt,conclusion,
    nil,[prdctn,[type,indpnt],
    [class,conclusion],[form,nil],
    [closing, Conclusion], Name],In,Out) :-
        split_input(In,In1,In2,Out),
        (esign_off(In1,Conclusion) &
        ep_name(In2,human,Name).
```

IAP emerged consistently also in the the second phase of the translation, where IRs are mapped to sentences in the target language. The rule below is an example:

```
s_prdctn(indpnt,Pc,fin,
    [prdctn, [type, indpnt],
    [class, Pc], [form, fin],P1,P2]):-
(s_prop1(dpnt,adv,fin,_M,_S_a1,_S_g1,P1) &
s_prop1(indpnt,Pc,fin,_Pm,_S_a2,_S_g2,P2)),
(Pc = dcl; Pc == imp; Pc = int).
```

No significant or-parallelism was detected in these examples (as indicated, for example, in table 3). In the next tables, *E-to-C* (*E-to-S*, *E-to-G*) indicates translation from English to Chinese (Spanish, German).

Query	ACE Agents		
	1	2	4
E-to-C	322669	290402 (1.11)	251682 (1.29)

Table 3: Or-parallelism in ULTRA (Sequent, ms.)

Table 4 presents the performance figures achieved running the parallelized version of ULTRA on three separate examples, translating the same text from English to three different target languages, Chinese, Spanish, and German. In most cases the improvement in execution time due to exploitation of parallelism is excellent, confirmed by the speedup curves (fig. 3). The parallel overhead is extremely low (around 5%).

The automatic annotation performed by the ACE compiler was rather slow, due to the size and organization of the application—a single module of over 35,000 lines of Prolog code. A modular reorganization of the code and the use of incremental analysis techniques (Hermenegildo *et al.* 1995) will improve the speed of annotation. The annotator is written in Prolog, so the annotation process itself can be parallelized.

Comparison with Other Work

Experience shows that NLP applications are highly parallel in nature. Although considerable research has been proposed in using parallelism for NLP (see (Adriaens & Hahn 1994) for a review of approaches to parallel NLP),

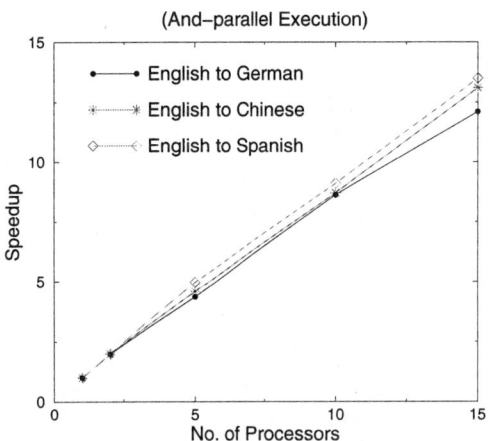

Figure 3: Speedups for ULTRA System

most of the approaches are based on ad-hoc and hand-made parallelization of NLP applications.

There has been research in the past in parallelizing the parsing phase of NLP (Devos et al. 1988), including some that use a logic programming approach (Matsumoto 1986; Trehan & Wilk 1988). More recently, the Eu-PAGE systems (Manousopoulou et al. 1997) has been proposed, a parser generator capable of producing parallel parsers (based on PVM). However, not much parallelism has been extracted from other phases of NLP systems. The main exception to this is the PUNDIT system (Hirschman et al. 1988) which exploits (only) or-parallelism from an NLP system coded in Prolog running on a simulated parallel environment. The PUNDIT system is about 3,000 lines long. Thus, our proposed work can be seen as taking the work done on the PUNDIT system further and exploiting both or- and and-parallelism from NLP programs. It should be noted that almost all work on parallel NLP (including the PUNDIT system) relies on explicit parallelization of the NLP system by the programmer. Our research results in this respect are distinctive in that: (i) we exploit parallelism from NLP applications implicitly or with limited programmer intervention, and (ii) we have been successful in parallelizing a significantly larger NLP application (it should be noted that in the PUNDIT system, the developers of the original system were the ones who did the parallelization; the same is true of other parallel NLP systems), whereas in our case system development and parallelization was decoupled.

Goals executed	ACE agents						
	1	2	3	5	10	15	18
E-to-G	562740	282339 (1.99)	190115 (2.96)	128509 (4.38)	65283 (8.62)	46507 (12.1)	37768 (14.9)
E-to-C	322669	160100 (2.0)	108642 (2.97)	70145 (4.6)	37088 (8.7)	24631 (13.1)	20817 (15.5)
E-to-S	91519	45756 (2.0)	30505 (3.0)	18370 (4.98)	10057 (9.1)	6779 (13.5)	5684 (16.1)

Table 4: Execution Times for ULTRA (Sequent Symmetry, times in ms.)

Conclusions and Future Work

In this paper we presented two case studies of parallel execution of large NLP applications—Artwork and ULTRA. In both cases we have taken advantage of the fact that the applications have been developed using logic programming, and logic programming is particularly suited to both automatic and semi-automatic exploitation of parallelism inherent in the application. In both cases we relied on the use of automatic compile-time analysis and run-time tools to extract parallelism (either directly or to supply information to the programmer to achieve this goal). Thus, the exploitation of parallelism required only a limited understanding of the behaviour and structure of the programs.

Our results show that the use of logic programming allows one to go beyond just the parallelization of the parsing phase of NLP systems, which has been the sole focus of most of the previous efforts. That is, it also allows the exploitation of parallelism from the semantic and discourse processing phases—which are typically the more computationally intensive.

In the case of ULTRA the goal of parallelization was quickly achieved with limited effort, thanks to the clean and declarative programming style adopted by the programmers who developed the system, necessitated by the requirement that computations be reversible (Farwell & Wilks 1991). In the case of Artwork the system had been developed following a more "imperative" approach in the code organization. We invested some effort in reorganizing some parts of the code and this proved effective in increasing the amount of and-parallelism. Our experience confirms the fact that adoption of an elegant, declarative style for program development not only makes the code more clear and readable, it also leads to an increase in the amount of parallelism inherent in the application exposed.

We are currently studying the possibility of using parallelism to improve the precision of the results produced by Artwork. For tractability, the rules for resolving temporal ambiguity are distinct from the rules for resolving speech act ambiguity. The temporal rules are applied in a first pass through the data, and the speech act rules are applied to the results of the first pass. This way, Artwork avoids considering all possible combinations of temporal and speech act features. However, the speech-act information cannot assist the system in resolving the temporal ambiguity. With a parallel implementation, more combinations can be processed, and this allows to perform a limited amount of integrated temporal and speech act processing.

References

Adriaens, G., and Hahn, U. 1994. *Parallel Natural Language Processing*. Ablex Publishing.

Ali, K., and Karlsson, R. 1990. The Muse Or-parallel Prolog.. In *NACLP*. MIT Press.

M. Carlson and G. Gupta (eds.) 1996. *Journal of Logic Progr.* 29(1-3).

DeGroot, D. 1984. Restricted AND-Parallelism. In *Conf. on 5th Generation Computer Systems*.

Devos M. et al. 1988. The Parallel Expert Parser. In *Proceedings of COLING*.

Farwell, D., and Wilks, Y. 1991. ULTRA: A multilingual machine translator. In *Mach. Transl. Summit*.

Gupta, G., Pontelli, E. et al. 1994. ACE: And/Or-parallel Copying-based Execution of Logic Programs. In *Proc. ICLP'94*, 93–109. MIT Press.

Hermenegildo, M. et al. 1995. Incremental analysis of logic programs. In *ICLP95*. MIT Press.

Hirschman L. et al. 1988. Or-parallel Speedup in Natural Language Processing. In *ICLP88*. MIT Press.

Levin, L. et al. 1995. Using Context in the Machine Translation of Spoken Language. In *Proc. Theoretical and Methodological Issues in Machine Translation*.

Manousopoulou A. et al. 1997. Automatic Generation of Portable Parallel Natural Language Parsers. In *ICTAI*. IEEE Computer Society.

Matsumoto, Y. 1986. A Parallel Parsing System for Natural Language Analysis. In *Int. Conf. on Logic Programming*. Springer Verlag.

Pereira, F. and Shieber, S.M. 1987. *Prolog and Natural-Language Analysis*. Cambridge University Press.

Pontelli, E. 1997. *High-Performance Parallel Execution of Prolog Programs*. Ph.D. Dissertation, NMSU.

Pontelli, E., Gupta, G. et al. 1997. Automatic Compile-time Parallelization of Prolog Programs for DAP. In *ICLP97*. MIT Press.

Reithinger, N. et al. 1995. Utilizing statistical dialogue act processing in verbmobil. In *ACL*, 116–122.

Rosé, C. et al. 1995. Discourse processing of dialogues with multiple threads. In *Proceedings of ACL*, 31–38.

Trehan, R. et al. 1988. A Parallel Chart Parser for the CCND Languages. In *ICLP88*. MIT Press.

M. Walker and J. Moore (eds.) 1997. *Computational Linguistics* 23(1).

Wiebe J. et al. 1996. ARTWORK: Discourse Processing in Machine Translation of Dialog. Technical Report MCCS96294, Computing Research Laboratory.

Wiebe J. et al. 1997. An Empirical Approach to Temporal Reference Resolution. In *Proceedings 2nd Conference on Empirical Methods in NLP*.

Metacognition in Software Agents Using Classifier Systems[1]

Zhaohua Zhang
Stan Franklin
Dipankar Dasgupta

Institute for Intelligent Systems
The University of Memphis
Memphis, Tennessee, 38152, USA

Abstract

Software agents "living" and acting in a real world software environment, such as an operating system, a network, or a database system, can carry out many tasks for humans. Metacognition is very important for humans. It guides people to select, evaluate, revise, and abandon cognitive tasks, goals, and strategies. Thus, metacognition plays an important role in human-like software agents. Metacognition includes metacognitive knowledge, metacognitive monitoring, and metacognitive regulation. Conscious Mattie (CMattie), "living" in a Unix machine, automatically reads and understands email concerning seminars (in natural language), and composes and distributes weekly seminar schedule announcements. CMattie implements Baar's global workspace theory of consciousness and some other cognitive theories concerning metacognition, episodic memory, emotions, and learning. Thus, the CMattie project has its cognitive science side (cognitive modeling) as well as its computer science side (intelligent software). This paper describes a case study of the design and implementation of modeling metacognition in software agents like CMattie by using a classifier system.

Keywords: Agent architectures, Genetic algorithms, Software agents, Cognitive modeling, Reinforcement learning

1 Introduction

Software agents are software entities "living" and acting in a real world software environment, such as an operating system, a network, or a database system, and carrying out many tasks for humans. They sense their environment thru their sensors, and act on that environment with their effectors. Their actions effect what they sense in the future, and are in the service of their own drives (Franklin and Graesser 1997). With the rapid development in computer networks, database systems and operating systems in recent years, developing software agents to manage resources in operating systems and information retrieval in network environments, etc. has drawn much more attention. Thus, the research on agent theories, architectures, mechanisms and languages has become much more important.

Copyright © 1998, American Association for Artificial Intelligence (www.aaai.org). All rights reserved.
[1] Partially supported under NSF SBR-9730314

There is still some debate regarding exactly how to define metacognition (Flavell 1976). However most researchers seem to agree that it should include knowledge of one's own knowledge and cognitive processes, and the ability to actively monitor and consciously regulate them. The concepts of self-monitoring, self-evaluation, self-regulation, self-control, self-instruction, self-consciousness, and meta-attention all belong to metacognition. Metacognition is very important for humans. It guides people to select, evaluate, revise, and abandon cognitive tasks, goals, and strategies (Hacker 1997). Implementing metacognition in software agents can be very exciting and challenging. If we want to build more human-like software agents, we need to build metacognition into them. By doing this, we provide agents a meta-system that allows them to overcome internal disorders, to choose an efficient strategy, and to self-regulate.

Conscious Mattie (CMattie) is the successor of Virtual Mattie (Franklin et al. 1996, Zhang et al. 1998, Song and Franklin forthcoming). Virtual Mattie[2] (VMattie) is a less intelligent clerical agent with the same domain as CMattie. CMattie's name derives from the fact that she implements the global workspace theory of consciousness (Baars 1988 1997), along with some other cognitive theories concerning metacognition, episodic memory, emotion, learning, etc. Baar's global workspace theory is a cognitive model of the human conscious experience. CMattie is expected to be more intelligent, more flexible and more adaptive than VMattie. Several functional modules are being added to improve her performance. CMattie's architecture and mechanisms make her "think" and act more like humans do. This paper focuses on a case study of building metacognition into CMattie.

CMattie's brain consists of two parts, the A-brain and the B-brain (Minsky 1985). The A-brain performs all cognitive activities. Its environment is the outside world, a dynamic, but limited, real world environment. The B-brain, sitting on top of the A-brain, monitors and regulates the A-brain. The B-brain performs all metacognitive activities, and its environment is the A-brain, that is, the A-brain's activities. Figure 1 depicts an overview of CMattie's architecture. In this paper, we will discuss only

---

[2] VMattie is currently being Beta-tested.

the mechanism of the B-brain and the interaction between some relevant modules in the A-brain and the B-brain. We describe a case study of the design and implementation of metacognition using a classifier system. This system allows the B-brain to satisfy one of the meta-drives of the B-brain, "Stopping any endless loop in which the A-brain finds itself." The endless loop here means that the A-brain repeats itself in an oscillatory fashion. In particular, the B-brain monitors the understanding process of the A-brain, and acts when any oscillation problem occurs. The classifier system allows the B-brain to monitor, to act, and to learn a correct action to stop an endless loop in the A-brain.

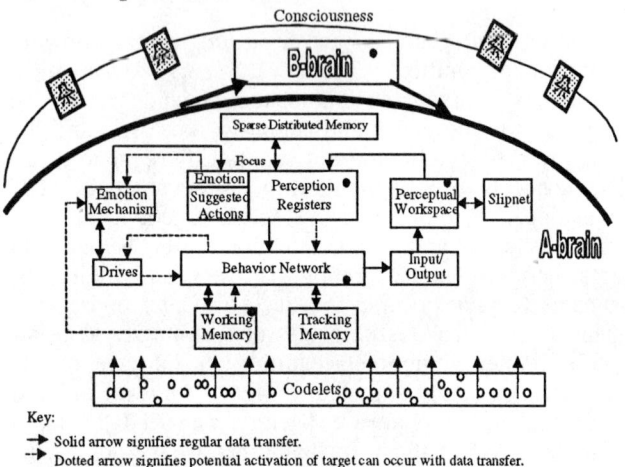

Figure 1: Overview of CMattie's Architecture

2 Problems

Metacognition plays an important role in reading comprehension in humans. Metacognitive monitoring and regulation increase the degree of one's understanding (Ortero 1997). CMattie's reading comprehension consists of understanding incoming email messages concerning seminars in natural language. Metecognition directs CMattie to a higher degree of understanding in that she can handle oscillation problems during her understanding phase.

At present, CMattie's natural language understanding occurs in two stages (Zhang et al. 1998). First, the incoming message is classified as one of the nine message types. This job is done with the help of the slipnet (Hofstadter and Mitchell 1994), an associative memory (see Figure 1 and Figure 3). The nine message types are: Initiate a seminar, Speaker topic, Cancel a seminar session, Conclude a seminar, Change of time, Change of place, Change of topic, Add to mailing list, and Remove from mailing list. For a given incoming message, the nine message-type nodes in the slipnet will have different activation levels. The one with the highest activation level is selected as the proposed message type, a "winner takes all" strategy. But all the other message-type nodes retain their activations and are candidates for the next selection, if the current winner proves to be wrong. The appropriate template is then chosen based on the message type, and placed in the perceptual workspace (see Figure 1). Each message type corresponds to one template. Different message types have different slots in their templates. Figure 2 shows the Speaker-Topic Message template. Codelets (processors) then begin to fill the slots (e.g. speaker name, title of the talk, time of the seminar, date, place, email address of sender, etc.) in the template. If any mandatory slots (e.g. speaker name) are finally not filled, the chosen template, and therefore the proposed message type, is not correct. So the message type with the next highest activation level is chosen as the new proposed message type, the corresponding template is chosen, and its slots are filled. The process repeats until there is a proposed message type with all the mandatory template slots filled. This proposed message type is correct and so is the information in the template. The A-brain performs all the above activities. But if CMattie's A-brain tries to understand an irrelevant message and does not realize that she does not have enough knowledge to do so, the B-brain takes over. It detects the situation and does something to prevent her from repeatedly looking for a message type. For example, a one-node loop could continually circle around a single message type. A classifier system can act as the action selection mechanism for the B-brain. In this particular case, the B-brain monitors whether there is an oscillatory thinking (endless loop) during the A-brain's understanding process, and learns how much activation to send to the nine message-type nodes in the slipnet so that the endless loop is stopped. Figure 3 depicts how the B-brain interacts with the A-brain during the understanding process.

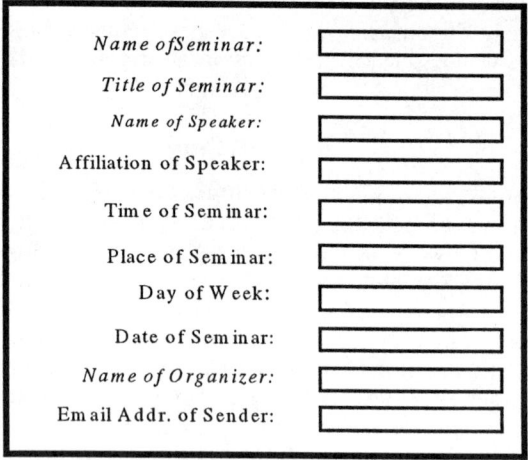

Figure 2: Speaker-topic Message Template
(Italic shows mandatory slots)

3 Mechanism of the B-brain

A classifier system (Holland and Reitman, 1978) is an adaptive system that learns to cope with an environment. Condition-action rules are coded as fixed-length string rules (classifiers) and can be evolved using genetic algorithms (Holland 1975). The Classifier System in the B-brain is composed of several modules: Inner Perception, Encoder, Message List, Classifier Store, Decoder, Evaluator, Genetic Algorithm and Inner Actions (see the B-brain in figure 3).

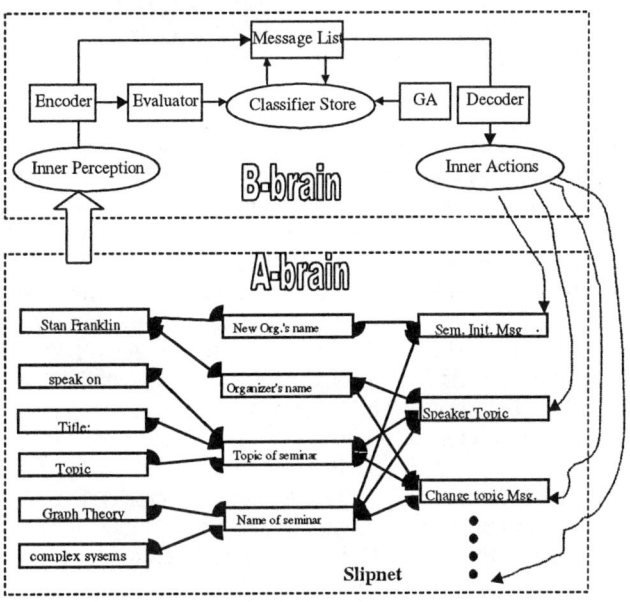

Figure 3: Interaction between the A-brain and the B-brain during the Understanding Process

The Inner Perception Module implements metacognitive monitoring. It consists of sensors and detectors. Detectors differ from sensors in that they do some inferences. Sensors get the raw data from the A-brain, and detectors put them into internal representations. For example, sensors provide information about the current proposed message type or trial template during the understanding process in the A-brain, and detectors check whether there is a loop in the understanding process. So perception can be conceptualized as sensation plus inference. In our case, an inner percept could be of a three-node loop, or a nine-node loop, etc. The inner perception is the B-brain's internal representation of the current state of the A-brain.

An inner percept is then fed to **the Encoder** of the classifier system. The Encoder will encode it to a finite-length string. The B-brain can have ten percepts in binary representation. No loop is encoded as 0000, a one-node loop as 0001, a two-node loop as 0010, etc.[3] After an inner percept is encoded as a string percept, it is put in the **Message List**. This string percept is actually the environment message (or the current state of the A-brain sensed by the B-brain).

The classifier store contains a population of classifiers. Each classifier consists of a condition, an action and a strength, such as 0100 : 001011011110100110, 3.3333. The condition part is a template capable of matching internal string percepts, 0000, 0001, 0010, 0011, 0100, 0101, 0110, 0111, 1000, 1001. The action part consists of sending activation to each message-type node in the A-brain. There are four different levels of activation: low (00), medium low (01), medium high (10), high (11). So the length of an action string is 2*9=18. (nine message-type nodes, each needing 2 bits to represent four levels of activation). The strength serves as a performance measure of the classifier, and ranges from 0 to 9. Since the lengths of the condition part and action part are 4 and 18 respectively, the total number of possible classifiers, ignoring strength, is 2^{22}. The above classifier is interpreted as "if the percept is a four-node loop, then send low activation to initiate-seminar node, medium high activation to speaker-topic node, etc., and this classifier has strength 3.3333."

An initial classifier population of thirty is randomly generated. The strength of each individual is assigned a single value, say 0.5. No domain-specific heuristic knowledge is used to "prime" the initial population. Notice that the strength of a classifier is not the actual performance measure at first. In the beginning, the B-brain has no idea about which rule is good, or which rule is bad. After it takes some actions on the A-brain, and gets feedback (**The Evaluator** changes the strength of a fired classifier), it will have a better idea. The B-brain gradually learns good rules, in other words, a correct action taken on the A-brain in some situations.

At each time step only one classifier acts on the A-brain. Only this classifier is evaluated and its strength updated. All the other unfired classifiers keep their current strengths. New classifiers produced by crossover take the average of their parents' strengths. If the population is too large, the chance of each classifier being fired is low. Convergence will slow down. Experiments show that populations of size over forty are slow to converge, and populations of size less than twenty take longer to stop a loop since there are fewer possible structures. Thirty proved a suitable size for the population and is used by this system.

Once a classifier's condition is matched to the current inner percept, that classifier becomes a candidate to post its action to the **Message List**. It is not possible to let all matched classifiers post their actions there. The length of the message list in this system is ten. The probability of a matched classifier posting its action in the message list is proportional to its strength. The action on the message list that acts on the A-brain is selected at random. A classifier with a high strength does not mean its action is correct. It only means this action is close to the right action. When a correct action is performed, the classifier system will stop since the loop is stopped. On the other hand, some classifiers have high strength because they make the loop smaller. However, we should not give them advantage over others because they cannot stop the loop. If we choose the one with the highest strength every time, some

---

[3] Binary strings 1010 to 1111 are not used by the system. The classifiers with these condition parts will be deleted by the system.

classifiers with better actions may not have a chance to be fired, and a chance to be evaluated. In the classifier system, only when a classifier is fired and its action is performed, it is evaluated. Randomly selecting an action from the message list gives every active classifier a chance to perform its action and to be evaluated. If no classifiers' condition matches a percept, then some classifiers with lower strengths are selected, and their condition parts changed to match the current percept.

A selected string action is decoded by **the Decoder**. As discussed earlier, 00 is decoded as low, 01 medium low, 10 medium high, and 11 high. Later, **the Inner Actions Module** sends activation to the message-type nodes in the A-brain. The actual activation levels are 0.5 (low), 1.5 (medium low), 2.5 (medium high) and 3.5 (high). The Evaluator decides whether the action provided by a fired classifier is good or bad.

The Evaluator is implemented by a reinforcement learning algorithm (Barto, Sutton, and Brouwer, 1981). It assigns reward or punishment to classifiers based on the next inner percept sensed from the A-brain. Notice that the B-brain has no teacher. In order to see how good or how bad its current action is, it has to see what the next percept is. If after an action is taken, the loop in the A-brain becomes smaller than before, this action gets some reward. If the loop in the A-brain is stopped, this action is a correct action and the classifier system stops.

The bucket brigade algorithm (Holland and Reitman, 1978) is not used in this situation since it is for distributing credit among classifiers. In this system, a good action or a bad action results from a single classifier in each sense-select-cycle. There is no need to distribute reward or punishment.

A sense-select-act cycle is a cycle during which the B-brain senses from the A-brain, selects an action (provided by a fired classifier), and performs the action on the A-brain. However, if the B-brain cannot stop a loop in the A-brain in twenty sense-select-act cycles, the **Genetic Algorithm Module** is activated to evolve new, possibly better classifiers. Classifier's strength is used as a fitness measure.

Genetic algorithms are search algorithms based on natural evolution. In this system, the selection is proportional to each classifier's strength. Only two classifiers with the same condition can participate in a crossover. This allows searching for new actions for a given percept (condition part). Suppose for a given situation in the A-brain, no current classifier has a correct action, crossover may generate a new and correct action to deal with such a situation. The crossover position (point) for each pair of classifiers is randomly generated. The strength of the offspring is the average of its parents' strengths. The rates of crossover and mutation are 1.0 and 0.2 respectively in this system.

In addition to crossover and mutation, this classifier system produces new classifiers using probability vectors (Baluja, Sukthankar, and Hancock, 1997). A probability vector is used to maintain statistics about the correct action string. One probability vector serves all the classifiers with a given condition. There are eighteen numbers in each probability vector since there are eighteen bits in the action part of the classifier. For example, the probability vector for condition 0100 may start as: <0.5, 0.5, 0.5, 0.5, ...0.5>. This means that, in the beginning, the B-brain has no idea about the correct action string. It could be 0 or 1 in each bit position with the same probability. After a classifier 0100 : 011000101100111010 is fired and an action 011000101100111010 acts on the A-brain, suppose the Evaluator gives a middle reward to this action. The probability vector will be updated to close to 011000101100111010 since this action got a reward. It could be updated as <0.25, 0.75, 0.75, 0.25, ... >. This means the first bit of the correct action string would be more like 0, and second bit 1, etc. Later, if a classifier 0100 : 111001101110111010 is fired and gets a punishment, the probability vector will be updated in the opposite direction. The formula used to update a probability vector is as follows: (Let LR represent the learning rate and i the position in a vector or a string)

Pvector[i] = Pvector[i]*(1-LR) + WinnerVector[i]*LR, when the winner gets a reward.

Pvector[i] = Pvector[i]*(1-LR) - WinnerVector[i]*LR, when the winner gets a punishment.

In this way, the B-brain takes every opportunity to learn the probability vector, and keeps a record of such learning. The B-brain updates its probability vector whenever an action is taken. Thus the new classifiers produced by using probability vectors are more likely to be correct.

The system keeps nine different probability vectors, one for each of the nine conditions. When a new classifier is generated from a probability vector, its condition is then associated with the vector. Its action has a 1 in a particular location with the probability found in that location in the vector. The strength of the new classifier is the average strength of the population.

In most GA-based applications, every individual in the population is evaluated at every time step (or generation). In a classifier system, only one individual is chosen and evaluated. So the B-brain must take every opportunity to learn from the feedback of each action. The probability vectors are very helpful in keeping track of what a right action should be. They help the B-brain to learn quickly.

To keep the population at a constant size, new classifiers replace similar members with lower strengths (De Jong 1975).

4 Experimental Results

The system is implemented in JAVA on a Unix workstation. During twenty test runs[4] of the classifier system, on average, the B-brain learned to stop an

---

[4] Each run used a message which could make CMattie in an oscillatory thinking state.

oscillatory thinking in the A-brain at the 70th sense-select-act-cycle. The fastest case was at the 37th cycle, and the slowest at the 279th cycle. The average clock time for each run is about two minutes.

By an environment, in this context, we mean a particular situation in which an oscillatory thinking (endless loop) is going on in the A-brain during the understanding process. The nine message-type nodes in the slipnet have certain activation levels. The B-brain tries to stop the endless loop by sending different levels of activation to the message-type nodes. In different environments, the A-brain reacts differently to the inner actions from the B-brain. Since the B-brain evaluates classifiers based on any change of the looping state in the A-brain, the A-brain indirectly provides reinforcement to the B-brain. Working in an environment allows the B-brain to find a classifier to stop the endless loop in this particular situation.

The system was tested in two different environments. In both environments, the B-brain successfully learned a that could stop the endless loop classifier in about the 70th sense-select-act cycle.

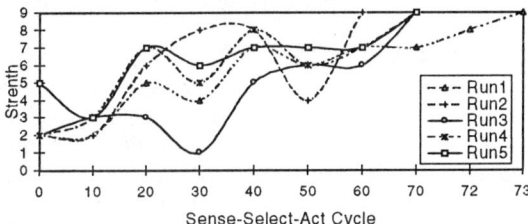

Figure 4: Winner Strenth on Five Runs (in Environment1)
Winner is the fired classifer at each sense-select-act cycle and its action is selected to act on the A-brain. Its strength reprents its fitness (performance)

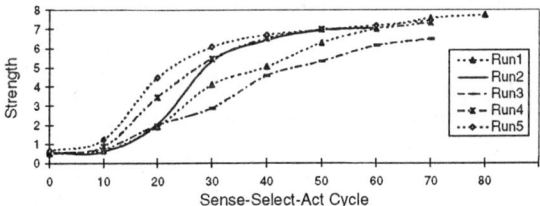

Figure 5: Average Strength of the population on Five Runs (in Environment 1)

We chose five runs from environment 1 and three runs from environment 2 to illustrate the winning classifiers' strength and the average strength of the population at different cycles (shown in Figures 4, 5, 6, and 7). As discussed earlier, at each sense-select-act cycle, one classifier is chosen as the winner and its action is taken on the A-brain. Later it is evaluated and assigned a strength (fitness). In both environment 1 and environment 2, we found that the average strength of the population increased with more sense-select-act cycles. This indicates that the average performance of individual classifiers in the population increased. The overall trend of the winning classifier's strength also increased with more sense-select-act cycles, but sometimes it went down for a while before finally going up.

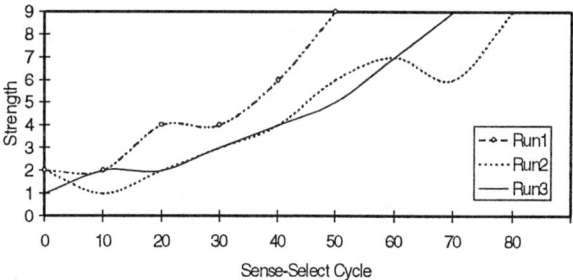

Figure 6: Winner Strength on Three Runs (in Environment2)

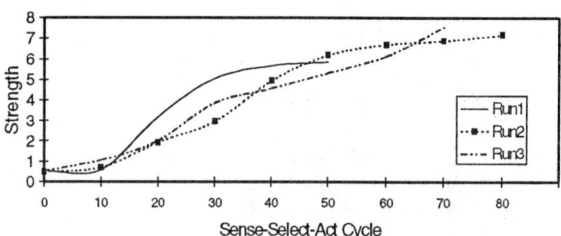

Figure 7: Average Strength of the Population on Three Runs (in Environment 2)

Table 1 and Table 2 show the learned correct classifiers that stopped the endless loops in the A-brain on five different runs in environment 1 and three different runs in environment 2. They also show the sense-select-cycle at which the right actions are performed on each run.

Table 1: Learned Classifiers on Five Runs (in Environment 1)

	Cycle	Learned Correct Classifier
Run1	73	0001 : 000000000000000000
Run2	57	0101 : 000000000000000000
Run3	67	0011 : 000000000000000000
Run4	70	0001 : 000000000000000000
Run5	69	0010 : 000000000000000000

Table 2: Learned Classifier on Three Runs (in Environment 2)

	Cycle	Learned Correct Classifier
Run1	45	0011 : 010000000000000000
Run2	76	0001 : 010000000000000000
Run3	69	0101 : 010000000000000000

In environment 1, the correct action is that the B-brain should send very low activation (0.5) to every message-type-node in the slipnet in any looping state (one-node loop, etc) so as to get rid of the endless loop. For example, on run 1, at 73rd sense-select-act cycle, the B-brain learned a correct classifier: 0001: 000000000000000000.

This means if there is a one-node loop in the A-brain, then send 0.5 activation to all the message-type nodes in the slipnet.

In environment 2, the correct action is that the B-brain should send medium low (1.5) activation to seminar-initial-message-type node and very low activation (0.5) to the other eight message-type-nodes in the slipnet in any looping states. If all the message types have low activation (below certain threshold), the A-brain can realize that the incoming email is an irrelevant message and won't oscillate.

5 Conclusions and Future Work

In this paper, we have used a classifier system to implement the B-brain in order to solve the oscillatory thinking problem in the A-brain. From this case study, we can draw the following conclusions:
- The classifier system proved to be a powerful on-line learning control mechanism, that learns and adapts to its environment.
- A classifier system may be a suitable mechanism for learning metacognitive knowledge by metacognitive monitoring and regulation.
- Classifier systems may converge more slowly than other GA-based applications since only one action is performed and evaluated at each sense-select-act cycle.
- A good way to scale a classifier system is to make it a multiple classifier system so that it distributes several learning tasks to several individual classifier systems.
- Using probability vectors is an efficient approach to speeding up learning in a classifier system.

In future work we will scale this system up to monitor and regulate more activities in the A-brain. We also want to explore a fuzzy classifier system and compare it with a classifier system.

References

Baluja, Sukthankar, and Hancock (1997) Prototyping Intelligent Vehicle Modules Using Evolutionary Algorithms, in Dasgupta, D. and Michalewica, Z. (Eds.) *Evolutionary Algorithms in Engineering Applications*, Springer-Veriag, 1997, pp 241-257.

Baars, Bernard, J. (1988) *A Cognitive Theory of Consciousness*, Cambridge: Cambridge University Press.

Baars, Bernard, J. (1997) *In the Theater of Consciousness*, Oxford: Oxford University Press, Inc.

Barto, A.G., Sutton, R. S., and Brouwer, P. S. (1981). Associative Search Network: a Reinforcement Learning Associative Memory, *Biological Cybernetics*, 40(3): 201-211.

De Jong, K.A. (1975) An Analysis of the Behavior of a Class of Genetic Adaptive Systems, Doctoral dissertation, University of Michigan.

Flavell, John, H. (1976) Metacognitive Aspects of Problem Solving, In L.B. Resnick (Ed.), *The Nature of In Intelligence*. Hillsdale, NJ: Erlbaum.

Franklin, Stan (1995), *Artificial Minds*, Cambridge: MA: MIT Press.

Franklin, Stan, Art Graesser, Brent Olde, Hongjun Song, and Aregahegn Negatu (1996) Virtual Mattie—an Intelligent Clerical Agent, *AAAI Symposium on Embodied Cognition and Action*, Cambridge MA.

Franklin, Stan and Art Graesser (1997), Is it an Agent, or just a Program?: A Taxonomy for Autonomous Agents, *Intelligent Agents III*, Springer-Verlag, 21-35

Gilber, A.H. and Bell, F. (1995), Adaptive Learning of Process Control and Profit Optimization Using a Classifier System, *Evolutionary Computation* 3(2): 177-198, MIT Press.

Goldberg, David, E., (1989) *Genetic Algorithms in Search, Optimization and Machine Learning*, Addison Wesley Longman, Inc.

Hacker, Douglas, (1997), Metacognitive: Definitions and Empirical Foundations, In Hacker, D., Dunlosky, J., Graesser A. (Eds.) *Metacogniton in Educational Theory and Practice*. Hillsdale, NJ: Erlbaum, in press.

Hofstadter, D. R. and M. Mitchell, (1994), The Copycat Project: A model of mental fluidity and analogh-making. In Holyoak, K.J. & Barnden, J. A. (Eds.) *Advances in Connectionist and Neural Computation Theory*, Vol. 2: Analogical connections. Norwood, NJ: Ablex.

Holland, J. H. (1975). *Adaptation in Natural and Artificial Systems*. Ann Arbor: University of Michigan Press.

Holland, J. H. and Reitman, J. S. (1978). Cognitive Systems Based on Adaptive Algorithms. In D. A. Waterman & F. Hayey-Roth (Eds.), *Pattern Directed Inference Systems* (pp. 313 -329). New York: Academic Press.

Maes, Pattie (1990), How to do the right thing, *Connection Science*, 1:3.

Minsky, Marvin (1985), *Society of Mind*, New York: Simon and Schuster.

Ortero, Jose (1997) Influence of Knowledge Activation and Context on Comprehension Monitoring of Science Texts, In Hacker, D., Dunlosky, J., Graesser A. (Eds.) *Metacogniton in Educational Theory and Practice*. Hillsdale, NJ: Erlbaum, in press.

Sloman, Aaron (1996) What Sort of Architecture is Required for a Human-like Agent?, *Cognitive Modeling Workshop*, AAAI96, Portland Oregon.

Song, Hongjun and Stan Franklin (forthcoming), Action Selection Using Behavior Instantiation

Wilson, Stewart W. (1994), ZCS: A Zeroth Level Classifier System, *Evolutionary Computation*, MIT Press.

Zhang, Zhaohua, Stan Franklin, Brent Olde, Art Graesser and Yun Wan (1998), Natural Language Sensing for Autonomous Agents In Proceedings of *International IEEE Joint Symposia on Intelligence and Systems'98*.

Agents That Work in Harmony by Knowing and Fulfiling Their Obligations

Mihai Barbuceanu
Enterprise Integration Laboratory
University of Toronto
4 Taddle Creek Road, Rosebrugh Building,
Toronto, Ontario, Canada, M5S 3G9
mihai@ie.utoronto.ca

Abstract

Societies constrain the behavior of agents by imposing multiple, often contradictory, obligations and interdictions amongst them. To work in harmony, agents must find ways to satisfy these constraints, or to break less important ones when necessary. In this paper[1], we present a solution to this problem based on a representation of obligations and interdictions in an organizational framework, together with an inference method that also decides which obligations to break in contradictory situations. These are integrated in an operational, practically useful agent development language that covers the spectrum from defining organizations, roles, agents, obligations, goals, conversations to inferring and executing coordinated agent behaviors in multi-agent applications. One strength of the approach is the way it supports negotiation by exchanging deontic constraints amongst agents. We illustrate this and the entire system with a negotiated solution to the feature interaction problem in the telecommunications industry.

Introduction and Motivation

Working together in harmony requires that everybody fulfils their obligations and respects everybody else's rights. In other words, it requires that everybody respects the social laws of their community. To build agents that can be trusted to work with and on behalf of humans in organizations requires the same thing, that agents know and fulfil their obligations while respecting the rights and authority of humans and of other agents in the organzation. Multiple symultaneous obligations and interdictions require agents to find the right behavior that achieves the goals induced by obligations without violating the interdictions. Often, there is no way to find the right behavior without violating less important obligations or interdictions in order to ensure the more important ones are fulfilled. Current models of collective behavior often oversimplify this situation. The Cohen-Levesque account of teamwork (Levesque, Cohen & Nunes 90) for example, and the implemented systems based on it (Jennings 95;

Tambe 97) assume that all members of a team have essentially a single, implicit, obligation towards a common mutual goal.

In this paper we build on a different model of social interaction, one that explicitely represents and integrates multiple obligations.

1. At the social level, our model assumes that societies and organizations constrain the social behavior of agents by imposing social laws, representable as networks of mutual obligations and interdictions amongst agents. Not fulfilling an obligation or interdiction is sanctioned by paying a cost or by a loss of utility, which allows an agent to apply rational decision making when choosing what to do. Social laws are objective forces motivating social behavior and to a large extent determine the 'attitudes' at the individual agent level. Agents 'desire' and 'intend' the things that are requested by their current obligations, knowing that otherwise there will be a cost to pay.

2. At the individual agent decision level, each agent decides what behavior to adopt to satisfy the applicable social laws as well as its own goals and priorities. In particular, at this level agents determine how to solve conflicting obligations and interdictions.

3. Having decided on the general behavior in terms of what to do or not, agents need to plan/schedule the activities that compose the selected behavior. This determines the precise sequencing of actions to be executed, consistent with time, resource and possibly other constraints on action execution.

4. Finally, actions have to be executed as planned, with provisions for handling exceptions and violations. These may be dealt with at any of the above levels, for example by retrying, replanning, deciding on different actions or even (in an extreme case that we do not deal with) trying to modify the social laws.

To integrate obligations in this framework we rely on (1) a representation - semantically founded on dynamic deontic logic - of social laws as obligations, permissions and interdictions among the roles that agents play in an organization and (2) a constraint propagation reasoning method allowing agents to infer the applicable obliga-

---

[1]Copyright ©1998, American Association for Artificial Intelligence (www.aaai.org). All rights reserved.

tions and to decide among conflicting ones. The approach is fully implemented and operational, being integrated in a coordination language that supports agent development along the entire spectrum from organization and role specification, definition of social obligations and interdictions, agent construction, proactive and interactionist agent behavior according to the applicable social laws and to the agent's own conversation plans. An important consequence of the approach is the way it supports negotiation as exchange of obligations and interdictions among agents. We illustrate this, and the entire system, with an agent negotiated solution to the feature interaction problem in the telecommunications industry, one of the industries we work with directly in applying our system. We end with conclusions, a review of related work and future work hints.

Representing and Reasoning about Obligation

Intuitively, an agent a1 has an obligation towards an agent a2 for achieving a goal G iff the non-performance by a1 of the required actions allows a2 to apply a sanction to a1. The sanction is expressed as a cost or loss of utility. Agent a2 (who has authority) is not necessarily the beneficiary of executing G by the obliged agent (you may be obliged to your manager for helping a colleague), and one may be obliged to oneself (e.g. for the education of one's children).

Semantics. We model obligations, permissions and interdictions (OPI-s) using the reduction of deontic logic to dynamic logic due to (Meyer 88) in a multi-agent framework. Briefly, we define obligation, interdiction and permission as follows, where V_α^{ij} denotes a violation by i of a constraint imposed by j wrt action or goal α (associated with a cost to be paid):

- $F^{ij}\alpha \equiv [\alpha]^i V_\alpha^{ij}$: i is forbidden by j to execute α. An agent is forbidden to do α iff in any state resulting after executing α the violation predicate holds.
- $P^{ij}\alpha \equiv \neg F^{ij}\alpha$: i is permitted by j to execute α. Permission is the same as non-interdiction.
- $O^{ij}\alpha \equiv F^{ij}(-\alpha)$: i is obliged by j to execute α. Obligation is an interdiction for the negation of the action (forbidden not to do α).

As shown by (Meyer 88), this reduction eliminates the paradoxes that have plagued deontic logic for years and moreover, leads to a number of theorems which, as will be shown immediately, are the first step toward applying an efficient constraint propagation method to reason about OPI-s in action networks. Both of these are necessary for applying this model to real applications.

The main theorems that we use are as follows (indices dropped for clarity), where ; denotes sequential composition, $\cup$ nondeterministic choice and & parallel composition of actions.

$\models F(\alpha;\beta) \equiv [\alpha]F\beta$ (1)
$\models F(\alpha \cup \beta) \equiv F\alpha \wedge F\beta$ (2)
$\models (F\alpha \vee F\beta) \supset F(\alpha\&\beta)$ (3)
$\models O(\alpha;\beta) \equiv (O\alpha \wedge [\alpha]O\beta)$ (4)
$\models (O\alpha \vee O\beta) \supset O(\alpha \cup \beta)$ (5)
$\models O(\alpha \& \beta) \equiv (O\alpha \wedge O\beta)$ (6)
$\models P(\alpha;\beta) \equiv <\alpha> P\beta$ (7)
$\models P(\alpha \cup \beta) \equiv (P\alpha \vee P\beta)$ (8)
$\models P(\alpha \& \beta) \supset (P\alpha \wedge P\beta)$ (9)
$\models O(\alpha \cup \beta) \wedge F\alpha \wedge P\beta \supset O\beta$ (10).

In words, these theorems tell us that: (1) A sequence is forbidden iff after executing the first action the remaining subsequence is forbidden. (2) A choice is forbidden iff all components are also forbidden. (3) If at least one component of a parallel composition is forbidden, the parallel composition is forbidden as well. (4) A sequence is obliged iff the first action is obliged and after exccuting it the remaining subsequence is obliged as well. (5) If at least one component of a choice is obliged, the choice is also obliged. (6) A parallel composition is obliged iff all components are obliged. (7) A sequence is permitted iff there is a way to execute the first action after which the remaining subsequence is permitted. (8) A choice is permitted iff at least one component of it is permitted. (9) If a parallel composition is permitted, then all components must be permitted. (10) If a choice is obliged and one component is forbidden while the other is permitted, then the permitted component is obliged.

While providing an understanding of what OPI-s are in a dynamic framework where agents' behavior can be described with sequential, parallel and choice compositions, this model does not allow to compare obligations in conflicting situations. Next, we show (1) how the model can be given a constraint propagation formulation and (2) how in this format it can be extended to handle conflict resolution.

Deontic Constraint Propagation. We start with representing possible behavior as acyclic networks where nodes represent goals, and arcs relate goals to subgoals. Figure 1 shows a somewhat arbitrary such network in which par1 and par2 are parallel goals, seq1 to seq4 are sequences, g1 to g5 are atomic and ch1 is a choice. All subgoals of ch1 except g2 are negated in ch1, shown by having their connecting arcs to ch1 labeled with a '-'. That means that ch1 is a choice between *not doing* g1, doing g2, not doing g3, etc.

Assume we have initially asserted (forbidden ch1) and (obliged par2). For each of these assertions the propagation process traverses the network along supergoal and subgoal links and applies the theorems listed previously. Thus, (obliged par2) implies (obliged seq3) and (obliged seq4) cf. theorem (6). Forbidding ch1 makes each component forbidden, cf. (2). But as g1 is negated in ch1, this means -g1 is forbidden, hence g1 is obliged, and similarly g3, g4, g5. Since g2 is forbidden (being non-negated in ch1) it follows that seq1 and seq2 will become eventually forbidden, cf. (1). Then par1 will also become forbidden, cf. (3).

Integrating violation costs. With violation costs, the propagation process can no longer be described by Meyer's theorems in their given form. The purpose of

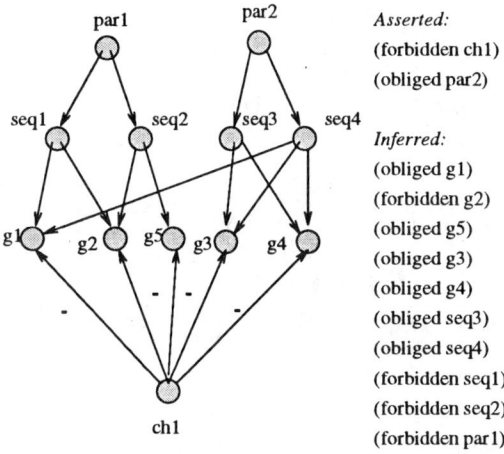

	Asserted:
	(forbidden ch1)
	(obliged par2)
	Inferred:
	(obliged g1)
	(forbidden g2)
	(obliged g5)
	(obliged g3)
	(obliged g4)
	(obliged seq3)
	(obliged seq4)
	(forbidden seq1)
	(forbidden seq2)
	(forbidden par1)

Figure 1: Deontic propagation in a goal network.

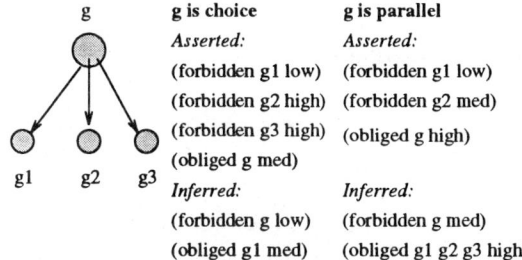

g is choice	g is parallel
Asserted:	Asserted:
(forbidden g1 low)	(forbidden g1 low)
(forbidden g2 high)	(forbidden g2 med)
(forbidden g3 high)	(obliged g high)
(obliged g med)	
Inferred:	Inferred:
(forbidden g low)	(forbidden g med)
(obliged g1 med)	(obliged g1 g2 g3 high)

Figure 2: Deontic propagation with costs and conflicts.

violation costs is to allow us to compare obligations and, in conflicting cases, select those that incur a smaller cost to pay. Consider figure 2 and assume **g** is a choice. Asserting all its subgoals forbidden with violation costs as shown, results in propagating **g** as forbidden (cf. theorem (2)) with a violation cost that is the *minimum* of the violation costs of subgoals (in our case `low`). This *minimum cost propagation rule* (from subgoals to supergoal) is justified because to execute a choice, at least one subgoal must be executed. If **g** is asserted as obliged with a cost greater than the minimum interdiction cost of subgoals, then at least the minimum cost subgoal can be turned to obliged with the obligation cost of **g**. In figure 2, since **g** is obliged with cost `med`, there is only one subgoal with a smaller interdiction cost, **g1**, and this is turned into obliged with cost `med`, thus solving the conflict by having the agent execute **g1**. If there is more than one subgoal with smaller interdiction costs than the obligation cost of **g**, any of them are executable as part of the choice, and the agent has freedom to choose from among them.

Assume now **g** is a parallel goal. To execute a parallel goal, all subgoals must be executed. Thus, if some subgoals are forbidden, (which would make **g** forbidden as well cf. (3)) **g** must be obliged with a cost higher than the *maximum* interdiction cost of subgoals in order to become overall obliged, and in this case all forbidden subgoals become obliged with this cost. This situation justifies the *maximum cost propagation rule* (from subgoals to supergoal), and is illustrated in the figure. If **g** was a sequential goal, then the previous propagation would have taken place in the same way, using the maximum cost propagation from subgoals to supergoal. But in this case the execution semantics would be quite different in that sequences can not be executed with time overlapping of their subgoals, while parallel goals can. This is explained later on, when we address the issue of action scheduling.

This scheme works with both *quantitative* and *qualitative* violation costs by means of a cost abstract data type allowing each agent to define the nature of violation costs it uses.

Deontic Propagation Algorithm. The propagation algorithm uses Mayer's theorems extended with cost propagation as above, formulated as a collection of propagation rules inside a recursive invocation mechanism. In figure 3 we show one example of such an extended propagation rule. The rule is activated when (1) a subgoal **gi** of a choice type goal **g** has been propagated as forbidden, (2) **g** is obliged, (3) all its subgoals are forbidden, (4) **s0** is the sum of all obligation costs on **g** (derived from all independent obligations placed on **g**), (5) **g-min** and **c-min** are the subgoal with smallest interdiction cost and that cost respectively and finally (6) **g-min** is the only subgoal whose interdiction cost is smaller than **s0**. In this case, **g-min** becomes obliged or, if it occurs negated in **g**, forbidden.

Labelings consist of multiple, independently justified propositions of type (`obliged <goal> <cost>`) or (`forbidden <goal> <cost>`). These propositions are stored in a LTMS (McAllester 80) and are justified by the other propositions that make the rules applicable. This allows us to implement non-monotonic reasoning and to provide explanations of every labeling in the system.

The propagation process propagates one input deontic assertion at a time. For each assertion, all goals reachable from the goal of the input assertion along both supergoal and subgoal links are visited at most once. For each visited goal, all rules are checked and those applicable are executed. A goal is never visited more than once for the same initial assertion because any subsequent visit would produce either identical labelings or incorrect ones, circularly justified.

Action Scheduling. Knowing which actions are obliged and which are forbidden is not sufficient for execution. The agent also needs to know the relative order of actions and the allowed time windows for execution. These however, depend on different constraints about resource usage and capacity, action duration, time horizons and the execution semantics of composed actions. To deal with these, we first include in the representation of each action (1) an execution time window specified as an interval `[earliest-start, latest-end]`, and (2) a specification of the duration of atomic ac-

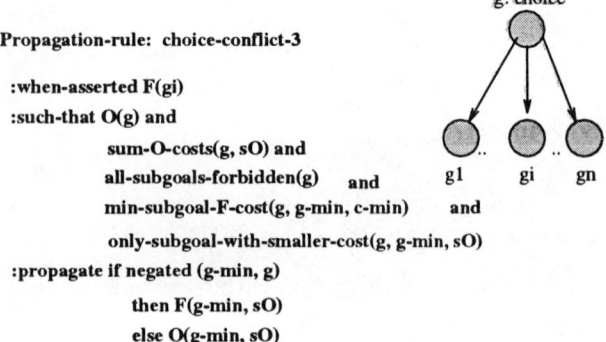
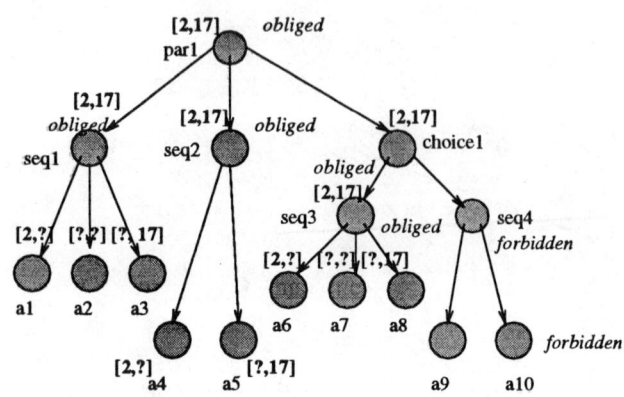

```
Propagation-rule: choice-conflict-3
  :when-asserted F(gi)
  :such-that O(g) and
           sum-O-costs(g, sO) and
           all-subgoals-forbidden(g) and
           min-subgoal-F-cost(g, g-min, c-min) and
           only-subgoal-with-smaller-cost(g, g-min, sO)
  :propagate if negated (g-min, g)
              then F(g-min, sO)
              else O(g-min, sO)
```

Figure 3: Deontic propagation rule.

Resources and usage: r1(a1, a4, a7), r2(a2, a5, a8, a10), r3(a3, a6)
Action duration: a1(3), a2(4), a3(5), a4(3), a5(5), a6(4), a7(3), a8(3)
a9(4), a10(6)

Figure 4: Action network to be scheduled

tions. The time window contains the time limits (in a discrete model of time) within which the action can be executed consistently with all other constraints, and is computed by scheduling as explained immediately.

Second, for composed actions, we define the following execution semantics. For parallel actions, all subactions are constrained to be executed within the time-window of the parallel (super)action, with temporal overlapping allowed. For choices, only the chosen (obliged) subactions must be executed within the time-window specified by the choice (super)action, also with overlapping allowed. For sequences, all subactions must be executed within the time-window of the sequence (super)action, without temporal overlapping amongst subactions. Note that these temporal constraints operate outside the deontic propagation framework which assumes that all obligations and interdictions hold for the entite time horizon (including all action time windows). Third, we assume finite capacity of resources, in that a resource can be used by a given finite number of actions at any moment.

Consider now the action network shown in figure 4 with the given durations and associated resource usage (all resources can support only one action at a time). Suppose that the time window for par1 is given, $time - window(par1, [2, 17])$. Assume also that (obliged par1) and (forbidden a10). Deontic propagation determines (obliged seq1), (obliged seq2), (obliged seq3) and (forbidden seq4). But in what order should the agent execute the obliged actions? This can only be determined by scheduling the obliged actions in a way that considers all the resource, duration and order constraints. In our system, we solve the problem by endowing the agent with a constraint based scheduler of the type described e.g. in (Beck 97). Its output is a complete ordering of actions that is consistent with all input constraints, plus the allowed execution time windows for each action, as implied by the ordering.

The Coordination Language

Having presented the representation and reasoning mechanisms for OPI-s, we now show how these are integrated and used within an implemented, practical coordination language for multi-agent system development.

Organizations, Agents and Roles. Organizations are systems that constrain the actions of member agents by imposing mutual obligations and interdictions. The association of obligations and interdictions is mediated by the *roles* agents play in the organization. For example, when an agent joins a software production organization in the `system administrator` role, he becomes part of a speci fic constraining web of mutual obligations, interdictions and permissions - *social constrai nts or laws* - that link him as a `system administrator` to `developers`, `managers` and every other role and member of the organization. Not fulfilling an obligation or interdiction is sanc tioned by paying a cost or by a loss of utility, which allows an agent to apply rational d ecision making when choosing what to do.

Our coordination language allows organizations to be described as consisting of a set of roles filled by a number of agents. In the example in figure 5 `customer`, `developer`, `help-desk-attendant` etc. are roles filled respectively by agents `Customer`, `Bob`, etc.

An agent can be a member of one or more organizations and in each of them it can play one or more roles. An agent is aware of the existence of some of the other agents in specific roles, but not necessarily of all of them. Each agent has its local store of beliefs (its `database`).

A *role* describes a major function together with the obligations, interdictions and permissions attached to it. Roles can be organized hierarchically (for example `developer` and `development-manager` would be both `development-member` roles) and subsets of them may be declared as disjoint in that the same agent can not

```
(def-organization O1
  :roles ((customer Customer)
          (developer Bob)
          (help-desk-attendant Bob)
          (development-manager Alice)
          (help-desk-manager John)))
(def-agent 'Bob
  :database 'bob-db
  :acquaintances '((Alice development-manager)
                   (John help-desk-manager)))
(def-role 'help-desk-manager
  :super-roles '(help-desk-member)
  :max-agents 1)
```

Figure 5: Organizations, agents and roles

perform them (like help-desk-member and customer). For each role there may be a minimum and a maximum number of agents that can perform it (e.g. minimum and maximum 1 president).

Situations. A situation is a specific combination of occuring events and agent's local state in which the agent acquires obligations and/or interdictions and starts acting in accordance with these. Situations are generically defined in terms of roles, rather than in terms of specific agents. That means that any set of agents that play the specified roles can be involved in the situation, if all conditions are met.

Consider the situation in figure 6. This is a description of a situation in which an agent in the help-desk-attendant role (the acting party) acquires an obligation to accept work from the agent in the help-desk-manager role (the authority party). The beneficiary is someone in the client role. According to the definition, this happens when the help-desk-attendant receives a request in this sense from the help-desk-manager such that the help-desk-attendant knows the sender of the request as a help-desk-manager and the help-desk-attendant is currently idle. Situations are always described from the viewpoint of the acting party (here the help-desk-attendant). If the above conditions are met, the help-desk-attendant will add two new beliefs to its context, namely it is not idle anymore and that the help-desk-manager has requested work. These beliefs justify the agent to believe that it has an obligation to accept the requested work. This is described by the agent creating a new LTMS clause, as shown in the :add-clause slot. To deal with this request from its manager, the agent stores the beliefs relevant to this request in a special propositional space (or :pspace) of its database, named at-work. This enables the agent to differentiate the beliefs related to this request from other beliefs and to reason separately in chosen spaces (context switching). To help with this,

```
(def-situation 'accept-help-desk-work-s
  "attendant must accept work when idle"
  :acting 'help-desk-attendant
  :authority 'help-desk-manager
  :beneficiary 'customer
  :received
   '(request :from (help-desk-manager ?manager)
             :receiver-role help-desk-attendant
             :content do-help-desk-attending)
  :such-that
   '(and(believes ?agent '(now-doing idle)
                  :pspace 'at-work)
        (known-to-me-as ?agent ?manager
                        'help-desk-manager))
  :beliefs-in
   '(list (proposition 'not 'now-doing 'idle)
          (proposition 'requested-hdw ?manager)
          :pspace 'at-work)
  :add-clause
   '(clause
     (conse 'obliged 'accept-hd-work :cost 8)
     (ante 'not 'now-doing 'idle)
     (ante 'requested-hdw ?manager)))
```

Figure 6: A Situation

spaces can also inherit beliefs from other spaces. Finally, any situation becomes an entry in the agent's agenda, guaranteeing that it will be dealt with by the agent.

Conversation Plans. An agent's possible behaviors in a given situation are described by one or more *conversation plans*. To choose one of them, the agent evaluates specific conditions in the context of the given situation. We borrow the idea of conversation plans from (Barbuceanu & Fox 97), as descriptions of both how an agent *acts locally* and *interacts* with other agents by means of communicative actions. A conversation plan consists of states (with distinguished initial and final states) and rule governed transitions together with a control mechanism and a local data base that maintains the state of the conversation. The execution state of a conversation plan is maintained in *actual conversations*.

For example, the conversation plan in figure 7 shows how the Customer interacts with the help-desk-attendant when requesting assistance. After making the request for assistance, the customer-conversation goes to state requested where it waits for the help-desk-attendant to either accept or reject. If the help-desk-attendant accepts to provide assistance, the interaction enters an iterative phase in which the Customer asks questions and the help-desk-attendant responds. This cycle can end only when the Customer decides to terminate it. In each non-final state *conversation rules* specify how the agent interprets incoming messages, how it updates its status and how it responds with outgoing messages. The language in which messages are expressed is a lib-

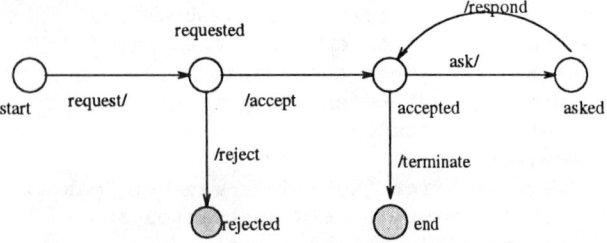

Figure 7: The Customer-conversation

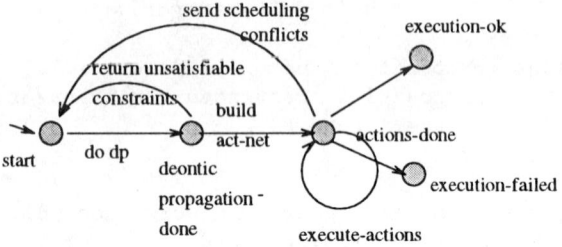

Figure 8: Conversation plan doing deontic propagation, scheduling and action execution

eral form of KQML (Finin 92), but any communicative action language is usable.

To see how conversation plans are used to specify agents' behavior in given situations, the conversation plan in figure 8 shows a generic behavior involving both interaction and local reasoning that an agent would use in a situation when it is requested to satisfy a set of obligations and interdictions from another agent. This plan shows how an agent receives a set of obligations and interdictions that another agent requestes it to satisfy, performs deontic propagation (going to state `deontic-propagation-done`) and, if no requested constraints are violated, plans and schedules the required actions (going to state `act-net-done`). Then it executes the planned/scheduled actions in rule `execute-actions`. If no execution failure occurs, the plan ends in state `execution-ok`, otherwise it ends in `execution-failed`. If during deontic propagation the agent determines that it can not satisfy some of the requested constraints, or if actions can not be scheduled or planned, the violated constraints may be sent back to the sender for revision.

The Action Executive executes scheduled actions according to the specified time windows. The time windows produced by scheduling satisfy the ordering conditions imposed by sequences and parallel compositions (e.g. two consecutive elements of a sequence have time windows that do not allow overlapping, while two elements of a parallel compositions have time windows that may overlap). For this reason, the Executive only needs to pick up atomic actions and choices for execution, making sure time windows are obeyed. When a component action of an obliged sequence is about to be executed, the Executive propagates the component action as obliged and, after executing it, propagates the remaining subsequence as obliged (cf. theorem 4, section 2). This may have as effect new obliged or forbidden actions, in which case we have to reschedule the remaining actions. Similarly, after a component action of a forbidden sequence has been executed, the remaining subsequence is propagated as forbidden (cf. theorem 1, section 2), with the same possible consequences. This shows how much intertwined deontic propagation, scheduling and execution actually are.

To execute an action, either a one-shot method is invoked, or a full conversation plan is initiated. In particular, conversation plans for choices may initiate exchanges with other agents and more complex decision making to determine which alternative to execute (if several are permitted). The architecture allows conversation plans to be suspended in any state, waiting for conditions or events to happen and be resumed when the waited for events or conditions have happened. Conversation plans are always executed incrementally, in a multi-threaded fashion in that each time only at most one state transition is executed, after which the next action is tackled. The Executive is first invoked inside conversation plans tackling situations, as shown in figure 8.

Control Architecture. Each agent operates in a loop where: (1) Events are sensed, like the arrival of messages expressing requests from other agents. (2) Applicable situations are activated updating the agent's beliefs, possibly creating new propositional spaces. (3) Agent selects an entry from the agenda. This is either a new situation, for which a plan is retrieved and initiated, or one that is under processing, in which case its execution continues incrementally, as shown above.

Coordination by Exchanging Deontic Constraints

A basic building block of social interaction is the ability of agents to request things from other agents and to execute other agents requests. Requests normally consist of things an agent wants another to do or to refrain from doing. Thus, they can be described as sets of obligations and interdictions an agent wants another to satisfy. Suppose B receives a message from A containing such a set of obligations and interdictions. By propagating these locally, together with its own obligations and interdictions and with other obligations and interdictions it is committed to, B will determine which of them it can satisfy and which it can't. Both sets are then revealed to A, perhaps with some explanations for the reasons for failure attached. A may now revise its request in various ways. It may drop constraints, it may add constraints, or it may raise or lower costs (e.g. to make B violate other constraints). The revised set of constrains is sent back to B, which will repeat the same cycle. The process may end with both agents agreeing on a set of constraints that A still wants and B can satisfy, or may terminate before any agreement is reached.

To illustrate the use of this approach, we consider the feature interaction problem, a general service creation problem in the telecommunications industry (Cameron 96), on which we are working with industrial partners. We assume A and B are agents responsible for establishing voice connections amongst their users. The creation and administration of connections can use various levels of functionality, or *features*, that provide different services to subscribers or the telephone administration.

Here are a few examples for the features that are usually available (modern telecommunication services may have many hundreds of such features): (1) *Incoming Call Screening*: the calee will refuse all calls from callers in an incoming call screening list. (2) *Call Forward*: the calee will forward the incoming call to another number. (3) *Recall*: if the calee is busy, the caller will be called back later when the calee becomes available. (4) *Outgoing Call Screening*: the caller does not allow to be connected to some specified directory numbers.

The feature interaction problem is that often combinations of features interact in undesired ways, affecting the intended functionality of the provided services. In our example, *Incoming Call Screening* and *Recall* may conflict if *Recall* is done without checking that the number belongs to the incoming call screening list - we shouldn't call back numbers that are not accepted in the first place. Similarly, *Call Forward* and *Outgoing Call Screening* may conflict if a caller is forwarded to a number that it does not wish to be connected to.

The deontic propagation framework can be used to solve such interactions in a principled manner. When agent A wishes to connect to agent B, it sends to B a set of constraints that specify A's relevant features that B must consider. For example, if A has *Outgoing Call Screening*, it will send to B a list of interdictions about the numbers that it doesn't want to be connected to. If B has *Call Forward*, A's interdictions will be used to forbid forwarding to A's undesired numbers.

For illustration, figure 9 shows the inferences performed by a calee B when receiving a call from A. A has *Outgoing Call Screening* for number #1, and B has *Incoming Call Screening* with A in its incoming call screening list (meaning B does not want to talk to A directly). The set of constraints that A sends to B is {(obliged accept-call :from A :cost 5) (forbidden forward :from A :to #1 :cost 9)}.

In response to this message, a situation becomes applicable within B that posts an obligation for B to execute Process Incoming Call. A generic plan that can be used in this situation (shown in figure 8) performs deontic propagation, schedules and then executes the action network. Incoming Call Screening is scheduled first and executed by retrieving and activating a plan for it. The plan places an interdiction for Accept Call and Recall in the current context, because A is on the black list. Deontic propagation activated again by

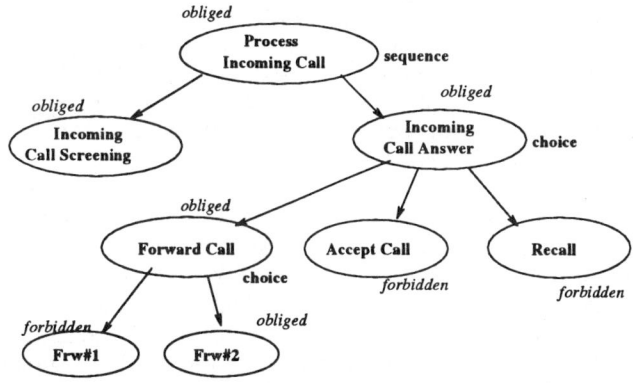

Figure 9: Deontic propagation applied to feature interaction.

the plan infers that Forward Call is obliged. As this is a choice whose first subgoal Frw#1 (forward to #1) is forbidden by the caller, deontic propagation also infers that the second subgoal, Frw#2 (forward to #2) is obliged. That leaves Frw#2 as the only obliged subgoal in the action network. Its execution completes the execution of the action network. In conclusion, we have obtained the desired behavior: B does not accept the call and does not set a callback to A if busy. B forwards the call to its second number, because the first is not acceptable to A.

Suppose now that A has Outgoing Call Screening to both #1 and #2. In this case A sends to B interdictions for both numbers. Deontic propagation will reveal that B can not forward the call (theorem 2) as both alternatives of the choice are now forbidden. B will then reply with a meesage in which it states that the interdictions on both #1 and #2 can not be satisfied. A is then free to choose: either it drops one of these or it drops the entire call. Alternatively, if A has enough authority it may increase the cost of obliging B to accept the call, in order to force B to override its own interdiction of talking to A directly. In this case B would have to accept the call and, if busy, commit to recalling.

Conclusions and Related Work

We believe we have demonstrated the feasibility of agents that can represent social constraints in the form of obligations and interdictions and that can efficiently reason about them to find courses of action that either do not violate them or violate them in a 'necessary' way as imposed by the participating agents authorities or priorities. We have shown how an initially 'theoretical' representation of obligation founded on dynamic deontic logic could be extended with violation costs, reformulated as a constraint propagation method and integrated in a *practically useful* agent development language that covers the spectrum from the definition of organizations, roles, agents, obligations, goals, conversations, to inferring and executing actual, coordinated agent behaviors in applications. One consequence of the approach is that it allows agents to be 'talked to' by giving them a list of obligations and interdictions and then trusting the agent to figure out how to actually fulfil them, including which of them to break if necessary! In particular, agents can talk to each other in this way, leading to a clean approach to negotiation which we have illustrated in the context of service provisioning in telecommunications.

Social constraints have been addressed to some extent previously. In discourse modeling, (Traum &Allen 94) make a strong case for the need of obligations, together with intentions and goals, to understand social interaction. (Jameson & Weis 95) extended their approach with penalty costs and time limitations on obligations. None of them uses the principled deontic constraint propagation method we use, and the requirements of natural language dialogue are different (more complexity, more dynamic conversation turns, but also less quality of service guarantees) from those of artificial agent interaction. (Werner 89) describes a theory of coordination within social structures built from roles among which permissions and responsibilities are defined. (Shoham & Tennenholtz 95) study very general computational properties of social laws. (Castelfranchi 95) stresses the importance of obligations in organizations but does not advance operational architectures. AOP (Shoham 93) defines obligations locally, but does not really exploit them socially. (Boman 97) uses norms to improve local decison making, but not coordination.

On the application side, we are currently exploring the space of negotiation strategies based on the deontic constraint exchange approach. In telecommunications for example, we are looking at strategies that limit and control the amount of information disclosed in exchanges (e.g. if the caller does not want the calee to know that it does not want to be forwarded to a certain number, how should the negotiation proceed?). Also, we are applying the approach to global supply chain management where many horizontal and vertical levels of interaction have to be managed among agents with many different rights and obligations. On the system development side, we are working on the direct integration of time in the deontic propagation process, allowing to infer obligations and interdictions for specific time intervals, rather than assuming that all obligations apply to the entire horizon. By further allowing action sequences to be produced by planning systems we aim at a more complete architecture that integrates social laws reasoning with classical planning and scheduling.

Acknowledgments

This research is supported, in part, by the Manufacturing Research Corporation of Ontario, Natural Science and Engineering Research Council, Digital Equipment Corp., Mitel Corp., Micro Electronics and Computer Research Corp., Spar Aerospace, Carnegie Group and Quintus Corp.

References

Barbuceanu, M. and Fox, M. S. 1997. Integrating Communicative Action, Conversations and Decision Theory to Coordinate Agents. *Proceedings of Automomous Agents'97*, 47-58, Marina Del Rey, February 1997.

Beck, C. et al. Texture-Based Heuristics for Scheduling Revisited. *Proceedings of AAAI-97*, 241-248, July 1997, Providence RI.

Boman, M. 1997. Norms as Constraints on Real-Time Autonomous Agent Action. In *Multi-Agent Rationality*, Boman and Van de Welde (eds) Springer Verlag.

Cameron, E.J., N.D. Griffeth, Y.J. Lin, M.E. Nilson, W.K. Schnure, and H. Velthuijsen. A Feature Interaction Benchmark for for IN and Beyond. In L.G. Bouma and H. Velthuijsen, editors, *Feature Interactions in Telecommunication Systems*, 1-23, Amsterdam, May 1996. IOS Press.

Castelfranchi, C. 1995. Commitments: From Individual Intentions to Groups and Organizations. *Proceedings of ICMAS-95*, AAAI Press, 41-48.

Levesque, H, Cohen, P.R. and Nunes, J. On Acting Together. *Proceedings of AAAI'90*, Menlo Park, CA.

Finin, T. et al. 1992. Specification of the KQML Agent Communication Language. The DARPA Knowledge Sharing Initiative, External Interfaces Working Group.

Jameson, A. and Weis, T. 1995. How to Juggle Discourse Obligations. *Proceedings of the Symposium on Conceptual and Semantic Knowledge in Language Generation*, Heidelberg, November 1995.

Jennings, N. 1995. Controlling Cooperative Problem Solving in Industrial Multi-Agent Systems Using Joint Intentions. *Artificial Intelligence* 75.

McAllester, D. 1980. An Outlook on Truth Maintenance. Memo 551, MIT AI Laboratory.

Meyer, J. J. Ch. 1988. A Different Approach to Deontic Logic: Deontic Logic Viewed as a Variant of Dynamic Logic. *Notre Dame J. of Formal Logic* 29(1) 109-136.

Shoham, Y. 1993. Agent-Oriented Programming. *Artificial Intelligence* 60, 51-92.

Shoham, Y. and Tennenholtz, M. 1995. On Social Laws for Artificial Agent Societies: Off-line Design. *Artificial Intelligence* 73 231-252.

Tambe, M. 1997. Agent Architectures for Flexible, Practical Teamwork. *Proceedings of AAAI'97*, Providence, RI, 22-28.

Traum, D.R. and Allen, J.F. 1994. Discourse Obligations in Dialogue Processing. *Proceedings of the 32th Annual Meeting of the ACL*, Las Cruces, NM, 1-8.

Werner, E. 1989. Cooperating Agents: A Unified Theory of Communication and Social Structure. In L. Gasser and M.N. Huhns (eds), *Distributed Artificial Intelligence Vol II* 3-36, Pitman.

What is Wrong With Us?
Improving Robustness Through Social Diagnosis

Gal A. Kaminka and **Milind Tambe**
Information Sciences Institute and Computer Science Department
University of Southern California
4676 Admiralty Way, Marina del Rey, CA 90292
{galk, tambe}@isi.edu

Abstract[1]

Robust behavior in complex, dynamic environments mandates that intelligent agents autonomously monitor their own run-time behavior, detect and diagnose failures, and attempt recovery. This challenge is intensified in multi-agent settings, where the coordinated and competitive behaviors of other agents affect an agent's own performance. Previous approaches to this problem have often focused on single agent domains and have failed to address or exploit key facets of multi-agent domains, such as handling team failures. We present SAM, a complementary approach to monitoring and diagnosis for multi-agent domains that is particularly well-suited for collaborative settings. SAM includes the following key novel concepts: First, SAM's failure detection technique, inspired by social psychology, utilizes other agents as information sources and detects failures both in an agent and in its teammates. Second, SAM performs social diagnosis, reasoning about the failures in its team using an *explicit model of teamwork* (previously, teamwork models have been employed only in prescribing agent behaviors in teamwork). Third, SAM employs *model sharing* to alleviate the inherent inefficiencies associated with representing multiple agent models. We have implemented SAM in a complex, realistic multi-agent domain, and provide detailed empirical results assessing its benefits.

Introduction

Attaining robustness in face of uncertainty in complex, dynamic environments is a key challenge for intelligent agents (Toyama and Hager 1997). This problem is exacerbated in complex multi-agent environments due to the added requirements for communication and coordination. Example domains include virtual environments for training (Tambe et al. 1995), robotic soccer (Kitano et al. 95), potential multi-robotic space missions, etc. The inherent explosion of state space complexity in these dynamic environments inhibits the ability of any designer, human or machine (i.e., planners), to specify the correct response in each possible state in advance (Atkins et al. 1997). For instance, it is generally difficult to predict when sensors will return unreliable answers, communication messages get lost, etc. The agents are therefore presented with countless opportunities for failure, and must autonomously monitor and detect failures in their run-time behavior, then diagnose and recover from them, i.e., agents must display *post-failure robustness* (Toyama and Hager 1997).

Previous approaches to monitoring and diagnosis (e.g., Doyle et al. 1986, Williams and Nayak 1996) have often focused on a single agent that utilizes designer-supplied information, either in the form of explicit execution-monitoring conditions, or a model of the agent itself. This information allows the agent to compare its *actual* behavior with the *ideal* behavior to detect failures. While powerful in themselves, these methods have several limitations in multi-agent dynamic environments.

First, these approaches are geared towards detecting and diagnosing failures in a single agent's own behaviors. They do not consider failures in other agents even when those affect the agent's own performance. For instance, a teammate's failure can change the ideal behavior expected of an agent, but this can only be known if the agent can detect teammates' failures.

Second, these single-agent approaches cannot capture team-level failures, where the failures may not be all in a single individual, but rather are distributed among a number of agents in a team. In this case diagnosis and recovery imply not only correcting the individual failure, but also re-establishing coordination at the team-level.

Third, the single-agent perspective in these approaches prevents them from utilizing other agents as sources of knowledge to compensate for possible failures in some of an agent's own sensors, i.e., to use whatever information is sensed about other agents to infer the failing sensors' results[2]. For example, a driver may not see an obstacle on the road, but if s/he sees another car swerve, s/he can infer the presence of the obstacle.

Fourth, these previous approaches are hard to scale up to complex, multi-agent environments. In particular, since agents in such environments adjust their behavior flexibly to respond to their actual circumstances, it becomes increasingly hard to specify the correct behavior. For instance, specifying a target range for monitoring the velocity of a car becomes difficult if we are to take into

---

[1] Copyright © 1998, American Association for Artificial Intelligence (www.aaai.org). All rights reserved.

[2] This relies on the reliability sensors recognizing the other agents. If all sensors fail, little can be done.

account some of the possible responses of the driver, e.g., acceleration beyond the speed limit or slowing down to avoid hitting another car.

To alleviate such limitations of the existing approaches, we have developed SAM (Socially Attentive Monitoring), a new approach to failure detection, diagnosis and recovery. SAM *complements* existing approaches by addressing the difficulties and exploiting the opportunities in multi-agent environments. It is particularly relevant for collaborative (teamwork) settings, that are ubiquitous in multi-agent environments. SAM allows detection of failures in the monitoring agent and its peers by a technique inspired by Social Comparison Theory (Festinger 1954). The key idea is that agents compare their own behavior, beliefs, goals, and plans to those of other agents, reason about the differences in belief and behavior (not necessarily imitating the others), and draw useful conclusions regarding the correctness of their own actions or their peers'. While information about other agents' beliefs can be obtained via communication, such communication can be a significant overhead or risk (in hostile environments). Instead, SAM uses plan recognition to infer other agents' beliefs, goals, and plans from their observable actions (communicating only if necessary and feasible). Thus, SAM would be applicable in the car swerving example discussed above. To reduce inefficiency in keeping track of other agents' beliefs/plans, SAM utilizes *model sharing* for efficient reasoning with such models.

Upon detecting a possible failure, SAM performs diagnosis using an *explicit teamwork model* to establish the exact difference in beliefs between the agents and the significance of the difference. Explicit teamwork models have begun to be used in multi-agent domains for teamwork flexibility (Jennings 1995; Tambe 1997). SAM exploits these models--and the guarantees they provide-- in a novel way, running them in reverse for diagnosis. A detailed diagnosis enables SAM to recover.

SAM complements previous work on execution monitoring and diagnosis by alleviating key weaknesses mentioned above. First, social comparison allows agents to detect failures in their peers' behavior, diagnose the failures, and recover either by adjusting own behavior or influencing the failing agents (e.g., by communicating with the failing agents). Second, SAM utilizes an explicit teamwork model to facilitate diagnosis and recovery at the team-level (re-establishing team coordination), and not just at the individual level. Third, SAM enables an agent to compensate for some of its failures to sense the environment directly, by sensing other agents' behaviors, from which SAM infers missing information about the environment. Finally, SAM complements the models or conditions normally specified by the designer with information gained from other agents. These other agents behave flexibly in their environment and thus effectively provide a model that matches the particular state the agent is facing. However, SAM has to address the possibility that these other agents may be behaving erroneously.

Motivation and Examples

The motivation for our approach comes from our application domain which involves developing automated pilot agents for participation in a commercially-developed battlefield simulation (Tambe et al. 1995). This real-world environment is complex and dynamic, with uncertainties such as unscripted behaviors of other agents, unreliable communications and sensors, possibly incomplete mission and task specifications, etc. These qualities present the agents with never-ending opportunities for failure, as anticipation of all possible internal and external states is impossible for the designer. Two example failures may serve to illustrate. The first failure involved a scenario where a team of three helicopter pilot agents was to fly to a specified landmark position. Having reached this position, one of the team members, whose role was that of a *scout*, was to fly forward towards the enemy, verifying its position. The scout's two teammates (role: *attackers*) were to land and wait for its return to the specified position. All of the pilot agents were explicitly provided conditions to monitor for the landmark. However, due to an unexpected sensor failure, one of the attackers failed to sense the landmark marking the waiting position. So while the other attacker correctly landed, the failing attacker continued to fly forward with the scout, following the original plan which called for flying in formation! The failing attacker had clearly seen that the other attacker had landed, but it did not use this information to infer the position of the landmark. Furthermore, the other attacker and the scout did not complain to the failing attacker about its failure. In a second example, a similar team of three helicopters was to take off from the home base and head towards their battle position. One of the agents unexpectedly did not receive the correct mission specification, so while two of the agents began to fly out as planned, the failing agent kept hovering in place at the starting position indefinitely. Again, none of the agents complained about the unusual performance of the team.

We have collected dozens of such failure reports during the last two years. While it is generally easy for the human designer to correct these failures once they occur, it is hard to anticipate them in advance. These failures occur despite significant development and maintenance efforts. Given the complexity of the dynamic environment, predicting all possible states and all possible interactions is impossible. Furthermore, these failures are not negligible. Rather, they are very obvious (to the human observer) catastrophic failures, for both individual agents and the team. In the second example above, not only was the single agent stuck behind unable to participate in the mission, but the remaining agents were unable to carry out the mission by themselves.

Furthermore, these failures are not due to a lack of domain expertise, as the domain experts expect some common sense handling of such failures even in the most structured military procedure. Indeed, by exercising social common sense, an agent may at least detect that something may be wrong. Social clues, such as (in the examples above) noticing that teammates are leaving while the agent is hovering in place, or that a team-member has landed while the team was flying in formation, would have been sufficient to infer that something may be wrong.

Social Monitoring: Detecting Failures

SAM is composed of three processes: (i) a failure detection process, which involves comparison with peers, in particular teammates, to detect the possibility of failure, (ii) a diagnosis process to confirm the detected failure and perform detailed diagnosis, and (iii) a recovery process. We begin in this section by describing SAM's failure detection process, which is inspired by Social Comparison Theory (Festinger 1954) from social psychology. The first three axioms of this theory are as follows: (1) Every agent has a drive to evaluate its opinions and abilities; (2) If the agent can't evaluate its opinions and abilities objectively, then it compares them against the opinions and abilities of others; (3) Comparing against others decreases as the difference with others increases.

The numerous failure reports we have collected empirically demonstrate the very real need of agents in dynamic, unpredictable domains to evaluate themselves by monitoring their execution (first axiom). Current approaches emphasizing the designer as a source of information against which to compare the agent's performance fit naturally under the title of objective sources for the agent's self-evaluation. SAM's detection technique is inspired by the remaining parts of the axioms-- allowing the agent to compare its own abilities and opinions (i.e., behavior, beliefs, and goals) to those of others, and considering the weight put on these comparisons (third axiom).

SAM's monitoring technique is an operationalization of this descriptive social comparison process. To detect possible failures, SAM compares the monitoring agent's own state and the state of other agents -- where an agent's state may include its beliefs, goals, behaviors, etc. However, as implied by the third axiom of social comparison theory, differences with other agents are meaningful only to the extent that the other agents are *socially similar*. If other agents' states are expected to be dissimilar to the agent's state, they may be unable to contribute relevant information towards the monitoring of the agent's own performance. Also, hostile agents may intentionally want to use deception in order to influence the agent's decision making to advance their own agendas.

To address this issue, SAM currently limits its comparison to the agent's teammates only, as these tend to work on common goals and related sub-plans, and can be assumed to be non-hostile (given the ubiquity of teamwork in multi-agent domains, this is not a limiting assumption). Differences with team members' states may imply a *possible* failure in either agent. For instance, in the second helicopter example above, the agent left hovering at the starting point could detect a possible failure by comparing its own state with teammates' states.

SAM's capabilities may differ depending on what state information about teammates is compared, e.g., internal beliefs and goals vs. observable behavior. In general, the information compared should satisfy a trade-off between two criteria: (i) For efficiency, only limited information should be maintained about other agents and compared, and (ii) For maximized monitoring capabilities, the information should capture as much as possible of the agents' beliefs, goals, and internal control processes, since we can only hope to detect discrepancies in the actual agent-attributes we are comparing.

Our agents' design is based on reactive plans (operators) (Firby 1987, Newell 1990), which form a decomposition hierarchy that controls each agent. Operator hierarchies provide a good trade-off between the criteria considered above, as they are both compact enough to be reasoned about efficiently, while being central to the agent behavior (capturing its decision process). We therefore chose operator hierarchies for our comparison purpose. Figure 1 presents a small portion of such a hierarchy. Each operator in the hierarchy has preconditions for selecting it, application conditions to apply it, and termination conditions. The design of the hierarchical plans uses the STEAM framework (Tambe 1997) for maintaining an explicit model of teamwork. Following this framework, operators may be team operators (that explicitly represent the joint activities of the team) or individual (specific to one agent). In Figure 1, boxed operators are team operators, while other operators are individual. The filled arrows signify the operator hierarchy currently in control, while dotted arrows point to alternative operators which may be used. In the figure, the agent is currently executing the execute-mission team operator which is its highest-level team operator, and has chosen (jointly with its team) to execute the fly-flight-plan operator, for flying with the team through the different mission-specified locations.

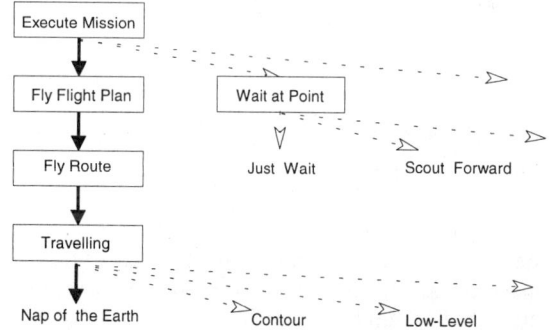

Figure 1. An example operator hierarchy.

To compare its own operator hierarchy with other agents' hierarchies, an agent must acquire knowledge about the others. Such knowledge can be acquired in two ways: it can be communicated by the other agents or it can be inferred by the monitoring agent based on its observation of the other agents via plan recognition. The choice to prefer one method over the other (or use a combination of both) is dependent on the (i) cost and (ii) expected reliability of these methods, which changes across domains.

In many realistic domains, continuous communication involves significant cost, both in overhead and risk. For example, in our battlefield simulation domain, the cost of communications is very high, as the agents operate in a hostile environment and expose themselves to risks by communicating with each other. In contrast, the cost of plan recognition is relatively low, being mostly a computational cost rather than a survival risk. In addition, in a team context, plan recognition is often quite reliable due to assumptions that can be made about the behavior of other agents, since they are team members. Our estimates of reliability and the cost make plan recognition an attractive choice for acquiring knowledge of others.

We use the $RESC_{team}$ (Tambe 1996) method for plan-recognition, but different techniques may be used interchangeably, as long as they provide the needed information and representation. $RESC_{team}$ provides real-time plan recognition capabilities, constructing operator hierarchies (in the recognizing agent's memory) that correspond to the other agents' currently executing reactive operators. The monitoring agent therefore has unified access not only to its own hierarchies, but also to the (inferred) operator hierarchies of other team members, constructed by $RESC_{team}$. In figure 2 below, the left hierarchy is the hierarchy actually in control of the agent. The right one is inferred by $RESC_{team}$ to be currently executed by another agent.

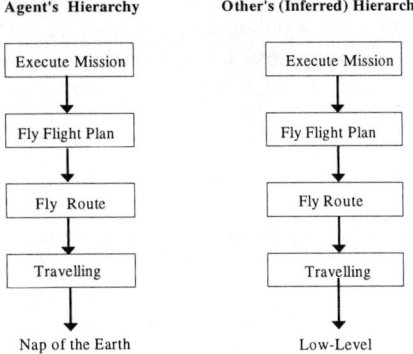

Figure 2. Two example hierarchies in the agent's memory.

Comparing the agents' operator hierarchies involves a top-down comparison of the operators in equal depths of the hierarchies (hierarchies of different lengths are also considered different). In figure 2, the difference that would be detected is between the two leaf nodes, since all operators above them are identical.

Any such difference indicates a possible failure, if teammates were supposed to be executing similar operators in the first place. Before we discuss further diagnosis of this failure (next Section), we address here one inherent inefficiency in this failure detection method--it potentially needs to keep track of the operator hierarchies of all other teammates. To alleviate this inefficiency, we rely on *model-sharing*--the use of shared hierarchies for team operators (Tambe 1996). Team operators at equal depths (the agent's own, and those inferred of others), which should be identical for all team-members, are shared in the agent memory. Thus, only individual operators are maintained separately. When team-operator differences occur (see next section), SAM unshares the hierarchies at the point at which they differ to allow reasoning about the differences to continue, without having to maintain separate hierarchies needlessly. Model sharing thus maintains conceptually different hierarchies, while limiting the actual computational overhead.

Social Diagnosis and Recovery

While SAM's detection process indicates possibilities of failures, its diagnosis process verifies the failure and generates an explanation for it utilizing social knowledge sources (other agents and the explicit teamwork model). These sources determine the expected similarity between the agents involved, and thus determine whether, and to what degree, the difference in operators is truly an indication of failure. In particular, differences can be detected at the team level (the monitoring agent and its teammates are not executing the same team operator), or individual level. The extent of the diagnosis and recovery depends on the type of difference detected.

Team-Operator Differences

In the case of team-operator differences, SAM's failure diagnosis is driven by explicit models of teamwork. Such models have recently emerged as a promising approach to provide greater flexibility in teamwork (Jennings 1995; Tambe 1997). In particular, they alleviate the need for domain-specific coordination plans.

The key idea in SAM is based on the observation that teamwork models specify how a team should work in general. Thus, tracing back through such a model can help confirm and diagnose team failures. In particular, teamwork models contain domain-independent axioms that prescribe general responsibilities for team members and the team. These axioms in turn have been derived from teamwork theories, such as joint intentions (Levesque et al. 1990) and SharedPlans (Grosz and Kraus, 1996). Our basic idea is to backchain through these axioms to diagnose the failure. For instance, one axiom of the joint intentions framework mandates that a persistent (committed) team goal cannot be abandoned unless there exists mutual belief in the team goal being irrelevant, achieved, or unachievable. Thus, if the agent discovers a goal has been abandoned by others, it can infer they believe mutual belief has been established in the goal's irrelevancy, achievement, or unachievability.

In our implementation, the agents utilize one such explicit model of teamwork, STEAM (Tambe 1997), for their collaborative execution of team operators. STEAM ensures that team operators are established jointly by the team via attainment of mutual belief in their preconditions, and terminated jointly by attaining mutual belief in the team-operator's termination conditions (either achievement, unachievability, or irrelevancy conditions). In theory, team operators must therefore *always be identical* for all team members. However, given the well recognized difficulty of establishing mutual belief in practice (Halpern and Moses 1990), differences in team operators unfortunately do occur. Furthermore, for security or efficiency, team members sometimes deliberately reduce communication, and inadvertently contribute to such team-operator differences. For instance, agents may assume that an external object in team members' visual range (such as a landmark) is visible to all, and may not communicate about it.

Given STEAM's guarantees that the team operator must always be identical, any team-operator differences detected by SAM therefore imply not only a possibility but a certainty of team coordination failure. Having established this certainty in the failure, SAM's team-level diagnosis next attempts to identify the exact differences between its own beliefs and its teammates' beliefs that have led them to execute different team operators--this aspect of diagnosis is key for recovery, and it proceeds as follows. First, given a difference between the monitoring agent's **T1** team operator and the other team-members' **T2** team operator, SAM infers that the entire team was initially executing **T1** (since no differences were detected earlier). However, now teammates have begun executing **T2**[3]. Therefore, SAM infers that the teammates believe that one or more of the disjunctive preconditions necessary for selection and execution of **T2** were satisfied. Furthermore, SAM infers that teammates believe that one or more of the disjunctive termination conditions of **T1** have been achieved. Typically, the intersection between these two sets of possible beliefs determines the actual set of beliefs that the teammates hold that are different at this point[4]. In addition, the teamwork model guarantees SAM that this is the only real difference that has led to the teammates' executing **T2**. Of course, this intersection idea can be applied to both team and individual operator differences, but it is of particular importance for team-level failures given the guarantees provided by the teamwork model.

In the example of the agent's failure to detect a key landmark, SAM infers that the other agents are carrying out the wait-at-point operator (one attacker lands, while the scout goes forward). Once this discrepancy is noted ("I am executing fly-flight-plan, they are executing wait-at-point"), SAM determines that since the other agents have terminated "fly-flight-plan" they have either met with an enemy, or reached the landmark. From their current choice of "wait-at-point" operator (whose preconditions include reaching the landmark), SAM infers that the teammates believe that they have indeed reached the landmark. Thus, given the guarantees of teamwork models, the difference in team operators is elaborated by the diagnosis process to infer specific differences in team members' beliefs.

SAM next continues to backchain through the teamwork model, attempting to glean further information about the belief difference. To begin with, it infers if this difference of beliefs among team members is one that causes the operator in question to be achieved, unachievable, or irrelevant. SAM can then diagnose the failure in further detail. For instance, in a different failure scenario, the scout was shot down but this was known only to some agents in the team. They then began to communicate as part of a replan procedure to take over the role of the dead scout. The agents that did not see the scout crash failed to understand why these messages were sent, and chose to ignore them, therefore causing a failure in coordination. However, using SAM, the monitoring agent indirectly determines that the scout is no longer functioning when it receives communication messages from its peers calling for a replan. In particular, SAM first infers that the other agents are executing a "replan" team-coordination operator. This triggers a difference with the agent's own "wait-at-point". SAM then infers that the preconditions for a replan have become true, which means that there was a failure in "wait-at-point" which made it unachievable (as opposed to achieved or irrelevant). The only possible reason for this is that the scout cannot complete its mission.

Recovery is greatly facilitated by better diagnosis. Currently, SAM's recovery assumes that the agent's perception is incomplete, but not inconsistent. For example, an agent's sensors may fail to detect the landmark (a "don't know" response), but would not erroneously say it is there when it isn't. Thus, SAM's diagnosis that teammates have come to believe in something which the monitoring agent does not know about (or vice versa) enables the monitoring agent to recover by adopting this belief (or in the reverse case, by letting others know about this belief). The above assumption is made only in the recovery stage, not in the detection or diagnosis stages, and removing it is a topic for future work.

In the example of the failure to detect the landmark, once the agent diagnoses the problem that the other agents have detected the landmark (making the "fly-flight-plan" achieved), it recovers completely by adopting the other agents' belief. This adoption of belief makes the preconditions for its own "wait-at-point" operator true, and it re-establishes mutual belief with the team, completely resolving the problem.

Individual Operator Differences

In service of team operators different agents may work on different individual operators. Thus, a difference in individual operators may not necessarily signify failure. Individual operators do not carry with them the responsibilities for mutual belief that team operators do, and also none of the guarantees provided by a teamwork model. Therefore, SAM consults additional information about the agents causing the difference which can help in determining whether the difference is justified or not, prior to embarking on the diagnosis of the exact set of differences in beliefs. Agents working towards similar

---

[3] The case where the team did not switch but the monitoring agent did is also possible, but is not described here for brevity
[4] Empty intersection cases are a topic for future work.

goals have similar *social roles* or *status*. For example, in a soccer game there are field players and a goalie which have different roles within the team. Agents with similar roles serve as better sources of information for plan-execution monitoring than agents with different roles. In some cases, SAM may choose to completely eliminate some agents which are too socially dissimilar from further consideration even at the detection level, so that differences in choice of individual operators will no longer signify possible failures. At the team level, however, these agents are still very much considered.

SAM will therefore choose to fully diagnose only differences with agents of similar role/status, assigning appropriate discounted weight to the explanation generated. The example where a failing agent was stuck in place while its team-members have taken off and were flying away serves to illustrate. Here, the agent compares its chosen method-of-flight operator to the method-of-flight chosen by its comrades. This comparison is meaningful since at least one of the comrades has a similar role and status. The comparison indicates to the failing agent that it is not acting like its team-mates - that a failure may have occurred (see leaf operators in Figure 2). The process of diagnosis here results in SAM's inferring that the reason for the difference is that the mission specification of the flight-method (which is a precondition for selecting a particular method) is different between the agents. However, it is highly improbable that two different mission specifications were intentionally sent out to two agents in a team (domain-specific knowledge). Therefore, the monitoring agent communicates with teammates and their commander to possibly resolve this problem.

Results and Evaluation

Our agent, including SAM, is implemented completely in the Soar integrated AI architecture (Newell 1990). About 1200 rules are used to implement the agent, including the military procedures, teamwork capabilities (STEAM), and plan-recognition capabilities (RESC$_{team}$). Approximately 60 additional rules implement SAM, forming an add-on layer on top of the procedures making up the agent.

SAM can resolve a significant portion of the team and individual failures in our collected failure reports, too numerous to discuss here in detail. We have therefore chosen to illustrate SAM's strengths and limitations via systematic experimentation with variations of the landing point failure described above. Here, we systematically tested SAM's capabilities in all possible permutations of the original scenario, i.e., all possible pairings of agents' failures and roles. To make things tougher, only a single agent deployed SAM. Thus, in our experiments SAM had to detect and diagnose failures not only in the monitoring agent, but also in one or more of its teammates.

In the first set of experiments, our SAM-executing agent (called SAM in the tables below) plays its original role of an *attacker* (Table 1). The other agents (other-1 and other-2) also play their original role. For further variations in failure scenarios, we set up another set of experiments, where SAM plays the other role involved in the scenario, that of the scout (see Table 2).

The first column in the tables is experiment number. The next three columns note the three agent/roles in the experiments. Entries marked "Fail" indicate that in the given experiment (row), the agent in question has failed to detect the landing point, and thus continued execution of "fly-flight-plan". The "Detect" column marks "Yes" in experiments in which SAM was successful in detecting a difference in operators indicating possible failure (and "No" otherwise). The Diagnose column similarly indicates whether SAM's diagnosis procedure was successful at generating an explanation of the failure. Recovery was successful in all cases where a diagnosis was generated.

Exp #	**attack SAM**	attack other1	scout other2	Detect	Diagnose
1	-	-	-	N/A	N/A
2	Fail	-	-	Yes	Yes
3	-	Fail	-	Yes	Yes
4	Fail	Fail	-	No	No
5	-	-	Fail	Yes	Yes
6	Fail	-	Fail	Yes	Yes
7	-	Fail	Fail	Yes	Yes
8	Fail	Fail	Fail	No	No

Table 1. SAM - attacker, other-1 - attacker, other-2 - scout

Exp #	attack other1	attack other2	**scout SAM**	Detect	Diagnose
9	-	-	-	N/A	N/A
10	Fail	-	-	Yes	Yes
11	-	Fail	-	Yes	Yes
12	Fail	Fail	-	Yes	Yes
13	-	-	Fail	Yes	Yes
14	Fail	-	Fail	Yes	No
15	-	Fail	Fail	Yes	No
16	Fail	Fail	Fail	No	No

Table 2. SAM - scout, other-1 and other-2 - attackers.

In experiments 1 and 9 no failure occurred (a "-" in columns 2-4), and SAM's capabilities were not applicable. There are thus 14 cases where at least one agent fails. Of those, SAM detected a failure in 11, and generated a diagnosis for 9.

Experiment 2 is the original failure scenario. Here, as mentioned in the previous section, SAM detected a difference between its own "fly-flight-plan" and the other agents' "wait-at-point" and through diagnosis, realized the other agents believe the landmark is detected. It then recovered from the failure by adopting this belief, compensating for its own sensors' failure to detect the landmark. Experiment 13 is analogous, except that here SAM is playing the scout. SAM proves successful there as well.

There are 6 cases (experiments 3, 5, 7, 10-12) where a reverse difference occurs, in which the agent running SAM has detected the landmark successfully, but one or more other agents did not (and are continuing with "fly-flight-plan"). In all but one of these, a diagnosis is completed and recovery facilitated. This is a particularly strong result, since here a single agent deploying SAM is detecting a failure in one or more of its peers' perceptions.

In cases where two out of the three agents fail, SAM does better in detecting failures when working as the scout (capturing all of the cases 12,14,15), than when working as the attacker (not capturing all of 4,6,7). This is due to the fact that as a scout, even when SAM was failing, usually one of the two attackers would unambiguously signify detecting it by landing. In contrast, in case 4, when SAM was failing as an attacker, the scout is the only agent that did not fail. Here, since the scout continues to fly out to the battle position, and since SAM has not seen the landmark, SAM's plan-recognition fails to detect the scout's internal operator shift to "wait-at-point". Instead, SAM believes that the scout is continuing with "fly-flight-plan", and so no operator difference is generated. This shows a limitation of relying exclusively on plan-recognition in SAM, since plan-recognition may sometimes fail. Indeed, cases 14 and 15 further illustrate this point. These cases are also difficult to diagnose given the ambiguity in plan-recognition. Here, when one attacker detected the landmark and landed, while the other continued to fly along, the team was essentially split, and SAM's plan-recognition failed to unambiguously infer whether the team as a whole was running "fly-flight-plan" or "wait-at-point". It could only identify that each of the other agents was running a different operator, and thus only detected the failure (but did not diagnose it).

Although SAM is sensitive to plan-recognition ambiguity, this difficulty is alleviated since it focuses on teams and team-members. This constrains very much the space of possible hypotheses, and reduces the chance for ambiguity. Indeed, as the results of the experiments clearly show, there was only one case of detection failure and only two cases of diagnosis failure due to ambiguity.

SAM's two other failures at detection are both in cases where all three agents have failed together - which is another limitation of SAM. When all agents fail together, no differences in observed behavior or inferred operators occur, and so no failure is detected.

The combined results of the two sets of experiments demonstrate that just two agents running SAM--the scout and an attacker--are sufficient to detect failure, fully diagnose, and recover in *all 12 cases* where at least one agent behaves correctly (i.e., all cases except for those where all agents fail together).

Although we deliberately point out SAM's limitations and strengths as they show in the 14 experiments, its performance should also be compared to that of the techniques focusing only on single-agent perspective. Those would fail to even detect a failure in all 14 cases, even with all three agents running a diagnosis system. This is due to their lack of social attention to other agents. They consider only the agent's own sensors that are supposed to detect the landmark, but ignore the sensors telling them about what other agents are doing. Thus, they cannot diagnose or recover from failures in other agents.

A reviewer of this paper suggested contrasting these results with an evaluation of SAM running with no condition monitoring in place. In this case, none of the agents can detect the landmark, and so SAM will fail to detect the problem. This is to be expected, as SAM is a complementary technique, and does not consider the task-specific sensors that the condition monitors do.

SAM's results should also be contrasted with those achieved with imitation (Bakker and Kuniyoshi 1996). Imitation is a very special case of the general SAM method -- by choosing to always adapt the others' view, SAM leads to imitation. However, imitation works only in the presence of a *correct* role-model. The scout has a unique role in the team, and so has no role-model to imitate. Thus, imitation would be inadequate in all experiments in table 2. The attacker has a role model (the other attacker) and would manage to land correctly in experiments 2 and 6, but would also imitate its role-model when the role-model is failing (experiments 3 and 7).

Finally, to evaluate SAM's plan-recognition efficiency provided by model sharing, we compare the number of operators selected during a typical mission by an agent running with two other full hierarchies (as in a team with three agents), to that of the same agent doing modeling but using model-sharing for efficiency. The agent not using model-sharing keeps track of 57 different operators during the course of a typical mission. The latter agent, running with model sharing, keeps track of only 34 different operators--a two-fold computational savings.

The results demonstrate that SAM is a useful technique for detecting and diagnosing failures, able to capture failures in the agent running SAM and in its teammates, facilitating recovery not only of an individual agent, but of the team as a whole.

Related Work

We have already discussed some key related work—imitation and previous work on monitoring and diagnosis—earlier in the paper. In addition, SAM is related to work on multi-agent coordination and teamwork, although it generalizes to also detect failures in execution of individual operators, which are outside the scope of coordination. Particularly relevant are *observation-based* methods, which use plan recognition rather than communications for coordination. Huber and Durfee (1996) do not assume an explicit model of teamwork, but rather view collaboration as emergent from opportunistic agents, which coordinate with others when it suits their individual goals. These agents do not have the guarantees of maximal social similarity at the team level, and while they possibly will find the detected differences useful, they cannot be certain of failures, nor facilitate team recovery (since the other agent may simply have left the team opportunistically). Work on teamwork (Jennings 1995, Tambe 1997) concentrates on maintaining identical joint goals to prevent miscoordination, while the focus of SAM is on detecting when the goals do differ. Indeed. SAM is useful as a diagnosis component for general teamwork models, allowing a general teamwork replanner to take over the recovery process.

Atkins et al. (Atkins et al. 1997) attack a similar problem of detecting states for which the agent does not have a plan ready. They offer a classification of these states, and provide planning algorithms that build tests for these states. However, their approach considers only the individual agents and not teams. It thus suffers from the same limitations as other single agent approaches in being unable to detect modeled states which have not been sensed correctly.

Summary and Future Work

This paper presents SAM, a novel system for failure detection, diagnosis and recovery in large-scale, dynamic, multi-agent domains. SAM is not only able to detect failures in the individual agent deploying it, but also in that agent's peers--even if they are not deploying SAM themselves. SAM additionally diagnoses and recovers from failures at the team level -- it thus truly performs social diagnosis, spanning failures distributed in a number of agents rather than in one particular individual.

Key novel aspects of SAM include: (a) a new failure detection method, able to detect previously undetectable failures in the monitoring agent, and in its peers, (b) a social diagnosis method, able to diagnose failures in behavior of agents and agent-teams, based on an explicit teamwork model, and (c) a model-sharing technique for limiting the inefficiencies inherently associated with keeping track of multiple agent models. Finally, SAM exploits a novel synergy among three different agent components, specifically plan-recognition, teamwork, and monitoring components. These general principles would appear to be applicable in many domains such as those mentioned in the introduction.

In our work, we have implemented SAM in a complex, realistic multi-agent environment and conducted a careful and systematic evaluation of its benefits and limitations, demonstrating SAM's applicability in different single- and multiple-failure scenarios. We demonstrated that SAM was able to diagnose almost all failures in these cases, but approaches focusing on single-agent perspective have failed to even detect the failures.

Many areas are open for future work. Further exploration of Social Comparison Theory or the uses of model-based teamwork diagnosis is high on our agenda. We also plan to investigate further individual-operator differences, which do not enjoy the guarantees and diagnostic power of team-level failures.

Acknowledgments

This research was supported in part by NSF Grant IRI-9711665, in part by subcontract 090881-96-06 from Sverdrup Technologies, and in part by AFOSR contract #F49620-97-1-0501. Special thanks to K. Ushi.

References

Atkins, E. M.; Durfee, E. H.; and Shin, K. G. 1997. Detecting and reacting to unplanned-for world states, in *Proceedings of the Fourteenth National Conference on Artificial Intelligence (AAAI-97)*. pp. 571-576.

Bakker, P.; and Kuniyoshi, Y. 1996. Robot see, robot do: An overview of robot imitation. *AISB Workshop on Learning in Robots and Animals*, Brighton, UK.

Doyle R. J., Atkinson D. J., Doshi R. S., Generating perception requests and expectations to verify the execution of plans, in *Proceedings of AAAI-86*.

Festinger, L. 1954. A theory of social comparison processes. *Human Relations*, 7, pp. 117-140.

Firby, J. 1987. An investigation into reactive planning in complex domains. In *Proceedings of the National Conference on Artificial Intelligence (AAAI-87)*.

Grosz, B.; and Kraus, S. 1996. Collaborative Plans for Complex Group Actions. In *Artificial Intelligence*. Vol. 86, pp. 269-358.

Halpern, J. Y. and Moses, Y. 1990. Knowledge and Common Knowledge in a Distributed Environment., in *Distributed Computing* 37(3), pp. 549-587.

Huber, M. J.; and Durfee, E. H. 1996. An Initial Assessment of Plan-Recognition-Based Coordination for Multi-Agent Teams. In *Proceedings of the Second International Conference on Multi-Agent Systems.*.

Jennings, N. 1995. Controlling Cooperative Problem Solving in Industrial Multi-Agent System Using Joint Intentions. *Artificial Intelligence*. Vol. 75 pp. 195-240.

Kitano, H; Asada, M.; Kuniyoshi, Y.; Noda, I.; and Osawa, E. 1995. RoboCup: The Robot World Cup Initiative. In *Proceedings of IJCAI-95 Workshop on Entertainment and AI/Alife*.

Levesque, H. J.; Cohen, P. R.; Nunes, J. 1990. On acting together, in *Proceedings of the National Conference on Artificial Intelligence (AAAI-1990)*, Menlo Park, California, AAAI Press.

Newell A., 1990. *Unified Theories of Cognition*. Harvard University Press.

Tambe, M.; Johnson W. L.; Jones, R.; Koss, F.; Laird, J. E.; Rosenbloom, P. S.; and Schwamb, K. 1995. Intelligent Agents for interactive simulation environments. *AI Magazine*, 16(1) (Spring).

Tambe, M. 1996. Tracking Dynamic Team Activity, in *Proceedings of the Thirteenth National Conference on Artificial Intelligence (AAAI-96)*.

Tambe, M. 1997. Towards Flexible Teamwork, in *Journal of Artificial Intelligence Research*, Vol. 7. pp. 83-124.

Toyama, K.; and Hager, G. D. 1997. If at First You Don't Succeed..., in *Proceedings of the Fourteenth National Conference on Artificial Intelligence (AAAI-97)*. pp. 3-9.

Williams, B. C.; and Nayak, P. P. 1996. A Model-Based Approach to Reactive Self-Configuring Systems. In *Proceedings of the Thirteenth National Conference on Artificial Intelligence (AAAI-96)*.

Artificial Intelligence and Education

Procedural help in Andes: Generating hints using a Bayesian network student model

Abigail S. Gertner and **Cristina Conati** and **Kurt VanLehn**
Learning Research & Development Center
University of Pittsburgh
gertner+@pitt.edu, conati@pogo.isp.pitt.edu, vanlehn+@pitt.edu

Abstract

One of the most important problems for an intelligent tutoring system is deciding how to respond when a student asks for help. Responding cooperatively requires an understanding of both what solution path the student is pursuing, and the student's current level of domain knowledge. Andes, an intelligent tutoring system for Newtonian physics, refers to a probabilistic student model to make decisions about responding to help requests. Andes' student model uses a Bayesian network that computes a probabilistic assessment of three kinds of information: (1) the student's general knowledge about physics, (2) the student's specific knowledge about the current problem, and (3) the abstract plans that the student may be pursuing to solve the problem. Using this model, Andes provides feedback and hints tailored to the student's knowledge and goals.

Introduction

Many different kinds of computer programs have to decide how to respond when their users ask for help, and some must even decide when help is needed. Both of these tasks involve a great deal of uncertainty, especially in the case of Intelligent Tutoring Systems (ITS), where there is uncertainty about both the student's intentions and what the student knows about the task domain.

The problem we address in this paper is how to decide what to say when a student needs help solving a problem, given observations of what the student has done already. Our solution uses a probabilistic model of the student's knowledge and goals to decide between alternatives. We have developed a procedure that searches the solution space of the problem the student is working on to find a proposition that is both part of the solution path the student is probably pursuing, and that the student is unlikely to know. This proposition will be the subject of the help given to the student. Furthermore, we use a theory of hinting to model the effect of the help that has been given on the student's mental state. This framework for responding to help requests is implemented in Andes, an ITS for Newtonian physics.

Copyright ©1998, American Association for Artificial Intelligence (www.aaai.org). All rights reserved.

Andes' tutor uses *coached problem solving* (VanLehn 1996), a method of teaching cognitive skills in which the tutor and the student collaborate to solve problems. In coached problem solving, the initiative in the student-tutor interaction changes according to the progress being made. As long as the student proceeds along a correct solution, the tutor merely indicates agreement with each step. When the student stumbles on part of the problem, the tutor helps the student overcome the impasse by providing hints that lead the student back to a correct solution path. In this setting, a critical problem for the tutor is to interpret the student's actions and the line of reasoning that the student is following so that it can conform its hints to that line of reasoning.

This paper first describes how Andes' probabilistic student model is created and how it represents various aspects of the student's mental state while solving a problem. We then demonstrate how Andes uses this student model to generate hints that are both relevant and appropriate to the student's understanding of the domain.

The Andes Tutoring System

Andes has a modular architecture, as shown in Figure 1. The left side of Figure 1 shows the authoring environment. Prior to run time, a problem author creates both the graphical description of the problem, and the corresponding coded problem definition. Andes' problem solver uses this definition to automatically generate a model of the problem solution space called the *solution graph*.

The right side of the figure shows the run-time student environment. The student interface, known as the Workbench, sends student entries to the Action Interpreter, which looks them up in the solution graph and provides immediate feedback as to whether the entries are correct or incorrect. More detailed feedback is provided by Andes' Help System. Both the Action Interpreter and the Help System refer to the student model to make decisions about what kind of feedback and help to give the student. The most important part of the student model is a Bayesian network (Pearl 1988) that is constructed and updated by the Assessor, and provides probabilistic estimates of the student's goals, beliefs, and knowledge (Conati et al. 1997). The student model also contains information about what problems the student has worked on, what interface features they have

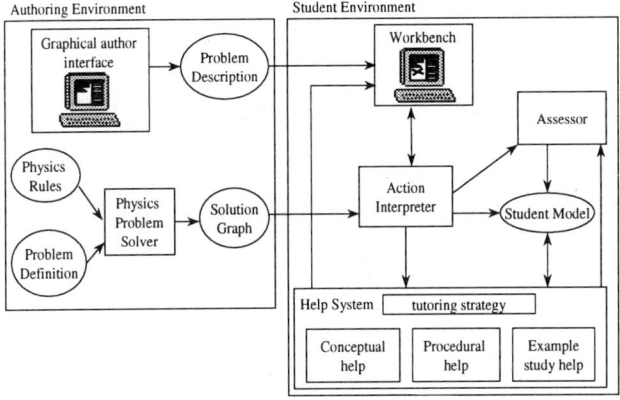

Figure 1: The Andes System Architecture. Rectangles are system modules, ellipses are data structures.

used, and what help they have received from the system in the past.

The Andes Student Modeling Framework

Inferring an agent's plan from a partial sequence of observable actions is a task that involves inherent uncertainty, since often the same observable actions can belong to different plans. In coached problem solving, two additional sources of uncertainty increase the difficulty of the plan recognition task. First, coached problem solving often involves interactions in which most of the important reasoning is hidden from the coach's view. Second, there is additional uncertainty regarding what domain knowledge the student has and can bring to bear in solving problems. While substantial research has been devoted to using probabilistic reasoning frameworks to deal with the inherent uncertainty of plan recognition (Charniak & Goldman 1993; Huber, Durfee, & Wellman 1994; Pynadath & Wellman 1995), none of it encompasses applications where much uncertainty concerns the user's planning and domain knowledge. On the other hand, probabilistic approaches to student modeling mostly assume certainty in plan recognition and use probabilistic techniques to model uncertainty about knowledge (Anderson *et al.* 1995; Jameson 1995).

Andes uses a framework for student modeling that performs plan recognition while taking into account both the uncertainty about the student's plans and the uncertainty about the student's knowledge state (Conati *et al.* 1997). By integrating these two kinds of information, Andes' student model is able to perform three functions: *plan recognition*, *prediction* of the student's future goals and actions, and *long-term assessment* of the student's domain knowledge. The framework uses a Bayesian network to represent and update the student model on-line, *during* problem solving (see Conati *et al.*, 1997, for a discussion of the issues involved in using Bayesian networks for on-line student modeling). In the following two sections we describe the structure of the student model and how it is created.

Generating the solution graph

Like its two predecessors, OLAE (Martin & VanLehn 1995) and POLA (Conati & VanLehn 1996), Andes automatically constructs its Bayesian networks from the output of a problem solver that generates all the acceptable solutions to a problem. We have based Andes' problem solver's rules on the representation used by Cascade (VanLehn, Jones, & Chi 1992), a cognitive model of knowledge acquisition developed from an analysis of protocols of students studying worked example problems. The rules are being developed in collaboration with three physics professors who are the domain experts for the Andes project.

In addition to knowledge about the qualitative and quantitative physics rules necessary to solve complex physics problems, Andes' problem solver has explicit knowledge about the abstract plans that an expert might use to solve problems, and about which Andes will tutor students. Thus, given an initial description of the problem situation and a problem-solving goal, Andes produces a hierarchical dependency network including, in addition to all acceptable solutions to the problem in terms of qualitative propositions and equations, the abstract plans for generating those solutions. This network, called the *solution graph*, represents Andes' model of the solution space.

For example, consider the problem statement shown in Figure 2. The problem solver starts with the top-level goal of finding the final velocity of the car. From this goal, it forms the sub-goal of using a kinematics equation, which involves several quantities including the car's acceleration and displacement. Since the acceleration of the car is unknown, the problem solver forms a sub-goal to find it, which in turn leads to a goal of using Newton's second law applied to the car.

When all applicable rules have fired, the result is a partially ordered network of propositions leading from the top-level goal to a set of equations that are sufficient to solve for the sought quantity. This network, including all propositions and the rules that were used to generate them, is saved as the solution graph. Figure 3 shows a section of the solution graph for this problem, showing the relationship between the goals of finding the final velocity and finding the acceleration, and the actions that address those goals.

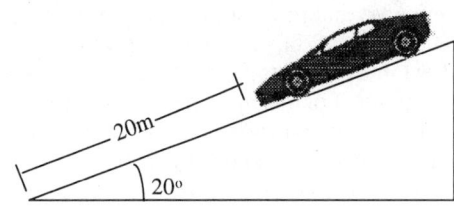

A 2000kg car at the top of a 20° inclined driveway 20m long slips its parking brake and rolls down. Assume that the driveway is frictionless. At what speed will it hit the garage door?

Figure 2: A physics problem.

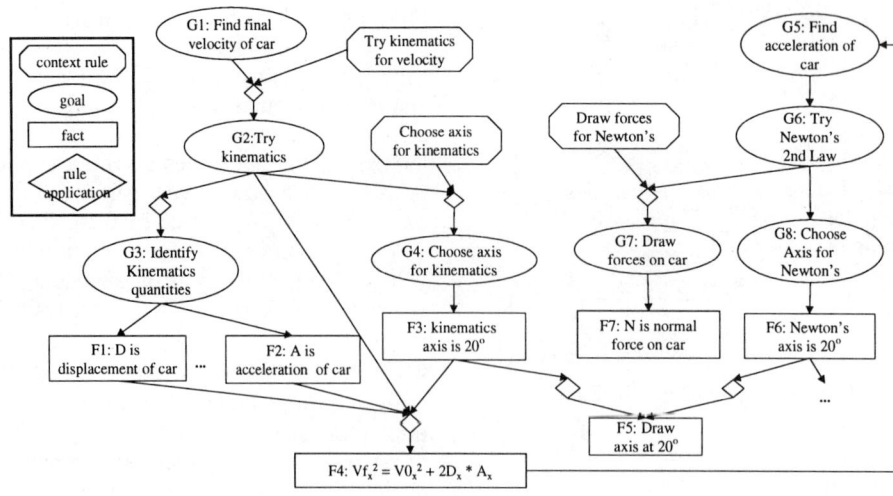

Figure 3: A solution graph segment for the car problem. Some rule nodes have been left out for readability.

The Assessor's Bayesian Network

The Assessor's Bayesian network is automatically generated each time the student selects a new problem. The structure of the Bayesian network is taken directly from the structure of the solution graph. The network contains five kinds of nodes, shown in Figure 3 using different shapes:

1. *Context-Rule nodes* model the ability to apply a rule in a specific problem solving context in which it may be used.

2. *Fact nodes* represent the probability that the student knows a fact that is part of the problem solution.

3. *Goal nodes* represent the probability that the student has been pursuing a goal that is part of the problem solution.

4. *Rule-Application nodes* represent the probability that the student has applied a piece of physics knowledge represented by a context-rule to derive a new fact or goal.

5. *Strategy nodes* (not shown in Figure 3) correspond to points where the student can choose among alternative plans to solve a problem.

To convert the solution graph into a Bayesian network, it is first annotated with prior probabilities for all the top level nodes – the rule nodes and propositions that were given in the problem statement. All other nodes are given a conditional probability table describing the relationship between the node and its parents. For example, each rule-application node has as parents exactly one rule node, corresponding to the rule that is being applied, and one or more goal and/or fact nodes, corresponding to the propositions that must be true in order to apply the rule. The conditional probability table of a rule-application node captures the assumption that the student will likely do the consequent action if all of the antecedent knowledge (Rule, Goals, and Facts) is available, but if any of the knowledge is not available, the student cannot apply the rule.

When a student performs an action in the Andes Workbench, the Action Interpreter determines which fact or goal nodes in the solution graph, if any, correspond to that action. If one or more are identified, the Assessor is told to set the value of those nodes to True, and the entire network is then re-evaluated to reflect the effects of the new observation.

In general, evidence that a fact is known causes the probabilities of the antecedents of the corresponding node(s) in the solution graph to go up, indicating the model's *explanation* for the new evidence. Likewise, the probabilities of goals and facts that are consequences of knowing the fact will also go up, corresponding to the model's *prediction* of future actions that have become more likely as a result of observing the evidence. If the student asks for help, Andes can use the probabilities produced by the Assessor to inform its decisions regarding the part of the solution graph about which to begin hinting.

Procedural help: deciding what to say

In a Wizard of Oz experiment designed to provide information about the kinds of help students using Andes might need (VanLehn 1996), students solved problems on an interface similar to Andes, requesting help by sending a message to a human tutor. In this experiment, the most common help request students made was of the form, "I'm stuck. What should I do next?" (27 occurrences out of 73 help requests). The part of Andes' help system that answers this kind of help request is called the Procedural Helper.

In most tutoring systems, such as Anderson's model tracing tutors (Anderson *et al.* 1995), it is easy to decide what the topic of a hint should be because the student is only allowed to follow one solution path. If there are several correct paths through the solution space, the tutor asks the student which one the student wants to pursue. Thus, the tutor always knows what path the student is on, and when she indicates that she is stuck, the only possible hint is to point to the next performable step on that path.

In the physics task domain, however, there are many correct solution paths because inferences can be done in many different orders. In some problems, there may be more than one alternative solution strategy that may be brought to bear, resulting in the application of different physics laws and the use of different equations. Thus, it is impractical to keep asking the student which path she is following. In fact, our own informal analyses of tutoring transcripts indicate that human tutors rarely ask students what their goals are before giving a hint. Moreover, Andes seldom forces students explicitly to enter all the steps of a derivation in the interface. These properties of the domain make it very difficult to know what path the student is pursuing, and where along that path the student was when she got stuck.

Nonetheless, it would be extremely infelicitous if Andes gave hints intended to help a student along one part of the solution path when the student is actually focusing on a different part of the path, or possibly going down a different path altogether. Thus, Andes uses its Bayesian network to infer which part of the solution the student is working on and where she got stuck. This is a form of probabilistic plan recognition, and it is one of the main reasons for using Bayesian networks in Andes.

As with any plan recognition task, Andes needs an inductive bias to guide the search through the solution space for the student's most likely solution path. The bias that Andes uses is to assume that the student traverses the solution graph in depth-first order when generating a solution. This means that if a student has just identified the displacement of the car in Figure 3 (node F1 in the diagram), they would not be expected to go on to draw an axis (node F5) until they had also identified the car's acceleration (node F2). Following this assumption, Andes searches the solution graph depth-first for paths that begin with the student's most recent action.

Since we are trying to identify an appropriate part of the solution to give a hint about, we want to determine where the student is probably getting stuck. In other words, we have to find a node that the student is not likely to have in mind already. The depth-first traversal of the solution graph therefore will terminate whenever it reaches a node whose probability is below a certain threshold (currently 0.8). The search will also terminate if it reaches a node that must be entered before continuing with the rest of the solution because it is a precondition for applying any other rule along that path.

The result of this traversal is a set of paths through the solution graph, each beginning with the student's most recent action, and terminating with a node that has a probability of less than .8, or that must be entered. In our example (Figure 3), suppose that the last action observed is F5. Additionally, suppose the probabilities of F3, F6, G2, G3, G4, G6, and G8 are above .8, and the probabilities of F1, F2, F7, and G7 are below .8. The set of paths found in the part of the graph that is shown will be:

1. F5 → F3 → G4 → G2 → G3 → F1
2. F5 → F3 → G4 → G2 → G3 → F2
3. F5 → F6 → G8 → G6 → G7

Next, Andes must choose one of these paths as the one it will use to guide the student. To do this, it looks at the joint probability of all the nodes in each path *except* the last node, which is the one that the student is supposed to be stuck on. The path with the highest value is chosen as being the most likely to represent the student's current path, and thus the best candidate for procedural help.

In the absence of additional evidence, if the rules associated with kinematics have higher prior probability than the rules associated with Newton's law, then paths 1 and 2 will be chosen over the third path. However, since these two paths are identical except for the last node, they will have exactly the same joint probability. In such a situation, we need a metric to decide which of the last nodes in each path is the best candidate for a hint, given that both are on paths that the student is probably pursuing. We choose the node with the lowest probability, because it is the one that the student is most likely to be stuck on.

If, on the other hand, the student has performed some actions associated with the Newton's law plan, such as drawing a vector for the weight of the car (not shown in Figure 3), the third path will be more likely, and node G7 will therefore be selected as the topic of the hint to be generated.

Generating hints from BN nodes

Evidence from studies of the performance of human tutors suggests that one of the main reasons human tutors are effective is that they are able to let students do most of the work in correcting errors and overcoming impasses, while providing just enough guidance to keep them on a productive solution path (Merril *et al.* 1992). Likewise, in generating help from the target node selected by the procedure described above, Andes tries to encourage the student to solve the problem on her own by giving hints, rather than by directly telling her what actions to perform.

Andes' Procedural Helper uses templates to generate hints from nodes in the solution graph. For each goal and fact in its knowledge base, Andes has an associated *sequence* of hint templates, ranging from quite general to very specific. Slots in the templates are filled in with descriptions of the appropriate objects in the problem situation. When guiding a student towards a particular goal, Andes begins by using the most general templates to encourage the student to generate the next solution step with as little extra information as possible.

For example, suppose that Andes has selected node G7 from Figure 3, representing the goal of drawing all of the forces on the car, as the topic of its next hint as described in the previous section. The templates associated with this goal are:[1]

(3 *"Think about what you need to do in order to have a complete free body diagram for [   ]."* body)

---

[1]The numbers before each template indicate the specificity of the hint. The arguments after each template string tell the system how to fill in the corresponding slots, indicated by square brackets.

(5 *"Draw all the forces acting on [   ] as part of your free body diagram."* body)

Choosing the first template from this list, and substituting the appropriate descriptions of objects or quantities from the problem into the slots, Andes would generate the hint,

Hint 1 *"Think about what you need to do in order to have a complete free body diagram for [the car]."*

If the student does not know what to do after receiving the first general hint, she can select a follow-up question by clicking one of three buttons:

- Explain Further: Andes will display the next hint in the hint sequence, which gives slightly more specific information about the proposition represented by the node.

- How do I do that?: Andes finds a child of the hint node that has not yet been addressed, and gives a hint about that node. If there is more than one child node, it chooses the one with the lowest probability, assuming that is the node the student is most likely to be stuck on.

- Why?: Andes displays a canned description of the rule that was used by the problem solver to derive that node.

In the above example, after seeing Hint 1, clicking on the "Explain Further" button results in the hint,

Hint 2 *"Draw all the forces acting on [the car] as part of your free body diagram."*

which is a more specific description of the goal in question. Clicking "How do I do that?" after Hint 1, on the other hand, might result in the hint,

Hint 3 *"Do you know of any [other] forces acting on [the car]?"*

which points to a sub-goal of drawing the forces on the car, namely drawing the normal force (the word "other" is used optionally if at least one force has already been drawn).

The discourse model

Another important consideration when generating hints is the current discourse context. In particular, Andes should avoid giving a hint that the student has already seen. Therefore for each node in the solution graph, Andes keeps a record of what hints about that node it has given the student. When the hint selection algorithm selects a node that has already been mentioned, the Procedural Helper tries to give a more specific hint than was given last time. If the most specific hint available has already been given, Andes will repeat it.

Andes also uses its representation of what the student has done so far to generate referring expressions. For example, if the student has defined the acceleration of the car as A, Andes will refer to it by the variable A, rather than with its description. So Hint 1 above would be, "To find A, try using a principle that mentions acceleration."

Updating the student model after a hint

An ITS must take into account the hints that it has given when interpreting the student's actions and updating the student model. Typically, a student will ask for hints down to a certain level of specificity before taking the action suggested by the hint. Thus, the student modeler should interpret student actions taken in response to a hint differently depending on that hint's specificity.

This problem has been solved differently in different ITS's. Many tutors, e.g. (Anderson *et al.* 1995), assume that hints affect the knowledge directly. For instance, strong hints may cause the student to learn the knowledge required to make the action. Thus, it does not matter whether a student's correct entry was preceded by a strong hint, a weak hint or no hint at all. If they make a correct entry, then they probably know the requisite knowledge. This seems a bit unrealistic to us, especially when the last possible hint is so specific that it essentially tells the student what to enter (as often occurs in Andes, the Andersonian tutors, and many others). Perhaps the most elaborate and potentially accurate method of interpreting hints is used by the SMART ITS (Shute 1995), which uses a non-linear function derived from reports by experts, that boosts the level of mastery by different amounts depending on the specificity of the hint and the level of mastery before the hint was given.

Our approach attempts to be more principled by modeling a simple "theory" of hints directly in the Bayesian network. The theory is based on two assumptions:

- Hints from Andes' Procedural Helper are worded so as to remind the student of the requisite knowledge, rather than teach it. (Teaching missing pieces of knowledge is handled by the Conceptual Help system, which is not discussed here.) Thus, procedural hints do not directly cause students to master knowledge.

- A strong hint increases the chance that the student can guess the next action rather than derive it from her knowledge. Thus, a hint can cause an entry directly.

In other words, hints affect actions directly but not domain knowledge.

This mini-theory of hints is encoded in the Bayesian network as follows. Whenever a hint has been given for a node, a new node is attached to the network as its parent, representing the fact that a hint was given. The conditional probability table on the target node is modified so that the target node may be true if it was derived either via the application of a known rule, or via guessing based on the hint. Moreover, the higher the specificity level of the hint, the more likely that the target node is true (The specificy levels are the numbers that appear at the beginning of the hint templates shown earlier). In operation, this means that when the student makes the corresponding entry, the hint node "explains away" some of that evidence, so the probability of mastery of the requisite knowledge is not raised as much as it would be if the student made that entry without receiving a hint.

Evaluations of Andes

In the Fall semester of 1997, an earlier version of Andes was used in a formative evaluation by students in the introductory physics course at the US Naval Academy. About

160 students were asked to use Andes in their dorm rooms to do their physics homework for three weeks. Students were given a short pre- and post-test to assess the effect of using Andes on their understanding of physics concepts. Only 85 students ended up using the system enough to evaluate their test results. A multiple regression for these students, with post-test score as the dependent variable, shows a small but significant positive effect of the number of times a student asked for help ($p < .05$, $R^2 = .016$). The only other variable to have a significant effect on post-test score was the student's pre-test score.

The small size of the effect of asking for help, together with reports from students that the hints did not always seem relevant to what they were thinking about at the time they asked for help, led us to revise the plan recognition algorithm to its present form. In the version of Andes used in the first evaluation, the plan recognition strategy was simply to assume that the goal node with the highest probability in the entire network was the one the student was addressing. However, since there is no temporal information represented in the Bayesian network, this meant that the system was ignoring evidence about *when* actions had been done. The version of the procedural help system described in this paper addresses this problem by using the student's most recent action as the starting point in its search for the next hint target.

Preliminary results from 25 students who used the new version of Andes in the Spring semester show that the number of help requests per problem went up from 0.19 in the Fall to 0.52 in the Spring. Test results for these students are not yet available as of this writing.

As the project moves forward, we will continue to gather data from such formative evaluations. These evaluations are invaluable in both assessing the effectiveness of the system and suggesting new directions and improvements.

Future work and conclusions

There are several areas of future work planned for the Andes ITS. These include:

- Improved language generation: for instance, using discourse cues and more sophisticated surface generation to improve the coherence and grammaticality of the output.

- Tutorial planning: a new project (CIRCLE) is looking at the problem of deciding what kind of response to give to the student at any given time (e.g. a hint vs. an longer explanatory subdialog vs. no response).

In this paper we have presented a framework for generating responses to help requests that is particularly relevant to domains in which there is uncertainty about the user's mental state. We would argue that this uncertainty exists to some degree in most domains for which help systems are implemented. Our Procedural Help module performs three functions: it decides on the most effective topic for its help, it generates a hint about that topic taking into account the previous discourse context, and it updates its model of the user's mental state as a result of having received the hint. Furthermore, the integration of these abilities with a general knowledge assessment tool means that Andes can adapt its help as the student's level of knowledge changes over time.

Acknowledgements

The authors would like to thank Patricia Albacete, Zhendong Niu, Kay Schulze, Stephanie Siler, Bob Shelby, and Mary Wintersgill for their many ongoing contributions to this work. This research is supported by ARPA's Computer Aided Education and Training Initiative under grant N660001-95-C-8367, by ONR's Cognitive Science Division under grant N00014-96-1-0260, and by AFOSR's Artificial Intelligence Division under grant F49620-96-1-0180.

References

Anderson, J.; Corbett, A.; Koedinger, K.; and Pelletier, R. 1995. Cognitive tutors: Lessons learned. *The Journal of the Learning Sciences* 4(2):167–207.

Charniak, E., and Goldman, R. P. 1993. A Bayesian model of plan recognition. *Artificial Intelligence* 64:53–79.

Conati, C., and VanLehn, K. 1996. POLA: a student modeling framework for Probabilistic On-Line Assessment of problem solving performance. In *Proceedings of the 5th International Conference on User Modeling*.

Conati, C.; Gertner, A. S.; VanLehn, K.; and Druzdzel, M. J. 1997. On-line student modeling for coached problem solving using Bayesian networks. In *Proceedings of UM-97, Sixth International Conference on User Modeling*, 231–242. Sardinia, Italy: Springer.

Huber, M.; Durfee, E.; and Wellman, M. 1994. The automated mapping of plans for plan recognition. In *Proceedings of the 10th Conference on Uncertainty in Artificial Intelligence*, 344–351.

Jameson, A. 1995. Numerical uncertainty management in user and student modeling: an overview of systems and issues. *User Moldeing and User-Adapted Interaction* 3-4(5):193–251.

Martin, J., and VanLehn, K. 1995. Student assessment using Bayesian nets. *International Journal of Human-Computer Studies* 42:575–591.

Merril, D. C.; Reiser, B. J.; Ranney, M.; and Trafton, J. G. 1992. Effective tutoring techniques: A comparison of human tutors and intelligent tutoring systems. *The Journal of the Learning Sciences* 3(2):277–305.

Pearl, J. 1988. *Probabilistic Reasoning in Intelligent Systems: Networks of Plausible Inference*. San Mateo, Calif: Morgan Kaufman.

Pynadath, D. V., and Wellman, M. P. 1995. Accounting for context in plan recognition, with application to traffic monitoring. In *Proceedings of the 11h Conference on Uncertainty in Artificial Intelligence*, 472–481.

Shute, V. J. 1995. SMART: Student modeling approach for responsive tutoring. *User Modeling and User-Adapted Interation* 5:1–44.

VanLehn, K.; Jones, R. M.; and Chi, M. T. H. 1992. A model of the self-explanation effect. *The Journal of the Learning Sciences* 2(1):1–59.

VanLehn, K. 1996. Conceptual and meta learning during coached problem solving. In Frasson, C.; Gauthier, G.; and Lesgold, A., eds., *Proceedings of the 3rd International Conference on Intelligent Tutoring Systems ITS '96*. Springer. 29–47.

Generating Coordinated Natural Language and 3D Animations for Complex Spatial Explanations*

Stuart G. Towns and **Charles B. Callaway** and **James C. Lester**

Multimedia Laboratory
Department of Computer Science
North Carolina State University
Raleigh, NC 27695-7534
{sgtowns, cbcallaw, lester}@eos.ncsu.edu

Abstract

Dynamically providing students with clear explanations of complex spatial concepts is critical for a broad range of knowledge-based educational and training systems. This calls for a realtime solution that can dynamically create 3D animated explanations that artfully integrate well-chosen speech with rich visualizations. Unfortunately, planning the integrated creation of 3D animation and spatial linguistic utterances in realtime requires coordinating the visual presentation of 3D objects and generating appropriate spatial phrases that accurately reflect the relative position, orientation, and direction of the objects presented. We present a visuo-linguistic framework for generating multimedia spatial explanations combining 3D animation and speech that complement one another. Because 3D animation planners require spatial knowledge in a geometric form and natural language generators require spatial knowledge in a linguistic form, a realtime multimedia planner interposed between the visual and linguistic components can serve as a mediator. This framework has been implemented in CINESPEAK, a multimedia explanation generator consisting of a visuo-linguistic mediator, a 3D animation planner, and a realtime natural language generator with a speech synthesizer. CINESPEAK has been used in conjunction with a prototype 3D learning environment in the domain of physics to generate realtime multimedia explanations of three dimensional electromagnetic fields, forces, and electrical current.

Introduction

As multimedia technologies reach ever higher levels of sophistication, knowledge-based learning environments and intelligent training systems can create increasingly effective educational experiences. Moreover, if learning environments could leverage the growing body of work on intelligent multimedia systems in the form of knowledge-based 2D graphics generation (Roth, Mattis, & Mesnard 1991; Mittal et al. 1995), automated static 3D graphics production (Wahlster et al. 1993; Feiner 1985; Seligmann & Feiner 1991; Feiner & McKeown 1993), and 3D animation generation (Bares & Lester 1997; Butz & Krüger 1996; Christianson et al. 1996; Karp & Feiner 1993), they could fluently generate multimedia explanations that clearly communicate complex concepts. A critical functionality required in many domains is the ability to unambiguously communicate spatial knowledge. Learning environments for the basic sciences frequently focus on physical structures and the fundamental forces that act on them in the world, and training systems for technical domains often revolve around the structure and function of complex devices. Explanations of electromagnetism, for example, must effectively communicate the complex spatial relationships governing the directions and magnitudes of multiple vectors representing currents and electromagnetic fields, many of which are orthogonal to one another.

Because text-only spatial explanations are notoriously inadequate for expressing complex spatial relationships, realtime multimedia spatial explanation generation could contribute significantly to a broad range of learning environments and training systems. This calls for a computational model of multimedia explanation generation for complex spatial knowledge. Unfortunately, planning the integrated creation of 3D animation and spatial linguistic utterances in realtime requires coordinating the visual presentation of 3D objects and generating appropriate spatial phrases that accurately reflect the relative position, orientation, and direction of the objects presented. Although a number of projects have studied the automated coordination of natural language and 2D graphics (Feiner & McKeown 1993), previous work on knowledge-based 3D animation either avoids accompanying narration altogether (Butz & Krüger 1996; Christianson et al. 1996; Karp & Feiner 1993), employs canned audio clips in conjunction with generated 3D graphics (Bares &

---

*Support for this work was provided by a grant from the NSF (Faculty Early Career Development Award IRI-9701503), the IntelliMedia Initiative of North Carolina State University, The William S. Kenan Institute for Engineering, Technology and Science, and an industrial gift from Novell, Inc. Copyright ©1998, American Association of Artificial Intelligence (www.aaai.org). All rights reserved.

Lester 1997), or focuses on either basic coordination issues (Wahlster *et al.* 1993) or on the challenges of incorporating animated characters (André & Rist 1996) rather than on coordinating the generation of language and visualizations for complex 3D spatial relationships.

To address this problem, we have developed the visuo-linguistic explanation planning framework for generating multimedia spatial explanations combining 3D animation and speech that complement one another. Because 3D animation planners require spatial knowledge in a geometric form and natural language generators require spatial knowledge in a linguistic form, a realtime multimedia planner interposed between the visual and linguistic components serves as a mediator. This framework has been implemented in CineSpeak, a multimedia explanation generator consisting of a media-independent explanation planner, a visuo-linguistic mediator, a 3D animation planner, and a realtime natural language generator with a speech synthesizer. CineSpeak has been used in conjunction with PhysViz (Figure 1), a prototype 3D learning environment in the domain of physics, to generate realtime multimedia explanations of three dimensional electromagnetic fields, forces, and electrical current.

Spatial Explanation Generation

A critical functionality of knowledge-based learning environments and training systems (Burton & Brown 1982; Hollan, Hutchins, & Weitzman 1987; Lesgold *et al.* 1992) is automatically providing students with clear explanations of spatial phenomena. For the same reason that in psycho-social frameworks of comprehension, hearers interpret linguistic events in concrete contexts, speakers (and hence, spatial explanation generators) must carefully consider the physical context in which utterances are generated (Fillmore 1975). Generating clear spatial explanations therefore entails addressing six fundamental problems, each of which can be illustrated with the difficulties presented by an explanation system for the domain of physics that must communicate the basic principles of electromagnetism:

- *Complementarity of 3D Animation and Speech:* Because of the conceptual complexity of spatial knowledge, even three-dimensional animations without accompanying explanatory speech are too limiting. For example, explanations of how to apply the right-hand rule[1] to solve E&M problems require both (1) spoken natural language about how the fingers and thumb correspond respectively to the current and magnetic force and (2) visual demonstrations of the spatial relationships bearing on the alignment of the thumb and fingers with the particular orientations of forces, fields, and current in the world. While previous work has addressed the coordination of 2D graphics and natural language (Maybury 1994; Feiner & McKeown 1993), work on 3D animation generation either does not address natural language generation issues (Bares & Lester 1997; Butz & Krüger 1996; Christianson *et al.* 1996; Karp & Feiner 1993) or does not explore natural language generation capabilities required of complex spatial knowledge (Wahlster *et al.* 1993; André & Rist 1996).

- *Physical Context Impact on Visuo-Linguistic Utterances:* Because of the inherent difficulties in linguistically expressing spatial relationships, generating spatial natural language poses enormous difficulties. While foundational work has studied generating spatial natural language, e.g., scene description generation (Novak 1987) and spatial layout description generation (Sibun 1992), the interplay between relative and absolute coordinate systems must be carefully monitored. For example, in explaining how magnets induce a field that flows from the north pole of a magnet to a south pole of another magnet, and explaining how current in a wire flows from positive electrodes to negative ones, the relative directions that the field and current travel in a physical environment depend on the absolute locations of the poles and electrodes. The language employed to realize this message is therefore highly dependent on (1) the orientation of objects in the world and (2) the students' perspective on these objects, e.g., whether she is viewing them from in front, to the side, or behind.

- *Synchronization of 3D Animation and Speech:* Just as in the coordination of natural language and 2D graphics (Maybury 1994; Feiner & McKeown 1993) when the timing of events must be considered, the timing of visual cues and events must be synchronized with the relevant spatial utterances for 3D. For example, in explaining how a particular section of a wire has a magnetic force acting on it, when the speech refers to that section of the wire, the animation might highlight that region when the reference to it is spoken.

- *Dual Representation of Geometric and Linguistic Spatial Knowledge:* While we are far from a comprehensive theory of spatial reasoning, which must included techniques for determining individuation, relative position, and relative orientation of objects (Davis 1990; Gapp 1994), integrated 3D spatial explanations combining animation with speech must exploit two types of representations of space. Animation planners for 3D visualizations reason most easily with geometric representations, while natural language generators require spatial representations that can enable them to map spatial relations to grammatically appropriate realizations.

---

[1]The *right hand rule* is a mnemonic device for determining the three dimensional orthogonal spatial relationships that hold between current, magnetic fields, and the resulting magnetic force they induce.

Figure 1: Explaining electromagnetism in the PHYSVIZ learning environment

Generating Coordinated 3D Spatial Explanations

As a student interacts with a 3D learning environment, they manipulate the 3D scene in which the the objects of interest are arranged. For example, a 3D learning environment for the domain of physics might include current-carrying wires and magnetic fields surrounding the poles of magnets. When the student poses a query (Figure 2), a media-independent explanation planner uses it to construct a plan for communicating that goal. By inspecting a knowledge base of domain concepts and using its explanation knowledge about how to communicate, it forms an explanation plan specifying the temporal order in which atomic presentation units should be conveyed. Critically, none of these specifications include low-level geometric or linguistic knowledge; they are restricted to references to domain objects and processes. A visuo-linguistic mediator examines the leaves of the plan and parcels out the specifications to a 3D animation planner and a natural language generator. To the animation planner, the mediator passes visual communicative goals that specify the objects that should be featured. It exploits knowledge of the scene geometries and the 3D models occupying the virtual world to create animation plans. To the language generator, the mediator passes linguistic communicative goals that specify the concepts to be realized in speech. It exploits a grammar capable of producing spatial utterances involving concepts related by direction and orientation and a lexicon with spatial entries to create the appropriate text.

To the great extent possible, the mediator requests both the animation planner and the language generator to run to completion. Because the animation planner makes determinations about the final positions of models, and hence the relative orientations of objects in visualizations, it can run undisturbed. However, because the language generator frequently requires up-to-date knowledge about the positions and orientations of the featured 3D models in order to generate appropriate spatial phrasings, it often must inform the mediator that its knowledge about spatial relationships is incompletely specified. The mediator consults the animation planner's world model and supplies the natural language generator with the necessary spatial features.

The 3D animation specifications and the natural language specifications of the explanation plans are passed to the media realization engines. The 3D animation specifications are passed to the animation renderer, while the text produced by the natural language generator is passed to a speech synthesizer. Visualizations and speech are synchronized in an incremental fashion and presented in atomic presentation units as dictated by the structure of the initial media-independent plan. They are presented in realtime within the 3D learning environment, and the process repeats each time the student poses another query.

Explanation Plan Construction and Visuo-Linguistic Mediation

Given a communicative goal to explain some complex spatial phenomenon, the media-independent explanation planner constructs an explanation plan that will be used in each of the upcoming phases. Using the by-now classic top-down decomposition approach to explanation generation (Suthers 1991; Cawsey 1992; Hovy 1993; Moore 1995), the media explanation determines the following:

- *Explanatory Content:* By extracting relevant propositions from the domain knowledge base, it identifies the key knowledge (spatial and otherwise) to include in the final explanation. For example, when a request to explain how the right-hand rule is used to determine the direction of the magnetic force acting on the wire, it then examines the knowledge base to find the inputs (current and magnetic field), the sub-events (finger pointing and finger curling), and the outputs (the direction of the force).

- *Multimedia Rhetorical Structure:* It must then impose a temporal structure on the knowledge identified above. In the same manner that text has a discourse structure, multimedia explanations have an analogous structure that specifies the order in which to present content in the 3D animations and spoken utterances. For example, the content identified in the example above is organized in the structure depicted in the second level of the explanation plan shown in Figure 3.

- *3D Animation Specifications:* Each of the content specifications is annotated with visual presentation specifications. To maintain the high degree of modularity essential for such multi-faceted computations, it is critical that the media-independent explanation

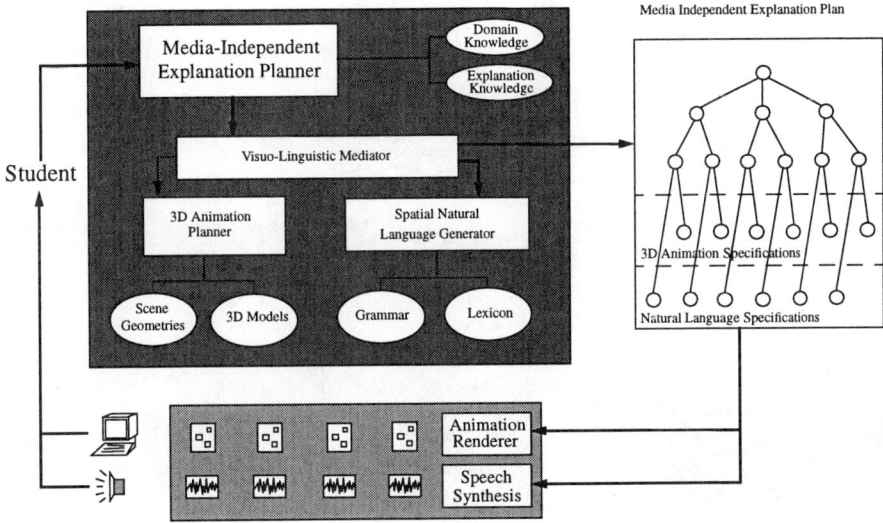

Figure 2: The Visuo-Linguistic Multimedia Explanation Framework

planner not be concerned with *any* of the complexities of 3D animation generation. To accomplish this, the explanation planner expresses its presentation needs with very high-level visual specifications. For example, to visually present the magnetic field, the explanation planner creates the visual annotation (`show-object magnetic-field`) to request that the animation planner create a clear shot of the magnetic field.

- *Linguistic Specifications:* Each of the content specifications of the explanation plan is also annotated with linguistic presentation specifications. As above, all details of natural language generation will be delegated to the linguistic component, so the explanation planner formulates the linguistic requirements without itself considering grammatical or lexicalizaton issues.

Once the media-independent explanation plan has been constructed, the visuo-linguistic mediator coordinates the integrated generation of visual and linguistic expressions of spatial knowledge in the content determined above. However, achieving the desired integration while preserving the modularity of the media planners is complicated by the fact that it (a) has no detailed knowledge of scene geometry and (b) has no detailed knowledge of linguistic techniques for realizing spatial knowledge in appropriate phrases. To address these problems, the mediator conducts itself as follows.

(1) The mediator issues recommendations to the natural language generator by formulating as much of a linguistic specification as it can. (2) If it encounters no spatial uncertainties, i.e., features in the evolving specifications with values that cannot be determined without detailed knowledge of scene geometries, its task is complete and no arbitration is required. Because of the dynamic nature of the virtual camera that "films" the animations, it is likely that spatial uncertainties will arise. For example, if the camera is filming a motor in the PHYSVIZ environment from a front view, from the student's perspective, the current in the wire appears to flow to the left, so the utterance should communicate the notion of "leftward." In contrast, if the camera is filming exactly the same apparatus from a rear view, from the student's perspective, the current in the wire appears to flow to the right, so the utterance should communicate be express a "rightward" direction of flow. It is therefore the responsibility of the mediator to determine the correct orientations and inform the natural language generator. (3) To do so, on an as-needed basis, it requests spatial information from the animation planner, which computes spatial knowledge from scene geometries in its developing animation plan. (4) It next delivers the new spatial knowledge to the natural language generator. (5) Finally, it issues orders for both the animation planner and natural language generator to undertake their respective tasks.

3D Animation Planning

When the animation planner is invoked with high-level visual communication goals, its task is to construct a 3D visualization that clearly communicates the spatial concepts and relations. These include *positions* of objects, such as the north magnetic pole being on top of the motor, *orientations*, such as a magnetic field facing downwards, and *relative orientations*, such as the current in the wire being orthogonal to the magnetic field. Because animated explanations should focus students' attention on the most critical concept at each moment in the explanation (Rieber 1990), the animation planner must carefully lay out the low-level visual specifications which will be passed to the renderer.[2] Planning

---

[2]The 3D animation planner is the result of a long term effort to develop a general-purpose pedagogical 3D animation generator (Bares & Lester 1997).

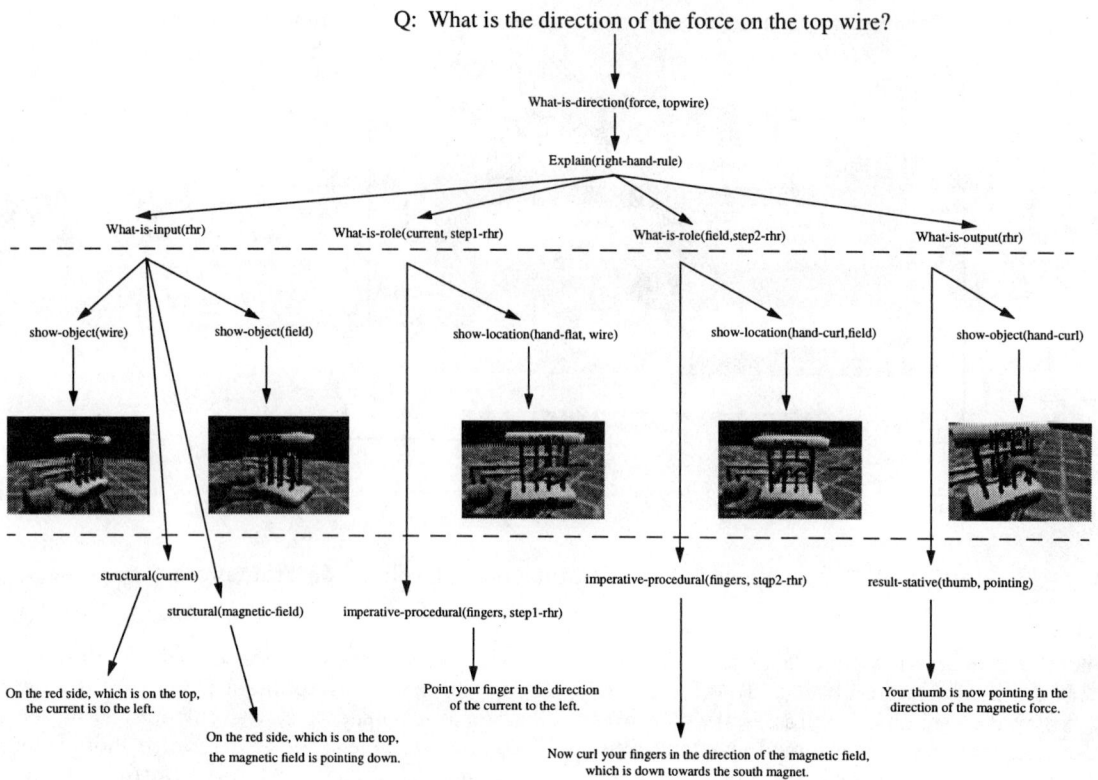

Figure 3: Example 3D multimedia explanation plan

animated explanations is a synthetic process of organizing the raw materials of 3D wire frame models and scene geometries and planning "camera shots" of the virtual camera:

1. *3D Model Selection:* Given a query which specifies a question type, e.g., (explain-function ?X), and a target concept, e.g. battery, the explanation system uses the ontological indices of the knowledge base to retrieve the relevant *concept suite*. Indicating the most relevant visual and auditory elements, a concept suite is defined by a sequence of concepts, each of which is either an object, e.g., Electrode or a process, e.g., Current-Flow. The animation planner then selects the relevant wireframe models and introduces them into the virtual scene.

2. *Camera Shot Planning:* Through judicious camera shot selection, explanations can direct students' attention to the most important aspects of a scene, even in complex scenes presenting a number of objects in motion, and provide visual context. While high and far shots present more information (Mascelli 1965), close-up shots are useful for centering on a single subject (Millerson 1994). To provide visual context, it initially selects far shots for unfamiliar objects, unfamiliar processes, and tracking moving objects. It selects close-ups for presenting the details of familiar objects.

3. *Time Map Construction:* A time map houses parallel series of 3D coordinate specifications for all object positions and orientations, visual effects, and camera positions and orientations, with which the renderer can construct a frame of the explanation for every tick of the clock. These frames will be rendered with the accompanying narration in realtime, creating a continuous immersive visualization in which rich 3D explanations mesh seamlessly with the student's exploration of the environment.

Generating Spatial Natural Language Utterances

Given the spatial linguistic specifications created by the visuo-linguistic mediator, the natural language generator must utilize its grammar and lexicon to create sentences realizing the given content. The natural language generator copes with difficulties of producing spatial text by exploiting knowledge about position, direction, and orientation. It avoids utterances that otherwise would be spatially ambiguous by distinguishing the basic categories of spatial relationships that bear on objects in a three dimensional world. For example, the physics testbed for electromagnetism requires the language generator to ontologically discern the following in order to avoid spatial ambiguity:

- *Positions*: left-side, top-side, bottom-side, right-side, center.

- *Orientations*: `facing-up`, `facing-down`, `facing-left`, `facing-right`, `facing-toward`, `facing-away-from`.
- *Relative Orientations*: `perpendicular`, `parallel`, `oblique`.
- *Rotations*: `clockwise`, `counterclockwise`.
- *Curl Directions*: `curl-towards`, `curl-away-from`, `curl-up`, `curl-down`, `curl-left`, `curl-right`.

This family of spatial primitives enables the generator to appropriately adjudicate between a broad range of ambiguous candidate realizations. For example, although the position `left-side` and the orientation `facing-left` will be realized with the same lexicalization ("left"), the former case will occupy part of a noun phrase and the latter will be adverbial. With the linguistic specifications in hand, the natural language generator's sentence planner exploits the spatial ontology to map the given ontological concepts (e.g., `facing-left`) to the appropriate semantic role necessary to correctly realize the linguistic specification. For example, specifications frequently include features for relative position and pointing direction. These serve as cues to the natural language generator that enable it to distinguish the appropriate semantic roles. To illustrate, Figure 4 shows the result of a specification mapped to a *functional description* (Elhadad 1992). In this specification, the concept of left-side is realized as a locative semantic role because it had been marked in the specification as being a position type. If the primary actor had instead been a direction rather than a position, it would have been mapped not to a locative role but rather to a predicate-modifying adverb.

After the sentence planner constructs functional descriptions, it passes them to a unification-based surface generator (Elhadad 1992) to yield the surface string, which is itself passed to a speech synthesizer and delivered in synchronization with the actions of the associated 3D visualization. This process is repeated for each leaf of the explanation plan as the planner walks across the specifications in a left-to-right order. When the final verbal and visual elements of the explanation have been constructed, they are presented to the student, and the planner awaits the student's next question.

An Implemented Multimedia Explanation Generator

All of the components of the spatial explanation framework have been implemented in a realtime explanation planner that constructs integrated 3D animations and speech for complex three dimensional spatial phenomena. Given queries about directions, orientations, and spatial roles of forces, it generates 3D visualizations, produces coordinated natural language utterances, and synchronizes the two. The explanation planner is implemented in a heterogeneous computing environment consisting of two PentiumPro 200s and a Sparc Ultra communicating via TCP/IP socket protocols over

```
((CAT CLAUSE)
 (CIRCUM
    ((LOCATION
       ((POSITION FRONT)
        (CAT PP)
        (PREP ((LEX ''on'')))
        (NP ((CAT COMMON)
             (DEFINITE YES)
             (LEX ''side'')
             (DESCRIBER ((CAT ADJ)
                         (LEX ''red'')))
             (QUALIFIER
               ((CAT CLAUSE)
                (RESTRICTIVE NO)
                (SCOPE {^ PARTIC LOCATED})
                (PROC ((TYPE LOCATIVE)))
                (PARTIC ((LOCATION
                           ((CAT PP)
                            (PREP === ''on'')
                            (NP ((CAT COMMON)
                                 (COUNTABLE NO)
                                 (LEX ''top'')))))))
                (MOOD SIMPLE-RELATIVE)))))))))
 (PROC ((TYPE LOCATIVE)))
 (PARTIC
    ((LOCATED ((CAT COMMON)
               (DEFINITE YES)
               (LEX ''current'')))
     (LOCATION ((CAT PP)
                (PREP === ''to'')
                (NP ((CAT COMMON)
                     (DEFINITE YES)
                     (LEX ''left side'')))))))
```

Figure 4: Example function description: current

an Ethernet. Both the media-independent explanation planner and mediator were implemented in the CLIPS production system. The 3D animation planner was implemented in C++. The spatial natural language generator was implemented in Harlequin Lispworks and employs the FUF surface generator and SURGE (Elhadad 1992), a comprehensive unification-based English grammar. The animation renderer was created with the OpenGL rendering library, and the speech synthesis module employs the Truetalk synthesizer. With regard to efficiency issues, the media-independent explanation planner, mediator, and animation planner operate in a small number of milliseconds; the natural language generator requires approximately 2–8 seconds, with the bulk of the time consumed by unification.

The PHYSVIZ Testbed

To study CINESPEAK's explanation planning behaviors, it has been incorporated into PHYSVIZ, a prototype 3D learning environment for the domain of high school physics. Physics presents a particularly challenging set of communicative requirements because many fundamental physics concepts are exceptionally hard to visualize. For typical physics students, attempting to understand these concepts by studying static two-dimensional graphics typically yields a less-than-satisfying learning experience. Focusing on concepts of electromagnetism, PHYSVIZ exploits a library of 3D models representing a battery, wires, magnets, and magnetic fields. It also includes a virtual 3D hand that can be used to explain the right-hand rule for determining the direction of magnetic forces. PHYSVIZ was developed by a multidisciplinary design team that included an experienced high school physics teacher. In a numerous sessions spanning a semester, the physicist was posed detailed questions about electromagnetism. His verbal responses and his diagrammatic reasoning guided the design of the 3D models in the learning environment.

Example Explanation Planning Episode

To illustrate CineSpeak's behavior, suppose a student interacting with PhysViz constructs the query, "What is the direction of the force on the top of the wire?" The media independent explanation planner determines that it should create an explanation of the right-hand rule to respond to the question. There are four major steps in explaining the right-hand rule, which will be explained sequentially. It first explains the inputs, the current and the magnetic field and eventually proceeds on to the outcome of the right-hand's rule application, which is that the direction of the magnetic force is equivalent to the resulting orientation of the thumb. This content and the sequential organization are housed in the leaves of the media-independent explanation plan.

The mediator now coordinates the planning of animation and speech. First, the animation planner creates a 3D visualization plan consisting of specifications for the relevant 3D models (the wire, the magnetic field, and the virtual hand), their orientations, and relevant camera views that clearly depict these objects. Next, the mediator creates specifications for the natural language generator, continuing until an impasse is reached resulting from a dearth of up-to-date spatial information. It notes that the relative orientation of the current's direction is from right to left for this particular camera view. It requests and receives this information from the animation planner. It continues in this fashion until complete linguistic specifications have been created. It then passes the full specifications to the natural language generator, which creates a functional description for each.

Finally, the animation plan is passed to the renderer while the text string is passed to the speech synthesizer. As the renderer constructs a 3D visualization depicting the virtual hand pointing in the direction of the current (which it determines is to the left of the screen based on the student's vantage point), the speech synthesizer says, "Point your fingers in the direction of the current to the left." After explaining how the hand curls in the direction of the magnetic field, it concludes by visually demonstrating how the virtual hand's direction and orientation are used to determine the direction of the magnetic force on the top section of the wire while it says, "Your thumb is now pointing in the direction of the magnetic force."

Focus Group Study

To investigate the effectiveness with which CineSpeak generates clear 3D explanations of spatial phenomena, in addition to replicating the physicist's communication techniques (albeit in 3D but with more limited natural language phrasing), we conducted an informal focus group study with nine college-age subjects drawn from both technical and non-technical backgrounds. They were introduced to the PhysViz learning environment interface and briefly grounded in the basic concepts. Because many people unfamiliar with computer-generated speech frequently find it difficult to understand, subjects were first exposed to sample utterances produced by the speech synthesizer. Bearing in mind the caveat that the study was quite informal, results were nevertheless very encouraging:

- *Viewing perspectives:* Subjects unanimously liked the viewing perspectives chosen in the course of explanations and the dynamic highlighting of objects being referred to in the speech.

- *Timing and Synthesis:* Undoubtedly the most problematic aspect of the explanation stemmed from implementation limitations. Most subjects found the long delays between utterances, which were caused primarily by the time spent by the surface generator on unification, to be bothersome and the quality of the speech to be much less than ideal.

- *Superiority of Coordinated Multiple Media:* Perhaps the most telling finding was that the more redundancy between visual cues and verbal utterances, the more subjects understood the concepts. For example, explanations of current do not include visualizations of it other than the mere presence of the wire; explanations of current and its orientation were generated solely with verbal phrasings and an occasional use of the virtual hand. In contrast, explanations of magnetic fields, which employed both visual representations in the form of 3D arrows and magnets as well as verbalizations of the field orientation, were much more easily understood. Because subjects, unprompted, eagerly voiced their strong preferences for the latter over the former, the differences were particularly striking. This finding is consistent with a growing body of empirical evidence on the effectiveness of multiple modalities in intelligent multimedia interfaces, e.g., (Oviatt 1997).

Conclusion

The visuo-linguistic explanation generation framework can be used to create 3D multimedia explanations of complex spatial phenomena. By exploiting a mediator that serves as an intermediary between a 3D animation planner utilizing geometric spatial knowledge and a natural language generator that utilizes linguistic spatial knowledge, the visuo-linguistic explanation framework takes advantage of the strengths of both types of representations to generate clear spatial explanation combining 3D animations and complementary speech. In combination, well-designed visualizations integrated with spatial utterances effectively communicate complex three-dimensional phenomena. While this work provides a strong computational foundation for generating integrated 3D animations and natural language, much remains to be done, particularly with regard to generating 3D spatial explanations of highly dynamic phenomena. This entails extending the animation planner's ability to render 3D models exhibiting more complex behaviors, the natural language generator's dynamic spatial linguistic coverage, and the visuolinguistic mediator's arbitration strategies for coordinating more dynamic spatial knowledge. We will be pursuing these activities in our future work.

Acknowledgements

The authors gratefully acknowledge Dr. Loren Winters of the North Carolina School of Science and Mathematics for collaboration on all aspects of the PHYSVIZ learning environment, William Bares for his generous assistance in integrating the RAPID 3D animation and cinematography system, and Luke Zettlemoyer for his work in preparing the manuscript.

References

André, E., and Rist, T. 1996. Coping with temporal constraints in multimedia presentation planning. In *Proceedings of the Thirteenth National Conference on Artificial Intelligence*, 142–147.

Bares, W. H., and Lester, J. C. 1997. Realtime generation of customized 3D animated explanations for knowledge-based learning environments. In *AAAI-97: Proceedings of the Fourteenth National Conference on Artificial Intelligence*, 347–354.

Burton, R. R., and Brown, J. S. 1982. An investigation of computer coaching for informal learning activities. In Sleeman, D., and Brown, J. S., eds., *Intelligent Tutoring Systems*. London: Academic Press. 79–98.

Butz, A., and Krüger, A. 1996. Lean modeling—the intelligent use of geometrical abstraction in 3D animations. In *Proceedings of the Twelfth European Conference on Artificial Intelligence*, 246–250.

Cawsey, A. 1992. *Explanation and Interaction: The Computer Generation of Explanatory Dialogues*. MIT Press.

Christianson, D. B.; Anderson, S. E.; He, L.-W.; Salesin, D. H.; Weld, D. S.; and Cohen, M. F. 1996. Declarative camera control for automatic cinematography. In *Proceedings of the Thirteenth National Conference on Artificial Intelligence*, 148–155.

Davis, E. 1990. *Representations of Commonsense Knowledge*. San Mateo, CA: Morgan Kaufmann.

Elhadad, M. 1992. *Using Argumentation to Control Lexical Choice: A Functional Unification Implementation*. Ph.D. Dissertation, Columbia University.

Feiner, S. K., and McKeown, K. R. 1993. Automating the generation of coordinated multimedia explanations. In Maybury, M. T., ed., *Intelligent Multimedia Interfaces*. Menlo Park, CA: AAAI Press/The MIT Press. chapter 5, 117–138.

Feiner, S. 1985. APEX: An experiment in the automated creation of pictorial explanations. *IEEE Computer Graphics and Applications* 29–37.

Fillmore, C. 1975. *Santa Cruz Lectures on Deixis 1971*. Available from Indiana University Linguistics Club.

Gapp, K.-P. 1994. Basic meanings of spatial relations: Computation and evaluation in 3D space. In *Proceedings of the Eleventh National Conference on Artificial Intelligence*, 1393–1398.

Hollan, J. D.; Hutchins, E. L.; and Weitzman, L. M. 1987. STEAMER: An interactive, inspectable, simulation-based training system. In Kearsley, G., ed., *Artificial Intelligence and Instruction: Applications and Methods*. Reading, MA: Addison-Wesley. 113–134.

Hovy, E. H. 1993. Automated discourse generation using discourse structure relations. *Artificial Intelligence* 63:341–385.

Karp, P., and Feiner, S. 1993. Automated presentation planning of animation using task decomposition with heuristic reasoning. In *Proceedings of Graphics Interface '93*, 118–127.

Lesgold, A.; Lajoie, S.; Bunzo, M.; and Eggan, G. 1992. SHERLOCK: A coached practice environment for an electronics trouble-shooting job. In Larkin, J. H., and Chabay, R. W., eds., *Computer-Assisted Instruction and Intelligent Tutoring Systems: Shared Goals and Complementary Approaches*. Hillsdale, NJ: Lawrence Erlbaum. 201–238.

Mascelli, J. 1965. *The Five C's of Cinematography*. Cine/Grafic Publications, Hollywood.

Maybury, M. T. 1994. Planning multimedia explanations using communicative acts. In *Proceeding of AAAI-91*, 65–66.

Millerson, G. 1994. *Video Camera Techniques*. Focal Press, Oxford, England.

Mittal, V.; Roth, S.; Moore, J. D.; Mattis, J.; and Carenini, G. 1995. Generating explanatory captions for information graphics. In *Proceedings of the International Joint Conference on Artificial Intelligence*, 1276–1283.

Moore, J. D. 1995. *Participating in Explanatory Dialogues*. MIT Press.

Novak, H.-J. 1987. Strategies for generating coherent descriptions of object movements in street scenes. In Kempen, G., ed., *Natural Language Generation*. Dordrecht, The Netherlands: Martinus Nijhoff. 117–132.

Oviatt, S. 1997. Multimodal interactive maps: Designing for human performance. *Human-Computer Interaction* 12:93–129.

Rieber, L. 1990. Animation in computer-based instruction. *Educational Technology Research and Development* 38(1):77–86.

Roth, S. F.; Mattis, J.; and Mesnard, X. 1991. Graphics and natural language as components of automatic explanation. In Sullivan, J. W., and Tyler, S. W., eds., *Intelligent User Interfaces*. New York: Addison-Wesley. 207–239.

Seligmann, D. D., and Feiner, S. K. 1991. Automated generation of intent-based 3D illustrations. *Computer Graphics* 25(4):123–132.

Sibun, P. 1992. Generating text without trees. *Computational Intelligence* 8(1):102–122.

Suthers, D. D. 1991. A task-appropriate hybrid architecture for explanation. *Computational Intelligence* 7(4):315–333.

Wahlster, W.; André, E.; Finkler, W.; Profitlich, H.-J.; and Rist, T. 1993. Plan-based integration of natural language and graphics generation. *Artificial Intelligence* 63:387–427.

Automated Reasoning

Reasoning under inconsistency based on implicitly-specified partial qualitative probability relations: a unified framework

S. Benferhat[1] D. Dubois[1] J. Lang[1] H. Prade[1] A. Saffiotti[2] P. Smets[2]

[1] IRIT, Université Paul Sabatier
118 Route de Narbonne
Toulouse 31062 Cedex 4, France
{benferhat, dubois, lang, prade}@irit.fr

[2] IRIDIA, Université Libre de Bruxelles
50 av. F. Roosevelt
B-1050 Bruxelles, Belgium
{psmets, asaffio}@ulb.ac.be

Abstract

Coherence-based approaches to inconsistency handling proceed by selecting preferred consistent subbases of the belief base according to a predefined method which takes advantage of explicitly stated priorities. We propose here a general framework where the preference relation between subsets of the belief base is induced by a system of constraints directly expressed by the user. Postulates taking their source in the qualitative modelling of uncertainty, either probabilistic or possibilistic, are used for completing the implicit specification of the preference relations. This enables us to define various types of preference relations, including as particular cases several well-known systems such as Brewka's preferred sub-theories or the lexicographical system. Since the number of preferred consistent subbases may be prohibitive, we propose to compile the inconsistent belief base into a new one from which it is easier to select one preferred consistent subbase.

1. Introduction

Inconsistency may appear when a plausible consequence, obtained under incomplete information, has to be revised because further information is available. This issue has been extensively investigated in the nonmonotonic reasoning literature. In this paper we rather view inconsistency as being caused by the use (and the fusion) of multiple sources of information. Coherence-based approaches (Rescher; 1976) (Benferhat et al., 1995a) to inconsistency have two main steps, as shown in Fig. 1: i) build one or several preferred consistent subbases of the belief base **K**, and ii) use classical entailment on these subbases.

A preference relation between subbases is a reflexive and transitive relation $\geq$ on 2^K. Thus specifying it *explicitly* would need, in the extreme case, $O(2^{2*|K|})$ space which is not reasonable. It is why we have to *implicitly* specify a "small" set of constraints bearing on sets of formulas, which can be completed into a preference relation over 2^K using a set of postulates.

Two kinds of such constraints have been considered:

(a) *priority* constraints, which are qualitative in essence, and which consist in specifying an ordering relation *on the formulas in K*, from which the preference relation on 2^K is induced. This is the case with Nebel (1991; 1994)'s syntax-based entailment, Brewka(1989)'s preferred sub-theories, Williams(1996)'s approach to belief revision, Geffner(1992)'s conditional entailment, the lexicographical system (Benferhat et al., 1993), (Lehmann, 1995), etc.

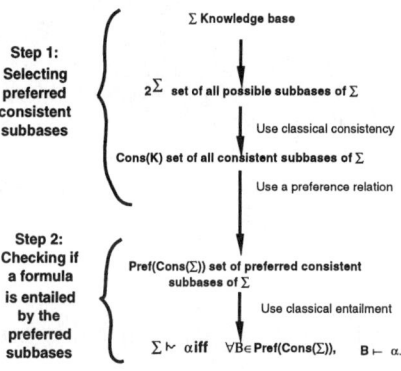

Figure 1

(b) *numerical* constraints, which consist in attaching to each formula a numerical weight which can be a probability degree (infinitesimal or not), a possibility degree (Dubois et al., 1994), a penalty value (Dupin et al., 1994), or an infinitesimal belief degree in belief functions theory (Benferhat et al., 1995b).

However, all these methods for specifying preferences implicitly lack flexibility on the way the preference relation is induced from the constraints, since the set of postulates is fixed once for all and is not a part of the representation language. In the first part of the article (Sections 2-4) we propose a general representation framework for coherence-based reasoning, which encompasses the well-known systems mentioned above. This framework offers a lot of flexibility, and for instance makes it possible to the user to define, a system which lays between Brewka's preferred sub-theories and the lexicographical system.

In the second part of the paper, we deal with the problem of representing the preferred consistent subbases compactly, in order to perform task 2 (see Fig. 1) efficiently. For this purpose we propose a compilation technique which transforms **K** into a new belief base $\mathbb{C}(\mathbf{K})$ (with some additional formulas). This combination technique is inspired from the one recently introduced in the possibilistic logic setting (Benferhat et al., 1997). We show that this syntactic combination of belief bases offers a method for tackling inconsistency in the sense that any plausible conclusion inferred from **K** using some existing inconsistency-tolerant consequence relation, is also a consequence from a unique consistent subbase of $\mathbb{C}(\mathbf{K})$.

This paper emphasizes the syntactic aspects of the approach, while a companion paper (Benferhat et al., 1998) develops the semantical issues and concentrates on preference relations which are total orders.

2. Specifying preferences implicitly

In this paper, we only consider a propositional language. The symbol $\vdash$ represents the classical consequence relation, Greek letters $\alpha, \beta, \ldots$, represent formulas.

Let $\mathcal{S} = \{s_1, \ldots, s_n\}$ be a set of sources (all the s_i are different). A belief base $\mathbf{K} = \{\phi(s_i) \mid s_i \in \mathcal{S}\}$ associated to $\mathcal{S}$ is a multiset of the formulas ϕ provided by the sources s_i. For the sake of simplicity, we simply write ϕ_i instead of $\phi(s_i)$. The same belief can be present several times in **K** if it comes from different sources and this explains why we consider **K** as a multiset. However $\mathcal{S}$ is not a multiset but a set since all s_i are different. Thus, instead of working with $2^{\mathbf{K}}$, which would lead to ambiguities (since **K** is a multiset), we prefer to work with $2^{\mathcal{S}}$ having in mind that s_i is associated to ϕ_i.

Def. 1: A partially qualitative positive probability (PQPP) relation $\geq$ on $2^{\mathcal{S}}$ is a relation satisfying the following postulates: Let $X, Y, Z \subseteq \mathcal{S}$,

A1. $\geq$ is reflexive and transitive;
A2. $X \supsetneq Y$ implies $X > Y$; ($\supsetneq$ means strict inclusion)
A3. If X, Y, Z are disjoint subsets then :
$$X \cup Y \geq X \cup Z \Leftrightarrow Y \geq Z;$$
where : $X > Y$ means that $X \geq Y$ and not $Y \geq X$.

The intuitive meaning of $X \geq Y$ (resp. $X > Y$) is that the set of sources in X is at least as preferred/prioritary/reliable as (resp. strictly more prioritary than) the set of sources in Y. Note that we do not require $\geq$ to be connected ($\geq$ is generally a partial order only), which entails that there may be incomparable subsets of $\mathcal{S}$. The incomparability relation should not be confused with the equivalence (or indifference) relation defined by: X and Y are equivalent (denoted by $X \approx Y$) iff $X \geq Y$ and $Y \geq X$. The relation $\geq$ is a kind of partially ordered qualitative probability (Lehmann, 1996), where all non-empty events have a "non-null" probability value due to A2. The cancellation property A3 is close to the one of comparative probabilities (Fishburn, 1986), although we remain in the qualitative framework.

Now, what has to be first specified is a set of constraints $\mathcal{C}$ bearing on the preference relation; the latter is induced from $\mathcal{C}$ by applying axioms A1-A2-A3 repeatedly. $\mathcal{C}$ consists of inequalities and strict inequalities, i.e., $\mathcal{C} = \{X_i > Y_i, i=1,\ldots,n\} \cup \{X_j \geq Y_j, j=1,\ldots,m\}$. An equivalence statement $X \approx Y$ is specified by the two weak inequalities $X \geq Y$ and $Y \geq X$. $\mathcal{C}$ is said to be consistent if there exists a PQPP-preference relation $\geq$ compatible with $\mathcal{C}$ (i.e., $\geq$ extends $\mathcal{C}$, namely $\geq$ satisfies all the inequalities of $\mathcal{C}$). The preference relation induced by $\mathcal{C}$ will be the closure of $\mathcal{C}$ by A1-A3, i.e., the smallest preference relation $\geq$ extending $\mathcal{C}$. The following proposition states that for each consistent set of constraints $\mathcal{C}$, there exists a unique closure of $\mathcal{C}$:

Proposition 1: If $\mathcal{C}$ is consistent with the axioms A1-A3 then there exists a unique PQPP preference relation, denoted by $\geq_{\mathcal{C}}$, such that for any PQPP preference relation $\geq$, we have: $\geq$ extends $\mathcal{C} \Leftrightarrow \geq$ extends $\geq_{\mathcal{C}}$.

$\geq_{\mathcal{C}}$ will be called the closure of $\mathcal{C}$. When $\mathcal{C}$ is consistent with the axioms A1-A3, then $\geq_{\mathcal{C}}$ can be constructed in the following way: let $R_{\mathcal{C}} = \{(I,J); I \leq J \in \mathcal{C} \text{ or } I < J \in \mathcal{C}\}$ and $R_C = \{(I, J); I \subseteq J\}$. Now, complete $R_{\mathcal{C}} \cup R_C$ by considering $R = \{(I \cup M, J \cup M); \forall I, J, M \text{ disjoint subsets}, (I,J) \in R_{\mathcal{C}} \cup R_C\}$. Finally, take the transitive closure of R.

<u>Example 1</u>: Let $\mathcal{S} = \{s1, s2, s3, s4\}$. Let $\mathcal{C} = \{\{s1\} > \{s2,s3\}, \{s2\} \approx \{s3\}\}$. The closure of $\mathcal{C}$ is shown in Fig. 2 (reflexivity and transitivity are not represented for the sake of clarity). For instance $\{s1, s4\} >_{\mathcal{C}} \{s2, s3, s4\}$ is obtained from $\{s1\} > \{s2,s3\}$ and postulate A3.

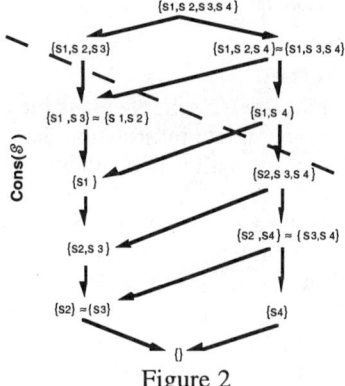

Figure 2

3. PQPP-preference-based entailment

Roughly speaking, > helps selecting preferred subbases of **K** by removing all those which are not maximal. $X > Y$ means that, in order to restore the consistency of **K**, we prefer to maintain the set of beliefs supported by the sources in X rather than to maintain the set of beliefs supported by the sources in Y. In this way, the condition A2 becomes very natural since it corresponds to the idea of minimal change : we try to maintain as many pieces of information from **K** as possible. A3 simply means that only the formulas which differ between Y and Z should be taken into account to distinguish between Y and Z.

Now, coherence-based entailment of a formula α from an initial specification is defined by taking the intersection of the theories implied by all $\geq_{\mathcal{C}}$ – preferred subbases (those that are $\mathcal{C}$-maximal). Given a family $\mathcal{B}$ of subsets of $\mathcal{S}$, and a preference relation $\geq$, we define Max($\mathcal{B}$, $\geq$) in the usual way: Max($\mathcal{B}, \geq$)={X$\in \mathcal{B}$ ∄Y$\in \mathcal{B}$ such that Y>X}. The minimum operator Min can be defined in a similar way. For X$\subseteq \mathcal{S}$, we note $\mathbf{AND}(X)=\wedge\{\phi_i\in K | s_i\in X\}$ the conjunction of formulas provided by the sources in X.

Def. 2: X is said to be consistent iff $\mathbf{AND}(X)$ is consistent (in the sense of classical logic). We note Cons($\mathcal{S}$)={X$\subseteq \mathcal{S}$ such that $\mathbf{AND}(X)$ is consistent} the set of all consistent subbases of **K**.

Def. 3: $\mathbf{K},\mathcal{C} \vdash \alpha$ iff $\forall X\in$ Max(Cons($\mathcal{S}$), $\geq_{\mathcal{C}}$), we have $\mathbf{AND}(X)\vdash\alpha$.

Example 1 (continued): Let $\mathbf{K}=\{\phi_1, \phi_2, \phi_3, \phi_4\}$ and $\mathcal{S}=\{s_1, s_2, s_3, s_4\}$ with $\phi_1=a$, $\phi_2=\neg a\vee b$, $\phi_3=\neg a\vee\neg b$, $\phi_4=\neg a\wedge c$. Referring to Fig. 2, the preferred consistent subsets of $\mathcal{S}$ are: Max(Cons($\mathcal{S}$), $\geq_{\mathcal{C}}$) = {{s_1,s_2}, {s_1,s_3}, {s_2, s_3, s_4}}. We have: $\mathbf{AND}(\{s_1,s_2\}) \equiv a\wedge b$; $\mathbf{AND}(\{s_1,s_3\}) \equiv a\wedge\neg b$; $\mathbf{AND}(\{s_2, s_3, s_4\}) \equiv \neg a\wedge c$, therefore we have $\mathbf{K},\mathcal{C} \vdash a\vee c$, but $\mathbf{K},\mathcal{C} \nvdash a$ (since $\mathbf{AND}(\{s_2, s_3, s_4\})\nvdash a$). ∎

Note that $\vdash$ is nonmonotonic w.r.t. **K** and monotonic w.r.t. $\mathcal{C}$:

Prop. 2: If $\mathcal{C}'\supseteq\mathcal{C}$ then $\forall\alpha$, $\mathbf{K},\mathcal{C} \vdash \alpha$ implies $\mathbf{K},\mathcal{C}'\vdash\alpha$.

This is due to the fact that $\mathcal{C}'\supseteq\mathcal{C}$ implies that Max(Cons($\mathcal{S}$), $\geq_{\mathcal{C}}$) is included in Max(Cons($\mathcal{S}$), $\geq_{\mathcal{C}'}$). The non-monotonicity of $\vdash$ w.r.t. **K** is shown below:

Example 1 (continued)

Let $\mathbf{K}'=\mathbf{K}\cup\{\phi_5\}$ and $\mathcal{S}'=\mathcal{S}\cup\{s_5\}$ be the result of adding $\phi_5=\neg a\wedge\neg c$ to the belief base of Example 1. The set $\mathcal{C}$ is the same as the one given in Example 1 (thus there is no explicit constraints on s_5). The preferred consistent subsets of $\mathcal{S}'$ are: Max(Cons($\mathcal{S}'$), $\geq_{\mathcal{C}}$) = {{s_1,s_2}, {s_1,s_3}, {s_2, s_3, s_4}, {s_2,s_3,s_5}}. We can check that we have: $\mathbf{K}',\mathcal{C} \nvdash a\vee c$, since $\mathbf{AND}(\{s_2,s_3,s_5\})\nvdash a\vee c$. ∎

4. Recovering coherence theories

This section shows that the entailment based on PQPP-relations allows us to recover several well-known systems. Coherence-based theories generally assume first a stratification of $\mathcal{S}$ which is a partition $\{\mathcal{S}_1,...,\mathcal{S}_p\}$ of $\mathcal{S}$. We note s_{ik} the k-th source (according to an arbitrary numbering) in $\mathcal{S}_i$. This stratification expresses a total pre-order between the sources: $\forall s_{ik},s_{jl}\in\mathcal{S}$, $s_{ik} > s_{jl}$ iff i>j, i.e., the lower is the number of the stratum, the less

prioritary it is. There are two well-known criteria to rank-order Cons($\mathcal{S}$): Let X,Y$\in$ Cons($\mathcal{S}$):

- *inclusion-based ordering* defined by X >$_{\text{Incl}}$ Y iff ∃i such that X$\cap\mathcal{S}_i\supsetneq$Y$\cap\mathcal{S}_i$ and for any j>i, X$\cap\mathcal{S}_j$=Y$\cap\mathcal{S}_j$.

- *lexicographic ordering* defined by X >$_{\text{lex}}$ Y iff ∃i such that |X$\cap\mathcal{S}_i$|>|Y$\cap\mathcal{S}_i$| and for any j>i, |X$\cap\mathcal{S}_j$|=|Y$\cap\mathcal{S}_j$|, and X$\approx_{\text{lex}}$Y iff for any i, |X$\cap\mathcal{S}_i$|=|Y$\cap\mathcal{S}_i$|.

The >$_{\text{Incl}}$-maximal consistent elements are called preferred subtheories in (Brewka, 1989) and >$_{\text{lex}}$-maximal consistent elements are called lexicographically preferred subbases in (Benferhat et al., 1993), (Lehmann, 1995).

There are also some other coherence theories which associate positive integer numbers c_i (resp. symbolic weights w_i, unknown but ordered) to the sources s_i. An example of a system which uses such assignments is the (symbolic) penalty logic proposed in (Dupin et al., 1994), which rank-orders Cons($\mathcal{S}$) in the following way:

- *(symbolic) penalty-based ordering* defined by X >$_{\text{pen}}$ Y (resp. X >$_{\text{spen}}$ Y) iff $\sum\{c_i | s_i\notin X\} < \sum\{c_j | s_j\notin Y\}$ (resp. $\sum\{w_i | s_i\notin X\} < \sum\{w_j | s_j\notin Y\}$).

Clearly, X >$_{\text{spen}}$ Y implies X >$_{\text{pen}}$ Y. Symbolic penalty logic is equivalent to an infinitesimal version of belief functions (Benferhat et al., 1995b).

The necessary conditions for recovering the previous systems are summarized in Fig. 3, see (Benferhat et al., 1998):

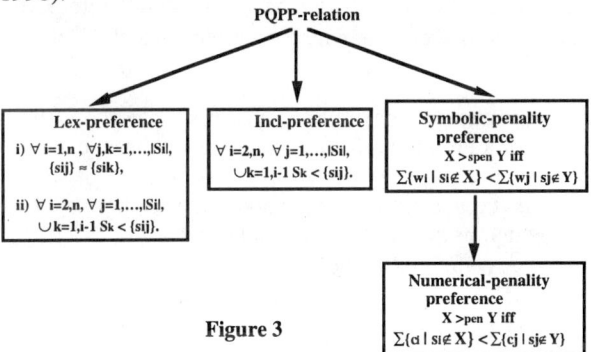

Figure 3

A natural question suggested by the above picture is: can penalty logic be a numerical representation of PQPP-relations? Namely, we may wonder if for any PQPP-relation > there exists a set of weights c_i associated to the sources s_i such that X > Y iff $\sum\{c_i | s_i\notin X\} < \sum\{c_j | s_j\notin Y\}$. The answer is no, and we can use the same counter-example given by Kraft, Pratt and Seidenberg (1959) where they show that qualitative probability relations cannot be represented by a probability distribution. Let $\mathcal{S}=\{s_1,s_2,s_3,s_4,s_5\}$ and $\varepsilon=1$. Let $c_1=400-\varepsilon$, $c_2=100-\varepsilon$, $c_3=300-\varepsilon$, $c_4=200$ and $c_5=600$. Then

define $\geq$ in the following way:
. for any couple $(X,Y) \neq (\{s_1,s_2,s_3\}, \{s_4,s_5\})$:
$$X \geq Y \quad \text{iff} \quad \Sigma\{c_j \mid s_j \notin X\} \leq \Sigma\{c_j \mid s_j \notin Y\}$$
. $\{s_1,s_2,s_3\} > \{s_4,s_5\}$ (although $c_4+c_5 > c_1+c_2+c_3$)

It can be shown that $\geq$ cannot be represented by any numerical penalty logic. This is due to the following facts:
• Note that the qualitative preference relation $\geq$ satisfies the following inequalities:
$\{s_1, s_4, s_5\} > \{s_2,s_3,s_4,s_5\}$, $\{s_3, s_4, s_5\} > \{s_1,s_2,s_5\}$,
$\{s_2,s_4,s_5\} > \{s_1,s_3,s_4\}$, $\{s_1,s_2,s_3\} > \{s_4,s_5\}$,
and that there is no $\{c_1,c_2,c_3,c_4,c_5\}$ integer costs which satisfy the above inequalities. Indeed, $c_2+c_3 < c_1$, $c_1+c_2 < c_3+c_4$, $c_1+c_3 < c_2+c_5$ implies $c_1+c_2+c_3 < c_4+c_5$.
• The preference relation is a PQPP-relation. Indeed, the penalty ordering defined from the above numerical numbers satisfies the axioms A1-A3, and changing the direction of the link $\{s_1,s_2,s_3\} < \{s_4,s_5\}$ has no incidence on the satisfaction of axioms since there is no $X \neq \{s_1,s_2,s_3\}$, $X \neq \{s_4,s_5\}$ such that $\{s_4,s_5\} \geq X \geq \{s_1,s_2,s_3\}$.

Apart from the well-known systems recovered by our general framework, we may define a variety of other systems by specifying a set of constraints for a specific problem:

Example 2: multi-agent preferences + Pareto ordering
   Agent A: expresses a belief base K_A, $\mathcal{S}_A$, and a set of constraints $\mathcal{C}_A$ which induces a preference relation $\geq_A$. Similarly for Agent B we have (K_B, $\mathcal{S}_B$, $\mathcal{C}_B$, $\geq_B$). Letting $K = K_A \cup K_B$ and adding the axioms:
$$\forall X \subseteq \mathcal{S}, \forall Y \subseteq \mathcal{S}, X \geq Y \text{ iff } X_A \geq X_B \text{ and } Y_A \geq Y_B$$
with $X_A = X \cap \mathcal{S}_A$ and $X_B = X \cap \mathcal{S}_B$, we get a Pareto-like global preference relation, where the preference of A and B are not commensurable. ∎

Some systems, in particular systems based on the selection of a unique preferred consistent subbase, cannot be recovered using PQPP-relations. An example of such systems is the possibilistic logic approach (Dubois et al., 1994), which uses a stratification and where the ordering on Cons($\mathcal{S}$) is defined in the following way:
- "best out" ordering: defined by $X >_{B_o} Y$ if Max$\{i \mid \exists s \in \mathcal{S}_i \text{ and } s \notin X\} <$ Max$\{j \mid \exists s' \in \mathcal{S}_j \text{ and } s' \notin Y\}$ with the convention Min$\emptyset = 0$.

Possibilistic logic can be recovered using the following postulates: (A1), (A'2) $Y \subseteq X \Rightarrow X \geq Y$ and (A'3) $Y \geq Z \Rightarrow X \cup Y \geq X \cup Z$, instead of A1-A3. A'3 is the main axiom of qualitative possibility theory (Dubois et al., 1994). See (Dubois et al., 1992) for an explicit possibilistic handling of the sources.

5. Compiling inconsistent belief bases
Coherence-based approaches take blindly into account all the beliefs in K and compute the set of preferred consistent subsets of K although some beliefs are not used in inferences. For instance, consider the belief base $K = \{\alpha, \neg\alpha, \beta\}$ where all the beliefs are assumed to be equally reliable. This belief base is inconsistent and admits two preferred consistent subsets $A = \{\alpha, \beta\}$ and $B = \{\neg\alpha, \beta\}$. We can easily check that for any formula ψ, we have both $A \vdash \psi$ and $B \vdash \psi$ iff $\beta \vdash \psi$. This means that we can ignore the two beliefs $\{\alpha, \neg\alpha\}$ without changing the set of plausible consequences of K in the sense of preferred consistent subbases inference.

Generalizing this idea, we propose an alternative way for recovering coherence theories. This is done in two steps:
• The first step consists in transforming the belief base K into a new belief base denoted by $\mathbb{C}(K)$, from which it is easier to select one preferred consistent subbase.
• The second step, presented in Section 6, consists in selecting one consistent subset $BC(K)$ in $\mathbb{C}(K)$ such that: $K, \mathcal{C} \vdash \alpha$ iff $BC(K) \vdash \alpha$.

The belief base $\mathbb{C}(K)$ is obtained by viewing the couple $(2^{\mathcal{S}}, \geq_{\mathcal{C}})$ as a prioritized belief base. We note $OR(X) = \vee \{\phi_i \in K \mid s_i \in X\}$ the disjunction of the original formulas in K provided by the sources in X. More formally, $\mathbb{C}(K)$ is defined in the following way:

Def. 4: $\mathbb{C}(K)$ is a maximal subbase of $\{OR(X) \mid X \subseteq \mathcal{S}\}$ which does not contain neither tautologies nor subsumed formulas.

Def. 5: Let $\mathcal{B} \subseteq 2^{\mathcal{S}}$, and $B = \{OR(X) \mid X \subseteq \mathcal{B}\}$. A formula $OR(Y)$ is said to be subsumed by B iff $\exists OR(X) \in B$ such that $X \geq Y$ and $OR(X) \vdash OR(Y)$.

$\mathbb{C}(K)$ is not unique in general, however all $\mathbb{C}(K)$ are equivalent in the sense that in the second step all the selected consistent subbases are classically equivalent.

Example 1 (continued): Let $K = \{\phi_1, \phi_2, \phi_3, \phi_4\}$ with $\phi_1 = a$, $\phi_2 = \neg a \vee b$, $\phi_3 = \neg a \vee \neg b$, $\phi_4 = \neg a \wedge c$. After removing tautologies from $\{OR(X) \mid X \subseteq \mathcal{S}\}$ we get $\{\phi_1, \phi_2, \phi_3, \phi_4, \phi_1 \vee \phi_4, \phi_2 \vee \phi_4, \phi_3 \vee \phi_4\}$ with:
$$\phi_1 \vee \phi_4 \equiv a \vee c; \phi_2 \vee \phi_4 \equiv \neg a \vee b; \phi_3 \vee \phi_4 \equiv \neg a \vee \neg b;$$
Note that ϕ_2 is subsumed by $\phi_2 \vee \phi_4$ since $\phi_2 \vee \phi_4 \vdash \phi_2$ and $\{s_2, s_4\} > \{s_2\}$ and that ϕ_3 is also subsumed by $\phi_3 \vee \phi_4$ since $\phi_3 \vee \phi_4 \vdash \phi_3$ and $\{s_3, s_4\} > \{s_3\}$. Therefore:
$$\mathbb{C}(K) = \{\phi_1, \phi_4, \phi_1 \vee \phi_4, \phi_2 \vee \phi_4, \phi_3 \vee \phi_4\}. \quad \blacksquare$$

In (Benferhat et al., 1998) an incremental way has been proposed for computing $\mathbb{C}(K)$. This is possible by applying an associative and commutative binary combination operator, denoted by $\Diamond$. We briefly recall the definition of this operator. Let $K_1 = \{OR(X_i) \mid X_i \subseteq \mathcal{S}, i = 1, k\}$ and $K_2 = \{OR(Y_j) \mid Y_j \subseteq \mathcal{S}, j = 1, m\}$. Then $K_1 \Diamond K_2$ is defined by:
$$K_1 \Diamond K_2 = K_1 \cup K_2 \cup \{OR(X_i \cup Y_j) \mid X_i \in K_1, Y_j \in K_2, OR(X_i \cup Y_j) \text{ is not a tautology}\}.$$

As it can be seen, the operator ◊ introduces new disjunctions of formulas which are not necessarily subsumed (in the sense of Def. 5). Let $K=\{\phi_i | i=1,n\}$ be a belief base. Let $K_i=\{\phi_i\}$ be a one formula belief base. Then we can show that $\mathbb{C}(K)$ is equivalent to $K_1 ◊ ... ◊ K_n$.

6. Selecting a consistent subbase in $\mathbb{C}(K)$

In the previous section, an inconsistent belief base **K** has been compiled into a new belief base $\mathbb{C}(K)$. We recall that all formulas of $\mathbb{C}(K)$ are of the form **OR(X)**, with $X \subseteq \mathcal{S}$. In this section, we select a classical consistent subset of $\mathbb{C}(K)$, denoted by **BC(K)**, such that: $K, \breve{C} \vdash \alpha$ iff $BC(K) \vdash \alpha$. Formulas in **BC(K)** are called accepted beliefs and roughly speaking represent pieces of information in $\mathbb{C}(K)$ which are not attacked by any minimally inconsistent subset of $\mathbb{C}(K)$. The following definitions are needed in order to formally define the notion of accepted beliefs.

Def. 6: A subbase B of $\mathbb{C}(K)$ is said to be minimally inconsistent if $B \vdash \bot$ and $\forall OR(X) \in B, B-\{OR(X)\} \not\vdash \bot$.

Let Nogood($\mathcal{S}$) be the set of all minimally inconsistent subbases of $\mathbb{C}(K)$.

Def. 7: A formula **OR(X)** of $\mathbb{C}(K)$ is said to *escape* from a minimally inconsistent subbase B if $\exists OR(Y) \in B$ such that $X >_{\breve{C}} Y$.

Finally, accepted beliefs are defined by:

Def. 8: A formula **OR(X)** of $\mathbb{C}(K)$ is said to be accepted in $\mathbb{C}(K)$ iff $\forall B \in$ Nogood(K), **OR(X)** escapes from B.

The following proposition shows that the entailment $\vdash$ can be recovered using accepted beliefs (a similar result is proved in (Benferhat et al., 1998)) :

Proposition 3: Let **BC(K)** be a subbase of $\mathbb{C}(K)$ such that any formula **OR(X)** of **BC(K)** is accepted in $\mathbb{C}(K)$. Then: $K, \breve{C} \vdash \alpha$ iff $BC(K) \vdash \alpha$.

Fortunately, we do not need to compute all the minimal inconsistent subsets of $\mathbb{C}(K)$ for computing **BC(K)**. We will distinguish two cases:

. If the PQPP-preference relation is complete (i.e., $\forall X, Y \subseteq \mathcal{S}$, we have either $X \geq_{\breve{C}} Y$ or $Y \geq_{\breve{C}} X$), then it is enough to compute a subset of $\mathcal{S}$, denoted Incons($\mathcal{S}$). Then, $OR(X) \in BC(K)$ iff $X > Incons(\mathcal{S})$. This case is largely developed in (Benferhat et al., 1998). An efficient procedure for computing Incons($\mathcal{S}$) is also provided.

. If the PQPP-preference relation is not complete, we only need to consider a subset of the set of minimal inconsistent subbases of $\mathbb{C}(K)$, denoted Nogood*($\mathcal{S}$).

This section focuses on the case where the PQPP-preference relation is not complete. Computing **BC(K)** is then more tricky, even if we do not need to compute all the minimal inconsistent subbases of $\mathbb{C}(K)$. The following definitions and propositions give tools for facilitating the computing of **BC(K)**. The first improvement is to notice that we can restrict ourselves only to the minimal elements in each minimally inconsistent subbase, namely:

Proposition 4: **OR(X)** in $\mathbb{C}(K)$ is accepted iff $\forall B \in$ Nogood($\mathcal{S}$), $\exists OR(Y) \in Min(B)$ such that $X >_{\breve{C}} Y$.

To make further improvements, we need to extend the definition of $>_{\breve{C}}$ in the following way: Let A,B∈ Nogood($\mathcal{S}$):

$Min(A) \geq_{\breve{C}} Min(B)$ iff $\forall J \in A, \exists I \in B$, s.t., $J \geq I$.

This extension is defined in a way that any ordering that complete $\geq_{\breve{C}}$ (and in this case the minimum is equivalent to one element) satisfies $Min(A) \geq_{\breve{C}} Min(B)$.

We will denote by Nogood*($\mathcal{S}$) the set of all non-dominated minimally inconsistent subbases, namely:

$$Nogood^*(\mathcal{S}) = \{A \mid \not\exists B, \text{ s.t. } B \geq_{\breve{C}} A\}$$

Such a Nogood*($\mathcal{S}$) is not unique (for instance if Nogood($\mathcal{S}$) contains two elements A and B with $Min(A) \geq_{\breve{C}} Min(B)$ and $Min(A) \geq_{\breve{C}} Min(B)$ then we can either remove A or B). The following proposition shows that in order to check if a formula is accepted or not, it is enough to use Nogood*($\mathcal{S}$) instead of Nogood($\mathcal{S}$):

Proposition 5: **OR(X)** in $\mathbb{C}(K)$ is accepted iff $\forall B \in$ Nogood*($\mathcal{S}$), **OR(X)** escapes from B.

The following improvement is important for computing Nogood*($\mathcal{S}$) more easily :

Proposition 6: Let A be a minimally inconsistent subbase, and let **OR(X)** be a belief of $\mathbb{C}(K)$ such that $\forall OR(Y) \in A, Y \geq X$. Then any minimally inconsistent subbase B containing **OR(X)** is such that $Min(A) \geq_{\breve{C}} Min(B)$.

On the basis on the previous propositions, the following algorithm presents a way to compute Nogood*($\mathcal{S}$). It is all the more efficient as it starts with a minimally inconsistent subbase made of the most important beliefs in $\mathbb{C}(K)$.

```
Function: Computing-Nogood*(𝒮)
    Input: ≥_C , ℂ(K), 𝒮   Output: Nogood*(𝒮)
Begin
    • Nogood*(𝒮)=∅;
    • Let A a minimal inconsistent subbase of ℂ(K) ;
    While (A≠∅) do Begin
        • Minimize A: Remove from A, OR(X) if
          ∃OR(Y)∈ A, s.t. X>_C Y
        • Remove from ℂ(K) each OR(X)
          s.t. ∀OR(Y)∈ A, Y≥_C X
        • Nogood*(𝒮) = Nogood*(𝒮) ∪ A
        • Minimize Nogood*(𝒮): remove dominated
          elements
        • Let A a minimal inconsistent subbase of
          ℂ(K) s.t. ∄B∈Nogood*(𝒮) with
          Min(B)≥_C Min(A)
    end
    Return (Nogood*(𝒮))
end {Function}
```

<u>Example 1</u> (continued) We recall that: $\mathbb{C}(K)=\{\phi_1, \phi_4, \phi_1 \vee \phi_4, \phi_2 \vee \phi_4, \phi_3 \vee \phi_4\}$, with: $\phi_1=a$, $\phi_4=\neg a \wedge c$, $\phi_1 \vee \phi_4 \equiv a \vee c$; $\phi_2 \vee \phi_4 \equiv \neg a \vee b$; $\phi_3 \vee \phi_4 \equiv \neg a \vee \neg b$. Let us compute the consistent subbase **BC(K)** by first computing Nogood*(𝒮). We develop the previous algorithm. Let A = $\{\phi_1, \phi_2 \vee \phi_4, \phi_3 \vee \phi_4\}$ be a minimal inconsistent subbase of ℂ(K). Neither ϕ_4 nor $\phi_3 \vee \phi_4$ are removed form ℂ(K) since for instance we have neither $\{s1\} \geq \{s4\}$ nor $\{s1\} \geq \{s3, s4\}$. At this step Nogood*(𝒮)={$\{\phi_1, \phi_2 \vee \phi_4, \phi_3 \vee \phi_4\}$} and ℂ(K)={$\phi_1, \phi_4, \phi_1 \vee \phi_4, \phi_2 \vee \phi_4, \phi_3 \vee \phi_4$}. Let us run again the previous algorithm. There is only one other minimal inconsistent subbase which is: A={ϕ_1, ϕ_4}. However, A is not considered since:
 Min ($\{\phi_1, \phi_2 \vee \phi_4, \phi_3 \vee \phi_4\}$) ≥ Min ($\{\phi_1, \phi_4\}$).
Therefore: Nogood*(𝒮) = {$\{\phi_1, \phi_2 \vee \phi_4, \phi_3 \vee \phi_4\}$}.
Lastly the set of accepted beliefs is:
 BC(K) = $\{\phi_1 \vee \phi_4\} \equiv \{a \vee c\}$
and we can easily check that:
 $\forall \alpha, K, \tilde{C} \vdash \alpha$ iff **BC(K)** $\vdash \alpha$. ∎

The proposed approach is incremental, contrary to coherence based approaches, in the sense that if a new belief ϕ provided by the source s_ϕ is added to the original belief base **K**, with a new set of constraints $\tilde{C}_\phi$ to be added to $\tilde{C}$, then $\mathbb{C}(K \cup \{\phi\})$ is recovered from $\mathbb{C}(K)$. This is done by first computing **K*=BC(K)** ◊ {ϕ}. Then if **K*** is consistent then **BC(K∪{ϕ})=K***, otherwise **BC(K∪{ϕ})** contains accepted beliefs in **K***.

7. Concluding remarks

Several well-known prioritized inconsistency handling methods have been unified into a powerful framework. A qualitative treatment of the priorities is provided by an implicit specification of the priority ordering through user-originated constraints and general postulates. Then a knowledge "compilation" technique enables us to explicit all the formulas useful for the inference process, which amounts to select the consistent subpart of the new belief base obtained by compilation. This subpart is composed of all the accepted formulas (i.e., those which escape from any minimally inconsistent subset of formulas of the belief base).

8. References

S. Benferhat, C. Cayrol, D. Dubois, J. Lang, H. Prade (1993) Inconsistency management and prioritized syntax-based entailment. Proc. of IJCAI'93, pp. 640-645.

S. Benferhat , D. Dubois, H. Prade (1995a) How to infer from inconsistent beliefs without revising?. Proc. of IJCAI'95, 1449-1455.

S. Benferhat, A. Saffiotti and P. Smets (1995b). Belief functions and default reasoning. Proc. of the 11th Conf. on Uncertainty in Artificial Intelligence, pp. 19-26.

S. Benferhat , D. Dubois, H. Prade (1997) From semantic to syntactic approaches to information combination in possibilistic logic. In Aggregation and Fusion of Imperfect Information, (B. Bouchon-Meunier, ed.), Physica Verlag, pp. 141-151.

S. Benferhat, D. Dubois, J. Lang, H. Prade, A. Saffiotti, P. Smets (1998) A general approach for inconsistency handling and merging information in prioritized knowledge bases. To appear in Proc. of KR-98.

G. Brewka (1989) Preferred subtheories: an extended logical framework for default reasoning. Proc. IJCAI'89, 1043-1048.

D. Dubois, J. Lang, H. Prade (1992) Dealing with multi-source information in possibilistic logic. Proc. 10th European Conf. on Artif. Intelligence (ECAI'92), 38-42.

D. Dubois, J. Lang, H. Prade (1994) Possibilistic logic. In: Handbook of Logic in Artif. Int. and Logic Progr., Vol. 3 (D.M. Gabbay et al., eds.), Oxford Univ. Press, 439-513.

F. Dupin de St Cyr , J. Lang , T. Schiex (1994) Penalty logic and its link with Dempster-Shafer theory. Proc. of the 10th Conf. on Uncertainty in Artif. Intellig., 204-211.

C. H. Kraft, J. W. Pratt, A. Seidenberg (1959) Intuitive probability on finite sets. Ann. Math. Statist. 30, 408-419.

P. Fishburn (1986) The axioms of subjective probabilities. statistical science 1, 335-358.

H. Geffner, Default Reasoning:Causal and Conditional Theories. MIT Press, Cambridge, MA, 1992.

D. Lehmann (1995) Another perspective on default reasoning. Annals of Mathematics and Artificial Intelligence, 15, pp. 61-82.

D. Lehmann (1996) Generalized qualitative probability: Savage revisited. In Procs. of 12th Conf. on Uncertainty in Artificial Intelligence (UAI-96), pp. 381-388.

B. Nebel(1991), Belief revision and default reasoning : syntax-based approaches. Proc. of KR'91, 417-428.

B. Nebel (1994) Base revision operator ans schemes: semantics representation and complexity. Proc. 11th European Conf. on AI, 341-345.

N. Rescher (1976) Plausible reasoning. Van Gorcum, Amsterdam.

M.A. Williams (1996). Toward a practical approach to belief revision: reason-based change. Proc. KR'96, 412-420.

Belief Revision with Unreliable Observations

Craig Boutilier*
Dept. Computer Science
University of British Columbia
Vancouver, British Columbia
Canada, V6T 1W5
cebly@cs.ubc.ca

Nir Friedman[†‡]
Computer Science Division
387 Soda Hall
University of California
Berkeley, CA 94720
nir@cs.berkeley.edu

Joseph Y. Halpern[§]
Dept. Computer Science
Cornell University
Ithaca, NY 14850
halpern@cs.cornell.edu

Abstract

Research in belief revision has been dominated by work that lies firmly within the classic AGM paradigm, characterized by a well-known set of postulates governing the behavior of "rational" revision functions. A postulate that is rarely criticized is the *success postulate*: the result of revising by an observed proposition φ results in belief in φ. This postulate, however, is often undesirable in settings where an agent's observations may be imprecise or noisy. We propose a semantics that captures a new ontology for studying revision functions, which can handle noisy observations in a natural way while retaining the classical AGM model as a special case. We present a characterization theorem for our semantics, and describe a number of natural special cases that allow ease of specification and reasoning with revision functions. In particular, by making the *Markov assumption*, we can easily specify and reason about revision.

1 Introduction

The process by which an agent revises its beliefs when it obtains new information about the world, that is, the process of *belief change*, has been the focus of considerable study in philosophy and artificial intelligence. One of the best known and most studied theories of belief change is the classic *AGM theory of belief revision* of Alchourrón, Gärdenfors and Makinson [2, 18]. Recent years have seen many extensions and refinements of the AGM paradigm, including the distinction between *revision* and *update* [23, 32], the proposal of models that combine the two [8, 15], and the acceptance of the notion that epistemic states are much richer than simple belief sets [4, 17, 27, 29].

All of these advances can be viewed as refinements of the AGM paradigm, for none contradict the basic, if—in retrospect—somewhat limited, view of revision proffered by AGM. However, as noted in [14], there are reasons to question some of their rationality postulates, even some that have been viewed as "beyond controversy". One example is the *success postulate*, which asserts that when an agent revises its beliefs based on new information φ, the resulting belief set should contain φ; that is, the revision should "succeed" in the incorporation of the new information. Generally, this requires that, in order to accept φ, the agent give up some of its old beliefs to remain consistent.

As argued in [14], to justify the success postulate (or any other postulate), we must carefully consider the particular process we hope to characterize as well as the ontology adopted in that characterization. Gärdenfors [18] provides one interpretation of belief revision for which the success postulate is appropriate. Under this interpretation, the agent's beliefs consist of those propositions the agent accepts as being true and the agent revises by φ only if it accepts φ as being true. In this case, the success postulate holds almost by definition.

In much work on revision, it is implicitly assumed that an agent should revise by φ after observing φ. The reasonableness of this assumption depends in part on the language being used. For example, if the agent is a robot making observations and φ talks about the reading of a sensor—for example, saying that a particular sensor had a high reading—then the success postulate may again be deemed acceptable. Of course, the relationship between the propositions that talk about the robot's sensors and more interesting propositions that talk about what is actually true in the "external" world must be modeled if the robot is to draw useful inferences [8]. The relationship will generally be complicated because of sensor noise, unreliability, and so on. One may instead wish to model a situation of this type by assuming the robot can directly observe the truth values of external propositions, but that these direct observations may be corrupted. Adopting this ontology, the success postulate is no longer reasonable: an observed proposition may contradict such strongly held beliefs that the robot has no choice but to dismiss the observation as incorrect.[1]

As another example where the success postulate may be questionable, imagine an agent conducting a market survey

---

*This work was supported by NSERC Research Grant OGP0121843 and IRIS-II Project IC-7, and was undertaken while the author was visiting the University of Toronto. Thanks also to the generous support of the Killam Foundation.

[†]Current address: Institute of Computer Science, The Hebrew University, Givat Ram, Jerusalem 91904, Israel. nir@cs.huji.ac.il

[‡]Work was supported in part by ARO under the MURI program "Integrated Approach to Intelligent Systems", grant number DAAH04-96-1-0341.

[§]Work was supported in part by NSF under grant IRI-96-25901 and by the Air Force Office of Scientific Research under grant F49620-96-1-0323.

Copyright 1998, American Association for Artificial Intelligence (www.aaai.org). All rights reserved.

---

[1] As we shall see, "dismiss" is too strong a word, for an observation that is not incorporated into the agent's belief set will still have an impact on its epistemic state, for instance, by predisposing it to the future acceptance of that proposition.

by having people fill in on-line questionnaires. By sending several different questionnaires to the same person, the agent can obtain multiple observations of, say, the person's salary. None of these observations may be the person's actual salary; in fact, the agent might believe that most people tend to exaggerate their salaries when filling out such questionnaires.

Notice also that the success postulate imposes an overwhelming bias toward accepting the most recently observed propositions. An agent that observes a sequence of propositions containing some number of φs and $\neg\varphi$s is bound to accept φ or $\neg\varphi$ depending on which it observed most recently, regardless of any feature of the actual history of observations. For instance, the robot will ignore the fact that twice as many φ observations as $\neg\varphi$ observations were made; and our survey agent must ignore the fact that men tend to inflate their reported salaries over time and accept the most *inaccurate* observation. Clearly what is required is a model of revision that lets us understand when the success postulate is reasonable and allows us to discard it when it is not.

In this paper, we propose a model of belief revision that deals with imprecise observations by adopting the second ontology mentioned above. We assume that an agent has access to a stream of observed propositions, but that it is under no obligation to incorporate any particular observed proposition into its belief set. Generally, a proposition will be accepted only if the likelihood that the proposition is true given the agent's current sequence of observations "outweighs" the agent's prior belief that it was false. The basic intuitions are drawn from the standard Bayesian model of belief change. Roughly speaking, once we have represented in our model the correlation between a given stream of observations and the truth of various propositions, we can simply condition on the observations. The key point is that conditioning on the event of *observing* φ is very different from conditioning on the event φ. After conditioning on φ, the probability of φ is 1; after conditioning on observing φ, the probability of φ depends on the prior probability of φ and the correlation between the observation and φ actually being true.

To use these ideas in the context of belief revision, we must use a more qualitative measure of uncertainty than probability—here we adopt Spohn's [31] *ranking functions*. Nevertheless, the basic intuitions are drawn from the standard probabilistic approach. Indeed, it is remarkable how little work is needed to apply these intuitions in a qualitative setting. This emphasizes how small the gap is between belief revision and probability kinematics. We note, however, that our model differs from qualitative adaptations of Jeffrey's Rule [22] devised for belief revision [11, 19, 31] (see Section 2 for further discussion).

The rest of this paper is organized as follows. In Section 2, we discuss the AGM model, and describe *generalized revision functions* for dealing with sequences of observations. In Section 3, we present our basic framework, which is taken from Friedman and Halpern [16, 17]. We define *observation systems* that allow unreliable observations, show how conditioning can be used to effect belief revision, and characterize the class of generalized revision functions determined by observation systems. In Section 4, we consider the important class of observation systems that satisfy the *Markov assumption*, allowing revision functions to be specified concisely and naturally. In Section 5, we consider two further special cases where (a) observations are more likely to be true than false; and (b) observations are known to be accurate. We conclude with a brief discussion of related and future work.

2 The AGM Theory of Belief Revision

Throughout, we assume that an agent has a deductively closed *belief set* K, a set of sentences drawn from some logical language reflecting the agent's beliefs about the current state of the world. For ease of presentation, we assume a classical propositional language, denoted $\mathcal{L}$, and consequence operation Cn. The belief set K will often be generated by some finite knowledge base KB (i.e., $K = Cn(KB)$). The identically true and false propositions are denoted $\top$ and $\bot$, respectively. Given a set of possible worlds W and $\varphi \in \mathcal{L}$, we denote by $[\![\varphi]\!]$ the set of φ-worlds, the elements of W satisfying φ.[2]

Given a belief set K, an agent will often obtain information φ not present in K. In this case, K must be *revised* to incorporate φ. If φ is consistent with K, one expects φ to simply be added to K. More problematic is the case when $K \vdash \neg\varphi$; certain beliefs must be given up before φ is adopted. The *AGM theory* provides a set of postulates governing this process. We use K_φ^* to denote the *revision* of K by φ. Of interest here is the following:

(R2) $\varphi \in K_\varphi^*$.

R2 is the success postulate mentioned in the introduction; it says that φ is believed after revising by φ. We refer the reader to [18] for the remaining postulates and a discussion of the AGM theory.

Unfortunately, while the postulates constrain possible revisions, they do not dictate the precise beliefs that should be retracted when φ is observed. An alternative model of revision, based on the notion of *epistemic entrenchment* [18], has a more constructive nature. Given a belief set K, we can characterize the revision of K by ordering beliefs according to our willingness to give them up. If one of two beliefs must be retracted in order to accommodate some new fact, the less entrenched belief will be relinquished, while the more entrenched persists.

Semantically, an entrenchment relation (hence a revision function) can be modeled by associating with each set of possible worlds a plausibility, in any of a number of ways [5, 10, 17, 20]. For the purposes of this paper, we adopt Spohn's *ordinal conditional functions* or κ-rankings [19, 31]. A function $\kappa : W \to \mathbf{N} \cup \{\infty\}$ assigns to each world a ranking reflecting its plausibility: if $\kappa(w) < \kappa(v)$ then w is more plausible than v. We insist that $\kappa^{-1}(0) \neq \emptyset$, so that maximally plausible worlds are assigned rank 0. If $\kappa(w) = \infty$, we say w is *impossible*. If $U \subseteq W$, then $\kappa(U) = \min_{u \in U} \kappa(u)$.

Following [4, 16, 27, 29], we distinguish the agent's *epistemic state* from its belief set. We define the form of the epistemic state carefully in Section 3. For now we simply require that it includes a ranking κ. This ranking then determines the agent's belief set K as follows:

$$K = \{\varphi \in \mathcal{L} : \kappa^{-1}(0) \subseteq [\![\varphi]\!]\}. \tag{1}$$

Thus, the formulas in K are precisely those that are true in all worlds of rank 0.

The ranking κ also induces a revision function: to revise by φ an agent adopts the most plausible φ-worlds as epistemically possible. Thus, using $\min(\varphi, \kappa)$ to denote this set, we have

$$K_\varphi^* = \{\psi \in \mathcal{L} : \min(\varphi, \kappa) \subseteq [\![\psi]\!]\}$$

---

[2] In our setting, we can safely identify the possible worlds with valuations over $\mathcal{L}$, although in general we must distinguish the two.

If $\llbracket\varphi\rrbracket \cap W = \emptyset$, we set $\min(\varphi, \kappa) = \emptyset$ and $K_\varphi^* = \mathcal{L}$ (the inconsistent belief set). It is normally assumed that $\llbracket\varphi\rrbracket \cap W \neq \emptyset$ for every satisfiable φ — thus every satisfiable proposition is accorded some degree of plausibility. It is well-known that this type of model induces the class of revision functions sanctioned by the AGM postulates [5, 19, 20].

We define *conditional plausibility*, for $U, V \subseteq W$ and $\kappa(U) \neq \infty$, as:

$$\kappa(V|U) = \kappa(V \wedge U) - \kappa(U).$$

Intuitively, this denotes the degree to which V would be considered plausible if U were believed.

These notions are strongly reminiscent of standard concepts from probability theory. Indeed, the role of $+$ in probability is assumed by min in the theory of rankings, while the role of $\times$ is assumed by $+$ (so, in the definition of conditioning, division becomes subtraction). In fact, a κ-ranking can be interpreted as a semi-qualitative probability distribution. Using the ε-*semantics* of Adams [1], Goldszmidt and Pearl [19] show how one can interpret the κ values of propositions as "order of magnitude" probabilities.

It has been remarked by a number of authors that models of revision based on epistemic entrenchment or κ-rankings are not strong enough to adequately capture *iterated revision* [4, 16, 27, 29]. Specifically, while these models determine the content of a new belief set when φ is observed, given an epistemic state, they do not determine the new epistemic state (or ranking) associated with the new belief set. To deal with iteration semantically, we need a way of determining a new epistemic state, given an observation [7, 9, 26, 30]. Spohn's *conditioning* operation [31] does just this. When an observation φ is made, all $\neg\varphi$-worlds are deemed impossible and removed from the ranking (or set to ∞). The remaining φ-worlds retain their relative plausibilities, with the resulting ranking κ_φ^* renormalized; formally we have

$$\kappa_\varphi^*(w) = \begin{cases} \kappa(w) - \kappa(\varphi) & \text{if } w \models \varphi \\ \infty & \text{if } w \not\models \varphi. \end{cases} \quad (2)$$

Thus each observation determines not just a revised belief set, but a new epistemic state which can be used to model subsequent revisions.

Spohn also proposed a more general model of revision called α-*conditioning*. Rather than accepting an observed proposition φ with certainty, φ is accepted with degree α, with $\neg\varphi$-worlds retaining a certain plausibility. This model can be viewed as a way of dealing with noisy observations (and has been developed further in [11, 19]). In fact, this model is a qualitative analogue of *Jeffrey's Rule* [22] for probabilistic belief update. Jeffrey's rule is a generalization of conditioning where a piece of evidence can be accepted with a given probability.

Goldszmidt and Pearl [19] argue that Jeffrey's rule is unreasonable since it requires that the observation φ is associated with the agent's posterior degree of belief in φ. As an alternative, they propose *L-conditioning*, where the strength associated with observing φ conveys the difference in the *evidential support* that the observation gives to worlds that satisfy φ and to worlds that satisfy $\neg\varphi$. They use a qualitative version of Bayes' rule that combines this support with the agent's prior ranking of φ and $\neg\varphi$ to get a *posterior* ranking over both propositions. Then they apply Jeffrey's rule to update the ranking over worlds to match this posterior.

The approach we propose is different from and, in a sense, more general, than both of these qualitative update rules. Unlike Jeffrey's rule, we do not assume that there is any doubt that φ has been observed but, as we said earlier, we distinguish observing φ from φ being true. Like Goldszmidt and Pearl's approach, our approach relies on Bayes rule to combine the evidence with a prior rankings. However, unlike their approach, we assume that the evidence provides support for each possible world (rather than to the propositions φ and $\neg\varphi$), and thus we do not have to appeal to Jeffrey's rule. In this sense, our proposal has more in common with probabilistic *observation models* that are standard in decision and control theory [3, 24].

A general way of thinking about iterated revision is not to think of revision functions as mapping from (belief set, observation) pairs to belief sets, but as mapping from finite observation sequences to belief sets. More precisely, assume that an agent's observations are drawn from language $\mathcal{L}$. We use $\langle \varphi_1, \varphi_2, \cdots, \varphi_n \rangle$ to denote the length n sequence consisting of $\varphi_1, \varphi_2, \ldots$; and $\langle\rangle$ denotes the length-0 sequence. Let $\mathcal{O}$ denote the set of all finite sequences of observations, and let $\mathcal{B}$ denote the set of all belief sets over $\mathcal{L}$.

Definition 2.1: A *generalized revision function* B is a mapping $B : \mathcal{O} \to \mathcal{B}$.

This definition deals naturally with iterated revision. Furthermore, there is no need to specify an initial belief set: the agent's prior beliefs are captured by the belief set $B(\langle\rangle)$.[3]

3 An Ontology for Imprecise Observations
3.1 Observation Systems

In this section, we present a framework that allows us to describe what is true in the world, what the agent observes, and the plausibility of these observations. The framework is essentially that of Friedman and Halpern [17, 16], which in turn is based on the multi-agent framework of [21]. We briefly review the details here; further discussion and motivation can be found in [12].

The key assumption in the multi-agent system framework is that we can characterize the system by describing it in terms of a *state* that changes over time. Formally, we assume that at each point in time, the agent is in some *local state*. Intuitively, this local state encodes the information the agent has observed thus far and its ranking. There is also an *environment*, whose state encodes relevant aspects of the system that are not part of the agent's local state. In this case, the relevant information is simply the *state of the world*. A *global state* (s_e, s_a) consists of the environment state s_e and the local state s_a of the agent. A *run* of the system is a function from time (which here ranges over $\mathbf{N}$) to global states. Thus, if r is a run, then $r(0), r(1), \ldots$ is a sequence of global states that completely describes a possible system execution. A *system* consists of a set of runs that dictates all the possible behaviors of the system.

Given a system $\mathcal{R}$, we refer to a pair (r, m) consisting of a run $r \in \mathcal{R}$ and a time m as a *point*. If $r(m) = (s_e, s_a)$, we define $r_a(m) = s_a$ and $r_e(m) = s_e$. A *(ranked) interpreted system* is a tuple $\mathcal{I} = (\mathcal{R}, \kappa, \pi)$, consisting of a system $\mathcal{R}$, a ranking κ on the runs in r, and an *interpretation* π, which associates with each point a truth assignment for $\mathcal{L}$. The ranking κ represents the agent's initial ranking of runs. Notice that in the previous section, the agent simply ranks possible worlds; here the agent ranks the relative plausibility

---

[3]Our definition of generalized revision functions is similar to that of Lehmann [26].

of entire "evolutions" of both its local state and the environment state. Of course, in general, it is infeasible for the agent to come up with a complete ranking over all possible runs. Later, we discuss some simplifying assumptions that make obtaining such a ranking more feasible.

To capture belief revision, we consider a special class of interpreted systems called *observation systems*.[4] We assume that the agent makes observations, which are characterized by formulas in $\mathcal{L}$, and that its local state consists of the sequence of observations that it has made. We also assume that the environment state is a truth assignment for $\mathcal{L}$, reflecting the actual state of the world. As observed by Katsuno and Mendelzon [23], the AGM postulates assume that the world is *static*; to capture this, we require that the environment state does not change over time. An *observation system* (OS) is a ranked interpreted system $(\mathcal{R}, \kappa, \pi)$ that satisfies the following three assumptions for every point (r, m):

- The environment state $r_e(m)$ is a truth assignment to the formulas in $\mathcal{L}$ that agrees with π at (r, m) (that is, $\pi(r, m) = r_e(m)$), and $r_e(m) = r_e(0)$.
- The agent's state $r_a(m)$ is a sequence of the form $\langle \varphi_1, \ldots, \varphi_m \rangle$ of formulas in $\mathcal{L}$; and if $m \geq 1$ and $r_a(m) = \langle \varphi_1, \ldots, \varphi_m \rangle$, then $r_a(m-1) = \langle \varphi_1, \ldots, \varphi_{m-1} \rangle$.
- If $\vec{\varphi}$ is a sequence $\langle \varphi_1, \ldots, \varphi_m \rangle$ of observations such that $r_a(m) = \vec{\varphi}$ for some run r, then $\kappa(\llbracket Obs(\vec{\varphi}) \rrbracket) \neq \infty$, where $\llbracket Obs(\vec{\varphi}) \rrbracket = \{r' : r'_a(m) = \vec{\varphi}\}$. Intuitively, this says that any sequence of observations that actually arises in the system is initially considered possible.

Notice that the form of the agent's local state makes explicit an important implicit assumption: that the agent remembers all of its previous observations. Its local state "grows" at every step.[5]

We introduce the following notation before proceeding. Since the environment state is fixed throughout a given run r, we use r_e to denote this state, dropping the time index from $r_e(m)$. We use the notation $\llbracket C \rrbracket$ to denote the set of runs in $\mathcal{R}$ that satisfy condition C. In particular:

- For any length-m observation sequence $\vec{\varphi}$, $\llbracket Obs(\vec{\varphi}) \rrbracket = \{r : r_a(m) = \vec{\varphi}\}$ denotes the set of runs in $\mathcal{R}$ in which $\vec{\varphi}$ is the initial sequence of observations.
- For any $\psi \in \mathcal{L}$, $\llbracket Obs^m(\psi) \rrbracket = \{r : r_a(m) = \vec{\varphi} \cdot \psi$, for some length-$(m-1)$ sequence $\vec{\varphi}\}$ is the set of runs in which ψ is the mth observation.
- For any $\psi \in \mathcal{L}$, $\llbracket \psi \rrbracket = \{r : r_e \models \psi\}$ is the set of runs in which the (fixed) environment state satisfies ψ
- For any truth assignment w, $\llbracket w \rrbracket = \{r : r_e = w\}$ is the set of runs whose (fixed) environment state is w.
- For any length-m sequence $\vec{\varphi}$ and truth assignment w, $\llbracket w, Obs(\vec{\varphi}) \rrbracket = \{r : r_e = w, r_a(m) = \vec{\varphi}\}$.

We stress again the difference between $\llbracket Obs^m(\psi) \rrbracket$ and $\llbracket \psi \rrbracket$. The former is the event of observing ψ at time m; the latter is the event of ψ being true.

In the analysis of the AGM framework in [16], an extra requirement is placed on OSs: it is required that, in any run r, if $r_a(m) = \langle \varphi_1, \ldots, \varphi_m \rangle$, then $\varphi_1 \wedge \ldots \wedge \varphi_m$ is true according to the truth assignment at $r_e(m)$. This requirement forces the observations to be accurate; if φ is observed, then it must be true of the world. It is precisely this requirement that we drop here to allow for noisy observations. The initial κ ranking specifies (among other things) the likelihood of such noisy observations.

We can now associate with each point (r, m) a ranking $\kappa^{r,m}$ on the runs. We take $\kappa^{r,0} = \kappa$, and define

$$\kappa^{r,m+1}(U) = \kappa^{r,m}(U \mid \llbracket Obs(r_a(m+1)) \rrbracket)$$

for each subset U of runs. Thus, $\kappa^{r,m+1}$ is the result of conditioning $\kappa^{r,m}$ on the observations the agent has made up to the point $(r, m+1)$. Because the agent has perfect recall, it is easy to see that conditioning on the sequence of observations $r_a(m+1)$ is equivalent to conditioning on the last observation φ'. More precisely,

Lemma 3.1: *If $r_a(m+1) = \langle \varphi_1, \ldots, \varphi_{m+1} \rangle$, then*

$$\kappa^{r,m+1}(U) = \kappa^{r,m}(U \mid \llbracket Obs^{m+1}(\varphi) \rrbracket).$$

It is immediate from the definition that $\kappa^{r,m}$ depends only on the agent's local state $r_a(m)$; if $r_a(m) = r'_a(m)$, then $\kappa^{r,m} = \kappa^{r',m}$. Thus, we usually write $\kappa^{\vec{\varphi}}$ to denote the ranking $\kappa^{r,m}$ such that $r_a(m) = \vec{\varphi}$. We take the agent's *epistemic state at the point* (r, m) to consist of its local state $r_a(m)$ and the ranking $\kappa^{r,m}$. Since the ranking is determined by the local state, we can safely identify the agent's epistemic state with its local state. We note that we can generalize our model by embedding the agent's κ-rankings in the local state without difficulty, allowing different initial rankings in different situations. For simplicity of exposition, we consider only a fixed ranking.

The beliefs an agent holds about the world at any point (r, m) are determined by the runs it considers most plausible at that point. Mirroring (1), we define the agent's belief set $Bel(\mathcal{I}, r, m)$ at point (r, m) in a system $\mathcal{I}$ as

$$Bel(\mathcal{I}, r, m) = \{\varphi \in \mathcal{L} : ((\kappa^{r,m})^{-1}(0) \subseteq \llbracket \varphi \rrbracket\}. \quad (3)$$

Again, notice that an agent's belief set depends only on its local state; that is, if $r_a(m) = r'_a(m')$, then $Bel(\mathcal{I}, r, m) = Bel(\mathcal{I}, r', m')$. However, it may well be that the agent has the same belief set at two points where it has quite distinct local states; moreover, revisions of these belief sets can proceed differently. Thus, an observation system $\mathcal{I}$ defines a generalized revision function that maps epistemic states to belief sets:

$$B_\mathcal{I}(\vec{\varphi}) = \begin{cases} Bel(\mathcal{I}, r, m) & \text{for } (r, m) \text{ such that } r_a(m) = \vec{\varphi} \\ Cn(\bot) & \text{if } \kappa(\llbracket Obs(\vec{\varphi}) \rrbracket) = \infty. \end{cases}$$

Example 3.2 As an example of an OS, consider the marketing survey example discussed in the introduction. Suppose our marketing agent sends three different surveys to one person. In each of them, the respondent must mark his salary, in multiples of ten thousand. Initially, the agent considers the person's annual salary to be either $30,000, $40,000, or $50,000, each equally plausible. The agent also knows how plausible various observation sequences for these three surveys are—if the person's salary is $10,000x$, he will report one of the following sequences:

- $\langle x+1, x+2, x+3 \rangle$: the incremental exaggerator
- $\langle x+2, x+2, x+2 \rangle$: the consistent exaggerator

---

[4]Observation systems are a special case of the *belief change systems* considered in [13, 16].

[5]This is analogous to the assumption of *perfect recall* in game theory [28] and distributed computing [12].

- $\langle x, x+1, x+1 \rangle$: the reluctant exaggerator
- $\langle x, x, x \rangle$: the non-exaggerator.

The agent considers it most likely that the survey recipient is an incremental or consistent exaggerator, less likely that he is a reluctant exaggerator, and quite implausible that he is a non-exaggerator. The ranking of any run with environment state (salary) $x \in \{3, 4, 5\}$ and sequence of survey answers $\langle x_1, x_2, x_3 \rangle$ is: 0 if the sequence follows the incremental or consistent pattern (given state x); 1 if it follows the reluctant pattern; 2 if it is unexaggerated; and 3 if it follows any other pattern. In addition, for $x \notin \{3, 4, 5\}$, we set κ of any run r with $r_e = x$ to be 3.

In the resulting system $\mathcal{I}$, the agent's initial belief set, $B_{\mathcal{I}}(\langle\rangle)$, is $Cn(x \in \{3, 4, 5\})$. The agent's belief set after getting a response of 6 to the first survey, $B_{\mathcal{I}}(\langle 6 \rangle)$, is $Cn(x \in \{4, 5\})$. This observation rules out the most plausible runs where the agent's actual salary is \$30,000, since they are incompatible with the agent being an incremental or consistent exaggerator. After then observing 7, the agent's belief set is $B_{\mathcal{I}}(\langle 6, 7 \rangle) = Cn(x = 5)$; he believes that he is dealing with an incremental exaggerator. Finally, if he then observes 7 again, his belief set is $B_{\mathcal{I}}(\langle 6, 7, 7 \rangle) = Cn(x = 6)$; he believes that he is dealing with a reluctant exaggerator. ∎

3.2 Expressive Power

We now examine properties of the revision functions induced by OSs, and the expressive power of OSs. We might ask whether the (ordinary) revision function determined by $B_{\mathcal{I}}$ satisfies the AGM postulates. The answer is, of course, no. Not surprisingly, the success postulate is not satisfied, for an agent may observe ψ and still believe $\neg\psi$ (as illustrated in our example above).

With respect to expressive power, we might ask whether all possible generalized revision functions (mapping observation sequences to belief sets) can be represented by OSs. This is not the case in general, but a particular class of revision functions does correspond to OSs.

We say that an observation is *unsurprising* if it does not cause the agent to retract any of its previous beliefs. That is, its belief set after the observation is a superset of its prior belief set. We impose the following rationality postulate on generalized revision functions:

(O1) For any finite observation sequence $\vec{\varphi}$ there exists a nonempty set of observations $Plaus(\vec{\varphi})$ such that

$$Cn(\cap\{B(\vec{\varphi} \cdot \psi) : \psi \in Plaus(\vec{\varphi})\}) = B(\vec{\varphi}).$$

According to O1, for every observation sequence $\vec{\varphi}$, there is a set $Plaus(\vec{\varphi})$ of observations, each of which is unsurprising with respect to the belief set $B(\vec{\varphi})$. To see this, note that O1 implies that if $\psi \in Plaus(\vec{\varphi})$, then $B(\vec{\varphi}) \subseteq B(\vec{\varphi} \cdot \psi)$, that is, the agent retains all of its beliefs after observing ψ. Moreover, this set of unsurprising observations "covers" the possibilities embodied by the belief set, in that any formula consistent with $B(\vec{\varphi})$ must be consistent with $B(\vec{\varphi} \cdot \psi)$ for some $\psi \in Plaus(\vec{\varphi})$.

With O1, we now can show the desired characterization theorems.

Theorem 3.3: *For any OS $\mathcal{I}$, the revision function $B_{\mathcal{I}}$ induced by $\mathcal{I}$ satisfies O1.*

Theorem 3.4: *Let B be an revision function satisfying O1. There exists an OS $\mathcal{I}$ such that $B = B_{\mathcal{I}}$.*

This shows that κ-rankings over runs are sufficient to represent any coherent revision function (i.e., satisfying O1) and thus can be viewed as a suitable semantics for revision based on unreliable observations.

4 Markovian Observation Models

To this point, we have placed few restrictions on the initial κ ranking on runs. This generality can cause several problems. First, the specification of such a κ ranking can be onerous, requiring (potentially) the individual ranking of all possible observation histories with respect to all possible truth assignments. Second, maintaining and updating such an explicit model imposes severe computational demands. Fortunately, there are a number of natural assumptions that can be made about the form of the observation model that make both the specification and reasoning tasks much more tractable.

Very often the state of the world completely determines the plausibility of various observations at a given point in time. In such a case, the history of past observations is irrelevant to the determination of the plausibility of the next observation if the state of the world is known. For instance, our agent conducting market surveys may know that a respondent provides independent salary reports at different points in time, the plausibility of a particular report being determined solely by the respondent's actual salary, not by their previous reports. In such a case, the "exaggeration patterns" described above no longer make sense. Instead the agent might assess the plausibility of a respondent reporting $x + k$ given that his salary is x.

We say an OS $\mathcal{I} = (\mathcal{R}, \kappa, \pi)$ is *Markovian* if it captures this intuition, which can be expressed formally as follows.

Definition 4.1: The OS $\mathcal{I} = (\mathcal{R}, \kappa, \pi)$ is *Markovian* if

(a) the likelihood of observing φ is independent of history and depends only on the state of the world, i.e., for all m, length-m sequences $\vec{\psi}$, and worlds w, we have

$$\kappa(\llbracket Obs^{m+1}(\varphi) \rrbracket \mid \llbracket w, Obs(\vec{\psi}) \rrbracket) = \kappa(\llbracket Obs^{m+1}(\varphi) \rrbracket \mid \llbracket w \rrbracket).$$

(b) the likelihood of observing φ is independent of time, given the state of the world, i.e., for all m and m', we have

$$\kappa(\llbracket Obs^m(\varphi) \rrbracket \mid \llbracket w \rrbracket) = \kappa(\llbracket Obs^{m'}(\varphi) \rrbracket \mid \llbracket w \rrbracket).$$

The Markov assumption is standard in the probabilistic literature and has been argued to be widely applicable [25]. It is also adopted implicitly in much work in reasoning about action, planning, control and probabilistic inference with respect to system dynamics. Although it plays a key role in the observation models adopted in control theory and probabilistic reasoning [3, 24], it has received little attention in this respect within the qualitative planning literature.

The Markov assumption is also very powerful, allowing us to specify a ranking over runs relatively compactly. We need specify only two components: a *prior ranking* over worlds, i.e., $\kappa(\llbracket w \rrbracket)$ for each truth assignment w, and a family of *conditional observation rankings* of the form $\kappa(\llbracket Obs^\star(\varphi) \rrbracket \mid \llbracket w \rrbracket)$ for any observation φ and world w (we use the $\star$ to indicate that the observation plausibility is independent of m). Note that our conditional observation rankings differ dramatically from the general model, requiring that we rank individual observations, not infinite sequences of observations. These two components, however, determine the κ-ranking over runs.

Lemma 4.2: *Let $\mathcal{I} = (\mathcal{R}, \kappa, \pi)$ be a Markovian OS. Then the plausibility of the run $(w, \langle \varphi_1, \varphi_2, \ldots \rangle)$ is given by*

$$\kappa(w, \langle \varphi_1, \varphi_2, \cdots \rangle) = \kappa(\llbracket w \rrbracket) + \sum_{j=1}^{\infty} \kappa(\llbracket Obs^\star(\varphi_j) \rrbracket | \llbracket w \rrbracket). \quad (4)$$

Note that the infinite sum in the lemma may be ∞; this simply means that the run $(w, \langle \varphi_1, \varphi_2, \cdots \rangle)$ is impossible.

We can also easily characterize the ranking of an agent who has observed $\vec{\psi} = \langle \psi_1, \ldots, \psi_m \rangle$ at time m:

$$\kappa^{\vec{\psi}}(w, \langle \varphi_1, \varphi_2, \cdots \rangle) = \begin{cases} \infty \text{ if } \vec{\psi} \neq \langle \varphi_1, \ldots, \varphi_m \rangle \\ \kappa^{\vec{\psi}}(\llbracket w \rrbracket) + \sum_{j=m+1}^{\infty} \kappa(\llbracket Obs^\star(\varphi_j) \rrbracket | \llbracket w \rrbracket) \text{ otherwise.} \end{cases} \quad (5)$$

Thus, after observing $\vec{\psi}$, the agent's posterior over runs retains its Markovian structure, except that instead of using $\kappa(\llbracket \alpha \rrbracket)$, the prior over truth assignments, the agent now uses its posterior over truth assignments.

Example 4.3: We now reexamine the survey example. It is easy to verify that the system described in the previous example is not Markovian.[6] Instead, imagine that the agent believes a respondent with salary $\$x$ is most likely reply $x+2$, then $x+1$ then x, regardless of the number of times they are questioned. This can be modeled in a Markovian OS by (e.g.) assessing $\kappa(\llbracket Obs^\star(x+2) \rrbracket | \llbracket x \rrbracket) = 0$, $\kappa(\llbracket Obs^\star(x+1) \rrbracket | \llbracket x \rrbracket) = 1$, $\kappa(\llbracket Obs^\star(x) \rrbracket | \llbracket x \rrbracket) = 2$, and a rank of 3 to all other observations. Given an initial ranking over worlds, this fixes a ranking over runs. ∎

From a computational perspective, the Markov assumption admits further advantages, particularly if we are interested in modeling the agent's beliefs about propositions. We see from (5) that if the agent cares only about runs that extend the observations seen so far, then the term $\kappa^{\vec{\psi}}(\llbracket w \rrbracket)$ summarizes the influence of the past observations on current and future beliefs. This means that instead of examining an *arbitrarily long* sequence of past observations, the agent can reconstruct its beliefs using its posterior over truth assignments.

The following theorem shows how the agent can update this ranking of assignments when a new observation is made.

Theorem 4.4: *Let $\mathcal{I} = (\mathcal{R}, \kappa, \pi)$ be a Markovian OS. Then*

$$\kappa^{\vec{\psi} \cdot \varphi}(\llbracket w \rrbracket) = \kappa(\llbracket Obs^\star(\varphi) \rrbracket | \llbracket w \rrbracket) + \kappa^{\vec{\psi}}(\llbracket w \rrbracket) - \min_{\{w: \kappa^{\vec{\psi}}(\llbracket w \rrbracket) \neq \infty\}} (\kappa(\llbracket Obs^\star(\varphi) \rrbracket | \llbracket w \rrbracket) + \kappa^{\vec{\psi}}(\llbracket w \rrbracket)).$$

This is the qualitative analogue of standard Bayesian update of a probability distribution using Bayes rule. Since $\kappa^{\vec{\psi} \cdot \varphi}(\llbracket \sigma \rrbracket) = \min_{w \in \llbracket \sigma \rrbracket}(\kappa^{\vec{\psi} \cdot \varphi}(\llbracket w \rrbracket))$ for $\sigma \in \mathcal{L}$, this theorem shows that all we need to know to compute $\kappa^{\vec{\psi} \cdot \varphi}(\llbracket \sigma \rrbracket)$ is $\kappa^{\vec{\psi}}(\llbracket w \rrbracket)$ for each world w, together with the transition likelihoods. Thus, in many cases, the information an agent needs needs to be able to do revision in this setting, given

---
[6]Note that this example can be captured by a Markovian system if we model the state of the world so that it encodes the recipient's response history as well as her salary.

---

the Markov assumption, is feasible. Of course, it is still nontrivial to *represent* all this information. But this is precisely the same problem that arises in the probabilistic setting; we would expect the techniques that have proved so successful in the probabilistic setting (for example, Bayesian networks) to be applicable here as well [19].

4.1 Expressive Power of Markovian Systems

One property that immediately follows from the definition of a Markovian OS is the fact that the *order* in which the observations from a sequence are made does not influence the beliefs of the agent; only their presence and quantity do. This suggests the following *exchangability* postulate:

(O2) For any finite observation sequence $\varphi_1, \ldots, \varphi_m$ and for any permutation ρ of $1, \ldots, m$

$$B(\langle \varphi_1, \ldots, \varphi_m \rangle) = B(\langle \varphi_{\rho(1)}, \ldots, \varphi_{\rho(m)} \rangle).$$

It is easy to verify that O2 is sound in Markovian OSs.

Theorem 4.5: *For any Markovian OS $\mathcal{I}$, the revision function $B_\mathcal{I}$ induced by $\mathcal{I}$ satisfies O2.*

Unfortunately, O1 and O2 do not suffice to characterize the properties of revision functions in Markovian systems. As we show in the full paper, we can construct revision functions that satisfy both O1 and O2 yet cannot be modeled by a Markovian OS. The question of what conditions are needed to completely characterize Markovian OSs remains open.

5 Credible Observation Models

We have not (yet) put any constraints on the plausibility of observations in different runs. Thus, we can easily construct systems that obey the "opposite" of the success postulate. Consider, for example, a Markovian system where an observation φ is maximally plausible in a world where $\neg \varphi$ holds, and impossible otherwise. That is,

$$\kappa(\llbracket Obs^\star(\varphi) \rrbracket | \llbracket \alpha \rrbracket) = \begin{cases} 0 & \text{if } \alpha \models \neg \varphi \\ \infty & \text{if } \alpha \models \varphi. \end{cases}$$

It is easy to verify that in this system, after observing φ, the agent believes $\neg \varphi$.

Of course, this behavior runs counter to our intuition about the role of observations. In this section we examine conditions that attempt to capture the intuition that observations carry useful information about the true state of the world.

We start by considering a very simple condition. We say that an OS is *informative* if an agent is more likely to make accurate observations (ones that are true of the environment state) than inaccurate ones.

Definition 5.1: A Markovian OS $\mathcal{I} = (\mathcal{R}, \kappa, \pi)$ is *informative* if for all $\varphi, \psi \in \mathcal{L}$ and environment states w, if $w \models \varphi \wedge \neg \psi$, then $\kappa(\llbracket Obs^\star(\varphi) \rrbracket | \llbracket w \rrbracket) < \kappa(\llbracket Obs^\star(\psi) \rrbracket | \llbracket w \rrbracket)$.

Informativeness is clearly a nontrivial requirement, and it does seem to go some of the way towards capturing the intuition that observations are usually not misleading. Unfortunately, informative systems need not satisfy even a weak form of success. Consider the OS $\mathcal{I}$ where there are two environment states, p and $\neg p$, such that $\kappa(\llbracket Obs^\star(\top) \rrbracket | \llbracket p \rrbracket) = \kappa(\llbracket Obs^\star(\top) \rrbracket | \llbracket \neg p \rrbracket) = 0$, $\kappa(\llbracket Obs^\star(p) \rrbracket | \llbracket p \rrbracket) = 3$, $\kappa(\llbracket Obs^\star(\neg p) \rrbracket | \llbracket p \rrbracket) = 4$, $\kappa(\llbracket Obs^\star(\neg p) \rrbracket | \llbracket \neg p \rrbracket) = 1$, $\kappa(\llbracket Obs^\star(p) \rrbracket | \llbracket \neg p \rrbracket) = 2$, and $\kappa(\llbracket Obs^\star(\bot) \rrbracket | \llbracket p \rrbracket) =$

$\kappa([\![Obs^\star(\bot)]\!] \mid [\![\neg p]\!]) = \infty$. In this system, the only observation the agent is likely to make is the trivial observation $\top$; both p and $\neg p$ are unlikely. $\mathcal{I}$ is informative, since p is more likely to be observed than $\neg p$ if p is true (and $\neg p$ is more likely to be observed than p if $\neg p$ is true). Unfortunately, the agent is still more likely to observe p when p is false than when p is true. Suppose now that the initial ranking is such that both environment states are equally plausible, i.e., $\kappa([\![p]\!]) = \kappa([\![\neg p]\!]) = 0$. It is easy to verify that after m successive observations of p, we have

$$\kappa([\![p, Obs(\langle p, \ldots, p\rangle)]\!]) = 3m$$
$$\kappa([\![\neg p, Obs(\langle p, \ldots, p\rangle)]\!]) = 2m.$$

Thus, $B_\mathcal{I}(\langle p, \ldots, p \rangle) = Cn(\neg p)$. Moreover, observing more instances of p only strengthens the belief that p is false.

In our marketing example, this type of situation might arise if we take into account that respondents may be unresponsive (i.e., provide no salary information). Suppose that people with a salary of over $100,000 are most likely to be unresponsive, while people with a salary of $90,000 are more likely to report "10" than those that actually have a salary of $100,000. (The system is informative as long as people with a salary of $90,000 are more likely to report "9" than "10.") If we take p to denote "10 or more," then this situation is modeled by the system $\mathcal{I}$ above. With each observation "10," our agent (correctly) assesses $90,000 to be more likely.

Informativeness fails to lead to the recovery of the success postulate because it requires only that we compare the plausibilities of different observations at the same environment state. For an observation φ to provide evidence that increases the agent's degree of belief in φ, we must compare the plausibility of the observation across different states. This suggests the following definition.

Definition 5.2: A Markovian OS $\mathcal{I} = (\mathcal{R}, \kappa, \pi)$ is *credible* if, for all φ and environment states w, v such that $w \models \varphi$ and $v \models \neg \varphi$, we have $\kappa([\![Obs^\star(\varphi)]\!] \mid [\![w]\!]) < \kappa([\![Obs^\star(\varphi)]\!] \mid [\![v]\!])$

Intuitively, credibility says that an observation φ provides stronger evidence for *every* φ-world than it does for *any* $\neg \varphi$-world. In the example above, this requirement is not satisfied, for an observation "10" is most likely to be made in a state where $90,000 holds.

This requirement allows OSs to satisfy certain weak variants of the success postulate.

(O3) If $\neg \varphi \notin B(\vec{\psi})$, then $\varphi \in B(\vec{\psi} \cdot \varphi)$.

(O4) For all finite observation sequences $\vec{\psi}$ such that $\neg \varphi \notin B(\vec{\psi} \cdot \vec{\psi}')$ for some $\vec{\psi}'$, there is a number n such that $\varphi \in B(\vec{\psi} \cdot \varphi^n)$, where φ^n denotes n repetitions of φ.

Condition **O3** says that if φ is considered plausible (i.e., the agent does not believe $\neg \varphi$), then observing φ suffices to convince the agent that φ is true. Condition **O4** says that if φ is compatible with observing $\vec{\psi}$ (in that there is some sequence of observations that would make φ plausible), then the agent will believe φ after some number of φ observations.

Theorem 5.3: *If $\mathcal{I}$ is credible, then $B_\mathcal{I}$ satisfies O3 and O4.*

We can relate informativeness and credibility by requiring an additional property. Suppose that we think of each observation as arising from an experiment that tests the truth or falsity of a particular proposition. Specifically, after experiment E_φ, the agent observes either φ or $\neg \varphi$. In general, whether or not a particular experiment is performed will depend on the state. An OS is *experiment-independent* if the likelihood that a particular experiment is chosen is independent of the state.

Definition 5.4: The Markovian OS $\mathcal{I} = (\mathcal{R}, \kappa, \pi)$ is *experiment-independent* if, for every observation φ, there is a constant κ_φ such that $\min(\kappa([\![Obs^\star(\varphi)]\!] \mid [\![w]\!]), \kappa([\![Obs^\star(\neg \varphi)]\!] \mid [\![w]\!])) = \kappa_\varphi$ for all w.

We can think of κ_φ as the likelihood that the experiment for φ is performed (since the experiment will result in observing either φ or $\neg \varphi$). The OS $\mathcal{I}$ described above is not experiment-independent since both observations p and $\neg p$ are less plausible in state p than in state $\neg p$.

While the assumption of experiment-independence does not seem very natural, together with informativeness it implies credibility.

Lemma 5.5: *If $\mathcal{I} = (\mathcal{R}, \kappa, \pi)$ is informative and experiment-independent Markovian OS, then $\mathcal{I}$ is credible.*

Credibility, while allowing for O3 and O4, is still not strong enough to recover the success postulate. For this, we require a yet stronger assumption: we need to assume that all observations are known to be correct; that is, it must be impossible to make an inaccurate observation.

Definition 5.6: A Markovian OS is *accurate* if $\kappa([\![Obs^\star(\varphi)]\!] \mid [\![w]\!]) = \infty$ whenever $w \not\models \varphi$.

In our example, accuracy requires that when our agent observes, say, "10," the respondent's salary is in fact $100,000, and the agent is aware of this fact. It is thus impossible to observe two contradictory propositions in any sequence.

Accuracy almost implies informativeness and credibility, but doesn't quite: if observing both φ and $\neg \varphi$ is impossible, the system is accurate but neither informative nor credible. However, as long as $\min(\kappa([\![Obs^\star(\varphi)]\!] \mid [\![w]\!]), \kappa([\![Obs^\star(\neg \varphi)]\!] \mid [\![w]\!])) < \infty$ for all $\varphi \in \mathcal{L}$ and environment states w, then accuracy implies both properties. More significantly, accuracy implies the success postulate.

Theorem 5.7: *If $\mathcal{I}$ is an accurate Markovian OS, then $B_\mathcal{I}$ satisfies R2, that is, $\varphi \in B_\mathcal{I}(\vec{\psi} \cdot \varphi)$.*

Accuracy is not enough by itself to recover all of the AGM postulates. As we show in the full paper, we need both accuracy and a strong form experiment-independence, which says that all experiments are quite likely (and equally likely) to be performed; that is, $\kappa_\varphi = 0$ for all φ.

The key point here is that, while we can impose conditions on OSs that allow us to recover the full AGM model, it should be clear that these requirements are not always met by naturally-occurring OSs. Notions such as informativeness, credibility and accuracy are often inapplicable in many domains (including our running example of a marketing agent). The framework of OSs (and Markovian OSs in particular) provides a convenient and coherent model for examining the assumptions that hold in a given application domain and determining the precise form a revision function should take.

6 Concluding Remarks

We have described a general ontology for belief revision that allows us to model noisy or unreliable observations and relax the success postulate in a natural way. By imposing the Markov assumption, we obtained OSs that can be easily and naturally described. These give rise to agents whose epistemic state can be encoded in the "usual" way: as a ranking over worlds. Further assumptions about the quality of the observation model allow us to recover the success postulate (and a weaker version of it); this illustrates the general nature of our framework. The emphasis on semantics, as opposed to postulates, has allowed us to readily identify these assumptions and examine their consequences.

There is considerable related work that we survey in detail in a longer version of this paper. Lehmann [26] describes a model where observation sequences are treated as epistemic states in order to deal effectively with iterated revision. Two proposals impact strongly on this paper. Friedman and Halpern [16] use interpreted systems to model both revision and update, and examine the Markov assumption in this context. Boutilier [6, 8] develops a less general model for revision and update (taking the Markov assumption as given) and considers several methods for modeling noisy observations. All of this work (with the exception of [8]) essentially takes the success postulate as a given. Spohn's method of α-conditioning [31], a generalization of the notion of conditioning rankings defined above, was one of the first revision models to explicitly account for strength of evidence. However, α-conditioning does not provide an account of how strength of evidence might be derived. Our model allows us to do this in a natural way, by adapting well-known techniques from probability theory.

Important future research on observation systems includes the incorporation of system dynamics that allows the environment state to change, the development of suitable languages and logics for reasoning with noisy observations, and the syntactic characterization of special cases of OSs (in particular, Markovian OSs). We hope to report on this in future work.

Acknowledgements

The authors are grateful to Daniel Lehmann for comments on a draft of this paper.

References

[1] E. W. Adams. *The Logic of Conditionals*. D.Reidel, 1975.

[2] C. Alchourrón, P. Gärdenfors, and D. Makinson. On the logic of theory change: Partial meet contraction and revision functions. *J. Sym. Logic*, 50:510–530, 1985.

[3] K. J. Aström. Optimal Control of Markov Decision Processes with Incomplete State Estimation. *J. Math. Analysis and Applications*, 10:174–205, 1965.

[4] C. Boutilier. Normative, subjunctive and autoepistemic defaults: Adopting the Ramsey test. In *Proc. 3rd Inter. Conf. on Principles of Knowledge Representation and Reasoning*, pp. 685–696, 1992.

[5] C. Boutilier. Unifying default reasoning and belief revision in a modal framework. *Artificial Intelligence*, 68:33–85, 1994.

[6] C. Boutilier. Generalized update: Belief change in dynamic settings. In *Proc. 14th Inter. Joint Conf. on AI*, pp. 1550–1556, 1995.

[7] C. Boutilier. Iterated revision and minimal revision of conditional beliefs. *J. Phil. Logic*, 25(3):262–305, 1996.

[8] C. Boutilier. A unified model of qualitative belief change: A dynamical systems perspective. *Artificial Intelligence*, 98(1–2):281–316, 1998.

[9] A. Darwiche and J. Pearl. On the logic of iterated belief revision. *Artificial Intelligence*, 89:1–29, 1997.

[10] D. Dubois and H. Prade. Belief change and possibility theory. In Peter Gärdenfors, ed., *Belief Revision*. Cambridge University Press, 1992.

[11] D. Dubois and H. Prade. Belief revision with uncertain inputs in the possibilistic setting. In *Proc. 12th Conf. on Uncertainty in AI*, pp. 236–243, 1996.

[12] R. Fagin, J. Y. Halpern, Y. Moses, and M. Y. Vardi. *Reasoning about Knowledge*. MIT Press, 1995.

[13] N. Friedman. *Modeling Beliefs in Dynamic Systems*. PhD thesis, Stanford University, 1997.

[14] N. Friedman and J. Y. Halpern. Belief revision: A critique. In *Proc. 6th Inter. Conf. on Principles of Knowledge Representation and Reasoning*, pp. 421–431, 1996.

[15] N. Friedman and J. Y. Halpern. A qualitative Markov assumption and its implications for belief change. In *Proc. 12th Conf. on Uncertainty in AI*, pp. 263–273, 1996.

[16] N. Friedman and J. Y. Halpern. Modeling belief in dynamic systems. Part II: revision and update. Submitted for publication. A preliminary version appears in *Proc. 4th Inter. Conf. on Principles of Knowledge Representation and Reasoning*, 1994, pp. 190–201.

[17] N. Friedman and J. Y. Halpern. Modeling beliefs in dynamic systems. part I: Foundations. *Artificial Intelligence*, 95:257–316, 1997.

[18] P. Gärdenfors. *Knowledge in Flux: Modeling the Dynamics of Epistemic States*. MIT Press, 1988.

[19] M. Goldszmidt and J. Pearl. Qualitative probabilities for default reasoning, belief revision, and causal modeling. *Artificial Intelligence*, 84:57–112, 1996.

[20] A. Grove. Two modellings for theory change. *J. Phil. Logic*, 17:157–170, 1988.

[21] J. Y. Halpern and R. Fagin. Modelling knowledge and action in distributed systems. *Distributed Computing*, 3(4):159–179, 1989.

[22] R. C. Jeffrey. *The Logic of Decision*. University of Chicago Press, 1983.

[23] H. Katsuno and A. O. Mendelzon. On the difference between updating a knowledge database and revising it. In *Proc. 2nd Inter. Conf. on Principles of Knowledge Representation and Reasoning*, pp. 387–394, 1991.

[24] R. E. Kalman. A New Approach to Linear Filtering and Prediction Problems. *J. Basic Eng.*, 82:35–45, 1960.

[25] J. G. Kemeny and J. L. Snell. *Finite Markov Chains*. Van Nostrand, 1960.

[26] D. Lehmann. Belief revision, revised. In *Proc. 14th Inter. Joint Conf. on AI*, pp. 1534–1540, 1995.

[27] I. Levi. Iteration of conditionals and the Ramsey test. *Synthese*, 76(1):49–81, 1988.

[28] M. J. Osborne and A. Rubinstein. *A Course in Game Theory*. MIT Press, 1994.

[29] H. Rott. Conditionals and theory change: Revisions, expansions, and additions. *Synthese*, 81(1):91–113, 1989.

[30] H. Rott. Belief change using generalized epistemic entrenchment. *J. Logic, Language and Information*, 1(1):45–78, 1992.

[31] W. Spohn. Ordinal conditional functions: A dynamic theory of epistemic states. In W.L. Harper and B. Skyrms, eds., *Causation in Decision, Belief Change and Statistics*, vol. 2, pp. 105–134. D. Reidel, 1987.

[32] M. Winslett. *Updating Logical Databases*. Cambridge University Press, 1990.

Toward Design as Collaboration

Susan L. Epstein

Department of Computer Science
Hunter College and The Graduate School of The City University of New York
New York, NY 10021 USA
epstein@roz.hunter.cuny.edu

Abstract

In design, multiple disparate goals must be addressed simultaneously. It is the thesis of this work that problems in two-dimensional layout design can be solved by collaboration among single-goal, intelligent agents, each responsible for a class of objects and responsive to explicit metrics. In this model, each agent produces conflict-free designs for its own class of objects, and then, when objects conflict with each other in the combined design, the agents that own those objects address the conflicts. A limitedly rational implementation demonstrates its efficacy for park layout design in the two-dimensional plane.

Two-dimensional Layout Design

Design problems typically entail large search spaces and multiple, ill-defined goal tests (Goel and Pirolli 1989). As a result, design has been regarded as a domain (CAD/CAM) in which computers assist people rather than work alone. This paper's primary contributions are a model for autonomous two-dimensional layout design as collaboration among a set of agents, and a limitedly rational architecture for this model. Drawing upon research on human experts, the model devotes considerable effort to the selection of an initial high-quality state likely to include multiple constraint violations, and then seeks to remove them.

The problem in two-dimensional layout design is to position a set of two-dimensional objects within a prespecified outline to meet a set of restrictions (*criteria*). In the park design problem of Table 1, for example, 13 objects must be located precisely on a grid. Criteria that must be satisfied are called *constraints*. In Table 1, only the object criteria and C_5 are constraints. Table 1's task is non-trivial; about 1.3×10^{26} placements abide by the object constraints.

A *solution* to a two-dimensional layout design problem positions all the objects and satisfies all the constraints. Typically there are many solutions; it is the multiple, vague goal tests make design problems particularly difficult (Goel and Pirolli 1992). Those tests are represented here as non-required criteria called *principles*. (There are 7 in Table 1.) Principles are important to a designer, but in some unspecified combination. As a result, design is not an optimization problem, yet designers speak of solutions that are "better" or "worse" (Goel and Pirolli 1992). Thus in a

Copyright © 1998, American Association for Artificial Intelligence (www.aaai.org). All rights reserved.

Table 1: A park design problem.

Task: Place on a 20 × 40 discrete grid the following objects:

PF_1: a 7 × 7 playing field	P_1: a 5 × 3 pond	B_1: a 5 × 10 building
PF_2: a 5 × 2 playing field	P_2: a 3 × 2 pond	B_2: a 2 × 2 building
PF_3: a 5 × 2 playing field		

F_1: a 6 × 7 forest	R_1: a road of width 1
F_2: a 4 × 2 forest	R_2: a road of width 1
	R_3: a road of width 1
	R_4: a road of width 1

Goal: Satisfy all constraints and respond to all principles as well as possible.

Object constraints:
  PF_1 boundary is ≥ 0.1 away from all edges.
  PF_3 center is within 0.8 of the park's center.
  B_1 boundary is against some edge.
  B_2 center is within 0.5 of the park's center.
  P_1 boundary is ≥ 0.3 away from all edges.
  P_2 center is within 0.3 of the park's center.
  F_1 center is within 0.4 of the park's center.
  F_2 boundary is within 0.1 of some edge.
  R_1 runs from the eastern grid edge.
  R_2 runs from the western grid edge.
  R_3 runs from the northern grid edge.
  R_4 runs from the southern grid edge.
  R_1, R_2, R_3, and R_4 are connected.

Intra-class principles:
  C_1: Total road length should be small.
  C_2: Fields should not adjoin each other.
  C_3: Ponds' centers should be ≤ .2 of the grid apart.
  C_4: Buildings' centers should be ≤ .6 of the grid apart.

Inter-class constraint:
  C_5: Objects may not overlap.

Inter-class principles:
  C_6: Buildings should be adjacent to roads.
  C_7: Every building should have a view, i.e., be within 2 units of a pond or forest.

Secondary inter-class principle:
  C_8: Minimize the total Manhattan distance of all empty grid positions to their nearest road.

two-dimensional layout design problem, how well a solution meets all the principles becomes a metric on its quality. The goal is to find a high-quality solution.

Object Categories and a Collaborative Model

Two-dimensional layout design problems usually categorize the objects to be instantiated (Goel and Pirolli 1992). Table 1, for example, partitions its objects into five *classes*, sets of functionally and/or structurally similar objects: ponds, playing fields, forests, buildings, and roads. (The remainder of the park is intended to be open grassy space.) Design criteria can be categorized with respect to these classes. An *object criterion* describes how a single object relates to the grid, such as "the boundary of B_1 is against some edge." An *intra-class criterion* restricts two or more objects of the same class. For example, in Table 1 the intra-class criterion "Total road length should be small" describes a desirable property for the set of roads. An *inter-class criterion* restricts two or more objects of different classes. For example, in Table 1 the inter-class criterion "Buildings should be adjacent to roads" describes how each building should relate to some road.

To cast two-dimensional layout design as a state space search, let a description that positions every objects be a *complete state*; otherwise it is a *partial state*. In addition, let a state be *legal* if it violates no constraints; otherwise it is *illegal*. A two-dimensional layout design problem can then be addressed as search for a path from a partial, legal state through a space of legal states to a complete legal state. Using this single-goal approach, a designer would locate one object at a time on the grid until all objects were present, and backtrack as necessary. (Constraint satisfaction programming, *CSP*, is addressed in the final section.)

Human design experts, however, do not search this way. They consider a set of objects or parts of objects and how they relate to each other, typically in an illegal state (Schraagen 1993). In addition, a human expert's first state is likely to be a compendium of a number of legal partial states, each for an entire class of objects (Schraagen 1993). Since there are usually many different possible states, the human designer selects, both initially and during search, states that meet metrics for good design. A metric applicable to legal partial states and limited to a single agent's objects is an intra-class principle. A metric applicable to complete states and pertaining to objects of more than one agent is an inter-class principle.

In light of the human approach, this paper proposes a collaborative model that addresses two-dimensional layout design as a task for a set of agents, each of which advocates on behalf of a single object class. For example, five separate agents would collaborate on the problem in Table 1. Problem solving in this model is search for a path through a space that also includes both illegal and partial states. This collaborative model for two-dimensional layout design begins search from an initial state that respects the principles of each agent. Each agent produces an *ideal framework*, a legal partial state for all its objects that is

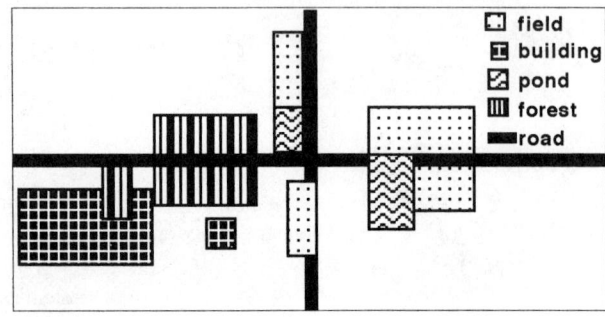

Figure 1: An initial state with 6 conflicts for Table 1.

highly-rated by its principles. For Table 1, where C_1 is the only all-road principle, one ideal road framework is four orthogonal roads from the center of the grid to the edges. The union of the agents' ideal frameworks is a complete, initial state, such as Figure 1, and likely to be illegal.

Since agents produce legal partial states, a *conflict* arises in this model only when two or more agents violate an inter-class constraint, as when objects overlap in Figure 1. A conflict is uniquely identified by its set of objects. There are 6 distinct conflicts in Figure 1: between the large field and the large pond, the large field and the eastern road, the small forest and the large building, the large forest and the western road, a small field and the southern road, and the strip contested by the large pond, the large field, and the eastern road.

Collaboration among agents in this model can be either explicit or implicit. Explicit collaboration would be negotiation over a conflict. Implicit collaboration is achieved by the influence of shared inter-class principles on decision making. For now, the latter is the primary focus. Consider, for example, the conflict between the large building and the small forest in Figure 1. One way to resolve it is to relocate either or both objects. When the forest agent considers a forest relocation, it will prefer those that abide by C_7. The building agent, meanwhile, will prefer building relocations that abide by C_4, C_6, and C_7. (Consideration of the secondary principle C_8 is postponed, as discussed later.) Because the strength with which each agent suggests a relocation reflects how well that proposal meets the agent's principles, the strongest suggestion represents a decision that best addresses both mutual and individual goals.

The CD Architecture and FLO

CD (Collaborative Design) is a limitedly rational architecture which applies the collaborative model to two-dimensional layout design problems. The CD program for park design is called *FLO*, after park designer Frederick Law Olmstead. Although CD is not restricted to parks, for clarity the examples here are all drawn from runs with FLO. A CD-based system begins with partially specified objects already categorized into classes. CD's task is to specify them fully. For example, Table 1 restricts each object's location in the grid; a solution locates all of them precisely.

CD assigns the full specification of the objects in any

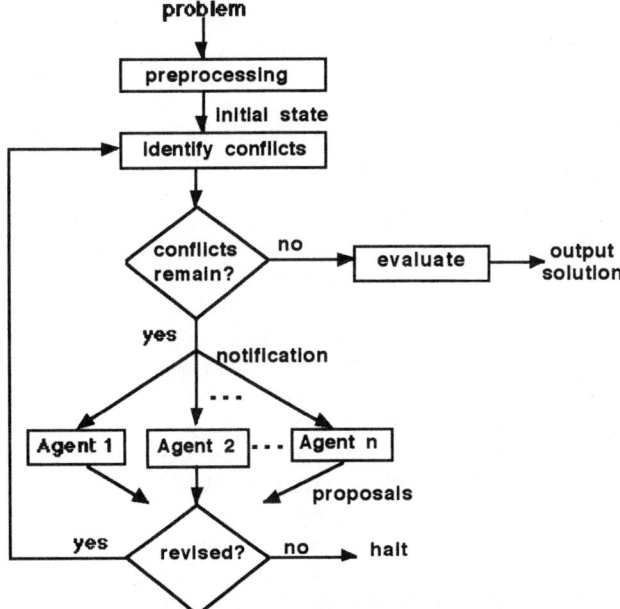

Figure 2: An overview of the CD solution process.

one class to a limitedly rational agent. The current problem state describes the objects' specifications, and represents the agent's environment. Each agent computes and executes responses to that environment in the form of proposals that specify its own objects further or differently and abide by constraints.

Figure 2 sketches the CD solution process (*trial*). When a problem is first presented, CD constructs an initial state. Objects that conflict there notify their respective agents. An agent whose object is in conflict with another's tries to construct *proposals*, recommendations that address the conflict. A proposal includes the agent's name, the conflict it addresses, the action it proposes, and comments on how well the proposal abides by the agent's principles.

Until some state is conflict-free or there are no proposals, CD selects the proposal that has the best comments and addresses the most *severe* conflict. In FLO, that is the conflict that involves the most objects and the most grid locations, and engenders the fewest proposals. Implementation of the selected proposal creates a new state, and the cycle in Figure 2 repeats. CD is non-deterministic because ties among equally good choices are made at random. Typically, therefore, CD runs multiple trials, and all the agents evaluate each output solution.

Throughout a trial, each CD agent has access to three kinds of procedures, listed in Table 2. An *originator* is restricted to a single agent and formulates proposals to address a conflict in which its agent's object is involved. A *commentator* evaluates how well the state resulting from a proposal will satisfy a particular metric. A commentator restricted to a single agent represents an intra-class principle; a commentator shared among a set of agents represents an inter-class principle. FLO's road agent, for example, has a C_1 commentator to support short roads, and a C_6 commentator (shared with the building agent) to encourage roads

Table 2: Procedures available to a CD agent

Type	Role
Originator	Propose conflict resolution
Commentator	Evaluation metric
Secondary commentator	High-cost evaluation metric

near buildings. A *secondary commentator*, such as C_8, also applies a metric to a state, but one so costly that its application is restricted to preprocessing and solution evaluation only. The remainder of this section details the construction of the initial state and proposal generation.

The initial state

CD devotes substantial effort to construction of an initial state, as diagrammed in Figure 3. To begin, each agent produces several ideal frameworks, descriptions including only that agent's objects and their locations. In this phase, an agent considers only its own objects and abides by all relevant constraints. The agent rates each of its ideal frameworks with its commentators of both kinds, and forwards the top-rated ones.

CD uses the best ideal frameworks from each agent to produce several complete states. Each is a *combined ideal*, the union of one ideal framework from each agent. Figure 1 was a combined ideal, the union of an ideal framework for Table 1 from each of FLO's five agents.

The combined ideal with the fewest conflicts is called the *candidate*. In a candidate, any agent that has more than $x\%$ of its resources in conflict is labeled an *offender*. For example, all but the building agent are 25% offenders in Figure 1. From its store of ideal frameworks, each offender offers several highly-rated alternatives. CD replaces the of-

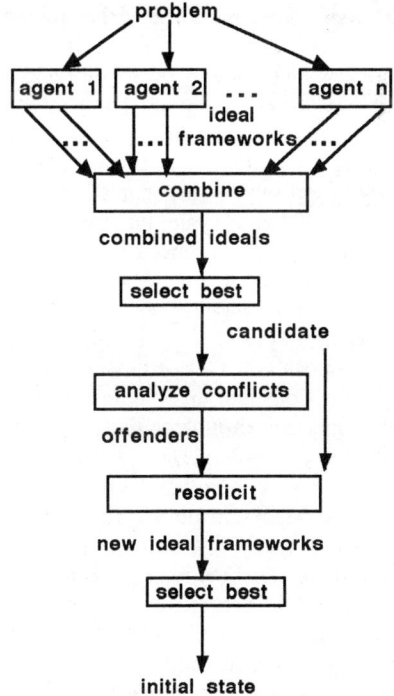

Figure 3: Initial state construction in CD.

Automated Reasoning 137

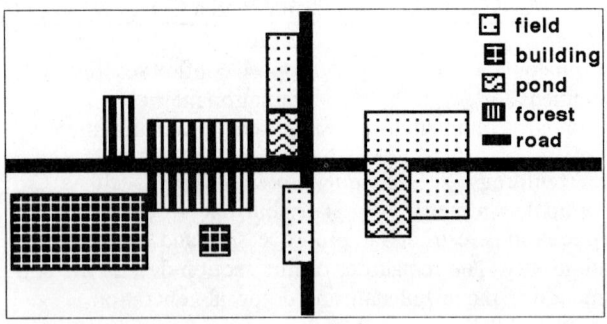

Figure 4: A revision of Figure 1 with 5 conflicts.

fender's ideal framework in the candidate with whichever alternative produces the fewest conflicts. For example, FLO substituted another forest ideal framework in Figure 1 to produce the new combined ideal in Figure 4, with 5 conflicts instead of 6. Every offender is given only one opportunity to resubmit ideal frameworks. CD uses the initial state only as a good starting point, and then goes on to address the remaining conflicts differently.

Proposal generation and limited rationality

As in Figure 2, until the current state is a solution, objects notify their agents when they are involved in one or more conflicts. Each notified agent formulates a set of proposals to address those conflicts. An agent may propose either to *resolve* (eliminate) a conflict between two objects or to *ameliorate* (reduce the number of objects in) a conflict among three or more objects. In the state of Figure 4, for example, two agents reacted to the conflict involving a small field and the southern road. The field agent proposed relocating the field so that it did not conflict with any other object, and the road agent proposed either relocating the southern road or diverting it around the field. Conflicts among more than two agents may be ameliorated first, and then resolved. For example, the pond agent might propose to ameliorate the three-agent conflict over the strip in Figure 4 by relocating the pond. If that proposal were implemented, the large field would then conflict only with the eastern road, and, in the next cycle, the road agent and the field agent could address that reduced conflict. CD always prefers resolution, however, to amelioration.

There are usually more ways to resolve or ameliorate a conflict than a design system should explore. To control the number of proposals, a CD originator suggests only constraint-abiding actions that involve its own objects. For each agent, FLO has one originator that relocates one of that agent's objects. For example, in Figure 4 the western road could shift to any of the other 19 rows. All but 5 of those, however, would still conflict with some other object. Rather than propose many substandard relocations, the road agent's originators enforce relevant constraints. Thus in Figure 4 any road relocation proposal would shift the western road to a clear row and connect it to at least one other road. An originator is forbidden to propose an action that would return to an equivalent prior state. Each agent may have any number of originators. In addition to its five relocators, FLO has a road originator that reroutes a specific road around a specific object.

On two-dimensional layout design problems, even constraint-abiding originators are likely to generate far too many proposals. Therefore CD makes each agent *limitedly rational* by imposing two prespecified limits: one on its total computation time per cycle, and another on the number of proposals it may produce about any one state.

After an agent's originators produce their proposals, its commentators rate how well each prospective new state would meet the agent's principles. Unlike ideal framework construction, comment construction affords the agent a view of the entire state, not just its own objects. Although commentators are not subject to resource constraints the way originators are, care must be taken to guard against system slowdown from those that are resource-hungry. For example, although an efficient implementation discourages roads along the edges of the grid, the commentator for Table 1's C_8 is still costly enough to substantially degrade system performance. C_8 would slow down any system whenever it was evaluated. It is more economical, therefore, to exclude it during search. Such a secondary commentator is applied with the ordinary commentators only to rate combined ideals during generation ("select best" in Figure 3) and to compare solutions ("evaluate" in Figure 2). Empirically, however, high-quality solutions are less likely as more commentators are made secondary; only the most costly should be relegated to this category.

Empirical Results and Discussion

Several performance measures apply in two-dimensional layout design. The system should be able to address multiple problems. Solutions should be achieved quickly and fit criteria well. Easier problems should be easier to solve. Speed can be measured as elapsed problem-solving (clock) time, or as number of decision cycles.

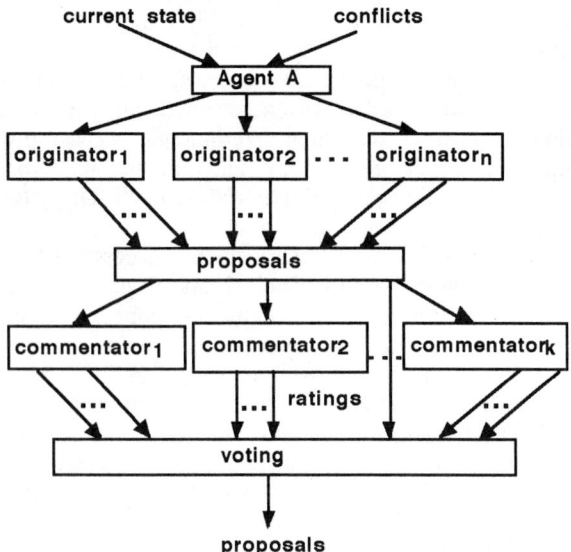

Figure 5: Proposal solicitation from a CD agent.

Table 3: Partial specification of a small park design problem. See Table 1 for intra-class and inter-class principles.

Task: Place on a 10 × 20 discrete grid the following objects:
- PF: a 4 × 2 playing field
- B: a 3 × 3 building
- R_1: a road of width 1
- R_3: a road of width 1
- P: a 4 × 3 pond
- F: a 2 × 1 forest
- R_2: a road of width 1
- R_4: a road of width 1

Goal: Satisfy all constraints and respond to all principles as well as possible.

Object constraints:
- PF center is within 0.8 of the park's center.
- F center is within 0.1 of some edge.
- R_3 runs from the northern grid edge.
- B center is within 0.5 of the park's center.
- R_1 runs from the eastern grid edge.
- R_4 runs from the southern grid edge.
- P center is within 0.2 of the park's center.
- R_2 runs from the western grid edge.
- R_1, R_2, R_3, and R_4 are connected.

CD and FLO are both implemented in Common Lisp. All combined ideals, initial and intermediate states, plus proposals and ratings, can be made transparent to the user. FLO was tested on both the larger problem of Table 1 and on the small problem partially specified in Table 3. Both problems use the intra-class and inter-class principles in Table 1. Each run consisted of 10 trials on the same problem. The results shown in Table 4 are averaged over 10 runs, where "size" counts complete states conforming to all object constraints. Figure 6 shows the top-rated solution to the small problem; it satisfies all the criteria of Table 1.

Table 4: Results on 10 trials for two problems with FLO.

	Small problem	Larger problem
Size	3.9×10^{11}	1.3×10^{26}
Offenders	2.20	1.36
Solutions	9.3	7.3
Cycles to solution	2.1	10.0
Time per trial	7.33 seconds	136.9 seconds

In a typical trial on the larger problem, the combined ideals ranged from 19 to 6 conflicts; the best was Figure 1, with 4 offenders. Only the forest agent's alternative ideal framework improved that candidate, making the initial state Figure 4 with 5 conflicts. After 4 revisions (the last solved 2 conflicts), FLO arrived at the solution in Figure 7(a), with a road bent around the southernmost field. Another solution from the same run, Figure 7(b), rates lower because the large building has a poor view. The remainder of this section addresses the primary issues in two-dimensional layout design within the collaborative model envisioned here: search, optimality, speed, and generality.

Search

CD executes a satisficing search guided by explicit principles through the space of complete states. CD finds highly-rated solutions so quickly in so large a space because it prunes search several ways. Search begins with a state a highly-rated by the commentators and with the prospect of a short solution path (number of conflicts). The originators prevent searching some predictably illegal states, while limited rationality controls the branch factor. The commentators bias search in the direction of highly-rated states. Agents proffer only high-rated proposals, and one that promises to resolve some most severe conflict is chosen.

On a finite number O of objects in a finite grid, CD is guaranteed to halt. The system does not cycle through the same set of states (shift one or more objects back and forth repeatedly) because the originators do not make such proposals. In addition, each object is treated as if it has finitely many possible locations on the grid, so that there are finitely many proposals to consider. Let C be the number of conflicts in the initial state, and $obj(c_i)$ be the number of objects involved in conflict c_i. Clearly $obj(c_i) \leq O$ for $i = 1, 2, \ldots, C$. Since CD never introduces new conflicts, and since it either halts or reduces or ameliorates at least one

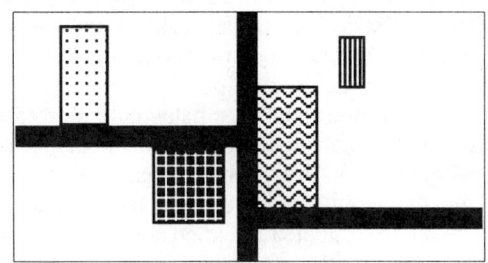

Figure 6: FLO's best solution to the small problem.

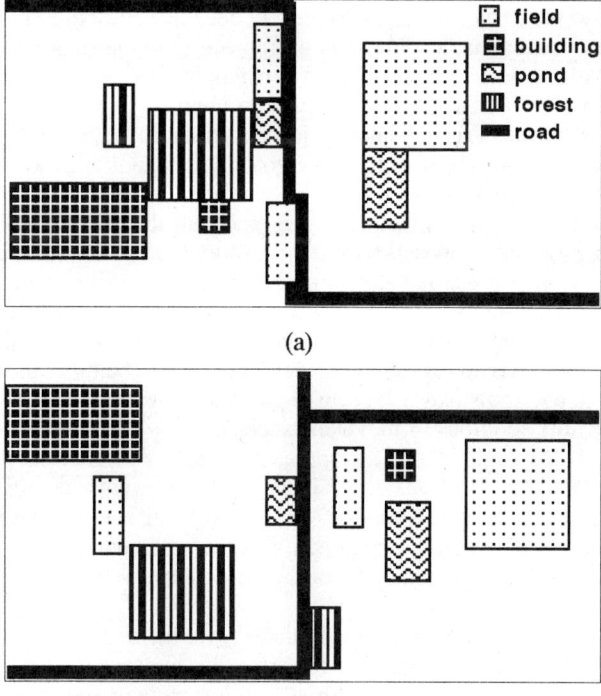

Figure 7: Two solutions to the problem in Table 1.

conflict on each iteration, the maximum number of iterations before it halts is:

$$\sum_{i=1}^{C} [obj(c_i) - 1] < O \cdot C$$

OC is an overestimate of the distance to solution, since a single proposal can resolve more than one conflict.

Like many satisficing systems, CD is not guaranteed to find a solution. This is why a run is a set of trials, as it often is in hill climbing. During some trials, an illegal state engenders no proposals, so the program produces no solution. Typically these are "nearly good enough" states with only one or two conflicts remaining. Four approaches to these states are under investigation. First, under limited rationality, a constructive proposal may be overlooked. CD could provide originators with increasing resource limits if a state has only a few conflicts remaining, in a kind of iterative broadening. Second, after the initial state, CD never proposes to introduce additional conflicts. It could allow an originator to introduce a proposal that addresses one conflict at the price of introducing another that is expected to be easier to resolve. Care would be required to preserve halting. Third, CD never violates object criteria, but human designers frequently do (e.g., cost overruns). CD could modify an object's description (e.g., size or shape) within some prespecified limits. Finally, CD's proposal system supports collaboration based on shared principles, but does not provide for direct communication between agents. It could also have agents negotiate a mutual conflict together.

Optimality and high-quality solutions

As discussed in the introduction, the two-dimensional layout designer must satisfy only constraints and may merely "do well" on principles. Since CD does hill-climbing only on constraints, a solution is guaranteed to be optimal only with respect to them. FLO, for example, only guarantees no overlap in a solution to a park problem.

The use of a single non-object constraint in FLO was deliberate. All the principles are goals in design, but making more of them required is not necessarily constructive. That further constrains the generators, and runs the risk of finding too few proposals within the resource limits. Thus there is no guarantee that any commentator will rate an eventual solution highly, only that the solution process will prefer to pass through states the commentator rates more highly than some alternatives, all other decision factors being equal. Enough trials (say 10) seem to guarantee a variety of high-quality solutions from which to select.

Uncertainty about an optimal value for a criterion is characteristic of design problems, but it prevents identification of an optimal design. C_8, for example, is normed on an overestimate; its maximum value is unknown. As a result, solutions can only be better than others, as Figure 7(a) is on C_8, never "best."

Human designers typically tinker with their solutions. In Figure 7(a), for example, lowering the western road one unit is likely to improve the C_8 rating without impacting the other ratings. A tweaking phase is therefore planned for CD, where a solution will be repeatedly improved by hill-climbing through legal states. Additional or refined principles could also further improve the designs of Figure 7.

Speed

Including illegal states substantially enlarges the search space. CD's ideal framework is a highly-rated, albeit illegal, initial state. To test the impact of a refined initial state, FLO was run on the small problem using a single combined ideal without testing for offenders. Compared to the data reported above, there was a 51% reduction in the number of solutions, running time approximately tripled, and the number of iterations to a solution increased by 81%. Clearly, some computational effort on the initial state is worthwhile, but how much does it merit?

In extensive empirical testing, a variety of values for parameter settings were tried on the small problem, measuring both total computation time and the fraction devoted to construction of the initial state. Number of ideal frameworks generated (1–10), number of combined ideals (1–8), percentage of conflicted resources defining an offender (25-75%), and number of alternatives submitted by an offender (1-5) were tested in many combinations, varying one at a time. In these experiments the initial state almost always needed revision. Up to 6 or 7, more combined ideal frameworks made it more likely that the problem would be solved and that the overall solution time would be low, but it also increased the percentage of total computation time devoted to the initial state. Lower percentages for the offender definition also improved the number of solutions, without any impact on either time. Finally, the number of alternatives submitted by an offender appeared to have little impact as long as it was at least 3. Under the settings used here (10 ideal frameworks, 7 combined ideals, 3 alternatives from 25% offenders), FLO devoted 36% of its computation time to the initial state on the small problem, and 21.3% on the larger problem.

Could FLO have done as well with smaller resource limits on the originators? Table 4's data was generated with limits of 10 seconds and 10 proposals, but some originators (notably the road agent's) used far less. In a run where the originators were held to 5 seconds and 5 proposals, FLO solved the larger problem about as often and the solutions were about the same quality. At the 95% confidence level for statistical significance, however, problem solving required more time (166.0 seconds) because the commentators spent considerably more time evaluating the proposals.

AI research has long recognized that a generate-and-test approach like CD's derives power when intelligence is moved from the tester into the generator. In an earlier version, originators proposed relocations whether or not they produced a conflict, and thereby substantially slowed the program. Forcing the roads to interconnect is a kind of embedded intelligence, too. Additional domain-specific routines (e.g., one that would perceive large chunks of "clear" space quickly and investigate relocation alternatives within them) could further speed performance.

In a parallel implementation, CD agents and shared

commentators would be relegated to separate processors, and proposals computed quickly would be considered first. Caution would be advised, however, since a quickly developed proposal is often to a conflict that is easier to resolve, one less worthy of immediate attention.

If the grid is made larger, the number of alternative locations for objects of the same size increases, so that an intuitively easier problem (the same size objects in more space) could require more computation (more proposals to generate and comment upon). CD's limited rationality prevents this. Although such limited rationality could make it more difficult to discover a solution, the quality of FLO's solutions as rated by the commentators does not deteriorate, and it solves problems much faster with these limits in place. Preliminary testing on a still larger problem in a 30 × 90 grid indicates that FLO should scale nicely.

Two speedup techniques applied here are domain-dependent. First, certain symmetries of the two-dimensional plane produce equally valid object placement for ideal frameworks with relatively little additional computation time. Therefore, FLO symmetrically transforms an offending ideal framework and any proffered alternatives to produce more alternatives quickly. Second, relocators site an object according to its alternatives. Because its object criteria are static, FLO can compute all possible locations for an object as constrained by its object criteria only once, when the problem is defined.

Generality

CD is not limited to parks; it is intended for many two-dimensional layout domains. The design criteria for buildings, for example, also includes object criteria (e.g., room dimensions), intra-class criteria (e.g., "keep the plumbing along a central core" or "provide electrical power to every room,") and inter-class criteria (e.g., "do not place an outlet too near running water"). A variety of other domains is under active consideration.

Within any domain, CD is highly modular. It accommodates any number of object classes and their agents, any grid size, and any number of objects. Each agent may have any number of originators and commentators, each with its own resource limits. Thus, if the solutions are unsatisfactory with respect to some unelucidated principle, it is easy enough to add it.

If, on the other hand, solutions are unsatisfactory with respect to some principles P already present, there are several ways to give them more influence. CD normalizes each commentator's ratings in a range before they are submitted. Thus one could bias the system with a higher range for P. If, for example, road costs are a particular concern, increase C_1's range. Similarly, CD normalizes the proposal strengths of each agent in a range, so one could assign a higher range to an agent that included P. If, for example, playing fields are the park's primary function, increase the field agent's range. Alternatively, CD runs multiple trials on a problem. One could rate those solutions on P and identify the best, or further perturb the solution top-rated by P in ways that P preferred.

This proposed model and the CD architecture are likely to succeed only if the design space meets the following conditions:
• Objects are readily categorizable.
• Each principle quantifies a single aspect of good design.
• Non-secondary commentators are relatively efficient.
• There are easy to find ideal frameworks for each class.
• There are many solutions of varying quality.

These are all typical of two-dimensional layout design space, although other design spaces may also fit this description. If ideal frameworks score equally under some perturbation (e.g., the symmetries applied in FLO), or static object criteria conserve originator time, so much the better.

Related and Future Work

An underlying assumption in CD is that explicit knowledge can control the combinatorics of search in a very large space, an assumption shared by human designers. Although CD is not intended as a full cognitive model of the human design process, it does simulate many features identified by psychological studies of experts in architecture, mechanical engineering, and instructional design (Goel and Pirolli 1992). Like these human experts, CD has distinct problem solving phases (ideal frameworks, initial state, iteration), decomposition into modules (object classes and their agents), incremental development with limited commitment, little deductive inference, and a variety of evaluation methods (CD's commentators and secondary commentators) not traditional in many other AI domains.

CD is a satisficing architecture; like people, it solves problems "well enough" rather than optimally (Simon 1981). There is ample support in the psychology literature for satisficing behavior in a variety of domains and for multiple rationales like CD's commentators (Biswas, Goldman, Fisher, Bhuva, and Glewwe 1995; Crowley and Siegler 1993). Failure-driven conflict resolution, such as the repeated refinements described for CD, has proved successful in a variety of other domains (Collins, Birnbaum, and Krulwich 1989).

Because it requires a group of logically distinct processing agents to address the same problem, CD can be classified as distributed AI, in particular as a multi-agent system (Bond and Gasser 1988). The architecture seeks to realize collective system properties (good design) within a fixed environment (Durfee and Rosenschein 1994). CD is a step toward organizational cognition, where individual agents are responsive both to their own objects and those of other agents (Gasser 1993). CD is also an example of distributed constraint satisfaction, a newly-emerging research area (Armstrong and Durfee 1997). AI in design has received substantial attention (e.g., (Gero and Sudweeks 1996)), but the collaborative model for two-dimensional layouts presented here is novel to the best of the author's knowledge.

Although preliminary indications are that CD and FLO are efficient, a comparison of these results with those of other methods, particularly CSP, is in order. Each FLO object would be represented as a variable whose possible values represented its legal alternative locations. The overlap constraint renders the graph complete. CSP could also play an important role in the formulation of ideal frameworks. Economics-based negotiation is another likely method to consider (Pennock and Wellman 1996). In FLO, the resources are the distinct grid squares for which agents would compete. The author hopes to attract specialists in both areas to these problems. Although other techniques exist, most notably in operations research and numerical methods, their cost for these problems appears prohibitive.

Two of Olmstead's New York City parks (Central Park and Prospect Park, often cited as examples of outstanding design) are intended as further test cases. FLO soon will have originators to rotate objects and to interchange the locations of same-class objects. Several commentators that encourage additional aesthetic properties, such as even distribution of vacant space, are also under development.

CD agents are reactive; they sense conflicts in the grid and respond to them with proposals. An intention shared among agents is thus far represented only as a common decision making principle. An important next step is to enable CD agents to communicate directly with one another. This should be particularly valuable in situations where only joint action (for example, shifting objects of different classes simultaneously) will resolve a conflict.

CD is a direct descendant of FORR, a general architecture for learning and problem solving (Epstein 1994). CD can be thought of as a set of FORR-based agents, each of which has a set of FORR-like Advisors (the procedures of Table 2). A CD agent, however, has originators so that it is not compelled to comment on all possible actions as a FORR-based agent is. FORR's more sophisticated learning and search approaches should eventually migrate to CD.

Meanwhile, this paper has shown how a collaborative model for two-dimensional layout design can both constrain search and impose aesthetic design criteria. The model capitalizes on collaboration among agents to clarify the process description, to organize search, and to find a good initial state. The CD architecture provides a limitedly rational version of this model which distinguishes between a resource-limited search for good ideas (originators) and good reasons to support them (commentators). CD makes conflict and collaboration transparent to the user, solves easier problems more quickly, and produces a variety of high-quality solutions even though it tolerates constraint violations during search. FLO, the implementation for park design, is fast, modular, and offers a broad set of high-quality solutions.

Acknowledgments

This work was supported in part by NSF grant #9423085, PSC-CUNY #666318. Thanks to Jack Gelfand and the anonymous reviewers for their constructive suggestions.

References

Armstrong, A. and Durfee, E. H. 1997. Dynamic Prioritization of Complex Agents in Distributed Constraint Satisfaction Problems. In *Proceedings of the Fifteenth International Joint Conference on Artificial Intelligence*, 620-625. Morgan Kaufmann.

Biswas, G., Goldman, S., Fisher, D., Bhuva, B. and Glewwe, G. 1995. Assessing Design Activity in Complex CMOS Circuit Design. In P. Nichols, S. Chipman, & R. Brennan (Ed.), *Cognitively Diagnostic Assessment*, Hillsdale, NJ: Lawrence Erlbaum.

Bond, A. H. and Gasser, L. 1988. An Analysis of Problems and Research in DAI. In A. H. Bond, & L. Gasser (Ed.), *Readings in Distributed AI*, 3-35. CA: Morgan Kaufmann.

Collins, G., Birnbaum, L. and Krulwich, B. 1989. An Adaptive Model of Decision-Making in Planning. In *Proceedings of the Eleventh International Joint Conference on Artificial Intelligence*, 511-516. Morgan Kaufmann.

Crowley, K. and Siegler, R. S. 1993. Flexible Strategy Use in Young Children's Tic-Tac-Toe. *Cognitive Science*, 17 (4): 531-561.

Durfee, E. H. and Rosenschein, J. S. 1994. Distributed Problem Solving and Multi-Agent Systems: Comparisons and Examples. In *Proceedings of the Thirteenth International Distributed AI Workshop*, 94-104.

Epstein, S. L. 1994. For the Right Reasons: The FORR Architecture for Learning in a Skill Domain. *Cognitive Science*, 18 (3): 479-511.

Gasser, L. 1993. Social Knowledge and Social Action: Heterogeneity in Practice. In *Proceedings of the Thirteenth International Joint Conference on Artificial Intelligence*, 751-757. Chambéry, France: Morgan Kaufmann.

Gero, J. S. and Sudweeks, F. (1996). *Artificial Intelligence in Design '96*. Kluwer Academic Publishers,

Goel, V. and Pirolli, P. 1989. Motivating the Notion of Generic Design within Information Processing Theory: The Design Problem Space. *AI Magazine*, 10 : 19-36.

Goel, V. and Pirolli, P. 1992. The Structure of Design Problem Spaces. *Cognitive Science*, 16 : 395-429.

Pennock, D. M. and Wellman, M. 1996. Toward a Market Model for Bayesian Inference. In *Proceedings of the Twelfth Conference on Uncertainty in Artificial Intelligence*, 405-413.

Schraagen, J. M. 1993. How Experts Solve a Novel Problem in Experimental Design. *Cognitive Science*, 17 (2): 285-309.

Simon, H. A. 1981. *The Sciences of the Artificial* (second ed.). Cambridge, MA: MIT Press.

An Architecture for Exploring Large Design Spaces

John R. Josephson[1], B. Chandrasekaran[1], Mark Carroll[1], Naresh Iyer[1],
Bryon Wasacz[2,3], Giorgio Rizzoni[2], Qingyuan Li[2], David A. Erb[4,5]

The Ohio State University, Columbus Ohio, 43210 USA
[1] - Computer and Information Science Department
[2] - Mechanical Engineering Department
[3] Present address: Motorola SPS, Austin, TX, 78735 USA
[4] – Center for Automotive Research
[5] Present address: ERB Professional Services,
Upper Arlington, OH, 43221 USA

{jj|chandra|carroll|niyer}@cis.ohio-state.edu,
RA6734@email.sps.mot.com, rizzoni.1@osu.edu,
li-q@rclsgi6.eng.ohio-state.edu, dave_erb@mindspring.com

Abstract

We describe an architecture for exploring very large design spaces, for example, spaces that arise when design candidates are generated by combining components systematically from component libraries. A very large number of candidates are methodically considered and evaluated. This architecture is especially appropriate during the stage of conceptual design when high-level design decisions are under consideration, multiple evaluation criteria apply, and a designer seeks assurance that good design possibilities have not been overlooked. We present a filtering technique based on a dominance criterion that can be used to select, from millions of design candidates, a relatively small number of promising candidates for further analysis. The dominance criterion is lossless in that it insures that each candidate not selected is inferior to at least one of the selected candidates. We also describe an interactive interface in which the selected designs are presented to the designer for analysis of tradeoffs and further exploration. In our current implementation, the computational load is distributed among a large number of workstations in a client-server computing environment. We describe the results of experiments using the architecture to explore designs for hybrid electric vehicles. In a recent experiment more than two million distinct designs were evaluated.

Motivation

Design can be considered to start from a specification of properties and behavior that an artifact is intended to satisfy. It typically ends when the designer is able to describe a set of components and their interconnection, and a mode of use by a user (Chandrasekaran, 1990). If an instance of the artifact is constructed with the components in the specified inter-component relationships, and if a user interacts with it as described in the mode of use, then the artifact's properties and behavior are supposed to satisfy the given specifications.

Design, like all problem solving, can be formulated as a search in a problem space (Nilsson, 1971; Newell, 1980). Except in routine design tasks, the design process usually involves considering alternative configurations of components, alternative components, and various parameter values. The design candidates that arise during this process are usually evaluated using multiple criteria. Due to time and other resource limitations, designers usually consider only a narrow range of the possible combinations of components and configurations.

At times, the design problem may be formulated explicitly as a parameter optimization problem, and well-known optimization techniques may be applied (Wilde, 1978). Most commonly, these techniques are variations of hill climbing. Given a design candidate, the direction of change in which the gain in a performance measure is largest is first ascertained, a new design candidate is chosen in that direction, and this process is repeated until changes in any direction result in a decrease in the performance measure. However, this optimization technique is not always applicable. When design candidates are generated by changes of components and configurations, which may be unordered, there may be no adjacency relationship to exploit in the space of design candidates. Moreover, hill climbing techniques, by

---

Copyright © 1998, American Association for Artificial Intelligence (www.aaai.org). All rights reserved.

requiring that a single evaluation function be defined, preclude explicit, local reasoning about tradeoffs among multiple performance criteria. In general, it is hard to use symbolic knowledge in numerical optimization schemes and thus they are not very good for early-stage design.

In this paper we describe a kind of design-space exploration that explicitly considers large numbers of design candidates, sampling widely from all regions of the design space. This exploration tells the designer how the design candidates in the space behave with respect to the various evaluation criteria, and helps to identify candidates or regions with interesting properties. Exhaustive exploration would be ideal, where all possible design candidates are examined. However, exhaustiveness is not essential for this kind of design exploration to be useful. What is needed is that all regions of the design space are sampled sufficiently to develop an understanding of the characteristics of the design space, which may well call for considering a very large number of design candidates. This kind of exploration may set the stage for a more detailed exploration of selected areas of the design space. Thus, this kind of exploration is especially appropriate for the conceptual design stage.

Because of the need to examine a very large number of candidates, this kind of design-space exploration may require substantial computing power. Fortunately, conceptual design is a relatively small part of the overall design process. Thus, allocation of substantial computing resources for this stage of design may be justified in view of its importance, especially as computing power is becoming more affordable. This kind of design space exploration has natural parallelism that can be exploited to distribute the computational burden; in our experiments we used a large collection of networked workstations to provide the needed computing power.

Overview of the Architecture

The overall architecture is that of an interactive decision-support architecture for design, as shown in Figure 1. A component/configuration library is available for generating design candidates. The user can specify constraints. The Good-Design Seeker generates design candidates by selecting components from the library and composing them, according to configuration templates (generic devices), to satisfy the given constraints. Several design critics evaluate each design candidate. Each critic assesses a candidate design from the point of view of a particular aspect of performance. One might focus on cost, another on convenience of use, yet a third on diagnosability, and so on. A critic might use an evaluation function based on the conclusions of other critics.

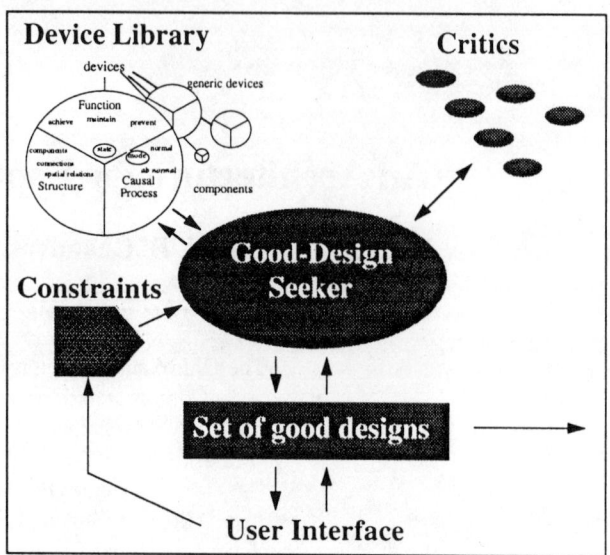

Figure 1. Decision-support architecture for design

The total number of design candidates might be quite large, so, for the designer to make effective use of the information from the critics, it would be desirable to have some form of filtering that selects a relatively small number of designs that are worth examining further. As it happens, we have discovered a lossless filtering criterion, i.e., one for which there are guarantees that there is no danger of excluding good designs. This will be described in a following section. In initial experiments, with real data, this filtering criterion has shown quite good performance, as will be described.

The designer is presented with the design candidates that survive the filtering process. Since a large number of candidates may yet remain, it is important to develop effective ways to aid the designer in investigating the properties of the surviving designs. Thus, the user interface is an important part of the architecture. We have discovered user-interface elements that are very useful. In particular, visualizing the set of surviving designs by way of interactive, connected, tradeoff diagrams enables the user to zoom in on subsets with desirable tradeoff characteristics, and so reduce the number of designs for further investigation to a manageable few. These will be described in a later section.

The scope of our project includes many issues in the design of component libraries and design critics that will not be discussed in this paper. In this paper, we will emphasize issues related to the exploration of large design spaces, using multiple criteria of evaluation. Besides a high-level conceptual description of the architecture, we will also describe our most recent implementation of it, which distributes the computation over a network of workstations, using otherwise idle machines, and has achieved explorations that consider more than two million candidates.

Good-Design Seeker

Design candidates are generated by systematically considering the members of a set of preset configurations or "generic devices." For each generic device, alternative component substitutions from a device library are systematically considered, and for components, various parameter values are considered chosen from a set of user-specified landmark values.

Design candidates are checked against any constraints that might rule them out. We have considered two sets of user-supplied constraints: one set is applied to partially specified designs and the other is applied to fully specified designs. Partial designs are created on the way to creating fully instantiated design candidates, and arise when not all of the components in a configuration have yet been chosen, or not all the parameter values. Sometimes partial designs may be checked against constraints with little computational cost. For example, if there is a constraint on total weight, a partially specified design may be rejected as soon its weight exceeds the limit, thus avoiding the substantial amount of work involved in generating and evaluating refinements of the design. Constraints that apply to fully specified designs are used to eliminate candidates. Such constraints might be used to eliminate implausible combinations or unacceptable performance.

Prior to constraint checking, designs are sent to various design critics, and each design is annotated with the conclusions from the critics. These conclusions can be used by the constraints, and are the basis for design filtering, which selects a subset of candidates to present to the designer. Dominance filtering is an important type of design filtering, and may be applied after generating and evaluating all candidates, or incrementally, as candidates are being generated and evaluated.

Dominance Filtering

We say that design candidate A **dominates** candidate B if A is superior or equal to B with respect to every criterion of evaluation and distinctly superior with respect to at least one criterion. Dominated designs need not be considered further - they may be filtered out. Among the designs that survive the dominance-filtering process, none is clearly superior to another. These designs are retained for further analysis.

To develop an intuition about what the dominance filter does, let us consider a geometric representation. Figure 2 illustrates the situation when there are only two evaluation criteria C_1 and C_2. Larger values of C_1 and C_2 are more desirable. Let M_1 be a design candidate. If another design candidate M_2 falls in region R_1, it can be eliminated, since M_1 would be clearly superior to M_2 on both criteria. If it falls in Region R_4, M_1 can be eliminated since M_2 would best M_1 on both criteria. If M_2 falls in Regions R_2 or R_3, both M_1 and M_2 need to be retained for the next stage since neither would be superior to the other with respect to all criteria of evaluation. This 2-dimensional description of dominance filtering generalizes to situations where there are more than two criteria; similar behavior will occur in the appropriate multidimensional space.

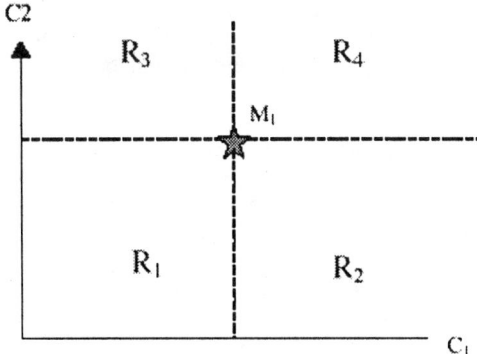

Figure 2. Illustration of dominance filtering.

Our algorithm for dominance filtering keeps a list of retained candidates, to which new candidates are compared. New candidates are compared serially to the items on the list. If the new candidate is dominated by some from the list, then there is no need to compare with the remaining elements in the list, and the new candidate is discarded, which contributes to efficiency. If the new candidate dominates a candidate in the retained list, the comparison still needs to continue with the other candidates in the list, since the new candidate may dominate some others as well. The final surviving set is independent of the order in which the candidates are generated and compared. Another probable source of efficiency in our implementation is that if a design on the list beats a new one, the dominator is moved to the front of the list. The idea is that this design is more likely to beat other new designs as well, in comparison with others on the list, and it will probably be efficient to consider it early when evaluating new candidates. We have not experimentally verified that moving designs up the list this way enhances efficiency, but it seems plausible and is implemented at little cost.

The Size of the Surviving Set. Let f be the fraction of the total design space that survives dominance pruning. If f is small, then the task of the designer is much eased. She only needs to consider a relatively small number of designs for further analysis while retaining assurance that the results speak about the entire design space. What kinds of values for f might one expect? This is an empirical question. We will describe experimental results which show that it is reasonable to expect small values of f in at least some real-world domains.

In a given domain, the value of f would, as a rule, increase as the number of evaluation criteria increases. That is, the probability that a design candidate is worse than another in all N dimensions of criticism will get smaller as N increases. However, f may become smaller as the size of the design space increases, say by considering parameter changes at finer resolutions. To see why, one can generalize from Figure 2 and consider each design to be a point in N-dimensional space, N being the number of criteria we are considering in dominance checking. The surviving set will be on the surface of the region of space wherein the designs lie. As more points (designs) are added within or near the region of designs in the N-dimensional space, the total number of designs should increase at a faster rate than the number of designs on its surface. We will describe some experiments that explored how f tends to decrease as the number of designs increases.

Adding or Removing Evaluation Criteria. Suppose we have a surviving set of candidates after exploration and dominance filtering. Now suppose the problem specification changes, and one of the criteria is no longer relevant. Is there a simple way to construct the new surviving set from the previous one? If A dominates B in, say, N dimensions of criticism, of course A will still dominate B in $N-1$ dimensions. Thus, the elements of the surviving set for N dimensions will still dominate the previously pruned candidates in $N-1$ dimensions as well. Thus, the dominance algorithm simply needs to be re-run among the members of the N-dimension surviving set to compute the $N-1$-dimension surviving set.

On the other hand, if the problem statement changes and a new criterion is added, the solution is not so simple. That A dominates B in N dimensions is no guarantee that A will still dominate B in $N+1$ dimensions. Maybe B happens to be better than A in the new dimension of criticism. This means that the new surviving set cannot be simply computed from the old surviving set. The dominance algorithm must again consider all the elements of the design space.

Independence of criteria. Dominance checking does not require evaluation criteria to be independent. In general, if the values according to two criteria are positively correlated, we can expect that use of these criteria will not increase the size of the surviving set as much as two independent criteria might. However, if values according to two criteria are negatively correlated (as they might well be when the designer is interested in investigating performance tradeoffs) we can expect the size of the surviving set to be larger than it would be if the criteria were independent.

Accuracy of Models. When we consider whether or not A is superior or equal to B with regard to every criterion, and superior in at least one, it is important to consider that the models upon which critics are based will have limited accuracy. The dominance filter can be adapted to take into account suspected model inaccuracy. A constant ε may be introduced for each critic such that A and B are considered to perform equally well with regard to the criterion of that critic if, as evaluated by the critic, the performance of the two differs by less than ε. Weakening the stringency of filtering in this way reduces the chances that a good design is mistakenly filtered out because of modeling inaccuracies. On the other hand, increasing ε for any critic will typically increase f, the surviving fraction. In choosing the value of ε for a particular critic, we express our estimate of the accuracy of the domain model used by that critic. Thus, choosing a value for ε gives a domain expert the opportunity to express a meta-knowledge judgment about the accuracy of the computer-based model.

Distributed Computing

Suppose that the design space has a million candidates, that we have five critics, and that each critic needs one tenth of a second for evaluating a candidate (all reasonable numbers). The total time on a serial machine for performing exhaustive evaluation will be about 6 days. Because of time requirements of this sort, we developed a novel computational architecture that employs Modula-3 (Cardelli, et. al., 1990) network objects (Birrell, et. al., 1994) to make use of the distributed computing environments that are presently commonly available in engineering institutions. A client-server architecture is employed that uses idle workstation time (in our case, often over 150 machines at a time) to allow the criticism of candidate designs to proceed in parallel.

The Exploration Interface

Even if dominance filtering is quite effective, one would expect hundreds if not thousands of designs to survive after exploring a design space consisting of, say, hundreds of thousands of design candidates. These would be designs where none would be clearly superior to another, based on the criteria that were used. What is a designer to make of so many designs, and how to help her narrow the choices? Clearly, additional knowledge is needed about choosing among designs, knowledge that was not incorporated during the search. If the additional knowledge were available in the form of new critics that were not used, the best way to proceed would be to do the search again using the new critics. (As we noted, the surviving set is quite sensitive to the addition of new critics.) Similarly, if the designer knew in advance how to weight the different criteria to form a composite evaluation, she might have used this composite evaluation to perform some form of optimization. However, we think that there is an important opportunity at the conceptual-design stage to develop a sense of the tradeoffs that arise from multiple criteria.

Our current visualization environment presents the designer with a set of tradeoff diagrams. Each diagram is a two-dimensional scatter plot, where the axes are a pair of design criteria, and all the surviving designs are plotted in that space. For example, if there are three critics with corresponding design criteria C_1, C_2, and C_3, up to three plots will be generated, one each for C_1-C_2, C_2-C_3, and C_3-C_1. Each design candidate will be represented in each of these plots. The designer can select any region in any of the plots and the design candidates that fall in the selected region in one diagram space will be highlighted in the other plots. The designer can thus easily observe how design candidates that look interesting in one of the diagrams fare with respect to other tradeoffs. Note that, in general, candidates that are contiguous in one of the plots will not necessarily be contiguous in the other plots.

Typically, a designer will explore the surviving designs by identifying regions or individual candidates that appear to have interesting properties in one diagram, selecting them, and examining their properties in the other diagrams. For example, the designer might note in one diagram that a small number of designs seem to have high evaluations in both dimensions. She might select this region. The interface would then highlight in the other diagrams the candidates in the selected region in the first diagram. If their performance is satisfactory with respect to the other dimensions, she might mark that subset as worthy of further attention. A particularly important function of visual analysis is to see if there are regions in the diagrams where, for a relatively small sacrifice in performance in one dimension, a large gain is available in the other dimension. This sort of visual analysis gives the designer some understanding of the structure of the design space, and locates opportunities for favorable design tradeoffs.

One cannot anticipate all the forms of visual analyses that a designer might make using the tradeoff diagrams, nor imagine all of the kinds of insights that might be gained. In our experiments, we have found that the designers first note certain interesting properties in one region of one of the diagrams, think about what they noticed, and generate explanations for what struck them as interesting. At this point, they are able to make additional hypotheses about relationships in other diagrams and regions. In addition to identifying a small number of design candidates for further analysis, designers end up with a deeper understanding of the design space.

The number of possible tradeoff plots increases approximately with the square of the number of criteria. So, one must not demand that the designer consider all plots at once, but instead let the user choose which plots to see. Even if she never examines the results according to a particular criterion, it has still entered into dominance calculations. Dominance checking does not depend on the exploration environment. It is plausible that in many fields the number of criteria will not need to be very large.

While we are currently experimenting with tradeoff diagrams, the issue of how to effectively present exploration results to the designer is wide open. Certainly users should be able to select a subset of designs and throw them into a special Examination Set (ExamSet) for closer inspection. We have implemented this kind of selection for rectangular regions on tradeoff plots; users would like the ability to use the mouse to lasso regions of arbitrary shape. The user might want to create more than one such ExamSet and might want to union, or intersect, or pull a subset from any of them. The user should be able to look at any available ExamSet through multiple, cross-updating tradeoff plots, and other inspectors. We also envision providing the user with a set of abstraction agents (Abstractors) able to automatically form certain interesting generalizations about the designs in any chosen ExamSet. One such Abstractor should gather statistics on the design choices that are represented in the ExamSet, and if any choice is represented by more than 50% of the designs, it should produce a comment of the form:

X% of the designs in <ExamSet> are designs where <design choice>.

For example, "88% of the designs in ExamSet-1 are designs where engine = Volkswagen #2." or "All of the designs in ExamSet-2 are designs where configuration = parallel-hybrid." This should be very useful to the designer in understanding and exploring the implications of the search results.

Ways of displaying and interacting with data in higher dimensions would be worth investigating. (See, for example, Tufte, 1983, 1990.) Automated clustering algorithms could identify interesting properties in the higher-dimensional spaces (Jain and Dubes, 1988). Higher-dimensional spatial analysis algorithms might be applied to identify outliers (Yip and F. Zhao, 1996). Outliers tend to have interesting properties, good or bad, or they may point to broken domain models or buggy software. Conversely, the absence of outliers should give the user some confidence in the fidelity of domain models and reassure the user that no especially good design possibilities have been overlooked.

Experimental Results

We will now describe a set of experiments that we have conducted in a real-world domain. At this point, no especially surprising designs have been discovered using the architecture. However, users have reacted favorably and remarked that designers can use tools such as this to explore the design space on their own and not merely go by the intuitions and gut-feelings of whatever strongly opinionated and highly vocal people they happen to be working with. The goal in reporting these experiments is to show how the proposed architecture works in practice, to describe some of what we have learned about the technology, to demonstrate candidate generation and filtering, and to show how the user interface works for interactive exploration. We also wish to draw attention to the significantly large design-space sizes the technology can already handle.

The Domain. The domain in which we performed our experiments was that of hybrid electric vehicles. Hybrid electric vehicles are automobiles that use both an electrical motor and an internal-combustion (IC) engine as power sources. (See Wouk, 1997, for an introduction to the problem area.) Electrical motors are attractive as power source partially because of the potential for using the motor as a generator during braking and thus recapturing the kinetic energy of the vehicle. They also have good emission properties, making them attractive for city use. On the other hand, they have limited range because of the limitations of current battery technology. Hybrid vehicles use an IC engine to extend range, either to move the vehicle when battery power is low, or to recharge the batteries. An interesting issue in the design of hybrid vehicles is the control policy, which is the formula that decides when to use which source of power for movement and when to activate the IC to charge the batteries.

The domain has a number of attractive features for exercising our architecture. The underlying design space is not simply generated by parametric variations; for example, there are four distinct vehicle configurations. There are also several criteria for evaluating performance, and no simple way to combine them a priori into a weighted composite objective function. Moreover, there are well-defined mathematical models for the various design criticisms of interest. With several alternative components to be considered for each component choice point within a configuration alternative, the design space grows combinatorially and rapidly. When we include consideration of alternative control-policy parameters, the combinatorial explosion of design alternatives is even more dramatic. Modeling of hybrid-electric vehicles is described in Baumann, et. al. (1988); details of the domain models used in our experiments are available in Wasacz (1997) and Li (1998).

The most basic components are the four vehicle configurations, or types of vehicles: IC engine only; Electric motor only; Parallel hybrid; Serial hybrid. Once a commitment has been made to a particular configuration, there is a further need to specify the set of components required by that configuration, and parameter values associated with the various components. This set is different for each of the four types, although some of the components are common to each type. First, we describe components and parameters common to all of the vehicle types.

Transmission, of which the available types are: Automatic, Manual or CVT (continuously variable). For manual transmissions there is a choice of the number of gears (3, 4, or 5-speed) and the corresponding gear ratios. Choice of Shift Speeds for manual transmissions determines various performance characteristics. Also: Downshift Speed, which is the vehicle speed at which a lower gear ratio is chosen for manual and automatic transmissions.

The following components and parameters must be specified for some vehicle types but not others:

Electric motors in different sizes (small, medium and large) and their respective weights,

IC engines varied by their sizes (small, medium or large) and their corresponding weights, torque-speed characteristics and fuel-efficiency maps,

Batteries, which include the number of cells in the pack with their respective weights,

Speed reduction ratio, which refers to the gear ratio between the electric motor and the axle and,

Control policy, which is applicable only to hybrid vehicles and is varied in terms of four parameters, the high and low values of vehicle velocities and high and low values of the state of charge at which the switch is made from primary reliance on one engine to primary reliance on another.

The user supplies a set of plausible choices for each of these components, and the Good-Design Seeker explores them all. Candidates are generated by first selecting a vehicle configuration from the four choices, then systematically going through all relevant combinations of component choices and parameter-value choices. Constraints are applied at this stage, as described earlier. The design space size can be made to grow very large by stepping component changes through very small increments, e.g., small changes in cutoff speeds or gear ratios. The reader will note that we were careful in our experiments not to artificially inflate the sizes of the spaces to be explored by using unreasonably small steps of variation. Once interesting regions of space are explored during a first round of processing, finer distinctions may be made in selected areas of the space and additional explorations, similar to the first but at greater resolution, may be undertaken.

Design Critics. The following design critics were employed in the experiments we report here: Maximum acceleration, top speed, city-driving efficiency, and highway-driving efficiency. Maximum acceleration was calculated as the time to reach 60 MPH. We also included experimental city-driving and highway-driving range critics, but did not use them in dominance checking. The details of how the vehicles were modeled for computing these various performance characteristics are beyond the scope of this paper. Briefly, dynamical models of vehicle performance in the form of differential equations were constructed using well-understood vehicle-modeling methods. The equations were simulated temporally, i.e., the values of the operating parameters were determined as a function of time using appropriately chosen time increments. City and highway driving models imposed contours of desired velocities that were incorporated into the simulations. The models were simulated using Matlab and Simulink, widely available application packages, especially appropriate for simulating complex systems governed by differential equations. Of course, city and highway efficiency are correlated, and these are somewhat inversely correlated with both top speed and maximum acceleration.

Dominance Filtering. So far, we have run a series of experiments, progressively exploring larger spaces. In Table 1, we present results for our largest run to date (made in March 1998), and "fake" smaller runs constructed from random sampling of the results of this run. This insures that our investigation of dominance filtering is not skewed by recent improvements in the simulation models used by the critics. This experiment used the four critics mentioned in the previous section.

Experiment	Designs Considered	Survivors	Percentage survivors
A	1,798	71	3.949
B	17,711	173	0.977
C	179,874	556	0.309
D	1,796,025	1,078	0.060

TABLE 1. Effectiveness of dominance filtering as the size of the space increases.

Note that dominance filtering appears to be quite effective in eliminating a large fraction of the design space. In this case, a small design space was cut by well more than an order of magnitude, and the largest was cut by more than three orders of magnitude. If these results are representative of what can be expected, dominance filtering will be a practical way to help reduce the complexity of explicitly comparing very large numbers of design alternatives.

In order to investigate how the surviving fraction behaves with respect to the number of dimensions of comparative criticism, the dominance algorithm was run on a set of 17,711 candidates corresponding to Experiment B of Table 1 using subsets of two and three criteria each. Table 2 summarizes the results for two criteria each, while Table 3 does the same for three criteria. The entries in these tables represent the numbers of surviving designs. In Table 2, the rows and columns indicate the two criteria. (Since the situation is symmetric, only the top half of the table is filled.) In Table 3, the column heading indicates which one of the four criteria is not used.

	MPG (City)	Max Accel.	Top Speed
MPG (Highway)	2	24	18
MPG (City)		36	18
Max Accel.			10

TABLE 2. Effectiveness of dominance filtering for two criteria. Number of surviving designs is shown

Not used:	MPG (Highway)	MPG (City)	Max Accel.	Top Speed
	103	83	35	76

TABLE 3. Effectiveness of dominance filtering for three criteria. Number of surviving designs is shown.

The data in both tables, and the fact that 173 designs survived with four criteria, support the hypothesis that, as the number of criteria increases, the tendency is for the effectiveness of dominance filtering to decrease. That is, a larger percentage of the candidates survive. However, we have observed that sometimes the size of the surviving set decreases as criteria are added. This presumably occurs because designs that were regarded as equally valued in the original set are now regarded as differently valued because the extra criterion allows some to dominate others.

Scale of computation. In our largest experiment (Experiment D in Table 1), 2,152,698 designs were evaluated, of which 1,796,025 were fully specified. Fully specified designs were evaluated according to four performance criteria, which required multiple simulations of each design. Dominance filtering reduced the number to 1,078 best designs for human analysis. 207 workstations were used as clients during the experiment; from zero to 159 were running at any one time. The experiment used 164 hr. 41 min. of wall-clock time, 14 hr. 54 min. of CPU time on the server, for generation and evaluation, and approximately 4.5 hr. of wall-clock time for dominance filtering performed as serial post processing. We note that our experiment used idle workstation in a university computer science department during the last week of classes of the term. Presumably, the wall-clock time would have been less at any other time. Approximately half of the computation was accomplished over the weekend.

Exploration Interface. Figure 3 shows one of the six tradeoff diagrams from Experiment D obtained by considering the four criteria two at a time. In each diagram, each point that is plotted corresponds to a design that survived the strict dominance test. The user can use the pointing device to select subsets for further examination, save and load such subsets and further narrow them.

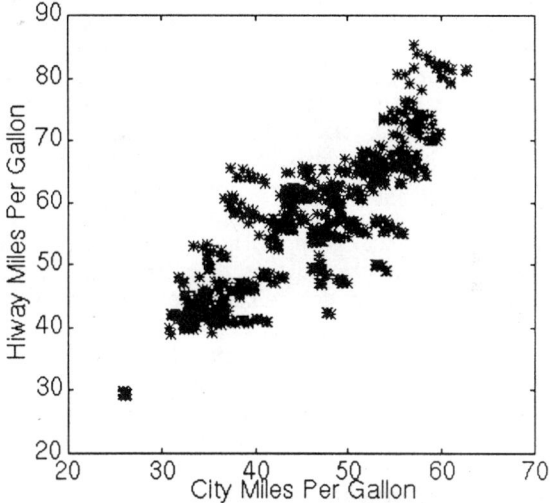

Figure 3. One of the tradeoff diagrams from Experiment D

Through the series of experiments, a striking phenomenon was the usefulness of the visualization interface for debugging domain models and ensuring sufficient realism. The diagrams quickly revealed designs with implausible performance characteristics; for example, at one stage of model development we saw vehicles with unreasonably high top speeds. On one occasion, it was noticed that for several designs, the values of city driving efficiency were higher than those for highway driving efficiency, which is quite unreasonable. On another occasion, stratification of points in tradeoff diagrams alerted us that time steps for the acceleration simulations had been set too coarsely. It is clear that visual exploration of this sort helps to ensure model accuracy. The tradeoff diagrams show the results of exercising the models over an extremely broad range of combinations of inputs. Model inaccuracies are given every opportunity to betray their presence through anomalies that appear in visualizations of the results.

Discussion

"Exploration" is a term that has been often used in the design literature, but with no single meaning. For example, for Navinchandra (1991), exploration consists of deviating "... from the beaten path to generate unconventional solutions to problems." Sometimes exploration is contrasted with search: exploration is supposed to be examining a space without any specific goal, while search is supposed to be examining a space for a specific object. We use the term "exploration" in the sense of examining a region thoroughly to develop an understanding of it.

In this paper, we have suggested that large-scale exploration can make a significant contribution at the stage of conceptual design. We have presented a software architecture for large-scale exploration. The architecture is comprised of: a Good-Design Seeker, which systematically generates and evaluates large numbers of candidate designs using multiple criteria, filters that pass only superior designs, and a visualization environment that enables designers to investigate tradeoffs among the superior designs and select subsets for further analysis. The Good-Design Seeker may use component substitution and exhaustive methods similar in spirit to drug discovery by "combinatorial chemistry" (Economist 1998). Filtering based on dominance is practical to implement and promises to reduce the number of alternatives to be considered from vast to manageable; it has been remarkably effective in a small number of relatively realistic experiments in one domain. The visualization environment presents the user with the results of multi-criterial evaluation, without forcing the evaluation to a single criterion. Tradeoffs are displayed and the user is able to bring human evaluation and judgment to bear in choosing designs for further investigation.

Additionally, we have demonstrated at least one way to make the demanding computations practical: distribute the criticism of designs over a network of workstations (potentially as large a pool as there are friendly hosts on the Internet). We conjecture that very large-scale exploration of the space of design alternatives has been so computationally demanding that even the possibility of it has remained outside the thought processes of design practice, even within the computer-supported design community. We believe that computing technology today has advanced to where such large-scale explorations are practical for many design domains. We have presented experimental results that lend strong early encouragement to claims of practicality.

Acknowledgments

This material is based upon work supported by The Office of Naval Research under Grant No. N00014-96-1-0701. The support of ONR and the DARPA RaDEO program are gratefully acknowledged. Standard disclaimers apply.

References

Baumann, B., Rizzoni, G., Washington, G.: 1998, Society of Automotive Engineers Technical paper 981061, SAE Special Publication 1356, Electronic Engine Controls 1998: Sensors, Actuators, and Development Tools.

Birrell, A., Nelson, G., Owicki, S., and Wobber, E.: 1994, Network Objects, DEC Systems Research Center.

Cardelli, L., Donahue, J., Glassman, L., Jordan, M., Kalsow, B., and Nelson, G.: 1990, Modula-3 Report (revised), Nov 89, including a final update insert, Twelve Changes to Modula-3 dated Dec 1990, DEC Systems Research Center.

Chandrasekaran, B.: 1990, Design Problem Solving: A task analysis, *AI Magazine*, **11**(4), 59-71.

Economist 1998, Combinatorial Chemistry, *The Economist*, March 14th 1998.

Jain, A., Dubes, R.: 1988, *Algorithms for clustering data*, Prentice Hall, Englewood Cliffs, NJ.

Li, Qingyuan: (1998) "Development And Refinement of a Hybrid Electric Vehicle Simulator and Its Application in Design Space Exploration," M.S. Thesis, Department of Mechanical Engineering, the Ohio State University.

Navinchandra, D.: 1991 *Exploration and Innovation in Design: Towards a Computational Model*, Springer-Verlag, New York.

Newell, A.: 1980, Reasoning, Problem Solving and Decision Process: The problem space as a fundamental category, in *Attention and Performance VIII*, R. Nickerson (ed.), Lawrence Erlbaum, Hillsdale, NJ

Nilsson, N.: 1971, *Problem-Solving Methods in Artificial Intelligence*, McGraw Hill, New York.

Tufte, E.: 1983, *The Visual Display of Quantitative Information*, Graphics Press, Cheshire, Conn.

Tufte, E.: 1990, *Envisioning Information*, Graphics Press, Cheshire, Conn.

Wasacz, B.: 1997, Development and Application of A Hybrid Electric Vehicle Simulator, MS thesis, Department of Mechanical Engineering, The Ohio State University

Wilde, D. J.: 1978, *Globally Optimal Design*, Wiley, New York.

Wouk, V.: 1997, Hybrid Electric Vehicles, *Scientific American*, October 1997, 70-74.

Yip, K. and Zhao, F.: 1996, Spatial aggregation: theory and applications, *Journal of Artificial Intelligence Research*, 5:1-26.

Constructing the Correct Diagnosis When Symptoms Disappear

Nancy E. Reed
Department of Computer and Information Science
Linköpings Universitet, S-581 83 Linköping, SWEDEN
nanre@ida.liu.se

Abstract

When multiple defects (also called diseases or faults) are present, there is a possibility of *interactions* between the defects. When defects interact, the *cues* (data obtainable) for a combination of defects is not a simple sum of the cues observable for the component defects. Expected cues may be missing, altered, or new cues may appear. Each of these alterations of cues makes diagnosis more difficult, as the correct defect combination may not even be considered (triggered) by a diagnostic system. We present an algorithm for heuristic solution construction that integrates multiple types of information about the case. Solutions are evaluated based on how many of the abnormal cues are accounted for, with a method that combines cues that may be altered due to interactions between defects. The method can account for cues that combine with one another in three basic ways, set union, additively and ordered dominance (some values mask other values) or with a combination of those basic ways.

For the solution space of one task, diagnosing congenital heart defects, we considered seven major defects and found the solution space (exhaustive) was reduced by approximately 50% because some of the defects could not physically occur together. Experimental results on cases from hospital files demonstrate the effectiveness of the heuristic solution construction algorithm to generate the correct solution early which reduced the number of solutions explored (compared to an exhaustive search) even further on most cases. With the computational power of current workstations, even cases requiring exploration of this entire solution space required less than 4 minutes of CPU time per case.

Introduction

Cue refers to a piece of data available about the case (observed) or one expected from a defect. Cues may be either normal (expected of a normal patient) or abnormal (also called *symptoms*). Cues include test results, patient interviews, physical exams, and the patient's history. *Single defect* refers to a single physical abnormality. *Disease* or *fault* are terms also used frequently.

Each defect has a name that uniquely identifies it. *Multiple defect* refers to the coexistence of two or more physical abnormalities (defects), independent of any causal relationship(s). A multiple defect with a unique name will be called a *complex* defect.

Diagnosing multiple defects continues to be a difficult problem in many domains, especially medical domains. When multiple defects might be present, the number of potential solutions to each problem is greatly increased. Multiple defects are *interacting* when the cues from the multiple defect case are not set additive (Patil 1988) when compared to the cues for the component defects. Diagnosis is even more difficult if the defects interact. In particular, when defects interact, expected abnormal cues may be combined, missing, or altered, and new abnormal cues may appear.

Bylander, et al. (1991) have shown that abduction problems are in general intractable. One exception is finding one best explanation for an ordered, independent, monotonic abduction problem. Interacting defects are clearly not in the tractable category, since cues may cancel. As a result, solutions to multiple defect problems will continue to require a great deal of computational power. Within these constraints, a combination of efficient heuristic solution construction algorithms and increasingly powerful computers allows us to tackle interesting diagnostic problems, one of which is described in this paper.

Diagnostic Control Algorithm

This is a decision-support approach to diagnosis, in other words, the goal is not "a diagnosis", but rather to produce evidence that compares alternative solutions. This approach uses a ranking of solutions based on how many of the abnormal cues in the case are accounted for and identifying which one(s) are not. Any solutions accounting for all or almost all of the abnormal cues can be considered potential diagnoses.

This approach applies to multiple interacting defects and synthesizes ideas from a number of diagnostic approaches including set covering (Peng and Reggia 1990), recognition-based reasoning (Thompson *et al.* 1983; Johnson *et al.* 1988) and abduction and hypothesis assembly (Bylander *et al.* 1991; Fischer 1991;

Josephson and Josephson 1994).

This computational model uses two primary modes of reasoning. First, a forward chaining style including recognition-based reasoning is performed until all cues have been accepted. Then, an abductive style consisting of alternating solution construction and evaluation is performed until an adequate solution is found or all alternatives have been considered (Reed 1995; Reed et al. 1997). Heuristics are used in the construction of alternative solutions to focus on the most promising solutions first.

The modules applicable when new cues are available include two *identify features* modules and two *recognize defect* modules for recognition-based reasoning (RBR) described next. The *identify solution type* module searches for cues that can focus problem solving on a subset of the solution space. The solution type may be identified as a single defect, a named defect, a complex defect, a multiple defect, or some combination of those types. The *identify essential defects* module searches for cues that are only produced by one specific defect. These are also called pathognomonic cues. If a cue can only be caused by one defect and that cue appears, then the corresponding defect must be a component of the solution. These defects are called *essential* (Fischer 1991).

The two recognition-based reasoning (RBR) modules applicable when new cues are available propose and evaluate hypotheses (Thompson et al. 1983; Johnson et al. 1988). The *propose hypotheses* module activates physiological and defect hypotheses based on observed cues in the case. The *review hypotheses* module evaluates all active hypotheses with new information as it becomes available. Hypotheses can be in exactly one of four states, *dormant* (inactive), *proposed* (believed relevant), *accepted* (believed true), and *rejected* (believed false). All hypotheses start in a dormant state, meaning they are not currently considered relevant to the case. The other three states all describe active hypotheses. Evidence is gathered to support or oppose active hypotheses. If enough positive evidence accumulates, a proposed hypothesis will be accepted. If enough negative evidence accumulates, a proposed or accepted hypothesis will be rejected. Rejecting a hypothesis is final. Once rejected, a hypothesis cannot change state.

The second step of the control algorithm is to evaluate the current solution. If the RBR modules accept one defect after all observed cues have been processed, that solution is considered the "current solution" and is evaluated using a metric described in the next section. If the current solution explains all abnormal cues (or at least some specified cutoff value), then that is the only solution evaluated and the problem is considered solved.

In all other cases, when recognition-based reasoning (RBR) accepts no defects or more than one defect, or if the accepted defect does not explain all the abnormal cues, then solutions are constructed and evaluated by the *construct solutions* and *evaluate solutions* modules, respectively.

Evaluating Solutions

The metric used to compare solutions is called *evidence points* and is defined below (Reed et al. 1997). Solutions are evaluated based on the ratio of explained to total abnormal cues. For a case C and a solution S, the abnormal cues observed in the case ($Obs._C$) and expected for the defects in the solution ($Exp._S$). The best solutions are those that have the highest evidence point ratios (meaning the fewest unexplained abnormal cues). The evidence point (EP) formula is shown next.

$$EvidencePoints(C, S) =$$

$$\frac{\sum Explained\ Abnormal(Obs._C\ or\ Exp._S)}{\sum Explained\ Abnormal + \sum Unexplained\ Abnormal}$$

Cues are categorized as either important or ignored. Important abnormal expected cues for each defect are classified in one of two categories - *required* or *optional*. Required expected cues are "always" present in a case when the defect is present (unless they are missing or altered due to interactions between defects). Optional expected cues are often present in cases when the defect is present, but their absence does not need a reason. Ignored cues are those that are either not important for determining a diagnosis or are not useful for discriminating between defects. Ignored cues are not included in the evaluation of solutions using the evidence points metric.

EP calculations generalize to solutions containing more than one defect and account for interactions between defects as follows. The EP calculations *cluster* cues. Cues of the same type from the case and all defects in the solution are considered together. Each type of cue has a specific combination method. The methods currently available include three basic ways - set union, additively, and ordered dominance (where "stronger" values mask other values), or a combination of the three basic ways based on characteristics of the cue, case or domain. These combination methods allow the correct interpretation of altered cues due to interacting defects.

When a case is presented, it is assumed that all abnormal cues of the important types are included, as is usually done by physicians documenting a case. If the observation of a specific cue is not possible, that cue is given a value of *unknown* for that case. Unknown cues and all expected cues of the same type are not included in the EP formula when solutions are evaluated.

Heuristic Solution Construction

Candidate solutions are constructed using the heuristic algorithm summarized in Table 1. First, solutions containing one defect (single or complex) are explored, then those with two defects, etc, up to the *maximum number of defects per solution*, which is domain dependent. Heuristic solution construction makes use of the defects proposed and accepted by the recognition-based reasoning (RBR) modules and any essential defects or solution type identified (all modules active on new cues).

In both heuristic and exhaustive search modes, solution construction and evaluation will stop when either the *first* sufficient solution or *all* solutions up to the same number of defects as the first have been constructed and evaluated. If no solutions explaining enough abnormal cues are found, processing continues until all heuristic or exhaustive solutions have been constructed and evaluated (up to the maximum number of defects per solution).

Heuristically generated solutions are constructed using the following modules: *include essential defects, cover cues, add associated defects, match solution type, eliminate incompatible defects,* and *eliminate duplicate solutions.* The *add essential defects* module makes sure that any essential defects identified are included in the solutions constructed. The *cover cues* module includes defects that explain significant abnormal observed cues in the case as identified by the RBR modules (accepted, proposed, or rejected defect hypotheses).

1. Construct 1 defect solutions in this order:
   Essential defects.
   RBR *accepted* defects.
   RBR *proposed* (including rejected) defects.
2. **For** NumDef = 2 **to** MaxDefPerSoln **do**
   Start with solutions of (NumDef -1) defects,
   form solutions containing NumDef defects by
     adding defects in the following order:
       essential defects.
       RBR accepted defects
       RBR proposed defects.
       associated defects (Common,Occasional,Rare):
     Remove duplicate solutions.
     Remove solutions of incompatible type(s).
     Remove solutions with incompatible defects.
   End For

Table 1: Heuristic solution construction algorithm.

The *add associated defects* module finds and adds defects that co-occur with a minimum of some specified frequency with some defect already under consideration to a solution. The frequencies that defects occur with other defects are classified into four categories, common, occasional, rare, and never. For each pair of defects, D_i and D_j, the rate that D_j occurs when defect D_i is present is contained in a database. Defects that never occur together can be due to the physical properties of the defects. Often the frequency that D_k appears when D_l is present is the same as that of D_l appearing when D_k is present. These appear as symmetrical entries in the matrix. However, it is possible that the frequencies will be different due to the fact that D_k and D_l can occur with greatly different frequencies.

The *eliminate duplicates*, *match solution type*, and *eliminate incompatibles* modules prune unproductive solutions that may be generated and should be self explanatory.

Exhaustive Solution Construction

Exhaustive solution construction mode, when selected, first constructs and evaluates solutions using the heuristic module. Then all solutions not constructed in the heuristic mode are constructed and evaluated. The exhaustive mode may also be automatically invoked if the heuristic mode did not find any solutions capable of explaining all or most of the important abnormal cues.

Example Domain

This section describes characteristics of the domain of pediatric cardiology. There is a standard set of data collected in this domain including history, physical exam, blood tests, cardiac auscultation, X-ray, and EKG data. Based on consultation with an expert, we chose between 2 and 5 important types of cues in each of 4 critical test areas (cardiac auscultation, EKG, physical exam, and X-ray). Cues in other areas were ignored.

Defects

In this domain, four kinds of physical defects can occur – communication defects (holes), obstructions near valves (or insufficiencies), absent or mis-connected vessels, and electromechanical defects. Electromechanical defects (other than secondary manifestations of other defects) were excluded from this investigation. They are covered in the work of others including Bratko et al. (1989) and Downing and Widman (1991).

The 7 common defects selected for this study are described next. Aortic Stenosis (AS) and Pulmonary Stenosis (PS) are valvular defects (obstructions) that restrict the flow of blood through the aortic or pulmonary valves, respectively. Atrial Septal Defect (ASD) and Ventricular Septal Defect (VSD) are communication defects, where blood flows between two normally unconnected chambers of the heart (the upper two and lower two respectively).

Tetralogy of Fallot (TF) is a complex defect with four components: VSD, PS, the aorta usually overrides the VSD, and right ventricular hypertrophy (thickening of the chamber wall) is present. Total Anomalous Pulmonary Venous Connection (TAPVC) is another complex defect. It occurs when all the vessels from the lungs connect to the right atrium instead of the left atrium. A hole in the atrial septum (ASD) is necessary with this defect, otherwise oxygenated blood could not flow to the body.

Partial Anomalous Pulmonary Venous Connection (PAPVC) is when some, but not all, of the vessels are mis-connected as in TAPVC. There need not be a hole in the atrial septum with this defect, therefore it is considered a single defect. The maximum number of (named) defects per case is considered to be three.

Defect associations and incompatibilities

Figure 1 shows the association relationships among the 7 cardiac defects examined in this study. The diagonal of the figure is crossed out since each defect can occur only once in a patient. In the top row, ASD and VSD occasionally occur with AS, while PAPVC, PS, and TAPVC rarely occur with AS. TF never occurs with AS. PS and VSD never occur with TF because they are part of the definition of TF. Similarly with ASD and TAPVC.

	ASSOCIATED DEFECT						
DEFECT	Aortic Stenosis	Atrial Septal Defect	Partial APVC	Pulmonary Stenosis	Total APVC	Tetralogy of Fallot	Ventricular Septal Defect
Aortic Stenosis	✕	O occasional	R rare	R rare	R rare	N never	O occasional
Atrial Septal Defect	O occasional	✕	C common	C common	N never	C common	C common
Partial APVC	R rare	C common	✕	R rare	N never	R rare	R rare
Pulmonary Stenosis	R rare	C common	R rare	✕	R rare	N never	C common
Total APVC	R rare	N never	N never	R rare	✕	R rare	R rare
Tetralogy of Fallot	N never	C common	R rare	N never	R rare	✕	N never
Ventricular Septal Defect	O occasional	C common	R rare	C common	R rare	N never	✕

Figure 1: Defect association relationships identified.

Some of the 7 defects are incompatible, they do not or cannot (physically) occur together, and are identified by an N in a cell of Figure 1. Ignoring the order of defects in a solution and using the maximum of 3 defects per case, a maximum of 37 possible combinations of defects can occur, 7 containing single (including complex) defects, 16 with 2 defects, and 14 with 3 defects.

In a domain with no incompatible defects (and 7 single defects where the order of defects is again ignored), there would be 63 possible combinations to search (7 single defects, 21 combinations of 2 defects, and 35 combinations of 3 defects). The search space is reduced by almost half (41% fewer) due to characteristics of the domain.

If the maximum of 3 defects per case is lifted, the reduction in the number of possible solutions is even greater - there are only 44 possible solutions containing the above defects consistent with the incompatibilities - an additional 6 possibilities with 4 defects and 1 possible combination of 5 defects. If there were no incompatible defects, there would be 127 possible solutions. The number of solutions to explore is reduced by over 65% due to the defect incompatibilities of this domain.

Tests on Hospital Cases

The diagnostic algorithm has been implemented and a knowledge base constructed for the task of diagnosing congenital heart defects. The knowledge base contains the 7 common defects described above (5 single and 2 complex). A total of 78 cases with single, complex, and multiple defects were available from hospital files for knowledge base construction and testing. Each case contained 1, 2, or 3 of the 7 defects as determined by surgery or cardiac catheterization (performed after the initial expert diagnosis). Approximately one-third of the cases were used for knowledge base construction and the other two-thirds (53 cases) were used in a "blind" test. On these cases, the original expert diagnosis is compared to the results obtained using recognition-based reasoning alone (RBR) and to the results obtained using the computational model with the heuristic solution construction (HSC) algorithm (which includes the RBR modules). It should be noted that the experts saw the patients in person while both RBR and HSC used selected information from the written records. Therefore, the experts had access to more information about the cases.

	Result	Expert	RBR	HSC
S	Correct or ranks high	32	18	30
S	UTD or partial	1	10	0
S	Incorrect or ranks low	0	5	3
C	Correct or ranks high	4	2	4
C	UTD or similar defect	2	2	1
C	Incorrect or ranks low	0	2	1
M	Correct or ranks high	8	0	7
M	UTD, or near the top	5	7	3
M	Incorrect or ranks low	1	7	4

S - single, C - complex, M - multiple, UTD - Unable to diagnose.

Table 2: Results on all 53 test cases.

Table 2 summarize the results on all the test cases. In the 33 single defect cases (S), the experts correctly identified all but 1 case where the expert gave a partially correct diagnosis. RBR alone correctly diagnosed approximately half (18) of the cases, incorrectly diagnosed 5 cases and was unable to come to a conclusion in the rest. HSC was almost as good as the experts, ranking the correct diagnosis as the best single defect solution (29/33) or very close (1/33) in approximately 90% of the cases. The center of the table shows the results on the 6 complex defect test cases (C). The experts gave the correct diagnosis in 2/3 of the cases and diagnosed a clinically similar defect to the actual defect in the other cases. RBR correctly diagnosed 1/3 of the cases, diagnosed incorrect defects in another 1/3 of the cases and was unable to diagnose the remaining 1/3. HSC ranked the correct solution at or close to the top in 2/3 of the cases and ranked a clinically similar defect higher in 1 case, again approaching the level of the experts.

On the 14 multiple defect cases (M) shown at the bottom of the table, the experts gave the correct diagnosis in over half (8) of the cases, gave alternative or partial diagnoses in approximately 1/3 (5) of the cases and incorrectly diagnosed the remaining case (with clinically very similar defects). RBR did not correctly diagnose any cases. In half of the cases, RBR diagnosed incorrect defects, in the remaining half of the cases no conclusion was reached. HSC ranked the correct solution at or near the top in half of the cases, in approximately 1/4 (3) of the cases, the correct solution ranked reasonably high, while in the remaining cases, the correct solution was not near the top. On the case misdiagnosed by the experts, HSC ranked the same incorrect, but clinically similar solution well above the correct solution (which was ranked low).

The RBR knowledge base was updated during the construction phase, but was not originally designed for multiple defects. This clearly shows as none of the multiple defect cases were correctly diagnosed by RBR. The same RBR knowledge base was used in HSC, however, and contributed to the correct diagnosis of 7 multiple defect cases, which is detailed in the next section.

In the cases where the correct solutions did not rank at the top, we analyzed all unexplained abnormal cues (missed points in the EP formula) and determined that they were due to either atypical cues present in the case, or inaccurate expected cues in the knowledge base. More knowledge base development effort can reduce or eliminate the second category. Atypical cues will always be a hazard when working with real data. The EP metric's evaluation of cases is used to highlight these "unexplained" cues to bring them to the attention of the user. Even including these unexplained abnormal cues, the HSC algorithm demonstrates a large improvement from a previous method, RBR alone, applied to the cases and approached the level of the original expert diagnoses.

Generating the correct solution

To improve the percentage of correct solutions generated by HSC in the future, we next analyze the test cases above to determine which reasoning methods generated the correct solutions.

Results on the 53 test cases are shown in Table 3. RBR activated (accepted, proposed, or rejected) the correct solution in the majority of the cases (29/33 or 88%), although only reached the correct diagnosis in about half (18). On one case, both the correct defect and an incorrect defect were accepted.

In general, this means that RBR is very good at activating the correct defect on single defect cases. It is not infallible, however. The evaluation of solutions with the EP metric gives something like a "second opinion" on potential solutions and resulted in a much higher number of correct diagnoses being rated at or near the top compared to other solutions (Table 2). However, po-

Solution Generation	S	C	M
RBR accepted (all)	18	2	0
RBR accepted (1 of 2 or 3)	N/A	N/A	3
RBR accepted (2 of 1, 2 or 3)	1	N/A	0
RBR accepted incorrect	2	2	2
RBR accepted correct+incorrect	1	0	1
RBR rejected (1 of 1, 2 or 3)	2	0	1
RBR proposed all	6	0	2
RBR proposed (1 of 1, 2 or 3)	2	0	1
RBR proposed (2 of 2 or 3)	N/A	0	1
RBR proposed only incorrect	0	2	3
No defects proposed	2	0	0
Associated defects	N/A	N/A	2

S - single, C - complex, M - multiple

Table 3: Correct solutions generated on all 53 test cases.

tential solutions must be constructed before they can be evaluated. In cases where no defects were proposed, or the proposed defects did not explain very much of the data, all possible single defects were evaluated (exhaustive search).

In the complex and multiple defect cases, RBR activated the correct defect in 2/3 of the complex cases and at least one of the component defects in all but 3 (11/14) of the multiple defect cases. In two multiple defect cases, associated defects were necessary to construct the correct solutions since only one component defect was activated by RBR. In one case, one correct defect was proposed, and in the other, one correct defect was accepted by RBR. The other component of the correct solution was not proposed by RBR in either case. Both second defects were commonly associated with a defect under consideration. Unfortunately, in one of the cases, a single defect explained all the case cues, so this single defect solution would be preferred over a two defect solution (which was correct). The other case contained one atypical cue that was not explained by the correct two-defect solution, although the correct solution was the best two-defect solution. Two three-defect solutions (supersets of the correct solution) were able to explain all the observed cues in that case.

Discussion

Generating and testing large numbers of potential solutions to one problem has been computationally prohibitive until recently. We use a combination of heuristics to focus on the most promising solutions first, combined with reasonably fast computers. The experiments reported were performed using sun 4 (40 Mhz Sparc) workstations running Unix BSD 4.3 and Lucid Common Lisp. The fastest of the 53 problems mentioned above were solved in 3 seconds of CPU time. Even when all possible (37) solutions were explored and verbose printout was requested (generating 30-50 pages of text per case), the longest cases took less than 4 minutes of CPU time.

HSC performed very well and explored only one or a very few solutions on most single-defect cases, where there is no possibility of interactions between defects. More time and computation was focused on cases that were more difficult - ones containing multiple defects or presenting atypical cues. Effort is reduced in the evaluation of all solutions because only "important" cues are processed (14 types in the domain investigated). In addition, only cues of the same type are matched in clusters to calculate the EP, so there is no exponential growth there. The amount of time spent was well within the limits of current systems, and increasingly larger problems will be feasible as computer power doubles every few years.

Other successful approaches to the diagnosis of multiple interacting defects include model-based reasoning (de Kleer and Williams 1987; Reiter 1987), qualitative reasoning (Bratko et al. 1989; Downing and Widman 1991), complete simulation models (Wu 1991; Jang 1993) and probabilistic reasoning based on variations of Bayes theory (Kleiter 1992; Szolovits and Pauker 1993; Heckerman et al. 1995).

The significant differences and advantages of this computational model center on correctly explaining cues modified due to interactions between defects, especially in domains where complete simulation models are not available or cannot feasibly be constructed. All defects in a solution are evaluated in a cluster, when necessary, to explain abnormal cues in this method. Other methods, like symptom clustering, group cues together and explain them with one disease, but do not use a combinations of defects to explain one cue (with the exception of some additive combinations). For probabilistic methods, the interaction between defects means that the probability of an abnormal cue is altered compared to the probability calculated from the component defects. Thus the collection and use of additional statistics is necessary for each combination of defects and each type of cue where interactions are present.

Future work is planned to experiment on larger sets of defects and to explore the usefulness of different weights associated with each type of cue, giving more (or less) importance to selected cues.

Summary

Multiple interacting defects occur in many domains. On real problems, the entire search space of solutions may not need to be explored except on the most difficult cases. In the domain examined, we found that the number of possible solutions was greatly reduced, by almost half, due to incompatible defects. There were also a relatively small number (3) of maximum defects per solution. Current computational resources easily processed even an exhaustive generation and evaluation of solutions. Other domains may produce similar results.

References

Ivan Bratko, I. Mozetič, and N. Lavrač. *KARDIO: A Study in Deep and Qualitative Knowledge for Expert Systems*. MIT Press, Cambridge, MA, 1989.

Tom Bylander, D. Allemang, M. C. Tanner, and J. R. Josephson. The computational complexity of abduction. *Artificial Intelligence*, 49:25–60, 1991.

Johan de Kleer and B. C. Williams. Diagnosing multiple faults. *Artificial Intelligence*, 32(1):97–130, 1987.

K. L. Downing and L. E. Widman. Extending model-based diagnosis to medicine. In *5th Workshop on Qualitative Reasoning*, pp. 263–273, Austin, TX, 1991.

Olivier Fischer. *Cognitively Plausible Heuristics to Tackle the Computational Complexity of Abductive Reasoning*. PhD thesis, Ohio State University, 1991.

David Heckerman, J. S. Breese, and K. Rommelse. Decision-theoretic troubleshooting. *Communicaitons of the ACM*, 38(3):49–57, 1995.

Y. Jang. *HYDI: A hybrid System with Feedback for diagnosing Multiple Disorders*. PhD thesis, MIT, 1993.

Paul E. Johnson, J. B. Moen, and W. B. Thompson. Garden path errors in diagnostic reasoning. In L. Bolc and M.J. Coombs, editors, *Expert System Applications*, pp. 395–427. Springer-Verlag, 1988.

John R. Josephson and S. G. Josephson, editors. *Abductive Inference: Computation, Philosophy, Technology*. Cambridge University Press, 1994.

Gernot D. Kleiter. Bayesian diagnosis in expert systems. *Artificial Intelligence*, 54(1):1–32, 1992.

Ramesh S. Patil. Artifical intelligence techniques for diagnostic reasoning in medicine. In Shrobe and the AAAI, editors, *Exploring Artificial Intelligence*, pp. 347–379, San Mateo, CA, 1988. Morgan Kaufmann.

Yun Peng and James A. Reggia. *Abductive Inference Models for Diagnostic Problem-Solving*. Springer-Verlag, New York, N.Y., 1990.

N. E. Reed, M. Gini, P. E. Johnson, and J. H. Moller. Diagnosing congenital heart defects using the fallot computational model. *Artificial Intelligence in Medicine*, 10:25–40, 1997.

N. E. Reed. *Diagnosing Multiple Interacting Defects with Cue Combination Descriptions*. PhD thesis, University of Minnesota, June 1995.

Raymond Reiter. A theory of diagnosis from first principles. *Artificial Intelligence*, 32:57–95, 1987.

Peter Szolovits and S. G. Pauker. Categorical and probabilistic reasoning in medicine revisited. *Artificial Intelligence*, 42:167–180, 1993.

W. B. Thompson, P. E. Johnson, and J. B. Moen. Recognition-based diagnostic reasoning. In *Proc. 8th IJCAI*, pp. 236–238, Karlsruhe, W. Germany, 1983.

Thomas D. Wu. A problem decomposition method for efficient diagnosis and interpretation of multiple disorders. *Comp. Meth. and Prog. in Biomed.*, 35:239–250, 1991.

Structured Representation of Complex Stochastic Systems

Nir Friedman*
Computer Science Division
387 Soda Hall
U.C. Berkeley
Berkeley, CA 94720
nir@cs.berkeley.edu

Daphne Koller
Computer Science Department
Stanford University
Gates Building, 1A
Stanford, CA 94305-9010
koller@cs.stanford.edu

Avi Pfeffer
Computer Science Department
Stanford University
Gates Building, 1A
Stanford, CA 94305-9010
avi@cs.stanford.edu

Abstract

This paper considers the problem of representing complex systems that evolve stochastically over time. *Dynamic Bayesian networks* provide a compact representation for stochastic processes. Unfortunately, they are often unwieldy since they cannot explicitly model the complex organizational structure of many real life systems: the fact that processes are typically composed of several interacting subprocesses, each of which can, in turn, be further decomposed. We propose a hierarchically structured representation language which extends both dynamic Bayesian networks and the *object-oriented Bayesian network* framework of [9], and show that our language allows us to describe such systems in a natural and modular way. Our language supports a natural representation for certain system characteristics that are hard to capture using more traditional frameworks. For example, it allows us to represent systems where some processes evolve at a different rate than others, or systems where the processes interact only intermittently. We provide a simple inference mechanism for our representation via translation to Bayesian networks, and suggest ways in which the inference algorithm can exploit the additional structure encoded in our representation.

1 Introduction

Consider the problem of representing and reasoning about a complex system such as a computer network, a factory, or a busy highway system. We may be interested in estimating the current status of the system, in predicting its behavior over the near future, or in understanding the cause for a certain sequence of observations. These applications, as well as many others, have some common characteristics. First, they require that we represent the system and its evolution over several time points. Second, there is significant uncertainty over the projected evolution of the system, leading us to prefer stochastic models, which provide an explicit representation for the various possibilities and their likelihoods. Finally, the system represented is usually quite complex. It is composed of several subprocesses that interact with each other; the subprocesses can, in turn, be decomposed into yet

---
*Current address: Institute of Computer Science, The Hebrew University, Givat Ram, Jerusalem 91904, Israel. nir@cs.huji.ac.il.

Copyright 1998, American Association for Artificial Intelligence (www.aaai.org). All rights reserved.

finer grained processes. Thus, for example, a computer network is usually composed of several sub-networks, each of which is composed of servers and clients, and so on.

How do we represent such a stochastic dynamic system? A standard approach, in the AI literature, is to use a *dynamic Bayesian network (DBN)* [3]. A DBN is a temporally-extended version of a Bayesian network (BN) [11], and shares many of the same advantages. It provides a natural representation of the different states of the process via a set of time-indexed random variables, clear and coherent probabilistic semantics for our uncertainty, and a compact representation of our probabilistic model using a set of *conditional independence assumptions* (including the Markov assumption).

Unfortunately, despite their appealing properties, DBNs are not ideally suited for the type of task that concerns us here. In many real-life domains, including the ones above, the high-level processes are structured entities, each composed of lower-level processes. These processes interact, thereby probabilistically influencing each other. However, most of the "activity" of a process is internal to it, and therefore encapsulated from the rest of the world. Simon [13] has observed that this type of hierarchical decomposition of complex systems in terms of weakly interacting subsystems is extremely common. For example, in a highway system [6], most of the activity inside a car is local to it; only limited aspects, such as lane occupancy and speed, influence other cars on the highway. DBNs do not support the notion of a process, far less the ability to refer to its interactions with others. Our inability to refer to components of the process also prevents us from declaratively reusing parts of the model that occur more than once. For example, if our computer network uses many servers of the same type, we would like to utilize the same model for all of them.

Our earlier work on the *Object-Oriented Bayesian Network (OOBN)* framework [9] addresses these problems for the case of static models. This framework supports decomposition and modularity by defining the domain in terms of a set of *objects*. An object has attributes, which can be simple variables (such as the speed of a car), or complex attributes which are themselves objects (e.g., the car's engine). Complex objects can depend on other objects via a set of *input* attributes, and can affect other objects via a set of *output* attributes. By defining classes of objects, the OOBN framework also supports reuse of model fragments for multiple objects.

Unfortunately, the basic OOBN framework cannot be directly applied to the task of representing interacting processes. An OOBN object is a black box that does not interact with the rest of the world except via its inputs and outputs. Its probability model is a stochastic mapping from the inputs to the outputs. To avoid a cyclic mapping, the framework requires that objects can be ordered so that the inputs of an object precede it in the ordering. Obviously, this requirement prohibits us from describing interacting objects, where each takes as input some of the other's outputs.

To avoid these shortcomings, we define a new representation, called *dynamic OOBNs (DOOBNs)*, which applies the hierarchical decomposition approach of OOBNs to evolving processes. We allow a process to be hierarchically decomposed into subprocesses, which interact repeatedly over time. We show how we can perform inference in our framework using standard inference tools for BNs and OOBNs.

Our representation allows us to obtain many of the advantages of OOBNs in the temporal setting. We can easily provide modular and reusable specifications of hierarchical, composable Markov models. DOOBNs also allow us to explicitly represent important properties of process-based systems that cannot naturally be described using DBNs. In particular, our framework supports a natural representation for processes that are changing with different *time granularity* and for processes with *sparse interactions*. As we show, the explicit representation of such properties allows us to model the system in terms of a smaller number of variables, thereby potentially making inference more efficient.

2 Object-oriented Bayesian networks

We begin with a brief overview of the OOBN framework [9], on which our current work is based. An OOBN is a hierarchically structured probabilistic model, based on Bayesian networks (BNs). BNs provide a concise representation of a joint probability distribution over a set of variables. A BN is a directed acyclic graph whose nodes are the random variables and whose edges are direct probabilistic dependencies between them. Each variable is associated with a conditional probability table (CPT), encoding the local dependence of a variable on its parents. The complete joint distribution over the set of variables is defined as the product of the conditional probability of each node given its parents [11].

OOBNs extend BNs by allowing structured objects, which are hierarchically composed of other objects. Specifically, an object has a set of attributes. Some of these are simple, and correspond to nodes in a traditional BN. Others are complex, and take other objects as their value. The value of an object is a tuple consisting of the values of all its attributes.

Definition 2.1 : A *simple type* is an enumerated set $\{a_1, \ldots, a_n\}$; a *value* for a simple type τ is any element of τ. A *complex type* is a tuple $\tau = \langle A_1 : \tau_1, \ldots, A_n : \tau_n \rangle$; a value for τ is a tuple $\langle A_1 : v_1, \ldots, A_n : v_n \rangle$ where each v_i is a value for τ_i. The elements A_i are called *attributes* of τ. We require that types are stratified, i.e., non-recursive.

We use the term *object* to denote an entity in the domain. A *simple object* has a simple type. A *complex object* has a complex type τ, and three subsets $\mathcal{I}, \mathcal{V}$ and $\mathcal{O}$ of the attributes of τ, where $\mathcal{I}, \mathcal{V}$ are a disjoint partition of $\{A_1, \ldots, A_n\}$, and $\mathcal{O} \subseteq \mathcal{V}$. The sets $\mathcal{I}, \mathcal{V}$, and $\mathcal{O}$ are called *input* attributes, *value* attributes, and *output* attributes.

The type of an object X is denoted $\mathcal{T}(X)$. An object also has an *output type*, denoted $\mathcal{OT}(X)$. The output type of a simple object τ is simply τ itself. The output type of a complex object X with output attributes $\mathcal{O} = \{A_{j_1}, \ldots, A_{j_k}\}$ is defined as $\mathcal{OT}(X) = \langle A_{j_1} : \mathcal{OT}(\tau_{j_1}), \ldots, A_{j_k} : \mathcal{OT}(\tau_{j_k}) \rangle$. An *attribute chain* for an object X is a (possibly empty) chain $\rho = A_1.A_2.\cdots.A_j$ such that A_1 is an attribute of X, A_2 is an attribute of $X.A_1$, and so on. ∎

Aside from its type, the specification of a complex object includes a *probability model* that describes the conditional probability of value attributes, given the input attributes.

Definition 2.2: Let X be a complex OOBN object with type τ. A probability model $\mathcal{P}$ for X defines the following for each $X.A_i \in \mathcal{V}(X)$.

- If τ_i is simple, $\mathcal{P}$ specifies for A_i a set of *parents* $Par(A_i) = \{\rho_1, \ldots, \rho_k\}$ and a CPT. For each j, ρ_j must be an attribute chain of X such that $X.\rho_j$ is simple. The CPT for A_i maps from joint values of $Par(A_i)$ to distributions over τ_i.
- If τ_i is complex, $\mathcal{P}$ associates with A_i a probability model $\mathcal{P}_i$ and an *input binding* that for each $I \in \mathcal{I}(X_i)$ assigns some object $Y.\rho$ such that $\mathcal{OT}(Y.\rho) = \mathcal{T}(I)$.[1] ∎

The probabilistic model of an object defines the way in which its attributes depend on each other. In order for the probability distribution to be well-defined, it is important that there are no cycles in the dependency graph.

Definition 2.3: The *dependency graph* $\mathcal{G}(X)$ associated with an OOBN object X is a directed graph with a node for each of the attributes of X, and an edge from B to A if

- A is a simple attribute, and $B.\rho \in Par(A)$.
- A is complex, and $B.\rho$ is assigned to one of A's inputs.

An OOBN object X is *well defined* if $\mathcal{G}(X)$ is acyclic. ∎

Given this acyclicity requirement, the probabilistic model for an OOBN object is guaranteed to define a coherent conditional probability distribution.

Theorem 2.4: [9] *The probability model for a well defined OOBN object defines a conditional probability distribution over its value attributes given its input attributes.*

The OOBN framework also allows *classes* of objects to be defined. A class defines the set of attributes for a complex object as well as its probabilistic model. Multiple objects can therefore be defined from the same class, allowing reuse of model components. The encapsulation properties of the OOBN language allow objects from the same class to be used in a variety of contexts. An *OOBN model* is simply a complex OOBN object without input and output attributes. By building on the reusable class definitions, very large structured models can be constructed from a set of modular components.

It is easy to see that an OOBN that has only simple attributes is essentially a Bayesian network. In general, Koller and Pfeffer show how to "unwind" complex OOBN objects into a "flat" Bayesian network that is equivalent to it, in a precise sense. We briefly review this construction.

---

[1]Input binding results in objects having several names. For example, if $\mathcal{P}$ binds $X.A$ to $X.B.I$, then $X.A$ and $X.B.I$ refer to the same object.

Let X be an OOBN object. We define $\mathcal{S}(X)$ to be the set of simple attributes of X as follows. If X has simple type, then $\mathcal{S}(X) = \{X\}$. If X has complex type, then $\mathcal{S}(X) = \cup\{\mathcal{S}(X.A) : A \in \mathcal{V}(X)\}$. Let $\mathcal{B}$ be an OOBN. It is easy to prove that an assignment of values to $\mathcal{S}(\mathcal{B})$ uniquely determines the value of $\mathcal{B}$. Thus, a distribution over $\mathcal{S}(\mathcal{B})$ determines a distribution over the (complex) value of $\mathcal{B}$.

Definition 2.5: Let $\mathcal{B}$ be an OOBN. The *induced network* $BN(\mathcal{B})$ is a Bayesian network over $\mathcal{S}(\mathcal{B})$, such that the parents of each $X \in \mathcal{S}(\mathcal{B})$ are $Par(X)$ and the conditional probability $P(X \mid Par(X))$ is the CPT of X in $\mathcal{B}$. ∎

Koller and Pfeffer show that the induced network is well-defined and captures the distribution defined by $\mathcal{B}$:

Theorem 2.6: [9] *Let $\mathcal{B}$ be an OOBN, then $P_\mathcal{B}(\mathcal{S}(\mathcal{B}))$, the distribution $\mathcal{B}$ defines over simple attributes, is the same as $P_{BN(\mathcal{B})}(\mathcal{S}(\mathcal{B}))$.*

The construction of the induced network allows us to use any standard BN inference algorithm to answer queries about the distribution described by an OOBN. However, OOBNs give us the ability to represent models that are much larger and more complex, thereby raising the problem of inference in these very large networks. Luckily, we can exploit the encapsulation properties of OOBNs to guide the application of inference procedures on the induced BN. That is, the input and output attributes of an object "shield" its internals from rest of the OOBN. More precisely, we can define as follows:

Definition 2.7: The *interface* of an OOBN object X, denoted $Interface(X)$, contains all the simple attributes in $\mathcal{I}(X)$ or in $\mathcal{O}(X)$. Note that the interface of a simple object is the object itself. ∎

The interface of X can be used to separate the inference for simple objects within X from the inference in the rest of the model. In particular, we can divide the inference process for $BN(\mathcal{B})$ into a separate computation for each complex object X, one which need only look at the simple variables in $Interface(X) \cup \bigcup_{A \in \mathcal{V}(X)} Interface(A)$. Koller and Pfeffer define a cost function $Cost(X)$ that measures the complexity of this computation for an object X, one which is (in the worst-case) exponential in the number of simple variables in $Interface(X) \cup \bigcup_{A \in \mathcal{V}(X)} Interface(A)$. They show that

Theorem 2.8: [9] *The complexity of the inference in $BN(\mathcal{B})$ is $O(\sum_X Cost(X))$.*

This result is important, since it provides guarantees about the complexity of inference in an OOBNs based on properties of the object classes that are used to construct it.[2]

3 Interacting objects

While OOBNs are useful for describing hierarchical models of objects, they are limited by their inability to describe interacting processes that mutually influence each other. Consider, for example, a pair of computational processes, e.g., a client process and a server process, who go through several rounds of communication. If we were to draw a high-level

---

[2]Note that one of the complex objects is the OOBN $\mathcal{B}$ itself. In particular, if the OOBN corresponds to a standard BN, then $Cost(\mathcal{B})$ is simply the cost of inference in the BN.

dependency graph, as above, we would see that the state of each process depends on that of the other.

Introducing cycles into an OOBN may lead to an incoherent probability model, just as it does for BNs. However, a cyclic description of a process at a high level may obscure an acyclic process at a finer level of granularity. In the client-server example, it is clear that there are many possible acyclic models at the finer model: the client sends the server a request, the server in turn sends a result to the client, influencing its next query, and so on.

We could, of course, accommodate such models simply by dropping the acyclicity requirement for the dependency graph of an object. In order to guarantee coherence of our model, we could simply test, on a case-by-case basis, whether an OOBN object defined an acyclic model at the lowest level of granularity, i.e., whether $BN(\mathcal{B})$ is acyclic.

This approach, while straightforward, defeats the purpose of providing modular, composable models of objects. There would be no guarantee that a set of objects, each of which has a coherent model of its own, would compose into a coherent object at a higher level. We therefore take a different approach, that allows an object to provide guarantees about its own internal ordering. Each output of an object X will declare the inputs on which it depends. When X is used in a higher-level object, the only thing required to ensure an acyclic process is that no output of X can influence any of the inputs on which it depends. In other words, the output cannot be used before the inputs on which it depends are supplied.

Definition 3.1: An *interacting object* X is an OOBN object, as before, except that $\mathcal{P}$ associates complex attributes with *interacting* objects, and that $\mathcal{P}(X)$ defines a *dependency model* d_X which is a function from $\mathcal{O}(X)$ to subsets of $\mathcal{I}(X)$. ∎

Intuitively, if X is an interacting object, the value of an output attribute $X.O$ depends only on the inputs specified in $d_X(O)$.

To ground this intuition, consider the interacting OOBN in Figure 1(a), representing a simple client/server system. There are two computations to be processed, and two servers available to process them. An allocator receives requests from each of the computations and decides what job to send to each server. The two servers each have the simple attribute FREE, indicating whether the server is available for computation, and the complex output attribute RESULT, which in turn has the simple attributes COMPLETE and SIZE. The servers also take as input the complex attribute JOB, which has simple attributes PRIORITY and COMPLEXITY. Presumably, the servers will also have various other complex attributes representing their components, such as their processors, memory and hard drive, but they are not shown in this simple model. Note that we can use the same model to describe the two server objects, and similarly for the computation objects. A computation object has the simple output attribute SUCCESS, the complex value attribute RESULT (of the same type as SERVER.RESULT), and a complex attribute QUERY. It also has a simple input RESPONSE, which is a notification from the allocator as to which process, if any, is serving its request.

The model of Figure 1(a) is not a legal OOBN, since there are numerous cycles: for example, between each computation and the allocator, and between each server and the allocator. All the cycles are broken, however, because the QUERY output of the computation objects and the FREE output of the server objects do not depend on any

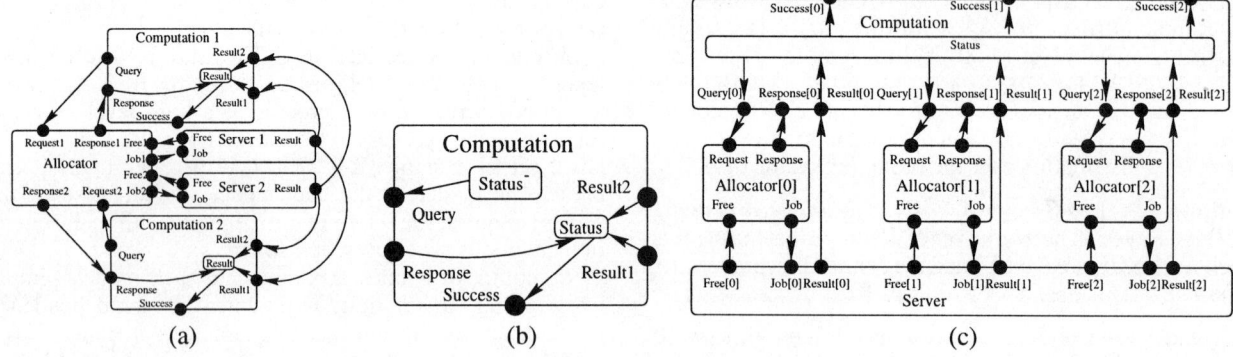

Figure 1: (a) A high-level picture of an interacting OOBN. (b) The DOOBN model for a computation object. (c) The interacting OOBN for 3 time slices of the client-server DOOBN.

of their inputs. The model can express this fact by asserting that their dependency lists are empty. The dependency list for COMPUTATION.SUCCESS, on the other hand, is {RESPONSE, RESULT1, RESULT2}.

Recall that the dependency graph of an OOBN object ensures that the probability model of the object does not contain cycles. Since an OOBN treats an enclosed object as a black box, Definition 2.3 assumes that all outputs of an object are dependent on all of its inputs. We now modify this definition to use the declared dependency model of the contained objects of X to get a more refined representation of the dependencies among attributes. To do so, however, we need to define the graph over input/output attributes of objects rather than over complete objects.

Definition 3.2: The *dependency graph* $\Gamma(X)$ of an interacting object X is a directed graph whose nodes are the input attributes of X, the simple value attributes of X, and the input and output attributes of complex value attributes of X. There is an edge from node ν to node μ in $\Gamma(X)$ if:

1. $\nu.\rho \in Par(\mu)$, for a simple attribute μ.
2. μ is of the form $A.I$ (where we use I to denote input attributes and O to denote output attributes), and some expression of the form $\nu.\rho$ is assigned to $A.I$ by $\mathcal{P}(X)$.
3. μ is of the form $A.I$, ν is of the form $B.O$, and B was assigned to $A.I$.
4. μ is of the form $C.I$, ν is of the form $C.O$, and I is in $d_{X.C}(O)$. ∎

The cases (1) and (2) are similar to the cases we saw in Definition 2.3, except that in case (2) the edge points to $A.I$ rather than to A as a whole. Case (3) deals with situations in which an entire top-level attribute B is assigned to $A.I$; there, any of B's output attributes may be used within A, so we must have an edge between each of them and $A.I$. Case (4) simply reflects the dependencies reported by the complex attributes. This graph allows us to state the basic definitions that force an interacting object to define a coherent probability distribution.

Definition 3.3: An object X is said to *respect* d_X if, whenever there is a causal path in $\Gamma(X)$ from an input attribute $X.I$ to an output attribute $X.O$ or to one of $X.O$'s attributes (if $X.O$ is complex), then $I \in d_X(O)$. An interacting object X is *coherent* if $\Gamma(X)$ is acyclic, X respects d_X, and all complex attributes of X are also coherent. ∎

We can now state the main theorem of this section:

Theorem 3.4: *If X is a coherent interacting object, then X defines a conditional probability distribution over its value attributes given its input attributes.*

Thus, the use of declarative dependency models allows us to extend OOBNs for interacting objects, without requiring other changes to the representation. The main difference is that the semantics of an interactive object is no longer in terms of one stochastic map from inputs to outputs, but rather as a more complex collection of such mappings. In spite of the different semantics, we still perform inference by constructing the induced BN; in fact, the construction of Definition 2.5 applies unchanged.

Theorem 3.5: *Let $\mathcal{B}$ be a coherent interacting OOBN. Then, the network $BN(\mathcal{B})$ is well-defined, and $P_\mathcal{B}(\mathcal{S}(\mathcal{B}))$ is the same as $P_{BN(\mathcal{B})}(\mathcal{S}(\mathcal{B}))$.*

As for OOBNs, the ability to construct a ground-level BN provides us with an inference algorithm for the richer representation. More importantly, the encapsulation properties of objects also remain unchanged. Technically, it is easy to show that the value of an object X is independent of the remaining objects in the OOBN (those not enclosed in X) given values for X's inputs and outputs. Thus, as for OOBNs, we can utilize the structure encoded in our representation to provide guidance to the inference algorithm. Using the same definitions for *Interface* and *Cost*, we can thus show:

Theorem 3.6: *The complexity of the inference in $BN(\mathcal{B})$ is $O(\sum_X Cost(X))$.*

4 Dynamic OOBNs

Interacting OOBNs allow us to describe complex interacting objects. Yet, they are still unwieldy for dealing with tasks such as modeling a computer network or a freeway system, which involve *repetitive* interactions. In this section we introduce a compact representation for such domains.

Let us reconsider the example of the previous section, but now under the assumption that the computations are long-lived: they generate a stream of queries and wait for one to be answered before sending the next. In each round, the allocator will attempt to dispatch incoming queries to the servers. The servers themselves may take several rounds to process a query.

To capture such repetitious interaction patterns between objects, we define *dynamic OOBNs* (DOOBNs), which have the same relationship to OOBNs as dynamic Bayesian networks (DBNs) have to BNs. In a DOOBN, we have dynamic objects whose state—the values of its objects—changes over time. We define the dynamics of the object using a standard *Markov assumption*, i.e., that the future state of the process is independent of its past given its future. As usual, this assumption allows us to represent the process via a *transition model* that describes the conditional probability of the current state given the current inputs and the previous state.

The objects in a DOOBN are of two kinds: *persistent* and *transient*. A persistent object exists for the entire duration of the system; its state changes over time, but its state at one time point can influence its state in the future. We often refer to persistent objects as *processes*. A transient object X, on the other hand, has a limited lifetime; every time the system changes, X is replaced by a new object of the same type. In our running example, the computation and server objects have state, and so they are persistent. On the other hand, queries and results, which are communicated between the various units, are transient. They are replaced by new queries and results every round of communication.

Definition 4.1: A *dynamic object* X is declared to be either *transient* or *persistent*. A transient object is exactly an interacting OOBN object. A persistent object is defined in the same manner as an interacting object, except that it also allows parents of simple attributes and inputs of complex attributes to be of the form $A.\rho^-$, where A is a value attribute of X. Additionally, the model $\mathcal{P}$ of a persistent object can associate attributes with either persistent or transient objects. However, input and outputs attributes must be transient.

The dependency graph $\Gamma(X)$ for a dynamic object X is the same as that for an interacting object. The definitions of when X respects d_X and when X is coherent are the same for dynamic objects as for interacting objects. ∎

Intuitively, the attribute $A.\rho^-$ refers to the value of the object that was assigned to $A.\rho$ at the preceding point in time. (Recall that $A.\rho$ must be a transient object.) To make this definition precise, we assume that a process changes state at fixed time intervals, each of which is called a time slice. Thus, $A.\rho^-$ is simply the value of A at the previous time slice. We now get the following as a corollary of Theorem 3.4.

Theorem 4.2: *If X is a coherent dynamic object, then X defines a conditional probability distribution over its value attributes given its input attributes and its previous value.*

Figure 1(b) shows the DOOBN model for a computation object. Since the computation is persistent, it may itself contain persistent attributes, and in fact the STATUS attribute, representing the accumulated result of computation, is persistent. STATUS has, among other things, the simple attribute WORK-TO-GO. The current query depends on the status at the previous time slice, while the status at the current time slice is affected by the current result.

To fully describe an evolving process, we must provide a starting point as well as a transition probability.

Definition 4.3: A *Dynamic OOBN* (DOOBN) is a pair $\mathcal{D} = \langle \mathcal{D}_0, \mathcal{D}_\rightarrow \rangle$, where $\mathcal{D}_\rightarrow$ is a dynamic object without inputs, and $\mathcal{D}_0$ is an (interacting) OOBN object of the same type as $\mathcal{D}_\rightarrow$. For simplicity, we also assume that $\mathcal{D}_0$ and $\mathcal{D}_\rightarrow$ have the same dependency model d. ∎

Intuitively, $\mathcal{D}_\rightarrow$ describes the transition probability from one time slice to the next, while $\mathcal{D}_0$ is an OOBN (that therefore lacks the A^- attributes) that describes the distribution over the initial state. As a whole the DOOBN model describes a complex Markov process, where the value of the process at each step is of type $\mathcal{T}(\mathcal{D}_\rightarrow)$.

To reason about such a process, we need to reason about the values of the process at different points in time. To do so, we *unroll* the DOOBN into an interacting OOBN that has many copies of the same objects, one for each time slice. To unroll a DOOBN for N time slices, we unroll each of its attributes. A transient object is duplicated N times; a persistent one is unrolled recursively. The inputs and outputs are then connected appropriately by the enclosing object.

Definition 4.4: Let $\mathcal{D}$ be a DOOBN, let X be a persistent object in $\mathcal{D}$, and let $N > 0$ be the number of non-initial time slices. The unrolled object $\mathcal{U}_N(X)$ is an interacting OOBN object defined as follows:

- If A is a transient attribute of X, then $\mathcal{U}_N(X)$ contains an attribute $A[0]$—a copy of $X.A$ in $\mathcal{D}_0$—and N attributes $A[1], \ldots, A[N]$, each of which is a copy of $X.A$. If $\mathcal{D}_\rightarrow$ (or $\mathcal{D}_0$ for $k = 0$) assigns $B.\rho$ to $A.I$ or a parent $B.\rho$ to A, then $\mathcal{U}_N(X)$ assigns $\sigma_k(B.\rho)$ to $A[k].I$ or to $Par(A[k])$ respectively. If A is simple, the CPT of $A[k]$ is the same as that of A.
- If A is a persistent attribute of X, then $\mathcal{U}_N(X)$ contains the single attribute $\mathcal{U}_N(A)$. If $B.\rho$ is assigned to $A.I$ in X, then a *time k snapshot* $\sigma_k(B.\rho)$ is assigned to $\mathcal{U}_N(A).I[k]$.
- The dependency list $d_{\mathcal{U}_N(X)}(O[k]) = \{I[j] : j < k, I \in \mathcal{I}(X)\} \cup \{I[k] : I \in d_X(O)\}$.

The definition of $\sigma_k(B.\rho)$ is straightforward: $\sigma_k(B.\rho^-) = \sigma_{k-1}(B.\rho)$; if B is transient, $\sigma_k(B.\rho) = B[k].\rho$; otherwise, letting $\rho = O.\rho'$, $\sigma_k(B.\rho) = B.O[k].\rho'$. ∎

At its most basic, the construction generates a copy of each simple attribute for each time slice. These attributes are encapsulated in a way that matches the process structure: persistent attributes are represented by a single long-lived subobject, while transient attributes have a separate object for each time slice. Figure 1(c) shows part of the interacting OOBN for 3 time slices of the DOOBN for our example.

Theorem 4.5: *If $\mathcal{D} = \langle \mathcal{D}_0, \mathcal{D}_\rightarrow \rangle$ is a DOOBN where $\mathcal{D}_0$ is a coherent interacting OOBN object and $\mathcal{D}_\rightarrow$ is a coherent DOOBN object, then $\mathcal{U}_N(\mathcal{D})$ is a coherent interacting OOBN.*

If we now take the resulting interacting OOBN, and apply the transformation described in Theorem 3.5, we obtain a BN with $N + 1$ time slices, each containing the simple attributes in $\mathcal{D}_\rightarrow$; These are connected appropriately both within and between time slices. This transformation is illustrated in Figure 2, which shows two time slices of the BN constructed from the DOOBN for our example. (For simplicity, the model for the size of the result has been omitted.) Recall that the same simple attribute can have a number of names, because values are passed from the outputs of one object to the inputs of another. In the BN, we use the name of the attribute at the time it is created. For example, COMP.STATUS.WORKTOGO depends on COMP.RESULT.COMPLETE, which is the

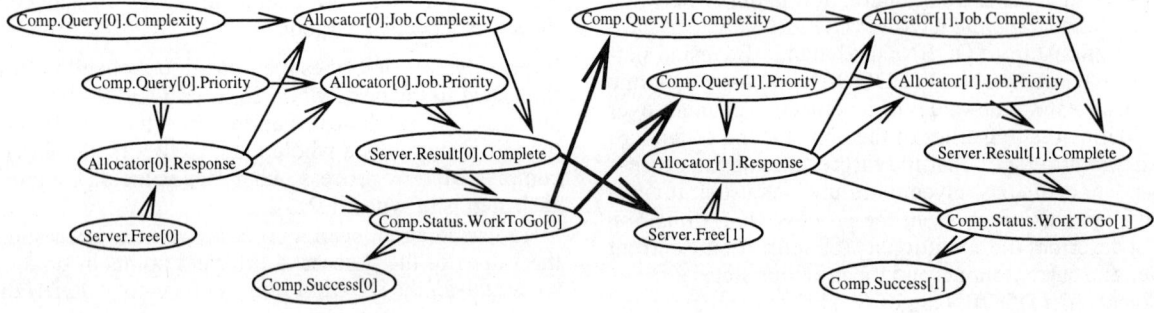

Figure 2: The DBN for 2 time slices of the client-server DOOBN. Edges between the time slices are shown in bold.

same as SERVER.RESULT.COMPLETE. This is represented by an edge from SERVER.RESULT.COMPLETE to COMP.STATUS.WORKTOGO in each time slice.

Since the BN was built from an interacting OOBN, Theorem 3.6 on the cost of inference still applies. Since the number of objects in an N-time slice interacting OOBN is linear in N, one might think that the cost of inference is also linear in N. Unfortunately, this is not the case—the cost of inference in the subobjects grows exponentially with N. The reason is that the interface to a persistent object contains $N+1$ copies of its inputs and outputs, and the cost of reasoning in an OOBN is exponential in the size of the largest interface.

Of course, there is no requirement that we use the guidance given to us by object boundaries in performing the inference. After all, the resulting BN structure is a familiar one: it is exactly the type of structure that we obtain by unrolling a DBN for N time slices; perhaps we can employ standard DBN inference algorithms. As we mentioned above, the key to most BN algorithms is the separation of the inference problem into two pieces using a set of variables that render the pieces conditionally independent (e.g., the interface of an object in OOBNs). DBN inference algorithms, even the most sophisticated [8], rely on the same basic idea. Largely, DBN inference algorithms focus on *Markovian separators*, which separate the future of the process from its past. Unfortunately, in order to render the future and past independent, our separator must contain some set of variables that block all paths through which influence can flow. In Figure 1(c), for example, a Markovian separator would have to "cut" both the computation process and the server process, rendering their future independent of their past. This separator would have to contain (at least) all the simple variables in these processes whose value at the previous time step is referenced. For complex processes the number of such variables may be quite large. The inference algorithm has to maintain a joint distribution over the separator, rendering the cost exponential in the number of variables in it.[3] Since we are interested in reasoning about fairly complex systems, using Markovian separators is often infeasible.

It would appear that we are faced with two unpalatable alternatives. We can either use a method that is exponential in the number of time slices, or one that is exponential in the size of a time slice. If both are large, neither option will be feasible. This problem also occurs in traditional DBNs, and approximate algorithms for DBN inference is an important area of current research [4, 7, 2]. The work of Boyen and Koller [2] is particularly relevant to our discussion, as it explicitly utilizes a decomposition of a complex process into weakly interacting subprocesses. They utilize this decomposition to approximate the joint distribution over a Markovian separator by assuming that the states of the subprocesses are independent. They then provide bounds on the error incurred by approximation using the degree to which the different subprocesses interact. In their current work, the decomposition of the process into subprocesses is given as input to their algorithm, presumably by some user. Our DOOBN representation makes this structure explicit, allowing their algorithm to take advantage of the process structure automatically.

5 Time granularity

By making the notion of a process explicit, we obtain the ability to refer directly to its properties and distinguish them from the properties of other processes in the system. In particular, our framework gives us the tools to avoid one of the main deficiencies of the DBN representation. In a standard DBN model, we begin by picking some fixed granularity of time, and then generating multiple instances of each state variable in our domain, one instance for each time slice. For example, in the traffic surveillance application of [6], accurate tracking requires that the locations of vehicles be modeled at the rate of 30 time slices a second. All other variables in the system are therefore modeled at the same level of granularity. However, most of these variables, e.g., the weather or the alertness of the driver, evolve much more slowly than the car's location. Clearly, had the presence of the location variables not forced them to do so, it would not have occurred to the designers of [6] to model these other variables so finely.

What we want is a framework that allows us to model different parts of the system at different levels of time granularity. One could imagine trying to extend the DBN framework directly in order to achieve this goal. For example, we could annotate each variable with a time granularity, using

---
[3]One might think that, in highly structured processes, it would be possible to use conditional independence to decompose the joint over the separator. Unfortunately, this is not the case. Except for the first few time slices, all of the variables in a Markovian separator are correlated. Intuitively, for almost any two variables, there is an influence path leading back through earlier time slices, that renders them dependent.

that number to dictate the frequency with which it is modeled. Aside from leading to unwieldy notation, such a solution suffers from a serious knowledge engineering problem: DBNs provide no notion of a high-level process consisting of several variables; thus, if we decide to change the time granularity at which one of our processes is modeled we have to manually change the annotation on all of the relevant variables.

We now describe how to represent such situations by making a small extension to the basic DOOBN model. We simply add an optional additional granularity argument, $\delta(X)$, to each persistent attribute X in the DOOBN, that denotes how frequently we should model the process represented by X. If X is not labeled with a granularity value, it simply inherits its granularity value from its enclosing object.

Let us analyze the behavior of a process containing processes at different granularities by examining our transformation from Definition 4.4. The number of times that a transient object is duplicated depends on $\delta(X)$, where X is the enclosing process. We start with one copy at time 0; each instance lasts for exactly δ seconds, at which point a new instance is generated from the appropriate transition probability model. Thus, the kth "time slice" of the object maintains its value over the half open interval $[k\delta, (k+1)\delta)$.

In this context, it no longer makes sense to index time-specific instances of an object A with a natural number k representing its time slice. Instead, we use $A[t_1, t_2]$ to index an object by the interval over which its holds. We use the notation $A[t]$ as a shorthand reference to the (unique) time indexed object $A[t_1, t_2]$ for which $t \in [t_1, t_2)$.

The probability distribution over the values of a transient object depends on values of other objects, both from the current time and from the previous time. To understand the nature of this dependence, consider the (imaginary) process by which a new value for A is chosen at time t_1. A parent B of A represents a dependence of $A[t_1, t_2]$ on a contemporaneous variable. Thus, the appropriate parent for $A[t_1, t_2]$ would be $B[t_1]$—the value of B at the time A's value is selected. On the other hand, a parent of the form B^- represents a dependence of A on the value of B at a preceding moment in time. We choose to interpret B^- as referring to the closest preceding moment, i.e., $B[t_1 - \epsilon]$ for arbitrarily small ϵ. Intuitively, A looks at the value of $B.\rho$ immediately before t_1, and then changes its value at t_1. Clearly, this interpretation is not the only legitimate one. In particular if some of A's inputs evolve much more quickly than A, we may wish to have A depending on an their earlier values, or perhaps on some appropriate aggregate value. Space limitations prevent us from discussing these ideas, but the extensions are straightforward and introduce no new subtleties. We now formalize this intuition by extending Definition 4.4.

Definition 5.1: Let X be a persistent DOOBN object, and let $T > 0$ be some time point. Let δ be the time granularity of X and $N = \lfloor T/\delta \rfloor$. The unrolled object $\mathcal{U}_T(X)$ is simply $\mathcal{U}_N(X)$, with the following changes:

- Any attribute in $\mathcal{U}_N(X)$ of the form $A[k]$ is renamed to $A[k\delta, (k+1)\delta]$.
- The function σ_k is replaced by the function $\sigma_t(B.\rho)$, defined as follows: if B is transient, $\sigma_t(B.\rho) = B[t].\rho$; otherwise, letting $\rho = O.\rho'$, $\sigma_t(B.\rho) = B.O[t].\rho'$. $\sigma_t(B.\rho^-)$ is defined to be $\sigma_{t-\epsilon}(B.\rho)$ for an ϵ so small that $\sigma_{t-\epsilon}(B.\rho) = \sigma_{t-\epsilon'}(B.\rho)$ for any $\epsilon' \in (0, \epsilon)$. ∎

Theorem 5.2: If $\mathcal{D} = \langle \mathcal{D}_0, \mathcal{D}_\rightarrow \rangle$ is a DOOBN with time granularities where $\mathcal{D}_0$ is a coherent interacting OOBN object and $\mathcal{D}_\rightarrow$ is a coherent DOOBN object, then $\mathcal{U}_T(\mathcal{D})$ is a coherent interacting OOBN.

The proof is based on defining the set of time points at which some object in the model determines its value. Although this set of time points no longer has regular structure, it is still finite. The same techniques as in the previous section can be used to show that the probability model over the variables at these time points is acyclic, and that the conditional distribution is well-defined given the values at the previous time point.

If we now take the resulting interacting OOBN, and apply the transformation into a BN described in Theorem 3.5, the result is still a BN, but it is no longer a standard DBN. Variables that evolve more slowly have fewer copies than their more volatile counterparts. The dependencies between variables are resolved automatically by our construction process.

While modeling processes at their appropriate granularity is a worthwhile goal on its own, it can also provide some help with the inference task. As we saw in the previous section, using the OOBN structure to perform inference in a DOOBN is exponential in the number of time slices. However, if some processes evolve much more slowly than others, their interfaces will be fairly small. Therefore, it may make sense to use interface-based separators, at least for slowly changing processes. The resulting fragments might involve fewer processes, and thus would allow for efficient use of Markovian separators. A combined approach that uses both kinds of separators suggests itself. This topic deserves a full investigation, which is beyond the scope of this paper.

6 Sparsely interacting processes

Up to now, we have assumed that the interaction between processes is regular; at each point in time, they receive inputs from other processes, change their state, and export their outputs. Clearly, this type of regular communication is not an aspect of all systems. In our client/server example, it is reasonable to assume that a server output representing the size of the query result influences the client state only if the client has issued a query to the server at some previous time point, and if the server has just indicated that the processing is complete. If queries are only issued rarely and their processing takes a variable amount of time, the interaction model is far from regular. As another example, consider modeling cars traveling on a highway. While the behavior of one car is definitely influenced by attributes of others, this influence might be intermittent; e.g., a driver might examine the status of cars on the left only when he tries to change lanes.

Such situations are represented very naturally in the *transition system* framework of Manna and Pnueli [10]. There, each process can take one of several possible transitions, which affect its state. However, each transition is associated with a *guard*, which may or may not be true in a given state. A transition is said to be *enabled* in a state if its guard is true at that state; at a given state, a process can only take a transition if it is enabled. In our client/server example, we may have an additional *processing-complete* variable in the server and a *query-issued* variable in the client. The transition which updates the client's state based on the query results would be enabled only if both of these variables are true.

We can extend this idea to our probabilistic framework by using the techniques of Boutilier et al. [1]. They define a notion of *context specific independence (CSI)*, which corresponds to situations in which the variables on which some variable depends are different in different situations (or contexts). They also show how these situations can be represented explicitly within the language, by using structured CPT models such as trees. In our example, the state of the client object will only depend on the server's other output variables if both of these variables are true.

Boutilier et al. also propose ways in which the CSI structure can be exploited to speed up BN inference. We believe that these ideas can be extended to DOOBN models, allowing our inference algorithm to take advantage of sparse interaction between the processes. We conclude this section by sketching one possible mechanism by which computational advantage can be gained.

Recall that applying the OOBN inference idea to models generated from DOOBNs led us to consider the use of process interfaces to decompose the BN computation. When interactions between the processes are sparse, the actual "information" content of the interface is much smaller. For example, assume that our client is unlikely to issue very many queries to the server, perhaps because it intersperses queries with other (lengthy) tasks. We can define an *active interaction* to be a state in which both the *query-issued* and *processing-complete* variables are true, so that the client state is influenced by the server. At a time slice where there is no active interaction, none of the other server outputs affect the client; otherwise, the client state depends on some set of ℓ variables describing the query results. If we know that there are exactly k "active interactions" in N time slices, there are only $\binom{N}{k}$ interaction patterns, and a total of $\binom{N}{k} 2^{k\ell}$ possible interactions between the server and the client. Using a process of *global conditioning* [12], we can do a case analysis on the different possible interactions, thereby separating the client and server processes. The cost of this separation is $\binom{N}{k} 2^{k\ell}$, which (for small k) is exponentially smaller than the $2^{N\ell}$ required without using the sparsity. We can also extend these ideas to situations where we have no specified bound on the number of interactions. If we only know that "runs" where there are many queries are highly improbable, most of the probability mass would be on those runs where the interaction pattern is sparse. The bounded conditioning algorithm of [5] can then be used to restrict attention only to runs with sparse interaction.

7 Conclusion

In this paper, we have presented a new language for representing complex dynamic systems with uncertainty. The language supports structured hierarchical representations of systems in terms of interacting subprocesses, and allows large models to be constructed from modular, reusable components. Our language can express important aspects of complex systems, such as the different rates at which various processes evolve, and the sparse interactions that take place between processes. Our framework also allows additional features to be incorporated easily; for example, we may be able to represent asynchronous stochastic systems by extending our time granularity framework to allow for stochastic models of when processes *wake up*.

We provide an inference algorithm for answering queries over models in our language by converting them to Bayesian networks. Unfortunately, as with standard DBNs, inference in DOOBNs can be extremely costly. However, as our discussion above illustrates, the types of structure that can be expressed in our language can potentially lead to improved inference algorithms. We believe that approximations are crucial for inference in large complex processes, and we hypothesize that the encapsulation structure of our representation can guide approximation methods such as these of [4, 2]. We plan to examine these issues in future work.

Acknowledgments Part of this work was done while Nir Friedman was at Stanford. This work was supported by ARO under the MURI program "Integrated Approach to Intelligent Systems", grant number DAAH04-96-1-0341, by ONR contract N66001-97-C-8554 under DARPA's HPKB program, by DARPA contract DACA76-93-C-0025 under subcontract to Information Extraction and Transport, Inc., and through the generosity of the Sloan Foundation and the Powell Foundation.

References

[1] C. Boutilier, N. Friedman, M. Goldszmidt, and D. Koller. Context-specific independence in Bayesian networks. In *Proc. UAI*, 1996.

[2] X. Boyen and D. Koller. Tractable inference for complex stochastic processes. Submitted to UAI '98, 1998.

[3] T. Dean and K. Kanazawa. A model for reasoning about persistence and causation. *Comp. Int.*, 5(3), 1989.

[4] Z. Ghahramani and M. I. Jordan. Factorial hidden Markov models. *Machine Learning*, 29, 1997.

[5] E.J. Horvitz, H.J. Suermondt, and G.F. Cooper. Bounded conditioning: Flexible inference for decisions under scarce resources. In *Proc. UAI*, 1989.

[6] T. Huang, D. Koller, J. Malik, G. Ogasawara, B. Rao, S.J. Russell, and J. Weber. Automatic symbolic traffic scene analysis using belief networks. In *AAAI*, 1994.

[7] K. Kanazawa, D. Koller, and S.J. Russell. Stochastic simulation algorithms for dynamic probabilistic networks. In *Proc. UAI*, 1995.

[8] U. Kjaerulff. A computational scheme for reasoning in dynamic probabilistic networks. In *Proc. UAI*, 1992.

[9] D. Koller and A. Pfeffer. Object-oriented Bayesian networks. In *Proc. UAI*, 1997.

[10] A. Manna and A. Pnueli. *Temporal Verification of Reactive Systems*. Springer Verlag, 1995.

[11] J. Pearl. *Probabilistic Reasoning in Intelligent Systems*. Morgan Kaufmann, 1988.

[12] R. Shachter, S. Andersen, and P. Szolovits. Global conditioning for probabilisitic inference in belief networks. In *Proc. UAI*, pp. 514–522, 1994.

[13] H. Simon. *The Sciences of the Artificial*. MIT Press, 1981.

Solving Very Large Weakly Coupled Markov Decision Processes

**Nicolas Meuleau, Milos Hauskrecht,
Kee-Eung Kim, Leonid Peshkin
Leslie Pack Kaelbling, Thomas Dean**[*]

Computer Science Department, Box 1910
Brown University, Providence, RI 02912-1210
{nm, milos, kek. ldp, lpk, tld}@cs.brown.edu

Craig Boutilier[†]

Department of Computer Science
University of British Columbia
Vancouver, BC V6T 1Z4, Canada
cebly@cs.ubc.ca

Abstract

We present a technique for computing approximately optimal solutions to stochastic resource allocation problems modeled as Markov decision processes (MDPs). We exploit two key properties to avoid explicitly enumerating the very large state and action spaces associated with these problems. First, the problems are composed of multiple tasks whose utilities are independent. Second, the actions taken with respect to (or resources allocated to) a task do not influence the status of any other task. We can therefore view each task as an MDP. However, these MDPs are weakly coupled by resource constraints: actions selected for one MDP restrict the actions available to others. We describe heuristic techniques for dealing with several classes of constraints that use the solutions for individual MDPs to construct an approximate global solution. We demonstrate this technique on problems involving thousands of tasks, approximating the solution to problems that are far beyond the reach of standard methods.

1 Introduction

Markov decision processes [12, 16] have proven tremendously useful as models of stochastic planning and decision problems. However, the computational difficulty of applying classic dynamic programming algorithms to realistic problems has spurred much research into techniques to deal with large state and action spaces. These include function approximation [4], reachability considerations [8] and aggregation techniques [11, 6, 7].

One general method for tackling large MDPs is *decomposition* [10, 15, 17, 5]. An MDP is either specified in terms of a set of "pseudo-independent" subprocesses [17] or automatically decomposed into such subprocesses [5]. These subMDPs are then solved and the solutions to these subMDPs are merged, or used to construct an approximate global solution. These techniques can be divided into two broad classes: those in which the state space of the MDP is divided into regions to form subMDPs, so that the MDP is the union (in a loose sense) of the subMDPs [10, 15]; and those in which the subMDPs are treated as concurrent processes, with their (loosely) cross-product forming the global MDP. In this paper, we focus on the latter form of decomposition: it offers great promise by allowing one to solve subMDPs that are exponentially smaller than the global MDP. If these solutions can be pieced together effectively, or used to guide the search for a global solution directly, dramatic improvements in the overall solution time can be obtained.

The problems we address here are sequential stochastic resource allocation problems. A number of different tasks, or objectives, must be addressed and actions consist of assigning various resources at different times to each of these tasks. We assume that each of these tasks is *additive utility independent* [13]: the utility of achieving any collection of tasks is the sum of rewards associated with each task. In addition, we assume that state space of the MDP is formed from a number of features that, apart from resources, are relevant only to a specific task. Furthermore, an assignment of resources to one task has no bearing on the features relevant to any other task. This means that each task can be viewed as an independent subprocess whose rewards and transitions are independent of the others, given a fixed action or policy (assignment of resources).[1]

Even this degree of independence, however, does not generally make it easy to find an optimal policy. Resources are usually constrained, so the allocation of resources to one task at a given point in time restricts the actions available for others at every point in time. Thus, a complex optimization problem remains. If there are no resource constraints, the processes are completely independent. They can be solved individually, and an optimal global solution determined by concurrent execution of the optimal local policies; solution time is determined by the size of the subMDPs. With resource constraints, local optimal solutions can be computed, but merging them is now non-trivial. The question of how best to exploit local solutions to determine a global policy is the subject of

---

[*]This work was supported in part by DARPA/Rome Labs Planning Initiative grant F30602-95-1-0020 and in part by NSF grants IRI-9453383 and IRI-9312395

[†]This work was supported by NSERC Research Grant OGP0121843 and IRIS-II Project IC-7, and was undertaken while the author was visiting Brown University. Thanks also to the generous support of the Killam Foundation.

[0]Copyright ©1998, American Association for Artificial Intelligence (www.aaai.org). All rights reserved.

[1]This model can be applied more generally to processes where the action can be broken into several components, each affecting a different process independently; resource allocation is a specific example of this.

this paper. We note that in resource allocation problems, the action space is extremely large (every possible assignment of resources to tasks), making other standard approximation methods such as neurodynamic programming [4] unsuitable.

Singh and Cohn [17] treat a version of this problem, in which there are constraints on the feasible joint action choices. As they observe, the value functions produced in solving the subMDPs can be used to obtain upper and lower bounds on the global value function. These bounds are used to improve the convergence of value iteration (via a form of *action elimination* [16]) for the global MDP. Unfortunately, their algorithm requires explicit state-space and action-space enumeration, rendering it impractical for all but moderate-sized MDPs.

We take a different approach in this paper: we are willing to sacrifice optimality (assured in Singh and Cohn's algorithm) for computational feasibility. To do this, we develop a several greedy techniques to deal with variants of this problem (in which the types of resource constraints differ). A hallmark of these heuristic algorithms is their division into two phases. An *off-line phase* computes the optimal solutions and value functions for the subMDPs associated with individual tasks. In an *on-line* phase, these value functions are used to compute a gradient for a heuristic search to assign resources to each task based on the current state. Once an action is taken, these resource assignments are reconsidered in light of the new state entered by the system.

This problem formulation was motivated by a military air campaign planning problem in which the tasks correspond to targets, and in which there are global constraints on the total number of weapons available as well as instantaneous constraints (induced by the number of available aircraft) on the number of weapons that may be deployed on any single time step. Actions have inherently stochastic outcomes and the problem is fully observable. This type of problem structure is fairly general, though, and can also be seen in domains such as stochastic job shop scheduling, allocation of repair crews to different jobs, disaster relief scheduling, and a wide variety of bandit-type problems [3].

We are able to solve problems of this type involving hundreds of tasks (with a state space exponential in this number) and thousands of resources (with an action space factorial in this number). Such problems are far beyond the reach of classic dynamic programming techniques and typical approximation methods such as neurodynamic programming.

In Section 2 we discuss some relevant background on MDPs and define our specific problem class formally. In Section 3, we describe *Markov task decomposition* (MTD) as a means of breaking down large, loosely coupled decision processes and describe, in very general terms, how solutions for the subMDPs might be used to construct a global solution in the presence of various types of action constraints. In Section 4, we describe the air campaign planning problem in some detail, and show how particular characteristics of this problem make it especially well-suited to both MTD and our heuristic policy construction methods. Section 5 demonstrates the results of MTD applied to very large instances of this problem. We conclude in Section 6 with some remarks on the reasons for MTD's success and future work.

2 Markov Task Sets

A (finite) *Markov decision process* is a tuple $\langle S, A, T, R \rangle$ where: S is a finite set of states; A is a finite set of actions; T is a transition distribution $T : S \times A \times S \to [0, 1]$, such that $T(s, a, \cdot)$ is a probability distribution over S for any $s \in S$ and $a \in A$; and $R : S \times A \times S \to \mathbb{R}$ is a bounded reward function. Intuitively, $T(s, a, w)$ denotes the probability of moving to state w when action a is performed at state s, while $R(s, a, w)$ denotes the immediate utility associated with the transition $s \rightsquigarrow w$ under action a. More generally, both the probabilities and rewards maybe *non-stationary*, depending also on the time at which the action is performed or the transition is made.

Given an MDP, the objective is to construct a *policy* that maximizes expected accumulated reward over some horizon of interest. We focus on *finite horizon* decision problems. Let H be our horizon: the aim is construct a non-stationary policy $\pi = \langle \pi^0, \cdots, \pi^{H-1} \rangle$, where $\pi^t : S \to A$, whose value

$$V_\pi^H(s) = E(\sum_{t=0}^{H-1} R(s^t, \pi^t(s^t), s^{t+1}))$$

is maximum. Standard dynamic-programming methods [2, 16] can be used to compute a sequence of optimal k-stage-to-go value functions up to the horizon of interest, from which an optimal policy can be derived.

We consider a special form of MDP suitable for modeling the stochastic resource allocation problems described in the introduction. A *Markov task set* (MTS) of n tasks is defined by a tuple $\langle \mathcal{S}, \mathcal{A}, \mathcal{R}, \mathcal{T}, c, M_g, M_r \rangle$, where

- $\mathcal{S}$ is a vector of state spaces, $S_1, \ldots, S_n$, where each S_i is the set of primitive states of Markov task i;
- $\mathcal{A}$ is a vector of action spaces, $A_1, \ldots, A_n$, where each A_i is a set of integers from 0 to some limit, describing the allocation of an amount of resource to task i;[2]
- $\mathcal{R}$ is a vector of reward functions $R_1, \ldots, R_n$, where $R_i : S_i \times A_i \times S_i \times \text{Time} \to \mathbb{R}$, specifying the reward conditional on the starting state, resulting state and action at each time;[3]
- $\mathcal{T}$ is a vector of state transition distributions, $T_1, \ldots, T_n$, where $T_i : S_i \times A_i \times S_i \to [0, 1]$, specifying the probability of a task entering a state given the previous state of the task and the action;
- c is the cost for using a single unit of the resource;
- M_l is the instantaneous (local) resource constraint on the amount of resource that may be used on a single step;
- M_g is the global resource constraint on the amount of the resource that may be used in total.

We again assume a finite horizon H.[4] An MTS induces an MDP in the obvious way: the state space consists of the

---

[2]It may be possible to extend this work to apply to real-valued amounts of resources and to multiple resource types.

[3]If reward values are stationary the time index may be omitted.

[4]Our techniques may be extended to other optimality criteria, such as infinite-horizon discounted or average reward.

cross product of the individual state spaces and the available resources; the action space is the set of resource assignments, with an assignment being feasible at a state only if its sum exceeds neither M_l nor the total resources available at that state; rewards are determined by summing the original component rewards and action costs; and transition probabilities are given by multiplying the (independent) individual task probabilities (with the change in resources being determined by the action).

Instead of formulating this "flat" MDP explicitly, we retain the factored form as much as possible. The goal, then, is to find an optimal non-stationary policy $\pi^* = \langle \pi^0, \ldots, \pi^{H-1} \rangle$, where $\pi^t = \langle \pi_1^t, \ldots, \pi_n^t \rangle$ and each $\pi_i^t : S \to A_i$ is a *local policy* for task i, that maximizes

$$E\left[\sum_{t=0}^{H-1}\sum_{i=1}^{n} T(s_i^t, \pi_i^t(s^t), s_i^{t+1}) R_i(s_i^t, \pi_i^t(s^t), t) - c \cdot \pi_i^t(s^t)\right]$$

subject to the constraints

$$\forall t < H, \sum_{i=1}^{n} \pi_i^t(s^t) \leq M_l \text{ and } \sum_{t=0}^{H-1}\sum_{i=1}^{n} \pi_i^t(s^t) \leq M_g$$

For simplicity, we have described MTSs involving only a single resource type. In general, there may be multiple resources, each of which has a cost and may be subject to local and global constraints. In Section 4 we present a problem with two resources with interrelated constraints. Note that MTSs allow one to model both reusable resources, such as machines on a shop floor (with local but no global constraints,) and consumable resources, such as raw materials (that have global and possibly induced local constraints).

Finding an optimal policy is a very hard problem even for small MTSs, because the equivalent MDP is very large. It is, for all practical purposes, impossible to solve exactly unless the number of tasks, the individual state spaces and the available resources are very small. The major source of difficulty is that the decision to apply a resource to a given task influences the availability of that resource (either now or in the future) for other tasks. Thus, the tasks, while exhibiting tremendous independence, still have strongly interacting solutions. A "local policy" for each task must take into account the state of each of the other tasks, precluding any state-space reduction in general[5]. We now turn our attention to approximation strategies that limit the scope of these interactions.

3 Markov Task Decomposition

Our approximation strategy for MTSs is called *Markov task decomposition* (MTD).

The MTD method is divided into two phases. In the first, *off-line phase*, value functions are calculated for the individual tasks using dynamic programming. In the second, *on-line phase*, these value functions are used to calculate the next action as a function of the current state of all processes.

---

[5]If there are no resource constraint, the sub-processes can be solved individually and the local policies can be defined as mappings $\pi_i^t : S_i \to A_i$.

3.1 Global Constraints Only

We will first consider the case in which there is only a global resource constraint, but no limit on the total number of resources applied on a single step.

In the off-line phase, we compute the *component value functions* $V_i(s_i, t, m)$ where s_i is the current state of task i, $0 \leq t \leq H$ is the time step, and m is the number of resources remaining:

$$V_i(s_i, t, m) = \max_{a \leq m} \sum_{s_i' \in S_i} T_i(s_i, a, s_i')[R_i(s_i, a, s_i', t) + V_i(s_i', t+1, m-a)] - c \cdot a \quad (1)$$

where $V_i(s_i, H, m) = 0$. This is the expected cumulative reward of the optimal policy for task i starting in state s_i at time t using at most m resources. In other words, if we ignored all other tasks and had m resources to allocate to task i, we would expect this value. It is useful to note that, even at the last stage, it may be suboptimal to spend all (or even any) of the remaining resources.

It is relatively simple to compute V_i using dynamic programming as long as we have some way of tightly bounding the values of m and t that must be considered. In Section 4, we describe a domain for which tight bounds on these quantities are available.

With these V_i in hand, we proceed to the on-line phase. We are faced with a particular situation, described by the current state $s = \langle s_1, \ldots, s_n \rangle$, remaining global resources m_g, and time-step t. We must calculate $a = \langle a_1, \ldots, a_n \rangle$, the action to be taken (i.e., the resources to be spent) at the current time step (where a_i is applied to task i). Since we are ignoring instantaneous constraints, we require only that $\sum_i a_i \leq m_g$. However, allocating all resources at the current time step will generally not be optimal. Optimal allocation would be required to take into account future contingencies, their probabilities and the value of holding back resources for these future contingencies.

Rather than solve this complex optimization problem, we rely on the fact that the local value functions V_i give us some idea of the value of assigning $m_i \leq m_g$ resources to task i at time t. Furthermore, V_i implicitly determines a policy for task i, telling us how many of the resources $a_i \leq m_i$ should be used at the current step t. Thus, MTD works in the following loop, executed once per decision stage:

(a) Using the functions $V_i(s_i, t, \cdot)$, heuristically assign resources m_i to task i such that $\sum_{i \leq n} m_i \leq m_g$.

(b) Use V_i and m_i to determine a_i, the action to be taken currently w.r.t. task i; that is

$$a_i = \arg\max_{a \leq m_i} \sum_{s_i' \in S_i} T_i(s_i, a, s_i')[R_i(s_i, a, s_i', t) + V_i(s_i', t+1, m_i - a)] - c \cdot a$$

(c) Execute action $a = \langle a_1, \ldots, a_n \rangle$, observe resulting state $s = \langle s_1, \ldots, s_n \rangle$, and compute remaining resources $m_g' = m_g - \sum_{i \leq n} a_i$.

The one component of MTD that has been left open is the heuristic allocation of resources to tasks. Doing this well will generally require specific domain knowledge. We describe a greedy approach in Section 4 below that works extremely well in the air campaign planning domain, though the fundamental characteristics of this problem hold true of a wide class of problem domains.

This approach is plausible, but even if the m_i are chosen optimally with respect to the criteria described above, the policy produced will generally be suboptimal for the following reasons.[6] We estimate the utility of an allocation m_i to task i using V_i, which is exactly the utility of solving task i with m_i resources; clearly,

$$\hat{V}(s,t,m) = \sum_{i=1}^{n} V_i(s_i, t, m_i)$$

is a lower bound on V^*; it is the value we would achieve if we made the allocations at step t and never re-evaluated them. In particular, given m_i resources for task i, MTD allocates a_i resources to the task at the current stage based only on V_i. The optimal Bellman equations indicate that an optimal allocation a_i must not only take into account the future course of task i, but also reason about future contingencies regarding other tasks, and assess the value of reallocating some of these resources to other tasks in the future.

3.2 Adding Instantaneous Constraints

It is quite difficult to incorporate local constraints in a satisfying way. An obvious strategy is to simply enforce the constraint that $\sum_{i=1}^{n} a_i \leq M_l$ to the on-line phase of MTD. This will result in the generation of admissible policies, but they may be of poor quality—$\hat{V}$ is likely to be a serious overestimate of the value function. This is because the allocations m_i determined by the V_i in step (a) above may be based on the assumption that more than M_l resources can be used in parallel.

Despite the potential drawbacks, we pursue a strategy of this type in the application described in Section 4. This type of strategy has the appeal of computational simplicity and leads to reasonably good results in our domain. However, more complex strategies for dealing with instantaneous constraints can easily be accommodated within the MTD framework. Such strategies will be the subject of future study.

4 Example: Air Campaign Planning

In the simplified air campaign planning problem, tasks correspond to targets and there are two resource types: weapons and planes. The status of a target is either damaged or undamaged: $S_i = \{d, u\}$. Each target has a window of availability $[t_i^s, t_i^e]$, whose length is denoted $w_i = t_i^e - t_i^s + 1$, and a reward r_i; if it is damaged during the window, then the reward r_i is received:

$$R_i(s_i, a_i, s_i', t) = \begin{cases} r_i & \text{if } t_i^s \leq t \leq t_i^e \text{ and } s_i = u \text{ and } s_i' = d \\ 0 & \text{otherwise} \end{cases}$$

With probability p_i, a single weapon will damage target i; a "noisy-or" model is assumed for multiple weapons, in which a single "hit" is sufficient to damage the target and individual weapons' hit probabilities are independent. That is,

$$T_i(s_i, a_i, s_i') = \begin{cases} 0 & \text{if } s_i = d \text{ and } s_i' = u \\ 1 & \text{if } s_i = d \text{ and } s_i' = d \\ q_i^{a_i} & \text{if } s_i = u \text{ and } s_i' = u \\ 1 - q_i^{a_i} & \text{if } s_i = u \text{ and } s_i' = d \end{cases}$$

where $q_i = 1 - p_i$ is the probability of a weapon missing the target. There is a cost, c, per weapon used.[7] Each plane has a capacity K_p (which we take to be fixed for simplicity) and can carry only up to K_p weapons. A plane loaded with a weapons and assigned to a target will deliver all a weapons. We will consider a variety of different constraints. In Section 4.3 we treat the case in which the only constraint is a global constraint on the total number of weapons, M_g. In Section 4.4 we treat the case in which the only constraint is a local constraint on the number of planes, M_l, that can be used at a single stage. Since each plane can only carry a limited number of weapons, any constraint on planes induces a constraint on weapons. This is a more sophisticated type of local constraint than previously. Now, each action must satisfy:

$$\sum_{i=1}^{n} \lceil a_i / K_p \rceil \leq M_l$$

Finally, we combine global weapon constraints with local plane constraints in Section 4.5.

4.1 Calculating Component Value Functions

The following discussion is somewhat brief and informal; a formal discussion with detailed derivations will be provided in a forthcoming technical report.

Within this problem, the component value functions can be considerably simplified. First, since every state in which the target has been damaged has value 0, we need only compute value functions for the state in which the target is undamaged. Second, since there is only a restricted window of opportunity for each target i, we need only compute the value function for a horizon equal to the number of time steps w_i in the target's window of opportunity. Since window lengths are typically much shorter than the horizon for the entire problem, this considerably simplifies the dynamic programming problem: we need only compute $V_i(u, m, t)$ for $t_i^s \leq t \leq t_i^e$, and then we apply:

$$V_i(u, m, t) = \begin{cases} V_i(u, m, t_i^s) & \text{if } t < t_i^s \\ 0 & \text{if } t > t_i^e \end{cases}$$

Another factor that strongly influences the "shape" of the local value functions (and ultimately, our heuristic algorithm) is the noisy-or transition model. Because of this, the probability of damaging the target of any policy that uses m weapons in no more than g steps, depends only on m (not on when the weapons are used) and is equal to $1 - q_i^m$. Policies may differ in expected utility, however, depending on how they choose to allocate weapons over time, which affects the expected number of weapons used. If $w_i \geq m$ then it is never optimal to send more than one weapon at a time. Otherwise,

---

[6] Note that the policy produced by MTD is constructed incrementally; indeed, it isn't a policy *per se* since it only plans for states that are actually reached.

[7] We ignore the cost per plane in the present paper.

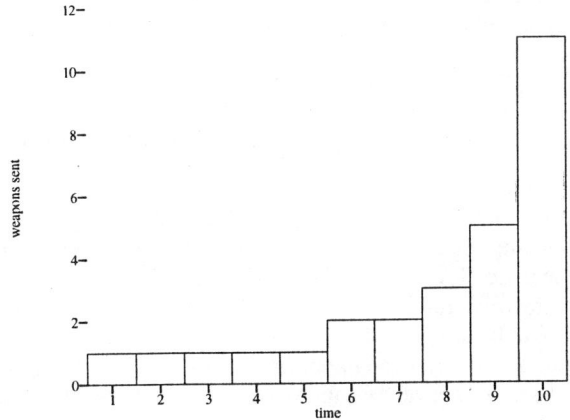

Figure 1: An instance of optimal policy for single-target problem: number of weapon sent if the target is still undamaged at time t, as a function of t ($p_i = 0.25$, $r_i = 90$, $w_i = 10$ and $c = 1$).

the optimal policy sends an increasing number of weapons at each step, in the case that the weapons on the previous step failed to damage the target.

Figure 1 shows an example of such a single target policy with a given window, reward and hit probability (it is optimal for any allocation of weapons greater than the cumulative total shown).

Furthermore, we can show that $V_i(u, m, t)$ increases monotonically with m until a point $m^*_{i,t}$, at which point it remains constant: $m^*_{i,t}$ is the point at which marginal utility of resource allocation becomes zero, and where the marginal utility of resource use is negative (the cost of a weapon exceeds the value of the small increase in success probability, so even if it is allocated, it will not be used). This implies that we need only compute $V_i(u, m, t)$ for $m \leq m^*_{i,t}$, again significantly reducing the effort needed to compute V_i.

For each target i, each $t \in [t^s_i, t^e_i]$, and each $m \leq m^*_{i,t}$, we will compute $V_i(u, m, t)$ and store these results in a table to be used in the on-line phase of MTD. We can do this using the dynamic programming equation

$$V_i(u, m, t) = \max_{0 \leq a \leq m} \left[(1 - q^a_i) r_i - c_w a + q^a_i V_i(u, m-a, t+1) \right],$$

where $V_i(u, m, t^e_i + 1) = V_i(u, 0, t) = 0$. The value of spending b' weapons can be described using three terms: the first is the expected reward due to damaging the target on the current time step, the second is the cost of using a weapons, and the third is the future value of trying to damage the target with $m - a$ weapons left.

4.2 No Resource Constraints

If there are no resource constraints, the on-line phase of MTD is not required. The tasks are completely decoupled and the optimal policy π^t is described by the component value functions (recall that $\pi^t_i(d) = 0$; no action is required for a damaged target):

$$\pi^t_i(u) = \arg\max_{a_i} (1 - q^{a_i}_i) r_i - c_w a_i + q^{a_i}_i V_i(u, m^*_{i,t+1}, t+1) \quad (2)$$

(for any t within i's window). This requires a simple search over values of a_i, bounded by $a_i \leq m^*_{i,t}$.

4.3 Weapon (Global) Constraints Only

With constraints on the number of weapons available, the on-line phase is crucial. We have the component value functions V_i at our disposal, and are given the current state s of all targets, the number of weapons remaining m_g, and the time t. Our goal is to choose m_i—the weapons to assign to each target i with state $s_i = u$ and such that $t \leq t^f_i$—according to step (a) of the on-line algorithm in Section 3.1; that is, to maximize $\sum V_i(u, m_i, t)$.

To do this, we adopt a greedy strategy. Define

$$\Delta V_i(u, m, t) = V_i(u, m+1, t) - V_i(u, m, t) \quad (3)$$

to be the marginal utility of assigning an additional weapon to target i, given that m weapons have already been assigned to it. We assign weapons one by one to the target that has the highest value $\Delta V_i(u, m, t)$ given its current assignment of weapons (i.e., gradient ascent on $\sum V_i$). This proceeds until all m_g weapons have been assigned or $\Delta V_i(u, m, t) \leq 0$ for all i. The concavity of the local value functions assures:

Proposition 1 *The process described above chooses b_i to maximize $\sum V_i(u, m_i, t)$.*

Despite this, as we argued above, this does not necessarily result in an optimal policy. However, in this domain, the empirical results are impressive, as we discuss in Section 5.

4.4 Plane (Instantaneous) Constraints Only

Even with an unlimited number of weapons (or as many as required to reach zero marginal utility), we generally have to deal with constraints on the number of simultaneously deliverable weapons (i.e., number of planes available). The strategy we adopt is similar to the one above, except we greedily allocate planes instead of weapons. The one subtlety lies in the fact that it may not be optimal to load a plane to capacity (recall, that all weapons on a plane are delivered).

We proceed at time t by allocating planes one by one to active targets. We assume (optimistically) that all targets in the future can be allocated their optimal number of weapons (this is optimistic because of future plane constraints, not because of weapon availability); in other words, for computational reasons, we deal with plane constraints only at the current stage. Assume we have assigned n_i planes and $a_i \leq n_i \cdot K_p$ weapons to target i so far. For each active target i, we compute a'_i, the number of bombs that the new plane would carry:

$$a'_i = \min\{K_p, \pi^t_i(u) - K_p \cdot n_i\}$$

where $\pi^t_i(u)$ is given by (2). This can be used to compute the marginal expected utility of assigning a new plane to any active target:

$$\Delta V_i = q^{a_i}_i \left(1 - q^{a'_i}_i\right) r_i - c_w a'_i + \\ q^{a_i}_i \left(q^{a'_i}_i - 1\right) V_i(u, m^*_{i,t+1}, t+1).$$

As in the case of global constraints only, we assign planes to active targets greedily until $\sum n_i = M_l$ or $\Delta V_i \leq 0$ for all i. Note that marginal utility is associated with increasing the number of planes, not weapons as in the previous section.

4.5 Weapon and Plane Constraints

Our approach in this case will necessarily be more complicated. We begin by assigning weapons to targets using the greedy strategy outlined in Section 4.3; no plane constraints are accounted for. The result is an assignment of resources m_i to each target. An action $a = \langle a_1, \cdots, a_n \rangle$ is determined for the current stage, and we assign n_i planes to each target at the current stage that will suffice to carry the a_i weapons. This action may be infeasible however if $\sum n_i > M_l$ (more planes are required to carry out action a than are available). We thus begin a greedy deallocation-reallocation process.

Deallocation requires that we remove certain weapons from the current assignment a. We do this by greedily removing the assigned planes one by one until $\sum n_i = M_l$ (note that i need only range over active targets). Intuitively, we proceed as follows: first we compute the number of weapons a'_i that would be removed from target i if we deallocated a single plane; we compute the change in utility that would accompany this deallocation if we were to "optimally" reallocate these weapons to a new target (or possibly the same target, but forced to be used at a later stage); and then we deallocate the plane and perform the reallocation that results in the smallest decrease in utility. However, we will see that this requires some care.

At any point in time, we have a list of (active) targets which have had planes deallocated. For any such target i, we may consider assigning new weapons to it that have been deallocated from some target j. But since we do not want to consider providing a new plane for i at the *current* stage (one has just been taken away), we compute ΔV_i, the marginal utility of adding a weapon to i, as follows:

$$\Delta V_i = q_i^{a_i}\left[V_i(m_i - a_i + 1, t+1) - V_i(m_i - a_i, t+1)\right] \quad (4)$$

That is, we consider that this weapon must be used at some time *after* the current stage. For any target that has not had a plane deallocated, ΔV_i is computed as in (3). We let $\Delta_n V_i$ denote the change in utility if we assign n new weapons (instead of 1).

Let $a'_i = a_i - (m_i - 1)K_p$ be the number of weapons that will be removed from (active) target i if one of its n_i planes is deallocated to satisfy the instantaneous constraint. Then compute δV_i, the value of reallocating the a'_i weapons optimally: we do this by adding i to the deallocated list (temporarily) and simulating the greedy algorithm described in Section 4.3.[8] The only difference is that we use (4) as the measure of marginal utility for any target on the deallocated list. Notice that weapons taken from i can be reallocated to i, but the value of this reallocation is derived from using these at *later* stages. If d_j weapons are assigned to target j, where $\sum d_j = a'_i$, then $\delta V_i = \sum \Delta_{d_j} V_j$.

The quantities δV_i will be used to determine which target will have a plane deallocated. For any active target i, define

$$\nabla V_i = q_i^{a_i - a'_i}\left(q_i^{a'_i} - 1\right)r_i + c_w a'_i + \\ q_i^{a_i - a'_i}\left(1 - q_i^{a'_i}\right)V_i(m_i - a_i, t+1) + \delta V_i$$

This is the (negative) change in expected value by deallocating a'_i weapons (i.e., one plane) from target i.[9] We deallocate by choosing the target i with the largest ∇V_i. Once selected, a plane is deallocated from i, and the a'_i weapons are reallocated greedily. In fact, the d_j values used in the computation of δV_i can be stored and used for this purpose (the simulated reallocation can now be imposed).

We note that if any weapons are reallocated to an active target j, it may cause j to require an additional plane (in fact, this can occur for several active targets). To deal with this we simply allocate new planes. While the deallocation of one plane may cause the allocation of more planes, this process will eventually terminate, since no deallocated target can ever be reallocated weapons for *current* use.[10]

5 Empirical Results

To validate our heuristics, we tried them on several randomly-generated instances of the air campaign problem, and compared them to:

- the optimal policy calculated by flat DP
- the greedy policy that applies the action with highest expected immediate reward
- a "semi-greedy" policy that applies the action $\pi_i^t(u)$ given by (2) to each active target i, without regard to potential interactions

The calculation of the optimal policy by DP is infeasible for problems of moderate size. For instance, the solution time for a problem with 5 targets and 50 weapons is on the order of 10 minutes; for 6 targets and 60 weapons, up to 6 hours; and beyond that was not practically computable. In contrast, the execution time for MTD is shown in Figure 2. Without instantaneous constraints, MTD can solve a problem with thousands of targets and tens of thousands of weapons in under 15 minutes. A problem of 1000 targets, 10,000 weapons and 100 planes (imposing such constraints) can be solved in about 35 minutes.

We compare the quality of solutions produced by MTD with the optimal solutions produced by DP in Figure 3, though we are restricted to very small problems (5 tasks, with no instantaneous constraints; and 7 task, with instantaneous constraints) because of the computational demands of DP. We also compared the greedy and semi-greedy strategies.[11] The performance of MTD is encouraging, closely tracking optimal, though the performance of the greedy and semi-greedy

---

[8] By simulating, we mean that we compute the reallocation that would take place if we actually reallocated the weapons from i; this won't necessarily take place if we decide to deallocate a plane from some other target.

[9] Note that ∇V_i is not equal to $V_i(u, m_i - a'_i, t) - V_i(u, m_i, t)$.

[10] We are currently exploring more sophisticated strategies that prevent this from happening.

[11] For all but DP, whose solution has a known value, the results show average reward obtained over 1000 simulations of the process, as a function of M_g (initial global resources).

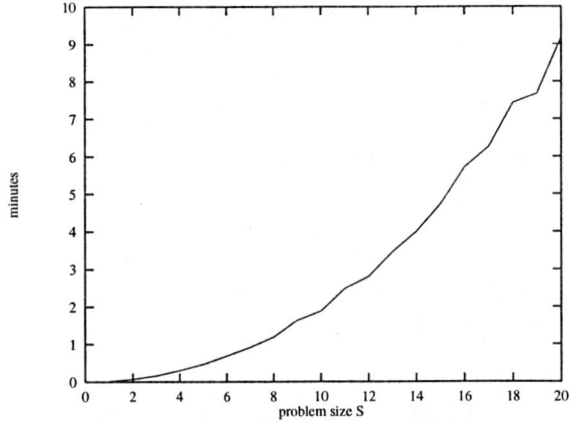 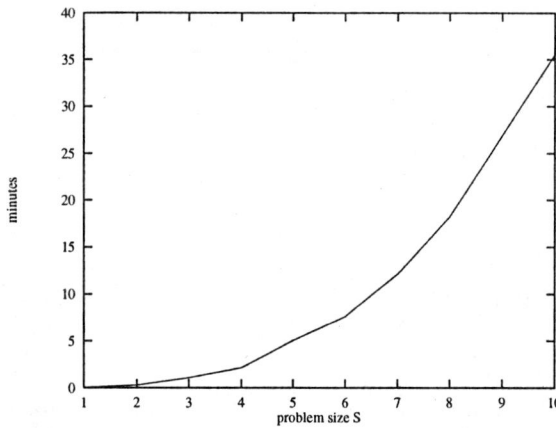

Figure 2: Complexity of MTD: time of execution as a function of the problem size S. A problem of size S has $100S$ targets, $1000S$ weapons and $10S$ planes. The graph on left shows the time to solve a problem with no local constraints. The graph on the right shows the time for a problem with local constraints (given by $10S$ planes).

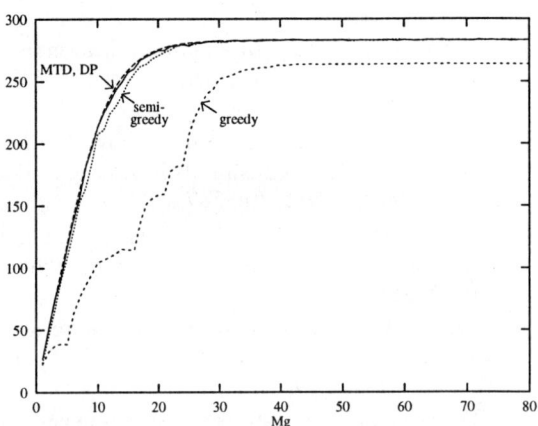 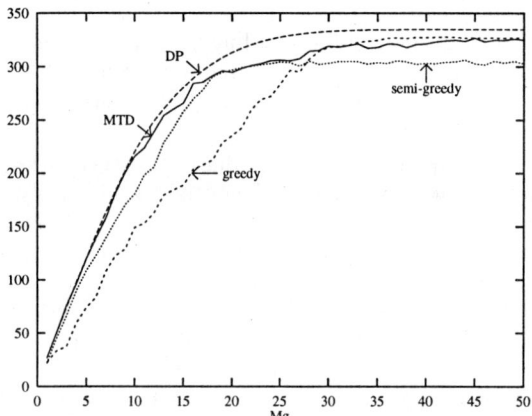

Figure 3: Comparison of the quality of policies generated by MTD, optimal DP, greedy and semi-greedy strategies on small test problems. The graph on left shows results for a 5-task problem with no local constraints. The graph on the right describes a 7-task problem with local constraints. Values are averaged over 1000 runs.

policies suggests these problems are not difficult enough to differentiate these from MTD.

On much larger problems, MTD compares much more favorably to both greedy methods, with Figure 4 showing their performance on 100 target (with instantaneous constraints) and 300 target (no constraints) problems. The policy produced by MTD performs substantially better than the greedy and semi-greedy policy. Such problems are well beyond the reach of classic DP.

6 Conclusions

We have presented the method of Markov task decomposition for solving large weakly coupled MDPs, in particular, stochastic resource allocation problems. We described several instantiations of this technique for dealing with different forms of resource or action constraints. The empirical results for the air campaign problem are extremely encouraging, demonstrating the ability for MTD techniques to solve problems with thousands of tasks.

Three key insights allowed us to approximately solve large MDPs in this fashion. The first is the ability to decompose the process into pseudo-independent subprocesses, and construct optimal policies and value functions for these subMDPs feasibly. Often special features of the domain (in this case, the noisy-or dynamics and limited windows) can be exploited to solve these subMDPs effectively. The second is that these value functions can offer guidance in the construction of policies that account for the interactions between processes. Again, special domain features (here, the convexity of the value functions) can offer guidance regarding the appropriate heuristic techniques. The third is the use of on-line policy construction to alleviate the need to reason about many fu-

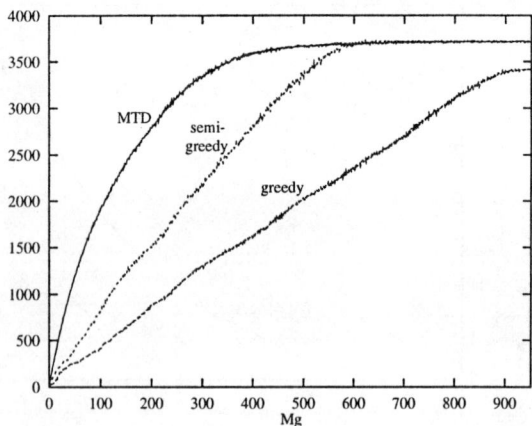
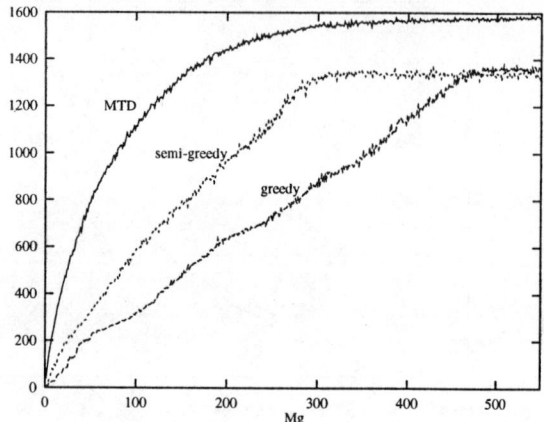

Figure 4: Comparison of the quality of policies generated by MTD, greedy and semi-greedy strategies on large test problems. The graph on left shows results for a 200-task problem with no local constraints. The graph on the right describes a 100-task problem with local constraints. Values are averaged over 100 runs.

ture contingencies. While on-line methods are popular [1], crucial to the success of the on-line component of MTD is the ability to quickly construct good actions heuristically using the component value functions.

MTD is a family of algorithms that exploit specific structure in the problem domain to make decisions effectively. It requires that the problem be specified in a specific form, taking advantage of utility independence and probabilistic independence in action effects. Much recent research has focussed on using representations for MDPs that make some of this structure explicit and automatically discovering appropriate problem abstractions and decompositions [9, 6, 14, 11, 5]. The extent to which effective Markov task decompositions can be automatically extracted from suitable problem representations remains an interesting open question.

References

[1] A. G. Barto, S. J. Bradtke, and S. P. Singh. Learning to act using real-time dynamic programming. *Artificial Intelligence*, 72:81–138, 1995.

[2] R. E. Bellman. *Dynamic Programming*. Princeton University Press, Princeton, 1957.

[3] D. A. Berry and B. Fristedt. *Bandit Problems: Sequential Allocation of Experiments*. Chapman and Hall, London, 1985.

[4] D. P. Bertsekas and J.. N. Tsitsiklis. *Neuro-dynamic Programming*. Athena, Belmont, MA, 1996.

[5] C. Boutilier, R. I. Brafman, and C. Geib. Prioritized goal decomposition of markov decision processes: Toward a synthesis of classical and decision theoretic planning. *Proc. IJCAI-97*, pp.1156–1163, Nagoya, 1997.

[6] C. Boutilier, R. Dearden, and M. Goldszmidt. Exploiting structure in policy construction. *Proc. IJCAI-95*, pp.1104–1111, Montreal, 1995.

[7] T. Dean and R. Givan. Model minimization in markov decision processes. *Proc. AAAI-97*, pp.106–111, Providence, 1997.

[8] T. Dean, L. P. Kaelbling, J. Kirman, and A. Nicholson. Planning under time constraints in stochastic domains. *Artificial Intelligence*, 76:35–74, 1995.

[9] T. Dean and K. Kanazawa. A model for reasoning about persistence and causation. *Computational Intelligence*, 5(3):142–150, 1989.

[10] T. Dean and S. Lin. Decomposition techniques for planning in stochastic domains. *Proc. IJCAI-95*, pp.1121–1127, Montreal, 1995.

[11] R. Dearden and C. Boutilier. Abstraction and approximate decision theoretic planning. *Artificial Intelligence*, 89:219–283, 1997.

[12] R. A. Howard. *Dynamic Programming and Markov Processes*. MIT Press, Cambridge, 1960.

[13] R. L. Keeney and H. Raiffa. *Decisions with Multiple Objectives: Preferences and Value Trade-offs*. Wiley, New York, 1978.

[14] A. E. Nicholson and L. P. Kaelbling. Toward approximate planning in very large stochastic domains. *AAAI Spring Symp. on Decision Theoretic Planning*, pp.190–196, Stanford, 1994.

[15] D. Precup and R. S. Sutton. Multi-time models for temporally abstract planning. In M. Mozer, M. Jordan and T. Petsche editor, *NIPS-11*. MIT Press, Cambridge, 1998.

[16] M. L. Puterman. *Markov Decision Processes: Discrete Stochastic Dynamic Programming*. Wiley, New York, 1994.

[17] S. P. Singh and D. Cohn. How to dynamically merge markov decision processes. In M. Mozer, M. Jordan and T. Petsche editor, *NIPS-11*. MIT Press, Cambridge, 1998.

Speech Recognition with Dynamic Bayesian Networks

Geoffrey Zweig and Stuart Russell
Computer Science Division, UC Berkeley
Berkeley, California 94720
{zweig,russell}@cs.berkeley.edu

Abstract

Dynamic Bayesian networks (DBNs) are a useful tool for representing complex stochastic processes. Recent developments in inference and learning in DBNs allow their use in real-world applications. In this paper, we apply DBNs to the problem of speech recognition. The factored state representation enabled by DBNs allows us to explicitly represent long-term articulatory and acoustic context in addition to the phonetic-state information maintained by hidden Markov models (HMMs). Furthermore, it enables us to model the short-term correlations among multiple observation streams within single time-frames. Given a DBN structure capable of representing these long- and short-term correlations, we applied the EM algorithm to learn models with up to 500,000 parameters. The use of structured DBN models decreased the error rate by 12 to 29% on a large-vocabulary isolated-word recognition task, compared to a discrete HMM; it also improved significantly on other published results for the same task. This is the first successful application of DBNs to a large-scale speech recognition problem. Investigation of the learned models indicates that the hidden state variables are strongly correlated with acoustic properties of the speech signal.

Introduction

Over the last twenty years, probabilistic models have emerged as the method of choice for large-scale speech recognition tasks in two dominant forms: hidden Markov models (Rabiner & Juang 1993), and neural networks with explicitly probabilistic interpretations (Bourlard & Morgan 1994; Robinson & Fallside 1991). Despite numerous successes in both isolated-word recognition and continuous speech recognition, both methodologies suffer from important deficiencies. HMMs use a single state variable to encode all state information; typically, just the identity of the current phonetic unit. Neural networks occupy the opposite end of the spectrum, and use hundreds or thousands of hidden units that often have little or no intuitive meaning.

Our work is motivated by the desire to explore probabilistic models that are expressed in terms of a rich yet well-defined set of variables, and dynamic Bayesian networks provide the ideal framework for this task: with a single set of formulae expressed in a single program, probabilistic models over arbitrary sets of variables can be expressed and computationally tested. By decomposing the state information into a set of variables, DBNs require fewer parameters than HMMs to represent the same amount of information. In the context of speech modeling, DBNs provide a convenient method for defining models that maintain an explicit representation of the lips, tongue, jaw, and other speech articulators as they change over time. Such models can be expected to model the speech generation process more accurately than conventional systems. One particularly important consequence of including an articulatory model is that it can handle *coarticulation* effects. One of the main reasons these occur is that the inertia of the speech articulators which is acquired in the generation of one sound modifies the pronunciation of following sounds. In addition, DBNs are able to model the correlations among multiple acoustic features at a single point in time in a way that has not previously been exploited in discrete-observation HMMs.

We have implemented a general system for doing speech recognition in the Bayesian network framework, including methods for representing speech models, efficient inference methods for computing probabilities within these models, and efficient learning algorithms for training the DBN model parameters from observations. The system has been tested on a large-vocabulary isolated-word recognition task. We found that a large improvement results from modeling correlations among acoustic features within a single time frame. A further increase results from modeling the temporal correlations among acoustic features across time frames. Analysis of the learned parameters shows that the two kinds of models capture different aspects of the speech process.

Problem Background

The task of a statistical speech recognition system is to learn a parametric model from a large body of

---

Copyright 1998, American Association for Artificial Intelligence (www.aaai.org). All rights reserved.

training data, and then to use the model to recognize the words in previously unheard utterances. Since the number of words in a natural language is large, it is impossible to learn a specific model for every word. Instead, words are expressed in terms of a small number of stereotypical atomic sounds or phonemes—English, for example, is often modeled in terms of 40 to 60 phonemes. Models for each phoneme are learned, and whole-word models are created by concatenating the models of the word's constituent phonemes. So, for example, the word "cat" might have the phonetic transcription /k ae t/.

In order to model coarticulatory effects, expanded phonetic alphabets are often used, in which there is a unique symbol for each phoneme in the context of surrounding phonemes. In left-context biphone alphabets, there is a phonetic unit for each phoneme in the left-context of every possible preceding phoneme. In right-context biphone alphabets, there is a unit for each phoneme in the right-context of every possible following phoneme. Triphone modeling is a particularly common scheme in which there is a unit for each phoneme in the context of all possible preceding *and* following phonemes. The phonetic units found in these (and other) alphabets are often referred to as *phones*. Theoretically, the use of biphones squares the number of atomic units, and the use of triphones cubes the number; in practice, only the commonly occurring combinations are modeled.

It is often beneficial to break each phonetic unit into two or more substates. In a two-state-per-phone system, for example, each phone is broken into an initial sound and a final sound, thus doubling the total number of phonetic units.

Whatever the precise form of the phonetic alphabet, the training data consists of a collection of utterances, each of which has an associated phonetic transcription. Each utterance is broken into a sequence of overlapping time frames, and the sound is processed to generate the acoustic features $o_1, o_2, \ldots, o_n$. One or more acoustic features may be extracted from each frame, and we use the notation o_i to refer to the features extracted from the ith frame regardless of number. A phonetic transcription or word model, M, is also associated with each utterance.

Statistical Speech Recognition

The main goal of a statistical speech recognition system is to estimate the probability of a word model M given a sequence of acoustic observations $\mathbf{o}$. (We focus on isolated word recognition, and the results generalize to connected word recognition.) This can be rewritten with Bayes' rule as: $P(M|\mathbf{o}) = \frac{P(\mathbf{o}|M)P(M)}{P(\mathbf{o})}$. This is desirable because it decomposes the problem into two subproblems: $P(M)$ can be estimated from a language model that specifies the probability of the occurrence of different words, and $P(\mathbf{o}|M)$ can be estimated with a model that describes how sounds are generated. Since $P(\mathbf{o})$ is a constant with respect to word models, different models M_i can be compared by computing just $P(\mathbf{o}|M_i)P(M_i)$. Computation of $P(M)$ is straightforward in the case of isolated words, and we focus on the estimation of $P(\mathbf{o}|M)$, i.e., the probability of the observation sequence given the word.

This probability distribution is not usually estimated directly. Instead, statistical models typically use a collection of hidden state variables $\mathbf{s}$, which are intended to represent the state of the speech generation process over time. Thus we have

$$P(\mathbf{o}|M) = \sum_{\mathbf{s}} P(\mathbf{o}, \mathbf{s}|M)$$

In addition, the observation generated at any point is usually assumed to depend only on the state of the process, so we have

$$P(\mathbf{o}|M) = \sum_{\mathbf{s}} P(\mathbf{s}|M) P(\mathbf{o}|\mathbf{s})$$

We refer to the specification of $P(\mathbf{s}|M)$ as the pronunciation model, and to the specification of $P(\mathbf{o}|\mathbf{s})$ as the acoustic model.

HMMs

A hidden Markov Model is a simple representation of a stochastic process of the kind described above. The hidden state of the process is represented by a single state variable s_i at each point in time, and the observation is represented by an observation variable o_i (Figure 1). Furthermore, a Markovian assumption is made, so that we can decompose the probability over the state sequence as follows (leaving implicit the dependence on M):

$$P(\mathbf{o}, \mathbf{s}) = P(s_1) P(o_1|s_1) \prod_{i=2}^{n} P(s_i|s_{i-1}) P(o_i|s_i)$$

In the case of speech, the state variable is usually identified with the *phonetic state*, i.e., the current phone being uttered. Thus, the pronunciation model is contained in the probability distribution $P(s_i|s_{i-1}, M)$ which designates the transition probabilities among phones, and consequently the distribution over phone sequences for a particular word. The acoustic model is the probability distribution $P(\mathbf{o}|\mathbf{s})$, and is independent of the particular word. Both of these models are assumed independent of time.

The conditional probability parameters in HMMs are usually estimated by maximizing the likelihood of the observations using the EM algorithm. Once trained, the HMM is used to recognize words by computing $P(\mathbf{o}|M_i)$ for each word model M_i. For details, the reader is referred to (Rabiner & Juang 1993).

In this paper, we will be concerned with *discrete* observation variables, which can be created from the actual signal by the process of *vector quantization* (Rabiner & Juang 1993). In order to allow for a wide range of sounds, it is common to generate several discrete observation variables o_i^j at each point in time, each of which has a fairly small range (say 256 values). To

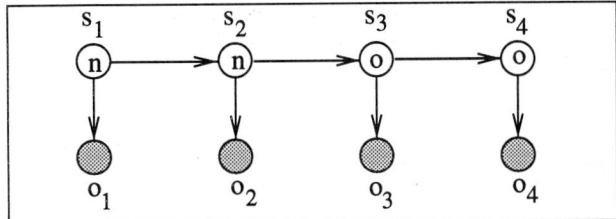

Figure 1: A DBN representation of an HMM. There is a distinct state and observation variable at each point in time. A node in the graph represents a variable, and the arcs leading into a node specify the variables on which it is conditionally dependent. A valid assignment of values to the state variables for the word "no" is shown. Observation variables are shaded. This simple picture ignores the issues of parameter tying and phonetic transcriptions.

keep the number of parameters manageable with these multiple observation streams, a further conditional independence assumption is typically made (Lee 1989):

$$P(o_i|s_i) = \prod_j P(o_i^j|s_i)$$

Bayesian Networks

A Bayesian network is a general way of representing joint probability distributions with the chain rule and conditional independence assumptions. The advantage of the Bayesian network framework over HMMs is that it allows for an arbitrary set of hidden variables **s**, with arbitrary conditional independence assumptions. If the conditional independence assumptions result in a sparse network, this may result in an exponential decrease in the number of parameters required to represent a probability distribution. Often there is a concomitant decrease in the computational load (Smyth, Heckerman, & Jordan 1997; Ghahramani & Jordan 1997; Russell *et al.* 1995).

More precisely, a Bayesian network represents a probability distribution over a set of random variables $V = V_1, .. V_n$. The variables are connected by a directed acyclic graph whose arcs specify conditional independence among the variables, such that the joint distribution is given by

$$P(v_1, \ldots, v_n) = \prod_i P(v_i | Parents(V_i))$$

where $Parents(V_i)$ are the parents of V_i in the graph. The required conditional probabilities may be stored either in tabular form or with a functional representation. Figure 1 shows an HMM represented as a Bayesian network. Although tabular representations of conditional probabilities are particularly easy to work with, it is straightforward to model observation probabilities with mixtures of Gaussians, as is often done in HMM systems.

When the variables represent a temporal sequence and are thus ordered in time, the resulting Bayesian network is referred to as a dynamic Bayesian network (DBN) (Dean & Kanazawa 1989). These networks maintain values for a set of variables X_i at each point in time. X_{ij} represents the value of the ith variable at time j. These variables are partitioned into equivalence sets that share time-invariant conditional probabilities.

Bayesian Network Algorithms. As with HMMs, there are standard algorithms for computing with Bayesian networks. In our implementation, the probability of a set of observations is computed using an algorithm derived from (Peot & Shachter 1991). Conditional probabilities can be learned using gradient methods (Russell *et al.* 1995) or EM (Lauritzen 1995). We have adapted these algorithms for dynamic Bayesian networks, using special techniques to handle the deterministic variables that are a key feature of our speech models (see below). A full treatment of these algorithms can be found in (Zweig 1998).

DBNs and Speech Recognition

Like HMMs, our DBN speech models also decompose into a pronunciation model and an acoustic model. However, our acoustic model includes additional state variables that we will call "articulatory context" variables; the intent is that these may capture the state of the articulatory apparatus of the speaker, although this will not be the case in all of our models. These variables can depend on both the current phonetic state and the previous articulatory context. Mathematically, this can be expressed by partitioning the set of hidden variables into phonetic and articulatory subsets: $\mathcal{S} = \mathcal{Q} \cup \mathcal{A}$. Then, $P(\mathbf{o}, \mathbf{s}|M) = P(\mathbf{o}, \mathbf{q}, \mathbf{a}|M) = P(\mathbf{q}|M)P(\mathbf{o}, \mathbf{a}|\mathbf{q})$. The Bayesian network structure can be thought of as consisting of two layers: one that models $P(\mathbf{q}|M)$, and one that models $P(\mathbf{o}, \mathbf{a}|\mathbf{q})$. Figure 2 illustrates a DBN structured for speech recognition in this manner. In the following two sections, we discuss the pronunciation model and acoustic model in turn.

Pronunciation Model. In (Zweig & Russell 1997; Zweig 1998), it is shown that the DBN model structure we use can represent any distribution over phone sequences that can be represented by an HMM. For the purposes of simplifying the presentation in this paper, we will make two additional assumptions. The first is that each word model consists of a linear sequence of phonetic units; so, for example, "cat" is assumed always to be pronounced /k ae t/ without any variation in the phonetic units present or their order. The second assumption concerns the average durations of phones, and is that the probability that there is a transition between two consecutive phones q_1 and q_2 is given by a phone-dependent transition probability, t_{q_1}.

The index node in Figure 2 keeps track of the position in the phonetic transcription; all words go through the same sequence of values $1, 2, \ldots, k$ where k is the

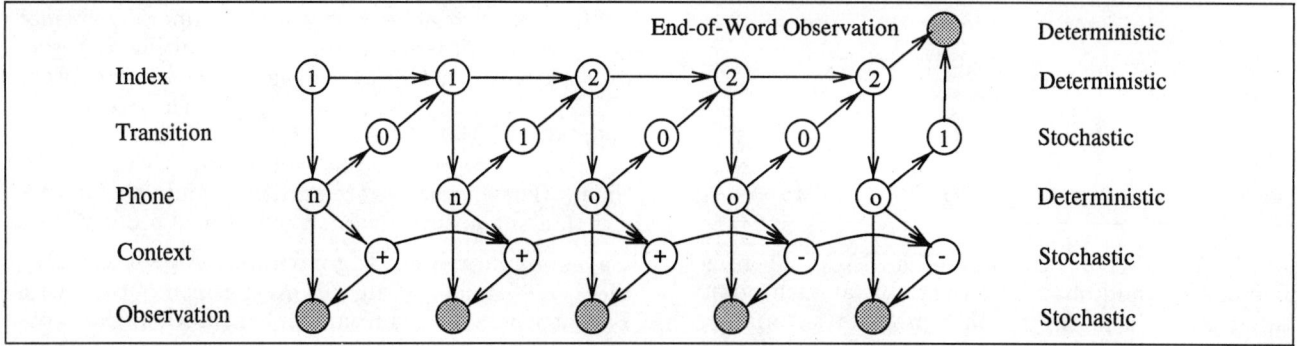

Figure 2: A DBN for speech recognition. The index, transition, phone, and end-of-word variables encode a probability distribution over phonetic sequences. The context and observation variables encode a distribution over observations, conditioned on phonetic sequence. A valid set of variable assignments is indicated for the word "no." In this picture, the context variable represents nasalization. The vowel /o/ is not usually nasalized, but in this case coarticulation causes nasalization of its first occurrence.

number of phonetic units in the transcription. An assignment of values to the index variables specifies a time-alignment of the phonetic transcription to the observations. For a specific pronunciation model, there is a deterministic mapping from the index of the phonetic unit to the actual phonetic value, which is represented by the phone variable. This mapping is specified on a word-by-word basis. There is a binary transition variable that is conditioned on the phonetic unit. When the transition value is 1, the index value increases by 1, which can be encoded with the appropriate conditional probabilities.

The distinction between phonetic index and phonetic value is required for parameter tying. For example, consider the word "digit" with the phonetic transcription /d ih jh ih t/. The first /ih/ must be followed by /jh/, and the second /ih/ must be followed by /t/; thus there must be a distinction between the two phone occurrences. On the other hand, the probability distribution over acoustic emissions should be the same for the two occurrences; thus there should not be a distinction. It is impossible to satisfy these constraints with a single set of conditional probabilities that refers only to phonetic values or index values.

The conditional probabilities associated with the index variables are constrained so that the index value begins at 1 and then must either stay the same or increase by 1 at each time step. A dummy end-of-word observation is used to ensure that all sequences with non-zero probability end with a transition out of the last phonetic unit. This binary variable is "observed" to have value 1, and the conditional probabilities of this variable are adjusted so that $P(EOW = 1|index = last, transition = 1) = 1$, and the probability that $EOW = 1$ is 0 in all other cases. Conditioning on the transition variable ensures an unbiased distribution over durations for the last phonetic unit.

In Figure 2, deterministic variables are labeled. Taking advantage of the deterministic relationships is crucial for efficient inference.

Acoustic Model. The reason for using a DBN is that it allows the hidden state to be factored in an arbitrary way. This enables several approaches to acoustic modeling that are awkward with conventional HMMs. The simplest approach is to augment the phonetic state variable with one or more variables that represent articulatory-acoustic context. This is the structure shown in Figure 2.

The context variable serves two purposes, one dealing with long-term correlations among observations across time-frames, and the other with short-term correlations within a time-frame. The first purpose is to model variations in phonetic pronunciation due to coarticulatory effects. For example, if the context variable represents nasalization, it can capture the coarticulatory nasalization of vowels. Depending on the level of detail desired, multiple context variables can be used to represent different articulatory features. Model semantics can be enforced with statistical priors, or by training with data in which the articulator positions are known.

The second purpose is to model correlations among multiple vector-quantized observations within a single time-frame. While directly modeling the correlations requires a prohibitive number of parameters, an auxiliary variable can parsimoniously capture the most important effects.

Network Structures Tested. In our experiments, we tested networks that varied only in the acoustic model. All the DBN variants had a single binary context variable, and differed in the conditional independence assumptions made about this variable. We used the following model structures (see Figure 3):

1. An "articulator" network in which the context variable depends on both the phonetic state and its own past value. This can directly represent phone-dependent articulatory target positions and inertial constraints.

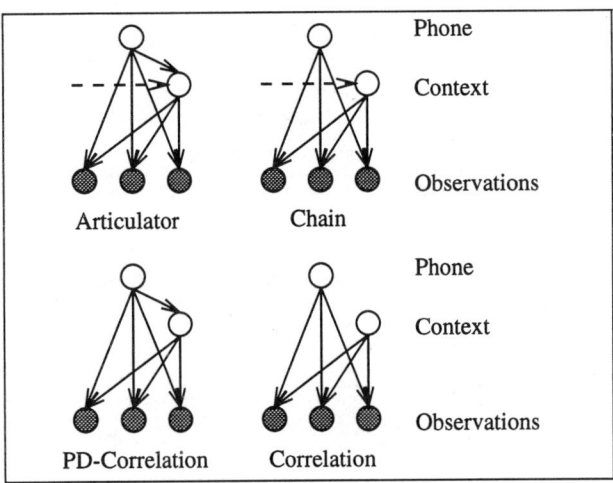

Figure 3: Acoustic models for the networks tested. Three acoustic observations were made in each time frame. The dotted arcs represent links to the previous time frame.

2. A "chain" network in which the phonetic dependence is removed. This structure can directly represent phone-independent temporal correlations.

3. A "phone-dependent-correlation" network (PD-Correlation) which results from removing the temporal links from the articulator network. This can directly model phone-dependent intra-frame correlations among multiple acoustic features.

4. A "correlation" network which further removes the phonetic dependence. This is only capable of modeling intra-frame observation correlations in the most basic way.

The articulator network was initialized to reflect voicing, and the chain network to reflect temporal continuity.

Experimental Results

Database and Task

As a test-bed, we selected the Phonebook database, a large-vocabulary, isolated-word database compiled by researchers at NYNEX (Pitrelli *et al.* 1995). The words were chosen with the goal of "incorporating all phonemes in as many segmental/stress contexts as are likely to produce coarticulatory variations, while also spanning a variety of talkers and telephone transmission characteristics." These characteristics make it a challenging data set.

The data was processed in 25ms windows to generate 10 mel-frequency cepstral coefficients (MFCCs) (Davis & Mermelstein 1980) and their derivatives every 8.4ms. MFCCs are generated by computing the power spectrum with an FFT; then the total energy in 20 different frequency ranges is computed. The cosine transform of the logarithm of the filterbank outputs is computed, and the low-order coefficients constitute the MFCCs. MFCCs represent the shape of the short-term power spectrum in a manner inspired by the human auditory system.

The MFCCs were vector-quantized using a size-256 codebook. Their derivatives were quantized in a second codebook. The C_0 and delta-C_0 coefficients were quantized separately with size-16 codebooks, and concatenated to form a third 256-valued data stream. We performed mean-cepstral subtraction for C_1 through C_{10}, and speaker normalization for C_0 (Lee 1989). The effect of mean-cepstral subtraction is to remove the transmission characteristics of telephone lines. Speaker normalization scales C_0 to the overall power level of a speaker by subtracting the maximum value, so that the resulting values can be compared across utterances.

We experimented with DBN models using both context-independent and context-dependent phonetic units. In both cases, we started from the phonetic transcriptions provided with Phonebook, ignoring the stressed/unstressed distinction for vowels.

In the case of context-independent units, i.e., simple phonemes, we used four distinct states for each phoneme: an initial and final state, and two interior states.

To generate the context-dependent transcriptions, we replaced each phoneme with two new phonetic units: one representing the beginning of the phoneme in the left-context of the preceding phoneme, and one representing the end of the phoneme in the right-context of the following unit. For example, the /ae/ in /k ae t/ becomes /(k − ae) (ae − t)/. To prevent the proliferation of phonetic units, we did not use context-dependent units that were seen fewer than a threshold number of times in the training data. If a context-dependent unit was not available, we used a context-independent phoneme-initial or phoneme-final unit instead. Finally, we found it beneficial to repeat the occurrence of each unit twice. Thus, each phoneme in the original transcription was broken into a total of four substates, comparable to context-independent phonemes. The effect of doubling the number of occurrences of a phonetic unit is to increase the minimum and expected durations in that state.

We report results for two context-dependent phonetic alphabets: one in which units occurring at least 250 times in the training data were used, and one in which units occurring at least 125 times were used. In both cases, the alphabet also contained context-independent units for the initial and final segments of each of the original phonemes. The two alphabets contained 336 and 666 units respectively. Thus the number of parameters in the first case is comparable to the context-independent-alphabet system with an auxiliary variable; the number of parameters in the second case is comparable to the number that arises when an auxiliary variable is added to the first context-dependent system.

Note that the notion of context in the sense of a context-dependent alphabet is different from that rep-

Network	Parameters	Error Rate
Baseline-HMM	127k	4.8%
Correlation	254k	3.7%
PD-Correlation	254k	4.2%
Chain	254k	3.6%
Articulator	255k	3.4%

Figure 4: Test results with the basic phoneme alphabet; $\sigma \approx 0.25\%$. The number of independent parameters is shown to 3 significant figures; all the DBN variants have slightly different parameter counts.

resented by the context variable in Figures 2 and 3. Context of the kind expressed in an alphabet is based on an idealized pronunciation template; the context-variable represents context as manifested in a specific utterance.

The training subset consisted of all *a, *h, *m, *q, and *t files; we tuned the various schemes with a development set consisting of the *o and *y files. Test results are reported for the *d and *r files, which were not used in any of the training or tuning phases. The words in the Phonebook vocabulary are divided into 75-word subsets, and the recognition task consists of identifying each test word from among the 75 word models in its subset. There were 19,421 training utterances, 7291 development utterances and 6598 test utterances. There was no overlap between training and test words or training and test speakers.

Performance

Figure 4 shows the word-error rates with the basic phoneme alphabet. The results for the DBNs clearly dominate the baseline HMM system. The articulatory network performs slightly better than the chain network, and the networks without time-continuity arcs perform at intermediate levels. However, most of the differences among the augmented networks are not statistically significant.

These results are significantly better than those reported elsewhere for state-of-the-art systems: Dupont *et al.* (1997) report an error rate of 4.1% for a hybrid neural-net HMM system with the same phonetic transcription and test set, and worse results for a more conventional HMM-based system. (They report improved performance with transcriptions based on a pronunciation dictionary from CMU.)

Figure 5 shows the word error rates with the context-dependent alphabets. Using a context-dependent alphabet proved to be an effective way of improving performance. For about the same number of parameters as the augmented context-independent phoneme network, performance was slightly better. However, augmenting the context-dependent alphabet with an auxiliary variable helped still further. We tested the best performing augmentation (the articulator structure) with the context-dependent alphabet, and obtained a significant performance increase. Increasing the alphabet size

Network	Parameters	Error Rate
CDA-HMM	257k	3.2%
CDA-Articulator	515k	2.7%
CDA-HMM	510k	3.1%

Figure 5: Test results with the context-dependent alphabets (CDA); $\sigma \approx 0.20\%$. In the first two systems, each context-dependent unit occurred at least 250 times in the training data; in the third, the threshold was 125. This resulted in alphabet sizes of 336 and 666 respectively.

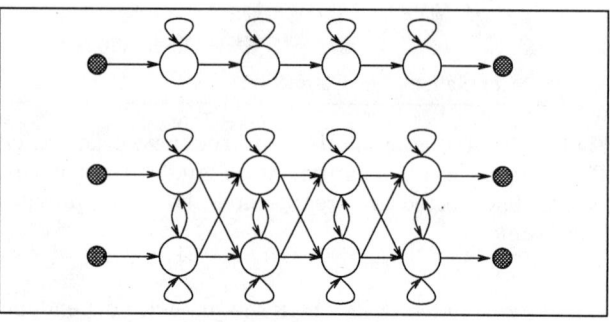

Figure 6: A 4-state HMM phone model (top), and a corresponding HMM model with a binary context distinction (bottom). In the second HMM, there are two states for each of the original states, representing context values of 0 and 1. The shaded nodes represent notional initial and final states in which no sound is emitted. Phone models are concatenated by merging the final state(s) of one with the initial state(s) of the other. The more complex model must have two initial and final states to retain memory of the context across phones. These graphs specify possible transitions between HMM states, and are not DBN specifications.

to attain a comparable number of parameters did not help as much.

In terms of computational requirements, the "Baseline-HMM" configuration requires 18M of RAM, and can process a single example through one EM iteration 6X faster than real time on a SPARC Ultra-30. The "Articulator" network requires 28M of RAM and runs 2X faster than real time.

Cross-Product HMM. Acoustic and articulatory context can be incorporated into an HMM framework by creating a distinct state for each possible combination of phonetic state and context, and modifying the pronunciation model appropriately. This is illustrated for a binary context distinction in Figure 6. In the expanded HMM, there are two new states for each of the original states, and the transition model is more complex: there are four possible transitions at each point in time, corresponding to all possible combinations of changing the phonetic state and changing the context value. The number of independent transition parameters needed for the expanded HMM is 6 times the number of original phones. The total number of independent transition and context parameters needed in the articulatory DBN is 3 times the number of phones. In the chain DBN, it is equal to the number of phones.

We tested the HMM shown in Figure 6 with the basic phoneme alphabet and two different kinds of initialization: one reflecting continuity in the context variable (analogous to the Chain-DBN), and one reflecting voicing (analogous to the Articulator-DBN). The results were 3.5 and 3.2% word-error respectively, with 255k parameters. These results indicate that the benefits of articulatory/acoustic context modeling with a binary context variable can also be achieved by using a more complex HMM model. We expect this not to be the case as the number of context variables increases.

Discussion

The presence of a context variable unambiguously improves our speech recognition results. With basic phoneme alphabets, the improvements range from 12% to 29%. Statistically, these results are highly significant; the difference between the baseline and the articulator network is significant at the 0.0001 level. With the context-dependent alphabet, we observed similar effects.

Having learned a model with hidden variables, it is interesting to try to ascertain exactly what those variables are modeling. We found striking patterns in the parameters associated with the context variable, and these clearly depend on the network structure used. The $C_0/\delta C_0$ observation stream is most strongly correlated with the context variable, and this association is illustrated for the articulator network in Figure 7. This graph shows that the context variable is likely to have a value of 1 when C_0 has large values, which is characteristic of vowels. The same information is shown for the correlation network in Figure 8; the pattern is obviously different, and less easily characterized. Although we initialized the context variable in the articulator network to reflect known linguistic information about the voicing of phonemes (on the assumption that this might be the most significant single bit of articulator state information), the learned model does not appear to reflect voicing directly.

For the networks with time-continuity arcs, the parameters associated with the context variable indicate that it is characterized by a high degree of continuity. (See Figure 9.) This is consistent with its interpretation as representing a slowly changing process such as articulator position.

Conclusion

In this paper we demonstrate that DBNs are a flexible tool that can be applied effectively to speech recognition, and show that the use of a factored-state representation can improve speech recognition results. We explicitly model articulatory-acoustic context with an auxiliary variable that complements the phonetic state

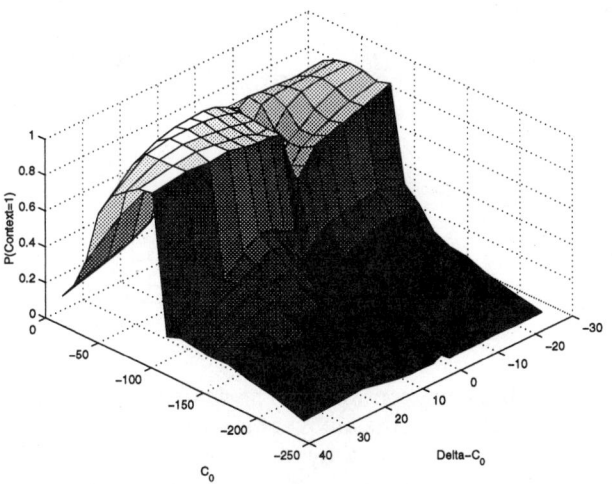

Figure 7: Association between the learned context variable and acoustic features for the articulatory network. C_0 is indicative of the overall energy in an acoustic frame. The maximum value in an utterance is subtracted, so the value is never greater than 0. Assuming that each mel-frequency filter bank contributes equally, C_0 ranges between its maximum value and about 50 decibels below maximum.

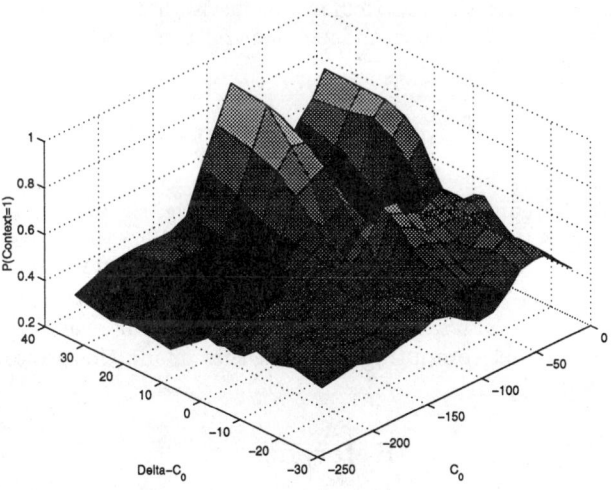

Figure 8: Association between the learned context variable and acoustic features for the correlation network. This shows a quite different pattern from that exhibited by the articulator network. (For clarity, the surface is viewed from a different angle.)

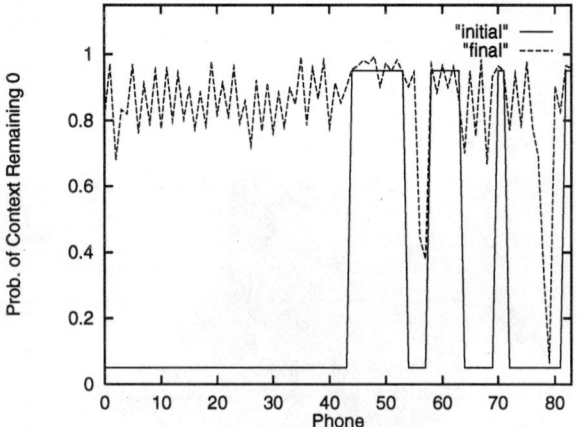

Figure 9: Learning continuity. The solid line shows the initial probability of the auxiliary state value remaining 0 across two consecutive time frames as a function of the phone. The variable was initialized to reflect voicing, so low values reflect voiced phones. The dotted line indicates the learned parameters. The learned parameters reflect continuity: the auxiliary variable is unlikely to change regardless of phone. This effect is observed for all values of the auxiliary chain. To generate our recognition results, we initialized the parameters to less extreme values, which results in fewer EM iterations and somewhat better word recognition.

variable. The use of a context variable initialized to reflect voicing results in a significant improvement in recognition. We expect further improvements from multiple context variables. This is a natural approach to modeling the coarticulatory effects that arise from the inertial and quasi-independent nature of the speech articulators.

Acknowledgments

This work benefited from many discussions with Nelson Morgan, Jeff Bilmes, Steve Greenberg, Brian Kingsbury, Katrin Kirchoff, and Dan Gildea. The work was funded by NSF grant IRI-9634215, and ARO grant DAAH04-96-1-0342. We are grateful to the *International Computer Science Institute* for making available the parallel computing facilities that made this work possible.

References

Bourlard, H., and Morgan, N. 1994. *Connectionist Speech Recognition: A Hybrid Approach.* Dordrecht, The Netherlands: Kluwer.

Davis, S., and Mermelstein, P. 1980. Comparison of parametric representations for monosyllabic word recognition in continuously spoken sentences. *IEEE Transactions on Acoustics, Speech, and Signal Processing* 28(4):357–366.

Dean, T., and Kanazawa, K. 1989. A model for reasoning about persistence and causation. *Computational Intelligence* 5(3):142–150.

Dupont, S.; Bourlard, H.; Deroo, O.; Fontaine, V.; and Boite, J.-M. 1997. Hybrid HMM/ANN systems for training independent tasks: Experiments on PhoneBook and related improvements. In *ICASSP-97*, 1767–1770. Los Alamitos, CA: IEEE Computer Society Press.

Ghahramani, Z., and Jordan, M. I. 1997. Factorial hidden Markov models. *Machine Learning* 19(2/3).

Lauritzen, S. L. 1995. The EM algorithm for graphical association models with missing data. *Computational Statistics and Data Analysis* 19:191–201.

Lee, K.-F. 1989. *Automatic speech recognition: The development of the SPHINX system.* Dordrecht, The Netherlands: Kluwer.

Peot, M., and Shachter, R. 1991. Fusion and propagation with multiple observations. *Artificial Intelligence* 48(3):299–318.

Pitrelli, J.; Fong, C.; Wong, S.; Spitz, J.; and Leung, H. 1995. Phonebook: A phonetically-rich isolated-word telephone-speech database. In *ICASSP-95*, 101–104. Los Alamitos, CA: IEEE Computer Society Press.

Rabiner, L. R., and Juang, B.-H. 1993. *Fundamentals of Speech Recognition.* Prentice-Hall.

Robinson, A., and Fallside, F. 1991. A recurrent error propagation speech recognition system. *Computer Speech and Language* 5:259–274.

Russell, S.; Binder, J.; Koller, D.; and Kanazawa, K. 1995. Local learning in probabilistic networks with hidden variables. In *IJCAI-95*, 1146–52. Montreal, Canada: Morgan Kaufmann.

Smyth, P.; Heckerman, D.; and Jordan, M. 1997. Probabilistic independence networks for hidden Markov probability models. *Neural Computation* 9(2):227–269.

Zweig, G., and Russell, S. J. 1997. Compositional modeling with dpns. Technical Report UCB/CSD-97-970, Computer Science Division, University of California at Berkeley.

Zweig, G. 1998. *Speech Recognition with Dynamic Bayesian Networks.* Ph.D. Dissertation, University of California, Berkeley, Berkeley, California.

Multimodal Reasoning for Automatic Model Construction

Reinhard Stolle and Elizabeth Bradley[*][†]
University of Colorado at Boulder
Department of Computer Science
Boulder, Colorado 80309-0430
{stolle,lizb}@cs.colorado.edu

Abstract

This paper describes a program called PRET that automates system identification, the process of finding a dynamical model of a black-box system. PRET performs both structural identification and parameter estimation by integrating several reasoning modes: qualitative reasoning, qualitative simulation, numerical simulation, geometric reasoning, constraint reasoning, resolution, reasoning with abstraction levels, declarative meta-level control, and a simple form of truth maintenance.

Unlike other modeling programs that map structural or functional descriptions to model fragments, PRET combines hypotheses about the mathematics involved into candidate models that are intelligently tested against observations about the target system.

We give two examples of system identification tasks that this automated modeling tool has successfully performed. The first, a simple linear system, was chosen because it facilitates a brief and clear presentation of PRET's features and reasoning techniques. In the second example, a difficult real-world modeling task, we show how PRET models a radio-controlled car used in the University of British Columbia's soccer-playing robot project.

Introduction

Models are powerful tools that are used to understand physical systems. The abstraction level of a model is an essential part of its power as a reasoning aid. Abstract models are simple: they account for major properties of the physical system. Less-abstract models are more complicated, allowing them to capture the features of the physical system more accurately and in more detail, but at the cost of increased complexity during model construction and usage. Typically, in this abstraction hierarchy, the model of choice is the one that is just detailed enough to account for the properties and perspectives that are of interest for the task at hand.

[*] Supported by NSF NYI #CCR-9357740, ONR #N00014-96-1-0720, and a Packard Fellowship in Science and Engineering from the David and Lucile Packard Foundation.

[†] Copyright (c) 1998, American Association for Artificial Intelligence (www.aaai.org). All rights reserved.

The process of inferring an internal model of a system's dynamics from external observations—often called *system identification*—is a routine and difficult problem faced by engineers in a variety of domains (Astrom & Eykhoff 1971; Ljung 1987). The first stage of the system identification process, *structural identification*, identifies the form of the model, or skeleton of the equation, such as $a\ddot{\theta} + b\sin\theta = 0$ for a simple pendulum. In the second system identification stage, *parameter estimation*, the parameter values a and b are determined.

The program PRET (Bradley & Stolle 1996) automates both stages of the system identification process; it finds a system of ODEs that models a given physical system. Inputs are *observations* about that system, user-supplied *hypotheses* about the desired model, and *specifications*. Fig. 1 shows a physical system that consists of two masses and three springs and the call that instructs PRET to construct a model of that system. It is important to note that this simple linear example does not by any means exercise PRET's power.

Observations are measured automatically by sensors and/or interpreted by the user; they may be symbolic or numeric and take on a variety of formats and degrees of precision. For example, an observation might inform PRET that the system to be modeled is autonomous; another observation could state that the state variable q oscillates and that this oscillation is damped. Observations can also be physical measurements made directly and automatically on the system (Bradley & Easley 1998). Hypotheses about the physics involved, e.g., a hypothesis about friction, are supplied to PRET by the user; these may conflict and need not be mutually exclusive, whereas observations are always held to be true. Finally, specifications indicate the quantities of interest and their resolutions— for example, a specification might impose a microsecond resolution over 120 seconds of system evolution.

When modeling physical systems, human engineers make use of a variety of well-established modeling techniques. A modeler's reasoning about a given physical system and possible candidate models takes place at an abstract level first and resorts to more detailed reasoning later in the modeling process. PRET's goal is to mimic this strategy and attempt to find the right

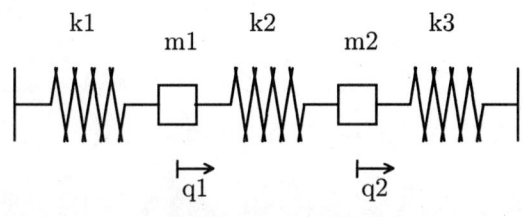

```
(find-model
  (domain mechanics)
  (state-variables <q1> <q2>)
  (point-coordinates <q1> <q2>)
  (hypotheses
    (<force> (* m1 (deriv (deriv <q1>))))
    (<force> (* m2 (deriv (deriv <q2>))))
    (<force> (* k1 <q1>))
    (<force> (* k2 (- <q1> <q2>)))
    (<force> (* k3 <q2>))
    (<force> (* r1 (deriv <q1>)))
    (<force> (* r2 (square (deriv <q1>))))
    (<force> (* r3 (deriv <q2>)))
    (<force> (* r4 (square (deriv <q2>)))))
  (observations
    (autonomous)
    (oscillation <q1>)
    (oscillation <q2>)
    (numeric (<time> <q1> <q2>)
      ((0 .1 .1) (.1 .1099 .1103) ... )))
  (specifications
    (resolution <q1> absolute 1e-3 (0 1))
    (resolution <q2> absolute 1e-3 (0 1))))
```

Figure 1: A `find-model` call that instructs PRET to model the `Springs&Masses` system shown above. In this example, the user first sets up the problem, then hypothesizes nine different force terms, makes four observations about the position coordinates q_1 and q_2, and finally specifies resolutions and ranges.

model at the right abstraction level as quickly as possible. Therefore, the challenge in designing PRET was to work out a formalism that meets two requirements: first, it must facilitate easy formulation of the various reasoning techniques; and second, it must allow PRET to reason about which techniques are appropriate in which situation. This paper describes PRET's reasoning modes, how they are integrated, and how they solve these problems.

The next section gives a brief overview of PRET. In the following section, we present the various reasoning modes, their interaction, and their integration, and give two examples that illustrate how PRET works. Finally, we give an evaluation, point to problems and future directions, and discuss related work.

Overview of PRET

PRET incorporates two types of knowledge:
- *Domain rules* that apply in individual domains, such as Kirchhoff's voltage law for electronic circuits, and
- *ODE rules* that capture mathematical precepts that are true for all ODEs, such as the definition of an equilibrium point.

The high-level control flow of PRET is a variant of "generate-and-test." In the "generate" phase, the domain rules are used to construct candidate models from the user's hypotheses. Since PRET tries to find a model that accounts for all observations without being more complex than necessary, candidate models are generated in order of increasing complexity. In the "test" phase, PRET uses its ODE rules to generate new knowledge about the physical system and about the current candidate model. A model is valid if the known facts about the system to be modeled are consistent with the known facts about the model. Any inconsistency is a reason to discard the model. Currently, the first model in this generate-and-test sequence that is consistent with the observations is returned as the result.

PRET judges models according to the opportunistic paradigm "valid if not proven invalid:" if a model is bad, there must be a reason for it. Or, conversely, if there is no reason to discard a model, it is a valid model. Therefore, PRET's central task is to quickly find inconsistencies between a candidate model and the target system. The remainder of the paper focuses on the techniques that PRET uses to accomplish this task.

Reasoning Modes

In order to find inconsistencies between candidate models and the target system quickly, PRET employs a number of very different techniques. None of these techniques is new; human engineers routinely use them when modeling dynamical systems, and every one has been used in at least one automated modeling tool (see the Related Work section). The particular set of techniques used here, the multimodal reasoning framework that integrates them, and the system architecture that lets PRET decide which one is appropriate in which situation, make the approach taken here different—and powerful. This particular combination of tactics—designed for and focused upon a particular problem domain—constitutes the novel contributions of the work described in this paper.

Using the paradigm "valid if not proven invalid," it is important to rule out invalid candidate models as quickly as possible. To accomplish this, PRET uses abstract knowledge first and detailed knowledge later. In order to achieve this behavior, PRET chooses among, invokes, and interprets the results of several reasoning modes. In the following subsections, we describe these reasoning modes and show how PRET orchestrates their selection, invocation, and interactions.

Qualitative Reasoning

Reasoning about abstract features of the physical system or the candidate model is typically faster than reasoning about their detailed properties. Therefore, PRET uses a "high-level first" strategy: it tries to rule out a model by purely *qualitative* techniques before advancing to more expensive semi-numerical or numerical techniques. Often, only a few steps of inexpensive qualitative reasoning (QR) suffice to quickly discard a model. Some of these qualitative rules in turn make use of other tools, e.g., symbolic algebra facilities from the commercial package Maple. For example, PRET's ODE theory includes the qualitative rule that oscillating linear systems must be of at least second order. If the user's observations imply an oscillation, any model whose order is less than two can be discarded without performing more-complex operations such as, for example, a numerical integration of the model.

PRET's QR features are not only important for accelerating the search for inconsistencies between the physical system and the model; they also allow the user to express incomplete information (Kuipers 1992). For example, the user might not know the exact value of a friction coefficient, but he or she might know that it is constant and positive. This example also shows the importance and power of interaction among the various reasoning modes. A qualitative result about the sign of a parameter can be used by the constraint reasoner, and vice versa. PRET's logic inference system is designed to facilitate exactly this type of interaction (see Section "Storing and Reusing Intermediate Results").

Geometric Reasoning

Verification of a *valid* candidate model with respect to a numeric observation requires point-by-point comparison with a numeric integration of the ODE (see the section entitled "Parameter Estimation and Numerical Simulation"). However, *invalid* models can often be ruled out without such an expensive numeric procedure; many inappropriate models, for instance, can be discarded by reasoning about purely qualitative information that can be inferred inexpensively from numeric information. In order to achieve this behavior, PRET processes the observations—curve fitting, recognition of linear regions, and so on—using Maple functions and simple phase-portrait analysis techniques, both of which yield high-level results that can then be used much as qualitative observations are (Bradley & Easley 1998).

Qualitative Simulation

Before PRET resorts to the numerical level, it attempts to establish contradictions quickly and cheaply by reasoning about the qualitative states of the physical system (Kuipers 1992). PRET's qualitative envisioning module constrains the possible ranges of parameters in the candidate model. If the constraints become inconsistent—i.e., the range of a parameter becomes the empty set—the model is ruled out. Currently, the qualitative states contain only sign information $(-, 0, +)$. For example, for the model $ax + by = 0$ the state $(x, y) = (+, +)$ constrains (a, b) to the possibilities $(+, -)$ or $(0, 0)$ or $(-, +)$.

PRET does not do full qualitative simulation (Kuipers 1986). Instead, it only envisions the state space of all possible combinations of qualitative values of state variables and parameters. This strategy is faster than full qualitative simulation, but it is also less accurate; it may let invalid models pass the test. These invalid models are later ruled out by the numeric simulator. However, for the models that do fail the qualitative envisioning test, this test is much cheaper than a numeric simulation and point-by-point comparison would be.

Parameter Estimation and Numerical Simulation

If the observations contain a numerical time series, the model must match the time series to within the resolution specified in the find-model call. If a candidate model cannot be discarded by qualitative means, PRET integrates the model (an ODE system) with fourth-order Runge-Kutta, comparing the result to the numeric time-series observation. Typically, however, models contain parameters whose values must be determined before the numeric integration can take place. For example, for the model $a\ddot{\theta} + b\sin\theta = 0$ of a simple pendulum the parameter values a and b must be determined. Parameter estimation for nonlinear systems is a (very difficult) global optimization task; PRET solves this problem by combining qualitative reasoning and local numerical methods (an orthogonal distance regression-based nonlinear least-squares solver, specifically). The nonlinear parameter estimation reasoner (NPER) that implements these ideas is described in (Bradley, O'Gallagher, & Rogers 1997).[1] The NPER uses knowledge derived during the structural identification phase to guide the parameter estimation process—for example, using constraint reasoning (e.g., the sign of a friction coefficient) or the results of the qualitative envisionment to choose good initial values, thereby avoiding local minima in the regression landscape.

Constraint Reasoning

Often, information *between* the purely qualitative and the purely numeric levels is also available. If a linear system oscillates, for example, the imaginary parts of at least one pair of the roots of its model's characteristic polynomial must be nonzero. Thus, if the model $a\ddot{x} + b\dot{x} + cx = 0$ is to match an oscillation observation, the coefficients must satisfy the inequality $4ac > b^2$. PRET uses expression inference to merge and simplify such *constraints*. However, this approach works only for linear and quadratic expressions and some special cases of higher order. We are investigating techniques for reasoning about more-general expressions, e.g., (Faltings & Gelle 1997). For example, if the candidate model

---

[1] How to use qualitative reasoning (QR) to navigate in the parameter space for models of one particular class of *linear* systems is exemplified in (Capelo, Ironi, & Tentoni 1996).

$\ddot{x} + a\dot{x}^4 + b\dot{x}^2 = 0$ is to match a `conservative` observation, the coefficients a and b must take on values such that the divergence $-4a\dot{x}^3 - 2b\dot{x}$ is zero, below a certain resolution threshold, for the specified range of interest of x.

SLD-based resolution

PRET's search for an inconsistency between the observations and a particular candidate model is based on SLD resolution. The language in which observations and the ODE theory are expressed is that of generalized Horn clause intuitionistic logic (GHCIL) (McCarty 1988). Roughly, GHCIL clauses are Horn clauses that also allow embedded implications in their bodies.

The special atomic formula `falsum` may only appear as the head of a clause. Such clauses express fundamental reasons for inconsistencies, e.g., that a system cannot be oscillating *and* non-oscillating at the same time. This concept of *negation as inconsistency* (Gabbay & Sergot 1986) is the only form of negation in our paradigm. Negation as failure, for example, which is the standard form of negation in PROLOG, is particularly undesirable for our purposes. Since we do not require the user to supply all possible[2] observations, the absence of knowledge cannot be used to generate new knowledge.

A model is ruled out if and only if a contradiction exists between a mathematical property of the physical system (e.g., a sensor observation that includes an oscillation (`oscillation <x>`)) and a mathematical property of the model (e.g., (`no-oscillation <x>`), derived from a root-locus analysis of an ODE model). For every candidate model, PRET combines basic facts about the target system, basic facts about the candidate model, and basic facts and rules from the ODE theory into one set of clauses, and then checks that set for inconsistency, i.e., tries to derive `falsum` from it.

The basic facts about the target system are the observations. They have two potential sources—the user and the sensors—and may be *descriptive*, *graphical*, or *numeric*. The former use special descriptive keywords, the second are sketches drawn on a computer screen with a mouse, and the third simply specify data points. Only the first and the last are currently implemented. The basic facts about the current model are obtained by a collection of SCHEME[3] "model observer" functions that identify mathematical properties of the model, e.g., "the ODE is linear in x." These functions essentially implement the basic operations found in any differential equations text.

In the course of trying to prove the `falsum`, PRET's inference engine expands both sets of properties by applying the ODE rules; for example, if the system is known to be autonomous, its model cannot explicitly contain the variable `<time>`. This is one of the advantages of the declarative reasoning framework: an expert user of PRET can easily extend and specialize the ODE theory represented in the knowledge base.

The special predicate `scheme-eval` provides the link between the inference engine and PRET's model observer functions. It also provides the link to all modules that implement other reasoning modes.

For a more detailed discussion of PRET's logic system, see (Stolle & Bradley 1996).

Declarative Meta Level Control

The *control strategy* of a SLD resolution theorem prover is defined by the function that selects the literal that is resolved and by the function that chooses the resolving clause. PRET provides meta-level language constructs that allow the implementer of the ODE theory to specify the *control strategy* that is to be used (Davis 1980; Gallaire & Lasserre 1982; Beckstein, Stolle, & Tobermann 1996). The intuition here is, again, that the search should be guided towards a cheap and quick proof of a contradiction. As an example, consider the following (simplified) excerpt from the knowledge base.

$$\begin{aligned} stable &\leftarrow linear,\ all\_roots\_in\_left\_half\_plane. \\ stable &\leftarrow non\_linear,\ stable\_in\_all\_basins. \\ hot(L) &\leftarrow linear,\ goal(L, stable). \end{aligned}$$

A linear dynamical system has a unique equilibrium point, and the stability of that point—and therefore of the system as a whole—can be determined by examining the system's eigenvalues: a simple symbolic manipulation of the coefficients of the equation. *Nonlinear* systems can have arbitrary numbers of equilibrium sets, which are expensive to find and evaluate. Thus, if a system is known to be linear, its *overall* stability is easy to establish, whereas evaluating the stability of a nonlinear system is far more complicated and expensive. Therefore, PRET's meta control predicate `hot` is used in this example to prioritize a stability check in the case where this check is cheap and easy—i.e., if the system is known to be linear.

For a more detailed discussion of PRET's meta control constructs, see (Hogan, Stolle, & Bradley 1998).

Reasoning at Different Abstraction Levels

Every rule in the ODE theory is assigned a natural number that indicates its level of abstraction: the lower the *abstraction level number*, the more abstract the rule. Whereas the meta predicates described in the previous paragraph specify *dynamic* control, the ODE rule abstraction levels express *static* control information. The theorem prover proceeds to a higher abstraction level number only if the attempt to prove the `falsum` with ODE rules with lower abstraction level numbers fails. For example, the `scheme-eval-rule` that triggers numerical integration has a higher abstraction level number than the `scheme-eval-rule` that calls the qualitative simulation.

PRET tries to build complete proofs on a more-abstract level before even considering less-abstract

---

[2]Here, *possible* means *expressible with the implemented observation vocabulary*.

[3]PRET is written in SCHEME.

rules. Since abstract reasoning usually involves less detail, this approach leads to short and quick proofs of the falsum whenever possible.

Storing and Reusing Intermediate Results

PRET reuses previously derived knowledge in three ways. First, knowledge about the physical system is global, whereas knowledge about a candidate model is local to that model. Therefore, PRET reuses knowledge that is independent of the current candidate model.

Second, knowledge is reused within the process of reasoning about one particular model. Every time the reasoning proceeds to a less-abstract level, PRET needs all information that has already been derived at the more abstract level. To avoid duplication of effort, PRET stores this information rather than rederiving it. The user declares a number of predicates as *relevant* (Beckstein & Tobermann 1992) which causes all succeeding subgoals with this predicate to be stored for later reuse.[4] Currently, PRET recognizes special cases and generalizations of previously proved formulae, but it maintains no contexts or labels for intermediate results.

Finally, other—non-logic-based—reasoning modes typically use knowledge that has been generated by previous inferences, which may in turn have triggered other reasoning modules. To facilitate this, PRET gives these modules access to the set of formulae that have been derived so far. As described above, for example, the nonlinear parameter estimation reasoner (NPER) uses knowledge derived in the structural identification phase.

Example Applications

In this section we trace PRET's actions on the example of Fig. 1. The four friction forces are omitted here for space reasons, and the numeric observation has the form (numeric (<time> <q1> <q2>) (eval *data*)). The keyword eval causes the variable *data* to be evaluated in the calling environment. Bound to this variable is a time series that was generated by Runge-Kutta integration of the system

$$\ddot{q}_1 = -0.1\,q_1 - 0.2\,(q_1 - q_2)$$
$$\ddot{q}_2 = 0.2\,(q_1 - q_2) - 0.3\,q_2.$$

The first candidate model is $k_1 q_1 = 0$. A SCHEME function called on the ODE establishes the fact (order <q1> 0) which expresses that the order of the highest derivative of q_1 in this model is zero. This fact conflicts with facts inferred from the observation (oscillation <q1>), so this model is ruled out. The way PRET handles this first candidate model demonstrates the power of its abstract-reasoning-first approach; only a few steps of inexpensive qualitative reasoning suffice to let it quickly discard the model.

PRET tries all combinations of <force> hypotheses at single point coordinates, but all these models are ruled out for qualitative or numeric reasons. It then proceeds with ODE systems that consist of *two* force balances—one for each point coordinate. One example of a candidate model of this type is

$$k_1 q_1 + m_1 \ddot{q}_1 = 0$$
$$m_2 \ddot{q}_2 = 0$$

None of the implemented rules discards this model by purely qualitative means, so PRET invokes its nonlinear parameter estimation reasoner (NPER) which finds no appropriate values for the coefficients k_1, m_1, and m_2 such that any ODE solution matches the numeric time series. Therefore, this candidate model is also ruled out.[5] After having discarded a variety of candidate models in a similar manner, PRET tries the model

$$k_1 q_1 + k_2(q_1 - q_2) + m_1 \ddot{q}_1 = 0$$
$$k_3 q_2 + k_2(q_1 - q_2) + m_2 \ddot{q}_2 = 0$$

Again, it calls the NPER, this time successfully. It then substitutes the returned parameter values for the constants k_1, k_2, k_3, m_1, and m_2 and integrates the resulting ODE system with fourth-order Runge-Kutta, comparing the result to the numeric time-series observation. The difference between the integration and the observation stays within the specified resolution, so the numeric comparison yields no contradiction and this candidate model and the parameter values are returned as the answer.

We have chosen the simple spring-mass example of Fig. 1 to make this presentation brief and clear. Linear systems of this type are easy to model; no engineer would use a software tool to do generate-and-test and guided search to find an ODE model of a system so simple and well-understood. This example is representative neither of PRET's power nor of its intended applications—nonlinear, high-dimensional, black-box dynamical systems. Modeling these types of systems is where PRET's mixture of exact and approximate techniques, quantitative and qualitative reasoning, and precise and heuristic knowledge becomes truly powerful.

PRET has also been successfully used to solve a real-world problem: modeling the radio-controlled (R/C) cars used in the University of British Columbia's soccer-playing robot project. These commercially acquired cars cannot be controlled without an accurate ODE model of their dynamics—something that is not part of the specifications sheet. The sensor data consists of the car's position in an (x, y)-plane and its heading (orientation) θ.

PRET goes through the structural identification process that we have already seen in the Springs&Masses

---

[4] The set of previously derived relevant formulae is currently implemented as a hash table.

[5] In certain cases, this approach may result in a departure from the paradigm *valid if not proven invalid*; unless we trust that the parameter estimator *always* finds a set of coefficients if such a set exists, this amounts to *negation as failure*. This is the appropriate decision here because a user who supplies a numeric time series is certainly interested in a numerically accurate ODE model.

example, using force balances to assemble hypotheses into models, examining hypothesis combinations in order of increasing complexity, and discarding models that are inconsistent with the observations, always taking advantage of its abstract-reasoning-first approach. The result, in this example, is the model:

$$\dot{x} = v\cos\theta$$
$$\dot{y} = v\sin\theta$$
$$\dot{\theta} = \rho v$$
$$\dot{v} = \alpha + \gamma v$$

where v is the car's velocity, θ its orientation, ρ the position of the steering wheel, α acceleration, and γ friction. Following the structural identification phase, PRET calls the NPER; as in the previous example, qualitative knowledge derived during the earlier phases of the modeling process are used during parameter estimation—for example, symbolic algebra, constraint propagation, and divided differences are used to compute the initial values and bounds that are passed to the local least-squares solver that lies at the heart of the NPER.

PRET's solution to the modeling problem surprised the University of British Columbia analyst. The model did not match his intuition because he had omitted some important information from the specification—including the fact that the car *started from rest*. In order to work around noise in sensor data, PRET's NPER is designed to filter data and adjust boundary conditions; in this case, this reasoning led to a numerically successful ODE model with a negative initial condition for the velocity—a conflict with the expert's implicit mental model of the situation. Some reflection on this discrepancy led the analyst to realize that the system dynamics might include a delay. Thus, the correct find-model call for this example should contain an observation that the initial velocity was zero and a hypothesis that incorporates a delay between the application of force and the acceleration of the car.

We include this anecdote to emphasize that PRET is an engineer's tool, not a scientific discovery system. Its goal is to construct the simplest ODE that accounts for the observations and specifications that are *explicit* in the find-model call, not to infer physics that the user left implicit. The interaction between human expert and automated modeling tool was unexpectedly fruitful in this example; not only did PRET construct an accurate model of the target system, but it actually helped the expert identify what was wrong with the observations and model fragments that he suggested. For a more detailed discussion see (Bradley, O'Gallagher, & Rogers 1997).

Evaluation and Future Work

PRET's declarative knowledge representation system is well-suited for encoding ODE theory and control knowledge. Mathematical truths about ODEs are naturally expressed as logical implications. Since the person who implements or maintains this knowledge base is an expert in mathematics and/or engineering—not in logic programming—an approach where control knowledge is separated from object level knowledge and represented declaratively is ideal for this application.

The model tester's cheap-first strategy works well on most junior/senior-level engineering textbook examples and even, as described in the previous section, on some research-level problems. Candidate models that do not trigger qualitative envisioning or numeric parameter estimation and simulation are ruled out symbolically in less than a second,[6] even though the SCHEME code is uncompiled and mostly unoptimized. The time needed for qualitative envisionment and parameter estimation ranges between seconds and minutes, and this is inescapable: a human modeler would face the same expenses when resorting to these techniques. PRET's design goal is not to speed up these techniques, but to avoid them whenever possible.

Currently, the model generator (which was not the focus of this paper) is impractical if more than about ten hypotheses are under consideration, since the number of possible models grows exponentially with the number of hypotheses. This problem can even arise if there are only a few hypotheses in the find-model call, as PRET resorts to power series expansions in state variables if it runs out of user-provided hypotheses, and such methods can generate dozens or hundreds of ODE fragments in no time at all. We are investigating solutions to this complexity problem that preferentially select promising hypothesis combinations. Hypotheses could be explicitly prioritized by the user, for instance, or PRET could use case-based reasoning and a repertoire of typical hypothesis combinations (e.g., coriolis and centripetal forces usually appear together, and both have recognizable forms). Other existing modeling tools use energy-based approaches and/or bond graphs (Karnopp & Rosenberg 1975) to find structural models (Amsterdam 1992). This approach may be useful in our case: typical bond graphs and bond graph fragments may help select terms from a large number of hypotheses. It is not clear, however, how similarity of system behavior (the *solution* of an ODE) translates to similarity of the involved model *fragments*.

Developing a more sophisticated way of navigating in the space of possible models is an important, interesting, and promising task. Since the state of PRET's inference engine is represented explicitly, it is trivial to generate explanations (proof trees) for failures of models. These explanations can then be used to guide the generation of better models. In the literature this approach has been termed *discrepancy-driven refinement* (e.g., (Addanki, Cremonini, & Penberthy 1991)).

---

[6]Several algebraic operations call Maple; interaction with this package is realized through file I/O which can, in sum, take longer than a second. In principle, however, SCHEME could communicate with Maple without file I/O, or the algebraic operations could be implemented in SCHEME directly.

More research is also needed concerning the form in which the user provides hypotheses and observations. In other modeling programs, this input is called *scenario description*. Since PRET's intended target systems are high-dimensional black-box systems, a modeling task's "scenario" must be described in mathematical terms—state variables, ODE fragments, etc.—rather than in terms of traditional qualitative physics—U-tubes, capacitors, springs, and so on. In the R/C car modeling task, for example, the formulation of the ODE makes use of two reference frames simultaneously. PRET's actual formulation of the model is much more complicated. Allowing the user to express hypotheses in appropriate reference frames—and transforming smoothly between different reference frames—is a current focus of our research effort. This is a fundamentally difficult problem; learning how to select the appropriate reference frame in which to reason is one of the most important and difficult concepts one learns in a physics course, so it is not surprising that this is a difficult (perhaps even impossible) task to automate well.

Related Work

The work described in this paper draws upon ideas and techniques from almost a dozen areas of mathematics, engineering, and computer science; citing more than the few most important and/or most closely related publications in each of these areas would yield an excessive bibliography, so this section—particularly the paragraph on the very active area of reasoning about physical systems—is necessarily abridged. For space reasons, references to related work that appear in the body of the paper will not be repeated here.

In general, *modeling* underlies most approaches to reasoning about physical systems. Strictly speaking, every formalization of the properties of a physical system constitutes a *model* of that system. The spectrum of models ranges from those that use a language that is very close to the physics (e.g., QPT/QPE (Forbus 1984)) to models that use a language that is well suited to describe the system mathematically (e.g., ODEs). QSIM (Kuipers 1986) is a qualitative realization of the mathematics end of this spectrum. PRET resides somewhere in the middle. Its inputs are partially expressed in terms of physics and its reasoning uses concepts from physics. However, its output—the model of the physical system that it constructs—is purely mathematical: an ODE. This choice makes PRET both precise and broadly applicable, as all domains of science and engineering use ODE models.[7] It also imposes some constraints—notably continuity—on the types of systems to which PRET can be applied. There has been recent attention to discontinuities in physical system models; see, for example, (Mosterman & Biswas 1996). PRET models the continuous sections between discontinuities.

Most automated modeling programs (Forbus 1984; Addanki, Cremonini, & Penberthy 1991; Falkenhainer & Forbus 1991; Amsterdam 1992; Kuipers 1993; Nayak 1995) use domain knowledge in order to map a structural description of the system to model fragments. PRET, however, uses only general mathematics in its analysis and does not rely on knowledge specific to the domain in question. Also, PRET's aim is not to discover the underlying physics of the system, but rather to find the simplest ODE that is consistent with the observed behavior. We emphasize, once again, that PRET is not a scientific discovery program (Langley *et al.* 1987) whose goal is to discover new physical phenomena; it is an engineering tool that identifies (already understood) phenomena and models them.

In other automated modeling systems, one of the important features of the formalized domain theory is that it suggests how structural components of the physical system map to candidate model fragments. PRET's true targets are physical systems that do not have a well-defined domain theory, such as complex industrial devices and processes.[8] The R/C car was a first step in this direction; the next test case, on which we are currently working, is a complex machine tool that takes a plastic blank and a prescription and automatically produces an eyeglass lens.

PRET aims to integrate quantitative and qualitative information. Many good papers have reported work in this area, among which are (Williams 1991; Kay & Kuipers 1993).

Statically ordering rules according to their expected computational complexity is a common strategy in rule-based systems, and dynamic meta control has been in use for two decades (Gallaire & Lasserre 1979; Davis 1980). However, we are not aware of any automated modeling program that uses *dynamic* meta control to choose among various reasoning techniques.

Recently, there has been an interesting discussion on the need of domain-dependent control information in *any* application. Theoretically, there is no need for domain-dependent control because control knowledge can be factorized into domain-independent control information and domain-dependent modal information that encodes the structure of the search space (Ginsberg & Geddis 1991). While this elegant result is true for logic programming in general, our particular project (and others as well, e.g., (Minton 1996)) suggested a different approach. Having to think about control in terms of the structure of the search space is exactly what we want to avoid. The implementer of the knowledge base should instead approach it from the viewpoint of his/her domain—in our case as an engineer: which rules are more abstract than others, which rules or goals trigger expensive calls to other packages, and so on.

---

[7] Many of these domains also use partial differential equation models. PRET is not designed to work with PDEs, but it *can* produce useful ODE truncations of PDE-governed systems, thus automating another hard and useful part of the modeling art.

[8] In (Münker *et al.* 1997), chemical processes are modeled using a PRET-like approach.

Conclusion

System identification (SID) is a necessary first step in many control-theory problems; without a reasonable model of the dynamics, very few systems admit any form of control. PRET automates the system identification process by building an AI layer on top of a set of the kinds of traditional SID techniques that human experts use to solve these problems: regression, curve-fitting, matrix methods, fast-fourier transforms and filtering, root-locus plots, etc. Integrating a collection of techniques like this—a heterogeneous group that is diverse both in methods and in reasoning levels—was an important design goal for the inference system described in this paper. The successful design of that framework allows PRET to intelligently assess the task at hand, and then automatically choose, invoke, and interpret the results of appropriate lower-level methods.

Acknowledgements

Matt Easley, Apollo Hogan, Brian LaMacchia, Agnes O'Gallagher, Janet Rogers, Ray Spiteri, and Tom Wrensch contributed ideas, code, and/or R/C car data to this project. We would also like to thank the reviewers and the QR community for helpful comments.

References

Addanki, S.; Cremonini, R.; and Penberthy, J. S. 1991. Graphs of models. *Artif. Intell.* 51:145–177.

Amsterdam, J. 1992. *Automated Qualitative Modeling of Dynamic Physical Systems*. Ph.D. Dissertation, MIT.

Astrom, K. J., and Eykhoff, P. 1971. System identification — a survey. *Automatica* 7:123–167.

Beckstein, C., and Tobermann, G. 1992. Evolutionary logic programming with RISC. In *4th Intl. Workshop on Logic Programming Environments*.

Beckstein, C.; Stolle, R.; and Tobermann, G. 1996. Meta-programming for generalized horn clause logic. In *META-96*.

Bradley, E., and Easley, M. 1998. Reasoning about sensor data for automated system identification. *Intelligent Data Analysis*. In press. Also in *IDA-97*.

Bradley, E., and Stolle, R. 1996. Automatic construction of accurate models of physical systems. *Annals of Mathematics and Artif. Intell.* 17:1–28.

Bradley, E.; O'Gallagher, A.; and Rogers, J. 1997. Global solutions for nonlinear systems using qualitative reasoning. In *QR-97*.

Capelo, A. C.; Ironi, L.; and Tentoni, S. 1996. The need for qualitative reasoning in automated modeling: A case study. In *QR-96*.

Davis, R. 1980. Meta-rules: Reasoning about control. *Artif. Intell.* 15(3).

Falkenhainer, B., and Forbus, K. D. 1991. Compositional modeling: Finding the right model for the job. *Artif. Intell.* 51:95–143.

Faltings, B., and Gelle, E. 1997. Local consistency for ternary numeric constraints. In *IJCAI-97*.

Forbus, K. D. 1984. Qualitative process theory. *Artif. Intell.* 24:85–168.

Gabbay, D. M., and Sergot, M. J. 1986. Negation as inconsistency I. *J. Logic Progr.* 3(1):1–36.

Gallaire, H., and Lasserre, C. 1979. Controlling knowledge deduction in a declarative approach. In *IJCAI-79*.

Gallaire, H., and Lasserre, C. 1982. Metalevel control for logic programs. In Clark, K., and Tärnlund, S., eds., *Logic Programming*. London: Academic Press.

Ginsberg, M., and Geddis, D. 1991. Is there any need for domain-dependent control information? In *AAAI-91*.

Hogan, A.; Stolle, R.; and Bradley, E. 1998. Putting declarative meta control to work. Technical Report CU-CS-856-98, University of Colorado at Boulder.

Karnopp, D., and Rosenberg, R. 1975. *System Dynamics: A Unified Approach*. New York: John Wiley & Sons.

Kay, H., and Kuipers, B. 1993. Numerical behavior envelopes for qualitative models. In *AAAI-93*.

Kuipers, B. J. 1986. Qualitative simulation. *Artif. Intell.* 29(3):289–338.

Kuipers, B. J. 1992. *Qualitative Reasoning: Modeling and Simulation with incomplete knowledge*. Reading, MA: Addison-Wesley.

Kuipers, B. J. 1993. Reasoning with qualitative models. *Artif. Intell.* 59:125–132.

Langley, P.; Simon, H. A.; Bradshaw, G. L.; and Zytkow, J. M., eds. 1987. *Scientific Discovery: Computational Explorations of the Creative Process*. Cambridge, MA: MIT Press.

Ljung, L., ed. 1987. *System Identification; Theory for the User*. Englewood Cliffs, N.J.: Prentice-Hall.

McCarty, L. T. 1988. Clausal intuitionistic logic I. Fixed-point semantics. *J. of Logic Progr.* 5:1–31.

Minton, S. 1996. Is there any need for domain-dependent control information? A reply. In *AAAI-96*.

Mosterman, P. J., and Biswas, G. 1996. A formal hybrid modeling scheme for handling discontinuities in physical system models. In *AAAI-96*.

Münker, B.; Hellinger, S.; Schaich, D.; and King, R. 1997. Application of QR techniques within an integrated tool for automated modelling of chemical reaction systems. In *QR-97*.

Nayak, P. 1995. *Automated Modeling of Physical Systems*. Berlin: Springer. LNCS 1003.

Stolle, R., and Bradley, E. 1996. A customized logic paradigm for reasoning about models. In *QR-96*.

Williams, B. C. 1991. A theory of interactions: unifying qualitative and quantitative algebraic reasoning. *Artif. Intell.* 51:39–94.

Discovering Admissible Simultaneous Equations of Large Scale Systems

Takashi Washio and Hiroshi Motoda

Institute of Scientific and Industrial Research, Osaka University
8-1 Mihogaoka,
Ibaraki, Osaka, 567, Japan
washio@sanken.osaka-u.ac.jp

Abstract

SSF is a system to discover the structure of simultaneous equations governing an objective process through experiments. SSF combined with another system SDS to discover a quantitative formula of a complete equation derives the quantitative model consisting of simultaneous equations reflecting the first principles underlying in the objective process. The power of SSF comes from the use of the complete subset structure in a set of simultaneous equations which can be experimentally identified. The theoretical foundations of the structure identification and the algorithm of SSF are described, and its efficiency and practicality are demonstrated and discussed with large scale working examples. This work is to promote the research of scientific discovery to a novel and promising direction, since the conventional equation discovery systems could not handle such a simultaneous equation process.

Introduction

A challenging task to find regularities in the data is discovering quantitative formulae of scientific laws from experimental measurements. Langley and others' BACON systems (P.W. Langley & Zytkow 1987) are the most well known as a pioneering work. They founded the succeeding BACON family. FAHRENHEIT (Koehn & Zytkow 1986), ABACUS (Falkenhainer & Michalski 1986) and IDS (Nordhausen & Langley 1990) and etc. are such successors that use basically similar algorithms to BACON in searching for a complete equation governing the measured data in a continuous process. However, one of the drawbacks of the BACON family is their complexity in the search of equation formulae. Another drawback is the considerable amount of ambiguity in their results for noisy data even for the relations among small number of quantities (Schaffer 1990; Huang & Zytkow 1996).

To alleviate these difficulties, some systems, e.g. ABACUS and COPER (Kokar 1986), utilize the information of the unit dimension of quantities to prune the meaningless terms. However, their applicability is limited only to the case where the quantity dimension is known. SDS is a quantitative model discovery system developed based on some novel principles(Washio & Motoda 1997). It utilizes the constraints of *scale-type* and *identity* both of which highly constrain the generation of candidate terms. Since the knowledge of scale-types is widely obtained in various domains, SDS is applicable to non-physics domains including psychophysics, sociology and etc. In addition, an extra strong mathematical constraint named *triplet checking* is introduced to check the validity of those bi-variate equations. By these constraints, the complexity of the algorithm remains quite low, and the high robustness against the noise in the measurements is provided.

In spite of these efforts, many of the practical and large scale processes have not been covered yet. This is because such processes consist of multiple mechanisms, and are represented by multiple equations in terms of given quantities. Some past studies have partially addressed this issue. The aforementioned FAHRENHEIT and ABACUS identify each operation mode of the objective process and transition conditions among those modes, and they derives an equation to represent each mode. For example, they can discover state equations of water for solid, liquid and gas phases respectively from experimental data. However, many processes such as large scale electric circuits are represented by simultaneous equations. The model representation in form of simultaneous equations is essential to grasp the dependency structure among the multiple mechanisms in the processes (Iwasaki & Simon 1986; Murota 1987). An effort to develop a system called LAGRANGE has been made to automatically discover dynamical models represented by simultaneous equations(Dzeroski & Todorovski 1994). It enumerates candidate models of an objective process based on a set of observations by using inductive logic programming technique. However, many redundant representations of the process are derived in high computational complexity, while the soundness of the solutions is not guaranteed.

The primary objective of this study is to establish a

method to discover admissible simultaneous equations governing a large scale process while maintaining the advantage of the recent scientific discovery approaches such as SDS. We set two assumptions on the feature of the objective process to be analyzed. One is that the objective process can be represented by a set of quantitative, continuous, complete and under-constrained simultaneous equations for the quantity ranges of our interest. Another is that all of the quantities in every equation can be measured, and all of the quantities except one dependent quantity can be controlled in every equation to their arbitrary values in the range under experiments while satisfying the constraints of the other equations. These assumptions are common in the past BACON family except the features associated with the simultaneous equations. The following studies have been conducted under these assumptions.

(1) Characterization of under-constrained simultaneous equations in terms of invariant structure of dependency among quantities.

(2) Algorithm to derive the invariant structure through experiments to control the objective process.

(3) Principle and algorithm to apply conventional scientific discovery approaches to separately derive each equation.

(4) Performance evaluation and demonstration of our proposing framework through various examples.

Based on the algorithm and the theory obtained in the studies from (1) to (3), we developed a tool program named "*Simultaneous Structure Finder (SSF)*". In the evaluation and demonstration of the study (4), SSF is combined with the aforementioned SDS, since SDS has an excellent feature to discover each complex equation appearing in large scale processes.

Basic Principle to Discover Simultaneous Equations

Insights Through an Example

First, we show an analysis of a simple process represented by under-constrained simultaneous equations to provide some important insights on the basic principle proposed in this research. Figure 1 depicts an electric circuit consisting of two parallel resistances and a battery. It can be modeled by the following equations.

$$V_1 = I_1 R_1 \; [1], \; V_2 = I_2 R_2 \; [2],$$
$$V_e = V_1 \; [3] \text{ and } V_e = V_2 \; [4], \quad (1)$$

where R_1, R_2:two resistances,
V_1, V_2:voltage differences across resistances,
I_1, I_2:electric current going through resistances
and V_e:voltage of a battery.

Another model of this circuit can be given.

$$I_1 R_1 = I_2 R_2 \; [1], \; V_2 = I_2 R_2 \; [2],$$
$$V_e = V_1 \; [3] \text{ and } V_e = V_2 \; [4]. \quad (2)$$

Both representations give correct behaviors of the circuit. However, the former seems more natural and

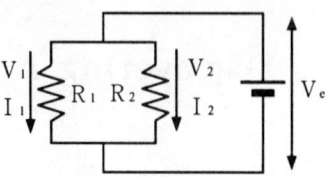

Figure 1: An circuit of parallel resistances.

comprehensive than the latter in spite of their quantitative equivalence. This may be due to the different configuration of quantities in each equation system. The configuration of the quantities in a set of simultaneous equations is represented by an "*incidence matrix*" T where its rows correspond to the mutually independent equations and its columns to the quantities. If the j-th quantity appears in the i-th equation, then the (i,j) element of T, i.e., T_{ij}, is 1, and otherwise T_{ij} is 0 (Murota 1987). The following two expressions represent the incidence matrices T_1 for Eqs.(1) and T_2 for Eqs.(2) respectively.

$$T_1 = \begin{bmatrix} V_e & V_1 & V_2 & I_1 & I_2 & R_1 & R_2 \\ 0 & 1 & 0 & 1 & 0 & 1 & 0 \\ 0 & 0 & 1 & 0 & 1 & 0 & 1 \\ 1 & 1 & 0 & 0 & 0 & 0 & 0 \\ 1 & 0 & 1 & 0 & 0 & 0 & 0 \end{bmatrix} \quad (3)$$

$$T_2 = \begin{bmatrix} 0 & 0 & 0 & 1 & 1 & 1 & 1 \\ 0 & 0 & 1 & 0 & 1 & 0 & 1 \\ 1 & 1 & 0 & 0 & 0 & 0 & 0 \\ 1 & 0 & 1 & 0 & 0 & 0 & 0 \end{bmatrix} \quad (4)$$

More strictly speaking, when a subset consisting of n independent equations containing n undetermined quantities are obtained by exogenously specifying the values of some extra quantities in the under-constrained simultaneous equations, the values of those n quantities are determined by solving the equations in the subset. In terms of an incidence matrix, exogenous specification of a quantity value corresponds to eliminating the column of the quantity. Accordingly, the partial solvability of the under-constrained simultaneous equations can be restated as when each of n columns come to contain nonzero element in some of n rows by eliminating some extra columns in an incidence matrix, the quantities corresponding to the n columns are determined. Such an equation subset corresponding to the n rows is called a "*complete subset*" of order n in this paper. In the former model of the electric circuit, if we exogenously specify the values of V_e and R_1, the first, the third and the forth rows of T_1 come to contain the three nonzero columns of V_1, V_2 and I_1. Thus these equations form a complete subset of order 3, and the three quantities are determined while the others, I_2 and R_2, are not. On the other hand, if the identical specification on V_e and R_1 is made in the latter model, no complete subset of order 3 is obtained, since every combination of three rows in T_2 contains more than three nonzero columns. In the real electric circuit, the validity of the consequence derived by the former model is clear. In fact, the former model gives correct answers for any combinations of quantities exogenously specified, while the latter becomes erroneous in some cases. The model having the incidence matrix which always derives valid interpretations of the determination of quantities of an objective process is named "*structural form*" in this paper.

Characterizing Simultaneous Equations

Now, more strict formalization and characterization of under-constrained simultaneous equation processes are given. For the basis of the formalization, some fundamental definitions are introduced first.

Definition 1 (incidence matrix) *Given a set of mutually independent simultaneous equations which is a model of an objective process, $E = \{eq_i | i = 1, ...M\}$, containing a set of quantities, $Q = \{q_j | j = 1, ..., N\}$, a matrix T is called an "incidence matrix" for E and Q, where $T_{ij} = 1$ if $q_j(\in Q)$ appears in $eq_i(\in E)$, otherwise $T_{ij} = 0$. Here, T_{ij} is an (i,j) element of T.*

Definition 2 (complete subset) *Given an incidence matrix T, after applying elimination of a set of columns, $RQ(\subset Q)$, let a set of nonzero columns of $T[CE, Q - RQ]$ be $NQ(\subseteq Q - RQ)$, where $CE \subseteq E$, and $T[CE, Q - RQ]$ is a sub-incidence matrix for equations in CE and quantities in $Q - RQ$. CE is called a "complete subset" of order n, if $|CE| = |NQ| = n$. Here, $|\bullet|$ stands for the cardinality of a set.*

Based on these definitions, some characteristics of a complete subset are derived.

Theorem 1 (symmetry theorem) *Given a complete subset CE of order n under the elimination of a set of columns RQ in T where $|RQ| = m$, let a set of nonzero columns in $T[CE, Q]$ be CQ, where $T[CE, Q]$ is a sub-incidence matrix for equations in CE and all quantities in Q. Under the elimination of any subset RQ_i of CQ where $|RQ_i| = m$ and $i = 1, ..., {}_{(n+m)}C_m$, CE is a complete subset of order n.*

Proof. Because NQ is a set of nonzero columns of $T[CE, Q - RQ]$, $CQ = RQ + NQ$. $|CQ| = m + n$, since $|RQ| = m$ and $|NQ| = n$ by definition of a complete subset. For the elimination of any $RQ_i(\subset CQ)$ where $|RQ_i| = m$ and $i = 1, ..., {}_{(n+m)}C_m$, the rest of $NQ_i = CQ - RQ_i$ has the cardinality $(m+n) - m$, i.e., $|NQ_i| = n$. Thus, CE is a complete subset of order n for the elimination of any RQ_i. ∎

Theorem 2 (invariance theorem) *Given a transform $f : U_E \to U_E$ where U_E is the entire universe of equations. When CE is a complete subset of order n in T, $f(CE)$ is also a complete subset of order n, if $f(CE)$ for $CE \subset U_E$ maintains the number of equations and the nonzero column structure, i.e., $|CE| = |f(CE)|$ and $CQ = CQ_f$, where CQ_f is a set of nonzero columns in $T[f(CE), Q]$.*

Proof. Because of $CQ = CQ_f$, an identical set of nonzero columns NQ is obtained by eliminating RQ in both $T[CE, Q]$ and $T[f(CE), Q]$. When CE is a complete subset of order n, $|CE| = n$, and thus if $|CQ| = |CQ_f| = m + n$, then $|NQ|$ can be n by choosing RQ to be $|RQ| = m$. Under such a RQ, $|CE| = |f(CE)| = |NQ| = n$, and $f(CE)$ satisfies the condition of a complete subset of order n. ∎

Remark 1 *The "symmetry theorem" indicates that given an objective simultaneous equation process, every complete subset can be identified independent of the choice of quantities to be exogenously controlled in the experiment, as far as it controls the required number m of the quantities involved in each subset. An efficient, complete and sound search algorithm can be developed based on this feature of a complete subset.*

Remark 2 *Our assumption on the controllability of the quantities admits one dependent quantity which can not be directly controlled in an equation. The "symmetry theorem" is the theoretical basis to correctly derive every complete subset and obtain valid quantitative form of each equation through the experiment. If a dependent quantity exits in a complete subset, the other controllable quantities in the subset can be used to constrain the subset and make up identical states.*

Remark 3 *Given a model of an objective process, various simultaneous equation formulae maintaining the equivalence of the quantitative relations and the dependency structure among quantities can be derived by limiting the equation transform f of the "invariance theorem" to the quantitative manipulation such as substitution and arithmetic operation among equations.*

In the example of the aforementioned electric circuit, if the value of V_e is exogenously specified in Eqs.(1), i.e., the first column of T_1 is eliminated, the third and forth rows of T_1 become to involve only two nonzero columns. Consequently, the set of equations $\{V_e = V_1[3], V_e = V_2[4]\}$ in Eqs.(1) is known to be a complete subset of order 2. These equations can be transformed by the linear algebra as follows while keeping their quantitative equivalence.

$$V_e = 2V_1 - V_2 \ [3], V_e = -V_1 + 2V_2 \ [4]. \quad (5)$$

For this third model, the following incidence matrix is obtained.

$$T_3 = \begin{array}{c} \\ \end{array} \begin{array}{cccccc} V_e & V_1 & V_2 & I_1 & I_2 & R_1 & R_2 \end{array} \\ \left[\begin{array}{ccccccc} 0 & 1 & 0 & 1 & 0 & 1 & 0 \\ 0 & 0 & 1 & 0 & 1 & 0 & 1 \\ 1 & 1 & 1 & 0 & 0 & 0 & 0 \\ 1 & 1 & 1 & 0 & 0 & 0 & 0 \end{array} \right] \quad (6)$$

By applying the elimination of the first column for V_e similarly to the case of T_1, the third and forth rows of T_3 become to involve only two nonzero columns, and thus the complete subset of order 2 consisting of the these two rows still remains in this new model.

As the complexity of the algorithm to enumerate all forms of a complete subset admitted by the transform f faces the combinatorial explosion, our approach identifies only one specific form defined bellow.

Definition 3 (canonical form of a complete subset) *Given a complete subset CE of order n, the "canonical form" of CE is the form where all elements of the nonzero columns CQ in its incidence matrix $T[CE, Q]$ are 1.*

An example of the canonical form of a complete subset is eq.5. Because every admissible form is mathematically equivalent with the others, the identification of the canonical form is sufficient, and the others can be derived by applying appropriate f to the form.

Though each complete subset represents a basic mechanism to determine the values of quantities in a given simultaneous equation process, some complete subsets are not mutually independent in many cases. For instance, the following four complete subsets can be found in the example of Eqs.(1).

$$\{[3], [4]\}(n=2), \quad \{[1], [3], [4]\}(n=3),$$
$$\{[2], [3], [4]\}(n=3), \quad \{[1], [2], [3], [4]\}(n=4) \quad (7)$$

The number in [ ] indicates each equation and n the order of the subset. They mutually have many overlaps, and the complete subsets having higher order represent the redundant mechanism with the lower subsets. The following theorem characterizes the dependency among complete subsets.

Theorem 3 (lattice theorem) *Given a model of an objective process consisting of equations E, the set of all complete subsets of the model, i.e., $L = \{\forall CE_i \subseteq E\}$, forms a lattice of the sets, where $CE_i \cup CE_j \in L$ and $CE_i \cap CE_j \in L, \forall CE_i, CE_j \in L$.*

Proof. Omitted. ∎

Theorem 4 (modular lattice theorem) *Given a model of an objective process consisting of equations E, the set of complete subsets of the model, i.e., $L = \{\forall CE_i \subseteq E\}$, forms a modular lattice of the sets for the order of the complete subsets, i.e., $n(CE_i \cup CE_j) = n(CE_i) + n(CE_j) - n(CE_i \cap CE_j)$ where n is the order of a given complete subset.*

Proof. The order of a complete subset is equal to its cardinality by definition. Because of the relation $|CE_i \cup CE_j| = |CE_i| + |CE_j| - |CE_i \cap CE_j|$, the relation among the order in the theorem is clear. ∎

Based on the modular lattice structure among complete subsets, the independent component and its order of each complete subset can be defined as follows.

Definition 4 (independent component of a complete subset) *The independent component DE_i of the complete subset CE_i is defined as*

$$DE_i = CE_i - \bigcup_{\substack{\forall CE_j \subset CE_i \\ \text{and } CE_j \in L}} CE_j.$$

The set of essential quantities DQ_i of CE_i which do not belong to any other complete subsets but involved only in CE_i is also defined as

$$DQ_i = CQ_i - \bigcup_{\substack{\forall CE_j \subset CE_i \\ \text{and } CE_j \in L}} CQ_j,$$

where CQ_i is a set of nonzero columns of $T(CE_i)$. The order δn_i and the freedom δm_i of DE_i are defined as

$$\delta n_i = |DE_i| \text{ and } \delta m_i = |DQ_i| - |DE_i|.$$

Remark 4 *An "independent component" of a complete subset represents an independent mechanism to determine the values of some quantities under a given dependency structure among quantities in a set of simultaneous equations. The values of quantities appearing only within an independent component DE_i can be changed with the δm_i degree of freedom without violating any other constraints.*

In the example of Eq.(7), the three independent components are derived.

$$\begin{aligned}
DE_1 &= \{[3], [4]\} - \phi = \{[3], [4]\}, \\
\delta n_1 &= 2 - 0 = 2, \\
DE_2 &= \{[1], [3], [4]\} - \{[3], [4]\} = \{[1]\}, \\
\delta n_2 &= 3 - 2 = 1, \\
DE_3 &= \{[2], [3], [4]\} - \{[3], [4]\} = \{[2]\}, \\
\delta n_3 &= 3 - 2 = 1.
\end{aligned} \quad (8)$$

Because of the monotonic structure of set inclusion in the modular lattice, a bottom up and greedy search is applicable without facing very high complexity of the algorithm to derive every independent component.

Because each independent component DE_i is a subset of the complete subset CE_i, the nonzero column structure of DE_i also follows the invariance theorem. Consequently, the subset of the canonical from of CE_i is applicable to represent DE_i. Based on this consideration, the definition of the canonical form of the simultaneous equations representing an given objective process is introduced.

Definition 5 (canonical form of simultaneous equations) *The "canonical form" of a set of simultaneous equations consists of the equations in $\cup_{i=1}^{b} DE_i$ where each equation in DE_i is represented by the canonical form in the complete subset CE_i, where b is the total number of DE_i.*

The incidence matrix of the model of the electric circuit can be derived in the canonical form T_4 based on the result of Eq.(8).

$$T_4 = \begin{array}{c} \begin{array}{cccccccc} V_e & V_1 & V_2 & I_1 & I_2 & R_1 & R_2 \end{array} \\ \left[\begin{array}{ccccccc} 1 & 1 & 1 & 1 & 0 & 1 & 0 \\ 1 & 1 & 1 & 0 & 1 & 0 & 1 \\ 1 & 1 & 1 & 0 & 0 & 0 & 0 \\ 1 & 1 & 1 & 0 & 0 & 0 & 0 \end{array}\right] \end{array} \quad (9)$$

If the canonical form of simultaneous equations are experimentally derived to reflect the actual dependency structure among quantities in the objective process, then the model must be a "*structural form*". Thus, the following terminology is introduced.

Definition 6 (structural canonical form) *If the canonical form of simultaneous equations is derived to be a "structural form", then the form is named "structural canonical form".*

The incidence matrix T_4 which has been obtained from a structural form T_1 corresponds to the structural canonical form for the example.

Algorithm of SSF and its Implementation

Under our aforementioned assumption on the measurements and the controllability of quantities, the bottom up and greedy algorithm indicated in Fig.2 has been developed and implemented into SSF. SSF requires a list of the quantities for the modeling of the objective process and their actual measurements. Starting from the set of control quantities having small cardinality, this algorithm tests if values of any quantities become to be fully under control. If such controlled quantities are found, the collection of the control quantities and the controlled quantities are considered as a newly found complete subset $|CE_i|$. Then, based on the definition 4, its $|DE_i|$, $|DQ_i|$, δn_i and δm_i are derived and stored. Once any independent components are derived, only δm_i of the quantities in every $|DQ_i|$ and the quantities which do not belong to any $|DQ_i|$ are used for control. Though the complexity of this algorithm is NP-hard, this constraint by $|DQ_i|$ significantly reduces the computation amount. as shown in the latter section. The constraint of $|DQ_i|$ does not miss any complete subset to search due to the monotonic lattice structure among complete subsets.

The conventional systems to discover a complete equation can not directly accept the knowledge of the structural canonical form for the discovery. The problem to derive quantitative knowledge of the simultaneous equations must be decomposed into sub-problems to derive each equation individually. Accordingly, an algorithm to decompose the entire problem into such small problems is also implemented into SSF. As previously stated in Definition 4, the values of the quantities within an independent component of each complete subset are mutually constrained in the order δn_i degree. Accordingly, the constraints within the independent component disable the bi-variate tests among the quantities of an equation in the structural canonical form, if the order δn_i is more than one. However, this difficulty is removed if the $(\delta n_i - 1)$ quantities are eliminated by the substitution of the other $(\delta n_i - 1)$ equations within the independent component. The reduction of the number of quantities by (δn_i-1) in each equation enables to control each quantities as if it is in

(S1) Let $Q = \{q_k | k = 1, ..., N\}$ be a set of quantities to appear in the model of an objective process. Set $X = \{x_k | x_k = q_k$, for all but directly controllable $q_k \in Q\}$, $DE = \phi$, $DQ = \phi$, $N = \phi$, $M = \phi$, $h = 1$ and $i = 1$.

(S2) Choose $C_j \subset DQ_j \in DQ$ for some DQ_j and also $C_x \subseteq X$, and take their union $C_{hi} = ... \cup C_j \cup ... \cup C_x$, while maintaining $|C_j| \leq \delta m_j$ and $|C_{hi}| = h$. Control all $x_k \in C_{hi}, k = 1, ..., |C_{hi}|$ in an experiment.

(S3) Let a set of all quantities which values are determined be $D_{hi} \subseteq (Q - C_{hi})$. Set $DE_{hi} = C_{hi} + D_{hi}$, $DQ_{hi} = DE_{hi} - \cup_{\forall DE_{h'i'} \subset DE_{hi} \atop DE_{h'i'} \in DE} DE_{h'i'}$, $\delta n_{hi} = |D_{hi}| - \sum_{\forall DE_{h'i'} \subset DE_{hi} \atop DE_{h'i'} \in DE} \delta n_{h'i'}$, and $\delta m_{hi} = |DQ_{hi}| - \delta n_{hi}$. If $\delta n_{hi} > 0$, then add DE_{hi} to the list DE, DQ_{hi} to the list DQ, δn_{hi} to the list N, δm_{hi} to the list M and $X = X - DQ_{hi}$.

(S4) If all quantities are determined, i.e., $D_{hi} = Q - C_{hi}$, then go to (S5), else if any more C_{hi} where $|C_{hi}| = h$ does not exist, $h = h + 1, i = 1$ and go to (S2), else $i = i + 1$ and go to (S2).

(S5) The contents of the lists DE, DQ and N represent the sets of quantities involved in independent components, the sets of essential quantities and their orders respectively.

Figure 2: Algorithm for structural canonical form

a complete equation. This elimination of quantities is essential to enable the application of the equation discovery system based on the bi-variate test. The reduction of quantities in equations provides further advantage, since the computation amount required in the equation search strongly depends on the number of quantities. In addition, the less degree of freedom of the objective equation in the search introduces more robustness against the noise in the data and the numerical error in the data fitting. The algorithm for the problem decomposition of SSF minimizes the number of quantities involved in each equation based on the admissible equation transform stated in the invariance theorem. Once quantitative form of each equation is obtained by the equation discovery system, then those forms can be transformed again into the different forms requested by the users.

Figure 3 indicates the algorithm to transform a structural canonical form to minimize the number of quantities in each equation. This algorithm uses the list of the complete subsets and their order resulted in the algorithm of Fig.2. The quantities involved in each equation are eliminated by the equations in the other complete subset in (S2). In the next (S3), the quantities involved in each equation are eliminated by the other equation within the same complete subset, if the order of the subset is more than one. The quantities to eliminate in (S2) and (S3) are selected by lexicographical order in the current SSF. This selection can be more

(S1) Let DE, DQ and N be the lists obtained in the algorithm of Fig.2.

(S2) For $i = 1$ to $|DE|$ {
  For $j = 1$ to $|DE|$ where $j \neq i$ {
    If $DE_i \supset DE_j$ where $DE_i, DE_j \in DE$ {
      $DE_i = DE_i - DQ'_j$,
      where DQ'_j is arbitrally, and
      $DQ'_j \subset DQ_j \in DQ$ and $|DQ'_j| = N_j$.}}}

(S3) For $i = 1$ to $|DE|$ {
  For $j = 1$ to N_i {
    $DE_{ij} = DE_i - DQ_{ij}$,
    where DQ_{ij} is arbitrally, and
    $DQ_{ij} \subset DQ_i \in DQ$ and $|DQ_{ij}| = N_i - 1$.}}

(S4) Every DE_{ij} shows the list of quantities contained in a transformed equation.

Figure 3: Algorithm for minimization.

tuned up based on the information of the sensitivity to noise and error of each quantities in the future.

Outline of SDS

The information required by SDS besides the knowledge given by SSF and the actual measurements is the scale-type of each quantity (Washio & Motoda 1997). The scale-types of measured quantities reflect the rules of the assignment of numerals to objects in the measurement process. The representative scale-types of the quantitative measurements are interval scale, ratio scale and absolute scale. Examples of the interval scale quantities are temperature in Celsius and musical tone where the origins of their scales are not absolute. Examples of the ratio scale quantities are physical mass and absolute temperature where each has an absolute zero point. The absolute scale quantities are dimensionless quantities.

The two important theorems called "extended Buckingham Π-theorem" and "extended product theorem" provide the basis of the equation search of SDS. Former states that any meaningful complete equation $\phi(x_1, x_2, x_3, ...) = 0$ consisting of the arguments of interval, ratio and absolute scale-types can be decomposed into an equation $F(\Pi_1, \Pi_2, ..., \Pi_{n-w}) = 0$ called an "ensemble equation," where n is the number of arguments of ϕ, w is the basic number of bases in $x_1, x_2, x_3....$, respectively. For all i, Π_i is an absolute scale-type quantity. Latter presents the following multiple formulae named "regimes" to represent Πs by interval and ratio scale-type quantities.

$$\Pi = (\prod_{x_i \in R} |x_i|^{a_i})(\prod_{I_k \subseteq I} (\sum_{x_j \in I_k} b_{kj}|x_j| + c_k)^{a_k})$$

$$\Pi = \sum_{x_i \in R} a_i \log|x_i| + \sum_{I_k \subseteq I} a_k \log(\sum_{x_j \in I_k} b_{kj}|x_j| + c_k) + \sum_{x_\ell \in I_g \subseteq I} b_{g\ell}|x_\ell| + c_g$$

where R and I are sets of ratio and interval scale type quantities, respectively. *all* coefficients except Π are constants and $I_k \cap I_g = \phi$. SDS initially seeks the relations of regimes represented in the extended product theorem through the bi-variate data fitting. Because "*scale-type constraint*" admits only these formulae as valid relations, the relations discovered by this approach have high possibility to represent first principle governing the objective process.

After all regime formulae are derived, SDS starts to seek the relation of ensemble equation by using "*identity constraint*". The basic principle of the identity constraints comes by answering the question that "*what is the relation among Θ_h, Θ_i and Θ_j, if $a(\Theta_j)\Theta_h + \Theta_i = b(\Theta_j)$ and $a(\Theta_i)\Theta_h + \Theta_j = b(\Theta_i)$ are known?*" The following answer is easily proven.

$$\Theta_h + \alpha_1 \Theta_i \Theta_j + \beta_1 \Theta_i + \alpha_2 \Theta_j + \beta_2 = 0$$

This principle is generalized to various relations among multiple terms.

Once a triplet of bi-variate relations is identified for a set of three quantities by using the aforementioned constraints, a certain consistency checking among the three relations called "*triplet test*" is applied to remove invalid relations due to the noise and error of data fitting.

The superior abilities of SDS have been confirmed of its low complexity, high robustness, high scalability and wide applicability (Washio & Motoda 1997). This is because of the introduction of these new types of mathematical constraints and tests.

Evaluation of SSF combined with SDS

The program of SSF has been developed in the environment of a numerical processing shell named MATLAB (Mat 1992). The knowledge of an equation in the structural canonical form discovered by SSF is transferred to SDS, and SDS executes its experiments based on the transferred knowledge and the knowledge of the scale-types of quantities. This process is iterated for each equation. The objective processes are provided by simulation in this research.

The performance of SSF has been evaluated in terms of the validity of its results and the computational complexity through some examples including quite large scale processes. In addition, the performance of the SDS combined with SSF is also checked through the same examples. The examples we applied are summarized as follows.

(1) Two parallel resistances and a battery
This is depicted in Fig.1, and has been already explained in the previous sections. Its model consists of 4 equations and 7 quantities as shown in Eqs.1.

(2) Heat conduction at walls of holes
Given a large solid material having two vertical holes, gas goes into those holes, and condensed to its liquid phase during the flow in the holes by providing its heat energy to the walls of the holes. In these holes, the heat conduction process are represented by the following 8 equations involving 17 quantities(Kalagnanam,

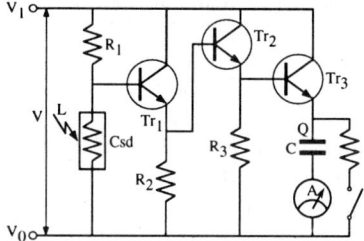

Figure 4: A circuit of photo meter.

Henrion, & Subrahmanian 1994).

$$\omega = 0.9423 \left(\frac{vsk^3}{L\mu}\right)^{1/4}, \quad \dot{H} = \dot{H}_1 + \dot{H}_2$$
$$\Delta T_1 = T_f - T_{w1}, \quad \Delta T_2 = T_f - T_{w2}$$
$$h_1 = \Delta T_1^{-1/4}\omega, \quad h_2 = \Delta T_2^{-1/4}\omega \quad (10)$$
$$\dot{H}_1 = 2\pi\gamma L h_1 \Delta T_1, \quad \dot{H}_2 = 2\pi\gamma L h_1 \Delta T_2$$

Here, v, s, k, μ are the latent heat per volume, density, heat conductance, viscosity in liquid phase of the fluid. L is the length of the holes, T_f temperature of the fluid, T_{w1} and T_{w2} temperature of walls of two holes. $\dot{H}$ is the total rate of heat conduction from the fluid to the wall material.

(3) A circuit of photo-meter

Figure 4 depicts a circuit of photo-meter to measure the rate of increase of photo intensity within a time period. The model of this system is represented by 14 equations involving 22 quantities. The contents of equations are not shown due to the limited space.

(4) Reactor core of power plant

A model of nuclear fission reaction process, heat removal of nuclear fuel, and heat and mass balance of reactor coolant is tested. This model involves 24 equations and 60 quantities.

Table 1 is the summary of the specifications of each problem size, complexity and robustness against noise. T_{scf} is to derive the structural canonical form and T_{min} to minimize the number of quantities appearing in each equation. T_{tl} and T_{av} are the total and the average time per equation required by SDS. T_{scf} shows strong dependency to the parameter m and n, i.e., the size of the problem. This is natural, since the algorithm to derive structural canonical forms is NP-hard to the size. T_{scf} also moderately depends on the difference between the numbers of quantities and equations in the model, i.e. $n - m$. This seems reasonable because the large number of $n - m$ represents the high degree of freedom of the objective simultaneous equations. This also exponentially increases the search space. In contrast, T_{min} shows very slight dependency to the size of the problem, and the absolute value of the required time is negligible. This observation is also highly consistent with the theoretical view that its complexity should be only $O(n^2)$. The total time T_{tl} required by SDS seems not to strongly depend on the size of the problem. This consequence is also very natural, because SDS handles each equations separately. The required time of SDS should be proportional to the number of equations in the model. Instead, the efficiency of the SDS more sensitively depends on the average number of quantities involved in an equation. This tendency becomes clearer by comparing T_{av} with av. In the past study, the complexity of SDS is known to be around $O(n^2)$. The relation between T_{av} and av roughly follows this claim. Thus, T_{tl} may vary almost in $O(mn^2)$. In short summary, the complexity of SSF shown in the result of T_{scf} seems to be crucial for a large scale problem, However, the performance shown in the Table 1 may be sufficient for numbers of engineering problems.

Table 1: Statistics on complexity and robustness

Ex.	m	n	av	T_{scf}	T_{min}	T_{tl}	T_{av}	NL
(1)	4	7	2.5	3	0.00	206	52	35
(2)	8	17	3.9	1035	0.05	725	91	29
(3)	14	22	2.6	1201	0.05	773	55	31
(4)	26	60	4.0	42395	0.11	3315	128	26

m: number of equation, n: number of quantities, av: average number of quantities/equation, T_{scf}: CPU time (sec) to derive structural canonical form, T_{min}: CPU time to derive minimum quantities form, T_{tl}: CPU time to derive all equations by SDS, T_{av}: average CPU time per equation by SDS, NL: limitation of % noise level of SDS.

The last column of Table 1 shows the influence of the noise to the result of SSF+SDS, where Gaussian noise is artificially introduced to the measurements. The noise does not affect the computation time in principle. The result showed that 25-35% of relative noise amplitude to the absolute value of each quantity was acceptable at the maximum under which 8 times per 10 trials of SSF+SDS successfully give the correct structure and coefficients of all equations with statistically acceptable errors. The noise sensitivity dose not increase significantly, because SSF focuses on a complete subset which is a small part of the entire system. Similar discussion holds for SDS. The robustness of SDS combined with SSF against the noise is sufficient for practical application.

Finally, the validity of the results are checked. In the example (1), SSF derived the expected structural canonical form shown in Eq.9. Then SSF gave the following form of minimum number of quantities to SDS. Here, each equation is represented by a set of quantities involved in the equation.

$$\{V_e, R_1, I_1\}, \{V_e, R_2, I_2\}, \{V_e, V_1\}, \{V_e, V_2\} \quad (11)$$

As a result, SDS derived the following answer.

$$V_e = I_1 R_1 \ [1], V_e = I_2 R_2 \ [2],$$
$$V_e = V_1 \ [3] \text{ and } V_e = V_2 \ [4], \quad (12)$$

This is equivalent with Eq.1 not only in the sense of the invariance theorem but also the quantitativeness. In the example (2), SSF derived the following structural canonical form.

$$\{\dot{H}, \dot{H}_1, \dot{H}_2\}, \{\omega, v, s, k, L, \mu\},$$
$$\{\Delta T_1, T_f, T_{w1}\}, \{\Delta T_2, T_f, T_{w2}\},$$
$$\{h_1, \Delta T_1, \omega\}, \{h_2, \Delta T_2, \omega\}, \quad (13)$$
$$\{\dot{H}_1, \Delta T_1, \gamma, L, h_1, \omega\}, \{\dot{H}_2, \Delta T_2, \gamma, L, h_2, \omega\}.$$

Then, by the elimination of ω in the last two equations by substituting the fifth and the sixth equations, SSF gave the form of minimum number of quantities which configuration is identical with the original. Then, SDS successfully reconstructed the equations in Eqs.10. Similarly almost original equations could be reconstructed in the other examples, and they have been confirmed to be equivalent to the original in the sense of the invariant theorem and quantitativeness.

Discussion and Related Work

The form of the process models in which the appearance of quantities are minimized resulted by SSF is quite close to the configuration of our familiar models in many cases. This might be because the less connection links among equations through quantities clarify the process represented by each equations, and hence the models obtained by SSF and SDS can provide comprehensive knowledge of the objective processes.

As mentioned in the introduction, the conventional equation discovery systems can derive only one or a few complete equation(s) with high computational complexity. SSF and its background theory, not only to overcome this limitation, provide generic tool and measure which can be combined with any conventional equation discovery systems. Moreover, the background theory can be used in more generic manner to identify various simultaneous structures embedded in real systems. It can be applied to some discrete systems as far as the systems have structures to propagate states through simultaneous constraints.

The basic theory of complete subsets in simultaneous equations can be seen as an extension of the causal ordering theory (Iwasaki & Simon 1986). A complete subset involves many candidates of self-contained subsets. A part of a complete subset becomes a self-contained subset once the exogenous specification of the values of some quantities is given. The structural form introduced in this research is also an extension of structural equations (Iwasaki & Simon 1986). Our theory gives more precise definition and characterization of structural equations.

Conclusion

The research presented here characterized underconstrained simultaneous equations in terms of complete subsets, and provided an algorithm to derive the structure through experiments. In addition, an algorithm to apply conventional scientific discovery to simultaneous equations are established. These are implemented into a generic tool named SSF, and its significant performance under the combination with a discovery system SDS have been readily confirmed.

A remained but important problem is to establish more efficient algorithm of SSF.

References

Dzeroski, S., and Todorovski, L. 1994. Discovering Dynamics: From Inductive Logic Programing to Machine Discovery. *Journal of Intelligent Information Systems* 3:1–20.

Falkenhainer, B., and Michalski, R. 1986. Integrating Quantitative and Qualitative Discovery: The ABACUS System. *Machine Learning* 367–401.

Huang, K., and Zytkow, J. 1996. Robotic discovery: the dilemmas of empirical equations. In *Proceedings of the Fourth International Workshop on Rough Sets, Fuzzy Sets, and Machine Discovery*.

Iwasaki, Y., and Simon, H. 1986. Causality in Device Behavior. *Artificial Intelligence* 3–32.

Kalagnanam, J.; Henrion, M.; and Subrahmanian, E. 1994. The Scope of Dimensional Analysis in Qualitative Reasoning. *Computational Intelligence* 10(2):117–133.

Koehn, B., and Zytkow, J. 1986. Experimenting and theorizing in theory formation. In *Proceedings of the International Symposium on Methodologies for Intelligent Systems*, 296–307. ACM SIGART Press.

Kokar, M. 1986. Determining Arguments of Invariant Functional Descriptions. *Machine Learning* 403–422.

The Math Works, Inc. 1992. *MATLAB Reference Guide*.

Murota, K. 1987. Systems Analysis by Graphs and Matroids - Structural Solvability and Controllability. *Algorithms and Combinatorics* 3.

Nordhausen, B., and Langley, P. 1990. An Integrated Approach to Empirical Discovery. In *Computational Models of Scientific Discovery and Theory Formation*. San Mateo, California: Morgan Kaufman Publishers.

P.W. Langley, H.A. Simon, G. B., and Zytkow, J. 1987. *Scientific Discovery; Computational Explorations of the Creative Process*. Cambridge, Massachusetts: MIT Press.

Schaffer, C. 1990. A Proven Domain-Independent Scientific Function-Finding Algorithm. In *Proceedings Eighth National Conference on Artificial Intelligence*. AAAI Press/The MIT Press.

Washio, T., and Motoda, H. 1997. Discovering Admissible Models of Complex Systems Based on Scale-Types and Identity Constraints. In *Proceedings of the Fifteenth International Joint Conference on Artificial Intelligence*.

Decompositional, Model-based Learning and its Analogy to Diagnosis

Brian C. Williams and William Millar [†]
NASA Ames Research Center, MS 269-2
Moffett Field, CA 94305 USA
E-mail: {williams, millar}@ptolemy.arc.nasa.gov

Abstract

A new generation of sensor rich, massively distributed autonomous system is being developed, such as smart buildings and reconfigurable factories. To achieve high performance these systems will need to accurately model themselves and their environment from sensor information. Accomplishing this on a grand scale requires automating the art of large-scale modeling. To this end we have developed *decompositional, model-based learning (DML)*. DML takes a parameterized model and sensed variables as input, decomposes it, and synthesizes a coordinated sequence of "simplest" estimation tasks. The method exploits a rich analogy between parameter estimation and consistency-based diagnosis. Moriarty, an implementation of DML, has been applied to thermal modeling of a smart building, demonstrating a significant improvement in learning rate.

A new generation of sensor rich, massively distributed, autonomous systems is being developed, such as networked building energy systems, autonomous space probes, and biosphere-like life support systems, that have the potential for profound environmental and economic change (Williams & Nayak 1996). To achieve high performance, these *immobile robots* will need to develop sophisticated regulatory systems that accurately and robustly control their complex internal functions. To accomplish this immobots will exploit a vast nervous system of sensors to accurately estimate models of themselves and their environment on a grand scale. Handling these large scale model estimation tasks requires high-level reasoning methods that coordinate a large set of traditional adaptive processes. Decompositional, model-based learning (DML) and its implementation Moriarty address this problem, providing a high-level reasoning method that generates and coordinates a set of nonlinear estimation codes, by exploiting a rich analogy to ATMS-based prime implicant generation(de Kleer 1986) and consistency-based diagnosis (e.g., (de Kleer & Williams 1987)).

[†]Caelum Research Corporation.

Large-scale Model-Estimation

Moriarty emerged out of work on the *Responsive Environment*, an intelligent building control system developed within the Ubiquitous Computing project at Xerox PARC, and is currently being developed to support a biosphere-like habitat for Mars.

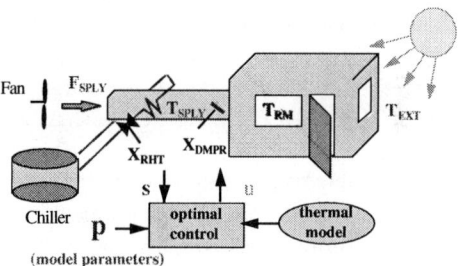

Figure 1: Office heating through an airduct.

Environmental control is made difficult by the overwhelming number of control variables, the tight coupling between control variables, and the slow response time of room temperature. Model-based control offers a natural solution, using a global model to adaptively predict where the optima lies. An informal evaluation of a non-linear, model-based controller using Xerox's responsive environment testbed suggests that energy savings in excess of 30% are conceivable (Zhang, Williams, & Elrod 1993).

The bottleneck is acquiring a model tailored to an individual building. Generic thermal models are available for complete buildings (e.g., the DOE2 simulator models), but these models are complex, containing on the order of thousands of equations and parameters for buildings with one hundred or more offices.

The technical challenge involves estimating the values of these parameters from sensor data, such as thermal conductance through walls and thermal capacity of an office's air space. An immobile robot can estimate its parameters by adjusting their values until the model best fits the sensor data. More precisely,

Definition 1 A *system model* is a set of algebraic equations $e(c; v) = 0$ over constants c and variables v. An *embedded system model* is a system model with unknown parameters $p \subset c$, sensed variables $s \subset v$, and sensor data D. An *estimator* (for p) is a function $f(x; p)$, where $x \subset s$, and such that $f(x; p) = 0$ follows from the system model.

Given an embedded system model and estimator $f(x; p)$, we can estimate p by solving, for example, the non-linear optimization problem,

$$p^* = arg \min_{p} \sum_{x_i \in D_x} f(x_i; p)^2.$$

A broad set of non-linear estimation codes are, of course, standard tools of the trade, used by physical scientists to extract parameters of physical phenomena. We make no contribution here to these basic algorithms. We simply note that the performance of these basic codes on non-linear physical models can quickly become inadequate as the dimension of the problem grows.

For example, consider office thermal modeling (Williams & Millar 1996) in figure 1. Heat flow into an office through a duct is regulated using a damper to control airflow via X_{dmpr}, and a radiator like device, called a reheat, to control air temperature via X_{rht}. Heat also flows from the sun, equipment, through walls and doorways. The thermal model of a single office consists of fourteen equations involving seventeen state variables and eleven parameters. About a third of the equations are nonlinear, such as,

$$F_{dmpr} = \left(\frac{\rho_{dmpr}(X_{dmpr})}{R_{dct}} \right) \sqrt{P_{dct}},$$

which relates air flow through the damper to duct pressure and duct air resistance as a function of damper position. Nine of the state variables are sensed, including temperature T, flow rate F, air pressure P, damper and reheat valve position X. Seven of the eleven parameter values are unknown and must be estimated. Estimating all seven parameters at once requires solving a 7-dimensional, nonlinear optimization problem involving a multi-modal objective space. Using arbitrary initial values, a Levenberg-Marquardt algorithm was applied repeatedly to this problem, but consistently became lost in local minima and did not converge after several hours.

Estimation Plans

To estimate parameters of higher dimensional systems a skilled modeler massages the physical equations into

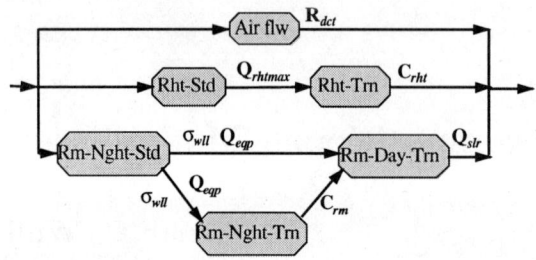

Figure 2: Model-estimation plan for a single office.

a tractable set of smaller parameter estimation tasks, coordinates their invocation and combines their results. For large modeling tasks that are an international priority, such as earth ecosystem modeling, an army of modelers can be employed at great cost. For the important, but more modest tasks performed by immobile robots, this army must be automated if high performance and robustness are to be achieved. The open research problem that we address through Moriarty is to automate the modeler's process of synthesizing these estimation plans. Moriarty automates key aspects of how a community of modelers decomposes, simplifies and coordinates large scale model estimation tasks, and generates code to perform the parameter estimation.

The problem of decomposing and coordinating estimation tasks is not one that has received significant attention in the statistics or machine learning literature. The classical estimation literature offers a vast number of techniques, many available as subroutines in Matlab or Splus, for online and offline estimation of various families of linear and nonlinear estimation problems, using a variety of different objective criteria. However these techniques do not generate the codes that setup and coordinate these subroutines. The Bayesian learning community makes extensive use of graphical models to strongly bias estimation, hence improving convergence (Buntine 1994; Spiegelhalter & Lauritzen 1990) and qualitative reasoning (QR) work exploits monotonicity constraints as a bias (Kay & Ungar 1993). However, research, for example, in graphical models and QR is only beginning to look at the model decomposition process (Shachter, Anderson, & Poh 1990; Stolle & Bradley 1996).

An estimation plan for the office model is shown above in figure 2. Each octagon in the diagram is an *estimation action* that is defined by an estimator of the form $y = f(x; p)$, applied to a subset of the sensors, parameters, and sensor data. The arc labels identify those parameters whose values are estimated in the preceding action. For example, the top octagon labeled "Air flw" produces an estimate for parameter

R_{dct}, the air resistance in the duct, using the estimator,

$$F_{ext} = (\rho_{lkg} + \rho_{dmpr}(X_{dmpr}))\frac{\sqrt{P_{dct}}}{R_{dct}}$$

derived from three equations in the office model pertaining to airflow. Note again that an estimator contains only *sensed* variables. This action exploits previously estimated parameters as constants (ρ_{lkg} and the coefficients of function $\rho_{dmpr}(X_{dmpr})$). The six estimators in the plan each contain only one or two unknown parameters, reducing the original seven dimensional problem to several problems of at most two dimensions.

Generating Estimation Plans

Consider a common sense account of the basic steps Moriarty uses to generate an estimation plan. First, Moriarty generates a set of possible estimation actions from the model. It then selects a subset of these actions sufficient to estimate all parameters, and coordinates the passing of estimated parameter values between these actions. Possible actions are generated in two steps: decomposition and simplification.

In the decomposition step, subsets of the model and sensors are identified that are sufficiently constrained to define an estimation problem, and are each turned into an estimator. For example, the estimator for the "Air flw" action described above was derived from the following air flow equations in $\mathbf{e}(\mathbf{c}; \mathbf{v})$,

$$\begin{aligned}
F_{ext} &= F_{lkg} + F_{dmpr}, \\
F_{lkg} &= \left(\frac{\rho_{lkg}}{R_{dct}}\right)\sqrt{P_{dct}}, \\
F_{dmpr} &= \left(\frac{\rho_{dmpr}(X_{dmpr})}{R_{dct}}\right)\sqrt{P_{dct}}.
\end{aligned}$$

In the thermal example, Moriarty's decomposition step automatically generates eight possible estimation actions in total, each containing as few as one parameter or as many as all seven. Three of these actions are "Air flw" (with single parameter R_{dct}), "Rht" (with two parameters Q_{rhtmax} and C_{rht}), and "Rm" (with four parameters, σ_{wll}, Q_{eqp}, C_{rm} and $Q_{slr}(t)$). It is purely coincidental that the parameter sets for these actions are disjoint.

These three actions are sufficient to estimate all seven model parameters. If we were to produce an estimation plan based on this alone, the result would have a single action for each of the three primary parallel paths in figure 2. While any subset of the possible actions that estimate all seven parameters could be chosen to form a plan, the above three actions contain the fewest parameters individually.

The simplification step is optional, and is not developed here technically; however, we summarize its result here, as it makes the coordination step of our example more interesting. This step produces one or more simplified versions of each estimation action that contain fewer parameters, by identifying conditions on the data such that influences by one or more parameters become negligible. For example, consider the estimator for action "Rm":

$$\frac{dT_{rm}}{dt} = \frac{C_0 F_{sply}(T_{sply} - T_{rm})}{C_{rm}} + \frac{Q_{eqp} + Q_{slr}(t) + \sigma_{wll}(T_{ext} - T_{rm})}{C_{rm}}$$

This estimator is simplified by noticing that solar effect $Q_{slr}(t)$ is negligible at night time, when the sun is down (action "Rm-Nght"), while it is significant during the day (action "Rm-Day-Trn"). Action "Rm-Nght" is generated from "Rm" by restricting the data set to data taken at night. This allows $Q_{slr}(t)$ to be eliminated, reducing the number of parameters in the estimator from four to the three parameters σ_{wll}, Q_{eqp} and C_{rm}. Six additional estimators are generated – "Rm-Nght-Std", "Rm-Nght-Trn", "Rm-Day-Std", "Rm-Day-Trn", "Rht-Std" and "Rht-Trn" – by applying similar simplifications to estimators "Rm-Nght", "Rm-Day" and "Rht" that focus on transient and steady state behaviors. Six of the resulting estimators are those appearing in the plan of figure 2. Note that these simplified estimators are currently generated manually. The algorithm we are currently developing to automate this simplification step is based on *caricatural modeling*, described in (Williams & Raiman 1994).

Having generated these possible estimation actions, the coordination step selects and sequences a subset of the estimation actions to further simplify the search performed by each action. The parameter value estimated by an action, such as "Rm-Nght-Std", can be fed as a constant to a later action, such as "Rm-Day-Trn", reducing the dimensionality of the later action. Alternatively, an estimated parameter value can be exploited as an *initial* bias to the later action, by constraining its random restarts for the parameter based on the confidence in the previous estimate. The first policy more dramatically reduces the dimensionality of later actions, while the second policy can enable more refined estimates. We are currently evaluating the trade-offs. The plan in figure 2 treats passed parameter estimates as constants in later actions. For example, "Rm-Nght-Trn" is left only with C_{rm} as an unknown parameter.

Moriarty generates a "simplest" estimation plan using a greedy algorithm. This algorithm determines the next action to perform as follows: first, the action must have a minimal (but positive) number of unknown parameters; second, if two estimators have equal numbers of new parameters, then the action is selected that contains the fewest number of sensed variables. The first condition drives the convergence time downwards by reducing the dimensionality of the search space, while the second condition improves accuracy, by reducing the combined sensor error introduced.

The decomposition step automatically generates eight estimators F1-F8, characterized later in the experiments section. Invoking the greedy algorithm on these estimators generates a plan with three parallel actions, "Air-flw", "Rht" and "Rm", with one, two and four parameters, respectively. More interestingly, given the six estimators mentioned above under decomposition and simplification, the greedy algorithm generates the plan shown in figure 2, with each estimator containing at most two unknown parameters. The remaining sections turn to the details of decomposition.

Model Decomposition

The decomposition step determines a set of possible estimation actions that can be coordinated within an estimation plan. Estimation actions are generated by decomposing the model into a set of potentially overlapping sub-models, called *dissents*, and then by generating an estimator from each dissent. In this section we develop DML's concepts of *dissent* and *support*, and the role they play in the generation of estimation actions. As discussed later, dissent and support are inspired by the consistency-based diagnosis concepts of *conflict* and *environment*, respectively (de Kleer & Williams 1987; de Kleer, Mackworth, & Reiter 1992).

The office example is too complex for pedagogical purposes. Instead we introduce a modification of the standard polycell example from diagnosis. This example (figure 3) consists of five equations, one for each of the three multipliers M1, M2, M3 and two adders A1, A2. M1, for example, denotes the equation $x = a \times b$. The goal is to estimate unknown parameters b, d, f, s and t given sensed variables a, c, e, u and v. Variables x, y and z are dependent.

Recall that an estimation action solves an optimization problem that minimizes *disagreement* between a subset of the observables and a subset of the model. For a disagreement to exist the submodel must be *overdetermined*, given the sensed variables; that is, there must be at least two ways of uniquely determining the same value. We call an overdetermined submodel a *dissent*, and a submodel that uniquely determines a variable its *support*. More precisely,

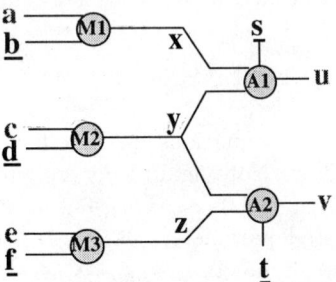

Figure 3: Polycell with $\mathbf{e} = \{M1, M2, M3, A1, A2\}$, $\mathbf{p} = \{b, d, f, s, t\}$ and $\mathbf{s} = \{a, c, e, u, v\}$.

Definition 2 Given a system model $S = \langle \mathbf{e}, \mathbf{s} \rangle$ with equations $\mathbf{e}(\mathbf{c}; \mathbf{v}) = \mathbf{0}$ and sensed variables $\mathbf{s}$, a *dissent* of S is a subsystem $\langle \mathbf{e_d}, \mathbf{s_d} \rangle$ of S, such that $\mathbf{e_d}(\mathbf{c}; \mathbf{v}) = \mathbf{0}$ is overdetermined given $\mathbf{s_d}$. $\langle \mathbf{e_d}, \mathbf{s_d} \rangle$ is a *minimal dissent* if no proper subsystem $\langle \mathbf{e'}, \mathbf{s'} \rangle$ of $\langle \mathbf{e_d}, \mathbf{s_d} \rangle$ exists such that $\langle \mathbf{e'}, \mathbf{s'} \rangle$ is a dissent of S.

Definition 3 Given system model $S = \langle \mathbf{e}, \mathbf{s} \rangle$ with variables $\mathbf{v}$, a *support* for variable $v_s \in \mathbf{v}$ is a subsystem $\langle \mathbf{e'}, \mathbf{s'} \rangle$ of S, such that $\langle \mathbf{e'}, \mathbf{s'} \rangle$ determines v_s, and no proper subsystem of $\langle \mathbf{e'}, \mathbf{s'} \rangle$ determines v_s.

Note that a pair of support for variable v_s provides two means of determining v_s. Hence the union of the pair overdetermine v_s, and constitutes a dissent $\langle \mathbf{e}_{s1} \cup \mathbf{e}_{s2}, \mathbf{s}_{s1} \cup \mathbf{s}_{s2} \rangle$. We exploit this fact in the next section to generate dissents from a set of support.

The goal of decomposition is to generate a set of "simplest" estimation actions. A minimal dissent captures the intuition of "simplest" subproblem for two reasons. First, minimality increases convergence rate, by minimizing the number of parameters appearing in each dissent's equations $\mathbf{e}(\mathbf{c}; \mathbf{v}) = \mathbf{0}$, and hence the dimensionality of the optimization problem. In addition, minimality improves accuracy by minimizing the number of sensed variables $\mathbf{s}$ per estimation, and hence the amount of noise introduced.

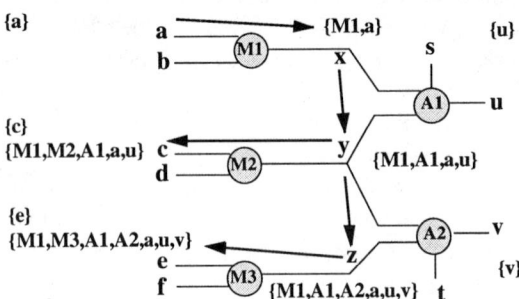

Figure 4: Examples of support in Polycell.

Returning to the example, figure 4 shows several examples of support for polycell. Note first the trivial support at each sensed variable: a sensed variable is its own support. Next, beginning with trivial support at a, u and v, and moving out towards c and e, a support is provided for each variable along the way. For example, y has support $\{M1, A1, a, u\}$. Note also that c and e each have pairs of support. The union of each pair comprises a (minimal) dissent, D1 and D2 respectively. A final dissent, not shown, results in D1–D3:

D1: $\{M1, M2, A1, a, c, u\} \Rightarrow b, d, s$
D2: $\{M1, M3, A1, A2, a, e, u, v\} \Rightarrow b, f, s, t$
D3: $\{M2, M3, A2, c, e, v\} \Rightarrow d, f, t$

To the left of the arrow is the set of equations and sensed variables for each dissent. To the right is the set of parameters mentioned in the dissent's equations, hence, those that can be estimated using that dissent.

Next, defining an estimation action represented by a minimal dissent $\langle \mathbf{e_d}, \mathbf{s_d} \rangle$ involves generating an estimator $\mathbf{y} = f(\mathbf{x}; \mathbf{p})$ and setting up a corresponding optimization problem. For example, dissent D1 consists of equations M1, M2, A1:

$$x = a \times b$$
$$y = c \times d$$
$$u = x + y + s.$$

Solving for u in D1 produces $u = a \times b + c \times d + s$, resulting in the estimation action,

$$\mathbf{p}^* = arg \min_{\mathbf{p}} \sum_{\langle a_i, c_i, u_i \rangle T \in D} (u_i - [b \times a_i + d \times c_i + s])^2$$

where the parameters are $\mathbf{p} = \langle b, d, s \rangle^T$.

As discussed in the next section, to address tractability, Moriarty only generates those dissents composed of equations that are free of simultaneities. Solving this set of equations, to generate an estimator, is straightforward (see (Williams & Millar 1996)).

The Support Maintenance System

To generate support and (minimal) dissents we need conditions for identifying when a subsystem is uniquely determined or (minimally) over-determined, respectively. An appropriate choice of conditions hinges upon the computational price one is willing to pay.

A standard presumption, made by causal ordering research (e.g., see (Iwasaki & Simon 1986)), and frequently used for analyzing models of nonlinear physical systems, is that n independent model equations and exogenous variables uniquely determine n unknowns.

Assumption 1 *Given system $\langle \mathbf{e}, \mathbf{s} \rangle$ with variables $\mathbf{v}$, let $\langle \mathbf{e}', \mathbf{s}' \rangle$ be any of its subsystems, $\mathbf{v}'$ its variables, $n = |\mathbf{e}'|$, $m = |\mathbf{s}'|$ and $l = |\mathbf{v}'|$. We assume that subsystem $\langle \mathbf{e}', \mathbf{s}' \rangle$ is (a) overdetermined if $n + m > l$, (b) dissenting if $n + m = l + 1$, (c) uniquely determined if $n + m = l$, and (d) underdetermined if $n + m < l$.*

Note that this condition holds universally for linear systems, and is true of many *physical* systems.

The power of this condition is that it is trivial to evaluate; for example, it is far easier than identifying minimal dissents with a series of subset tests, or solving the system of equations. In addition, the condition doesn't require knowledge of the form of an equation, just the variables each equation interacts with. Moriarty uses this condition to decompose a graph of interactions into estimation subproblems, without restriction on, or further knowledge about, the form of the underlying equations. This is in the spirit of graphical learning methods, such as (Buntine 1994; Shachter, Anderson, & Poh 1990).

To generate minimal dissents, recall that a dissent is the union of two support for some variable. Hence minimal dissents can be generated from a set of support, by computing all such unions, and selecting those that satisfy condition (b). Furthermore, if the equations of the system are invertible, then it follows trivially that all dissents can be generated just from the support of the sensed variables $\mathbf{s}$.

To generate support we exploit an analogy to the concept of *prime implicant*, from propositional logic. A (theory) implicant for proposition p is a set of literals whose conjunction entails p, given propositional theory T. The implicant is prime if the set of literals is minimal under subset. While a support determines a variable's value, an implicant entails a proposition. The sensed variables of a support are analogous to the literals of the implicant, and the equations of a support are analogous to the subset of the theory that, together with the implicant, entails p.

An assumption-based truth maintenance system (de Kleer 1986) is an example of a restricted form of prime implicant algorithm that has proven useful in practice. The ATMS generates implicants that are comprised of a distinguished set of literals, called *assumptions,* given a theory that is horn. The implicants generated by the ATMS are referred to as *environments*.

Moriarty generates candidate support by exploiting the analogy to ATMS environments, and then uses condition (c) to quickly test that the candidate is uniquely determined, and hence constitutes a support. ATMS environments are generated by propagating them locally through a network of horn clauses, starting at the literals denoting assumptions, combining and then propagating a new set of environments after each traversal of a clause. Analogously, Moriarty generates a support by propagating them locally through the network of equations, starting at the sensed variables, combining and then propagating a new set of support after each traversal of an equation. A single path of propagation for polycell is shown in figure 4.

The propagation algorithm is called a support maintenance system (SMS), to highlight its analogy to an ATMS. The SMS uses the function *CreateDecomposition* to kick off propagation, by adding to each sensed variable v a trivial support $\{v\}$, indicating that v is independent. For polycell, this type of support is added to sensed variables a, c, e, u, and v.

CreateDecomposition($\langle e, s \rangle$)
/* system model $\langle \mathbf{e}, \mathbf{s} \rangle$ */
Initialize *dissents* to empty
for each $s_i \in \mathbf{s}$
   $trivialSupport = \{\{\}, \{s_i\}\}$
   AddSupport(s_i, trivialSupport)
return *dissents*

After recording a new support, *AddSupport* tries to propagate the new support through successive local equations (partial results for propagating from a are shown in figure 4). For example, support $\{a\}$ propagates through $M1$ to x, creating new support $\{M1, a\}$. In addition, if a non-trivial support is being added to a sensed variable, then it is turned into a dissent. For example, when the support $\{M1, M2, A1, a, u\}$ is added to sensed variable c, the dissent $\{M1, M2, A1, a, c, u\}$ is generated.

AddSupport(v, $\langle \mathbf{e}, \mathbf{s} \rangle$)
/* variable v, support $\langle \mathbf{e}, \mathbf{s} \rangle$ */
Add $\langle \mathbf{e}, \mathbf{s} \rangle$ to the support of v
for each $e_i \in$ set of equations involving v
  if $e_i \notin \mathbf{e}$ then
    for each $co \in$ *CausalOrientations(e_i, v)*
      Propagate(v, $\langle \mathbf{e}, \mathbf{s} \rangle$, co)
if $\mathbf{e} \neq \{\}$ and *Sensed?(v)* then
  Add $\langle \mathbf{e}, \mathbf{s} \cup \{v\} \rangle$ to *dissents*

Propagation requires an equation that acts as a conduit, a variable to be propagated to (called the *effect*) and a set of variables that support this effect (called the *cause*). The function *CausalOrientations* generates the set of all ways the equation e can be oriented about a cause variable v to determine a new effect variable y, from complementary, cause variables $\mathbf{x}$. For polycell, given cause variable x and equation $A1$, y or u may be selected as effects, with the remaining variable and x acting as the cause.

CausalOrientations(e, v)
/* equation e, cause variable v */
$\mathbf{v}$ = set of variables in e
return $\{\langle y, e, \mathbf{x} \rangle | y \in \mathbf{v}, \mathbf{x} = \mathbf{v} - \{y\}, v \in \mathbf{x}\}$

The core of the algorithm is *Propagate*, which passes a new support through an equation e to effect y. It uses the function *WeaveSupport* to take the union of a newly added support to a variable v, with a support for each of the other causes $(\mathbf{x} - \{v\})$, producing a composite subsystem c. Within WeaveSupport, S denotes a set of new support, S_2 is the set of support for one of the other cause variables, h, and S_c represents the set of all composite support constructed. Propagate then adds e to each composite c in S_c to produce candidate support S_w for effect v. For example, suppose Propagate is given new support $\{M1, a\}$ for x, and equation $A1$, with effect y and causes $\{u, x\}$. WeaveSupport selects the support $\{u\}$ for u, combines this with the new support to produce $\{M1, a, u\}$. Propagate then adds $A1$ to produce the new support $\{M1, A1, a, u\}$ for y. The effects of each propagate are indicated by arrows in figure 4.

Note that there are cases where a support being generated by Propagate or WeaveSupport is thrown away. First, to avoid circularities, propagate will not propagate through an equation mentioned in the new support. Likewise, it will not add a composite support to an effect if the effect is mentioned in that support. For WeaveSupport note that the union of a set of support may either be uniquely determined or overdetermined, depending on the sharing of variables and equations between the support being combined. The later case is ruled out by the "Overdetermined?" test, in the construction of S'_c.

Propagate(v, $\langle \mathbf{e}, \mathbf{s} \rangle$, $\langle y, e, \mathbf{x} \rangle$)
/* equation e, y its effect, $\mathbf{x}$ its causes,
   $v \in \mathbf{x}$, support $\langle \mathbf{e}, \mathbf{s} \rangle$ */
if $e \notin \mathbf{e}$ then
  $S_w = WeaveSupport(v, \{\langle \mathbf{e}, \mathbf{s} \rangle\}, e, \mathbf{x})$
  for each $\langle \mathbf{e}_w, \mathbf{s}_w \rangle \in S_w$
    if $y \notin$ set of variables in $\mathbf{e}_w$ then
      AddSupport(y, $\langle \mathbf{e}_w \cup \{e\}, S_w \rangle$)
end

WeaveSupport(v, S, e, $\mathbf{x}$)
/* equation e, its causes $\mathbf{x}$, $v \in \mathbf{x}$,
   & its supporters S */
if $\mathbf{x}$ is empty, then
  return S
else
  h = a variable in $\mathbf{x}$
  $R = \mathbf{x} - \{h\}$
  if $h = v$, then
    return *WeaveSupport(ϕ, S, e, R)*
  else
    $S_2 = \{\langle \mathbf{e}, \mathbf{s} \rangle | \langle \mathbf{e}, \mathbf{s} \rangle \in Support(h), e \notin \mathbf{e}\}$

$$S_c = \{\langle \mathbf{e} \cup \mathbf{e}_2, \mathbf{s} \cup \mathbf{s}_2\rangle|$$
$$\langle \mathbf{e}, \mathbf{s}\rangle \in S, \langle \mathbf{e}_2, \mathbf{s}_2\rangle \in S_2\}$$
$$S'_c = \{s|s \in S_c, \neg Overdetermined?(s)\}$$
return *WeaveSupport(v,S'_c,e,R)*

The SMS is sound, since after weaving support the SMS checks and records support only if they are uniquely determined according to condition (c). With respect to completeness, we return to the analogy. For an ATMS, the set of environments generated by local propagation is incomplete for general clausal theories. However, it is complete for horn clause theories. Analogously, if a support is a system of simultaneous equations, then it will not be identified through the above local propagation algorithm, since the simultaneity represents a codependence between variables. The algorithm does, however, generate all support that are *simultaneity-free*. Soundness and completeness are evaluated further in (Williams & Millar 1996).

Analogy to Diagnosis

In addition to the analogy between support and prime implicants, there exists a strong analogy between model-estimation and consistency-based diagnosis, and their respective decomposition methods. Model-estimation and consistency-based diagnosis problems identify a set of *parameter values* and *modes*, respectively, that *minimize disagreement* between the model and the observables. In diagnosis, each mode is discrete and finite. Treating polycell as a diagnosis problem, the mode variables are M1, M2, M3, A1 and A2, each with the two modes OK and not-OK. In estimation, parameter values can be a mixture of continuous and discrete.

Both problems involve measuring a disagreement between model and observables. In estimation, the disagreement is usually a continuous error defined by a *Euclidean metric*. The error is to be minimized by the estimated parameters. In consistency-based diagnosis, logical disagreement can be framed using a *discrete metric*, which treats the distance between two values u and v as 1 unless they are equal, in which case the distance is 0. Diagnosis amounts to searching for a set of modes that bring the disagreement between model and observables to 0.

Turning to the decomposition process, a simplest diagnostic subproblem is a minimal subset of the component models and observed values that are inconsistent. This is loosely the concept of a *minimal conflict*, which is a minimal set of components, whose nominal models disagree with the observables (de Kleer & Williams 1987).* For example, assuming polycell has the values $a = 3, b = 2, c = 3, d = 2, e = 3, f = 2$,

---
*The subtle, although important, difference is that a

$u = 10$ and $v = 12$, then there are two minimal conflicts, $\{M1, M2, A1\}$, and $\{M1, M3, A1, A2\}$.

Shifting to estimation, we replace logical inconsistency (a conflict) with a system being overdetermined (a dissent). There is an important distinction between conflict and dissent. The inconsistency indicated by a conflict is unequivocal, while a dissent merely indicates the potential for error, hence, our use of a more mild term – "dissent" – in naming this form of disagreement. For example, polycell has three dissents, but only two conflicts. There is no conflict corresponding to dissent D3. The reason is that the potential for disagreement in D3, is not realized for the particular values assigned to the sensed variables in the diagnosis example, hence no conflict exists.

As we've already seen, this analogy continues down into the concepts of support, environment and their respective generation. This suggests the opportunity for developing a rich unification of large-scale model-based learning and diagnostic methods.

Experiments and Discussion

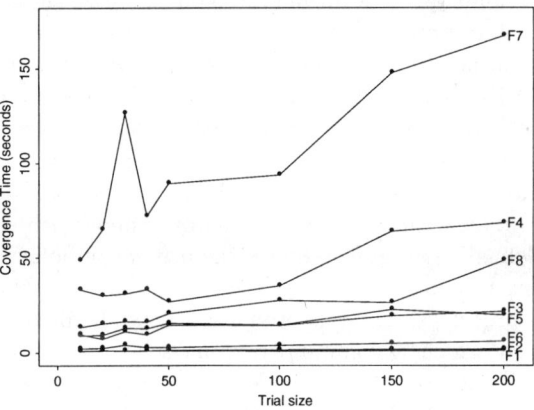

Figure 5: Convergence rate vs data size for the generated estimators F1–F8.

Moriarty implements all of DML except for the optional simplification step, using Mathematica for symbolic manipulation and Splus for statistical analysis. Consider Moriarty's performance on the office thermal example (figure 5) using dissent generation, but without the simplification step. Moriarty generates eight estimators, F1 – F8, in the decomposition step, and sequences them to produce $\langle F2, F1, F6\rangle$, which correspond to the "Air-Flw," "Rht," and "Rm" estimation actions. We compare the performance of the eight

---
conflict doesn't include the subset of observed values that are involved in the inconsistency.

estimators by running them against sensor data sets ranging in size from 10 to 200, shown above. The y axis denotes time required to converge on a final estimate of parameters involved in the dissent. The plot labeled F7 is for the original seven dimensional estimator, while plots F2, F1, and F6 are the three estimators in Moriarty's sequence. Higher dimensional estimators, like F7, tend to fail to converge given arbitrary initial conditions, hence ball-park initial parameter estimates were supplied to allow convergence in the higher dimensional cases. Decomposition leads to significant speed-up even when good initial estimates were available. For example, at trial size 200, the original estimator requires 166 seconds, while the total time to estimate all parameters using F2, F1, and F6 is under 9 seconds. This represents a speed up by a factor of 14.

In addition the sequence requires less data to converge. This is important for self-modeling systems that use online estimation to quickly track time-varying parameters. Employing the rule of thumb that the data set size should be roughly ten fold the dimension of the parameter space, F7 would require around 70 data points, while the F2, F1, F6 sequence requires only 40. The anomalous slow down in the convergence rate of F7 at 25 data points is attributed to insufficient data. Finally, although not included, parameter accuracy, measured by the confidence interval of each parameter is also improved using the generated sequence.

To summarize, a model-based approach is essential for regulating systems of the size of most immobile robots. Embodying an immobile robot with self-modeling capabilities requires the use of symbolic reasoning to coordinate a large set of autonomic estimation processes. This coordination should mimic the way in which a community of modelers decompose, simplify and coordinate modeling problems on a grand challenge scale. DML automates one aspect of this rich model decomposition and analysis planning process, by exploiting an analogy between model estimation, prime implicant generation and consistency-based diagnosis, and by introducing the concepts of dissent, support, and support maintenance system, analogous to conflicts, environment and the ATMS. Turning to the future, we are beginning to develop Moriarty to support a "biosphere-like" habitat, called a closed loop ecological life support system, and an *insitu* propellant plant for NASA's Mars exploration program.

Acknowledgements

Thanks to Sonia Leach and the Responsive Environment team at Xerox PARC – Zhang Ying, Scott Elrod and Joseph O'Sullivan for their support. Jim Kurien and Pandu Nayak provided valuable feedback.

References

Buntine, W. L. 1994. Operations for learning with graphical models. *Journal of Artificial Intelligence Research* 2:159–225.

de Kleer, J., and Williams, B. C. 1987. Diagnosing multiple faults. *Artificial Intelligence* 32(1):97–130.

de Kleer, J., and Williams, B. C. 1989. Diagnosis with behavioral modes. In *Proceedings of IJCAI-89*, 1324–1330.

de Kleer, J.; Mackworth, A.; and Reiter, R. 1992. Characterizing diagnoses and systems. *Artificial Intelligence* 56:197–222.

de Kleer, J. 1986. An assumption-based TMS. *Artificial Intelligence* 28(1):127–162.

Iwasaki, Y., and Simon, H. 1986. Theories of causal ordering: Reply to de Kleer and Brown. *Artificial Intelligence* 29:63–72.

Kay, H., and Ungar, L. 1993. Deriving monotonic function envelopes from observations. *Seventh International Workshop on Qualitative Reasoning*.

Shachter, R.; Anderson, S.; and Poh, K. 1990. Directed reduction algorithms and decomposable graphs. In *Proceedings of the Sixth Conference on Uncertainty in Artificial Intelligence*, 237–244.

Spiegelhalter, D., and Lauritzen, S. 1990. Sequential updating of conditional probabilities on directed graphical structures. *Networks* 20:579–605.

Stolle, R., and Bradley, E. 1996. Automatic construction of accurate models of physical systems. *Annals of Mathematics and Artificial Intelligence*.

Williams, B. C., and Millar, B. 1996. Automated decomposition of model-based learning problems. In *Proceedings of the Tenth International Workshop on Qualitative Reasoning, AAAI Technical Report WS-96-01*, 265–273.

Williams, B. C., and Nayak, P. P. 1996. Immobile robots: AI in the new millennium. *AI Magazine* 17(3):16–35.

Williams, B. C., and Raiman, O. 1994. Decompositional modeling through caricatural reasoning. In *Proceedings of AAAI-94*, 1199–1204.

Zhang, Y.; Williams, B. C.; and Elrod, S. 1993. Model estimation and energy-efficient control for building management systems. Technical report, Xerox PARC.

What can Knowledge Representation do for Semi-Structured Data?

Diego Calvanese, Giuseppe De Giacomo, Maurizio Lenzerini

Dipartimento di Informatica e Sistemistica
Università di Roma "La Sapienza"
Via Salaria 113, 00198 Roma, Italy
{calvanese,degiacomo,lenzerini}@dis.uniroma1.it

Abstract

The problem of modeling semi-structured data is important in many application areas such as multimedia data management, biological databases, digital libraries, and data integration. Graph schemas (Buneman *et al.* 1997) have been proposed recently as a simple and elegant formalism for representing semistructured data. In this model, schemas are represented as graphs whose edges are labeled with unary formulae of a theory, and the notions of conformance of a database to a schema and of subsumption between two schemas are defined in terms of a simulation relation. Several authors have stressed the need of extending graph schemas with various types of constraints, such as edge existence and constraints on the number of outgoing edges. In this paper we analyze the appropriateness of various knowledge representation formalisms for representing and reasoning about graph schemas extended with constraints. We argue that neither First Order Logic, nor Logic Programming nor Frame-based languages are satisfactory for this purpose, and present a solution based on very expressive Description Logics. We provide techniques and complexity analysis for the problem of deciding schema subsumption and conformance in various interesting cases, that differ by the expressive power in the specification of constraints.

Introduction

The ability to represent data whose structure is less rigid and strict than in conventional databases is considered a crucial aspect in modern approaches to data modeling, and is important in many application areas, such as biological databases, digital libraries, data integration, and access to web databases (Abiteboul 1997; Buneman *et al.* 1997; Christophides *et al.* 1994; Mendelzon, Mihaila, & Milo 1997; Quass *et al.* 1995). Consider, for example, the set of home pages designed by the faculties for a University web site. Since different home pages may vary considerably one from another, it is extremely hard to describe their structure in a rigid form such as the one imposed, say, by relational databases. Indeed, we need structuring mechanisms that are much more flexible than traditional data models.

Following (Abiteboul 1997), we define semi-structured data as data that is neither raw, nor strictly typed as in conventional database systems. BDFS (Basic Data model For Semi-structured data) (Buneman *et al.* 1997) is a formal and elegant data model, based on graphs with labeled edges, where information on both the values and the schema for the data are kept. The labels of edges in the schemas are formulae of a certain theory $\mathcal{T}$, and the notion of a database D being coherent to a schema $\mathcal{S}$ is given in terms of a special relation, called simulation, between the graph representing the database and the graph representing the schema. Roughly speaking, a simulation is a correspondence between the edges of D and those of $\mathcal{S}$ such that, whenever there is an edge labeled a in D, there is a corresponding edge in $\mathcal{S}$ labeled with a formula satisfied by a (but not necessarily vice-versa). The notion of simulation is less rigid than the usual notion of satisfaction, and suitably reflects the need of dealing with less strict structures of data.

In (Buneman *et al.* 1997), the authors point out that, for several tasks related to data management, it is important to be able to reason about schemas, in particular to check subsumption between two schemas, which is the task of deciding whether every database conforming to one schema always conforms to another schema. They also present algorithms for, and analyze the complexity of checking subsumption in BDFS.

Several papers indicate that in many applications there is the need to extend the BDFS model with different types of constraints. Indeed, in (Buneman *et al.* 1997) all the properties of the schema are expressed in terms of the structure of the graph, and therefore, there is no possibility of specifying additional conditions, such as existence of edges or bounds on the number of edges emanating from a node, or imposing that a certain subgraph is well-founded.

Our intuition suggests that Knowledge Representation (KR) techniques should be very useful for the above purpose. After all, the problem deals with *representing* constraints, and *reasoning* about schemas with constraints. The basic goal of the work reported in this paper was to verify this intuition, and we present here the following results of our investigation:

- We analyze the appropriateness of various KR formalisms for representing and reasoning about graph schemas extended with constraints, and demonstrate that neither First Order Logic, nor Logic Programming nor Frame-based languages are satisfactory for this purpose.

- We show that very expressive Description Logics (DLs), such as the ones studied in (De Giacomo & Lenzerini 1996; Calvanese 1996; De Giacomo & Lenzerini 1997), are the right tools for modeling and reasoning about semi-structured data with constraints. In particular, we propose to express constraints in terms of DLs formulae associated to nodes of the schema. A formula on a node u imposes a condition that, for every database D conforming to $\mathcal{S}$, must be satisfied by every node of D simulating u.

Copyright ©1998, American Association for Artificial Intelligence (www.aaai.org). All rights reserved.

- We consider languages for specifying constraints with different expressive power, and present several results on the corresponding reasoning problems. We show that adding various types of local constraints (i.e. constraints that impose conditions only on the edges emanating from a node) does not increase the complexity of reasoning. On the other hand, we present an intractability result for the case of non-local constraints. Finally, we study the case where the constraints are expressed in a very powerful DL, namely, $\mu\mathcal{ALCQ}$ (De Giacomo & Lenzerini 1997), that allows for imposing complex conditions on the schema, such as well-foundedness of subgraphs. We present a technique for checking subsumption in this case, showing that the problem is decidable in double exponential time.

Our presentation starts with a brief description of both BDFS, and the description logic $\mu\mathcal{ALCQ}$.

Preliminaries

In this section, we describe the basic characteristics of the BDFS model for semi-structured data and the description logic $\mu\mathcal{ALCQ}$.

The BDFS Data Model

The data model BDFS, which is the basis of our investigation, is an edge-labeled graph model of semi-structured data, where labels are unary formulae of a first order language $\mathcal{L}_\mathcal{T}$. The language $\mathcal{L}_\mathcal{T}$ is constituted by a set of predicates, including the equality predicate "=", and one constant for every element of a universe $\mathcal{U}$.

A schema in BDFS always refers to a complete and decidable theory $\mathcal{T}$ on $\mathcal{U}$. In other words, $\mathcal{T}$ is the set of first order formulae which are true (or valid) for the elements of $\mathcal{U}$, and it is decidable to check whether a formula p in $\mathcal{L}_\mathcal{T}$ is valid in $\mathcal{T}$ (in notation, $\mathcal{T} \models p$).

Definition 1 *A BDFS $\mathcal{T}$-schema is a rooted connected graph whose edges are labeled with unary formulae of $\mathcal{L}_\mathcal{T}$. A $\mathcal{T}$-database is a rooted connected graph whose edges are labeled with constants of $\mathcal{T}$.*

For any rooted graph G, we denote the root of G by $root(G)$, the set of nodes of G by $Nodes(G)$, and the set of edges of G by $Edges(G)$. We denote an edge from node u to node v labeled by a with $u \xrightarrow{a} v$.

In order to establish if a database is coherent with a schema, or if a schema is more general than another schema, the notions of conformance and subsumption are defined as follows.

Definition 2 *A $\mathcal{T}$-database D conforms to a BDFS $\mathcal{T}$-schema S, in notation $D \preceq S$, if there exists a simulation from D to S, i.e. a binary relation $\trianglelefteq$ from the nodes of D to those of S satisfying: (1) $root(D) \trianglelefteq root(S)$, (2) $u \trianglelefteq u'$ implies that for each edge $u \xrightarrow{a} v$ in D, there exists an edge $u' \xrightarrow{p} v'$ in S such that $\mathcal{T} \models p(a)$, and $v \trianglelefteq v'$.*

Definition 3 *If S and S' are two BDFS $\mathcal{T}$-schemas, then S' subsumes S, in notation $S \sqsubseteq S'$, if for every $\mathcal{T}$-database D, $D \preceq S$ implies $D \preceq S'$. S is equivalent to S' if $S \sqsubseteq S'$ and $S' \sqsubseteq S$.*

In (Buneman *et al.* 1997), an algorithm is presented for checking subsumption (and also conformance, being a $\mathcal{T}$-database a special case of $\mathcal{T}$-schema). The algorithm essentially looks for the greatest simulation between the nodes of the two schemas, and works in time $O(m^{O(1)} \cdot t_\mathcal{T}(m))$, where m is the size of the two schemas and $t_\mathcal{T}(x)$ is the time needed to check whether a formula of size x is valid in $\mathcal{T}$. In general it is meaningful not to consider $\mathcal{T}$ to be part of the input of the problem (Buneman *et al.* 1997). Therefore, whenever $t_\mathcal{T}(m)$ may be assumed to be independent of m, $t_\mathcal{T}(m)$ can be replaced by a constant (e.g. when m is polynomial in the size $|S|$ of a $\mathcal{T}$-schema S, which is considerably smaller than $|\mathcal{T}|$).

If not specified otherwise, we also make the assumption that the theory $\mathcal{T}$ is not part of the input to the reasoning problems addressed in the paper (namely, consistency and subsumption).

The Description Logic $\mu\mathcal{ALCQ}$

Description logics (DLs) allow one to represent a domain of interest in terms of *concepts* and *roles*. Concepts model classes of individuals, while roles model relationships between classes. We concentrate on the DL $\mu\mathcal{ALCQ}$ studied in (De Giacomo & Lenzerini 1997), where a correspondence was shown with a well-known logic of programs, called *modal mu-calculus* (Kozen 1983; Streett & Emerson 1989), that has been recently investigated for expressing temporal properties of reactive and parallel processes (Stirling 1996; Emerson 1996). $\mu\mathcal{ALCQ}$ can be viewed as a well-behaved fragment of first-order logic with fixpoints (Park 1970; Abiteboul, Hull, & Vianu 1995). We make use of the standard first-order notions of scope, bound and free occurrences of variables, closed formulae, etc., treating μ and ν as quantifiers.

The primitive symbols in $\mu\mathcal{ALCQ}$ are *atomic concepts*, (concept) *variables*, and *atomic roles* (in the following called simply *roles*). Concepts are formed according to the following syntax:

$$C ::= A \mid \neg C \mid C_1 \sqcap C_2 \mid (\geq n R.C) \mid \mu X.C \mid X$$

where A denotes an atomic concept, R a role, n a natural number, and X a variable, and the restriction is made that every free occurrence of X in $\mu X.C$ is in the scope of an even number of negations.

We introduce the following abbreviations: $C_1 \sqcup C_2$ for $\neg(\neg C_1 \sqcap \neg C_2)$, $\top$ for $A \sqcup \neg A$, $\bot$ for $\neg\top$, $\exists R.C$ for $(\geq 1 R.C)$, $\forall R.C$ for $\neg\exists R.\neg C$, $(\leq n R.C)$ for $\neg(\geq n+1 R.C)$, $(= n R.C)$ for $(\leq n R.C) \sqcap (\geq n R.C)$, and $\nu X.C$ for $\neg\mu X.\neg C[X/\neg X]$ (where $C[X/\neg X]$ is the concept obtained by substituting all free occurrences of X with $\neg X$).

An *interpretation* $\mathcal{I} = (\Delta^\mathcal{I}, \cdot^\mathcal{I})$ consists of an *interpretation domain* $\Delta^\mathcal{I}$, and an *interpretation function* $\cdot^\mathcal{I}$, which maps every atomic concept to a subset of $\Delta^\mathcal{I}$, and every atomic role to a subset of $\Delta^\mathcal{I} \times \Delta^\mathcal{I}$. The presence of free variables does not allow us to extend the interpretation function $\cdot^\mathcal{I}$ directly to every concept of the logic. For this reason we introduce valuations. A *valuation* ρ on an interpretation $\mathcal{I}$ is a mapping from variables to subsets of $\Delta^\mathcal{I}$. Given a valuation ρ, we denote by $\rho[X/\mathcal{E}]$ the valuation identical to ρ except for the fact that $\rho[X/\mathcal{E}](X) = \mathcal{E}$.

Let $\mathcal{I}$ be an interpretation and ρ a valuation on $\mathcal{I}$. We assign meaning to concepts of the logic by associating to $\mathcal{I}$

and ρ an *extension function* $\cdot_\rho^{\mathcal{I}}$, mapping concepts to subsets of $\Delta^{\mathcal{I}}$, as follows:

$$\begin{aligned}
X_\rho^{\mathcal{I}} &= \rho(X) \subseteq \Delta^{\mathcal{I}} \\
A_\rho^{\mathcal{I}} &= A^{\mathcal{I}} \subseteq \Delta^{\mathcal{I}} \\
(\neg C)_\rho^{\mathcal{I}} &= \Delta^{\mathcal{I}} - C_\rho^{\mathcal{I}} \\
(C_1 \sqcap C_2)_\rho^{\mathcal{I}} &= (C_1)_\rho^{\mathcal{I}} \cap (C_2)_\rho^{\mathcal{I}} \\
(\geq n\, R.C)_\rho^{\mathcal{I}} &= \{s \in \Delta^{\mathcal{I}} \mid \\
&\quad \#\{s' \mid (s,s') \in R^{\mathcal{I}} \text{ and } s' \in C_\rho^{\mathcal{I}}\} \geq n\} \\
(\mu X.C)_\rho^{\mathcal{I}} &= \bigcap\{\mathcal{E} \subseteq \Delta^{\mathcal{I}} \mid C_{\rho[X/\mathcal{E}]}^{\mathcal{I}} \subseteq \mathcal{E}\}
\end{aligned}$$

Observe that $C_{\rho[X/\mathcal{E}]}^{\mathcal{I}}$ can be seen as an operator from subsets $\mathcal{E}$ of $\Delta^{\mathcal{I}}$ to subsets of $\Delta^{\mathcal{I}}$, and that, by the syntactic restriction enforced on variables, such an operator is guaranteed to be monotonic wrt set inclusion. The constructs $\mu X.C$ and $\nu X.C$ denote respectively the *least fixpoint* and the *greatest fixpoint* of the operator. The extension of closed concepts is independent of the valuation, and therefore for closed concepts we do not consider the valuation explicitly.

A $\mu\mathcal{ALCQ}$ knowledge base is a finite set of *axioms* $C_1 \sqsubseteq C_2$ where C_1 and C_2 are closed concepts of $\mu\mathcal{ALCQ}$. An interpretation $\mathcal{I}$ satisfies an axiom $C_1 \sqsubseteq C_2$, if $C_1^{\mathcal{I}} \subseteq C_2^{\mathcal{I}}$. $\mathcal{I}$ is a *model* of a knowledge base Γ, if $\mathcal{I}$ satisfies all axioms in Γ. A closed concept C is *satisfiable* in a knowledge base Γ if there exists a model $\mathcal{I}$ of Γ such that $C^{\mathcal{I}} \neq \emptyset$.

Theorem 4 *(De Giacomo & Lenzerini 1997) Satisfiability of closed $\mu\mathcal{ALCQ}$ concepts in $\mu\mathcal{ALCQ}$ knowledge bases is an EXPTIME-complete problem.*

Which KR Formalism for Semi-Structured Data Modeling?

In this section we discuss how the technology of KR can contribute to the problem of modeling semi-structured data with constraints.

We start our investigation by verifying whether First Order Logic (FOL) is suited for representing BDFS schemas. We observe that, in principle, FOL would be an interesting tool, because it would allow expressing very complex constraints on the schema. However, we need to check if FOL is able to model the notions of BDFS schemas, databases, and simulation.

A reasonable approach to expressing BDFS schemas in FOL is based on the following observations:

- If $u_1, \ldots, u_N$ are the nodes of the schema, we make use of predicate symbols, $n_1, \ldots, n_N$ and *edge*, where $n_i(x)$ means that x is a node (the n_i corresponding to the root is called the root predicate), and $edge(x, y, z)$ means that there is an edge from x to y labeled with z. The fact that the label z satisfies the formula F of $\mathcal{T}$ is represented by $F(z)$.

- We represent the schema $\mathcal{S}$ by means of a set $FOL(\mathcal{S})$ of suitable formulae. For example, the fact that a node u_i has two outgoing edges to u_j and u_k labeled with P_1 and P_2, is represented by the formula

$$\forall x\, (n_i(x) \Leftrightarrow (\forall y \forall z\, edge(x,y,z) \supset \\ ((P_1(z) \wedge n_j(y)) \vee (P_2(z) \wedge n_k(y)))))$$

- An interpretation of $FOL(\mathcal{S})$ is obtained by choosing a so-called pre-interpretation that assigns a truth value to every ground formula of the form $edge(x, y, z)$, and then extending it to an interpretation by computing the extension of the predicates $n_1, \ldots, n_N$ on the basis of the formulae in $FOL(\mathcal{S})$.

- Given a logical model M of $FOL(\mathcal{S})$, if we traverse the relation *edge* in M starting from one object satisfying the root predicate, we should obtain a structure that corresponds to a database conforming to $\mathcal{S}$, and, on the contrary, every database conforming to $\mathcal{S}$ should correspond to a logical model of $FOL(\mathcal{S})$ in which the extension of the root predicate is not empty.

Consider, for example, the BDFS schema $\mathcal{S}_1$ with two nodes u_1 and u_2, and one edge from u_1 to u_2 labeled with P. The corresponding set $FOL(\mathcal{S}_1)$ of formulae in FOL is:

$$\{\, \forall x\, (n_1(x) \Leftrightarrow (\forall y \forall z\, edge(x,y,z) \supset (P(z) \wedge n_2(y)))), \\ \forall x\, (n_2(x) \Leftrightarrow (\neg \exists y \exists z\, edge(x,y,z))) \,\}$$

Consider the database D_1 with two nodes d and e and an edge from d to e labeled with t such that $P(t)$ is valid in $\mathcal{T}$. It is easy to see that D_1 conforms to $\mathcal{S}_1$, and that it corresponds to the pre-interpretation where $edge(d, e, t)$ is true, which is extended to a model of $FOL(\mathcal{S}_1)$ such that $d \in n_1$ and $e \in n_2$. Observe that the empty database with just one node and no edges also conforms to $\mathcal{S}_1$ and corresponds to the pre-interpretation where $edge(x, y, z)$ is always false. This is correctly captured by $FOL(\mathcal{S}_1)$.

On the other hand, consider a schema $\mathcal{S}_2$ with one node u and one edge from u to u labeled with P. The set $FOL(\mathcal{S}_2)$ is simply

$$\{\, \forall x\, (n(x) \Leftrightarrow (\forall y \forall z\, edge(x,y,z) \supset (P(z) \wedge n(y)))) \,\}$$

and it is easy to see that there is at least one model of $FOL(\mathcal{S}_2)$ which does not correspond to any database conforming to $\mathcal{S}_2$. Indeed, consider a pre-interpretation I assigning true to $edge(d, d, t)$, with $P(t)$ valid in $\mathcal{T}$. Clearly, such a pre-interpretation can be extended to a model of $FOL(\mathcal{S}_2)$ simply by letting the extension of n be empty. However, since d is not in the extension of n, the resulting model does not reflect the fact that the database corresponding to I conforms to $\mathcal{S}_2$.

The above example shows a general problem that FOL has in representing BDFS schemas. The first order semantics is intrinsically too liberal for capturing the notion of simulation. Indeed, in order to reflect such a notion, we need a type of semantics that forces an object o to be in the extension of a predicate n_i whenever there is no evidence that it cannot satisfy such predicate. We observe that the greatest fixpoint semantics (Baader 1996) satisfies exactly this property. Thus, FOL extended with fixpoints would be suitable, but FOL itself is not.

For the same reason, one can verify that neither Logic Programming languages under the completion semantics (Lloyd 1987), nor Frame-based languages are suited for modeling BDFS schemas. In particular, the difficulties arise when BDFS schemas with cycles are taken into account (see the schema $\mathcal{S}_2$ in the example above). On the contrary, schemas without cycles may be modeled correctly, for example by using KR systems such as CLASSIC (Borgida & Patel-Schneider 1994). Note, however, that the assumption of acyclicity of semi-structured data schemas is too restrictive in practice.

The above observations tell us that, in order to use the KR technology for modeling and reasoning about semi-structured data with constraints, we must resort to KR formalisms that are able:

- to model graphs with no limitations on cycles;
- to interpret such graphs by making use of the greatest fixpoint semantics;
- to express complex constraints on the graphs;
- to provide reasoning procedures for computing the subsumption relation between schemas.

Below we show that $\mu\mathcal{ALCQ}$ has exactly the above characteristics. However, as a first step, we need to formally define graph schemas with constraints and the associated reasoning tasks.

Schemas with Constraints

We address the problem of extending the BDFS data model in order to express constraints on the graph representing a schema. We conceive a constraint for a BDFS schema $\mathcal{S}$ as a formula associated to a node u of the schema. The formula is expressed in a certain language $\mathcal{L}$, and its role is to impose a condition that, for every database D conforming to $\mathcal{S}$, must be satisfied by every node of D simulating u. In other words, constraints are used to impose additional conditions on the schema, with respect to those already implied by the structure of the graph.

Definition 5 *A $\mathcal{T}$-schema with $\mathcal{L}$-constraints is a pair $\mathcal{S} = (\mathcal{G}, \mathcal{C})$, where $\mathcal{G}$ is a BDFS $\mathcal{T}$-schema, and $\mathcal{C}$ is a total function from the nodes of $\mathcal{G}$ to formulae of a constraint language $\mathcal{L}$.*

Definition 6 *A $\mathcal{T}$-database D conforms to a $\mathcal{T}$-schema with $\mathcal{L}$-constraints $\mathcal{S} = (\mathcal{G}, \mathcal{C})$, in notation $D \preceq \mathcal{S}$, if there exists a constraint-consistent simulation, i.e. a binary relation $\trianglelefteq$ from the nodes of D to those of $\mathcal{G}$ satisfying: (1) $root(D) \trianglelefteq root(\mathcal{G})$, (2) $u \trianglelefteq u'$ implies that (2.1) u satisfies $\mathcal{C}(u')$, and (2.2) for each edge $u \xrightarrow{a} v$ in D, there exists an edge $u' \xrightarrow{q} v'$ in $\mathcal{S}$ such that $\mathcal{T} \models q(a)$, and $v \trianglelefteq v'$.*

Since constraints may contradict each other, or may even be incompatible with the structure of the graph, the notion of consistency becomes relevant.

Definition 7 *For a $\mathcal{T}$-schema with $\mathcal{L}$-constraints $\mathcal{S} = (\mathcal{G}, \mathcal{C})$, a node $u \in Nodes(\mathcal{G})$ is consistent if there is at least one $\mathcal{T}$-database which conforms to $(\mathcal{G}', \mathcal{C})$, where $\mathcal{G}'$ is equal to $\mathcal{G}$ except that $root(\mathcal{G}') = u$. $\mathcal{S}$ is consistent, if $root(\mathcal{G})$ is consistent.*

The notion of subsumption remains unchanged.

We consider now different constraint languages, and study consistency and subsumption checking for schemas with constraints. Being conformance a special case of subsumption, we do not explicitly deal with conformance.

Local Constraints

We first consider a language $\mathcal{L}_l$ in which only local constraints can be expressed, i.e. only constraints on the edges directly emanating from a node. $\mathcal{L}_l$ is inspired by DLs with number restrictions and its formulae have the following syntax (γ, γ_1 and γ_2 denote constraints, and p denotes a formula of $\mathcal{T}$):

$$\gamma ::= \top \mid \exists p \mid \neg \exists p \mid \exists^{\leq 1} p \mid \gamma_1 \wedge \gamma_2$$

Intuitively, a constraint of the form $\exists p$ on a node u, called *edge-existence constraint*, imposes that u has at least one outgoing edge $u \xrightarrow{a} v$ such that $\mathcal{T} \models p(a)$, while a constraint of the form $\exists^{\leq 1} p$, called *functionality-constraint*, imposes that u has at most one such outgoing edge. More precisely, let $\mathcal{S} = (\mathcal{G}, \mathcal{C})$ be a $\mathcal{T}$-schema with $\mathcal{L}_l$-constraints. and D a $\mathcal{T}$-database. Then a node u of D *satisfies* a constraint γ, in notation $u \models_c \gamma$, if the following conditions are satisfied:

$$
\begin{array}{lll}
u \models_c \top & \text{always} \\
u \models_c \exists p & \text{iff} & \exists u \xrightarrow{a} v \in Edges(D). \, \mathcal{T} \models p(a) \\
u \models_c \neg \exists p & \text{iff} & \forall u \xrightarrow{a} v \in Edges(D). \, \mathcal{T} \models \neg p(a) \\
u \models_c \exists^{\leq 1} p & \text{iff} & \#\{u \xrightarrow{a} v \in Edges(D) \mid \mathcal{T} \models p(a)\} \leq 1 \\
u \models_c \gamma_1 \wedge \gamma_2 & \text{iff} & (u \models_c \gamma_1) \wedge (u \models_c \gamma_2)
\end{array}
$$

Note that we can view a $\mathcal{T}$-database D as a $\mathcal{T}$-schema $(D, \mathcal{C})$ with constraints, where $\mathcal{C}(u) = \top$ for every node u of D (such a schema is always consistent).

Checking the consistency of a schema amounts to visiting the graph and removing nodes that violate constraints, which can be detected by a local check. An algorithm for subsumption is obtained essentially by incorporating local checks for constraint violations into the algorithm of (Buneman *et al.* 1997).

Theorem 8 *Consistency and subsumption of $\mathcal{T}$-schemas with $\mathcal{L}_l$-constraints, can be checked in polynomial time in the size of the schemas.*

Non-Local Constraints

Next we consider languages in which the constraints are not local, i.e. they can express conditions on edges that are not directly connected to the node labeled with the constraint. We show that even in a simple non-local constraint language, namely $\mathcal{L}_{\mathcal{ALE}}$ inspired by the DL $\mathcal{ALE}$ (Donini *et al.* 1992), consistency and subsumption of $\mathcal{T}$-schemas become intractable.

The formulae of $\mathcal{L}_{\mathcal{ALE}}$ have the following syntax:

$$\gamma ::= \top \mid \exists p \uparrow \gamma \mid \forall p \uparrow \gamma \mid \gamma_1 \wedge \gamma_2$$

where the additional rules for the satisfaction of constraints of $\mathcal{L}_{\mathcal{ALE}}$ in a node u of a $\mathcal{T}$-database are:

$$
\begin{array}{lll}
u \models_c \exists p \uparrow \gamma & \text{iff} & \exists u \xrightarrow{a} v \in Edges(D). \, (\mathcal{T} \models p(a) \wedge v \models_c \gamma) \\
u \models_c \forall p \uparrow \gamma & \text{iff} & \forall u \xrightarrow{a} v \in Edges(D). \, (\mathcal{T} \models p(a) \supset v \models_c \gamma)
\end{array}
$$

Observe that $\mathcal{L}_{\mathcal{ALE}}$ is not local since the constraints imposed on one node may imply other constraints on adjacent nodes. By exploiting this property and the hardness results in (Donini *et al.* 1992), we can show that consistency checking is coNP-hard.

Theorem 9 *Checking the consistency of a $\mathcal{T}$-schema $\mathcal{S}$ with $\mathcal{L}_{\mathcal{ALE}}$-constraints is coNP-hard in the size of $\mathcal{S}$, even if $\mathcal{T}$ is empty, i.e. all edges of $\mathcal{S}$ are labeled with* **true**.

By observing that checking consistency can be reduced to checking subsumption wrt an inconsistent schema, we immediately get that subsumption is NP-hard. Theorem 9 shows also that consistency stays coNP-hard, even if $\mathcal{T}$ can be used as an oracle for validity. The complexity of checking consistency in the presence of non-local constraints lies in the necessity to verify whether a database may exist, whose topology is determined by the constraints. Since $\mathcal{T}$ cannot predict anything about the possible topologies of databases, the validity checker of $\mathcal{T}$ cannot be used to "hide" a potentially exponential calculation. Note that this is different from

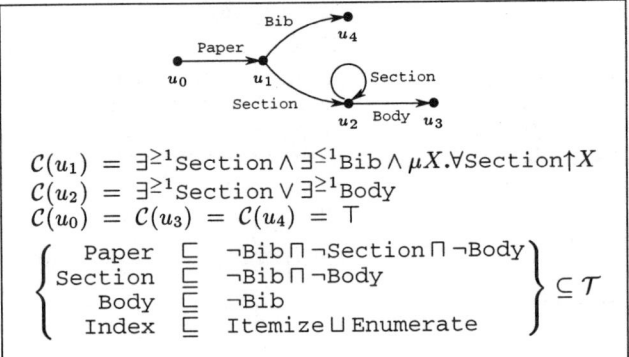

$$\begin{aligned}
\mathcal{C}(u_1) &= \exists^{\geq 1}\mathtt{Section} \wedge \exists^{\leq 1}\mathtt{Bib} \wedge \mu X.\forall \mathtt{Section}{\uparrow}X \\
\mathcal{C}(u_2) &= \exists^{\geq 1}\mathtt{Section} \vee \exists^{\geq 1}\mathtt{Body} \\
\mathcal{C}(u_0) &= \mathcal{C}(u_3) = \mathcal{C}(u_4) = \top
\end{aligned}$$

$$\left\{\begin{array}{rcl}
\mathtt{Paper} &\sqsubseteq& \neg\mathtt{Bib} \sqcap \neg\mathtt{Section} \sqcap \neg\mathtt{Body} \\
\mathtt{Section} &\sqsubseteq& \neg\mathtt{Bib} \sqcap \neg\mathtt{Body} \\
\mathtt{Body} &\sqsubseteq& \neg\mathtt{Bib} \\
\mathtt{Index} &\sqsubseteq& \mathtt{Itemize} \sqcup \mathtt{Enumerate}
\end{array}\right\} \subseteq \mathcal{T}$$

Figure 1: A $\mathcal{T}$-schema with $\mathcal{L}_\mu$-constraints

the case of local constraints, where the aspects related to the topology enforced by the constraints can be embedded in an appropriate formula of $\mathcal{T}$.

Fixpoint Constraints

We now extend our framework to a very expressive constraint language, which is a variant of $\mu\mathcal{ALCQ}$, and show decidability of consistency and subsumption.

The constraint language $\mathcal{L}_\mu$ is the set of *closed* formulae constructed according to the following syntax (p denotes a formula of $\mathcal{T}$, n a positive integer, and X a variable):

$$\begin{array}{rcl}
\gamma &::=& X \mid \exists^{\geq n} F \mid \neg\gamma \mid \gamma_1 \wedge \gamma_2 \mid \mu X.\gamma \\
F &::=& p \mid {\uparrow}\gamma \mid \neg F \mid F_1 \wedge F_2
\end{array}$$

with the restriction that every free occurrence of X in $\mu X.\gamma$ is in the scope of an even number of negations.

We introduce the abbreviations: $\gamma_1 \vee \gamma_2$ for $\neg(\neg\gamma_1 \wedge \neg\gamma_2)$, $\top$ for $\gamma \vee \neg\gamma$, and $\forall p{\uparrow}\gamma$ for $\neg\exists^{\geq 1}(p \wedge {\uparrow}\neg\gamma)$.

Let D be a $\mathcal{T}$-database, and $\mathcal{M}$ be a model of $\mathcal{T}$. A *valuation* ρ on D is a mapping from variables to subsets of $Nodes(D)$. We denote by $\rho[X/\mathcal{E}]$ the valuation identical to ρ except for $\rho[X/\mathcal{E}](X) = \mathcal{E}$. For each node $u \in Nodes(D)$, we define when u *satisfies a constraint* γ *under a valuation* ρ, in notation $\rho, u \models_c \gamma$, as follows:

$$\begin{array}{lll}
\rho, u \models_c X & \text{iff} & u \in \rho(X) \\
\rho, u \models_c \exists^{\geq n} F & \text{iff} & \#\{u \xrightarrow{a} v \in Edges(D) \mid \\
& & \quad \rho, u \xrightarrow{a} v \models_c F\} \geq n \\
\rho, u \models_c \neg\gamma & \text{iff} & \rho, u \not\models_c \gamma \\
\rho, u \models_c \gamma_1 \wedge \gamma_2 & \text{iff} & (\rho, u \models_c \gamma_1) \wedge (\rho, u \models_c \gamma_2) \\
\rho, u \models_c \mu X.\gamma & \text{iff} & \forall \mathcal{E} \subseteq Nodes(D). (\forall v \in Nodes(D). \\
& & \rho[X/\mathcal{E}], v \models_c \gamma \supset \rho[X/\mathcal{E}], v \models_c X) \supset \rho[X/\mathcal{E}], u \models_c X
\end{array}$$

where

$$\begin{array}{lll}
\rho, u \xrightarrow{a} v \models_c p & \text{iff} & \mathcal{T} \models p(a) \\
\rho, u \xrightarrow{a} v \models_c {\uparrow}\gamma & \text{iff} & \rho, v \models_c \gamma \\
\rho, u \xrightarrow{a} v \models_c \neg F & \text{iff} & \rho, u \xrightarrow{a} v \not\models_c F \\
\rho, u \xrightarrow{a} v \models_c F_1 \wedge F_2 & \text{iff} & (\rho, u \xrightarrow{a} v \models_c F_1) \wedge (\rho, u \xrightarrow{a} v \models_c F_2)
\end{array}$$

Since the constraints in $\mathcal{L}_\mu$ are closed formulae, satisfaction is independent of the valuation, and we denote it simply by $u \models_c \gamma$.

Example The schema shown in Figure 1 represents a set of web pages such as those generated by "latex2html" when translating a LaTeX article containing nested sections and possibly a bibliography. The connections between the pages are represented by the graph, whereas the content of the pages is modeled by $\mathcal{T}$. Notice the use of constraints to state complex conditions on the structure of the allowed databases. In particular, the constraint $\mu X.\forall \mathtt{Section}{\uparrow}X$ associated with u_1 rules out all databases that have loops in the connections of the various sections.

Checking Subsumption for $\mathcal{L}_\mu$ We develop now a technique for checking subsumption of $\mathcal{T}$-schemas with $\mathcal{L}_\mu$-constraints, which works in the case where the theory $\mathcal{T}$ can be expressed in terms of axioms of $\mu\mathcal{ALCQ}$. In order to illustrate the features of the technique, we further assume that $\mathcal{T}$ is interpreted over a fixed finite universe $\mathcal{U}$, includes only unary predicates, one distinct constant $c(d)$ for each element $d \in \mathcal{U}$, and is presented as a finite set containing either $p(a)$ or $\neg p(a)$ for each predicate p and constant a[1].

The formulae of $\mathcal{T}$ that label the edges of a $\mathcal{T}$-schema are boolean combinations of atomic formulae in the language of $\mathcal{T}$ and of expressions of the form $(self = a)$, where a is a constant of $\mathcal{T}$. We define when a formula $p(a)$ labeling an edge is valid in $\mathcal{T}$, in notation $\mathcal{T} \models p(a)$, as follows:

$$\begin{array}{lll}
\mathcal{T} \models (self = a')(a) & \text{iff} & a = a' \\
\mathcal{T} \models \neg p(a) & \text{iff} & \mathcal{T} \not\models p(a) \\
\mathcal{T} \models (p_1 \wedge p_2)(a) & \text{iff} & \mathcal{T} \models p_1(a) \wedge \mathcal{T} \models p_2(a)
\end{array}$$

It is immediate to view a $\mathcal{T}$-database as a $\mathcal{T}$-schema, simply by replacing each edge label a by $(self = a)$. Therefore, as in BDFS, conformance is a special case of subsumption.

The technique we use for checking subsumption is based on a reduction to unsatisfiability in $\mu\mathcal{ALCQ}$ knowledge bases. Differently from the previous cases, in what follows we consider $\mathcal{T}$ to be part of the input to subsumption checking.

Given two $\mathcal{T}$-schemas $\mathcal{S}_1$ and $\mathcal{S}_2$, we reduce the problem of deciding whether $\mathcal{S}_1 \sqsubseteq \mathcal{S}_2$, to the problem of deciding the unsatisfiability of the $\mu\mathcal{ALCQ}$ concept $\Phi_{\mathcal{S}_1} \sqcap \neg\Phi_{\mathcal{S}_2}$ in the $\mu\mathcal{ALCQ}$ knowledge base $\Gamma_\mathcal{T}$, where $\Gamma_\mathcal{T}$, $\Phi_{\mathcal{S}_1}$, and $\Phi_{\mathcal{S}_2}$ are defined as follows.

$\Gamma_\mathcal{T}$: **encoding of $\mathcal{T}$ and of the general properties of BDFS graphs** To encode the general properties of BDFS graphs, $\Gamma_\mathcal{T}$ exploits *reification* of edges, as used in (Buneman et al. 1997). Specifically, we use a special role $\mathbf{E}$ and split each labeled edge $u \xrightarrow{a} v$ into two edges $u \xrightarrow{\mathbf{E}} e_{uv} \xrightarrow{\mathbf{E}} v$, by introducing an intermediate node e_{uv} labeled by a. $\Gamma_\mathcal{T}$ contains the following axioms (T_N, T_E, and T_D are new atomic concepts, and $\mathbf{L}$ is a new role):

$$\begin{array}{rclcrcl}
\top &\sqsubseteq& \mathsf{T}_N \sqcup \mathsf{T}_E \sqcup \mathsf{T}_D & \quad & \mathsf{T}_N &\sqsubseteq& \neg\mathsf{T}_E \\
\mathsf{T}_E &\sqsubseteq& \neg\mathsf{T}_D & & \mathsf{T}_D &\sqsubseteq& \neg\mathsf{T}_N \\
\mathsf{T}_N &\sqsubseteq& \forall\mathbf{E}.\mathsf{T}_E \\
\mathsf{T}_E &\sqsubseteq& \multicolumn{5}{l}{\forall\mathbf{E}.\mathsf{T}_N \sqcap (=1\,\mathbf{E}.\top) \sqcap \forall\mathbf{L}.\mathsf{T}_D \sqcap (=1\,\mathbf{L}.\top)}
\end{array}$$

Intuitively, these axioms partition the interpretation domain into objects denoting nodes (T_N), edges (T_E), and constants of $\mathcal{T}$ (T_D), and specify the correct links for those object denoting nodes and edges.

In addition, in order to encode the theory $\mathcal{T}$, we introduce one concept C_p for each predicate of $\mathcal{T}$, and one concept O_a (called an *object-concept*) for each constant a of $\mathcal{T}$, and, for each pair C_p, O_a we add to $\Gamma_\mathcal{T}$ the axiom:

---

[1] We point out that we restrict ourselves to such simple kinds of theories for the sake of simplicity, but our approach works when $\mathcal{T}$ has a more general form.

$$\top_D \sqcap O_a \sqsubseteq C_p \quad \text{if} \quad \mathcal{T} \models p(a)$$
$$\top_D \sqcap O_a \sqsubseteq \neg C_p \quad \text{if} \quad \mathcal{T} \models \neg p(a)$$

Observe that, $|\Gamma_\mathcal{T}|$ is linear in $|\mathcal{T}|$.

$\Phi_\mathcal{S}$: **encoding of the schema** $\mathcal{S}$ In order to define the encoding $\Phi_\mathcal{S}$ of a $\mathcal{T}$-schema $\mathcal{S} = (\mathcal{G}, \mathcal{C})$ we define a mapping ψ from constraint expressions to $\mu\mathcal{ALCQ}$ formulae as follows:

$$\psi(X) = X$$
$$\psi(\exists^{\geq n} F) = (\geq n \mathbf{E}.\psi(F)) \qquad \psi(p) = \forall \mathbf{L}.p$$
$$\psi(\neg\gamma) = \neg\psi(\gamma) \qquad \psi(\uparrow\gamma) = \forall \mathbf{E}.\psi(\gamma)$$
$$\psi(\gamma_1 \wedge \gamma_2) = \psi(\gamma_1) \sqcap \psi(\gamma_2) \qquad \psi(\neg F) = \neg\psi(F)$$
$$\psi(\mu X.\gamma) = \mu X.\psi(\gamma) \qquad \psi(F_1 \wedge F_2) = \psi(F_1) \sqcap \psi(F_2)$$

We construct for each node $u \in Nodes(\mathcal{G}) = \{u_1, \ldots, u_h\}$ a *characteristic* $\mu\mathcal{ALCQ}$ *concept* χ_u as follows[2]: Consider the set of mutual recursive equations, one for each node u_i in $Nodes(\mathcal{G})$

$$X_{u_1} \equiv \top_N \sqcap \psi(\mathcal{C}(u_1)) \sqcap \forall \mathbf{E}.(\top_E \sqcap \bigsqcup_{u_1 \xrightarrow{p} v} (\forall \mathbf{L}.p \sqcap \forall \mathbf{E}.X_v))$$
$$\ldots$$
$$X_{u_h} \equiv \top_N \sqcap \psi(\mathcal{C}(u_h)) \sqcap \forall \mathbf{E}.(\top_E \sqcap \bigsqcup_{u_h \xrightarrow{p} v} (\forall \mathbf{L}.p \sqcap \forall \mathbf{E}.X_v))$$

and eliminate, one at the time, each of the above equations, except the one for X_{u_i} as follows: Eliminate the equation $X_{u_j} = C_j$ and substitute each occurrence of X_{u_j} in the remaining equations by $\nu X_{u_j}.C_j$. Let $X_{u_i} = C_i$ be the resulting equation. The concept χ_{u_i} is $\nu X_{u_i}.C_i$. The encoding $\Phi_\mathcal{S}$ of $\mathcal{S}$ is $\Phi_\mathcal{S} = \chi_{root(\mathcal{G})}$.

Observe that, in the worst case, $|\Phi_\mathcal{S}|$ is exponential with respect to $|\mathcal{S}|$.

Properties of the encoding The following three properties of the encoding establish decidability and complexity of checking subsumption between two $\mathcal{T}$-schemas with $\mathcal{L}_\mu$-constraints $\mathcal{S}_1$ and $\mathcal{S}_2$.

Theorem 10 $\mathcal{S}_1$ *is subsumed by* $\mathcal{S}_2$ *if and only if there is no model of* $\Gamma_\mathcal{T}$ *that satisfies* $\Phi_{\mathcal{S}_1} \sqcap \neg \Phi_{\mathcal{S}_2}$ *and interprets every object-concept as a singleton.*

Theorem 11 *Let* $\Gamma_\mathcal{T}$, $\Phi_{\mathcal{S}_1}$, *and* $\Phi_{\mathcal{S}_2}$ *be as defined above. Then there exists a* $\mu\mathcal{ALCQ}$ *knowledge base* Γ' *whose size is polynomial in* $|\Gamma_\mathcal{T}| + |\Phi_{\mathcal{S}_1}| + |\Phi_{\mathcal{S}_2}|$ *such that:* $\Phi_{\mathcal{S}_1} \sqcap \neg\Phi_{\mathcal{S}_2}$ *is satisfied in a model of* $\Gamma_\mathcal{T}$ *that interprets every object-concept as a singleton, if and only if* $\Phi_{\mathcal{S}_1} \sqcap \neg\Phi_{\mathcal{S}_2}$ *is satisfiable in* Γ'.

Theorem 12 *Checking whether* $\mathcal{S}_1$ *is subsumed by* $\mathcal{S}_2$ *is EXPTIME-hard and decidable in time* $O(2^{p(|\Gamma_\mathcal{T}|+|\Phi_{\mathcal{S}_1}|+|\Phi_{\mathcal{S}_2}|)})$.

Since $|\Phi_\mathcal{S}|$ may be exponential with respect to $|\mathcal{S}|$, it follows that subsumption checking in the presence of $\mathcal{L}_\mu$-constraints can be done in deterministic double exponential time with respect to the size of the two schemas.

---

[2] This construction is analogous to the one used in Process Algebra for defining a characteristic formula of a process (Steffen & Ingólfsdóttir 1994), i.e. a formula which is satisfied by exactly all processes that are equivalent to the process under bisimulation. In a certain sense, we may say that $\Phi_\mathcal{S}$ characterizes, exactly all databases that conform to $\mathcal{S}$.

Conclusions

The result of our investigation is that very expressive DLs are interesting tools for modeling and reasoning about semi-structured data with constraints. The analysis presented in the paper shows that the complexity of subsumption rises even when simple non-local constraints are added to BDFS. This justifies our approach that aims at adding as much expressive power as possible in specifying the constraints, without loosing decidability.

Acknowledgments This work was partly supported by ESPRIT LTR Prj. No. 22469 DWQ and the Italian Space Agency.

References

Abiteboul, S.; Hull, R.; and Vianu, V. 1995. *Foundations of Databases*. Addison Wesley Publ. Co., Reading, Massachussetts.

Abiteboul, S. 1997. Querying semi-structured data. In *ICDT-97*, 1–18.

Baader, F. 1996. Using automata theory for characterizing the semantics of terminological cycles. *Ann. of Math. and AI* 18:175–219.

Borgida, A., and Patel-Schneider, P. F. 1994. A semantics and complete algorithm for subsumption in the CLASSIC description logic. *J. of Artificial Intelligence Research* 1:277–308.

Buneman, P.; Davidson, S.; Fernandez, M.; and Suciu, D. 1997. Adding structure to unstructured data. In *ICDT-97*, 336–350.

Calvanese, D. 1996. Finite model reasoning in description logics. In *KR-96*, 292–303.

Christophides, V.; Abiteboul, S.; Cluet, S.; and Scholl, M. 1994. From structured documents to novel query facilities. In *ACM SIGMOD*, 313–324.

De Giacomo, G., and Lenzerini, M. 1996. TBox and ABox reasoning in expressive description logics. In *KR-96*, 316–327.

De Giacomo, G., and Lenzerini, M. 1997. A uniform framework for concept definitions in description logics. *J. of Artificial Intelligence Research* 6:87–110.

Donini, F. M.; Hollunder, B.; Lenzerini, M.; Spaccamela, A. M.; Nardi, D.; and Nutt, W. 1992. The complexity of existential quantification in concept languages. *Artif. Intell.* 2–3:309–327.

Emerson, E. A. 1996. Automated temporal reasoning about reactive systems. In *Logics for Concurrency: Structure versus Automata*, volume 1043 of *LNCS*. Springer-Verlag. 41–101.

Kozen, D. 1983. Results on the propositional μ-calculus. *Theor. Comp. Sci.* 27:333–354.

Lloyd, J. W. 1987. *Foundations of Logic Programming (Second, Extended Edition)*. Springer-Verlag.

Mendelzon, A.; Mihaila, G. A.; and Milo, T. 1997. Querying the World Wide Web. *Int. J. on Digital Libraries* 1(1):54–67.

Park, D. 1970. Fixpoint induction and proofs of program properties. In *Machine Intelligence*, volume 5. Edinburgh University Press. 59–78.

Quass, D.; Rajaraman, A.; Sagiv, I.; Ullman, J.; and Widom, J. 1995. Querying semistructured heterogeneous information. In *DOOD-95*, 319–344. Springer-Verlag.

Steffen, B., and Ingólfsdóttir, A. 1994. Characteristic formulae for processes with divergence. *Information and Computation* 110:149–163.

Stirling, C. 1996. Modal and temporal logics for processes. In *Logics for Concurrency: Structure versus Automata*, volume 1043 of *LNCS*. Springer-Verlag. 149–237.

Streett, R. E., and Emerson, E. A. 1989. An automata theoretic decision procedure for the propositional μ-calculus. *Information and Computation* 81:249–264.

Modeling Web Sources for Information Integration*

Craig A. Knoblock, Steven Minton, Jose Luis Ambite, Naveen Ashish
Pragnesh Jay Modi, Ion Muslea, Andrew G. Philpot, and Sheila Tejada

Information Sciences Institute, Integrated Media Systems Center,
and Department of Computer Science
University of Southern California
4676 Admiralty Way,
Marina del Rey, CA 90292

Abstract

The Web is based on a browsing paradigm that makes it difficult to retrieve and integrate data from multiple sites. Today, the only way to do this is to build specialized applications, which are time-consuming to develop and difficult to maintain. We are addressing this problem by creating the technology and tools for rapidly constructing information agents that extract, query, and integrate data from web sources. Our approach is based on a simple, uniform representation that makes it efficient to integrate multiple sources. Instead of building specialized algorithms for handling web sources, we have developed methods for mapping web sources into this uniform representation. This approach builds on work from knowledge representation, machine learning and automated planning. The resulting system, called Ariadne, makes it fast and cheap to build new information agents that access existing web sources. Ariadne also makes it easy to maintain these agents and incorporate new sources as they become available.

Introduction

The amount of data accessible via the Web and intranets is staggeringly large and growing rapidly. However, the Web's browsing paradigm does not support many information management tasks. For instance, the only way to integrate data from multiple sites is to build specialized applications by hand. These applications are time-consuming and costly to build, and difficult to maintain.

This paper describes Ariadne,[1] a system for extracting and integrating data from semi-structured web sources. Ariadne enables users to rapidly create "information agents" for the Web. Using Ariadne's modeling tools, an application developer starts with a set of web sources — semi-structured HTML pages, which may be located at multiple web sites — and creates a unified view of these sources. Once the modeling process is complete, an end user (who might be the application developer himself) can issue database-like queries as if the information were stored in a single large database. Ariadne's query planner decomposes these queries into a series of simpler queries, each of which can be answered using a single HTML page, and then combines the responses to create an answer to the original query.

The modeling process enables users to integrate information from multiple web sites by providing a clean, well-understood representational foundation. Treating each web page as a relational information source — as if each web page was a little database — gives us a simple, uniform representation that makes query planning straightforward. The representation is not very expressive, but we compensate for that by developing intelligent modeling tools that help application developers map complex web sources into this representation.

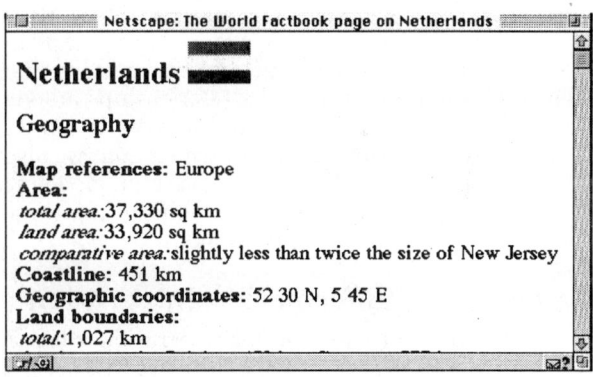

Figure 1: A CIA Factbook page

We will illustrate Ariadne by considering an example application that involves answering queries about the world's countries. An excellent source of data is the CIA World Factbook, which has an HTML page for each country describing that country's geography, economy, government, etc. The top of the factbook page for the Netherlands is shown in Figure 1.[2] Some

---

*Copyright ©1997, American Association for Artificial Intelligence (www.aaai.org). All rights reserved.

[1] In Greek mythology, Ariadne was the daughter of Minos and Pasiphae who gave Theseus the thread that let him find his way out of the Minotaur's labyrinth.

[2] All the web sources in our examples are based on real sources that Ariadne handles, but we have simplified some of them here for expository purposes.

of the many other relevant sites include the NATO site, which lists the NATO member countries, as shown in Figure 2, and the World Governments site, which lists the head of state and other government officers for each country (not shown due to space limitations). Consider queries such as "What NATO countries have populations less than 10 million?" and "List the heads of state of all the countries in the Middle East". Since these queries span multiple countries and require combining information from multiple sources, answering them by hand is time consuming. Ariadne allows us to rapidly put together a new application that can answer a wide range of queries by extracting and integrating data from prespecified web sources.

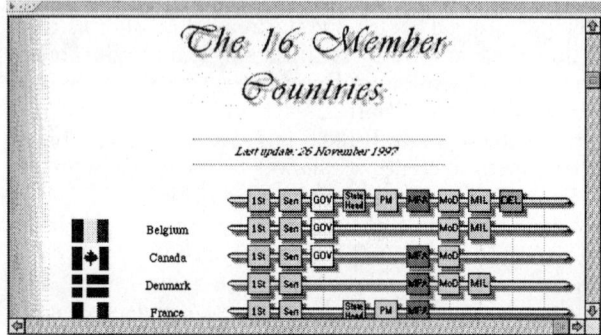

Figure 2: NATO members page

In the following section we describe our basic approach to query planning, where a unifying domain model is used to tie together multiple information sources. We then describe the details of our modeling approach: how we represent and query individual web pages, how we represent the relationships among multiple pages in a single site, and how we integrate data that spans multiple sites. In each section, we also describe the AI methods that are used in modeling and query processing, and how the uniform representational scheme supports these methods.

Approach to Information Integration

Ariadne's approach to information integration is based heavily on the SIMS mediator architecture (Arens *et al.* 1996; Knoblock 1995). SIMS enables users to obtain information from multiple heterogeneous information sources. The framework consists of two parts: 1) a query planner/executor that determines how to efficiently process a query given the set of available information sources and 2) wrappers that provide uniform access to the information sources so that they can be queried as if they were SQL databases. The SIMS framework was designed with specific types of information sources in mind, primarily databases and knowledge bases (and to some extent programs), but as we will explain, the approach can be extended to handle web sources.

One of the most important ideas underlying SIMS is that for each application there is a unifying *domain model* that provides a single ontology for the application. The domain model is represented using the Loom knowledge representation system (MacGregor 1988) and is used to describe the contents of each information source. Given a query in terms of the domain model, the system dynamically selects an appropriate set of sources and then generates a plan to efficiently produce the requested data.

To illustrate this, let us first suppose that the information in the three web sites described earlier, the CIA World Factbook, the World Governments site, and the NATO members page, are each available in three separate databases, along with a fourth database containing a map for each country. To define a new information agent, one would first define a domain model that contains the set of terms that the user might want to query about. An example domain model is shown in Figure 3. The model contains four classes with some relations between them, e.g., 'NATO Country' is a subclass of 'Country', and 'Country' has a relation called 'Head-of-State' which points to a class with the same name. We then use the domain model to describe each of the individual information sources. This provides the glue for answering queries that span multiple sources. For example, the figure shows that the CIA factbook is a source for information about Countries, and the World Governments database is a source for Heads of State. Each class has a set of attributes (e.g., total area, latitude, population, etc.) which may be available from one or more sources.

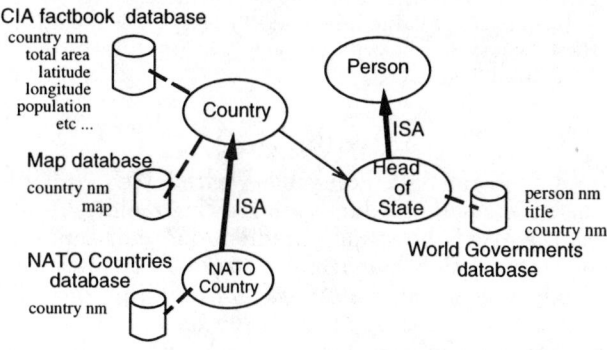

Figure 3: Domain Model with Database Sources

Query Processing

Queries are presented to the system in terms of the domain model. For example, a query might be "List the heads of state of all the countries whose population is less than ten million."[3] The system then decomposes the query into subqueries on the individual sources, such as the World Governments and Factbook

---

[3] In actuality, queries are phrased in the Loom KR language, the same language used to express the domain theory. We use English translations for clarity.

sources, producing a partially-ordered query plan consisting of a series of relational operators, i.e., joins, selects, projects, remote subqueries, etc.

The SIMS query planner (Knoblock 1995) was designed primarily for database applications, but database applications typically involve only a small number of databases, while web applications can involve accessing many more sources. Since the SIMS planner did not scale well to large numbers of sources, we developed an approach capable of efficiently constructing very large query plans. We addressed this problem by combining preprocessing techniques with a local-search method for query planning.

In Ariadne, query processing is broken into a preprocessing phase and a query planning phase. In the first phase the system determines the possible ways of combining the available sources to answer a query. Since sources may be overlapping (i.e., an attribute may be available from several sources) or replicated, the system must determine an appropriate combination of sources that can answer the query. The Ariadne source selection algorithm (Ambite et al. 1998) preprocesses the domain model so that the system can efficiently and dynamically select sources based on the classes and attributes mentioned in the query.

In the second phase, Ariadne generates a plan using a method called Planning-by-Rewriting, developed by Ambite and Knoblock (Ambite and Knoblock 1997; 1998). This approach takes an initial, suboptimal plan and then attempts to improve it by applying rewriting rules. In the case of query planning, producing an initial, suboptimal plan is straightforward; we can generate an initial plan in $O(n)$ time, where n is the length of the query, based on a depth-first parse of the query. The rewriting process iteratively improves the query via a local search process that can change both the sources used to answer a query and the order of the operations on the data.

Consider the processing required to retrieve all NATO countries that have a population of less than 10 million. Using the domain model in Figure 3, the source selection step would determine that the NATO source is the only source for the class of NATO countries. This source provides only the names of the NATO countries and not their populations. However, the population information can be extracted from the Factbook source since it provides data for a superclass of NATO countries. The reasoning to combine sources in this way is done efficiently by precomputing the way sources can be combined before any queries are processed.

The next step in the example is to construct a plan for efficiently retrieving and combining the data. In this case, the system might first construct an initial plan that retrieves the data from the NATO source, separately retrieves the names and population for all countries from the Factbook source, and then combines the data locally, which is very costly since the Factbook source is quite large. This initial, suboptimal plan is then improved in a series of rewriting steps that would order the retrieval of the NATO source before the factbook source so that only population data on the NATO countries would need to be retrieved. The optimized plan would then be executed, returning only Denmark, which has a population of just over 5 million.

Because Ariadne combines an efficient source selection algorithm with an efficient, anytime planning algorithm, the system can produce query plans for web environments in a robust, efficient manner. Ariadne's development was aided by the fact that the relational algebra is very simple and well understood, so that we could concentrate on the issues involved in searching for a plan, rather than on the underlying plan representation, which simply consists of a partially ordered set of relational operators. To move to the Web, we only needed one extension to the basic representation, which was the inclusion of "binding patterns" (Kwok and Weld 1996). That is, unlike database sources, web sources may have input/output constraints (e.g., a stock quote server requires a ticker symbol in order to retrieve a stock quote). This is a small extension that is naturally handled by the source selection algorithm and planning operators.

In the remainder of the paper we consider in more detail the modeling issues involved in creating a database-like view of the Web.

Modeling the Information on a Page

The previous section describes how the planner decomposes a complex query into simple queries on individual information sources. To treat a web page as an information source so that it can be queried, Ariadne needs a wrapper that can extract and return the requested information from that type of page. While we cannot currently create such wrappers for unrestricted natural language texts, many information sources on the Web are *semistructured*. A web page is semistructured if information on the page can be located using a concise formal grammar, such as a context-free grammar. Given such a grammar, the information can be extracted from the source without recourse to sophisticated natural language understanding techniques. For example, a wrapper for pages in the CIA factbook would be able to extract fields such as the Total Area, Population, etc. based on a simple grammar describing the structure of factbook pages.

Our goal is to enable application developers to easily create their own wrappers for web-based information sources. To construct a wrapper, we need both a semantic model of the source that describes the fields available on that type of page and a syntactic model, or grammar, that describes the page format, so the fields can be extracted. Requiring developers to describe the syntactic structure of a web page by writing a grammar by hand is too demanding, since we want to make it easy for relatively unsophisticated users to develop applications. Instead, Ariadne has a "demonstration-oriented user interface" (DoUI) where users show the system what information to extract from example pages. Underlying the interface is a machine learning system for inducing grammar rules.

Figure 4 shows how an application developer uses the interface to teach the system about CIA factbook pages, producing both a semantic model and a syntactic model of the source. The screen is divided into two parts. The upper half shows an example document, in this case the Netherlands page. The lower half shows a semantic model, which the user is in the midst of constructing for this page. The semantic model in the figure indicates that the class Country has attributes such as Total Area, Coastline, Latitude, Longitude, etc. The user constructs the semantic model incrementally, by typing in each attribute name and then filling in the appropriate value by cutting and pasting the information from the document. In doing so, the user actually accomplishes two functions. First, he provides a name for each attribute. Notice that he can choose the same names as used in the document (e.g., "Total area") or he can choose new/different names (e.g., "Latitude"). As we will explain later, the attribute names have significance, since they are the basis for integrating data across sources.

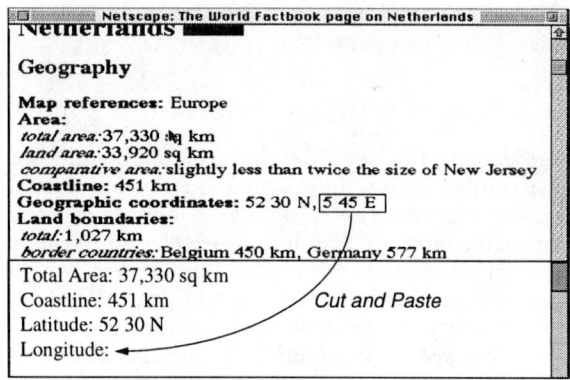

Figure 4: Creating a Wrapper by Demonstration

The second function achieved by the user's demonstration is to provide examples so that the system can induce the syntactic structure of the page. Ideally, after the user has picked out a few examples for each field, the system will induce a grammar sufficient for extracting the required information for all pages of this type. Unfortunately, grammar induction methods may require many examples, depending on the class of grammars being learned. However, we have observed that web pages have common characteristics that we can take advantage of, so that a class of grammars sufficient for extraction purposes can be rapidly learned in practice.

More specifically, we can describe most semistructured web pages as *embedded catalogs*. A *catalog* is either a homogeneous list, such as a list of numbers, (1,3,5,7,8), or a heterogeneous tuple, such as a 3-tuple consisting of a number, a letter, and a string, (1,A,"test"). An *embedded* catalog is a catalog where the items themselves can be catalogs. As an example, consider a CIA factbook page (see Figure 1). The top level consists of an 8-tuple distinguished by section headings: Geography, People, etc. The Geography section is a tuple consisting of Map References, Area, Coastline, etc. These can be decomposed further if necessary; Coastline is a tuple consisting of a number and the string "km".

Because web pages are intended to be human readable, special markers often play a role identifying the beginning or ending of an item in an embedded catalog, separating items in a homogeneous list, and so on. These distinguishing markers can be used as landmarks for locating information on a page. For instance, to find the longitude, simply skip down to the heading "Geography", then to "Geographic Coordinates:", and then skip past the first comma.

A *landmark grammar* describes the position of a field via a sequence of landmarks, where each landmark is itself described by a deterministic finite automaton. Our recent work (Muslea *et al.* 1998) shows that in practice, a subclass of landmark grammars (linear, augmented landmark grammars) can be learned rapidly for a variety of web pages using a greedy covering algorithm. There are several reasons for this. Firstly, because web pages are intended to be human readable, there is often a *single* landmark that distinguishes or separates each field from its neighbors. Therefore the number of landmarks for a field in an embedded catalog will generally be equal to its "depth" in the catalog. Since most catalogs are very shallow, this means that the length of the grammar rules to be learned will be very small, and learning will be easy in practice. Secondly, during the demonstration process, users traverse a page from top-to-bottom, picking out the positive examples of each field. Any position on the page that is not marked as a positive example is implicitly a negative example. Thus, for every positive example identified by the user, we obtain a huge number of negative examples that the covering algorithm can use to focus its search.

The modeling tool we have described enables unsophisticated users to turn web pages into relational information sources. But it has a second advantage as well. If the format of a web source changes in minor respects, the system could induce a new grammar by reusing examples from the original learning episode, without any human intervention (assuming the underlying content has not changed significantly). This is a capability we are currently exploring.

Modeling the Information in a Site: Connections between Pages

The previous section showed how Ariadne extracts information from a web page to answer a query. However, before extracting information from a page, Ariadne must first locate the page in question. Our approach, described in this section, is to model the information required to "navigate" through a web site, so that the planner can automatically determine how to locate a page.

For example, consider a query to our example information agent asking for the population of the Netherlands. To extract the population from the factbook's page on the Netherlands, the system must first find the URL for that page. A person faced with the same task would look at the index page for the factbook, shown in Figure 5, which lists each country by name together with a hypertext link to the page in question. In our approach, Ariadne does essentially the same thing. The index page serves as an information source that provides a URL for each country page. These pages in turn serve as a source for country-specific information.

Figure 5: CIA Factbook Index

To create a wrapper for the index page, the developer uses the approach described in the last section, where we illustrated how a wrapper for the factbook's country pages is created. There is only one difference: this wrapper only wraps a single page, the index page. The developer creates a semantic model indicating that the index page contains a list of countries, each with two attributes, country-nm and country-URL.[4] The learning system induces a grammar for the entire page after the developer shows how the first few lines in the file should be parsed.

As the wrappers for each source are developed, they are integrated into the unifying domain model. Figure 6 shows the domain model for the completed geopolitical agent. (Notice that we have substituted web source wrappers for the hypothetical databases used previously.) To create the domain model, the developer specifies the relationship between the wrappers and the domain concepts. For instance, the developer specifies that the Factbook country wrapper and the Factbook index wrapper are both information sources for "country" information, and he identifies which attributes are keys (i.e., unique identifiers). In the example, "country-nm" and "country-URL" are both keys. Binding constraints specify the input and output of

---

[4] During the demonstration, a special copy command is used to obtain a URL from a hyperlink, as opposed to grabbing text.

each wrapper (shown by the small directional arrows in Figure 6). The country page wrapper takes a country-URL, and acts as a source for "total area", "population", "latitude", etc. The index wrapper takes a country name[5] and acts as a source for "country-URL". Given the domain model and the binding constraints, the system can now construct query plans. For instance, to obtain the population of a country given its name, the planner determines that the system must first use the country name to retrieve the country-URL from the index page wrapper, and then use the country-URL to retrieve the population data from the country page wrapper.

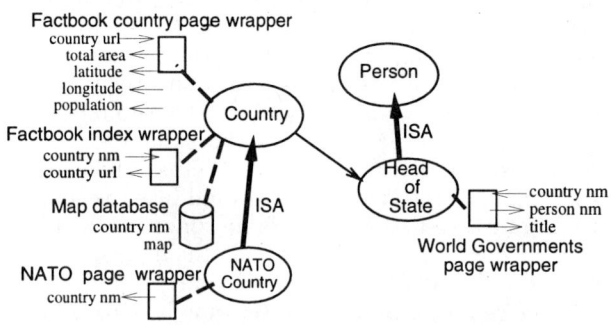

Figure 6: Domain Model with Web Sources

Explicitly modeling 'navigation' pages, such as the factbook index, as information sources enables us to reuse the same modeling tools and planning methodology underlying the rest of the system. The approach works well in part because there are only two common types of navigation strategies used on the Web – direct indexing and form-based retrieval. We have already seen how index pages are handled; form-based navigation is also straightforward. A wrapper for an HTML form simply mimics the action of the form, taking as input a set of attributes, each associated with a form parameter name, and communicating with the server specified in the form's HTML source.

When the resulting page is returned, the wrapper extracts the relevant attributes in the resulting page. Imagine, for instance, a form-based front end to the factbook, where the user types in a country name and the form returns the requested country page. To create a wrapper for this front end, the developer would first specify that the parameter associated with the type-in box would be filled by a "country-nm". He would then specify how the system should extract information from the page returned by the form using the approach described in the last section.

The Factbook example described in this section illustrates our basic approach to modeling navigation pages. Many web sites are more complex than the factbook. The approach still works, but the models

---

[5] No URL is needed as input to the index page wrapper since the URL of the index page is a constant.

become more involved. For instance, indexes can be hierarchical, in which case each level of the hierarchy must be modeled as an information source. Imagine the top-level factbook index was a list of letters, so that clicking on a letter "C" would produce an index page for countries starting with "C" (a "subindex"). We would model this top level index as a relation between letters and subindex-URL's. To traverse this index, we also need an information source that takes a country name and returns the first letter of the name (e.g., a string manipulation program). Thus, altogether four wrappers would be involved in the navigation process, as shown in Figure 7. Given a query asking for the Netherlands' population, the first wrapper would take the name "Netherlands", call the string manipulation program, and return the first letter of the name, "N". The second wrapper would take the letter "N", access the top level index page, and return the subindex-URL. The third wrapper would take the subindex-URL and the country name, access the subindex page for countries starting with "N", and return the country-URL. Finally, the last wrapper would take the country-URL and access the Netherlands page. The advantage of our approach is that all these wrappers are treated uniformly as information sources, so the query planner can automatically determine how to compose the query plan. Furthermore, the wrappers can be semi-automatically created via the learning approach described earlier, except for the string manipulation wrapper, which is a common utility.

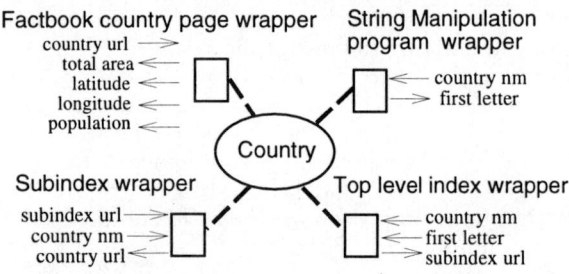

Figure 7: Domain Model with Hierarchical Index

Modeling Information Across Sites

Within a single site, entities (e.g., people, places, countries, companies, etc.) are usually named in a consistent fashion. However, across sites, the same entities may be referred to with different names. For example, the CIA factbook refers to the "Vatican City" while the World Governments site refers to "The Holy See". Sometimes formatting conventions are responsible for differences, such as "Denmark" vs. "Denmark, Kingdom of". To make sense of data that spans multiple sites, we need to be able to recognize and resolve these differences.

Our approach is to select a primary source for an entity's name and then provide a mapping from that source to each of the other sources where a different naming scheme is used. An advantage of the Ariadne architecture is that the mapping itself can be represented as simply another wrapped information source. One way to do this is to create a *mapping table*, which specifies for each entry in one data source what the equivalent entity is called in another data source. Alternatively, if the mapping is computable, it can be represented by a *mapping function*, which is a program that converts one form into another form.

Figure 8 illustrates the role of mapping tables in our geopolitical information agent. The Factbook is the primary source for a country's name. A mapping table maps each factbook country name into the name used in the World Governments source (i.e., WG-country-nm). The mapping source contains only two attributes, the (factbook) country name and the WG-country-nm. The NATO source is treated similarly. So, for example, if someone wanted to find the Heads of State of the NATO countries, the query planner would retrieve the NATO country names from the NATO wrapper, map them into (factbook) country names using the NATO mapping table, then into the World Government country names using the World Governments mapping table, and finally retrieve the appropriate heads of state from the World Governments wrapper.

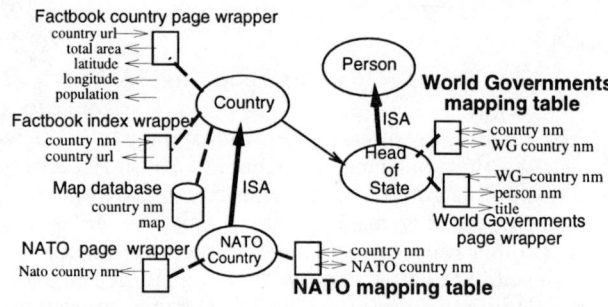

Figure 8: Domain Model with Mapping Tables

Currently, mapping tables and functions must be created manually, but we are developing a semi-automated method for building mapping tables and functions by analyzing the underlying data in advance. The basic idea is to use information retrieval techniques to provide an initial mapping (e.g., (Cohen 1998)), and then use additional data in the sources to resolve any remaining ambiguities via statistical learning methods (e.g., (Huang and Russell 1997)). For example, both the Factbook and the World Governments sources list the title of the Heads of State.[6] This information can help determine that the Factbook's "North Korea" and "South Korea" refer respectively to the World Government's "Democratic Republic of Korea"

---

[6]The Factbook lists the name of the Heads of State as well but, unlike the World Governments site, the information is often out of date. This is one reason why the World Governments site is useful.

and "Republic of Korea", rather than the other way around. Our approach can also be used to automatically update mapping tables when new sources are released. For instance, each year a new version of the CIA factbook is released, and sometimes countries have new names, or countries merge or split. These name confusions can often be resolved using geographical information (e.g., land area, latitude and longitude).

Applications

Below we list some Ariadne applications we are developing, illustrating the generality of our approach:

World-Wide Geographic Information Server: We are collaborating with another group that is building a geographic information system that integrates a variety of map-based information sources. These sources include satellite images, detailed street maps, parcel data, historical aerial photographs, etc. We are using Ariadne to extract geographically referenced data from the Web and integrate it with map data. We have built a system using Ariadne that extracts restaurant data from the Zagats Restaurant Reviews site, feeds the restaurant address into a geocoder, and then places the restaurant on an aerial map. Other web sources that we plan to incorporate include census data, US Geological Survey data, and real estate data from the Multiple Listing Service.

Electronic Catalog Access: We are applying Ariadne to provide access to online electronic catalogs for the Defense Logistics Agency. One implemented application provides real-time access to pricing and availability data from the General Services Administration web pages. This application accesses only a single site, but retrieves pricing data for parts by extracting and integrating data from multiple pages in the site.

Financial Information Agent: We have done initial work on an agent that accesses stock quote servers, stock exchange sources, and the SEC's EDGAR Archives (which contains copies of financial filings, such as annual reports, by publicly traded companies and mutual funds). By integrating these sources, the agent could answer queries such as "Find all airline companies whose stock has risen more than thirty percent in the last year" and "Find all people who serve as directors of two or more companies located in Los Angeles". Using the modeling tools described earlier, users could also include their own personal financial data sources, tailoring the system to their needs.

Related Work

There is large body of relevant literature on information integration (Wiederhold 1996), but the most closely related work focuses specifically on the problems of information integration on the Web, such as Information Manifold (Levy *et al.* 1996), Occam (Kwok and Weld 1996), Infomaster (Genesereth *et al.* 1997), and InfoSleuth (Bayardo Jr. *et al.* 1997). These systems focus on a variety of issues, including the problems of representing and selecting a relevant set of sources to answer a query, handling binding patterns, and resolving discrepancies among sources. All of this work is directly relevant to Ariadne, but the issue addressed in this paper that has not been addressed previously is how one represents the information within a single page, across pages at a site, and across sites to support web-based information integration.

Another closely related body of work is on the extraction of data from web sources (Hammer *et al.* 1997; Doorenbos *et al.* 1997; Kushmerick 1997). The focus of all of these systems are on building wrappers for semi-structured sources. The systems either take a template-based specification of a source, as in (Hammer *et al.* 1997), or learn the structure of the source by example and then compile a wrapper that provides access to the source, as in (Kushmerick 1997). Our work on inducing wrappers takes the latter approach. The induction method is not only very general, but is also integrated into the larger Ariadne development system so that the learned wrappers can be used directly by the query planner.

Discussion

There are many examples of impressive AI systems based on relatively simple representational schemes. In the realm of planning, recent examples include SATplan (Kautz and Selman 1996) and Graph-plan (Blum and Furst 1995); the former employs a propositional CSP approach, the latter, a graph-based search. In machine learning, propositional learning schemes (e.g., decision trees) have been dominant. Though it is often difficult to understand exactly what a simple representational scheme buys you computationally, one thing seems clear: systems with simple representations are often easier to design and understand.

We believe that Ariadne is successful, in terms of the broad applicability of the approach, because it combines a simple representation scheme with sophisticated modeling tools that map web information sources into this simple representation. Ariadne capitalizes on a representation scheme adopted from database systems, where the world consists of a set of relations (or tables) over objects, and simple relational operators (retrieve, join, etc.) are composed to answer queries. This representation makes it straightforward to integrate multiple databases using an AI planner. Ariadne's planner can efficiently search for a sequence of joins, selections, etc. that will produce the desired result without needing to do any sophisticated reasoning about the information sources themselves.

The Web environment is much richer than the database world, of course. What makes Ariadne possible are the modeling tools that enable a user to create a database-like view of the Web. Where our approach becomes challenging (and could break down) is in situations where the "natural" way to represent a web source is not possible due to limitations of the underlying representation.

One such limitation is that Ariadne cannot reason about recursive relations. (To do this properly would require query plans to contain loops.) This has many practical ramifications. For example, consider web pages that have a 'more' button at the bottom, such as Alta Vista's response pages. It would be natural to represent each 'more' button as a pointer to the next page in a list, but there is no way to do this without a recursive relation. Instead, we can build knowledge about 'more' buttons in our wrapper generation tools, so the process of following a 'more' buttons is done completely within a wrapper, hiding the complexity from the query planner.

Another ramification of the planner's inability to reason about recursive relations shows up with hierarchical indexes like Yahoo, where there is no fixed depth to the hierarchy. The natural way to model such pages is with a parent-child relation. Instead, the alternative is to build a more sophisticated wrapper that computes the transitive closure of the parent-child relationship, so that we can obtain all of a node's descendants in one step.

There is an obvious tension between the expressiveness of the representation and the burden we place on the modeling tools. Our approach has been to keep the representation and planning process simple, compensating for their weaknesses by relying on smarter modeling tools. As we have described, the advantage is that we can incrementally build a suite of modeling tools that use machine learning, statistical inference, and other AI techniques, producing a system that can handle a surprisingly wide range of tasks.

Acknowledgements

This work was supported in part by USC's Integrated Media Systems Center (IMSC) - an NSF Engineering Research Center, by the U.S. Air Force under contract number F49620-98-1-0046, by the Rome Laboratory of the Air Force Systems Command and the Defense Advanced Research Projects Agency (DARPA) under contract number F30602-97-2-0352, by the Defense Logistics Agency, DARPA, and Fort Huachuca under contract number DABT63-96-C-0066, and by a research grant from General Dynamics Information Systems. The views and conclusions contained in this paper are the authors' and should not be interpreted as representing the official opinion or policy of any of the above organizations or any person connected with them.

References

Ambite, J.L. and Knoblock, C.A. 1997. Planning by rewriting: Efficiently generating high-quality plans. In *Proceedings of AAAI-97*.

Ambite, J.L. and Knoblock, C.A. 1998. Flexible and scalable query planning in distributed and heterogeneous environments. In *Proceedings of AIPS-98*.

Ambite, J.L.; Knoblock, C.A.; Muslea, I.; and Philpot, A. 1998. Compiling source descriptions for efficient and flexible information integration. Technical report, USC Information Sciences Inst.

Arens, Y.; Knoblock, C.A.; and Shen, W.M. 1996. Query reformulation for dynamic information integration. *Journal of Intelligent Information Systems*, 6(2/3):99–130.

Bayardo Jr., R.J.; Bohrer, W.; Brice, R.; Cichocki, A.; Fowler, J.; Helal, A.; Kashyap, V.; Ksiezyk, T.; Martin, G.; Nodine, M.; Rashid, M.; Rusinkiewicz, M.; Shea, R.; Unnikrishnan, C.; Unruh, A.; and Woelk, D. 1997. Infosleuth: Agent-based semantic integration of information in open and dynamic environments. In *Proceedings of ACM SIGMOD-97*.

Blum, A. and Furst, M. 1995. Fast planning through planning graph analysis. In *Proceedings of IJCAI-95*.

Cohen, W.W. 1998. Integration of Heterogeneous Databases without Common Domains using Queries Based on Textual Similarity. In *Proceedings of ACM SIGMOD-98*.

Doorenbos, R.B.; Etzioni, O.; and Weld, D.S. 1997. A scalable comparison-shopping agent for the world-wide web. In *Proceedings of the First International Conference on Autonomous Agents*.

Genesereth, M.R.; Keller, A.M.; and Duschka, O.M. 1997. Infomaster: An information integration system. In *Proceedings of ACM SIGMOD-97*.

Hammer, J.; Garcia-Molina, H.; Nestorov, S.; Yerneni, R.; Breunig, M.; and Vassalos, V. 1997. Template-based wrappers in the TSIMMIS system. In *Proceedings of ACM SIGMOD-97*.

Huang, T. and Russell, S. 1997. Object Identification in a bayesian context. In *Proceedings of IJCAI-97*.

Kautz, H. and Selman, B. 1996. Pushing the envelope: Planning, propositional logic, and stochastic search. In *Proceedings of AAAI-96*.

Knoblock, C.A. 1995. Planning, executing, sensing, and replanning for information gathering. In *Proceedings of IJCAI-95*.

Kushmerick, N. 1997. *Wrapper Induction for Information Extraction*. PhD thesis, Computer Science Dept., University of Washington.

Kwok, C.T. and Weld, D.S. 1996. Planning to gather information. In *Proceedings of AAAI-96*.

Levy, A.Y.; Rajaraman, A.; and Ordille, J.J. 1996. Query-answering algorithms for information agents. In *Proceedings of AAAI-96*.

MacGregor, R. 1988. A deductive pattern matcher. In *Proceedings of AAAI-88*.

Muslea, I.; Minton, S.; and Knoblock, C.A. 1998. Wrapper induction for semistructured, web-based information sources. In *Proceedings of the CONALD-98 Workshop on Learning from Text and the Web*.

Wiederhold, G. 1996. *Intelligent Integration of Information*. Kluwer.

An Ontology for Transitions in Physical Dynamic Systems*

Pieter J. Mosterman
Inst. of Robotics and System Dynamics
DLR Oberpfaffenhofen
P.O. Box 1116
D-82230 Wessling
Pieter.J.Mosterman@dlr.de

Feng Zhao
Department of Computer and
Information Science
The Ohio State University
Columbus, OH 43210
fz@cis.ohio-state.edu

Gautam Biswas
Department of Computer Science
Box 1679, Sta B
Vanderbilt University
Nashville, TN 37235
biswas@vuse.vanderbilt.edu

Abstract

Physical systems often exhibit complex nonlinear behaviors in continuous time at multiple temporal and spatial scales. Abstractions simplify behavioral analysis and help focus on dominant system behaviors by defining sets of equivalent behavior types called *modes*. System behavior evolves in continuous modes with discrete transitions between modes. Subtle interactions between the continuous behaviors and discrete transitions need to be captured by well-defined hybrid modeling and analysis semantics. This paper presents a taxonomy of transition modes, and develops a formal semantics for transition conditions that lead to efficient and physically consistent simulation algorithms for physical systems.

Introduction

Physical system behaviors, governed by the principles of *conservation of energy* and *continuity of power* (Mosterman & Biswas 1998), are continuous but can operate at multiple temporal and spatial scales. When analyzing gross behavior the details of fast nonlinear changes are often insignificant. Consider the bouncing clutch in Fig. 1. With the clutch, Sw_1, in the open position, the mass m_1 applies a gravitational force causing the latch and inertia I_1 to rotate. At a predetermined angle $\theta_{contact}$, the latch collides with the fixed pinions, but the torsional elasticity in the connecting rod, I_1, results in further movement after collision before the angular velocity ω_I of the inertia reverses. For the modeler interested in overall behaviors, the collision process can be abstracted to generate an instantaneous reversal in velocity.

Hybrid modeling techniques simplify complex continuous nonlinear behaviors to piecewise continuous behaviors interspersed with discrete transitions. Fast nonlinear behavior effects are replaced by discrete transitions to alleviate numerical problems caused by the

---
* Copyright ©1998, American Association of Artificial Intelligence (www.aaai.org). All rights reserved.

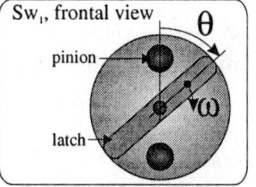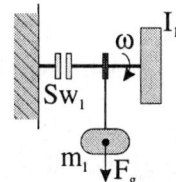

Figure 1: **Elastic collision of a braking clutch.**

steep gradients. Model generation is simplified by eliminating parasitic parameters that are abstracted away. Discrete transitions are linked to *configuration changes* in the system model, and result in the system operating in a number of different *modes*. *Hybrid systems* are becoming increasingly popular in analyzing embedded systems (physical systems with discrete controllers) and complex physical systems that exhibit fast nonlinear behaviors (Alur *et al.* 1994; Guckenheimer & Johnson 1995; Mosterman & Biswas 1996; 1997). Hybrid system models combine continuous behaviors governed by ordinary differential equations (ODEs) or differential and algebraic equations (DAEs) with discrete transitions defined by finite state machines or Petri nets.

Compositional modeling approaches are adopted to model discrete changes as local switching functions defined by system variables crossing threshold values. A local transition can trigger additional changes which continue till no further local transition functions are active, and the system behavior resumes continuous evolution in time. Sometimes system variables in the new continuous mode are at their threshold values, and the mode is departed in an infinitesimally small time interval resulting in a new sequence of discrete changes (Mosterman & Biswas 1997). In other situations, the system *chatters*, i.e., it exhibits quick oscillations between two modes of operation (Mosterman, Zhao, & Biswas 1997; Zhao & Utkin 1996).

We build on two existing strands of work that stud-

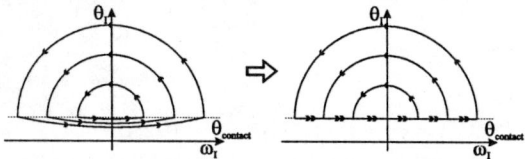

Figure 2: **Bouncing clutch phase space.**

ied individual mode transitions: (i) analysis of hybrid systems models with instantaneous mode and state vector changes (Mosterman & Biswas 1996), and (ii) analysis of hybrid system models which exhibit *chattering* (Mosterman, Zhao, & Biswas 1997; Zhao 1995; Zhao & Utkin 1996). This paper develops a taxonomy of transitions in hybrid models of complex physical systems, and a unified semantics that combines the continuous interior and boundary modes with mythical, pinnacle, and sliding behavior modes. These semantics are translated into a behavior generation algorithm, whose effectiveness is demonstrated by simulation results. The principal contribution of this work is a systematic treatment of transition behavior in hybrid systems.

Phase Space Description Formalism

The state vector of a continuous system defines an n-dimensional space called the *phase space*. Individual behaviors of the system can be described as trajectories in the phase space.

Discontinuities in Phase Space

A common approach to simplify behaviors at multiple scales is to replace a complex trajectory by piecewise continuous segments, where the system of equations describing the behavior in each segment is simpler than the original nonlinear equations. However, this introduces switching functions into the system model, and discontinuities may occur in the system variables at switching points. The phase space behavior representation of the bouncing clutch, illustrated in Fig. 2 shows the nonlinear behavior of I_1's velocity upon collision (left) being replaced by an instantaneous transition (right), indicated by the double-headed arrows.

Hybrid System Definition

Hybrid systems combine continuous and discrete behaviors (Mosterman & Biswas 1997). A hybrid model can be formally defined in terms of I, a discrete indexing set with $\alpha \in I$, defining the modes of the system. Piecewise behavior trajectories $\mathcal{F}_\alpha$ are a continuous, C^2, flow on a possibly open subset V_α of $\Re^n$, called a *chart* (Fig. 3) (Guckenheimer & Johnson 1995). The

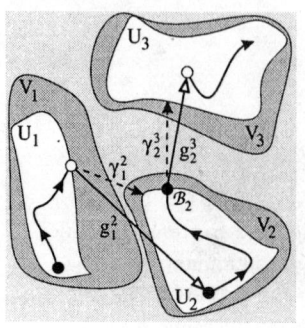

Figure 3: **A planar hybrid system.**

sub-domain of V_α where a continuous flow in time occurs is called a *patch*, $U_\alpha \subset V_\alpha$. Behavior at time t is specified by the state vector $x_\alpha(t)$, a location in chart V_α in mode α. Mode change is specified by the discrete switching function γ_α^β, a *threshold function* on V_α. If $\gamma_\alpha^\beta \leq 0$ then the system transitions from mode α to β. The change in state is defined by the mapping $g_\alpha^\beta : V_\alpha \to V_\beta$. The piecewise continuous level curves $\gamma_\alpha^\beta = 0$ define patch boundaries. If a flow $\mathcal{F}_\alpha$ includes the level curve, it contains the *boundary point*, $\mathcal{B}_\alpha$ (see patch 2 in Fig 3).

Modes of Hybrid System Behavior

Behavior discontinuities in hybrid models of physical systems have been attributed to two general abstraction techniques: (i) *time scale* and (ii) *parameter* abstraction (Mosterman & Biswas 1997; Mosterman, Zhao, & Biswas 1997). These discontinuities may manifest as jumps in system variable values and discrete switches in the fields that govern behaviors in individual modes. A formal semantics governs mode and state vector changes associated with transitions.

Hybrid Modeling of Physical Systems

Time scale abstractions model complex behaviors over small time intervals by discontinuous changes at points in time. An example is a bouncing rubber ball, where the ball velocity is modeled to reverse instantaneously upon collision with the floor. In reality, the initial kinetic energy of the ball is stored on impact as elastic energy within the ball and the floor for a very small time period, and then returned back as kinetic energy to the ball, which causes it to fly back up. Time scale abstraction reduces the process of energy storage and return to a point in time. Parameter abstractions, on the other hand, eliminate small, parasitic dissipation and storage parameters from the system model. In case of a steel ball, the elasticity coefficient of the ball may be small enough to be ignored. The implication is

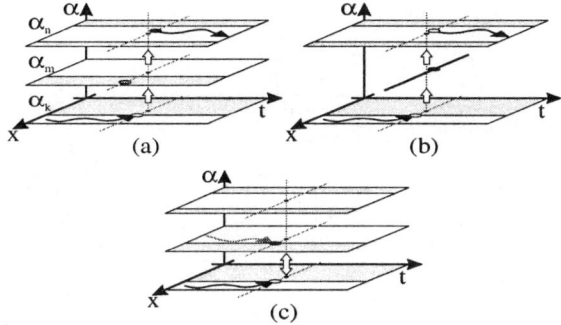

Figure 4: (a) Mythical, (b) Pinnacle, and (c) Sliding modes.

that the collision between the floor and ball becomes non-elastic (there is no energy storage at collision), and the ball comes to rest at the point of contact. A closer study of the two abstraction forms reveals a number of transition behaviors that require particular semantics. Fig. 4 illustrates the different transition mode behaviors (**x** represents the state vector and α represents the mode of operation).

Mythical Modes

Consider the two clutch freewheeling system (Fig. 5) where the bodies and connecting rod are assumed to be rigid (no elasticity) and small component parameters are abstracted away. The dissipation or small deformation effects in the connecting rod that are active upon collision are not modeled. Simulation results, illustrating the torsional force F_I and angular velocity ω_I appear in Fig. 6. Initially, brake Sw_1 is open and Sw_2 is closed. The weight m_1 produces an angular velocity, ω_I in inertia I_1. At 0.2 s, the rotation causes Sw_1 to close. At this point both Sw_1 and Sw_2 are closed, and ω_I is forced to 0. This causes a force in Sw_2 that moves the latch away from the pinion. Sw_2 opens, I_1 is free to rotate, and ω_I stays at a nonzero value.

The intermediate configuration, where the angular velocity was forced to 0, is mythical, i.e., it does not exist in real time. Fig. 4a illustrates a trajectory that transitions from a real mode α_k to an intermediate mythical mode α_m, and then to a real mode α_n where behavior evolves continuously. The instantaneous transitions do not affect the state vector, therefore, the angular velocity of I_1, ω_I, after the configuration changes equals its value before (Fig. 6), which is consistent with real behavior. Note that the intermediate mythical configuration defines the mode change sequence. Mythical modes also occur in hybrid models of a diode-inductor circuit and the collision of a free-

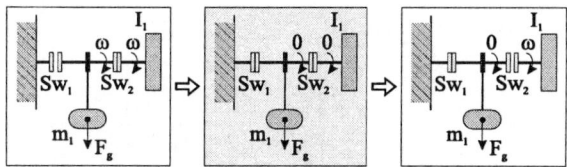

Figure 5: **Mythical mode in analyzing a freewheeling clutch.**

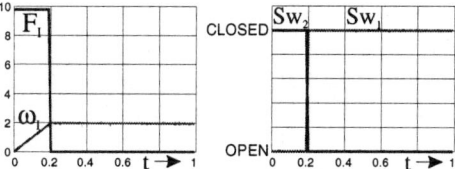

Figure 6: **A mythical configuration has no representation in real time.**

falling thin rod with the ground (Mosterman & Biswas 1997).

Pinnacles

Consider the system in Fig. 7 with significant torsional elasticity in the connecting rod. This causes a perfectly elastic collision between the latch and pinion when Sw_1 closes. The latch and I_1's rotation toward the pinions is a continuous behavior. The collision, governed by the rotational analog of Newton's elastic collision rule, satisfies $\omega_I^+ = -\epsilon\omega_I$, where ϵ represents the coefficient of restitution ($= 1$ for a perfectly elastic collision). This collision rule captures the torsional compression and expansion of the connecting rod on collision into a behavior at a point in time, called a pinnacle. Change in the state vector at that point in time is governed by algebraic equations, which hold only for that point. Simulation results in Fig. 8 illustrate Sw_1 closing at 0.6 s, causing momentum transfer and instantaneous reversal of angular velocity ω_I at a point in time. A pinnacle manifests as a jump in the state vector, after which the system behavior evolves in a continuous trajectory (Fig. 4b).

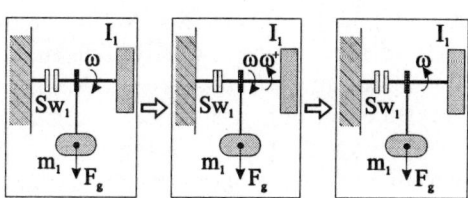

Figure 7: **A pinnacle due to an elastic collision.**

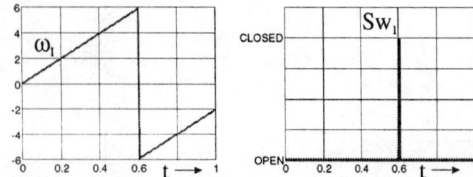

Figure 8: **Pinnacles occur at a point in time.**

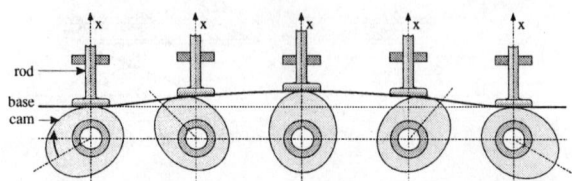

Figure 9: **A cam mechanism opens a valve.**

Sliding Mode

Sliding mode behavior occurs when a phase space transition chatters between two modes. If a transition leads the system to the boundary region of an adjoining mode, and the direction of the field vector is toward the first mode, the system may switch from the second mode back to the boundary of the first. If the gradient of the field is again toward the second mode, the first transition may repeat. If this phenomenon continues, one observes chattering behavior (i.e., the system goes back and forth between two modes in Fig. 4c). This is best-handled by introducing sliding mode behavior on the surface that defines the boundary of the two modes.

Sliding mode behavior is illustrated for the cam-follower system in Fig. 9. The cam mechanism translates rotational motion into a linear displacement to open and close valves in the engine cylinders. Typically, a spring mechanism ensures contact between the rod and rotating cam but the high velocities of operation (up to several thousands of revolutions per minute) and wear of the spring can cause the rod to bounce on and off the cam.

When the deceleration of the cam causes the rod to disconnect, it may reconnect within an infinitesimal period of time. This chattering behavior, an artifact of the numerical time step, can slow down the simulation process. The sliding mode algorithm replaces chattering by *equivalent dynamics* to derive the nonlinear behavior from the linearized phase space under the assumption of small physical inertial and hysteresis effects (Mosterman, Zhao, & Biswas 1997). Fig. 10 shows the simulation behavior of a cam-follower mechanism. The simulation results on the left do not apply equivalent dynamics. The cam and rod alternately have equal and nonequal velocities. When the rod disconnects from the cam the velocity difference builds up. However, because the cam decelerates, at the next simulation time step a nonelastic collision occurs and the rod and cam velocities are instantaneously forced to equal values. The simulation on the right applies equivalent dynamics to remove this simulation artifact. The system slides on the switching surface $v_{rod} = v_{cam}$ and there is no error due to chattering. This conforms

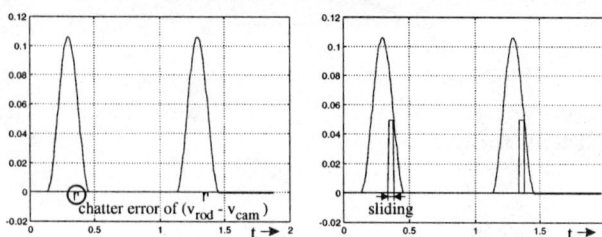

Figure 10: **Sliding mode simulation during an interval of time.**

with true physical behavior, where unmodeled higher order physical phenomena such as adhesive forces between the rod and cam would result in the rod and cam having the same velocity.

An Ontology for Transitions

Starting from the three modes defined above, a formal characterization of mode transitions can be derived by focusing on the mechanisms active during the transition process. This is best derived from a mathematical hybrid system model. An implemented simulation algorithm applies the mode taxonomy to invoke the correct semantics for generating physically consistent behaviors.

The Mathematical Model

The mathematical model defines a switching function, γ_α^β, with parameters the state vector x_α, prior to the jump and x_α^+, the state vector immediately after the jump. The semantics of transitions is specified by the recursive relation between γ_α^β and g_α^β

$$\begin{cases} x_{\alpha_k}^+ = g_{\alpha_k}^{\alpha_i}(x_{\alpha_k}) \\ \gamma_{\alpha_i}^{\alpha_{i+1}}(x_{\alpha_k}, x_{\alpha_k}^+) \leq 0 \end{cases} \quad (1)$$

Note the α_k subscript of x_{α_k} in $g_{\alpha_k}^{\alpha_i}$. In physical systems, continuous behavior is completely specified by the state. Therefore, the state mapping is independent of the departed mode, i.e., g_α^β is independent of α. This results in the general sequence

$$\underbrace{\begin{cases} x^+ = g^{\alpha_1}(x) \\ x = x^+ \\ \dot{x} = f_{\alpha_1}(x,t) \end{cases}}_{\alpha_1} \xrightarrow{\gamma_{\alpha_1}^{\alpha_2}(x,x^+)} \underbrace{\begin{cases} x^+ = g^{\alpha_2}(x) \\ x = x^+ \\ \dot{x} = f_{\alpha_2}(x,t) \end{cases}}_{\alpha_2} \xrightarrow{\gamma_{\alpha_2}^{\alpha_3}(x,x^+)}$$

$$\cdots \xrightarrow{\gamma_{\alpha_{m-1}}^{\alpha_m}(x,x^+)} \underbrace{\begin{cases} x^+ = g^{\alpha_m}(x) \\ x = x^+ \\ \dot{x} = f_{\alpha_m}(x,t) \end{cases}}_{\alpha_m} \quad (2)$$

In this sequence, each mode, α, may be departed when any of the three assignment statements is executed. The resultant computational model, illustrated in Fig. 11, distinguishes the three cases.

(a) *Transition to mythical mode* (Fig. 11a): This occurs when $x^+ = g^{\alpha_i}(x)$ leads to $\gamma_{\alpha_i}^{\alpha_i+1}(x,x^+) \leq 0$. The immediate transition bypasses the *integrator* ($\int$), therefore, the state vector x remains unchanged through the transition (also see Fig. 4a).

(b) *Transition to pinnacle* (Fig. 11b): This occurs when $x = x^+$ results in $\gamma_{\alpha_i}^{\alpha_i+1}(x,x^+) \leq 0$. Updating state vector x causes a mode transition. Therefore, mode α_i only exists at a point in time but the state vector can change with the transition (Fig. 4b).

(c) *Transition to continuous mode* (Fig. 11c): In this case after the transition and update $x = x^+$, $\forall_{\alpha_n} \gamma_{\alpha_m}^{\alpha_n}(x,x^+) > 0$. Therefore, f_{α_m} is active. Three situations may occur:

- *Interior mode:* Behavior evolution is continuously governed by a field, f_{α_m}. In Fig. 12a the system transitions from one continuous mode α_k to a second continuous mode α_m.
- *Boundary:* A transition occurs after an infinitesimal period of time, which indicates a patch boundary was reached (see Fig. 12b), and the newly established mode switches to another mode within an infinitesimal period of time.
- *Sliding mode:* A transition occurs after an infinitesimal period of time and the newly established mode switches back to the current one within an infinitesimal period of time (Fig. 4c).

Pinnacles and continuous modes are referred to as *real* modes because they change the state vector x stored in the integrator ($\int$). Interior modes, boundary modes and sliding modes are *continuous* because the gradient of the field vector defines the behavior evolution process. Note that there is a distinct difference between the pinnacle and boundary modes. Pinnacles, caused by time scale abstraction, define behaviors by an algebraic equation that causes a jump in phase space. As soon as the *a priori* state vector is updated, the pinnacle is departed. Boundary behaviors are governed by gradients of continuous flow. After the state vector is updated, the boundary is active. It is departed after behavior evolves over an infinitesimal

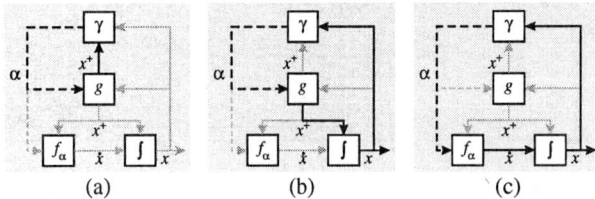

Figure 11: **Classes of modes of operation.**

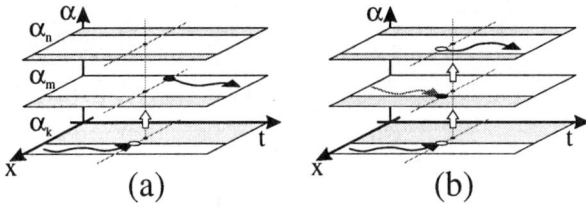

Figure 12: **(a) Interior mode and (b) boundary mode.**

amount of time along the field gradient (Mosterman & Biswas 1997).

The described mode transitions may appear in combination with one another. For example, in the cam-follower system, collision effects occur between the cam and the pushing rod that opens valves. These collisions introduce pinnacles in phase space that are traversed in between sliding modes.

The Simulation Algorithm

Simulation of hybrid models requires special semantics for mythical, pinnacles, and sliding modes. Starting from an interior mode α_k and a transition from α_k to α_m with $x_{\alpha_k}(t)^+ = g^{\alpha_m}(x_{\alpha_k})$, Table 1 specifies the conditions that have to be satisfied for each of these modes.[1] A mythical mode is detected when the new state vector x^+ is beyond the patch of the newly inferred mode. This requires an instantaneous transition governed by invariance of state (see Table 2) (Mosterman & Biswas 1997). For pinnacles, algebraic relations govern system behavior. No continuous behavior evolution occurs. In a new mode for which continuous evolution is specified, an immediate transition may occur when the system is advanced over an infinitesimal time interval. This implies that the transition moved the system onto a boundary point instead of the interior of a patch (Fig. 12). If repeated transitions occur between two modes chattering behavior governed by equivalence dynamics is observed (Mosterman, Zhao, & Biswas 1997).

---

[1] The function $\gamma_\alpha^\beta(x,x^+)$ is replaced for clarity reasons by $\gamma_\alpha^\beta(x^+)$ for sliding modes because $x^+ = x$.

Mode Class	Criteria
mythical mode	$\exists \alpha_n (\gamma_{\alpha_m}^{\alpha_n}(x_{\alpha_k}(t), x_{\alpha_k}(t)^+) \leq 0$
pinnacle	$\exists \alpha_n (\gamma_{\alpha_m}^{\alpha_n}(x_{\alpha_k}(t)^+, x_{\alpha_k}(t)^+) \leq 0$
sliding mode	$\exists \delta t_1 (\delta t_1 < \epsilon)(\gamma_{\alpha_m}^{\alpha_k}(x_{\alpha_m}(t+\delta t)) \leq 0) \wedge$ $\exists \delta t_2 (\delta t_2 < \epsilon)(\gamma_{\alpha_k}^{\alpha_m}(x_{\alpha_k}(t+\delta t)) \leq 0)$

Table 1: **Classification scheme and guards.**

Mode Class	Semantics
mythical mode	invariance of state
pinnacle	no continuous evolution
sliding mode	equivalence of dynamics

Table 2: **Semantics governing particular mode transition behavior.**

A high level description of the simulation algorithm appears as Algorithm 1. The input is the mathematical hybrid system model, and the output a behavior trajectory that includes mode transitions. A forward Euler numerical approximation function, $timeStep(\alpha, x)$ evolves behavior along field gradients. When a transition condition occurs ($\gamma_\alpha^\beta \leq 0$), the function $recursion(\alpha, x)$, which implements Eq. (1) is invoked. When recursion terminates, the state vector is updated ($x = x^+$). This may cause a further change implying a pinnacle. The pinnacle may be followed by mythical modes. When mode changes terminate in a new continuous mode, the sliding mode condition in Table 1 is checked by the function $slide(\alpha, x)$. If satisfied, equivalence dynamics approximates system behavior until behavior moves away from the switching surface. The system continues to evolve until a new transition condition is detected. Applications to the braking clutch and cam-follower system were illustrated earlier.

Algorithm 1 Hybrid Simulation Algorithm

Require: $\alpha, x, f_\alpha, \gamma_\alpha^\beta, g_\alpha^\beta$
  while time < end time **do**
    $x = timeStep(\alpha, x)$
    $[\alpha^+, x^+] = recursion(\alpha, x)$
    if $\alpha^+ \neq \alpha$ **then**
      repeat
        $\alpha = \alpha^+$
        $x = x^+$
        $[\alpha^+, x^+] = recursion(\alpha, x)$
      until $\alpha^+ = \alpha$
      $[\alpha, x] = slide(\alpha, x)$
    end if
  end while

Conclusions

A systematic study of abstractions provides a formal methodology for hybrid modeling of physical systems. The models operate in multiple piecewise continuous regions represented by patches in phase space. Transitions between patches give rise to modes of behavior classified as: (i) mythical, (ii) pinnacle, (iii) interior, (iv) boundary, and (v) sliding. Formal definitions for transitions between modes are developed that allow the specification of self-consistent simulators for hybrid systems. Our simulator has been applied to generate behaviors for a number of physical examples. It handles the idiosyncrasies of each transition type as well as combinations of transitions well. Future research will focus on applying this framework to verification problems in control. As phase space dimensions increase, verifying the sliding mode guards becomes a more challenging task.

Acknowledgements: Pieter Mosterman is supported by a grant from the DFG Schwerpunktprogramm KONDISK. Feng Zhao is supported in part by ONR YI grant N00014-97-1-0599, NSF NYI grant CCR-9457802, and a Xerox grant to the Ohio State University. Gautam Biswas is supported by grants from PNC, Japan and Hewlett-Packard, Co.

References

Alur, R.; et al., 1994. The algorithmic analysis of hybrid systems. In *Proc. of the 11th Intl. Conf. on Analysis and Optimization of Discrete Event Systems*, 331–351.

Guckenheimer, J., and Johnson, S. 1995. Planar hybrid systems. In *Hybrid Systems II*, vol. 999, 202–225.

Mosterman, P. J., and Biswas, G. 1996. A Formal Hybrid Modeling Scheme for Handling Discontinuities in Physical System Models. In *AAAI-96*, 985–990.

Mosterman, P. J., and Biswas, G. Formal Specifications for Hybrid Dynamical Systems. In *IJCAI-97*, 568–573.

Mosterman, P. J., and Biswas, G. 1998. A theory of discontinuities in dynamic physical systems. *Journal of the Franklin Institute* 335B(6):401–439.

Mosterman, P. J.; Zhao, F.; and Biswas, G. 1997. Model semantics and simulation for hybrid systems operating in sliding regimes. In *AAAI Fall Symp. on Model Directed Autonomous Systems*, 48–55.

Zhao, F., and Utkin, V. I. 1996. Adaptive simulation and control of variable-structure control systems in sliding regimes. *Automatica: IFAC Journal* 32(7):1037–1042.

Zhao, F. 1995. Qualitative reasoning about discontinuous control systems. In *Proc. of IJCAI-95 Engineering Problems for Qualitative Reasoning Workshop*, 83–93.

A New Architecture for Automated Modelling

Neil Smith[*]

Department of Computing and Information Sciences
De Montfort University, Milton Keynes, UK

Abstract

Existing automated modelling systems either rely on large, complex libraries or require complete access to the modelled system's behaviour, neither of which is desirable. To address these problems, a simpler architecture for modelling knowledge is described, based on the separation between ideal models of components and corrections that can be applied to these ideal models. The use of this architecture to develop accurate model boundaries is described, based on consideration of interactions within such ideal models. A novel algorithm for refining models is also proposed. This algorithm considers behavioural differences between models and applies the corrections that cause the greatest differences in behaviour. Finally, some models generated by this method are shown to be parsimonious.

Introduction

Existing automated modelling systems can be divided into two broad categories on the basis of how they develop models (Schut & Bredeweg, 1996). Model composition systems (*e.g.* Falkenhainer & Forbus (1991) and Iwasaki & Levy (1994)) are characterised by possessing a library of complex model fragments that are combined to form the model. This model composition process is controlled by applicability conditions in the model fragment library. In contrast, model induction systems (*e.g.* Addanki, Cremonini, & Penberthy (1991) and Amsterdam (1992)) have a very simple library structure, with model development occurring by comparing the behaviour of the model to that of the referent system.

These approaches have contrasting and complementary advantages and disadvantages. The libraries used in model composition systems are complex and difficult to develop (owing to the need to ensure that the applicability conditions are consistent). Such libraries are also restricted in flexibility: the modelling system is restricted to consider only those combinations of simplifications that are contained in the library. However, the structure of the modelling library is used to guide the development of the model boundary.

Model induction systems, on the other hand, use much simpler knowledge bases. As there are no separate submodels, there are no applicability conditions. Simplifying assumptions can be asserted and retracted independently.

---

[*] Current Address: CISMG, Cranfield University, Shrivenham, Swindon, SN6 7LA, UK. neil.smith@rmcs.cranfield.ac.uk

Copyright © 1998, American Association for Artificial Intelligence (www.aaai.org). All rights reserved.

Model revision is performed by comparing the behaviour of the model to that of the referent system and using differences in behaviour to select the best alteration to make to the model. This approach is very flexible, but has the major constraint that the referent system's behaviour must be specified. In addition, model induction systems are incapable of determining a model boundary, but instead model everything in the referent system.

These considerations indicate a need to develop a modelling methodology that combines the benefits of the model composition and model induction approaches while eliminating their drawbacks. The structure of the modelling knowledge should be much simpler than compositional libraries while retaining sufficient sophistication to allow the modeller to identify the model boundary. The modeller should perform model revision based on the behaviour of the model, but this revision should be not be based on information beyond what is in a normal task definition.

In this paper, we describe AIM, an automated modeller that has many of these features. We describe the architecture used in AIM to contain the modelling knowledge and show how this provides the power and flexibility desired. We then describe how AIM uses this architecture with a novel modelling algorithm to generate parsimonious models, and give some results showing this. Finally, we discuss some limitations of this approach.

Architecture of AIM

AIM is a component-centred modelling system, where discrete, separate components communicate with each other only through connections between specified ports. Knowledge in AIM is strictly partitioned between knowledge about physical *components* (stored in the component library) and knowledge about various models of these components (called *m-components*, and stored in the m-component library). Each of the libraries is organised into a hierarchy of frames, which allows AIM to infer default values for parameters that are not specified in the system description. The component library is used to store all the physical parameters relating to actual components, while the m-component library stores all the information relating to how these components can be represented in a model. A separately defined surjective function, with a domain including all components in the library, maps components to m-components. This function takes account of the state of the component and the type of interaction to which it is subjected.

M-components are similar to model fragments in that they are partial representations of a component's behaviour. Each m-component only specifies the component's

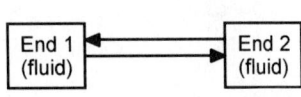
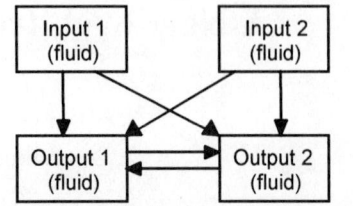

1a: Intra-actions in a `fluidPipe`   1b: Intra-actions in a sample `bathtub`

Figure 1: Intra-actions

response to interactions of a specified type when the component is in a specified state. For instance, the fluid flow properties of a steel pipe would be represented by a `fluidPipe` m-component; the same pipe's electrical properties would be represented by an `electricalConductor` m-component. A single m-component may represent many types of component: for instance, a `linearBlock` m-component can represent almost any free object subjected to a force.

The behaviour of an m-component is described by a fragment of a bond graph (Rosenberg & Karnopp, 1983) contained in the m-component. When the model is generated, these bond graph fragments are merged to produce a bond graph representation of the model; the bond graph is used to produce the state equations that yield the system's behaviour. The parameters that govern an m-component's behaviour (*e.g.* a `linearBlock`'s mass) are determined by the physical parameters of the component the m-component represents.

When an m-component is used in a model to represent a component, an effect (an interaction in a specified energy domain) at one port of a component will not necessarily cause similar effects at all other ports of the same component. To reflect this, each m-component has a set of intra-actions, which specify which of the m-component's other ports are affected by an effect at any one port. Intra-actions do not themselves indicate any causal direction within the m-component; they describe the possible causal orientations the m-component can support. Causal directions within an m-component are only defined when the m-component is placed in a model and the casual ordering of the whole model determined.

Intra-actions are normally symmetric, to reflect the symmetric nature of the relationships between effects in a component, *i.e.* the symmetric relationship between fluid flow rates at either end of a `fluidPipe` (figure 1*a*). However, the relationships between some effects are non-symmetric and the m-component's intra-actions reflect this. For example, the water flow rate from a tap into a bath affects the flow rate from the plughole, but the converse is not true (figure 1*b*). This information is used by AIM when it determines the model boundary; this is described in the next section.

M-components differ from model fragments in that an m-component only represents the *ideal* model of a component, *i.e.* a model in which all simplifying assumptions have been made. However, not all of these assumptions are valid in all circumstances: the viscosity of fluid in a pipe will be negligible if the fluid flows slowly and the model is only used to represent a small time scale. In other situations, the viscosity might be significant, and the basic `fluidPipe` m-component will need to be augmented to include the effects of fluid viscosity. This is achieved in AIM through the mechanism of corrections, which can be added to m-components to reflect the retraction of these simplifying assumptions. All corrections in AIM are examples of fitting approximations (Weld, 1992).

Corrections have a very similar structure to m-components. Each correction has at least one port, the attachment port, that controls how the correction is added to the m-component (though note that corrections attach to an m-component's body, rather than one of its ports). Some corrections, *e.g.* heating in an electrical resistor, introduce additional ports and intra-actions to the m-component to which they attach. The inclusion of such corrections can expand the model boundary, but a detailed examination of such corrections is outside the scope of this paper. Each correction contains a bond graph fragment that is merged into the bond graph of the m-component to which it applies. Corrections have various parameters that are defined by the physical parameters of the component to which they relate.

As each correction represents the retraction of a simplifying assumption, a correction can only be applied once to a particular instantiated m-component. However, the same correction can be applied to an arbitrary number of different instantiations of the same m-component, and can even be applied to different types of m-component. The application of corrections to one m-component is independent of the application of that correction to any other m-component in the model. The *correction candidates* of a model are all those corrections that can validly be added to the model, *i.e.* are not already present in the model.

This architecture for the modelling knowledge used in AIM allows for the combination of the benefits of the model composition and model induction approaches. The component-centred approach to modelling, combined with the m-components' intra-actions, provides the sophistication required to accurately determine the model boundary in response to a specified task definition. The separation of the corrections from the m-components allows AIM the freedom to select only the simplifying assumptions that are appropriate in this model.

Generating models

AIM requires three inputs before modelling can begin: a system description, a task definition, and a significance

```
function find_parsimonious_model (sd, voi, cd, ε)
% sd: system description
% voi: variables of interest
% cd: causal direction specified in task
% ε: significance threshold value
% m, m', m_next: models
% R(m): correction candidates of m
% r: correction

begin
    m = coherent (expand_boundary (sd, ∅, voi, cd))
    repeat
        R(m) = all valid correction candidates for m
        J_max = 0
        for each r ∈ R(m)
            m' = coherent (expand_boundary (sd, m + r,
                    intra-actions(r, attach_port, cd), cd))
            J = ϑ(m, m')      % difference in behaviour
            if J > J_max,
                J_max = J
                m_next = m'
            end
        end
        if J_max ≪ λ    % J_max is significant
            m = m_next
        end
    until J_max ≪ λ ∨ R(m) = {}
    if R(m) = {}
        return nil    % cannot guarantee an adequate model
    else
        return m
    end
end
```

Figure 2: AIM's Algorithm

threshold value. The system description is given in terms of the components that make up the system and the connections between them. The task definition defines both the variables of interest and a causal direction. The causal direction indicates whether the model created should either describe the effects these variables have on the system, or describe what factors in the system affect these variables. This information is used in the model boundary analysis. The significance threshold value defines when AIM should regard two models' behaviours as significantly different.

AIM generates a single output: the model. The model consists of a 3-tuple of (m-components, connections, corrections), where m-components is a set of instantiated m-components; connections is a set of connections, each connection consisting of a domain of interaction and a set of ports at that connection; and corrections is a set of instantiated corrections. If a component is subjected to many effects, it may be represented in the model by several m-components.

Models are developed in AIM in a two-stage process. The first stage determines the model boundary, which identifies the physical and behavioural extent of the model. The model boundary defines the initial model. AIM then moves on to test all the simplifying assumptions made in the initial, idealised model and, by adding corrections, retracts those assumptions that are unjustified. The process repeats until AIM determines that all the remaining simplifying assumptions are justified; when this occurs, modelling stops. This algorithm is shown in figure 2. Models are generated for only a single operating region: different operating regions of a system will require different models. In addition, as AIM is purely a model builder, AIM cannot control the transitions between distinct models.

The discussion below of AIM's algorithm will be illustrated by showing how AIM generates a model of a water-filled syringe (figure 3). The model is intended to show all the effects of a force applied by the finger.

Finding the model boundary

The determination of the model boundary focuses on the ports in the model and what other ports in the system are either affected by these ports, or are needed to explain effects at these ports. As additional ports are identified, the model boundary expands to include the m-components to which these ports belong. The algorithm, shown in figure 4, centres on the *boundary analysis queue*. This stores details of all the ports in the model (with their corresponding effects) that are currently on the model boundary. However, there can be no ports on a correctly-drawn model boundary as any ports on the boundary represent an underspecified effect: each port forms part of a junction, and the effects at a junction depend on all the ports at that junction. For example, the consideration of the current on one lead at an electrical junction requires the consideration of the electrical properties of all the other leads at that junction. Therefore, the boundary analysis continues until the boundary analysis queue becomes empty.

The boundary identification process starts by identifying the ports and effects referred to in the task definition and placing these in the boundary analysis queue. In the example of the syringe, the boundary analysis queue will initially contain the single port/effect combination (finger, end, linearMechanical).

Boundary expansion performed port by port, as shown in figure 4. When several ports are connected, an effect at one port requires AIM to consider the same effect at all the connected ports (providing the connection supports the inter-action). All the connected ports are added to the boundary analysis queue and the connection is added to the model. For instance, because the finger touches the end of the plunger handle, this latter port will be added to the boundary analysis queue. However, if a port already exists in the model as part of a connection, the connection must already have been processed and AIM does not process this connection again.

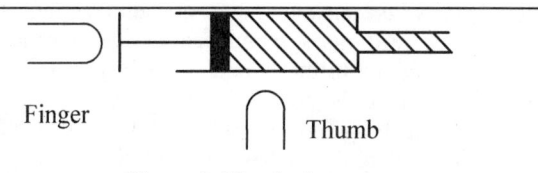

Figure 3: The Syringe

```
function expand_boundary (sd, initmodel, baq, cd)
% m: model
% bap: boundary analysis port
% p: port
% cp, mp: additional ports
% mc : m-component

begin
  m = initmodel
  while baq ≠ {}
    bap = dequeue (baq)
    if bap ∉ m
      cp = system ports connected to bap
      enqueue (baq, cp)
      m = m + cp
    end
    mc = correct_m-component (bap, sd)
    if mc ∉ m ∨ ¬(∃p such that [p ∈ m ∧
         p ∈ intra-actions (mc, bap, ¬cd)]
      mp = intra-actions (mc, bap, cd)
      enqueue (baq, mp)
      m = m + mc
    end
  end
  return m
end
```

Figure 4: Algorithm for finding the model boundary

AIM also needs to determine the correct m-component to use to represent each component in the model. The component is identified directly from the port description. The combination of port description, effect, and component type and state (found from the system description) is sufficient to specify the correct m-component to use to represent that component.

AIM checks whether this port requires further processing by examining the m-component's intra-actions. If the current port was placed in the boundary analysis queue through the analysis of other ports of this m-component (*i.e.* if there exists in the model a port of the current m-component whose consideration would have caused this port to be included), AIM can move on to the next port in the boundary analysis queue. If not, details of the m-component, and the component to which it relates, are added to the model.

The m-component's intra-actions are then used to determine which of the component's other ports have effects that are significant in the model. The causal information in the task description indicates whether to use the intra-actions entering the port (to find the ports that affect the port in question) or the intra-actions leaving the port (to find the ports affected by this port). This only becomes significant where an m-component's intra-actions are not symmetric. All ports mentioned in the relevant intra-actions are added to the boundary analysis queue. In the syringe, the finger is modelled as an exogenous application of force, and so has no intra-actions. The plunger handle, modelled as a rigid bar, has a symmetric intra-action that relates mechanical effects at the ends to each other: the finger pressing at one end of the handle prompts AIM to consider the effects of the other end of the handle on the plunger.

The components found to be inside the model boundary in the syringe example, together with their m-components, are shown in table 1. Note that all the components are represented by ideal models, and note that the atmosphere surrounding the syringe is explicitly included in the model boundary.

Refining the model

The initial model, found during the identification of the model boundary, is likely not to be sufficient to address the task specified. The model is made adequate by the addition of corrections. Corrections can be added for two reasons: to ensure coherence in the model, or to reduce the behavioural difference between the model and the referent system.

A model is said to be *incoherent* if it does not yield a complete set of state equations[1]; this normally reflects a physically impossible situation in the model. The initial model of the syringe, shown in table 1, would predict an infinite velocity for the ram, due to the lack of friction or other similar phenomena in the model. Such errors in the model are removed by the addition of corrections. The function **coherent**, described by Smith (1998), identifies the corrections that could potentially eliminate the error and selects the one that has the greatest effect on the model's behaviour. In the syringe example, this correction is the friction between the plunger and the cylinder.

However, the main reason for including corrections in a model is to reduce the behavioural difference between the model and the referent system. We take the view that models are always intended, at some level, to explain the behaviour of the referent system. This allows us to define a model as adequate for a task if the behaviour of the model is not significantly different from the behaviour of interest of the referent system.

If we assume that AIM's libraries contain all possible corrections (thus ignoring any closed world assumption), the behaviour of a model can be brought as close as desired to that of the referent system by the inclusion of corrections in the model. Normally, only a few of the possible corrections will have significant effects on the model's behaviour; the objective of modelling is to identify which corrections fall into this category. A model that contains all the significant corrections will be adequate for the specified task. An adequate model that contains no other corrections is parsimonious.

The problem is how to assess the effect of each correction candidate on the behavioural difference between the model and the referent system. Model induction systems do this by generating the behaviour of the model and com-

---

[1] State equations are found from the bond graph representation of the model. This reliance on bond graphs restricts the level of granularity of models.

Component	Modelled as
Finger	Source of force
Thumb	Not modelled
Ram	Rigid, massless bar
Plunger	Watertight, rigid, frictionless plunger
Cylinder	Rigid container of inviscid fluid
Nozzle	Rigid container of inviscid fluid
Atmosphere	Source of (zero) pressure

Table 1: M-components of the Syringe

paring it to a trace of the referent system's behaviour, provided as part of the problem specification. This requires that the referent system's behaviour be known.

Alternatively, AIM could produce a "most complex" model to produce a behaviour trace against which other models are compared. Unfortunately, this model would be formed under an arbitrary closed world assumption. Additionally, a model that contains all the corrections available under this closed world assumption might not be coherent. To make it coherent, AIM would have to arbitrarily eliminate corrections to ensure the model's coherence. Finally, increasing the knowledge in the modeller would increase the complexity of the initial model. If the additional complexity is not needed in the parsimonious model, including it only serves to increase the cost of modelling.

Instead of the above approaches, AIM takes the novel step of using the behaviour of an existing model as the base against which refinements are compared. When a model is generated, its behaviour is found. When each correction candidate is assessed, the model is revised to include this correction and the behaviours of the base model and the revised model are compared. This revision and comparison is repeated for all the model's correction candidates. If no correction causes a significant change in the model's behaviour, the model is deemed adequate and modelling stops. If the largest change in behaviour is significant, then the correction that caused that change is included in the model. This revised model becomes the current model and the process repeats. This approach relies on the effects of corrections on the model's behaviour being nearly independent, and on the insignificant correction assumption (see below).

AIM's search strategy through the space of possible models is similar to a steepest ascent hill climbing search. If the effects of corrections on the model's behaviour were truly independent, the order of inclusion of the significant corrections would be irrelevant. However, while corrections' effects are nearly independent, they are not truly independent. This has the result that if AIM is given a choice between two correction candidates, both of which have a significant effect on the model's behaviour but with one having a larger effect than the other, AIM should first include the correction candidate with the largest effect and reassess the model.

Whichever correction candidate is chosen, there is a chance that the remaining correction candidate will not have a significant effect on the modified model. If the corrections' effects are nearly independent, a correction candidate with a large effect will continue to have a large, significant effect, ensuring that this correction is included in a later refinement of the model. However, the small effect of the other correction candidate might become insignificant in a later model, meaning that this correction might not be included. In this case, this correction is not necessary to form an adequate model, and should not be included in the final, parsimonious model. This consideration leads to AIM's steepest ascent hill climbing search strategy. By including early the corrections with the largest effects on behaviour, AIM defers decisions on correction candidates with smaller effects until their impact becomes clearer.

In AIM's current implementation, behaviours are generated by simple numerical methods and compared using an extension of the integral-absolute error performance index (Palm, 1983). However, any method of generating and comparing behaviours will suffice for AIM's algorithm to work so long as behavioural differences can be found, ordered, and tested for significance.

Rather than compare the behaviours of all variables in the model, AIM selects a subset of variables to track, depending on the structure of the model and the causal direction in the task definition (if the model is to explain how the specified variables are affected, only these variables are tracked; if the effect of the specified variables on the rest of the model is to be found, all state variables and outputs are tracked). If there are n tracked variables in the base model, of which $v_i(t)$ is the ith tracked variable in the base model and $v_i'(t)$ is the corresponding variable in the modified model, the difference in behaviour over the period $[0, \tau]$ is given by:

$$\vartheta(m, m') = \max_{1 \leq i \leq n} \left(\frac{\int_0^\tau |v_i'(t) - v_i(t)| \, dt}{\int_0^\tau |v_i(t)| \, dt} \right)$$

where the performance index is normalised to give a measure of the relative difference in behaviour.

To show how AIM includes these corrections in the model, consider the simplest coherent model of the syringe (the model shown in table 1, with the addition of the plunger friction correction to ensure model coherence). If the cylinder is made of steel, the remaining correction with the largest effect is the inertia of the water in the nozzle: including this correction gives a performance index of 0.01218. Given a significance threshold value of 0.1, this is an insignificant effect. Therefore, the simplest model, excluding this correction, is deemed adequate. However, if the cylinder is made from soft rubber, the deformation of the cylinder is has the largest effect of all the corrections with a significant performance index of 0.2186. Following the algorithm in figure 2, this means that this correction is added to the model and refinement must continue.

The Insignificant Correction Assumption

AIM uses the insignificant correction assumption to determine when modelling is to stop. Modelling stops when the current model, m, is adequate. m is adequate iff the performance index between m and the referent system S is insignificant, *i.e.* $\vartheta(m, S) \ll 1$ ($x \ll 1 \leftrightarrow x < \varepsilon$, where ε is the significance threshold value).

Turning attention to the mythical most complex model m_∞ (for which $\vartheta(m_\infty, S) \equiv 0$), there are some corrections r in m_∞ for which $\vartheta(m_\infty - r, m_\infty) \ll 1$. Such corrections are termed *insignificant*, as they have no significant effect on the behaviour of the most complex model. I is the set of all such insignificant corrections:

$$I = \{r \in R : \vartheta(m_\infty - r, m_\infty) \ll 1\}$$

where R is the set of all corrections.

If we assume that the effects of all corrections on the behaviour of the model are independent, it is true that:

$$\vartheta(m_\infty - I, m_\infty) \ll 1$$

which means that $m_\infty - I$ is an adequate model.

The insignificant correction assumption states that no insignificant correction has a significant effect on the behaviour of any model:

$$\forall r \in I, \vartheta(m, m + r) \ll 1$$

Therefore, given $R(m)$ is the set of valid correction candidates for m:

$$\forall r \in R(m), \vartheta(m, m + r) \ll 1 \rightarrow R(m) \subseteq I$$
$$\leftrightarrow m \supseteq m_\infty - I$$
$$\rightarrow \vartheta(m, m_\infty) \ll 1$$
$$\leftrightarrow \vartheta(m, S) \ll 1$$

This allows AIM to detect an adequate model by examining the effects of the remaining corrections on the behaviour of that model. If no correction candidate has a significant effect on the behaviour of the model, all the correction candidates must be insignificant; therefore, the model is adequate.

However, the assumption that all corrections have totally independent effects on the model's behaviour is not wholly true. In linear systems, corrections will generally have independent effects, but in order to allow for synergistic effects between corrections, the independence relation is weakened to:

$$\vartheta(m_\infty - I, m_\infty) \ll 1/\lambda$$

which means that m is adequate when:

$$\forall r \in R(m), \vartheta(m, m + r) \ll \lambda$$

Cylinder	Force	Corrections
Steel	Constant	Plunger friction*
Steel	Varying	Plunger friction* Nozzle fluid inertia Plunger leakage
Rubber	Constant	Plunger friction* Cylinder deformation Nozzle fluid drag* Nozzle fluid inertia
Rubber	Varying	Plunger friction* Cylinder deformation Nozzle fluid drag* Nozzle fluid inertia

Table 2: Corrections added to the Syringe
* Correction added to ensure model coherence.

The value to use for λ seems to be problem dependent, but an investigation of the combined effects of corrections (Smith, 1998) suggests that using $\lambda = \frac{1}{2}$ is reasonable.

Results

AIM's libraries contain approximately 40 components, 40 m-components, and 20 corrections. AIM has been used to generate models for several systems, including a cascaded tank system, a heat exchanger, and a simple tachometer, each containing about a dozen components. Each system was modelled under a variety of different conditions; the results are described by Smith (1998). However, only the syringe system (figure 3) is discussed here.

In order to accurately describe the effect of the force applied by the finger, the basic model of the syringe (table 1) is augmented with various corrections; these are shown in table 2. However, if the physical parameters in the system description are altered, different corrections will be appropriate in different circumstances. Table 2 shows how the necessary corrections change depending on whether the finger exerts a constant or rapidly varying force, and whether the syringe cylinder is made from steel or soft rubber. The corrections are shown in the order in which they were added to the model (*i.e.* the most significant correction first). All models were built under the same significance threshold value (ε) of 0.1.

To determine whether these models are adequate, a very complex model was built manually and the behaviours of the generated models were compared to this complex model. The results are shown in the third column of table 3. In addition, the precursors of these models were also compared to the complex model and the results of these comparisons can be found in the fourth column of table 3.

As can be seen from these results, the models produced

Cylinder	Finger Force	$\vartheta(m, m_\infty)$	$\vartheta(m_-, m_\infty)$
Steel	Constant	0.089516	—
Steel	Varying	0.023991	0.451486
Rubber	Constant	0.035248	0.728074
Rubber	Varying	0.031973	1.01271

Table 3: Performance Indices for Syringe Models

by AIM are adequate ($\vartheta(m, m_\infty) \ll 1$, i.e. $\vartheta(m, m_\infty) < \varepsilon$) while the precursor models are not ($\vartheta(m_-, m_\infty) \not< 0.1$). This means that AIM produced the simplest adequate, i.e. parsimonious, models.

Related Work

Nayak & Joskowicz (1996) describe a typical model composition system, whose modelling knowledge base shares many features with AIM. Model fragments are organised into hierarchies to allow the reuse of modelling knowledge, and articulation rules (similar to AIM's intra-actions) are used to infer what effects are induced in a component in response to a given effect. However, the modelling algorithm is entirely reliant on the structure of the modelling library to guide the modelling process. This is only achieved at the cost of embedding modelling assumptions throughout the library. This is shown in the different but overlapping hierarchies of model fragments, and in the arbitrary nature of the structural and behavioural preconditions governing when model fragments can be used. Smith (1998a) shows how most of these embedded assumptions can be avoided.

In contrast, MM (Amsterdam, 1992) is a typical model induction system that depends wholly on behavioural considerations. However, MM compares qualitative behaviours, which greatly reduces MM's ability to resolve qualitatively similar but quantitatively different behaviours. AIM's quantitative method of behavioural comparison allows it to produce models more appropriate to the specified task. In addition, while MM is able to correctly identify the different behaviourally significant regions within the system (the lumping problem), little attention is paid to the determination of the model boundary.

DME (Iwasaki & Levy, 1994) is a model composition system that uses relevance reasoning to guide modelling. Each model fragment contains a set of modelling assumptions under which it is valid. As the model boundary expands, these assumptions are asserted and retracted, which can prompt the modeller to revise earlier decisions. DME's performance depends critically on the correctness of these assumptions. Iwasaki & Levy do not guarantee this is the case, and instead offer the library coherence assumption. AIM's simpler knowledge base structure obviates the need to make any such coherence assumptions when developing the libraries, and AIM ensures the coherence of models as they are being built.

Williams & Raiman (1994) have produced Charicatures, a radically different modelling system based on the simplification of the equations that represent the most complex model. Their major contribution is their exploration of the concept of a model's domain of validity, which describes the situations in which the model can be used with confidence. This is used to indicate when model transitions are required. However, focusing solely on the equations is a very shallow approach as it ignores the physics that underlies the algebraic formulation. This restricts the application of Charicatures to situations that have already been modelled as algebraic systems.

Conclusions

We have described AIM, an automated modelling system that uses a novel architecture to provide both power and flexibility during the modelling process. AIM implements an algorithm that does not rely on external sources of information or fine structure in the modelling knowledge to guide and halt modelling. Instead, AIM compares the behaviours of successive models, including corrections that cause significant changes in the model's behaviour. We have shown that this approach to modelling usually generates parsimonious models.

However, this approach relies on the insignificant correction assumption and assumptions about the independence of corrections. Tests on other systems have shown that, occasionally, these assumptions are not sophisticated enough to always ensure parsimonious models. In addition, AIM's reliance on fitting approximations restricts the types of corrections that can be made.

References

Addanki, S., Cremonini, R., Penberthy, J. S. (1991), Graphs of Models, *Artificial Intelligence* **51**:145–177.

Amsterdam, J. (1992), Automated Modeling of Physical Systems, in Falkenhainer, B & Stein, J. L. (eds.), *Automated Modelling, DCS* **41**, American Society of Mechanical Engineers, pp. 21–30.

Falkenhainer, B., Forbus, K. (1991), Compositional Modeling: Finding the Right Model for the Job, *Artificial Intelligence* **51**:95–143.

Iwasaki, Y., Levy, A. Y. (1994), Automated Model Selection for Simulation, *Proceedings AAAI-94*, pp. 1183–1190.

Nayak, P. P., Joskowicz, L. (1996), Efficient Compositional Modeling for Generating Causal Explanations, *Artificial Intelligence* **83**:193–227.

Palm, W. J. (1983), *Modeling, Analysis, and Control of Dynamic Systems*, New York: J. Wiley & Sons.

Rosenberg, R. C., Karnopp, D. C. (1983), *Introduction to Physical System Dynamics*, New York: McGraw-Hill.

Schut, C., Bredeweg, B. (1996), An Overview of Approaches to Qualitative Model Construction, *Knowledge Engineering Review* **11**(1):1–25.

Smith, N. (1998), Reducing the Need for Assumptions in the Automated Modelling of Physical Systems, PhD thesis, School of Computing, De Montfort University.

Smith, N. (1998a), Handling Assumptions in Automated Modelling, *Working Notes of the 12th International Workshop on Qualitative Reasoning*.

Weld, D. S. (1992), Reasoning about Model Accuracy, *Artificial Intelligence* **56**:225–300.

Williams, B. C., Raiman, O. (1994), Decompositional Modeling Through Charicatural Reasoning, *Proceedings AAAI-94*, pp. 1199–1204.

Qualitative Analysis of Distributed Physical Systems with Applications to Control Synthesis *

Christopher Bailey-Kellogg **Feng Zhao**
Xerox Palo Alto Research Center
3333 Coyote Hill Road, Palo Alto, CA 94304   U.S.A.
{kellogg,zhao}@parc.xerox.com

Abstract

Many important physical phenomena, such as temperature distribution, air flow, and acoustic waves, are described as continuous, distributed parameter fields. Analyzing and controlling these physical processes and systems are common tasks in many scientific and engineering domains. However, the challenges are multi-fold: distributed fields are conceptually harder to reason about than lumped parameter models; computational methods are prohibitively expensive for complex spatial domains; the underlying physics imposes severe constraints on observability and controllability.

This paper develops an ontological abstraction and a structure-based design mechanism, in a framework collectively known as **spatial aggregation** (SA), for reasoning about and synthesizing distributed control schemes for physical fields. The ontological abstraction models a physical field as a hierarchy of networks of spatial objects. SA applies a small number of generic operators to a field to compute concise structural descriptions such as iso-contours, gradient trajectories, and influence graphs. The design mechanism uses these representations to find feasible control configurations. We illustrate the mechanism using a thermal control problem from industrial heat treatment and demonstrate that the active exploitation of structural knowledge in physical fields yields a significant computational advantage.

Introduction

Continuous, distributed parameter fields are common physical phenomena: consider the temperature field in a building, the air flow around an airplane wing, or the noise from a copy machine. There are enormous practical benefits to reasoning about and controlling these physical processes and systems. For instance, the drag on an airplane can be reduced by analyzing and controlling the air flow around the wings. Temperature in a "smart" building can be regulated to maximize occupant comfort while minimizing energy consumption. Because of the rapid advance in micro-fabrication technology that can integrate and produce micro-electro-mechanical system (MEMS) devices on a massive scale,

---
* Copyright 1998, American Association for Artificial Intelligence (www.aaai.org). All rights reserved.

we are becoming increasingly reliant on large networks of sensors, actuators, and computational elements to augment our ability to interact with and control the physical environment (Berlin 1994).

However, there is enormous challenge in controlling and optimizing physical fields using networks of sensors and controllers. The difficulties arise from three sources. First, a distributed parameter field is conceptually harder to reason about and model than a lumped parameter system such as a circuit. Spatial topology, metric, material properties and physical laws all come into play, in addition to the combinatorial structures. The underlying physical processes might be nonlinear and defy analytic, closed form solution. Second, numerical methods developed for designing and controlling physical fields require solving large systems of equations and hence are prohibitively expensive for large, irregular geometric domains and highly non-uniform phenomena. Third, physical laws constrain the ability of spatially distributed, local agents to sense and affect the environment (Seidman 1996). Local sensors and control elements measure and interact with small neighborhoods around them. Macroscopic consequences are aggregated from local actions. Consequently, the design, programming, and coordination of distributed computational agents immersed in physical media require abstraction mechanisms, inference methods, and programming languages different from those for reasoning about and controlling centralized, lumped parameter models.

In this paper, we develop an ontological abstraction for physical fields and a structure-based design mechanism for reasoning about and synthesizing distributed control schemes for physical fields. The ontological abstraction builds neighborhood relations and equivalence classes and describes the structure and behavior of a field in multiple layers of spatial objects. The design mechanism finds a feasible control design for a physical field specifying control placement and associated actions that meet given design objectives; it employs data types and generic operators to manipulate and transform objects. The ontological abstraction, generic operators, and reasoning mechanisms are collectively called **spatial aggregation** (SA); we have implemented the spatial aggregation language (SAL) to support modular programming in this framework. To determine control placement, SA transforms higher-level control objectives into local control actions using divide-and-conquer, exploiting physical constraints of fields manifested as locality, continuity, and spatial and temporal scales. SA then optimizes control design using an *influence graph* that explicitly encodes dependencies between spatial objects. This work has significantly extended the previously developed SA framework for data interpretation (Yip & Zhao 1996; Bailey-Kellogg, Zhao, & Yip 1996) to address new problems arising from control and optimization of distributed parameter physical fields.

SA differs from existing numerical design and optimization methods in several important ways. Traditionally, detailed, labor-intensive numerical simulations are employed to elaborate consequences of global models for physical systems. In contrast, our objective is to construct a qualitative physics model for physical fields so that behaviors of the fields can be inferred using a small number of operations on a discrete representation and explained in terms of object interaction and evolution. SA constructs explicit structural descriptions for fields from discretizations, measurements, or other sources. These structural descriptions can be abstracted and articulated to support a variety of inference, explanation, tutoring, and design tasks. For instance, SA exploits the knowledge of structure to solve for both structural and parametric design problems, while most existing numerical methods address parametric optimization only.

The remainder of the paper proceeds as follows. First we present key elements in the field ontology. Then we show how the ontology helps extract structures from physical fields. We describe algorithms that use the structures uncovered in a field to design distributed control structures and to optimize parameters for such structures. We provide empirical evidence supporting our approach. Finally, we discuss related work.

Field Ontological Abstraction

Fields abstract a wide range of continuous, distributed physical phenomena such as temperature, velocity, and image data. Formally, a field maps one continuum to another. A temperature field in a room maps location to temperature, i.e., $R^3 \to R^1$. Many important reasoning and controlling tasks for physical fields require compact structural and behavioral descriptions of the fields.

Consider a problem from manufacturing: heat treatment of a metal sheet (Jaluria & Torrance 1986), as shown in Figure 1[1]. As part of the manufacturing pro-

[1] A similar problem arises from temperature control in semiconductor manufacturing, in which the oven temperature over a surface of semiconductor wafer must be regulated by a set of spatially distributed heating lamps to ensure high yield. This is a challenging control problem in rapid thermal processing (RTP) of semiconductor wafers because temper-

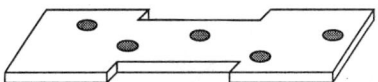

Figure 1: Industrial heat treatment of a metal sheet. The control objective is to heat the material to a desired temperature at a small number of locations, shown as dark circles, so as to minimize temperature fluctuation across the material.

cess, the temperature distribution over the sheet must be regulated at some desired profile over a period of time to minimize damage to the material. To describe the thermal process in the metal sheet, we need to specify physical laws, geometry, material properties, and boundary conditions. In addition, the control objective specifies a desired thermal profile over the material.

Physical laws governing fields are described by partial differential equations. For instance, the physical process of isotropic, steady-state heat diffusion is governed by the Poisson equation:

$$k\nabla^2\phi + \dot{Q} = 0$$

where ∇^2 is the Laplace operator, ϕ is the temperature, k is material conduction coefficient, and $\dot{Q}$ is the source value representing heat per unit time and volume. The Poisson equation also governs other physical phenomena such as gravity and electrostatics. In fluid dynamics, the motion of fluid is governed by the Navier-Stokes equation, another well-known partial differential equation.

A physical field exhibits multiple temporal and spatial scales due to physical properties of the domain, geometry, boundary conditions, and external forces. Mechanical vibrations travel at the speed of sound in a piece of material. Temperature decays with varying rates along different directions, determined by material property and geometric shape. Acoustic waves mix and reflect, according to wave lengths and boundary conditions. The scales and locality permit a continuous, distributed parameter field to be abstracted as a set of discrete objects by suppressing irrelevant details. Consequently, the field can be understood by interpreting a compact structural and behavioral representation. Figure 2 illustrates the spatial objects used in a weather map, where points denote sampled data, curves represent isobars connecting points of equal pressure, and regions indicate low pressure cells. We need to develop abstractions that explicitly model the field structure so that other programs can exploit such knowledge for analysis and design tasks.

SA provides the **field ontology** that represents a physical field as a network of spatial objects (Yip & Zhao 1996; Bailey-Kellogg, Zhao, & Yip 1996). Each spatial object comprises a geometric description for its

ature non-uniformity often leads to chip defects (Kailath & others 1996).

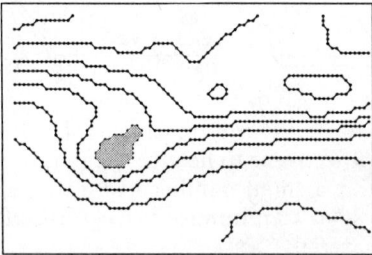

Figure 2: Spatial objects in a meteorological map: sample points, isobar curves, and a region of low pressure.

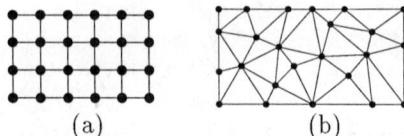

Figure 3: A field modeled by a network of local spatial objects: (a) A regular finite difference grid of objects; (b) A finite element mesh of triangle objects. Higher-dimensional fields can be likewise modeled.

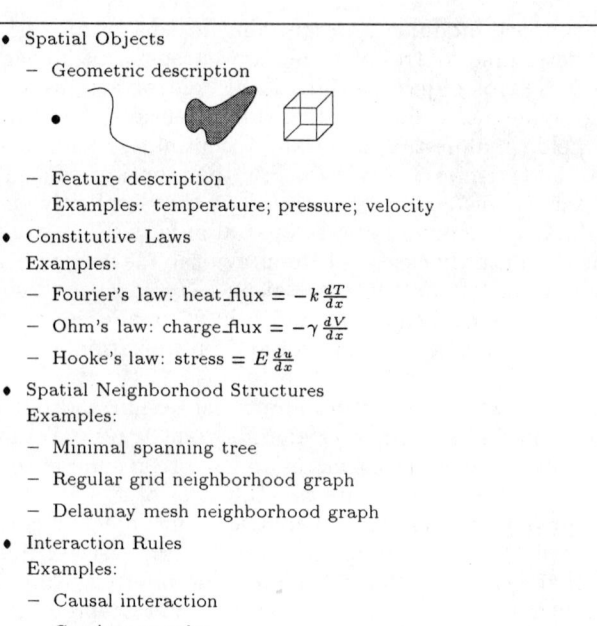

Table 1: Spatial Aggregation field ontology.

spatial extent and a feature description for its values. For instance, a spatial object in a temperature field describes a location and the temperature at that location. A *neighborhood graph (N-graph)* encodes spatial adjacencies among the objects. The spatial objects are governed by interaction rules relating neighboring objects. Table 1 summarizes the major elements of the SA ontology.

Two field discretizations, a regular grid of points (Figure 3(a)) for a relatively uniform spatial domain, or a triangular mesh of elements (Figure 3(b)) for a more complex domain, are particularly useful for the control and optimization tasks discussed in this paper. Each spatial object abstracts geometry and physics over a finite region. Local constraints, derived from a finite difference approximation to the Laplace operator at grid points or conservation properties over elements in a mesh, govern the evolution of the objects. The field values are determined by a local relaxation method that iteratively updates spatial objects using the local constraints. While the finite difference and finite element methods commonly used in engineering and science for numerically approximating a field (Vichnevetsky 1981) also build and manipulate such discretizations, SA subsumes many of the same operations and provides additional mechanisms for reasoning about and exploiting important structures in the fields (e.g. the isobars and low pressure cell in Figure 2). SA also supports multi-level approaches (Briggs 1987) that use solutions at coarse levels to guide solutions at finer levels. Note that, unlike standard multi-level approaches, SA does not require uniformity of objects at various levels.

Qualitative Field Descriptions

Building upon the spatial object abstraction, SA provides an aggregation-disaggregation algorithm for reasoning about structures in physical fields. Figure 4 illustrates the bi-directional mapping between lower- and higher-level objects within each spatial aggregation layer (Yip & Zhao 1996; Bailey-Kellogg, Zhao, & Yip 1996). SA employs a sequence of such bi-directional mappings to mediate the input fields and higher-level compact descriptions. In the aggregation process, SA operators `aggregate`, `classify`, and `redescribe` build a hierarchy of increasingly more abstract spatial object neighborhood graphs (N-graphs) and equivalence classes. During disaggregation, the operator `disaggregate` opens up higher-level aggregate objects to permit control over finer component objects of the field. The SA operator `update` establishes local update rules to propagate information among neighbors. Additional operators act on the objects, fields, and N-graphs, to search, map, filter, update, form correspondences, and maintain consistency.

The spatial aggregation operators provide powerful building blocks for developing programs for analysis and control of distributed physical fields. The operators modularize user-specified domain-specific knowledge and abstract away many low-level implementation details. In the following subsections we will show how these operators extract structures from physical fields; in later sections these structures will be used for control design.

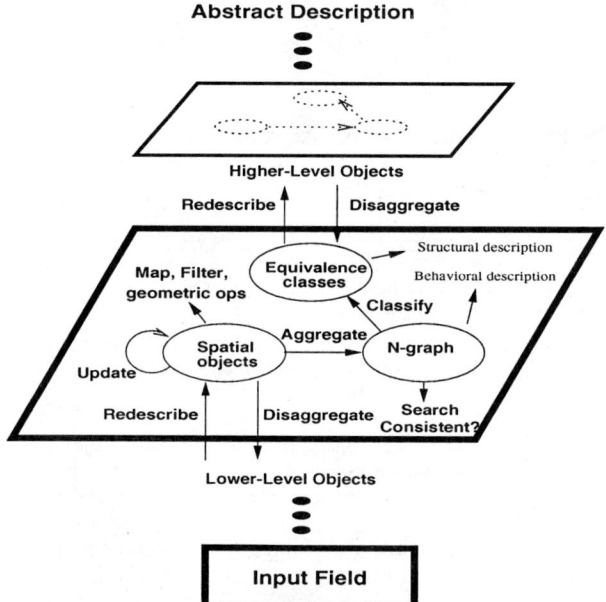

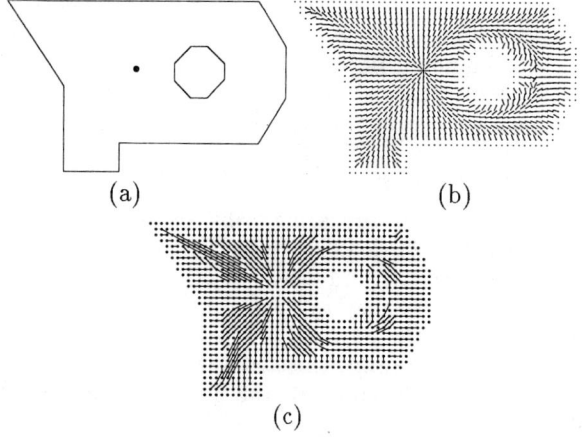

Figure 5: A complex thermal domain: (a) Geometry and heat source location; (b) Directions of the resulting temperature gradient field; (c) Gradient trajectories aggregated by SA operators.

Figure 4: Spatial aggregation and disaggregation support bidirectional mapping between lower- and higher-level spatial objects. SA aggregates lower-level objects to form a neighborhood graph, classifies them into equivalence classes, and redescribes the classes as higher-level objects. Reciprocally, SA disaggregates higher-level objects into component objects.

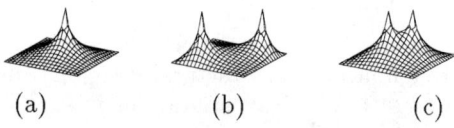

Figure 6: Thermal hills around sources; the vertical axis represents temperature value. (a) A single source. (b) Two fairly independent sources. (c) Two tightly coupled sources.

Field Terrain

In many cases, it is helpful to abstract the "terrain" of a data-massive input field into more qualitative structures. For example, meteorologists often find isobars and low pressure cells (Figure 2) a more convenient description than raw pressure data. The section below on control design will demonstrate the utility of isotherms in designing thermal control structures.

While iso-surfaces are often used to abstract the terrain of a field, we will also make use of a dual structure derived from the corresponding gradient field. The gradient field is a field with vectors based on spatial derivatives at each point; the vectors are orthogonal to iso-surfaces. For example, consider the problem in Figure 5(a): an irregularly-shaped metal sheet has a hole near its right end and a single heat source near the center of mass. Figure 5(b) shows the temperature gradient field directions (lengths normalized for visibility), computed from a pointwise description of the temperature. SA operators `aggregate` the gradient vectors based on adjacency of the points (e.g. relate a point to its 4 adjacent neighbors) and `classify` them into equivalence classes based on similarity in vector direction. The equivalence classes can be `redescribed` as higher-level objects, trajectories, as in Figure 5(c). These trajectories show the structure of steepest-descent paths through the terrain.

Influence Graph

A heat source influences the temperature distribution in a field through heat propagation. Figure 6(a) shows the influence of a source on regions around the source through a "thermal hill": the temperature decays away from the source. However, the coupling among multiple sources in controlling a thermal field necessitates the need for sharing information among sources during control parameter optimization, depending on the coupling strength (Figure 6(b) and Figure 6(c)).

We introduce the *influence graph* to record the dependencies between control sources and spatial objects in the field. For a design problem with field nodes F and source nodes S, an influence graph is a triple (V, E, w) with vertices $V = F \cup S$, edges $E = S \times F$, and edge weights $w : E \rightarrow \mathcal{R}$ such that $w((s, f))$ is the field value at f given a unit source at s. Hence, the graph edges record a normalized influence from each source to each field node; Figure 6(a) can be considered a pictorial representation of the edge weights for an influence graph from one source. In many *distributed* physical phenomena described by the Poisson equation, despite nonlinearities in the spatial variables such as non-uniform conduction characteristics and irregular geometries, the field is linearly dependent upon control sources and boundary conditions. Hence, the effects of sources can be combined through a superposition of influence hills. Influence graphs explicate the crucial dependencies between sources and thermal field objects, while hiding other possibly nonlinear effects.

Structure-Based Control Synthesis

For control and optimization tasks, the input to SA is a physical field modeled as a collection of spatial objects, a control objective, and a set of optimality constraints. SA determines a spatially distributed control that effectively steers the physical process to meet the desired criteria[2]. To determine the structure and parameters of the distributed control, i.e., the number, location, and values of control sources, one needs to search the large design space subject to structural and performance constraints:

- Structural constraints: geometry, physical properties, boundary conditions.
- Performance constraints: desired profile, optimality conditions on solutions, restriction on control sources (placement and strength).

Although many numerical methods exist for the parametric design problems, structural design has remained an ad hoc practice. SA structural design exploits physical scales of the field to determine the number and locations of distributed control. Similarly, SA parametric design exploits the knowledge of dependencies to optimize control values.

As an example, consider again the temperature regulation problem for a piece of material (Figure 1). The temperature field is represented by thermal spatial objects indicating locations and temperature values. A grid or mesh (Figure 3) explicates spatial adjacencies. The control objective is to establish a uniform temperature distribution over the entire field, using a small set of discrete heat sources, subject to constraints on the number of control sources, maximum source output, and acceptable temperature fluctuations. This global control objective can be formulated locally by constraining each thermal object to have a temperature within some error tolerance of its desired temperature. The available control authority consists of point sources, each of which regulates temperature in a local neighborhood. The design task is to determine the number, locations, and values of heat sources required to satisfy the objective.

Field Decomposition

Physical fields possess locality. For instance, after examining the thermal field in a dumbbell-shaped material heated at the heavy ends (Figure 7), we discover that the isotherms are more sparse along the narrow

---

[2]A dual problem concerns placement of sensors for maximum observability. We will only consider the controllability problem in this paper and note that the observability problem can be likewise solved.

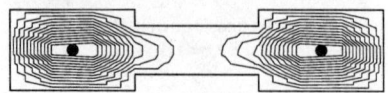

Figure 7: Temperature distribution in the dumbbell-shaped material, heated at the centers of heavy ends. The temperature gradient is described by isotherms.

```
while control error is too large
    for each unsatisfactory control region r
        disaggregate:
            generate candidate control partitions:
                find weak coupling directions
                partition r
            optimize control locations/values
            replace control with best configuration
    update field values
```

Figure 8: Algorithm for disaggregation-based control configuration design.

channel of the dumbbell, indicating a very small temperature decay. Intuitively, the heat flux is constrained by the narrow geometry of the channel. More formally, physics tells us this direction corresponds to the weakest coupling direction of the temperature field[3]. In order to control the field using a collection of decentralized sources, the field must be decoupled into constituent regions. The qualitative structural description computed by SA formalizes the physical intuition of coupling to permit principled and programmed trade-offs among different design choices.

The control structure design is accomplished by an iterative disaggregation process; the algorithm is outlined in Figure 8. Given a source configuration, the algorithm *disaggregates* a source that does not adequately control its region, replacing it with multiple more localized sources that better control subregions. To disaggregate, it makes use of the physical knowledge illustrated in Figure 7: sparse isotherms, or small gradients, indicate weak coupling. In Figure 7, the best way to decouple the field is to split the dumbbell in half into two ends. By placing new sources along directions of weak coupling, the algorithm divides and conquers the problem. At each step, multiple possible disaggregations are considered, and the one with the best error profile is chosen.

Weak coupling directions are computed using the gradient structures discussed in the section on field terrain abstractions. The trajectories indicate possible directions of interest; the algorithm calculates average gradient magnitudes along those directions and chooses as candidates those with small gradient vector magnitudes. In the example of Figure 5, an implementation of the algorithm chooses directions of weak coupling

---

[3]To be precise, this gives the smallest positive eigenvalue of the Laplacian graph of the field (Spielman & Teng 1996).

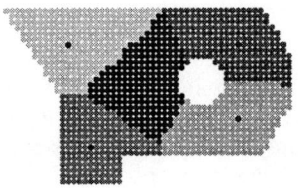

Figure 9: Decomposition of a complex thermal domain.

that yield the disaggregated source structure shown in Figure 9.

The use of physical structures (gradient-trajectory N-graph) allows spatial aggregation to design a control structure that decomposes a field into components that can be controlled relatively independently by a distributed set of sources.

Control Optimization

Once a source placement has been designed, the actions for the sources must be optimized. While algorithms for multi-parameter optimization exist (Press *et al.* 1986), they are computationally expensive for large problems and difficult to parallelize for distributed applications.

The basic optimization algorithm follows the structure of many standard multi-parameter optimizers: repeatedly adjust each source's value[4] in the direction that minimizes error. We will show how physical knowledge, in the form of an influence graph, can significantly improve the performance of numerical optimization. In particular, the influence graph will be used (1) to dramatically speed up the computation in optimization, and (2) to cooperate among distributed optimization processes for the sources.

Efficient field evaluation

During each step of an iterative optimization process, the field is evaluated using the relatively expensive, iterative relaxation method on the spatial objects. However, recall that an influence graph caches field information for normalized sources. Thus the field value for a spatial object can be calculated by simply summing the influences of edges coming into the node, weighted by the control source values[5]. The computation is extremely fast. Since the field has to be recomputed at every step of optimization, the influence graph results in a drastic speed-up in computation.

Cooperation among distributed optimization processes

While we want to independently optimize sources, in reality there is coupling — the heat from one source affects the temperature in the region which another source is trying to optimize, as shown in Figure 6(b) and (c). Since the influence graph records dependence of field nodes on sources, it guides the search through the large design space to make appropriate use of cooperation among independent source optimization processes.

When a source is adjusted, it must estimate the error due to that adjustment. One approach is to consider only the region assigned to the source by the structure design, but that ignores the influence on the other regions. Alternatively, a source can consult the entire temperature field, but that requires much communication. Better yet, we can recompute those field nodes strongly affected by a source more frequently. If a source only weakly affects a temperature node, we need not assign it much blame/credit for the error at that node. The influence graph is used to compute source-field communication frequency as a function of the amount of influence.

Structural knowledge can also be used to indicate the potential need for joint source optimization. For example, the influence graph indicates regions strongly influenced by multiple sources, in turn suggesting the need for cooperative optimization of the sources. This can help avoid ridges in the optimization landscape.

Performance

The design algorithms, when applied to several problems, result in competitive designs and run-time performance.

Control structure design through field decomposition is extremely fast; the design time is dominated by the parametric optimization that must be performed at each step. For example, in an implementation using the C++-based SA library on a 100-MHz Pentium system with Linux and gcc, it takes about 8 seconds to classify and redescribe the gradient trajectories on the 1103-node P-shaped field in Figure 5. As previously mentioned, there are no standard structure-design algorithms against which to compare the results, but on a variety of problems, the SA-based design consistently outperformed anything we hand-designed.

As expected, using influence graphs to solve for fields given new source configurations results in enormous savings. For example, on the system and field described above, it takes about 49 seconds to iteratively solve for the temperature, while it takes less than 0.02 seconds to solve directly with an influence graph. Since the solving must be performed at each iteration, the savings add up quickly.

Finally, parametric design successfully uses influence graphs to guide distributed source optimization. Table 2 summarizes results for parametric design on a regular 20x20 discretized thermal field. The first two optimizers (Gauss-Newton and Broyden-Fletcher-Golfarb-Shanno) are Matlab's implementations of two standard global multi-parameter optimization algorithms (Simplex search optimization was omitted because it failed to converge within 300 steps on all of these tests.)

---

[4] Position can also be optimized in this manner, but space prohibits detailed discussion of extensions to handle that.

[5] The influence graph essentially pre-computes and caches the inverse of the capacitance matrix of the field *in a decentralized fashion*, and is particularly efficient when sources are sparse. Boundary conditions can be treated the same as sources.

	GN	BFGS	SA1	SA2	SA3
4-corner					
# iterations	19	14	21	19	17
# communic.	24624	18144	27216	10572	2332
error	.2028	.2028	.2028	.2037	.2281
4-center					
# iterations	20	14	24	21	19
# communic.	25920	18144	31104	21004	6980
error	.3459	.3459	.3459	.3463	.3621
16-tiled					
# iterations	56	213	36	49	46
# communic.	290304	1104192	186624	161790	50535
error	.1164	.1164	.1167	.1181	.1189

Table 2: Parametric design performance data.

The SA-based optimizers use an implementation with default parameters and varying amounts of communication: SA1 updates each field object based on each source every iteration, while SA2 and SA3 update field objects with frequency proportional to influence, with two different constants of proportionality. The optimizers were run on three different tests: four sources near the corners of the grid, four sources near the center of the grid, and sixteen sources tiled over the grid. Three performance results are shown for each test: the number of iterations for convergence, the total source-field node communication[6], and the average squared error across the thermal field. Actual run-time is roughly proportional to the number of communications.

These results show that on prototypical multi-parameter optimization problems, the SA structure-based design competes well with other optimization techniques in both speed and error, and can drastically reduce the amount of communication among distributed optimization processes. In problems with larger domains, there will be even fewer field nodes strongly influenced by a source (depending of course on geometry, material properties, and so forth), providing even greater potential savings.

Discussion

Spatial aggregation exploits physical knowledge to build multi-layer spatial aggregates that can be used to automatically generate explanations for why higher-level control decisions are made. For instance, the field geometry might induce a weak gradient direction; hence, SA refines spatial objects along that direction in order to decouple the field. In contrast, traditional numerical simulations require humans to interpret and explain the results.

Traditionally, qualitative physics has focused on lumped parameter models of physical systems. For instance, the device ontology describes an electrical circuit as a network of components, while abstracting away

---

[6]In the Matlab-based routines, essentially each source communicates with each non-boundary field node each iteration.

the spatial dimension (DeKleer & Brown 1984). However, many important physical phenomena are modeled as spatially distributed parameter systems. The SA field ontology describes such physical phenomena by encapsulating the important spatial information in the spatial objects and the neighborhood structures, permitting efficient reasoning about these phenomena.

Unlike control design for lumped parameter linear systems, few analytic design techniques have been developed for distributed control of large physical fields (Sandell Jr. et al. 1978). In practice, the design is often accomplished by brute-force numerical simulations. SA offers a powerful modeling framework and an alternative mechanism for synthesizing decentralized control. The multi-resolutional SA model is particularly useful for formulating structural design problems that are not well addressed by numerical methods.

Doumanidis (Doumanidis 1997) addressed the problem of control parameter optimization for distributed parameter systems. He introduced a first-order approximation to local effects of heat sources during the optimization. However, his approach ignored effects of geometries and how a field can be decomposed using the structural knowledge.

The design techniques introduced here rely on two important pieces of physical knowledge: locality and linear superposability of control. Locality makes it possible to decouple a field and separately consider a source's effects on strongly-influenced nodes and on weakly-influenced nodes. We note that certain problems, such as heat transfer with highly conductive materials, may not possess strong locality; such problems are less amenable to a decompositional approach. Many physical processes (e.g. heat conduction, gravity, electrostatics, and incompressible fluid flow) are linear in control. This fact makes it possible, for example, to calculate temperature as a sum of influences from different heat sources. Influence graphs encapsulate other possibly nonlinear irregularities in physical fields, exposing linear dependence on source values. Extensions to transient problems make a direct use of spatiotemporal structures; for example, an influence graph would represent the influence of a source's heat at a given time on thermal field objects at various points in time.

Many other interesting papers have studied problem decomposition and interaction among sub-problems. For instance, the parti-game algorithm decomposes high-dimensional state-spaces for learning control strategies (Moore & Atkeson 1995). Similarly, Bradley and Zhao presented several methods for synthesizing nonlinear control laws in phase spaces (Bradley & Zhao 1993); their methods partition phase spaces into manageable subspaces. Bertsekas uses adaptive aggregation in dynamic programming to group states and their dependencies into meta-states according to residual errors (Bertsekas & Castanon 1989). Williams and Millar (Williams & Millar 1996) and Clancy and Kuipers (Clancy & Kuipers 1997) present two different methods for decomposing large models and reasoning about the interactions of sub-components. Our work differs from these in that it uses structural knowledge (e.g. isotherms and influence graphs) of distributed parameter fields to guide decomposition and cooperation.

Other researchers have developed related frameworks and systems for reasoning about spatial, analogue representations of the physical world. Williams and Nayak discussed model-based methods for modeling, configuring and programming distributed physical systems (Williams & Nayak 1996). Lundell presented a qualitative model for distributed parameter physical fields (Lundell 1996). Forbus et al. developed the Metric Diagram/Place Vocabulary (MD/PV) framework for qualitative spatial reasoning (Forbus, Nielsen, & Faltings 1991). In computer scene analysis, Hummel and Zucker formalized a class of problems called relaxation labeling that computes a consistent labeling for a network of objects (Hummel & Zucker 1983). In comparison to the above work, the SA framework focuses on structure recovery and control of spatial fields. It differs from relaxation labeling in that SA builds multi-layer spatial aggregates to exploit a variety of spatial and temporal constraints. It also differs from many neural net based learning and optimization methods in that SA explicitly models and exploits field topological structures. This paper develops SA mechanisms for controlling physical fields that significantly extend the framework developed in (Yip & Zhao 1996; Bailey-Kellogg, Zhao, & Yip 1996).

Conclusions

This paper advances the state-of-the-art in qualitative physics and spatial reasoning in several ways. It has developed the SA ontological abstraction for distributed parameter physical fields and a structure-based design mechanism for synthesizing placement and parameters for distributed control of the fields. SA extracts meaningful structures from continuous fields so that design decisions can be articulated using discrete spatial objects. SA introduces the influence graph to manage the search space during optimization and to avoid repeatedly recomputing field values. Because spatial aggregates comprise mixed numeric, geometric, and symbolic descriptions, we expect SA to take advantage of and complement the arsenal of existing numerical methods.

This research addresses several scientific and engineering concerns central to artificial intelligence. We expect SA to shed light on bi-directional mappings between macroscopic decisions and local actions in biological and engineered systems. In addition, SA aims to systematize design principles and programming methodologies for interpreting and controlling distributed parameter physical fields, and to provide useful tools for practicing engineers.

Acknowledgments

The work is supported in part by ONR YI grant N00014-97-1-0599, NSF NYI grant CCR-9457802, and a Xerox grant to the Ohio State University.

References

Bailey-Kellogg, C.; Zhao, F.; and Yip, K. 1996. Spatial aggregation: language and applications. In *Proceedings of AAAI*.

Berlin, A. 1994. MEMS-based active structural strengthening technology. In *Proceedings of Government Microcircuit Applications Conference*.

Bertsekas, D., and Castanon, D. 1989. Adaptive aggregation methods for infinite horizon dynamic programming. *IEEE Trans. on Automatic Control* 34.

Bradley, E., and Zhao, F. 1993. Phase-space control system design. *IEEE Control Systems* 13(2):39-47.

Briggs, W. 1987. *A Multigrid Tutorial*. Lancaster Press.

Clancy, D. J., and Kuipers, B. 1997. Model decomposition and simulation: A component based qualitative simulation algorithm. In *Proceedings of AAAI*.

DeKleer, J., and Brown, J. 1984. A qualitative physics based on confluences. *Artificial Intelligence* 24.

Doumanidis, C. C. 1997. In-process control in thermal rapid prototyping. *IEEE Control Systems*.

Forbus, K.; Nielsen, P.; and Faltings, B. 1991. Qualitative spatial reasoning: the CLOCK project. *Artificial Intelligence* 51.

Hummel, R., and Zucker, S. 1983. On the foundations of relaxation labeling processes. *IEEE Trans. on Pattern Analysis and Machine Intelligence* 5(3).

Jaluria, Y., and Torrance, K. 1986. *Computational Heat Transfer*. Hemisphere Publishing.

Kailath, T., et al. 1996. Control for advanced semiconductor device manufacturing: A case history. In Levine, W., ed., *The Control Handbook*. CRC Press.

Lundell, M. 1996. A qualitative model of physical fields. In *Proceedings of AAAI*.

Moore, A., and Atkeson, C. 1995. The parti-game algorithm for variable resolution reinforcement learning in multidimensional state-spaces. *Machine Learning* 21.

Press, W. H.; Flannery, B. P.; Teukolsky, S. A.; and Vetterling, W. T. 1986. *Numerical Recipes: the Art of Scientific Computing*. Cambridge University Press.

Sandell Jr., N.; Varaiya, P.; Athans, M.; and Safonov, M. 1978. Survey of decentralized control methods for large scale systems. *IEEE Trans. on Automatica Control* 23(2).

Seidman, T. 1996. Control of the heat equation. In Levine, W., ed., *The Control Handbook*. CRC Press.

Spielman, D., and Teng, S. 1996. Spectral partitioning works: Planar graphs and finite element meshes. Technical Report UCB CSD-96-898, UC Berkeley.

Vichnevetsky, R. 1981. *Computer Methods for Partial Differential Equations, Vol. 1*. Prentice-Hall.

Williams, B. C., and Millar, B. 1996. Automated decomposition of model-based learning problems. In *Proc. 10th International Workshop on Qualitative Reasoning*.

Williams, B., and Nayak, P. 1996. Immobile robots: AI in the new millenium. *AI Magazine* 17(3).

Yip, K. M., and Zhao, F. 1996. Spatial aggregation: theory and applications. *J. Artificial Intelligence Research* 5.

Qualitative simulation as a temporally-extended constraint satisfaction problem *

Daniel J. Clancy
Caellum/NASA Ames Research Center, MS 269-3
Moffett Field, CA 94035 USA
clancy@ptolemy.arc.nasa.gov

Benjamin J. Kuipers
Computer Science Department
University of Texas at Austin
Austin, Texas 78712
kuipers@cs.utexas.edu

Abstract

Traditionally, constraint satisfaction problems (CSPs) are characterized using a finite set of constraints expressed within a common, shared constraint language. When reasoning across time, however, it is possible to express both temporal and state-based constraints represented within multiple constraint languages. Qualitative simulation provides an instance of this class of CSP in which, traditionally, all solutions to the CSP are computed. In this paper, we formally describe this class of *temporally-extended* CSPs and situate qualitative simulation within this description. This is followed by a description of the DecSIM algorithm which is used to incrementally generate all possible solutions to a temporally-extended CSP. DecSIM combines problem decomposition, a tree-clustering algorithm and ideas similar to directed arc-consistency to exploit structure and causality within a qualitative model resulting in an exponential speed-up in simulation time when compared to existing techniques.

Introduction

Traditionally, constraint satisfaction problems (CSPs) are characterized using a finite set of constraints expressed within a common, shared constraint language (Tsang 1993). When reasoning across time, however, it is possible to express both temporal and state-based constraints represented within multiple constraint languages. A *state-based constraint* specifies restrictions between variables that must hold at any given point in time while a *temporal constraint* specifies restrictions that occur across time. Qualitative simulation provides an instance of this class of *temporally-extended* constraint satisfaction problems.

---

*This work has taken place in the Qualitative Reasoning Group at the Artificial Intelligence Laboratory, The University of Texas at Austin and was supported in part by NSF grants IRI-9504138 and CDA 9617327, by NASA grants NAG 2-994 and NAG 9-898, and by the Texas Advanced Research Program under grant no. 003658-242. Copyright ©1998, American Association for Artificial Intelligence (www.aaai.org). All rights reserved.

Qualitative simulation (Forbus 1984; Kuipers 1994) reasons about the behavior of a class of dynamical systems using a branching time description of alternating time-point and time-interval states. The model specifies a finite set of variables and constraints. Each constraint specifies valid combinations of variable values for any given point in time (*i.e.* state-based constraints). Continuity constraints are then used to restrict the valid transitions between states. For example, if in a time-point state S_1 the variable X is increasing and has a value $X*$, then immediately following S_1, X must be greater than $X*$ and increasing. The continuity constraints correspond to temporal restrictions. The use of temporal constraints within qualitative simulation has been further generalized within the TeQSIM algorithm to allow the specification of an arbitrary temporal constraint (Brajnik & Clancy 1996; 1997). TeQSIM uses a propositional linear-time temporal logic (PLTL) (Emerson 1990) that combines propositional state-formulae specifying either qualitative or quantitative information about a state with temporal operators such as *next*, *eventually*, *always*, and *until*. Each qualitative behavior generated during simulation corresponds to a solution to the CSP defined by the composition of the state-based constraints with the temporal constraints.

Viewing qualitative simulation as a temporally-extended CSP is beneficial because it allows us to explore how advances within the CSP literature can be used to improve the techniques applied during simulation. In addition, it describes a new class of constraint satisfaction problems that has not been extensively explored within the CSP literature. While conceptually a traditional temporal CSP can be used to express state-based constraints, by separating the two sets of constraints we are able to exploit inherent structure that exists within the state-based constraints to reduce the overall complexity of finding a solution.

The DecSIM qualitative simulation algorithm efficiently computes all possible solutions to this class of

CSPs by building upon and extending existing research within the constraint satisfaction literature.[1] DecSIM provides a sound, but potentially incomplete algorithm that solves instances within this class of CSPs exponentially faster than the techniques currently used within the qualitative reasoning literature. This speed-up facilitates the application of qualitative simulation techniques to larger, more realistic problems.

Qualitative simulation explicitly computes all possible solutions to the temporally–extended CSP defined by the model. If two variables are completely unconstrained with respect to each other, then the set of all possible solutions contains the cross–product of the possible values for each variable. For QSIM this results in combinatoric branching when the temporal ordering of a set of events is unconstrained by the model.

DecSIM uses a divide and conquer approach to reduce the complexity of a simulation by exploiting structure within the qualitative model. DecSIM decomposes the state–based CSP, P_M, defined by the qualitative model M into a set of smaller sub–problems. Each sub–problem contains a subset of the variables in P_M while shared variables represent the constraints between sub–problems. DecSIM explicitly computes all solutions only for each sub–problem. In addition, however, DecSIM must also ensure that each partial solution participates in at least one solution to the original CSP. This task is characterized as a separate global CSP. Note that for each partial solution DecSIM is only required to compute a *single* solution to this global CSP as opposed to explicitly enumerating all possible solutions as is effectively done by QSIM. Furthermore, causality is used along with a tree-clustering algorithm to simplify the task of identifying this solution. The primary technical innovation provided by the DecSIM algorithm is the application of these basic concepts to a temporally–extended CSP ensuring that both the state-based and the temporal continuity constraints are satisfied. In this paper, we describe the DecSIM algorithm and present both theoretical and empirical results demonstrating the benefits provided by DecSIM when compared to techniques currently used to perform a simulation. In addition, we provide a formal characterization of a temporally-extended CSP thus laying the ground work for future research to explore how work within fields such as qualitative reasoning, planning, constraint satisfaction and reasoning about action can potentially be integrated.

Definitions and concepts

Qualitative simulation uses an imprecise, structural model describing a class of dynamical systems to derive a description of all qualitatively distinct behaviors consistent with the model.[2] In its basic form, a model, called a qualitative differential equation (QDE), is defined by the tuple $<V, Q, I, C>$ where V is a set of variables, Q a discrete set of values for each variable, I is an initial state, and C a set of state–based constraints on the variables in V.

The constraints are abstractions of mathematical relationships restricting the valid combinations of values for the variables in the constraint. The behavior of the system is described by a tree of qualitative states in which each path consists of alternating time–point and time–interval states. Each qualitative state provides a value for all of the variables within the model along with a value for a special variable representing time.

A qualitative model defines a traditional, state–based CSP. During simulation, however, this CSP is extended across time as each variable is assigned a value at successive time-point and time-interval states. These variable assignments must satisfy both the state–based constraints as well as any implicit or explicit temporal constraints. A temporally-extended CSP is defined by extending the definitions that are commonly used to define a traditional CSP.

Definition 1 (Temporally–extended CSP)
A temporally–extended CSP is defined by the tuple $<V, D, C_s, C_t, closed>$ where

- *V is a set of variables,*
- *D defines the domain for each variable,*
- *C_s is the set of state-based constraints,*
- *C_t is a set of temporal constraints, and*
- closed *is a domain-specific boolean predicate that is used to determine whether or a temporal sequence can be extended further.*

A *label* is an assignment of a value to a variable at a particular point within the temporal sequence. Thus, a label is defined by the tuple $<v, d_v, t>$ where v is a variable, d_v is a value for the variable and t is a non-negative integer corresponding to the "location" of the value assignment within the temporal sequence. A label with the value of $t = 0$ corresponds to the

---

[1] An earlier version of the DecSIM algorithm was published in (Clancy & Kuipers 1997) with preliminary results. Since that publication, the algorithm has been significantly generalized, resulting in stronger theoretical claims and experimental results.

[2] In this presentation, we focus on the representation used by the QSIM qualitative simulation algorithm. These concepts can also be applied to alternative representations (Forbus 1984; de Kleer & Brown 1985) that have been proposed within the literature.

initial state within a temporal sequence.[3] An *extended label* (also called a *variable history*) corresponds to a sequence $(<v,d_v^1,t>, <v,d_v^2,t+1>, \ldots, <v,d_v^m,t+m>)$ of consecutive labels while a *rooted extended label* is an extended label with $t=0$. A *compound label* is a set of labels $(<v_1,d_{v_1},t>, <v_2,d_{v_2},t>, \ldots <v_n,d_{v_n},t>)$ providing values to multiple variables in the same time-state while an *extended compound label* is simply a set of extended labels for multiple variables.

A *solution* to the temporally-extended CSP corresponds to an extended compound label that satisfies both the state-based and the temporal constraints. The formal definition of a solution, however, needs to account for the potentially infinite nature of a temporal sequence. To address this issue, the domain specific boolean predicate *closed* is used.

Definition 2 (Partial and Full Solutions) *A fully extended solution is an extended compound label that satisfies all of the constraints as well as the* closed *predicate. Conversely, a partially extended solution is an extended compound label that satisfies all of the constraints but fails to satisfy the* closed *predicate.*

How the *closed* predicate is defined depends upon the domain. Within qualitative simulation, a solution is fully extended if either a cycle is detected, a transition condition occurs or the last state is quiescent (*i.e.* in a steady state). On the other hand, if planning were viewed as a temporally-extended CSP, then a solution is fully extended when the final state satisfies the goal condition. One of the reasons that it is important to define the *closed* predicate is that in qualitative simulation a partially-extended solution is eliminated from the solution set if it is determined that there does not exist a consistent extension to the solution.

Given a qualitative model and an initial state, qualitative simulation can be mapped to a temporally-extended CSP in a straight-forward manner by mapping the variables, their domains and the state-based constraints directly from one problem to the next and then by deriving the temporal constraints from the continuity constraints applied when performing a simulation.[4] Qualitative simulation then attempts to find all possible solutions to the temporally-extended CSP given some limit on either the length of a temporal sequence or the overall set of compound labels within the solution set. Thus, the complexity of the problem is completely determined by the size of the solution space. Since larger models tend to be more loosely constrained, simulation of these models often results in intractable branching and an exponential number of solutions. Thus, a state-based representation is inherently limited in its ability to represent and reason about the behavior of an imprecisely defined dynamical system.

The DecSIM Algorithm

DecSIM modifies the representation used to describe the solution space generated during qualitative simulation thus providing a more compact representation and a more efficient simulation algorithm. DecSIM exploits the fact that larger systems can often be decomposed into a number of loosely connected subsystems due to inherent structure that exists within the model. By decomposing the model, DecSIM is able to address one of the primary sources of complexity — combinatoric branching due to the complete temporal ordering of the behaviors of unrelated variables.

Component Generation

Given a model M with a set of variables V and an initial state I, DecSIM uses a partitioning $\{V_1, V_2, \ldots V_n\}$ of the variables in the model to generate a *component* for each partition. Currently, the partitioning of the variables is provided as an input to the DecSIM algorithm.[5] A separate behavioral description (*i.e.* set of solutions) is explicitly generated for each component. The interaction between components is represented via shared variables called *boundary variables*. For each partition V_i, DecSIM generates a component C_i containing two types of variables: **within-partition variables** are the variables specified in V_i, and **boundary variables** are variables contained in other partitions that have a *direct causal influence* on the within-partition variables.

DecSIM identifies boundary variables using an extension of Iwasaki's (1988) causal ordering algorithm to transform the model into a hybrid directed/undirected hypergraph called the *causal graph*. A variable v_i is said to have a *direct causal influence* on a variable v_j if there exists either an undirected hyperedge in the causal graph relating v_i and v_j or if there exists a di-

---

[3]In our definition of a temporally-extended CSP, we do not restrict the semantic interpretation of a point within this sequence. In qualitative simulation, a temporal progression will alternate between time-point and time-interval states, however, other interpretations can be used for different domains.

[4]To describe the problem addressed by TeQSIM, the set of temporal constraints are extended to include any temporal logic expressions contained within the model. Currently, however, DecSIM does not handle arbitrary temporal constraints as can be expressed using TeQSIM.

[5]Various techniques for automating this process have been considered; however, up to this point, we have focused on the simulation algorithm since partitioning the variables is a fairly straight-forward extension of the model-building process.

rected hyperedge extending from v_i and terminating in v_j.[6]

Each component C_i defines a qualitative model, in which the variables correspond to the union of the within–partition and boundary variables for the component and the constraints correspond to the set of constraints in the original model relating the variables contained in the component. Furthermore, the relationship between components defined by the shared boundary variables defines a labeled directed graph called the *component graph* defined as follows.

Definition 3 (Component graph) *Given a set of related components* $\{C_1, C_2, \ldots, C_n\}$ *the* component graph *is a labeled, directed graph with a node corresponding to each component. The edges are defined as follows:*

- *An edge exists from component C_i to node C_j if and only if there exists a variable v such that v is a within–partition variable in C_i and a boundary variable in C_j.*
- *An edge from C_i to C_j is labeled with the set of boundary variables in C_j that are classified as within–partition variables in C_i.*

Local and global consistency

The core QSIM algorithm is used to derive a separate behavioral description, called a *component tree*, for each component. The terms *component behavior* and *component state* are used to refer to a behavior and a state within a component tree respectively.

Definition 4 (Local consistency) *A component behavior for component C_i is* locally consistent *if and only if it is a solution to the CSP defined by C_i.*

In addition, however, each component behavior must be consistent with respect to the rest of the model. To determine if a component behavior participates in a complete solution to the original CSP, DecSIM must solve a separate *global* CSP in which the "variables" correspond to components, the "variable values" to component behaviors, and the "constraints" to the restrictions represented by the variables that are shared between components.

A component behavior b_i is *globally consistent* if and only if there exists a set of component behaviors $B = \{b_{C_1}, b_{C_2}, \ldots, b_{C_n}\}$ containing b_i such that B is a solution to the global CSP.[7] Thus, DecSIM must determine if a set of component behaviors are compatible with respect to the variables that are shared between components.

Definition 5 (Compatible behaviors) *A set of component behaviors* $B = \{b_{C_1}, b_{C_2}, \ldots, b_{C_n}\}$ *are* compatible *if and only if the behaviors can be combined to form at least one composite behavior describing all of the variables within each component behavior.*

Conceptually, behavior composition is equivalent to a multi-way join as it is used in the relational database literature.

Definition 6 (Behavior composition) *Given a set of component behaviors* $B = \{b_{C_1}, b_{C_2}, \ldots, b_{C_n}\}$, $\mathcal{B}$ *is a* composite *behavior for B if and only if $\mathcal{B}$ describes all of the variables in $\bigcup_{i=1}^{n} V_{C_i}$ and for i from 1 to n and $\Pi_{V_{C_i}}(\mathcal{B}) = b_i$ where $\Pi_{V_{C_i}}$ is the projection of a behavior onto the variables in V_{C_i}.*[8]

The set of all composite behaviors is essentially the cross-product of the component behaviors, minus the combinations filtered out by the global consistency constraints. Thus, if the components are weakly connected, this set can be quite large.

Since each behavior is actually a temporal sequence, determining if a set of component behaviors is compatible is not simply a straight–forward comparison of the variable values. DecSIM addresses this issue by maintaining a many-to-many mapping between states within components related in the component graph. Two states are mapped to each other if and only if the behaviors terminating in these two states are compatible. This mapping allows DecSIM to evaluate the global consistency of a set of behaviors by comparing the final states within the behaviors with respect to this mapping.

The mapping is generated as each component behavior is incrementally extended. If components A and B are related via shared variables, then state S_A maps to component state S_B if and only if S_A and S_B are equivalent with respect to any shared variables, and either S_A and S_B are initial states, the predecessor of S_A maps to the predecessor of S_B, the predecessor of S_A maps to S_B, or S_A maps to the predecessor of S_B.

By maintaining the many-to-many mapping between compatible states in related components, DecSIM translates the global CSP in which the variable values correspond to component *behaviors* into a CSP, called the *component graph CSP*, in which the variable values correspond to qualitative *states*. This translation enables DecSIM to evaluate the global consistency

---

[6]The algorithm used to generate the causal graph is potentially incomplete in which case the causal relationship between any two variables may be incomplete thus resulting in an undirected hyperedge in the causal graph.

[7]Throughout this paper, subscripts are used to identify the component to which a state, behavior or set of variables belong.

[8]Please refer to (Clancy 1997) for a formal definition of the projection operator as it applies to a qualitative behavior.

of a state based upon local inferences with respect to the temporal progression of the behaviors.

Definition 7 (Component graph CSP) *The component graph CSP is defined by the tuple $<V, D, C>$ such that*

- *the variables V correspond to components,*
- *the domain for each variable is the set of qualitative states defined in the component tree for the corresponding component (D is the set of domains for each variable),*
- *the constraints C are defined by the many-to-many mapping maintained between related components. If components C_i and C_j are related in the component graph, then a constraint exists between the corresponding variables within the component graph CSP that is satisfied for two states s_{C_i} and s_{C_j} if and only s_{C_i} and s_{C_j} are linked by the many-to-many mapping relating these components.*

Specification of this global CSP on qualitative states allows us to define global consistency with respect to a qualitative state as opposed to an entire behavior.

Definition 8 (Globally consistent) *A component state is globally consistent if and only if the state is both locally consistent and participates in a solution to the component graph CSP.*

Performing the simulation

When performing a simulation, DecSIM iterates through the components incrementally simulating the leaf states in each component tree. DecSIM uses QSIM to generate the successors of each component state, thus ensuring that each state is locally consistent. In addition, however, DecSIM must ensure that each state is also globally consistent.

Determining whether a component state is globally consistent for a fully simulated set of component behaviors is a straight-forward constraint satisfaction problem given the characterization that has been provided. DecSIM, however, incrementally generates each component behavior. Thus, it is possible that as component behaviors are extended, a solution to the component graph is generated containing a state already within a component tree that had previously not been globally consistent. In other words, a state s not being globally consistent at a given point during the simulation does not imply that s is globally *inconsistent*. DecSIM addresses this issue using two techniques: 1) successors of a component state s are only computed if s is determined to be globally consistent, and 2) the identification of a state as globally consistent must be propagated through the component graph CSP by identifying all solutions to the component graph that contain at least one state whose status with respect to global consistency had previously been undetermined.

The first condition ensures that globally inconsistent states are not simulated while the second condition ensures that all globally consistent solutions are still computed given the first restriction.

The algorithm used to test a state for global consistency exploits causality and structure within the component graph CSP to reduce the complexity of finding a solution. First, a tree-clustering algorithm (Dechter & Pearl 1988; 1989) is used to transform the component graph CSP into an acyclic *cluster graph* by grouping components that are included within a cycle into a single node within the cluster graph. This transformation significantly reduces the time required to find a solution to the component graph by allowing DecSIM to use constraint propagation between clusters as opposed to computing a complete solution to the CSP. Second, causality is used to further reduce the complexity of this process by asserting the independence of causally upstream components from those components that are strictly downstream with respect to the causal ordering.

Two primary benefits are provided by DecSIM with respect to a standard QSIM simulation. First, by transforming the component graph into an acyclic cluster graph, the worst case complexity required to find a solution to the component graph CSP is exponential in the size of the largest cluster as opposed to overall size of the component graph. Second, DecSIM is only required to find a single solution to the component graph for each component behavior as opposed to computing all possible solutions as is required by a standard QSIM simulation.

An Example

The benefits provided by DecSIM can be demonstrated using a simple model of a sequence of cascaded tanks. Two versions of this model will be used during the discussion. In the simpler version, a simple cascade is used while in the more complex version a feedback loop exists by which the inflow to the top tank is controlled by the level in the bottom tank (see figure 1).

When performing a standard QSIM simulation of a simple N-tank cascade, a total of 2^{N-1} behaviors are generated enumerating all possible solutions to the CSP. Many of these solutions, however, simply provide different temporal orderings of unrelated events. DecSIM, however, eliminates these distinctions generating a separate behavioral description, each containing a total of three behaviors, for each tank. By using causality, we are able to reason about the behavior of the upstream tanks independently of the downstream

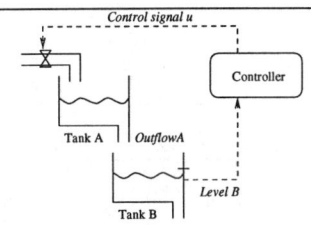

(a) Controlled two tank cascade

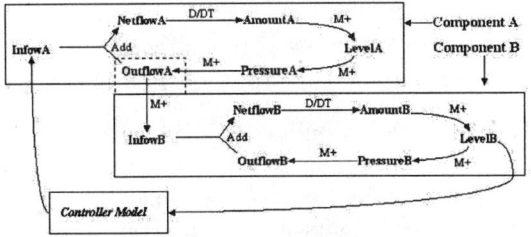

(b) Causal graph and variable partitioning

The qualitative model of a controlled two tank cascade (a) is partitioned into three components: tankA, tankB and the controller. DecSIM generates a causal graph of the model (b) that is used to identify the boundary variables. The variable partitioning is identified by the solid boxes within the causal graph. Boundary variables are variables in other partitions that are causally upstream. Thus, OutflowA is a boundary variable for component B and therefore included in the component; however, InflowB is not a boundary variable for component A.

Figure 1: Controlled two tank cascade

tanks. Thus, the overall complexity of the simulation is linear in the number of tanks. In the controlled version of the N-tank cascade, a feedback loop connects the upstream and downstream tanks. DecSIM, however, is still able to provide significant improvements in the overall simulation time due to its ability to partition the problem into smaller sub-problems and reason about the interaction between sub-problems independently. For an 8 tank cascade, DecSIM generates an average of 28 behaviors for each component while QSIM generates a total of 1071 behaviors. Table 1 displays the simulation time for a number of variations on this example.

Theoretical Results

Traditional techniques for qualitative simulation, while both sound and complete with respect to the CSP defined by the model, are unable to scale to larger problems.[9] DecSIM, on the other hand, trades completeness for efficiency. The following results are established in (Clancy & Kuipers 1998).

---

[9] Note the *incompleteness* of qualitative simulation is with respect to the set of real valued trajectories described by the behavioral description and not the CSP.

Theorem 1 (DecSIM Soundness Guarantee)
Given a consistent qualitative model M and a decomposition of the model into components $\{C_1, C_2, \ldots C_m\}$, for all solutions B to the temporally-extended CSP defined by M, DecSIM generates the set of partial solutions $\{b_1, b_2, \ldots, b_n\}$ such that for $i : 1 \leq i \leq n$ :: $\Pi_{V_i}(B) = b_i$.[10]

Theorem 2 (DecSIM Completeness Guarantee)
Given a consistent model M and a decomposition of the model into components $\{C_1, C_2, \ldots C_m\}$ such that there does not exist a cycle of size 3 or greater in the component graph CSP, for all partial solutions b_i generated by DecSIM describing the subset of variables V_i, there exists a corresponding solution to the temporally-extended CSP defined by M such that $b_i = \Pi_{V_i}(B)$.

Note that the completeness theorem includes a restriction on the maximum cycle size within the component graph CSP. Except for this one limitation and the temporal ordering of behaviors in separate components, the behavioral description generated by DecSIM is identical to the description generated by QSIM. Temporal ordering information (which is intentionally omitted), however, is still available since DecSIM implicitly represents this information via the constraints represented by the mapping maintained between component states.

Incompleteness The source of the incompleteness comes from the characterization of the component graph CSP as a CSP over qualitative states as opposed to qualitative behaviors. This translation is essential if DecSIM is to efficiently determine if a component state is globally consistent; however, it may result in the introduction of component behaviors that do not have a corresponding behavior within the behavioral description generated by QSIM. The problem encountered is analogous to the distinction between constraint propagation and constraint satisfaction with respect to the temporal continuity constraints. Before allowing a state S_A to participate in a solution to the component graph CSP, DecSIM requires that its predecessor participate in a solution. However, it does not check to ensure that the solution containing S_A satisfies the continuity constraints with respect to a solution containing the predecessor of S_A. To do this, DecSIM would be required to maintain a record of solutions to the component graph CSP to ensure that a proposed solution is continuous with a solution identified for the preceding time-step. For many models, this may require DecSIM to compute *all* solutions for a cluster

---

[10] $\Pi_{V_i}(B)$ is the projection of the solution onto the subset of variables V_i where component C_i is assumed to describe the set of variables V_i.

within the component graph thus eliminating the computational efficiency benefits provided by DecSIM for the behavior of the system within this cluster.

In practice, the incompleteness of the algorithm has not been a problem for a number of reasons. First, the conditions under which the incompleteness of the algorithm is encountered is quite restricted and only occurs when two components are closely related. In fact, we have yet to encounter this problem in any of the models that have been tested. In addition, we have developed an algorithm that can be used to identify when this problem occurs which can be run following completion of a simulation. Finally, qualitative simulation already encounters a problem with behaviors being generated that do not correspond to a real-valued trajectory of a dynamical system described by the model. Thus, techniques using qualitative simulation already must account for possible spurious behaviors. In the end, as is often the case, a trade-off exists between completeness and the overall computational complexity of the algorithm. [11] A traditional state–based approach is inherently limited in its ability to scale to larger problems and thus at times we may be required to sacrifice completeness guarantees when reasoning about these problems.

Computational complexity

The overall complexity of a standard QSIM simulation is determined by the size of the representation that is being computed. The worst case size of the behavioral description is exponential in the number of variables within the model. DecSIM reduces the size of the solution space by decomposing the model. For DecSIM, the worst case size is simply exponential in the number of variables in the largest component. DecSIM, however, must also reason about the global consistency of a component state by solving the component graph CSP. Thus, the overall benefits provided by DecSIM depend upon the topology of the model and the degree to which it lends itself to decomposition along with the variable partitioning selected by the modeler.

The following two conclusions (Clancy 1997) define the relationship between DecSIM and QSIM with respect to the complexity of a simulation for a model that is decomposed into k partitions: 1) as the degree of overlap between components approaches zero, the size of the total solution space is reduced by an exponential factor k where k is the number of components within the decomposed model; and 2) as the degree of

---

[11] We are currently in the process of developing a proof to establish that this trade-off is an inherent limitation when computing all possible solutions to a temporally–extended CSP.

# of Tanks	Cascade		Chained		Loop	
	Qsim	DecS	Qsim	DecS	Qsim	DecS
2	0.20	0.815	3.07	6.79	0.757	5.58
3	0.62	1.6	10.9	19.90	16.14	8.14
4	2.2	3.12	37.5	25.98	89.41	12.6
5	7.09	5.49	139	36.71	493.8	23.2
6	21.9	6.32	676	62.40	2758	48.7
7	71.5	8.39	1633	70	14474	116
8	236	11.6	8101	77	nc	442

nc = Resource limitation prevented completion

Table 1: Simulation Time Results: DecSIM vs QSIM

overlap approaches a fully connected constraint graph for the component graph CSP, the size of the set of behaviors generated by DecSIM is within a factor of k of a standard QSIM simulation. In practice, the savings provided by a DecSIM simulation are quite pronounced as is demonstrated by our empirical results. The primary source of these savings is the fact that DecSIM is only required to compute a *single* solution to the component graph CSP (*i.e.* to ensure that each component behavior is consistent with at least one global solution) as opposed to computing all solutions (as QSIM does for the non-decomposed model).

Empirical Evaluation

Empirical evaluation has been used to measure the benefits provided by a DecSIM simulation with respect to a standard QSIM simulation. Both DecSIM and QSIM were tested on a set of "extendible" models. An extendible model is a model composed of a sequence of identical components thus enabling the incremental extension of the model to facilitate an evaluation of the asymptotic behavior of the algorithm. The models used were variations on the cascaded tanks example described in figure 1. Three different versions were used; each with a different topology for the component graph CSP. A simple *cascade* topology, a *loop* topology in which the top tank is controlled by the bottom tank, and a *chain* topology in which the outflow for tank n is controlled by the level for tank $n + 1$.

For all three models, DecSIM performed exponentially better than QSIM. Table 1 shows the simulation time results as the number of tanks are varied while figure 2(a) plots the results for the loop configuration comparing QSIM to DecSIM. The benefits provided by DecSIM are even more pronounced for the other two topologies. Figure 2(b) provides a comparison of the results from the DecSIM simulation for all three topologies. Note the dependence of the computational complexity on the topology of the model. In the loop configuration, the component graph CSP is composed of a single, large cycle. Thus, it is more likely to en-

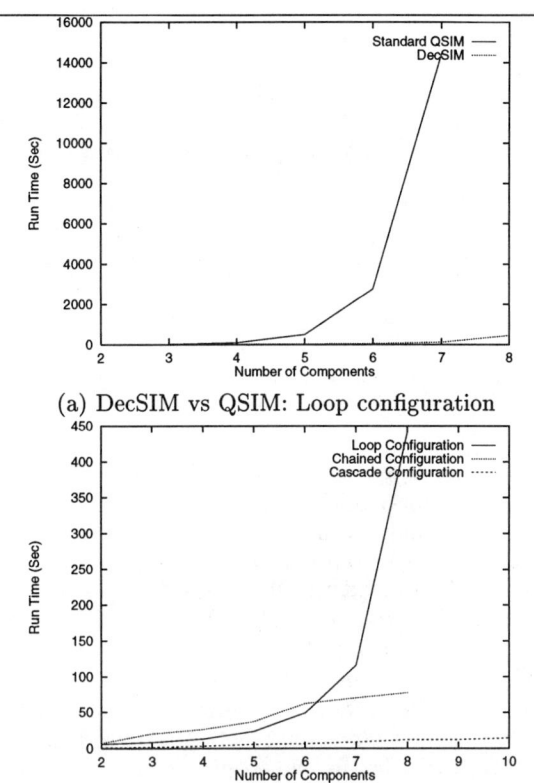

(a) DecSIM vs QSIM: Loop configuration

(b) DecSIM on different versions of the N-tank cascade

Figure 2: DecSIM results

counter backtracking when determining if a component state is globally consistent. Thus, the complexity of the simulation becomes exponential in the number of tanks. DecSIM, however, still performs significantly better than QSIM. For the simple N-tank cascade the complexity is linear in the number of tanks.

Conclusions

In this paper, we have characterized qualitative simulation as the composition of a state–based and a temporal–based CSP. Furthermore, we have shown that the state–based representation that is traditionally used when performing a simulation is inherently limited thus restricting the degree to which techniques based upon qualitative simulation can scale to larger, more realistic problems. DecSIM provides an alternative simulation algorithm that addresses this problem by decomposing the model into components. Decomposition eliminates combinatoric branching due to the complete temporal ordering of behaviors for unrelated variables contained in separate components. Thus, the complexity of the simulation is determined by the inherent complexity of the problem specification as opposed to an artifact of the inference mechanism used to perform simulation. Furthermore, characterizing qualitative simulation as a general class of CSPs allows the ideas presented here to be applied within a broader context. Hopefully, the concept of a temporally-extended CSP can help integrate ideas from fields such as qualitative simulation, planning and reasoning about action to provide a more unified representation that can be used to reason about both autonomous and non–autonomous change within the physical world.

References

Brajnik, G., and Clancy, D. J. 1996. Temporal constraints on trajectories in qualitative simulation. In Clancey, B., and Weld, D., eds., *Proc. of the Thirteenth National Conference on Artificial Intelligence*. AAAI Press. To appear.

Brajnik, G., and Clancy, D. J. 1997. Focusing qualitative simulation using temporal logic: theoretical foundations. *Annals of Mathematics and Artificial Intelligence*. To appear.

Clancy, D. J., and Kuipers, B. J. 1997. Model decomposition and simulation: A component based qualitative simulation algorithm. In Kuipers, B. J., and Webber, B., eds., *Proc. of the Fourteenth National Conference on Artificial Intelligence*. AAAI Press.

Clancy, D. J., and Kuipers, B. 1998. Divide and conquer: A component–based qualitative simulation algorithm. Technical Report forthcoming, Artificial Intelligence Laboratory, The University of Texas at Austin.

Clancy, D. J. 1997. Solving complexity and ambiguity problems in qualitative simulation. Technical Report AI-TR97-264, Artificial Intelligence Laboratory, The University of Texas at Austin.

de Kleer, J., and Brown, J. S. 1985. A qualitative physics based on confluences. In Hobbs, J. R., and Moore, R. C., eds., *Formal Theories of the Commonsense World*. Norwood, New Jersey: Ablex. chapter 4, 109–183.

Dechter, R., and Pearl, J. 1988. Tree-clustering schemes for constraint processing. In *Proceedings of the Seventh National Conference on Artificial Intelligence*. Los Altos, CA.: Morgan Kaufman.

Dechter, R., and Pearl, J. 1989. Tree-clustering for constraint networks. *Artificial Intelligence* 38:353–366.

Emerson, E. 1990. Temporal and modal logic. In van Leeuwen, J., ed., *Handbook of Theoretical Computer Science*. Elsevier Science Publishers/MIT Press. 995–1072. Chap. 16.

Forbus, K. 1984. Qualitative process theory. *Artificial Intelligence* 24:85–168.

Iwasaki, Y. 1988. Causal ordering in a mixed strcuture. In *Proc. of the Seventh National Conference on Artificial Intelligence*, 313–318. AAAI Press / The MIT Press.

Kuipers, B. 1994. *Qualitative Reasoning: modeling and simulation with incomplete knowledge*. Cambridge, Massachusetts: MIT Press.

Tsang, E. 1993. *Foundations of Constraint Satisfaction*. San Diego, CA: Academic Press.

Backtracking Algorithms for Disjunctions of Temporal Constraints[*][†]

Kostas Stergiou   Manolis Koubarakis

Department of Computation
UMIST
P.O. Box 88
Manchester M60 1QD, U.K.
{stergiou,manolis}@co.umist.ac.uk

Abstract

We extend the framework of simple temporal problems studied originally by Dechter, Meiri and Pearl to consider constraints of the form $x_1 - y_1 \leq r_1 \vee \ldots \vee x_n - y_n \leq r_n$, where $x_1 \ldots x_n, y_1 \ldots y_n$ are variables ranging over the real numbers, $r_1 \ldots r_n$ are real constants, and $n \geq 1$. We have implemented four progressively more efficient algorithms for the consistency checking problem for this class of temporal constraints. We have partially ordered those algorithms according to the number of visited search nodes and the number of performed consistency checks. Finally, we have carried out a series of experimental results on the location of the hard region. The results show that hard problems occur at a critical value of the ratio of disjunctions to variables. This value is between 6 and 7.

Introduction

Reasoning with temporal constraints has been a hot research topic for the last fifteen years. The importance of this problem has been demonstrated in many areas of artificial intelligence and databases, e.g., planning, scheduling, spatio-temporal databases, geographical information systems and medical information systems.

The class of quantitative temporal constraints has been studied originally by (Dechter et al., 1989) in the framework of *simple temporal problems* (STPs) where constraints are of the form $x - y \leq c$ where x and y are real variables and c is a real constant, and *temporal constraint satisfaction problems* (TCSPs) where constraints are disjunctions of formulas $l \leq x - y \leq u$ involving the *same pair* of real variables x and y ($\bar{l}$ and u are real constants). (Schwalb and Dechter, 1997) studied the performance of local consistency algorithms for processing TCSPs on hard problems in the transition region.

This paper continues the work on quantitative temporal constraints, but can also be seen as a *successful* transfer of methodology (theoretical and practical!) from binary CSPs to a non-binary temporal reasoning problem. We extend the framework of STPs studied originally by (Dechter et al., 1989) to consider constraints of the form $x_1 - y_1 \leq r_1 \vee \ldots \vee x_n - y_n \leq r_n$, where $x_1 \ldots x_n, y_1 \ldots y_n$ are variables ranging over the real numbers, $r_1 \ldots r_n$ are real constants, and $n \geq 1$. The reader should note that we do not restrict the variables in the disjuncts to be the same pair as (Dechter et al., 1989) do in the framework of TCSPs. The added generality is useful in many problems including temporal planning, job shop scheduling and temporal constraint databases.

We have implemented four progressively more efficient algorithms for the consistency checking problem for this class of temporal constraints (backtracking, backjumping, forward checking and forward checking with backjumping)[1]. We will only present the most efficient of these algorithms, which is forward checking with backjumping. Following the methodology of (Kondrak and van Beek, 1997), we have proved the correctness of all of the above algorithms, and partially ordered them according to the number of visited search nodes and the number of performed consistency checks. We have studied the performance of the above algorithms experimentally using randomly generated sets of data. We also present a series of experimental results on the location of the hard region and investigate the transition from the region where almost all problems are soluble to the region where almost no problem is soluble.

The organization of this paper is as follows. First, we present some basic definitions and describe the problem in detail. Then, we present forward checking with backjumping and the minimum remaining values heuristic. In what follows, we briefly discuss the theoretical evaluation of the algorithms and then present the results of our empirical analysis. Finally, we conclude and discuss future work.

---

[*] This work was carried out in the context of project CHOROCHRONOS funded by the Training and Mobility of Researchers programme of ESPRIT IV.

[†] Copyright © 1998, American Association for Artificial Intelligence (www.aaai.org). All rights reserved.

[1] The codes for the algorithms are available from the first author.

Preliminaries

We consider time to be linear, dense and unbounded. *Points* will be our only time entities. Points are identified with the real numbers. The set of real numbers will be denoted by $\mathcal{R}$.

Definition 1 A *temporal constraint* is a disjunction of the form $x_1 - y_1 \leq r_1 \vee \ldots \vee x_n - y_n \leq r_n$, where $x_1 \ldots x_n, y_1 \ldots y_n$ are variables ranging over the real numbers, $r_1 \ldots r_n$ are real constants, and $n \geq 1$. A temporal constraint containing only one disjunct will be called *non-disjunctive*. Temporal constraints with more than one disjuncts will be called *disjunctive*.

Example 1 The following are examples of temporal constraints:

$$x_1 - y_1 \leq 2, \quad x_1 - y_1 \leq 5 \ \vee x_2 - y_2 \leq -2$$

Definition 2 Let C be a set of temporal constraints in variables $x_1, \ldots, x_n$. The *solution set* of C, denoted by $Sol(C)$, is

$$\{(\tau_1, \ldots, \tau_n) : (\tau_1, \ldots, \tau_n) \in \mathcal{R}^n \text{ and for every } c \in C,$$
$$(\tau_1, \ldots, \tau_n) \text{ satisfies } c\}.$$

Each member of $Sol(C)$ is called a *solution* of C. A set of temporal constraints is called *consistent* if and only if its solution set is nonempty.

The consistency checking problem for a set of m temporal constraints in n variables can be equivalently restated as a m-ary *meta*-CSP, where disjunctions can be viewed as variables, and the disjuncts of each disjunction as the possible values of the corresponding variable. The m-ary constraint between the variables is that all values that are part of an assignment to variables must be simultaneously satisfied. The consistency of a given set C of temporal constraints can be decided in two steps. First, we check the consistency of the subset of non-disjunctive constraints. This is done using the incremental directional path consistency algorithm IDPC of (Chleq, 1995). If the subset of non-disjunctive constraints is consistent, we consider the subset of disjunctive constraints as well. Now C is consistent if for each disjunction there exists one disjunct that can be added to the subset of non-disjunctive constraints so that the new set of constraints produced is still consistent.

The Algorithm

First we introduce some necessary terminology. Some of it is similar to the terminology of (Gerevini and Schubert, 1995). The given set of disjunctions will be denoted by D. $D(i)$ and $D(i,j)$ will represent the i-th disjunction and the j-th disjunct of the i-th disjunction, respectively. The set of non-disjunctive constraints will be represented by a labelled directed graph and will be denoted by G. We call the set of selected disjuncts an *instantiation* of D in G. When a constraint is consistently added to G we say that it has been *instantiated*, and when a constraint is retracted from G that it has been *uninstantiated*. The *current disjunction* is the disjunction chosen for instantiation at each step of the algorithm. The *past disjunctions* are the disjunctions that have been already instantiated. The *future disjunctions* are the disjunctions that have not yet been instantiated. Each disjunct can be in one of three possible states at any time. It can be *available*, *current* or *eliminated*. A disjunct is available if it is neither current nor eliminated. A disjunct is current if it is part of the currently attempted instantiation of D. A disjunct becomes eliminated when it is tried and fails. A *dead-end* is a situation when all the disjuncts of the current disjunction are rejected.

A general strategy in CSPs is to preprocess the set of constraints prior to the search. Preprocessing tries to reduce the search space that backtracking algorithms explore, and in that way improve their efficiency (Dechter and Meiri, 1994). The set of disjunctions D can be reduced to an equivalent smaller subset by applying three simple *pruning rules* prior to the execution of the search algorithm:

1. If a disjunction $D(i)$ contains a disjunct that is subsumed by a single constraint in G then disjunction $D(i)$ can be eliminated from D.
2. If a disjunction $D(i)$ is subsumed by another disjunction $D(j)$ then $D(i)$ can be eliminated from D.
3. If a disjunct $D(i,j)$ is inconsistent relative to G then it can be eliminated from disjunction $D(i)$.

The worst-case complexity of preprocessing is $O(|N||D|^2|d|^2nW^2)$ where $|N|$ is the number of non-disjunctive constraints, $|D|$ is the number of disjunctions, $|d|$ is the maximum number of disjuncts in a disjunction, n is the number of variables, and W is the width of graph G (Dechter et al., 1989). After the preprocessing rules have been applied, the disjunctions are ordered in ascending order of domains.

FC-BJ (Prosser, 1993) is a hybrid search algorithm that combines the forward move of FC with the backward move of BJ. In that way, the advantages of both algorithms are exploited. In the context of our problem, FC-BJ will attempt to instantiate a disjunct from each disjunction, starting with the first. First, the current disjunct $D(i,j)$ will be added to G using a version of the IDPC algorithm of (Chleq, 1995). IDPC adds constraints to a given directional path consistent constraint graph, propagates them in the graph, and enforces directional path consistency again. Then, all disjuncts of the future disjunctions will be checked for consistency using the same version of IDPC. If a disjunct fails it will be "removed" from the disjunction it belongs to. If during the *filtering* of the domains, one of the future disjunctions is annihilated then the disjuncts that were removed due to $D(i,j)$ will be restored, the attempted instantiation will be rejected, and the next disjunct of the current disjunction $D(i)$ will be tried. In case there are no more disjuncts left in $D(i)$,

FC-BJ will backjump to one of the past disjunctions that are responsible for the dead-end, uninstantiate its instantiated disjunct and try the next available one. Here is an example that shows how FC-BJ works.

Example 2 Suppose that we want to determine the consistency of the following set of disjunctions:

$$D(1) \quad x_2 - x_1 \leq 5 \ \vee \ x_3 - x_4 \leq 6$$
$$D(2) \quad x_3 - x_1 \leq 4 \ \vee \ x_3 - x_4 \leq 5$$
$$D(3) \quad x_5 - x_4 \leq -6 \ \vee \ x_3 - x_4 \leq 4$$
$$D(4) \quad x_1 - x_3 \leq 0 \ \vee \ x_3 - x_4 \leq 2$$
$$D(5) \quad x_3 - x_5 \leq 2 \ \vee \ x_1 - x_3 \leq -6$$
$$D(6) \quad x_1 - x_2 \leq -8 \ \vee \ x_4 - x_3 \leq 1$$

FC-BJ will first try to instantiate $D(1)$. Disjunct $D(1,1)$ is instantiated and its forward checking causes the elimination of $D(6,1)$. $D(2,1)$ is instantiated and its forward checking causes the elimination of $D(5,2)$. $D(3,1)$ and $D(4,1)$ are instantiated without affecting any future disjunctions. The forward checking of $D(5,1)$ causes the elimination of $D(6,2)$. Since there are no more available disjuncts in $D(6)$, $D(5,1)$ is rejected. This leaves $D(5)$ with no available disjuncts. Therefore, FC-BJ has reached a dead-end.

FC-BJ will backjump to the deepest past disjunction that precludes a disjunct of $D(5)$. This disjunction can be discovered by reasoning as follows. Disjunct $D(5,2)$ is eliminated because of the forward checking of $D(2,1)$. Therefore, we can say that the *culprit* for the elimination of $D(5,2)$ is disjunction $D(2)$. $D(5,1)$ is eliminated because its forward checking results in the annihilation of $D(6)$. The disjunctions responsible for the elimination of $D(5,1)$ are the past disjunctions whose instantiations, together with $D(5,1)$, cause the annihilation of $D(6)$. Disjunct $D(6,1)$ is eliminated because of the forward checking of $D(1,1)$. Thus, the culprit for the elimination of $D(6,1)$ is $D(1)$. $D(6,2)$ is eliminated because it is in conflict with a constraint that is derived from constraints $D(5,1)$ and $D(3,1)$. Therefore, $D(3)$ is responsible for the elimination of $D(6,2)$. The past disjunctions responsible for the annihilation of $D(6)$, and thus for the elimination of $D(5,1)$, are $D(1)$ and $D(3)$. FC-BJ will backjump to the deepest disjunction that precludes either $D(5,1)$ or $D(5,2)$ (i.e., to $D(3)$). If $D(3)$ is uninstantiated, the forward checking of $D(5,1)$ will not cause the elimination of $D(6,2)$, which means that $D(5,1)$ will be consistent. Finally, $D(6,2)$ will be consistently instantiated, and the algorithm will terminate.

For each inconsistent disjunct $D(i,j)$ there can be more than one set of past disjunctions that is responsible for its rejection. FC-BJ will discover *only one* of these sets. We call this set the *culprit set* of $D(i,j)$. FC-BJ tries to select the deepest possible disjunction to backjump to when a dead-end is encountered. Therefore, if there is a dead-end at $D(i)$, FC-BJ will select the deepest disjunction among the disjunctions in the culprit sets of the disjuncts of $D(i)$. The main difficulty in adapting FC-BJ to the domain of temporal constraints was identifying the culprit set of a disjunct. When an inconsistency is encountered during the consistency checking of disjunct $D(i,j)$, the cause of the inconsistency cannot be identified immediately. This is due to the constraint propagation involved in the consistency check. In order to solve this problem, we use *dependency pointers* which connect each constraint with the constraints it is derived from. In that way we can "roll back" the changes for each of the constraints involved in the inconsistency until we reach the instantiated disjuncts of past disjunctions. These disjunctions have caused the inconsistency and will form the culprit set of $D(i,j)$.

It is well known that backtracking algorithms for CSPs benefit significantly from *dynamic variable ordering* techniques (Dechter and Meiri, 1994; Bacchus and van Run, 1995)). The most popular dynamic variable ordering heuristic is the *minimum remaining values* (MRV) heuristic (also known as the *fail-first* heuristic). In the context of the problem we are studying, the MRV heuristic suggests that at each step we select to instantiate the disjunction that has the fewest available disjuncts. Due to the forward checking that FC-BJ does, we can find the future disjunction with the fewest available disjuncts simply by counting the disjuncts in each future disjunction. The one with the fewest available disjuncts is selected as the next disjunction to be instantiated. Ties are broken randomly.

Theoretical Evaluation

We have analyzed theoretically the behaviour of the algorithms we have developed. Our analysis is similar to Kondrak and van Beek's theoretical evaluation of the basic backtracking algorithms for binary CSPs (Kondrak and van Beek, 1997). Among other results, they were able to partially order the algorithms according to two standard peformance measures: the number of search tree nodes visited, and the number of consistency checks performed. We proved that the results of (Kondrak and van Beek, 1997) for binary CSPs are also valid for our non-binary problem. First, we proved eight theorems that specify the sufficient and necessary conditions for nodes to be visited by BT, BJ, FC and FC-BJ. The proofs are similar to the corresponding proofs for binary CSPs (Kondrak and van Beek, 1997), and can be found in (Stergiou, 1997). Based on these theorems we were able to partially order the algorithms according to the search tree nodes they visit. We proved that BJ never visits more nodes than BT, FC never visits more nodes than BJ, and FC-BJ never visits more nodes than FC. BT and BJ perform exactly one consistency check at each node. This means that BJ never performs more consistency checks than BT. The fact that FC and FC-BJ perform the same consistency checks at each node means that FC-BJ never performs more consistency checks than FC. A relationship between the backward checking algorithms and the forward checking algorithms with respect to the number of performed consistency checks cannot be established.

Experimental Results

In this section we present extensive results from the experimental evaluation of the search algorithms. The algorithms were tested using randomly generated sets of data. First, we made a comparison of the algorithms with respect to the number of search tree nodes visited, the number of consistency checks performed, and the CPU time used. Then, we tried to investigate the phase transition in the problem we study. (Cheeseman et al., 1991; Prosser, 1996; Smith and Dyer, 1996; Selman et al., 1996; Gent and Walsh, 1996; Crawford and Auton, 1996) showed that for many NP-complete problems, hard problems occur arround a critical value of a control parameter. The control parameter in our problem is the ratio r of disjunctions to variables. We have chosen this parameter because of the similarities between our problem has and SAT problems. In SAT problems the control parameter used is the ratio of clauses to variables which transfered to our problem corresponds to the ratio of disjunctions to variables.

The Random Generation Model

The random problem generation model used is in some ways similar to the *fixed clause length model* for SAT, as described in (Selman et al., 1996). For each set of problems there are four parameters: the number of constrained variables n, the number of disjuncts per disjunction k, the number of disjunctions m, and the maximum integer value L. Therefore, each problem is described by the 4-tuple $<k,n,m,L>$. As in the fixed clause length model for SAT we have kept k fixed. We have only examined problems with $k = 2$, since this is the most interesting class in planning and scheduling applications. Many such problems can be formulated as sets of disjunctions with $k = 2$. Problems with two disjuncts per disjunction are NP-complete, in constrast with 2-SAT problems.

For given n, m, L, a random instance is produced by randomly generating m disjunctions of length 2. Each disjunction, $D(i) \equiv x_1 - y_1 \leq r_1 \vee x_2 - y_2 \leq r_2$, is constructed by randomly generating each disjunct $x_j - y_j \leq r_j$ in the following way:

1. Two of the n variables are randomly selected with probability $1/n$. It is made sure that the two variables are different.

2. r_j is a randomly selected integer in the interval $[0, L]$. r_j is negated with probability 0.5.

3. If the pair of variables in $D(i, 1)$ is the same as in $D(i, 2)$ then it is made sure that r_1 is not equal to r_2 so that the disjuncts are different.

The experiments were carried out using a PC with a Pentium processor at 100 Mhz with 16 Mb of RAM.

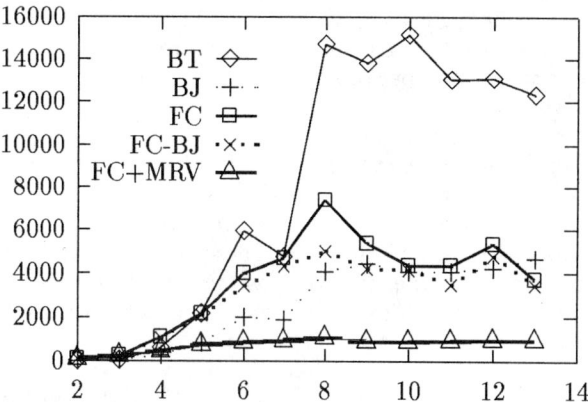

Figure 1: The median number of consistency checks as a function of the ratio of disjunctions to variables

Comparison of the Algorithms

The empirical evaluation presented here helped us to estimate quantitatively the differences between the algorithms. We evaluated the performance of BT, BJ, FC, FC-BJ, FC+MRV, and FC-BJ+MRV on randomly generated sets of problems involving 5 variables. Figure 1 shows the *median* number of consistency checks performed by each algorithm. There is no curve representing FC-BJ+MRV because the number of consistency checks for FC-BJ+MRV was only slightly less than the corresponding number for FC+MRV. Each data point gives the median number of consistency checks for 100 instances of the $<2, 5, m, 100>$ problem, where m is the number of disjunctions.

As expected, FC+MRV and FC-BJ+MRV are by far the best algorithms and BT is by far the worst. It seems that BJ performs less consistency checks than FC and FC-BJ. This is caused by the forward checking that FC and FC-BJ do. For small values of r most of the problems are solved after very few, if any, backtracks. Therefore, for small problems there are no real gains by the forward checking of FC and FC-BJ. Experiments with 10 or more variables showed that this is not true for larger problems. We should note that for values of r greater than 7, the mean consistency checks performed by BJ are marginally more than the ones performed by the forward checking algorithms. This is caused by a few hard instances in which BJ performs poorly. The results with respect to the number of visited nodes and CPU time used are similar.

The Hard Problems

For many NP-complete problems there is a problem parameter such that the hardest problems tend to be those for which the parameter is in a particular range (Cheeseman et al., 1991). In both 3-SAT problems (Selman et al., 1996; Gent and Walsh, 1996; Crawford and Auton, 1996) and binary CSPs (Prosser, 1996; Smith and Dyer, 1996) *under-constrained* problems appear to be easy to solve because they generally have many solutions. *Over-constrained* problems also appear to be easy because such problems generally have no solutions, and a sophisticated algorithm is able to quickly identify dead-ends and abandon most or all the branches in the search tree. The hardest problems generally occur in the region where there is a *phase transition* from easy problems with many solutions to easy problems with no solutions. These problems are very important for the accurate evaluation of the performance of algorithms. The region in which hard problems occur is called the *hard region*.

In order to locate the hard region, we experimented with sets of disjunctions involving 10, 12, 15, and 20 variables. The problems created were solved using FC+MRV. We did not use FC-BJ+MRV because our experiments with 5 variables, and also additional experiments with 8, 10 and 12 variables showed that FC-BJ+MRV is only slightly better than FC+MRV[2]. All the other algorithms were unacceptably slow at solving problems with 10 or more variables. Figure 2 shows the number of consistency checks performed by FC+MRV for problems with 10, 12, 15 and 20 variables. Figure 3 shows the median and mean number of consistency checks for problems with 20 variables. The curve representing the consistency checks for 10 variables starts to rise sharply at $r = 5$, reaches its peak at $r = 7$, and then slowly falls away. The curves representing the consistency checks for 12 and 15 variables follow the same pattern, with the difference that their peak is reached at $r = 6$. The curve representing the median consistency checks for 20 variables is similar to the corresponding curve for 10 variables in the sense that it reaches its peak at $r = 7$. Note, though, that the curve for 20 variables is much sharper than the one for 10 variables.

These observations suggest that the hardest problems occur in the region where the ratio of disjunctions to variables is between 6 and 7. Figure 2 also shows that the hard region becomes narrower as the number of variables is increased. We should note that the curves representing the median number of visited nodes and the CPU time used are similar to the corresponding curves in Figure 2. The difference is that the number of consistency checks declines slower than the number of visited nodes for $r > 7$. As we shall see later, most of the problems with r more than 7 have no solutions. In this case, FC+MRV is able to discover dead-ends soon and thereby avoid visiting redundant nodes. This results in the decline of the median number of visited nodes. The median number of consistency checks declines relatively slower because as the number of disjunctions rises, FC+MRV has to do more forward checking early in the search, and therefore perform more consistency checks. The mean number of

---

[2] Actually, in most of the generated instances FC+MRV and FC-BJ+MRV performed exactly the same number of consistency checks and visited the same number of nodes.

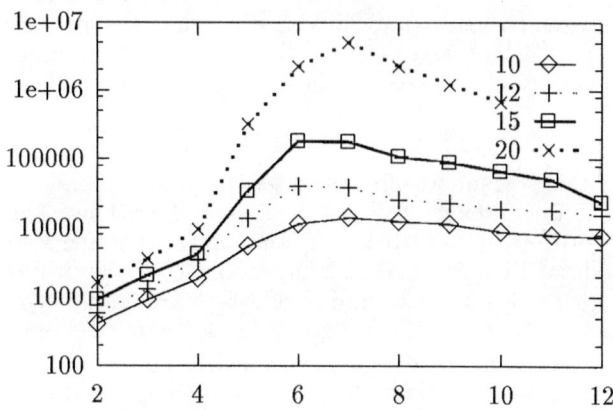

Figure 2: The median number of consistency checks for problems with 10, 12, 15 and 20 variables as a function of the ratio of disjunctions to variables

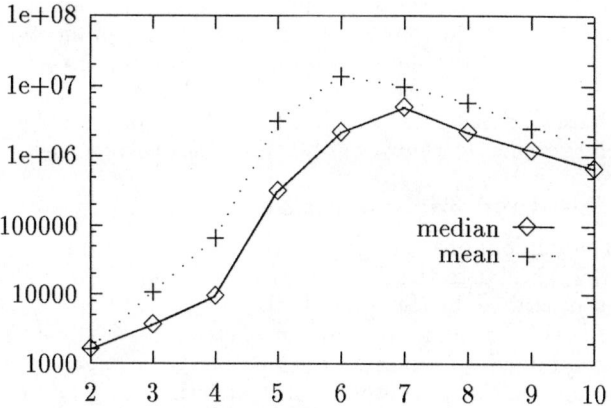

Figure 3: The median and mean number of consistency checks for 20 variables as a function of the ratio of disjunctions to variables

consistency checks is by far greater than the median (Figure 3). The location of the peak of the mean curve is at $r = 6$, which means that it does not coincide with the peak of the median curve. This is due to a few exceptionally hard problems that occured at $r = 6$. Similar results regarding the differences between medians and means were observed for 10, 12, and 15 variables.

The Transition from Soluble to Insoluble Problems

Figure 4 shows the proportion of satisfiable problems for 5, 10, 12, 15, and 20 variables as a function of r. Each data point represents the number of consistent instances out of 100 instances. As we can see, at small ratios ($r < 4$) almost all problems are satisfiable and at high ratios ($r > 7$) almost all problems are unsatisfiable. There is a range of r values over which the proportion of satisfiable problems abruptly changes from almost 100% to almost 0%. This transition region from

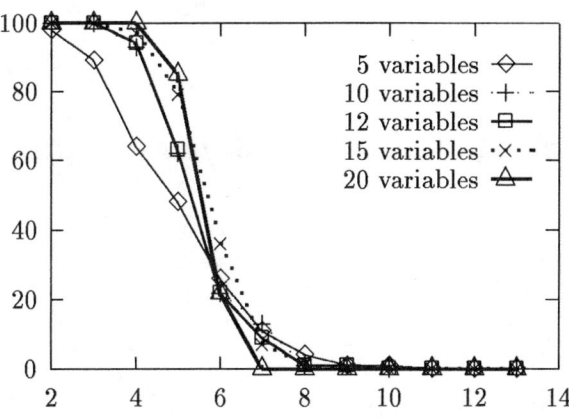

Figure 4: The percent satisfiable problems as a function of the ratio of disjunctions to variables

soluble to insoluble problems becomes narrower as the number of variables increases. For 10, 12 and 15 variables the transition region appears to occur at values of r between 4 and 7. For 20 variables the proportion of satisfiable problems at $r = 5$ is 85% and at $r = 6$ it is 22%. This suggests that the phase transition from soluble to insoluble problems occurs in this area.

As we saw previously, the hard region occurs at values of r between 6 and 7. For 10 variables the hardest problems occur at $r = 7$. At this point the proportion of satisfiable problems is 13%. For 12 variables the hardest problems occur at $r = 6$ where the proportion of satisfiable problems is 22%. For 15 variables the proportion of satisfiable problems at $r = 6$ is 36% and at $r = 7$ it is 7%. For 20 variables the hardest problems occur at $r = 7$ where all the generated problems are unsatisfiable. It seems therefore, that the hard region does not coincide with the transition from soluble to insoluble problems. Unlike SAT problems and binary CSPs, problems near the *50%-satisfiability* point are easy. The hardest problems occur in a region where there are very few, if any, soluble problems. In Figures 2 and 3 we can see that for values of r greater than 7 problems become easy again. This means that the problems follow the expected pattern: easy with many solutions, hard, easy with no solutions. The difference with SAT problems and binary CSPs is that the hard problems occur in the area where there are very few soluble problems. This may be due to high variance in the number of solutions (Smith and Dyer, 1996).

Future Work

We have developed backtracking algorithms for a class of disjunctive temporal constraints, and presented theoretical and experimental results concerning the behaviour of these algorithms. For future work we would like to develop tie breaking heuristics for variable ordering and discover even more efficient algorithms for determining the consistency of the studied class of temporal constraints. For this, we plan to consider *local search* algorithms similar to min-conflicts and GSAT. Local search algorithms have recently received a lot of attention in the AI literature and have produced surprising results.

Acknowledgements

We would like to thank Patrick Prosser, Ian Gent, and Toby Walsh for their help and comments.

References

Bacchus, F. and van Run, P. (1995). Dynamic variable ordering in csps. In *Proc. CP-95*, pages 258–275.

Cheeseman, P., Kanefsky, B., and Taylor, W. (1991). Where the really hard problems are. In *Proc. IJCAI-95*, volume 1, pages 331–337.

Chleq, N. (1995). Efficient algorithms for networks of quantitative temporal constraints. In *Proc. CONSTRAINTS-95*, pages 40–45.

Crawford, J. and Auton, D. (1996). Experimental Results on the Crossover Point in Random 3-SAT. *Artificial Intelligence*, 81:31–57.

Dechter, R. and Meiri, I. (1994). Experimental Evaluation of Preprocessing Algorithms for Constraint Satisfaction Problems. *Artificial Intelligence*, 68:211–241.

Dechter, R., Meiri, I., and Pearl, J. (1989). Temporal Constraint Networks. In *Proc. KR-89*, pages 83–93.

Gent, I. P. and Walsh, T. (1996). The Satisfiability Constraint Gap. *Artificial Intelligence*, 81:59–80.

Gerevini, A. and Schubert, L. (1995). Efficient Algorithms for Qualitative Reasoning about Time. *Artificial Intelligence*, 74:207–248.

Kondrak, G. and van Beek, P. (1997). A Theoretical Evaluation of Selected Backtracking Algorithms. *Artificial Intelligence*, 89:365–387.

Prosser, P. (1993). Hybrid Algorithms for the Costraint Satisfaction Problem. *Computational Intelligence*, 9(3):268–299.

Prosser, P. (1996). An Empirical Study of Phase Transitions in Binary Costraint Satisfaction Problems. *Artificial Intelligence*, 81:81–109.

Schwalb, E. and Dechter, R. (1997). Processing Disjunctions in Temporal Constraint Networks. *Artificial Intelligence*, 93:29–61.

Selman, B., Mitchell, D., and Levesque, H. (1996). Generating Hard Satisfiability Problems. *Artificial Intelligence*, 81:17–29.

Smith, B. and Dyer, M. (1996). Locating the Phase Transitions in Constraint Satisfaction Problems. *Artificial Intelligence*, 81:155–181.

Stergiou, K. (1997). Backtracking algorithms for checking the consistency of disjunctions of temporal constraints. Technical report, Department of Computation, UMIST.

Fast Transformation of Temporal Plans for Efficient Execution

Ioannis Tsamardinos
Intelligent Systems Program
University of Pittsburgh
Pittsburgh, PA 15260
tsamard@cs.pitt.edu

Nicola Muscettola
Recom Technologies.
NASA Ames Research Center
Moffett Field, CA 94035
mus@ptolemy.arc.nasa.gov

Paul Morris
Caelum Research.
NASA Ames Research Center
Moffett Field, CA 94035
pmorris@ptolemy.arc.nasa.gov

Abstract

Temporal plans permit significant flexibility in specifying the occurrence time of events. Plan execution can make good use of that flexibility. However, the advantage of execution flexibility is counterbalanced by the cost during execution of propagating the time of occurrence of events throughout the flexible plan. To minimize execution latency, this propagation needs to be very efficient. Previous work showed that every temporal plan can be reformulated as a dispatchable plan, i.e., one for which propagation to immediate neighbors is sufficient. A simple algorithm was given that finds a dispatchable plan with a minimum number of edges in cubic time and quadratic space. In this paper, we focus on the efficiency of the reformulation process, and improve on that result. A new algorithm is presented that uses linear space and has time complexity equivalent to Johnson's algorithm for all-pairs shortest-path problems. Experimental evidence confirms the practical effectiveness of the new algorithm. For example, on a large commercial application, the performance is improved by at least two orders of magnitude. We further show that the dispatchable plan, already minimal in the total number of edges, can also be made minimal in the maximum number of edges incoming or outgoing at any node.

Introduction

In a control system that distinguishes a deliberative layer (*planner*) and a reactive layer (*executive*) (Pell *et al.* 1997; Bonasso *et al.* 1997; Wilkins *et al.* 1995; Drabble, Tate, & Dalton 1996; Simmons 1990; Musliner, Durfee, & Shin 1993; Bresina *et al.* 1993), the function of a plan is to provide robust and effective directives to the executive on how to control a system toward desired behaviors. To be robust against uncertainty in the execution environment a plan must be *flexible*, i.e., must specify a set of possible acceptable behaviors. The executive should be able to choose among such behaviors on the basis of the actual execution conditions. To be effective a plan must be *localized*, i.e., it must be possible for the executive to locally process the constraints in the plan and quickly decide which action to execute next.

To obtain flexibility one can explicitly represent in the plan the relationship between a set of plan parameters as a network of constraints. When receiving the constraint network, the executive will iteratively pick one variable and decide which value to assign to it. To make this decision the executive needs to propagate to the current variable the consequence of the value assignments that have already been made.

Relying on explicit constraint propagation during execution can be costly. In fact, the greater the time needed to propagate through the constraint network, the higher will be the total time needed by the executive to decide when and how to execute a task. It can be shown that this decision time determines the intrinsic uncertainty on the exact time of occurrence of any event in the plan (Muscettola *et al.* 1998). The more precise we want the execution of a plan to be, the less propagation an execution algorithm should perform. This is particularly important when plans are used in mission critical applications (Pell *et al.* 1997; Carpenter, Driscoll, & Hoyme 1994) for which the executive must guarantee to operate within a specific time bound.

Fortunately for certain classes of constraints one can rely on the special nature of the execution constraint propagation process in order to significantly speed it up. In the rest of the paper we will focus on flexible plans that represent temporal information as a Simple Temporal Network (STN) (Dechter, Meiri, & Pearl 1991). In previous work (Muscettola, Morris, & Tsamardinos 1998) we described a simple dispatcher, i.e., an execution algorithm that maximally localizes execution propagation in STNs. We showed that any STN can be transformed into an equivalent one that is both *dispatchable* and *minimum*. An STN is dispatchable if a dispatcher can generate all assignments of time to time variables that are consistent with the constraints in the STN. A dispatchable STN is minimum if it contains the minimum number of constraints among all dispatchable

Copyright ©1998, American Association for Artificial Intelligence (www.aaai.org). All rights reserved.

networks.

The main focus in the previous paper was to establish the existence of the transformation to a minimum dispatchable network. A simple algorithm was given that performs the transformation in $O(N^2)$ space and $O(N^3)$ time, where N is the number of variables in the original STN. While this is fine for problems of moderate size (hundreds of nodes), it becomes unworkable for large graphs (tens of thousands of nodes) that may occur in some applications.

In this paper we give a new transformation algorithm that, when applied to an input STN with N nodes and E edges, uses space linear in the size of the input and output STNs and $O(NE + N^2 \ln N)$ time. For problems in which E is roughly proportional to N the new algorithm can yield very big improvements over our previous one. In particular, as discussed later in the paper, our current implementation can solve a large problem from a commercial domain in minutes using tens of megabytes of memory while best estimates for the older algorithm yield processing times of several days and memory usage of tens of gigabytes.

We also revisit the concept of minimality for a dispatchable network. It may be argued that to achieve the best execution performance with a dispatcher, it is not sufficient for a dispatchable STN to have a minimum number of edges. Among all such networks it is possible to select a *fastest dispatchable* network as the one that also minimizes the maximum in/out degree, i.e., the number of temporal constraints that enter/exit a variable in the STN. To this end we present an additional $O(N^2 \ln N)$ time transformation step that when applied to the output of our new transformation algorithm, yields a fastest dispatchable network.

The rest of the paper is organized as follows. The first section summarizes the results of our previous work and provides the background for the rest of the paper. The next section formally describes the new algorithm, while the succeeding sections justify the algorithm and discuss experimental results for random and natural problems. A further section describes the additional transformation to yield the fastest dispatchable network, and the final section concludes the paper.

Temporal Network Dispatchability

In this section we summarize the main results of our previous work. See (Muscettola, Morris, & Tsamardinos 1998) for details and proofs.

Recall that Simple Temporal Networks (Dechter, Meiri, & Pearl 1991) are directed graphs where each node is an *event* or *time point* (e.g., time points A and B) and each edge AB is marked with a bound delay $[d, D]$. The interpretation of each edge is that if T_A and T_B are the times of occurrence of A and B respectively, then in a consistent execution $d \leq T_B - T_A \leq D$. It has been shown (Dechter, Meiri, & Pearl 1991) that finding the ranges of execution times for each event's *time bounds*, is equivalent to solving two single-source shortest-path problems (Cormen, Leiserson, & Rivest

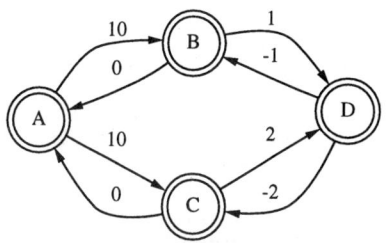

Figure 1: Distance Graph.

1990) on a simple transformation of the STN graph. Figure 1 shows such a distance graph obtained from a simple plan with two tasks BD and CD of fixed durations, respectively 1 and 2 time units, that synchronize at the end (event D) and must start within 10 time units of a time origin (event A). From now on, any time we refer to an STN, we will mean the transformed distance graph.

The simplest algorithm that can select occurrence times for events at execution is a *dispatcher* (figure 2). Unfortunately STNs may not always be correctly executed by a dispatcher. For example, since the network in figure 1 does not contain an explicit edge of length 1 to synchronize C and B, it is possible for the dispatcher to select B before C, yielding an inconsistent execution.

The STNs that can always be correctly executed by a dispatcher are called *dispatchable*. It is always possible to transform any STN into an equivalent dispatchable STN. Trivially, it can be shown that the all-pairs shortest-path graph ($\mathcal{APSP}$) (Cormen, Leiserson, & Rivest 1990) derived from the original STN is dispatchable. However, this would be the largest dispatchable network for the problem. We are interested in finding small dispatchable networks, in fact, networks that contain the minimum total number of edges, or *minimal dispatchable* STNs.

In order to find the minimal number of edges in a dispatchable graph, we look for edges that are *dominated* in $\mathcal{APSP}$, i.e., whose propagations are subsumed by those of some other edge in all possible executions. It has been shown in our previous paper that, for execution purposes, upper and lower bounds can be independently propagated. In fact, it is sufficient to propagate upper bounds through non-negative edges and lower bounds through negative edges (in the reverse direction (Dechter, Meiri, & Pearl 1991)). So, dominance relations between lower-bound links (*lower-domination*) can be checked separately from those between upper-bound links (*upper-domination*). It was also shown that removal of a dominated edge does not affect the dominance relation between other pairs of edges.

The following fundamental filtering theorem applies.

Theorem 1 (Triangle Rule) *Consider an $\mathcal{APSP}$ derived from a consistent STN.*

```
TIME DISPATCHING ALGORITHM:
  1. Let
       A = {start_time_point}
           current_time = 0
       S = {}
  2. Arbitrarily pick an event TP in A such
     that current_time is in TP's time bound;
  3. Set TP's execution time to current_time
     and add TP to S;
  4. Propagate the time of execution
     to its IMMEDIATE NEIGHBORS in the distance
     graph;
  5. Put in A all events TPx such that all
     negative edges starting from TPx have a
     destination that is already in S;
  6. Wait until current_time has advanced to
     some time between
         min{lower_bound(TP) : TP in A}
     and
         min{upper_bound(TP) : TP in A}
  7. Go to 2 until every event is in S.
```

Figure 2: The Dispatching Execution Controller.

(1) A non-negative edge AC is upper-dominated by another non-negative edge BC if and only if $|AB| + |BC| = |AC|$.

(2) A negative edge AC is lower-dominated by another negative edge AB if and only if $|AB| + |BC| = |AC|$.

The transformation algorithm that we proposed in our previous work is quite simple: it applies the triangle rule in all possible ways to the $\mathcal{APSP}$ obtained from the original STN. Since this algorithm relies on all shortest paths being known in advance, it requires $O(N^2)$ space. Moreover, the time needed by the algorithm is dominated by applying the filtering rule (constant time) over all possible triples of nodes, yielding a time complexity of $O(N^3)$.

Fast Filtering Algorithm

The algorithm sketched in the previous section precomputed $\mathcal{APSP}$ and then applied the dispatchability filtering step. However we can do better if we interleave filtering with the process of computing the shortest-paths. The algorithm we propose is a modification of the Johnson's all-pairs shortest-path algorithm and its overall structure is described in figure 3. The references to lines of JOHNSON in the figure refer to the line numbering in the description of Johnson's algorithm at page 569 of (Cormen, Leiserson, & Rivest 1990).

In the rest of the paper we will discuss the formal details of how steps 2, 3.b, 3.c and 3.d work and why. Here we want to give some general observations that will help frame the rest of the discussion.

The first observation is that it is possible to exploit to our advantage any amount of "rigidity" present in the temporal network. Step 2 examines the graph G and identifies all the sets of time points that are rigidly

```
FAST-DISPATCHABILITY-MINIMIZATION (G)

  1. Run Bellman-Ford pre-processing step
     of Johnson's algorithm
     [ lines 1-7 of JOHNSON]
  2. [RIGID COMPONENTS PROCESSING]
     Identify all rigid components in G.
     For each rigid component RC;
       a) find a single node representative for
          MIN(RC) and contract G so that all
          nodes in RC are represented by MIN(RC).
       b) output the minimum dispatchable graph for RC.
     Call the contracted graph obtained after this
     step CONTR_G.
  3. [DAG DISPATCHABILITY MINIMIZATION]
     For each node A in CONTR_G;
       a. Run Dijkstra's algorithm on CONTR_G
          with A as the source [ lines 9-11 of JOHNSON]
       b. Do a preliminary depth-first search
          of the predecessor graph computed at step a.
          to collect the nodes into reverse-postorder.
       c. [UPPER-DOMINATES MINIMIZATION]
          Find and output all non UPPER-BOUND dominated
          edges with source in A;
       d. [LOWER-BOUND DOMINATES MINIMIZATION]
          Find and output all non LOWER-BOUND dominated
          edges in G with source in A;
```

Figure 3: Fast Dispatch Minimization Algorithm.

connected, i.e., such that once the execution time of one of them is fixed, we know exactly when all the others in the set must execute. Given this we will show that the entire set can be represented in the minimization process by a single node, without loss of information. The complexity of this step (beyond the propagation already required by Johnson's Algorithm) is $O(N + E)$, where N and E are the numbers of nodes and edges, respectively, in the input graph. This is well within the Johnson bounds.

Once the graph has been contracted, step 3 uses single-source distance information to scan the graph for dominated edges in a systematic way. The key data structure in this process, and in the rigidity analysis in step 2, is the *predecessor graph*, which is a subgraph of the distance graph that retains only the edges that participate in shortest paths from the current source. We will show that one important consequence of step 2 is that all predecessor graphs of CONTR_G are DAGs. This means the non-dominated edges can be found through a fixed number of depth-first searches in CONTR_G, making the overall cost of filtering $O(N^2 + NE)$ where N and E are the numbers of nodes and edges in CONTR_G. This is also within the bounds of Johnson's algorithm.

Finally, we observe that the algorithm only requires space needed to store the input graph G, and the output minimal dispatchable graph. Moreover, steps 2.b, 3.c and 3.d can output the edges incrementally, so they do not actually need to be stored in main memory. This is a significant space improvement with respect to the previous approach, which required $O(N^2)$ space to store the intermediate all-airs shortest-path graph obtained by Johnson's Algorithm.

The result is an algorithm that, as we shall see, makes it practical to apply the filtering process to enormous networks where it would be infeasible to use the cubic filtering algorithm.

Notation

We use upper case italics to denote nodes in a temporal network or distance graph. Edges and paths are denoted by lower italics. The shortest-path distance from node X to node Y is denoted by $|XY|$. In the context of a single-source distance computation from an origin node S, the shortest-path distance from S to any node X is denoted by $d(X)$. The All-Pairs Shortest-Path graph is denoted by $\mathcal{APSP}$. We will use XY to denote an edge from X to Y in $\mathcal{APSP}$.

Predecessor Graph

The central data structure needed for steps 2 and 3 is the *predecessor graph*. The predecessor graph is a generalization of the *predecessor tree* generated by a single-source shortest-path algorithm (Cormen, Leiserson, & Rivest 1990). The predecessor tree is constructed while finding *some* shortest-path from a source node to every other node. The predecessor graph, on the other hand, concisely represents information on *all* shortest-paths from the source node.

Definition 1 *Given a consistent distance graph, the* predecessor graph *with respect to an origin node S, denoted by $\mathcal{P}(S)$, is the subgraph defined by the set of all edges on shortest paths from S.*

The next result gives a characterization that allows edges to be checked locally for membership in the predecessor graph.

Theorem 2 *An edge from node X to node Y is in $\mathcal{P}(S)$ if and only if*

$$d(Y) = d(X) + b(X,Y)$$

where $b(X,Y)$ is the length of the edge, and $d(X)$ and $d(Y)$ are the shortest-path distances from S to X and Y, respectively.

Proof Let e be the edge from X to Y.

Suppose the distance equation $d(Y) = d(X) + b(X,Y)$ holds. Then the path from S to Y that passes through X and along e has length equal to the shortest-path distance to Y. Thus, e is on a shortest path.

Conversely, suppose e is on a shortest path p from S. Without loss of generality, we may assume e is the last edge in p. Then $d(Y) = \text{length}(p)$. Let p' be the part of p that does not include the final edge e. Since any subpath of a shortest path is itself a shortest path, we have $d(X) = \text{length}(p')$. It follows that $d(Y) = d(X) + b(X,Y)$. □

Corollary 2.1 *Every path in $\mathcal{P}(S)$ is a shortest path. Moreover, the length of such a path from X to Y in $\mathcal{P}(S)$ is given by $d(Y) - d(X)$.*

Proof Consider a path p from a node X to a node Y. If we sum the distance equations from Theorem 2 for each edge in the path, we obtain $d(Y) = d(X) + l(p)$, where $l(p)$ is the length of p. It follows that p is a shortest path, since otherwise we could derive a smaller value for $d(Y)$ by choosing a shorter alternative to p. It also follows that $l(p) = d(Y) - d(X)$. □

Dominance

As noted before, we need to systematically apply the Triangle Rule to all triangles in $\mathcal{APSP}$ for which the triangle equality among distances applies. The following theorem allows us to precisely pinpoint these triangles among the $O(N^3)$ possible triangles in $\mathcal{APSP}$. This observation is a key element in the efficiency of the proposed algorithm.

Theorem 3 *Let A, B, and C be nodes in a consistent distance graph. Then the equation $|AC| = |AB| + |BC|$ holds if and only if there is a path from B to C in $\mathcal{P}(A)$.*

Proof

Suppose the equation $|AC| = |AB| + |BC|$ holds. Then there is a shortest path from A to C that passes through B. By definition, all the edges on this path are in $\mathcal{P}(A)$. In particular, the subpath from B to C is in $\mathcal{P}(A)$.

Conversely, suppose $\mathcal{P}(A)$ includes a path from B to C. By Corollary 2.1, this is a shortest path and its length is $d(C) - d(B)$. Thus, $|BC| = d(C) - d(B) = |AC| - |AB|$. The result follows. □

We now construct specific tests for upper and lower dominance. The edges considered for elimination or retention in the following theorems are edges in the implicit $\mathcal{APSP}$. The algorithm does not build the full $\mathcal{APSP}$ but only outputs an edge in $\mathcal{APSP}$ according to the values of the upper and lower dominance tests. The implicit edge AC of $\mathcal{APSP}$ is considered by examining the properties of the node C with respect to $\mathcal{P}(A)$.

First we derive a test for lower-dominance of negative edges.

Theorem 4 *A negative edge AC is lower-dominated by a negative edge AB if and only if there is a path from B to C in $\mathcal{P}(A)$.*

Proof Immediate by the Triangle Rule (Theorem 1) and Theorem 3. □

Note that in the case where $\mathcal{P}(A)$ is a DAG, this means that the edge AC associated with a negative-distance node C may be eliminated if and only if there is another negative-distance node B that precedes C. This suggests an algorithm that traverses the DAG, collecting minimal negative nodes for retention. (Although predecessor graphs are not acyclic in general, step 2 of the algorithm reduces them to DAGs for the benefit of step 3.)

The next theorem gives a condition for determining whether a non-negative edge is upper-dominated.

Theorem 5 *A non-negative edge AC is upper-dominated if and only if there is a node B, distinct from A and C, such that $|AB| \leq |AC|$ and there is a path from B to C in $\mathcal{P}(A)$.*

Proof

Suppose $|AB| \leq |AC|$ and there is a path from B to C in $\mathcal{P}(A)$. By Theorem 3, $|AC| = |AB| + |BC|$. It follows that $|BC| \geq 0$. By the Triangle Rule, AC is then upper-dominated by $|BC|$.

The argument in the converse is just the reverse. (Note that if AC is upper-dominated by BC, then $|BC|$ is non-negative by definition.) □

The above conditions can be used to decide in time $O(N+E)$ which edges emanating from a node A should be retained in the output graph. While traversing $\mathcal{P}(A)$, the algorithm propagates two pieces of information. The first datum indicates whether a negative-distance node has been encountered at a predecessor node. The second datum keeps track of the minimum distance value for all the predecessor nodes other than A itself. These data are used to determine whether the implicit edge AC corresponding to a node C is dominated. If $|AC|$ is negative, this depends on the first datum in the manner dictated by Theorem 4. If $|AC|$ is non-negative, then Theorem 5 shows that the edge is dominated if and only if the minimum distance value for the predecessors does not exceed the distance value for C (i.e., $|AC|$).

The above algorithm correctly identifies the edges to include in the output, provided the nodes are visited in an order that ensures the propagated values are calculated correctly. In the case where the predecessor graph is acyclic, a reverse-postorder traversal is guaranteed to visit all ancestors before a given node. In the case where the predecessor graph is not initially a DAG, we will see that the strongly-connected components can be effectively contracted to single points, resulting in a DAG. This is considered in the next section.

Identifying and Using Rigid Components

An important concept for our analysis concerns a situation where two nodes have a connection with no slack. More formally, two points X and Y are *rigidly-related* if in the distance graph we have $|XY| + |YX| = 0$.

It is easy to verify that, given a consistent distance graph, the property of being rigidly-related determines an equivalence relation. We call each equivalence class a *rigid component* ($\mathcal{RC}$). We will see that constructing a dispatchable graph can be simplified if these can be identified; in that case the problem can be reduced to one where each $\mathcal{RC}$ is contracted to a single point.

Identifying Rigid Components

Before considering the contraction process in detail, we address the issue of how to identify each $\mathcal{RC}$. For this, we offer the following result.

Theorem 6 *Given a consistent distance graph, and a single-source propagation from an arbitrary node S that reaches every node in the graph, each $\mathcal{RC}$ of the distance graph coincides with a strongly-connected component (Cormen, Leiserson, & Rivest 1990) of the predecessor graph $\mathcal{P}(S)$ (and vice versa).*

Proof: Suppose X and Y are rigidly-related. Consider a shortest path from the source to X. This can be extended by a shortest path to Y and then back again to X. Since $|XY| + |YX| = 0$, this is also a shortest path to X. Thus, the predecessor graph includes a path from X to Y and vice versa, so X and Y are in the same strongly-connected component.

Conversely, suppose X and Y are in the same strongly-connected component of the predecessor graph. Then there is a path from X to Y in $\mathcal{P}(S)$. By Corollary 2.1, $|XY| = d(Y) - d(X)$. Similarly, $|YX| = d(X) - d(Y)$. It follows that X and Y are rigidly-related. □

The theorem states that we can find all $\mathcal{RC}$ subgraphs by doing a single-source propagation from a suitable starting point in the distance graph. Since Johnson's Algorithm requires an initial run of Bellman-Ford to set up a "potential-function" value at every node, it is convenient to use this to determine the strongly-connected components and hence $\mathcal{RC}$ subgraphs. There is a well-known algorithm (Cormen, Leiserson, & Rivest 1990) for computing strongly-connected components (SCCs) that runs in time linear in the number of edges. This has two parts, an initial depth-first search to collect the nodes in reverse-postorder, and a secondary traversal to trace out each SCC. For our purposes, it is necessary to do some further processing on every SCC. It is convenient to piggy-back this on the part that traces out the SCC.

Rigid Component Contraction

In order to contract a $\mathcal{RC}$ to a single-point for further processing, it is necessary to choose some point in the $\mathcal{RC}$ as a representative or *leader*. The algorithm selects a *minimum point* for this purpose, that is, a node X such that $d(X)$ is minimum over the $\mathcal{RC}$, where $d(X)$ is the distance from the origin node of the single-source propagation.

Once a leader is selected, some further issues arise. To prepare the $\mathcal{RC}$ for contraction, we need to modify the input graph so that all incoming and outgoing edges of the $\mathcal{RC}$ are replaced by equivalent edges to/from the leader. This is accomplished by appropriately modifying the edge lengths. Second, in order to justify the contraction, we need to show that the $\mathcal{RC}$ can be represented by the leader as far as output edges are concerned. We do this by demonstrating that potential output edges to/from the interior of the $\mathcal{RC}$ are dominated by those to/from the leader. There will also be edges in the output that correspond to internal edges of the $\mathcal{RC}$. These are identified and collected prior to the contraction. This step can be accomplished by considering the $\mathcal{RC}$ in isolation, and simply consists of arranging the $\mathcal{RC}$ nodes in a doubly-linked chain.

Rigid Component Edge Rearrangement

We now consider the preparation step that rearranges the input graph by redirecting the outgoing and incoming edges of each $\mathcal{RC}$ to the leader node.

Theorem 7 *Suppose X and Y are rigidly-related with $|XY| = b$. Then (1) an edge YZ of length u is equivalent to an edge XZ of length $u + b$, and (2) an edge ZY of length v is equivalent to an edge ZX of length $v - b$.*

Proof: The given rigid relation corresponds to the equation $T_Y = T_X + b$. In its presence, the inequality $T_Z - T_Y \leq u$ is equivalent to $T_Z - T_X \leq u + b$. A similar argument works for (2). □

Notice that if two nodes in the $\mathcal{RC}$ are connected to the same node Z outside the $\mathcal{RC}$, then the theorem provides two replacement inequalities of the form $T_Z - T_X \leq u1$ and $T_Z - T_X \leq u2$. In this case, one of the inequalities is subsumed, and we need only retain the edge corresponding to $T_Z - T_X \leq \min(u1, u2)$. Thus, the replacement process allows us to recognize and remove some logically redundant edges in the distance graph.

After the edge replacement, the only connection the $\mathcal{RC}$ has to the rest of the graph is through the leader node.

Rigid Component Edge Elimination

In this section we prove dominance properties for edges entering or exiting nodes in a $\mathcal{RC}$. In particular we see that all edges that start or end with an "interior" node are dominated. An interior node is a node in $\mathcal{RC}$ other than the leader (minimum mode).

Lemma 1 *Suppose L and A belong to the same $\mathcal{RC}$, and B is any other node. Then $|AB| = |AL| + |LB|$ and $|BA| = |BL| + |LA|$.*

Proof:

From the properties of shortest-path graphs, the triangle inequalities $|AB| \leq |AL| + |LB|$ and $|LB| \leq |LA| + |AB|$ must hold. The second inequality can be rewritten as $|AB| \geq |LB| - |LA|$. Since $|LA| = -|AL|$, we have $|AB| \geq |LB| + |AL|$. Combining this with the first inequality gives $|AB| = |AL| + |LB|$.

The proof of the second condition is similar. □

The following result permits the elimination from the output of edges to/from interior nodes of an $\mathcal{RC}$. The proof requires an assumption that there are no *zero-related* pairs of nodes in the distance graph. (Two nodes X and Y are zero-related if $|XY| = |YX| = 0$.) This is actually not a significant restriction because zero-related nodes must be executed simultaneously, and so they may be collapsed to a single node. The system described in this paper detects zero-related nodes during the $\mathcal{RC}$ identification phase and automatically collapses them.

Theorem 8 *Assume a consistent distance graph with no zero-related pairs. Suppose L and A are distinct nodes in a rigid component, where L is the leader of the $\mathcal{RC}$, and suppose B is a node not in the $\mathcal{RC}$. Then the edges AB and BA are always dominated.*

Proof:

We will consider only AB. The dominance proof for BA is analogous. By lemma 1, we have $|AB| = |AL| + |LB|$. We distinguish two cases, depending on whether $|AB|$ is negative or non-negative.

Suppose first that $|AB|$ is negative. Note that $|AL|$ is also negative (assuming there are no zero-related pairs) since L is the minimum node of the $\mathcal{RC}$. Since $|AB| = |AL| + |LB|$, the Triangle Rule (Theorem 1) allows us to conclude $|AB|$ is lower-dominated by $|AL|$.

Now suppose $|AB|$ is non-negative. Since $|AB| = |AL| + |LB|$ and $|AL|$ is negative, it follows that $|LB|$ is non-negative. Then $|LB|$ upper-dominates $|AB|$ by the Triangle Rule. □

We have shown that output edges to and from non-leader nodes of the $\mathcal{RC}$ to the rest of the graph are dominated, and so may be eliminated from the final output. Edges in the output graph that are entirely within the $\mathcal{RC}$ can be generated independently of the rest of the graph, and may be dumped immediately. (One valid arrangement consists of edges that connect the nodes of the $\mathcal{RC}$ in a doubly-linked chain.) Thus, the non-leader nodes play no essential role in further processing of the input graph, and so may be deleted. The effect is the same as contracting the $\mathcal{RC}$ to a single node. (Note, however, that this may entail an arbitrary choice of which edges to eliminate in cases of mutual dominance. We will see in a later section that there may be reason to redistribute some of the unfiltered edges to the $\mathcal{RC}$ interior as a postprocessing step.)

Consequences of Contraction

An obvious benefit of the $\mathcal{RC}$ contraction process is that it may reduce the size of the network, but this is not its primary purpose. Because of the equivalence of rigid components and strongly-connected components, removal of the former will also eliminate the latter. Thus, subsequently determined predecessor graphs are acyclic (DAGs) This facilitates dominance identification. For example, reverse-postorder traversals can be used to ensure that parents are visited before children in descents through the predecessor graph. These traversals require only linear time (in the number of edges).

Another consequence is that the dominance relations are simplified by eliminating mutual-dominating edges. To see this we need the following result.

Theorem 9 *(1) Suppose AC and BC are two non-negative edges in $\mathcal{APSP}$. Then AC and BC mutually dominate each other if and only if A and B are rigidly-related.*

(2) Suppose AC and AB are two negative edges in the $\mathcal{APSP}$. Then AC and AB mutually dominate each other if and only if B and C are rigidly-related.

	Input Graph		Output Graph		
Nodes	Edges	Degree	Edges	Degree	Time
Grid-SSquare family data					
257	768	16	744.8	12	1.18
1025	3072	32	2997.4	22.8	29.66
4097	12288	64	12010	45.4	878.64
Grid-SWide family data					
257	768	32	745.6	21.8	1.13
1025	3072	128	2982.5	90.8	18.57
4097	12288	512	11905.4	377.4	302.13
Grid-SLong family data					
257	768	8	746.2	5.2	1.08
1025	3072	8	3002.2	5.8	17.17
4097	12288	8	12028.4	5.8	297.22
Grid-NHard family data					
257	2166	12	570	4	3.33
1025	9944	12	2311.8	4.2	165.06
4097	40904	12	9235.8	5	12272.7

Table 1: Data from random generated networks.

	Input Graph			Output Graph		
Nodes	Edges	Deg.	#RC	Edges	Deg.	Time
61	133	24	37	106	18	0.02
63	135	26	35	104	17	0.02
42	84	11	28	64	11	0.01
85	194	48	46	153	27	0.03
59487	192790	1151	7111	190733	4104	2230

Table 2: Data from natural plans.

The proof is omitted for brevity, but is an easy consequence of combining the triangle conditions associated with the mutual dominance relations. The theorem shows that mutually dominating edges imply nontrivial rigid components. Thus, in a graph where the $\mathcal{RC}$ subgraphs are contracted, the dominance relation becomes asymmetric. This removes any danger of inadvertently eliminating both edges in a mutually-dominating pair.

Experimental Results

The algorithm was implemented in Lisp and the experiments were run on an Ultra-2 Sparc. We experimented with five natural temporal plans as well as 60 randomly generated ones. Four out of the five natural plans were generated by the planner/scheduler of the Remote Agent control architecture (Pell *et al.* 1997) and were relatively small, averaging about 60 nodes. The fifth plan was taken from an an avionics processor schedule for a commercial aircraft provided by Honeywell (Carpenter, Driscoll, & Hoyme 1994) and was much larger, having about 60,000 nodes.

For the generation of the random networks we used the same code as in (Cherkassky, Goldberg, & Radzik 1996), where a variety of shortest paths algorithms are evaluated on a number of different families of randomly generated networks. We chose the four families of networks that most approximate STNs found in natural plans: Grid-SSquare, Grid-SWide, Grid-SLong, and Grid-NHard. For every family and every different size of the initial network we generated 5 network instances. The averages for a number of different statistics are reported in table 1. The initials in tables 1 and 2 stand for: **Nodes**, the number of nodes in the input and output graphs; **Edges**, the number of edges; **Degree**, the maximum out-degree; **Time**, the time in seconds for the filtering algorithm to run; and **#RC**, the number of rigid components in the input graph. All statistics are within 15% of the reported average.

From the results of tables 1 and 2 we observe that the number of edges in the output graph is much smaller than the worst case corresponding to the $\mathcal{APSP}$, which has $N(N-1)$ directed edges. In fact, in our experiments, the output graph was slightly smaller than the input graph—an indication of some redundancy in the latter.

A second observation is that the performance of the algorithm is greatly improved relatively to the old cubic algorithm. A 60,000 nodes network, such as the one displayed in table 2, would take at least an estimated 48.7 days to be filtered (counting only memory accesses, assuming an extremely fast memory cycle of 5ns) and would use about 14.14 GBytes of memory (assuming 4 bytes per edge). The new algorithm filtered the network in about 37 minutes using 25.3 MBytes of memory. Out of these only 204.7 KBytes are used for data structures other than the input graph.

Minimizing the Outdegree

The foregoing sections of this paper have addressed the issue of producing a dispatchable network with a minimum number of edges. However, the time needed for propagation by the dispatching controller (Step 4 in Figure 2) depends on the *indegree* and *outdegree* of the node, i.e., the number of edges to or from the node. Thus, to optimize the Real-Time execution guarantee we need to minimize the *maximum* indegree and outdegree in the network. In this section, we briefly sketch how this can be done for the outdegree within the framework developed in this paper. A similar analysis can be used to minimize the maximum indegree.

Out of all the edge-minimal dispatchable networks, we seek one that minimizes the maximum outdegree. (Notice that we need only consider the edge-minimal dispatchable networks. If a dispatchable network has a small maximum outdegree but does not have a minimum number of edges, we can eliminate edges from it until it is edge-minimal.) The different edge-minimal networks correspond to different choices of which edge to eliminate in cases of mutual dominance. Theorem 9 shows that mutual dominance is associated with the rigid components. Within the framework of the Fast-Filtering algorithm, we can ensure minimality in terms of maximum outdegree by judiciously choosing which edges to keep among those outgoing from the nodes in each $\mathcal{RC}$.

Consider an $\mathcal{RC}$ with leader L. The algorithm as presented resolves mutual dominance in a way that assigns to L all outgoing edges from the $\mathcal{RC}$ (in the final output graph). To assure minimality of maximum outdegree, we need instead to redistribute those out-edges as evenly as possible among the nodes of the $\mathcal{RC}$. The redistribution actually involves choosing alternate members of mutual dominating pairs, but we visualize it as "moving" the out-edges from the minimum node to the other nodes of the $\mathcal{RC}$. An examination of the mutual dominance conditions associated with an $\mathcal{RC}$ shows that only non-negative out-edges may be moved, and they may only be moved over the range in which they remain non-negative. During the move algorithm a number of internal nodes of $\mathcal{RC}$ will be "poorest," i.e., will have a minimum number of out-edges. It is easy to see that a greedy algorithm that moves edges with the shortest ranges first, and moves them to one of the currently "poorest" nodes will provide an optimal distribution. Since the range depends on the edge length, this requires sorting the list of out-edges according to length. Finding a "poorest" node involves searching the $\mathcal{RC}$ within the allowable range. Adopting conservative upper bounds for these operations, the complexity for the redistribution is $\sum_i(E_i \log E_i + E_i * K_i)$ where E_i is the number of out-edges from the leader, and K_i is the number of nodes, of the i-th $\mathcal{RC}$ in an enumeration of all $\mathcal{RC}$ subgraphs. Note that $E_i < N$ and $\sum_i K_i = N$, where N is the total number of nodes. Thus, an upper bound on the complexity is given by $O(N^2 \log N)$, which fits within the bound of Johnson's Algorithm.

Conclusion

We have presented a sophisticated algorithm for reformulating temporal plans so that they may be executed with local propagation. With linear space and time complexity equivalent to Johnson's Algorithm, this is a substantial improvement over the previous simpler quadratic space and cubic time algorithm.

Acknowledgments. We thank Marc Ringer and Mark Boddy of the Honeywell Technology Center who provided us with the avionics processor schedule that motivated much of this research. Participation by the first author was supported by the National Science Foundation under grants IRI-9258392 and IRI-9619579.

References

Bonasso, R. P.; Kortenkamp, D.; Miller, D.; and Slack, M. 1997. Experiences with an architecture for intelligent, reactive agents. *Journal of Experimental and Theoretical Artificial Intelligence* 9(1).

Bresina, J.; Drummond, M.; ; and Kedar, S. 1993. Reactive, integrated systems pose new problems for machine learning. In Minton, S., ed., *Machine Learning Methods for Planning*. San Mateo, California: Morgan Kaufmann.

Carpenter, T.; Driscoll, K.; and Hoyme, K. C. J. 1994. Arinc 659 scheduling: Problem definition. In *Proceedings of 1994 IEEE Real Time System Symposium*. IEEE.

Cherkassky, B.; Goldberg, A.; and Radzik, T. 1996. Shortest paths algorithms: Theory and experimental evaluation. *Mathematical Programming* 73:129–174.

Cormen, T.; Leiserson, C.; and Rivest, R. 1990. *Introduction to Algorithms*. Cambridge, MA: MIT press.

Dechter, R.; Meiri, I.; and Pearl, J. 1991. Temporal constraint networks. *Artificial Intelligence* 49:61–95.

Drabble, B.; Tate, A.; and Dalton, J. 1996. O-plan project evaluation experiments and results. Oplan Technical Report ARPA-RL/O-Plan/TR/23 Version 1, AIAI.

Muscettola, N.; Morris, P.; Pell, B.; and Smith, B. 1998. Issues in temporal reasoning for autonomous control systems. In Wooldridge, M., ed., *Proceedings of the Second Int'l Conference on Autonomous Agents*. ACM Press.

Muscettola, N.; Morris, P.; and Tsamardinos, I. 1998. Reformulating temporal plans for efficient execution. In *Proc. of Sixth Int. Conf. on Principles of Knowledge Representation and Reasoning (KR'98)*.

Musliner, D.; Durfee, E.; and Shin, K. 1993. Circa: A cooperative, intelligent, real-time control architecture. *IEEE Transactions on Systems, Man, and Cybernetics* 23(6).

Pell, B.; Bernard, D. E.; Chien, S.; Gat, E.; Muscettola, N.; Nayak, P. P.; Wagner, M.; and Williams, B. 1997. An autonomous spacecraft agent prototype. *Autonomous Robotics*.

Simmons, R. 1990. An architecture for coordinating planning, sensing, and action. In *Procs. DARPA Workshop on Innovative Approaches to Planning, Scheduling and Control*, 292–297. San Mateo, CA: DARPA.

Wilkins, D. E.; Myers, K. L.; Lowrance, J. D.; and Wesley, L. P. 1995. Planning and reacting in uncertain and dynamic environments. *Journal of Experimental and Theoretical Artificial Intelligence* 7(1):197–227.

An Algorithm to Evaluate Quantified Boolean Formulae *

Marco Cadoli, Andrea Giovanardi, Marco Schaerf

Dipartimento di Informatica e Sistemistica
Università di Roma "La Sapienza"
Via Salaria 113, I-00198 Roma, Italy
email: (cadoli|giovanardi|schaerf)@dis.uniroma1.it

Abstract

The high computational complexity of advanced reasoning tasks such as belief revision and planning calls for efficient and reliable algorithms for reasoning problems harder than NP. In this paper we propose Evaluate, an algorithm for evaluating *Quantified Boolean Formulae*, a language that extends propositional logic in a way such that many advanced forms of propositional reasoning, e.g., reasoning about knowledge, can be easily formulated as evaluation of a QBF. Algorithms for evaluation of QBFs are suitable for the experimental analysis on a wide range of complexity classes, a property not easily found in other formalisms. Evaluate is based on a generalization of the Davis-Putnam procedure for SAT, and is guaranteed to work in polynomial space. Before presenting Evaluate, we discuss all the abstract properties of QBFs that we singled out to make the algorithm more efficient. We also briefly mention the main results of the experimental analysis, which is reported elsewhere.

Introduction

Interest in algorithms for the SAT problem has been constant in the AI community. SAT is obviously relevant to AI, and, being the prototypical NP-complete problem, challenges our ability to cope with large knowledge bases. Usage of algorithms for SAT for reasoning tasks different from classical propositional reasoning has been recently emphasized in the literature. For example, real-world problems such as constraint-based planning can be encoded in SAT (Kautz & Selman 1996), and theorem provers for modal logic can use SAT solvers as black boxes (Giunchiglia & Sebastiani 1996).

Anyway, optimizing algorithms for SAT is not enough for the goals of Knowledge Representation: theoretical analysis showed that advanced forms of reasoning such as belief revision, non-monotonic reasoning, reasoning about knowledge, and STRIPS-like planning, have computational complexity higher that the complexity of SAT, cf. e.g., (Eiter & Gottlob 1992) which shows Σ_2^p- and PSPACE-complete reasoning problems. This calls for efficient and reliable algorithms for reasoning problems harder than NP.

In this paper we propose Evaluate, an algorithm for evaluating a *Quantified Boolean Formula* (QBF). Intuitively, QBFs extend propositional logic in a way similar to the extension from first- to second-order logic: in QBFs propositional variables can be quantified over, either existentially, or universally. As an example, $\forall x_1 \exists x_2 \ (x_1 \vee x_2) \wedge (\neg x_1 \vee \neg x_2)$ means "for each truth assignment to x_1 there exists a truth assignment to x_2 such that $(x_1 \vee x_2) \wedge (\neg x_1 \vee \neg x_2)$ is true". The above QBF is indeed true: if $x_1 =$ true then x_2 can be assigned to false; if $x_1 =$ false then x_2 can be assigned to true; in both cases $(x_1 \vee x_2) \wedge (\neg x_1 \vee \neg x_2)$ is true. The *evaluation problem* for a QBF is to decide whether a given QBF is true or not. QBFs are both harder to cope with, and much more expressive, than pure propositional logic. In fact, many advanced forms of reasoning such as reasoning about knowledge using modal logics, temporal and description logics, can be easily formulated as evaluation of a QBF.

Evaluation of QBFs is similar to SAT also because it is the prototypical problem complete for an important complexity class, i.e., PSPACE. Other reasoning problems, e.g., satisfiability of modal formulae in the system K, are PSPACE-complete too, but syntactically restricted QBFs offer complete problems for other complexity classes relevant to KR such as Σ_2^p and Σ_3^p. Therefore, algorithms for evaluation of QBFs are very suitable for the experimental analysis on a wide range of complexity classes, a property not easily found in other formalisms.

To the best of our knowledge, the only published algorithm for evaluation of QBFs appears in (Büning, Karpinski, & Flögel 1995), and is based on resolution. Evaluate is based on a generalization of the Davis-Putnam (DP) procedure for SAT, and is guaranteed to work in polynomial space. Implementations of DP are still among the most efficient complete algorithms for SAT. Like DP, Evaluate exploits the idea of performing unit propagation as much as possible, and resorts to branching when all other simplifying rules fail. Of course, the different nature of evaluation of QBF and SAT forced us to use specific rules in the design of Eval-

---

* Copyright 1998, American Association for Artificial Intelligence (www.aaai.org). All rights reserved.

uate, e.g., variables bound by the external quantifier must be dealt with before others. In particular, some rules do not affect soundness and/or completeness, but rather efficiency of the algorithm. As an example, if a QBF has a non-tautologous clause in which all literals are universally quantified, then it is false.

We implemented the algorithm in C++ and performed an extensive analysis of its performances for the evaluation of randomly generated QBFs. The analysis, which is reported in (Cadoli, Giovanardi, & Schaerf 1997), is the first of its kind. In particular, we were able to find patterns for *shift of crossover point* (the point at which half of the instances evaluate to true), *phase transition* (sharp differences between instances close to the crossover point from instances far from it), and *easy-hard-easy* distribution. Some of the result generalize those shown in (Selman, Mitchell, & Levesque 1996) for SAT, while others do not. Moreover, the richer structure of QBFs raises the possibility of analyzing experimental behavior for parameters that do not have any counterpart in the propositional case (e.g., number of quantifiers alternations in a QBF).

The purpose of this paper is to present Evaluate. To this end we also discuss all the properties of QBFs that we singled out to make it more efficient. We also briefly mention the main results of the experimental analysis.

Quantified Boolean Formulae

A QBF has the form

$$Q_1 x_1 \cdots Q_n x_n E(x_1, \ldots, x_n) \qquad (1)$$

where E is a propositional formula involving the propositional variables $x_1, \ldots, x_n$ and every Q_i ($1 \leq i \leq n$) is either an existential quantifier $\exists$ or a universal one $\forall$. The expression $\exists x_i \phi$ is an abbreviation for "there exists a truth assignment to x_i such that ϕ is true". Analogously, $\forall x_i \phi$ is an abbreviation for "for each truth assignment to x_i, ϕ is true". Inverting quantifiers in a QBF may change its truth value. As an example, inverting quantifiers in $\forall x_1 \exists x_2 \ (x_1 \vee x_2) \wedge (\neg x_1 \vee \neg x_2)$ yields $\exists x_1 \forall x_2 \ (x_1 \vee x_2) \wedge (\neg x_1 \vee \neg x_2)$, which is indeed false (cf. Introduction).

Given a generic QBF, we can group in the same set all consecutive variables having the same quantifier. In such a format, each quantifier is applied to a set of variables rather than to a single propositional variable. Moreover, the sequence of quantifiers alternates: an existential quantifier follows a universal quantifier and vice-versa.

A *kQBF* (with k constant integer) is a QBF in which the quantifiers are applied to k disjoint sets of variables and the sequence of quantifiers alternates; sometimes we will add a subscript denoting the type of the most external quantifier in the formula. For example, if X_1, X_2, and X_3 are mutually disjoint sets of propositional variables, then the formula $\exists X_1 \forall X_2 \exists X_3 \ E(X_1, X_2, X_3)$ is a 3QBF$_\exists$. SAT coincides with the evaluation problem for 1QBF$_\exists$. Evaluating a QBF is inherently more difficult than deciding satisfiability of a propositional formula: the evaluation problem for a QBF is PSPACE-complete, and plays the role of prototypical problem for such a class. The problem of evaluating a kQBF$_\exists$ is Σ_k^p-complete, whereas the problem of evaluating a kQBF$_\forall$ is Π_k^p-complete, Σ_k^p and Π_k^p being the classes at the k-th level of the Polynomial Hierarchy.

In the rest of this paper we refer to QBFs in *Conjunctive Normal Form* (CNF), i.e., QBFs of the form (1) in which the boolean formula E is a conjunction of *clauses*, each one being a disjunction of *literals* —a negated or non-negated variable. In this case E is called *matrix* of the formula. A QBF is said to be in *hCNF* if every clause contains exactly h literals.

Considering QBF in CNF is not a restriction, since the problem of evaluating such formulae is still PSPACE-complete. With respect to kQBFs, the evaluation problem of kQBFs in 3CNF is complete for the same complexity class of the general case if the most internal quantifier is an existential. As a consequence, in the following we will consider kQBFs of the form

$$Q_1 X_1 \cdots \exists X_k \ E(X_1, \ldots, X_k) \qquad (2)$$

in which $E(X_1, \ldots, X_n)$ is in CNF, the most internal quantifier is existential and the sequence of quantifiers alternates. Fixing the type of the most internal quantifier makes the use of subscripts in, e.g., kQBF$_\exists$ useless. As an example, a 2QBF has the form $\forall X_1 \exists X_2 \ E(X_1, X_2)$, while a 3QBF has the form $\exists X_1 \forall X_2 \exists X_3 \ E(X_1, X_2, X_3)$.

We now show some relevant properties of QBFs that are of interest in the development of the algorithm.

Definition 1 *Given a kQBF of the form (2), we define the sets Σ and Π as follows:*

$$\Sigma = X_k \cup X_{k-2} \cup \cdots$$

$$\Pi = X_{k-1} \cup X_{k-3} \cup \cdots$$

that is, Σ is the union of all the sets of existentially quantified variables, while Π collects all the universally quantified variables.

Example 1 *Let F be the QBF*

$$\forall W \exists Z \forall X \exists Y \ [(x_1 \vee \neg y_1 \vee z_1) \wedge (y_1) \wedge \\ (w_1 \vee \neg w_2 \vee \neg z_1) \wedge (\neg x_2) \wedge \\ (y_2 \vee \neg w_1 \vee \neg x_1) \wedge (\neg y_2 \vee z_1)]$$

Then $\Pi = W \cup X = \{w_1, w_2, x_1, x_2\}$, while $\Sigma = Z \cup Y = \{z_1, y_1, y_2\}$.

Using the sets Σ and Π, we can partition the matrix $E(X_1, \ldots, X_k)$ of any kQBF of the form (2) into three matrices:

1. $H(\Sigma)$, containing the clauses in which only variables of Σ occur;

2. $G(\Pi)$, containing the clauses in which only variables of Π occur;

3. $L(\Sigma, \Pi)$, containing the remaining clauses.

Therefore, any such kQBF can be rewritten as:

$$Q_1 X_1 \cdots \exists X_k \ [H(\Sigma) \wedge G(\Pi) \wedge L(\Sigma, \Pi)] \quad (3)$$

Example 2 *Referring to Example 1:*

$$\begin{aligned} H(\Sigma) &\equiv (y_1) \wedge (\neg y_2 \vee z_1) \\ G(\Pi) &\equiv (\neg x_2) \\ L(\Sigma,\Pi) &\equiv (x_1 \vee \neg y_1 \vee z_1) \wedge (w_1 \vee \neg w_2 \vee \neg z_1) \wedge \\ & \quad (y_2 \vee \neg w_1 \vee \neg x_1) \end{aligned}$$

Lemma 1 (Trivial falsity on Π) *A QBF F of the form (3) is false if $G'(\Pi) \neq \emptyset$, where $G'(\Pi)$ is obtained from $G(\Pi)$ by deleting all tautological clauses.*

Proof. Let us assume that $G'(\Pi)$ is non-empty. Then there exists at least one non tautological clause $C = l_1 \vee \cdots \vee l_m$, where $l_1, \ldots, l_m$ are literals. The truth assignment $l_i = false$ for $i = 1, \ldots, m$ makes G false. Since all variables corresponding to the literals $l_1, \ldots, l_m$ are universally quantified, F is false. □

Notice that the formula in Example 1 is trivially false since $G'(\Pi)$ is non empty $(\neg x_2)$. The simple check required in Lemma 1 can be accomplished in time linear in the size of the matrix. As a consequence, in all the interesting cases we always have that $G(\Pi) = \emptyset$. In the following we assume that this is the case. Thus, the generic form of a QBF becomes:

$$Q_1 X_1 \cdots \exists X_k \ [H(\Sigma) \wedge L(\Sigma, \Pi)] \quad (4)$$

Lemma 2 (Trivial falsity on Σ) *A QBF F of the form (4) is false if $H(\Sigma)$ is unsatisfiable.*

Proof. If $H(\Sigma)$ is unsatisfiable, there are no truth assignments to the existentially quantified variables that can make the matrix true. Therefore, F is false. □

A corollary of Lemma 2 is that, if a unit clause occurs in $H(\Sigma)$, then it is useless to try to falsify it. In other words, the unit propagation rule of the Davis-Putnam algorithm is also applicable to QBFs when applied to variables in Σ. On the contrary, unit propagation is ruled out for variables in Π by Lemma 1. In fact, if there exists a unit clause whose only variable belongs to Π then the QBF is false.

Example 3 *Let F be the following QBF:*

$$\begin{aligned} F = \forall X \exists Y \ & [y_2 \wedge (\neg y_1 \vee y_2 \vee y_3) \wedge (\neg y_2 \vee y_1) \wedge \\ & (x_1 \vee x_2 \vee y_3) \wedge (\neg y_1 \vee x_1 \vee \neg x_2)] \end{aligned}$$

F is false: in fact, $H(Y) \equiv y_2 \wedge (\neg y_1 \vee y_2 \vee y_3) \wedge (\neg y_2 \vee y_1)$ must be satisfiable (Lemma 2), and therefore, $y_2 = true$. By unit propagation $y_1 = true$ and F can be simplified as

$$\forall X \exists Y [(x_1 \vee x_2 \vee y_3) \wedge (x_1 \vee \neg x_2)]$$

Now there exists a clause $(x_1 \vee \neg x_2)$ with all variables in Π. Thus, by Lemma 1, F is false.

Lemma 3 (Trivial truth) *A QBF F of the form (4) is true if $H(\Sigma) \wedge L'(\Sigma)$ is satisfiable, where $L'(\Sigma)$ is obtained from $L(\Sigma, \Pi)$ by deleting all variables in Π.*

Proof. All models of $L'(\Sigma)$ are also models of $L(\Sigma, \Pi)$. Let us assume $H(\Sigma) \wedge L'(\Sigma)$ is satisfiable, and M is one of its models. M makes $H(\Sigma) \wedge L(\Sigma, \Pi)$ true for any truth assignment to the letters in Π. Therefore, F is true. □

Example 4 *The following QBF*

$$\begin{aligned} \forall W \exists Z \forall X \exists Y \ & [(\neg w_1 \vee x_2 \vee y_1) \wedge (\neg x_1 \vee y_2 \vee z_3) \wedge \\ & (\neg x_2 \vee w_1 \vee \neg z_1) \wedge (x_1 \vee z_2 \vee y_1) \wedge \\ & (\neg z_2 \vee \neg y_2 \vee y_1)] \end{aligned}$$

is trivially true. In fact, $H(\Sigma) \wedge L'(\Sigma) \equiv y_1 \wedge (y_2 \vee z_3) \wedge (\neg z_1) \wedge (z_2 \vee y_1) \wedge (\neg z_2 \vee \neg y_2 \vee y_1)$ is satisfiable since the model $y_1 = true$, $y_2 = true$, $z_1 = false$ satisfies it.

Lemma 3 presents a sufficient condition which is not necessary. For example, the QBF $\forall X \exists Y[(x_1 \vee y_1) \wedge (\neg x_1 \vee \neg y_1)]$ is true while $L'(\Sigma) \equiv y_1 \wedge \neg y_1$ is unsatisfiable. Notice that verifying the condition of the above lemma requires to perform a satisfiability test. Nevertheless, our experimental analysis has shown that the presence of this test makes the algorithm **Evaluate** more efficient.

There are other conditions that can help us to simplify QBFs. Following the terminology used for the Davis-Putnam procedure, we call literal l *monotone* if its complementary literal does not appear in the matrix E of the QBF. Monotone literals are important because we can immediately assign them a value without any need for branching. The truth value we need to assign them is a function of the set to which they belong. In the following, when we assign a truth value to a literal, we implicitly assign the opposite truth value to the complementary literal.

Lemma 4 (Monotone literals in Σ) *Given a QBF F of the form (2) and a monotone literal $l \in \Sigma$, then F is true if and only if $F' = Q_1 X_1 \cdots \exists X_k \ E'(X_1, \ldots, X_k)$ is true, where $E'(X_1, \ldots, X_k)$ is obtained from $E(X_1, \ldots, X_k)$ by replacing l with true.*

Due to the lack of space we omit this and the following proofs.

Lemma 5 (Monotone literals in Π) *Given a QBF F of the form (2) and a monotone literal $l \in \Pi$, then F is true if and only if $F' = Q_1 X_1 \cdots \exists X_k \ E'(X_1, \ldots, X_k)$ is true, where $E'(X_1, \ldots, X_k)$ is obtained from $E(X_1, \ldots, X_k)$ by replacing l with false.*

The conditions of Lemmata 4 and 5 can be checked in polynomial time. There is one more simple situation (whose conditions can be checked in polynomial time) where we can avoid considering all assignments to a variable.

Lemma 6 (Forced assignment for Σ) *Let F be a QBF of the form (2) and C a clause in E such that:*

1. *there exists a literal $l \in X_i \subseteq \Sigma$ in C, and*
2. *all other literals of C belong to the set $X_{i+1} \cup X_{i+3} \cup \cdots \cup X_{k-1} \subseteq \Pi$.*

Algorithm Evaluate
Input: a kQBF CNF formula F of the form (2)
Output: *true* if F is true, *false* otherwise.

```
boolean Evaluate (QBF F)
  { while (F contains a tautological clause C)
        remove C from F;
    if (F is a Π-formula) return Π_Evaluate(F);
    else return Σ_Evaluate(F);
  }
```

Figure 1: The Evaluate algorithm

Then the formula F is true if and only if the formula $F' = Q_1 X_1 \cdots \exists X_k E'(X_1, \ldots, X_k)$ is true, where $E'(X_1, \ldots, X_k)$ is obtained from $E(X_1, \ldots, X_k)$ by substituting all occurrences of l with *true*.

The Algorithm

The algorithm Evaluate is shown in Figure 1. For solving a QBF, Evaluate performs successive simplifications on the original formula, using techniques such as propagation and backtracking, and performing partial evaluation of subformulae obtained in this way. As a matter of fact, Evaluate makes use of two recursive procedures Σ_Evaluate and Π_Evaluate that interact each other and cooperate in evaluating the input formula. Σ_Evaluate is a procedure that works on a QBF in which the most external quantifier is existential (Σ-formulae). Dually, Π_Evaluate works on Π-formulae, that is, formulae in which the most external quantifier is universal. The matrix of both Σ- and Π-formulae is in CNF.

The main procedure Evaluate takes as input a QBF F and returns its truth value. As a matter of fact, it performs two simple actions: first of all, all tautological clauses in F (if any) are removed. Notice that the elimination of tautological clauses can be performed once and for all: in fact, none of the successive manipulations that the algorithm makes on the input formula can create a tautological clause. Then, Evaluate invokes either Σ_Evaluate or Π_Evaluate according to whether F is a Σ-formula or a Π-formula.

Figure 2 shows the procedure Π_Evaluate. The procedure takes in input a Π-formula and returns its truth value; it is at the same time an iterative and recursive procedure, that works as follows.

Base of recursion. First of all, Π_Evaluate checks whether the input formula F is formed by all existentially quantified variables; in this case, F is indeed a 1QBF and then for evaluating it is sufficient to invoke any procedure for SAT (cf. line (1)) –the Davis-Putnam algorithm in our implementation. Successively, Π_Evaluate verifies whether F is *trivially* true by using Lemma 3. To this end, it computes the 1QBF G, obtained by removing from F all the universally quantified variables (cf. (2)), and checks its satisfiability. To check whether G is satisfiable, Π_Evaluate makes use of a procedure for SAT (cf. (3)). If G is satisfiable, the input

Procedure Π_Evaluate
Input: a Π-formula of the form:
$F = \forall X_1 \exists X_2 \cdots \forall X_{k-1} \exists X_k \ E(X_1, \ldots, X_k)$
Output: *true* if F is true, *false* otherwise.

```
boolean Π_Evaluate (QBF F)
(1)  { if (all the variables in F are existentially quantified)
         return SAT(F);
(2)    remove from F all the universally quantified
       variables, thus obtaining the formula G;
(3)    if (SAT(G)) return true;
(4)    while (there are uninstantiated variables in X_1)
(5)      { if (E is an empty set of clauses)
(6)          return true;
(7)        if (E contains an empty clause)
(8)          return false;
(9)        if (there is a clause made of all
             universally quantified variables in E)
(10)         return false;
(11)       if (there is a unit clause c formed by
             a literal l ∈ Σ in E)
(12)         { assign true to l;
(13)           simplify F with l = true;
             }
(14)       else if (there is a monotone literal l ∈ Σ in E)
(15)         { assign true to l;
(16)           simplify F with l = true;
             }
(17)       else if (there is a monotone literal l ∈ Π in E)
(18)         { assign false to l;
(19)           simplify F with l = false;
             }
(20)       else if (there is a clause c including a literal
             l ∈ X_h ⊆ Σ in E and all other literals
             of c are in X_{h+1} ∪ ⋯ ∪ X_{k-1} ⊆ Π)
(21)         { assign true to l;
(22)           simplify F with l = true;
             }
(23)       else
(24)         { choose a literal l ∈ X_1;
(25)           QBF OldF = F;
(26)           assign false to l;
(27)           simplify F with l = false;
(28)           if (Π_Evaluate(F) == false)
                 return false;
(29)           else
(30)             { F = OldF;
(31)               assign true to l;
(32)               simplify F with l = true;
(33)               return Π_Evaluate(F);
                 }
             }
       } /* while */
(34)   return Σ_Evaluate(F);
     }
```

Figure 2: The Π_Evaluate procedure

formula F is true, and then Π_Evaluate can stop and return *true* (cf. (3)). We could use an incomplete, faster algorithm for testing satisfiability of G, but experiments showed that a sound and complete procedure for SAT results in a more efficient evaluation of the QBF.

Iteration and forced assigments. If F is not trivially true, the algorithm proceeds iteratively: during the generic iteration, the formula F is simplified by means of truth values assignments to one or more of its variables. The assignments made by Π_Evaluate can be of two kinds: *forced* and *unforced*. A *forced assignment* to a variable x in F causes F to be simplified in an other QBF G such that F is true *if and only if G is true*. Thus, forced assignments are very important, since they simplify the evaluation process without making backtracking necessary.

Unforced assignments are performed on variables that belong to X_1, that is, the most external set of variables in the input formula F (cf. the input of Π_Evaluate). Unforced assignment generally require the use of backtracking, as we will see later.

Turning back to the algorithm, simplifications on F are performed until one of the following cases is verified:

1. Simplifications made on F cause all the variables in X_1 to be instantiated (cf. (4)); in this case X_1 is empty, and F is indeed a Σ-Formula. For evaluating F, Π_Evaluate invokes the Σ_Evaluate procedure (cf. (34)).

2. Simplifications made on F cause the matrix E to be empty (cf. (5)); this means that all clauses in E have been satisfied, and so F is true. As a consequence, the algorithm stops returning *true* (cf. (6)).

3. Simplifications made on F cause the matrix E to contain an empty clause (cf. (7)); in this case F is trivially false and the algorithm stops returning *false* (cf. (8)).

4. Simplifications made on F cause the matrix E to contain a clause formed by all universally quantified variables (cf. (9)). By Lemma 1 the formula F is false. So, the algorithm stops returning *false* (cf. (10)).

If none of the above cases is verified, Π_Evaluate checks whether it is possible to perform forced assignments on variables in F. Using Lemmata 3, 4, 5, 6, and unit propagation (using Lemma 2), we have characterized four different situations where forced assignments can be performed (cf. statements from (11) to (22)).

Branch. If no forced assignments can be performed, Π_Evaluate simplifies the input formula by means of an unforced assignment made on a variable x in X_1 (cf. statements between (24) and (33)). Since there is no way for excluding neither the value *true* nor the value *false* for x, the evaluation of F is splitted in the evaluation of the two subformulae obtained assigning respectively *false* and *true* to x. Since x is a universally quantified variable, F is true if and only if both these subformulae are true. The instantiation of x is indeed a branch in the evaluation process of F; for this reason, we call x the *branch variable*, whereas the literals corresponding to x are called *branch literals*.

Three heuristics for choosing the branch literal were adopted. In increasing efficiency, they are: 1) random, 2) try to maximize the number of Horn/dual-Horn clauses after simplification (using on ideas of (Crawford & Auton 1993)), and 3) privilege those variables having the maximum number of occurrences in short clauses and, among them, variables that appear most frequently in the matrix of the input formula (using ideas of the SAT-solver "Böhm" as described in (Buro & Büning 1993)).

After having chosen the branch variable and a particular branch literal (cf. (24)), the actual structure of F is saved for future backtracking (cf. (25)). Successively, Π_Evaluate is recursively invoked on the formula obtained assigning *false* to the branch literal l (cf. (26), (27) and (28)). If the result of the recursive call of Π_Evaluate is *false*, the procedure can stop and return *false* (cf. (28)). Otherwise, Π_Evaluate backtracks and restores the old structure of F (cf. (30)). The formula F is then simplified assigning *true* to the branch literal (cf. (31) and (32)). Lastly, the procedure returns the result obtained applying recursively Π_Evaluate on F (cf. (33)).

The procedure Σ_Evaluate is very similar to Π_Evaluate, and so is omitted. As a matter of fact, Σ_Evaluate differs from Π_Evaluate only in case of branch: now X_1 is a set of existentially quantified variables. While in Π_Evaluate a logical AND between the two recursive calls is performed, in Σ_Evaluate is necessary to perform a logical OR between them.

Experimental results

In (Cadoli, Giovanardi, & Schaerf 1997) we present in detail an experimental analysis of the complexity of valuating randomly generated kQBF instances. Here we briefly recall these results together with some new ones. In our tests, we have generated kQBF instances according to two different models: *Fixed Clause Length* (FCL) and *Constant Probability* (CP); both of them are well-known in the literature (cf. e.g., (Selman, Mitchell, & Levesque 1996)).

In the FCL model each formula is generated so that all clauses are different, non-tautologous, and contain exactly h literals, not all of them universally quantified. If V is the set of all propositional variables in the formula (that is $V = X_1 \cup \cdots \cup X_k$), then a clause is produced by randomly choosing h different variables in V and negating each one with probability 0.5. The CP model has the same parameters of the FCL model, except for h, which represents in this case the average number of literals per clause in the formula. The empty clause and unit clauses are disallowed.

The results we obtained can be summarized as follows:

- If clauses are long enough, e.g., 6CNF, evaluation is more difficult for 3QBF than 2QBF, and for 2QBF than 1QBF.

- Phase transition phenomena for the percentage of true instances as a function of the #clauses/#variables per set ratio exists in all the examined cases (2QBF-3/4/5/6CNF, 3QBF-3/6CNF) of QBF.

- An easy-hard-easy pattern for the average difficulty of the instances as a function of the #clauses/#variables per set ratio has been observed in the following cases: 2QBF-5/6CNF, and 3QBF-6CNF. In particular, we noticed a correlation between the location of the hardest instances and the crossover point for 2QBF-6CNF and 3QBF-6CNF. The easy-hard-easy pattern, instead, has not been observed in all the other cases (2QBF-3/4CNF, and 3QBF-3CNF)

- The number of clauses at the crossover point is not a linear function of the number of variables (as it was for 1QBF); in all the cases in which we could examine a wide range for the number of variables per set (2QBF-3/4CNF, and 3QBF-3CNF), we have verified that the number of clauses at the crossover point is proportional to the square root of the number of variables per set

- As in the 1QBF case, instances generated according to the CP model are, on average, much easier than those generated by means of the FCL model.

- In all the considered cases, the true instances are the easiest for kQBF with k odd, whereas the easiest instances are the false ones for kQBF with k even.

- Unbalancing the number of existentially-quantified and universally-quantified variables has remarkable effects on the difficulty of kQBF instances; if the $\exists$-variables are increased and the $\forall$-variables are decreased, the instances become much harder with respect to the instances where their number is balanced. An opposite phenomenon has been observed when the $\forall$-variables are increased and the $\exists$-variables are decreased.

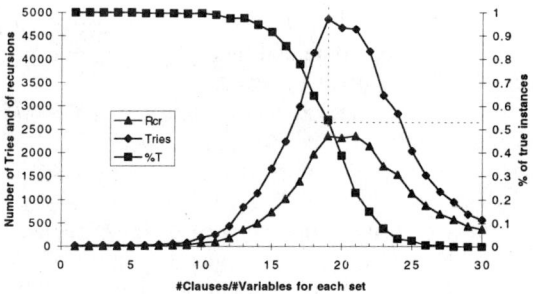

Figure 3: Results for 3QBF-6CNF

To give an example of the results we obtained, we report in Figure 3 the percentage of true instances, the average number of truth values assignment made to the variables before being able to evaluate the formula (tries), and the average number of recursions, as a function of the #clauses/#variables per set ratio. The total number of variables is 30 (10 variables per set), the number of clauses varies from 10 to 300, with a step of 10, and 500 experiments for each setting of the parameters were run. The curves regarding the number of tries and recursions show an easy-hard-easy pattern, with the hardest instances being associated with the crossover point. At the peak, evaluation takes about 10 seconds on average on a 75MHz/32MB SPARC10.

Conclusions and Future Work

In this paper we have presented Evaluate, an algorithm to evaluate quantified boolean formulae. This algorithm can help us in understanding the computational structure of all problems that belong to the classes captured by QBFs, i.e., each level of the Polynomial Hierarchy and PSPACE. We do not claim Evaluate is the best conceivable algorithm, but it can benefit from advancements in technology of algorithms for SAT, because it uses the black-box principle. We singled out some cases which appear in practice to require more computational resources, hence made a first step in the development of algorithms which are efficient in the average case. This is also one step for our long-term goal to characterize, from the experimental point of view, the most widely accepted KR formalisms. In order to substantiate this claim, we are currently experimenting on the usage of our algorithm to solve decision problems that are not in NP, such as satisfiability of modal formulae. To this end, we have found reductions that map a modal formula into a QBF.

References

Büning, H. K.; Karpinski, M.; and Flögel, A. 1995. Resolution for quantified boolean formulas. *Information and Computation* 117:12–18.

Buro, M., and Büning, H. K. 1993. Report on a SAT competition. *EATCS Bulletin* 49:143–151.

Cadoli, M.; Giovanardi, A.; and Schaerf, M. 1997. Experimental analysis of the computational cost of evaluating quantified boolean formulae. In *Proc. of AI*IA-97*, number 1321 in LNAI, 207–218. Springer-Verlag.

Crawford, J. M., and Auton, L. D. 1993. Experimental results on the crossover point in satisfiability problems. In *Proc. of AAAI-93*, 21–27.

Eiter, T., and Gottlöb, G. 1992. On the complexity of propositional knowledge base revision, updates and conterfactuals. *Artif. Intell.* 57:227–270.

Giunchiglia, F., and Sebastiani, R. 1996. A SAT-based decision procedure for $\mathcal{ALC}$. In *Proc. of KR-96*, 304–314.

Kautz, H. A., and Selman, B. 1996. Pushing the envelope: planning, propositional logic, and stochastic search. In *Proc. of AAAI-96*, 1194–1201.

Selman, B.; Mitchell, D.; and Levesque, H. 1996. Generating Hard Satisfiability Problems. *Artif. Intell.* 81:17–29.

Two forms of dependence in propositional logic: controllability and definability

Jérôme Lang
IRIT-UPS
118 route de Narbonne
31062 Toulouse Cedex, France
e-mail: lang@irit.fr

Pierre Marquis
CRIL/Université d'Artois
rue de l'Université – S.P. 16
62307 Lens Cedex, France
e-mail: marquis@cril.univ-artois.fr

Abstract

We investigate two forms of dependence between variables and/or formulas within a propositional knowledge base: *controllability* (a set of variables X controls a formula Γ if there is a way to fix the truth value of the variables in X in order to achieve Γ to have a prescribed truth value) and *definability* (X defines a variable y if every truth assignment of the variables in X enables us finding out the truth value of y). Several characterization results are pointed out, complexity issues are analyzed, and some applications of both notions, including decision under incomplete knowledge and/or partial observability, and hypothesis discrimination, are sketched.

Introduction

For many reasoning tasks which make use of propositional logic, exhibiting structure can be of a great help. By "structure" we mean some relationships that exist between some sets of variables and/or formulas within a propositional knowledge base Σ. A nice example of such structure, which has received much attention recently, is *independence* (Darwiche 1997) (Lakemeyer 1997) and related structural properties such as relevance (Lakemeyer 1995), or causal independence (Darwiche & Pearl 1994). Revealing independence relations in Σ not only helps understanding Σ better but also is a great help for making easier some reasoning tasks such as satisfiability, deduction, abduction or diagnosis (Darwiche 1997). Apart from independence other kinds of structural properties are worth investigating, especially different kinds of *dependence* involving sets of variables and/or formulas. In this paper, two particular forms of dependence are studied:

- *controllability*: a set of variables X controls a formula Γ w.r.t. Σ if it is always possible to fix the values of some of the variables in X in order to achieve Γ to have a given truth value (true or false); the particular case where one is only interested in Γ being true corresponds to achieving a *goal* and relates to qualitative decision making under incomplete knowledge.

- *definability*: a set of variables X defines a variable y w.r.t. Σ if whatever the observed values of all variables of X are, they enable us finding out the truth value of y. This notion has many applications, including designing test policies in order to discriminate among hypotheses (such as plausible diagnoses).

For these two kinds of dependence, several definitions are introduced together with their specific interest, some characterizations are given, computational complexity issues are investigated, and some applications ranging from decision under partial observability to fault isolation in model-based diagnosis, are also sketched. As to definability, this paper completes a companion paper (Lang & Marquis 1998) in several directions, including the practical computation of definability relations.

Formal Preliminaries

Let PS be a countable set of propositional variables and $PROP_{PS}$ the propositional language built up from PS, the connectives and the boolean constants $true$ and $false$. For $X \subseteq PS$, $PROP_X$ denotes the sublanguage of $PROP_{PS}$ generated from the variables of X only. Elements (resp. subsets) of PS are denoted $x, y,$ etc. (resp. $X, Y,$ etc). Full instantiations of variables of $X \subseteq PS$ (called X–worlds) are denoted by ω_X and their set is denoted Ω_X. Σ denotes a finite propositional knowledge base, i.e., a conjunctively-interpreted finite set of propositional formulas from $PROP_{PS}$. $Var(\Sigma)$ is the set of propositional variables appearing in formula Σ.

For every formula Φ and every $x \in PS$, $\Phi_{x \leftarrow 0}$ (resp. $\Phi_{x \leftarrow 1}$) is the formula obtained by replacing in Φ every occurence of x by $false$ (resp. $true$).

Given a propositional knowledge base Σ, the set of prime implicants modulo Σ of a formula Φ over $PROP_X$ will be denoted by $PI_\Sigma^X(\Phi)$; this set is defined by $PI_\Sigma^X(\Phi) = max(\{PI(\Sigma \Rightarrow \Phi) \cap PROP_X\}, \models)$ where $PI(\Phi)$ denotes the set of prime implicants of Φ for every formula Φ. $PI^X(\Phi)$ ($= PI_{true}^X(\Phi)$) denotes the subset of $PI(\Phi)$ consisting of the terms built upon X, only. $IP(\Phi)$ denotes the set of prime implicates of Φ. For instance, if $\Sigma = \{a \vee b, \neg a \wedge c \Rightarrow e, d \Leftrightarrow e\}$ then $PI_\Sigma^{\{a,b,c,d\}}(e) = \{d, \neg a \wedge c, \neg a \wedge \neg b\}$, $PI_\Sigma^{\{a,c\}}(e) = \{\neg a \wedge c\}$, $PI_\Sigma^{\{b,c\}}(e) = \emptyset$, $PI_\Sigma^{\{a,b,c,d\}}(a \vee b) = \{true\}$, $IP(\Sigma) = \{a \vee b, a \vee \neg c \vee e, \neg d \vee e, d \vee \neg e, a \vee \neg c \vee d\}$.

In this paper we refer to some complexity classes above NP and coNP, details about which can be found in Papadimitriou's textbook (Papadimitriou 1994).

Conditional controllability

Let Σ be a propositional knowledge base, $X, Z \subseteq PS$, and Γ be a formula. Intuitively, X positively controls Γ given Z w.r.t. Σ means that for any observed Z-world ω_Z there is a X-world ω_X which certainly achieves Γ. A very intuitive interpretation of positive controllability relates to decision under incomplete knowledge and partial observability: Z is the set of observable variables, Ω_Z the observation space, X the set of controllable variables, Ω_X the action space (an action being the composition of elementary actions, an elementary action assigning a variable of X to either *true* or *false*), and Γ the goal.

Controllability in a logical setting has not received much attention so far. The first approach we know is in (Boutilier 1994) where an action model for qualitative decision theory is based on a partition between controllable and uncontrollable variables. While inspired by the latter, this study extends it in several directions, especially regarding to observability and complexity (some of our results applying to Boutilier's framework). Controllability appears also in the independent choice logic (Poole 1997), where each variable is assigned a specific agent controlling it, and in (Fargier, Lang, & Schiex 1996) in a constraint satisfaction framework.

We may think of defining conditional positive controllability as follows:

X positively controls Γ given Z w.r.t. Σ iff $\forall \omega_Z \in \Omega_Z$ $\exists \omega_X \in \Omega_X$ such that $\omega_Z \wedge \omega_X \wedge \Sigma \models \Gamma$.

Now, there are two points which must be considered before going further:

1. *What if $\omega_Z \wedge \Sigma$ is inconsistent?* This means that observation ω_Z is impossible: it can merely not happen. Hence assigning an action to ω_Z is needless.

2. *What if $\omega_Z \wedge \Sigma$ is consistent and $\omega_Z \wedge \omega_X \wedge \Sigma$ is inconsistent?* This is more difficult to interpret, or at least more ambiguous. The most intuitive interpretation is that when ω_Z is observed, the action ω_X is simply not available[2].

We now have the elements for defining formally conditional controllability and related notions:

Definition 1 (conditional controllability)
Let $\Sigma, \Gamma \in PROP_{PS}$ and $X, Z \subseteq PS$.
- X **positively controls** Γ *given Z w.r.t. Σ (denoted by $X \ll_\Sigma^Z \Gamma^+$) iff $\forall \omega_Z \in \Omega_Z$ s.t. $\omega_Z \wedge \Sigma$ is consistent $\exists \omega_X \in \Omega_X$ s.t. (i) $\omega_Z \wedge \omega_X \wedge \Sigma$ is consistent and (ii) $\omega_Z \wedge \omega_X \wedge \Sigma \models \Gamma$.*
- X **fully controls** Γ *given Z w.r.t. Σ (denoted by $X \ll_\Sigma^Z \Gamma$) iff both $X \ll_\Sigma^Z \Gamma^+$ and $X \ll_\Sigma^Z (\neg \Gamma)^+$.*

---
[2]As noticed by Fargier (personal communication), in the case where it is guaranteed that any action can always be performed then the specification of the decision problem *must* be s.t. for any ω_Z, if $\omega_Z \wedge \Sigma$ is consistent, then for every ω_X, $\omega_Z \wedge \omega_X \wedge \Sigma$ is consistent.

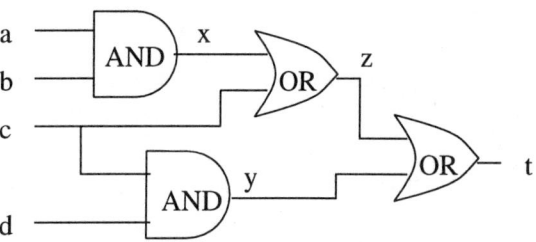

Figure 1: A circuit.

Positive controllability intuitively means that there is a way to fix the values of variables in X in order to make the goal Γ true; full controllability means that both Γ and $\neg \Gamma$ can be achieved. Note that the technical difference between this definition of positive controllability and the definition given above without consistency conditions does not rely on whether impossible observations are taken into account or not; indeed, if $\omega_Z \wedge \Sigma$ is inconsistent, then $\exists \omega_X$ s.t. $\omega_Z \wedge \omega_X \wedge \Sigma \models \Gamma$ is trivially satisfied (any ω_X does the job). So the only difference is requiring the action ω_X assigned to an observation to be available, i.e. consistent with the observation and the knowledge base.

As an illustration, let us consider the circuit depicted on Figure 1. Let $\Sigma = \{x \Leftrightarrow a \vee b, y \Leftrightarrow (b \Leftrightarrow \neg c), z \Leftrightarrow (x \Leftrightarrow \neg y)\}$. We have $\{a, c\} \ll_\Sigma^{\{b\}} x^+$ but *not* $\{a, c\} \ll_\Sigma^{\{b\}} x$; we also have $\{a, c\} \ll_\Sigma^{\{b\}} y$ and $\{a, c\} \ll_\Sigma^{\{b\}} z$. Note that we do *not* have $\{a, c\} \ll_\Sigma^\emptyset y^+$ (nor $(\neg y)^+$, nor z^+, nor $(\neg z)^+$) (we only have $\{a, c\} \ll_\Sigma^\emptyset x^+$).

Now, positive controllability can be characterized by means of prime implicants (similar results follow easily for other forms of controllability).

Proposition 1
$X \ll_\Sigma^Z \Gamma^+$ iff $\forall \omega_Z \in \Omega_Z$ s.t. $\omega_Z \wedge \Sigma$ is consistent, $\exists \delta \in PI_\Sigma^{X \cup Z}(\Gamma) \setminus PI^{X \cup Z}(\neg \Sigma)$ s.t. $\delta \supseteq \omega_X$ and $\delta \supseteq \omega_Z$.

As already said, a practical application area of controllability is decision under incomplete knowledge and partial observability: $\mathcal{P} = \langle X, Z, \Sigma, \Gamma \rangle$ can be seen as a logical specification of a qualitative, single-step decision problem with incomplete knowledge and partial observability. The set of possible observations is $PossObs(\mathcal{P}) = \{\omega_Z \in \Omega_Z \mid \omega_Z \wedge \Sigma \text{ is consistent}\}$ and a *sound policy* for $\mathcal{P}$ is a mapping π from $PossObs(\mathcal{P})$ to Ω_X such that $\forall \omega_Z \in PossObs(\mathcal{P})$, (i) $\omega_Z \wedge \pi(\omega_Z) \wedge \Sigma$ is consistent, and (ii) $\omega_Z \wedge \pi(\omega_Z) \wedge \Sigma \models \Gamma$. Clearly, X positively controls Γ given Z w.r.t. Σ iff there exists a sound policy for $\mathcal{P}$.

We turn now to complexity issues. We first give a straightforward result which avoids studying separately positive and full controllability.

Proposition 2
$X \ll_\Sigma^Z \Gamma^+$ iff $X \cup \{new\} \ll_\Sigma^Z \Gamma \wedge new$, where $new \in PS \setminus (Var(\Sigma) \cup Var(\Gamma) \cup X \cup Z)$.

This reduction from full to positive controllability is clearly polynomial, and a polynomial reduction from positive to full controllability is a trivial consequence of the definitions. Thus, both notions are polynomially related. Consequently:

Corollary 1 (FULL) CONDITIONAL CONTROLLABILITY *and* POSITIVE CONDITIONAL CONTROLLABILITY *are in the same complexity classes.*

Since the reduction given by Proposition 2 preserves the restrictions that are considered in the following (i.e., $Z = \emptyset$ and $X \cup Z = Var(\Sigma)$), both problems remain in the same complexity classes for each of these restrictions. Accordingly, in the rest of the section, we will mainly focus on the complexity of full conditional controllability.

Proposition 3
CONDITIONAL CONTROLLABILITY *is* Π_3^p-*complete*

We are now going to investigate some particular restrictions of controllability, each of which corresponds to a particular type of decision problem. We start with *unconditional controllability*, obtained by letting $Z = \emptyset$.

Proposition 4
UNCONDITIONAL CONTROLLABILITY *is* Σ_2^p-*complete.*

Intuitively, unconditional controllability means that there is no observable variable – thus the action to be undertaken must be taken unconditionally, which corresponds to non-observability. Interestingly, UNCONDITIONAL POSITIVE CONTROLLABILITY can be abductively characterized; indeed, $X \ll_\Sigma^\emptyset \Gamma^+$ holds iff there exists an abductive explanation for Γ given Σ, where the set of possible individual hypotheses is the set of literals built up from X. Accordingly, the Σ_2^p-completeness of UNCONDITIONAL POSITIVE CONTROLLABILITY is recovered as a consequence of Theorem 4.2 from (Eiter & Gottlob 1995). Thanks to such an abductive characterization, the complexity of many restricted subcases of UNCONDITIONAL POSITIVE CONTROLLABILITY can be easily derived from (Eiter & Gottlob 1995).

Another particular case is obtained by letting $X \cup Z = Var(\Sigma)$. We call the corresponding problem *ceteris paribus* controllability.

Proposition 5
CETERIS PARIBUS CONTROLLABILITY *is* Π_2^p-*complete.*

Propositions 4 and 5 are similar to some complexity results in (Fargier, Lang, & Schiex 1996) for mixed constraint satisfaction. Intuitively, *ceteris paribus* conditional controllability means that all variables are either controllable or observable (full observability). *Ceteris paribus* controllability has been first proposed by Boutilier (Boutilier 1994) for $\Sigma = \emptyset$. His appealing characterization of controllability (X controls Γ iff $PI^X(\Gamma) \neq \emptyset$ and any $\delta \in PI(\Gamma)$ mentions a variable of X) is equivalent to ours when $\Sigma = \emptyset$, using the fact that Γ is equivalent to the disjunction of all its (standard) prime implicants. Despite the additional restriction $\Sigma = \emptyset$, the complexity of checking this form of *ceteris paribus* controllability does not fall down.

Proposition 6
Boutilier's controllability is Π_2^p-*complete.*

Definability

Definitions and characterizations

Definability is a stronger form of dependence than controllability: while the latter states that there is a way to fix a variable y to the desired truth value, definability imposes that for every X–world, the truth value of y is determined. The computational complexity of definability has been investigated in a companion paper (Lang & Marquis 1998); herefater, the focus is mainly led on the practical computing of definability. We start by a series of definitions concerning *definability* and later on we give a closely related definition, *hypothesis discriminability*.

Definition 2 (definability) *(Lang & Marquis 1998)*
Let $\Sigma \in PROP_{PS}$, $X \subseteq PS$ and $y \in PS$.

- X **defines** y *w.r.t.* Σ *(denoted by $X \sqsubseteq_\Sigma y$) iff* $\forall \omega_X \in \Omega_X, \omega_X \wedge \Sigma \models y$ or $\omega_X \wedge \Sigma \models \neg y$.

- X **defines minimally** y *w.r.t.* Σ *iff* $X \sqsubseteq_\Sigma y$ *and no proper subset of X does it.*

- X **defines nontrivially** y *w.r.t.* Σ *iff* $X \sqsubseteq_\Sigma y$ *and Σ is consistent.*

- X *is a* **basis** *for y w.r.t.* Σ *iff* X *defines minimally and nontrivially y w.r.t.* Σ.

While every X–world that is not consistent with Σ can be considered impossible, requiring $\omega_X \wedge \Sigma$ to be consistent in the definition above would be useless since $\omega_X \wedge \Sigma \models y$ and $\omega_X \wedge \Sigma \models \neg y$ hold whenever $\omega_X \wedge \Sigma$ is inconsistent. When no X-world consistent with Σ can be found, Σ is inconsistent. In this case, definability trivializes, i.e., $X \sqsubseteq_\Sigma y$ holds for every X and every y, and no basis for y can be pointed out.

Clearly enough, the four definability relations given above can be easily extended to sets Y of variables by $X \sqsubseteq_\Sigma Y$ iff $X \sqsubseteq_\Sigma y$ for every $y \in Y$, as well as to formulas Γ (replacing y by Γ in the definitions above, see (Lang & Marquis 1998) for details).

As an illustration, let us step back to our example (Fig. 1). We have $\{a,b\} \sqsubseteq_\Sigma x$, $\{b,c\} \sqsubseteq_\Sigma y$, $\{a,b,c\} \sqsubseteq_\Sigma \{x,y,z\}$; note that $\{a,b,c\}$ defines minimally z and also $\{x,y\}$ w.r.t. Σ but *not* x nor y. Here is the list of all bases for y w.r.t. Σ: $\{y\}$, $\{b,c\}$, $\{x,z\}$ and $\{a,b,z\}$; for z we get the following bases: $\{z\}$, $\{a,b,c\}$, $\{x,y\}$, $\{a,b,y\}$, $\{x,b,c\}$ and $\{a,c,y\}$.

There is a clear link between (full) unconditional controllability and definability, which states that except in "pathological" cases, definability is stronger than unconditional controllability; indeed, $X \sqsubseteq_\Sigma y$ implies ($X \ll_\Sigma^\emptyset y$ or $\Sigma \models y$ or $\Sigma \models \neg y$). Furthermore, it is easily shown that if X defines *minimally* y w.r.t Σ, then X and y are marginally dependent in the sense of (Darwiche 1997) and that for any x

in X then $\{x\}$ is relevant to $\{y\}$ in the sense of (Lakemeyer 1997)[3].

While definability has been intensively studied in mathematical logic (see e.g., (Beth 1953)), propositional definability (and its computational complexity) has received much less attention in AI, up to now. Let us nevertheless mention that similar notions have been introduced in the recent literature on causal reasoning (Darwiche & Pearl 1994) (Geffner 1996b), and especially (Geffner 1996a) who proposes a framework for ramification which makes use of a causality principle

> the values that a variable may take (...) is a function of the values of its causes

that is very similar to our notion of definability[4]. Another closely related work is by Ibaraki et al. (Ibaraki, Kogan, & Makino 1998), where the focus is laid on functional dependencies for Horn knowledge bases (functional dependency is definability).

The fact that definability has not yet been fully investigated by the AI community is somewhat surprising since it proves helpful for many AI applications. For instance, when reasoning about change, a way to address the well-known *frame problem* consists in finding out fluents that can be derived from primitive ones (called a frame, or a defining family in our framework) within the knowledge base, and to apply change on reduced world descriptions (composed of primitive fluents) (Lifschitz 1990). Many formalisms for reasoning about change, adhere to this approach that has been implemented in various planning systems (e.g., in the early system BUILD (Fahlman 1974)). The notion of basis can also prove valuable in automated reasoning. For instance, identifying functionally dependent variables is a way to find out variable orderings that may prevent the Binary Decision Diagram (BDD) representation of a formula from an exponential size blowup (Hu & Dill 1993). More recently, (Kautz, McAllester, & Selman 1997) have shown how variable dependency can be exploited in local search for the satisfiability problem.

We now turn back to logical characterizations of definability. As a corollary of Beth's theorem (Beth 1953) (stated in the more general framework of first-order logic), we get the equivalence between the *implicit* form of definability given above and the following *explicit* form: X (explicitly) defines y w.r.t. Σ iff there is a formula Φ_y s.t. $Var(\Phi_y) \subseteq X$ and $\Sigma \models (\Phi_y \Leftrightarrow y)$; when it exists, Φ_y is clearly unique up to Σ–equivalence (i.e., every Φ'_y s.t. $\Sigma \wedge \Phi_y \equiv \Sigma \wedge \Phi'_y$ holds does the job).

For instance, considering our circuit example again, we know that $\{a, b, c\} \sqsubseteq_\Sigma z$; the corresponding formula Φ_z is Σ–equivalent to $(a \vee b) \Leftrightarrow (b \Leftrightarrow c)$.

---
[3] Similar results would hold with a notion of *minimal* controllability which is omitted for considerations of space.

[4] From a practical point of view, in the literature on causal reasoning, *searching* for bases is a priori useless – they are induced from the causal structure of the knowledge base.

Interestingly, whenever X defines nontrivially y, the explicit definition of y from X in Σ can be derived thanks to the following result, that makes use of the notion of *forgetting* introduced by Lin and Reiter (Lin & Reiter 1994). Let us recall that $forget(\Sigma, X)$ is defined inductively by: (i) $forget(\Sigma, \emptyset) = \Sigma$; (ii) $forget(\Sigma, \{x\}) = (\Sigma_{x \leftarrow 0} \vee \Sigma_{x \leftarrow 1})$; (iii) $forget(\Sigma, X \cup \{x\}) = forget(forget(\Sigma, X), \{x\})$.

Proposition 7
$X \sqsubseteq_\Sigma y$ iff $\Sigma \models (\Phi_y \Leftrightarrow y)$, where $\Phi_y \in PROP_X$ is defined by $\Phi_y \equiv forget(\Sigma, Var(\Sigma) \setminus (X \cup \{y\}))_{y \leftarrow 1}$.

The above result proves particularly helpful when Σ is given by its prime implicates. In this situation, $forget(\Sigma, Var(\Sigma) \setminus (X \cup \{y\}))$ can be computed efficiently by selecting from $IP(\Sigma)$ the prime implicates from $PROP_{X \cup \{y\}}$ (see Lemma 8 from (Lakemeyer 1995)). Once this formula has been computed, provided that Σ is consistent, the truth value of y can be computed in linear time as the truth value of $forget(\Sigma, Var(\Sigma) \setminus (X \cup \{y\}))_{y \leftarrow 1}$ for every $\omega_X \in \Omega_X$.

Definability can be characterized in several other ways. In (Lang & Marquis 1998), we show how checking definability comes down to a deduction check thanks to Padoa's method (Padoa 1903). Hereafter, we show how definability can also be characterized by means of prime implicants (where $\bigvee PI_\Sigma^X(y)$ denotes the disjunction of all prime implicants in $PI_\Sigma^X(y)$).

Proposition 8
$X \sqsubseteq_\Sigma y$ iff $\Sigma \models (\bigvee PI_\Sigma^X(y)) \vee (\bigvee PI_\Sigma^X(\neg y))$.

Of course, in the general case $PI_\Sigma^X(y)$ and $PI_\Sigma^X(\neg y)$ can be exponentially long. However, provided that these prime implicants have been computed off-line (and that Σ is consistent), the truth value of y can be computed in polynomial time for every X–world.

Computing bases

In this section, we propose an algorithm for computing bases. The following result shows that computing a basis (resp. the set of all bases) for sets Y of variables comes down to compute it (resp. them) for each variable individually.

Proposition 9 $X \sqsubseteq_\Sigma \{y_1, \ldots, y_p\}$ iff $\exists X_1, \ldots, X_p$ s.t. $X = X_1 \cup \ldots \cup X_p$ and $X_i \sqsubseteq_\Sigma y_i$ for every $i \in \{1, \ldots, p\}$.

As a corollary, $\text{Bases}(Y)$ denoting the set of all bases for Y w.r.t. Σ, $\text{Bases}(\{y_1, \ldots, y_p\})$ is the minimization w.r.t. set inclusion of $\{\cup_{i=1..p} B_i \mid B_i \in \text{Bases}(\{y_i\})\}$.

Thanks to Proposition 9, focusing on bases for individual variables is sufficient; this is the purpose of the algorithm below. Without any loss of generality, we assume that X is contained in a fixed set of "relevant" variables V^*. The utility of V^* is to focus on relevant bases, only; for instance, in a discriminability problem, V^* is the set of testable variables.

This is a greedy algorithm which considers all the variables of X in any order and throws them away when they are not necessary for forming a basis from the current set of relevant variables.

Proposition 10 *Provided that the function* Defines *returns true iff X defines y w.r.t. Σ, the algorithm returns a V^*-relevant basis for y w.r.t. Σ if there exists one, "failure" otherwise.*

There are several possible ways to implement the function Defines. In the case where the syntactic restrictions on Σ makes definability testable in polynomial time, the search for a V^*-relevant basis is itself polynomial because it consists in $|V^*|$ definability tests (plus one consistency test). In the general case, an approach to compute Defines that takes advantage of Proposition 8 consists in compiling Σ under the form of its prime implicants. Thus, the prime implicant lists $PI_\Sigma^{V^*}(y), PI_\Sigma^{V^*}(\neg y)$ and $PI^{V^*}(\neg \Sigma)$ (for identifying impossible V^*-worlds) are computed off-line. These lists are updated each time a variable is picked up (namely, prime implicants mentioning these variables are filtered out from the lists). Now, Defines makes use of this updated prime implicant lists and explores a search tree the leaves of which correspond to (partial or complete) instantiations over X, labelled by the corresponding value of y whenever possible. Not only this function checks whether X defines y but it also generates a "definition tree" for y from X.

```
Begin
If Σ is inconsistent
then return "failure";
X ← V*;
If not(Defines(X, y))
then return "failure"
else
    Z ← X;
    Repeat
        pick a x in Z;
        Z ← Z \ {x};
        if Defines(X \ {x}, y)
        then X ← X \ {x};
    Until Z = ∅;
    Return X;
End
```

Clearly enough, the worst case complexity of this algorithm is high. The contrary would be surprising, since the corresponding decision problem is hard:

Proposition 11 *(Lang & Marquis 1998)*
The results are synthesized in the following table[5]:

definability	standard	+ minimality
standard	coNP-complete	BH$_2$-complete
+ Σ consistent	BH$_2$-complete	BH$_2$-complete

Fortunately, some tractable restrictions exist. Especially, as a consequence of Propositions 33 and 34 from (Lang & Marquis 1998), our algorithm for computing a basis for y runs in time polynomial in the size of V^* plus the size of Σ whenever Σ is a set of binary clauses, or a renamable Horn formula or a DNF formula.

---

[5]BH$_2$ (also known as DP) is the class of all languages L such that $L = L_1 \cap L_2$, where L_1 is in NP and L_2 in coNP.

Hypothesis discriminability

We investigate now a notion, slightly generalizing definability, which has many practical applications ranging from fault isolation in diagnosis to decision under partial observability. Intuitively, given a set of hypotheses variables $H = \{h_1 \ldots h_n\}$, X discriminates H w.r.t. Σ if knowing the truth values of variables of X helps finding out *one of the h_i being true*. This statement may look strange – one may have preferred to read "finding out *which one of the h_i is true*". However, while for many problems hypotheses are mutually exclusive w.r.t. Σ ($\forall h_i \neq h_j, \Sigma \models \neg(h_i \wedge h_j)$) and covering all possible cases ($\Sigma \models h_1 \vee \ldots \vee h_n$), this is not always the case (see below).

Definition 3 *A* **discrimination problem** *consists in a consistent knowledge base Σ, $X \subseteq PS$ and a set of hypotheses variables $H = \{h_1, \ldots h_n\}$. X* **discriminates** *H w.r.t. Σ iff $\forall \omega_X \in \Omega_X \exists h \in H$ s.t. $\omega_X \wedge \Sigma \models h$. X* **discriminates minimally** *H w.r.t. Σ iff X discriminates H w.r.t. Σ and no proper subset of X does it.*

Clearly, each variable x of X corresponds to an available test, and performing this test consists in measuring the truth value of x.

There is a straightforward link between hypothesis discriminability and definability, in presence of exclusive and covering hypotheses. Indeed, in this restricted case, finding out a true variable h_i is exactly as hard as finding out the truth value of all the h_k's in H, since for any $k \neq i$ we have $\Sigma \wedge h_i \models \neg h_k$. Thus hypothesis discriminability is more general than definability. However, there is no complexity gap between both problems:

Proposition 12
HYPOTHESIS DISCRIMINABILITY *is* coNP-*complete.*

Thus, when dealing with mutually exclusive and covering hypotheses, defining families can be used to design minimal test inputs (Struss 1994) (McIlraith 1994) in order to isolate faulty components in model-based diagnosis (in this case hypotheses are candidate diagnoses, and testable variables correspond most often to available measurements). Note that McIlraith's notions of relevant or necessary tests (McIlraith 1994) have some counterparts in our framework (for instance, a necessary test corresponds to a variable without which the hypotheses space cannot be discriminated). Lastly, the algorithm for computing bases described above can be used to design conditional test policies (where tests are performed sequentially and conditioned by the outcomes of previous tests – see (Lang 1997)).

Another application of hypothesis discrimination is *decision making (and planning) under partial observability*. The logical formulation of a (one-stage) decision problem consists in a description of the initial state by a propositional formula, a fixed set $\mathcal{A}$ of available actions together with the descriptions of their (context-dependent) effects – for instance by a list of STRIPS-like expressions) and a set of goals (described for instance by a set of literals). These data enable computing, for each action a, the context h_a in which performing a certainly leads to a goal state. In order to find out a satisfying action, we need to discriminate between the h_a's, by observing enough of the initial state, knowing that some variables are measurable and some are not. This is a discrimination problem, and without the assumption that hypotheses are exclusive nor covering all possible situations; this is important because it is generally useless to find out the truth value of all the h_a's once any of them has been shown up true – which makes it different (and easier) than computing a defining family for $\{h_a, a \in \mathcal{A}\}$. Now, having in mind that both conditional controllability and hypothesis discrimination could be applied to qualitative decision under partial observability, one may wonder why the complexities do not coincide. Why the latter is much easier then the former relies on the fact that the "context" of each action is precomputed and part of the input, but also on the structure of the decision space: the set of possible decisions is 2^X (thus exponentially large) for the former while it is fixed (and thus has a constant size) for the latter.

Conclusion

In this paper, a variety of results for conditional controllability, definability, and closely related problems such as hypothesis discrimination, have been pointed out.

Regarding computational complexity, definability appears to be much easier than controllability. The high complexity of controllability is not surprising since decision under incomplete knowledge with succinct representations (such as logic) is hard. For instance, Fargier et al. (Fargier, Lang, & Schiex 1996) give two notions of consistency of a "mixed CSP" that are close to our notions of *ceteris paribus* and unconditional controllability, and show them (respectively) Π_2^p-complete and in Σ_2^p. Our results are also related (to some extent) to recent results about the complexity of probabilistic planning with succinct representations (Littman 1997); in particular, the latter problem is **PSPACE**-complete if the number of stages is polynomially bounded (and **EXPTIME**-complete otherwise); since our notions of controllability correspond more or less to "one-stage" planning under (qualitative) uncertainty, we can expect that the complexity of controllability would climb up in the polynomial hierarchy (up to **PSPACE**) if polynomially many stages were allowed.

It is clear that controllability and definability are two strong forms of dependence. We believe that relating them to various notions of relevance can be useful. The companion paper (Lang & Marquis 1998) is a first step in this direction.

Acknowledgements

We would like to thank Hélène Fargier for helpful discussions about controllability. The second author has been partly supported by the "IUT de Lens" and a "Contrat d'objectifs de la Région Nord/Pas-de-Calais".

References

Beth, E. 1953. On padoa's method in the theory of definition. *Indigationes mathematicae* 15:330–339.

Boutilier, C. 1994. Toward a logic for qualitative decision theory. In *Proc. KR'94*, 75–86.

Darwiche, A., and Pearl, J. 1994. Symbolic causal networks. In *Proc. AAAI'94*, 238–244.

Darwiche, A. 1997. A logical notion of conditional independence: properties and applications. *Artificial Intelligence* 97:45–82.

Eiter, T., and Gottlob, G. 1995. The complexity of logic-based abduction. *JACM* 42(1):3–42.

Fahlman, S. 1974. A planning system for robot construction tasks. *Artificial Intelligence* 5:1–49.

Fargier, H.; Lang, J.; and Schiex, T. 1996. Mixed constraint satisfaction: a framework for decision making under incomplete knowledge. In *Proc. AAAI'96*, 175–180.

Geffner, H. 1996a. Causality, constraints and the indirect effects of actions. In *Proc. AAAI'97*, 208–222.

Geffner, H. 1996b. A formal approach for causal modeling and argumentation. In *Proc. FAPR'96*, 208–222.

Hu, A., and Dill, D. 1993. Reducing bdd size by exploiting functional dependencies. In *Proc. ACM/IEEE DAC'93*, 266–271.

Ibaraki, T.; Kogan, A.; and Makino, K. 1998. Functional dependencies in horn theories. In *Proc. AI&Math'98*.

Kautz, H.; McAllester, D.; and Selman, B. 1997. Exploiting variable dependency in local search (abstract). In *Proc. IJCAI'97 (poster session)*, 57.

Lakemeyer, G. 1995. A logical account of relevance. In *Proc. IJCAI'95*, 853–859.

Lakemeyer, G. 1997. Relevance from an epistemic point of view. *Artificial Intelligence* 97:137–167.

Lang, J., and Marquis, P. 1998. Complexity results for independence and definability in propositional logic. In *Proc. KR'98*. to appear.

Lang, J. 1997. Planning to discriminate diagnoses. In *Proc. DX'97*, 135–139.

Lifschitz, V. 1990. Frames in the space of situations (research note). *Artificial Intelligence* 46:365–376.

Lin, F., and Reiter, R. 1994. Forget it! In *Proc. AAAI Fall Symposium on Relevance*, 154–159.

Littman, M. 1997. Probabilistic planning: representation and complexity. In *Proc. AAAI'97*, 748–754.

McIlraith, S. 1994. Generating tests using abduction. In *Proc. KR'94*, 449–460.

Padoa, A. 1903. Essai d'une théorie algébrique des nombres entiers, précédé d'une introduction logique à une théorie déductive quelquonque. In *Bibliothèque du Congrès International de Philosophie*, 309–365.

Papadimitriou, C. H. 1994. *Computational complexity*. Addison-Wesley.

Poole, D. 1997. The independent choice logic for modelling multiple agents under uncertainty. *Artificial Intelligence* 94(1):7–56.

Struss, P. 1994. Testing for the discrimination of diagnoses. In *Proc. DX'94*, 312–320.

Anytime Approximate Modal Reasoning

Fabio Massacci
Dipartimento di Informatica e Sistemistica
Università di Roma "La Sapienza"
via Salaria 113, I-00198 Roma
email:massacci@dis.uniroma1.it

Abstract

Propositional modal logics have two independent sources of complexity: unbounded logical omniscience and unbounded logical introspection. This paper discusses an approximation method to tame both of them, by merging propositional approximations with a new technique tailored for multi-modal logics. It provides both skeptical and credulous approximations (or approximation that are neither of the two).

On this semantics we build an anytime proof procedure with a simple modification to classical modal tableaux. The procedure yields approximate proofs whose precision increases as we have more resources (time, space etc.) and we analyze its semantical and computational "quality guarantees". [*]

Introduction

The study of tractability of logical inference has received a major attention in AI. For propositional logic the obstacle to tractability is *unbounded logical omniscience*: given a knowledge base we can always derive all its logical consequences. Modal logics have another source of intractability, *unbounded logical introspection*: we can reason about our beliefs about somebody's belief about...

Logical omniscience has received most attentions and, as noted out in (Fagin, Halpern, & Vardi 1995), it has been tamed essentially by weakening the "omniscience" or by weakening the "logical".

The first approach is based on *inference procedures which are tractable but incomplete* such as unit resolution (del Val 1994) or boolean constraint propagation (Dalal 1996a). We can also restrict inferences to a subset of formulae as in (Dalal & Etherington 1992). In this way we have a complete procedure for a subset of the language and a sound but incomplete (yet tractable) system for the whole language.

Completeness for the whole language can be recovered by lemmaizing off-line (*knowledge compilation*) or on-line (*analytic cut*). We compute all answers of the tractable inference mechanism and store them for future retrieval.

The technique of (Selman & Kautz 1996) only included Horn lemmas and was complete only for horn relaxations of the original problem. New systems use general clauses as lemmas (del Val 1994; Dalal 1996a). Then we can start an incremental knowledge compilation by imposing incremental bounds on the size of the clauses used as lemmas and construct an anytime reasoning procedure following (Dean & Boddy 1988; Russel & Zilberstein 1991). Since the number of lemmas grows exponentially, the result may be a blow-up of the knowledge base (Selman & Kautz 1996).

An incremental construction can also be done by lemmaizing on-line (Crawford & Kuipers 1989; Dalal 1996a) i.e. by using cut (also called "Socratic completeness").

The dual approach is weakening the "logical" and keeping the "omniscience" in a logic weaker than classical logic. Typically one uses a variant of Belnap's four valued logic as done by Levesque (1984) and further studied, for example, in (Fagin, Halpern, & Vardi 1995; Lakemeyer 1994,1996; Schaerf & Cadoli 1995).

We can construct *incremental approximations* with the techniques of (Fagin & Halpern 1988) and (Schaerf & Cadoli 1995): we consider a subset of the propositional variables as interesting, i.e. deserving a classical interpretation, while the rest of propositions is given a three-valued interpretation. By increasing the set of interesting variables we can regain completeness in an incremental fashion. In (Schaerf & Cadoli 1995) we find sound & incomplete and complete & unsound reasoning while (Fagin & Halpern 1988) is limited to sound & incomplete reasoning.

We still have a problem of computational complexity since tractability results are restricted to special normal forms. In the general case, "approximate" logical consequence in classical logic corresponds to the "exact" logical consequence in relevance logic, which is CO-NP-complete (Fagin, Halpern, & Vardi 1995; Schaerf & Cadoli 1995).

Most works cited above use modal operators for explicit (tractable) beliefs and implicit (intractable) beliefs. Yet tractability results are usually restricted to sentences of the form $\mathbf{K}_a A \supset \mathbf{K}_b B$ where A and B are propositional formulae. When full introspection is allowed by Lakemeyer (1994,1996), it is only for modal logic K45 which is in NP (Halpern & Moses 1992). In a nutshell, the expressivity of modal operators is not used. It is not a case that the problem of unbounded logical introspection is hardly mentioned.

The development of tractable inference systems for $\mathcal{ALC}$ (a variant of modal logic K) has been done by (Patel-Schneider 1989) where a four-valued semantics is adopted for tractability. The study of incremental approximations has been made in (Schaerf & Cadoli 1995) where approxi-

---
[*]Copyright 1998, American Association for Artificial Intelligence (www.aaai.org). All rights reserved.

mation is essentially an incremental rewriting procedure.

In the rest of the paper, we present the intuitions behind our proposal and recall some preliminaries. Then we develop an approximation for the propositional part of the reasoning, an approximation for the modal part and combine the two. Finally we show how to transform a traditional tableau calculus due to Fitting (1983) into an anytime deduction procedures for which we discuss the semantical and computational quality of the approximation.

Semantical Intuitions

The main intuition behind our approximate semantics stems from the observation, following (Russel & Zilberstein 1991), that the difficulty behind unbounded logical omniscience and introspection is not the "logical", nor the "omniscience" nor the "introspection" but the "unbounded".

This difficulty is caused by the egalitarian attitude of classical modal logic: all propositional atoms are equal, all possible worlds are equal. So, we must consider a potentially exponential number of propositional assignments (unbounded logical omniscience) for a potentially exponential number of worlds (unbounded logical introspection).

Therefore, logical inference has an "all-or-nothing" behavior: either we have considered (implicitly or explicitly) all worlds and all propositions and then we can answer "A is a theorem" or we don't know what to say.

The idea behind *anytime reasoning* is that it should be possible to interrupt our reasoning process at any time and get *approximate answers* whose quality improves with time and which eventually converge to the exact answer. For instance, suppose that the exact computation requires time 2^{cn} in the worst case. An anytime reasoner gives a first approximate answer in time 2^{c1} and then improves the the answer in time 2^{c2} and so on until the exact answer is obtained or the process is interrupted. In the worst case n steps are required for completion (although we may be luckier). Anyhow, if we interrupt the process at time t we obtain the approximate answer provided at the kth checkpoint such that $2^{ck} \le t < 2^{c(k+1)}$. See (Dean & Boddy 1988; Russel & Zilberstein 1991) for further details.

What is difficult to grasp is the meaning of approximate answer for logical inference: what is an approximate proof or an approximate counter model?

Consider the propositional case; suppose that we have coded a planning problem in propositional logic (Kautz & Selman 1992) and that we are looking for a plan (a model for the KB). To approximate logical omniscience, we start by considering just few atoms as describing *interesting* properties and therefore deserving a classical interpretation. Other variables stand for *unknown* properties and so are the formula composed with them. They don't specify properties of "interesting models". Other atoms corresponds to *incoherent* properties and do not contribute to "interesting proofs".

When we start the search for an approximate model, we process interesting formulae as usual. Each time we find an unknown formula we conclude the branch of the search with failure: at this level of approximation, interesting models (plans) do not require to give truth values to unknown propositions. When we meet incoherent formulae we simply ignore them, we assume that we can fix them later. Thus we do not consider incoherent formulae in the (approximate) proof that a plan does not exist; only contradictions between interesting formulae matter.

From the viewpoint of inference, the presence of incoherent propositions leads to more models (we assume these formulae are approximately satisfied) and thus fewer proofs than classical logic (sound approximations). Unknown formulae yield fewer models (these formulae cannot be approximately satisfied) and thus more proofs (complete approximation). By suitably combining interesting, unknown and incoherent propositions we can reconstruct the tractable cases of (Levesque 1984; Schaerf & Cadoli 1995; Fagin, Halpern, & Vardi 1995) and many more.

This technique is not sufficient for modal logics because of the (possibly exponential) number of possible worlds. The key observation is that interesting worlds should not be "too remote" from the real world i.e. they should be reachable with few introspection steps. We curtail the "unbounded" logical introspection by imposing that "too many" steps of introspection always lead outside interesting worlds.

Again, we divide worlds into three sets: incoherent, unknown and interesting worlds. In incoherent worlds we enforce any kind of statement, including contradictory statements, while at unknown worlds we do not enforce any statement whatsoever.

So we can define the notion of k-skeptical and k-credulous agents: a k-skeptical agent is logical omniscient and able of introspective reasoning but only up to k levels of introspection. Afterwards, she will give up and assume that an incoherent world is reached. The dual attitude will be taken by a credulous agent.

Note that the notion of incoherent and unknown worlds is substantially different from the notion of "impossible" world used in the literature (Levesque 1990). The notion of impossible world refers to "inaccessible" worlds, i.e. worlds which are not reachable via the accessibility relation $\mathcal{R}_a$. Our notion is closer to the "non-normal" worlds introduced by Kripke (see (Fitting 1983)) and the "incoherent" and "incomplete" worlds of (Fagin, Halpern, & Vardi 1995)[page 212], although our use and formalization is different.

We have defined two independent approximations: one for the propositional part of the logic and an approximation for the modal part. These approximations can be combined in many ways. For example, we known that incoherent formulae are approximately satisfied in interesting worlds and interesting formulae never hold in unknown worlds. So what happens to incoherent formulae in unknown worlds?

One choice is to make the propositional part predominant: incoherent proposition always hold in a world, no matter which world. The opposite choice gives more importance to worlds: unknown worlds never satisfies a formula, no matter which formula. In the latter case the propositional approximation is a secondary approximation and the modal one is a primary approximation. This is our choice, mainly because it makes computations simpler.

We are only left with the last step: an anytime algorithm.

We decided to pick a traditional system off-the-shelves and transform it into an anytime procedure based on our semantics. The idea is to use a refutation procedure and change the termination conditions: devise complete approximations by accepting more (unknown) formulae as approximately contradictory, devise sound approximation by accepting more (incoherent) formulae as approximately satisfiable.

Preliminaries on Modal Logics

An introduction can be found in (Fitting 1983; Halpern & Moses 1992). We construct *modal formulae* A, B from atomic propositions $p \in \mathcal{P}$ and agent names $a \in \mathcal{A}$:

$$A, B ::= p \mid \neg A \mid A \wedge B \mid \mathbf{K}_a A$$

We use signed formulae so that the α, β, π, ν notation of Fitting (1983) can be used for other connectives. A *signed formula* φ, ψ is a pair $\mathbf{t}.A$ or $\mathbf{f}.A$. The intuitive interpretation is that A is respectively true and false.

The semantics is based on *Kripke models* i.e. triples $\langle W, \{\mathcal{R}_a\}_{a \in \mathcal{A}}, \mathcal{I} \rangle$ where W is a non empty set, whose elements are called *worlds*, $\{\mathcal{R}_a\}_{a \in \mathcal{A}}$ is a family of binary *accessibility relations* over W, and $()^\mathcal{I}$ is function, called *valuation* from propositional letter to subset of worlds. Intuitively the worlds in $(p)^\mathcal{I} \subseteq W$ are those where p is true.

Let $\mathcal{M}$ be a model, w a world in $\mathcal{M}$, and φ a signed formula, the forcing relation $w \Vdash \varphi$ is defined below:

$w \Vdash \mathbf{t}.p$	if	$w \in (p)^\mathcal{I}$
$w \Vdash \mathbf{t}.\neg A$	if	$w \Vdash \mathbf{f}.A$
$w \Vdash \mathbf{t}.A \wedge B$	if	$w \Vdash \mathbf{t}.A$ and $w \Vdash \mathbf{t}.B$
$w \Vdash \mathbf{t}.\mathbf{K}_a A$	if	$\forall v \in W : w\mathcal{R}_a v$ implies $v \Vdash \mathbf{t}.A$
$w \Vdash \mathbf{f}.p$	if	$w \notin (p)^\mathcal{I}$
$w \Vdash \mathbf{f}.\neg A$	if	$w \Vdash \mathbf{t}.A$
$w \Vdash \mathbf{f}.A \wedge B$	if	$w \Vdash \mathbf{f}.A$ or $w \Vdash \mathbf{f}.B$
$w \Vdash \mathbf{f}.\mathbf{K}_a A$	if	$\exists v \in W : w\mathcal{R}_a v$ and $v \Vdash \mathbf{f}.A$

When $w \Vdash \varphi$ holds we say that *"w satisfies φ in $\mathcal{M}$"*. We say that $\langle W, \{\mathcal{R}_a\}_{a \in \mathcal{A}}, \mathcal{I} \rangle$ is *model* for A iff every world in W satisfies $\mathbf{t}.A$; it is a *counter model* for A if there is world $w \in W$ which satisfies $\mathbf{f}.A$.

Our definition of logical consequence is a modal extension of the propositional definition in (Dalal 1996b).

Definition 1 *A formula A is a* logical consequence *of KB (in symbols $KB \models A$) iff every model for KB is not a counter model for A. If $\emptyset \models A$ we say that A is* valid.

Just Propositional Approximation

For the propositional approximation assume an *approximate partition* (for short ap) of the set of propositional atoms $\mathcal{P}$ into three sets: *unknown* propositions $unk(\mathcal{P})$, *interesting* propositions $int(\mathcal{P})$, and *incoherent* propositions $inc(\mathcal{P})$.

We only change the forcing relation $\Vdash$ for propositions:

$w \Vdash \mathbf{t}.p$	if	$p \in inc(\mathcal{P})$
	elseif	$p \in int(\mathcal{P})$ & $w \in (p)^\mathcal{I}$
$w \Vdash \mathbf{f}.p$	if	$p \in inc(\mathcal{P})$
	elseif	$p \in int(\mathcal{P})$ & $w \notin (p)^\mathcal{I}$

The corresponding logical consequence is $\models^{ap}$.

Combined with our key definition of logical consequence, this is enough to limit logical omniscience to interesting formulae. We can use incoherent formulae for sound but incomplete (i.e. skeptical) reasoning and unknown formulae for complete but unsound (i.e. credulous) reasoning.

For instance with incoherent concepts we may be incomplete: if $q \in int(\mathcal{P})$ and $p \in inc(\mathcal{P})$ we have

$$\not\models^{ap} \mathbf{K}_a(p \supset q) \wedge \mathbf{K}_a p \supset \mathbf{K}_a q \ .$$

With unknown concepts we may draw unsound conclusions. If $q \in int(\mathcal{P})$ and $p \in unk(\mathcal{P})$ then

$$\models^{ap} \mathbf{K}_a(p \vee q) \supset \mathbf{K}_a q \ .$$

What is interesting is the presence of formulae which mixes interesting, unknown, and incoherent propositions. It turns out that we can evaluate the overall nature of a formula in polynomial time (see the section on tableaux).

Just Modal Approximation

For the modal approximation we partition the worlds of a Kripke model into interesting worlds $int(W)$, incoherent worlds $inc(W)$, and unknown worlds $unk(W)$.

At first there is a constraint on the accessibility relation: *from an incoherent (unknown) world we only access incoherent (unknown) worlds*. Formally, $w\mathcal{R}_a v$ and $w \in inc(W)$ implies that $v \in inc(W)$. Dually $w\mathcal{R}_a v$ and $w \in unk(W)$ implies $v \in unk(W)$.

The next step is a revision of the forcing relation for propositional atoms (the rest is unchanged):

$w \Vdash \mathbf{t}.p$	if	$w \in inc(W)$
	elseif	$w \in int(W)$ & $w \in (p)^\mathcal{I}$
$w \Vdash \mathbf{f}.p$	if	$w \in inc(W)$
	elseif	$w \in int(W)$ & $w \notin (p)^\mathcal{I}$

Now, we can prove that if one only see incoherent worlds then everything is believed (the world satisfies $\mathbf{t}.\mathbf{K}_a A$ for all A) and everything unbelieved(the world also satisfies $\mathbf{f}.\mathbf{K}_a A$). If all worlds nearby are unknown then nothing is believed and nothing is unbelieved.

To approximate the introspection capabilities of an agent, we consider first the single agent case.

A *bounded agent* as a triple $\langle a, k_a, type \rangle$ where k_a is an integer and $type$ is either c (for credulous) or s (for skeptical). We say that agent a is k_a-*skeptical* in the former case and k_a-*credulous* in the latter.

A simple method for bounding introspection is to say that if a is k_a-skeptical (credulous) then every simple $\mathcal{R}_a$ path with more than $k_a + 1$ worlds terminates into an incoherent (unknown) world. Unfortunately, this definition is too strong: as in (Fagin, Halpern, & Vardi 1995), skeptical agents would believe too few valid formulae and credulous agents would believe too many invalid formulae because we have only specified the "maximal" distance between the "real world" and incoherent or unknown worlds. Without a minimal distance, the "real" world may be too close to uninteresting worlds.

To avoid this problem we introduce *realistic worlds*:

Definition 2 *Let $\langle a, k_a, type \rangle$ be a bounded agent and $\langle W, \{\mathcal{R}_a\}_{a \in \mathcal{A}}, \mathcal{I} \rangle$ be an approximate model with a partition of worlds. A world $w \in W$ is k_a-realistic if it is an interesting world and if*

- $k_a = 0$ *and a is skeptical then $w\mathcal{R}_a v$ implies $v \in inc(W)$;*

- $k_a{=}0$ and a is credulous then $w\mathcal{R}_a v$ implies $v{\in}unk(W)$;
- $k_a > 1$ then $w\mathcal{R}_a v$ implies that v is $k_a - 1$-realistic.

So, in the definition of forcing for π formulae

$$w \Vdash \mathbf{f}.\mathbf{K}_a A \text{ iff } \exists v \in W : w\mathcal{R}_a v \ \& \ v \Vdash \mathbf{f}.A \quad (1)$$

if w is a k_a-realistic world then v is a $k_a - 1$-realistic world. Each time we satisfy a false belief $\mathbf{f}.\mathbf{K}_a A$ we get closer to unknown and incoherent worlds.

We upgrade the notion of counter model: given a bounded agent $\langle a, k_a, type\rangle$, a model $\langle W, \{\mathcal{R}_a\}_{a\in\mathcal{A}}, \mathcal{I}\rangle$ is an *approximate counter model* for A if there is a k_a-realistic world $w \in W$ which satisfies $\mathbf{f}.A$. The rest is unaltered and we denote the corresponding logical consequence as $\models^{k_a-type}$.

Some examples can be helpful to clarify the semantics. For 1-skeptical agents plain logical omniscience holds:

$$\models^{1-s} \mathbf{K}_a(p \supset q) \wedge \mathbf{K}_a p \supset \mathbf{K}_a q \quad (2)$$

although unbounded logical omniscience may not hold:
$$\not\models^{1-s} \mathbf{K}_a(\mathbf{K}_a(p \supset q) \wedge \mathbf{K}_a p) \supset \mathbf{K}_a \mathbf{K}_a q$$

The situation is reversed for 1-credulous agents: (2) holds but unsound formulae may become approximately valid.
$$\models^{1-c}_L \mathbf{K}_a(\mathbf{K}_a p \vee \mathbf{K}_a q) \supset \mathbf{K}_a \mathbf{K}_a q$$

Still, 1-credulous agents remain sound if the reasoning does not require introspection over 1 level of modal nesting:
$$\not\models^{1-c}_L (\mathbf{K}_a \mathbf{K}_a p \vee \mathbf{K}_a q) \supset \mathbf{K}_a q$$

With many agents around reasoning may remain hard. Using the same techniques of (Halpern & Moses 1992) we can prove that *deciding approximate validity remains* PSPACE-*hard if we only bound self-introspection*. The trick is to use $\mathbf{K}_a\mathbf{K}_b A$ formulae to reason about mutual beliefs.

For bounding mutual introspection, we introduce the notion of *family of bounded agents* as the set $\mathcal{F} = \{\langle a, k_a, type_a\rangle\}_{a\in\mathcal{A}}$. We assume that there is only one triple in $\mathcal{F}$ for every agent a and we say that agent a is k_a-skeptical if $\langle a, k_a, s\rangle \in \mathcal{F}$ and it is k_a-credulous if $\langle a, k_a, c\rangle \in \mathcal{F}$.

Definition 3 *Let $\mathcal{F}$ be a family of bounded agents and $\langle W, \{\mathcal{R}_a\}_{a\in\mathcal{A}}, \mathcal{I}\rangle$ be an approximate model with a partition of worlds. A world $w \in W$ is $\mathcal{F}$-realistic if it is an interesting world and for every agent a in the family*

- $k_a = 0$ and a is skeptical then $w\mathcal{R}_a v$ implies $v{\in}inc(W)$;
- $k_a{=}0$ and a is credulous then $w\mathcal{R}_a v$ implies $v{\in}unk(W)$;
- if $k_a > 0$ then $w\mathcal{R}_a v$ implies that v is $\mathcal{F}/a$-realistic.

where the family $\mathcal{F}/a$ is obtained by $\mathcal{F}$ by setting for all agents *the bound to $k_a - 1$ and the type to $type_a$.*

Hence, in (1) we converge towards incoherent or unknown worlds no matter the path we follow. This definition has a intuitive motivation: when passing from w to v we are performing an introspection step for the agent a. Loosely speaking it is a who is now reasoning about the beliefs of other agents in his own head. If a is skeptical so he will reason skeptically when reasoning about other agents.

We can prove that if A has counter model for KB then it has a counter model with at most $2^{k_m} + 3$ worlds where k_m is the maximum bound for every agent in family $\mathcal{F}$.

Combined Approximation

We choose the modal approximation as the primary approximation. This requires a revision of the forcing relation:

$w \Vdash \mathbf{t}.p$ if $w\in inc(W)$
 elseif $w \in int(W) \ \& \ p \in inc(\mathcal{P})$
 elseif $w \in int(W) \ \& \ p \in int(\mathcal{P}) \ \& \ w \in (p)^\mathcal{I}$

$w \Vdash \mathbf{f}.p$ if $w \in inc(W)$
 elseif $w \in int(W) \ \& \ p \in inc(\mathcal{P})$
 elseif $w \in int(W) \ \& \ p \in int(\mathcal{P}) \ \& \ w \notin (p)^\mathcal{I}$

Approximate Tableaux

We use *prefixed tableaux* by Fitting (1983) and present only the aspects we need for the anytime reasoner.

The basic component is a prefixed signed formula $\sigma : \varphi$ where σ is an alternating sequence of integers and agent names called *prefix* and defined as $\sigma ::= 1 \mid \sigma.a.n$.

The basic intuition is that σ is a "name" for a world where φ is satisfied. The key advantage for this representation is that the name explicitly codes the introspection steps from the "real" world denoted by 1 to the world σ.

The rest of the machinery is pretty standard: a *tableau* for proving that A is a logical consequence of KB is a tree where the root is labelled by $1 : \mathbf{f}.A$ and where nodes are added and labelled by prefixed signed formulae according tableau rules (Fitting 1983). A *branch* $\mathcal{B}$ is a path from the root to the leaf. Intuitively, each branch is a tentative model and the tableau construction is an attempt to construct a counter model for A. If we fail (because we find a contradiction in each branch) then A is a logical consequence; if we succeed (because we have reduced all formulae in a branch without finding contradictions) then we have the required counter model.

The simplest way to plug our approximation semantics onto this machinery is to change the rules that terminates the search by accepting branches which are only approximately contradictory or approximately reduced.

We need to lift the interesting, unknown and incoherent meaning that we have given to atoms and worlds to general prefixed formulae in a quick way.

So, we construct a *superficial valuation* of a formula, i.e. a function $\mathrm{V}(a, k, \varphi)$ with values in the set $\{inc, unk, int\}$. The first argument is the agent a for which the formula is evaluated, the second the current bound of introspection and the last is the signed formula. If the agent is not specified we use the wild card $*$.

For propositional letters we have

$$\begin{array}{l}\mathrm{V}(\_,\_,\mathbf{t}.p) \\ \mathrm{V}(\_,\_,\mathbf{f}.p)\end{array} = \left\{\begin{array}{ll} int & \text{if } \in int(\mathcal{P}) \\ unk & \text{if } p \in unk(\mathcal{P}) \\ inc & \text{if } p \in inc(\mathcal{P})\end{array}\right.$$

We use $\_$ as a don't care condition.

The function is defined inductively on the propositional and modal connectives. For negation we have that $\mathrm{V}(a, k, \mathbf{t}.\neg A) = \mathrm{V}(a, k, \mathbf{f}.A)$ and similarly for $\mathbf{f}.\neg A$. The other cases are shown in Table 1 and Fig. 1. We use the variable X to represent the table in compact form so in the third line of the $\mathbf{t}.A \wedge B$-table we have that if $\mathrm{V}(\_,\_,\mathbf{t}.B) = X$ then $\mathrm{V}(\_,\_,\mathbf{t}.A \wedge B) = X$.

t.A	t.B	t.A∧B	f.A	f.B	f.A∧B
unk	X	unk	unk	X	X
X	unk	unk	inc	X	inc
inc	X	X	X	inc	inc
int	int	int	int	int	int

Table 1: Superficial Valuation

$$V(a, 0, \text{f.}\mathbf{K}_a A) = \begin{cases} inc & \text{if } a \text{ is skeptical} \\ unk & \text{if } a \text{ is credulous} \end{cases}$$

$$V(a, k+1, \text{f.}\mathbf{K}_a A) = V(a, k, \text{f.}A)$$

$$V(a, 0, \text{t.}\mathbf{K}_a A) = \begin{cases} inc & \text{if } a \text{ is skeptical} \\ int & \text{if } a \text{ is credulous} \end{cases}$$

$$V(a, k+1, \text{t.}\mathbf{K}_a A) = \begin{cases} inc & \text{if } V(a, k, \text{t.}A) = inc \\ int & \text{otherwise} \end{cases}$$

Figure 1: Meaning of Formulae for Bounded Agents

The intuition behind the superficial evaluation is simple. Consider negation: if a formula is interesting, then also its negation is interesting. On the other case if a formula represents a unknown concept also its negation is an unknown concept. In the case of disjunction, if one disjunct of a formula is unknown then the overall status of the formula will be given by the remaining disjunct.

If the bound or the agent is not yet specified, we use the wild card $*$ as a symbol and the equations below, where $\langle a, k_a, type \rangle \in \mathcal{F}$:

$$V(*, *, \text{f.}\mathbf{K}_a A) = V(a, k_a, \text{f.}\mathbf{K}_a A)$$
$$V(*, *, \text{t.}\mathbf{K}_a A) = V(a, k_a, \text{t.}\mathbf{K}_a A)$$

We define the *first step of introspection* as $\text{first}(1) = *$ and $\text{first}(1.a_1.n_1.\ldots a_k.n_k) = a_1$ and say that σ *belongs to an agent* a whenever $\text{first}(\sigma) = a$. Intuitively, this means that a is the "main" agent responsible for the chain of introspective reasoning which lead to the world σ. The *length* of a prefix, denoted by $|\sigma|$ is the number of introspection steps, i.e. $|1| = 0$ and $|1.a_1.n_1.\ldots a_k.n_k| = k$.

Intuitively, each time we pass from σ to $\sigma.b.n$ we are performing an introspection step. So the length of σ tells how many introspection steps that we have already done. If σ belongs to an agent a with bound k_a then we are only left with $k_a - |\sigma|$ introspection steps.

Once $V()$ is defined we simply need to compute $V(\text{first}(\sigma), k_{\text{first}(\sigma)} - |\sigma|, \varphi)$ and reduce it only if it is interesting. Moreover we consider it classically contradictory with $\sigma : \overline{\varphi}$ only if both formulae are interesting. In all other cases an approximate decision (without search) is taken.

Formally we revise the definition of reduced formulae and contradictory branches from (Fitting 1983):

Definition 4 *Let $\mathcal{F}$ be a family of bounded agents and ap an approximate partition. The prefixed formula $\sigma : \varphi$ is approximately reduced iff*

- *it is interesting and reduced according the classical definition*
- *or $\sigma = 1$ and $V(*, *, \varphi) = inc$;*

Input The modal formulae KB and A, and a time limit
Output A tableau $\mathcal{T}_k$

1. **choose** an approximate partition so that the set of interesting variables $I_0 = int(\mathcal{P})$ is small (e.g. logarithmic in the size of KB and A);
2. **choose** a family of bounded agents $\mathcal{F}_0 = \{\langle a, k_a, type_a \rangle\}_{a \in \mathcal{A}}$ where k_a is a small constant, and decide whether $type_a$ is credulous or skeptical;
3. **compute** an approximate tableau $\mathcal{T}_k$;
4. **if** the approximate tableau $\mathcal{T}_k$ is a classical proof or a classical counter model **then** stop;
5. **else if** not timeout
   (a) **find** the part of $\mathcal{T}_k$ where non classical reduction or closure rules have been applied
   (b) **increase** the precision so that one approximately reduced or contradictory formula change status by
       - either enlarging the set of interesting variables from I_k to I_{k+1} generating a new partition ap_{k+1};
       - or increasing the bound k_a for an agent a in the family $\mathcal{F}_k$ generating a new family $\mathcal{F}_{k+1}$;
   (c) **return to** (3) for a new $\mathcal{T}_{k+1}$;

Figure 2: Anytime Deduction Algorithm

- *or σ belongs to a and $V(a, k_a - |\sigma|, \varphi) = inc$.*

Definition 5 *Let $\mathcal{F}$ be a family of bounded agents and ap an approximate partition. A branch $\mathcal{B}$ is approximately contradictory iff*

- *$\mathcal{B}$ is contradictory for interesting formulae according the classical definition,*
- *or $\sigma = 1$ and $V(*, *, \varphi) = unk$,*
- *or σ belongs to a and $V(a, k_a - |\sigma|, \varphi) = unk$.*

If all tableaux branches are contradictory according the classical definition we have a *classical proof*. In a similar way a branch yields a *classical countermodel* if it is not contradictory and fulfils the classical definition.

We have now the formal machinery to construct an approximating sequence of proofs of increasing precision with the anytime algorithm in Fig. 2.

If we time out after $\mathcal{T}_k$, we have available either an approximate proof (all branches of $\mathcal{T}_k$ are approximately closed) or an approximate counter model (an open branch of $\mathcal{T}_k$). With enough resources we can arrive at a stage where every agents in $\mathcal{F}_k$ has a bound k_a sufficiently large to guarantee that a classical proof (or counter model) is found.

For what regard the *semantical direction* of the approximation, we can increase the soundness of the procedure by increasing the bound of credulous agents or by decreasing the number of unknown proposition. Increasing the bound of skeptical agents or decreasing the number of incoherent proposition increase the completeness.

Quality of Approximation

Now we analize the quality of the approximation:

Theorem 1 (Approx. Soundness and Completeness)
Given an approximate partition and a family of bounded agents, the formula A is an approximate logical consequence of KB iff it has a approximate tableau proof.

The standard soundness proof would proceed by induction showing that if there is a contradictory branch then we can unwind the contradiction down to atomic level. The only difficulty is to rule out "contradictory" incoherent formulae.

For the completeness the hard part is construction of the model from a reduced but not contradictory branch. It is similar to the traditional construction (Fitting 1983) with two tweaks: use two extra worlds (one subsuming all unknown worlds and one for all incoherent worlds) and consider only interesting propositions for the valuation $()^{\mathcal{I}}$.

The next result shows that, given enough resources we are guaranteed to find the correct (classical) answer:

Theorem 2 (Convergence Guarantee) *For every A and KB there is a k_0 such that for all $k \geq k_0$, $\mathcal{T}_k$ is a classical tableau proof for A iff $KB \models A$.*

The last step is proving the anytime complexity guarantee. At first we note that the verification of $V(a, k, \varphi)$ takes polynomial time in the size of A and KB.

Without restrictions, we cannot guarantee that the timing of the computation of $\mathcal{T}_k$ and $\mathcal{T}_{k+1}$ respects the anytime guarantees from (Dean & Boddy 1988; Russel & Zilberstein 1991). We need the following assumptions:

- for generating ap_{k+1} and $\mathcal{F}_{k+1}$, apply a polynomial time algorithm to not interesting parts of $\mathcal{T}_k$;

- apply rules for constraint propagation (Massacci 1998) before other rules and apply rule for reducing $\mathbf{t}.A \wedge B$ formulae before other rules.

Then we can prove an *anytime guarantee* on the performance of the algorithm as follows: every branch has 2^{k_b} prefixes where k_b is the maximum bound of the family of bounded agents and for each prefix we can generate a number of branches which is exponential in the number of occurrences of interesting propositions.

This is not a good bound since occurrences of interesting formulae may be many. To improve the bound we consider *modal atoms* i.e. signed formulae $\mathbf{f}.A$ (or $\mathbf{t}.A$) where A where either $A = \mathbf{K}_a B$ or A is an atomic proposition.

If A is a modal atom such that both $\sigma : \mathbf{t}.A$ and $\sigma : \mathbf{f}.A$ are interesting, then we apply the cut rule to $\sigma : \mathbf{t}.A$ and $\sigma : \mathbf{f}.A$. Then, the systematic application of constraint propagation before other rules eliminate the atom from the branch. So an induction on the number of modal atoms provide the required anytime guarantee using the number (not the number of occurrences) of interesting modal atoms.

Conclusions

We have proposed an approximation technique for propositional modal logic which encompasses both propositional and modal aspects. The approximations makes it possible to tame unbounded logical omniscience and unbounded logical introspection both in the single and multi-agent case.

With this approximation it is possible to define skeptical (sound) approximations, credulous (complete) approximations and mixed approximations where some agents reason in a skeptical way and other agents in a credulous way.

We designed an anytime procedure which uses an *existing* deduction procedure (prefixed tableau) and we have discussed the "quality guarantees" of this approximate anytime deduction mechanism.

There are a number of open problems such as the extension to first order logic, the definition of a measure theory for the approximation, the developement of heuristics for the incremental selection of interesting propositions.

References

Crawford, J., & Kuipers, B. 1989. Towards a theory of access-limited logic for knowledge representation. In *Proc. of KR-89*, 67–78.

Dalal, M., & Etherington, D. 1992. Tractable approximate deduction using limited vocabularies. In *Proc. of the 9th Canadian Conf. on AI (AI-92)*, 206–221.

Dalal, M. 1996a. Anytime families of tractable propositional reasoners. In *Proc. of AI and Math. (AI/MATH-96)*, 42–45.

Dalal, M. 1996b. Semantics of an anytime family of reasoners. In *Proc. ECAI-96*, 360–364.

Dean, T., and Boddy, M. 1988. An analysis of time-dependent planning. In *Proc. AAAI-88*, 49–54.

del Val, A. 1994. Tractable databases: How to make propositional unit resolution complete through compilation. In *Proc. of KR-94*, 551–561.

Fagin, R., & Halpern, J. 1988. Belief, awareness, and limited reasoning. *AIJ* 34:39–76.

Fagin, R.; Halpern, J.; and Vardi, M. 1995. A nonstandard approach to the logical omniscience problem. *AIJ* 79:203–240.

Fitting, M. 1983. *Proof Methods for Modal and Intuitionistic Logics*. Reidel.

Halpern, J., and Moses, Y. 1992. A guide to completeness and complexity for modal logics of knowledge and belief. *AIJ* 54:319–379.

Kautz, H., & Selman, B. 1992. Planning as satisfiability. In *Proc. ECAI-92*, 359–363.

Lakemeyer, G. 1994, 1996. Limited reasoning in first-order knowledge bases. *AIJ* 71:1994 and *AIJ* 84:209–255, 1996.

Levesque, H. 1984. A logic of implicit and explicit belief. In *Proc. of AAAI-84*, 198–202.

Levesque, H. 1988. Logic and the complexity of reasoning. *J. of Philosophical Logic* 17:355–389.

Levesque, H. 1990. All I know, a study in autoepistemic logic. *AIJ* 42.

Massacci, F. 1998. Constraint propagation in propositional and modal tableaux. In *Proc. TABLEAUX-98*.

Patel-Schneider, P. 1989. A four-valued semantics for terminological logic. *AIJ* 38:319–351.

Russel, S., & Zilberstein, S. 1991. Composing real-time systems. In *Proc. IJCAI-91*, 212–217.

Schaerf, M., and Cadoli, M. 1995. Tractable reasoning via approximation. *AIJ* 74:1–62.

Selman, B., & Kautz, H. 1996. Knowlege compilation and theory approximation. *JACM* 43:193–224.

Algorithms for propositional KB approximation

Yacine Boufkhad

CRIL Université d'Artois
Rue de l'université SP-16 62307
Lens cedex 03 FRANCE
email: boufkhad@cril.univ-artois.fr

Abstract

One of the obstacles to the effective compilation of propositional knowledge bases (KBs) using Horn approximations, as introduced by (Selman & Kautz 1991), is the lack of computationally feasible methods for generating Horn bounds. In this paper new algorithms for generating Horn Greatest Lower Bounds (GLB) that can apply to large size KBs, are presented. The approach is extended through a more general target language: the renamable Horn class. The conditions under which a renamable Horn formula is a renamable Horn GLB of a KB are established and algorithms for computing it are derived. These algorithms can be used in the other approaches based on computation of Horn or renamable lower bounds as (Boufkhad et al. 1997). The efficiency of these algorithms and the tightness with respect to the KB in terms of number of models of the bounds, are experimentally evaluated. The renamable Horn GLB proves to be closer to the KB than the Horn GLB.

Introduction

Given a satisfiable Knowledge Base (in short; KB) Σ for which the propositional deduction is intractable, a knowledge compilation approach consists in transforming Σ into one or several tractable formulae so that the subsequent queries are answered efficiently from the tractable formulae. Many approaches to knowledge compilation have been proposed (Reiter & De Kleer 1987; Selman & Kautz 1991; del Val 1994; Dechter & Rish 1994; Marquis 1995). In particular, (Selman & Kautz 1991; 1996) have proposed to approximate a KB through a greatest lower bound (GLB), which is the weakest Horn theory that entails Σ, and a lowest upper bound (LUB) which is the strongest Horn theory entailed by Σ. Answering queries from a GLB of Σ (Σ_{glb}) and the LUB (Σ_{lub}) is done in this way: for a clause c, if $\Sigma_{glb} \not\models c$ then $\Sigma \not\models c$ and if $\Sigma_{lub} \models c$ then $\Sigma \models c$ otherwise, the answer is "don't know". The nice feature is that queries $\Sigma_{glb} \models^? c$ and $\Sigma_{lub} \models^? c$ can be answered in linear time since Σ_{glb} and Σ_{lub} are Horn (Dowling & Gallier 1984). The size, the quality and algorithms for generating LUB have been studied in (Cadoli 1993; del Val 1995; Selman & Kautz 1996). It has been shown that the size of the LUB is in general exponential w.r.t. the size of the KB. On the other hand, the size of a GLB is always smaller than the size of the original formula (Selman & Kautz 1996) and the complexity of the problem of generating a GLB is in P^{NP} (Cadoli 1993).

An other approach to compilation using tractable lower bounds is proposed in (Boufkhad et al. 1997). It consists in transforming a KB into an equivalent disjunction of tractable formulae. Each formula being a lower bound of the KB falling into a list of target tractable classes.

Although the compilation step is viewed as an off-line process for which time is not a critical parameter, finding comptationally feasible algorithms allowing large size KBs to be handled remains an important open issue. In this paper, new algorithms for generating Horn and renamable Horn GLBs are introduced. The basic algorithm for generating a Horn GLB is based on the Davis and Putnam procedure (Davis & Putnam 1960). When the KBs are too large for a systematic search to be considered, an incomplete method is used to preprocess the KB and make it easier for compilation. Using this method, Horn GLBs of large KBs can be actually computed.

As an even more important contribution, GLBs are then investigated within the more general class of renamable Horn. The conditions under which a renamable Horn formula is a renamable Horn GLB ($\mathcal{RH}$-GLB) of a KB Σ are established. Then an algorithm for generating a $\mathcal{RH}$-GLB is provided. Finally, the tightness of these bounds is explored experimentally with respect to the KB, in terms of the number of models. As can be expected from the generality of the renamable Horn class the $\mathcal{RH}$-GLB proves to be a tighter bound than the Horn GLB.

The above procedures can also be used to compute more efficiently the tractable covers of the KB as defined in

(Boufkhad *et al.* 1997).

In this paper, interpretations and models are represented by the sets of literals they satisfy. Implicants and prime implicants are defined in the usual way. The KB to be compiled is a set Σ of clauses (in CNF). The KB Σ is assumed to be satisfiable.

This paper[1] is organized in three sections. In the first one, a new algorithm for generating Horn GLB is introduced and some improvements w.r.t. the processing of large KBs described. The second section is concerned with the renamable Horn case and the third one presents the experimental evaluation of algorithms and the comparative evaluation of the quality of the two types of GLBs.

Generating Horn GLBs

The basic algorithm

Let us give some useful preliminary definitions. A clause is Horn iff it contains at most one positive literal. A set of clauses is Horn if every clause is Horn. A Horn GLB of a Knowledge base Σ is a Horn formula Σ_{glb} s.t. there is no other Horn formula H s.t. $\Sigma_{glb} \not\equiv H$ and $\Sigma_{glb} \models H \models \Sigma$.

First, Selman and Kautz's approach to compute Horn GLB is based on the *Horn strengthening* concept. A Horn strengthening of a clause C is a clause obtained by removing all but one positive literal of C. Example: the clause $\neg a \vee \neg b \vee c \vee d \vee e$. The Horn strengthenings of this clause are $\neg a \vee \neg b \vee c$, $\neg a \vee \neg b \vee d$ and $\neg a \vee \neg b \vee e$. A Horn strengthening of a set of clauses Σ is a set of Horn strengthenings of clauses of Σ. For every Horn GLB Σ_{glb} of Σ there exists a Horn strengthening H s.t. $H \equiv \Sigma_{glb}$ (Selman & Kautz 1996). The difficulty of finding a Horn GLB comes from the possibly large number of Horn strengthenings of a set of clauses.

To overcome this drawback, implicants of Σ will be used to strengthen Σ so that the search of a GLB of Σ collapses into the search of a GLB of this strengthened Σ. To this end, a concept of *I-Strengthening* is introduced, which itself is based on the Horn strengthening. For a partial interpretation I and a clause C satisfied by I, the I-Strengthening of C is defined as the clause obtained by removing from C every positive literal l s.t. $I \not\models C^H$ where C^H is the Horn strengthening of C containing l. The I-Strengthening of a set of clauses Σ entailed by I is the formula formed by the I-Strengthening of its clauses. Example: the same clause in the previous example is taken. For the partial interpretation $I = \{a, b, \neg d, c\}$ the I-strengthening of C is $\neg a \vee \neg b \vee c$ since I does not satisfy the second and the third Horn strengthening of C (see previous example). For $I' = \{\neg a, b, \neg d\}$ the I'-strengthening of C is C itself since I' satisfies every Horn strengthening of C.

---
[1] A long version of this paper, including proofs, is available.

Accordingly, any Horn GLB of Σ can be computed as a Horn GLB of the I-strengthening of Σ, provided that I is an implicant of Σ that entails this GLB. Indeed:

Proposition 1 *Let Σ be a set of clauses, I an implicant of Σ and Γ a Horn GLB of Σ. $I \models \Gamma$ iff Γ is a Horn GLB of the I-strengthening of Σ.*

The idea of the generation procedure of a Horn GLB consists in searching for implicants of Γ, after initializing Γ with Σ. Each time an implicant is found, Γ is replaced by its I-strenghtning. Consequently the remaining part of the search is restricted to the Horn Strengthenings that are entailed by I. This process is repeated on Γ until Γ is Horn or all its implicants have been visited. In the latter case, all the Horn strengthenings of Γ are equivalent.

Let us now describe the procedure that generates a Horn GLB of a set Σ of clauses. A systematic search of implicants is done using the DP procedure. DP procedure has already been used in compilation (Schrag 1996; Boufkhad *et al.* 1997). As an important difference with DP, the formula for which DP searches for implicants is not the same all along the tree. Every time an implicant I is found, the current formula is replaced by its I-strengthening.

GLB(Σ)
input: a set of clauses $\Sigma = \{C_1, C_2, ..., C_p\}$
output: a Horn GLB.
begin
  $\Gamma \leftarrow$ **DP_GLB**($\Sigma, \emptyset$);
  return any Horn-strengthenings of Γ;
end

DP_GLB(Γ, I)
input: a set of clauses Γ and a partial interpretation I
output: a strengthening of Γ.
begin
  if unit propagation shows $\Gamma \wedge I$ is inconsistent
    then return Γ;
  if ($I \models \Gamma$) **then return** I-Strengthening of Γ;
  $l \leftarrow$ **ChooseLiteral**($\Gamma \wedge I$);
  $\Gamma \leftarrow$ **DP_GLB**($\Gamma, I \cup \{l\}$);
  if Γ is Horn **then return** Γ;
  $\Gamma \leftarrow$ **DP_GLB**($\Gamma, I \cup \{\neg l\}$);
  return Γ;
end

Theorem 1 *Let Σ be a set of clauses, **GLB**(Σ) delivers a Horn GLB of Σ.*

Interestingly enough, **GLB** is an anytime procedure in the sense that if interrupted, it returns a Horn strengthening of Γ which is a Horn LB that includes at least the implicants encountered so far by **DP_GLB**. An other advantage of this procedure is that it allows to choose which models to include in the Horn GLB to be generated.

Let us now compare the efficiency of GLB with the original algorithm **Generate_GLB** by Selman and Kautz. **Generate_GLB** enumerates all possible Horn strengthenings of the set of clauses and chooses the weakest one. The number N of iteration steps needed by **Generate_GLB** is thus the number of Horn strengthenings of a formula, which depends on the numbers of non Horn clauses and of positive literals in these clauses. This is, let $|P(C_i)|$ be the number of positive literals in the clause C_i: $N = \prod_{C_i \in \Sigma} |P(C_i)|$. In general, this number is so huge that this algorithm is actually intractable. Conversely, when the number of non Horn clauses is very small **Generate_GLB** might behave better than **GLB**. An extreme example requires the presence of only one non Horn clause with 2 positive literals and a large number of Horn clauses with an exponential number of models: **Generate_GLB** needs only two steps to decide which Horn strengthening to choose, while **GLB** needs a large amount of time to find a GLB. Because this situation can happen in the course of execution of **GLB**, the number of steps needed by **Generate_GLB** to give a Horn GLB of the current formula Γ is computed before every recursive call to **DP_GLB**. If this number is sufficiently small, **DP_GLB** is interrupted and switches to **Generate_GLB** to finish the computation process.

Preprocessing large formulae

In **DP_GLB**, each time an implicant is found, it strengthens the formula Γ making it more constrained and thus easier for the remaining search process. When the formula is too large, even finding just one model is too hard for this method. To overcome this drawback, a logically incomplete but efficient procedure is used for finding a model and strengthening the formula until it becomes sufficiently constrained for being processed by **DP_GLB**. Generating Horn GLB of large size KBs will consist in looping over the following 3 steps until the formula is sufficiently constrained to be easy for procedure **GLB**. Γ is initialized with the KB Σ:

1. Use a logically incomplete procedure (e.g. a local search one) for finding a model I of Γ (in our experimentations we used the local search method (Mazure, Saïs, & Grégoire 1997)).

2. Drop literals from I successively until I is a prime implicant of Γ.

3. Replace Γ by its I-strengthening.

Many criteria can be used to decide whether a formula is sufficiently constrained for being easy enough for **GLB**. In our experimentations the number of unit and binary clauses in the formula has been chosen. After this preprocessing **GLB** is called with the resulting formula as an input.

Generating Renamable Horn GLBs

The general framework for theory approximation defined in (Selman & Kautz 1996) leaves freedom for choice of representation languages other than Horn. The renamable Horn class (Lewis 1978; Henschen & Wos 1974) is one of these possible target languages. Let us stress that it includes the Horn, reverse Horn and satisfiable binary classes.

Renaming a variable x in a set of clauses Σ consists in replacing every occurrence of x by $\neg x$ and vice versa. A renaming function w.r.t an interpretation r, denoted by $\mathcal{R}_r$, maps the formula Σ into an other formula $\mathcal{R}_r(\Sigma)$ obtained by renaming in Σ every variable having its positive literal in r. When used in a renaming function, the interpretation r is said to be a renaming. It can be noted that $\mathcal{R}_r(\mathcal{R}_r(\Sigma)) = \Sigma$. Example: $\Sigma = \{x \vee \neg y, y \vee z\}$ and $r = \{\neg x, y, z\}$ then $\mathcal{R}_r(\Sigma) = \{x \vee y, \neg y \vee \neg z\}$. A set of clauses Σ is renamable Horn if there exists a renaming r s.t. $\mathcal{R}_r(\Sigma)$ is Horn, in this case r is said to be a Horn renaming of Σ. Testing whether a CNF formula Σ is renamable Horn can be done in time linear in the size of Σ (Aspvall 1980).

A $\mathcal{RH}$-GLB of a set of clauses Σ is a renamable Horn formula Σ_{rh-glb} s.t. $\Sigma_{rh-glb} \models \Sigma$ and there is no other renamable Horn formula H s.t. $H \not\equiv \Sigma_{rh-glb}$ and $\Sigma_{rh-glb} \models H \models \Sigma$. There is a close connection between Horn and renamable Horn LBs. Indeed, considering a set of clause Σ and a renaming r, every horn LB of $\mathcal{R}_r(\Sigma)$ is a renamable Horn LB of Σ. This is why, in the following, there is a need to use the procedure **GLB** to generate a renamable Horn GLB.

Due to the larger scope of the renamable Horn class, generating bounds should be more difficult and expensive than in the Horn case. However, tighter bounds could be expected.

The algorithm for computing a $\mathcal{RH}$-GLB can be summarized in this way: The formula Λ is initialized to $false$. Then the renamings r are successively considered: if there exists H a Horn GLB of $\mathcal{R}_r(\Sigma)$ that improves Λ (i.e. $\Lambda \models \mathcal{R}_r(H)$) then Λ is replaced by $\mathcal{R}_r(H)$.

By these successive improvements of Λ, after testing all the renamings, we are sure that there is no better renamable Horn LB than Λ.

Since for a set of propositional variables V there are $2^{|V|}$ possible renamings, and for each renaming r there is in general an exponential number of Horn GLBs of $\mathcal{R}_r(\Sigma)$, the search space of $\mathcal{RH}$-GLBs of Σ is huge. It is then essential to restrict this search space in order to allow the generation of a $\mathcal{RH}$-GLB to be achieved in reasonable time. The following results established here, give the means for dramatically reducing this search:

- It is sufficient to consider only the renamings that are models of Σ.
- It can be tested in polynomial time, whether renaming w.r.t. a model m can give a better bound than the current one.
- When a model m verifies the latter condition, it is sufficient to generate only one Horn GLB H of $\mathcal{R}_m(\Sigma)$ provided that the current bound entails $\mathcal{R}_m(H)$.

Thanks to the next proposition, the first point of the previous list is established:

Proposition 2 *Let Σ be a set of clauses and K a satifiable renamable Horn LB of Σ. There exists a model m of Σ and a renamable Horn Lower bound Λ of Σ having m as a Horn renaming s.t. $K \equiv \Lambda$.*

If K of the previous proposition has a model among its Horn renamings then the statement is trivial. Otherwise, the formula Λ is obtained by removing from K every opposite occurrence of the literals satisfied by a unit propagation performed on Λ.

The preceding proposition stated for any renamable Horn LB, holds in particular for a $\mathcal{RH}$-GLB. Then every $\mathcal{RH}$-GLB is equivalent to a renamable Horn formula that has a model among its Horn renamings. Thus, in searching for a $\mathcal{RH}$-GLB of Σ it is sufficient to consider only the models of Σ as renamings.

Let us consider a model m for renaming, if H is a Horn LB of $\mathcal{R}_m(\Sigma)$ then $\mathcal{R}_m(H)$ is a renamable Horn LB of Σ. Consequently, only Horn GLBs of $\mathcal{R}_m(\Sigma)$ can correspond to renamable Horn GLBs of Σ. Indeed:

Proposition 3 *Let Σ be a set of clauses and Σ_{rh-glb} one of its renamable Horn GLBs. For every Horn renaming r of Σ_{rh-glb}, $\mathcal{R}_r(\Sigma_{rh-glb})$ is a Horn GLB of $\mathcal{R}_r(\Sigma)$.*

Let us now consider a renamable Horn LB K. Checking whether renaming w.r.t some model m improves K (i.e. whether there is a Horn GLB Γ of $\mathcal{R}_m(\Sigma)$ s.t. $K \models \mathcal{R}_m(\Gamma)$) could require to generate every Horn GLB Γ of $\mathcal{R}_m(\Sigma)$ and to check if $K \models \mathcal{R}_m(\Gamma)$. This is avoided by the next proposition that establishes the conditions under which, renaming w.r.t a model m can improve K. Since a Horn GLB of $\mathcal{R}_m(\Sigma)$ is equivalent to a Horn Strengthening (Selman & Kautz 1996) then K must entail at least one Horn strengthening of $\mathcal{R}_m(\Sigma)$.

Proposition 4 *Let Σ be a set of clauses, m one of its models and K a renamable Horn LB of Σ. There exists a Horn GLB Γ of $\mathcal{R}_m(\Sigma)$ s.t. $K \models \mathcal{R}_m(\Gamma)$ iff for every clause C of $\mathcal{R}_m(\Sigma)$ there is a Horn Strengthening C^H of C s.t. $\mathcal{R}_m(K) \models C^H$.*

Interestingly, since K is renamable Horn, the above condition can be checked in linear time in the size of K and C.

When the conditions defined in the proposition 4 are fulfilled by a model m, the procedure **GLB** defined in the previous section can be used to generate a Horn GLB Λ of $\mathcal{R}_m(\Sigma)$ s.t. $\mathcal{R}_m(K) \models \Lambda$. To ensure that $\mathcal{R}_m(K) \models \Lambda$, the parameter given to **GLB** is a strengthening of $\mathcal{R}_m(\Sigma)$ similar to the I-strengthening defined in the previous section. For this, the definition of the I-strengthening is generalized in this way: for a formula F, the F-strengthening of a clause C is the clause obtained from C by removing every positive literal l s.t. $F \not\models C^H$ where C^H is the Horn strengthening of C containing l. Clearly, and for the same reasons that in proposition 1, every Horn GLB of the $\mathcal{R}_m(K)$-strengthening of $\mathcal{R}_m(\Sigma)$ is entailed by $\mathcal{R}_m(K)$.

To summarize the above results, let us give a partial description of the algorithm for computing a $\mathcal{RH}$-GLB. Let M denotes the set of the models of Σ. The formula Λ is initialized to $false$.

for every model m in M
    if $\mathcal{R}_m(\Lambda)$ entails some Horn strengthening of $\mathcal{R}_m(\Sigma)$
    then
        $\Sigma' \leftarrow \mathcal{R}_m(\Lambda)$-strengthening of $\mathcal{R}_m(\Sigma)$;
        $\Lambda' \leftarrow \mathbf{GLB}(\Sigma')$;
        $\Lambda \leftarrow \mathcal{R}_m(\Lambda)$

It is assumed in the partial procedure given above, that the set of models of Σ has been computed. In our implementation, a Davis and Putnam procedure is used to sytematically search for models. As models are found the above partial procedure is used to improve the current bound.

By generalizing the condition given in proposition 4, it is possible to prune the DP search tree at a node where the current partial interpretation cannot improve the current bound through one of its models (if any). Let us consider a partial interpretation I and a renamable Horn LB K, we address the question: Is it possible to extend I to a renaming that improves K? A small modification to proposition 4 allows, in some cases, to answer efficiently negatively this question. Let us consider a clause C and rename it using the renaming function $\mathcal{R}'_I$ defined in this way: for every literal l in C if l or $\neg l$ is in I then rename it the usual way, otherwise rename it negatively. Let us denote by C^H the clause s.t. $\mathcal{R}'_I(C^H)$ is a Horn strengthening of $\mathcal{R}'_I(C)$. Example: $C = \neg a \vee \neg b \vee c \vee d$ and $I = \{a, \neg b, \neg c\}$ then $\mathcal{R}'_I(C) = a \vee \neg b \vee c \vee \neg d$, then $C^H = \neg b \vee c \vee d$ is s.t. $\mathcal{R}'_I(C^H)$ is a Horn strengthening of $\mathcal{R}'_I(C)$. Clearly, if there is no Horn strengthening $\mathcal{R}'_I(C^H)$ s.t. $K \models C^H$ then the answer to the above question is no. This is because no full interpretation obtained from I, can rename negatively more literals than does I using the renaming function described above. This method allows us to prune the search by skipping all the models (if any) in the considered partial interpretation.

Automated Reasoning   283

Let us now describe the complete procedure that generates a $\mathcal{RH}$-GLB of a set Σ of clauses. Similarly to **GLB**, **RH_GLB** performs a single call to a procedure **DP_RH_GLB** that develops a DP like tree. A formula Λ is initialized to *false* and then is improved everytime a model of Σ that can improve it is found. At each step, **DP_RH_GLB** tests if the current partial interpretation can produce a renaming that improves Λ, in the negative case **DP_RH_GLB** backtracks allowing for a significant pruning (in the next procedures, Λ is a global variable).

RH_GLB(Σ)
input: a set of clauses $\Sigma = \{C_1, C_2, ..., C_p\}$
output: a $\mathcal{RH}$-GLB.
begin
  $\Lambda \leftarrow false$;
  DP_RH_GLB($\Sigma,\emptyset$);
  return Λ;
end.

DP_RH_GLB(Σ,I);
input: a formula Σ and a partial interpretation I
output: none.
begin
  if unit propagation shows that $\Sigma \wedge I$ is inconsistent
    then return;
  for every clause C
    if there is no Horn strengthening $\mathcal{R}'_I(C^H)$
      of $\mathcal{R}'_I(C)$ s.t. $\Lambda \models C^H$ **then return**;
  if I is a model of Σ
    then
      $\Sigma' \leftarrow \mathcal{R}_I(\Lambda)$-strengthening of $\mathcal{R}_I(\Sigma)$;
      $\Lambda' \leftarrow$ **GLB(Σ')**;
      $\Lambda \leftarrow \mathcal{R}_I(\Lambda')$;
      return;
  $l \leftarrow$ **ChooseLiteral**;
  DP_RH_GLB($\Sigma,I \cup \{l\}$);
  DP_RH_GLB($\Sigma,I \cup \{\neg l\}$);
end.

Theorem 2 *Let Σ be a set of clauses, **RH_GLB(Σ)** delivers a renamable Horn GLB of Σ.*

Interestingly, the procedure **RH_GLB** is anytime. If interrupted, it returns the current formula Λ which is a renamable Horn LB of Σ.

Experimental results
Generation of GLB

In (Kautz & Selman 1994; Selman & Kautz 1996) the experimental evaluation of knowledge compilation using theory approximation has been done using unit clause bounds. To our best knowledge, actual computations of

k #vars	#clauses	#instances (#fails)	CPU Prep.	CPU GLB
3-cnf 1000	3800	100 (0)	0.5s	1s
	4000	100 (0)	0.8s	1s
	50	100 (0)	61s	0.5s
4-cnf 300	2700	100 (23)	2s	324s
	2800	100 (13)	4s	173s
	2900	100 (0)	84s	108s

Table 1: Generation of Horn GLBs of randomly generated 3-CNF formulae of 1000 variables and 4-CNF formulae of 300 variables.

instance	#variables	#clauses	T_H	T_R
as2-yes.cnf	96	954	0.1s	55s
as3-yes.cnf	96	954	0.1s	26s
as6-yes.cnf	184	2277	12s	-
as8-yes.cnf	84	974	0.2s	140s
as10-yes.cnf	216	2780	265s	-
as11-yes.cnf	112	1312	1s	78s
as12-yes.cnf	72	1012	0.1s	43s
as14-yes.cnf	92	758	0.1s	123s

Table 2: Experiment on Asynchronous circuits design instances.

Horn bounds have never been performed. This is why the experimental results given in this section are not compared with other methods. As an illustration of the efficiency of the algorithms for generating GLB on large size KBs, we tested them on large random k-CNF formula on a Pentium 200MHz. These instances have been generated around the hard region (Mitchell, Selman, & Levesque 1992; Dubois *et al.* 1996). Table 1 reports the results on 3-CNF instances of 1000 variables and 4-CNF instances of 300 variables. Up to one hour was allocated for each formula. CPU times are presented separately for preprocessing and for the **GLB** procedure.

Table 2 reports the results of CPU computation time of Horn GLBs (T_H) and renamable Horn lower bounds (T_R) on 15 benchmarks coming from asynchronous circuits design (available at dimacs.rutgers.edu/pub/sat-files/ by anonymous ftp). The table reports only the benchmarks for which computation was possible. To let experiments be done in reasonable time, the renamable Horn lower bound is computed using **RH_GLB** which is interrupted, the first time a renamable Horn LB better than the Horn GLB computed is found.

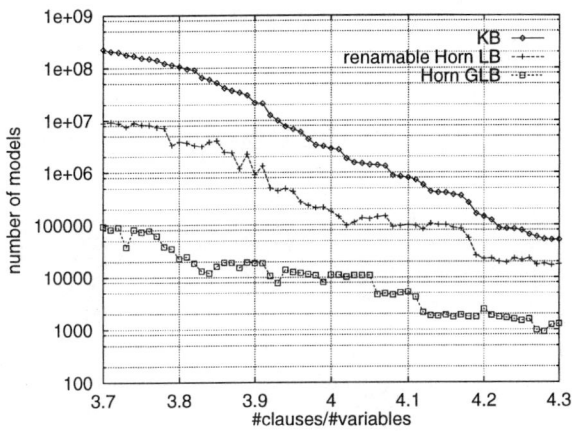

Figure 1: Number of models of Horn LBs, renamable Horn GLBs and KBs.

Quality of the lower bounds

Results obtained on random 3-CNF instances of 100 variables and for ratio #clauses/#variables ranging from 3.7 to 4.3 are represented in Figure 1. Each point of each curve is the mean number of models on a sample of 1000 instances. For the renamable Horn case, only lower bounds have been computed. In spite of that the renamable Horn LBs approximates better the KB than does the Horn GLB.

Conclusion

The renamable Horn class proves to be an interesting target language in propositional KB approximation. It can actually also improve the quality of upper bounds. Let us stress that the algorithms described in this paper can be easily modified to generate more compact tractable covers in the framework defined in (Boufkhad et al. 1997). An interesting issue for further research is to investigate the computational complexity of generating the renamable Horn bounds.

Aknowledgment

This work has been supported in part by the Ganymede II project of the "Contrat de plan Etat/Nord-Pas-de-Calais". Special thanks to Eric Grégoire for his useful comments that helped to improve this paper.

References

Aspvall, B. 1980. Recognizing disguised nr(1) instances of the satisfiability problem. *J. Algorithms* 1:97–103.

Boufkhad, Y.; Grégoire, E.; Marquis, P.; Mazure, B.; and Saïs, L. 1997. Tractable cover compilations. In *Proc. IJCAI'97*, 122–127.

Cadoli, M. 1993. Semantical and computational aspects of horn approximations. In *Proc. IJCAI'93*, 39–44.

Davis, M., and Putnam, H. 1960. A computing procedure for quantification theory. *JACM* 7:201–215.

Dechter, R., and Rish, I. 1994. Directional resolution: The davis-putnam procedure, revisited. In *Proc. KR'94*, 134–145.

del Val, A. 1994. Tractable databases: How to make propositional unit resolution complete through compilation. In *Proc. KR'94*, 551–561.

del Val, A. 1995. An analysis of approximate knowledge compilation. In *Proc. IJCAI'95*, 830–836.

Dowling, W., and Gallier, J. 1984. Linear time algorithms for testing the satisfiability of propositional horn formulae. *Journal of Logic Programming* 1(3):267–284.

Dubois, O.; Andre, P.; Boufkhad, Y.; and Carlier, J. 1996. Sat vs. unsat. In 2nd *DIMACS Implementation Challenge*, volume 26 of *DIMACS Series*. American Mathematical Society. 415–436.

Henschen, L., and Wos, L. 1974. Unit refutations and horn sets. *JACM* 21:590–605.

Kautz, H., and Selman, B. 1994. An empirical evaluation of knowledge compilation by theory approximation. In *AAAI'94*, 155–161.

Lewis, H. 1978. Renaming a set of clauses as a horn set. *JACM* 25:134–134.

Marquis, P. 1995. Knowledge compilation using theory prime implicates. In *Proc. IJCAI'95*, 837–843.

Mazure, B.; Saïs, L.; and Grégoire, E. 1997. Tabu search for SAT. In *AAAI'97*. 281–285.

Mitchell, D.; Selman, B.; and Levesque, H. 1992. Hard and easy distribution of sat problems. In *AAAI'92*, 459–465.

Reiter, R., and De Kleer, J. 1987. Foundations of assumption-based truth maintenance systems: Preliminary report. In *Proc. AAAI'87*, 183–188.

Schrag, R. 1996. Compilation for critically constrained knowledge bases. In *Proc. AAAI'96*, 510–515.

Selman, B., and Kautz, H. 1991. Knowledge compilation using horn approximations. In *Proc. AAAI'91*, 904–909.

Selman, B., and Kautz, H. 1996. Knowledge compilation and theory approximation. *JACM* 43(2):193–224.

A Non-Deterministic Semantics for Tractable Inference

James M. Crawford
i2 Technologies
909 E. Las Colinas Blvd.
12th Floor
Irving, TX 75038

David W. Etherington
Computational Intelligence Research Laboratory
University of Oregon
1269 University of Oregon
Eugene, OR 97403-1269

Abstract

Unit resolution is arguably the most useful known algorithm for tractable reasoning in propositional logic. Intuitively, if one knows a, b, and $a \wedge b \supset c$, then c should be an obvious implication. However, devising a tractable semantics that allows unit resolution has proven to be an elusive goal. We propose a 3-valued semantics for a tractable fragment of propositional logic that is inherently non-deterministic: the denotation of a formula is not uniquely determined by the denotation of the variables it contains. We show that this semantics yields a tractable, sound and complete, decision procedure. We generalize this semantics to a family of semantics, tied to Dalal's notion of intricacy, of increasing deductive power and computational complexity.

Introduction

Despite the recent advances in propositional reasoning power [Selman, Kautz, & Cohen 1993; Crawford & Auton 1996; Bayardo & Miranker 1996; Bayardo & Schrag 1997], knowledge-bases of the size required for common-sense reasoning are still far beyond the reach of complete reasoners. This means that, for the foreseeable future, common-sense reasoners will necessarily be based on tractable, classically-incomplete inference algorithms.

Many such algorithms have been proposed, and these algorithms are generally reasonably easy to understand procedurally. However, understanding inference procedurally is no substitute for understanding what sort of models of the world implicitly underlie the inference. This kind of deeper understanding is the domain of semantics. A sound and complete semantics for an inference algorithm tells us what it means for the world to be consistent with a theory, and thus gives a clearer picture of what the inference algorithm is, and is not, assuming about the world.

Early attempts at devising a semantics for tractable limited deduction [Patel-Schneider 1990; Frisch 1987] were oriented toward limiting potentially unbounded "chaining," i.e., inferences such as deducing b from a and $(a \supset b)$, or deducing $(a \supset c)$ from $(a \supset b)$ and

---

Copyright 1998, American Association for Artificial Intelligence (www.aaai.org). All rights reserved.

$(b \supset c)$. It was assumed that such inferences were the source of intractability. While this restriction did, in fact, produce polynomial-time reasoners, the resulting preclusion of unit propagation was a significant restriction. Unit propagation is a powerful, yet computationally cheap, reasoning technique [Schrag & Crawford 1996], and its loss severely limited the utility of these systems.

As a case in point, in a recent paper we attempted to develop a tractable reasoner by restricting inference to a limited context and pruning deductions that branched beyond the bounds of the context [Etherington & Crawford 1996]. Paradoxically, our experimental results showed that such context limitation actually degrades performance in certain cases, making it harder to detect inconsistency. Analysis of the data shows that pruning inference can block unit propagation that would pass outside the context, and this propagation can help quickly detect contradictions in theories with significant numbers of unit clauses. The loss of unit propagation can overwhelm the benefits gained by restricting inference. Such observations have led us to investigate mechanisms for avoiding this problem.

Crawford and Kuipers [1989; 1991] approached tractable deduction by limiting chaining to defined "access paths" in the knowledge base. Intuitively, when attempting to deduce a, the focus of attention is restricted to only rules for deriving a. If such a rule says that a follows from b then attention is extended to b, and then to c if b follows from c, and so on. The essential idea here is the same as unit resolution: follow "linear" chains of inference but do not perform reasoning by cases. Reasoning by cases (i.e., considering the effects of choosing each of several alternatives and then concluding whatever holds in all cases) was then permitted by a dialectical process of making assumptions that then enabled further access-limited reasoning.

Recently, Dalal has furthered this approach, developing a family of tractable deduction systems that do not sacrifice unit propagation [Dalal 1996a]. The essential insight that underlies his work, Crawford and Kuipers', and ours is that it is reasoning by cases, not chaining or disjunction per se, that makes propositional reasoning intractable. However, Dalal's systems have been limited to theories in clausal form. We present a semantics for tractable propositional deduction that corresponds in many respects to Dalal's systems, but extends naturally to non-clausal formulae and to limited, tractable, first-order reasoners.

Model Theory

As have previous authors, we begin by basing our semantics on three truth values: **t**, **f**, and **u**. Intuitively we can imagine **u** as corresponding to 0.5 in an integer programming encoding of a propositional formula. In such an encoding **t** maps to 1, **f** maps to 0, $x \vee y$ and $x \wedge y$ map to $x + y$ and $x * y$, respectively, over the 3-element domain. This gives the initial truth table shown in Table 1.

x	y	$\neg y$	$x \vee y$	$x \wedge y$
u	t	f	t	u
u	f	t	u	f
u	u	u	t	f

Table 1: A simple 3-valued truth table[1]

This is essentially the semantics used by Dalal [1996b][2] but extended to include conjunction (Dalal deals only with clausal theories, first converting non-clausal theories to clausal form).

Unfortunately there is a problem with this semantics: determining satisfiability is NP-complete for non-clausal theories. To see this, observe that we can take any theory and conjoin it with:

$$(x \wedge x') \vee (\neg x \wedge \neg x')$$

for each variable x in the theory, where x' is a unique new variable. These additional clauses force all the variables to take the values **t** or **f**, and thus force the semantics to behave classically. Dalal avoided this problem by dealing only with clausal theories, but we must face it if we are to achieve tractability while allowing general propositional formulae.

There is an additional, more subtle, problem with the initial semantics given above. Every non-unit clause evaluates to **t** when its constituent literals are valued **u**, which means that uncertainty about the constituents does not carry over into uncertainty about their disjunction, which seems peculiar. For example, consider the theory consisting of the clauses $(x \vee y)$, $(x \vee \neg y)$, $(\neg x \vee y)$, and $(\neg x \vee \neg y)$. If we focus on all models in which $x = y = \mathbf{u}$ then all four of these clauses evaluate to **t**. This is, in a sense, more non-classical than we want to be. Furthermore, if x is changed from **u** to **t** then the truth value of $\neg x \vee y$ goes from **t** to **f**. This is even more unfortunate since, ideally, increased certainty about variable values should translate into increased certainty about clause values. To put this another way, as variables values are refined from non-classical to classical values we would like to see the set of models also refine toward the classical models. We formalize this notion of compositional refinement below.

We can address both semantic and tractability issues by adopting a nondeterministic semantics. In order to allow unit propagation without allowing arbitrary reasoning by cases, it is necessary to develop a mechanism that can allow, for example, $(a \vee b)$ and $(\neg b \vee c)$ to evaluate to **t**, without forcing $(a \vee c)$ to do so too. Clearly, the truth values for a and c must be weaker than **t**, and b cannot be classically valued. However, setting all three atoms to **u** and applying the above semantics won't work either, since all three clauses would evaluate to **t**. Allowing nondeterminism in the semantics for $\vee$ and $\wedge$ provides a way around this dilemma. Intuitively, this nondeterminism reflects the fact that it is computationally too expensive, in general, to work out all the ramifications of uncertainty about particular facts.

x	y	$\neg y$	$x \vee y$	$x \wedge y$
u	t	f	t	u
u	f	t	u	f
u	u	u	t u	f u

Table 2: A nondeterministic truth table[3]

The modified truth table in Table 2 constitutes such a nondeterministic semantics for propositional logic. Multiple values in a cell indicate a non-deterministic choice in interpretation construction. Thus if $x = y = \mathbf{u}$ then $x \vee y$ will take on the value **u** in some interpretations and the value **t** in others. This solves the tractability problem above because there are models that set $x = x' = \mathbf{u}$, choose $x \wedge x' = \mathbf{u}$ and $\neg x \wedge \neg x' = \mathbf{u}$, and then choose to evaluate the disjunction of the two as **t**. This approach also solves the semantic problem because if $x = y = \mathbf{u}$ then there will be models in which $x \vee y$ is **t** and others in which it is **u**. Thus when x and y are refined to **t**, we can regard the classical model produced as a refinement of the non-classical model that set $\neg x \vee \neg y$ to **u**. In the formal development below we precisely define this notion of compositional refinement and show that it holds in general for the semantics defined by Table 2.

The following definitions make the details of the above discussion precise. Except as explicitly noted, we will use lowercase letters to represent propositional variables, and Greek letters to represent propositional formulae. Theories will be defined in terms of the primitive connectives, $\wedge$, $\vee$, and $\neg$, although we will occasionally use $(\alpha \supset \beta)$ as shorthand for $(\neg \alpha \vee \beta)$. We will restrict our attention to propositional theories in negation-normal form (all negations pushed in as far as possible), and use T and T' to represent propositional

---

[1] The purely classical cases are omitted for succinctness.
[2] For details see the "related work" section.
[3] We assume the obvious generalization of this truth table for n-ary disjunctions and conjunctions: $x_1 \vee \ldots \vee x_m$ is valued **t** if some x_i is true, false if all x_i are false, **u** if exactly one x_i is **u**, and **t u** otherwise. Conjunctions are handled similarly.

theories.

Definition 1 *A basic assignment for a propositional theory, T, is an assignment of $\mathbf{t}$, $\mathbf{f}$, or $\mathbf{u}$ to the propositional variables of T.*

Definition 2 *A 3-interpretation, M, for a theory, T, consists of a basic assignment for T together with an assignment to the subformulae of T that respects Table 2. We write $M(\alpha)$ for the value assigned by M to α.*

Definition 3 *M is a 3-model for a formula, α, (written $M \Vvdash \alpha$) if M is a 3-interpretation for α and $M(\alpha) = \mathbf{t}$. M is a 3-model for a theory, T, (written $M \Vvdash T$) if M is a 3-interpretation for T and $\forall \alpha \in T. M \Vvdash \alpha$.*

To give the reader a feel for how the semantics is applied, as well as some of its properties, consider the following examples, where a, b, and c are literals. To invalidate a reasoning schema, we must show a model where the premises are all $\mathbf{t}$, but the conclusion is $\mathbf{u}$ or $\mathbf{f}$ (i.e., *not* $\mathbf{t}$). If such a model does not exist, the schema is valid.

Example 1 (Unit propagation) *Unit propagation allows us to conclude b from a and $a \supset b$. Consider a basic assignment where a is $\mathbf{t}$. To make $a \supset b$ (i.e. $\neg a \vee b$) $\mathbf{t}$, b must be $\mathbf{t}$—i.e., the conclusion must be true. Hence the schema is valid.*

Unit propagation is a simple form of modus ponens. We now show that the general form of modus ponens is not valid under our semantics.

Example 2 (Failure of modus ponens) *We first construct a model where $a \vee b$ and $(a \vee b) \supset (b \vee c)$ are both $\mathbf{t}$. Start with the basic assignment $a = b = c = \mathbf{u}$, and for the first formula choose $\mathbf{u} \vee \mathbf{u}$ to be $\mathbf{t}$. The second formula is a notational shorthand for $(\neg a \wedge \neg b) \vee (b \vee c)$. We can choose $(\neg \mathbf{u} \wedge \neg \mathbf{u}) \vee (\mathbf{u} \vee \mathbf{u})$ to be $\mathbf{t}$ (choose $\mathbf{u} \mathbf{f} \vee \mathbf{u} \mathbf{t}$ as $\mathbf{u} \vee \mathbf{u}$, which reduces to $\mathbf{u} \mathbf{t}$ and choose this to be $\mathbf{t}$). However, $(b \vee c)$ evaluates to $\mathbf{u} \vee \mathbf{u}$, which can be $\mathbf{u}$.*

Finally, we show that chaining fails in general.

Example 3 (Failure of chaining) *Given premises $(a \vee b)$ and $(\neg b \vee c)$, the basic assignment $a = b = c = \mathbf{u}$ can make both true (let $\mathbf{u} \vee \mathbf{u}$ be $\mathbf{t}$ in both cases). However, in the case of $(a \vee c)$, $\mathbf{u} \vee \mathbf{u}$ can also be $\mathbf{u}$.*

The third truth value, $\mathbf{u}$, represents ambiguities in models that could potentially be refined away, thus reducing uncertainty. This refinement process only restricts the possibilities available, it never creates new alternatives. This is important, since it means that a model containing $\mathbf{u}$'s should never lead us to dismiss as impossible the "true" model of the world. We can formally capture this idea with the notion of compositional refinement. The essential idea here is that if we refine the basic assignment (by taking some variable from $\mathbf{u}$ to $\mathbf{t}$ or $\mathbf{f}$) we must be able to find, for each model consistent with the new assignment, a "parent" that was consistent with the old assignment:

Definition 4 *An assignment A' is a refinement of an assignment A iff A' differs from A only in that some variables assigned to $\mathbf{u}$ by A are assigned to $\mathbf{t}$ or $\mathbf{f}$ by A'. Refinement relations between interpretations are defined similarly.*

Theorem 5 (Compositional Refinement)
Assume that A is the basic assignment for some 3-model of a theory T. For any refinement A' of A, if M' is a 3-model of T with basic assignment A', then there is some model M of T with basic assignment A such that M' is a refinement of M.

One important corollary of this result is that if V is the set of propositional variables valued classically ($\mathbf{t}$ or $\mathbf{f}$) by A, then any formula valued $\mathbf{t}$ in all models of T with basic assignment A will also be valued $\mathbf{t}$ in all classical models of T and V.

Proof Theory

Two of the rules of inference used most commonly in tractable reasoners are unit resolution and unit subsumption. Unit resolution allows x to be deduced from $(x \vee y \vee z)$, $\neg y$, and $\neg z$. Unit subsumption allows $(x \vee y \vee z)$ to be deduced from x. In terms of proof rules, these can be written (for δ, δ_i literals, α, β formulae) as:

$R1$: *unit subsumption* $\quad \dfrac{T \Vdash \delta}{T \Vdash \delta \vee \alpha}$

$R2$: *unit resolution* $\quad \begin{array}{c} T \Vdash \delta_1 \vee \ldots \vee \delta_m \\ T \Vdash \neg \delta_1 \\ \vdots \\ T \Vdash \neg \delta_{m-1} \\ \hline T \Vdash \delta_m \end{array}$

To this we add the obvious rule that a theory's constituent terms can be deduced from the theory, and a rule for contradictory theories:

$R3$: *containment* $\quad \dfrac{\alpha \in T}{T \Vdash \alpha}$

$R4$: *contradiction* $\quad \begin{array}{c} T \Vdash \delta \\ T \Vdash \neg \delta \\ \hline T \Vdash \alpha \end{array}$

(where by $\alpha \in T$ we mean that T is a conjunction of formulae, one of which is α). We also need the following rules for handling conjunctions in the non-clausal case:

$R5$: $\wedge$-*elimination* $\quad \dfrac{T \Vdash \alpha \wedge \beta}{T \Vdash \alpha}$

$R6$: $\wedge$-*introduction* $\quad \begin{array}{c} T \Vdash \alpha \\ T \Vdash \beta \\ \hline T \Vdash \alpha \wedge \beta \end{array}$

This set of rules is slightly weaker than the tractable inference theory BCP defined by Dalal [1996b], as it must be to preserve tractability in the non-clausal case. It is, however, precisely equivalent to the the semantics defined above:

Theorem 6 $T_1 \Vdash T_2$ iff $T_1 \models T_2$.

In a real sense the core of this proof theory is unit resolution. This observation is captured in the following proposition.

Proposition 7 *A propositional theory, T, has a 3-model iff unit propagation over T does not produce both a literal and its negation.*

To see why this must hold, note that we can construct an interpretation, I, for a theory, T, using the following algorithm:

Unit propagate T to completion. Assign $\mathbf{t}$ to each variable appearing positively in a unit clause (or a top-level unit conjunct), and $\mathbf{f}$ to each variable appearing negatively in a unit clause in the resulting theory. Assign $\mathbf{u}$ to the remaining variables. Beginning with the most deeply nested connectives, using the truth table of Table 2, choose the greatest allowable truth value ($\mathbf{t} > \mathbf{u} > \mathbf{f}$) to assign.

If no variable is assigned both $\mathbf{t}$ and $\mathbf{f}$, then I is a 3-model for T.

Discussion

Using non-deterministic truth tables does introduce some interesting behavior. The primary difference from classical semantics hinges on an issue we call "pegging." Consider the formula:

$$(x \vee y) \wedge (x \vee y \vee z)$$

The non-deterministic nature of the semantics above allows the first clause to take on the truth value $\mathbf{t}$ and the second (subsumed) clause to take on the value $\mathbf{u}$. In a sense an interpretation has no memory of the decisions that are made on the value of formulae. As a result, the value assigned to $x \vee y$ in one part of the theory is not pegged to the value assigned to subsuming clause in another part of the theory. We have explored a variety of "pegged" versions of this semantics, and found them all to be incoherent or intractable (or both). While this is not a proof that no suitable pegged version could be found, pegging *seems* to provide a back-door entry for intractability, and we have decided to content ourselves with an unpegged semantics. This is, however, an area that deserves further study.

It is also interesting to note that some of the truisms of classical model theory do not hold for this semantics. In particular, there are theories, T, for which $M(T) \cap M(\neg T) \neq \emptyset$. For example, $(a \vee c) \wedge (b \vee d)$ shares a model where $a = b = c = d = \mathbf{u}$ with $(\neg a \wedge \neg c) \vee (\neg b \vee \neg d)$. Similarly, there are theories, T, for which $M(T) \cup M(\neg T) \neq M(\emptyset)$ (no variable appearing in a unit clause in T can be valued $\mathbf{u}$).

Perhaps most disturbing, however, is that certain transformations that preserve classical equivalence do not preserve equivalence under our new semantics. For example, conversion to clausal form may change the set of interpretations. Thus, $(a \wedge b) \vee (a \wedge c)$ can be valued $\mathbf{t}$, $\mathbf{f}$, or $\mathbf{u}$ when $a = b = c = \mathbf{u}$, but $(a \wedge (b \vee c))$ can be only valued $\mathbf{f}$ or $\mathbf{u}$.

A Family of Tractable Semantics

The semantics described so far allows for sound but classically incomplete tractable inference from a set of premises. This notion of inference essentially amounts to avoiding reasoning by cases. In some circumstances, however, such reasoning is essential. We thus seek a way of reintroducing a limited form of reasoning by cases without at the same time losing tractability. One obvious way to do this is to limit the "depth" of reasoning by cases. Our goal is to allow assumptions to be made that allow "lemmas" to be derived that further the inference process, but to restrict the complexity of these lemmas to avoid a combinatorial explosion.

Essentially, we allow k assumptions to be made. If a set of assumptions allows us to derive a contradiction, we deduce the negation of that set of assumptions. An interesting question is then, "What level of nesting is required to reach a particular conclusion, α?" This depth corresponds to how difficult it is to deduce α, and is essentially analogous to Dalal's notion of *intricacy* [Dalal 1996a].

Using this notion of nested assumptions, we define a hierarchical family of semantics corresponding to computationally more expensive reasoning systems.

Definition 8 $M \models_0 T$ iff $M \models T$.
For $k > 0$, $M \models_k T$ iff $M \models T$ and, for all clauses, γ, such that $|\gamma| \leq k$ and $M(\gamma) = \mathbf{u}$:
$\exists M'. \; M' \models_{(k-|\gamma|)} (T \wedge \gamma)$, and
$\exists M'. \; M' \models_{(k-|\gamma|)} (T \wedge \neg \gamma)$.
If $M \models_k T$, we say M is a k-model for T and T is k-satisfiable.

Basically, a k-model is forced to be "honest" about the possible truth values of clauses with no more than k literals, in the sense that they cannot be labeled $\mathbf{u}$ without explicitly allowing the possibility that the actual value may be either of $\mathbf{f}$ and $\mathbf{t}$.

We define a notion of entailment in the obvious way.

Definition 9
$T \Vdash_k \alpha$ iff $M(\alpha) = \mathbf{t}$ for all k-models, M, of T.

To generate a sound and complete proof theory we augment the proof theory given earlier with the following rules (for clauses γ and formulae α and β):

$R7$: *base case* $\qquad \dfrac{T \Vdash \alpha}{T \Vdash_k \alpha}$

$R8$: *contradiciton* $\qquad \dfrac{T, \neg\gamma \Vdash \mathbf{f} \quad |\gamma| \leq k}{T \Vdash_k \gamma}$

$R9$: *weak modus ponens*
$$\frac{T \Vdash_k \alpha \quad T \wedge \alpha \Vdash_k \beta \quad |\alpha| \leq k}{T \Vdash_k \beta}$$

Theorem 10 (Soundness+Completeness)
If $T \Vdash_k \gamma$ then $T \models_k \gamma$. If T is k-satisfiable and $T \models_k \gamma$ then $T \Vdash_k \gamma$.

The complexity of determining whether $T \Vdash_k \gamma$ is polynomial in the sizes of T and γ, but it increases exponentially with k. We conjecture that when k equals the number of variables in T, the $\Vdash$ relation is classically complete, but we have not yet proven this.

Related Work

Cadoli and Schaerf [1992] present a semantics in which chaining is restricted to a set S of literals in the theory. In the clausal case, entailment can be determined in PTIME for fixed S. However, their approach differs from ours in that unit resolution is allowed only within S, not throughout the theory. Based on our earlier experience, described in the introduction, however, we expect this restriction to be a significant limitation.

The basic idea of limiting the depth of assumption nesting goes back at least to Access-Limited Logic (ALL) [Crawford & Kuipers 1989] and Socratic sequent systems [McAllester, Givan, & Fatima 1989]. The results reported here grew out of our attempts to semantically characterize ALL.

The first attempt to define a semantics for such limited inference is Dalal's recent work [Dalal 1996b]. Dalal's semantics assigns real numbers in the range $[0,1]$ to all variables in the theory, and assigns $1 - x$ to $\neg x$. The value of any clause is the sum of the values in the clause. E.g., if $x = 0.4$ and $y = 0.8$ then $(x \vee y) = 1.2$. A theory is satisfied by a model if the model makes every clause in the theory ≥ 1.

The precise relationship between our two semantics is given by the following results.

Let $\models_D$ mean "models under Dalal's semantics". We can define a mapping g from his models to ours by:

$$\begin{aligned} g(M)(x) &= \mathbf{t} & \text{if } M(x) = 1 \\ g(M)(x) &= \mathbf{f} & \text{if } M(x) = 0 \\ g(M)(x) &= \mathbf{u} & \text{otherwise} \end{aligned}$$

then for any disjunction:

$$\begin{aligned} g(M)(x_1 \vee ... x_k) &= \mathbf{t} & \text{if } M(x_1 \vee ... x_k) \geq 1 \\ g(M)(x_1 \vee ... x_k) &= \mathbf{f} & \text{if } M(x_1 \vee ... x_k) = 0 \\ g(M)(x_1 \vee ... x_k) &= \mathbf{u} & \text{otherwise} \end{aligned}$$

Note that we can do this only because our semantics is non-deterministic (i.e., sometimes taking $\mathbf{u} \vee \mathbf{u}$ to $\mathbf{u}$ and sometimes taking it to $\mathbf{t}$). Since Dalal handles only clausal theories directly[4] this completely defines the mapping g.

Lemma 11 $M \models_D T$ iff $g(M) \models T$.

---
[4]Non-clausal theories are converted to clausal form.

To map the other way we take any model M under our semantics and map:

$$\begin{aligned} h(M)(x) &= 1 & \text{if } M(x) = \mathbf{t} \\ h(M)(x) &= 0 & \text{if } M(x) = \mathbf{f} \\ h(M)(x) &= 0.5 & \text{if } M(x) = \mathbf{u} \end{aligned}$$

Since Dalal's semantics is compositional this completely defines the mapping h. The correspondence in this case is more limited since we must restrict our attention to models that are deterministic.

Lemma 12 If M always maps $\mathbf{u} \vee \mathbf{u}$ to $\mathbf{t}$ then $M \models T$ iff $h(M) \models_D T$.

Dalal defines $T_1 \models_D T_2$ iff all models of T_1 do not assign T_2 the value $\mathbf{f}$. This is different from our (we believe more intuitive) requirement that T_2 takes the value $\mathbf{t}$ in all models of T_1. Still, one can show the following relationship:

Theorem 13 If $T_1 \models T_2$ then $T_1 \models_D T_2$.

The converse is not true. Take $T_1 = (x \vee y)$ and $T_2 = (x \vee y \vee z)$. $T_1 \models_D T_2$ (in fact, $T_1 \models T_2$). However, our semantics allows models that map $(x \vee y)$ to $\mathbf{t}$ and $(x \vee y \vee z)$ to $\mathbf{u}$ (this is, in fact, a necessary consequence of our lack of pegging).

Our extension to $\models_k$ is also quite similar to Dalal's. Our proof rules $R7$ and $R9$ are identical to his. The differences in the base semantics necessitated our addition of rule $R8$ (for Dalal our rule $R8$ is a special case of rule $R9$).

Conclusions and Future Work

We have presented a nondeterministic 3-valued semantics for propositional logic, and have shown that it is equivalent to a tractable proof theory based on unit resolution. The semantics has the virtue that it supports compositional refinement: increasing certainty about the truth values of the atomic formulae leads to increased certainty about those of general formulae. It also has the unusual property that the truth value of a formula is not uniquely determined by the truth value of the terms in the formula.

We then generalized our semantics to a family of semantics for a range of tractable inference mechanisms similar to that proposed by Dalal. For each member of the family we described a set of sound and complete proof rules.

We have been exploring extensions of our approach to the first-order case, where it shows promise in providing a tractable notion of context-limited first-order reasoning. The extension is non-trivial because in classical first-order logic, unit-resolution alone is undecidable. Intuitively this is because one can write axioms saying things like, "Every man has a father who is a man," which force infinite chains of "linear" inferences. The reason these chains do not seem to bother commonsense reasoning seems to be that we focus our attention on a limited set of objects that we are reasoning about and let this focus "grey out" around the edges (e.g.

we will think about John and perhaps be aware of his father, but we will only mentally instantiate John's father's father if we have some reason to believe he is significant).

Semantically we capture this notion of a focus of attention by introducing an explicit model-theoretic context object at the first-order level; all universal quantifications are scoped to just objects in the context and witnesses for existential quantifiers are required to be in the context or to have an unknown (u) relationship to the context. One nice property of this extension is that the truth value u plays a similar role in propositional reasoning and in first-order reasoning—in both cases it marks the points at which reasoning was cut off because of computational limits. Variables bound to u are primary targets for reasoning by cases—the source of intractability in propositional logic. Domain objects with an unknown relationship to the context are targets for extending the context since they represent existential witnesses that are not fully instantiated.

The details of the first-order case will be described in a future paper.

Acknowledgments

We would like to thank Mukesh Dalal and members of CIRL for productive discussions, as well as the anonymous referees for their helpful comments.

This work was sponsored in part by the National Science Foundation (NSF) under grant number IRI-94-12205, and by the Defense Advanced Research Projects Agency (DARPA) and the Air Force Research Laboratory (AFRL) under agreement numbers F30602-95-1-0023 and F30602-97-1-0294. The U.S. Government is authorized to reproduce and distribute reprints for Governmental purposes notwithstanding any copyright annotation thereon. The views, findings, and conclusions contained herein are those of the authors and should not be interpreted as necessarily representing the official policies or endorsements, either expressed or implied, of the NSF, DARPA, AFRL, or the U.S. Government.

References

Bayardo, R. J., and Miranker, D. P. 1996. A complexity analysis of space-bounded learning for the constraint satisfaction problem. In *Proceedings of the Twelfth National Conference on Artificial Intelligence (AAAI-96)*, 298–304.

Bayardo, R. J., and Schrag, R. C. 1997. Using CSP look-back techniques to solve real-world sat instances. In *Proceedings of the Thirteenth National Conference on Artificial Intelligence (AAAI-97)*, 203–208.

Cadoli, M., and Schaerf, M. 1992. Tractable reasoning via approximation. In *Proceedings of the AAAI Workshop on Tractable Reasoning*, 12–15.

Crawford, J. M., and Auton, L. D. 1996. Experimental results on the crossover point in random 3SAT. *Artificial Intelligence* 81:13–59.

Crawford, J., and Kuipers, B. 1989. Towards a theory of access-limited logic for knowledge representation. In *Proceedings of the First International Conference on Principles of Knowledge Representation and Reasoning (KR'89)*, 67–78.

Crawford, J., and Kuipers, B. 1991. ALGERNON – A tractable system for knowledge-representation. In *AAAI Spring Symposium on Implemented Knowledge Representation and Reasoning Systems*.

Dalal, M. 1996a. Anytime families of tractable propositional reasoners. In *Proceedings of the Fourth International Symposium on Artificial Intelligence and Mathematics (AI/MATH-96)*, 42–45.

Dalal, M. 1996b. Semantics of an anytime family of reasoners. In *Proceedings of the European Conference on Artificial Intelligence (ECAI-96)*, 360–364.

Etherington, D., and Crawford, J. 1996. Toward efficient default reasoning. In *Proceedings of the Twelfth National Conference on Artificial Intelligence (AAAI-96)*, 627–632.

Frisch, A. 1987. Inference without chaining. In *Proceedings of the Tenth International Joint Conference on Artificial Intelligence (IJCAI-87)*, 515–519.

McAllester, D.; Givan, R.; and Fatima, T. 1989. Taxonomic syntax for first order inference. In *Proceedings of the First International Conference on Principles of Knowledge Representation and Reasoning (KR'89)*, 289–300.

Patel-Schneider, P. F. 1990. A decidable first-order logic for knowledge representation. *Journal of Automated Reasoning* 6:361–388.

Schrag, R., and Crawford, J. 1996. Implicates and prime implicates in random 3SAT. *Artificial Intelligence* 81:199–222.

Selman, B.; Kautz, H.; and Cohen, B. 1993. Local search strategies for satisfiability testing. In *Proceedings 1993 DIMACS Workshop on Maximum Clique, Graph Coloring, and Satisfiability*, 521–523.

Computing Intersections of Horn Theories for Reasoning with Models*

Thomas Eiter

Institut für Informatik
Universität Gießen
Arndtstraße 2, D-35392 Gießen
eiter@informatik.uni-giessen.de

Toshihide Ibaraki

Dept. Applied Mathematics & Physics
Graduate School of Informatics,
Kyoto University, Kyoto 606
ibaraki@kuamp.kyoto-u.ac.jp

Kazuhisa Makino

Dept. Systems & Human Science
Graduate School of Engineering Science,
Osaka University, Toyonaka, Osaka 560
makino@sys.es.osaka-u.ac.jp

Abstract

We consider computational issues in combining logical knowledge bases represented by their characteristic models; in particular, we study taking their logical intersection. We present efficient algorithms or prove intractability for the major computation problems for Horn knowledge bases. We also consider an extension of Horn theories, for which negative results are obtained. They indicate that generalizing the positive results beyond Horn theories is not immediate.

Introduction

More recently, model-based reasoning has been proposed as an alternative to the traditional approach of representing and accessing a logical knowledge base through formulas, cf. (Dechter & Pearl 1992; Kautz, Kearns, & Selman 1993; 1995; Kavvadias, Papadimitriou, & Sideri 1993; Khardon & Roth 1996; 1997). In this approach, a logical knowledge base KB is represented by a subset S of its models, which are commonly called *characteristic models*, rather than by a set of formulas. Reasoning from KB becomes then as easy as to test whether a given query α is true in all models of S; for suitable α, this can be decided efficiently. Note that it has also be shown that abduction from a KB represented by its characteristic models can be done in polynomial time (Kautz, Kearns, & Selman 1993; Khardon & Roth 1996), while this problem is intractable under formula representation (Selman & Levesque 1990; Eiter & Gottlob 1995).

This time speed up comes at the price of space; indeed, the formula-based and the model-based approach are orthogonal, in the sense that while a KB may have small representation in the one formalism, it can be exponentially larger sized in the other. The intertranslatability of the two approaches, in particular for Horn theories, has been addressed in (Kautz, Kearns, & Selman 1993; 1995; Kavvadias, Papadimitriou, & Sideri 1993; Khardon 1995; Khardon & Roth 1996).

*We gratefully acknowledge the partial support of the Scientific Grant in Aid by the Ministry of Education, Science and Culture of Japan (Grant 06044112). The major part of this research was conducted while the first author visited Kyoto University in 1995 and 1998. Copyright © 1998, American Association for Artificial Intelligence (www.aaai.org). All rights reserved.

A number of techniques for efficient model-based representation of various fragments of propositional logic have been devised, cf. (Kautz, Kearns, & Selman 1995; Khardon & Roth 1996; 1997). However, little attention has been paid so far on the important issue of how under this representation different knowledge bases $KB_1, \ldots, KB_n$ can be combined into a single KB.

The semantical issue of combining knowledge bases has been studied in the recent literature, see e.g. (Baral, Kraus, & Minker 1991; Subrahmanian 1994; Liberatore & Schaerf 1998), and we do not pick up the same issue here; rather, we are interested in tools for operations at the technical level.

In this context, a principal operation is taking the logical intersection of $KB_1, \ldots, KB_n$, i.e., the resulting knowledge base KB should have the models which are common to all KB_i's. While this operation is easily accomplished under formula-based representation (just take $KB := \bigcup_i KB_i$), this task appears to be much more complicated under model-based representation. In fact, it is a priori not clear, how from the characteristic models of the individual KB_i's the characteristic models of KB can be efficiently constructed, and what the complexity of this problem is; even an efficient algorithm for simply deciding the consistency of KB is unclear.

In this paper, we study the problems of computing characteristic as well as arbitrary models of the logical intersection $\Sigma = \Sigma_1 \cap \cdots \cap \Sigma_n$ of propositional theories Σ_i. We focus on Σ_i's which are Horn theories, as such theories are frequently encountered in the context of knowledge representation, and have received the major attention in (Dechter & Pearl 1992; Kautz, Kearns, & Selman 1993; 1995; Khardon 1995; Khardon & Roth 1996). In particular, we consider the following main problems.

Problem MODEL

Input: Sets of characteristic models $M_i \subseteq \{0,1\}^n$, representing Horn theories $\Sigma_i, i = 1, 2, \ldots, l$.

Output: Model v in $\Sigma = \bigcap_{i=1}^{l} \Sigma_i$ if $\Sigma \neq \emptyset$; else, "No".

Problem CMODEL

Input: Sets of characteristic models $M_i \subseteq \{0,1\}^n$, representing Horn theories $\Sigma_i, i = 1, 2, \ldots, l$.

Output: A characteristic model v in $\Sigma = \bigcap_{i=1}^{l} \Sigma_i$ if $\Sigma \neq \emptyset$; otherwise, "No".

Problem ALL-MODELS
Input: Sets of characteristic models $M_i \subseteq \{0,1\}^n$, representing Horn theories Σ_i, $i = 1, 2, \ldots, l$.
Output: All models v in $\Sigma = \bigcap_{i=1}^{l} \Sigma_i$.

Problem ALL-CMODELS
Input: Sets of characteristic models $M_i \subseteq \{0,1\}^n$, representing Horn theories Σ_i, $i = 1, 2, \ldots, l$.
Output: All characteristic models v in $\Sigma = \bigcap_{i=1}^{l} \Sigma_i$.

Notice that problem MODEL contains the consistency problem of Σ as a special case; if we have an efficient algorithm for MODEL, then we can use it for an efficient check whether Σ is consistent, i.e., $\Sigma \neq \emptyset$. Such a consistency test is another principal operation. Note that by the results of (Dowling & Gallier 1984), problem MODEL and the consistency check can be done in linear time under formula representation.

Obviously, problem MODEL is not harder than problem CMODEL, since any procedure for the latter can be used for the former. However, it remains to see whether the computation of an arbitrary model can be done more efficiently.

Problem ALL-MODELS generalizes the first problem, and is of interest for the issue of producing all models of Σ. Ideally, the models are generated one at a time, so that we can stop any time when no further models are desired. Such a procedure is valuable e.g. in case-based reasoning, if one tries to find a "model" of the reality which fits a given description.

Problem ALL-CMODELS is the counterpart for CMODEL. Here, we are interested in the complete output, as it is the requested representation of Σ in terms of its characteristic models.

From the results in (Kautz, Kearns, & Selman 1993), it easily follows that the output size of problem ALL-MODELS may be exponential in the input size, even if $l = 1$. However, it was unknown whether a similar result holds for ALL-CMODELS. In this paper, we show this by an example in which the output of ALL-CMODELS has 2^n models, while $l = 2$ and $|M_1| = |M_2| = 2n$.

Since ALL-MODELS and ALL-CMODELS may have exponential output, they are clearly not solvable in polynomial time. Observe that our latter result improves on (Gogic, Papadimitriou, & Sideri 1998, Theorem 6), which states that for $l = 2$, ALL-CMODELS is not polynomial unless P = NP.

However, this does not rule out the possibility of an algorithm which enumerates the models with *polynomial delay* (Johnson, Yannakakis, & Papadimitriou 1988), i.e., the next model is always output in time polynomial in the input size, and the algorithm stops in polynomial time after the last output. Any such algorithm runs in *polynomial total time* (Johnson, Yannakakis, & Papadimitriou 1988), i.e., polynomial in the *combined* size of input and output. As ALL-MODELS outputs more models than ALL-CMODELS, there appear more chances of having a polynomial total time algorithm for ALL-MODELS; we shall see in this paper that this is in fact the case.

Detailed Proofs of all results are given in the full paper, which contains more results (Eiter, Makino, & Ibaraki 1998).

Preliminaries

We assume a standard propositional language with atoms $x_1, x_2, \ldots, x_n$, where each x_i takes either value 1 (true) or 0 (false). Negated atoms are denoted by $\overline{x}_i$.

A *model* v is a vector in $\{0,1\}^n$, whose i-th component is denoted by v_i. For models v, w, we denote by $v \leq w$ the usual componentwise ordering, i.e., $v_i \leq w_i$ for all $i = 1, 2, \ldots, n$, where $0 \leq 1$; $v < w$ means $v \neq w$ and $v \leq w$. As usual, $v \geq w$ is the reverse ordering. For $B \subseteq \{1, \ldots, n\}$, we denote by x^B the model v such that $v_i = 1$, if $i \in B$ and $v_i = 0$, if $i \notin B$, for all $i = 1, \ldots, n$.

A *theory* is any set $\Sigma \subseteq \{0,1\}^n$ of models; its cardinality is denoted by $|\Sigma|$. By $\min(\Sigma)$ and $\max(\Sigma)$ we denote the sets of minimal and maximal models in Σ under $<$, respectively, where $v \in \Sigma$ is *maximal* (resp., *minimal*) model in Σ, if there is no $w \in \Sigma$ such that $w > v$ (resp., $w < v$).

A propositional clause $C = \ell_1 \vee \cdots \vee \ell_k$ is *Horn*, if at most one literal ℓ_i is positive, and a CNF is *Horn*, if it contains only Horn clauses. A theory Σ is *Horn*, if there exists a Horn CNF representing it.

Horn theories Σ have a well-known model-theoretic characterization. Denote by $v \wedge w$ componentwise AND of vectors $v, w \in \{0,1\}^n$, and by $Cl_\wedge(S)$ the closure of $S \subseteq \{0,1\}^n$ under $\wedge$. Then, Σ is Horn, if and only if $\Sigma = Cl_\wedge(\Sigma)$. Note that as a consequence, any Horn theory Σ has the *least* (i.e., unique minimal) model $v = \bigwedge_{w \in \Sigma} w$, i.e., $\min(\Sigma) = \{v\}$.

E.g., consider $\Sigma_1 = \{(0101), (1001), (1000)\}$ and $\Sigma_2 = \{(0101), (1001), (1000), (0001), (0000)\}$. Then, for $v = (0101)$, $w = (1000)$, we have $w, v \in \Sigma_1$, while $v \wedge w = (0000) \notin \Sigma_1$; hence Σ_1 is not Horn. On the other hand, $Cl_\wedge(\Sigma_2) = \Sigma_2$, thus Σ_2 is Horn.

For any Horn theory Σ, a model $v \in \Sigma$ is called *characteristic* (Kautz, Kearns, & Selman 1993) (or *extreme* (Dechter & Pearl 1992)), if $v \notin Cl_\wedge(\Sigma \setminus \{v\})$. The set of all characteristic models of Σ, the *characteristic set of* Σ, is denoted by $C^*(\Sigma)$. Note that every Horn theory Σ has a unique characteristic set $C^*(\Sigma)$ and that $\max(\Sigma) \subseteq C^*(\Sigma)$. E.g., $(0101) \in C^*(\Sigma_2)$, while $(0000) \notin C^*(\Sigma_2)$; it holds that $C^*(\Sigma_2) = \Sigma_1$.

Finding Some Model

We start with the following lemma, which is useful for solving problem MODEL.

Lemma 1 *Let $\Sigma_i \subseteq \{0,1\}^n$, $i = 1, 2, \ldots, l$, be Horn theories, and let $\Sigma = \bigcap_{i=1}^{l} \Sigma_i$. Then any $v \in \Sigma$ satisfies*

$$v \geq \bigvee_{i=1}^{l} \left(\bigwedge_{w \in C^*(\Sigma_i)} w \right). \tag{1}$$

Proof. First note that $v = \bigwedge_{w \in Q_1} w = \bigwedge_{w \in Q_2} w = \ldots = \bigwedge_{w \in Q_l} w$ holds for some $Q_i \subseteq C^*(\Sigma_i)$, $i = 1, 2, \ldots, l$, by the definitions of v and $C^*(\Sigma_i)$. Then we have $v \geq \bigwedge_{w \in C^*(\Sigma_i)} w$ for all i, and hence (1). □

Based on the lemma, a model of Σ is found as follows.

Clearly, Σ has no model, if some Σ_i is empty; if not, then consider the least models $v_1, \ldots, v_l$ of $\Sigma_1, \ldots, \Sigma_l$. If they all coincide, then $v = v_1$ is a model of Σ, which is the output. Otherwise, exploiting Lemma 1, we look at the least upper bound of $v_1, \ldots, v_l$ as a new candidate u for a model; in fact, any $v \in \Sigma$ must satisfy $u \leq v$. Since v must be generated from characteristic models in each Σ_i, we can discard all characteristic models which for sure do not contribute in that. Since the resulting theories are Horn, we can iterate and build a chain $C : u^{(1)} < u^{(2)} < \cdots < u^{(k)}$ such that either $u^{(k)}$ is found to be a model of Σ, or $\Sigma = \emptyset$ is detected.

The formal description of this algorithm is as follows.

Algorithm MODEL

Input: Characteristic sets $M_i = C^*(\Sigma_i)$, representing Horn theories $\Sigma_i \subseteq \{0,1\}^n$, $i = 1, \ldots, l$.

Output: Model $v \in \Sigma = \bigcap_{i=1}^{l} \Sigma_i$ if $\Sigma \neq \emptyset$; else, "No".

Step 0. for each $i = 1, 2, \ldots, l$ do $Q_i := M_i$;

Step 1. if $Q_i = \emptyset$ for some i then output "No" and halt;

Step 2. if $\bigwedge_{w \in Q_1} w = \bigwedge_{w \in Q_2} w = \ldots = \bigwedge_{w \in Q_l} w$
then output $v = \bigwedge_{w \in Q_1} w$ and halt;

Step 3. $u := \bigvee_{i=1}^{l} (\bigwedge_{w \in Q_i} w)$;
for each $i = 1, \ldots, l$ do $Q_i := \{w \in Q_i \mid w \geq u\}$;
goto Step 1. □

Example 1 Let $M_1 = C^*(\Sigma_1) = \{(0110), (0011), (1010)\}$ and $M_2 = C^*(\Sigma_2) = \{(1110), (0111), (0011)\}$.

In step 2, we have $\bigwedge_{w \in Q_1} = (0010)$ and $\bigwedge_{w \in Q_2} = (0010)$; hence, $v = (0010)$ is output. Note that $\Sigma = \{(0110), (0010), (0011)\}$; thus, output of $v = (0010)$ is correct. □

An analysis of its run time gives the following result.

Theorem 1 Problem MODEL can be solved in $O(n^2 \sum_{i=1}^{l} |M_i|)$ time. □

In fact, algorithm MODEL finds a distinguished model of Σ; it is not hard to see from its working that the output is the *least model* of Σ. Thus,

Corollary 1 Algorithm MODEL finds the least model v of $\Sigma = \bigcap_{i=1}^{l} \Sigma_i$ in $O(n^2 \sum_{i=1}^{l} |M_i|)$ time if $\Sigma \neq \emptyset$, and outputs "No" if $\Sigma = \emptyset$. □

Algorithm MODEL has run time about size of the input times the number of propositional atoms, and is thus almost quadratic in the worst case.

In the full paper, we describe an improved version MODEL+ which runs in $O(n \sum_{i=1}^{l} |M_i|)$ time, i.e., in linear time. This is achieved by using appropriate data structures, including cross-reference lists and counters which help in avoiding that the same bit of the input is examined more than a constant number of times. We only note the result.

Proposition 1 Given the characteristic sets $C^*(\Sigma_i)$ of Horn theories $\Sigma_i \subseteq \{0,1\}^n$, $i = 1, 2, \ldots, l$, deciding consistency and computing the least model of $\Sigma = \bigcap_{i=1}^{l} \Sigma_i$ is possible in $O(n \sum_{i=1}^{l} |M_i|)$ time, i.e., in linear time. □

Finding Some Characteristic Model

Also problem CMODEL can be solved in polynomial time.

Basically, we can proceed as follows. We construct the least model u of $\Sigma = \bigcap_i \Sigma_i$ as a candidate in $C^*(\Sigma)$; this is possible using algorithm MODEL. Then, two cases arise:

(i) $u \in C^*(\Sigma)$; in this case, we can output u and stop.

(ii) $u \notin C^*(\Sigma)$; here, u is replaced by a new larger candidate model $u' > u$, $u' \in \Sigma$, and the process is continued.

Since any chain of models $u = u^{(1)} < u^{(2)} < \ldots < u^{(k)}$ is bounded, the algorithm eventually finds some characteristic model (as any maximal model is characteristic) and halts. The problem is recognizing which case applies, and to select in (ii) a proper u'. It can be seen that $u \in C^*(\Sigma)$ holds, if (but not only if) the following condition holds. Let $Q_i = \{v > u \mid v \in M_i\}$ and $P_{ij} = \{w \in Q_i \mid w_j = 1\}$.

$$\forall j : u_j = 0 \implies \bigcap_{i=1}^{l} Cl_\wedge(P_{ij}) = \emptyset \qquad (2)$$

On the other hand, if for some j, (2) is violated, then any model $v \in Cl_\wedge(P_{ij})$ is a model of Σ with $v > u$; since some characteristic model $\geq v$ exists, we can safely select $u' = v$ and replace each M_i by the set $\{w \geq u' \mid w \in P_{ij}\}$.

Example 2 Let again $M_1 = C^*(\Sigma_1) = \{(0110), (0011), (1010)\}$ and $M_2 = C^*(\Sigma_2) = \{(1110), (0111), (0011)\}$.

The least model of $\Sigma = \Sigma_1 \cap \Sigma_2$ is $u = u^{(1)} = (0010)$. Thus, we have $Q_1^{(1)} = M_1$ and $Q_2^{(1)} = M_2$. For $j = 2$, we have $P_{12}^{(1)} = \{(0110)\}$ and $P_{22}^{(1)} = \{(1110), (0111)\}$; hence, $(0110) \in Cl_\wedge(P_{12}^{(1)}) \cap Cl_\wedge(P_{22}^{(1)})$ violates (2). Thus, we set $u^{(2)} = (0110)$ and continue; we set $M_1^{(2)} := \{(0110)\}$ and $M_2^{(2)} := \{(1110), (0111)\}$. Then, we obtain $Q_1^{(2)} = \emptyset$ and $Q_2^{(2)} = \{(1110), (0111)\}$. Consequently, for each j, $P_{1j}^{(2)}$ is empty, which means that condition (2) is true; hence, $v = u^{(2)}$ is output. Note that $C^*(\Sigma) = \{(0110), (0011)\}$; thus, output of $v = (0110)$ is correct. □

Improving the above method, we can save on time by exploiting the observation that if some j with $u_j = 0$ satisfies (2), then we need not check if (2) holds for this j later again. Indeed, this means that there exists no $w' \in \Sigma$ such that $w' \geq u$ and $w'_j = 1$.

Formally, our algorithm can be written as follows.

Algorithm CMODEL
Input: Characteristic sets $M_i = C^*(\Sigma_i)$ of Horn theories $\Sigma_i \subseteq \{0,1\}^n$, $i = 1, 2, \ldots, l$.
Output: A model $v \in C^*(\Sigma)$, where $\Sigma = \bigcap_{i=1}^{l} \Sigma_i$, if $\Sigma \neq \emptyset$; otherwise, "No".

Step 1. find the least model u in Σ;
   if no such u exists **then** output "No"
   else for each $i = 1, 2, \ldots, l$ **do**
      $Q_i := \{w \in M_i \,|\, w \geq u\}$;

Step 2. **for** each $j = 1, 2, \ldots, n$ **do**
   if $u_j = 0$ **then begin**
      for each $i = 1, 2, \ldots, l$ **do**
         $P_{ij} := \{w \in Q_i \,|\, w_j = 1\}$;
      if $\bigcap_{i=1}^{l} Cl_\wedge(P_{ij}) \neq \emptyset$ **then begin**
         find a model w' in $\bigcap_{i=1}^{l} Cl_\wedge(P_{ij})$;
         $u := w'$;
         for each $i = 1, 2, \ldots, l$ **do**
            $Q_i := \{w \in P_{ij} \,|\, w \geq u\}$;
      end;
   end;

Step 3. output the model $v := u$. □

An analysis of the running time of this algorithm yields the following result.

Theorem 2 *Problem* CMODEL *can be solved in* $O(n^2 \sum_{i=1}^{l} |M_i|)$ *time.* □

From the working of this algorithm, we see that it outputs some particular characteristic model, namely a maximal model of Σ. We thus obtain the following result.

Corollary 2 *Algorithm* CMODEL *finds a maximal model v in $\Sigma = \bigcap_{i=1}^{l} \Sigma_i$ in $O(n^2 \sum_{i=1}^{l} |M_i|)$ time if $\Sigma \neq \emptyset$, and outputs "No" if $\Sigma = \emptyset$.* □

The fact that we can *compute* some characteristic model fast does not automatically mean that we can *recognize* any characteristic model fast; nonetheless, this task can be solved in polynomial time. The key for this result is the following lemma.

Lemma 2 *Let Σ be a Horn theory and v be a model in Σ. Then $v \notin C^*(\Sigma)$ holds if and only if $v \neq (11 \cdots 1)$ and $v = \bigwedge_{w \in \min(\Sigma_v)} w$, where $\Sigma_v = \{w \in \Sigma \,|\, w > v\}$.* □

Exploiting this Lemma, we construct the following algorithm for characteristic model checking.

Algorithm CHECK-CMODEL
Input: Characteristic sets $M_i = C^*(\Sigma_i)$ of Horn theories $\Sigma_i \subseteq \{0,1\}^n$, $i = 1, \ldots, l$, and a model $v \in \Sigma = \bigcap_{i=1}^{l} \Sigma_i$.
Output: "Yes", if $v \in C^*(\Sigma)$, otherwise, "No".

Step 0. **if** $v = (1 \cdots 1)$ **then** output "Yes" and halt **else** $S := \emptyset$;

Step 1. **for** each j with $v_j = 0$ **do begin**
   for each $i = 1, 2, \ldots, l$ **do**
      $Q_i^{(j)} := \{w \in M_i \,|\, w \geq v, w_j = 1\}$;
   if $\bigcap_{i=1}^{l} Cl_\wedge(Q_i^{(j)}) \neq \emptyset$ **then begin**
      $w^{(j)} :=$ least model in $\bigcap_{i=1}^{l} Cl_\wedge(Q_i^{(j)})$;
      $S := S \cup \{w^{(j)}\}$;
   end;
end;

Step 2. **if** $v = \bigwedge_{w^{(j)} \in S} w^{(j)}$ **then** output "No"
   else output "Yes". □

Example 3 Let as above $M_1 = C^*(\Sigma_1) = \{(0110), (0011), (1010)\}$ and $M_2 = C^*(\Sigma_2) = \{(1110), (0111), (0011)\}$, and suppose $v = (0110)$.

Then, in step 1 of CHECK-CMODEL, $S := \emptyset$; in step 2, j takes values 1 and 4. For $j = 1$, we obtain $Q_1^{(1)} := \emptyset$ and $Q_2^{(1)} := \{(1110)\}$, hence $Cl_\wedge(Q_1^{(1)}) \cap Cl_\wedge(Q_2^{(1)}) = \emptyset$, and S is unchanged. For $j = 4$, we have $Q_1^{(4)} = \emptyset$ again and $Q_2^{(4)} = \{(0111)\}$; hence $S = \emptyset$ is not changed. In step 3, the check $v = \bigwedge_{w^{(j)} \in S} w^{(j)}$ yields false (for empty S, $\bigwedge_{w \in S} w = (11\ldots1)$); hence the output is "Yes". Note that $v = (0110)$ is indeed a characteristic model of Σ. □

An analysis of the running time of the algorithm yields the following result.

Theorem 3 *Given the characteristic sets $C^*(\Sigma_i)$ of Horn theories $\Sigma_i \subseteq \{0,1\}^n$, $i = 1 \ldots, l$, and a model $v \in \Sigma = \bigcap_{i=1}^{l} \Sigma_i$, checking if $v \in C^*(\Sigma)$ is possible in $O(n^2 \sum_{i=1}^{l} |M_i|)$ time.* □

ALL-CMODELS and ALL-MODELS

It is known that for a Horn theory Σ, the number $|\Sigma|$ of its models may be exponential in $|C^*(\Sigma)|$. Thus the output size of ALL-MODELS may be exponential in the input size. For ALL-CMODELS, we derive an analogous result.

Claim 1 *For every $n \geq 1$, there exist Horn theories Σ_1 and Σ_2 such that $|C^*(\Sigma_1)| = |C^*(\Sigma_2)| = 2n$ and $|C^*(\Sigma)| = 2^n$, where $\Sigma = \Sigma_1 \cap \Sigma_2$.*

Proof. (Sketch) Fix n, and define $S_1, S_2 \subseteq \{0,1\}^{4n}$ as follows. Let $V_i = \{i*n + j \,|\, j = 1, \ldots n\}$, for $i = 0, \ldots, 3$ and $V = \bigcup_{i=0}^{3} V_i = \{1, \ldots, 4n\}$. Then,

$S_1 = \{x^{V \setminus (V_2 \cup \{j, 3n+j\})}, x^{V \setminus (V_2 \cup \{n+j, 3n+j\})} \,|\, 1 \leq j \leq n\}$,
$S_2 = \{x^{V \setminus (V_3 \cup \{j, 2n+j\})}, x^{V \setminus (V_3 \cup \{n+j, 2n+j\})} \,|\, 1 \leq j \leq n\}$.

E.g., for $n = 2$, we have

$S_1 = \{(01110001), (11010001), (10110010), (11100010)\}$,
$S_2 = \{(01110100), (11010100), (10111000), (11101000)\}$.

Observe that $|S_1| = |S_2| = 2n$. Since $S_1 = \max(S_1)$ and $S_2 = \max(S_2)$, there are Horn theories Σ_1 and Σ_2 such that $C^*(\Sigma_1) = S_1$ and $C^*(\Sigma_2) = S_2$. Define

$S = \{x^B \,|\, B \subseteq V_0 \cup V_1, j \in B \equiv n+j \notin B, 1 \leq j \leq n\}$.

For $n = 2$, we have

$S = \{(00110000), (10010000), (01100000), (11000000).$

Observe that $|S| = 2^n$. It can be shown that $S = C^*(\Sigma)$. Since $|S| = 2^n$, the claim is verified. □

Hence, a polynomial time algorithm in the input size for ALL-CMODELS is impossible, which improves (Gogic, Papadimitriou, & Sideri 1998, Theorem 6).

However, even the remaining hope for a polynomial total time algorithm is unlikely to come true, since the following related problem is intractable.

Lemma 3 *The problem* ADD-CMODEL: *Given characteristic sets $C^*(\Sigma_i)$ of Horn theories $\Sigma_i \subseteq \{0,1\}^n$, $i = 1, \ldots, l$ and $S \subseteq C^*(\Sigma)$, where $\Sigma = \bigcap_{i=1}^{l} \Sigma_i$, decide if some $v \in C^*(\Sigma) \setminus S$ exists; is NP-hard, even for $l = 2$.*

Proof. (Sketch) We prove NP-hardness by a reduction from the satisfiability problem (SAT) (Garey & Johnson 1979); we define for a given CNF formula $\Phi = \bigwedge_{i=1}^{m} C_i$ on n atoms polynomially computable sets M_1, M_2, and S of vectors in $\{0,1\}^{n+2m}$, such that $M_1 = C^*(\Sigma_1)$, $M_2 = C^*(\Sigma_2)$ and $S \subseteq C^*(\Sigma_1 \cap \Sigma_2)$. Moreover, $S = C^*(\Sigma_1 \cap \Sigma_2)$ holds iff Φ is unsatisfiable. □

Theorem 4 *There is no polynomial total time algorithm for problem* ALL-CMODELS, *unless* P=NP.

Proof. Assume there is an algorithm A for ALL-CMODELS with polynomial running time $p(I, O)$, where I is the input length and O the output length. We solve ADD-CMODEL using A: Execute A until either (i) it halts or (ii) time $p(I, |S|)$ is reached. In case (i), output "Yes" if A outputs some vector in $C^*(\Sigma) \setminus S$; otherwise, "No". In case (ii), output "Yes", since it implies $C^*(\Sigma) \setminus S \neq \emptyset$. Hence, ADD-CMODEL is solvable in time polynomial in I and $|S|$, which contradicts Lemma 3 unless P=NP. □

In the full paper, we also show that *approximating* $C^*(\Sigma)$ is hard; unless P = NP, there are no polynomial total time algorithms for computing a polynomially larger superset or a polynomial fraction of $C^*(\Sigma)$, respectively.

Contrary to ALL-CMODELS, problem ALL-MODELS has a polynomial total time algorithm. As we show that it is possible to check whether a *partial* vector $v \in \{0, 1, ?\}^n$, where '?' represents unknown, can be completed to a model $w \in \Sigma$ in polynomial time, we can apply the method of dynamic lexicographic ordering (Dechter & Itai 1992) to enumerate all models with polynomial delay. The algorithm uses a bookkeeping vector $mark \in \{0,1\}^n$ and a subroutine PART-MODEL, which has the following specification:

Procedure PART-MODEL

Input: Characteristic sets M_i of Horn theories $\Sigma_i \subseteq \{0,1\}^n$, $i = 1, 2, \ldots, l$, and a list $b_1, b_2, \ldots, b_r$ of values $b_i \in \{0, 1\}, 1 \leq i \leq r \leq n$.

Output: Model $w \in \Sigma = \bigcap_{i=1}^{l} \Sigma_i$ such that $w_i = b_i$ holds for all $i = 1, 2 \ldots, r$, if one exists; "No," otherwise. □

This algorithm can be implemented to run in $O(n |\sum_{i=1}^{l} |M_i|)$ time. The main algorithm is then as follows.

Algorithm ALL-MODELS

Input: Characteristic sets $M_i = C^*(\Sigma_i)$ of Horn theories $\Sigma_i \subseteq \{0,1\}^n, i = 1, 2, \ldots, l$.

Output: All models $v \in \Sigma = \bigcap_{i=1}^{l} \Sigma_i$, if $\Sigma \neq \emptyset$; otherwise, "No".

Step 1. call MODEL to find some model $v \in \Sigma$;
  if the answer is "No", **then** output "No" and halt
  else begin output v;
    $mark := (00\ldots0)$; $i := n$
  end;

Step 2. if $mark_i = 0$ **then begin**
    call PART-MODEL($\Sigma_1, .., \Sigma_l, v_1, .., v_{i-1}, 1 - v_i$);
    if a model w is returned **then**
      begin output w;
      set $v := w$; $mark_i := 1$;
      for $j = i + 1$ to n do $mark_j := 0$;
      $i := n + 1$
    end
  end;

Step 3. if $i = 1$ **then** halt
  else begin $i := i - 1$; **goto** Step 2 **end**. □

Example 4 Let again $M_1 = C^*(\Sigma_1) = \{(0110), (0011), (1010)\}$ and $M_2 = C^*(\Sigma_2) = \{(1110), (0111), (0011)\}$.

In Step 1, the call to MODEL returns the least model of Σ, which is $v = (0010)$; this model is output and $mark$ is initialized to (0000) and $i := 4$.

In Step 2, PART-MODEL is called for the list $0, 0, 1, 1$ of b_i values (we omit $\Sigma_1, \ldots, \Sigma_l$, which may be accessed as global variables). The model (0011) is returned, which is output and assigned to v; $mark$ is updated to (0001) and i is set to 5 and decreased to 4 in Step 3, where the computation returns to Step 2.

In Step 3, i is decreased to 3, and in next iteration of Step 2, PART-MODEL is called for the b_i values $0,0,0$. The answer is "No", and hence i is decreased to 2 in Step 3. Subsequently, in Step 2 PART-MODEL is called for the b_i values $0,1$. The model $w = (0110)$ is returned, which is output; $v := (0110)$, $mark := (0100)$, and $i := 5$.

In the next 2 iterations, PART-MODEL is called for b_i values $0,1,1,1$ and $0,1,0$, respectively, for which "No" is returned; after decreasing i to 1, PART-MODEL is called again for B_i value 1, which also returns "No". Hence, in Step 3 $i = 1$ is true, and the algorithm stops.

Thus, the models output are: $(0010), (0110)$, and (0011); these are precisely the models in Σ. □

The analysis of the time complexity of ALL-MODELS, gives us the next result.

Theorem 5 *Algorithm* ALL-MODELS *is a polynomial delay algorithm for* ALL-MODELS, *where the delay is* $O(n^2 \sum_{i=1}^{l} |M_i|)$. □

Further Results and Conclusion

As shown in (Kautz, Kearns, & Selman 1993), a striking advantage of characteristic models is that both deduction

$\Sigma \models \alpha$ of a CNF formula α and abduction of a query letter q from the characteristic models of a Horn theory is possible in polynomial time. In the full paper, we show the following results:

Theorem 6 *Deductive inference $\Sigma \models \alpha$ of a CNF formula α from $\Sigma = \bigcap_{i=1}^{l} \Sigma_i$, given α and the characteristic sets $M_i = C^*(\Sigma_i)$ of the Horn theories $\Sigma_i \subseteq \{0,1\}^n$ for input, is feasible in $O(nm \sum_{i=1}^{l} |M_i|)$ time, where m is the number of clauses in α;*

Theorem 7 *Abduction of a letter q from $\Sigma = \bigcap_{i=1}^{l} \Sigma_i$, given α and the characteristic sets $M_i = C^*(\Sigma_i)$ of the Horn theories $\Sigma_i \subseteq \{0,1\}^n$ and a given set A of assumptions is NP-complete.* □

The results show that deduction scales up gracefully from a single Horn KB to the intersection of multiple Horn KBs, while this is not the case for abduction; it indicates that the tractability result in (Kautz, Kearns, & Selman 1993) is not very robust.

Characteristic models have been generalized to Non-Horn theories by making use of *monotone theory* (Bshouty 1995) in (Khardon & Roth 1996). This approach is promising, since many advantages of Horn theories carry over to Non-Horn theories. In this direction, we investigate in the full paper the class $\mathcal{C}_{EH}$ of *extended Horn* theories, which contains Horn and *reverse* Horn theories, i.e., theories which become Horn by negating all propositions. For this class, we establish the following result.

Theorem 8 *Problem MODEL for class $\mathcal{C}_{EH}$ is NP-hard, even if $l = 2$.* □

We prove this result by a reduction from the EXACT-HITTING-SET problem (Garey & Johnson 1979).

Corollary 3 *For class $\mathcal{C}_{EH}$, problem CMODEL is NP-hard, and there exist no polynomial total time algorithms for ALL-MODELS and ALL-CMODELS, unless P=NP.* □

Moreover, also deduction and abduction for $\mathcal{C}_{EH}$ are intractable. This indicates that a generalization of characteristic models is not immediately computationally feasible for combining knowledge bases. Moreover, an investigation of relevant classes besides Horn theories which are benign for combination remains to be done.

Further operations in combining theories Σ_i may be needed; e.g., taking the union $\Sigma' = \bigcup_i \Sigma_i$. Notice that Σ' is not necessarily Horn, if all Σ_i are Horn; in that case, Σ' may be approximated by Horn theories (Kautz, Kearns, & Selman 1995; Kavvadias, Papadimitriou, & Sideri 1993).

Our further and future work addresses these and other issues; e.g., we investigate into conditions for Horn Σ' which may serve as a basis for suitable algorithms.

Acknowledgments. We thank the referees for their helpful comments on this paper.

References

Baral, C.; Kraus, S.; and Minker, J. 1991. Combining Multiple Knowledge Bases. *IEEE Transactions on Knowledge and Data Engineering* 3(2):208–220.

Bshouty, N. H. 1995. Exact Learning Boolean Functions via the Monotone Theory. *Information and Computation* 123:146–153.

Dechter, R., and Itai, A. 1992. Finding All Solutions if You can Find One. Technical Report ICS-TR-92-61, University of California at Riverside.

Dechter, R., and Pearl, J. 1992. Structure Identification in Relational Data. *Art. Intelligence* 58:237–270.

Dowling, W., and Gallier, J. H. 1984. Linear-time Algorithms for Testing the Satisfiability of Propositional Horn Theories. *J. Logic Programming* 3:267–284.

Eiter, T., and Gottlob, G. 1995. The Complexity of Logic-Based Abduction. *JACM* 42(1):3–42.

Eiter, T.; Makino, K.; and Ibaraki, T. 1998. Computing Intersections of Horn Theories for Reasoning with Models. TR 9803, Institut für Informatik, Universität Gießen, Germany.

Garey, M., and Johnson, D. S. 1979. *Computers and Intractability*. New York: W. H. Freeman.

Gogic, G.; Papadimitriou, C.; and Sideri, M. 1998. Incremental Recompilation of Knowledge. *J. Artificial Intelligence Research* 8:23–37.

Johnson, D. S.; Yannakakis, M.; and Papadimitriou, C. H. 1988. On Generating All Maximal Independent Sets. *Information Processing Letters* 27:119–123.

Kautz, H.; Kearns, M.; and Selman, B. 1993. Reasoning With Characteristic Models. In *Proc. AAAI-93*.

Kautz, H.; Kearns, M.; and Selman, B. 1995. Horn Approximations of Empirical Data. *Artificial Intelligence* 74:129–245.

Kavvadias, D.; Papadimitriou, C.; and Sideri, M. 1993. On Horn Envelopes and Hypergraph Transversals. In *Proc. ISAAC-93*, LNCS 762, 399–405.

Khardon, R., and Roth, D. 1996. Reasoning with Models. *Artificial Intelligence* 87(1/2):187–213.

Khardon, R., and Roth, D. 1997. Defaults and Relevance in Model-Based Reasoning. *Artificial Intelligence* 97(1/2):169–193.

Khardon, R. 1995. Translating between Horn Representations and their Characteristic Models. *J. Artificial Intelligence Research* 3:349–372.

Liberatore, P., and Schaerf, M. 1998. Arbitration (or How to Merge Knowledge Bases). *IEEE Transactions on Knowledge and Data Engineering* 10(1), 1998.

Selman, B., and Levesque, H. J. 1990. Abductive and Default Reasoning: A Computational Core. In *Proc. AAAI-90*, 343–348.

Subrahmanian, V. 1994. Amalgamating Knowledge Bases. *ACM Trans. on Database Syst.* 19(2):291–331.

Constraint Satisfaction and Search

The Branching Factor of Regular Search Spaces

Stefan Edelkamp
Institut für Informatik
Am Flughafen 17
79110 Freiburg
edelkamp@informatik.uni-freiburg.de

Richard E. Korf
Computer Science Department
University of California
Los Angeles, Ca. 90095
korf@cs.ucla.edu

Abstract

Many problems, such as the sliding-tile puzzles, generate search trees where different nodes have different numbers of children, in this case depending on the position of the blank. We show how to calculate the asymptotic branching factors of such problems, and how to efficiently compute the exact numbers of nodes at a given depth. This information is important for determining the complexity of various search algorithms on these problems. In addition to the sliding-tile puzzles, we also apply our technique to Rubik's Cube. While our techniques are fairly straightforward, the literature is full of incorrect branching factors for these problems, and the errors in several incorrect methods are fairly subtle.

Introduction

Many AI search algorithms, such as depth-first search (DFS), depth-first iterative-deepening (DFID), and Iterative-Deepening-A* (IDA*) (Korf 1985) search a problem-space tree. While most problem spaces are in fact graphs with cycles, detecting these cycles in general requires storing all generated nodes in memory, which is impractical for large problems. Thus, to conserve space, these algorithms search a tree expansion of the graph, rooted at the initial state. In a tree expansion of a graph, each distinct path to a given problem state gives rise to a different node in the search tree. Note that the tree expansion of a graph can be exponentially larger than the underlying graph, and in fact can be infinite even for a finite graph.

The time complexity of searching a tree depends primarily on the *branching factor* b, and the *solution depth* d. The solution depth is the length of a shortest solution path, and depends on the given problem instance. The branching factor, however, typically converges to a constant value for the entire problem space. Thus, computing the branching factor is an essential step in determining the complexity of a search algorithm on a given problem, and can be used for selecting among alternative problem spaces for the same problem.

The branching factor of a node is the number of children it has. In a tree where every node has the same branching factor, this is also the branching factor of the tree. The difficulty occurs when different nodes at the same level of the tree have different numbers of children. In that case, we can define the branching factor at a given depth of the tree as the ratio of the number of nodes at that depth to the number of nodes at the next shallower depth. In most cases, the branching factor at a given depth converges to a limit as the depth goes to infinity. This is the *asymptotic branching factor*, and the best measure of the size of the tree.

In the remainder of this paper, we present some simple examples of problem spaces, including sliding-tile puzzles and Rubik's Cube, and show how to compute their asymptotic branching factors, and how not to. We formalize the problem as the solution of a set of simultaneous equations, which can be quite large in practice. As an alternative to an analytic solution, we present an efficient numerical technique for determining the exact number of nodes at a given depth, and for estimating the asymptotic branching factor to a high degree of precision. Finally, we present some data on the branching factors of various sliding-tile puzzles.

Example Problem Spaces

The Five Puzzle

Our first example is the Five Puzzle, the 2 × 3 version of the well-known sliding-tile puzzles (see Figure 1). There are five numbered square tiles, and one empty position, called the "blank". Any tile horizontally or vertically adjacent to the blank can be slid into the blank position. The goal is to rearrange the tiles from some random initial configuration into a particular goal configuration, such as that shown at right in Figure 1.

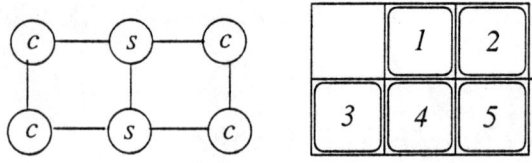

Figure 1: Side and corner states in the Five Puzzle.

The branching factor of a node in this space depends on the position of the blank. There are two different types of locations in this puzzle, "side" or s positions, and "corner" or c positions (see Figure 1). Similarly, we refer to a node or state where the blank is in an s or c position as an s or c node or state. For simplicity at first, we assume that the parent of a node is also generated as one of its children, since all operators are invertible. Thus, the branching factor of an s node is three, and the branching factor of a c node is two. Clearly, the asymptotic branching factor will be between two and three.

The exact value of the branching factor will depend on f_s, the fraction of total nodes at a given level of the tree that are s nodes, with $f_c = 1 - f_s$ being the fraction of c nodes. For a given level, f_s will depend on whether the initial state is an s node or a c node, but we are interested in the limiting value of this ratio as the depth goes to infinity, which is independent of the initial state.

Equal Likelihood The simplest hypothesis is that f_s is equal to 2/6 or 1/3, since there are two different s positions for the blank, out of a total of six possible positions. This gives an asymptotic branching factor of $3 \cdot 1/3 + 2 \cdot 2/3 = 2.333$. Unfortunately, this assumes that all possible positions of the blank are equally likely, which is incorrect. Intuitively, the s positions are more centrally located in the puzzle, and hence overrepresented in the search tree.

Random-Walk Model A better hypothesis is the following. Consider the six-node graph at left in Figure 1. In a long random walk of the blank over this graph, the fraction of time that the blank spends in any particular node will eventually converge to an equilibrium value, subject to a minor technicality. If we divide the six positions into two sets, consisting of 1, 3, and 5 verses 2, 4, and the blank in Figure 1, every move takes the blank from a position in one set to a position in the other set. Thus, at even depths the blank will be in one set, and at odd depths in the other. Since the two sets are completely symmetric, however, we can ignore this issue in this case.

The equilibrium fraction from the random walk is easy to compute. Since s nodes have degree three, and c nodes have degree two, the equilibrium fraction of time spent in an individual s state versus an individual c state must be in the ratio of three to two (Motwani & Raghavan 1995). Since there are twice as many c states as s states, c states are occupied 4/7 of the time and s states are occupied 3/7 of the time. This gives a branching factor of $3 \cdot 3/7 + 2 \cdot 4/7 \approx 2.42857$, which differs from the value of 2.3333 obtained above.

Unfortunately, this calculation is incorrect as well. While the random-walk model accurately predicts the probability of being in a particular state given a long enough random walk down the search tree, if the tree has non-uniform branching factor, this is not the same as the relative frequencies of the different states at that level of the tree. For example, consider the simple tree fragment in Figure 2. If we randomly sample the three leaf nodes at the bottom, each is equally likely to appear. However, in a random walk down this tree, the leftmost leaf node will be reached with probability 1/2, and the remaining two nodes with probability 1/4 each.

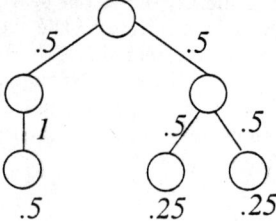

Figure 2: Tree with Nonuniform Branching Factor.

The Correct Answer The correct way to compute the equilibrium fraction f_s is as follows. A c node at one level generates an s node and another c node at the next level. Similarly, an s node at one level generates another s node and two c nodes at the next level. Thus, the number of c nodes at a given level is two times the number of s nodes plus the number of c nodes at the previous level, and the number of s nodes is the number of c nodes plus the number of s nodes at the previous level. Thus, if there are nf_s s nodes and nf_c c nodes at one level, then at the next level we will have $2nf_s + nf_c$ c nodes and $nf_s + nf_c$ s nodes at the next level. Next we assume that the fraction f_s converges to an equilibrium value, and hence must be the same at the next level, or

$$f_s = \frac{nf_s + nf_c}{nf_s + nf_c + 2nf_s + nf_c} =$$

$$\frac{f_s + 1 - f_s}{f_s + 1 - f_s + 2f_s + 1 - f_s} = \frac{1}{f_s + 2}$$

Cross multiplying results in the quadratic equation $f_s^2 + 2f_s - 1 = 0$, which has positive root $\sqrt{2} - 1 \approx .4142$. This gives an asymptotic branching factor of $3f_s + 2(1 - f_s) = 3(\sqrt{2} - 1) + 2(2 - \sqrt{2}) = \sqrt{2} + 1 \approx 2.4142$.

The assumption we made here is that the parent of a node is generated as one of its children. In practice, we wouldn't generate the parent as one of the children, reducing the branching factor by approximately one. It is important to note that the reduction is not exactly one, since pruning the tree in this way changes the equilibrium fraction of s and c states. In fact, the branching factor of the five puzzle without generating the parent as a child is 1.3532, as we will see below.

Rubik's Cube

As another example, consider Rubik's Cube, shown in Figure 3. In this problem, we define any 90, 180, or 270 degree twist of a face as a single move. Since there are six different faces, this suggests a branching factor of 18. However, it is immediately obvious that we shouldn't twist the same face twice in a row, since the same result can be obtained with a single twist. This reduces the branching factor to $5 \cdot 3 = 15$ after the first move.

The next thing to notice is that twists of opposite faces are independent of one another, and hence commutative. Thus, if two opposite faces are twisted in sequence, we restrict them to be twisted in one particular order, to eliminate the identical state resulting from twisting them in the opposite order. For each pair of opposite faces, we label one a "first" face, and the other a "second" face, depending on an arbitrary order. Thus, Left, Up and Front might be the first faces, in which case Right, Down, and Back would be the second faces. After a first face is twisted, there are three possible twists of each of the remaining five faces, for a branching factor of 15. After a second face is twisted, however, there are three possible twists of only four remaining faces, leaving out the face just twisted and its corresponding first face, for a branching factor of 12. Thus, the asymptotic branching factor is between 12 and 15.

To compute it exactly, we need to determine the equilibrium frequencies of first (f) and second (s) nodes, where an f node is one where the last move made was a twist of a first face. Each f node generates six f nodes and nine s nodes as children, the difference being that you can't twist the same face again. Each s node generates six f nodes and six s nodes, since you can't twist the same face or the corresponding first face immediately thereafter. Let f_f be the equilibrium fraction of f nodes at a given level, and $f_s = 1 - f_f$ the equilibrium fraction of s nodes. Since we assume that this equilibrium fraction eventually converges to a constant, the fraction of f nodes at equilibrium must be

$$f_f = \frac{6f_f + 6f_s}{6f_f + 6f_s + 9f_f + 6f_s} =$$

$$\frac{6f_f + 6(1 - f_f)}{15f_f + 12(1 - f_f)} = \frac{6}{3f_f + 12} = \frac{2}{f_f + 4}$$

Cross multiplying gives us the quadratic equation $f_f^2 + 4f_f - 2 = 0$, which has a positive root at $f_f = \sqrt{6} - 2 \approx .44949$. This gives us an asymptotic branching factor of $15f_f + 12(1 - f_f) \approx 13.34847$.

Figure 3: Rubik's Cube.

The System of Equations

The above examples required only the solution of a single quadratic equation. In general, a system of simultaneous equations is generated. As a more representative example, we use the Five Puzzle with predecessor elimination, meaning that the parent of a node is not generated as one of its children. To eliminate the inverse of the last operator applied, we have to keep track of the last two positions of the blank. Let cs denote a state or node where the current position of the blank is on the side, and the immediately previous position of the blank was in an adjacent corner. Define ss, sc and cc nodes analogously.

Figure 4 shows these different types of states, and the arrows indicate the children they generate in the search tree. For example, the double arrow from ss to sc indicates that each ss node in the search tree generates two sc nodes.

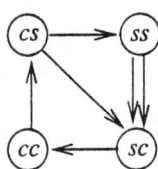

Figure 4: The graph of the Five Puzzle with predecessor elimination.

Let $n(t, d)$ be the number of nodes of type t at depth d in the search tree. Then, we can write the following recurrence relations directly from the graph in figure 4. For example, the last equation comes from the fact that there are two arrows from ss to sc, and one arrow from cs to sc.

$$n(cc, d+1) = n(sc, d)$$
$$n(cs, d+1) = n(cc, d)$$
$$n(ss, d+1) = n(cs, d)$$
$$n(sc, d+1) = 2n(ss, d) + n(cs, d)$$

Note that we have left out the initial conditions. The first move will either generate an ss node and two sc nodes, or a cs node and a cc node, depending on whether the blank starts on the side or in a corner, respectively. The next question is how to solve these recurrences.

Numerical Solution

The simplest way is to iteratively compute the values of successive terms, until the relative frequencies of the different types of states converge. At a given search depth, let f_{cc}, f_{cs}, f_{ss} and f_{sc} be the number of nodes of the given type divided by the total number of nodes at that level. Then we compute the ratio between the total nodes at two successive levels to get the branching factor. After about a hundred iterations of the equations above we get the equilibrium fractions $f_{cc} = .274854$, $f_{cs} = .203113$, $f_{ss} = .150097$, and $f_{sc} = .371936$. Since the branching factor of ss and cs states is two, and the branching factor of the others is one, this gives us the asymptotic branching factor $f_{cc} + 2f_{cs} + 2f_{ss} + 1f_{sc} = .274854 + .406226 + .300194 + .371936 = 1.35321$. If q is the number of different types of states, four in this case, and d is the depth to which we iterate, the running time of this algorithm is $O(dq)$.

Analytical Solution

To solve for the branching factor analytically, we assume that the fractions converge to a set of equilibrium fractions that remain the same from one level to the next. This fixed point assumption gives rise to a set of equations, each being derived from the corresponding recurrence. Let b be the asymptotic branching factor. If we view, for example, f_{cc} as the normalized number of cc nodes at depth d, then the number of cc nodes at depth $d+1$ will be bf_{cc}. This allows us to directly rewrite the recurrences above as the following set of equations. The last one expresses the fact that all the normalized fractions must sum to one.

$$bf_{cc} = f_{sc}$$
$$bf_{cs} = f_{cc}$$
$$bf_{ss} = f_{cs}$$
$$bf_{sc} = 2f_{ss} + f_{cs}$$
$$1 = f_{cc} + f_{cs} + f_{ss} + f_{sc}$$

We have five equations in five unknowns. As we try to solve these equations by repeated substitution to eliminate variables, we get larger powers of b. Eventually we can reduce this system to the single quartic equation, $b^4 - b - 2 = 0$. It is easy to check that $b \approx 1.35321$ is a solution to this equation.

While quartic equations can be solved in general, this is not true of higher degree polynomials. In general, the degree of the polynomial will be the number of different types of states. The Fifteen Puzzle, for example, has six different types of states.

General Formulation

In this section we abstract from the above examples to exhibit the general structure of the equations and their fixed point. We begin with an adjacency matrix representation P of the underlying graph $G = (V, E)$. For Figure 4, the rows P_j of P, with $j \in \{cc, cs, ss, sc\}$, are $P_{cc} = (0, 1, 0, 0)$, $P_{cs} = (0, 0, 1, 1)$, $P_{ss} = (0, 0, 0, 2)$ and $P_{sc} = (1, 0, 0, 0)$. Without loss of generality, we label the vertices V by the first $|V|$ integers, starting from zero. We represent the fractions of each type of state as a distribution vector F. In our example, $F = (f_{cc}, f_{cs}, f_{ss}, f_{sc})$. We assume that this vector converges in the limit of large depth, resulting in the equations $bF = FP$, where b is the asymptotic branching factor. In addition, we have the equation $\sum_{i \in V} f_i = 1$, since the fractions sum to one. Thus, we have a set of $|V| + 1$ equations in $|V| + 1$ unknown variables.

The underlying mathematical issue is an eigenvalue problem. Transforming $bF = FP$ leads to $0 = F(P - bI)$ for the identy matrix I. The solutions for b are the roots of the characteristic equation $det(P - bI) = 0$ where det is the determinant of the matrix. In the case of the Five Puzzle we have to calculate

$$det \begin{pmatrix} -b & 1 & 0 & 0 \\ 0 & -b & 1 & 1 \\ 0 & 0 & -b & 2 \\ 1 & 0 & 0 & -b \end{pmatrix} = 0$$

which simplifies to $b^4 - b - 2 = 0$.

Note that the assumption of convergence of the fraction vector and the asymptotic branching factor is not true in general, since for example the asymptotic branching factor in the Eight Puzzle of Figure

5 alternates between two values, as we will see below. Thus, here we examine the structure of the recurrences in detail. Let n_i^d be the number of nodes of type i at depth d in the tree, and n^d be the total number of nodes at depth d. Let N^d be the count vector $(n_0^d, n_1^d, ..., n_{|V|-1}^d)$. Similarly, let f_i^d be the fraction of nodes of type i out of the total nodes at depth d in the tree, and let F^d be the distribution vector $(f_0^d, f_1^d, ..., f_{|V|-1}^d)$ at level d in the tree. In other words, $f_i^d = n_i^d/n^d$, for all $i \in V$. We arbitrarily set the initial count and distribution vectors, F^0 and N^0 to one for i equal to zero, and to zero otherwise. Let the node branching factor b_k be the number of children of a node of type k, and let B be the vector of node branching factors, $(b_0, b_1, ..., b_{|V|-1})$. In terms of P the value b_k equals $\sum_{j \in V} p_{k,j}$, with the matrix element $p_{k,j}$ in row k and column j denoting the number of edges going from state k to state j. We will derive the iteration formula $F^d = F^{d-1}P/F^{d-1}B$ to determine the distribution F^d given F^{d-1}. For all $i \in V$ we have

$$
\begin{aligned}
f_i^d &= n_i^d/n^d \\
&= \frac{N^{d-1}(P^T)_i}{\sum_{j \in V} N^{d-1}(P^T)_j} \\
&= \frac{\sum_{j \in V} n_j^{d-1} p_{j,i}}{\sum_{j \in V} \sum_{k \in V} n_k^{d-1} p_{k,j}} \\
&= \frac{\sum_{j \in V} f_j^{d-1} n^{d-1} p_{j,i}}{\sum_{k \in V} \sum_{j \in V} f_k^{d-1} n^{d-1} p_{k,j}} \\
&= \frac{F^{d-1}(P^T)_i}{\sum_{k \in V} f_k^{d-1} \sum_{j \in V} p_{k,j}} \\
&= F^{d-1}(P^T)_i / F^{d-1}B.
\end{aligned}
$$

It is not difficult to prove that the branching factor of depth $d+1$ equals $F^d \cdot B$. Therefore, if the iteration formula reaches equilibrium F the branching factor b reaches equilibrium as well. In this case b equals $F \cdot B$ and we get back to the formula $bF = PF$ as cited above. Even though we have established a neat recurrence formula, up to now we have not found a full answer to the convergence of the simulation process to determine the asymptotic branching factor. A solution to this problem might be found in connections to homogenous Markov processes (Norris 1997), where we have a similar iteration formula $F^d = QF^{d-1}$, for a well defined stochastic transition matrix Q.

Experiments

Here we apply our technique to derive the branching factors for square sliding-tile puzzles up to 10×10. Table 1 plots the odd and even asymptotic branching factors in the $(n^2 - 1)$-puzzle with predecessor elimination. As n goes to infinity, the values in both columns will converge to three, the asymptotic branching factor of an infinitely large sliding-tile puzzle, with predecessor elimination.

n	$n^2 - 1$	even depth	odd depth
3	8	1.5	2
4	15	2.1304	2.1304
5	24	2.30278	2.43426
6	35	2.51964	2.51964
7	48	2.59927	2.64649
8	63	2.6959	2.6959
9	80	2.73922	2.76008
10	99	2.79026	2.79026

Table 1: The asymptotic branching factor for the (n^2-1)-Puzzle.

To understand the even-odd effect, consider the Eight Puzzle, shown in Figure 5. At every other level of the search tree, all states will be s states, and all these states will have branching factor two, once the parent of the state has been eliminated. The remaining levels of the tree will consist of a mixture of c states and m states, which have branching factors of one and three, respectively. We leave the analytic determination of the branching factor at these levels as an exercise for the reader.

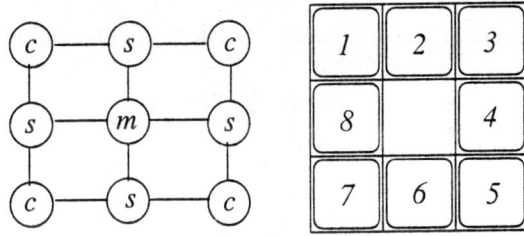

Figure 5: Side and Corner and Middle States in the Eight Puzzle.

In general, if we color the squares of a sliding-tile puzzle in a checkerboard pattern, the blank always moves from a square of one color to one of the other color. For example, in the Eight Puzzle, the s states will all be one color, and the rest will be the other color. If the two different sets of colored squares are entirely equivalent to each other, as in the five and fifteen puzzles, there will be a single branching factor at all levels. If the different colored sets of squares are different however, as in the Eight Puzzle, there will be different odd and even branching factors. In general, a rectangular sliding-tile puzzle will have a single branching factor if at least one of its dimensions is even, and alternating branching factors if both dimensions are odd.

Application to FSM Pruning

So far, we have pruned duplicate nodes in the sliding-tile puzzle search trees by eliminating the inverse of the last operator applied. This pruning process can be represented and implemented by the finite state machine (fsm) shown in Figure 6. A node represents the last operator applied, and the arcs include all legal operators, except for the inverse of the last operator applied. Thus, the FSM gives the legal moves in the search space, and can be used to prune the search.

However, even more duplicates can be eliminated by the use of a more complex FSM. For example, there is cycle of twelve moves in the sliding-tile puzzles that comes from rotating the same three tiles in a two by two square pattern. Taylor and Korf (Taylor & Korf 1993) show how to automatically learn such duplicate patterns and express them in an FSM for pruning the search space. For example, they generate an FSM with 55,441 states for pruning duplicate nodes in the Fifteen Puzzle. An incremental learning strategy for FSM pruning is addressed by Edelkamp (Edelkamp 1997).

The techniques described here can be readily applied to determine the asymptotic branching factor of these pruned spaces. Since the number of different types of nodes is so large, only the numerical simulation method is practical for solving the resulting system of equations. For example, we computed a branching factor of 1.98 for the above mentioned FSM, after about 50 iterations of the recurrence relations. This compares with a branching factor of 2.13 for the Fifteen Puzzle with just inverse operators eliminated.

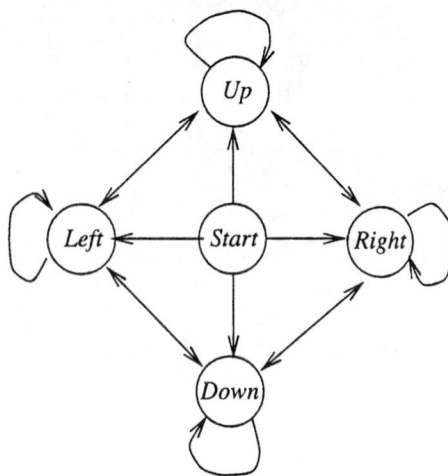

Figure 6: An automaton for predecessor elimination in the sliding tile puzzle.

Conclusions

We showed how to compute the asymptotic branching factors of search trees where different types of nodes have different numbers of children. We begin by writing a set of recurrence relations for the generation of the different node types. These recurrence relations can then be used to determine the exact number of nodes at a given depth of the search tree, in time linear in the depth. They can also be used to estimate the asymptotic branching factor very accurately. Alternatively, we can rewrite the set of recurrence relations as a set of simultaneous equations involving the relative frequencies of the different types of nodes. The number of equations is one greater than the number of different node types. For relatively small numbers of node types, we can solve these equations analytically, by finding the roots of the characteristic equation of a matrix, to derive the exact asymptotic branching factor. We give asymptotic branching factors for Rubik's Cube, the Five Puzzle, and the first ten square sliding-tile puzzles.

Acknowledgments S. Edelkamp is supported by DFG within graduate program on human and machine intelligence. R. Korf is supported by NSF grant IRI-9619447. Thanks to Eli Gafni and Elias Koutsoupias for helpful discussions concerning this research.

References

Edelkamp, S. 1997. Suffix tree automata in state space search. In *KI-97*, 381–385.

Korf, R. E. 1985. Depth-first iterative-deepening: An optimal admissible tree search. *Artificial Intelligence* 27:97–109.

Motwani, R., and Raghavan, P. 1995. *Randomized Algorithms.* Cambridge University Press, Cambridge, UK.

Norris, J. R. 1997. *Markov Chains.* Cambridge University Press, Cambridge, UK.

Taylor, L. A., and Korf, R. E. 1993. Pruning duplicate nodes in depth-first search. In *AAAI-93*, 756–761.

Complexity Analysis of Admissible Heuristic Search

Richard E. Korf
Computer Science Department
University of California, Los Angeles
Los Angeles, CA 90095
korf@cs.ucla.edu

Michael Reid
Department of Mathematics
Brown University
Providence, RI 02912
reid@math.brown.edu

Abstract

We analyze the asymptotic time complexity of admissible heuristic search algorithms such as A*, IDA*, and depth-first branch-and-bound. Previous analyses relied on an abstract analytical model, and characterize the heuristic function in terms of its accuracy, but do not apply to real problems. In contrast, our analysis allows us to accurately predict the performance of these algorithms on problems such as the sliding-tile puzzles and Rubik's Cube. The heuristic function is characterized simply by the distribution of heuristic values in the problem space. Contrary to conventional wisdom, our analysis shows that the asymptotic heuristic branching factor is the same as the brute-force branching factor, and that the effect of a heuristic function is to reduce the effective depth of search, rather than the effective branching factor.

Introduction

We consider the asymptotic time complexity of heuristic search algorithms, such as A* (Hart et al 1968), iterative-deepening-A* (IDA*) (Korf 1985), and depth-first branch-and-bound (DFBnB), that are guaranteed to return optimal solutions. All these algorithms use the same cost function, $f(n) = g(n) + h(n)$, applied to each node n of the search space, where $g(n)$ is the cost of reaching node n from the initial state, and $h(n)$ is an estimate of the cost of reaching a goal from node n. $h(n)$ is *admissible* if it never overestimates the cost of reaching a goal from node n. These algorithms are only guaranteed to find an optimal solution, if their heuristic function is admissible (Hart et al 1968).

The time complexity of these algorithms depends primarily on the quality of the heuristic function. For example, if the heuristic returns zero for every state, these algorithms become brute-force searches, with time complexity that is exponential in the solution cost. Alternatively, if the heuristic always returns the exact cost to reach a goal, the time complexity is linear in the solution depth, assuming ties among f values are broken in favor of smaller h values (Pearl 1984). Realistic cases fall between these two extremes.

Copyright © 1998, American Association for Artificial Intelligence (www.aaai.org). All rights reserved.

Previous Work

Most previous work on this problem (Pohl 1977, Gaschnig 1979, Pearl 1984) was based on an abstract model of the problem space and heuristic function. The model is a tree with no cycles, where every node has exactly b children. Every edge has unit cost, and there is a single goal node at depth d.

The heuristic function is characterized by its error as an estimator of actual solution cost. For example, two common assumptions are that the heuristic suffers from constant absolute error, or constant relative error. This model predicts that a heuristic with constant relative error results in linear time complexity, while constant absolute error results in exponential time complexity (Pohl 1977, Gaschnig 1979).

The main limitation of these analyses is the characterization of the heuristic function in terms of its error. In order to determine the accuracy of the heuristic on even a single state, we need to know the optimal cost to a goal from that state, which requires a great deal of computation. Doing this for a large number of states is impractical for large problems. In other words, we can't determine the accuracy of real heuristics. As a result, we cannot predict the performance of these algorithms on real problems.

Overview

This requires a different approach, which is the subject of this paper. We begin with the conditions for node expansion by any admissible search algorithm. Next, we give an alternative characterization of a heuristic, which is simply the distribution of heuristic values over the problem space. Then we specify the assumptions of our analysis. The main result is the number of node generations as a function of the distribution of the heuristic, the depth of search, and the branching factor of the problem space. Finally, we compare our analytic predictions with actual data on both Rubik's Cube and sliding-tile puzzles, using well-known heuristics. One of the implications of this analysis is that, contrary to current belief, the effect of a heuristic function is to decrease the effective depth of search, rather than the effective branching factor.

Conditions for Node Expansion

We measure asymptotic time complexity by the number of node generations, which is b times the number of node expansions, where b is the branching factor. This assumes that a node can be generated and evaluated in constant time. While some implementations of A* require logarithmic time to select the best node to expand next, and some heuristic functions require more than constant time to evaluate, these additional costs are usually polynomial, however, and depend on particular implementation choices. The dominant factor in time complexity, however, is the number of node generations, which is usually exponential in solution cost, and relatively independent of the particular admissible algorithm chosen and its implementation. The set of nodes expanded can be characterized by their cost, relative to the optimal solution cost. We begin with the conditions for node expansion by A*, then consider IDA* and depth-first branch-and-bound.

A heuristic function $h(n)$ is *consistent* if for any node n and any neighbor n', $h(n) \leq k(n,n') + h(n')$, where $k(n,n')$ is the cost of the edge from n to n' (Pearl 1984). Consistency is similar to the triangle inequality of metrics, and is usually satisfied in practice. If $h(n)$ is consistent, then $f(n) = g(n) + h(n)$ is monotonically nondecreasing along any path from the root node. Thus, the sequence of costs of nodes expanded by A* starts at the heuristic value of the start state, and stays the same or increases until it reaches the cost of an optimal solution. Some nodes with the optimal solution cost may be expanded, until a goal node is chosen for expansion, at which point the algorithm terminates. This means that all nodes n whose cost $f(n) < c$ will be expanded, where c is the optimal solution cost, and no nodes n whose cost $f(n) > c$ will be expanded. In other words, $f(n) < c$ is a sufficient condition for A* to expand node n, and $f(n) \leq c$ is a necessary condition. For a worst-case analysis, we adopt the necessary condition.

If the heuristic function is inconsistent, then the conditions for node expansion are more complex. However, most naturally occurring admissible heuristic functions are consistent (Pearl 1984). Furthermore, an inconsistent but admissible heuristic is easily transformed into a consistent admissible heuristic, which is more accurate than the original one (Mero 1984).

An easy way to understand the node expansion condition is that any admissible search algorithm must continue to expand every possible solution path until its cost is guaranteed to exceed the cost of an optimal solution, lest it lead to a better solution. Thus, while this condition was originally derived for A*, it also applies to IDA* and depth-first branch-and-bound.

On the final iteration of IDA*, the one that finds a goal, the cost threshold will equal c, and in the worst case, IDA* will expand all nodes n whose cost $f(n) \leq c$. If the number of nodes grows exponentially with cost, the previous iterations will not effect the asymptotic time complexity of IDA* (Korf, 1985).

For depth-first branch-and-bound (DFBnB), once an optimal solution is found, the upper bound on solution cost will equal c. From then on, DFBnB will expand only those nodes with $f(n) < c$. Until then, while the upper bound exceeds c, DFBnB will expand some nodes with $f(n) > c$. However, locally ordering the internal nodes of the search tree by cost often results in finding an optimal solution fairly quickly, with most of the time spent verifying that the solution is indeed optimal. Thus, we measure the asymptotic time complexity of all three algorithms by the number of nodes n whose total cost $f(n) = g(n) + h(n) \leq c$, where c is the cost of an optimal solution.

Characterization of the Heuristic

The previous analyses characterized the heuristic function in terms of its accuracy of estimating optimal costs. As mentioned above, this is very hard to determine for a real heuristic, since obtaining optimal solutions is computationally very expensive.

By contrast, we characterize a heuristic by the distribution of heuristic values over all nodes in the problem space. In other words, all we need to know is the number of nodes that have heuristic value zero, one, two, etc. Equivalently, we specify this distribution by a set of parameters $P(x)$, which is the fraction of total nodes in the problem space whose heuristic value is less than or equal to x. We refer to this set of values as the *overall distribution* of the heuristic function, assuming that every state in the problem space is equally likely. For all values of x greater than or equal to the maximum value of the heuristic, $P(x) = 1$.

The overall distribution is easily obtained for most real heuristics. For heuristics that are implemented by table-lookup, or *pattern databases* (Culberson and Schaeffer 1996), the distribution can be determined exactly from the table. Alternatively, another way to view $P(x)$ is as the probability that a state s chosen randomly and uniformly from all states in the problem space has $h(s) \leq x$. Thus, by random sampling of the problem space, we can determine the overall distribution to any desired degree of accuracy.

For heuristics that are the maximum of several different heuristics, we can compute the overall distribution of the entire heuristic from the distributions of the individual heuristics by assuming that the individual heuristic values are independent of one another. The resulting distribution will be accurate to the extent that the independence assumption is warranted.

Note that the characterization of a heuristic function in terms of its distribution is not a measure of the accuracy of the function. In particular, it says nothing about the correlation of heuristic values with actual costs, and hence doesn't require the computation of optimal solutions to any problem instances. As a result, the overall distribution is much easier to determine in practice than the accuracy of a heuristic function.

The Equilibrium Distribution

While the overall distribution is the easiest to understand, the complexity of a search algorithm depends on a potentially different distribution called the *equilibrium distribution*. The equilibrium distribution is the distribution of heuristic values at a given depth of a brute-force search, in the limit of large depth.

In some cases, such as a Rubik's Cube problem space where a 180-degree twist is a single move, the equilibrium distribution is the same as the overall distribution. The reason is that in this problem space, ignoring any special significance attached to the standard goal state, every state is equivalent to every other state, in the sense that there exists an automorphism of the problem space that maps any state to any other state.

In general, however, the equilibrium distribution may not equal the overall distribution, for example in bipartite problem-space graphs. A bipartite graph is one where the set of nodes can be divided into two subsets so that every edge goes between nodes in different subsets. For example, the problem spaces of the sliding-tile puzzles, shown in Figure 1, are bipartite. Every legal move takes the blank from an odd-numbered position to an even-numbered position. If our underlying problem space is bipartite, then the heuristic values may converge to two different equilibrium distributions, one at even levels of the tree and the other at odd levels.

Figure 1: Eight and Fifteen Puzzles

For example, the familiar Manhattan distance heuristic function for the sliding-tile puzzles is computed by measuring the distance of each tile from its goal location in grid units, and summing these values over all tiles, except the blank. This heuristic is both admissible and consistent. Since the Manhattan distance always increases or decreases by one with every move, at a given level of the search tree, the Manhattan distance of all nodes have the same even-odd parity. Thus, there are two different equilibrium heuristic distributions, one for odd values and one for even values.

Another reason for a discrepancy between the equilibrium and overall distributions is if the problem space contains different types of states. For example, in Eight Puzzle states where the distance to the goal and hence Manhattan distance is even, the blank could either be in the center or a corner location. The overall distribution assumes that any position of the blank is equally likely, but in a deep brute-force search, the blank is more likely to be in the center position than in any one of the corners (Edelkamp and Korf 1998). In this case, the equilibrium distribution of odd heuristic values is computed by combining the separate overall distributions for corner and center states, weighted by their relative asymptotic frequencies.

The equilibrium distribution is not a property of a problem, but of a problem space. For example, eliminating the parent of a node as one of its children in a problem with invertible operators will affect the equilibrium distribution. As another example, the Rubik's Cube problem space that allows only 90-degree twists as primitive operators is a bipartite graph, whereas the space that allows single 180-degree twists is not bipartite. The equilibrium distribution is defined by a brute-force search of a particular problem space, and is not affected by any pruning of the tree. Thus, it is independent of cost threshold and initial state.

In a bipartite graph, we treat even and odd levels of the search separately. For simplicity of exposition, however, we will use $P(x)$ to refer to a single equilibrium distribution. If it can't be determined exactly, it may be approximated by the overall distribution.

Complexity Analysis

Basic Assumptions

First, we assume that our algorithm doesn't detect states that have been previously generated. Thus, multiple nodes that correspond to the same state of the problem are counted separately in our analysis. This is true of linear-space algorithms such as IDA* and DF-BnB. While A* checks for previously generated states, the resulting space complexity makes it impractical for large problems. Next, we assume that all edges have unit cost, and hence the cost of a solution is the number of edges in the solution path. We also assume that the heuristic function is integer valued. Given an admissible non-integer valued heuristic, we simply round up to the next larger integer. We also assume that the heuristic is consistent. This implies that the heuristic value of a parent is at most one greater than the heuristic value of its children.

Given these assumptions, our task is to determine $N(b, d, P)$ the asymptotic worst-case number of nodes generated by an admissible search algorithm on a tree with branching factor b, solution depth d, and a heuristic characterized by the equilibrium distribution $P(x)$. As explained above, this is the number of children of nodes n for which $f(n) = g(n) + h(n) \leq d$.

An Example Search Tree

To understand the derivation of our main result, consider Figure 2. It shows a schematic representation of a search tree generated by an iteration of IDA* to depth 8. The vertical axis represents the depth of a node below the start, and the horizontal axis represents the heuristic value. Each box represents not an individual node, but an entire set of nodes with the same depth and heuristic value, indicated by the number in the node. The arrows represent the relationship between parent and child node sets. Since the heuristic is assumed to be consistent, and furthermore, in our example problems all operators are invertible, each parent node can only generate children with heuristic values one less, one greater, or equal to that of the parent, but this latter condition is not required by our analysis. Solid boxes represent "fertile" nodes which are expanded in this iteration, while dotted boxes represent "sterile" nodes that are not expanded, because their total cost exceeds the cutoff depth. The thick diagonal line separates the fertile and sterile nodes. In this particular example, the maximum value of the heuristic is 4, and the cutoff depth d is 8 moves. We arbitrarily chose 3 for the heuristic value of the start state.

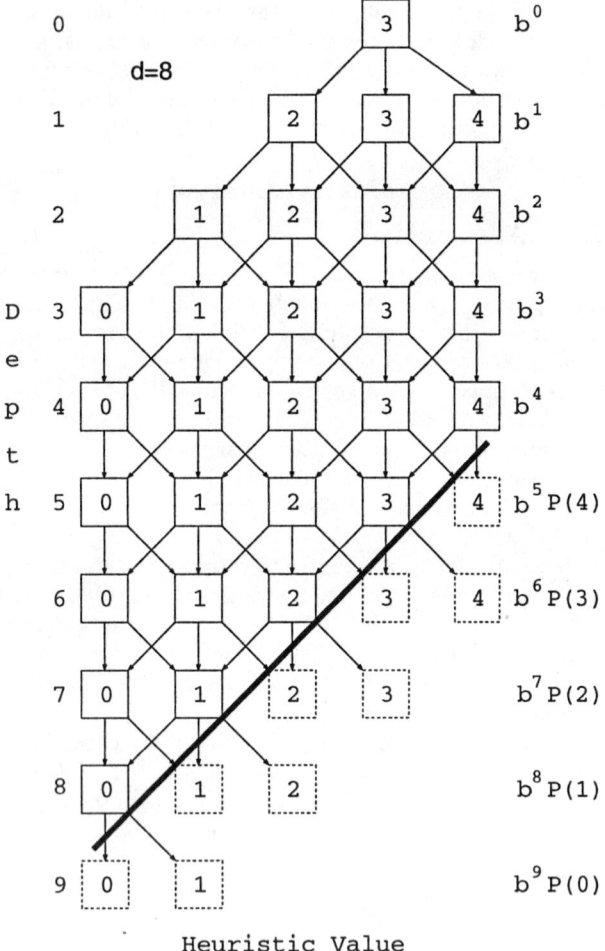

Figure 2: Sample Graph for Analysis Result

Nodes Generated as a Function of Depth

At depth 0, there is a single start state. This root node generates b children, whose heuristic values range from 2 to 4, inclusive. Each of these nodes generate b nodes, whose heuristic values will range from 1 to 4, giving a total of b^2 nodes at depth 2. Since the cutoff depth is 8, in the worst-case, all nodes n whose total cost $f(n) = g(n) + h(n) \leq 8$ will be expanded. Since 4 is the maximum heuristic value, all nodes down to depth $8 - 4 = 4$ will be expanded, and hence all nodes down to depth 5 will be generated, as in a brute-force search. Down to this depth, the number of nodes at depth d will be b^d. Note that $P(4) = 1$, and hence $b^5 P(4) = b^5$, since 4 is the maximum heuristic value. In general, down to depth $d - m$, where d is the cutoff depth and m is the maximum heuristic value, all nodes are expanded, and up to depth $d - m + 1$, all nodes are generated. Asymptotically in the limit of large depth, the distribution of heuristic values will have converged to the equilibrium distribution by this point.

The total number of nodes at depth 6 is b times the number of fertile nodes at depth 5. The fertile nodes at depth 5 are those with $f(n) = g(n) + h(n) = 5 + h(n) \leq 8$, or $h(n) \leq 3$. Since the heuristic distribution at depth 5 is assumed to be the equilibrium distribution, the fraction of all the nodes at depth 5 with $h(n) \leq 3$ is $P(3)$. Since the total number of nodes at depth 5 is b^5, the number of fertile nodes at depth 5 is $b^5 P(3)$, and the total number of nodes at depth 6 is $b^6 P(3)$.

While there are nodes at depth 6 with all possible heuristic values, their distribution is not equal to the equilibrium distribution. In particular, the nodes with heuristic values 3 and 4 are underrepresented compared to the equilibrium distribution. The reason is that such nodes are normally generated by parents with heuristic values from 2 to 4. At depth 5, however, the nodes with heuristic value 4 are sterile, and hence their offspring are missing from depth 6, reducing the number of nodes at depth 6 with heuristic values 3 and 4.

The number of nodes at depth 6 with $h(n) \leq 2$ is completely unaffected by this pruning, however, since their parents are the nodes at depth 5 with $h(n) \leq 3$, all of which are fertile. In other words, the number of nodes at depth 6 with $h(n) \leq 2$ is exactly the same as in a brute-force search to depth 6, or $b^6 P(2)$.

Similarly, the number of nodes at depth 7 is b times the number of fertile nodes at depth 6. The fertile nodes at depth 6 are those with $h(n) \leq 2$. Thus, the number of nodes at depth 7 is $b \cdot b^6 P(2) = b^7 P(2)$.

Due to consistency of the heuristic function, all the possible parents of fertile nodes are themselves fertile. Thus, the absolute numbers of nodes to the left of the diagonal line is exactly the same as in a brute-force search. In other words, the heuristic pruning of the tree has no effect on the fertile nodes, even though the distribution of the sterile nodes is affected. This is the key idea behind this analysis. If the heuristic were inconsistent, then the distribution of fertile nodes would change at every level where pruning occurred, making the analysis much more complex.

In general, the number of fertile nodes at depth i is

$b^i P(d-i)$, and the total number of nodes at depth i is b times the number of fertile nodes at depth $i-1$, or $bb^{i-1}P(d-(i-1))$ or $b^i P(d-i+1)$. The total number of nodes generated by the iteration in the worst case is

$$N(b,d,P) = \sum_{i=1}^{d+1} b^i P(d-i+1)$$

Heuristic Branching Factor

The *heuristic branching factor* is the ratio of the number of nodes generated in an iteration to depth d, compared to an iteration to depth $d-1$. One immediate consequence of our analysis is that the heuristic branching factor is the same as the brute-force branching factor b. This conflicts with results from previous analyses based on an abstract model (Pearl, 1984), which predict that the effect of a heuristic function is to reduce the heuristic branching factor, and hence the overall complexity, from $O(b^d)$ to $O(a^d)$, where $a < b$. Our analysis, however, shows that the effect of the heuristic is to reduce the effective depth of search, rather than the branching factor, from $O(b^d)$ to $O(b^{d-k})$, for some constant k.

Comparison with Experimental Data

We tested our analysis by predicting the nodes generated by IDA* on Rubik's Cube and sliding-tile puzzles, using well-known heuristics. In the above analysis, we used b^d to represent the number of nodes at depth d in a brute-force search. In our predictions below, we replaced the b^d terms in our formula by the actual numbers of nodes at level d. These numbers are computed in time linear in the depth, by expanding a set of recurrence relations governing the generation of different types of nodes (Edelkamp and Korf 1998).

Rubik's Cube

We first tried to predict results previously obtained on Rubik's Cube (Korf 1997). We use a problem space which allows 180-degree twists as single moves, we disallow two consecutive twists of the same face, and we only allow opposite faces to be twisted in succession in one order, since twists of opposite faces are independent and hence commutative. This space has a brute-force branching factor of about 13.34847. The median optimal solution depth is 18 moves.

The heuristic we used is the maximum of three different pattern databases (Culberson and Schaeffer 1996). It is admissible and consistent, with a maximum value of 11 moves, and a mean value of about 8.9 moves. We calculated the overall distribution of the individual heuristics exactly, then assumed independence of the three heuristics to calculate the overall distribution of the combined heuristic. We ignored goal states, completing the search iterations to various depths.

In Table 1, the left-most column shows the search depth, the center column gives the node generations

Depth	Theoretical	Experimental	Error
10	1,510	1,501	.596%
11	20,169	20,151	.089%
12	269,229	270,396	.433%
13	3,593,800	3,564,495	.815%
14	47,971,732	47,916,699	.115%
15	640,349,193	642,403,155	.321%
16	8,547,681,506	8,599,849,255	.610%
17	114,098,463,567	114,773,120,996	.591%

Table 1: Nodes Generated by IDA* on Rubik's Cube

predicted by our analysis, the next column shows the average number of nodes generated by IDA* for a single iteration to the given depth, and the last column gives the error. For depths 10 through 12 we averaged 1000 random problem instances, for depths 13 through 16 we used 100 instances, and for depth 17 we used 25 problem instances, due to computational limits.

The theory predicts the data to within 1% in every case. The remaining error may be due to noise, or the independence assumption among the three different heuristics. The experimental heuristic branching factor between the last two levels is 13.34595.

Eight Puzzle

We ran a similar experiment on the Eight Puzzle, using the Manhattan distance heuristic. Its maximum value is 22 moves, and its mean value is 14 moves. The Eight Puzzle contains only 181,440 solvable states, so the heuristic distributions were computed exactly. Three different distributions were used, depending on the whether the blank is in the center, a corner, or a side position. This gives us the exact equilibrium distributions. The number of nodes at a given depth of the tree depends on the initial position of the blank, and this is also taken into account. The average optimal solution length is 22 moves, and the maximum is 31 moves, assuming the goal has the blank in a corner.

Table 2 shows a comparison of the number of nodes predicted by our analysis for a given depth, to the number of nodes actually generated by a single iteration of IDA* to the same depth, ignoring any solutions encountered. For even depths, each experimental data point is the average of all 100,800 problem instances at an even depth from the goal, and for the odd depths is the average of all 80,640 problem instances at an odd depth. Since both the average numbers of node generations and the heuristic distributions are exact, the model predicts the experimental data exactly.

Fifteen Puzzle

We ran the same experiment on the Fifteen Puzzle, again using Manhattan distance. The average optimal solution length is 52.6 moves. Since this puzzle contains over ten trillion solvable states, we can't compute the heuristic distribution exactly. Rather, we used a

Depth	Theoretical	Experimental	Error
20	793	793	0.0%
21	1,490	1,490	0.0%
22	2,386	2,386	0.0%
23	4,480	4,480	0.0%
24	7,170	7,170	0.0%
25	13,442	13,442	0.0%
26	21,509	21,509	0.0%
27	40,344	40,344	0.0%
28	64,553	64,553	0.0%
29	121,020	121,020	0.0%
30	193,634	193,634	0.0%

Table 2: Nodes Generated by IDA* on Eight Puzzle

Depth	Theoretical	Experimental	Error
40	118,847	108,685	8.55%
41	253,193	234,588	7.35%
42	539,403	502,267	6.88%
43	1,149,144	1,077,126	6.27%
44	2,448,134	2,313,858	5.48%
45	5,215,496	4,936,650	5.35%
46	11,111,071	10,632,238	4.31%
47	23,670,978	22,591,563	4.56%
48	50,428,548	48,752,514	3.32%
49	107,432,751	103,255,669	3.89%
50	228,874,246	223,159,051	2.50%

Table 3: Nodes Generated by IDA* on Fifteen Puzzle

random sample of ten billion states, that were generated in a way that guaranteed they were solvable, to approximate the overall distribution. Six different distributions were used, for each combination of the blank in a middle, corner, or side position, and at odd and even depths from the goal. The mean heuristic value is about 37 moves, and the maximum is 62 moves.

Table 3 is similar to Tables 1 and 2. Each line is the average of 10,000 random solvable problem instances, whose solution depths are the same parity as the search depth. There is enormous variation in the nodes generated in individual problem instances, for depth 50 ranging from 2 nodes to over 38 billion, for example. The agreement between theory and experiment improves almost monotonically with increasing depth, as expected for an asymptotic result. At depth 50, the error between theory and experiment is within 2.5%.

Conclusions and Further Work

We presented the first analysis of the time complexity of admissible heuristic search that predicts performance on real problems. Our characterization of the heuristic is simply the distribution of heuristic values, information that is easily obtained by random sampling. We compared our analytic predictions with experimental data on Rubik's Cube, the Eight Puzzle, and the Fifteen Puzzle, getting agreement within 1% for Rubik's Cube, exact agreement for the Eight Puzzle, and less than 2.5% for the Fifteen Puzzle on typical solution lengths. Contrary to previous results, our analysis and experiments indicate that the asymptotic heuristic branching factor is the same as the brute-force branching factor, and hence the effect of a heuristic is to reduce the effective depth of search, rather than the effective branching factor.

We presented an asymptotic analysis for a fixed-size problem as the solution length grows large. The asymptotic results provide excellent predictions at typical solution depths. Ideally, we would like to predict the performance of a fixed heuristic as the problem size increases. For example, what is the asymptotic performance of the Manhattan distance heuristic on sliding-tile puzzles, as the puzzle grows large? This remains an open problem for future research.

Acknowledgments

We would like to thank Eli Gafni, Elias Koutsoupias, and Mitchell Tsai for several helpful discussions. R. Korf is supported by NSF grant IRI-9619447.

References

Culberson, J.C., and J. Schaeffer, Searching with pattern databases, in *Advances in Artificial Intelligence*, Gordon McCalla (Ed.), Springer Verlag, 1996.

Edelkamp, S. and R.E. Korf, The branching factor of regular search spaces, *Proceedings of the National Conference on Artificial Intelligence (AAAI-98)*, Madison, WI, July, 1998.

Gaschnig, J. *Performance measurement and analysis of certain search algorithms*, Ph.D. thesis. Department of Computer Science, Carnegie-Mellon University, Pittsburgh, Pa., 1979.

Hart, P.E., N.J. Nilsson, and B. Raphael, A formal basis for the heuristic determination of minimum cost paths, *IEEE Transactions on Systems Science and Cybernetics*, Vol. SSC-4, No. 2, July 1968, pp. 100-107.

Korf, R.E., Depth-first iterative-deepening: An optimal admissible tree search, *Artificial Intelligence*, Vol. 27, No. 1, 1985, pp. 97-109.

Korf, R.E., Finding optimal solutions to Rubik's Cube using pattern databases, *Proceedings of the Fourteenth National Conference on Artificial Intelligence (AAAI-97)*, Providence, RI, July, 1997, pp. 700-705.

Mero, L., A heuristic search algorithm with modifiable estimate, *Artificial Intelligence*, Vol. 23, 1984, pp. 13-27.

Pearl, J. *Heuristics*, Addison-Wesley, Reading, MA, 1984.

Pohl, I., Practical and theoretical considerations in heuristic search algorithms, *Machine Intelligence 8*, 1977, pp. 55-72

On the Conversion between Non-Binary and Binary Constraint Satisfaction Problems

Fahiem Bacchus
Department of Computer Science
University Of Waterloo
Waterloo, Ontario, Canada, N2L 3G1
fbacchus@logos.uwaterloo.ca

Peter van Beek
Department of Computing Science
University of Alberta
Edmonton, Alberta, Canada, T6G 2H1
vanbeek@cs.ualberta.ca

Abstract

It is well known that any non-binary discrete constraint satisfaction problem (CSP) can be translated into an equivalent binary CSP. Two translations are known: the dual graph translation and the hidden variable translation. However, there has been little theoretical or experimental work on how well backtracking algorithms perform on these binary representations in comparison to their performance on the corresponding non-binary CSP. We present both theoretical and empirical results to help understand the tradeoffs involved. In particular, we show that translating a non-binary CSP into a binary representation can be a viable solution technique in certain circumstances. The ultimate aim of this research is to give guidance for when one should consider translating between non-binary and binary representations. Our results supply some initial answers to this question.

Introduction

The lion's share of work on constraint satisfaction problems (CSPs) has restricted its attention to binary CSPs, where all constraints are between two variables. This work has generated a great deal of knowledge about the theory and practice of solving CSPs. Unfortunately, it is not always straightforward to generalize this knowledge to non-binary CSPs. The well known fact that any non-binary discrete CSP can be converted into an equivalent binary CSP is usually used as a justification for restricting attention to binary CSPs. Implicitly, the assumption has been that when faced with a non-binary CSP we can simply convert it into a binary CSP, and then apply the best techniques for solving the binary equivalent.

The field has not completely ignored the issue of non-binary CSPs, however, as there has been work in both the constraint programming and the traditional CSP communities that addresses direct solution techniques for non-binary CSPs. In particular, two of the most successful techniques for solving binary problems, backtracking combined with forward checking and backtracking combined with arc consistency, have been generalized to the non-binary case (Mac77; VH89).

Hence, there are at least two options when it comes to dealing with non-binary CSPs: apply one of the standard translations to convert it to a binary CSP and then solve it using binary CSP techniques, or apply one of the direct solution techniques for non-binary CSPs. A potential advantage of translating to the binary is that much more is known about solving binary CSPs: more useful heuristics are known, more polynomial-time special cases have been identified, and more algorithms are known[1]. On the other hand it is unknown whether or not these techniques are useful when applied to the CSPs that arise from translating non-binary CSPs. Surprisingly little work has been done on examining the effectiveness of the translation technique, or on comparing these two options. The work presented here addresses this problem.

There are at least two good reasons for looking more carefully at the issue of translating non-binary CSPs into binary CSPs. First, non-binary CSPs appear quite frequently when modeling real problems. In this case the issue is how to solve these problems most efficiently, and as we show there are certain cases where translating to the binary produces significant performance gains and cases where it produces a degradation in performance. The second reason is that, as noted above, a common justification for focusing solely on binary CSPs is the fact that non-binary CSPs can be translated into binary CSPs. Hence, it is important to study the properties of these translations so as to better understand the legitimacy of focusing on the binary case.

Two general methods are known for converting non-binary CSPs to binary CSPs: the dual graph method and the hidden variable method. The dual graph representation comes from the relational database community and was introduced to the CSP community by Dechter and Pearl (DP89). Earlier, Freuder (Fre78) had used an incremental version of the method in an algorithm for finding all solutions to a CSP. The hidden variable translation has an even longer history. Rossi et al. (RPD89) credit Peirce (Pei33) with first showing that binary relations have the same expressive power as non-binary relations. Peirce's method for representing non-binary relations with a collection of binary relations forms the foundation of the hidden variable method. Dechter (Dec90) shows how to represent any non-binary relation with binary relations using hidden variables

---

[1] For example, algorithms such as minimal forward checking (DM94) and lazy arc consistency (SRGV96) are currently only applicable to binary CSPs.

that have bounded domain sizes. Rossi et al. (RPD89) discusses both the hidden and the dual conversion methods and examined whether a non-binary CSP and its binary representation are equivalent under various definitions of equivalence.

We present both empirical and theoretical results that help us understand the properties of the dual graph and hidden variable representations. Our results compare the number of nodes visited and the number of constraint checks executed by the forward checking algorithm (FC), when applied to a non-binary CSP and to its binary equivalents. The results indicate that for most problems the non-binary representation is the most efficient representation. However, there is a class of problems, when the constraints are tight or restrictive, for which the binary translations can be more efficient by orders of magnitude. Also, we examine a specialized algorithm for the hidden representation, which we call FC^+. This algorithm has the advantage that it provably never performs more than a polynomial factor worse than FC on the non-binary representation, and it can often perform exponentially better.

The ultimate aim of this research is to provide guidance for efficiently solving a CSP representation of a problem. Given a problem, there is always the question of how to formulate it as a CSP. Ideally, the problem is modeled in the most natural way and the machine automatically solves it in the most efficient way. When presented with a particular instance of a non-binary CSP, should the machine convert it to a binary representation before solving? To answer this question we need a better understanding of the tradeoffs involved in such a conversion.

Background

We first define constraint satisfaction problems (CSP) and then briefly review backtrack search, the dual graph translation, and the hidden variable translation.

Definition 1 [CSPs] A constraint satisfaction problem consists of a finite set of *variables*, $\mathcal{V} = \{V_1, \ldots, V_n\}$; for each variable $X \in \mathcal{V}$ a finite domain of *values*, $Dom(X) = \{x_1, \ldots, x_k\}$; and a finite collection of *constraints*, $\mathcal{C} = \{C_1, \ldots, C_m\}$. Each constraint $C \in \mathcal{C}$ is a constraint over some set of variables $Vars(C)$. The size of this set is known as the arity of the constraint. Non-binary CSPs are CSPs that contain constraints with arity greater than 2. Every constraint C can be viewed as being a subset of the product of the domains of the variables in $Vars(C)$ (i.e., C is the set of tuples that satisfy the constraint).

We say that a set of assignments to variables $\mathcal{A} = \{X_1 \leftarrow x_1, \ldots, X_\ell \leftarrow x_\ell\}$ is *consistent* with a constraint C if (i) it assigns a value to all of the variables of C (i.e., $Vars(C) \subseteq \{X_1, \ldots, X_\ell\}$) and (ii) the tuple of values assigned by $\mathcal{A}$ to the variables of C is a member of C (i.e., the assignment satisfies the constraint). A *solution* to a CSP is a set of assignments to all n variables $\{V_1 \leftarrow v_1, \ldots, V_n \leftarrow v_n\}$ that is consistent with each of the m constraints. The notation $\|C\|$ is used to denote the size of a set C.

Example 1 Consider the 3-SAT problem, $(X_1 \vee X_2 \vee X_6) \wedge (\neg X_1 \vee X_3 \vee X_4) \wedge (\neg X_4 \vee \neg X_5 \vee X_6) \wedge (X_2 \vee X_5 \vee \neg X_6)$.

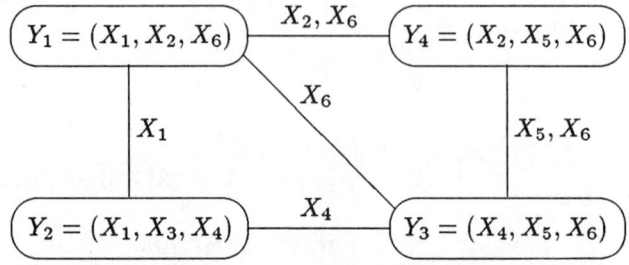

Figure 1: Binary CSP resulting from the dual method

In the non-binary CSP representation of the 3-SAT problem there is a variable for each boolean variable $X_1, \ldots, X_6$, each variable has the domain of values $\{0, 1\}$, and there is a 3-ary constraint for each clause in the formula to ensure that each clause evaluates to 1. For example, the constraint on the first clause contains the tuples, $R_{\{X_1,X_2,X_6\}} = \{(0,0,1), (0,1,0), (0,1,1), (1,0,0), (1,0,1), (1,1,0), (1,1,1)\}$, where the tuple $(0,0,0)$ does not appear in the constraint since the assignment $X_1 \leftarrow 0, X_2 \leftarrow 0, X_6 \leftarrow 0$ does not satisfy the clause.

CSPs are often solved using a backtracking algorithm. Here we restrict our attention to the widely used forward checking backtracking algorithm (FC) (HE80; McG79), which has been generalized to handle non-binary CSPs. Following Van Hentenryck (VH89) we say that a k-ary constraint, $k \geq 2$, is *forward checkable* if $k - 1$ of its variables have been instantiated and the remaining variable is uninstantiated. At a node in the search tree, the new variable assigned at that node causes some (possibly empty) set of constraints to become forward checkable. For each newly forward checkable constraint, FC forward checks the remaining unassigned variable. For each unpruned value of that unassigned variable FC checks whether or not that value along with the node's assignments is consistent with the constraint, pruning those values that are inconsistent. If this process causes the unassigned variable to have all of its domain values pruned, FC backtracks.

We now present the dual graph and hidden variable translations for converting non-binary CSPs into binary ones. In the dual translation, the constraints of the original problem become variables in the new representation. We refer to these variables, which represent the constraints, as *c-variables* and the original variables simply as variables. The domain of each c-variable is exactly the set of tuples that satisfy the original constraint and there is a binary constraint between two c-variables iff the original constraints share some variables. The binary constraints prohibit pairs of tuples in which shared variables receive different values.

Example 2 In the dual graph representation of the CSP in Example 1, there are four variables $Y_1, \ldots, Y_4$, one for each 3-ary constraint (or clause) in the original problem (see Figure 1). For example, the variable Y_1 corresponds to the non-binary constraint $R_{\{X_1,X_2,X_6\}}$ and the domain of Y_1 contains the tuples $(0, 0, 1), \ldots, (1, 1, 1)$. The binary constraints enforce that the ordinary variables appearing in more than

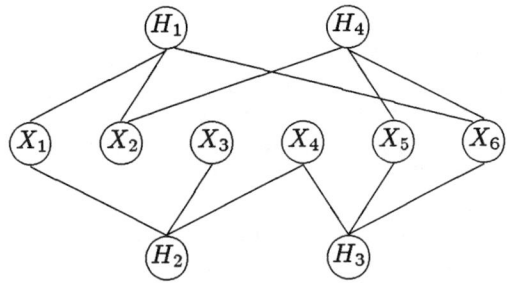

Figure 2: Binary CSP resulting from the hidden method

one c-variable have the same value.

In the hidden representation, the set of variables includes all of the variables of the original problem (with no changes to their domains) plus a new set of "hidden" or *h-variables* variables. For each constraint C_i in the original problem we add an h-variable H_i. The domain of H_i consists of a unique identifier for every tuple in C_i. The new representation contains only binary constraints, and these are constructed as follows. For every h-variable H_i we impose a binary constraint between H_i and each of the variables in $Vars(C_i)$. Say that H_i and X_k are thus constrained. Every value of H_i corresponds to a tuple of values for the variables in $Vars(C_i)$ and thus defines a unique value for X_k. Hence the binary constraint between H_i and X_k consists of a unique value for X_k for every value of H_i. (Note that the constraint is not functional in the other direction as a value for X_k may be compatible with many values of H_i.)

Example 3 In the hidden variable representation of the CSP in Example 1 there are ten variables: the six original variables $X_1, \ldots, X_6$ and four hidden variables, one for each constraint in the original problem (see Figure 2). For example, the constraint $R_{\{X_1,X_2,X_6\}}$ has a corresponding h-variable, H_1, whose domain can be the set $\{1, 2, \ldots, 7\}$ (a unique identifier for each of the seven tuples in the constraint). We can define a correspondence between the values of H_1 and the tuples in $R_{\{X_1,X_2,X_6\}}$ as follows:

$1 \mapsto (0,0,1), 2 \mapsto (0,1,0), 3 \mapsto (0,1,1), 4 \mapsto (1,0,0),$
$5 \mapsto (1,0,1), 6 \mapsto (1,1,0), 7 \mapsto (1,1,1).$

We then impose a constraint between the pairs of variables $\{X_1, H_1\}, \{X_2, H_1\}$, and $\{X_6, H_1\}$, giving the binary constraints,

$C_{\{X_1,H_1\}} = \{(0,1),(0,2),(0,3),(1,4),(1,5),(1,6),(1,7)\},$
$C_{\{X_2,H_1\}} = \{(0,1),(1,2),(1,3),(0,4),(0,5),(1,6),(1,7)\},$
$C_{\{X_6,H_1\}} = \{(1,1),(0,2),(1,3),(0,4),(1,5),(0,6),(1,7)\}.$

For example, for $C_{\{X_1,H_1\}}$, the value 3 for H_1 corresponds to the tuple $(0,1,1)$ in which $X_1 = 0$. Hence, $H_1 = 3$ is only compatible with $X_1 = 0$.

Theoretical Comparisons

We first consider the space requirements of the dual and hidden representations. Most CSP algorithms can deal with constraints represented either intensionally, as a function, or extensionally, as a list of compatible tuples or as a boolean array that stores for each possible assignment to the constrained variables a flag indicating whether or not that assignment is compatible. However, the more effective backtracking algorithms, such as FC, use storage proportional to the size of the domains of the variables to keep track of which domain values have been pruned during search. This means that when the dual and hidden representations "make the constraints into variables" they require extra storage of size equal to the total number of tuples in all of the constraints: $\sum_{i=1}^{m} \|C_i\|$.

As well, the dual and hidden representations require additional space to store their binary constraints. Fortunately, the constraints in both can be represented as simple functions, and thus impose only a small additional space requirement. For example, in the hidden representation, to check if $H_i \leftarrow h$ is compatible with $X_k \leftarrow x$, we simply find the tuple of assignments corresponding to h and then check to see if this tuple assigns x to X_k. The pair of assignments are compatible if and only if this is the case. If the original constraints are represented extensionally, as a list of satisfying tuples, then this operation can be done in constant time. However, if the original constraints are intensionally represented we have a space-time tradeoff. We can convert the intensional representation to an extensional one, and pay the space required to store the list of satisfying tuples. Or we can dynamically compute the tuple corresponding to h by iterating over the possible assignments of the constrained variables to find the h'th satisfying tuple. Since this has to be done every time we check a constraint, it will usually not be practical. Hence, we may also assume that we have an extensional representation of the original constraints. Of course, this will be an *additional* space requirement only when the original constraints are represented intensionally.

We now show analytic bounds on the differences in the number of nodes visited and consistency checks performed by the FC algorithm applied to a non-binary CSP and to the corresponding binary CSPs. For ease of exposition, we assume that FC runs until all solutions have been found or it is proven that no solution exists. One issue to address is that of properly accounting for checking k-ary constraints. Clearly, checking if a set of assignments $\{X_1 \leftarrow x_1, \ldots, X_k \leftarrow x_k\}$ satisfies an k-ary constraint must take at least k operations. This is true whether or not the constraint is represented intensionally as a function (where the function must consider all k values), or extensionally as an boolean array (where we will require k operations to index into an k-dimension array). Hence, we will charge k constraint checks for every check of an arity k constraint. To be consistent with this measure we charge the check of a binary constraint as 2 constraint checks (such a check requires at least 2 operations). Note that our counts for binary constraint checks are thus twice what is traditionally counted as a constraint check. This way of accounting for constraint checks allows us to properly compare the fundamental operations performed when solving the non-binary CSP and the corresponding binary CSPs.

Dual Graph Representation. The relative cost of FC on the non-binary CSP and the dual CSP depends on the cardinalities of the constraints and on the structure of the underlying constraint graph.

Example 4 shows that when the constraints have many satisfying tuples, the dual can be exponentially worse in terms of number of consistency checks. However, as Example 5 shows, when the constraints have few satisfying tuples, the dual can also be exponentially better. In such cases, FC on the original may have to visit a large number of assignments prior to being able to check a constraint, whereas FC on the dual only examines assignments that are known to be consistent with some constraint.

Example 4 Consider the non-binary CSP with n Boolean variables $X_1, \ldots, X_n$ and n constraints given by $\{X_1, \neg X_1 \vee X_2, \neg X_1 \vee \neg X_2 \vee X_3, \cdots, \neg X_1 \vee \cdots \vee \neg X_{n-1} \vee X_n\}$. In this CSP, nodes in the backtrack tree for the dual representation have exponentially many children and there is exactly one solution node. FC applied to this problem would visit n nodes and perform $O(n^2)$ consistency checks, whereas FC applied to the dual of this problem would visit n nodes and perform $O(2^n)$ consistency checks.

Example 5 Consider the non-binary CSP with n Boolean variables $X_1, \ldots, X_n$ and n constraints given by $\{X_1 \wedge \cdots \wedge X_{n-1}, X_1 \wedge \cdots \wedge X_{n-2} \wedge X_n, \cdots, X_2 \wedge \cdots \wedge X_n\}$; i.e., all n possible ways of forming a conjunction of $n-1$ variables. In this CSP, nodes in the backtrack tree for the dual have a single child and there is exactly one solution node. FC applied to this problem would visit 2^{n-1} nodes and perform $O(n2^n)$ consistency checks, whereas FC applied to the dual of this problem would visit n nodes and perform $O(n^2)$ consistency checks.

When visiting a node in the search tree for the original CSP, FC ensures that there exists a *single* extension of the current set of assignments that satisfies all of the forward checkable constraints. With FC on the dual, we have a different guarantee, that for every remaining constraint there exists *some* extension of the current set of assignments (to the original variables) that is consistent with it; there need not be a single extension satisfying multiple constraints. This means that FC on the original CSP checks for a stronger condition on a smaller number of constraints, while FC on the dual checks for a weaker condition on a larger set of constraints. An analysis of examples suggests that as the number of constraints m grows, it becomes increasingly likely that FC on the original CSP will detect deadends in the search earlier than FC on the dual, and that as m decreases, the converse situation becomes increasingly likely. How this works out in practice is an experimental question which we examine in the next section.

Hidden Variable Representation. We now turn our attention to the hidden representation. First, we demonstrate that, as with the dual, FC on the original CSP and FC on its hidden representation are incomparable: the algorithm can perform exponentially better or worse depending on the particular problem. Examples 6 and 7 illustrate this point.

Example 6 Consider a CSP containing the constraint C over some set of variables $\{X_1, X_2, \ldots\}$. Furthermore, say that there is no tuple in C in which $X_1 = 0$ and $X_2 = 0$. FC applied to the non-binary CSP is unable to detect that every node containing these assignments is a dead end: it can only forward check on the constraint C when all but one of C's variables have been instantiated. On the other hand, FC applied to the hidden is able to detect all of these dead ends: at every such node the h-variable corresponding to C will experience a domain wipe out.

Example 7 Consider a CSP containing two constraints C_1 and C_2 both over the set of variables $\{X_1, X_2, X_k\}$. Say that $C_1 = \{(0,0,0), (1,1,1)\}$ and $C_2 = \{(0,0,1), (1,1,1)\}$. FC applied to the non-binary CSP is able to detect that every node containing the assignments $X_1 = 0$ and $X_2 = 0$ is a dead end: at such nodes the domain of X_k will experience a domain wipe out when we forward check both C_1 and C_2. FC applied to the hidden, on the other hand, is unable to detect a dead end at every such node: assignments to ordinary variables can prune the domains of h-variables but not the domains of other ordinary variables.

These two examples can be used to construct CSPs where FC applied to the non-binary representation performs exponentially better than FC applied to the hidden and vice versa. There is a way, however, of improving FC on the hidden so that it can still perform exponentially better but can only be outperformed by a bounded amount. The intuition behind the improvement comes from Example 7. When FC on the hidden CSP visits a node in which $X_1 = 0$ and $X_2 = 0$ it will reduce the domains of the two h-variables H_1 and H_2 (corresponding to constraint C_1 and C_2 respectively) to the singleton set $\{1\}$, where 1 corresponds to the first satisfying tuple of the constraints. At this point if we continue constraint propagation so that we restore arc-consistency between H_1 and X_k and between H_2 and X_k we would detect the same dead end that FC on the non-binary does.

We can define the following enhancement to FC.

Definition 2 [FC$^+$] FC$^+$ is a backtracking algorithm designed to run on the hidden representation. It operates exactly like FC, except that after forward checking prunes the domain of any h-variable we additionally prune the domains of any uninstantiated variables constrained by that h-variable so as to remove values whose support has been lost. As usual we backtrack if any future variable experiences a domain wipe out.

This enhancement to FC is similar in spirit to those developed by Nadel (Nad89). It fits between standard forward checking and full maintenance of arc-consistency in terms of the amount of constraint propagation it performs. However, we can make the algorithm more efficient than the generic algorithms presented by Nadel because every value for an h-variable functionally determines the values of all the ordinary variables it is constrained with. When we instantiate an ordinary variable we forward check any h-variables it is constrained with in the normal manner. This operation requires a binary constraint check for every domain value of the h-variable. Say that h-variable H_i has had some of its values pruned. FC^+ must then check the domains of all of the unassigned ordinary variables H_i is constrained with. Say that $\{X_1, \ldots, X_k\}$ are the k unassigned variables constrained by H_i. We can restore arc-consistency between H_i and each of these variables by iterating *once* over the remaining domain of H_i. Every unpruned value of H_i supports a unique value for each of the X_j, and in $2k$ operations per value (k binary checks each requiring 2 operations) of H_i we can accumulate the set of still supported values for each of the X_j. Finally, in a second phase we iterate through the domains of the X_j pruning all values not marked as still supported by the first phase.

Counting all of these operations as primitive constraint checks, and using the simplifying assumption that each of the variables in the original non-binary CSP has an identical domain size, we obtain the following result.

Proposition 1 *Given any variable ordering strategy for the non-binary CSP, there exists an ordering strategy such that FC^+ applied to the hidden representation will never visit more nodes than FC applied to the non-binary CSP, and it will perform at most $\max_{i=1}^{m}((Arity(C_i) + 1)\|C_i\| + Arity(C_i))$ as many checks.*

The variable ordering employed is exactly the same as that used by FC on the non-binary representation. In particular, we delay instantiating all the h-variables until all of the ordinary variables are instantiated. Once all of the ordinary variables have been instantiated, and we have not experienced a domain wipe-out, each h-variable will have its domain reduced down to one value. In fact the values assigned to the other variables constitute a solution, so search can be terminated prior to visiting any of the h-variables.

These results shed some light on the hidden representation. We see that using the hidden imposes an overhead over direct use of the non-binary representation. Although this overhead is only a multiplicative factor, it can be orders of magnitude: non-binary constraints can often contain a large number of satisfying tuples. On the other hand, if we employ the FC^+ algorithm we can potentially save an exponential amount of work by visiting exponentially fewer nodes. When this potential is realized the savings can outweigh the multiplicative overhead. In the next section we show empirically that both outcomes are possible, and we provide some guidelines as to when conversion to the hidden might be effective.

Experimental Comparisons

We now show some experimental results comparing FC on the representations. Throughout this section, FC refers to an implementation of the forward checking algorithm which dynamically orders the variables by selecting as the next variable to instantiate the variable with the minimum remaining values (ties are broken by choosing the variable that participates in the most constraints) and FC^+ refers to an implementation of the algorithm of Definition 2 for the hidden variable method. In FC^+ we also employ the minimum remaining values heuristic. In particular, we allow h-variables to be instantiated prior to ordinary variables, if they are selected by the heuristic[2]. Finally, we count the checks performed by FC and FC^+ in the manner described in the previous section with one refinement: when solving the dual, we charged one constraint check for each shared variable. For example, with reference to Figure 1, checking the constraint between Y_1 and Y_2 costs one and checking the constraint between Y_1 and Y_4 costs two.

To systematically examine the effect of the cardinalities of the constraints and the number of constraints on the cost of solving a non-binary CSP and its corresponding binary representations, we use the following model of a random non-binary CSP. A random CSP has n variables each with domain size of d, and m constraints each with arity k and t satisfying tuples. Each constraint is over a subset of variables chosen with uniform probability from the $\binom{n}{k}$ possible subsets, and each constraint contains $0 \leq t \leq d^k$ tuples chosen at random.

Dual Graph Representation. Figure 3 shows the effect of the number of tuples in the constraints and the number of constraints on the cost of solving a random non-binary CSP and its dual. Specifically, for each parameter settings we generated and solved an ensemble of non-binary problems and their dual representations (a minimum of 30 problems in each ensemble). We then took the ratio of the median consistency checks needed to solve the dual representations over the median consistency checks needed to solve the non-binary CSPs. Finally, we constructed the contour lines shown in the figures using cubic spline interpolation on our data points. For example, the left most contour lines in the figures represent the points in the space of random problems where solving the dual was $10\times$ faster (in terms of consistency checks) than solving the non-binary CSP, and everything to the left of the left most line means the dual was *at least* $10\times$ faster. The experiments show that the dual can be an efficient representation.

We now consider two classes of problems, random 3-SAT and crossword puzzles, and show that the maps constructed from our experimental results over the space of random non-binary problems have predictive power and so provide guidance for selecting between the non-binary and dual CSP models of a problem. The results for random 3-SAT are shown in Table 1. It can be seen that the cost ratios for solving the original CSP and its dual representation fit well with the predictions of the order of magnitude curves (see Figure 3, $k = 3$, at the point 7/8 on the x-axis (each of the constraints has 7 out of the 8 possible tuples)). This provides some evidence that the experimental predictions scale for larger n. The results for 20 crossword puzzles (Gin93) are shown in Table 2. In the non-binary formulation of crossword puzzles there is a variable for each letter to be filled in and the constraints are the words in the Unix dictionary. There are few constraints and each constraint allows few of the possible tuples: at most 4000 out of the 26^k possible tuples for $k = 3, ..10$, where 10 is the length of the longest word in the puzzles to be filled. The order of magnitude

---

[2] We delay instantiating any h-variables all of whose constrained variables have already been assigned. When this happens the h-variable has become redundant and need not be further considered.

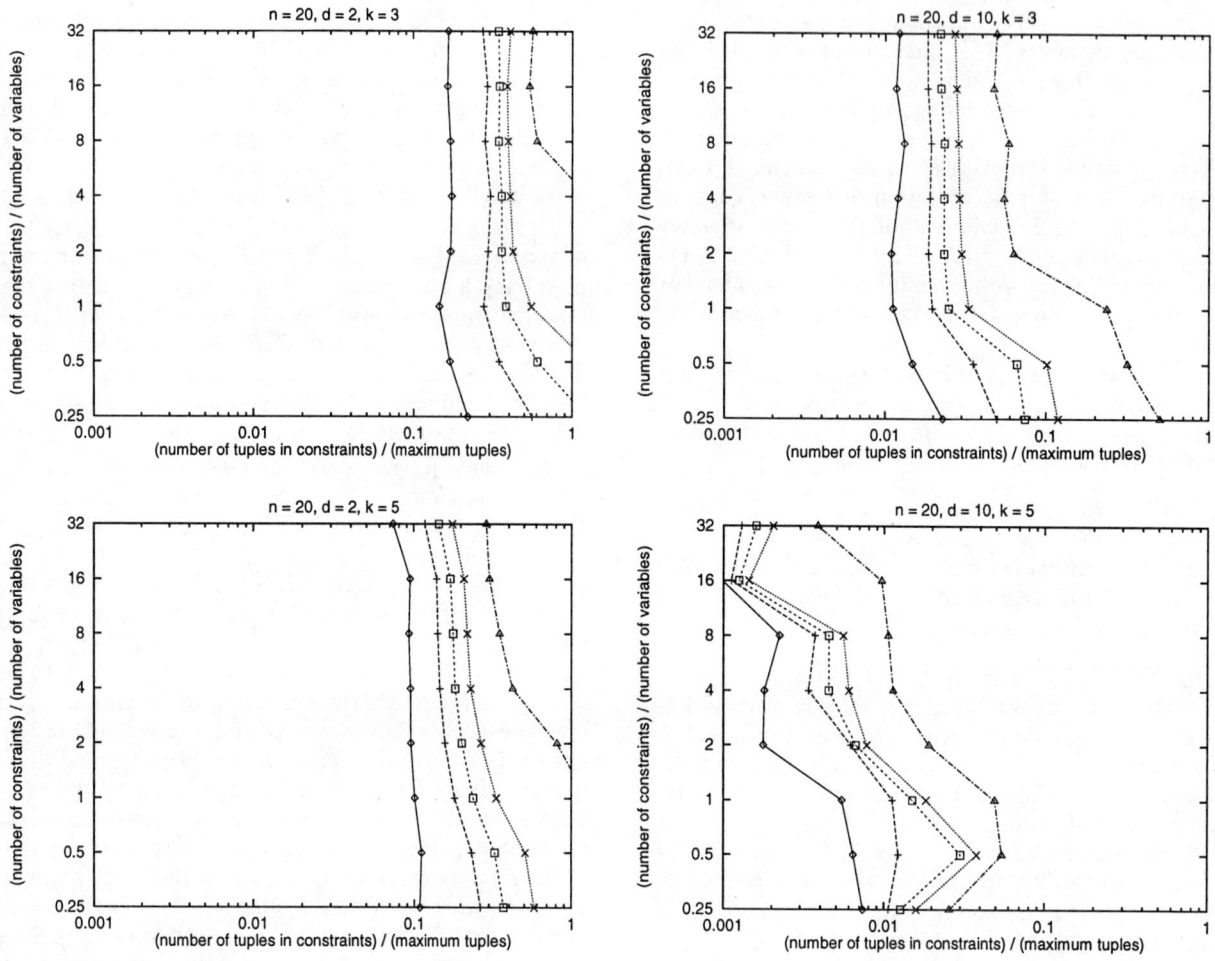

Figure 3: Order of magnitude curves for median cost of dual and original CSP when $n = 20$, $d = 2, 10$, and $k = 3, 5$. From left to right the curves mean: (i) dual is 10× better, (ii) dual is 2× better, (iii) dual and non-binary cost the same, (iv) dual is 2× worse, and (v) dual is 10× worse.

Table 1: Effect of the ratio of clauses to variables (m/n) on the ratio of the average number of consistency checks performed to solve the dual representation over the average number of consistency checks performed to solve the non-binary representation (cost rat.), when finding first solution to random 3-SAT problems with 100 Boolean variables.

m/n	1/4	1/2	1	2	4	8	16	32
cost rat.	0.9	1.5	2.5	4.2	31	33	38	44

curves predict that the dual representation should be more and more efficient as the length of the words in the puzzle grows. This is indeed the case and on the larger problems the dual is at least 1000 times faster.

Hidden Variable Representation. Figure 4 shows the basic behavior of the hidden variable representation on random CSPs. Over a wide range of different values for n, d, k, and m, we have found that it is the number of satisfying tuples in the constraint that determines the relative effectiveness of the hidden variable CSP. To determine which representation is superior, the hidden variable or the original non-binary, we plot the ratio of the average number of constraint checks performed by each algorithm. We run a sufficient number of problems at each data point to obtain averages that have two statistically significant digits. To present the data most effectively we plot the log (base 10) of this ratio: at zero the representations have approximately the same performance, positive numbers represent the number of orders of magnitude the hidden outperforms the non-binary, while negative number similarly represent the number of orders of magnitude the non-binary outperforms the hidden.

The plot shows three sample problem classes, each specified by the numbers $\langle n, d, k, m, t \rangle$. For each problem class we vary the number of satisfying tuples in each constraint from near 0% to near 100%. In the first two problem classes the number of constraints is 10% or less the total possible, while for the last class the number of constraints is 90% the total possible. The graphs show what we have also seen in

Table 2: Number of consistency checks performed when finding one solution to crossword puzzles. The absence of an entry indicates that the problem could not be solved within 5×10^8 consistency checks. For the dual problem, n is the number of variables and m is the number of constraints; for the non-binary problems, m is the number of variables and n is the number of constraints.

puzzle	original cc's	dual cc's	size n	size m
1	52	292	4	3
2	138	3,267	6	8
3	185	11,404	8	14
4	208	10,481	12	14
5	12,509	18,686	10	19
6	12,636	19,876	14	21
7	556,660	28,962	14	23
8	5,780,710	27,656	20	30
9	——	47,167	26	41
10	——	224,258	18	35
11	——	29,777	24	40
12	——	729,125	18	38
13	28,446,460	50,281	28	52
14	——	72,307	34	65
15	——	254,381	28	62
16	——	258,780	46	95
17	——	178,885	68	135
18	——	248,877	88	180
19	——	587,826	86	177
20	——	——	80	187

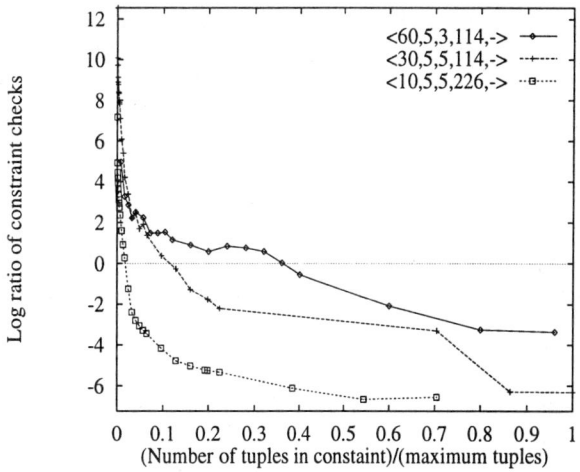

Figure 4: Log of the number of constraints checks performed by FC$^+$ on the hidden divided by the number of constraint checks performed by FC on the non-binary.

other problem classes: if the constraints have few satisfying tuples the hidden variable CSP can outperform the non-binary CSP by many orders of magnitude; the performance advantage of the hidden variable CSP decreases as we increase the number of satisfying tuples in the constraints and there is some threshold beyond which the non-binary becomes more effective; and finally, as our theory predicts the potential gain of the non-binary over the hidden is much less than the other way around. These results makes sense in terms of what FC$^+$ is doing. As the constraints have fewer and fewer satisfying tuples the FC$^+$ is able to detect a larger and larger number of extra deadends over FC running on the non-binary.

It is important to note that hard problems exist at all values of t. In particular, the hidden variable representation can be superior on hard problems: when the constraints contain a small number of satisfying tuples we can generate hard problems by increasing n or by decreasing m, both of these changes decrease the number of constraints each variable participates in. In Figure 5 we plot the average number of constraint checks required by FC$^+$ to solve the hidden variable CSP and the average number of checks required by FC to solve the equivalent non-binary CSP. In this plot we vary the number of constraints m. The graph shows something like the classic easy/hard/easy regions (smoothed out to some extent by our use of a log scale) as the varying number of constraints change the problems from solvable to unsolvable, and we see that although FC$^+$ on the hidden variable CSP never finds this particular problem class very difficult it becomes quite difficult for FC on the non-binary: at the peak (when we have a total of 10 constraints) it requires about 30 million checks on average to solve a problem vs. an average of 16 thousand checks for the hidden. More importantly is the fact that in this peak area FC on the non-binary requires in excess of 500 million checks on 3% of the problems while using the hidden the *same problems* were solved using less than 35 thousand checks. This phenomenon seems to be related to the exceptionally hard problems reported by Smith and Grant in (SG95). In particular, it indicates that for this problem class the distribution of constraint checks performed by FC$^+$ displays a lower variance as well as a lower mean.

Conclusions and Future Work

We examined how well the FC algorithm performs on a non-binary CSP in comparison to its performance on binary translations of the CSP.

Our experiments show that the dual graph representation can be more efficient by orders of magnitude, when the number of constraints is low relative to the number of variables, and the constraints are restrictive. As well, for the hidden variable representation, we showed that a modified forward checking algorithm which we call FC$^+$, can sometimes perform exponentially better than simply using FC on the non-binary, and sometimes it can be outperformed by a bounded (but sometimes large) amount. We have also provided better insights into the behavior and nature of the two binary translations. Translating a non-binary CSP involves some overhead, and we view this work as providing some initial intuitions as to when such a translation is worthwhile. Empirically, we have shown that the number of satisfying tuples in the constraints is perhaps the most important factor in determining how worthwhile the translation is.

An important question that we have not addressed here is

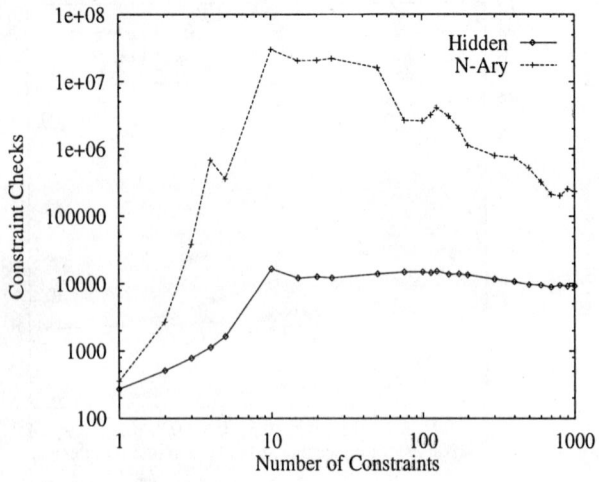

Figure 5: Number of constraints checks performed by the two algorithms on the problem class $\langle 30, 5, 5, -, 40 \rangle$.

the relationship between the two binary translations. When is the dual representation to be preferred to the hidden variable representation and vice versa? Are there any theoretical results that can be proved about their relative behaviour? We intend to address these questions in future work.

One thing, however, we feel that our data has demonstrated is that the translation to the binary has promise as a solution technique for non-binary CSPs. In the end, however, it could well be that insights about when these translations perform better, can be carried over directly to the non-binary case, so that improved methods for solving non-binary CSPs can be developed that avoid the overhead of the translation entirely. It should be clear, however, that studying and understanding these binary translations is an essential prerequisite to achieving such insights.

Acknowledgments

This work was supported by the Canadian Government through their NSERC and IRIS programs.

References

[Dec90] R. Dechter. On the expressiveness of networks with hidden variables. In *Proceedings of the Eighth National Conference on Artificial Intelligence*, pages 556–562, Boston, Mass., 1990.

[DM94] M. J. Dent and R. E. Mercer. Minimal forward checking. In *Proceedings of the Sixth IEEE International Conference on Tools with Artificial Intelligence*, pages 432–438, New Orleans, LA, 1994.

[DP89] R. Dechter and J. Pearl. Tree clustering for constraint networks. *Artificial Intelligence*, 38:353–366, 1989.

[Fre78] E. C. Freuder. Synthesizing constraint expressions. *Comm. ACM*, 21:958–966, 1978.

[Gin93] M. L. Ginsberg. Dynamic backtracking. *J. of Artificial Intelligence Research*, 1:25–46, 1993.

[HE80] R. M. Haralick and G. L. Elliott. Increasing tree search efficiency for constraint satisfaction problems. *Artificial Intelligence*, 14:263–313, 1980.

[Mac77] A. K. Mackworth. On reading sketch maps. In *Proceedings of the Fifth International Joint Conference on Artificial Intelligence*, pages 598–606, Cambridge, Mass., 1977.

[McG79] J. J. McGregor. Relational consistency algorithms and their application in finding subgraph and graph isomorphisms. *Inform. Sci.*, 19:229–250, 1979.

[Nad89] B. A. Nadel. Constraint satisfaction algorithms. *Computational Intelligence*, 5:188–224, 1989.

[Pei33] C. S. Peirce. In C. Hartshorne and P. Weiss, editors, *Collected Papers, Vol. III*. Harvard University Press, 1933. Cited in: F. Rossi, C. Petrie, and V. Dhar, 1989.

[RPD89] F. Rossi, C. Petrie, and V. Dhar. On the equivalence of constraint satisfaction problems. Technical Report ACT-AI-222-89, MCC, Austin, Texas, 1989. A longer version of (RPD90), with more details and results on the hidden variable method.

[RPD90] F. Rossi, C. Petrie, and V. Dhar. On the equivalence of constraint satisfaction problems. In *Proceedings of the 9th European Conference on Artificial Intelligence*, pages 550–556, Stockholm, Sweden, 1990.

[SG95] B. M. Smith and S. A. Grant. Sparse constraint graphs and exceptionally hard problems. In *Proceedings of the Fourteenth International Joint Conference on Artificial Intelligence*, pages 646–651, Montreal, 1995.

[SRGV96] T. Schiex, J.-C. Régin, C. Gaspin, and G. Verfaillie. Lazy arc consistency. In *Proceedings of the Thirteenth National Conference on Artificial Intelligence*, pages 216–221, Portland, Oregon, 1996.

[VH89] P. Van Hentenryck. *Constraint Satisfaction in Logic Programming*. MIT Press, 1989.

Generalizing Partial Order and Dynamic Backtracking

Christian Bliek

Artificial Intelligence Laboratory
Swiss Federal Institute of Technology
IN-Ecublens, 1015 Lausanne, Switzerland
cbliek@lia.di.epfl.ch

Abstract

Recently, two new backtracking algorithms, *dynamic backtracking* (DB) and *partial order dynamic backtracking* (PDB) have been presented. These algorithms have the property to be additive on disjoint subproblems and yet use only polynomial space. Unlike DB, PDB only imposes a partial search order and therefore appears to have more freedom than DB to explore the search space. However, both algorithms are not directly comparable in terms of flexibility. In this paper we present new backtracking algorithms that are obtained by relaxing the ordering conditions of PDB. This gives them additional flexibility while still being additive on disjoint subproblems. In particular, we show that our algorithms generalize both DB and PDB.

Introduction

Most sound and complete algorithms for solving constraint satisfaction problems are based on backtracking. Intelligent backtrackers record information regarding dead ends to avoid encountering them again. This approach was first used in *dependency directed backtracking* (DDB) where the subset of the current assignments that caused the dead end are recorded in a nogood (Stallman & Sussman 1977). By avoiding this subset of assignments, the efficiency of the subsequent search can be increased. Unfortunately, since the number of accumulated nogoods increases monotonically, DDB has an exponential space complexity.

To address this problem, recent backtrackers eliminate nogoods that are no longer relevant to the current assignments. By doing so, the space complexity remains polynomial. One of the standard techniques that has adopted this approach is *conflict based backjumping*[1] (CBJ) (Prosser 1993). When a dead end is encountered CBJ jumps back to the variable that participated in the dead end and was instantiated last. However, by doing so CBJ erases all assignments and nogoods that were obtained since. The search effort to solve disjoint subproblems is therefore multiplicative, not additive.

[1]This algorithm also appears in (Ginsberg 1993) where it is called *backjumping*.

Copyright © 1998, American Association of Artificial Intelligence (www.aaai.org). All rights reserved.

To overcome this drawback, *dynamic backtracking* (DB) reutilizes intermediate search information (Ginsberg 1993). Upon backtracking, it only removes the assignment of the backtrack variable and the nogoods that depend on it. This gives DB the property to be additive on disjoint subproblems. However, the forced reordering undoes the choices performed by variable selection heuristics. Experiments indicate that this negative effect often outweighs the benefits (Baker 1994).

CBJ and DB can be considered as classical backtrack search algorithms. The search consists in extending a consistent partial set of assignments until a solution is found. An alternative approach is to consider a complete set of assignments that is incrementally modified until all constraints are satisfied. During the search, a partial order on the variables is imposed to guarantee termination. This approach was first introduced by *partial order backtracking* (POB) (McAllester 1993). In (Ginsberg & McAllester 1994) this algorithm is slightly generalized and is referred to as PDB. Like DB, PDB has the property to be additive on disjoint subproblems.

The advantage of PDB with respect to DB is that it allows to reorder all variables and not just the "future" variables. It therefore appears to be much more flexible in terms of exploration of the search space. Nevertheless, DB and PDB are not directly comparable in terms of flexibility. In fact, in (McAllester 1993), it was raised as an open question whether a more general algorithm could be devised. In this paper we present two new intelligent backtrackers that are obtained by relaxing the ordering conditions of PDB. This gives them additional flexibility while still being additive on disjoint subproblems. In particular, we show that our algorithms generalize both DB and PDB.

Background

To avoid redundant search, intelligent backtrackers record nogoods. A nogood γ is a subset of assignments of values v_j to variables x_j which are incompatible:

$$\neg(x_1 = v_1 \wedge \cdots \wedge x_k = v_k) \qquad (1)$$

DDB accumulates all nogoods it encounters and hence suffers from an exponential space complexity. To keep the space complexity polynomial, some nogoods need to be removed during the search. In this paper we will follow the approach used by PDB which is outlined below.

We refer the reader to (McAllester 1993) and (Ginsberg & McAllester 1994) for a more detailed presentation.

At all times a complete set of assignments of the variables is considered. These assignments are incrementally modified until all constraints are satisfied. This search process is driven by the addition of new nogoods. New nogoods are added when the current assignments violate a constraint or when backtracking occurs. To satisfy a new nogood, one of its variable assignments, say x_k, needs to be changed. This is represented explicitly by rewriting expression (1) for γ as:

$$x_1 = v_1 \wedge \cdots \wedge x_{k-1} = v_{k-1} \to x_k \neq v_k$$

We will refer to this expression as the ordered nogood $\vec{\gamma}$. Here $x_1 = v_1$ through $x_{k-1} = v_{k-1}$ are called the *antecedent* and $x_k \neq v_k$ the *conclusion* of $\vec{\gamma}$. As soon as the value of x_k changes, all nogoods that have x_k as antecedent variable are removed. This means that the current assignments match all the antecedents of each nogood. Note that some assignments do not appear in any nogood antecedent. If desired, these assignments may be changed in addition to the one of x_k. We therefore say that an assignment is *acceptable* for a set of nogoods if all the antecedents are matched and none of the conclusions are violated. Observe that with this approach, a variable assignment can be ruled out by at most one nogood. There are therefore at most nd nogoods, where n is the number of variables and d the maximum domain size. Since each nogood requires $\mathcal{O}(n)$ space, the overall space complexity is $\mathcal{O}(n^2 d)$.

Backtracking occurs when for a given variable, say y, all values v_1 through v_d are ruled out by nogoods $\Sigma_i \to y \neq v_i$. In this case a new nogood is generated by the following inference rule:

$$\frac{\Sigma_1 \to y \neq v_1 \\ \vdots \\ \Sigma_d \to y \neq v_d}{\neg (\Sigma_1 \wedge \ldots \wedge \Sigma_d)} \quad (2)$$

New nogoods either correspond to constraint violations or are obtained by the above inference rule. This means that all steps in the inference process are valid. So when the empty nogood is obtained it can safely be concluded that the problem has no solution. It must be emphasized that this is true regardless of any considerations concerning variable ordering or nogood removal.

Each nogood eliminates a new section of the search space. Since DDB accumulates nogoods and the size of the search space is bounded, DDB will terminate. However, when nogoods are removed during the search, termination is no longer guaranteed. CBJ and DB therefore impose a total order on the assigned variables. By doing so, the portion of the search space ruled out by the new nogood includes the portions that were ruled out by the nogoods that are removed. As a result the size of the eliminated search space increases monotonically which ensures termination.

$\vec{\gamma}$	x_1	x_2	x_3	Γ
	2	2	2	
$x_2 = 2 \to x_1 \neq 2$	1	2	2	$\{x_2 = 2 \to x_1 \neq 2\}$
$x_3 = 2 \to x_2 \neq 2$	1	1	2	$\{x_3 = 2 \to x_2 \neq 2\}$
$x_1 = 1 \to x_3 \neq 2$	1	1	1	$\{x_1 = 1 \to x_3 \neq 2\}$
$x_2 = 1 \to x_1 \neq 1$	2	1	1	$\{x_2 = 1 \to x_1 \neq 1\}$
$x_3 = 1 \to x_2 \neq 1$	2	2	1	$\{x_3 = 1 \to x_2 \neq 1\}$
$x_1 = 2 \to x_3 \neq 1$	2	2	2	$\{x_1 = 2 \to x_3 \neq 1\}$
$\vdots$		$\vdots$		$\vdots$

Table 1: Search states of a simple search algorithm.

The inference made by an ordered nogood is directed. The value of the conclusion variable y is ruled out based on the assignments of the antecedent variables x_j. In a traditional backtrack tree search x_j will therefore precede y in the variable ordering. This relative ordering condition will be denoted by $x_j < y$. One may wonder if, to ensure termination, it is not sufficient to eliminate the possibility for cyclic inferences. This can be done by requiring that the set of conditions $x_j < y$ is acyclic. We hereby impose only a partial search order. Unfortunately, the answer is no. Consider the problem with three variables x_1, x_2 and x_3 each with values 1 and 2 and with constraints as depicted in figure 1. Table 1 shows the states of the search. The first column shows the nogood $\vec{\gamma}$ added at each step, the second column shows the current assignments and the third column Γ contains the current set of nogoods. Observe

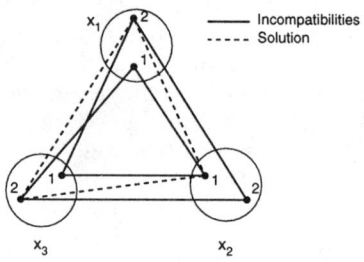

Figure 1: Example problem.

that the search process will cycle indefinitely, although $x_1 = 2, x_2 = 1$ and $x_3 = 2$ is a solution. The problem is that search information is deleted when nogoods are removed. As the example shows, this makes it possible for the search process to "chase its tail".

The relative ordering conditions corresponding to the ordered nogoods are consequently not sufficient to ensure termination. PDB therefore imposes additional relative ordering conditions, called *safety conditions*. The idea is to retain some of the ordering conditions of the nogoods that have been removed. The order selected for new nogoods is now required to respect both types of ordering conditions. That is, the resulting set of conditions may not be cyclic.

In the example above, when $x_2 = 2 \to x_1 \neq 2$ is deleted, PDB imposes the safety condition $x_2 < x_1$. Now we can no longer add $x_1 = 1 \to x_3 \neq 2$ as it would cause a cycle. Instead, we rewrite it as $x_3 = 2 \to x_1 \neq 1$. This now prompts us to change the value of x_1 to 2, hereby obtaining a solution.

General Partial Order Backtracking

While DB imposes a total variable order, only a partial variable order is required by PDB. Nevertheless, PDB is not a generalization of DB. We illustrate this point with an example. Consider a problem where each variable has three values. Suppose, as illustrated on top in figure 2, that the values (shown as •) for x_1, x_2 and x_3

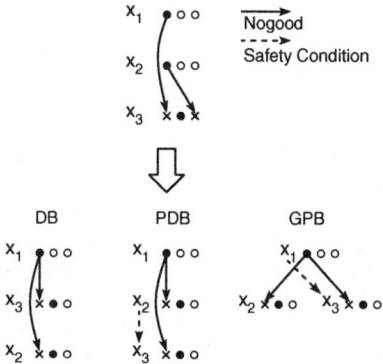

Figure 2: Backtracking with DB, PDB and GPB.

are not ruled out (shown as ×) by any nogood. Suppose further that x_1 and x_2 rule out all values of a fourth variable x_4 (not shown). At this point, we need to backtrack. So we use inference rule (2) to generate a new nogood involving x_1 and x_2. Let us select x_2 as conclusion and remove the nogood based on it. The first value of x_2 is now eliminated. As depicted on the bottom of figure 2, DB will hereby be forced to change the relative order of x_2 and x_3, whereas PDB has no choice but to keep the same order. In terms of flexibility both algorithms are therefore not comparable. However, it turns out that the safety condition $x_2 < x_3$ can be relaxed. Below we describe a new algorithm called *general partial order backtracking* or GPB that exploits this fact. As illustrated on the bottom of figure 2, in this case GPB only requires that $x_1 < x_3$. Observe that for GPB both the order of DB and the one of PDB are admissible.

PDB specifies explicitly how the set of safety conditions changes with the addition of each nogood. However, it is not needed to do so explicitly. We can abstract from the details on how safety conditions actually change and instead describe general conditions, called *transition conditions*, that need to be respected. We will do so in the following way. By transitivity, a set of safety conditions S implies a set of ordering conditions that will be denoted by $<_S$. Instead of specifying which safety conditions $<$ have to be present, we specify which ordering conditions $<_S$ have to be verified. We

then do not need to concern ourselves with how safety conditions actually imply these ordering conditions.

We consider the addition of a single nogood. Let S and S' be the set of safety conditions, before and after the addition of this nogood. Similarly, let Γ and Γ' be the set of ordered nogoods before and after the nogood is added. Let the conclusion variable of the added nogood be y and let $Z = \{z \mid y <_S z\}$. The transition conditions we require are:

1. only ordering conditions of the type $q <_S z$ with $z \in Z$ may disappear,
2. for every variable x for which $x <_{S'} y$, we have for all $z \in Z$, $x <_{S'} z$ and
3. for every ordered nogood in Γ' with antecedent variables x_j and conclusion variable y, we have $x_j <_{S'} y$.

Aside from the generalization of the formulation, the main difference with respect to PDB is that we no longer require that $y <_{S'} z$ for all $z \in Z$.

GPB has a main search loop and a backtrack procedure similar to PDB. The difference between the two resides in the conditions imposed on S. We use X to denote a complete set of assignments.

Algorithm GPB

Until X is a solution or the empty nogood is derived;
   select a nogood γ corresponding to a constraint violation,
   Backtrack γ,
   change X to be acceptable for Γ.

Backtrack γ

   Select a conclusion variable y of γ respecting S.
   Add $\vec{\gamma}$ to Γ and remove from Γ all nogoods which have y as antecedent variable.
   Modify S so that the transition conditions are satisfied.
   If the live domain[2] of y is empty
      infer a new nogood ρ and
      Backtrack ρ.

In the next section we prove that the properties of GDB concerning termination and systematicity still hold for GPB. In the subsequent section, we demonstrate that GPB is a generalization of both DB and PDB.

Properties of GPB

GPB goes through a sequence of states, called *partial order states*, each of which is described by a set of safety conditions S and a set of nogoods Γ. The transition between two subsequent states is performed by a top level call to the procedure Backtrack, including recursive calls if any. A state described by a total order and a complete set of assignments will be called a *total order state*. A total order state is an *instance* of a partial order state if its total order respects the safety conditions S and if its set of assignments is acceptable for

---

[2] The live domain of a variable is the set of values of its domain that is not ruled out by a conclusion of a nogood.

the set of nogoods Γ of the partial order state. We can now present the main result of this section:

Theorem 1 *For every sequence of partial order states σ^k, there exists a sequence of total order states σ_j^k so that σ_j^k is an instance of σ^k and so that the sequence σ_j^k is visited during the execution of a systematic backtrack algorithm.*

Note that this is a stronger property than what was previously shown for GDB in (Ginsberg & McAllester 1994). In fact, their result is a consequence of this theorem and is presented in corollary 1.

We first present three lemmas that allow us to prove theorem 1. In the lemmas we will consider the addition of a single nogood. That is, recursive calls of the procedure Backtrack are treated individually. The first lemma is adapted from (Ginsberg & McAllester 1994, lemma 5.5), the two remaining ones appear to be new.

Let α be the situation before, and β the situation after the addition of a single nogood. Take any total order that respects the ordering conditions in β. In this order, let s be the last variable before any variable in $Z \cup \{y\}$, S_1 be the set of variables up to and including s, and let S_2 be the remaining variables. Furthermore, let S_1^β be the ordering of S_1 according to the chosen order in β, and S_2^α an ordering of S_2 that respects the ordering conditions in α. The first two lemmas allow us to construct an order in α for any order in β. In particular, lemma 2 shows that this order can be constructed as depicted in figure 3.

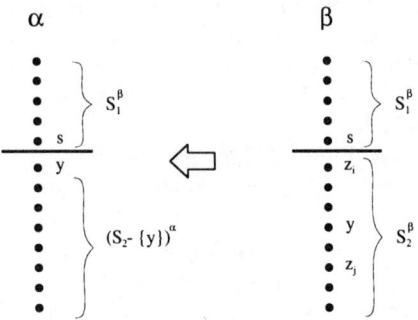

Figure 3: Orders before and after backtracking

Lemma 1 *The order $S_1^\beta; S_2^\alpha$ respects the ordering conditions in α.*

Proof: Transition condition 1 ensures that only ordering conditions of the type $q <_S z$ with $z \in Z$ disappear. Since by construction $Z \subseteq S_2$, we know that only ordering conditions of the type $q <_S s_2$ with $s_2 \in S_2$ are removed. Based on this we can verify that all ordering conditions in α are satisfied by $S_1^\beta; S_2^\alpha$. Let us distinguish 4 types of ordering conditions:

1. $s_1' <_S s_1''$ with $s_1' \in S_1$ and $s_1'' \in S_1$. No ordering conditions of the type $q <_S s_1$ with $s_1 \in S_1$ have been removed between α and β. So the ordering conditions between elements in S_1 are the same in α as in β. They are therefore satisfied by S_1^β.

2. $s_2' <_S s_2''$ with $s_2' \in S_2$ and $s_2'' \in S_2$. For the elements of S_2 an order S_2^α is used. This order respects the ordering conditions of α by definition.

3. $s_1 <_S s_2$ with $s_1 \in S_1$ and $s_2 \in S_2$. In $S_1^\beta; S_2^\alpha$, the elements s_1 precede the elements s_2 by construction. All ordering conditions of the type $s_1 <_S s_2$ are therefore satisfied by the proposed order.

4. $s_2 <_S s_1$ with $s_1 \in S_1$ and $s_2 \in S_2$. This type of ordering conditions is not present in β, and was not removed when going from α to β. This means that it could not be present in α.

$\square$

Lemma 2 *The order $S_1^\beta; y; (S_2 - \{y\})^\alpha$ respects the ordering conditions in α.*

Proof: By lemma 1 we know that $S_1^\beta; S_2^\alpha$ respects the ordering conditions in α. So it suffices to show that y can be taken as first element in S_2^α. We prove this by contradiction. Suppose y could not be taken as first element in S_2^α. This would mean that there exists an ordering condition of the type $x <_S y$ with $x \in S_2 - \{y\}$. By transition condition 1, this ordering condition could not have been removed when going from α to β. Now by transition condition 2, in β we will also have $x <_S z$ with $z \in Z$. But this would mean that x precedes both y and z. If this were the case, x would have been part of S_1, which is a contradiction. $\square$

Theorem 1 and its proof refer to a systematic backtrack algorithm. For this purpose let us consider a backtrack search algorithm with dynamic variable reordering. The elementary step of the algorithm is to process a single nogood. Consider the addition of a new nogood with conclusion y. First, all nogoods are removed that have y or subsequent variable as antecedent variable. Then the search tree is further explored to find a next set of assignments. If the live domain of y is not empty, a complete set of assignments that satisfies all nogoods will be found. Otherwise, the partial set of assignments up to and excluding y is used. Lemma 3 shows that this algorithm is systematic in the sense that any total set of assignments can at most be visited once. Furthermore, when a value of a variable y is ruled out by a nogood we can choose to instantiate any future variable next[3].

As before, let α and β be the situation before and after the addition of a single nogood. In lemma 3 and in the proof of theorem 1 assignments will be denoted as follows. X_1^β and X_2^β are the assignments in β for the variables in S_1 and S_2 respectively, and $(X_2 - \{y = v\})^\alpha$ are the assignments for the variables in $S_2 - \{y\}$ in α.

Lemma 3 *The transition from the partial set of assignments $X_1^\beta, y = v$ with search order $S_1^\beta; y; (S_2 -$*

---

[3]This is in fact the modification that was applied to DBI in (Ginsberg 1993, page 32).

$\{y\})^\alpha$ to the partial set of assignments X_1^β with search order $S_1^\beta; S_2^\beta$ is systematic.

Proof: The set of nogoods with conclusion variable in S_1 has not been changed. X_1^β is therefore a consistent partial set of assignments for S_1 in α. Now the variables in S_1 are ordered according to S_1^β and precede y. The addition of the nogood $\vec{\gamma}$ therefore rules out the portion $X_1^\beta, y = v$ of the search space. The nogoods that will be dropped by the addition of $\vec{\gamma}$ have $y = v$ or subsequent assignments as antecedent. Since the conclusion variable of these nogoods is in $S_2 - \{y\}$, the portion they ruled out is therefore a strict subset of the portion $X_1^\beta, y = v$ ruled out by $\vec{\gamma}$. As a result the set of possible assignments is a strict subset of the one before the addition of the nogood. □

Proof of Theorem 1: Let α and β now denote two subsequent partial order states of GPB. We first show that for any total order state β_j in β we can construct a total order state α_i in α, so that β_j can be reached from α_i by a systematic transition. This construction is illustrated in figure 4. Consider first the case where only

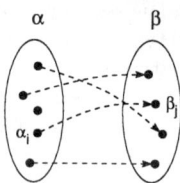

Figure 4: Transitions between instances of subsequent states.

one nogood is added in the transition between α and β. By lemma 2 we know that for each order $S_1^\beta; S_2^\beta$ in β we can construct the order $S_1^\beta; y; (S_2 - \{y\})^\alpha$ in α. Now by lemma 3 the transition between $X_1^\beta, y = v$ ordered according to $S_1^\beta; y; (S_2 - \{y\})^\alpha$ and X_1^β, X_2^β ordered according to $S_1^\beta; S_2^\beta$ is systematic. This means that for α_i we can take as assignments $X_1^\beta, y = v, (X_2 - \{y = v\})^\alpha$ and as order $S_1^\beta; y; (S_2 - \{y\})^\alpha$. If more than one nogood is added between α and β, this reasoning can be applied recursively.

We can now repeat this constructive argument for any sequence of partial order states σ^k visited by GPB. By doing so we obtain sequence of total order states σ_j^k which are visited during the execution of a systematic backtrack algorithm (see figure 5). □

Corollary 1 GPB *terminates and visits at most* $\prod_{i=1}^{n} d_i$ *states, where d_i is the domain size of variable x_i.*

Let us illustrate the level of systematicity implied by theorem 1. Consider for example the problem of finding all solutions to a given CSP. In this case the algorithm needs to be modified in the following way. Instead of

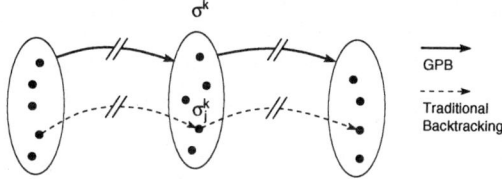

Figure 5: Sequence of instances visited by a systematic backtrack algorithm.

aborting the search when a solution is found, the solution is stored and a new nogood is generated that rules out exactly this set of assignments. Now, by theorem 1 this nogood will also be encountered in the execution of an underlying traditional backtrack algorithm. Since this algorithm is systematic it will not revisit this set of assignments. Hence it is not possible to encounter this nogood more than once. As a result, GPB will enumerate every solution to the CSP exactly once.

Nevertheless, GPB can revisit the same set of assignments. So, like PDB, it is not systematic in the traditional sense. To see this, consider the problem with three variables x_1, x_2 and x_3 each with values 1 and 2. Table 2 shows a possible sequence of states in which the same set of assignments is revisited twice.

$\vec{\gamma}$	x_1	x_2	x_3	S	Γ
	1	1	1		
$x_2 = 1 \to x_3 \neq 1$	2	1	2		$\{x_2 = 1 \to x_3 \neq 1\}$
$x_1 = 2 \to x_2 \neq 1$	2	2	2	$\{x_1 < x_3\}$	$\{x_1 = 2 \to x_2 \neq 1\}$
$x_1 \neq 2$	1	1	1		$\{x_1 \neq 2\}$

Table 2: GPB is not systematic in the traditional sense.

However, we can make it systematic. All we need to do is to restrict[4] GPB to change only assignments in Z. Let us call this algorithm GPB'.

Theorem 2 GPB' *is systematic.*

Proof: Consider the proof of theorem 1. Now with GPB' only the assignments in Z are allowed to be modified. The assignments in S_1 will therefore remain unchanged. As a result, the assignments constructed for the proof of theorem 1 will be the ones which are actually visited by GPB'. Since the traditional backtrack algorithm visiting these assignments is systematic, GPB' is systematic as well. □

GPB is additive on disjoint subproblems for the same reason as PDB is. The variables appearing in the same nogood are connected. This is the case for nogoods that are generated by constraint violations and is inductively

---

[4]The difference between POB and PDB is that in POB only the value of the conclusion variable is changed. POB therefore satisfies the proposed restriction and is systematic.

true for the nogoods generated by inference rule (2). Nogoods are only removed when their antecedents are ruled out by the conclusion of some other nogood. We consequently have no interaction between nogoods of disjoint subproblems.

Observe that lemma 3 would allow us to also remove the nogoods with antecedent variables in Z. By doing so we would obtain a new algorithm for which theorem 1 holds. Note that an ordering relation can only exist between variables that have been connected by a nogood. This modified algorithm therefore still enjoys the additivity property.

Instances of GPB

In this section we demonstrate that **GPB** is more general than **DB** and **PDB** in two ways. We first show that both algorithms are instances of **GPB** in the sense that they correspond with a specific choice for representing and manipulating S. Then we present an instance of **GPB**, called **GPB$_t$**, from which **DB** and **GDB** can be obtained by making heuristic choices.

DB[5] distinguishes instantiated variables i from uninstantiated variables u. All possible ordering conditions of the type $i <_S u$ are therefore implied. Furthermore, **DB** assumes a total order on instantiated variables. This means that for every pair of variables i_k and i_l, we have a condition of the type $i_k <_S i_l$, if i_l follows i_k in the total order. When a new nogood is added with conclusion variable y, **DB** effectively uninstantiates y. By doing so, all ordering conditions of the type $y <_S z$ are removed, which is in accordance with transition condition 1. Now, let x be an instantiated variable that precedes y in the total order and let z be a variable that follows y. With **DB**, x will still precede z after the reordering, whether z was an instantiated variable or a future variable. As required by transition condition 2, the ordering conditions of the type $x <_{S'} z$ are therefore satisfied. Transition condition 3 is verified since all nogoods either respect the ordering conditions $i_k <_S i_l$, or the ordering conditions $i <_S u$.

PDB manipulates safety conditions directly. When a nogood is added with conclusion variable y, it removes safety conditions of the type $q < z$ for each $z \in Z$, where $Z = \{z \mid y <_S z\}$. By doing so, only ordering conditions of the type $q' <_S z$ can disappear. Transition condition 1 is therefore verified. Then it adds the safety condition $y < z$ for every $z \in Z$. This means that for each x for which $x <_{S'} y$ we have $y < z$ and hence $x <_{S'} z$. So that transition condition 2 is satisfied as well. Since **PDB** explicitly respects the set of ordering conditions corresponding to the ordered nogoods, transition condition 3 is satisfied.

---

[5]Since all nogoods with antecedents in Z may safely be removed, the same reasoning can be used to show that **GDB** (McAllester 1993) is an instance of **GPB**.

There are many other ways to guarantee that transition conditions are verified. Consider the two following instances:

GPB$_s$ The transition conditions can be coded explicitly by modifying **PDB** in the following way. Instead of adding the safety condition $y < z$ for every $z \in Z$, we can add the safety condition $x < z$ for every $x < y$. This means that no relative ordering between y and z is imposed (see figure 2).

GPB$_t$ A different way of representing safety conditions is to associate with every nogood a set of variables called a *trail*. For a given nogood let the antecedent variables be x_i, the conclusion variable be c and the trail variables be t_j. We now associate two sets of safety conditions $\overline{S}$ and $\underline{S}$ with the nogoods. In $\overline{S}$ a nogood defines for each x_i the safety conditions; $x_i < c$ and $x_i < t_j$ for every t_j. In $\underline{S}$ a nogood defines for each x_i; $x_i < c$ and for each t_j; $c < t_j$.

Algorithm **GPB$_t$** proceeds as follows. When a new nogood is added, a conclusion variable y is selected that respects $\overline{S}$. As before, the new set of nogoods Γ' is obtained by removing from Γ all nogoods which have y as antecedent variables. Now let $Z = \{z \mid y <_{\underline{S}} z\}$ as obtained from the set of nogoods Γ. Each $z \in \overline{Z}$ is removed from the trail of all nogoods. Finally, each $z \in Z$ is added to the trail of those nogoods who either have y in their trail or as conclusion variable.

Observe that if Z was defined by $\overline{S}$, we obtain algorithm **GPB$_s$**. However, we are free to use $\underline{S}$ to define Z, since lemma 1 and lemma 2 will still hold. Indeed, referring to their proof, this eliminates some orders in β but not in α.

GPB$_t$ generalizes both **DB** and **PDB** in the sense that these algorithms can obtained by defining a specific heuristic. Let us see why this is the case. In **GPB$_t$** we can choose to extend a consistent partial assignment. The corresponding variables are the instantiated variables of **DB**. Now when a new nogood is added we may effectively uninstantiate its conclusion y and place it in the set of future variables. Indeed, subsequent nogoods need only to respect $\overline{S}$, not $\underline{S}$. This means that **DB** can be obtained by making specific heuristic choices in **GPB$_t$**. Similarly, we can also make heuristic choices in **GPB$_t$** so that it behaves as **PDB**. In particular, since $\overline{S}$ is less restrictive than $\underline{S}$, we can always order new nogoods as is done in **PDB**. If we do so, $\underline{S}$ of **GPB$_t$** will be the same as S of **GDB** and Z will be the same as in **GDB**.

Flexible Partial Order Backtracking

It turns out that the transition conditions of **GPB** can be further relaxed. By doing so we obtain an algorithm that enjoys even more freedom than **GPB** to explore the search space. We therefore call this algorithm *flexible partial order backtracking* or **FPB**. **FPB** is almost identical to **GPB**. The only difference is that transition condition 2 is now replaced by:

2. For every antecedent variable a_j in $\vec{\gamma}$, we have $a_j <_S z$ for all $z \in Z$.

The added flexibility of **FPB** comes at a price. Although we are able to show that the algorithm terminates, it no longer enjoys the properties concerning systematicity.

To prove that **FPB** terminates we will show that monotonic progress is made according to some measure. The flexibility of **FPB** requires us to introduce a new measure called the *maximum space size tuple*. The *space size* of a variable x_j with respect to a set of nogoods Γ and a given order $x_1; \ldots; x_n$ is defined to be $\sigma_j = \prod_{j \leq k} D_k(\Gamma, j)$ where $D_k(\Gamma, j)$ is the live domain of x_k with respect to the nogoods in Γ whose antecedent variables x_i have $i \leq j$. The *space size tuple* with respect to a given order and set of nogoods Γ is the tuple $\langle \sigma_1, \ldots, \sigma_n \rangle$. The *maximum space size tuple* is the tuple which is lexicographically the largest over all admissible orderings.

As before, let α and β be the situations before and after a nogood $\vec{\gamma}$ is added. Take any total order that respects the ordering conditions in β. Now in this order, let a be the last antecedent variable of $\vec{\gamma}$.

Lemma 4 *For any order in β there exists an order in α that agrees with it up to and including a.*

Proof: Since transition condition 1 still holds, lemma 1 applies. Furthermore, we know that $a \in S_1$ since $a <_S y$ and $a <_S z$. Hence the order $S_1^\beta; S_2^\alpha$ respects the ordering conditions in α and agrees with the order $S_1^\beta; S_2^\beta$ up to and including a. □

Theorem 3 **FPB** *terminates.*

Proof: To prove termination we show that the maximum space size tuple decreases with each backtrack. No nogoods with antecedent variables before or including a were deleted. Ignoring the effect of $\vec{\gamma}$ on the space size tuples, by lemma 4 we would have that for every space size tuple in β there exists a space size tuple in α whose entries agree up to and including σ_a. But now we added a nogood $\vec{\gamma}$, whose conclusion variable is y and whose last antecedent variable is a. This will reduce $D_y(\Gamma, a)$ by one, and hence reduce σ_a. The maximum space size tuple of β therefore has to be smaller than the maximum space size tuple of α. □

As shown in theorem 3, the algorithm terminates. However, it is not systematic in that a set of assignments can be visited more than once. This is true even we if we restrict **FPB** to change only assignments in Z. In fact, if we use the same modification as with **GPB** to find all solutions, **FPB** may enumerate solutions more than once.

Summary and Future Work

The main goal of this paper is to show that polynomial space backtrackers can yet be made more flexible. We have presented an algorithm, called **GPB**, that generalizes both **PDB** and **DB**. We have proven that **GPB** enjoys the same properties as **PDB** concerning termination and systematicity. Then we presented an algorithm, called **FPB**, which is even more flexible than **GPB**. However, in this case, the extra flexibility came at a price. Although we showed that **FPB** terminates, the algorithm can visit more states than **GPB**.

The next step is to investigate how heuristics can translate this added flexibility into increased efficiency. On the one hand, the performance of existing heuristics may improve. For example, we would expect that using **GPB** we can adhere to the local gradient heuristic of **GSAT** more often than with **PDB** (Ginsberg & McAllester 1994). On the other hand, new heuristics will need to be developed. For example, it is not clear how to best order new nogoods, or how the next constraint violation should be selected.

The overhead of **GPB** is similar to the one of **PDB**. However, to date little has been done to devise efficient representations and algorithms for maintaining nogoods and ordering conditions during the search. In our opinion this technical aspect also deserves some attention.

Acknowledgments

I would like to thank David McAllester for pointing out that **PDB** can be viewed as lifted classical backtracking. Thanks also to Gilles Trombettoni for his constructive comments on a draft of this paper.

This research work is supported through the ERCIM Fellowship Programme. It was performed in part at IIIA–CSIC in Bellaterra, Spain, sponsored by the European Commission and in part at LIA–EPFL in Lausanne, Switzerland sponsored by the Swiss National Science Foundation under project number 21-50237.97.

References

Baker, A. 1994. The hazards of fancy backtracking. In *AAAI'94: Proceedings of the Twelfth National Conference on Artificial Intelligence*, 288–293.

Ginsberg, M., and McAllester, D. 1994. GSAT and dynamic backtracking. In Doyle, J.; Sandewall, E.; and Torasso, P., eds., *KR'94: Proceedings of the Fourth International Conference on Principles of Knowledge Representation and Reasoning*, 226–237.

Ginsberg, M. 1993. Dynamic backtracking. *Journal of Artificial Intelligence Research* 1:25–46.

McAllester, D. 1993. Partial order backtracking. Research Note, Artificial Intelligence Laboratory, MIT. ftp://ftp.ai.mit.edu/people/dam/dynamic.ps.

Prosser, P. 1993. Hybrid algorithms for the constraint satisfaction problem. *Computational Intelligence* 9(3):268–299.

Stallman, R., and Sussman, G. 1977. Forward reasoning and dependency directed backtracking in a system for computer-aided circuit analysis. *Artificial Intelligence* 9:135–196.

On the Computation of Local Interchangeability in Discrete Constraint Satisfaction Problems

Berthe Y. Choueiry
Knowledge Systems Laboratory
Stanford University
Stanford, CA, 94305-9020
choueiry@ksl.stanford.edu

Guevara Noubir
Data Communications Group
Centre Suisse d'Electronique et de
Microtechnique (CSEM), Rue Jaquet-Droz 1
CH-2007 Neuchâtel, Switzerland
guevara.noubir@csemne.ch

Abstract

In [4], Freuder defines several types of interchangeability to capture the equivalence among the values of a variable in a discrete constraint satisfaction problem (CSP), and provides a procedure for computing one type of local interchangeability. In this paper, we first extend this procedure for computing a weak form of local interchangeability. Second, we show that the modified procedure can be used to generate a conjunctive decomposition of the CSP by localizing, in the CSP, independent subproblems. Third, for the case of constraints of mutual exclusion, we show that locally interchangeable values can be computed in a straightforward manner, and that the only possible type of local interchangeability is the one that induces locally independent subproblems. Finally, we give hints on how to exploit these results in practice, establish a lattice that relates some types of interchangeability, and identify directions for future research.

1 Introduction

Interchangeability among the values of a variable in a *Constraint Satisfaction Problem* (CSP) captures the idea of 'equivalence' among these values and was first formalized by Freuder [4]. Choueiry and Faltings [2] show that interchangeability sets are abstractions of the CSP with the following advantages: (1) The reduction of the computational complexity of a problem, and the improvement of the performance of the search technique used to solve it. (2) The identification of elementary components for interaction with the users.

This paper studies the computation of local interchangeability, and is organized as follows. In Section 2, we first review the definitions of a CSP and interchangeability; we discuss the advantages drawn from computing interchangeable sets; then we restate the procedure introduced in [4] for computing a strong type of local interchangeability. In the rest of the paper we describe our contributions. In Section 3.1, we extend the above mentioned procedure; we show that this extension enables the computation of a weak

Copyright ©1998, American Association for Artificial Intelligence (www.aaai.org). All rights reserved.

form of interchangeability (Section 3.2) as well as the identification of locally independent subproblems (Section 3.3); then we describe how these interchangeable sets are organized in a hierarchy (Section 3.4). Further, we sketch how to use their properties in practice (Section 4), and show that, for the case of constraints of mutual exclusion, local interchangeability can be easily computed, and is equivalent to identifying locally independent subproblems (Section 5). Finally, we introduce a lattice that situates various contributions reported in the literature (Section 6), and draw directions for future research (Section 7).

We intentionally restrict ourselves here to presenting the concepts, hinting on their usefulness, and illustrating them on simple problems. Although we have already identified several properties useful for problem solving, we do not discuss them here for lack of space.

2 Definitions

A CSP is defined by $\mathcal{P} = (\mathcal{V}, \mathcal{D}, \mathcal{C})$, where $\mathcal{V} = \{V_1, V_2, \ldots, V_n\}$ is the set of variables, $\mathcal{D} = \{D_{V_1}, D_{V_2}, \ldots, D_{V_n}\}$ the set of domains (*i.e.*, sets of values) associated with the variables, and $\mathcal{C}$ is the set of constraints that apply to the variables. A constraint C_{V_i, V_j}, applicable to two variables V_i and V_j, restricts the combination of values that can be assigned simultaneously to V_i and V_j, and thus defines a relation $R_{V_i, V_j} \subseteq D_{V_i} \times D_{V_j}$, which is the set of tuples allowed by C_{V_i, V_j}. When the relation is exactly the Cartesian product of the variable domains (*i.e.*, $R_{V_i, V_j} = D_{V_i} \times D_{V_j}$), the corresponding constraint is said to be *universal*. To solve a CSP is to assign one value to each variable such that all constraints are simultaneously satisfied. A CSP is commonly represented by a *constraint graph* in which the variables are represented by nodes, the domains by node labels, and the constraints by edges that link the relevant nodes. Universal constraints are omitted from the constraint graph. In this document, we restrict our study to discrete binary CSPs: each domain D_{V_i} is a finite set of discrete values, and each constraint applies to two variables. We define the *neighborhood* of a set of variables $\mathcal{S}$, denoted $\texttt{Neigh}(\mathcal{S})$, to be the set of variables adjacent to $\mathcal{S}$ in the constraint graph.

2.1 Interchangeability

Freuder introduces several types of value interchangeability for a CSP variable. Below, we recall those relevant to our study, while illustrating each of them on the list coloring problem of Fig. 1.

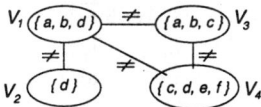

Figure 1: *An example of a list coloring problem.*

Definition 2.1 *Full interchangeability:* A value b for a CSP variable V_i is fully interchangeable (FI) with a value c for V_i if and only if every solution to the CSP that assigns b to V_i remains a solution when c is substituted for b in V_i and vice versa.

Two FI values b and c can be switched for variable V_i in any solution regardless of the constraints that apply to V_i. In Fig. 1, d, e, and f are fully interchangeable for V_4. Indeed, we inevitably have $V_2 = d$, which implies that V_1 cannot be assigned d in any consistent global solution. Consequently, the values d, e, and f can be freely permuted for V_4 in any global solution. No efficient general algorithm for computing FI has to date been reported: in fact, determining FI may require computing all solutions. Neighborhood interchangeability (NI) only considers local interactions, and can thus be efficiently computed:

Definition 2.2 *Neighborhood interchangeability:* A value b for a CSP variable V_i is neighborhood interchangeable (NI) with a value c for V_i if and only if for every constraint C on V_i:

$$\{x \mid (b,x) \text{ satisfies } C\} = \{x \mid (c,x) \text{ satisfies } C\}$$

In Fig. 1, e and f are NI for V_4. NI and FI are special cases of k-interchangeability, which introduces gradually levels of full interchangeability in all subproblems of size k, moving from NI for $k = 2$ (local), towards FI for $k = n$ (global). k-interchangeability (including FI and NI) is concerned with changing values of one variable, while keeping those of all other variables unchanged. Another type of interchangeability introduced in [4], partial interchangeability, allows a subset of the variables ($\mathcal{A} \subseteq \mathcal{V}$) to be affected when switching the values of V_i, while the rest of the 'world' ($\mathcal{V} - V_i - \mathcal{A}$) remains the same. Informally, partial interchangeability is about extending a boundary (which is the set of variables $\mathcal{S}$ affected by the switching operation) by *weakening* the requirement on what may be affected.

Definition 2.3 *Partial Interchangeability:* Two values are partially interchangeable (PI) with respect to a subset $\mathcal{A}$ of variables if and only if any solution involving one implies a solution involving the other, with possibly different values for variables in $\mathcal{A}$.

In Fig. 1, a and b are PI for V_1 with respect to the set $\mathcal{A} = \{V_3\}$. There is no known efficient algorithm for computing the PI-sets for a CSP variable. In addition to the difficulty of computing PI, one also needs to specify the set $\mathcal{A}$, which is not a straightforward task.

In this paper, we extend the polynomial algorithm for computing NI to efficiently compute a localized version of PI, which we call NPI and define in Section 3.2. Notice that FI corresponds to PI with $\mathcal{A} = \emptyset$; and similarly, NI corresponds to NPI with $\mathcal{A} = \emptyset$. Fig. 2 illustrates the relations between these types of interchangeability (from local to full, and from strong to weak). Informally, a variable V_i affects the problem

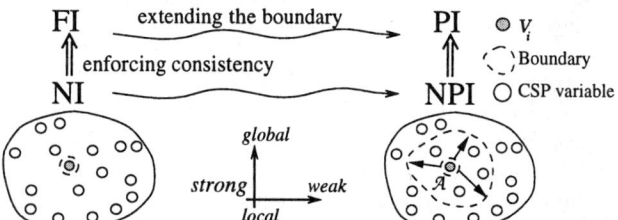

Figure 2: *Interchangeability.* Partial ($\leadsto$): from strong to weak. Full ($\Rightarrow$): from local to global.

'through' the constraints that link V_i to other variables in the problem, thus through V_i's neighborhood. Two values x and y that are NI for V_i 'affect' $\text{Neigh}(\{V_i\})$ in exactly the same fashion. They are bound to carry the same effect on the whole problem, and are inevitably FI for V_i. More formally, Freuder shows that NI is a sufficient but not a necessary condition for FI. (Indeed, in the example of Fig. 1, d and e for V_4 are FI but not NI.) It is easy to show that the same relation holds between NPI and PI.

We introduce the relation $\equiv_\mathcal{C}$ that links values x and y, variables V_i and V_j in $\mathcal{S} \subseteq \mathcal{V}$, and the constraints $\mathcal{C}$ of the CSP to indicate that the variable-value pairs (V_i, x) and (V_j, y) are compatible with exactly the same variable-value pairs in $\text{Neigh}(\mathcal{S})$.

$$(x, V_i, \mathcal{S}) \equiv_\mathcal{C} (y, V_j, \mathcal{S}) \qquad (1)$$

If x and y are NI for V_i, we have $(x, V_i, \{V_i\}) \equiv_\mathcal{C} (y, V_i, \{V_i\})$; if they are PI, we have $(x, V_i, \{V_i\} \cup \mathcal{A}) \equiv_\mathcal{C} (y, V_i, \{V_i\} \cup \mathcal{A})$. This relation is symmetric and transitive, because it is in essence a relation of equivalence.

2.2 Advantages of interchangeable values

We identify three main ways to use interchangeable values in practice:

1. Strongly interchangeable values can be replaced by one 'meta-value'.

2. An asymmetric type of interchangeability, called substitutability (see Definition 5.4), can be used to accommodate unquantifiable constraints or subjective preferences.

3. Partial interchangeability localizes the effect of modifications to some variables and identifies *compact*

families of partial solutions: qualitatively equivalent solutions can be generated by modifying the values of the indicated variables only.

Classical enumerative methods fail to organize the solution space in such a compact manner: they present solutions in a jumble without showing similarities and differences between alternative solutions. In particular, they fail to identify the boundaries within which the effect of a change remains local. In practice, these characteristics can be used as follows, beyond and including search:

In interactive problem solving. Interchangeable sets can be used to help the human decision-maker view alternative choices in a concise way [2]. More specifically, meta-values can be used to avoid displaying too much information to the user; substitutability allows the compliance to users' preferences; and finally, partial interchangeabilities delimit the extent of certain modifications, so that the users can modify a solution locally to cope with change in a dynamic environment.

In search. Interchangeability sets can be used (1) to monitor the search process to remain as local as possible, by compacting the solution space representation and by grouping solution families, and (2) to enhance the performance of both backtracking and consistency checking by removing redundant values, as shown in [1; 7].

In explanation. Interchangeability identifies groups of objects (sets of variables and sets of values) to become the basic components for a concept generation process aimed at providing explanation. In real-world applications, it is reasonable to suspect that the set of objects discovered to be interchangeable share common characteristics [4]. In [2], a concept generation procedure uses background knowledge, in the form of concept hierarchies, to generate dynamically concise descriptions of the interchangeable sets.

2.3 The discrimination tree

Below, we recall the procedure, introduced in [4], for computing the NI-sets for a variable by building its discrimination tree (DT). The complexity of this procedure is $O(nd^2)$, where n is the size of $\mathcal{V}$, and d the size of the largest domain. It is important, in this procedure, that variables and values be ordered in a canonical way.

Algorithm 1 DT for V_i (D_{V_i}, $\text{Neigh}(\{V_i\})$)

Create the root of the discrimination tree
Repeat for each value $v \in D_{V_i}$:
  Repeat for each variable $V_j \in \text{Neigh}(\{V_i\})$:
    Repeat for each $w \in D_{V_j}$ consistent with v for V_i:
    Move to if present, construct and move to if not,
    a child node in the tree corresponding to '$V_j = w$'.
  Add '$V_i, \{v\}$' to annotation of the node (or root),
  Go back to the root of the discrimination tree.

The collection of the annotations in the discrimination tree of a variable V_i yields the following set:

$$\text{DT}(V_i) = \{d_{1i}, d_{2i}, \ldots, d_{ki}\} \qquad (2)$$

where $1 \leq k \leq |D_{V_i}|$ is the number of annotations in the tree, and $d_{1i}, d_{2i}, \ldots, d_{ki}$ determine a partition of D_{V_i}. The NI-sets of V_i are expressed as follows:

$$\text{NI}(V_i) = \{d_{ki} \in \text{DT}(V_i) \text{ such that } |d_{ki}| > 1\} \qquad (3)$$

Although this was not explicitly stated in [4] or in other papers on this topic, there may be in general any number of NI-sets per variable. In Fig. 3, we show the graph and constraints of a simple CSP. The anno-

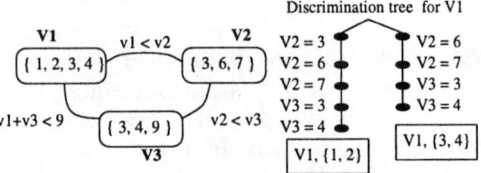

Figure 3: *Left:* CSP. *Right:* DT for V_1.

tations in the discrimination tree for V_1 are: $\text{DT}(V_1) = \{\{1,2\},\{3,4\}\}$. In this case, $\text{NI}(V_1) = \text{DT}(V_1)$. As for V_2 and V_3, we have $\text{DT}(V_2) = \{\{3\},\{6,7\}\}$, $\text{NI}(V_2) = \{\{6,7\}\}$, $\text{DT}(V_3) = \{\{3\},\{4\},\{9\}\}$ and $\text{NI}(V_3) = \emptyset$.

3 Weakening local interchangeability

First, we extend the DT associated with a variable to be a joint discrimination tree (JDT) associated with a set of variables. We identify the interchangeability sets determined by the JDT, and discuss a special case in which the discovered sets induce locally independent subproblems. Then we show that the annotations of the JDT determine partitions of the variable domains that are organized in a hierarchy.

3.1 Joint discrimination tree (JDT)

We extend Algorithm 1, and apply it to a set $\mathcal{S}$ of variables in order to identify how these variables, when considered together and regardless of the constraints that apply among them, interact through their neighborhood with the rest of the problem. The generalization to a set of variables is straightforward and is obtained by replacing the second argument of Algorithm 1, $\text{Neigh}(\{V_i\})$, by $\text{Neigh}(\mathcal{S})$ and repeating this algorithm for each of the variables in $\mathcal{S}$ while using the same tree structure. Given a set $\mathcal{S}$ of size s, the time complexity of the algorithm is $O(s(n-s)d^2)$ and the space complexity for storing the tree is $O((n-s)d)$, where n is the size of $\mathcal{V}$, and d the size of the largest domain. The annotations of the *joint discrimination tree* (JDT) of a set $\mathcal{S} = \{V_1, V_2, \ldots, V_k\} \subseteq \mathcal{V}$ yield[1]:

$$\begin{aligned}\text{JDT}(\mathcal{S}) = \{ \ &\{(V_1, d_{11}), (V_2, d_{12}), \ldots, (V_k, d_{1k})\}, \quad (4)\\ &\{(V_1, d_{21}), (V_2, d_{22}), \ldots, (V_k, d_{2k})\}, \ldots,\\ &\{(V_1, d_{m1}), (V_2, d_{m2}), \ldots, (V_k, d_{mk})\} \ \}\end{aligned}$$

It is important to highlight the following:

---
[1] When $\mathcal{S} = \{V_i\}$, a comparison of Expressions (2) and (4) yields: $\text{JDT}(\{V_i\}) = \{\{(V_i, d_{ki})\} \,|\, d_{ki} \in \text{DT}(V_i)\}$.

- In order to comply with Expression (4), the annotations in this tree that do not contain a variable-domain pair for every variable in $\mathcal{S}$ are completed with all pairs of a missing variable and an empty domain for this variable.
- In Expression (4), m denotes the number of annotations in the tree ($1 \leq m \leq \sum_{i=1}^{i=k} |D_{V_i}|$).
- $\forall V_j \in \mathcal{S}$, the sets d_{ij} for $1 \leq i \leq m$ determine a partition of D_{V_j}.
- Since all variable-value pairs in any annotation in the JDT for $\mathcal{S}$ are compatible with exactly the same value-variables pairs in $\text{Neigh}(\mathcal{S})$, we have $\forall V_k \in \mathcal{S}$, $\forall 1 \leq i \leq m$, and $\forall x, y \in d_{ik}$:

$$(x, V_k, \mathcal{S}) \equiv_c (y, V_k, \mathcal{S}) \qquad (5)$$

and, using the same notation, $\forall V_k, V_h \in \mathcal{S}$, $\forall x, y$:

$$\exists 1 \leq i \leq m, x \in d_{ik}, y \in d_{ih} \iff (x, V_k, \mathcal{S}) \equiv_c (y, V_h, \mathcal{S}) \qquad (6)$$

Fig. 4 shows an example of a CSP along with the JDT of $\mathcal{S} = \{V_1, V_2\}$. We have:

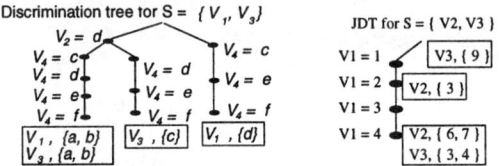

Figure 4: *Left:* CSP. *Right:* JDT for $\mathcal{S} = \{V_1, V_2\}$.

$$\text{JDT}(\{V_1, V_2\}) = \{\{(V_1, 10), (V_2, \emptyset)\}, \qquad (7)$$
$$\{(V_1, \{2,3\}), (V_2, \{3,4,5\})\}\}$$

Fig. 5 shows, to the left, the JDT for $\mathcal{S} = \{V_1, V_3\}$ of the CSP of Fig. 1, and, to the right, the JDT for $\mathcal{S} = \{V_2, V_3\}$ of the CSP of Fig. 3. We have:

$$\text{JDT}(\{V_1, V_3\}) = \{\{(V_1, \{a,b\}), (V_3, \{a,b\})\}, \qquad (8)$$
$$\{(V_1, \{d\}), (V_3, \emptyset)\}, \{(V_1, \emptyset), (V_3, \{c\})\}\}$$
$$\text{JDT}(\{V_2, V_3\}) = \{\{(V_2, \{6,7\}), (V_3, \{3,4\})\}, \qquad (9)$$
$$\{(V_2, \{3\}), (V_3, \emptyset)\}, \{(V_2, \emptyset), (V_3, \{9\})\}\}$$

Figure 5: *Left:* JDT for $\mathcal{S} = \{V_1, V_3\}$ of CSP of Fig. 1. *Right:* JDT for $\mathcal{S} = \{V_2, V_3\}$ of CSP of Fig. 3.

3.2 Neighborhood partial interchang. (NPI)

For any element of the set $\text{JDT}(\mathcal{S})$ in Expression (4), such as $\{(V_1, d_{m1}), (V_2, d_{m2}), \ldots, (V_k, d_{mk})\}$, for any $V_i \in \{V_1, V_2, \ldots, V_k\}$, if d_{mi} for V_i is the empty set, there seems to be no obvious way profitably to use this element of the $\text{JDT}(\mathcal{S})$ in practice. The same is true when all d_{mi} are singletons (i.e., $\forall 1 \leq i \leq k, |d_{mi}| = 1$).

In all other cases, any $x, y \in d_{mi}$ are partially interchangeable (PI) for V_i by construction of the JDT

and, according to Definition 2.3, $\mathcal{A} = \mathcal{S} - \{V_i\}$ in this case. Since these d_{mi} sets are computed locally, i.e. considering only $\text{Neigh}(\mathcal{S})$, they are only subsets of the 'complete' PI-sets, and the elements of each d_{mi} are said to be *neighborhood partially interchangeable* (NPI) for V_i. Thus the definition[2]:

$$\text{NPI}(\mathcal{S}) = \{\{(V_1, d_{m1}), (V_2, d_{m2}), \ldots, (V_k, d_{mk})\} \in \text{JDT}(\mathcal{S})$$
$$\text{such that } (\forall 1 \leq i \leq k, d_{mi} \neq \emptyset) \land$$
$$(\exists 1 \leq i \leq k, |d_{mi}| > 1) \} \qquad (10)$$

The extension of Algorithm 1 to a set of variables yields powerful results: For a given $\mathcal{S}$, it efficiently and simultaneously determines the NPI-sets for all the variables in $\mathcal{S}$. Obviously, if one is interested in the NPI-sets of a subset of $\mathcal{S}$, this procedure needs to iterate only over the variables of the subset.

Using Expression (8), we have, for the example of Fig. 4, $\text{NPI}(\{V_1, V_2\}) = \{\{(V_1, \{2,3\}), (V_2, \{3,4,5\})\}\}$. For the following two expressions, we have respectively: $\text{NPI}(\{V_1, V_3\}) = \{\{(V_1, \{a,b\}), (V_3, \{a,b\})\}\}$ and $\text{NPI}(\{V_2, V_3\}) = \{\{(V_2, \{6,7\}), (V_3, \{3,4\})\}\}$.

3.3 Subproblem identification

Sometimes a discrimination tree exhibits a branch worth singling out from the other branches in the tree. In Fig. 6, we show in a constraint graph of a CSP, the set $\mathcal{S} = \{V_1, V_2, \ldots, V_k\}$, and $\text{Neigh}(\mathcal{S}) = \{V_{n1}, V_{n2}, \ldots, V_{nl}\}$; we also sketch the JDT for $\mathcal{S}$. Consider the path in this figure whose leaf node is

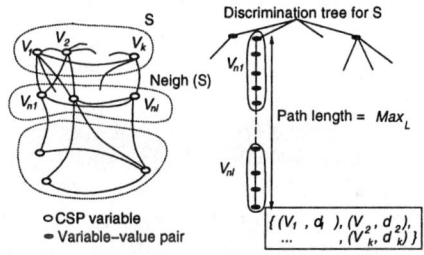

Figure 6: *Left:* Constraint graph. *Right:* Discrimination tree with a path of maximal length.

annotated with $\{(V_1, d_1), (V_2, d_2), \ldots, (V_k, d_k)\}$. When the length of this path (from the root to the leaf) is equal to the sum of the sizes of all the variable domains in $\text{Neigh}(\mathcal{S})$ (i.e., $\sum_{i=n1}^{i=nl} |D_{V_i}|$, denoted Max_L), this indicates that $\forall V_i \in \mathcal{S}$, any value in d_i is consistent with *all* the values of the variables in $\text{Neigh}(\mathcal{S})$. As long as we deliberately assign to V_i values exclusively chosen from d_i, no consistency checks with the variables in $\text{Neigh}(\mathcal{S})$ need be carried out. This appears as if all the constraints between $\mathcal{S}$ and $\text{Neigh}(\mathcal{S})$ have been replaced by universal constraints. We can thus generate a disjunctive decomposition[3] of the CSP into

---

[2]When $\mathcal{S} = \{V_i\}$, a comparison of Expressions (2) and (10) yields: $\text{NPI}(\{V_i\}) = \{\{(V_i, d_{ki})\} \mid d_{ki} \in \text{NI}(V_i)\}$.

[3]Note that, according to the terminology introduced in [5], this decomposition is consistent, simplifying, complete, and non-redundant.

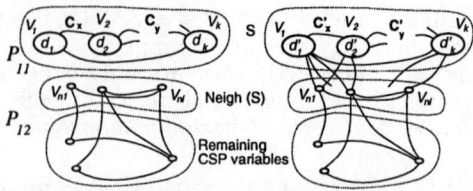

Figure 7: Left: $\mathcal{P}_1$. Right: $\mathcal{P}_2$.

the two CSPs $\mathcal{P}_1$ and $\mathcal{P}_2$ shown in Fig. 7. $\forall V_i \in \mathcal{S}$, D_{V_i} is replaced by d_i in $\mathcal{P}_1$, and by $d'_i = D_{V_i} - d_i$ in $\mathcal{P}_2$. Naturally, the constraints among the variables in $\mathcal{S}$, and also between $\mathcal{S}$ and Neigh($\mathcal{S}$), need to be updated accordingly, which is a trivial task. Further, we can generate a conjunctive decomposition of $\mathcal{P}_1$ into two subproblems: $\mathcal{P}_{11}$ containing the variables in $\mathcal{S}$ (and their new domains and updated constraints) and $\mathcal{P}_{12}$ containing the variables in $(\mathcal{V} - \mathcal{S})$. The advantage of this conjunctive decomposition is obvious. A solution to $\mathcal{P}_1$ can be obtained by simply 'concatenating' any solution to $\mathcal{P}_{11}$ and any solution to $\mathcal{P}_{12}$, both of which are smaller than $\mathcal{P}_1$, and the complexity of solving $\mathcal{P}_1$ is reduced to that of solving the bigger subproblem. Hence, we considerably reduce the complexity of solving $\mathcal{P}_1$, and as a result $\mathcal{P}$. Because we use local analysis (i.e., the JDT for $\mathcal{S}$) to determine that $\mathcal{P}_{11}$ is an independent subproblem of $\mathcal{P}_1$, we choose to call $\mathcal{P}_{11}$ a *neighborhood independent subproblem* (NIS). Moreover, at most one path of the JDT for $\mathcal{S}$ can be of maximal length.

Theorem 3.1 *The locally independent subproblem for a given set $\mathcal{S}$ is unique.*

Proof: Any path in the tree that is of maximal length must contain nodes for all variable-value pairs in the neighborhood of $\mathcal{S}$. If two such paths exist, they necessarily consist of exactly the same nodes, which is impossible according to the construction rule of Algorithm 1. □

The set NIS($\mathcal{S}$) is defined to be the element of the set JDT($\mathcal{S}$) that annotates a path in the tree of length Max_L. In the example of Fig. 4, NIS($\{V_1, V_2\}$) = $\emptyset$. In the example of Fig. 3, NIS($\{V_2, V_3\}$) = $\{(V_2, \{6, 7\}), (V_3, \{3, 4\})\}$, and NIS($\{V_1, V_3\}$) = $\{(V_1, \{1, 2\}), (V_3, \{9\})\}$. Note how the JDT reveals nontrivial independent subproblems that would, otherwise, have remained unnoticed.

3.4 Hierarchical structure of domain partitions

As stated in Section 3.1 and Expression (4), $\forall V_k \in \mathcal{S}$, the sets d_{ik} for $1 \leq i \leq m$ determine a partition of D_{V_k}. If we were to extend the set $\mathcal{S}$ for which the discrimination tree is built to a set $\mathcal{S}'$ ($\mathcal{S} \subset \mathcal{S}'$), the sets d_{ik} for variable V_k can only increase in size. In fact, for $\mathcal{S} \subset \mathcal{S}' \subset \mathcal{V}$ and for $V_k \in \mathcal{S}$, any element of the partition of D_{V_k} determined by JDT($\mathcal{S}'$) is either an element or a union of elements of the partition of

D_{V_k} determined by JDT($\mathcal{S}$). The sign $\oplus$ below denotes exclusive OR (i.e., XOR). More formally:

Property 3.2 $\forall V_k \in \mathcal{S}$ we have:

$\exists s_1, s_2 \in \text{JDT}(\mathcal{S}) \mid (V_k, d_{ik}) \in s_1; (V_k, d_{jk}) \in s_2$
$\iff \begin{cases} (\exists s'_1, s'_2 \in \text{JDT}(\mathcal{S}') \mid (V_k, d_{ik}) \in s'_1, (V_k, d_{jk}) \in s'_2) \\ \oplus \\ (\exists s' \in \text{JDT}(\mathcal{S}') \mid (V_k, d_{lk} \supseteq d_{ik} \cup d_{jk}) \in s') \end{cases}$

Indeed, the set Neigh($\mathcal{S}'$) contains no more nodes from the set Neigh($\{V_k\}$) than does the set Neigh($\mathcal{S}$), plus some nodes that are not connected to V_k. This means that JDT($\mathcal{S}'$) cannot discriminate more among the values in D_{V_k} than does JDT($\mathcal{S}$). This fact yields a hierarchical representation of the partitions of D_{V_k} of increasingly coarser granularity as JDT($\mathcal{S}'$) is gradually expanded to encompass more variables including V_k. One such hierarchy is illustrated in Fig. 8.

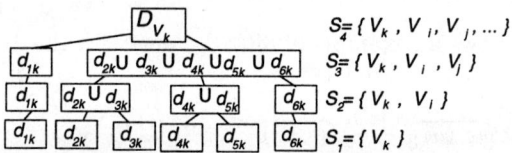

Figure 8: *A hierarchy of partitions of the domain of variable V_k, $D_{V_k} = d_{1k} \cup d_{2k} \cup \ldots \cup d_{6k}$.*

Moreover, when $\mathcal{S}$ is enlarged to $\mathcal{S}'$, the respective domain partitions of two or more variables are either maintained or reduced by union. Informally, this appears as if the lines in Expression (4) were either 'conserved' or 'unified,' as far as the 'old' variables are concerned. Consider two variables $V_k, V_h \in \mathcal{S}$. Consider two sets of the partition determined by JDT($\mathcal{S}$) on D_{V_k}, respectively on D_{V_h}. Let these sets be d_{ik} and d_{jk}, respectively d_{ih} and d_{jh}, as in:

$$\text{JDT}(\mathcal{S}) = \{\ldots, \{\ldots, (V_k, d_{ik}), (V_h, d_{ih}), \ldots\}, \quad (11)$$
$$\ldots, \{\ldots, (V_k, d_{jk}), (V_h, d_{jh}), \ldots\}, \ldots\}$$

Property 3.3 $\forall V_k, V_h \in \mathcal{S}$ we have:

$\exists s_1, s_2 \in \text{JDT}(\mathcal{S}) \mid$
$\quad (V_k, d_{ik}), (V_h, d_{ih}) \in s_1; (V_k, d_{jk}), (V_h, d_{jh}) \in s_2$
$\iff \begin{cases} (\exists s'_1, s'_2 \in \text{JDT}(\mathcal{S}') \mid \\ \quad (V_k, d_{ik}), (V_h, d_{ih}) \in s'_1; (V_k, d_{jk}), (V_h, d_{jh}) \in s'_2) \\ \oplus \\ (\exists s' \in \text{JDT}(\mathcal{S}') \mid \\ \quad (V_k, d_{lk} \supseteq d_{ik} \cup d_{jk}), (V_k, d_{lh} \supseteq d_{ih} \cup d_{jh}) \in s') \end{cases}$

This property can be extended to any number of variables in a straightforward manner.

4 Use of JDT-sets in practical applications

The practical benefit drawn from building the joint discrimination tree of a set of variables is two-fold: identification of independent subproblems and of partial interchangeability sets.

1. The advantage of isolating subproblems is obviously a reduction of the overall computational complexity of the problem, when these subproblems can be successfully solved.

   In case the independent subproblem is found to be insoluble, the combination of variables and variable domains can be remembered as a *compact no-good* set. The identified unsolvable subproblem can serve as a component in the 'factor out failure' decomposition scheme proposed in [6] or to improve the performance of backtracking during traditional search.

2. The benefit of computing partially interchangeable sets of values for a set of variables $S \subset V$ becomes apparent when one tries to explore alternative solutions to the CSP that may require updating the values of the variables in S while keeping the values of the variables outside S unchanged. The idea of localizing the effect of a modification is very important in several practical applications such as scheduling and resource allocation, where one tries to keep the stability of a global solution while locally adjusting a partial solution to accommodate unforeseen events. Thus, partial interchangeability sets can serve as a basis for *reactive* strategies, such as rescheduling.

Starting from the interchangeability sets of a variable V_i with $S = \{V_i\}$, one can compute the JDT for an increasingly larger 'environment' that encompasses V_i. Alternatively, starting from a large environment, one can gradually refine it by restricting the computations to a subset of S. We are investigating strategies for guiding both of these processes. We have already studied some properties of these sets to be exploited while building such strategies. These results are not reported here for lack of space. Below, we give hints on how such strategies may proceed:

Enlarging S. We should be careful to enlarge S to include variables that share a common neighborhood this would allow us to increase the size of the NPI-set and to identify independent subproblems.

Refining S. Properties 3.2 and 3.3 can be used as the basis of consistency checking techniques more efficient than the traditional ones. Such strategies would operate at coarse levels of detail by using the output of a JDT computed over a relatively large set S to remove 'coarse' inconsistent combinations of values between the variables in S and the rest of the problem, then gradually refining S to check and filter finer combinations of values among variables.

5 Constraints of mutual exclusion

In general, as in the example of Fig. 3, it is necessary for determining local interchangeability to compute a discrimination tree. In this section, we study the constraints of mutual exclusion, as in coloring problems, which are widely used in practical applications (*e.g.*, resource allocation [2]). These constraints are naturally highly disjunctive, and propagation algorithms perform poorly in this case unless values are assigned to variables (*i.e.*, search is carried out). Indeed, when the sizes of variable domains are strictly greater than 1, arc-consistency fails to rule out any value. In this section, we show that, when the constraints that link S to Neigh(S) are constraints of mutual exclusion[4], local interchangeabilities can be easily determined and do not require the computation of a discrimination tree. Let $D_{\text{Neigh}} = \bigcup_{V_j \in \text{Neigh}(S)} D_{V_j}$.

Theorem 5.1 *When S and Neigh(S) are linked by constraints of mutual exclusion, $\forall V_i \in S$, $\forall x, y \in D_{V_i}$, and $x \neq y$, we have:*

$$(x, V_i, S) \equiv_c (y, V_i, S) \iff x, y \notin D_{\text{Neigh}} \quad (12)$$

Proof: Suppose that $y \in D_{\text{Neigh}}$, then $\exists V_j \in \text{Neigh}(S)$ such that $y \in D_{V_j}$. Since $x \neq y$, and C_{V_i, V_j} is a constraint of mutual exclusion, then $V_i = x$ is compatible with $V_j = y$. Since x, y are NI for V_i, this implies that $V_i = y$ is compatible with $V_j = y$, which is impossible because C_{V_i, V_j} is a constraint of mutual exclusion. Thus, $y \notin D_{\text{Neigh}}$. Similarly, $x \notin D_{\text{Neigh}}$.

Further, $\forall x, y \in D_{V_i}, x, y \notin D_{\text{Neigh}}$ means that both x and y for V_i are compatible with all the elements in D_{Neigh}; thus they are NI for V_i. $\square$

The results listed below can be easily proven using this theorem; the proofs are omitted because of the space limit. The following theorem indicates how NIS(S) is obtained without a discrimination tree.

Theorem 5.2 *When S and Neigh(S) are linked by constraints of mutual exclusion, we have:*

$$\text{NIS}(S) = \{(V_i, d_i), \forall V_i \in S, d_i = D_{V_i} - D_{\text{Neigh}}\} \quad (13)$$

For the example of Fig. 1, NIS($\{V_4\}$) = $\{(V_4, \{e, f\})\}$ and NIS($\{V_1, V_3\}$) = $\{(V_1, \{a, b\}), (V_3, \{a, b\})\}$. The following theorem states that the only kind of local interchangeability that can show up in this situation is the one that induces a locally independent subproblem.

Theorem 5.3 *When S and Neigh(S) are linked by constraints of mutual exclusion, we have:*

$$\text{NPI}(S) = \begin{cases} \{\text{NIS}(S)\} & \text{if } \exists (V_i, d_i) \in \text{NIS}(S) \text{ such that } |d_i| > 1 \\ \emptyset & \text{otherwise} \end{cases} \quad (14)$$

Freuder also introduced *neighborhood substitutability* (NSUB), which is 'one-way' neighborhood interchangeability[5] [4]:

Definition 5.4 *Neighborhood substitutability:* For two values b and c, for a CSP variable V, b is neighborhood substitutable (NSUB) for c if and only if for every constraint C on V:

$$\{i \mid (b, i) \text{ satisfies } C\} \supseteq \{i \mid (c, i) \text{ satisfies } C\}$$

---

[4]Note that the constraints in $\mathcal{C}$ need not all be constraints of mutual exclusion.

[5]Naturally, the concept local substitutability can be extended to apply to a set of variables, as we did for the concept of neighborhood interchangeability.

The following theorem states that, in the case of constraints of mutual exclusion, NSUB values necessarily induce a locally independent subproblem:

Theorem 5.5 *When V_i and $\text{Neigh}(\{V_i\})$ are linked by constraints of mutual exclusion, $\forall x, y \in D_{V_i}$, we have:*

$$x \text{ is NSUB for } y \iff x \in d_i \mid \text{NIS}(\{V_i\}) = \{(V_i, d_i)\} \quad (15)$$

6 Related work

In spite of its importance for practical applications and the challenge its poses for the development of theoretically new search mechanisms, interchangeability has received relatively little attention in contrast, for instance, to backtracking and consistency filtering. Below we review some contributions on this topic, draw the relations among them, and summarize these relations in the lattice of Fig. 9.

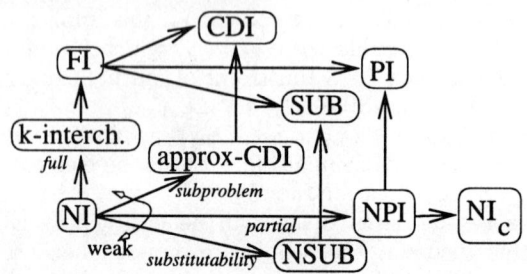

Figure 9: *A lattice of value interchangeability for a variable. Weak interchangeability (i.e., substitutability, partial, and subproblem [4]) and full interchangeability.*

6.1 On the conceptual side

We use the example of Fig. 10 to compare three types of interchangeability with respect to 'partial interchangeability' (see Fig. 9). The NI-sets are computed by iter-

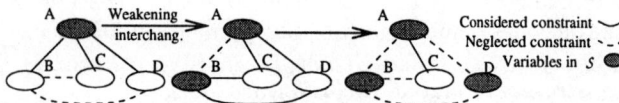

Figure 10: *Constraints for the computation of:* Left: NI for A. Center: NPI for $\{A, B\}$. Right: $\text{NI}_{C_{A,C}}$ for A.

ating over the neighborhood of a given variable, e.g. A in Fig. 10. This amounts to considering all the constraints that applies to A, namely: $C_{A,B}$, $C_{A,C}$, and $C_{A,D}$. NPI extends the boundaries within which change is permitted to comprise $\mathcal{S} = \{A, B\}$: it considers the constraints that apply to A or B, but not to A and B (i.e., $C_{A,C}$, $C_{A,D}$, $C_{B,C}$, and $C_{B,D}$). NPI for A is weaker than NI for A: an NI-set for A is always a subset of some NPI-set for $A \in \mathcal{S}$. In [7], Haselböck introduced a form of local interchangeability that is obtained from NI by considering, for A, only one constraint that apply to A, e.g $C_{A,C}$. We choose to call it 'NI for A according to $C_{A,C}$,' and denote it $\text{NI}_{C_{A,C}}(A)$. This is equivalent to extending the boundary to $\mathcal{S} = \text{Neigh}(\{A\}) - \{C\}$, and to iterating, in the JDT, only over the values of A. 'NI according to $C_{A,X}$' is thus weaker than NPI computed for any set $\mathcal{S}$ such that $A \in \mathcal{S}$ and $X \notin \mathcal{S}$: an NPI-set for $\mathcal{S}$ is always a subset of an element of $\text{NI}_{C_{A,X}}(A)$. Thus, NPI sits between NI and NI_C from three standpoints: conceptually, with regard to the computational cost, and also with respect to the size of the sets it defines (see Fig. 8).

In [9], Weigel *et al.* looked for interchangeability in subproblems induced from the original CSP by reducing the domains of a selected set of variables, which they called *Context Dependent Interchangeability* (CDI), as shown at the left of Fig. 11. Further, they proposed to approximate CDI-sets by a local form of CDI, denoted approx-CDI in Fig. 9, obtained by computing the NI-sets in the subproblems. The success of this strategy for weakening local interchangeability depends crucially on the selection of the induced subproblems. These NI-sets cannot be compared with NPI-sets since they are derived for distinct problems. They are conceptually a localized form of another type of weak interchangeability called *subproblem interchangeability* [4].

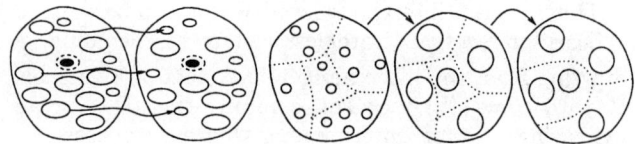

Figure 11: *Left:* Subproblem interchangeability by reduction of some variable domains. *Right:* Meta-interchangeability for variables.

In [8], Weigel and Faltings exploited NI-sets while constructing all solutions for a CSP. The iterative process is sketched at the right of Fig. 11. First, the variables are partitioned into subproblems, then each subproblem is replaced by a meta-variable that consists of all solutions to the subproblem (which are in fact partial solutions to the original problem). NI-sets are computed for each meta-variable, and the process iterates until a unique meta-variable is obtained, which represents all the solutions of the original CSP. This is a localized version of *meta-interchangeability* [4] for variables, not to be confused with k-interchangeability which requires full interchangeability in *all* subproblems of size k. As for approx-CDI, the choice of the subproblems is critical, and remains an open issue.

Most importantly, among all approaches explored for computing localized forms of weak interchangeability, our technique is the only one that gives full control of the coarseness of the interchangeability sets (through the selection, enlargement, and refinement of $\mathcal{S}$). This appears as if one can smoothly move along the axis labeled 'partial' in Fig. 9. In [4], Freuder gives an algorithm for computing, for any k, k-interchangeability for a variable (i.e., moving along the vertical axis in Fig. 9), which naturally has a higher time complexity than our technique (i.e., $O(n^{k-1}d^k)$ vs. $O(s(n-s)d^2)$).

6.2 Practical results

In [3], Choueiry et al. reported on various types of interchangeability discovered automatically by a decomposition heuristic, called VAD, for resource allocation. They showed how these sets are used for compacting the solution space and for supporting explanation and interaction with users. They also assessed the NI-sets discovered by this procedure with respect to the exact ones. Their evaluation of the interchangeabilities discovered by VAD can now, thanks to our results of Section 5, be extended to cover the case of NPI and NSUB-sets.

The practical usefulness of various kinds of local interchangeability has already been established on random problems for backtracking [1; 7], for arc-consistency [7], and for compacting solutions [8]. Freuder proved that "for any [k] there are cases in which preprocessing to remove redundant k-interchangeable values before backtracking, k-interchangeability preprocessing, will be cost effective" [4]. Since NPI is weaker than NI and than any level of k-interchangeability, it necessarily occurs more frequently, and the resulting benefits should be at least as good.

More generally, it is not clear whether one should search for 'symmetries' in random problems or in structured random problems, and whether this does not only reflect the power or shortcomings of the random generator itself. It seems to be more adequate to assess the usefulness of interchangeability in real-world problems, such as scheduling, configuration, and design. Since interchangeability is likely to be important in structured domains, it may greatly benefit practical applications. This has so far been shown for the case of resource allocation; experimentation with other application domains must be carried out.

7 Conclusions and Future directions

Interchangeability is known significantly to enhance search and backtracking, but has not yet been enough exploited for updating solutions. In this paper, we introduce NPI, which is weaker, and thus more frequent, than NI or FI. NPI is also an efficiently computable form of PI, which allows for local update of solutions in practical applications. We show how the procedure proposed by Freuder [4] is extended to compute the JDT-set, and thus identifying the NPI-sets and locally independent subproblems. We show how the JDT-sets are organized in a hierarchy, and give hints on how they can be exploited in practice. Further, we show that for the case of constraints of mutual exclusion, local interchangeability is easy to compute, and is equivalent to the existence of locally independent subproblems.

Our goal in this paper is to report the results summarized above and to draw the relations among the various types of interchangeability explored so far. Efforts now need to be invested in exploring strategies for selecting the sets of variables for which the JDT is built, and heuristics for monitoring the successive refinement or enlargement of these sets. We have already studied some properties of JDT-sets useful for this purpose, but do not report them here for lack of space. Another important issue is to combine the exploration of JDT-sets with the process of decomposing the CSP and solving it. Although we have not yet explored this, it should be possible to extend the techniques explored here to non-binary constraints by iterating, in the discrimination tree, over the constraints rather than over the domains of the neighboring variables. Further, and similarly to constraints of mutual exclusion, we believe that we must investigate the existence of constraint types for which interchangeability sets can be easily computed. We also believe that interchangeability may unveil novel strategies for domain splitting in a CSP involving continuous domains.

Acknowledgments

This work was started when the authors were at the Industrial Computing Lab. of the Swiss Federal Institute of Technology in Lausanne. B. Y. Choueiry is supported by a fellowship for advanced researchers from the Swiss-NSF.

References

[1] Brent W. Benson and Eugene C. Freuder. Interchangeability Preprocessing Can Improve Forward Checking Search. In *Proc. of the 10 th ECAI*, pages 28–30, Vienna, Austria, 1992.

[2] Berthe Y. Choueiry and Boi Faltings. Using Abstractions for Resource Allocation. In *IEEE 1995 International Conference on Robotics and Automation*, pages 1027–1033, Nagoya, Japan, 1995.

[3] Berthe Y. Choueiry, Boi Faltings, and Rainer Weigel. Abstraction by Interchangeability in Resource Allocation. In *Proc. of the 14 th IJCAI*, pages 1694–1701, Montreal, Canada, 1995.

[4] Eugene C. Freuder. Eliminating Interchangeable Values in Constraint Satisfaction Problems. In *Proc. of AAAI-91*, pages 227–233, Anaheim, CA, 1991.

[5] Eugene C. Freuder and Paul D. Hubbe. A Disjunctive Decomposition Control Schema for Constraint Satisfaction. In V. Saraswat and P. Van Hentenryck, editors, *Principles and Practice of Constraint Programming*, pages 319–335. MIT Press, Cambridge, MA, 1995.

[6] Eugene C. Freuder and Paul D. Hubbe. Extracting Constraint Satisfaction Subproblems. In *Proc. of the 14 th IJCAI*, pages 548–555, Montreal, Canada, 1995.

[7] Alois Haselböck. Exploiting Interchangeabilities in Constraint Satisfaction Problems. In *Proc. of the 13 th IJCAI*, pages 282–287, Chambéry, France, 1993.

[8] Rainer Weigel and Boi Faltings. Structuring Techniques for Constraint Satisfaction Problems. In *Proc. of the 15 th IJCAI*, pages –, Nagoya, Japan, 1997.

[9] Rainer Weigel, Boi Faltings, and Berthe Y. Choueiry. Context in Discrete Constraint Satisfaction Problems. In *12th European Conference on Artificial Intelligence, ECAI'96*, pages 205–209, Budapest, Hungary, 1996.

Supermodels and Robustness

Matthew L. Ginsberg
CIRL
1269 University of Oregon
Eugene, OR 97403-1269
ginsberg@cirl.uoregon.edu

Andrew J. Parkes
CIRL and CIS Dept.
1269 University of Oregon
Eugene, OR 97403-1269
parkes@cirl.uoregon.edu

Amitabha Roy
CIS Dept.
University of Oregon
Eugene, OR 97403
aroy@cs.uoregon.edu

Abstract

When search techniques are used to solve a practical problem, the solution produced is often brittle in the sense that small execution difficulties can have an arbitrarily large effect on the viability of the solution. The AI community has responded to this difficulty by investigating the development of "robust problem solvers" that are intended to be proof against this difficulty.

We argue that robustness is best cast not as a property of the problem solver, but as a property of the solution. We introduce a new class of models for a logical theory, called *supermodels*, that captures this idea. Supermodels guarantee that the model in question is robust, and allow us to quantify the degree to which it is so.

We investigate the theoretical properties of supermodels, showing that finding supermodels is typically of the same theoretical complexity as finding models. We provide a general way to modify a logical theory so that a model of the modified theory is a supermodel of the original. Experimentally, we show that the supermodel problem exhibits phase transition behavior similar to that found in other satisfiability work.

Introduction

In many combinatorial optimization or decision problems our initial concern is to find solutions of minimal cost, for example, a schedule with a minimal overall length. In practice, however, such optimal solutions can be very brittle. If anything out of our control goes wrong (call this a "breakage"), repairing the schedule might lead to a great increase in its final cost. If breakages are sufficiently common, we might well do better on average to use a suboptimal solution that is more robust. The difficulty with trading optimality for robustness is that robustness is difficult to quantify, and especially difficult to quantify in a practical fashion.

In building definitions that are useful for quantifying robustness, we need to be aware of the requirements of both the users and the producers of robust solutions.

Copyright © 1998, American Association for Artificial Intelligence (www.aaai.org). All rights reserved.

A user of robust solutions might be motivated by two distinct demands on the possibilities for repair:

1. Fast repair: A small set of changes must be repairable in polynomial time.

2. Small repair: The repaired solution should be close to the original model. In other words, it must be possible to repair a small set of changes with another small set of changes.

The condition of fast repair arises, for example, when something goes wrong in a production line and halting the line to perform exponential search might be far too costly. Demanding that small flaws can be addressed with small repairs is also common. A production line schedule might involve many people, each with a different list of tasks for the day. Constantly changing everyone's task list is likely to lead to far too much confusion. The ability to repair flaws with a small number of changes is a goal in itself, independent of the fact that this means repair is also likely to be fast.

As a producer of robust solutions, it might well be helpful if the measure of robustness were independent of the repair algorithm. An algorithm-independent characterization of robustness is useful not only because of its greater simplicity, but because it might support the use of intelligent search methods to find solutions with guaranteed levels of robustness. In contrast, algorithm-dependent notions of robustness imply that the search for robust solutions is likely to reduce to generate and test. This is because partial solutions might not carry enough information to determine whether the repair algorithm will succeed. For example, if we were to use local search for repair, it is already difficult to characterize the repairability of full solutions. Deciding whether a partial solution will extend to a repairable full solution might well be completely impractical. We are not implying that algorithm independence is essential, only that it might be very useful in practice.

This paper introduces the concept of *supermodels* as models that measure inherent degrees of robustness. In essence, a supermodel provides a simple way to capture the requirement that "for all small breakages there exists a small repair;" that repairs are also fast will be seen to follow from this. The supermodel definition also has the advantage that the robustness is inherently a property of the supermodel, and does not rely on assumptions about repair algorithms.

We will also see that despite the simplicity of the supermodel concept, there appears to be a surprisingly rich associated theory. Most importantly, there are many different interrelated classes of supermodel characterized by the amounts of breakage and repair that are allowed. This richness of structure with various degrees of robustness allows us to propose a framework under which robustness can be quantified, thereby supporting an informed tradeoff between optimality and robustness.

The first sections in the paper define supermodels and explore some theoretical consequences of the definition. For satisfiability, finding supermodels is in NP, the same complexity class as that of finding models. We give an encoding that allows us to find a particular kind of supermodel for SAT using standard solvers for SAT. Using this encoding, we explore the existence of supermodels in Random 3SAT, finding evidence for the existence of a phase transition, along with the standard easy-hard-easy transition in search cost.

Overall, the supermodel concept makes the task of finding robust solutions similar to that of finding solutions, rather than necessarily requiring special-purpose search technology of its own.

Supermodel Definitions

A first notion of solutions that are inherently robust to small changes can be captured as follows:

Definition 1: An (a,b)-supermodel is a model such that if we modify the values taken by the variables in a set of size at most a (breakage), another model can be obtained by modifying the values of the variables in a disjoint set of size at most b (repair).

The case $a = 0$ means that we never have to handle any breakages, and so all models are also $(0,b)$-supermodels. A less trivial example is a $(1,1)$-supermodel: This is a model that guarantees that if any single variable's value is changed, then we can recover a model by changing the value of at most one other variable.

We will typically take a and b to be small, directly quantifying the requirement for small repairs. Definition 1 also has a variety of attractive properties. Firstly, if finding models is in NP, and if a is taken to be a constant (independent of the problem size n) then finding (a,b)-supermodels is also in NP. This is because the number of possible breakages is polynomial $O(n^a)$. Secondly, if b is a constant, finding the repair is possible in polynomial time, since there are only $O(n^b)$ possible repairs. These observations are independent of the method used to make the repairs, depending only on the bounded size of the set of possible repairs.

We thus see that with a and b small constants, (a,b)-supermodels quantify our conditions for robustness and do so without worsening the complexity class of the problem (assuming we start in NP or worse).

In practice, the definition needs to be modified because not all variables are on an equal footing. We might not be able to account for some variables changing their value: some breakages might simply be irreparable, while others might be either very unlikely or impossible, and so not worth preparing for. To account for this, we use a "breakage set" that is a subset of the set of all variables, and will only attempt to guarantee robustness against changes of these variables. Similarly, repairs are likely to be constrained in the variables they can change; as an example, it is obviously impossible to modify a variable that refers to an action taken in the past. We therefore introduce a similar "repair set" of variables. We extend Definition 1 to

Definition 2: An (S_1^a, S_2^b)-supermodel is a model such that if we modify the values taken by the variables in a subset of S_1 of size at most a (breakage), another model can be obtained by modifying the values of the variables in a disjoint subset of S_2 of size at most b (repair).

It is clear that an (a,b)-supermodel is simply a (S_1^a, S_2^b)-supermodel in which the breakage and repair sets are unrestricted. We will use the term "supermodel" as a generic term for any (S_1^a, S_2^b)- or (a,b)-supermodel.

Different degrees of robustness correspond to variation in the parameters S_1, S_2, a and b. As we increase the size of the breakage set S_1 or the number of breaks a, the supermodels become increasingly robust. Robustness also increases if we decrease the size of the repair set S_2 or number of repairs b. Supermodels give us a flexible method of returning solutions with certificates of differing but guaranteed robustness. As an example,[1] consider the simple theory $p \vee q$. Any of the three models (p,q), $(\neg p, q)$ and $(p, \neg q)$ is a $(1,1)$-supermodel. Only the first model, however, is a $(1,0)$-supermodel. The supermodel ideas correctly identify (p,q) as the most robust model of $p \vee q$.

---

[1] for which we would like to thank Tania Bedrax-Weiss.

Theory

Let us now restrict our discussion to the case of propositional theories, so that breakage and repair will correspond to flipping the values of variables in the model from true to false or vice versa. We also focus on (a,b)-supermodels as opposed to the more general (S_1^a, S_2^b)-supermodels, and so breakage or repair might involve any variable of the theory.

We shall say that a theory Γ belongs to the class of theories SUPSAT(a,b) if and only if Γ has an (a,b)-supermodel. We will also use SUPSAT(a,b) to refer to the associated decision problem:

SUPSAT(a,b)
Instance: A clausal theory Γ
Question: Is $\Gamma \in $ SUPSAT(a,b) ?

We first prove that SUPSAT(a,b) is in NP for any constants a,b. Given an instance of a theory Γ with n variables, a nondeterministic Turing machine guesses a model and a table of which variables to repair for each set of variables flipped. The table has at most n^a entries, one for each possible possible breakage, and each entry is a list of at most b variables specifying the repair. It is obviously possible to check in polynomial time whether the assignment is a model and that all the repairs do indeed work.

In principle, a supermodel-finding algorithm could produce such a table as output, storing in advance all possible repair tuples. This would take polynomial space $O(n^a b)$ and reduce the time needed to find the repair to be a *constant*, $O(a)$. In practice, however, usage of $O(n^a b)$ memory is likely to be prohibitive.

We also have:

Theorem: SUPSAT$(1,1)$ is NP-hard.

Proof: We reduce SAT to SUPSAT$(1,1)$.

Let the clausal theory $\Gamma = C_1 \wedge C_2 \ldots \wedge C_m$ over n variables $V = \{x_1 \ldots x_n\}$ be an instance of SAT. We construct an instance of SUPSAT$(1,1)$ as follows: construct the theory Γ' over $n+1$ variables $V' = \{x_1, x_2 \ldots x_n, \alpha\}$ where

$$\Gamma' = (C_1 \vee \alpha) \wedge (C_2 \vee \alpha) \ldots (C_m \vee \alpha)$$

and α is a new variable not appearing in Γ. We prove that Γ has a model iff Γ' has a $(1,1)$-supermodel.

Suppose Γ had a model m. We construct a model for Γ' which will be a $(1,1)$-supermodel. Extend the assignment m to an assignment of Γ' by setting α to false. Clearly this assignment satisfies all clauses of Γ'. Suppose now we flip the value of a variable in V'. If we flip the value of some variable in $\{x_1 \ldots x_n\}$, we can repair it by setting $\alpha = $ true. If instead we flip the value of α from false to true, no repair is needed. Hence this assignment is indeed a model of Γ' such that on flipping the value of 1 variable, at most 1 repair is needed. Hence $\Gamma' \in $ SUPSAT$(1,1)$.

Next, suppose $\Gamma' \in $ SUPSAT$(1,1)$. By definition, it has a model m. If α is false in m observe that the restriction of m to $V = \{x_1, x_2 \ldots x_n\}$ is a model of Γ. If α is true, flip it to false. Since $\Gamma' \in $ SUPSAT$(1,1)$ we can repair it by flipping some other variable to get a model where α remains false. Restricting the repaired model to $V = \{x_1, x_2 \ldots x_n\}$ once again gives us a model for Γ. Thus Γ is satisfiable. **QED**.

It follows immediately from the definition that

$$\text{SUPSAT}(a,b) \subseteq \text{SUPSAT}(a,b+1) \qquad (1)$$

and

$$\text{SUPSAT}(a+1,b) \subseteq \text{SUPSAT}(a,b) \qquad (2)$$

since b repairs suffice for up to $a+1$ breaks, b repairs suffice for up to a breaks. In many cases we can prove that the inclusions in the above supermodel hierarchy are strict.

It is easy to show that the inclusion (1) is strict. i.e. SUPSAT$(a,b) \neq $ SUPSAT$(a,b+1)$. For example the following theory which consists of a chain of $b+2$ variables,

$$(x_1 \to x_2) \wedge (x_2 \to x_3) \ldots (x_{b+1} \to x_{b+2}) \wedge (x_{b+2} \to x_1)$$

belongs to SUPSAT$(a,b+1) - $SUPSAT$(a,b)$. The only models of this theory are those with all $b+2$ variables set to true or with all of them set to false. For any set of a flips, we need at most $b+1$ repairs, hence this theory is in SUPSAT$(a,b+1)$. If one variable value is flipped, we need exactly $b+1$ repairs. Since b repairs do not suffice, this theory is not in SUPSAT(a,b).

Using multiple chains and similar arguments, one can prove that the inclusion in (2) is strict whenever $a \leq b$. In general, however, the question of whether or not (2) is strict for all a,b is open.

Equations (1) and (2) induce a hierarchical structure on the set of all satisfiable theories. This gives a rich set of relative "strengths" of robustness with a fairly strong partial order among them.

Finding (1,1)-supermodels

We have shown the task of finding (a,b)-supermodels of a SAT problem to be in NP. It should therefore be possible to encode the supermodel requirements on a theory Γ as a new SAT CNF instance Γ_{SM} that is at most polynomially larger than Γ. In this section, we do this explicitly for (1,1)-supermodels in SAT, so that a model for Γ_{SM} has the property that if we are forced to flip any variable i there is another variable j that we can flip in order to recover a model of Γ. In other words, we will show how to construct Γ_{SM} such that Γ has a (1,1)-supermodel if and only if Γ_{SM} has a model. A model of Γ_{SM} will be a supermodel of Γ.

We are working with CNF so $\Gamma = \wedge_a C_a$ is a conjunction of clauses C_a. The basic idea underlying the encoding is to allow the assignment to remain fixed, instead flipping the variables as they appear in the theory.

Thus let Γ_i denote Γ in which all occurrences of variable i have been flipped, and let Γ_{ij} denote Γ in which all occurrences of the variables i and j have been flipped. Denoting the clauses with flipped variables similarly, $\Gamma_i = \wedge_a C_{ai}$ and $\Gamma_{ij} = \wedge_a C_{aij}$.

Now for a model to be a (1,1)-supermodel, if we flip a variable i, one of two conditions must hold. Either the model must be a model of the flipped theory, or there must be some different variable j for which the current model is a model of the doubly flipped theory. Hence, we must enforce

$$\forall i.\ \Gamma_i \vee (\exists j.\ j \neq i \wedge \Gamma_{ij}) \qquad (3)$$

Converting this to CNF by direct expansion would result in an exponential increase in size, and we therefore introduce new variables c and y that reify the flipped clauses and theories:

$$\begin{aligned} c_{ai} &\longleftrightarrow C_{ai} \\ c_{aij} &\longleftrightarrow C_{aij} \\ y_i &\longleftrightarrow \Gamma_i \\ y_{ij} &\longleftrightarrow \Gamma_{ij} \end{aligned}$$

These definitions are easily converted to a CNF formula Γ_{defs} via

$$\begin{aligned} \neg y_i &= \vee_a \neg c_{ai} \\ \neg y_{ij} &= \vee_a \neg c_{aij} \end{aligned}$$

The supermodel constraint (3) is now

$$\wedge_i (\neg y_i \vee \vee_{j \neq i} \neg y_{ij})$$

which is correctly in CNF. The complete encoding is

$$\Gamma_{SM} = \wedge_i (\neg y_i \vee \vee_{j \neq i} \neg y_{ij}) \wedge \Gamma \wedge \Gamma_{\text{defs}} \qquad (4)$$

If the original Γ had n variables and m clauses of length at most k then Γ_{SM} has $O(mn^2)$ variables, and $O(mn^2k)$ clauses of length at most $O(n)$.

As an example, consider once again the trivial theory $p \vee q$. The only clause is $C_0 = p \vee q$.

Flipping p, we get $C_{0p} = \neg p \vee q$. Flipping both gives $C_{0pq} = \neg p \vee \neg q$. For the defined variables, we have

$$c_{0p} \leftrightarrow (\neg p \vee q)$$

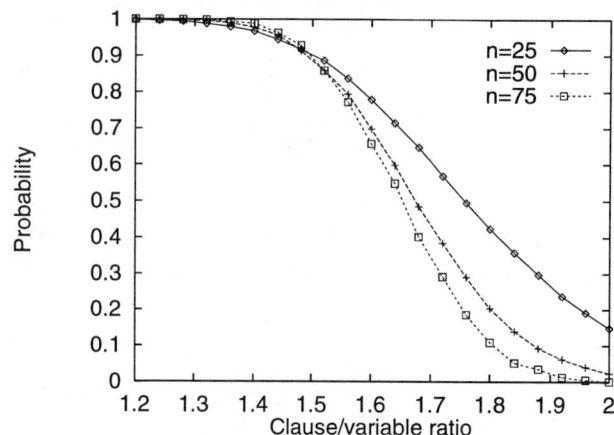

Figure 1: Probability of a Random 3SAT instance having a (1,1)-supermodel.

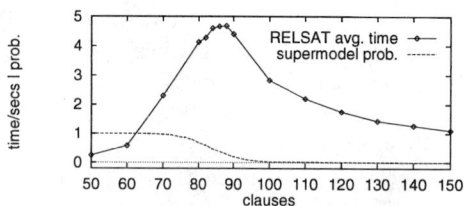

Figure 2: Easy-hard-easy transition at n=50. Time is for relsat(4) (Bayardo & Schrag 1997). For comparison we give the probability of finding a supermodel.

and similarly, together with $\neg y_p = \neg c_{0p}$ and similarly. The complete theory Γ_{SM} can now be constructed using (4). Note also that the general construction can easily be extended to (S_1^1, S_2^1)-supermodels simply by restricting the allowed subscripts in the c_{ai} and y_i.

Restricting a model of Γ_{SM} to the original variables will produce a (1,1)-supermodel of Γ. Since Γ_{SM} is just another SAT-CNF problem, we can solve it using a standard SAT solver. This solver itself need not know anything about supermodels, and can apply intelligent search techniques that are likely to be significantly more efficient than would be the case if were were to test for robustness in retrospect.

Phase Transitions

Phase transition, or "threshold", phenomena are believed to be important to the practical matter of finding solutions (Huberman & Hogg 1987, and others). This is in part because of the similarities to optimization: As we change the system, we change from many to relatively few to no solutions, and the cost of finding solutions simultaneously changes from easy to hard to easy again. The average difficulty peaks in the phase transition region, matching the intuition about finding

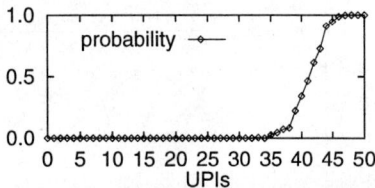

Figure 3: Probability of residual theory having a supermodel, as a function of number of UPIs. Instances are from the phase transition for satisfiability at n=50.

optimal solutions.

In this section, we briefly study the issue of supermodels and phase transitions for the case of Random 3SAT (Mitchell, Selman, & Levesque 1992). Instances are characterized by n variables, m clauses, and a clause/variable ratio $\alpha = m/n$. There is strong evidence that for large n, this system exhibits a phase transition at $\alpha \approx 4.2$ (Crawford & Auton 1996). Below this value, theories are almost always satisfiable; above it, they are almost always unsatisfiable.

We first consider whether or not SUPSAT(a, b) has similar phase transitions. Using the encoding of the previous section, we studied the empirical probability of Random 3SAT instances having a (1,1)-supermodel. Figure 1 gives the results, leading us to expect a phase transition at $\alpha \approx 1.5$. The apparent SUPSAT$(1, 1)$ transition thus occurs for theories that are very underconstrained. As seen in Figure 2, the time needed to solve the instances undergoes the usual easy-hard-easy transition.

Consider next the possible existence of supermodels at the satisfiability phase transition itself, $\alpha \approx 4.2$. We have just seen that there will almost certainly be no (1, 1)-supermodels at this phase transition. We also know that as we approach the transition, the number of prime implicates of the associated theory increases (Schrag & Crawford 1996), until at the transition itself, we have many instances with large numbers of unary prime implicates (UPIs) (Parkes 1997). Any model must respect these UPIs: if a variable in a UPI is changed then no repair is possible. Hence, any variables in UPIs must be excluded from the breakage set. Since flipping the value of a UPI can never be involved in a repair, these variables can also be excluded from the repair set. The simplest choice is thus to look for (S_1^a, S_2^b)-supermodels with

$$S_1 = S_2 = R = (V - \{v | v \text{ or } \neg v \text{ is a UPI}\})$$

Parkes called this set R the *residual variables* of the instance. Looking for an (R^a, R^b)-supermodel is equivalent to looking for an (a,b)-supermodel of the residual theory, which consists of the constraints remaining on the residual variables after accounting for the UPIs. Figure 3 shows that the residual theories tend to have (1,1)-supermodels in the so-called *single cluster instances*, instances with at least 80% UPIs. For $n = 50$, 80% or more of the variables appear in UPIs some 37% of the time.

The above experiments reflect two extremes. Demanding full (1,1)-supermodels forced us into a very underconstrained region. Conversely, instances from the critically constrained region having many UPIs can still have (S_1^a, S_2^b)-supermodels. In practice, it seems likely that realistic problems will require solutions with intermediate levels of robustness: not so robust as to be able to cater to any possible difficulty, but sufficiently robust as to require some sacrifice in optimality. The framework we have described allows to quantify the tradeoff between robustness and solution cost precisely.

Related Work

Since robustness has generally been viewed as a property of the solution *engine* as opposed to a property of the *solutions*, there has been little work on the development of robust solutions to AI problems. Perhaps the most relevant approach has been the attempt to use optimal Markov Decision Processes (MDPs) to find solutions that can recover from likely execution difficulties.

Unfortunately, it appears[2] that the cost of using MDPs to achieve robustness is extreme, in the sense that it is impractical with current technology to solve problems of interesting size. This is to be contrasted to our approach, where the apparent existence of a phase transition suggests that it will be practical to find near-optimal supermodels for problems of practical interest.

Of course, the supermodel approach is solving a substantially easier problem than is the MDP community. We do not (and at this point cannot) consider the differing likelihoods of various failures; a possible breakage is either in the set S_1 or it isn't. We also have no general framework for measuring the probabilistic cost of a solution; we simply require a certain degree of robustness and can then produce solutions that are optimal or nearly so given that requirement. On the other hand, our technology is capable of solving far larger problems and can be applied in any area where satisfiability techniques are applicable, as opposed to the currently restricted domains of applicability of MDPs (planning and scheduling problems, essentially).

A changing environment might also be modeled as a Dynamic Constraint Satisfaction Problem (DCSP) (Dechter & Dechter 1988); what we have called a "break" could instead be viewed as the dynamic addi-

---

[2]Steve Hanks, personal communication

tion of a unary constraint to the existing theory. The work in DCSPs aiming to prevent the solutions changing wildly from one CSP to the next (e.g. (Verfaillie & Schiex 1994, and others)) has similar motivations to our requirement for "small repairs", but DCSPs do not supply a way to select solutions to the existing constraints. Supermodels allow us to select the solutions themselves so as to partially guard against future changes of constraints requiring large changes to the solution. Conversely, DCSPs can handle changes that are more general than just one set of unary constraints, although we expect that the supermodel idea can be generalized in this direction.

MIXED-CSPs (Fargier, Lang, & Schiex 1996) allow variables to be controllable (e.g. our flight departure time) or uncontrollable (e.g. the weather). A system is consistent iff any allowed set of values for the uncontrollable variables can be extended to a solution by valuing the controllable variables appropriately. While this has some flavor of preserving the existence of models in the presence of other changes, MIXED-CSPs do not require that the model change be small: No attempt is made to select a model so that nearby worlds have nearby models. On a technical level, this is reflected in the MIXED-CSP consistency check being Π_2^P-complete as opposed to NP-complete for supermodels. Our observations about the phase transitions and reductions to SAT also give us significant practical advantages that are not shared by the MIXED-CSP approach.

Conclusions

This paper relies on two fundamental and linked observations. First, robustness should be a property not of the techniques used to solve a problem, but of the solutions those techniques produce. Second, the operational need for solutions that can be modified slightly to recover from small changes in the external environment subsumes the need for solutions for which the repairs can be found quickly. *Supermodels* are a generalization of the existing notion of a model of a logical theory that capture this idea of robustness and that allow us to quantify it precisely.

While the definition of a supermodel is simple, the associated mathematical structure appears to be fairly rich. There is a hierarchy of supermodels corresponding to varying degrees of robustness. Searching for a supermodel is of the same theoretical complexity as solving the original problem, and the experiments on finding supermodels bear this out, revealing a phase transition in the existence of supermodels that is associated with the usual easy-hard-easy transition in terms of computational expense.

Experimental results suggest that finding fully robust supermodels will in general involve substantial cost in terms of the quality of the overall solution. This can be dealt with by considering supermodels that are robust against a limited set of external changes, and we can quantify the expected cost of finding such supermodels as a function of the set of contingencies against which one must guard.

Acknowledgements

This work has been supported by the Air Force Research Laboratory and by the Defense Advanced Research Projects Agency under contracts F30602-95-1-0023 and F30602-97-1-0294. The U.S. Government is authorized to reproduce and distribute reprints for Governmental purposes notwithstanding any copyright annotation hereon. The views and conclusions contained herein are those of the authors and should not be interpreted as necessarily representing the official policies or endorsements, either expressed or implied, of DARPA, AFRL, or the U.S. Government.

The authors would like to thank the members of CIRL for many invaluable discussions related to the ideas we have presented.

References

Bayardo, R. J., and Schrag, R. C. 1997. Using CSP look-back techniques to solve real-world SAT instances. In *Proc. of AAAI-97*, 203–208.

Crawford, J. M., and Auton, L. D. 1996. Experimental results on the crossover point in random 3-SAT. *Artificial Intelligence* 81:31–57.

Dechter, R., and Dechter, A. 1988. Belief maintenance in dynamic constraint networks. In *Proc. of AAAI-88*, 37–42.

Fargier, H.; Lang, J.; and Schiex, T. 1996. Mixed constraint satisfaction: a framework for decision problems under incomplete knowledge. In *Proc. of AAAI-96*, 175–180.

Huberman, B. A., and Hogg, T. 1987. Phase transitions in artificial intelligence systems. *Artificial Intelligence* 33:155–171.

Mitchell, D.; Selman, B.; and Levesque, H. J. 1992. Hard and easy distributions of SAT problems. In *Proc. of AAAI-92*, 459–465.

Parkes, A. J. 1997. Clustering at the phase transition. In *Proc. of AAAI-97*, 340–345.

Schrag, R., and Crawford, J. M. 1996. Implicates and prime implicates in Random 3SAT. *Artificial Intelligence* 88:199–222.

Verfaillie, G., and Schiex, T. 1994. Solution reuse in Dynamic Constraint Satisfaction Problems. In *Proc. of AAAI-94*, 307–312.

"Squeaky Wheel" Optimization

David E. Joslin
i2 Technologies
909 E. Las Colinas Blvd.
Irving, TX 75039
dj@i2.com

David P. Clements
Computational Intelligence Research Laboratory
University of Oregon
Eugene, OR 97403-1269
clements@cirl.uoregon.edu

Abstract

We describe a general approach to optimization which we term "Squeaky Wheel" Optimization (SWO). In SWO, a greedy algorithm is used to construct a solution which is then analyzed to find the trouble spots, i.e., those elements, that, if improved, are likely to improve the objective function score. That analysis is used to generate new priorities that determine the order in which the greedy algorithm constructs the next solution. This Construct/Analyze/Prioritize cycle continues until some limit is reached, or an acceptable solution is found.

SWO can be viewed as operating on two search spaces: solutions and prioritizations. Successive solutions are only indirectly related, via the re-prioritization that results from analyzing the prior solution. Similarly, successive prioritizations are generated by constructing and analyzing solutions. This "coupled search" has some interesting properties, which we discuss.

We report encouraging experimental results on two domains, scheduling problems that arise in fiber-optic cable manufacturing, and graph coloring problems. The fact that these domains are very different supports our claim that SWO is a general technique for optimization.

Overview

We describe a general approach to optimization which we term "Squeaky Wheel" Optimization (SWO) (Clements *et al.* 1997). The core of SWO is a Construct/Analyze/Prioritize cycle, illustrated in Figure 1. A solution is constructed by a greedy algorithm, making decisions in an order determined by priorities assigned to the elements of the problem. That solution is then analyzed to find the elements of the problem that are "trouble makers." The priorities of the trouble makers are then increased, causing the greedy constructor to deal with them sooner on the next iteration. This cycle repeats until a termination condition occurs.

On each iteration, the analyzer determines which elements of the problem are causing the most trouble in the current solution, and the prioritizer ensures that

Copyright ©1998, American Association for Artificial Intelligence (www.aaai.org). All rights reserved.

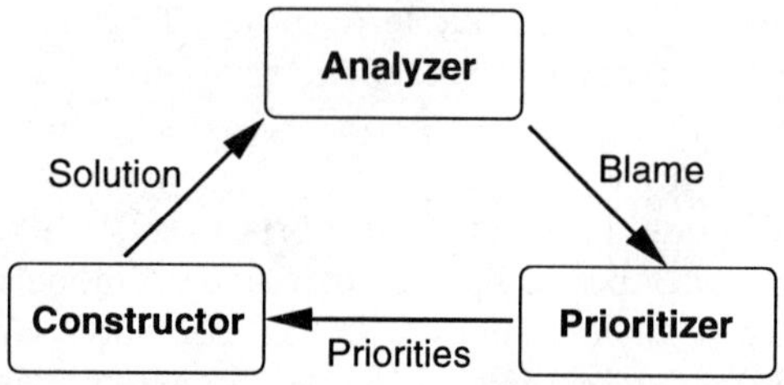

Figure 1: The Construct/Analyze/Prioritize cycle

the constructor gives more attention to those elements on the next iteration. ("The squeaky wheel gets the grease.") The construction, analysis and prioritization are all in terms of the elements that define a problem domain. In a scheduling domain, for example, those elements might be tasks. In graph coloring, those elements might be the nodes to be colored.

The three main components of SWO are:

Constructor. Given a sequence of problem elements, the constructor generates a solution using a greedy algorithm, with no backtracking. The sequence determines the order in which decisions are made, and can be thought of as a "strategy" or "recipe" for constructing a new solution. (This "solution" may violate hard constraints.)

Analyzer. The analyzer assigns a numeric "blame" factor to the problem elements that contribute to flaws in the current solution. For example, if minimizing lateness in a scheduling problem is one of the objectives, then blame would be assigned to late tasks.

A key principle behind SWO is that solutions can reveal problem structure. By analyzing a solution, we can often identify elements of that solution that work well, and elements that work poorly. This information about problem structure is local, in that it may only apply to the part of the search space currently under examination, but may be useful in determining what direction the search should go next.

Prioritizer. The prioritizer uses the blame factors assigned by the analyzer to modify the previous sequence of problem elements. Elements that received blame are moved toward the front of the sequence. The higher the blame, the further the element is moved.

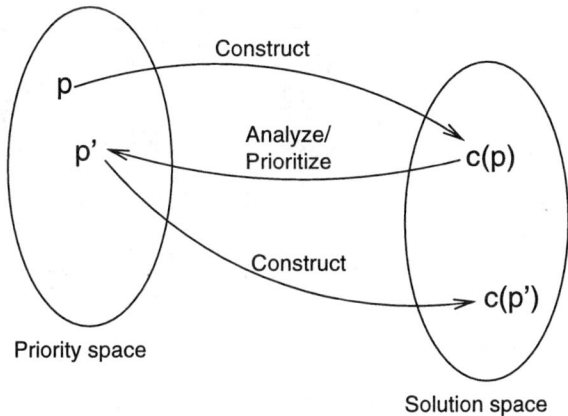

Figure 2: Coupled search spaces

The priority sequence plays a key role in SWO. As a difficult problem element moves forward in the sequence it is handled sooner by the constructor. It also tends to be handled better, thus decreasing its blame factor. Difficult elements rise rapidly to a place in the sequence where they are handled well. Once there, the blame assigned to them drops, causing them to slowly sink in the sequence as other parts of the problem that are not handled as well are given increased priority. Eventually, difficult elements sink back to the point where they are no longer handled well, causing them to receive higher blame and to move forward in the sequence again. Elements that are always easy to handle sink to the end of the sequence and stay there.

Real problems often combine some elements that are difficult to get right, plus others that are easy. In the scheduling problems presented below, some tasks can be assigned to just a few production lines, while others allow for much more flexibility. Some have due dates close to their release time, while others have a lot of leeway. It is sometimes possible to identify "difficult" elements of a problem with static analysis, but interactions can be complex, and elements that are causing difficulty in one part of the search space may be no trouble at all in another. Rather than trying to identify elements that are globally difficult by analyzing the entire problem, we analyze individual solutions in order to find elements that are *locally* difficult. Globally difficult elements tend to be identified over time, as they are difficult across wide parts of the search space.

It is useful to think of SWO as searching two coupled spaces, as illustrated in Figure 2. One search space is the familiar solution space, and the other is *priority space*. Moves in the solution space are made indirectly, via the re-prioritization that results from analyzing the prior solution. Similarly, successive prioritizations are generated by constructing and analyzing a solution, and then using the blame that results from that analysis to modify the previous prioritization.

One consequence of the coupled search spaces is that a small change in the sequence of elements generated by the prioritizer may correspond to a large change in the corresponding solution generated by the constructor, compared to the solution from the previous iteration. Moving an element forward in the sequence may change its state in the resulting solution. In addition, any elements that now occur after it in the sequence must accommodate that element's state. For example, in the scheduling domain, moving a task earlier in the priority sequence may allow it to find a better place in the schedule, with lower-priority tasks "filling in the gaps" after that task has been placed.

The result is a large move that is "coherent" in the sense that it is similar to what we might expect from moving the higher priority task, then propagating the effects of that change by moving lower priority tasks as needed. This single move may correspond to a large number of moves for a search algorithm that only looks at local changes to the solution, and it may thus be difficult for such an algorithm to find.

The fact that SWO makes large moves in both search spaces is one obvious difference between SWO and traditional local search techniques, such as WSAT (Selman, Kautz, & Cohen 1993). Another difference is that with SWO, moves are never selected based on their effect on the objective function. Instead, unlike hillclimbing techniques, each move is made in response to "trouble spots" found in the current solution. The resulting move may be uphill or downhill with respect to the objective function. In effect, SWO deals with local optima in the solution space by ignoring them.

In priority space the only "local optima" are those in which all elements of a solution are assigned equal blame. SWO tends to avoid getting trapped in local optima, because analysis and prioritization will always (in practice) suggest changes in the sequence, thus changing the solution generated on the next iteration. This does not guarantee that SWO will not become trapped in a small cycle, however. In our implementations we have introduced small amounts of randomness in the basic cycle. We also restart SWO periodically with a new initial sequence.

SWO for scheduling

This section describes an application of SWO to a fiber-optic production line scheduling problem, derived from data provided by Lucent Technologies. In this particular plant, a cable may be assembled on any one of 13 parallel production lines. For each cable type, only a subset of the production lines are compatible, and the time required to produce the cable will depend on which of the compatible lines is selected. Each cable also has a setup time, which depends on its own cable type and that of its predecessor. Setups between certain pairs of cable types are infeasible. Task preemption is not allowed, i.e. once a cable has started processing on a line, it finishes without interruption.

Each cable is assigned a release time and due date. Production cannot begin before the release time. The objective function includes a penalty for missing due dates, and a penalty for setup times.

Implementation

We describe the implementation in terms of the three main components of SWO:

Constructor. The constructor builds a schedule by adding tasks one at a time, in the order they occur in the priority sequence. A task is added by selecting a line and a position relative to the tasks already in that line. A task may be inserted between any two tasks already in the line or at the beginning or end of that line's schedule. Changes to the relative positions of the tasks already in the line are not considered. Each task in the line is then assigned to its earliest possible start time, subject to the ordering, i.e., a task starts at either its release time, or immediately after the previous task on that line, whichever is greater.

For each of the possible insertion points in the schedule, relative to the tasks already in each line, the constructor calculates the effect on the objective function, and the task is placed at the best-scoring location. Ties are broken randomly. After all tasks have been placed, the constructor applies SWO to the individual line schedules, attempting to improve the score for each line by reordering the cables that were assigned to it.

Analyzer. To assign blame to each task in the current schedule, the analyzer first calculates a lower bound on the minimum possible cost that each task could contribute to any schedule. For example, if a task has a release time that is later than its due date, then it will be late in every schedule, and the minimum possible cost already includes that penalty. Minimum possible setup costs are also included. For a given schedule, the blame assigned to each task is its "excess cost," the difference between its actual cost and its minimum possible cost. Excess lateness costs are assigned to tasks that are late, and excess setup costs are split between adjacent tasks.

Prioritizer. Once the blame has been assigned, the prioritizer modifies the previous sequence of tasks by moving tasks with non-zero blame factors forward in the sequence. Tasks are moved forward a distance that increases with the magnitude of the blame. To move from the back of the sequence to the front, a task must have a high blame factor over several iterations.

Our current implementation has considerable room for improvement. The analysis and feedback currently being used are very simple, and the construction of schedules could take various heuristics into account, such as preferring to place a task in a line that has more "slack," all other things being equal.

Experimental results

We have six sets of test data, ranging in size from 40 to 297 tasks, all with 13 parallel production lines. The largest problem was the largest that the manufacturer

Data Set	Best Obj	SWO Avg Obj	SWO Avg Time	TABU Obj	TABU Time	IP Obj	IP Time
40	1890	1890	48	1911	425	1934	20
50	3101	3156	57	3292	732	3221	175
60	2580	2584	87	2837	1325	2729	6144
70	2713	2727	124	2878	2046	2897	4950
148	8869	8927	431	10421	17260	—	—
297	17503	17696	1300	—	—	—	—

Table 1: Experimental results: scheduling

required in practice. We compare the following solution methods:

SWO Applies the SWO architecture to the problem, running for a fixed number of iterations and returning the best schedule it finds.

TABU Uses TABU search (Glover & Laguna 1997), a local search algorithm in which moves that increase cost are permitted to avoid getting trapped at local optima. To avoid cycling, when an "uphill" move is made, it is not allowed to be immediately undone.

IP Applies an Integer Programming (IP) solver, using an encoding described in (Clements et al. 1997).

On the 297 task problem, SWO was far more effective than either TABU or IP. TABU, for example, failed to find a feasible schedule after running for over 24 hours. On the smallest problems, TABU and IP were able to find solutions, but SWO outperformed both by a substantial margin.

Table 1 presents results on each problem for SWO, TABU and IP. For SWO, ten trials were run and the results averaged. The TABU and IP implementations were deterministic, so only the results of a single run are shown. The second column of the table shows the best objective function value we have ever observed on each problem. The remaining columns show the objective function value and running times for SWO, TABU and IP. All but the IP experiments were run on a Sun Sparcstation 10 Model 50. The IP experiments were run on an IBM RS6000 Model 590 (a faster machine).

The best values observed have been the result of combining SWO with IP, as reported in (Clements et al. 1997). In that work, SWO generated solutions, running until it had produced a number of "good" schedules. An IP solver was then invoked to re-combine elements of those solutions into a better solution. Although the improvements achieved by the IP solver were relatively small, on the order of 1.5%, it achieved this improvement quickly, and SWO was unable to achieve the same degree of optimization even when given substantially more time. While noting that the hybrid approach can be more effective than SWO alone, and much more effective than IP alone, here we focus on the performance of the individual techniques.

We also note that our very first, fairly naive implementation of SWO for these scheduling problems already outperformed both TABU and IP. Moreover, our improved implementation, reported above, is still fairly simple, and is successful without relying on domain-dependent heuristics. We take this as evidence that the effectiveness of our approach is not due to cleverness in the construction, analysis and prioritization techniques, but due to the effectiveness of the SWO cycle at identifying and responding to whatever elements of the problem happen to be causing difficulty in the local region of the search.

SWO for graph coloring

We have also applied SWO to a a very different domain, graph coloring. Here the objective is to color the nodes of a graph such that no two adjoining nodes have the same color, minimizing the number of colors.

Implementation

The priority sequence for graph coloring consists of an ordered list of nodes. The solver is always trying to produce a coloring that uses colors from the *target set*, which has one less color than was used to color the best solution so far.

Constructor. The constructor assigns colors to nodes in priority sequence order. If a node's color in the previous solution is still available (i.e. no adjacent node is using it yet), and is in the target set, then that color is assigned. If that fails, it tries to assign a color in the current target set, picking the color that is least constraining on adjacent uncolored nodes, i.e. the color that reduces the adjacent nodes' remaining color choices the least. If none of the target colors are available, the constructor tries to "grab" a color in the target set from its neighbors. A color can only be grabbed if all neighbor nodes with that color have at least one other choice within the target set. If multiple colors can be grabbed, then the least constraining one is picked. If no color in the target set can be grabbed then a color outside the target set is assigned.

Nodes that are early in the priority sequence are more likely to have a wide range of colors to pick from. Nodes that come later may grab colors from earlier nodes, but only if the earlier nodes have other color options within the target set.

Analyzer. Blame is assigned to each node whose assigned color is outside the target set. We ran experiments with several different variations of color-based analysis. All of them performed reasonably.

Prioritizer. The prioritizer modifies the previous sequence of nodes by moving nodes with blame forward in the sequence according to how much blame each received. This is done the same way it is done for the scheduling problems. The initial sequence is a list of nodes sorted in decreasing degree order, with some noise added to slightly shuffle the sort.

Data set	IG		SWO	
	Colors	Time	Colors	Time
DSJC125.5	18.9	4.2	18.4	2.7
DSJC250.5	32.8	11.3	31.7	11.8
DSJC500.5	58.6	30.3	56.3	51.7
DSJC1000.5	104.2	112.1	101.6	280.0
C2000.5	190.0	451.5	185.6	1446.4
C4000.5	346.9	1747.1	341.9	7184.6
R125.1	5.0	3.4	5.0	0.3
R125.1c	46.0	1.8	46.0	11.8
R125.5	36.9	3.1	36.0	5.7
R250.1	8.0	11.6	8.0	0.8
R250.1c	64.0	7.6	64.0	62.9
R250.5	68.4	13.8	65.0	27.1
DSJR500.1	12.0	35.0	12.0	3.0
DSJR500.1c	85.0	24.1	85.0	122.2
DSJR500.5	129.6	43.3	124.0	112.7
R1000.1	20.6	144.5	20.0	11.9
R1000.1c	98.8	80.7	101.4	556.6
R1000.5	253.2	170.5	239.0	801.3
flat300_20_0	20.2	6.2	25.3	20.7
flat300_26_0	37.1	12.7	36.0	15.9
flat300_28_0	37.0	15.8	35.8	16.5
flat1000_50_0	65.6	242.5	100.0	267.5
flat1000_60_0	102.5	144.7	100.2	265.2
flat1000_76_0	103.6	131.9	100.8	266.4
latin_sqr_10	106.7	99.0	111.4	486.7
le450_15a	17.9	28.1	15.0	8.9
le450_15b	17.9	26.9	15.0	9.4
le450_15c	25.6	24.0	21.3	9.4
le450_15d	25.8	22.5	21.4	9.6
mulsol.i.1	49.0	6.9	49.0	13.5
school1	14.0	17.4	14.0	11.8
school1_nsh	14.1	14.8	14.0	10.4

Table 2: Experimental results: graph coloring

Experimental results

We applied SWO to a standard set of graph coloring problems, including random graphs and application graphs that model register allocation and class scheduling problems. These were collected for the Second DIMACS Implementation Challenge (Johnson & Trick 1996), which includes results for several algorithms on these problems (Culberson & Luo 1996; Glover, Parker, & Ryan 1996; Lewandowski & Condon 1996; Morgenstern 1996). Problems range from 125 nodes with 209 edges to 4000 nodes with 4,000,268 edges.

(Glover, Parker, & Ryan 1996) is the only paper that uses a general search technique, TABU with branch and bound, rather than a graph coloring specific algorithm. This approach had the worst reported average results in the group. (Morgenstern 1996) used a distributed IMPASSE algorithm and had the best overall colorings, but also required that the target number of colors, as well as several other problem specific parameters be passed to the solver. (Lewandowski & Condon 1996) also found good solutions for this problem set. Their approach used a hybrid of parallel IMPASSE and systematic search on a 32 processor CM-5. (Culberson & Luo 1996) used an Iterated Greedy (IG) algorithm that bears some similarity to SWO. IG is the simplest algorithm in the group. It's solution quality falls between the IMPASSE algorithms and TABU but solves the entire set in 1 to 2 percent of the time taken by the other methods. Both IG and IMPASSE are discussed further under related work.

Table 2 compares SWO with the results for IG, the best serial algorithm in (Johnson & Trick 1996), and the only one with results for all 32 problems. The table shows average results and run times (in CPU seconds) of ten independent runs for each algorithm. Both algorithms terminated after 1000 iterations.

The times shown for IG are those reported in (Culberson & Luo 1996), normalized to our times using the DIMACS benchmarking program *dfmax*, provided for this purpose. Therefore, timing comparisons are only approximate. Our machine, a Pentium Pro 200Mhz workstation running Linux, ran the *dfmax r500.5* benchmark in 142.49 seconds, and their machine, a Sun Sparcstation 10/40, ran it in 192.60 seconds; in the table, we multiplied their times by 0.74.

As the table shows, SWO generally achieves better results than IG but, also generally, takes more time. The difference between them is less than 0.5 colors on 9 of the problems. Of those with a difference of 0.5 or greater, IG does better on 4 of the graphs and SWO does better on 19 of them.

We also note, as with the scheduling work, that our first, naive implementation produced respectable results. Even without color reuse, color grabbing, or the least constraining heuristic (the first free color found was picked), SWO matched IG on 6 problems and beat it on 10. However, on half of the remaining problems IG did better by 10 or more colors.

Related work

The importance of prioritization in greedy algorithms is not a new idea. The "First Fit" algorithm for bin packing, for example, relies on placing items into bins in decreasing order of size (Garey & Johnson 1979). Another example is GRASP (Greedy Randomized Adaptive Search Procedure) (Feo & Resende 1995). GRASP differs from our approach in several ways. First, the prioritization and construction aspects are more closely coupled in GRASP. After each element is added to the solution being constructed, the remaining elements are re-evaluated by some heuristic. Thus the order in which elements are added to the solution may depend on previous decisions. Second, the order in which elements are selected in each trial is determined only by the heuristic (and randomization), so the trials are independent. There is no learning from iteration to iteration in GRASP.

Doubleback Optimization (DBO) (Crawford 1996) was to some extent the inspiration for both SWO and another similar algorithm, Abstract Local Search (ALS) (Crawford, Dalal, & Walser 1998). In designing SWO, we began by looking at DBO, because it had been extremely successful in solving a standard type of scheduling problem. However, DBO is only useful when the objective is to minimize makespan, and is also limited in the types of constraints it can handle. Because of these limitations, we began thinking about the principles behind DBO, looking for an effective generalization of that approach. DBO can, in fact, be viewed as an instance of SWO. DBO begins by performing a "right shift" on a schedule, shifting all tasks as far to the right as they can go, up to some boundary. In the resulting right-shifted schedule, the left-most tasks are, to some extent, those tasks that are most critical. This corresponds to analysis in SWO. Tasks are then removed from the right-shifted schedule, taking left-most tasks first. This ordering corresponds to the prioritization in SWO. As each task is removed, it is placed in a new schedule at the earliest possible start time, i.e., greedy construction.

Like SWO, ALS was the result of an attempt to generalize DBO. ALS views priority space (to use the terminology from SWO) as a space of "abstract schedules," and performs a local search in that space. Unlike SWO, if a prioritization is modified, and the corresponding move in solution space is downhill (away from optimal), then the modified prioritization is discarded, and the old prioritization is restored. As is usual with local search, ALS also sometimes makes random moves, in order to escape local minima.

ALS, and also List Scheduling (Pinson, Prins, & Rullier 1994), are scheduling algorithms that deal with domains that include precedence constraints on tasks. Both accommodate precedence constraints by constructing schedules left-to-right temporally. A task cannot be placed in the schedule until all of its predecessors have been placed. In order for the analysis, prioritization and construction to be appropriately coupled, it is not sufficient to simply increase the priority of a task that is late, because the constructor may not be able to place that task until after a lot of other decisions have been made. Consequently, some amount of blame must be propagated to the task's predecessors.

In contrast, our schedule constructor is able to place tasks in any order because it commits to placing a task on a specific production line, and to a relative ordering on that line, without committing to a specific start time for each task. The ability for the constructor to make decisions in "best first" order allows the analysis and prioritization to be kept very simple, but obviously complicates the constructor. Our intuition is that it is more important to keep the analysis simple, with a constructor that is able to respond flexibly to the results of prioritization. We believe this approach also has the most potential for generalization.

The commercial scheduler OPTIFLEX (Syswerda 1994) uses a genetic algorithm approach to modify a sequence of tasks, and a constraint-based schedule constructor that generates schedules from those sequences.

OPTIFLEX can also be viewed as an instance of SWO, with a genetic algorithm replacing analysis. In effect, the "analysis" instead emerges from the relative fitness of the members of the population.

Two graph coloring algorithms also bear some similarity to SWO. Impasse Class Coloration Neighborhood Search (IMPASSE) (Morgenstern 1996; Lewandowski & Condon 1996), like SWO, maintains a target set of colors and produces only feasible colorings. Given a coloring, IMPASSE places any nodes that are colored outside of the target set into an impasse set. On each iteration a node is selected from the impasse set, using a noisy degree-based heuristic, and assigned a random color from the target set. Any neighbor nodes that are now in conflict are moved to the impasse set.

Iterated Greedy (IG) (Culberson & Luo 1996), like SWO, uses a sequence of nodes to create a new coloring on each iteration, and then uses that coloring to produce a new sequence for the next iteration. The method used to generate each new sequence differs from SWO. The key observation behind IG is that if all nodes with the same color in the current solution are grouped together in the next sequence (i.e. adjacent to each other), then the next solution will be no worse than the current solution. IG achieves improvement by manipulating the order in which the groups occur in the new sequence, using several heuristics.

Conclusions and future work

Our experience has been that it is fairly straightforward to implement SWO in a new domain, because there are usually fairly obvious ways to construct greedy solutions, and to analyze a solution to assign "blame" to some of the elements. Naive implementations of SWO tend to perform reasonably well.

We have found the view of SWO as performing a "coupled search" over two different search spaces to be very informative. It has been helpful to characterize the kinds of moves that SWO makes in each of the search spaces, and the effect this has on avoiding local optima, etc. We hope that by continuing to gain a deeper understanding of what makes SWO work we will be able to say more about the effective design of SWO algorithms.

Although the ability to make large, coherent moves is a strength of the approach, it is also a weakness. SWO is poor at making small "tuning" moves in the solution space, but the coupled-search view of SWO suggests an obvious remedy. SWO could be combined with local search in the solution space, to look for improvements in the vicinity of good solutions. Similarly, making small changes to a prioritization would generally result in smaller moves in the solution space than result from going through the full analysis and re-prioritization cycle. Yet another alternative is genetic algorithm techniques for "crossover" and other types of mutation to a pool of nodes, as is done in OPTIFLEX. Many hybrid approaches are possible, and we believe that the coupled-search view of SWO helps to identify some interesting strategies for combining moves of various sizes and kinds, in both search spaces, adapting dynamically to relative solution qualities.

While SWO uses fast, greedy algorithms for constructing solutions, and we have demonstrated its effectiveness on problems of realistic size, the greatest threat to the scalability of SWO is that it constructs a new solution from scratch on each iteration. An obvious solution to this problem is to develop an incremental version of SWO. The graph coloring solver, with its selective reuse of colors from the previous iteration, is a small step in this direction. It allows the constructor to avoid spending time evaluating other alternatives when the previous choice still works. More generally, it may be possible to look at the changes made to a prioritization, and modify the corresponding solution in a way that generates the same solution that would be constructed from scratch based on the new prioritization. It seems feasible that this could be done for some domains, at least for small changes to the prioritization, because there may be large portions of a solution that are unaffected.

A more interesting possibility is based on the view of SWO as performing local search plus a certain kind of propagation. A small change in priorities may correspond to a large change in the solution. For example, increasing the priority of one task in a scheduling problem may change its position in the schedule, and, as a consequence, some lower priority tasks may have to be shuffled around to accommodate that change. This is similar to what we might expect from moving the higher priority task, then propagating the effects of that change by moving lower priority tasks as well. This single move may correspond to a large number of moves in a search algorithm that only looks at local changes to the schedule, and may thus be difficult for such an algorithm to find.

Based on this view, we are investigating an algorithm we call "Priority-Limited Propagation" (PLP). With PLP, local changes are made to the solution, and then propagation is allowed to occur, subject to the current prioritization. Propagation is only allowed to occur in the direction of lower-priority elements. In effect, a small change is made, and then the consequences of that change are allowed to "ripple" through the plan. Because propagation can only occur in directions of decreasing priority, these ripples of propagation decrease in magnitude until no more propagation is possible. A new prioritization is then generated by analyzing the resulting solution. (It should be possible to do this analysis incrementally, as well.) The resulting approach is not identical to SWO, but has many of its interesting characteristics.

Another potential pitfall for SWO is that analysis, prioritization and construction must all work together to improve the quality of solutions. We have already discussed the complications that can arise when constraints are placed on the order in which the constructor can make decisions, as is the case for Line Scheduling and ALS, where construction is done strictly left-to-right. Without more complex analysis, the search spaces can effectively become uncoupled, so that changes in priority don't cause the constructor to fix problems discovered by analysis.

Another way the search can become uncoupled is related to the notion of "excess cost," discussed for the scheduling implementation. The calculation of excess cost in the analyzer turned out to be a key idea for improving the performance of SWO. However, problems sometimes have tasks that must be handled badly in order to achieve a good overall solution. One of the scheduling problems described previously has two such "sacrificial" tasks. Whenever a good solution is found, the analyzer assigns high blame to these sacrificial tasks, and the constructor handles them well on the next iteration. This means that the resulting solution is of poor overall quality, and it is not until other flaws cause other tasks to move ahead of the sacrificial tasks in the priority sequence that SWO can again, briefly, explore the space of good solutions. In such cases, to some extent the analysis is actually hurting the ability of SWO to converge on good solutions.

Ideally, we would like to generalize the notion of excess cost to recognize sacrificial tasks, and allow those tasks to be handled badly without receiving proportionate blame. For problems in which a task must be sacrificed in *all* solutions, it may be possible to use a learning mechanism that would accomplish this.

As the number of directions for future research suggests, we have only begun to scratch the surface of "Squeaky Wheel" Optimization.

Acknowledgments. The authors wish to thank Robert Stubbs of Lucent Technologies for providing the data used for the scheduling experiments. The authors also wish to thank George L. Nemhauser, Markus E. Puttlitz and Martin W. P. Savelsbergh with whom we collaborated on using SWO in a hybrid AI/OR approach. Many useful discussions came out of that collaboration, and without them we would not have had access to the Lucent problems. Markus also wrote the framework for the scheduling experiments and the TABU and IP implementations.

The authors also thank the members of CIRL, and James Crawford at i2 Technologies, for their helpful comments and suggestions. We would like to thank Andrew Parkes in particular for suggestions and insights in the graph coloring domain.

This effort was sponsored by the Air Force Office of Scientific Research, Air Force Materiel Command, USAF, under grant number F49620-96-1-0335; by the Defense Advanced Research Projects Agency (DARPA) and Rome Laboratory, Air Force Materiel Command, USAF, under agreements F30602-95-1-0023 and F30602-97-1-0294; and by the National Science Foundation under grant number CDA-9625755.

Most of the work reported in this paper was done while both authors were at CIRL.

References

Clements, D.; Crawford, J.; Joslin, D.; Nemhauser, G.; Puttlitz, M.; and Savelsbergh, M. 1997. Heuristic optimization: A hybrid AI/OR approach. In *Proceedings of the Workshop on Industrial Constraint-Directed Scheduling.*

Crawford, J.; Dalal, M.; and Walser, J. 1998. Abstract local search. Unpublished.

Crawford, J. M. 1996. An approach to resource constrained project scheduling. In *Artificial Intelligence and Manufacturing Research Planning Workshop.*

Culberson, J. C., and Luo, F. 1996. Exploring the k-colorable landscape with iterated greedy. In *(Johnson & Trick 1996)*, 245-284.

Feo, T. A., and Resende, M. G. 1995. Greedy randomized adaptive search procedures. *Journal of Global Optimization* 6:109-133.

Garey, M. R., and Johnson, D. S. 1979. *Computers and intractability: a guide to the theory of NP-completeness.* W. H. Freeman.

Glover, F., and Laguna, M. 1997. *Tabu Search.* Kluwer.

Glover, F.; Parker, M.; and Ryan, J. 1996. Coloring by tabu branch and bound. In *(Johnson & Trick 1996)*, 285-307.

Johnson, D. S., and Trick, M. A., eds. 1996. *Cliques, Coloring, and Satisfiability: Second DIMACS Implementation Challenge, 1993*, volume 26 of *DIMACS Series in Discrete Mathematics and Theoretical Computer Science.* American Mathematical Society.

Lewandowski, G., and Condon, A. 1996. Experiments with parallel graph coloring heuristics and applications of graph coloring. In *(Johnson & Trick 1996)*, 309-334.

Morgenstern, C. 1996. Distributed coloration neighborhood search. In *(Johnson & Trick 1996)*, 335-357.

Pinson, E.; Prins, C.; and Rullier, F. 1994. Using tabu search for solving the resource-constrained project scheduling problem. In *EURO-WG PMS 4 (EURO Working Group on Project Management and Scheduling)*, 102-106.

Selman, B.; Kautz, H. A.; and Cohen, B. 1993. Local search strategies for satisfiability testing. In *(Johnson & Trick 1996)*, 521-531.

Syswerda, G. P. 1994. Generation of schedules using a genetic procedure. U.S. Patent number 5,319,781.

Reversible DAC and Other Improvements for Solving Max-CSP

Javier Larrosa[*]
Univ. Pol. de Catalunya
Pau Gargallo 5,
08028 Barcelona
Spain
larrosa@lsi.upc.es

Pedro Meseguer[*]
IIIA-CSIC
Campus UAB
08193 Bellaterra
Spain
pedro@iiia.csic.es

Thomas Schiex
INRA
Chemin de Borde Rouge, BP 27
31326 Castanet-Tolosan Cedex
France
tschiex@toulouse.inra.fr

Gérard Verfaillie
ONERA-CERT
2 Av. E. Belin, BP 4025
31055 Toulouse Cedex 4
France
verfaillie@cert.fr

Abstract

Following the work of R. Wallace on Max-CSP, later improved by J. Larrosa and P. Meseguer, we tested a number of possible improvements of the usage of directed arc consistency for the *partial forward checking* algorithm (PFC). The main improvement consists in exploiting a non standard form of DAC, called *reversible DAC* where each constraint is exploited in a direction which is not necessarily determined by the variable ordering and can change dynamically during the search. Other improvements include: (i) avoiding some constraint checks when forward-checking by exploiting the constraint checks performed during DAC preprocessing (ii) using a dynamic variable ordering during the search, (iii) maintaining the directed arc-consistency counts during the search as values get deleted. These improvements have been assessed empirically on random CSP instances. Some of them lead to very large performance gains with respect to the initial algorithm.

Constraint Satisfaction Problems (CSP) consist in assigning values to variables under a given set of constraints. A solution is a total assignment that satisfies every constraint. In practice, such an assignment may not exist and it may be of interest to find a total assignment that best respects, in some sense, all the constraints. This type of problem is of interest in many applications and has been captured by general frameworks such as the Semiring or Valued CSP frameworks defined in (Bistarelli, Montanari, & Rossi 1995; Schiex, Fargier, & Verfaillie 1995). In this paper, we focus on the so-called Max-CSP problem where a solution is a total assignment that minimizes the number of violated constraints, but the reader should be aware that the algorithms presented here can easily be extended to the Valued CSP framework if needed.

The P-EFC3-DAC2 algorithm (Larrosa & Meseguer 1996), or PFC-DAC for short, is an improvement of the DAC based algorithm introduced in (Wallace 1995). It is among the best complete algorithms for Max-CSP. It is a branch and bound algorithm using forward-checking and directional arc consistency as a preprocessing step. To prune the search tree, a lower bound on the number of unsatisfied constraints is computed that takes into account (i) constraints between assigned variables using backward-checking (ii) constraints between assigned and unassigned variables using forward-checking and (iii) constraints between unassigned variables, using *directed arc consistency counts* (DAC). It needs a static variable ordering.

In this paper we present further improvements to this algorithm. The paper is organized as follows. In the next section, we present related algorithms for solving Max-CSP. We then provide preliminaries and definitions required in the sequel of the paper. Then, we consider the original PFC-DAC algorithm and present our improvements. The result of these improvements is finally assessed empirically on random Max-CSP instances, before the conclusion.

Related Work

The general scheme of most algorithms for solving Max-CSP is a *branch and bound* scheme. The algorithm performs a systematic traversal on the search tree where a node corresponds to a set of assigned (or *past*) variables and a set of unassigned (or *future*) variables. At each node, one future variable is selected (*current* variable) and all its feasible values are considered for instantiation. As search proceeds, branch and bound keeps track of the best solution obtained so far which is the total assignment which violates a minimum number of constraints in the explored part of the search tree. In order to avoid the exploration of the complete search tree, the algorithm computes at each node a *lower bound* on the cost of the best solution that could possibly be found under the current node. If this lower bound is larger than or equal to the cost of the best solution found so far (called the *upper bound*), the current line of search is abandoned because it cannot lead to a better solution that the current one. In practice, the efficiency of branch and bound algorithms depends on the quality of the lower bound which should be both as large and as cheap to compute as possible.

At a given node, the simplest lower bound one can imagine is defined by the number of constraints violated by the partial assignment associated with the node, also called the *distance* of the node. The PFC algorithm uses *forward checking* to improve this lower bound (see (Freuder & Wallace 1992) for a more detailed description). Further improvements have been introduced by the *Russian Doll Search* algorithm (Verfaillie, Lemaître, & Schiex 1996) or by algo-

---
[*]The research of Javier Larrosa and Pedro Meseguer is supported by the Spanish CICYT project TIC96-0721-C02-02

[†]Copyright (c) 1998, American Association for Artificial Intelligence (www.aaai.org). All rights reserved.

rithms using directed arc consistency.

The notion of *directed arc consistency* was first introduced by (Dechter & Pearl 1988), in the context of classical CSP. The use of DAC in Max-CSP to improve the lower bound of the PFC algorithm has been introduced in (Wallace 1995) and improved by (Larrosa & Meseguer 1996; Wallace 1996; Larrosa & Meseguer 1998). In a preprocessing step, *directed arc consistency counts* are computed for each value following a given variable ordering. This order must be used as a static variable ordering for variable instantiation in the DAC-based branch and bound algorithm.

Preliminaries

A discrete binary CSP is defined by a finite set of variables $X = \{1, \ldots, n\}$. Each variable $i \in X$ takes its values in a finite domain D_i and is subject to constraints R_{ij}. A constraint R_{ij} is a subset of $D_i \times D_j$ which defines the allowed pairs of values for variables i, j. We note n and e the number of variables and constraints and d the maximum cardinality of the domains D_i. In the sequel, $i, j, k \ldots$ denote variables, $a, b, c \ldots$ denote values, and a pair such as (i, a) denotes the value a of variable i.

It is usual, for arc-consistency algorithms, to associate with a given CSP a symmetric directed graph. For directed arc-consistency, we define a directed graph of the CSP to be a graph with one vertex i for each variable i and *only one* edge, either (i, j) or (j, i), for each constraint R_{ij}. Such a graph is not uniquely defined for a given CSP. Its edges will be denoted by EDGES(G). We will note PRED(i, G) (resp.SUCC(i, G)) the set of variables j such that (j, i) (resp. (i, j)) is an edge of G. We define DIRECTION(i, j, G) to be 1 is $(i, j) \in G$, -1 if $(j, i) \in G$ and 0 if there is no constraint between i and j.

Directed arc-consistency being defined up to a variable ordering, we define $G^{\succ}$, the directed graph induced by a variable ordering $\succ$, as the directed graph of the CSP such that $(i, j) \in$ EDGES(G) $\Rightarrow (i \succ j)$. $G^{\succ}$ is therefore the directed graph where all edges are oriented in a direction opposed to the variable ordering. The directed arc consistency count associated with value a of variable i, noted dac_{ia}, is defined as the number of variables in PRED($i, G^{\succ}$) which are *arc-inconsistent* with value (i, a) i.e., which have no value in their domain which is compatible with (i, a). All DAC can be simply precomputed in $O(ed^2)$ time and $O(nd)$ space. $\min_a(dac_{ia})$ is a lower bound on the number of inconsistencies that i will have with variables after i in the ordering in any total assignment.

The PFC-DAC algorithm (Larrosa & Meseguer 1996) is a branch and bound algorithm. It is described by functions PFC-DAC and LookAhead below. For future variables, the lower bound exploits the directed arc consistency counts defined above combined with so-called *inconsistency counts* introduced in the PFC algorithm (Freuder & Wallace 1992). Given a partial assignment, the inconsistency count associated with value a of a future variable i, noted ic_{ia}, is the number of constraints between any assigned variable and i that would be violated if value a is assigned to variable i (Freuder & Wallace 1992). If FV is the set of future variables, then the sum $\sum_{i \in FV} \min_a(ic_{ia} + dac_{ia})$ is a lower bound on the number of constraints that have to be violated between currently unassigned variables and all CSP variables in any total assignment extending the current partial assignment. This lower bound is used to prune branches (line 1.1) and to prune values (lines 2.1 and 2.2).

Function 1: PFC-DAC main function, S is the current partial assignment, d its distance, FV and FD are the future variables and their domains

PFC-DAC(S, d, FV, FD);
if $FV = \emptyset$ **then**
  if $(d < bestd)$ **then**
    $bestd := d$;
    $BestS := S$;
else
  $i :=$ SelectVariable(FV);
  $FV := FV - \{i\}$;
  $values :=$ SortValues(FD_i);
  while $(values \neq \emptyset)$ **do**
    $a :=$ First($values$);
    $newd := d + ic_{ia}$;
1.1   **if** $(newd + dac_{ia} + \sum_{j \in FV} \min_b(ic_{jb} + dac_{jb}) < bestd)$ **then**
      $newFD :=$ LookAhead(i, a, FV, FD);
      if not WipeOut($newFD$) **then**
        PFC-DAC($S \cup \{(i, a)\}, newd, FV, newFD$);
    $values := values - \{a\}$;

Function 2: PFC-DAC propagation function, (i, a) is the assignment to propagate, FV and FD are the future variables and their domains

LookAhead(i, a, FV, FD);
foreach $j \in FV$ **do**
  foreach $b \in FD_j$ **do**
2.1   **if** $(newd + \sum_{k \in FV - \{j\}} \min_c(ic_{kc} + dac_{kc}) + ic_{jb} + dac_{jb} \geq bestd)$ **then** Prune(j, b);
    else if Inconsistent(i, a, j, b) **then**
      Increment(ic_{jb});
2.2   **if** $(newd + \sum_{k \in FV - \{j\}} \min_c(ic_{kc} + dac_{kc}) + ic_{jb} + dac_{jb} \geq bestd)$ **then** Prune(j, b);

return *Updated domains*;

DAC Improvements

The basic procedure PFC-DAC for MAX-CSP can be improved in different ways, provided that the DAC preprocessing produces a data structure $GivesDac(i, a, j)$ that records the contribution of any variable j connected to i to the count dac_{ia}. The information contained in this data structure is used during search to perform the improvements detailed below. The size of this data structure is in $O(ed)$. In the following, we present four different and independent improvements on DAC usage.

1. Saving checks associated with DAC: If $GivesDac(i, a, j)$ is true ($i \prec j$), it means that no value of j is compatible with (i, a). When variable i becomes current and is assigned value a, we already know that the IC of every feasible value of variable j must be incremented by one (because (i, a) is arc-inconsistent with D_j), so IC updating of

j values can be done without any constraint check. In practice, instead of incrementing all ic_{jb}, we increase the current distance by 1 and prevent the updating of all ic_{jb} when $GivesDac(i,a,j)$ is true. This simple idea allows lookahead to reuse results obtained in DAC preprocessing, and saves the repetition of all the constraint checks associated with detected arc-inconsistencies.

2. Dynamic variable orderings: Original PFC-DAC requires to follow the same static order for variable selection that was used for DAC computation. However, this is no longer required, provided that individual contributions to DAC are available. Let i and j be variables such that GIVES-DAC(i,a,j) is true. DAC propagate the effect of R_{ij} from j to i, so the violation of this constraint is recorded in DAC of variable i. If variable j is instantiated before i, lookahead will propagate the possible violation of R_{ij} from j to i, incrementing some IC of i (and in particular, ic_{ia}). But this inconsistency has already been recorded in dac_{ia} using the *forward* edge (j,i), so adding $ic_{ia} + dac_{ia}$ would count twice the same inconsistency.

This problem can be overcome as far as the lookahead detects the situation and avoids redundant contributions to the lower bound. If we know that R_{ij} has been used from j to i, j can be safely instantiated before i as far as we prevent the updating of all ic_{ia} such that $GivesDac(i,a,j)$ is true. In this way, it is guaranteed that inconsistencies are counted only once, and IC and DAC of future values can be added to form a lower bound of inconsistencies for that value.

3. Reversible DAC:cd Te Originally (Wallace 1995) discarded the use of full arc-inconsistency counts because they could record the same inconsistency twice, so addition could not be safely used to compute lower bounds. Instead, he proposed directed arc-inconsistency counts, which do not suffer from this drawback. Following the work of (Dechter & Pearl 1988) on directed arc consistency, Wallace required a static variable ordering $\succ$, where DAC are computed in the direction of the corresponding edge in $G^\succ$. However, for lower bound computation, this restriction is arbitrary and can be removed. Each constraint can contribute to DAC in one of the two possible directions, to avoid inconsistency repetition, but the selected direction has not to be induced by a variable ordering.

With this idea in mind, given any directed graph G of a CSP, one can define directed arc inconsistency counts dac_{ia} based on this graph as the number of variables in PRED(i,G) which are arc-inconsistent with (i,a). The lower bound on the number of violated constraints that may exist in a complete assignment is defined as before as: $\sum_{i \in X} \min_a dac_{ia}$. During search, the lower bound $distance + \sum_{i \in FV} \min_a(ic_{ia} + dac_{ia})$ can be used, as far as DAC have their contributions from past variables removed,

At each node, one could try to find an optimal directed graph G, i.e., to determine an order for each future constraint that maximizes the lower bound. We have taken a simpler approach: to *locally* optimize G at each node during tree search using simple greedy heuristics. In our approach, we start from the graph inherited from the previous search state, and reverse constraints between future variables if it improves the lower bound. The process iterates until no such constraints can be found. When a constraint is reversed, DAC need to be appropriately modified. The *GivesDac* data-structure is suitable to do it efficiently.

As in the dynamic variable ordering case, forward edges may be met during assignment and again, if we know that R_{ij} is used from j to i, j can be safely instantiated before i as far as we prevent the updating of all ic_{ia} such that $GivesDac(i,a,j)$ is true.

4. Maintaining DAC: PFC-DAC requires a strong condition for variables to contribute to DAC counts: arc-inconsistencies need to hold before search starts, when no value is pruned. The PFC-DAC algorithm prunes future values during its execution. This implies that DAC counters, precomputed initially before search, are not updated during search. The maintaining DAC approach consists on keeping updated those DAC during search, taking into account current domains. This causes higher DAC to be computed, which leads to a higher lower bound: more branches may be pruned, more value deletions can occur, which are again propagated, etc. To perform maintaining DAC, any arc consistency algorithm (along with adequate data-structures) can be adapted to propagate the effect of value removal, either in one static direction of constraints (as in the basic PFC-DAC procedure), or in both directions, if the reversible DAC approach is taken.

Implementation

Each of the improvements introduced in this paper can be used alone. For the sake of simplicity and because of the limited space, we will define a version of the algorithm that includes all the refinements.

The data-structure $GivesDac(i,a,j)$ has been described in the previous section: $GivesDac(i,a,j)$ is true iff variable j contributes to dac_{ia}. It is needed for our three first improvements. In order to implement the fourth improvement (DAC maintainance), we have used AC4 like data-structures: $NSupport(i,a,j)$ contains the number of supports of value (i,a) on variable j and $LSupport(i,a,j)$ contains the list of all values (j,b) that are supported by (i,a). These data-structures have space complexity $O(ed)$ and $O(ed^2)$ respectively and are useless when DAC are not maintained. One can observe that $NSupport(i,a,j) = 0 \Leftrightarrow GivesDac(i,a,j)$ = true and therefore the $GivesDac$ data-structure is redundant with $NSupport$ and can be removed in this case.

Extra data structures have been introduced to easily maintain the quantities $\operatorname{argmin}_a(ic_{ia}+dac_{ia})$, $\min_a(ic_{ia}+dac_{ia})$ and the sum of these minima on future variables. All these quantities are respectively maintained in the arrays *MinIC-DACValue(i)*, *MinICDAC(i)* and in the variable *SumMinIC-DAC*. All these data structures are updated by a simple function noted UpdateMin in the sequel (not described here because of its simplicity).

The algorithm is embodied in the main function PFC-MRDAC-DVO. The reader should be aware that all context restoration mechanisms are not explicited in the code, for the sake of simplicity[1]. Before main function PFC-MRDAC-

---

[1] All context restorations are done using lists to memorize

Function 3: PFC-MRDAC main function, S is the current assignment, d its distance, FV and FD are the future variables and their domains and G is the current directed graph

PFC-MRDAC-DVO(S,d,FV,FD,G);
  if $FV = \emptyset$ then
    if $(d < bestd)$ then
      $bestd := d$;
      $BestS := S$;
  else
    $i := \text{SelectVariable}(FV)$;
    $FV := FV - \{i\}$;
    $SumMinICDAC := SumMinICDAC - MinICDAC(i)$;
    $values := \text{SortValues}(FD_i)$;
    while $(values \neq \emptyset)$ do
      $a := \text{First}(values)$;
3.1 $newd := d + ic_{ia} + dac_{ia}$;
      if $(newd + SumMinICDAC < bestd)$ then
        $newFD := \text{LookAhead}(i,a,FV,FD)$;
        if not $\text{WipeOut}(newFD)$ then
3.2 $newG := \text{GreedyOpt}(G)$;
          if $(newd + SumMinICDAC) < bestd$ then
3.3 $\text{PruneValues}(newd,i)$;
            PFC-MRDAC-DVO($S \cup \{(i,a)\}, newd, FV, newFD, newG$);
      $values := values - \{a\}$;

Function 4: PFC-MRDAC propagation function, (i,a) is the assignment to propagate, FV and FD are the future variables and their domains

LookAhead(i,a,FV,FD);
  foreach $j \in FV$ do
    $NewMin := \text{false}$;
    foreach $b \in FD_j$ do
      if $(newd + SumMinICDAC - MinICDAC(j) + ic_{jb} + dac_{jb} \geq bestd)$ then $\text{Prune}(j,b)$;
4.1 $\text{PropagateDel}(j,b,FV)$;
4.2   else if $(\text{DIRECTION}(i,j,G) = -1$ & $(\text{not GivesDac}(i,a,j)))$
      or
4.3 $(\text{DIRECTION}(i,j,G) = 1$ & $(\text{not GivesDac}(j,b,i)))$ then
        if $\text{Inconsistent}(i,a,j,b)$ then
          $\text{Increment}(ic_{jb})$;
4.4   if $MinICDAC(j) = ic_{jb} + dac_{jb}$ then
4.5 $NewMin := \text{true}$;
          if $(newd + SumMinICDAC - MinICDAC(j) + ic_{jb} + dac_{jb} \geq bestd)$ then
            $\text{Prune}(j,b)$;
4.6 $\text{PropagateDel}(j,b,FV)$;
4.7   if $NewMin$ then $\text{UpdateMin}(j)$;
  return $Updated\ domains$;

DVO is called, one should initialize data-structures dac and $GivesDac$ or ($NSupport$ and $LSupport$) if the fourth improvement is used. The initialization is straightforward and not described here. It can be performed in time $O(ed^2)$.

Compared to the initial PFC-DAC algorithm, line 3.1 has been modified in order to implement the first improvement. Lines 3.2 and 3.3 have been inserted to implement the reversible DAC improvement. The function GreedyOpt, used on line 3.2, implements the greedy optimization of the current directed graph. After this call, a new lower bound may be available and new values may be pruned. This is done by the PruneValues function on line 3.3.

The LookAhead function is in charge of propagating the assignment (i,a). Lines 4.4, 4.5 and 4.7 have been inserted to update the data-structure $MinICDAC$ and $SumMinICDAC$ when needed. Our three first improvements need to prevent the updating of ic_{jb} in some cases, because the corresponding costs have already been taken into account in PFC-MRDAC-DVO, on line 3.1. This is done by the test on lines 4.2 and 4.3. The last change in this function consists in calls to the new function PropagateDel on lines 4.1 and 4.6, which implements our fourth improvement: this function is in charge of propagating the deletion of value (j,b) on the previous line and updating the directed arc consistency counts.

This propagation is done using the AC4-like datastructures: the number of supports of all the feasible values which are supported by the value being deleted are decremented. If a value loses all its supports on one constraint and changes and later undo these changes upon backtrack.

if the correct direction of the constraint is used in the directed graph, the corresponding dac is incremented and the datastructures $MinICDAC$ and $SumMinICDAC$ updated by function UpdateMin if needed. One should note that function LookAhead and PropagateDel together do not completely "maintain DAC": if a deletion in LookAhead is propagated by PropagateDel, a deletion in PropagateDel is not propagated again. This appeared to be useless.

Function 5: Updating dac after deletions, (i,a) is the deleted value, FV is the set of future variables

PropagateDel(i,a, FV);
$NewMin := \text{false}$;
foreach $j \in FV$ do
  foreach $b \in LSupport(i,a,j)$ do
    if b is feasible then
      $\text{Decrement}(NSupport[j][b][i])$;
      if $NSupport[j][b][i] = 0$ & $\text{DIRECTION}(i,j) = 1$ then
        $\text{Increment}(dac_{jb})$;
        if $MinICDAC(j) = ic_{jb} + dac_{jb}$ then
          $\text{UpdateMin}(j)$;
          $NewMin := \text{true}$;

return $NewMin$;

The function GreedyOpt is in charge of optimizing the current directed graph G in order to improve the current lower bound. It is a simple greedy function: each edge is reversed (and the directed arc consistency counts modified accordingly). The lower bound is then recomputed and the change is kept only if it leads to an improvement. The function stops when no improvement could be obtained. Note that before edge (i,j) is reversed, a simple test is performed on line 6.1: this test is an obvious necessary condition for an improvement to be possible.

Function 6: Finding a "good" directed graph, G is the current directed graph

```
GreedyOpt(G);
Stop := false;
while not Stop do
    SaveMin := SumMinICDAC;
    foreach i, j ∈ FV s.t. (i, j) ∈ EDGES(G) do
        MinF := MinICDAC(i);
        ValMinF := MinICDACValue(i);
        MinT := MinICDAC(j);
        ValMinT := MinICDACValue(j);
        if (not GivesDac(j, ValMinT, i)) & GivesDac(i, ValMinF, j)
        then
            Reverse(i, j, G);
            UpdateMin(i);
            UpdateMin(j);
            if MinICDAC(i)+MinICDAC(j) < MinF + MinT then
                Reverse(i, j, G);
                UpdateMin(i);
                UpdateMin(j);
    if SaveMin = SumMinICDAC then
        Stop := true;
return Updated graph
```

Finally, the function PruneValues is in charge of value deletions once the lower bound has been improved by the GreedyOpt function. It can be considered as a simplified LookAhead function. Each value deletion is again propagated using function PropagateDel. Contrarily to function LookAhead however, a fix point is reached: value deletions are propagated until no new deletion occurs. This has been found to be useful in practice although gains are minor.

Function 7: Pruning values after a lower bound improvement, d is the current distance and FV is the set of future variables

```
PruneValues(d,FV);
Stop := false;
while not Stop do
    Copy := SumMinICDAC;
    foreach j ∈ FV do
        foreach b ∈ FD_j do
            if (d+ SumMinICDAC − MinICDAC(j) + ic_jb + dac_jb ≥ bestd) then
                Prune(j, b);
                PropagateDel(j, b, FV);
    if Wipe out then Empty := Stop := true;
    if Copy = SumMinICDAC then Stop := true;
return not Empty;
```

Experimental Results

We have evaluated the performance of our algorithms on over-constrained random CSP. A random CSP is characterized by $\langle n, d, p_1, p_2 \rangle$ where n is the number of variables, d the number of values per variables, p_1 the graph *connectivity* defined as the ratio of existing constraints, and p_2 the constraint *tightness* defined as the ratio of forbidden value pairs. The constrained variables and the forbidden value pairs are randomly selected (Prosser 1994). Using this model, we have experimented on the following problems classes:

1. $\langle 10, 10, \frac{45}{45}, p_2 \rangle$,
2. $\langle 15, 5, \frac{105}{105}, p_2 \rangle$,
3. $\langle 15, 10, \frac{50}{105}, p_2 \rangle$,
4. $\langle 20, 5, \frac{100}{190}, p_2 \rangle$,
5. $\langle 25, 10, \frac{37}{300}, p_2 \rangle$,
6. $\langle 40, 5, \frac{55}{780}, p_2 \rangle$.

Observe that (1) and (2) are highly connected problems, (3) and (4) are problems with medium connectivity, and (5) and (6) are sparse problems. For each problem class and each parameter setting, we generated samples of 50 instances.

Each problem is solved with three algorithms: PFC-DAC as described in (Larrosa & Meseguer 1996), PFC with reversible DAC and dynamic variable ordering (DVO), and PFC maintaining reversible DAC without DVO. We will refer to these algorithms as: PFC-DAC, PFC-RDAC-DVO and PFC-MRDAC, respectively. PFC-DAC and PFC-MRDAC use *forward degree*, breaking ties with *backward degree* (Larrosa & Meseguer 1996) as static variable ordering. PFC-RDAC-DVO uses *minimum domain* breaking ties with *graph degree* as dynamic variable ordering. We do not use DVO with PFC-MRDAC because we observed that it did not give any gain to the algorithm. Values are always selected by increasing IC+DAC. All three algorithms share code and data structures whenever it is possible. Experiments were performed using a Sun Sparc 2 workstation.

Figure 1 reports the average cost required to solve the six problem classes. Since the overhead produced by RDAC and MDAC is consistency check-free, we use CPU-time to compare search effort. As it can be observed, PFC-RDAC improves PFC-DAC in practically all problem classes. The gain grows with problem tightness. PFC-RDAC can be up to 900 times faster than PFC-DAC on the tightest sparse instances. Typical improvement ratios range from 1.5 to 20 for tightness greater than 0.6. Regarding the contribution of the individual improvements, we can state with no doubt that reversible DAC is the main responsible for the gain. Avoiding the repetition of checks associated with DAC, and using DVO have a limited effect that can cause improvement ratios from 1.2 to 2.

Regarding PFC-MRDAC, we observe that maintaining RDAC does only pay off on the tightest instances, and on the most sparse problems. On sparse problems PFC-MRDAC can be from 1.5 to 3 times faster than PFC-RDAC. This fact is understandable since we are using an AC4 based implementation. On loose constraints, lists of support are longer and supports are higher. Thus, propagating a deletion is more costly and is less likely to produce a new DAC contribution. We believe that moving to more elaborated local consistency algorithms (i.e. AC6-7) will increase the range of problems where maintaining RDAC pays off.

Regarding the number of visited nodes, Table 1 contains the average number for each algorithm on the hardest problem class for PFC-DAC. One can observe a decrease of an order of magnitude from PFC-DAC to PFC-RDAC-DVO (two orders for the $\langle 40, 5 \rangle$ class). Besides, from PFC-RDAC-DVO to PFC-MRDAC, the average number of visited nodes is divided by a constant between 2 and 5. Savings in CPU time are not as large as in visited nodes because improved algorithms perform more work per node than PFC-

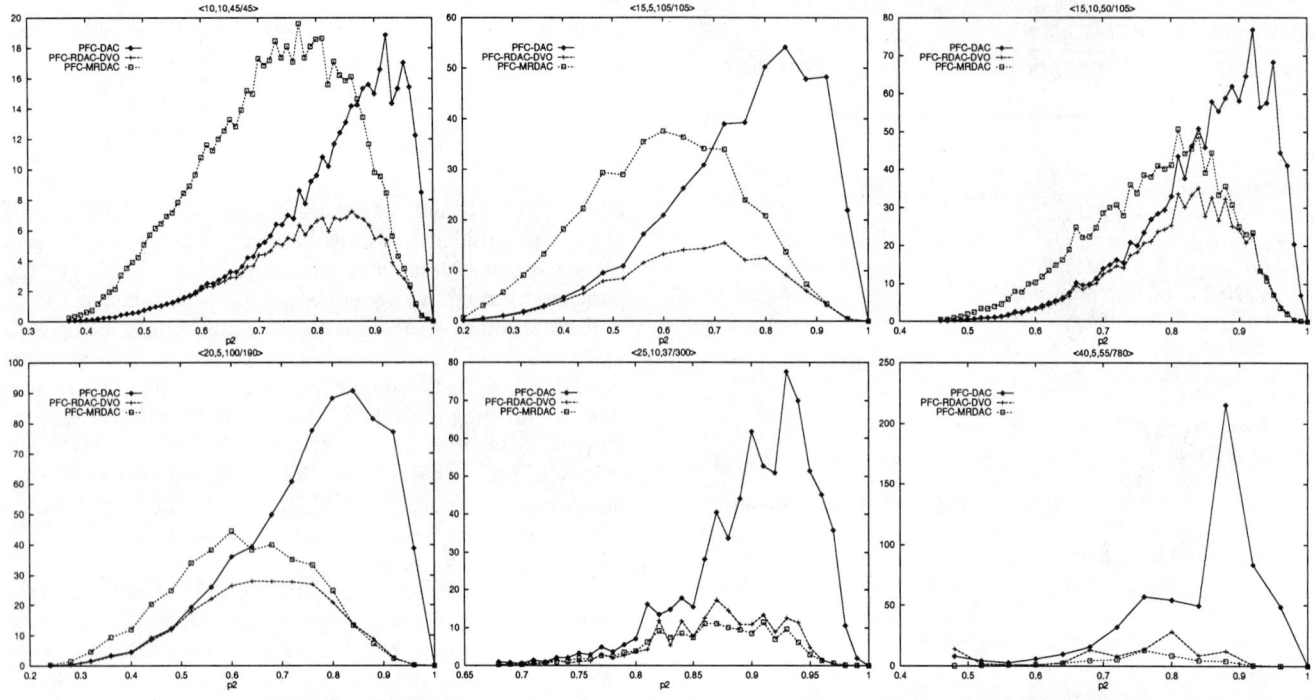

Figure 1: Measure of the cpu-time in various locations of the random CSP space

Random class	PFC DAC	PFC RDAC+DVO	PFC MRDAC
$\langle 10, 10, \frac{45}{45}, \frac{92}{100}\rangle$	191667	26706	12246
$\langle 15, 5, \frac{105}{105}, \frac{21}{25}\rangle$	565664	51241	23889
$\langle 15, 10, \frac{50}{105}, \frac{95}{100}\rangle$	442827	25943	10517
$\langle 20, 5, \frac{100}{190}, \frac{21}{25}\rangle$	748673	67555	24473
$\langle 25, 10, \frac{37}{300}, \frac{93}{100}\rangle$	412160	41672	15158
$\langle 40, 5, \frac{55}{780}, \frac{22}{25}\rangle$	1315303	44346	8287

Table 1: Visited nodes by the three algorithms on the hardest class for PFC-DAC.

DAC.

Conclusion

Several observations may be extracted from this work. Quite surprisingly, we have observed that the introduction of dynamic variable orderings, when it brings something, provides only very minor savings. This contradicts traditional wisdom in classical CSP and further studies are needed to check whether better DVO heuristics can be found.

Finally, the fact that reversible DAC is the improvement that brings the largest savings confirms the importance of the lower bound quality in branch and bound algorithms for Max-CSP. It is our feeling that lower bound quality remains the major issue in complete algorithms for Max-CSP. Considering the simplicity of the greedy optimization algorithm used in this paper for optimizing RDAC, there is probably an opportunity to still improve this lower bound.

References

Bistarelli, S.; Montanari, U.; and Rossi, F. 1995. Constraint solving over semirings. In *Proc. of the 14th IJCAI*.

Dechter, R., and Pearl, J. 1988. Network-based heuristics for constraint-satisfaction problems. *Artificial Intelligence* 34:1–38.

Freuder, E., and Wallace, R. 1992. Partial constraint satisfaction. *Artificial Intelligence* 58:21–70.

Larrosa, J., and Meseguer, P. 1996. Exploiting the use of DAC in Max-CSP. In *Proc. of CP'96*, 308–322.

Larrosa, J., and Meseguer, P. 1998. Partial lazy forward checking for max-csp. In *Proc. ECAI-98*.

Prosser, P. 1994. Binary constraint satisfaction problems: Some are harder than others. In *Proc. of the 11st ECAI*.

Schiex, T.; Fargier, H.; and Verfaillie, G. 1995. Valued constraint satisfaction problems: hard and easy problems. In *Proc. of the 14th IJCAI*, 631–637.

Verfaillie, G.; Lemaître, M.; and Schiex, T. 1996. Russian doll search. In *Proc. of AAAI-96*, 181–187.

Wallace, R. 1995. Directed arc consistency preprocessing. In Meyer, M., ed., *Selected papers from the ECAI-94 Workshop on Constraint Processing*, number 923 in LNCS. Berlin: Springer. 121–137.

Wallace, R. 1996. Enhancements of branch and bound methods for the maximal constraint satisfaction problem. In *Proc. of AAAI-96*, volume 1, 188–195. Portland, OR: AAAI Press/MIT Press.

Branch and Bound Algorithm Selection by Performance Prediction

Lionel Lobjois and Michel Lemaître

ONERA-CERT/DCSD - ENSAE
2, avenue Édouard Belin – BP 4025 – 31055 Toulouse cedex 4 – France
{Lionel.Lobjois,Michel.Lemaitre}@cert.fr

Abstract

We propose a method called *Selection by Performance Prediction* (SPP) which allows one, when faced with a particular problem instance, to select a Branch and Bound algorithm from among several promising ones. This method is based on Knuth's sampling method which estimates the efficiency of a backtrack program on a particular instance by iteratively generating random paths in the search tree. We present a simple adaptation of this estimator in the field of combinatorial optimization problems, more precisely for an extension of the *maximal constraint satisfaction* framework. Experiments both on random and strongly structured instances show that, in most cases, the proposed method is able to select, from a candidate list, the best algorithm for solving a given instance.

Introduction

The Branch and Bound search is a well-known algorithmic schema, widely used for solving combinatorial optimization problems. A lot of specific algorithms can be derived from this general schema. These can differ in many ways. For example, one can use different static or dynamic orderings for variables and values. Likewise, the computation of a lower bound (in the case of minimization) at each branch node is often a compromise between speed and efficiency of the induced cut, and several variants are potentially appropriate. Thus, each algorithm is a combination of several particular features. It is generally difficult to predict the precise behavior of a combinatorial algorithm on a particular instance. In actual practice, one can observe that the range of computation times used by the candidate algorithms to solve a particular instance is often very wide. Faced with a particular instance to be solved, often in a limited time, one must choose an algorithm without being sure of making the most appropriate choice. Bad decisions may lead to unacceptable running times.

Copyright © 1998, American Association for Artificial Intelligence (www.aaai.org). All rights reserved. This work was partially supported by the French Délégation Générale à l'Armement, under contract DRET 94/002 BC 47.
The authors thank Gérard Verfaillie and Thomas Schiex for helpful discussions during this work.

In this paper, we propose a method called *Selection by Performance Prediction* (SPP) to select, for each particular problem instance, the most appropriate Branch and Bound algorithm from among several promising ones. We restrict ourselves to the case of constraint optimization problems expressed in the Valued CSP framework (Schiex, Fargier, & Verfaillie 1995), which is an extension of the *maximal constraint satisfaction* framework, as explained in the next section. The proposed SPP method is based on an old and very simple idea (Knuth 1975) allowing one to statistically estimate the size of a search tree by iterative sampling. It gives surprisingly good results on both strongly structured and random problem instances. Estimating each candidate algorithm on the very instance to be solved is the key to a successful choice.

This paper is organized as follows. We first introduce the VCSP framework and describe Knuth's method of estimation. We show how this estimation can be used for Branch and Bound algorithms. Then we introduce the SPP method, and show some experimental results on both strongly structured and random problem instances. Lastly, after the review of some related works, we state our conclusions and discuss future directions.

Valued CSPs

A Constraint Satisfaction Problem (CSP) instance is defined by a triple (X, D, C), where X is a set of *variables*, D is a set of finite *domains* for the variables, and C is a set of *constraints*. A constraint is defined by a subset of variables on which it holds and by a subset of allowed tuples of values. A *solution* of an instance is a complete assignment — an assignment of values to all of the variables — which satisfies all of the constraints. Many CSP instances are so constrained that no solution exists. In this case, one can search for a solution maximizing the number of satisfied constraints. This is the maximal constraint satisfaction framework introduced by (Freuder & Wallace 1992). This framework can be further generalized by giving a weight or a *valuation* to each constraint, mirroring the importance one gives to its satisfaction. The cost of a complete assignment is the *aggregation* of the valuations of the unsatisfied constraints. We then search for a solution minimizing this cost. This extension of the CSP model is called the Valued CSP (VCSP) framework (Schiex, Fargier, & Verfaillie 1995). In this paper, we only consider Σ-VCSPs, for which the aggregation operator is the ordinary sum. Algorithms for maximal constraint satisfaction (Freuder & Wallace 1992; Larrosa & Meseguer 1996) are easily extended to VCSPs.

Knuth's method of estimation

Knuth's method (Knuth 1975) is based on a statistical estimation of the quantity $\varphi \stackrel{\text{def}}{=} \sum_{x \in \text{nodes}(T)} f(x)$, where T is any tree. Among other quantities this method can estimate the number of nodes in a search tree ($f(x) = 1$), or the total running time ($f(x)$ being the time spent on the node x).

Let $S = \langle x_1, x_2, \ldots \rangle$ be a random path from the root x_1 to a terminal node, in which the successor of each internal node is randomly selected according to a uniform distribution. Let $\hat{\varphi}(S) \stackrel{\text{def}}{=} \sum_{x_i \in S} w(x_i) f(x_i)$, where $w(x_i) \stackrel{\text{def}}{=} \prod_{k=1}^{i-1} d(x_k)$, and $d(x_k)$ is the number of successors of x_k. $\hat{\varphi}$ is an unbiased estimate of φ. This is formally expressed as $\mathbf{E}\hat{\varphi} = \varphi$ (the expected value of the random variable $\hat{\varphi}$ is φ). The variance of $\hat{\varphi}$ is

$$\mathbf{V}\hat{\varphi} = \sum_{x \in \text{nodes}(T)} w(x) \sum_{1 \le i \le j \le d(x)} \left(\varphi(x^{(i)}) - \varphi(x^{(j)}) \right)^2 \quad (1)$$

where $x^{(i)}$ is the ith successor of x, $\varphi(x) = \sum_{y \in \text{nodes}(T_x)} f(y)$, and T_x is the subtree rooted in x. The expression for the variance shows that it can be quite large, all the larger as the tree is unbalanced. Of course, one can get a better estimate of φ by repeatedly sampling the tree. Let $\hat{\varphi}_n$ be the mean of $\hat{\varphi}(S_i)$ over n successive random paths S_i. We still have $\mathbf{E}\hat{\varphi}_n = \varphi$, but the variance is now reduced to $\mathbf{V}\hat{\varphi}_n = \mathbf{V}\hat{\varphi}/n$. When sampling search trees, experiments show that the distribution of $\hat{\varphi}$ cannot be considered as a common one, hence it is difficult to provide a good confidence interval for $\hat{\varphi}$. However, Chebyshev's inequality[1] gives a confidence interval for φ with a probability of error less than $1/c^2$: $\Pr(|\hat{\varphi}_n - \varphi| \ge c\sqrt{\mathbf{V}\hat{\varphi}/n}) < 1/c^2$. In practice $\mathbf{V}\hat{\varphi}$ is unknown and must be estimated from the n random paths S_i using the well-known formula $\hat{\mathbf{V}}\hat{\varphi} = \frac{1}{n-1} \sum_{i=1}^{n} (\varphi(S_i) - \hat{\varphi}_n)^2$.

In his paper, Knuth suggests a refinement called *importance sampling*, in which the successor of a node is selected according to a weighted distribution (instead of a uniform one), the weight of each successor being an estimate of the corresponding $\varphi(x^{(i)})$. Knuth's method has been improved in different ways by (Purdom 1978) and (Chen 1992). These improvements are based on a deep knowledge of the structure of problem instances.

---

[1] It can be used because it does not make any assumption on the actual distribution of the random variable $\hat{\varphi}$.

```
DFBB(ub₀)
    c* ← ub₀
    success ← false
    SEARCH(1)
SEARCH(i)
    if i ≤ nb-variables
    then vᵢ ← VARIABLE-CHOICE(i)
         for each value k in Current-Domain[vᵢ]
             A[vᵢ] ← k
             PROPAGATE(i)
             b ← BOUND(i)
             if b < c* then SEARCH(i + 1)
             UNPROPAGATE(i)
    else success ← true
         A* ← A
         c* ← COST(A)
```

Figure 1: Depth First Branch and Bound search.

In this paper, we choose to keep close to the original and simplest prediction method.

Estimating the Performance of a Branch and Bound Algorithm

In this section, we will show how Knuth's estimation method can be used to predict the running time of a Depth First Branch and Bound algorithm for solving a particular VCSP instance. This prediction is based on the estimation of the number of nodes in the tree developed during the search.

Figure 1 shows the pseudo-code of a Depth First Branch and Bound algorithm. It looks for a complete assignment A^* of minimal cost c^* less than an initial upper bound ub_0. If such an assignment does not exist (because ub_0 is less than or equal to the optimal cost) then the algorithm ends with *success* equal to **false**. The current partial assignment, involving variables $v_1, v_2, \ldots v_i$, is stored in $A[1..i]$. PROPAGATE(i) is a procedure which, like forward-checking, propagates the choices already made for the assigned variables onto the domains of the unassigned ones. This propagation may result in value deletions in the domains of future variables, and thus may improve the subsequent lower bound computation. BOUND(i) returns a lower bound of the cost of any complete extension of the current partial assignment. UNPROPAGATE(i) simply restores the domains.

Figure 2 shows the pseudo-code of the procedure ESTIMATE-NB-NODES(ub_0, n) which estimates the number of nodes that will be developed by the call DFBB(ub_0). The procedure VARIABLE-CHOICE used in both SEARCH (figure 1) and SAMPLE (figure 2) chooses the next variable, using an appropriate heuristic. It should be stressed that the structure of the SAMPLE procedure is simply obtained from the structure of the SEARCH procedure by changing the **for** loop into a single random value choice.

```
ESTIMATE-NB-NODES($ub_0$,n)
    $c^* \leftarrow ub_0$
    $\hat{\varphi}_n \leftarrow 0$
    for $j = 1$ to $n$
        $w \leftarrow 1$
        $\hat{\varphi} \leftarrow 0$
        SAMPLE(1)
        $\hat{\varphi}_n \leftarrow \hat{\varphi}_n + \hat{\varphi}$
    $\hat{\varphi}_n \leftarrow \hat{\varphi}_n/n$
    return $\hat{\varphi}_n$
SAMPLE(i)
    if $i \leq$ nb-variables
    then $v_i \leftarrow$ VARIABLE-CHOICE(i)
        $k \leftarrow$ randomly select a value
            in Current-Domain[$v_i$]
        $A[v_i] \leftarrow k$
        $w \leftarrow w \cdot |$Current-Domain[$v_i$]$|$
        $\hat{\varphi} \leftarrow \hat{\varphi} + w$
        PROPAGATE(i)
        $b \leftarrow$ BOUND(i)
        if $b < c^*$ then SAMPLE($i + 1$)
        UNPROPAGATE(i)
```

Figure 2: Estimating the size of a DFBB search tree through iterative sampling.

```
SPP($\mathcal{I},\mathcal{L},t_\mu,t_s,ub_0$)
    for each $BB_i$ in $\mathcal{L}$
        $\hat{\mu} \leftarrow$ ESTIMATE-TIME-PER-NODE($\mathcal{I},BB_i,t_\mu,ub_0$)
        $\hat{\varphi}_n \leftarrow$ ESTIMATE-NB-NODES($\mathcal{I},BB_i,t_s,ub_0$)
        $time_i \leftarrow \hat{\mu} \cdot \hat{\varphi}_n$
    return $BB_i$ such as $time_i$ is minimal
```

Figure 3: The Selection by Performance Prediction (SPP) method.

As mentioned by Knuth in his paper, "the estimation procedure does not apply directly to branch-and-bound algorithms". To better understand this, one should note that SEARCH updates the current upper bound c^* each time it finds a better complete assignment, thus allowing for a better subsequent pruning of the search tree. On the contrary, SAMPLE never updates its initial upper bound: it estimates the size of a tree which would be generated by a search process in which the upper bound remained constant. Hence, the sampled search tree does not correspond exactly to the actual search tree.

Search efforts between the regular version and the constant upper bound version of a Branch and Bound algorithm can differ tremendously. One extreme case occurs when the initial upper bound is set to infinity: whereas the regular version finds good solutions and consequently prunes its search tree, the constant upper bound version has to explore all complete assignments. On the other hand, if the initial upper bound is less than or equal to the optimal cost, both versions develop exactly the same tree. Eventually, good estimates need low upper bounds. In practice, one can execute an incomplete method like a local search first in order to get a low upper bound of the optimal cost. This upper bound will help the estimation process as well as the resolution itself.

The SAMPLE procedure of figure 2 makes it possible to estimate the size (number of nodes) of the search tree. However, we are in fact more interested in an estimate of the running time. A simple way of estimating this running time is to estimate first the average time μ spent on a node. To do this, we run the target algorithm during a brief interval of time and then deduce an estimate of the average time per node. According to our experiments, such a simple procedure is sufficient to produce reasonable estimates.

Experiments with several instances and algorithms show that the variance of $\hat{\varphi}$ is generally very large. Hence, it seems difficult to produce useful confidence intervals for the number of developed nodes (and hence for the running time). The main contribution of this paper is to show empirically that the SPP method works well in practice despite this huge variance and the difference between sampled and actual search trees.

Selecting the Best Algorithm

In this section, we give a detailed description of the "Selection by Performance Prediction" method (SPP). Given an instance to be solved and a list of promising candidate Branch and Bound algorithms, we would like to select the best possible algorithm from among the candidates, that is, the algorithm which will solve the instance within the shortest time.

The principle of the method is very simple: we estimate the running time of each candidate algorithm on the instance; then we select the algorithm which gives the smallest expected running time. Figure 3 shows a pseudo-code of the proposed SPP method. $\mathcal{I}$ is the instance to be solved. $\mathcal{L}$ is the list of candidate algorithms. t_μ is the time allocated for estimating μ and t_s the time for estimating the size of each search tree. ub_0 is the initial upper bound used both for the actual search and for the estimation process.

ESTIMATE-TIME-PER-NODE($\mathcal{I},BB_i,t_\mu,ub_0$) runs the algorithm BB_i for a time t_μ on the instance $\mathcal{I}$ using ub_0 as initial upper bound. It returns an estimate $\hat{\mu}$ of the average running time per node for BB_i. ESTIMATE-NB-NODES($\mathcal{I},BB_i,t_s,ub_0$) samples during a time t_s the tree developed by the algorithm BB_i using ub_0 as constant upper bound. It returns the mean value $\hat{\varphi}_n$ of the n random paths that have been generated. ESTIMATE-NB-NODES is similar to ESTIMATE-NB-NODES of figure 1 (however, while SAMPLE in figure 2 is given a fixed n, ESTIMATE-NB-NODES is given instead a time limit).

Although the SPP method is very simple, it works surprisingly well in practice. Two reasons may explain this success. First, the estimator is unbiased: it produces on average good estimates despite a huge variance. Second, the method does not depend on absolute performance predictions: since it compares the constant upper bound version of each candidate algorithm, pessimistic estimates due to a poor upper bound are pessimistic for all algorithms.

Experiments

In this section, we describe some experiments of the SPP method both on random and strongly structured instances[2]. We selected four well known algorithms as candidates. Good descriptions of these algorithms can be found in (Freuder & Wallace 1992), (Wallace 1994) and (Larrosa & Meseguer 1996). BB_1 is a *forward-checking* (P-EFC3) with the widely used dynamic variable ordering: *minimum current domain* as first heuristic and *decreasing degree* to break ties. Its value ordering is *increasing IC* (Freuder & Wallace 1992). BB_2, BB_3 and BB_4 are *forward-checking* with *Directed Arc Consistency Counts* for lower bound computation (P-EFC3+DAC2 described in (Larrosa & Meseguer 1996)). They all use *increasing IC + DAC* as value ordering but they differ on their static variable ordering: BB_2 uses *decreasing forward degree* (FD in (Larrosa & Meseguer 1996)) with *max-cardinality* (Tsang 1993, p 179) as second criteria, BB_3 uses *minimum width* (Tsang 1993, p 164) and BB_4 uses *decreasing degree*. Our experience on several problems shows that these algorithms appear to be among the best Branch and Bound algorithms available today for strongly structured instances.

Since we are mainly interested in solving realistic problems, we chose for these experiments the field of Radio Link Frequency Assignment Problems (RLFAP) (Cabon *et al.* 1998). We used sub-instances of CELAR instances 6 and 7 which are probably the two most difficult instances of the set[3]. The next table summarizes some properties of these sub-instances:

name	# of variables	# of values	# of constraints	optimal cost
$\mathcal{I}_1$	16	44	207	159
$\mathcal{I}_2$	14	44	300	2669
$\mathcal{I}_3$	16	44	188	10310

In the following experiments, we address three different cases depending on the initial upper bound. The first case corresponds to the common situation in which ub_0 is an upper bound of the optimal cost provided by a simple local search. In the second case, ub_0 is the optimal cost itself. Such a situation may occur when the optimal cost is easily found by a local search but there is no proof of its optimality. In the last case, we try to prove that ub_0 is a lower bound of the optimal cost. This may be helpful to bound the optimal cost when it is impracticable (de Givry & Verfaillie 1997).

---

[2] All experiments have been done on a SUN Sparc5 with 64 Mo of RAM using CMU Common Lisp.

[3] The original instances and the sub-instances are available at ftp://ftp.cs.unh.edu/pub/csp/archive/code/benchmarks/FullRLFAP.tgz.

We ran SPP 5000 times on each instance using $\mathcal{L}=\{BB_1, BB_2, BB_3, BB_4\}$, $t_\mu = 1$ second and $t_s = 3$ seconds. In order to check predictions we then ran the complete algorithms using upper bounds given to SPP. The next table shows, for each instance and each algorithm, the running time in seconds of the complete search using the given upper bound and nbc, the number of times the algorithm was selected. For instance, algorithm BB_3 solved instance $\mathcal{I}_1$ to optimality in 377 seconds and was selected 4660 times among the 5000 runs of SPP:

	$\mathcal{I}_1$		$\mathcal{I}_2$		$\mathcal{I}_3$	
ub_0	159		2000		10413	
opt	159		2669		10310	
	time	nbc	time	nbc	time	nbc
BB_1	580000[6]	0	1200	4939	2116	441
BB_2	1961	170	18149	31	3200	229
BB_3	377	4660	40299	0	2162	881
BB_4	1015	170	18271	30	1010	3449

These experimental results are very encouraging: for all instances, SPP is able to find the best algorithm in the majority of runs. When it does not select the best algorithm, it generally selects a good one and rarely the worst. As could be guessed, SPP is unable to distinguish two algorithms which have close running times. More generally, the more the actual running times differ, the easier it is for SPP to select the best algorithm.

To give a more precise idea of the quality of the SPP method, we propose to compare it with two alternative approaches in terms of expected running time. The first approach, RANDOM, makes a random choice in the list of the candidate algorithms. When several algorithms seem to be suitable for the instance, one can pick one of them at random. The expected running time one obtains using this approach is simply the mean of the four running times. The second approach, INTERLEAVED, runs all the candidate algorithms in an interleaved way on the same processor as proposed in (Huberman, Lukose, & Hogg 1997; Gomes & Selman 1997). The first algorithm which finishes the search stops the others. For this approach, the expected running time is four times the running time of the best algorithm. We approximated the expected running time one obtains using SPP with the simple formula $\sum nbc_i \cdot t_i / \sum nbc_i$, where nbc_i is the number of times SPP selects algorithm BB_i and t_i is the actual running time of the complete solving using BB_i.

Figure 4 compares the running times of each algorithm and the expected running time using RANDOM, INTERLEAVED and SPP on our three instances. For SPP, we added the cost of the estimation process which is $4 \cdot (1+3) = 16$ seconds to the expected running time (this appears in a darker grey).

According to these experiments, SPP definitely outperforms RANDOM and INTERLEAVED approaches on these instances. In each case, the expected running

---

[6] This time is not the actual running time of BB_1 on $\mathcal{I}_1$, but an estimation using $t_\mu = 3$ minutes and $t_s = 1$ hour.

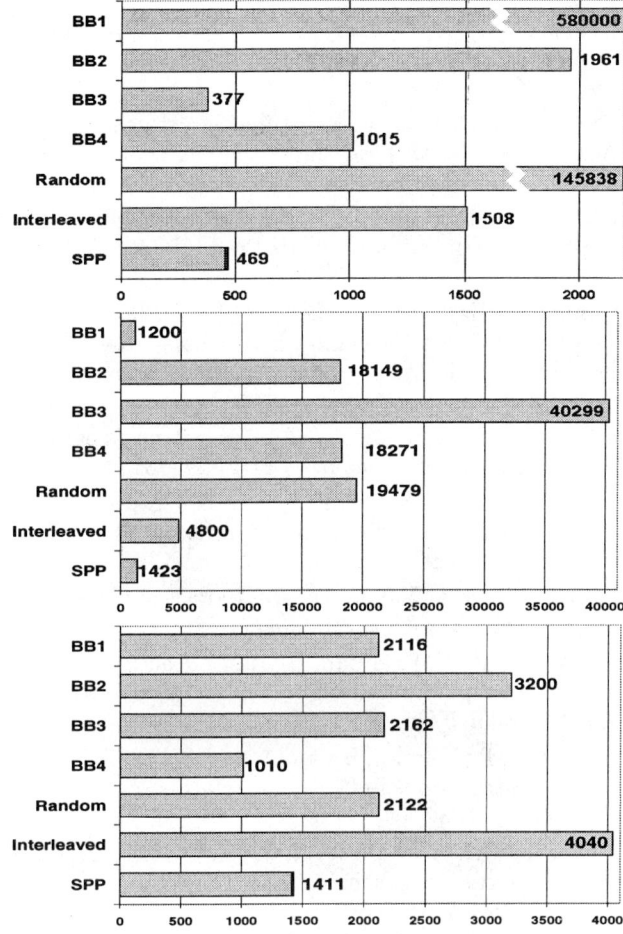

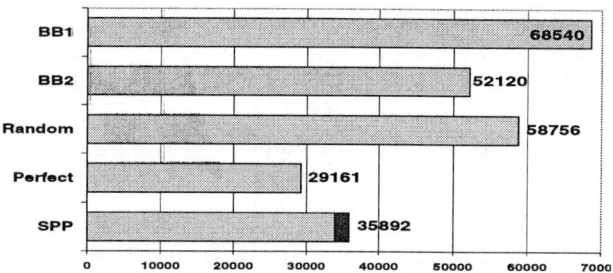

Figure 5: Cumulated running times on 238 random instances ($t_\mu = 1$, $t_s = 3$)

Figure 4: Expected running times using different approaches when solving instances $\mathcal{I}_1$, $\mathcal{I}_2$ and $\mathcal{I}_3$.

time using SPP is very close to the running time of the best algorithm: wrong selections have a small influence on the expected running time since they occur rarely.

To validate our approach on more instances, we experimented with the SPP method on a set of random instances. The goal of the experiment was to solve sequentially all instances of the set as quickly as possible. For this experiment, we chose to tackle the case where there are only two promising candidates for solving the whole set, neither algorithm clearly dominating the other. We restricted $\mathcal{L}$ to $\{BB_1, BB_2\}$ and generated 238 instances according to the model described in (Smith 1994) modified to allow valued constraints. These instances contain 20 variables and 10 values per variable; the graph connectivity is 50% and the tightness of each constraint is 90%. Constraints are uniformly valued in the set $\{1, 10, 100, 1000, 100000\}$. With such parameters, both algorithms have nearly equal chances to be the best.

For each instance, we first ran a simple Hill-Climbing to find an upper bound. Then we ran BB_1 and BB_2 on each instance with the given upper bound and recorded their running times: 103 instances were best solved by BB_1 as opposed to 135 for BB_2. Finally, we used approaches RANDOM and SPP to select an algorithm for each instance. Figure 5 shows the cumulated running times using, for each instance, algorithm BB_1, BB_2, the one selected by RANDOM, and the one selected by SPP[4]. To emphasize the performance of the SPP method, we also show the cumulated running times one would obtain using the hypothetical perfect selection method (a method which could choose the best algorithm for each instance).

One important point stressed by this last experiment is that it is better to use the algorithm selected by the SPP method for each instance, than to use the best algorithm on average for all instances. As a matter of fact, large experiments on a class of instances may indicate which algorithm is the best on average for this class. Nevertheless, our experimental results clearly show that each instance has to be solved with an appropriate algorithm. Moreover, SPP seems to be a very accurate selecting method since it is close to a perfect one, at least on this set of instances.

To summarize, experimental results confirm the interest of the SPP method. It allows one to use an appropriate algorithm, avoiding exceptional behaviors which can lead to unacceptable running times. Hence, it may save great amounts of time even when the best algorithm for the class of the instance is known.

Related work

(Bailleux & Chabrier 1996) estimate the number of solutions of constraint satisfaction problem instances by iterative sampling of the search tree.

In the context of a telescope scheduling application, (Bresina, Drummond, & Swanson 1995) use Knuth's sampling method to estimate the number of solutions which satisfy all hard constraints. But the main use of the sampling method is for statistically characterizing scheduling problems and the performance of schedulers. A "quality density function" provides a background against which schedulers can be evaluated.

---

[4] For SPP we added its running time which is $2 \cdot (1+3) = 8$ seconds per instance.

Works mentioned below do not make use of Knuth's estimator, but are related to this work in some way.

An adaptive method, aiming at automatically switching to good algorithms, has been proposed by (Borret, Tsang, & Walsh 1996). Despite similar goals, the adaptive method and the sampling method are different. The former one is based on a thrashing prediction computed during the regular execution of an algorithm. When such a thrashing is likely to occur, another algorithm is tried sequentially. Conversely, the SPP method, once its choice made, runs only one algorithm: the one which has the best chance of success.

Heading in yet a different direction, both (Gomes, Selman, & Crato 1997) and (Rish & Frost 1997) show that, in the case of random unsatisfiable CSPs, the *lognormal* distribution is a good approximation of the distribution of computational effort required by backtracking algorithms. We, too, observed a "heavy-tailed" distribution for the random variable $\hat{\varphi}$, but were unable to identify it. Note that the distribution of $\hat{\varphi}$ on a particular instance and the distribution of φ on a *class* of instances are two different distributions.

Algorithm portfolio design (Huberman, Lukose, & Hogg 1997; Gomes & Selman 1997) aims at combining several algorithms by running them in parallel or by interleaving them on a single processor.

(Minton 1996) addresses the problem of specializing general constraint satisfaction algorithms and heuristics for a particular application.

Conclusion and future work

We have proposed a simple method for selecting a Branch and Bound algorithm from among a set of promising ones. It is based on the estimation of the running times of those algorithms on the particular instance to be solved. We provided experimental results showing that the SPP method is a cheap and effective selection method. This efficient performance has been empirically demonstrated, in the field of constraint optimization problems, both on random and strongly structured problem instances.

Clearly, improvements on the proposed method must be sought in the estimation process itself. A better knowledge of the structure of problems to be solved would probably make it possible to better estimate running times. Improvements like *importance sampling* (Knuth 1975), *partial backtracking* (Purdom 1978) or *heuristic sampling* (Chen 1992) merit further investigations into the field of constraint optimization problems.

There is no doubt that this method can also be applied to inconsistent CSP instances, because a proof of inconsistency implies a complete search as well. Besides, it would be interesting to investigate the application of the proposed method to consistent CSP instances.

Experimental results clearly show that each instance is best solved with a particular algorithm. This confirms the interest of adapting general algorithms to suit each instance.

References

Bailleux, O., and Chabrier, J. 1996. Approximate Resolution of Hard Numbering Problems. In *Proc. AAAI-96*.

Borret, J. E.; Tsang, E. P. K.; and Walsh, N. R. 1996. Adaptive Constraint Satisfaction : The Quickest First Principle. In *Proc. ECAI-96*, 160–164.

Bresina, J.; Drummond, M.; and Swanson, K. 1995. Expected Solution Quality. In *Proc. IJCAI-95*, 1583–1590.

Cabon, B.; de Givry, S.; Lobjois, L.; Schiex, T.; and Warners, J. 1998. Benchmark Problems: Radio Link Frequency Assignment. *To appear in Constraints*.

Chen, P. 1992. Heuristic Sampling: a Method for Predicting the Performance of Tree Searching Programs. *SIAM Journal on Computing* 21(2):295–315.

de Givry, S., and Verfaillie, G. 1997. Optimum Anytime Bounding for Constraint Optimization Problems. In *Proc. AAAI-97*.

Freuder, E., and Wallace, R. 1992. Partial Constraint Satisfaction. *Artificial Intelligence* 58:21–70.

Gomes, C. P., and Selman, B. 1997. Practical aspects of algorithm portfolio design. In *Proc. of Third ILOG International Users Meeting*.

Gomes, C. P.; Selman, B.; and Crato, N. 1997. Heavy-Tailed Distributions in Combinatorial Search. In *Proc. CP-97*, 121–135.

Huberman, B. A.; Lukose, R. M.; and Hogg, T. 1997. An economics approach to hard computational problems. *Science* 275:51–54.

Knuth, D. 1975. Estimating the Efficiency of Backtrack Programs. *Mathematics of Computation* 29(129):121–136.

Larrosa, J., and Meseguer, P. 1996. Expoiting the Use of DAC in MAX-CSP. In *Proc. CP-96*, 308–322.

Minton, S. 1996. Automatically Configuring Constraint Satisfaction Programs : A Case Study. *Constraints* 1:7–43.

Purdom, P. 1978. Tree Size by Partial Backtracking. *SIAM Journal on Computing* 7(4):481–491.

Rish, I., and Frost, D. 1997. Statistical Analysis of Backtracking on Inconsistent CSPs. In *Proc. CP-97*, 150–162.

Schiex, T.; Fargier, H.; and Verfaillie, G. 1995. Valued Constraint Satisfaction Problems : Hard and Easy Problems. In *Proc. IJCAI-95*, 631–637.

Smith, B. 1994. Phase Transition and the Mushy Region in Constraint Satisfaction Problems. In *Proc. ECAI-94*, 100–104.

Tsang, E. 1993. *Foundations of Constraint Satisfaction*. London: Academic Press Ltd.

Wallace, R. 1994. Directed Arc Consistency Preprocessing. In *Proc. of the ECAI-94* Constraint Processing *workshop (LNCS 923)*. Springer. 121–137.

A fast algorithm for the bound consistency of alldiff constraints

Jean-Francois Puget
ILOG
9 Av. verdun
94253 Gentilly FRANCE
puget@ilog.fr

Abstract

Some n-ary constraints such as the alldiff constraints arise naturally in real life constraint satisfaction problems (CSP). General purpose filtering algorithms could be applied to such constraints. By taking the semantics of the constraint into account, it is possible to design more efficient filtering algorithms. When the domains of the variables are totally ordered (e.g. all values are integers), then filtering based on bound consistency may be very useful. We present in this paper a filtering algorithm for the alldiff constraint based on bound consistency whose running time complexity is very low. More precisely, for a constraint involving n variables, the time complexity of the algorithm is $O(nlog(n))$ which improves previously published results. The implementation of this algorithm is discussed, and we give some experimental results that prove its practical utility.

1. Introduction

Constraint programming systems are now routinely used to solve complex combinatorial problems in a wide variety of industries. These systems use filtering algorithms based on arc-consistency or bound consistency as subroutines. In real life CSP, n-ary constraints such as the alldiff constraint arise naturally. Although general purpose algorithms could be used, more efficient algorithms have been devised in the past years. These algorithm exploit the mathematical structure of the constraints. For instance Regin [5] proposed to apply graph theory for filtering the alldiff constraint.

In scheduling or time tabling problems, variables representing starting time of activities take their values in an ordered domain: the set of dates, usually represented by a number. In such problems, filtering based on the notion of bound consistency are very useful. In that case, domains are represented by intervals, and the purpose of filtering is to tighten the bounds of these intervals.

Copyright(c) 1998, American Association for Artificial Intelligence (www.aaai.org). All rights reserved.

The purpose of this paper is to propose a new bound consistency algorithm for one of the most widely used constraint, namely the alldiff constraint. This constraint involves a set of variables x_i, and simply states that the x_i are pairwise different. In other words, the same value cannot be assigned to two variables x_i and x_j, for any pair i,j. This constraint arises naturally in a wide variety of problems, ranging from puzzles (the n queens problem) to assignment problems, scheduling problems and time tabling problems.

More complex examples will be presented later on, but for the sake of clarity, let us consider a very simple time tabling problem, where a set of speeches must be scheduled during one day. Each speech lasts exactly one hour including questions, and only one conference room is available. Moreover, each speaker has other commitments, hence each speaker can only assist a fraction of the day, defined by an earliest and a latest possible time slot. Table 1 gives a particular instance of the problem.

Speaker	min	max
John	3	6
Mary	3	4
Greg	2	5
Susan	2	4
Marc	3	4
Helen	1	6

Table 1. A time tabling problem with 6 time slots.

This problem can easily be encoded as a CSP. We create one variable per speaker, whose value will be the period where he speaks. The initial domains of the variables are the availability interval for the speakers. Since two speeches cannot be held at the same time in the same conference room, the period for two different speakers must be different. The problem can thus be encoded as follows:

$x_1 \in [3,6], x_2 \in [3,4], x_3 \in [2,5], x_4 \in [2,4], x_5 \in [3,4], x_6 \in [1,6], alldiff(x_1, x_2, x_3, x_4, x_5, x_6)$

In this particular example, our algorithm deduces that in all solutions to this problem, x_1 must be assigned to 6, x_2 to 3 or 4, x_3 to 5, x_4 to 2, x_5 to 3 or 4, and x_6 to 1. Hence, the organizers of this event can tell John he will speak at 6, and that Mary can only chose between 3 and 4, for instance. A more realistic time tabling problem involves more than one constraint of course, but this example is sufficient for explaining our algorithm.

A number of filtering algorithms have been proposed for the alldiff constraint. The simplest approach is to consider the alldiff constraint as a set of $n(n+1)/2$ binary constraints: $\forall i < j, x_i \neq x_j$

It can easily be shown that applying arc consistency to this set of binary constraints amounts to apply the following inference rule: if x_i is assigned to a given value a, remove a from the domains of the other variables. This filtering is strong enough to solve easy problems such as the nqueens problem (see section 6). However, this filtering does no deductions in our time tabling example. Moreover, this simple filtering algorithm does not even check the satisfiability of the constraint. For instance, it does not reduce any domains in the following inconsistent problem.

$y_1 \in [1,2], y_2 \in [1,2], y_3 \in [1,2], alldiff(y_1, y_2, y_3)$

Following that remark, several researchers have proposed global filtering algorithms for the alldiff constraint. Regin proposed a graph theoretic approach the computes the arc consistency for the alldiff constraint in $O(n^{2.5})$ [5]. Leconte has proposed an algorithm that runs in $O(n^2)$[3]. This algorithm computes a consistency stronger than bound consistency, but weaker than arc-consistency. Both algorithms deduce the unfeasibility of the previous example, and make the correct deductions in our time tabling example.

We propose an algorithm that computes the bound consistency for the alldiff constraint running in $O(nlog(n))$ time, which improves the $O(n^2)$ complexity of Leconte's algorithm.

When the domains of all the variables appearing in an alldiff constraint are a subset of the interval $[1, n]$, we say that we have a permutation constraint. Bleuzen Guernalec and Colmerauer [1] have recently published an $O(nlog(n))$ algorithm for computing the bound consistency of the permutation constraint. Their algorithm however is not applicable to the general case of the alldiff constraint, contrarily to our work.

The rest of this paper is organized as follows. Section 2 contains a formalization of bound consistency, and the main theoretical result we use, namely Hall's theorem, is introduced. Section 3 presents the derivation of a simple $O(n^3)$ bound consistency algorithm. Using a mathematical property of the alldiff constraint, we derive an $O(n^2)$ algorithm in section 4. Section 5 shows how the previous algorithm can be modified in order to run in $O(nlog(n))$, which is the main contribution of the paper. Section 6 discusses the implementation of this algorithm, and provides experimental results that show its practical usefulness. We conclude by discussing some future directions of research.

2. Theoretical analysis

We will adopt the standard notations of constraint satisfaction problems (CSP). A CSP is defined by a set of variables x_i, a domain $\mathcal{D}$ and a set of constraints $\mathcal{C}$. A finite subset of $\mathcal{D}$ is associated to each variable x_i. This set is called the domain of the variable, and is noted $dom(x_i)$. A constraint c on the variables x_i is defined by a subset of the cartesian product $dom(x_1) \times ... \times dom(x_n)$, representing the set of admissible tuples. Finding a solution to a CSP amounts to select one value for each variable in its domain such that all constraints hold.

We will further assume that $\mathcal{D}$ is totally ordered. For instance D can represent the set of integers. In such a case, we define for each variable x_i its minimum value $min(x_i)$ and its maximum value $max(x_i)$. These values are called *the bounds* of the variable.

We will use the following definition for bound consistency: the constraint is bound consistent, if given any variable, each of its bound can be extended to a tuple satisfying the constraint:

Bound consistency A constraint $c(x_1, x_2, ..., x_n)$ is bound consistent iff for each variable x_i : $\forall a_i \in \{min(x_i), max(x_i)\}, \forall j \neq i, \exists a_j \in [min(x_j), max(x_j)], c(a_1, a_2, ..., a_n)$

For instance, our time tabling example is not bound consistent. Indeed, the min for x_1 is 1, and no solutions exists for $x_1 = 1$.

The following domains are bound consistent for the timetable example:

$x_1 = 6, x_2 \in [3,4], x_3 = 5, x_4 = 3, x_5 \in [3,4], x_6 = 1$

The definition above can be used to derive a bound consistency algorithm. However, the complexity of such an algorithm would be exponential in the number of variables appearing in the constraint.

A much faster algorithm is possible using some properties of the constraint we want to filter. Consider any set K of variables. We note by $\#(K)$ the cardinality of K, and $dom(K)$ the union of the domains of the variables in K: $dom(K) = \cup_{x \in K} dom(x)$. Since each variable in K will take one value, we need at least $\#(K)$ values for all the variables in K. In other words, if $\#(K) > \#(dom(K))$, then no solution can be found where all variables in K are assigned to different values. P. Hall [2] proved that this was a necessary and sufficient condition for the existence of a solution. The following corollary of his theorem can be stated in our setting.

Corollary to Hall's theorem: The constraint $alldiff(x_1, \ldots, x_n)$ has a solution if and only if there is no subset $K \subseteq \{x_1, \ldots, x_n\}$ such that $\#(K) > \#(dom(K))$.

If we look back at example 2, consider the set $K = \{y_1, y_2, y_3\}$. We have that dom(K)=$\{1,2\}$, hence $\#(K) > \#(dom(K))$, which proves that the problem has no solution.

Good filtering algorithms can be derived from Hall theorem. The main idea is the following. If there exists a set K such that $\#(K) = \#(dom(K))$, then we know that any assignment of the variables in K will use all the values in $dom(K)$. Hence these values are not possible for the variables not in K.

For instance, consider the set $K = \{x_2, x_4, x_5\}$ in our time tabling example. The domains of the variables in K are $[3,4], [2,4], [3,4]$, hence dom(K) = $\{2,3,4\}$. Then $\#(K) = \#dom(K)$, which implies that the values $\{2,3,4\}$ are not possible for the variables x_1, x_3 and x_6. Hence x_3 must be assigned to 5, and x_1 must be at least 5 for instance. Considering the set $K`=\{x_2,x_5\}$, we deduce that the values $\{3,4\}$ are not possible for x_1, x_3, x_4, x_6, hence x_4 is assigned to 2.

As we are mainly interested in intervals, let us introduce the following.

Definition: Hall Interval Given a constraint $alldiff(x_1, \ldots, x_n)$, and an interval I, let $vars(I)$ be the set of variables x_i such that $dom(x_i) \subseteq I$. We say that I is a Hall interval iff $\#(I) = \#(vars(I))$

In our time tabling example, the interval $[3,4]$ is a Hall interval, as it contains two variables x_2 and x_5.

Proposition 2: Given n variables, the number of Hall intervals can be at least n^2.

Proof: consider the following example:
$\forall i, 0 \leq i \leq n, dom(x_i) = [i-n, 0]$ $\forall i, n < i \leq 2n, dom(x_i) = [0, i-n]$

Then, any interval $I_{i,j} = [i-n, j-n]$ is a Hall interval. Indeed, $I_{i,j}$ contains the domains of all the variables $x_i, x_{i+1}, ..., x_j$, i. e. it contains $j-i+1$ variables. Its width is also $j-i+1$.

We can state the following result.

Proposition 3: The constraint $alldiff(x_1, \ldots, x_n)$ where no $dom(x_i)$ is empty is bound-consistent iff, for each interval I, $\#(vars(I)) \leq \#(I)$, and for each Hall interval I, $dom(x_i) \subseteq I$ or $\{min(x_i), max(x_i)\} \cap I = \emptyset$.

Proof: Let I be a Hall interval, and x_i a variable s.t. $dom(x_i)$ is not included in I. Suppose the constraint is bound consistent. By definition the constraint where $dom(x_i)$ is replaced by $min(x_i)$ has a solution. Applying Hall theorem to the set $vars(I)$ results immediately in $min(x_i) \notin I$. For the same reason, $max(x_i) \notin I$. Conversely, suppose that $min(x_i) \in I$ and the $dom(x_i)$ is not included in I. We have that $\#(I) = \#(vars(I))$. If $dom(x_i)$ is replaced by $min(x_i)$, $vars(I)$ is augmented with x_i, resulting in $\#(I) < \#(vars(I))$. From Hall theorem, this means that the new constraint has no solution. A similar reasoning with $max(x_i)$ concludes the proof.

Computing bound consistent domains can in fact be done in two passes. The algorithm that compute new min is applied twice: first to the original problem, resulting into new min bounds, second to the problem where variables are replaced by their inverse, deducing max bounds.

For instance, computing the max of all the variables in the time tabling example can be done by computing the min bounds of the following problem, obtained by replacing each x_i by its inverse z_i:
$\forall i, x_i = -z_i, z_1 \in [-6, -3], z_2, z_5 \in [-4, -3], z_3 \in [-5, -2], z_4 \in [-4, -2], z_5 \in [-4, -3], z_6 \in [-6, -1], alldiff(z_1, z_2, z_3, z_4, z_5, z_6)$

From this, our algorithm will compute the following new min for the variables z_i: $z_4 \geq -2$, $z_5 \geq -3$, $z_6 \geq -1$. This translates into the following new max for the variables x_i: $x_4 \leq 2$, $x_5 \leq 3$, $x_6 \leq 1$.

From now on, we will only consider the problem of updating the min bounds.

3. A $O(n^3)$ bound consistency algorithm

Using the results of the preceding section, a naive bound consistency algorithm can easily be devised. For all min ranging over minimal values of all variables, and for all max ranging over maximal values of all variables, consider the interval $I = [min, max]$. If $\#(I) < \#(vars(I))$, there is no solution. If I is a Hall interval, update the bounds that have to be changed.

At each loop, the algorithm treats one variable $x[i]$. The algorithm also maintains for each variable $x[j]$ s.t. $j < i$ a number $u^i[j]$ defined as follows:
$u^i[j] = min[j] + \#(\{k | k < i, min[k] \geq min[j]\}) - 1$
The algorithm computes the u^i numbers incrementally using the following relation:
$u^i[j] = u^{i-1}[j] + Bool(min[i] \geq min[j])$
where $Bool(exp)$ is equal to 1 if exp is true.

Proposition 4: : With the above notation, if $u^i[j] = max[i]$ then the interval $I = [min[j], max[i]]$ is a Hall interval.

Proof: The width of I is $\#(I) = max[i] - min[j] + 1$. The number of variables included in I is
$\#(\{k | max[k] \leq max[i], min[k] \geq min[j]\})$
which is greater than or equal to
$\#(\{k | k < i, min[k] \geq min[j]\})$
which is equal to $u[j] + 1 - min[j]$. If $u[j] = max[i]$ then the above number is equal to $\#(I)$ which concludes the proof.

```
% x is an array containing the variables
% u, min and max are arrays of integers
begin
    Sort(x) %in ascending max order
    for i=1 to n do
        min[i] = min(x[i])
        max[i] = max(x[i])
    for i=1 to n do
        Insert(i)
end
Insert(i)
    u[i] ← min[i]
    for j=1 to i-1 do
        if min[j] < min[i] then
            u[j] ← u[j] + 1
            if u[j] > max[i] then Failure
            if u[j] = max[i] then
                IncrMin(min[j],max[i],i)
        else  u[i] ← u[i] + 1
    if u[i] > max[i] then Failure
    if u[i] = max[i] then  IncrMin(min[i],max[i],i)
IncrMin(a,b,i)  % [a,b] is a Hall interval
    for j=i+1 to n do
        if min[j] ≥ a then post x[j] ≥ b+1
```

Algorithm 1: $O(n^3)$ filtering

For each such Hall interval, the algorithm updates the variables $x[j]$ with $j > i$.

In order to obtain what Leconte's algorithm computes, it is sufficient to change the function INCR-MIN(a,b,i) : remove $[a,b]$ from the domains of the variables not included in $[a,b]$. Clearly, this is stronger than bound consistency. Note also that Leconte's is more clever than this one, as it runs in $O(n^2)$.

Let's see how this algorithm behaves on the time tabling example. The first step is to sort the variables in ascending order of maximum, yielding $x[1] = x_2, x[2] = x_4, x[3] = x_5, x[4] = x_3, x[5] = x_1, x[6] = x_6$
Then the algorithm loops over these variables as follows.

INSERT(1)
max[1] ← $max(x_2) = 4$
min[1] ← $min(x_2) = 3$
u[1] ← 3
  INSERT(2)
max[2] ← $max(x_4) = 4$
min[2] ← $min(x_4) = 2$
u[2] ← 2
min[1] ≥ min[2] hence u[2] ← 3
  INSERT(3)
max[3] ← $max(x_5) = 4$
min[3] = ← $min(x_5) = 3$
u[3] ← 3

min[1] ≥ min[3] hence u[3] ← 4
Since u[3] = max[3], calls INCRMIN($3,4,3$)
which posts $x_1 ≥ 5$
min[2] < min[3] hence u[2] ← 4
Since u[2] = max[3], calls INCRMIN($2,4,3$)
which posts $x_1 ≥ 5$
and $x_3 ≥ 5$
  INSERT(4)
max[4] ← 5
u[4] ← 2
min[1] ≥ min[4] hence u[4] ← 3
min[2] ≥ min[4] hence u[4] ← 4
min[3] ≥ min[4] hence u[4] ← 5
since u[4]=max[4], call INCRMIN($2,5,4$)
which posts $x_1 ≥ 6$

Insert5 and Insert6
no more calls to INCRMIN .

4. A $O(n^2)$ bound consistency algorithm

Note that after proposition 2, any algorithm that loops over all Hall intervals has a complexity of at least $O(n^2 \times t(update))$.

It is in fact possible to update the minimum of all variables without examining all Hall intervals. Let's look again at our time tabling example. During the execution of INSERT(3), the algorithm discovers two Hall intervals, [2,4] and [3,4] corresponding to the sets of variables $\{x_2, x_5\}$, and $\{x_2, x_4, x_5\}$. We can observe that the updates due to the smaller one ($x_1 ≥ 5$) are contained in the updates of the largest one ($x_1 ≥ 5$ and $x_3 ≥ 5$). This is formalized as follows.

Proposition 5: With the notations of algorithm 1, if $[a,b]$ and $[a',b]$ are two Hall intervals such that $a < a'$, then INCRMIN(a',b,i) does not need to be called.

Proof: The variables updated by the call to INCRMIN(a',b,i) are the variables $x[j]$ such that $i+1 ≤ j ≤ n, min[j] ≥ a'$. The variables updated by the call to INCRMIN(a,b,i) are the variables $x[j]$ such that $i+1 ≤ j ≤ n, min[j] ≥ a$, which contains the previous set, since $a' ≥ a$.

The revised version of the INSERT function presented in algorithm 2 computes the largest Hall interval ending with $max[i]$ before calling the function INCRMIN

The algorithm obtained by replacing INSERT by INSERT2 runs in $O(n^2)$ time. Indeed, The function INSERT2 is called n times. In each call, the variables with index j smaller than i are visited once, whereas the variables with index j greater than i are visited at most once, when INCRMIN is called.

The behavior of algorithm 2 on the time tabling example is the same as for algorithm 1, except that INCRMIN is called at most once per call to INSERT2 in the main loop.

INSERT2(i)
  $u[i] \leftarrow min[i]$
  $bestMin \leftarrow n+1$
  for $j=1$ to $i-1$ do
    if $min[j] < min[i]$ then
      $u[j] \leftarrow u[j]+1$
      if $u[j] > max[i]$ then Failure
      if $u[j] = max[i]$ and $min[j] < bestMin$ then
        $bestMin \leftarrow min[j]$
    else $u[i] \leftarrow u[i]+1$

  if $u[j] > max[i]$ then Failure
  if $u[i] = max[i]$ and $min[i] < bestMin$ then
    $bestMin \leftarrow min[i]$

  if $bestIndex \leq n$ then
    INCRMIN($bestMin, max[i], i$)

Algorithm 2: $O(n^2)$ filtering

5. A $O(nLog(n))$ algorithm

The previous algorithm can still be improved. The main loop of the algorithm is unchanged, i.e. the variables are processed in ascending order of max, but the internals are changed.

% x is an array containing the variables
% u, rank, min and max are arrays of integers
begin
  SORT(x) % ascending max
  fill in min and max
  RANK(x)
  for $i=1$ to n do
    EXTRACT($x[i]$)
    INSERT3($x[i]$)
end

Algorithm 3: $O(nlog(n))$ filtering

The structure of the algorithm is similar to that of algorithm 2. it uses two main functions, INSERT3 and INCRMIN3 that are revised versions of INSERT2 and INCRMIN respectively.

After sorting the array x and filling the arrays min and max as before, the algorithm computes the rank of each variable, in the function RANK. This function sorts a copy of x in ascending order of min, then associates to each variable its rank in that ordering. The role of this rank will be explained later.

Then, we find the same main loop. The variables are processed in ascending order of max. For each of them, INSERT3 function is called. As in algorithm 2, INSERT3(i) calls INCRMIN3 for the largest Hall interval ending with $max[i]$ if any. N is a balanced binary tree whose leaves contain all the variables for which INSERT3 has not been called yet. Initially, the leaves of N are the n variables sorted in ascending order of

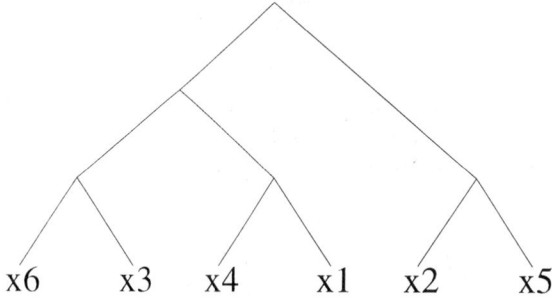

Figure 1: N tree in initial state.

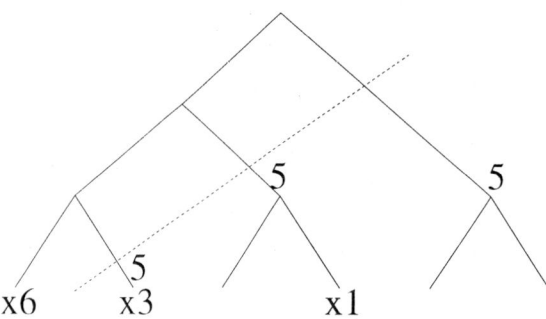

Figure 2: N tree after 3 iterations.

min. Each non terminal node o contains a pointer to its two children $o.left$ and $o.right$.

Figure1 represents N in its initial state for the timetabling example.

Within the function INSERT3, a call to INCRMIN3(a,b) stores the information that the variables appearing in N that have a min greater than or equal to a must have a min greater than b. In order to do so, each node o contains a number $o.newmin$, initially set to 0, that represents the new min computed by the algorithm for all the leaves below o. The function INCRMIN3(a,b) sets $newmin(o)$ to b for all the nodes o such that: all the leaves below o contain variables whose min is at least a, and the father of o has not been updated. In other words, INCRMIN3 only updates a "frontier" in N: all the leaves appearing on the right and below that frontier should be updated.

In our time tabling example, the first call to INCRMIN3 happens in the third call to INSERT3, after the processing of x_4, x_2 and x_5. Then INCRMIN3(2,4) is called on N. The effect of this call is depicted on figure 2. It will store 5 as a new min for the node containing x_3 and the node ancestor of x_1. The dotted line indicates the frontier drawn by this call. All the nodes below and on the right of that frontier will have a min greater than or equal to 5.

```
% N, P are a binary trees
INCRMIN3(a,b)
    o ← root of N
    while 1 do
        if o.min ≥ a then
            o.newmin ← b + 1
            return
        else
            o.right.newmin ← b + 1
            if o is a leaf then return
            o ← o.left

EXTRACT(y)
    o ← root of N
    nmin ← 0
    while o is not a leaf do
        if o.newMin > nmin then  nmin ← o.newMin
        o ← SELECT(o, y)
    if nMin > 0 then post y ≥ nmin

SELECT(o, y)
    if o.right.rank > y.rank then o ← o.left
    else o ← o.right
```

Algorithm 4: $O(n\log(n))$ filtering (cont'd)

The function EXTRACT(y) removes a variable y from N. It also traverses all the nodes on the path from the root of N to the leaf containing y, and collects the maximum $newmin$ on that path. It then posts the constraint $y \geq newmin$. It also uses the function SELECT(o,y), which returns the child node of o that contains y in one of its leaves. In order to implement SELECT, each node o also contains the rank $o.rank$ of its leftmost leaf. Then a simple test on the relative ranks of y and the right son of o is sufficient to decide whether y is below the left or the right son of o.

In our time tabling example, the fourth call of EXTRACT extracts x_3 from N, as depicted in figure 2. From the root to the node containing x_3, the maximum of the newmin is 5, hence $x_3 \geq 5$ is posted.

Note that each call to EXTRACT or INCRMIN3 traverses one path from the root of N to a leaf of N. It is a property of balanced binary trees that the length of such a path is at most $log(n)$. Thus, the functions EXTRACT(a) and INCRMIN3 run in $O(log(n))$ time.

Using similar ideas, the function INSERT3 can also be implemented in $O(log(n))$. In order to introduce its implementation, we need to define for each variable y the following number:

$y.u = min(y) + \#(\{z | z \notin N, min(z) \geq min(y)\})$

INSERT3 will update these numbers in a lazy way, using another balanced binary tree P. Initially, the leaves of P are empty. At the end of the algorithm, the leaves are all the variables, sorted in ascending order of min. The function INSERT3(y) inserts y in the $y.rank$ leaf of P. Each node o in P contains a number $o.u$ which is the

```
INSERT3(y)
    o ← root(P)
    INSERTAUX(y,o,0,0)
    if o.u ≥ max(y) then  INCRMIN3(o.min,o.u)
INSERTAUX(y,o,delta,count)
    if o is a leaf then
        o.u ← count + min(y)
        o.min ← min(y)
        o.count ← 1
        o.delta ← 0
    else
        delta ← delta + o.delta
        o.min ← o.min + delta
        o.count ← o.count + 1
        o.delta ← 0
        if o.min ≤ min(y) then  o.u ← o.u + 1
        if o.right.rank > y.rank then
            o.right.delta ← o.right.delta + delta
            count ← count + o.right.count
            INSERTAUX(y, o.left, delta, count)
        else
            o.left.delta ← o.left.delta + delta + 1
            INSERTAUX(y, o.right, delta, count)
        UPDATE(o)

UPDATE(o)
    uleft ← o.left.u + o.left.delta
    uright ← o.right.u + o.right.delta
    if uleft ≥ uright then
        o.u ← uleft
        o.min ← o.left.min
    else
        o.u ← uright
        o.min ← o.rigth.min
```

Algorithm 5: $O(n\log(n))$ filtering (cont'd)

maximum of $u(y)$ for the variables y appearing below o. o also contains the number $o.min$ which is the min of the variable y such that $y.u = o.u$. If there exists several such variables, the one with the smallest min is selected. Intuitively, $o.y$ is the best candidate for forming a Hall interval. When INSERT3($x[i]$) is called, then $y.u$ should be increased by 1 for all the variables appearing in P such that such that $min(y) < min(x[i])$. As the leaves are sorted by ascending order of min, it is sufficient to store this increment in the number $o.delta$, for nodes in that frontier. The only thing that remains to be computed is $x[i].u$. This number is equal to the number of variables y appearing in P such that $min(y) >= min(x[i])$. In order to do this, each node in P contains the number $o.count$ of variables below it. Then, when inserting $x[i]$, it is sufficient to sum up the numbers $o.count$ appearing on the right of the path to $x[i]$. Since a call to INSERT3 basically traverses one path from the root of P to one of its leaves, its complexity is $O(log(n))$.

6. Experimental results

In order to evaluate the actual usefulness of our work, we implemented algorithm 3 (let's call it algorithm A), and we compared it with 3 other algorithms on a set of various examples. The first algorithm (let's call it algorithm B) we considered is the basic one presented in the introduction: when a variable is assigned to a value, then this value is removed from the domain of all the other variables appearing in the constraint. Let's call Leconte's algorithm C and Regin's algorithm D. We chose to implement algorithm A using the Ilog Solver C++ library, as this library already provides an efficient implementation of algorithms B, C, and D. As all algorithms are implemented in the same library and run on the same computer, only their relative performance is of interest here. We report experiments running on a sparc 20 workstation.

Before presenting the results, we must say that our first implementation was not competitive at all: the overhead of manipulating binary trees was such that we obtained speedups only for constraints involving more than 10000 variables. After some further analysis of the algorithm, we decided to implement the following optimizations. The most effective optimization is to run algorithm B before, and to ignore the fixed variables. The second optimization is to treat all the variables having the same bounds in a single call to INSERT3. All in all, these two optimizations improved the algorithm enough to be competitive even on small problems. Similar optimizations are used in algorithm C.

Experiment 1 is to apply each algorithm to the theoretical example used in the proof of proposition 2. This example was designed to show the worst case behavior of each algorithm. The results are summarized in the table below. First column gives the size of the problem, whereas each subsequent column gives the running time of the algorithms on that problem. We see that algorithm A has an almost linear running time on this example. Algorithm C and D clearly are quadratic (running time is multiplied by 4 each time the problem size doubles).

size	A	B	C	D
100	0.01	0.01	0.03	.07
200	0.01	0.07	0.08	.3
400	0.02	0.27	0.33	1.2
800	0.08	1.05	1.3	4.7
1600	0.15	4.2	5.3	18.8
3200	0.33	16.9	21.4	75.6
6400	0.77	125.9	122.7	>200
12800	1.7	>200	>200	
25600	3.5			
52800	7.7			
102400	15.8			

In the rest of the examples, we apply a MAC like algorithm, i.e. a backtracking algorithm where local consistency is applied at each node of the search tree. We ran a first set of examples where our algorithm A is used for filtering the alldiff constraint appearing on the example. Then we ran the same set of experiments using algorithm B for the alldiff constraints, and so on. For each experiment we indicate the running time and also the number of backtracks needed to solve the problem.

The next experiment we consider it is to find all solutions of the nqueen problem, represented as follows, using 3n variables and 3 alldiff constraints.

$\forall i, 1 \leq i \leq n$, $x_i \in [1, n]$, $y_i \in [-n, n]$, $z_i \in [1, 2n]$, $y_i = x_i - i$, $z_i = x_i + i$, $alldiff(x)$, $alldiff(y)$, $alldiff(z)$

In the table below, the row beginning with time8 gives the running time for finding all the solutions of the 8 queens problem. The row beginning with bt8 indicates the number of backtracks for the same set of experiences. The rows time9 and bt9 give the same information for the 9 queens problem, and so on. We can see that algorithms A, C, and D are almost useless here because although their improved pruning reduces the number of backtracks the total running time is longer than when using algorithm B. We can also notice that our algorithm is quite as fast as algorithm C and produces the same amount of pruning.

queens	A	B	C	D
time8	.23	.17	.21	.26
time9	.86	.64	.84	.98
tim10	3.4	2.6	3.3	3.8
time11	15.1	11.3	14.8	16.9
time12	73.9	54.7	71.8	82
bt8	260	289	260	239
bt9	947	1111	949	854
bt10	4294	5072	4295	3841
bt11	18757	22124	18763	16368
bt12	87225	103956	87263	74936

Experiment 3 is to find one solution to the nqueen problem, using a first fail principle for variable ordering. This one involves as many variables as we want. We notice that as in experiment 2, algorithm B is the fastest. As the problem size grows, we also see that the smallest complexity of algorithm A pays off.

1stqueen	A	B	C	D
time50	.13	.09	.12	.28
time100	.49	.31	.54	1.54
time200	1.9	1.2	2.5	9.7
time400	8.1	4.7	14.0	68.1
time800	38.3	19.2	91.6	>100

Experiment 4 is to solve the Golomb [3] problem to optimality. A Golomb problem of size n, involves $n(n+1)/2$ variables appearing in an alldiff constraint, plus n^2 arithmetic constraints: $\forall i, 1 \leq i \leq n$, $x_i \in [1, 2^{n-1} - 1]$, $\forall i, j, i < j$, $y_{ij} = x_j - x_i$, $alldiff(y_{12}, ..., y_{n-1n})$, $minimize(x_n - x_1)$

In this example we see that in terms of pruning power, algorithm A is very similar to algorithm C, and lies between algorithms B and D. The speed difference between A and C, although small, increases with the size of the problem, due to the $nlog(n)$ vs. n^2 complexity of the algorithms.

Golomb	A	B	C	D
time8	1.02	2.38	1.10	1.44
time9	7.50	22.4	8.10	10.8
tim10	59.8	210.9	64.8	88.6
tim11	1288		1430	
bt8	697	2735	697	697
bt9	3740	19445	3740	3740
bt10	23464	140746	23464	23464
bt11	374888		374888	

Experiment 5 uses a sport league scheduling problem described in McAloon [4]. Problem of size n involves scheduling $2n$ teams, and has $n(n + 1)/2$ variables, $2n$ alldiff constraints involving n variables each, and one alldiff constraint involving $n(n + 1)/2$ variables. The use of algorithm B did not lead to a solution within 10 minutes for n greater than 8. As in the previous experiment, the relative speed of algorithm A vs algorithm C increases with the size of the problem.

ttabling	A	B	C	D
t8	0.14	1.0	0.13	0.27
t10	1.5		1.5	2.4
t12	.47		.48	2.8
t14	18.5		22.3	39.4
t16	8.0		9.5	30.7
bt8	32	767	32	32
bt10	417		417	417
bt12	41		41	41
bt14	3514		3514	3508
bt16	1112		1112	1110

Several conclusions can be drawn from the experiments above. Algorithm A and algorithm C have almost the same pruning power, although Leconte's algorithm computes a stronger consistency than bound consistency. On small problems the overhead of using binary trees is not very important. On larger problems, the logarithmic behavior pays off. The comparison with algorithm D is quite unfair, because this algorithm is not suited for ordered domains. We also noticed that on easy problems, such as the n queens problem, the use of sophisticated algorithms does not pay at all.

7. Conclusion

We presented a global filtering algorithm for a very useful n-ary constraint, the alldiff constraint. A mathematical analysis of the constraint led us to introduce the notion of Hall intervals. We then derived a simple $O(n^3)$ algorithm for bound consistency that looped over all Hall intervals. We then proved that some Hall intervals are not useful for computing bound consistency, thereby reducing the running time complexity of the algorithm to $O(n^2)$. We then showed that using balanced binary trees, the same algorithm could be implemented in $O(nlog(n))$ running time. The resulting algorithm has been implemented and tested on various examples including theoretical ones and complex real examples. Results show that the actual running time of the algorithm is competitive compared to some of the best known algorithms.

As noticed in [3], the alldiff constraint can be seen as a special case of the one resource scheduling problem. A potential line of research is to investigate whether our algorithm can be extended to that case.

Acknowledgements This paper benefited from numerous discussions with Jean-Charles Regin, Michel Leconte, and all the ILOG Solver development team. The anonymous referee's remarks (especially Ω) greatly improved the accuracy of the paper.

References

1. Noelle Bleuzen Guernalec and Alain Colmerauer.
   Narrowing a 2n-Bloc of sorting in O(nlog(n))
   In *proceedings of CP'97, pages 2-16*, Linz, Austria, 1997.

2. P. Hall.
   On representatives of subsets.
   Journal of the London Mathematical Society 10:26-30, 1935.

3. M. Leconte
   A Bounds-Based Reduction Scheme for Difference Constraints
   in *proc. of Constraints96*, Key West, Florida, 19 May 1996.

4. Ken McAloon, Carol Tretkoff and Gerhard Wetzel
   Sports league scheduling.
   In *proceedings of the third Ilog Solver User's conference*, Paris, 1997.
   Also available at http://www.ilog.com/ html/ products/ optimization/ customer_papers.htm

5. J-C. Régin.
   A filtering algorithm for constraints of difference in CSPs.
   In *proceedings of AAAI-94*, pages 362–367, Seattle, Washington, 1994.

Using Arc Weights to Improve Iterative Repair

John Thornton[1] and Abdul Sattar[2]

[1]School of Information Technology,
Griffith University Gold Coast,
Parklands Drive, Southport, Qld 4215, Australia
j.thornton@eas.gu.edu.au

[2]School of Computing and Information Technology,
Griffith University,
Kessels Road, Nathan, Qld, 4111, Australia
sattar@cit.gu.edu.au

Abstract

One of the surprising findings from the study of CNF satisfiability in the 1990's has been the success of iterative repair techniques, and in particular of weighted iterative repair. However, attempts to improve weighted iterative repair have either produced marginal benefits or rely on domain specific heuristics. This paper introduces a new extension of constraint weighting called Arc Weighting Iterative Repair, that is applicable outside the CNF domain and can significantly improve the performance of constraint weighting. The new weighting strategy extends constraint weighting by additionally weighting the connections or arcs between constraints. These arc weights represent increased knowledge of the search space and can be used to guide the search more efficiently. The main aim of the research is to develop an arc weighting algorithm that creates more benefit than overhead in reducing moves in the search space. Initial empirical tests indicate the algorithm does reduce search steps and times for a selection of CNF and CSP problems.

Introduction

One of the key findings in the study of Conjunctive Normal Form (CNF) satisfiability in the 1990's is that relatively simple iterative repair or local search techniques, like GSAT, are effective in finding answers to hard satisfiable CNF problems (Selman, Levesque and Mitchell 1992). A second finding is that the performance of such algorithms can be significantly improved by adding a simple clause or constraint weighting heuristic (Morris 1993, Selman and Kautz 1993, Cha and Iwama 1995). While research has been conducted into different implementations of weighting strategies (Frank 1996, 1997), the basic concept of constraint weighting has only been extended for solving CNF problems (Cha and Iwama 1996, Castell and Cayrol 1997). This paper is concerned with *domain independent* improvements to constraint weighting and is motivated by the success of constraint weighting in solving various Constraint Satisfaction Problems (CSPs) (eg Thornton and Sattar 1997).

The basic question for all non-trivial iterative repair algorithms is how to escape from a local minimum (a local minimum being defined as a solution from which no single change of variable value can lead to an improved solution). GSAT's answer is to make a series of random 'sideways' moves (ie moves to equivalent cost solutions) until either a maximum number of moves have been performed or a reduced cost solution is found. If the maximum number of moves ('maxflips') is reached then the algorithm is restarted from a random point (Selman, Levesque and Mitchell 1992). In contrast, constraint weighting works by adding a weight to each constraint (clause) that is violated at a local minimum and then continuing the search. The weighting changes the shape of the cost surface so that another solution is eventually preferred and the local minimum is exceeded. The cost surface itself is determined by summing the weights of all violated constraints at each solution point (Morris 1993).

Frank (1996, 1997) suggested several performance enhancing modifications to the weighting algorithm, including updating weights after each move (instead of at each minimum), only changing variables that are involved in a violation, using different functions to increase weights and allowing weights to decay over the duration of the search. Cha and Iwama (1996) produced significant performance improvements with their Adding New Clauses (ANC) heuristic, which instead of adding weights at a local minimum, adds a new clause for each violated clause (the new clause being the resolvent of the violated clause and one of it's neighbours). Castell and Cayrol (1997) suggest an extended weighting algorithm called Mirror which, in addition to weighting, has a scheme for 'flipping' variable values at each local minimum. However, both ANC and Mirror are domain dependent techniques, ANC relying on constraints being represented as clauses of disjunct literals and Mirror requiring Boolean variables. In addition the Mirror algorithm only appears useful for a small class of problem.

In this paper we present an enhanced weighting algorithm that can be incorporated into a domain independent iterative repair approach. The motivation is to improve the performance of weighting not just in the CNF domain but to investigate weighting as a general technique for solving CSPs. Specifically, the paper looks at whether there is any benefit in weighting the connections or arcs between violated constraints. An important aim of the research is to develop an arc weighting algorithm where the benefit of a more informed search outweighs the computational cost of

Copyright © 1998, American Association for Artificial Intelligence (www.aaai.org). All rights reserved.

updating and calculating the arc weights. The new approach is called Arc Weighting Iterative Repair (AWIR) and is tested on a set of CNF 3SAT problems and on a set of CSP scheduling problems.

Arc Weighting Iterative Repair

The Arc Weighting Iterative Repair algorithm extends the concept of a weighting algorithm to include weighting the connections or arcs that exist between constraints. A simple weighting algorithm builds up weights on individual constraints (clauses) each time a constraint is violated, either at a local minimum (Morris 1993) or each time a new variable value is chosen (Frank 1996). In either case the weights build up a picture of how hard a constraint is to satisfy and so represent knowledge or learning about the search space (Frank 1997). Within this framework, weighting the arcs between violated constraints represents learning about which *combinations* of constraints are harder to satisfy. For instance, consider the example in figure 1:

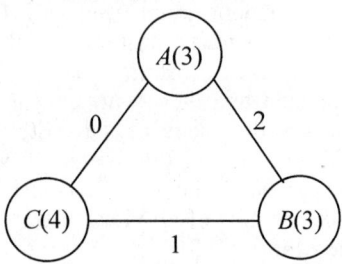

Figure 1: A Simple Constraint Weighting Scenario

The nodes A, B and C are three constraints in a hypothetical CSP. The values associated with A, B and C represent the current weights on each constraint. A constraint weight equals $(1 + v)$ where v is the number of times the constraint has already been violated in a local minima and 1 is the initial weight of the constraint. (ie $A(3)$ means constraint A has already been violated in 2 earlier local minima, plus 1 representing it's initial weight). The values on the arcs between constraints represent the number of times the two connected constraints have been *simultaneously* violated (ie the value 1 against arc BC represents that constraints B and C were once both violated in the *same* local minimum). Now consider the choice between two moves m_1 and m_2, such that m_1 violates constraints A and B and m_2 violates constraints A and C. The cost of m_1 for a simple weighting algorithm would be the sum of the weights on A and B ($3 + 3 = 6$) and the cost of m_2 would be the sum of the weights on A and C ($3 + 4 = 7$). Therefore m_1 would be preferred. However, an arc weighting algorithm would also consider that A and B have already been violated *together* in two previous minima, so the cost of m_1 includes the arc weight AB ($3 + 3 + 2 = 8$). The cost of m_2 still equals 7 as the arc weight $AC = 0$. Therefore, unlike simple weighting, arc weighting would prefer m_2. In accepting m_2 the search will move to the previously unexplored area where both A and C are violated, rather than re-exploring an AB violation. In this way, arc weighting can produce a more diverse search that is less likely to revisit previous solutions.

Looked at more formally, arc weighting operates on a graph $G = (V, E)$ where each vertex v_i represents a constraint (or clause) and each edge e_k represents a connection between two constraints v_i and v_j. The graph is complete in order to capture all information about violated constraint groups, hence an initial set of n constraints results in a set of $n(n - 1)/2$ edges. This means a CNF problem with 400 clauses will require 79,800 arcs! Typically an iterative repair algorithm calculates the cost of all candidate variable values before making a move. Clearly an arc weighting algorithm that checks all arcs for each variable value would be impractical with a significant number of constraints. Therefore the main challenge is to develop an efficient implementation of arc weighting without loss of arc information.

An Efficient Network Representation

The first step in representing the network graph is to realise that the only relevant arcs at a particular point in the search space are those existing between currently violated constraints that have also *already* been weighted (in the proposed algorithm, weighted constraints are those constraints that have been previously violated in a local minimum solution). Therefore the initial requirement is to build and maintain a list of currently violated, weighted constraints. This list (called CList) is generally short, but obviously changes according to the type of problem and the state of the search. Next arises the problem of how to represent and update the arc weights. This is done by first constructing an $n \times n$ array (called ArcArray) where element i,j represents the number of times constraints i and j have been violated together. The CList is then maintained in the following way: Each time a move is tested, all the newly violated and newly satisfied weighted constraints are added to a temporary list (TList). If the move appears promising (ie it satisfies at least one constraint that was previously violated) then the constraints in TList are merged with CList: Firstly CList is copied (as the move may still be rejected) then each newly *satisfied* constraint is removed from CList and the arc weights between the satisfied constraint and each remaining CList constraint are calculated from ArcArray and subtracted from the total cost for the current move. Then each newly *violated* constraint is added to CList and all the arc weights between it and the existing CList constraints are added to the total cost. According to the new total cost, the move is either accepted or rejected. If rejected, CList reverts to it's original state. This algorithm is shown in figure 2. Upon reaching a local minimum, the CList is reconstructed and the ArcArray counts updated accordingly (see figure 3).

Modifications to the Weighting Algorithm

As there is no 'standard' weighting approach, certain choices were made in the construction of the algorithm used in the study. Frank (1996) experimented with only

```
procedure Move(CList, ArcArray, TCost, OldValue, NewValue)
begin
    CopyList ← CList, Improve ← False,
    Counter ← 0, Diff ← 0
    for each constraint c_i that contains OldValue do
        CChange ← cost change from OldValue to NewValue for c_i
        if CChange < 0 then Improve ← True
        if c_i already weighted and CChange <> 0 then
            add c_i to TList, Counter ← Counter + 1
        end if
        Diff ← Diff + CChange
    end for
    if Improve = True and Counter > 0 then
        for each constraint c_i in TList do
            if c_i violated with OldValue then
                if c_i satisfied with NewValue then
                    delete c_i from CList
                    for each constraint c_j in CList do
                        Diff ← Diff - ArcArray[i][j](Cost(c_i) + Cost(c_j))
                end if
            else
                for each constraint c_j in CList do
                    Diff ← Diff + ArcArray[i][j](Cost(c_i) + Cost(c_j))
                insert c_i into CList
            end if
        end for
    end if
    if Diff < 0 then accept NewValue, TCost ← TCost + Diff
    else if Diff = 0 then randomly decide acceptance of NewValue
    if NewValue accepted then OldValue ← NewValue
    else CList ← CopyList
end
```

Figure 2: Move Selection Algorithm

```
procedure ArcWeightingIterativeRepair
begin
    set variables to initial assignments, CList ← Empty
    TCost ← cost of initial solution, ArcArray ← 0
    while unweighted cost of current solution > DesiredCost do
        if current state is not a local minimum then
            for each variable v_i involved in a constraint violation do
                OldValue_i ← StartValue_i ← current value of v_i
                for each domain value d_j of v_i do
                    if d_j <> StartValue_i then
                        Move(CList, ArcArray, TCost, OldValue_i, d_j)
                    end if
                end for
            end for
        else
            MoveSideways(), CList ← Empty
            for each constraint c_i in problem do
                if c_i currently violated then
                    proportionally increment weight of c_i
                    for each constraint c_j in CList do
                        ArcArray[i][j] ← ArcArray[i][j] + 1
                    end for
                    add c_i to CList
                end if
            end for
            TCost ← cost of current solution
        end if
    end while
end
```

Figure 3: The Arc Weighting Iterative Repair Algorithm

testing moves for variables that are currently involved in a constraint violation. This eliminates the possibility of many 'sideways' moves but significantly reduces the number of values tested before each move. Tests with this approach showed a significant speed up in search times for smaller problem instances, but a tendency for the algorithm to become 'lost' in larger problems and fail to find a solution. A compromise approach was developed that forces a move which changes the value of a variable not involved in a constraint violation each time a local minimum is encountered (represented by MoveSideways() in figure 3). For the test problems considered, this compromise performed better than either original approach.

Observation of the behaviour of the arc weighting algorithm indicated that it strongly favours solutions with only one constraint violation, and tends to cycle between these solutions (because there is zero arc weight for a single constraint violation). To remedy this behaviour an alternative weight allocation strategy was developed. Previously each constraint starts with a weight of one and is incremented by one each time it is violated at a local minimum. The new scheme distributes a fixed weight equal to the total number of constraints. If only one constraint is violated at a local minimum then it gets the full fixed weight, otherwise the weight is proportionally divided between all violated constraints. This 'proportional weighting' scheme significantly improves the performance of the arc weighting algorithm while causing the standard weighting algorithm to deteriorate. The overall arc weighting algorithm is shown in figure 3.

Experiments

The Arc Weighting Iterative Repair (AWIR) algorithm was primarily developed as a means of solving general (non-binary) CSPs. It is designed to accept problems in the form of sets of variables with domains and sets of constraints between the variables (Kumar 1992). Consequently the CNF formulas used in the study were transformed to equivalent CSPs in the following way: a 3SAT clause is modelled as a constraint between 3 variables, $\{x_1,x_2,x_3\}$, each with a domain of $\{0,1\}$ and corresponding coefficients $\{a_1,a_2,a_3\}$. These variables then form a constraint $a_1x_1 + a_2x_2 + a_3x_3 > b$ where a_ix_i corresponds to the ith literal in the clause such that $a_i = -1$ if the literal is negative, otherwise $a_i = 1$, and $b =$ -(total number of negative literals in clause).

The Arc Weighting Iterative Repair algorithm is compared to the same algorithm with the arc weighting features switched off. This standard algorithm is referred to as Weighted Iterative Repair (WIR). The aim of the study is to find whether any benefit is obtained from arc weighting over simple weighting, so no further algorithms are considered (for a comparison of weighting to other techniques see Cha and Iwama 1995; Thornton and Sattar 1997). The two weighting algorithms are tested on a set of 3SAT CNF problems and a set of real-world staff scheduling CSPs. Two classes of CNF problem are used:

- randomly generated 3SAT problems with a clause/variable ratio in the cross-over region of 4.3. These problems are prefixed with an r followed by the number of variables, ie $r100$ represents a randomly generated, satisfiable formula with 100 variables and 430 clauses.
- single solution SAT problems with a clause/variable ratio of 2.0 created using an AIM generator (see Cha and Iwama 1995). These problems are prefixed an o followed by the number of variables (as above).

The scheduling CSPs are based on real data used to roster nurses in a public hospital. The model has a variable for each staff member, with a domain of allowable schedules. Typically there are 25-35 variables each with a domain size of up to 5000 values. Therefore the structure of the problem differs significantly from the 2 value domain of the CNF problems. In addition, approximately 400 non-binary constraints are defined between variables expressing allowable levels of staff for each shift, and preferred shift combinations. Although the general problem is over-constrained, optimal solutions have been found using an integer programming (IP) approach (Thornton and Sattar, 1997). The IP solutions allow the problem to be formulated as a CSP, by defining each constraint to be satisfied when it reaches level attained in the optimum solution.

Performance Measures

For each category of problem, between 100 and 200 solutions were generated by each algorithm. The mean performance values for these solutions are reported in table 1. The Time column represents the mean execution time in seconds on a Sun Creator 3D-2000 and Std Dev is the standard deviation of the time. Loops is the mean number of iterations through the main program loop (the while loop in figure 3), Hills is the mean number of *improving* moves made by the algorithm and Minima is the mean number of local minima encountered. The staff scheduling problems are reported as ss.csp.

The study uses multiple performance measures to capture precise differences between the two algorithms. While previous research has concentrated on counting the number of 'flips' or moves (eg Cha and Iwama 1996, Frank 1996), this measure was found to be inadequate for comparing AWIR and WIR. As table 1 shows, for several problems the number of hill climbing moves made by AWIR exceeds WIR, while the AWIR execution time and number of itera-

Problem	Method	Time	Std Dev	Loops	Hills	Minima
$r100$	WIR	7.43	10.39	3955	3035	1398
	AWIR	6.04	7.90	2354	4218	637
$r200$	WIR	56.27	97.57	17171	9723	6614
	AWIR	20.91	27.02	4654	10839	1198
$r400$	WIR	342.23	202.10	61534	47383	22566
	AWIR	79.34	69.42	10779	31879	2684
$o100$	WIR	9.89	4.59	13322	5797	5101
	AWIR	6.41	3.49	7908	5796	2531
$o200$	WIR	88.25	45.25	66072	23557	26274
	AWIR	56.74	38.32	40618	27879	13316
ss.csp	WIR	144.35	250.38	207	390	69
	AWIR	74.02	97.68	136	475	38

Table 1: Comparison of mean performance values

Problem	Time	Std Dev	Loops	Hills	Minima
$r100$	.81	.76	.60	1.39	.46
$r200$	.37	.28	.27	1.11	.18
$r400$	.23	.34	.18	.67	.12
$o100$	.65	.76	.59	1.00	.50
$o200$	.64	.85	.62	1.18	.51
ss.csp	.51	.39	.66	1.22	.55

Table 2: Table 1 AWIR values as a proportion of WIR values

tions are actually less. This shows the number of moves is only a partial measure of the amount of 'work' done by the algorithms. The other dimension is the number of domain values tried (and hence the number of constraints tested) before a weighted cost improving move is found. This is analogous to the count of instantiations and consistency checks used in evaluating backtracking (eg see Haralick and Elliott 1980). The amount of 'work' done by each algorithm is therefore better captured in counting the main program iterations (Loops in table 1). However, the Loops measure does not capture the extra work done by the AWIR algorithm in maintaining the CList (see figure 2). For this reason, execution times are also recorded.

Analysis

The results show that the average solution times and the average number of iterations performed by the arc weighting algorithm are significantly less than for standard weighting. This supports the earlier hypothesis that arc weighting provides additional useful information about the search space. The time results also indicate that the benefits of arc weighting outweigh the costs of maintaining the constraint list (see figures 4 and 5).

Distinguishing Moves

Table 2 re-expresses the results from table 1, giving the AWIR values as a proportion of the WIR values, and more clearly shows the relative differences between the algorithms. In all cases the AWIR results are less than the

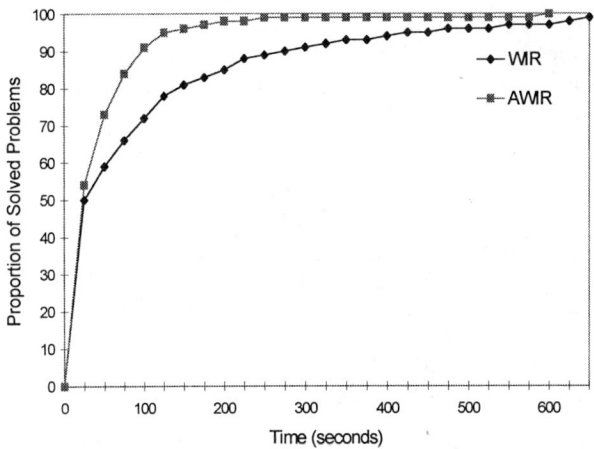

Figure 4: Proportion of solved problems by time

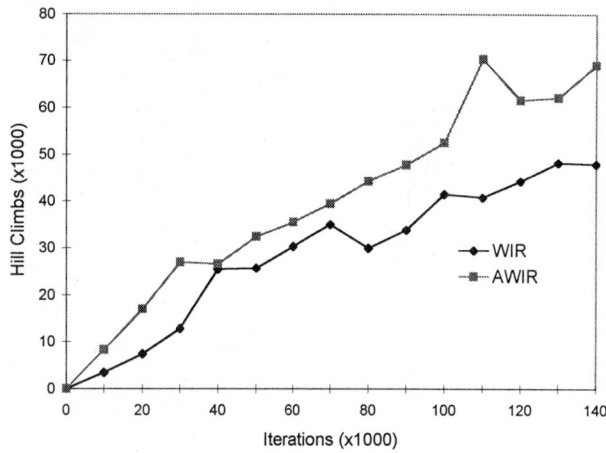

Figure 6: Comparison of hill climbing moves

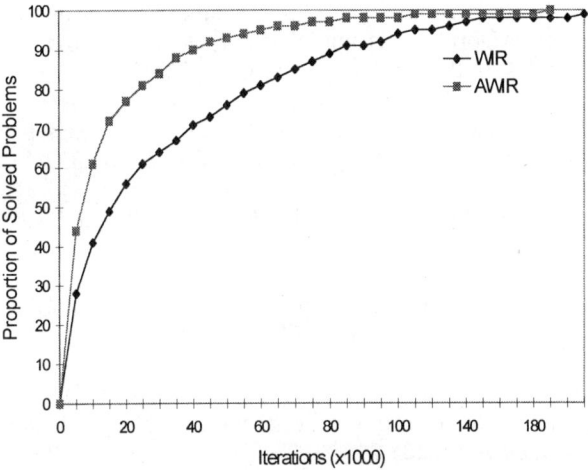

Figure 5: Proportion of solved problems by iterations

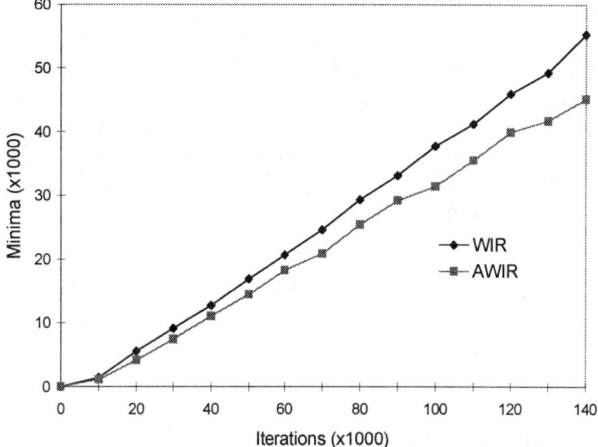

Figure 7: Number of minima by iterations

WIR results, except for the number of hill climbing or improving moves. The hill climb counts are shown in more detail in figure 6, which plots the average number of hill climbs performed, firstly for all problems completed in less than 10,000 iterations, then for problems completed between 10,000 and 20,000 iterations, and so on. As discussed earlier, the arc weighting information should incline the search to avoid visiting previously violated groups of constraints and hence to perform a more diverse search. The greater number of hill climbing moves combined with a reduced number of local minima for AWIR (see figure 7) indicate a more diverse search is occurring. More precisely, the hill climbing behaviour shows that, for a given number of iterations, AWIR is more likely to find a hill climbing move than WIR, because arc weighting is able to *distinguish* between moves that simple weighting would evaluate as having the same cost. Of course, the ability to distinguish between moves is only useful if the result, as in the present case, is a faster overall search.

Arc Weighting Costs

As would be expected, there is a greater proportional reduction in the number of program iterations than in the execution time for AWIR (compare figures 4 and 5). This reflects the cost to AWIR of using arc weights and is further analysed in table 3. Here the average number of iterations per second are calculated for each algorithm and problem class. The table shows the AWIR main loop is running at approximately 74% of the speed of WIR for the random CNF problems, increasing to 94% for the AIM problems. The probable explanation for this difference is the greater clause or constraint density for the random problems (4.3 in comparison to 2.0 for the AIM problems). The greater density would increase the average length of CList (figure 1) and hence add to AWIR's overhead. However, a larger CList indicates that arc weights are also giving more guidance to the search, and so a counterbalancing improvement in search efficiency would be expected (as the results demonstrate).

Problem	Method	Loops/Time	AWIR/WIR
r100	WIR	532.30	73.22%
	AWIR	389.74	
r200	WIR	305.15	72.94%
	AWIR	222.57	
r400	WIR	179.80	75.56%
	AWIR	135.86	
o100	WIR	1347.02	91.59%
	AWIR	1233.70	
o200	WIR	748.69	95.61%
	AWIR	715.86	
ss.csp	WIR	1.43	92.03%
	AWIR	1.32	

Table 3: Comparison of Iteration Speed

Divergence

A further property of AWIR is that solution times tend to be more predictable or less divergent than for WIR. This is shown in the execution time standard deviations and in the graph of figure 8, which plots the number of solutions found at various iteration ranges. As Cha and Iwama (1996) point out, reduced divergence is useful when using an iterative repair technique to indicate unsatisfiability.

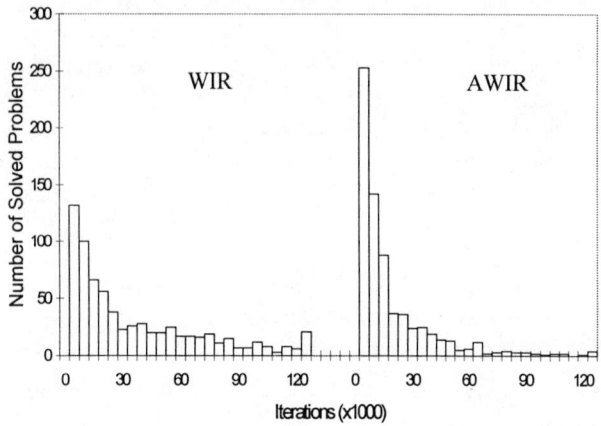

Figure 8: Number of solved CNF problems by iterations

Conclusions and Further Work

The main finding of this study is that arc weighing can improve the performance of a simple weighting algorithm on a range of different problems. While specialised algorithms like ANC may be more efficient for random CNF problems, arc weighting is domain independent and therefore is not tied to a particular problem formulation. This domain independence also means arc weighting can be used in conjunction with other techniques developed to improve simple weighting. The main technical contribution of the paper is the presentation of an efficient arc weighting algorithm, whose benefits have been shown to exceed the computational costs.

Ongoing research is concerned with a more extensive empirical evaluation of arc weighting and the integration of further performance enhancing strategies. The authors are also interested in applying weighting strategies in solving over-constrained problems.

Acknowledgments

The authors would like to acknowledge the encouragement and assistance of Byungki Cha and Paul Morris in providing the CNF test instances used in this study.

References

Castell, T., and Cayrol, M. 1997. Hidden Gold in Random Generation of SAT Satisfiable Instances. In Proceedings of AAAI-97, 372-377.

Cha, B., and Iwama, K. 1995. Performance Test of Local Search Algorithms Using New Types of Random CNF Formulas. In Proceedings of IJCAI-95, 304-310.

Cha, B., and Iwama, K. 1996. Adding New Clauses for Faster Local Search. In Proceedings of AAAI-96, 332-337.

Frank, J. 1996. Weighting for Godot. In Proceedings of AAAI-96, 338-343.

Frank, J. 1997. Learning Short-Term Weights for GSAT. In Proceedings of AAAI-97, 384-389.

Haralick, R., and Elliott, G. 1980. Increasing Tree Search Efficiency for Constraint Satisfaction Problems. *Artificial Intelligence*, 14, 263-313.

Kumar, V. 1992. Algorithms for Constraint Satisfaction Problems: A Survey. AI Magazine, Spring 1992: 32-43.

Morris, P. 1993. The Breakout Method for Escaping from Local Minima. In Proceedings of AAAI-93, 40-45.

Selman, B., and Kautz, H. 1993. Domain-Independent Extensions to GSAT: Solving Large Structured Satisfiability Problems. In Proceedings of IJCAI-93, 290-295.

Selman, B.; Levesque, H.; and Mitchell, D. 1992. A New Method for Solving Hard Satisfiability Problems. In Proceedings of AAAI-92, 440-446.

Thornton, J., and Sattar, A. 1997. Applied Partial Constraint Satisfaction using Weighted Iterative Repair. In Sattar, A. (ed.) *Advanced Topics in Artificial Intelligence*, LNAI 1342, 57-66: Springer-Verlag.

An Integer Local Search Method with Application to Capacitated Production Planning

Joachim P. Walser[1]
Programming Systems Lab
Univ. des Saarlandes, Postfach 151150
66041 Saarbrücken, Germany
walser@ps.uni-sb.de

Ramesh Iyer
i2 Technologies
909 East Las Colinas Boulevard
Irving, TX 75039
Ramesh_Iyer@i2.com

Narayan Venkatasubramanyan
i2 Technologies
909 East Las Colinas Boulevard
Irving, TX 75039
narayan@i2.com

Abstract

Production planning is an important task in manufacturing systems. We consider a real-world capacitated lot-sizing problem (CLSP) from the process industry. Because the problem requires discrete lot-sizes, domain-specific methods from the literature are not directly applicable. We therefore approach the problem with WSAT(OIP), a new domain-independent heuristic for integer optimization which generalizes the Walksat algorithm. WSAT(OIP) performs stochastic tabu search and operates on over-constrained integer programs. We empirically compare WSAT(OIP) to a state-of-the-art mixed integer programming branch-and-bound solver (CPLEX 4.0) on real problem data. We find that integer local search is considerably more robust than MIP branch-and-bound in finding feasible solutions in limited time, and branch-and-bound can only solve a sub-class of the CLSP with discrete lot-sizes. With respect to production cost, both methods find solutions of similar quality.

Introduction

Production planning is an important task in manufacturing systems and gives rise to a variety of optimization problems. Here we study a real-world lot-sizing problem from the process industry (manufacturing of chemicals, food, plastics, etc.). The problem is expressed as follows: given a set of products and a collection of customer orders with due dates, construct a minimal-cost production plan such that all orders are met in time without exceeding resource capacity. The total cost of a plan consists of inventory and labor costs.

The problem under consideration is similar to the well-studied capacitated lot-sizing problem (CLSP, see (Drexl & Kimms 1997) for a survey) but includes the requirement of discrete lot-sizes that prevents a direct application of domain-specific methods from the literature (Diaby *et al.* 1992; Kirca & Kökten 1994; Hindi 1996). We therefore approach the problem with a new domain-independent heuristic for integer optimization, WSAT(OIP), and empirically compare it to a commercial mixed integer programming (MIP) branch-and-bound solver (CPLEX 4.0).

The first part of the paper introduces the WSAT(OIP) heuristic and the constraint class on which it operates, over-constrained integer programs (OIPs). WSAT(OIP) is a straightforward extension of the WSAT($\mathcal{PB}$) heuristic (Walser 1997) from binary variables to variables ranging over finite integer domains. While both methods generalize the stochastic Walksat algorithm for propositional satisfiability (Selman, Kautz, & Cohen 1994), their refined strategy for move selection follows principles from tabu search (Glover & Laguna 1993). By using an algebraic problem specification as input, such *integer local search* methods are potentially applicable to a range of optimization problems of practical importance. This calls for investigating the effectiveness of such heuristics by empirical comparison with established methods.

The second part of the paper describes a case study of WSAT(OIP) on a large CLSP with discrete lot-sizes and fixed charges. We compare the experimental results on real data to CPLEX applied to a tight integer programming model. We find that MIP branch-and-bound can only solve a sub-class of the CLSP with discrete lot-sizes, namely the problem where fixed charges and lot-sizes are equal. Further, WSAT(OIP) is considerably more robust than CPLEX in finding feasible solutions in limited time, in particular as the capacity constraints are tightened. With respect to production cost, both methods find solutions of similar quality. We examine fixed-capacity and varied-capacity problems. Using a Lagrangean relaxation technique we provide lower bounds that prove that the fixed-capacity problems are solved with near-optimal overall cost. We show that substantial savings can be achieved by varying capacity.

Part I. Integer Local Search

Many domain-specific heuristics for problem classes like set-covering, generalized assignment, or time-tabling exist in the operations research literature. In contrast, only few general purpose heuristics for integer programming

---

[1]This study was carried out during a visit of the first author at i2 Technologies. Copyright ©1998, American Association for Artificial Intelligence (www.aaai.org). All rights reserved.

have been described that aim at covering a broader range of combinatorial problems. These heuristics are of two kinds, (i) approaches based on linear programming which relax the integrality constraints (Aboudi & Jörnsten 1994; Løkketangen, Jörnsten, & Storøy 1994; Glover & Laguna 1997; Balas & Martin 1980), and (ii) techniques in which local moves are performed directly in the space of integer solutions, such as simulated annealing (Connolly 1992; Abramson, Dang, & Krishnamoorthy 1996) and stochastic local search (Walser 1997). We will refer to the second class of heuristics as *integer local search* methods.

In this paper we generalize WSAT($\mathcal{PB}$) (Walser 1997) from 0-1 variables to finite domain integer variables, introducing WSAT(OIP). For reasons of its variable selection strategy, WSAT(OIP) operates on over-constrained integer programs (OIPs) instead of classical integer programs (Nemhauser & Wolsey 1988). Unlike integer programs (IPs), OIPs represent the overall optimization objective by competing sub-objectives instead of using a single objective function. Similarly as discussed in the context of constraint hierarchies (Borning, Freeman-Benson, & Wilson 1996), OIPs encode optimization objectives with soft constraints.

Over-Constrained Integer Programs

We define a constraint system of hard and soft inequalities and equations over integer variables as an *over-constrained integer program*. Here, we consider the special case where all constraints are linear and the system can be denoted in matrix notation as

$$\begin{aligned} A\mathbf{x} &\geq \mathbf{b} \\ C\mathbf{x} &\leq \mathbf{d} \quad (soft) \\ x_i &\in D_i. \end{aligned} \quad (1)$$

A and C are real valued coefficient matrices, $\mathbf{b}, \mathbf{d}$ are real-valued vectors, and $\mathbf{x}$ is the variable vector, all variables x_i ranging over finite integer domains D_i.[1] The objective is to minimize some measure of the overall violation of soft constraints, subject to the hard constraints. Given an evaluation function $\|.\|$ to measure the overall violation of soft constraints, (1) is interpreted as the following optimization problem.

$$\begin{aligned} \min \quad & \|C\mathbf{x} - \mathbf{d}\| \\ \text{subject to} \quad & A\mathbf{x} \geq \mathbf{b}, \ x_i \in D_i. \end{aligned} \quad (2)$$

The following sections describe WSAT(OIP), a local search heuristic to find approximately optimal solutions to over-constrained IPs.

---

[1] We will refer to a problem of the form (1) as being in *min normal form*. Every OIP minimization problem can be converted into min normal form by multiplying every 'incorrect' inequality (e.g. $\leq$ instead of $\geq$) by -1 and converting every equality into two inequalities. Input to WSAT(OIP) is not required to be in min-normal form.

The Variable Selection Cycle of WSAT(OIP)

WSAT(OIP) is an iterative repair heuristic. Starting with a random variable assignment, individual variable/value pairs are iteratively selected to be changed, thereby moving in the space of feasible and infeasible solutions. Generalizing from the Walksat algorithm (Selman, Kautz, & Cohen 1994), variable changes are selected in a two-stage process of first randomly selecting an unsatisfied (hard or soft) constraint for partial repair and within the constraint selecting a variable to be changed. The criterion for move selection is to perform hill-climbing on a *score* which reflects both the degree of infeasibility and the optimization objective.

A move of WSAT(OIP) consists of *triggering* the value of a finite domain integer variable to a smaller or greater value close to its current assignment. This extends WSAT($\mathcal{PB}$) in which Boolean variables are *flipped* (complemented). Occasionally, a restart with a new initial assignment takes place to escape from local optima, typically after a fixed number of moves. To describe the move selection strategy for over-constrained IPs in more detail, we first need a score definition. Given a particular assignment $\mathbf{x}$, we define a score to evaluate a system of the form (1) as

$$score(\mathbf{x}) = \|\mathbf{b} - A\mathbf{x}\|_\lambda + \|C\mathbf{x} - \mathbf{d}\| \quad (3)$$

We employ a simple evaluation function $\|.\|$ which scores each violated constraint in proportion to its degree of violation: $\|\mathbf{v}\| := \sum_i \max(0, v_i)$. Additionally, the score computation (3) uses a vector $\lambda \geq 0$ for weighting the violations of hard constraints, defined by $\|\mathbf{v}\|_\lambda := \sum_i \max(0, \lambda_i v_i)$. These weights can be statically assigned or dynamically updated during the search (Selman & Kautz 1993). The reported experiments were all performed with statically assigned weights.

Observation of the two-stage move selection strategy motivates the use of OIP encodings for integer local search: In the constraint/variable selection, the selected constraint induces a choice of moves leading towards a local goal (i. e. satisfying the constraint). In contrast with standard IP encodings, decision alternatives in OIPs are grouped together within one sub-objective and are evaluated in direct competition. We hypothesize that this helps to focus the search.

Local Moves

The remaining degrees of freedom are how to select a variable from within a clause and which new value to assign to it. The fundamental principle behind WSAT(OIP) is greediness: Select local moves that most improve the total score. Additionally, adaptive memory (Glover & Laguna 1993) and noise are employed to overcome local minima. Figure 1 outlines the variable selection strategy in detail. As has been reported for SAT local search (McAllester, Selman, & Kautz 1997; Parkes & Walser 1996), the details of the variable selection are important for performance. The described strategy includes a tabu mechanism (Glover

1. Randomly select an unsatisfied constraint α (with probability p_{hard} a hard constraint, and with $1 - p_{\text{hard}}$ a soft constraint).
2. From α, select all variables which can be changed such that α's score improves. For each such variable, select one or more α-improving values and compute the hypothetical total scores (finite domain integer variables are triggered up or down, Boolean variables are flipped).
3. From the selected variable-value pairs, remove the ones which are *tabu* (tabu-aspiration by score).
4. Of the remaining variable-value pairs, select one which most improves the total score, if assigned. Break ties according to i) *frequency* and ii) *recency*
5. Only if the total score cannot be improved: With probability p_{noise}, select a random α-improving non-tabu variable-value pair. With $1 - p_{\text{noise}}$, select the best possible one.

Figure 1: A move selection strategy for WSAT (OIP).

& Laguna 1993) with tenure of size t: No variable-value pair may be assigned that has been assigned in the previous t moves. Further, all ties between otherwise equivalent variable-value pairs are broken by a history mechanism: On ties, choose the move that was chosen i) least frequently, and then ii) longest ago. The experimental results section reports on parameter settings.

Part II. Production Planning

The problem under consideration can be classified as single-level, dynamic-demand capacitated lot-sizing problem (CLSP) with discrete lot-sizes and fixed charges. Given is a set of products and a number of customer orders (or forecasted demands) with due dates on a finite planning horizon. The goal is to compute a minimal-cost production plan such that all customer orders are met in time. No lateness or shortage of orders is permitted. Products (or *items*) can be produced in discrete periods of the planning horizon (weeks). Because production consumes resources and resources have limited capacity, items often have to be produced earlier than needed and carried to the period where they are shipped. Such carrying incurs inventory cost (opportunity cost of capital and storage cost) which is one of two cost factors in the problem considered here. Solving the CLSP optimally is known to be NP-hard (Bitran & Yanasse 1982). Table 1 specifies the problem parameters.

The CLSP considered here has two particularities: (i) Items can only be produced in predefined quantities (lots) and setup costs are compensated by economic production quantities (EPQs). At any time, production of item i is possible in quantities of 0 or $E_i + k \cdot L_i$, where $k \geq 0$, L_i is the

Index	Definition
i	Index for items/products.
t	Index for time periods.
Symbol	Definition
L_i	Lot-size of product i.
E_i	Economic production quantity of product i.
D_{it}	Demand of product i in time period t.
T_t	Total labor units available in time period t.
R_i	Unit labor requirement for product i.
C_i	Cost of carrying product i per unit/period.
Ω_{it}	Future demand of product i starting period t.
T	Number of periods.
N	Number of items.
S	cost per labor shift.

Table 1: Parameters for the CLSP with discrete lot-sizes and fixed charges (EPQs).

lot-size and E_i is the EPQ for item i (every EPQ is a multiple of the lot-size). (ii) The only resource is labor, available in either one or two shifts in any period. The amount of available labor has an associated cost (labor availability and consumption are expressed in cost units). Thus, production cost is equal to the sum of labor and inventory costs.

In the problem, labor capacity can be varied between one and two shifts. Because less capacity enforces earlier production of items, a tradeoff exists between labor and inventory costs. Because labor costs dominate inventory costs, reducing labor is critical to substantially save costs. However, due to practical considerations it is not acceptable to have too many labor level changes; thus the number of labor level changes considered was limited to 2 in our experiments. To optimize the overall problem, we take the approach to solve a series of capacitated lot-sizing problems with different 'labor profiles' and choose the best solution, as follows.

Labor Profiles Labor consumption varies between items and is expressed by parameters R_i in terms of resource consumption per production of one unit of item i. In any period t, the total labor consumption is limited by T_t, available in one or two shifts. One shift incurs a per-week cost of S, two shifts incur $2S$. A labor profile thus corresponds to a set $\{(t, T_t) \mid 1 \leq t \leq T, T_t \in \{S, 2S\}\}$. Possible labor profiles are restricted to the pattern 2-shifts/1-shift/2-shifts and can be denoted by an interval $[s_1, s_2]$ referring to periods $s_1 \ldots s_2$ on one shift, and periods $1 \ldots s_1 - 1$ and $s_2+1 \ldots T$ on two shifts. The cost of a labor profile $[s1, s2]$ is thus $(T - (s2 - s1 + 1)) \cdot 2S + (s2 - s1 + 1) \cdot S$.

Every labor profile has an optimal inventory cost. If labor could be freely varied, the labor availability would have to be modeled with problem variables. However, since the number of allowed labor profiles is small, we factored the labor variability out from the optimization problem and approached the problem by solving each permitted labor profile, optimizing one CLSP at a time. Possible shift boundaries $[s_1, s_2]$ were generated starting with $s_1 = 1$ and an initial one-shift period length l ($s_2 = s_1 + l - 1$). Iteratively, s_2 was then increased as long as WSAT (OIP) found feasible solutions for the resulting CLSP (for CPLEX, as long as infeasibility was not proved). If no feasible solution was found (for CPLEX, if infeasibility of the profile was proved), s_1 was increased to the next period and s_2 was reset.

The two different integer solvers require different algebraic models which are described in the following.

Integer Local Search Model

The integer local search model is straightforward. Production quantities per item and time period are expressed by finite domain variables p_{it} that range over the allowed production quantities (and are bounded by the summed future demand Ω_{it}):

$$p_{it} \in \{p \leq \Omega_{it} \mid p = 0 \lor p = E_i + k \cdot L\}$$

where $k = 0, 1, 2, \ldots$, for every item i and time period t and Ω_{it} is determined as $\Omega_{it} = \sum_{t \leq s \leq T} D_{is}$.

To formulate the constraints, we will make use of the abbreviation $S[i, t]$ representing the amount of product i carried in inventory in time period t (textually substituted in the constraints):

$$S[i, t] = \sum_{s=1}^{t} p_{is} - D_{is}$$

The formulation is as follows.

$$S[i, t] \geq 0 \quad \forall i, t \quad \text{(NOH)}$$

$$\sum_i R_i \cdot p_{it} \leq T_t \quad \forall t \quad \text{(CAP)}$$

$$\text{soft: } C_i \cdot S[i, t] \leq 0 \quad \forall i, t \quad \text{(INV)}$$

Negative-on-hand constraints (NOH) ensure that all orders are met in time. Capacity constraints (CAP) express that available labor capacity is not to be exceeded. The soft constraints (INV) express the competing objectives of minimizing inventory costs; for every item and time period, the inventory cost from carrying material has to be minimized. For every feasible solution, the resulting objective (the total inventory cost) is the summed violation of all soft constraints measured by our definition of $\|.\|$ in (2). Using finite domain variables to model production, the local search progresses by moving production up or down in allowed quantities induced by the violated constraints.

0-1 Integer Model The first modeling attempt used an over-constrained 0-1 integer model with a logarithmic encoding of production quantities ($E_i x_1 + L_i x_2 + 2 L_i x_3 + 4 L_i x_4 + \ldots$). In addition to the blowup of the number of

Sets	
SKU	Set of products (stock keeping units).
SKU_1	Set of products for which lot-size (L_i) is equal to economic production quantity (E_i).
SKU_2	Set of products for which lot-size is a multiple of economic production quantity.
Variables	
s_{it}	Amount of product i carried in inventory in time period t.
x_{it}	Amount of product i produced in time period t.
y_{it}	Number of lots of product i produced in time period t.
z_{it}	Binary variable which is unity if product i is produced in time period t.

Table 2: Sets and decision variables for the MILP model.

variables for this model, running WSAT ($\mathcal{PB}$) did not yield solutions of acceptable quality. We put this failure down to the fact that with a logarithmic encoding, a small change of production often requires a long sequence of local moves. For example, an increase from $2^k - 1$ to 2^k lots can only be achieved by flipping $k + 1$ variables. This appeared to be a strong hindrance of the search process.

Mixed Integer Programming Model

This section requires some familiarity with integer programming terminology, as covered for example in (Nemhauser & Wolsey 1988). The sets and variables defined in the mixed integer programming model (MILP) are given in tables 1 and 2. The problem formulation (P) is as follows.

$$\mathbf{P}: \min_{x_{it}, y_{it}, z_{it}, s_{it}} \sum_{i=1}^{N} \sum_{t=1}^{T} C_i s_{it} \quad (4)$$

subject to

$$x_{it} + s_{i,t-1} = D_{it} + s_{it} \quad \forall i, t \quad (5)$$

$$x_{it} = L_i y_{it} \quad \forall i \in SKU_1 \quad (6)$$

$$x_{it} = E_i z_{it} + L_i y_{it} \quad \forall i \in SKU_2 \quad (7)$$

$$E_i z_{it} \leq x_{it} \leq \Omega_{it} z_{it} \quad \forall i \in SKU_2 \quad (8)$$

$$\sum_{k=1}^{t} x_{ik} \geq L_i \lceil \sum_{k=1}^{t} D_{ik}/L_i \rceil \quad \forall i \in SKU_1, t \quad (9)$$

$$\sum_{k=1}^{t-1} x_{ik} \geq \sum_{k=1}^{t-1} D_{ik} z_{it} + \sum_{k=1}^{t} D_{ik}(1 - z_{it})$$
$$\forall i \in SKU_2, t \quad (10)$$

$$\sum_i R_i x_{it} \leq T_t \quad \forall t \quad (11)$$

$$z_{it} \in \{0, 1\}, y_{it} \text{ integer}$$

In the MILP model, equation (4) represents the sum of total inventory carrying costs. Equation (5) is the material balance in each time period and equations (6)-(7) determine the total production quantity of each product in time period t. Note that binary variables are only defined for $i \in SKU_2$. Equation (8) states that if z_{it} is non-zero, then the minimum amount (EPQ) must be produced, and cannot exceed the bound Ω_{it} (only for items in SKU_2).

Equations (9)-(10) represent constraints that tighten the relaxation gap between the integer solution and the LP relaxation of the problem. Equation (10) states that if product i is produced in period t, then the total amount produced up to period $t-1$ must meet the total demand up to period $t-1$. However, if the product is not made in period t, then the amount produced up to period $t-1$ must meet the demand up to period t. From our observation, this equation reduces the relaxation gap significantly and helps reduce the number of nodes branched on in a branch-and-bound solution method. Finally, equation (11) represents the labor constraints that link the problems across all products.

Due to the modelling of discontinuous integer values ($x_{it} \in \{0, E_i, E_i + L_i \ldots\}$) for items $i \in SKU_2$ with binary variables z_{it}, solving large problems is extremely expensive. We therefore attempted a Lagrangean relaxation technique (see (Beasley 1993) for an overview of Lagrangean relaxation) where the problem is decomposed by relaxing the equations (11) to obtain the value of binary variables and then solving problem (P) for fixed value of binary variables, thereby solving subproblems that are less expensive to solve in each step.

Lagrangean Relaxation Approach

The Lagrangean relaxation method used for solving the problem (P) relaxes the complicating constraints (11) using Lagrange multipliers, thus resulting in a relaxed problem that is decomposable for each i. The relaxed problem (PL) is as follows

$$\text{PL:} \min_{x_{it}, y_{it}, z_{it}, s_{it}} [\sum_{i=1}^{N} \sum_{t=1}^{T} C_i s_{it}] - \sum_{t=1}^{T} \lambda_t \sum_{i=1}^{N} (R_i x_{it} - T_t)$$

subject to Equations (5)-(10).

Thus, (PL) is a relaxation of (P) and represents a lower bound to the solution of (P). Since (PL) is decomposable with respect to i, each subproblem is combinatorially less complex, and can be solved to determine the variables z_{it}. Then, for fixed values of z_{it}, the problem (P) may be solved to determine a specific solution that is an upper bound to the solution of (P). We note that due to the discrete lot-sizes, the integer solution of (P) may result in slacks in equation (11) and therefore may result in all multipliers of value zero (to satisfy complementary slackness). Therefore, the multipliers λ_t for the next iteration were obtained from the LP relaxation of (P). The problem is then solved iteratively until the bounds converge. Note that the bounds are not guaranteed to converge as there may be a duality gap due to discrete nature of the problem.

Restricting the Problem: $L_i = E_i$

It is comparatively easier to solve the problem when x_{it} has no discontinuous discrete integer values. Thus, with the assumption $L_i := E_i \; \forall i \in SKU_2$, binary variables z_{it} and equations (8) and (10) can be eliminated from the formulation. Restricting a given problem instance increases the lot-sizes for all products in SKU_2, thereby reducing the set of feasible solutions. As we could not find solutions to the unrestricted problem with CPLEX, we used restricted models for all experiments with IP branch-and-bound. The restricted problem is a sub-class of the original problem.

Experimental Results

The experimental results reported in this section are based on a study of real data for 190 items and 52 weeks provided by a client of i2 Technologies from the process industry. The OIP model resulting from the given data is large: 7520 finite domain variables (average domain size 10) and 3047 constraints (average number of variables 30, 1525 constraints soft). To summarize the experimental results from the viewpoint of the client, what has the study achieved? (i) It found a solution which is provably within 1.4% of the optimal total cost for constant labor (two shifts), which (ii) shows that substantially cutting down cost requires reducing labor. (iii) It showed that labor can be reduced to one shift in up to 25 weeks with over 15% potential savings of total cost (or USD 1.9 million).

Comparison of Solvers

Table 3 reports the best solutions found by CPLEX and WSAT (OIP) in limited time and for different labor profiles. The table divides horizontally and vertically, distinguishing the original from the restricted model and the fixed-capacity from the varied-capacity case.

cost	real problem WSAT (OIP)	restricted problem CPLEX	WSAT (OIP)
profile	fixed capacity, two shifts (230K)		
labor	11,960,000	11,960,000	11,960,000
inventory	1,023,106	1,120,680	1,040,373
total	12,983,106	13,080,680	13,000,373
profile	one shift [28,52]	one shift [30,51]	
labor	9,085,000	9,430,000	9,430,000
inventory	1,961,049	1,715,043	1,819,634
total	11,046,049	11,145,043	11,249,634

Table 3: Computational results with WSAT (OIP) and CPLEX 4.0. The restricted model forces $L_i := E_i$.

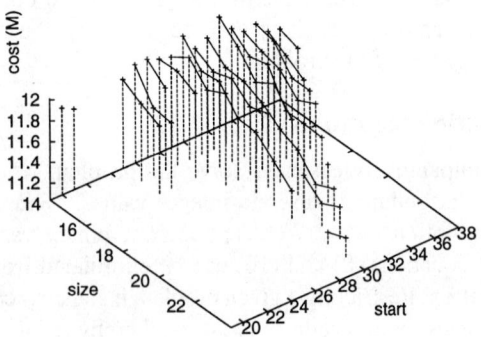

(a) CPLEX on the restricted MILP model.

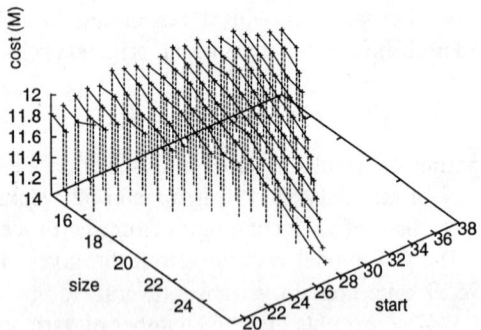

(b) WSAT (OIP) on the over-constrained IP model.

Figure 2: Solutions for various labor profiles. Each impulse represents the total cost of the best solution found at one labor profile (start/size coordinates correspond to profiles [start, start+size−1], the vertical axis is overall cost).

With respect to overall quality, the best solutions among all profiles obtained from both methods are approximately equal (WSAT (OIP) leading by less than 1% of the total cost, or USD 98,994). In the experiments, the runtime of WSAT (OIP) was limited to 10 minutes, CPLEX and was allowed 15 minutes for optimization and was cut-off after 30 minutes in case no feasible solution was found. All experiments were performed on a Sun Sparc Ultra II. Run-times were kept short because many labor profiles had to be examined to find solutions of good overall quality.

Figure 2 visualizes the experiments across different labor profiles. The right edge of the triangle reflects the fact that the size of the one-shift period must decrease as week 52 is approached, because the planning horizon is finite. On the restricted model, CPLEX could not find a solution with more than 22 one-shift periods in the given time while WSAT (OIP) was able to solve a problem with 25 one-shift periods. In general, CPLEX had difficulties to find feasible solutions as the labor constraints were tightened: Of 115 profiles solved by WSAT (OIP), CPLEX only solved 68 profiles (59%) within the given time limit (for comparison, WSAT (OIP) could still solve 100 given the restricted

model). For the profiles that could be solved with both methods, WSAT (OIP) found better solutions in 41 cases; CPLEX found better solutions in 22 cases, despite the fact that it was applied to the restricted model. In the cases where WSAT (OIP) [CPLEX] was better, on average it improved over CPLEX [WSAT (OIP)] by 3.7% [1.3%] with respect to pure inventory cost.

Parameters CPLEX was run with standard parameter settings. In all experiments with WSAT (OIP), the following parameters were used: Initial production was set to zero ($p_{zero} = 1$), and a number of 10 tries were performed, each with 100K moves. Allowed variable triggers were limited to 2 steps up or down the current variable value. Hard constraints were repaired with high priority ($p_{hard} = 0.9$). Random moves appeared to deteriorate the solution quality, therefore we set $p_{noise} = 0$. A long tabu tenure appeared to be important to find feasible solutions for problems with very tight capacity ($t = 100$). Constraint weights were critical to obtain good feasible solutions and were assigned statically: The hard NOH constraints were weighted with a large number, expressing a preference to keep NOH constraints satisfied. In contrast, CAP constraints were weighted below 1.0 so that temporarily violating them during the search was encouraged.

Lower Bounds

To assess the quality of the solutions, we applied bound reasoning based on Lagrangean relaxation as described above. We used a relaxed labor profile of constant 300K, which is over two shifts per week and therefore an unrealistic problem. For a precise estimate of the solution quality, table 4 reports pure inventory costs based on this profile for the different methods. Using Lagrangean decomposition, we found solutions to the relaxed labor profile, but unfortunately could not find solutions for realistic capacity constraints. Table 4 also indicates that WSAT (OIP) is still considerably away from the best Lagrangean relaxation based solution (3.4% of inventory costs). With respect to the overall cost of this profile, the difference vanishes (0.2%). The reported lower bound is valid also for the original problem with constant two-shift labor, because the 300K-problem is a relaxation of the original problem.

Solution/bound ($T_t = 300K$)	type	value
Best IP solution	restricted	986,780
Best solution from WSAT (OIP)	restricted	973,834
Best solution from WSAT (OIP)	original	942,511
Best Lagrangean solution	original	911,960
Best valid lower bound	original	839,875

Table 4: Solutions (inventory cost) based on a fixed-capacity labor profile of 300K in all weeks.

Conclusions

We have studied a real-world capacitated lot-sizing problem (CLSP) from the process industry. Because the problem includes discrete lot-size requirements not reported in the CLSP literature, existing domain-specific methods are not directly applicable. We therefore approached the problem with WSAT(OIP), a new domain-independent local search method for integer optimization. WSAT(OIP) operates on over-constrained integer programs and generalizes the WSAT($\mathcal{PB}$) heuristic. We experimentally compared the results to a commercial mixed integer programming solver.

While exact techniques for general purpose integer optimization (such as IP branch-and-bound) are widely researched and developed into industrial tools (such as CPLEX), few domain-independent heuristics for combinatorial optimization have been described. In this paper, we have presented a new local search heuristic for integer optimization and evaluated its performance on a capacitated production planning problem. Although the research on integer local search (ILS) is only at its beginning, the empirical results are promising: Integer local search can solve a CLSP with discrete lot-sizes of which a commercial MIP solver can only solve a sub-class. In terms of robustness, WSAT(OIP) is superior to CPLEX on the given data, in particular as the capacity constraints are tightened. The ILS model is simpler than the MIP model, and with respect to solution quality, the techniques are on par.

Acknowledgments

The first author is supported by a DFG (Deutsche Forschungsgemeinschaft) doctoral fellowship. We would like to thank Jimi Crawford for guidance and support in the course of this study. We are indebted to i2 Technologies, Ravi Gujar, Srinivasan Kumar, and the client from the process industry for making the publication of this study possible. Many thanks to the optimization teams of i2 Technologies and to Alexander Bockmayr, Martin Müller, Joachim Niehren, Gert Smolka, and Jörg Würtz for valuable suggestions and comments.

References

Aboudi, R., and Jörnsten, K. 1994. Tabu search for general zero-one integer programs using the pivot and complement heuristic. *ORSA Journal on Computing* 6(1):82–93.

Abramson, D.; Dang, H.; and Krishnamoorthy, M. 1996. A comparison of two methods for solving 0–1 integer programs using a general purpose simulated annealing algorithm. *Annals of Operations Research* 63:129–150.

Balas, E., and Martin, C. 1980. Pivot and complement – a heuristic for zero-one programming. *Management Science* 26:86–96.

Beasley, J. E. 1993. Lagrangean relaxation. In Reeves, C. R., ed., *Modern Heuristic Techniques for Combinatorial Problems*. Halsted Press. 70–150.

Bitran, G., and Yanasse, H. 1982. Computational complexity of the capacitated lot size problem. *Management Science* 28:1174–1186.

Borning, A.; Freeman-Benson, B.; and Wilson, M. 1996. Constraint hierarchies. In Jampel, M. B.; Freuder, E.; and Maher, M., eds., *Over-constrained Systems*. Springer.

Connolly, D. 1992. General purpose simulated annealing. *Journal of the Operational Research Society* 43:495–505.

Diaby, M.; Bahl, H.; Karwan, M.; and Zionts, S. 1992. A Lagrangean relaxation approach for very-large-scale capacitated lot-sizing. *Management Science* 38(9):1329–1340.

Drexl, A., and Kimms, A. 1997. Lot sizing and scheduling – survey and extensions. *European Journal of Operational Research* 99:221–235.

Glover, F., and Laguna, M. 1993. Tabu search. In Reeves, C. R., ed., *Modern Heuristic Techniques for Combinatorial Problems*. Halsted Press. 70–150.

Glover, F., and Laguna, M. 1997. General purpose heuristics for integer programming–part I & II. *Journal of Heuristics* 2/3(4/2):343–358/161–179.

Hindi, K. 1996. Solving a CLSP by a tabu search heuristic. *Journal of the Operational Research Society* 47:151–161.

Kirca, Ö., and Kökten, M. 1994. A new heuristic approach for the multi-item dynamic lot sizing problem. *European Journal of Operational Research* 75:332–341.

Løkketangen, A.; Jörnsten, K.; and Storøy, S. 1994. Tabu search within a pivot and complement framework. *Int. Transactions on Operations Research* 1(3):305–316.

McAllester, D.; Selman, B.; and Kautz, H. 1997. Evidence for invariants in local search. In *Proceedings AAAI-97*.

Nemhauser, G., and Wolsey, L. 1988. *Integer and Combinatorial Optimization*. Series in Discrete Mathematics and Optimization. Wiley-Intersience.

Parkes, A., and Walser, J. 1996. Tuning local search for satisfiability testing. In *Proceedings AAAI-96*, 356–362.

Selman, B., and Kautz, H. 1993. Domain-independent extensions to GSAT: Solving large structured satisfiability problems. In *Proceedings of IJCAI-93*.

Selman, B.; Kautz, H.; and Cohen, B. 1994. Noise strategies for improving local search. In *Proceedings AAAI-94*, 337–343.

Walser, J. 1997. Solving linear pseudo-boolean constraint problems with local search. In *Proceedings AAAI-97*.

Extending GENET to Solve Fuzzy Constraint Satisfaction Problems

Jason H. Y. Wong and Ho-fung Leung

Department of Computer Science and Engineering
The Chinese University of Hong Kong
Shatin, N.T., Hong Kong
{hywong,lhf}@cse.cuhk.edu.hk

Abstract

Despite much research that has been done on constraint satisfaction problems (CSP's), the framework is sometimes inflexible and the results are not very satisfactory when applied to real-life problems. With the incorporation of the concept of fuzziness, fuzzy constraint satisfaction problems (FCSP's) have been exploited. FCSP's model real-life problems better by allowing individual constraints to be either fully or partially satisfied. GENET, which has been shown to be efficient and effective in solving certain traditional CSP's, is extended to handle FCSP's. Through transforming FCSP's into $0-1$ integer programming problems, we display the equivalence between the underlying working mechanism of fuzzy GENET and the discrete Lagrangian method. Simulator of fuzzy GENET for single-processor machines is implemented. Benchmarking results confirm its feasibility in tackling CSP's and flexibility in dealing with over-constrained problems.

Introduction

A constraint satisfaction problem (CSP) (Mackworth 1977) involves finding an assignment of values to variables satisfying all constraints. Apart from the naive generate-and-test paradigm, two main approaches have been developed for solving CSP's. The first combines pure tree search with various degrees of constraint propagation. To improve the efficiency of search, techniques such as dependency-directed backtracking, value- and variable-ordering heuristics have been employed. Despite their extensive literature, these constructive methods still need to spend too much time on large-scale problems due to their exponential time complexity and thrashing behavior. In the second approach, repair-based methods are used. They consist of generating for all variables an initial, possibly inconsistent assignment. Variables are then repaired until all constraints are satisfied. This approach has efficiently solved problems such as the one million queens problem (Minton et al. 1990). Nevertheless, this method can get caught in local minima. By combining the min-conflicts heuristic repair method (Minton et al. 1990; 1992) with a learning strategy to escape local minima, Tsang and Wang (1992) proposed GENET, which is a generic neural network approach for solving CSP's with binary constraints.

The traditional CSP framework provides an elegant way to model problems with hard constraints. However, when applied to real-life problems, this framework is sometimes inflexible. Various proposals have been put forward in a direction to extend the original CSP model with soft constraints. Viewing a crisp constraint as the set of tuples for which the constraint holds, fuzzy set theory seems a natural choice as the tool for the extension. Several researchers have exploited this possibility by formalizing the concept of fuzzy constraint satisfaction problems (FCSP's). They suggest branch-and-bound algorithm as a substitution for backtracking tree search. Some existing techniques developed in the context of CSP's (for example, local consistency, value- and variable-ordering heuristics (Dubois, Fargier, & Prade 1993b; 1993a; Ruttkay 1994; Guesgen & Philpott 1995; Meseguer & Larrosa 1997)) are also adapted to boost search performance.

Inheriting the disadvantages from their counterparts in CSP algorithms, branch-and-bound searches are not efficient, either. Some researchers thus put their attention on stochastic algorithms and sacrifice completeness. One attempt is the emergent computation model CCM (Kanada 1995). Though not performing as good as tree search algorithms, CCM's sole dependency on local information lends itself to parallelization. Another attempt by Bowen and Dozier (1996a; 1996b) is the development of FMEHA1 and FMEHA2. Both of them are applications of evolutionary algorithms and have been tested on random FCSP's.

In this paper, we propose fuzzy GENET, a stochastic model for solving FCSP's based on GENET. Benchmarking results of GENET and fuzzy GENET exhibit similar performance on traditional CSP's. With the incorporation of the concept of fuzziness, fuzzy GENET excels GENET in the ability to deal with over-constrained problems.

This paper is organized as follows. After a short introduction of FCSP's in the next section, the fuzzy GENET model is revealed. We provide sufficient settings for the equivalence between the mechanism of fuzzy GENET and the discrete Lagrangian method (Shang & Wah 1998). Benchmarking results of fuzzy GENET on both CSP's and FCSP's are then presented. Finally, we conclude the paper and give the direction of our future work.

Fuzzy Constraint Satisfaction Problems

A *constraint satisfaction problem* (CSP) is defined as a tuple (Z, D, C^c). Z is a finite set of variables. D is a finite set of domains, one associated with each variable in Z. C^c is a set of constraints. Each k-ary constraint c^c is a crisp relation R^c among the variables of a subset $Z' = \{z_1, z_2, \ldots, z_k\}$ of Z. The *characteristic function* μ_{R^c} of R^c maps from $D_{z_1} \times D_{z_2} \times \ldots \times D_{z_k}$ to $\{0, 1\}$. A returned value of 1 signifies satisfaction and 0 violation. A binary CSP is a CSP with unary and binary constraints only. The assignment of value v to variable z is represented by a *label* v_z. A *compound label* is the simultaneous assignment of values to a set of variables. The goal of a CSP is to find a compound label for all variables in Z that satisfies all the constraints in C^c.

A *fuzzy constraint satisfaction problem* (FCSP) defined as (Z, D, C^f) differs from a CSP in the constraints involved. C^f is a set of fuzzy constraints. Each fuzzy constraint c^f is a fuzzy relation R^f among the variables of the subset $Z' = \{z_1, z_2, \ldots, z_k\}$ of Z. The *membership function* μ_{R^f} of R^f maps from $D_{z_1} \times D_{z_2} \times \ldots \times D_{z_k}$ to $[0, 1]$. μ_{R^f} assigns a *degree of satisfaction* $\alpha_{v_{z_1} v_{z_2} \ldots v_{z_k}} \in [0, 1]$ to each compound label $(v_{z_1} v_{z_2} \ldots v_{z_k})$ for variables in Z'. It is an indication of the extent $(v_{z_1} v_{z_2} \ldots v_{z_k})$ satisfies c^f. If it is equal to 0, $(v_{z_1} v_{z_2} \ldots v_{z_k})$ does not satisfy c^f at all. If it is 1, $(v_{z_1} v_{z_2} \ldots v_{z_k})$ fully satisfies c^f. An intermediate value between 0 and 1 signifies partial satisfaction.

The degree of satisfaction of a fuzzy constraint tells us to what extent it is satisfied. It is equal to the degree of satisfaction of the compound label chosen as the assignment. *Global satisfaction degree* $\alpha_P \in [0, 1]$ of an FCSP P shows its overall satisfaction. It is obtained from an aggregation of the degrees of satisfaction of all the fuzzy constraints by an operator f_α. In his first article about fuzzy set theory, Zadeh (1965) proposed to use min as f_α. Bellman and Zadeh (1970) later coined this as confluence of constraints, acquiring different meanings in different cases. With similar point of view, Zimmermann (1996) pointed out that the choice of appropriate aggregation operator largely depends on the context of the problem one deals with.

Threshold $\alpha_0 \in [0, 1]$ is a user-specified lower bound of the acceptable global satisfaction degree. The goal of an FCSP P is to find a compound label such that $\alpha_P \geq \alpha_0$.

Fuzzy GENET

Network Architecture

Fuzzy GENET is a neural network model for solving *binary* FCSP's. Each *label node* in the network represents one label using the same notation i_y. The state of a label node is either *on* or *off*. If a label node is on, it means that its corresponding assignment is being chosen. A *cluster* is the set of all label nodes that represents the labels of the same variable. A *connection* is placed between every pair of label nodes $(i_y j_z)$ of the two clusters of each binary fuzzy constraint (a *unary* fuzzy constraint is treated as a binary fuzzy constraint on the same variable). A 2-tuple is associated with each connection. The first component of the tuple is the degree of satisfaction of the compound label $(i_y j_z)$ according to the corresponding constraint. The second one is the *weight* $W_{i_y j_z}$ of the connection. Weights are initialized by

$$W_{i_y j_z} = \alpha_{i_y j_z} - 1 \qquad (1)$$

The *output* O_{i_y} of a label node i_y depends on its state. It is either 1 for on or 0 for off. The *input* I_{i_y} to i_y is the weighted sum of the outputs of all nodes connected to it. As only one label node in each cluster is permitted to be turned on at any time, every state of the network represents an assignment of a value to each variable in the network.

Convergence Procedure

The initial state of the fuzzy GENET network is *randomly* determined. One label node in each cluster is randomly selected to be turned on. In each convergence cycle, every label node calculates its input *asynchronously in parallel*. The node that receives the maximum input in each cluster will be turned on and the others will be turned off. Since there are only negative connections representing conflicting values, the winner in each cluster represents a value assigned to the corresponding variable with least constraint violations. After a number of cycles, the network will settle in a stable state. In a stable state, if $\alpha_P \geq \alpha_0$, an acceptable solution has been found. Otherwise, the network is trapped in a local minimum.

Care has to be taken when there is more than one winning node in a network update. If none of them is already on since the last update, one node will be *randomly* selected to be turned on. If one of them is already on, it will remain on. This is to avoid chaotic or cyclic wandering of the network states.

Learning Procedure

When fuzzy GENET settles in a local minimum, there are some active label nodes that still receive negative input, indicating that some constraints are violated. This happens because the state update of each cluster is only based on local decision and this does not necessarily lead to a global optimal solution. In such case, the state update rule would fail to make alternative choices.

To overcome these problems, a *heuristic learning rule* which updates the connection weights is used:
$$W_{i_y j_z}^{new} = W_{i_y j_z}^{old} + O_{i_y}^{old} O_{j_z}^{old}(\alpha_{i_y j_z} - 1) \quad (2)$$
To see how this rule works, suppose we have a network settled in local minimum. There must exist at least two active label nodes i_y and j_z connected by a negative weight. Also i_y and j_z must have the maximum input in their own cluster. However, their inputs will be reduced after every learning cycle, as long as the state of the network does not change. After sufficient number of cycles, either i_y or j_z will not win the competition in their own cluster. Hence, the state of the network will eventually find its way out of the local minimum.

The overall fuzzy GENET algorithm is shown in figure 1.

```
randomly turn on a label node per cluster
for each W_{i_y j_z} do
    set W_{i_y j_z} = α_{i_y j_z} - 1
end for
while α_P < α_0 do
    for each cluster do
        (asynchronously in parallel)
        turn on only node with maximum input
        and keep original state if needed
    end for
    if local minimum reached then
        for each W_{i_y j_z} do
            update W_{i_y j_z} :
            W_{i_y j_z}^{new} ← W_{i_y j_z}^{old} + O_{i_y}^{old} O_{j_z}^{old}(α_{i_y j_z} - 1)
        end for
    end if
end while
```

Figure 1: Fuzzy GENET algorithm $\mathcal{F}$

Fuzzy GENET can be seen as an extension to GENET. One way to model GENET using fuzzy GENET is by adopting the minimum function as the aggregation operator f_α and assigning 1.0 as the threshold α_0. Obviously, the invention of fuzzy GENET broadens the area of application of GENET by modifications conforming to the definition of FCSP.

Mechanism of Fuzzy GENET

Fuzzy GENET can tackle both binary CSP's and FCSP's. However, facing the same question to GENET, its underlying mechanism was not clear. Until recently, Choi and Lee (1998) have exploited the relationship between GENET and the Discrete Lagrangian Method. Their results shed light on our research as it has been mentioned above that GENET is an instance of fuzzy GENET. In this section, we employ a similar technique in search of an explanation of how fuzzy GENET works.

A $0-1$ Integer Programming Formulation of Binary FCSP's

To solve a binary FCSP, a fuzzy GENET network is built as explained in the previous section. The principles behind these rules of construction can be applied in transforming a binary FCSP into a $0-1$ *integer programming problem*. Consider a binary FCSP (Z, D, C^f). For all variables $z \in Z$, we introduce one $0-1$ variable x_{j_z} to represent each label j_z. Each x_{j_z} thus corresponds to the label node j_z in the fuzzy GENET network. They exhibit identical behavior by taking a value of 1 when j is assigned to z and 0 otherwise. The vector $(\ldots, x_{j_z}, \ldots)$ constitutes all the $0-1$ variables in the transformation and we adopt $\mathbf{x}$ as its representation for convenience. In the fuzzy GENET model, only one label node in each cluster can have output equal to 1. This imposes constraints on the $0-1$ variables:

$$c_z(\mathbf{x}) = 1 \quad \forall z \in Z \quad (3)$$

where $c_z(\mathbf{x})$ gives the number of x_{j_z}, $j \in D_z$, taking the value of 1.

For each 2-compound label of a binary fuzzy constraint in C^f, a connection is established in the fuzzy GENET network to encode its degree of satisfaction. Analogously, a constraint is introduced for each label $(i_y j_z)$ as follows:

$$g_{i_y j_z}(\mathbf{x}) \equiv a_{i_y j_z}(\mathbf{x})\sqrt{1 - \alpha_{i_y j_z}} = 0 \quad (4)$$

where $a_{i_y j_z}(\mathbf{x}) = \begin{cases} 1 & \text{if } x_{i_y} = x_{j_z} = 1 \\ 0 & \text{otherwise} \end{cases}$

The constraint is violated when both $0-1$ variables x_{i_y} and x_{j_z} takes a value of 1 and $\alpha_{i_y j_z} < 1$. Intuitively, this means that the 2-compound label $(i_y j_z)$ is chosen for instantiation but it fails to fully satisfy its corresponding binary fuzzy constraint. The reason for incorporating the factor $\sqrt{1 - \alpha_{i_y j_z}}$ into $g_{i_y j_z}$ will become clear in the following sections.

From the fuzzy GENET algorithm, we can see no explicit optimization of a particular function. So to complete the transformation, we set the objective function to be the constant function $f(\mathbf{x}) \equiv 0$. Finally, the corresponding $0-1$ integer programming problem for a binary FCSP is defined as follows:

$$\min f(\mathbf{x}) = 0$$

$$\text{subject to} \quad g_{i_y j_z}(\mathbf{x}) = 0 \quad \forall (i_y j_z) \in T$$

$$\text{and} \quad c_z(\mathbf{x}) = 1 \quad \forall z \in Z \quad (\mathcal{IP})$$

where $T = \{(i_y j_z) \mid y, z \in Z, i \in D_y, j \in D_z\}$.

Discrete Lagrangian Method Application

Lagrangian methods are well-known classical methods for solving continuous constrained optimization problems (Simmons 1975). Recently, Shang and Wah (1998) proposed the Discrete Lagrangian Method (DLM) that works in the discrete space. Applying DLM to problem ($\mathcal{IP}$), the Lagrangian function L is defined as

$$\begin{aligned} L(\mathbf{x}, \boldsymbol{\lambda}) &= f(\mathbf{x}) + \sum_{(i_y j_z) \in T} \lambda_{i_y j_z} g_{i_y j_z}(\mathbf{x}) \\ &= \sum_{(i_y j_z) \in T} \lambda_{i_y j_z} g_{i_y j_z}(\mathbf{x}) \end{aligned} \quad (5)$$

where $\boldsymbol{\lambda}$ is a vector of *Lagrange multipliers* $(\ldots, \lambda_{i_y j_z}, \ldots)$. Note that constraint 3 is missing in L. We will explain how it is enforced in the next section.

According to the Discrete Saddle-Point Theorem (Shang & Wah 1998), $\mathbf{x}^*$ is a minimum of ($\mathcal{IP}$) if and only if there exists some Lagrange multipliers $\boldsymbol{\lambda}^*$ such that $(\mathbf{x}^*, \boldsymbol{\lambda}^*)$ constitutes a *saddle point* of the associated Lagrangian function $L(\mathbf{x}, \boldsymbol{\lambda})$. In other words, we can apply a saddle point-seeking algorithm to obtain the minimum of ($\mathcal{IP}$). Based on its definition, $L(\mathbf{x}^*, \boldsymbol{\lambda}) \leq L(\mathbf{x}^*, \boldsymbol{\lambda}^*) \leq L(\mathbf{x}, \boldsymbol{\lambda}^*)$, a saddle point can be reached by performing a descent in the original variable space of $\mathbf{x}$ and an ascent in the Lagrange-multiplier space of $\boldsymbol{\lambda}$. So we end up with the following difference equations:

$$\begin{aligned} \mathbf{x}^{k+1} &= \mathbf{x}^k - \Delta_{\mathbf{x}} L(\mathbf{x}^k, \boldsymbol{\lambda}^k) \\ \boldsymbol{\lambda}^{k+1} &= \boldsymbol{\lambda}^k + \mathbf{g}(\mathbf{x}^k) \end{aligned} \quad (6)$$

where Δ_x is a *discrete gradient operator* and $\mathbf{g}(\mathbf{x}^k)$ is the vector of constraints $(\ldots, g_{i_y j_z}, \ldots)$.

Following Wah and Shang (1998), we translate equation 6 directly to the *generic discrete Lagrangian algorithm $\mathcal{G}$* as shown in figure 2. Notice that the algorithm is generic in the sense that several details for a real implementation are left unspecified.

```
set initial x and λ
while x not a solution, i.e., L(x, λ) > 0 do
    update x: x ← x − Δ_x L(x, λ)
    if condition for updating λ satisfied then
        update λ: λ ← λ + g(x)
    end if
end while
```

Figure 2: Generic discrete Lagrangian algorithm $\mathcal{G}$ for solving ($\mathcal{IP}$)

Equivalence Theorem

To construct the fuzzy GENET algorithm $\mathcal{F}$ by the generic discrete Lagrangian algorithm $\mathcal{G}$, we need the following five settings (ψ):

- initial $\mathbf{x}$: $\forall z \in Z, j \in D_z \quad x_{j_z} = O_{j_z}$
- initial $\boldsymbol{\lambda}$: $\forall (i_y j_z) \in T \quad \lambda_{i_y j_z} = \sqrt{1 - \alpha_{i_y j_z}}$

- acceptance condition for solution: $\alpha_P \geq \alpha_0$
- $\Delta_{\mathbf{x}} = \Delta_{\mathbf{x}}^{\mathcal{L}} \equiv (\{\Delta_{\mathbf{x}^z} \mid z \in Z\}, \Omega)$:

    $\Delta_{\mathbf{x}^z}$: *partial discrete gradient operator* that performs steepest descent in the x_{j_z} subspace, $\forall j \in D_z$. It exchanges the values of two variables x_{i_z} and x_{j_z}, $i, j \in D_z$ so that the Lagrangian L is minimized. In other words, its operation does not violate constraint 3. If there are two or more ways for the exchange, the choice follows that of algorithm $\mathcal{F}$.

    Ω: order of application of $\Delta_{\mathbf{x}^z}$'s. The same as the order of variable update in algorithm $\mathcal{F}$.

- condition for updating $\boldsymbol{\lambda}$: local minima in $\mathbf{x}$ space is reached

We call this resultant discrete Lagrangian algorithm $\mathcal{L}$ and it is shown in figure 3. Next, we state without prove two lemmas and the *equivalence theorem* between $\mathcal{L}$ and $\mathcal{F}$.

```
for z ∈ Z do
    randomly choose i ∈ D_z and set x_{i_z} = 1
    for each j ∈ D_z ∧ j ≠ i do
        set x_{j_z} = 0
    end for
end for
for each λ_{i_y j_z}, (i_y j_z) ∈ T do
    set λ_{i_y j_z} = √(1 − α_{i_y j_z})
end for
while α_P < α_0 do
    for each z ∈ Z do
        (asynchronously in parallel)
        update x : x ← x − Δ_{x^z}
    end for
    if local minimum reached then
        update λ: λ ← λ + g(x)
    end if
end while
```

Figure 3: Discrete Lagrangian algorithm $\mathcal{L}$

Lemma 1 *If currently, (i) $O_{j_z}^{old} = x_{j_z}^{old} \quad \forall z \in Z, j \in D_z$, (ii) $W_{i_y j_z}^{old} = -\lambda_{i_y j_z}^{old} \sqrt{1 - \alpha_{i_y j_z}} \quad \forall (i_y j_z) \in T$, (iii) $\mathcal{G}$ updates $\mathbf{x}$ once with $\Delta_{\mathbf{x}^v}$ and (iv) $\mathcal{F}$ updates the states of label nodes in cluster v once, then (i) $O_{j_z}^{new} = x_{j_z}^{new} \quad \forall z \in Z, j \in D_z$ and (ii) $W_{i_y j_z}^{new} = -\lambda_{i_y j_z}^{new} \sqrt{1 - \alpha_{i_y j_z}} \quad \forall (i_y j_z) \in T$.*

Corollary 1 *As v is only a generic variable, lemma 1 is true for all $z \in Z$. In other words, if currently, (i) $O_{j_z}^{old} = x_{j_z}^{old} \quad \forall z \in Z, j \in D_z$, (ii) $W_{i_y j_z}^{old} = -\lambda_{i_y j_z}^{old} \sqrt{1 - \alpha_{i_y j_z}} \quad \forall (i_y j_z) \in T$, (iii) $\mathcal{G}$ updates $\mathbf{x}$ with $\Delta_{\mathbf{x}} = \Delta_{\mathbf{x}}^{\mathcal{L}}$ and (iv) $\mathcal{F}$ performs once the convergence procedure, then (i) $O_{j_z}^{new} = x_{j_z}^{new} \quad \forall z \in Z, j \in D_z$ and (ii) $W_{i_y j_z}^{new} = -\lambda_{i_y j_z}^{new} \sqrt{1 - \alpha_{i_y j_z}} \quad \forall (i_y j_z) \in T$.*

Corollary 1 states that the equivalence between the state of a fuzzy GENET and the values of the parameters of its corresponding Lagrangian function is preserved if simultaneously $\mathcal{F}$ performs the convergence procedure once and $\mathcal{L}$ updates $\mathbf{x}$ with $\Delta \mathbf{x}$.

Lemma 2 *If currently, (i) $O_{j_z}^{old} = x_{j_z}^{old}$ $\forall z \in Z, j \in D_z$, (ii) $W_{i_y j_z}^{old} = -\lambda_{i_y j_z}^{old} \sqrt{1 - \alpha_{i_y j_z}}$ $\forall (i_y j_z) \in T$, (iii) $\mathcal{G}$ updates $\boldsymbol{\lambda}$ and (iv) $\mathcal{F}$ performs once the learning procedure, then (i) $O_{j_z}^{new} = x_{j_z}^{new}$ $\forall z \in Z, j \in D_z$ and (ii) $W_{i_y j_z}^{new} = -\lambda_{i_y j_z}^{new} \sqrt{1 - \alpha_{i_y j_z}}$ $\forall (i_y j_z) \in T$.*

Lemma 2 states that the equivalence between the state of a fuzzy GENET and the values of the parameters of its corresponding Lagrangian function is preserved if simultaneously $\mathcal{F}$ performs the learning procedure once and $\mathcal{L}$ updates $\boldsymbol{\lambda}$.

By corollary 1 and lemma 2, it is obvious that if the initial state of a fuzzy GENET is equivalent to the initial values of the parameters of its corresponding Lagrangian function, then $\mathcal{F}$ and $\mathcal{L}$ are equivalent. This fact is stated as the following theorem:

Theorem 1 *(Equivalence Theorem) If $\mathcal{G}$ is instantiated with the five settings (ψ), then it is equivalent to $\mathcal{F}$. That is, $\mathcal{L} \equiv \mathcal{F}$.*

Benchmarking Results

As mentioned above, fuzzy GENET is an extension of GENET. To illustrate this point, we have built a fuzzy GENET simulator and test the implementation on both binary CSP's and FCSP's. All the benchmarkings are performed on a SUN SPARCstation 10 model 30 running SunOS 4.1.4. Timing results for fuzzy GENET are the median of 100 runs.

The n-queens Problem

The n-queens problem is to place n queens on an $n \times n$ chess-board so that no two queens attack each other. A GENET simulator is built in this experiment. The timing results of GENET and fuzzy GENET are shown in table 1.

Table 1: Results on n-queens problem

n	GENET	Fuzzy GENET
10	0.06s	0.08s
20	0.48s	0.52s
30	2.09s	2.18s
40	7.27s	9.52s
50	12.49s	13.03s
60	23.04s	23.13s
70	32.03s	30.58s

Obviously, the results in table 1 illustrate that fuzzy GENET is almost as efficient as GENET in solving binary CSP's since fuzzy GENET and GENET are similar in handling crisp binary constraints.

The $n \times (n-1)$-queens Problem

In the $n \times (n - 1)$-queens problem (Guan 1994), n queens are placed on an $n \times (n-1)$ chess-board so that there exists at least one pair of queens attacking each other. We define that it is better for any two queens attacking each other to be separated by a greater vertical distance. Formally, the problem can be formulated as follows. There are n variables $\{v_1, \ldots, v_n\}$, each with a domain of $\{1, \ldots, n-1\}$. The degree of satisfaction for the fuzzy constraint $\texttt{noattack}(Q_{i_1}, Q_{i_2})$ that prohibits two queens on row i_1 and row i_2 from attacking each other is 1 if these two queens do not attack each other, and $\frac{|i_1 - i_2| - 1}{n-1}$ if they do. Therefore, when the vertical distance between two queens increases, $|i_1 - i_2|$ and the degree of satisfaction also increase.

The results of fuzzy GENET on the $n \times (n-1)$-queens problem are shown in table 2.

Table 2: Results on $n \times (n - 1)$ queens problem

threshold	0.9	0.8	0.7	0.6	0.5
20 × 19	0.40s	0.13s	0.10s	0.08s	0.05s
30 × 29	2.63s	0.88s	0.28s	0.22s	0.17s
40 × 39	5.03s	0.88s	0.33s	0.32s	0.32s
50 × 49	6.22s	1.70s	0.92s	0.77s	0.65s
60 × 59	9.28s	3.70s	1.85s	1.33s	1.32s
70 × 69	16.91s	4.54s	2.49s	2.10s	2.03s

Randomly Generated FCSP's

The suite of random FCSP's provided by Dozier (Bowen & Dozier 1996a; 1996b) can be viewed as a triple (n, d, t) where n is equal to 10 and represents the number of variables in the FCSP as well as the domain sizes. d is the network density and t is the average constraint tightness. Values of d and t are taken from the set $\{0.1, 0.3, 0.5, 0.7, 0.9\}$. Since 5 values can be assigned to d and t, there are 25 classes of randomly generated FCSP's. For each class there are 10 instances, making a total of 250. The truth value of each tuple permitted by a constraint has a randomly assigned value within $[0..1]$.

The results in table 3 show the median truth value obtained (in parentheses) and the median time required in seconds.

Table 3: Results on random FCSP's

t	.1	.3	.5	.7	.9
$d=.1$	.4(.92)	0.3(.89)	1.1(.85)	3.0(.71)	-(0)
$d=.3$	.6(.74)	0.8(.58)	1.7(.37)	5.2(.03)	-(0)
$d=.5$	1.0(.48)	0.9(.35)	1.3(.06)	-(0)	-(0)
$d=.7$	2.2(.33)	3.7(.16)	4.9(.01)	-(0)	-(0)
$d=.9$	3.2(.26)	3.9(.12)	-(0)	-(0)	-(0)

Comparing with results presented in (Bowen & Dozier 1996a; 1996b), the truth values obtained are similar. For the instances with tightness t tends to 0.9, it is believed that there are no solutions. Results of Bowen and Dozier (1996b) are not shown because what they counted was the number of evaluations performed by their genetic algorithms.

Conclusion and Future Work

In this paper, we have defined the fuzzy GENET model for solving binary FCSP's. Underlying mechanism of fuzzy GENET has also been shown to be based on the discrete Lagrangian method. Benchmarking results on both CSP's and FCSP's show its advantage over GENET.

The direction of our future work is two-fold. The first is to extend fuzzy GENET to solve *non-binary* fuzzy constraints (parallel to the work in (Lee, Leung, & Won 1995)) and try to give similar proof for its mechanism. The second is to exploit the vast freedom in the choice of parameters of the discrete Lagrangian method and sort out efficient *variants* of fuzzy GENET.

Acknowledgments

We would like to thank Kenneth M. F. Choi and Jimmy H. M. Lee for very useful discussions and inspiration. We would also like to thank Gerry Dozier for providing a set of random FCSP's for benchmarking purpose.

This work is supported by the Croucher Foundation Research Grant CF94/21.

References

Bellman, R. E., and Zadeh, L. A. 1970. Decision-Making in a Fuzzy Environment. *Management Science* 17-B(4):141–164.

Bowen, J., and Dozier, G. 1996a. Solving Randomly Generated Fuzzy Constraint Networks Using Iterative Microevolutionary Hill-Climbing. In *Proceedings of the First International Symposium on Soft Computing in Industry*.

Bowen, J., and Dozier, G. 1996b. Solving Randomly Generated Fuzzy Constraint Networks Using Evolutionary/Systematic Hill-Climbing. In *Proccedings of the Fifth IEEE International Conference on Fuzzy Systems*, volume 1, 226–231.

Choi, K. M. F., and Lee, J. H. M. 1998. A Lagrangian Reconstruction of a Class of Local Search Methods. Technical report, The Chinese University of Hong Kong.

Dubois, D.; Fargier, H.; and Prade, H. 1993a. Propagation and Satisfaction of Flexible Constraints. In Yager, R. R., and Zadeh, L. A., eds., *Fuzzy Sets, Neural Networks and Soft Computing*. Kluwer Academic Press.

Dubois, D.; Fargier, H.; and Prade, H. 1993b. The Calculus of Fuzzy Restrictions as a Basis for Flexible Constraint Satisfaction. In *Proceedings of the Second IEEE International Conference on Fuzzy Systems*, volume 2, 1131–1136.

Guan, Q. 1994. *Extending Constraint Satisfaction Problem Solving with Fuzzy Set Theory*. Ph.D. Dissertation, Technical University of Vienna.

Guesgen, H. W., and Philpott, A. 1995. Heuristics for Solving Fuzzy Constraint Satisfaction Problems. In *Proceedings of the Second New Zealand International Two-Stream Conference Artificial Neural Networks and Expert Systems*, 132–135.

Kanada, Y. 1995. Fuzzy Constraint Satisfaction Using CCM – A Local Information Based Computation Model. In *Proceedings of the Fourth IEEE International Conference on Fuzzy Systems*, volume 4, 2319–2326.

Lee, J. H. M.; Leung, H. F.; and Won, H. W. 1995. Extending GENET for Non-binary CSP's. In *Proceedings of the Seventh International Conference on Tools with Artificial Intelligence*, 338–343.

Mackworth, A. K. 1977. Consistency in Networks of Relations. *Artificial Intelligence* 8(1):99–118.

Meseguer, P., and Larrosa, J. 1997. Solving Fuzzy Constraint Satisfaction Problems. In *Proceedings of the Sixth IEEE International Conference on Fuzzy Systems*, volume 3, 1233–1238.

Minton, S.; Johnston, M. D.; Philips, A. B.; and Laird, P. 1990. Solving Large Scale Constraint Satisfaction and Scheduling Problems Using a Heuristic Repair Method. In *Proceedings of the Eighth National Conference on Artificial Intelligence*, 17–24.

Minton, S.; Johnston, M. D.; Philips, A. B.; and Laird, P. 1992. Minimizing Conflicts: A Heuristic Repair Method for Constraint Satisifaction and Scheduling Problems. *Artificial Intelligence* 58(1–3):161–205.

Ruttkay, Z. 1994. Fuzzy Constraint Satisfaction. In *Proccedings of the Third IEEE International Conference on fuzzy Systems*, volume 2, 1263–1268.

Shang, Y., and Wah, B. W. 1998. A Discrete Lagrangian-Based Global-Search Method for Solving Satisfiability Problems. *Journal of Global Optimization* 12(1):61–100.

Simmons, D. M. 1975. *Nonlinear Programming for Operations Research*. Englewood Cliffs, N.J. : Prentice Hall.

Tsang, E. P. K., and Wang, C. J. 1992. A Generic Neural Network Approach for Constraint Satisfaction Problems. In *Neural Network Applications*. Springer-Verlag. 12–22.

Zadeh, L. A. 1965. Fuzzy Sets. *Information and Control* 8:338–353.

Zimmermann, H.-J. 1996. *Fuzzy Set Theory – And its Applications*. Boston: Kluwer Academic Publishers, third edition.

Local Search for Statistical Counting

Olivier Bailleux

CRIL
Université d'Artois
rue de l'Université SP 16
F-62307 Lens Cedex, France
bailleux@cril.univ-artois.fr

Abstract

In this paper, statistical counting is introduced in the context of stochastic local search. From a sample of trajectories by independent local search computations, it is shown that interesting statistical information can be actually extracted about the search space, most notably an unbiased estimate of the number of solutions. Computational results for random #SAT instances are provided.

Introduction

The stochastic local search paradigm covers a large number of techniques that use a neighborhood relation and a so-called fitness function for exploring a search space. Typically, these techniques are used to address hard optimization and search problems (Selman & Kautz 1993) that cannot be solved by means of more standard methods. For example, some stochastic local search algorithms specialized for boolean satisfiability testing can solve positive instances of the boolean satisfiability problem (SAT) that are intractable for all known systematic approaches.

Generally speaking, a local search process tries to find out a solution by exploring a search landscape, i.e. a neighborhood graph labeled with a fitness (or cost) function.

The performance of a stochastic local search system depends on both the landscape and the search strategy. One of the simplest strategies for maximization problems is known as hill climbing. It consists in drawing each new configuration uniformly from the set of the current configuration neighbors that increase the fitness function. The drawback of this strategy is that the search stops at local extrema. The greedy search is a variant that choose each new configuration from those that maximize the fitness function (even if the fitness decreases). More sophisticated techniques, like simulated annealing (van Laarhoven & Aarts 1987), introduce a noise in order to escape from local extrema. Another technique, known as tabu search(Mazure, Saïs, & Grégoire 1997), deals with local extrema by storing the most recently visited configurations in a tabu list in order to avoid them during the next steps. Because they can be used on all discrete optimization and search problems, the strategies like tabu, simulated annealing or greedy search are called *metaheuristics*, in contrast with specialized local search algorithms that use specific problem features, like WSAT algorithm (Selman, Kautz, & Cohen 1994) for satisfiability testing.

Beyond assessing the efficiency of local search algorithms, some experimental studies have been conducted so far, relating the behavior of local search processes to topological properties of search landscapes. For example, see (Frank, Cheeseman, & Stutz 1997) for a study of landscapes related to random 3SAT instances.

Let us now recall the class #P and the concept of counting Turing machine (CTM) which was introduced by Valiant in (Valiant 1979). A CTM is a non deterministic Turing machine with an auxiliary device that "magically" outputs the number of accepting computations induced by the input. The time complexity of a CTM is defined as the time complexity of the related non deterministic Turing machine (with no auxiliary device). So, a CTM exhibits a polynomial time complexity iff there is a polynomial p such that the longest accepting computation induced by the set of all the inputs of size n takes at most $p(n)$ steps. The class #P is the set of functions that can be computed in polynomial time by a CTM. #SAT, the problem of counting the number of satisfying assignments of a boolean formula that is expressed in conjunctive normal form, is #P-Complete. The restriction of #SAT to the boolean formulae with only positive literals (#MONOTONE-SAT), and even to the monotone formulae with only binary clauses (#2-MONOTONE-SAT), remains #P-Complete.

The relation $PH \subseteq P^{\#P}$, where PH denotes the polynomial hierarchy (Garey & Johnson 1979) and $P^{\#P}$ denotes the set of problems that can be solved in deterministic polynomial time with a #P oracle, follows directly from Toda's theorem (Toda 1989). This relation shows the hardness of #P-Complete problems like #SAT, #MONOTONE-SAT, #2SAT. In (Roth 1996), D. Roth shows that for any constant $\varepsilon > 0$, approximating the number of satisfying assignments of a 2-MONOTONE boolean formula of n variables within $2^{n^{1-\varepsilon}}$ is NP-Hard. So, even approximate resolution of #2-MONOTONE-SAT is intractable under the assumption $P \neq NP$.

In (Bailleux & Chabrier 1996) and (Bailleux & Chabrier 1997), it is proposed to use a statistical exploration of a search tree for approximate resolution of numbering problems.

In this paper, a concept of statistical counting is introduced in the context of stochastic local search. From a sample of trajectories by independent local search computations, it is shown that interesting statistical information can be actually extracted about the search space, most notably an unbiased estimate of the number of solutions.

This approach can be used for the approximate resolution of hard numbering problems (typically #P-Hard problems). Despite a huge variance, a statistical lower bound of the solution can be obtain with a given probability of error.

The proposed method does not advance the state of the art in terms of efficiency or quality of estimates, at least for random #SAT instances. Our motivation is rather to show that, from a sample of solutions obtained through stochastic local search, global information about the search landscape can be derived. As a result, the local search paradigm is not necessarily restricted to satisfiability testing or solution searching, but could be *potentially* extended to statistical counting and search landscapes analysis.

The paper is organized as follows. In a first section, a lemma is presented, which makes the connection between the size of two partitions of a finite set and the mathematical expectation of a random variable defined on this set. Then the application of this lemma for statistical counting by making two partitions of the set of possible trajectories of a stochastic local search process is described. In a second section, computational results from random #SAT instances are provided.

Formal framework
Principle

In this section, a lemma is presented, which makes the connection between the sizes of two partitions E and F of a finite set Ω and the mathematical expectation of a random variable X defined on Ω.

Let W be a function that maps Ω into $[0,1]$ s.t. for each $f \in F$, $\sum_{t \in f} W(t) = 1$.
Let V be a function that maps Ω into $]0,1]$ s.t. for each $e \in E$, $\sum_{t \in e} V(t) = 1$.
Let X be a random variable on Ω s.t. for all $t \in \Omega$, $X(t) = \frac{W(t)}{V(t)}$ and the probability of t is $P(t) = \frac{1}{|E|} V(t)$.

Let $E[X]$ denote the mathematical expectation of X.

Lemma 1 $E[X] = \frac{|F|}{|E|}$.

Proof:
$$\begin{aligned}
E[X] &= \sum_{t \in \Omega} P(t) X(t) \\
&= \sum_{t \in \Omega} \frac{1}{|E|} W(t) \\
&= \frac{1}{|E|} \sum_{t \in \Omega} W(t) \\
&= \frac{1}{|E|} \sum_{f \in F} \sum_{t \in f} W(t) = \frac{|F|}{|E|}
\end{aligned}$$
□

Suppose that we know $|E|$ and are able to compute $V(t)$ and $W(t)$ for any $t \in \Omega$. Thanks to Lemma 1, we can estimate $|F|$ in the following manner: Let t be drawn from Ω according to the probability $P = \frac{1}{|E|} V$. Then $|E| \frac{W(t)}{V(t)}$ is an unbiased estimate of $|F|$.

Search landscape

A *search landscape* is the information a stochastic local search algorithm needs to address a problem instance. In the simplest case, a search landscape is a labeled graph (U, R, g) where U is the search space (a finite set of configurations), $R \subseteq U \times U$ is a neighborhood relation and g is a fitness (or cost) function which maps U into an ordered set (typically the set of integer numbers). When dealing with optimization problems, the fitness function is part of the problem itself. For search problems, a fitness (resp. cost) function that is maximal (resp. minimal) for solutions, only, must be pointed out.

Let us define a *trajectory* as a sequence of configurations $\alpha_1, ..., \alpha_n$, s.t. for each $i \in 2..n$, $(\alpha_{i-1}, \alpha_i) \in R$ (i.e. α_i is in the neighborhood of α_{i-1}). Then a local search process is simply a process that follows a trajectory in a search landscape.

Application to hill climbing

The main idea is to make two partitions E and F of the set Ω of all possible trajectories of a stochastic Hill Climbing process (HC).

For each $x \in U$, let $h(x)$ (resp. $l(x)$) denote the set of neighbors of x that increase (resp. decrease) the fitness function.

The process HC starts from a configuration uniformly drawn in the search space U. Each new configuration is drawn uniformly from the set $h(x)$, where x is the current configuration, until $h(x) = \emptyset$. Each run stops either at a local or a global extremum.

The first partition E consists in bringing together all the trajectories starting from the same configuration. Then $|E| = |U|$.

The second partition F consists in bringing together all the trajectories ending at the same global extremum. The trajectories ending at a *local* extremum are arbitrary dispatched in the sets assigned to the global extrema, in such a way that $|F|$ equals the number of global extrema.

Let $first(t)$ (resp. $last(t)$) denote the first configuration (resp. the last configuration) of a trajectory t. For each $t \in \Omega$, let $V(t)$ denote the probability that HC returns the trajectory t, given that the search starts from $first(t)$. Notice that $\frac{V}{|E|}$ is a probability on Ω and for each $e \in E$, $\sum_{t \in e} V(t) = 1$.

For a trajectory $t = (\alpha_1, \ldots, \alpha_n)$, $V(t)$ can be computed as follows:

$$\begin{cases} \text{if } n = 1 \text{ then } V(t) = 1 \\ \text{else } V(t) = \prod_{i=1}^{n-1} \frac{1}{|h(\alpha_i)|} \end{cases}$$

In order to take advantage from lemma 1, we need a function W s.t. for each $f \in F$, $\sum_{t \in f} W(t) = 1$. It must be possible to compute $W(t)$ for any $t \in \Omega$, whenever we want W to be actually useful.

Let PV be a "virtual" stochastic process (i.e. a process which will never run), starting from a given global extremum. At each step, PV considers the set $l(x)$, where x is the current configuration. When $l(x) = \emptyset$, the search stops. When $l(x) \neq \emptyset$, the search stops with probability Q, or continues from a new configuration, uniformly drawn in $l(x)$, with probability $1 - Q$.

We chose the following function W: For each $t = (\alpha_1, \ldots, \alpha_n) \in \Omega$, if t ends at a local extrema then $W(t) = 0$, else $W(t)$ is the probability that PV returns $\tilde{t} = (\alpha_n, \ldots, \alpha_1)$, given that the search starts from α_n.

Let S be the set of global extrema. For a trajectory $t = (\alpha_1, \ldots, \alpha_n)$, $W(t)$ can be computed as follows:

$$\begin{cases} \text{if } last(t) \notin S \text{ then } W(t) = 0 \\ \text{else } W(t) = \lambda(Q, t) \end{cases}$$

Where $Q \in [0, 1]$ is a constant and $\lambda(Q, t)$, is defined as:

$$\begin{cases} \text{if } n = 1 \text{ and } |l(\alpha_1)| \neq 0 \text{ then } \lambda(Q, t) = Q \\ \text{if } n = 1 \text{ and } |l(\alpha_1)| = 0 \text{ then } \lambda(Q, t) = 1 \\ \text{if } n > 1 \text{ then } \lambda(Q, t) = \frac{1-Q}{|l(\alpha_n)|} \lambda(Q, (\alpha_1, \ldots, \alpha_{n-1})) \end{cases}$$

Yet, assuming we know $|U|$, all the conditions are right for estimating $|S|$ from a sample $(t_1, \ldots, t_m)$ of trajectories achieved by m independent computations of HC. The value μ defined as follows is an unbiased estimate of $|S|$:

$$\mu = |U| \frac{1}{m} \sum_{i=1}^{m} \frac{W(t_i)}{V(t_i)}$$

Using Markov's inequality, we can compute a lower bound of $|S|$ with a given probability of error. Because the random variable X cannot take a negative value, we have: $P(X > \gamma E[X]) \leq \frac{1}{\gamma}$ for any constant $\gamma > 0$.

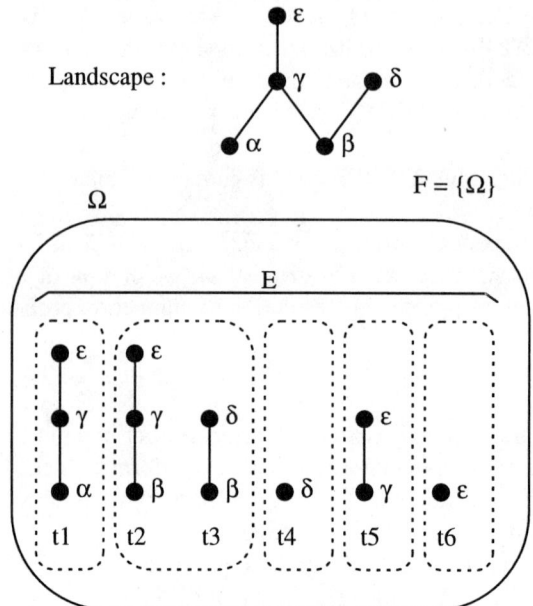

Figure 1: The set Ω and the partitions E and F for a simple landscape.

So, if $\mu_1, \ldots, \mu_n$ is a sequence of unbiased estimates of $|S|$, then we can claim that $\frac{1}{\gamma} \min\{\mu_1, \ldots, \mu_n\}$ is lower than $|S|$ with probability of error at most equals to $1/\gamma^n$.

Notice that if $Q = 1$ the only trajectories for which $X > 0$ are the ones that start directly from a global extremum ($first(t) = last(t) \in S$). So, the method collapses to the estimate of $|S|$ by uniform sampling from the search space. If $0 < Q < 1$, all the trajectories ending with a global extremum are taken into account. At last, if $Q = 0$, only the trajectories t for which $|l(first(t))| = 0$ are taken into account.

We suppose (and we show experimentally in the next section) that for a given landscape, quality of estimates depends on the value of Q. Actually, we have no way to determine the optimal value of Q for landscapes related to #P-complete (or even simpler) problems.

As an example, Figure 1 presents, for a simple landscape, the set Ω and the partitions E and F. For $Q = 0.5$, the following values are assigned by V (resp. W) to the trajectories $t_1, \ldots, t_6$:

	t_1	t_2	t_3	t_4	t_5	t_6
V	1	1/2	1/2	1	1	1
W	1/8	1/8	0	0	1/4	1/2

It follows that $E[X] = 1/5 = \frac{|F|}{|E|}$.

Computational results

Implementation for SAT

The Boolean Satisfiability Problem (SAT) is the problem to decide whether an equation $\phi = 1$ – where ϕ is a boolean formula in conjunctive normal form – has at least one solution (Cook 1971). So, a SAT instance is a formula $c_1 \wedge \ldots \wedge c_k$ where each c_i is a clause, i.e. a disjunction $v_1^{\varepsilon_1} \vee \ldots \vee v_r^{\varepsilon_r}$, where each literal v_i^0 (resp. v_i^1) denotes the complemented form (resp. the direct form) of the variable v_i.

The rSAT problem (i.e. the restriction of SAT to instances with r literals per clauses) is NP-Complete for $r > 2$. Thereby, 3SAT, one of the simplest NP-Complete problem, is often used to evaluate the solving algorithms efficiency.

The #rSAT problem (the numbering problem related to rSAT) is the problem to determine the number of solutions of an equation $\phi = 1$, where ϕ is a CNF boolean formula with at most r literals per clause. It is #P-complete for $r > 1$, even if ϕ is monotone.

In our experimentations, the landscape related to a formula ϕ on n variables is $L_\phi = (U, R, g)$, where $U = \{0,1\}^n$ and for all $x, y \in U$,

- $(x, y) \in R$ if and only if the Hamming distance $H(x, y) = 1$,

- $g(x)$ is the number of clauses satisfied by x.

Experimentations on tractable random #SAT instances

In this section, we give results obtained from instances for which systematic counting methods are usable. This allows us to compare each estimate with the related exact number of solutions.

Let us define a *reduced* clause as a clause each variable of which occurs at most one time.

Our benchmarks include 3SAT instances each clause of which is drawn uniformly from the set of all possible reduced clauses, for a given number of variables.

For tractability reasons, random 3SAT instances of at most 50 variables were addressed.

In the sequel, k/n will denote the ratio of the number of clauses by the number of variables of a 3SAT instance.

Let us define the *relative error* of an estimate μ, achieved from a sample of trajectories related to an instance of s solutions, as $|\mu - s|/s$.

Because a few estimates could exhibit a relative error much higher than others, we chose to use the average on the 15-85 percentile range (i.e. trimmed mean) of relative errors for evaluating the quality of a sample of estimates.

According to the parameter Q, Figure 2 (resp. 3) shows the relative error for random 3SAT instances of 30 (resp.

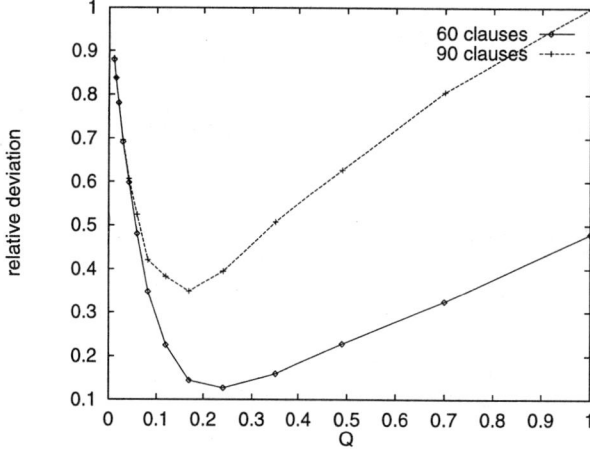

Figure 2: Random 3SAT instances, 30 variables. Relative error of estimates (Average on 15-85 percentile range, 500 mesures per point, 10000 trajectories per estimate).

50) variables with $k/n = 2$ and $k/n = 3$ (500 measures per point, 10000 trajectories per estimate).

Notice that in terms of exact counting, instances with $k/n = 2$ or 3 are much more difficult than instances with $k/n = 4.25$, usually used for evaluating search algorithms. For example, counting the solutions of random 50 variables 3SAT instances with a Davis and Putman procedure and Jeroslow's branching rule (Jeroslow & Wang 1990) requires on average 10^6 branches to be developed for $k/n = 2$, 10^4 for $k/n = 3$ and 200 for $k/n = 4.25$.

Empirically, the quality of estimates depends on the Q parameter. Local search based estimates are better than estimates based on uniform sampling, given that the best estimates are observed for $Q < 1$.

Experimentations on intractable random #SAT instances

In this section, we are interested in randomly generated instances of 200 variables for which we do not know any reference of usable exact counting method.

For several values of the ratio k/n, Figure 4 gives the average of estimated number of solutions of random 3SAT instances obtained on the one hand using our local search based method, on the other hand using uniform sampling from the search space. Theses results are compared with the theoretical expectation of the number of solutions (Simon & Dubois 1989), that is :

$$2^n \left(1 - \frac{1}{2^r}\right)^k$$

where $r = 3$ is the number of literals per clause, n is the number of variables and k is the number of clauses.

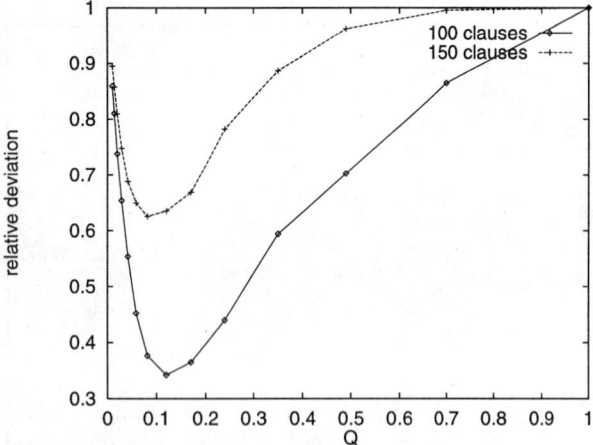

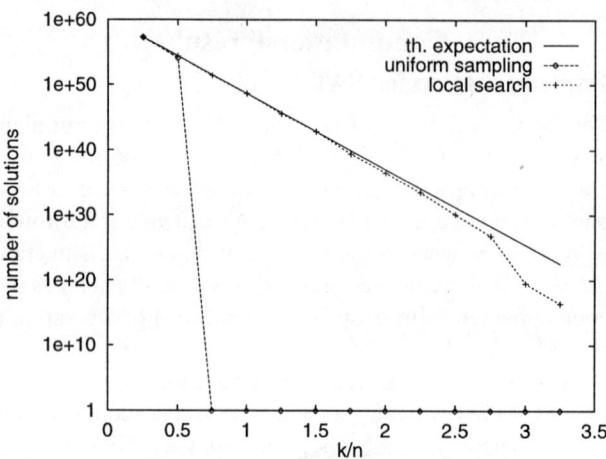

Figure 3: Random 3SAT instances, 50 variables. Relative error of estimates (Average on 15-85 percentile range, 500 mesures per point, 10000 trajectories per estimate).

Figure 4: Random 3SAT instances of 200 variables. Mathematical expectation of the number of solutions, local search based estimates and estimates by uniform sampling. 300 mesures per point, 10000 trajectories (resp. configurations) per mesure.

For each value of k/n, 300 estimates were computed. Each estimate was obtained by sampling 10^4 trajectories or 10^4 configurations, respectively.

Either way, the quality of estimates is getting worse when the number of solutions decreases, but this phenomenon occurs much more quickly with uniform sampling. Although these results are slightly worse than those obtained with a randomized David and Putman procedure, especially for $k/n > 3$ (Bailleux & Chabrier 1997), local search based sampling appears to be a better candidate than uniform sampling.

The fact that bad estimates are often *below* the theoretical expectation is typical of positive random variables with high dispersion.

Conclusion

In this paper, a stochastic local search based technique for estimating the number of global extrema in a search landscape has been proposed. It is based on a statistical analysis of a sample of trajectories achieved by a stochastic hill climbing process. It allows us to derive information on landscapes the density of global extrema of which is too low for an estimation by uniform sampling from the search space.

The estimates are unbiased but the variance, which can be very high, is unknown in the general case. So, we cannot obtain a confidence interval but a lower bound with a given (arbitrary low) probability of error.

Our experimentations on random #SAT instances show that there are landscapes for which stochastic local search sampling gives much better estimates than uniform sampling from the search space.

Although the proposed approach does not outperform existing statistical methods, at least for random 3SAT instances, it presents a theoretical and prospective interest.

As a research perspective, we plan to extend this approach to the estimation of other parameters of search landscapes, like the density of local extrema and the number of points with a given fitness. Another perspective is to extend the method in order to cover more efficient local search algorithms like GSAT or WSAT.

Acknowledgments

This work has been supported in part by the Ganymede II project of the "Contrat de plan Etat/Nord-Pas-de-Calais". Many thanks to Jean-Jacques Chabrier (Lirsia, Dijon, France), Yacine Boufkhad and Eric Grégoire (CRIL, Lens, France) for useful discussions and comments on this paper.

References

Bailleux, O., and Chabrier, J.-J. 1996. Approximate resolution of hard numbering problems. In *Proceedings of AAAI96*, 169–174.

Bailleux, O., and Chabrier, J.-J. 1997. Counting by statistics on search trees: Application to constraint satisfaction problems. *Intelligent Data Analysis* 1(4). http://www.elsevier.com/locate/ida.

Cook, S. 1971. The complexity of theorem-proving procedures. In *Proc. 3rd Ann. ACM Symp. on Theory of Computing*, 151–158.

Frank, J.; Cheeseman, P.; and Stutz, J. 1997. When gravity fails: Local search topology. *Journal of Artificial Intelligence Research* 7:249–281.

Garey, M. R., and Johnson, D. S. 1979. *Computers and Intractability*. W. H. Freeman and Compagny.

Jeroslow, R., and Wang, J. 1990. Solving propositional satisfiability problems. *Ann. Math. AI* 1:167–187.

Mazure, B.; Saïs, L.; and Grégoire, E. 1997. Tabu search for sat. In *Proceedings of AAAI97*, 281–285.

Roth, D. 1996. On the hardness of approximate reasoning. *Artificial Intelligence* 82:273–302.

Selman, B., and Kautz, H. 1993. An empirical study of greedy local search algorithms for satisfiability testing. In *Proceedings of the 11th National Conference on Artificial Intelligence*.

Selman, B.; Kautz, H.; and Cohen, B. 1994. Noises strategies for improving local search. In *Proceedings of AAAI94*, 337–343.

Simon, J. C., and Dubois, O. 1989. Number of solutions of satisfiability instances : application to knowledge bases. *International Journal of Pattern Recognition and Artificial intelligence* 3(1):53–65.

Toda, S. 1989. On the computational power of pp and +p. In *Proc. 30th IEEE Symp. on the Foundations of Computer Science*, 514–519.

Valiant, L. 1979. The complexity of enumeration and reliability problems. *SIAM J. Comput.* 8(3):410–421.

van Laarhoven, P. J. M., and Aarts, E. H. L. 1987. *Simulated annealing : Theory and Applications*. Kluwer Academic Publisher.

A Tractable Walsh Analysis of SAT and its Implications for Genetic Algorithms

Soraya Rana Robert B. Heckendorn Darrell Whitley
email:{rana,heckendo,whitley}@cs.colostate.edu

Abstract

Walsh Transforms measure all sources of nonlinear interactions for functions that have a bit representation. There can be exponentially many nonlinear interactions and exactly computing all Walsh coefficients is usually intractable for non-trivial functions. In this paper we will show that SAT problems evaluated as MAXSAT functions have a highly restricted set of nonzero Walsh coefficients and those coefficients can be computed in linear time with respect to the number of clauses. This analysis suggests why standard simple genetic algorithms should perform poorly on MAXSAT problems.

Introduction

Boolean Satisfiability (SAT) was the first problem proven to be NP-Complete. SAT problems consist of literals, defined as variables or negated variables, that are combined together using **and** ($\wedge$) and **or** ($\vee$). Typically, SAT problems are presented in conjunctive normal form which groups literals together into disjunctive clauses. A SAT problem is considered solved when an instantiation of variables is found such that the formula is true or it can be proven that no such instantiation exists. However, a function that provides only a 1 or 0 answer presents little information to guide a blackbox optimization algorithm. As a result, SAT problems are often expressed as MAXSAT problems where the goal is to maximize the number of satisfied clauses in the formula.

We prove that when SAT problems are evaluated as MAXSAT problems, it is possible to exactly compute the linear and nonlinear bit interactions of the function using Walsh analysis. Most importantly, this analysis can be done in linear time with the number of clauses, where the number of clauses is usually a multiple of the number of variables. Since MAXSAT is also NP-Complete, the proof that Walsh analysis can be performed in linear time is somewhat surprising. This means that if $P \neq NP$ then knowing the exact linear and nonlinear interactions of a function cannot be sufficient for inferring the global optimum.

Finally, schema averages, which are theoretically used by genetic algorithms to guide search, can be computed directly from the Walsh coefficients of a function. The limitations that exist on the Walsh coefficients for MAXSAT problems place limitations on the possible schema averages. We examine what these limitations reveal about the expected behavior of genetic algorithms in the MAXSAT problem domain.

Walsh Analysis

The **Walsh transform** is a discrete analog to the Fourier transform. It can be used to measure the bitwise nonlinearity that exists in functions whose domain is a bit representation. This nonlinearity is an important, but by no means the sole, feature in determining problem difficulty for stochastic search algorithms(Goldberg 1989a; 1989b; Reeves & Wright 1993).

Every real valued function f over an L-bit string, denoted $f : \mathcal{B}^L \rightarrow \mathcal{R}$, can be expressed as a Walsh polynomial. In this case, the role of the sines and cosines in Fourier transforms is played by an orthogonal basis of 2^L **Walsh functions** denoted by ψ_j, where $0 \leq j \leq 2^L - 1$ with each Walsh function being $\psi_j : \mathcal{B}^L \rightarrow \{-1, 1\}$. The function f can then be expressed as a weighted sum over the Walsh functions:

$$f(x) = \sum_{j=0}^{2^L-1} w_j \psi_j(x)$$

where the real valued weights w_j are called **Walsh coefficients**.

Operations on indices such as j act on the standard binary representation of j. A simple way to define a Walsh function is using a bitwise-AND of the function index and its argument. Let $bc(j)$ be a count of the number of 1 bits in string j then:

$$\psi_j(x) = (-1)^{bc(j \wedge x)}$$

Thus, if $bc(j \wedge x)$ is odd, then $\psi_j(x) = -1$ and if $bc(j \wedge x)$ is even, then $\psi_j(x) = 1$.

[0] Copyright ©1998, American Association for Artificial Intelligence (www.aaai.org). All rights reserved.

The 2^L Walsh coefficients can be computed by a Walsh transform:

$$w_j = \frac{1}{2^L} \sum_{i=0}^{2^L-1} f(i)\psi_j(i)$$

The Walsh transform, denoted W, acts as an invertible function analogous to a Fourier transform.

$$w_j = W(f(x)) \qquad f(x) = W^{-1}(w_j)$$

The calculation of Walsh coefficients can also be thought of in terms of matrix multiplication. Let $\vec{f}$ be a column vector of 2^L elements where the ith element is the value of the evaluation function $f(i)$. Similarly define a column vector $\vec{w}$ for the Walsh coefficients. If M is a $2^L \times 2^L$ matrix where $M_{i,j} = \psi_j(i)$ then:

$$\vec{w} = \frac{1}{2^L} \vec{f}^T M$$

An important property of Walsh coefficients is that w_j measures the contribution to the evaluation function by the interaction of the bits indicated by the positions of the 1's in j. Thus, w_{0001} measures the linear contribution to the evaluation function associated with bit b_0, while w_{0101} measures the nonlinear interaction between bits b_0 and b_2. (Bits are numbered right to left starting at 0.) In the next section we will use this decomposition of functions into Walsh coefficients to analyze the nonlinear structure of SAT problems.

Walsh Analysis of MAXSAT Problems

Computing a single Walsh coefficient of a function usually requires the enumeration of the entire function space. In general, this makes Walsh analysis impractical for problems of nontrivial size. However, we will show that the Walsh coefficients for MAXSAT problems can be generated directly from the clause information without evaluating any points in the search space. In fact, all the Walsh coefficients for a MAXSAT problem can be computed in $O(2^K C)$ time, where K is the number of unique variables in the largest clause and C is the number of clauses. Assuming K is a bounded constant, the time required to compute the Walsh coefficients is the same complexity as the time required to simply write down the SAT expression.

We generate the Walsh coefficients for MAXSAT problems by first generating the Walsh coefficients for a single clause. We then combine the Walsh information for the various clauses.

Walsh Coefficients for a Single Clause

Consider the example function consisting of a single clause $f(x) = \neg x_2 \vee x_1 \vee x_0$ where value of x_0 is given by the least significant bit in the string x and x_1 the next least significant bit, etc. Each function can only be false when the assignment of bit values causes every literal to be false. Since this can happen only in one way, the vector representing the function values $f(x)$ is composed of all 1's except for a single 0.

The explicit calculation of the Walsh coefficients for the example function is obtained using the matrix form of the Walsh transform. The computation $\vec{f}^T M$ is shown in equation 1. Notice the single zero in the function vector for assignment $x_2 = 1, x_1 = 0, x_0 = 0$.

$$\vec{w} = \frac{1}{8} \begin{bmatrix} 1 \\ 1 \\ 1 \\ 1 \\ 0 \\ 1 \\ 1 \\ 1 \end{bmatrix}^T \begin{bmatrix} 1 & 1 & 1 & 1 & 1 & 1 & 1 & 1 \\ 1 & -1 & 1 & -1 & 1 & -1 & 1 & -1 \\ 1 & 1 & -1 & -1 & 1 & 1 & -1 & -1 \\ 1 & -1 & -1 & 1 & 1 & -1 & -1 & 1 \\ 1 & 1 & 1 & 1 & -1 & -1 & -1 & -1 \\ 1 & -1 & 1 & -1 & -1 & 1 & -1 & 1 \\ 1 & 1 & -1 & -1 & -1 & -1 & 1 & 1 \\ 1 & -1 & -1 & 1 & -1 & 1 & 1 & -1 \end{bmatrix} \quad (1)$$

The first column of M is $\psi_0(x)$ and by definition of ψ_0 must always equal to 1. This means that the value of w_0 corresponds to the average fitness of all strings. The remaining coefficients are a summation of ± 1 terms with a single term zeroed out. This leads to the following lemma for computing the Walsh coefficients for a single disjunctive clause.

Lemma 1

Let f, $f : \mathcal{B}^K \to \mathcal{B}^1$ be a general disjunctive function corresponding to a single clause over K unique variables. Let $neg(f)$ return a K-bit string with 1 bits indicating which variables in the clause are negated. Then the Walsh coefficients for f are:

$$w_j = \begin{cases} \frac{2^K-1}{2^K} & \text{if } j = 0 \\ -\frac{1}{2^K}\psi_j(neg(f)) & \text{if } j \neq 0 \end{cases}$$

Proof:

For any function that is a single disjunctive clause over K unique variables there is exactly one setting of the variables that will result in the clause being false, i.e. $f(i) = 0$. This means that there will always be $2^K - 1$ function values that evaluate to 1 and only one that can be 0. Note that

$$w_j = \frac{1}{2^K} \sum_{i=0}^{2^K-1} f(i)\psi_j(i)$$

and since by definition $\forall x : \psi_0(x) = 1$, then the calculation of w_0 can be reduced to the constant:

$$w_0 = \frac{2^K - 1}{2^K}$$

Now consider how to compute w_j for $j > 0$. Let z be the string such that $f(z) = 0$. We know that all other strings will evaluate to 1. Therefore, we can simplify the expression for w_j:

$$w_j = \frac{1}{2^K} \sum_{i=0}^{2^K-1} f(i)\psi_j(i) = \frac{1}{2^K}\left(\left[\sum_{i=0}^{2^K-1} \psi_j(i)\right] - \psi_j(z)\right)$$

A general property of a Walsh transform for K-bit functions is that

$$\sum_{i=0}^{2^K-1} \psi_j(i) = 0 \qquad \forall j \neq 0.$$

Therefore

$$w_j = -\frac{1}{2^K}\psi_j(z) \qquad \forall j \neq 0 \qquad (2)$$

The value of z can be determined from the literals in the clause. Let $neg(f)$ return a K-bit number indicating which variables in clause are negated. For instance, $neg(\neg x_2 \vee x_1 \vee x_0) = 100$. Notice that $z = neg(f)$. Using this function, we can rewrite the equation for the Walsh coefficients.

$$w_j = -\frac{1}{2^K}\psi_j(neg(f)) \qquad \forall j \neq 0 \qquad (3)$$
$\square$

Tautological clauses may be removed or handled as a special case. All tautological clauses result in Walsh coefficients of 0 except for w_0 which is 1.

Walsh Coefficients for MAXSAT

An L-bit MAXSAT problem can be represented as a sum of C disjunctive clauses, f_i:

$$f(x) = \sum_{i=1}^{C} f_i(x)$$

where $f, f_1, f_2, ...f_C : \mathcal{B}^L \to \mathcal{R}$.

Since the Walsh transform can be performed by a simple linear transformation, we see that Walsh transform of a MAXSAT problem can be treated as a sum of the Walsh transforms of the individual clauses.

$$W(f(x)) = \sum_{i=1}^{C} W(f_i(x))$$

This implies that to compute the Walsh coefficient for a MAXSAT problem we merely have to sum over the Walsh coefficients for each clause calculated using Lemma 1. While this is actually how the Walsh coefficients can be computed, the f_i functions cannot be used directly with Lemma 1. Each clause f_i is passed an L-bit string as an argument but can utilize K_i literals, where K_i is bounded by a constant. This means, that unlike in Lemma 1, not all variables will be used in each clause and our argument for the existence of only one value z such that $f_i(z) = 0$ is no longer true. The theory presented in the previous section must be modified for extraneous variables. To facilitate this we introduce two new notations.

Let $i \subseteq j$ where $i, j \in \mathcal{B}^L$ denote i **is contained in** j such that wherever there is a 1 in i there is a 1 in j. A function **pack** is designed to map functions in L-bit space to functions in M-bit space: $pack : \mathcal{B}^L \times \mathcal{B}^L \to \mathcal{B}^M$ where $M \leq L$. The function $pack(x, m)$ extracts the values of M bits from the string x according to the L-bit mask m, where $bc(m) = M$. The values are extracted at locations corresponding to a 1 in m and compressed to form an M-bit string. For example: $pack(10101, 01101) \Longrightarrow 011$.

The next theorem shows that the only nonzero Walsh coefficients, w_j, for f_i occur when $j \subseteq m_i$ where m_i is a mask selecting the variables that occur in the clause.

Theorem 1
Let f_i be a function which is a single disjunctive clause of K_i unique variables drawn from a string of L variables i.e. $f_i : \mathcal{B}^L \to \mathcal{B}^1$. Let the mask m_i be a mask indicating which variables occur in the clause. Then

$$w_j = \begin{cases} 0 & \text{if } j \not\subseteq m_i \\ \frac{2^{K_i}-1}{2^{K_i}} & \text{if } j \subseteq m_i \text{ and } j = 0 \\ -\frac{1}{2^{K_i}}\psi_j(neg(f_i)) & \text{if } j \subseteq m_i \text{ and } j \neq 0 \end{cases}$$

Proof:
If we want to compute w_j for a given j then there are two cases: either the $j \not\subseteq m_i$ or $j \subseteq m_i$.

Consider first the case where $j \not\subseteq m_i$. Select a 1 bit from j that is not in m_i. This corresponds to selecting a variable that is not used in f_i. Let the assignment for that variable be found at position p in the L-bit string x, where x is the argument to the function. Now partition the set of all 2^L possible L-bit strings into two sets S_0 and S_1. S_0 is the set of those arguments that have a 0 in position p and S_1 is the set that have a 1 in that position. There is a one-to-one, onto mapping from S_0 to S_1 by flipping the 0 at position p to a 1. Let the function $T : S_0 \to S_1$ perform this mapping. Since the value at position p has no effect on the evaluation of f_i, we know if $x \in S_0$ then $f_i(x) = f_i(T(x))$. Hence,

$$\begin{aligned} w_j &= \tfrac{1}{2^L} \sum_{x=0}^{2^L-1} f_i(x)\psi_j(x) \\ &= \tfrac{1}{2^L}[\sum_{x \in S_0} f_i(x)\psi_j(x) + \sum_{y \in S_1} f_i(y)\psi_j(y)] \\ &= \tfrac{1}{2^L}\sum_{x \in S_0}[f_i(x)\psi_j(x) + f_i(T(x))\psi_j(T(x))] \\ &= \tfrac{1}{2^L}\sum_{x \in S_0}[f_i(x)\psi_j(x) + f_i(x)\psi_j(T(x))] \\ &= \tfrac{1}{2^L}\sum_{x \in S_0} f_i(x)[\psi_j(x) + \psi_j(T(x))] \end{aligned}$$

Since j by construction has a 1 in bit position p and we know that $T(x) \in S_1$ has 1 more bit than $x \in S_0$ then $bc(j \wedge x) + 1 = bc(j \wedge T(x))$. Therefore, $-\psi_j(x) = \psi_j(T(x))$ and the Walsh functions cancel so that

$$w_j = 0 \quad \text{if } j \not\subseteq m_i$$

Consider the second case where $j \subseteq m_i$. We now choose a bit position p outside of the bits set in m_i and thus also outside of the bits set by j. From above:

$$w_j = \frac{1}{2^L} \sum_{x \in S_0} f_i(x)(\psi_j(x) + \psi_j(T(x)))$$

However in this case j has a 0 at position p so $bc(j \wedge x) = bc(j \wedge T(x))$ and hence $\psi_j(x) = \psi_j(T(x))$.

$$w_j = \frac{1}{2^L} \sum_{x \in S_0} 2f_i(x)\psi_j(x)$$

Since the clause in f_i has K_i elements, there will be $L - K_i$ positions not overlapping with the 1 bits in m_i. This formula can simply be repeated $L - K_i$ times to account for all positions outside of mask m_i. We can create a reduced set S'_0 containing the 2^{K_i} strings with 1 bits inside the mask m_i, i.e., $x \subseteq m_i, \forall x \in S'_0$.

The simplified equation for w_j is:

$$w_j = 2^{L-K_i} \frac{1}{2^L} \sum_{x \in S'_0} f_i(x)\psi_j(x) = \frac{1}{2^{K_i}} \sum_{x \in S'_0} f_i(x)\psi_j(x) \quad (4)$$

In order to use Lemma 1 we need to compress the $\mathcal{B}^L$ space of f_i to $\mathcal{B}^{K_i}$ space by using the *pack* function. Let $f'_i : \mathcal{B}^{K_i} \to \mathcal{R}$ be the same clause as f_i but with the domain limited to just the variables in the clause. Specifically, define the values of f'_i as $f(x) = f'(pack(x, m_i)) \; \forall \; x \in S'_0$. Since $j \subseteq m_i$ we see that the following identity must hold:

$$\psi_{pack(j, m_i)}(pack(x, m_i)) = \psi_j(x) \quad (5)$$

Now we can translate equation 4 into

$$w_j = \frac{1}{2^{K_i}} \sum_{x \in S'_0} f'_i(pack(x, m_i)) \; \psi_{pack(j, m_i)}(pack(x, m_i))$$

We have now constrained the set of $x \in S'_0$ to the point where there exists only one value of x that will make f'_i zero. Thus, we have the same two cases as in Lemma 1. Either $j = 0$ in which case:

$$w_j = \frac{2^{K_i} - 1}{2^{K_i}} \quad \text{if} \; j \subseteq m_i \; \text{and} \; j = 0$$

or $j \neq 0$ and the reasoning of Lemma 1 can be applied. Let z be the L-bit string such that $f_i(z) = 0$.

$$w_j = -\frac{1}{2^{K_i}} \psi_{pack(j, m_i)}(pack(z, m_i))$$

The arguments to the Walsh function can now be simplified using the identity in equation 5 to

$$w_j = -\frac{1}{2^{K_i}} \psi_j(z)$$

The observations about the negation mask in equation 3 also apply here, being very careful to note that the negation mask is in $\mathcal{B}^L$. This yields:

$$w_j = -\frac{1}{2^{K_i}} \psi_j(neg(f_i)) \quad \text{if} \; j \subseteq m_i \; \text{and} \; j \neq 0$$

$\square$

An Example Computation

Table 1 shows an example of the application of this theory for a small MAXSAT function $f : \mathcal{B}^4 \to \mathcal{R}$ with $f(x) = f_1 + f_2 + f_3$ and

$$\begin{aligned} f_1 &= (\neg x_2 \vee x_1 \vee x_0) \\ f_2 &= (x_3 \vee \neg x_2 \vee x_1) \\ f_3 &= (x_3 \vee \neg x_1 \vee \neg x_0). \end{aligned}$$

x	w_i	$W(f_1)$	$W(f_2)$	$W(f_3)$	$W(f(x))$
0000	w_0	0.875	0.875	0.875	2.625
0001	w_1	−0.125	0	0.125	0
0010	w_2	−0.125	−0.125	0.125	−0.125
0011	w_3	−0.125	0	−0.125	−0.250
0100	w_4	0.125	0.125	0	0.250
0101	w_5	0.125	0	0	0.125
0110	w_6	0.125	0.125	0	0.250
0111	w_7	0.125	0	0	0.125
1000	w_8	0	−0.125	−0.125	−0.250
1001	w_9	0	0	0.125	0.125
1010	w_{10}	0	−0.125	0.125	0
1011	w_{11}	0	0	−0.125	−0.125
1100	w_{12}	0	0.125	0	0.125
1101	w_{13}	0	0	0	0
1110	w_{14}	0	0.125	0	0.125
1111	w_{15}	0	0	0	0

Table 1: Walsh Coefficients Broken Down by Clause.

Note that $w_0 = 2.625$, which is, as predicted, the average evaluation of f over all input strings. The linear, order-1 interactions are represented by w_1, w_2, w_4, and w_8 (each index has a single 1 bit when converted to a string). The order-2 nonlinear interactions are given by $w_3, w_5, w_6, w_9, w_{10}$ and w_{12} (each index has a pair of 1 bits when converted to a binary string). The third order nonlinear interactions are given by w_7, w_{11}, w_{13} and w_{14}. Since this is a 3-SAT problem, there can be no order 4 interactions, so $w_{15} = 0$. Other Walsh coefficients are zero due to cancellation of the constituent Walsh coefficients.

Notice that if f has L variables and C clauses the total number of possible Walsh coefficients is 2^L while an upper bound on the number of nonzero Walsh coefficients is $2^K C$ where $K = \max(K_i)$. Therefore, in general, the total number of Walsh coefficients that are zero grows exponentially as L increases.

The theorem we have presented allows us to determine which Walsh coefficients will be nonzero and compute a specific coefficient in at most $O(C)$ time. Furthermore, all Walsh coefficients can be computed in $O(2^K C)$ time because for each clause i, only the 2^{K_i} contributing coefficients need be computed. Finally, the maximum degree of bitwise nonlinearity (i.e. the maximum number of bits that interact to affect the evaluation function) is, as we would expect, limited to the number of variables in the longest clause.

Genetic Algorithms and MAXSAT

Genetic algorithms are population-based algorithms inspired by evolution. A population of strings is used to create a new population of strings through the use of **selection, recombination** and **mutation**. Each cycle of selection, recombination and mutation is considered one **generation**. Selection chooses individuals from a population that will be eligible for mating. Strings that are highly fit according to an evaluation function will have a better chance of being chosen for reproduction than a less fit string. Two strings are paired together through the use of a recombination operator that divides the parent strings into several pieces and then concatenates the pieces to form two new strings that will appear in the next population. Mutation then randomly flips a small number of bits in the new offspring.

Holland (1975) explains the computational behavior of genetic algorithms by arguing that genetic algorithms compare subpartitions of the search space and then allocate more trials to the subpartitions of the search space that have the highest fitness. These subpartitions are represented by **schemata**. Schemata are L-length strings defined using a trinary alphabet $\{0,1,*\}$ yielding 3^L possible schemata. The $*$ indicates a wildcard where either a 0 or 1 are allowed. The **order** of a schema is the number of positions that contain a 0 or 1. For instance, the schema *11* would contain 4 strings $\{0110, 0111, 1110, 1111\}$ and is an order-2 schema. For order-1 schemata such as **0** and **1**, if the current population is distributed such that strings with a 0 in the third position are on average better than those strings that contain a 1 in the third position, then more samples should be allocated to the schema **0** in the next population.

In some sense genetic algorithms stochastically hill-climb in the space of schemata rather than in the space of binary strings. As with other hill-climbing search strategies, a genetic algorithm can perform poorly if there is an absence of information or if that information is misleading (deceptive). However, it is usually difficult to statically analyze large functions to determine whether or not useful schema relationships exist. Computing the exact average fitnesses of low order schemata requires exponential time for most large problems. However, we can use Walsh coefficients to efficiently compute low order schema averages.

Functions α and β are defined on a schema, h, as per Goldberg (1989a):

$$\alpha(h)[i] = \begin{cases} 0 & \text{if } h[i] = * \\ 1 & \text{if } h[i] = 0 \text{ or } 1 \end{cases}$$

$$\beta(h)[i] = \begin{cases} 0 & \text{if } h[i] = * \text{ or } 0 \\ 1 & \text{if } h[i] = 1 \end{cases}$$

For example, consider $h = **01**$. Because schema h is a subset of strings, its fitness is the average fitness of all strings that belong in that subset. Rather than enumerating the subset of strings, the fitness of h can be computed using Walsh coefficients:

$$f(h) = \frac{1}{|h|} \sum_{x \in h} f(x) = \sum_{j \subseteq \alpha(h)} w_j \psi_j(\beta(h))$$

For all $j \subseteq \alpha(h)$ we see that $bc(j) \leq bc(\alpha(h))$. This implies that the highest order Walsh coefficient used in the formula has the same order as the schema.

The average fitness of schema $h = **01**$, depends only on Walsh coefficients w_0, w_4, w_8 and w_{12}.

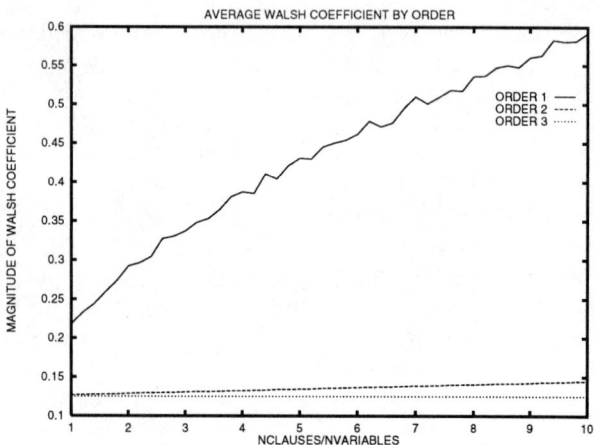

Figure 1: Average magnitudes of nonzero Walsh coefficients (excluding w_0).

Since $\alpha(**01**) = 001100$, the subset generated using α is $\{001100, 001000, 000100, 000000\}$ corresponding to the indices $\{12, 8, 4, 0\}$. The string generated by $\beta(**01**) = 000100$, so $\psi_4(000100) = -1$, $\psi_8(000100) = 1$ and $\psi_{12}(000100) = -1$. The sign of w_0 is always 1. So, $f(**01**) = w_0 - w_4 + w_8 - w_{12}$.

Schema Fitnesses for MAXSAT Problems

We have proven that the nonzero Walsh coefficients for MAXSAT problems are limited in number and maximum order. Since schema averages of varying order are generated as a summation of positive and negative Walsh coefficients, the limitations on the set of Walsh coefficients results in schema averages that will be very similar.

Consider the plot shown in Figure 1. The graph was generated using a set of randomly generated 100 variable 3-SAT problem instances. The ratio of clauses to variables ranged from 1 to 10 at increments of 0.2. Each point in the graph is the average of 30 problem instances. Each line tracks the average magnitude of all nonzero Walsh coefficients for order-1, order-2, and order-3 interactions.

Recall that any single clause in a 3-SAT problem contributes $\pm \frac{1}{2^3}$ to its nonzero Walsh coefficients. When combinations of variables co-occur in multiple clauses, the corresponding Walsh coefficient will be incremented or decremented by $\frac{1}{2^3}$. The final coefficient will either be zero or a multiple of 0.125.

Table 2 lists the number of nonzero Walsh coefficients that can occur for order-1, order-2, and order-3 interactions. In general, the maximum possible number of coefficients is $\binom{L}{k}$ for order-$k = 1, 2, 3$. However, the number of nonzero Walsh coefficients for a particular 3-SAT problem is limited. In the context of 3-SAT, the only way for 3 variables to interact is if all 3 variables occur in a clause. This means the number of nonzero order-3 Walsh coefficients is limited to the number of clauses in the problem. For any reasonable sized 3-SAT

Order	Max Possible	Max for MAX3SAT		
		100	500	1000
1	100	100	100	100
2	4950	300	1500	3000
3	161700	100	500	1000

Table 2: Upper bounds on the number of possible nonzero Walsh coefficients for an arbitrary function (Max Possible) and for a MAX3SAT problem with 100 variables and 100, 500, 1000 clauses.

problem, it is likely that the combinations of 3-variables will often be unique. Therefore the majority of the order-3 Walsh coefficients will be zero and any nonzero order-3 Walsh coefficients are likely to be ± 0.125.

The order-2 interactions result in higher Walsh coefficient magnitudes because as the number of clauses is increased, it becomes more likely for a pair of variables will co-occur in multiple clauses. Similarly, the magnitudes of the order-1 Walsh coefficients are larger because each individual variable occurs more often as the number of clauses is increased. As a general rule, the magnitudes of the Walsh coefficients will increase as it becomes more likely that a variable or variable combinations will reoccur in the problem.

An obvious observation from Figure 1 is that the size of the nonzero Walsh coefficients are minuscule (less than 0.6) compared to w_0 which is $\frac{7}{8}C$. For the 3-SAT problems in Figure 1, the C ranged from 100 to 1000 meaning that $87.5 \leq w_0 \leq 875$. Since all schema averages include the Walsh coefficient w_0, it will take many linear and nonlinear terms to induce any noticeable difference between schema averages. Consequently, the low order schema averages will all be near w_0. Of course, there will be some variation between low order schemata; the variation that occurs will largely be due to the linear Walsh coefficients. These differences will become more pronounced in higher order schemata. However, a genetic algorithm will have difficulty when there is little information in the low order schemata or if that information is misleading.

Conclusion

MAXSAT is commonly used as an evaluation function when general optimization techniques are applied to SAT problems. We have shown that all nonzero Walsh coefficients can be directly computed for MAXSAT in linear time as a function of the number of clauses. This result allows us to conclude that: If $P \neq NP$ then knowing the exact linear and nonlinear interactions of a function cannot be sufficient for inferring the global optimum in polynomial time. Furthermore, the Walsh coefficients that are generated for such functions are limited. The degree of bitwise nonlinearity that can exist in such problems is limited by the longest clause in the formula. The number of possible nonzero nonlinear Walsh coefficients is also limited by the number of clauses in the formula.

The Walsh analysis illustrates that the class of MAXSAT problems will result in little variation in schema averages. Furthermore, any differences that occur between lower level schemata are dominated by the linear order-1 schema information. If $P \neq NP$ then this order-1 schema information (as well as order-2 and order-3 schema information) cannot reliably guide search algorithms to a global optimum for MAXSAT. The misleading schema information makes MAXSAT unsuitable for optimization by traditional genetic algorithms. However, we cannot generalize this statement to other evaluation functions or other NP-Complete problems because modifying the evaluation function will result in different Walsh coefficients.

The Walsh analysis of MAXSAT problems is also related to polynomial time approximate algorithms for NP-Complete problems. This class of algorithms, sometimes called r-approximate algorithms (Trevisan 1997), is guaranteed to locate a solution that is at least a factor r, where $0 \leq r \leq 1$, from the optimum. It has been proven (Håstad 1997) that this factor cannot be higher than $\frac{7}{8}$ for satisfiable problem instances. The Walsh analysis proves that for *any* MAX3SAT problem, the average evaluation of all possible solutions to the problem is always $\frac{7}{8}$ times the number of clauses; thus, the polynomial time approximate algorithms cannot guarantee a solution that is better than average (unless $P = NP$). The relationship between the Walsh analysis of MAXSAT and polynomial time approximate algorithms will be explored in future work.

Acknowledgments

This work was supported by NSF grant IRI-9503366 and AFOSR grant F49620-97-1-0271. Soraya Rana was also supported by a National Physical Science Consortium fellowship awarded by NASA-SSC.

References

Goldberg, D. 1989a. Genetic algorithms and walsh functions: Part i, a gentle introduction. *Complex Systems* 3:129–152.

Goldberg, D. 1989b. Genetic algorithms and walsh functions: Part ii, deception and its analysis. *Complex Systems* 3:153–171.

Håstad, J. 1997. Some optimal inapproximability results. In *Proceedings of the 29th ACM Symposium on Theory of Computation*, 1–10.

Holland, J. 1975. *Adaptation in Natural and Artificial Systems*. University of Michigan Press.

Reeves, C., and Wright, C. 1993. Epistasis in genetic algorithms: An experimental design perspective. In Eshelman, L., ed., *Proceedings of the Seventh International Conference on Genetic Algorithms*, 217–224. Morgan Kaufmann.

Trevisan, L. 1997. Approximating satisfiable satisfiability problems. In *Proceedings of the 5th European Symposium on Algorithms*.

Hard Problems for CSP Algorithms

David G. Mitchell

Department of Computer Science, University of Toronto,
Toronto, Ontario, M5S 3G4, Canada
mitchell@cs.toronto.edu

Abstract

We prove exponential lower bounds on the running time of many algorithms for Constraint Satisfaction, by giving a simple family of instances on which they always take exponential time. Although similar lower bounds for most of these algorithms have been shown before, we provide a uniform treatment which illustrates a powerful general approach and has stronger implications for the practice of algorithm design.

Introduction

Finite-domain constraint satisfaction (CSP) is a popular problem solving technique in AI. A CSP instance is a set of variables, and a set of constraints on values assigned to them. Solving an instance requires finding an assignment which satisfies the constraints, or determining that no such assignment exists. In the usual formalizations this task is **NP**-complete, so a polynomial time algorithm exists if and only if **P=NP**. Since many practical problems amount to solving CSPs, we want to find the best algorithms we can, regardless of the truth of this proposition.

The literature on performance of CSP algorithms consists largely of experimental comparisons of variants of backtracking on benchmark instances. A few papers include proofs that one variant is never worse (and sometimes better) than another. These are valuable methods, but it may turn out that we are arguing over the best way to build ladders when we need rocketships. We habitually provide (rough) upper bounds for algorithms, but it is lower bounds that lead us to understand when and why algorithms do badly. Thus, lower bounds are more likely to lead us in fruitful directions, or at least away from some which are futile.

In this paper, we analyze a number of popular techniques for solving CSPs, and give a family of instances for which they take exponential time. We discuss differences between our bounds and some previous results, notably those from (Baker 1995), in Related Work. Our method involves showing a correspondence between the algorithm execution and proofs in the propositional calculus. That such correspondences exist seems to be conventional wisdom in the community, but we have never seen a coherent treatment of this in the literature, suggesting that it is not considered important. We hope with this paper to partially redress the former, and encourage re-consideration of the latter. In particular we will argue that proof-based analysis of algorithms, in addition to being a valuable tool for understanding existing algorithms, tells us something useful about what we ought to be doing next.

The properties we prove are for unsatisfiable instances, but the message about satisfiable instances is essentially the same[1]. When a backtrack-based algorithm takes a long time on a satisfiable instance it must be because, after making some unlucky assignments, it generated an unsatisfiable sub-problem that took a long time. If every unsatisfiable sub-problem generated was solved quickly, the algorithm would find a solution quickly. Our results apply also to unsatisfiable sub-problems generated in the process of solving a satisfiable instance.

Note that our lower bounds apply *independent of variable or value ordering heuristics*. (For unsatisfiable inputs, value ordering does not for matter for backtracking, but it does matter for better algorithms.) For a fully specified algorithm, it is often easy to construct hard inputs by tricking the ordering heuristic. This approach is inadequate in general, and we eliminate the issue by analyzing algorithms as families.

Method and Results

Here we address several of the most prominent methods in the literature. There are too many variants to be comprehensive, but our results apply to many others.

Let **R** be the following set of CSP algorithms.

{ Backtracking (BT)
Backmarking (BM) (Gashnig 1977),
Backjumping (BJ) (Gashnig 1978),
Graph-Based Backjumping (GBJ) (Dechter 1990),
Conflict-Directed Backjumping (CBJ)(Prosser 1993),
Forward Checking (FC) (Haralick and Elliot 1980),
Minimal Forward Checking (MFC)

Copyright ©1998, American Association for Artificial Intelligence (www.aaai.org). All rights reserved.

[1] We consider only complete algorithms. Incomplete methods are useful, but are not our concern here.

(Dent and Mercer 1994),
FC with CBJ (FC-CBJ) (Prosser 1993),
Maintaining Arc Consistency (MAC)
  (Sabin and Freuder 1994),
MAC with CBJ (MAC-CBJ) (Prosser 1995),
Learning (Dechter 1990)
Dynamic Backtracking (DB) (Ginsberg 1993) }

Let $Time_A(N)$ be the maximum execution time for algorithm A on an instance of size N. Recall that $\Omega(.)$ is the lower bound analog of $O(.)$. For $f, g : \mathbb{N} \mapsto \mathbb{N}$, $f(N) \in \Omega(g(N)) \Leftrightarrow \exists c > 0 \ s.t. \ \forall N > 0 \ f(N) \geq c \cdot g(N)$.

Theorem 1 *For every $A \in \mathbf{R}$, $Time_A(n) \in 2^{\Omega(n)}$.*

Theorem 1 says that for every algorithm in **R** there are infinitely many instances on which it takes takes time at least $2^{cn}, c > 0$ a constant, on every instance of size at least n. In fact, a single family of instances suffices for all the algorithms in **R**, and many others.

Proof: There are two main steps. First we define a class of "resolution bounded" CSP algorithms. The running time of a resolution bounded algorithm on instance Λ is at least as large as the length of a resolution refutation of a related formula $\phi(\Lambda)$. We then exhibit an infinite family of CSP instances, PH_n, such that any refutation of $\phi(PH_n)$ requires exponentially many clauses. This gives us,

Lemma 1 *Every resolution bounded CSP algorithm takes time at least $2^{\Omega(n)}$ on the instance family PH_n.*

In the second step we show that each algorithm in **R** is resolution bounded. To do this we describe modified versions of the algorithms which have the same time complexity as the originals, but also construct the clauses needed for a refutation of $\phi(\Lambda)$. This step gives us the second lemma.

Lemma 2 *Every $A \in \mathbf{R}$ is resolution bounded.*

Theorem 1 follows from Lemmas 2 and 1, which together show that there is an infinite family of instances on which every algorithm in **R** takes time $2^{\Omega(n)}$. ∎

In the next section, we define "resolution bounded", specify the family PH_n, and prove Lemma 1. In the following section, we prove Lemma 2, considering the algorithms case-by-case.

CSP and Resolution Bounds

Finite Constraint Satisfaction

As usual a CSP is a triple $\Lambda = \langle X, D, C \rangle$, but we treat C unconventionally. X is a set of variables. D is a function mapping each variable x to a finite set $D(x)$.

An assignment γ for a set of variables $U \subset X$, is a set of atoms of the form $x{:}a$, where $x \in X$ and $a \in D(x)$, and if $x{:}a$, $x{:}b$ are both in γ, then $a = b$. We write $vars(\gamma)$ for $\{x | \exists a, x{:}a \in \gamma\}$. Let Γ denote the set of all assignments for subsets of X. We model the constraints abstractly, as a function $C : \Gamma \mapsto \Gamma$. For an assignment γ, $C(\gamma)$ is a minimal subset of γ which violates a constraint, or $\emptyset$. ($C(.)$ can easily be defined over the usual formalizations of the constraint set.) We say assignment γ for X satisfies Λ if $C(\gamma) = \emptyset$.

Formula Corresponding to a CSP

We use the following common (e.g., (De Kleer 1989)) reduction from CSP to SAT. For each variable $x \in X$, we have $|D(x)|$ propositional variables to represent assignments of values to x. We write $x{:}a$ for the literal which, when true, corresponds to the CSP variable x being assigned value a. (So $x{:}a$ represents an assignment to a variable in the context of Λ, but a literal in the context of $\phi(\Lambda)$.) Three sets of clauses encode the properties of a CSP solution.

1. For each variable of Λ, a clause saying it is assigned a value from its domain. We will refer to such clauses as *domain clauses*.
2. For each $U \subseteq X$ and each assignment γ to U, if $C(\gamma) \neq \emptyset$, a clause expressing the corresponding restriction on truth assignments.
3. For each variable of Λ, a set of clauses saying that it gets at most one value.

For CSP Λ, we define the CNF formula $\phi(\Lambda)$ to be

$$\phi(\Lambda) = \bigwedge_{x \in X} \left(\bigvee_{a \in D(x)} x{:}a \right) \wedge \bigwedge_{C(\gamma) \neq \emptyset, \gamma \in \Gamma} \left(\bigvee_{x{:}a \in C(\gamma)} \overline{x{:}a} \right)$$

$$\wedge \bigwedge_{x \in X} \left(\bigwedge_{a \neq c \in D(x)} \left(\overline{x{:}a} \bigvee \overline{x{:}c} \right) \right).$$

Clearly $\phi(\Lambda)$ is satisfiable if and only if Λ is satisfiable.

Resolution Bounded Algorithms

The resolution rule for propositional clauses is

$$\frac{(x \vee X) \quad (\neg x \vee Y)}{(X \vee Y)}.$$

$(X \vee Y)$ is called the resolvent. A *resolution derivation* of a clause c from a set of clauses Δ is a sequence of clauses $c_1 \ldots c_m$ such that $c_m = c$ and each c_i is either in Δ or is a resolvent of two clauses c_j, c_k with $j, k < i$. The derivation is of size m. A *refutation* of Δ is a derivation of the empty clause () from Δ. A CNF formula is unsatisfiable if and only if it has a refutation. Sometimes we say a formula ϕ has a proof of size m, meaning there is a refutation of ϕ of size m.

For our analysis, a CSP algorithm takes a step for each explicit assignment of a value to a variable. If substantial processing occurs between assignments, we also count key steps in the relevant sub-program.

Definition: We say a CSP algorithm A is *resolution bounded* if for every unsatisfiable instance Λ, the number of steps taken by A on instance Λ is at least as large as the number of clauses in the shortest refutation of the formula $\phi(\Lambda)$.

Pigeon Hole Inputs

The pigeonhole principle says that you can't stuff $n+1$ pigeons into n holes, unless you put more than one pigeon in some hole. Writing $[n]$ to denote the set

$\{1 \ldots n\}$, the formal statement is that there is no one-to-one onto function $f : [n+1] \mapsto [n]$. We can encode the statement that such a function does exist as an unsatisfiable CSP PH_n as follows.

$$X = \{p_1, p_2, \ldots p_{n+1}\}$$
$$D(p_i) = \{h_1, h_2, \ldots h_n\}, \forall p_i \in X$$
$$C(\gamma) = \begin{cases} \{p_i{:}h_k, p_j{:}h_k\} & \text{if } \{p_i{:}h_k, p_j{:}h_k\} \subseteq \gamma, \\ & \text{and } i \neq j, \\ \emptyset & \text{otherwise.} \end{cases}$$

We can also encode this statement as a CNF formula, which we will call PHP_n.

$$\text{PHP}_n = \bigwedge_{1 \leq i \leq n+1} \left(\bigvee_{1 \leq j \leq n} p_i{:}h_j \right) \wedge \bigwedge_{\substack{1 \leq k \leq n \\ 1 \leq i < j \leq n+1}} \left(\overline{p_i{:}h_k} \vee \overline{p_j{:}h_k} \right)$$
$$\wedge \bigwedge_{1 \leq i \leq n+1} \left(\bigwedge_{1 \leq j \neq k \leq n} \left(\overline{p_i{:}h_j} \vee \overline{p_i{:}h_k} \right) \right)$$

This is the same as the formula that we get if we apply the transformation above to the CSP formulation. That is,

$$\text{PHP}_n = \phi(\text{PH}_n)$$

Resolution Lower Bounds

The first super-polynomial lower bounds for unrestricted resolution were given by Haken(Haken 1985), who showed that for large n there are no resolution refutations of PHP_n of size smaller than $2^{\Omega(n)}$. A simplified proof, with a slightly stronger lower bound, was recently given in (Beame and Pitassi 1996)[2].

Theorem 2 (Haken / Beame and Pitassi)
For sufficiently large n, any resolution proof of PHP_n requires at least $2^{n/20}$ clauses.

An examination of the proof shows that "sufficiently large" means $n \geq 1,867$. Unfortunately, space dictates that we only sketch the barest elements of the proof, which is not likely sufficient for the reader's intuition.
Proof ("Sketch"): Call a clause long if it has at least $n^2/10$ literals. Show that any refutation of PHP_n contains a long clause. Now, assume the existence of a refutation of PHP_n with fewer than $2^{n/20}$ clauses. By a process of successive restrictions it is possible to extract from this refutation a refutation of $\text{PNP}_{n'}$, where $n > n' > 0.671n$, which does not contain a long clause, thereby obtaining a contradiction. ■
Proof (of Lemma 1): Follows from theorem 2 and the definition of resolution bounded algorithm. ■

Observe that the lower bound result does not follow merely from Haken's theorem plus a correspondence between the algorithm execution and resolution proofs. Since the mapping of CSP inputs to CNF formulas is

---
[2] The cited papers use a slightly different formulation of PHP_n than we do, but the proof in (Beame and Pitassi 1996) goes through without modification for our version.

not onto, it is not necessarily the case that every unsatisfiable CNF formula has a refutation corresponding to the execution of an algorithm at hand. Thus, one needs to establish a CSP input family that does map onto a suitable CNF formula. It is fortuitous that the $\text{PH}n$ family behaves just as we want. To illustrate, if the only known resolution lower bounds were for random CNF formulas, the application of those bounds to CSP algorithms would be non-trivial.

Our lower bounds are expressed as an exponential in n, the number of holes, while the formula PHP_n is of size $\Theta(n^3)$. The exact nature of the lower bound depends on our assumptions about encoding of the input. Using N for input size, the lower bound for resolution proof size is $2^{\Omega(N^{1/3})}$. With a naive encoding, this will be the correct lower bound expressed in terms of input size. Since some more reasonable constraint languages can express PH_n in size linear in n, the implied lower bound for CSP algorithms is indeed $2^{\Omega(N)}$.

Algorithms and Refutations

Most complete CSP algorithms in the literature (including those in our set **R**), are refinements to backtracking. Backtrack-based algorithms attempt construct a solution by incrementally extending an assignment to a subset of the variables. Whenever a constraint is violated, a recent extension is retracted, and a different extension attempted.

The execution of a backtrack-based CSP algorithm corresponds to a depth-first search of a rooted tree of partial assignments. Each node corresponds to a variable, and each outgoing edge corresponds to one assignment of a value to that variable. Let $\text{T}(A, \Lambda)$ denote the search tree explored by algorithm A executing on unsatisfiable instance Λ. Associated with each node v is partial assignment γ_v, a variable x_v, and for each $a \in D(x_v)$, an outgoing edge corresponding to $x_v{:}a$. If $|D(x_v)| = k$, then v has k children, which we denote $v_1 \ldots v_k$, indexed in the order of execution.

The Refutation Corresponding to BT

The basic backtracking algorithm BT is given in Figure 1. The initial call is assumed to be $\text{BT}(\Lambda, \{\})$. Note that BT is really a family of algorithms, since it does not specify which variable, or which value, to choose next, and each possible way of choosing these induces one particular algorithm.

```
Procedure BT(Λ,γ)
    if C(γ) ≠ ∅ then return UNSAT
    elsif vars(γ) = X, then return SAT
    else
        pick some x ∈ X − vars(γ)
        for a ∈ D(x)
            if BT( Λ,γ ∪ {x:a}) =SAT then return SAT
        end for
    end if
    return UNSAT
```

Figure 1: Basic Backtracking Procedure, BT

We label each node v of $T(BT,\Lambda)$ with a clause c_v as follows. If v is a leaf, then γ_v violates a constraint, so let c_v be the clause from $\phi(\Lambda)$ expressing this constraint. If v is an internal node, then consider the k children of v, each of which is labeled with some clause c_i. If each of these clauses mentions x_v, then resolve all of these clauses against the domain clause for x_v and let c_v be the resulting clause. If some c_i does not mention x_v, and therefore the above sequence of resolution steps cannot be carried out, then let c_v be any such c_i, say the first one computed.

Lemma 3 *For every node v of $T(BT,\Lambda)$, if c_v is the label of node v, and n_v is the number of nodes in the subtree rooted at v, then*

1) *There is a resolution derivation of c_v from $\phi(\Lambda)$ of size less than n_v and,*
2) $c_v \subseteq \{\overline{x{:}a} | x{:}a \in \gamma_v\}$. *(I.e., c_v mentions a subset of assignments in γ_v.)*

Proof: If v is a leaf then $C(\gamma_v) \neq \emptyset$. So we have that $c_v = \{\overline{x{:}a} | x{:}a \in C(\gamma_v)\} \subseteq \{\overline{x{:}a} | x{:}a \in \gamma_v\}$. Also $c_v \in \phi(\Lambda)$, so the number of resolution steps needed to derive it is $0 < 1$.
If v is an internal node, then each child v_i of v is labeled with some clause c_i which, by inductive hypothesis, has the desired properties. If each of the c_i includes some $\overline{x_v{:}a_i}$, then resolve all of these clauses against the domain clause for x_v, $(\vee_{a \in D(x_v)}\, x_v{:}a) \in \phi(\Lambda)$ to obtain c_v. This operation can be carried out, because all the c_i contain only negated literals, so all signs match up as required. Now, $c_v = \cup_i (c_i - \overline{x_v{:}a_i}) \subseteq \{\overline{x{:}a} | x{:}a \in \gamma_v\}$, and the number of resolvents is the sum of those to construct the child clauses plus the number of child clauses, which is less than n_v. If one or more of the c_i do not mention any $\overline{x_v{:}a_i}$, then let c_v be such a c_i with smallest index i, and we are done. ∎

Lemma 4 *BT is resolution bounded.*

Proof: Follows from Lemma 3 and the definition of resolution bounded. ∎

Figure 2 shows a modified backtracking algorithm BTR which generates the clauses for our refutation of $\phi(\Lambda)$. On a given instance, the execution of BT and BTR are exactly the same, except that when BT returns UNSAT, BTR returns $\langle$UNSAT; $c\rangle$, where c is the clause labeling the corresponding node in $T(BT,\Lambda)$.

Backmarking

Backmarking (BM) (Gashnig 1977) is a technique to reduce the number of explicit consistency checks performed by backtracking. This does not affect the set of partial assignments examined, so resolution boundedness of BM follows from that of BT. (Explicit consistency checks are hidden in our function $C(.)$, since we can treat them as having no cost.)

Backjumping

Our labeling scheme for node v of the tree for BT allowed that a clause c_i from some child of a node v

```
Procedure BTR(Λ,γ)
    if C(γ) ≠ ∅ then return ⟨UNSAT; {x:a | x:a ∈ C(γ)}⟩
    elsif vars(γ) = X then return SAT
    else
        pick some x ∈ X − vars(γ)
        α ← (∨_{a∈D(x)} x:a)
        for a ∈ D(x)
            if BTR(Λ, γ ∪ {x:a}) = ⟨UNSAT; β⟩ then
                α ← res(α, β, x:a).
            else
                return SAT.
            end if
        end for
    end if
    return ⟨UNSAT; α⟩
```

Where,
$$res(\alpha, \beta, a) = \begin{cases} \text{resolvent of } \alpha \text{ and } \beta, & \text{if } a \in \alpha \text{ and } \overline{a} \in \beta \\ \beta, & \text{if } a \in \alpha \text{ and } \overline{a} \notin \beta \\ \alpha, & \text{if } a \notin \alpha \end{cases}$$

Figure 2: Computing Resolvents while Backtracking

might not mention x_v. In this case, we labeled v with the first such c_i. Stated another way, at a point where the algorithm BTR is assigning values to variable x_v, one of the recursive calls may return a clause which does not mention any assignment to x_v. This will happen when x did not appear in any of the constraints violated at the leaves in the subtree rooted at v. In this case, none of the other clauses from children of v are used in the refutation. Since such a c_i is a certificate that no extension of γ_v can be a solution, there is no point in exploring other assignments to x_v without first backtracking and reassigning a "previous" variable.

The algorithm RBJ (for Resolvent-Based Backjumping) shown in Figure 3 refines BT in accordance with this observation. If the clause returned by a recursive call does not mention the current variable, then RBJ immediately returns, passing this derived clause up to previous invocations. This passing up continues until a node is reached with a branching variable that occurs in the clause.

```
Procedure RBJ(Λ,γ)
    if C(γ) ≠ ∅ then return ⟨UNSAT; {x:a | x:a ∈ γ}⟩
    elsif vars(γ) = X then return SAT
    else
        pick some x ∈ X − vars(γ)
        α ← (∨_{a∈D(x)} x:a)
        for a ∈ D(x)
            R ← RBJ(Λ, γ ∪ {x:a})
            if R = ⟨UNSAT : β⟩ then
                if x:a ∈ β then
                    α ← res(α, β, x:a)
                else
                    return ⟨UNSAT; β⟩
                end if
            else
                return SAT.
            end if
        end for
    end if
    return ⟨UNSAT; α⟩
```

Figure 3: RBJ: Resolvent-Based Backjumping

The strategy RBJ just described sounds like conflict-directed backjumping (CBJ), and indeed they are equivalent. The standard description of CBJ adapts BT by making use of a *conflict set*, conflicts(x), for each variable x. Each time the algorithm reaches a node where x will be assigned values, the set conflicts(x) is set to $\emptyset$. When assigning a value to x violates a constraint with some already-assigned variable y, y is added to conflicts(x), and a new value is tried for x. If all values for x have been tried, then CBJ jumps back to the "latest" (i.e., most recently set) variable in conflicts(x). If this variable is y, then conflicts(y) is set to conflicts(y)$\cup$ conflicts(x) $- y$.

Lemma 5 *RBJ and CBJ are resolution bounded.*

Proof: It is clear that the lemma is true for RBJ, so it remains to show that RBJ and CBJ are equivalent. For this, it is sufficient to show that, when both algorithms are at nodes with the same corresponding truth assignments, they agree on whether to jump back or search another branch.

Label the tree T(CBJ,Λ), as follows. When CBJ backjumps from node v to node h, label each vertex on the path $v \ldots h$ with the set conflicts(x_v). Consider two nodes v, u of T(CBJ,Λ) and T(RBJ,Λ), respectively, such that $x_v = x_u$ and $\lambda_v = \lambda_u$. CBJ and RBJ do the same thing provided the label of v is the same $vars(c_u)$. If v is a leaf, this obvious. Assume v is not a leaf. Then if some child has a label which does not mention x_v, the label of v is the first such label encountered, and otherwise is is the union of all labels from v's children, less x_v. The clause c_u is constructed in the same manner from clauses labeling its children, so by inductive hypothesis we are done. ∎

Lemma 6 *Backjumping (BJ) and Graph-Based Backjumping (GBJ) (Gashnig 1978; Dechter 1990) are resolution bounded.*

Proof: The sub-trees pruned from the BT tree by BJ and GBJ are a subset of those pruned by RBJ. ∎

Forward Checking

Forward Checking (FC) modifies BT to reduce the number of nodes searched by doing extra consistency checks. When a variable is assigned a value, FC checks the constraints of all unassigned variables, and removes from their domains any values not consistent with the current assignment. If the domain of some future variable becomes empty, the current assignment is inconsistent, and backtracking takes place.

Our modified FC works as follows. For each variable x, we maintain a clause δ_x, which corresponds to the domain reductions that FC has performed on x. Initially $\delta_x = (\vee_{a \in D(x)} x{:}a)$. At a node v, when we assign the value a to x_v, we check the consistency of $x_v{:}a$ with each value c available for each unassigned variable y. If $C(\{x_v{:}a, y{:}c\}) \neq \emptyset$, then we let $\delta_y = Res(\delta_y, (\overline{x_v{:}a}, \overline{y{:}c}))$, and remove c from $D(y)$. (These two operations are undone when backtracking occurs.) If at some point $D(y)$ becomes empty, then δ_y no longer mentions y at all, but consists of a set of negated atoms which is falsified by the current assignment. Thus, the algorithm returns $\delta(y)$ as the clause for the current node.

Lemma 7 *FC and MFC are resolution bounded.*

Proof: Our modified FC simulates the original, and constructs resolvents from clauses in $\phi(\Lambda)$ such that whenever FC returns earlier than BT because of an empty domain, a resolvent is available for use in the refutation which is falsified by the current assignment. This clause is one of the possible clauses that could be returned (depending ordering strategy) by BT in searching the eliminated subtree.

The domain reductions made at each node by Minimal Forward Checking are a subset of those made FC, and can be carried out with a similar strategy. ∎

Arc Consistency

A CSP instance is arc consistent if, for every pair of variables x and y, for every $a \in D(x)$, there is at least one $c \in D(y)$ which is consistent, i.e., such that $C(\{x{:}a, y{:}c\}) = \emptyset$. We say that c supports $x{:}a$ at y. If there is no value c that supports $x{:}a$ at y, then no solution gives x the value a. Arc consistency filtering transforms a CSP instance into an arc consistent instance by repeatedly deleting domain elements with no support at some other variable.

We use Mohr and Henderson's AC-4 arc consistency algorithm, which has running time of optimal order(Mohr and Henderson 1986). Figure 4 shows our version, which constructs the set of clauses we need. The scheme is a generalization of that used for FC, and can in fact be further generalized to k-consistency filtering for arbitrary k.

The algorithm uses 4 data structures. $Supports[x{:}a]$ is the set of $y{:}c$ supported by a at x. $Number[x{:}a, y]$ stores the number of values which support $x{:}a$ at y. $Clause[x{:}a, y]$ is a clause which reflects the changes made to $Number[x{:}a, y]$. Initially $Clause[x{:}a, y] = (\vee_{c \in D(y)} y{:}c)$, the domain clause for y. There is also a stack S, which stores derived atoms which must be propagated. We assume the set E of pairs (x, y) of variables between which there is a constraint is available. $Supports[x{:}a]$ and E are used for efficiency, but have no role in constructing resolvents.

The initial pruning stage works as follows. For each $x{:}a$, it checks every $y{:}c$ to see how many values b support $x{:}a$ at y. Whenever $C(\{x{:}a, y{:}c\}) = \emptyset$, c supports $x{:}a$ at y. Whenever $C(\{x{:}a, y{:}c\}) \neq \emptyset$, the clause $Clause[x{:}a, y]$ is resolved with $\{\overline{x{:}a}, \overline{y{:}c}\}$, and the result becomes the new value of $Clause[x{:}a, y]$. After performing all checks for $x{:}a$, $Number[x{:}a, y]$ is the same as the number of occurrences of y in $Clause[x{:}a, y]$. If $Number[x{:}a, y] = 0$, then a is removed from $D(x)$ and $\overline{x{:}a}$ is pushed onto the stack. If this happens, $Clause[x{:}a, y] = (\overline{x{:}a})$, so the new domain clause for x, which does not include a, can be obtained by one more resolution step.

```
Procedure AC-4R(Λ)
  // initialize data structures
  for x ∈ X, a ∈ D(x)
    Supports[x:a] ← ∅
    for (x, y) ∈ E
      Number[x:a, y] ← 0
      Clause[x:a, y] ← (∨_{c∈D(y)} y:c)
    end for
  end for

  // initial pruning
  for (x, y) ∈ E
    for a ∈ D(x), c ∈ D(y)
      if C({x:a, y:c}) ≠ ∅ then
        Number[x:a, y] += 1
        Supports[y:c] ∪= {x:a}
      else
        Clause[x:a, y] ← Res(Clause[x:a, y], (x:a ∨ y:c))
      end if
    end for
    if Number[x:a, y] = 0 then
      D(x) ← D(x) − {a}
      S.Push(Clause[x:a, y])
    end if
  end for

  // propagation
  while not(Empty)
    (y:c) ← S.Pop()
    for x:a ∈ Supports[y:c]
      Number[x:a, y] −= 1
      Clause[x:a, y] ← Res(Clause[x:a, y], (y:c))
      if Number[x:a, y] = 0 and a ∈ D(x) then
        D(x) ← D(x) − {a}
        S.Push(Clause[x:a, y])
      end if
    end for
  end while
```

Figure 4: AC-4R

In the propagation stage, negated atoms – which identify values which have been eliminated from domains – are popped from the stack. When $\overline{y:c}$ is popped, $Number[x:a, y]$ and $Clause[x:a, y]$ are modified for each $x:a \in Supports[y:c]$. Further domain reductions may occur, with attendant computation of resolvents, and their effects also propagated. When the propagation phase completes, we have one of two possibilities. If some domain has been made empty, then the empty clause has been derived by resolution. Otherwise, we have an arc-consistent version Λ' of the original instance Λ, and a resolution derivation of the clauses in $\phi(\Lambda')$ from the clauses in $\phi(\Lambda)$.

A number of algorithms employ arc consistency filtering during backtracking, either at selected nodes or at all nodes (Nadel 1989; Sabin and Freuder 1994; Prosser 1995, for example). We will consider a generic and unrefined version of this idea, from which it should be clear that the same idea applies to most if not all of the variants in the literature.

Lemma 8 *Any algorithm which consists of backtracking (possibly with backjumping refinements) modified by performing k-consistency filtering before some or all branching operations, then A is resolution bounded.*

Proof (Sketch): Consider a path from the root to a leaf in the search tree for the algorithm. As the search progresses down the path, assignments to variables are made, and simplified instances are created by consistency filtering. The result of consistency filtering is reduced domains for some variables. First prove by induction downward that by carrying out the sequence of resolution steps specified by AC-4R (or a generalization of it for $k > 2$), we can derive shortened domain clauses corresponding to all reductions in domains performed by the consistency filtering operations. Then construct the refutation by induction from the bottom up as before. Because reduced domain clauses are available, there is no need for clauses from the sub-trees pruned by consistency filtering.

Note one subtlety in the downward construction. We cannot derive exactly the clauses that correspond to the reduced instance, since we cannot directly model the assignment operation with a resolution step. We carry out the sequence of resolution steps which correspond to consistency filtering operations as described for AC-4R, but the propositions corresponding to assignments made on the path still appear in the "reduced domain clauses". Fortunately, these are handled by the upward construction of the refutation, as in the versions without consistency filtering. ∎

Storing No-goods

A number of CSP algorithms make use of recording no-goods – often called learning – while doing backtracking ((Dechter 1990) for example).

Lemma 9 *Any of the above methods, when enhanced by no-good recording, is resolution bounded.*

Proof (Idea): A no-good corresponds exactly to a negative clause generated while constructing our refutation. Storing no-goods corresponds to caching these resolvents, and checking them against the current assignment each time an extension is made to it. ∎

Lemma 10 *Dynamic Backtracking (Ginsberg 1993) is resolution bounded.*

Proof (Idea): Storing no-goods is the primary control mechanism of dynamic backtracking. Space precludes a proof here, but a proof in our style can be easily obtained by adapting Baker's proof of a slightly different property, and Ginsberg's completeness proof (Baker 1995; Ginsberg 1993). ∎

Discussion

Related Work

We should begin by noting that even stronger lower bounds than ours (something like $n!$), can be obtained for some of these algorithms by applying known properties of local consistency (Dechter 1992, qv.). Our interest in the proof-based analysis is that we believe it can be more generally applied, and that it tells us something different about the algorithms (even when studying the same inputs).

There are many connections between resolution and backtracking algorithms in the literature. For propositional satisfiability, which is equivalent to CSPs with domain size two, the correspondence between resolution and the Davis-Putnam procedure is well known. de Kleer(De Kleer 1989) points out that (paraphrasing) if Λ' is the result of applying k-consistency filtering to Λ, then $\phi(\Lambda')$ can be obtained from $\phi(\Lambda)$ by resolution. However, his paper does not address complexity. Our point is that carrying out the resolution steps has computationally the same cost as running an optimal consistency filtering algorithm. Mackworth (Mackworth 1991) discusses logical representations of CSP instances and resolution, but does not draw connections to standard CSP algorithms or discuss algorithm complexity. Bayardo and Schrag (Bayardo Jr. and Schrag 1997) employed the relation between resolvents and CBJ for satisfiability, but did not discuss it in the context of general CSPs. The correspondence between no-goods and negative clauses appears, at least implicitly, in many papers.

The work closest to ours in both spirit and technique is in Chapter 5 of Baker's thesis (Baker 1995). There lower bounds are shown for backtracking (plus learning and backjumping) and dynamic backtracking using inputs with bounded induced width (Dechter and Pearl 1988). Since the PH_n inputs have unbounded width, these bounds provide information ours don't. However, the bounds obtained are weaker than ours ($O(n^{\log n})$), and apply to fewer algorithms. (Since the inputs used have short proofs, some resolution bounded procedures will solve them in polytime). Moreover, the inputs used to obtain these results are less natural than PH_n (see below). Baker defines a CSP variant of resolution, based only on no-good clauses, and then uses restricted versions of this system to obtain the lower bounds. The correspondence to propositional resolution is easy to see, not all algorithms will have convenient simulations, and the simulations for some will not be as tight as ours (e.g., the analogous notion of resolution-bounded is weaker), since not all propositional refutations can be represented.

Some Practical Considerations

A reasonable treatment of the relevance of these bounds to actually using algorithms in practice is beyond the scope of this paper, but we have a few brief comments to make along these lines.

Asymptotic results sometimes tell us little about instances of practical size, but these results are not asymptotic (other than that we use the standard asymptotic notation). The lower bound from (Beame and Pitassi 1996) holds for $n > 1,867$, which is not large for a real-world problem. $PH_{1,867}$ requires at least $2^{94} \approx 10^{29}$ steps, which is beyond hopeless for the for-seeable future. Moreover, this proven bound is likely much smaller than the best that can be achieved in practice. The shortest known refutation for PHP_n requires $(n-1)(n+2)2^{n-3}$ clauses, which even for PH_{100} is more than 10^{33} steps.

While it may be unlikely that one encounters PH_n inputs in practice, the problem is in essence quite natural. Whenever a problem requires finding a matching between two sets, a pigeonhole-like sub-problem can arise. Such matchings are central to a whole range of assignment, timetabling and scheduling problems. In hard instances of such problems, an unsolvable matching problem is exactly what we expect to obtain after a few bad choices have been made. It is important here to realize that the difficulty of the PH_n problems is much more general than this particular encoding of matching. For example, it sounds easier to spot the mistake of trying to squeeze far too many pigeons into a set of holes, rather than just one too many. But in fact, for resolution-bounded algorithms, it is just as hard (Buss and Turán 1988) Moreover, the same problem arises for more general matching problems to the extent that even having a solution to PH_n supplied for free (as an axiom or sub-routine, say) does not help (Ajtai 1988; Beame and Pitassi 1993).

Determining the extent to which problems of this sort actually occur in applications is an empirical question we cannot address here, but the proliferation of workshops on solving hard instances of the sorts of problems mentioned above is suggestive.

Proofs and Algorithms

Most of this paper is devoted to analysis of common CSP algorithms in terms of propositional calculus and resolution proofs, and using this analysis to prove exponential lower bounds for the algorithms. However, the technique of proof-based analysis can be applied to much more than what we have covered here. One role is a tool in understanding why certain algorithms do badly. Although there is considerable range in sophistication of the algorithms we have looked at, in some sense they all do badly for the same reason. Of course, they have important differences, which are reflected by other inputs, and even here we can learn something from proofs. For example, BT and CBJ correspond to the restriction to tree-like proofs, whereas methods which use consistency filtering or no-good recording have additional power which can be obtained by constructing DAG-like proofs.

From our speculations in the previous subsection it would follow that the resolution-bounded nature of almost all current algorithms is a major obstacle to progress. We conjecture that performance improvements of more than an order of magnitude beyond the current state, on a wide range of instances, will not occur until we break the "resolution barrier". (To see what sort of challenge this is, try to think up an algorithm which could conceivably be practical, but which you are convinced is not resolution bounded.)

A nice thing about viewing algorithms as proof-constructors is that there is a wide range of other proof systems available, most of which are more powerful than resolution. Most of these are not reasonable candidates for practical implementation, but they do provide a suite of potential tools for development.

The prevalence of resolution is in part a result of it's close relationship to backtracking, and in part a result of it being a week enough proof system that it is not too hard to find complete strategies which are can be practically implemented. Much stronger proof systems, such as extended resolution (for which no non-trivial lower bounds are known), do not offer much promise for practical implementation. In the middle ground are systems like the cutting planes system, which is stronger than resolution in that there are polynomial size proofs for the pigeonhole formulas, yet week enough that it is possible to base practical algorithms on it (as demonstrated by the mathematical programming community).

Concluding Remarks

We have shown, for a wide range CSP algorithms, a correspondence between execution on unsatisfiable instances (or sub-instances) and the construction of a resolution refutation for a related propositional formula. Using this property, we have shown that the simple family of instances PH_n, which encodes a version of the pigeonhole principle, induces exponential lower bounds on the runtime of the algorithms. The algorithms addressed include many of the most popular and successful algorithms in the literature.

For veterans in the area none of this will be surprising. Our main goal has been to make more explicit and precise the basics of what we consider to be a powerful but very under-utilized tool. There is probably more to be learned via this route even for existing algorithms. More importantly, we conjecture that what it has told us already has significant implications for how we should be approaching the task of designing better algorithms. That is, that the study of propositional proof systems and their complexity should be an integral part of this activity.

References

M. Ajtai. The complexity of the pigeonhole principle. In *Proc. FOCS-88*, pages 346–355, 1988.

Andrew B. Baker. *Intelligent Backtracking on Constraint Satisfaction Problems: Experimental and Theoretical Results*. PhD thesis, University of Oregon, 1995.

Roberto J. Bayardo Jr. and Robert C. Schrag. Using CSP look-back techniques to solve real-world SAT instances. In *Proc. AAAI-97*, 1997.

Paul Beame and Toniann Pitassi. An exponential separation between the matching principle and the pigeonhole principle. Technical Report 93-04-07, Dept. of Computer Science and Engineering, University of Washington, 1993.

Paul Beame and Toniann Pitassi. Simplified and improved resolution lower bounds. In *Proc. FOCS-96*, pages 274–282, 1996.

Samuel R. Buss and Györy Turán. Resolution proofs of generalized pigeonhole principles. *Theoretical Computer Science*, 62:311–317, 1988.

Johann De Kleer. A comparison of ATMS and CSP techniques. In *Proc. IJCAI 89*, pages 290–296, 1989.

R. Dechter and J. Pearl. Network-based heuristics for constraint satisfaction problems. *Artificial Intelligence*, 34:1–38, 1988.

Rina Dechter. Enhancement schemes for constraint processing: Backjumping, learning, and cutset decomposition. *Artificial Intelligence*, 41:273–312, 1990.

Rina Dechter. From local to global consistency. *Artificial Intelligence*, 55:87–107, 1992.

M.J. Dent and R.E. Mercer. Minimal forward checker. In *Proceedings, 6th INtl. Conf. on Tools with Artificial Intelligence.*, pages 432–438, New Orleans, 1994.

J. Gashnig. A general backtracking algorithm that eliminates most redundant tests. In *Proceedings, of the Intl. Joint Conf on Artificial Intelligence*, page 457, 1977.

J. Gashnig. Experimental case studies of backtrack vs. waltz-type vs. new algorithms for satisficing assignment problems. In *Proc. of the Canadian Artificial Intelligence Conference*, pages 268–277, 1978.

Matthew L. Ginsberg. Dynamic backtracking. *Journal of Artificial Intelligence Research*, 1:25–46, 1993.

A. Haken. The intractability of resolution. *Theoretical Computer Science*, 39:297–308, 1985.

R.M. Haralick and G.L. Elliot. Increasing tree search efficiency for constraint satsifaction problems. *Artificial Intelligence*, 14:263–313, 1980.

A.K. Mackworth. The logic of constraint satisfaction. Technical Report 91-26, Department of Computer Science, University of British Columbia, 1991.

R. Mohr and T.C. Henderson. Arc and path consistency revisited. *Artificial Intelligence*, 28:225–233, 1986.

Bernard A. Nadel. Constraint satisfaction algorithms. *Computational Intelligence*, 5:188–224, 1989.

Patrick Prosser. Hybrid algorithms for the constraint satisfaction problem. *Computational Intelligence*, 9(3):268–299, August 1993. (Also available as Technical Report AISL-46-91, Stratchclyde, 1991).

Patrick Prosser. MAC-CBJ: maintaining arc consistency with conflict-directed backjumping. Technical Report 95/177, Dept. of Comp. Sci., Unversity of Strathclyde, 1995.

Daniel Sabin and Eugene C. Freuder. Contradicting conventional wisdom in constraint satisfaction. In *Proc. PPCP-94. Appears as LNCS-874.*, pages 10–19, 1994. Also appears in Proc. ECAI-94.

The Constrainedness Knife-Edge

Toby Walsh
APES Group
Department of Computer Science
University of Strathclyde
Glasgow, Scotland
tw@cs.strath.ac.uk

Abstract

A general rule of thumb is to tackle the hardest part of a search problem first. Many heuristics therefore try to branch on the most constrained variable. To test their effectiveness at this, we measure the constrainedness of a problem during search. We run experiments in several different domains, using both random and non-random problems. In each case, we observe a constrainedness "knife-edge" in which critically constrained problems tend to remain critically constrained. We show that this knife-edge is predicted by a theoretical lower-bound calculation. We also observe a very simple scaling with problem size for various properties measured during search including the ratio of clauses to variables, and the average clause size. Finally, we use this picture of search to propose some branching heuristics for propositional satisfiability.

Introduction

Empirical studies of search procedures usually focus on statistics like run-time or nodes visited. It can also be productive to use the computer as a "microscope", looking closely at the running of the search procedure. To illustrate this approach, we measure the constrainedness of problems during search. A general purpose heuristic in many domains is to branch on the most constrained variable. For example, in graph coloring, the Brelaz heuristic colors a node with the fewest available colors, tie-breaking on the number of uncolored neighbours (Brelaz 1979). How effective are heuristics at identifying the most constrained variable? How constrained are the resulting subproblems? To answer such questions, we measured the constrainedness of problems during search in several different domains using both random and non-random problems.

We obtained similar results with a wide variety of algorithms and heuristics. In each case, we observed a constrainedness "knife-edge". Under-constrained problems tend to become less constrained as search deepens, over-constrained problems tend to become more constrained, but critically constrained problems from the region inbetween tend to *remain* critically constrained. We also observe a simple scaling with problem size for various properties measured during search including the ratio of clauses to variables. The existence of a constrainedness knife-edge helps to explain the hardness of problems from the phase transition. It also suggests some new branching heuristics for satisfiability. Similar microscopic studies that look closely inside search may be useful in other domains.

Constrainedness within satisfiability

There has been considerable interest in encoding problems into satisfiability and solving them either with local search procedures like GSAT (Selman, Levesque, & Mitchell 1992) or with the Davis-Putnam procedure (Bayardo & Schrag 1997). We therefore began our experiments by looking at how the constrainedness of satisfiability problems varies during search. The constrainedness of a satisfiability problem depends on several factors including the clause length (longer clauses are less constraining than shorter ones) and the number of clauses mentioning a variable (increasing the number of clauses makes the variable more constrained). We decided therefore to measure both the ratio of clauses to variables, and the average clause length during search for the popular random 3-SAT problem class (Mitchell, Selman, & Levesque 1992).

We use the Davis-Putnam procedure with unit propagation but no pure literal deletion. We branch with MOM's heuristic, picking the literal that occurs most often in the minimal size clauses. Depth is measured by the number of assignments. Similar results are obtained when depth is measured by the number of branch points, and with other heuristics including random branching. In each experiment, we simply follow the heuristic down the first branch, averaging over 1000 problems. To reduce variance, we use the same ensemble of problems in all experiments. We adopt the convention that initial parameters are in capitals and that values measured during search are in lower case.

---

[1]Copyright (c) 1998, American Association for Artificial Intelligence (www.aaai.org). All rights reserved.

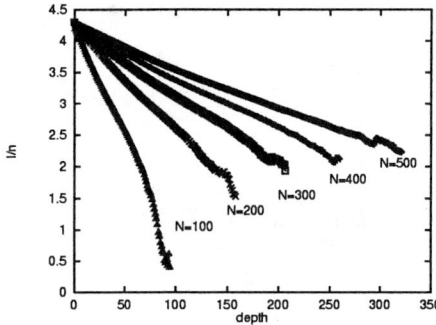

Figure 1: Ratio of clauses to variables, l/n on the heuristic branch against the depth.

In Figure 1, we plot the ratio of clauses to variables down the heuristic branch for random 3-SAT problems from the middle of the phase transition with an initial clause to variable ratio, $L/N = 4.3$. As search progresses, this ratio drops approximately linearly. However, it drops less rapidly for larger problems. Since not all heuristic branches extend to large depths, there is some noise at the end of each graph. Other experiments show that the rate of decay of l/n increases as we increase the initial ratio of clauses to variables, L/N. In Figure 2, we rescale the x-axis linearly with problem size, N. This rescaling shows that the gradient of l/n is inversely proportional to N. Such a simple scaling result is very unexpected. It may be useful in a theoretical analysis of the Davis Putnam procedure.

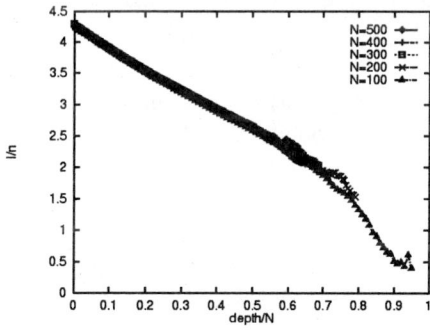

Figure 2: Ratio of clauses to variables, l/n on the heuristic branch against the fractional depth.

As the ratio of clauses to variables drops during search, we might expect that problems become less constrained. However, the average clause length also decreases as search deepens, tightening the constraints on variables. In Figure 3, we show that, just like the ratio of clauses to variables, the average clause length

is invariant if depths are scaled linearly with problem size, N. This simple scaling result may also be useful in a theoretical analysis of the Davis Putnam procedure. Other experiments show that the average clause length decreases as we decrease the initial ratio of clauses to variables, L/N. Which of these two factors wins? Does the decrease in clause size tighten the constrainedness faster than the decrease in the ratio of clauses to variables loosens it? To answer such questions, we need a more precise measure of constrainedness.

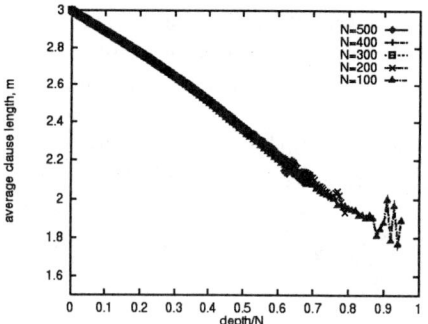

Figure 3: Average clause length, m on the heuristic branch against the fractional depth.

An approximate theory

(Gent *et al.* 1996) proposes an approximate theory for estimating the constrainedness of an ensemble of problems. This theory focuses on just two factors: the size of the problems, and the expected number of solutions. Problems which are large but which have a small number of solutions tend to be over-constrained. On the other hand, problems which are small but which have a large number of solutions tend to be under-constrained. Whilst this theory ignores important factors like problem structure and symmetries, its predictions are often surprisingly accurate. For instance, the theory predicts the location of a phase transition in number partitioning with just a 4% error (Gent & Walsh 1996).

If each problem in an ensemble has a state space with 2^N states, of which $\langle Sol \rangle$ are expected to be solutions, then the constrainedness, κ of the ensemble is defined by,

$$\kappa =_{\text{def}} 1 - \frac{\log_2(\langle Sol \rangle)}{N}$$

This parameter lies within the interval $[0, \infty)$. If $\kappa = 0$, problems in the ensemble are completely under-constrained and every state is a solution. If $\kappa = \infty$, problems in the ensemble are completely over-constrained and no states are solutions. If $\kappa < 1$, problems are under-constrained and are typically soluble. If

$\kappa > 1$, problems are over-constrained and are typically soluble. Around $\kappa \approx 1$, there tends to be a phase transition as problems can be both soluble and insoluble. The hardest problems to solve often occur around such transitions (Cheeseman, Kanefsky, & Taylor 1991).

Constrainedness knife-edge

We can use this definition of constrainedness to determine whether the decrease in average clause size outweighs the decrease in the ratio of clauses to variables. To estimate κ during search, we assume that the current subproblem is taken from an ensemble in which problems have the same number of clauses, the same number of variables, and the same distribution of clause lengths. If there are l_i clauses of length i, then as each clause of length i rules out the fraction $(1-\frac{1}{2^i})$ of the 2^n possible truth assignments,

$$\langle Sol \rangle \approx 2^n \cdot \prod_i (1 - \frac{1}{2^i})^{l_i}$$

Hence,

$$\kappa \approx -\sum_i \frac{l_i}{n} \cdot \log_2(1 - \frac{1}{2^i})$$

Note that for a random 3-SAT problem, κ is directly proportional to L/N, the ratio of clauses to variables.

In Figure 4, we plot the estimated constrainedness down the heuristic branch for random 3-SAT problems. For $L/N < 4.3$, problems are under-constrained and soluble. As search progresses, κ decreases as problems become more under-constrained and obviously soluble. For $L/N > 4.3$, problems are over-constrained and insoluble. As search progresses, κ increases as problems become more over-constrained and obviously insoluble. At $L/N \approx 4.3$ problems are on the *knife-edge* between solubility and insolubility. As search progresses, κ is roughly constant. Each successive branching decision gives a subproblem which has the same constrainedness as the original problem, neither more obviously satisfiable, nor more obviously unsatisfiable. Only deep in search does κ eventually break one way or the other.

As with the ratio of clauses to variables, and the average clause length, graphs of the constrainedness during search coincide if depths are scaled linearly with problem size, N. We have also observed similar knife-edge behaviour with a random heuristic, and with an anti-heuristic (that is, one which always branching against the heuristic) except that values of κ are slightly greater.

Figure 4 suggests an interesting analogy with statistical mechanics. At the phase boundary in physical systems, problems tend to be "self-similar". That is,

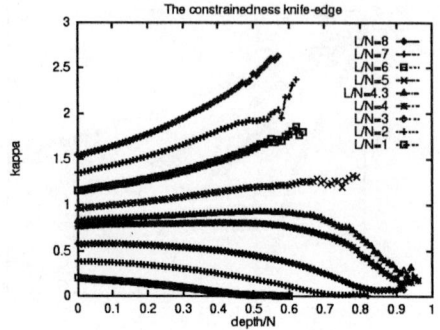

Figure 4: The estimated constrainedness, κ down the heuristic branch for random 3-SAT problems with 100 variables and varying initial ratio of clauses to variable.

they look similar at every length scale. At the phase boundary in computational systems, problems also display a form of self-similarity. Branching decisions give subproblems that look neither more or less constrained. This helps to explain why such problems are difficult to solve. Branching decisions tell us very little about the problem, giving subproblems that are neither more obviously soluble nor more obviously insoluble. We will often have to search to a large depth either for a solution or for a refutation. By comparison, branching on an over-constrained problem gives a subproblem that is often even more constrained and hopefully easier to show insoluble, whilst branching on an under-constrained problem gives a subproblem that is ofen even less constrained and hopefully easier to solve.

Lower bound on constrainedness

When we branch into a subproblem, the number of solutions remaining cannot increase. The expected number of solutions, $\langle Sol \rangle$ cannot therefore increase. This provides a lower bound on κ that is a good qualitative estimate for how the constrainedness actually varies during search. Let κ_i be the value of κ at depth i. Then,

$$\kappa_0 = 1 - \frac{\log_2(\langle Sol \rangle)}{N}$$

Hence,

$$\log_2(\langle Sol \rangle) = N(1 - \kappa_0)$$

Thus,

$$\kappa_i \geq 1 - \frac{\log_2(\langle Sol \rangle)}{N - i}$$
$$= 1 - \frac{N(1 - \kappa_0)}{N - i}$$
$$= \frac{N\kappa_0 - i}{N - i}$$

We can improve this bound slightly by noting that κ is bounded below by zero. Hence,

$$\kappa_i \geq \max(0, \frac{N\kappa_0 - i}{N - i})$$

In Figure 5, we plot this bound on κ for random 3-SAT problems with 100 variables and varying initial ratio of clauses to variable, L/N. We see that the behaviour of κ during search observed in Figure 4 is similar to that predicted by the bound.

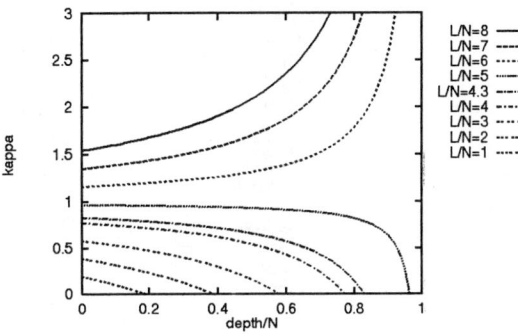

Figure 5: Lower-bound on the constrainedness, κ down a branch for random 3-SAT problems with 100 variables and varying initial ratio of clauses to variable.

Non-random problems

The existence of a constrainedness knife-edge helps to explain the difficulty of solving *random* problems at the phase transition in solubility. Branching decisions give subproblems which are neither more obviously soluble or insoluble. We are forced therefore to search to a large depth either for a solution or for a refutation. Phase transition behaviour has also been observed in problems which are not purely random. For instance, (Gent & Walsh 1995) identifies phase transition behaviour in traveling salesperson problems using real geographical data, in graph coloring problems derived from university exam time-tables, and in Boolean induction and synthesis problem. As a fourth example, (Gomes & Selman 1997) demonstrate phase transition behaviour in the quasi-group completion problem. Does the existence of a constrainedness knife-edge help to explain the difficulty of solving problems at the phase boundary in such non-random problems?

To answer this question, we ran some experiments with graph coloring problems from the DIMACS benchmark library. We used the register allocation problems as these are based on real code. To color the graphs, we use a forward checking algorithm with the Brelaz heuristic to pick the next node to color (Brelaz 1979), and Geelen's promise heuristic to choose one of the m possible colors (Geelen 1992). To estimate κ, we assume that the graph is drawn from an ensemble in which graphs have the same number of nodes, the same available colors, and the same number of edges as in the current subproblem. If V is the set of uncolored nodes, E is the set of edges between uncolored nodes, and m_i is the set of colors remaining for node i then there are $\prod_{i \in V} |m_i|$ possible colorings of the nodes, and each edge $\langle i,j \rangle \in E$ rules out $|m_i \cap m_j|$ of the $|m_i|.|m_j|$ pairs of colors between nodes, i and j. Thus,

$$N = \log_2(\prod_{i \in V} |m_i|) = \sum_{i \in V} \log_2(|m_i|)$$

$$\langle Sol \rangle \approx \prod_{i \in V} |m_i| . \prod_{\langle i,j \rangle \in E} (1 - \frac{|m_i \cap m_j|}{|m_i|.|m_j|})$$

Hence,

$$\kappa \approx -\frac{\sum_{\langle i,j \rangle \in E} \log_2(1 - \frac{|m_i \cap m_j|}{|m_i|.|m_j|})}{\sum_{i \in V} \log_2(|m_i|)}$$

In Figure 6, we plot the estimated constrainedness down the heuristic branch for a typical register allocation problem. Despite the fact that this plot is

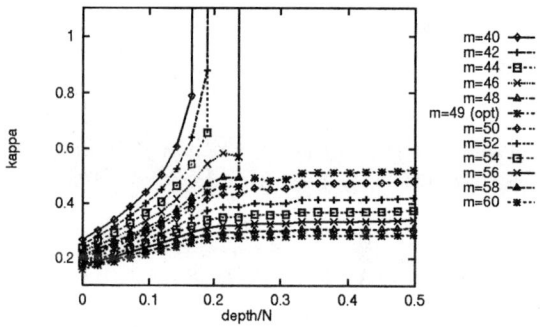

Figure 6: Estimated constrainedness down the heuristic branch for a typical register allocation problem from the DIMACS library using a forward checking algorithm. The problem instance ("zeroin.i.1.col") has 211 nodes, 4100 edges, and needs $m = 49$ colors. For $m \leq 48$, the estimate for κ becomes infinite before the end of search as the problem becomes arc inconsistent.

for a *single* problem instance, we observe a "knife-edge". With less than 49 colors, the problem is over-constrained and insoluble. As search progresses, the constrainedness increases rapidly. Each branching decision results in a subproblem that is more obviously insoluble. With more than 49 colors, the problem is under-constrained and soluble. As search progresses, the constrainedness only increases slightly.

Each branching decision gives a subproblem that is of similar constrainedness and difficulty to solve. Similar behaviour is seen with the other register allocation problems in the DIMACS library.

Constrainedness within optimization

Phase transition behaviour is not restricted to decision problems like propositional satisfiability. Certain optimization problems like number partitioning and the traveling salesperson problem also exhibit phase transitions (Gent & Walsh 1996; Zhang & Korf 1996). Do we observe a constrainedness knife-edge when solving such optimization problems?

To explore this question, we ran some experiments with the CKK optimization procedure for number partitioning (Korf 1995). Given a bag of N number, we wish to find a partition into two bags that minimizes Δ, the difference between the sum of the two bag. (Gent & Walsh 1996) shows that for partitioning n numbers drawn uniformly at random from $(0, l]$, $\kappa \approx log_2(l)/n$. To estimate κ during search, we assume that the numbers left are taken from such an ensemble and that their size, l is twice the sample average. In Figure 7, we plot this estimate for the constrainedness during search. For comparison, we also plot the lower bound on κ using the same scales. We again observe a constrainedness knife-edge. Although there is not a transition between soluble and insoluble problems (since there is always an optimal partition), there is now a transition between optimization problems with perfect partitions (that is, in which $\Delta \leq 1$) and those without, and verifying the optimality of a partition with $\Delta > 1$ can be costly.

Constrainedness as a heuristic

Knowledge about the existence of a constrainedness knife-edge may help us design more effective search procedures. For instance, for soluble problems, it suggests that we should try to get off the knife-edge as quickly as possible by branching into the subproblem that is as under-constrained as possible. That is, as suggested in (Gent et al. 1996), we should branch into the subproblem that minimizes κ. To test this thesis, we implemented a branching heuristic for the Davis-Putnam procedure that branches on the literal which gives the subproblem with smallest κ. In Table 1, we show that this heuristic performs well on hard and satisfiable random 3-SAT problems.

For insoluble problems, the existence of a constrainedness knife-edge suggests that we should branch into the sub-problem that is as over-constrained as possible. That is, we should branch into the subproblem that maximizes κ. Initial experiments suggest

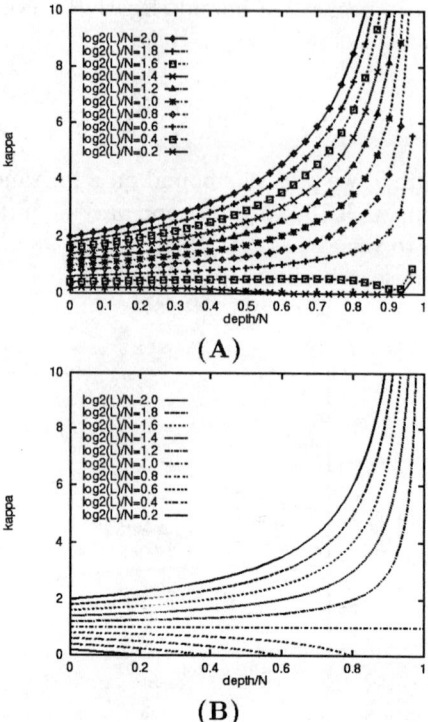

Figure 7: The constrainedness, κ down the heuristic branch for number partitioning problems with $N = 30$ numbers, and varying L. (A) estimated κ. (B) theoretical lower-bound to same scale.

that this heuristic is effective on hard and unsatisfiable random 3-SAT problems. For instance, for 50 variable unsatisfiable problems at $L/N = 4.3$, the median nodes searched using this heuristic is 2,575 compared to 3,331 nodes for MOM's heuristic, and 7,419 nodes for the heuristic that minimizes κ. On the other hand, maximizing κ is less effective on hard and satisfiable problems. For 50 variable satisfiable problems at $L/N = 4.3$, the median nodes searched when maximizing κ is 1,487 compared to 164 nodes with MOM's heuristic, and 104 nodes with the heuristic that minimizes κ. An adaptive heuristic that switches between minimizing and maximizing κ depending on an estimate of the solubility of the problem may therefore offer good performance.

Related work

Most theoretical studies of the Davis-Putnam procedure have used the easier constant probability model. One notable exception is (Yugami 1995) which computes the average-case complexity of the Davis-Putnam procedure for the random 3-SAT problem class. Freeman has studied experimentally the running of the

N	MOM	KAPPA
25	11	1
50	164	104
75	1129	580
100	3903	1174

Table 1: Median nodes searched by the Davis-Putnam procedure for satisfiable random 3-SAT problems at $L/N = 4.3$, branching either with MOM's heuristic, or to minimize the constrainedness (KAPPA).

Davis-Putnam procedure on random 3-SAT problems (Freeman 1996). Unlike here, where the focus is on the heuristic branch, Freeman computes averages across all branches in the search tree. He identifies an "unit cascade", a depth in the search tree where unit propagation greatly simplifies the problem. The ineffectiveness of unit propagation above this depth helps to explain the hardness of problems at the phase transition.

Gent and Walsh have studied experimentally the running of local search procedures for satisfiability (Gent & Walsh 1993). They show that various properties like the percentage of clauses satisfied, and the number of variables offered to flip are invariant if depths are scaled linearly with problem size. This mirrors the result here on the scaling of the constrainedness, the ratio of clauses to variables and the average clause size. Such simple scaling results may be useful in the theoretical analysis of these search procedures.

Conclusions

We have measured how the constrainedness of problems varies during search in several different problem domains: both decision problems like propositional satisfiability and graph coloring, and optimization problems like number partitioning. Our experiments have used both random and non-random problems. In each case, we observed a constrainedness "knife-edge" in which critically constrained problems tended to remain critically constrained. The existence of a constrainedness knife-edge helps to explain the hardness of problems from the phase transition. We have shown that a lower-bound calculation predicts this knife-edge theoretically. We have also observed a very simple scaling with problem size for various properties measured during search like the constrainedness, the ratio of clauses to variables, and the average clause size. Finally, we have used the existence of a constrainedness knife-edge to propose some branching heuristics for propositional satisfiability. We conjecture that similar microscopic studies that look closely inside search may be useful in other domains.

Acknowledgments

I wish to thank members of the APES group, especially Barbara Smith and Ian Gent, for their comments and criticisms. The author is supported by EPSRC award GR/K/65706.

References

Bayardo, R., and Schrag, R. 1997. Using CSP lookback techniques to solve real-world SAT instances. In *Proceedings of the 14th National Conference on AI*.

Brelaz, D. 1979. New methods to color the vertices of a graph. *Commincations of ACM* 22:251–256.

Cheeseman, P.; Kanefsky, B.; and Taylor, W. 1991. Where the really hard problems are. In *Proceedings of the 12th IJCAI*, 331–337.

Freeman, J. 1996. Hard random 3-SAT problems and the Davis-Putnam procedure. *Artificial Intelligence* 81(1-2):183–198.

Geelen, P. 1992. Dual viewpoint heuristics for binary constraint satisfaction problems. In *Proceedings of the 10th ECAI*, 31–35.

Gent, I., and Walsh, T. 1993. An empirical analysis of search in GSAT. *Journal of Artificial Intelligence Research* 1:23–57.

Gent, I., and Walsh, T. 1995. Phase transitions from real computational problems. In *Proceedings of the 8th Int. Symp. on Artificial Intelligence*, 356–364.

Gent, I., and Walsh, T. 1996. Phase transitions and annealed theories: Number partitioning as a case study. In *Proceedings of ECAI-96*.

Gent, I.; MacIntyre, E.; Prosser, P.; and Walsh, T. 1996. The constrainedness of search. In *Proceedings of the 13th National Conference on AI*.

Gomes, C., and Selman, B. 1997. Problem structure in the presence of perturbations. In *Proceedings of the 14th National Conference on AI*, 221–226.

Korf, R. 1995. From approximate to optimal solutions: A case study of number partitioning. In *Proceedings of the 14th IJCAI*.

Mitchell, D.; Selman, B.; and Levesque, H. 1992. Hard and Easy Distributions of SAT Problems. In *Proceedings of the 10th National Conference on AI*, 459–465.

Selman, B.; Levesque, H.; and Mitchell, D. 1992. A New Method for Solving Hard Satisfiability Problems. In *Proceedings of the 10th National Conference on AI*, 440–446.

Yugami, N. 1995. Theoretical analysis of Davis-Putnam procedure and propositional satisfiability. In *Proceedings of the 14th IJCAI*, 282–288.

Zhang, W., and Korf, R. 1996. A study of complexity transitions on the asymmetic traveling salesman problem. *Artificial Intelligence* 81(1-2):223–239.

Heuristic Search in Cyclic AND/OR Graphs

Eric A. Hansen and Shlomo Zilberstein
Computer Science Department
University of Massachusetts
Amherst, MA 01003
{hansen,shlomo}@cs.umass.edu

Abstract

Heuristic search algorithms can find solutions that take the form of a simple path (A*), a tree or an acyclic graph (AO*). We present a novel generalization of heuristic search (called LAO*) that can find solutions with loops, that is, solutions that take the form of a cyclic graph. We show that it can be used to solve Markov decision problems without evaluating the entire state space, giving it an advantage over dynamic-programming algorithms such as policy iteration and value iteration as an approach to stochastic planning.

Introduction

One of the most widely-used frameworks for problem-solving in artificial intelligence is state-space search. A state-space search problem is defined by a set of states, a set of operators that map states to successor states, a start state, and a set of goal states. The objective is to find a sequence of operators that transforms the start state into a goal state and also optimizes some measure of the cost, or merit, of the solution.

Two well-known heuristic search algorithms for solving state-space search problems are A* and AO* (Nilsson 1980). A* finds a solution that takes the form of a sequence of operators leading from a start state to a goal state. AO* finds a solution that has a conditional structure and takes the form of a tree, or more generally, an acyclic graph. However no heuristic search algorithm has been developed that can find a solution that takes the form of a cyclic graph, that is, a solution with loops.

For many problems that can be formalized in the state-space search model, it does not make sense for a solution to contain loops. For example, a loop in a solution to a theorem-proving problem represents circular reasoning. A loop in a solution to a problem-reduction problem represents a failure to reduce it to primitive subproblems. However there are some problems for which it does make sense for a solution to contain loops. These include problems that can be formalized as Markov decision processes (MDPs), a framework widely used for stochastic planning in artificial intelligence (Dean *et al.* 1995; Barto *et al.* 1985; Tash and Russell 1994; Dearden and Boutilier 1997). A stochastic planning problem includes operators (or actions) that transform a state into one of several possible successor states, with each possible state transition occurring with some probability. A solution is usually cast in the form of a mapping from states to actions called a *policy*. A policy is executed by observing the current state and taking the action prescribed for it. A solution represented in this way implicitly contains both branches and loops. Branching is present because the state that stochastically results from an action determines the next action. Looping is present because the same state may be revisited under a policy. (As an example of a plan with a conditional loop, consider an operator that has its desired effect with probability less than one and otherwise has no effect; an appropriate plan might be to repeat the action until it "succeeds.")

A policy for an MDP can be found using a dynamic programming algorithm such as policy iteration or value iteration. A disadvantage of dynamic programming is that it evaluates the entire state space; in effect, it finds a policy for every possible starting state. By contrast, heuristic search finds a policy for a particular starting state and uses an admissible heuristic to focus the search and remove from consideration regions of the state space that can't be reached from the start state by an optimal solution. For problems with large state spaces, heuristic search has an advantage over dynamic programming because it can find an optimal solution for a particular start state without evaluating the entire state space.

This advantage is well-known for problems that can be solved by A* or AO*. In fact, an important theorem about the behavior of A* is that (under certain condi-

---

Copyright ©1998, American Association for Artificial Intelligence (www.aaai.org). All rights reserved.

tions) it evaluates the minimal number of states among all algorithms that find an optimal solution using the same heuristic (Dechter and Pearl 1985) and a related result has been established for AO* (Chakrabarti et al. 1988). In this paper, we generalize heuristic search to find solutions with loops and show that the resulting algorithm can solve stochastic planning problems that are formalized as MDPs without evaluating the entire state space.

Background

We begin by reviewing AND/OR graphs and the heuristic search algorithm AO* for solving problems formalized as acyclic AND/OR graphs. We then briefly review MDPs and show that they can be formalized as cyclic AND/OR graphs.

AND/OR graphs

We formalize a state-space search problem as a graph in which each node represents a problem state and each arc represents the application of an operator to a state. Let S denote the set of all possible states; in this paper, we assume it is finite. Let $s \in S$ denote a start state that corresponds to the root of the graph and let $S^G \subseteq S$ denote a set of goal states that occur at the leaves of the graph. Let A denote a finite set of operators (or actions) and let $A(i)$ denote the set of operators applicable to state i.

Following Martelli and Montanari (1978) and Nilsson (1980), we view an AND/OR graph as a hypergraph. Instead of arcs that connect pairs of nodes as in an ordinary graph, a hypergraph has *hyperarcs* or *k-connectors* that connect a node to a set of k successor nodes. A k-connector can be interpreted in different ways. In problem-reduction search, it is interpreted as the transformation of a problem into k subproblems. Here we interpret a k-connector as a stochastic operator that transforms a state into one of k possible successor states. Let $p_{ij}(a)$ denote the probability that applying operator a to state i results in a transition to state j. A similar interpretation of AND/OR graphs is made by Martelli and Montanari (1978) and Pattipati and Alexandridis (1990), among others.

In AND/OR graph search, a "solution" is a generalization of the concept of a path in an ordinary graph. Starting from the start node, it selects exactly one operator (outgoing connector) for each node. Because a connector can have multiple successor nodes, a solution can also be viewed as a subgraph called a *solution graph*. Every directed path in the solution graph terminates at a goal node.

We assume a cost function assigns a cost to each hyperarc; let $c_i(a)$ denote the cost for the hyperarc that corresponds to applying operator a to state i. We also assume each goal state has a cost of zero. The cost of a solution graph for a given state is defined recursively as the sum of the cost of applying the operator prescribed for that state and the weighted sum of the cost of the solution graphs for each of its successor states, where the weight is the probability of each state transition. A minimal-cost solution graph is found by solving the following system of recursive equations,

$$f^*(i) = \begin{cases} 0 \text{ if } i \text{ is a goal node} \\ \text{else } min_{a \in A(i)} \left[c_i(a) + \sum_{j \in S} p_{ij}(a) f^*(j) \right] \end{cases}$$

where f^* denotes the optimal *cost-to-go function* and $f^*(i)$ is the optimal cost for state i. For an acyclic AND/OR graph, a special dynamic programming algorithm called backwards induction solves these equations efficiently by evaluating each state exactly once in a backwards order from the leaves to the root.

AO*

Unlike dynamic programming, heuristic search can find an optimal solution graph without evaluating the entire state space. Therefore a graph is not usually supplied explicitly to a search algorithm. We refer to G as the *implicit graph*; it is specified implicitly by a start node s and a successor function. The search algorithm works on an *explicit graph*, G', that initially consists only of the start node. A tip or leaf node of the explicit graph is said to be terminal if it is a goal node and nonterminal otherwise. A nonterminal tip node can be expanded by adding to the explicit graph its outgoing connectors and any successor nodes not already in the explicit graph.

Heuristic search works by repeatedly expanding the best partial solution until a complete solution is found. A *partial solution graph* is a subgraph of the explicit graph that starts at s and selects exactly one hyperarc for each node. It is defined similarly to a solution graph, except that a directed path may end at a nonterminal tip node. For every nonterminal tip node i of a partial solution graph, we assume there is an admissible heuristic estimate $h(i)$ of the minimal-cost solution graph for it. A heuristic evaluation function h is said to be *admissible* if $h(i) \leq f^*(i)$ for every node i. We can recursively calculate an admissible heuristic estimate $f(i)$ of the optimal cost of any node i in the explicit graph as follows:

$$f(i) = \begin{cases} 0 \text{ if } i \text{ is a goal node} \\ h(i) \text{ if } i \text{ is a nonterminal tip node} \\ \text{else } min_{a \in A(i)} \left[c_i(a) + \sum_{j \in S} p_{ij}(a) f(j) \right] \end{cases}$$

1. The explicit graph G' initially consists of the start node s.

2. *Forward search:* Expand the best partial solution graph as follows:

   (a) Identify the best partial solution graph and its nonterminal tip nodes by searching forward from the start state and following the marked action for each state.

   (b) If the best partial solution graph has no nonterminal tip nodes, goto 4.

   (c) Else expand some nonterminal tip node n and add any new successor nodes to G'. For each new tip node i added to G' by expanding n, if i is a goal node then $f(i) = 0$; else $f(i) = h(i)$.

3. *Dynamic programming:* Update state costs as follows:

   (a) Identify the ancestors in the explicit graph of expanded node n and create a set Z that contains the expanded node and all its ancestors.

   (b) Perform backwards induction on the nodes in Z by repeating the following steps until Z is empty.

   i. Remove from Z a node i such that no descendent of i in G' occurs in Z.

   ii. Set $f(i) := \min_{a \in A(i)} \left[c_i(a) + \sum_j p_{ij}(a) f(j) \right]$ and mark the best action for i. (When determining the best action resolve ties arbitrarily, but give preference to the currently marked action.)

   (c) Goto 2.

4. Return the solution graph.

Figure 1: AO*

Figure 1 outlines the algorithm AO* for finding a minimal-cost solution graph in an acyclic AND/OR graph. It interleaves forward expansion of the best partial solution with a dynamic programming step that uses backwards induction. As with all heuristic search algorithms, three classes of states can be distinguished. The implicit graph contains all possible states. The explicit graph contains all states that are generated and evaluated at some point in the course of the search. The solution graph contains those states that are reachable from the start state when a optimal solution is followed.

The version of AO* we have outlined is described by Martelli and Montanari (1973). Others have described slightly different versions of AO* (Martelli and Montanari 1978; Nilsson 1980; Bagchi and Mahanti 1983). One difference is to use a pathmax operation in step (3bii), as follows:

$$f(i) := \max \left(f(i), \min_{a \in A(i)} \left[c_i(a) + \sum_{j \in S} p_{ij}(a) f(j) \right] \right).$$

If the heuristic is admissible but not consistent, this ensures that state costs increase monotonically. Another difference is to try to limit the number of ancestors on which dynamic programming is performed by not considering the ancestors of a node unless the cost of the node has changed and the node can be reached by marked connectors. To simplify exposition, we have also omitted from our outline of AO* a solve-labeling procedure that is usually included to improve efficiency. Briefly, a node is labeled solved if it is a goal node or if all of its successor nodes are labeled solved. Labeling nodes as solved improves the efficiency of the forward search step of AO* because it is unnecessary to search below a solved node for nonterminal tip nodes.

Markov decision processes

MDPs are widely used in artificial intelligence as a framework for decision-theoretic planning and reinforcement learning. Here we note that an infinite-horizon MDP can be formalized in a straightforward way as a cyclic AND/OR graph. The cycles in the graph make infinite-horizon behavior possible. Let each node of the graph correspond to a state of the MDP and let each k-connector correspond to an action with k possible outcomes. The transition probability function and cost function defined earlier are the same as those for MDPs. A solution to an MDP generally takes the form of a mapping from states to actions, δ, called a policy.

Closely related to heuristic search problems are a class of infinite-horizon MDPs called *stochastic shortest-path problems* (Bertsekas 1995). (The name reflects an interpretation of costs as arc lengths.) Stochastic shortest-path problems have a start state and a set of absorbing states that can be used to model goal states. A policy is said to be *proper* if it ensures the goal state is reached from any state with probability 1.0. For a proper policy, the undiscounted infinite-horizon cost for each state i is finite and can be computed by solving the following system of $|S|$ equations in $|S|$ unknowns:

$$f^\delta(i) = c_i(\delta(s)) + \sum_{j \in S} p_{ij}(\delta(s)) f^\delta(j). \quad (1)$$

In the rest of this paper we make the simplifying assumption that all possible policies are proper. The results of this paper do not depend on this assumption. When it cannot be made, other optimality criteria – such as discounted cost over an infinite horizon or average cost per transition – can be adopted to ensure every state has a finite expected cost under every policy (Bertsekas 1995).

A policy δ is said to dominate a policy δ' if $f^\delta(i) \leq f^{\delta'}(i)$ for every state i. An optimal policy dominates every other policy and its cost-to-go function, f^*, satisfies the following Bellman optimality equation:

$$f^*(i) = \min_{a \in A(i)} \left[c_i(a) + \sum_{j \in S} p_{ij}(a) f^*(j) \right].$$

Policy iteration is a well-known method for solving infinite-horizon MDPs. After evaluating a policy using equation (1), it improves it by performing the following operation for each state i:

$$\delta(i) := \arg\max_{a \in A(i)} \left[c_i(a) + \sum_{j \in S} p_{ij}(a) f^\delta(j) \right].$$

Policy evaluation and policy improvement are repeated until the policy cannot be improved, which signifies that it is optimal. Another algorithm for solving MDPs is value iteration. Each iteration, it improves the estimated cost-to-go function f by performing the following operation for each state i,

$$f(i) := \max_{a \in A(i)} \left[c_i(a) + \sum_{j \in S} p_{ij}(a) f(j) \right].$$

However policy iteration and value iteration must evaluate all states to find an optimal policy. Therefore they can be computationally prohibitive for MDPs with large state sets. We try to overcome this limitation by using heuristic search to limit the number of states that must be evaluated.

LAO*

LAO* is a simple generalization of AO* that can find solutions with loops. Like AO*, it has two principal steps: a forward search step and a dynamic programming step. The forward search step is the same as in AO* except that it allows a solution graph to contain loops. Forward search of a partial solution graph now terminates at a goal node, a nonterminal tip node, or a loop back to an already expanded node of the current partial solution graph.

The problem with allowing a solution graph to contain loops is that the backwards induction algorithm of the dynamic programming step of AO* can no longer

---

1. The explicit graph G' initially consists of the start node s.

2. *Forward search:* Expand the best partial solution graph as follow:.

   (a) Identify the best partial solution graph and its nonterminal tip nodes by searching forward from the start state and following the marked action for each state.

   (b) If the best partial solution graph has no nonterminal tip nodes, goto 4.

   (c) Else expand some nonterminal tip node n and add any new successor nodes to G'. For each new tip node i added to G' by expanding n, if i is a goal node then $f(i) = 0$; else $f(i) = h(i)$.

3. *Dynamic programming:* Update state costs as follows:

   (a) Identify the ancestors in the explicit graph of expanded node n and create a set Z that contains the expanded node and all its ancestors.

   (b) Perform policy iteration on the nodes in set Z until convergence or else perform value iteration on the nodes in set Z for one or more iterations. Mark the best action for each state. (When determining the best action resolve ties arbitrarily, but give preference to the currently marked action.)

   (c) Goto 2.

4. Return the solution graph.

Figure 2: LAO*

be applied. However dynamic programming can still be performed by using policy iteration or value iteration algorithms for infinite-horizon MDPs. This simple generalization of AO* creates the algorithm LAO* that is summarized in Figure 2. In the rest of this section we discuss some of the issues that must be considered to implement it efficiently.

Policy iteration

We begin by considering the use of policy iteration to perform the dynamic programming step of LAO*. The advantage of using policy iteration is that it computes an exact cost for each node of the explicit graph, based on the heuristic estimates at the tip nodes.

Policy iteration is performed on the set of nodes that includes the expanded node and all of its ancestors in the explicit graph. Some of these nodes may have successor nodes that are not in this set of nodes but are still part of the explicit graph; in other words, policy iteration is not necessarily (or usually) performed on the entire explicit graph. The costs of these successor nodes can be treated as constants in the dynamic programming step because they cannot be affected by any change in the cost of the expanded node or its ancestors. The dynamic programming step of AO* exploits this reasoning as well.

Performing policy iteration on this set of nodes may change the best action for some states and, by doing so, change the best partial solution graph; the backwards induction algorithm of AO* can have the same effect. Because multiple iterations of policy iteration may be necessary to converge, it is important to stress that policy iteration must be performed on all of the nodes in this set until convergence. This is necessary to ensure that all nodes in the explicit graph have exact, admissible costs, including those that are no longer part of the best partial solution graph.

It is straightforward to show that LAO* shares the properties of AO* and other heuristic search algorithms. Given an admissible heuristic evaluation function, all state costs in the explicit graph are admissible after each step and LAO* converges to an optimal policy without (necessarily) evaluating the entire state space.

Theorem 1 *If the heuristic evaluation function h is admissible and policy iteration is used to perform the dynamic programming step of LAO*, then:*

1. $f(i) \leq f^*(i)$ *for every state i, after each step of LAO**

2. $f(i) = f^*(i)$ *for every state i of the best solution graph, when LAO* terminates*

3. *LAO* terminates after a finite number of iterations*

Proof: (1) The proof is by induction. Every node $i \in G$ is assigned an initial heuristic cost estimate and $h(i) \leq f^*(i)$ by the admissibility of the heuristic evaluation function. The forward search step expands the best partial solution graph and does not change the cost of any nodes and so it is sufficient to consider the dynamic programming step. We make the inductive assumption that at the beginning of this step, $f(i) \leq f^*(i)$ for every node $i \in G$. If all the tip nodes of G' have optimal costs, then all the nontip nodes in G' must converge to their optimal costs when policy iteration is performed on them by the convergence proof for policy iteration. But by the induction hypothesis, all the tip nodes of G' have admissible costs. It follows that the nontip nodes in G' must converge to costs that are as good or better than optimal when policy iteration is performed on them only.

(2) The search algorithm terminates when the best solution graph for s is complete, that is, has no unexpanded nodes. For every state i in this solution graph, it is contradictory to suppose $f(i) < f^*(i)$ since that implies a complete solution that is better than optimal. By (1) we know that $f(i) \leq f^*(i)$ for every node in G'. Therefore $f(i) = f^*(i)$.

(3) It is obvious that LAO* terminates after a finite number of iterations if the implicit graph G is finite, or equivalently, the number of states in the MDP is finite. (When the state set is not finite, it may still converge in some cases.) □

Because policy iteration is initialized with the current state costs, it may converge quickly. Nevertheless it is a much more time-consuming algorithm than the backward induction algorithm used by AO*. The backwards induction algorithm of AO* has only linear complexity in the size of the set of nodes on which dynamic programming is performed. Each iteration of policy iteration has cubic complexity in the size of this set of nodes and more than one iteration may be needed for policy iteration to converge.

Value iteration

An alternative is to use value iteration in the dynamic programming step of AO*. A single iteration of value iteration is computationally equivalent to the backwards induction algorithm of AO* and states can be evaluated in a backwards order from the expanded node to the root of the graph to maximize improvement. However the presence of loops means that state costs are not exact after value iteration. Therefore LAO* is no longer guaranteed to identify the best partial solution graph or to expand nodes in a best-first order. This disadvantage may be offset by the improved efficiency of the dynamic programming step, however, and it is straightforward to show that state costs remain admissible and converge in the limit to optimality.

Theorem 2 *If the heuristic evaluation function h is admissible and value iteration is used to perform the dynamic programming step of LAO*, then:*

1. $f(i) \leq f^*(i)$ *for every node i at every point in the algorithm*

2. $f(i)$ *converges to* $f^*(i)$ *in the limit, for every node i of the best solution graph*

Proof: (1) The proof is by induction. Every node $i \in G$ is assigned an initial heuristic cost estimate and $f(i) = h(i) \leq f^*(i)$ by the admissibility of the heuristic evaluation function. We make the inductive hypothesis that at some point in the algorithm, $f(i) \leq f^*(i)$

for every node $i \in G$. If a value iteration update is performed for any node i,

$$\begin{aligned} f(i) &= \min_{a \in A(i)} \left[c_i(a) + \sum_{j \in S} p_{ij}(a) f(j) \right] \\ &\leq \min_{a \in A(i)} \left[c_i(a) + \sum_{j \in S} p_{ij}(a) f^*(j) \right] = f^*(i), \end{aligned}$$

where the last equality restates the Bellman optimality equation.

(2) Because the graph is finite, LAO* must eventually find a complete solution graph. In the limit, the nodes is this solution graph must converge to their exact costs by the convergence proof for value iteration. The solution graph must be optimal by the admissibility of the costs of all the nodes in the explicit graph. □

When value iteration is used, convergence to optimal state costs is asymptotic. If bounds on optimal state costs are available, however, it may be possible to detect convergence to an optimal solution after a finite number of steps by using the bounds to prune actions that can be proved suboptimal.

Forward search

We briefly mention some ways in which the efficiency of LAO* can be affected by the forward search step.

As with AO*, the fringe of the best partial solution graph may contain many unexpanded nodes and the choice of which to expand next is nondeterministic. That is, LAO* works correctly no matter what heuristic is used to select which nonterminal tip node of the best partial solution graph to expand next. A well-chosen node selection heuristic can improve performance, however. Possibilities include expanding the node with the highest probability of being reached from the start state or expanding the node with the least cost.

It is also possible to expand several nodes at a time in the forward search step. This risks expanding some nodes unnecessarily but can improve performance when the dynamic programming step is more expensive than the forward search step.

Like all heuristic search algorithms, the efficiency of LAO* depends crucially on the heuristic evaluation function that guides the search. The more accurate the heuristic, the fewer states need to be evaluated to find an optimal solution, that is, the smaller the explicit graph generated by the search algorithm. Dearden and Boutilier (1997) describe a form of abstraction for MDPs that can create admissible heuristics of varying degrees of accuracy.

An ϵ-admissible version of AO* has been described that increases the speed of AO* in exchange for a bounded decrease in solution quality (Chakrabarti et al. 1988). An analogous ϵ-admissible version of LAO* may find an ϵ-optimal solution by evaluating a fraction of the states that LAO* would have to evaluate to find an optimal solution.

For some problems it may be possible to store all nodes visited by the best solution graph in memory, but impossible to store the entire explicit graph in memory. For such problems, it may be useful to create a memory-bounded version of LAO* modeled after memory-bounded versions of AO* (Chakrabarti et al. 1989).

Related Work

LAO* closely resembles some recently developed algorithms for solving stochastic planning problems formalized as MDPs.

Barto, Bradtke, and Singh (1995) describe an algorithm called real-time dynamic programming (RTDP) that generalizes Korf's learning real-time heuristic search algorithm (LRTA*) to MDPs (Korf 1990). They show that under certain conditions, RTDP converges (asymptotically) to an optimal solution without evaluating the entire state space. This parallels the principal result of this paper and LAO* and RTDP solve the same class of problems. The difference is that RTDP relies on trial-based exploration – a concept adopted from reinforcement learning – to explore the state space and determine the order in which to update state costs. By contrast, LAO* finds a solution by systematically expanding a search graph in the manner of heuristic search algorithms such as A* and AO*.

Dean et al. (1995) describe a related algorithm that performs policy iteration on a subset of the states of an MDP, using various methods to identify the most relevant states and gradually increasing the subset until eventual convergence (or until the algorithm is stopped). The subset of states is called an *envelope* and a policy defined on this subset of states is called a *partial policy*. Adding states to an envelope is very similar to expanding a partial solution in a search graph and the idea of using a heuristic to evaluate the fringe states of an envelope has also been explored (Tash and Russell 1994; Dearden and Boutilier 1997). However this algorithm is presented as a modification of policy iteration (and value iteration), rather than a generalization of heuristic search. In particular, the assumption is explicitly made that convergence to an optimal policy requires evaluating the entire state space.

Both of these algorithms are motivated by the problem of search (or planning) in real-time and both allow it to be interleaved with execution; the time constraint on search is often the time before the next action needs to be executed. Both Dean et al. (1995) and Tash and Russell (1994) describe decision-theoretic approaches to optimizing the value of search in the interval between actions. These algorithms can be viewed as real-time counterparts of LAO*. In fact, the relationship between LAO*, the envelope approach to policy and value iteration, and RTDP mirrors (closely, if not exactly) the relationship between A*, RTA*, and LRTA* (Korf 1990). Thus LAO* fills a gap in the taxonomy of search algorithms.

RTDP and the related envelope approach to policy and value iteration represent a solution as a mapping from states to actions, albeit an incomplete mapping called a partial policy; this reflects their derivation from dynamic programming. LAO* represents a solution as a cyclic graph (or equivalently, a finite-state controller), a representation that generalizes the graphical representations of a solution used by search algorithms like A* (a simple path) and AO* (an acyclic graph); this reflects its derivation from heuristic search. The advantage of representing a solution in the form of a graph is that it exhibits reachability among states explicitly and makes analysis of reachability easier.

Conclusion

We have presented a simple generalization of AO*, called LAO*, that can find solutions with loops. It can be used to solve state-space search problems that are formalized as cyclic AND/OR graphs, a class of problems that includes MDPs as an important case. Like other heuristic search algorithms, LAO* can find an optimal solution for a given start state without evaluating the entire state space.

LAO* has been implemented and tested on several small MDPs. Future work will study the factors that affect its efficiency by testing it on various large MDPs. The principal contribution of this paper is conceptual. It provides a foundation for recent work on how to solve MDPs more efficiently by focusing computation on a subset of states reachable from a start state. Our derivation of LAO* from AO* clarifies the relationship of this work to heuristic search. It also suggests that a rich body of results about heuristic search may be generalized in an interesting way for use in solving MDPs more efficiently.

Acknowledgments.

Support for this work was provided in part by the National Science Foundation under grants IRI-9624992, IRI-9634938 and INT-9612092.

References

Bagchi, A. and Mahanti, A. 1983. Admissible Heuristic Search in AND/OR Graphs. *Theoretical Computer Science* 24:207–219.

Barto, A.G.; Bradtke, S.J.; and Singh, S.P. 1995. Learn to Act using Real-Time Dynamic Programming. *Artificial Intelligence* 72:81–138.

Bertsekas, D. 1995. *Dynamic Programming and Optimal Control.* Athena Scientific, Belmont, MA.

Chakrabarti, P.P.; Ghosh, S.; & DeSarkar, S.C. 1988. Admissibility of AO* When Heuristics Overestimate. *Artificial Intelligence* 34:97-113.

Chakrabarti, P.P; Ghosh, S.; Acharya, A.; & DeSarkar, S.C. 1989. Heuristic Search in Restricted Memory. *Artificial Intelligence* 47:197-221.

Dean, T.; Kaelbling, L.P.; Kirman, J.; and Nicholson, A. 1995. Planning Under Time Constraints in Stochastic Domains. *Artificial Intelligence* 76:35–74.

Dearden, R. and Boutilier, C. 1997. Abstraction and Approximate Decision-Theoretic Planning. *Artificial Intelligence* 89:219–283.

Dechter, R. and Pearl, J. 1985. Generalized Best-First Search Strategies and the Optimality of A*. *Journal of the ACM* 32:505–536.

Korf, R. 1990. Real-Time Heuristic Search. *Artificial Intelligence* 42:189–211.

Martelli, A. and Montanari, U. 1973. Additive AND/OR Graphs. In Proceedings of the Third International Joint Conference on Artificial Intelligence, 1–11. Stanford, CA.

Martelli, A. and Montanari, U. 1978. Optimizing Decision Trees Through Heuristically Guided Search. *Communications of the ACM* 21(12):1025–1039.

Nilsson, N.J. 1980. *Principles of Artificial Intelligence.* Palo Alto, CA: Tioga Publishing Company.

Pattipati, K.R. and Alexandridis, M.G. 1990. Application of Heuristic Search and Information Theory to Sequential Fault Diagnosis. *IEEE Transactions on Systems, Man, and Cybernetics* 20(4):872–887.

Tash, J. and Russell, S. 1994. Control Strategies for a Stochastic Planner. In Proceedings of the Twelth National Conference on Artificial Intelligence, 1079–1085. Seattle, WA.

Single-Agent Search in the Presence of Deadlocks

Andreas Junghanns, Jonathan Schaeffer

Department of Computing Science
University of Alberta
Edmonton, Alberta
CANADA T6G 2H1
Email: {andreas, jonathan}@cs.ualberta.ca

Abstract

Single-agent search is a powerful tool for solving a variety of applications. Most of the application domains used to explore single-agent search techniques have the property that if you start with a solvable state, at no time in the search can you reach a state that is unsolvable. In this paper we address the implications that arise when state transitions can lead to unsolvable (deadlock) states. Deadlock states are partially responsible for the failure of our attempts to solve positions in the game of Sokoban. In this paper, we introduce *pattern search*, a real-time learning algorithm that identifies the minimal conditions (pattern) necessary for a deadlock, and applies that knowledge to eliminate provably irrelevant parts of the search tree. Identification of deadlock patterns is equivalent to correcting the heuristic lower bound of a position to infinity. Generalizing pattern searches to find arbitrary lower bound increases yields a powerful new search enhancement. In the game of Sokoban, pattern searches result in a 15-fold reduction of the cost of each additional IDA* iteration.

Keywords: single agent search, heuristic search, Sokoban, deadlocks, IDA*

Introduction

Single-agent search (A*) has been extensively studied in the literature. There are a plethora of enhancements to the basic algorithm that allows one to tailor the algorithms to the problem domains to maximize program performance. The result is an impressive reduction in the search effort required to solve challenging applications (see (Korf 1997) for a recent example). However, the applications used to illustrate the advances in single-agent search efficiency are "easy" in the sense that they have some (or all) of the following properties:
1) effective, inexpensive lower-bound estimators,
2) small branching factor in the search tree, and
3) moderate solution lengths.

The sliding-tile puzzles are the best known examples of these problems. Problem domains such as these also have the important property that given a solvable starting state, every move preserves the solvability, but not necessarily the optimality of the solution.

Sokoban is a popular one-player game. The rules of the game are quite simple. Littered throughout the playing area, consisting of rooms and passageways, are *stones* (shown as circular discs) and *goals* (shaded squares). There is a *man* whose job it is to move each stone to a goal square. The man can only push one stone at a time and must push from behind the stone. A square can only be occupied by one of a wall, stone or man at any time (Junghanns & Schaeffer 1998).

Since you cannot pull a stone, a single move can transform the problem from being solvable to being unsolvable. Many of these so-called deadlock states are trivial to identify and avoid in the search. However some require extensive analysis to prove their existence; the search trees may be so large that they are essentially unsolvable by traditional search methods.

Sokoban is a difficult domain for many reasons:
1) it has a complex lower-bound estimator ($O(n^3)$, given n goals (Kuhn 1955)),
2) the branching factor is large and variable (potentially over 100),
3) the solution may be very long (some problems require over 500 moves to solve optimally), and
4) some reachable states are unsolvable (deadlock).

For sliding-tile puzzles, there are algorithms for generating a non-optimal solution. In Sokoban, because of the presence of deadlock, often it is very difficult to find *any* solution.

Our previous attempts to solve Sokoban problems using standard single-agent search techniques are reported in (Junghanns & Schaeffer 1998). There, using our program *Rolling Stone*, we compare the different techniques and their usefulness with respect to the search efficiency when solving Sokoban problems. Even though each of the five standard single-agent search enhancements we investigated resulted in significant improvements (often several orders of magnitude in search-tree size reduction), at the time we were able to only solve 20 problems of a 90-problem test suite (http://xsokoban.lcs.mit.edu/xsokoban.html).

Copyright 1998, American Association for Artificial Intelligence (www.aaai.org). All rights reserved.

We concluded that the standard techniques are insufficient to make further progress in the domain of Sokoban. Additional search enhancements are needed to enable us to solve significantly more of the problems from the test set. Since large portions of the search are wasted searching problem configurations with deadlocks present, we speculated that the detection of these deadlocks could lead to significant efficiency gains. The techniques suggested in this paper are a direct result of those observations.

In this paper, we introduce a new search enhancement that dynamically finds deadlocks and improved lower bounds. *Pattern search* is a real-time learning algorithm that identifies the minimal conditions necessary for a deadlock, and applies that knowledge to eliminate provably irrelevant parts of the search tree. By devoting a portion of the search effort to learning properties about the search space, the program trades off search-tree size versus acquired knowledge. In the game of Sokoban, the additional knowledge gained by the pattern searches improves the program's search efficiency. The average growth rate of the tree is a factor of 15 times smaller per IDA* (Korf 1985) iteration. This results in 29 solved Sokoban problems, and significant progress towards solving many more.

Pattern Searches

In general, establishing the presence of deadlock can be quite involved. The deadlock may require as few as one and as many as all the stones on the board. Proving that a pattern of stones creates a deadlock will require a search to verify that no possible solution path exists. Ideally, having discovered a deadlock pattern, any state containing that pattern will now be assigned the correct lower bound of infinity.

This section describes our *pattern searches*. We describe how we prove the presence of deadlock by identifying that the properties needed to prevent deadlock are not present. A pattern search results in a minimal pattern which is saved and used throughout the search. In effect, the program learns the deadlock patterns and eliminates any search path leading to a position containing a deadlock pattern.

A deadlock implies a lower bound of infinity. While trying to prove/disprove a deadlock, we may be able to show that our lower bound is too low. Even if a deadlock is not present, we may uncover a pattern that allows the search to improve its admissible lower bound.

Basic Idea

By definition, a deadlock is a configuration of stones such that not all of the stones can reach a goal. If we make a move A-B, we might introduce a deadlock. If this deadlock was not present before the move, then the moved stone, now on square B, must be part of that pattern. This is the initial stone used for the pattern search. The pattern search will perform small searches with a subset of stones on the board to determine if a deadlock was introduced.

```
PatternSearch( From, To ) {
  clear TestMaze;
  set StonePath = {To};
  for( i=1; i <= MAX_PATTERN_SIZE
       AND NOT EffortLimit(); i++ ) {
    if( stone s on a square in StonePath )
      add closest s to TestMaze
    else if( stone s on a square in ManPath )
      add closest s to TestMaze
    else break;
    solution = PIDA*( TestMaze, SolLength,
        ManPath, StonePath );
    /* Test for a deadlock */
    if( solution == NO AND NOT EffortLimit() ) {
      GeneralizeAndAddPattern( TestMaze, infty );
      break;
    }
    /* Test for a lower bound increase */
    if( solution == YES ) {
      lb = LowerBound( TestMaze );
      if( SolLength > lb )
        GeneralizeAndAddPattern( TestMaze,
            SolLength - lb );
    }
  }
}
```

Figure 1: Pseudo Code for Pattern Searches

In the following, we will refer to two different mazes: the *original maze*, which is the maze with all the stones at the position after the move, and the *test maze* which will be used for the pattern searches.

A pattern search iterates on the number of stones in the test maze. We start by putting only the stone that was moved to B in the test maze. PIDA* (see below) is called to solve this test maze. It either returns in failure (no solution, hence deadlock), or it finds a solution. In the latter case, we are interested in the set of squares that are used by the stones and the man to effect the solution: the squares occupied by the stones(s) on their path to the goal(s) (StonePath), and the squares touched by the man while pushing the stone(s) to a goal(s) (ManPath). In effect, these sets of squares are preconditions for the solution to work.

The ManPath and StonePath are used to determine which stone from the original maze to include next in the test maze. A stone in the original maze on a square that is on one of the squares in ManPath or StonePath conflicts with the solution. The stone in StonePath closest to square B (the square the stone was moved to in the original maze) is included next. If such a stone does not exist, the stone on ManPath closest[1] to square A is used. If none of those exists, the pattern search returns without finding a deadlock.

After including the next stone, PIDA* is called again,

---

[1] *Closest* is always with respect to the distance of either the stone or the man to the conflicting stone. These distance measures are possibly different due to the more restricted movement of the stones.

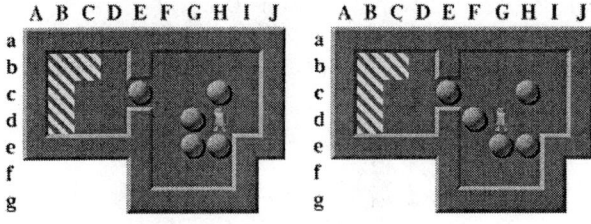

Figure 2: Deadlock example

returning with a solution determination and the two conflict sets. If deadlock has not been found, then the conflict sets are used to add another stone to the test maze. If any of the returning searches indicates a longer solution length than the lower bound estimate of the position, the current pattern is stored with a corresponding lower-bound increase. Figure 1 shows the pseudo code.

The notion of bit (stone) patterns is similar to the Method of Analogies (Adelson-Velskiy, Arlazarov, & Donskoy 1975). Pattern searches are a conflict-driven top-down proof of correctness, while the Method of Analogies is a bottom-up heuristic approximation.

Example

Figure 2 shows a simple position, before and after the move *Gd-Fd*. The question is whether this move introduces a deadlock. Figure 3 shows how the test maze is built. Since the last move ended up on square *Fd*, the test maze is initialized with this single stone (Figure 3a). A PIDA* search reveals a 5-move solution (*Fd-Fc-Ec-Dc-Cc-Bc*), and sets ManPath to the squares needed by the man (*Gd-Ge-Fe-Fd-Gd-Gc-Fc-Ec-Dc-Cc*), and StonePath to the squares used by the stone (*Fd-Fc-Ec-Dc-Cc-Bc*). Since there is a solution, we continue the pattern search.

The original maze has a stone on one of the squares that the stone moved over (square *Ec*) which now gets included in the test maze (Figure 3b). PIDA* will solve the test maze with the two stones and again find a solution. The ManPath is (*Gd-Gc-Fc-Ec-Dc-Dd-Cd-Cc-Dc-Ec-Fc-Gc-Gd-Ge-Fe-Fd-Gd-Gc-Fc-Ec-Dc-Cc*) and the StonePath is (*Ec-Dc-Cc-Cb Fd-Fc-Ec-Dc-Cc-Bc*). This time there are no stones in conflict with StonePath. However, there is a conflict with the ManPath, square *Ge*. This stone is added to the test maze (Figure 3c) and another search is commenced. A solution will be found, requiring a fourth stone to be added (Figure 3d).

The fourth call to PIDA* will return no solution and announce a deadlock with this pattern of four stones. Identifying the critical stones to examine has been driven by whether they conflict with a potential solution. The irrelevant parts of the maze (such as the stone on *Hc*) are ignored.

Generalizing the Patterns

The fewer stones in a deadlock pattern, the more likely it will match an arbitrary position and be used to eliminate futile branches of the search. A *minimal deadlock pattern* is a deadlock pattern from which no stone can be removed without making the remaining pattern solvable. The attentive reader will have noticed that only three stones are needed to guarantee deadlock in Figure 3; the stone on *Ec* is unnecessary. Before saving the deadlock pattern, our program will attempt to minimize the number of stones in it.

The deadlock set minimization routine takes an N-stone pattern and considers each of the possible N-1-stone sub-patterns. Each of the N-1-stone sub-patterns is searched to verify whether removing that stone preserves the deadlock. If the deadlock still exists, then the removed stone was not part of the minimal deadlock set and is removed from the deadlock pattern.

Customizing IDA* for Pattern Searches

If the pattern searches used the same IDA* procedure and lower bound estimator as in *Rolling Stone*, the search would be prohibitively large and slow. Instead, we use a special version of IDA* (PIDA*) that is customized for pattern searches, allowing for additional optimizations that dramatically improve the search efficiency. By relaxing the rules of Sokoban and introducing new goal criteria, the resulting search will be more efficient and will still return an admissible lower bound on the solution.

One optimization is to remove stones from the test maze once they reach a goal square or a man-reachable square. This comes from the observation that most deadlocks result in a number of stones getting *crowded* together. Hence, if a stone "breaks free", we assume we no longer need to consider it in that search sub-tree. Another optimization is to relax what we consider a goal state. Now, goal states are also positions where the man can reach all squares and at least one conflict with the current StonePath was found already.

These shortcuts simplify the search leading to large savings in the cost of a pattern search (from thousands of nodes to an average of 50). However, this comes at the cost of possibly missing a deadlock. In practice, the reduced search effort more than compensates for the few missed opportunities.

Since stones get removed from the board when they reach a goal square, the best lower bound heuristic is not appropriate (see (Junghanns & Schaeffer 1998)). A cheaper heuristic can be used: the sum of the shortest distances of each stone to its closest goal. When a stone moves, this lower bound is easily updated. This results in large savings in the cost per node compared to the original $O(n^3)$ lower bound. Since the number of stones is small in a pattern search, most search-related routines are fast, because their cost depends on the number of stones in the maze.

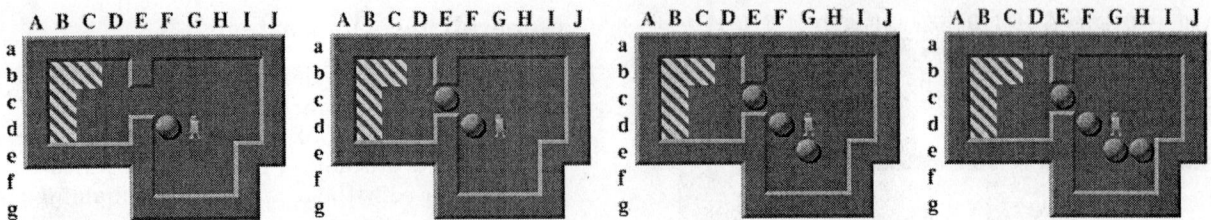

Figure 3: Sequence of test mazes as passed to PIDA* (a, b, c and d)

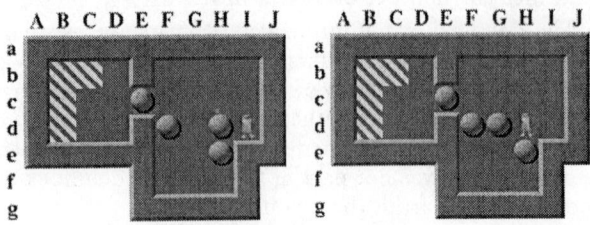

Figure 4: Penalty Example

Tradeoffs

Pattern searches can be costly. There are three main factors involved in their cost: the frequency of the pattern searches, a bound on the size of a pattern search, and a bound on the deadlock pattern size.

Frequency of Pattern Searches: We cannot afford to do a pattern search at every node in the IDA* search. We use some simple heuristics for deciding when to invest in a deadlock search.

The pattern search is always done for a node for which a deadlock search has not been previously done before (as retrieved from the transposition table) and the amount of effort spent below that node on a previous iteration exceeds a threshold. For our experiments, we use a threshold of 50 nodes, a number that reflects the size of a typical pattern search. Furthermore, if a stone is pushed onto an articulation point of the underlying graph structure of the maze, if the stone blocks an area for the man that was previously accessible, or if the stone pushed has no more legal moves, the pattern search is executed. These heuristics ensure the execution of pattern searches where the possibility of erroneous lower bounds is high.

Size of the Pattern Search: Pattern searches are restricted to a maximum effort of 1000 nodes. If the threshold is reached, the search is aborted.

Pattern Size: Deadlock patterns are restricted to 8 stones. This is an artificial limitation, but we have not fully explored the tradeoffs of finding larger deadlock patterns, versus the effort required to find them.

Generalizing Pattern Searches

The presence of a deadlock pattern in a position means the lower bound increases to infinity. Can we find patterns that allow us to increase the lower bound by an arbitrary amount, not just infinity?

Assume there are three stones in the test maze and PIDA* starts its first iteration but fails to find a solution. Hence PIDA* proved that this pattern cannot be solved with the number of moves that the heuristic lower bound indicated. In other words, the lower bound is wrong.

Some of the shortcuts used in the pattern searches are not appropriate when searching for a lower bound increase. Thus a second search routine is used to look for patterns that allow for arbitrary lower bound increases. If the first pattern search fails (looking for a deadlock), the second pattern search is executed, possibly finding a pattern that allows us to improve the lower bound.

In Figure 4, after the move *Hd-Gd* a pattern search looking for a deadlock will fail. A pattern search looking to improve the lower bound will uncover that the solution requires the non-optimal moves *Fd-Fe* and *Gd-Hd*, proving that the lower bound is off by four moves.

Storage and Retrieval of Patterns

To incorporate the deadlock and penalty patterns into the search, we need to save the patterns found and use them to match positions in the search. The pattern matching is complicated by the fact that you need to match not only the stones, but also the man position. With each pattern of stones the squares are stored which the man in the test maze cannot reach. To increase the usefulness of the information found by the pattern searches, we use the *multi-insert* technique. Instead of the root node only, the top two ply of the pattern search nodes are stored.

To match a pattern, the test maze must have the stones in the same places as the pattern and the man must not be able to reach any of the non-reachable squares stored together with the pattern. Since several patterns might match, stones that were used to match a pattern are not used when looking for a second pattern to match, to avoid double penalization. To maximize the penalties, the pattern matching starts with the highest penalty patterns.

This is similar to Ginsberg's Partition Search idea (Ginsberg 1996) where the entries of a hash table were generalized to hold information about sets of problem states. In *Rolling Stone* a pattern is the information about the lower-bound increase of the set of problem states in which this pattern is present.

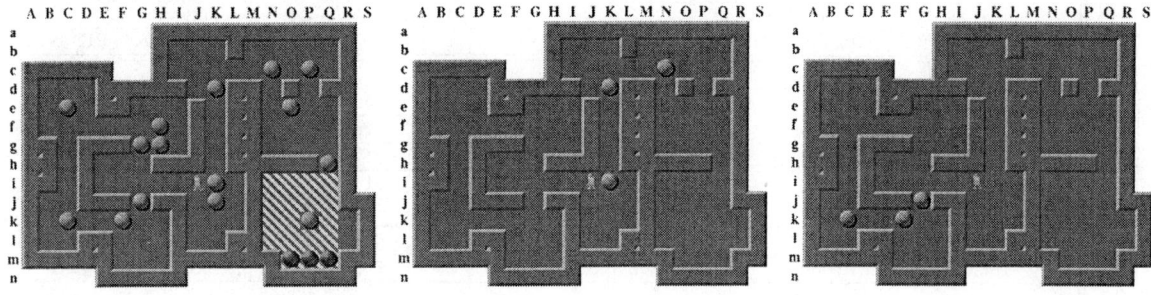

Figure 5: Maze #30 receives a penalty of 38 (24+14) after 2 patterns were matched

Experimental Results

Figure 5 shows maze #30 with a stone configuration that arises during the search. Two penalty patterns were successfully matched, resulting in an increase of 38 (14+28) to the lower bound.

Given 20 million nodes of search effort, our program can currently solve 29 problems of the 90 problem test suite. Without the pattern searches, only 22 problems can be solved[2]. Table 1 shows the results of searching these problems. Each column is labeled according to which of the three features is enabled: penalty searches (pen), deadlock searches (dl) and multi-insert (mi), where + and - mean enabled and disabled, respectively. Two node numbers are given: the IDA* nodes and the IDA* + PIDA* nodes.

Except for the small searches, the cost of performing the additional PIDA* searches is offset by the reduction in the IDA* search nodes. Problem 53 is an example. Previously, with 20,000,000 nodes of search, we were unable to solve this problem. Now the search is accomplished with only 177 IDA* nodes and a total of 1,229 nodes. Clearly, the pattern searches dominate the search cost, but the knowledge uncovered allows us to solve the problem where we failed previously.

Analysis of the data shows that the average growth rate of the search tree from iteration to iteration in an IDA* search decreased from 84,669 to 5,559 due to the pattern searches. Although this represents a significant reduction in search effort (a factor of 15 per iteration), it demonstrates how resistant the problem is to search. Decreasing the growth rate of the search tree size generally increases the number of iterations that the main IDA* search can perform in the same time. For example, on 13 of the remaining 61 problems 3 or more additional IDA* iterations were accomplished (the maximum was 9 extra iterations). Since the average increase of the tree size to the next iteration is 5,559, even 3 iterations are significant improvements.

Pattern searches are a gamble: you invest search effort (PIDA* nodes) expecting to find useful knowledge. A failed pattern search costs roughly 50 nodes. A successful pattern search typically costs over 1,000 nodes, because of the additional difficulty of the search and the cost of minimizing the pattern. Only 12% of the pattern searches are successful at discovering something useful. Although this sounds low, the results show the value of the discovered knowledge. Problem #21 is one example of where the gamble does not pay off. Even though the tree size (IDA*) is reduced to about 33%, including the PIDA* nodes quadruples the total number of nodes searched.

The results reported here are not the best numbers that can be achieved. There are numerous parameters in the search, each of which can be tuned for maximal performance. In Table 1, the PIDA* nodes dominate the cost of the search for some problems. Some additional heuristics for deciding when to do pattern searches can result in further improvements in the search efficiency.

Furthermore, examination of the results shows that lower-bound increases are more beneficial then the deadlock patterns. More is to be gained by improving the lower bound than by identifying deadlock states.

Conclusions and Future Work

Sokoban is a challenging puzzle – for both man and machine. The traditional enhanced single-agent search algorithms are inadequate to solve the entire 90-problem test suite, even with their dramatic impact on the search tree size.

The property of deadlocks in a search space adds considerable complexity to the search. The previously introduced deadlock tables (Junghanns & Schaeffer 1998) are beneficial for local deadlock detection, but inadequate to handle non-trivial situations. Pattern searches can detect global deadlock scenarios and are able to improve the lower bound considerably, resulting in a substantial improvement in search efficiency.

Further work is needed to identify when deadlocks are likely to occur and either avoid them or invest the resources to verify their existence. Detecting deadlocks is critical to any real-time application.

The pattern searches were based on demonstrating whether there existed a scenario by which all the stones in a position subset could reach their goals, and in how

---

[2] We previously reported 20 problems solved. Increasing the utility of the goal macros allowed the standard version to solve two more problems.

#	-dl -pen -mi	+dl -pen -mi		+dl +pen -mi		+dl +pen +mi	
	IDA*	IDA*	IDA*+PIDA*	IDA*	IDA*+PIDA*	IDA*	IDA*+PIDA*
1	53	53	125	50	410	50	412
2	224	210	1,137	149	3,090	149	3,329
3	393	188	3,734	97	7,231	97	11,753
4	394	310	3,488	187	1,878	187	1,879
5	1,768,356	16,071	110,709	2,813	61,608	2,664	66,658
6	207	168	427	139	2,234	139	3,008
7	30,118	20,833	138,685	2,818	61,879	2,743	61,017
9	198,667	121,868	207,833	7,619	162,999	8,647	160,833
17	10,108	1,676	9,512	1,103	23,771	821	22,588
21	374,843	330,273	2,112,792	145,939	1,668,636	109,913	1,231,217
38	312,017	104,255	128,451	75,244	117,770	75,244	118,835
43	> 20,000,000	> 13,431,042	> 20,000,000	13,834	2,223,154	10,661	2,337,712
51	50,675	97,299	99,754	133	2,564	133	6,042
53	> 20,000,000	177	368	177	1,184	177	1,229
55	> 20,000,000	> 13,198,858	> 20,000,000	4,527,930	12,482,548	4,462,920	12,301,510
57	3,078,112	215,541	521,533	176,413	780,398	79,792	608,261
62	127,434	821,533	872,317	2,036	21,395	440	18,711
63	3,137,313	415,401	2,293,790	25,200	1,086,424	18,024	742,490
65	1,333	1,333	2,272	980	3,848	1,355	4,242
68	> 20,000,000	> 19,519,926	> 20,000,000	203,966	8,214,930	145,528	6,260,529
70	> 20,000,000	> 9,189,442	> 20,000,000	> 619,739	> 20,000,000	185,820	3,639,142
72	> 20,000,000	> 13,142,686	> 20,000,000	49,279	145,276	1,701	49,962
73	> 20,000,000	> 19,011,026	> 20,000,000	29,586	45,309	29,586	45,318
78	75	75	267	75	882	75	882
79	4,474	3,799	5,504	1,970	13,163	1,957	10,555
80	2,430	109	2,981	98	9,555	98	10,534
81	305,185	16,655	50,344	1,991	28,502	1,908	21,333
82	162,517	151,720	717,656	230	32,395	471	49,323
83	1,198	90	2,883	90	7,204	90	7,271
∑	>149,566,126	> 89,812,617	>127,286,562	> 5,889,885	> 47,210,237	5,141,390	27,796,575

Table 1: Experimental Data

many moves. There are other proof conditions that can be tried. One promising avenue for proving that deadlock is not being introduced is the reversible move. For example, assume that in position P move A-B is made. It may be easy to verify that there is a sequence of moves that effectively unmakes the move A-B (possibly as simple as B-A) resulting in all the stones and the man being back as they were in position P. If this can be shown, then this is a proof that deadlock was not introduced by A-B. This property can be verified with a search where the goal conditions are changed.

Although pattern searches can be enhanced to make them more efficient, it appears they are inadequate to successfully solve all 90 Sokoban test positions. This is the subject of ongoing research.

Acknowledgements

The authors would like to thank the German Academic Exchange Service, the Killam Foundation and the Natural Sciences and Engineering Research Council of Canada for their support. This paper benefited from interactions with Yngvi Bjornsson, Russ Greiner, Peter van Beek and from the referees' comments.

References

Adelson-Velskiy, G.; Arlazarov, V.; and Donskoy, M. 1975. Some methods of controlling the tree search in chess programs. *Artificial Intelligence* 6(4):361–371.

Ginsberg, M. 1996. Partition search. In *AAAI-96*, 228–233.

Junghanns, A., and Schaeffer, J. 1998. Sokoban: Evaluating standard single-agent search techniques in the presence of deadlock. In *Proceedings AI-98*. To appear in Springer-Verlag's *Lecture Notes in Computer Science* series.

Korf, R. 1985. Depth-first iterative-deepening: An optimal admissible tree search. *Artificial Intelligence* 27(1):97–109.

Korf, R. 1997. Finding optimal solutions to Rubik's Cube using pattern databases. In *AAAI-97*, 700–705.

Kuhn, H. 1955. The Hungarian method for the assignment problem. *Naval Res. Logist. Quart.* 83–98.

Complete Anytime Beam Search

Weixiong Zhang
Information Sciences Institute and Computer Science Department
University of Southern California
4676 Admiralty Way, Marina del Rey, CA 90292
Email: zhang@isi.edu

ABSTRACT

Beam search executes a state-space search, but may abandon nonpromising search avenues in order to reduce complexity. Although it has existed for more than two decades and has been applied to many real-world problems, beam search still suffers from the drawback of possible termination with no solution or a solution of unsatisfactory quality. In this paper, we first propose a domain-independent heuristic for node pruning, and a method to reduce the possibility that beam search will fail. We then develop a complete beam search algorithm. The new algorithm can not only find an optimal solution, but can also reach better solutions sooner than its underlying search method. We apply complete beam search to the maximum boolean satisfiability and the symmetric and asymmetric Traveling Salesman Problems. Our experimental results show that the domain-independent pruning heuristic is effective and the new algorithm significantly improves the performance of its underlying search algorithm.

1 Introduction

Beam search [2] executes a state-space search algorithm [16], but may use heuristic rules to discard nonpromising search alternatives that appear to lead to a solution of unsatisfactory quality. Heuristic pruning keeps the size of the *beam*, the remaining search alternatives, as small as possible, in order to possibly find a solution quickly. The idea of beam search is simple, and has been successfully applied to many different problems, such as learning [4], jobshop scheduling [5], speech recognition [12], planning [14], and vision [19].

Despite the fact that beam search has existed for more than two decades and has been applied to many real-

Copyright ©1998, American Association for Artificial Intelligence (www.aaai.org). All rights reserved.

world applications, it has not been carefully studied. Beam search is a heuristic technique used to reduce search complexity. It has, however, a serious drawback of possible termination with no solution or a solution of unsatisfactory quality. In other words, beam search is an *incomplete algorithm* that is not guaranteed to find a solution even if one exists. The pruning power and possibility of finding a solution depend on the accuracy of the pruning rules used. Effective heuristic rules are generally problem dependent, and their effectiveness comes from deep understanding of the problem domains. In practice, it is difficult to find effective heuristic rules that can strike the right balance of finding a desired goal and using the minimal amount of computation.

In this paper, we first propose a domain-independent heuristic pruning rule that uses only heuristic node evaluations (Section 3), and a method to increase the possibility that beam search finds a solution (Section 4). We then develop a complete anytime beam search algorithm that is able to continuously find better solutions and eventually reach an optimal solution (Section 5). We apply complete anytime beam search to the maximum boolean satisfiability and the symmetric and asymmetric Traveling Salesman Problems, and investigate the anytime feature of the new algorithm on these real problems (Section 6). We discuss related work in Section 7, and finally conclude in Section 8.

2 Beam Search

Beam search runs a state-space search method, such as best-first search (BFS) or depth-first search (DFS). What sets beam search apart from its underlying search is the use of heuristic rules to prune search alternatives before exploring them. Note that these heuristic pruning rules are different from the pruning rule based on monotonic node costs and an upper bound α on the cost of an optimal goal. To make the paper self contained, we list beam search in Table 1, where R represents the set of heuristic pruning rules, and $c(n)$ is the cost of n.

Beam search can use any strategy, such as best first or depth first, to select a node at line 3 of Table 1. The

Table 1: Beam search.

```
BeamSearch(problem, R, α)
 1.  open ← {problem};
 2.  WHILE (open ≠ ∅)
 3.    n ← a node in open;
 4.    If (n is a desired goal) exit;
 5.    If (n is a goal & c(n) < α) α ← c(n);
 6.    Remove n from open;
 7.    Generate all children of n;
 8.    Discard a child n' if c(n') ≥ α;
 9.    Discard n' if pruned by a rule in R;
10.    Insert remaining children into open.
```

Table 2: Complete beam search algorithm.

```
CompleteBeamSearch(problem, R, α)
  DO
    Call BeamSearch(problem, R, α);
    Weaken heuristic pruning rules in R;
  WHILE (no desired goal found & a rule ∈ R
         applied in the last iteration)
```

only difference between beam search and its underlying search method is line 9 of Table 1, where heuristic pruning rules are used to prune nodes. The algorithm terminates in two cases. It may stop when a required goal node is reached at line 4. It may also terminate when no node is left for further exploration, which is a failure if a goal exists. This failure makes beam search *incomplete*, an unfavorable feature for practical use.

3 Domain-Independent Pruning Rule

Whether or not beam search can find a solution depends on the heuristic pruning rules it uses. Accurate heuristic rules can provide strong pruning power by eliminating the nodes that do not need to be explored. On the other hand, effective heuristic pruning rules are generally domain dependent and require a deep understanding of problem domains.

In this research, we are interested in domain-independent heuristic pruning rules. We propose one such pruning rule in this section. It uses information of static heuristic evaluations of the nodes in a state space. Without loss of generality, we assume that heuristic node evaluation function is monotonically nondecreasing with node depth.

Consider a node n and its child node n' in a state space. Let $c(n)$ be the static heuristic evaluation or static node cost of n. If $c(n')$ exceeds $c(n)$ by δ, i.e., $c(n') > c(n) + \delta$, then n' is discarded, where δ is a predefined, positive parameter. Thus, a smaller δ represents a stronger pruning rule. This heuristic pruning rule was derived from the intuition that if a child node has a significantly large cost increase from its parent, it is more likely that the child may lead to a goal node with a large cost. The effectiveness of this rule will be examined in Section 6.

4 Reducing Failure Rate

The use of heuristic pruning rules in beam search is a two-edged sword. On one side, it reduces the amount of search, solving some problems in reasonable time. On the other side, however, it runs the risk of missing a solution completely, making it incomplete and inapplicable to some applications. When beam search fails to find a solution, its heuristic pruning rules abandon too many search alternatives. The pruned nodes are deadend nodes, which do not have children, as far as beam search is concerned.

The idea of increasing the possibility of reaching a goal node is to reduce the possibility of creating deadends. When a node has children, the pruning may be too strong if all its child nodes are discarded. Instead of abandoning all children based on the pruning rules, keeping at least one child will prevent treating the current node as a deadend. We call this a modification rule, a meta rule that governs how the pruning rules should be used. To find a high-quality goal node, the modification rule chooses to explore the child node that has the minimum cost among all the children.

5 Complete Anytime Beam Search

We have developed a *complete beam search algorithm* (CBS) using a technique called *iterative weakening* [18]. The algorithm is simple and straightforward. It iteratively runs a series of beam searches using weaker heuristic pruning rules in subsequent iterations.

5.1 The algorithm

Specifically, the algorithms runs as follows. It first runs the original beam search. If a desired solution is found, the algorithm terminates. Otherwise, the heuristic pruning rules are weakened, and the algorithm runs another iteration of beam search. This iterative process continues until a required solution has been found, or no heuristic pruning rule was applied in the last iteration. The latter case means that either no required solution exists, or the solution found so far is optimal, because the last iteration runs the underlying BFS or DFS (which is guaranteed to find an optimal solution). This case also means that this algorithm is complete. Table 2 lists the complete beam search algorithm.

When domain-specific pruning rules are used, we can reduce the number of pruning criteria or remove individual components in pruning rules to reduce their pruning power. For the domain-independent pruning rule suggested in Section 3, we can increase the parameter δ to make the rule weak. Recall that a child node n' will be pruned if its cost $c(n')$ is greater than the cost of its parent $c(n)$ by δ. By increasing δ, we reduce the possibility of pruning the child node.

5.2 Anytime feature

Anytime algorithms [3] are an important class of algorithms for real-time problem solving. An anytime algorithm first finds a solution quickly, and then successively improves the quality of the best solution found so far, as long as more computation is available. CBS is an anytime algorithm for solving combinatorial optimization problems. The state spaces of combinatorial optimization problems, such as those considered in Section 6, have leaf nodes that are goal states. When solving these problems, CBS can find a solution quickly in an early iteration, and continuously find better solutions in subsequent iterations.

When using best-first search (BFS) as its underlying search method, CBS turns BFS into an anytime search algorithm. Note that BFS does not provide a solution until its termination [16]. By using heuristic pruning rules, an iteration of CBS searches a small portion of the state space that is examined by the full BFS, and may obtain a suboptimal solution quickly. With weaker pruning rules, a larger portion of the state space will be explored in order to find better solutions. By repeatedly using weaker pruning rules, CBS can incrementally find better solutions until it visits an optimal solution.

Now consider depth-first search (DFS). DFS is an anytime algorithm by nature [22], as it systematically explores leaf nodes of a state space. Based on our experiments on random search trees, CBS significantly improves DFS' anytime feature, finding better solutions sooner. The real challenge is whether complete beam search can outperform DFS on real problems. This question will be favorably answered in the next section.

6 Applications

In this section, we apply the complete beam search (CBS) algorithm and the domain-independent heuristic pruning rule of Section 3, plus the modification rule of Section 4, if necessary, to three NP-complete [15] combinatorial optimization problems, the maximal boolean satisfiability and the symmetric and asymmetric Traveling Salesman Problems. The purpose of this experimental study is to examine the anytime feature of CBS and the effectiveness of the domain-independent pruning rule. In our experiments, we use DFS as CBS' underlying search method, and compare CBS' performance profile [23] against that of DFS.

The performance profile of an algorithm characterizes the quality of its output as a function of computation time. Denote $prof(A, t)$ as the performance profile of algorithm A. We define $prof(A, t)$ as

$$prof(A, t) = 1 - error(A, t), \qquad (1)$$

where $error(A, t)$ is the error of solution cost of A at time t relative to the optimal solution cost. During the execution of A, $prof(A, t) \leq 1$; and at the end of its execution, $prof(A, t) = 1$. In our experiments, we compare $prof(CBS, t)$ against $prof(DFS, t)$.

Our domain-independent heuristic pruning rule uses a parameter δ. In order to set the value of δ properly, we need information about how much the cost of a node will increase from that of its parent. It would be ideal if we knew the distribution of cost differences between nodes and their parents for a given application. Such information has to be collected or learned from the problems to be solved. This can be done in two ways. The first is offline sampling. If some sample problems from an application domain are available, we can first solve these problems using BFS or DFS, and use the costs of the nodes encountered during the search as samples to calculate an empirical distribution of node-cost differences. The second method is online sampling, which can be used when sample problems are not provided. Using this sampling method, the first iteration of CBS does not apply heuristic pruning rules until a certain number of nodes have been generated. In our experiments presented in the rest of this section, we use the online sampling method and DFS as CBS' underlying search method. In our implementation, CBS does not use pruning rules until it has reached the first leaf node. All the nodes generated in the process of reaching the first leaf node are used as initial samples for computing an empirical distribution.

Using the empirical distribution of node-cost differences, we can set parameter δ. What value of δ to use in the first iteration and how it is updated from one iteration to the next are critical factors that directly determine CBS' performance. In general, these factors must be dealt with on a case by case basis, depending on the applications. In our experiments on the following three combinatorial problems, the initial δ is set to a value δ_I such that a node-cost difference is less than δ_I with probability p equal to 0.1. The next iteration increases probability p by 0.1, and so forth, until the heuristic pruning rule has not been used in the latest iteration or probability p is greater than 1.

Due to space limitations, in the following discussions we will be brief on our implementations of DFS on the three problems.

6.1 Maximum boolean satisfiability

We are concerned with boolean 3-satisfiability (3-Sat), a special case of the constraint-satisfaction problem (CSP). A 3-Sat involves a set of boolean variables, and

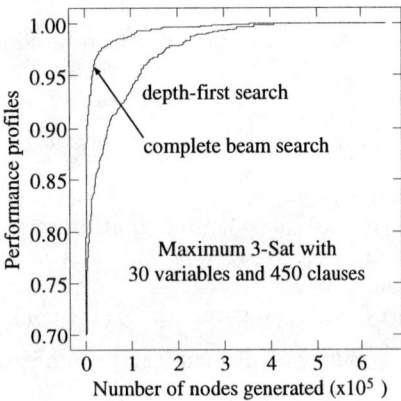

Figure 1: CBS vs. DFS on maximum 3-Satisfiability.

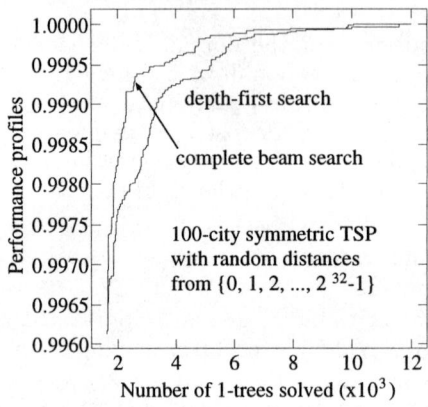

Figure 2: CBS vs. DFS on the symmetric TSP.

a set of disjunctive clauses of 3 literals (variables and their negations) which defines constraints of acceptable combinations of variables. There are many practical CSPs in which no value assignment can be found that does not violate a constraint; see [6] for discussion and references therein. In this case, one option is to find an assignment such that the total number of satisfied constraints is maximized. In our experiment, we consider maximum 3-Sat.

Maximum 3-Sat can be optimally solved by DFS as follows. The root of the search tree is the original problem with no variable specified. One variable is then chosen and set to either true or false, thus decomposing the original problem into two subproblems. Each subproblem is then simplified as follows. If the selected variable is set to true, a clause can be removed if it contains this variable. A clause can also be discarded if it contains the negation of a variable that is set to false. Furthermore, a variable can be deleted from a clause if the negation of the literal is set to true. Since the two values of a variable are mutually exclusive, so are the two subproblems generated. Therefore, the state space of the problem is a binary tree without duplicate nodes. The cost of a node is the total number of clauses violated, which is monotonically nondecreasing with the depth of the node. In our implementation of DFS, we use the *most occurrence heuristic* to choose a variable; in other words, we choose an unspecified variable that occurs most frequently in the set of clauses.

We generated maximum 3-Sat problem instances by randomly selecting three variables and negating them with probability 0.5 for each clause. Duplicate clauses were removed. The problem instances we used have a large ratio of the number of clauses to the number of variables (clause to variable ratio), since random 3-Sat problems with a small clause-to-variable ratio are generally satisfiable [13].

In our experiments, we studied the effects of the modification rule proposed in Section 4, which will explore the best child node if the two children of a node are pruned by the heuristic pruning rule. On random 3-Sat, CBS without the modification rule cannot compete with DFS. This is due to two factors. The first is the small branching factor 2 of the state space, so that deadend nodes can be easily generated if the modification rule is not applied. The second is that the initial value of δ is too small, thus most early iterations of CBS cannot find a solution at all. However, CBS with the modification rule is significantly superior to DFS.

Figure 1 shows the experimental result of CBS using the modification rule on 3-Sat with 30 variables and 450 clauses, averaged over 100 random problem instances. The vertical axis presents the performance profiles of CBS and DFS, and the horizontal axis is the number of nodes generated. The comparison has an almost identical picture when the horizontal axis is plotted in terms of CPU time on a SUN Sparc 2 machine, as the time spent for online sampling is negligible. Figure 1 shows that CBS significantly improves the anytime performance of DFS, finding better solutions sooner.

6.2 The symmetric TSP

Given n cities $\{1, 2, ..., n\}$ and a cost matrix $(c_{i,j})$ that defines a cost between each pair of cities, the *Traveling Salesman Problem* (TSP) is to find a minimum-cost tour that visits each city once and returns to the starting city. When the cost from city i to city j is the same as that from city j to city i, the problem is the *symmetric TSP* (STSP).

In our implementation of DFS, we use the Held-Karp lower bound function [9] to compute node costs. This function iteratively computes a Lagrangian relaxation on the STSP, with each step constructing a 1-tree. A 1-tree is a minimum spanning tree (MST) [15] on $n-1$ cities plus the two shortest edges from the city not in the MST to two cities in the MST. Note that a complete TSP tour is a 1-tree. If no complete TSP tour has been found after a predefined number of steps of Lagrangian relaxation, which is $n/2$ in our experiment, the problem

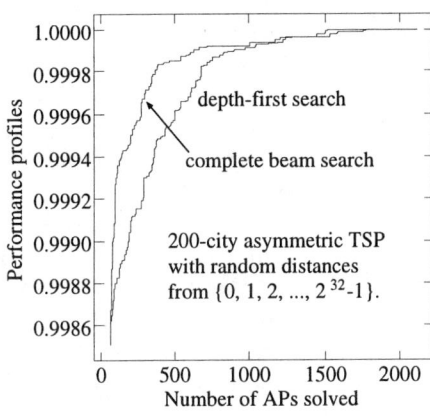

Figure 3: CBS vs. DFS on the asymmetric TSP.

is decomposed into at most three subproblems using the Volgenant and Jonker's branching rule [20]. Under this decomposition rule, the state space of the STSP is a tree without duplicate nodes.

We generated STSP problem instances by uniformly choosing a cost between two cities from $\{0, 1, 2, \cdots, 2^{32} - 1\}$. The experiment results show that CBS without the modification rule of Section 4 is substantially degenerated from DFS, due to the same reasons described in Section 6.1, on maximum 3-sat.

Figure 2 shows the experimental result of CBS with the modification rule on 100-city random STSPs, averaged over 100 problem instances. The vertical axis still presents the performance profiles of CBS and DFS. The horizontal axis is the numbers of 1-trees solved by both algorithms. We do not use the number of tree nodes generated as a time measure, because generating a node requires the solution of one to $n/2$ 1-trees based on Lagrangian relaxation, and the CPU time is proportional to the number of 1-trees solved. Figure 2 shows that CBS improves DFS on random STSPs.

6.3 The asymmetric TSP

When the cost from city i to city j is not necessarily equal to that from city j to city i, the TSP is the *asymmetric TSP* (ATSP). The most efficient approach known for optimally solving the ATSP is subtour elimination, with the solution to the assignment problem (AP) as a lower-bound function [1]. The AP is to assign to each city i another city j, with the cost from i to j as this assignment, such that the total cost of all assignments is minimized. An AP is a relaxation on the ATSP without the requirement of a complete tour. See [1] for the details of this algorithm. In short, the problem space of subtour elimination can be represented by a tree with maximum depth less than n^2. We used this algorithm in our experiments.

It is worth mentioning that the branching factor of an ATSP state space is large, proportional to the number of cities. Therefore, the modification rule of Section 4 does not matter much. In fact, the experimental result of CBS with the modification rule is slightly worse than that without the modification rule.

We used random ATSP in our experiments. The costs among cities were uniformly chosen from $\{0, 1, 2, \cdots, 2^{32} - 1\}$. Figure 2 shows the experimental results of CBS without the modification rule on 200-city random ATSP, averaged over 100 instances. Figure 3 shows that CBS outperforms DFS on random ATSPs.

7 Related Work and Discussions

A restricted version of beam search was defined in [21], which runs breadth-first search, but keeps a fixed number of nodes active on each depth. The definition used in this paper follows that in [2] and is more general. The most closely related work on beam search is the early applications of beam search to various problems which demonstrated its effectiveness [2, 4, 5, 12, 14, 19].

CBS is a combination of beam search heuristics and iterative weakening [18]. Iterative weakening directly follows iterative deepening [11] and iterative broadening [7]. They all repeatedly apply a search process, but with stronger or weaker parameters in different passes. It has been shown that a given set of search policies should be applied in an increasing order of the search complexities that these policies incur [18].

CBS bears a close similarity to iterative broadening. Briefly, iterative broadening first carries out a search with a breadth limit of two, and if it fails, the algorithm repeats the search with breadth limit of three, and so on, until it finds a solution. Early passes of both algorithms comb through the state space for better solutions, and they gradually extend the coverage of their exploration by increasing the search breadth. The difference between these two algorithms is that iterative broadening extends its search breadth in a predetermined fashion, while CBS broadens its search depending on how heuristic pruning rules are weakened. If we treat the way that search breadth is extended in a predefined way as a special heuristic, iterative broadening can then be considered as a special case of CBS.

CBS using the domain-independent pruning rule of Section 3 is symmetric to Epsilon search [17]. In Epsilon search, a node with a cost no greater than its parent's cost plus ϵ is treated as if it has the same cost as its parent, so as to force an early exploration of the node, while in CBS a node with cost greater than its parent's cost plus δ is considered as if it has an infinitely large cost, so as to postpone the exploration of the node.

Anytime algorithms are important tools for problem solving in a real-time setting and with resource constraints [3, 10, 23]. Although it is well known that many search methods, such as depth-first search and local search, can be used as anytime algorithms, little work has been done to improve their anytime performance, except that of [8, 17]. In [8], non-admissible heuristic search runs as an anytime algorithm. CBS is more similar to Epsilon search [17], since both manipulate state space during their searches.

8 Conclusions

In this paper, we made beam search heuristics into a complete search algorithm, called complete beam search (CBS), by using the iterative weakening technique. CBS can not only find an optimal solution, but it also reaches better solutions sooner than its underlying search method. CBS is an anytime algorithm for solving combinatorial optimization problems. We also proposed a domain-independent node pruning heuristic. We applied CBS and the domain-independent heuristic pruning rule to three NP-complete optimization problems, the maximum boolean satisfiability and the symmetric and asymmetric Traveling Salesman Problems. Our experimental results show that the domain-independent pruning rule is effective, and CBS significantly improves the efficiency and anytime performance of its underlying depth-first search.

Acknowledgments

This research was partially funded by NSF Grant IRI-9619554. Thanks to the anonymous reviewers for their insightful comments and for bringing [18] to my attention, and to Sheila Coyazo for proof reading this paper.

References

[1] E. Balas and P. Toth. Branch and bound methods. In E.L. Lawler *et al.*, editor, *The Traveling Salesman Problem*, pages 361–401. John Wiley & Sons, Essex, 1985.

[2] R. Bisiani. Search, beam. In S. C. Shapiro, editor, *Encyclopedia of Artificial Intelligence*, pages 1467–1468. Wiley-Interscience, 2nd edition, 1992.

[3] T. Dean and M. Boddy. An analysis of time-dependent planning. In *Proc. AAAI-88*, pages 49–54, St. Paul, MN, Aug. 1988.

[4] G. Dietterich and R. S. Michalski. Inductive learning of structural descriptions: Evaluation criteria and comparative review of selected methods. *Artificial Intelligence*, 16:257–294, 1981.

[5] M. S. Fox. *Constraint Directed Search: A Case Study of Job-Shop Scheduling*. PhD thesis, Carnegie Mellon University, 1983.

[6] E. C. Freuder and R. J. Wallace. Partial constraint satisfaction. *Artificial Intelligence*, 58:21–70, 1992.

[7] M. L. Ginsberg and W. D. Harvey. Iterative broadening. *Artificial Intelligence*, 55:367–383, 1992.

[8] E. A. Hansen, S. Zilberstein, and V. A. Danilchenko. Anytime heuristic search: First results. Technical Report CMPSCI 97-50, CSD, University of Massachusetts, Sept. 1997.

[9] M. Held and R. M. Karp. The Traveling Salesman Problem and minimum spanning trees: Part II. *Mathematical Programming*, 1:6–25, 1971.

[10] E. J. Horvitz. Reasoning about beliefs and actions under computational resource constraints. In *Proc. of the 3rd Workshop on UAI*, 1987.

[11] R. E. Korf. Depth-first iterative-deepening: An optimal admissible tree search. *Artificial Intelligence*, 27:97–109, 1985.

[12] K.-F. Lee. *Large-Vocabulary Speaker-Dependent Continuous Recognition: The Sphinx System*. PhD thesis, Carnegie Mellon University, 1988.

[13] D. Mitchell, B. Selman, and H. Levesque. Hard and easy distributions of SAT problems. In *Proc. AAAI-92*, pages 459–465, San Jose, CA, July 1992.

[14] N. Muscettola, S. F. Smith, G. Amiri, and D. Patak. Generating space telescope observation schedules. Technical Report CMU-RI-TR-89-28, Carnegie Mellon University, 1989.

[15] C. H. Papadimitriou and K. Steiglitz. *Combinatorial Optimization: Algorithms and Complexity*. Prentice-Hall, Englewood Cliffs, NJ, 1982.

[16] J. Pearl. *Heuristics: Intelligent Search Strategies for Computer Problem Solving*. Addison-Wesley, Reading, MA, 1984.

[17] J. C. Pemberton and W. Zhang. Epsilon-transformation: Exploiting phase transitions to solve combinatorial optimization problems. *Artificial Intelligence*, 81:297–325, 1996.

[18] F. J. Provost. Iterative weakening: Optimal and near-optimal policies for the selection of search bias. In *Proc. AAAI-93*, pages 769–775, 1993.

[19] S. Rubin. *The ARGOS Image Understanding System*. PhD thesis, Carnegie Mellon University, 1978.

[20] T. Volgenant and R. Jonker. A branch and bound algorithm for the symmetric traveling salesman problem based on the 1-tree relaxation. *European Journal of Operations Research*, 9:83–89, 1982.

[21] P. H. Winston. *Artificial Intelligence*. Addison-Wesley, second edition, 1992.

[22] W. Zhang. Truncated branch-and-bound: A case study on the asymmetric TSP. In *Proc. AAAI 1993 Spring Symp.: AI and NP-Hard Problems*, pages 160–166, 1993.

[23] S. Zilberstein and S. J. Russell. Optimal composition of real-time systems. *Artificial Intelligence*, 82:181–213, 1996.

Boosting Combinatorial Search Through Randomization

Carla P. Gomes*
Computer Science Department
Cornell University
Ithaca, NY 14853
gomes@cs.cornell.edu

Bart Selman
Computer Science Department
Cornell University
Ithaca, NY 14853
selman@cs.cornell.edu

Henry Kautz
AT&T Labs
180 Park Avenue
Florham Park, NJ 07932
kautz@research.att.com

Abstract

Unpredictability in the running time of complete search procedures can often be explained by the phenomenon of "heavy-tailed cost distributions", meaning that at any time during the experiment there is a non-negligible probability of hitting a problem that requires exponentially more time to solve than any that has been encountered before (Gomes *et al.* 1998a). We present a general method for introducing controlled randomization into complete search algorithms. The "boosted" search methods provably eliminate heavy-tails to the right of the median. Furthermore, they can take advantage of heavy-tails to the left of the median (that is, a non-negligible chance of very short runs) to dramatically shorten the solution time. We demonstrate speedups of several orders of magnitude for state-of-the-art complete search procedures running on hard, real-world problems.

Introduction

The time required by complete search methods to solve similar combinatorial problems can be surprisingly variable. Two problem instances may be identical, except for the order in which the variables are numbered. A particular complete search algorithm may solve the first in seconds, yet require hours or days to solve the second. Even for a single problem instance, a seemingly trivial change in a detail of the search algorithm may drastically alter the solution time. In addition, in many domains there are problem instances that can be quickly solved by incomplete methods, but apparently cannot be solved by complete methods, even methods guided by powerful heuristics.

This unpredictability in the running time of a complete algorithm undermines one of the main reasons that one may choose to employ such a method, namely the desire for a guarantee that the algorithm will determine whether or not each problem instance in fact has a solution. It is desirable, therefore, to find ways to improve the robustness and predictability of these algorithms.

---

*Carla P. Gomes is also a Research Associate at the Air Force Research Laboratory, Rome, NY, USA.
Copyright (c) 1998, American Association for Artificial Intelligence (www.aaai.org). All rights reserved.

This paper discusses a general technique for improving complete search methods by introducing a controlled amount of *randomization*. The technique actually takes advantage of the variability of the underlying search method in order to find solutions more quickly and with less variance in solution time. We demonstrate the effectiveness of this strategy on SAT and CSP algorithms, in the domains of logistics planning, circuit synthesis, and round-robin scheduling. Solutions times are reduced by an order of magnitude or more, and some instances are solved for the first time by a method other than local search.

We will show that the unpredictability in running times for combinatorial algorithms can often be explained by a phenomenon called a "heavy-tailed cost distribution" (Gomes *et al.* 1998a). In our preliminary experiments, we plotted the solution times for a deterministic search algorithm running on a random distribution of scheduling problem instances. We noticed that at any time during the experiment there was a non-negligible probability of hitting a problem that required exponentially more time to solve than any that had been encountered before. This so-called "heavy-tail" phenomena causes the mean solution time to increase with the length of the experiment, and to be infinite in the limit.

Previous authors have noted the occurrence of seemingly exceptionally hard problems in fixed problem distributions (Gent and Walsh 1994; Smith and Grant 1996). However, we further discovered that when a small amount of randomization was introduced into the heuristic used by the search algorithm, then, on some runs, the instances were solved quickly. Thus, the "hardness" did not reside in the instances, but rather in the combination of the instance with the details of the deterministic algorithm. When we plotted the solution times for many runs of the randomized complete algorithm (with different random seeds) on a *single* problem instance, we discovered the same heavy-tailed distribution as we had seen before on a collection of instances.

This observation led us to realize that a deterministic search algorithm can be viewed as a *single run* of a randomized algorithm. The unpredictability of deterministic,

Problem	Solver	Deterministic soln. time	Randomized mean soln. time
logistics.d	Satz	108 min	95 sec
3bit-adder-32	Satz	> 24 hrs	165 sec
3bit-adder-31	Satz	> 24 hrs	17 min
round-robin 14	ILOG	411 sec	250 sec
round-robin 16	ILOG	> 24 hrs	1.4 hrs
round-robin 18	ILOG	> 48 hrs	$\approx$ 22 hrs
block-world.d	Satz	30 min	23 min

Table 1: Comparison of speed of original deterministic algorithms and randomized versions on test-bed problems.

complete algorithms is thus explained by the variance one would expect in any one run of a randomized algorithm. Furthermore, by analyzing the shape of the cost distribution we developed simple techniques that provably *reduce* the mean solution time.

For our experiments, we used known hard problem instances from scheduling, planning, and circuit synthesis, and a state of-the-art satisfiability engine (Satz, by Li and Anbulagan (1997)), and a highly efficient CSP solver built using the ILOG C++ constraint programming library (Puget and Leconte 1995). It is important to note that in both cases the underlying deterministic complete search engines are among the fastest (and on many problems, *the* fastest) in their class. Thus, the techniques discussed in this paper extend the range of complete methods to problems that were previously beyond their reach. For a preview of our main results, see Table 1. The table shows how our randomization strategy enabled us to solve several previously unsolved problem instances, and other instances were solved up to an order of magnitude faster. Given the techniques' simplicity and generality, our approach can be easily adapted to improve the performance of other backtrack-style search methods used in planning, scheduling, and other tasks of interest to AI.

Problem Domains

Our problem domains are timetable scheduling, planning, and circuit synthesis. The first is formalized as a CSP problem, and the latter two as propositional satisfiability.

Timetabling consists in determining whether there exists a feasible schedule that takes into consideration a set of pairing and distribution constraints. More specifically, we consider problems derived from sports scheduling applications. The literature in this area is growing, and one can begin to get a sense of the range and mathematical difficulty of the problems encountered (McAloon *et al.* 1997; Nemhauser and Trick 1997; and Schreuder 1992). Here we consider the timetabling problem for the classic "round-robin" schedule: every team must play every other team exactly once. The problem is formally defined as follows:
1. There are N teams (N even) and every two teams play each other exactly once.
2. The season lasts $N - 1$ weeks.
3. Every team plays one game in each week of the season.
4. There are $N/2$ periods and, each week, every period is scheduled for one game.
5. No team plays more than twice in the same period over the course of the season.

Up to 8-team problems are relatively simple and can be done by brute force. However, the combinatorics of this scheduling problem are explosive. For an N team league, there are $N/2 \cdot (N-1)$ matchups (i, j) with $0 \leq i < j < N$ to be played. A schedule can be thought of as a permutation of these matchups. So, for N teams the search space size is $(N/2 \cdot (N - 1))!$, *i.e.*, the search space size grows as the factorial of the square of $N/2$. Published algorithms for this problem all scale poorly, and the times for our *deterministic* solver (as shown in Table 1) are among the best (see also Gomes *et al.* 1998b).

The second domain is planning. Kautz and Selman (1996) showed that propositional SAT encodings of difficult STRIPS-style planning problems could be efficiently solved by SAT engines. While both a complete backtrack-style engine and an incomplete local-search engine worked well on moderate-sized problems, the largest problems from the domain of logistics scheduling could only be solved by local search. However, it turns out that the deterministic version of Satz can solve all of the logistics instances from that paper in less than 2 minutes. Therefore we constructed a still-larger planning problem, labeled "logistics.d". This domain involves moving packages on trucks and airplanes between different locations in different cities. While the largest logistics problem from the Kautz and Selman (1996) paper involved 1,141 variables, "logistics.d" involves 2,160 variables.

The final domain is circuit synthesis. Kamath *et al.* (1993) developed a technique for expressing the problem of synthesizing a programmable logic array (PLA) as a propositional satisfiable problem. The statement of the problem includes a table specifying the function to be computed, and an upper-bound on the number of gates that may appear in the circuit. In general, these problems become more difficult to solve as the number of gates is reduced, until the limit is reached where the instance is unsatisfiable. These problems are quite hard to solve with complete SAT procedures, and have been used as part of the test-beds for numerous SAT competitions and research studies. The problems considered in this paper, "3bit-adder-32" and "3bit-adder-31" are (as one would guess) based on synthesizing a 3-bit adder using 32 and 31 gates respectively. Although Selman and Kautz (1993) solve the instances using local search, no one has previously solved either using a backtrack-style procedure.

Randomizing Complete Search Engines

We now consider general techniques for adding randomization to complete, systematic, backtrack-style search procedures. Such a procedure constructs a solution incrementally. At each step a heuristic is used to select an operation to be applied to a partial solution, such as assigning a value to an unassigned variable. Eventually either a complete solution is found, or the algorithm determines that the current partial solution is inconsistent. In the latter case, the algorithm backtracks to an earlier point in its search tree.

If several choices are heuristically determined to be equally good, then a deterministic algorithm applies some fixed rule to pick one of the operations; for example, to select the lowest-numbered variable to assign. The most obvious place to apply randomization, therefore, is in this step of tie-breaking: if several choices are ranked equally, choose among them at random. Even this simple modification can dramatically change the behavior of a search algorithm, as we will see in the section on CSP below.

However, if the heuristic function is particular powerful, it may rarely assign more than one choice the highest score. To handle this, we can introduce a "heuristic equivalence" parameter to the algorithm. Setting the parameter to a value H greater than zero means all choices who receive scores within H-percent of the highest score are considered equally good. This expands the choice-set for random tie-breaking.

With these changes each run of the search algorithm on a particular instance will differ in the order in which choices are made and potentially in time to solution. As we will discuss in detail below, it can be advantageous to terminate searches which appear to be "stuck", exploring a part of the space far from a solution. Therefore we will also introduce a "cutoff" parameter, that limits search to a specified number of backtracks. When the cutoff is reached, the algorithm is restarted at the root of the search tree.

We should note that introducing randomness in the branching variable selection does not effect the completeness of the backtrack-style search. Some basic bookkeeping (only linear space) ensures that the procedures do not revisit any previously explored part of the search space, which means that we can still determine inconsistencies, unlike local search methods. The cutoff parameter does limit the size of the space that can be searched exhaustively between restarts. In practice, we gradually increase the cutoff, to allow us to determine inconsistencies, if necessary.

A variable-order randomization and restart strategy was employed in Crawford and Baker's (1994) "probing" algorithm for SAT. Despite the fact that it performed no backtracking at all, it was shown to solve a number of examples. Even though, the "power of randomization" in combinatorial search has been informally recognized by others (for recent work in scheduling domains, see e.g., Bresina 1996 and Oddi and Smith 1997), our work provides the first explanation for the potential success of this kind of strategy, in terms of heavy-tailed distributions (Gomes et al. 1998a). As we will see, our data also shows that there is often a clear optimal cutoff value; simply probing down with unit propagation but no backtracking can be ineffective. For example, in Table 3 we have a 0% success rate for a cutoff value of 2. More recently, Bayardo and Schrag (1997) introduced a backtrack-style solver, rel-sat, that included randomized tie-breaking and restarts, but with only a fixed, high cutoff value. The focus of that work was on the backtracking technique, rather than the effect of restarts.

The first complete search algorithm we randomized was a CSP solver. ILOG SOLVER is a powerful C++ constraint programming library (Puget and Leconte 1995). For the round-robin scheduling problems discussed below, we used the library to build a deterministic, backtrack-style CSP engine. (See Dechter (1991) and Freuder and Mackworth (1994) for an overview of basic CSP algorithms.) It employs the first-fail heuristic for variable assignment, which selects the variables with the smallest domain first; ties are broken lexicographically. The performance of this deterministic version already matches or exceeds all the published results on solving these types of problems. We then randomized the solver by breaking ties randomly, and adding a cutoff parameter (Gomes et al. 1998b).

The second algorithm we randomized was for propositional satisfiability. One of the fastest complete search engines for propositional satisfiability testing is the Satz system of Li and Anbulagan (1997). Satz is a version of the Davis-Putnam-Loveland procedure (Davis et al. 1962), with a heuristic based on choosing a branch variable that maximizes a function of the number of the unit propagations performed when it is set positively or negatively. Satz is the fastest deterministic SAT procedure we have found for the instances discussed in this paper. It can often solve smaller instances of these types with less than 100 backtracks. Because its heuristic usually chooses a single branching variable without ties, we added a heuristic equivalence parameter to enlarge the choice-set.

Heavy-Tailed Cost Distributions

In previous work (Gomes *et al.* 1998a), we show that the tail behavior of randomized complete backtrack style methods is often best modeled using distributions which asymptotically have tails of the Pareto-Lévy form, *viz.*

$$\Pr\{X > x\} \sim C.x^{-\alpha}, \quad x > 0 \qquad (1)$$

where $\alpha > 0$ is a constant (Mandelbrot 1960; and Samorodnitsky 1994). These are heavy-tailed distributions, *i.e.*, distributions whose tails have a *power law decay*. The constant α is called the *index of stability* of the distribution. For $\alpha < 2$, moments of X of order less than α are finite while all higher order moments are infinite, *i.e.*, $\alpha = \sup\{a > 0 : \mathrm{E}|X|^a < \infty\}$. For example, when $\alpha = 1.5$, the distribution has a finite mean but no finite variance. With $\alpha = 0.6$, the distribution has neither a finite mean nor a finite variance.

If a Pareto-Lévy tail is observed, then the rate of decrease of the distribution is a power law. (Standard distributions exhibit exponential decay.) From (1), we have $1 - F(x) = \Pr\{X > x\} \sim C.x^{-\alpha}$, so the complement-to-one of the cumulative distribution, $F(x)$, also decays according to a power law. Given the power law decay of the complement-to-one of the cumulative distribution of a heavy-tailed random variable, its log-log plot should show an approximately linear decrease in the tail. Moreover, the slope of the observed linear decrease provides an estimate of the index α.

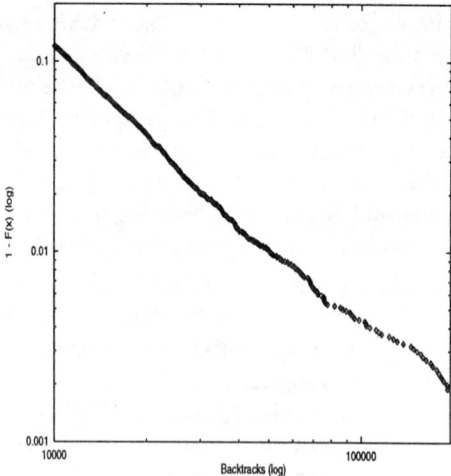

Figure 1: Log-log plot of the tail of 12 team round-robin scheduling.

Figure 1 shows the log-log plot of the tail ($X > 10,000$) of the complement-to-one of the cumulative distribution, 1-$F(x)$, for our 12 team round-robin problem. The linear nature of the tail in this plot directly reveals heavy-tails of the Pareto-Lévy type.

To complement our visual check of heavy-tailed behavior of Figure 1, we calculate the maximum likelihood estimate of the index of stability (the value of α): For our round-robin scheduling problem, for $N = 12$, we obtain $\alpha = 0.7$, which is consistent with the hypothesis of infinite mean and infinite variance, since $\alpha \le 1$.[1]

So far, we have identified heavy-tailed behavior of the cost distribution to the right of the median. The heavy tail nature shows that there is a computationally significant fraction of very long runs, decaying only at a polynomial rate. The strategy of running the search procedure with a cutoff near the median value of the distribution clearly avoids these long runs in the tail.

However, our experiments in Gomes (1998a) also suggest a heavy tail phenomenon on the left-hand side of the median value of the cost distribution, which means that the success rate for a solution only increases polynomially with the number of backtracks. This explains how a relatively low cutoff value still gives a sufficiently high success rate to allow us to solve a problem instance. For example, for our round-robin scheduling problems with $N = 16$, we observed several runs that took less than 200 backtracks, compared to a median value of around 2,000,000. For $N = 18$, we ran with a cutoff of 500,000 and solved the instance after 20 tries. Each try took about 1 hour, and the successful run took 350,632 backtracks.

Tails on the left are also characterized by an index of stability. Based on our data (Gomes 1998a), we conjecture that α for the tail on the left is less than 1.0 on hard combinatorial search problems. This conjecture has strong implications in terms of algorithm design: It means that in order to obtain the minimal expected run time, a preferred strategy consists of relatively short runs of a randomized backtrack-style procedure.

We do not wish to give the impression that *every* search problem gives rise to a heavy-tailed distribution. In fact, doing so would give rise to the suspicion that the distributions we found were an artifact of our methodology, rather than a real phenomena of the problem domain! One domain in which we have *not* found heavy-tails is on blocks-world planning problems. The hardest blocks-world problem from Kautz and Selman (1996) is blocks-world.d, and it can be solved by deterministic Satz in 30 minutes. We ran the randomized version of Satz on this instance at a wide range of cutoff values and heuristic equivalence settings.

---

[1]Of course, the computational cost of complete backtrack-style algorithms has a finite upper-bound. However, since we are dealing with NP-complete problems, this upper-bound is exponential in the size of the problem, which means that *de facto*, for realistic-size hard instances, it can be treated as infinite for practical purposes: no practical procedure can explore the search full space.

The optimal equivalence parameter setting was 30%. However, over a range of cutoff values, there was no evidence of a heavy-tailed distribution, and, therefore, randomization only slightly increases the effectiveness of Satz: the mean cost is 23 minutes. Further studies are needed to determine exactly what characteristics of combinatorial search problems lead to heavy-tailed behavior.

Boosting Performance by Randomization and Restarts

So far, we have discussed how heavy-tailed probability distributions underlie the large variability observed when running a randomized backtrack-style procedure on a variety of problem instances. We can obtain more efficient and more predictable procedures by running the search up to a certain cutoff point and then restarting at the root of the tree. Restarts clearly prevent the procedure from getting trapped in the long tails on the right of the distribution. In addition, a very low cutoff value can also be used to exploit the heavy-tails to the left of the median, and will allow us to solve previously unsolved problem instances after a sufficient number of restarts. In Table 1, the mean solution times in the "Randomized" column are based on empirically determined near-optimal cutoff values. For each randomized solution time the standard deviation is of the same order of magnitude as the mean. This is to be expected because the distribution is geometric, as will be shown in the next section. Without restarts, of course, the variance and mean tend to infinity to a first approximation.

We will now discuss these results in more detail.

Our deterministic CSP procedure on the round-robin scheduling problem gives us us a solution for $N = 14$ in about 411 seconds. (Experiments ran on a 200MHz SGI Challenge.) We could not find a solution for $N = 16$ and $N = 18$. Apparently, the problem quickly becomes very difficult, even for moderate values of N. The subtle interaction between global and local constraints makes the search for a globally consistent solution surprisingly hard.

For problems for which we can empirically determine the overall cost profile, we can calculate an *optimal* cutoff value to minimize the expected cost of finding a solution. Our main interest, however, is in solving previously unsolved instances, such as the $N = 16$ and $N = 18$ case. These problems are too hard to obtain a full cost distribution. For example, for $N = 16$, running with a cutoff of 1,000,000 gives a success rate of less than 40%, so we do not even reach the median point of the distribution. Each run takes about 2 hours to complete. (We estimate that the median value is around 2,000,000. Our deterministic procedure apparently results in a run that still lies to the right of the expected median cost.) In order to find a good cutoff value for very hard problem instances, the best available strategy is a trial-and-error process, where one experiments with vari-

cutoff	succ. rate	mean cost ($\times 10^6$)
200	0.0001	2.2
5,000	0.003	1.5
10,000	0.009	1.1
50,000	0.07	0.7
100,000	0.06	1.6
250,000	0.21	1.2
1,000,000	0.39	2.5

Table 2: Solving the 16-team robin-robin scheduling problem for a range of cutoff values.

cutoff	succ. rate	mean cost
2	0.0	>300,000
4	0.00003	147,816
8	0.0016	5,509
16	0.009	1,861
32	0.014	2,405
250	0.018	13,456
16000	0.14	107,611
128000	0.32	307,550

Table 3: Solving the logistics.d problem for a range of cutoff values.

ous cutoff values, starting at relatively low values, since the optimal cutoff for these problems tends to lie below the median value of the distribution. This can be seen from Table 2, which gives the expected cost (backtracks) for finding a solution for $N = 16$ for a range of cutoff values. The optimal cutoff is around 5.10^4, resulting in an expected cost per solution of 7.10^5 backtracks (≈ 1.4 hrs). For the $N = 18$ case, we ran with a cutoff of 5.10^5, and found a solution after approximately 22 hours.[2]

Table 3 gives the performance of Satz for a range of cutoff values on the logistics.d instance. Again, there is a clear optimal value: In this case, it's surprisingly low, 16 backtracks. Despite the low success rate (less than 1%) at this cutoff value, the overall performance is close to optimal here, requiring around 1,800 backtracks total per solution, which takes around 95 seconds. Compare this with the 108 minutes for the deterministic version of Satz. It's important to note that the 108 minutes run is not just an "unlucky" determinist run. Given the shape of the underlying heavy-tailed distribution, most runs take more than 100,000 backtracks (over 1 hour). The trick is to exploit the fact that we

---

[2]Since the submission of this paper, a lot of progress has been made in terms of solving larger instances (McAloon *et al.* in preparation). By using multiple threads on a 14 processor Sun system, 26 and 28 teams schedules were generated, which is the record as of this writing (Wetzel and Zabatta, 1998). We believe these numbers can be improved upon with our randomization technique.

have a non-negligible probably of solving the instance in a *very* short run. Our fast restart strategy exploits this.

See Table 1 for other improvements due to randomization. Until now, the 3bit-adder problems had not been solved by any backtrack-style procedure. On the blockworld problem, we obtain little improvement, which can be attributed to the absence of heavy-tails as discussed above.

These results show that introducing a stochastic element into a backtrack-style search procedure, combined with an appropriate restart strategy, can significantly enhance the procedure's performance. In fact, as we see here, it allows us to solve previously unsolved problem instances.

A Formal Analysis of Restarts

In this section we formalize the strategy of restarts S of a complete stochastic procedure A. We derive the probability distribution of S assuming the full knowledge of the probability distribution of A. We demonstrate that the probability distribution associated with S does not exhibit heavy tails. Furthermore, S has a finite mean and variance, even if the stochastic procedure A has an infinite mean and variance.

Let us consider a complete stochastic procedure and associate with it the random variable A, where A is the number of backtracks that it takes to find a solution or prove that it does not exist. Let us now consider the following stochastic strategy for running A: run A for a fixed number of backtracks c (the cutoff); if A finds a solution or proves it does not exist, then our stochastic strategy has also found a solution (or proved that it does not exist) and it stops. Otherwise, restart A from the beginning, using an independent random seed, for another c backtracks, and so on. Define S as the number of backtracks that the stochastic strategy of restarts of A with cutoff c takes to find a solution or prove that it does not exist. Let's assume that we know $P[A \leq c]$, *i.e.*, the probability that the stochastic procedure A will find a solution or prove that it does not exist in no more than c backtracks. The sequence of runs of A executed by our restart strategy are independent, and therefore they can be seen as a sequence of Bernoulli trials, in which the success consists in finding a solution (or proving that it doesn't exist) before the end of the run.

It's convenient to also define a random variable R, giving the number of restarts until a solution is found (or the instance is shown inconsistent). Note that $R = \lceil S/c \rceil$. R follows a *geometric distribution* with parameter $p = P[A \leq c]$. The probability of the tail of S, $P[S > s]$, is given by

$$P[S > s] = (1-p)^{\lfloor s/c \rfloor} P[A > s \bmod c]$$

Taking into consideration that $R = \lceil S/c \rceil$ and that it follows a geometric distribution (exponential decay; finite mean and variance), it follows that the tail of the distribution of S also exhibits exponential decay and S has a finite mean and variance.

We should emphasize that when adopting a low cutoff the strategy of restarts partially eliminates the heavy tail on the left: the lower the cutoff, the shorter the tail. This is true since the distribution of S exhibits exponential decay for $S >$ cutoff.

Conclusions

Building on our previous work on heavy-tailed behavior in combinatorial search (Gomes et al. 1998a), we have shown that performance of complete, backtrack-style search algorithms on hard real-world problems can be greatly enhanced by the addition of randomization combined with a rapid restart strategy. Speedups of several orders of magnitude were observed, and some test problem instances were solved for the first time by any backtrack-style procedure.

The success of our approach is based on exploiting the heavy-tailed nature of the cost distributions. We saw that in most of the domains we found that "outliers" on *both* sides of the median occur with a relatively high frequency. Heavy-tails to the right of the median cause the mean solution time to grow without bounds. Adding cutoffs and restarts to the search algorithm, however, both theoretically and empirically eliminate the heavy-tail and bound the mean. Heavy-tails to the left of the mean can be exploited by performing many rapid restarts with short runs, leading to a further dramatic decrease in expected solution time.

We applied the randomization techniques to two state-of-the-art search engines for CSP and propositional satisfiability. We were able to solve hard round-robin scheduling instances of up to size 18, when the corresponding deterministic version could only handle instances up to size 14. In the domain of planning as satisfiability, we extended the range of logistics problems that could be solved by complete methods from problems containing 1,141 variables to ones involving 2,160 variables (solved with mean cost of 95 seconds).

It would be interesting to explore our randomization approach in context of other backtrack-style approaches, such as dynamic backtracking (Ginsberg 1993). We believe that the generality of the approach will lead to further advances in planning, scheduling, diagnosis, game-playing, and other areas of AI.

Acknowledgments The first author is sponsored by the Air Force Research Laboratory, Air Force Materiel Command, USAF, under agreement number F30602-98-1-0008 and the Air Force Office of Scientific Research, under the New World Vistas Initiative, AFOSR NWV project 2304, LIRL 97RL005N25. The second author is supported by an NSF Faculty Early Career Development Award. The views and conclusions contained herein are those of the authors and should not be interpreted as necessarily representing the official policies or endorsements, either expressed or implied, of the Air Force Research Laboratory or the U.S. Government.

References

Alt, H., Guibas, L., Mehlhorn, K., Karp, R., and Wigderson A. (1996). A method for obtaining randomized algorithms with small tail probabilities. *Algorithmica*, 16, 1996, 543–547.

Bayardo, Roberto J., and Schrag, Robert C. (1997). Using CSP look-back techniques to solve real-world SAT instances. *Proc. AAAI-97*, New Providence, RI, 1997, 203–208.

Bresina, J. (1996) Heuristic-biased stochastic sampling. *Proc. AAAI-96*, Portland, OR, 1996.

Crawford, J. M., and Baker, A. B. (1994). Experimental results on the application of satisfiability algorithms to scheduling problems. *Proc. AAAI-94*, Seattle, WA, 1092–1097.

Davis, M., Logemann, G., and Loveland, D. (1962). A machine program for theorem proving. *Comm. ACM*, 5, 1962, 394–397.

Dechter, R. (1991). Constraint networks. *Encyclopedia of Artificial Intelligence* John Wiley, New York (1991) 276-285.

Freuder, E. and Mackworth, A., eds. (1994). *Constraint-based reasoning.* MIT Press, Cambridge, MA.

Gent, Ian P. and Walsh, Toby (1994). Easy problems are sometimes hard. *Artificial Intelligence*, (70)1-2, 335–345.

Ginsberg, M. (1993). Dynamic Backtracking. *Journal of Artificial Intelligence*, Vol. 1, 25–46.

Gomes, C.P. and Selman, B. (1997). Problem structure in the presence of perturbations. *Proc. AAAI-97*, New Providence, RI, 221–226.

Gomes, C.P., Selman, B.,and Crato, N. (1998a). Heavy-Tailed Phenomena in Combinatorial Search, 1998. (submitted for publication)

Gomes, C.P. and Selman, B., McAloon, K., and Tretkoff C. (1998b). Randomization in Backtrack Search: Exploiting Heavy-Tailed Profiles for Solving Hard Scheduling Problems. To appear in: *Proc. AIPS-98*.

Kamath, A.P., Karmarkar, N.K., Ramakrishnan, K.G., and Resende, M.G.C. (1993). An Interior Point Approach to Boolean Vector Function Synthesis. *Proc. 36th MSCAS*, 185–189.

Kautz, H. and Selman, B. (1996). Pushing the envelope: planning, propositional logic, and stochastic search. *Proc. AAAI-1996*, Portland, OR.

Li, Chu Min and Anbulagan (1997). Heuristics based on unit propagation for satisfiability problems. *Proc. IJCAI-97*, Kyoto, Japan, 1997.

Luby, M., Sinclair A., and Zuckerman, D. (1993). Optimal speedup of Las Vegas algorithms. *Information Process. Lett.*, 17, 1993, 173–180.

Mandelbrot, Benoit, B. (1960). The Pareto-Lévy law and the distribution of income. *International Economic Review* 1, 79–106.

McAloon, K., Regin, J-C., Tretkoff C. and Wetzel G. (1998). Constraint-Based Programming for Sports League Scheduling. Manuscript in preparation 1998.

McAloon, K., Tretkoff C. and Wetzel G. (1997). Sports League Scheduling. *Proceedings of Third Ilog International Users Meeting*, 1997.

Nemhauser, G., and Trick, M. (1997). Scheduling a major college basketball conference. Georgia Tech., Technical Report, 1997.

Oddi A. and Smith, S. (1997) Stochastic procedures for generating feasible schedules. *Proc. AAAI-97*, New Providence, RI, 1997.

Puget, J-F., and Leconte, M. (1995). Beyond the Black Box: Constraints as objects. *Proceedings of ILPS'95*, MIT Press, 513–527.

Samorodnitsky, Gennady and Taqqu, Murad S. (1994). *Stable Non-Gaussian Random Processes: Stochastic Models with Infinite Variance*, Chapman and Hall, New York.

Schreuder, J. A. M. (1992). Combinatorial Aspects of Construction of Competition Dutch Professional Football Leagues, *Discrete Applied Mathematics* 35 (1992) 301-312.

Selman, B. and Kautz, H. (1993). Domain-independent extensions to GSAT: solving large structured satisfiability problems. *Proc. IJCAI-93*, Chambéry, France, 290–295.

Smith, B. and Grant S.A. (1996). Sparse constraint graphs and exceptionally hard problems. *IJCAI-95*, 646–651, 1995. Full version in AIJ (Hogg et al. 1996).

Wetzel, G. and Zabatta, F. (1998). CUNY Graduate Center CS Technical Report, 1998.

Which Search Problems Are Random?

Tad Hogg

Xerox Palo Alto Research Center
Palo Alto, CA 94304, U.S.A.
hogg@parc.xerox.com

Abstract

The typical difficulty of various NP-hard problems varies with simple parameters describing their structure. This behavior is largely independent of the search algorithm, but depends on the choice of problem ensemble. A given problem instance belongs to many different ensembles, so applying these observations to individual problems requires identifying which ensemble is most appropriate for predicting its search behavior, e.g., cost or solubility. To address this issue, we introduce a readily computable measure of randomness for search problems called "approximate entropy". This new measure is better suited to search than other approaches, such as algorithmic complexity and information entropy. Experiments with graph coloring and 3-SAT show how this measure can be applied.

Introduction

Search is ubiquitous in AI. Hence the importance of developing rapid predictions of behavior, e.g., a problem's search cost or solubility. Such predictions could help select among alternate heuristics or problem formulations, decide whether to collect additional domain knowledge, or construct portfolios [12, 16]. A significant step toward this goal was the recognition of regularities, such as phase transitions, in many search ensembles, i.e., classes of problems with an associated probability for each to occur [5, 24, 8, 11, 14, 28]. These observations have also led to new heuristics [6, 10, 20]. Two key difficulties limit the application of this work to individual searches. First, the variance of ensemble behaviors is often very large, limiting the accuracy of predictions based on ensemble averages. Second, every problem is a member of many ensembles, with differing typical behaviors. So it is difficult to know which ensemble best applies to a particular problem.

This paper addresses the second difficulty by introducing a new measure of randomness particularly well-suited for search through its connection to the underlying problem structure [28]. This measure is then applied to distinguish typical instances of different search ensembles and to elucidate questions raised by a previous study of problem structure based on algorithmic complexity [27]. The results also give additional insight into the nature of the large variances.

Copyright © 1998, American Association for Artificial Intelligence (www.aaai.org). All rights reserved.

Quantifying Randomness

When is a problem a typical member of an ensemble? This question's conceptual difficulty is seen with bit sequences [4, 17]: in the ensemble of random 10-bit sequences, 0101010101 and 0101110001 each appear with probability 2^{-10} but differ in their regularity. One way to quantify this difference is *algorithmic complexity*: irregular sequences are those that cannot be produced by a program substantially shorter than the sequence itself [4, 7]. However, this measure is not readily computable and applies only to asymptotically long sequences. Another approach is the *entropy* of the sequence probabilities [7, 26]. While readily computed, it applies to the process generating the sequences rather than to a resulting instance. Thus its usefulness is limited since different processes can produce the same instance. E.g., the first 10-bit sequence given above could also be produced by alternating 0 and 1 bits, a process with lower entropy than random generation.

A practical measure must be readily computable, meaningful even for fairly small instances, and defined by an instance itself rather than the, possibly unknown, process that created it. One measure with these properties is *approximate entropy* (ApEn) of sequences [21]. In this paper we apply ApEn to search problems. Specifically, this section defines ApEn for any discrete structure by comparing its component parts, generalizing a technique previously introduced for hierarchies [15]. Sequences and graphs are examples of such structures, whose parts are, respectively, subsequences and subgraphs. The next section describes how these ideas apply to combinatorial searches.

Let C be a structure of size n with N parts, $\{c_1, \ldots, c_N\}$, of size $m \leq n$. Let $R(c, c')$ be an equivalence relation among the parts, identifying the set of D *distinct* parts $\{d_1, \ldots, d_D\}$ of size m. Let n_i be the number of times the ith distinct part d_i appears in C, and $f_i = n_i/N$ its frequency, for $i = 1, \ldots, D$. These frequencies define

$$\Phi^{(m)} = -\sum_{i=1}^{D} f_i \ln f_i \qquad (1)$$

The approximate entropy (ApEn) for size m is

$$\text{ApEn}(m) = \Phi^{(m+1)} - \Phi^{(m)} \qquad (2)$$

and characterizes the log-likelihood two parts of size $m+1$ are equivalent given that they each contain equivalent parts of size m [21].

For sequences [21], R tests for identical subsequences. Both sequences given above have 5 0's and 5 1's so $\Phi^{(1)} = \ln 2$. For $m = 2$, the regular sequence has 5 copies of 01 and 4 of 10, so $\Phi^{(2)} = -\frac{5}{9}\ln\frac{5}{9} - \frac{4}{9}\ln\frac{4}{9}$ or 0.69. The irregular sequence has 2 copies each of 00, 10 and 11, and 3 of 01, giving $\Phi^{(2)} = -3\frac{2}{9}\ln\frac{2}{9} - \frac{3}{9}\ln\frac{3}{9}$ or 1.37.

Randomness of Search Problems

To apply ApEn to search, we focus on constraint satisfaction problems (CSPs) [18] consisting of n variables and the requirement to assign a value to each variable to satisfy given constraints. Searches examine various *assignments*, which give values to some of the variables. These assignments, and their consistency relationships, form the *deep structure* of the CSP, which is fully specified by the inconsistent assignments directly specified by the constraints, i.e., the *minimized nogoods* [28].

Using ApEn with CSPs requires specifying the parts to use and an equivalence relation among them. A natural choice relevant for search is to use subproblems defined by sets of m variables. A subproblem's constraints and minimized nogoods are just those from the full problem involving only the subproblem's m variables. Subproblems can be compared in various ways. A simple method labels their variables from 1 to m in the same order as they appear in the full problem. Two subproblems are then considered equivalent when they have the same number of minimized nogoods (indicating the degree to which problems are constrained), and the same sets of variables involved together in these nogoods. That is, for each subset of $\{1,\ldots,m\}$, the corresponding variables in the two subproblems must appear together in at least one nogood of each subproblem, or not appear in any nogoods. Alternatively, each set of variables that appears together in at least one nogood can be viewed as a hyperedge in a hypergraph [1] whose nodes are the subproblem's variables. From this viewpoint, the equivalence relation requires both identical constraint hypergraphs and the same number of minimized nogoods.

A problem with n variables has $N = \binom{n}{m}$ subproblems with m variables. Because the number of subproblems grows rapidly with m, it is important that significant distinctions between problems are readily apparent even with small values of m. In fact, for studies of sequences [22] as well as the experiments on search problems reported here, values of 3 or 4 for m suffice, even for significantly different problem sizes. This use of small m makes approximate entropy tractably computable for search problems[1].

When ApEn varies over a small range, it is convenient to use

$$\text{def}(m) = \text{ApEn}_{\max} - \text{ApEn}(m) \qquad (3)$$

---

[1]Although not used in this paper, a faster, but approximate, estimate of the f_i values is possible from sampling only some of the m variable subproblems.

where $\text{ApEn}_{\max}$ is the maximum value of $\text{ApEn}(m)$ for a given *class* of problems, and is the same for *all* ensembles defined on that class of problems.

Examples

Most empirical studies of search use random ensembles, with constraints selected randomly from among all possibilities. Ensembles emphasizing more realistic structures have quantitatively different behaviors [13]. In many cases the constraints arise from physical interactions whose strength decrease with distance. In others, some variables are more critical and hence more tightly constrained than others. These cases have clustered constraints: some sets of variables are more constrained than expected from random generation. Thus we examine ApEn in random and clustered ensembles for two well-studied problems: graph coloring and satisfiability.

Graph Coloring

A graph coloring problem consists of a graph, a specified number of colors, and the requirement to find a color for each node in the graph such that adjacent nodes (i.e., nodes linked by an edge in the graph) have distinct colors. Viewed as a CSP, each node in the graph is a variable. The minimized nogoods are pairs of adjacent nodes assigned the same color. With b colors, each edge gives b such nogoods. Thus the number of constraints is uniquely determined by the number of edges e in the graph, or the average degree: $\gamma \equiv 2e/n$. In this paper we use $b = 3$ colors, in which case the hardest problems are concentrated near $\gamma = 4.5$ for random graphs [5].

A subproblem with m variables defines a subgraph with each edge adding b minimized nogoods. Hence the subproblem equivalence relation tests for identical subgraphs so ApEn is determined by the number of times each distinct subgraph with m nodes appears in the graph.

For example, $m = 2$ gives $D = 2$ distinct 2–node subgraphs: those with and without an edge. The number of subgraphs with an edge equals the number of edges e in the full graph, giving a frequency $f = e/\binom{n}{2}$. The other distinct subgraph, without an edge, has frequency $1 - f$. Thus, $\Phi^{(2)} = -f \ln f - (1-f) \ln (1-f)$ which is 0.185 for every 100–node graph with $\gamma = 4.5$. Because $\Phi^{(2)}$ depends only on e, we must use $\Phi^{(m)}$ with $m \geq 3$ to distinguish graphs with the same n and e. Thus we use def(2), which involves $\Phi^{(3)}$, in our experiments.

The random graph ensemble [2] takes each graph with n nodes and e edges as equally likely. A clustered ensemble [13] can be formed by grouping the nodes into a binary tree, which induces an ultrametric distance between each pair of nodes, i.e., the number of levels up the tree required to reach a common ancestor. A clustered graph is generated by choosing edges between nodes at ultrametric distance d with relative probability p^d. Random graphs result when $p = 1$, while $p < 1$ makes edges more likely between nearby nodes, giving a hierarchical clustering which shifts the location of the phase transition [13].

To evaluate search cost, we used conflict-directed backtracking based on the Brelaz heuristic [3] which assigns the most constrained nodes first (i.e., those with the most distinctly colored neighbors), breaking ties by choosing nodes with the most uncolored neighbors (with any remaining ties broken randomly). For each node, the smallest color consistent with the previous assignments is chosen first, with successive choices made when the search is forced to backtrack. As a simple optimization, we never change the colorings for the first two selected nodes to avoid unnecessarily repeating the search with a permutation of the colors. When forced to backtrack we jump back to the most recent node involved in the conflict [9, 23], a form of conflict directed backjumping. We measure the search cost by the number of assignments examined until the first solution is found or, when no solutions exist, until no further possibilities remain.

k-SAT

The satisfiability problem consists of a propositional formula in n binary variables, and the requirement to find an assignment to the variables that makes the formula true. The formula is usually represented as a conjunction of clauses, each of which is a disjunction of some variables, possibly negated. For k-SAT problems, each clause has k variables. The minimized nogoods correspond to the clauses in the formula: each clause excludes a single assignment to the k variables that appear in the clause [28]. For 3-SAT, the hardest problems are concentrated near $c = 4.2n$, where c is the number of clauses [8].

If $m = k$, each set of m variables is either together in a clause or not, so each such subproblem has one of two possible constraint hypergraphs. Since the m variables could appear in more than one clause, the subproblems can have differing numbers of nogoods. Thus, unlike graph coloring, k-SAT can have different $\Phi^{(m)}$ values even when m is the same size as the problem constraints.

In the class of all the 4-variable 2-SAT problems, an example is one with the two clauses $v_2 \vee v_3$ and $v_2 \vee \neg v_4$ so v_1 is unconstrained. For $m = 3$, there are 4 subproblems. The first, with variables 1, 2 and 3, contains only the first clause, involving the second and third subproblem variables, so the subproblem has a single nogood. The second subproblem, with variables 1, 2 and 4, contains only the second clause, again involving the second and third subproblem variables, and one nogood. When these subproblems' variables are labeled from 1 to 3, the second subproblem has the same variables in clauses as the first, so they satisfy the equivalence relation since they also both have one nogood. The third subproblem, with variables 1, 3 and 4, has no clauses, and is thus distinct from the first two. Finally, the fourth subproblem, with variables 2, 3 and 4, contains both clauses, has two nogoods and is distinct from all the other subproblems. Thus three distinct subproblems exist, with the first appearing twice and the rest appearing once, giving frequencies $f_1 = \frac{2}{4}$ and $f_2 = f_3 = \frac{1}{4}$. Hence, $\Phi^{(3)} = -\frac{2}{4} \ln \frac{2}{4} - 2\left(\frac{1}{4} \ln \frac{1}{4}\right)$ or $\frac{1}{2} \ln 8$. This example also illustrates that not all variables need appear in the constraints.

The random k-SAT ensemble selects the specified number of clauses randomly. For a clustered ensemble, we suppose that half the variables are more likely to be involved in clauses than the others. Specifically, for 3-SAT, we select half the clauses from among those that involve only the first $n/2$ variables, and then take the remaining clauses from among those that involve at least one of the second half of the variables. This results in a different form of clustering than the multilevel hierarchical clustering graph ensemble, allowing a broader range of empirical evaluation of ApEn behavior.

The SAT problems were solved with GSAT [25], an incomplete search method, to contrast with the exhaustive backtrack method used for the graph coloring experiments. In its simplest form, GSAT consists of a number of trials, which start from a randomly selected assignment and proceed in a series of steps. At each step, we count the number of conflicts in the neighbors of the current assignment and move to a neighbor with the fewest conflicts. If the search reaches a local minimum or a prespecified limit on the number of steps, a new trial is started. In the searches reported here, this limit was twice the number of variables in the problem. We performed 1000 trials to repeatedly find solutions, which allows estimating the average cost to find a solution by the total number of steps in all the trials divided by the number of times a solution was found. For the cases used here, typically several hundred trials for each problem found a solution.

Applications

Having introduced ApEn for search, we illustrate its use with two problems (graph coloring and SAT), ensembles (random and clustered), and search methods (complete and incomplete). Experiments with other combinations and problem sizes than those reported here gave similar results.

Identifying Typical Instances

ApEn distinguishes typical instances of random or clustered ensembles as shown in Figs. 1 and 2 for graph coloring and SAT, respectively. These figures show the cumulative distribution, i.e., the fraction of a sample of instances for which def(m) exceeds each value. The distributions are well separated. This separation is particularly significant for the small SAT problems in Fig. 2, in spite of the larger spread due to the small size. A similar distinction is seen with larger values of m in both the graph coloring and SAT problems. Thus ApEn distinguishes typical

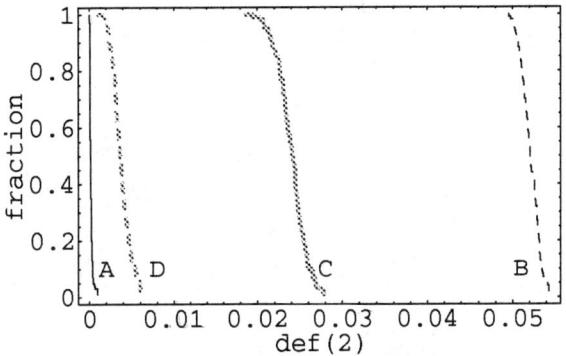

Fig. 1. Cumulative def(2) distribution for 100-node graphs with $\gamma = 4.5$, defined with respect to the largest value of ApEn(2) for such graphs: ApEn$_{max}$ = 0.3698. The curves each have 100 graphs but from different ensembles: random (A, solid black) and hierarchically clustered with p equal to 0.1 (B, dashed black), 0.5 (C, solid gray) and 2.0 (D, dashed gray).

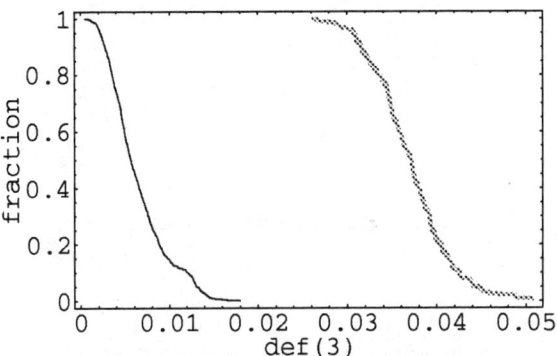

Fig. 2. Cumulative def(3) distribution for 3-SAT problems with 20 variables and 80 distinct clauses, defined with respect to the largest value of ApEn(3) for such problems: ApEn$_{max}$ = 0.7731. The curves each have 100 instances but from different ensembles: random (black) and clustered (gray).

instances of different ensembles that have significantly different transition points and typical search costs [13].

The subproblem equivalence relation used here is based on a single, arbitrary, ordering of the variables. An alternative allows permutations of the variables when comparing subproblems. For graph coloring, this amounts to testing for isomorphic, rather than identical, subgraphs. Although isomorphism is a more natural comparison of subproblems, it is more expensive to compute and, as a coarser grouping of subproblems, less able to distinguish ensembles. Repeating Fig. 1 using isomorphism has less distinct distributions, but is otherwise qualitatively similar.

Defining ApEn using problem structure is important for discriminating among ensembles. This is seen by comparison with another representation commonly used in discussions of algorithmic complexity [7], but which completely ignores problem structure. Specifically, a graph's edges are a particular subset of all possible edges among its nodes. These subsets can be ordered, e.g., lexicographically [19]. Each graph then corresponds to the position, in this ordering, of its set of edges. Viewing this integer position index as a sequence of bits, allows

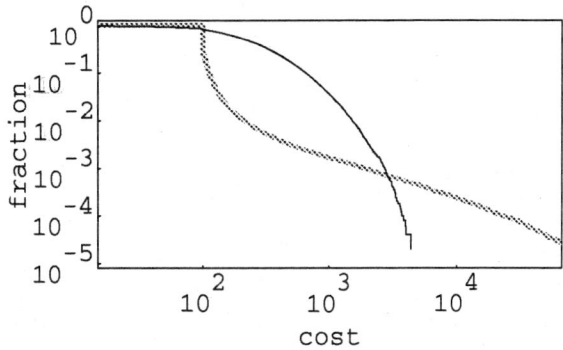

Fig. 3. Cumulative search cost distribution for 100-node random graphs with $\gamma = 3.5$ (gray) and 4.5 (black) using the Brelaz heuristic, on a log-log scale. Median costs are 100 and 215, respectively.

ApEn to be computed [21], giving another definition of ApEn for graphs. Experiments similar to those of Fig. 1 show this representation does *not* distinguish the ensembles. This dependence on the representation is similar to that reported for digit sequences [21], and indicates the problem sizes here are not large enough for algorithmic complexity to be usefully applied: asymptotically, such changes in representation do not affect compressibility [7].

Are Hard Cases Atypical?

Within a given ensemble, the search cost varies considerably among the instances. An example is shown in Fig. 3. This behavior led to a claim that the rare high cost instances are distinctly nonrandom compared to other members of the ensemble, and the exceptionally hard cases are part of a finite set of exceptions that does not persist to larger problem sizes [27]. An alternate view is the exceptionally high costs are due to the search algorithm making unlucky choices early in the search, resulting in exhaustive search of many assignments before returning to correct the early mistake. In this case, the high costs would be due to the algorithm choices rather than intrinsic characteristics of the problem instances [24].

To examine this question with ApEn for the random graph ensemble, we generated graphs that fully sample the cost distributions of Fig. 3. Specifically, we first generated 100 random graphs. We then examined additional graphs, collecting only those with a cost of at least 1000, until a second set of 100 graphs was created. This process was repeated with minimum costs of 10^4 and 10^5 for $\gamma = 3.5$, and minimums of 5000 and 10^4 for $\gamma = 4.5$, giving a total of 400 graphs for each value of γ, with representatives from the high cost tail of the distributions. The result, in Fig. 4, shows no correlation between the cost and ApEn. Using isomorphic instead of identical subgraphs for the equivalence relation gives qualitatively similar behavior. For SAT problems, the distribution of GSAT search costs is shown in Fig. 5. These costs are also uncorrelated with ApEn, as shown in Fig. 6.

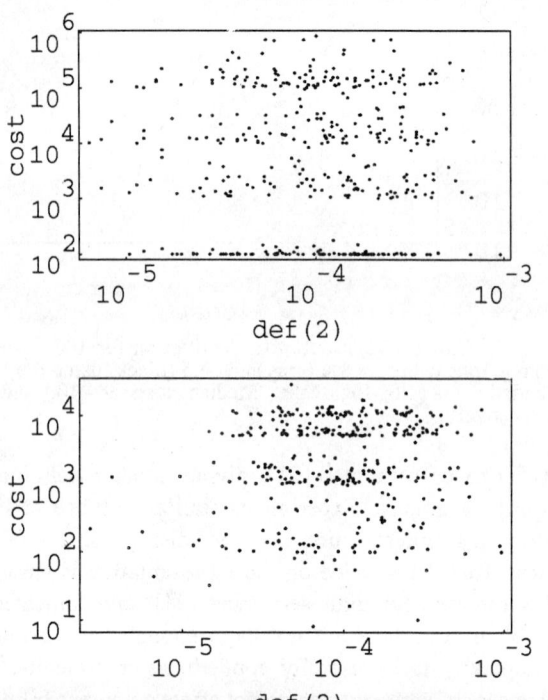

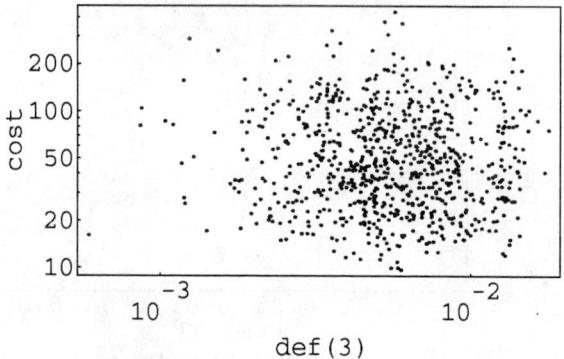

Fig. 6. Average search cost of GSAT vs. def(3) for soluble cases of random 3-SAT instances with 20 variables and 80 clauses, on a log-log scale. Similar behavior is seen using def(4).

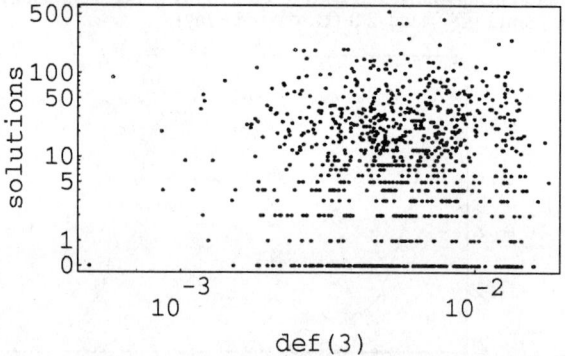

Fig. 4. Graph coloring search cost vs. def(2) for 100–node random graphs with $\gamma = 3.5$ (top) and 4.5 (bottom) on a log-log scale. Maximum ApEn(2) for graphs with 175 and 225 edges is 0.305771 and 0.369815, respectively. Vertical groupings of the points reflect the cost distribution sampling described in the text. Qualitatively similar plots are seen using def(3).

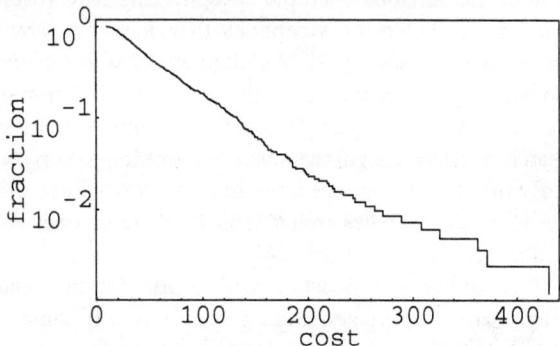

Fig. 7. Number of solutions vs. def(3) for random 3-SAT on a log-log scale (except for the problems with 0 solutions included at the bottom of the plot). Similar behavior is seen using def(4).

Fig. 5. Cumulative search cost distribution for GSAT on random soluble 3-SAT problems for 20 variables and 80 clauses.

Similar plots for the clustered ensembles of graph coloring and SAT show the same qualitative behavior: no correlation within an ensemble, but distinct clusterings of cost and ApEn values for the different ensembles.

The small SAT problems examined here allow an exhaustive count of solutions, giving the behavior shown in Fig. 7. Again there is no correlation with the ApEn values. This suggests that further global characteristics of the search problem, determined with exhaustive analysis of state space, such as the number of local minima, would also not be correlated with the ApEn value.

These results on search cost and number of solutions suggest that no additional readily computable problem parameters will distinguish most instances with very different values of these properties within a single ensemble. Instead, much of the high variance is likely to be an intrinsic property of ensembles for which instances can be generated without intractable computations such as exponential search. Furthermore, the results are consistent with the observation mentioned above that rare exceptionally high cost cases in an ensemble are primarily due to algorithm choices rather than intrinsic instance complexity.

Discussion

By distinguishing ensembles, ApEn may improve the use of the phase transition location as a heuristic [6, 10, 20]. For example, it could detect when choices appear to be typical of the ensemble used to design the heuristic, thus giving some indication of the reliability of the heuristic in different situations during the search. ApEn could also estimate the likely applicability of such heuristics based on different ensembles, either to select which one to use or to create [7] a portfolio [12, 16] of methods. ApEn's focus on problem instances complements probabilistic analyses of ensemble averages. Whether ApEn is useful in these contexts remains to be investigated.

ApEn can be generalized to a broader range of situations, such as search problems with continuous parameters, e.g., weights on links in a graph. Requiring exact matches between such values will not distinguish nearly equal values from significantly different ones. One approach to such cases is coarse graining, where the continuous parameter values are grouped into a few discrete bins. Alternatively, one can introduce a metric on the parts, and count the proportion of the parts within a given threshold distance of each one, as was studied for sequences [21].

Another modification, giving a more sensitive comparison of a problem instance and an ensemble, is replacing $\Phi^{(m)}$ by the disparity [7] $\sum f_i \ln(f_i/p_i)$ where p_i is the ensemble probability that a size m subproblem is of distinct type i. The disparity is nonnegative and equals zero only when $f_i = p_i$, i.e., the observed frequencies match those expected for the ensemble.

Applying approximate entropy to search has some arbitrariness in the choices of problem representation and the equivalence relation. With choices based on the deep structure of problems, ApEn readily discriminates ensembles even when the problems are too small for asymptotic behaviors. It thus provides a readily computable measure, directly relevant for search, that can help apply insights from ensemble analyses to individual problems.

Acknowledgments

I thank Don Kimber and Rajan Lukose for helpful discussions.

References

1. C. Berge. *Graphs and Hypergraphs*. North-Holland, Amsterdam, 1973.
2. B. Bollobas. *Random Graphs*. Academic Press, NY, 1985.
3. Daniel Brelaz. New methods to color the vertices of a graph. *Communications of the ACM*, 22(4):251–256, 1979.
4. G. Chaitin. Randomness and mathematical proof. *Scientific American*, 232:47–52, May 1975.
5. Peter Cheeseman, Bob Kanefsky, and William M. Taylor. Where the really hard problems are. In J. Mylopoulos and R. Reiter, editors, *Proceedings of IJCAI91*, pages 331–337, San Mateo, CA, 1991. Morgan Kaufmann.
6. Scott H. Clearwater and Tad Hogg. Problem structure heuristics and scaling behavior for genetic algorithms. *Artificial Intelligence*, 81:327–347, 1996.
7. Thomas M. Cover and Joy A. Thomas. *Elements of Information Theory*. John Wiley, New York, 1991.
8. James M. Crawford and Larry D. Auton. Experimental results on the crossover point in random 3SAT. *Artificial Intelligence*, 81:31–57, 1996.
9. Rina Dechter. Enhancement schemes for constraint processing: Backjumping, learning, and cutset decomposition. *Artificial Intelligence*, 41:273–312, 1990.
10. Ian P. Gent, Ewan MacIntyre, Patrick Prosser, and Toby Walsh. The constrainedness of search. In *Proc. of the 13th Natl. Conf. on Artificial Intelligence (AAAI96)*, pages 246–252, Menlo Park, CA, 1996. AAAI Press.
11. Ian P. Gent and Toby Walsh. An empirical analysis of search in GSAT. *J. of AI Research*, 1:47–59, 1993.
12. C. P. Gomes and B. Selman. Algorithm portfolio design: Theory vs. practice. In *Proc. of UAI-97*, 1997.
13. Tad Hogg. Refining the phase transitions in combinatorial search. *Artificial Intelligence*, 81:127–154, 1996.
14. Tad Hogg, Bernardo A. Huberman, and Colin Williams. Phase transitions and the search problem. *Artificial Intelligence*, 81:1–15, 1996.
15. B. A. Huberman and T. Hogg. Complexity and adaptation. *Physica*, 22D:376–384, 1986.
16. Bernardo A. Huberman, Rajan M. Lukose, and Tad Hogg. An economics approach to hard computational problems. *Science*, 275:51–54, 1997.
17. Donald E. Knuth. *The Art of Computer Programming*. Addison-Wesley, Reading, MA, 1969.
18. Alan Mackworth. Constraint satisfaction. In S. Shapiro, editor, *Encyclopedia of Artificial Intelligence*, pages 285–293. Wiley, NY, 1992.
19. A. Nijenhuis and H. S. Wilf. *Combinatorial Algorithms for Computers and Calculators*. Academic Press, New York, 2nd edition, 1978.
20. David M. Pennock and Quentin F. Stout. Exploiting a theory of phase transitions in three-satisfiability problems. In *Proc. of the 13th Natl. Conf. on Artificial Intelligence (AAAI96)*, pages 253–258, Menlo Park, CA, 1996. AAAI Press.
21. Steve Pincus and Rudolf E. Kalman. Not all (possibly) "random" sequences are created equal. *Proc. Natl. Acad. Sci. USA*, 94:3513–3518, 1997.
22. Steve Pincus and Burton H. Singer. Randomness and degrees of irregularity. *Proc. Natl. Acad. Sci. USA*, 93:2083–2088, 1996.
23. Patrick Prosser. Hybrid algorithms for the constraint satisfaction problem. *Computational Intelligence*, 9(3):268–299, 1993.
24. Bart Selman and Scott Kirkpatrick. Critical behavior in the computational cost of satisfiability testing. *Artificial Intelligence*, 81:273–295, 1996.
25. Bart Selman, Hector Levesque, and David Mitchell. A new method for solving hard satisfiability problems. In *Proc. of the 10th Natl. Conf. on Artificial Intelligence (AAAI92)*, pages 440–446, Menlo Park, CA, 1992. AAAI Press.
26. Claude E. Shannon and Warren Weaver. *The Mathematical Theory of Communication*. Univ. of Illinois Press, Chicago, 1963.
27. Dan R. Vlasie. The very particular structure of the very hard instances. In *Proc. of the 13th Natl. Conf. on Artificial Intelligence (AAAI96)*, pages 266–270, Menlo Park, CA, 1996. AAAI Press.
28. Colin P. Williams and Tad Hogg. Exploiting the deep structure of constraint problems. *Artificial Intelligence*, 70:73–117, 1994.

A^* with Bounded Costs

Brian Logan and Natasha Alechina
School of Computer Science, University of Birmingham
Birmingham B15 2TT UK

{b.s.logan,n.alechina}@cs.bham.ac.uk

Abstract

A key assumption of all problem-solving approaches based on utility theory, including heuristic search, is that we can assign a utility or cost to each state. This in turn requires that all criteria of interest can be reduced to a common ratio scale. However, many real-world problems are difficult or impossible to formulate in terms of minimising a single criterion, and it is often more natural to express problem requirements in terms of a set of constraints which a solution should satisfy. In this paper, we present a generalisation of the A^* search algorithm, A^* with bounded costs (ABC), which searches for a solution which best satisfies a set of prioritised soft constraints, and show that, given certain reasonable assumptions about the constraints, the algorithm is both complete and optimal. We briefly describe a route planner based on ABC and illustrate the advantages of our approach in a simple route planning problem.

Introduction

Heuristic search is one of the classic techniques in AI and has been applied to a wide range of problem-solving tasks including puzzles, two player games, and path finding problems. A key assumption of all problem-solving approaches based on utility theory, including heuristic search, is that we can assign a *utility* or *cost* to each state. This in turn requires that all criteria of interest can be reduced to a common ratio scale. For example, in a game of chess it is assumed that all the pieces and their positions on the board can be given a value on a common scale. Similarly, in decision theory, it is assumed that, for example, the inconvenience of carrying an umbrella and the discomfort of getting wet can be expressed as commensurable (dis)utilities. However, many real-world problems are difficult or impossible to formulate in terms of minimising a single criterion, and it is often more natural to view such problems in terms of a set of prioritised soft constraints. By prioritised we mean that it is more important to satisfy some constraints than others. For example, while not getting wet and not carrying an umbrella is clearly preferable, we may also prefer being dry with an umbrella to being wet without one. Soft constraints are constraints which can be satisfied to a greater or lesser degree, for example how long we have to spend in the rain, or the number of items we have to carry.

In this paper, we present a generalisation of the A^* search algorithm, A^* with bounded costs (ABC), which searches for a solution which best satisfies a set of prioritised soft constraints, and show that, given certain reasonable assumptions about the constraints, the algorithm is both complete and optimal. We briefly describe an implemented route planning system based on ABC and illustrate the advantages of ABC compared to A^* in a simple route planning problem.

The work reported in this paper was originally motivated by difficulties in applying classical search techniques to agent route planning problems, and we shall use this as a motivating example throughout the paper. However, the problems we identify with utility based approaches, and the solutions we propose, are equally applicable to other search problems.

An example: route planning

Consider, for example, the problem of an agent playing the game of hide-and-seek which has to plan a route from its current position to home base in a complex environment consisting of hills, valleys, impassable areas and so on. The plan should satisfy a number of criteria, for example, it should be concealed from the agent's opponents, it should be as short as possible and be executable given the agent's current resources (e.g., fuel or energy).

The route planning task can be formulated as the problem of finding a *minimum-cost* (or low-cost) route between two locations in a digitised map, where the cost of a route is an indication of its quality (Campbell *et al.* 1995). In this approach, planning is seen as a search problem in space of partial plans, allowing many of the classic search algorithms such as A^* (Hart, Nilsson, & Raphael 1968) or variants such as A^*_ϵ (Pearl 1982) to be applied. However, while such planners are complete and optimal (or optimal to some bound ϵ), it can be difficult to formulate the route planning task in terms of minimising a single criterion.

One way of incorporating multiple criteria into the planning process is to define a cost function for each criterion and use, e.g. a weighted sum of these functions as the function to be minimised. For example, we can define a 'visibility cost' for being exposed and combine this with cost functions for the time and energy required to execute the plan

---

Copyright ©1998, American Association for Artificial Intelligence (www.aaai.org). All rights reserved.

to form a composite function which can be used to evaluate alternative plans. However the relationship between the weights and the solutions produced is complex, and it is often not clear how the different cost functions should be combined to give the desired behaviour across all magnitude ranges for the costs. This makes it hard to specify what kinds of plans a planner should produce and hard to predict what it will do in any given situation; small changes in the weight of one criterion can result in large changes in the resulting plans. Changing the cost function for a particular criterion involves changing not only the weight for that cost, but the weights for all the other costs as well. Moreover, if different criteria are more or less important in different situations, we need to find sets of weights for each situation.

At best the amount of, e.g., time or energy, we are prepared to sacrifice to remain hidden is context dependent. In general, the properties which determine the quality of a solution are incommensurable. For example, the criteria may only be ordered on an ordinal scale, with those criteria which determine the feasibility of a solution being preferred to those properties that are merely desirable. It is difficult to see how to convert such problems into a multi-criterion optimisation problem without making ad-hoc assumptions.

State space search with prioritised soft constraints

In the remainder of this paper we describe a new search algorithm, A^* with bounded costs (ABC), which searches for a solution which best satisfies a set of prioritised soft constraints (Logan 1997). In effect, we replace the optimisation problem solved by A^* with a satificing or constraint satisfaction problem which allows optimisation as a special case. For example, rather than finding the least cost plan on the basis of a weighted sum of the time required to execute the plan and its visibility, we might specify a route that takes time less than t and is at least 50% concealed, or a route that requires no more than e units of energy to execute and minimises visibility. This approach provides a means of more clearly specifying problems and more precisely evaluating solutions. For example, a plan can be characterised as satisfying some costraints and only partially satisfying or not satisfying others.

We define an ABC search problem as consisting of:

- a set of states and operators as for A^*;
- a set of *cost functions*, one for each criterion on which solutions are to be evaluated;
- a set of *constraints* on acceptable values for each cost;
- a preference ordering over sets of constraint values; and
- a preference ordering over costs.

A *solution* to an ABC search problem is a path from the start state to a goal state.

Path constraints

A *cost* is a measure of path quality relative to some criterion, and can be anything for which an ordering relation can be defined: e.g., numbers, booleans, or more generally a label from an ordered set of labels (e.g., 'tiny', 'small', 'medium', 'large', 'huge') etc. A *cost function* is a function which takes a path and returns an estimate of the cheapest completion of the path to a goal state. A cost function is *admissible* if it never over-estimates the true cost of the cheapest completion of a path to a goal state. A cost function is *increasing* (resp. *decreasing*) if every operator application costs at least some minimum positive (resp. negative) amount d.

A *constraint* is a relation between a cost and a set of acceptable values for the cost, for example the boolean value '*true*', '$= 100$', an open interval such as '< 10', '> 20', or '$\leq O + \epsilon$' (i.e. within ϵ of the optimum value O).

An important class of constraints are upper/lower bound constraints which define an upper or lower bound on some property of the solution, such as the time required to execute a plan, its degree of visibility etc. Another kind of constraint which we consider in detail, since they allow us to formulate ABC as a generalisation of A^*, are optimisation constraints which require that some property of the solution be minimised or maximised, or more generally should lie within ϵ of the minimum or maximum value (for example that a plan should be as short as possible).

Upper bound/minimisation constraints on increasing admissible cost functions and lower bound/maximisation constraints on decreasing admissible cost functions are termed *admissible*. The latter are precise mirror images of the former, and for the ease of exposition we assume that admissible constraints bound increasing functions.

Path ordering

A path which satisfies all the constraints is termed *valid*. If the problem is over-constrained, there will be no solution which satisfies all the constraints. In such situations, it is often possible to distinguish among the invalid solutions, as the violation of some (sets of) constraints will be preferable to others.

Combinations of possible constraint values define a set of *path equivalence classes*, with those paths which satisfy the same constraints falling in the same equivalence class. We assume that there exists a preference ordering over these equivalence classes. A path p_a is *preferred* to a path p_b if the equivalence class of p_a precedes the equivalence class of p_b in this ordering. For example we may prefer paths which satisfy the greatest number of constraints, or paths which satisfy constraints which determine the feasibility of the solution to those which satisfy constraints defining properties which are merely desirable. In what follows, we assume that this ordering is at least a pointwise ordering, that is, if a path p_a satisfies the same constraints as p_b plus at least one more constraint, it is preferred to p_b.

We can use this ordering over equivalence classes without having an explicit ordering over the constraints. However, in many situations, it is often more natural to *prioritise* the constraints and use this ordering to generate the ordering on the path equivalence classes. For example, we could define a total order over the constraints and use this to partition paths into eqivalence classes on the basis of the number of important constraints they satisfy, by comparing the value of each constraint in order until we find a constraint which is satisfied by only one of the paths. This is essentially lexicographic ordering on fixed length boolean strings in which *true* is preferred to *false*.[1]

If the problem is under-constrained, there may be many valid solutions. In such cases, it is often possible to define a notion of how well a path satisfies a constraint, which can be used to order the solutions. For example, we may prefer paths which over-satisfy the constraints, i.e., where there is some 'slack' between the cost of a path and the bound on the cost defined by a constraint. In the case of route plans, solutions which over-satisfy time or energy constraints are often more robust in the face of unexpected problems during the execution of the plan.

The preference ordering on costs depends on the constraints associated with the costs. In general, if v_1 and v_2 are values and k_1, k_2 constants, then v_1 is preferred to v_2 if:

Form of constraint on cost v	Cost ordering
$v < O_e + \epsilon$	$v_1 < v_2$
$v < k_1$	$v_1 < v_2$
$v > k_1$	$v_1 > v_2$
$v = k_1$	$\|k_1 - v_1\| < \|k_2 - v_2\|$

Combined orderings on cost values define a pointwise ordering over costs, i.e., a path p_a is preferred to a path p_b if it has the same or 'better' values on all cost functions. A special case of the pointwise ordering is a dominance ordering. One path p_a *dominates* another path p_b if both paths terminate in the same state, and there is at least one cost f_i such that $f_i(p_a) < f_i(p_b)$ and there is no cost f_j such that $f_j(p_a) > f_j(p_b)$.

Many refinements of the pointwise ordering of costs are possible. For example, we could order the equivalence classes using the costs for the most important constraint or the cost for the most important violated constraint. If the constraints are ordered lexicographically, it is often more natural to use a lexicographic ordering over the costs which reflects the constraint ordering. We will refer to all such refinements as *slack orderings*.

The slack ordering allows us to sub-order paths within a path equivalence class, with those paths which have the greatest slack being the most preferred. Conversely, for violated constraints, the sub-ordering may favour paths which are closer to satisfying the constraint. This can be useful in the case of 'soft' constraints, where minor violations are acceptable.

Slack ordering also allows us to define *relative optimisation constraints*, which are reqirements that some cost f be minimised or maximised, given that some more important constraints are satisfied. A relative minimisation constraint has the form $f < \infty$ and is assumed to be always satisfied, but the slack ordering associated with the constraint prefers the paths with the minimal cost on f within every equivalence class.

The constraint and slack orderings over paths are used to direct the search and control backtracking.[2] The dominance ordering is used to decide which newly generated paths to keep and which to discard.

A^* with bounded costs

The search strategy of ABC is similar to A^*. We use two lists, an OPEN list of unexpanded nodes (paths) ordered using the preference ordering, and a CLOSED list containing all non-dominated expanded nodes. At each step, we take the first node from the OPEN list and put it on CLOSED. Call this node n. If n is a valid solution and all the constraints are admissible we return the path and stop. Otherwise we generate all the successors of n, and for each successor we cost it and determine its equivalence class. We remove from OPEN and CLOSED all paths dominated by any of the successors of n and discard any successor which is dominated by any path on OPEN or CLOSED. We add any remaining successors to OPEN, in order, and recurse (see Figure 1).

If the constraints are admissible, the first solution found will satisfy the greatest number of more important constraints; if slack ordering is used, this solution is also the most preferred with respect to the slack ordering. If the constraints are not admissible, we can never be sure we have found the optimum solution without an exhaustive search: even if we have a solution which satisfies all the constraints, there may be another solution which is prefereable with respect to the slack ordering.

```
OPEN ← [start]
CLOSED ← []

repeat
    if OPEN is empty return false

    remove n, the least member of the first
    non-empty equivalence class, from OPEN
    and place it on CLOSED

    if n is a solution then return n

    otherwise for every successor, n', of n

        cost n' and determine its equivalence
        class

        remove from OPEN and CLOSED all paths
        dominated by n'

        if n' is dominated by any path on OPEN
        or CLOSED, discard n'

        otherwise add n' to OPEN, in order
```

Figure 1: The ABC algorithm

---

[1] It is clear that, in the general case, this ordering cannot be produced using a weighted sum cost function.

[2] Favouring paths which over-satisfy the constraints has the additional advantage of reducing the likelihood that the path will violate the constraint as the length of the path increases, reducing the amount of backtracking. (If the cost functions are admissible, the estimated cost of a path will typically increase as the path is expanded.)

We end this section by stating two theorems about the formal properties of ABC, the proofs of which we omit due to lack of space.

Given reasonable assumptions about the constraints, it can be shown that ABC is both complete and optimal. By *complete* we mean that if a solution exists, it will be found after a finite number of steps. By an *optimal solution* we mean a solution in the highest non-empty equivalence class with respect to the constraint ordering which is also most preferred with respect to the slack ordering. An algorithm is optimal if it returns an optimal solution. Note that there may be several different optimal solutions.

Theorem 1 *ABC with admissible constraints is complete.*

Theorem 2 *ABC with admissible constraints is optimal.*

Proofs of these theorems can be found in (Logan & Alechina 1998)

Comparison of ABC and A^*

ABC is a strict generalisation of A^*: with a single admissible optimisation constraint its behaviour is identical to A^*. Indeed, ABC can be seen as A^* with two partial orderings on paths: a dominance ordering to determine which paths to discard and a preference ordering to determine which paths to expand first.

As might be expected, the additional flexibility of ABC involves a certain overhead compared with A^*. The preference ordering of paths requires the comparison of k constraint values for each pair of paths, where k is the number of constraints. If slack ordering is used, we must also perform an additional $\log m$ comparisons of k cost values, where m is the number of paths in the equivalence class. In addition, we must update the constraint values of the paths in the OPEN list when we obtain a better estimate of the optimum value for an optimisation constraint.

There is also a storage overhead associated with this approach. For each path we must now hold k constraint values in addition to the k costs from which the constraint values are derived. More importantly, we must remember all the non-dominated paths to each state visited by the algorithm rather than just the minimum cost path as with A^* since: (a) it may be necessary to 'trade off' slack on a more important constraint to satisfy another, less important constraint; and (b) it may not be possible to satisfy all the constraints, in which case we must backtrack to a path in a lower equivalence class. In some cases remembering all the non-dominated paths can be a significant overhead. However, there are a number of ways round this problem, including more intelligent initial processing of the constraints and discretising the Pareto surface. For example we can require that the algorithm retain no more than l paths to any given state, by discarding any path which is sufficiently similar to an existing path to that state. In the limit, this reduces to A^* where we only remember one path to each state.

Route planning with prioritised soft constraints

In this section, we present an example application of the ABC algorithm and compare it to conventional approaches based on weighted sum cost functions. We describe a simple route planner based on ABC for an agent which plays the game of 'hide-and-seek' in complex environments. The goal of the agent is to get from the start point to home base subject to a number of constraints, e.g., that the route should take less than t timesteps to execute or that the route should be hidden from the agent's opponents, and the function of the planner is to return a plan which best satisfies these constraints.

The current implentation of the route planner supports seven constraint types which bound the time and effort taken to execute the plan or require that certain cells be visted or avoided (for example *concealed route* constraints enforce a requirement that none of the steps in the plan be visible by the agent's opponents).[3] However, for reasons of brevity, we shall consider only time and energy constraints here. Time constraints establish an upper bound on the time required to execute the plan assuming the agent is moving at a constant speed of one cell per timestep. Energy constraints bound a non-linear 'effort' function which returns a value expressing the ease with which the plan could be executed—the cost function is based on the 3D distance travelled with an additional non-linear penalty for going uphill.

In the following example, we consider the problem of planning from coordinates (50, 10) to (10, 45) in an 80×80 grid of spot heights representing a 10km $\times$ 10km region of Southern California. The terrain model is shown in Figure 2 (lighter shades of grey represent higher elevations).[4] We use a lexicographic ordering over constraints and costs, with the time constraint being more important than the energy constraint. The time taken to execute the plan should be less than 100 timesteps ($t < 100$) and the energy cost should be less than 15,000 units ($e < 15,000$). There is a conflict between the two constraints, in that shorter plans involve traversing steeper gradients and so require more energy to execute.

Figure 2 shows the plan returned by the ABC planner. The plan requires 63 timesteps and 14,736 units of energy to execute, i.e. it just satisfies the energy constraint. A straight line path would have given maximum slack on the first (time) constraint, but the planner has traded slack on the more important constraint to satisfy the second, less important, constraint (energy). In fact this plan has the greatest slack on the time constraint while still satisfying the energy constraint. Finding the plan requires the generation 29,107 nodes and 9,195 insertions into the OPEN list, and takes about about 40 seconds of CPU time on a Sun UltraSparc (300 MHz). As a rough comparison, with only the energy constraint (i.e., equivalent to A^* with energy as the cost function), the planner requires about 2.5 seconds of

---

[3]Note that the current implementation of the planner does not support optimisation constraints.

[4]We are grateful to Jeremy Baxter at DERA Malvern for providing the terrain model.

CPU time to find a plan, generates 6,110 nodes and performs 2,363 insertions into the OPEN list.

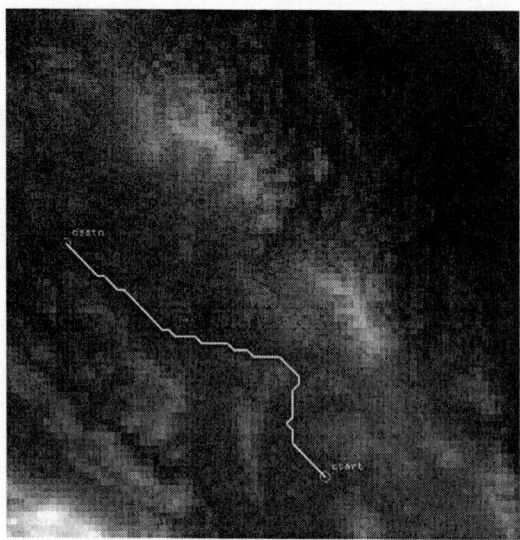

Figure 2: Planning with two constraints.

Unfortunately, it is not possible to compare the performance of ABC with A^* in other than trivial cases, e.g., when there is a single optimisation constraint, because we can't reduce the dominance and preference orderings used by ABC to the single ordering required by A^*. If, for example, we attempted to solve the above problem with A^* using a weighted sum cost function of the form $w_1 t + w_2 e$, we must ensure that the ratio of w_1 to w_2 is greater than the maximal value of

$$\frac{|e(p_a) - e(p_b)|}{|t(p_a) - t(p_b)|}$$

for any two plans p_a and p_b. But then a planner minimising $w_1 t + w_2 e$ will never trade off slack on the first constraint to satisfy the second one. The following example illustrates this point, and also explains why ABC must remember all non-dominated paths to each visited state.

Suppose that there are two plans, p_a and p_b to a point n, both satisfying the time and energy constraints, that is, $t(p_a) < T, e(p_a) < E,$ and $t(p_b) < T, e(p_b) < E$, where T and E are upper bounds on time and energy respectively. Suppose further that $t(p_a) < t(p_b)$ and $e(p_a) > e(p_b)$. Given that

$$\frac{w_1}{w_2} > \frac{e(p_a) - e(p_b)}{t(p_b) - t(p_a)},$$

we have

$$w_1 t(p_a) + w_2 e(p_a) < w_1 t(p_b) + w_2 e(p_b),$$

that is, p_a is cheaper than p_b.

However if it subsequently turns out that no completion of p_a through n will satisfy the energy constraint but there exists a completion of p_b which satisfies both constraints, we cannot backtrack to p_b since A^* retains only the (estimated) cheapest solution through n. A^* collapses both costs into a single value which is used to determine both the preference ordering and whether one plan dominates another. The resulting loss of completeness means we cannot use A^* to trade one constraint off against another (Logan 1997).

Another possible way of solving the example problem using A^* would be to use a partial order on the set of plans. Suppose we have some partial order on plans, which is at least the dominance ordering. Given two plans to the same point, p_a and p_b such that p_a satisfies the time and energy constraints, and p_b takes less time to execute but violates the energy constraint, then if p_a and p_b are comparable in this ordering, then p_a is preferred to p_b. If A^* uses this ordering to decide which plans to discard, then only p_a will be retained. However, if all extensions of p_a violate the first constraint, while there exists an extension of p_b which satisifies it, then the optimal solution will never be found. Conversely if A^* uses only the dominance ordering then the first solution found may not be optimal.

Related work

Our work has similarities with work in both optimisation (e.g., heuristic search for path finding problems and decision theoretic approaches to planning) and constraint satisfaction (e.g., planning as satisfiability). ABC is a strict generalisation of A^*: with a single optimisation constraint its behaviour is identical to A^*. However unlike heuristic search and decision theoretic approaches, we do not require that all the criteria be commensurable. The emphasis on non-dominated solutions has some similarities with Pareto optimisation which also avoids the problem of devising an appropriate set of weights for a composite cost function. However the motivation is different: the aim of Pareto optimisation is to return some or all of the non-dominated solutions for further consideration by a human decision maker. In contrast, when slack ordering is used, ABC will return the most preferred solution from the region of the Pareto surface bounded by the the constraints which are satisfied in the highest equivalence class. If an optimal solution is not required (i.e., a slack ordering is not used), the algorithm will return any solution which satisfies the constraints; such a solution will not necessarily be Pareto optimal.

ABC also has a number of features in common with boolean constraint satisfaction techniques. However, algorithms for boolean CSPs assume that: (a) all constraints are either true or false, (b) all constraints are equally important (i.e., the solution to an over-constrained CSP is not defined), and (c) the number of variables is known in advance. Considerable work has been done on partial constraint satisfaction problems (PCSP), e.g., (Freuder & Wallace 1992), where the aim is to find a solution satisfying the greatest number of most important constraints. Dubois et al. (Dubois, Fargier, & Prade 1996) introduce Fuzzy Constraint Satisfaction Problems (FCSP), a generalisation of boolean CSPs, which support prioritisation of constraints and preference among feasible solutions. In addition, FCSPs allow uncertainty in parameter values and ill-defined CSPs where the set of constraints which define the problem is not precisely known. However, in common with more conventional techniques, both PCSP and FCSP assume that the number of variables is known in advance. In many cases this assumption is violated, for example, in route planning the number of steps in the plan is not normally known in advance. Several authors, for example (Kautz & Selman 1996; Liatsos & Richards 1997), have described iterative techniques which can be applied when the number of variables is unknown. However, to date, these techniques have been applied to problems which are considerably smaller than the route planning problems we consider, which typically involve more than 100,000 states and plans of more than 500 steps. Moreover these techniques are incapable of handling prioritised or soft constraints.

Like A^*, ABC requires monotonic cost functions and good heuristics. However it has many of the advantages of PCSP/FCSPs and iterative techniques: it can handle prioritised and soft constraints (though not uncertain values or cases in which the set of constraints which define the problem is not precisely known) and problems where the number of variables is not known in advance.

Conclusions and further work

In this paper, we have presented a new approach to formulating and solving multi-criterion search problems with incommensurable criteria.

We have argued that it is often difficult or impossible to formulate many real world problems in terms of minimising a single weighted sum cost function. By using an ordered set of prioritised soft constraints to represent the requirements on the solution we avoid the difficulties of formulating an appropriate set of weights for a composite cost function. Constraints provide a means of more clearly specifying problem-solving tasks and more precisely evaluating the resulting solutions: a solution can be characterised as satisfying some constraints (to a greater or lesser degree) and only partially satisfying or not satisfying others.

We have described a new search algorithm, A^* with bounded costs, which searches for a solution which best satisfies a set of prioritised soft constraints, and shown that for an important class of constraints the algorithm is complete and optimal. The utility of our approach and the feasibility of the ABC algorithm has been illustrated by an implemented route planner which is capable of planning routes in complex terrains satisfying a variety of constraints.

The present work is the first step in the development of a hybrid approach to search with prioritised soft constraints. It raises many new issues related to preference orderings over solutions ('slack ordering') and the relevance of different constraint orderings for different kinds of problems. More work is also necessary to characterise the performance implications of ABC relative to A^*. However, we believe that the increase in flexibility of our approach outweighs the increase in computational cost associated with ABC.

Acknowledgements

We wish to thank Aaron Sloman and the members of the Cognition and Affect and EEBIC (Evolutionary and Emergent Behaviour Intelligence and Computation) groups at the School of Computer Science, University of Birmingham for useful discussions and comments. This research is partially supported by a grant from the Defence Evaluation and Research Agency (DERA Malvern).

References

Campbell, C.; Hull, R.; Root, E.; and Jackson, L. 1995. Route planning in CCTT. In *Proceedings of the Fifth Conference on Computer Generated Forces and Behavioural Representation*, 233–244. Institute for Simulation and Training.

Dubois, D.; Fargier, H.; and Prade, H. 1996. Possibility theory in constraint satisfaction problems: Handling priority, preference and uncertainty. *Applied Intelligence* 6:287–309.

Freuder, E. C., and Wallace, R. J. 1992. Partial constraint satisfaction. *Artificial Intelligence* 58:21–70.

Hart, P. E.; Nilsson, N. J.; and Raphael, B. 1968. A formal basis for the heuristic determination of minimum cost paths. *IEEE Transactions on Systems Science and Cybernetics* SSC–4(2):100–107.

Kautz, H., and Selman, B. 1996. Pushing the envelope: Planning, propositional logic, and stochastic search. In *Proceedings of the Thirteenth National Conference on Artificial Intelligence, AAAI-96*, 1194–1201. AAAI Press/MIT Press.

Liatsos, V., and Richards, B. 1997. Least commitment—an optimal planning strategy. In *Proceedings of the 16th Workshop of the UK Planning and Scheduling Special Interest Group*, 119–133. University of Durham.

Logan, B., and Alechina, N. 1998. A^* with bounded costs. Technical Report CSRP-98-09, School of Computer Science, University of Birmingham.

Logan, B. 1997. Route planning with ordered constraints. In *Proceedings of the 16th Workshop of the UK Planning and Scheduling Special Interest Group*, 133–144. University of Durham.

Pearl, J. 1982. A^*_ϵ — an algorithm using search effort estimates. *IEEE Transactions on Pattern Analysis and Machine Intelligence* 4(4):392–399.

Stochastic Node Caching for Memory-bounded Search

Teruhisa Miura and **Toru Ishida**

Department of Social Informatics, Kyoto University,
Kyoto 606-8501, Japan
{ miura, ishida }@kuis.kyoto-u.ac.jp

Abstract

Linear-space search algorithms such as IDA* (Iterative Deepening A*) cache only those nodes on the current search path, but may revisit the same node again and again. This causes IDA* to take an impractically long time to find a solution. In this paper, we propose a simple and effective algorithm called *Stochastic Node Caching* (SNC) for reducing the number of revisits. SNC caches a node with the best estimate, which is currently known of the minimum estimated cost from the node to the goal node. Unlike previous related research such as MREC, SNC caches nodes selectively, based on a fixed probability. We demonstrate that SNC can effectively reduce the number of revisits compared to MREC, especially when the state-space forms a lattice.

Introduction

Linear-space search algorithms such as IDA* (Korf 1985) perform a series of depth-first search iterations, gradually extending the search depth. Since they cache only nodes on the current search path, the amount of memory required by them is only linear to the depth of the current search path. By the virtue of small memory requirement, IDA* can solve some problems that A* cannot. Nevertheless, there are problems that neither A* and IDA* can solve; A* runs out of memory and IDA* takes an impractically long time as it cannot avoid revisiting the same node.

There have been several efforts to deal with such problems, by using a limited amount of memory to store information needed to avoid revisits. Among such efforts, MREC(Sen & Bagchi 1989) is a generalization of IDA* that uses a limited amount of memory to cache generated nodes. It caches as many nodes as possible, until the memory limit is reached; at that point, MREC starts iterative deepening in the same manner as IDA* from the cached nodes. Unfortunately, the efficiency of MREC's memory usage is sometimes poor, since the nodes generated and cached at the beginning of search are not necessarily the ones that are visited most.

In this paper, we propose a new mechanism called *Stochastic Node Caching* (SNC) that can effectively reduce the number of revisits. In contrast to MREC which caches

---

Copyright ©1998, American Association for Artificial Intelligence (www.aaai.org). All rights reserved.

nodes greedily, SNC caches nodes *selectively*. Whenever it expands a node, it decides whether to keep the node in memory by flipping a (possibly biased) coin. This selective caching allows SNC to store, with high probability, only nodes that are visited most frequently.

To evaluate the power of SNC, we apply MREC and SNC to the multiple sequence alignment problem. We show that, compared with MREC, SNC can reduce effectively the total number of revisits in the multiple sequence alignment problem wherein the state-space forms a lattice.

Previous Work

Before going into the details of SNC, we describe IDA* and MREC algorithms, upon which SNC is based. We use the following notations in this section.

n_s	Start node.
n_i	Successor of node n.
M	Maximum number of cached nodes.
N	Current number of cached nodes.
$c(n, n_i)$	Cost from node n to node n_i.
$g(n)$	Cost from the start node n_s to node n along the current search path.
$h(n)$	Estimated cost from node n to the goal node. A value of the estimate function for node n if not cached, and a value kept in memory for node n if cached.
$f(n)$	Estimated cost from the start node n_s through node n to the goal node.
θ	Global variable. θ is the node cutoff threshold for the current iteration.
θ'	Global variable. θ' is the node cutoff threshold for the next iteration.

IDA* IDA* performs a series of depth-first search iterations, increasing the threshold value θ. θ is used to prune branches during each iteration. For the next iteration, the value is increased to the minimum cost of all nodes that were generated but not expanded in the last iteration. Therefore, IDA* can eventually find the minimum cost path to a goal node. The IDA* algorithm is described as follows.

SEARCH (n_s)
  $\theta := h(n_s)$
  $\theta' := \infty$
  repeat until a goal node is found
    IDA*$(n_s, 0)$
    $\theta := \theta'$
    $\theta' := \infty$
  end repeat

IDA*$(n, g(n))$
  for each successor n_i of n **do**
    $f(n_i) := g(n) + c(n, n_i) + h(n_i)$
    if n_i is a goal node and $f(n_i) \leq \theta$ **then stop**
    if $f(n_i) \leq \theta$ **then**
      IDA*$(n_i, g(n) + c(n, n_i))$
    else if $f(n_i) < \theta'$ **then** $\theta' := f(n_i)$
    end if
  end do

MREC MREC is a generalization of IDA* that uses a limited memory pool for caching nodes. Let M be the number of nodes that can be stored in the pool. When $M = 0$, MREC is identical to IDA*.

The two major differences between MREC and IDA* are as follows.

1. *Cached nodes:*
   MREC caches every node n_i with $h(n_i)$ when node n is expanded. IDA* caches only nodes on the current search path.

2. *Selection of a node to be expanded:*
   MREC memorizes $h(n_i)$ with n_i and uses it for selecting a node to be expanded. MREC expands node n_i if $f(n_i) = g(n) + c(n, n_i) + h(n_i)$ is less than the threshold value θ. IDA* expands nodes from left to right.

The estimated cost $h(n)$, which is memorized with node n, is used not to revisit the descendants of node n. After searching the descendants of node n, MREC updates $h(n)$ to $\min_i\{c(n, n_i) + h(n_i)\}$. Thus, $h(n)$ is equal to the maximum lower bound of estimated costs from node n to the goal node. After the number of cached nodes N reaches M, MREC performs iterative deepening in the manner identical to IDA* from the frontier nodes.

In this paper, however, we use a modified version of MREC, where the algorithm caches only expanded nodes, not generated ones.

The algorithm is as follows.

SEARCH (n_s)
  $\theta := h(n_s)$
  $\theta' := \infty$
  repeat until a goal node is found
    MREC$(n_s, 0)$
    $\theta := \theta'$
    $\theta' := \infty$
  end repeat

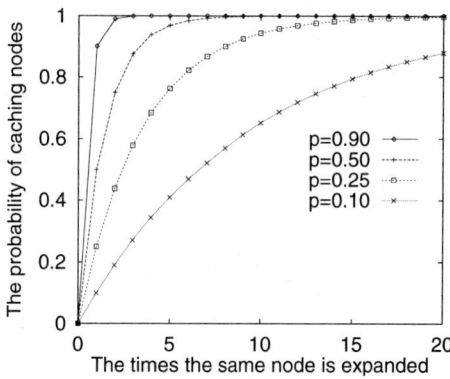

Figure 1: The probability of a node being cached

MREC$(n, g(n))$
  cutoff := ∞
  if $N < M$ **then** cache n with $h(n)$
  for each successor n_i of n **do**
    $f(n_i) := g(n) + c(n, n_i) + h(n_i)$
    if n_i is a goal node and $f(n_i) \leq \theta$ **then stop**
    if $f(n_i) \leq \theta$ **then**
      MREC$(n_i, g(n) + c(n, n_i))$
    else if $f(n_i) < \theta'$ **then** $\theta' := f(n_i)$
    end if
    if $h(n_i) + c(n, n_i) < $ *cutoff* **then**
      cutoff := $h(n_i) + c(n, n_i)$
    end if
  end if
  $h(n) := $ *cutoff*

Stochastic Node Caching

The aim of SNC is to efficiently reduce the number of revisits. Just like MREC, SNC has the memory that can store up to M nodes. It takes an additional parameter p, which is the probability of a node being cached every time it is expanded. It follows that the overall probability of a node being stored after it is expanded t times is $1 - (1 - p)^t$; the more frequently the same node is expanded, the higher the probability of it being cached becomes. Figure 1 shows the probability of a node being cached versus the number of times the node is expanded for various values of p. SNC is identical to IDA* and MREC when $p = 0$ and $p = 1$, respectively.

Let RANDOM be a function that returns a real number from zero to one at random. The SNC algorithms is as follows.

SEARCH (n_s)
  $\theta := h(n_s)$
  $\theta' := \infty$
  repeat until a goal node is found
    SNC$(n_s, 0)$
    $\theta := \theta'$
    $\theta' := \infty$
  end repeat

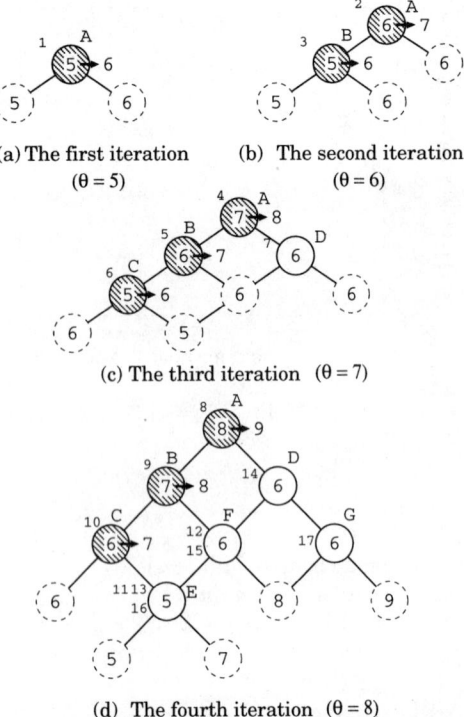

(a) The first iteration ($\theta = 5$)
(b) The second iteration ($\theta = 6$)
(c) The third iteration ($\theta = 7$)
(d) The fourth iteration ($\theta = 8$)

Figure 2: Search behavior of MREC

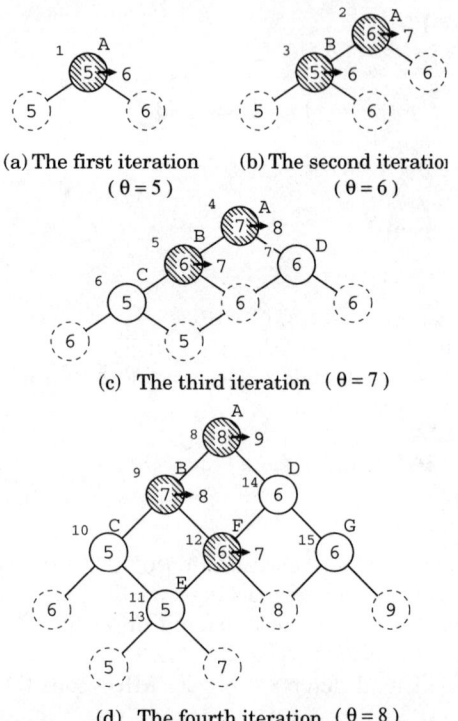

(a) The first iteration ($\theta = 5$)
(b) The second iteration ($\theta = 6$)
(c) The third iteration ($\theta = 7$)
(d) The fourth iteration ($\theta = 8$)

Figure 3: Search behavior of SNC

```
SNC(n, g(n))
  cutoff := ∞
  if N < M and RAND ≤ p then
    cache n with h(n)
  end if
  for each successor n_i of n do
    f(n_i) := g(n) + c(n, n_i) + h(n_i)
    if n_i is a goal node and f(n_i) ≤ θ then stop
    if f(n_i) ≤ θ then
      SNC(n_i, g(n) + c(n, n_i))
    else if f(n_i) < θ' then θ' := f(n_i)
    end if
    if h(n_i) + c(n, n_i) < cutoff then
      cutoff := h(n_i) + c(n, n_i)
    end if
  end if
  h(n) := cutoff
```

The difference between SNC and MREC is as follows.

- *Selection of a node to be cached:*
  MREC always caches as many expanded nodes as possible, while SNC stochastically caches expanded nodes.

This difference in the two algorithms results in a difference in the total number of visits. Figures 2 and 3 illustrate the search behaviors of the two algorithms when $M = 3$. In these examples, we assume unit cost for each edge. The shaded circles represent the cached node. The hollow circles represent the expanded nodes and the dashed circles represent the generated but not expanded nodes. The digits in the circles represent $h(n)$ at the current iteration. The digits on the right side of the arrow represent $h(n)$ after searching the descendants of node n. The digits on the left side of the circle represent the order of visiting a node.

In Figure 2(a),(b) and (c), MREC caches the first three nodes (A, B and C) in order of their expansion. On the other hand, SNC is less likely to cache node C as shown in Figure 3(c), because of its stochastic behavior. In this case, SNC is more likely to cache node F, which is visited more often than node C. By caching node F, SNC can avoid visiting descendants of node F afterwards. In Figure 2(d), for example, MREC visits node E and F, after visiting node D. On the other hand, SNC does not visit node E and F, as shown Figure 3(d).

Because of the stochastic caching, SNC does not cache always a node with its ancestors unlike MREC. SNC's search frontier is a jumbled collection of nodes in the search space.

Evaluation

Example Problems

We applied the MREC and SNC algorithms to the *Multiple sequence alignment* problem. This problem is of extracting the common features among several sequences. Multiple sequence alignment is used in various ways for biological sequence analysis. Protein sequences that have a similar biological function tend to share a common pattern. The alignment for sequences of such proteins is useful for predicting the function or the three-dimensional structure of a protein. If the sequence of the protein which has an unknown function is similar to an alignment, the protein is likely to have the same function and three-dimensional structure as proteins with the same sequence alignment. It is important to align as many sequences as possible, since it will greatly improve the reliability of the alignment. (Boguski *et al.* 1992).

A biological sequence is composed of alphabetic characters representing its constituents. For example, the protein sequence consists of 20 amino acids. The following figure shows a part of the aligned sequences.

```
Hal  VNKMDLVD--YGESEYKQVVEEV-KDLLTQVRFDSENAK
Met  VNKMDTVN--FSEADYNELKKMIGDQLLKMIGFNPEQIN
Tha  INKMDATSPPYSEKRYNEVKADA-EKLLRSIGFK-D-IS
Thc  VNKMDMVN--YDEKKFKAVAEQV-KKLLMMLGYK-N-FP
Sul  INKMDLADTPYDEKRFKEIVDTV-SKFMKSFGFDMNKVK
Ent  VNKMDAIQ--YKQERYEEIKKEI-SAFLKKTGYNPDKIP
Pla  VNKMDTVK--YSEDRYEEIKKEV-KDYLKKVGYQADKVD
```

Hyphens, or gaps, are inserted into the sequences so that the same character occupy the same column.

We formulate the multiple sequence alignment problem as a search problem (Carrillo & Lipman 1988; Ikeda & Imai 1994). The following notations are used.

d	Number of sequences to be aligned.
S_k	k-th sequence.
$L(S_1, \ldots, S_d)$	State-space which is a d-dimensional lattice. k-th axis corresponds to S_k. This lattice is the Cartesian product of the d sequences.
$L(S_i, S_j)$	Two dimensional lattice which is the projection of $L(S_1, \ldots, S_d)$ on the plane determined by S_i and S_j.
γ	Path in $L(S_1, \ldots, S_d)$
γ_{ij}	Path in $L(S_i, S_j)$. It is the projection of γ on $L(S_i, S_j)$.
s	The start node.
t	The goal node.
t_{ij}	Node in $L(S_i, S_j)$. It is the projection of the goal node t on $L(S_i, S_j)$.
u, v	Node in $L(S_1, \ldots, S_d)$.
u_{ij}	Node in $L(S_i, S_j)$. It is the projection of u on $L(S_i, S_j)$.
$c(u, v)$	Cost of the edge (u, v) in $L(S_1, \ldots, S_d)$.
$c(u_{ij}, v_{ij})$	Cost of the edge (u_{ij}, v_{ij}) which is the projection of (u, v) on $L(S_i, S_j)$.
$m(\gamma)$	Cost of γ.
$m(\gamma_{ij})$	Cost of γ_{ij}.
$h^*_{ij}(v_{ij})$	Cost of the shortest path from v_{ij} to the goal node t_{ij} in $L(S_i, S_j)$.

We can define the multiple sequence alignment problem as the problem of finding the shortest path from the start node to the goal node in the d-dimensional lattice $L(S_1, S_2, \ldots, S_d)$. The cost of the path in the d-dimensional lattice is defined as follows.

$$m(\gamma) = \sum_{1 \leq i \leq j \leq d} m(\gamma_{ij}).$$

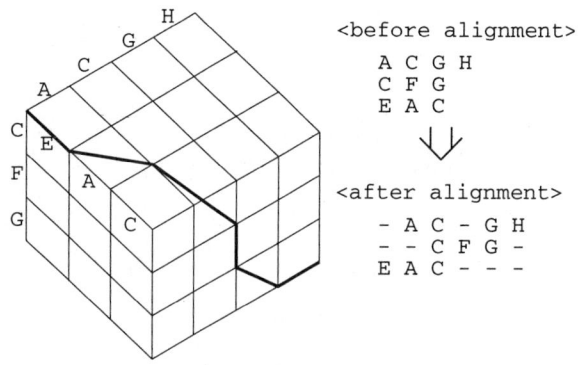

Figure 4: State-space representation

The cost of the edge in this lattice is defined as follows.

$$c(u, v) = \sum_{1 \leq i \leq j \leq d} c(u_{ij}, v_{ij}),$$

where the cost of the edge $c(u_{ij}, v_{ij})$ is given by the PAM-250 matrix(Dayhoff, Schwartz, & Orcutt 1978) which represents the mutation distance between two amino acids or characters. The number of operators is usually $2^d - 1$, because a general node on the lattice $L(S_1, \ldots, S_d)$ has $2^d - 1$ descendant nodes.

Figure 4 depicts the state-space representation of the multiple sequence alignment problem of three sequences $S_1 = $ ACGH, $S_2 = $ CFG and $S_3 = $ EAC. In this 3-dimensional lattice, the top left-hand corner is the start node and the bottom right-hand corner is the goal node. A path from the start node to the goal node determines an alignment of the three sequences; for example, the path drawn with bold line in Figure 4 corresponds to the following alignment.

```
S₁  -AC-GH
S₂  --CFG-
S₃  EAC---
```

In this example, the cost of the path is calculated by

$$\begin{aligned} m(\gamma) &= m(\gamma_{12}) + m(\gamma_{13}) + m(\gamma_{23}) \\ &= c(-,-) + c(\text{A},-) + c(\text{C},\text{C}) + c(-,\text{F}) \\ &\quad + c(\text{G},\text{G}) + c(\text{H},-) + \cdots. \end{aligned}$$

Using this formulation, Ikeda *et al.* (Ikeda & Imai 1994) successfully applied the A* algorithm to the multiple sequence alignment problem. Though it could align up to seven sequences, there is little or no hope of it solving more than seven sequences by A* because of its large memory requirement. Therefore, we first applied the linear-space search algorithm IDA* to this problem. We used the same cost function(the PAM-250 matrix and the gap cost of 8) and the same seven sequences[1] as in Ikeda *et al*'s experiments.

---

[1] These are elongation factor TU(EF-TU) of Haloarcula marismortui and Methanococcus vannielii, and elongation factor 1α(EF-1α) of Thermoplasma acidophilum, Thermococcus celer, Sulfolobus acidocaldarius, Entamoeba histolytica and Plasmodium falciparum.

Table 1: The number of visited nodes: protein sequence alignment problem

M	MREC	SNC		
		$p = 0.1$	$p = 0.01$	$p = 0.001$
5000	1,932,448,612	1,588,688,060(0.82)	1,418,349,564(0.73)	1,856,357,576(0.96)
2000	12,099,281,720	10,755,536,884(0.89)	5,894,480,820(0.49)	4,972,223,330(0.41)
1000	34,684,660,730	32,337,946,952(0.93)	20,402,428,944(0.59)	12,683,118,881(0.37)

The average sequence length is 430. These sequences are elongation factors from various species, obtained from the Genbank database [2]. The heuristic estimate function in Ikeda et al's experiment is constructed as

$$h(v) = \sum_{1 \le i \le j \le d} h^*_{ij}(v_{ij}),$$

where h^*_{ij} is calculated by the dynamic programming for each pair of S_i and S_j before the search algorithm is applied.

After several trials, we found that IDA* could align only four sequences in our computing environment, owing to the large number of revisits. Thus, this is not a toy problem for either A* or IDA*.

Results

We applied the two algorithms MREC and SNC to the multiple sequence alignment problem. We measured their performance by the cumulative number of visited nodes, to which the running time of the algorithms is proportional.

As mentioned before, we used a modified version of MREC that caches expanded nodes, not generated ones. The reason for this modification is to ensure fair comparison with SNC; in the problem like multiple sequence alignment in which branching factor is large and the edge costs have many significant digits, the original MREC caches a lot of nodes that will never be visited. In addition, since we evaluate the performance with respect to the number of visits, not the number of expansions, this modification does not work disadvantageously for MREC; it only improves the efficiency of MREC's memory usage.

The following are observed.

Table 1 shows the result of aligning seven protein sequences. The figure in a parenthesis shows the ratio of SNC value for MREC's corresponding value. In this case, each node has $2^7 - 1$ predecessors and successors. Because there is an enormous number of paths through the same node, linear-space search visits the same node again and again. These results show that SNC reduces the number of revisits effectively compared to MREC. The advantage of SNC over MREC increases as the cache size M decreases. When $M = 1000$ and $p = 0.001$, SNC reduces the number of visits by 63% compared to MREC. In other words, SNC can solve this problem three times faster than MREC.

The major results obtained from the above experiments are as follows.

[2]http://www.genome.ad.jp

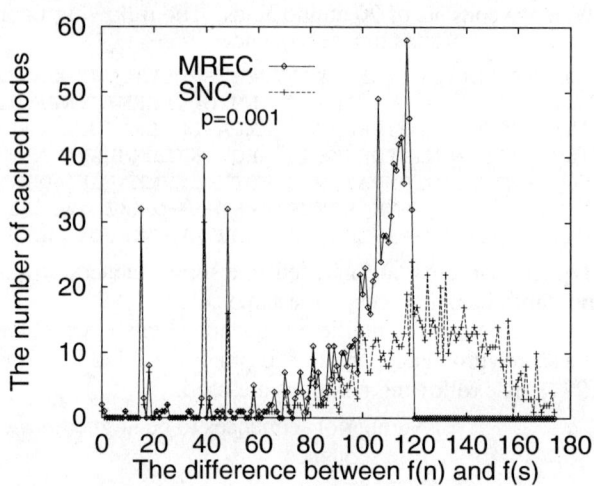

Figure 5: The locations of cached nodes: Protein sequence alignment ($M = 1000$)

1. *SNC can cache nodes that are far from the root node.*
   Figure 5 shows the location of the cached nodes in the search space. The x-axis shows the difference between the initial estimated cost for node n and that for the start node, i.e., $f(n) - f(s)$. The y-axis shows the number of cached nodes of which $f(n) - f(s)$ value correspond to x-value. The difference between the initial estimate cost $f(s)$ for the start node and the optimal cost $f^*(t)$ to the goal node is 244 in this problem. The value of $f(n) - f(s)$ is 0 and 244 when n is the start and the goal node, respectively. Both algorithms expand nodes in ascending order of initial estimated cost $f(n)$. As shown in Figure 5, SNC can cache nodes that are far from the root node. MREC caches nodes in the order of node expansion. On the other hand, SNC caches only nodes that are visited for many times. As a result, SNC can avoid to revisit such nodes that are visited for many times.

2. *The probability of node caching determines the performance of SNC.*
   When the probability of node caching is low, SNC can cache nodes which are located far from the start node. Thus, SNC may reduce revisits by the effect of caching such nodes. Until MREC caches the maximum number of nodes, however, SNC visits more nodes and cannot outperform MREC, because SNC only caches a part of

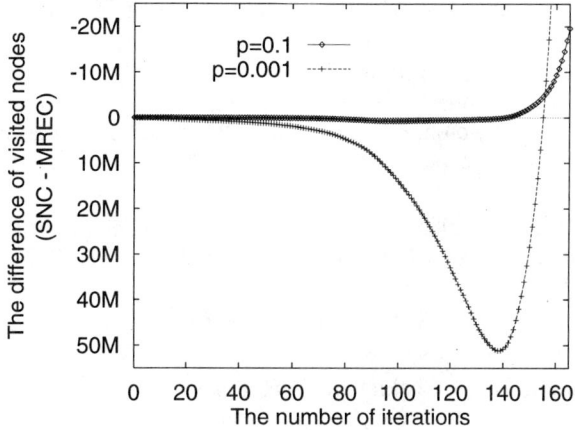

Figure 6: The difference of visited nodes (SNC − MREC) Protein sequence alignment($M = 1000$)

nodes cached by MREC. This tradeoff affects the overall performance of SNC. In the protein sequence alignment problem($M = 1000$), MREC caches M nodes at the 89th iterations, and then MREC performs IDA* for descendants of the cached frontier nodes. Most of nodes cached by SNC after that time are not cached by MREC. Figure 6 shows the difference in the numbers of nodes visited by SNC and MREC. In general, the difference increases until some point of time, then decreases. Finally, the number of nodes visited by SNC becomes less than that by MREC.

3. *SNC improves the search efficiency for such a problem where the number of revisits is enormous using linear-space search algorithms*

   In the seven sequence alignment problem, each node has $2^7 - 1$ successors. Furthermore, the value of $f(n) - f(s)$ varies between 0 to 244. Since linear-space search algorithms perform depth-first search for each value of $f(n)$, the number of iterations is large in the alignment problem. As a result, on average, IDA* visits each node at least 40,000 times for the seven sequence alignment problem.

   For such problems, SNC can reduce the number of revisits efficiently by caching nodes selectively. On the other hand, SNC may be less effective in the case where linear-space search does not visit the same node many times.

Related Work

There has been a lot of work on memory-bounded search. The work can be classified as follows.

1. Algorithms based on A* but use the limited-memory (MA*).

2. Algorithms that reduce revisits in the iterative deepening.

   (a) Globally control the node expansion (RBFS, Tayler and Korf's method).

   (b) Control the number of iterations in IDA* (IDA*_CR, DFS*).

   (c) Cache nodes and utilize them to avoid revisits (MREC, SNC).

The mechanism of SNC can be applied to algorithms based on the iterative deepening, that is, all of the classes 2(a),(b) and (c). We briefly refer to other memory-bounded search algorithms.

MA* (Chakrabarti *et al.* 1989)

The MA* algorithm dynamically caches the best nodes that were generated within memory constraints. MA* maintains the two sets OPEN and CLOSED nodes, just as A*. Until MA* caches the maximum number of nodes, it behaves like A*. When the number of cached nodes reaches the limit, MA* begins to prune the node with the highest cost in the OPEN set.

Though it surpasses MREC in the light of efficient usage of memory, it is reported that the overhead of maintaining these two sets are prohibitively expensive compared to the algorithms based on iterative deepening(Korf 1993).

RBFS (Korf 1993)

Korf proposed a linear-space best-first search algorithm, called Recursive Best-First Search. This algorithm explores nodes in a best-first order and expands fewer nodes than IDA* with a nondecreasing cost function. RBFS can be combined with MREC. The mechanism of SNC is also compatible with RBFS.

Tayler and Korf's method (Taylor & Korf 1993)

Tayler and Korf developed a method using a finite-state machine for pruning duplicate nodes. Unlike MREC and SNC, this method does not cache nodes, but keeps the structure of the state-space as the finite-state machine. At first, the method learns the finite-state machine. The learning phase consists of two steps. First, a small breadth-first search in the state-space is performed and a set of operator strings that produce duplicate nodes is detected. The operator strings represent portions of node generation paths. It then constructs the finite-state machine that recognizes such operator strings. This method prunes duplicate nodes by its finite-state machine.

This method is effective for problems in which a string of operators has the same cost at any node, such as 15-puzzle. In the space of the multiple sequence alignment problems, the edge costs have many significant digits, since it depends on which characters correspond to its edge. Because of this, the same string of operators does not always take the same value. Consequently, this method may not be effective for problems such as the multiple sequence alignment, though SNC mechanism can be incorporated in this method as well.

IDA*_CR (Sarkar *et al.* 1991)

IDA*_CR tries to decrease revisits by reducing the number of iterations of IDA*. Each iteration of IDA*_CR is depth-first branch-and-bound search, not depth-first search as in IDA*. At first, IDA*_CR performs an iteration with the initial estimate for the start node, $f(s)$, as the upper bound for cutoff. Then IDA*_CR performs iterations, as increasing the upper bound for cutoff. By introducing the idea of SNC, IDA*_CR can reduce revisits in each iteration.

DFS* (Vempaty, Kumar, & Korf 1991)

Unlike IDA*_CR, DFS* performs depth-first search iterations. DFS* sets the threshold of the next iteration to the value larger than the minimum cost of all nodes which were generated but not expanded on the last iteration. When the solution is found, DFS* performs the depth-first branch and bound with the cost of this solution as its initial upper bound to find the optimal solution. By introducing the idea of SNC, DFS* can also reduce revisits in each iteration.

Conclusions

We have proposed *Stochastic Node Caching* (SNC) to reduce the number of node revisits, the most serious disadvantage of linear-space search. It caches nodes stochastically, not deterministically. To demonstrate the effectiveness of this method, we applied SNC and MREC to the multiple sequence alignment problem. We found that SNC can effectively reduce the total number of node visits compared to MREC. The greatest effects are obtained in the case where the state-space includes many paths to the same node (especially a lattice), and in the case where linear-space search performs a large number of iterations of depth-first search. For the multiple sequence alignment problem, for example, SNC visits only one-third the number of nodes visited by MREC.

We may use frequency of visits explicitly as part of the SNC scheme. SNC may be revised in order to swap out cached nodes by frequency. This idea is similar to MA*. The overhead of maintaining cached nodes by MA* seems to be expensive in the multiple sequence alignment problem too. We will have to apply approximate techniques to the SNC scheme. We will evaluate and compare SNC with various selective caching techniques in our future research.

Acknowledgments

We would like to thank Yasuhiko Kitamura, Hideyuki Nakanishi, and Masashi Shimbo for comments that greatly improved this paper.

References

Boguski, M. S.; Caballero, L.; Eisenberg, D.; Elliston, K.; Luthy, R.; Rice, P. M.; and States, D. J. 1992. *Sequence Analysis Primer*. UWBC Biotechnical Resource Series. Oxford University Press.

Carrillo, H., and Lipman, D. 1988. The multiple sequence alignment problem in biology. *SIAM Journal Applied Mathematics* 48:1073–1082.

Chakrabarti, P. P.; Ghose, S.; Acharya, A.; and de Sarkar, S. C. 1989. Heuristic search in restricted memory. *Artificial Intelligence* 41:197–221.

Dayhoff, M. O.; Schwartz, R. M.; and Orcutt, B. C. 1978. *Atlas of protein sequence and structure*, volume 5. Washington DC: National Biomedical Research Foundation. 345–352.

Ikeda, T., and Imai, H. 1994. Fast A* algorithms for multiple sequence alignment. In Miyano, S.; Akutsu, T.; Imai, H.; Gotoh, O.; and Takagi, T., eds., *Proceedings of Genome Informatics Workshop 1994*, 90–99. Tokyo, Japan: Universal Academy Press.

Korf, R. E. 1985. Depth-first iterative-deepening: An optimal admissible tree search. *Artificial Intelligence* 27:97–109.

Korf, R. E. 1993. Linear-space best-first search. *Artificial Intelligence* 62:41–78.

Sarkar, U. K.; Chakrabarti, P. P.; Ghose, S.; and Sarkar, S. C. D. 1991. Reducing reexpansions in iterative-deepening search by controlling cutoff bounds. *Artificial Intelligence* 50:207–221.

Sen, A. K., and Bagchi, A. 1989. Fast recursive formulations for best-first search that allow controlled use of memory. In *Proceedings of the Eleventh International Joint Conference on Artificial Intelligence*, 297–302.

Taylor, L. A., and Korf, R. E. 1993. Pruning duplicate nodes in depth-first search. In *Proceedings of the eleventh National Conference on Artificial Intelligence (AAAI-93)*, 756–761.

Vempaty, N. R.; Kumar, V.; and Korf, R. E. 1991. Depth-first vs best-first search. In *Proceedings of the ninth National Conference on Artificial Intelligence (AAAI-91)*, 434–440.

A Feature-based Learning Method for Theorem Proving

Matthias Fuchs
Automated Reasoning Project
Australian National University
Canberra ACT 0200, Australia
Matthias.Fuchs@anu.edu.au

Abstract

Automated reasoning or theorem proving essentially amounts to solving search problems. Despite significant progress in recent years theorem provers still have many shortcomings. The use of machine-learning techniques is acknowledged as promising, but difficult to apply in the area of theorem proving. We propose here to learn search-guiding heuristics by employing features in a simple, yet effective manner. Features are used to adapt a heuristic to a solved source problem. The adapted heuristic can then be utilized profitably for solving related target problems. Experiments have demonstrated that the approach not only allows for significant speed-ups, but also makes it possible to prove problems that were out of reach before.

Introduction

Theorem proving in general confronts us with undecidable problems. Such problems necessitate a search in infinite search spaces. Automated theorem provers (ATPs) traverse these spaces guided by heuristics in order to find proofs. Advanced implementation techniques and (problem-specific) search-guiding heuristics account for the impressive performance of state-of-the-art ATPs. However, ATPs can hardly rival a mathematician when it comes to proving "challenging" theorems. Unlike a mathematician, current state-of-the-art ATPs lack the ability to learn and hence tackle each problem as a complete novice. Everything they "know" about a problem (domain) has essentially been hard-coded into the heuristics. But learning is a key element in human problem-solving. Hence, the use of machine-learning (ML) techniques is advisable.

Integrating ML techniques with an ATP is a difficult task. In many areas of AI the use of ML is thriving because the assumption that *"small changes of the problem specification cause small changes of the solution"* is often satisfied. In theorem proving, however, a petty-looking variation of a problem can alter its solution (i.e., proof) tremendously. Therefore,

[0]Copyright © 1998, American Association for Artificial Intelligence (www.aaai.org). All rights reserved.

learning methods based on *analogous proof transformation* (Brock, Cooper, & Pierce 1988; Bundy 1988; Kolbe & Walther 1994; Melis 1995) in general have severe difficulties. In particular failures of the transformation process, so to speak "breakdowns in analogy", necessitate sophisticated *recovery mechanisms* (Brock, Cooper, & Pierce 1988) or *patching strategies* (Kolbe & Walther 1995). Such extensions, however, cannot reduce the fundamental difficulties of analogous proof transformation. Therefore, it is mostly applied to inductive theorem proving where the inherent proof structures provide a suitable platform.

An alternative and promising approach is to learn by integrating acquired knowledge into the search-guiding heuristics (Suttner & Ertel 1990; Fuchs 1995; Denzinger & Schulz 1996; Fuchs 1997a). That is, the ATP still conducts a search, but the search is guided by a *learned* heuristic which, in some way, exploits experiences made in previous successful runs of the ATP.

This approach has several advantages. First of all, a learned heuristic can be used like any other heuristic. Hence, there is no need for creating new systems or even for major modifications of existing ones if learned heuristics are employed. Furthermore, the approach is able to handle vague knowledge much better than analogy-based methods can. This ability is crucial for learning in connection with theorem proving. It originates from an abstract representation of knowledge and the fact that a search is conducted (as opposed to a possibly deterministic transformation process).

In this paper we present a method for learning heuristics that centers on the use of *features*. Each feature represents a syntactic property of facts. Using this abstract level of representation, learning amounts to detecting deviations w.r.t. previous experience and thus to predict usefulness (of a fact) depending on the degree of deviation. Our method will be described and employed in the context of *saturation-based* ATPs.

Saturation-based Theorem Proving

Theorem provers can attempt to accomplish a task in various ways. We focus here on so-called *saturation-based* theorem provers. This type of theorem proving is very common and is employed by provers based on the resolution method (e.g., (Chang & Lee 1973)) or the Knuth-Bendix completion procedure (e.g., (Bachmair, Dershowitz, & Plaisted 1989)). The principle working method of such a prover is to infer *facts* (e.g., first-order clauses or equations) by applying given rules of inference, starting with a given set Ax of *axioms*, until the *goal* λ_G (the theorem to be proved) can be shown to be a logical consequence of Ax. A proof problem $\mathcal{A}$ is hence specified by $\mathcal{A} = (Ax, \lambda_G)$.

The prover maintains two sets of facts, the set F^A of *active facts* and the set F^P of *passive* or *potential facts*. In the beginning, $F^A = \emptyset$ and $F^P = Ax$. In the *selection* or *activation step* a fact $\lambda \in F^P$ is selected, removed from F^P, and put into F^A unless there is a fact $\lambda' \in F^A$ that subsumes λ (in symbols $\lambda' \triangleleft \lambda$) in which case λ is simply discarded. Note that $\lambda \equiv \lambda'$ (syntactic identity modulo renaming variables) implies $\lambda' \triangleleft \lambda$ (and of course $\lambda \triangleleft \lambda'$). If λ is indeed activated (put into F^A), all (finitely many) inferences involving λ are applied exhaustively, and inferred facts are added to F^P. Facts in F^P are known to be inferable from F^A, but are not considered to be actually inferred.

The activation step is the only inherently indeterministic step in the proof procedure just sketched. Commonly, a heuristic $\mathcal{H}$ is employed to resolve the indeterminism at the (inevitable) expense of introducing search. $\mathcal{H}$ associates a natural number $\mathcal{H}(\lambda) \in \mathbb{N}$ (a *weight*) with each $\lambda \in F^P$. The fact with the smallest weight $\mathcal{H}(\lambda)$ is next in line for activation. Ties are usually broken in compliance with the FIFO strategy.

The search-guiding heuristic $\mathcal{H}$ is pivotal for efficiency. The quality of $\mathcal{H}$ can be measured in terms of redundant search effort. The sequence $\mathcal{S} \equiv \lambda_1; \ldots; \lambda_n$ of facts activated by $\mathcal{H}$ describes the search behavior of $\mathcal{H}$. Assuming that such a *search protocol* $\mathcal{S}$ represents a successful search, the last fact λ_n of $\mathcal{S}$ concluded the proof. By tracing back the application of inference rules starting with λ_n we can identify all those facts that actually contributed to concluding the proof. These facts constitute the set P of *positive facts*. The remaining facts constitute the set N of *negative facts* and represent redundant search effort. P and N together represent the proof experience which methods for learning heuristics can make use of.

Basics of Learning Heuristics

Most methods for learning heuristics attempt to learn from one *source problem* $\mathcal{A}_S$ solved in the past. (We are only aware of one method (Denzinger & Schulz 1996) that is designed to exploit a large number of source problems.) These methods create a search-guiding heuristic $\mathcal{H}_{\mathcal{A}_S}$ which is adapted to or specialized in solving $\mathcal{A}_S$. $\mathcal{H}_{\mathcal{A}_S}$ can then be profitably employed to solve *target problems* which are "similar" to $\mathcal{A}_S$. Similarity is an important issue for all learning methods. It is required to detect a source problem $\mathcal{A}_S$ which is "similar enough" to a given target problem $\mathcal{A}_T$

so that $\mathcal{H}_{\mathcal{A}_S}$ is useful for proving $\mathcal{A}_T$. We shall address this topic in the context of our experiments.

When $\mathcal{A}_S$ was solved, the ATP at hand employed a heuristic $\mathcal{H}$. As described in the preceding section, the successful search conducted by $\mathcal{H}$ provides us with sets P and N. P and N are pivotal for learning. Essentially, in order to create a $\mathcal{H}_{\mathcal{A}_S}$ adapted to $\mathcal{A}_S$, $\mathcal{H}_{\mathcal{A}_S}$ should give "small" weights to facts in P (recall that facts with smaller weights are activated earlier) and "big" weights to facts in N. In (Fuchs 1995), the parameters of a given heuristic are fine-tuned using a genetic algorithm so as to distinguish positive facts from negative ones. In (Suttner & Ertel 1990), P and N are used for training a neural network. After training, the network can be used as a "fuzzy" classifier in order to predict whether a fact may be positive or negative. The heuristic described in (Fuchs 1997a) explicitly uses P and assigns small weights to facts in P if they appear during the search for a proof of a target problem. These very principles are also pursued by our learning method presented in the subsequent section.

A Feature-based Learning Method

Let $\mathcal{A}_S$ be a source problem and $\mathcal{H}$ be the heuristic employed to prove $\mathcal{A}_S$. Let furthermore P and N be the sets of positive and negative facts stemming from the search conducted by $\mathcal{H}$. In order to create a heuristic $\mathcal{H}_{\mathcal{A}_S}$ adapted to $\mathcal{A}_S$ we propose to add a *penalty weight* to the weight computed by $\mathcal{H}$:

$$\mathcal{H}_{\mathcal{A}_S}(\lambda) = \mathcal{H}(\lambda) + pw(\lambda).$$

For reasons that will become clear as we proceed and to comply with the principles introduced in the preceding section, the penalty weight pw is to satisfy the conditions $pw(\lambda) = 0$ for all $\lambda \in P$ and $pw(\lambda) \geq 0$ for all other facts λ. Thus, $\mathcal{H}_{\mathcal{A}_S}(\lambda) = \mathcal{H}(\lambda)$ for all $\lambda \in P$ and $\mathcal{H}_{\mathcal{A}_S}(\lambda) \geq \mathcal{H}(\lambda)$ for all other facts.

Let P' and N' be the sets of positive and negative facts resulting from the search for a proof of $\mathcal{A}_S$ conducted by $\mathcal{H}_{\mathcal{A}_S}$. Without giving a formal proof it holds true that $P' = P$ and $N' \subseteq N$. In the extreme case, by giving sufficiently large penalty weights to all $\lambda \notin P$, we can achieve $N' = \emptyset$. That is, $\mathcal{H}_{\mathcal{A}_S}$ activates only $\lambda \in P$ and does not incur any redundant search effort.

The design of $\mathcal{H}_{\mathcal{A}_S}$ has the advantage that we do not have to worry about the facts which $\mathcal{H}$ never activated. These facts are also negative facts in the sense that they obviously do not contribute to the proof found by $\mathcal{H}$ or $\mathcal{H}_{\mathcal{A}_S}$. Since $\mathcal{H}_{\mathcal{A}_S}(\lambda) = \mathcal{H}(\lambda)$ for all $\lambda \in P$ and $\mathcal{H}_{\mathcal{A}_S}(\lambda) \geq \mathcal{H}(\lambda)$ else, facts that were not activated by $\mathcal{H}$ will also not be activated by $\mathcal{H}_{\mathcal{A}_S}$. Note that parameter adaptation (Fuchs 1995) and neural networks (Suttner & Ertel 1990) which in a way "mix up" weights do have serious difficulties with previously unseen negative facts and need to deal with this problem.

There are of course many ways to create a pw that satisfies the conditions above. When designing pw, we should, however, keep in mind that the main purpose of $\mathcal{H}_{\mathcal{A}_S}$ does not consist in being profitable for solving $\mathcal{A}_S$; $\mathcal{A}_S$ has already been solved. It is more important that it is useful for future target problems. Hence we need to achieve a certain degree of *flexibility*. That is, we have to avoid to create a $\mathcal{H}_{\mathcal{A}_S}$ that is overspecialized in solving $\mathcal{A}_S$ and therefore possibly has very limited capabilities for proving target problems (except for those which are very similar to $\mathcal{A}_S$).

Consequently, we have to find a suitable compromise between focusing on the source proof—represented by P—and a sufficient degree of abstraction from P. The most common method in AI systems to deal with such a task is to represent each object in question (a fact λ in our case) with a feature-value vector. This takes care of the abstraction requirement because such a vector reflects only certain aspects of a fact. A focus on the source proof can be attained by using some kind of a distance measure. We shall now present the details of our approach.

Let $f_1, \ldots, f_k$ be k *features*. Each f_i maps a fact λ to its integer *feature value* $f_i(\lambda) \in \mathbb{Z}$. Such a feature value describes a syntactic property of λ, e.g., the number of distinct variables occurring in λ. The *feature-value vector* $FV(\lambda)$ of λ is given by $FV(\lambda) = (f_1(\lambda), \ldots, f_k(\lambda)) \in \mathbb{Z}^k$. For each feature f_i, we introduce a set $\emptyset \neq V_i \subseteq \mathbb{Z}$ of *permissible feature values*. Each V_i contains those feature values that are considered desirable for feature f_i. The *minimal feature-value difference*

$$\Delta_i(\lambda) = \min(\{|f_i(\lambda) - v| \mid v \in V_i\}) \in \mathbb{N}$$

allows us to measure by how much $f_i(\lambda)$ of a fact λ deviates from the values in V_i. We recruit the V_i from P:

$$V_i = \{f_i(\lambda) \mid \lambda \in P\}.$$

Thus the $\Delta_i(\lambda)$ measure deviation from the feature values of the facts that contributed to the source proof. Note that $\Delta_1(\lambda) = \cdots = \Delta_k(\lambda) = 0$ for all $\lambda \in P$. The penalty weight pw is based on the Δ_i:

$$pw(\lambda) = \sum_{i=1}^{k} c_i \Delta_i(\lambda), \quad c_i \in \mathbb{N}.$$

Note that in using $\sum c_i \Delta_i(\lambda)$ instead of, e.g., a (weighted) Euclidean distance of feature-value vectors, features are in a way uncoupled. That is, it is possible for a $\lambda \notin P$ that $\Delta_1(\lambda) = \cdots = \Delta_k(\lambda) = 0$ although there is no $\lambda' \in P$ so that $FV(\lambda) = FV(\lambda')$. Each feature is considered individually which reduces specialization in the source proof and thus increases the flexibility of the approach. Note also that, as required, $pw(\lambda) = 0$ for all $\lambda \in P$ and $pw(\lambda) \geq 0$ otherwise.

The coefficients c_i determine the influence of the Δ_i on the penalty weight. Hence, they are crucial for the performance of $\mathcal{H}_{\mathcal{A}_S}$. Obviously, $pw(\lambda) = 0$ for all $\lambda \in P$ regardless of the coefficients. Consequently, only the $\lambda \notin P$ with $\Delta_i(\lambda) \neq 0$ for at least one $i \in \{1, \ldots, k\}$ are affected by modifying coefficients. If $c_1, \ldots, c_k$ are chosen "sufficiently large", all these negative facts will receive a penalty weight that will cause them to disappear from the search.

But since it is not our goal to merely speed up the search for the known proof of $\mathcal{A}_S$, we have to use a moderate and judicious way to choose coefficients in order to ensure a good chance for $\mathcal{H}_{\mathcal{A}_S}$ to be useful for a wider range of target problems (flexibility). In order to find some middle course in this inherent dilemma between flexibility and specialization, we content ourselves with raising coefficients until "satisfactorily many" negative facts have received a "sufficiently large" penalty weight, while the total weight computed by $\mathcal{H}_{\mathcal{A}_S}$ should be kept as low as possible. In other words, we want a certain percentage of the $\lambda \in N$ to have a weight $\mathcal{H}_{\mathcal{A}_S}(\lambda)$ that *only just* suffices to make them disappear from the search. Thus, they will not (all) be completely out of reach in case a proof of a problem $\mathcal{A}_T$ related to $\mathcal{A}_S$ requires them. In the following we shall make these ideas more precise.

Let $w_{\max}^+$ be the maximal weight of positive facts:

$$w_{\max}^+ = \max(\{\mathcal{H}_{\mathcal{A}_S}(\lambda) \mid \lambda \in P\}).$$

(Note that $w_{\max}^+$ is independent of $c_1, \ldots, c_k$ since $\mathcal{H}_{\mathcal{A}_S}(\lambda) = \mathcal{H}(\lambda)$ for all $\lambda \in P$.) If $c_1, \ldots, c_k$ are chosen so that $pw(\lambda)$ causes $\mathcal{H}_{\mathcal{A}_S}(\lambda) > w_{\max}^+$ for a $\lambda \in N$, then this fact will not be activated anymore when searching for the proof of $\mathcal{A}_S$ using $\mathcal{H}_{\mathcal{A}_S}$. Such a $\lambda \in N$ is said to be *edged out*. Obviously, only the following set $E \subseteq N$ can be edged out:

$$E = \bigcup_{i=1}^{k} \mathcal{N}_i, \qquad \mathcal{N}_i = \{\lambda \in N \mid \Delta_i(\lambda) \neq 0\}.$$

If $\lambda \in \mathcal{N}_i$, then $pw(\lambda)$ is affected by increasing c_i. Note that the $\mathcal{N}_i$ are not necessarily pairwise disjoint.

Increasing c_i by $1 \leq \varepsilon_i \in \mathbb{N}$ will raise the weight of negative facts by at most $\varepsilon_i \cdot d_i^{max}$, where d_i^{max} is the maximal feature-value difference regarding feature f_i:

$$d_i^{max} = \max(\{\Delta_i(\lambda) \mid \lambda \in N\}).$$

The negative facts $\mathcal{E}_i(\varepsilon_i)$ that are edged out on account of raising c_i by ε_i can be determined as follows. (To this end we have to make $\mathcal{H}_{\mathcal{A}_S}$'s dependence on c_i explicit to facilitate the notation.)

$$\mathcal{E}_i(\varepsilon_i) = \{\lambda \in \mathcal{N}_i \mid \quad \mathcal{H}_{\mathcal{A}_S}(\lambda, c_i) \leq w_{\max}^+ \ \wedge \\ \mathcal{H}_{\mathcal{A}_S}(\lambda, c_i + \varepsilon_i) > w_{\max}^+\}.$$

Since our goal is to edge out as many negative facts as possible, but to keep the increase of their weights low,

$$a_i = \begin{cases} \frac{|\mathcal{E}_i(\varepsilon_i)|}{\varepsilon_i \cdot d_i^{max}}, & \varepsilon_i \cdot d_i^{max} \geq 1 \\ -\infty, & \varepsilon_i \cdot d_i^{max} = 0 \end{cases}$$

measures how well we achieved this trade off. The c_i associated with the maximal a_i is then to be raised by ε_i. Since it is desirable to increase coefficients in a

```
input:    H, P, N, f_1,...,f_k, e, n_1,...,n_k
compute w^+_max and V_1,...,V_k with P
compute E and N_i for 1 ≤ i ≤ k with N
determine I using n_1,...,n_k
compute d_i^max for all i ∈ I
m := 0     'number of negative facts edged out so far'
c_1 := ··· := c_k := 0
while m < |E| ∧ m/|N| < e do
{
     compute minimal ε_i for each i ∈ I
     determine E_i(ε_i) for each i ∈ I
     compute a_i for each i ∈ I
     determine j so that a_j = max({a_i | i ∈ I})
     c_j := c_j + ε_j
     m := m + |E_j(ε_j)|
}
output:   c_1,...,c_k
```

Figure 1: Algorithm CFC

step-by-step manner (starting with $c_1 = \cdots = c_k = 0$), ε_i should be minimal, i.e.,

$$\varepsilon_i = \min(\{\varepsilon \mid \mathcal{E}_i(\varepsilon) \neq \emptyset\}), \quad \min(\emptyset) := 0.$$

Computing the a_i and raising the respective c_i is iterated until all $\lambda \in E$ have been edged out or a satisfactory fraction $e \in [0;1]$ of *all* negative facts in N has been edged out. Hence, the fraction of negative facts actually edged out is equal to $\min(\{e, |E|/|N|\})$.

So far we take into account all features when computing coefficients. It makes sense to exclude a feature f_i if the associated set $\mathcal{N}_i$ is rather small, i.e., by increasing c_i we can only expect to get rid of a (relatively) small number of negative facts. Hence we risk edging out negative facts that might be useful for proving similar problems, but we gain little. Therefore, we refine the procedure for determining the coefficients by enabling it to exclude features f_i if $|\mathcal{N}_i|/|N| < n_i$ for given thresholds $n_i \in [0;1]$. We let

$$I = \{i \mid 1 \leq i \leq k \wedge |\mathcal{N}_i|/|N| \geq n_i\}$$

and then consider only those features f_i where $i \in I \subseteq \{1,\ldots,k\}$. (That is, $c_i = 0$ for $i \notin I$.)

Figure 1 summarizes the procedure just described in algorithmic form. The input of algorithm CFC ("*Compute Feature Coefficients*") consists of the heuristic $\mathcal{H}$ used to solve a source problem $\mathcal{A}_S$, the sets P and N originating from the successful search conducted by $\mathcal{H}$, the features $f_1,\ldots,f_k$, and the thresholds e and $n_1,\ldots,n_k$. As output, CFC produces the coefficients $c_1,\ldots,c_k$ essentially by employing a hill-climbing procedure using the a_i as gradient information.

Naturally, the choice of features has a strong influence on what can be achieved with $\mathcal{H}_{\mathcal{A}_S}$. The main demand on the features is to be distinctive with respect to positive and negative facts. In other words,

for most of the negative facts $\lambda \in N$ there should be at least one feature f_i with $f_i(\lambda) \notin V_i$. Note that CFC has certain *feature-selection* capabilities, namely by excluding features on account of the threshold n_i or, more implicitly, by letting the respective $c_i = 0$. Hence, an "abundance" of features is not harmful since ineffective features can be excluded.

Similar to parameter adaptation (Fuchs 1995) and the neural network approach (Suttner & Ertel 1990), our approach distinguishes a *learning phase* and an *application phase*. During the learning phase (which is executed *once* for each $\mathcal{H}$ and $\mathcal{A}_S$ since it is independent of future target problems), algorithm CFC produces the coefficients required by $\mathcal{H}_{\mathcal{A}_S}$. In *every* application phase $\mathcal{H}_{\mathcal{A}_S}$ uses these coefficients. (We assume that the respective sets of permissible feature values are also available for $\mathcal{H}_{\mathcal{A}_S}$ at any time.)

Experiments

We conducted our experimental studies with the ATPs CODE (Fuchs & Fuchs 1997a) and DISCOUNT (Avenhaus, Denzinger, & Fuchs 1995). CODE is a prover specialized in problems of *condensed detachment*, i.e., problems related to the study of logic calculi with a modus ponens style inference rule. DISCOUNT is an equational reasoning system based on the unfailing Knuth-Bendix completion procedure.

For all experiments, CODE employed $k = 11$ features. For CODE, a fact is a first-order term. Hence, features such as the number of distinct variables or certain function symbols occurring in a term were among the 11 features. Due to space limitations, it is impossible to give a detailed presentation of the features. Such a presentation requires many technical details and background knowledge on logic calculi in order to be meaningful. Therefore, we kindly refer the reader to (Fuchs 1997b). The same goes for the features used by DISCOUNT. We want to point out that, assuming a reasonable familiarity with the respective calculi, the features provided by us are straight forward.

For both CODE and DISCOUNT the threshold parameters were set as follows: $e = 0.8$ and $n_1 = \cdots = n_k = 0.1$. In the experiments, the chosen features allowed for edging out at least 80% of the negative facts, i.e., $|E|/|N| \geq 0.8$. (In most cases, $|E|/|N| < 1$.) Various experiments showed that the above parameter setting is satisfactorily close to optimal in most cases.

The problems to be solved by the ATP systems were taken from the TPTP (Sutcliffe, Suttner, & Yemenis 1994) version 1.2.1. The TPTP is a large publicly accessible collection of standardized problems for ATPs. As such, it serves as a platform for a meaningful comparison of results and ensures a unique use of problem names and specifications.

Table 1 displays the results of CODE in the TPTP problem domain LCL (*logic calculi*). All the problems CODE can handle are in this domain. From the 112 available problems, we selected a batch of related prob-

Table 1: Experiments with CoDe.

Target $\mathcal{A}_T$	Source $\mathcal{A}_S$	$\mathcal{H}_{\mathcal{A}_S}$	$\mathcal{H}^*$
LCL040-1	LCL064-1	8s	—
LCL042-1	LCL045-1	21s	—
LCL060-1	LCL059-1	23s	91s
LCL068-1	LCL069-1	5s	35s
LCL071-1	LCL070-1	14s	45s
LCL114-1	LCL113-1	24s	—
LCL116-1	LCL113-1	40s	—

Table 2: Experiments with DISCOUNT.

Target $\mathcal{A}_T$	Source $\mathcal{A}_S$	$\mathcal{H}_{\mathcal{A}_S}$	$\mathcal{H}^*$
ROB008-1	ROB003-1	88s	—
ROB009-1	ROB003-1	140s	—
ROB022-1	ROB003-1	76s	—
ROB023-1	ROB003-1	24s	76s

lems that CoDe has (severe) difficulties solving without falling back on learning techniques.

The first two columns of Table 1 show the names of the target and source problems, respectively. (The names are "TPTP names".) The third column lists the run-times needed by $\mathcal{H}_{\mathcal{A}_S}$ for solving the respective target problems. $\mathcal{H}$ stands for the heuristic which solved the respective source problems. Hence, each $\mathcal{H}_{\mathcal{A}_S}$ was generated as described in the preceding section using $\mathcal{H}$ and the search for a proof of the respective source problem $\mathcal{A}_S$ conducted by $\mathcal{H}$. Run-times are approximate CPU time on a SPARCstation ELC. These times merely represent the run-times of application phases. That is, they do not include the run-times of the respective learning phases. The time required by the learning phase (i.e., by algorithm CFC), however, is less than one second and can consequently be ignored.

The last column shows the *best* run-times of a range of "conventional" (i.e., non-learning) heuristics. $\mathcal{H}$ was among these heuristics which are variations of the same *generic* heuristic of CoDe obtained by using different parameter settings. The entry '—' denotes failure to find a proof before exceeding a time-out of one hour.

The results in Table 1 demonstrate that besides considerable speed-ups (factor 3-7), $\mathcal{H}_{\mathcal{A}_S}$ also allows for solving problems that are out of reach for conventional heuristics. Note that CoDe is believed to be currently the best ATP for problems of condensed detachment that outperforms other ATPs even when it employs only conventional heuristics (Fuchs & Fuchs 1997a). Hence it is not at all easy for $\mathcal{H}_{\mathcal{A}_S}$ to attain improvements. This circumstance underlines the contributions of our approach to advancing the state-of-the-art.

Table 2 shows the results of our experiments with DISCOUNT. It is organized like Table 1. All problems are taken from the domain ROB (*Robbins algebra*) although there are further domains DISCOUNT can be applied to. Note that such a limited selection of problems does not indicate a weakness of our approach. It indicates, however, that the TPTP is not adapted to the needs of learning ATPs: Most domains of the TPTP are collections of hard, but rather unrelated problems. In particular a *didactic* arrangement of problems is not an issue in the TPTP. Such an arrangement, however, is perfectly natural for human learning and is also fundamental for a sensible use of machine learning. Starting out with simple problems, more and more difficult ones can be solved by learning ("bootstrapping", cp. (Denzinger, Fuchs, & Fuchs 1997)). Nonetheless, the TPTP is an excellent point of reference for evaluating new methods for reasons given above.

The entries in columns 3 and 4 of Table 2 are again approximate CPU time in seconds, this time obtained on a SPARCstation 10. As before in connection with CoDe, our approach enables DISCOUNT to significantly improve its performance.

Finally, we want to sketch how source problems were selected. Selection was based on the following similarity criterion for problems. Given a source problem $\mathcal{A}_S = (Ax_S, \lambda_S)$ and a target problem $\mathcal{A}_T = (Ax_T, \lambda_T)$, $\mathcal{A}_S$ is considered to be the more similar to $\mathcal{A}_T$ the more axioms in Ax_S have a counterpart in Ax_T. A "counterpart" denotes an identical or a more general axiom. Similarity is considered to be even higher if λ_T is identical to or an instance of λ_S. The basic idea of this similarity criterion derives from the fact that "more and possibly more general axioms allow for inferring more theorems". In case there are several source problems which are equally similar to a target problem, then the "most difficult" of these source problems is selected. Difficulty corresponds to the run-time (or a related measure) required to solve the respective problem. During our experiments this selection technique was applied by the user. Recent research has shown that an automation of the technique produces excellent results (Fuchs & Fuchs 1997b).

Discussion

Machine-learning techniques appear to play a key role in advancing the state-of-the-art in theorem proving. In this paper we presented a method for learning search-guiding heuristics based on features. In this approach, a comparison of feature values results in a penalty weight which is used to adapt a heuristic to a source problem solved by this very heuristic. The adapted heuristic can then be utilized to tackle target problems which are similar to the source problem.

The success of the approach depends on the suitability of the available features. This is a general difficulty for feature-based methods in AI. For classification tasks it is a common practice to provide a choice of features which seem to be relevant to the task. We essentially did the same. The built-in capability of our approach for feature selection could be supported by more sophisticated methods for feature selection or even feature extraction (e.g., (Sherrah, Bogner, & Bouzerdoum 1997; Yang & Honavar 1997)).

Experiments have demonstrated that learning heuristics as proposed here can result in significant improvements of theorem proving systems. Besides prominent speed-ups, it is also possible to solve problems that were out of reach before. This constitutes a significant contribution of machine learning to advancing the state-of-the-art in theorem proving. The price we have to pay for this is rather small: The time spent on learning (i.e., executing algorithm CFC) is negligible. This is definitely not the case for (Fuchs 1995) and (Suttner & Ertel 1990) which need to run a genetic algorithm or train a neural network, respectively. The additional effort an adapted heuristic spends on computing feature values and feature-value differences is also insignificant compared to the gains on account of a reduced search effort.

Our approach is related to instance-based learning (Aha, Kibler, & Albert 1991). Note, however, that the uncoupled use of features distinguishes our approach from commonly used variants of the nearest-neighbor rule. An application of "standard" instance-based learning methods for theorem proving is an interesting and promising area for further studies. Furthermore, our approach exhibits some of the main characteristics of explanation-based learning (Ellman 1989): analytic learning (extraction of positive and negative facts), generalization (use of features), and the use of a single example (single source problem).

References

Aha, D.; Kibler, D.; and Albert, M. 1991. Instance-based learning algorithms. *Machine Learning* 6:37–66.

Avenhaus, J.; Denzinger, J.; and Fuchs, M. 1995. DISCOUNT: A system for distributed equational deduction. In *Proc. 6th Conference on Rewriting Techniques and Applications (RTA-95)*, LNCS 914, 397–402. Springer.

Bachmair, L.; Dershowitz, N.; and Plaisted, D. 1989. Completion without failure. In *Colloquium on the Resolution of Equations in Algebraic Structures*. Academic Press.

Brock, B.; Cooper, S.; and Pierce, W. 1988. Analogical reasoning and proof discovery. In *Proc. 9th Conference on Automated Deduction (CADE-9)*, LNCS 310, 454–468. Springer.

Bundy, A. 1988. The use of explicit plans to guide inductive proofs. In *Proc. 9th Conference on Automated Deduction (CADE-9)*, LNCS 310, 111–120. Springer.

Chang, C., and Lee, R. 1973. *Symbolic Logic and Mechanical Theorem Proving*. Academic Press.

Denzinger, J., and Schulz, S. 1996. Learning domain knowledge to improve theorem proving. In *Proc. 13th Conference on Automated Deduction (CADE-13)*, LNAI 1104, 62–76. Springer.

Denzinger, J.; Fuchs, M.; and Fuchs, M. 1997. High performance ATP systems by combining several AI methods. In *Proc. 15th International Joint Conference on Artificial Intelligence (IJCAI-97)*, 102–107. Morgan Kaufmann.

Ellman, T. 1989. Explanation-based learning: A survey of programs and perspectives. *ACM Computing Surveys* 21(2):163–221.

Fuchs, D., and Fuchs, M. 1997a. CODE: A powerful prover for problems of condensed detachment. In *Proc. 14th Conference on Automated Deduction (CADE-14)*, LNAI 1249, 260–263. Springer.

Fuchs, M., and Fuchs, M. 1997b. Applying case-based reasoning to automated deduction. In *Proc. 2nd International Conference on Case-based Reasoning (ICCBR-97)*, LNAI 1266, 23–32. Springer.

Fuchs, M. 1995. Learning proof heuristics by adapting parameters. In Prieditis, A., and Russell, S., eds., *Machine Learning: Proceedings of the Twelfth International Conference (ML-95)*, 235–243. Morgan Kaufmann.

Fuchs, M. 1997a. Flexible re-enactment of proofs. In *Proc. 8th Portuguese Conference on Artificial Intelligence (EPIA-97)*, LNAI 1323, 13–24. Springer.

Fuchs, M. 1997b. *Learning Search Heuristics for Automated Deduction*. Ph.D. Dissertation. Hamburg: Verlag Dr. Kovač. ISBN 3-86064-623-0.

Kolbe, T., and Walther, C. 1994. Reusing proofs. In *Proc. 11th European Conference on AI (ECAI-94)*, 80–84.

Kolbe, T., and Walther, C. 1995. Patching proofs for reuse. In *Proc. 8th European Conference on Machine Learning (ECML-95)*, LNCS 912, 303–306. Springer.

Melis, E. 1995. A model of analogy-driven proof-plan construction. In *Proc. 14th International Joint Conference on Artificial Intelligence (IJCAI-95)*, 182–189. Morgan Kaufmann.

Sherrah, J.; Bogner, R.; and Bouzerdoum, A. 1997. The evolutionary pre-processor: Automatic feature extraction for supervised classification using genetic programming. In *Proc. 2nd International Conference on Genetic Programming (GP-97)*, 304–312. Morgan Kaufmann.

Sutcliffe, G.; Suttner, C.; and Yemenis, T. 1994. The TPTP problem library. In *Proc. 12th Conference on Automated Deduction (CADE-12)*, LNAI 814, 252–266. Springer.

Suttner, C., and Ertel, W. 1990. Automatic acquisition of search-guiding heuristics. In *Proc. 10th Conference on Automated Deduction (CADE-10)*, LNAI 449, 470–484. Springer.

Yang, J., and Honavar, V. 1997. Feature subset selection using a genetic algorithm. In *Proc. 2nd International Conference on Genetic Programming (GP-97)*, 380–385. Morgan Kaufmann.

Learning Investment Functions for Controlling the Utility of Control Knowledge

Oleg Ledeniov and Shaul Markovitch
Computer Science Department
Technion, Haifa, Israel
{olleg,shaulm}@cs.technion.ac.il

Abstract

The utility problem occurs when the cost of the acquired knowledge outweighs its benefits. When the learner acquires control knowledge for speeding up a problem solver, the benefit is the speedup gained due to the better control, and the cost is the added time required by the control procedure due to the added knowledge. Previous work in this area was mainly concerned with the costs of matching control rules. The solutions to this kind of utility problem involved some kind of selection mechanism to reduce the number of control rules. In this work we deal with a control mechanism that carries very high cost regardless of the particular knowledge acquired. We propose to use in such cases explicit reasoning about the economy of the control process. The solution includes three steps. First, the control procedure must be converted to anytime procedure. Second, a resource-investment function should be acquired to learn the expected return in speedup time for additional control time. Third, the function is used to determine a stopping condition for the anytime procedure. We have implemented this framework within the context of a program for speeding up logic inference by subgoal ordering. The control procedure utilizes the acquired control knowledge to find efficient subgoal ordering. The cost of ordering, however, may outweigh its benefit. Resource investment functions are used to cut-off ordering when the future net return is estimated to be negative.

Introduction

Speedup learning is a sub-area of machine learning where the goal of the learner is to acquire knowledge for accelerating the speed of a problem solver (Tadepalli & Natarajan 1996). Several works in speedup learning concentrated on acquiring *control knowledge* for controlling the search performed by the problem solver. When the cost of using the acquired control knowledge outweighs its benefits, we face the so called *Utility Problem* (Minton 1988; Markovitch & Scott 1993). Existing works dealing with the utility of control knowledge are based on a model of control rules whose main associated cost is the time it takes to match their preconditions. Most of the existing solutions for this problem involve *filtering* out control rules that are estimated to be of low utility (Minton 1988; Markovitch & Scott 1993; Gratch & DeJong 1992). Others try to restrict the complexity of the preconditions (Tambe, Newell, & Rosenbloom 1990).

In this work we deal with a different setup where the control procedure has potentially very high complexity regardless of the specific control knowledge acquired. In this setup, the utility problem can become significant since the cost of using the control knowledge can be higher than the time it saves on search. Filtering is not useful for such cases, since deleting control knowledge will not necessarily reduce the complexity of the control process. We propose to use a three step framework for dealing with this problem. First, convert the control procedure into an *anytime* procedure. Then learn the *resource investment function* which predicts the saving in search time for given resources invested in control decision. Finally, run the anytime control procedure minimizing the sum of the control time and the expected search time.

This framework is demonstrated through a learning system for speeding up logic inference. The control procedure is the Divide-and-Conquer (DAC) subgoal ordering algorithm (Ledeniov & Markovitch 1998). The learning system learns costs and number of solutions of subgoals to be used by the ordering algorithm. A good ordering of subgoals will increase the efficiency of the logic interpreter. However, the ordering procedure has high complexity. We employ the above framework by first making the DAC algorithm anytime. We then learn a resource investment function for each goal pattern. The functions are used to stop the ordering procedure before its costs become too high. We demonstrate experimentally how the ordering time decreases without harming significantly the quality of the resulting order.

Learning Control Knowledge for Speeding up Logic Inference

In this section we describe our learning system which performs off-line learning of control knowledge for speeding up logic inference. The problem solver is a Prolog interpreter for pure Prolog. Thus the goal of the learning system is to speed up the SLD-resolution search of the AND-OR tree.

The Control Procedure
The control procedure orders AND nodes of the AND-OR search tree. When the current goal is unified with a rule head, the set of subgoals of the rule body, under the current binding, is given to our DAC algorithm to find a low-cost ordering.

The algorithm produces candidate orderings and estimates their cost using the equation (Smith & Genesereth 1985):

$$Cost(\langle A_1, A_2, \ldots A_n \rangle) = \sum_{i=1}^{n} \sum_{b \in Sols(\{A_1,\ldots A_{i-1}\})} Cost(A_i|_b) = \sum_{i=1}^{n} \left[\left(\prod_{j=1}^{i-1} \overline{nsols}(A_j)|_{\{A_1\ldots A_{j-1}\}} \right) \times \overline{cost}(A_i)|_{\{A_1\ldots A_{i-1}\}} \right], \quad (1)$$

where $\overline{cost}(A)|_\mathcal{B}$ is the *average cost* (number of unifications) of proving a subgoal A under all the solutions of a set of subgoals $\mathcal{B}$, $\overline{nsols}(A)|_\mathcal{B}$ is the *average number of solutions* of A under all the solutions of $\mathcal{B}$. For each subgoal A_i, its average cost is multiplied by the total number of solutions of all the preceding subgoals.

The main idea of the DAC algorithm is to create a special AND-OR tree, called the *divisibility tree* (DT), which represents the partition of the given set of subgoals into subsets, and to perform a traversal of this tree. The partition is performed based on dependency information. We call two subgoals that share a free variable *dependent*. A leaf of the tree represents an independent set of subgoals. An AND node represents a subset that can be partitioned into subsets that are mutually independent and each of the AND branches corresponds to the DT of one of the partitions. An OR node represents a dependent set of subgoals. Each OR branch corresponds to an ordering where one of the subgoals in the subset is placed first. The selected first subgoal binds some of the variables in the remaining subgoals. For each node of the tree, a set of *candidate orderings* is created, and the orderings of an internal node are obtained by combining orderings of its children. For different types of nodes in the tree, the combination is performed differently. In (Ledeniov & Markovitch 1998), we prove several sufficient conditions that allow us to discard a large number of possible ordering combinations, therefore the obtained sets of candidate orderings are generally small. Candidate orderings are propagated up the DT. A candidate of an OR-node is generated from a candidate of *one* of its children, while a candidate of an AND-node is constructed by merging candidates of *all* its children. The last step of the algorithm is to return the lowest cost candidate of the root according to Equation 1. In most practical cases the new algorithm works in polynomial time. For more details about the DAC algorithm see (Ledeniov & Markovitch 1998).

The Learning Component
The learning system either performs on-line learning using the user queries, or performs off-line learning by generating training queries based on a distribution learned from past user queries. The ordering algorithm described above assumes the availability of correct values of average cost and number of solutions for various literals. The learning component acquires this control knowledge while solving the training queries.

Storing control values separately for each literal is not practical, for several reasons. The first is the large space required by this approach. The second reason is the lack of generalization: the ordering algorithm is quite likely to encounter literals which were not seen before, and whose real control values are thus unknown.

The learner therefore acquires control values for *classes* of literals rather than for separate literals. The more refined are the classes, the smaller is the variance of real control values inside each class, the more precise are the $\overline{cost}$ and $\overline{nsols}$ estimations that the classes assign to their members, and the better orderings we obtain. One easy way to define classes is by *modes* or *binding patterns* (Debray & Warren 1988): for each argument we denote whether it is free or bound.

Class refinement can be obtained by using more sophisticated tests on the predicate arguments than the simple "bound-unbound" test. For this purpose we can use *regression trees* – a sort of decision trees that classify to continuous numeric values (Breiman *et al.* 1984; Quinlan 1986). Two separate regression trees are stored for every program predicate, one for its $\overline{cost}$ values, and one for the $\overline{nsols}$. For each literal whose $\overline{cost}$ or $\overline{nsols}$ is required, we address the corresponding tree of its predicate and perform recursive descent in it, starting from the root. Each tree node contains a test which applies to the arguments of the literal. Since we store separate trees for different predicates, we do not need tests that apply to the predicate names. A possible regression tree for estimation of number of solutions for predicate `father` is shown in Figure 1.

The tests used in the nodes can be *syntactic*, such as "is the first argument bound?", or *semantic*, such as "is the first argument male?". If we only use the test *"is argument i bound?"*, then the classes of literals defined by regression trees coincide with the classes defined by binding patterns. Semantic tests require logic inference. For example, the semantic test above invokes the predicate `male` on the first argument of the literal. Therefore these tests must be as "cheap" as possible, otherwise the retrieval of control values will take too much time.

Ordering and the Utility Problem
To test the effectiveness of our ordering algorithm, we experimented with it on various domains, and compared its performance to other ordering algorithms. Most experiments were performed on randomly created

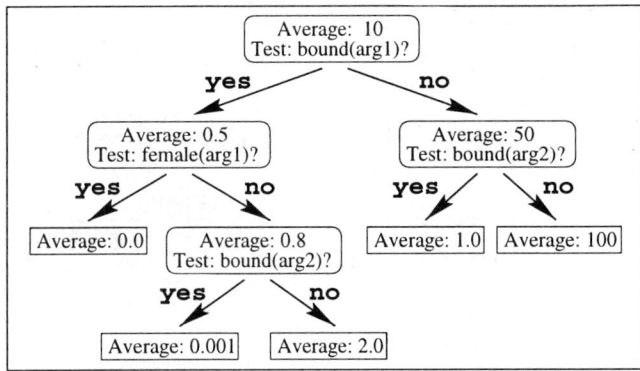

Figure 1: A regression tree for estimation of number of solutions for father(arg1,arg2).

artificial domains. We also tested the performance of the system on several real domains.

All the experiments described below consist of a training session, followed by a testing session. Training and testing sets of queries are randomly drawn from a fixed distribution. During the training session the learner acquires the control knowledge for literal classes. During the testing session the problem solver proves the queries of the testing set using different ordering algorithms. The goal of ordering is to reduce the time spent by the Prolog interpreter when it proves queries of the testing set. This time is the sum of the time spent by the ordering procedure (*ordering time*) and the time spent by the interpreter (*inference time*).

In order to ensure statistical significance of results of comparison of different ordering algorithms, we experimented with many different domains. For this purpose, we created a set of artificial domains, each with a small fixed set of predicates, but with random number of clauses in each predicate, and with random rule lengths. Predicates in rule bodies, and arguments in both rule heads and bodies are randomly drawn from fixed distributions. Each domain has its own training and testing sets (these two sets do not intersect). Since the domains and the query sets are generated randomly, we repeated each experiment 100 times, each time with a different domain.

The following ordering methods were tested:

- *Random:* Each time we address a rule body, we order it randomly.

- *Best-first search*: over the space of prefixes. Out of all prefixes that are permutation of each other, only the cheapest one is retained. A similar algorithm was used Markovitch and Scott (1989).

- *Adjacency:* A best-first search with adjacency restriction test added. The adjacency restriction requires that two adjacent subgoals always stand in the cheapest order. A similar algorithm was described by Smith and Genesereth(1985).

- *The DAC algorithm* using binding patterns for learning.

- *The DAC algorithm* using regression trees with syntactic tests.

Table 1 shows the results obtained. The results clearly show the advantage of the DAC algorithm over other ordering algorithms. It produces much shorter inference time than the random ordering method. It requires much shorter ordering time than the other deterministic ordering algorithms. Therefore, its total time is the best. The results with regression trees are better than the results with binding patterns. This is due to the better accuracy of the control knowledge that is accumulated for a more refined classes.

It is interesting to note that the random ordering method performs better than the *best-first* and the *adjacency* methods. The inference time that these method produce is much better than the inference time when using random ordering. However, they require very long ordering time which outweighs the inference time gain. This is a clear manifestation of the utility problem where the time required by the control procedure outweighs its benefit. The DAC algorithm has much better ordering performance. However, its complexity is $O(n!)$ in the worst case. Therefore, it is quite feasible to encounter the utility problem even when using the efficient ordering procedure.

To study this problem, we performed another experiment where we varied the maximal length of rules in our randomly generated domains and tested the effect of the maximal rule length on the utility of learning. Rules with longer bodies require much longer ordering time, but also carry a large potential benefit.

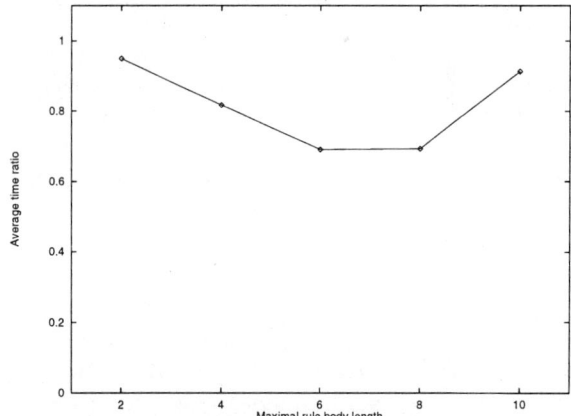

Figure 2: The effect of rule body length on utility.

The graph in Figure 2 plots the average time saving of the ordering algorithm: for each domain we calculate the ratio of its total testing time with the DAC algorithm and with the random method. For each maximal body length, a point on the graph shows the average

Ordering Method	Unifications	Reductions	Ordering Time	Inference Time	Total Time	Ord.Time / Reductions
Random	86052.06	27741.52	8.191	27.385	35.576	0.00029
Best-first	8526.42	2687.39	657.973	2.933	660.906	0.24
Adjacency	8521.32	2686.96	470.758	3.006	473.764	0.18
DAC - binding patterns	8492.99	2678.72	8.677	2.895	11.571	0.0032
DAC - regression trees	2454.41	859.37	2.082	1.030	3.112	0.0024

Table 1: The effect of ordering algorithm on the tree sizes and the CPU time (mean results over 100 artificial domains).

over 50 artificial domains. For each domain, testing with the random method was performed 20 times, and the average result was taken.

The following observations can be made:

1. For short rule bodies, the DAC ordering algorithm performs only a little better than the static random method. When bodies are short, little permutations are possible, thus the random method often finds good orderings.

2. For middle-sized rule bodies, the utility of the DAC ordering algorithm grows. Now the random method errs more frequently (there are more permutations of each rule body, and less chance to pick a cheap permutation). At the same time, the ordering time is not too large yet.

3. For long rule bodies, the utility again decreases, and the average time ratio nearly returns to the 1.0 level. Although the tree sizes are now reduced more and more (compared to the sizes of the random method), the additional ordering time grows notably, and the overall effect of ordering becomes almost null.

These results show that risk of encountering the utility problem exists even with our efficient ordering algorithm. In the following section we present a methodology for controlling the cost of the control mechanism by explicit reasoning about its expected utility.

Controlling the Utilization of Control Knowledge

The last section showed an instance of the utility problem which is quite different from the one caused by the matching time of control rules. There, the cost associated with the usage of control knowledge could be reduced by filtering out rules with low utility. Here, the high cost is an inherent part of the control procedure and is not a direct function of the control knowledge.

For cases such as the above, we propose to use a a methodology with the following three steps. First, make the control procedure anytime. Then acquire the resource-investment function that predicts the expected reduction in search time as a result of investing more control time. Finally, execute the anytime control procedure with a termination criterion based on the resource investment function. In this section, we will show how this three-step methodology can be applied to our DAC algorithm.

Anytime Divide-and-Conquer Algorithm

The DAC algorithm propagates the set of all candidate orderings in a bottom-up fashion to the root of the DT. Then it uses Equation (1) to estimate the cost of each candidate and finally returns the cheapest candidate. The anytime version of the algorithm works differently:

- Find first candidate, compute its cost.
- Loop until a termination condition holds (and while there are untried candidates):
  - Find next candidate, compute its cost.
  - If it is cheaper than the current minimal one – update the current cheapest candidate.
- Return the current cheapest candidate.

In the new framework, we do not generate all candidates exhaustively (unless the termination condition never holds). This algorithm is an instance of **anytime algorithm** (Boddy & Dean 1989): it always has a "current" answer ready, and at any moment can be stopped and return its current answer.

The new algorithm visits each node of the DT several times: it finds its first candidate, then pass this candidate to higher levels (where it participates in mergings and concatenations). Then, if the termination condition permits, the algorithm re-enters the node, finds its next candidate and exits with it, and so on. The algorithm stores for each node some information about the last candidate created. Note that all the nodes of a DT never physically co-exist simultaneously, since in every OR-node only one child is maintained at every moment of time. Thus, if the termination condition occurs in the course of the execution, some OR-branches of the DT are not created.

Using Resource-Investment Functions

The only part of the above algorithm that remains undefined is the termination condition which dictates when the algorithm should stop exploring new candidates and return the currently best candidate. Note that if this condition is removed or is always false then all candidates are created, and the anytime version becomes equivalent to the original DAC algorithm.

The more time we dedicate to ordering, the more candidates we create, and the cheaper becomes the best current candidate. This functional dependence can be expressed by a *resource-investment function* (*RIF* for shorthand).

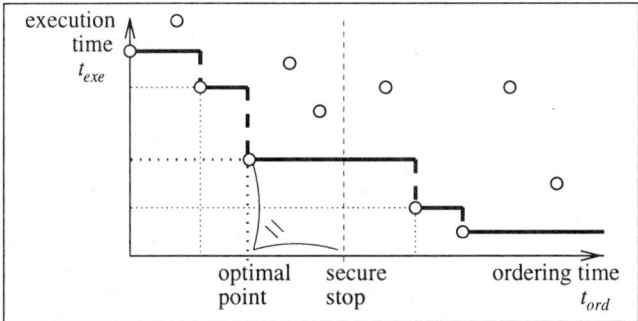

Figure 3: A resource-investment function.

An example of a RIF is shown in Figure 3: the x-axis (t_{ord}) corresponds to the ordering time spent, small circles on the graph are candidate orderings found, and the y-axis (t_{exe}) shows the estimated execution time of the cheapest candidate seen till now.

For each point (candidate) on the RIF, we can define $t_{all} = t_{ord} + t_{exe}$, the total computation time which is the sum of the ordering time it takes us to reach this point and the time it takes to execute the currently cheapest candidate. There exists a point (candidate) for which this sum is minimal ("optimal point" in Figure 3). This is the best point to terminate the anytime ordering algorithm: if we stop before it, execution time of the chosen candidate will be large, and if we stop after it, the ordering time will be large. In each of the two cases the total time spent on this rule will increase.

But how can we know that the current point on the RIF is optimal? We have only seen the points before it (to the left of it), and cannot predict how the RIF will behave further. If we continue to explore the current RIF until we see all the candidates (then we surely can detect the optimal point), all the advantages of an early stop are lost. We cannot just stop at the point where t_{all} starts to grow, since there may be several local minima of t_{all}.

However, there is a condition that guarantees that optimal point can not occur in the future. If the current ordering time t_{ord} becomes greater than the currently minimal t_{all}, there is no way that the optimal point will be found in later stage. Since t_{ord} can only grow thereafter, and t_{exe} is positive, t_{all} cannot become smaller than the current minimum. So using this termination condition guarantees that the current known minimum is the global minimum. It also guarantees that, if we stop at this point, the total execution time will be $t_{ord}^{opt} + 2 \cdot t_{exe}^{opt}$, where ($t_{ord}^{opt}, t_{exe}^{opt}$) are the coordinates of the point with minimal t_{all} (the "optimal point" in Figure 3). Now the total time is less than twice the optimal one.

We can maintain a variable t_{all}^{opt} and update it after the cost of a new candidate is computed. The termination condition therefore becomes:

$$\text{TerminationCondition} :: t_{ord} \geq t_{all}^{opt} \quad (2)$$

where t_{ord} is the time spent in the current ordering. The point where these two value become equal is shown as the "secure stop" point in Figure 3.

Although the secure-point-stop strategy promises us that no more than twice the minimal effort is spent, we would surely prefer to stop at the optimal point. A possible solution is to *learn* the optimal point, basing on RIFs produced on the previous orderings of this rule. The RIF learning is performed in parallel with the learning of control values. We learn and store a RIF for each rule and for each binding pattern of the rule head, as a set of (t_{ord}, t_{exe}) pairs accumulated during training. Instead of binding patterns we can use classification trees, where attributes are rule head arguments, and tests are the same as for regression trees that learn control knowledge. Before we start ordering a rule, we use the learned tree to estimate the optimal stop point for this rule. Assume that this point is at time t_{opt}. Then the termination condition for the anytime algorithm is

$$\text{TerminationCondition} :: t_{ord} \geq t_{opt} \quad (3)$$

where t_{ord} is the time spent in the current ordering.

Experimentation

We have implemented the anytime algorithm, with both terminal conditions 2 (the *current-RIF* method) and 3 (the *learned-RIF* method). The results are shown in Table 2. As we see, the tree sizes did not change significantly, but the ordering time decreased. The average time of ordering one rule (the rightmost column of the table) also decreased strongly, which shows that much less ordering is performed, and this does not lead to worse ordering results.

We then repeated the second experiment, distributing domains by their maximal body lengths, and computing the average utility of ordering separately for each maximal body length. The upper graph in Figure 4 is the same as in Figure 2. The new graph for the anytime algorithm with learned RIFs is shown in dotted line. We can see that using the resource-sensitive ordering algorithm reduced the utility problem by controlling the costs of ordering long rules.

Conclusions

This paper presents a technique for dealing with the utility problem when the complexity of the control procedure that utilizes the learned knowledge is very high regardless of the particular knowledge acquired. We propose to convert the control procedure into an anytime algorithm and perform explicit reasoning about

Ordering Method	Unifications	Ordering Time	Inference Time	Total Time	Ord.Time Reductions
complete ordering	2467.95	1.668	1.039	2.707	0.001931
current RIF	2338.15	0.686	0.999	1.685	0.000833
learned RIFs	2340.37	0.569	1.027	1.595	0.000690

Table 2: Comparison of the uncontrolled and controlled ordering methods.

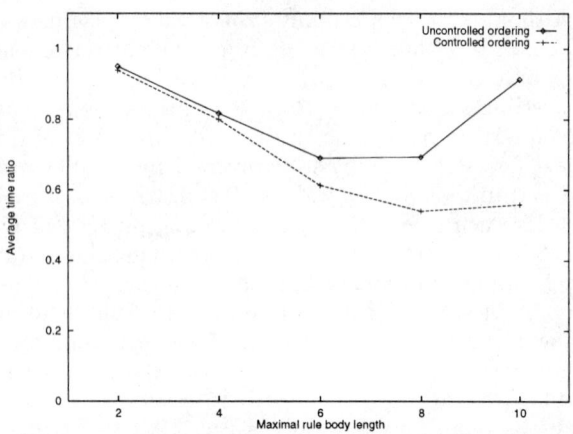

Figure 4: The effect of rule body length on utility.

the utility of investing additional control time. This reasoning uses the *resource investment function* of the control process which can be either learned, or built during execution.

We show an example of this type of reasoning in a learning system for speeding up logic inference. The system orders sets of subgoals for increased inference efficiency. The costs of the ordering process, however, may exceed its potential gains. We describe a way to convert the ordering procedure to be anytime. We then show how to reason about the utility of ordering using a resource investment function during the execution of the ordering procedure. We also show how to learn and use resource investment functions. The methodology described here can be used also for other tasks such as planning. There, we want to optimize the total time spent for planning and execution of the plan. Learning resource investment functions in a way similar to the one described here may increase the efficiency of the planning process.

References

Boddy, M., and Dean, T. 1989. Solving time-dependent planning problems. In *Proceedings of the Eleventh International Joint Conference on Artificial Intelligence*, 979–984. Los Altos, CA: Morgan Kaufmann.

Breiman, L.; Friedman, J. H.; Olshen, R. A.; and Stone, C. J. 1984. *Classification and Regression Trees*. Wadsworth International Group.

Debray, S. K., and Warren, D. S. 1988. Automatic mode inference for logic programs. *The Journal of Logic Programming* 5:207–229.

Gratch, J., and DeJong, D. 1992. COMPOSER: A probabilistic solution to the utility problem in speed-up learning. In *Proceedings of the Tenth National Conference on Artificial Intelligence*, 235–240. San Jose, California: American Association for Artificial Intelligence.

Ledeniov, O., and Markovitch, S. 1998. The divide-and-conquer subgoal-ordering algorithm for speeding up logic inference. Technical Report CIS9804, Technion.

Markovitch, S., and Scott, P. D. 1989. Automatic ordering of subgoals – a machine learning approach. In *Proceedings of North American Conference on Logic Programming*, 224–240.

Markovitch, S., and Scott, P. D. 1993. Information filtering: Selection mechanisms in learning systems. *Machine Learning* 10(2):113–151.

Minton, S. 1988. *Learning Search Control Knowledge: An Explanation-Based Approach*. Boston, MA: Kluwer.

Quinlan, J. R. 1986. Induction of decision trees. *Machine Learning* 1:81–106.

Smith, D. E., and Genesereth, M. R. 1985. Ordering conjunctive queries. *Artificial Intelligence* 26:171–215.

Tadepalli, P., and Natarajan, B. K. 1996. A formal framework for speedup learning from problems and solutions. *Journal of Artificial Intelligence Research* 4:419–443.

Tambe, M.; Newell, A.; and Rosenbloom, P. 1990. The problem of expensive chunks and its solution by restricting expressiveness. *Machine Learning* 5(3):299–348.

Fast Probabilistic Modeling for Combinatorial Optimization

Shumeet Baluja
baluja@cs.cmu.edu
Justsystem Pittsburgh Research Center &
Carnegie Mellon University

Scott Davies
scottd@cs.cmu.edu
School of Computer Science
Carnegie Mellon University

Abstract

Probabilistic models have recently been utilized for the optimization of large combinatorial search problems. However, complex probabilistic models that attempt to capture inter-parameter dependencies can have prohibitive computational costs. The algorithm presented in this paper, termed COMIT, provides a method for using probabilistic models in conjunction with fast search techniques. We show how COMIT can be used with two very different fast search algorithms: hillclimbing and Population-based incremental learning (PBIL). The resulting algorithms maintain many of the benefits of probabilistic modeling, with far less computational expense. Extensive empirical results are provided; COMIT has been successfully applied to jobshop scheduling, traveling salesman, and knapsack problems. This paper also presents a review of probabilistic modeling for combinatorial optimization.

1 Background

Within the past few years, there have been several novel methods proposed for probabilistic modeling for combinatorial optimization. Unlike methods such as hillclimbing, which progress by sampling solutions neighboring the current solution, probabilistic methods explicitly maintain statistics about the search space by creating models of the good solutions found so far. These models are sampled to generate the next query points to be evaluated. The sampled solutions are then used to update the model, and the cycle is continued.

By maintaining a population of points, genetic algorithms (GAs) can be viewed as creating *implicit* probabilistic models of the solutions seen in the search. GAs attempt to implicitly capture dependencies between parameters and the solution quality by maintaining a population of solutions. Samples are generated by applying randomized recombination operators to high-performance members of the population [Goldberg, 1989][Holland, 1975][De Jong, 1975]. Unlike the models explored in this paper, however, no explicit information is kept about which groups of parameters contribute to the quality of candidate solutions. One of the first steps towards making the GA's model more explicit was the "Bit-Based Simulated Crossover (BSC)" operator [Syswerda,1993]. Instead of combining pairs of solutions, population-level statistics were used to generate new solutions. The BSC operator works as follows. For each bit position[1], the number of members which contain a one in that bit position is counted. Each member's contribution is weighted by its fitness with respect to the target optimization function. The same process is used to count the number of zeros. Instead of using traditional crossover operators to generate new solutions, BSC generates new query points by stochastically assigning each bit's value by the probability of having seen that value in the previous population (the value specified by the weighted count) [Syswerda, 1993].

BSC used a population of solutions from which the sampling statistics were entirely rederived after each generation. In contrast, Population-based incremental learning (PBIL) incrementally adjusts its sampling statistics after each generation [Baluja, 1995]. Rather than being based on population-genetics, PBIL is very similar to a cooperative system of discrete learning automata in which the automata choose their actions independently, but all automata receive a common reinforcement dependent upon all their actions [Thathachar & Sastry, 1987]. Unlike most previous studies of learning automata, which have commonly addressed optimization in noisy but very small environments, PBIL was used to explore large deterministic spaces. The algorithm maintains a real-valued probability vector from which solutions are generated. As search progresses, the values in the probability vector are gradually shifted to represent high-evaluation solution vectors. This algorithm will be described in detail in Section 4.

Note that the probabilistic model created in PBIL is extremely simple. *There are no inter-parameter dependencies modeled; each bit is examined independently.* Although this simple probabilistic model was used, PBIL was very successful when compared to a variety of standard genetic algorithm and hillclimbing algorithms on

---

Copyright (c) 1998, American Association for Artificial Intelligence (www.aaai.org). All rights reserved.

1. Note that in this paper, we will discuss combinatorial optimization with the solutions represented as binary vectors. However, all of the results can be trivially extended to higher cardinality alphabets.

numerous benchmark and real-world problems [Baluja, 1997][Greene, 1996]. A more theoretical analysis of PBIL can be found in [Juels, 1997][Kvasnicka *et al.*, 1995][Hohfeld & Rudolph, 1997].

The most immediate way in which the PBIL algorithm can be improved is to create mechanisms that capture inter-parameter dependencies. One of the first extensions to PBIL along these lines was termed *Mutual Information Maximization for Input Clustering (MIMIC)* [De Bonet *et al.*, 1997]. MIMIC captured a heuristically chosen set of the pairwise dependencies between the solution parameters. MIMIC maintained the top N% of all previously generated solutions, from which it calculated pair-wise conditional probabilities. MIMIC used a greedy search to generate a chain in which each variable was conditioned on the previous variable. The first variable in the chain, X_1, was chosen to be the variable with the lowest unconditional entropy $H(X_1)$. When deciding which subsequent variable X_{i+1} to add to the chain, MIMIC selected the variable with the lowest conditional entropy $H(X_{i+1} | X_i)$. As with PBIL, after creating the full chain, it randomly generated more samples from the distribution specified by this chain. The entire process was then repeated.

In [Baluja & Davies, 1997a], MIMIC's probabilistic model was extended to a larger class of dependency graphs: trees in which each variable is conditioned on at most one parent. As shown in [Chow and Liu, 1968], a simple algorithm can be employed to select the *optimal* tree-shaped network for a maximum-likelihood model of the data. In experimental comparisons, MIMIC's chain-based probabilistic models typically worked significantly better than PBIL's simpler models. The tree-based graphs typically worked significantly better than MIMIC's chains. Thus, using more accurate probabilistic models increased the probability of generating new candidate solutions in promising regions of the search space. Tree-Based graphs are the basis of the probabilistic models used in this study, and will be returned to in Section 2.

An extension of pair-wise dependency modeling is arbitrary dependency modeling. Bayesian networks [Pearl, 1988] are a popular method for efficiently representing dependencies and independencies in probability distributions. Bayesian networks are directed acyclic graphs in which each variable is represented by a vertex, and dependencies between variables are encoded as edges. As in the tree-based algorithm, the networks model probability distributions of the form shown in Equation (1).

$$P_B(X_1,...,X_n) = \prod_{i=1}^{n} P_B(X_i | \Pi_{X_i}) \qquad (1)$$

where Π_{X_i} is the set of X_i's parents in B and n is the number of nodes. The tree-shaped networks described in the previous paragraph are a special case of Bayesian networks in which each node in the graph has at most one parent. PBIL may be thought of as employing a degenerate Bayesian network in which the graph has no edges. Unfortunately, when we move toward models in which variables can have more than one parent, the problem of finding an optimal network with which to model a set of data becomes NP-complete [Chickering, *et al.*, 1995]. However, search heuristics have been developed for automatically learning Bayesian networks from data (for example [Heckerman, *et al.*, 1995]). A common approach is to perform hill-climbing over network structures, starting with a relatively simple network. This approach was used for combinatorial optimization in [Baluja & Davies, 1997b]. The empirical results with Bayesian networks showed a noticeable improvement over tree-based optimization in some problems that exhibit complicated dependencies. However, this benefit is achieved through significantly more computational effort. In other problems in which only a few dependencies must be modeled, the tree-based model performed as well as the Bayesian network.

Thus far, all of the approaches that model dependencies have been used for optimizing relatively small problems (with search spaces smaller than 2^{256}). Extending these models to large problems is challenging because of the severe computational expense of modeling the dependencies between a large number of variables. On the other hand, when using less computationally expensive search algorithms, it is a common procedure to restart them with random initialization points in the hope that they will find better local optima. After performing several such restarts, there is information to be gained by analyzing the various local optima found in multiple search runs and looking for features they have in common.

One learning-based approach to selecting good starting points for hillclimbing was presented in [Boyan & Moore, 1997]. The algorithm attempts to map a set of user-supplied features of the state space to a single value. This value represents the quality of solutions that were found by hill-climbing runs passing through states with similar features. The algorithm then uses this "value function" to select promising starting points for future hillclimbing runs.

In this paper, we utilize probabilistic methods to model the solutions obtained by faster search algorithms. This contrasts with the approach of [Boyan and Moore, 1997] since an explicit probabilistic model is used to model only the top-performing solutions gathered through all of the fast searches. Further, the model is based directly on the parameters of the solution encoding; *no high-level attributes of the problem are provided to the algorithm*. These models are then sampled to intelligently select new starting points for further searches. The resulting algorithm, termed COMIT (*C*ombining *O*ptimizers with *M*utual *I*nformation *T*rees), gains most of the benefits of modeling the dependencies in the search space at a significantly reduced computational cost.

In the next section, we describe the COMIT algorithm, and give details of how the probabilistic model is created. In Section 3, we illustrates the use of COMIT with search techniques, such as hillclimbing, that maintain only a single solution from which new solutions are generated. Section 4 demonstrates how COMIT can be integrated with algorithms that themselves model probability distributions of possible solutions, such as PBIL. Extensive empirical results are provided in both sections. Finally, Section 5 presents conclusions and directions for future research.

2 The COMIT Algorithm

The basic premise of the COMIT algorithm is that probabilistic models can be used to intelligently select starting points for fast search algorithms such as hillclimbing or PBIL. The model is created based upon good solutions gathered from all previous searches. The general procedure is shown in Figure 1.

Specifically, once we have chosen a model P'(X_1...X_n) of the set, **S**, of previously found good solutions, P' is used to stochastically generate a number of candidate solutions. The best of these newly generated solutions are used to initialize the fast-search algorithm. Once the fast-search has terminated, up to MAX_INFLUENCE solutions in **S** are replaced by better solutions generated during the run; the size of **S** is kept constant. The MAX_INFLUENCE parameter is important, and must be set by considering the size of **S**. If MAX_INFLUENCE is set too high, too much weight may be given to a single fast-search run, resulting in premature convergence. If it is too low, then previously found good solutions may not carry enough weight; this causes the algorithm to put too much emphasis on random exploration. The process is repeated until a termination condition is met. The next section describes in detail how the probabilistic model of the good solutions is generated.

2.1 Modeling Dependencies in the COMIT algorithm

Suppose we have a set of good solutions, **S**, found from previous fast-search runs. We wish to discover what inter-parameter dependencies are exhibited by the bit strings in **S**, and use this information to generate good starting points for future hillclimbing runs. To do this, we try to model a probability distribution P(**X**) = P(X_1, ..., X_n) over bit-strings of length n, where X_1, ..., X_n are variables corresponding to the values of the bits. We try to learn a simplified model P'(X_1, ..., X_n) of the empirical probability distribution P(X_1, ..., X_n) entailed by the bitstrings in **S**. As in [Baluja & Davies, 1997a], we restrict our model P'(X_1, ..., X_n) to the following form:

$$P'(X_1...X_n) = \prod_{i=1}^{n} P\left(X_i | \Pi_{X_i}\right) \quad (2)$$

where Π_{X_i} is X_i's single "parent" variable. We require that there be no cycles in these "parent-of" relationships: formally, there must exist some permutation $m = (m_1, ..., m_n)$ of $(1, ..., n)$ such that $(\Pi_{X_i} = X_j) \Rightarrow m(i) < m(j)$ for all i. (The "root" node, X_R, will not have a parent node; however, this case can be handled with a "dummy" node X_0 such that P(X_R | X_0) is by definition equal to P(X_R).) In other words, we restrict P' to factorizations representable by Bayesian networks in which each node (except X_R) has one parent, *i.e.*, tree-shaped graphs. As described earlier, more complete Bayesian Networks could be used; however, trees were used because of computational limitations.

A method for finding the optimal model within these restrictions is given in [Chow and Liu, 1968]. A complete weighted graph **G** is created in which every variable X_i is represented by a corresponding vertex V_i, and in which the weight W_{ij} for the edge between vertices V_i and V_j is set to the mutual information I(X_i,X_j) between X_i and X_j:

$$I(X_i, X_j) = \sum_{a,b} P(X_i = a, X_j = b) \cdot \log \frac{P(X_i = a, X_j = b)}{P(X_i = a) \cdot P(X_j = b)} \quad (3)$$

The empirical probabilities of the form P(X_i = a) and P(X_i = a, X_j = b) are computed directly from **S** for all combinations of i, j, a, and b (a & b are binary assignments to X_i & X_j). Once these edge weights are computed, the maximum spanning tree of **G** is calculated, and this tree deter-

---

- Initialize dataset **S** with random solutions from uniform distribution
- While termination condition is not met:
  - Create probabilistic model of **S**.
  - Use model to stochastically generate **K** solutions. Evaluate new solutions.
  - Execute fast-search procedure, initialized with the best solutions generated from the model.
  - Replace up to MAX_INFLUENCE bitstrings in **S** with better bitstrings found during the fast-search run just executed.

USER DEFINED CONSTANTS (values used in this study)
|**S**|: Constant size of the dataset **S** (**1000**)
MAX_INFLUENCE: max number of bitstrings to replace in **S** with better strings from a single fast-search run (100).

Figure 1: Overview of the COMIT algorithm.

mines the structure of the network used to model the original probability distribution. Since the edges in **G** are undirected, a decision must be made about the directionality of the dependencies with which to construct P′; however, all such orderings conforming to the restrictions described earlier model identical distributions.

Among all trees, this produces a tree that maximizes:

$$\sum_{i=1}^{n} I(X_{m(i)}, X_{m(p(i))}) \qquad (4)$$

this minimizes the Kullback-Leibler divergence, $D(P\|P')$, between P (the true empirical distributions exhibited by **S**) and P′ (the distribution modeled by the network):

$$D(P \| P') = \sum_{X} P(X) \log \frac{P(X)}{P'(X)} \qquad (5)$$

As shown in [Chow & Liu, 1968], this produces the tree-shaped network that maximizes the likelihood of **S**, under the assumption that the members of **S** were generated independently and identically distributed. Our optimization algorithm violates this assumption since many highly correlated members are added to the dataset from any single fast-search run; however, the use of the **MAX_INFLUENCE** parameter limits this correlation.

This tree generation algorithm, summarized in Figure 2, runs in time $O(|S|*n^2)$, where |S| is the size of **S** and **n** is the number of bits in the solution encoding.

Generate an optimal dependency tree:
- Set the root to an arbitrary bit X_{root}
- For all other bits X_i, set bestMatchInTree[X_i] to X_{root}.
- While not all bits have been added to the tree:
  - Of all the bits not yet in the tree, pick bit X_{add} with the maximum mutual information I(X_{add}, bestMatchInTree[X_{add}]), using **S** to estimate the relevant probability distributions.
  - Add X_{add} to tree, with bestMatchInTree[X_{add}] as parent.
  - For each bit X_{out} not in the tree,
    if I(X_{out}, bestMatchInTree[X_{out}]) < I(X_{out}, X_{add}).
    then set bestMatchInTree[X_{out}]=X_{add}.

Figure 2: Procedure for generating the dependency tree.

---

3 Using COMIT with Hillclimbing

This section illustrates the use of COMIT with search techniques, such as hillclimbing, that maintain a single solution from which new solutions are generated. The algorithm uses a tree-shaped probabilistic network, **T**, to model a set, **S**, of previously found good solutions. **T** is then sampled to generate **K** new solutions, of which the highest-evaluation solution is used as the starting point of a hillclimbing run. Up to **MAX_INFLUENCE** solutions in **S** are replaced

---

- Initialize dataset **S** with random solutions from uniform distribution
- While termination condition is not met:
  - Create a tree-shaped probabilistic network **T** that models **S**.
  - Use **T** to stochastically generate **K** solutions. Evaluate these **K** new solutions.
  - Start hillclimbing run initialized with the single best of the **K** solutions.
  - Replace up to **MAX_INFLUENCE** bitstrings in **S** with better bitstrings found during the hillclimbing run just executed.

USER DEFINED CONSTANTS (values used in this study)
|S|: Constant size of the dataset **S**. (1000)
MAX_INFLUENCE: max number of bitstrings to replace in **S** with better strings from a single fast-search run (100).

Figure 3: Overview of the COMIT algorithm with hillclimbing.

---

with better solutions from this run, and the process is repeated. The algorithm is summarized in Figure 3.

3.1 Algorithm Details

__Hillclimbing (HC):__ The baseline search technique is next-ascent stochastic hillclimbing. The hillclimbing algorithm used has three notable properties. First, it allows moves to solutions with higher or equal evaluation; this is extremely important for hillclimbing to work well in many complicated spaces, since this allows it to explore plateaus. Second, before restarting, up to **PATIENCE** evaluations are allowed that are worse than the best evaluation seen so far in the run. Evaluations which are equal to the best evaluation seen so far are not counted towards the **PATIENCE** count. This parameter has a large impact on the effectiveness of hillclimbing in large search spaces. Therefore, for each problem, multiple settings were tried for this parameter. The range of values was (1*|X|) to (10*|X|), where |X| is the length of the solution encoding. The results with the best setting of the **PATIENCE** parameter are reported. Third, the hillclimbing algorithm used is a next-ascent hillclimber; as soon as a better solution is found, it is accepted. This contrasts with steepest-ascent hillclimbing, which searches all possible single-bit changes and accepts the one with the largest improvement. On the problems explored here, steepest ascent hillclimbing did not work as well.

__COMIT:__ We experiment with two versions of the COMIT algorithm: one with **K** set to 100 (termed COMIT-100), which samples the tree 100 times before selecting the best point; and one with K=1000 (termed COMIT-1000). These evaluations are counted against the total allowed.

__Augmented Hillclimbing (AHC):__ The fact that COMIT-*K* examines **K** points before choosing one to use for hillclimbing is a possible confounding factor in determining how effective COMIT is in comparison to HC. To ensure that it is not simply the process of selecting these **K** before hillclimbing that gives performance gains, we augment hillclimbing as follows. Before the beginning of each run, AHC-*K* examines **K** *randomly* chosen points from which it selects the best one as the starting position. (The difference between this and COMIT is that COMIT samples **K** points from the dependency tree). Two versions of AHC are examined: AHC-100, and AHC-1000.

Note that all of the parameters of all of the algorithms were tuned on the 100-city TSP problem, and were held constant for all runs and all problems.

3.2 Results

For each algorithm on each problem, we try multiple settings of the **PATIENCE** parameter. The setting of the **PATIENCE** parameter that gives the best result is reported here. The results reported are the average of at least 25 runs of the entire algorithm. Each algorithm is given 200,000 function evaluations on each problem. Because of space limitations, the full description of the problems cannot be given here. However, brief descriptions are given in Appendix A. The results are shown in Table I. In the first line of each cell in the table, the numerical results are presented. In the second line, the rank (1[best]..5[worst]) of each algorithm is given. Also given for HC, AHC-100 and AHC-1000 is whether the difference between the results achieved is significantly different from that of COMIT-100 and COMIT-1000, respectively. The significance is measured by the Mann-Whitney test (a non-parametric equivalent to the t-test) at the 95% confidence interval.

Table I: COMIT with Hillclimbing

	Size of Problem in Bits (Goal: MAX or MIN)	HC ($\neq$C100, $\neq$C1000) (95% Conf. Interval)	AHC-100 ($\neq$C100, $\neq$C1000) (95% Conf. Interval)	AHC-1000 ($\neq$C100, $\neq$C1000) (95% Conf. Interval)	COMIT-100	COMIT-1000
Knapsack 512 elem.	512 (MAX)	3238 5 (Y,Y)	3377 3 (Y,Y)	3335 4 (Y,Y)	6684 1	6259 2
Knapsack 900 elem.	900 (MAX)	3403 5 (Y,Y)	3418 4 (Y,Y)	3488 3 (Y,Y)	7733 1	7182 2
Knapsack 1200 elem.	1200 (MAX)	5226 5 (Y,Y)	5270 4 (Y,Y)	5280 3 (Y,Y)	13052 1	12829 2
Jobshop-enc 1 10x10	500 (MIN)	998 5 (Y,Y)	988 4 (Y,Y)	982 3 (N,Y)	978 2	970 1
Jobshop-enc 2 10x10	700 (MIN)	965 5 (Y,Y)	961 4 (Y,Y)	957 3 (N,N)	954 2	953 1
Jobshop-enc 2 20x5	700 (MIN)	1207 5 (Y,Y)	1201 4 (Y,Y)	1199 3 (N,N)	1196 2	1196 1
Binpack (10^{-3}) 8 bins, 168 el.	504 (MIN)	1.70 5 (N,Y)	1.58 3 (N,N)	1.62 4 (N,N)	1.56 2	1.45 1
Binpack (10^{-2}) 16 bins, 200 el.	800 (MIN)	1.54 5 (Y,Y)	1.50 4 (Y,Y)	1.38 3 (Y,Y)	1.11 1	1.24 2
Summation Cancellation	675 (MIN)	64 5 (Y,Y)	61 4 (Y,Y)	59 3 (Y,Y)	54 2	52 1
TSP 100 city	700 (MIN)	1629 5 (Y,Y)	1599 4 (Y,Y)	1573 3 (Y,Y)	1335 1	1336 2
TSP 200 city	1600 (MIN)	15119 3 (N,N)	15286 5 (N,N)	15100 1 (N,N)	15189 4	15117 2
TSP 150 city	1200 (MIN)	11451 5 (Y,Y)	11247 3 (Y,Y)	11290 4 (Y,Y)	9812 2	9077 1

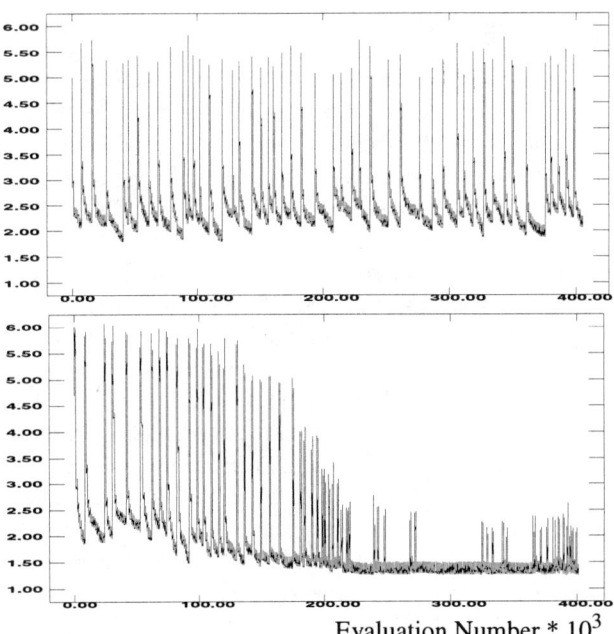

Figure 4: These graphs show the values of every evaluation performed by the HC (top) and COMIT (bottom) algorithms for the TSP domain. The object is to minimize the tour length. Note that these runs are extended to 400,000 evaluations.

In almost every problem examined, COMIT significantly improves the performance over hillclimbing. Only in one problem (200-city TSP) did one of the COMIT runs (COMIT-100) not perform as well as HC. However, the difference in performance was not statistically significant.

To provide some intuition about how the COMIT algorithm progresses, Figure 4 shows the values of each evaluation performed by the HC and COMIT-1000 algorithm in the TSP domain. There are four features that should be noticed. First, the spikes in the evaluations correspond to the beginning of hillclimbing runs. In the COMIT graph, the spikes also represent the **K** samples generated by sampling the tree. Second, for the COMIT algorithm, the random initial samples in the dataset **S** were entirely removed by evaluation #90,000 (this approximately corresponds to the number of evaluations used in the first 10 hillclimbing runs; each run contributed 100 samples to the dataset, and the size of **S** is 1000). Third, the magnitude of the spikes in the COMIT plot gradually decreases; this corresponds to the COMIT algorithm learning to seed the hillclimbing runs with high-quality solutions. Fourth, and most importantly, the final solutions found at each hillclimbing run have improved over standard hillclimbing, even before the HC runs are started at noticeably better solutions. This indicates that by using the interparameter dependency models to generate starting points, the hillclimbing runs are started in basins of the search space that lead to high-evaluation solutions.

4 Using COMIT with PBIL

The previous section demonstrated that relatively complex probabilistic models can be used in conjunction with search techniques, such as hillclimbing, that maintain only a single solution from which new solutions are generated. In this section, we examine how to integrate COMIT with other algorithms that themselves model probability distributions of possible solutions. As described in Section 1, PBIL only maintains unconditional probabilities; no inter-parameter dependencies are modeled. A vector, **P**, specifies the probability of generating a 1 in each bit position. Initially, all values in **P** are set to 0.5. A number of solution vectors are generated by stochastically sampling **P**; each bit is sampled independently of all the others. The probability vector is then moved towards the generated solution vector with the highest evaluation according to Equation 6. The update rule is similar to the updates used in unsupervised competitive learning [Hertz, et al. 1991].

$$ProbabilityVector_{t+1, i} = \qquad (6)$$
$$(1 - \alpha) \cdot ProbabilityVector_{t, i} + \alpha \cdot BestSolutionVector_i$$

$ProbabilityVector_{t,i}$ is the value of the probability vector at time t, for parameter i. $BestSolutionVector_i$ is the value of parameter i in the vector being used to update the probability vector. α is a learning rate parameter that determines how much each new datapoint changes the value of the probability vector. The basic version of the PBIL algorithm and its parameters are shown in Figure 5. The final result of the PBIL algorithm is the best solution generated throughout the search. The version used here extended this as suggested in [Baluja, 1997]: first, a mutation operator was added. This randomly selects positions in the probability vector to alter. The motivation for using a mutation operator is to preserve diversity in the generated solutions; therefore, the mutation operator always moves the probabilities to higher-entropy states (closer to 0.5). Second, instead of only moving towards the best solution, the probability vector was also moved away from the worst solution in the positions in which the best and worst solutions differed.

In the experiments conducted with COMIT in this section, three algorithms were compared. The first algorithm, which we use as a baseline, is PBIL. The parameters are set as follows: α=.15, M=1, N=50, MUT_PROB = 0.02, MUT_SHIFT= 0.05; these parameters are also used for the second and third algorithms. The second algorithm tested is COMIT-PBIL. COMIT-PBIL is identical to the version of COMIT used for hillclimbing except for the following differences: PBIL is used instead of hillclimbing; each PBIL run is terminated after 5000 evaluations without improvement. At the beginning of a PBIL run, each entry of the probability vector, **P**, is initialized to the average value of

```
****** Initialize Probability Vector ******
for i :=1 to LENGTH do P[i] := 0.5;

while (NOT termination condition)
    ***** Generate Samples *****
    for i :=1 to N do
        solution_vectors[i] := generate_vector_with_probabilities (P);
        evaluations[i] :=Evaluate_Solution (solution_vectors[i]);

    best_solution_vectors =
        sort_solutions_best_to_worst (solution_vectors,evaluations);

    **** Update Probability Vector towards best solutions ****
    for i := M downto 1 do
        for j :=1 to LENGTH do
            P[j] := P[j] * (1.0 - α) + best_solution_vectors[i][j]* (α);

    **** Mutation - Always move towards 0.5 ****
    for i := 1 to LENGTH do
        if (random (0,1) < MUT_PROB) then
            if (P[i] > 0.5) P[i] := P[i]*(1.0 - MUT_SHIFT);
            else P[i] := P[i]*(1.0 - MUT_SHIFT) + MUT_SHIFT
```

Return the best solution generated throughout the entire search.

PBIL CONSTANTS:
N: # of vectors generated before update of the probability vector.
α: the learning rate, how fast to exploit the search performed.
M: number of vectors in the population that are used to update P.
LENGTH: # of bits in the solution encoding (problem dependent).
MUT_PROB: probability of "mutating" each bit position.
MUT_SHIFT: amount a mutation alters the value in the bit position

Figure 5: Basic PBIL algorithm for a binary alphabet.

that position in the top 10% of the solutions generated by sampling the tree-based model 1000 times. As described in Section 2, the tree-based model is created from the data-set **S**, which contains the good solutions returned from multiple PBIL searches. As before, the size of **S** is 1000 and **MAX_INFLUENCE** is 100. The algorithm is shown in Figure 6. The third algorithm tested is PBIL with restarts; after 5,000 evaluations are conducted with no improvement, the algorithm is restarted. This test is to ensure that it is the probabilistic modeling (of COMIT) that is responsible for the increase in performance, not simply the fact that PBIL is being restarted. The parameters for all of the algorithms were tuned on the 100-city TSP problem, and no parameter changes were made for any other problem.

- Initialize dataset **S** with random solutions from uniform distribution
- While termination condition is not met:
  - Create a tree-shaped probabilistic network **T** that models **S**.
  - Use **T** to stochastically generate **K** solutions. Evaluate new solutions.
  - Select top **C**% of the **K** generated solutions.
  - Initialize PBIL's **P** vector to unconditional probabilities in selected solutions.
  - Execute PBIL run. Replace up to **MAX_INFLUENCE** bitstrings in **S** with better bitstrings found during the PBIL run just executed.

USER DEFINED CONSTANTS (values used in this study)
|S|: Constant size of the dataset **S**. **(1000)**
MAX_INFLUENCE: max number of bitstrings to replace in **S** with better strings from a single fast-search run (100).
C: Percentage of **K** generated solutions used to initialize **P**. (10)

Figure 6: Overview of the COMIT algorithm for PBIL.

The results are shown in Table II. Each experiment was given 600,000 evaluations. The results reported are the average of at least 50 experiments per algorithm, per problem. In the first line of each cell in the table, the numerical results are presented. In the second line, the rank (1[best]..3[worst]) of each algorithm is given. Also given for PBIL with no-restarts and random restarts is whether the difference between the results is significantly different from those of COMIT-PBIL.

Table II: COMIT with PBIL

	Size of Problems in Bits (Goal: Maximize or Minimize)	PBIL - No Restart ($\neq$ to COMIT at 95% conf)	PBIL - Restart ($\neq$ to COMIT at 95% conf)	COMIT-PBIL
Knapsack 512 elem.	512 (MAX)	7823 2 (Y)	7765 3 (Y)	7872 1
Knapsack 900 elem.	900 (MAX)	9601 2 (Y)	9402 3 (Y)	10134 1
Knapsack 1200 elem.	1200 (MAX)	14668 2 (Y)	13768 3 (Y)	18014 1
Jobshop-enc 1 10x10	500 (MIN)	982 3 (Y)	963 2 (N)	961 1
Jobshop-enc 2 10x10	700 (MIN)	959 3 (Y)	943 2 (Y)	940 1
Jobshop-enc 2 20x5	700 (MIN)	1188 3 (Y)	1176 2 (Y)	1170 1
Binpack (10^{-3}) 8 bins, 168 el.	504 (MIN)	1.4 1 (Y)	2.8 2 (N)	2.8 3
Binpack (10^{-2}) 16 bins, 200 el.	800 (MIN)	8.3 1 (Y)	9.6 2 (N)	10.0 3
Summation Cancellation	675 (MIN)	25 1 (Y)	33 2 (N)	33 3
TSP 100 city	700 (MIN)	1331 2 (Y)	1518 3 (Y)	1021 1
TSP 200 city	1600 (MIN)	17148 2 (Y)	21858 3 (Y)	14870 1
TSP 150 city	1200 (MIN)	11035 2 (Y)	13698 3 (Y)	9078 1

In summary, in the majority of the problems examined, the COMIT-PBIL approach was significantly better than PBIL, both with and without restarts. This is encouraging, since PBIL has itself often outperformed standard genetic algorithms and hillclimbing techniques on similar problems [Baluja, 1997]. Two exceptions to this are the binpacking problem and the summation cancellation problem. In both of these problems, COMIT's choice of restarting points did not hurt performance; however, not restarting PBIL at all led to better performance.

5 Conclusions & Future Work

We have shown that probabilistic models can be used to combine the information gathered from runs of fast search algorithms. By using a model of the interparameter dependencies in previously found good solutions, new starting points for the fast search algorithm are chosen. In most of the problems examined, this has led to the discovery of significantly better final solutions.

One can imagine that COMIT lies in the middle of a continuous spectrum, with the ends representing never using a probabilistic model (as is done with hillclimbing) and always using a probabilistic model (as is done in [Baluja & Davies, 1997]). In the Tree-based algorithm described in [Baluja & Davies, 1997a], all of the candidate generation is done by sampling the model, and the high-evaluation points are added directly back into **S**. The empirical results with COMIT have demonstrated that even infrequent use of the probabilistic model is advantageous. An immediate direction for future research is to determine if there is any performance loss incurred by using the complex probabilistic models only for the initialization of searches when compared to always using the probabilistic model (which is extremely computationally expensive). In the preliminary tests conducted, the COMIT algorithm was often able to perform as well as the Tree-Based algorithm. Quantifying the difference in performance and computational expense is currently being researched.

Because different search algorithms have different sampling procedures, each may explore different regions of the solution space. By allowing all of the search algorithms to contribute solutions to the dataset from which dependencies are modeled, COMIT provides a simple method for combining multiple different search algorithms.

Since the probabilistic model is updated infrequently by COMIT, it may be feasible to replace the dependency-tree model with more sophisticated but computationally expensive models, such as general Bayesian networks. It will be interesting to determine if automatically learning networks with hidden variables [Friedman, 1997] would improve optimization performance. It will also be interesting to examine whether it is possible to explicitly use the fact that the samples modeled are *not* independent, as is assumed by the probabilistic models used here.

We illustrated how to incorporate COMIT with PBIL and hillclimbing. Although not reported here, we have used COMIT to restart genetic algorithm (GA) based searches. This combination improved the performance over the GA alone. However, neither the GA nor COMIT-GA were typically able to perform as well as the hillclimbing and PBIL approaches presented here. COMIT requires no change to be used with other search algorithms such as simulated annealing or TABU search [Glover, 1989]. In addition to these general search techniques, it can also be used with randomized search techniques designed to address specific problems, such as WALKSAT [Selman *et. al*, 1996].

References

Baluja, S. (1997) "Genetic Algorithms and Explicit Search Statistics," *Advances in Neural Information Processing System*s 9, 1996. Mozer, M.C., Jordan, M.I., & Petsche, T. (Eds). MIT Press.

Baluja, S. (1995),"An Empirical Comparison of Seven Iterative and Evolutionary Heuristics for Static Function Optimization" Technical Report CMU-CS-95-193, Carnegie Mellon University, Pittsburgh, PA.

Baluja, S. & Davies, S. (1997a) "Using Optimal Dependency-Trees for Combinatorial Optimization: Learning the Structure of the Search Space", *Proc. 1997 International Conference on Machine Learning.* pp 30-38.

Baluja, S. & Davies, S. (1997b) "Probabilistic Modeling for Combinatorial Optimization", *Pre-Print*.

Boyan, J. & Moore, A. (1997) "Using Prediction to Improve Global Optimization", to appear in *Sixth Intl. Wkshp. on AI & Statistics*.

Chickering, D., Geiger, D., and Heckerman, D. (1995) "Learning Bayesian networks: Search methods and experimental results," *Proc.of Fifth Conference on Artificial Intelligence and Statistics*

Chou. C. and Liu, C. (1968) Approximating discrete probability distributions with dependence trees. *IEEE Trans. on Info. Theory*, 14:462-467.

De Bonet, J., Isbell, C., and Viola, P. (1997) "MIMIC: Finding Optima by Estimating Probability Densities," *Advances in Neural Information Processing Systems*, 1996. Mozer, M.C., Jordan, M.I, & Petsche, T. (Eds).

Fang, H.L., Ross, P. & Corne, D. "A Promising GA Approach to Job-Shop Scheduling, Rescheduling and Open-Shop Scheduling Problems". In *Proc. Int. Conf. on GAs-95*. S. Forrest, (ed). Morgan Kaufmann.

Friedman (1997) "Learning Belief Networks in the Presence of Missing Values and Hidden Variables," *Proc. 1997 International Conference on Machine Learning.* pp 125-133.

Glover, F. (1989) "Tabu-Search - Part I", *ORSA Journal on Computing* 1:190-206.

Greene, J.R. (1996) "Population-Based Incremental Learning as a Simple Versatile Tool for Engineering Optimization". In *Proceedings of the First International Conf. on EC and Applications.* pp. 258-269.

Heckerman, D., Geiger, D., and Chickering, D. (1995) "Learning Bayesian networks: The combination of knowledge and statistical data," *Machine Learning* 20:197-243.

Hertz, J., Krogh A., & Palmer R.G. (1991), *Introduction to the Theory of Neural Computing*. Addison-Wesley, Reading, MA.

Hohfeld, M. & Rudolph, G. (1997) "Towards a Theory of Population-Based Incremental Learning", *International Conference on Evolutionary Computation*. pp. 1-5.

Juels, A. (1996) *Topics in Black-box Combinatorial Optimization*. Ph.D. Thesis, University of California - Berkeley.

Kvasnica, V., Pelikan, M, Pospical, J. "Hill Climbing with Learning (An Abstraction of Genetic Algorithm). *In Proceedings of the First International Conference on Genetic Algorithms (MENDEL, '95)*. pp. 65-73.

Muth & Thompson (1963) *Industrial Scheduling* Prentice Hall International. Englewood Cliffs, NJ.

Pearl, J. (1988) *Probabilistic Reasoning in Intelligent Systems*. Morgan Kaufmann.

Selman, B. Kautz, H. & Cohen, B. (1996) "Local Search Strategies for Satisfiability Testing", in Johnson & Trick (eds) Cliques, Coloring and Satisfiability, DIMANCS VOlume 26 521-532.

Syswerda, G. (1989) "Uniform Crossover in Genetic Algorithms," *Int. Conf. on Genetic Algorithms 3.* 2-9.

Syswerda, G. (1993) "Simulated Crossover in Genetic Algorithms," in (ed.) Whitley, D.L., Foundations of Genetic Algorithms 2, Morgan Kaufmann Publishers, San Mateo, CA. 239-255.

Thathachar, M, & Sastry, P.S. (1987) "Learning Optimal Discriminant Functions Through a Cooperative Game of Automata", *IEEE Transactions on Systems, Man, and Cybernetics*, Vol. 17, No. 1.

APPENDIX A: Problem Descriptions

Due to space limitations, only brief descriptions of the problems are given here. Details can be found in the referenced reports.

1. Traveling Salesman Problems (TSP)

The encoding used in this study requires a bit string of size $N\log_2 N$ bits, where N is the number of cities in the problem. Each city is assigned a substring of length $\log_2 N$ bits; the value of these bits determines the order in which the city is visited. See [Syswerda, 1989] for details. Three problem were attempted: 100, 200 and 150 city.

2. Jobshop Scheduling Problems

Two standard test problems are attempted, a 10-job, 10-machine problem and a 20-job, 5-machine problem. A description of the problems can be found in [Muth & Thompson, 1963]. The first problem is encoded in two ways. The first encoding is commonly used with genetic algorithms; see [Fang et. al, 1993].

The second encoding [Baluja, 1995] is very similar to the encoding used in the Traveling Salesman Problem. The drawback of this encoding is that it uses more bits than the previous one. Nonetheless, empirically, it revealed improved results. Each job is assigned M entries of size $\log_2(J*M)$ bits. The total length of the encoding is $J*M*\log_2(J*M)$. The value of each entry (of length $\log_2(J*M)$) determines the order in which the jobs are scheduled. The job that contains the smallest valued entry is scheduled first, etc. The order in which the machines are selected for each job depends upon the ordering required by the problem specification.

3. Knapsack Problem

In this problem, there is a bin of limited capacity, and **M** elements of varying sizes and values. The goal is to select the elements that yield the greatest summed value without exceeding the capacity of the bin. A penalty is given to solutions that exceed the maximum capacity; the encoding was taken from [Baluja, 1995]. Three versions of the problem were attempted with 512, 900, and 1200 elements.

4. Bin Packing/Equal Piles

In this problem there are **N** bins of varying capacities and **M** elements of varying sizes. The goal is to pack the bins with elements as tightly as possible, so that the size of the bins closely matches the total size of the elements assigned to the bins. The solution is encoded in a bit string of length $M*\log_2 N$. Each element is assigned to a bin (which is encoded in $\log_2 N$ bits). These problems were generated so that there was an assignment of elements which matched the capacities of the bins exactly. Two version of this problem are explored, the first with 8 bins and 168 elements, and the second with 16 bins and 200 elements.

5. Summation Cancellation

In this problem, there is very strong parameter interdependence. The parameters in the beginning of the solution string have a large influence on the quality of the solution. The goal is to minimize the magnitudes of cumulative sums of the parameters. The problem had 75 parameters, and each parameter was represented with 9 bits, encoded in standard base-2, with the values uniformly spaced between -2.56 and +2.56. It is set as a maximization problem by using the reciprocal of the function.

$$-2.56 \le s_i \le 2.56 \quad y_i = s_i + y_{i-1} \quad f = \frac{1.0}{C + \left|\sum_1^N |y_i|\right|}$$

$$i = 1...N \quad i = 2...N$$

$$y_1 = s_1 \quad C = \frac{1}{100000}$$

Highest Utility First Search Across Multiple Levels of Stochastic Design

Louis Steinberg

J. Storrs Hall*

Brian D. Davison

Department of Computer Science, Rutgers University
New Brunswick, NJ 08903
{lou,davison}@cs.rutgers.edu

Abstract

Many design problems are solved using multiple levels of abstraction, where a design at one level has combinatorially many children at the next level. A stochastic optimization methods, such as simulated annealing, genetic algorithms and multi-start hill climbing, is often used in such cases to generate the children of a design. This gives rise to a search tree for the overall problem characterized by a large branching factor, objects at different levels that are hard to compare, and a child-generator that is too expensive to run more than a few times at each level. We present the Highest Utility First Search (HUFS) control algorithm for searching such trees. HUFS is based on an estimate we derive for the expected utility of starting the design process from any given design alternative, where utility reflects both the intrinsic value of the final result and the cost in computing resources it will take to get that result. We also present an empirical study applying HUFS to the problem of VLSI module placement, in which HUFS demonstrates significantly better performance than the common "waterfall" control method.

INTRODUCTION

Some parts of some problems are naturally decomposed into successive levels of abstraction. E.g., in designing a microprocessor, we might start with an instruction set, implement the instructions as a series of pipeline stages, implement the set of stages as a "netlist" defining how specific circuit modules are to be wired together, etc.

There are typically a combinatorially large number of ways a design at one level can be implemented at the next level down, but only a small, fixed set of levels, maybe a dozen or two at the extreme. Thus the search space is a tree with depth of a dozen or two but with huge, branching factors. Furthermore, the partial solutions at different levels are entirely different types of things, and it is hard to come up with heuristic evaluation functions that allow us to compare, say, a set of

[0]Copyright ©1998, American Association for Artificial Intelligence (wwww.aaai.org). All rights reserved.
[0]Current address: Institute for Molecular Manufacturing, 123 Fremont Ave, Los Altos, CA, josh@imm.org

pipeline stages and a netlist. The huge branching factor and the disparate types at different levels make it hard to apply standard tree-search algorithms such as A* or Branch-and-Bound to this search space.

Recently, a number of techniques for stochastic optimization have been shown to be useful for specific levels of such problems. These techniques include simulated annealing (Ingber 1996), genetic algorithms(Michalewicz 1996; Goldberg 1989), and random-restart hill climbing(Zha *et al.* 1996). A design at one level is translated into a correct but poor design at the next level, and a stochastic optimizer is used to improve this design. An inherent feature of a stochastic method is that it can be run again and again on the same inputs, each time potentially producing a different answer. Thus, these optimizers generate a much smaller tree of greatly enhanced quality. However, even this tree has a large branching factor (in the thousands for examples we have looked at), and the cost of generating a single descendant is so high we cannot possibly generate more than a few at each level, so there is still the problem of controlling the search within the smaller tree.

In practice, human engineers faced with a design task that has this structure often take a very simple "waterfall" approach: they work from top down, using CAD tools such as optimizers to generate only a few (often one) alternatives at a given level. They choose the best design at this level by some heuristic that compares alternatives *within* a level, and use this best design as the (only) parent from which to generate designs at the next level down.

This paper presents an alternative to the waterfall control method, called "Highest Utility First Search" (HUFS). HUFS applies ideas from the decision theory(Tribus 1969) to explore the tree of alternatives in a much more flexible manner than waterfall. We will describe HUFS and present empirical data from one example design task showing that HUFS can be a significant improvement over waterfall search.

HUFS is based on the idea that a good control method is not one that finds the best design, but one that gives the best tradeoff between computation cost and design quality, and that therefore control decisions should be based on an analysis of the *utility*, of each possible computation, i.e. the value of the result minus the cost of doing the computation.

In our context, we can use the notion of the utility of a computation to define the utility of a design alternative. The utility of a design alternative d, which we will refer to as $Udesign(d)$, is the expected utility of a design process that starts with d as input and returns a ground-level design from among the descendants of d. I.e., the utility of d is the expected difference between the value of the final design we will get if we use d as our starting point and the cost of the computation it will take to get this design. (This formulation of utility was taken from (Russell & Wefald 1991).)

The basic idea of HUFS is very simple:

Find the design alternative d_{opt} with the highest $Udesign$, among all the design alternatives you currently have on all the levels, and generate one child from d_{opt}, that is, run the appropriate level's optimizer with d_{opt} as input. Repeat this process until d_{opt} is a ground-level design, then stop and return d_{opt} as the result

To do his, however, we need some way of estimating $Udesign(d)$. Below we will explain how HUFS does this and will present HUFS in more detail. We will then describe our empirical test of HUFS, and then discuss related work. In order to provide a concrete example to use in these sections, we will first describe the design problem we have used as the main testbed for our research on HUFS.

The Example Problem: Module Placement

The initial example problem that we have been using to drive our work is the problem of positioning rectangular circuit modules on the surface of a VLSI chip: a given set of rectangles must be placed in a plane in a way that minimizes the area of the bounding box circumscribed around the rectangles plus a factor that accounts for the area taken by the wires needed to connect the modules in a specified way.

The input to the placement problem is a "netlist". A netlist specifies a set of modules, where each module is a rectangle of fixed size along with a set of "ports". A port is simply a location within the rectangle where a wire may be connected. In addition to giving the modules, a netlist specifies which ports of which modules must be connected by wires.

The output from a placement problem is a location and orientation for each module. Modules may be rotated by any multiple of 90 degrees and/or reflected in X, Y, or both. The modules' rectangles may not overlap.

We break the placement process into two stages. First we choose a structure called a "slicing tree". A slicing tree is a binary tree. Each leaf is a module to be placed. Each non-leaf node represents the commitment to place a particular group of modules next to another group, in a given relative position. The slicing tree does not determine the reflections, however. The module or group of modules that correspond to any node in the tree can still be replaced by their reflections in X and/or Y. Reflecting a module cannot change the circuit's bounding box area but it can change wire lengths and thus wire area.

The optimizer for slicing trees starts by generating a random binary tree. We define a set of neighbors as those trees that can be reached from the current tree by choosing two nodes and interchanging the subtrees rooted at those nodes. At each step of the optimizer, we generate the neighbors of the current tree in a random order until we find a neighbor that is better than the current tree. When we find a better one, we make that the current tree and repeat. If no neighbor is better, the optimizer halts.

The second stage of the placement process converts a slicing tree into a full, specific placement by choosing a set of reflections for each node in the slicing tree and then optimizing the reflections, Reflections are optimized in the same way that slicing trees are, with one set of reflections defined to be a neighbor of another if they can be reached from each other by reflecting one node of the slicing tree in one dimension.

Expected Utility and Highest Utility First Search

This section will first explain the process HUFS uses to estimate $Udesign(d)$, the expected utility of design using alternative d as the starting point. We will see that some of the information HUFS uses in this process is not directly provided by HUFS' input, so we will then explain how HUFS gets this additional information. Finally, we will give the HUFS algorithm.

Calculating $Udesign(d)$

Let us start by considering a simplified case. We will focus on a single-level problem such as that of generating full placements from a slicing tree. Also we will assume that HUFS has all of the following information:

- The *cost*, c, of the CPU time to run the optimizer once. We assume that each run has the same fixed cost.

- A heuristic *Score function* $S(f)$, where f is a full placement. S gives an estimate of how good a design f is. We assume a lower score is a better design.

- A *Utility function*, $U(s)$, that represents utility we place on having a child with score s. This utility needs to be in the same units as c. We will assume that utilities are non-negative. Since a larger utility is better, $U(s)$ is monotonic decreasing.

- The *Child-Score Distribution*, $G(s)$. This is a probability distribution. It gives the probability that if we generate a full placement its score will be s. G will depend on which slicing tree we are using as input to the optimizer, but for the moment let us assume that we are dealing with one specific slicing tree and that we know its G.

Since for now we are considering a single level problem, there is no question of which optimizer to run or which input to give it — there is only one optimizer, and only one possible slicing tree to use as input. All that needs to be chosen is whether to do another run or to stop and declare the best design we have so far to be our final answer.

To make this choice, we consider the utility of doing one more run. If the utility of doing that one run is positive, i.e., if the utility of doing the run exceeds the cost, it clearly makes sense to do that run, and if not it makes sense to stop. We assume we know c, the cost of a run, so to determine the utility we just need to determine the utility of the run. We call this utility the *expected incremental utility*, EIU, of doing a run. It is the average expected increase in utility (based on the information we have now) from the best design we have now to the best design we will have after the run.

The better the current best score is, the less likely it is that another run will do better, so the EIU depends on the best score we have so far. If s_b is the current best score and N is a random variable representing the score we will get on the next run,

$$\begin{aligned} EIU(s_b) &= E(\max(U(s_b), U(N)) - U(s_b)) \\ &= \sum_s G(s)(\max(0, U(s) - U(s_b))) \end{aligned}$$

Where E is Expected Value and s ranges over all possible child scores. (Note that the probability that $N = s$ is just $G(s)$.) Since U is monotonic decreasing,

$$\begin{aligned} EIU(s_b) &= \sum_s G(s)\max(0, U(s) - U(s_b)) \\ &= (\sum_{s<s_b} G(s)U(s)) - U(s_b)\sum_{s<s_b} G(s) \end{aligned}$$

Note that s_b cannot increase as we do more runs, and that as s_b decreases, $EIU(s_b)$ cannot increase. Therefore, once the EIU is less than c it will stay less than c for all further runs, so the expected utility of doing any number of further runs is negative, and the rational control decision at this point is to stop.

In other words, if we define the *threshold score* s_t to be such that $EIU(s_t) = c$, then the optimal strategy for a single-level problem is to continue generating children until we get one whose score is less than s_t.

Now, given the stopping criterion, we can calculate expected values for U^f, the utility of the resulting full placement, and for C, the total cost of the optimizer runs. From these we will calculate an expected value for the utility of the overall process. Note the distinction between U^f, the utility of *having* the final design,

and $U(d)$, the utility of doing the work to *compute* the design, which is $U^f - C$.

The final full placement is the first one we find whose score is less than s_t, so the Expected Value of its utility is the average over these scores of $U(s)$, weighted by the *relative* probability of each score, i.e., the probability of getting that score given that we got some score less than s_t:

$$E(U^f) = \sum_{s<s_t} U(s)G(s) / \sum_{s<s_t} G(s)$$

The chance of finding a score under s_t in one run is $\sum_{s<s_t} G(s)$ so the average number of runs to find such a score is $1/\sum_{s<s_t} G(s)$ and the Expected Value of C is

$$E(C) = c / \sum_{s<s_t} G(s)$$

The Expected Utility of the overall design process is $E(U^f - C)$ but because the scores of successive children are independent, and the cost of a single optimizer run is a constant and therefore independent of the score of the child it produces, U^f and C are independent, and $E(U^f - C) = E(U^f) - E(C)$. so

$$Udesign(d) = \frac{\sum_{s<s_t} U(s)G(s)}{\sum_{s<s_t} G(s)} - \frac{c}{\sum_{s<s_t} G(s)}$$

A curious property to note is that $EIU(s_t) = c$ implies (by algebra on the formula above for EIU) that

$$U(s_t) = \frac{\sum_{s<s_t} U(s)G(s) - c}{\sum_{s<s_t} G(s)}$$

which is just $Udesign(d)$. That is, the utility of the design process is just the utility of the threshold score s_t. Since we stop for any score better than s_t the expected utility of the score we stop at will be better than $U(s_t)$. But the expected utility of the design process is the expected utility of the design we stop with minus the expected cost of the runs, and subtracting the cost of the runs brings us exactly back to $U(s_t)$.

In general, then, the expected utility of generating a final ground-level design from a design alternative d at the next higher abstraction level is

$$Udesign(d) = U(s_t(G, U, c))$$

where $s_t(G, U, c)$ is the score such that $(\sum_{s<s_t} U(s)G(s)) - U(s_t)\sum_{s<s_t} G(s) = c$

That is, the utility of a given non-ground object is determined by its G.

In this subsection we have shown how to compute $Udesign(d)$ from G, U, and c in a single-level case. However, in general we do not know a priori what G is. Different slicing trees have different Gs, and it is not reasonable to ask that their Gs be provided as inputs to HUFS. Therefore, HUFS has to estimate the Gs for itself. In following subsections we will discuss how it does so, and then show how the approach we have discussed for a single-level problem can be extended to multiple levels. Before we cover these topics, however, we will explain the notational conventions we use in the rest of this paper.

We will number the abstraction levels from the lowest level to the highest, with ground-level designs (e.g. full placements) being at level 0. So a slicing tree is at level 1 and a netlist at level 2. We will use superscripts to denote levels. Thus for our example problem either d^{tree} or d^1 would refer to a slicing tree design alternative, while d^0 would be a full placement.

The distribution $G(s)$ depends not only on the level but on which specific parent we are generating from. We will let $G(s|d)$ be the child-score distribution for d, that is,

$$G(s|d) = P(S(d') = s | d' \text{ is a child of d})$$

We will use similar notation with other probability distributions we mention.

Estimating G

In general, we will not know the exact G for any design alternative. Instead, we make a heuristic estimate of the G. If from this estimate it appears worthwhile to generate children we do so, and as we see the scores of these children we update our estimate using a Bayesian method. This section will describe how we form our initial of the G and how we update it.

We model the Gs for a given level as all coming from some parameterized family of distributions, e.g. the family of normal distributions with parameters specifying the mean and standard deviation. We assume the family is specified as part of the input to HUFS. Given the family we can specify a particular G by a tuple r containing a value for each of the family's parameters. Thus, $r = <10, 2>$ might represent a normal distribution with mean 10 and standard deviation 2. Also, we define the function $R(d)$ to mean the R tuple that corresponds to $G(d|d)$, the G of design alternative d.

The user specifies the family of distributions by giving the function $G(s|r)$, where,

$$G(s|r) = P(S(child) = s | R(parent(child)) = r)$$

For example, if the family is the normal distributions, $G(s| <\mu, \sigma>) = e^{-(s-\mu)^2/(2\sigma^2)} / \sqrt{2\Pi}\sigma$.

The problem of determining $G(s|d)$ then becomes the problem of determining $R(d)$. We cannot determine exactly what $R(d)$ is, but we can estimate the probability that $R(d) = r$ for any specific r. This is equivalent to estimating the probability that $G(s|d)$ is any given member of the family of distributions. We define the probability distribution $H(r|d)$ to be the probability that $R(d) = r$. We make an initial estimate of $H(r|d)$ and use it to make our initial estimate of $G(s|d)$, then as we see scores of d's children we update our estimate of $H(r|d)$ and use it to get our updated estimate of $G(s|d)$.

Our initial estimate is based on the parent's score. Just as we assumed we have a heuristic score function, S^0, on the children, we assume we have a similar function, S^1, on the parents. In our example, S^1, i.e.

$S^{tree}(t)$, is the sum of the module area from the tree and an estimate of wire area based on the number of tree edges between modules that must be connected.

So, in addition to the $G(s|r)$, the user needs to provide a function

$$H(r|s) = P(R(d) = r | S(d) = s)$$

Continuing our example, if $H(<10, 2> | 100) = 0.1$, then a parent whose score is 100 has probability 0.1 of having a child distribution with mean 10 and standard deviation 2.

When we generate children from d, we update our estimate of $H(r|d)$ by using $H(r|S(d))$ (that is, $H(r|s)$ where $s = S(d)$) as our prior estimate and $H(r|d)$ as our posteriori estimate, and the standard Bayesian formula (Tribus 1969),

$$sP(R(d) = r | \text{child scores} = s_1 \ldots s_n) =$$
$$\frac{P(R(d) = r)P(\text{child scores} = s_1 \ldots s_n | R(d) = r)}{P(\text{child scores} = s_1 \ldots s_n)}$$

i.e.,

$$H(r|d) = \frac{H(r|s) \prod_{i=1}^n G(s_i|r)}{\int H(r'|s) \prod_{i=1}^n G(s_i|r') dr'}$$

Now, given our estimate of $H(r|d)$, we can estimate $G(s|d)$ as

$$G(s|d) = \int H(r|d) G(s|r) dr$$

Since $G(s|d)$ is only an estimate of the true G, and especially since it is an estimate that is changed as a result of generating children, the control strategy of stopping when $EIU(s_b) < c$ is not necessarily the optimal rational strategy. In the previous subsection, where we assumed a known, fixed G, once the EIU was less than c, further optimizer runs could never increase the EIU, so there could be no point in continuing. Here, however, even if the current G is less than c another optimizer run could change the CSD in a way that increases the EIU, and thus making it rational to continue.

One way to look at this situation is to say that doing an optimizer run gets you an improved estimate of the parent's H, that doing so has utility, and this utility may justify doing an optimizer run even when the EIU by itself does not. We would like to find a method to include this utility in our accounting, but for now it is ignored.

In summary, we can estimate a design alternative's $G(s|d)$ from its $H(r|s)$, its score, and the scores of any children we have generated. From the alternative's $G(S|d)$ we can estimate its $Udesign$. So far, however, we have assumed we had a single-level problem.

Multiple Levels: Estimating $Udesign$

Now we turn to the task of calculating $Udesign$ for a multi-level problem. If we knew U^{i-1}, S^{i-1}, c^{i-1}, and $G(s^{i-1}|d^i)$ we could apply our single level method to compute $Udesign(d^i)$:

$$Udesign(d^i) = U^{i-1}(s_t(G(s^{i-1}|d^i), U^{i-1}, c^{i-1}))$$

where $s_t(G(s|d), U, c)$ is the score such that

$$\left(\sum_{s<s_t} U(s)G(s|d)\right) - U(s_t)\sum_{s<s_t} G(s|d) = c$$

In fact, we assume we are given S^{i-1} and c^{i-1} as part of the input to HUFS. We can use the method discussed in the previous subsection to estimate $G(s^{i-1}|d^i)$ from $G(s^{i-1}|r^i)$, $H(r^i|s^i)$, and S^i, all of which we assume are provided to HUFS, and from the scores of any children of d^i we have generated.

The only difficulty is in determining U^{i-1}. Since a ground-level design is the output the user is asking the design system for, we assume the user can tell us what a such a design is worth, so we assume U^0 is supplied to HUFS. But even if we know what, e.g., a full placement is worth, how can we determine the utility of a design alternative at a higher level, e.g. a slicing tree?

In fact, in and of itself a slicing tree has no utility — it only has utility as a starting point for generating placements. Thus it makes sense to define its utility in terms of the utility of the placement we would ultimately end up with if we started with this slicing tree. Of course, we have to subtract from this utility the cost of getting from the slicing tree to that placement. But the utility of the resulting placement minus the cost of finding it is just the utility of the slicing tree. So, the utility of a slicing tree is just its *Udesign*.

Now, when calculating $U^{tree}(s)$ we may not have a specific tree whose utility is s. For instance, in calculating s_t we integrate $U(s)$ over a range of values of s. Thus, what we need is $U^{tree}(s)$, which takes a tree score, not a tree, as its argument. In other words, we need to be able to calculate the a priori utility a hypothetical tree *would* have if its score were some given s. Since we know nothing about this tree but its score, we estimate its $H(r|d)$ by just applying this level's $H(r|s)$ to the score. In general for a design alternative d^i with no children,

$$G(s^{i-1}|s^i) = \int H(r|s^i)G(s^{i-1}|r)dr$$

where s^{i-1} is the child score whose probability we are calculating, and s^i is a parent score.

From $G(s^{i-1}|s^i)$ we can calculate the utility of a d^i whose score is s:

$$U(d^i|s) = U(d^{i-1}|s_t(G(s^i-1|s^i), U^{i-1}, c^{i-1}))$$

So we can compute U^{tree} from $H(r^{tree}|s^{tree}$, $U(d^{placement}|s)$, and $c^{placement}$. Given a netlist L, we can compute an a priori $H(r^{netlist}|L)$ for L from L's score and $H(r^{netlist}|s^{netlist}$, and update $H(r^{netlist}|L)$ from the scores of the trees we generate from L. From $H(r^{netlist}|L)$ we can compute $G(s^{tree}|L)$, and from that, from the function U^{tree}, and from the cost c^{tree} of generating a slicing tree we can compute a threshold score $s_t(L)$ for generating slicing trees from netlist L. This allows us to compute $Udesign(L) = U^{tree}(s_t(L))$.

Furthermore, our definition of U^{tree} allows us to combine the two single-level analyses (one for generating trees from netlists and one for generating placements from trees) to show that $Udesign(L)$ is not only the utility of generating trees from L, it is also the utility of the whole multi-level process of generating placements from L. (See (Steinberg, Hall, & Davison 1998) for this proof.)

Thus, in general, for level $i > 0$,

$$U^i(s) = U^{i-1}(s_t(G(s^{i-1}|s)), U^{i-1}, c^{i-1}))$$

The HUFS Algorithm

The HUFS algorithm is a best first search where "best" means "largest *Udesign*". We start with a single, top-level design alternative representing the initial problem specifications. At each step, we find the design alternative with the largest *Udesign*, generate one child from it, and compute the child's *Udesign*.

Now that the parent design alternative has a new child, we recompute the Bayesian update of the parent's $H(r|d)$ using all the child scores including this new one, and compute a revised utility, and hence a new *Udesign*, for the parent from the new $H(r|d)$. This new utility for the parent is used in turn to revise the $H(r|d)$ of *its* parent, and so on — we propagate the change in utility through all the ancestors of the new child.

Note that our formula for the utility of an alternative implicitly assumes that it and the alternatives below it will be designed with a modified waterfall search, going down level by level but using utilities to decide when to go to the next level. search. If we are using full HUFS, we should be able to get a higher quality design and/or take less time to do the design, and thus the utility of an alternative will be higher than the value of this formula. Ideally, HUFS should be adjusted to take this into account.

Empirical Evaluation

We now turn to the empirical studies we did to evaluate HUFS.

We will first discuss our implementation of HUFS on the example problem described above, then we will discuss the waterfall control method we used as our standard of comparison, and finally the tests we ran and their results.

HUFS for the Placement Problem

To implement HUFS for the placement problem, we needed the costs of the optimizers, the value function for placements, the score functions at all levels, and the $G(s|r)$ and $H(r|s)$ for each optimizer. As will be seen, we actually tested HUFS for a range of costs, although we kept the costs of the two levels equal. We rather arbitrarily set $U^{placement}(s) = 10^6 - s$. The score functions were all simple heuristics based on the information available in a design at each level. See (Steinberg, Hall, & Davison 1998) for more details.

In order to provide netlists both for calibrating the Gs and Hs and as test data for our experiments, we wrote a program to generate netlists with the modules'

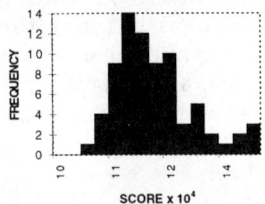 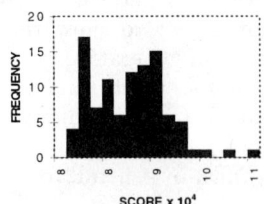

Figure 1: Child Score Distributions (G) for Two Netlists

heights and widths, the number and location of ports, and the specific interconnections all chosen randomly. All netlists in these tests had 20 modules.

To get data to determine the $G(s|r)$s and $H(r|s)$s we generated 8 netlists and ran the respective optimizers to generate 30 slicing trees each from these netlists, and 30 placements each from 8 of these slicing trees.

Figure 1 shows the actual distribution of child scores for two netlists. That is, these are the scores of the slicing trees that are the netlists' children. The distributions of child scores for slicing trees were similar. We modeled the distributions with a very simple family we call the "triangle distributions". These are piecewise linear functions, with three parameters: l, m, and r. The function is a line sloping up from 0 probability at score $m - l$ to a peak probability at score m, and then a line sloping down from there to 0 probability at score $m + r$.

From the calibration data we saw no reason not to use normal distributions for the $H(r|s)$'s, so we set the a priori probability of a parameter vector $<l, m, r>$ to

$$H(<l,m,r>|s) =$$
$$Z(s, lm(s), ld) * Z(s, mm(s), md) * Z(s, rm(s), rd)$$

where $Z(s, m, d)$ is the normal distribution function with mean m and standard deviation d applied to score s. The functions $lm(s)$, etc, are linear functions of s (except for mm of the distribution of placements, which needed a quadratic function to fit the data well.) The parameters ld, etc., are constants. The values for these constants and for the coefficients of the mean functions were determined by fitting to the data we had collected. We then ran HUFS 5 times on each of the 8 netlists, and adjusted the parameters slightly (e.g., we had underestimated md). At that point we froze the parameters and proceeded to test HUFS.

HUFS is implemented in Common Lisp and takes about 15 seconds on a Sun Ultrasparc I to update the Hs after an optimizer has been run and then to choose the next design alternative to generate children from.

As a standard for comparison we used a waterfall search. This process took a netlist, generated some prespecified number of slicing trees from it, and chose the one that had the lowest score. It then generated the same number of placements from the chosen slicing tree, and chose the placement with the lowest score as its final result. We had the waterfall search generate equal numbers of children at each level because some preliminary experiments indicated that, for a given total number of children generated, the quality of the resulting designs was optimal when the ratio of children at the two levels was roughly one to one, and that the quality was quite insensitive to the precise ratio.

The Test

To test HUFS we ran it and waterfall on a set of 19 random netlists, which did not include any of the netlists we used for calibration. To save time, the tests were run on pre-generated data. For each netlist we generated 50 slicing trees, and for each of these 50 trees we generated 100 placements. When we ran HUFS or waterfall with this data, instead of calling the optimizer to generate a slicing tree we chose randomly (with replacement) one of the trees we had pre-generated for this netlist, and similarly for generating a placement from a tree.

Using this test data, we tested HUFS for each of 4 different settings of c, the cost per run of the optimizer: 1600, 3200, 6400 and 12800. The setting of 1600, for instance, means that the cost of doing one additional optimizer run would be justified by an increase in the value of our final placement of 1600. Given our $V^{placement}$, this means a decrease in placement score of 1600.

For each setting of c, we ran HUFS 100 times on each netlist, and took both the average score of the 100 resulting placements and also the "95th percentile" scores — the score that was achieved or surpassed by 95 percent of the runs. We believe the 95th percentile score is a more realistic measure than the average score. An engineer normally only designs a given circuit once, so the primary measure of merit should be the quality a tool can be *counted on* to produce each time it is used. We then averaged the 95th percentile scores of the separate netlists to obtain a combined 95th percentile score for the test set, and similarly we averaged the average scores. We did not take the 95th percentile of the separate netlist scores because some netlists are inherently harder than others to place, and it was not clear how adjust for this in determining what the 95th percentile netlist was.

To compare HUFS with waterfall we started with 2 optimizer runs per waterfall trial (i.e., one per level) and did 1000 trials on each of the 19 test netlists. As with HUFS we took the average (over the 19 netlists) of the 95th percentile (over the 1000 runs for a netlist) score. We repeated this with 4 optimizer runs per waterfall (2 per level), then 6, etc., until there were enough runs that waterfall achieved the same overall score that HUFS had gotten. Finally, we re-did the tests using averages in place of 95th percentile scores.

Figure 2 plots the 95th percentile results. Successive points from left to right represent results for the successive values of c, with 1600 on the left. Note that the designs are better, and hence optimizer runs higher, to the left.

Table 1 presents the same data. The column labeled

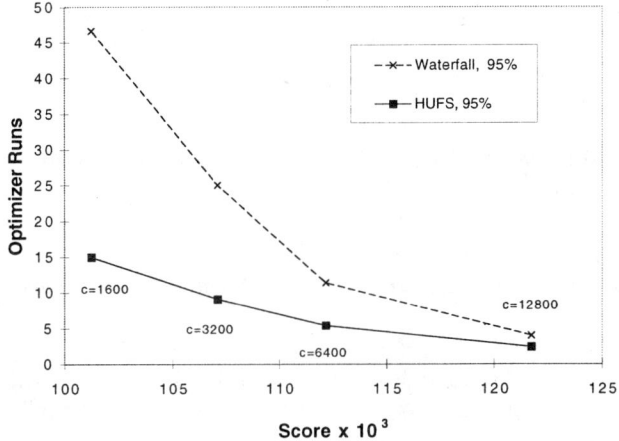

Figure 2: Optimizer runs vs. 95th percentile score for HUFS and waterfall

c	HUFS Score	HUFS Runs	Waterfall Runs	HUFS/WF Runs
1600	101252.	15.6	50.0	0.31
3200	107086.	8.8	26.0	0.34
6400	112174.	5.6	12.0	0.47
12800	121729.	2.3	6.0	0.38

Table 1: Optimizer runs vs. 95th percentile score for HUFS and waterfall

"HUFS/WF" is the ratio of the number of optimizer runs taken by HUFS to those taken by waterfall for the same score. Table 2 gives the results using averages instead of 95th percentiles.

As can be seen from the data, HUFS produces an equivalent quality design using 30% to 70% of the optimizer runs compared to waterfall. These results demonstrate that, at least for this particular problem, HUFS is a significant improvement over waterfall. Furthermore, HUFS did this well even though we modeled the score distributions as "triangle" distributions, which did not correspond very closely to the actual distributions, and we used few enough optimizer runs in the calibration phase that calibration was very feasible.

Related Work

The two bodies of literature that are most relevant to our work on HUFS are the work on utility-based meta-reasoning by Russell and Wefald reported in (Russell & Wefald 1991) and the work on monitoring anytime algorithms by Zilberstein and colleagues. Another relevant paper is (Etzioni 1991).

The key points that Russell and Wefald make are that it is often impossible due to time constraints for a problem solver to do all computations that are relevant to the problem it is solving, and therefore it can be useful to reason explicitly about the utility of alternate computations, and to use this reasoning to guide the choice of which computations to actually do. They also note that this utility can often be expressed as the difference between an *intrinsic utility* of the solution itself and a *time cost* that accounts for the decreased in utility as delay increases. Both our focus on utility and our formulation of utility as value minus cost of computation time were inspired by this work.

Russell and Wefald also present applications of their ideas to game-tree search and to problem solving (state-space) search. However, these problems do not have the large branching factors and different types of objects at each level of the search tree, and the specific methods they use do not apply to our problem here.

Hansen and Zilberstein (Hansen & Zilberstein 1996a), (Hansen & Zilberstein 1996b) are concerned with *anytime algorithms* (Boddy & Dean 1994). An anytime algorithm is one that can be stopped after working for a variable amount of time. If it is stopped after working for a short time, it will give lower quality results than if it is stopped after working for a longer time. The single-level problem discussed above, i.e. repeated execution of one stochastic optimizer, is thus an anytime algorithm — if there is more time, more runs can be done and the average quality of the result will be better, and if there is less time fewer runs can be done and the quality will be worse.

(Hansen & Zilberstein 1996a) defines the "myopic expected value of computation" (myopic EVC) which is equivalent in our terms to $EIV - c$, and their rule for stopping, stop when myopic EVC is negative, is equivalent to our rule, stop when $EIV < c$. However, Hansen and Zilberstein are concerned with the general case of anytime algorithms (and also with the cost of the monitoring, which we do not consider), and thus do not derive any more specific formula for myopic EVC. They also do not consider multi-level systems.

(Zilberstein 1993) and (Zilberstein & Russell 1996) also define a stopping rule similar to ours and prove that, under conditions similar to those that hold in our single-level case, it is optimal.

It is worth noting that while repeated stochastic optimization can be seen as an anytime algorithm, HUFS as a whole is not an anytime algorithm. If it is stopped before any ground-level design is produced, then it gives no answer at all. It would be interesting to see if HUFS could be turned into an anytime algorithm.

Etzioni (Etzioni 1991) describes an approach to a planning problem that is quite different from our problem here, but he uses a notion called "marginal utility".

c	HUFS Score	HUFS Runs	Waterfall Runs	HUFS/WF Runs
1600	92523.	15.6	26.0	0.60
3200	96272.	8.8	12.0	0.73
6400	99978.	5.6	8.0	0.70
12800	107958.	2.3	4.0	0.57

Table 2: Optimizer runs vs. average score for HUFS and waterfall

Marginal utility is the incremental value divided by the incremental cost, and is analogous to our $EIV - c$ but is based on a model of utility as "return on investment" rather than our model of utility as "profit". He also includes an interesting learning component to estimate means of distributions for cost and value.

Summary

In summary, we have presented a method for searching a tree where

- the branching factor is very large,
- the nodes at different level are different types of entities, hard to compare with each other, and
- we have a method of generating random children of a node, but it is too expensive to run more than a few times per level of the tree.

as is the case with design systems that work by translating a design down through a hierarchy of abstraction levels, using stochastic optimization to generate children of a node. This search is based on optimizing the utility of the result, i.e. the value of the final design produced minus the cost of the computation time it took to produce it.

Our search control method, Highest Utility First Search (HUFS), is based on a method for estimating, for any design alternative in the tree, what the average utility of our final design will be if we start with this alternative and produce the final design from it. At each point where we must choose a design alternative to translate and optimize, we simply choose the alternative with the highest estimated utility. When this alternative is at the lowest level abstraction level, i.e. is a leaf of the tree, we stop and return this alternative as our result.

We presented HUFS and its implementation for a two-level system that solves the problem of placing circuit modules on a VLSI chip, and showed that HUFS performed significantly better than the waterfall approach of working in a strict top-down, level by level manner. See (Steinberg, Hall, & Davison 1998) for further details and discussions of such issues as the scalability of HUFS and problems with the models of value and time cost used in HUFS.

Finally, we believe the general approach of combining a utility-based analysis with statistical measures such as G shows great promise for many kinds of search problems, and we plan to explore the broader application of this approach.

Acknowledgements

The work presented here is part of the "Hypercomputing & Design" (HPCD) project; and it is supported (partly) by ARPA under contract DABT-63-93-C-0064. The content of the information herein does not necessarily reflect the position of the Government and official endorsement should not be inferred.

Thanks are due to Saul Amarel, Robert Berk, Haym Hirsh, Sholmo Zilberstein, and the anonymous reviewers for for comments on earlier drafts.

References

Boddy, M., and Dean, T. 1994. Deliberation scheduling for problem solving in time-constrained environments. *Artificial Intelligence* 67:245–285.

Etzioni, O. 1991. Embedding decision-analytic control in a learning architecture. *Artificial Intelligence* 49:129–159.

Goldberg, D. E. 1989. *Genetic Algorithms in Search, Optimization, and Machine Learning*. Reading, Mass.: Addison-Wesley.

Hansen, E., and Zilberstein, S. 1996a. Monitoring anytime algorithms. *SIGART Bulletin Special Issue on Anytime Algorithms and Deliberation Scheduling* 7(2):28–33.

Hansen, E., and Zilberstein, S. 1996b. Monitoring the progress of anytime problem-solving. In *Proceedings of the 13th National Conference on Artificial Intelligence*, 1229–1234.

Ingber, L. 1996. Adaptive simulated annealing (ASA): Lessons learned. *Control and Cybernetics* 25(1):33–54.

Michalewicz, Z. 1996. *Genetic Algorithms + Data Structures = Evolution Programs*. New York: Springer-Verlag.

Russell, S., and Wefald, E. 1991. *Do the Right Thing*. MIT Press.

Steinberg, L.; Hall, J. S.; and Davison, B. 1998. Highest utility first search: a control method for multi-level stochastic design. Technical Report HPCD-TR-59, High Perfomance Computing and Design Project, Department of Computer Science, Rutgers University, New Brunswick, NJ.

Tribus, M. 1969. *Rational Descriptions, Decisions and Designs*. New York: Pergamon Press.

Zha, G.-C.; Smith, D.; Schwabacher, M.; Rasheed, K.; Gelsey, A.; and Knight, D. 1996. High performance supersonic missile inlet design using automated optimization. In *AIAA Symposium on Multidisciplinary Analysis and Optimization '96*.

Zilberstein, S., and Russell, S. 1996. Optimal composition of real-time systems. *Artificial Intelligence* 82(1-2):181–213.

Zilberstein, S. 1993. *Operational Rationality Through Compilation of Anytime Algorithms*. Ph.D. Dissertation, University of California at Berkeley.

Evolvable Hardware

Evolvable Hardware Chip for High Precision Printer Image Compression

Hidenori Sakanashi[1], Mehrdad Salami[1], Masaya Iwata[1], Shogo Nakaya[2]
Tsukasa Yamauchi[2], Takeshi Inuo[2], Nobuki Kajihara[2] and Tetsuya Higuchi[1]

[1] Electrotechnical Laboratory
1-1-4 Umezono, Tsukuba 305-0047, Japan
{h_sakana, m_salami, miwata, higuchi}@etl.go.jp

[2] RWCP Adaptive Device NEC Laboratory

Abstract

This paper describes a data compression chip for the high-precision electrophotographic printer using Evolvable Hardware (EHW). EHW is a new hardware paradigm which combines Genetic Algorithm (GA) and reconfigurable hardware technology such as FPGA (Field Programmable Gate Array). In EHW, GA is used to search for the most desirable hardware structure to a given task. If the task requirement changes, GA is invoked to get a better hardware structure and EHW is reconfigured that way. In data compression, EHW is used to implement the most adequate compression method directly in hardware according to the characteristics of the target image. The EHW-based compression chip attains approximately twice the compression compared with the international standard called JBIG. This chip is the first EHW-chip to lead to a commercial product.

Introduction

The electrophotographic (EP) printing is the next generation technology in printing and publishing industry to print books with a high-precision photo quality.

One A4-size EP image of 1200 dpi requires 70 MBytes for storage, and the EP printer processes hundreds different pages with the speed of 100 page/min. It means that, for printing a book with 100 pages, 7 giga bytes of image data must be transferred to the printer in the speed of 1800 Mbyte/min. On the other hand, the data transfer speed of the usual hard-disk drive is only 300 Mbyte/min. Thus, the EP printers must employ data compression techniques. They are required (1) to compress image data efficiently, and (2) to reconstruct the compressed data very fast. However, the traditional techniques are insufficient both in the compression ratios and the decompression speed.

This paper proposes a data compression chip using Evolvable Hardware (EHW) that enables on-line reconfiguration of the hardware structure. In EHW, genetic algorithm determines how the hardware structure should be reconfigured whenever a new hardware structure is needed for a better performance. EHW can adaptively reconfigure its hardware structure to compress the target images more efficiently. Besides, it can change compression method during compressing one image. As a consequence, we obtained three times higher compression rate than that of the current

Copyright © 1998, American Association for Artificial Intelligence (www.aaai.org). All rights reserved.

printing machine, and five times faster compression speed than the exhaustive search method with similar performances. Moreover, EHW can meet the speed requirement of the printer because the expansion of data is done by EHW hardware. This chip is determined to be adopted in a commercial EP printer.

In the rest of this paper, section 2 explains the foundation of EHW. The data compression in EP printing is mentioned in section 3. In section 4, the data compression method adopting EHW is described in detail, and the results of computational simulations show that EHW exhibits the superior performance to the other methods. Section 5 shows the design of a chip implementing based on this method[†], and section 6 concludes this paper.

Evolvable Hardware

This section explains genetic algorithm (GA) and Evolvable Hardware (EHW) in which GA is combined with the reconfigurable hardware.

Genetic Algorithm

Genetic Algorithm (GA) was proposed to model adaptation of natural and artificial systems through evolution (Holland 1975), and is well known as one of the most powerful search procedures (Goldberg 1989). The canonical GA has a population of chromosomes, each of them is obtained by encoding a point in the search space. Usually, they are represented by the strings of binary characters.

At an initial state, chromosomes in the population are generated at random, and processed by many operations, such as *evaluation*, *selection*, *crossover* and *mutation*. The latter three operations are called the genetic operations, and one cycle of the evaluation and the genetic operation is counted as a generation. The evaluation assigns the fitness values to the chromosomes, which indicates how well the chromosomes perform as solutions of the given problem. According to the fitness values, the selection determines which chromosomes can survive into the next generation. The crossover chooses some pairs of chromosomes, and exchanges their sub-strings at random. Finally, the mutation randomly picks some positions in

---

[†] Mitsubishi Heavy Industry Ltd. will use a similar architecture as a basis for the data compression chip in the next model of their electrophotographic printer.

the chromosome and flips their values.

The major advantages of GA are its robustness and superior search performance in many type of problems without a prior knowledge (Davis 1991). However, it is rarely reported that GA is used for industrial applications or commercial products, because of the cost for fitness evaluation. If the evaluation can be executed very quickly by the specific hardware device, however, the most serious problem of GA can be solved, and we can use GA more effectively. Evolvable Hardware is based on this concept, and utilizes the robust capability of GA by reducing its computational cost.

Brief Summary of Evolvable Hardware

Evolvable Hardware (EHW) is a hardware device which is built on software-reconfigurable devices, e.g. PLD (Programmable Logic Device) and FPGA (Field Programmable Gate Array). The hardware structure of EHW can be reconfigured autonomously by using GA in order to attain better hardware performance in a changing environment (Higuchi et al. 1992). The hardware structure is determined by downloading a binary bit string into the device. This string is called *architecture bits*, and it is regarded as chromosome of GA as shown in Fig.1. Once a good chromosome is found by GA, it will be downloaded into software-reconfigurable devices.

EHW inherits two important features: fast computation of hardware device and adaptability of GA. EHW has three advantages over the traditional hardware and software systems (Yao and Higuchi 1996): First, as mentioned above, EHW can *autonomously* improve the performance by changing its hardware configuration with GA. Second, it processes the information much faster than the software system, and can realize the *real-time* computation. Third, the reconfigurable-device can change its functionality in an *on-line* fashion during execution. EHW can also deal with a new application area to which the inflexible traditional hardware systems are not efficient (Murakawa et al. 1996, Bennett et al. 1996). In particular, EHW exhibits a superior performance in dynamically changing environment because it can reconfigure its hardware structure to adapt to the changes. The image compression is also one of them. Depending on the nature of the image data to be compressed, EHW implements the most effective compression configuration in its hardware structure.

Electrophotographic Printing

This section describes the motivation to apply EHW to the

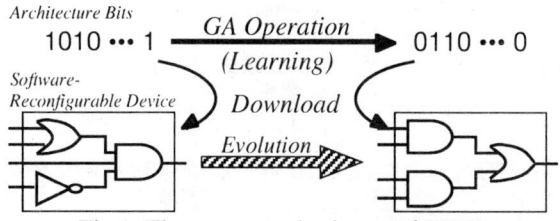

Fig.1: The conceptual scheme of EHW.

electrophotographic (EP) printer as the data compression system.

Electrophotographic Printing, Halftone Dot Image and Data Compression

EP printing is a new technology in the field of printing and publication, and we can easily have many printed matters of photo-quality at anytime with very low cost. The EP printer is required to be much smaller than the offset printers, and to work much faster than color copier.

In the EP printing, the original data created on the desktop publishing (DTP) systems is divided into four halftone dot images, which are binary image data and correspond to four colors (cyan, magenta, yellow and black). In halftone images, gray levels are represented using binary pixel patterns. The total size of the four images is much larger than the size of the data in the DTP system. One A4-size color image of 1200 dpi requires about 70 Mbytes for storage. A digital printer prints hundreds sets of hundreds different pages in the speed of 100 page/min. Therefore, it must have huge memory devices and very fast data-transfer bus. In order to reduce the costs for storage and communication, the halftone dot images must be compressed as much as possible and the compressed data must be expanded faster than the printing speed. Besides, the images must be compressed in the lossless way in which the expanded data is completely the same as the original data.

Many techniques have been proposed for lossless image compression in the field of information processing. Some of them are realized only by software, but they cannot satisfy the speed requirement of the EP printer. The others are implemented in a chip and work very fast in compression and decompression. They are used in various industrial products, such as facsimile. However, they are not suitable for the EP printer, because their adaptation mechanisms are too simple for the complex characteristics of the halftone dot image. It is very difficult for them to realize the efficient compression and the fast compression & decompression, simultaneously.

Therefore, this paper proposes to apply EHW to the EP printer as the data compression unit. Since EHW is implemented in a chip, it can compress and decompress image data very quickly. Moreover, since EHW has powerful ability of adaptation caused by GA, the compression chip with EHW can efficiently compress the halftone dot images in the printer.

Compression of Halftone Dot Image

Currently, the EP printer uses the data compression chips based on Lempel-Ziv method. Its advantage is fast compression and decompression, but its compression ratio is poor because Lempel-Ziv method is not theoretically optimized for compressing image data.

Image data consists of many pixels, and each pixel tends to tightly relate with its neighboring pixels. Then, we can predict the pixel value using the values of its neighboring pixels, and we don't have to represent the pixel if

Table 1: Two components of the proposed method and their two function modes.

		Learning Mode	Compression Mode
Template Generator	Statistical Calculation Genetic Algorithm	Search for best template	---
	Template Memory	Store discovered templates	Output stored templates
Data Compressor		Calculate compression ratio	Output compressed data

the prediction is correct. Namely, the precision of prediction strongly influences the compression ratio. The pattern of the values of pixels used for prediction is called the *context*. The large context allows the precise expectation, but it increases the computational cost. Therefore, we must carefully select the *template* which is a set of relative locations of the reference pixels from the currently coded pixel. However, the different images have different optimal templates, and the template may have to change even in one image to improve the compression ratio.

JBIG (Joint Bi-level Image coding experts Group), which is the international standard method specialized to bi-level image data, basically adopts the method mentioned above (CCITT 1993). It has a template consisting of 10 reference pixel positions (Fig.2). In the figure, black and hatched rectangles respectively represent the positions of a currently coded pixel and the reference pixels. A hatched rectangle with thick edges, called the *adaptive template*, can move in the area indicated by the rectangles with crosses during compressing one image to capture any variable structure that might exist in the image, using the simple statistical calculation (Sayood 1996).

JBIG is developed to mainly compress the binary facsimile images, but the halftone dot images of EP printing have quite different characteristics. In the halftone dot images, the adjacent pixels don't relate with each other strongly. Therefore, JBIG can not compress those images well, because (1) the configuration of template is not suitable, and (2) the simple mechanism to move the adaptive template can not work well (Forchhammer 1993). Therefore, to resolve the above two difficulties, EHW is applied to the data compression system of the EP printer. The chip implementing this method will compress the halftone dot images much better than others without affecting the compression speed. The next section explains this approach in details.

Lossless Image Data Compression by Genetic Algorithm

As shown in Fig.3, the proposed method in this paper consists of two parts, the template generator (TG) part with GA and the data compressor (DC) part (Salami 1998). This section explains them, and shows the result of simulations.

Data Compressor Part

This system has two operating modes, the learning mode and the compression mode (Table 1). In both modes, the image data is divided into units named the *stripe*, consisting of L lines of an image. In the learning mode, DC part searches for the optimal template of each stripe by GA, and the discovered templates are stored in the memory. Using those templates discovered in the learning mode, the compression mode compresses the image data. In the compression mode, GA doesn't work for generating templates, and the stored templates are used for compressing the corresponding stripes.

DC part also consists of 2 components, the context selector and QM-Coder (Pennebaker et al. 1988). The context selector determines the contexts corresponding to the coded pixels, using the template sent from TG part (as mentioned in the next sub-section). Fig.4 illustrate an example of the template. Similar to Fig.2, black and hatched rectangles respectively represent the positions of a currently coded pixel and the reference pixels. QM-Coder sequentially encodes all pixels in a stripe using the contexts corresponding to them.

DC part is much more flexible than JBIG. It can change the relative locations of *all* reference pixels, while JBIG changes only one. Besides, the pixels can separately move within much wider area of 32x8 (Fig.4). Because of the these enhancements in the context selection, this system can easily deal with the halftone dot image where the adjacent pixels don't relate with each other. It can also compress the ordinal facsimile images similar to JBIG.

Template Generator Part

As mentioned in the previous section, the compression ratio is strongly influenced by the template specifying which pixels are used to generate contexts. TG part searches for the optimal template in every stripe using GA.

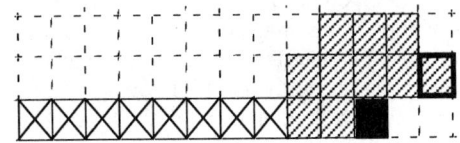

Fig.2: Configuration of reference pixels (template) of JBIG.

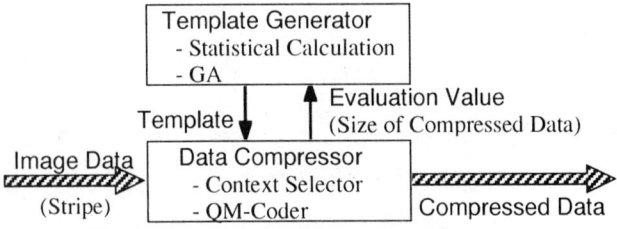

Fig.3: Framework of the proposed system.

A template is defined to have 10 pixel locations, and each location is selected from the 32x8 area. One location can be represented by 8 bits ($2^8 = 32 \times 8$), and 80 bits are required to indicate a template with 10 locations. In the rest of this paper, the 8 bits specifying one location is called the *slot*.

In the learning mode, the initial population of GA is generated using the *initial template*, which is prepared by the simple statistical calculation on the first stripe, based on the following steps:

1. The default template of JBIG is set as the initial template.
2. The compression ratio is calculated by using the initial template.
3. Among 10 slots in the initial template, the most useless slots are determined. (The most useless slots specifies the position of the reference pixel which records the largest compression ratio even if it is removed from the template.)
4. Among all possible locations in the 32x8 area, the most efficient location is selected. (The most efficient location records the largest compression ratio when it is assigned to the previously selected slot.)
5. The new template is created by assigning the selected location to the selected slot.
6. If the compression ratio using the new template is better than the initial template, the initial template will be exchanged by the new template and go to step-3.
7. Finish the procedure.

The discovered initial template is copied to one chromosome in the population of GA, and its mutated copies are assigned to other chromosomes. This procedure is simple and the result of the statistical calculation is not always the best template, but it accelerates the search speed of GA, compared with the random initial population.

The initial template discovered by the statistical calculation is stored in the template memory and GA runs from the second stripe. In each stripe, the chromosomes in the population are sent to the context selector one by one as templates and the size of the compressed stripe from QM-Coder will be returned as the fitness value. The number of generations for one stripe is represented by the parameter G, and GA searches for the optimal template minimizing the size of the compressed stripe. The best template discovered by GA is stored in the template memory, and GA moves to the next stripe. The stored templates in the template memory are used for compressing their corresponding stripe in the compression mode.

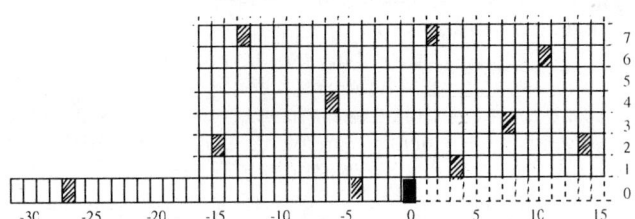

Fig.4: Configuration of reference pixels (template) of the proposed system.

Enhanced Representation

From the viewpoint of GA, the data compression is a nonstationary problem because the target stripe for compression changes periodically. It is well known that the nonstationary problem is difficult for GA (Grefenstette 1992). Using the structured GA (Dasgupta and McGregor 1992), therefore, chromosome representation is enhanced to allow GA effectively follows the changing environment.

The basic idea of this enhancement is to keep the previously good templates in the population even if the environment changes suddenly. In one image, there may be many local areas with similar textures, and their optimal templates tend to have many common locations of reference pixels. Hence, it is important for the chromosomes in the population to keep the previously good locations for the next stripes.

The enhanced representation have $M \geq 10$ locations of the reference pixels (slots), and M additional bits indicating which slots are active to generate a template (Fig.5). The inactive slots are never influenced by the genetic operations except the selection, and can keep the previously good locations. The active slots are changed to search for the better locations of the reference pixels. Additionally, two more genetic operations are introduced to handle the inactive slots, *slot copy* and *slot swap*. Using slot copy, the contents of one randomly selected active slot is copied to one of the inactive slots. The slot swap operation chooses one active slot and one inactive slot at random, and exchange their activation bits. These two additional operations of the slot copy and the slot swap correspond to memorization and remembrance. The probabilities that a chromosome is changed by these operators are given by two parameters, the slot-copy ratio and the slot-swap ratio.

Simulation Results

This section shows the results of some computational simulations, before explaining the the architecture of the EHW chip implemented for the data compression.

For the simulation, we prepare a printer image (halftone dot image; JIS/ISO standard color image data N2), and 8 facsimile images (standard images of CCITT (International Telegraph and Telephone Consultative Committee)). The printer image is divided in 8 sub-images, and they are compressed separately.

In order to compare the performance of the proposed system, the following 4 methods are also applied to the images: (1) JBIG, (2) Lempel-Ziv method ("compress" command of Unix), (3) the statistical method, and (4) the sequentially exhaustive search. Among them, the simple statistical method (3) are same as the proposed method, but it doesn't use GA. In the method (3), after the statistical calculation in the first stripe, the same template is used for compressing the following stripes. In the method (4), only

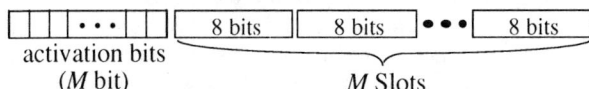

Fig.5: Enhanced representation of chromosome.

Table 2: Compression ratios of various method.

	Printer Image	Fax Image
(1) Lempel-Ziv	3.34	8.41
(2) JBIG	3.35	14.67
(3) Statistical calculation	6.38	19.49
(4) Exhaustive search	6.61	---
Proposed method	6.52	19.82

Table 3: Parameter setting of the proposed system.

Total generation	162	Population size	20
Tournament size	2	Crossover ratio	0.8
Mutation ratio	0.03	Number of slots	15
Slot-copy ratio	0.1	Slot-swap ratio	0.1
Number of lines in one stripe (L)			40
Number of slots in enhanced representation (M)			15

one location in a template can be optimized by the exhaustive search. The search area is same as the proposed method. The reason why two or more locations can not be changed at once is to avoid the combinatorial explosion.

Table 2 shows the compression ratios of the above methods. The parameter setting of the proposed system and GA is shown in Table 3. Unfortunately, the compression ratio of the proposed method on the printer image is worse than the method (4), but it can finish the compression much faster than the method (4), as mentioned below. The following 3 important facts can be concluded from the simulations: First, among method (1), (2) and (3), the method (3) shows the best performance for compressing both images. This fact means that the enhanced context selector introduced for the halftone dot images can deal with the ordinal facsimile images. Namely, the proposed context selector has the ability to process the general image data.

Next, the proposed method can exhibit better compression ratio than the method (3). The only difference between their procedures is that the proposed method executes GA after the second stripe. The improvement of the performance demonstrates the efficiency of the adaptability of GA during compressing one image. Under the parameter setting of Table 3, the difference between two methods are very small, but the compression ratio of the proposed method is expected to improve by more generations and larger population. When it is implemented in the hardware, we may ignore such increased computational costs.

Finally, the proposed method presents less compression ratio for compressing the printer data than the method (4). Table 4 shows the more detailed results, and we can understand the proposed method exhibits better compression ratio on 4 out of 8 images. It means that the search performance of the GA is not always inferior to the sequential exhaustive search method. Moreover, from the viewpoint of the computational cost, the proposed method can finish the task about *ten times* faster than the exhaustive search.

Data Compression Chip

We are developing the data compression chip based on the method explained in the previous sections.

Fig.6 illustrates the architecture of the EHW data-compression chip. The chip mainly consists of NEC V830 RISC processor (32 bit, 100 MHz), the data compression hardware, and 3 registers. Through the registers, V830 and the compression hardware can communicate with each other. V830 controls the chip, runs GA calculation in the learning mode, and interfaces with the host computer.

The data compression hardware have 5 components and 3 controllers (Fig.7). The image data is temporally stored in the line memory of 10240 bits x 10 lines and sent to the reference buffer. It sequentially send the currently coded pixels and extracts the corresponding 32x8 pixels sent to the context generator. Using the template, the context generator creates contexts from the received 32x8 pixels. The contexts are sent to QM-Coder with the currently coded pixels. In the compression mode, QM-Coder sends a sequence of the compressed data to the external data storage and outputs the size of the compressed data to V830 in the learning mode.

Those components are configured to process the image data as fast as possible, because it must calculate the evaluation values of GA in the learning mode. In the case of the computer simulation in the previous section, the evaluation of chromosomes in the population spent about 95% of the total computational time. Therefore, by implementing the data compression part in hardware, the total speed of this chip including the learning mode becomes drastically fast. For example, in the above simulations, the proposed method spent about fifty minuets for learning and compressing a 1184x6464 image on the Ultra Sparc Station (144 MHz). On the contrary, assuming that QM-Coder works at 40 MHz, the hardware can finish the same process within a minute. The volume of the hardware for the proposed system is greater than JBIG system, but the extra hardware allows the system to search for the optimal template adaptively. This chip can not expand the compressed data yet, but we are starting to design the new chip which can compress the image data and expand the compressed data.

Conclusions

This paper described a data compression chip for the high-precision electrophotographic printer using Evolvable Hardware (EHW), which is a new hardware paradigm combining Genetic Algorithm and the reconfigurable hardware. The computer simulations showed that the EHW-based system can exhibits much better compression ratios than the international standard.

The salient contribution of this paper is to reveal the true importance of hardware reconfigurability. While software-reconfigurable devices have been mainly used for prototyping and reducing manufacturing costs, our EHW-chip demonstrates that hardware reconfigurability is indispensable for satisfying severe performance requirements. Thus, this paper represents a new direction for reconfigurable computing.

Table 4: Compression ratio of Exhaustive search and proposed method in divided printer images.

	1	2	3	4	5	6	7	8	Average
Exhaustive search	15.66	6.34	4.47	4.50	4.86	6.02	7.6	25.00	6.61
Proposed method	16.08	6.566	4.57	4.55	4.74	5.81	6.77	23.48	6.52

Acknowledgements

This work is supported by MITI Real World Computing Project (RWCP). We thank Dr. Otsu and Dr. Ohmaki in Electrotechnical Laboratory, and Dr. Shimada in RWCP for their support.

Reference

Bennett III, F. H., Koza, J. R., Andre, D. and Keane, M. A. 1996. Evolution of a 60 Decibel Op Amp Using Genetic Programming, *Evolvable Systems: From Biology to Hardware*, 455-469, Springer.

Dasgupta, D. and McGregor, D. R. 1992. Nonstationary Function Optimization using the Structured Genetic Algorithm. *Parallel Problem Solving from Nature*, 2: 145-154. Elsevier.

Davis, L. ed. 1991. *Handbook of Genetic Algorithms*: Van Nostrand Reinhold.

Forchhammer, S. 1993. Adaptive Context for JBIG Compression of Bi-Level Halftone Images, Proc. of the 1993 Data Compression Conference: 431 IEEE Computer Society Press.

Goldberg, D. E. 1989. *Genetic Algorithms in Search, Optimization and Machine Learning*: Addison-Wesley.

Higuchi, T., Niwa, T., Tanaka, T., Iba, H., de Garis, H. and Furuya, T. 1992. Evolvable Hardware with Genetic Learning, *Proc. of Simulated Adaptive Behavior*. The MIT Press.

Holland, J. H. 1975. *Adaptation in Natural and Artificial Systems*: University of Michigan Press.

Grefenstette, J. J. 1992. Genetic Algorithms for changing environment. *Parallel Problem Solving from Nature*, 2: 137-144, Elsevier.

International Telegraph and Telephone Consultative Committee (CCITT). 1993. *Progressive Bi-level Image Compression*, Recommendation T.82.

Murakawa, M., et al.. 1996. On-line Adaptation of Neural Networks with Evolvable Hardware, *Proc. of the 7th International Conference on Genetic Algorithms*, pp.792-799, Morgan Kaufmann.

Pennebaker, W. B., Mitchell, J. L., Langdon Jr., G. G. and Arps, R. B. 1988. An overview of the basic principles of the Q-coder. *IBM Journal of Research & Development* 32 (6): 717-726.

Salami, M. et al.. 1998. On-Line Compression of High Precision Printer Images by Evolvable Hardware. *Proc. of the 1998 Data Compression Conference*. IEEE Computer Society Press.

Yao, X. and Higuchi, T. 1998. Promises and Challenges of Evolvable Hardware. *IEEE Transactions on Systems, Man, and Cybernetics*, Part C, 28 (4).

Sayood, L. 1996. *Introduction to Data Compression*. 475: Morgan Kaufmann.

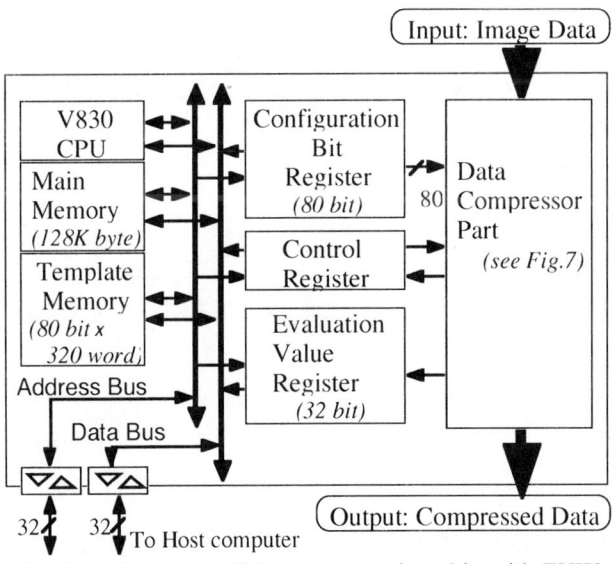

Fig.6: Architecture of data compression chip with EHW.

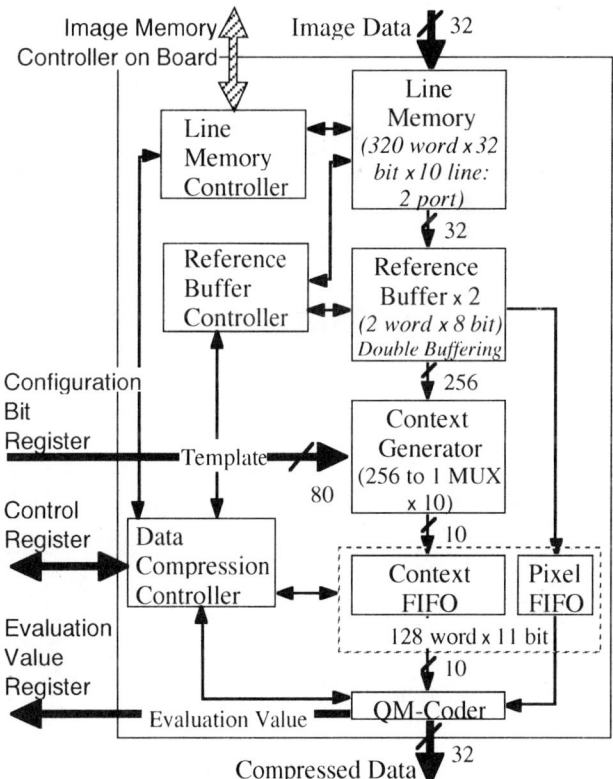

Fig.7: Architecture of data compressor part.

Game Playing

Opponent Modeling in Poker

Darse Billings, Denis Papp, Jonathan Schaeffer, Duane Szafron
Department of Computing Science
University of Alberta
Edmonton, Alberta Canada T6G 2H1
{darse, dpapp, jonathan, duane}@cs.ualberta.ca

Abstract

Poker is an interesting test-bed for artificial intelligence research. It is a game of imperfect knowledge, where multiple competing agents must deal with risk management, agent modeling, unreliable information and deception, much like decision-making applications in the real world. Agent modeling is one of the most difficult problems in decision-making applications and in poker it is essential to achieving high performance. This paper describes and evaluates *Loki*, a poker program capable of observing its opponents, constructing opponent models and dynamically adapting its play to best exploit patterns in the opponents' play.

Introduction

The artificial intelligence community has recently benefited from the tremendous publicity generated by the development of chess, checkers and Othello programs that are capable of defeating the best human players. However, there is an important difference between these board games and popular card games like bridge and poker. In the board games, players always have complete knowledge of the entire game state since it is visible to both participants. This property allows high performance to be achieved by brute-force search of the game trees. Bridge and poker involve imperfect information since the other players' cards are not known; search alone is insufficient to play these games well. Dealing with imperfect information is the main reason why research about bridge and poker has lagged behind other games. However, it is also the reason why they promise higher potential research benefits.

Until recently, poker has been largely ignored by the computing science community. However, poker has a number of attributes that make it an interesting domain for mainstream AI research. These include imperfect knowledge (the opponent's hands are hidden), multiple competing agents (more than two players), risk management (betting strategies and their consequences), agent modeling (identifying patterns in the opponent's strategy and exploiting them), deception (bluffing and varying your style of play), and dealing with unreliable information (taking into account your opponent's deceptive plays). All of these are challenging dimensions to a difficult problem.

Copyright © (1998) American Association of Artificial Intelligence (www.aaai.org). All rights reserved.

There are two main approaches to poker research. One approach is to use simplified variants that are easier to analyze. However, one must be careful that the simplification does not remove challenging components of the problem. For example, Findler (1977) worked on and off for 20 years on a poker-playing program for 5-card draw poker. His approach was to model human cognitive processes and build a program that could learn, ignoring many of the interesting complexities of the game.

The other approach is to pick a real variant, and investigate it using mathematical analysis, simulation, and/or ad-hoc expert experience. Expert players with a penchant for mathematics are usually involved in this approach (Sklansky and Malmuth 1994, for example).

Recently, Koller and Pfeffer (1997) have been investigating poker from a theoretical point of view. They implemented the first practical algorithm for finding optimal randomized strategies in two-player imperfect information competitive games. This is done in their *Gala* system, a tool for specifying and solving problems of imperfect information. Their system builds trees to find the optimal game-theoretic strategy. However the tree sizes prompted the authors to state that "...we are nowhere close to being able to solve huge games such as full-scale poker, and it is unlikely that we will ever be able to do so."

We are attempting to build a program that is capable of beating the best human poker players. We have chosen to study the game of Texas Hold'em, the poker variation used to determine the world champion in the annual World Series of Poker. Hold'em is considered to be the most strategically complex poker variant that is widely played.

Our initial experience with a poker-playing program was positive (Billings et al. 1997). However, we quickly discovered how adaptive human players were. In games played over the Internet, our program, *Loki*, would perform quite well initially. Some opponents would detect patterns and weaknesses in the program's play, and they would alter their strategy to exploit them. One cannot be a strong poker player without modeling your opponent's play and adjusting to it.

Although opponent modeling has been studied before in the context of games (for example: Carmel and Markovitch 1995; Iida et al. 1995; Jansen 1992), it has not yet produced tangible improvements in practice. Part of the reason for this is that in games such as chess, opponent modeling is not critical to achieving high performance. In poker, however, opponent modeling is essential to success.

This paper describes and evaluates opponent modeling in *Loki*. The first sections describe the rules of Texas

Hold'em and the requirements of a strong Hold'em program as it relates to opponent modeling. We then describe how *Loki* evaluates poker hands, followed by a discussion of how opponents are modeled and how this information is used to alter the assessment of our hands. The next section gives some experimental results. The final section discusses ongoing work on this project. The major research contribution of this paper is that it is the first successful demonstration of using opponent modeling to improve performance in a realistic game-playing program.

Texas Hold'em

A hand of Texas Hold'em begins with the *pre-flop*, where each player is dealt two *hole cards* face down, followed by the first round of betting. Three community cards are then dealt face up on the table, called the *flop*, and the second round of betting occurs. On the *turn*, a fourth community card is dealt face up and another round of betting ensues. Finally, on the *river*, a fifth community card is dealt face up and the final round of betting occurs. All players still in the game turn over their two hidden cards for the *showdown*. The best five card poker hand formed from the two hole cards and the five community cards wins the pot. If a tie occurs, the pot is split. Texas Hold'em is typically played with 8 to 10 players.

Limit Texas Hold'em uses a structured betting system, where the order and amount of betting is strictly controlled on each betting round.[1] There are two denominations of bets, called the small bet and the big bet ($2 and $4 in this paper). In the first two betting rounds, all bets and raises are $2, while in the last two rounds, they are $4. In general, when it is a player's turn to act, one of five betting options is available: fold, call/check, or raise/bet. There is normally a maximum of three raises allowed per betting round. The betting option rotates clockwise until each player has matched the current bet or folded. If there is only one player remaining (all others having folded) that player is the winner and is awarded the pot without having to reveal their cards.

Requirements for a World-Class Poker Player

We have identified several key components that address some of the required activities of a strong poker player. However, these components are not independent. They must be continually refined as new capabilities are added to the program. Each of them is either directly or indirectly influenced by the introduction of opponent modeling.

Hand strength assesses how strong your hand is in relation to the other hands. At a minimum, it is a function of your cards and the current community cards. A better hand strength computation takes into account the number of players still in the game, position at the table, and the history of betting for the hand. An even more accurate calculation considers the probabilities for each possible opponent hand, based on the likelihood of each hand being played to the current point in the game.

Hand potential assesses the probability of a hand improving (or being overtaken) as additional community cards appear. For example, a hand that contains four cards in the same suit may have a low hand strength, but has good potential to win with a flush as more community cards are dealt. At a minimum, hand potential is a function of your cards and the current community cards. However, a better calculation could use all of the additional factors described in the hand strength computation.

Betting strategy determines whether to fold, call/check, or bet/raise in any given situation. A minimum model is based on hand strength. Refinements consider hand potential, pot odds (your winning chances compared to the expected return from the pot), bluffing, opponent modeling and trying to play unpredictably.

Bluffing allows you to make a profit from weak hands,[2] and can be used to create a false impression about your play to improve the profitability of subsequent hands. Bluffing is essential for successful play. Game theory can be used to compute a theoretically optimal bluffing frequency in certain situations. A minimal bluffing system merely bluffs this percentage of hands indiscriminately. In practice, you should also consider other factors (such as hand potential) and be able to predict the probability that your opponent will fold in order to identify profitable bluffing opportunities.

Unpredictability makes it difficult for opponents to form an accurate model of your strategy. By varying your playing strategy over time, opponents may be induced to make mistakes based on an incorrect model.

Opponent modeling allows you to determine a likely probability distribution for your opponent's hidden cards. A minimal opponent model might use a single model for all opponents in a given hand. Opponent modeling may be improved by modifying those probabilities based on collected statistics and betting history of each opponent.

There are several other identifiable characteristics which may not be necessary to play reasonably strong poker, but may eventually be required for world-class play.

The preceding discussion is intended to show how integral opponent modeling is to successful poker play. Koller and Pfeffer (1997) have proposed a system for constructing a game-theoretic optimal player. It is important to differentiate an *optimal* strategy from a *maximizing* strategy. The optimal player makes its decisions based on game-theoretic probabilities, without regard to specific context. The maximizing player takes into account the opponent's sub-optimal tendencies and adjusts its play to exploit these weaknesses.

In poker, a player that detects and adjusts to opponent weaknesses will win more than a player who does not. For example, against a strong conservative player, it would be correct to fold the probable second-best hand. However, against a weaker player who bluffs too much, it would be

---

[1] In No-limit Texas Hold'em, there are no restrictions on the size of bets.

[2] Other forms of deception (such as calling with a strong hand) are not considered here.

an error to fold that same hand. In real poker it is very common for opponents to play sub-optimally. A player who fails to detect and exploit these weaknesses will not win as much as a better player who does. Thus, a maximizing program will out-perform an optimal program against sub-optimal players because the maximizing program will do a better job of exploiting the sub-optimal players.

Although a game-theoretic optimal solution for Hold'em would be interesting, it would in no way "solve the game". To produce a world-class poker program, strong opponent modeling is essential.

Hand Assessment

Loki handles its play differently at the pre-flop, flop, turn and river. The play is controlled by two components: a hand evaluator and a betting strategy. This section describes how hand strength and potential are calculated and used to evaluate a hand.

Pre-flop Evaluation

Pre-flop play in Hold'em has been extensively studied in the poker literature (Sklansky and Malmuth 1994). These works attempt to explain the play in human understandable terms by classifying all the initial two-card pre-flop combinations into a number of categories. For each class of hands a suggested betting strategy is given, based on the category, number of players, position at the table, and type of opponents. These ideas could be implemented as an expert system, but a more systematic approach would be preferable, since it could be more easily modified and the ideas could be generalized to post-flop play.

For the initial two cards, there are {52 choose 2} = 1326 possible combinations, but only 169 distinct hand types. For each one of the 169 possible hand types, a simulation of 1,000,000 poker games was done against nine random hands. This produced a statistical measure of the approximate *income rate* (profit expectation) for each starting hand. A pair of aces had the highest income rate; a 2 and 7 of different suits had the lowest. There is a strong correlation between our simulation results and the pre-flop categorization given in Sklansky and Malmuth (1994).

Hand Strength

An assessment of the strength of a hand is critical to the program's performance on the flop, turn and river. The probability of holding the best hand at any time can be accurately estimated using enumeration techniques.

Suppose our hand is A♦-Q♣ and the flop is 3♥-4♣-J♥. There are 47 remaining unknown cards and therefore {47 choose 2} = 1,081 possible hands an opponent might hold. To estimate hand strength, we developed an enumeration algorithm that gives a percentile ranking of our hand (Figure 1). With no opponent modeling, we simply count the number of possible hands that are better than, equal to, and worse than ours. In this example, any three of a kind, two pair, one pair, or A-K is better (444 cases), the remaining A-Q combinations are equal (9 cases), and the rest of the hands are worse (628 cases). Counting ties as half, this corresponds to a percentile ranking, or hand strength (HS), of 0.585. In other words, there is a 58.5% chance that our hand is better than a random hand.

```
HandStrength(ourcards,boardcards)
{ ahead = tied = behind = 0
  ourrank = Rank(ourcards,boardcards)
  /* Consider all two card combinations of  */
  /* the remaining cards.                   */
  for each case (oppcards)
  { opprank = Rank(oppcards,boardcards)
     if(ourrank>opprank)         ahead += 1
     else if(ourrank=opprank)    tied  += 1
     else /* < */                behind += 1
  }
  handstrength = (ahead+tied/2)
                 / (ahead+tied+behind)
  return(handstrength)
}
```

Figure 1. HandStrength calculation

The hand strength calculation is with respect to one opponent but can be extrapolated to multiple opponents by raising it to the power of the number of active opponents. Against five opponents with random hands, the adjusted hand strength (HS_5) is $.585^5$ = .069. Hence, the presence of additional opponents has reduced the likelihood of our having the best hand to only 6.9%.

Hand Potential

In practice, hand strength alone is insufficient to assess the quality of a hand. Consider the hand 5♥-2♥ with the flop of 3♥-4♣-J♥. This is currently a very weak hand, but there is tremendous potential for improvement. With two cards yet to come, any heart, Ace, or 6 will give us a flush or straight. There is a high probability (over 50%) that this hand will improve to become the winning hand, so it has a lot of value. In general, we need to be aware of how the potential of a hand affects the effective hand strength.

We can use enumeration to compute this positive potential (Ppot), the probability of improving to the best hand when we are behind. Similarly, we can also compute the negative potential (Npot) of falling behind when we are ahead. For each of the possible 1,081 opposing hands, we consider the {45 choose 2} = 990 combinations of the next two community cards. For each subcase we count how many outcomes result in us being ahead, behind or tied (Figure 2).

The results for the example hand A♦-Q♣ / 3♥-4♣-J♥ versus a single opponent are shown in Table 1. The rows are labeled by the status on the flop. The columns are labeled with the final state after the last two community cards are dealt. For example, there are 91,981 ways we could be ahead on the river after being behind on the flop. Of the remaining outcomes, 1,036 leave us tied with the best hand, and we stay behind in 346,543 cases. In other words, if we are behind a random hand on the flop we have roughly a 21% chance of winning the showdown.

In Figure 2 and Table 1, we compute the potential based on two additional cards. This technique is called two-card lookahead and it produces a $Ppot_2$ of 0.208 and an $Npot_2$ of 0.274. We can do a similar calculation based on one-card lookahead ($Ppot_1$) where there are only 45 possible upcoming cards (44 if we are on the turn) instead of 990 outcomes. With respect to one-card lookahead on the flop, $Ppot_1$ is 0.108 and $Npot_1$ is 0.145.

```
HandPotential(ourcards,boardcards)
{ /* Hand potential array, each index repre-  */
  /* sents ahead, tied, and behind.           */
  integer array HP[3][3]        /* initialize to 0 */
  integer array HPTotal[3]      /* initialize to 0 */

  ourrank = Rank(ourcards,boardcards)
  /* Consider all two card combinations of    */
  /* the remaining cards for the opponent.    */
  for each case(oppcards)
  { opprank = Rank(oppcards,boardcards)
    if(ourrank>opprank)           index = ahead
    else if(ourrank=opprank)      index = tied
    else /* < */                  index = behind
    HPTotal[index] += 1

    /* All possible board cards to come.      */
    for each case(turn,river)
    { /* Final 5-card board */
      board = [boardcards,turn,river]
      ourbest = Rank(ourcards,board)
      oppbest = Rank(oppcards,board)
      if(ourbest>oppbest)       HP[index][ahead]+=1
      else if(ourbest=oppbest)  HP[index][tied]+=1
      else  /* < */             HP[index][behind]+=1
    }
  }
  /* Ppot: were behind but moved ahead.       */
  Ppot = (HP[behind][ahead]+HP[behind][tied]/2
                           +HP[tied][ahead]/2)
         / (HPTotal[behind]+HPTotal[tied])
  /* Npot: were ahead but fell behind.        */
  Npot = (HP[ahead][behind]+HP[tied][behind]/2
                           +HP[ahead][tied]/2)
         / (HPTotal[ahead]+HPTotal[tied])
  return(Ppot,Npot)
}
```

Figure 2. HandPotential calculation

5 Cards	7 Cards				
	Ahead	Tied	Behind	Sum	
Ahead	449005	3211	169504	621720 =	628x990
Tied	0	8370	540	8910 =	9x990
Behind	91981	1036	346543	439560 =	444x990
Sum	540986	12617	516587	1070190 =	1081x990

Table 1. A♦-Q♣ / 3♥-4♣-J♥ potential

These calculations provide accurate probabilities that take every possible scenario into account, giving smooth, robust results. However, the assumption that all two-card opponent hands are equally likely is false, and the computations must be modified to reflect this.

Betting Strategy

When it is our turn to act, how do we use hand strength and hand potential to select a betting action? What other information is useful and how should it be used? The answers to these questions are not trivial and this is one of the reasons that poker is a good test-bed for artificial intelligence. The current betting strategy in *Loki* is unsophisticated and can be improved (Billings et al. 1997).

It is sufficient to know that betting strategy is based primarily on two things:
1. *Effective hand strength* (EHS) includes hands where we are ahead, and those where we have a Ppot chance that we can pull ahead:
$$EHS = HS_n + (1 - HS_n) \times Ppot$$
2. *Pot odds* are your winning chances compared to the expected return from the pot. If you assess your chance of winning to be 25%, you would call a $4 bet to win a $16 pot (4/(16+4) = 0.20) because the pot odds are in your favor (0.25 >= 0.20).

Opponent Modeling

In strategic games like chess, the performance loss by ignoring opponent modeling is small, and hence it is usually ignored. In contrast, not only does opponent modeling have tremendous value in poker, it can be the distinguishing feature between players at different skill levels. If a set of players all have a comparable knowledge of poker fundamentals, the ability to alter decisions based on an accurate model of the opponent may have a greater impact on success than any other strategic principle.

Having argued that some form of opponent modeling is indispensable, the actual method of gathering information and using it for betting decisions is a complex and interesting problem. Not only is it difficult to make appropriate inferences from certain observations and then apply them in practice, it is not even clear how statistics should be collected or categorized.

Weighting the Enumeration

Many weak hands that probably would have been folded before the flop, such as 4♥-J♣, may form a very strong hand with the example flop of 3♥-4♣-J♥. Giving equal probabilities to all starting hands skews the hand evaluations compared to more realistic assumptions. Therefore, for each starting hand, we need to define a probability that our opponent would have played that hand in the observed manner. We call the probabilities for each of these 1,081 subcases *weights* since they act as multipliers in the enumeration computations.[1]

The use of these weights is the first step towards opponent modeling since we are changing our computations based on the relative probabilities of different cards that our opponents may hold. The simplest approach to determining these weights is to treat all opponents the same, calculating a single set of weights to reflect "reasonable" behavior, and use them for all opponents. An initial set of weights was determined by ranking the 169 distinct starting hands and assigning a probability commensurate with the strength (income rate) of each hand (as determined by simulations).

There are two distinct ways to improve the accuracy of the calculations based on these weights. First, an opponent's betting actions can be used to adjust the

---

[1] The probability that an opponent holds a particular hand is the weight of that subcase divided by the sum of the weights for all the subcases.

weights. For example, if an opponent raises on the flop, the weights for stronger hands should be increased and the weights for weaker hands should be decreased. We call this *generic* modeling since the model is identical for all opponents in the same situation. Second, we can maintain a separate set of weights for each opponent, based on their betting history. We call this technique *specific* modeling, because it differentiates between opponents.

Each opponent is assigned an array of weights indexed by the two-card starting hands. Each time an opponent makes a betting action, the weights for that opponent are modified to account for the action. For example, a raise increases the weights for the strongest hands likely to be held by the opponent given the flop cards, and decreases the weights for the weaker hands. This means that at any point during the hand, the weight reflects the relative probability that the opponent has that particular hand.

If these weights are used for opponent modeling, the algorithms of Figures 1 and 2 are only slightly modified. Each of the increments ("+= 1") is replaced with the code "+= Weight[oppcards]". There are two problems that must be solved to make this form of opponent modeling work. First, what should the initial weights be? Second, what transformation functions should be applied to the weights to account for a particular opponent action?

Computing Initial Weights

The initial weights are based on the starting hands each opponent will play. The most important observed information is the frequency of folding, calling and raising before the flop. We deduce the mean (μ, representing the median hand) and variance (σ, for uncertainty) of the threshold needed for each player's observed action. These are interpreted in terms of income rate values, and mapped onto a set of initial weights for the opponent model.

Suppose an opponent calls 30% of all hands, and this translates to a median hand whose income rate is +200 (roughly corresponding to an average of 0.2 bets won per hand played). If we assume a σ that translates to an income rate of +/-100, then we would assign a weight of 1.0 to all hands above +300, a weight of 0.01 to all hands below +100, and a proportional weight for values between +100 and +300. The median hand at +200 is thus given a 0.50 weight in the model. A weight of 0.01 is used for "low" probabilities to avoid labeling any hand as "impossible". While this approach will not reveal certain opponent-specific tendencies, it does provide reasonable estimates for the probability of each possible starting hand.

To classify the opponent's observed actions, we consider the action (fold, check/call, bet/raise) taken by the opponent, how much the action cost (bets of 0, 1, or > 1) and the betting round in which it occurred (pre-flop, flop, turn, river). This yields 36 different categories. Some of these actions do not normally occur (e.g. folding to no bet) and others are rare. Each betting action an opponent makes results in one of these categories being incremented. These statistics are then used to calculate the relevant frequencies.

Re-weighting

Each time an opponent makes a betting action, we modify the weights by applying a transformation function. For simplicity we do not do any re-weighting on the pre-flop, preferring to translate income rates into weights. For the betting rounds after the flop, we infer a mean and variance (μ and σ) of the threshold for the opponent's observed action. However, we can no longer map our μ and σ to a list of ranked starting hands. Instead, we must rank all of the five card hands that are formed from each starting hand and the three community cards. To do this, we use EHS.

For example, based on observed frequencies, we may deduce that an opponent needs a median hand value of 0.6 to call a bet, with a lower bound of 0.4 and an upper bound of 0.8. In this case, all hands with an EHS greater than 0.8 are given re-weighting factors of 1.0. Any hand with a value less than 0.4 is assigned a re-weighting factor of 0.01, and a linear interpolation is performed for values between 0.4 and 0.8. Figure 3 shows the algorithm used for computing the re-weighting factors for a given μ and σ.

Recall that EHS is a function of both HS and Ppot. Since $Ppot_2$ is expensive to compute, we currently use a crude but fast function for estimating potential, which produces values within 5% of $Ppot_2$, 95% of the time. Since these values are amortized over the 1,081 five-card hands, the overall effect of this approximation is small.

For each five-card hand, the computed re-weighting factor is multiplied by the initial weight to produce the updated weight. The process is repeated for each observed betting decision during the hand. By the last round of betting, a certain opponent may have only a small number of hands that have relatively high weights, meaning that the program has zeroed in on a narrow range of possible hands.

Table 2 illustrates how the re-weighting is performed on some selected examples for a flop of 3♥-4♣-J♥, with $\mu=0.60$ and $\sigma=0.20$. The context considers an opponent who called a bet before the flop and then bet after the flop. For each possible hand we note the initial weight (Weight), unweighted hand rank (HR), hand strength (HS_1), approximate $Ppot_2$ (~PP_2), effective hand strength (EHS), the re-weighting factor based on $\mu = 0.6$ and $\sigma = 0.2$ (Rwt), and the new overall weight (Nwt).

```
constant   low_wt   0.01
constant   high_wt  1.00

Reweight(μ,σ,weight,boardcards)
{ /* interpolate in the range μ +- σ. */
  for each case(oppcards)
  { EHS=EffectiveHandStrength(oppcards,boardcards)
    reweight = (EHS-μ+σ)/(2*σ)
    /* Assign low weights below (μ-σ). */
    if(reweight<low_wt)  reweight = low_wt
    /* Assign high weights above (μ+σ). */
    if(reweight>high_wt) reweight = high_wt
    weight[subcase] = weight[subcase]*reweight
  }
}
```

Figure 3. Computing the re-weighting factors

Hand	Weight	HR	HS$_1$	~PP$_2$	EHS	Rwt	Nwt	Comment
J♣ 4♥	0.01	0.993	0.990	0.04	0.99	1.00	0.01	very strong, but unlikely
A♣ J♣	1.00	0.956	0.931	0.09	0.94	1.00	1.00	strong, very likely
5♥ 2♥	0.20	0.004	0.001	0.35	0.91	1.00	0.20	weak, but very high potential
6♠ 5♠	0.60	0.026	0.006	0.21	0.76	0.90	0.54	weak, good potential
5♠ 5♥	0.70	0.816	0.736	0.04	0.74	0.85	0.60	moderate, low potential
5♠ 3♠	0.40	0.648	0.671	0.10	0.70	0.75	0.30	mediocre, moderate potential
A♣ Q♦	1.00	0.585	0.584	0.11	0.64	0.60	0.60	mediocre, moderate potential
7♠ 5♠	0.60	0.052	0.012	0.12	0.48	0.20	0.12	weak, moderate potential
Q♠ T♠	0.90	0.359	0.189	0.07	0.22	0.01	0.01	weak, little potential

Table 2. Re-weighting various hands after a 3♥-4♣-J♥ flop ($\mu = 0.6$, $\sigma = 0.2$)

Consider the case of Q♠ T♠. In the pre-flop this is a fairly strong hand, as reflected by its income rate of +359 and weighting of 0.90. However, these cards do not mesh well with the flop cards, resulting in low hand strength (0.189) and low potential (0.07). This translates to an effective hand strength of 0.22. Given that observations of the opponent show that they will only bet with hands of strength $\mu=0.60$ (+/-$\sigma=0.20$), we assign this a re-weighting of 0.01 (since $0.22<\mu-\sigma$). Hence, we will consider this hand to be unlikely for this opponent from this point on.

The opponent's decisions may actually be based on a different metric than EHS, resulting in an imperfect model. New techniques can improve the results, but the current method does capture much of the information conveyed by the opponent's actions.

In competitive poker, opponent modeling is more complex than portrayed here. One also wants to fool the opponent into constructing a poor model. For example, early in a session a strong poker player may try to create the impression of being very conservative, only to exploit that image later when the opponents are using incorrect assumptions. In two-player games, the M* algorithm allows for recursive definitions of opponent models, but it has not been demonstrated to improve performance in practice (Carmel and Markovitch 1995).

Experiments

Self-play simulations offer a convenient method for the comparison of two or more versions of the program. Our simulations use a duplicate tournament system, based on the same principle as duplicate bridge. Since each hand can be played with no memory of preceding hands, it is possible to replay the same deal, but with the participants holding a different set of hole cards each time. Our tournament system simulates a ten-player game, where each deal is replayed ten times, shuffling the seating arrangement so that every participant has the opportunity to play each set of hole cards once. This arrangement greatly reduces the "luck element" of the game, since each player will have the same number of good and bad hands. The differences in the performance of players will therefore be based more strongly on the quality of the decisions made in each situation. This large reduction in natural variance means that meaningful results can be obtained with a much smaller number of trials than in a typical game setting. Nevertheless, it is important to not over-interpret the results of one simulation.

Figure 4 shows the results of self-play simulations between several versions of *Loki* playing $2/$4 Hold'em. Two copies of five different programs played 100,000 hands. The average profit is plotted against the number of hands played. Each data point is the average of the two programs of that type.

We started with our previous best version of *Loki*, representing a basic player (BPM). BPM uses a crude system for assigning initial weights, so some generic modeling is done for the pre-flop hand selection[1] but there is no re-weighting. To add diversity to the simulated game, the betting parameters of *Loki* were modified to include two additional styles of play (BPT and BPL). BPT is a "tight" (conservative) player, while BPL is a "loose" (more liberal) player, but are otherwise identical to BPM. Two opponent modeling variations of BPM were then added (GOM and SOM). GOM uses generic opponent modeling with re-weighting, and the default models for the opponent are based on how GOM itself plays. SOM uses specific opponent modeling with re-weighting, starting with the GOM defaults but basing its decisions entirely on observed behavior after 20 data points have been collected.

Very quickly, the two opponent modeling programs asserted their superiority over the non-modeling versions. GOM is able to exploit the basic players, as expected, because its model of how they play is accurate, and is used to make better decisions. GOM might not perform as well against players with very different styles of play, because its model would be less accurate, but it would be better than using no modeling at all.

SOM is more successful using observed frequencies rather than a good default model. Against players with very different styles of play, as typically seen in human competition, SOM's advantage over GOM will be magnified.

Another experiment was performed with a single copy of SOM against nine copies of BPM. After 100,000 hands the SOM version was ahead roughly $5,000, while the BPM player had lost more than $550 on average. The advantage

---
[1] This feature was not removed because having no information at all would be a large handicap.

of good opponent modeling is clear – *Loki* with opponent modeling is a stronger program than without it.

Loki has also been tested in more realistic games against human opposition. For this purpose, the program participates in an on-line poker game, running on the Internet Relay Chat (IRC). Human players connect to IRC and participate in games conducted by dedicated server programs. No real money is at stake, but bankroll statistics on each player are maintained. Both the new opponent modeling versions of *Loki* and the previous versions with no re-weighting win consistently when playing on the IRC server. The natural variance in these games is very high, and the results depend strongly on which players happen to be playing. Consequently, not enough information has been gathered to safely conclude that the opponent modeling versions of *Loki* are outperforming the previous best program in these games.

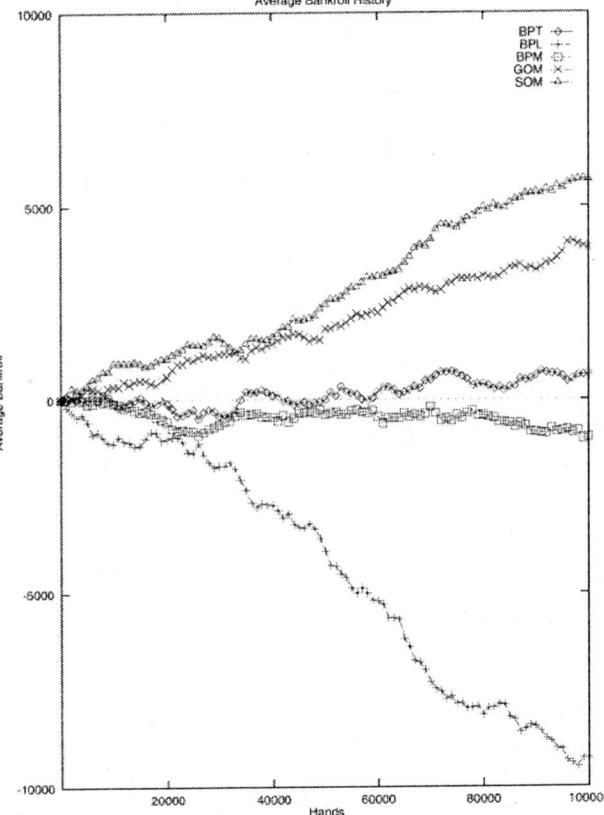

Figure 4. Experiments with different versions of *Loki*.

Conclusions and Work in Progress

Loki successfully uses opponent modeling to improve its play. This is the first demonstration of beneficial opponent modeling in a high-performance game-playing program.

However, it does not necessarily follow that opponent modeling will be just as successful in games against human players as it was in the closed experiments. Humans are also very good at opponent modeling, and can be less predictable than the players in these simulations. We have not yet investigated modeling opponents who vary their strategy over time.

Specific opponent modeling was hampered by the crude method used for collecting and applying observed statistics. Much of the relevant context was ignored for simplicity, such as combinations of actions within the same betting round. A more sophisticated method for observing and utilizing opponent behavior would allow for a more flexible and accurate opponent model.

Poker is a complex game. Strong play requires the player to excel in all aspects of the game. Developing *Loki* seems to be a cyclic process. We improve one aspect of the program until it becomes apparent that another aspect is the performance bottleneck. That problem is then tackled until it is no longer the limiting factor, and a new weakness in the program's play is revealed. We have made our initial foray into opponent modeling and are pleased with the results, although it is far from a completed subject. It is now apparent that the program's betting strategy is the major cause for concern. Hence we will now focus our efforts on that topic, and opponent modeling will be revisited in the future.

Acknowledgments

We gratefully thank the referees for their insightful comments. Regretfully, some of their excellent suggestions were omitted due to space constraints.

This research was supported by the Natural Sciences and Engineering Council of Canada.

References

Billings, D., Papp, D., Schaeffer, J. and Szafron, D. 1997. Poker as a Testbed for AI Research, AI'98. To appear.

Carmel, D. and Markovitch, S. 1995. Incorporating Opponent Models into Adversary Search. AAAI, 120-125.

Findler, N. 1977. Studies in Machine Cognition Using the Game of Poker. *CACM* 20(4):230-245.

Iida, H., Uiterwijk, J., van den Herik, J. and Herschberg, I. 1995. Thoughts on the Application of Opponent-Model Search. In *Advances in Computer Chess 7*, University of Maastricht, 61-78.

Jansen, P. 1992. Using Knowledge about the Opponent in Game-Tree Search. Ph.D. diss., Dept. of Computer Science, Carnegie-Mellon University.

Koller, D. and Pfeffer, A. 1997. Representations and Solutions for Game-Theoretic Problems. *Artificial Intelligence* 94(1-2), 167-215.

Sklansky, D. and Malmuth, M. 1994. *Hold'em Poker for Advanced Players*. Two Plus Two Publishing.

Finding Optimal Strategies for Imperfect Information Games*

Ian Frank
Complex Games Lab
Electrotechnical Laboratory
Umezono 1-1-4, Tsukuba
Ibaraki, JAPAN 305
ianf@etl.go.jp

David Basin
Institut für Informatik
Universität Freiburg
Am Flughafen 17
Freiburg, Germany
basin@informatik.uni-freiburg.de

Hitoshi Matsubara
Complex Games Lab
Electrotechnical Laboratory
Umezono 1-1-4, Tsukuba
Ibaraki, JAPAN 305
matsubar@etl.go.jp

Abstract

We examine three heuristic algorithms for games with imperfect information: Monte-carlo sampling, and two new algorithms we call *vector minimaxing* and *payoff-reduction minimaxing*. We compare these algorithms theoretically and experimentally, using both simple game trees and a large database of problems from the game of Bridge. Our experiments show that the new algorithms both out-perform Monte-carlo sampling, with the superiority of payoff-reduction minimaxing being especially marked. On the Bridge problem set, for example, Monte-carlo sampling only solves 66% of the problems, whereas payoff-reduction minimaxing solves over 95%. This level of performance was even good enough to allow us to discover five errors in the expert text used to generate the test database.

Introduction

In games with imperfect information, the actual 'state of the world' may be unknown; for example, the position of some of the opponents' playing pieces may be hidden. Finding the optimal strategy in such games is NP-hard in the size of the game tree (see *e.g.*, (Blair, Mutchler, & Liu 1993)), and thus a heuristic approach is required to solve non-trivial games of this kind.

For any imperfect information game, we will call each possible outcome of the uncertainties (*e.g.*, where the hidden pieces might be) a possible *world state* or *world*. Figure 1 shows a game tree with five such possible worlds $w_1, \cdots, w_5$. The squares in this figure correspond to MAX nodes and the circles to MIN nodes. For a more general game with n possible worlds, each leaf node of the game tree would have n payoffs, each corresponding to the utility for MAX of reaching that node in each of the n worlds.[1]

*Copyright ©1998, American Association for Artificial Intelligence (www.aaai.org). All rights reserved.

[1] For the reader familiar with basic game-theory, (von Neumann & Morgenstern 1944; Luce & Raiffa 1957), Figure 1 is a compact representation of the extensive form of a particular kind of two-person, zero-sum game with imperfect information. Specifically, it represents a game tree with a single chance-move at the root and n identically shaped subtrees. Such a tree can be 'flattened', as in Figure 1, by

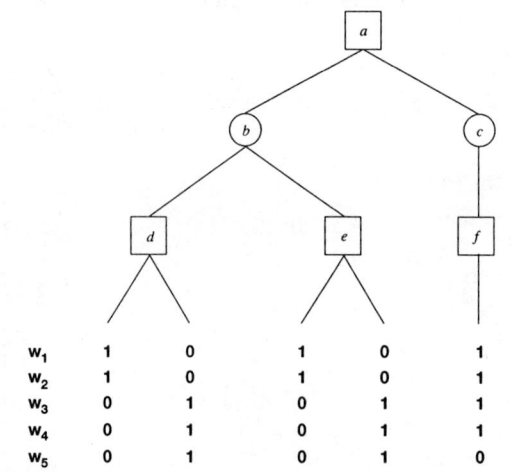

Figure 1: A game tree with five possible worlds

If both MAX and MIN know the world to be in some state w_i then all the payoffs corresponding to the other worlds can be ignored and the well-known minimax algorithm (Shannon 1950) used to find the optimal strategies. In this paper we will consider the more general case where the state of the world depends on information that MAX does not know, but to which he can attach a probability distribution (for example, the toss of a coin or the deal of a deck of cards). We examine this situation for various levels of MIN knowledge about the world state.

We follow the standard practice in game theory of assuming that the best strategy is one that would not change if it was made available to the opponent (von

assigning payoff n-tuples to each leaf node so that the ith component is the payoff for that leaf in the ith subtree. It is assumed that the only move with an unknown outcome is the chance move that starts the game. Thus, a single node in the flattened tree represents between 1 and n *information sets*: one if the player knows the exact outcome of the chance move, n if the player has no knowledge.

Neumann & Morgenstern 1944). For a MIN player with *no* knowledge of the world state the situation is very simple, as an expected value computation can be used to convert the multiple payoffs at each leaf node into a single value, and the standard minimax algorithm applied to the resulting tree. As MIN's knowledge increases, however, games with imperfect information have the property that it is in general important for MAX to prevent MIN from 'finding out' his strategy, by making his choices probabilistically. In this paper, however, we will restrict our consideration to *pure* strategies, which make no use of probabilities. In practice, this need not be a serious limitation, as we will see when we consider the game of Bridge.

We examine three algorithms in detail: Monte-carlo sampling (Corlett & Todd 1985) and two new algorithms we call *vector minimaxing* and *payoff-reduction minimaxing*. We compare these algorithms theoretically and experimentally, using both simple game trees and a large database of problems from the game of Bridge. Our experiments show that Monte-carlo sampling is out-performed by both of the new algorithms, with the superiority of payoff-reduction minimaxing being especially marked.

Monte-carlo Sampling

We begin by introducing the technique of Monte-carlo sampling. This approach to handling imperfect information has in fact been used in practical game-playing programs, such as the QUETZAL Scrabble program (written by Tony Guilfoyle and Richard Hooker, as described in (Frank 1989)) and also in the game of Bridge, where it was proposed by (Levy 1989) and recently implemented by (Ginsberg 1996b).

In the context of game trees like that of Figure 1, the technique consists of guessing a possible world and then finding a solution to the game tree for this complete information sub-problem. This is much easier than solving the original game, since (as we mentioned in the Introduction) if attention is restricted to just one world, the minimax algorithm can be used to find the best strategy. By guessing different worlds and repeating this process, it is hoped that an action that works well in a large number of worlds can be identified.

To make this description more concrete, let us consider a general MAX node with branches $M_1, M_2, \cdots$ in a game with n worlds. If e_{ij} represents the minimax value of the node under branch M_i in world w_j, we can construct a scoring function, f, such as:

$$f(M_i) = \sum_{j=1}^{n} e_{ij} \Pr(w_j), \qquad (1)$$

where $\Pr(w_j)$ represents MAX's assessment of the probability of the actual world being w_j. Monte-carlo sampling can then be viewed as selecting a move by using the minimax algorithm to generate values of the e_{ij}s, and determining the M_i for which the value of $f(M_i)$ is greatest. If there is sufficient time, all the e_{ij} can be generated, but in practice only some 'representative' sample of worlds is examined.

As an example, consider how the tree of Figure 1 is analysed by the above characterisation of Monte-carlo sampling. If we examine world w_1, the minimax values of the left-hand and the right-hand moves at node a are as shown in Figure 2 (these correspond to e_{11} and e_{21} for this tree). It is easy to check that the

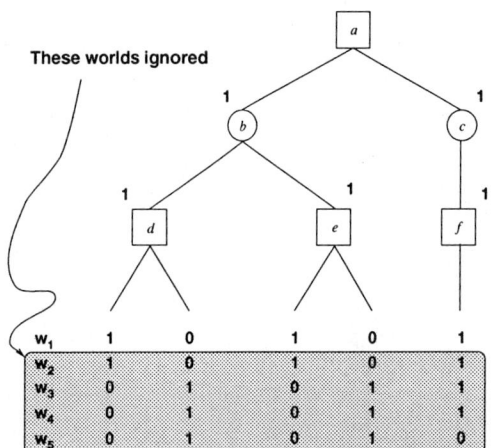

Figure 2: Finding the minimax value of world w_1

minimax value at node b is again 1 if we examine any of the remaining worlds, and that the value at node c is 1 in worlds w_2, w_3, and w_4, but 0 in world w_5. Thus, if we assume equally likely worlds, Monte-carlo sampling using (1) to make its branch selection will choose the left-hand branch at node a whenever world w_5 is included in its sample. Unfortunately, this is not the best strategy for this tree, as the right-hand branch at node a offers a payoff of 1 in four worlds. The best return that MAX can hope for when choosing the left-hand branch at node a is a payoff of 1 in just three worlds (for any reasonable assumptions about a rational MIN opponent).

Note that, as it stands, Monte-carlo sampling identifies pure strategies that make no use of probabilities. Furthermore, by repeatedly applying the minimax algorithm, Monte-carlo sampling models the situation where both MIN and MAX play optimally in each individual world. Thus, the algorithm carries the implicit assumption that both players *know* the state of the world.

Vector Minimaxing

That Monte-carlo sampling makes mistakes in situations like that of Figure 1 has been remarked on in the literature on computer game-playing (see, *e.g.*, (Frank 1989)). The primary reason for such errors has also recently been formalised as *strategy fusion* in (Frank &

Basin 1998). In the example of Figure 2, the essence of the problem with a sampling approach is that it allows *different choices* to be made at nodes d and e in *different worlds*. In reality, a MAX player who does not know the state of the world must make a *single choice* for all worlds at node d and another single choice for all worlds at node e. Combining the minimax values of separate choices results in an over-optimistic analysis of node b. In effect, the false assumption mentioned above that MAX knows the state of the world allows the results of different moves — or strategies — to be 'fused' together.

We present here an algorithm that removes the problem of strategy fusion from Monte-carlo sampling by ensuring that at any MAX node a single branch is chosen in all worlds. This algorithm requires the definition of a payoff vector, $\vec{K}(\nu)$, for leaf nodes of the game tree, ν, such that $\vec{K}[j](\nu)$ (where $\vec{K}[j]$ is the jth element of the vector $\vec{K}$) takes the value of the payoff at ν in world w_j ($1 \leq j \leq n$). Figure 3 defines our algorithm, which we call *vector minimaxing*. It uses payoff vectors to identify a strategy for a tree t, where $sub(t)$ computes the set of t's immediate subtrees.

Algorithm *vector-mm(t)*:
Take the following actions, depending on t.

Condition	Result
t is leaf node	$\vec{K}(t)$
root of t is a MIN node	$\min_{t_i \in sub(t)} \text{vector-mm}(t_i)$
root of t is a MAX node	$\max_{t_i \in sub(t)} \text{vector-mm}(t_i)$

Figure 3: The vector minimaxing algorithm

In this algorithm, the normal min and max functions are extended so that they are defined over a set of payoff vectors. The max function returns the single vector $\vec{K}$, for which

$$\sum_{j=1}^{n} \Pr(w_j)\vec{K}[j] \qquad (2)$$

is maximum, resolving equal choices randomly. In this way, vector minimaxing commits to just *one* choice of branch at each MAX node, avoiding strategy fusion (the actual strategy selected by the algorithm is just the set of the choices made at the MAX nodes).

As for the min function, it is possible to define this as the dual of the max function, returning the single vector for which (2) is minimum. However, this would result in modelling the simple situation, described in the Introduction, where MIN, like MAX, has no knowledge of the state of the world. Instead, we therefore say that for a node with m branches and therefore m

payoff vectors $\vec{K}_1, \cdots, \vec{K}_m$ to choose between, the min function is defined as:

$$\min_{i} \vec{K}_i = (\min_{i} \vec{K}_i[1], \min_{i} \vec{K}_i[2], \cdots, \min_{i} \vec{K}_i[n]). \qquad (3)$$

That is, the min function returns a vector in which the payoff for each possible world is the lowest possible. This models a MIN player who has *complete* knowledge of the state of the world, and uses this to choose the best branch in each possible world. As we pointed out in the previous section, this is the same assumption that is implicitly made by Monte-carlo sampling. We use the assumption again as it represents the most conservative approach: modelling the strongest possible opponents provides a lower bound on the payoff that can be expected when the opponents are less informed. Also, we shall see later that this assumption is actually used by human experts when analysing some imperfect information games.

As an example of vector minimaxing in practice, Figure 4 shows how the algorithm would analyse the tree of Figure 1, using ovals to represent the vectors produced at each node. The branches selected at MAX nodes by the max operator (assuming equally likely worlds) are highlighted in bold, showing that the right-hand branch is correctly chosen at node a.

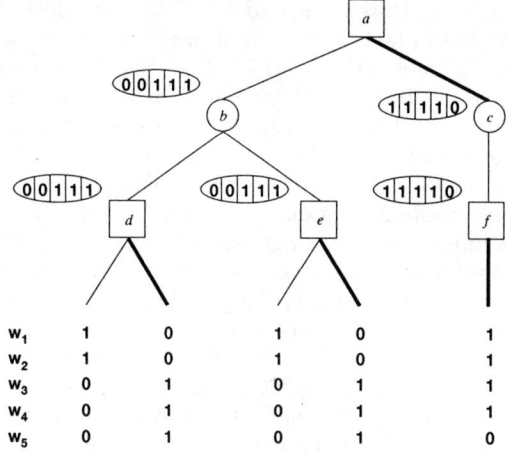

Figure 4: Vector minimaxing applied to example tree

Payoff-reduction Minimaxing

Consider Figure 5, which depicts a game tree with just three worlds. If we assume that MIN has complete knowledge of the world state in this game (as implicitly modelled by Monte-carlo sampling and vector minimaxing) the best strategy for MAX is to choose the left-hand branch at node d and the right-hand branch at node e. This guarantees a payoff of 1 in world w_1.

In the figure, however, we have annotated the tree to show how it is analysed by vector minimaxing. The branches in bold show that the algorithm would choose the right-hand branch at both node d and node e. The vector produced at node b correctly indicates that when MAX makes these selections, a MIN player who knows the world state will always be able to restrict MAX to a payoff of 0 (by choosing the left branch at node b in world w_1 and the right branch in worlds w_2 and w_3). Thus, at the root of the tree, both subtrees have the same analysis, and vector minimaxing never wins on this tree.

Applying Monte-carlo sampling to the same tree, in the limiting case where all possible worlds are examined, we see that node b has a minimax value of 1 in world w_1, so that the left-hand branch would be selected at the root of the tree. However, the same selections as vector minimaxing will then be made when subsequently playing at node d or node e. Thus, despite both modelling the situation where MIN has complete knowledge of the actual world state, neither Monte-carlo sampling nor vector minimaxing choose the best strategy against a MIN player with complete information on this tree.

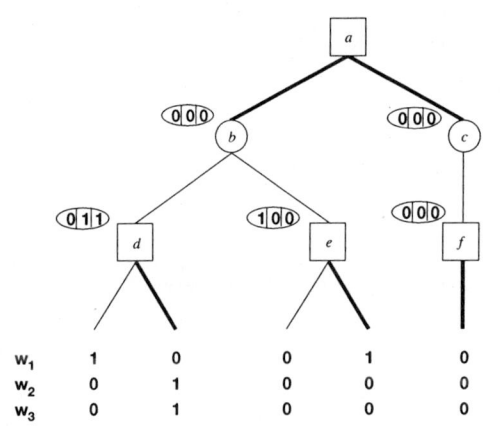

Figure 5: Example tree with three worlds

The difficulty here is that MIN can *always* restrict MAX to a payoff of 0 in worlds w_2 and w_3 by choosing the right-hand branch at node b. Thus, at node d the payoffs of 1 under the right-hand branch will never actually be realised, and should be ignored. Effectively, and perhaps counterintuitively, the analysis of node d is dependent on first correctly analysing node e. This is an example of how imperfect information games can not be solved by search algorithms that are 'compositional' (*i.e.*, algorithms that determine the best play at an internal node ν of a search space by analysing only the *local* subtree beneath ν). Such algorithms do not take into account information from other portions of the game tree. In particular, they do not recognise that under some worlds the play may never actually reach any given internal node, ν. At such nodes, they may therefore mistakenly select moves on the basis of high expected payoffs in world states that are in fact of no consequence at that position in the tree (as happens in Figure 5). This problem, which is more difficult to eliminate than strategy fusion, has been formalised as *non-locality* in (Frank & Basin 1998).

We propose here a new algorithm that lessens the impact of non-locality by reducing the payoffs at the frontier nodes of a search tree. As in the case of Montecarlo sampling and vector minimaxing, the assumption in this algorithm is that MIN plays as well as possible in each individual world. However, this time we implement this assumption by reducing the payoff in any given world w_k to the maximum possible (minimax) return that can be produced when the game tree is examined as a single, complete information search tree in world w_k. The resulting algorithm, which we call *payoff-reduction minimaxing*, or *prm*, is shown in its simplest form in Figure 6 (it can be implemented more efficiently, for example by combining steps 2 and 3 together).

Algorithm $prm(t)$:
Identifies strategies for game trees, t

1. Conduct minimaxing of each world, w_k, finding for each MIN node its minimax value, m_k, in that world.

2. Examine the payoff vectors of each leaf node. Reduce the payoffs p_k in each world w_k to the minimum of p_k and all the m_k of the node's MIN ancestors.

3. Apply the *vector-mm* algorithm to the resulting tree.

Figure 6: Simple form of the *prm* algorithm

The reduction step in this algorithm addresses the problem of non-locality by, in effect, parameterising the payoffs at each leaf node with information on the results obtainable in other portions of the tree. By using minimax values for this reduction, the game-theoretic value of the tree in each individual world is also left unaltered, since no payoff is reduced to the extent that it would offer MIN a better branch selection at any node in any world.

As an example, let us consider how the algorithm would behave on the tree of Figure 5. The minimax value of node c is zero in every world, but all the payoffs at node f are also zero, so no reduction is possible. At node b, however, the minimax values in the three possible worlds are 1, 0, and 0, respectively. Thus, all the payoffs in each world at nodes d and e are reduced to at most these values. This leaves only the two payoffs of 1 in world w_1 as shown in Figure 7, where the strategy selection subsequently made by vector-minimaxing has also been highlighted in bold. In this tree, then, the *prm* algorithm results in the correct strategy being chosen. In the next section, we examine how often this holds in general.

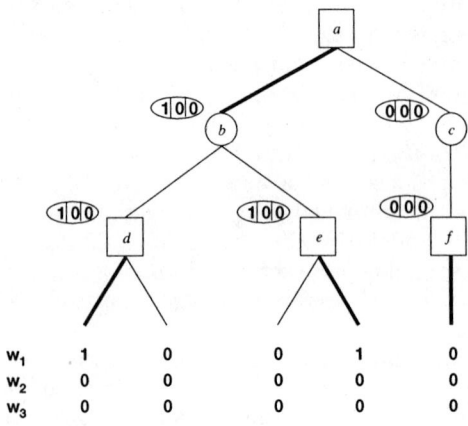

Figure 7: Applying *vector-mm* after payoff reduction

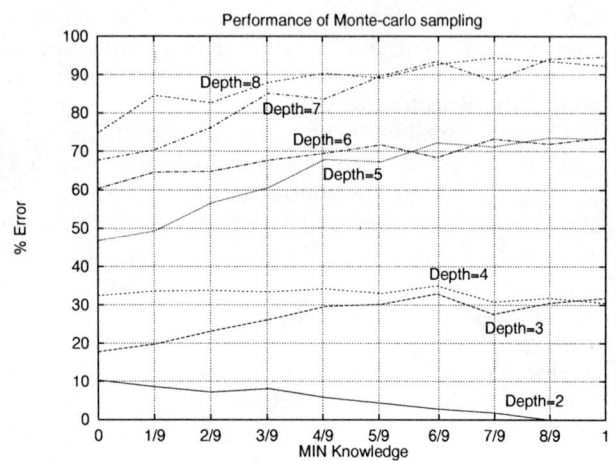

Experiments on Random Trees

We tested the performance of Monte-carlo sampling, vector minimaxing and payoff-reduction minimaxing on randomly generated trees. For simplicity, the trees we use in our tests are complete binary trees, with $n = 10$ worlds and payoffs of just one or zero. These payoffs are assigned by an application of the Last Player Theorem (Nau 1982), so that the probability of there being a forced win for MAX in the complete information game tree in any individual world is the same for all depths of tree.[2]

We assume that MAX has no information about the state of the world, so that each world appears to have the equally likely probability of $1/n$ (in our tests, $1/10$). For MIN's moves, on the other hand, we assume that for i ($0 \leq i < n$), the rules of the game allow MIN to identify the actual world state in i cases. In each of these (randomly selected) i worlds, MIN can therefore make branch selections based on the actual payoffs in that particular world, and will only require an expected value computation for the remaining $n - i$ worlds. We define the level of knowledge of such a MIN player as being $i/(n-1)$.

The graphs of Figure 8 show the performance of each of the three algorithms on these test game trees. These graphs were produced by carrying out the following

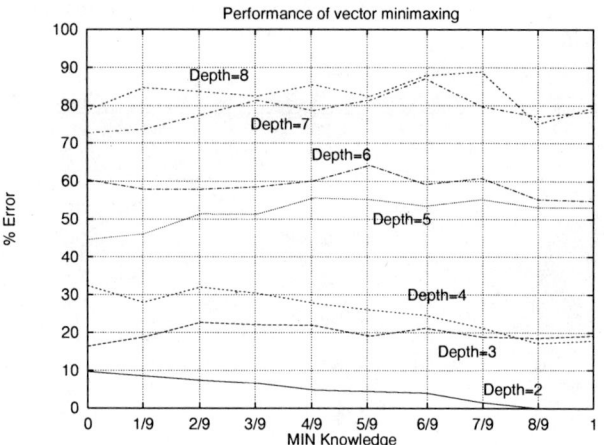

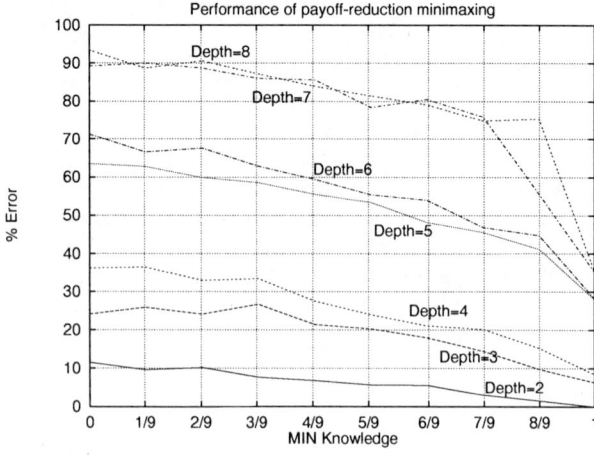

Figure 8: The error in Monte-carlo sampling, vector minimaxing and payoff-reduction minimaxing, for trees of depth 2 to 8

---

[2]The Last Player Theorem introduces a probability, p, that governs the assignment of leaf node payoffs as follows: if the last player is MAX, choose a 1 with probability p; if the last player is MIN, choose a 1 with probability $1-p$. For complete information binary trees with a MAX node at the root, (Nau 1982) shows that if $p = (3 - \sqrt{5})/2 \approx 0.38197$ the probability of any node having a minimax value of 1 is constant for all sizes of tree ($1 - p$ for MAX nodes, and p for MIN nodes). For lower values of p, the chance of the last player having a forced win quickly decreases to zero as the tree depth increases. For higher values, the chance of a forced win for the last player increases to unity.

steps 1000 times for each data point of tree depth and opponent knowledge:

1. Generate a random test tree of the required depth.
2. Use each algorithm to identify a strategy. (For each algorithm, assume that the payoffs in *all* worlds can be examined.)[3]
3. Compute the payoff of the selected strategies, for an opponent with the level of knowledge specified.
4. Use an inefficient, but correct, algorithm (based on examining every strategy) to find an optimal strategy and payoff, for an opponent with the level of knowledge specified.
5. For each algorithm, check whether they are in error (*i.e.*, if any of the values of the strategies found in Step 3 are inferior to the value of the strategy found in step 4, assuming equally likely worlds).

Our results demonstrate that vector minimaxing out-performs Monte-carlo sampling by a small amount, for almost all levels of MIN knowledge and tree depths. This is due to the removal of strategy fusion. However, even when strategy fusion is removed, the problem of non-locality remains, to the extent that the performance of vector minimaxing is only slightly superior to Monte-carlo sampling. A far more dramatic improvement is therefore produced by the *prm* algorithm, which removes strategy fusion and further reduces the error caused by non-locality. When MIN has no knowledge on the state of the world, *prm* actually *introduces* errors through its improved modelling of the assumption that MIN will play as well as possible in each world. However, as MIN's knowledge increases, this assumption becomes more accurate, until for levels of knowledge of about 5/9 and above, the *prm* algorithm out-performs both Monte-carlo sampling and vector minimaxing. When MIN's knowledge of the world state is 1 the performance advantage of *prm* is particularly marked, with the error of *prm* for trees of depth 8 being just over a third of the error rate of Monte-carlo sampling.

To test the performance advantage of *prm* on larger trees, we extended the range of our tests to cover trees of depth up to 13 (the largest size that our algorithm for finding optimal solutions could handle), with the opponent knowledge fixed at 1. The results of this test are shown in Figure 9. When the trees reach depth 9, Monte-carlo sampling and vector minimaxing have error rates of 99.9% and 96%, whereas *prm* still identifies the optimal strategy in over 40% of the trials. For trees of depth 11 and over, where Monte-carlo sampling and vector minimaxing *never* find a correct solution, *prm* still performs at between 40% and 30%.

---

[3]Note that in general, examining all the payoffs may not be possible, but just as Monte-carlo sampling deals with this problem by selecting a subset of possible worlds, vector minimaxing and *prm* can also be applied with vectors of size less than n.

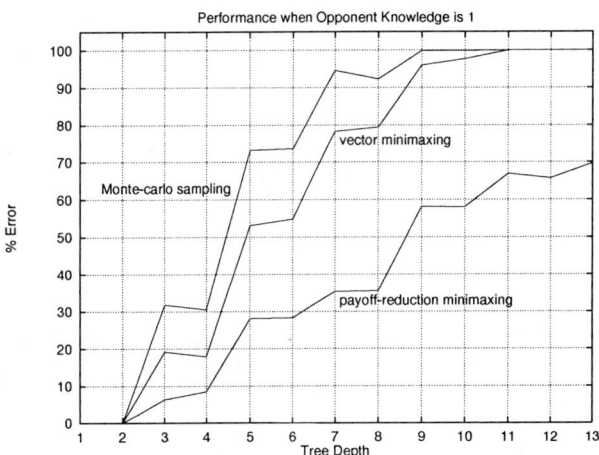

Figure 9: Superiority of payoff-reduction minimaxing, with opponent knowledge of 1, trees of depth up to 13

The ability to find optimal solutions when the opponents have full knowledge of the world state is highly significant in games with imperfect information. For instance, we have already pointed out that the payoff obtainable against the strongest possible opponents can be used as a lower bound on the expected payoff when the opponents are less informed. We have also noted that the other extreme, where MIN has *no* knowledge, is easily modelled (thus, it is not significant that all the algorithms in Figure 8 perform badly when MIN's knowledge is zero). Most significant of all, however, is that the assumption that the opponents know the state of the world is, in fact, made by human experts when analysing real games with imperfect information. We examine an example of this below.

Experiments on the Game of Bridge

As we mentioned earlier, Monte-carlo sampling has in fact been used in practical game-playing programs for games like Scrabble and Bridge. Bridge is of particular interest to us here as we have shown in previous work (Frank & Basin 1998) that expert analysis of single-suit Bridge problems is typically carried out under the *best defence* assumption that the opponents know the exact state of the world (*i.e.*, the layout of the hidden cards). Further, Bridge has been heavily analysed by human experts, who have produced texts that describe the optimal play in large numbers of situations. The availability of such references provides a natural way of assessing the performance of automated algorithms.

To construct a Bridge test set, we used as an expert reference the Official Encyclopedia of Bridge, published by the American Contract Bridge League (ACBL 1994). This book contains a 55-page section presenting optimal lines of play for a selection of 665 single-suit problems. Of these, we collected the 650 examples that gave *pure* strategies for obtaining the maximum possible payoff against best defence.[4] Using the FINESSE Bridge-playing system (Frank, Basin, & Bundy 1992; Frank 1996), we then tested Monte-carlo sampling, vector minimaxing and *prm* against the solutions from the Encyclopedia. In each case, the expected payoff of the strategy produced by the algorithms (for the maximum possible payoff) was compared to that of the Encyclopedia, producing the results summarised in Figure 10.

Algorithm	Correct	Incorrect
Monte-carlo sample	431 (66.3%)	219 (33.7%)
Vector minimaxing	462 (71.1%)	188 (28.9%)
The *prm* algorithm	623 (95.8%)	27 (4.2%)

Figure 10: Performance on the 650 single-suit Bridge problems from the Encyclopedia

As before, these results demonstrate that vector minimaxing is slightly superior to Monte-carlo sampling, and that the *prm* algorithm dramatically outperforms them both. In terms of the expected loss if the entire set of 650 problems were to be played once (against best defence and with a random choice among the possible holdings for the defence) the *prm* algorithm would be expected to lose just 0.83 times, compared to 16.97 and 12.78 times for Monte-carlo sampling and vector minimaxing, respectively.

The performance of *prm* was even good enough to enable us to identify five errors in the Encyclopedia (in fact, these errors could also have been found with the other two algorithms, but they were overlooked because the number of incorrect cases was too large to check manually). Space limitations prevent us from presenting more than the briefest summaries of one of these errors here, in Figure 11. In our tests, the line of play generated for this problem has a probability of success of 0.266 and starts by leading small to the Ten.

More Experiments on Random Trees

To understand why the performance of all the algorithms is better on Bridge than on our random game trees, we conducted one further test. The aim of this experiment was to modify the payoffs of our game trees so that each algorithm could identify optimal strategies with the same success rate as in Bridge. We achieved

---
[4]The remaining fifteen examples split into four categories: six problems that give no line of play for the maximum number of tricks, four problems involving the assumption of a *mixed* strategy defence, four for which the solution relies on assumptions about the defenders playing sub-optimally by not *false-carding*, and one where there are restrictions on the resources available.

K T 8 x x

J x x

For four tricks, run the Jack. If this is covered, finesse the eight next. Chance of success: 25%

Figure 11: Problem 543 from the Bridge Encyclopedia

this by the simple expedient of parameterising our trees with a probability, q, that determines how similar the possible worlds are. To generate a tree with n worlds and a given value of q:

- first generate the payoffs for n worlds randomly, as in the original experiment, then
- generate a set of payoffs for a dummy world w_{n+1},
- and finally, for each of the original n worlds, overwrite the complete set of payoffs with the payoffs from the dummy world, with probability q.

Trees with a higher value of q tend to be easier to solve, because an optimal strategy in one world is also more likely to be an optimal strategy in another. Correspondingly, we found that by modifying q it was possible to improve the performance of each algorithm. What was unexpected, however, was that the value of q for which each algorithm performed at the same level as in Bridge roughly coincided, at $q \approx 0.75$. For this value, the error rates obtained were approximately 34.1%, 31.5% and 6.1%, as shown in Figure 12. Thus, on two different types of game we have found the relative strengths of the three algorithms to be almost identical. With this observation, the conclusion that similar results will hold for other imperfect information games becomes more sustainable.

Efficiency Issues

All of the algorithms we have presented execute in time polynomial in the size of the game tree. In our tests, the *prm* algorithm achieves its performance gains with a small, constant factor, slowdown in execution time. For example, to select a strategy on 1000 trees of depth 13 takes the *prm* algorithm 571 seconds, compared to 333 seconds for vector minimaxing and 372 seconds for the Monte-carlo sampling algorithm (all timings obtained on a SUN UltraSparc II running at 300MHz). Over all depths of trees, the *prm* algorithm ranges between 1.08 and 1.39 times as expensive as our implementation of Monte-carlo sampling. Similarly for the Bridge test set, *prm* takes an average of 11.9 seconds to solve each problem, compared to 1.9 seconds for vector minimaxing and 4.1 seconds for Monte-carlo sampling.

However, the efficiency of the implementations was not our major concern for the current paper, where

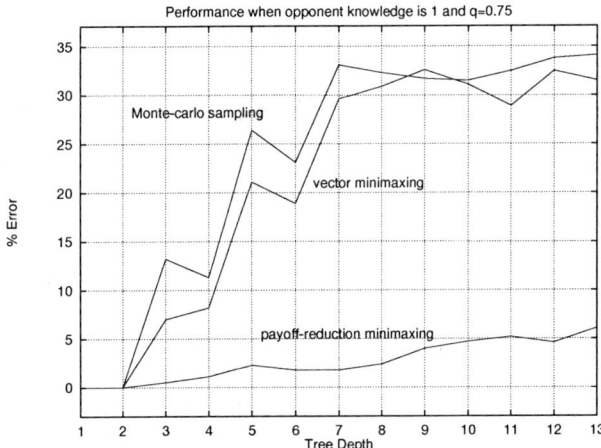

Figure 12: Superiority of payoff-reduction minimaxing on random game trees where the optimal strategy in one world is more likely to be optimal in another

we were interested instead in producing a qualitative characterisation of the relative strengths of the different algorithms. Thus, the data presented in this paper was obtained without employing any of the well-known search enhancement techniques such as alpha-beta pruning or partition search (Ginsberg 1996c).

Note, though, that it is possible to quite simply incorporate the alpha-beta algorithm into the vector minimaxing framework via a simple adaptation that prunes branches based on a pointwise $\geq$ (or $\leq$) comparison of vectors. Whether this kind of enhancement can improve the efficiency of *prm* to the point where it can tackle larger problems such as the full game of Bridge is a topic for further research. In this context, it is noteworthy that the 66.3% performance of Monte-carlo sampling in our single-suit tests correlates well with the results reported by (Ginsberg 1996a), where the technique was found to solve 64.4% of the problems from a hard test set of complete deals. Combined with the results of the previous sections, this extra data point strengthens the suggestion that the accuracy of *prm* will hold at 95% on larger Bridge problems.

Conclusions and Further Work

We have investigated the problem of finding optimal strategies for games with imperfect information. We formalised *vector minimaxing* and *payoff-reduction minimaxing* by discussing in turn how the problems of strategy fusion and non-locality affect the basic technique of Monte-carlo sampling. We tested these algorithms, and showed in particular that payoff-reduction minimaxing dramatically outperforms the other two, both on simple random game trees and for an extensive set of problems from the game of Bridge. For these single-suit Bridge problems, *prm*'s speed and level of performance was good enough to allow us to detect errors in the analysis of human experts.

The application of *prm* to larger, real-world games, as well as the further improvement of its accuracy, are important topics for further research. We are also investigating algorithms that solve weakened forms of the best defence model, for example taking advantage of mistakes made by less-than-perfect opponents.

References

ACBL. 1994. *The Official Encyclopedia of Bridge*. 2990 Airways Blvd, Memphis, Tennessee 38116-3875: American Contract Bridge League, Inc., 5th edition.

Blair, J.; Mutchler, D.; and Liu, C. 1993. Games with imperfect information. In *Games: Planning and Learning, 1993 AAAI Fall Symposium*, 59–67.

Corlett, R., and Todd, S. 1985. A Monte-carlo approach to uncertain inference. In Ross, P., ed., *Proceedings of the Conference on Artificial Intelligence and Simulation of Behaviour*, 28–34.

Frank, I., and Basin, D. 1998. Search in games with incomplete information: A case study using bridge card play. *Artificial Intelligence*. To appear.

Frank, I.; Basin, D.; and Bundy, A. 1992. An adaptation of proof-planning to declarer play in bridge. In *Proceedings of ECAI-92*, 72–76.

Frank, A. 1989. Brute force search in games of imperfect information. In Levy, D., and Beal, D., eds., *Heuristic Programming in Artificial Intelligence 2*. Ellis Horwood. 204–209.

Frank, I. 1996. *Search and Planning under Incomplete Information: A Study using Bridge Card Play*. Ph.D. Dissertation, Department of Artificial Intelligence, Edinburgh. Also to be published by Springer Verlag in the Distinguished Dissertations series.

Ginsberg, M. 1996a. GIB vs Bridge Baron: results. Usenet newsgroup *rec.games.bridge*. Message-Id: <56cqmi$914@pith.uoregon.edu>.

Ginsberg, M. 1996b. How computers will play bridge. *The Bridge World*. Also available for anonymous ftp from dt.cirl.uoregon.edu as the file /papers/bridge.ps.

Ginsberg, M. 1996c. Partition search. In *Proceedings of AAAI-96*, 228–233.

Levy, D. 1989. The million pound bridge program. In Levy, D., and Beal, D., eds., *Heuristic Programming in Artificial Intelligence*. Ellis Horwood. 95–103.

Luce, R. D., and Raiffa, H. 1957. *Games and Decisions—Introduction and Critical Survey*. New York: Wiley.

Nau, D. S. 1982. The last player theorem. *Artificial Intelligence* 18:53–65.

Shannon, C. E. 1950. Programming a computer for playing chess. *Philosophical Magazine* 41:256–275.

von Neumann, J., and Morgenstern, O. 1944. *Theory of Games and Economic Behaviour*. Princeton University Press.

Information Extraction

Learning to Extract Symbolic Knowledge from the World Wide Web

Mark Craven[†]   Dan DiPasquo[†]   Dayne Freitag[†]   Andrew McCallum[‡†]

Tom Mitchell[†]   Kamal Nigam[†]   Seán Slattery[†]

[†]School of Computer Science
Carnegie Mellon University
Pittsburgh, PA 15213-3891
⟨firstname⟩.⟨lastname⟩@cs.cmu.edu

[‡]Just Research
4616 Henry Street
Pittsburgh, PA 15213

Abstract

The World Wide Web is a vast source of information accessible to computers, but understandable only to humans. The goal of the research described here is to automatically create a *computer understandable* world wide knowledge base whose content mirrors that of the World Wide Web. Such a knowledge base would enable much more effective retrieval of Web information, and promote new uses of the Web to support knowledge-based inference and problem solving. Our approach is to develop a trainable information extraction system that takes two inputs: an ontology defining the classes and relations of interest, and a set of training data consisting of labeled regions of hypertext representing instances of these classes and relations. Given these inputs, the system learns to extract information from other pages and hyperlinks on the Web. This paper describes our general approach, several machine learning algorithms for this task, and promising initial results with a prototype system.

Introduction

The rise of the World Wide Web has made it possible for your workstation to retrieve any of 200 million Web pages for your personal perusal. The research described here is motivated by a simple observation: although your workstation can currently *retrieve* 200 million Web pages, it currently *understands* none of these Web pages. Of course this is because Web pages are written for human consumption and consist largely of text, images, and sounds. In this paper we describe a research effort with the long term goal of automatically creating and maintaining a computer-understandable knowledge base whose content mirrors that of the World Wide Web.

Such a "World Wide Knowledge Base" would consist of computer understandable assertions in symbolic, probabilistic form, and it would have many uses. At a minimum, it would allow much more effective information retrieval by supporting more sophisticated queries

Copyright © 1998, American Association for Artificial Intelligence (www.aaai.org). All rights reserved.

than current keyword-based search engines. Going a step further, it would enable new uses of the Web to support knowledge-based inference and problem solving.

How can we develop such a world wide knowledge base? The approach explored in our research is to develop a *trainable* system that can be taught to extract various types of information by automatically browsing the Web. This system accepts two types of inputs:

1. An ontology specifying the classes and relations of interest. An example of such an ontology is provided in the top half of Figure 1. This particular ontology defines a hierarchy of classes including **Person**, **Student**, **Research.Project**, **Course**, etc. It also defines relations between these classes such as **Advisors.Of** (which relates an instance of a **Student** to the instances of **Faculty** who are the advisors of the given student).

2. Training examples that represent instances of the ontology classes and relations. For example, the two Web pages shown at the bottom of Figure 1 represent instances of **Course** and **Faculty** classes. Furthermore, this pair of pages represents an instance of the relation **Courses.Taught.By** (i.e., the **Courses.Taught.By** Jim includes **Fundamentals.of.CS**).

Given such an ontology and a set of training examples, our system attempts to learn general procedures for extracting new instances of these classes and relations from the Web.

To pursue this problem, we must make certain assumptions about the mapping between the ontology and the Web.

- We assume that each instance of an ontology class is represented by one or more contiguous segments of hypertext on the Web. By "contiguous segment of hypertext" we mean either a single Web page, or a contiguous string of text within a Web page, or a collection of several Web pages interconnected by hyperlinks. For example, an instance of a **Person** might be described by a single page (the person's home page), or by a reference to the person in a string of text in an arbitrary Web page, or by a collection of interconnected Web pages that jointly describe the person.

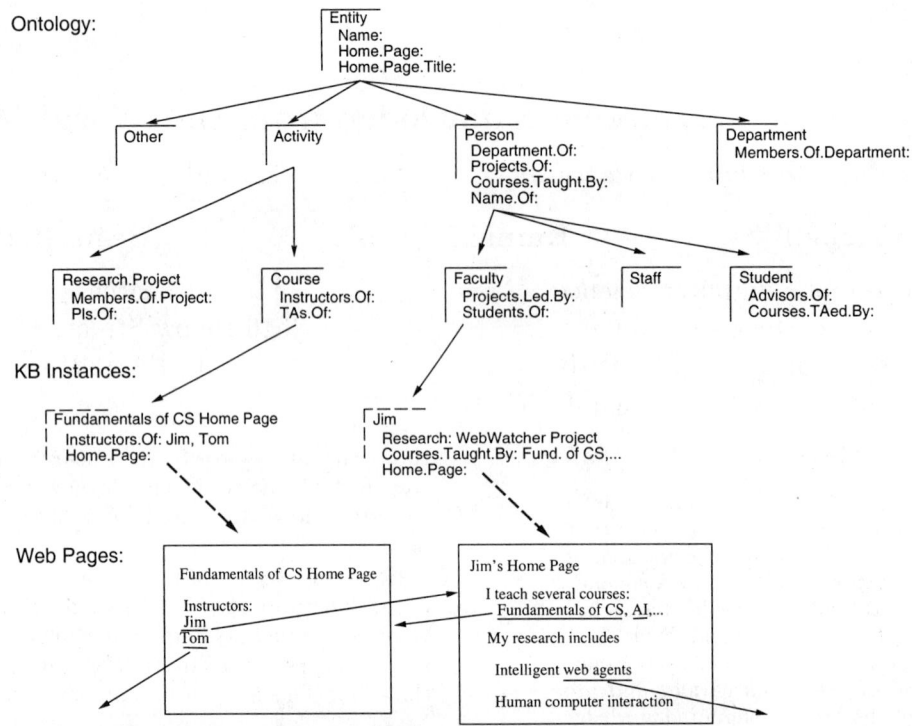

Figure 1: The inputs and outputs of the WEBKB system. The top part of the figure shows an ontology that defines the classes and relations of interest. The bottom part shows two Web pages identified as training examples of the classes **Course** and **Faculty**. Together, these two pages also constitute a training example for the relations **Instructors.Of** and **Courses.Taught.By**. Given the ontology and a set of training data, WEBKB learns to interpret additional Web pages and hyperlinks to add new instances to the knowledge base, such as those shown in the middle of the figure.

- We assume that each instance R(A,B) of a relation R is represented on the Web in one of three ways. First, the instance R(A,B) may be represented by a segment of hypertext that *connects* the segment representing A to the segment representing B. For example, the hypertext segment shown at the bottom of Figure 1 connects the segment representing **Jim** with the segment representing **Fundamentals.of.CS**, and it represents the relation **Instructor.Of.Course(Fundamentals.of.CS, Jim)**. Second, the instance R(A,B) may alternatively be represented by a contiguous segment of text representing A that *contains* the segment that represents B. For example, the relation instance **Research.Of(Jim, Human.Computer.Interaction)** is represented in Figure 1 by the fact that Jim's home page contains the phrase "Human computer interaction" in a specific context. Finally, the instance R(A,B) may be represented by the fact that the hypertext segment for A satisfies some learned model for relatedness to B. For example, we might extract the instance **Research.Of(Jim, Artificial.Intelligence)** by classifying Jim's page using a statistical model of the words typically found in pages describing AI research.

In addition to these assumptions about the mapping between Web hypertext and the ontology, we make several simplifying assumptions in our initial research reported in this paper. We plan to lift the following assumptions in the future as our research progresses.

- We assume that each class instance is represented by a single Web page (e.g., a person is represented by their home page). If an instance happens to be described by multiple pages (e.g., if a person is described by their home page plus a collection of neighboring pages describing their publications, hobbies, etc.), our current system is trained to classify only the primary home page as the description of the person, and to ignore the neighboring affiliated pages.

- We assume that each class instance is represented by a *single* contiguous segment of hypertext. In other words, if the system encounters two non-contiguous Web pages that represent instances of the same class, it creates two distinct instances of this class in its knowledge base.

Given this problem definition and our current set of assumptions, we view the following as the three primary learning tasks involved in extracting knowledge-base instances from the Web: (i) recognizing class instances by classifying bodies of hypertext, (ii) recognizing relation instances by classifying chains of hyperlinks, (iii) recognizing class and relation instances by extracting small fields of text from Web pages. We discuss each of these tasks in the main sections of the paper. Additional details concerning the methods and experiments described in this paper can be found elsewhere (Craven *et al.* 1998). After describing approaches to these three tasks, we describe experiments with a system that incorporates learned classifiers for each task.

Experimental Testbed

As a testbed for our initial research, we have investigated the task of building a knowledge base describing computer science departments. As shown in Figure 1, our working ontology for this domain includes the classes **Department, Faculty, Staff, Student, Research.Project, Course,** and **Other**. Each of the classes has a set of slots defining relations that exist among instances of the given class and other class instances in the ontology.

We have assembled two data sets for the experiments reported here. The first is a set of pages and hyperlinks drawn from four CS departments. The second is a set of pages from numerous other computer science departments. The four-department set includes 4,127 pages and 10,945 hyperlinks interconnecting them. The second set includes 4,120 additional pages.

In addition to labeling pages, we also hand-labeled relation instances. Each of these relation instances consists of a pair of pages corresponding to the class instances involved in the relation. For example, an instance of the **Instructors.Of.Course** relation consists of a **Course** home page and a **Person** home page. Our data set of relation instances comprises 251 **Instructors.Of.Course** instances, 392 **Members.Of.Project** instances, and 748 **Department.Of.Person** instances.

Finally, we also labeled the name of the owner of pages in the **Person** class. This was done automatically by tagging any text fragment in the person's home page that matched the name as it appeared in the hyperlink pointing to the page from the index page. These heuristics were conservative, and thus we believe that, although some name occurrences were missed, there were no false positives. From a set of 174 **Person** pages, this procedure yielded 525 distinct name occurrences.

Recognizing Class Instances

The first task for our system is to identify new instances of ontology classes from the text sources on the Web. In this section we address the case in which class instances are represented by Web pages; for example, a given instance of the **Student** class is represented by the student's home page.

In the first part of this section we discuss a statistical approach to classifying Web pages using the words found in pages. In the second part of this section we discuss learning first-order rules to classify Web pages. Finally, we consider using information from URLs to improve our page classification accuracy.

Statistical Text Classification

Our statistical page-classification method involves building a probabilistic model of each class using labeled training data, and then classifying newly seen pages by selecting the class that is most probable given the evidence of words describing the new page.

As is common in learning text classifiers, the probabilistic models we use ignore the sequence in which the words occur. These models are often called *unigram* or *bag-of-words* models because they are based on statistics about single words in isolation.

The approach that we use for classifying Web pages is the *naive Bayes* method, with minor modifications based on Kullback-Leibler Divergence. More precisely, we classify a document d as belonging to class c' according to the following rule:

$$c' = \underset{c}{\operatorname{argmax}} \left[\frac{\log \Pr(c)}{n} + \sum_{i=1}^{T} \Pr(w_i|d) \log \left(\frac{\Pr(w_i|c)}{\Pr(w_i|d)} \right) \right]$$

where n is the number of words in d, T is the size of the vocabulary, and w_i is the ith word in the vocabulary. $Pr(w_i|c)$ thus represents the probability of drawing w_i given a document from class c, and $Pr(w_i|d)$ represents the frequency of occurrence of w_i in document d.

This method makes exactly the same classifications as naive Bayes, but produces classification scores that are less extreme, and thus better reflect uncertainty than those produced by naive Bayes.

When estimating the word probabilities, $\Pr(w_i|c)$, we use a smoothing method that prevents words from having zero probability and provides more robust estimates for infrequently occurring words. We have found that we get more accurate classifications when using a restricted vocabulary size, and thus we limit our vocabulary to 2000 words in our experiments. The vocabulary is selected by ranking words according to their average mutual information with respect to the class labels.

We evaluate our method using a four-fold cross-validation methodology. We conduct four runs in which we train classifiers using data from three of the universities in our data set (plus the auxiliary set of pages mentioned in the previous section), and test the classifiers using the university held out. On each iteration we hold out a different university for the test set.

Along with each classification, we calculate an associated measure of confidence which is simply the classification score described in the formula above. By setting a minimum threshold on this confidence, we can select a point that sacrifices some coverage in order to obtain increased accuracy. Given our goal of automatically extracting knowledge base information from the Web, it is desirable to begin with a high-accuracy classifier, even if we need to limit coverage to only 10% of the pages available on the Web. The effect of trading off coverage for accuracy is shown in Figure 2. The horizontal axis on this plot represents *coverage*: the percentage of pages for a given class that are correctly classified as belonging to the class. The vertical axis represents *accuracy*:

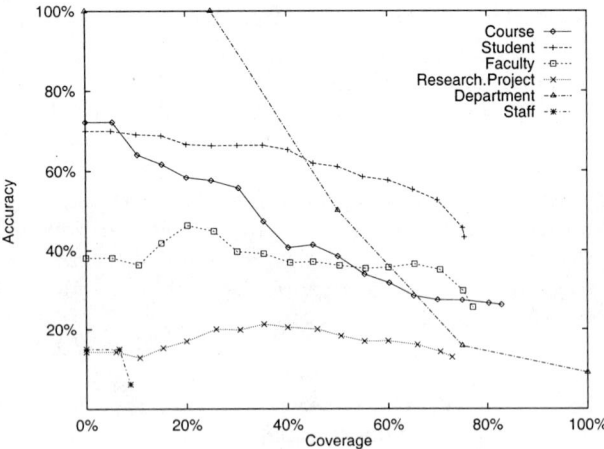

Figure 2: Accuracy/coverage for statistical classifiers.

the percentage of pages classified into a given class that are actually members of that class. To understand these results, consider, for example, the class **Student**. If we accepted our classifiers' decisions every time they predicted **Student**, they would be correct 43% of the time. As we raise the confidence threshold for this class, however, the accuracy of our predictions rises. For example, at a coverage of 20%, accuracy reaches a level of 67%.

Nearly all of the misclassifications made by our statistical text classifiers involve two types of mistakes. First, the classifiers often confuse different subclasses of **Person**. For example, although only 9% of the **Staff** instances are correctly assigned to the **Staff** category, 80% of them are correctly classified into the more general class of **Person**. As this result suggests, not all mistakes are equally harmful; even when we fail to correctly classify an instance into one of the leaf classes in our ontology, we can still make many correct inferences if we correctly assign it to a more general class.

Second, the most common form of mistake involves classifying **Other** pages into one of the "core" classes; only 35% of **Other** instances are correctly classified. The low level of classification accuracy for the **Other** class is largely explained by the nature of the class. Many of the instances of the **Other** class have content, and hence word statistics, very similar to instances in one of the core classes. For example, whereas the home page for a course will belong to the **Course** class, "secondary" pages for the course, such as a page describing reading assignments, will belong to the **Other** class. Although the content of many of the pages in the **Other** class might suggest that they properly belong in one of the core classes, our motivation for not including them in these classes is the following. When our system is browsing the Web and adding new instances to the knowledge base, we want to ensure that we do not add multiple instances that correspond to the same real-world object. For example, we should not add two new instances to the knowledge base when we encounter a course home page and its secondary page listing the reading assignments. Because of this requirement, we have framed our page classification task as one of correctly recognizing the "primary" pages for the classes of interest. We return to this issue shortly.

One of the interesting aspects of Web page classification, in contrast to conventional flat-text classification, is that redundancy of hypertext naturally suggests a variety of different representations for page classification. In addition to classifying a page using the words that occur in the page, we have also investigated classification using (a) the words that occur in hyperlinks (i.e. the words in the anchor text) that point to the page, and (b) the words that occur only in the HTML title and headings fields of the page. For some classes, these methods provide more accurate predictions than the approach described above. Space limitations preclude us from discussing these results in detail. In the next section, however, we describe another approach to Web page classification that exploits the special properties of hypertext.

First-Order Text Classification

The hypertext structure of the Web can be thought of as a graph in which Web pages are the nodes of the graph and hyperlinks are the edges. The method for classifying Web pages discussed above considers the words in either a single node of the graph or in a set of edges impinging on the same node. However, such methods do not allow us to learn models that take into account features as the pattern of connectivity around a given page, or the words occurring in neighboring pages. It might be profitable to learn, for example, a rule of the form "A page is a **Course** home page if it contains the words *textbook* and *TA* and is linked to a page that contains the word *assignment*." Rules of this type, which are able to represent general characteristics of a graph, require a first-order representation. In this section, we consider the task of learning to classify pages using an algorithm that is able to induce first-order rules.

The learning algorithm that we use in this section is FOIL (Quinlan & Cameron-Jones 1993). FOIL is a greedy covering algorithm for learning function-free Horn clauses. The representation we provide to the learning algorithm consists of the following background relations:

- has_*word*(Page): Each of these Boolean predicates indicates the pages in which the word *word* occurs.

- link_to(Page, Page): This relation represents the hyperlinks that interconnect the pages in the data set. The first argument is the page on which the link occurs, and the second is the page to which it is linked.

We apply FOIL to learn a separate set of clauses for six of the seven classes considered in the previous section. We do not learn a description of the **Other** class, but instead treat it as a default class.

When classifying test instances, we calculate an associated measure of confidence along with each prediction. The confidence of a prediction is determined

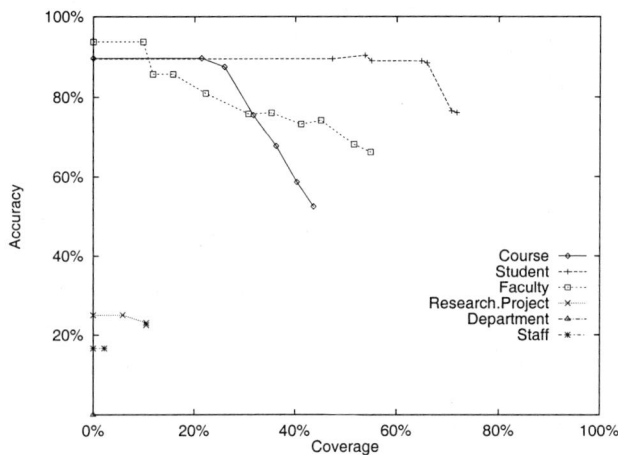

Figure 3: Accuracy/coverage for FOIL classifiers.

student(A) :- not(has_data(A)), not(has_comment(A)),
    link_to(B,A), has_jame(B), has_paul(B), not(has_mail(B)).
Test Set: 126 Pos, 5 Neg

faculty(A) :- has_professor(A), has_ph(A), link_to(B,A),
    has_faculti(B).
Test Set: 18 Pos, 3 Neg

Figure 4: Two of the rules learned by FOIL for classifying pages, and their test-set accuracies.

by an *m*-estimate (Cestnik 1990) of the error-rate of the clause making the prediction. The resulting Accuracy/Coverage plot is shown in Figure 3. Comparing this figure to Figure 2, one can see that for several of the classes, the first-order rules are significantly more accurate than the statistical classifiers, although in general, their coverage is not quite as good.

The Student class provides an interesting illustration of the power of a first-order representation for learning to classify Web pages. Figure 4 shows the most accurate rule learned for this class for one of the training/test splits. Notice that this rule refers to a page (bound to the variable B) that has two common first names on it (*paul* and *jame*, the stemmed version of *james*). This rule (and similar rules learned with the other three training sets) has learned to exploit "student directory" pages in order to identify student home pages. As this example shows, Web-page classification is different than ordinary text classification in that neighboring pages may provide strong evidence about the class of a page.

Identifying Multi-Page Segments

As discussed above, our representational assumption is that each class instance in the knowledge base corresponds to some contiguous segment of hypertext on the Web. This allows, for example, that a particular student might be represented by a single Web page, or by a cluster of interlinked Web pages centered around their home page. In the experiments reported thus far, we

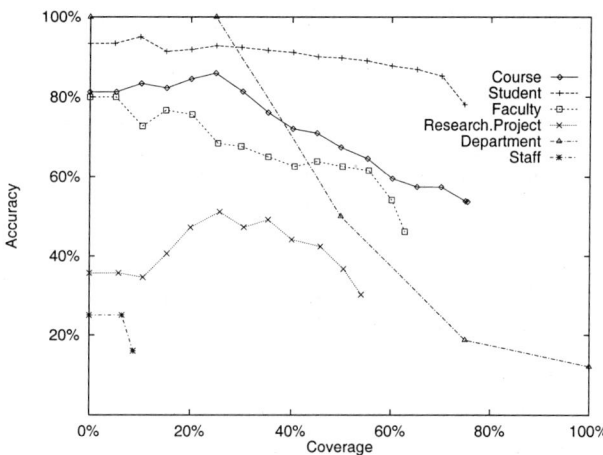

Figure 5: Accuracy/coverage for the statistical text classifiers after the application of URL heuristics.

have effectively made a simpler assumption: that each instance is represented by a single Web page. In fact, in labeling our training data, we encountered a variety of students (and instances of other classes) that were described by a several interlinked Web pages rather than a single page. In these cases we hand labeled the primary home page as Student, and labeled any interlinked pages associated with the same student as Other.

To relax this simplifying assumption we must use methods for identifying sets of interlinked pages that represent a single knowledge base instance. Spertus (1997) has described regularities in URL structure and naming, and presented several heuristics for discovering page groupings and identifying representative home pages. We use a similar, slightly expanded, heuristic approach.

The impact of using the URL heuristics with our statistical text classifiers is summarized in Figure 5. Comparing these curves to Figure 2 one can see the striking increase in accuracy for any given level of coverage across all classes. Also note some degradation in total coverage. This occurs because some pages that were previously correctly classified have been misidentified as being secondary pages.

Recognizing Relation Instances

In the previous section we discussed the task of learning to extract instances of ontology classes from the Web. Our approach to this task assumed that the class instances of interest are represented by whole Web pages or by clusters of Web pages. In this section, we discuss the task of learning to recognize *relations* of interest that exist among extracted class instances. The hypothesis underlying our approach is that relations among class instances are often represented by *hyperlink paths* in the Web. Thus, the task of learning to recognize relation instance involves inducing rules that characterize the prototypical paths of the relation.

```
members_of_project(A,B) :- research_project(A), person(B),
    link_to(C,A,D), link_to(E,D,B),
    neighborhood_word_people(C).
Test Set:   18 Pos, 0 Neg

department_of_person(A,B) :- person(A), department(B),
    link_to(C,D,A), link_to(E,F,D), link_to(G,B,F),
    neighborhood_word_graduate(E).
Test Set:   371 Pos, 4 Neg
```

Figure 6: Two of the rules learned for recognizing relation instances, and their test-set accuracies.

Because this task involves discovering hyperlink paths of unknown and variable size, we employ a learning method that uses a first-order representation for its learned rules. The representation consists of the following background relations:

- class(Page) : For each *class* from the previous section, the corresponding relation lists the pages that represent instances of *class*. These instances are determined using actual classes for pages in the training set and predicted classes for pages in the test set.

- link_to(Hyperlink, Page, Page) : This relation represents the hyperlinks that interconnect the pages in the data set.

- has_word(Hyperlink) : This set of relations indicates the words that are found in the anchor (i.e., underlined) text of each hyperlink.

- all_words_capitalized(Hyperlink) : The instances of this relation are those hyperlinks in which all of the words in the anchor text start with a capital letter.

- has_alphanumeric_word(Hyperlink) : The instances of this relation are those hyperlinks which contain a word with both alphabetic and numeric characters.

- has_neighborhood_word(Hyperlink) : This set of relations indicates the words that are found in the "neighborhood" of each hyperlink. The neighborhood of a hyperlink includes words in a single paragraph, list item, table entry, title or heading in which the hyperlink is contained.

We learn definitions for the members_of_project(Page, Page), instructors_of_course(Page, Page), and department_of_person(Page, Page) target relations. In addition to the positive instances, our training sets include approximately 300,000 negative examples.

The algorithm we use for learning to recognize relation instances is similar to FOIL. Unlike FOIL however, our method does not simply use a hill-climbing search when learning clauses. We have found that such a hill-climbing strategy is unable to learn rules for paths consisting of more than one hyperlink. The search process that our method employs instead consists of two phases. In the first phase, the "path" part of the clause is learned, and in the second phase, additional literals are added to the clause using a hill-climbing search.

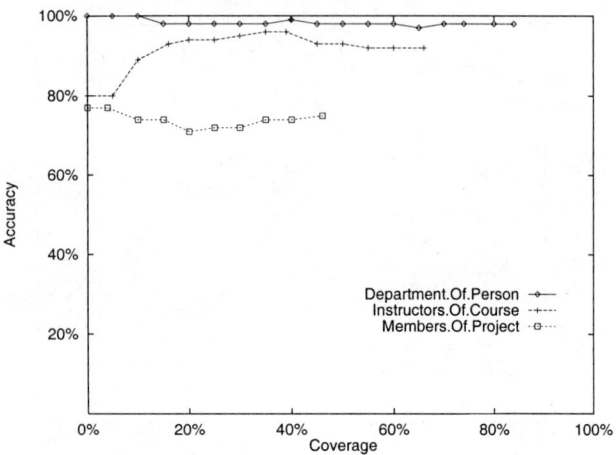

Figure 7: Accuracy/coverage for learned relation rules.

Our algorithm for constructing the path part of a clause is a variant of Richards and Mooney's (1992) *relational pathfinding* method.

Figure 6 shows one of the learned clauses for each of the Members.Of.Project and Department.Of.Person relations. Each of these rules was learned on more than one of the training sets, therefore the test-set statistics represent aggregates over the four test sets. The rule shown for the Members.Of.Project relation describes instances in which the project's home page points to an intermediate page which points to personal home pages. The hyperlink from the project page to the intermediate page must have the word *people* near it. This rule covers cases in which the members of a research project are listed on a subsidiary "members" page instead of on the home page of the project. The rule shown for the Department.Of.Person relation involves a three-hyperlink path that links a department home page to a personal home page. The rule requires that the word "graduate" occur near the second hyperlink in the path. In this case, the algorithm has learned to exploit the fact that departments often have a page that serves as a graduate student directory, and that any student whose home page is pointed to by this directory is a member of the department.

Along with each of our predicted relation instances, we calculate an associated confidence in the prediction. Using these confidence measures, Figure 7 shows the test-set accuracy/coverage curves for the three target relations. The accuracy levels of all three rule sets are fairly high. The limited coverage levels of the learned rules is due primarily to the limited coverage of our page classifiers since all of the learned rules include literals which test predicted page classifications.

Extracting Text Fields

In some cases, the information we want to extract will not be represented by Web pages or relations among pages, but instead it will be represented by small fragments of text embedded in pages. This type of task is commonly called *information extraction*. In this section we discuss our approach to learning rules for such information-extraction tasks.

We have developed an information-extraction learning algorithm called SRV which is a hill-climbing, first-order learner in the spirit of FOIL. Input to the algorithm is a set of pages labeled to identify instances of the field we want to extract. Output is a set of information-extraction rules. The extraction process involves examining every possible text fragment of appropriate size to see whether it matches any of the rules.

In our particular domain, a positive example is a labeled text fragment – a sequence of tokens – in one of our training documents; a negative example is any unlabeled token sequence having the same size as some positive example. During training we assess the goodness of a predicate using all such negative examples.

The representation used by our rule learner includes the following relations:

- length(Fragment, Relop, N): The learner can specify the length of a field, in terms of number of tokens, is less than, greater than, or equal to some integer.

- some(Fragment, Var, Path, Attr, Value): The learner can posit an attribute-value test for some token in the sequence (e.g., "the field contains some token that is capitalized"). One argument to this predicate is a variable. Each such variable binds to a distinct token. Thus, if the learner uses a variable already in use in the current rule, it is specializing the description of a single token; if the variable is a new one, it describes a previously unbound token. The learner has the option of adding an arbitrary path of relational attributes to the test, so that it can include literals of the form, "some token which is followed by a token which is followed by a token that is capitalized."

- position(Fragment, Var, From, Relop, N): The learner can say something about the position of a token bound by a *some*-predicate in the current rule. The position is specified relative to the beginning or end of the sequence.

- relpos(Fragment, Var1, Var2, Relop, N): Where at least two variables have been introduced by *some*-predicates in the current rule, the learner can specify their ordering and distance from each other.

As in the previous experiments, we follow the leave-one-university-out methodology. The data set for the present experiment consists of all **Person** pages in the data set. The unit of measurement in this experiment is an individual page. If SRV's most confident prediction on a page corresponds exactly to some instance of the page owner's name, or if it makes no prediction for a page containing no name, its behavior is counted as correct. Otherwise, it is counted as an error.

Figure 8 shows a learned rule and its application to a test case. Figure 9 shows the accuracy-coverage curve for SRV on the name-extraction task. Under the criteria

```
ownername(Fragment) :- some(Fragment, B, [], in_title, true),
    length(Fragment, <, 3),
    some(Fragment, B, [prev_token], word, "gmt"),
    some(Fragment, A, [], longp, true),
    some(Fragment, B, [], word, unknown),
    some(Fragment, B, [], quadrupletonp, false)
```

Last-Modified: Wednesday, 26-Jun-96 01:37:46 GMT

`<title>`Bruce Randall Donald`</title>`

```
<h1>
<img
src="ftp://ftp.cs.cornell.edu/pub/brd/images/brd.gif">
<p>
Bruce Randall Donald<br>
Associate Professor<br>
```

Figure 8: **Top:** An extraction rule for name of home page owner. This rule looks for a sequence of two tokens, one of which (A) is in a HTML title field and longer than four characters, the other of which (B) is preceded by the token **gmt**, unknown from the training data, and not a four-character token. **Bottom:** An example HTML fragment which the above rule matches.

described above, it achieves 65.1% accuracy when all pages are processed. A full 16% of the files did not contain their owners' names, however, and a large part of the learner's error is because of spurious predictions over these files. If we consider only the pages containing names, SRV's performance is 77.4%.

The Crawler

The previous sections have considered the tasks of learning to recognize class and relation instances in an off-line setting. In this section, we describe an experiment that involves evaluating our approach in a novel, on-line environment.

We have developed a Web-crawling system that populates a knowledge base with class and relation instances as it explores the Web. The system incorporates trained classifiers for the three learning tasks discussed previously: recognizing class instances, recognizing relation instances, and extracting text fields. Our crawler employs a straightforward strategy to browse the Web. It maintains a priority queue of pages to be explored. Each time it processes a Web page, it considers adding the URLs of the hyperlinks found on this page to the queue. One of these URLs is added if (1) the current page led to the creation of a new instance in the knowledge base, and (2) the URL is within the domain allowed by a user-specified parameter.

To evaluate the performance of our crawler, we trained a set of classifiers using all of the data in our four-university set and the auxiliary set, and then gave the system the task of exploring a fifth Web site: the computer science department at Carnegie Mellon Uni-

	Student	Faculty	Person	Project	Course	Dept.	Instruct.Of	Members.Of.Project	Department.Of
Extracted	180	66	246	99	28	1	23	125	213
Correct	130	28	194	72	25	1	18	92	181
Accuracy	72%	42%	79%	73%	89%	100%	78%	74%	85%

Table 1: Page and relation classification accuracy when exploring the CMU computer science department Web site.

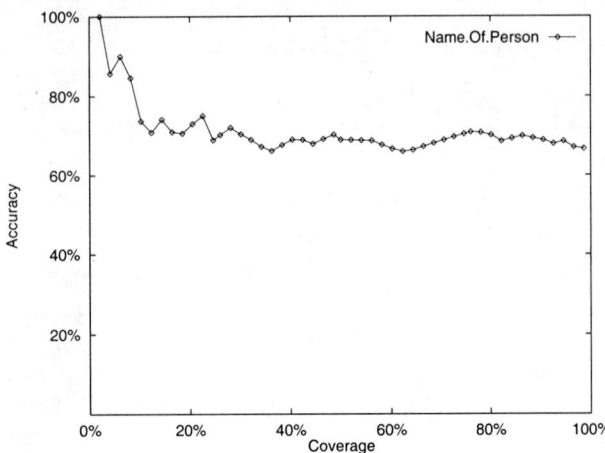

Figure 9: Accuracy/coverage for learned name-extraction rules.

versity. After exploring 2722 Web pages at this site, the crawler extracted 374 new class instances and 361 new relation instances for its knowledge base. The accuracy of the crawler over this run is summarized in Table 1. The name extractor produced a name for each of the 246 extracted **Person** instances. Among the 194 pages that actually represented people, 73% of the names were correctly identified. Overall its accuracy was 57%.

This experiment confirms that the learned classifiers described earlier in this paper can be used to accurately populate a knowledge base in an on-line setting.

Related Work

Our work builds on related research in several fields, including text classification (e.g. Lewis *et al.*, 1996), information extraction (e.g. Soderland, 1996), and Web agents (e.g. Shakes & Etzioni, 1996). Space limitations preclude us from describing this work in detail; the interested reader is referred elsewhere (Craven *et al.* 1998) for a comprehensive discussion of related work.

Conclusions

We began with the question of how to automatically create a computer-understandable world-wide knowledge base whose content mirrors that of the World Wide Web. The approach we propose in this paper is to construct a system that can be trained to automatically populate such a knowledge base.

The key technical problem in our proposed approach is to develop accurate learning methods for this task.

We have presented a variety of approaches that take advantage of the special structure of hypertext by considering relationships among Web pages, their hyperlinks, and specific words on individual pages and hyperlinks.

Based on the initial results reported here, we are optimistic about the future prospects for automatically constructing and maintaining a symbolic knowledge base by interpreting hypertext on the Web. Currently, we are extending our system to handle a richer ontology, and we are investigating numerous research issues such as how to reduce training data requirements, how to exploit more linguistic and HTML structure, and how to integrate statistical and first-order learning techniques.

Acknowledgments

This research is supported in part by the DARPA HPKB program under contract F30602-97-1-0215.

References

Cestnik, B. 1990. Estimating probabilities: A crucial task in machine learning. In Aiello, L., ed., *Proc. of the 9th European Conf. on Artificial Intelligence*.

Craven, M.; DiPasquo, D.; Freitag, D.; McCallum, A.; Mitchell, T.; Nigam, K.; and Slattery, S. 1998. Learning to extract symbolic knowledge from the World Wide Web. Technical report, CMU CS Dept.

Lewis, D.; Schapire, R. E.; Callan, J. P.; and Papka, R. 1996. Training algorithms for linear text classifiers. In *Proc. of the 19th Annual Int. ACM SIGIR Conf.*

Quinlan, J. R., and Cameron-Jones, R. M. 1993. FOIL: A midterm report. In *Proc. of the 12th European Conf. on Machine Learning*.

Richards, B. L., and Mooney, R. J. 1992. Learning relations by pathfinding. In *Proc. of the 10th National Conf. on Artificial Intelligence*.

Shakes, J. Langheinrich, M., and Etzioni, O. 1996. Dynamic reference sifting: a case study in the homepage domain. In *Proc. of 6th Int. World Wide Web Conf.*

Soderland, S. 1996. *Learning Text Analysis Rules for Domain-specific Natural Language Processing*. Ph.D. Dissertation, University of Massachusetts. Department of Computer Science Technical Report 96-087.

Spertus, E. 1997. ParaSite: Mining structural information on the Web. In *Proc. of the 6th Int. World Wide Web Conf.*

Information Extraction from HTML: Application of a General Machine Learning Approach*

Dayne Freitag
Department of Computer Science
Carnegie Mellon University
5000 Forbes Avenue
Pittsburgh, PA 15213
dayne@cs.cmu.edu

Abstract

Because the World Wide Web consists primarily of text, information extraction is central to any effort that would use the Web as a resource for knowledge discovery. We show how information extraction can be cast as a standard machine learning problem, and argue for the suitability of relational learning in solving it. The implementation of a general-purpose relational learner for information extraction, SRV, is described. In contrast with earlier learning systems for information extraction, SRV makes no assumptions about document structure and the kinds of information available for use in learning extraction patterns. Instead, structural and other information is supplied as input in the form of an extensible token-oriented feature set. We demonstrate the effectiveness of this approach by adapting SRV for use in learning extraction rules for a domain consisting of university course and research project pages sampled from the Web. Making SRV Web-ready only involves adding several simple HTML-specific features to its basic feature set.

The World Wide Web, with its explosive growth and ever-broadening reach, is swiftly becoming the default knowledge resource for many areas of endeavor. Unfortunately, although any one of over 200,000,000 Web pages is readily accessible to an Internet-connected workstation, the information *content* of these pages is, without human interpretation, largely inaccessible.

Systems have been developed which can make sense of highly regular Web pages, such as those generated automatically from internal databases in response to user queries (Doorenbos, Etzioni, & Weld 1997) (Kushmerick 1997). A surprising number of Web sites have pages amenable to the techniques used by these systems. Still, most Web pages do not exhibit the regularity required by they require.

There is a larger class of pages, however, which are regular in a more abstract sense. Many Web pages come from collections in which each page describes a single entity or event (e.g., home pages in a CS department; each describes its owner). The purpose of such a page is often to convey essential facts about the entity it

describes. It is often reasonable to approach such a page with a set of standard questions, and to expect that the answers to these questions will be available as succinct text fragments in the page. A home page, for example, frequently lists the owner's name, affiliations, email address, etc.

The problem of identifying the text fragments that answer standard questions defined for a document collection is called *information extraction* (IE) (Def 1995). Our interest in IE concerns the development of machine learning methods to solve it. We regard IE as a kind of text classification, which has strong affinities with the well-investigated problem of document classification, but also presents unique challenges. We share this focus with a number of other recent systems (Soderland 1996) (Califf & Mooney 1997), including a system designed to learn how to extract from HTML (Soderland 1997).

In this paper we describe SRV, a top-down relational algorithm for information extraction. Central to the design of SRV is its reliance on a set of *token-oriented* features, which are easy to implement and add to the system. Since domain-specific information is contained within this features, which are separate from the core algorithm, SRV is better poised than similar systems for targeting to new domains. We have used it to perform extraction from electronic seminar announcements, medical abstracts, and newswire articles on corporate acquisitions. The experiments reported here show that targeting the system to HTML involves nothing more than the addition of HTML-specific features to its basic feature set.

Learning for Information Extraction

Consider a collection of Web pages describing university computer science courses. Given a page, a likely task for an information extraction system is to find the title of the course the page describes. We call the title a *field* and any literal title taken from an actual page, such as "Introduction to Artificial Intelligence," an *instantiation* or *instance* of the title field. Note that the typical information extraction problem involves multiple fields, some of which may have multiple instantiations in a given file. For example, a course page might

---

Copyright © 1998, American Association for Artificial Intelligence (www.aaai.org). All rights reserved.

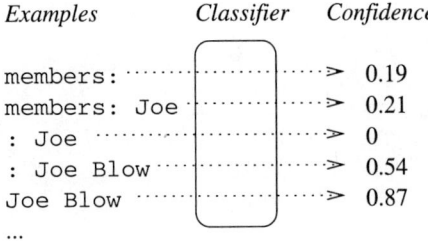

Figure 1: Information extraction as text classification. Above, a hypothetical fragment of text from a document describing a research project. Below, some of the corresponding *examples*. Each is assigned a number by a classifier designed to recognize, say, project members. This illustration assumes that any fragment containing two or three tokens (terms or units of punctuation) is an example, but the actual range in example lengths depends on the task.

include, in addition to the title, the official course number and the names of the instructors. In traditional IE terms, this collection of tasks is a *template*, each field a *slot*, and each instantiation a *slot fill*.

The general problem of information extraction involves multiple sub-tasks, such as syntactic and semantic pre-processing, slot filling, and anaphora resolution (Cardie 1997). The research reported here addresses only the slot filling problem, and we use the term *information extraction* to refer to this problem. In all results we report, therefore, our system is attempting to solve the following task: *Find the best unbroken fragment (or fragments) of text to fill a given slot in the answer template*. Note that this task is attempted for each field in isolation. A solution to this task, simple as it may seem, could serve as the basis for a large number of useful applications, involving both Web and non-Web documents. Moreover, our focus allows us to study more carefully the behavior of the machine learning approaches we develop.

Extraction as Text Classification

Information extraction is a kind of text classification. Figure 1 shows how the problem of finding instances of a "project member" field can be re-cast as a classification problem. Every candidate instance in a document is presented to a classifier, which is asked to accept or reject them as project members, or more generally, as in the figure, to assign a score to each, the size of which is its confidence that a fragment is a project member.

In contrast with the document classification problem, where the objects to classify (documents) have clear boundaries, the IE problem is, in part, to *identify* the boundaries of field instances, which always occur in the context of a larger unit of text. One way to implement a learned classifier for Figure 1 would be to treat each fragment as a mini-document and use a bag-of-words technique, as in document classification. There is reason to believe, however, that this would not yield good results. The terms in a fragment by themselves do not typically determine whether it is a field instance; its relation to surrounding context is usually of great importance.

Relational Learning

Relational learning (RL), otherwise known as inductive logic programming, comprises a set of algorithms suited to domains with rich relational structure. RL shares with traditional machine learning (ML) the notion of a universe consisting of class-labeled instances and the goal of learning to classify unlabeled instances. However, in contrast with traditional ML, in which instances are represented as fixed-length attribute-value vectors, the instances in a relational universe are embedded in a domain theory. Instance attributes are not isolated, but are related to each other logically. In a typical covering algorithm (e.g., CN2 (Clark & Niblett 1989)), predicates based on attribute values are greedily added to a rule under construction. At each step the number of positive examples of some class is heuristically maximized while the number of negative examples is minimized. Relational learners are rule learners with on-the-fly feature derivation. In addition to simple attribute-value tests, a relational learner can also logically derive new attributes from existing ones, as, for example, in FOIL (Quinlan 1990).

SRV

Our learner must induce rules to identify text fragments that are instances of some field. When presented with an instance of the field, these rules must say "yes"; when given any other term sequence drawn from the document collection, they must say "no." The set of positive examples for learning, therefore, is simply the set of field instances. Because the set of all possible text fragments is intractably large, however, we make the assumption that field instances will be no smaller (in number of terms) than the smallest, and no larger than the largest seen during training. Any non-field-instance fragment from the training document collection which matches these criteria is considered a negative example of the field and counted during induction.

Features In a traditional covering algorithm, the learner is provided with a set of features, defined over examples, which it can use to construct predicates. Unfortunately, multi-term text fragments are difficult to describe in terms of simple features. In contrast, individual terms (or tokens), lend themselves much more readily to feature design. Given a token drawn from a document, a number of obvious feature types suggest themselves, such as length (e.g., single_character_word),

word	punctuationp	sentence_punctuation_p
capitalized_p	all_upper_case	all_lower_case
numericp	singletonp	hybrid_alpha_num_p
doubletonp	tripletonp	quadrupletonp
longp	**prev_token**	**next_token**

Table 1: SRV "core" token features. The two features in bold face are relational features.

character type (e.g., **numeric**), orthography (e.g., **capitalized**), part of speech (e.g., **verb**), and even lexical meaning (e.g., **geographical_place**). Of course, a token is also related to other tokens by a number of different kinds of structure, and this structure suggests other, relational feature types, such as adjacency (e.g., **next_token**) and linguistic syntax (e.g., **subject_verb**).

SRV differs from existing learning systems for IE by requiring and learning over an explicitly provided set of such features. These features come in two basic varieties: *simple* and *relational*. A simple feature is a function mapping a token to some discrete value. A relational feature, on the other hand, maps a token to another token. Figure 1 shows some of the features we used in these experiments. We call these the "core" features, because they embody no domain-specific assumptions.

Search SRV proceeds as does FOIL, starting with the entire set of examples—all negative examples and any positive examples not covered by already induced rules—and adds predicates greedily, attempting thereby to "cover" as many positive, and as few negative examples as possible. An individual predicate belongs to one of a few predefined types:

- length(Relop N): The number of tokens in a fragment is less than, greater than, or equal to some integer. Relop is one of $<$, $>$, or $=$. For example, length($=$ 3) accepts only fragments containing three tokens.

- some(Var Path Feat Value): This is a feature-value test for some token in the sequence. An example is some(?A [ ] capitalizedp true), which means "the fragment contains some token that is capitalized." One argument to this predicate is a variable. For a rule to match a text fragment, each distinct variable in it must bind to a distinct token in the fragment. How the Path argument is used is described below.

- every(Feat Value): Every token in a fragment passes some feature-value test. For example, every(numericp false) means "every token in the fragment is non-numeric."

- position(Var From Relop N): This constrains the position of a token bound by a some-predicate in the current rule. The variable From takes one of two values, fromfirst or fromlast. These values control whether the position is specified relative to the beginning or end of the sequence. For example, position(?A fromfirst $<$ 2) means "the token bound to ?A is either first or second in the fragment."

- relpos(Var1 Var2 Relop N): This constrains the ordering and distance between two tokens bound by distinct variables in the current rule. For example, relpos(?A ?B $=$ 1) means "the token bound to ?A immediately precedes the token bound to ?B."

At every step in rule construction, all documents in the training set are scanned and every text fragment of appropriate size counted. Every legal predicate is assessed in terms of the number of positive and negative examples it covers.[1] That predicate is chosen which maximizes the gain metric used in FOIL.

Relational paths Relational features are used only in the Path argument to the some predicate. This argument can be empty, in which case the some predicate is asserting a feature-value test for a token actually occurring within a field, or it can be a list of relational features. In the latter case, it is positing both a relationship about a field token with some other nearby token, as well as a feature value for the other token. For example, the assertion:

some(?A [prev_token prev_token] capitalized true)

amounts to the English statement, "The fragment contains some token preceded by a capitalized token two tokens back." There is no limit to the number of relational features the learner can string together in this way. Thus, it is possible in principle for the learner to exploit relations between tokens quite distant from each other. In practice, SRV starts each rule by considering only paths of length zero or one. When it posits a some-predicate containing a path, it adds to its set of candidate paths all paths obtained by appending any relational feature to the path used in the predicate. In this way, it builds its notion of field context outward with each rule.

Validation In the experiments reported here, each rule in a learned rule set is validated on a hold-out set. A randomly selected portion (one-third, in this case) of the training data is set aside for validation prior to training. After training on the remaining data, the number of matches and correct predictions over the validation set is stored with each rule. In order to get as much out of the training data as possible, this procedure—training and validation—is repeated three times, once for each of three partitions of the training data. The resulting validated rule sets are concatenated into a single rule set, which is used for prediction. Figure 2 summarizes all the steps involved in training SRV.

During testing, Bayesian m-estimates are used to assess a rule's accuracy from the two validation numbers (Cestnik 1990). All rules matching a given fragment are used to assign a confidence score to SRV's extraction of the fragment. If C is the set of accuracies for matching

---

[1] For example, a *position*-predicate is not legal unless a *some*-predicate is already part of the rule. See the following discussion for restrictions on how the relational component of the *some*-predicate is used.

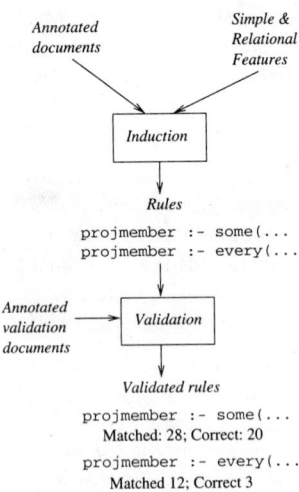

in_title	in_a	in_h
in_h1	in_h2	in_h3
in_list	in_tt	in_table
in_b	in_i	in_font
in_center	in_strong	in_em
in_emphatic	after_br	after_hr
after_p	after_li	after_td
after_th	after_td_or_th	
table_next_col	**table_prev_col**	
table_next_row	**table_prev_row**	
table_row_header	**table_col_header**	

Table 2: HTML features added to the core feature set. Features in bold face are relational.

Figure 2: Input/output of the SRV algorithm.

rules, then the combined confidence is $1 - \prod_{c \in C}(1-c)$. We found in practice that this yields better results than, say, taking the score of the single matching rule of highest confidence.

SRV and FOIL It is important to distinguish between SRV and FOIL, the general-purpose learning algorithm on which it is based. FOIL takes as input a set of Horn clauses, which define both the set of training examples, as well as the structure of the search space. SRV, in contrast, takes a document collection tagged for some field and a set of *features* (see Figure 2). Although it might be possible to get some of the functionality of SRV by encoding a field extraction problem in first-order logic (an ungainly encoding at best), it is doubtful that FOIL would perform as well, and it certainly would perform less efficiently. In addition to heuristics SRV shares with FOIL, it encompasses many additional heuristics which render its search through typically huge negative example sets tractable. Examples are handled implicitly, on a token-by-token basis; because a token is generally shared by many examples (see Figure 1), this permits a much more rapid accounting than if examples were explicitly given. And SRV's exploration of relational structure is restricted in a way that makes sense for the IE problem; in contrast with traditional ILP systems, for example, it cannot infer recursive rules.

Experiments

To test our system, we sampled a set of pages from the Web and tagged them for relevant fields. This section describes the data set and the approach we took to adapting SRV for HTML.

Adapting SRV for HTML

Making SRV able to exploit HTML structure only involved the addition of a number of HTML-specific features to its default set. Table 2 shows the features we added to the core set for these experiments. The *in* features return true for any token occurring within the scope of the corresponding tag. The *after* features return true only for the single token following the corresponding tag. The feature in_emphatic is a disjunction of in_i, in_em, in_b, and in_strong. In addition, several relational features were added which capture relations between tokens occurring together in HTML tables.

Data

For these experiments we sampled and labeled course and research project pages from four university computer science departments: Cornell, University of Texas, University of Washington, and University of Wisconsin. Course pages were labeled for three fields: course title, course number, and course instructor. Course instructor was defined to include teaching assistants. Project pages were labeled for two fields: project title and project member. After collection and tagging, we counted 105 pages in our course collection and 96 in our research project collection.

Procedure

To gauge the performance of SRV, we partitioned each of the two data sets into training and testing sets several times and averaged the results. We tried SRV using the core features shown in Table 1, and again with this same set augmented with the HTML features shown in Table 2. We also performed separate experiments for each of two ways of partitioning: *random partitions*, in which a collection (course or project) was randomly divided into training and testing sets of equal size; and *leave-one-university-out* (LOUO) partitioning, in which pages from one university were set aside for testing and pages from the other three university were used for training. Using random partitioning, we split each data set 5 times into training and testing sets of equal size. The numbers reported for these experiments represent average performance over these 5 sessions. Using LOUO partitioning, the numbers reported represent average performance over a 4-fold experiment, in which each single experiment involves reserving the pages from one university for testing.

		Full		≈ 80%		≈ 20%	
		Acc	Cov	Acc	Cov	Acc	Cov
		\multicolumn{6}{c}{Course Title}
ran	html	45.7	94.4	53.8	80.4	100.0	19.6
ran	core	33.0	91.1	37.2	79.9	51.1	20.1
unv	html	48.5	96.6	55.7	79.5	83.3	20.5
unv	core	30.8	93.2	32.9	79.5	31.6	20.5
		\multicolumn{6}{c}{Course Number}
ran	html	84.0	100.0	87.2	80.1	91.7	19.9
ran	core	84.1	98.3	86.9	80.1	89.6	19.9
unv	html	79.2	95.7	81.1	73.4	87.0	22.3
unv	core	52.1	95.7	65.8	75.5	77.3	20.2
		\multicolumn{6}{c}{Project Title}
ran	html	26.3	99.5	31.0	79.9	50.0	20.1
ran	core	7.7	99.0	8.2	79.4	9.8	20.6
unv	html	34.0	97.5	39.2	80.0	81.2	20.0
unv	core	9.9	93.8	11.3	80.0	6.3	20.0

Table 3: SRV performance on "one-per-document" fields. The label *ran* stands for random partitioning; *unv* stands for leave-one-university-out partitioning. Rows labeled *core* show SRV's performance using the feature set shown in Table 1; those labeled *html* used the same feature set augmented with the features shown in Table 2.

Field			Full		≈ 20%	
			Prec	Rec	Prec	Rec
Course Instr.	ran	html	21.6	55.9	63.6	20.1
Course Instr.	ran	core	20.6	53.2	47.7	20.1
Course Instr.	unv	html	13.9	47.2	37.7	19.9
Course Instr.	unv	core	16.6	47.2	55.0	20.4
Project Member	ran	html	30.0	41.0	66.4	20.0
Project Member	ran	core	26.2	35.2	46.0	20.0
Project Member	unv	html	29.1	42.8	64.1	20.1
Project Member	unv	core	26.7	35.9	52.6	20.1

Table 4: SRV performance on the "many-per-document" fields.

Results

We distinguish between two kinds of IE task, depending on whether a field is likely to have only one or multiple instantiations in a document. For example, a research project page refers to a single project, so can have only a single project title, even though the project title may occur (and be tagged) multiple times in the page. On the other hand, a project typically has multiple members.

The former case, "one-per-document" (OPD), is obviously a much simpler IE task than the latter. Although a system, heuristic or learned, may recognize multiple project titles in a page, we can simply take the single most confident prediction and have done with it. In the case of project member, a "many-per-document" (MPD) field, a system will ideally extract every occurrence. The answer of the system in this case to the extraction task must be to return every prediction it makes for a document.

Table 3 shows the performance of SRV on the three OPD fields: course title, course number, and project title. Here, the unit of performance is a single file. Accuracy (*Acc*) is the number of files for which a learner correctly identifies a field instance, divided by the number of files for which it made a prediction. Coverage (*Cov*) is the number of files containing instances for which any prediction was made.

It is common in machine learning and information retrieval to try to exploit the spread in the confidence of learner predictions by trading off coverage for increased accuracy. Perhaps by sacrificing all predictions except those with confidence greater than x, for instance, we can realize accuracy much higher than baseline. The standard way of measuring the feasibility of such a trade-off is with an accuracy-coverage (or precision-recall) graph. To construct such a graph, we sort all learner predictions by confidence, then, for various n from 1 to 100, plot the accuracy of the $n\%$ most confident predictions. In lieu of such graphs, we have included two additional columns in Table 3, one for accuracy at approximately 80% coverage and one for approximately 20% coverage. [2]

Table 4 shows SRV performance on the two MPD fields: course instructor and project member. The unit of performance in this table is the individual prediction and field instance. Because the accuracy and coverage statistics bear a strong relationship to the standard IR notions of *precision* and *recall*,[3] and in order to emphasize the different way of measuring performance, we use different labels for the columns. *Prec* is the number of correctly recognized field instances divided by the total number of predictions. *Rec* is the number of correctly recognized field instances divided by the total number of field instances. Because this is a fundamentally harder task than in Table 3, in no case does SRV achieve 80% coverage; thus, only a 20% column is presented. By the same token, the accuracy-coverage trade-off is perhaps more crucial here, because it shows the effect of discarding all the low-confidence predictions that are naturally filtered out in the OPD setting.

Finally, Table 5 shows the performance of two strawman approaches to the task. The `Rote` learner simply memorizes field instances it sees in the training set, making a prediction on any test sequences that match an entry in its learned dictionary and returning a confidence that is the probability, based on training statistics, that a sequence is indeed a field instance. We take this learner to be the simplest possible machine learning approach to the problem. We have found in other

---

[2] Actual coverages are listed, because it is often impossible to choose a confidence cut-off that yields exactly the desired coverage.

[3] Field instances correspond to "relevant" documents, incorrect predictions to irrelevant ones.

Field	Part.	Rote Acc	Rote Cov	Guess Acc
Course Title	rand	44.3	49.5	1.3
	univ	36.2	47.7	1.4
Course Number	rand	44.4	28.8	3.1
	univ	0.0	0.0	2.9
Project Title	rand	18.8	21.6	8.3
	univ	28.6	7.5	8.5
		Prec	Rec	Prec + Rec
Course Instr.	rand	69.4	11.5	0.9
	univ	0.0	0.0	0.9
Project Member	rand	70.3	10.7	7.1
	univ	44.1	2.0	7.6

Table 5: Performance of two simple baseline strategies.

```
coursenumber :-
  length(= 2),
  every(in_title false),
  some(?A [previous_token] in_title true),
  some(?A [] after_p false),
  some(?B [] tripleton true)
```

```
<title> Course Information CS213 </title>
<h1> CS 213 C++ Programming </h1>
```

Figure 3: A learned rule for course number with some sample matching text. This rule matched 11 examples in the validation set with no false positives.

contexts that it performs surprisingly well in a small number of "naturally occurring" IE problems.

The Guess column shows the expected performance of a random guesser, given unrealistically optimistic assumptions. The learner is "told" how many field instances occur in a test file and what their lengths are. For each instance it is allowed to make one guess of the appropriate length. Because it always makes exactly as many predictions as there are test field instances, its precision and recall are equal on MPD fields.

Discussion

Not surprisingly, SRV performs better than the baseline approaches in all cases. This is especially apparent for the OPD fields. Note that, although Rote may appear to have comparable accuracies in some cases, these accuracy figures show only performance over "covered" files. In cases where SRV and Rote accuracies appear comparable, Rote coverage is generally much lower.

As expected, the addition of HTML features generally yields considerable improvement, especially at the high precision end of the curve. HTML information appears to be particularly important for recognizing project titles. The single exception to this trend is the course instructor problem in the LOUO setting. It appears that formatting conventions for a course page are relatively specific to the department from which it comes, as page templates are passed around among instructors and re-used from semester to semester. SRV takes advantage of the resulting regularities, and its performance suffers when some of the rules it learns do not generalize across university boundaries.

SRV performs best by far on the course number field, even in the LOUO case, where (as the results for Rote indicate) memorization yields no benefit. Figure 3 shows one HTML-aware rule responsible for this good performance. The core results show that much of its performance on this field is attributable to the strong orthographic regularities these numbers exhibit.

As noted above, Rote is sometimes a viable approach. This appears to be true for the course title field, for which Rote achieves reasonable performance at surprisingly high coverage levels. This is obviously an effect of the generic character of course titles. The title "Introduction to Artificial Intelligence" is quite likely to be a course title, wherever it is encountered, and is probably used at many universities without variation. Rote's high coverage for this field allows us to measure its accuracy at the approximate 20% level: 80.6% accuracy at 16.4% coverage, in the random-split experiments, and 57.9% at 20.5% coverage, in the LOUO experiments. Armed with HTML-specific features, SRV achieves much better accuracy at this coverage level for both partitioning methods.

A comparison between Table 3 and Table 4 makes the difficulty of the MPD extraction problem evident. Of course, the lower performance in Table 4 is also due to the fact that names of people are being extracted—probably a more difficult task for an automated system than fields made up of common English terms—and that formatting conventions for course instructors and project members vary more than for, say, course titles. Note, however, that if we can be satisfied with only finding 20% of the names of instructors and project members (in the case of random partitioning), we can expect about two-thirds of our predictions to be correct.

A comparison between the two partitioning methods shows, not surprisingly, that random partitioning makes for an easier learning task than LOUO partitioning. This is especially apparent for Rote on the person-name fields; faculty members tend to teach multiple courses, and researchers at a university become involved in multiple projects. But Web formatting conventions also tend to be shared within a department, so we might hope that SRV could benefit from intra-department regularities. Surprisingly, this is not uniformly evident. In the case of project title, SRV actually does worse in all three columns. This effect is probably in part due to differences in training set size between the two partitioning regimes (half of the data in random vs. three-fourths of the data, on average, in LOUO).

Related Work

Soderland originally showed the viability of a covering (rule learning) approach to the slot filling problem (Soderland 1996). More recently, Califf and Mooney have demonstrated a similar system with relational extensions (Califf & Mooney 1997). In both of these systems, rules are patterns which stipulate what must occur in and around field instances, and both systems generalize by starting with maximally specific patterns and gradually dropping constraints. Generalization is halted when a rule begins to accept too many negative examples.

This "bottom-up" search represents an efficient and useful approach, but it must rely on heuristics to control how constraints are dropped. Typically, there are many ways in which a rule can be generalized so that it does not cover negative examples. In contrast, top-down search is entirely controlled by the distribution of positive and negative examples in the data. SRV does this in part with the aid of a set of features, which are separate from the core algorithm. In the two bottom-up systems discussed here, the features are implicit and entangled with the search heuristics.

Soderland describes modifications which must be made to CRYSTAL, his learning system for IE, in order to use it for HTML (Soderland 1997). CRYSTAL's assumption that text will be presented in sentence-sized chunks must be satisfied heuristically. How this segmentation is performed depends in part on the domain and requires manual engineering. In contrast, because SRV searches at the token level, it requires no modifications to be retargeted. *Exploiting* HTML structure only involves the addition of several new HTML-specific features to its basic feature set. These feature are only additional information, and SRV does not require them in order to work with HTML.

It is common to report the performance of an IE system in terms of two summary numbers, precision and recall, and the systems described above adhere to this convention. In SRV, we have added a mechanism whereby these numbers can be varied to achieve the balance most advantages for the particular application.

Conclusion

Proceeding from general considerations about the nature of the IE problem, we have implemented SRV, a relational learner for this task. Adapting SRV for HTML requires no heuristic modifications to the basic algorithm; instead, HTML structure is captured by the addition of simple, token-oriented features. There is clear evidence that, armed with such features, SRV achieves interesting and effective generalization on a variety of tasks in two HTML domains.

Among the contributions made by this work are:

- **Increased modularity and flexibility.** Domain-specific information is separate from the underlying learning mechanism. This permits, among other things, the rapid adaptation of the system for use with HTML.
- **Top-down induction.** SRV demonstrates the feasibility of conducting learning for IE in the direction from general to specific.
- **Accuracy-coverage trade-off.** In contrast with other work in this area, the learning framework includes a mechanism for associating confidence scores with predictions. This allows the system to trade coverage for increased accuracy.

With the introduction of SRV, and other IE systems like it, we can begin to address the larger problem of designing artificially intelligent agents for mining the World Wide Web.

Acknowledgments Thanks to the other members of the WebKB project at CMU, whose data collection made this work possible. This research was supported in part by the DARPA HPKB program under contract F30602-97-1-0215.

References

Califf, M. E., and Mooney, R. J. 1997. Relational learning of pattern-match rules for information extraction. In *Working Papers of ACL-97 Workshop on Natural Language Learning*.

Cardie, C. 1997. Empirical methods in information extraction. *AI Magazine* 18(4):65–79.

Cestnik, B. 1990. Estimating probabilities: A crucial task in machine learning. In *Proceedings of the Ninth European Conference on Artificial Intelligence*.

Clark, P., and Niblett, T. 1989. The CN2 induction algorithm. *Machine Learning* 3(4):261–263.

Defense Advanced Research Projects Agency. 1995. *Proceedings of the Sixth Message Understanding Conference (MUC-6)*, Morgan Kaufmann Publisher, Inc.

Doorenbos, R.; Etzioni, O.; and Weld, D. S. 1997. A scalable comparison-shopping agent for the world-wide web. In *Proceedings of the First International Conference on Autonomous Agents*.

Freitag, D. 1998. Toward general-purpose learning for information extraction. In *Proceedings of COLING-ACL '98*. In submission.

Kushmerick, N. 1997. *Wrapper Induction for Information Extraction*. Ph.D. Dissertation, University of Washington. Tech Report UW-CSE-97-11-04.

Quinlan, J. R. 1990. Learning logical definitions from relations. *Machine Learning* 5(3):239–266.

Soderland, S. 1996. *Learning Text Analysis Rules for Domain-specific Natural Language Processing*. Ph.D. Dissertation, University of Massachusetts. CS Tech. Report 96-087.

Soderland, S. 1997. Learning to extract text-based information from the world wide web. In *Proceedings of the 3rd International Conference on Knowledge Discovery and Data Mining*.

Towards Text Knowledge Engineering

Udo Hahn & Klemens Schnattinger

Computational Linguistics Group
Text Knowledge Engineering Lab
Freiburg University
Werthmannplatz 1, D-79085 Freiburg, Germany
http://www.coling.uni-freiburg.de

Abstract

We introduce a methodology for automating the maintenance of domain-specific taxonomies based on natural language text understanding. A given ontology is incrementally updated as new concepts are acquired from real-world texts. The acquisition process is centered around the linguistic and conceptual "quality" of various forms of evidence underlying the generation and refinement of concept hypotheses. On the basis of the quality of evidence, concept hypotheses are ranked according to credibility and the most credible ones are selected for assimilation into the domain knowledge base.

Introduction

Knowledge engineering is still an expert task. Though a variety of architectures have been proposed to date (Buchanan *et al.* 1983), the dominating paradigm for the process of eliciting and maintaining domain ontologies continues to focus on the interactive knowledge transfer from humans to machines (Stefik 1995). Some experimental activities tried to make use of machine learning methods in order to induce knowledge from structured data repositories (Morik *et al.* 1993), but even fewer efforts were targeted at unstructured natural language texts as a source for automating knowledge engineering processes (Gomez & Segami 1990).

We propose here such a text-based knowledge acquisition methodology, in which domain knowledge bases are continuously enhanced as a by-product of text understanding processes – hence, *text knowledge engineering*. New concepts are acquired taking two sources of evidence into account: background knowledge of the domain the texts are about, and linguistic patterns in which unknown lexical items occur. Domain knowledge serves as a comparison scale for judging the plausibility of newly derived concept descriptions in the light of prior knowledge. Linguistic knowledge assesses the strength of the interpretative force that can be attributed to the grammatical construction in which new lexical items occur. Our model makes explicit the kind of qualitative reasoning that is behind such a learning process.

This is, then, a knowledge-intensive model of concept acquisition, tightly integrated with the non-learning mode of text understanding. The "plain" text understanding mode

[0]Copyright ©1998, American Association for Artificial Intelligence (www.aaai.org). All rights reserved.

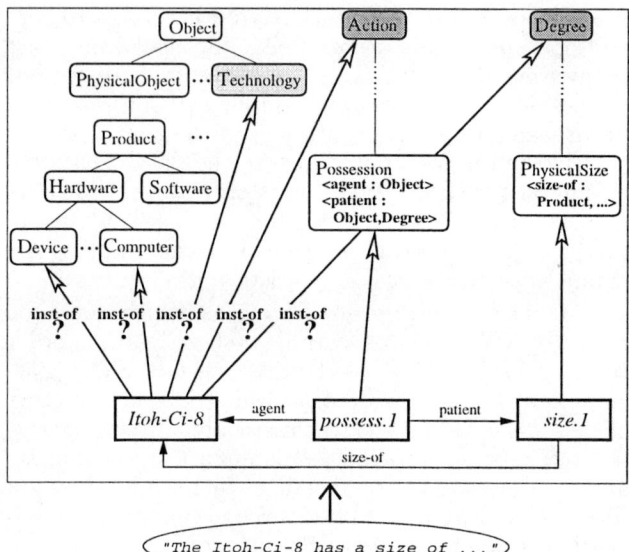

Figure 1: A Sample Scenario

can be considered the instantiation and continuous role filling of *single concepts* already available in the knowledge base. Under learning conditions, a *set of alternative concept hypotheses* are managed for each unknown item, with each hypothesis denoting a newly created conceptual interpretation tentatively associated with the unknown item.

For illustration purposes, consider the following scenario as depicted in Fig. 1. Suppose, your knowledge of the information technology domain tells you nothing about an *Itoh-Ci-8*. Imagine, one day your favorite technology magazine features an article starting with *"The Itoh-Ci-8 has a size of ..."*. Has your knowledge increased? If so, what did you learn from just this phrase?

The text knowledge acquisition process starts upon the reading of the unknown lexical item *"Itoh-Ci-8"*. In this initial step, the corresponding hypothesis space incorporates all the top level concepts available in the ontology for the new lexical item *"Itoh-Ci-8"*. So, the concept ITOH-CI-8 may be a kind of an OBJECT, an ACTION, a DEGREE, etc. As a consequence of processing the noun phrase *"The Itoh-Ci-8"* as the grammatical subject of the verb *"has"*, ITOH-CI-8 is related via the AGENT role to the ACTION

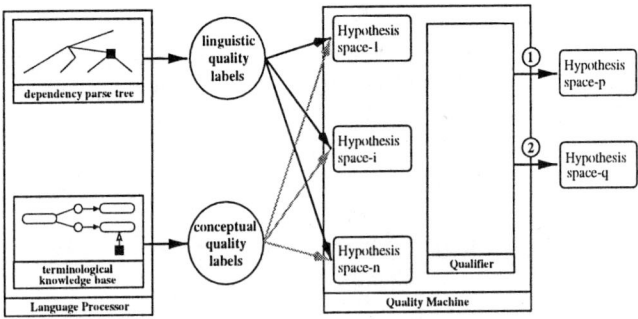

Figure 2: Architecture for Text Knowledge Engineering

concept POSSESSION, the concept denoted by *"has"* (lexical ambiguities, e.g., for the verb *"has"*, lead to the creation of alternative hypothesis spaces). Since POSSESSION requires its AGENT to be an OBJECT, ACTION and DEGREE are no longer valid concept hypotheses. Their cancellation (cf. the darkly shaded boxes) yields significant reduction of the huge initial hypothesis space. The learner then aggressively specializes the remaining single hypothesis to the immediate subordinates of OBJECT, viz. PHYSICALOBJECT and TECHNOLOGY, in order to test more restricted hypotheses which – according to more specific constraints – are easier falsifiable.

In addition, the *linguistic* constraints for the verb *"has"* indicate that the grammatical direct object relation is to be interpreted in terms of a conceptual PATIENT role. Accordingly, the phrase *"...has a size of..."* is processed such that $size.1$ is the PATIENT of the POSSESSION relationship. Also, AGENT and PATIENT are both restricted by specific *conceptual* constraints. These come into play in the subsequent semantic interpretation step, where possible conceptual relations between the AGENT and PATIENT are tried.

A straightforward translation of the basic conceptual relations contained in the utterance above yields the following terminological expressions:

(P1) $size.1$: PHYSICALSIZE
(P2) $size.1$ SIZE-OF *Itoh-Ci*-8

Assertion P1 indicates that $size.1$ is an instance of the concept class PHYSICALSIZE and P2 relates $size.1$ and *Itoh-Ci*-8 via the binary relation SIZE-OF.

Given the conceptual roles attached to PHYSICALSIZE, the system recognizes that all specializations of PRODUCT can be related to the concept PHYSICALSIZE (via the role SIZE-OF), while for TECHNOLOGY no such relation can be established. So, we prefer the conceptual reading of ITOH-CI-8 as a kind of a PRODUCT over the TECHNOLOGY hypothesis (cf. the grey-shaded boxes).

A Model of Text Knowledge Engineering

The methodology and corresponding system architecture for text knowledge elicitation is summarized in Fig. 2. It depicts how linguistic and conceptual evidence are generated and combined to continuously discriminate and refine the set of concept hypotheses (the unknown item yet to be learned is characterized by the black square).

The *language processor* (for an overview, cf. Hahn, Schacht, & Bröker (1994)) yields structural dependency information from the grammatical constructions in which an unknown lexical item occurs in terms of the corresponding *parse tree*. The kinds of syntactic constructions (e.g., genitive, apposition, comparative), in which unknown lexical items appear, are recorded and assessed later on relative to the credit they lend to a particular hypothesis. The conceptual interpretation of parse trees involving unknown lexical items in the *terminological knowledge base* (cf. Woods & Schmolze (1992) for a survey of terminological, KL-ONE-style knowledge representation) is used to derive *concept hypotheses*, which are further enriched by conceptual annotations reflecting structural patterns of consistency, mutual justification, analogy, etc. This kind of initial evidence, in particular its predictive "goodness" for the learning task, is represented by corresponding sets of *linguistic* and *conceptual quality labels*. Multiple concept hypotheses for each unknown lexical item are organized in terms of a corresponding *hypothesis space*, each subspace holding different or further specialized concept hypotheses.

The *quality machine* estimates the overall credibility of single concept hypotheses by taking the available set of quality labels for each hypothesis into account. The final computation of a preference order for the entire set of competing hypotheses takes place in the *qualifier*, a terminological classifier extended by an evaluation metric for quality-based selection criteria. The output of the quality machine is a ranked list of concept hypotheses. The ranking yields, in decreasing order of significance, either the most plausible concept classes which classify the considered instance or more general concept classes subsuming the considered concept class (cf. Schnattinger & Hahn (1996) for details of this metareasoning process).

Linguistic Quality Labels

Linguistic quality labels reflect structural properties of phrasal patterns or discourse contexts in which unknown lexical items occur — we assume here that the type of grammatical construction exercises a particular interpretative force on the unknown item and, at the same time, yields a particular level of credibility for the hypotheses being derived therefrom. As a concrete example of a high-quality label, consider the case of APPOSITION. This label is generated for constructions such as *".. the printer @A@ .."*, with *"@..@"* denoting the unknown item. The apposition almost unequivocally determines *"@A@"* (considered as a potential noun)[1] to denote a PRINTER. This assumption is justified independent of further conceptual conditions, simply due to the nature of the linguistic construction being used. Still of good quality but already less constraining are occurrences of the unknown item in a CASEFRAME construction as illustrated by *".. @B@ has a size of .."*. In this example, case frame specifications of the verb *"has"* that relate to its AGENT role carry over to *"@B@"*. Given its final

---

[1] Such a part-of-speech hypothesis can be derived from the inventory of valence and word order specifications underlying the dependency grammar model we use (Hahn, Schacht, & Bröker 1994).

semantic interpretation, "@B@" may be anything that has a size. Considering an utterance like *"The Itoh-Ci-8 has a size of .."*, we may hypothesize that, in an information technology domain, at least, the concept ITOH-CI-8 can tentatively be considered a PRODUCT (which IS-A PHYSICALOBJECT and, hence, always provides a HAS-SIZE relation).

Depending on the type of the syntactic construction in which the unknown lexical item occurs, different hypothesis generation rules may fire. As in a sample phrase such as *"The switch of the Itoh-Ci-8 .."*, genitive noun phrases place only a few constraints on the item to be acquired. In the following, let *target* be the unknown item (*"Itoh-Ci-8"*) and *base* be the known item (*"switch"*), whose conceptual relation to the target is constrained by the syntactic relation in which their lexical counterparts co-occur. The main constraint for genitives says that the target concept fills (exactly) one of the n roles of the base concept. Since the correct role cannot yet be decided upon, n alternative hypotheses have to be posited (unless additional constraints apply), and the target concept has to be assigned as a filler of the i-th role of base in the corresponding i-th hypothesis space. As a consequence, the classifier is able to derive a suitable concept hypothesis by specializing the target concept (initially TOP, by default) according to the value restriction of the base concept's i-th role. Additionally, this rule assigns a syntactic quality label to each i-th hypothesis indicating the type of syntactic construction in which target and base co-occur.

After the processing of *"The Itoh-Ci-8 has a size of .."*, the target ITOH-CI-8 is already predicted as a PRODUCT. Prior to continuing with the phrase *"The switch of the Itoh-Ci-8 .."*, consider some fragments of the conceptual representation for SWITCHes:

(P3) SWITCH-OF $\doteq$ $_{\text{SWITCH}}|\text{PART-OF}|_{\text{HARDWARE}}$
(P4) SWITCH $\doteq$
  $\forall$HAS-PRICE.PRICE $\sqcap$
  $\forall$HAS-WEIGHT.WEIGHT $\sqcap$
  $\forall$SWITCH-OF. $\begin{pmatrix} \text{OUTPUTDEV} \sqcup \text{INPUTDEV} \sqcup \\ \text{STORAGEDEV} \sqcup \text{COMPUTER} \end{pmatrix}$

The relation SWITCH-OF is defined by P3 as the set of all PART-OF relations which have their domain restricted to SWITCH and their range restricted to HARDWARE. In addition, (P4) reads as "all fillers of HAS-PRICE, HAS-WEIGHT, and SWITCH-OF roles must be concepts subsumed by PRICE, WEIGHT, and the disjunction of (OUTPUTDEV $\sqcup$ INPUTDEV $\sqcup$ STORAGEDEV $\sqcup$ COMPUTER), respectively". So, three roles have to be considered for relating the target ITOH-CI-8, as a tentative PRODUCT, to the base concept SWITCH. Two of them, HAS-PRICE and HAS-WEIGHT, are ruled out due to the violation of a simple integrity constraint (PRODUCT does not denote a unit of measure). Therefore, only the role SWITCH-OF must be considered. Due to the definition of SWITCH-OF (cf. P3), ITOH-CI-8 is immediately specialized to HARDWARE by the classifier. Since the classifier aggressively pushes the hypothesizing to be maximally specific, four distinct hypotheses are immediately created due to the specific range restrictions of the role SWITCH-OF expressed in (P4), the definition of the concept SWITCH, viz. OUTPUTDEV, INPUTDEV, STORAGEDEV and COMPUTER, and they are managed in four distinct hypothesis spaces, h_1, h_2, h_3 and h_4, respectively. We sketch their contents roughly in the following concept descriptions (note that for *Itoh-Ci-8* we also include parts of the implicit IS-A hierarchy):

$(Itoh\text{-}Ci\text{-}8 : \text{OUTPUTDEV})_{h_1}, (Itoh\text{-}Ci\text{-}8 : \text{DEVICE})_{h_1}, ..,$
$(switch.1 \text{ SWITCH-OF } Itoh\text{-}Ci\text{-}8)_{h_1}$
$(Itoh\text{-}Ci\text{-}8 : \text{INPUTDEV})_{h_2}, (Itoh\text{-}Ci\text{-}8 : \text{DEVICE})_{h_2}, ..,$
$(switch.1 \text{ SWITCH-OF } Itoh\text{-}Ci\text{-}8)_{h_2}$
$(Itoh\text{-}Ci\text{-}8 : \text{STORAGEDEV})_{h_3}, (Itoh\text{-}Ci\text{-}8 : \text{DEVICE})_{h_3}, ..,$
$(switch.1 \text{ SWITCH-OF } Itoh\text{-}Ci\text{-}8)_{h_3}$
$(Itoh\text{-}Ci\text{-}8 : \text{COMPUTER})_{h_4}, (Itoh\text{-}Ci\text{-}8 : \text{HARDWARE})_{h_4}, ..,$
$(switch.1 \text{ SWITCH-OF } Itoh\text{-}Ci\text{-}8)_{h_4}$

Conceptual Quality Labels

Conceptual quality labels result from comparing the representation structures of a concept hypothesis with those of alternative concept hypotheses or already existing representation structures in the underlying domain knowledge base from the viewpoint of structural similarity, compatibility, etc. The closer the match, the more credit is lent to a hypothesis. For instance, a very positive conceptual quality label such as M-DEDUCED is assigned to multiple derivations of the same concept hypothesis in different hypothesis (sub)spaces. Positive labels are also assigned to terminological expressions which share structural similarities, though they are not identical. The label C-SUPPORTED, e.g., is assigned to any hypothesized relation $R1$ between two instances when another relation, $R2$, already exists in the knowledge base involving the same two instances, but where the role fillers occur in "inverted" order (note that $R1$ and $R2$ need not necessarily be semantically inverse relations such as with *"buy"* and *"sell"*). This rule of *"cross"* support captures the inherent symmetry between concepts related via quasi-inverse conceptual relations.

Quality annotations of the conceptual status of concept hypotheses are derived from qualification rules. For instance, the rule for the label M-DEDUCED applies to the case where the same assertion is deduced in at least two different hypothesis spaces (cf. h_1 and h_2 in the expression below). That assertion, e.g., $(Itoh\text{-}Ci\text{-}8 : \text{DEVICE})_{h_1}$ in the example below, is then annotated by a high-quality label. In technical terms, an instance of the quality label M-DEDUCED is created (for a formal specification of several qualification rules, including the representation of and metareasoning with quality assertions, cf. Hahn, Klenner, & Schnattinger (1996)). Considering our example, for ITOH-CI-8 the concept hypotheses OUTPUTDEVice, INPUTDEVice and STORAGEDEVice were derived independently of each other in different hypothesis spaces. Hence, DEVICE, as their common superconcept, has been *multiply* derived by the classifier in each of these spaces, too. Accordingly, this hypothesis is assigned a high degree of confidence by issuing the conceptual quality label M-DEDUCED:

$(Itoh\text{-}Ci\text{-}8 : \text{DEVICE})_{h_1} \wedge (Itoh\text{-}Ci\text{-}8 : \text{DEVICE})_{h_2}$
$\Longrightarrow$
$(Itoh\text{-}Ci\text{-}8 : \text{DEVICE})_{h_1} : \text{M-DEDUCED} \quad .. \quad ..$

Quality-Based Classification

Whenever new evidence for or against a concept hypothesis is brought forth in a single learning step all concept hypotheses are reevaluated. First, weak or even untenable hypotheses are discarded. A quality-based selection among the remaining hypothesis spaces is grounded in *threshold levels* (later on referred to as **TH**). Their definition takes linguistic evidence into account. At the first threshold level, all hypothesis spaces with the maximum of APPOSITION labels are selected. If more than one hypothesis is left to be considered, only concept hypotheses with the maximum number of CASEFRAME assignments are approved at the second threshold level. Those hypothesis spaces that have fulfilled these threshold criteria will then be classified relative to two different *credibility levels* (later on referred to as **CB**). The first level of credibility contains all hypothesis spaces which have the maximum of M-DEDUCED labels, while at the second level (again, with more than one hypothesis left to be considered) those are chosen which are assigned the maximum of C-SUPPORTED labels. A comprehensive terminological specification of the underlying qualification calculus is given by Schnattinger & Hahn (1996).

For an illustration, consider the first utterance, once again: *"The Itoh-Ci-8 has a size of .."*. An assignment of the syntactic quality label CASEFRAME is triggered only in those hypothesis spaces where the unknown item is considered a PHYSICALOBJECT (cf. Table 3, learning step 1). The remaining hypotheses (cf. Table 3, learning step 2) cannot be annotated by CASEFRAME, since the concepts they represent (e.g., MENTALOBJECT, NORM) have no property such as PHYSICALSIZE. As a consequence, their hypothesis spaces are ruled out by the criterion set up at the second threshold level, and the still valid concept hypothesis PHYSICALOBJECT is further refined as PRODUCT. As far as the sample phrase *"The switch of the Itoh-Ci-8 .."* is concerned, four more specific hypothesis spaces are generated from the PRODUCT hypothesis, three of which stipulate a DEVICE hypothesis. Since the conceptual quality label M-DEDUCED has been derived by the classifier, this result yields a ranking with these three DEVICE hypotheses preferred over the one associated with COMPUTER (cf. Table 3, learning step 3).

Evaluation

In this section, we present some data from an empirical evaluation of the text knowledge acquisition system. We start with a consideration of canonical performance measures (such as recall, precision, etc.) and then focus on the more pertinent issues of learning accuracy and the learning rate. Due to the given learning environment, the measures we apply deviate from those commonly used in the machine learning community. In concept learning algorithms like IBL (Aha, Kibler, & Albert 1991) there is no hierarchy of concepts. Hence, any prediction of the class membership of a new instance is either true or false. However, as such hierarchies naturally emerge in terminological frameworks, a prediction can be more or less precise, i.e., it may approximate the target concept at different levels of specificity. This is captured by our measure of *learning accuracy* which takes

	Phrase	Semantic Interpretation
1.	The *Itoh-Ci-8 has*	(possess.1, agent, Itoh-Ci-8)
2.	a *size* of ..	(possess.1, patient, size.1)
		↦ (size.1, size-of, Itoh-Ci-8)
		↦ (Itoh-Ci-8, has-size, size.1)
3.	The *switch* of the *Itoh-Ci-8* ..	(switch.1, switch-of, Itoh-Ci-8)
		↦ (Itoh-Ci-8, has-switch, switch.1)
4.	The *housing* from the *Itoh-Ci-8* ..	(housing.1, case-of, Itoh-Ci-8)
		↦ (Itoh-Ci-8, has-case, housing.1)
5.	*Itoh-Ci-8* with a *main memory* ..	(memory.1, memory-of, Itoh-Ci-8)
		↦ (Itoh-Ci-8, has-memory, memory.1)
6.	*Itoh-Ci-8's LED lines* ..	(LED-line.1, part-of, Itoh-Ci-8)
		↦ (Itoh-Ci-8, has-part, LED-line.1)
7.	*Itoh-Ci-8's toner supply* ..	(tonerSupply.1, part-of, Itoh-Ci-8)
		↦ (Itoh-Ci-8, has-part, tonerSupply.1)
8.	*Paper cassette* of the *Itoh-Ci-8* ..	(paperSupply.1, part-of, Itoh-Ci-8)
		↦ (Itoh-Ci-8, has-part, paperSupply.1)
9.	*Itoh-Ci-8* with a *resolution rate* ..	(resolution.1, rate-of, Itoh-Ci-8)
		↦ (Itoh-Ci-8, has-rate, resolution.1)

Table 1: Interpretation Results of a Text Featuring *"Itoh-Ci-8"*

into account the conceptual distance of a hypothesis to the goal concept of an instance, rather than simply relating the number of correct and false predictions, as in IBL.

In our approach, learning is achieved by the refinement of *multiple* hypotheses about the class membership of an instance. Thus, the measure of *learning rate* we propose is concerned with the reduction of possible hypotheses as more and more *information* becomes available about one particular new instance. In contrast, IBL-style algorithms consider only one concept hypothesis per learning cycle and their notion of *learning rate* relates to the increase of correct predictions as more and more *instances* are being processed.

The knowledge base on which we performed our experiments contained 325 concept definitions and 447 conceptual relations. The upper-level concepts of that ontology were taken from Nirenburg & Raskin (1987). We considered a total of 101 texts (= **SizeofTestSet** below) randomly selected from a corpus of information technology magazines. For each of them, 5 to 15 learning steps were considered. A *learning step* captures the final result of all semantic interpretation processes being made at the level of hypothesis spaces after new textual input has been supplied in which the item to be learned occurs. In order to clarify the input data available for the learning system, cf. Table 1. It consists of nine single learning steps for the unknown item *"Itoh-Ci-8"* that occurred while processing the entire text. Each learning step is associated with a particular natural language phrase in which the unknown lexical item occurs and the corresponding semantic interpretation data.

Canonical Performance Measures

In a first series of experiments, we neglected the incrementality of the learner and evaluated our system in terms of its *bare off-line* performance. By this we mean its potential to determine the correct concept description at the end of each text analysis considering the outcome of the final learning step only. Following previous work on evaluation measures for learning systems (Hastings 1994), we distinguish here the following parameters:

- **Hypothesis** denotes the set of concept hypotheses derived by the system as the final result of the text understanding process for each target item;

Information Extraction 527

	CAMILLE	–	TH	CB
Correct	*	100	100	99
OneCorrect	*	21	26	31
ConceptSum	*	446	360	255
RECALL := $\frac{\text{Correct}}{\text{SizeofTestSet}}$	44%	99%	99%	98%
PRECISION := $\frac{\text{Correct}}{\text{ConceptSum}}$	22%	22%	28%	39%
PARSIMONY := $\frac{\text{OneCorrect}}{\text{SizeofTestSet}}$	14%	21%	26%	31%

Table 2: Performance Measures

- **Correct** denotes the number of cases in the test set in which **Hypothesis** contains the correct concept description for the target item;
- **OneCorrect** denotes the number of cases in the test set in which **Hypothesis** is a singleton set which contains the correct concept description only;
- **ConceptSum** denotes the number of concepts generated for all of the target items considering the entire test set.

Measures were taken under three experimental conditions (cf. Table 2). In the second column (indicated by –), we considered the contribution of only the terminological reasoning component to the concept acquisition task, the third column contains the results of incorporating the (linguistic) threshold criteria (denoted by **TH**), while the fourth one incorporates (linguistic as well as conceptual) credibility criteria (designated by **CB**). The data indicate a surprisingly high recall rate. The slight drop for **CB** (98% relative to 99%) is due to an incidental selection fault during processing. The values for precision as well as those for parsimony are consistently in favor of the full qualification calculus (**CB**).

In an attempt to relate these results of the quality-based learner to a system close in spirit to our approach, we chose CAMILLE (Hastings 1994), considering versions 1.0, 1.2, 2.0, and 2.1, and the results reported for recall, precision, and parsimony in the assembly line and the terrorism domain (cf. Table 2, column one). Not surprisingly, the precision of our terminological reasoning component, the LOOM system (MacGregor 1994), is equal to CAMILLE's,[2] but our system outperforms CAMILLE significantly on the evaluation dimensions **TH** and **CB** with respect to any of the performance measures we considered. Unlike CAMILLE, our learner also consistently improves as more and more information becomes available for an unknown target item (cf. the following section).

---

[2]Hastings (1994, page 71) mentions that "... classifier systems [like LOOM] provide a very similar inference mechanism to CAMILLE's." This statement is backed up by our precision data which exhibit equal values for our system and CAMILLE. Hastings (ibid.) also rightly observes that "... they [the classifier systems] stop short of inferring the best hypotheses." The specialization procedure developed for CAMILLE resembles the one underlying our system. Contrary to Hasting's approach, however, we evaluate the different, more specific hypotheses with respect to linguistic and conceptual evidence and arrive at a ranked list of hypotheses based on **TH** and **CB** criteria. This way, more specific hypotheses simultaneously pass an evidential filtering mechanism that significantly increases the system's learning performance.

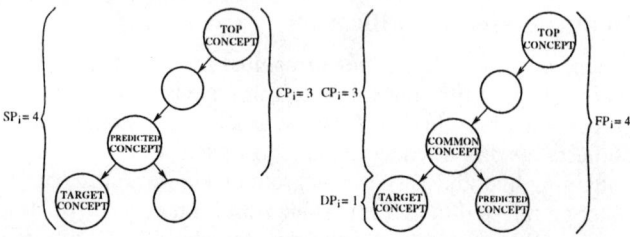

Figure 3: LA for an Underspecified Concept Hypothesis

Figure 4: LA for a Slightly Incorrect Concept Hypothesis

Learning Accuracy

In a second series of experiments, we investigated the *learning accuracy* of the system, i.e., the degree to which it correctly predicts the concept class which subsumes the target concept to be learned. Learning accuracy (LA) is defined as (n being the number of concept hypotheses for the target):

$$LA := \sum_{i \in \{1...n\}} \frac{LA_i}{n} \text{ with}$$

$$LA_i := \begin{cases} \frac{CP_i}{SP_i} & \text{if } FP_i = 0 \\ \frac{CP_i}{FP_i + DP_i} & \text{else} \end{cases}$$

SP_i specifies the length of the *shortest path* (in terms of the number of nodes being traversed) from the TOP node of the concept hierarchy to the maximally specific concept subsuming the instance to be learned in hypothesis i; CP_i specifies the length of the path from the TOP node to that concept node in hypothesis i which is *common* both to the shortest path (as defined above) and the actual path to the predicted concept (whether correct or not); FP_i specifies the length of the path from the TOP node to the predicted (in this case *false*) concept ($FP_i = 0$, if the prediction is correct), and DP_i denotes the node *distance* between the predicted false node and the most specific common concept (on the path from the TOP node to the predicted false node) still correctly subsuming the target in hypothesis i. Sample configurations for concrete LA values involving these parameters are depicted in Fig. 3, which illustrates a correct, yet too general prediction with $LA_i = .75$, while Fig. 4 contains a false prediction with $LA_i = .6$. Though the measure is sensitive to the depth of concept graphs, it produced adequate results in the technology domain we considered. As the graphs in knowledge bases for "natural" domains typically have an almost canonical depth that ranges between seven to ten nodes from the most general to the most specific concept, our measure seems to generalize to other domains as well.[3]

Given the LA measure from above, Table 3 and Table 4 illustrate how alternative concept hypotheses for ITOH-CI-8 develop in accuracy from one step to the other. The numbers in brackets in the column **Concept Hypotheses** indicate

---

[3]We tested the WORDNET lexical database (Fellbaum 1998), a common-sense ontology, in order to determine concept paths of maximal length. In the computer domain, the maximum path length amounts to eight nodes. For the entire ontology, the maximum path length of eleven nodes was found in the biology domain. The data were collected by one of our colleagues, Katja Markert.

Concept Hypotheses	LA –	LA TH	LA CB
PHYSICALOBJECT(176)	0.30	0.30	0.30
MENTALOBJECT(0)	0.16	0.16	0.16
INFORMATIONOBJECT(5)	0.16	0.16	0.16
MASSOBJECT(0)	0.16	0.16	0.16
NORM(3)	0.16	0.16	0.16
TECHNOLOGY(1)	0.16	0.16	0.16
MODE(5)	0.16	0.16	0.16
FEATURE(0)	0.16	0.16	0.16
	∅:0.18	∅:0.18	∅:0.18
Learning Step 1			
PRODUCT(136)	0.50	0.50	0.50
MENTALOBJECT(0)	0.16		
INFORMATIONOBJECT(5)	0.16		
MASSOBJECT(0)	0.16		
NORM(3)	0.16		
TECHNOLOGY(1)	0.16		
MODE(5)	0.16		
FEATURE(0)	0.16		
	∅:0.20	∅:0.50	∅:0.50
Learning Step 2			
COMPUTER(5)	0.50	0.50	
OUTPUTDEV(9)	0.80	0.80	0.80
STORAGEDEV(5)	0.55	0.55	0.55
INPUTDEV(2)	0.55	0.55	0.55
	∅:0.60	∅:0.60	∅:0.63
Learning Step 3			

Table 3: Learning Steps 1 to 3 for the Sample Text

for each hypothesized concept the number of concepts subsumed by it in the underlying knowledge base (cf. also our notion of learning rate, as introduced below); **LA CB** gives the accuracy rate for the full qualification calculus including threshold and credibility criteria, **LA TH** for threshold criteria only, while **LA –** depicts the accuracy values produced by the terminological reasoning component without incorporating any quality criteria. As can be read off from both tables, the full qualification calculus produces either the same or even more accurate results on average, equally many or fewer hypothesis spaces (indicated by the number of rows), and derives the correct prediction more rapidly (in step 6) than the less knowledgeable variants (in step 9).

The data also illustrate the continuous specialization of concept hypotheses achieved by the terminological classifier, e.g., from PHYSICALOBJECT in step 1 via PRODUCT in step 2 to OUTPUTDEVICE, PRINTER, and LASERPRINTER in step 3, 4, and 5, respectively. The overall learning accuracy – due to the learner's aggressive specialization strategy – may even temporarily decrease in the course of hypothesizing (e.g., from step 3 to 4 or step 5 to 6 for **LA –**, as well as for **LA TH**), but the learning accuracy value for the full qualification calculus (**LA CB**) always increases.

Fig. 5 depicts the learning accuracy curve for the entire data set (101 texts). We also have included the graph depicting the growth behavior of hypothesis spaces (Fig. 6). For both data sets, we distinguish again between the measurements for **LA –**, **LA TH** and **LA CB**. In Fig. 5, we start from LA values in the interval between 48% to 54% for **LA –**/**LA TH** and **LA CB**, respectively, in the first learning step, whereas the number of hypothesis spaces (**NH**) range between 6.2 and 4.5 (Fig. 6). In the final step, learning accuracy rises up from 79%, 83% to 87% for **LA –**, **LA TH** and **LA CB**, respectively, and the **NH** values reduce to 4.4, 3.6 and 2.5 for each of the three criteria, respectively.

Concept Hypotheses	LA –	LA TH	LA CB
NOTEBOOK(0)	0.43	0.43	
PORTABLE(0)	0.43	0.43	
PC(0)	0.43	0.43	
WORKSTATION(0)	0.43	0.43	
DESKTOP(0)	0.43	0.43	
PRINTER(3)	0.90	0.90	0.90
VISUALDEV(2)	0.66	0.66	0.66
LOUDSPEAKER(0)	0.66	0.66	0.66
PLOTTER(0)	0.66	0.66	0.66
RW-STORE(2)	0.50	0.50	0.50
RO-STORE(1)	0.50	0.50	0.50
MOUSE(0)	0.50	0.50	
KEYBOARD(0)	0.50	0.50	
	∅:0.54	∅:0.54	∅:0.65
Learning Step 4			
NOTEBOOK(0)	0.43	0.43	
PORTABLE(0)	0.43	0.43	
PC(0)	0.43	0.43	
WORKSTATION(0)	0.43	0.43	
DESKTOP(0)	0.43	0.43	
LASERPRINTER(0)	1.00	1.00	1.00
INKJETPRINTER(0)	0.75	0.75	0.75
NEEDLEPRINTER(0)	0.75	0.75	0.75
	∅:0.58	∅:0.58	∅:0.83
Learning Step 5			
NOTEBOOK(0)	0.43	0.43	
PORTABLE(0)	0.43	0.43	
PC(0)	0.43	0.43	
WORKSTATION(0)	0.43	0.43	
DESKTOP(0)	0.43	0.43	
LASERPRINTER(0)	1.00	1.00	1.00
	∅:0.53	∅:0.53	∅:1.00
Learning Step 6,7,8			
LASERPRINTER(0)	1.00	1.00	1.00
	∅:1.00	∅:1.00	∅:1.00
Learning Step 9			

Table 4: Learning Steps 4 to 9 for the Sample Text

The pure terminological reasoning machinery always achieves an inferior level of learning accuracy and generates more hypothesis spaces than the learner equipped with the qualification calculus. Also, the inclusion of conceptual criteria (**CB**) supplementing the linguistic criteria (**TH**) helps a lot to focus on the relevant hypothesis spaces and to further discriminate the valid hypotheses (on the range of 4% of precision). Note that an already significant plateau of accuracy is usually reached after the third step (*viz.* 67%, 73%, and 76% for **LA –**, **LA TH**, and **LA CB**, respectively, in Fig. 5; the corresponding numbers of hypothesis spaces being 6.1, 5.1, and 3.7 for **NH –**, **NH TH**, and **NH CB**, respectively, in Fig. 6). This indicates that our approach not only yields competitive accuracy rates (a mean of 87%) but also finds the most relevant distinctions in a very early phase of the learning process, i.e., it requires only a *few* examples.

Learning Rate

The learning accuracy focuses on the predictive power of the learning procedure. By considering a third type of measure, the *learning rate*, we supply data from the step-wise reduction of alternatives for the learning process. Fig. 7 depicts the mean number of transitively included concepts for all considered hypothesis spaces per learning step (each concept hypothesis denotes a concept which transitively subsumes various subconcepts). Note that the most general concept hypothesis, in our example, denotes OBJECT which currently includes 196 concepts. In general, we observed a

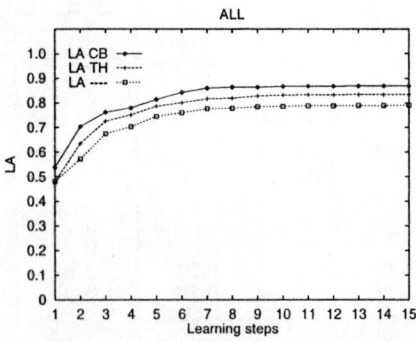
Figure 5: Learning Accuracy (LA)

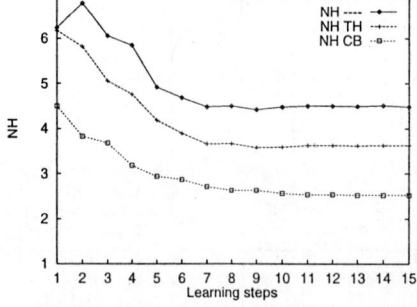
Figure 6: Number of Hypotheses (NH)

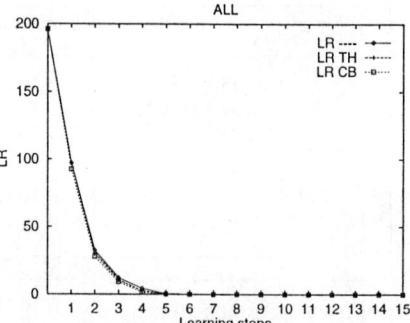
Figure 7: Learning Rate (LR)

strong negative slope of the curve for the learning rate. After the first step, slightly less than 50% of the included concepts are pruned (with 93, 94 and 97 remaining concepts for **LR CB**, **LR TH** and **LR –**, respectively). Again, learning step 3 is a crucial point for the reduction of the number of included concepts (ranging from 16 to 21 concepts). Summarizing this evaluation experiment, the quality-based learning system exhibits significant and valid reductions of the predicted concepts (up to two, on the average).

Related Work

Our approach bears a close relationship to the work of Granger (1977), Mooney (1987), Berwick (1989), Rau, Jacobs, & Zernik (1989), Gomez & Segami (1990), Hastings (1994), and Moorman & Ram (1996), who all aim at the automated learning of word meanings from context using a knowledge-intensive approach. But our work differs from theirs in that the need to cope with *several competing* concept hypotheses and to aim at a *reason-based selection* in terms of the *quality* of arguments is not an issue in these studies. Learning from real-world texts usually provides the learner with only sparse and fragmentary evidence such that multiple hypotheses are likely to be derived and a need for a hypothesis evaluation arises.

The work closest to ours has been carried out by Rau, Jacobs, & Zernik (1989) and Hastings (1994). They also generate concept hypotheses from linguistic and conceptual evidence. Unlike our approach, the selection of hypotheses depends only on an ongoing discrimination process based on the availability of these data but does not incorporate an inferencing scheme for reasoned hypothesis selection. The difference in learning performance for Rau *et al.*'s system – in the light of our evaluation study (cf. Fig. 5, final learning step) – amounts to 8%, considering the difference between **LA -** (plain terminological reasoning) and **LA CB** values (terminological metareasoning based on the qualification calculus). Similarly strong arguments hold for a comparison of our results with Hasting's (1994) approach at the precision dimension, with an even greater advantage for the full qualification calculus (39%) over terminological-style reasoning in the CAMILLE System (22%). Hence, our claim that we produce competitive results.

Note that the requirement to provide learning facilities for real-world text knowledge engineering also distinguishes our approach from the currently active field of information extraction (IE) (Appelt *et al.* 1993). The IE task is defined in terms of a *pre-fixed* set of templates which have to be instantiated (i.e., filled with factual knowledge items) in the course of text analysis. In particular, no new templates have to be created. This step would correspond to the procedure we described in this contribution.

In the field of knowledge engineering from texts, our system constitutes a major achievement through the complete automatization of the knowledge elicitation process (cf. also Gomez & Segami (1990)). Previous studies mainly dealt with that problem by either hand-coding the content of the textual documents (Skuce *et al.* 1985), or providing semi-automatic, interactive devices for text knowledge acquisition (Szpakowicz 1990), or using lexically oriented statistical approaches to text analysis (Shaw & Gaines 1987).

Conclusion

Knowledge-based systems provide powerful forms of reasoning, but it takes a lot of effort to equip them with the knowledge they need by means of manual knowledge engineering. In this paper, we have introduced an alternative solution based on the fully automatic processing of expository texts. This text knowledge engineering methodology is based on the incremental assignment and evaluation of the quality of linguistic and conceptual evidence for emerging concept hypotheses. No specialized learning algorithm is needed, since learning is a (meta)reasoning task carried out by the classifier of a terminological reasoning system. However, strong heuristic guidance for selecting between plausible hypotheses comes from the different quality criteria. Our experimental data indicate that, given these heuristics, we achieve a high degree of pruning of the search space for hypotheses in very early phases of the learning cycle.

The procedure for text knowledge engineering was tested on a medium-sized knowledge base for the information technology domain. The choice of a single domain reduces the number of possible conceptual ambiguities when concept hypotheses are created, in particular when compared with common-sense ontologies such as WORDNET (Fellbaum 1998). However, one might envisage partitioning mechanisms in order to control the activation of reasonable portions of a knowledge base and thus escape from a prohibitive explosion of the number of alternatives to be pursued.

Actually, we also like to contrast our text knowledge engineering approach to standard machine learning algorithms like ID3, k-nearest neighbor and Bayesian classifers. Initial evidence from current experiments indicates that either the number of hypotheses they generate become prohibitively large, even in the medium-sized knowledge base we use (especially for k-nearest neighbor), or the learning accuracy drops down very seriously (e.g., for ID3). The outcome of these experiments might clarify the usefulness of standard ML algorithms for the text knowledge engineering task.

It should also be obvious that the accuracy of our text knowledge engineering procedure is dependent on the input supplied by the parser. This is particularly true of false semantic interpretations (cf. Table 1), which directly misguide the reasoning process of the learner. Missing data, however, are far less harmful, since the knowledge acquisition procedure needs only a few examples to narrow down the search space, as has become evident from the evaluation study.

In our experiments, learning was restricted to the case of a single unknown concept in the entire text. Generalizing to n unknown concepts can be considered from two perspectives. When hypotheses of another target item are generated and assessed relative to an already given base item, no effect occurs. When, however, two targets (i.e., two unknown items) have to be related, then the number of hypotheses that have to be taken into account is equal to the product of the number of hypothesis spaces associated with each of them. In the future, we intend to study such test cases, too. Fortunately, the number of hypothesis spaces decreases rapidly (cf. Fig. 6) as does the learning rate (cf. Fig. 7) so that the learning system should remain within feasible bounds.

Acknowledgements. We would like to thank our colleagues in the CLIF group for fruitful discussions and instant support, in particular Joe Bush who polished the text as a native speaker. K. Schnattinger is supported by a grant from DFG (Ha 2097/3-1).

References

Aha, D.; Kibler, D.; and Albert, M. 1991. Instance-based learning algorithms. *Machine Learning* 6:37–66.

Appelt, D.; Hobbs, J.; Bear, J.; Israel, D.; and Tyson, M. 1993. FASTUS: a finite-state processor for information extraction from real-world text. In *IJCAI'93 – Proceedings 13th International Joint Conference on Artificial Intelligence.*, 1172–1178. San Mateo, CA: Morgan Kaufmann.

Berwick, R. 1989. Learning word meanings from examples. In Waltz, D., ed., *Semantic Structures. Advances in Natural Language Processing.* L. Erlbaum. 89–124.

Buchanan, B.; Barstow, D.; Bechtal, R.; Bennett, J.; Clancey, W.; Kulikowski, C.; Mitchell, T.; and Waterman, D. 1983. Constructing an expert system. In Hayes-Roth, F.; Waterman, D.; and Lenat, D., eds., *Building Expert Systems.* Reading, MA: Addison-Wesley. 127–167.

Fellbaum, C., ed. 1998. *WordNet: An Electronic Lexical Database.* Cambridge, MA: MIT Press.

Gomez, F., and Segami, C. 1990. Knowledge acquisition from natural language for expert systems based on classification problem-solving methods. *Knowledge Acquisition* 2(2):107–128.

Granger, R. 1977. FOUL-UP: a program that figures out meanings of words from context. In *IJCAI'77 – Proc. of the 5th Intl. Joint Conf. on Artificial Intelligence.*, 172–178.

Hahn, U.; Klenner, M.; and Schnattinger, K. 1996. Learning from texts: a terminological metareasoning perspective. In Wermter, S.; Riloff, E.; and Scheler, G., eds., *Connectionist, Statistical and Symbolic Approaches to Learning for Natural Language Processing.* Springer. 453–468.

Hahn, U.; Schacht, S.; and Bröker, N. 1994. Concurrent, object-oriented natural language parsing: the PARSETALK model. *International Journal of Human-Computer Studies* 41(1/2):179–222.

Hastings, P. 1994. *Automatic Acquisition of Word Meaning from Context.* Ph.D. Dissertation, Computer Science and Engineering Department, University of Michigan.

MacGregor, R. 1994. A description classifier for the predicate calculus. In *AAAI'94 – Proceedings 12th National Conference on Artificial Intelligence.*, 213–220. Menlo Park, CA: AAAI Press & Cambridge, MA: MIT Press.

Mooney, R. 1987. Integrated learning of words and their underlying concepts. In *CogSci'87 – Proceedings of the 9th Annual Conference of the Cognitive Science Society*, 974–978. Hillsdale, NJ: L. Erlbaum.

Moorman, K., and Ram, A. 1996. The role of ontology in creative understanding. In *CogSci'96 – Proceedings of the 18th Annual Conference of the Cognitive Science Society*, 98–103. Mahwah, NJ: L. Erlbaum.

Morik, K.; Wrobel, S.; Kietz, J.-U.; and Emde, W. 1993. *Knowledge Acquisition and Machine Learning: Theory, Methods, and Applications.* London: Academic Press.

Nirenburg, S., and Raskin, V. 1987. The subworld concept lexicon and the lexicon management system. *Computational Linguistics* 13(3/4):276–289.

Rau, L.; Jacobs, P.; and Zernik, U. 1989. Information extraction and text summarization using linguistic knowledge acquisition. *Information Processing & Management* 25(4):419–428.

Schnattinger, K., and Hahn, U. 1996. A terminological qualification calculus for preferential reasoning under uncertainty. In *KI'96 – Proceedings 20th Annual German Conference on Artificial Intelligence*, 349–362. Springer.

Shaw, M., and Gaines, B. 1987. KITTEN: knowledge initiation and transfer tools for experts and novices. *International Journal of Man-Machine Studies* 27(3):251–280.

Skuce, D.; Matwin, S.; Tauzovich, B.; Oppacher, F.; and Szpakowicz, S. 1985. A logic-based knowledge source system for natural language documents. *Data & Knowledge Engineering* 1(3):201–231.

Stefik, M. 1995. *Introduction to Knowledge Systems.* San Francisco, CA: Morgan Kaufmann.

Szpakowicz, S. 1990. Semi-automatic acquisition of conceptual structures from technical texts. *International Journal on Man-Machine Studies* 33:385–397.

Woods, W., and Schmolze, J. 1992. The KL-ONE family. *Computers & Mathematics with Applications* 23:133–177.

Answering Questions for an Organization Online

Vladimir A. Kulyukin   Kristian J. Hammond   Robin D. Burke

Intelligent Information Laboratory,
Department of Computer Science,
University of Chicago
1100 E. 58th St., Chicago, IL 60637
kulyukin@cs.uchicago.edu

Abstract

The World Wide Web continues to challenge organizations to make online access to their expertise convenient for their clients. One means of expertise access that many clients find convenient in everyday life is asking natural language questions of the organization. To support it online, we developed an approach to building organization-embedded question-answering intermediaries, called Information Exchange systems. These systems use their knowledge of the organization's structure to answer the clients' questions and to acquire new expertise from the organization's experts. Our approach uses techniques of hierarchical and predictive indexing, combined term weighting, abstraction-based retrieval, and negative evidence acquisition. We illustrate our approach with the Chicago Information Exchange system, an Information Exchange application embedded in one university's computer science department.

Introduction

The World Wide Web (WWW) continues to challenge organizations to make online access to their expertise convenient for their clients. Standard approaches to expertise access such as query languages, knowledge-intensive natural language understanders, and intelligent browsers may be inappropriate for organizations that must answer questions from diverse groups of clients. A query language is a skill that many clients may not possess nor have the time to acquire. A knowledge-intensive approach demands expensive knowledge engineering and may not scale up to multiple domains. An intelligent browser is inappropriate for clients whose questions are not expressible with the available interface options.

Our approach to online access to an organization's expertise is to employ *organization-embedded question answering*. A question-answering system is a search intermediary between the organization's clients and experts. The intermediary is organization-embedded inasmuch as it knows the organization's units and their areas of expertise. The clients are provided with a natural language interface to the organization. The intermediary answers their questions by retrieving answers to similar questions or by transferring them to relevant experts. As the experts answer the incoming questions, their answers are stored for future use.

The Problem

We implemented our approach in the Chicago Information Exchange system (CIE), an Information Exchange system (IES) embedded in one university's computer science department. The class of problems addressed by CIE is best described through an example:

> X is a CS undergraduate enrolled in CS115, which uses Scheme. X finds the textbook for the class terse and wants to know if there is another book that he could read, too. How does the CS Department make sure that X gets the answer quickly? How can it see to it that once the answer is available it can be reused?

Our objective is to develop a technology for building question-answering systems that organizations can easily embed into their information infrastructures. We see this technology as applicable in organizations that receive questions on large sets of topics via the WWW.

An Outline of a Solution

Each IES goes through two stages of deployment: *organization modelling* and *expertise acquisition*. Organization modelling relies on the fact that many organizations are structured as single- or multiple-inheritance hierarchies of units (Solomon 1997; Simon 1976). Since each unit handles a specific area of expertise, the collective expertise of the organization is represented as a hierarchy of topics, each of which corresponds to one such area. Figure 1 gives part of CIE's hierarchy of topics. During the expertise acquisition stage, the organization's experts open *information accounts* under the topics about which they want to answer questions. Opening an information account is a protocol by which an expert becomes known to the system through a brief online interview.

Copyright ©1998, American Association for Artificial Intelligence (www.aaai.org). All rights reserved.

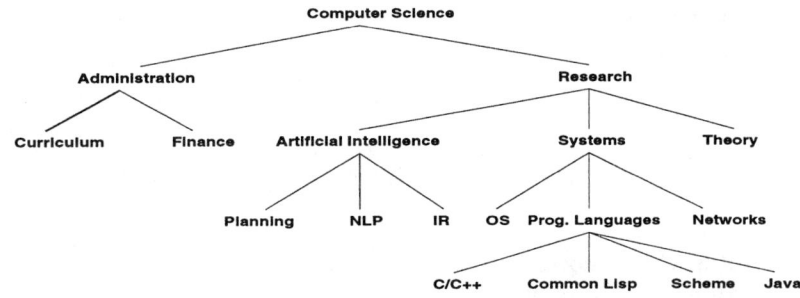

Figure 1: CIE's Hierarchy of Topics

An expert is described by three free-text documents: the description of expertise on the topic from the information account, the collection of question-answer pairs (Q&A's), and the collection of questions classified by the expert as nonrelevant. A topic is described by its subtopics and experts.

The vector space retrieval model is used (Salton and McGill 1983). A collection of documents is a vector space whose dimensions are the documents' terms. Each document is a vector of the weights assigned to its terms. A client's question is a vector in the same space. The document vectors closest to it are retrieved. In addition, several indexing and retrieval techniques are essential to the Information Exchange architecture:

- **Hierarchical Indexing:** The system builds its memory of the organization so as to be searchable by questions. The hierarchy of topics and experts is turned into a hierarchy of vector spaces. Each node in the hierarchy becomes a vector in the space consisting of the vectors of the node's siblings. A topic becomes a vector containing the weights of the terms from its subtopics and experts. An expert becomes a vector containing the weights of the terms from the Q&A collection and the expertise description. Each Q&A becomes a vector containing the weights of the terms from the question, the answer, and the terms found during predictive indexing. Each collection of nonrelevant questions becomes a vector space associated with its expert.

- **Predictive Indexing:** The clients and experts often use different terms to describe the same content. When an expert answers a question, the related terms from a general purpose semantic network are added to the Q&A vector during indexing. If a related term is seen in a question, it triggers the Q&A's retrieval. Information retrieval (IR) researchers proposed several term expansion techniques for similar purposes (Voorhees 1994; Salton and Lesk 1971). Predictive indexing is different insomuch as it is completely automated, goes beyond synonymy and inclusion, and is not based on a single-domain thesaurus.

- **Combined Term Weighting:** A term's weight combines its semantic and statistical properties. Our semantic metric uses the term's part of speech, polysemy, and the closeness of its relation to a term in an expert's question. Our statistical metrics rely on the term's frequency distribution in the collection (Salton and McGill 1983) and its pattern of occurrence in the documents (Bookstein, Klein, and Raita 1998).

- **Abstraction-Based Retrieval:** The system seeks to imitate the behavior of a human search intermediary whose goal is to answer a client's question on the level of abstraction comfortable for the client. The question "How is case-based reasoning used in planning?" is answered on the level of artificial intelligence (AI) by the question "What is case-based reasoning?" whose answer mentions planning in passing. Alternatively, it is answered on the level of planning by the question "What is a case-based planner?" whose answer contains a detailed discussion of case-based planning.

- **Negative Evidence Acquisition:** Relevance feedback is used in IR systems to adjust the term weights in document vectors in response to clients' evaluations (Brauen 1971). But, relevance feedback requires multiple iterations before the term weights improve significantly. Since the experts do not want to receive the same nonrelevant question repeatedly, the experts are indexed by the questions they specify as nonrelevant. When there is a match on a nonrelevant question, the expert is no longer considered. Negative evidence acquistion complements relevance feedback and allows the system to learn from its failures (Hammond 1989).

How CIE Works

CIE is built on four assumptions about indexing and retrieval of free-text expertise. First, expertise on a topic is a collection of Q&A's (Kulyukin, Hammond, and Burke 1996). Second, questions are used as indices into Q&A collections. Third, no answers are generated from scratch: the old answers are reused; the new answers are obtained from the experts when needed. Fourth, the question-answering environment is friendly.

The first three assumptions make CIE a case-based retriever (Kolodner 1993): a Q&A is a case codified for reuse; a question is a cue from the environment that triggers the retrieval of an answer. The fourth assumption allows CIE to trust feedback from its clients and experts.

Computation of Terms

The terms are computed from the expertise descriptions, Q&A's, and nonrelevant questions. To convert an expertise description, a Q&A's answer, or a nonrelevant question into a term vector, CIE removes from it the terms in its stoplist and applies a greedy morphological analysis to the nonstoplisted words. Our stoplist extends the stoplist derived by Francis and Kucera (1982).

The morphological analysis is based on the morphological component of WordNet, a semantic network of English words and phrases (Miller 1995).[2] The goal is to convert a word to its base form, e.g., the base of "computers" is "computer." The analysis is greedy, because it stops as soon as a conversion rule obtains a base form, which is tagged with the part of speech whose conversion rule obtained it. The parts of speech are nouns, verbs, adjectives, and adverbs. If all rules fail, the word is tagged as a noun.

Computing terms from the question of a Q&A is different. To do the predictive indexing of the question, CIE uses a spreading activation technique (Cohen and Kjeldsen 1987) based on WordNet. WordNet consists of four subnets organized by the four parts of speech. Each subnet has its own relations. For example, nouns have antonymy, the *isa* relation, and three *part-of* relations. WordNet's basic unit is *a synset*, which contains words and phrases interchangeable in a context, e.g., "computer" and "data_processor."

The spreading activation routine uses all four parts of speech, but for each part of speech a subset of relations is used. For nouns, *isa* is used: "machine" is a "computer." For verbs, *entailment* is used: "to limp" entails "to walk." For adjectives, *similarity* is used: "wet" is similar to "watery." No relation is used for adverbs.

The activation routine takes a word and a depth integer specifying how many links away from the origin word the activation is to spread. Each term found during the spread is annotated with its part of speech and the depth at which it was found. Integers 1, 2, 3, and 4 encode nouns, verbs, adjectives, and adverbs, respectively. Thus, "device12" means that "device" is a noun found at depth 2. The origin word's depth is 0. Terms like "device12" are called *annotated* or *a-terms*.

One advantage of predictive indexing is that no activation is spread during retrieval. Instead, the retriever does the *depth expansion* of each a-term in the client's question. For example, if the question contains "machine10" and the depth is 2, "machine11" and "machine12" are added to the question vector, provided that they are dimensions of the current vector space. If an expert's question contains "computer10," and "machine11" is added to the Q&A vector during predic-

---
[2] WordNet is a trademark of Princeton University.

534   Information Extraction

tive indexing, the question vector and the Q&A vector match on "machine11."

Computation of Term Weights

The semantic weight of an a-term a is computed by the WordNet weight function, $\omega_{wn}(a, r)$, given by $\omega_{wn}(a, r) = \rho(a)/(\pi(a)r^{\delta(a)})$, where $\rho(a)$ assigns an intrinsic weight to each part of speech: 1.0 to nouns, 0.75 to verbs, and 0.5 to adjectives and adverbs; $\pi(a)$ gives a's polysemy; $\delta(a)$ gives a's depth; the rate of decay, r, indicates how much a's weight depreciates with depth. Thus, a's semantic weight is inversely related to its polysemy and its distance from the activation's origin.

The statistical weight combines two metrics. The first metric is known as *tfidf* (Salton and McGill 1983). Let D be the total number of documents in a collection $\mathcal{C}$. Let $\phi(a, \kappa_i)$, $1 \leq i \leq D$, be a's frequency of occurrence in the i-th document κ_i. Put $\tilde{d}_i = 1$ if $\phi(a, \kappa_i) > 0$, and 0, otherwise. Put $D_a = \sum_{i=1}^{D} \tilde{d}_i$. For a's *tfidf* weight in κ_i, put $\omega_{tfidf}(a, \kappa_i) = \phi(a, \kappa_i) log(D/D_a)$. The second metric is based on *condensation clustering* (CC) (Bookstein, Klein, and Raita 1998). CC values indexing terms by their patterns of occurrence in a sequence of textual units, e.g., sentences, paragraphs, pages, chapters, and documents. Assuming the sequence proceeds from topic to topic, the terms pertinent to a topic cluster in the units that cover it, while terms that do not bear content appear to be randomly distributed over the units.

Put $\tau(a, \mathcal{C}) = \sum_{i=1}^{D} \phi(a, \kappa_i)$. For the expectation of D_a, put $E(D_a) = DE(\tilde{d}_i)$. Since $\forall (1 \leq i \leq D)(\tilde{d}_i \in \{0, 1\})$, $E(\tilde{d}_i) = 1 - (1 - 1/D)^{\tau(a, \mathcal{C})}$. For a's CC weight in $\mathcal{C}$, put $\omega_{cc}(a, \mathcal{C}) = D_a/E(D_a)$. When a's weight is computed with respect to κ_i, a's local importance is factored in through the product of $\omega_{cc}(a, \mathcal{C})$ and $\phi(a, \kappa_i)$. If a bears content, $\omega_{cc}(a, \mathcal{C})$ is likely to be smaller than 1. Hence, for a's CC weight in κ_i, put $\omega_{tfcc}(a, \kappa_i, \mathcal{C}, \theta) = -\phi(a, \kappa_i) log(\omega_{cc}(a, \mathcal{C}))$ if $1 - D_a/E(D_a) > \theta$, and 0, otherwise, where $0 \leq \theta < 1$. Let α_1, α_2, and α_3 denote how much importance is given to each metric. The total weight of a in D is given by $\omega_{wn}^{\alpha_1}(\omega_{tfidf}^{\alpha_2} + \omega_{tfcc}^{\alpha_3})$.

Retrieval

Given a client's question, the retriever starts in the top vector space. The client's question Q is turned into a vector of term weights $\vec{Q} = (q_1, ..., q_n)$, where n is the dimension of the current space and each q_i is the weight of an a-term from the question or an a-term added during the depth expansion. The similarity between $\vec{Q}$ and a vector $\vec{V} = (v_1, ..., v_n)$ is the cosine of the angle between them. The similarities between $\vec{Q}$ and the vectors in the current space are thresholded.

If the top retrieved vector is a topic vector, the search proceeds into the vector space under it, which becomes the current vector space. If it is an expert vector, it goes into the expert's nonrelevant collection. If no similarities are found with any nonrelevant questions, the retriever iterates through the Q&A vectors. If there is a similarity with a nonrelevant question, the expert is no longer considered. Thus, the memory of past failures helps the retriever not to make the same mistake twice.

When several vectors match, the client is asked for his or her search preferences. If the client is unable to determine the relevancy of a topic, the client can examine the description of the topic and the list of experts on it. To determine the relevancy of an expert, the client can see the expert's information account under a specific topic. The client can also search another topic or e-mail his or her question to an expert. Thus, in addition to finding answers to their questions, the clients get insights into the organization's information infrastructure.

The retrieval from an expert's Q&A space is done with the relevance feedback technique similar to the one proposed by Aalbersberg (1992). The Q&A's are retrieved one by one. At each retrieval, the new question vector is formed from the previous question vector and the vector of the previously retrieved Q&A. If the Q&A was relevant, the weights of its terms are slightly increased in the new question vector; if it was nonrelevant, they are slightly decreased. Our technique differs from Aalbersberg's in that the number of negative interactions that the client can have with the retriever is limited. If the client is not satisfied within a certain number of iterations, the client is advised to browse the Q&A collection, contact the expert, or move the search elsewhere. One advantage of this approach is that the retriever knows when to give up.

Upon receiving a client's question, the expert can tell the system that it is nonrelevant, in which case the system adjusts its weights both locally and globally. The local adjustment is made by adding the question vector to the nonrelevant collection. The global adjustment is made by modifying the weights in the vectors on the path from the root down to the expert vector. Since there was a retrieval failure, the idea is to reward the differences between the question vector and the path vectors and to punish their similarities. For the question vector $\vec{Q}$ and each path vector $\vec{H}$ the weights of the common terms are decreased, while the weights of the different ones are increased. This technique is similar to the one proposed by Brauen (1971). However, Brauen's technique takes no action when the term is present in the question vector and absent in a document vector. In our case, these terms are added to the expert's nonrelevant collection.

After the expert answers the client's question, the new Q&A is added to the expert's Q&A collection and then e-mailed to the client. The terms in the Q&A and the terms found during predictive indexing become new dimensions of the expert's Q&A space where the Q&A vector of their weights is added. During the next hierarchical indexing, these terms become dimensions in each vector space that is traversed from the root to the expert vector.

Evaluation

Recall and precision are two evaluation techniques used in many IR systems (Salton and McGill 1983). Recall is the percentage of relevant documents retrieved by a client's question; precision is the percentage of the retrieved documents that are relevant. The information seeking behavior that these measures capture is that of a client who is interested in retrieving all relevant answers.

We observed that the information seeking behavior of the CIE clients is different. A typical CIE client wants to find the first relevant answer fast. One way to measure this is to count the number of interactions the client has with the system before the answer is found. For each test question, we compute the number of interactions that occur as the system searches for the first relevant answer. The number of interactions is averaged over all test questions. Hence, the measure is called the *average number of interactions* (ANI).

We evaluated CIE's ANI with 105 questions about Common Lisp and AI. The questions were obtained from 20 CS undergraduates. Each undergraduate was asked to write 10 questions about Common Lisp and AI that he or she would like to submit to CIE. Out of these 200 questions, a human judge selected the questions that had at least one relevant answer in the system's Q&A collections. In computing term weights, θ was set to .0, α_1 was set to 1.0, α_2 and α_3 were each set to .5.

We first measured the number of interactions it takes a client to find the first relevant answer. Five subjects with a CS background were each given a random sample of size 10 taken without replacement from the test questions. For each question the subjects reported the number of interactions they went through to find the first relevant answer. The following interactions were counted: submitting a question, selecting a topic from multiple topics, requesting a topic's description, selecting an expert from multiple experts, requesting an expert's expertise on a topic, and requesting another Q&A to be retrieved.

The results are summarized in Figure 2. We explain the differences in ANI by the differences in the term ambiguity of different samples. The questions given to the fourth subject had the lowest term ambiguity because most terms identified the correct topic uniquely. For example, in the question "How does garbage collection work in Lisp?", the terms "garbage10" and "lisp10" led to the retrieval of the vectors on the path to the topic of Common Lisp. The questions given to the second subject had the highest term ambiguity, because many terms were indicative of multiple topics. For instance, the terms of the question "Do Lisp process schedulers use the round robin algorithm?" retrieved the topics of Common Lisp, Operating Systems, and Theory. Thus, the second subject had to interact with the system on multiple occasions to clarify her search preferences.

We also experimented with the relative importance of ω_{tfidf} and ω_{tfcc} to see whether the results would

subject	1	2	3	4	5
ani	1.2	3.2	2.5	1.0	3.1

Figure 2: Average Number of Navigation Interactions

Num. of Q&A's/α_2, α_3	20	40	60	80	100	120	140
$\alpha_2 = .7; \alpha_3 = .3$	3.1	2.9	7.5	7.7	8.1	8.6	8.2
$\alpha_2 = .3; \alpha_3 = .7$	6.4	7.2	4.3	4.1	4.7	4.4	4.3

Figure 3: Average Number of Q&A Interactions

confirm our hypothesis that in small collections ω_{tfidf} is a better discriminator than ω_{tfcc}. We chose a Q&A collection of 140 Q&A's about Common Lisp and AI written by a CIE expert. To simulate a dynamically growing collection, we split it into Q&A subsets whose cardinalities were multiples of 20: the first 20 questions, the first 40 questions, etc. For each Q&A subset, we chose the subset of the 105 test questions answered in it. For each question, an ordered list of matches was computed, and the number of nonrelevant Q&A's before the first relevant one was counted. The number of nonrelevant Q&A's was averaged for every Q&A set. The activation depth was 2; α_1 was 1.0. The values of α_2 and α_3 were set to .7 and .3, respectively, in the first experiment, and to .3 and .7, respectively, in the second.

The ANI numbers are given in Figure 3. The table shows that on collections of 20 and 40 Q&A's the metric that valued ω_{tfidf} higher than ω_{tfcc} achieved smaller ANI's, while the metric valuing ω_{tfcc} higher than ω_{tfidf} was more successful on larger collections.

Discussion

How to access online expertise with question answering is an area of active research both in AI and IR (Burke et al. 1997; Kupiec 1993). We share with this research the belief that a good way to make online access to expertise convenient for clients is to allow them to use their language skills. However, our research objective is different. We focus on developing a deployable question-answering technology that organizations can benefit from today.

CIE has much in common with FAQ Finder, a system that provides a natural language interface to the Usenet files of frequently asked questions (Burke et al. 1997). But, while the two systems are similar, because they both combine semantic and statistical techniques in indexing and retrieval, they differ in several respects. CIE predicts indexing features during indexing; FAQ Finder computes them during retrieval. Spreading activation in CIE uses all four parts of speech and several semantic relations; spreading activation in FAQ Finder is restricted to the *isa* relations among nouns. The Information Exchange architecture allows CIE to continuously integrate feedback from the clients and the experts; FAQ Finder does not utilize users' evaluations. CIE treats failures as opportunities to acquire new expertise; FAQ Finder has no explicit notion of failure.

Our approach has its closest precedent in retrievers of case-based reasoning (CBR) systems (Kolodner 1993; Hammond 1989). A CBR system solves new problems by retrieving solutions to similar problems solved in the past. CIE answers new questions by retrieving answers to similar questions answered previously. One unique feature of CIE is that it is a social agent embedded in a real organization (Kulyukin 1998). Its job is to service two user groups with different interests: the clients who are interested in finding fast answers and the experts who want to reduce their question-answering burden. CIE achieves its objective by allowing its memory of the organization to be driven by continuous feedback from its environment.

Conclusion

We presented an approach to building organization-embedded question-answering systems. We outlined the Information Exchange architecture that underlies these systems. One such system is CIE, an Information Exchange application embedded in one university's computer science department. CIE provides clients with online access to the department's expertise by answering their natural language questions. Instead of generating answers from scratch, CIE retrieves the answers to similar questions answered before. When the retrieved answers fail, CIE solicits new answers from the organization's experts. We presented a new metric for computing term weights that uses semantic and statistical properties of terms. We evaluated the metric in several experiments.

Acknowledgments

The authors would like to express their profound gratitude to Dr. Abraham Bookstein of the University of Chicago's Center for Information and Language Studies for his help with several drafts of this paper. They would also like to thank the three anonymous reviewers for their insightful and constructive comments.

References

Aalbersberg, I. J. 1992. Incremental Relevance Feedback. In Proceedings of the 15th Annual International SIGIR Conference, 11-21.

Bookstein, A.; Klein, S. T.; and Raita, T. 1998. Clumping Properties of Content-Bearing Words. *Journal of the American Society for Information Science* 49(2):102-114.

Brauen, T. L. 1971. Document Vector Modification. In G. Salton, editor, *The SMART Retrieval System: Experiments in Automatic Document Processing*, 456-484. Englewood Cliffs, NJ: Prentice-Hall, Inc.

Burke, R. D.; Hammond, K. J.; Kulyukin, V.; Lytinen, S. L.; Tomuro, N.; and Schoenberg, S. 1997. Question Answering from Frequently Asked Question Files: Experiences with the FAQ Finder System. *AI Magazine* 18(2):57-66.

Cohen, P. R., and Kjeldsen, R. 1987. Information Retrieval by Constrained Spreading Activation in Semantic Networks. *Information Processing & Management* 23:255-268.

Francis, W., and Kucera, H. 1982. *Frequency Analysis of English Usage.* New York: Houghton Mufflin.

Hammond, K. J. 1989. *Case-Based Planning: Viewing Planning as a Memory Task.* San Diego, CA: Academic Press, Inc.

Kolodner, J. 1993. *Case-Based Reasoning.* San Mateo, CA: Morgan Kaufmann.

Kulyukin, V. 1998. An Interactive and Collaborative Approach to Answering Questions for an Organization. In Proceedings of the ASIS-98 Mid Year Conference.

Kulyukin, V.; Hammond, K.; and Burke, R. 1996. Automated Analysis of Structured Online Documents. In Proceedings of the AAAI-96 Workshop on Internet-Based Information Systems.

Kupiec, J. 1993. MURAX: A Robust Linguistic Approach for Question Answering Using an On-line Encyclopedia. In Proceedings of the 16th International SIGIR Conference.

Miller, G. A. 1995. WordNet: A Lexical Database for English. *Communications of the ACM* 38(11):39-41.

Salton, G., and Lesk, M. E. 1971. Computer Evaluation of Indexing and Text Processing. In G. Salton, editor, *The SMART Retrieval System: Experiments in Automatic Document Processing*, 143-180. Englewood Cliffs, NJ: Prentice-Hall, Inc.

Salton, G., and McGill, M. 1983. *Introduction to Modern Information Retrieval.* New York: McGraw-Hill.

Simon, H. A. 1976. *Administrative Behavior: A Study of Decision-Making Processes in Administrative Organizations.* 3rd ed. New York: The Free Press.

Solomon, P. 1997. Discovering Information Behavior in Sense Making: III. The Person. *Journal of the American Society for Information Science* 48(12):1127-1138.

Voorhees, E. M. 1994. Query Expansion Using Lexical-Semantic Relations. In Proceedings of ACM SIGIR Conference.

Integrated Artificial Intelligence Systems

BIG: A Resource-Bounded Information Gathering Agent [*][†]

Victor Lesser   Bryan Horling   Frank Klassner   Anita Raja
Thomas Wagner   Shelley XQ. Zhang

Computer Science Department
University of Massachusetts
Amherst, MA 01003

Abstract

Effective information gathering on the WWW is a complex task requiring planning, scheduling, text processing, and interpretation-style reasoning about extracted data to resolve inconsistencies and to refine hypotheses about the data. This paper describes the rationale, architecture, and implementation of a next generation information gathering system – a system that integrates several areas of AI research under a single research umbrella. The goal of this system is to exploit the vast number of information sources available today on the NII including a growing number of digital libraries, independent news agencies, government agencies, as well as human experts providing a variety of services. The large number of information sources and their different levels of accessibility, reliability and associated costs present a complex information gathering coordination problem. Our solution is an information gathering agent, BIG, that plans to gather information to support a decision process, reasons about the resource tradeoffs of different possible gathering approaches, extracts information from both unstructured and structured documents, and uses the extracted information to refine its search and processing activities.

Introduction

The vast amount of information available today on the World Wide Web (WWW) has great potential to improve the quality of decisions and the productivity of consumers. However, the WWW's large number of information sources and their different levels of accessibility, reliability and associated costs present human decision makers with a complex information gathering planning problem that is too difficult to solve without high-level filtering of information. In many cases, manual browsing through even a limited portion of the *relevant* information obtainable through advancing information retrieval (IR) and information extraction (IE) technologies (Callan, Croft, & Harding 1992; Larkey & Croft 1996; Cowie & Lehnert 1996; Lehnert & Sundheim 1991) is no longer effective. The time/quality/cost tradeoffs offered by the collection of information sources and the dynamic nature of the environment lead us to conclude that the user cannot (and should not) serve as the detailed controller of the information gathering (IG) process. Our solution to this problem is to integrate different AI technologies, namely scheduling, planning, text processing, and interpretation problem solving, into a single information gathering agent, BIG (resource-Bounded Information Gathering), that can take the role of the human information gatherer.

Information Gathering as Interpretation

Our approach to the IG problem is based on two observations. The first observation is that a significant portion of human IG is itself an intermediate step in a much larger *decision-making process*. For example, a person preparing to buy a car may search the Web for data to assist in the decision process, e.g., find out what car models are available, crash test results, dealer invoice prices, reviews and reliability statistics. In this information search process, the human gatherer first *plans* to gather information and reasons, perhaps at a superficial level, about the time/quality/cost trade-offs of different possible gathering actions before actually gathering information. For example, the gatherer may know that Microsoft CarPoint site has detailed and varied information on the models but that it is slow, relative to the Kelley Blue Book site, which has less varied information. Accordingly, a gatherer pressed for time may choose to browse the Kelley site over CarPoint, whereas a gatherer with unconstrained resources may choose to browse-and-wait for information from the slower CarPoint site. Human gatherers also typically use information learned during the search to refine and recast the search process; perhaps while looking for data on the new Honda Accord a human gatherer would come across a positive review of the Toyota Camry and would then broaden the search to include the Camry. Thus the human-centric process is both top-down and bottom-up, structured, but also opportunistic. The final result of this semi-structured search process is a decision or a suggestion of which product to purchase, accompanied by the extracted information and raw supporting documents.

The second observation that shapes our solution is that WWW-based IG is an instance of the *interpretation problem*. Interpretation is the process of constructing high-level models (e.g. product descriptions) from low-level data (e.g. raw documents) using feature-extraction methods that can produce evidence that is incomplete (e.g. requested documents are unavailable or product prices are not found) or inconsistent (e.g. different documents provide different prices for the

---

[*] Copyright (c) 1998, American Association for Artificial Intelligence (www.aaai.org). All rights reserved.

[†] This material is based upon work supported by the Department of Commerce, the Library of Congress, and the National Science Foundation under Grant No. EEC-9209623, and by the National Science Foundation under Grant No.s IRI-9523419 and IRI-9634938, and the Department of the Navy and Office of the Chief of Naval Research, under Grant No. N00014-95-1-1198. The content of the information does not necessarily reflect the position or the policy of the Government or the National Science Foundation and no official endorsement should be inferred.

same product). Coming from disparate sources of information of varying quality, these pieces of uncertain evidence must be carefully combined in a well-defined manner to provide support for the interpretation models under consideration.

In recasting IG as an interpretation problem, we face a search problem characterized by a generally combinatorially explosive state space. In the IG task, as in other interpretation problems, it is impossible to perform an exhaustive search to gather information on a particular subject, or even in many cases to determine the total number of instances (e.g. particular word processing programs) of the general subject (e.g. word processing) that is being investigated. Consequently, any solution to this IG problem needs to support reasoning about tradeoffs among resource constraints (e.g. the decision must be made in 1 hour), the quality of the selected item, and the quality of the decision process (e.g. comprehensiveness of search, effectiveness of IE methods usable within specified time limits). Because of the need to conserve time, it is important for an interpretation-based IG system to be able to save and exploit information about pertinent objects learned from earlier forays into the WWW. Additionally, we argue that an IG solution needs to support *constructive problem solving*, in which potential answers (e.g. models of products) to a user's query are incrementally built up from features extracted from raw documents and compared for consistency or suitability against other partially-completed answers – and the number of potential answers is not known *a priori*.

In connection with this incremental model-building process, an interpretation-based IG problem solution must also support sophisticated scheduling to achieve *interleaved* data-driven and expectation-driven processing. Processing for interpretation must be driven by expectations of what is reasonable, but, expectations in turn must be influenced by what is found in the data. For example, during a search to find information on word processors for Windows95, with the goal of recommending some package to purchase, an agent finding Excel in a review article that also contains Word 5.0 might conclude based on IE-derived expectations that Excel is a competitor word processor. However, scheduling of methods to resolve the uncertainties stemming from Excel's missing features would lead to additional gathering for Excel, which in turn would associate Excel with spreadsheet features and would thus change the expectations about Excel (and drop it from the search when enough of the uncertainty is resolved). Where possible, the scheduling should permit parallel invocation of IE methods or requests for WWW documents.

To illustrate our objective, consider a simple sketch of BIG in action. A simplified control flow view of this sketch is shown in Figure 1. A client is interested in finding a drawing program for Windows95. The client submits goal criteria that describe desired software characteristics and specifications for BIG's search-and-decide process. The search parameters are *quality importance = 80%, time importance = 20%, soft time deadline of 20 minutes, hard cost limitation of 0*. This translates into emphasizing quality over duration, a preference for a response in 20 minutes if possible, and a hard constraint that the search use only free information. The product parameters are: *product price: $200 or less, plat-*

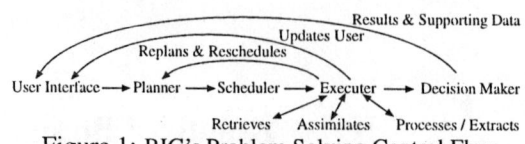

Figure 1: BIG's Problem Solving Control Flow

form: Windows95, usefulness importance rating 100 units, future usefulness rating 25, product stability 100, value 100, ease of use 100, power features 25, enjoyability 100. The client is a middle-weight home-office user who is primarily concerned with using the product today with a minimum of hassles but who also doesn't want to pay too much for power user features. Upon receipt of the criteria, BIG first invokes its planner to determine what information gathering activities are likely to lead to a solution path; activities include retrieving documents from known drawing program makers such as Corel and MacroMedia as well as from consumer sites containing software reviews, such as the Benchin Web site. Other activities pertain to document processing options for retrieved text; for a given document, there are a range of processing possibilities each with different costs and different advantages. For example, the heavyweight information extractor pulls data from freeformat text and fills templates and associates certainty factors with the extracted items. In contrast, the simple and inexpensive pattern matcher attempts to locate items within the text via simple grep-like behavior. These problem solving options are then considered and weighed by the task scheduler that performs quality/cost/time trade-off analysis and determines a course of action for BIG. The resulting schedule is then executed; multiple retrieval requests are issued and documents are retrieved and processed. Data extracted from documents at the MacroMedia site is integrated with data extracted from documents at the Benchin site to form a product description object for MacroMedia Freehand. However, when BIG looks for information on Adobe Illustrator at the Benchin site it also comes across products such as the Bible Illustrator for Windows, and creates product description objects for these products as well. After sufficient information is gathered, and the search resources nearly consumed, BIG then compares the different product objects and selects a product for the client. In this case, BIG's data indicates that the "best" product is MacroMedia Freehand though the academic version is the specific product that is below our client's price threshold. (The regular suggested retail price is $595.) BIG returns this recommendation to the client along with the gathered information and the corresponding extracted data.

Though the sketch above actually illustrates one of the problem areas of BIG's text processing, that is identifying special versions of products, it illustrates one of the cornerstones of our approach to the information explosion – we believe that retrieving relevant documents is not a viable end solution to the information explosion. The next generation of information systems must use the information to make decisions and thus provide a higher-level client interface to the enormous volume of on-line information. Our work is related to other agent approaches (Wellmen, Durfee, & Birmingham 1996) that process and use gathered information, such as the WARREN (Decker *et al.* 1997) portfolio management system or the original BargainFinder (Krulwich 1996) agent or Shopbot (Doorenbos, Etzioni, & Weld 1997), both of which work to find the best available price for a music CD. However, our research differs in its direct representation of, and reasoning about, the time/quality/cost trade-offs of alternative ways to gather information, its ambitious use of gathered information to drive further gathering activities, its bottom-up and top-down directed processing, and its explicit representation of sources-of-uncertainty associated with both inferred and extracted information. Our time/quality/cost trade-off approach is similar to formal methods (Etzioni *et al.* 1996) for reasoning about gathering information, except that our trade-off analysis focuses on problem solving actions (including text processing) and other agent activities rather than simply focusing on the trade-offs of different information resources, i.e., our work addresses both agent control level and information value.

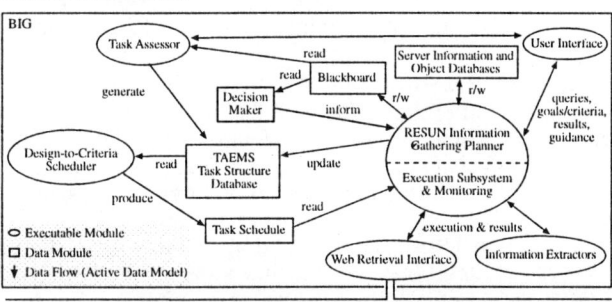

Figure 2: The BIG Agent Architecture

The BIG Agent Architecture

The overall BIG agent architecture is shown in Figure 2. The agent is comprised of several sophisticated components that are complex problem-solvers and research subjects in their own rights. The integration of such complex components is a benefit of our research agenda. By combining components in a single agent, that have hereto been used individually, we gain new insight and discover new research directions for the components. The most important components, or component groups, follow in rough order of their invocation in the BIG agent.

Task Assessor The task assessor is responsible for formulating an initial information gathering plan and then for revising the plan as new information is learned that has significant ramifications for the plan currently being executed. The task assessor is not the execution component nor is it the planner that actually determines the details of how to go about achieving information gathering goals; the task assessor is a component dedicated to managing the high-level view of the information gathering process and balancing the end-to-end top-down approach of the agent scheduler (below) and the opportunistic bottom-up RESUN planner (also below). The task assessor receives an initial information gathering goal specification from an external decision maker, which can be a human or another sophisticated automated component, and then formulates a family of plans for gathering the necessary information. The task assessor has a model of the goals that can be achieved by the RESUN planner and the performance characteristics and parameters of the actions that RESUN will employ to achieve the goals. The task assessor combines this knowledge with previously learned information stored in the server and object databases (below) and generates a set of plans that delineates alternative ways to go about gathering the information and characterizes the different possibilities statistically in three dimensions quality, cost, and duration, via discrete probability distributions. The task assessor encodes the plans in the TÆMS (Decker & Lesser 1993) generic, domain-independent task modeling framework. The TÆMS models then serve as input to the agent scheduler and other agent control components that will be added in the future (e.g., a multi-agent coordination module).

Object Database Used initially by the task assessor when determining possible courses of action, the object database is also used by the RESUN planner during information gathering sessions. As the planner creates information objects they are stored in the object database for use during future information gathering sessions. The stored objects may be incomplete and may have uncertainties attached to them, however, the uncertainties and incompletions can be filled in the next time the object is used to address a query. Through the object database and the server information database (below), BIG learns during problem solving. Information and resources learned and discovered are stored for subsequent information gathering activities. The issue of aging stored data and a detailed discussion on learning are beyond the scope of this paper.

Server Information Database The server database is used by the task assessor to help generate its initial list of information gathering options and again during the actual search process by the RESUN planner when the information gathering activities actually take place. The database is used to seed the initial search and is queried as new products are discovered. The database contains records identifying both primary and secondary information sources on the Web. Accompanying the sources are attributes that describe the sources' retrieval times and costs, their quality measures (see below), keywords relevant to the sources, and other related items. The database is constructed by an offline Web spider and modified during the search process to reflect newly discovered sites and data. This object has information aging concerns similar to those of the object database.

TÆMS Modeling Framework The TÆMS (Decker 1996) task modeling language is used to hierarchically model the information gathering process and enumerate alternative ways to accomplish the high-level gathering goals. The task structures probabilistically describe the quality, cost, and duration characteristics of each primitive action and specify both the existence and degree of any interactions between tasks and primitive methods. For instance, if the task of *Find-Competitors-for-WordPerfect* overlaps with the task of *Find-Competitors-for-MS-Word* (particular bindings of the general *Find-Competitors-for-Software-Product* task) then the relationship is described via a mutual facilitation and a degree of the facilitation specified via quality, cost, and duration probability distributions. TÆMS task structures are stored in a common repository and serve as a domain independent medium of exchange for the domain-independent agent control components; in the single agent implementation of BIG, TÆMS is primarily a medium of exchange for the scheduler, below, the task assessor, and the RESUN planner.

Design-to-Criteria Scheduler Design-to-Criteria (Wagner, Garvey, & Lesser 1997; 1998) is a domain independent real-time, flexible computation (Horvitz, Cooper, & Heckerman 1989; Dean & Boddy 1988; Russell & Zilberstein 1991) approach to task scheduling. The Design-to-Criteria task scheduler reasons about quality, cost, duration and uncertainty trade-offs of different courses of action and constructs custom satisficing schedules for achieving the high-level goal(s). The scheduler provides BIG with the ability to reason about the trade-offs of different possible information gathering and processing activities, in light of the client's goal specification (e.g., time limitations), and to select a course of action that best fits the client's needs and the current problem solving context. The scheduler receives the TÆMS models generated by the task assessor as input and the generated schedule, containing parallelism where appropriate, is returned to the RESUN planner for execution.

RESUN Planner The RESUN (Carver & Lesser 1991; 1995) (pronounced "reason") blackboard based planner/problem solver directs information gathering activities. The planner receives an initial action schedule from the scheduler and then handles information gathering and processing activities. The strength of the RESUN planner is that it identifies, tracks, and plans to resolve sources-of-uncertainty (SOUs) associated with blackboard objects, which in this case correspond to gathered information and hypotheses about the information. For example, after processing a software review, the planner may pose the hypothesis that Corel Wordperfect is a Windows95 wordprocessor, but associate a SOU with that hypothesis that identifies the uncertainty associated with the extraction technique used. The planner may then decide to resolve that SOU by using a different extraction technique or finding corroborating evidence elsewhere. RESUN's control mechanism is fundamentally opportunistic – as new evidence and information is learned, RESUN may elect to work on whatever particular aspect of the information gathering problem seems most fruitful at a given time. This behavior is at odds with the end-to-end resource-addressing trade-off centric view of the scheduler, a view necessary for BIG to meet deadlines and address time and resource objectives. Currently RESUN achieves a subset of the possible goals specified by the task assessor, but selected and sequenced by the scheduler. However, this can leave little room for opportunism if the goals are very detailed, i.e., depending on the level of abstraction RESUN may not be given room to perform opportunistically at all. This is a current focus of our integration effort. In the near term we will complete a two-way interface between RESUN and the task assessor (and the scheduler) that will enable RESUN to request that the task assessor consider new information and replan the end-to-end view accordingly.

Relatedly, we will support different levels of abstraction in the plans produced by the task assessor (and selected by the scheduler) so we can vary the amount of room left for RESUN's run-time opportunism and study the benefits of different degrees of opportunism within the larger view of a scheduled sequence of actions.

Web Retrieval Interface The retriever tool is the lowest level interface between the problem solving components and the Web. The retriever fills retrieval requests by either gathering the requested URL or by interacting with with both general (e.g., InfoSeek), and site specific, search engines. Through variable remapping, it provides a generic, consistent interface to these interactive services, allowing the problem solver to pose queries without knowledge of the specific server's syntax. In addition to fetching the requested URL or interacting with the specific form, the retriever also provides server response measures and preprocesses the html document, extracting other URLs possibly to be explored later by the planner.

Information Extractors The ability to process retrieved documents and extract structured data is essential both to refine search activities and to provide evidence to support BIG's decision making. For example, in the software product domain, extracting a list of features and associating them with a product and a manufacturer is critical for determining whether the product in question will work in the user's computing environment, e.g., RAM limitations, CPU speed, OS platform, etc. BIG uses several information extraction techniques to process unstructured, semi-structured, and structured information. The information extractors are implemented as knowledge sources in BIG's RESUN planner and are invoked after documents are retrieved and posted to the blackboard. The information extractors are:

textext-ks This knowledge source processes unstructured text documents using the BADGER (Soderland et al. 1995) information extraction system to extract particular desired data. The extraction component uses a combination of learned domain-specific extraction rules, domain knowledge, and knowledge of sentence construction to identify and extract the desired information. This component is a heavy-weight NLP style extractor that processes documents thoroughly and identifies uncertainties associated with extracted data.

grep-ks This featherweight KS scans a given text document looking for a keyword that will fill the slot specified by the planner. For example, if the planner needs to fill a product name slot and the document contains "WordPerfect" this KS will identify WordPerfect as the product, via a dictionary, and fill the product description slot.

cgrepext-ks Given a list of keywords, a document and a product description object, this middleweight KS locates the context of the keyword (similar to paragraph analysis), does a word for word comparison with built in semantic definitions thesaurus and fills in the object accordingly.

tablext-ks This specialized KS extracts tables from html documents, processes the entries, and fills product description slots with the relevant items. This KS is trained to extract tables and identify table slots for particular sites. For example, it knows how to process the product description tables found at the Benchin review site.

quick-ks This fast and highly specialized KS is trained to identify and extract specific portions of regularly formatted html files. For example, many of the review sites use standard layouts.

Decision Maker After product information objects are constructed BIG moves into the decision making phase. In the future, BIG may determine during decision making that it needs more information, perhaps to resolve a source-of-uncertainty associated with an attribute that is the determining factor in a particular decision, however, currently BIG uses the information at hand to make a decision. Space precludes full elucidation of the decision making process, however, the decision is based on a utility calculation that takes into account the user's preferences and weights assigned to particular attributes of the products and the confidence level associated with the attributes of the products in question.

Currently, all of these components are implemented, integrated, and undergoing testing. However, we have not yet fully integrated all aspects of the the RESUN planner at this time. In terms of functionality, this means that while the agent plans to gather information, analyzes quality/cost/duration trade-offs, gathers the information, uses the IE technology to break down the unstructured text, and then reasons about objects to support a decision process, it does not respond opportunistically to certain classes of events. If, during the search process, a new product is discovered, the RESUN planner may elect to expend energy on refining that product and building a more complete definition, however, it will not generate a new top down plan and will not consider allocating more resources to the general task of gathering information on products. Thus, while the bindings of products to planned tasks are dynamic, the allocations to said tasks are not. This integration issue is currently being solved. We return to this issue later in the paper.

BIG in Action

To provide a more concrete example of how BIG operates, let us walk through a sample run. The domain for this example is word processing software, where a client uses the system to find the most appropriate package, given a set of requirements and constraints. The query process begins with a user specifying search criteria, which includes such elements as the duration and cost of the search as well as desired product attributes, such as genre, price, quality and system requirements. In this example, the client desires to search for a word processor for the Macintosh costing no more than 200 dollars, and would like the search process to take about ten minutes and cost less than five dollars. The user also describes the importance of product price and quality by assigning weights to these product categories, in this case the client specified a 50/50 split between price and quality. Space precludes an in depth discussion of the product quality fields, but they include items like usefulness, future usefulness, stability, value, ease of use, power, and enjoyability.

Once these parameters are specified the query begins. The task assessor starts the process by first analyzing the user's parameters and then, using its knowledge about RESUN's problem solving options and its own top-down understanding of reasonable ways to go about performing the task, it generates a TÆMS task structure believed to be capable of achiev-

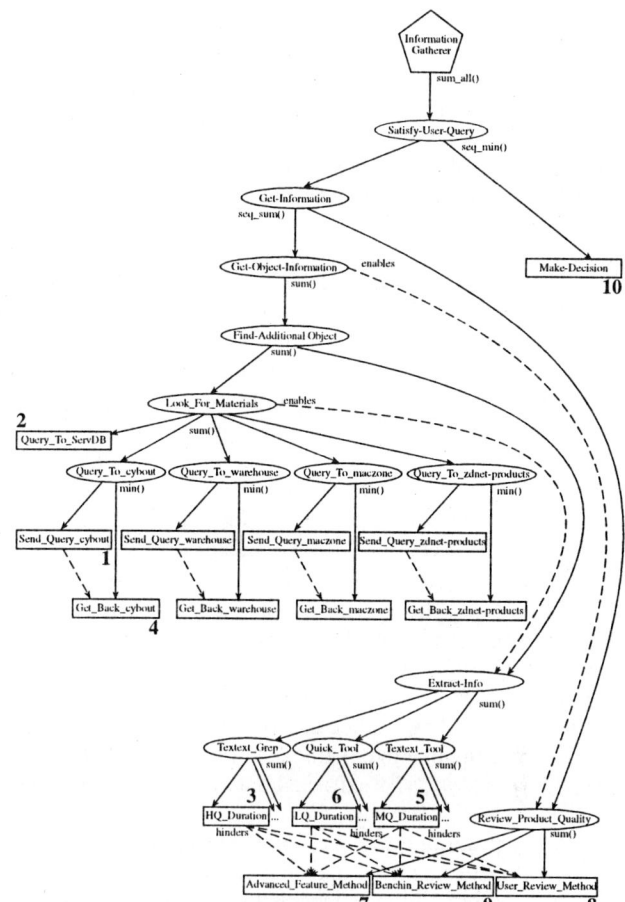

Figure 3: BIG's TÆMS Task Structure for the 10 Min. Case

ing the query. Although not used in this example, knowledge learned in previous problem solving episodes may be utilized during this step by querying a database of previously discovered objects and incorporating this information into the task structure. The task structure produced for our example query can be seen in Figure 3. Note that sets of outcomes are associated with each method, where each outcome has a probability of occurring and is described statistically via discrete probability distributions in terms of quality, cost, and duration. This detail is omitted from the figure for clarity.

Once constructed, the task structure is passed to the scheduler which makes use of the user's time and cost constraints to produce a viable run-time schedule of execution. Comparative importance rankings of the search quality, cost and duration, supplied by the client, are also used during schedule creation. The sequence of primitive actions chosen by the scheduler for this task structure is also shown in Figure 3. The numbers near particular methods indicate their assigned execution order. Again, space precludes a detailed schedule with its associated probability distributions.

The schedule is then passed to the RESUN planner/executor to begin the process of information gathering. Retrieval in this example begins by submitting a query to a known information source called "cybout." While this information is being retrieved, a second query is made and completed to the local server database information source.

This second action results in 400 document descriptions being placed on the blackboard, from which three are selected for further action. These three documents are then retrieved and processed in turn with a high-quality, high-duration sequence of information extraction tools. Before actual processing takes place, a quick search of each document's content for the product genre provides a cheap method of ensuring relevance – we envision this document preclassification step becoming more involved in the future. Three objects, one from each document, are found during the high-quality examination and placed on the blackboard. By this time, the initial query to cybout has completed and is retrieved, which results in an additional 61 documents being posted to the blackboard. Six more documents are then selected and retrieved for medium-quality, medium-duration extraction/processing. Four of these, though, fail the product genre search test and are discarded before processing takes place. Examination of the remaining two reveals two more products, which are added to the blackboard. A similar low-quality, low-duration process then adds two more objects.

At this point the system has a total of seven competing product objects on the blackboard which require more discriminating information to make accurate comparisons. To do this, three known review sites are queried for each object, each of which may produce data which is added to the object, but not combined with existing data for the given object (discrepancy resolution of extracted data is currently handled at decision time). After this, the final decision making process begins by pruning the object set of products which have insufficient information to make an accurate comparison. The data for the remaining objects is then assimilated, with discrepancies resolved by generating an average, each point being weighted by the quality of the source. A final product quality is then computed for each object, taking into account the gathered information, the quality of this information and the user's requirements. From this set the product with the highest expected quality is selected as the final recommendation. A confidence measure of this decision is also calculated based on the quality of each product and the certainty of the information. This information can be seen for several trials in Figure 4

Looking at Figure 4 in more detail one can obtain a reasonable view of how the system operates under different time constraints. In the first column of data we can see information relating to the duration of each search. Given is the user's requested duration, the duration expected by the schedule produced from the task structure and the actual execution time. Discrepancies may arise between the requested and scheduled times because of both how the task assessor creates the task structure and how the scheduler interprets it. For instance, valid 10 minute runs were available in the 600 second query, but a 743 second path was chosen because of its greater likelihood of producing high quality results. This sort of time/quality tradeoff is controlled in part by the parameters set in the user interface. The differences seen between the scheduled and actual time is caused simply by the fact that it is difficult to accurately predict the response time of remote services in the face of capricious network traffic.

The decision quality column reflects the number and qualities of the information sources used to generate the final decision. This attribute is based on the number of products considered, the number of documents used to obtain information and the quality rankings of these pages. The quality of the retrieved documents is based on knowledge about the quality of the source, which is generated by prior human examination. Unknown sites are ranked as medium quality. The product number and information coverage values increase given more scheduled time, as one would expect. The information quality values, however, may seem un-intuitive, since medium and low quality sources were used despite the fact that the quality of the information contained is known *a priori*. Such sites may be selected for retrieval for two reasons: they may respond quickly, and our set of tools may be able to analyze them particularly well. So a number of such sources may be used relatively cheaply, and still be useful when examined in conjunction with a high-quality source.

The decision confidence values describe how confident the system is in the information extraction and decision making processes. Information accuracy, supplied by the information processing tool, is the degree of belief that the actual extracted information is correctly categorized and placed in the information objects. Information confidence, generated by the decision maker, reflects the likelihood that the selected product is the optimal choice given the set of products considered. This value is based on the quality distributions of each product, and represents the chance that the expected quality is correct. It should be noted that both these values are not dependent on the scheduled time. The accuracy does not change because our current information extraction tools do not produce different results with more execution time. Decision confidence, on the other hand, is based on the quality of the individual products, which are independent of execution time themselves, thus making the confidence independent.

The final decision of which product to recommend represents the sum of all these earlier efforts. The successes and failures of earlier processes are thus manifested here, which may lead to unpredictable results. For instance, in the five minute run, the system suggests that Adobe Acrobat will fulfill the client's word processing needs. This sort of error can be caused by the misinterpretation of an information source. Specifically, the phrase "word processing" was found associated with this package in a product description, which caused it to be accidentally included in the list of possible products. The subsequent 10 and 20 minute runs produced more useful results, both recommending the same word processor. After 40 minutes, though, the system has again selected a non-word processing package. This was also caused by a misunderstood product description, and was compounded by the fact that it was low-cost and well reviewed. It should also be noted, though, that the second and third place packages in this run were both highly rated word processors, namely ClarisWorks Office and Corel WordPerfect.

The final 5 minute query was performed after the 40 minute run, and made use of the previously generated objects when creating the initial task structure. These objects were also used to initially seed the object level of the RESUN blackboard. In this final search, more information was found on these objects, which decreased the expected qual-

Duration (seconds)						Decision Quality		Decision Confidence		Product retrieved
Requested	Scheduled	Actual	Num. products	Info. coverage		Info. quality		Accuracy	Info. confidence	
300	572	550	3	11		5 High 0 Medium 6 Low		1.461	0.830	Acrobat 3.0 Upg. from Acrobat Pro MAC CD platform: MAC price: $59.95　　　　　quality: 2.1
600	743	860	7	21		12 High 0 Medium 9 Low		1.068	0.860	Nisus Writer 5.1 Upgrade from 2.0, 3.0 or 4.0 CD ROM platform: Macintosh price: $34.95　　　　　quality: 2.7
1200	1163	942	11	25		9 High 8 Medium 8 Low		1.073	0.860	Nisus Writer 5.1 Upgrade from 2.0, 3.0 or 4.0 CD ROM platform: Macintosh price: $34.95　　　　　quality: 2.7
2400	2819	2543	23	76		28 High 16 Medium 32 Low		1.070	0.850	The Big Thesaurus V2.1 platform: Macintosh price: $27.95　　　　　quality: 2.9
Using previously learned information										
300	572	386	21	10		5 High 0 Medium 5 Low		1.058	0.710	Nisus Writer 5.1 Upgrade from 5.0 CD ROM platform: Macintosh price: $29.95　　　　　quality: 2.7

Figure 4: Five Different Results: Four with Different Time Allotments and the Fifth Generated by Using Previously Learned Knowledge

ity of the 40 minute search's erroneously selected product, The Big Thesaurus, to 2.3 from 2.9. This small amount of extra information was sufficient for the system to discount this product as a viable candidate, which resulted in a much better recommendation in a shorter period of time, i.e., the recommendation of Nisus Writer. One may also see a dramatic difference when comparing these results with the initial 5 minute query, which had similar information coverage but many fewer products to select from, which produced a lower quality decision and selected a non-word processor product.

Integration Lessons and Future Work

The integration of the different AI problem solvers in BIG, namely the RESUN planner, the Design-to-Criteria scheduler, the BADGER information extraction system, with each other and the web retriever agents, the different data storage mechanisms and process modeling systems, is a major accomplishment in its own right. The integration of these systems and tools has enabled us to study the systems in a different light than they have been studied in a stand-alone research environment. For example, the software product domain, one of BIG's IG areas, is a new domain for the BADGER extractor that required new training and new methods for handling documents, e.g., reviews and product comparisons, that are structured differently from the genres of documents dealt with in the past (e.g., terrorist articles and medical reports). We also have an interesting extraction problem when dealing with complimentary, but not competitor products. For example, when searching for word processors BIG is likely to come across supplementary dictionaries, word processor tutorials, and even document exchange programs like Adobe Acrobat. These can be misleading to the extraction tools and to BIG in general because they are referenced much like a competitor product and the documents about these products often contain terminology that further supports the notion that they are competitors rather than complimentary products. We are experimenting with enhancements to our information extraction systems to cope with this and planning to use a tf/idf style document classifier (Callan 1996) to prequalify documents before running the extraction system on them.

We have also learned new things about the Design-to-Criteria scheduler and discovered some modeling problems with applying the TÆMS task modeling framework to this application. For example, in the information gathering task structures there is a notion of search activities producing some number of documents to process, and document processing time is tied to this number of documents; additionally, the final decision making process is tied to the number of documents that are processed because with each processed document, there is some probability that it will lead to new information objects that must be considered at decision time. This dependency is data-driven and TÆMS only models certain types of domain problem solving states. We have been able to model this task adequately using existing modeling constructs, but, inaccuracies in the models sometimes lead to less-than-perfect expectations. The solution is the addition of a database resource in TÆMS that can record and model the state information pertaining to the number of documents retrieved, the number of documents processed, and the number of information objects to be considered at decision time. A secondary enhancement is the creation of new TÆMS non-local-effects to model soft task interactions, e.g., *hinders* and *facilitates*, that have an additive, rather than power-multiplier, effect.

Another major integration issue is the balance between a top-down end-to-end view of problem solving and a reactive, opportunistic view. These two views are embodied by the scheduler and the RESUN planner respectively. The scheduler designs schedules to meet real-time and real-resource performance criteria by scheduling activities from start to finish. RESUN, on the other hand, is an opportunistic problem solver that responds to newly learned information and performs processing on whatever hypothesis seems most significant at a given time step. Currently, BIG uses little of RESUN's opportunistic control to react to changes in the problem solving state. We are working on integrating the two way feedback loop between the planner, task assessor, and scheduler, that will enable the system to react, where appropriate, to changes in the problem solving state. The major issue is identifying when it is beneficial to incur the cost of rescheduling BIG's planned actions and potentially disrupting finish time guarantees that have been communicated to the client. This tension between opportunistic, bottom-up, data-driven control and top-down process-centric control is one of the major open questions in BIG but also potentially our largest gain in terms of the ability to effectively retrieve, process, and make decisions with Web-based information. Relatedly, we also intend to study a slightly different view of BIG's control as an anytime process.

As we have discussed, the integration of these components in BIG, and the view of the IG problem as an interpretation task, has given BIG some very strong abilities. First there is the issue of information fusion. BIG does not just retrieve documents. Instead BIG retrieves information, extracts data from the information, and then combines the extracted data with data extracted from other documents to build a more complete model of the product at hand. RESUN's evidential framework enables BIG to reason about the sources of uncertainty associated with particular aspects of product object and to even work to find corroborating or negating evidence to resolve the SOUs. BIG also learns from previous problem solving episodes and reasons about resource tradeoffs. As shown, given different allotments of cost and time, and even different desired quality levels, BIG can analyze its options and plan to achieve the decision goal while meeting the client's search criteria. Though cost is not an issue spotlighted in the examples in this paper, cost on the web is a reality. For example, in the automotive product domain different sites charge different amounts for information such as invoice prices, and some sites are free, but offer less timely and less precise information.

In terms of limitations and extensibility, many of the components used in the system, such as the web retrieval interface and some of the information extractors like grep-ks and tablext-ks, are generic and domain independent. However, certain aspects of the system require domain specific knowledge and adapting BIG to operate in another domain, perhaps the auto-purchase domain, would require the addition of specific knowledge about the particular domain. For example, information extractors such as BADGER, cgrepext-ks and quickext-ks require supervised training to learn extraction rules and make use of semantic dictionaries to guarantee a certain level of performance. (Though we tested the system on the related domain of computer hardware and found it to work well considering no hardware related documents were in the training corpus.) Additionally, both the server and object databases, being persistent stores of the system's past experiences, are inherently domain dependent, rendering most of this knowledge useless and possibly distractive when used in other scenarios.

References

Callan, J. P.; Croft, W. B.; and Harding, S. M. 1992. The INQUERY retrieval system. In *Proceedings of the 3rd Intl. Conf. on Database and Expert Systems Applications*, 78–83.

Callan, J. P. 1996. Document filtering with inference networks. In *Proceedings of the 19th Intl. ACM SIGIR Conference on Research and Development in Information Retrieval*, 262–269.

Carver, N., and Lesser, V. 1991. A new framework for sensor interpretation: Planning to resolve sources of uncertainty. In *Proceedings of the Ninth National Conference on Artificial Intelligence*, 724–731.

Carver, N., and Lesser, V. 1995. The DRESUN testbed for research in FA/C distributed situation assessment: Extensions to the model of external evidence. In *Proceedings of the 1st Intl. Conf. on Multiagent Systems*.

Cowie, J., and Lehnert, W. 1996. Information extraction. *Communications of the ACM* 39(1):80–91.

Dean, T., and Boddy, M. 1988. An analysis of time-dependent planning. In *Proceedings of the Seventh National Conference on Artificial Intelligence*, 49–54.

Decker, K. S., and Lesser, V. R. 1993. Quantitative modeling of complex environments. *International Journal of Intelligent Systems in Accounting, Finance, and Management* 2(4):215–234.

Decker, K.; Pannu, A.; Sycara, K.; and Williamson, M. 1997. Designing behaviors for information agents. In *Proceedings of the 1st Intl. Conf. on Autonomous Agents*, 404–413.

Decker, K. S. 1996. Task environment centered simulation. In Prietula, M.; Carley, K.; and Gasser, L., eds., *Simulating Organizations: Computational Models of Institutions and Groups*. AAAI Press/MIT Press.

Doorenbos, R.; Etzioni, O.; and Weld, D. 1997. A scalable comparision-shopping agent for the world-wide-web. In *Proceedings of the 1st Intl. Conf. on Autonomous Agents*, 39–48.

Etzioni, O.; Hanks, S.; Jiang, T.; Karp, R.; Madani, O.; and Waarts, O. 1996. Optimal information gathering on the internet with time and cost constraints. In *Proceedings of the Thirty-seventh IEEE Symposium on Foundations of Computer Science (FOCS)*.

Horvitz, E.; Cooper, G.; and Heckerman, D. 1989. Reflection and action under scarce resources: Theoretical principles and empirical study. In *Proceedings of the 11th Intl. Joint Conf. on Artificial Intelligence*.

Krulwich, B. 1996. The BargainFinder Agent: Comparison price shopping on the Internet. In Williams, J., ed., *Bots and Other Internet Beasties*. SAMS.NET. http://bf.cstar.ac.com/bf/.

Larkey, L., and Croft, W. B. 1996. Combining classifiers in text categorization. In *Proceedings of the 19th Intl. Conf. on Research and Development in Information Retrieval (SIGIR '96)*, 289–297.

Lehnert, W., and Sundheim, B. 1991. A performance evaluation of text analysis technologies. *AI Magazine* 12(3):81–94.

Russell, S. J., and Zilberstein, S. 1991. Composing real-time systems. In *Proceedings of the 12th Intl. Joint Conf. on Artificial Intelligence*, 212–217.

Soderland, S.; Fisher, D.; Aseltine, J.; and Lehnert, W. 1995. Crystal: Inducing a conceptual dictionary. In *Proceedings of the 14th Intl. Joint Conf. on Artificial Intelligence*, 1314–1321.

Wagner, T.; Garvey, A.; and Lesser, V. 1997. Complex Goal Criteria and Its Application in Design-to-Criteria Scheduling. In *Proceedings of the 14th National Conf. on Artificial Intelligence*, 294–301.

Wagner, T.; Garvey, A.; and Lesser, V. 1998. Criteria-Directed Heuristic Task Scheduling. *International Journal of Approximate Reasoning, Special Issue on Scheduling*.

Wellmen, M.; Durfee, E.; and Birmingham, W. 1996. The digital library as community of information agents. *IEEE Expert*.

Design Principles for Intelligent Environments

Michael H. Coen

MIT Artificial Intelligence Lab
545 Technology Square
Cambridge, MA 02139
mhcoen@ai.mit.edu

Abstract

This paper describes design criteria for creating highly embedded, interactive spaces that we call Intelligent Environments. The motivation for building these systems is to bring computation into the real, physical world to support what is traditionally considered non-computational activity. We describe an existing prototype space, known as the Intelligent Room, which was created to experiment with different forms of natural, multimodal human-computer interaction. We discuss design decisions encountered while creating the Intelligent Room and how the experiences gained during its use have shaped the creation of its successor.

1. Introduction

This paper describes design criteria for creating highly embedded, interactive spaces that we call *Intelligent Environments* (IEs). The motivation for building IEs is to bring computation into the real, physical world. The goal is to allow computers to participate in activities that have never previously involved computation and to allow people to interact with computational systems the way they would with other people: via gesture, voice, movement, and context.

We describe an existing prototype space, known as the *Intelligent Room*, which is a research platform for exploring the design of intelligent environments. The Intelligent Room was created to experiment with different forms of natural, multimodal human-computer interaction (HCI) during what is traditionally considered non-computational activity. It is equipped with numerous computer vision, speech and gesture recognition systems that connect it to what its inhabitants are doing and saying.

Our primary concern here is how IEs should be designed and created. Intelligent environments, like traditional multimodal user interfaces, are integrations of methods and systems from a wide array of subdisciplines in the Artificial Intelligence (AI) community. Selecting the modal components of an IE requires a careful strategic approach because of the *a priori* assumption that the IE is actually going to be embedded in the real-world. In particular, there is a need for the use of synergy (Cohen [4]) to allow imperfect modalities to reinforce and support each other.

We discuss below the design of our laboratory's Intelligent Room and how experiences gained during its use have shaped the creation of its successor. Given the increasingly widespread interest in highly interactive, computational environments (Bobick et al. [3]), (Coen [6,7,8]), (Cooperstock et al. [10]), (Lucente et al. [17]), we hope these experiences will prove useful to other IE designers and implementers in the AI community.

Some of the earliest work in this area has been done wholly outside the AI community. This is primarily due to the perception that AI has little to offer in the way of robust, ready for the real world systems. We contend that Intelligent Environments not only would benefit from AI subdisciplines ranging from knowledge representation to computer vision, but they would be severely limited without them.

Outline

Section 2 describes some sample interactions with and applications of the Intelligent Room. These range from an intelligent command post to a reactive living room. Comparison to other HCI paradigms, such as ubiquitous computing, and other embedded computational environments is contained in section 3. Section 4 presents the Intelligent Room's physical infrastructure. Sections 5 and 6 detail the Intelligent Room's visual and spoken language modalities. We document the rationales that influenced our approach, system limitations, and solutions we are pursuing in the development of the next generation Intelligent Room currently under construction in our laboratory.

2. Room Interactions

Our approach with the Intelligent Room has been to create a platform for HCI research that connects with real-world phenomena through several computer vision and speech

---

This material is based upon work supported by the Advanced Research Projects Agency of the Department of Defense under contract number F30602—94—C—0204, monitored through Rome Laboratory. Additional support was provided by the Mitsubishi Electronic Research Laboratories.

Copyright © 1998, American Association for Artificial Intelligence (www.aaai.org). All rights reserved.

recognition systems. These allow the room to watch where people are moving, under certain circumstances where they are pointing, and to listen to a fairly wide variety of spoken language utterances.

The Intelligent Room supports a variety of application domains. One of these is a command center for planning hurricane disaster relief in the Caribbean. This makes use of two interactive projected displays that respond to both finger pointing and laser pointing gestures. A sample interaction with the disaster relief center is:

User: *"Computer, <pause> stay awake."*
[The room will now listen for utterances without requiring they be prefaced by the word *Computer*.]
User: *"Show me the Virgin Islands."*
Room: *"I'm a showing the map right next to you."* [Room shows map on video display *closest* to the user.]
User: [now points at St. Thomas.] *"Zoom in. How far away is Hurricane Marilyn?"*
Room: *"The distance between Hurricane Marilyn and the city of Charlotte Amalie located in St. Thomas is 145 miles."*
User: *"Where's the nearest disaster field office?"*
[Room highlights them on the map.]
Room: *"The St. Thomas disaster field office is located one mile outside of Charlotte Amalie. Michael, there is a new weather forecast available. Do you want to see it?"*
User: *"Yes, show me the satellite image."*

We are currently developing a next generation of the Intelligent Room, called *Hal* (after the computer in the movie, *2001: A space odyssey*). Hal is furnished like a combination home/office and supports a wider range of activities than the original Intelligent Room. A scenario that currently runs within Hal is:

> I walk into Hal and lie down on the sofa after shutting the door. Hal sees this, dims the lights, closes the curtains, and then puts on Mozart softly in the background. Hal then asks, *"Michael, what time would you like to get up?"*

The goal of implementing these types of scenarios is to explore and help define what an intelligent environment should be, what sensory capabilities it needs, and to determine what roles such environments could potentially play in our lives. In the process, these scenarios provide insight into both how AI systems can participate in the real world and directions for further research in the subdisciplines whose systems contribute to the creation of intelligent environments.

3. Motivation

Intelligent environments are spaces in which computation is seamlessly used to enhance ordinary activity. One of the driving forces behind the emerging interest in highly interactive environments is to make computers not only genuinely user-friendly but also essentially invisible to the user. The user-interface primitives of these systems are not menus, mice and windows but gesture, speech, affect, and context. Their applications are not spreadsheets and word processing but intelligent rooms and personal assistants.

Intelligent environments are both embedded and multimodal and thereby allow people to interact with them in natural ways. By being embedded, we mean these systems use cameras for eyes, microphones for ears, and ever-increasingly a wide-range of sophisticated sensing technologies to connect with real-world phenomena. Computer vision and speech recognition/understanding technologies can then allow these systems to become fluent in natural forms of human communication. People speak, gesture, and move around when they communicate. For example, by embedding user-interfaces this way, the fact that people tend to point at what they are speaking about is no longer meaningless from a computational viewpoint and we can build systems that make use of this information. In some sense, rather than make computer-interfaces for people, we want to make people-interfaces for computers.

Coupled with their natural interfaces is the expectation that these systems are not only highly interactive (i.e. they talk back when spoken to) but also that they are useful for ordinary activities. They should enable tasks historically outside the normal range of human-computer interaction by connecting computers to phenomena (such as someone walking into a room) that have traditionally been outside the purview of contemporary user-interfaces.

Why this isn't Ubiquitous Computing

Intelligent environments require a highly embedded computational infrastructure; they need many connections with the real world in order to participate in it. However, this does not imply that computation need be everywhere in the environment nor that people must directly interact with any kind of computational device. Our approach is to advocate minimal hardware modifications and "decorations" (e.g., cameras and microphones) in ordinary spaces to enable the types of interactions in which we are interested. Rather than use the computer-everywhere model of ubiquitous computing – where for example, chairs have pressure sensors that can register people sitting in them or people wear infrared-emitting badges so they can be located in a building – we want to enable unencumbered interaction with non-augmented, non-computational objects (like chairs) and to do so without requiring that people attach high-tech gadgetry to their bodies (as opposed to the approach in [24,25]).

AI-based approaches have much to offer these environments. For example, although a pressure sensor on a chair may be able to register that someone has sat down, it is unlikely to provide other information about that person, e.g., her identity. Visual data from a single camera can provide far more information than simple sensing technologies. This includes the person's identity, position, gaze direction, facial expression, gesture, and activity ([13,

25,17,30,12]). While there has yet to be a coherent system that unifies all of these capabilities, many prototypes are currently under development. Furthermore, enhancing the capabilities of a computer vision system often requires modifying only the software algorithms that process incoming images and not the room's sensory components. Also, because the room senses at a distance, objects, in particular people and furniture, do not need to be physically augmented and/or wired for the room to become aware of them.

Other related work

The DigitalDesk project (Wellner [26], Newman et al. [19]) was an early and influential system that had a bird's eye view of a desktop through an overhead video camera. It recognized and responded to predetermined hand gestures made by users while interacting with real paper documents on the surface of a desk. The Intelligent Room has a desktop environment directly motivated by the DigitalDesk, which recognizes a wider range of complex hand gestures (Dang [11]).

Other substantial efforts towards highly interactive environments include an automated teleconferencing office (Cooperstock et al. [10]) and an immersive fictional theater (Bobick et al. [3]). Each of these projects makes use of embedded computation to enable unusual human-computer interactions, e.g., vision-based person tracking. However their modal processing is extraordinarily specific to their applications, and the applicability of such carefully tuned systems to other domains is unclear. The Classroom 2000 project (Abowd et al. [1]) is an educational environment that automatically creates records linking simultaneous streams of information, e.g. what the teacher is saying while a student is writing down her notes on a digital pad.

Mozer ([18]) describes a house that automatically controls basic residential comfort systems, such as heating and ventilation, by learning patterns in its occupants behavior.

Related user-interface work such as Cohen et al. [5] uses multimodal interface technology to facilitate human interaction with a preexisting distributed simulator. In doing so, it provides a novel user-interface to a complex software system, but it is one that requires tying down the user to a particular computer and a specific application. We are interested in creating new environments that support never before conceived of applications – applications that historically have not involved computation.

4. The Intelligent Room

The Intelligent Room occupies a 27'x37' room in our laboratory. Approximately half of this space is laid out like an ordinary conference room, with a large table surrounded by chairs. (See Figure 1.) This section has two bright, overhead LCD projectors in addition to several

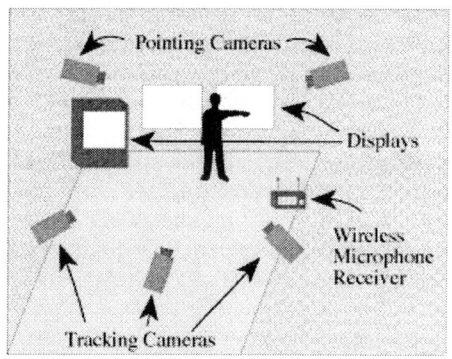

Figure 1 – A skeletal view of the conference area in the Intelligent Room

video displays. There is also an array of computer controlled video equipment which is discussed below. Mounted at various places in the conference area are twelve video cameras, which are used by computer vision systems.

Separated from the conference area by a small partition and occupying the rest of the room are most of the workstations that perform the room's computation. The section of the room is not interactive, but having it adjacent to the interactive conference area simplifies wiring, implementation and debugging.

The Intelligent Room contains an array of computer controlled devices. These include steerable video cameras, VCRs, LCD projectors, lights, curtains, video/SVGA multiplexers, an audio stereo system, and a scrollable LCD sign. The room's lighting is controlled through several serially interfaced X-10 systems. Many of the room's other devices have serial ports that provide both low-level control and status information, e.g., our VCRs can report their present position on a videotape to give us random access to video clips. The room can also generate infrared remote control signals to access consumer electronics items (namely, objects that don't have serial ports).

Room Controller

When the Intelligent Room was in the early stages of it design and construction, the most challenging research problems appeared to be developing its computer vision and speech recognition/understanding systems. What was not obvious is that interconnecting all of the rooms many subsystems and coordinating the flows of information among the room components was a non-trivial problem. Developing a software architecture that allowed the room to run in real-time and cope with vagaries of its real-world interactions emerged to be one of the room's chief research problems.

What emerged from an iterative development process is a modular system of software agents known collectively as the *Scatterbrain* (described in detail in Coen [6]). The Scatterbrain currently consists of approximately 50 distinct, intercommunicating software agents that run on ten different networked workstations. These agents' primary task is to connect various components of the room (e.g., tracking and speech recognition systems) to each other and to internal and external stores of information (e.g., a person locator or an information retrieval system). Essentially, the Scatterbrain agents are intelligent *computational glue* for interconnecting all of the room's components and moving information among them.

5. Room Vision Systems

Person Tracking

The Intelligent Room can track up to four people moving in the conference area of the room at up to 15Hz. The room's person tracking system (DeBonet [13]) uses two wall-mounted cameras, each approximately 8' from the ground. (A debugging window from the system showing the view from one of the cameras is shown in Figure 2.)

We initially decided that incorporating a tracking system in the Intelligent Room was essential for a number of reasons. It gives the room the ability to know where and how many people are inside it, including when people enter or exit. The room is able to determine what objects people are next to, so for example, it can show data on a video display someone is near. A person's location in the room also provides information about what she is doing. For example, someone moving near a video display while others are seated around the conference table might indicate she is giving a presentation.

The tracking data are useful for supplying information to other systems in the room including, to our surprise, our speech understanding system. It was clear from the start that tracking could disambiguate other room modalities, for example, by providing a foveal area for gesture recognition. However, its use in providing contextual information to the room's speech recognizer is a revealing example of how one modality can be used to help overcome the weaknesses of another. In this case, where people are in the room can sometimes provide information about what they are likely to say (see section 6).

The tracking system works via background segmentation and does 3D reconstruction through a neural network. The output image from each camera is analyzed by a program that labels and identifies a bounding box around each occupant in the room. This information is then sent through a coordination program that synchronizes the findings from the individual cameras and combines their output using a neural network to recover a 3D position for each room occupant. People are differentiated in the system using color histograms of their clothing, which the room builds when they first come inside. Because the room's configuration is fairly static and the cameras used for tracking are stationary, the tracking system can build a model of the room's relatively slowly changing background to compare with incoming images.

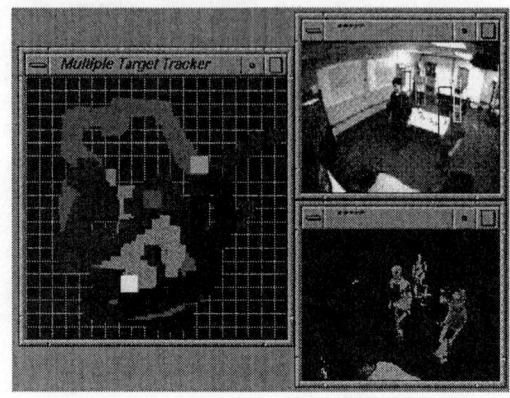

Figure 2 - Tracking System Debug Window

The tracking subsystem also controls three steerable cameras. These can be used to follow individuals as they move about the room or to select optimal views of people given their position and previous knowledge of room geometry, e.g. where people likely face when standing in particular areas of the room.

This approach differs from the overhead tracking system described in Bobick et al. [3]. Their domain had 27' high ceilings, for which it is quite reasonable to look for people from a single camera bird's eye perspective. Rooms with ordinary height ceilings do not make this possible, so a stereo vision system seems necessary for performing background segmentation.

Pointing

The Intelligent Room's two overhead LCD video projectors display next to each other on one of the room's walls. Each can display SVGA output from one of the room's workstations or composite signals from any of the room's video sources, e.g., a VCR. These projected displays support both finger and laser pointing interactions. For example, the room can track the finger of a person who is pointing within four inches of the wall where images are displayed. Alternatively, the person can use a laser pointer to interact with the display from a distance. Both of these pointing systems also allow displayed screen objects to be selected (i.e. clicked) or moved (i.e. dragged).

Additionally, the pointing systems allow people to treat the displays like virtual whiteboards. The room can draw a visible trail on top of a displayed image that follows the continuous path of a motile pointing gesture. This allows people to overlay handwritten text and drawings on top of whatever information the room is displaying. These can then be automatically recalled at a later date, for example, when the room shows this information again.

The finger pointing system uses two cameras mounted parallel to the wall on either side of the displays. It makes use of only three scan lines from each camera image to explore the region closest to the wall's surface. The laser pointing system uses a camera roughly orthogonal to the plane of the display wall to locate the laser's distinctive signature on the wall's surface. These systems run at approximately 15-20Hz, depending on the precise type of interaction, and provide resolution per display ranging from approximately 640x480 for laser pointing to 160x120 for finger pointing. Although the pointing systems are sufficiently responsive for discrete pointing and dragging events, handwriting recognition using the above mentioned drawing feature does not seem practical with out at least doubling the sampling frequency.

Interactive Table

Through a ceiling mounted camera, the room can detect hand-pointing gestures and newly placed documents on the surface of the conference table. The gesture recognition system has been used to support a wide variety of functions (described in Dang [11]). We found, however, that making gestures over the surface of a table was not a particularly natural form of interaction and required extensive practice to master. As has been widely observed in the graphical user interface community, we found that increased novelty in an interface does not necessarily lead to increased utility. This is even more pertinent in domains like the Intelligent Room, which stress natural modes of interaction.

One useful application of this system, however, allows people to place Post-It™ notes on the surface of the table and assign to them particular functions, such as dimming the lights or announcing the current time. Touching a given note then evokes its assigned behavior from the Intelligent Room. As a mnemonic, the function of each note can be handwritten upon it, giving the table the feeling of a virtual, very non-standard control panel. The room is oblivious to any written information on these notes, as long as it doesn't interfere with the color segmentation that allows individual notes to be recognized.

Issues

Our person tracking system uses a neural network to perform 3D reconstruction. The tracking network is trained by laying a masking tape coordinate system on the room's floor and then training the network by having a person stand at each intersection of the axes. (The grid was roughly 10x20.) Although non-network approaches to 3D reconstruction are possible, such as directly calculating the reverse projective transformation, they would all likely require a user-intensive preliminary learning period to determine the transformation between room and image space. Thus, installing our tracking system is labor intensive and requires some familiarity with how it operates.

Another difficulty with this approach is that the system is enormously sensitive to any deviation from its training conditions. For example, if one of the cameras is moved by so much as 1cm, the tracking system fails to function. Although automatic recalibration might be possible by using natural or artificial environmental fiducials, in practice these are either difficult to detect or highly intrusive when added to the environment. Thus, cameras being moved or rotated requires retraining the neural network, something a non-technical user would never want to do.

It is not accidental that so much computer vision research around the world is performed in rooms without windows. Computer visions systems, particularly ones that rely on background segmentation, can be extraordinarily sensitive to environmental lighting conditions. For example, early in the Intelligent Room's development, ambient light coming through a newly opened door could completely disrupt all of the room's vision systems. While this was an early design flaw, in general it can be extremely difficult to compensate for changing lighting conditions.

Shadows are also particularly difficult phenomena to cope with and we took great pains to avoid them. We disabled some of the room's overhead fluorescent lighting and used upward pointing halogen floor lamps instead. Additionally, we selected a fairly dark colored carpet, which is better at shadow masking. The tracking system also used a color correction mechanism for shadow elimination. However, a static color correction scheme was only partially useful because the tracking cameras were affected by the dynamic lighting of the projected video displays.

Solutions

Our research agenda for computer vision systems for Hal has changed drastically from the approach used in the Intelligent Room. Rather than incorporating the state of the art in visually based interactions, we have become far more interested in robust vision systems that require little calibration and are essentially self-training.

We have enabled the room's vision systems to reinforce one another. For example, our multi-person tracker may temporarily lose people when they occlude one another or blend into the background. One way to help offset this is to have the finger pointing system provide information useful for tracking. Someone finger pointing at the projected display must be standing somewhere near that position on the room's floor. By knowing where someone is pointing, the tracker can focus its attention on that section of the room. Conversely, the tracking system allows the room to identify the person who is pointing at the wall. By determining which tracked person is closest to the pointed at position, the room can distinguish among its inhabitants during finger pointing gestures.

Various devices in the room can also interact with its vision systems. The software agents that control the room's drapes and electrical lights notify the vision systems before they do anything that might affect the room's ambient lighting. This allows each vision system either to recalibrate or to deactivate itself until conditions favorable to its correct operation are restored and also avoids incorrect event recognition due to luminosity changes.

Although dynamic person tracking seemed essential during the design of the Intelligent Room, it became clear in retrospect that the vast majority of the tracking system's output is thrown away. Few applications need or can make use of real-time trajectory information for the room's occupants. Rather, what is particularly important is to know where someone is when she stops moving (i.e. next to or sitting on some piece of furniture) or when she has crossed a particular threshold (i.e. the room's doorway).

It is far easier and computationally less demanding to build systems that provide these kind of relatively slowly changing data without resorting to real-time occupant tracking. They look for people at rest in places where they are expected to be found, such as sitting on a couch or standing by a display, or for people crossing through a narrow, well-defined region such as a doorway.

We have implemented and experimented with several such systems, which we call *static person locators* and *threshold detectors*. These include a template-based *couch detector*, which locates people either sitting or lying down on a chair or sofa. This system is easily trained and quite robust. We have also implemented a dedicated *doorway tracker* for distinctly determining when someone enters or leaves the room, and thereby it also keeps track of how many people are currently present. Both of these systems are algorithmically quite simple and far less sensitive to environmental variations than our initial tracking system. They have proved quite robust, and their initial detection accuracy in varying light conditions and over a wide range of individuals is over 90%.

We are also creating generic chair locators using a ceiling mounted vision system. Our assumption is that occlusion of a chair provides evidence that someone is sitting in it, and this person can be located using prior knowledge of the chair's position. This system will use low dimension eigenspaces for approximating object manifolds under varying pose and lighting conditions (Stauffer [21]). The advantage to this approach is that the system need not be given in advance an explicit model of the chairs it will be locating. The system can construct object manifolds itself by having a user rotate any new types of chairs she brings inside.

6. Speech Interactions

Among the earliest decisions regarding the Intelligent Room was that it should support spoken language interactions. In particular, we were interested in allowing these interactions to be unimodal – i.e. ones that did not tie the user to a video display to verify or correct utterances recognized by the system nor require a keyboard for selecting among possible alternative utterances. We also wanted to avoid simply creating a keyboard replacement that allowed speech commands to substitute for actions ordinarily performed by typing or mouse clicking. Finally, we wanted to allow interaction with multiple applications simultaneously and thus not have interactions that monopolized the user. In the process, we have tried to allow the Intelligent Room to engage in dialogs with users to gather information, correct misunderstandings, and enhance recognition accuracy.

People in the Intelligent Room wear wireless lapel microphones that transmit to the speech understanding system described below. By default, the room ignores the spoken utterances of its inhabitants, which are generally directed to other people within the room. This state is known as "the room being asleep."[1] To obtain the room's attention, a user stops speaking for a moment and then says the word *"Computer"* out loud. The room immediately responds with an audible, quiet chirp from an overhead speaker to indicate it is paying attention. The user then has a two second window in which to begin speaking to the room. If the room is unable to recognize any utterances starting within that period, it silently goes back to sleep until explicitly addressed again. However, if what the user says is recognized, the room responds with an audible click and then under most circumstances it returns to sleep. This hands- and eyes-free style of interaction coupled with audio feedback allows a user to ignore the room's *computational presence* until she explicitly needs to communicate with it. There is no need to do anything other than preface spoken utterances with the cue *Computer* to enable verbal interaction. Thus, a user can interact with the room easily, regardless of her proximity to a keyboard or monitor.

The Intelligent Room is capable of addressing users via the Festival Speech Synthesis System (Black et al. [2]). Utterances spoken by the room are also displayed on a scrollable LCD sign in case a user was unable to understand what was said. The room uses its speech capability for a variety of purposes that include conducting dialogs with users and getting its occupant's attention without resorting to use of a visual display. Sometimes, the room chooses to respond vocally to a question because its video displays are occupied by what it considers high priority information. For example, if a user asks, *"What's the weather forecast for New York City?"* the room can simply read the forecast to the user, rather than put up a weather map containing forecast information if its displays are occupied.

For processing spoken utterances, we use both the Summit (Zue et al. [27]) and DragonDictate speech recognition systems in parallel. Each of these has different strengths and used together they have fairly robust performance. The Summit system recognizes continuous speech and is particularly adept at handling syntactic variability during recognition. By entering bigram models, it is fairly straightforward to build topically narrow but syntactically unconstrained sets of recognizable utterances. Bigram models, however, make it quite difficult to exclude particular statements from being erroneously recognized by the system and require that we heavily post process

---

1 The room's vision systems continue to function and respond to users even when it is not listening for verbal input.

Summit's output. This is performed primarily by the START natural-language information retrieval system (Katz [15]).

DragonDictate is a commercially available system primarily used for discrete speech dictation, meaning that users must pause after each word. This, when coupled with its relatively low word accuracy, would be an intolerable speech interface to the room. However, DragonDictate also supports explicit construction of continuous speech, context-free recognition grammars. Via a special library, it also provides complete control over low-level aspects of its behavior to external applications, which makes it ideal for incorporating into other systems.

Issues

There is a tradeoff between making the room's recognition grammars sufficiently large so that people can express themselves somewhat freely versus making the grammars small enough so that the system runs with high accuracy and in real-time. We tuned DragonDictate's performance by creating sets of specialized grammars for different room contexts and having the room's software agent controller dynamically activate different subsets of grammars depending on the context of the activity in the Intelligent Room (Coen et al. [9]). This allows us to overcome the combinatorial increase in parsing time due to incorporating natural syntactic variability in the recognition grammars.

Instead of keeping a single enormous recognition grammar active, the room keeps subsets of small grammars active in parallel, given what it currently expects to hear. The key assumptions here are that certain types of utterances are only likely to be said under particular circumstances, and these are circumstances among which the room is capable of distinguishing. These may be related to where someone is spatially, the history of her previous interactions (i.e. what room applications are active), how she is gesturing, what devices in the room are doing, etc. At the simplest level, this can range from the implausibility of someone saying *"stop the video,"* when none is playing, to more complex dependencies, such as the meaninglessness of someone asking *"What's the weather there?"* if no geographic entity has somehow been brought to the room's attention.

We have generalized the notion of linguistic context to include the state of and goings on in the room and have put this contextual knowledge into the room's software agents rather than its linguistic data structures. For example, if the room starts showing a video clip, the agent that controls the showing of videos activates the grammars that involve VCR operation. When the clip stops, these grammars are in turn deactivated. More interesting cues can involve the location of someone inside the room. The fact that someone has moved near an interactive displayed map causes the room to pay attention to spoken utterances involving geographic information. Thus, information from the room's other systems can help overcome computational limitations in the room's speech recognition and understanding systems.

Verbal interactions can also be extremely useful for dealing with the room's other modalities. They can be used to gather information about what the room is observing, to modify internal representations of its state, or to correct a perceptual error. It is also of enormous benefit to be able to verbally interact with the room's vision systems while developing or debugging them, because it is generally impossible to manually interact with them at a workstation while remaining in the cameras' fields of view.

7. Conclusion

Our experience with the Intelligent Room has led us to reevaluate many of our initial assumptions about how a highly interactive environment should be designed. Intelligent environments need to be more than rough assemblages of previously existing systems. In particular, careful selection and communication among modalities can lead to synergistic reinforcement and overall, a more reliable system. The modalities must also be carefully selected in order to make the environment easy to install, maintain, and use under a wide range of environmental conditions.

Systems that dynamically adjust to the room's activity, such as our speech understanding system, and systems that can train themselves and avoid extensive manual calibration, are essential to an IE's success. We hope the issues addressed in this paper will both stimulate further discussion and prove useful to other designers of intelligent environments.

8. Acknowledgements

Development of the Intelligent Room has involved the efforts of many people. This includes Professors Tomas Lozano-Perez, Rodney Brooks, and Lynn Stein. Graduate students who have been or are involved in the room include Mark Torrance, Jeremy De Bonet, Chris Stauffer, Sajit Rao, Darren Phi Bang Dang, JP Mellor, Gideon Stein, Michael Coen, Josh Kramer, Brenton Phillips, Mike Wessler, and Luke Weisman. Postdocs associated with the project include Kazuyoshi Inoue and Polly Pook. Many undergraduates have been or are currently working on it. These include Kavita Thomas, Nimrod Warshawsky, Owen Ozier, Marion Groh, Joanna Yun, James Clark, Victor Su, Sidney Chang, Hau Hwang, Jeremy Lilley, Dan McGuire, Shishir Mehrotra, Peter Ree, and Alice Yang.

References

1. Abowd, G., Atkeson, C., Feinstein, A., Hmelo, C., Kooper, R., Long, S., Sawhney, N., and Tani, M. Teach and Learning a Multimedia Authoring: The Classroom 2000 project. *Proceedings of the ACM Multimedia'96 Conference.* 1996.

2. Black, A. and Taylor, P. Festival Speech Synthesis System: system documentation (1.1.1) Human Communication Research Centre Technical Report HCRC/TR-83. University of Edinburgh. 1997.
3. Bobick, A.; Intille, S.; Davis, J.; Baird, F.; Pinhanez, C.; Campbell, L.; Ivanov, Y.; Schütte, A.; and Wilson, A. Design Decisions for Interactive Environments: Evaluating the KidsRoom. *Proceedings of the 1998 AAAI Spring Symposium on Intelligent Environments.* AAAI TR SS-98-02. 1998.
4. Cohen, P., "The role of natural language in a multimodal interface," *Proceedings of User Interface Software Technology (UIST'92) Conference*, Academic Press, Monterey, California, 1992.
5. Cohen, P., Chen, L., Clow, J., Johnston, M., McGee, D., Pittman, K., and Smith, I. Quickset: A multimodal interface for distributed interactive simulation, *Proceedings of the UIST'96 Demonstration Session*, Seattle. 1996.
6. Coen, M. Building Brains for Rooms: Designing Distributed Software Agents. *Proceedings of the Ninth Conference on Innovative Applications of Artificial Intelligence. (IAAI97).* Providence, R.I. 1997. http://www.ai.mit.edu/people/mhcoen/brain.ps
7. Coen, M. Towards Interactive Environments: The Intelligent Room (a short paper). *Proceedings of the 1997 Conference on Human Computer Interaction (HCI'97).* Bristol, U.K. 1997.
8. Coen, M. (ed.) *Proceedings of the 1998 AAAI Spring Symposium on Intelligent Environments.* AAAI TR SS-98-02. 1998.
9. Coen, M; Thomas, K; Weisman, L; Groh, M; and Yee, A. A Natural Language Modality for an Embedded Multimodal Environment. Forthcoming.
10. Cooperstock, J; Fels, S.; Buxton, W. and Smith, K. Environments: Throwing Away Your Keyboard and Mouse. *Commmunications of the ACM.* 1997.
11. Dang, D. Template Based Gesture Recognition. SM Thesis. Massachusetts Institute of Technology. 1996.
12. Davis, J. and Bobick, A. The representation and recognition of action using temporal templates. *Proceedings Computer Vision and Pattern Recognition (CVPR'97).* pp.928-934. 1997.
13. DeBonet, J. Multiple Room Occupant Location and Identification.1996. http://www.ai.mit.edu/people/jsd/jsd.doit/Research/HCI/Tracking_public
14. Druin, A.; and Perlin, K. Immersive Environments: a physical approach to the computer interface. *Proceedings of the Conference on Human Factors in Computer Systems (CHI'94)*, pages 325-326, 1994.
15. Katz, B. Using English for Indexing and Retrieving. In *Artificial Intelligence at MIT: Expanding Frontiers.* Winston, P.; and Shellard, S. (editors). MIT Press, Cambridge, MA. Volume 1. 1990.
16. Lien, J., Zlochower, A., Cohn, J., Li, C., and Kanade, T. Automatically Recognizing Facial Expressions in the Spatio-Temporal Domain. *Proceedings of the Workshop on Perceptual User Interfaces (PUI'97).* Alberta, Canada. pp.94-97. 1997.
17. Lucente, M.; Zwart, G.; George, A. Visualization Space: A Testbed for Deviceless Multimodal User Interface. *Proceedings of the AAAI 1998 Spring Symposium on Intelligent Environments.* AAAI TR SS-98-02. 1998.
18. Mozer, M. The Neural Network House: An Environment that Adapts to its Inhabitants. *Proceedings of the AAAI 1998 Spring Symposium on Intelligent Environments.* AAAI TR SS-98-02. 1998.
19. Newman, W. and Wellner, P. A Desk Supporting Computer-based interaction with paper. *Proceedings of the Conference on Human Factors in Computing Systems (CHI'92).* p587-592. 1992.
20. Saund, E. Example Line Drawing Analysis for the ZombieBoard Diagrammatic User Interface. http://www.parc.xerox.com/spl/members/saund/lda-example/lda-example.html. 1996.
21. Stauffer, C. Adaptive Manifolds for Object Classification. 1996. http://www.ai.mit.edu/people/stauffer/Projects/Manifold/
22. Stiefelhagen, R., Yang, J., and Waibel, A. Tracking Eyes and Monitoring Eye Gaze. *Proceedings of the Workshop on Perceptual User Interfaces (PUI'97).* Alberta, Canada. pp.98-100. 1997.
23. Torrance, M. Advances in Human-Computer Interaction: The Intelligent Room. *Working Notes of the CHI 95 Research Symposium*, May 6-7, Denver, Colorado. 1995.
24. Want, R.; Schilit, B.; Adams, N.; Gold, R.; Petersen, K.; Goldberg, D.; Ellis, J.; and Weiser, M. The ParcTab Ubiquitous Computing Experiment. Xerox Parc technical report.
25. Weiser, M. The Computer for the 21st Century. *Scientific American.* pp.94-100, September, 1991.
26. Wellner, P. The DigitalDesk Calculator: Tangible Manipulation on a Desk Top Display, *Proceedings of UIST'91.* pp.27-33. 1991.
27. Zue, V. Human Computer Interactions Using Language Based Technology. *IEEE International Symposium on Speech, Image Processing & Neural Networks.* Hong Kong. 1994

Cooperating with people: the Intelligent Classroom

David Franklin

Department of Computer Science
University of Chicago
1100 E. 58th, Chicago IL 60637
franklin@cs.uchicago.edu

Abstract

People frequently complain that it is too difficult to figure out how to get computers to do what they want. However, with a computer system that actually tries to understand what its users are doing, people can interact in ways that are more natural to them. We have been developing a system, the Intelligent Classroom, that does exactly this. The Intelligent Classroom uses cameras and microphones to sense a speaker's actions and then infers his intentions from those actions. Finally, it uses these intentions to decide what to do to best cooperate with the speaker. In the Intelligent Classroom, the speaker need not worry about how to operate the Classroom; he may simply go about his lecture and trust the Classroom to assist him at the appropriate moments.

Introduction

This paper describes a method for integrating computer vision, plan recognition and autonomous robotics research to construct cooperative systems that people can interact with in a natural and intuitive manner. In particular, the paper describes the Intelligent Classroom and the elements of its design that allow it to cooperate with a speaker as he gives a presentation.

This cooperation is first shown through its interaction with the speaker. The Classroom uses video cameras to observe the motion and gestures of the speaker and uses microphones to recognize a small vocabulary of utterances. Using what it observes, the Classroom attempts to infer what the speaker is trying to do and then acts based on what it believes the speaker would like it to do. By doing this, the Classroom will encourage speakers to incorporate whatever media is most appropriate to their presentations; it will support a wide range of media types (such as video tapes, Powerpoint or HTML slides, or the display output from a laptop computer) and allow a speaker to easily control them through natural gestures and speech. One of our primary goals in designing the Classroom is for speakers to only require

Copyright ©1998, American Association for Artificial Intelligence (www.aaai.org). All rights reserved.

a brief (no more than five minute) introduction to the facility before their presentations.

Also, the Classroom will provide speakers with an easy way of producing fair quality videos of their presentations. Based on what it has inferred about the speaker's intentions the presentation cameras pan, tilt and zoom to best capture what is important at every moment in the lecture. This will allow interesting lectures to be shown on cable TV, videos of entire classes to be distributed, and lectures to be broadcast in support of distance learning – extending learning beyond the confines of a traditional classroom.

An Integrated AI domain

For the Intelligent Classroom to be successful (as outlined in the introduction) there are a few things that it must do. It must:

- use real sensors (cameras and microphones) to produce information that the plan recognizer can use.

- use this sensory data to infer the speaker's goals (requiring an extensive library describing the plans that the speaker might attempt).

- use the results of this plan recognition to determine what actions to take.

The problem of how to sense what is going on in the Classroom, while very important to the success of the project, will only be discussed briefly in this paper. Some of the more interesting issues are discussed in (Franklin & Flachsbart 1998). This paper focuses on how to understand what the speaker is trying to do, and how to use this understanding to produce cooperative behavior.

To infer the speaker's intentions, the Classroom uses plan recognition techniques to suggest (and reject) possible explanations for the speaker's actions. (Each plan in the Classroom's library describes the actions the speaker will take in pursuing it and also provides temporal constraints.) The Classroom follows along as the speaker progresses through his plan and it takes action at the moments that it deems appropriate.

Scenarios

The following scenarios outline a few of the sorts of cooperative behavior to be implemented in the Intelligent Classroom. They show the sorts of sequences of actions the Classroom could identify and what it would do in response.

What is the speaker doing?

> The Classroom observes the speaker walk away from the podium and over to the chalkboard. As he is walking, the camera zooms out to follow him and, once he has reached the chalkboard and stopped, the Classroom adjusts the lights and sets the camera to show the portion of the chalkboard he is likely to write on.

In this example, the Classroom recognizes that the speaker is planning to write on the chalkboard. The plan for writing on the chalkboard might consist of: (1) moving towards the chalkboard, (2) stopping in front of the chalkboard, (3) picking up a piece of chalk, and (4) writing on the chalkboard. After observing the first two steps, the Classroom infers that the speaker wants to write on the chalkboard.

At all times, the Classroom considers the perceived intentions of the speaker in deciding what it should do. Before the start of this example, the Classroom believes that the speaker intends to speak at the podium for a while. In response to this, it has decided to zoom in on the speaker's face to capture his facial expressions as he speaks. When it sees that he intends to write, it adjusts the camera in response.

What is the speaker asking me to do?

> The speaker is in the midst of lecturing from a set of slides when a member of the audience asks a question pertaining to the previous slide. The speaker points to the light switch, gestures upwards, and says "Let's go back to the previous slide." The Classroom brings up the lights a bit and displays the earlier slide. The camera briefly shows the slide and then pans over to the speaker as he begins to answer the question.

In this example, the speaker is essentially telling the Classroom what he would like for it to do. So, while in the first example, the speaker was just going about lecturing and letting the Classroom figure out how to help, in this example, the Classroom can view the speaker's actions as direct commands. The gesture where the speaker points to the light switch and moves his hands upwards is understood as a command to bring up the lights and the utterance "go back to the previous slide" is also treated as a command.

Although the speaker's actions in this example appear to be of a very different nature than those in the first example, the Classroom uses the same mechanism to produce the cooperative behavior. The Classroom uses the speaker's actions to recognize what the speaker is trying to do (for example, that the speaker wants the lights to be brought up) and uses these inferred intentions to determine what action to take in order to be cooperative.

Following the presentation outline

> The speaker is lecturing from a set of slides and notices that he is running out of time. He says "Let's skip ahead to the video." The Classroom plays the video and, when it has finished, displays the slide that would have followed the video under normal circumstances. After discussing a few more slides, the speaker says "Let's skip ahead to the conclusion." The Classroom displays the "Conclusion" slide and the speaker finishes his presentation.

A presentation outline tells the Classroom what the key events (slides, videos, desired camera shots) in a presentation are and what order they will occur in. It allows the Classroom to anticipate what will happen next and can even instruct the Classroom to take particular actions without being explicitly told to by the speaker. If the speaker has provided the Classroom with a presentation outline[1], the Classroom will follow along with it while the speaker gives his presentation; if the speaker deviates from the outline, the Classroom detects that and follows the speaker.

In the example above, the speaker needs to speed up his lecture and so decides to skip portions of what he had intended to present. He lets the Classroom know this by what he says. The Classroom associates the phrases "the video" and "the conclusion" with particular places in the outline and is therefore able to keep up with the speaker.

Design issues

In order to produce cooperative behavior, an agent must not only perform the appropriate actions, but perform them at the right time. As a result, even when the Intelligent Classroom knows what the speaker is trying to do, it still must carefully synchronize its actions with the speaker's. For example, when the speaker goes to the chalkboard to write, there are two very different camera techniques that the Classroom must use: one for when he walks and the other for when he writes. If, when the speaker was walking, the Classroom were to frame him as if he were writing, the resulting footage would appear ludicrous. Because of this need for synchronization, the Intelligent Classroom produces unique challenges that cannot be easily solved using existing plan representation. We will now describe a new way of representing plans that facilitates synchronization and show how cooperative behavior can be produced using them.

---

[1] The Classroom will have a large library of default behaviors that will be sufficient for typical presentations. Through a presentation outline, a speaker can tell the Classroom how to respond to particular events in his presentation.

```
(define-plan (move-to-cboard-and-lecture)
  :main-actor
    (person ?lector)
  :roles
    ((intelligent-classroom ?classroom))
  :accomplishes
    ((do ?lector (lecture-at-cboard)))
  :processes
    ((_p1 ?lector
          (lector-move-to-cboard-and-lecture))
     (_p2 ?classroom
          (observe-lector-move-to-cboard-and-lecture ?lector)))
  :synchronization
    ((starts (_p1 _1) (_p2 _1))
     (equals (_p1 _3) (_p2 _2))))

(define-process (lector-move-to-cboard-and-lecture)
  :main-actor
    (person ?lector)
  :roles
    ((chalkboard ?cboard)
     (chalk ?chalk))
  :steps
    ((_1 (achieve (at ?lector ?cboard))
         (wait-for (at ?lector ?cboard) _2))
     (_2 (achieve (holding ?lector ?chalk))
         (wait-for (holding ?lector ?chalk) _3))
     (_3 (do _write (write-on-cboard-and-lecture))
         (wait-for (_write :done) :done)))
  :time-constraints
    ((duration (30 300 3000))
     (process-duration (_1) (0 5 30))
     (process-duration (_2) (0 5 30))))

(define-process (observe-lector-move-to-cboard-and-lecture ?l)
  :main-actor
    (classroom ?class)
  :roles
    ((person ?l))
  :steps
    ((_1 (do (track-moving-person ?l)))
     (_2 (do _track (track-person-write-and-lecture ?l)))))
```

Figure 1: Plan and process definitions for the Intelligent Classroom

Plan representation

In order to be clear as to what our plan representation means, we define some terms. A *process* is a sequence of actions that will be executed by a single agent (such as the speaker or the Classroom). Using this definition, a STRIPS plan for stacking blocks would be considered a process. We have developed a language for describing processes that have simultaneous actions and conditional branching. A *plan* is a set of processes (often to be executed by a number of different agents) that, when executed together correctly, accomplish a particular goal. In the Intelligent Classroom, many plans have some processes executed by the speaker and other processes executed by the Classroom. It is important to note that this is not really a new definition of plan – any plan that has a step of the form "wait for this event to happen" is implicitly representing processes external to its main actor. This definition simply makes these external processes explicit.

Figure 1 shows a simple plan and two of its processes that represent a speaker's plan for going to the chalkboard and writing. The plan definition details who the actors are, what the plan accomplishes, what processes need to be executed, and how they should be synchronized. The first item under :processes states that a process labeled _p1, executed by ?lector and named lector-move-to-chalkboard-and-lecture is a part of this plan. The first item under :synchronization indicates that step _1 of process _p1 needs to start at the same moment as step _1 of process _p2. The second item indicates that step _3 of process _p1 must occur over the same time interval as step _2 of process _p2.

The process definitions describe who the actors are (the :main-actor is the actor who executes the process), what steps will be executed in the running of the process, and how long different parts of the process should take to run. For the process lector-move-to-chalkboard-and-lecture, the first item under :steps states that the first step (labeled _1) in running this process is to achieve the goal of being at the chalkboard, and once this goal is achieved, to go on to the step labeled _2. For the same process, the first item under :time-constraints states that the process must take between 30 and 3000 seconds to run, and will typically take 300 seconds. (The "typical" values can be used to predict how long a process should take.) The other two items indicate how long the steps _1 and _2 must take to execute.

Process manager

Crucial to producing cooperative behavior, the *process manager* is responsible for monitoring the progress of all the processes going on in the Classroom. For example, the Classroom views the presentation outline provided by the speaker as a process; as the speaker goes through his lecture, the process manager keeps track of his place in the presentation outline.

Figure 2 shows the important structures in the process manager. At the highest level, there is a set of active processes. In each process, the steps are treated as the states of a finite automaton; to monitor a process, the process manager keeps track of which step the process is in. The process manager will advance a process to a different state when it observes one of the events that the process is waiting for. For example, the process is currently in step 2 and if the process designated by _track signals failure, the process will go on to step 1.

When a process moves to a new step, the process manager spawns processes for each of the actions (propositions to achieve or processes to do) given in the step definition. Then, while these subprocesses run, the original process waits for any of the events given in the step definition to occur. Finally, when such an event occurs, the process manager halts all of the subprocesses and advances the process based on which event occurred.

There are two types of events that a process may wait on: a memory proposition becoming true and a process sending a particular signal. Processes send signals when they start, when they are done, and sometimes to communicate important events they have observed. In addition, the Intelligent Classroom is always performing some basic sensing to keep track of where the speaker is; this default sensing will also signal events.

When the process manager receives a signal, it attempts to explain it through one of the processes it is monitoring (find a process that is waiting for that signal). If no explanation can be found, the system will

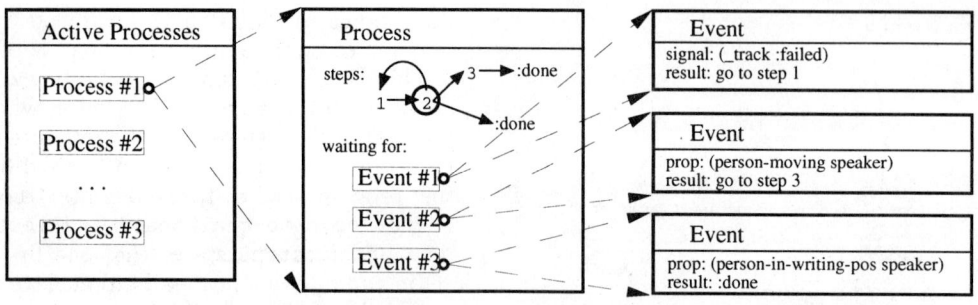

Figure 2: Important structures in the process manager

hypothesize new processes that could explain the signal. When new processes are hypothesized, it is likely that most of them are actually incorrect[2]. So, the process manager needs to deal with sets of processes, and be able to reject processes as future sensory data contradicts their presence. One way that a process can be rejected is if its temporal constraints are violated. Each step in a process has a shortest, expected and longest completion time associated with it. Using this information, the process manager computes the interval that any given event should occur in. If the system fails to sense this event in this interval, a temporal constraint has been violated and the process can be removed from consideration.

Monitoring other agent's processes

There may be many processes making up a given plan, but the Intelligent Classroom itself will be running only some of them. In order for the Classroom to stay synchronized with the other processes, it must monitor these external processes as well as its own. For example, if the speaker's process is "walk to the chalkboard and write something," the Classroom will need to observe him as he walks, notice when he stops, and perhaps detect that he is actually writing.

To accomplish this, the Classroom must run observation steps that parallel the action steps in other agent's processes. The Classroom executes steps in processes where it is the main actor and performs observation steps in processes where it is not. For steps that cannot be observed (for example, if the lecturer mentally chooses which color chalk to use), it uses the step's typical completion time to determine when to expect the next step.

---

[2] Were the system to use a measure of likelihood, many of the hypothesized processes could be eliminated immediately. We have not yet committed to any particular technique for determining likelihood. In the short term, we will provide "reasonableness" tests for every process: memory queries that indicate whether it would be reasonable for an agent to run this process in the current situation.

Plan recognition and cooperation

Most of the work of plan recognition is accomplished by the process manager as it recognizes what processes the agents in the Intelligent Classroom are executing. In fact, by most definitions, the process manager is actually doing traditional plan recognition. However, given how we define "plan", the system must perform one additional step to recognize plans rather than processes. As mentioned previously, a plan consists of a number of processes, being executed by at least one agent. Plan recognition, given a set of active processes, is accomplished by finding a plan that both explains and is consistent with the processes. A process is explained by a plan if the process matches one of the processes in the plan definition and is consistent if none of the plan's synchronization or time constraints are violated by it.

Due to the linear nature of lectures, we hope to be able to avoid the problem of having to consider sets of plans (this would render plan recognition intractable.) Instead we will address two ways that we expect a speaker to go from one plan to another: through interruptions and through abandonment. With interruptions, the speaker temporarily suspends his current plan to pursue another, while with abandonment, he never resumes the old one. The Classroom will maintain a stack of suspended plans which will aid it in following along as the speaker interrupts and then resumes or abandons his plans.

Most of the plans to be recognized in the Intelligent Classroom contain a process that has the Classroom as its main actor. This means that a speaker, in executing his part of a plan, expects the Classroom to do its part of the plan: to cooperate. Cooperation, as might be expected, is achieved through being aware of what the agents around you are trying to do and then seeing how you fit into their plans. To do this, the Classroom must know what plans and processes the speaker is executing and exactly how far each of the processes has progressed. Otherwise, the Classroom will frequently perform the right actions, but at the wrong time and hinder rather than help the speaker. The synchronization declarations in the plan definitions tell the Classroom how to synchronize its actions with those of other agents.

Ambiguity in plan recognition

Any system that uses the results of plan recognition to affect what actions it takes must deal with the problem of ambiguity: the system often needs to take action before it has determined exactly what the other agent is doing. Because the Intelligent Classroom always needs to be producing video footage, this is always the case. For example, consider what really should happen when the speaker walks towards the chalkboard. There are at least two processes that the speaker might be executing: he could be going to the chalkboard to write, or he could be going there to lecture. While he is walking, the Classroom cannot tell which of these processes he is running. But, at the same time, the Classroom must continue to film him.

In situations like this, the Classroom has to act on what it can infer: in this example, the Classroom can only determine that the speaker plans to go somewhere to do something. The Classroom's process in this plan involves filming the speaker as he moves and finally stops somewhere. Then, as the Classroom narrows down the speaker's possible plans, it is able to take more specific actions.

Plan ambiguity occurs in the Classroom when it hypothesizes a set of processes for the speaker (based on an observed action). This ambiguity is resolved by repeatedly substituting a process (for which each process in the set is a specialization) for the whole set. This process will be the one that the Classroom acts on. As processes from the process set are eliminated, the Classroom is able to select increasingly specific processes to represent the set until, finally, it knows the precise process that the speaker is executing.

To support this technique of further specifying processes as it is executing them, the Classroom will rely on a hierarchy of plans and processes(Kautz & Allen 1986). The processes will be defined so that, when the Classroom is executing a general process, it can switch to a more specific version of the process, starting the specific process at the point where the general process left off. For this example, when the speaker begins writing on the board, the Classroom use the more specific plan and will immediately start framing him as someone writing on the chalkboard.

Dealing with the physical world

The first several parts of this section describe only the high-level operation of the Intelligent Classroom. But, like any other physically embodied system, the Classroom must be able to sense what is going on around it and to physically take action. To facilitate this, the Classroom architecture consists of two components: the high-level execution system described in this paper, and a control system that links together reactive skills and vision modules to form tight control loops(Firby et al. 1995). As a part of the control system, we use the Gargoyle modular visual system(Prokopowicz et al. 1996) and have implemented Perseus' tracking

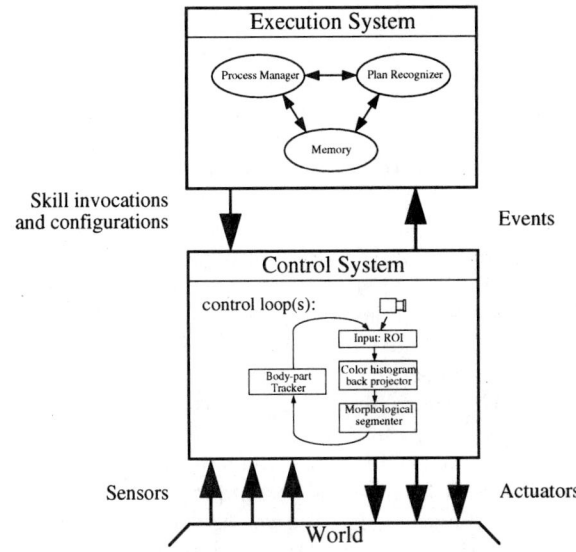

Figure 3: The Intelligent Classroom's Architecture

algorithms(Kahn et al. 1996) with it(Flachsbart 1997), allowing the Classroom to locate and track the speaker's head, hands and feet.

The lower-level processes tell the control system how to build control loops for specific tasks, and then observe them. When necessary, these processes can modify the control loops' behavior by setting parameters or even swapping in new skills or vision modules. (Gargoyle was specifically designed to facilitate building and adapting these sorts of dynamic control loops.) This allows the high-level system to aid the sensing system by giving it useful contextual information. For example, if the Classroom dims the lights, it can adjust the parameters of the appropriate vision modules so that the vision system does not suddenly go blind. Figure 3 shows the system architecture we use for the Intelligent Classroom. (There is a simple control loop displayed in the control system.) (Franklin & Flachsbart 1998) discusses the architecture in greater detail and outlines how contextual information can be used to dynamically configure the control loops.

In addition to aiding computer vision, situational context is needed to help with speech recognition. The speech recognizer can use contextual information to restrict what it listens for. Also, to prevent the Classroom from acting on speech that is simply part of the presentation, the Classroom will only "listen" when the speaker is addressing it[3].

---

[3]We are considering two possible techniques that the speaker may use to indicate that he is addressing the Classroom: (1) preceding all voice commands with "Computer" or "Classroom" and (2) facing a computer monitor that will serve as the "embodiment" of the Classroom.

Related work

The design of the Intelligent Classroom has been influenced by the work of researchers in several AI disciplines: plan recognition, process-based execution monitoring, knowledge representation and robotics (discussed earlier). In this section we describe the research that has most strongly influenced our design.

This research got its start through an effort to extend DMAP(Martin 1993) to do plan recognition. We have extended the DMAP notion of concept predictions to deal with events – allowing us to not only explain what we observe, but also to know what to look for. We have also taken seriously the DMAP commitment that a system's memory should not be treated as a list of facts and beliefs, but rather that the memory should be used to control how the system works.

The process manager's technique of building explanations for what it observes is based in part on PAM(Wilensky 1981). Both build representations of what is going on incrementally: first trying to explain new input based on current hypotheses of what is happening and then, only when that fails, proposing new hypotheses. Also, both represent what the different agents are doing and why. Our representation of plans and processes has been influenced in many ways by Schank's representation of scripts(Schank & Abelson 1977).

The idea of viewing the operation of the world as the interaction of a set of concurrent processes is adapted from (Earl & Firby 1997). They have also looked at ways to learn what events should be observed (and when) through the repeated execution of processes.

The view of processes as being sequences of steps where each step has a number of conditions that it waits for (signals from other processes or memory propositions becoming true) is taken from Firby's work on RAPs(Firby 1994).

Finally, it is important to contrast this work with Georgia Tech's Classroom 2000 project(Brotherton & Abowd 1998). The Classroom 2000 utilizes ubiquitous computing techniques to record everything that happens during a lecture and then integrates the events and provides a web-based interface to them. The Classroom 2000 does not try to understand what the lecturer does – given the researcher's goals, it does not need to.

Conclusion

This paper outlines a technique for effectively cooperating with people through building understandings of what they are doing and deciding what actions would be helpful. We discuss how, in order to cooperate in this way, a system must explicitly represent the processes people execute, and follow along while they execute them. Further, we describe how these techniques are used in a particular integrated system: the Intelligent Classroom.

It is important to note that the Classroom is not fully implemented yet; the facility itself is currently under construction. However, the algorithms described in this paper have been implemented and tested on a system prototype that uses real cameras but virtual actuators.

Beyond the Intelligent Classroom, we hope that the techniques presented in this paper will prove useful in many other domains where human-computer interaction is involved: from games (where the system may attempt to thwart a player's intentions) to providing better help for desktop computer applications.

Acknowledgments

Thanks to R. James Firby, Kristian Hammond, Joshua Flachsbart, Alain Roy and the anonymous reviewers for insightful discussions regarding this research and for helpful comments on the paper.

References

Brotherton, J. A., and Abowd, G. D. 1998. Rooms take note: Room takes notes! In *AAAI Technical Report SS-98-02*.

Earl, C., and Firby, R. J. 1997. Combined execution and monitoring for control of autonomous agents. In *1st International Conference on Autonomous Agents*.

Firby, R. J.; Kahn, R. E.; Prokopowicz, P. N.; and Swain, M. J. 1995. An architecture for vision and action. In *Proceedings of IJCAI-95*.

Firby, R. J. 1994. Task networks for controlling continuous processes. *2nd International Conference on AI Planning Systems*.

Flachsbart, J. 1997. Gargoyle: Vision in the intelligent classroom. Master's thesis, University of Chicago.

Franklin, D., and Flachsbart, J. 1998. All gadget and no representation makes jack a dull environment. In *AAAI Technical Report SS-98-02*.

Kahn, R. E.; Swain, M. J.; Prokopowicz, P. N.; and Firby, R. J. 1996. Gesture recognition using the perseus architecture. *Computer Vision and Pattern Recognition*.

Kautz, H. A., and Allen, J. F. 1986. Generalized plan recognition. In *Proceedings of AAAI-86*.

Martin, C. E. 1993. Direct memory access parsing. Technical report, University of Chicago (CS-93-07).

Prokopowicz, P. N.; Kahn, R. E.; Firby, R. J.; and Swain, M. J. 1996. Gargoyle: Context-sensitive active vision for mobile robots. In *Proceedings of AAAI-96*.

Schank, R., and Abelson, R. 1977. *Scripts Plans Goals and Understanding*. Lawrence Erlbaum. chapter 3.

Wilensky, R. 1981. *Inside Computer Understanding*. Lawrence Erlbaum Associates, Inc. chapter 7.

Integrating AI Components for a Military Planning Application

Marie A. Bienkowski
SRI International
Menlo Park, CA 94025
bienk@erg.sri.com

Louis J. Hoebel
General Electric CRD
Niskayuna, NY 12309
hoebel@crd.ge.com

Abstract

We integrated three mature AI reasoning systems and several legacy military systems in order to provide human planners with advanced capabilities in a military planning domain. The integration demonstrates the operation of a diverse set of AI applications that present a unified system to a human planner in a realistic and meaningful context. We began with an operational planning support system and integrated into it AI components that filled technology gaps. These components, drawn from AI research laboratories, were a generative planner, a temporal reasoner and plan visualizer, and a knowledge-based plan critiquer. The resulting system uses a shared representation to support plan authoring, consistency checking, feasibility analysis, replanning, and visibility into the plan. The support provided is flexible and user controlled. We describe lessons learned from the simultaneous application and integration of mature AI research software, and for individual system components, primarily as they relate to the representation of plans.

Introduction

Military planning support systems demand end-to-end functionality that can be provided by the integration of separately developed components, including AI and legacy systems. Pursuing both application and integration requires tailoring tools to the requirements of a user while making the integration appear seamless through a combination of common interfaces and the use of shared representations and reasoning tasks. The challenges for integration multiply when we consider the need of the end-to-end system to augment rather than supplant human reasoning and to support an existing military work process.

The system described in this paper had, as its genesis, a manual plan authoring tool, the Air Campaign Planning Tool (ACPT), which the U.S. Air Force (USAF) developed after the air war in the Persian Gulf to capture their experiences in developing and executing the air campaign. ACPT was designed to support a new military planning paradigm called "strategy-to-task." Strategy-to-task planning involves articulating high-level military strategies down to specific actions or tasks. It is a complex human endeavor, and the goal of the integrated system we describe was to combine technology into an end-to-end planning system to better support it. As a standalone application, ACPT lacks support for the time-consuming and complex tasks of generating consistent and complete plans. ACPT also lacks support for generating qualitatively different plans to address the same high-level campaign objectives and then estimating the feasibility of these plans. Additional system requirements were for military planners to be able to (1) achieve a coherent view of a plan that includes its structure, resources, and timeline, (2) understand the results of changes in the plan, (3) manage dependencies, and (4) perform "what-if" analyses.

The planning system we describe is called the IFD4 system because it resulted from a year-long effort called the Integrated Feasibility Demonstration 4 (IFD4). IFD4 was the fourth major demonstration effort of the [D]ARPA/Rome Laboratory (RL) Planning and Scheduling Initiative (ARPI). ARPI is a multiyear program, begun in 1990, for the development of the next generation of knowledge- and constraint-based planning and scheduling technology (Fowler, Cross, and Owens 1995). As is typical of a feasibility demonstration (see Bienkowski and Edwards, 1996), the IFD4 system as it was demonstrated in 1996 is not in current use. Instead, based on the favorable reviews it received from government sponsors and the military end users, parts of the system and system concept were transitioned to other programs within DARPA in early 1997. The IFD4 system concept and software modules were also used for a 1997 ARPI demonstration on planning and evaluation of multiple alternative plans using advice, visualization, and simulation. Also, some IFD4 concepts and code have been included in deployed versions of ACPT.

The IFD4 system development team[1] integrated several AI reasoning systems in order to meet the demands of the strategy-to-task planning application. The IFD4 system started with ACPT and a campaign analysis tool. ACPT provides an excellent user interface to a text-based plan editor and database, and provides a way for users to organize an air campaign hierarchically from high-level military

---

Copyright © 1998, American Association for Artificial Intelligence (www.aaai.org). All rights reserved.

[1] The integration described in this paper was accomplished by several companies: SRI International, General Electric Corporate Research Division (GE CRD), Information Sciences Institute (ISI), and ISX Corporation. Personnel contributing to the effort are called out in the acknowledgements. Direction was provided by DARPA and Rome Laboratory.

objectives to low-level strikes on targets. The campaign analysis tool is a deployed USAF tool called the Conventional Targeting Effectiveness Model (CTEM), and it calculates detailed planning actions for target strikes. The team extended these by integrating INSPECT, a plan critiquing system; SIPE-2, a generative planner; and the Tachyon temporal reasoner and its derivative presentation agent, the Plan Viewing Tool (PVT)[2].

The IFD4 integration had several significant outcomes in addition to the transitions mentioned above. It resulted in extensions to ACPT and the development of new tools derived from existing technology. It also produced a first attempt at a shared representation for plans, and a large knowledge base for air campaign support planning. These developments were driven both by user requirements and technology limitations.

In the next section we introduce the domain and air campaign planning. We then describe the component technologies and their interactions in the IFD4 system. The final section of the paper summarizes the general lessons learned.

Manual Air Campaign Planning

A human planner following strategy-to-task planning (Warden 1989) to develop an air campaign uses guidance from a commanding military authority, and objectives from political and military authorities, to create a prioritized set of tasks that are traceable back to high-level strategies. The detailed air campaign is a set of strikes on targets over time. Air campaign planning is largely a manual process supported by paper maps with overlay drawings.

Campaign planners find it difficult to keep track of the myriad details of a large operation over many days. Military plans, in general, are unlike the short-lived plans which are created then executed in most AI planning domains, and are more like those found in factory scheduling because of setup time and resources contentions. The dependencies among the actions in campaign plans, which are indispensable for providing plan justifications and for analyzing hypothetical modifications to plans, can be difficult to recall at execution time. Situations and operating constraints change hourly, and there is an adversarial component that makes the outcome of events uncertain. This latter feature differentiates campaign planning from transportation planning. Numerous and sometimes vague constraints (e.g., reduce enemy morale) must be met. In terms of size (i.e., the number of terminal or atomic action nodes) and complexity (number of planning levels and resources), military air campaigns dwarf the planning domains typically investigated by AI planning researchers. (Lee and Wolverton, 1998, describe the knowledge base; Weld, 1994, presents typical research domains.)

We have learned that the application of AI tools to this domain can support human planners' tasks but not automate them. Unlike typical AI planning applications, then, the task is not to generate and execute a plan, e.g., for moving blocks on a table or trucks on a roadway. Instead, the domain experts on the IFD4 project team, drawn from Checkmate (a USAF office responsible for contingency air campaign planning) helped us understand what they needed to create better air campaign plans. The integration performed for IFD4 was motivated by the need to provide the user with end-to-end connectivity throughout their planning process. The plan representation underlying the IFD4 system enables the human planner to keep track of the detailed dependencies in the plan, enables the construction of feasible plans, and supports analysis and review. The human planner retains interactive control over the planning operations.

Military campaign planning can be likened to any situation where crisis response personnel are attacking an adversary: fighting forest fires (uncertain outcome of actions), oil spill emergency response (evaluating alternatives and contingencies), logistics and transportation (optimizing use of resources), and humanitarian relief efforts (estimation of plan feasibility).

ACPT provides support for air campaign planning by allowing human planners to enter objectives and objective descriptions as text strings, and to manually link the objectives to subordinate air tasks. The goals of IFD4 were to (1) provide a user-controlled system that automated as much of the process as was possible; (2) capture, maintain, communicate, and apply assumptions and constraints as they are developed and changed; and (3) provide analysis and viewing of the plan.

Early in the IFD4 development cycle, candidate technologies for integration with ACPT were presented by ARPI technologists to Checkmate planners. Based on the capabilities of the technologies, user requirements were solicited. The resulting system development was conducted with military planners from Checkmate as team members. Checkmate also provided the end user evaluation criteria, and critiqued proposed user interfaces (an instance of user-centered design, as in DeBellis and Haapala 1995). Technical evaluation criteria for the integration were to (1) make the system operation appear seamless to the user beginning from ACPT, (2) function on a 2-3 day plan with up to 500 targets, (3) manage a shared plan representation among all components, and (4) show end-to-end operation on a demonstration script that began and ended with ACPT.

Components

The IFD4 system is unique in two ways. First, it utilizes existing, independently developed AI modules to supplement a deployed, manual plan authoring tool, ACPT. Second, it integrates capabilities from several AI reasoning systems to produce a plan construction, critiquing and viewing system within ACPT. In this section, we describe the individual components and their IFD4 roles. Figure 1 shows the functional integration

---

[2] SIPE-2 is a trademark of SRI International. Tachyon and INSPECT are products of GE CRD, and ISI, respectively.

accomplished in IFD4.

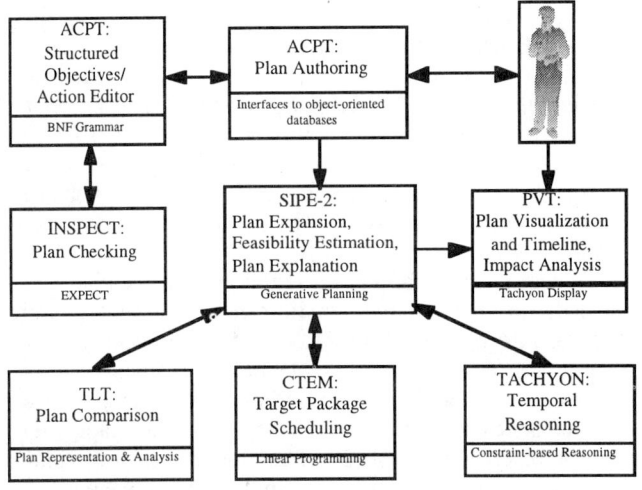

Figure 1: Functional Architecture

ACPT

The capabilities provided by ACPT include viewing commanders' guidance and scenario data, defining objectives for the air campaign, and assigning target sets to objectives. ACPT supports the use of modeling tools such as CTEM to assess the effectiveness of a plan. ACPT outputs a prioritized target list, a plan that includes required forces, and a schedule for force movement. It relies on an objectives hierarchy—a linked set of objectives that range from the national level down to a specific tactical course of action.

ACPT is implemented in an architecture that relies on specialized classes to provide operations such as wrappers for transparent data access, and plan entry and presentation (Bienkowski and Edwards 1996). This architecture allows ACPT to interface with other, supporting tools such as plan analysis and critiquing tools.

ACPT provided a baseline planning support capability from which to develop the IFD4 system. The core of ACPT is its representation of air objectives. As a result of IFD4, ACPT could better represent objectives using a grammar that was developed for use with INSPECT (see below); this includes representations such as measures of success, actions, restrictions, percentage complete, and review status.

INSPECT

In the IFD4 system, the task of INSPECT is to check the consistency and completeness of aspects of the emerging and final campaign plan (Valente, Gil, and Swartout 1996). INSPECT produces an agenda of problems in the air campaign plan (ordered from most to least serious), provides an explanation of each problem, and suggests fixes. The problems checked include completeness of objective, reasonableness of plan structure, and availability of resources. The user can control how INSPECT operates by selecting automatic or on-demand checks and by choosing which problems it checks.

INSPECT is generated from EXPECT, a general knowledge acquisition architecture (Swartout and Gil 1996). EXPECT represents problem solving and factual knowledge, and supports interactions and user changes to the knowledge base. INSPECT is an instance of an expert system that knows the basic errors and fixes in building air campaign plans.

During the integration of INSPECT with ACPT, the developers saw an opportunity for improving the unstructured and semantically empty terms of the objectives representation in ACPT. A structured representation for objectives (specified by a grammar) and a structured, template-driven objectives editor was added to ACPT (Valente, Swartout, and Gil 1996). The development of this structured representation and its enthusiastic acceptance by ACPT users was a major success of IFD4.

SIPE-2

In the IFD4 system, ACPT and INSPECT operate in tandem to create and validate an air campaign plan that is specified to a certain level of detail. SIPE-2 provides an estimation of the feasibility of this air campaign. Using a plan from ACPT, it fills in the details that are needed to execute the plan down to the level of flying missions and refueling planes. SIPE-2 relies on external programs for temporal reasoning (Tachyon) and target scheduling (CTEM). Before, after, or during planning, goals and resources can be interactively added to or deleted from the plan. This feature provides the ACPT user with a what-ifing capability (Bienkowski 1997).

SIPE-2 is a partial-order planner that supports planning at multiple levels of abstraction (Wilkins 1988). SIPE-2's plan representation goes beyond the ACPT objective hierarchy. It automatically captures the hierarchical relationship among goals and subgoals or actions, the interdependencies among goals and actions, and the rationale for planning choices. SIPE-2 also has an efficient representation of constraints, resources, and causal rules.

Using plan critics that operate at the end of a planning level, SIPE-2 can supplement its goal and action representation with temporal information from Tachyon, and force packaging results from CTEM. SIPE-2 can produce various outputs from the plan representation, including that used by PVT.

SIPE-2 relies on an extensive knowledge base of plan operations. Its IFD4 knowledge base covers gaining and maintaining air superiority over both friendly and enemy territory, force application against weapons of mass destruction, and support requirements (refueling, reconnaissance, and protection from air and ground threats). The knowledge base also represents the results of an intelligence analysis of the situation, which focuses SIPE-2's planning on the most important parts of the situation.

TLT

TLT, a simple plan comparison tool, was the last addition to the IFD4 system, and was developed in response to critiques of the early demonstrations. TLT generates a simple table of differences in resource usage based on a traversal of the SIPE-2 plan representations and resource annotations. This table provides a view of the quantitative difference between two qualitatively different plans. SIPE-2 generates the different plans either as a result of a reduction in resources (as shown in IFD4) or by means of a user controlling its plan expansion with high-level advice for operator selection (Myers 1996). This work led to an investigation of the relationship between plan explanation and advice.

CTEM

CTEM is an analytical tool based on an optimizing scheduler and resource allocator. CTEM takes information about resources (strike aircraft and weapons); targets (location and type); and preferences (e.g., the desired level of destruction) and assigns resources to targets over days. It schedules specific missions by pairing a strike aircraft with munitions required to destroy a target to a certain level of destruction.

CTEM produces force requirements estimations and schedules at such an accuracy level that Checkmate routinely uses it for feasibility assessments of strike missions. Therefore, we used CTEM within the feasibility estimation computed by SIPE-2 for the IFD4 system. SIPE-2 plans the air campaign to the target level, then CTEM's results on that target set are incorporated into SIPE-2's plan representation. SIPE-2 generates a planning problem—provide support for this strike mission—from the mission list output by CTEM. SIPE-2 then generates support missions for each strike mission generated by CTEM.

Tachyon

Tachyon is an implementation of a constraint-based model for representing and reasoning about time (Stillman, Arthur, and Farley 1996). The Tachyon model contains events and interevent constraints and is capable of reasoning about both qualitative and quantitative aspects of time, including convex and nonconvex constraints (Allen 1983).

Tachyon is employed in the IFD4 system both as a temporal constraint reasoner for the generation of plans by SIPE-2 and as the means for constructing hierarchical, time-based views of the plan in PVT. PVT thus has all of Tachyon's capabilities including search and temporal what-if analysis.

Plan Viewing Tool

An early requirement of the IFD4 system was to provide visibility into a plan. We initially thought that this could be provided by existing tools, such as the plan graph layout used in SIPE-2. We discovered that these views did not highlight the critical plan elements for the air campaign planning task, mainly the time phasing of the operation. Consequently, a new tool was developed to meet Checkmate's requirements. This tool, based on a Tachyon display which shows the temporal scope of actions on a timeline, displayed resource status indicators that showed how the campaign looked in relation to resources for specific objectives The indicators that showed if a resource was sufficiently supplied (green), in transit (yellow) or unavailable (red).

PVT was used in IFD4 to present a view of the plan that included its parent-child relationship, resources, and temporal information. A user could view the plan at one level or drill down to subordinate tasks. Tachyon's query capabilities enabled the user to find plan elements that used a particular resource. In the IFD4 system, this capability was combined with SIPE-2 replanning an existing plan using new resources in order to show how replanning of goals given different resources affects the execution or timeline of a plan. In the IFD4 example, the effects of the resource change create tasks that are not accomplished until after a specific time has passed.

Component Interactions

A military planner begins the construction of an air campaign plan by developing a set of air objectives based on high-level commander's guidance, including national and political objectives. The planner uses the objectives editor to create a set of air objectives and to link them both to high-level objectives (e.g., show of force) and to lower-level tasks that achieve the objective. The use of the structured objectives editor allows human planners to create well-defined objectives so that the meaning of an objective is the same for different planners. Objectives typically have many tasks and may share tasks with other objectives; ACPT provides a connectivity viewer to make these connections visible.

ACPT objectives are stored in an object-oriented database, and components such as INSPECT and SIPE-2 download the plan from the database via an agent which manages the distributed requests to the ACPT database via remote procedure calls.

INSPECT uses the structured representation creating from the objectives editor for plan critiquing. It can provide assistance at any point during plan development. It provides a critique of the plan structure and an agenda of errors and inconsistencies. These range from warnings that air tasks have no parent air objective, to cautions about proper resource use, temporal sequencing, and the number of air tasks on a single objective. An agenda manager, another extension to ACPT resulting from the IFD4 integration, provides the management and display of the INSPECT plan critiques. As a result of the evaluation conducted during IFD4, we have learned that INSPECT's plan critiquing improves plan quality and allows the planner to concentrate on the planning task without unwarranted intrusion.

After constructing a mixed set of air objectives, air tasks, and targets in ACPT, the planner may choose to conduct a feasibility estimation. SIPE-2 estimates feasibility by showing that a complete plan, which includes support missions and resource assignments, can be generated. SIPE-2 completes the plan (in IFD4, SIPE-2 planned the air superiority part of a full air campaign plan) by generating objectives, tasks, and notional target lists. SIPE-2 generates a set of primitive actions, executable by a group of aircraft or other air assets, that provide protection to friendly aircraft and critical areas from all enemy threats.

SIPE-2 interacts with CTEM to schedule missions and assign resources. CTEM uses SIPE-2-supplied information about targets and the resources available to calculate the type and number of strike assets (either aircraft with munitions or missiles) and schedules the strikes based on task priority and resource availability. SIPE-2 incorporates these results into its plan.

Once strike recommendations are made by CTEM, SIPE-2 continues planning to determine the support requirements of each mission. These include defense (against both hostile aircraft and missiles), refueling, and reconnaissance.

To complete the feasibility estimation, now that the ACPT-provided plan is complete, SIPE-2 collects all missions, and passes them to a resource allocation module. This module allocates resources to missions in a non-optimized, greedy manner. If resources become exhausted, limited alternatives are explored and resource shortfalls may be identified.

As SIPE-2 is generating a complete plan, it uses Tachyon to propogate temporal constraints at the end of every planning level. Tachyon reads a file of constraints and performs temporal reasoning; SIPE-2 then incorporates the updated temporal constraints. Our decision to use CTEM for part of SIPE-2's feasibility estimation shows how use of legacy systems can introduce inflexibility into an end-to-end capability. CTEM fixes the temporal information for use of the strike assets in the SIPE-2 plan but does not accept temporal constraints as input. Thus, temporal reasoning that SIPE-2 did before calling CTEM would have to be discarded. After CTEM's results are in SIPE-2's plan, Tachyon cannot reason about CTEM-contributed temporal information, because it has no access to the rationale for CTEM's temporal decisions.

The next step in campaign planning, as supported by the IFD4 system, is to examine plan details using PVT. Missions with resource shortfalls are annotated by SIPE-2 so they can be highlighted in PVT. All parent links are passed through to allow PVT to propagate resource shortfall information upwards through the goal hierarchy (this required translating SIPE-2's directed acyclic graph representation to PVT's dependency-lattice syntax). This permits display of all higher-level goals that may fail due to resource shortages detected at lower levels. Mission scheduling information is also passed to PVT and propagated upwards. This allows display of the duration of all goals and missions, and identification of schedule overruns.

PVT shows resource status indicators for objectives, tasks, and missions. The status indicators are shown individually at the lowest level and are aggregated for tasks and objectives. In IFD4, the PVT query mechanism was used to check for missions using specific planes, then the SIPE-2 feasibility estimation was redone without those planes available. The results were shown in a new PVT display, and could also be shown using TLT.

Our users wished us to address two aspects of replanning in the SIPE-2 feasibility estimation: resource modification and task addition. Resource modification resulted in the same higher plan abstraction levels, but different schedules and low-level actions. For task addition, the original plan is retained and additional actions are generated, but using only the resources that remain available after the original plan has been completed. We have learned through repeated application of SIPE-2 in military planning domains that its plan representation provides the technical support for replanning, but is not amenable to arbitrary plan editing by humans.

Lessons Learned

Earlier, we listed a set of technical evaluation criteria for the IFD4 integration. We were somewhat unsuccessful in making the system operation appear seamless to the user beginning from ACPT. the lack of complete success was due to the time it took to generate complex displays and to the difficulty of passing planning commands (e.g., delete this resource) among components.

SIPE-2 was able to generate a 3 day plan with up to 363 targets in about 3 minutes. To support this domain, one change was made to SIPE-2. SIPE-2 previously had an n-squared algorithm (where n is the number of choice points in the plan) for determining which actions are in the current alternative plan. Plans in this domain can have thousands of choice points, so this algorithm was replaced by a linear one that orders the choice points.

The IFD4 system was able to use a hybrid plan representation among all components. INSPECT replaced the text-string representation within ACPT with a structured objectives representation based on a grammar, and SIPE-2 extended ACPT's objectives hierarchy with a more complete action and dependency representation. SIPE-2 also incorporated results into its plan representation from CTEM and Tachyon, and produces outputs from its plan representation for PVT.

We almost achieved end-to-end operation on a demonstration script that began and ended with ACPT. The missing link was a method for connecting the ACPT structured objectives representation and the SIPE-2 representation. Consequently, only a few air objectives could be passed from ACPT to SIPE-2, and plan additions could not be returned from SIPE-2 to ACPT.

System integration can be challenging, but we have learned that often it is only through integration that component technologies can be subjected to the feedback that comes from application. Gaps discovered in the integration can lead to new applications for existing technologies, as in the case of PVT, or the creation of new technologies, as in TLT.

A particularly important lesson is that the investment in knowledge acquisition and modeling, while time consuming and costly, pays off by testing the scalability of technology (as in the case of SIPE-2 in IFD4) and may point out useful research issues and near-term applications. Active involvement of the domain experts, both in rapid prototyping and knowledge acquisition, substantially enhances the entire project.

Both developers and users benefit from increased formalization of representations. The formal grammar in IFD4 helps users create meaningful air objectives and also increases INSPECT's ability to provide automated support. This can lead to future payoffs: we are now seeing increased formilization of all aspects of the objective description and a subsequent expansion of the breadth of INSPECT's critiques. Also SIPE-2's generation and maintenance of a hybrid plan representation should be seen as a constructive proof that one need not develop formal representations for each new application.

A final lesson learned is that integration led to standard representations and visualizations of the plan in a way that promoted plan sharing between the human planner and the automated systems. The IFD4 system supports a planning paradigm that explicates links in the plan between high- and low-level actions, and offers a plan development style that supports the user's manual process.

Acknowledgments

David Wilkins provide valuable comments on this paper. The IFD4 development team was Gary Edwards, Jim Shoop, Gregg Menin, Joe Roberts, and Anna Griffith of ISX Corp.; Yolanda Gil, Andre Valente, and Bill Swartout of the ISI; David Wilkins, Tom Lee, Ann Tamaru, and John Mark Agosta of SRI; Jon Stillman, Rick Arthur, and James Farley of GE CRD; Tom Garvey of DARPA; Bill Cotsworth, the CTEM developer; and MAJs Mike Cardenas, Jim Hutto, Mark Aldred, and Steve Cunico of Checkmate. Finally, IFD4 would have been impossible without the support and vision of COL Robert Plebanek of Checkmate.

References

Allen, J. 1983. Maintaining knowledge about temporal intervals. *Communications of the ACM*, 26(11):832-843.

Bienkowski, M., and desJardins, M. 1994. Planning-Based Integrated Decision Support Systems. In Proceedings of the 1994 Conference on AI Planning Systems. 196–201.

Bienkowski, M., and Edwards, G. 1996. Demonstrating the Operational Feasibility of New Technologies: The ARPI IFDs. In Tate, A. ed. *Advanced Planning Technology: Technological Achievements of the ARPA/Rome Laboratory Planning Initiative*. Menlo Park, CA: AAAI Press.

Bienkowski, M. 1997. SOCAP-ACPT Technology Integration and Application. Technical Report, ITAD-7112-AR-97-095, SRI International.

DeBellis, M. and Haapala, C. 1995. User-Centric Software Engineering. *IEEE Expert: Intelligent Systems and their Applications*. 10(1):34-41.

Fowler, N. III; Cross, S.; and Owens, C. 1995. The ARPA-Rome Knowledge-Based Planning and Scheduling Initiative. *IEEE Expert: Intelligent Systems and their Applications*. 10(1):4-9.

Lee, T., and Wolverton, M. 1998. Air and Maritime Campaign Support Mission Knowledge Base. SRI International. Forthcoming.

Myers, K. 1996. Strategic advice for hierarchical planners. In Proceedings of the Fifth International Conference on Principles of Knowledge Representation and Reasoning. San Francisco, CA: Morgan Kaufmann.

Stillman, J., Arthur, R., and Farley, J. 1996. Temporal Reasoning for Mixed-Initiative Planning. In Tate, A. ed. *Advanced Planning Technology: Technological Achievements of the ARPA/Rome Laboratory Planning Initiative*. Menlo Park, Calif.: AAAI Press.

Swartout, W. and Gil, Y. EXPECT: A User-Centered Environment for the Development and Adaptation of Knowledge-Based Planning Aids. In Tate, A. ed. *Advanced Planning Technology: Technological Achievements of the ARPA/Rome Laboratory Planning Initiative*. Menlo Park, CA: AAAI Press.

Valente, A., Swartout, W., and Gil, Y. 1996. A representation and library for objectives in air campaign plans, Technical Report, USC-ISI.

Valente, A., Gil, Y., and Swartout, W. 1996. INSPECT: an intelligent system for air campaign plan evaluation based on EXPECT, Technical Report, USC-ISI.

Warden, J.A., III. 1989. *The Air Campaign*. McLean, VA: Pergamon-Brassey's International Defense Publishers.

Wilkins, D.E. 1988. *Practical Planning: Extending the Classical AI Planning Paradigm*. San Francisco, CA: Morgan Kaufmann Publishers, Inc.

Weld, D. 1994. "An Introduction to Least Commitment Planning." AI Magazine. 15(4):27-61.

Wilkins, D.E. and Myers, K 1995. A common knowledge representation for plan generation and reactive execution. *Journal of Logic and Computation*. 5:731-761.

TRIPS: An Integrated Intelligent Problem-Solving Assistant

George Ferguson and **James F. Allen**
Department of Computer Science
University of Rochester
Rochester, NY 14627-0226
{ferguson,james}@cs.rochester.edu

Abstract

We discuss what constitutes an integrated system in AI, and why AI researchers should be interested in building and studying them. Taking integrated systems to be ones that integrate a variety of components in order to perform some task from start to finish, we believe that such systems (a) allow us to better ground our theoretical work in actual tasks, and (b) provide an opportunity for much-needed evaluation based on task performance. We describe one particular integrated system we have developed that supports spoken-language dialogue to collaboratively solve planning problems. We discuss how the integrated system provides key advantages for helping both our work in natural language dialogue processing and in interactive planning and problem solving, and consider the opportunities such an approach affords for the future.

Content areas: AI systems, natural language understanding, planning and control, problem solving, user interfaces

Introduction

It is an interesting time to be an AI researcher. Computer speeds and capacities have increased to the point that tasks that used to take days can now be done in seconds. The pervasive role of computers in everyday life has emphasized the need for people and computers to co-exist and, one hopes, complement rather than hinder each other. Within the field of AI itself, we now have a solid understanding of many of the core issues. AI concepts like search, planning, learning, natural language, and so on have mature theoretical underpinnings and extensive practical histories. In many cases we understand just how hard some of these problems are to solve, and in these cases we often have a good understanding of how approximate solutions can be found and what the tradeoffs are in using them.

Supported by these two trends, it is now possible to build AI systems that actually perform tasks that people find difficult (and that require intelligence, however exactly you define it) in reasonable amounts of time. A good example is Deep Blue (Hamilton & Garber 1997), which, despite some controversy, certainly counts as a highly successful, working AI system that leverages both of the trends described above. But on a smaller scale, researchers are starting to report on experiences with building AI systems that solve some task from start to finish, whether it is answering questions using a database, large-scale planning and scheduling of shipments, or autonomous robots and robotic assistants.

This paper argues first for the utility of building end-to-end systems that integrate a variety of capabilities in the performance of some task. We discuss some of the dimensions along which such integration can take place, and how the different aspects of integrated systems interact in the design, implementation, and operation of the system. We then describe in detail one particular implemented, integrated system: TRIPS, the Rochester Interactive Planner System. This system integrates speech recognition, natural language understanding, discourse processing, planning and plan recognition, and much more in order to provide the human user with an interactive, intelligent problem-solving assistant in a transportation/logistics domain. TRIPS is fully functional and will be demonstrated at AAAI in the Intelligent Systems Demonstrations program.

Integrated Systems

We start with what it means to be an integrated AI system. The AI part seems straightforward: the system should perform some task or tasks that people find to require intelligence. As for integration, we feel that there are two important dimensions to consider. First, the system can integrate the functionality of multiple more specialized components in the performance of the task. In an integrated AI system, these components are things like planners, natural language parsers, learning algorithms, speech recognizers, temporal reasoners, logic engines, and so on. These are AI technologies that do not themselves solve a task, but that provide services necessary to do so. The second, less obvious, dimension to consider is the integration between the AI system and the person or people using it. Most, if not all, fielded AI systems have to interact with people at some time. It is in our interests to make this interaction as natural for the people as possible, both to increase the acceptance of the AI technology and to leverage people's skills in the performance of the task. So an integrated system, to us, is one that both integrates multiple capabilities in service of a task and integrates its functions with those of its human users.

Why then should AI researchers want to build integrated AI systems? The first benefit is that it gets us to the "criti-

Copyright ©1998, American Association for Artificial Intelligence (www.aaai.org). All rights reserved.

cal mass" of an end-to-end system, rather than toy programs in toy domains. This has two huge advantages. First, the task grounds the research. For example, natural language understanding has to be *about* something, planning has to be *for* something, and so on. Second, end-to-end performance allows evaluation using task-based metrics. AI systems are notoriously difficult to evaluate in isolation—what does it mean for an NLU system to "understand" a sentence? Task-based metrics allow us to compare different approaches, components, or architectures. They also allow us to compare the system's performance to that of people on the same task, which is surely the ultimate test of an intelligent system.

The second benefit of building integrated AI systems is less clearcut but just as significant. The need to integrate disparate components often forces us to broaden our perspective, add functionality, increase robustness, and so on. This makes one-off, *ad hoc* solutions less likely, since it is unlikely that the same shortcuts will serve different components equally well. For example, a planner might prefer not to reason about time, but an NLU system might absolutely require it. Integration requires a clear understanding of the representations being used and clear specification of component interfaces, both of which are issues that the AI community is well-positioned to address.

Finally then, if integrated AI systems are desirable research goals, how do we build them? We cannot be definitive on this point, of course. But one methodological principle has been useful in our research, to be described below. This is the need to clearly define the task that the system is to perform. Without a crisp task definition and a definition of what it means to "do better," evaluation is impossible. Further, the task should support a range of incrementally more difficult problems, allowing us to bootstrap the system-building process by building a simple system for a simple task, then increasing the complexity of the task and improving the system. Task-based evaluation throughout provides a guide to what is working and what isn't. A corollary of this is that we have to choose hard enough tasks and big enough problems. Integrated systems using current AI technologies are already, in fact, capable of performing some very challenging tasks.

TRIPS: The Rochester Interactive Planning System

We next describe a particular integrated AI system that we have developed based on the previous observations. TRIPS, the Rochester Interactive Planning System, is the latest in a series of prototype collaborative planning assistants. Our research plan is to design and build a series of progressively more sophisticated systems working in progressively more realistic domains. TRIPS builds on our experiences with the TRAINS system (Ferguson *et al.* 1996; Allen *et al.* 1995; Ferguson, Allen, & Miller 1996), but (a) functions in a more complicated logistics domain compared to TRAINS' simple route-planning domain, (b) supports the construction of much more complex plans than TRAINS could produce or understand, and (c) embodies a more complex model of col-

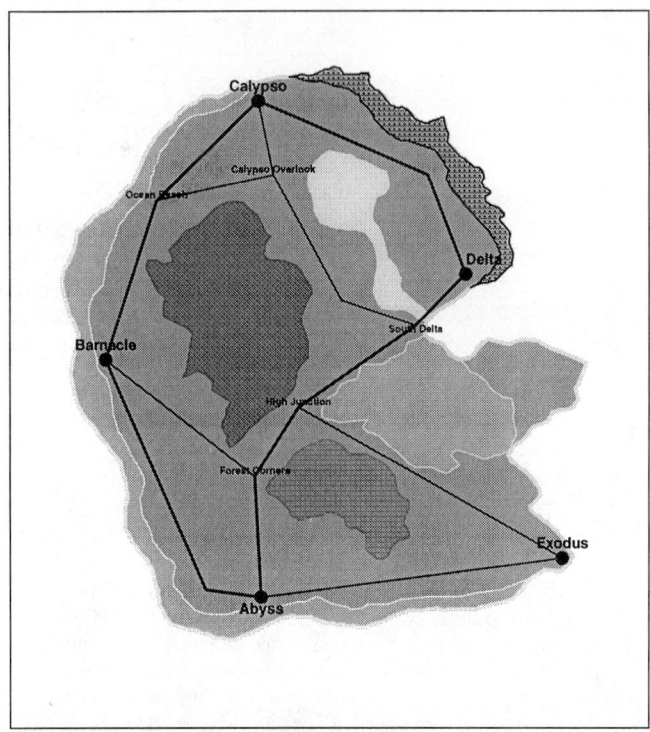

Figure 1: Map of Pacifica

laborative problem-solving than TRAINS. All three of these developments required significant analysis, redesign, and reimplementation (the extension of the domain *per se* was perhaps the most straightforward part). TRIPS does build directly on TRAINS, however, reusing many of the components and all of the infrastructure directly.

TRIPS is an assistant to a human manager. The two of them collaborate to construct plans in crisis situations. Our example scenario involves the island of Pacifica (see Figure 1), which is in the path of an approaching hurricane. Because of the hurricane, the population must be evacuated to one of the cities (the "safe" city) and from there presumably to safety. The manager's task is to plan the evacuation, using a variety of vehicles (with varying capabilities) at his or her disposal. There may be a variety of constraints placed on the final plans, such as time, cost, weather-related factors, and so on. The important features of this scenario as a research environment are: (a) it is clear what the task is and when it is completed (*i.e.*, we can easily describe tasks to people, they can know when they're done, and we can verify that); (b) the relative quality of the solution is easily measured (in terms of time, violated constraints, or some measure of robustness, for example); and (c) it is easy to vary the complexity of the task from trivially solvable to problems that people would have difficulty solving and, in fact, that TRIPS could not solve on its own (*e.g.*, increase numbers of people, change numbers and types of vehicles, modify road network, and so on). The first two aspects make evaluation possible, the final aspect lets us work incrementally on progressively harder problems.

> **0:00 H:** Hello.
> **0:02 S:** Hi there.
> **0:03 H:** Show me a map of Pacifica.
> **0:07 S:** Ok. *Displays large map of the island of Pacifica*
> **0:08 H:** Where are the people?
> **0:11 S:** There are two groups of people at Exodus, two at Calypso, two at Barnacle, and one group of people at Abyss. *Displays a bar chart showing the numbers of people in the cities. This chart is updated as the conversation progresses to show the state of the world given the plan under consideration.*
> **0:17 H:** And where are the transports?
> **0:19 S:** There are two trucks and one helicopter at Delta. *Displays a chart showing vehicle status and contents (also updated through the conversation)*
> **0:24 H:** Use a truck to get the people from Calypso to Delta.
> **0:31 S:** Your wish is my command. *Displays a construction window with a timeline view of the plan under development, with the vehicles on the vertical axis and time horizontally. The map is also updated to show the route taken to Calypso and back.*
> **0:34 H:** How long will that take?
> **0:37 S:** It will take six hours and forty-two minutes.
> **0:43 H:** What if we went along the coast instead?
> **0:47 S:** That option would take ten hours and twenty-seven minutes. *Displays another construction window showing the option alongside the original plan.*
> **0:53 H:** Forget it.
> **0:55 S:** Ok. *Deletes second construction window from the display.*
> **1:05 H:** Use the other truck to get the people from Exodus to Delta.
> **1:13 S:** Ok. *Adds the new task to the original construction window, using a different color, and updates the map. In this case, the task is clearly seen to take more than ten hours.*
> **1:22 H:** Let's use the helicopter instead.
> **1:34 S:** Ok. *Changes the construction window view of this task and updates the map display.*
>
> **1:38 H:** Now send truck one to Barnacle.
> **1:41 S:** Your wish is my command. *Adds a third task to the construction window (in a third color) and updates the map.*
> **1:44 H:** Pick up the people there.
> **1:48 S:** Ok. *Updates displays*
> **1:50 H:** Go on to Abyss.
> **1:54 S:** Ok. *Updates displays*
> **1:57 H:** And take the people there to Delta.
> **2:05 S:** Ok. *Updates displays*
> **2:10 H:** That looks good.
> **2:12 S:** Glad to be of service.
>
> *We now suppose that the manager learns of a change in road status from an external source, and informs the system so that the plan can be adjusted. Delta Bridge crosses the inlet between Delta and South Delta.*
>
> **2:18 H:** Delta bridge is out.
> **2:21 S:** Ok. The highlighted actions may need to be revised. *Flashes Delta Bridge in red, and highlights actions whose routes use the bridge in red in the construction window.*
> **2:37 H:** Send truck two along the coast instead.
> **2:39 S:** Ok. *Displays new route (to Calypso and back) on the map and updates the construction window (longer trips).*
> **2:42 H:** Have the other truck stop at South Delta instead.
> **3:02 S:** Ok. *Display new route (along coast to Barnacle, then to Abyss, then to South Delta) and updates the construction window.*
> **3:06 H:** Unload the people there.
> **3:13 S:** Ok. *Updates displays*
> **3:18 H:** And use the helicopter to get the people from South Delta to Delta.
> **4:03 S:** No problem. *Multiple flights with the helicopter are added to the third task in the construction window and the map is updated to show them.*

Figure 2: Example Dialogue

Example Dialogue

An example dialogue is presented in Figure 2. This is a verbatim transcript of an actual session, annotated to describe the graphical displays generated by TRIPS. The times shown are wall time—the actual time of each utterance. The exact times are not important,[1] but note that most utterances are understood within a few seconds, including speech recognition and all processing. This level of responsiveness is required to maintain an effective dialogue with the user.

TRIPS System Architecture

The organization of TRIPS is shown in Figure 3. Modules communicate by exchanging KQML messages (Finin *et al.* 1993) using our own central message-passing Input Manager (not shown in the figure). Most modules are in fact separate Unix processes, and TRIPS can run on any combination of machines that can run the individual modules. The TRIPS infrastructure allows any program that can read standard input and write standard output to exchange messages.

---

[1]This session was run using two Sun Ultra 1 workstations with 167 MHz SPARC processors.

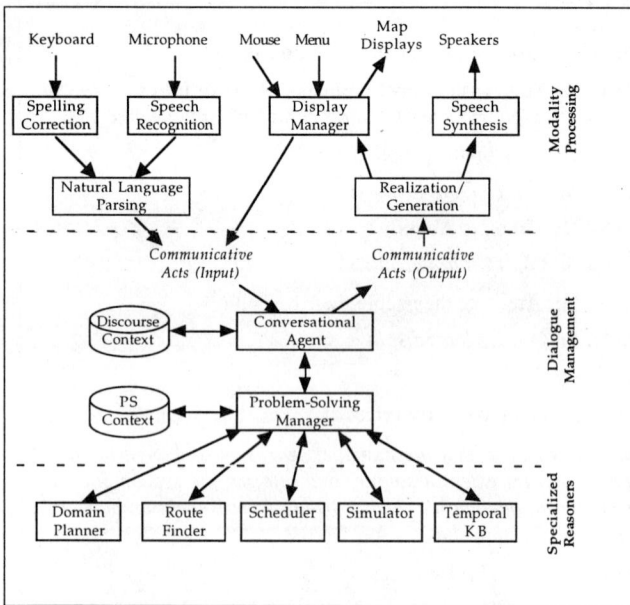

Figure 3: TRIPS System Architecture

As shown in the figure, the components of TRIPS can be divided into three groups:

1. **Modality Processing**: This includes speech recognition and generation, graphical displays and gestures, typed input, and so on. All modalities are treated uniformly. For input, words and gestures are parsed into meaning representations based on treating them as communicative acts. For output, communicative acts generated by the system are realized using speech or graphics.

2. **Dialogue Management**: These components are the core of TRIPS, and are responsible for managing the ongoing conversation, interpreting user communication in context, requesting and coordinating specialized reasoners to address the needs of the conversation, and selecting what communicative actions to perform in response.

3. **Specialized Reasoners**: These components provide the "brains" of TRIPS, in the sense of being able to solve hard problems such as planning courses of actions, scheduling sets of events, or simulating the execution of plans. The goal here is to provide a form of plug-and-play interoperability, where new or improved specialized reasoners (including, for example, network-based sources or agents) can be easily added to the suite of resources at TRIPS' disposal.

Space obviously precludes discussing all these components here. The robust speech recognition work is described in (Ringger & Allen 1996b; 1996a). Descriptions of the approach to robust language understanding can be found in (Allen et al. 1996). The approach to planning, which is interesting for its emphasis on plan modification and its use of an expressive, temporal world model, is described in (Ferguson & Allen 1998). The rest of this section will concentrate on the dialogue management components of TRIPS, namely the Conversational Agent and the Problem Solving Manager, since it is these that really effect the integration in TRIPS. In both cases, the contexts shown in the figure support the incremental specification and development so necessary for effective integration.

Interaction as Conversation

The Conversational Agent coordinates all system activity as it interacts with the user. The key idea for integrating various different input and output modalities is that all user interaction is viewed as *communicative acts*, a generalization of speech acts. As a consequence, all communication between the Conversational Agent and the modality processing modules is in terms of possible communicative acts that have been or should be performed. TRIPS supports a wide range of speech acts, ranging from direct requests (*e.g., show me the map*), questions (*where are the transports?*), assertions (*The bridge is out*), suggestions (*Let's use a helicopter instead*), acceptances and rejections (*ok, no*), as well as a range of social acts including thanks, apologies, and greetings. In addition, there are a limited range of gestural acts such as pointing and dragging screen objects using the mouse. The modality processing modules typically produce a set of possible *surface acts* based on the form of the act. The Conversational Agent then combines these interpretations with the discourse context in order to determine the *intended acts*, and then in coordination with the problem solving manager, determines the system's response, which again is expressed in terms of communicative acts.

Since the task in TRIPS is interactive problem solving, most of the acts that are performed relate to different problem solving operations. The operations most common in TRIPS include introducing a new task or subtask to the plan, modifying or deleting an existing task, defining all or part of a solution for a task, modifying an existing solution, or evaluating all or part of the plan. As well, as is common in human-human problem-solving, either the person or the system can create alternate solutions (options) for comparison purposes, remove an option from consideration, or adopt a particular option. Note that the problem solving operation involved is orthogonal to the communicative act used to communicate it. For example, one might request a modification to a plan, suggest a modification, accept or reject a modification, or promise to do a modification.

The Conversational Agent is driven by a set of rules that identify possible interpretations intended by the user and plan a system response for each. These interpretation/response pairs are then ranked and the system's response is selected. Currently, this selection process is based on a static ranking of the strength and reliability of the rules. In the future, more complex deliberation processes will be introduced that allow the system to generate a wider range of responses, including taking the initiative in the conversation if desired.

Integration as Collaborative Problem-Solving

While the Conversational Agent coordinates the interpretation of communicative acts and chooses system responses, it does not have direct knowledge of the task or current state of the problem solving process. This information is handled by the Problem Solving Manager, which maintains an abstract representation of the task and the current solution (or solutions) under consideration, and coordinates reasoning by the specialized reasoners when necessary. The key idea supporting the PSM in this is a very general representation of plan-related information, including a hierarchical task structure, explicit representation of the possible solutions under consideration, and a temporal knowledge base that represents the world over time relative to different solutions.

The abstract plan representation is general purpose and is used for a wide range of purposes including: providing the context for recognition of the user's intentions, driving displays that summarize the state of the world and/or plan, answering queries about the plan, building the commands and context required by the specialized reasoners, and integrating and managing the results from all the specialized reasoners. Note that while it supports a wide range of purposes, this representation is not typically used directly in any planning process. Rather the PSM converts the general representation into specific commands to each specialized reasoner using a representation that that reasoner understands. It then converts the results returned back into the general representation for use by other components. A key feature of this representation is that it allows the system to represent and reason about plans that it could not have generated on its own. This allows the user to incrementally develop plans that are more complex than the TRIPS planner can generate.

To support the interpretation processes in the conversational agent, the PSM and conversational agent interact using a propose-evaluate-confirm protocol. The conversational agent suggests a possible problem solving action, say to modify a certain subtask by using a different vehicle. The PSM then evaluates this interpretation based on *coherence* (*i.e.*, did this operation make sense in the current problem solving context) and *feasibility* (*i.e.*, could the requested operation be performed). Based on these evaluations, the CA chooses a particular set of interpretations and then informs the PSM so it can update its context for the next interaction. In order to evaluate each interpretation, the PSM may invoke the specialized reasoners as necessary to perform the actual reasoning required.

Consider a brief example from the sample dialogue, when the user says *Let's use the helicopter instead*. From its surface form, this utterance is interpreted as a suggestion to use the helicopter in some unspecified part of the plan instead of some other (also unspecified) vehicle. The CA uses coherence heuristics to explore the most likely possibility: that the modification should apply to the last subtask being discussed, namely getting the people from Exodus to Delta. It asks the PSM to evaluate modifying this plan by replacing something with the helicopter. The PSM uses its abstract representation of the plan to find likely objects that the helicopter could replace in this task, in this case the truck mentioned in the previous interaction. It then calls the Planner with the task to replace this truck with the helicopter in this task. The Planner performs this operation and returns a revised plan. This plan, however, is quite different from the previous solution. Rather than making one trip with the truck, the plan now involves making two trips with the helicopter (due to different vehicle capacities). The PSM then calls the Router to instantiate routes for the helicopter for its two trips, and then invokes the Scheduler to produce a nominal plan that can be used to generate a display. Since all these operations were performed successfully, the PSM returns to the CA an evaluation saying that this interpretation ranks high on both coherence and feasibility. The CA has no other viable options, and so notifies the PSM that this is the interpretation selected. The PSM updates its problem solving state to reflect the new plan, and updates the world model used to drive the plan display. The CA executes the response corresponding to this interpretation, causing display updates and a spoken confirmation.

Related Work

Few integrated systems have been constructed that have the robustness and depth of TRIPS. In most other work, either the interface to the system is highly constrained, or the task that the system performs is highly constrained. For example, most speech-based query systems (such as the ATIS systems (DARPA 1989–1991)) may handle a wide range of questions but only do one thing—answer queries about a trip. The system does not have to explicitly reason about what needs to be done as the task is fixed in advance, and remains constant during the interaction. Nevertheless, such systems do fit the criteria we laid out for an integrated system to the extent that they truly handle a task that a person would have in obtaining travel information.

Other systems provide a richer back end task but limit the interface. The Circuit Fix-it Shop (Smith, Hipp, & Biermann 1995), for instance, handles a complex task of diagnosing and repairing circuits, but the user must use one of a fixed set of sentences. The COLLAGEN system (Rich & Sidner 1997) involves an architecture with some strong similarities to our approach, but the interface is quite constraining and cumbersome for a person to use as it does not support natural language, and only supports plan modification by chronological backtracking. In both of these systems however, as in TRIPS, treating the interaction as a *dialogue* between the system and the user provides the *context* required to integrate system functions and coordinate system behaviours.

In fact, one of the earliest integrated systems is still one of richest to date. This is the Basic Agent (Vere & Bickmore 1990), in which a person could interact in natural language with a submarine robot in a simulated world. This system lacked a compelling task to be accomplished, however, and the interactions were more of the flavor of demonstrating the capabilities of the system. Nonetheless, the Basic Agent integrated a wide range of capabilities within a system that could be used effectively by a person.

Conclusions and Future Work

Integrated systems like TRIPS take time and effort to build. What have we gained from the experience?

First, we can evaluate performance by having people solve problems. In work on TRIPS' predecessor TRAINS, we developed a methodology for testing groups of naive users solving a set of predefined problems (Sikorski & Allen 1996; Stent & Allen 1997). The results were encouraging (90% of sessions resulting in success), but these were mostly a reflection of the simplicity of the TRAINS task. We have not yet evaluated TRIPS on its more complex task and domain, but applying the same methodology, we expect to be able to show that people can solve problems faster with TRIPS than with another person. We hope to report those results in the near future. The point for this paper, however, is that this experiment could not even be conceived without an integrated, end-to-end system with which to work.

Second, the emphasis on integrating multiple specialized reasoners at the problem-solving level has had several benefits. The drive towards integration has resulted in a very general shared representation of plans, objectives, domain objects, and the like. This representation is used by a range of components from natural language understanding to planning and simulation. And of course, the integration of multiple specialized reasoners allows us to plug new technologies into TRIPS or interact with external agents. The key to making this more generally effective is the specification of component or agent *capabilities* so that meta-reasoners like the TRIPS PSM can task them and understand their responses. Specifying and using such capabilities is an active area of our current research.

Finally, the close, intuitive integration between person and computer in TRIPS has several benefits. Viewing the interaction as a conversation is far more natural for the person than learning arcane command languages or GUIs. This will translate into more effective performance with less training (as we hope to show in our evaluation experiments). The closely-integrated, mixed-initiative interaction is also easier for the computer, since it is possible for it to indicate when it can't solve a problem and literally ask for help. The generality of the representations described above ensures that the system can understand and use suggestions that it would never have come up with by itself. The emphasis for the specialized reasoners then changes from complete but impractical reasoning, to flexible and expressive but almost certainly incomplete forms of reasoning.

In the end, the whole, integrated system is greater than the sum of its parts. TRIPS allows the human and the system to collaboratively solve harder problems than either could solve on their own.

Acknowledgements

The TRIPS development team includes Eric K. Ringger, Lucian Galescu, Donna Byron, Amanda Stent, and Myroslava Dzikovska, in addition to the authors. Neal Lesh developed the TRIPS simulator. Further thanks are due to the "Big Picture" group at Rochester, especially Len Schubert, and to the members of the original TRAINS group from which TRIPS emerged.

TRIPS is funded in part by ARPA/Rome Laboratory contract no. F30602-95-1-1088, ONR grant no. N00014-95-1-1088, and NSF grant no. IRI-9623665.

References

Allen, J. F.; Schubert, L. K.; Ferguson, G.; Heeman, P.; Hwang, C. H.; Kato, T.; Light, M.; Martin, N. G.; Miller, B. W.; Poesio, M.; and Traum, D. R. 1995. The TRAINS project: A case study in defining a conversational planning agent. *Journal of Experimental and Theoretical AI* 7:7–48.

Allen, J. F.; Miller, B. W.; Ringger, E. K.; ; and Sikorski, T. 1996. A robust system for natural spoken dialogue. In *Proceedings of the 1996 Annual Meeting of the Association for Computational Linguistics (ACL-96)*, 62–70.

DARPA. 1989–1991. *Proceedings of the DARPA Speech and Natural Language Workshops*, San Mateo, CA: Morgan Kaufmann.

Ferguson, G., and Allen, J. F. 1998. From planners to plan management via a hybrid planning architecture. To appear as a University of Rochester CS Dept. Technical Report.

Ferguson, G.; Allen, J.; and Miller, B. 1996. TRAINS-95: Towards a mixed-initiative planning assistant. In Drabble, B., ed., *Proceedings of the Third Conference on Artificial Intelligence Planning Systems (AIPS-96)*, 70–77.

Ferguson, G.; Allen, J. F.; Miller, B. W.; and Ringger, E. K. 1996. The design and implementation of the TRAINS-96 system: A prototype mixed-initiative planning assistant. TRAINS Technical Note 96-5, Department of Computer Science, University of Rochester, Rochester, NY.

Finin, T.; Weber, J.; Wiederhold, G.; Genesereth, M.; Fritzson, R.; McKay, D.; McGuire, J.; Pelavin, R.; Shapiro, S.; and Beck, C. 1993. Specification of the KQML agent-communication language. Draft.

Hamilton, S., and Garber, L. 1997. Deep blue's hardware-software synergy. *IEEE Computer* 30(10).

Rich, C., and Sidner, C. L. 1997. COLLAGEN: When agents collaborate with people. In *First International Conference on Autonomous Agents*, 284–291.

Ringger, E. K., and Allen, J. F. 1996a. Error correction via a post-processor for continuous speech recognition. In *Proceedings of the 1996 IEEE International Conference on Acoustics, Speech, and Signal Processing (ICASSP-96)*.

Ringger, E. K., and Allen, J. F. 1996b. A fertility channel model for post-correction of continuous speech recognition. In *Proceedings of the 1996 International Conference on Speech and Language Processing (ICSLP-96)*.

Sikorski, T., and Allen, J. 1996. A task-based evaluation of the TRAINS-95 dialogue system. In *Proceedings of the ECAI Workshop on Dialogue Processing in Spoken Language Systems*.

Smith, R. W.; Hipp, D. R.; and Biermann, A. W. 1995. An architecture for voice dialog systems based on prolog-styletheorem proving. *Computational Linguistics* 21(3):281–320.

Stent, A. J., and Allen, J. F. 1997. TRAINS-96 system evaluation. TRAINS Technical Note 97-1, Department of Computer Science, University of Rochester, Rochester, NY.

Vere, S., and Bickmore, T. 1990. A basic agent. *Computational Intelligence* 6(1):41–60.

Knowledge Representation

Knowledge Intensive Exception Spaces

Sarabjot S. Anand, David W. Patterson, John G. Hughes
School of Information and Software Engineering
University of Ulster at Jordanstown,
Newtownabbey, County Antrim,
Northern Ireland
e-mail: {ss.anand, wd.patterson, jg.hughes}@ulst.ac.uk

Abstract

In this paper we extend the concept of exception spaces as defined by Cost and Salzberg (Cost and Salzberg, 1993), in the context of exemplar-based reasoning. Cost et al. defined exception spaces based on the goodness, in terms of performance, of an exemplar. While this is straightforward when using exemplars for classification problems, such a definition does not exist for regression problems. Thus, firstly we define a measure of goodness of an exemplar. We then use this measure of goodness to compare the effectiveness of exception spaces with a variant that we introduce, called Knowledge Intensive Exception Spaces or KINS. KINS remove the restriction on the geometric shape of exception spaces as defined by Cost et al. We provide a rationale for KINS and use a data set from the domain of colorectal cancer to support our hypothesis that KINS are a useful extension to exception spaces.

Introduction

Instance-based Reasoning (Aha, 1990) (or Exemplar-based (Cost and Salzberg, 1993) or Nearest Neighbour algorithms (Cover, 1967)) employ the principle of lazy learning. These algorithms delay generalisation until a prediction or query instance is presented to them. Thus, they are characterised by large storage requirements, small learning time requirement, large prediction time and robustness in dealing with noise.

Early algorithms using the Nearest Neighbour paradigms suffered from the curse of dimensionality (the presence of a number of irrelevant attributes) which had the dual effect of increased execution time of the algorithm as well as decreased predictive accuracy. These algorithms, known as the 1-Nearest Neighbour (1-NN) retrieved the most similar exemplar (based on the Euclidean distance metric) and allocated the class of the retrieved instance to the target instance, thus, they were not very effective at handling noise.

Since then a number of extensions have been proposed to make these algorithms more robust. Variants of the 1-NN algorithm have been developed along a number of different dimensions. The k-dimension generalises the prediction to be based on more than one of the nearest neighbours, introducing the need for techniques for using a number of possible outcomes (each associated with a different neighbour) to be combined into one. Thus, the concepts of the "most common" and "voting" based prediction techniques were developed. The votes associated with each of the neighbours are based on the distance between the target and retrieved instance, using a kernel function defined on the distance metric. Developments along this dimension lead to better noise tolerance and can be thought of as a generality control on the algorithm. The value of k is normally set using cross-validation (Wetteschereck, Aha and Mohari, 1997).

The attribute weights dimension attempts to deal with the curse of dimensionality. These variants of the k-NN are also known as the *weighted Nearest Neighbour algorithm (wk-NN)*. Wetterchek et al. (Wetteschereck, Aha and Mohari, 1997) provide a survey of various techniques for attribute weight selection for use in conjunction with the k-NN algorithm.

The exemplar weights dimension further enhances the accuracy and noise tolerance of the k-NN algorithm. The idea is to weight each exemplar based on its ability to reliably predict the outcome attribute of an unseen instance (Salzberg, 1990). Reliable exemplars are given small weights (close to 1) while unreliable instances are given large weights (> 1). The rationale is that unreliable exemplars represent either noise or "exceptions" - thus, an exemplar weight greater than 1 is assigned to define a small area within the feature space where generally accepted rules do not apply. Rather than using a continuous exemplar weight (Cost and Salzberg, 1993), Aha et al. (Aha and Kibler, 1989) suggest that exemplars should only be used if they have proven themselves on classifying training examples. The advantage of the approach by Cost et al. however, is that it defines a clustering of the exemplars identifying exceptional exemplars. Such identification of exceptional exemplars may be used to identify optimal exemplar or case bases (Anand et al., 1998).

The distance metric dimension attempts to remove deficiencies within traditional distance metrics especially with respect to handling symbolic attributes. Initial approaches to handling symbolic attributes were based around their conversion into a set of binary attribute values - one attribute for each symbol within the original

---

[1] Copyright © 1998, American Association of Artificial Intelligence (www.aaai.org). All rights reserved.

symbolic attribute. However, there are a number of problems with this approach. Firstly, there is an unnecessary increase in the number of attributes in the data set ("dimensionality explosion"). Secondly, the intuitive notion of attribute weights as signifying the significance of the attribute within the classification (or regression) problem was lost for the symbolic attribute as a weight was now associated with each value. Thus, it was not possible to compare the significance, for example, of Age versus site of tumour in predicting months of survival in cancer. Anand et al (Anand and Hughes, 1998) have already shown how using symbolic attributes can lead to biased retrieval of neighbours by utilising the overlap distance metric. Enhanced distance metrics that attempt to remove this bias, representing a truer neighbour representation, are enhancements along this dimension (Stanfill and Waltz, 1986, Anand and Hughes 1998, Cost and Salzberg, 1993).

This paper revisits and extends the exemplar weighting ideas presented by Cost et al. (Cost and Salzberg, 1993) and is as a proposed enhancement along the exemplar weights dimension.

Application Domain

The authors have recently been working towards building a prognostic model for colorectal cancer (Anand et al., 1998a). The data set consists of 134 colorectal cancer patients. All patients in this study presented with colorectal cancer between 1973 and 1983 in the Royal Victoria Hospital and the Belfast City Hospital, Belfast, Northern Ireland.

Attribute	Type	Ordered
Sex	Categorical	No
Pathological Type	Categorical	No
Polarity	Categorical	Yes
Tubule Configuration	Categorical	Yes
Tumour Pattern	Categorical	No
Lymphocytic Infiltration	Categorical	Yes
Fibrosis	Categorical	Yes
Venous Invasion	Categorical	Yes
Mitotic Count	Categorical	Yes
Penetration	Categorical	Yes
Differentiation	Categorical	Yes
Dukes Stage	Categorical	Yes
Age	Continuous	Yes
Obstruction	Categorical	No
Site	Categorical	No

Table 1: Description of Attributes in the Data Set

Complete clinical and pathological data were collected on these patients. For each case, details of age, sex, site and obstruction were collected. Histopathological grading according to Jass (Jass, 1987) and Dukes staging (Dukes, 1932) of each tumour was carried out by the same pathologist. Fifteen clinico-pathological features were recorded for each patient. These are described in Table 1.

The objective was to use these features to induce a regression model that could predict the number of months the patient is expected to survive after diagnosis of colorectal cancer. Such a model, if accurate, could help in treatment planning and effective management of cancer patients.

Knowledge Intensive Exception Spaces

Cost et al. (Cost and Salzberg, 1993) suggested a scheme for exemplar weighting according to their performance history. In their scheme, the weight assigned to an exemplar was the ratio of the number of uses of the exemplar, to the number of correct uses of the exemplar.

The definition of a correct use of an exemplar is obvious in the case of a classification problem i.e. every time an exemplar is used to classify the target example into a correct class. However, in the case of a regression problem, such a definition is a little more difficult. In this section we will firstly discuss how we defined such a measure of goodness for regression problems. We then describe the concept of knowledge intensive exception spaces or KINS giving the rationale behind them and describing their geometrical interpretation and use.

Defining Goodness of Use of Exemplars

An initial cross-validation run of the k-NN algorithm using the Euclidean distance metric, retrieving five closest neighbours and using a voting scheme for making a prediction resulted in individual neighbour predictive errors shown in Figure 1. The k-NN algorithm used forms part of the MKS data mining toolkit (Anand et al, 1997) under development within the authors' laboratory.

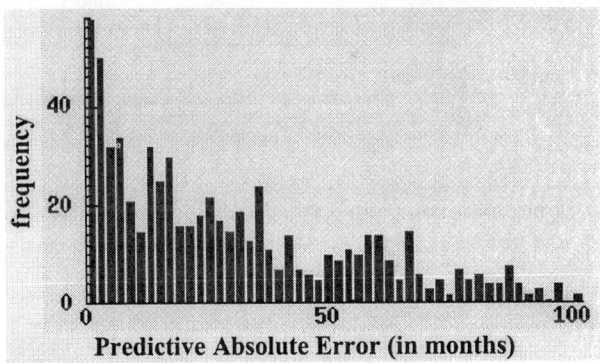

Figure 1: Distribution of Predictive Errors

The distribution of errors may be described using the statistical measure of spread namely quartiles. A *goodness membership function (gmf)* is defined on the quartiles as the degree to which a retrieval of an exemplar producing an error within that quartile may be regarded as a good use of the exemplar. For example, a membership function defined by the values {1, 0.7, 0.3, 0} would imply that a retrieval of an exemplar when it produces an error in the first quartile is certainly good, the second quartile is 0.7 in magnitude of goodness and the third quartile is 0.3 in magnitude of goodness. Thus when calculating the goodness value or weight of the exemplar we now use the formula:

$$w_x = \frac{\sum_{i=1}^{4} n_x^i}{\sum_{i=1}^{4} \mu_i * n_x^i}$$

where, μ_i is the membership value for quartile i
and n_x^i is the no. of retrievals of x in quartile i

We refer to this as the *Weighted Quartile Measure* for allocating exemplar weights.

To illustrate the use of the above measure of goodness as well as to illustrate the effect of the definition of the gmf on performance of the measure we now use three different gmf definitions and see their effect on the exemplar base for colorectal cancer. The gmfs are defined as :

M1: {1, 0, 0, 0}; M2: {1, 1, 0, 0} and M3: {1, 0.7, 0.3, 0}
M1 identifies a usage of an exemplar as good only if it produces an error within the first quartile of the error distribution. M2 identifies as good usage of an exemplar any retrieval that produces an error less than the mean absolute error of the initial k-NN run, while M3 identifies good exemplar usage with varying degrees of magnitude for the first three quartiles.

Exemplar #	Error (in months)	Quartile	Mean Abs. Error
69	11	1	Good
69	0	1	Good
69	35	3	Bad
69	25	2	Good
69	9	1	Good
69	67	4	Bad
69	42	4	Bad

Table 2: Example Usage of an Exemplar

Given the usage of exemplar #69 in Table 2, the weights associated with the exemplar using these gmfs would be:
Using M1: $w_x = 7/3 = 2.33$
Using M2: $w_x = 7/4 = 1.75$
Using M3: $w_x = 7/(3*1+1*0.7+1*0.3+2*0) = 1.75$

Now let us observe the effect that using these different gmfs has on the usage of exemplars in the exemplar-base. Table 3 shows a sample of exemplar weights from the exemplar-base.

As can be seen from Table 3, the stricter weighting regime used in M1 results in higher weights for most exemplars. M2 and M3 produce similar weights, lower than those of M1.

Using M1, exemplar 17, 56 and 59 were not retrieved anymore. Table 4 summarises the exemplar usage for our examples in Table 3 when using weights based on M1. As can be seen, the reduction in usage of exemplars assigned large weights has resulted in an unwarranted increase in the incorrect usage of previously "good" exemplars like exemplar #8. Similar increases can be observed when using M2 and M3-based exemplar weights (Table 5 and 6).

Exemplar # \ gmf	M1	M2	M3
8	1	1	1
17	3	2	1.67
40	2	1	1.17
49	1.75	1.16	1.4
50	1.8	1.14	1.26
56	4	4	4
59	4	2	2

Table 3 Exemplar Weights for a subset of Exemplars

Exemplar # \ Quartile	1	2	3	4
8	5	5	4	11
17	0	0	0	0
40	1	0	0	0
49	2	1	1	1
50	0	1	0	0
56	0	0	0	0
59	0	0	0	0

Table 4: Exemplar Usage using M1-based Exemplar Weights

Exemplar # \ Quartile	1	2	3	4
8	2	5	0	0
17	0	0	0	0
40	14	14	0	0
49	6	6	0	0
50	6	7	0	0
56	0	0	0	0
59	1	1	0	0

Table 5: Exemplar Usage using M2-based Exemplar Weights

Exemplar # \ Quartile	1	2	3	4
8	3	5	1	11
17	0	0	0	0
40	9	4	1	2
49	4	1	1	1
50	7	5	0	3
56	0	0	0	0
59	1	1	0	1

Table 6: Exemplar Usage using M3-based Exemplar Weights

An important conclusion of these preliminary results is that the weighted quartile method for measuring goodness of an exemplar is a useful technique to use when defining exception spaces. However, if the membership function is not chosen sensibly the results can be sub-optimal as we saw in the case of the M1 and M3. While M2 produced the best results, in terms of the distribution of errors on the four error quartiles, there is no guarantee that its definition is optimal. Thus a useful addition to the weighted quartile technique would be its coupling with some kind of optimiser like a genetic algorithm.

Local Exemplar Weights

As described by Cost et al., exemplar weights can be graphically represented as circular boundaries (assuming a 2-dimensional space) defined around exceptional exemplars. The weight assigned to the exemplar defines the radius of the circular boundary using an inverse relationship i.e. the larger the assigned weight, the smaller the radius of the circle. For the exemplar to be retrieved the target example must fall within its boundary region.

The use of a 'global' exemplar weight results in the restriction on the boundary area around the exemplar being circular. We now study the validity of this restriction and present a less rigid boundary to be defined around each exemplar. We refer to this as local exemplar weights as the weights associated with the exemplar vary based on different *retrieval circumstances*. The resulting exception spaces are called *Knowledge INtensive exception Spaces or KINS*, as their definition utilises knowledge about the exemplar performance under various circumstances.

As shown in Table 2, most exemplars are not "globally" bad predictors. As in the case of Exemplar #69, there are three of the seven instances where the exemplar has been used to produce low errors and to discriminate against it by associating a global weight may result in a wholly inappropriate exemplar being retrieved instead in cases where Exemplar #69 was actually appropriate. This can be seen from Tables 3, 4, 5 and 6. Thus, what is required is a method to identify the circumstances where Exemplar #69 is appropriate and when it is not and only assign a large weight to it when its use is inappropriate.

While attribute weights attempt to reconfigure the exemplar space so as to best fit the real-world process being modelled, the reason why exemplars may still be retrieved inappropriately has its roots within the use of the distance metric. Consider the following example where two exemplars are retrieved for the same target example. While one exemplar differs from the target on the attributes "Dukes Stage", "Configuration" and "Site", the other differs on "Tumour Pattern" and "Mitotic Count". It may be the case that due to the global summation used by the Euclidean distance metric, the two exemplars have the same distance from the target associated with them. However, the retrieval of the first exemplar may be wholly inappropriate as in this particular part of the exemplar space, the distance of the target from the exemplar with regards to "Dukes Stage" may invalidate its use. Thus, let us investigate the individual attribute distances for each use of Exemplar #69. Table 7 shows these distances. Columns relate to individual retrievals of Exemplar# 69.

Using these distances as independent variables we may now use a classifier to discover a set of rules that would discriminate between the different Error Quartiles that the usage of the exemplar will result in. The following rules were generated for exemplar #69 using the implementation of C4.5 (Quilan, 1992) within the CLEMENTINE Data Mining Toolkit[2]:

```
if age <= 0.01
then Quartile = 1
if venous = 0 and age > 0.01
then Quartile = 3
if venous > 0 and age > 0.01
then Quartile -> 4
Default: Quartile -> 1
```

The rule can now be interpreted as follows: Exemplar #69 is a good exemplar to use if the Age attribute is a near exact match. However, if this in not the case the use of the exemplar produces an error within the third quartile if venous invasion is a perfect match and if it doesn't match either then the error will be in the fourth quartile.

Now an exemplar weight consists of a quadruple representing a weight for each Error Quartile. Note once again that these weights need to be optimised to get the best results. Assume the quadruple to be (1,2,3,4), which by no means is optimal. Even with such a sub-optimal set of weights the results obtained were very encouraging (see next section). Note that a smaller weight is associated with the first quartile and the weights function monotonically increases as the error quartile increases. These rules and the quartile weights together define KINS.

Using such KINS implies that now when a target example is presented to the exemplar-base the following set of steps are followed to retrieve the nearest neighbours. Firstly, the Euclidean distance is calculated between the target example and each exemplar. Next, the attribute distances used in this calculation are used for predicting the Error Quartile or the "appropriateness" of the exemplar to be used in the present context. Finally, the weight associated with the predicted Quartile is multiplied with the Euclidean distance to arrive at a final distance measure for the exemplar.

Now, let us have a closer look at the geometric interpretation of KINS. Consider the case of an exemplar that always produces errors in the same quartile. Without loss of generality we may assume this quartile to be quartile 3. In this case, the only significant weight assigned to the exemplar is 3. As described by Cost et al., such a weight may be represented as a circular region around the exemplar. Thus, exception spaces are a special case of KINS when errors produced by the exemplar always lie in the same quartile of the error distribution. In the more general case, the definition of KINS is based on the inter-attribute distances, and exception spaces of different sizes are drawn around the exemplar. For example, if the age attribute of the target example is only at a small distance from exemplar #69 (<= 0.01), a very large space,

---

[2] The CLEMENTINE Toolkit is a registered trademark of Integral Solutions Limited, Basingstoke, England.

Attribute	Use#1	Use#2	Use#3	Use#4	Use#5	Use#6	Use#7
Sex	0	0	0	0	0	0	0
Pathological Type	0	0	0	0	0	0	0
Polarity	0	0	0	0	0	0	0
Tubule Configuration	0	0	0.111	0	0	0	0
Tumour Pattern	0	0	0	0	0	0	0
Lymphocytic Infiltration	0	0	0	0.25	0	0	0
Fibrosis	0.25	0	0.25	0	0	0	0
Venous Invasion	0	0	0	0.56	0	0.062	0.062
Mitotic Count	0.027	0.25	0.25	0.11	0	0.027	0.027
Penetration	0	0.062	0	0	0	0.062	0.062
Differentiation	0	0	0.25	0	0	0	0.25
Dukes Stage	0.062	0.25	0.062	0.062	0.062	0.25	0.062
Age	0.0008	0.0008	0.02	0.016	0.058	0.36	0.024
Obstruction	1	0	0	0	0	0	0
Site	0	0	0	0	0	0	0
Error Quartile	1	1	3	1	3	4	4

Table 7 Attribute Distances for each use of Exemplar #69

encompassing the entire exemplar space is defined. However, if age > 0.01 and venous invasion is a perfect match, the region defined as #69's exception space is much smaller. If Venous Invasion isn't an exact match, an even smaller space is defined. Thus, KINS define a much more complex space around exemplars than exception spaces, equivalent to a set of exception spaces.

Experimental Results

Initial tests to observe the effectiveness of KINS used the Euclidean distance metric, no attribute weights, a voting based prediction mechanism and 5 as the value of k. Tenfold cross validation was used to arrive at the Mean Absolute Errors shown in Table 8. The three gmfs defined in the previous section were used as variants of the Exception Spaces. The aim being, to highlight the effect of the gmf definition on the performance of the algorithm. As can be from Table 8, the definition of the gmf does have an effect on the predictive accuracy of the model. Three variants of KINS were also tested using different exemplar weights for the error quartiles. Once again the weights do seem to have an effect on the predictive accuracy of the model but these differences seem to be much less significant than those in the case of Exception Spaces.

An interesting observation of the results in Table 8 is the large decrease in mean absolute error by using any form of exemplar weighting. This can be partly attributed to the nature of the data set, which is very sparse. Therefore, using no attribute weights was expected to produce large errors in prediction. Using a genetic algorithm to produce an optimal set of attribute weights arrived at the attribute weights shown in Table 9 (Anand and Hughes, 1998). The varied attributes weights explain the high error rate when using an unweighted k-NN.

Exemplar Weight Technique	Variant	Mean Absolute Error
None	-	31.91
Exception Spaces	M1	25.91
	M2	24.64
	M3	25.33
KINS	{1,2,3,4}	21.76
	{1,1,3,4}	21.67
	{1,1.5,3,4}	21.59

Table 8: Mean Absolute Error using different Exemplar Weighting Techniques

Attribute	Weight
Sex	0.74
Pathological Type	0.14
Polarity	0.06
Tubule Configuration	0.22
Tumour Pattern	0.19
Lymphocytic Infiltration	0.53
Fibrosis	0.7
Venous Invasion	0.61
Mitotic Count	0.46
Penetration	0.99
Differentiation	0.03
Dukes Stage	0.72
Age	0.51
Obstruction	0.72
Site	0

Table 9: Attribute Weights generated using a Genetic Algorithm

Table 10 summarises the results produced using exemplar weights along with the attribute weights in Table 9. An interesting result here is that when no exemplar weights are used the mean absolute error arrived at using attribute weights is lower than the mean absolute error produced using exception spaces in both the unweighted and weighted cases. However, even when using the optimal attribute weights, the mean absolute error achieved by the KINS is lower.

Exemplar Weight Technique	Variant	Mean Absolute Error
None	-	23.21
Exception Spaces	M1	25.72
	M2	26.23
	M3	25.28
KINS	{1,2,3,4}	19.09
	{1,1,3,4}	18.94
	{1,1.5,3,4}	18.73

Table 10: Mean Absolute Error using different Exemplar Weighting Techniques

Conclusions and Future Work

In this paper we revisited exception spaces as defined by Cost and Salzberg. We re-enforced the advantages of assigning weights to exemplars, introducing a method for doing so in the case of regression problems. We then introduced a generalisation of exception spaces called KINS and provided empirical proof of how the definition and use of KINS within lazy learning can prove advantageous in terms of improved accuracy of the developed model.

The results presented in this paper are by no means an end in itself. The authors believe that the results presented in the paper have left a number of open questions that need answered as well as suggesting a number of further developments to the definition of KINS. Extensions to KINS include optimising the weights used for each quartile. Also the optimisation of the goodness membership function needs to be undertaken to enable a true measurement of the advantage of defining KINS rather than simple exception spaces.

The definition of KINS has its disadvantages that need to be further quantified. These include possible Overfitting of the model produced and increased training costs. Another interesting question that is worth asking is whether the increased training costs still justify such an algorithm being termed as a lazy learning algorithm as well as the loss in terms of the advantages that accrue from lazy learning.

Acknowledgements

The authors would like to thank Dr. Peter Hamilton, Royal Victoria Hospital, for providing the data set used in the study as well as for his continued support and domain expertise during the course of this research.

References

Aha, D.; and Kibler, D. 1989. Noise Tolerant instance-based learning algorithms. In *Proceedings of the 11th International Joint Conference on Artificial Intelligence*, 794-799. Melno Park, Calif..

Aha, D. 1990. A study of instance-based algorithms for supervised learning tasks, Ph.D. diss., University of California, Irvine.

Anand, S. S.; Scotney, B. W.; Tan, M. G.; McClean, S. I.; Bell, D. A.; Hughes, J. G.; and Magill, I. C. 1997. Designing a Kernel for Data Mining. *IEEE Expert* 12(2): 65 - 74.

Anand, S. S.; Patterson, D.; Hughes, J. G.; and Bell, D. A. 1998. Discovering Case Knowledge using Data Mining. In *Proceedings of the Pacific-Asia Conference in Knowledge Discovery and Data Mining*, Springer-Verlag,

Anand, S. S.; Hamilton, P.; Smith, A. E.; and Hughes, J. G. 1998a. Intelligent Systems for the Prognosis of Colorectal Cancer Patients. In *Proceedings of CESA Special Session on Intelligent Prognostic Systems*.

Anand, S. S.; and Hughes, J. G. 1998. Hybrid Data Mining Systems: The Next Generation. In *Proceedings. of the Pacific-Asia Conference in Knowledge Discovery and Data Mining*, Springer-Verlag.

Cost, S.; and Salzberg, S. 1993. A Weighted Nearest Neighbour Algorithm for Learning with Symbolic Features. *Machine Learning* 10: 57-78.

Cover, T.; and Hart, P. 1967. Nearest Neighbour Pattern Classification, *IEEE Transactions on Information Theory*, 13(1): 21-27.

Dukes, C. E. 1932. The classification of cancer of the rectum. *J Pathol Bacteriol*. 35: 323-332.

Jass, J.; Love, S.; and Northover, J. 1987. A new prognostic classification for rectal cancer. *Lancet*. 1333-1335.

Quinlan, J. R. 1992. *C4.5: Programs for Machine Learning*, Morgan Kaufmann Publishers.

Salzberg, S. 1990. *Learning with nested generalised exemplars*, Norwell, MA: Kluwer Academic Publications.

Stanfill, C.; and Waltz, D. 1986. Towards Memory-based Reasoning. *Communications of the ACM*. 29(12): 1213-1228.

Wettschereck, D. 1994. A study of distance-based machine learning algorithms, Ph.D. diss., Oregon State University.

Wettschereck, D.; Aha, D.; and Mohri, T. 1997. A Review of Empirical Evaluation of Feature Weighting Methods for a Class of Lazy Learning Algorithms, *Artificial Intelligence Review Journal*.

Probabilistic frame-based systems

Daphne Koller
Computer Science Department
Stanford University
Gates Building, 1A
Stanford, CA 94305-9010
koller@cs.stanford.edu

Avi Pfeffer
Computer Science Department
Stanford University
Gates Building, 1A
Stanford, CA 94305-9010
avi@cs.stanford.edu

Abstract

Two of the most important threads of work in knowledge representation today are frame-based representation systems (FRS's) and Bayesian networks (BNs). FRS's provide an excellent representation for the organizational structure of large complex domains, but their applicability is limited because of their inability to deal with uncertainty and noise. BNs provide an intuitive and coherent probabilistic representation of our uncertainty, but are very limited in their ability to handle complex structured domains. In this paper, we provide a language that cleanly integrates these approaches, preserving the advantages of both. Our approach allows us to provide natural and compact definitions of probability models for a class, in a way that is local to the class frame. These models can be instantiated for any set of interconnected instances, resulting in a coherent probability distribution over the instance properties. Our language also allows us to represent important types of uncertainty that cannot be accomodated within the framework of traditional BNs: uncertainty over the set of entities present in our model, and uncertainty about the relationships between these entities. We provide an inference algorithm for our language via a reduction to inference in standard Bayesian networks. We describe an implemented system that allows most of the main frame systems in existence today to annotate their knowledge bases with probabilistic information, and to use that information in answering probabilistic queries.

1 Introduction

Frame representation systems (FRS's) are currently the primary technology used for large scale knowledge representation in AI [8, 3, 7]. Their modular organization according to cognitively meaningful entities and their ability to capture patterns common to many individuals provide a convenient language for representing complex structured domain models. One of the most significant gaps in the expressive power of this type of framework is its inability to represent and reason with uncertain and noisy information. Uncertainty is unavoidable in the real world: our information is often inaccurate and always incomplete, and only a few of the "rules" that we use for reasoning are true in all possible cases.

In the "propositional" setting, this problem has largely been resolved over the past decade by the development of

Copyright 1998, American Association for Artificial Intelligence (www.aaai.org). All rights reserved.

probabilistic reasoning systems, and particularly Bayesian networks [10]. A Bayesian network (BN) is a representation of a full joint distribution over a set of random variables; it can be used to answer queries about any of its variables given any evidence. A BN allows a complex distribution to be represented compactly by using the locality of influence in our model of the world. But, like all propositional systems, the applicability of BNs is largely limited to situations that can be encoded, in advance, using a fixed set of attributes. Thus, they are inadequate for large-scale complex KR tasks.

Building on our recent work [6, 5], we propose a representation language that integrates frame-representation systems and Bayesian networks, thereby providing the first bridge between these two very different threads of work in KR. The key component in our representation is the annotation of a frame with a probability model. This probability model is, broadly speaking, a BN representing a distribution over the possible values of the slots in the frame. That is, each simple slot in the frame is annotated with a local probability model, representing the dependence of its value on the values of related slots. For example, in a frame representing a PhD student, the value of the slot *years-to-graduation* may depend on the slot *year* and the slot chain *advisor.picky*.

As we can see even from this simple example, by building on standard FRS functionality, our approach provides significantly more expressive power than traditional BNs. For example, by allowing the probability model of a slot to depend on a slot chain, we allow the properties of one instance in the model to depend on properties of other related instances. We can also use the standard class hierarchy of the FRS to allow the probability model of a class to be used by multiple instances of that class, and to allow inheritance of probability models from classes to subclasses, using the same mechanism in which slot values are currently inherited. Finally, by making domain individuals first-class citizens in our framework we can also express a new and important type of uncertainty called *structural uncertainty*. We can have a probabilistic model expressing our uncertainty about the set of entities in our model, e.g., the number of PhD students in a department. We can also represent uncertainty about relations between entities, e.g., which of several conferences a paper appeared in.

We provide a probabilistic inference algorithm for our language based on an approach known as *knowledge-based model construction*. The algorithm takes a knowledge base in our language, including a set of instances, and generates a standard BN which can then be queried effectively for our beliefs about the value of any slots.

Our probability model is expressed using standard frame representation techniques such as facets and value restrictions. This property is important, since it allows our approach to be used with virtually any frame system, and thereby to annotate existing KBs with probabilistic information. In particular, we have implemented a system based on our approach, capable of interacting with most existing FRS's via *OKBC* [2], an emerging standard for FRS interoperability.

Our work is a signficant improvement over previous approaches to combining first-order logic and Bayesian networks. Most of the attempts in this direction (e.g., [12, 11, 9]) use probabilistic Horn clauses as the basic representation. The choice of Horn clauses as an underlying language already dictates some of the properties of the representation, e.g., its inability to encapsulate an object and its properties within a cognitively meaningful frame. Moreover, the use of structural uncertainty in this framework typically causes combinatorial blowup of the resulting models, leading most approaches to outlaw it entirely. Our framework also overcomes some major limitations of our earlier proposals [6, 5], by allowing both structural uncertainty (absent in the first) and probabilistic dependencies between instances (absent in the second). It also provides the crucial ability, absent in both, to create complex models containing many instances that are connected to each other in a variety of ways.

2 Basic representation

We begin with some basic terminology for frame systems. The terminology varies widely from system to system. In this paper we adopt the language and basic knowledge model of the OKBC protocol [2].

The basic unit of discourse in a frame system is a *frame*. A frame has a set of *slots*, each of which may have *slot values* or *fillers*. Formally, a slot represents a binary relation on frames; if the filler of slot A in frame X is frame Y, then the relation $A(X, Y)$ holds. In general slots may be single-valued or multi-valued. In this section we assume that slots are single-valued. This assumption will be relaxed in Section 4. A *slot-chain* is a sequence of zero or more slots separated by periods. A slot-chain represents a binary relation: the slot-chain $A.\sigma$ where A is a slot and σ is a slot-chain denotes the relation $\{(X, Z) \mid A(X, Y) \wedge \sigma(Y, Z)\}$. A slot in a frame may have associated *facets*. A facet is a ternary relation: if the facet value of facet F on slot A in frame X is Y, then the relation $F(X, A, Y)$ holds. A standard facet is value-type, which specifies a value restriction on the values of a slot. The value-type of a slot will be called its *type*.

The two main types of frames are *class frames*, representing sets of entities, and *instance frames*. The class frames are organized in an is-a hierarchy, where one class may be a *subclass* of another (its *superclass*). The slots of a class frame may be *own slots*, which describe a property of the class itself, and *template slots*, which are slots inherited by all instances and subclasses of the class. The facets associated with template slots are *template facets*, and are also inherited. An instance or subclass may override the values of inherited slots or facets.

Probabilistic information is incorporated into a frame KB by annotating class frames with local probabilistic models. A class frame that has been so annotated is called a *p-class*. A p-class has a set of template slots, each with a value-type facet. Depending on the type, a slot is either *simple* or *complex*. The type of a complex slot is another p-class. The type of a simple slot is an explicitly enumerated list of possible values for the slot. For example, the phd-student p-class may have a simple slot *year*, whose type is {*1st, 2nd, 3rd, 4th–6th, tenured*}, and a complex slot *advisor* whose type is the p-class professor. A p-class may also have other slots that do not participate in the probability model, whose type is neither of the above. For example, phd-student may also have the slot *name*, which does not have an associated probability model. This feature allows existing KBs to be annotated with probabilistic information, without requiring a complete redesign of the ontology.

A simple slot is very much like a node in a Bayes net. It has a range of values, a set of parents, and a CPT. A p-class specifies a probability model for its simple slots using two special-purpose facets: parents and distribution. Facets are a natural place to put a probability model, since such a model can be viewed as a generalization of a value restriction: not only does it specify a range of possible values, but also a distribution over that range. The parents facet lists the slots on which the value of this slot depends. Each parent is specified by a slot-chain referring to some other simple slot. More precisely, let X be a p-class and A a simple slot. The parents facet of A is a list of slot chains $[\sigma_1, \ldots, \sigma_n]$, such that $X.\sigma_i$ refers to a simple slot. For example, in the phd-student p-class, *year* may have the parent [*age*], while the parents of *years-to-graduation* may be [*year, advisor.picky*]. The distribution facet specifies the conditional probability distribution over values of the slot given values of its parents. The conditional distribution is specified using a conditional probability table (CPT) as in Bayesian networks. For each combination of values of its parents, the CPT provides a probability distribution over values of the slot. For the purposes of this paper, we assume that the CPTs are represented as fully specified functions of parent values. More compact representations such as noisy-or can easily be accomodated within our framework.

The probability model of a complex slot is simply described by its p-class Y. However, each complex slot A also has an additional facet called imports, whose value is a list of slots in Y. This list, called the *import list* of A, is the list of slots of Y that are visible within X. We require that if $A.B.\sigma$ (for a possibly empty slot chain σ) is a slot chain appearing within X, then B must be in the import list of A.

Once a probability model has been specified for a p-class, the p-class can be used just like any other class frame. One can create instances of the class, which will inherit all of its template slots and facets. In particular, the probability distribution over values of slots of the instance will be as described in the p-class. Similarly, the inheritance mechanism of a frame system can be used to make one p-class a subclass of another. A subclass can extend the definition of the superclass as well as overwrite parts of it. In particular, a subclass can redefine the probability model of one or more of the slots. For example, we can define associate-professor to be a subclass of professor, and overwrite the distribution over *salary* to one that is appropriate to the more specific class. Another important aspect of subtyping is that an instance of a subclass is also an instance of the superclass, so that it can fill a slot whose type is the superclass. For example, in a particular instance of phd-student, the value of the *advisor* slot may be specified to be an instance whose class is associate-professor.

Values can be assigned to an own slot of an instance frame either directly or by assignment to a template slot at the class level. Both types of assignments are interpreted in the same way. An assignment to a simple slot is interpreted as observing the value of the slot, thereby conditioning the probability distribution for the instance. This conditioning process may result in a change in our beliefs for other related slots. Consider, for example, a subclass graduating-phd-student of phd-student which assigns 1 to the slot *years-to-graduation*. Then the conditioning process will result in a new probability model for any instance I of this subclass; in particular, our beliefs about $I.year$ and $I.advisor.picky$ will both change, as will our beliefs about other related slots.

An assignment to a complex slot specifies that the value of that slot is another particular instance. Thus, complex networks of inter-related frames can be created, such as students who share an advisor, and students of different advisors in the same department. Such an assignment at the class level results in all of the class instances having the same frame as their value for that slot.

One of the features of a probabilistic frame system is that related frames can influence each other. We have already seen one mechanism for such interactions: since a parent of a slot is a slot-chain, the value of a simple slot may be influenced probabilistically by the value of a slot in another frame. This mechanism, however, only allows a frame to be influenced by related frames, but not to influence them in turn. We resolve this difficulty by utilizing a basic feature of most FRS's—*inverse slots*.

Let X and Y be two class frames, A a slot of X with type Y, and B a slot of Y with type X. Then A and B are *inverse slots* if, for every instance I of X, if $I.A = J$ then $J.B = I$, and vice versa. Thus, we view an assignment of a specific instance frame J to a slot $I.A$ as encompassing the corresponding assignment of I to $J.B$. For that reason, we do not allow assignments of values to slots such as A at the class level; otherwise, for any given frame J of class Y, the value of $J.B$ would be the set consisting of every frame of class X, a model which is too unwieldy to deal with.

Inverse slots allow either of the frames to refer to slots in the other, thereby allowing probabilistic dependencies in both directions. Allowing such intertwined dependencies without restriction could lead to horribly complex interactions between two frames. In particular, it could lead to a cyclic chain of influences that has no coherent probability model. Therefore, one of the two inverse slots—say $X.A$—is designated to be the *primary* direction while the other—$Y.B$—is *secondary*. Similarly, X is called the primary frame, while Y is the secondary frame. A primary inverse slot such as A in X has a parents facet just like a simple slot, i.e., it is a list of slot-chains in X. Intuitively, the parents of A are the only slots of X that are *exported* to Y via B. More precisely, the parent list of A in X must be identical to the import list of B in Y. Thus, the flow of influence between the two frames is neatly regulated: The parents of A in X can influence any of the slots in Y; some of those can, in turn, influence other slots in X that are "downstream" from A.

For example, suppose we decide that the *thesis* slot of phd-student should be an inverse slot, with its inverse being the *author* slot of phd-thesis. The slot *thesis* is designated to be primary, and is given the parent *field* in phd-student. Then *field* is visible within the phd-thesis class, so that for example, *jargon-content* may depend on *author.field*. Other slots of phd-student may depend on slots of thesis; thus, for example, *job-prospects* may depend on *thesis.quality*, which would therefore have to be on the import list of *thesis*.

Inverse slots serve a dual purpose in our language. As we said, they allow bidirectional dependencies between two instances. But they also allow our probabilistic models to be *multicentered*. If, as above, $X.A$ and $Y.B$ are inverses, and we define an instance from class X, it immediately implies the existence of a corresponding instance from class Y. Alternatively, we could start modeling with an object of class Y, and guarantee that the corresponding X will exist. Thus, we can define a model centered around whatever entities are of interest to us in our context.

3 Semantics

In this section we present a semantics for probabilistic frame knowledge bases. For a given KB with a set of class and instance frames, our semantics defines a probability distribution over the slot values of the instance frames (and of some other related instance frames). In order to define a coherent probability distribution, our frame KB must satisfy several conditions. The basic theme of the conditions is familiar from the realm of Bayesian networks: our dependency model must be acyclic. However, since there may be complicated chains of dependencies both within a frame and between frames, and on both the class and instance levels, we need to develop some tools to reason about dependencies.

Definition 3.1: A *dependency* is a pair $X.A \leftarrow Y.B$, where X and Y are frames (not necessarily distinct), A is a slot of X and B is a slot of Y. We say that $X.A \leftarrow Y.B$ holds if

- A is a simple slot of X, $Y = X$ and $B.\sigma$ is a parent of A;
- A is a complex slot of X, B is in the import list of A, and Y is either an instance frame assigned to $X.A$ or the p-class frame which is the value type of $X.A$. ∎

Intuitively, a dependency $X.A \leftarrow Y.B$ asserts that for every instance frame I consistent with X there exists an instance frame J consistent with Y such that $I.A$ depends on $J.B$. (If X is itself an instance frame I, then only I is consistent with X; if X is a class, then any instance of that class is consistent with X.) Note however, that our definition of dependencies only considers the first slot in a chain on which a slot depends; thus, it makes only a first-level partition of dependency. It is a conservative overestimate of the true dependency model, since if $X.A \leftarrow Y.B$, it is not necessarily the case that $X.A$ depends on every slot-chain

$Y.B.\sigma$. While it is fairly straightforward to refine our notion of dependency, we have found our definition to be adequate for most purposes.

Definition 3.2: A *dependency chain* is a list $X_1.A_1 \leftarrow X_2.A_2 \leftarrow \cdots$ such that, for each i, $X_i.A_i \leftarrow X_{i+1}.A_{i+1}$. A *dependency cycle* is a dependency chain that begins and ends with the same slot. ∎

Dependency cycles reflect potential problems with our model. (Although, as indicated by our discussion above, some correct models may appear to be problematic simply because of our overestimate for probabilistic dependencies.) A dependency cycle containing $I.A$, where I is an instance frame, corresponds to a possible chain of dependencies through which $I.A$ depends on itself. Such a cyclic dependency, if it exists, prevents us from defining a coherent probability model. A dependency cycle containing $X.A$ for some class X means that for every instance I_1 of X there is some instance I_2 of X such that $I_1.A$ depends on $I_2.A$. In some cases, I_1 and I_2 are necessarily the same instance; such cases are called *truly cyclic*. In others, however, they are distinct instances of the class X. These cases can also be problematic, as they may represent an infinite dependency chain beginning with $I_1.A$: $I_1.A$ depends on $I_2.A$ which depends on some $I_3.A$, etc. Such models also do not typically have well-defined probabilistic semantics.

We conclude from this discussion that we want to disallow all dependency cycles.[1] Some types of dependency cycles are easy to prevent using purely local considerations. Specifically, we can build, for each class X, a *dependency graph* for X. This graph contains all the slots of X, with an edge from B to A if the dependency $X.A \leftarrow X.B$ holds. Clearly, if we want to avoid dependency cycles, this graph should be acyclic. Indeed, our care in designing the dependency model for inverse slots implies that if we make all class dependency graphs acyclic, we avoid any truly cyclic dependency chains at the class level. Formally, if we define a *class-level dependency chain* to be one in which all the X_i's are p-classes, we obtain the following theorem:

Theorem 3.3: *If we have a knowledge base in which all class dependency graphs are acyclic, then there are no truly cyclic class-level dependency chains.*

However, as we discussed, even dependency chains that are not truly cyclic can result in incoherent models. In addition, we have not eliminated instance-level dependency chains that are truly cyclic. Unfortunately, the general problem is not so easy to prevent using purely local constraints. However, we can detect whether or not the KB contains a dependency cycle by building a more global directed graph $\mathcal{G}$, called the *dependency graph* of the KB. The nodes of $\mathcal{G}$ are all $X.A$ where X is a p-class or named individual frame and A is a slot of X. There is an edge from $Y.B$ to $X.A$ if the dependency $X.A \leftarrow Y.B$ holds. Clearly, the KB contains a dependency cycle iff $\mathcal{G}$ is cyclic.

For a KB that contains no dependency cycles, our goal now is to define a probability distribution over instantiations

---

[1] Note that we are not disallowing infinite reference chains (chains of related instances), unless they imply infinite dependency chains.

to frames, i.e., assignments of values to the slots of the frames. Several issues combine to make such a definition difficult.

The most obvious idea is to follow the approach taken in the semantics of Bayesian networks: we determine a set of random variables, and define a distribution over their joint value space. Unfortunately, our framework is too rich to make this approach appropriate. As we mentioned, the set of instance frames that we can potentially refer to may be infinite. While one might be able to circumvent this particular problem, a more serious one manifests when we enrich our language with structural uncertainty in Sections 4 and 5. Then, the set of instance frames can also vary probabilistically, in a way that both depends on and influences the values of other random variables in the model.

We therefore define our semantics via a data generating process, that randomly samples values for the various frames in the model. The random sampling process implicitly defines a distribution over the different possible value assignments: the probability of a value assignment is the probability with which it is generated by the process. Note that, although a random sampling process can also be used as a stochastic algorithm for approximate inference, we are not proposing this approach; our sampling process is purely a thought experiment for defining the distribution. In Section 6, we show how a more standard process of exact inference can be used to effectively answer queries relative to this distribution.

The sampling process builds value assignments to slots of frames incrementally, as the different components are required. By allowing such partial assignments, we bypass the problem of going off on infinite sampling chains. The assumption of finite dependency chains guarantees that the sampling chains required to sample the value of any simple slot will always terminate.

Definition 3.4: A partial value ϑ for an instance frame is an assignment of values (of the appropriate type) to some subset of its simple slots, an assignment of instance frames (from the appropriate p-class) to some subset of its complex slots, and a partial value for each of these assigned instances. ∎

One final subtlety arises in the sampling construction. Some instance frames may have specific values pre-assigned to some of the their slots. Such an assignment can be done via an explicit statement for a named instance frame, or via a process of inheritance from a template slot of a class to which the instance belongs. As we explained in Section 2, the semantics of such assignments is to condition the distribution. To obtain the right semantics, we make the obvious modification to our data generating process. If, during the sampling process, a value is generated for a slot which is inconsistent with the observed value, we simply discard the entire partial value generated up to that point. It is easy to see [4] that the relative probability with which a partial value is generated in this data generating process is exactly the same as its probability conditioned on the observed slot values.

As we discussed, our sampling procedure builds up a partial value ϑ piece by piece, as the pieces are needed. Our main procedure, shown in Figure 1, is **Sample**(I, A), which samples the value of a single simple slot A of a single instance frame I. In order to sample A from the correct distribution, it must backward chain and sample other slots on which the

```
Sample(I, A)                          ComplexValue(I, σ)
  If A has a value in ϑ then return     If σ is empty then
  Foreach parent σ of A                   Return I
    If σ is a slot B in I then          /* σ is of the form B.σ' */
      Sample(I, B)                      If I.B is assigned a value J in ϑ then
    Else /* σ is of the form σ'.C */      Let K := J
      Let J := ComplexValue(I, σ')      Else if I.B is pre-assigned a value J then
      Sample(J, C)                        Extend ϑ with I.B = J
  Choose(I, A)                            Let K := J
                                        Else
Choose(I, A)                              Let Y be value-type(B)
  Choose a value v for A                  Create a new instance K of p-class Y
    according to P(A | Pa(A))             Extend ϑ with I.B = K
  Extend ϑ with I.A = v                 If B has an inverse B' in K then
  If A has a pre-assigned value v' then   Extend ϑ with K.B' = I
    If v' ≠ v then fail                 Return ComplexValue(K, σ')
```

Figure 1: Data generating sampling model

value of A depends. **ComplexValue**(I, σ) determines the value of the complex slot-chain $I.\sigma$, if necessary creating new instance frames to represent the values of complex slots. When the procedure returns, the partial value ϑ (a global variable in the procedure) contains a value for $I.A$.

Lemma 3.5: *If the dependency graph is acyclic, then* **Sample**(I, A), *executed from a partial value ϑ defines a probability distribution over extensions of ϑ with a value assigned to $I.A$. Furthermore, the distribution does not depend on the order in which the parents of A are examined.*

Proof: The basic steps in the proof are as follows. To prove the first part of the theorem, it suffices to show that the sampling algorithm terminates. This proof proceeds using a simple inductive argument over the length of dependency chains. To prove that the distribution is independent of the order, we observe that a simple slot is always generated from the same conditional distribution, regardless of when it is sampled, and that the failure conditions are also applied universally. ∎

We can now define a **SampleKB** procedure that uses **Sample**(I, A) to sample values for the slots of all named instances in the KB. If any call to **Sample** fails, the entire sampling process needs to be restarted. Once a value has been assigned to all simple slots of named instances, we have accounted for all evidence in the model, and therefore further sampling of other slots cannot possibly fail. Therefore the distribution we have obtained over the slots we have sampled is the final one.

Theorem 3.6: *If the dependency graph is acyclic then* **SampleKB** *defines a probability distribution over partial values ϑ which have values assigned to all simple slots $I.A$ for all named instances I.*

4 Multivalued slots and number uncertainty

To this point, we have assumed that every slot is single-valued. However, slots that take on multiple values are a fundamental concept in frame systems. The ai-professor p-class may have a multi-valued *papers* slot of type ai-paper. To simplify our discussion, we require multi-valued slots to be complex, and all values of the slot must be of the same p-class, as specified in the slot's value-type.

To allow other slots in a frame X to depend on the properties of a multi-valued slot A, we must present a way for a slot to depend on a set of slots. As the elements in the set cannot be referred to individually, we must refer instead to the properties of the set.

Definition 4.1: A *quantifier slot* for a multi-valued slot A has the form $\forall(A.\sigma : e)$, $\exists(A.\sigma : e)$, $\leq n(A.\sigma : e)$ or $\geq n(A.\sigma : e)$, where σ is a slot chain of A and e is an element of the value type of $A.\sigma$. The value-type of a quantifier slot is the set $\{true, false\}$. ∎

Given a set of values for A, the value of a quantifer slot on $A.B$ has precisely the meaning that one would expect; for example, if for at least 10 values I of the *papers* slot $I.impact$ has the value *high*, then the value of $\geq 10(papers.impact : high)$ is *true*. Note that the CPT of a quantifier slot is well-defined for any number of values of its multi-valued slot. On the other hand, no other slot can depend directly on the multi-valued slot, thereby avoiding the problem of defining general CPTs with a variable number of parents. A quantifier slot, on the other hand, is treated in the same way as a simple slot, so it may be used as a parent of another slot. Thus, for example, the *will-get-tenure* slot of the assistant-professor class may depend on the above quantifier slot.

So far, we have not specified the number of values that a given multi-valued slot can take. In many cases, e.g., the number of papers, this number is not fixed. Therefore, we would like to be able to model situations in which different numbers of papers are possible, and to represent our beliefs in these various possibilities. In other words, we would like to allow *structural uncertainty*—uncertainty over the set of entities in the world and the relationships between them. Uncertainty over the number of values of a multi-valued slot is a type of structural uncertainty called *number uncertainty*.

We can extend our language to represent number uncertainty by associating with each multivalued slot A of X a new *number slot num*(A), which ranges over some set of natural numbers $\{0, 1, \ldots, n\}$ (we assume that the number of values of every slot is bounded). The slot *num*(A) is treated just like any other simple slot; it has parents and distribution facets that describe its probability model. Thus, the number of values of A in X can depend on values of other slots of X and of related frames, and it can also be the parent of another slot. For example, ai-professor will have a *num*(*papers*) slot, whose value ranges from 0 to 50; *num*(*papers*) may depend on *productivity* and in turn influence *tired*.

As with the case of single-valued slots, a specific value I may be asserted for a multi-valued slot A of both a p-class and a named individual. We interpret such assignments as asserting that one of A's values is I. It does not prevent A from having other values; in fact, multiple values may be asserted for the slot. Such assignments do not eliminate our number uncertainty for this slot, but any case where the slot has fewer than the number of asserted fillers is eliminated; thus, we must condition *num*(A) to be at least the asserted number. To assert that A has only the values mentioned, we would need to explicitly assert a value for *num*(A).

It is interesting to examine the interaction between multi-valued slots and inverses. Assume that the *advisees* slot has an inverse *advisor* within the phd-student frame. If we now have a student instance frame I, then we automatically assert at least one value—the value I—for the *advisees* slot in the instance frame $I.advisor$. Thus, even if we have no other information whatsoever about this instance frame, it will not be a generic member of the professor class. The very fact that the professor is someone's advisor modifies its distribution by conditioning it on the fact that $num(advisees) \geq 1$. Note that the inverse slot may also be multi-valued. Many-many relations give rise to potentially infinite reference chains. For example, a paper may have several authors, who have all written several papers, and so on. However, due to the restrictions on the flow of influence between primary and secondary inverses, an infinite reference chain of this sort cannot lead to an infinite dependency chain.

Number uncertainty can be incorporated into our semantics quite easily. We need to add number and quantifier slots into the dependency graph. Number slots are treated just like simple slots: there is an edge into $X.num(A)$ for each of the parents of $num(A)$ in X. If $X.Q$ is a quantifier slot over $X.A$, there is an edge from $X.A$ to $X.Q$. Finally, we must make the value of $X.A$ depend both on $X.num(A)$ and the properties it imports from each of its fillers. If $X.A$ imports B, then we have $X.A \leftarrow Y.B$, where Y is the type of A, and $X.A \leftarrow I.B$ for every asserted value I of $X.A$.

The sampling process can easily be modified to account for multi-valued slots. When a multi-valued slot A needs to be sampled for the first time, we sample first a value n for $num(A)$. Let m be the number of asserted values for A. If $n < m$, the sample fails. Otherwise, $n - m$ new instances of the type of A are created, and the set of values of A is set to be the m asserted fillers and the $n - m$ new instances. Theorem 3.6 continues to hold.

5 Reference uncertainty

As we said, structural uncertainty allows us to represent distributions over models with different structures. Number uncertainty allows us to vary the *set* of instances in our model. In this section, we describe *reference uncertainty*, which allows us to vary the relations between the instances. For example, we may want the *conference* slot of the AI-paper class to be AAAI with probability 0.3, and another generic AI conference with probability 0.7; note that AAAI is not the value of a simple slot, but an instance frame itself. We extend our language to accomodate reference uncertainty by allowing some complex slots to be *indirect*. Each indirect slot A is associated with a *reference slot ref(A)*, a simple slot whose value dictates the value of the indirect slot.

Definition 5.1: If A is an indirect slot of type Y in p-class X, then $ref(A)$ is a simple slot in X whose value type is an enumerated set $\mathcal{R}$, each of whose values ρ is either: a named individual of type Y, a slot-chain of X whose type is Y, or the class Y itself.

In any instance I of X, the value of A is defined in terms of the value of $ref(A)$: if the value of $ref(A)$ is a named individual J, $I.A = J$; if the value of $ref(A)$ is a slot-chain σ, then $I.A = I.\sigma$; if $ref(A)$ is the p-class Y, then the value of A is a new instance of Y. ∎

A reference slot is treated just like any other simple slot, so it has parents and a CPT, and can influence other simple slots. A value can be assigned to a reference slot from within its value-type, and the value of the indirect slot will be determined by it. An indirect slot is treated like any other single-valued complex slot; it has an import list, and other slots can depend on the slots it imports. For technical reasons, we do not allow direct assignments to indirect slots, nor do we allow them to have inverses.

As with number uncertainty, reference uncertainty can be incorporated quite easily into our semantics. We need to add reference and indirect slots to the dependency graph. A reference slot is treated like any other simple slot; thus, its only dependencies are on its parents. An indirect slot A clearly depends on $ref(A)$, so we have $A \leftarrow ref(A)$. Since A is a complex slot, it also depends on the slots that it imports. However, because of reference uncertainty, we do not know the frame from which it imports those slots. Let B be some slot on the import list of A. To be safe, we need to account for every possible value ρ of $ref(A)$. Thus, for each $\rho \in \mathcal{R}$, if ρ is a named individual I, we have $X.A \leftarrow I.B$; if ρ is a slot chain $C.\sigma$, we have $X.A \leftarrow X.C$; if ρ is the class Y, we have $X.A \leftarrow Y.B$, denoting the fact A may import B from some instance of Y.

The sampling process requires a small change to Assign-Complex to deal with indirect slots. When AssignComplex is called with an indirect slot, we first sample the value of the corresponding reference slot in the usual manner, and then assign the value of the indirect slot in the manner determined by the value of the reference slot. With this change, Theorem 3.6 continues to hold.

6 Inference

In the preceding sections, we presented a representation language and semantics for probabilistic frame systems. To complete the story, we now present a simple inference algorithm for answering probabilistic queries in such a system. Our algorithm can handle any instance-based query, i.e., queries about the values of slots of instances. For simplicity, we restrict attention to simple slots of named instances, as other queries can easily be reduced to these. The algorithm, called **ConstructBN**, is based on *knowledge-based model construction* [12], the process of taking a KB and deriving a BN $\mathcal{B}$ representing the same probability model. Standard BN inference can then be used to answer queries.

Nodes in the Bayes net $\mathcal{B}$ have the form $I.\sigma.A$ where I is an instance frame (not necessarily named), σ is a possibly empty slot chain, and A is a simple slot. The algorithm works by backward chaining along dependency chains, constructing the appropriate nodes in the BN if they do not already exist. More specifically, the algorithm maintains an open list $\mathcal{L}$ of nodes to be processed. Initially, $\mathcal{L}$ contains only the simple slots of named instances. In each iteration, the algorithm removes a node from $\mathcal{L}$, and processes it. When a node is removed from $\mathcal{L}$, it is processed in one of three ways: as a simple slot, as a slot chain, or as a quantifier slot.

Simple slots $I.A$ are processed as follows. For each parent $I.\sigma$, an edge is added from $I.\sigma$ to $I.A$ by a call to AddParent$(I.A, I.\sigma)$; if $I.\sigma$ is not already in $\mathcal{B}$, this routine adds $I.\sigma$ to $\mathcal{B}$ and $\mathcal{L}$. (Note that the parent list of any simple non-quantifier slot is fixed.) When all parents have been added, the CPT is constructed from the distribution facet of A.

A slot chain $I.B.\tau$ is processed as follows:

ProcessComplex($I.B.\tau$)
  If B is indirect then
    ProcessIndirect($I.B.\tau$)
  Else
    If B is assigned a value J in I then $K = J$
    Else $K = X[I.B]$, where X is the type of B in I
    AddParent($I.B.\tau, K.\tau$)
    Set CPT of $I.B.\tau$ to copy the value of $K.\tau$

Essentially, if B is assigned a named individual J in I, then $I.B = J$. Otherwise, $I.B = X[I.B]$, an instance of X that does not appear anywhere else in the KB; roughly, $X[I.B]$ serves the role of a Skolem function. Either way, the value of $I.B$ is known to be some other frame K, so that $I.B.\tau$ is equal to $K.\tau$. We make $K.\tau$ a parent of $I.B.\tau$, and define the CPT to enforce this equality. These intermediate nodes along the slot chain are introduced to monitor the flow of values through complex slots. They are needed because the flow becomes complicated when the chain contains indirect slots. Intermediate variables that are spurious can easily be eliminated in a simple post-processing phase.

If B is indirect, then the value of $I.B$ could be one of several frames, depending on the value of the reference slot $I.ref(B)$. For any value ρ of $I.ref(B)$, let $K[\rho]$ denote the frame which is the value of $I.B$. The value of $I.B.\sigma$ is equal to the value of $K[\rho].\sigma$. In other words, $I.ref(B)$ selects the value of $I.B.\sigma$ from a set of possibilities. Therefore, the node $I.B.\sigma$ is a *multiplexer* node [1]; it has as parents the node $I.ref(B)$ and all nodes $K[\rho].B.\sigma$, and it uses the value of $I.ref(B)$ to select, as its value, the value of one of its appropriate parents.

ProcessIndirect($I.B.\tau$)
  AddParent($I.B.\tau, I.ref(B)$)
  For each value ρ of $I.ref(B)$
    If ρ is a named individual J then $K[\rho] = J$
    If ρ is the slot chain σ then $K[\rho] = I.\sigma$
    If ρ is the class Y then $K[\rho] = Y[I.C]$
    AddParent($I.B.\tau, K[\rho].\tau$)
  Set CPT for $I.B.\tau$ to select the value of $K[I.B].\tau$

It remains to deal with the cases introduced by number uncertainty. Since a multi-valued slot A can only be used by quantifier slots, these are the only slots which we need to consider. Consider a quantifier slot $I.Q$ over $A.\sigma$. The value of $I.Q$ is fully determined by $I.num(A)$ and the value of σ in each of the possible values of A. Let n be the maximum number of such values, and suppose that A is assigned m values $J[1], \ldots, J[m]$ in I. In addition to these, there can be up to $n - m$ other instances that are values for A; we build a frame for each of them, $J[m+1], \ldots, J[n]$. The node $I.Q$ depends on $I.num(A)$ and on the appropriate subset of the variables $J[i].\sigma$; i.e., if $num(A)$ is k, then only $J[1], \ldots, J[k]$ will influence $I.Q$. The exact form of the dependence will depend on the form of the quantifier. For example, a $\forall$ quantifier slot will be a deterministic conjunction of the appropriate subset of its parents.

ProcessQuantifier($I.Q$) /* a quantifier over $A.\sigma$ */
  AddParent($I.Q, I.num(A)$)
  Let n be the maximum value of $I.num(A)$
  Let $J[1], \ldots, J[m]$ be the assigned values to $I.A$
  For $i = m + 1$ to n
    $J[i] = X[i][I.A]$, where X is the type of $I.A$

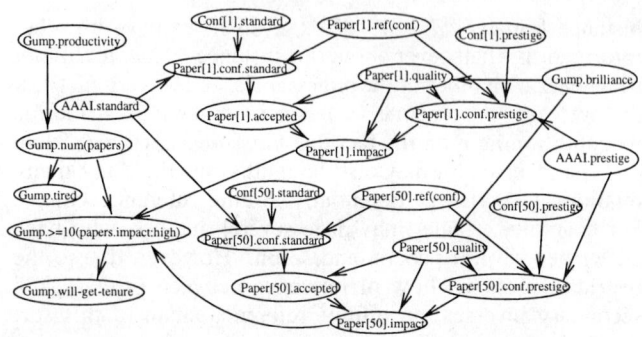

Figure 2: Part of the constructed BN for Prof. Gump's tenure case. Models for only two of the fifty possible papers are shown. Paper[i] is shorthand for paper[Gump.*papers*][i], and Conf[i] is short for conf[paper[Gump.*papers.conference*][i]].

  For $i = 1$ to n
    AddParent($I.Q, J[i].\sigma$)
  Set the CPT for $I.Q$ to depend on $J[1].\rho, \ldots, J[num(A)].\sigma$

To illustrate the algorithm, Figure 2 shows part of the BN constructed for a KB concerning the tenure case of one Prof. F. Gump, an instance of ai-assistant-professor. The node Gump.*will-get-tenure* depends on Gump.≥ 10(*papers.impact:high*). The latter is a quantifier slot, so it has as parents Gump.*num*(*papers*) and the *impact* slot of each of the 50 possible papers. Now, assume that the class paper has *impact* depending on *conference.prestige*. This dependence is duplicated for each of the 50 possible papers. The slot *conference* is indirect, so that for each i (using the shorthand of the figure) Paper[i].*conf.prestige* has the parent Paper[i].*ref(conf)* and the *prestige* slot of the possible values of that reference, which are AAAI and *conf*[i].

Looking over the overall structure of the algorithm, we see that there is a correspondence between the structure of the dependency graph $\mathcal{G}$ and that of the BN $\mathcal{B}$. We can define a mapping φ from nodes of $\mathcal{B}$ to nodes of $\mathcal{G}$ as follows: $\varphi(I.A.\sigma)$ is $I.A$ if I is a named individual, and $X.A$ otherwise for X the p-class of I. Intuitively, the node $X.A$ in $\mathcal{G}$ is a representative for all the nodes $I.A$ where I is a generic instance of X.

Lemma 6.1: *If there is an edge from node μ_1 to node μ_2 in $\mathcal{B}$, then there is an path from $\varphi(\mu_1)$ to $\varphi(\mu_2)$ in $\mathcal{G}$.*

In other words, $\mathcal{G}$ serves as a template for the dependencies in $\mathcal{B}$. Many edges in $\mathcal{B}$ may map to the same path in $\mathcal{G}$, but any cycle or infinite dependency in $\mathcal{B}$ will necessarily map to a cycle in $\mathcal{G}$ (because $\mathcal{G}$ is finite). This property is the basis for the following theorem.

Theorem 6.2: *If the dependency graph is acyclic,* **ConstructBN** *terminates and the constructed Bayes net is acyclic.*

This construction also provides us with an alternative specification for the distribution defined by a probabilistic frame KB. Intuitively, the BN corresponds to the prior distribution defined by the KB. In particular, the CPT of a *num*(A) slot can ascribe a positive probability to *num*(A) = 0, despite the fact that one or more values have been asserted for A in the

KB. In order for $\mathcal{B}$ to represent the distribution defined by our semantics, we must condition it on all of our observations. Specifically, we assert the value for any simple slot whose value was assigned in the KB, and lower bounds on the value of $num(A)$ corresponding to the number of values asserted for A (including indirectly via inverses).

Theorem 6.3: *Let $\mathcal{S}$ be the set of simple slots of named individuals, and $\mathcal{E}$ the evidence on simple slots and number slots derived from the KB. Then $\Pr_\mathcal{B}(\mathcal{S} \mid \mathcal{E})$ is the same as the distribution over $\mathcal{S}$ defined by our semantics.*

We have implemented our approach within a system that contains the following functionality: A graphical network-based editor/browser can be used to annotate a frame KB with the facets encoding its probability model. The editor/browser interacts with the underlying FRS using OKBC, thus allowing its use with many of the existing frame systems (e.g., [3, 8, 7]). Our inference component also connects to the FRS via OKBC; it extracts the relevant information about frames, instances, and their probabilistic models, constructs the BN corresponding to the KB, and utilizes the BN to answer probabilistic queries. The system has been integrated successfully with the Ontolingua frame system [3] and was used for representing simple models of vehicle movement patterns in a military setting. Our experience with the system showed that even very simple models with three or four simple p-classes could be used to generate fairly complicated BNs (with hundreds of nodes) involving several interacting entities.

7 Discussion and conclusions

In this paper, we have described the first integration between two of the most dominant threads of work in KR. Our language provides a clean synthesis between the probabilistic reasoning component and standard frame reasoning capabilities. From the perspective of frame systems, our system allows existing frame KBs to be annotated with probabilistic models, greatly increasing the ability of frame systems to express meaningful knowledge in real-world applications. We have also provided an inference algorithm capable of answering probabilistic queries about instances, thereby providing a significant increase to the inferential ability of such systems. From the perspective of probabilistic modeling, our language provides the tools for the construction of probabilistic models for very large complex domains, significantly scaling up our ability to do uncertain reasoning.

Our language has given us the exciting capability of creating highly expressive probabilistic models with structural uncertainty. Clearly, we have only scratched the surface of this idea. For example, it is easy to add uncertainty over the type of an object, e.g., to define a probability distribution with which a professor is an assistant, associate, and full professor. It is also easy to combine number and reference uncertainty, allowing, for example, the advisor of a student to be selected from the set of faculty members in the CS department. These are two of many possible extensions that can now be considered.

Another important issue which we have partially resolved is the inference problem for probabilistic frame-based models. We have shown how we can reduce the problem to that of reasoning in a standard BN, but this approach does not make full use of the structure encoded in our representation. In particular, it fails to exploit encapsulation of frames within other frames and the reuse of class models among several objects. These ideas are put to good use in [6, 5], and it is an important research topic to apply them in our richer framework. We believe that by exploiting these features in our inference as well as in our representation, we will be able to effectively represent and reason in large uncertain domains.

Acknowledgments This work was supported by ONR contract N66001-97-C-8554 under DARPA's HPKB program, by DARPA contract DACA76-93-C-0025 under subcontract to Information Extraction and Transport, Inc., and through the generosity of the Powell Foundation and the Sloan Foundation.

References

[1] C. Boutilier, N. Friedman, M. Goldszmidt, and D. Koller. Context-specific independence in Bayesian networks. In *Proc. UAI*, 1996.

[2] V.K. Chaudhri, A. Farquhar, R. Fikes, P.D. Karp, and J.P. Rice. Open knowledge base connectivity 2.0.2. Available from http://www.ai.sri.com/~okbc, 1998.

[3] A. Farquhar, R. Fikes, and J. Rice. The Ontolingua server: A tool for collaborative ontology construction. Technical report, Stanford KSL 96-26, 1996.

[4] M. Henrion. Propagation of uncertainty in Bayesian networks by probabilistic logic sampling. In *Proc. UAI*, 1988.

[5] D. Koller, A. Levy, and A. Pfeffer. P-classic: A tractable probabilistic description logic. In *Proc. AAAI*, 1997.

[6] D. Koller and A. Pfeffer. Object-oriented Bayesian networks. In *Proc. UAI*, 1997.

[7] D.B. Lenat and R.V. Guha. *Building Large Knowledge-Based Systems: Representation and Inference in the CYC Project*. Addison-Wesley, 1990.

[8] R. MacGregor. The evolving technology of classification-based knowledge representation systems. In J. Sowa, editor, *Principles of semantic networks*, pages 385–400. Morgan Kaufmann, 1991.

[9] L. Ngo and P. Haddawy. Answering queries from context-sensitive probabilistic knowledge bases. *Theoretical Computer Science*, 1996.

[10] J. Pearl. *Probabilistic Reasoning in Intelligent Systems*. Morgan Kaufmann, 1988.

[11] D. Poole. Probabilistic Horn abduction and Bayesian networks. *Artificial Intelligence*, 64(1):81–129, November 1993.

[12] M.P. Wellman, J.S. Breese, and R.P. Goldman. From knowledge bases to decision models. *The Knowledge Engineering Review*, 7(1):35–53, November 1992.

Logical representation and computation of optimal decisions in a qualitative setting †

Didier Dubois, Daniel Le Berre, Henri Prade, Régis Sabbadin
IRIT - Université Paul Sabatier - 31062 Toulouse Cedex (France)
e-mail: {dubois, leberre, prade, sabbadin}@irit.fr

Abstract

This paper describes a logical machinery for computing decisions based on an ATMS procedure, where the available knowledge on the state of the world is described by a possibilistic propositional logic base (i.e., a collection of logical statements associated with qualitative certainty levels). The preferences of the user are also described by another possibilistic logic base whose formula weights are interpreted in terms of priorities and formulas express goals. Two attitudes are allowed for the decision maker: a pessimistic uncertainty-averse one and an optimistic one. The computed decisions are in agreement with a qualitative counterpart to classical expected utility theory for decision under uncertainty.

Introduction

In classical decision theory under uncertainty, the preferences of the decision maker are directly expressed by means of a utility function, while a probability distribution on the possible states of the world represents the available, uncertain information about the situation under consideration. However, it seems reasonable to allow for a more granular expression of both the preferences and the available knowledge about the world, under the form, e.g., of logical expressions from which it would be possible to build the utility and the uncertainty functions.

Many works are concerned with qualitative decision theory under uncertainty. Some approaches consider only all-or-nothing notions of utility and plausibility (Bonet and Geffner (1996)); others use in addition a preference ordering on consequences (Brafman and Tennenholtz (1997)). Boutilier (1994) also uses a plausibility ordering, but focuses only on the most plausible states. Tan and Pearl (1994) use two integer-valued rankings for preference and plausibility and compare

---

† This article is dedicated to the memory of Thierry Castell, our colleague and friend, who accidentally died in August 1997. He significantly contributed to the development of the MPL algorithm.

Copyright ©1998, American Association for Artificial Intelligence (www.aaai.org). All rights reserved.

actions pairwise, according to the relative plausibilities of the subsets in which one action "dominates" the other. This pairwise comparison is not representable by a utility function, and the associated preference relation is not generally transitive. A similar kind of pairwise comparison was also studied in (Dubois, Fargier and Prade (1997)).

In the following, we propose two syntactic approaches based on possibilistic logic, the first one being more cautious than the second, for computing optimal decisions. Here gradual uncertainty and preferences are expressed by means of two distinct possibilistic propositional logic bases (which are stratified bases). Then, the semantics underlying the two syntactic approaches are shown to be in agreement with the two qualitative utility functions advocated in (Dubois and Prade (1995)). Then, we recall some background on the ATMS framework, and it is shown how to encode a decision problem as one of label computation. Then a procedure called MPL is described for computing optimal decisions in terms of labels. It relies on a modified Davis and Putnam (1960) (1962) semantic evaluation algorithm, described in (Castell et al. (1996), (1998)). Two algorithms based on the use of this procedure, are proposed for computing optimistic and pessimistic optimal decisions respectively. A preliminary version of the logical representation of decision problems used in the following was presented in a workshop paper (Dubois et al. (1997a)). A longer version of the present paper, explaining all the computational details and providing all the proofs of the propositions is to be published (Dubois et al. (1998)).

Qualitative decision in stratified propositional bases

In this article, upper case letters ($K, D, P, H, \ldots$) denote sets of propositional formulas that can possibly be literals. For any set A of formulas, $A^\wedge$ denotes the logical conjunction of the formulas in A and $A^\vee$, the logical disjunction. If $H = \{l_i\}$ is a set of literals, $\sim H = \{\neg l_i, l_i \in H\}$.

A decision problem under uncertainty can be cast in a logical setting in the following way. A vocabulary

V of propositional variables contains two kinds of variables: decision variables and state variables. Let V_D be the set of decision variables which are controllable, that is, their value can be fixed by the decision-maker. The propositional variables outside V_D are state variables. Making a decision amounts to fixing the truth value of every decision variable (or possibly just a part of them). On the contrary state variables are fixed by nature, and their value is a matter of knowledge by the decision maker. He/she has no control on them (although he/she may express preference about their values).

Let K be a knowledge base (here in propositional logic) describing what is known about the world including constraints relating the decision variables. Let P be another propositional base describing goals delimiting the preferred states of the world. K, and P are assumed to be finite, as is the logical propositional language L under consideration. To get a flavour of the decision procedures, assume first that K and P are classical logic bases, and preferences are all-or-nothing. The aim of the decision problem, described in the logical setting, is to try to make all formulas in the goal set P true by acting on the truth-value of decision variables which control the models of K and P. A good decision $d^\wedge$ (from a pessimistic point of view) is a conjunction of decision literals that entails the satisfaction of every goal in P, when formulas in K are assumed to be true. Therefore, d should satisfy

$$K^\wedge \wedge d^\wedge \vdash P^\wedge. \qquad (1)$$

Moreover, the allowed decisions must be such that $K^\wedge \wedge d^\wedge$ be consistent, for if it is not the case, (1) is trivially satisfied. Under an optimistic point of view, we may just look for decisions d which are consistent with the knowledge base and the goals,

$$K^\wedge \wedge d^\wedge \wedge P^\wedge \neq \bot. \qquad (2)$$

Note that (2) is verified as soon as (1) is. (2) which is over-optimistic should be used only if there is no solution to (1).

In the logical form of decision problems, the knowledge base may be pervaded with uncertainty, and the goals may not have equal priority. Let us enrich our logical view of the decision problem, by assigning levels of certainty to formulas in the knowledge base, and levels of priority to the goals. Thus we obtain two stratified logical bases that model gradual knowledge and preferences. It has been shown (e.g., Dubois et al. (1994)) that a possibility distribution encodes the semantics of a possibilistic logic base, i.e., a stratified base whose formulas are gathered into several layers according to their levels of certainty or priority. In the following we focus on how a decision problem can be stated, expressing knowledge and preferences in terms of stratified bases. Then we will show that the corresponding semantics can be represented by the qualitative utility introduced in (Dubois and Prade (1995)).

In the whole paper it is assumed that certainty degrees and priority degrees are commensurate, and assessed on the same (*finite*, as is the language under consideration) linearly ordered scale[1] S. The top element of S will be denoted $\mathbf{1}$, and the bottom element, $\mathbf{0}$. Knowledge and preferences are stored in two distinct possibilistic bases. The knowledge base is $K = \{(\phi_i, \alpha_i)\}$ where $\alpha_i \in S$ ($\alpha_i > \mathbf{0}$) denotes a level of certainty, and the ϕ_i's are formulas in L where decision literals may appear. The base expressing preferences or goals is $P = \{(\psi_i, \beta_i)\}$, where $\beta_i \in S$ ($\beta_i > \mathbf{0}$) is a level of priority, and the ψ_i are formulas of L (where decision literals may also appear).

Let K_α (resp. P_β) denote the set of formulas with certainty at least equal to α (resp. the formulas with priority at least equal to β). Note that we only consider layers of K (or P) such that $\alpha > \mathbf{0}$ and $\beta > \mathbf{0}$ since $K_\mathbf{0} = P_\mathbf{0} = L$. In the following we also use the notations $K_{\overline{\alpha}}$ and $P_{\overline{\beta}}$ (with $\alpha < \mathbf{1}$ and $\beta < \mathbf{1}$), for denoting the set of formulas with certainty or priority *strictly* greater than α or β respectively. In particular $K_{\overline{\mathbf{0}}}$ and $P_{\overline{\mathbf{0}}}$ are the sets of formulas in K and P respectively, without their certainty levels. Since the scale S is finite, $K_{\overline{\alpha}} = K_{\alpha'}$, where α' is the level of S just above α (the same holds for P).

Making a decision amounts to choosing a subset d of the decision set $D = \{l_i\}$ where the l_i are distinguished positive literals of the language L. Our objective is to rank-order decisions, which will be done by using a utility function $U : 2^D \to S$ such that d is not preferred to d' iff $U(d) \leq U(d')$. In the following, we will use two different functions: U_* which agrees with a pessimistic view, and U^* which agrees with an optimistic one.

In the first case (pessimistic view), we are interested in finding a decision d (if it exists) such that

$$K_\alpha^\wedge \wedge d^\wedge \vdash P_\beta^\wedge \qquad (3)$$

with α high and β low, i.e., such that the decision d together with the most certain part of K entails the satisfaction of the goals, even those with low priority. d is implicitly assumed to be included in the most certain part of $K \cup d$ (certainty level equal to $\mathbf{1}$). Moreover, $K_\alpha^\wedge \wedge d^\wedge$ should be consistent for the α's satisfying (3). One way of guaranteeing this consistency requirement is to assume $K_{\overline{\mathbf{0}}}^\wedge \wedge d^\wedge$ is consistent. By convention, utility $\mathbf{0}$ is assigned to every decision d that is not consistent with K. Besides, observe that the values of the β satisfying (3) are necessarily such that $\beta > \mathbf{0}$ (since $P_\mathbf{0}^\wedge = L$ is inconsistent). Let n be the order reversing map of scale S. Namely if S is $\mathbf{0} = \alpha_0 < \ldots < \alpha_n = \mathbf{1}$ then $n(\alpha_i) = \alpha_{n-i}$.

---

[1] An attempt to relax this assumption has been made in (Dubois, Fargier and Prade (1997)). These authors point out that working without the commensurability assumption leads to a decision method close to rational inference machinery in non-monotonic reasoning. Unfortunately, that method also proves to be either very little decisive or to lead to very risky decisions.

Ideally, d, along with the most certain part of K only ($K_{\bar{1}}$), should entail every goal in P, even the least preferred ones ($P_{\bar{0}}$). Such a decision should have a maximal utility ($\mathbb{1}$). The worst case would be when a decision is unable, even with the whole knowledge($K_{\bar{0}}$) to entail even only the most preferred formulas of P ($P_{\bar{1}}$). Such a decision should have a utility of $\mathbb{0}$.

It can be proved that the solution of the problem of maximizing α and minimizing β in (3) satisfies $\beta = \overline{n(\alpha)}$. Thus, the pessimistic utility of decision d, defined at the syntactic level, shall take the form:

Definition 1
$U_*(d) = \max\{\alpha / K_\alpha^\wedge \wedge d^\wedge \vdash P_{\overline{n(\alpha)}}^\wedge, K_\alpha^\wedge \wedge d^\wedge \neq \bot\}$ and if $\{\alpha > \mathbb{0}, K_\alpha^\wedge \wedge d^\wedge \vdash P_{\overline{n(\alpha)}}^\wedge$ and $K_\alpha^\wedge \wedge d^\wedge \neq \bot\}$ is empty, then $U_*(d) = \mathbb{0}$.

If now we consider the optimistic case, we are interested in finding a decision d such that:

$$K_\alpha^\wedge \wedge d^\wedge \wedge P_\beta^\wedge \neq \bot \qquad (4)$$

with α and β as low as possible: The preferred states are among the most plausible ones and are also consistent with the decision. The optimistic utility of d is thus given by

Definition 2
$U^*(d) = \max\{n(\alpha) / K_\alpha^\wedge \wedge d^\wedge \wedge P_\alpha^\wedge \neq \bot\}$
and $U^*(d) = \mathbb{0}$ if $\{\alpha < \mathbb{1}, K_\alpha^\wedge \wedge d^\wedge \wedge P_\alpha^\wedge \neq \bot\} = \emptyset$.

Observe that $U^*(d) = \mathbb{1}$ iff $K_{\bar{0}}^\wedge \wedge d^\wedge \wedge P_{\bar{0}}^\wedge \neq \bot$, that is if the decision is consistent with every goal and piece of knowledge. This is of course over-optimistic in the sense that it assumes that goals will be attained as soon as their negation cannot be proved: however (4) can be useful to discriminate solutions d, d' to (3) such that $U_*(d) = U_*(d')$.

Possibilistic semantics of decision in stratified bases

Let us present the semantics underlying the logical expression of decision problems we have adopted. Interpreting the α_i's (which are attached to the layers of K) as the degrees of necessity of the formulas in the corresponding layers of $K \cup d$, we compute a possibility distribution π_{K_d} over Ω (the set of all the interpretations of the language L), expressing the semantics of $K \cup d$ (see, e.g., (Dubois et al. (1994))): $\forall \omega \in \Omega$,
$\pi_{K_d}(\omega) = \min_{(\phi_i, \alpha_i) \in K / \omega \models \neg \phi_i} n(\alpha_i)$ if $\omega \models d^\wedge$, and
$\pi_{K_d}(\omega) = \mathbb{1}$ if $\{\phi_i / \omega \models \neg \phi_i\} = \emptyset$ and $\omega \models d^\wedge$, and
$\pi_{K_d}(\omega) = \mathbb{0}$ if $\omega \not\models d^\wedge$.

The possibility distribution π_{K_d} rank-orders the interpretations according to their level of possibility/plausibility induced by the levels of certainty of the formulas in K. This semantics agrees with the idea that an interpretation ω is all the less possible as it violates formulas with an higher level of certainty. Note that since $K_{\bar{0}}^\wedge \wedge d^\wedge$ is consistent, π_{K_d} is normalized,

i.e., there exists at least an interpretation ω with degree $\pi_{K_d}(\omega) = \mathbb{1}$.

From P, interpreting the β_i attached to the layers of P as degrees of priority of the formulas in P, we build a utility function μ over Ω in a similar way (ω is all the more satisfactory as it violates no goal with a high priority):
$\mu(\omega) = \min_{(\psi_j, \beta_j) \in P, \omega \models \neg \psi_j} n(\beta_j)$
and $\mu(\omega) = \mathbb{1}$ if $\{\psi_j / \omega \models \neg \psi_j\} = \emptyset$.

The two utility functions U_* and U^* defined precedently can be expressed in terms of the possibility distribution π_{K_d} and the utility function μ:

Proposition 1 *Semantic expressions of the utilities.*
$U_*(d) = \max_{\alpha / K_\alpha^\wedge \wedge d^\wedge \vdash P_{\overline{n(\alpha)}}^\wedge} \alpha = \min_{\omega \in \Omega} \max(n(\pi_{K_d}(\omega)), \mu(\omega))$.

$U^*(d) = \max_{\alpha / K_\alpha^\wedge \wedge d^\wedge \wedge P_\alpha^\wedge \neq \bot} n(\alpha) = \max_{\omega \in \Omega} \min(\pi_{K_d}(\omega), \mu(\omega))$.

The semantic expression of $U_*(d)$ is exactly the qualitative utility function introduced in (Dubois and Prade (1995)). These utility functions have been also justified in a Savage-like setting in (Dubois et al. (1997b)). Note that S is an ordinal scale, and decisions computed as above are robust since only min, max and the order reversing function of S are used. The ranking of decisions is insensitive to any bijective monotonic transformation of S.

Maximizing $U_*(d)$ means finding a decision d whose highly plausible consequences are among the most preferred ones. $U_*(d)$ is small as soon as it exists a possible consequence which is both highly plausible and bad with respect to preferences. This is clearly an uncertainty-averse and thus a pessimistic attitude. When π_d is the characteristic function of a set A, $U_*(d)$ reduces to: $U_*(d) = min_{\omega \in A} \mu(\omega)$, which is the Wald criterion, that evaluates the worth of a decision as the worst-case utility. The other utility function $U^*(d)$ corresponds to an *optimistic* attitude since $U^*(d)$ is high as soon as it exists a possible consequence of d which is both highly plausible and highly prized. The two utility functions may not be opposed one against the other; the optimistic utility function should be used to refine the pessimistic one, when the latter proves not to be decisive.

A question may be raised as to the meaning of the different levels of preference or certainty that are assigned to each sentence. It is clear that the *preference* ordering can be directly given by the decision maker. The *uncertainty* ordering may be assessed by a unique agent classifying the sentences into layers of different levels of certainty. In case the knowledge is given by multiple sources, we can suppose that they have levels of reliability (which may be different), and thus rank the sentences according to the levels of reliability of the sources which provide them (all the information given by a source having the same reliability). On the contrary if the sources are equally reliable, but each of them has its own ordering, we have to suppose that there exists a common agreement on the meaning of the layers of each source, so as to be able to merge the layers of the different sources. Besides, System Z (Pearl (1990)) may also help to rank order pieces of generic conditional knowledge by taking the specificity of formulas into account (Benferhat et al. (1997)).

Computation of decisions

The similarity is striking between the two modes of decision under uncertainty and the two modes of diagnostic reasoning, namely abductive and consistency-based diagnosis solutions (e.g., Console, de Kleer (1992)). It is then tempting to encode a logical decision problem under uncertainty by means of techniques coming from the theory of assumption-based truth maintenance systems (ATMS) initiated by (De Kleer (1986)).

In this section, we give some algorithms based on the use of the MPL procedure (which stands for *Modèles Préférés et Littéraux* in French) described in (Castell et al. (1996)) to solve qualitative possibilistic decision problems.

The MPL procedure

The MPL procedure introduced in (Castell et al. (1996)) does the following: given a logical formula ϕ in conjunctive normal form, involving two types of literals, it computes its projection by restricting to one type of literals; and this projection is the most informative such consequence of ϕ, expressed in disjunctive normal form. It is shown that nogoods in an ATMS are easily obtained by means of this procedure.

Principle of the MPL algorithm A (Davis and Putnam (1960)) algorithm enumerates the interpretations of a knowledge base K until it finds a model (consistent case) if any (the inconsistent case is when it finds no model). So doing, it is obvious that searching for models is closely related to finding a disjunctive normal form for a knowledge base, since it is easy to exhibit models of a DNF. Let H be a *consistent* set of literals ($\forall l_i \in H, \neg l_i$ does not belong to H). $V_H \subseteq V$ is the set of variables involved in H. Davis and Putnam's algorithm builds a binary search tree over V, starting with the instanciation of the variables in V_H. At each node it branches on the truth value of a variable. An interpretation I over V is then a path from the root node to a leaf of the tree. Equivalently, it is a set of literals. For any interpretation I we can define its restriction over the set H by: $R_H(I) = I \cap H$. If I is a model of K, $R_H(I)$ is called H-restricted model of K.

The MPL algorithm tries to find (if it exists) a H-restricted model of K, whereas the Davis and Putnam's one searches for a complete one (or a V-restricted one, stated differently). Moreover if it finds one, it is minimal with respect to set inclusion. It is so because the algorithm goes *depth-first* through the binary tree starting with literals in $\sim H$, building the current interpretation I by adding to it literals of $\sim H$ and checking its consistency with K. If $\{l_i, l_i \in \sim H\}$ is consistent with K, then $R_H(I) = \sim H \cap H = \emptyset$ is of course minimal. If it is not the case, it is at least guaranteed that the first model I found is such that $R_H(I)$ is minimal (because of the depth-first aspect of the algorithm and the fact that the $\sim H$ part of it is explored first). Moreover, the MPL algorithm aims at computing *every* H-restricted model of K. In order to perform this computation, it does not stop after the first model is found, but instead it goes through the whole tree. As soon as a (minimal) H-restricted model $R_H(I)$ is found, the clause $C = \vee_{l \in R_H(I)} \neg l$ is added to K in order to eliminate every other H-restricted models containing $R_H(I)$ (since they are not minimal), and the exploration of the tree goes on from the same point. In this way, the whole set of minimal H-restricted models of K, denoted $MP_H(K)$, is found.

The computation of $MP_H(K^\wedge)$ is performed by a call to the procedure MPL (see Castell et al. (1996)). MPL has three arguments: K, KA and H, KA being the set of clauses that are added during the run of MPL (it contains the C clauses described above). We get that $MP_H(K^\wedge) = MPL(K, KA = \{\}, H)$, and KA contains exactly $\neg MP_H(K^\wedge)$ which is a CNF form of the nogoods after a call to $MPL(K, KA = \{\}, H)$. Note that KA is generally initially empty except, as we will see, when MPL is used for performing a label computation.

Application to ATMS Indeed, the basic elements of an ATMS, labels, nogoods, will be efficiently computed by the MPL() algorithm, without any minimization step contrary to De Kleer's original one, due to the following properties (first proposed in (Castell et al. (1996)).

Proposition 2 *The set of nogoods of a knowledge base K with respect to a set of hypotheses H is exactly $MP_H(\neg MP_{\sim H}(K^\wedge))$.*

Proof: E is a nogood iff $K^\wedge \vdash (\sim E)^\vee$ and E is minimal $\Leftrightarrow MP_{\sim H}(K^\wedge) \vdash (\sim E)^\vee \Leftrightarrow E^\wedge \vdash \neg MP_{\sim H}(K^\wedge)$. So, the DNF form of the nogoods satisfies the property.

Proposition 3 *Let K be a set of clauses and H a set of hypotheses. Let ϕ be a formula. The label of ϕ exactly contains the elements of $MP_H(\neg MP_{\sim H}(K^\wedge \wedge \neg \phi))$ that are not among the nogoods of K.*

Proof: Similar to the one above, as $label(\phi) = nogoods(K^\wedge \wedge \neg \phi)$.

We remove the nogoods from the label because every formula is a logical consequence of an inconsistent one. This is done by initializing KA with the set of nogoods, in the MPL algorithm.

Proposition 4 *Let K be a set of clauses. Let ϕ and ψ two formulas. The label of $\phi \wedge \psi$ is exactly $MP_H(\neg MP_{\sim H}(K^\wedge \wedge \neg \phi) \wedge \neg MP_{\sim H}(K^\wedge \wedge \neg \psi))$ (except nogoods of K).*

Proof: $MP_H(\neg MP_{\sim H}(K^\wedge \wedge \neg(\phi \wedge \psi))) = MP_H(\neg MP_{\sim H}((K^\wedge \wedge \neg \phi) \vee (K^\wedge \wedge \neg \psi))) =$

$MP_H(\neg(MP_{\sim H}(K^\wedge \wedge \neg\phi) \vee (K^\wedge \wedge \neg\psi))) =$
$MP_H(\neg MP_{\sim H}(K^\wedge \wedge \neg\phi) \wedge \neg MP_{\sim H}(K^\wedge \wedge \neg\psi)).$

Owing to Prop. 4, an MPL-based ATMS is able to compute the label of a phrase (a conjunction of literals) or a clause. So we can compute the label of each preference clause in a simple way. Let us point out the fact that *only the function* MPL() *is used to compute labels and nogoods*. Difficult operations like subsumption are not explicitly performed for these computations.

The main advantage of the MPL-technique is its ability to compute the label of a unique literal without computing the labels of the other literals as with de Kleer's technique. Moreover, an MPL-based ATMS can be applied on any set of clauses (CNF formula) and can compute in the same way the label of a literal, a disjunction or a conjunction of literals. The label computation presupposes a computation of the nogoods, in order to remove from the label the inconsistent environments. Nogoods and labels are computed in the same way, from the knowledge base (K) for nogoods, and from the knowledge base augmented with the negation of the formula, ($K^\wedge \wedge \neg\phi$), for the label of this formula.

Computation of optimal decisions via MPL

Optimistic decisions The use of MPL to solve an optimistic decision problem is easy. Assuming that K and P are CNF representations of knowledge and preference bases [2] of the decision problem, *good* decisions d can be obtained by a call to MPL:

Proposition 5 $K^\wedge \wedge d^\wedge \wedge P^\wedge \neq \bot$ iff $\exists E \in MPL(K \cup P, \{\}, D)$ s.t. $E \subseteq d$.

A good (optimistic) decision is then a consistent superset of an element from $MPL(K \cup P, \{\}, D)$.
Let $K^\wedge = \phi_1 \wedge \phi_2 \ldots \wedge \phi_n$ and $P^\wedge = \psi_1 \wedge \psi_2 \wedge \ldots \wedge \psi_m$. Finding d maximizing $U^*(d) = n(\alpha)$ such that: $K_{\overline{\alpha}}^\wedge \wedge d^\wedge \wedge P_{\overline{\alpha}}^\wedge \neq \bot$ (cf Definition 2) is equivalent to finding $MPL(K_{\overline{\alpha}} \cup P_{\overline{\alpha}}, \{\}, D) \neq \{\}$ minimizing α.
This method has one requirement: $K^\wedge \wedge P^\wedge$ must be a CNF formula, so $P^\wedge$ must be a CNF formula, that is P must contain only clauses.

Pessimistic optimal decisions We propose to translate the *pessimistic* decision problem into a problem tractable by an ATMS. Let us define the set of assumption symbols $\mathcal{H} = D$. Then, assume that K is the knowledge base of the decision problem in conjunctive normal form and consider the goal base P as a formula $P^\wedge$. Using the symbols in $\mathcal{H}$, a decision d is a subset of $\mathcal{H}$. For any decision d such that $K^\wedge \wedge d^\wedge \vdash P^\wedge$ and $K^\wedge \wedge d^\wedge \neq \bot$ there is at least one element E of $label_K(P)$ according to the assumption set $\mathcal{H}$ such that $E \subseteq d$.

---

[2] A stratified possibilistic knowledge base can always be put in an equivalent base of weighted clauses (Dubois et al. (1994)), since necessity measures are min-decomposable for conjunction.

Proposition 6 $K^\wedge \wedge d^\wedge \vdash P^\wedge$ and $K^\wedge \wedge d^\wedge \neq \bot$ iff $\exists E \in label_K(P)$ s.t. $E \subseteq d$.

A good (pessimistic) decision is then a superset of an element from $label_K(P)$. In the following we will only look for decisions which are minimal for set inclusion. Let $K^\wedge = \phi_1 \wedge \phi_2 \ldots \wedge \phi_n$ and $P^\wedge = \psi_1 \wedge \psi_2 \wedge \ldots \wedge \psi_m$. Finding all decisions d maximizing α such that: $K_\alpha^\wedge \wedge d^\wedge \vdash P_{\overline{n(\alpha)}}^\wedge$ and $K_\alpha^\wedge \wedge d^\wedge \neq \bot$ is equivalent to finding $label_{K_\alpha}(P_{\overline{n(\alpha)}}) \neq \emptyset$ maximizing α.

Algorithm 1: COMPUTE_PESSIMISTIC_DECISION

Data: K the knowledge base, P the preference base, and D the set of decision symbols.
Result: Utility of the best pessimistic decisions, set of the best pessimistic decisions.
begin
  $\alpha \leftarrow \mathbb{1}$ % we consider the most certain layer ;
  $S \leftarrow \{\}$;
  while $S = \{\}$ *and* $\alpha > \mathbb{0}$ **do**
    % we must first compute the nogoods of K ;
    $NG' \leftarrow MPL(K_\alpha, \{\}, \sim D)$;
    $NG \leftarrow \sim MPL(\neg NG', \{\}, D)$;
    % NG contains the nogoods of K_α ;
    $S' \leftarrow MPL(K_\alpha \cup \sim P_\mathbb{1}, \{\}, \sim D)$;
    $S \leftarrow \sim MPL(\neg S', \sim NG, D)$;
    % S contains the label of $P_\mathbb{1}$;
    $\beta \leftarrow \mathbb{1}$;
    while $\beta > n(\alpha)$ *and* $S \neq \{\}$ **do**
      $S' \leftarrow S' \wedge MPL(K_\alpha \cup \sim P_{(\beta)}, \{\}, \sim D)$;
      $S \leftarrow MPL(\neg S', \sim NG, D)$;
      % S contains the label of P_β ;
      $\beta \leftarrow \underline{\beta}$;
    if $S = \{\}$ **then** $\alpha \leftarrow max(\underline{\alpha}, n(\beta))$;
  return $< \alpha, S >$;
end

where $P_{(\beta)} = P_\beta - P_{\overline{\beta}}$ is the set of goals with priority level β, $\underline{\alpha}$ denotes the level (either of certainty or of priority) of the next non-empty layer below α.

We need to compute the nogoods, and then the required label. The restriction here is to have $K^\wedge \wedge (\sim P)^\wedge$ as a CNF formula, so $P^\vee$ being a DNF formula. Since P is a CNF, this procedure will accept only P as a single clause or a single phrase (both are CNF and DNF form). Thus, we have to use a particularity of MPL to compute the label of a conjunction of formulas: the label of a conjunction $\psi \wedge \phi$ can be performed from the two first steps needed to compute the label of both ψ and ϕ (Prop. 4). This approach allows to stop label computation as soon as the intermediate label is empty.

One of the major advantages of our approach is that we only need to implement the MPL algorithm. An efficient implementation of MPL entails an efficient implementation of the decision algorithm. Thanks to the relation between the MPL algorithm and the Davis and Putnam algorithm, some improvements on the latter can be used in the former (heuristics for instance). The anytime aspect of the MPL algorithm can also be pointed out here. If you stop the algorithm before its normal end, you can obtain a subset of the set of optimal decisions. This can be used for instance if we only need a single optimal decision, or the utility of the optimal decision(s).

Concluding remarks

The main contribution of this paper has been to describe a logical machinery for decision-making, implementing the qualitative possibilistic utility theory, in the framework of possibilistic logic. A link between this logical machinery and the ATMS framework has been pointed out, which allowed to adapt some efficient algorithms proposed in this framework to possibilistic qualitative decision making.

Besides, in (Le Berre and Sabbadin (1997)), another logical machinery has been presented, in the diagnosis and repair framework. There, probabilities are assigned to assumptions, and numerical rewards to goals, leading to a variant of the expected-utility criterion, based on belief functions.

References

Benferhat, S.; Dubois, D.; and Prade, H. 1997. Nonmonotonic reasoning, conditional objects and possibility theory. *Artificial Intelligence* 92:259–276.

Bonet, B., and Geffner, H. 1996. Arguing for decisions : a qualitative model of decision making. In Horwitz, E., and Jensen, F., eds., *Proc. of the 12th Conf. on Uncertainty in Artificial Intelligence (UAI'96)*, 98–105. Portland, Oregon: Morgan Kaufman.

Boutilier, C. 1994. Toward a logic for qualitative decision theory. In Doyle, J.; Sandewall, E.; and Torasso, P., eds., *Proc. of the Fourth Int. Conf. on Principles of Knowledge Representation and Reasoning (KR'94)*, 75–86. Bonn, Germany: Morgan Kaufman.

Brafman, R., and Tennenholtz, M. 1997. On the axiomatization of qualitative decision criteria. In *Proc. of the 14th National Conf. on Artificial Intelligence (AAAI'97)*, 76–81. Providence, R. H.: AAAI Press / MIT Press.

Castell, T.; Cayrol, C.; Cayrol, M.; and Le Berre, D. 1996. Efficient computation of preferred models with Davis and Putnam procedure. In *Proc. of the 12th European Conf. on Artificial Intelligence (ECAI'96)*, 354–358. Budapest: Wiley.

Castell, T.; Cayrol, C.; Cayrol, M.; and LeBerre, D. 1998. Modèles p-restreints. applications à l'inférence propositionnelle. In *Proc. 11eme Congrès Reconnaissance des Formes et Intelligence Artificielle (RFIA'98)*, pp. 205–214. Clermont-Ferrand, France.

Console, L., and de Kleer, J., eds. 1992. *Readings in Model-Based Diagnosis*. San Mateo CA: Morgan Kaufmann.

Davis, H., and Putnam, L. 1960. A computing procedure for quantification theory. *J. of the Assoc. Comp. Mach.* 7:201–215.

Davis, H.; Logemann, G.; and Loveland, D. 1962. A machine program for theorem proving. *Commun. Assoc. Comp. Mach.* 5:394–397.

De Kleer, J. 1986. An assumption based truth maintenance system, and extending the atms. *Artificial Intelligence* 28:127–162, 163–196.

Dubois, D., and Prade, H. 1995. Possibility theory as a basis for qualitative decision theory. In *Proc. of the 14th Int. Joint Conf. in Artif. Intelligence (IJCAI'95)*, 1925–1930. Montreal, Canada: Morgan Kaufman.

Dubois, D.; Le Berre, D.; Prade, H.; and Sabbadin, R. 1998. Using possibilistic logic for modeling qualitative decision. *Fundamenta Informaticae*. To appear.

Dubois, D.; Fargier, H.; and Prade, H. 1997. Decision-making under ordinal preferences and uncertainty. In *Proc. of the 13th Conf. on Uncertainty in Artificial Intelligence (UAI'97)*, 157–164. Providence R. H.: Morgan Kaufman.

Dubois, D.; Lang, J.; and Prade, H. 1994. Automated reasoning using possibilistic logic: Semantics, belief revision, and variable certainty weights. *IEEE Trans. on Knowledge and Data Engineering* 6(1):64–69.

Dubois, D.; Prade, H.; and Sabbadin, R. 1997a. A possibilistic logic machinery for qualitative decision. In *AAAI 1997 Spring Symposium Series (Qualitative Preferences in Deliberation and Practical Reasoning)*, 47–54.

Dubois, D.; Prade, H.; and Sabbadin, R. 1997b. Towards axiomatic foundations for decision under qualitative uncertainty. In *Proc. of the 7th World Congress of the Inter. Fuzzy Systems Association (IFSA'97)*, 441–446. Prague, Czech Republic: Academia Verlag.

Le Berre, D., and Sabbadin, R. 1997. Decision-theoretic diagnosis and repair: representational and computational issues. In *Proc. of the 8th International Workshop on Principles of Diagnosis (DX'97)*, 141–145. Le Mont-Saint-Michel, France: M.O. Cordier, ed.

Pearl, J. 1990. System Z: A natural ordering of defaults with tractable applications to default reasoning. In *Proc. of the 3rd Conf. on Theoretical Aspects of Reasoning About Knowledge (TARK'90)*, 121–135. Morgan Kaufman.

Tan, S. W., and Pearl, J. 1994. Qualitative decision theory. In *Proc. of the 12th National Conf. on Artificial Intelligence (AAAI'94)*, 928–933. Seattle WA: AAAI Press / MIT Press.

A Fuzzy Description Logic

Umberto Straccia

I.E.I - C.N.R.
Via S. Maria, 46
I-56126 Pisa (PI) ITALY
straccia@iei.pi.cnr.it

Abstract

Description Logics (DLs, for short) allow reasoning about individuals and concepts, *i.e.* set of individuals with common properties. Typically, DLs are limited to dealing with crisp, well defined concepts. That is, concepts for which the problem whether an individual is an instance of it is a yes/no question. More often than not, the concepts encountered in the real world do not have a precisely defined criteria of membership: we may say that an individual is an instance of a concept only to a certain degree, depending on the individual's properties. Concepts of this kind are rather vague than precise. As fuzzy logic directly deals with the notion of vagueness and imprecision, it offers an appealing foundation for a generalisation of DLs to vague concepts.

In this paper we present a general fuzzy DL, which combines fuzzy logic with DLs. We define its syntax, semantics and present constraint propagation calculi for reasoning in it.

Introduction

Description Logics (DLs, for short) provide a logical reconstruction of the so-called frame-based knowledge representation languages[1]. *Concepts, roles* and *individuals* are the basic building blocks of these logics. Concepts are expressions which collect the properties, described by means of roles, of a set of individuals. From a first order point of view, concepts can be seen as unary predicates, whereas roles are interpreted as binary predicates. A *knowledge base* (KB) typically contains a set of *assertions*. An assertion states either that an individual a is an instance of a concept C (written $C(a)$), or that two individuals a and b are related by means of a role R (written $R(a,b)$). A basic inference task with knowledge bases is *entailment* and amounts to verify whether the individual a is an instance of the concept C w.r.t. the KB Σ (written $\Sigma \models C(a)$).

Typically, DLs are limited to dealing with crisp concepts. However, many useful concepts that are needed by an intelligent system do not have well defined boundaries. That is, often it happens that the concepts encountered in the real world do not have a precisely defined criteria of membership, *i.e.* they are *vague concepts* rather than precise concepts. For instance, Tall is such a concept: we may say that an individual tom is an instance of the concept Tall only to a certain degree $n \in [0,1]$ depending on tom's height.

Fuzzy logic directly deals with the notion of vagueness and imprecision using fuzzy predicates. Therefore, it offers an appealing foundation for a generalisation of DLs in order to dealing with such vague concepts.

The aim of this work is to present a general fuzzy DL, which combines fuzzy logic with DLs. In particular we will extend DLs by allowing expressions of the form $\langle C(a)\,n \rangle$ ($n \in [0,1]$), *e.g.* $\langle \text{Tall}(\text{tom})\,.7 \rangle$, with intended meaning "the membership degree of individual a being an instance of concept C is at least n".

Extending DLs with fuzzy features has already be done in the past. For instance, in (Yen 1991) the very limited DL $\mathcal{FL}^-$ (Brachman & Levesque 1984) has been extended with some fuzzy features. In particular, it allows the definition of fuzzy concepts and the only supported reasoning mechanism is determining subsumption[2]. Unfortunately, it does not allow reasoning in presence of assertions. Recently, (Meghini, Sebastiani, & Straccia 1997) proposed a fuzzy DL as a tool for modelling multimedia document retrieval[3]. But this work was rather at a preliminary stage and no reasoning algorithm was given.

We present a more general framework in the sense that it is based both on the DL $\mathcal{ALC}$, a significant and expressive representative of the various DLs, and on sound and complete constraint propagation calculi for reasoning in it. This allows us to adapt it easily to the different DLs presented in the literature. Moreover, we will show that the additional expressive power has no impact from a computational complexity point of view. This is important as the nice trade-off between computational complexity and expressive power of DLs contributes to their popularity.

Finally, note that most existing work in extending DLs for uncertainty management lie in the category of probabilistic extension like *e.g.* (Heinsohn 1994; Jäger 1994; Koller, Levy, & Pfeffer 1997) with some exceptions like (Hollunder 1994). Even though these

---

Copyright ©1998, American Association for Artificial Intelligence (www.aaai.org). All rights reserved.

[1]See the DL Web Home Page: http://dl.kr.org/dl.

[2]Roughly, a concept D subsumes a concept C iff from a first order point of view, $\forall x. C(x) \rightarrow D(x)$ is logically valid.

[3]The idea to use DLs in the context of multimedia document retrieval has been proposed in (Gobel, Haul, & Bechhofer 1996) too.

probabilistic extensions enlarge the applicability of DLs they do not directly address the issue of reasoning about individuals and vague concepts. Moreover, reasoning in a probabilistic framework is generally a harder task, from a computational point of view, than the relative non probabilistic case (see *e.g.* (Roth 1996) for an overview) and thus, the computational problems have to be addressed carefully like in (Koller, Levy, & Pfeffer 1997).

In the following sections we first introduce crisp $\mathcal{ALC}$, then we extend it to the fuzzy case. Thereafter, we will present constraint propagation calculi for reasoning in it.

A quick look to $\mathcal{ALC}$

The specific DL we will extend with fuzzy capabilities is $\mathcal{ALC}$, a significant representative of the best-known and most important family of DLs, the $\mathcal{AL}$ family.

We assume three alphabets of symbols, called *primitive concepts* (denoted by A), *primitive roles* (denoted by R) and *individuals* (denoted by a and b). The *concepts* (denoted by C and D) of the language $\mathcal{ALC}$ are formed out of primitive concepts according to the following syntax rules[4]:

$$
\begin{array}{rll}
C, D \longrightarrow & \top & \text{(top concept)} \\
& \bot & \text{(bottom concept)} \\
& A | & \text{(primitive concept)} \\
& C \sqcap D | & \text{(concept conjunction)} \\
& C \sqcup D | & \text{(concept disjunction)} \\
& \neg C | & \text{(concept negation)} \\
& \forall R.C | & \text{(universal quantification)} \\
& \exists R.C & \text{(existential quantification)}
\end{array}
$$

An *interpretation* $\mathcal{I}$ is a pair $\mathcal{I} = (\Delta^\mathcal{I}, \cdot^\mathcal{I})$ consisting of a non empty set $\Delta^\mathcal{I}$ (called the *domain*) and of an *interpretation function* $\cdot^\mathcal{I}$ mapping different individuals into different elements of $\Delta^\mathcal{I}$, primitive concepts into subsets of $\Delta^\mathcal{I}$ and primitive roles into subsets of $\Delta^\mathcal{I} \times \Delta^\mathcal{I}$. The interpretation of complex concepts is defined in the usual way: $\top^\mathcal{I} = \Delta^\mathcal{I}, \bot^\mathcal{I} = \emptyset, (C \sqcap D)^\mathcal{I} = C^\mathcal{I} \cap D^\mathcal{I}, (C \sqcup D)^\mathcal{I} = C^\mathcal{I} \cup D^\mathcal{I}, (\neg C)^\mathcal{I} = \Delta^\mathcal{I} \setminus C^\mathcal{I}, (\forall R.C)^\mathcal{I} = \{d \in \Delta^\mathcal{I} : \forall d'. (d, d') \in R^\mathcal{I} \text{ implies } d' \in C^\mathcal{I}\}$, and $(\exists R.C)^\mathcal{I} = \{d \in \Delta^\mathcal{I} : \exists d'. (d, d') \in R^\mathcal{I} \text{ and } d' \in C^\mathcal{I}\}$. For instance, the concept Tall $\sqcap$ Student denotes the set of tall students.

An *assertion* (denoted by α) is an expression of type $C(a)$ (a is an instance of C), or an expression of type $R(a, b)$ (a is related to b by means of R). For instance, (Tall $\sqcap$ Student)(tom) asserts that tom is a tall student, whereas Friend(tim,tom) asserts that tom is a friend of tim.

The semantics of assertions is specified by saying that the assertion $C(a)$ (resp. $R(a, b)$) is *satisfied* by $\mathcal{I}$ iff $a^\mathcal{I} \in C^\mathcal{I}$ (resp. $(a^\mathcal{I}, b^\mathcal{I}) \in R^\mathcal{I}$). A set Σ of assertions will be called a *knowledge base* (KB). An interpretation $\mathcal{I}$ satisfies (*is a model of*) a KB Σ iff $\mathcal{I}$ satisfies each element in Σ. A KB Σ *entails* an assertion α (written $\Sigma \models \alpha$) iff every model of Σ also satisfies α. For instance, if Σ is {(Tall $\sqcap$ Student)(tom), Friend(tim,tom)} then

---
[4]Through this work we assume that every metavariable has an optional subscript.

$\Sigma \models (\exists \text{Friend.Tall})(\text{tim})$, *i.e.* tim has a tall friend. Notice that $\Sigma \models R(a, b)$ iff $R(a, b) \in \Sigma$.

Fuzzy $\mathcal{ALC}$

From a syntax point of view, in *fuzzy* $\mathcal{ALC}$ we are dealing with *fuzzy assertions* (denoted with γ), *i.e.* expressions of type $\langle \alpha\, n \rangle$, where α is an $\mathcal{ALC}$ assertion and $n \in [0, 1]$.

From a semantics point of view, we will follow Zadeh's semantics. According Zadeh's work about fuzzy sets (Zadeh 1965), a *fuzzy set* X with respect to a set S is characterized by a membership function $\mu_X : S \to [0, 1]$, assigning a X-membership degree, $\mu_X(s)$, to each element s in S. This membership degree gives us an estimation of the belonging of s to X. Typically, if $\mu_X(s) = 1$ then s definitely belongs to X, while $\mu_X(x) = .7$ means that s is "likely" to be an element of X. Moreover, according to Zadeh, the membership function has to satisfy three well-known restrictions. For all $s \in S$ and for all fuzzy sets X, Y with respect to S: $\mu_{X \cap Y}(s) = \min\{\mu_X(s), \mu_Y(s)\}$, $\mu_{X \cup Y}(s) = \max\{\mu_X(s), \mu_Y(s)\}$, and $\mu_{\overline{X}}(s) = 1 - \mu_X(s)$, where $\overline{X}$ is the complement of X in S, *i.e.* $S \setminus X$[5].

In fuzzy $\mathcal{ALC}$, a concept is interpreted as a fuzzy set. Therefore, concepts and roles become *imprecise* (or *vague*). According to this view, the intended meaning of *e.g.* $\langle C(a)\, n \rangle$ we will adopt is: "the membership degree of individual a being an instance of concept C is at least n". Similarly for roles. Hence, *e.g.* $\langle \text{Tall}(\text{tom})\, .7 \rangle$ means that the degree of tom being Tall is at least $.7$, *i.e.* tom is likely tall; $\langle \text{Tall}(\text{tom})\, 1 \rangle$ means that tom is tall, whereas $\langle \neg \text{Tall}(\text{tom})\, 1 \rangle$ means that tom is not tall.

A *fuzzy interpretation* is now a pair $\mathcal{I} = (\Delta^\mathcal{I}, \cdot^\mathcal{I})$, where $\Delta^\mathcal{I}$ is, as for the crisp $\mathcal{ALC}$ case, the *domain*, whereas $\cdot^\mathcal{I}$ is an *interpretation function* mapping (*i*) individuals as for the crisp case; (*ii*) $\mathcal{ALC}$ concepts into a membership degree function $\Delta^\mathcal{I} \to [0, 1]$, and (*iii*) $\mathcal{ALC}$ roles into a membership degree function $\Delta^\mathcal{I} \times \Delta^\mathcal{I} \to [0, 1]$. Therefore, if C is a concept then $C^\mathcal{I}$ will naturally be interpreted as the *membership degree function* of the fuzzy concept (set) C w.r.t. $\mathcal{I}$, *i.e.* if $d \in \Delta^\mathcal{I}$ is an object of the domain $\Delta^\mathcal{I}$ then $C^\mathcal{I}(d)$ gives us the degree of being the object d an element of the fuzzy concept C under the interpretation $\mathcal{I}$. Similarly for roles. Additionally, $\cdot^\mathcal{I}$ has to satisfy the following equations: for all $d \in \Delta^\mathcal{I}$

$$
\begin{array}{rll}
\top^\mathcal{I}(d) & = & 1 \\
\bot^\mathcal{I}(d) & = & 0 \\
(C \sqcap D)^\mathcal{I}(d) & = & \min\{C^\mathcal{I}(d), D^\mathcal{I}(d)\} \\
(C \sqcup D)^\mathcal{I}(d) & = & \max\{C^\mathcal{I}(d), D^\mathcal{I}(d)\} \\
(\neg C)^\mathcal{I}(d) & = & 1 - C^\mathcal{I}(d) \\
(\forall R.C)^\mathcal{I}(d) & = & \min_{d' \in \Delta^\mathcal{I}}\{\max\{1 - R^\mathcal{I}(d, d'), C^\mathcal{I}(d')\}\} \\
(\exists R.C)^\mathcal{I}(d) & = & \max_{d' \in \Delta^\mathcal{I}}\{\min\{R^\mathcal{I}(d, d'), C^\mathcal{I}(d')\}\}.
\end{array}
$$

Just note that w.r.t. the $\forall$ connective, $(\forall R.C)^\mathcal{I}(d)$ is the result of viewing $\forall R.C$ as the first order formula

---
[5]Other membership functions have been proposed in the literature. The interested reader can consult *e.g.* (Dubois & Prade 1980; Kundu & Chen 1994).

$\forall y.R(x,y) \to C(y)$, where $F \to G$ is $\neg F \vee G$[6] and the universal quantifier $\forall$ is viewed as a conjunction over the elements of the domain. Similarly, for the $\exists$ connective $(\exists R.C)^{\mathcal{I}}(d)$ is the result of viewing $\exists R.C$ as $\exists y.R(x,y) \wedge C(y)$, where the existential quantifier $\exists$ is considered a disjunction over the elements of the domain (see e.g. (Lee 1972)).

It is easily verified that for all interpretations $\mathcal{I}$ and individuals $d \in \Delta^{\mathcal{I}}$, $(\neg(C \sqcap D))^{\mathcal{I}}(d) = (\neg C \sqcup \neg D)^{\mathcal{I}}(d)$ and $(\neg(\forall R.C))^{\mathcal{I}}(d) = (\exists R.\neg C)^{\mathcal{I}}(d)$.

An interpretation $\mathcal{I}$ satisfies a fuzzy assertion $\langle C(a)\,n \rangle$ (resp. $\langle R(a,b)\,n \rangle$) iff $C^{\mathcal{I}}(a^{\mathcal{I}}) \geq n$ (resp. $R^{\mathcal{I}}(a^{\mathcal{I}},b^{\mathcal{I}}) \geq n$). An interpretation $\mathcal{I}$ satisfies (is a model of) a set of fuzzy assertions Σ, i.e. a fuzzy KB, iff $\mathcal{I}$ satisfies each element of Σ. A fuzzy KB Σ fuzzy entails a fuzzy assertion γ (written $\Sigma \approx \gamma$) iff every model of Σ also satisfies γ. Given a fuzzy KB Σ and an assertion α, we define the maximal degree of truth of α with respect to Σ (written $Maxdeg(\Sigma, \alpha)$) to be $\max\{n > 0 : \Sigma \approx \langle \alpha\,n \rangle\}$ ($\max \emptyset = 0$). Notice that $\Sigma \approx \langle \alpha\,n \rangle$ iff $Maxdeg(\Sigma, \alpha) \geq n$.

Example 1 Suppose we have two images i1 and i2 regarding tim, tom and joe. i1 and i2 have been indexed as follows: $\Sigma_{\text{i1}} = \{\langle \text{About(i1,tim)}\,.9 \rangle, \langle \text{Tall(tim)}\,.8 \rangle, \langle \text{About(i1,tom)}\,.6 \rangle, \langle \text{Tall(tom)}\,.7 \rangle\}$, $\Sigma_{\text{i2}} = \{\langle \text{About(i1,joe)}\,.6 \rangle, \langle \text{Tall(joe)}\,.9 \rangle\}$. Moreover, let $\Sigma_{\text{B}} = \{\langle \text{Student(tim)}\,1 \rangle, \langle \text{Student(tom)}\,1 \rangle, \langle \text{Student(joe)}\,1 \rangle, \langle \text{Image(i1)}\,1 \rangle, \langle \text{Image(i2)}\,1 \rangle\}$. We define $\Sigma_1 = \Sigma_{\text{i1}} \cup \Sigma_{\text{B}}$ and $\Sigma_2 = \Sigma_{\text{i2}} \cup \Sigma_{\text{B}}$. Our intention is to retrieve all images in which there is a tall student. This can be formalised by means of the query concept $C = \text{Image} \sqcap \exists \text{About.(Student} \sqcap \text{Tall)}$. It can easily verified that $Maxdeg(\Sigma_1, C(\text{i1})) = .8$, whereas $Maxdeg(\Sigma_1, C(\text{i2})) = .6$. Therefore, we will retrieve both images and rank i1 before i2. ∎

Some properties

The following properties are easily verified: for all concepts C, D and for all $n, m \in [0,1]$, $\{\langle C(a)\,n \rangle, \langle \neg C(a)\,m \rangle\}$ is satisfiable iff $n \leq 1 - m$ and

$$Maxdeg(\emptyset, (\neg C \sqcup C)(a)) = .5 \quad (1)$$
$$\{\langle C(a)\,m \rangle, \langle (\neg C \sqcup D)(a)\,n \rangle\} \approx \langle D(a)\,n \rangle, \text{ if } m > 1 - n \quad (2)$$

Relation (2) is a sort of modus ponens over concepts. Similarly for $\forall$, the semantics of the $\forall$ connective gives us a sort of modus ponens over roles: if $k = \min\{n, m\}$ then

$$\{\langle R(a,b)\,m \rangle, \langle (\forall R.C)(a)\,n \rangle\} \approx \langle C(b)\,n \rangle, \text{ if } m > 1 - n \quad (3)$$
$$\{\langle (\exists R.D)(a)\,m \rangle, \langle (\forall R.C)(a)\,n \rangle\} \approx \langle (\exists R.D \sqcap C)(a)\,k \rangle,$$
$$\text{ if } m > 1 - n. \quad (4)$$

It is natural to ask whether there is a relation between $\models$ and $\approx$. As first, given a fuzzy KB Σ, let $\overline{\Sigma}$ be the

---

[6] In the literature, several different definitions of the fuzzy implication connective $\to$ has been proposed. See e.g. (Kundu & Chen 1994) for a discussion.

(crisp) KB $\overline{\Sigma} = \{\alpha : \langle \alpha\,n \rangle \in \Sigma\}$. Since every "crisp" interpretation is a fuzzy interpretation, the following proposition is easily verified.

Proposition 1 Let Σ be a fuzzy KB and let α be an assertion. For all $n > 0$, if $\Sigma \approx \langle \alpha\,n \rangle$ then $\overline{\Sigma} \models \alpha$. ⊣

Proposition 1 states that there cannot be fuzzy entailment without entailment. For instance, w.r.t. Example 1 we have $\Sigma_1 \approx \langle C(\text{i1})\,.8 \rangle$ and $\overline{\Sigma_1} \models C(\text{i1})$. Unfortunately, the converse of Proposition 1 is not true in the general case. For instance, $\{\langle C(a)\,.3 \rangle, \langle (\neg C \sqcup D)(a)\,.6 \rangle\} \not\approx \langle D(a)\,n \rangle$ for all $n > 0$, whereas $\{C(a), (\neg C \sqcup D)(a)\} \models D(a)$.

A simple result concerning the "converse" relation between $\approx$ and $\models$ is the following. Let Σ be a crisp KB: we define $\tilde{\Sigma} = \{\langle \alpha\,1 \rangle : \alpha \in \Sigma\}$.

Proposition 2 If $\Sigma \models \alpha$ then $\tilde{\Sigma} \approx \langle \alpha\,1 \rangle$. ⊣

A closer relationship holds whenever we consider normalized fuzzy KBs. We will say that a fuzzy assertion $\langle \alpha\,n \rangle$ is normalized if $n > .5$. A fuzzy KB is normalized if every fuzzy assertion in it is. If we consider normalized fuzzy KBs only, then from (Lee 1972) it follows that

Proposition 3 If Σ is normalized then there is $n \geq .5$ such that $\Sigma \approx \langle \alpha\,n \rangle$ iff $\overline{\Sigma} \models \alpha$. ⊣

For instance, $\{\langle C(a)\,.6 \rangle, \langle (\neg C \sqcup D)(a)\,.7 \rangle\} \approx \langle D(a)\,.7 \rangle$ and and $\{C(a), (\neg C \sqcup D)(a)\} \models D(a)$ hold. The reason relies on the fact that for $m, n > .5$, the condition $m > 1 - n$ in (2) – (4) is always true.

Deciding fuzzy entailment

Deciding whether $\Sigma \approx \langle \alpha\,n \rangle$ requires a calculus. We will develop a calculus in the style of the constraint propagation method, as this method is usually proposed in the context of DLs (see, e.g. (Buchheit, Donini, & Schaerf 1993)). The calculus extends the propositional framework described in (Chen & Kundu 1996) to the DL case.

Consider a new alphabet of variables. An Interpretation is extended to variables by mapping these into elements of the interpretation domain. An object (written w) is either an individual or a variable. A constraint (written τ) is an expression of the form $w{:}C$ or $(w_1, w_2){:}R$, where w, w_1, w_2 are objects, C is an $\mathcal{ALC}$ concept and R is a role. A fuzzy constraint (written σ) is an expression having one of the following forms: $\langle \tau \geq n \rangle$, $\langle \tau > n \rangle$, $\langle \tau \leq n \rangle$, $\langle \tau < n \rangle$. An interpretation $\mathcal{I}$ satisfies a fuzzy constraint $\langle w{:}C \text{ rel } n \rangle$ (resp. $\langle (w_1, w_2){:}R \text{ rel } n \rangle$) ($rel \in \{\geq, >, \leq, <\}$) iff $C^{\mathcal{I}}(w^{\mathcal{I}})$ rel n (resp. $R^{\mathcal{I}}(w_1^{\mathcal{I}}, w_2^{\mathcal{I}})$ rel n). $\mathcal{I}$ satisfies a set S of fuzzy constraints iff $\mathcal{I}$ satisfies every element of it. In the following we will reduce the fuzzy entailment problem to the unsatisfiability problem of a set of fuzzy constraints. Given a fuzzy KB Σ, let

$$S_{\Sigma} = \{\langle a{:}C \geq n \rangle | \langle C(a)\,n \rangle \in \Sigma\} \cup \{\langle (a,b){:}R \geq n \rangle | \langle R(a,b)\,n \rangle \in \Sigma\}. \quad (5)$$

It follows then that[7]

---

[7] Notice that $Maxdeg(\Sigma, R(a,b)) = \max\{n : \langle R(a,b)\,n \rangle \in \Sigma\}$.

$$\Sigma \models \langle C(a)\, n\rangle \text{ iff } S_\Sigma \cup \{\langle a{:}C < n\rangle\} \text{ not satisfiable.} \quad (6)$$

Our calculus, determining whether a set S of fuzzy constraints is satisfiable or not, is based on a set of constraint propagation rules transforming a set S of fuzzy constraints into "simpler" model preserving sets S_i until either all S_i contains a clash (indicating that from all the S_i no model of S can be build) or some S_i is completed and clash-free, that is, no rule can be further be applied to S_i and S_i contains no clash (indicating that from S_i a model of S can be build).

A set of fuzzy constraints S contains a *clash* iff it contains either $\langle w{:}\bot \geq n\rangle$ with $n > 0$, or $\langle w{:}\bot > n\rangle$, or $\langle w{:}\bot < 0\rangle$, or $\langle w{:}\top \leq n\rangle$ with $n < 1$, or $\langle w{:}\top < n\rangle$, or $\langle w{:}\top > 1\rangle$, or S contains a conjugated pair of fuzzy constraints. Each entry in the table below says us under which condition the row-column pair of fuzzy constraints is a *conjugated pair*.

	$\langle \tau < m \rangle$	$\langle \tau \leq m \rangle$
$\langle \tau \geq n \rangle$	$n \geq m$	$n > m$
$\langle \tau > n \rangle$	$n \geq m$	$n \geq m$

Given a fuzzy constraint σ, with σ^c we indicate a conjugate of σ (if there exists one). Just notice that a conjugate of a fuzzy constraint may be not unique, as there are could be infinitely many. For instance, both $\langle a{:}C < .6\rangle$ and $\langle a{:}C \leq .7\rangle$ are conjugates of $\langle a{:}C \geq .8\rangle$.

Concerning the rules, for each connective $\sqcap, \sqcup, \neg, \forall$ and $\exists$ there is a rule for each relation $rel \in \{\geq, >, \leq, <\}$, *i.e.* there are 20 rules. We will restrict our presentation to the set $rel \in \{\geq, \leq\}$. The rules for the case $rel \in \{>, <\}$ are quite similar. The rules can take the following two forms:

$$\Phi \to \Psi \text{ if } \Gamma \qquad \Phi \Rightarrow \Psi \text{ if } \Gamma \qquad (7)$$

where Φ and Ψ are sequences of fuzzy constraints and Γ is a condition. Both rules fire only if the condition Γ holds and if the current set S of fuzzy constraints contains fuzzy constraints matching Φ. After execution, the first deletes the fuzzy constraints matching Φ from S, while the second keeps them. Both forms add the constraints from Ψ to S after firing. In order to prevent infinite application of the second type of rules, we assume that each instantiation of the rules is applied only once. The rules are the following:

$(\neg_\geq)$ $\langle w{:}\neg C \geq n\rangle \to \langle w{:}C \leq 1-n\rangle$
$(\neg_\leq)$ $\langle w{:}\neg C \leq n\rangle \to \langle w{:}C \geq 1-n\rangle$

$(\sqcap_\geq)$ $\langle w{:}C \sqcap D \geq n\rangle \to \langle w{:}C \geq n\rangle, \langle w{:}D \geq n\rangle$
$(\sqcup_\leq)$ $\langle w{:}C \sqcup D \leq n\rangle \to \langle w{:}C \leq n\rangle, \langle w{:}D \leq n\rangle$

$(\sqcup_\geq)$ $\langle w{:}C \sqcup D \geq n\rangle \to \langle w{:}C \geq n\rangle \mid \langle w{:}D \geq n\rangle$
$(\sqcap_\leq)$ $\langle w{:}C \sqcap D \leq n\rangle \to \langle w{:}C \leq n\rangle \mid \langle w{:}D \leq n\rangle$

$(\forall_\geq)$ $\langle w_1{:}\forall R.C \geq n\rangle, \sigma^c \Rightarrow \langle w_2{:}C \geq n\rangle$
   if σ is $\langle (w_1, w_2){:}R \leq 1-n\rangle$
$(\exists_\leq)$ $\langle w_1{:}\exists R.C \leq n\rangle, \sigma^c \Rightarrow \langle w_2{:}C \leq n\rangle$
   if σ is $\langle (w_1, w_2){:}R \leq n\rangle$

$(\exists_\geq)$ $\langle w{:}\exists R.C \geq n\rangle \to \langle (w,x){:}R \geq n\rangle, \langle x{:}C \geq n\rangle$
   if x new variable
$(\forall_\leq)$ $\langle w{:}\forall R.C \leq n\rangle \to \langle (w,x){:}R \geq 1-n\rangle, \langle x{:}C \leq n\rangle$
   if x new variable
$$(8)$$

An instance of the $(\forall_\geq)$ rule is *e.g.*

$$\langle a{:}\forall R.C \geq .8\rangle, \langle (a,b){:}R \geq .7\rangle \Rightarrow \langle b{:}C \geq .8\rangle,$$

where σ is $\langle (a,b){:}R \leq .2\rangle$ and $\sigma^c = \langle (a,b){:}R \geq .7\rangle$ is a conjugate of σ.

A set of fuzzy constraints S is said to be *complete* if no rule is applicable to it. Any complete set of fuzzy constraints S_2 obtained from a set of fuzzy constraints S_1 by applying the above rules is called a *completion* of S_1. Due to the presence of the rules $\sqcup_\geq, \sqcup_>, \sqcap_<$ and $\sqcap_\leq$, more than one completion can be obtained. These rules are called *nondeterministic rules*. All other rules are called deterministic rules.

Example 2 Consider $\gamma = \langle (\exists R.D \sqcap C)(a)\, .6\rangle$ and $\Sigma = \{\langle (\exists R.D)(a)\, .7\rangle, \langle (\forall R.C)(a)\, .6\rangle\}$. We show that $\Sigma \models \gamma$, confirming (4), by verifying that all completions of $S = S_\Sigma \cup \{\langle a{:}\exists R.D \sqcap C < .6\rangle\}$ contain a clash. In fact, we have the following two sequences.

(1)	$\langle a{:}\exists R.D \geq .7\rangle$	Hypothesis:S
(2)	$\langle a{:}\forall R.C \geq .6\rangle$	
(3)	$\langle a{:}\exists R.D \sqcap C < .6\rangle$	
(4)	$\langle (a,x){:}R \geq .7\rangle, \langle x{:}D \geq .7\rangle$	$(\exists_\geq) : (1)$
(5)	$\langle x{:}C \geq .6\rangle$	$(\forall_\geq) : (2), (4)$
(6)	$\langle x{:}D \sqcap C < .6\rangle$	$(\exists_<) : (3), (4)$
	$\Omega_1 \mid \Omega_2$	

where the two sequences Ω_1 and Ω_2 are respectively

(7a)	$\langle x{:}D < .6\rangle$	$(\sqcap_<) : (6)$
(8a)	clash	$(4), (7a)$

and

(7b)	$\langle x{:}C < .6\rangle$	$(\sqcap_<) : (6)$
(8b)	clash	$(5), (7b)$. ∎

Soundness, completeness and complexity

It is easily verified that the above rules are sound, *i.e.* if S_1 is satisfiable then there is a satisfiable completion S_2 of S_1 and, thus, S_2 contains no clash. Vice-versa, completeness, *i.e.* if there is a completion S_2 of S_1 containing no clash then S_1 is satisfiable, can be shown by building an interpretation $\mathcal{I}$ from S_2 satisfying S_1. Roughly, given a clash-free completion S_2 of S_1 we consider $N_1[\tau] = \max\{n : \langle \tau \geq n\rangle \in S_2\}$, and $N_2[\tau] = \max\{n : \langle \tau > n\rangle \in S_2\}$. Since S_2 is clash-free, it follows that there is $\epsilon > 0$ such that the interpretation $\mathcal{I}$, (i) with domain $\Delta^\mathcal{I}$ being the set of objects appearing in S_2, (ii) $w^\mathcal{I} = w$ for all $w \in \Delta^\mathcal{I}$ and (iii) $\top^\mathcal{I}(w^\mathcal{I}) = 1$, $\bot^\mathcal{I}(w^\mathcal{I}) = 0$, $A^\mathcal{I}(w^\mathcal{I}) = \max\{N_1[w{:}A], N_2[w{:}A] + \epsilon\}$, $R^\mathcal{I}(w_1^\mathcal{I}, w_2^\mathcal{I}) = \max\{N_1[(w_1, w_2){:}R], N_2[(w_1, w_2){:}R] + \epsilon\}$, satisfies both S_2 and S_1. It can be shown that

Proposition 4 *A set of fuzzy constraints S is satisfiable iff there exists a clash free completion of S.* ⊣

From a computational complexity point of view, it is easily verified that termination of the above algorithm is guaranteed. Moreover, from Proposition 2 and from PSPACE-completeness of the entailment problem in crisp $\mathcal{ALC}$ (Schmidt-Schauß & Smolka 1991), PSPACE-hardness of the fuzzy entailment problem follows. It can be verified that *trace rules* as in (Schmidt-Schauß & Smolka 1991) can be defined. Therefore,

Proposition 5 *Let Σ be a fuzzy KB and and let γ be a fuzzy assertion. Determining whether $\Sigma \models \gamma$ is a PSPACE-complete problem.* ⊣

Computing the maximal degree of truth

The problem of determining $Maxdeg(\Sigma, \alpha)$ is important, as computing $Maxdeg(\Sigma, \alpha)$ is in fact the way to answer a query of type "to which degree is α (at least) true, given the (vague) facts in Σ ?". An easy algorithm can be given in terms of a sequence of fuzzy entailment tests. It is based on the observation that $Maxdeg(\Sigma, \alpha) \in \{0, .5, 1\} \cup N_\Sigma$, where $N_\Sigma = \{n : \langle A\, n \rangle \in \Sigma\}$. The algorithm is described below.

Algorithm $Max(\Sigma, \alpha)$
Let Σ be a set of $\mathcal{ALC}$ fuzzy assertions, let α be an assertion. Set $Min := 0$ and $Max := 2$.

1. Pick $n \in N_\Sigma \cup \{.5, 1\}$ such that $Min < n < Max$. If there is no such n, then set $Maxdeg(\Sigma, \alpha) := Min$ and exit.
2. If $\Sigma \models \langle \alpha\, n \rangle$ then set $Min = n$ and go to Step 1, else set $Max = n$ and go to Step 1. ∎

By a binary search on N_Σ the value of $Maxdeg(\Sigma, \alpha)$ can be determined in at most $\log |N_\Sigma + 1|$ fuzzy entailment tests. As checking fuzzy entailment is time consuming, this approach may be unfeasible.

In the extended version of this work, we present an alternative method for computing $Maxdeg(\Sigma, \alpha)$ performing the fuzzy entailment test only *once*. Essentially, the method extends the ideas described in (Straccia 1997) to our DL context.

Roughly, in order to determine $Maxdeg(\Sigma, C(a))$, we start with a set of constraints of the form $S = S_\Sigma \cup \{\langle a : C < \lambda \rangle\}$, where λ is a new variable symbol. Thereafter, we apply to S constraint propagation rules similar to those in (8) until each derived set S_i of constraints is completed. Finally, we are looking for the *maximal value* $n \in [0, 1]$ such that for each of the completions S_i, the constraint set $S_i[\lambda/n]$ (if not empty) contains a clash, where $S_i[\lambda/n]$ is the set obtained by replacing each occurrence of λ by n.

Concerning computational complexity, it can be shown that the problem of determining $Maxdeg(\Sigma, \alpha)$ inherits the result of determining (fuzzy) entailment, and thus, determining $Maxdeg(\Sigma, \alpha)$ is a PSPACE-complete problem.

Dealing with terminological axioms

We shortly show how to dealing with *terminological axioms*. In DLs, a general terminological axiom assumes the form $C \Rightarrow D$, where C and D are concepts. From a first-order point of view, $C \Rightarrow D$ is viewed as the formula $\forall x. C(x) \rightarrow D(x)$. For instance, `Ferrari` $\Rightarrow$ `SportCar` $\sqcap \exists$`Ownedby.CarFanatic` states that a Ferrari is a sport car which is owned by a car fanatic. When we switch to the fuzzy case, the simple form of *fuzzy terminological axiom* we allow is $\langle C \Rightarrow D\, n \rangle$, where $n \in [0, n]$. The semantics is given coherently to the above first order view of $C \Rightarrow D$: an interpretation $\mathcal{I}$ satisfies $\langle C \Rightarrow D\, n \rangle$ iff $\min_{d \in \Delta^\mathcal{I}} \{(\neg C \sqcup D)^\mathcal{I}(d)\} \geq n$. As for the $\forall$ connective, $F \rightarrow G$ is viewed as $\neg F \vee G$. It is easily verified that $\{\langle C(a)\, m \rangle, \langle C \Rightarrow D\, n \rangle\} \models \langle D(a)\, n \rangle$ if $m > 1 - n$, which is similar to (2).

We will say that D subsumes C with degree n w.r.t. Σ (written $\Sigma \models \langle C \Rightarrow D\, n \rangle$) iff all models of Σ are models of $\langle C \Rightarrow D\, n \rangle$. $Maxdeg(\Sigma, C \Rightarrow D)$ is the maximal degree n such that $\Sigma \models \langle C \Rightarrow D\, n \rangle$. For instance, if Σ is $\{\langle A \Rightarrow C .6 \rangle, \langle B \Rightarrow D .7 \rangle\}$, then it can be verified that $Maxdeg(\Sigma, A \sqcap B \Rightarrow C \sqcap D) = .6$. Notice that $Maxdeg(\emptyset, C \Rightarrow C) = .5$, according to (1).

Example 3 Consider Example 1. Suppose we add $\{\langle \texttt{Student} \sqcap (\texttt{Male} \sqcup \texttt{Tall}) \Rightarrow \texttt{TallStudent} .7 \rangle, \langle \texttt{Male(tim)}\, 1 \rangle, \langle \texttt{Male(tom)}\, 1 \rangle, \langle \texttt{Male(joe)}\, 1 \rangle\}$ to the background KB Σ_B. Suppose the query concept C is $\texttt{Image} \sqcap \exists\texttt{About.TallStudent}$. It can be verified that $Maxdeg(\Sigma_1, C(\texttt{i1})) = .7$, whereas $Maxdeg(\Sigma_1, C(\texttt{i2})) = .6$. ∎

From a calculus point of view, we make the following assumptions: (i) $\langle C \Rightarrow D\, n \rangle$ is considered a constraint too; and (ii) given Σ, then S_Σ is defined as usual except that additionally we add $\langle C \Rightarrow D\, n \rangle$ to S_Σ for each $\langle C \Rightarrow D\, n \rangle \in \Sigma$. Just note that, w.r.t. subsumption, we have that $\Sigma \models \langle C \Rightarrow D\, n \rangle$ iff $S_\Sigma \cup \{\langle (\neg C \sqcup D)(a) < n \rangle\}$ not satisfiable, where a is a new individual. Moreover, we will make the following *restrictions*: (i) the fuzzy terminological axioms in a fuzzy KB Σ have to be of the form $\langle A \Rightarrow C\, n \rangle$ (if A then C) or $\langle A := C\, n \rangle$ (A iff C), where A is a primitive concept; and (ii) *we do not allow cycles*. Here, $\langle A := C\, n \rangle$ is a macro for $\langle A \Rightarrow C\, n \rangle$ and $\langle C \Rightarrow A\, n \rangle$. This restriction guarantees us soundness, completeness and termination of the deduction process[8].

The rules are the following:

$$(\Rightarrow_R) \quad \langle A \Rightarrow C \geq n \rangle, \sigma^c \Rightarrow \langle w : C \geq n \rangle$$
$$\text{if } \sigma = \langle w : A \leq 1 - n \rangle$$
$$(\Rightarrow_L) \quad \langle C \Rightarrow A \geq n \rangle, \sigma^c \Rightarrow \langle w : C \leq 1 - n \rangle \quad (9)$$
$$\text{if } \sigma = \langle w : A \geq n \rangle$$

Example 4 Let $\Sigma = \{\langle A \Rightarrow C .6 \rangle, \langle B \Rightarrow D .7 \rangle\}$ and consider $\delta = A \sqcap B \Rightarrow C \sqcap D$. It is easily verified that $Maxdeg(\Sigma, \delta) = .6$. We show that $\Sigma \models \langle \delta .6 \rangle$ by verifying that all completions of $S = S_\Sigma \cup \{\langle a : \neg(A \sqcap B) \sqcup (C \sqcap D) < .6 \rangle\}$ contain a clash. By applying rules (8) and (9), we have the following two sequences.

---

[8]Unfortunately, the technique used in (Buchheit, Donini, & Schaerf 1993) in order to reason in presence of axioms of the form $C \Rightarrow D$ is not directly applicable in the fuzzy case. This remains an open problem yet.

$$
\begin{array}{lll}
(1) & \langle A \Rightarrow C \ .6 \rangle & \text{Hypothesis}{:}S \\
(2) & \langle B \Rightarrow D \ .7 \rangle & \\
(3) & \langle a{:}\neg(A \sqcap B) \sqcup (C \sqcap D) < .6 \rangle & \\
\hline
(4) & \langle a{:}\neg(A \sqcap B) < .6 \rangle, \langle a{:}(C \sqcap D) < .6 \rangle & (\sqcup_<) : (3) \\
(5) & \langle a{:}A \sqcap B > .4 \rangle & (\neg_<) : (4) \\
(6) & \langle a{:}A > .4 \rangle, \langle a{:}B > .4 \rangle & (\sqcap_>) : (5) \\
(7) & \langle a{:}C \geq .6 \rangle & (\Rightarrow_R) : (1), (6) \\
(8) & \langle a{:}D \geq .7 \rangle & (\Rightarrow_R) : (2), (6) \\
& \Omega_1 \quad | \quad \Omega_2 &
\end{array}
$$

where the two sequences Ω_1 and Ω_2 (which determine the two c-completions S_1 and S_2, respectively) are

$$
\begin{array}{lll}
(9a) & \langle a{:}C < .6 \rangle & (\sqcap_<) : (4) \\
(10a) & \text{clash} & (9a), (7)
\end{array}
$$

and

$$
\begin{array}{lll}
(9b) & \langle a{:}D < .6 \rangle & (\sqcap_<) : (4) \\
(10b) & \text{clash} & (9b), (8)
\end{array}
$$

respectively. ∎

A further extension (which we roughly address here without working it out formally) is to allow terminological axioms in which the membership function is specified explicitly. These axioms are of the form $A =_\mu \mu_A(f_1, \ldots, f_n)$, where A is a primitive concept, f_i are features (*i.e.* functional roles) and μ_A is a fuzzy membership function defined on a *concrete domain* (called *universe of discourse* in (Yen 1991)) such that μ_A depends on the features f_i (see (Baader & Hanschke 1991) for the formal aspects about concrete domains). For instance, the concept Tall could be defined as Tall $=_\mu \mu_\text{Tall}(\text{height})$, where μ_Tall is defined as a lambda abstraction on reals such that it relies on the height of an individual: *e.g.* $\lambda x. \min\{(x/200)^2, 1\}$. Therefore, if Σ contains both $\text{height}(\text{tom}) = 180$ and the above axiom, then we may infer that $\langle \text{Tall}(\text{tom}) .81 \rangle$, where $.81 = \mu_\text{Tall}(\text{height}(\text{tom})) = (\lambda x. \min\{(x/200)^2, 1\})(\text{height}(\text{tom})) = \min\{(180/200)^2, 1\}$.

Conclusions and Future Work

We have presented a fuzzy DL which enables us to reason in presence of imprecise concepts. In particular, syntax, semantics and sound and complete algorithms for reasoning in it has been presented. The complexity results shows that the additional expressive power has no impact from a computational complexity point of view. This work can be used as a basis both for extending existing DL based systems and for further research. In particular, the case of considering general terminological axioms (including cycles) and role-forming rules should be worked out. Another interesting point is to understand the impact of fuzziness on the computational complexity: is it always true that the upper bound of the complexity is the same as in the crisp case?

Acknowledgements

This work is funded by the European Community ESPRIT project FERMI 8134. Thanks go to C. Meghini, F. Sebastiani and the reviewers for their suggestions and comments.

References

Baader, F., and Hanschke, P. 1991. A schema for integrating concrete domains into concept languages. In *Proc. of the 12th Int. Joint Conf. on Artificial Intelligence (IJCAI-91)*, 452–457.

Brachman, R. J., and Levesque, H. J. 1984. The tractability of subsumption in frame-based description languages. In *Proceedings of AAAI-84, 4th Nat. Conf. on Artificial Intelligence*, 34–37.

Buchheit, M.; Donini, F. M.; and Schaerf, A. 1993. Decidable reasoning in terminological knowledge representation systems. In *Proc. of the 13th Int. Joint Conf. on Artificial Intelligence (IJCAI-93)*, 704–709.

Chen, J., and Kundu, S. 1996. A sound and complete fuzzy logic system using Zadeh's implication operator. In *Proc. of the 9th Int. Sym. on Methodologies for Intelligent Systems (ISMIS-96)*, LNAI 1079, 233–242.

Dubois, D., and Prade, H. 1980. *Fuzzy Sets and Systems*. New York, NJ: Academic Press.

Gobel, C. A.; Haul, C.; and Bechhofer, S. 1996. Describing and classifying multimedia using the description logic GRAIL. In *Proceedings of the SPIE Conference on Storage and Retrieval for Still Images and Video Databases IV (SPIE-96)*, 132–143.

Heinsohn, J. 1994. Probabilistic description logics. In *Proceedings of the 10th Conference on Uncertainty in Artificila Intelligence*, 311–318.

Hollunder, B. 1994. An alternative proof method for possibilistic logic and its application to terminological logics. In *10th Annual Conference on Uncertainty in Artificial Intelligence*.

Jäger, M. 1994. Probabilistic reasoning in terminological logics. In *Proceedings of KR-94, 5th International Conference on Principles of Knowledge Representation and Reasoning*, 305–316.

Koller, D.; Levy, A.; and Pfeffer, A. 1997. P-CLASSIC: A tractable probabilistic description logic. In *Proc. of the 14th Nat. Conf. on Artificial Intelligence (AAAI-97)*, 390–397.

Kundu, S., and Chen, J. 1994. Fuzzy logic or Lukasiewicz logic: A clarification. In *Proc. of the 8th Int. Sym. on Methodologies for Intelligent Systems (ISMIS-94)*, LNAI 869, 56–64.

Lee, R. C. T. 1972. Fuzzy logic and the resolution principle. *Journal of the ACM* 19(1):109–119.

Meghini, C.; Sebastiani, F.; and Straccia, U. 1997. Reasoning about the form and content for multimedia objects (extended abstract). In *Proceedings of AAAI 1997 Spring Symposium on Intelligent Integration and Use of Text, Image, Video and Audio*, 89–94.

Roth, D. 1996. On the hardness of approximate reasoning. *Artificial Intelligence* 82:273–302.

Schmidt-Schauß, M., and Smolka, G. 1991. Attributive concept descriptions with complements. *Artificial Intelligence* 48:1–26.

Straccia, U. 1997. A four-valued fuzzy propositional logic. In *Proc. of the 15th Int. Joint Conf. on Artificial Intelligence (IJCAI-97)*, 128–133.

Yen, J. 1991. Generalizing term subsumption languages to fuzzy logic. In *Proc. of the 12th Int. Joint Conf. on Artificial Intelligence (IJCAI-91)*, 472–477.

Zadeh, L. A. 1965. Fuzzy sets. *Information and Control* 8(3):338–353.

OKBC: A Programmatic Foundation for Knowledge Base Interoperability [1] [2]

Vinay K. Chaudhri
SRI International
333 Ravenswood Avenue
Menlo Park, CA 94025
vinay@ai.sri.com

Adam Farquhar
Knowledge Systems Laboratory
Stanford University
Stanford, CA, 94309
axf@ksl.stanford.edu

Richard Fikes
Knowledge Systems Laboratory
Stanford University
Stanford, CA 94309
fikes@ksl.stanford.edu

Peter D. Karp[3]
Pangea Systems
4040 Campbell Ave
Menlo Park CA 94025
pkarp@PangeaSystems.com

James P. Rice
Knowledge Systems Laboratory
Stanford University
Stanford, CA 94309
rice@ksl.stanford.edu

Abstract

The technology for building large knowledge bases (KBs) is yet to witness a breakthrough so that a KB can be constructed by the assembly of prefabricated knowledge components. Knowledge components include both pieces of domain knowledge (for example, theories of economics or fault diagnosis) and KB tools (for example, editors and theorem provers). Most of the current KB development tools can only manipulate knowledge residing in the knowledge representation system (KRS) for which the tools were originally developed. Open Knowledge Base Connectivity (OKBC) is an application programming interface for accessing KRSs, and was developed to enable the construction of reusable KB tools. OKBC improves upon its predecessor, the Generic Frame Protocol (GFP), in several significant ways. OKBC can be used with a much larger range of systems because its knowledge model supports an *assertional view* of a KRS. OKBC provides an explicit treatment of entities that are not frames, and it has a much better way of controlling inference and specifying default values. OKBC can be used on practically any platform because it supports network transparency and has implementations for multiple programming languages. In this paper, we discuss technical design issues faced in the development of OKBC, highlight how OKBC improves upon GFP, and report on practical experiences in using it.

Introduction

In the construction of a new knowledge base (KB), significant productivity gains can be obtained by reusing existing knowledge components. These components include pieces of domain knowledge (for example, theories of economics or fault diagnosis) and KB development tools (for example, editors and theorem provers). To support reuse of domain knowledge, the knowledge sharing community has undertaken various efforts, including the development of shared portable ontologies (Farquhar, Fikes, & Rice 1997) and the development of well-defined languages for knowledge interchange (Genesereth & Fikes 1992). There has been, however, less emphasis on the reuse of KB development tools. A significant amount of effort is invested in building customized tools for specific knowledge representation systems (KRSs). These tools work only with a single KRS, and the development effort is wasted if the KRS is no longer used. A KRS developer usually does not have the choice of using off-the-shelf tools and is forced to develop tools on her own.

Open Knowledge Base Connectivity (OKBC) is an application programming interface (API) for KRSs that has been developed to address the problem of KB tools reusability. The name OKBC was chosen to be analogous to ODBC (Open Database Connectivity), as used in the database community (Geiger 1995).

An API specifies the *operations* that can be used to access a system by an application program. When specifying an API for a KRS, some assumptions must be made about the representation used by that KRS. Such assumptions are made explicit in the *OKBC knowledge model*. As it can be too restrictive to enforce the same semantics for all operations in an API across all KRSs, OKBC supports *behaviors* to allow for differences among KRSs. Behaviors are a tool to achieve flexibility in specifying OKBC operations. Thus, the OKBC specification consists of three components: a knowledge model, a collection of operations to access a KRS, and a collection of behaviors.

A KRS can be *bound* to OKBC by defining a mapping from OKBC to the native API of that KRS. To achieve interoperability, a KB tool accesses a KRS using only OKBC operations. Such a tool is isolated from the peculiarities of the KRS and can be used with any KRS that has been bound to OKBC. The interoperability achieved by using OKBC is at the level of the OKBC knowledge model. For example, the OKBC knowledge model defines the concept of a *class* that has the same interpretation across all OKBC bindings. OKBC does

---

[1] Copyright ©1998, American Association for Artificial Intelligence (www.aaai.org). All rights reserved.

[2] OKBC implementations in Lisp, C and Java may be obtained from http://ontolingua.stanford.edu/okbc/.

[3] The work presented in this paper was done while the author was at SRI International.

not guarantee, however, that a particular class (e.g., Person) defined in KBs residing in two different KRSs represents identical concepts.

OKBC is a successor to the Generic Frame Protocol (GFP) (Karp, Myers, & Gruber 1995) and improves upon GFP in two significant ways. First, OKBC supports a larger class of KRSs because its knowledge model includes an *assertional view* of a KRS, provides an explicit treatment of entities that are not frames, and has a much better way of controlling inference and specifying default values. Second, OKBC can be used on practically any platform and with a substantially larger range of applications because it supports network transparency, multiple programming languages, and a remote procedure language.

Two conclusions can be drawn from the design experience of OKBC. First, an expressiveness vs. generality tradeoff emerged. The expressiveness of the knowledge model must be controlled so that it can work with a range of KRSs. If the knowledge model is too expressive, it becomes difficult to define OKBC bindings for systems that have limited representational power. If the knowledge model is insufficiently expressive, the OKBC bindings for systems with more representational power will not expose their capabilities. Second, the protocol was augmented by two features to support variability among KRSs: additional returned values and behaviors. Wherever it is not feasible to legislate certain requirements, KRSs can expose the difference either globally by setting the value of a *behavior* or locally by returning an additional value from an operation.

This paper is devoted to the discussion of the technical issues faced in the design of OKBC. It is not intended to be a comprehensive description of OKBC, which may be found elsewhere (Chaudhri *et al.* 1997; Rice & Farquhar 1998). The paper is organized along the two major classes of enhancement in OKBC: expanding the range of supported KRSs, and expanding the range of supported applications. We also discuss practical experiences in using OKBC.

The OKBC Knowledge Model

The OKBC knowledge model is designed to include representational features supported by several KRSs (Karp 1992). It includes constants, frames, slots, facets, classes, individuals, and knowledge bases. Classes and individuals form two disjoint partitions of a KB (see Figure 1). A *class* is defined as a set of entities. Each of the entities in a class is said to be an *instance* of that class. An *individual* is an entity that is not a set.

Any entity has associated with it a collection of *own* slots. Own slots describe the direct properties of an entity. For example, if the age of Fred is 42, then **age** is an own slot of **Fred**. Own slots and their values are not inherited. A class has associated with it a collection of *template* slots. Template slots describe properties of the instances of a class (own slots of a class describe the properties of the class itself). Template slots are inherited by subclasses of a class; a template slot on a class becomes an own slot on each instance of the class.

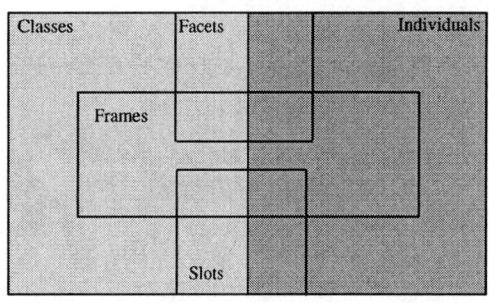

Figure 1: The OKBC knowledge model defines that classes and individuals form disjoint partitions of a KB. It does not commit to whether classes, individuals, slots, and facets are represented as frames. It also does not commit to whether slots and facets should be represented as classes or individuals.

Own facets describe the properties of slots associated with an entity, for example, cardinality or range. A template slot of a class has associated with it a collection of *template* facets that describe own facets for the corresponding own slot of each instance of the class.

Orthogonal to the knowledge-level distinction between classes and individuals is the notion of a *frame*. A frame is a data structure that is typically used to represent a single entity and the slots and facets associated with it. The decision as to which entities are represented as frames is driven primarily by implementation considerations; historically, KRSs have made different decisions about it. The OKBC knowledge model does not legislate which entities are frames (see Figure 1). For example, in a given KRS, classes may or may not be represented as frames. Even if classes are generally represented as frames, OKBC allows for a subset of classes not to be represented as frames. Indeed, it is common for KRSs to excluded unnamed sets, such as {1, 2, 4}, and primitive data structures, such as numbers and strings, from the set of frames.

The OKBC knowledge model does not legislate whether slots and facets should be represented as classes or individuals. In some KRSs, a slot (or more generally, a relation) denotes a set of tuples. In such systems, a slot is therefore also a class. In other KRSs, the space of classes and slots are disjoint. In such systems, a slot is also an individual. As shown in Figure 1, the knowledge model allows for a slot or a facet to be either a class or an individual.

A KB is a collection of classes, individuals, frames, slots, slot values, facets, facet values, frame-slot associations, and frame-slot-facet associations and sentences. Multiple KBs may be represented in a KRS.

OKBC supports operations that apply to specific frames in a KB (for example, querying the values of a slot of a frame), operations that apply to a KRS but not to any specific KB (for example, getting a list of all the KBs defined using a specific KRS), and operations that apply neither to a KRS nor to a KB (for example, establishing a connection to a knowledge server).

Expanding the range of supported KRSs

Although GFP was successfully used in several projects at Stanford University's Knowledge Systems Laboratory (KSL) (Farquhar, Fikes, & Rice 1997; Farquhar et al. 1996) and at SRI International (Paley, Lowrance, & Karp 1997; Karp et al. 1996), it lacked the power and flexibility needed in a generic API. Most of the enhancements considered here address the deficiencies encountered while GFP was used at KSL and SRI.

Support for assertions

GFP was found to be inadequate for use with KRSs that prefer to view a KB as a collection of logical sentences, as well as systems that have a knowledge model more expressive than the knowledge model of GFP. To address these problems, we introduced a *tell/ask* interface that supports an *assertional view* of a KB.

The design approach for supporting OKBC was analogous to the one adopted in KRYPTON (Brachman, Fikes, & Levesque 1983). An OKBC KB supports two alternative and isomorphic views of a KB: a frame-oriented view and an assertional view. (The frame-oriented view was called the *terminological component* in KRYPTON.) While defining the assertional view of a KB, we took a lowest common denominator approach: an assertion language with an expressive power roughly equivalent to an object-oriented frame language is defined. For other assertions, support is provided, but no portability claims are made.

Assertion Language OKBC defines an assertion language (AL) for declarative specification of knowledge. The AL is a first-order language with conjunction and predicate symbols, but without disjunction, explicit quantifiers, function symbols, negation, or equality. The predicate symbols of the OKBC AL are `class`, `individual`, `primitive`, `instance-of`, `type-of`, `subclass-of`, `slot-of`, `facet-of`, `template-slot-of`, `template-facet-of`, `own-slot-value`, `own-facet-value`, `template-slot-value`, and `template-facet-value`. For example, (`instance-of John Person`) means that John is an instance of the class `Person`. For convenience, (`instance-of John Person`) may be written as (`Person John`).

A well-formed formula (WFF) of the AL is an atomic formula constructed by enclosing one of the predicate symbols followed by a number of terms in parentheses. The terms of the AL are constants and variables. The conjunction of two WFFs of the AL is a WFF.

OKBC provides the **tell**, **ask** and **untell** operations to query and update a KB using the AL. OKBC guarantees that only ground WFFs can be **tell**ed or **untell**ed. Any WFF may be **ask**ed.

OKBC specifies the effect of **tell**ing any WFF of the AL to a KB by identifying an equivalent set of OKBC operations that does not include **tell**. For example, the operation (**tell** (`instance-of` frame class)), which asserts *frame* to be an instance of *class*, is equivalent to the operation (**add-instance-type** frame class). **Ask**ing any WFF of the AL is similarly equivalent to a set of OKBC operations not including **ask**. For example, the operation (**ask** (`instance-of ?x` class)) is equivalent to the operation (**get-class-instances** class).

Assertions not guaranteed to be supported by OKBC To handle assertions outside of the AL, OKBC defines the operations **tellable** and **askable**. The OKBC operation **tellable** determines which sentences may be acceptable to **tell** for a specific KB. Before using **tell** with an arbitrary formula, an application can check whether a formula is **tellable**. If the formula is not **tellable**, the application cannot safely assert that formula using **tell**.

For example, consider the WFFs (`age John 30`) and (`friend John Sally`). It is straightforward to assert them using either **tell** or **add-slot-value**. An application may, however, wish to assert the disjunction, (`or (age John 30) (friend John Sally)`), which is not a WFF of the AL. An OKBC binding for a KRS is free to accept this formula, and an application can check for this by using the **tellable** operation. If a formula is **tellable** for a KRS, the **tell** operation can be used to communicate that formula to the KRS. Using this mechanism, a KB may accept formulae that contain quantifiers, functions, or higher arity predicates.

There is no equivalence between using **tell** with arbitrary formulae and a set of OKBC operations that do no use **tell**. Use of such formulae may, therefore, not be portable across different OKBC bindings.

Handling entities that are not frames

As discussed above, KRSs make different assumptions about which entities are represented as frames. These differences influence the semantics of operations that systematically process frames in a KB (for example, **get-kb-frames**, **get-kb-individuals**, **get-kb-classes** that respectively return all the frames, classes, and individuals in a KB). These operations could be specified by saying that they respectively return all the frames, classes, and individuals in a KB. Because of differences in which entities are represented as frames, this simplicity can be deceptive.

Not all entities are frames As shown in Figure 1, not all classes in a KB are necessarily represented as frames. Given such differences, it is not obvious how to define the operation **get-kb-classes**. Should it return only those classes that are frames? Should it return all sets in a KB?

Returning only those classes that are frames is a problem for KRSs that do not represent all classes as frames. Some of the non-frame classes can be important to a client application. Defining **get-kb-classes** to return all the sets is also problematic because the results of one OKBC operation cannot necessarily be passed to another operation, making an application program more complex. The complexity occurs because it is generally not possible to perform operations such as creating slots and adding slot values to entities that are not frames. Thus, if **get-kb-classes** were to return classes that are not frames, an application program would need to identify those classes that are not frames and treat them differently. A possible solution to this problem is to require a KRS to appear as if it represents every class as a frame. This is not reasonable, however, because it is unnatural and can make the implementation extremely inefficient.

To address this problem, we introduced an extra argument, **selector**, to **get-kb-classes** and similar operations. When the value of **selector** is :frames, only those classes that are frames are returned, and when its value is :all, all classes are returned. For a system in which all classes are represented by frames, **get-kb-classes** returns identical results for these two values of **selector**. We expect many applications to use :frames as a value for the **selector** argument, because it has the desirable property that the union of **get-kb-classes** and **get-kb-individuals** equals the result of **get-kb-frames**. A third legal value for this argument is :system-default, which gives a KRS the freedom to use the most efficient or natural method of computing **get-kb-classes**.

Not all entity categories are frames As shown in Figure 1, not all KRSs represent all categories of entities as frames. Consider two KRSs: KRS1, which represents slots as frames, and KRS2, which does not. Furthermore, consider KB1, stored in KRS1, and KB2, stored in KRS2, both of which were created using an identical set of OKBC creation operations. Calling an operation such as **get-kb-frames** will return different results on KB1 and KB2. This may make it more difficult for an application to work portably with both KBs, but it is acceptable if OKBC provides a mechanism to detect the difference. The :are-frames behavior allows a KRS to indicate which categories of entities are represented as frames.

The values of the :are-frames behavior constitute a set of the following keywords: :class, :slot, :facet, and :individual. If the values of :are-frames contain an entity category, it implies that frames may be used to represent them. In most KRSs, classes and instances of those classes are represented as frames, and therefore we expect the most common set of values for :are-frames to be at least {:class, :individual}. If two KRSs have different values for the behavior :are-frames, we can expect to get a different list of frames by executing **get-kb-frames** on these KBs.

Controlling KRS inference

One area in which KRSs differ widely is in the inference mechanisms that they support and in the methods available to control the inference mechanisms. It is critical for applications to have some means of controlling the type and cost of inferences that a KRS performs in response to a retrieval operation. Unfortunately, there is not yet widespread agreement on either the inference mechanisms or the parameters used to control them. This makes it impossible for OKBC to provide a rich KRS-independent method for controlling inference. Instead, OKBC provides a restricted method for specifying which inferences should be performed in retrieval operations, as well as methods for a KRS to indicate the degree to which the specifications have been satisfied. OKBC does not provide means to specify limits on computing time in performing those inferences.

OKBC retrieval operations support an **inference-level** argument that takes one of the following three values: :direct, :taxonomic, or :all-inferable. When **inference-level** is :direct, *at least* the directly asserted non redundant values are returned. When **inference-level** is :taxonomic, *at least* the directly asserted and inherited values are returned. The inherited values are computed using at least the taxonomic inheritance axioms defined by the knowledge model. For example, a taxonomic inheritance axiom for slot values states that if a template slot S of a class C has value V, then for all instances of C, the own slot S has value V, and for all subclasses of C, the template slot S has value V. Similar inheritance axioms are defined for facet values, and for the class/subclass and class/instance relationships. When **inference-level** is :all-inferable, values inferable by any means supported by the KRS are returned, including any values inferable at the :taxonomic inference level.

With an **inference-level** value of :direct, returning exactly the directly asserted values may impose a high burden on some systems such as forward chaining systems that do not maintain a distinction between directly asserted and inferred values. To permit flexibility in such cases, we use the following two techniques.

First, the **inference-level** argument defines the lower bound on the values that may be returned. For example, when the **inference-level** is :direct, *at least* the directly asserted values are returned, but a KRS is not prevented from returning additional values. Second, any OKBC operation accepting the **inference-level** argument returns two additional values, called **exact-p** and **more-status**. The value of **exact-p** is *true* if it is known that exactly the :direct (or :taxonomic) values are returned. An OKBC implementation that always returns *false* as the value of **exact-p** is compliant. The value of **more-status** is either *false*, which indicates that there are known to be no more results, or :more, which indicates that there may still be more results but the KRS was unable to find out how many more, or an integer, which indicates how many more values exist.

By specifying the inference level in terms of the lower bound on the result and returning two additional values, **exact-p** and **more-status**, we were able to permit flexibility in the specification and also be accurate.

Handling defaults

In the absence of any widely accepted model of defaults (Brewka, Dix, & Konolige 1997), OKBC incorporates only simple provisions for default values of slots and facets. Template slots and template facets have a set of *default values* associated with them. Intuitively, these default values inherit to instances unless the inherited values are logically inconsistent with other assertions in the KB, the values have been removed, for example, at the instance, or the default values have been explicitly overridden by other default values. OKBC does not require a KRS to determine the logical consistency of a KB, nor does it guarantee a means of explicitly overriding default values. Instead, OKBC leaves the inheritance of default values unspecified. That is, no requirements are imposed on the relationship between default values of template slots and facets and the values of the corresponding own slots and facets. The default values on a template slot or template facet are simply available to the KRS to use in whatever way it chooses when determining the values of own slots and facets. The slot or facet values that are not default values are referred to as "known true" values. Operations on slot and facet values take a **value-selector** argument that allows a user to choose between only default values and monotonic ("known true") values.

Expanding the range of applications

The OKBC implementation was heavily influenced by pragmatic considerations, for example, the need to support different programming languages and efficient operation over a network. Network operation is necessary because many applications are developed using a client-server model, and because knowledge sharing should not be restricted to sharing of KBs on the same machine or within the same institution.

Network transparency is achieved using an abstraction called a *connection* that encodes the actual location of an OKBC KB and mediates communication between an OKBC application and the KB. To communicate with a KB, an application program first establishes a connection to the KRS in which the KB resides and subsequently, with each OKBC operation, the program must indicate the connection that should be used in executing it. Some OKBC operations take an explicit connection argument, whereas others derive the connection from a KB argument. Thus, once a connection is established, a user need not be aware of the actual location of the KB or whether the KB is being accessed from the same address space as the application or over the network.

The network substrate in the OKBC implementation plays an important role in supporting multiple programming languages, as it allows OKBC applications to manipulate KBs through a network connection that appears and operates just like a local KB. Client-side implementations for OKBC exist for Lisp, C, and Java.

To improve efficiency in a networked environment, OKBC defines an implementation-language-independent *procedure language*. The procedure language allows an application writer to combine several OKBC operations into a single procedure or set of procedures. These procedures can be recursive, and are transmitted over a network to achieve a substantial performance boost. For example, computing the information necessary to display a complete class graph for a KB may require calling at least two OKBC operations for each class (one to get its subclasses, and the other one to get a printable representation of the class name). This could result in many thousands of invocations of OKBC operations. With the procedure language, all the invocations can be done within a single procedure, and only a single network call is needed.

OKBC operations on large KBs may return many values. If only a portion of the result is necessary, significant speedup can be obtained by retrieving only the desired part of the result. OKBC supports enumerator operations that allow an application to retrieve the result in batches. For C++ and Java, enumerators are a common programming idiom. Operations are defined on enumerators to get the **next** element, to determine if an enumerator **has-more** elements, to **fetch** a list of elements, to **prefetch** a batch of elements, and to **free** an enumerator.

Experiences in using OKBC

Defining a metric to measure the success of a generic API is difficult. We will argue that OKBC has been successful in its goal of enabling the construction of interoperable tools by presenting empirical evidence based on the definition of OKBC bindings for several KRSs. We also consider a small case study of building an interoperable tool using OKBC.

OKBC bindings

Defining OKBC bindings for a KRS means implementing a subset of OKBC operations by using calls to the native API of that KRS (Rice & Farquhar 1998). OKBC bindings for several systems have been defined by our research groups at KSL and SRI. At SRI, OKBC bindings were defined for LOOM (MacGregor & Burstein 1991), Theo (Mitchell *et al.* 1989), SIPE-2 (Wilkins 1988), and Ocelot (Paley, Lowrance, & Karp 1997). At KSL, OKBC bindings were defined for Ontolingua (Farquhar, Fikes, & Rice 1997), Abstract Theorem Prover (ATP) (a theorem prover developed at KSL), CML (Farquhar *et al.* 1996), Tuple-KB (Rice & Farquhar 1998), file system KB, and CLOS. The University of Southern California's Information Sciences Institute has now produced its own version of an OKBC binding for LOOM. An OKBC binding for Cyc (Lenat & Guha 1990) has been defined by Cycorp.

OKBC was recently licensed by Pangea Systems Inc. (see http://www.panbio.com) in support of its projects in the area of bioinformatics. It is used extensively in several ongoing projects at Stanford and SRI, and has been adopted by DARPA's HPKB program (see http://www.teknowledge.com/HPKB/). OKBC server implementations in Lisp and Java and client implementations in Lisp, C, and Java may be obtained from http://ontolingua.stanford.edu/okbc/.

The KRSs for which OKBC bindings were defined fall into three categories: systems with a knowledge model that closely match the OKBC knowledge model, systems with knowledge models more expressive than the OKBC knowledge model, and systems with a knowledge model less expressive than the OKBC knowledge model. Defining OKBC bindings for systems that have a knowledge model closely matching the OKBC knowledge model is straightforward. We discuss how we handled the systems in the other two categories.

Binding a less expressive KRS A compliant OKBC binding must implement all the OKBC operations. Many OKBC users are interested in only a subset of the functionality specified by OKBC, because their KRSs have knowledge models less expressive than the OKBC knowledge model. Instead of excluding such systems, OKBC defines compliance classes that allow a KRS to specify which subset of OKBC functionality it supports. By reviewing numerous KRS bindings, we developed the following compliance classes: :facets-supported, :user-defined-facets, :read-only, and :monotonic. A KRS in the :facets-supported class supports facets, in the :user-defined-facets class it supports user-defined facets, in the :read-only class it supports at least all the read operations, and in the :monotonic class it supports at least all the operations that monotonically update a KB.

For example, consider the OKBC bindings for the Unix file system: directories are mapped to classes, subdirectory relationships are mapped to subclass relationships, and the files in a directory that themselves are not directories are mapped to individuals. For such a binding, there is no natural way to create new facets. Therefore, the OKBC bindings for a Unix directory system will not satisfy the :user-defined-facets compliance class. If a user does not have write permissions on a file system, it can still be compliant in the :read-only compliance class. An implementation of OKBC bindings for a file system is included in the OKBC source distribution (Rice & Farquhar 1998).

Binding a more expressive KRS The ATP system, developed at KSL, is a model elimination theorem prover that supports full first-order logic (FOL), provides limited support for axiom schema definitions, and is designed to handle a large number of ground facts efficiently. It provides a good example of a system with a knowledge model that is much more expressive than that of OKBC. Defining an OKBC binding for ATP presented several interesting design choices.

Because ATP is not a frame-oriented system, there is considerable freedom in deciding which objects should correspond to frames. We considered two possibilities. The first possibility is to introduce a specific class "frame", all of whose instances are frames. The second possibility is to make every object, function, and relation constant a frame (ATP allows for predications over relation and function constants). The first choice makes it harder to use the OKBC binding with an arbitrary ATP KB that does not include axioms for the class "frame". The second choice makes the ATP notion of a frame slightly more inclusive than many KRSs. For example, ATP would have a frame representing the number 42. Copying the frame representing the number 42 to a KRS that provides data structures for all frames can easily result in a frame data structure being allocated for 42, rather than using the built-in machine representation that the target KRS would prefer. Nonetheless, we chose to model all constants as frames.

ATP supports many ways of representing the basic relationships used by OKBC. Consider the subclass relationship between the class dog and the class mammal. This can be represented by the implication (=> (dog ?x) (mammal ?x)), or by the WFF (subclass-of dog mammal) of the AL. Because we expected querying and asserting subclass relationships to be a common operation, we wanted it to be efficient. ATP provides an efficient mechanism for storing ground facts. To exploit this efficient representation, all WFFs of the AL are implemented using ground facts. In addition to being efficient for OKBC's basic queries, this simplifies the deletion of frames.

For **inference-level**, OKBC defines the values: :direct, :taxonomic, and :all-inferable. We implemented this by using the multiple theories feature of ATP to place all of the taxonomic inference axioms in a separate theory. For inference level :direct, ATP looks only at the ground facts; for inference level :taxonomic, ATP uses the facts together with the taxonomic axioms; and for inference level :all-inferable, all available axioms are used.

For ATP, any FOL sentence is both **tellable** and **askable**. Some surprises may arise when a sentence is told that it is equivalent to some WFF in the AL, but has a different form. For example, the relationship between dog and mammal can be asserted in the implication, (=> (dog ?x) (mammal ?x)), instead of using the corresponding WFF of the AL, (subclass-of dog mammal). As long as the inference level is :all-inferable, the expected inferences are drawn (for example, a dog will be a mammal). At the :taxonomic inference level, however, the implication would not be used, and the inference would not be drawn.

Interoperable tools built using OKBC

At least two browsing and editing tools have been built using OKBC: the Generic Knowledge Base Editor (GKB-Editor) (Paley, Lowrance, & Karp 1997) and the Java Ontology Tool (JOT). GKB-Editor is a tool for graphically browsing and editing KBs and is written using Common Lisp. JOT is a Java-based tool for viewing and editing the contents of KBs and was written using a commercial off-the-shelf widget package. For the purpose of the current discussion, we say that a browser has been "successfully tested" with a KRS if it is able to display the class-subclass relationships and all the contents of frames.

GKB-Editor was initially developed and tested with Ocelot. After the initial testing with Ocelot, GKB-Editor was tested with Ontolingua. One of the differences between Ontolingua and Ocelot is the value of the :frame-names-required behavior. Ocelot sets the value of the :frame-names-required behavior to *true*; Ontolingua sets it to *false*. Browsing with the GKB-Editor substantially depends on frame names. Therefore, porting the GKB-Editor to Ontolingua required us to assign fictitious names to frames in Ontolingua. Since the fictitious names have no significance to a user, they are never displayed, and instead the pretty names of the frames are shown. Except for this difficulty with frame names, we were able to test the GKB-Editor with Ontolingua successfully. In addition to Ocelot and Ontolinugua, GKB-Editor has been successfully tested with LOOM and Theo. In fact, it is being used in conjunction with LOOM in a natural language generation project at the Technical University of Berlin (Stede & Umbach 1998).

JOT was initially developed and tested with Ontolingua and Tuple-kb. It was successfully tested with Ocelot without any difficulty. JOT demonstrates the language independence of OKBC, as one can use it freely and transparently to browse and edit tightly coupled KBs implemented in Java, network-based Java KBs, and numerous different KBs written in Common Lisp. Much of this editor's operation is done by means of remote procedures. This experiment shows that tools written using OKBC, such as JOT, really do interoperate with a wide range of KRSs.

Limitations of OKBC

The goal of OKBC is to enable the construction of reusable KB tools, that is, the application programs that access a KRS to perform browsing, editing, or reasoning tasks. Empirical evidence has shown that it has been successful in meeting this goal. Potential users of OKBC are usually concerned with whether they can successfully use OKBC in their projects. Here, we identify some of the commitments and sacrifices that they may need to make to use OKBC successfully.

To construct a new OKBC binding for a KRS, it is necessary to identify the knowledge model used by the KRS and define a mapping between it and the OKBC knowledge model. By providing both frame-oriented and assertional views of a KB, OKBC is capable of supporting a wide range of systems. Some systems do not easily admit to either of these views. While an OKBC binding can be defined for such systems, some users may not find it to be an intuitive or natural mapping. OKBC bindings work best when the knowledge model of the KRS closely matches that of OKBC.

OKBC bindings isolate a KB tool from many of the peculiarities of a KRS, but certainly cannot cover all of them. Therefore, porting a KB tool to a new KRS usually requires some additional effort. For example, Ocelot supports a slot type called :unique. The slots of this type are inherited by subclasses and instances, but their values are not inherited. For the GKB-Editor to handle this peculiarity, a small amount of Ocelot-specific code had to be added. Similarly, ATP provides operations to return the proof that a value satisfied some query, but OKBC does not currently provide any operations for specifically extracting proofs.

OKBC is neither the lowest, nor the highest common denominator protocol. It cannot hope to expose all of the functionality of every system, but it exposes what we believe most applications want. In addition, the protocol is specifically designed to be extensible by means of the behavior mechanism so that clients and servers can negotiate the use of a more powerful functionality than is provided by the protocol.

OKBC does not solve the problem of semantic KB interoperation. For example, using the OKBC operation **get-slot-values**, an application may query the salary of a person from two different systems, but there is no guarantee that the returned values will be semantically identical — one system may return annual salary and the other system may return monthly salary. Semantic interoperation is beyond the scope of OKBC.

OKBC is a functional interface to a KB (Brachman, Fikes, & Levesque 1983) and does not specify the data structures that should be used to implement its knowledge model. Using OKBC, an application cannot manipulate internal data structures of a KRS that are used to implement frames.

Summary and Conclusions

We have shown how OKBC provides an effective interface between diverse software tools and KRSs. The OKBC knowledge model is inspired by an extensive study of existing KRSs. OKBC defines a comprehensive set of operations for accessing a KB. The semantics of those operations are precise, yet flexible enough to support both frame-oriented and assertional interaction.

For supporting variability among KRSs, behaviors and additional return values proved to be central techniques. Wherever it is not feasible to legislate certain requirements, KRSs can expose their differences from the OKBC knowledge model either globally by setting the value of a *behavior*, or locally by returning an additional value from an operation. For example, support for frame names can be advertised by using the :frame-names-required behavior, and the degree of conformity to the :inference-level argument is exposed by an extra return value.

Design experience with OKBC suggests the existence of an "expressiveness vs. generality" tradeoff that is similar to the "expressiveness vs. tractability" tradeoff (Levesque & Brachman 1987). Some of the KRSs with which we have used OKBC are highly expressive and would require OKBC to support an equally expressive knowledge model to expose their full functionality. A highly expressive knowledge model, however, makes defining OKBC bindings for KRSs with limited functionality difficult and time consuming. Throughout the design of OKBC, this tradeoff was a guiding principle for carefully controlling the expressiveness of the knowledge model. We believe that expressiveness vs. generality is a fundamental tradeoff in knowledge sharing.

OKBC represents a major advance over its predecessor GFP. OKBC supports a larger class of KRSs: its knowledge model includes an assertional view of a KRS, provides an explicit treatment of KB entities that are not frames, has a stronger method to control inferences and has a better method for specifying default values. Unlike GFP, OKBC can be used on practically any platform and with a substantially larger range of applications because it supports network transparency, multiple programming languages, and a remote procedure language.

In summary, OKBC substantially advances our ability to achieve interoperability between KRSs and client-side KB tools. Its success is shown by its use with a broad range of systems, one of which is being used in a commercial environment. Availability of OKBC implementations in multiple programming languages makes it an attractive choice for the developers of applications that make use of the content and services provided by KRSs. They can have increased confidence that their applications will interoperate with multiple KRSs. With the availability of OKBC-compliant tools, KRS developers will be able to use off-the-shelf knowledge components that are not the primary focus of their work. We believe that OKBC makes a modest contribution toward achieving plug-and-play operation between KB tools and KRSs.

Acknowledgments

At Stanford University, this work was supported by the Department of Navy contracts titled *Technology for Developing Network-based Information Brokers* (Contract Number N66001-96-C-8622-P00004) and *Large-Scale Repositories of Highly Expressive Reusable Knowledge* (Contract Number N66001-97-C-8554). At SRI International, it was supported by a Rome Laboratory contract titled *Reusable Tools for Knowledge Base and Ontology Development* (Contract Number F30602-96-C-0332) and a DARPA contract entitled *Ontology Construction Toolkit*. The protocol has undergone revisions based on input from many people, including Fritz Mueller, Karen Myers, S. Paley, and Bob MacGregor.

References

Brachman, R.; Fikes, R.; and Levesque, H. 1983. KRYPTON: A functional approach to knowledge representation. *IEEE Computer* 16(10):67–73.

Brewka, G.; Dix, J.; and Konolige, K. 1997. *Non Monotonic Reasoning*. Cambridge University Press.

Chaudhri, V. K.; Farquhar, A.; Fikes, R.; Karp, P. D.; and Rice, J. P. 1997. Open Knowledge Base Connectivity 2.0. Technical Report KSL-98-06, Available from Knowledge Systems Laboratory, Stanford University.

Farquhar, A.; Iwasaki, Y.; Fikes, R.; and Bobrow, D. G. 1996. A compositional modeling language. In *Proceedings of the 1996 Qualitative Reasoning Workshop*.

Farquhar, A.; Fikes, R.; and Rice, J. P. 1997. A Collaborative Tool for Ontology Construction. *International Journal of Human Computer Studies* 46:707–727.

Geiger, K. 1995. *Inside ODBC*. Microsoft Press.

Genesereth, M. R., and Fikes, R. E. 1992. Knowledge Interchange Format, Version 3.0 Reference Manual. Technical Report Logic-92-1, Computer Science Department, Stanford University.

Karp, P.; Riley, M.; Paley, S.; and Pellegrini-Toole, A. 1996. EcoCyc: Electronic Encyclopedia of *E. coli* Genes and Metabolism. *Nuc. Acids Res.* 24(1):32–40.

Karp, P.; Myers, K.; and Gruber, T. 1995. The Generic Frame Protocol. In *Proceedings of the 1995 International Joint Conference on Artificial Intelligence*, 768–774.

Karp, P. 1992. The Design Space of Frame Knowledge Representation Systems. Technical Report 520, SRI International Artificial Intelligence Center.

Lenat, D., and Guha, R. 1990. *Building Large Knowledge-Based Systems: Representation and Inference in the CYC Project*. Addison-Wesley.

Levesque, H., and Brachman, R. 1987. Expressiveness and tractability in knowledge representation and reasoning. *Computational Intelligence* 3(2):78–93.

MacGregor, R., and Burstein, M. 1991. Using a description classifier to enhance knowledge representation. *IEEE Expert* 6(3):41–46.

Mitchell, T.; Allen, J.; Chalasani, P.; Cheng, J.; Etzioni, E.; Ringuette, M.; and Schlimmer, J. 1989. Theo: A framework for self-improving systems. In *Architectures for Intelligence*. Erlbaum. 323–355.

Paley, S. M.; Lowrance, J. D.; and Karp, P. D. 1997. A generic knowledge base browser and editor. In *Proceedings of the Ninth Conference on Innovative Applications of Artificial Intelligence*.

Rice, J. P., and Farquhar, A. 1998. OKBC: A Rich API on the Cheap. Technical Report KSL-98-09, Available from Knowledge Systems Laboratory, Stanford University.

Stede, M., and Umbach, C. 1998. Dimlex: A lexicon of discourse markers for text generation and understanding. Technical report, Technical University of Berlin, submitted for publication.

Wilkins, D. 1988. *Practical Planning: Extending the Classical AI Planning Paradigm*. San Mateo, CA: Morgan-Kaufmann Publishing.

Usability Issues in Knowledge Representation Systems

Deborah L. McGuinness
AT&T Labs—Research
180 Park Avenue
Florham Park, NJ 07932
dlm@research.att.com

Peter F. Patel-Schneider
Bell Labs Research
600 Mountain Avenue
Murray Hill, NJ 07974
pfps@research.bell-labs.com

Abstract

The amount of use a knowledge representation system receives depends on more than just the theoretical suitability of the system. Some critical determiners of usage have to do with issues related to the representation formalism of the system, some have to do with non-representational issues of the system itself, and some might be most appropriately labeled public relations. We rely on over eight years of industrial application experiences using a particular family of knowledge representation systems based on description logics to identify and describe usability issues that were mandatory for our application successes.

Introduction

Determining whether a knowledge representation system is suitable for a particular use and, in fact, is used is driven by a number of important issues including the standard issues of expressive adequacy and computational complexity and more general issues concerning usability. We believe that while expressivity and computational aspects are critical to application success, usability issues play an equally important role in determining whether a knowledge representation system is suitable for a particular use, or, indeed, suitable for any use at all. If a knowledge representation system does not "sweat these details", it will not be used in most domains.

The usability issues that we will consider in this paper fall into three general categories. The first group has to do with the access to the knowledge in the system. One element of this access is the standard interface to the system, where new information is told to the system and queries are asked of it. Some foundational aspects of this have been well studied, for example in work by Levesque (Levesque 1982). In our work, we focus on the issues concerning the acquisition of knowledge for the system, the presentation of the results of queries, the explanation of these results, and recovery from inconsistent states of knowledge. Although there has been some work on these issues, they are much less studied than the standard interface and, arguably, no implemented system has adequate support in all of these areas.

The second group encompasses the general technical, but non-representational aspects, of the system. One element

Copyright © 1998, American Association for Artificial Intelligence (www.aaai.org). All rights reserved.

of this group is the theoretical running time of the algorithms used to process updates and queries. Again, this element has been well-studied, particularly in description logics where there are many papers describing algorithms for description-logic inference and their theoretical running times (Buchheit, Donini, & Schaerf 1993; Donini *et al.* 1991). Other non-representational aspects include the actual response time to updates and queries experienced, the programming interface that the system presents, and the prosaic, but important, issue of which platforms the system runs on. Again, these issues have received much less study than the theoretical running times of the algorithms. (One study of actual response time, and the improvement thereof, was performed by Baader *et al.* (1992).)

This paper would not be complete without mentioning the most vital issues having to do with how much the system is used. These issues are not typically considered part of the field of knowledge representation, and are thus somewhat outside the scope of a technical paper. The issues referred to here are, of course, advertising and approvals. If a system is unknown or not understood then it will not be used, and if a system is not on the list of approved systems for a particular organization then it will not be used in that organization.

We will describe and analyze these three groups of issues with respect to the usability of knowledge representation systems. This will be done in the context of the CLASSIC family of knowledge representation systems developed at AT&T (Borgida *et al.* 1989; Brachman *et al.* 1991; Patel-Schneider *et al.* 1991). This family is based on expressively-limited description logics (also called terminological logics) (Baader *et al.* 1991); expressively-limited to ensure good computational properties, description-logic-based because of the desirable representational properties of description logics. There are two currently-supported members of the family, LISP CLASSIC (Resnick *et al.* 1995) and NEOCLASSIC (Patel-Schneider *et al.* 1997), and one older member C-CLASSIC (Weixelbaum 1991). We will be referring to characteristics of both of the current members in this paper, as currently neither dominates the other in the characteristics we are concerned with here.

Our experiences with CLASSIC may be of interest to the community for two main reasons. First, CLASSIC is the implemented system most similar to the description logic community-generated specification for description logics(Patil *et al.* 1992) and thus provides a representative basis for description logics. Second, arguably, CLASSIC has had the longest lived and most extensive industrial application history of any description logic-based system.

The CLASSIC family, and Description Logics in general, have been used in a number of classes of applications. We will mention one here as a motivational example for the some of the concerns we discuss. This class of applications has to do with configuration (Wright *et al.* 1993; Rychtyckyj 1996; McGuinness, Resnick, & Isbell 1995; McGuinness & Wright 1998).

In a typical configuration problem, a user is interested in entering a small number of constraints and obtaining a complete, correct, and consistent parts list. Given a configuration application's domain knowledge and the base description logic inference system, the application can determine if the user's constraints are consistent. It can then calculate the deductive closure of the user-stated knowledge and the background domain knowledge to generate a more complete description of the final parts list. For example, in a home theater demonstration configuration system (McGuinness, Resnick, & Isbell 1995), user input is solicited on the quality a user is willing to pay for and the typical use (audio only, home theater only, or combination), and then the application deduces all applicable consequences. This typically generates descriptions for 6-20 subcomponents which restrict properties such as price range, television diagonal, power rating, etc. A user might then inspect any of the individual components possibly adding further requirements to it which may, in turn, cause further constraints to appear on other components of the system. Also, a user may ask the system to "complete" the configuration task, completely specifying each component so that a parts list is generated and an order may be completed.

This home theater configurator example is fairly simple but it is motivated by real world application uses in configuring very large pieces of transmission equipment where objects may have thousands of parts and subparts and one decision can easily have hundreds of ramifications. It was complicated applications such as these that drove our work on access to information.

Some of the above mentioned usability issues have been discussed in separate papers, and they have played at prominent role in at least one major presentation (Brachman 1992), but there are new issues and new insights in this paper, springing from five years of additional experience and evolution of the CLASSIC family of applications. If some of these issues had not been addressed, the family of applications would have been discontinued commercially. This paper brings together these issues in one place and directly comments on their role in the usability of knowledge representation systems.

Knowledge Access Concerns

The first group of concerns addresses access to the knowledge in the system. This is not the basic "tell-and-ask" access, but instead is access to other knowledge, including how the system produces knowledge, or control of the access to knowledge. We also consider issues having to do with information overload, acquisition of domain knowledge, and error handling.

Explanation

Many research areas which focus on deductive systems (such as expert systems and theorem proving) have determined that explanation modules are required for even simple deductive systems to be usable by people other than their designers. Description Logics have at least as great a need for explanation as other deductive systems since they typically provide similar inferences to those found in other fields and also support added inferences particular to description logics. They provide a wide array of inferences (Borgida 1992) which can be strung together to provide complicated chains of inferences. Thus conclusions may be puzzling even to experts in description logics when application domains are unfamiliar or when chains of inference are long. Additionally, naive users may require explanations for deductions which may appear simple to knowledgeable users. Both sets of needs became evident in work on a family of configuration applications and necessitated an automatic explanation facility.

The main inference in description logics is subsumption—determining when membership in one class necessitates membership in another class. For example, PERSON is subsumed by MAMMAL since anything that is a member of the class PERSON must be a member of the class MAMMAL. Almost every inference in description logics can be rewritten using subsumption relationships and thus subsumption explanation forms the foundation of an explanation module (McGuinness & Borgida 1995).

Although subsumption in most implemented description logics is calculated procedurally, it is preferable to provide a declarative presentation of the deductions because a procedural trace typically is very long and is littered with details of the implementation. We proposed and implemented a declarative explanation mechanism which relies on a proof-theoretic representation of the deductions. All the inferences in a description logic system can be represented declaratively by a proof rules which state some (optional) antecedent conditions and deduce some consequent relationship. The subsumption rules may be written so that they have a single subsumption relationship in the denominator. For example, if PERSON is subsumed by MAMMAL, then it follows that something that has all of its children restricted to be PERSONs must be subsumed by something that has all of its children restricted to be MAMMALs. This can be written more generally (with C representing PERSON, D representing MAMMAL, and p representing child) as the all restriction rule below:

$$\text{All restriction} \quad \frac{\vdash C \Rightarrow D}{\vdash (\text{all } p \ C) \Rightarrow (\text{all } p \ D)}$$

Using a set of proof rules that represent description logic inferences, it is possible to give a declarative explanation of subsumption conclusions in terms of proof rule applications and appropriate antecedent conditions. This basic foundation can be applied to all of the inferences in description logics, including all of the inferences for handling constraint propagation and other individual inferences. There is a wealth of techniques that one can employ to make this basic approach more manageable and meaningful for users (McGuinness 1996; McGuinness & Borgida 1995).

In analyzing user needs and help desk query logs, although we found explanation of all deductions to be important, we found a small set of inferences which were the most critical to be explained. Without some automatic support for explaining this set, the system was not usable. These inferences include inheritance (if A is an instance of B and B is a subclass of C, then A "inherits" all the properties of C), propagation (if A fills a role r on B, and B is an instance of something which is known to restrict all of its fillers for the r role to be instances of D, then A is an instance of D), rule firing (if I is an instance of E and E has a rule associated with it that says that anything that is an E must also be an F, then I is an instance of F), and contradiction detection (e.g., I can not be an instance of something that has at least 3 children and at most 2 children). We believe at a minimum, these inferences need to be explained for application uses which exploit deductive closure such as configuration. Application developers may also find it useful to do special purpose handling of such inferences. In the initial development version, explanation was only provided for these inferences in an effort to minimize development costs. The two current implementations contain complete explanation. One demonstration system incorporates special handling for the most heavily used inferences providing natural language templates for presentations of explanations aimed at lay people.

Error Handling

Since one common usage of deductive systems is for contradiction detection, handling error reporting and explanation is critical to usability. This usage is common in applications where object descriptions can easily become over-constrained. For example, one could generate a non-contradictory request for a high quality home theater system that costs under a certain amount. The description could later become inconsistent as more information is added. For example, a required large screen television could violate a low total price constraint. Understanding evolving contradictions such as this challenges many users and leads them to request special error explanation support. Informal studies with internal users and external academic users indicate that adequate error support is crucial to the usability of the system.

Error handling could be viewed simply as a special case of inference where the conclusion is that some object is found to be described by the a special concept typically called bottom or nothing. For example, a concept is incoherent if it has conflicting bounds on some role:

Bounds Conflict $\quad \dfrac{\vdash C \Rightarrow (\mathsf{atleast}\ m\ r) \quad \vdash C \Rightarrow (\mathsf{atmost}\ n\ r) \quad n < m}{\vdash C \Rightarrow \mathsf{NOTHING}}$

If an explanation system is already implemented to explain proof theoretic inference rules, then explaining error conditions is *almost* a special case of explaining any inference. There are two issues that are worth noting, however. The first is that information added to one object in the knowledge base may cause another object to become inconsistent. In fact, information about one object may impact another series of objects before a contradiction is discovered at some distant point along an inference chain. Typical description logic systems require consistent knowledge bases, thus whenever they discover a contradiction, they use some form of truth maintenance to revert to a consistent state of knowledge, removing conclusions that depend on the information removed from the knowledge base. Thus, it is possible, if not typical, for an error condition to depend upon some conclusion that was later removed. A simple minded explanation based solely on information that is currently in the knowledge base would not be able to refer to these removed conclusions. Thus, any explanation system capable of explaining errors will need access to the current state of the knowledge base as well as to its inconsistent state.

Because of the added complexity resulting from the distinction between the current (consistent) state and the inconsistent state of the knowledge base and because of the importance of error explanation, we believe system designers will want to support special handling of error conditions. For example, in most of the implementations, users typically ask for explanations of a particular object property or relationships between objects. Under error conditions, users had more trouble identifying an appropriate query to ask, thus we included a simple explanation command that finds the last error encountered and generates an explanation of the contradiction. This way the user requires no knowledge (other than the explanation error command name) in order to ask for help.

Another issue of importance to error handling is the completeness or incompleteness of the system. If a system is incomplete then it may miss deductions. Thus, it is possible for an object to be inconsistent if all of the logically implied deductions were to be made but, because the system was incomplete, it missed some of these deductions and thus the object remains consistent in the knowledge base. In order for users to be able to use a system that is incomplete, they may need to be able to explain not only error deductions but deductions that were missed because of incomplete reasoning. An approach that completes the reasoning with respect to a particular aspect of an object is described in (McGuinness 1996). Given the completed information, the system can then explain missed deductions.

Pruning

If a knowledge representation system makes it easy to generate and reason with complicated objects, users may find naive object presentations to be much too complex to handle. In order to make a system more usable, there needs to be some way of limiting the amount of information presented about complicated objects. For example, in the stereo demonstration application, a typical stereo system description may generate four pages of printout. The information contained in the description may be clearly meaningful information such as price ranges and model numbers for components but it may also contain descriptions of where the component might be displayed in the rack and which superconcepts are related to the object. In certain contexts it is desirable to print just model numbers and prices, and in other contexts it is desirable to print price ranges of components. We believe it is critical to provide support for encoding domain independent and domain dependent information which can be used along with contextual information to determine what information to print or explain.

In CLASSIC there is a meta language for describing what is interesting to either print or explain on a class by class basis. Any subclass or instance of the class will then inherit the meta description and thus will inherit "interestingness" properties from its parent classes. The meta language essentially captures the expressive power of the base description logic with some carefully chosen epistemic operators to allow contextual information (such as known fillers or closed roles) to impact decisions on what to print.

The meta language has been used to reduce object presentation and explanation by an order of magnitude in at least one application. This reduction was required for the application to be able to include object presentation. The algorithms of the basic approach are included in (McGuinness 1996), the theory of a generalized approach are presented in (Borgida & McGuinness 1996).

Knowledge Acquisition

If an application is expected to have a long life-cycle, then acquisition and maintenance of knowledge become major issues for usability. There are two kinds of knowledge acquisition which are worth considering: (i) acquisition of additional knowledge once a knowledge base is in place, and (ii) acquisition of original domain knowledge. A complete environment will address both concerns, however the original acquisition of knowledge is a much more general and difficult problem and conveniently enough, is not the activity that users will find themselves doing repeatedly while maintaining a project.

We believe, with knowledge of the domain and appropriate analysis of evolution, it is possible to build a knowledge evolution environment suitable for extending knowledge bases. In a fairly domain specific manner, we considered the evolution support environment for configurators. We looked at the information that was typically added and found generally only certain classes had new subclasses added to them as product knowledge evolved. We also found that instances were typically populated in particular patterns. While CLASSIC provides no general support for such additions, one domain specific environment was produced in an application family that supported specific subclass and instance addition. Also, in related work, Gil(Gil & Melz 1996) has analyzed planning-based uses of another description logic-based system and systematically supports knowledge base evolution with respect to the known plan usage. The more general problem that does not rely on domain or reasoning knowledge has been addressed in the editor work (Paley, Lawrence, & Karp 1997) for the general frame protocol. The general work, of course, is broader yet shallower with respect to reasoning implications.

Other Technical Concerns

The computer science concerns that affect the suitability of a knowledge representation system have to do with the behavior of the system as a computer program or routine, ignoring its status as a representer of knowledge. The most-studied aspect of this collection of concerns has to do with the computational analysis of the basic algorithms embodied in the system, in particular their worst-case complexity. Because this worst-case complexity has been so well studied, we will not say anything about it further, except to state that it *is* important in determining the suitability of a knowledge representation system for particular task.

Efficiency

Although the worst-case complexity of knowledge representation systems has been well-studied, there are other resource-consumption issues that are important for determining the suitability of a knowledge representation system. These concerns are generally more prosaic, but perhaps even more important, than the concerns about worst-case complexity. For example, it is necessary to know the usual resource consumption of the most-frequently called operations of the knowledge representation system or those operations that are called at critical time in the operation of the whole system.

The CLASSIC family has been particularly aggressive in ensuring that queries to the system are fast, working under the assumption that the most-common operations are queries. Most queries in CLASSIC are simply retrievals of data stored by the system, as CLASSIC responds to the addition of knowledge by computing most of its consequences. (There are other reasons to compute all consequences that have been seen earlier.) Further, the performance of the addition of knowledge to the system is optimized over the retraction or change of knowledge.

CLASSIC achieves these characteristics of fastest queries, fast additions, and slower retractions and changes by retaining data structures that record the current set of consequences and also record, on a fairly granular level, which knowledge affects other knowledge. This is not full truthmaintenance data, which would be prohibitively expensive to compute (and store), but is just enough to make additions cheap. It also serves to make retractions and changes somewhat cheaper than they otherwise would be, but this effect is much less than the change in the speed up additions of knowledge.

Application Programming Interface

One other aspect of a knowledge representation system that is vitally important for its suitability in any real application is its application programming interface, or how it can be accessed by other computer programs. In the vast majority of applications, the knowledge representation system has to serve as a tightly integrated component of a much larger overall system. For this to be workable, the knowledge representation system must provide a full-featured interface for the use of the rest of the system.

The NEOCLASSIC system, which is programmed in C++, and is expected to be part of a larger C++ program, provides a very wide application programming interface. (LISP CLASSIC has a similar wide application programming interface.) There are, of course, the usual calls to add and retract knowledge and to query for the presence of particular knowledge. In addition to this interface, there is a large interface that lets the rest of the system receive and process the actual data structures used inside NEOCLASSIC to represent knowledge, but without allowing these structures to be modified outside of NEOCLASSIC.[1] This interface allows for much faster access to the knowledge stored by NEOCLASSIC, as many accesses just retrieve fields from a data structure. Further, direct access to data structures allows the rest of the system to keep track of knowledge from NEOCLASSIC without having to keep track of a "name" for the knowledge querying using this name. (In fact, it is in this way possible to dispense with any notion of querying by name.)

There are also ways to obtain the data structures that are used by NEOCLASSIC for other purposes, including explanation. We have used this facility to write graphical user interfaces to present explanations and other information.

A less-traditional interface that is provided by both LISP CLASSIC and NEOCLASSIC is a notification mechanism, or hooks. This mechanism allows programmers to write functions that are called when particular changes are made in the knowledge stored in the system or when the system infers new knowledge from other knowledge. Hooks for the retraction of knowledge from the system are also provided. These hooks allow, among other things, the creation of a graphical user interface that mirrors (some portion or view of) the knowledge stored in the representation system.

Others in the knowledge representation community have recognized the need for common APIs, (e.g., the general frame protocol(Chaudhri et al. 1997) and the open knowledge base connectivity(Chaudhri et al. 1998)) and translators exist between the general frame protocol API specification and CLASSIC.

Platforms

A third important aspect concerns the platforms on which the knowledge representation system runs. This encompasses not only the machines and operating systems, but also the language in which the system is written (if it is visible), the version of the libraries that the system uses, and the mechanism for linking to the system. Many applications have needs for a particular operating system or language, and cannot utilize tools not available in this context.

CLASSIC has been made available on a reasonable number of platforms. The underlying language of a member of the CLASSIC family is visible, not just because of the application programming interface which is, of necessity, language-specific, but also because programmers can write functions to extended the expressive power of the system, and these functions have to be written in the underlying language of the system.

CLASSIC is currently available in two different languages: LISP and C++. The C++ member is the more recent, and the reimplementation used C++ precisely to make CLASSIC available for a larger number of applications. This was done even though C++ is not the ideal language in which to write a representation system.

The members of the CLASSIC family have also been written in a platform-independent manner. This has required not using some of the nicer capabilities of the underlying language or of particular operating systems. For example, NEOCLASSIC does not use C++ exceptions, partly because few C++ compilers supported this extension to the language. LISP CLASSIC runs on various LISP implementations and on various operating systems, including most versions of Unix, MacOS, and Windows. NEOCLASSIC runs under four C++ compilers and on both Unix and Windows NT.

Public Relations Concerns

Researchers sometimes underestimate the varied public relations aspects involved with making a system usable. Barriers to usability come in many forms: potential users who are unaware of a system's existence will not use it; potential users who do not understand how a system can meet the users needs are unlikely to use it; potential users who do not have enough understanding to visualize an abstract solution to their problem using a new system are unlikely to depend on the new system over tools they understand and can predict; and finally potential users who have a limited set of approved tools which does not include the new system are unlikely go to the effort of getting the new system approved for their internal use. In order to address these issues, description logic system designers need to devise ways to make their systems known to likely users, educate those users about the possible uses, provide support for teaching users how to use them for some standard and leveragable uses, and either obtain approval for their systems or provide ammunition for users to gain approval.

In experiences with CLASSIC, the following tools have been employed to overcome the above stated barriers to usability.

Documentation: Beyond the standard research papers, users demanded usage guidelines aimed at non-PhD researchers. In an effort to educate people on when a description logic-based system might be useful, what its limitations were, and how one might go about using one in a simple application, a long paper was written with a running (executable) example on how to use the system (Brachman et al. 1991).

Demonstration Applications: Motivated by the need to help users understand a simple reasoning paradigm and by the need to have a quick prototyping domain for showing off novel functionality which exploits the strengths of the underlying system, a few demonstration systems were developed. The first developed was a simple application that captures

---

[1]Of course, as C++ does not have an inviolable type system, there are mechanisms to modify these structures. It is just that any well-typed access cannot.

"typical" reasoning patterns in an accessible domain. This one system has been used in dozens of universities as a pedagogical tool and test system. While this application was appropriate for many students, an application more closely resembling some actual applications was needed to (i) give more meaningful demonstrations internally and to (ii) provide concrete suggestions of new functionality that developers might consider using in their applications. This led to a more complex application with a fairly serious graphical interface (McGuinness, Resnick, & Isbell 1995). Both of these applications have been adapted for the web.[2]

It was only when a demonstration system that was clearly isomorphic to the developer's applications was available that there could be effective providing of clear descriptions and implemented examples of the functionality that we believed should be incorporated into development applications.

Course Materials: Motivated by the need to grow a larger community of people trained in knowledge representation in general and description logics in particular, we collaborated with a training center to generate a course. Independently, at least one university developed a similar course and a set of five running assignments to help students gain experience using the system. We collaborated on the tutorial to support the educators and to gather feedback from the students.

Talks: The value of personal introduction to topics can not be underestimated. We have given numerous general talks about knowledge representation, the use of description logics, and some of their more successful application areas. Many other colleagues have acted similarly and we now see description logics being a topic of discussion in some related technical communities such as databases and configuration.

Standard Tool Use: We believe it is imprudent to ignore the business community's demands of common standard implementation languages, reasonable support, and standard platform toolkits. The business world was accommodated by providing a development version of the system written in C. (Although the research LISP implementation is still the academic system of choice, all of the commercial applications could only use the C version, essentially because it was written in a language that developers and their management felt comfortable with.) More recently, it has been found difficult to develop extensions in one system and rely on another organization to import those extensions into a development system, so we decided to support one version of CLASSIC for *both* research and development use. This led to the development of NEOCLASSIC which is written in C++. This addresses the issue of maintaining an implementation in a widely accepted language.

The issue of getting CLASSIC included in the standard approved platform for application development remains outstanding. One reason for this is that it entails providing evidence of the equivalent of commercially competitive support for the product.

Summary

Although a knowledge representation system must have sufficient expressive power and appropriate computational complexity to be considered for use in applications, there are many other issues that also determine whether it will be used. These issues involve access to the knowledge stored in the system, such as explanation and presentation of the knowledge, other technical issues, such as efficiency and programming interfaces, and non-technical issues, such as publicity and demos. If these issues are not addressed appropriately, a knowledge representation system will not be used in real applications.

The majority of the efforts over the last several years of development of the CLASSIC family have been spent on these issues. Explanation and presentation components have been built, efficiency has been improved, large application programming interfaces have been constructed, and courses and demos have been designed. The entire system has even been reimplemented in C++. Together, these efforts have made the CLASSIC family much more acceptable for use in applications.

In fact, these issues were vitally important for the use of CLASSIC in the PROSE configuration system in AT&T (Wright *et al.* 1993). Before PROSE could be fielded, there had to be a version of CLASSIC written in C, with a large application programming interface, that supported recovery from inconsistent states of knowledge and the examination of these states. Before PROSE could be widely used, there had to be an explanation component, and considerable promotion had to be done. Without the development of a special purpose knowledge acquisition tool, the project would not have been continued. Arguably, it is precisely because of the work presented in this paper that we have maintained some of, if not *the* longest lived[3] commercial applications of description logics.

Acknowledgments

We are indebted to the rest of the CLASSIC group for their contributions in the design, implementation, and applications of CLASSIC. Major contributors in all aspects of CLASSIC include Alex Borgida and Lori Alperin Resnick. Others who have impacted portions of this work include Merryll Abrahams, Ron Brachman, Charles Foster, Charles Isbell, Elia Weixelbaum, and Jon Wright.

---

[2] The web version of our wines demonstration system was provided by Chris Welty and is available at http://untangle.cs.vassar.edu/wines. We collaborated with Charles Isbell, Matt Parker, and Chris Welty to produce the web version of our stereo configurator, which is is available at http://taylor.vassar.edu/stereo-demo/.

[3] CLASSIC-based configurators are still in use in Lucent and some have projected life spans into the year 2000, NCR has a commercially deployed CLASSIC-based knowledge discovery tool, and AT&T has deployed CLASSIC-based knowledge enhanced search applications(McGuinness 1998).

References

Baader, F.; Bürckert, H.-J.; Heinsohn, J.; Hollunder, B.; Müller, J.; Nebel, B.; Nutt, W.; and Profitlich, H.-J. 1991. Terminological knowledge representation: A proposal for a terminological logic. German Research Center for Artificial Intelligence (DFKI), Saarbrücken, Germany.

Baader, F.; Hollunder, B.; Nebel, B.; Profitlich, H.-J.; and Franconi, E. 1992. An empirical analysis of optimization techniques for terminological representation systems, or, making KRIS get a move on. In *Proceedings KR-92*, 270–281. Morgan Kaufmann.

Borgida, A., and McGuinness, D. L. 1996. Inquiring about frames. In *Proceedings KR-96*, 340–349. Morgan Kaufmann.

Borgida, A.; Brachman, R. J.; McGuinness, D. L.; and Resnick, L. A. 1989. CLASSIC: A structural data model for objects. In *Proceedings SIGMOD-89*, 59–67. Association for Computing Machinery.

Borgida, A. 1992. From type systems to knowledge representation: Natural semantics specifications for Description Logics. *International Journal of Intelligent and Cooperative Information Systems* 93–126.

Brachman, R. J.; McGuinness, D. L.; Patel-Schneider, P. F.; Resnick, L. A.; and Borgida, A. 1991. Living with CLASSIC: When and how to use a KL-ONE-like language. In Sowa, J., ed., *Principles of Semantic Networks: Explorations in the representation of knowledge*. San Mateo, California: Morgan-Kaufmann. 401–456.

Brachman, R. J. 1992. "Reducing" CLASSIC to practice: Knowledge representation theory meets reality. In *Proceedings KR-92*, 247–258. Morgan Kaufmann.

Buchheit, M.; Donini, F. M.; and Schaerf, A. 1993. Decidable reasoning in terminological knowledge representation systems. *Journal of Artificial Intelligence Research* 1:109–138.

Chaudhri, V. K.; Farquhar, A.; Fikes, R.; Karp, P. D.; and Rice, J. 1997. The generic frame protocol 2.0. Technical report, Artificial Intelligence Center, SRI International, Menlo Park, CA.

Chaudhri, V. K.; Farquhar, A.; Fikes, R.; and Karp, P. D. 1998. Open knowledge base connectivity 2.0. Technical report, Technical Report KSL-09-06, Stanford University KSL.

Donini, F. M.; Lenzerini, M.; Nardi, D.; and Nutt, W. 1991. The complexity of concept languages. In *Proceedings KR-91*, 151–162. Morgan Kaufmann.

Gil, Y., and Melz, E. 1996. Explicit representations of problem-solving strategies to support knowledge acquisition. In *Proceedings AAAI-96*, 469–476.

Levesque, H. J. 1982. The logic of incomplete knowledge bases. In Brodie, M. L.; Mylopoulos, J.; and Schmidt, J. W., eds., *On Conceptual Modelling: Perspectives from Artificial Intelligence, Databases, and Programming Languages*. New York: Springer-Verlag. 165–186.

McGuinness, D. L., and Borgida, A. 1995. Explaining subsumption in Description Logics. In *Proceedings IJCAI-95*, 816–821.

McGuinness, D. L., and Wright, J. R. 1998. Conceptual modeling for configuration: A description logic-based configurator platform. *Artificial Intelligence for Engineering Design, Analysis, and Manufacturing Journal - Special Issue on Configuration*.

McGuinness, D. L.; Resnick, L. A.; and Isbell, C. 1995. Description Logic in practice: A CLASSIC application. In *Proceedings IJCAI-95*, 2045–2046.

McGuinness, D. L. 1996. *Explaining Reasoning in Description Logics*. Ph.D. Dissertation, Department of Computer Science, Rutgers University. Also available as Rutgers Technical Report Number LCSR-TR-277.

McGuinness, D. L. 1998. Ontological Issues for Knowledge-Enhanced Search. In *roceedings of Formal Ontology in Information Systems*. Also to appear in Frontiers in Artificial Intelligence and Applications, IOS-Press, Washington, DC, 1998.

Paley, S. M.; Lawrence, J. D.; and Karp, P. D. 1997. A generic knowledge-base browser and editor. In *Proceedings AAAI-97*, 1045–1051.

Patel-Schneider, P. F.; McGuinness, D. L.; Brachman, R. J.; Resnick, L. A.; and Borgida, A. 1991. The CLASSIC knowledge representation system: Guiding principles and implementation rationale. *SIGART Bulletin* 2(3):108–113.

Patel-Schneider, P. F.; Resnick, L. A.; McGuinness, D. L.; Weixelbaum, E.; Abrahams, M.; and Borgida, A. 1997. NeoClassic user's guide: Version 1.0. AI Principles Research Department, AT&T Labs—Research.

Patil, R. S.; Fikes, R. E.; Patel-Schneider, P. F.; Mckay, D.; Finin, T.; Gruber, T.; and Neches, R. 1992. The DARPA knowledge sharing effort: Progress report. In *Proceedings KR-92*, 777–788. Morgan Kaufmann.

Resnick, L. A.; Borgida, A.; Brachman, R. J.; McGuinness, D. L.; and Patel-Schneider, P. F. 1995. CLASSIC description and reference manual for the COMMON LISP implementation: Version 2.3. AI Principles Research Department, AT&T Bell Laboratories.

Rychtyckyj, N. 1996. DLMS: An evaluation of KL-ONE in the automobile industry. In *Proceedings KR-96*, 588–596. Morgan Kaufmann.

Weixelbaum, E. S. 1991. C-Classic reference manual release 1.0. AT&T Bell Laboratories.

Wright, J. R.; Weixelbaum, E. S.; Brown, K.; Vesonder, G. T.; Palmer, S. R.; Berman, J. I.; and Moore, H. H. 1993. A knowledge-based configurator that supports sales, engineering, and manufacturing at AT&T network systems. In *Proceedings IAAI-93*, 183–193. American Association for Artificial Intelligence.

Representing Scientific Experiments: Implications for Ontology Design and Knowledge Sharing

Natalya Fridman Noy and Carole D. Hafner

College of Computer Science
Northeastern University
Boston, MA 02115
{natasha, hafner}@ccs.neu.edu

Abstract

As part of the development of knowledge sharing technology, it is necessary to consider a variety of domains and tasks in order to ensure that the shared framework is widely applicable. This paper describes an ontology design project in experimental molecular biology, focusing on extensions to previous ontological models and frame-based formalisms that allow us to handle problems in the representation of experimental science knowledge. We define *object histories*, which are used to track substances through a series of experimental processes, including those which transform their participants from one category to another. We define object and process *complexes* – temporary configurations with features of their own. We present extensions to a frame-based formalism to support these features. Additional features of our frame formalism include *slot groups* for identifying sets of relations with common properties, and partial filler restrictions that combine knowledge of the most likely slot values with the ability to handle unexpected values. We demonstrate how these extensions enable the use of (relatively) domain independent inference rules, support intelligent information retrieval, and improve the quality of query interfaces; and we describe the translation of our formalism into Ontolingua.

Introduction

The field of ontology development has become very active in recent years on the premise that it will encourage and enable knowledge sharing and reuse (Fikes et al. 1991). It is generally accepted that building an ontology for any real-world domain is a difficult task, and this task could be greatly facilitated if it were possible to reuse and modify ontologies created by others. For example, a model for representing biology experiments could take advantage of general ontologies of time and space, whose axioms would support inferences such as: if process A occurred before a process B, then every substep of A occurred before every substep of B; or: a DNA molecule that is part of a chromosome inside the cell nucleus is also located inside the cell nucleus.

Copyright © 1998, American Association for Artificial Intelligence (www.aaai.org). All rights reserved.

ARPA has sponsored a knowledge-sharing effort to develop methodology and software for the sharing and reuse of knowledge. Two results of this effort were: the Knowledge Interchange Format (KIF) (Genesereth and Fikes 1992), a computer-oriented language for knowledge interchange based on first-order logic and augmented by meta-knowledge and non-monotonic reasoning rules; and Ontolingua (Farquhar, Fikes, and Rice 1996; Gruber 1992) – a language for defining ontologies that provides a frame-like syntax in addition to full first-order logic of KIF. Ontolingua has become a de-facto standard for representing ontologies. The Ontolingua Server (http://www-ksl-svc.stanford.edu:5915/), maintained by the Knowledge Systems Laboratory at Stanford University, contains tools for designing and analyzing ontologies as well as a large shared Ontology library.

In addition to standard formalisms and tools for knowledge sharing, some common ontological foundations are needed, so that intelligent agents can use a common vocabulary in a way that is consistent (but not necessarily complete) with respect to each agent's knowledge. Agreement on a shared ontological framework among researchers is crucial to enable different groups working on ontology design in different domains to communicate with each other and share their results (Gruber 1993; Guarino, Carrara, and Giaretta 1994). As part of the process of developing such a shared framework, it will be necessary to experiment with a variety of domains and tasks, in order to ensure that the shared framework is widely applicable.

This paper describes an ontology design project in the domain of molecular biology experiments, focusing on several areas where standard formalisms, tools, or frameworks needed to be extended. Our primary goal was to develop a representation framework for biology experiments described in the literature, which would be capable of supporting intelligent (i.e. semantic-based) question answering. This ontology provides support for inferences about complex substances, participants, conditions and effects of processes that can be used for information retrieval, planning, simulation, and other tasks. We believe that the challenges we faced, and the solutions we found, are relevant to other domains, particularly experimental sciences.

Experiments described in molecular biology papers are similar to cooking recipes. First, the ingredients (chemicals, bacteria, plasmids, etc.) are listed, followed by a description of the processes performed on the ingredients (mix, spin, separate, analyze, etc.) Thus, substances and processes are central to any ontology of experimental sciences. Some processes occur naturally, such as bacteria growth; others (experimental procedures) are set up and controlled by an experimenter. All processes take substances as their inputs and then change or observe some of their properties, destroy them, transform them into a different substance, etc. The substances themselves can be quite complex: they can be objects with elaborate internal structure, populations of molecules or cells, or mixtures of other substances. Sometimes this conglomerate will have a name of its own, and sometimes it will be just a temporary configuration of other substances. Processes also range from simple, "atomic" events, to complex configurations of events and actions dependent on each other.

Below we describe some extensions to previous ontological models and frame-based formalisms that allow us to handle problems in the representation of experimental science knowledge. We then demonstrate how these extensions enable the use of (relatively) domain independent inference rules, support intelligent information retrieval, and improve the quality of query interfaces. Finally, we describe the translation of our formalism to Ontolingua.

Elements of an ontological framework for experimental sciences

Representing knowledge about experiments, and molecular biology experiments in particular, presents its own unique challenges. Many of these are described in (Fridman Noy 1997). In this section, we describe elements of our ontological framework that address some of these challenges: *object histories, object complexes* and *process complexes*.

Object Histories

One of the major challenges in representing processes in experimental sciences is representing effects of transformations, in particular transformations that can change the category of their participants (called *category conversions*). When batter is baked, for instance, the batter object "migrates" to a different category, cake. The stuff the object was made from is still the same, but its classification has changed. From the standpoint of a knowledge model, we could represent this migration as the original participant (in this case, batter) ceasing to exist and the new object (cake) coming into existence. This, however, is not an accurate reflection of the way people think about the situation: there needs to be a link between the original object and the newly created one. For instance, when one asks if there is sugar in the cake, if this link exists, it can be inferred that since sugar was in the batter, it is now in the cake (possibly, in some transformed form). The fundamental notion in knowledge representation that every individual object is defined as an instance of a category seems incompatible with a universe where objects can gradually change their category as a result of a transformation. Thus, a straightforward process model that represents inputs (participants) and outputs (objects that come into existence) is inadequate for modeling conversions, because a) it does not represent the fact that the inputs no longer exist and b) it does not represent the relationship between the outputs and the original inputs, one of the most important relationships being the fact that the stuff the inputs were made from is now the stuff the outputs are made from.

Our solution to this problem is introducing *Object Histories*. The idea of histories was suggested in (Hayes 1990) and is used in Qualitative Physics (Collins and Forbus 1987; Forbus 1984). However, it is generally assumed that objects do not change their category or identity. We extend the notion of object histories to account for these changes and to trace substances as they go through processes, including category conversions. In our ontology an Object History for an object A consists of: information about the process that "gave life" to A; a list of complex objects that A was part of; a list of processes that A participated in; information about the process that destroyed A and substances that it was transformed into. This information does not need to be complete in order to be used for inferencing and query answering. For instance, in the earlier example of batter and cake, an object history for a sugar object can include batter, then the mix and beat processes, bake process, cake object, possibly an eat process (that would probably destroy the sugar, as we may not want to consider what becomes of sugar after we eat it).

Object Complexes

Another useful structure we introduce to represent biology experiments is Complexes – joining of several objects in a temporary configuration that, taken as a whole, has meaningful properties. The idea of a Complex was inspired by Individual Views in Qualitative Process Theory (Forbus 1984). The example Forbus uses is the *Contained-Liquid* Individual View. This Individual View describes liquid in a container and relations imposed on both objects (liquid and container) by this binding. For an example of a Complex from molecular biology, consider a binding complex that arises in gene transcription and includes a site on DNA ("promoter binding site") and an enzyme. The immediate significance of this chemical binding complex is a precondition for the gene transcription process.

Note that there is a subtle distinction between the relations of Participants in a Complex to each other and relation between a whole and its parts: the existence of a whole in the latter case generally is not contingent on the existence of its parts, i.e. a car without a wheel is still a car. It is different for a Complex. For example, in the *Contained-Liquid* example, if there is no liquid, or no container, the instance of a *Contained-Liquid* Complex does not exist.

Treating Complexes as first-class objects in the Things hierarchy, allows us to sub-categorize Complexes depending on the relations between their components: for example, we have such categories as `Containment Complex` (when one participant in a `Complex` contains all the others), or `Attachment Complex` (where participants are `attached` to each other).

Process Complexes

Similar to `Complexes` for objects, there are `Process Complexes` that represent a set of events that can be viewed as a whole with aggregate properties. In our ontology there are several sub-categories of `Process Complexes`, based on how sub-processes in it are related to each other. Firstly, sub-steps in a `Complex` could be sequential or parallel (i.e. executed simultaneously). Sub-class `Sequence Complex` represents a simple sequence of `Processes`. Sub-class `Combination Complex` is used to represent `Complexes` with parallel, dependent substeps. `Chromatography` is an example of the latter `Complex`. In many instances of chromatography its substeps, adding a substance at one end of a column and eluting it from the other end, are dependent since in order for something to be eluted from the bottom of the column, something needs to be added at the top. The rates of addition and elution are directly proportional: the more you add, the more substance is eluted.

Another sub-class of `Process Complex` is `Technique Complex`. This class is used to represent a complex of a main process and a technique used to achieve it. In a sense, the main process is the goal for the technique process, and the technique is the means of executing the main process. In this case, inputs and outputs of the two processes (the main one and the technique) are the same. Descriptions could be different though. Consider, for example a process "harvest by centrifugation". Harvest is the goal-process and centrifugation is a technique. Both processes have cells in growth medium as their input and cells without the medium as their output.

Extensions to frame-based formalism

The formalism that we used to represent our ontology is described in full in (Fridman Noy 1997). Here we present some of its more interesting features (mainly, slot groups, axiom groups and complex value restrictions) and show how they help to handle the structures described above. We demonstrated the formality and portability of this formalism in (Fridman Noy 1997) by translating it to Ontolingua. Some of the features of this translation are described below. We demonstrate that not everything can be translated *directly* into Ontolingua, but show how still to store the information so that it can be extracted later.

We took a standard frame-based formalism (see, for example, (Minsky 1981) or (Chaudhri et al. 1997)) as a basis and then extended it. So, each frame consists of a category name, a super-category name, and a list of slots and slot groups (slot groups are introduced and described below).

```
Process Chromatography: Combination Complex
   Participants:
      object instance-of Tangible-Thing
   Substeps:
      load-process instance-of Combine
      elute-process instance-of Separate
```

Figure 1. Partial definition of a `Chromatography` *process as a sub-category of a* `Combination Complex`

Slot groups

In order to capture various aspects of object and category change that are then automatically translated into object histories, as well as represent complexes (both, object complexes and process complexes), we introduce *slot groups*. Slot groups add an extra dimension to slot definitions when necessary. This allows slots that have similar ontological function to be grouped together. This semantic role can then be employed in the inference rules and axioms. The slot group `Participants` in a process is a good example of this phenomenon. Each member of a `Participant` slot group is a slot in itself, with its own name that can be referred to in axioms and inference rules (e.g., `object`, `growth-medium`) and value restrictions. At the same time, we can refer to all the process `Participants` as a whole. Similarly, some processes have a slot group for newly created objects. When an instance frame of such a process is created in a knowledge base, we automatically create frames (and corresponding object histories) for the new objects. At the same time, axioms representing effects of a process can contain conditions on properties of each of these newly created objects.

A slot group consists of a slot group name followed by a list of slot definitions, where each slot has a name and, possibly, some value restrictions (described later).

```
<slot-group> ::= slot-group-name: {<slot >}*
<slot>       ::= slot-name [value-restriction]
```

Specific slot groups and the inferences they license are determined by the ontology. The number of slot groups is usually small and reflects only very high-level assumptions about the data. As an example we will describe here some of the slot groups used in our ontology.

Each `Process` has a `Participant` group that contains objects participating in the process. They are differentiated inside by various roles reflected in the corresponding slot names (e.g., `solution`, `catalyst`, etc.).

`Substeps` in a `Process Complex` is also a slot group. For example, in `Chromatography`, which is a sub-class of `Combination Complex` consisting of two simultaneous inter-related processes (loading into a column and eluting from a column), the two substeps with their corresponding roles are: `load-process` and `elute-process` (see Figure 1).

A number of slot groups are used to trigger corresponding updates in object histories by the inference rules. For example:
- `Objects-created`: list of new objects created as a result of a process, their categories and value restrictions.

```
Process Transform : Process
  Participants:
      original instance-of Tangible-Thing
      catalyst instance-of Chemical
  Objects-created:
      new instance-of Tangible-Thing
  Objects-converted:
      conversion (original, new)
```

Figure 2. Sample definition of a Transform process.

Instances of each of these objects are created. This, in turn, triggers creation of corresponding object histories.
- Objects-converted: list of *conversion* slots. The value of each slot is a pair: original object (or list of objects), and the object it was converted into.

Consider, for example, a simple transformation process that transforms some *original* substance into some *new* substance (a chemical reaction with a catalyst present, for instance) presented in Figure 2. Here an instance of Tangible Thing is created (new) along with an instance of its object history. An instance of this Transform process will be put as the final process in the original's object history and as the first process in the new's object history. In the object history of new it would also be noted that it was derived from original.

Axiom groups

Most frame-based formalisms allow a set of axioms to be associated with a concept definition. Axioms can be used to specify restrictions on the values of the slots that cannot be specified by simple slot restrictions, such as conditions involving dependencies among the values of several slots. Usually an axiom associated with a frame stipulates that a condition must be true for any instance of the concept. However, in modeling knowledge about processes, it is useful to distinguish axioms that describe preconditions of a process and axioms that describe process' effects.

For instance, an effects axiom for a mix process can state that all the inputs are now ingredients in the mixture and any process applied to the mixture (such as heating) is indirectly applied to the original inputs also. Then, if a user asks whether a certain sugar (assuming it was put into the mixture) was ever heated, the answer will be positive. However, if the mixture was heated before the sugar was added to it, then the answer should be negative.

We realize this distinction between axioms by allowing two groups of axioms in a process frame: one preceded by a keyword Conditions and the other by a keyword Effects. This distinction can then be used by inference rules.

Specifying slot value restrictions

Another feature of our frame-based formalism is an expanded way of specifying value restrictions for a slot.

Figure 3 shows a sample definition of the category DNA. DNA, for example, can be *chromosomal*, *genomic*, or some other, unspecified, type. So, the Type slot has a list of fillers with ellipsis that indicates an open value set. DNA can be *synthesized* or come from bacteria. Thus, the Source slot can either contain the filler value *synthesized* (or some other, unspecified filler), or an instance of a Bacteria class. For the Composition slot possible fillers are limited to: single-stranded or double-stranded. A DNA molecule might not be labeled radioactively (in which case, the filler for the last slot is *no*), or it might be labeled by some radioactive label (which should then fill the value of the slot).

The use of open value sets for slot fillers accomplishes several things: Having a list of specific expected fillers can help in natural-language processing, since they can be used to infer the presence of a frame from the presence of one of its fillers (for instance, the presence of DNA from the use of *genomic*). The list of specific fillers also can be used to provide users with a set of suggested values to choose from when interactively specifying a query. On the other hand, allowing other possible values accounts for evolving domains (which experimental sciences certainly are): if new values are invented, they would easily fit into the existing knowledge base, since there was no strict limit on what can fill the slot.

In our formalism we also allow for various combinations of restrictions on slot values. The value restriction on a slot is either a list of possible filler values or specification of a category that the slot value should belong to, or both.

```
<value restriction> ::=
    <list of fillers> | <class restriction> |
    <list of fillers> or <class restriction>
<class restriction> ::=
    instance-of class-name {or class-name}*
```

If a list of fillers for a slot value is specified and it is not followed by ellipsis, the range of values for the slot is limited to the values from this list. If ellipsis follows the list of fillers, the slot can take on other values as well (in the latter case, the list of fillers usually represents the most likely values):

```
<list of fillers> ::= {filler-value }+ [...]
```

This added richness in specification is used in the query interface for providing an easier way for the user to fill in query frames.

```
Thing DNA : Nucleic-Acid
  Type         chromosomal  genomic  ...
  Source       synthesized  ...      or
               instance-of bacteria
  Composition
               single-stranded  double-stranded
  Labeled-or-not   no           or
                   instance-of label
```

Figure 3. Sample definition of the category DNA. It has four simple slots with various kinds of value restrictions.

> **Growth of Cells and Protein Purification.** The *cheW* and *cheA* plasmids were expressed in *E. coli* mutant strain RP3098 (a Δ*flhA-flhD* mutant), which was provided by J.S. Parkinson (University of Utah). Cells were grown at 30°C in L broth...
> CheW purification is based on the procedure described by Stock *et al.* (14) with the following modifications. Cells were harvested by centrifugation at 5000rpm (Beckman JA 10 rotor) for 5 min, resuspended in a small volume of buffer containing 10 mM Mes (pH 6.0), 100 mM NaCl, 0.5 mM EDTA, and 50 μM phenylmethylsulfonyl fluoride, and then broken by French press. The lysate was ultracentrifuged at 50,000 rpm (Beckman Ti 60 rotor) for 1 hr to remove cellular debris. Protein was precipitated from the supernatant by adding $(NH_4)_2SO_4$ to 40% saturation and pelleted by centrifugation.... CheW was >99% pure as determined by Coomassie Blue staining.

Figure 4. A potential target for retrieval (an excerpt from (Gegner and Dahlquist 1991)).

Using the framework for inference and query answering

Inference using slot groups

The slot groups and axiom groups in an ontology should be small in number and relatively domain independent. This means that knowledge about slot groups can be expressed in high-level inference rules that do not depend on specific frame attributes. We will present here a few examples of inference rules that use slot groups.[1]

For the first example consider again the Transform process in Figure 2, with slot groups: Participants, Objects-created, Objects-converted. Each slot group triggers corresponding updates in the object histories. For instance, each Participant has an instance of the Transform process added to its object history:

```
(=> (Process ?x)                            (1)
  (∀ (?y)
    (=> (member-of ?y (Participants ?x))
        (member-of ?x
          (Processes (Object-history ?y))))))
```

For members of the Objects-created group, a new instance and object history are created, with the Transform process as the creator:

```
(=> (Process ?x)                            (2)
  (∀ (?y)
    (=> (member-of ?y (Objects-created ?x))
        (= (Creator-Process (Object-history ?y))
           ?x))))
```

Another example involves Process Complexes. In a Combination Complex, all the Substeps occur at the same time and temperature (recall, that Combination Complex consists of a number of simultaneous inter-related substeps). This can be expressed with the following rule:

```
(=> (Combination-Complex ?x)                (3)
  (∀ (?y ?z)
    (=> (and (member-of ?y (Substeps ?x))
             (member-of ?z (Substeps ?x)))
        (= (duration ?x) (duration ?y)
           (duration ?z)))))
```

That is, knowing the duration for either the whole Combination Complex, or any of its Substeps, allows us to fill in this value for all the others. The same can be stated for the temperature of these processes, or, say, Object in a Technique Complex and its Substeps. This rule does not rely on the roles of specific Substeps, which are themselves slots in the Process Complex frame.

Inference in query answering

Intelligent Information Retrieval was the initial goal of our ontology design effort, so the extent to which the ontology supports inferencing for this type of retrieval is an important measure of our success. In this section we will show how the knowledge encoded in our ontology and described in the previous section can be used to answer queries more intelligently. Two retrieval heuristics are described here: indirect match of transformants and technique abstraction.

Example paragraph

The queries below will be illustrated by an excerpt from (Gegner and Dahlquist 1991) presented in Figure 4. This excerpt describes a sequence of steps to purify CheW protein from a certain strain of *E. coli* bacteria (namely, strain RP3098).

The sequence starts out with a strain of *E. coli* bacteria which is grown to get the necessary number of cells. The grown cells contain CheW protein which now needs to be purified. The purification process consists of first breaking the cell walls to create *lysate* (an unstructured mixture of pieces of the walls and cell elements) and then gradually removing substances other than CheW from the mixture and achieving higher and higher concentration of CheW in the mixture that remains. Along the way, various substances (buffers, chemicals) are added to the mixture and then removed, carrying some of the unwanted stuff away with them. In the end, all that is left is a mixture 99% of which is CheW protein.

We will now describe two queries that can be answered better by using the inference rules presented in the previous section. As will be discussed in these examples, this approach increases the *recall* of the information retrieval as compared to other knowledge-based systems by utilizing the more extensive information stored in our knowledge base. At the same time, this approach also increases the *precision* of information retrieval compared to statistical, keyword-based systems that would bring many incorrect

---

[1] We present declarative inference rules here; they get their operational semantics when used in the inference engine

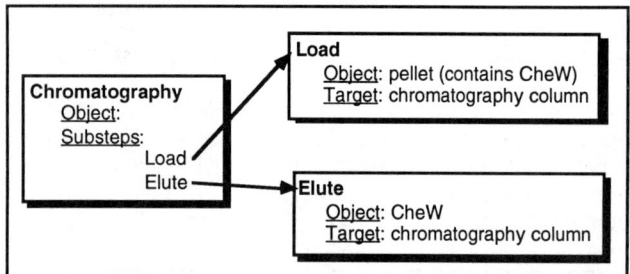

Figure 5. Illustration of implicit technique recognition. Arrows represent reference pointers in this case.

answers based only on presence and/or proximity of words in a sentence or paragraph.

Indirect match of transformants

Consider the following query:

Show me the papers that describe RP3098 cells being ultracentrifuged.

In the paragraph in Figure 4 the ultracentrifugation process was applied to the lysate (and not to the RP3098 cells). So, this paper might not be brought up as an answer. However, since the lysate is a direct transformant of the cells and thus the ultracentrifugation was indirectly applied to the cells, it could be desirable to present this paragraph as an answer to the query above. In our system, when an instance of a `break` process that produced the lysate, is created, the object history for this instance of `lysate` is updated to contain the `cells` as the `Original-object` for the lysate. Thus, when the `lysate` is put as an `object` in the `ultracentrifugation` frame, it can be easily inferred, that this process is applied to the direct transformant of the `cells`.

Technique abstraction

Consider the following sentence from Figure 4:

The pellet was ... loaded onto a Whitman DE-52 column. Protein was eluted from the column with a linear gradient of ...

Even though it is not explicitly mentioned here, this sequence of events describes a chromatography process. Chromatography is the *complex* of these experiment substeps (see Figure 5). It is easy to imagine a query pertaining to this technique:

Show me the papers where chromatography was used in the process of purifying CheW

So, this paper should be retrieved as the result. However, this answer is possible only if we consider the `Chromatography Combination Complex`, the presence of which could be inferred by the presence of two other processes, `load` and `elute`. Besides, the object of the two process (load and elute) - the protein, would be automatically placed in the object of the Process Complex, by a rule similar to rule (3) in the previous section.

Using the framework for user interaction

To evaluate the practical usefulness of the ontology, we implemented a proof-of-concept prototype of an intelligent information retrieval system: M&M Query System, designed to assist biologists in accessing on-line texts of the Materials and Methods sections of research papers.

First, research papers in the database are annotated with frames based on the corresponding knowledge model (in turn, using the features described here). Frames along with the texts of papers they are linked to, are stored in a database. This database can then be used by biologists to search for specific information in the papers. After a query is entered (in the form of a concept list or filled-in frames), it is presented to the search engine that matches it to the frames in the knowledge base. The result comes back in the form of a list of relevant papers. The user can then choose any paper (or papers) to be displayed. To point out the more relevant part of the paper and to provide simple feedback of why this particular paper was brought up, the parts of the paper associated with the frame are highlighted.

One of the query modes in our system is *frame fill-in query*, where a user is given a (possibly simplified) frame for a concept s/he is interested in. The user then specifies some of the values in the frame slots to restrict the search field. These values are matched with the ones in the frame database. This query mode makes use of some of the features of our frame formalism. Figure 6 presents an example of such a query. There are several ways in which the domain knowledge (specified when classes are defined) is used to assist the user in filling out slot values: for instance, if the class definition specifies a list of fillers for a specific slot, this list appears in the pop-up menu next to the slot; any value from this list can be chosen as a fill-in; if there is a class restriction on the slot, the list of these categories can be presented to the user as well. Otherwise, s/he can browse the list of all categories to fill in the value for the slot

An important feature of this interface is that it does not depend on the specific knowledge in the knowledge base. Any frame-based knowledge model, as long as it follows

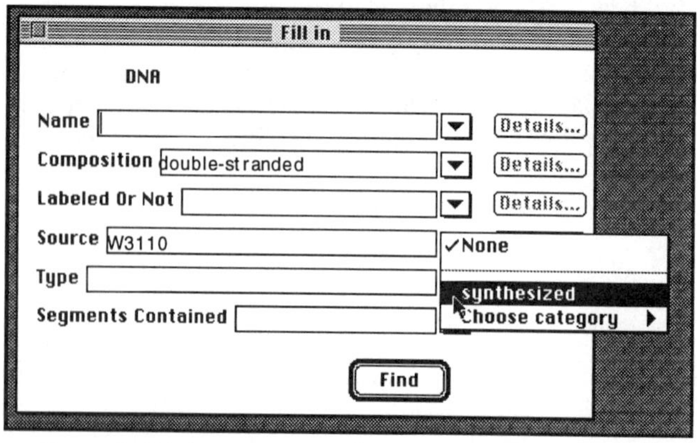

Figure 6. A frame fill-in dialog for a DNA class (short form).

```
(DEFINE-FRAME DNA
      :OWN-SLOTS
      ((ARITY 1) (DOCUMENTATION "Describes properties of DNA")
       (INSTANCE-OF CLASS)
       (SUBCLASS-OF NUCLEIC-ACID))
      TEMPLATE-SLOTS
    ((SOURCE (SLOT-FILLERS '(synthesized)) (MORE-FILLERS-ALLOWED TRUE) (VALUE-TYPE BACTERIA))
     (TYPE (SLOT-FILLERS '(chromosomal genomic)) (MORE-FILLERS-ALLOWED TRUE))
     (COMPOSITION (SLOT-FILLERS '(double-stranded single-stranded)))
     (LABELED-OR-NOT (SLOT-FILLERS '(no)) (VALUE-TYPE LABEL))))
```

Figure 7. Ontolingua definition for DNA class from Figure 3 (http://www-ksl-svc.stanford.edu:5915/doc/ontolingua/reference-manual).

the formalism, can be plugged in this system and the user will be guided through the new hierarchies and new frames.

Translation to Ontolingua

To validate the formality and portability of our formalism, we translated the ontology into Ontolingua (Farquhar, Fikes, and Rice 1996) which has become a standard repository for ontologies for knowledge sharing.

As described above, Ontolingua supports a frame-based formalism, and, thus, it lends itself easily as a translation target for our formalism. Although not all the features of our formalism could be translated directly into Ontolingua, the information could still be stored (in most cases, using facets) and then extracted back if necessary.

Facets in Ontolingua are relations associated with the slots that allow specification of various constraints on the slots. For instance, commonly used Ontolingua facets include Slot-Value-Type to specify the class the slot values should belong to, or Slot-Cardinality to constrain the cardinality of a slot. We add a set of extra facets to encode features that can be expressed in our formalism but not in the standard frame formalism. These features include slot belonging to a particular slot group, list of possible slot fillers, etc. Figure 7, for instance, demonstrates how the DNA category from Figure 3 is represented in Ontolingua directly. In this example, every slot has a facet added to it. We associate a facet Slot-Fillers with a slot if a list of fillers is available. The value of the facet is the list itself. If fillers not from the list are allowed (denoted by ellipsis in our formalism), a facet More-Fillers-Allowed with a true value is added to the slot (e.g., Source slot in Figure 7).

The formalism features described in this paper require two groups of extra facets:

- For each slot group, there is a facet <Slot-Group-Name>-Group-Member for specifying a slot group that a slot belongs to. When a slot belongs to a certain slot group, the corresponding facet is then associated with this slot and is given a True value. Since the number of slot groups is limited and is one of characteristics of an ontology, these facets should be defined before defining any of the other frames in a knowledge base.
- Facets are used to specify restrictions on slot values that go beyond simple class restriction. Slot-fillers facet specifies the list of slot-fillers for a slot. When the facet is associated with a slot, its value is a list of possible fillers. A facet More-Fillers-Allowed is added to a slot and given a value True if values not from the Slot-Fillers list could also be used for the slot (open value set).

There were a few other facets that were necessary to encode all the information that our formalism allows to specify, in Ontolingua. Even though this encoding did not allow these features to be available directly (since Ontolingua does not have provisions for them), all of them could be stored in it and then extracted back when necessary. That is, frames encoded in our formalism can be ported into Ontolingua and exported back without loss of information

Related work

Recently a number of research groups have created ontologies for different domains and purposes. In (Fridman Noy and Hafner 1997) we summarize and compare the contents, structure, design and evaluation methodologies and applications of ten projects representing the range of current work. The features of our ontology described in this paper address issues that were not fully or not at all addressed in these earlier projects.

In addition to research explicitly aimed at ontology design, research in Qualitative Physics (Collins and Forbus 1987; Hayes 1990); and in particular Qualitative Process Theory (Forbus 1984) has influenced our ontology framework. Our idea of Complexes is related to the notion of Individual Views from QPT. Reifying this notion to be a first-class object in the hierarchy of Things allows us to sub-categorize Complexes based on relations between their components. We also extend this notion into the Process sub-ontology and introduce Process Complexes. Our use of Object Histories extends the classic notion of histories to account for the fact that objects change not only their properties, but also their categories as a result of processes. Object histories in our model trace substances through *category conversions* as well as other processes.

Some work in description logic explores the idea of extending frame-based formalisms for more elaborate description of possible slot-fillers (see, for example, (Brachman et al. 1991)). We believe that our approach simplifies these specifications as compared to, say, CLASSIC, at the same time allowing for the richness of open-value sets to assist in natural-language processing and to account for evolving domains. Our treatment of process configurations also shares some characteristics with the *components* in (Clark and Porter 1997), which are abstract "mini-theories", or patterns of interactions between concepts. Each *component* consists of participants, their roles, and axioms. However, *components* are not related in hierarchical fashion (which makes re-use of parts of the descriptions more difficult).

Conclusions

In this paper we presented extensions to previous ontological models and standard frame-based formalism that are necessary to adequately represent knowledge about scientific experiments described in the literature. We also showed how these extensions can improve the quality of query answering and user interfaces.

The ontology elements described here include object histories, and object and process complexes. The formalism extensions are based on the ontology that we developed and include slot groups, axiom groups, and complex value restrictions on the slots. Slot groups are used to represent object and process complexes (temporary configurations with features of their own) and object histories (used to trace substances through processes including the processes that change categories of their participants). Axiom groups are used to distinguish between conditions that need to be true for a process to take place and those that are true after the process. All these features of the ontology are, in turn, used by an inference engine for query answering.

This formalism was used in an a prototype of an Intelligent Information Retrieval System (M&M Query System).

As foundations for shared ontologies and formalisms are considered, the requirements of such a large and important domain as experimental sciences should certainly be considered and accounted for in such an effort.

Acknowledgments

The authors thank the reviewers for their feedback. This research was supported in part by the National Science Foundation under grants IRI-9117030 and IRI-9633661.

References

Brachman, R. J., McGuiness, D. L., Patel-Schneider, P. F., Resnik, L. A., and Borgida, A. 1991. Living with CLASSIC: When and how to use KL-ONE-like language. *Principles of Semantic Networks*. J. F. Sowa, ed.: Morgan Kaufmann: 401-456.

Chaudhri, V., Farquhar, A., Fikes, R., Karp, P., and Rice, J. 1997. The Generic Frame Protocol 2.0, Technical Report, KSL-97-05, Knowledge Systems Laboratory, Stanford University

Clark, P. and Porter, B. 1997. Building Concept Representations from Reusable Components. In Proceedings of Fourteenth National Conference on Artificial Intelligence, 369-376. Providence, RI: AAAI Press.

Collins, J. W. and Forbus, K. D. 1987. Reasoning About Fluids Via Molecular Collections. In Proceedings of Sixth National Conference on Artificial Intelligence, 590-594. Seattle, WA: AAAI Press.

Farquhar, A., Fikes, R., and Rice, J. 1996. The Ontolingua Server: a Tool for Collaborative Ontology Construction. In Proceedings of Tenth Knowledge Acquisition for Knowledge-Based Systems Workshop. Banff, Canada.

Fikes, R., Cutkosky, M., Gruber, T., and Baalen, J. v. 1991. Knowledge Sharing Technology Project Overview, KSL 91-71, Knowledge System Laboratory, Stanford University

Forbus, K. D. 1984. Qualitative Process Theory. *Artificial Intelligence* 24: 85-168.

Fridman Noy, N. 1997. Knowledge Representation for Intelligent Information Retrieval in Experimental Sciences. Ph.D. diss., College of Computer Science, Northeastern University.

Fridman Noy, N. and Hafner, C. 1997. The State of the Art in Ontology Design: A Survey and Comparative Review. *AI Magazine* 18(3): 53-73.

Gegner, J. A. and Dahlquist, F. W. 1991. Signal transduction in bacteria: CheW forms a reversible complex with the protein kinase CheA. *Proceedings National Academy Sciences* 88: 750-754.

Genesereth, M. R. and Fikes, R. E. 1992. Knowledge Interchange Format, Version 0.3, Reference Manual, Logic-92-1, Knowledge Systems Laboratory, Stanford University

Gruber, T. R. 1992. Ontolingua: A Mechanism to Support Portable Ontologies, Knowledge Systems Laboratory, Stanford University

Gruber, T. R. 1993. Toward Principles for the Design of Ontologies Used for Knowledge Sharing, KSL 93-04, Knowledge Systems Laboratory, Stanford University

Guarino, N., Carrara, M., and Giaretta, P. 1994. Formalizing Ontological Commitments. In Proceedings of Twelfth National Conference on Artificial Intelligence (AAAI '94), 560-568. Seattle, Washington: AAAI Press/ The MIT Press.

Hayes, P. J. 1990. Naive Physics I: Ontology for liquids. *Readings in Qualitative Reasoning about Physical Systems*. D. S. Weld and J. de Kleer, eds.: Morgan Kaufmann, San Mateo, CA: 484-502.

http://www-ksl-svc.stanford.edu:5915/ Stanford KSL Network Services. Palo Alto, CA: Stanford University Knowledge Systems Laboratory.

http://www-ksl-svc.stanford.edu:5915/doc/ontolingua/reference-manual Ontolingua System Reference Manual: Knowledge Systems Lab, Stanford University.

Minsky, M. 1981. A Framework for Representing Knowledge. *Readings in Knowledge Representation*. R. Brachman and H. Levesque, eds.: Morgan Kaufmann Publishers, INC: 245-262.

An Action Language Based on Causal Explanation: Preliminary Report

Enrico Giunchiglia
DIST — Università di Genova
Viale Causa 13
16145 Genova, Italy

Vladimir Lifschitz
Department of Computer Sciences
University of Texas at Austin
Austin, TX 78712, USA

Abstract

Action languages serve for describing changes that are caused by performing actions. We define a new action language $\mathcal{C}$, based on the theory of causal explanation proposed recently by McCain and Turner, and illustrate its expressive power by applying it to a number of examples. The mathematical results presented in the paper relate $\mathcal{C}$ to the Baral—Gelfond theory of concurrent actions.

Introduction

Representing properties of actions has been the subject of many papers and two recent books (Sandewall 1995), (Shanahan 1997). One direction of work makes use of "action languages," such as $\mathcal{A}$ (Gelfond & Lifschitz 1993) and its dialects. An action language serves for describing the effects of actions on fluents. The meaning of a set of propositions in an action language can be represented by a "transition diagram."

In this paper we define a new action language $\mathcal{C}$, based on the theory of causal explanation proposed in (McCain & Turner 1997) and extended in (Lifschitz 1997a). The main idea of this theory (Geffner 1990) is to distinguish between the claim that a formula is true and the stronger claim that there is a *cause* for it to be true. This idea leads to a semantics for "causal rules" of the form

$$F \leftarrow G \qquad (1)$$

where F and G are formulas of classical logic. This rule expresses that there is a cause for F if G is true.

The distinction between being true and being caused is used here to define the syntax and semantics of a language for representing transition diagrams. We use the new language $\mathcal{C}$ to formalize a number of examples of reasoning about action, relate $\mathcal{C}$ to causal logic, and compare it with $\mathcal{A}$ and with the extension of $\mathcal{A}$ proposed by Baral and Gelfond [1997] for describing the concurrent execution of actions.

In this preliminary report, discussion is limited to the propositional fragment of $\mathcal{C}$, in which all fluents are truth-valued, and neither fluents nor actions are allowed to have parameters. The full language is described in a forthcoming paper.

Copyright 1998, American Association for Artificial Intelligence (www.aaai.org). All rights reserved.

Language $\mathcal{C}$

Syntax and Semantics

A *propositional signature* is a set of propositional atoms. An *interpretation* of a propositional signature σ is a truth-valued function defined on σ.

Consider a propositional signature σ partitioned into the *fluent symbols* σ^{fl} and the *action symbols* σ^{act}. An *action* is an interpretation of σ^{act}. We will identify an action symbol A with the action that assigns the value t to A and the value f to all other action symbols. Such actions will be called *elementary*. An action can be viewed as a set of elementary actions—as the set of all action symbols to which it assigns t. Intuitively, to execute an action a means to execute concurrently all elementary actions that belong to a.

There are two kinds of propositions in $\mathcal{C}$: *static laws* of the form

$$\textbf{caused } F \textbf{ if } G \qquad (2)$$

and *dynamic laws* of the form

$$\textbf{caused } F \textbf{ if } G \textbf{ after } H, \qquad (3)$$

where F, G, H are formulas of σ such that F and G do not contain action symbols. In a proposition of either kind, the formula F will be called its *head*.

An *action description* is a set of propositions.

Consider an action description D. A *state* is an interpretation of σ^{fl} that satisfies $G \supset F$ for every static law (2) in D. A *transition* is any triple $\langle s, a, s' \rangle$ where s, s' are states and a is an action; s is the *initial* state of the transition, and s' is its *resulting* state. A formula F is *caused* in a transition $\langle s, a, s' \rangle$ if it is

- the head of a static law (2) from D such that s' satisfies G, or
- the head of a dynamic law (3) from D such that s' satisfies G and $s \cup a$ satisfies H.

A transition $\langle s, a, s' \rangle$ is *causally explained* according to D if its resulting state s' is the only interpretation of σ^{fl} that satisfies all formulas caused in this transition.

The *transition diagram* represented by an action description D is the directed graph which has the states of D as nodes, and which includes an edge from s to s' labeled a for every transition $\langle s, a, s' \rangle$ that is causally explained according to D.

Two abbreviations are useful. A dynamic law of the form[1]

caused F **if** *True* **after** H

will be written as

caused F **after** H.

Such propositions can be used to describe a direct effect of an elementary action. In this case F is the formula that is made true by executing this action (no matter what other elementary actions are performed concurrently), and H is the conjunction of the elementary action with the preconditions for its effect. Second, a dynamic law of the form

caused F **if** F **after** F

will be written as

inertial F.

Such propositions can be used to express the commonsense law of inertia understood as in (McCain & Turner 1997): if F has remained true then there is a cause for this.

We will combine a group of propositions

inertial F_1, **inertial** F_2, ...

into

inertial $F_1, F_2 \ldots$.

Example

Let $\sigma^{fl} = \{P, Q\}$, $\sigma^{act} = \{A\}$, and let D consist of the propositions

$$\begin{aligned}&\textbf{inertial } P, \neg P, Q, \neg Q,\\ &\textbf{caused } P \textbf{ after } Q \wedge A.\end{aligned} \qquad (4)$$

The second line of (4) tells us that P is made true by the execution of A if the precondition Q is satisfied (as, for instance, in the familiar shooting example which corresponds to *Dead* as P, *Loaded* as Q, and *Shoot* as A).

According to the definitions above, (4) is shorthand for

$$\begin{aligned}&\textbf{caused } P \textbf{ if } P \textbf{ after } P,\\ &\textbf{caused } \neg P \textbf{ if } \neg P \textbf{ after } \neg P,\\ &\textbf{caused } Q \textbf{ if } Q \textbf{ after } Q,\\ &\textbf{caused } \neg Q \textbf{ if } \neg Q \textbf{ after } \neg Q,\\ &\textbf{caused } P \textbf{ if } \textit{True} \textbf{ after } Q \wedge A.\end{aligned} \qquad (5)$$

In this action description, there are 4 states (PQ, $P\overline{Q}$, $\overline{P}Q$, $\overline{P}\,\overline{Q}$)[2] and 2 actions ($A$ and $\overline{A}$). Consequently there are $4 \times 2 \times 4 = 32$ transitions. Out of these, 8 transitions are causally explained: $\langle \overline{P}Q, A, PQ \rangle$ and the transitions of the form $\langle s, a, s \rangle$ where $s \neq \overline{P}Q$ or $a \neq A$.

---

[1] *True* stands for *False* $\supset$ *False*, where *False* is a 0-place connective assumed to be available in the language of propositional logic.

[2] We represent a propositional interpretation by listing the literals that are satisfied by it. $\overline{L}$ is the literal complementary to L.

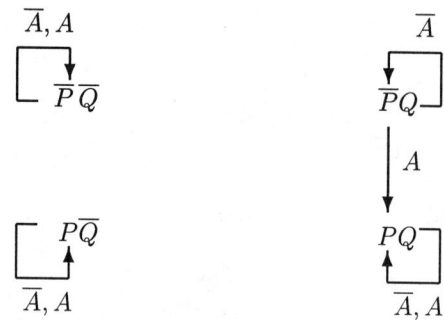

Figure 1: Transition diagram for action description (4).

Figure 1 shows the corresponding transition diagram. We can see from it that each of the actions A, $\overline{A}$ can be executed in any state in exactly one way.

To check that the transition $\langle \overline{P}Q, A, PQ \rangle$ is causally explained, note that the formulas caused in this transition are the heads Q, P of the 3rd and 5th propositions in (5), and that the resulting state PQ of the transition is the only interpretation that satisfies both heads.

As another illustration of the definition, let us verify that $\langle \overline{P}Q, \overline{A}, PQ \rangle$ is not causally explained. The only formula caused in this transition is the head Q of the 3rd proposition in (5). It is satisfied by more than one interpretation.

The mathematical theory presented in the next section makes it easier to compute the causally explained transitions in examples like this.

Relation to $\mathcal{A}$

"Effect propositions" of the language $\mathcal{A}$ from (Gelfond & Lifschitz 1993) are essentially part of the new language $\mathcal{C}$. They correspond to dynamic laws of the form

caused L **after** $F \wedge A$ \qquad (6)

where L is a literal, F a formula that does not contain action symbols, and A an action symbol. Propositions of this form will be called $\mathcal{A}$-propositions.

An action description D is an $\mathcal{A}$-description if it is the union of the set of propositions

inertial $P, \neg P$

for all fluent symbols P with a set of $\mathcal{A}$-propositions. For instance, (4) is an $\mathcal{A}$-description. Proposition 1 below shows that the transitions causally explained by an $\mathcal{A}$-description are characterized by the semantics that is given to effect propositions in the definition of $\mathcal{A}$.

To state this theorem, we need the following definitions. Let D be an $\mathcal{A}$-description. For any state s, action a and literal L of the fluent signature, we say that executing a in s causes L if D includes a dynamic law (6) with the head L such that $a \cup s$ satisfies $F \wedge A$. A transition $\langle s, a, s' \rangle$ is an $\mathcal{A}$-transition for D if s' satisfies every literal L such that

- executing a in s causes L, or
- executing a in s does not cause $\overline{L}$, and s satisfies L.

Proposition 1 *For any $\mathcal{A}$-description D, a transition is an $\mathcal{A}$-transition for D iff it is causally explained according to D.*

Note that this characterization is applicable to a transition $\langle s, a, s' \rangle$ even when a is not elementary, although such transitions are not covered by the semantics of $\mathcal{A}$.

Computing Causally Explained Transitions

According to (Lifschitz 1997a), a *causal theory* is a finite set of rules (1), with some of the nonlogical constants of the underlying language designated as *explainable*. In this paper we only need the special case when the language is propositional.

The semantics of causal theories is defined in (Lifschitz 1997a) by a translation that turns these theories into formulas of classical logic. A *model* of a causal theory T is an interpretation that satisfies the translation of T. A *theorem* of T is a formula that is entailed by the translation of T.

The formula representing T in classical logic is stronger than the conjunction of the material implications $G \supset F$ for all rules (1) of T; it contains an additional conjunctive term which makes the translation nonmonotonic (and which is similar in this sense to the minimality condition in the definition of circumscription). Details can be found in (Lifschitz 1997a); it is not necessary to know them to understand the computational procedure described below.

In the first of the next two subsections we define, for any positive integer n, a translation ct_n that turns any finite action description D into a causal theory. The models of $ct_n(D)$ correspond to "histories" of length n—to the paths of length n in the transition diagram represented by D. In particular, the models of $ct_1(D)$ correspond to the transitions causally explained according to D. The second subsection describes the process of literal completion, proposed in (McCain & Turner 1997) and generalized in (Lifschitz 1997a), which can be used to find the models of such theories.

Representing Histories in Causal Logic

The translation $ct_n(D)$ of an action description D is defined as follows. Its signature σ_n consists of $n+1$ disjoint copies σ_i^{fl} ($0 \leq i \leq n$) of the fluent signature σ^{fl} and n disjoint copies σ_i^{act} ($0 \leq i < n$) of the action signature σ^{act}. For any formula F of the original signature σ, by F_i we denote the result of replacing every atom in F by the corresponding atom from σ_i^{fl} or from σ_i^{act}. Intuitively, the subscript i represents time. For any fluent symbol P, the atom P_i expresses that P holds at time i. For any action symbol A, the atom A_i expresses that A is among the elementary actions executed between times i and $i+1$.

The rules of $ct_n(D)$ are

$$F_i \leftarrow G_i \qquad (0 \leq i \leq n)$$

for all static laws (2) in D, and

$$F_{i+1} \leftarrow G_{i+1} \wedge H_i \qquad (0 \leq i < n)$$

for all dynamic laws (3) in D. The explainable symbols of $ct_n(D)$ are the atoms from σ_i^{fl} for all $i > 0$.

For instance, the result of applying the translation ct_1 to action description (4) is the causal theory whose rules are

$$\begin{aligned} P_1 &\leftarrow P_1 \wedge P_0, \\ \neg P_1 &\leftarrow \neg P_1 \wedge \neg P_0, \\ Q_1 &\leftarrow Q_1 \wedge Q_0, \\ \neg Q_1 &\leftarrow \neg Q_1 \wedge \neg Q_0, \\ P_1 &\leftarrow True \wedge Q_0 \wedge A_0 \end{aligned} \qquad (7)$$

and whose explainable symbols are P_1 and Q_1.

Proposition 2 below shows that there is a one-to-one correspondence between the models of $ct_n(D)$ and the paths of length n in the transition diagram represented by D. To define this correspondence, we need the following notation. Let I be an interpretation of σ_n. For any $i \leq n$, the interpretation $State_i[I]$ of σ^{fl} is defined by the condition: for every fluent symbol P,

$$State_i[I](P) = I(P_i).$$

For any $i < n$, the interpretation $Action_i[I]$ of σ^{act} is defined by the condition: for every action symbol A,

$$Action_i[I](A) = I(A_i).$$

Proposition 2 *For any finite action description D and positive integer n, an interpretation I of σ_n is a model of $ct_n(D)$ iff each of the triples*

$$\langle State_i[I], Action_i[I], State_{i+1}[I] \rangle \qquad (0 \leq i < n)$$

is a transition causally explained by D.

For instance, the claim that $\langle \overline{P}Q, A, PQ \rangle$ is a transition causally explained by (4) can be equivalently expressed by saying that the interpretation $\overline{P_0}Q_0 A_0 P_1 Q_1$ is a model of causal theory (7). The problem of computing all transitions that are causally explained by (4) is equivalent to the problem of finding all models of (7).

Literal Completion

The formula of classical logic that represents the meaning of a causal theory contains, generally, bound second-order variables. In case of a propositional causal theory, these variables are propositional and can be always eliminated, although the formula can become much longer in the process.

There is a special case, however—the case of "definite" theories—when a modification of the process of completion familiar from logic programming (Clark 1978) allows us to construct a short formula that is equivalent to the given causal theory and has no new higher-order variables.

In the propositional case, a causal theory T is *definite* if the head F of every rule $F \leftarrow G$ of T is a literal or contains no explainable symbols. For instance, (7) is definite. Generally, if the head of every proposition in an action description D is a literal then $ct_n(D)$ is a definite causal theory.

Literal completion differs from Clark's completion in that the "completed definition" of any explainable symbol P consists of *two* equivalences, one "positive" and one "negative." The positive completion formula is obtained from the rules whose head is P in exactly the same way as in (Clark 1978). The negative completion formula is generated in a similar way from the rules whose head is $\neg P$. In addition, for every rule $F \leftarrow G$ whose head F does not contain explainable symbols, there is a corresponding completion formula, which is simply the material implication $G \supset F$. The conjunction of all completion formulas for a definite causal theory T is equivalent to the formula representing T in classical logic.

For instance, the set of completion formulas for causal theory (7) consists of the positive definition of P_1
$$P_1 \equiv (P_1 \wedge P_0) \vee (Q_0 \wedge A_0), \tag{8}$$
the negative definition of P_1
$$\neg P_1 \equiv \neg P_1 \wedge \neg P_0, \tag{9}$$
the positive definition of Q_1
$$Q_1 \equiv Q_1 \wedge Q_0 \tag{10}$$
and the negative definition of Q_1
$$\neg Q_1 \equiv \neg Q_1 \wedge \neg Q_0. \tag{11}$$
Causal theory (7) is equivalent to the conjunction of these formulas.

To simplify this conjunction, note that (9) can be rewritten as
$$P_0 \supset P_1, \tag{12}$$
and (10), (11) can be rewritten as
$$Q_1 \supset Q_0,$$
$$Q_0 \supset Q_1.$$
In the presence of (12), (8) is equivalent to
$$P_1 \equiv P_0 \vee (Q_0 \wedge A_0). \tag{13}$$
The last formula entails (12). Consequently, the conjunction of (8)–(11) is equivalent to the conjunction of (13) and
$$Q_1 \equiv Q_0. \tag{14}$$
We conclude that causal theory (7) is equivalent to the conjunction of (13) and (14). These formulas define P_1 and Q_1 in terms of P_0, Q_0 and A_0. Consequently, (7) has 8 models, corresponding to the interpretations of $\{P_0, Q_0, A_0\}$. These models represent the 8 transitions shown in Figure 1.

The same procedure is applicable when $n > 1$. The result of applying the translation ct_n to action description (4) consists of $5n$ rules
$$P_{i+1} \leftarrow P_{i+1} \wedge P_i,$$
$$\neg P_{i+1} \leftarrow \neg P_{i+1} \wedge \neg P_i,$$
$$Q_{i+1} \leftarrow Q_{i+1} \wedge Q_i,$$
$$\neg Q_{i+1} \leftarrow \neg Q_{i+1} \wedge \neg Q_i,$$
$$P_{i+1} \leftarrow Q_i \wedge A_i$$

for all $i < n$, with $P_1, \ldots, P_n, Q_1, \ldots, Q_n$ explainable. (We dropped the trivial conjunctive term *True* in the last rule.) The literal completion of this theory is equivalent to the conjunction of $2n$ formulas
$$P_{i+1} \equiv P_i \vee (Q_i \wedge A_i),$$
$$Q_{i+1} \equiv Q_i$$
for all $i < n$. The models of this set of formulas represent paths of length n in the graph shown in Figure 1.

Example: Loading and Shooting
The Shooting Domain
The shooting scenario from (Hanks & McDermott 1987) involves three actions: *Load*, *Wait* and *Shoot*. In $\mathcal{C}$, there is no need to introduce *Wait* as an elementary action, because it can be identified with the empty set of elementary actions. On the other hand, since there is an action in $\mathcal{C}$ that includes both *Load* and *Shoot*, we may wish to postulate that these two elementary actions cannot be executed concurrently. For any conjunction H of action symbols, we will write

nonexecutable H

for

caused *False* **after** H.

The shooting domain is characterized by the propositions

inertial *Loaded*, $\neg$*Loaded*, *Alive*, $\neg$*Alive*,
caused *Loaded* **after** *Load*,
caused $\neg$*Alive* **after** *Loaded* $\wedge$ *Shoot*, (15)
caused $\neg$*Loaded* **after** *Shoot*,
nonexecutable *Load* $\wedge$ *Shoot*.

Computing Causally Explained Transitions
The ct_1 translation of (15) is a definite causal theory. (The head of the rule corresponding to the last line of (15) is *False* and consequently does not contain explainable symbols.) Having simplified the set of completion formulas for this translation, we get:

$$Loaded_1 \equiv Load_0 \vee (Loaded_0 \wedge \neg Shoot_0),$$
$$Alive_1 \equiv Alive_0 \wedge \neg(Loaded_0 \wedge Shoot_0), \tag{16}$$
$$\neg(Load_0 \wedge Shoot_0).$$

The first two of these formulas define $Loaded_1$ and $Alive_1$ in terms of
$$Loaded_0, Alive_0, Load_0, Shoot_0. \tag{17}$$
Consequently, the edges of the transition diagram for (15) correspond to the interpretations of (17) that satisfy the last of formulas (16). Any proper subset of the set of elementary actions $\{Load, Shoot\}$ can be executed in any state in exactly one way.

More generally, the ct_n translation of (15) is equivalent to the conjunction of the formulas

$$Loaded_{i+1} \equiv Load_i \vee (Loaded_i \wedge \neg Shoot_i),$$
$$Alive_{i+1} \equiv Alive_i \wedge \neg(Loaded_i \wedge Shoot_i), \tag{18}$$
$$\neg(Load_i \wedge Shoot_i)$$

for all $i < n$.

Temporal Reasoning

The "Yale Shooting Problem" (Hanks & McDermott 1987) and the "Stanford Murder Mystery" (Baker 1991) correspond to propositional reasoning problems involving formulas (18). In the first case, the goal is to establish that $\neg Alive_3$ is entailed by

$$Load_0, \neg Shoot_0,$$
$$\neg Load_1, \neg Shoot_1,$$
$$\neg Load_2, Shoot_2$$

conjoined with formulas (18) for all $i < 3$. The second problem is to establish that $Loaded_0$ is entailed by

$$Alive_0,$$
$$\neg Load_0, \neg Shoot_0,$$
$$\neg Load_1, Shoot_1,$$
$$\neg Alive_2$$

conjoined with formulas (18) for all $i < 2$. Both claims can be easily verified.

Expressive Possibilities of $\mathcal{C}$

Action Preconditions

In action description (15), $Loaded$ is a "fluent precondition" for the action $Shoot$: if it is not satisfied then the action is still possible to execute, although its effect on the fluent $Alive$ is not guaranteed. We may wish to treat $Loaded$ as an "action precondition," that is to say, to postulate that the action $Shoot$ is nonexecutable when $Loaded$ is false.

It is convenient to extend the notation previously introduced as follows: if H is a conjunction of action symbols and F is a formula that does not contain action symbols, we will write

nonexecutable H **if** F

for

caused $False$ **after** $H \wedge F$.

In the following modification of (15), $Loaded$ is an action precondition for $Shoot$:

inertial $Loaded, \neg Loaded, Alive, \neg Alive,$
caused $Loaded$ **after** $Load,$
caused $\neg Alive$ **after** $Shoot,$
caused $\neg Loaded$ **after** $Shoot,$
nonexecutable $Shoot$ **if** $\neg Loaded,$
nonexecutable $Load \wedge Shoot.$

The ct_1 translation of this domain description is equivalent to

$Loaded_1 \equiv Load_0 \vee (Loaded_0 \wedge \neg Shoot_0),$
$Alive_1 \equiv Alive_0 \wedge \neg Shoot_0,$
$Shoot_0 \supset (Loaded_0 \wedge \neg Load_0).$

Indirect Effects and Implicit Preconditions

So far we have not had a chance to use static laws—propositions of form (2). As observed in (Lin 1995) and (McCain & Turner 1995), a static law can play two roles in reasoning about action. First, postulating **caused** F **if** G may allow us to conclude that an action has an indirect effect: any action that causes G to become true will also indirectly cause F to become true. Second, we may be able to conclude that an action has an implicit precondition: an action that causes F to become false is not executable if G is true (unless it causes G to change its truth value also).

For instance, if an object is submerged in water then there is a cause for it to be wet. The action of putting a puppy in water causes it to be in water; consequently, it has an indirect effect: it will make the puppy wet. The action of drying a puppy with a towel causes it to be dry; consequently, it has an implicit precondition: it is impossible to dry a puppy with a towel when it is in water.

This example can be formalized in $\mathcal{C}$ as follows:

inertial $InWater, \neg InWater, Wet, \neg Wet,$
caused $InWater$ **after** $PutInWater,$ (19)
caused $\neg Wet$ **after** $DryWithTowel,$
caused Wet **if** $InWater.$

The states of action description (19) are the interpretations of the fluent signature $\{InWater, Wet\}$ that satisfy

$$InWater \supset Wet;$$

there are 3 such interpretations. To find the causally explained transitions, we write out the completion formulas for the ct_1 translation of (19) and simplify them. The result can be written in the form

$InWater_1 \equiv InWater_0 \vee PutInWater_0,$
$Wet_1 \equiv (Wet_0 \wedge \neg DryWithTowel_0) \vee PutInWater_0,$
$InWater_0 \supset Wet_0,$
$DryWithTowel_0 \supset (\neg InWater_0 \wedge \neg PutInWater_0).$

The first two formulas characterize $InWater_1$ and Wet_1 in terms of the other atoms; they show that any action can be performed in at most one way. The second disjunctive term in the second line represents the indirect effect of $PutInWater$ on Wet. The third line says that the initial state of a transition is indeed a state. The last line shows that the action $DryWithTowel$ can be executed only when $InWater$ is false—this is the implicit precondition mentioned above—and also that this action cannot be executed concurrently with $PutInWater$.

Nondeterminism

When Jack goes to work, he can walk there or, if his car is in his garage, he can drive. The action $GoToWork$ always makes the fluent $JackAtWork$ true; it will also make the fluent $CarInGarage$ false if Jack chooses to drive. One of the two effects of $GoToWork$ is nondeterministic.

We will use

possibly caused F **after** H

as an abbreviation for

caused F **if** F **after** H.

The example above can be formalized as follows:

inertial $JackAtWork, \neg JackAtWork$,
inertial $CarInGarage, \neg CarInGarage$,
caused $JackAtWork$ **after** $GoToWork$,
possibly caused $\neg CarInGarage$
        after $CarInGarage \wedge GoToWork$,
nonexecutable $GoToWork$ **if** $JackAtWork$.

The ct_1 translation of this action description is equivalent to

$JackAtWork_1 \equiv JackAtWork_0 \vee GoToWork_0$,
$\neg GoToWork_0 \supset (CarInGarage_1 \equiv CarInGarage_0)$,
$CarInGarage_1 \supset CarInGarage_0$,
$\neg(JackAtWork_0 \wedge GoToWork_0)$.

The nondeterministic behavior of $CarInGarage$ is described by the two formulas in the middle. After performing the action $GoToWork$ in a state in which $CarInGarage$ is true, this fluent can either remain true or become false. The corresponding transition diagram has two edges that are labeled $GoToWork$ and begin in the state in which $JackAtWork$ is false and $CarInGarage$ is true.

Regarding the abbreviation **possibly caused** we can observe that

inertial F

is identical to

possibly caused F **after** F.

Noninertial Fluents

In all examples so far, every literal in the fluent signature was postulated to be inertial. In some useful action descriptions this is not the case.

We would not assume inertia, first of all, for a fluent that is explicitly defined in terms of other fluents. Imagine, for instance, that we want to enhance the shooting domain by saying that the potential victim is in danger if he is alive and the gun is loaded. This idea can be formalized by adding $InDanger$ to the fluent signature, and adding the static law

caused $InDanger \equiv (Alive \wedge Loaded)$ **if** $True$. (20)

to action description (15). This amounts to adding the formulas

$InDanger_i \equiv Alive_i \wedge Loaded_i \quad (i = 0, 1)$

to the formulas of classical logic representing the ct_1 translation of (15).

There is no need to assume inertia for the new fluent in this example. Actually, adding

inertial $InDanger, \neg InDanger$

to (15) along with (20) would have led to unintuitive results. (The execution of $Load$ in the state in which $Loaded$ is false and $Alive$ is true would be nondeterministic: it would be possible for both fluents to be affected.)

Note that the head of (20) is not a literal, so that the literal completion method is not applicable to the corresponding causal theory. But this proposition can be equivalently replaced here by a pair of propositions whose head are literals:

caused $InDanger$ **if** $Alive \wedge Loaded$,
caused $\neg InDanger$ **if** $\neg(Alive \wedge Loaded)$.

Second, there are fluents whose values tend to change in a specific way, rather than remain unchanged. Consider, for instance, a pendulum that moves from its leftmost position to the rightmost and back, with each swing taking one unit of time. We want to describe the action of holding the pendulum steady in its current position for the duration of one unit of time. In the following action description, $Right$ is a fluent symbol, and $Hold$ is an action symbol:

possibly caused $Right$ **after** $\neg Right$,
possibly caused $\neg Right$ **after** $Right$,
caused $Right$ **after** $Right \wedge Hold$,
caused $\neg Right$ **after** $\neg Right \wedge Hold$.
      (21)

The first two lines of (21) are similar to the inertia assumption but different: if the pendulum has changed its position then there is a cause for this. The "normal" behavior of an unloaded gun is to remain unloaded; the "normal" behavior of a pendulum in the leftmost position is to move to the rightmost position.

The completion formulas for the ct_1 translation of (21) are equivalent to

$Right_1 \equiv (Hold_0 \equiv Right_0)$.

The pendulum is in the rightmost position in two cases: if it was in this position earlier and was held there, and if it was in the leftmost position earlier and was not held there.

Finally, some fluents have a "default" value that they take unless an action causes them to take a different value. A spring-loaded door is closed unless someone has just opened it; its behavior is not described by inertia. For any formula F without action symbols, let

default F

stand for the static law

caused F **if** F

—if F holds then there is a cause for this. Several propositions of this form can be combined like inertia propositions.

A spring-loaded door is characterized by the following action description:

default $Closed$,
caused $\neg Closed$ **after** $OpenDoor$.

Its ct_1 translation is equivalent to

$Closed_1 \equiv \neg OpenDoor_0$.

The door is closed unless it has just been opened.

Interaction between Concurrent Actions

Pednault [1987] considers lifting the opposite ends of a table upon which various objects have been placed. If one end of the table has been raised, a cup on the table falls off. But if both ends are lifted simultaneously, the cup remains fixed.

Formalizing (a modification of) this example in the situation calculus is discussed in Section 8.3.2 of (Gelfond, Lifschitz, & Rabinov 1991). Baral and Gelfond [1997] expressed Pednault's example in their action language $\mathcal{A}_C$ (see the next section). Turner [1996] formalized it using a static law, and our representation of this example in $\mathcal{C}$ is based on the same idea.

We describe the positions of the two ends of the table by the fluents $Up1$ and $Up2$. By default, these fluents are false, that is, normally the two sides are not in their up position. These fluents can be made true by performing the actions $Raise1$ and $Raise2$. The fluent $OnTable$ indicates that the cup is on the table. This last fluent is inertial.

Our formalization of the lifting example consists of the following propositions:

> **inertial** $OnTable, \neg OnTable$,
> **default** $\neg Up1, \neg Up2$,
> **caused** $Up1$ **after** $Raise1$,
> **caused** $Up2$ **after** $Raise2$,
> **caused** $\neg OnTable$ **if** $\neg(Up1 \equiv Up2)$.

The ct_1 translation of this action description is equivalent to

$Up1_1 \equiv Raise1_0$,
$Up2_1 \equiv Raise2_0$,
$OnTable_1 \equiv OnTable_0 \wedge (Raise1_0 \equiv Raise2_0)$,
$OnTable_0 \supset (Up1_0 \equiv Up2_0)$.

Embedding $\mathcal{A}_C$ into $\mathcal{C}$

In this section we analyze the relationship between the treatment of concurrency in two action languages—$\mathcal{A}_C$ from (Baral & Gelfond 1997) and the new language $\mathcal{C}$—by embedding the former into the latter.

The Language $\mathcal{A}_C$

The main idea of $\mathcal{A}_C$ is that the effects of a set of elementary actions are "inherited" from its subsets, and that this inheritance is defeasible.

To specify an action description in the language $\mathcal{A}_C$, just as in case of $\mathcal{C}$, we first select a set of fluent symbols σ^{fl} and a set of action symbols σ^{act}. An *action* is a finite subset of σ^{act}.

An *action description* in the language $\mathcal{A}_C$ is a set of propositions of the form

$$a \text{ causes } L \text{ after } F, \qquad (22)$$

where a is an action, L a literal of the fluent signature, and F a formula of the fluent signature. We will abbreviate (22) as $\langle a, L, F \rangle$.

The semantics of $\mathcal{A}_C$ is defined as follows. Consider an action description D in this language. A *state* is an interpretation of the fluent signature. For any action a, state s and literal L of the fluent signature, we say that executing a in s *causes* L if there exists a proposition $\langle a', L, F \rangle$ in D such that

- $a' \subseteq a$,
- s satisfies F, and
- there is no proposition $\langle a'', \overline{L}, G \rangle$ in D such that

$$a' \subset a'' \subseteq a$$

and s satisfies G.

Thus a proposition (22) of the Baral—Gelfond language tells us what the effect of the supersets of a might be; in case of conflict, the "more specific" proposition applies. Finally, we say that a state s' is the *result* of executing a in s if s' satisfies every literal L such that

- executing a in s causes L, or
- executing a in s does not cause $\overline{L}$, and s satisfies L.

It is clear that, for any a and s, there can be at most one such resulting state s'.

Consider, for instance, an $\mathcal{A}_C$ description of the form

$$\begin{array}{l} \{A_1\} \text{ causes } L \text{ after } F_1, \\ \{A_1, A_2\} \text{ causes } \overline{L} \text{ after } F_2. \end{array} \qquad (23)$$

If a does not include A_1 then the execution of a in any state s has no effect on s. If a includes A_1 but not A_2, and s satisfies F_1, then the resulting state s' satisfies L. If a includes both A_1 and A_2, and s satisfies F_1, then s' satisfies $\overline{L}$ or L depending on whether or not s satisfies F_2.

The characterization of $\mathcal{A}_C$ above differs from (Baral & Gelfond 1997) in a number of details. Baral and Gelfond require that F in (22) be a conjunction of literals, and write **if** instead of **after**. Their language includes "v-propositions" that we do not discuss here; our version is the "action description component" (Lifschitz 1997b) of theirs.

First Translation from $\mathcal{A}_C$ into $\mathcal{C}$

Consider a finite action description D in the language $\mathcal{A}_C$. We will define the corresponding action description $c_1(D)$ in $\mathcal{C}$. To simplify notation, we will identify an action a with the conjunction of the action symbols that belong to it. The description $c_1(D)$ consists of the dynamic laws

$$\textbf{caused } L \textbf{ after } (a \wedge F) \wedge \bigwedge_{\substack{a', G: \\ \langle a', \overline{L}, G \rangle \in D,\, a \subset a'}} \neg(a' \wedge G) \qquad (24)$$

for all propositions (22) in D, and of the inertia propositions

$$\textbf{inertial } P, \neg P \qquad (25)$$

for all fluent symbols P.

Knowledge Representation 629

For instance, the translation of (23) into $\mathcal{C}$ includes

caused L **after** $A_1 \wedge F_1 \wedge \neg(A_1 \wedge A_2 \wedge F_2)$,
caused $\overline{L}$ **after** $A_1 \wedge A_2 \wedge F_2$

and the inertia propositions.

The following theorem shows that the translation c_1 preserves the meaning of action descriptions.

Proposition 3 *For any finite action description D in the language $\mathcal{A}_C$, a state s' is the result of executing an action a in a state s iff $\langle s, a, s' \rangle$ is a transition causally explained by $c_1(D)$.*

Second Translation from $\mathcal{A}_C$ into $\mathcal{C}$

The translation c_1 is applicable to finite descriptions only: without this restriction, the set of conjunctive terms in (24) can be infinite. Furthermore, c_1 is not "elaboration tolerant," in the sense that adding a proposition to D requires, generally, that some of the propositions in $c_1(D)$ be modified. We therefore define a second translation c_2 in which these defects are corrected.

The fluent signature of $c_2(D)$ includes, along with every fluent symbol P of the description D, the atoms P^a for all actions a such that D includes a proposition (22) with $|L| = P$.[3] Intuitively, P^a means that the given action description "allows" a to modify P.

The translation $c_2(D)$ consists of the following propositions:

- for each proposition (22) in D, the dynamic law

  caused L **if** $|L|^a$ **after** $a \wedge F$

  and, for all propositions $\langle a', \overline{L}, G \rangle$ in D such that $a' \subset a$, the dynamic law

  caused $\neg |L|^{a'}$ **after** $a \wedge F$;

- for each of the additional fluent symbols P^a, the static law

  default P^a;

- the inertia propositions (25) for each fluent symbol P from D.

For example, the new translation of (23), with $|L|^{\{A_1\}}$ and $|L|^{\{A_1, A_2\}}$ abbreviated as P_1 and P_2, consists of the propositions

caused L **if** P_1 **after** $A_1 \wedge F_1$,
caused $\overline{L}$ **if** P_2 **after** $A_1 \wedge A_2 \wedge F_2$,
caused $\neg P_1$ **after** $A_1 \wedge A_2 \wedge F_2$,
default $P_i \quad (i = 1, 2)$

and the inertia propositions (25) for all fluent symbols P from (23).

Proposition 4 *For any action description D in the language $\mathcal{A}_C$, a state s' is the result of executing an action a in a state s iff there exists a transition $\langle s_1, a, s'_1 \rangle$ causally explained by $c_2(D)$ such that s and s' are the results of restricting s_1 and, respectively, s'_1 to the fluent signature of D.*

---

[3] By $|L|$ we denote the atom contained in the literal L.

Acknowledgements

We are grateful to Norman McCain and Hudson Turner for useful discussions on the subject of this paper. This work was partially supported by National Science Foundation under grant IRI-9306751.

References

Baker, A. 1991. Nonmonotonic reasoning in the framework of situation calculus. *Artificial Intelligence* 49:5–23.

Baral, C., and Gelfond, M. 1997. Reasoning about effects of concurrent actions. *Journal of Logic Programming* 31.

Clark, K. 1978. Negation as failure. In Gallaire, H., and Minker, J., eds., *Logic and Data Bases*. New York: Plenum Press. 293–322.

Geffner, H. 1990. Causal theories for nonmonotonic reasoning. In *Proc. AAAI-90*, 524–530.

Gelfond, M., and Lifschitz, V. 1993. Representing action and change by logic programs. *Journal of Logic Programming* 17:301–322.

Gelfond, M.; Lifschitz, V.; and Rabinov, A. 1991. What are the limitations of the situation calculus? In Boyer, R., ed., *Automated Reasoning: Essays in Honor of Woody Bledsoe*. Kluwer. 167–179.

Hanks, S., and McDermott, D. 1987. Nonmonotonic logic and temporal projection. *Artificial Intelligence* 33(3):379–412.

Lifschitz, V. 1997a. On the logic of causal explanation. *Artificial Intelligence* 96:451–465.

Lifschitz, V. 1997b. Two components of an action language. *Annals of Mathematics and Artificial Intelligence* 21:305–320.

Lin, F. 1995. Embracing causality in specifying the indirect effects of actions. In *Proc. IJCAI-95*, 1985–1991.

McCain, N., and Turner, H. 1995. A causal theory of ramifications and qualifications. In *Proc. IJCAI-95*, 1978–1984.

McCain, N., and Turner, H. 1997. Causal theories of action and change. In *Proc. AAAI-97*, 460–465.

Pednault, E. 1987. Formulating multi-agent, dynamic world problems in the classical planning framework. In Georgeff, M., and Lansky, A., eds., *Reasoning about Actions and Plans*. San Mateo, CA: Morgan Kaufmann. 47–82.

Sandewall, E. 1995. *Features and Fluents*, volume 1. Oxford University Press.

Shanahan, M. 1997. *Solving the Frame Problem: A Mathematical Investigation of the Common Sense Law of Inertia*. MIT Press.

Turner, H. 1996. Splitting a default theory. In *Proc. AAAI-96*, 645–651.

Abductive Planning with Sensing

Matthew Stone

Department of Computer and Information Science
University of Pennsylvania
200 South 33rd St, Philadelphia PA 19104-6389
matthew@linc.cis.upenn.edu

Abstract

In abductive planning, plans are constructed as reasons for an agent to act: plans are demonstrations in logical theory of action that a goal will result assuming that given actions occur successfully. This paper shows how to construct plans abductively for an agent that can sense the world to augment its partial information. We use a formalism that explicitly refers not only to time but also to the information on which the agent deliberates. Goals are reformulated to represent the successive stages of deliberation and action the agent follows in carrying out a course of action, while constraints on assumed actions ensure that an agent at each step performs a specific action selected for its known effects. The result is a simple formalism that can directly inform extensions to implemented planners.

Introduction

In this paper, we take a view of planning as ABDUCTION: A plan is (or at least comes with) a logical demonstration that a desired goal will be achieved, assuming the agent follows a specified course of action. To build a plan is simply to prove the goal, abductively assuming the occurrence of appropriate actions as necessary. In this framework, special-purpose planning algorithms, as in (McAllister and Rosenblitt, 1991; Penberthy and Weld, 1992), have been faithfully reconstructed and then extended to richer kinds of action using frameworks such as the event calculus (see e.g. (Shanahan, 1997)) and explanation closure (see e.g. (Ferguson, 1995)).

In existing abductive planning frameworks, and indeed most implemented planners, the plan shows that the agent can now commit to a specified sequence of actions that will achieve the goal. But a rational agent need not make all its decisions immediately. It can just as well defer choices of future actions to later steps of deliberation. Plans can and should guide these later steps of deliberation, but only if they anticipate the NEW reasons to act afforded by the agent's increased future information.

Traditional theories of action and knowledge (Moore, 1985; Morgenstern, 1987; Davis, 1994) suggest that searching for plans becomes vastly more complicated when this increasing information is taken into account. The problem is that these theories are based on NAMING plans, using object-level terms that must be specified in advance without reference to the agent's knowledge. This introduces two new and artificial search problems.

The first problem is that actions must be described indirectly in the plan. For example, suppose an agent plans to look up Bill in the phone book, then call him. From the agent's point of view, when it makes the call, it will just dial some number n. But since the value of n is settled in a future situation, n cannot be included in a term that specifies the plan fully in advance. Instead, the plan must include a characterization that indirectly describes this action, like *dialing Bill's phone number*. This means that even after the right action is found, a planner still has to search to find an independent description strong enough to show that the action achieves its intended effects.

The second problem is that planners must reason about FOLLOWING THE PLAN, not simply about acting in the world. Not every description corresponds to an action or plan that the agent can carry out: the description might appeal to a fact that the agent will not know. To avoid this, plan reasoning must map out the control structure of the plan in advance and compare the knowledge required by that control structure and the knowledge the agent can expect to have, at each step of execution.

One approach is to avoid these problems using heavy limitations on the syntax and semantics of parameterized actions (Levesque, 1996; Goldman and Boddy, 1996; Golden and Weld, 1996). This paper takes a very different approach. We simply add the idea of CHOICE directly into the characterization of achieving a goal. Any future situation offers the agent a number of concrete actions to take. To choose one of these, an agent simply consults its knowledge of these actions to find a good one. Thus, in our basic formulation, a plan is a demonstration that a goal state will follow a series of such feasible choices.

This definition allows plans to be constructed in which each choice is represented as it will be made. This is even true for the new, parametric actions that become available with more information. This account thus dispenses with object-level descriptions of actions and reasoning about following plans; instead, the account parameterizes actions using local Skolem constants, corresponding to the run-time variables of implemented planners. At the same time, the proof itself specifies how choices depend on one another. For example, conditional plans are realized as proofs that use case analysis to reason separately about alternative states of knowledge for the agent. Thus, proof search allows the control structure of the plan to be derived incrementally—in a way that mirrors the introduction and exploration of branches of alternative executions in implemented planners.

Choice and Future Reasons to Act

In this section, we introduce a characterization of reasons to act that explicitly refers to the successive stages of information in which an agent deliberates and chooses its future actions. This characterization can be formulated in intuitive language, as follows. A reason to choose a particular next action consists of a demonstration that this choice is the first step in a sequence of steps of deliberation and action—where the agent knows at each state what action to do next, and does it—which allows the agent to achieve its goals, thanks to a specified set of causal connections.

Choice

We derive and formalize our characterization by a running example, the bomb-in-the-toilet problem, which goes as follows: Given that one of two packages is a bomb, and that R can defuse a bomb-package by dunking it, how can R defuse the bomb? The solution is for R to successively dunk both packages (two actions); the one-action plan in which R dunks whatever package is the bomb is not a solution, because R cannot choose to carry it out.

We start with a purely temporal theory, in which a plan is a formal demonstration, constructed according to some theory of events and their consequences, that a sequence of actions will achieve some goal. We assume this demonstration takes the form of a deduction $\mathcal{D}$ with conclusion:

$$T, I, P \longrightarrow G \qquad (1)$$

This notation indicates that in the deduction $\mathcal{D}$, the formulas in T, I and P are used to derive the formula G. The deductive approach matches previous work on knowledge and action, and suggests an explanation-closure approach to reasoning about inertia, as in (Reiter, 1991; Scherl and Levesque, 1993) for example. G is a logical statement that some goal or goals hold at various points in the future. T is a theory describing the causal effects of actions in the domain. I describes the initial conditions for the planning problem (and perhaps further available information about future conditions and events). P records assumptions describing the occurrence and interactions of actions in the plan. In this framework, the basic problem of building a plan is to find an appropriate set of actions in P by abductively assuming premises, given the specification of T, I and G.

(1) provides a model in which the agent makes a SINGLE CHOICE OF ACTION, and evaluates the consequences of that choice of action in the different possibilities compatible with what it knows. Given a choice of P, we can make assumptions for the sake of argument; for example we can consider the different cases for which package is the bomb. However, assumptions in P are made once-and-for-all and cannot depend on what is assumed for the sake of argument; thus, P cannot name *whatever package is the bomb*.

A logic of knowledge can make the idea of choice explicit. We treat a single-choice, single-step plan as a proof of

$$[\text{K}]T, [\text{K}]I \longrightarrow \exists a[\text{K}]([\text{K}]\mathbf{h}a \supset [\text{N}][\text{K}]G) \qquad (2)$$

($[\text{K}]p$ represents that the agent knows p; $[\text{N}]p$, that p is true after one step of time; $\mathbf{h}a$ means that a is the next event to happen.) The goal formula says that the agent knows, of some concrete action a, that if a patently occurs, then as a result G will patently hold—in philosophical shorthand: the agent KNOWS WHAT WILL ACHIEVE G (Hintikka, 1971). The assumed theory T and facts I are now explicitly represented as part of the agent's knowledge. (2) matches (1) because of the wide scope of $\exists a$. Like P in (1), a here must specify a concrete action that cannot depend on assumptions in the argument assessing a's known result.

Moore's definition of ability to act (Moore, 1985) also works by giving a quantifier wide scope over a modal operator. However, Moore's definition also includes a requirement that an agent knowingly select its concrete action under a given abstract description, d. Moore's condition can be reformulated in our notation for comparison:

$$[\text{K}]T, [\text{K}]I \longrightarrow \exists a[\text{K}](a = d \wedge ([\text{K}]\mathbf{h}a \supset [\text{N}][\text{K}]G)) \qquad (3)$$

The equation $a = d$ greatly increases the complexity of building a proof, by introducing cumbersome reasoning about known equalities between terms. Since we have grounded (2) in (1), we discover that it is not essential to derive an abstract description d, and then perform the equational reasoning to show $a = d$; naming the action abstractly does not help analyze an agent's ability to choose an appropriate action from among its concrete options.

Dependent Choice

The definition in (2) allows us to specify not only ambiguities in the state of the world but also ambiguities in the information that the agent might have. If what the agent knows is specified partially, proofs will permit an agent's chosen action to depend on its knowledge. By supporting correct reasoning about these dependent choices, proofs already allow us to describe conditional plans and plans with parameterized actions. There is thus no need for explicit, object-level constructs describing the structure of complex plans. Moreover, we continue to avoid the explicit abstract description of actions and plans using terms in the language. This allows us to maintain a very simple definition of achieving a goal by a sequence of choices.

To describe our representation of dependent choices, we return to the bomb-in-the-toilet scenario. If we suppose that the agent knows which package is the bomb, we can conclude that the agent knows enough to defuse the bomb. The agent can dunk the package it knows is the bomb.

Formally, this inference might play out in one of two ways. We can add the condition $[\text{K}]b1 \vee [\text{K}]b2$ to say that the agent knows whether package one is the bomb or whether package two is. Using case analysis, we can prove

$$[\text{K}]T, [\text{K}]I, [\text{K}]b1 \vee [\text{K}]b2 \longrightarrow \exists a[\text{K}]([\text{K}]\mathbf{h}a \supset [\text{N}][\text{K}]G)$$

If the agent knows package one is the bomb, it can conclude that dunking package one will defuse the bomb; otherwise, it must know that package two is the bomb and be able to conclude that dunking it will defuse the bomb.

This proof instructs the agent to make a CONDITIONAL choice of action, depending on what it knows. To see that this proof implicitly represents a conditional choice, imagine how the agent might use the proof directly to select an action while executing a plan. According to our specification, the agent will have one of two facts as part of its concrete knowledge: either $[K]b1$ or $[K]b2$. The proof maps out the reasoning that shows what to do in either case. Thus, the agent need only match its concrete knowledge against the cases in the proof to find which applies, then extract the appropriate component. For practical execution, we might want to use such analysis in advance, to recover an explicit conditional from a proof. Nevertheless, for efficient search, we must represent dependent choices implicitly rather than explicitly. Case analysis can be performed incrementally in proof search, so it is straightforward to derive the conditions for performing different actions piece-by-piece, as needed. Moreover, logical case analysis always interacts correctly with scope of quantifiers, so there is no possibility of proposing a conditional expression that could not form the basis of the agent's choice.

The other alternative is to add the condition $\exists x[K]bomb(x)$, to say that the agent knows what the bomb is. Then we prove that the agent has a plan by picking a witness c that the agent knows is a bomb and showing that the agent knows dunking c defuses the bomb. We can regard this proof as instructing the agent to make a PARAMETERIZED choice of action, depending on what it knows.

Again, as with an abstract, symbolic description of a parameterized action, this proof has enough information for the agent to choose a successful action. If the partial specification of its knowledge is correct, its concrete knowledge includes a fact $[K]bomb(x)$ for some object x. The proof spells out what to do with that value x: use it in place of the arbitrary witness c that the proof assumed. Doing so allows the agent to derive from the proof a concrete reason for a specific action. Again, by comparison with an explicit description, we see that the logical treatment, in terms of scope, naturally guarantees that only information the agent has can affect its choices. There could be no possibility of proposing a described action whose referent the agent did not know.

Sequenced Choice

We can call these arguments indirect assessments of an agent's plan. Indirect assessments allow an agent to determine the options available to itself in the future. Here is an example. Suppose we equip an agent R with a bomb-detector in the initial bomb-in-the-toilet scenario. R can describe what would hold after it used the bomb detector in the indefinite way just outlined: R would know which package is the bomb. Therefore, in the next step, R could choose to defuse the bomb. Thus, R already knows that in two steps of deliberation and action (choosing first to detect and then to dunk) the bomb will be defused.

This argument gives R an indirect reason to use the bomb detector now. The proofs we accept as plans must have a staged structure to reflect this staged introduction of future reasons to act. We should represent R's goal thus:

$$\exists a[K]([K]ha \supset [N]\exists a'[K]([K]ha' \supset [N][K]G))$$

This fits R's argument. R first chooses a based on what R knows now. R's choice of a must enable R to choose a good action a' in the next step, based on what R knows then. There, R will choose a' by reasoning that a' brings about G. In all, G is nested under three $[K]$ operators. Each inserts a boundary corresponding to a new stage of deliberation as R assesses its progress toward the goal. Each may be preceded by an existential quantifier for any action selected at that stage.

We can generalize this to longer plans using a recursive definition. At each step, we identify an action to do next based on information then available, and assume this action occurs; we then make sure that any remaining actions will be identified when needed, until the goal is finally achieved. We use $can(G, n)$ to denote the condition whose proof constitutes a plan to achieve the goal G in n further steps of action; $can(G, n)$ is defined inductively:

$$can(G, 0) \equiv [K]G$$
$$can(G, n+1) \equiv \exists a_n[K]([K]ha_n \supset [N]can(G, n))$$

This recursive definition directly reflects the staged process by which successive actions are selected and taken.

In describing the knowledge an agent needs to follow a plan p, (Davis, 1994) uses a similar staged definition. Simplifying somewhat, and adapting the notation of (3), the agent satisfies $can(G,p)$ to follow p and achieve G:

$$\exists a_n[K](a_n = next(p) \wedge ([K]ha_n \supset [N]can(G, rest(p))))$$

As with Moore, this presupposes an overall abstract description of the course of action being carried out and appeals to complicated reasoning to determine the *next* action to match that course of action. We have seen that we can give a logical analysis of what an agent can choose to do without separately constructing or reasoning about such a description of a plan.

Formalizing Knowledge and Time

This section and the next section consider the construction of plan-proofs. For a (k-step) plan we need proofs of

$$[K]T, [K]I \longrightarrow can(G, k)$$

Such proofs can in fact be constructed in a very similar way to plan-proofs in a purely temporal theory.

This section describes the underlying logic. We adapt the model of (Moore, 1985) to introduce a type distinction between possible worlds and states in time. We capture the same inference schemes as Moore, but can apply recently-developed equational translation methods for efficient modal reasoning, e.g. (Ohlbach, 1991).

Each world in our models is populated by three sorts of entities. There are the ordinary INDIVIDUALS that are named by first-order terms in the language (like actions and objects). Then there are STATES, naming particular possible times in the history of the world. Finally there are UPDATES that describe possible ways a state could evolve in one moment of time. If s is a state and τ is an update, then $s;\tau$ names the state denoting the result of performing update τ in state s. Temporal operators are interpreted as quantifiers over updates; thus [N]p is true at state s in world w if for any update τ in w, p is true at $(s;\tau)$ in w. Each world resolves all ambiguities about a particular state. But what could happen later is still up in the air. You can think of the states of the world as recording the REAL POSSIBILITIES of how things could turn out in that world: so each world is like a situation calculus model.

The worlds themselves are related by EPISTEMIC TRANSITIONS. If w is a world and α is an epistemic transition, then in w, for all the agent knows, it could be in $w;\alpha$. Thus, [K]p is true at state s in world w if for any transition α, p is true in state s at world $w;\alpha$. By including an identity transition 1 with w; $1 = w$, we ensure that no fact can be known unless it is true. We ensure that an agent is aware of the facts it knows by closing transitions under an operator of composition, $\star$: $w;(\alpha \star \beta) = w;\alpha;\beta$.

The entities in $w;\alpha$ include all the entities—individuals, states, and updates—in w, but may include others. A consequence of these increasing domains is the constraint of memory that [K][N]$p \supset$ [N][K]p but not vice versa. Here is why. The new entities indicate the agent's potentially limited knowledge about what exists—and what can happen. For all the agent knows now, the future might include any CONCEIVABLE POSSIBILITY—found by looking in each world $w;\alpha$ at states of the form $s;\tau'$ with τ' an update in $w;\alpha$. This corresponds to the semantics of [K][N]p. But as time passes, only the REAL POSSIBILITIES can actually be reached; the agent's knowledge in real possibilities is found by looking in each world $w;\alpha$ at states of the form $s;\tau$ with τ an update in w. This corresponds to the semantics of [N][K]p. Since there can only be more values for τ' than for τ, what an agent knows now about future alternatives is always less than what it will know about them.

The model is set up for PREFIX theorem-proving techniques for modal logic (Wallen, 1990; Ohlbach, 1991). Instead of proving that worlds and states are related by accessibility, prefix techniques use terms for worlds and states that directly encode accessibility. We follow (Ohlbach, 1991) in presenting prefix techniques by means of a semantics-based translation to classical logic (with sorts and equality), where modal operators are replaced by explicit quantifiers over transitions and updates. After translation, modal reasoning follows directly from the classical case.

The only trick in the translation is the handling of the increasing domains of individuals across possible worlds. We use compound terms $t@w$ where w names the world at which the referent for t is first defined—the DOMAIN of t. As arguments of relations involving individuals and states, any constant symbol or free variable t is immediately translated as $t@w_0$, where w_0 represents the real world. Bound variables are assigned an appropriate domain as quantifiers are translated. This translation depends on whether the quantifier is instantiated or Skolemized. At a world w, Skolemized quantifiers introduce a term $t@w$ that cannot be assumed to exist before w. So at Skolemized quantifiers we replace (argument occurrences of) the old bound variable x by a new term $x@w$. Other quantifiers are instantiated; at a world w

$$[R(t_1,\ldots,t_k)]^{d,w,\pm} \equiv R(t_1,\ldots,t_k,d,w)$$
$$[A \wedge B]^{d,w,\pm} \equiv [A]^{d,w,\pm} \wedge [B]^{d,w,\pm}$$
$$[\neg A]^{d,w,\pm} \equiv \neg [A]^{d,w,\mp}$$
$$[[K]A]^{d,w,\pm} \equiv \forall \alpha [A]^{d,w;\alpha,\pm}$$
$$[[N]A]^{s@v,w,+} \equiv \forall \tau \forall u(u \leq w \supset [A]^{s;\tau@u,w,+})$$
$$[[N]A]^{s@v,w,-} \equiv \forall \tau [A]^{s;\tau@w,w,-}$$
$$[\forall x A]^{d,w,+} \equiv \forall e \forall u(u \leq w \supset [A[e@u/x]]^{d,w,+})$$
$$[\forall x A]^{d,w,-} \equiv \forall e [A[e@w/x]]^{d,w,-}$$

Figure 1: Translation $[\cdot]^{\cdot,\cdot,\pm}$ to classical logic

they may take on any value $t@u$, provided that this t exists at w (given it first exists at u). To meet the proviso, we must find a path $u;v = w$, showing that u is a prefix of w, written $u \leq w$. So at instantiated quantifiers we replace the old bound variable x by a new term $x@u$ where u is a new restricted variable over worlds.

For completeness, the translation that we have just outlined informally is given precisely in Figure 1. The translation turns a modal formula A into a classical formula $[A]^{s_0@w_0,w_0,\pm}$ depending on the initial state s_0, the real world w_0 and whether A is assumed (+) or to be proved (-). It looks more complicated than it is: the translation just annotates terms and quantifiers with explicit domains and annotates atomic relations with an explict world and state of evaluation. The translation requires us to reason with the equations

$$E \equiv w;(\alpha \star \beta) = w;\alpha;\beta, \quad w;1 = w$$

Using this translation, a plan is just a classical deduction with the following conclusion:

$$E, [[K]T, [K]I]^{s_0@w_0,w_0,+} \longrightarrow [can(G,k)]^{s_0@w_0,w_0,-}$$

Abduction

In this section, we recast this DEDUCTIVE approach to planning as an ABDUCTIVE problem, in which action occurrences are assumed as needed. The recursive definition of *can* already outlines a sequence of assumptions with a common content: at a particular stage of action and deliberation, the agent selects and performs an appropriate action. More precisely, proving $can(G,k)$ introduces, in lock-step with the introduction of temporal transitions, action assumptions that all take the form

$$\forall \beta.\mathbf{h}(\; \underbrace{e_i@u_i}_{\text{real action}}\;,\; \underbrace{t_i@m_i}_{\text{real state}}\;,\; \underbrace{m_i;a_i;\beta}_{\text{known world}}\;) \quad (4)$$

Here $u_i \leq m_i$. m_i represents the agent's view of what is REAL when the action is chosen; $t_i@m_i$ is a real state introduced at m_i by a goal quantifier; and e_i is some real action. Meanwhile, because the assumption is applicable at any world $m_i;a_i;\beta$, it can contribute only to what is KNOWN at m_i. By encoding the evaluation of a CONCRETE action for KNOWN effects, this form concisely distills the notion of choice.

Because the assumptions are indistinguishable, we can make them as needed. Thus, we can offer a purely abductive presentation of the proof search problem for building a plan to achieve G after k steps of deliberation and action. We simply prove $([K][N])^k[K]G$, making action assumptions of the form in (4) where necessary. This abductive approach eliminates ambiguities in proof search: there is only one way to assume a new action but there are many ways to match a sequence of uninstantiated actions (assumed independently). It also helps strengthen the connection between this theory and implemented planners: implemented planners also add actions one by one, as necessary.

The derivation of this abductive characterization in part depends on how formulas are represented using Skolem terms, logic variables and unification, according to a particular theorem-proving technique. We prefer to follow a LOGIC PROGRAMMING proof search strategy, as characterized in e.g. (Miller et al., 1991; Baldoni et al., 1993). In logic programming proofs, the first actions taken are always to decompose goals; this matches the strategies of special-purpose planning algorithms, and moreover allows modal operators in planning goals to be processed by introducing fresh constants independent of actions. (On the use of constrained constants for Skolem terms more generally, see (Bibel, 1982).) As we prove $can(G, k)$ by this strategy, the formula is decomposed level-by-level. Level n requires us to decompose a goal translated from $\exists a[K]([K]\mathbf{h}a \supset [N]\ldots)$; the implication introduces a new assumption of the form in (4).

This explains the source of the assumptions in (4). But is abduction sufficiently restricted? Suppose an assumption instantiates the sequence t_i to a particular time $s_j @ w_j$. Then e_i first exists at some world $u_i \leq w_j$. If the assumption contributes to the ultimate proof of G, moreover, a_i can only equal α_j. Thus the instantiated assumption could just as well have been explicitly made in decomposing the formula $can(G, k)$.

Key Examples

The last three sections have outlined a logical approach to planning based on an analysis of an agent's ability to choose. To plan, an agent describes its goal in a form that indicates that the goal can be reached after a sequence of steps not only of action (corresponding to temporal updates) but also of deliberation and choice (corresponding to modal transitions). At each step, an agent must choose a concrete next action based on its known properties; this restriction corresponds directly to constraints which distinguish the possible worlds where actions and times are defined from the worlds where action assumptions can be used.

Run-time variables and knowledge preconditions

In this section, we first show how our framework allows the results of one action to provide parameters for later actions—unlike (Levesque, 1996; Goldman and Boddy, 1996). We return to the example of the bomb-in-the-toilet, formalized as in figure 2. The agent knows there is a bomb, knows it has a detector and knows it can dunk. The agent must defuse something in two steps. (In figure 2, [H]p abbreviates that p is true indefinitely; explanation closure axioms are omitted as this proof goes through without them.) This translates

1   $[K]\exists b.bomb(b)$
2   $\exists a[K][H]\forall x(bomb(x) \wedge \mathbf{h}a \supset [N][K]bomb(x))$
3   $[K]\forall x \exists d[K][H](bomb(x) \wedge \mathbf{h}d \supset [N]defused(x))$

Figure 2: Bomb-in-the-toilet with detector.

into the goal:

$defused(b(\alpha)@w_0; \alpha,\ s_0; \tau; \tau'@w_0; \alpha; \alpha',\ w_0; \alpha; \alpha'; \beta)$

$b(\alpha)$ Skolemizes b; other first-order terms will be Skolemized similarly; here, $b(\alpha)$ could also be found by unification during proof search. The proof requires two actions:

$\forall \beta.\mathbf{h}(a@w_0,\ s_0@w_0,\ w_0; \alpha; \beta)$
$\forall \beta.\mathbf{h}(d(\alpha, b(\alpha))@w_0; \alpha,\ s_0; \tau@w_0; \alpha,\ w_0; \alpha'; \beta)$

The first assumption considers the result of the immediate real action a of using the detector, assessed in worlds $w_0; \alpha$ compatible with what we know initially. The second assumption considers the result of dunking the hypothetical object $b(\alpha)$—a real action in world $w_0; \alpha$—in worlds $w_0; \alpha; \alpha'$ compatible with what we know after one step. The reader can readily flesh out this proof along the outlines suggested earlier, after first computing the translation and Skolemization of the clauses of figure 2.

Note how we represent the choice of dunking $b(\alpha)$ directly. The agent will learn from using the detector that $b(\alpha)$ is a bomb; the proof relies on the fact that the agent has this knowledge. Encoding this into the proof is enough—for, as we saw earlier, this is enough information to allow the agent later to extract what to do, by matching its concrete knowledge against the abstract knowledge the proof supposes. So we need not describe the dunking, as do (Moore, 1985; Morgenstern, 1987; Davis, 1994).

A comparison is instructive with a representative implemented planning language with similar plans, SADL (Golden and Weld, 1996). In their plans for such examples, sensing introduces a RUN-TIME VARIABLE storing the observed value; these run-time variables can be then appear as arguments to later actions. The terminology suggests some inherent departure from logic. On the contrary, such variables correspond exactly to Skolem terms like $b(\alpha)$, naming new abstract entities that exist only at remote worlds. Recognizing this logical status for run-time variables explains why such variables are treated existentially and why—in view of the "knowledge precondition" that only concrete actions can be chosen—they can serve as parameters only to actions chosen in future deliberation. At the same time, it confirms our contention that an agent's internal representation of its future actions need not be a timeless, abstract description of that action.

Knowledge preconditions for actions and plans

The next example shows, as (Golden and Weld, 1996) argue, that actions may have to be performed with different knowledge in different circumstances. However, it also shows that this variation is a natural component of a logical approach to planning—not an argument against it.

Consider a domain with a safe. If the agent dials the combination to the safe, the safe patently opens; if the agent

4 $[\textsc{k}]\forall sv\exists o[\textsc{k}][\textsc{h}](closed(s) \wedge combo(s,v) \wedge \mathbf{h}o \supset$
    $[\textsc{n}][\textsc{k}]open(s)) \wedge$
    $[\textsc{k}][\textsc{h}](closed(s) \wedge \neg combo(s,v) \wedge \mathbf{h}o \supset$
    $[\textsc{n}][\textsc{k}]closed(s))$
5 $[\textsc{k}](closed(d_0))$
6 $[\textsc{k}]([\textsc{h}]combo(d_0,n_0) \vee [\textsc{h}]\neg combo(d_0,n_0))$
7 $[\textsc{k}]\forall s[\textsc{h}]\neg(open(s) \wedge closed(s))$

Figure 3: Safe problem

dials something else, the safe patently remains closed. The safe starts out closed, has a constant combination, and can't be open and closed at once. We formalize the situation in figure 3. Suppose the agent wants to open the safe d_0 in one step—in our theory, to build this plan requires proving:

$$open(d_0@w_0, s_0; \tau@w_0; \alpha, w_0; \alpha; \alpha')$$

This cannot be proved abductively unless the agent knows the combination to the safe. Let's add that assumption:

$$\exists v[\textsc{k}]combo(d_0, v)$$

Then we can assume the real action of dialing this combination for assessment according to what the agent knows:

$$\forall \beta.\mathbf{h}(o(1,d_0,v)@w_0, s_0@w_0, w_0; \alpha; \beta)$$

This allows us to complete the plan straightforwardly, by applying the first rule of clause 4.

By comparison, suppose the agent merely wants to determine in one step whether the combination to the safe is n_0 or not. This goal is represented in modal logic as $[\textsc{k}]combo(d_0,n_0) \vee [\textsc{k}]\neg combo(d_0,n_0)$. It translates into a planning problem to prove

$$combo(d_0@w_0, n_0@w_0, s_0; \tau@w_0; \alpha, w_0; \alpha; \alpha'; \beta) \vee$$
$$\neg combo(d_0@w_0, n_0@w_0, s_0; \tau@w_0; \alpha, w_0; \alpha; \alpha'; \gamma)$$

This is a weaker statement than the goal for the previous problem—for starters, it contains disjunction. We can prove this abductively—without assuming knowledge of what the combination of the safe is—by considering the known consequences of attempting to dial n_0:

$$\forall \beta.\mathbf{h}(o(1,d_0,n_0)@w_0, s_0@w_0, w_0; \alpha; \beta)$$

(The proof is interesting. As the reader can work out, it uses nested case analysis to ANTICIPATE the agent's ability to correctly EXPLAIN the observed results of dialing.)

Conclusion

This paper has laid a new, clean groundwork for bridging formal and implemented accounts of sensing and planning. Further ties can be expected. Our account is compatible with partial-order representations of time (and modality) as in planners—provided path equations are represented and solved by corresponding constraints (Stone, 1997). Prospects are also good for reasoning about inertia efficiently by adapting the threat-resolution techniques used in implemented planners. The obvious starting point would be to use argumentation or negation-as-failure as in (Ferguson, 1995; Shanahan, 1997) on a world-by-world basis.

Acknowledgments

Thanks to Doug DeCarlo, Chris Geib, Leora Morgenstern, David Parkes, Mark Steedman and Rich Thomason for comments and discussion. Supported by an IRCS graduate fellowship and NSF grant IRI95-04372, ARPA grant N66001-94-C6043, and ARO grant DAAH04-94-G0426.

References

M. Baldoni, L. Giordano, and A. Martelli. A multimodal logic to define modules in logic programming. In *ILPS*, pp 473–487, 1993.

W. Bibel. *Automated Theorem Proving*. Vieweg, 1982.

E. Davis. Knowledge preconditions for plans. *J. of Logic and Comp.*, 4(5):721–766, 1994.

G. M. Ferguson. *Knowledge Representation and Reasoning for Mixed-Initiative Planning*. PhD thesis, University of Rochester, 1995.

K. Golden and D. Weld. Representing sensing actions: the middle ground revisited. In *Proc. of KR*, 1996.

R. P. Goldman and M. S. Boddy. Expressive planning and explicit knowledge. In *Proc. of AIPS*, pp 110–117, 1996.

J. Hintikka. Semantics for propositional attitudes. In Linsky, *Reference and Modality*, pp 145–167. Oxford, 1971.

H. J. Levesque. What is planning in the presence of sensing? In *Proc. of AAAI*, pp 1139–1146, 1996.

D. McAllister and D. Rosenblitt. Systematic nonlinear planning. In *Proc. of AAAI*, pp 634–639, 1991.

D. Miller, G. Nadathur, F. Pfenning, and A. Scedrov. Uniform proofs as a foundation for logic programming. *Annals of Pure and Applied Logic*, 51:125–157, 1991.

R. C. Moore. A formal theory of knowledge and action. In Hobbs and Moore, *Formal Theories of the Commonsense World*, pp 319–358. Ablex, 1985.

L. Morgenstern. Knowledge preconditions for actions and plans. In *Proc. of IJCAI*, pp 867–874, 1987.

H. J. Ohlbach. Semantics-based translation methods for modal logics. *J. of Logic and Comp.*, 1(5):691–746, 1991.

J. S. Penberthy and D. S. Weld. UCPOP: a sound, complete partial order planner for ADL. In *Proc. of KR*, pp 103–114, 1992.

R. Reiter. The frame problem in the situation calculus: a simple solution (sometimes) and a completeness result for goal regression. In Lifschitz, *AI and Mathematical Theory of Computation*, pp 359–380. Academic Press, 1991.

R. B. Scherl and H. J. Levesque. The frame problem and knowledge-producing actions. In *Proc. of AAAI*, pp 689–695, 1993.

M. Shanahan. Event calculus planning revisited. In *Proc. of ECP 97*, LNAI 1348, pp 390–402. Springer, 1997.

M. Stone Efficient constraints on possible worlds for reasoning about necessity. Report IRCS 97-7, University of Pennsylvania.

L. A. Wallen. *Automated Proof Search in Non-Classical Logics*. MIT Press, 1990.

A Formal Methodology for Verifying Situated Agents

Phan Minh Dung
Department of Computer Science,
Asian Institute of Technology
PO Box 2754, Bangkok 10501, Thailand
dung@cs.ait.ac.th

Abstract

In this paper, we develop a formal methodology for verifying situated agents. The methodology consists of two elements, a specification language for specifying the agent capabilities to execute its actions in dynamic environments and a repertoire of proof methods by which the correctness of an agent, relative to its capabilities, can be formally verified.

Keywords: Planning and control: situated reasoning, plan execution, reactive control.

Introduction

In recent years there is a shift in AI from the classical paradigm of rational agents to the notion of reactive, situated agents that have an intelligent ongoing interaction with dynamic and uncertain environments (Agre et al 1987, Brooks 1991, Georgeff et al 1987, Kowalski et al 1996, Rosenschein et al 1995, Saffioti et al 1995, Shoham 1993). The correct construction of reliable situated agents is an important task in agent research nowadays.

Consider for example the following plan for a robotic agent to cross a busy motor way:

Wait until the road is clear then cross it.

Is it a correct plan to cross a busy road ? [1]

The correctness of this plan depends very much on the robot's capabilities. If the robot is fast enough to be able to finish crossing the road before a car could pass by then the above plan is correct. But it may not be correct for a slower robot.

The correctness of plans depends on the capabilities of the agents executing them. There is some debate in the literature on whether capability should be defined in mental terms or not (Cohen et al 1990, Lesperance et al 1995, Shoham, 1993, Thomas 1994). Here we will not take a stance on this issue. Our notion of capability is grounded fully in terms of actions and

---

Copyright ©1998, American Association for Artificial Intelligence (www.aaai.org). All rights reserved.

[1] By correctness we mean that the robot should not be run over by cars when executing this plan

states of automata-like agents. We define an agent's capability as sets of possible execution processes that can unfold during the execution of the agent's plans in interaction with the environment.

Let us look at the road crossing problem again. As crossing a road takes time, we follow the literature (Reiter 1996) in representing it as a sequence of two actions: *start-crossing;end-crossing* where the effects of *start-crossing* and *end-crossing* are *on-road* and *not on-road*, respectively.

For an agent to execute a plan in an uncertain environment is like to play a game with an unpredictable opponent where the moves of the agent are constrained by the plan while the environment can make its moves randomly. In the road crossing game, the environment has two actions *car-appear* and *car-pass-by* to its disposal where the action *car-appear* is executable in all situations (i.e. a car could appear anytime) with the effect that the fluent *car-coming* becomes true after a car appears. The action *car-pass-by* is executable only in those situations in which *car-coming* is true

Imagine a situation s where the agent is alive and on road while a car is coming. Formally s is represented by $s = \{alive, on\text{-}road, car\text{-}coming\}$. Further let p be a plan whose only action is *end-crossing*. Let us consider two possible scenarios in the game to execute this plan between the agent and the environment. In one scenario, the agent manages to make a move by executing the action *end-crossing* before the environment does anything. This scenario is represented by the sequence of state transitions: $s \xrightarrow{end\text{-}crossing} s'$ where $s' = \{alive, car\text{-}coming\}$. In the other scenario, the environment manages to make a move by executing the action *car-pass-by* before the agent could finish the action *end-crossing*. Afterwards the agent's action *end-crossing* is not defined anymore (as the agent has ceased to be alive). This scenario is represented by the sequence of state ! transitions: $s \xrightarrow{car\text{-}pass\text{-}by} s'' \xrightarrow{\perp} s''$ where $s'' = \{on\text{-}road\}$ and the label $\perp$ means that the game has been interrupted as the agent can not execute the action *end-crossing* any more.

Note that though both actions *end-crossing* and *car-pass-by* are executable in the situation s, the second scenario can not happen if the agent has the capability to finish crossing the road before any car could pass by.[2]

Formally, an agent's capability is represented by an capability function $\mathcal{C}$ which assigns to each plan p and state r, a set $\mathcal{C}(p,r)$ of possible execution processes of p, starting from r, which could unfold in the agent's game with the environment. For example, the agent's capability to finish crossing a road before a car could pass by in the situation s above is characterized by $\mathcal{C}(\text{end-crossing}, s) = \{s \xrightarrow{\text{end-crossing}} s'\}$

In this paper, we develop a formal methodology for verifying situated agents. The methodology consists of two elements, a specification language for specifying the agent capabilities to execute its actions in dynamic environments and a repertoire of proof methods by which the correctness of an agent, relative to its capabilities, can be formally verified.

Preliminaries

The methodology for representing actions in this paper is adopted from (Gelfond et al 1993). The language for describing the world consists of a set of propositional fluent names FLU and a set of action names ACT. A state of the world is represented by a subset of FLU. The set of all states is denoted by STA. The effects of an action A is determined by a partial transition function $T_A : STA \to STA$. We say that A is *executable* in s if $T_A(s)$ is defined.

Example 1 *The language for our road crossing problem is given by:* $FLU = \{\text{alive } (al), \text{on-road } (on), \text{car-coming } (cc)\}$, *and* $ACT = \{\text{car-appear } (ca), \text{car-pass-by } (cp), \text{start-crossing } (sc), \text{end-crossing } (ec)\}$. *The actions have effects according to their common-sense understanding:*

$$T_{sc}(s) = \begin{cases} s \cup \{on\} & \text{if } s \models al \land \neg on \\ undefined & \text{otherwise} \end{cases}$$

$$T_{ec}(s) = \begin{cases} s - \{on\} & \text{if } s \models al \land on \\ undefined & \text{otherwise} \end{cases}$$

$T_{ca}(s) = s \cup \{cc\}$ *for every s.*

$$T_{cp}(s) = \begin{cases} s - \{cc\} & \text{if } s \models cc \land \neg on \\ s - \{cc, al\} & \text{if } s \models cc \land on \\ undefined & \text{otherwise} \end{cases}$$

Reasoning about the effect of actions have been studied extensively in the literature (see Gelfond et all 93, Reiter 96 and the references therein). As our interest in this paper is not primarily about reasoning about action, we will not dwell further on this topic from now on.

---
[2] We assume that the agents always act with their best capability

Agent Capabilities

The world of our agent in this paper consists of the agent itself and its environment. Therefore the set of action names ACT is a disjoint union $ACT = ACT_{agent} \cup ACT_{env}$ of the set of the agent's actions ACT_{agent} and the set of environment actions ACT_{env}.

A *sequential plan* is defined as a sequence $A_0; \ldots; A_n$ of the agent's atomic actions $A_i \in ACT_{agent}$, $0 \leq i \leq n$.

Definition 1 *1. A (possibly infinite) global process e starting from s_0 is a sequence of the form*

$$s_0 \xrightarrow{A_0} s_1 \ldots \xrightarrow{A_n} s_{n+1} \ldots$$

such that for each $i \geq 0$, $A_i \in ACT$ and A_i is executable in s_i, and $s_{i+1} = T_{A_i}(s_i)$. The set of all states in e is denoted by St(e), i.e. $St(e) = \{s_0, \ldots, s_n, \ldots\}$.

2. A global process is called an environment process if for each $i \geq 0$, $A_i \in ACT_{env}$

3. The initial and final state of a global process e are denoted by initial(e) and final(e) respectively. We often write $s \overset{e}{\leadsto} s'$ to indicate that e is a global process with initial state s and final state s'. We also write $s \overset{e}{\leadsto}$ to indicate that e is a global process with initial state s.

4. For global processes e, e' such that final(e) = initial(e'), the concatenation of e and e', denoted by e.e', is defined as the global process

$initial(e) \overset{e}{\leadsto} final(e) \overset{e'}{\leadsto}$

For sets of global processes S,S', define $S.S' = \{e.e' \mid e \in S, e' \in S', final(e) = initial(e')\}$

To understand the definition of the crucial notion of plan execution process in the following definition, remember that for an agent to execute a plan in an uncertain environment is like to play a game with an unpredictable opponent where the moves of the agent are constrained by the plan while the environment can make its moves randomly.

Definition 2 *A possible execution process of a sequential plan p starting from a state $s_0 \in STA$ is defined inductively as follows:*

1. $p = A$ where $A \in ACT_{agent}$. Then a possible execution process of p starting from s_0 has

(a) either the form $s_0 \overset{e}{\leadsto} s_1 \xrightarrow{A} s_2$ where e is a finite environment process and A is executable in s_1, and $s_2 = T_A(s_1)$.[3]

(b) or the form $s_0 \overset{e}{\leadsto} s_1 \xrightarrow{\bot} s_1$ where e is a finite environment process and A is not executable in s_1.[4]

---
[3] In this case, the environment has already made the moves in e before the agent manages to actually perform A

[4] In this case, the environment has already made the moves in e before the agent is about to perform A which has become unexecutable.

2. $p = A; q$ where $A \in Act_{agent}$. Then a possible execution process of p starting from s_0 is

   (a) either an execution process of A from s_0 which is ended by an undefined action $\perp$

   (b) or of the form $e_1.e_2$ where e_1 is a successful execution process of A [5], and e_2 is a execution process of q starting from $final(e_1)$.

3. The set of all possible execution processes of p starting from $s \in STA$ is denoted by $Exe(p,s)$.

4. A plan execution process is interupted if it is ended by an undefined action $\perp$.

5. A plan execution process is successful if it is not interupted.

Two examples of possible execution processes of the plan $p = sc; ec$ in the road crossing example are:
$s_0 \xrightarrow{sc} s_1 \xrightarrow{ec} s_0$ and $s_0 \xrightarrow{sc} s_1 \xrightarrow{ca} s_2 \xrightarrow{ec} s_3$
where $s_0 = \{al\}$, $s_1 = \{al, on\}$, $s_2 = \{al, on, cc\}$, $s_3 = \{al, cc\}$.

Now we can define the crucial notion of capability.

Definition 3 *The capability of an agent is defined as a function that assigns to each pair (p,s) of a sequential plan p, and a state $s \in STA$ a set $\mathcal{C}(p,s) \subseteq Exe(p,s)$ such that the following properties are satisfied:*

1. *$\mathcal{C}(p,s)$ is a finite nonempty subset of $Exe(p,s)$*
2. *For any plans p_1, p_2: $\mathcal{C}(p_1; p_2) = \mathcal{C}(p_1).\mathcal{C}(p_2)$ where for any plan p, $\mathcal{C}(p) = \bigcup \{\mathcal{C}(p,s) \mid s \in STA\}$.*

Intuitively, $\mathcal{C}(p,s)$ represents the set of all possible execution processes which could occur when the agent is executing p from s. The first condition is motivated by the assumption that our agent can execute any executable action $A \in ACT_{agent}$ in a finite time interval, and to exlude *Zeno processes* in which there are infinitely many state-changes in a finite time interval. The motivation for the second condition should be intuitively clear.

In the road crosing example, our agent's capabilities to cross a clear road before any car could appear is represented by any capability function $\mathcal{C}$ satisfying $\mathcal{C}(sc; ec, s_0) = \{s_0 \xrightarrow{sc} s_1 \xrightarrow{ec} s_0\}$. Moreover, the incapability to finish crossing a road alive in the state $s_2 = \{al, on, cc\}$ is expressed by the following capability function: $\mathcal{C}(ec, s_2) = \{s \xrightarrow{cp} r \xrightarrow{\perp} r\}$ where $r = \{on\}$.

It is not difficult to see that the following lemma holds.

Lemma 1 *Two capability functions coincide on every plan if they coincide on the single action plans.*

This lemma shows that the capability of an agent to carry out a plan is fully determined by her capability to carry out the basic actions in the plan.

For later use, for each plan p, each fluent proposition φ, define $\mathcal{C}(p, \varphi) = \bigcup \{\mathcal{C}(p,s) \mid s \models \varphi\}$.

---
[5] See point 5 in this definition

A Language for Agent Capabilities

Agent capabilities are described by *ability propositions* of the form

executable p **when** φ **before** ψ

where φ, ψ are fluent propositions and p is a sequential plan. The informal semantics of such proposition is that whenever the agent starts executing p in a state satisfying φ, it will finish before ψ could become true.

For example, the proposition that the agent is capable to cross a clear road before any car could appear, is expressed by the following proposition:

executable $sc; ec$ **when** $\neg cc \wedge al \wedge \neg on$ **before** cc (1)

The semantics of the ability propositions is defined with respect to the capability functions as follows.

Definition 4 *Let $\mathcal{C}$ be a capability function and ϵ be an ability proposition of the form* **executable** p **when** φ **before** ψ.

1. *We say that $\mathcal{C}$ satisfies ϵ, written $\mathcal{C} \models \epsilon$, if for each $e \in \mathcal{C}(p, \varphi)$: e is successful and $\forall s' \in St(e), s' \not\models \psi$*

2. *$\mathcal{C}$ is said to be a model of a set of ability propositions if $\mathcal{C}$ satisfies each proposition in this set. A set of ability propositions is consistent if it has a model.*

3. *We say that ϵ follows from a set of ability propositions $\mathcal{E}$, written $\mathcal{E} \models \epsilon$ if each model of $\mathcal{E}$ is also a model of ϵ.*

In the road crossing example, any capability function $\mathcal{C}$ such that

$$\mathcal{C}(sc; ec, s_0) = \{s_0 \xrightarrow{sc} s_1 \xrightarrow{ec} s_0\} \qquad (2)$$

satisfies the ability proposition (1).

Reactive Plans

For each fluent proposition φ, we assume that ACT_{agent} contains an action $\varphi?$ to test whether φ holds in the current situation. Formally, the semantics of a test action $\varphi?$ is defined by

1. $T_{\varphi?}(s)$ is defined iff $s \models \varphi$
2. If $T_{\varphi?}(s)$ is defined then $T_{\varphi?}(s) = s$

Definition 5 *1. A conditional plan c has the form*
$\varphi \Longrightarrow p$
where φ, called the test of c and denoted by $test(c)$, is a fluent proposition and p, called the body of c and denoted by $body(c)$, is a sequential plan.

2. *A reactive plan is a finite (possibly empty) set of conditional plans. The disjunction of the tests of all the conditional plans in a reactive plan $\mathcal{R}$ is denoted by $cond(\mathcal{R})$.*

Reactive plans are executed in cycles. At the begin of each cycle, the test conditions of the conditional plans are checked. If none of them hold then the agent waits until some of them become true. If one of the test conditions holds (either at the first check or after waiting a while), then the body of the corresponding conditional plan is executed. If it is successful then a new cycle starts. If not, the execution of the reactive plan will be interrupted.

For an agent to operate safely in an environment, it seems necessary that it should possess a capability to sense any relevant change of the environment early enough to react accordingly. An agent is said to be *alert* if it has the capability to recognize every relevant change of the environment "instantly" (in the sense that during the sensing time the environment undergoes no significant change).

Definition 6 *A capability function C is said to be* alert *if for any fluent proposition φ*

$$C(\varphi?, s) = \{s \xrightarrow{\varphi?} s\} \text{ if } s \models \varphi$$
$$C(\varphi?, s) = \{s \xrightarrow{\perp} s\} \text{ if } s \models \neg\varphi$$

For simplicity and understandability, we will restrict ourself on alert agents when considering the execution of reactive plans.

Definition 7 *Let C be an alert capability function and $\mathcal{R} = \{\varphi_0 \Rightarrow p_0, \ldots, \varphi_n \Rightarrow p_n\}$ be a reactive plan.*

1. *A possible execution process e of $\mathcal{R}$ with respect to C starting from an initial state s_0 is defined as follows:*

   (a) *Case 1: $s_0 \models cond(\mathcal{R})$. Then for some k such that $s_0 \models \varphi_k$,*

      i. *either e has the form $e_0.e_1$ where e_0 is a successful execution process in $C(\varphi_k?; p_k, s_0)$, and e_1 is an execution process of $\mathcal{R}$ with respect to C starting from $final(e_0)$.*

      ii. *or e is an interrupted execution process in $C(\varphi_k?; p_k, s_0)$*

   (b) *Case 2: $s_0 \not\models cond(\mathcal{R})$. Then*

      i. *either e has the form $e_0.e_1$ where*
      - *e_0 is an environment process of the form*

      $$s_0 \xrightarrow{A_0} s_1 \ldots \xrightarrow{A_{m-1}} s_m$$

      such that for each $0 \leq i < m$, $s_i \not\models cond(\mathcal{R})$ and $s_m \models cond(\mathcal{R})$, and
      - *e_1 is an execution process of $\mathcal{R}$ with respect to C starting from s_m*

      ii. *or e is an infinite environment process such that for each state $s \in St(e)$, $s \not\models cond(\mathcal{R})$* [6].

      iii. *or e is a finite environment process such that for each $s \in St(e)$ $s \not\models cond(\mathcal{R})$ and there exists no executable environment action at $final(e)$* [7].

2. *A reactive plan execution process is interrupted if it is ended by an undefined action $\perp$.*

3. *A reactive plan execution process is successful if it is not interrupted.*

---

[6] This represents the case where the agent has to wait infinitely

[7] The agent also has to wait infinitely in this case

4. *The set of all execution processes of $\mathcal{R}$ wrt C starting from a state s is denoted by $Exec_C(\mathcal{R}, s)$ while $Exec_C(\mathcal{R}, \varphi)$ denotes the set of all execution processes of $\mathcal{R}$ wrt C starting from a state satisfying φ*

For example, consider again the road crossing example where the agent has the capability (2). Let $\mathcal{R}_0 = \{\neg cc \Rightarrow sc; ec\}$. Then $Exec_C(\mathcal{R}_0, s_0) = \{s_0 \xrightarrow{\neg cc?} s_0 \xrightarrow{sc} s_1 \xrightarrow{ec} s_0 \xrightarrow{\neg cc?} s_0 \xrightarrow{sc} s_1 \xrightarrow{ec} s_0 \longrightarrow \ldots\}$

Verification of Reactive Agents

We consider in this paper the verification of invariance formulas of the forms

$$\varphi \rightarrow \Box(\mathcal{R}, \psi)$$

which states that if the agent starts executing $\mathcal{R}$ (a reactive plan) in a state satisfying φ then ψ will always hold during the execution of $\mathcal{R}$.

We say that an alert capability function C *satisfies* a formula $\varphi \rightarrow \Box(\mathcal{R}, \psi)$, written $C \models \varphi \rightarrow \Box(\mathcal{R}, \psi)$, if for each execution process $e \in Exec_C(\mathcal{R}, \varphi)$, for each state $s \in St(e)$, $s \models \psi$.

For the verification of invariance formulas, we also need to consider verification conditions of the form

$$[\varphi]\, p\, [\psi]$$

which states that if the agent starts executing p (a sequential plan) in a state satisfying φ then it will terminate successfully in a state satisfying ψ.

We say that a capability function C *satisfies* a formula $[\varphi]\, p\, [\psi]$, written $C \models [\varphi]\, p\, [\psi]$, if each execution process $e \in C(p, \varphi)$ is successful and terminates in a state satisfying ψ.

Verifying $[\varphi]\, p\, [\psi]$

To prove the condition $[\varphi]\, p\, [\psi]$, we need another kind of conditions of the form

$$\{\varphi\}\, p\, \textbf{inv}\, \gamma\, \{\psi\}$$

which states that every successful execution process $e \in Exe(p, \varphi)$ satisfying the property that γ is invariant during it (i.e. $\forall s \in St(e): s \models \gamma$), terminates in a state satisfying ψ.

It is important to note that the validity of condition $\{\varphi\}\, p\, \textbf{inv}\, \gamma\, \{\psi\}$ does not depend on the agent's capabilities. They are therefore often referred to as *cap-free conditions*.

We can now give the rule for proving $[\varphi]\, p\, [\psi]$

- (SP)

$$\frac{\textbf{executable}\, p\, \textbf{when}\, \varphi\, \textbf{before}\, \gamma \quad \{\varphi\}\, p\, \textbf{inv}\, \neg\gamma\, \{\psi\}}{[\varphi]\, p\, [\psi]}$$

Lemma 2 *The rule (SP) is sound in the sense that for each capability function C, if $C \models$ **executable** p **when** φ **before** γ, and $\{\varphi\}\, p\, \textbf{inv}\, \neg\gamma\, \{\psi\}$ holds then $C \models [\varphi]p[\psi]$*

Proof Rules for Cap-Free Conditions

For each fluent proposition φ, define $T_A(\varphi) = \{T_A(s) \mid s \models \varphi\}$. Further we write $T_A(\varphi) \models \psi$ if each state in $T_A(\varphi)$ satisfies ψ.

The following notion of environment invariance plays an important role in the rules for proving cap-free conditions.

Definition 8 1. *A fluent proposition φ is said to be* environment invariant *with respect to γ starting from ψ if for each environment process e, if $initial(e) \models \psi$ and $\forall s \in St(e) : s \models \gamma$ then $\forall s \in St(e) : s \models \varphi$.*

2. *We often say that φ is environment invariant starting from ψ if $\gamma \equiv true$*

3. *We also say that φ is environment invariant if it is environment invariant starting from φ.*

We can now introduce the rules for proving cap-free conditions.

- (CF1)

$$\frac{\varphi \text{ is environment invariant wrt } \gamma \text{ starting from } \varphi \quad T_A(\varphi \wedge \gamma) \models \gamma \rightarrow \psi}{\{\varphi\} \, A \, \mathbf{inv} \, \gamma \, \{\psi\}}$$

- (CF2)

$$\frac{\{\varphi\} \, p \, \mathbf{inv} \, \gamma \, \{\phi\} \quad \{\phi\} \, q \, \mathbf{inv} \, \gamma \, \{\psi\}}{\{\varphi\} \, p;q \, \mathbf{inv} \, \gamma \, \{\psi\}}$$

- (CF3)

$$\frac{\varphi' \rightarrow \varphi, \, \{\varphi\} \, p \, \mathbf{inv} \, \gamma \, \{\psi\}, \, \psi \rightarrow \psi'}{\{\varphi'\} \, p \, \mathbf{inv} \, \gamma \, \{\psi'\}}$$

Lemma 3 *The proof system for cap-free conditions is sound.*

Proof Theory for Ability Propositions
Rules for Sequential Operator

- (CP1)

$$\frac{\text{executable } p;q \text{ when } \varphi \text{ before } \psi}{\text{executable } p \text{ when } \varphi \text{ before } \psi}$$

- (CP2)

$$\frac{[\varphi] \, p \, [\psi] \quad \text{executable } p \text{ when } \varphi \text{ before } \phi \quad \text{executable } q \text{ when } \psi \text{ before } \phi}{\text{executable } p;q \text{ when } \varphi \text{ before } \phi}$$

- (CP3)

$$\frac{\begin{array}{c}\text{executable } p; A \text{ when } \varphi \text{ before } \psi \\ \text{executable } p \text{ when } \varphi \text{ before } \gamma \\ [\varphi] \, p \, [\phi] \\ \{\phi\} A \, \mathbf{inv} \, \neg\psi [\neg\gamma] \\ \neg\gamma \text{ is environment invariant wrt } \neg\psi \text{ starting from } \phi\end{array}}{\text{executable } p; A \text{ when } \varphi \text{ before } \gamma}$$

Rule for Atomic Actions

- (CP4)

$$\frac{\begin{array}{c}\text{executable } A \text{ when } \varphi \text{ before } \gamma \\ \{\varphi\} \, A \, \mathbf{inv} \, \neg\gamma \, \{\neg\psi\} \\ \neg\psi \text{ is environment invariant wrt } \neg\gamma \text{ starting from } \varphi\end{array}}{\text{executable } A \text{ when } \varphi \text{ before } \psi}$$

Other Rules

- (CP5)

$$\frac{\text{executable p when } \varphi \text{ before } \psi \quad \text{executable p when } \varphi_1 \text{ before } \psi_1}{\text{executable p when } \varphi \wedge \varphi_1 \text{ before } \psi \vee \psi_1}$$

- (CP6)

$$\frac{\text{executable p when } \varphi \text{ before } \psi \quad \text{executable p when } \varphi_1 \text{ before } \psi_1}{\text{executable p when } \varphi \vee \varphi_1 \text{ before } \psi \wedge \psi_1}$$

- (CP7)

$$\frac{\text{executable p when } \varphi \text{ before } \psi \quad \varphi_1 \models \varphi, \, \psi_1 \models \psi}{\text{executable p when } \varphi_1 \text{ before } \psi_1}$$

For each set of ability proposition $\mathcal{E}$, let $\Gamma_\mathcal{E}$ be the set of rules obtained by adding to the rules for ability propositions a new rule of the form

- (CP8)

$$\frac{\epsilon \in \mathcal{E}}{\epsilon}$$

Lemma 4 *The proof system for the ability propositions is sound in the sense that for each set of ability propositions $\mathcal{E}$, if $\mathcal{E} \vdash_{\Gamma_\mathcal{E}} \epsilon$, then $\mathcal{E} \models \epsilon$*

Rule for Invariance Formulae

We can now give the rule for invariance formula.

- (IF)

$$\frac{\begin{array}{rl}\exists \phi : & \varphi \rightarrow \phi, \, \phi \rightarrow \psi \\ & \phi \text{ is environment invariant wrt } \neg cond(\mathcal{R}) \\ & \text{starting from } \phi \\ \forall c \in \mathcal{R}: & [\phi \wedge test(c)] \, body(c) \, [\phi] \\ & \text{executable } body(c) \text{ when } \phi \wedge test(c) \\ & \text{before } \neg\psi\end{array}}{\varphi \rightarrow \Box(\mathcal{R}, \psi)}$$

Lemma 5 *The rule (IF) is sound in the sense that for each alert capability function $\mathcal{C}$, for each reactive plan $\mathcal{R}$, if there exists ϕ such that folowing conditions are satisfied:*

- *$\varphi \rightarrow \phi$ and $\phi \rightarrow \psi$ are valid and ϕ is environment invariant wrt $\neg cond(\mathcal{R})$ starting from ϕ*
- *For each $c \in \mathcal{R}$, $\mathcal{C} \models [\phi \wedge test(c)] \, body(c) \, [\phi]$ and $\mathcal{C} \models$ executable $body(c)$ when $\phi \wedge test(c)$ before $\neg\psi$*

then $\mathcal{C} \models \varphi \to \Box(\mathcal{R}, \psi)$

Example 2
Let ϵ be the capability proposition (1). Further let $\mathcal{R}_0 = \{\neg cc \Rightarrow sc; ec\}$.
We want to prove: $\{\epsilon\} \vdash (al \land \neg on) \to \Box(\mathcal{R}_0, al)$

It is easy to see that $al \land \neg on$ is environment invariant. Using rule (CF1) we get

$$\vdash \{al \land \neg on\} \, sc \, \mathbf{inv} \, \neg cc \, \{al \land on\} \quad (3)$$

$$\vdash \{al \land on\} \, ec \, \mathbf{inv} \, \neg cc \, \{al \land \neg on\} \quad (4)$$

¿From (3,4) using rule (CF2) we get

$$\vdash \{al \land \neg on\} \, sc; ec \, \mathbf{inv} \, \neg cc \, \{al \land \neg on\} \quad (5)$$

Therefore, it is obvious from (CF3) and (5)

$$\vdash \{al \land \neg on \land \neg cc\} \, sc; ec \, \mathbf{inv} \, \neg cc \, \{al \land \neg on\} \quad (6)$$

Let $\mathcal{E} = \{\epsilon\}$, it follows from (CP8) $\mathcal{E} \vdash \epsilon$. Using rule (CP1) we have

$\mathcal{E} \vdash \mathbf{executable} \, sc \, \mathbf{when} \, \neg cc \land al \land \neg on \, \mathbf{before} \, cc$
$\hfill (7)$

Hence using (SP) and from (3,7), it follows:

$$\mathcal{E} \vdash [al \land \neg on \land \neg cc] \, sc \, [al \land on] \quad (8)$$

Using rule (CF3) and (3), we get

$$\vdash \{al \land \neg on \land \neg cc\} \, sc \, \mathbf{inv} \, \neg cc \, \{al \land on\} \quad (9)$$

Using (CP4) and (7,9), we get

$\mathcal{E} \vdash \mathbf{executable} \, sc \, \mathbf{when} \, \neg cc \land al \land \neg on \, \mathbf{before} \, \neg al$
$\hfill (10)$

Using (CF3), we get from (4)

$$\vdash \{al \land on\} \, ec \, \mathbf{inv} \, \neg cc \, \{al\} \quad (11)$$

Using (CP3), we get from (11,8,9), ϵ and the fact that al is environemt invariant wrt $\neg cc$ from $al \land on$:

$\mathcal{E} \vdash \mathbf{executable} \, sc; ec \, \mathbf{when} \, \neg cc \land al \land \neg on \, \mathbf{before} \, \neg al$
$\hfill (12)$

Using rule (SP), we can derive from ϵ and (6)

$$\mathcal{E} \vdash [al \land \neg on \land \neg cc] \, sc; ec \, [al \land \neg on] \quad (13)$$

Using rule (IF), where $\varphi \equiv al \land \neg on$, $\phi \equiv \varphi$, and $\psi \equiv al$, we can conclude from (12,13) and the fact that $al \land \neg on$ is environment invariant:

$\mathcal{E} \vdash (al \land \neg on) \to \Box(\mathcal{R}_0, al)$

Discussion

Reasoning about complex actions in dynamic environment where environment actions are allowed to occur randomly has also been studied in the literature lately (Baral et al 1998, De Giacomo et al 1997). But these works consider only agents with a capability $\mathcal{C}$ satisfying $\mathcal{C}(p, s) = Exe(p, s)$ for each p and s. In other words, their agents constitute a subset of the class of agents considered in this paper.

For simplification and ease of understanding, we have made an assumption that our agents are alert. In many real world applications, this assumption could be an oversimplification. Hence it is important to study agents which are not alert in the future. Integrating the framework of (Saffioti et al 1995) with ours could be promising here.

Acknowledgement

We would like to thank Bob Kowalski, Franchesca Toni, Marek Sergot, Rob Miller, Murray Shanahan, Fariba Sadri, Ber, Paolo Mancarella, Antonio Brogi for their many very valuable suggestions. We are also very grateful to the three anonymous referees for their constructive and helpful suggestions. The paper is partially supported by the EC Keep in Touch grant, LP-KRR.

References

Agre P.E., Chapman D., 1987, *Pengi: An Implementation of a Theory of activity*, Proc. of AAAI'87, pp 268-272

Brooks R., 1991, *Intelligence without Reasons* Proc. of IJCAI'91, pp 569-595

C. Baral and Son T.C. *Relating theories of actions and reactive control*, http://cs.utep.edu/chitta, 1998

Cohen P.R., Levesque H.J., 1990, *Intention is choice with commitment*, Artificial Intelligence 42, No 3, 213-261

De Giacomo G., Lesperance Y, Levesque H.J. *Reasoning about concurrent actions, prioritized interupts and exogenous actions i the situation calculus*, IJCAI-97.

M. Georgeff and A. Lansky, 1987 *Reactive reasoning and planning*, In AAAI 87.

M. Gelfond and V. Lifschitz., 1993, *Representing actions and change by logic programs*, Journal of Logic Programming, 17(2,3,4):301–323.

Kowalski R., Sadri F.,1996, *Towards a Unified Agent Architecture that Combines Rationality with Reactivity*, Proceedings of International Workshop on Logic in Databases, San Miniato, Italy, Springer Verlag.

Lesperance Y, Levesque H.J., 1995, *Indexical knowledge and robot action - a logical account*, Artificial Intelligence, Vol 73, Feb 1995, pp 117-148

Levesque H.J., Reiter R., Lesperance Y., Lin F., and Scherl R. *GOLOG: A Logic Programming Language for Dynamic Domains* Journal of LP, Vol 31, 1997

R. Reiter., 1996, *Natural actions, concurrency and continuous time in the situation calculus*, In L. Aiello, J. Doyle, and S. Shapiro, editors, KR 96, pages 2–13, 1996.

Rosenschein S.J, Kaelbling L.P., 1995, *A situated view of representation and control*, Artificial Intelligence, Vol 73, Feb 1995, pp 149-176

Saffioti A., Konolige K., Ruspini E. *A multivalued logic approach to integrating planning and control* Artificial Intelligence, Vol 76, 1995

Shoham Y., 1993, *Agent-oriented Programming*, Artificial Intelligence, Vol 60, Feb 1993, pp 51-92

Thomas S.R., 1994, *The PLACA agent programming language* Proc. of ECAI'94 Workshop (ATAL), LNAI 890, 1994

An Algebra for Cyclic Ordering of 2D Orientations

Amar Isli and Anthony G. Cohn
School of Computer Studies, University of Leeds
Leeds LS2 9JT, United Kingdom
{isli,agc}@scs.leeds.ac.uk
http://www.scs.leeds.ac.uk/spacenet/{isli,agc}.html

Abstract

We define an algebra of ternary relations for cyclic ordering of 2D orientations. The algebra (1) is a refinement of the CYCORD theory; (2) contains 24 atomic relations, hence 2^{24} general relations, of which the usual CYCORD relation is a particular relation; and (3) is NP-complete, which is not surprising since the CYCORD theory is. We then provide: (1) a constraint propagation algorithm for the algebra, which we show is polynomial, and complete for a subclass including all atomic relations; (2) a proof that another subclass, expressing only information on parallel orientations, is NP-complete; and (3) a solution search algorithm for a general problem expressed in the algebra.

Introduction

Qualitative spatial reasoning (QSR) has become an important and challenging research area of Artificial Intelligence. An important aspect of it is topological reasoning (e.g. (Cohn 1997)). However, many applications (e.g., robot navigation (Levitt & Lawton 1990), reasoning about shape (Schlieder 1994)) require the representation and processing of orientation knowledge. A variety of approaches to this have been proposed: the CYCORD theory (Megiddo 1976; Röhrig 1994; 1997), Frank's (1992) and Hernández's (1991) sector models and Schlieder's (1993) representation of a panorama.

In real applications, CYCORDs may not be expressive enough. For instance, one may want to represent information such as "objects A, B and C are such that B is to the left of A; and C is to the left of both A and B, or to the right of both A and B", which is not representable in the CYCORD theory. This explains the need for refining the theory, which is what we propose in the paper. Before providing the refinement, which is an algebra of ternary relations, we shall define an algebra of binary relations which is much less expressive (it cannot represent the CYCORD relation). Among other things, we shall provide a composition table for the algebra of binary relations. One reason for doing this first is that it will then become easy to understand how the relations of the refinement are obtained.

Copyright © 1998, American Association for Artificial Intelligence (www.aaai.org). All rights reserved.

We first provide some background on the CYCORD theory; then the two algebras. Next, we consider CSPs on cyclic ordering of 2D orientations. We then provide (1) a constraint propagation algorithm for the algebra of ternary relations, which we show is polynomial, and complete for a subclass including all atomic relations; (2) a proof that another subclass, expressing only information on parallel orientations, is NP-complete; and (3) a solution search algorithm for a general problem expressed in the algebra. Before summarising, we shall discuss some related work.

CYCORDs

Given a circle centred at O, there is a natural isomorphism from the set of 2D orientations to the set of points of the circle: the image of orientation X is the point P_X such that the orientation of the directed straight line (OP_X) is X. A CYCORD X-Y-Z represents the information that the images P_X, P_Y, P_Z of orientations X, Y, Z, respectively, are distinct and encountered in that order when the circle is scanned clockwise starting from P_X.

We now provide a brief background on the CYCORD theory, taken from (Megiddo 1976; Röhrig 1994; 1997). We consider a set $S = \{X_0, \ldots, X_n\}$:

Two linear orders $(X_{i_0}, \ldots, X_{i_n})$ and $(X_{j_0}, \ldots, X_{j_n})$ on S are called cyclically equivalent if: $\exists m \forall k (j_k = (i_k + m) mod(n+1))$. A total cyclic order on S is an equivalence class of linear orders on S modulo cyclic equivalence; X_{i_0}-$\ldots$-X_{i_n} denotes the equivalence class containing $(X_{i_0}, \ldots, X_{i_n})$. A closed partial cyclic order on S is a set T of cyclically ordered triples such that:

(1) X-Y-$Z \in T \Rightarrow X \neq Y$ (irreflexivity)
(2) X-Y-$Z \in T \Rightarrow Z$-Y-$X \notin T$ (asymmetry)
(3) $\{X$-Y-Z, X-Z-$W\} \subseteq T \Rightarrow X$-$Y$-$W \in T$ (transitivity)
(4) X-Y-$Z \notin T \Rightarrow Z$-Y-$X \in T$ (closure)
(5) X-Y-$Z \in T \Rightarrow Y$-Z-$X \in T$ (rotation)

The algebra of binary relations

The algebra is very similar to Allen's (1983) temporal interval algebra. We describe briefly its relations and its three operations.

Given an orientation X of the plane, another orientation Y can form with X one of the following qualitative configurations: (1) Y is equal to X (the angle (X, Y) is equal to 0); (2) Y is to the left of X (the angle (X, Y) belongs to $(0, \pi)$); (3) Y is opposite to X (the angle

(X, Y) is equal to π); (4) Y is to the right of X (the angle (X, Y) belongs to $(\pi, 2\pi)$). The configurations, which we denote by *(Y e X)*, *(Y l X)*, *(Y o X)* and *(Y r X)*, respectively, are Jointly Exaustive and Pairwise Disjoint (JEPD): given any two 2D orientations, they stand in one and only one of the configurations.

The algebra contains four atomic relations: e, l, o, r. A (general) relation is any subset of the set BIN of all four atomic relations (when a relation is a singleton set (atomic), we omit the braces in its representation). A relation $B = \{b_1, \ldots, b_n\}, n \leq 4$, between orientations X and Y, written $(Y\ B\ X)$, is to be interpreted as $(Y b_1 X) \vee \ldots \vee (Y b_n X)$.

The converse of an atomic relation b is the atomic relation $b^\smile$ such that: $\forall X, Y ((Y\ b\ X) \Leftrightarrow (X\ b^\smile\ Y))$. The converse $B^\smile$ of a general relation B is the union of the converses of its atomic relations: $B^\smile = \bigcup_{b \in B} \{b^\smile\}$.

The intersection of two relations B_1 and B_2 is the relation B consisting of the set-theoretic intersection of B_1 and B_2: $B = B_1 \cap B_2$.

The composition of two relations B_1 and B_2, written $B_1 \otimes_2 B_2$, is the strongest relation B such that: $\forall X, Y, Z ((Y B_1 X) \wedge (Z B_2 Y) \Rightarrow (Z B X))$.

The following tables give the converse $b^\smile$ of an atomic relation b (left), and the composition for atomic relations (right):

b	$b^\smile$
e	e
l	r
o	o
r	l

$\otimes_2$	e	l	o	r
e	e	l	o	r
l	l	{l,o,r}	r	{e,l,r}
o	o	r	e	l
r	r	{e,l,r}	l	{l,o,r}

Given three atomic binary relations b_1, b_2, b_3, we define the induced ternary relation $b_1 b_2 b_3$ as follows (see Figure 1(Top)(I)): $\forall X, Y, Z (b_1 b_2 b_3 (X, Y, Z) \Leftrightarrow (Y b_1 X) \wedge (Z b_2 Y) \wedge (Z b_3 X))$. The composition table above has 12 entries consisting of atomic relations, the remaining four consisting of three-atom relations. Therefore any three 2D orientations stand in one of the following 24 JEPD configurations: *eee, ell, eoo, err, lel, lll, llo, llr, lor, lre, lrl, lrr, oeo, olr, ooe, orl, rer, rle, rll, rlr, rol, rrl, rro, rrr*.

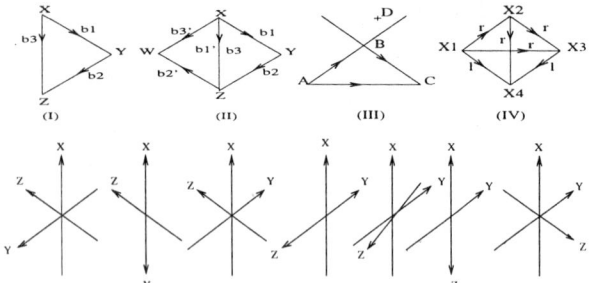

Figure 1: Illustrations.

Refining the CYCORD theory: The algebra of ternary relations

The algebra of binary relations introduced above cannot represent a CYCORD. However, if we use what we have called an *"induced ternary relation"*, we can easily define an algebra of ternary relations of which the CYCORD relation will be a particular relation.

Definition 1 (the relations) *An atomic ternary relation is any of the 24 JEPD configurations a triple of 2D orientations can stand in. We denote by TER the set of all atomic ternary relations: TER = {eee, ell, eoo, err, lel, lll, llo, llr, lor, lre, lrl, lrr, oeo, olr, ooe, orl, rer, rle, rll, rlr, rol, rrl, rro, rrr}. A (general) ternary relation is any subset T of TER:* $\forall X, Y, Z (T(X, Y, Z) \Leftrightarrow \bigvee_{t \in T} t(X, Y, Z))$.

As an example, a CYCORD *X-Y-Z* can be represented by the relation $CR = \{lrl, orl, rll, rol, rrl, rro, rrr\}$ (see Figure 1(Bottom)): $\forall X, Y, Z (X\text{-}Y\text{-}Z \Leftrightarrow CR(X, Y, Z))$.

Definition 2 (the operations) *The converse of an atomic ternary relation t is the atomic ternary relation* $t^\smile$ *such that:* $\forall X, Y, Z (t(X,Y,Z) \Leftrightarrow t^\smile(X, Z, Y))$. *The converse* $T^\smile$ *of a general ternary relation T is* $T^\smile = \bigcup_{t \in T} \{t^\smile\}$.

The rotation of an atomic ternary relation t is the atomic ternary relation $t^\frown$ *such that:* $\forall X, Y, Z (t(X,Y,Z) \Leftrightarrow t^\frown(Y, Z, X))$. *The rotation* $T^\frown$ *of a general ternary relation T is* $T^\frown = \bigcup_{t \in T} \{t^\frown\}$.

The following three tables provide the converse $t^\smile$ *and the rotation* $t^\frown$ *of an atomic ternary relation t:*

t	$t^\smile$	$t^\frown$	t	$t^\smile$	$t^\frown$	t	$t^\smile$	$t^\frown$
eee	eee	eee	lor	rol	olr	rer	rer	ell
ell	lre	lre	lre	ell	rer	rle	err	lel
eoo	ooe	ooe	lrl	lll	rrr	rll	lrr	lrl
err	rle	rle	lrr	rll	rrl	rlr	rlr	lll
lel	lel	err	oeo	oeo	eoo	rol	lor	orl
lll	lrl	lrr	olr	rro	llo	rrl	llr	rrl
llo	orl	lor	ooe	ooe	oeo	rro	olr	rrl
llr	rrl	llr	orl	llo	rro	rrr	rlr	rll

The intersection of two ternary relations T_1 and T_2 is the ternary relation T consisting of the set-theoretic intersection of T_1 and T_2: $\forall X, Y, Z (T(X, Y, Z) \Leftrightarrow T_1(X, Y, Z) \wedge T_2(X, Y, Z))$.

The composition of two ternary relations T_1 and T_2, written $T_1 \otimes_3 T_2$, is the most specific ternary relation T such that: $\forall X, Y, Z, W (T_1(X, Y, Z) \wedge T_2(X, Z, W) \Rightarrow T(X, Y, W))$.

Given four 2D orientations X, Y, Z, W and two atomic ternary relations $t_1 = b_1 b_2 b_3$ and $t_2 = b'_1 b'_2 b'_3$, the conjunction $t_1(X, Y, Z) \wedge t_2(X, Z, W)$ is inconsistent if $b_3 \neq b'_1$ (see Figure 1(Top)(II)). Stated otherwise, when $b_3 \neq b'_1$ we have $t_1 \otimes_3 t_2 = \emptyset$. Therefore, in defining composition for atomic ternary relations, we have to consider four cases: Case 1: $b_3 = b'_1 = e$ ($t_1 \in \{eee, lre, ooe, rle\}$ and $t_2 \in \{eee, ell, eoo, err\}$); Case 2: $b_3 = b'_1 = l$; Case 3: $b_3 = b'_1 = o$; Case 4: $b_3 = b'_1 = r$. The corresponding composition tables are given below (case 1, case 3, case 2 and case 4, respectively, from top to bottom, left to right). The entries E_1, E_2, E_3, E_4 stand for the relations $\{lel, lll, lrl\}$, $\{llr, lor, lrr\}$, $\{rer, rlr, rrr\}$, $\{rll, rol, rrl\}$, respectively. If T_1 and T_2 are general ternary relations: $T_1 \otimes_3 T_2 = \bigcup_{t_1 \in T_1, t_2 \in T_2} t_1 \otimes_3 t_2$.

Definition 3 (projection and cross product) *The 1st, 2nd and 3rd projections of a ternary relation T, which we shall refer to as* $proj_1(T), proj_2(T), proj_3(T)$, *respectively, are* the binary relations $proj_1(T) = \{b_1 \in BIN | (\exists b_2, b_3 \in BIN | b_1b_2b_3 \in T)\}$, $proj_2(T) = \{b_2 \in BIN | (\exists b_1, b_3 \in BIN | b_1b_2b_3 \in T)\}$, $proj_3(T) = \{b_3 \in BIN | (\exists b_1, b_2 \in BIN | b_1b_2b_3 \in T)\}$. The cross product of three binary relations B_1, B_2, B_3, written $B_1 \times B_2 \times B_3$, is the ternary relation $B_1 \times B_2 \times B_3 = \{b_1b_2b_3 | (b_1 \in B_1, b_2 \in B_2, b_3 \in B_3)\} \cap TER$.

$\otimes_3$	eee	ell	eoo	err	$\otimes_3$	oeo	olr	ooe	orl
eee	eee	ell	eoo	err	oeo	oeo	err	eee	ell
lre	lre	E_1	llo	E_2	llo	lre	E_1	llo	E_2
ooe	ooe	orl	oeo	olr	oeo	orl	olr	oor	orr
rle	rle	E_4	rro	E_3	rro	rro	E_3	rle	E_4

$\otimes_3$	lel	lll	llo	llr	lor	lre	lrl	lrr
ell	ell	ell	eoo	err	err	eee	ell	err
lel	lel	lll	llo	llr	lor	lre	lrl	lrr
lll	lll	lll	llo	E_2	lrr	lre	E_1	lrr
lrl	lrl	E_1	llo	llr	llr	lre	lrl	E_2
orl	orl	orl	oeo	olr	olr	ooe	orl	olr
rll	rll	E_4	rro	rrr	rrr	rle	rll	E_3
rol	rol	rrl	rro	rrr	rre	rle	rll	rlr
rrl	rrl	rrl	rro	E_3	rlr	rle	E_4	rlr

$\otimes_3$	rer	rle	rll	rlr	rol	rrl	rro	rrr
err	err	eee	ell	err	ell	ell	eoo	err
llr	llr	lre	lrl	E_2	lrl	E_1	llo	llr
lor	lor	lre	lrl	lrr	lel	lll	llo	llr
lrr	lrr	lre	E_1	lrr	lll	lll	llo	E_2
olr	olr	ooe	orl	olr	orl	orl	oeo	olr
rer	rer	rle	rll	rlr	rol	rrl	rro	rrr
rlr	rlr	rle	E_4	rlr	E_4	rlr	rro	E_3
rrr	rrr	rle	rll	E_3	rll	E_4	rro	rrr

CSPs of 2D orientations

A CSP of 2D orientations (henceforth 2D-OCSP) consists of (a) a finite number of variables ranging over the set 2DO of 2D orientations[1]; and (b) relations on cyclic ordering of these variables, standing for the constraints of the CSP. A binary (resp. ternary) 2D-OCSP is a 2D-OCSP of which the constraints are binary (resp. ternary). We shall refer to binary 2D-OCSPs as BOCSPs, and to ternary 2D-OCSPs as TOCSPs.

We now consider a 2D-OCSP P (either binary or ternary) on n variables $X_1, \ldots, X_n$.

Remark 1 (normalised 2D-OCSP) *If P is a BOCSP, we assume that for all i, j, at most one constraint involving X_i and X_j is specified. The network representation of P is the labelled directed graph defined as follows: (1) the vertices are the variables of P; (2) there exists an edge (X_i, X_j), labelled with B, if and only if a constraint of the form $(X_j B X_i)$ is specified. If P is a TOCSP, we assume that for all i, j, k, at most one constraint involving X_i, X_j, X_k is specified.*

Definition 4 (matrix representation) *If P is a BOCSP, it is associated with an $n \times n$-matrix, which we shall refer to as P for simplicity, and whose elements will be referred to as $P_{ij}, i, j \in \{1, \ldots, n\}$. The matrix P is constructed as follows: (1) Initialise all entries of P to the universal relation BIN: $P_{ij} := BIN, \forall i, j$; (2) $P_{ii} := e, \forall i$; (3) $\forall i, j$ such that P contains a constraint of the form $(X_j B X_i)$: $P_{ij} := P_{ij} \cap B$; $P_{ji} := P_{ij}^{\smile}$.*

If P is a TOCSP, it is associated with an $n \times n \times n$-matrix, which we shall refer to as P, and whose elements will be referred to as $P_{ijk}, i, j, k \in \{1, \ldots, n\}$.

The matrix P is constructed as follows: (1) Initialise all entries of P to the universal relation TER: $P_{ijk} := TER, \forall i, j, k$; (2) $P_{iii} := eee, \forall i$; (3) For all i, j, k such that P contains a constraint of the form $T(X_i, X_j, X_k)$: $P_{ijk} := P_{ijk} \cap T$; $P_{ikj} := P_{ijk}^{\smile}$; $P_{jki} := P_{ijk}^{\frown}$; $P_{jik} := P_{jki}^{\smile}$; $P_{kij} := P_{jki}^{\frown}$; $P_{kji} := P_{kij}^{\smile}$; (4) For all $i, j, i < j$: (a) $B := \bigcap_{k=1}^{n} proj_1(P_{ijk})$; (b) $P_{iij} := e \times B \times B$; $P_{iji} := P_{iij}^{\smile}$; $P_{jii} := P_{iji}^{\frown}$; (c) $P_{jji} := e \times B^{\smile} \times B^{\smile}$; $P_{jij} := P_{jji}^{\smile}$; $P_{ijj} := P_{jij}^{\frown}$.

Without loss of generality, we make the assumption that a TOCSP is closed under projection: $\forall i, j, k, l (proj_1(P_{ijk}) = proj_1(P_{ijl}))$.

Definition 5 *(Freuder 1982) An instantiation of P is any n-tuple of $[0, 2\pi)^n$, representing an assignment of an orientation value to each variable. A consistent instantiation, or solution, is an instantiation satisfying all the constraints. A sub-CSP of size k, $k \leq n$, is any restriction of P to k of its variables and the constraints on the k variables. P is k-consistent if every solution to every sub-CSP of size $k-1$ extends to every k-th variable; it is strongly k-consistent if it is j-consistent, for all $j \leq k$.*

1-, 2- and 3-consistency correspond to node-, arc- and path-consistency, respectively (Mackworth 1977; Montanari 1974). Strong n-consistency of P corresponds to global consistency (Dechter 1992). Global consistency facilitates the exhibition of a solution by backtrack-free search (Freuder 1982).

Remark 2 *A BOCSP is strongly 2-consistent. A TOCSP is strongly 3-consistent.*

We now assume that to the plane is associated a reference system (O, x, y); and refer to the circle centred at O and of unit radius as $\mathcal{C}_{O,1}$. Given an orientation z, we denote by $rad(z)$ the radius $(O, P_z]$ of $\mathcal{C}_{O,1}$, excluding the centre O, such that the orientation of the directed straight line (OP_z) is z. An orientation z can be assimilated to $rad(z)$.

Definition 6 (sector of a binary relation) *The sector, $sect(z, B)$, determined by an orientation z and a binary relation B is the sector of circle $\mathcal{C}_{O,1}$, excluding O, representing the set of orientations z' related to z by relation B: $sect(z, B) = \{rad(z') | z' B z\}$.*

Definition 7 *The projection, $proj(P)$, of a TOCSP P is the BOCSP P' having the same set of variables and such that: $\forall i, j, k, P'_{ij} = proj_1(P_{ijk})$. A ternary relation, T, is projectable if $T = proj_1(T) \times proj_2(T) \times proj_3(T)$. A TOCSP is projectable if for all i, j, k, P_{ijk} is a projectable relation.*

Definition 8 *Let B be a binary relation. The dimension of B is the dimension of its sector. B is convex if its sector is a convex part of the plane; it is holed if (1) it is equal to BIN, or (2) the difference $BIN \setminus B$ is a binary relation of dimension 1 (is equal to e, o or $\{e, o\}$). The subclass of all binary relations which are either convex or holed will be referred to as BCH.*

---

[1] The set 2DO is isomorphic to the set $[0, 2\pi)$.

A ternary relation is {convex,holed} if (1) it is projectable, and (2) each of its projections belongs to BCH. The subclass of all {convex,holed} ternary relations will be referred to as TCH.

Example 1 (the 'Indian tent') *The 'Indian tent' consists of a clockwise triangle (ABC), together with a fourth point D which is to the left of each of the directed lines (AB) and (BC) (see Figure 1(Top)(III)).*

The knowledge about the 'Indian tent' can be represented as a BOCSP on four variables, X_1, X_2, X_3 and X_4, representing the orientations of the directed lines (AB), (AC), (BC) and (BD), respectively. From (ABC) being a clockwise triangle, we get a first set of constraints: $\{(X_2 r X_1), (X_3 r X_1), (X_3 r X_2)\}$. From D being to the left of each of the directed lines (AB) and (BC), we get $\{(X_4 l X_1), (X_4 l X_3)\}$.

If we add the constraint $(X_4 r X_2)$ to the BOCSP, this clearly leads to an inconsistency. Röhrig (1997) has shown that using the CYCORD theory one can detect such an inconsistency, whereas this cannot be detected using classical constraint-based approaches such as those in (Frank 1992; Hernández 1991).

The BOCSP is represented graphically in Figure 1(Top)(IV). The CSP is path-consistent; i.e.: $\forall i, j, k (P_{ij} \subseteq (P_{ik} \otimes_2 P_{kj}))$.[2] However, as mentioned above, the CSP is inconsistent. Therefore:

Theorem 1 *Path-consistency does not detect inconsistency even for BOCSPs of atomic relations.*

The algebra of ternary relations is NP-complete:

Theorem 2 *Solving a TOCSP is NP-complete.*

Proof: We shall show that a TOCSP of atomic relations is polynomial. So, we need to prove that there exists a deterministic polynomial transformation of an NP-complete problem, e.g. a problem expressed in the CYCORD theory (Galil & Megiddo 1977), to a TOCSP. Such a problem, i.e., a conjunction of CYCORD relations, is so transformed by the rule illustrated in Figure 1(Bottom) transforming a CYCORD relation into a relation of the ternary algebra. ∎

A constraint propagation algorithm

A constraint propagation procedure, $s4c(P)$, for TOCSPs is given below. The input is a TOCSP P on n variables, given by its $n \times n \times n$-matrix. When the algorithm completes, P verifies: $\forall i, j, k, l(P_{ijk} \subseteq P_{ijl} \otimes_3 P_{ilk})$.

The algorithm makes use of a queue $Queue$. Initially, we can assume that all variable triples (X_i, X_j, X_k) such that $1 \leq i < j < k \leq n$ are entered into $Queue$. The algorithm removes one variable triple from $Queue$ at a time. When a triple (X_i, X_j, X_k) is removed from $Queue$, the algorithm eventually updates the relations on the neighbouring triples (triples sharing two variables with (X_i, X_j, X_k)). If such a relation is successfully updated, the corresponding triple is sorted, in

---
[2]This can be easily checked using the composition table for atomic binary relations.

such a way to have the variable with smallest index first and the variable with greatest index last, and the sorted triple is placed in $Queue$ (if it is not already there) since it may in turn constrain the relations on neighbouring triples: this is done by add-to-queue(). The process terminates when $Queue$ becomes empty.

```
1.   procedure s4c(P);
2.   repeat{
3.     get next triple (X_i, X_j, X_k) from Queue;
4.     for m := 1 to n{
5.       Temp := P_{ijm} ∩ (P_{ijk} ⊗_3 P_{ikm});
6.       if Temp ≠ P_{ijm}
7.         {add-to-queue(X_i, X_j, X_m); change(i,j,m,Temp);}
8.       Temp := P_{ikm} ∩ (P_{ikj} ⊗_3 P_{ijm});
9.       if Temp ≠ P_{ikm}
10.        {add-to-queue(X_i, X_k, X_m); change(i,k,m,Temp);}
11.      Temp := P_{jkm} ∩ (P_{jki} ⊗_3 P_{jim});
12.      if Temp ≠ P_{jkm}
13.        {add-to-queue(X_j, X_k, X_m); change(j,k,m,Temp);}
14.    }
15.  }
16.  until Queue is empty;
1.   procedure change(i,j,k,T);
2.     P_{ijk} := T; P_{jki} := T⌢; P_{kij} := P⌢_{jki};
3.     P_{ikj} := T⌣; P_{kji} := P⌢_{ikj}; P_{jik} := P⌢_{kji};
```

Theorem 3 *The constraint propagation algorithm runs into completion in $O(n^4)$ time.*

Proof (sketch). The number of variable triples (X_i, X_j, X_k) is $O(n^3)$. A triple may be placed in Queue at most a constant number of times (24, which is the total number of atomic relations). Every time a triple is removed from Queue for propagation, the algorithm performs $O(n)$ operations. ∎

Complexity classes

Theorem 4 *The propagation procedure $s4c(P)$ achieves strong 4-consistency for the input TOCSP P.*

Proof. A TOCSP is strongly 3-consistent (Remark 2). The algorithm clearly ensures 4-consistency, hence it ensures strong 4-consistency. ∎

We refer to the subclass of all 28 entries of the four composition tables of the algebra of ternary relations as CT. We show that the closure under strong 4-consistency, CT^c, of CT is tractable. We then show that the subclass $PAR = \{\{oeo, ooe\}, \{eee, oeo, ooe\}, \{eee, eoo, ooe\}, \{eee, eoo, oeo, ooe\}\}$, which expresses only information on parallel orientations, is NP-complete.

Definition 9 *Let S denote a subclass of the algebra of ternary relations. The closure of S under strong 4-consistency, or s4c-closure of S, is the smallest subclass S^c of the algebra such that: (1) $S \subseteq S^c$; (2) $\forall T_1, T_2 \in S^c(T_1\smile, T_1\frown, T_1 \cap T_2 \in S^c)$; and (3) $\forall T_1, T_2, T_3 \in S^c(proj_3(T_1) = proj_1(T_2) \wedge proj_1(T_1) = proj_1(T_3) \wedge proj_3(T_2) = proj_3(T_3) \Rightarrow T_3 \cap (T_1 \otimes_3 T_2) \in S^c)$.*

Theorem 5 *Let P be a TOCSP expressed in TCH. If P is strongly 4-consistent then it is globally consistent.*

The proof will use the specialisation to $n = 2$ of Helly's convexity theorem (Chvátal 1983):

Theorem 6 (Helly's Theorem) *Let S be a set of convex regions of the n-dimensional space $\mathbb{R}^n$. If every $n+1$ elements in S have a non empty intersection then the intersection of all elements of S is non empty.*

Proof of Theorem 5. Since P lies in the TCH subclass and is strongly 4-consistent, (1) it is equivalent to its projection, say P^{pr}, which is a $BOCSP$ expressed in BCH; and (2) P^{pr} is strongly 4-consistent.

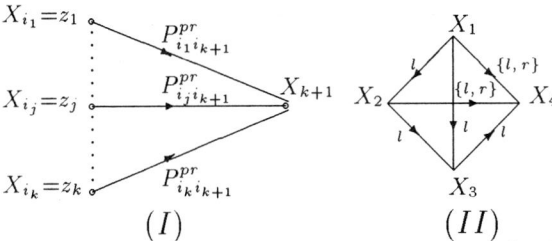

Figure 2: Illustration (I) of the proof; and (II) of non closure of TCH under strong 4-consistency.

So the problem becomes that of showing that P^{pr} is globally consistent. For this purpose, we suppose that the instantiation $(X_{i_1}, X_{i_2}, \ldots, X_{i_k}) = (z_1, z_2, \ldots, z_k), k \geq 4$, is a solution to a k-variable sub-CSP, say S, of P^{pr} whose variables are $X_{i_1}, X_{i_2}, \ldots, X_{i_k}$. We need to prove that the partial solution can be extended to any $(k+1)$st variable, say $X_{i_{k+1}}$, of P^{pr}.[3] This is equivalent to showing that the following sectors have a non empty intersection (see Figure 2(I) for illustration): $sect(z_1, P^{pr}_{i_1 i_{k+1}}), sect(z_2, P^{pr}_{i_2 i_{k+1}}), \ldots, sect(z_k, P^{pr}_{i_k i_{k+1}})$.

Since the $P^{pr}_{i_j i_{k+1}}, j = 1 \ldots k$, belong to BCH, each of these sectors is (1) a convex subset of the plane, or (2) almost equal to the surface of circle $C_{O,1}$ (its topological closure is equal to that surface). We split these sectors into those verifying condition (1) and those verifying condition (2). We assume, without loss of generality, that the first m verify condition (1), and the last $k - m$ verify condition (2). We write the intersection of the sectors as $I = I_1 \cap I_2$, with $I_1 = \bigcap_{j=1}^{m} sect(z_j, P^{pr}_{i_j i_{k+1}}), I_2 = \bigcap_{j=m+1}^{k} sect(z_j, P^{pr}_{i_j i_{k+1}})$.

Due to strong 4-consistency, every three of these sectors have a non empty intersection. If any of the sectors is a radius (the corresponding relation is either e or o) then the whole intersection must be equal to that radius since the sector intersects with every other two.

We now need to show that when no sector reduces to a radius, the intersection is still non empty:

Case 1: m=k. This means that all sectors are convex. Since every three of them have a non empty intersection, Helly's theorem immediately implies that the intersection of all sectors is non empty.

Case 2: m=0. This means that no sector is convex; which in turn implies that each sector is such that its topological closure covers the whole surface of $C_{O,1}$. Hence, for all $j = 1 \ldots k$: (1) $sect(z_j, P^{pr}_{i_j i_{k+1}})$ is equal to the whole surface of $C_{O,1}$ minus the centre ($P_{i_j i_{k+1}}$ is equal to BIN), or (2) $sect(z_j, P^{pr}_{i_j i_{k+1}})$ is equal to the whole surface of $C_{O,1}$ minus one or two radii ($P_{i_j i_{k+1}}$ is equal to $\{e, l, r\}$, $\{l, o, r\}$ or $\{l, r\}$). So the intersection of all sectors is equal to the whole surface of $C_{O,1}$ minus a finite number (at most $2k$) of radii. Since the surface is of dimension 2 and a radius is of dimension 1, the intersection must be non empty.

Case 3: $0 < m < k$. This means that some sectors (at least one) are convex, the others (at least one) are such that their topological closures cover the whole surface of $C_{O,1}$. The intersection I_1 is non empty due to Helly's theorem, since every three sectors appearing in it have a non empty intersection:

Subcase 3.1: I_1 **is a single radius, say** r. Since the sectors appearing in I_1 are less than π, there must exist two sectors, say s_1 and s_2, appearing in I_1 such that their intersection is r. Since, due to strong 4-consistency, s_1 and s_2 together with any sector appearing in I_2 form a non empty intersection, the whole intersection, i.e. I, must be equal to r.

Subcase 3.2: I_1 **is a 2-dimensional (convex) sector.** The intersection I_2 is the whole surface of $C_{O,1}$ minus a finite number (at most $2(k-m)$) of radii. Since a finite union of radii is of dimension 0 or 1, and that the intersection I_1 is of dimension 2, the whole intersection I must be non empty (of dimension 2).

The intersection of all sectors is non empty in all cases. The partial solution can hence be extended to variable $X_{i_{k+1}}$ (which can be instantiated with any orientation in the intersection of the k sectors). ∎

It follows from Theorems 3, 4 and 5 that if the TCH subclass is closed under strong 4-consistency, it must be tractable. Unfortunately, as illustrated by the following example, TCH is not so closed.

Example 2 *The BOCSP depicted in Figure 2(II) can be represented as the projectable TOCSP P whose matrix representation verifies:* $P_{123} = lll, P_{124} = l \times \{l, r\} \times \{l, r\}, P_{134} = P_{234} = l \times l \times \{l, r\}$. *Applying the propagation algorithm to P leaves unchanged $P_{123}, P_{134}, P_{234}$, but transforms P_{124} into the relation $\{lll, llr, lrr\}$, which is not projectable: this is done by the operation $P_{124} := P_{124} \cap (P_{123} \otimes_3 P_{134})$.*

∅	$l \times r \times r$	$r \times r \times r$	$\{l,r\} \times l \times l$
$e \times e \times e$	$o \times e \times o$	$l \times \{e,l,r\} \times l$	$r \times l \times \{e,l,r\}$
$e \times l \times l$	$o \times l \times r$	$l \times \{l,o,r\} \times r$	$r \times r \times \{l,o,r\}$
$e \times o \times o$	$o \times o \times e$	$r \times \{e,l,r\} \times l$	$l \times l \times \{l,o,r\}$
$e \times r \times r$	$o \times r \times l$	$r \times \{l,o,r\} \times l$	$r \times \{l,r\} \times r$
$l \times e \times l$	$r \times e \times r$	$\{e,l,r\} \times r \times r$	$l \times l \times \{l,r\}$
$l \times l \times l$	$r \times l \times e$	$\{l,o,r\} \times l \times r$	$l \times r \times \{e,l,r\}$
$l \times l \times o$	$r \times l \times l$	$\{e,l,r\} \times l \times l$	$r \times \{l,r\} \times l$
$l \times l \times r$	$r \times l \times r$	$\{l,r\} \times l \times r$	$l \times \{l,r\} \times l$
$l \times o \times r$	$r \times o \times l$	$\{l,r\} \times r \times r$	$r \times r \times \{l,r\}$
$l \times r \times e$	$r \times r \times l$	$\{l,o,r\} \times r \times l$	$l \times \{l,r\} \times r$
$l \times r \times l$	$r \times r \times o$	$\{l,r\} \times r \times l$	$r \times l \times \{l,r\}$
			$l \times r \times \{l,r\}$

Enumerating CT^c leads to 49 relations (see table above) all of which lie in TCH. Therefore:

Corollary 1 CT^c *is tractable.*

Proof. Immediate from Theorems 3, 4 and 5. ∎

Example 3 *Transforming the BOCSP of the 'Indian tent' into a TOCSP, say P', leads to $P'_{123} = rrr, P'_{124} = rrl, P'_{134} = rll, P'_{234} = rlr$. P' lies in CT^c,*

---

[3]Since the $TOCSP$ P is projectable, any solution to any sub-CSP of the projection P^{pr} is solution to the corresponding sub-CSP of P. This would not be necessarily the case if P were not projectable.

hence the propagation algorithm must detect its inconsistency. Indeed, the operation $P'_{124} := P'_{124} \cap (P'_{123} \otimes_3 P'_{134})$ leads to the empty relation, since $rrr \otimes_3 rll = rll$.

Theorem 7 *The subclass PAR is NP-complete.*

Proof. The subclass PAR belongs to NP, since solving a TOCSP of atomic relations is polynomial. We need to prove that there exists a (deterministic) polynomial transformation of an NP-complete problem (we consider 3-SAT: a SAT problem of which every clause contains exactly three literals) into a TOCSP expressed in PAR in such a way that the former is satisfiable if and only if the latter is consistent.

Suppose that S is a 3-SAT problem, and denote by: (1) $Lit(S) = \{\ell_1, \ldots, \ell_n\}$ the set of literals appearing in S; (2) $Cl(S)$ the set of clauses of S; (3) $BinCl(S)$ the set of binary clauses which are subclauses of clauses in $Cl(S)$. The TOCSP, P_S, we associate with S is as follows. Its set of variables is $V = \{X(c) | c \in Lit(S) \cup BinCl(S)\} \cup \{X_0\}$. X_0 is a truth determining variable: all orientations which are equal to X_0 correspond to elements of $Lit(S) \cup BinCl(S)$ which are true, the others (those which are opposite to X_0) to elements of $Lit(S) \cup BinCl(S)$ which are false. The constraints of P_S are constructed as follows: (a) for all pair $(X(p), X(\overline{p}))$ of variables such that $\{p, \overline{p}\} \subseteq Lit(S)$, p and $\overline{p}$ should have complementary truth values; hence $X(p)$ and $X(\overline{p}))$ should be opposite to each other in P_S: $\{oeo, ooe\}(X(p), X(\overline{p}), X_0)$; (b) for all variables $X(c_1), X(c_2)$ such that $c_1 \vee c_2$ is a clause of S, c_1 and c_2 cannot be simultaneously false; translated into P_S, $X(c_1)$ and $X(c_2)$ should not be both opposite to X_0: $\{eee, oeo, ooe\}(X(c_1), X(c_2), X_0)$; (c) for all variables $X(\ell_1 \vee \ell_2), X(\ell_1)$, if ℓ_1 is true then so is $(\ell_1 \vee \ell_2)$: $\{eee, eoo, ooe\}(X(\ell_1 \vee \ell_2), X(\ell_1), X_0)$; (d) for all other triple $(X, Y, Z) \in V^3$ of variables, add to P_S the constraint $\{eee, eoo, oeo, ooe\}(X, Y, Z)$.

The transformation is deterministic and polynomial. If M is a model of S, it is mapped to a solution of P_S as follows. X_0 is assigned any value of $[0, 2\pi]$. For all $\ell \in Lit(S)$, $X(\ell)$ is assigned the same value as X_0 if M assigns the value true to literal ℓ, the value opposite to that of X_0 otherwise. For all $(\ell_1 \vee \ell_2) \in BinCl(S)$, $X(\ell_1 \vee \ell_2)$ is assigned the same value as X_0 if either $X(\ell_1)$ or $X(\ell_2)$ is assigned the same value as X_0, the opposite value otherwise. On the other hand, any solution to P_S can be mapped to a model of S by assigning to every literal ℓ the value true if and only if the variable $X(\ell)$ is assigned the same value as X_0. ∎

A solution search algorithm

Since the constraint propagation procedure $s4c$ is complete for the subclass of atomic ternary relations (Corollary 1), it is immediate that a general $TOCSP$ can be solved using a solution search algorithm such as the one below, which is similar to the one provided by Ladkin and Reinefeld (1992) for temporal interval networks, except that (1) it instantiates triples of variables at each node of the search tree, instead of pairs of variables, and (2) it makes use of the procedure $s4c$, which achieves strong 4-consistency, in the preprocessing step and as the filtering method during the search, instead of a path consistency procedure. The other details are similar to those of Ladkin and Reinefeld's algorithm.

```
     Input: the matrix representation of a TOCSP P;
     Output: true if and only if P is consistent;
     function consistent(P);
1.     s4c(P);
2.     if(P contains the empty relation)return false;
3.     else
4.       if(P contains triples labelled with non atomic relations){
5.         choose such a triple, say (X_i, X_j, X_k);
6.         T := P_{ijk};
7.         for each atomic relation t in T{
8.           instantiate triple (X_i, X_j, X_k) with t (P_{ijk} := t);
9.           if(consistent(P))return true;
10.        }
11.        P_{ijk} := T;
12.        return false;
13.      }
14.      else return true;
```

Related work

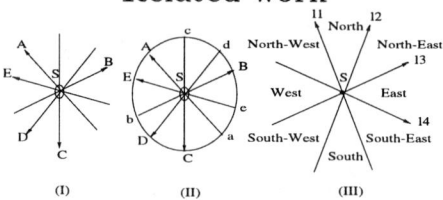

Figure 3: (I-II) The panorama of a location; and (III) Frank's system of cardinal directions.

Representing a panorama. Figure 3(I-II) illustrates the panorama of an object S with respect to five reference objects (landmarks) A, B, C, D, E in Schlieder's system (1993) (page 527). The panorama is described by the total cyclic order of the five directed straight lines $(SA), (SB), (SC), (SD), (SE)$, and the lines which are opposite to them, namely $(Sa), (Sb), (Sc), (Sd), (Se)$: (SA)-(Sc)-(Sd)-(SB)-(Se)-(Sa)-(SC)-(SD)-(Sb)-(SE). By using the algebra of binary relations, only the five straight lines joining S to the landmarks are needed to describe the panorama: $\{(SB)r(SA), (SC)r(SB), (SD)r(SB), (SD)r(SC), (SE)l(SB), (SE)l(SA)\}$; using the algebra of ternary relations, the description can be given as a 2-relation set: $\{rll((SA), (SB), (SE)), rrr((SB), (SC), (SD))\}$.

Because the algebra of binary relations contains the relations e(qual) and o(pposite), its use rules out an implicit assumption which seems to be made in Schlieder's system, which is that the object to be located (i.e., S) is supposed not to be on any of the straight lines joining pairs of the reference objects. Finally, note that Schlieder does not describe how to reason about a panorama description.

Sector models for reasoning about orientations. These models use a partition of the plane into sectors determined by straight lines passing through the reference object, say S. The sectors are generally equal, and the granularity of a sector model is determined by the number of sectors, therefore by the number of straight lines (n straight lines determine $2n$ sectors).

Determining the relation of another object relative to the reference object becomes then the matter of giving the sector to which the object belongs.

Suppose that we consider a model with $2n$ sectors, determined by n (directed) straight lines $\ell_1, \ldots, \ell_n$ which we shall refer to as reference lines. We can assume without loss of generality that (the orientations of) the reference lines verify: ℓ_j is to right of ℓ_i (i.e., $(\ell_j r \ell_i)$), for all $j \in \{2, \ldots, n\}$, for all $i \in \{1, \ldots, j-1\}$. We refer to the sector determined by ℓ_i and ℓ_{i+1}, $i = 1 \ldots n - 1$, as s_i, to the sector determined by ℓ_n and the directed line opposite to ℓ_1 as s_n. For each sector $s_i, i = 1 \ldots n$, the opposite sector will be referred to as s_{n+i}. Figure 3(III) illustrates these notions for Frank's (1992) system of cardinal directions, for which $n = 4$: $\ell_1, \ldots, \ell_4$ are as indicated in the figure; $s_1, \ldots, s_{2 \times 4}$ are North,North-East,East,South-East,South,South-West,West and North-West, respectively. Hernández's (1991) sector models can also benefit from this representation.

Suppose that a description is provided, consisting of qualitative positions of objects relative to the reference object S. S may be a robot for which the current panorama has to be given; the description may consist of sentences such as "landmark 1 is northeast, and landmark 2 south of the robot". Such a description can be translated into a *BOCSP* P in the following natural way. P includes all the relations described above on pairs of the reference lines. For each sentence such as the one above, the relations $(X_{(rob,1)} \, r \, \ell_2)$, $(X_{(rob,1)} \, l \, \ell_3)$, $(X_{(rob,2)} \, l \, \ell_1)$ and $(X_{(rob,2)} \, r \, \ell_2)$ are added to P. $X_{(rob,1)}$, for instance, stands for the orientation of the directed straight line joining the reference object 'robot' to landmark 1.

Summary and future work

We have provided a refinement of the theory of cyclic ordering of 2D orientations, known as CYCORD theory (Megiddo 1976; Röhrig 1994; 1997). The refinement has led to an algebra of ternary relations, for which we have given a constraint propagation algorithm and shown several complexity results.

A discussion of some related work in the literature has highlighted the following: (1) Existing systems for reasoning about 2D orientations are covered by the presented approach (CYCORDs (Megiddo 1976; Röhrig 1994; 1997) and sector models (Frank 1992; Hernández 1991)); (2) The presented approach seems more adequate than the one in (Schlieder 1993) for the representation of a panorama.

There has been much work on Allen's interval algebra (1983), e.g. Nebel and Bürckert's (1995) maximal tractable subclass. Most of this work could be adapted for the two algebras of 2D orientations we have defined.

Finally, a calculus of 3D orientations, similar to what we have presented for 2D orientations, might be developed.

Acknowledgements

The support of the EPSRC under grant GR/K65041, and also the CEC under the HCM network SPACENET are gratefully acknowledged. Our thanks are due to comments from the anonymous referees and members of the SPACENET community.

References

Allen, J. F. 1983. Maintaining knowledge about temporal intervals. *Comm. of the ACM* 26(11):832–843.

Chvátal, V. 1983. *Linear Programming*. New York: W.H. Freeman and Company.

Cohn, A. G. 1997. Qualitative spatial representation and reasoning techniques. In *Proc. KI*, LNAI 1303. Springer Verlag.

Dechter, R. 1992. From local to global consistency. *Art. Int.* 55:87–107.

Frank, A. U. 1992. Qualitative spatial reasoning with cardinal directions. *J. of VLC* 3:343–371.

Freuder, E. C. 1982. A sufficient condition for backtrack-free search. *J. of the ACM* 29:24–32.

Galil, Z., and Megiddo, N. 1977. Cyclic ordering is NP-complete. *TCS* (5):199–182.

Hernández, D. 1991. Relative representation of spatial knowledge: the 2-d case. In *Cognitive and Linguistic Aspects of Geographic Space*, Nato Advanced Studies Institute. Kluwer.

Ladkin, P., and Reinefeld, A. 1992. Effective solution of qualitative constraint problems. *Art. Int.* 57:105–124.

Levitt, T. S., and Lawton, D. T. 1990. Qualitative navigation for mobile robots. *Art. Int.* 44(2):305–360.

Mackworth, A. K. 1977. Consistency in networks of relations. *Art. Int.* 8:99–118.

Megiddo, N. 1976. Partial and complete cyclic orders. *Bull. Am. Math. Soc.* 82:274–276.

Montanari, U. 1974. Networks of constraints: Fundamental properties and applications to picture processing. *Information Sciences* 7:95–132.

Nebel, B., and Bürckert, H.-J. 1995. Reasoning about temporal relations: a maximal tractable subset of Allen's interval algebra. *J. of the ACM* 42(1):43–66.

Röhrig, R. 1994. A theory for qualitative spatial reasoning based on order relations. In *Proc. AAAI*.

Röhrig, R. 1997. Representation and processing of qualitative orientation knowledge. In *Proc. KI*, LNAI 1303. Springer Verlag.

Schlieder, C. 1993. Representing visible locations for qualitative navigation. In *Qualitative Reasoning and Decision Technologies: CIMNE*.

Schlieder, C. 1994. Qualitative shape representation. In Frank, A., ed., *Spatial conceptual models for geographic objects with undetermined boundaries*. London: Taylor and Francis.

The Temporal Analysis of Chisholm's Paradox

Leendert W.N. van der Torre

IRIT
Paul Sabatier University
118 Route de Narbonne
31062 Toulouse, France
TORRE@IRIT.FR

Yao-Hua Tan

EURIDIS
Erasmus University
P.O. Box 1738
3000 DR Rotterdam, the Netherlands
YTAN@FAC.FBK.EUR.NL

Abstract

Deontic logic, the logic of obligations and permissions, is plagued by several paradoxes that have to be understood before deontic logic can be used as a knowledge representation language. In this paper we extend the temporal analysis of Chisholm's paradox using a deontic logic that combines temporal and preferential notions.[0]

Introduction

Deontic logic is a modal logic in which Op is read as 'p ought to be (done).' Deontic logic has traditionally been used by philosophers to analyze the structure of the normative use of language. In the eighties deontic logic had a revival, when it was discovered by computer scientists that this logic can be used for the formal specification and validation of a wide variety of topics in computer science (for an overview and further references see (Wieringa & Meyer 1993)). For example, deontic logic can be used to formally specify soft constraints in planning and scheduling problems as norms. The advantage is that norms can be violated without creating an inconsistency in the formal specification, in contrast to violations of hard constraints. Another application is the use of deontic logic to represent legal reasoning in legal expert systems in artificial intelligence. Legal expert systems have to be able to reason about legal rules and documents such as for example a trade contract. Deontic notions are essential to represent the meaning of such rules or the content of such contracts. A recent topic is the relation between deontic logic and logics of desires and goals as these are developed in qualitative decision theory. First results seem to indicate that extensions of deontic logic can be used in this type of decision theory (Pearl 1993; van der Torre & Tan 1998a). Another recent development that is currently attracting a lot of attention is the use of deontic logic to specify intelligent agents for the Internet. For example, one of the major challenges in electronic commerce is to develop agents that can automatically draft, negotiate and process trade contracts. Since contracts are legal documents, these agents have to be able to perform deontic reasoning to handle these contracts (for a survey see (Kimbrough & Lee 1997)). Furthermore, deontic logic could be fruitful for the analysis and specification of normative issues about the Internet such as authorization, access regulation, and privacy maintenance (Conte & Falcone 1997).

With the increasing popularity and sophistication of applications of deontic logic the fundamental problems of deontic logic become more pressing. From the early days, when deontic logic was still a purely philosophical enterprise, it is known that it suffers from certain paradoxes. The most notorious one is the so-called Chisholm paradox. The conceptual issue of this paradox is how to proceed once a norm has been violated. Clearly, this issue is of great practical relevance, because in most applications norms are violated frequently. Usually it is stipulated in the fine print of a contract what has to be done if a term in the contract is violated. For example, if the delivery time is over due the responsible agent might be obliged to pay the extra transport and wharehousing costs that result from the delay. If the violation is not too serious, or was not intended by the violating party, the contracting parties usually do not want to consider this as a breach of contracts, but simply as a disruption in the execution of the contract that has to be repaired. Hence, Chisholm's paradox is an important benchmark example of deontic logic, and deontic logics incapable of dealing with it are considered insufficient tools to analyze deontic reasoning. The Chisholm set consists of the following four sentences.

1. 'α ought to be (done),'
2. 'if α is (done), then β ought to be (done),'
3. 'if α is not (done), then β ought not to be (done),'
4. 'α is not (done).'

The formalization of these sentences in Standard Deontic Logic (see below) is either inconsistent or the sentences are logically dependent. The Chisholm set is therefore called a *paradox*. Temporal deontic logic can consistently formalize the set

1'. 'α ought to be (done),'
2'. 'if α has been (done), then β ought to be (done),'
3'. 'if α has not been (done), then β ought not to be (done),'
4'. 'α has not been (done).'

---

[0]Copyright 1998, American Association for Artificial Intelligence (www.aaai.org). All rights reserved.

For most α and β the first set can be transformed to the second one without changing the meaning of the sentences. It has been argued that temporal deontic logic therefore *solves* the paradox (van Eck 1982; Loewer & Belzer 1983).[1] However, this 'solution' does not work for the original set given by Chisholm (1963), in which α is read as 'a certain man goes to the assistance of his neighbors' and β as 'the man tells his neighbors that he will come' (Vorobej 1986; Feldmann 1990; Smith 1994; Yu 1995). For example,

2. 'if a certain man goes to the assistance of his neighbors, then the man ought to tell his neighbors that he will come'

means something different than

2'. 'if a certain man has gone to the assistance of his neighbors, then the man ought to tell his neighbors that he will come.'

The representation $1'-4'$ assumes that the antecedent (condition) α occurs before the consequent (conclusion) β, but the contrary is the case for these specific α and β from the Chisholm set! The contribution of this paper is twofold. We introduce a new deontic logic, combining temporal and preferential notions, and we show how the temporal antecedent-before-consequent analysis of the paradox can be extended with preferences on sequences of actions to cover the original Chisholm set. Moreover, we start with a survey of the paradox in so-called Standard Deontic Logic and temporal deontic logic, and, to put our new formalization in context, we end with a formalization in preference-based deontic logic.

Standard Deontic Logic (SDL)

SDL is usually formalized by a normal modal system of type KD^2 according to the Chellas classification, although normal modal systems validate the counterintuitive theorem $O\top$, where $\top$ stands for any tautology like $p \vee \neg p$. We start with some terminology.

- A conditional obligation 'α ought to be (done) if β is (done)' is usually formalized in SDL by $\beta \to O\alpha$, and sometimes by $O(\beta \to \alpha)$.

- The conditional obligation $\beta \to O\alpha$ or $O(\beta \to \alpha)$ is called a *Contrary-To-Duty* (CTD or *secondary*) obligation of the (*primary*) obligation $O\alpha_1$ when β and α_1 are contradictory. The condition of a CTD obligation is only fulfilled if the primary obligation is violated.

- A conditional obligation $\beta \to O\alpha$ or $O(\beta \to \alpha)$ is an *According-To-Duty* (ATD) obligation of $O\alpha_1$ when β logically implies α_1. The condition of an ATD obligation is satisfied only if the primary obligation is fulfilled.

The Chisholm paradox can be represented in SDL by one of the following two sets of SDL formulas, where a is read as 'a certain man goes to the assistance of his neighbors' and t as 'he tells them that he will come.'

$$T_1 = \{Oa, O(a \to t), \neg a \to O\neg t, \neg a\}$$
$$T_2 = \{Oa, a \to Ot, \neg a \to O\neg t, \neg a\}$$

The second obligation is an ATD obligation and the third obligation is a CTD obligation, see Figure 1.

$$Oa \qquad\qquad Oa$$
$$\text{implies} \nearrow \qquad\qquad \text{inconsistent} \nearrow$$
$$O(a \to t) \qquad\qquad \neg a \to O\neg t$$

Figure 1: $O(a \to t)$ is an ATD, $\neg a \to O\neg t$ is a CTD

Both sets are problematic. T_1 derives two contradictory obligations, although the set of premises is intuitively consistent. Since SDL allows a kind of so-called deontic detachment, i.e. $\models_{SDL} (O\beta \wedge O(\beta \to \alpha)) \to O\alpha$, we have $T \models_{SDL} Ot$ from the first two sentences. Moreover, since SDL also allows factual detachment, i.e. $\models_{SDL} (\beta \wedge (\beta \to O\alpha)) \to O\alpha$, we have $T \models_{SDL} O\neg t$ from the last two sentences.

T_2 has logical redundant sentences, because $a \to Ot$ can be derived from $\neg a$,[3] and, more seriously, it does not derive the obligation 'the man ought to tell his neighbors that he will come and go to their assistance' $O(t \wedge a)$, not even from $\{Oa, a \to Ot\}$ (i.e. when the truth value of a is not yet fixed). In SDL the obligation $O(t \wedge a)$ is derived if and only if Ot is derived, because SDL has the theorem $O(\alpha \wedge \beta) \leftrightarrow (O\alpha \wedge O\beta)$. Ot cannot be deontically detached from the first two sentences of T_2 in

---

[1]Traditionally, the deontic paradoxes are understood as phenomena occurring in natural language which cannot be solved, only analyzed. However, several logicians have argued (though not very convincingly) that the deontic paradoxes are not paradoxes in natural language, but only 'paradoxes' in the logical formalization.

[2]System KD is closed under the inference rules modus ponens and necessitation and it satisfies besides the propositional theorems the axioms **K**: $O(\alpha \to \beta) \to (O\alpha \to O\beta)$ that says that the modal operator is closed under modus ponens and **D**: $\neg(O\alpha \wedge O\neg \alpha)$ that says that there are no conflicting obligations.

[3]Chisholm argued that this logical dependence is counterintuitive, and several logicians have demanded that a solution of the Chisholm paradox should represent the sentences such that they are logically independent. However, Tomberlin (1981) observes that the criterion is a 'rather glaring theoretical commitment' which 'would be a case of flagrant methodological question-begging.' Moreover, this logical dependence is easily solved by introducing a weaker notion of implication. For example, the two conditional obligations can be represented by $a > Ot$ and $\neg a > O\neg t$ where '>' is a so-called strict implication. For example, we can represent the obligations by $\Box(a \to Ot)$ and $\Box(\neg a \to O\neg t)$ where $\Box$ is a so-called alethic modal operator that satisfies at least axiom **T**: $\Box \alpha \to \alpha$ (reflexivity). This solves the logical dependence, because the formula $\neg \alpha \to (\alpha > \beta)$ is in contrast to the formula $\neg \alpha \to (\alpha \to \beta)$ not a theorem.

SDL, because we have $\not\models_{SDL} (O\beta \wedge (\beta \to O\alpha)) \to O\alpha$. The problem is that the following intuitive deontic reasoning pattern is not supported.

> Assume that although the man is able to go to the assistance of his neighbors, he has no intention of doing so. He argues: 'I ought to change my mind, tell them, and go to their assistance. So I ought to tell them. My present fulfillment of this obligation will help to make up for my sinfully not going to the assistance!'[4]

Summarizing, the SDL analysis of the Chisholm paradox (the inconsistency of T_1) is based on rejection of one of the detachment principles (e.g. rejection of deontic detachment in T_2). However, both principles seem intuitive in most cases. Rejection of one of the principles because they *seem* to be problematic in a *very few* cases is a solution that seems like overkill. These 'solutions' miss the point of the paradox. Since the problems are caused by the second obligation of the set, we prefer to call it an ATD paradox instead of, as it is usually called, a CTD paradox.

Many alphabetic variants of the Chisholm paradox have been proposed, see e.g. (van Eck 1982; Loewer & Belzer 1983). However, a crucial distinction with the original Chisholm set is that the consequents of the CTD and ATD obligation occur later than the primary obligation! For example, Section 79 subsection 4 of the United Nations Convention on Contracts for the International Sale of Goods reads as follows (see (Smith 1994, p.127)): "The party who fails to perform must give notice to the other party of the impediment and its effect on his ability to perform. If the notice is not received by the other party within a reasonable time after the party who fails to perform knew or ought to have known of the impediment, he is liable for damages resulting from such non-receipt." Here we have a double contrary-to-duty construction: first a contrary-to-duty obligation (to give notice), and then a prevision of what the consequences will be if that contrary-to-duty obligation remains unfulfilled (liability for damages). Obviously, there are many practical issues involved in representing such 'real' systems of norms, for example the formalization of domain knowledge (e.g. exact conditions when a party fails to conform), and the formalization of the protocols involved.[5] However, as far as we are concerned, a typical case between the parties A and B can be formalized by the SDL theory $T_3 = \{O_A p, p \to O_A \neg n, \neg p \to O_A n, \neg p\}$ where p stands for 'party A performs' and p for 'it gives notice to party B.' These SDL sentences have the same logical structure as the SDL sentences of T_2.

At first sight it may seem that a solution for T_3 also solves T_2. However, the two examples are not the same, because they have different temporal references. Their logical representations are only the same, because we left the temporal representation implicit. In the following section we show that this makes a fundamental difference.

Temporal Deontic Logic (TDL)

Since the late seventies, several temporal deontic logics and deontic action logics were introduced, which formalize satisfactorily a special type of CTD obligations, see for example (Thomason 1981; van Eck 1982; Loewer & Belzer 1983). In this section we illustrate the TDL analysis of the paradox using a logic recently proposed by Horty (Horty & Belnap 1995; Horty 1996), based on a seeing-to-it-that (stit) operator. A stit-frame $\langle Tree, <, Agent, Choice, Ought \rangle$ is based on a picture of moments ordered into a tree-like structure $(Tree, <)$, with forward branching representing the openness or indeterminacy of the future, and the absence of backward branching representing the determinacy of the past. $Choice_\alpha^m$ is the partition of the set of histories through moment m for agent α, which represents that at any moment in time, an agent can choose between several sets of histories. $Ought(m)$ is a subset of the set of histories through moment m, representing the good histories.

There are several ways to define actions and obligations in these stit-frames.[6] We say that two histories are m-indistinguishable if at moment m they are in the same equivalence class of the partition. A history is preferred to another one if all histories m-indistinguishable from the first are good, and there is a bad history m-indistinguishable from the second (Horty & Belnap 1995, p.592). Finally, we conditionalize on β by only considering histories in which β is true. We denote the

---

[4] In other words, the man ought to tell his neighbors that he will come, because *otherwise he will violate an obligation*. If he does not tell them and later he goes to the assistance, then he violates the second obligation. If he does not tell them and later he does not go, then he violates the first obligation. In the ideal state the man tells his neighbors that he will come and he goes. According to the semantics of SDL, the obligations $O(t \wedge a)$ and Ot should be derived.

[5] The most serious practical problem is caused by the fact that some norms are defined vaguely (called open texture) such that they are applicable in unforeseen circumstances. As a consequence, criminal law is more difficult to formalize than for example contract law.

[6] A simple definition in the style of SDL is the following. It is obligatory to see to it that α if and only if on all good histories $stit_H : \alpha$ is true (Horty & Belnap 1995, p.616). This is a very strong definition. For example, consider the choice between the two sets $\{h_1, h_2\}$ and $\{h_3, h_4\}$ where h_4 is the only bad history. It seems that we have to choose the first set, because then we always end up in a good history. However, this is not derived from the definition above, because we have $M, m, h_3 \not\models stit_H : \alpha$, whereas h_3 is a good history. The example hints at a definition based on comparing different choices by a so-called dominance function. It is obligatory to see to it that α if and only if all histories in which $stit_H : \alpha$ is true dominate histories in which $stit_H : \alpha$ is false. See (Horty 1996; Horty & Belnap 1995) for different notions of dominance.

obligations by O_{ABC}, because they presuppose that the Antecedent occurs Before the Consequent, as is illustrated by the example below.

Definition 1 (stit$_H$ and O_{ABC}) *A stit$_H$-frame $\langle Tree, <, Agent, Choice, Ought\rangle$ consists of a picture of moments ordered into a tree-like structure with forward branching and the absence of backward branching $(Tree, <)$, a set of agents Agent, a partition of the set of histories through moment m for agent α $Choice^m_\alpha(h)$, and a subset of the set of histories through moment m called Ought(m). Two histories are m-indistinguishable if at moment m they are in the same equivalence class of the partition $Choice^m_\alpha$. The agent sees to it that α at moment m on history h, denoted by $M, m, h \models$ stit$_H : \alpha$, if and only if all histories m-indistinguishable from h make α true, and there is a history through m that does not make α true. We have $M \models O_{ABC}(\text{stit}_H : \alpha \mid \beta)$ if and only if for all moments m and histories h_1, h_2 such that $M, m, h_1 \models \beta \wedge \text{stit}_H : \alpha$ and $M, m, h_2 \models \beta \wedge \neg\text{stit}_H : \alpha$ we have that all β-histories m-indistinguishable from h_1 are good and there is a bad β-history m-indistinguishable from h_2, and such m, h_1 and h_2 exist.*

Horty's logic satisfactorily formalizes the Convention on Contracts example, but not the assistance of neighbors example. Let M be the stit$_H$-model of $T = \{O_{ABC}(\text{stit}_H{:}p|\top), O_{ABC}(\text{stit}_H{:}\neg n|p), O_{ABC}(\text{stit}_H{:}n|\neg p)\}$ represented in Figure 2. We leave it implicit that this

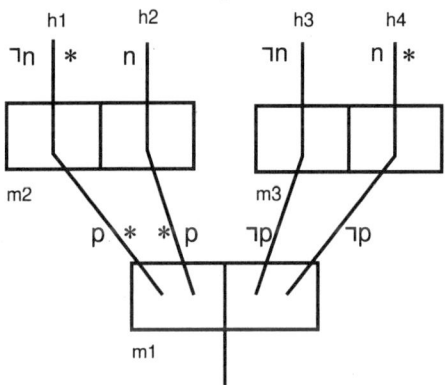

Figure 2: Convention on Contracts

model only represents the obligations of agent A. This figure should be read as follows. The upward direction represents the forward direction of time, and a box represents a partition of histories at a moment. Good histories are represented by an asterisk '*' (for the moment just below it).

First consider the action model. The tree structure represents that party A first has to choose between 'performing' p and 'not performing' $\neg p$, and secondly between 'giving notice' n and 'not giving notice' $\neg n$. At moment m_1 party A sees to it that p or it sees to it that $\neg p$. For example, we have $M, m_1, h_1 \models \text{stit}_H : p$,

because p is true on histories m_1-indistinguishable from h_1 (i.e. h_1 and h_2) and there is a history at m that does not make p true (histories h_3 and h_4). Analogously, at moment m_2 or m_3 it sees to it that n or it sees to it that $\neg n$. Given this action model, consider the deontic model. We have $M \models O_{ABC}(\text{stit}_H : p \mid \top)$ because at moment m_1 the histories h_3 and h_4 are bad histories, $M \models O_{ABC}(\text{stit}_H : \neg n | p)$ because at moment m_2 history h_2 is bad, and $M \models O_{ABC}(\text{stit}_H : n \mid \neg p)$ because at moment m_3 history h_3 is bad. Summarizing, history h_1 is the only good history, and history h_3 is a double-violation history. At each moment it is clear what should be done, because for each moment there is an obligation that prescribes the choice of party A.

Now consider the action model of the assistance of neighbors example represented in Figure 3. Notice that

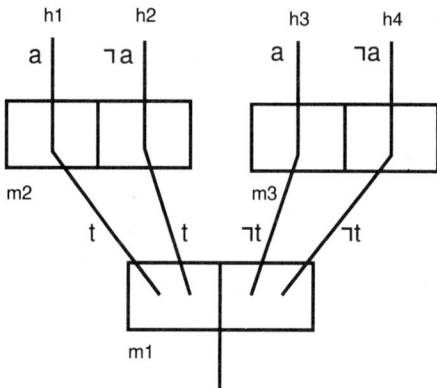

Figure 3: The Chisholm paradox

the deontic part of the model (i.e. $Ought(m)$) has not been specified in the figure. First, the agent has to choose between 'telling' t and 'not-telling' $\neg t$, and secondly the agent has to choose between 'going to the assistance' a and 'not-going to the assistance' $\neg a$. Given this action model, the problem is how to define the deontic part of the model such that the three obligations $O_{ABC}(\text{stit}_H : a \mid \top)$, $O_{ABC}(\text{stit}_H : t \mid a)$ and $O_{ABC}(\text{stit}_H : \neg t | \neg a)$ are true. The fundamental problem is that the model cannot validate the premises, regardless of the choice of $Ought(m)$. For example, we have $M \not\models O_{ABC}(\text{stit}_H : t|a)$, because once a is settled (moment m_2 or m_3) the man can no longer see to it that t. The truth value of t is already fixed.

There is an underlying problem in the action model. The man does not see to it that $(t \wedge a)$ at moment m_1 on history h_1, i.e. we have $M, m_1, h_1 \not\models \text{stit}_H : (t \wedge a)$, because not all histories m_1-indistinguishable from h_1 make $(t \wedge a)$ true. However, intuitively the man can see to it that $(t \wedge a)$ by first choosing h_1 and h_2 at moment m_1, and thereafter choosing h_1 at moment m_2. Moreover, the man is able to see to it that the ideal state is reached in this way. This intuitive deontic reasoning in the Chisholm paradox can be formalized, if the man can reason about sequences of actions. In the following section we show how this can be achieved.

Pref.-based Temporal Deontic Logic (PTDL)

In this section we analyze the Chisholm paradox in Preference-based Temporal Deontic Logic (PTDL). We show how the temporal deontic logic discussed in the previous section can be extended with preferential notions by formalizing a suggestion from Horty (Horty 1996, Section 7.1), see also (Horty 1997). To reason about preferred strategies we adapt the definitions introduced in the previous section in three ways.

$stit_H$ First, we adapt the definition of $stit_H$ such that strategies are taken into account. We define an action which not only considers the choices at a moment, but also the choices the agent can make in the future. We replace the definition of m-indistinguishable by a global definition of indistinguishable. We consider two histories indistinguishable if there is not any moment in which we can distinguish them. We call the operator $stit_S$, where 's' stands for strategies.

O_{ABC} Second, we adapt the definition of O_{ABC} with a notion of dominance for strategies. We therefore need to adapt $Ought$ of the $stit_H$-frame such that it represents a preference ordering on histories instead of a binary distinction between good and bad (Horty & Belnap 1995, p.617). We change the dominance function to the following one: a set of histories is preferred to a second one if each history in the first set is at least as good as each history in the latter set, and there is a history in the second set which is worse than all histories in the first set. This is an arbitrary choice, and other (more complicated) definitions may be preferred, see (Horty 1996, Section 7.2).

O_{ABC} Third, we also adapt the definition of O_{ABC} for a conditionalization on β such that the antecedent can be later than the consequent. We call a history a β-history if β is true at some moment of it. It is implicitly assumed that propositions formalize facts that cannot change over time. For example, we cannot write s for 'Ron is smoking,' but we have to use 'Ron is smoking at moment t.'

Definition 2 ($stit_S$ and O) A $stit_S$-frame $\langle Tree, <, Agent, Choice, Ought\rangle$ is a $stit_H$-frame, where $Ought(m)$ is a preference ordering on the set of histories through moment m. Two histories are indistinguishable if at any moment m they are m-indistinguishable. The agent sees to it that ($stit_S$) α at moment m on history h, denoted by $M, m, h \models stit_S : \alpha$, if and only if all histories indistinguishable from h make α true, and there is a history through m that does not make α true. We have $M \models O(stit_S : \alpha|\beta)$ if and only if for all moments m and all β-histories h_1, h_2 such that $M, m, h_1 \models stit_H : \alpha$ and $M, m, h_2 \models \neg stit_S : \alpha$ we have that all β-histories indistinguishable from h_1 are at least as good as each β-history indistinguishable from h_2, and there is a β-history indistinguishable from h_2 which is worse than each β-history indistinguishable from h_1, and such m, h_1 and h_2 exist.

Consider the set of conditional obligations $T = \{O(stit_S : a \mid \top), O(stit_S : t \mid a), O(stit_S : \neg t \mid \neg a), \neg a\}$ and let M be a model of T represented in Figure 3 with the $Ought$ ordering $h_1 > h_3 > h_4 > h_2$. We have $M, m_1, h_1 \models stit_S : (t \wedge a)$ and $M, m_2, h_1 \models stit_S : (t \wedge a)$. Moreover, we have $M \models O(stit_S : a \mid \top)$, because we have the obligation 'go to the assistance' deontically prefers history h_1 and h_3, $M \models O(stit_S : t \mid a)$, because the obligation 'tell that you go if you go' prefers history h_1 to h_3, and $M \models O(stit_S : \neg t \mid \neg a)$, because the obligation 'do not tell that you go if you do not go' prefers history h_4 to h_2. We have that the agent first ought to see to it that t and thereafter ought to see to it that a, $M \models O(stit_S : t \wedge a \mid \top)$, because history h_1 is preferred to all other histories. We do not have that the agent ought to see to it that t, $M \not\models O(stit_S : t \mid \top)$, because at m_1 history h_2 is not as good as history h_3 and h_4.

Summarizing, taking two moments together in consideration we can derive the obligation to tell as part of a more complex action, but there is not an obligation to tell simpliciter.

Preference-based Deontic Logic (PDL)

Hansson (1971) argues that the fundamental problem underlying the CTD paradoxes is that the type of possible world semantics of SDL is not flexible enough. In these semantics only two types of worlds are distinguished in a model; *actual* and *ideal* ones. The ideal worlds have to satisfy all obligations in a deontic theory T. Clearly, if these obligations contradict each other, then a problem arises. We must use more complicated value structures that somehow bear information about comparisons or gradations of value.

Definition 3 *Let $M = \langle W, \leq, V \rangle$ be a standard possible worlds model with W a nonempty set of worlds, $\leq$ a binary reflexive, transitive and connected accessibility relation, and V a valuation function of the propositions at the worlds. We have $M \models O_{HL}(\alpha|\beta)$ if and only if there is a world w_1 such that $M, w_1 \models \alpha \wedge \beta$ and for all worlds $w_2 \leq w_1$ we have $M, w_2 \models \beta \to \alpha$.*

A typical preference-based model M of the Chisholm set $T = \{O_{HL}(a \mid \top), O_{HL}(t \mid a), O_{HL}(\neg t \mid \neg a), \neg a\}$ is represented in Figure 4. This figure should be

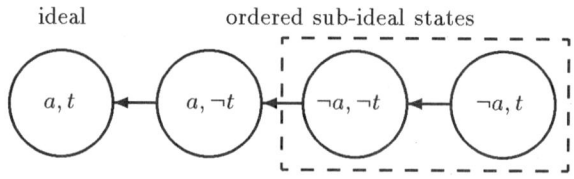

Figure 4: Preference relation of Chisholm's paradox

read as follows. A circle represents a nonempty set of worlds that satisfies the propositions written within them. An arrow represents strict preference for all the worlds represented by the circle. The transitive closure is left implicit. The dashed box represents the set of worlds which might be the actual world, see e.g. (Hansson 1971) for a discussion on the interpretation of circumstances in preference-based logics. We have $M \models O_{HL}(a \wedge t | \top)$ and $M \models O_{HL}(t | \top)$, because the logic has the theorem $\models O_{HL}(\alpha | \beta) \wedge O_{HL}(\beta | \top) \to O_{HL}(\alpha | \top)$.

In previous papers (Tan & van der Torre 1996; van der Torre & Tan 1997) we argued that PDL is the *minimal* logic to analyze CTDs. The analyses given in this paper are in accord with this arguments. In particular, it is clear that the PTDL analysis of the Chisholm paradox in the previous section is analogous to the PDL analysis, in the sense that a history is a world in which we added temporal structure explicitly. Moreover, the analysis of Chisholm's paradox in Hansson's PDL and the analysis in our new PTDL are both based on rejection of factual detachment. There are several ways in which our PTDL can be extended with alternative notions of factual detachment developed in TDL and PDL (for the latter see e.g. (van der Torre 1997)).

Conclusions

In previous work we introduced preference-based frameworks for deontic reasoning and in this paper we propose a deontic logic that combines preferential and temporal notions. We used the logic to analyze the backward version of Chisholm's paradox. We showed how the paradox can be analyzed if temporal and preferential notions are represented explicitly. Moreover, the analysis of the interaction between preferential and temporal notions is a first step towards the analysis of the dynamics of obligations. In (van der Torre & Tan 1998b) we discuss an alternative way to combine preferences and time by formalizing prescriptive obligations in update semantics. However, the logics are not expressive enough yet to formalize all aspects of preferences that change in time. This is subject of present research.

References

Chisholm, R. 1963. Contrary-to-duty imperatives and deontic logic. *Analysis* 24:33–36.

Conte, R., and Falcone, R. 1997. Icmas'96: Norms, obligations, and conventions. *AI Magazine* 18,4:145–147.

Feldmann, F. 1990. A simpler solution to the paradoxes of deontic logic. In Tomberlin, J., ed., *Philosophical perspectives 4: Action theory and Philosophy of Mind*. Atascadero: Ridgview.

Hansson, B. 1971. An analysis of some deontic logics. In Hilpinen, R., ed., *Deontic Logic: Introductory and Systematic Readings*. Dordrecht, Holland: D. Reidel Publishing Company. 121–147.

Horty, J., and Belnap, N. 1995. The deliberative stit: a study of action, omission, ability, and obligation. *Journal of Philosophical Logic* 583–644.

Horty, J. 1996. Agency and obligation. *Synthese* 108:269–307.

Horty, J. 1997. *Agency and Deontic Logic*. Preliminary draft.

Kimbrough, S., and Lee, R. 1997. Formal aspects of electronic commerce: research issues and challenges. *International Journal of Electronic Commerce* 1.

Loewer, B., and Belzer, M. 1983. Dyadic deontic detachment. *Synthese* 54:295–318.

Pearl, J. 1993. A calculus of pragmatic obligation. In *Proceedings of Uncertainty in Artificial Intelligence (UAI'93)*, 12–20.

Smith, T. 1994. *Legal expert systems: discussion of theoretical assumptions*. Ph.D. Dissertation, University of Utrecht.

Tan, Y.-H., and van der Torre, L. 1996. How to combine ordering and minimizing in a deontic logic based on preferences. In *Deontic Logic, Agency and Normative Systems. Proceedings of the Δeon'96. Workshops in Computing*, 216–232. Springer Verlag.

Thomason, R. 1981. Deontic logic as founded on tense logic. In Hilpinen, R., ed., *New Studies in Deontic Logic: Norms, Actions and the Foundations of Ethics*. D. Reidel. 165–176.

Tomberlin, J. 1981. Contrary-to-duty imperatives and conditional obligation. *Noûs* 16:357–375.

van der Torre, L., and Tan, Y. 1995. Cancelling and overshadowing: two types of defeasibility in defeasible deontic logic. In *Proceedings of the IJCAI'95*, 1525–1532.

van der Torre, L., and Tan, Y. 1997. The many faces of defeasibility in defeasible deontic logic. In Nute, D., ed., *Defeasible Deontic Logic*. Kluwer. 79–121.

van der Torre, L., and Tan, Y.-H. 1998a. Diagnosis and decision making in normative reasoning. *Artificial Intelligence and Law*. To appear.

van der Torre, L., and Tan, Y. 1998b. An update semantics for prima facie obligations. In *Proceedings of the ECAI'98*. To appear.

van der Torre, L. 1997. *Reasoning About Obligations: Defeasibility in Preference-based Deontic Logics*. Ph.D. Dissertation, Erasmus University Rotterdam.

van Eck, J. 1982. A system of temporally relative modal and deontic predicate logic and its philosophical application. *Logique et Analyse* 100:249–381.

Vorobej, M. 1986. Conditional obligaton and detachment. *Canadian Journal of Philosophy* 16:11–26.

Wieringa, R., and Meyer, J.-J. 1993. Applications of deontic logic in computer science: A concise overview. In Meyer, J.-J., and Wieringa, R., eds., *Deontic Logic in Computer Science*. Chichester, England: John Wiley & Sons. 17–40.

Yu, X. 1995. *Deontic Logic with Defeasible Detachment*. Ph.D. Dissertation, University of Georgia.

Temporal Reasoning with Qualitative and Quantitative Information about Points and Durations*

Rattana Wetprasit and Abdul Sattar
Knowledge Representation and Reasoning Unit
School of Computing and Information Technology
Griffith University, NATHAN, QLD 4111 AUSTRALIA
{rattana,sattar}@cit.gu.edu.au

Abstract

A duration is known as a time distance between two point events. This relationship has recently been formalized as the *point duration network* (PDN) in (Navarrete & Marin 1997). However, only the qualitative information about points and durations was considered. This paper presents an *augmented point duration network* (APDN) to represent both qualitative and quantitative information about point events. We further extend APDN to capture quantitative information about durations. We propose algorithms to solve reasoning tasks such as determining satisfiability of the network, and finding a consistent scenario with minimal domains. Thus, we present an expressively richer framework than the existing ones to handle both qualitative and quantitative information about points as well as durations.

Introduction

Temporal knowledge can be classified into two main categories: qualitative and quantitative (or metric) information. Relationships between events (e.g., Fred arrived at work before John) are considered as a class of qualitative information while numeric distance or an event instance (e.g., Fred took 15-20 minutes to get to work) is considered as quantitative information. Interval algebra (Allen 1983) and point algebra (Vilain & Kautz 1986) are two traditional models to represent and reason with qualitative information when events are considered as intervals and points, respectively. In (Dean & McDermott 1987) and (Dechter, Meiri, & Pearl 1991), two systems for handling metric information between point events were proposed. The integration of qualitative and quantitative information between point and interval events was attempted in (Meiri 1996) and (Kautz & Ladkin 1991).

In (Barber 1993), an object-oriented approach with two types of items: points and durations was introduced. This approach can represent qualitative and quantitative constraints between points and durations but no disjunction of the constraints is allowed. Recently, a point based bi-network to represent qualitative relationships among point events and durations, so called *point duration network* (PDN) has been proposed (Navarrete & Marin 1997). In their framework, a duration represents a time distance between two point events. The basic relations between two durations are: $\{<,>,=\}$, indicating a duration is either shorter, longer or equal to another duration.

In this paper, we examine the frameworks proposed for representing information about points and durations, in particular the recently proposed point duration network framework. Let us consider the example proposed in (Meiri 1996) with additional qualitative information about durations and quantitative information about points concerning Bob's traveling.

Example 1 John, Fred and *Bob* work for a company that has local and main offices in Los Angeles. They usually work at the local office, in which case it takes John less than 20 minutes and Fred 15-20 minutes to get to work. Twice a week John works at the main office, in which case his commute to work takes at least 60 minutes. Today John left home between 7:05-7:10 a.m., and Fred arrived at work between 7:50-7:55 a.m. We also know that Fred and John met at a traffic light on their way to work. *Since Bob lives close to the office, it takes him less time than Fred to go to work and today he leaves home before 7:45 a.m.* □

To the best of our knowledge, none of the existing frameworks can adequately handle this sort of information. We would like to have a system that can sufficiently represent qualitative as well as quantitative information about points and durations. For example, it should be able to deduce that *today Bob arrives at work not later than 8.05 a.m.* We also expect our system to retain the reasoning ability of the existing systems such as deducing that John arrived at the main office after 8.05 a.m., and he arrives at work at least 10 minutes after Fred.

In this paper, we present an augmented point duration network by introducing unary constraints to all point and duration variables. This new framework allows us to:

Copyright (c) 1998, American Association for Artificial Intelligence (www.aaai.org). All rights reserved.

1. represent and reason with both qualitative and quantitative constraints over point events and durations between points;
2. provide an expressively rich point duration network framework that can handle the disjunction of qualitative and quantitative (metric) constraints (dealing with possible uncertain knowledge); and
3. effectively use the existing techniques for point algebra networks and constraint satisfaction problems to solve the reasoning problems within these extended networks.

Our intuition behind constraining point and duration variables with unary constraints is that the quantitative information about when each point takes place indicates the instance of the corresponding point. The metric information about each pair of points specifies the distance between the two points, which is the instance of the corresponding duration. Therefore, the quantitative temporal information can be naturally represented by constraining the domains of points and durations. Let us consider the above example, if we anchor the beginning of the world, x_0, to 7:00 a.m., other time instances in the above story are represented with respect to x_0. Let us consider Fred's traveling. We denote F_1 and F_2 as the time that Fred leaves home and arrives at work respectively. From the given information that Fred arrives at work between 7:50-7:55 a.m., the domain of F_2 is restricted to the time interval (50,55). The time distance from F_1 to F_2 is also limited to (15,20) by the fact that Fred takes 15-20 minutes to get to work. By the distance property, we can simply infer that the domain of F_1 or the time that Fred leaves home is between (30,40) or 7:30-7:40 a.m.

Definitions

Before defining a point duration network, we first review the point algebra as the underlying structure of the proposed framework. Point algebra (PA) considers an event as a time instance, mapping to a rational number on an imaginary time line. The three possible basic relations that can hold between any two points is a set (T) of $\{<, >, =\}$. A PA network is a binary constraint network where the variables represent time points $x_1, ..., x_n$ having the same domain, i.e., the set of rational numbers $\mathcal{Q}$. The binary relation $R_{i,j}$ is a disjunction of the basic point relations in T.

We introduce qualitative and quantitative constraints which will be used in the augmented framework and the further extension.

Definition 1 A *qualitative constraint* between two objects O_i and O_j, in which both objects may be a pair of points or durations, is a disjunction of the form

$$(O_i r_1 O_j) \vee ... \vee (O_i r_k O_j)$$

where each of the r_i's is a basic relation in T.

Definition 2 A *quantitative constraint* is represented by a set of intervals[1]:

$$I = \{I_1, ..., I_k\} = \{[a_1, b_1], ..., [a_k, b_k]\}.$$

- If $a_l \neq b_l$ $(1 \leq l \leq k)$ and $k > 1$ then the constraint is classified as *multiple-interval*.
- If $a_l \neq b_l$ $(1 \leq l \leq k)$ and $k = 1$ then the constraint is classified as *single-interval*.
- If $a_l = b_l$ $(1 \leq l \leq k)$ and $k \geq 1$ then the constraint is classified as *discrete*.

There are two types of quantitative constraints:

1. A *unary constraint* quantitatively restricts the domain of a variable, say O_i, to the given set of intervals. Essentially, it represents the disjunction:

$$(a_1 \leq O_i \leq b_1) \vee ... \vee (a_k \leq O_i \leq b_k).$$

The three types of domains are multiple-interval, single-interval, and discrete, corresponding to the three classes of quantitative constraints.

2. A *binary constraint* represents the metric information between durations (for more detail see the further extension section).

Point Duration Network

The *point duration network* (PDN) was first formulated in (Navarrete & Marin 1997)[2]. A PDN consists of two binary networks: point and duration networks. Domains of point and duration variables are rational numbers, while the binary constraints in both networks are qualitative constraints. For example, $R_{ij,km} = \{\leq\}$, indicates that the duration from point i to j is equal to or shorter than the duration from k to m. The two networks are related by a set of ternary constraints specifying the relationship between points and durations.

Augmented Point Duration Network

We propose to augment the PDN framework with unary domain constraints to enforce the handling of both qualitative and quantitative information about points, and qualitative information about durations.

Definition 3 An *augmented point duration network* (APDN) is a structure $\Sigma_{APD} = \langle N_P, N_D, Rel(P, D) \rangle$, where

- N_P is a network consisting of a set (P) of point variables: $\{x_1, ..., x_n\}$; the domains of points: $\{D_1, ..., D_n\}$, which are restricted by unary constraints; and a set $(Rel(P))$ of binary relations over point variables,

$$Rel(P) = \{R_{i,j} \in 2^T \mid 1 \leq i, j \leq n\}.$$

---
[1] For simplicity, we assume closed intervals, but the same treatment can be applied to open and semi-open intervals as well. This is similar to a set of intervals for TCSP defined in (Dechter, Meiri, & Pearl 1991).
[2] In (Allen & Kautz 1985), the notion of duration was investigated in terms of one duration being a proportion of another.

- N_D is a network consisting of a set (D) of duration variables: $\{d_{ij} \mid 1 \leq i < j \leq n\}$; the domains of durations: $\{D_{12}, ..., D_{(n-1)n}\}$, which are restricted by unary constraints; and a set $(Rel(D))$ of binary relations over duration variables,

  $Rel(D) = \{R_{ij,km} \in 2^T \mid 1 \leq i,j,k,m \leq n\}$.

- $Rel(P, D)$ is a set of *ternary* constraints relating points and durations, where
  $Rel(P, D) = \{\triangle_{ij} \subseteq Q^3 \mid 1 \leq i, j \leq n\}$ such that
  $\triangle_{ij} = \{(X_i, X_j, D_{ij}) \in Q^3 \mid D_{ij} = |X_i - X_j|\}$.

The $Rel(P)$, $Rel(D)$, $Rel(P,D)$, and all unary constraints altogether are referred to as Σ_{APD}-constraints. When a domain of the network is restricted to a simple interval, we call it a *simple domain*.

A duration variable d_{ij} represents time elapsed between points x_i and x_j in an absolute value form, i.e., only d_{ij} $(i < j)$ is represented (not d_{ji}). The set of ternary constraints, $Rel(P, D)$, specifies instances of points and durations which are related to each other by the distance property $d_{ij} = |x_i - x_j|$.

Illustration: (Continued from Example 1) J_1, J_2, B_1, B_2 denote the time that John and Bob respectively leave home and arrive at the office. All given information can be represented in the APDN as shown in Figure 1. The beginning of the story is anchored at 7:00 a.m. Therefore, the information that John left home between 7:05-7:10 a.m. is represented as a single-interval domain of point J_1, i.e., (5,10), and the same treatment is applied for the time that Fred arrived at work (F_2), and Bob left home (B_1). The time that John takes in reaching, either his local office (less than 20 minutes), or the main office (at least 60 minutes), is represented by the multiple-interval domain of the duration node $J_1 J_2$. The information that Fred takes between 15-20 minutes to go to work is represented as the domain of the duration node $F_1 F_2$. The qualitative relation that *Bob takes less time than Fred to go to work* is specified by the constraint between durations $B_1 B_2$ and $F_1 F_2$. The incomplete qualitative information that *Fred and John met at a traffic light on their way to work* can be interpreted as either a *start, started by, during, contain, finish, finished-by, overlapped, overlapped-by, or equal* relationship between the two events of Fred and John going to work. This can be represented by a conjunction of relations between endpoints of the two intervals as in the point network of Figure 1.

Consistency and Minimality

Given an APDN, $\Sigma_{APD} = \langle N_P, N_D, Rel(P,D) \rangle$ with n point variables $(x_1, ..., x_n)$, and the domains of points $(D_1, ..., D_n)$. An assignment of all variables in N_P is the n-tuple of the form:

$A_P = ((x_1, X_1), ..., (x_n, X_n))$, $\quad X_i \in D_i$.

Similarly, the assignment of all $\frac{n(n-1)}{2}$ duration variables in N_D $(d_{12}, ..., d_{(n-1)n})$ with the domain constraints $(D_{12}, ..., D_{(n-1)n})$ is the tuple of the form:

$A_D = ((d_{12}, Y_{12}), ..., (d_{(n-1)n}, Y_{(n-1)n}))$, $\quad Y_{ij} \in D_{ij}$.

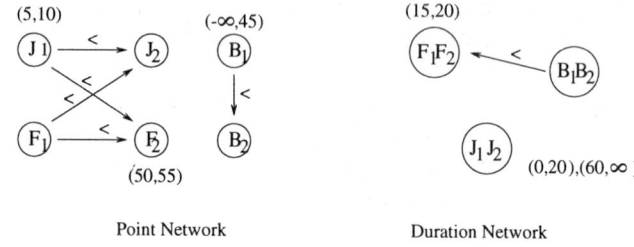

Figure 1: The graphical representation of Example 1

A pair $A(A_P, A_D)$ is *a solution* for the APDN iff it satisfies all the Σ_{APD}-constraints. An APDN is *consistent* iff there is a solution.

A value X_i is a feasible value for a variable x_i if there exists a solution in which $x_i = X_i$. The set of all feasible values of a variable is called the *minimal domain*. We can also say the same for the minimal domain of a duration variable.

A *simple APDN*, $\Sigma^S_{APD} = \langle N^S_P, N^S_D, Rel^S(P,D) \rangle$, is an APDN such that every qualitative constraint is a basic relation and every quantitative constraint is an element of the single-interval class.

Definition 4 *A consistent scenario of an APDN with minimal domains* is a consistent simple APDN where all constraints are minimal.

In next section, we present an algorithm to find a consistent scenario of APDN with minimal domains.

Reasoning with APDN

The useful reasoning tasks for an APDN are determining:

1. satisfiability of the network;
2. a consistent scenario with minimal domains; and
3. the minimal APDN.

The satisfiability problem is a special case of finding a consistent scenario of an APDN with minimal domains (or the minimal APDN). However, computing consistent scenarios of PDNs is an NP-complete problem (Navarrete & Marin 1997). Similarly, we cannot expect better computational complexity in the case of APDNs, as stated in the following theorem:

Theorem 5 *Deciding the satisfiability of an augmented point duration network (APDN) is an NP-complete problem.*

This theorem can be proved by showing that the APDN framework is an integration of the PDN framework and the *temporal constraint satisfaction problem* (TCSP) introduced in (Dechter, Meiri, & Pearl 1991). A TCSP network is a constraint network of point events with unary (domain) and binary quantitative constraints. Each constraint is represented by a set of intervals I defined in Definition 2.

We propose an algorithm for finding a consistent scenario of an APDN with minimal simple domains. To do so, instead of starting from the simple case, as proposed for PDN and TCSP, we allow non-atomic relations in point and duration networks with multiple-interval domains as input. Our goal is to prune the unnecessary search space before decomposing the main problem into several simple problems. This algorithm comprises two functions: CSAPDN and DomainMinimize.

Algorithm $CSAPDN\_MinD$
Input: An APDN
Output: A consistent scenario of APDN
with minimal simple domains
If CSAPDN($\Sigma_{APD}, \Sigma_{APD}^S$) then
if DomainMinimize(Σ_{APD}^S) then
the APDN is consistent.

The CSAPDN finds a consistent scenario of APDN, if succeed then DomainMinimize finds minimal simple domains with respect to the consistent scenario.

To demonstrate the functioning of our algorithm, the following simple example will be used through out this section:

Example 2 An APDN of four points $(p_1, ..., p_4)$ with qualitative and quantitative constraints as shown below:

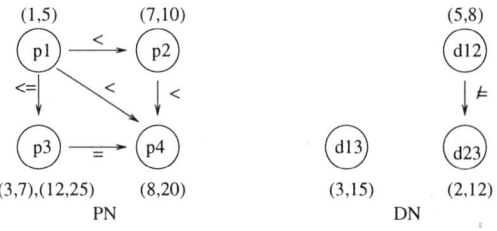

$\square$

Computing Consistent Scenarios

The core structure of CSAPDN is motivated by the algorithm CSPAN for finding a solution for PA networks (Van Beek 1992). Here, we need to consider the relationship between points and durations and also their domains.

The main description of CSAPDN is as follows:

Step 1 Since all nodes in the same class (if instantiated, they will have '=' relationship) must have the same domain, our first task is to identify all equivalent classes of nodes in the point and duration networks individually. This is the same as finding the *strongly connected components* (SCCs) in graphs for which the efficient algorithms by (Tarjan 1972) can be applied[3].

Illustration: In PN, points p_3 and p_4 are in the same SCC, while none of durations can be classified into the same class. Points p_1, p_3 and p_4 are not in the same class as '=' $\notin R_{1,4}$.

Step 2 From the SCCs in PN and DN, deduce more nodes that can be classified into same SCCs using the following properties:

---

[3]Nodes i and j belong to the same SCC if there exists a path from i to j and a path from j to i which contain only the edges labeled with '$\leq$' or '=', e.g., $i \leq j = i$.

- If two points i and j are in the same SCC then it implies: 1) For every point $k \neq i, j$, it must be $d_{ik} = |k-i| = |k-j| = d_{jk}$ (d_{ik} and d_{jk} must be in the same SCC); and 2) $d_{ij} = 0$ (d_{ij} must be in the same SCC as the null duration d_0).

- If two durations, ik and jk ($i \neq j$) are in the same SCC then points i and j must be in the same SCC. The same statement can also be made for ki and kj.

Illustration: Since points p_3 and p_4 are in the same SCC, then a) duration d_{34} has null distance; b) the distances from point p_1 to p_3 and p_4 are equal, or d_{13} and d_{14} are in the same SCC. This also applies to d_{23} and d_{24}. In the duration network, no further node can be grouped into SCC.

Step 3 Condense PN and DN by collapsing each SCC into a single node. The domain of each new node will be the intersection of all domains in the SCC, and the relation between a pair of the new nodes will be the intersection of the relations from nodes in one SCC to another SCC. Thus, the original APDN is reduced to the point and duration networks such that all nodes are in different SCCs. If any intersection results in empty set, the corresponding constraint is inconsistent.

Illustration: The point network then is reduced to three nodes: x_1, x_2, and x_3, while x_3 includes points p_3 and p_4. The reduced duration network consists of four nodes: y_0 with the null duration d_{34}, and y_{12}, y_{23} and y_{13} with the durations $(d_{12}), (d_{23}, d_{24})$ and (d_{13}, d_{14}) respectively. Relations and domain constraints are shown as follows (the direction of the arrow from node i to j indicates i *is less than* j, if not labeled otherwise). The interval $(3,7)$ on the domain of p_3, after intersection with domain of p_4, becomes empty set.

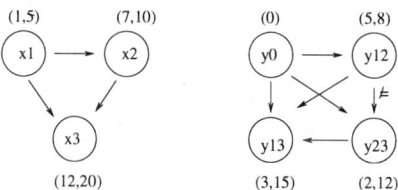

Step 4 Find a consistent scenario for the APDN, in other words, a pair of consistent scenarios of reduced networks for PN and DN that satisfy each other. This step is much like the function Exist_Solution proposed in (Navarrete & Marin 1997). We first find a consistent scenario for PN and DN independently. Then each duration in the consistent scenario of DN is instantiated with an integer d corresponding to the ordering of the durations. Using the distance property $x_j = x_i + d_{ij}$, the value of each point in PN is then calculated. If all relations between the point values in PN are satisfied then a consistent scenario for the APDN is found.

Illustration: We choose consistent scenarios of PN and DN as: $x_1 < x_2 < x_3$, and $y_0 < y_{12} < y_{23} < y_{13}$, $y_0 < y_{23}, y_0 < y_{13}, y_{12} < y_{13}$. Then without considering the domains of all nodes, we sequentially assign integers to all durations: $y_0 = 0, y_{12} = 1, y_{23} = 2$ and $y_{13} = 3$. By the distance property and the initial value

C	QUAN(C)
$<$	$(0, \infty)$
$\leq$	$[0, \infty)$
$=$	$[0]$
$>$	$(-\infty, 0)$
$\geq$	$(-\infty, 0]$
$\neq$	$(-\infty, 0), (0, \infty)$
$?$	$(-\infty, \infty)$

Table 1: The QUAN translation

$x_1 = 0$, we have $x_2 = x_1 + y_{12} = 1$ and $x_3 = 3$, which are consistent with their atomic relations in the consistent scenario. Therefore, the chosen consistent scenario of PN is consistent with the one for DN.

Computing Minimal Domains

The subfunction DomainMinimize takes the consistent scenario, $\Sigma_{APD}^S = \langle N_P^S, N_D^S, Rel^S(P, D) \rangle$, from the subfunction CSAPDN with (possible multiple-interval) domains as an input, and returns the minimal simple domains with respect to N_P^S and N_D^{S4}. A general description of this subfunction is as follows:

Step 1 Find the domains that are consistent with the qualitative relations of N_P^S and N_D^S individually by applying arc-consistency. In (Meiri 1996), the domains of a nonempty arc- and path-consistent CPA network (the PA network without '$\neq$' relation) over multiple-interval domains are shown to be minimal. A consistent scenario is certainly k-consistent ($k \leq n$)[5], and all qualitative labels are non-disjunctive constraints (no '$\neq$' relation). Therefore, acquiring an arc-consistent network at this step will result in all minimal domains of the corresponding network. The main operation of the arc-consistency algorithm REVISE((i, j)) makes arc (i, j) consistent by tightening the domain of node i according to the domain of node j and the qualitative constraint between i and j:

$$D_i := D_i \otimes (D_j - QUAN(C_{i,j}))$$

Function QUAN(C) transforms qualitative temporal constraints to quantitative constraints (Meiri 1996) (shown in Table 1).

Illustration: The consistent scenarios of N_P^S from the previous steps is already arc-consistent. Enforcing arc-consistency on N_D^S results in the updating of two domains: D_{23} and D_{13}. Consider arc (d_{23}, d_{12}), function REVISE((d_{23}, d_{12})) is expressed as: $D_{23} := D_{23} \otimes (D_{12} - QUAN(C_{23,12})) = (2, 12) \otimes ((5, 8) - (-\infty, 0)) = (2, 12) \otimes (5, \infty) = (5, 12)$. The domain of d_{23} has been updated, and thus all related arcs to d_{23} ((d_{12}, d_{23}),

---

[4] For simplicity, we will refer to a component in the reduced network of PN as a point node, and a component in the reduced network of DN as a duration node.

[5] As noted in (Meiri 1996), the notation of k-consistency here is slightly different from the orginal definition (Freuder 1978) since at this stage, we consider the consistency as per infinite domains.

(d_{13}, d_{23}) and (d_0, d_{23})) are added into queue. Then after the propagation terminates, the arc-consistent N_P^S and N_D^S are as shown below:

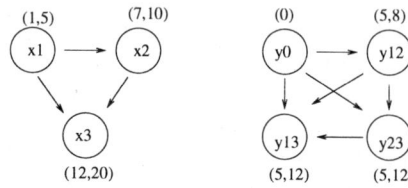

Step 2 Minimize the domains with respect to both N_P^S and N_D^S. As mentioned in relation to the proof of Theorem 5, the quantitative information represented in our framework is equivalent to the metric constraints represented in TCSP. A multiple-interval domain of a point p_i in N_P^S is equivalent to the unary constraint of a point in TCSP. This constraint is represented as the binary constraint between points p_i and p_0 (the beginning of the world) in TCSP, and implies the disjunction:

$$(a_1 \leq p_i - p_0 \leq b_1) \vee ... \vee (a_k \leq p_i - p_0 \leq b_k)$$

where $a_1, ..., a_k$ and $b_1, ..., b_k$ are endpoints of multiple intervals defined in Definition 2. The multiple-interval domain of a duration d_{ij} in N_D^S is equivalent to the metric constraint between points p_i and p_j in TCSP. This constraint represents the disjunction:

$$(a_1 \leq p_j - p_i \leq b_1) \vee ... \vee (a_k \leq p_j - p_i \leq b_k).$$

A special polynomial case of TCSP when all constraints are single intervals is called the *simple temporal problem* (STP) (Dechter, Meiri, & Pearl 1991). The minimal STP network can be found by applying Floyd-Warshall's All-Pairs-Shortest-Paths algorithm. (Dechter, Meiri, & Pearl 1991) also showed that applying the path-consistency algorithm (Mackworth 1977) to an STP network is identical to applying Floyd-Warshall's All-Pairs-Shortest-Paths algorithm. Here, when all unary constraints of the APDN are restricted to single intervals (simple domains), they form an equivalent STP network. Therefore, enforcing global path-consistency over all simple domains of N_P^S and N_D^S concurrently, results in all minimal simple domains of the consistent scenario of the APDN.

Looked at in the context of STP, the path-consistency conditions of the quantitative constraints in Σ_{APD}^S can be expressed as follows:

$$D_i = D_j - D_{ij} \quad (1)$$
$$D_j = D_i + D_{ij} \quad (2)$$
$$D_{ij} = D_j - D_i \quad (3)$$
$$D_{ij} = D_{ik} - D_{jk} \quad (4)$$

where $1 \leq i < j \leq n, 1 \leq k \leq n, k \neq i, j$. If the domain of a point is constrained (by Condition 1 or 2), we need to consider all other related domains (Conditions 1, 2 and 3). If the domain of a duration node is updated (by Condition 3 or 4), we examine Conditions 1, 2 and 4. We introduce three queues: QPD, QPP and QDD.

Elements in QPD represent the domain indices in Conditions 1, and 2, while QPP and QDD are for Conditions 3 and 4 respectively. The propagation of the four conditions over the domains of APDN is repeated until all domains are stable, or become empty indicating inconsistency.

While propagating such conditions, we maintain the consistency between each pair of domains and the atomic relations N_D^S by calling arc-consistency algorithm. Our modified version of arc-consistency algorithm determines only the arcs related to the updated domain. The algorithm also returns the indices of all affected nodes for further propagation.

When the propagation terminates, the resulting network is a consistent scenario of the APDN with minimal simple domains.

Illustration: For this example, initially QPD and QPP each consist of three elements: $(1,2), (1,3)$ and $(2,3)$. QDD has three elements: $(1,3,2), (1,2,3)$ and $(2,1,3)$.

With an element $(1,3)$ in QPD, the domain of d_3 is updated as follows: $D_3 \otimes (D_1 + D_{13}) = (12,20) \otimes ((1,5) + (5,12)) = (12,20) \otimes (6,17) = (12,17)$. Then the domains of all nodes connecting to p_3 in N_P^S are computed by arc-consistency algorithm, and elements $(1,3), (2,3)$ are added in QPD, and $(3,1), (3,2)$ in QPP. None of other elements in QPD updates other domains at this stage.

When consider QPP, the element $(1,3)$ updates the domain of d_{13} as follows: $D_{13} \otimes (D_3 - D_1) = (5,12) \otimes ((12,17) - (1,5)) = (5,12) \otimes (7,16) = (7,12)$. Then checking arc-consistency on the domains of all nodes connecting to d_{13} in N_D^S does not affect other domains. The elements $(1,3)$ are added in QPD, and $(1,3,2), (2,1,3)$ in QDD. The domain of d_{23} is also updated to $(5,10)$ by the condition $D_{23} \otimes (D_3 - D_2)$.

The domain of d_{12} is updated by the element $(1,3,2)$ from QDD as follows: $D_{12} \otimes (D_{13} - D_{23}) = (5,8) \otimes ((7,12) - (5,10)) = (5,8) \otimes (-3,7) = (5,7)$. Applying arc-consistency to N_D^S results in no change to other domains of the network. Then the elements $(1,2)$ are added in QPD, and $(1,2,3), (3,1,2)$ in QDD.

When the algorithm terminates, a consistent scenario with minimal simple domains of the given APDN is returned as:

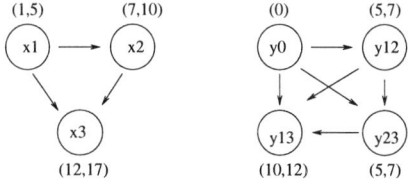

Our algorithm can handle the general problem without the restriction of atomic labels. However, if such restriction is applied, our algorithm solves the desired problem in polynomial time.

Theorem 6 *Finding a consistent scenario with minimal domains of a simple APDN is solvable in polynomial time, $O(nd^2)$, where n, d are the numbers of points and durations respectively.*

In (Navarrete & Marin 1997), deciding the satisfiability of point duration networks when only qualitative information is considered has the complexity of $O(d^2)$.

The minimal APDN can be computed by repeatedly finding all consistent scenarios with their corresponding minimal simple domains. Then taking union over all consistent scenarios and minimal domains. Of course, this task requires exponential time in worst case. It is worth noting here that a consistent scenario can have several sets of minimal simple domains depending upon the number of multiple intervals given. However, consistent scenarios can be found efficiently as our algorithm prunes much of the search space using both qualitative and quantitative constraints.

Further Extensions to APDN

The augmented point duration network framework proposed earlier in this paper allows only qualitative constraints labeling arcs in the duration networks. As a result, the metric constraints between durations cannot be handled. In this section, we propose a further extension to the APDN to address the problem when quantitative information between durations is allowed e.g., *Bob takes 30-45 minutes less than Fred to go to work*.

The proposed extension, a *fully quantified point duration network*, is an APDN, as defined earlier, except that the binary constraints between durations in the duration network are *quantitative*. The binary constraint, $C_{ij,km} \in I$, restricts the permissible values for the time differences between durations ij and km; it represents the disjunction:

$$(a_1 \leq d_{km} - d_{ij} \leq b_1) \vee ... \vee (a_k \leq d_{km} - d_{ij} \leq b_k).$$

This can be one of the three constraint classes in Definition 2.

When representing the binary constraints between durations:

- if the qualitative relation between a pair of durations $\{<, >, =\}$ is given, we transform the relation into metric constraint using Table 1;
- if both qualitative and quantitative information is given, the metric constraint is the intersection of the given quantitative constraint and the transformation of the qualitative constraint from Table 1; and
- if there is no binary constraint between a pair of durations provided, we allow the infinite range $(-\infty, \infty)$ label.

Example 3 Combining the information from Example 1 and *Bob takes 30-45 minutes less than Fred to go to work*, the fully quantified point duration network representing this information is shown in Figure 2. □

A *solution* and the *consistency* of a fully quantified point duration network can be defined as in APDN.

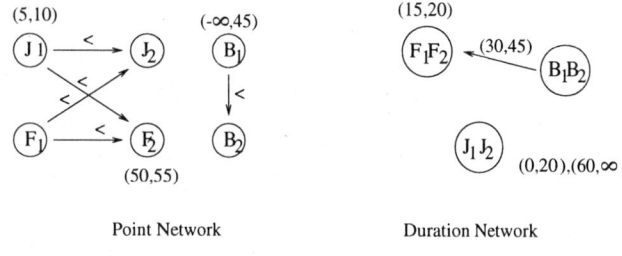

Figure 2: The graphical representation of the fully quantified problem

The main strategies for solving APDN introduced earlier are still useful for solving the consistency problem and finding a consistent scenario with minimal simple domains in a fully quantified point duration network. Here, we describe how the techniques proposed for APDN can be adapted to address the above problems.

Computing consistent scenarios

For APDN, after identifying the networks of all strongly connected components, we find a consistent scenario of the point network that is consistent to a consistent scenario of the duration network. Here, since all constraints in DN are quantitative constraints, we find a consistent scenario of PN that is consistent with a minimal simple DN (the DN with all constraints being single intervals and minimal). A minimal simple DN can be computed by applying the techniques for finding the minimal STP as proposed in (Dechter, Meiri, & Pearl 1991). We introduce a null duration d_0, and associate a directed edge-weighted graph, called a *distance graph*. The single-interval domain $[a, b]$ of duration d_{ij} represents a binary constraint:

$$a \leq d_{ij} - d_0 \leq b.$$

The metric constraint $[a, b]$ constrains the time difference between durations d_{ij} and d_{km} as follows:

$$a \leq d_{km} - d_{ij} \leq b.$$

Then applying *All-Pairs-Shortest-Paths* algorithm to the distance graph where arcs are weighted with the permissible values $[a, b]$. This results in the minimal distances between all pairs of nodes, thus the minimal simple duration network.

The consistency between a consistent scenario of PN and the minimal simple DN is determined by using a similar method as for APDN. The value of a point is $x_j = x_i + d_{ij}$ where d_{ij} in this case is the upper bound of the minimal domain of duration d_{ij}[6]. A consistent

[6]In (Dechter, Meiri, & Pearl 1991), the authors proved that for a minimal STP of n nodes with minimal domains, if d_{0i} and d_{i0} denote the upper and lower bounds of node i, there are two special solutions to the STP which are the tuples: $(d_{01}, ..., d_{0n})$ and $(-d_{10}, ..., -d_{n0})$. Here we can choose either one.

scenario of PN is consistent with the minimal simple DN if the atomic labels of the scenario are consistent with the point values computed by using the above equation.

Computing minimal domains

Since the domains of the minimal simple DN are already minimal, we initially apply the arc-consistency algorithm only to the consistent scenario of PN (N_P^S). Then minimizing the quantitative constraints with respect to both N_P^S and N_D^S becomes almost the same as in APDN (Step 2 of the subfunction DomainMinimize). The propagation of the four constraints (Conditions 1,2, 3 and 4) specifying the global path-consistency conditions of both N_P^S and N_D^S, and the treatment of N_P^S remain the same as for APDN. However, instead of performing arc-consistency on N_D^S when a duration domain is updated, we call the All-Pairs-Shortest-Paths algorithm to maintain the consistency of all constraints. After all constraints are stable, the resulting network is a consistent scenario of a fully quantified point duration network with minimal simple domains.

Theorem 7 *Finding a consistent scenario with minimal domains of a simple fully quantified point duration network is solvable in polynomial time, $O(d^3)$, where d is the number of durations.*

Since relations between durations can be translated into binary quantitative constraints, this results in the following theorem:

Theorem 8 *An augmented point duration network (APDN) is a special case of a fully quantified point duration network.*

Discussion

This section discusses some additional advantages of APDN and fully quantified PDN over the existing frameworks, in particular Meiri's qualitative and quantitative model (Meiri 1996).

The unary constraints in APDN and fully quantified PDN can be viewed as the metric constraints between pairs of points in TCSP. Let us consider our path-consistency algorithms in the context of TCSP. At the global domain minimizing step (corresponding to the propagating of Conditions 1, 2, 3, and 4), the algorithms determine the consistency of all possible length-two paths. If any arc (corresponding to a domain in APDN/fully quantified PDN) is updated, the algorithm ensures the arc-consistency of the corresponding PN or DN network by calling the arc-consistency algorithm. Generally, performing arc-consistency checks the consistency between domains of all pairs of nodes with respect to the constraints between each two corresponding nodes. Here, each domain of APDN specifies all permissible distances between two points as in TCSP. This means the arc-consistency algorithm checks the consistency between any two distances, or four points. Therefore, consistency between four points (cf. TCSP) is implicitly maintained in APDN/fully quantified PDN framework by ensuring path-consistency. Hence, the path-consistency in APDN/fully quantified PDN parallels 4-consistency in TCSP.

In (Meiri 1996), Allen's interval algebra relations, Vilain & Kautz's point algebra relations and quantitative information between points are represented in a hybrid network. Nodes of the network are either intervals or points. Arcs connecting nodes representing points are labeled with quantitative constraints, otherwise they are labeled with qualitative relations. Conceptually, this network combines the TCSP and Allen's interval algebra frameworks. However, this framework is not capable of capturing the qualitative and quantitative information about durations, such as the information about Bob, given in Example 1. This is crucial as it is a general type of information which arises in various applications. A technical example pointed out in (Kautz & Ladkin 1991) is the problem of translating metric constraints to Allen's interval relations as follows[7]:

Example 4 Given metric information about the durations of two intervals I and J: $3 < (I_2 - I_1) < \infty$ and $-\infty < (J_2 - J_1) < 2$, I_1, I_2 and J_1, J_2 denote the starting and ending points of intervals I and J respectively. The reasoning system should be able to infer that *I has longer duration than J*, thus *I cannot be during J*. □

In the APDN framework, the above information is represented as domain constraints of duration nodes $I_1 I_2$ and $J_1 J_2$. The proposed path-consistency algorithm will infer the single constraint that *"duration $I_1 I_2$ is longer than $J_1 J_2$"*. Hence, APDN can further infer *"I cannot be during J"*. Meiri's framework cannot represent and reason about the relation lengths of different durations. Therefore, it would be unable to conclude this final inference without first achieving 4-consistency.

Conclusion

Precisely, the contributions of this paper are:

- An augmented point duration network (APDN) which adequately handles both qualitative and quantitative information about point events.
- A further extension of the APDN framework to capture quantitative information about durations.
- The algorithms for finding a consistent scenario with minimal domains for both APDN and the extended frameworks.
- Identifying simple cases for which the time complexities of the proposed algorithms are polynomial.

Like other point-based approaches which are restricted to conjunctions of binary relations, the point duration network based model cannot handle the disjointedness of interval algebra (e.g., Interval A is either before or

---

[7](Kautz & Ladkin 1991) proved that to compute the strongest set of basic interval relations, metric constraints between four points (extreme points of two intervals) must be considered at a time.

after interval B). Our ongoing research is to investigate an APDN-based framework that can deal with full interval relations. One possibility is combining the APDN framework with the *generalized multi-point event* framework (GMPE) (Wetprasit, Sattar, & Khatib 1997). GMPE represents the disjunction of interval relations by using disjunction of matrices of relations between interval endpoints.

Acknowledgments

We thank Peter van Beek for his valuable comments which improved the preliminary version of this paper. Also, thanks to Michael Maher and the anonymous reviewers for their helpful comments.

References

Allen, J., and Kautz, H. 1985. A model of naive temporal reasoning. In J.Hobbs, and R.Moore., eds., *Formal Theories of the Commonsense World*. Ablex. 251–268.

Allen, J. 1983. Maintaining knowledge about temporal intervals. *Communication of the ACM* 26(11):832–843.

Barber, F. 1993. A metric time-point and duration-based temporal model. *SIGART Bulletin* 4(3):30–49.

Dean, T., and McDermott, D. 1987. Temporal data base management. *Artificial Intelligence* 32:1–55.

Dechter, R.; Meiri, I.; and Pearl, J. 1991. Temporal constraint networks. *Artificial Intelligence* 49:61–95.

Freuder, E. 1978. Synthesizing constraint expressions. *Communications of the ACM* 21(11):958–966.

Kautz, H., and Ladkin, P. 1991. Integrating metric and qualitative temporal reasoning. In *Proceedings of AAAI-91*, 241–246.

Mackworth, A. 1977. Consistency in networks of relations. *Artificial Intelligence* 8:99–118.

Meiri, I. 1996. Combining qualitative and quantitative constraints in temporal reasoning. *Artificial Intelligence* 87:343–385.

Navarrete, I., and Marin, R. 1997. Qualitative temporal reasoning with points and durations. In *Proceedings of the 15th International Joint Conference on Artificial Intelligence (IJCAI-97)*, 1454–1459.

Tarjan, R. 1972. Depth-first search and linear graph algorithms. *SIAM J. Comput.* 1:146–160.

Van Beek, P. 1992. Reasoning about qualitative temporal information. *Artificial Intelligence* 58:297–326.

Vilain, M., and Kautz, H. 1986. Constraint propagation algorithms for temporal reasoning. In *Proceedings of AAAI-86*, 377–382. San Mateo: Morgan Kaufman.

Wetprasit, R.; Sattar, A.; and Khatib, L. 1997. A generalised framework for reasoning with multi-point events. In *Lecture Notes in Computer Science 1345; Advances in Computing Science, Proceedings of the third Asian Computing Science Conference (ASIAN'97)*, 121–135. Kathmandu, Nepal: Springer.

Learning

Iterated Phantom Induction: A Little Knowledge Can Go a Long Way

Mark Brodie and Gerald DeJong
Department of Computer Science, Beckman Institute
University of Illinois at Urbana-Champaign
405 N Mathews Avenue, Urbana, IL 61801
m-brodie@cs.uiuc.edu

Abstract

We advance a knowledge-based learning method that augments conventional generalization to permit concept acquisition in failure domains. These are domains in which learning must proceed exclusively with failure examples that are relatively uninformative for conventional methods. A domain theory is used to explain and then systematically perturb the observed failures so that they can be treated as if they were positive training examples. The concept induced from these "phantom" examples is exercised in the world, yielding additional observations, and the process repeats. Surprisingly, an accurate concept can often be learned even if the phantom examples are themselves failures and the domain theory is only imprecise and approximate. We investigate the behavior of the method in a stylized air-hockey domain which demands a nonlinear decision concept. Learning is shown empirically to be robust in the face of degraded domain knowledge. An interpretation is advanced which indicates that the information available from a plausible qualitative domain theory is sufficient for robust successful learning.

1 Introduction
1.1 Learning in Failure Domains

In some domains negative examples are as helpful as positive ones. Negative examples can be viewed as positive examples of a different concept. Characterizing and then complementing that concept provides a characterization of the original target concept. However in other domains, which we call *failure domains*, characterizing a concept by means of negative examples may be difficult. A failure domain is a domain where negative examples are relatively uninformative and yet provide the only feedback available.

Consider the problem of learning a single salchow jump in ice skating. Until a skater's behavior is nearly correct all of the attempted jumps are crashing failures. Thus much of the skater's learning must occur exclusively with negative trials. Furthermore, failing to land the jump provides little information. There are so many alternative ways of failing that it hardly helps to enumerate them.

Failure domains should be difficult to learn. Yet the single salchow jump is learned quite quickly by the average dedicated skating student. How can this be? Perhaps the concept space is small, so that the learning problem requires only a few examples of any sort. But this is clearly not the case in the skating domain. A skater's trajectory is influenced by the positions, velocities, and accelerations of many body joints. Small changes in any of these variables may result in vastly different behaviors.

Perhaps the concept space, while large, is dense with goal concepts. After empirically ruling out a few, the student would then have a good chance of entertaining an acceptable hypothesis. But imparting just the right rotational momentum, twirling for the right interval, and stopping rotation while keeping one's balance on a knife edge is not a common occurrence in the space of possible skating behaviors.

A third possibility is to define the single salchow as a coaching problem. Certainly an insightful skating coach can greatly aid the student. However, no amount of prior coaching, reading, discussing, or mental exercise can result in the student's first attempt being even close to a success. There is no substitute for the initial spate of negative trials. Acquiring the jump remains quintessentially a learning problem for the student.

The salchow jump is only one illustration of a failure domain. Other examples include learning to walk, play the violin, land an airplane, cook a fluffy souffle, and write a successful AAAI paper. It is surprising that any of these tasks can be learned quickly, since the learner must initially rely solely on failures for guidance.

Conventional learning approaches encounter difficulties in domains of this type. For example, reinforcement learning (Kaelbling, Littman and Moore 1996) and genetic algorithms (Goldberg 1989) rely on extensive exploration of the world, which may consume exponentially many examples before any successes are encountered. Good performance in failure domains may require the use of prior domain knowledge, which can

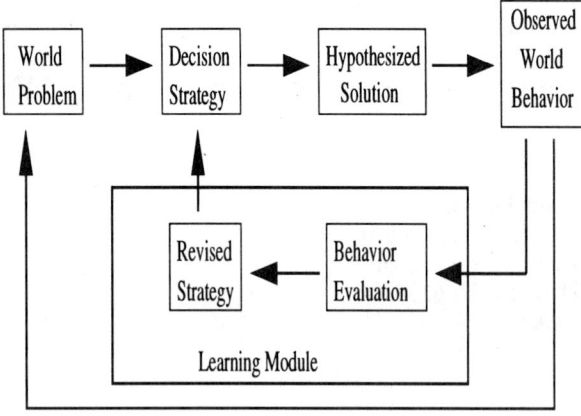

Figure 1: Interactive Learning

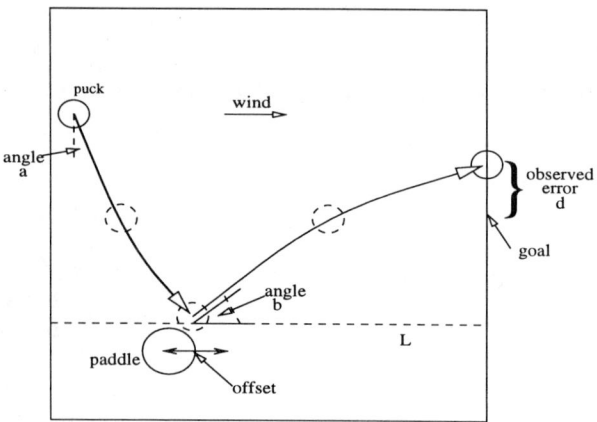

Figure 2: Air-Hockey

be difficult to express in the "vocabulary" of genetic operators, neural net topologies, initial Q table entries and the like, even if one knows a fair amount about the task of interest.

We have developed and tested a machine learning approach for one type of failure domain. Our approach grew from investigations of plausible explanation-based control (DeJong 1994), in which qualitative domain knowledge (Forbus 1984; Kuipers 1986) is combined with exploration of the world to generate decision-making concepts. We describe the methodology behind our approach, the implementation and performance of an algorithm, and suggest an interpretation of the results we have obtained.

1.2 "Phantom" Decisions

We call the approach "*phantom induction*". It uses an "on-line" learning paradigm (Natarajan 1991); problems are successively given to the learning system, which generates solutions according to its current decision strategy. Each hypothesized solution is tried out in the world. This usually yields a failure, but some information is gained by the system observing the world's reactions to its decisions. Periodically, after accumulating such traces of world behavior, the learning module revises its decision strategy. (see Figure 1).

A problem is described as a pair (w, g), where w is a world state and g the goal to be achieved. The system uses its current decision strategy f_c to generate a decision $f_c(w, g)$. When this hypothesized solution is tried out, the *observed error* is the difference between the goal and the actual outcome that occurs in the world.

Domain knowledge is employed to explain observed world behavior. The observed error is propagated through the explanation, resulting in a characterization of the decision error for the hypothesized solution. From this decision error and the actual decision a "phantom decision" d_{ph} is produced. According to the system's model of the world, choosing this phantom decision in place of the original decision would have yielded an adequate solution to the problem. Thus the observed failure $((w, g), f_c(w, g))$ is transformed into a "phantom" success $((w, g), d_{ph})$.

The phantom decision will achieve the goal only if the domain theory is correct. But if the system's domain knowledge is flawed the phantom decision is likely to yield a failure. Suppose these phantom points are nonetheless employed as if they were positive training examples. Using an inductive algorithm, a new decision strategy is generated from the collection of phantom observations. This process is iterated; given further problems, the system attempts to solve them using its new decision strategy; from the observed world behavior new phantom decisions are generated; these are added to the collection of phantom observations, which are used to generate another strategy.

It is noteworthy that domain knowledge is used to perturb the observed training examples into phantom training examples, without requiring any committment to a particular inductive algorithm. It is intuitively clear that the performance of this iterated phantom induction process will depend on the accuracy of the explanations. We conducted a sequence of experiments which show that the method can be successful even with a highly inaccurate domain theory. Surprisingly, convergence need not be uniform; intermediate strategies can perform dramatically worse than earlier strategies and yet these poorly-performing strategies must be exercised for the algorithm to converge to an adequate strategy. We propose and test an interpretation in which the success of the method is due to the interplay between experimentation with the world and knowledge-guided refinement.

2 The Domain

We constructed a failure domain using a simulated air-hockey table. The task is to guide an incoming puck to a goal position with a single deflection by a circular paddle (see Figure 2). In our experiments the goal position, the viscous deflection of the wind, the puck's point of release, and the puck's velocity are fixed but the puck's angle of release varies. The puck impacts the paddle along a horizontal line L across the air-hockey table. The paddle automatically tracks the position of the puck and positions itself to direct the puck back along its incoming path. Just before impact, the paddle is offset horizontally along L so as to deflect the puck in the direction of the goal. The offset is measured negatively to the left and positively to the right.

We use a discrete-time simulator of the air-hockey table to compute the "world" puck behavior, taking into account sliding friction, air resistance, and collision dynamics. The relationship between the puck's angle of release and the paddle offset needed to deflect it to the goal position is highly non-linear.

2.1 Domain Knowledge

Let f^* be the ideal strategy. This non-realizable function maps incoming puck angles to the correct offsets. The learning problem is to find a good (necessarily nonlinear) approximation to f^*.

A strategy f that imperfectly approximates f^* will generate errors. If a is a puck angle, the offset $f(a)$ will deflect the puck to a point distance d from the goal - d is the *observed error* (see Figure 2), measured positively above the goal and negatively below it.

Let e^* denote the ideal function which transforms each observed error for the employed strategy f into the correct decision error, so that using offset $f(a) + e^*(d, a)$ instead of offset $f(a)$ would have achieved the goal. This error function e^* is also highly nonlinear.

Knowledge of e^* would allow each failure to be transformed into a success. But knowledge of e^* requires a perfect domain theory. A system that possesses only an imperfect domain theory will be able to compute only some approximation of e^*, denoted by e. What characteristics should a domain theory possess so that the approximation e generated by its knowledge is still adequate to acquire a strategy f which is a good approximation to f^*?

Our investigation indicates that the following qualitative domain knowledge is sufficient:

- As the departing angle of the puck (angle b in Figure 2) increases, the value (not the absolute magnitude) of the observed error d increases.

- As the offset increases (i.e. moves to the right), angle b increases.

The system infers from this knowledge that the offset error is a monotonically decreasing function of the observed error; if the observed error is positive, the offset needs to be decreased, and the amount of decrement increases as the size of the observed error increases.

The inference of monotonicity is generated by the explanation. In a more complex domain different explanations might apply in different regions, generating a variety of constraints. In each region of the space phantom induction would proceed using the relevant inferred constraint.

Simple error functions approximating $e^*(d, a)$ that respect these qualitative constraints are linear in the first argument (the observed error d) and ignore the second argument (the puck angle a). Thus our experiments examine error functions of the form $e(d) = m \cdot d$, where m is a negative constant.

2.2 The Algorithm

The following algorithm instantiates the general phantom induction algorithm:

1. Initialize $f_0 = 0$.
2. Set $j = 0$.
3. For $i = 1$ to n:

   i: The environment generates a random puck angle a_i. This is the problem from our failure domain.

   ii: Apply the current strategy to compute the suggested paddle offset; $o_i = f_j(a_i)$.

   iii: Observe the puck behavior and note the observed error – the distance d_i between the final position of the puck and the goal.

   iv: Compute the estimated *decision error* from the observed error using the error function e; this is $e(d_i)$, the estimated error in the paddle offset.

   v: Compute the "phantom" offset $o_i + e(d_i)$ obtained by adding the estimated offset error to the offset o_i that was tried; this is the phantom decision that the system thinks would have, for puck angle a_i, driven the puck into the goal.

   vi: Add the "phantom point" $(a_i, o_i + e(d_i))$ to the set of training points.

4. Set $j = j + 1$.
5. Generate a new strategy f_j from the set of training points.
6. Measure the performance of f_j.
7. If the performance of f_j is satisfactory, exit and return f_j, otherwise return to Step 3.

3 Initial Experiments

We explored the algorithm's sensitivity to the accuracy of the error function e. In these experiments n is set to ten; thus each strategy is sampled for ten inputs before being replaced by a new strategy. The performance of each strategy is measured by computing the mean-squared observed error (msE) over an independent, randomly generated, test set of size 100, during which no phantom decisions are made and no learning takes place.

In the experiments we employ an instance-based approach (Aha et al. 1991; Atkeson 1991). Strategy values are computed by convolution of the phantom points, as follows: Given a puck angle, a Gaussian is centered at that puck angle. The paddle offset is computed as a weighted average of all the phantom observations, the weights being determined by the values of the Gaussian. In section 5 we consider alternative strategy generation methods.

Experiments 1-4 explore the algorithm's behavior as the slope m of the error approximation function varies. Figure 3 shows the results. The vertical scale plots the logarithm of the msE.

3.1 Experiment 1: Best Linear Error Function

Experiment 1 shows that using the best linear error function yields performance very similar to the performance using the perfect error function e^*.

As discussed in section 2.1, knowledge of the ideal error function e^* would yield the correct decision for each training example. Thus a collection of positive examples can be accumulated. This was tested in Experiment 1a and indeed performance converges rapidly to a low error level. The msE decreases quickly but does not fall to zero because of the complexity of the target function f^*.

In Experiment 1b the system uses as its decision error function the best linear approximation to e^*: $e^\dagger(x) = m^\dagger \cdot x$. It cannot accumulate positive examples as in Experiment 1a, but most of the phantom decisions will be quite close to the correct decisions. Thus a strategy based on these points should perform quite well. Figure 3 indeed shows that $e^\dagger$ results in performance almost as good as in the case of e^*.

Knowledge of e^* and $e^\dagger$ is unreasonable: e^* requires a perfect domain theory and $e^\dagger$ depends on the extent and distribution of the still-unseen observation errors. However, with these as standards of comparison, we can now investigate the consequences of systematically decreasing the accuracy of the error approximation function.

3.2 Experiment 2: Underestimating Error Function

Experiment 2 shows that using a smaller linear error function results in a slower convergence rate.

Suppose the system uses a linear decision error function which underestimates the decision error (when compared with the best linear approximation $e^\dagger$). In this case most of the phantom decisions will lie between the actual decision and the correct decision. So one would expect the error to fall slowly as the phantom decisions gradually approach the correct decisions.

Figure 3 shows the results of Experiment 2 with $m = m^\dagger/5$. When compared with the best linear approximation, we see that performance improves more slowly, as expected. Continuing the graph beyond the first 100 iterations would show that performance would eventually reach the same level as in Experiment 1.

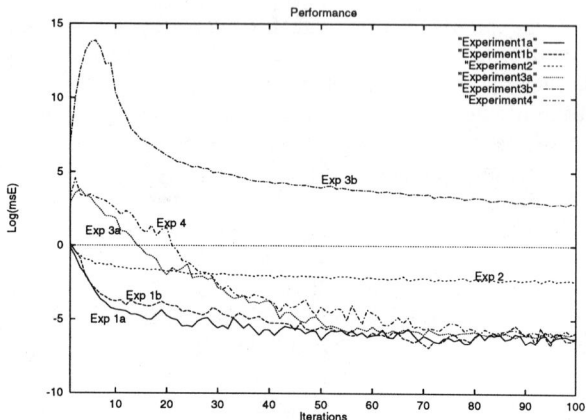

Figure 3: Experimental Results

3.3 Experiment 3: Overestimating Error Function

Experiment 3 shows that using a larger linear error function also results in convergence. This may seem surprising, because of the following argument:

Suppose the system uses a linear decision error function which overestimates the decision error (when compared with the best linear approximation $e^\dagger$). This could result in the method "overcompensating" for previous errors. Too see this, consider a puck angle a and suppose that the actual offset o_1 tried by the current strategy is smaller than the correct offset o^*. The observed error d_1 will correctly indicate that o^* lies above o_1, but since the estimated decision error is larger than the true decision error the phantom offset $o_1 + m \cdot d_1$ will be placed above o^*. If angle a is chosen again, the offset o_2 used by a new strategy will be too large. The observed error d_2 will correctly indicate that o^* lies below o_2, but the estimated decision error will again be too large (in magnitude), and the new phantom offset $o_2 + m \cdot d_2$ will lie below o^*. Errors may be magnified by this overcompensation effect and one might expect the algorithm to oscillate and possibly diverge.

Figure 3 includes results for two overestimates. Experiment 3a uses $m = 10m^\dagger$; the error rises briefly initially but then falls quickly to the convergence level. Experiment 3b uses $m = 50m^\dagger$; thus each phantom training point is placed about 50 times farther from the correct decision than it should be. Initially the observed error rises to a very large peak value (recall that the graph shows the logarithm of the msE; thus the actual peak error value in Experiment 3b is more than 12 orders of magnitude worse than the error generated by the initial strategy f_0). It then falls sharply and continues to converge slowly.

If the error function systematically overestimates the true decision error, the algorithm seems initially to diverge, with each strategy performing worse than its predecessor. However after some time performance begins to improve until once again a low error is reached.

It seems that instability *is* introduced but is then overcome. As the amount of overestimation increases, the msE rises for a longer time and to much larger values, but it always eventually decreases and converges.

3.4 Experiment 4: Random Error Function

Experiment 4 shows that using an error function which varies randomly between smaller and larger estimates results in little initial divergence followed by fairly rapid convergence.

Imperfect domain knowledge may not produce an error function which systematically over- or underestimates the decision error. Experiment 4 uses an error function which sometimes underestimates the decision error but at other times overestimates it. Here $e(d) = m_r \cdot d$ where m_r is uniformly distributed over $(m^\dagger/50, 50m^\dagger)$, so that the decision error fluctuates randomly between being too small and too large. Figure 3 shows that the observed error does not rise very much when compared with the systematic overestimate in Experiment 3b, and also converges much faster than the systematic underestimate in Experiment 2.

4 Interpretation

The results of Experiment 3 are somewhat surprising: successful learning occurs even when the decision errors are persistently over-estimated by large amounts. We now advance an interpretation of this phenomenon.

Let $e(d) = m \cdot d$ be the linear decision error function, a any puck angle, and f^* the "ideal" function that computes the correct offset. Without loss of generality set $f^*(a) = 1$, which amounts only to selecting the units in which the observed error is measured.

Iteration 1: Assume angle a is selected. If the observed error were accurate, $d = f^*(a) - f_0(a)$, which is 1, because the initial strategy f_0 is identically zero. Hence the estimated offset error is $e(d) = m \cdot d = m$, and a phantom point is placed at $(a, f_0(a) + e(d)) = (a, m)$.

Note that (depending on the exact value of m) this phantom point may be farther away from the correct value of 1 than the original guess of zero.

Iteration 2: After the first strategy is computed, angle a is selected again. There is a phantom point at (a, m), so $f_1(a) = m$. The offset error is $e(d) = m \cdot (f^*(a) - f_1(a)) = m \cdot (1 - m) \approx -m^2$ if we neglect lower order terms, which is justifiable if m is "large". A phantom point is placed at $(a, f_1(a) + e(d)) = (a, m - m^2) \approx (a, -m^2)$, neglecting lower order terms.

If m is large the phantom point at $-m^2$ is farther from the correct value (and on the opposite side) than the previous phantom point at m. It appears that the algorithm is diverging.

However, there are now 2 phantom points at a: (a, m) and $(a, -m^2)$. Since each strategy is computed by convolution of the phantom points, the next strategy will pass through the average of the 2 phantom points, so $f_2(a) = 1/2 \cdot (m + (-m^2)) \approx -m^2/2$.

Repeating this argument, we get:
$f_1(a) \approx m$,
$f_2(a) \approx -m^2/2$,
$f_3(a) \approx m^3/6$,
$f_4(a) \approx -m^4/24$,
and in general
$f_j(a) \approx (-1)^{j+1} \cdot (m^j/j!)$.

So the error, the distance between $f_j(a)$ and $f^*(a)$, behaves, approximately, like $m^j/j!$. This initially increases to a peak at $m = j$ and then decreases to zero as $j \to \infty$. This may explain why the msE in Experiment 3 first rises and then falls, and why the length and magnitude of the rise increase as the quality of the decision error approximation degrades.

5 Further Experiments: Alternative Strategy Generation Methods

In the previous experiments each strategy was computed by convolution of the training points. We now investigate whether robust convergence depends on this particular method of strategy generation. The analysis in section 4 ascribes the algorithm's stability to the averaging effect of convolution. Hence any method which also generalizes by "averaging" or smoothing the training points should yield similar results. We tested this by replacing convolution with other generalization techniques and repeating the experiments discussed previously.

Experiments 1-4 were repeated using each of the following generalization methods: convolution, regression, Fourier methods, and neural networks. We obtained similar results for each method in all the experiments. For space reasons we present only the results of Experiment 3b: an overestimating decision error function ($m = 50m^\dagger$). Figure 4 displays the performance of the different generalization strategies in this experiment. The error curves are quite similar.

5.1 Regression

Linear regression is a standard statistical smoothing scheme. We used cubic polynomials; each strategy is generated by fitting a cubic to the current set of phantom training points. The fitted cubic specifies the paddle offset for any puck angle. The learning algorithm proceeds exactly as before. The resulting curve is shown in figure 4 and displays the same behavior as in the case of convolution: the error initially rises to a high peak and then falls to convergence.

5.2 Fourier Methods

Fourier methods comprise another family of smoothing techniques. Here we apply a Fourier transform to the phantom training points, filter out the high-frequency components, and use an inverse transform to obtain a smoothed set of points. The strategy value

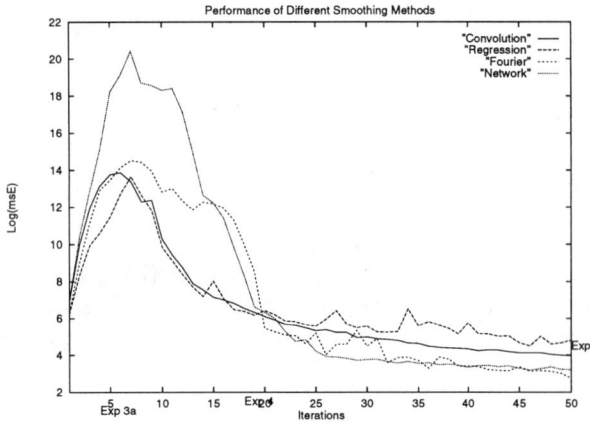

Figure 4: Different Smoothing Methods

is then computed by linear interpolation between adjacent smoothed points.

The results for convolution and regression also hold for Fourier methods. Figure 4 includes the performance of the Fourier technique in the same experiment. The characteristic error curve is apparent.

5.3 Neural Networks

Neural networks also encode a generalization of their input data. We discretized the continuous input data, chose a simple network structure and used standard back-propagation (Anguita 1993) to train the network on the set of phantom training points. After training the network constitutes the next strategy and iterated phantom induction proceeds as before.

This approach yields similar experimental results. Figure 4 includes the performance of the network. The peak of the error curve is considerably higher and performance converges more slowly, but the basic shape of the error curve is the same. Results are similar over a wide variety of network configurations.

6 Conclusions

We have shown robust empirical learning of a nonlinear decision concept. Each candidate decision strategy is embodied by a non-linear numeric function. Most of the learning must be accomplished without positive training data, and negative examples in domains such as this provide little information. The iterated phantom decision algorithm is still able to converge efficiently to an adequate decision strategy.

The approach constructs "phantom" training data through a knowledge-based alteration of the actual world observations. Each observed example is systematically perturbed by an amount and direction dictated by the explanation of its failure. Induction is performed to generate the candidate strategy which best describes the phantom training data. The selected strategy is then employed to solve additional problems, resulting in more phantom data which augment the training set, and the process repeats.

The main result of the paper is that iterated phantom induction converges quickly to a good decision strategy. Domain knowledge is required for the approach, but a simple qualitative domain theory suffices for convergence. A slope must be chosen to quantify the qualitative error function. Correctly approximating the slope results in quickest convergence. A slope which is too small attenuates the error feedback and slows learning. A slope which is too large magnifies the error, initially causing poor concepts to be used but, even when the observed error grows extremely large, further iterations overcome the error growth and the algorithm converges to an accurate decision strategy.

While our initial results are promising, much remains to be done. Future work will consider more complex domains in which the explanations play a more prominent role. It is also important to systematically compare iterated phantom induction with other learning approaches. The background knowledge used by phantom induction is employed in perturbing the training data and does not permeate the induction algorithm itself. This suggests a way of incorporating prior knowledge into a broad class of conventional induction algorithms.

7 Acknowledgements

This research was sponsored by the Office of Naval Research under grant N00014-94-1-0684.

References

Aha, D., D. Kibler, et al. 1991. Instance-Based Learning Algorithms. *Machine Learning* 6(1): 37-66.

Anguita, D. 1993. Neural Network Backpropagation. Software available by anonymous ftp from risc6000.dibe.unige.it. University of Geneva.

Atkeson, C. G. 1991. Using Locally Weighted Regression for Robot Learning. IEEE International Conference on Robotics and Automation, Sacramento.

DeJong, G. 1994. Learning to Plan in Continuous Domains. *Artificial Intelligence* 65: 71-141.

Forbus, K. 1984. Qualitative Process Theory. *Artificial Intelligence* 24: 85-168.

Goldberg, D. 1989. *Genetic Algorithms in Search, Optimization, and Machine Learning*. Addison-Wesley.

Kaelbling, L.P., Littman M.L., and Moore A.W. 1996. Reinforcement Learning: A Survey. *Journal of Artificial Intelligence Research* 4: 237-285.

Kuipers, B. J. 1986. Qualitative Simulation. *Artificial Intelligence* 29: 289-338.

Natarajan, B. 1991. *Machine Learning: A Theoretical Approach*. Morgan Kaufman.

SUSTAIN: A Model of Human Category Learning

Bradley C. Love and Douglas L. Medin
Northwestern University

> SUSTAIN (Supervised and Unsupervised STratified Adaptive Incremental Network) is a network model of human category learning. SUSTAIN is a three layer model where learning between the first two layers is unsupervised, while learning between the top two layers is supervised. SUSTAIN clusters inputs in an unsupervised fashion until it groups input patterns inappropriately (as signaled by the supervised portion of the network). When such an error occurs, SUSTAIN alters its architecture, recruiting a new unit that is tuned to correctly classify the exception. Units recruited to capture exceptions can evolve into prototypes/attractors/rules in their own right. SUSTAIN's adaptive architecture allows it to master simple classification problems quickly, while still retaining the capacity to learn difficult mappings. SUSTAIN also adjusts its sensitivity to input dimensions during the course of learning, paying more attention to dimensions relevant to the classification task. Shepard, Hovland, and Jenkins's (1961) challenging category learning data is fit successfully by SUSTAIN. Other applications of SUSTAIN are discussed. SUSTAIN is compared to other classification models.

Introduction

Some categories have a very simple structure, while others can be complex. Accordingly, learning how to properly classify items as members of category "A" or "B" can be almost trivial (e.g., the value of a single input dimension determines membership) or can be so difficult that no regularity is discovered (e.g., rote memorization of every category member is required to determine membership).

Classifications are harder to master when the decision boundary (in a multi-dimensional space of possible inputs) is highly irregular and when there are multiple boundaries (e.g., all the members of category "A" do not fall inside one contiguous region of the input space). Difficult classification problems (problems with complex decision boundaries) typically involve categories that have a complex internal structure, perhaps consisting of multiple prototypes (i.e., category subtypes) and a number of exceptions. Linguistic analyses have demonstrated that many categories have a rich internal structure (Lakoff, 1987). Very simple learning models will fail to master difficult categorizations with complex boundaries (i.e., categories with rich internal structure). For instance, a purely linear model, like the perceptron (Rosenblatt, 1958), will be unable to master a classification when the mapping from input features to category labels is nonlinear.

Interestingly, a complex nonlinear model, such as a back-propagation model (Rumelhart, Hinton, & Williams, 1986) with many hidden units, can learn complex decision boundaries but will perform poorly on a simple problem (e.g., a problem where the decision boundary is linear). In such cases, the more complex model will generalize poorly by over-fitting the training data. Thus, making a model too powerful or too weak is undesirable. Geman, Bienenstock, and Doursat (1992) termed this tradeoff between data fitting and generalization as the bias/variance dilemma. In brief, when a network is too simple it is overly biased and cannot learn the correct boundaries. Conversely, when a network is too powerful, it masters the training set, but the boundaries it learns are somewhat arbitrary and are highly influenced by the training sample, leading to poor generalization.

Unfortunately, the complexity of learning models is usually fixed prior to learning. For instance, in network models, the number of intermediate level processing units (which governs model complexity) must usually be chosen in advance. The problem may not be avoidable by treating the number of intermediate units as an additional parameter, because certain architectures may be preferable at certain stages of the learning process. For example, Elman (1994) provides computational evidence (which seems in accord with findings from developmental psychology) that beginning with a simple network and adding complexity as learning progresses improves overall performance.

Models with an adaptive architecture (like SUSTAIN), do not need to specify the number of intermediate units prior to learning. Some models (including SUSTAIN) begin with a small network and expand the network when necessary. Most methods expand the network when overall error (the difference between desired and observed output) is high. For example, the cascade-correlation model (Fahlman & Lebiere, 1990) expands the network vertically with additional intermediate layers, creating higher-order feature detectors. Other

---

Copyright ©1998, American Association for Artificial Intelligence (www.aaai.org). All rights reserved. B. C. Love was supported by the Office of Naval Research under the National Defense Science and Engineering Graduate Fellowship Program. We would like to thank the reviewers for their excellent comments. Correspondence concerning this research should be addressed to loveb@nwu.edu or Bradley C. Love, Department of Psychology, Northwestern University, Evanston, IL 60208

models expand horizontally when error is high (Ash, 1989; Azimi-Sadjadi, Sheedvash, & Trujillo, 1993).

Unlike the aforementioned models, SUSTAIN does not accrue units based on overall error. Instead, SUSTAIN adds a new intermediate level unit when the unsupervised part of the network clusters input patterns in a manner deemed inappropriate by the supervised part of the network. This happens when two input patterns (that differ) belong to the same cluster and the differences between the two input patterns proves critical for successfully mastering the classification. When such an error occurs, SUSTAIN splits the cluster into two clusters by adding an intermediate unit. Thus, intermediate level units in SUSTAIN encode the prototypes (a category can have multiple prototypes) and exceptions of the categories being learned. The method for adding units in SUSTAIN is psychologically motivated by the intuition that people ignore differences when they can (a bias towards simple solutions), but will note differences when forced to by environmental feedback. Additionally, intermediate level units in SUSTAIN are intended to be psychologically real. We claim that SUSTAIN acquires and modifies its prototypes and exceptions in a manner analogous to how people infer a category's internal structure.

Another aspect of networks that is usually fixed, but should vary depending upon the nature of the learning problem, is the activation function of an intermediate level unit. In backpropagation networks, the steepness of a hidden unit's sigmoidal shaped activation function is set as a parameter. In models where an intermediate level unit's activation function is viewed as a receptive field (e.g., Poggio & Girosi, 1990; Kruschke, 1992), the shape of a unit's receptive field is set as a parameter.

An intermediate level unit in SUSTAIN integrates the responses from multiple receptive fields (each subcateogry unit has a receptive field for each input dimension). SUSTAIN treats the shape of a receptive field as something to be learned, rather than as a parameter. SUSTAIN assumes that receptive fields are initially broadly tuned and are adjusted during the course of learning to maximize the receptive field's response to inputs. Intermediate units with peaked (narrow) receptive fields can be described as highly focused. Receptive fields that develop tighter tunings are capable of stronger responses to stimuli (see Figure 1). As an outcome of learning how to perform a classification, SUSTAIN learns which dimensions of the stimuli are relevant and should be attended to. Conceiving of attention as enhancing the tuning of cells is consistent with current work on the neural basis of attention (Treue & Maunsell, 1996).

An Overview of SUSTAIN

SUSTAIN consists of three layers: input, subcategory, and category. Input layer units take on real values to encode information about the environment (e.g., the encoding of a stimulus item that needs to be classified as belonging to category

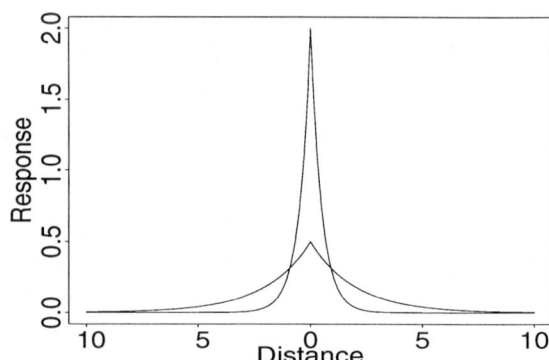

Figure 1. Both units respond maximally when a stimulus appears in the center of their receptive field (a .5 response for the broadly tuned unit; a 2.0 response for the tightly tuned unit). Compared to the broadly tuned unit, the tightly tuned unit's response is stronger to stimuli close to the center and is weaker for stimuli farther from the center (the crossover point occurs at a distance from center of .9 (approximately).

"A" or "B"). Units in the subcategory layer (the intermediate layer) encode the prototypes and exceptions of the category units. Subcategory units compete with one another to respond to patterns at the input layer with the winner (the subcategory unit that is most active) being reinforced. Weights are adjusted according to the Kohonen unsupervised learning rule for developing self-organizing maps (Kohonen, 1984). When a subcategory unit "wins" the centers of its receptive fields (there is a receptive field for each input dimension) move in the direction of the input pattern, minimizing the distance between the centers and the input pattern. This method is similar to a number of clustering techniques used for classification and pattern recognition, such as maximum-distance, K-means, and isodata (Tou & Gonzalez, 1974; Duda & Hart, 1972).

One novel aspect of our implementation is that this unsupervised learning procedure is combined with a supervised procedure. When a subcategory unit responds strongly to an input pattern (i.e., it is the winner) and has an excitatory connection to the inappropriate category unit (i.e., the subcategory unit predicts "A" and the correct answer is "B"), the network shuts off the subcategory unit and recruits a new subcategory unit that responds maximally to the misclassified input pattern (i.e., the new unit's receptive fields are centered upon the input pattern).[1]

The process continues with the new unit competing with the other subcategory units to respond to input patterns with the position of the winner's receptive fields being updated, as well as its connection to the category units by the one layer delta learning rule (Rumelhart et al., 1986). At a minimum,

---

[1] Initially the network only has one subcategory unit that is centered upon the first input pattern.

there must be as many subcategory units as category units when category responses are mutually exclusive.

Previous proposals that bear some resemblance to SUSTAIN include counterpropagation networks (Hecht-Nielsen, 1988) which are multilayer networks where the Kohonen learning rule is used for the bottom two layers. Simpson has explored a supervised version of the Kohonen network where the model does not determine which cluster is the winner, but is told (Simpson, 1989). This change greatly speeds up learning. Interestingly, our approach to clustering is not properly characterized as being either supervised or unsupervised. Clustering is unsupervised unless the network makes a serious clustering error (i.e., an incorrect prediction). A serious error leads to the creation of a new cluster; otherwise learning at the subcategory layer is completely unsupervised.

Another interesting aspect of SUSTAIN's subcategory units is that in addition to adjusting the centers (i.e., the position) of their receptive fields, the sensitivities (i.e., the shape) of their receptive fields also are adjusted in response to input patterns. Input units (i.e., dimensions of the input pattern) that provide consistent evidence (i.e., the position of the subcategory units' receptive fields for that dimension does not have to be adjusted often), develop tighter tunings (see Figure 1). These more reliable input dimensions receive more attention. SUSTAIN uncovers (and explicitly represents) which dimensions are relevant for classification.

Mathematical Formulation

Receptive fields have an exponential shape with a receptive field's response decreasing exponentially as distance from its center increases:

$$\alpha(\mu) = \lambda e^{-\lambda \mu} \quad (1)$$

where λ is the tuning of the receptive field, and μ is the distance of the stimulus from the center of the field. Arguments for activation dropping off exponentially can be found in (Shepard, 1987).

While receptive fields with different λ have different shapes, for any λ, the area "underneath" a receptive field is constant:

$$\int_0^\infty \alpha(\mu) d\mu = \int_0^\infty \lambda e^{-\lambda \mu} d\mu = 1. \quad (2)$$

For a given μ, the λ that maximizes $\alpha(\mu)$ can be computed by differentiating:

$$\frac{\partial \alpha}{\partial \lambda} = e^{-\lambda \mu}(1 - \lambda \mu). \quad (3)$$

These properties of exponentials prove useful in formulating SUSTAIN.

The activation of a subcategory unit is given by:

$$A_{H_j} = \frac{\sum_{i=1}^n (\lambda_i)^r e^{-\lambda_i \mu_{ij}}}{\sum_{i=1}^n (\lambda_i)^r} \quad (4)$$

where n is the number of input units, λ_i is the tuning of each subcategory unit's receptive field for the ith input dimension, μ_{ij} is the distance between the center of subcategory unit j's receptive field for the ith input unit and the output of the ith input unit (distance is simply the absolute value of the difference of these two terms), and r is an attentional parameter (always nonnegative). When r is high, input units with tighter tunings (units that seem relevant) dominate the activation function. Equation 4 sums the responses of the receptive fields for each input dimension and normalizes the sum. The activation of a subcategory unit is bound between 0 (exclusive) and 1 (inclusive).

Subcategory units compete to respond to input patterns and in turn inhibit one another. When many subcategory units are strongly activated, the output of the winning unit is less. Units inhibit each other according to:

$$O_{H_j} = \frac{(A_{H_j})^\beta}{\sum_{i=1}^m (A_{H_i})^\beta} A_{H_j} \quad (5)$$

where β is the lateral inhibition parameter (always nonnegative) and m is the number of subcategory units. When β is small, competing units strongly inhibit the winner. When β is high the winner is weakly inhibited. Units other than the winner have their output set to zero.[2]

After feedback is provided by the "experimenter", if the winner predicts the wrong category, its output is set to zero and a new unit is recruited:

for all j and k, if $(t_k O_{H_j} w_{jk} < 0)$, then recruit a new unit (6)

where t_k is the target value for category unit k and w_{jk} is the weight from subcategory unit j to category unit k. When a new unit is recruited its receptive fields are centered on the misclassified input pattern and the subcategory units' activations and outputs are recalculated.

If a new subcategory unit is not created, the centers of the winner's receptive fields are adjusted:

$$\Delta w_{ij} = \eta (O_{I_i} - w_{ij}) \quad (7)$$

where η is the learning rate, O_{I_i} is the output of input unit i. The centers of the winner's receptive fields move towards the input pattern according to the Kohonen learning rule. This learning rule centers the prototype (i.e., the cluster's center) amidst the members of the prototype.

Using our result from Equation 3, receptive field tunings are updated according to:

$$\Delta \lambda_i = \eta e^{-\lambda_i \mu_{ij}} (1 - \lambda_i \mu_{ij}). \quad (8)$$

Only the winning subcategory unit updates the value of λ_i. Equation 8 adjusts the shape of the receptive field for each

---

[2] The model (as specified) can have multiple winners. For instance, there could always be two winners. More complex schemes could also be considered for determining the number of winners. We do not explore any of these possibilities because they are less conceptually clear and the data does not demand it.

input so that each input can maximize its influence on subcategory units. Initially, λ_i is set to be broadly tuned. For example, if input unit i takes on values between -1 and 1, the maximum distance between the ith input unit's output and the position of a subcategory unit's receptive field (for the ith dimension) is 2, so λ_i is set to .5 because that is the optimal setting of λ_i for μ equal to 2 (i.e., Equation 8 equals zero).

Activation is spread from the winning subcategory unit to the category units:

$$A_{C_k} = O_{H_j} w_{jk} \qquad (9)$$

where A_{C_k} is the activation of the kth category unit and O_{H_j} is the output of the winning subcategory unit.

The output of a category unit is given by:

$$\text{if } (C_k \text{ is nominal and } |A_{C_k}| > 1), \text{ then } O_{C_k} = \frac{A_{C_k}}{|A_{C_k}|} \qquad (10)$$
$$\text{else } O_{C_k} = A_{C_k}$$

where O_{C_k} is the output of the kth category unit. If the feedback given to subjects concerning C_k is nominal (e.g., the item is in category "A" not "B"), then C_k is nominal. Kruschke (1992) refers to this kind of teaching signal as a "humble teacher" and explains when its use is appropriate.

When a subcategory unit is recruited, weights from the unit to the category units are set to zero. The one layer delta learning rule (Rumelhart et al., 1986) is used to adjust weights these weights:

$$\Delta w_{jk} = \eta(t_k - O_{C_k}) O_{H_j}. \qquad (11)$$

Note that only the winner will have its weights adjusted since it is the only subcategory unit with a nonzero output.

The following equation determines the response probabilities (for nominal classifications):

$$Pr(k) = \frac{(O_{C_k} + 1)^d}{\sum_{i=1}^{p}(O_{C_i} + 1)^d} \qquad (12)$$

where d is a response parameter (always nonnegative) and p is the number of category units. The category unit with the largest output is almost always chosen when d is large. In Equation 12, one is added to each category unit's output to avoid performing calculations over negative numbers. The Luce choice rule is a special case ($d = 1$) of this decision rule (Luce, 1963).

Empirically Testing SUSTAIN

Critiques of computational models have historically focused on what functions are learnable (e.g., Minsky & Papert, 1969). This trend continues with Hornik, Stinchcombe, and White (1990) proving that backpropagation networks are universal approximators (given enough hidden units) and Poggio and Girosi (1990) demonstrating similar results for their model. Unfortunately, researchers have not focused on the *time course* of learning. A more informative test of a model's performance requires examining which functions (i.e., classifications) a model can easily learn and which functions are difficult to master. For a model of human category learning, it is not sufficient to show that a model can learn some function (e.g., logical XOR), but one must show that a model can match the learning curves of human subjects over a variety of functions, using the same parameter values. As models become more sophisticated, fitting a diverse set of studies with the same parameter values may prove to be a useful test of models.

In accord with this stance, SUSTAIN is fit to a variety of human learning data (here we focus on Shepard et al. (1961)) using the same parameter values: $\eta = .1$, $\beta = 1.0$, $r = 3.5$, and $d = 8.0$ (Love & Medin, 1998). The parameters were determined by beginning with $\eta = .1$, $\beta = 1.0$, $r = 1.0$, and $d = 1.0$ and adjusting them by hand until a good qualitative fit of the data was achieved. Because each of SUSTAIN's parameters has an intuitive meaning, it was easy to fit the data. For example, when we noticed SUSTAIN was not sufficiently biased towards solutions focusing on a small number of input dimensions, the value of the attentional parameter r was increased. When we noticed overall accuracy was too low, the value of then decision parameter d was increased until SUSTAIN sufficiently stressed accuracy.

Modeling Shepard et al. (1961)

Shepard et al.'s (1961) classic experiments on human category learning provided challenging data to fit. Subjects learned to classify 8 objects that varied on three binary dimensions (shape, size, and color) into two categories (four items per category). On every trial, subjects assigned the stimulus to a category and feedback was provided. Subjects trained for 16 blocks (each object was shown twice per block in a random order) or until they completed two consecutive blocks without an error. Six different assignments of objects to categories were tested with the six problems varying in difficulty (Type I was the easiest to master, Type VI the hardest). The logical structure of the six problems is shown in Table 1. The Type I problem only requires attention along one input dimension, while the Type II problem requires attention to two dimensions (Type II is XOR with an irrelevant dimension). Types III-V require attention along all three dimensions but some regularities exist (Types III-V can be classified as rule plus exception problems). Type VI requires attention to all three dimensions and has no regularities across any pair of dimensions.

Nosofsky et al. (1994) replicated Shepard et al. (1961) with more subjects and traced out learning curves. Figure 2 shows the learning curves for the six problem types. The basic finding is that Type I is learned faster than Type II which is learned faster than Types III-V which are learned faster than VI. This data is particularly challenging for learning models as most models fail to predict Type II easier than Types III-V.

Table 1
The logical structure of the six classification problems tested in Shepard et al. (1961) is shown. The physical attributes (e.g., large, dark, triangle, etc.) were randomly assigned to an input dimension for each subject.

Input	I	II	III	IV	V	VI
111	A	A	B	B	B	B
112	A	A	B	B	B	A
121	A	B	B	B	B	A
122	A	B	A	A	A	B
211	B	B	A	B	A	A
212	B	B	B	A	A	B
221	B	A	A	A	A	B
222	B	A	A	A	B	A

The only models known to reasonably fit these data are ALCOVE (Kruschke, 1992) and RULEX (Nosofsky, Palmeri, & McKinley, 1994b). RULEX is designed to classify stimuli that can be represented by binary features, while ALCOVE is an exemplar based model.

SUSTAIN's fit of Nosofsky et al.'s data is also shown in Figure 2. While fitting the data (see Section Empirically Testing SUSTAIN), the same difficulty ordering of the six problem types was observed for all combinations of parameter values with the exception that for high values of d all six problem types were of equal difficulty (in this case SUSTAIN masters each problem within the first learning block).

How SUSTAIN Solves the Six Problems

SUSTAIN is not a black box and it is possible to understand how SUSTAIN solves a classification problem (perhaps gaining insight into the problem itself). Table 2 shows the number of subcategory units SUSTAIN recruited by problem type. The most common solution for the Type I problem was to create one unit for each category. Type I has a simple category structure (the value of first dimension determines membership). Accordingly, SUSTAIN solves the problem with only two subcategory units. Type II requires attention to two dimensions. SUSTAIN solved the Type II problem by allocating two units to each category. Each subcategory unit responded to two input patterns, largely ignoring the irrelevant dimension. Because category members are highly dissimilar (e.g., 121 and 212 are in the same category), SUSTAIN formed two clusters for each category (ignoring differences on the irrelevant dimension). Types III-V can be roughly characterized as imperfect rule plus exception categories. SUSTAIN solved these problems by uncovering regularities and memorizing exceptions (devoting a unit for one pattern). Type VI has no regularities that can be exploited, forcing SUSTAIN to "memorize" each pattern (i.e., SUSTAIN devoted a subcategory unit to each input pattern).[3]

The right column of Table 2 shows the mean λ value (averaged over the three input dimensions) at the end of the second block for each problem.[4] The sharpness of the mean tuning was positively correlated with the number of subcategory units recruited. Only one dimension develops a sharp tuning

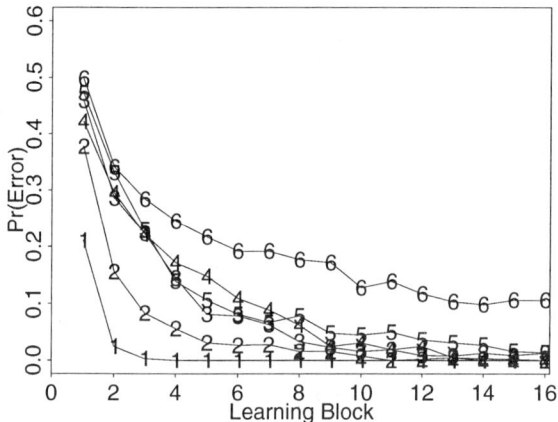

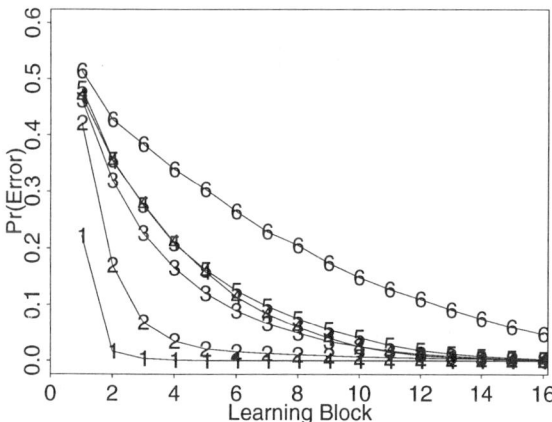

Figure 2. Each learning block consisted of two presentations of each stimulus (in a random order). Nosofsky et al.'s (1994) replication of Shepard et al. (1961) is shown on top. Below, SUSTAIN's fit of Nosofsky et al.'s (1994) data is shown (averaged over 10,000 runs on each problem).

---

[3]Occasionally, SUSTAIN recruited nine subcategory units (one more than the number of input patterns). This occurred when a subcategory unit responding to one input pattern was "stolen" by another input pattern belonging to the same category (i.e., the subcategory unit temporarily responded to two input patterns). Because no regularities exist in the Type VI problem, each subcategory unit can only encode one input pattern. The input pattern whose subcategory unit was "stolen" is forced to recruit a new subcategory unit.

[4]SUSTAIN's mean tunings are reported after two learning blocks because some runs reached criterion at that point. Differences in tunings between the six conditions are magnified when later blocks are examined.

Table 2
SUSTAIN's Final Architecture and mean λ (2nd block).

Problem Type	Mean Subcategory Units	Mean λ
I	2.2	2.0
II	4.3	2.8
III	5.9	3.0
IV	6.3	3.1
V	6.5	3.2
VI	8.2	3.5

in the Type I problem (the network learns the other two dimensions are irrelevant), while all three dimensions develop a sharp tuning in the Type VI problem (the network learns all three dimensions are highly relevant).

Discussion

SUSTAIN is an adaptive architecture, tailoring its architecture to the problem at hand. It is motivated by the basic psychological notion that people prefer general solutions and ignore distinctions when possible. SUSTAIN's potential is highlighted by its successfully fit of Shepard et al.'s (1961) six problem types. While this task uses binary input dimensions, SUSTAIN is not restricted to this input format. SUSTAIN has been successfully applied to Billman & Knutson's (1996) unsupervised learning data and Medin, Gerald, and Murphy's (1983) data on item and category learning where input patterns consist of attributes that are mulitvalued (Love & Medin, 1998).

References

Ash, T. (1989). Dynamic node creation in backpropagation networks. *Connection Science, 1*(4), 365–375.

Azimi-Sadjadi, M. R., Sheedvash, S., & Trujillo, F. O. (1993). Recursive dynamic node creation in multilayer neural networks. *IEEE Transactions on Neural Networks, 4*(2), 242–256.

Billman, D. & Knutson, J. (1996). Unsupervised concept learning and value systematicity: A complex whole aids learning the parts. *Journal of Experimental Psychology: Learning, Memory, & Cognition, 22*(2), 458–475.

Duda, R. O. & Hart, P. E. (1972). *Pattern Classification and Scene Analysis.* New York: Wiley.

Elman, J. L. (1994). Implicit learning in neural networks: The importance of starting small. In C. Umilta & M. Moscovitch (Eds.), *Attention and performance XV: Conscious and nonconscious information processing.*, pp. 861–888. Cambridge, MA: MIT Press.

Fahlman, S. E. & Lebiere, C. (1990). The cascade-correlation learning architecture. In D. S. Touretzky (Ed.), *Advances in Neural Information Processing Systems 2. Proceedings of the 1989 Conference*, pp. 524–532. San Mateo, CA: Morgan Kaufmann.

Geman, S., Bienenstock, E., & Doursat, R. (1992). Neural networks and the bias/variance dilemma. *Neural Computation, 4*(1), 1–58.

Hecht-Nielsen, R. (1988). Applications of counterpropagation networks. *Neural Networks, 1*(2), 131–139.

Hornik, K., Stinchcombe, M., & White, H. (1990). Universal approximation of an unknown mapping and its derivatives using multilayer feedforward networks. *Neural Networks, 3*(5), 551–560.

Kohonen, T. (1984). *Self-Organization and Associative Memory.* Berlin, Heidelberg: Springer. 3rd ed. 1989.

Kruschke, J. K. (1992). ALCOVE: An exemplar-based connectionist model of category learning. *Psychological Review, 99*(1), 22–44.

Lakoff, G. (1987). *Women, fire, and dangerous things: What categories reveal about the mind.* Chicago: University of Chicago Press.

Love, B. C. & Medin, D. L. (1998). A model of human category learning. In Preparation.

Luce, R. D. (1963). Detection and recognion. In R. D. Luce, R. R. Busg, & E. Galanter (Eds.), *Handbook of Mathematical Psychology*, pp. 103–189. New York: Wiley.

Medin, D. L., Gerald, G. I., & Murphy, T. D. (1983). Relationships between item and category learning: Evidence that abstraction is not automatic. *Journal of Experimental Psychology: Learning, Memory, & Cognition, 9*, 607–625.

Minsky, M. L. & Papert, S. (1969). *Perceptrons: An introduction to computational geometry.* Cambridge, MA: MIT Press.

Nosofsky, R. M., Gluck, M. A., Palmeri, T. J., McKinley, S. C., & Glauthier, P. (1994a). Comparing models of rule based classification learning: A replication and extension of Shepard, Hovland, and Jenkins (1961). *Memory & Cognition, 22*, 352–369.

Nosofsky, R. M., Palmeri, T. J., & McKinley, S. C. (1994b). Rule-plus-exception model of classification learning. *Psychological Review, 101*(1), 53–79.

Poggio, T. & Girosi, F. (1990). Regularization algorithms for learning that are equivalent to multilayer networks. *Science, 247*, 978–982.

Rosenblatt, F. (1958). The perceptron: A probabilistic model for information storage in the brain. *Psychological Review, 65*, 386–408.

Rumelhart, D. E., Hinton, G. E., & Williams, R. J. (1986). Learning representations by back-propagating errors. *Nature, 323*, 533–536.

Shepard, R. N. (1987). Toward a universal law of generalization for psychological science. *Science, 237*, 1317–1323.

Shepard, R. N., Hovland, C. L., & Jenkins, H. M. (1961). Learning and memorization of classifications. *Psychological Monographs, 75*(13, Whole No. 517).

Simpson, P. K. (1989). *Artificial Neural Systems.* Elmsford, NY: Pergamon Press.

Tou, J. T. & Gonzalez, R. C. (1974). *Pattern Recognition Principles.* Reading: Addison-Wesley.

Treue, S. & Maunsell, J. H. R. (1996). Attentional modulation of visual motion processing in cortical areas mt and mst. *Nature, 382*(6591), 539–541.

Optimal 2D Model Matching Using a Messy Genetic Algorithm

J. Ross Beveridge
Colorado State University
ross@cs.colostate.edu

Abstract

A Messy Genetic Algorithm is customized to find optimal many-to-many matches for 2D line segment models. The Messy GA is a variant upon the Standard Genetic Algorithm in which chromosome length can vary. Consequently, population dynamics can be made to drive a relatively efficient and robust search for larger and better matches. Run-times for the Messy GA are as much as an order of magnitude smaller than for random starts local search. When compared to a faster Key-Feature Algorithm, the Messy Genetic Algorithm more reliably finds optimal matches. Empirical results are presented for both controlled synthetic and real world line matching problems.

Introduction

How to create algorithms which recognize objects in imagery is one of the key problems facing researchers working in Computer Vision. A variety of approaches have emerged, including that of matching stored geometric models to features extracted from imagery. Some of the earliest work in Computer Vision adopted this paradigm (Roberts 1965), and many researchers have worked on refinements and extensions to the basic idea. Some of the most prominent work relating to this topic includes tree search (Grimson 1990), pose clustering (Stockman 1987), pose equivalence analysis (Cass 1992) and local search (Beveridge 1993). Also important is work on indexing techniques such as geometric hashing (Lamdan, Schwartz, & Wolfson 1990) and geometric invariants (J. Mundy and A. Zisserman (editors) 1992).

The specific task addressed in this paper is that of finding optimal matches between 2D models and image data where both model and data are expressed as sets of line segments. Image, or data, segments are typically extracted from imagery using one of several standard straight line extraction algorithms (Burns, Hanson, & Riseman 1986). Object models come from a variety of sources, including 3D CAD models and reference images. A match is characterized by both a discrete correspondence mapping between model and data segments as well as an associated geometric transformation which aligns the object model to the matched data. For the correspondence mapping, many-to-many matches are allowed. The alignment process will allow for variations in 2D orientation, position and size.

This paper contributes a new combinatorial optimization algorithm which finds matches faster and more reliably than any other technique known to the authors. This algorithm is an adaptation of a class of Genetic Algorithms called a Messy GA (Goldberg, Korb, & Deb 1989). What characterizes a Messy GA is the ability to operate on populations consisting of partial chromosomes. While representing a significant departure from the biological model of genetics, the ability to handle partial chromosomes makes the Messy GA ideal for manipulating partial matches.

Background

While the Messy GA is new to Computer Vision, it recapitulates some common ideas in a novel framework. One idea is to exploit small sets of pairwise matched model and data features: typically n-tuples where n equals 2, 3 or 4. For example, all Generalized Hough Transform (Davis & Yam 1980; Ballard 1981) and Pose Clustering (Stockman 1987) algorithms involve a step where n-tuples of paired features constrain or vote for transformations that align model to data. The Messy GA uses 3-tuples of spatially proximate pairs of model and data segments as an initial population.

How the Messy GA evolves a population of partial matches is suggestive of a clustering process, and it is tempting to compare the Messy GA with prior work on pose cluster (Stockman 1987; Olson 1994). The comparison is apt to the degree that both algorithms seek groups of paired features which imply a common alignment between the model and data. However, while pose clustering does this explicitly in the pose space, the Messy GA clusters pairs based upon a global evaluation of the consistency of the match.

Other significant works on matching 2D line mod-

---

[0] Copyright ©1998, American Association for Artificial Intelligence (www.aaai.org). All rights reserved.

els include (Grimson 1990) and (Cass 1992). Grimson has done perhaps the most thorough study of computational complexity. He has shown that tree search has $O(m^2 d^2)$ average case complexity for problems involving a single instance of an asymmetric object model. Here m is the number of model segments and d the number of data segments. If models are symmetric or more than one model instance is present, then tree search becomes exponential: $O(d^m)$ or $O(m^d)$ depending on formulation.

Pose equivalence (Cass 1992) analysis combines search in pose and correspondence space. For 2D problems involving rotation, translation and scale, pose equivalence analysis has an analytic worst-case complexity bound of $O(k^4 n^4)$. Here, $n = md$ and k is the number of sides on a convex polygon within which corresponding features must appear. The exponent 4 derives from the 4 degrees of freedom in a 2D similarity transform. The existence of this bound is significant, but the dependence upon n^4 precludes large problems in the worst case.

A final broad class of matching algorithms are those which look for a complete match by first seeking highly predictive n-tuples. For example, (Lowe 1985) uses general principles of perceptual organization to find localized features which predicted the presence of a modeled 3D object. (Huttenlocher & Ullman 1990) took a similar approach, but went further in formulating the idea of a ranked list of indexing features.

The Optimal Matching Problem

This paper will adopt the formulation of matching as a combinatorial optimization problem presented in (Beveridge 1993; J. Ross Beveridge & Steinborn 1997; J. Ross Beveridge & Graves 1997). The Messy GA uses constructs from both the Random Starts Local Search and Key-Feature algorithms presented in these papers. Consequently, it is best to present the Messy GA by first reviewing the problem formulation and these two other algorithms. For reasons of limited space, some details must be omitted and interested readers are directed to these other papers for additional background.

Optimal 2D Line Matching

Line matching determines the correspondence mapping between a set of model line segments M and data line segments D that minimizes a *match error function*. The match error is formulated as the sum of *fit* and *omission* errors. The fit error indicates how closely the model fits the data. The omission error measures the extent to which the model line segments are covered by the data. Match error may be written as:

$$E_{match} = \frac{1}{\sigma^2} E_{fit} + E_{omission} \quad (1)$$

The weighting coefficient σ controls the relative importance of the two error components and controls when it is better to omit versus include a data segment in a match. In general, σ is the maximum allowable distance in pixels between two segments which should be included in a match.

Anytime E_{match} is evaluated, evaluation begins by fitting the model to the data so as to minimize the *integrated squared perpendicular distance* between infinitely extended model lines and the bounded data line segments. Fitting is done subject to a 2D similarity transformation. The best-fit transformation is determined by solving for the roots of a second order polynomial and specifies a scaling, rotation and translation which best-fits the model the corresponding data. The fit error E_{fit} is a function of the residual squared error after fitting. The omission error $E_{omission}$ is a nonlinear function of the percentage of the model segments not covered by corresponding data segments after the model has been fit to the data.

The search space for matching is the power set C of all pairs S drawn from the set of model segments M and data segments D. Thus,

$$S \subset M \times D \quad C = 2^S \quad (2)$$

Matching seeks the optimal match $c^* \in C$ such that

$$E_{match}(c^*) \leq E_{match}(c) \quad \forall c \in C \quad (3)$$

Random Starts Local Search

Perhaps the simplest algorithm to find optimal matches is steepest-descent on a 'Hamming-distance-1' neighborhood. This neighborhood is so named because any correspondence mapping c may be represented by a bit-string of length n, where $n \in |S|$. A '1' in position j of the bit-string indicates that the jth pair in the set S is part of the match c. The n neighbors of c are generated by successively toggling each bit. Hence, the neighborhood contains all matches created by either 1) adding a single pair s not already in the match or 2) removing a single pair s currently in the match.

Steepest-descent local search using this neighborhood computes E_{match} for all n neighbors of the current match c, and moves to the neighbor yielding the greatest improvement: the greatest drop in E_{match}. Search terminates at a local optimum when no neighbor is better than the current match. Recall that in evaluating E_{match} the best global alignment of model to data is computed. Thus, all decisions about the relative worth of an individual pair of segments $s \in S$ is made in light of how this change alters the complete fit of the model to the currently matched data segments.

Because local search often becomes stuck at undesirable local optima, it is common to run multiple trials. Each trial is started from a randomly chosen initial match c_i. The random selection of c_i is biased to choose, on average, λ data segments for each model segment. Specifically, let h_m be the number of pairs in S which contain a model segment m. Each of these pairs is included in c_i with independent probability $\frac{\lambda}{h}$. Our experience suggests $\lambda = 4$ is a good choice, thus binding on average 4 data segments to each model segment.

Over t trials, the probability of failing to find a good match drops as an exponential function of t. Let P_s be the probability of finding a good solution on a single trial. The probability of failing to find a good match in t trials is:

$$Q_f = (1 - P_s)^t \quad (4)$$

More generally, given a set of training problem instances it is possible to derive an estimate t_s for the number of trials needed to solve these problems. Let P_s be the true probability of successfully finding the optimal match in a single trial. Now note that the maximum likelihood estimate $\hat{P}_s$ for this true probability is the ratio of the number of trials where the optimal match is found over the total number of trials run.

From $\hat{P}_s$, the required number of trials t_s needed to solve a particular problem to a preset level of confidence Q_s may be derived from equation 4:

$$t_s = \lceil \log_{\hat{P}_f} Q_f \rceil \quad Q_f = 1 - Q_s \quad \hat{P}_f = 1 - \hat{P}_s \quad (5)$$

Key-Feature Algorithm

The Random Starts Local Search algorithm just presented can be turned into a deterministic search algorithm by initiating search from k carefully selected key feature matches. Here our key features F will be based upon triples of paired model and data segments. If there are n possible pairings between model and data features in the set S, then there are n^3 possible triples. For typical problems presented below, $n \approx 1,000$. It is impractical to enumerate and rank $1,000,000,000$ triples; clearly, some filter must be used. We use a very general heuristic: Filtering by spatial proximity will generate on the order of n ranked triples.

To generate spatially proximate triples, first model and data segments are analyzed independently to find the nearest neighbors of each. For each model line $m_i \in M$, determine the closest two neighbors m_{i1} and m_{i2} as defined by Euclidean distance δ:

$$\delta(m_i, m_{i1}) \leq \delta(m_i, m_k) \; \forall \, m_k \in M - \{m_i\}$$
$$\delta(m_i, m_{i2}) \leq \delta(m_i, m_k) \; \forall \, m_k \in M - \{m_i, m_{i1}\}$$

Analogous nearest neighbors d_{j1} and d_{j2} for each data line segment $d_j \in D$ are found.

When matching segments M to D, each pair of segments $(m_i, d_j) \in S$ form two spatially proximate triples f_1 and f_2:

$$f_1 = ((m_i, d_j), (m_{i1}, d_{j1}), (m_{i2}, d_{j2}))$$
$$f_2 = ((m_i, d_j), (m_{i1}, d_{j2}), (m_{i2}, d_{j1}))$$

Since each of the n pairs of model and data segments in S leads to 2 triples, there are $2n$ spatially proximate triples in the initial set of key features F.

In keeping with the assumption that some key features are better than others, order the set F from lowest to highest match error;

$$F = \{f_1, f_2, \ldots f_{2n}\} \quad (6)$$
$$E(f_k) < E(f_l) \quad \text{iff} \quad k < l \quad (7)$$

The Key Feature Algorithm initiates local search independently from each of the k best triples in F. Moreover, since it is assumed that the triple is a good match, the neighborhood is restricted to consider only the addition of pairs $s \in S$. One question is how deep into the ranked set F to go. Our experiments take a conservative approach and use all $2n$ triples.

The Messy Genetic Algorithm

Messy Genetic Algorithms (Goldberg, Korb, & Deb 1989) differ from normal Genetic Algorithms in that they allow variable-length strings that may be under-specified or over-specified with respect to the problem being solved. For matching geometric models, this means they can operate over partial matches and so piece together larger and better matches.

A Messy GA typically has three phases:

1. Initialization.
2. Primordial Phase.
3. Juxtapositional phase.

In the initialization phase some procedure is used to enumerate a set of partial chromosomes. Next, in the primoridial phase, these partial chromosomes are evaluated using a fitness function and some subset of these found to be most fit are used to form the initial population. Finally, the juxtapositional phase is analogous to the normal cycle of selection and recombination used in a traditional GA.

For initialization, our Messy GA uses the same set of spatially proximate triples F defined above for the Key-Feature Algorithm. This customized initialization phase creates $2n$ triples to seed the initial population. Next, in the primordial phase, the triples are sorted by the match error E_{match} and some fraction of the best form the initial population. In the experiments presented here, all the $2n$ triples are used.

During juxtaposition, selection is used together with two operators: cut and splice. Cut 'cuts' the chromosome at random position. Splice 'attaches' two cut chromosomes together. These two operators are the equivalents of crossover in a traditional GA. In our matching problem, a chromosome h is a variable length set of pairs $h \subset S$ representing a match between model and data segments. Both the cut and splice operators pick the positions in the set representations where cutting and splicing take place with uniform probability. Hence, for example, if a set h contains 6 pairs of model and data segments, then cut will select one of the five possible break points with equal probability.

To select parents, the Messy GA uses a variant of the Genitor (Whitley & Starkweather 1990) algorithm which uses fitness ranking to bias selection and a monotinic replacement strategy. Selection based upon rank means that two parents are selected for recombination based upon their ranking in the population rather than upon the absolute difference in fitness between themselves and the others in the population. To make this process more efficient, the population is always maintained in sorted order from lowest to highest E_{match}. The current parameterization of the algorithm makes the most fit individual twice as likely to be selected as a parent as compared to the least fit individual.

Monotonic selection means that each time two parents are selected and used to create a child, that child is inserted back into the original ranked ordered population based upon its newly computed E_{match}. Afterward, the least fit individual is removed from the population. This means that if a child is inferior to all other individuals in the population, then that child is effectively discarded. This also means that the overall quality of the population will increase monotonically, since a worse individual can never displace one which is more fit.

To help drive the Messy Genetic Algorithm to a solution, every three generations the least fit individual in the population is dropped and the population size correspondingly shrinks by one. Every $f = \frac{p}{2}$ generations, an individual is selected from the population and local search is run using the selected match as an initial state. If the result is better than the worst currently in the population, then it is inserted back into the population. This periodic use of local search as part of the genetic search is of great practical benefit, and is consistent with other results suggesting hybridized algorithms of this type often out perform pure Genetic or Local Search (D. Whitley, J. Ross Beveridge, C. Graves and K. Mathias 1996).

Like Random Starts Local Search, the Messy Genetic Algorithm is a non-deterministic search algorithm. Consequently, the same technique of running multiple independent trials in order to increase the probability of seeing the best match applies. Further, the probability $\hat{P}_s$ that the Messy Genetic Algorithm will succeed on any given trial can again be estimated.

Messy GA Performance Compared to Alternative Search Algorithms

In comparing the new Messy GA to previous algorithms, two things are important: time required to solve a problem and probability any given problem is solved optimally. The Key-Feature Algorithm is deterministic, and hence characterizing its performance is relatively straight forward. The algorithm is run for all $2n$ Key-Features and the time required and quality of the resulting best match is recorded.

In contrast, the Messy GA and Random Starts Local Search algorithms are non-deterministic, and analysis begins by running a sufficient number of trials that it is possible to estimate the probability of finding an optimal solution in a given run or trial. Here 1,000 trials of Random Starts Local Search and 100 trials of the Messy GA are run. Of course, in some cases, the best is not found even in a great many empirical trials, and then this probability cannot be estimated and the algorithm is considered to have failed.

Here we present results comparing run-time and probability of solving a problem for a synthetic data set designed to test matching algorithms under a variety of controlled conditions. Results are also presented on an application domain considered by the authors to be challenging: matching line segments representing a horizon extracted from a digital terrain map to line segments extracted from an image of the same terrain.

Comparison on Controlled Synthetic Data

Figure 1 shows examples of 48 test problems created from six stick figure models. These six models have been chosen to test a matching algorithm under different conditions known to be problematic for at least some matching techniques. Included is a "Dandelion" with 16 fold partial symmetry and a "Leaf" in which the line segments approximate an underlying curved boundary. Also included is a simple three line segment "Pole" whose simplicity might be expected to cause problems for a Key-Feature approach.

To create the test data for each model, model segments are randomly scaled and placed in the data images and are potentially fragmented, skewed and omitted. Finally, random clutter and structured clutter are added to the data. In 24 problems, 0, 10, 20 and 30 additional clutter segments are randomly placed about the image for each model: Figure 1a. In the another 24 problems, 0, 1, 2 and 3 additional more highly corrupted model instances are added: Figure 1b. The smallest resulting search space contains 2^{12} matches, the largest $2^{1,296}$. This dataset is available through our website: http://www.cs.colostate.edu/~vision.

Optimal matches can be reliably found to all 48 problems using Random Starts Local Search (J. Ross Beveridge & Graves 1997). However, as shown in (J. Ross Beveridge & Steinborn 1997), the Key-Feature Algorithm only finds optimal solutions to 7 out of the 48 problems. Thus, while the Key-Feature Algorithm runs in perhaps a tenth of the time required by Random Starts Local Search, it does not reliably find optimal matches.

Like Random Starts Local Search, the Messy GA also finds the optimal match for all 48 problems, but it requires considerably less time to so. For the Messy GA, the average number of trials required t_s (equation 5) over the 48 problems is 2, the median is 1, the minimum is 1 and the maximum is 9. For Random Starts Local Search, the the average t_s is 111, the median is 42, the minimum is 5 and the maximum is 998.

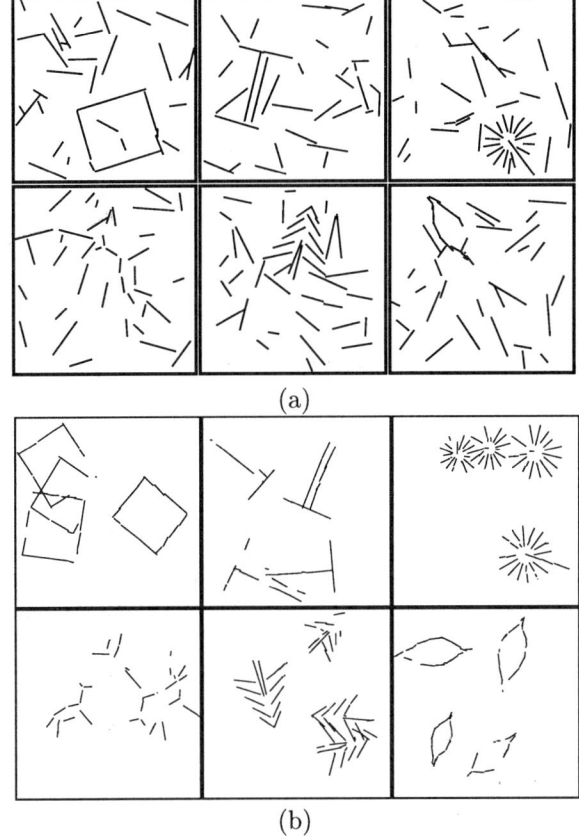

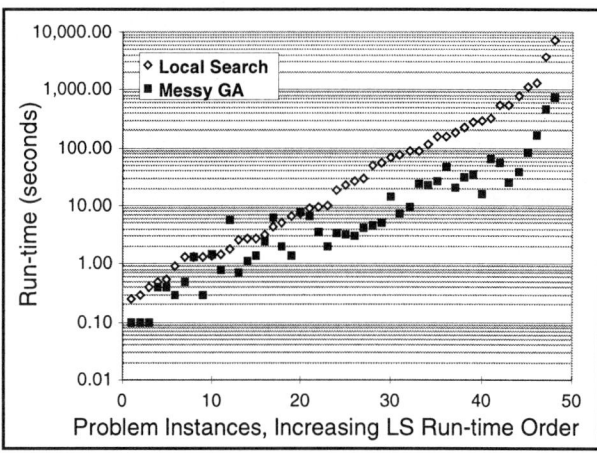

Figure 2: Comparison of run-times.

Figure 1: Test suite. a) Random clutter, b) Multiple model instances.

An estimate of the time required to solve each problem with 95% confidence is the average run-time per trial times the number of trials t_s. These run-times for a Sparc 20 are shown in Figure 2. On average, the Messy Genetic Algorithm is 5.9 times faster than Random Starts Local Search. Perhaps more importantly, the Messy Genetic Algorithm is doing better on the harder problems. Divide the problems into the the 24 solved quickly by Random Starts Local Search and the 24 requiring the most time. On the easier problems, the Messy Genetic Algorithm runs on average 2.5 faster. In contrast, for the harder 24 problems the Messy Genetic Algorithm runs 9.4 times faster. In other words, for the problems taking thousands of seconds to solve using Random Starts Local Search, the Messy Genetic Algorithm is dropping run-times by an order of magnitude.

Horizon Matching Comparison

An interesting application for optimal line matching has arisen in the context of the Unmanned Ground Vehicle (UGV) Program (Firschein & Strat 1997). It was found that when a mobile robot operating outdoors used a Satellite Global Positioning System (GPS), vehicle position was reliably known to within several meters. However, using an inertial guidance system to track vehicle orientation, errors of from 1 to 2 degrees were common. These errors generate uncertainty in camera pointing angle relative to the terrain, and even small orientation errors translate to large pixel errors.

For example, a 2 degree error equates to a 50 pixel error when using a 10 degree field of view camera and 512^2 images. If an algorithm could match the horizon as it is predicted to appear to the true horizon in the image, then this error in 3D orientation could be corrected. Moreover, because the horizon is a distant object and essentially all the uncertainty is in 3D pointing angle, the resulting matching task is essentially 2D. In other words, the predicted horizon need only be rotated and translated relative to the true horizon, and scaling is only required to account for minor inconsistencies in sensor calibration.

The Messy GA, Key-Feature and Random Starts Local Search algorithms have all been tested on a series of horizon matching problems of this type using imagery, terrain maps and sensor data from the UGV Demo C test site (Ray Rimey 1995). Imagery and example horizon features for one of the two UGV locations used to generate matching problems are shown in Figure 3. Figure 3a shows the CCD image captured from the UGV. Figure 3b shows a rendering of the terrain map based upon the estimated position and orientation of the vehicle. Figure 3c shows line segments extracted from the CCD image using the Burns algorithm (Burns, Hanson, & Riseman 1986). Figure 3d shows segments extracted from a thresholded version of the rendered terrain image using the same line extraction algorithm. The images are all 512 pixels across by 480 pixels high.

Horizon matching is important in the context of this paper because it is appears to generate challenging 2D matching problems of practical utility. One factor making horizon matching challenging is that horizons are relatively long and narrow structures which exhibit

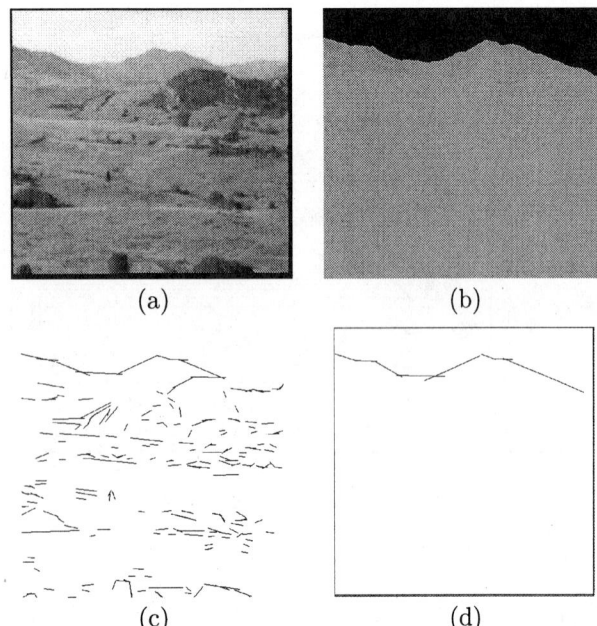

Figure 3: Horizon matching problem. a) CCD Image, b) rendered terrain map, c) segments extracted from image, d) segments extracted from rendered terrain.

Vehicle Location 1					
	μ	Min.	Max.	Med.	σ
n	364	247	469	371	62
Time:					
MGA	1,006	749	1,414	977	180
RSLS	1,180	480	1,870	1,140	371
KF	118	69	161	118	22
$\hat{P}_s$:					
MGA	0.97	0.56	1.00	1.00	0.09
RSLS	0.009	0.001	0.033	0.007	0.07

Vehicle Location 2					
	μ	Min.	Max.	Med.	σ
n	1085	456	2083	1140	429
Time::					
MGA	7,171	1,907	15,766	6,414	3,624
RSLS	8,137	1,230	27,040	7,400	6,105
KF	1,307	288	2,836	1,027	683
$\hat{P}_s$:					
MGA	0.57	0.01	1.00	0.49	0.40
RSLS	0.002	0.0	0.026	0.001	0.005

MGA: Messy GA
RSLS: Random Starts Local Search
KF: Key-Feature Algorithm

Table 1: Problem size n, run-time statistics and probabilities of success for the two vehicle locations.

significant amounts of self-similarity. In the limiting case of a flat horizon, the horizon becomes a line and the problem becomes ill-posed. Typically, a matching algorithm must select the best match out of many possible partial matches. It is also a domain in which allowing for a many-to-many mapping between model and data is important. This is because the horizon is in fact a curve which is approximated by line segments, and the break points in the model and data are almost certain to fall at different points.

Results for Two Vehicle Locations Data from two different vehicle locations were used to generate a total of 54 different optimal matching problems. For each location the terrain map was rendered for 27 perturbed camera pointing angles. The perturbations were: pan $-2°, 0°, +2°$, roll $-5°, 0°, +5°$ and tilt $-1°, 0°, +2°$. For each of the 54 matching problems, Random Starts Local Search was run for 1,000 trials, the Messy GA was run for 100 trials and the Key-Feature Algorithm was run from all $2n$ spatially proximate triples. These are conservative settings for all three algorithms, involving substantial amounts of run-time with the goal of giving the algorithm the fairest chance of finding the best match.

For vehicle location 1, all three algorithms found the optimal horizon line match. However, for vehicle location 2 (Figure 3), the Key-Feature Algorithm failed to find the optimal match on 3 out of the 27 problems and Random Starts Local Search failed on 9 out of the 27 problems. The Messy GA was the only algorithm to find the optimal match on all 54 problems.

Table 1 summarizes the problem sizes, run-times and measured probability of success $\hat{P}_s$ for the 27 matching problems arising out of each of the two vehicle locations. Run-time is measured in seconds on a Sun Sparc 20. Observe that 100 trials of the Messy GA takes time comparable to the 1,000 trials of Random Starts Local Search. Also observe that while the median $\hat{P}_s$ for vehicle location 2 is high, 0.49, the minimum value is 0.01. Thus, while 100 trials is more than needed on most problems, it is barely adequate for the hardest problem.

The Messy GA as Cordinated Search

The Key-Feature algorithm exemplifies a general heuristic applied widely in object recognition work. As indicated in (J. Ross Beveridge & Steinborn 1997), when the Key-Features are reliable predictors of an object, then Key-Feature matching is a very useful. However, in difficult problems where more and more Key-Features must be considered in order to guarantee finding an optimal match, one begins to observe wasted effort resulting from the fact that search to fill out the match from each Key-Feature is conducted in isolation.

The Messy GA is a technique for initiating a single coordinated search from a large set of Key-Features as opposed to many isolated searches. In the Messy GA, population dynamics introduce competition which tends to focus effort on more promising partial solutions and away from others. By operating within a single population, the Messy GA may also reduce the amount of effort spent repeatedly enumerating nearly identical solutions. Since it is reasonable to expect that a single coordinated search is more efficient than many isolated ones, it reasonable to conjecture that for difficult matching tasks the Messy GA will prove itself more efficient than Key-Feature approaches.

Conclusion

A new matching algorithm has been presented based upon a Messy Genetic Algorithm. This algorithm has been compared to both Random Starts Local Search and a Key-Feature Algorithm. On controlled synthetic data and real world data, the Messy GA performs better than either of these two alternative approaches. On the synthetic problems, the Messy GA finds optimal matches on all 48 test problems in run-time comparable to that needed by the Key-Feature Algorithm. However, the Key-Feature Algorithm finds sub-optimal matches in 7 out of the 48 problems. Matching horizons from rendered digital elevation maps to horizons in CCD imagery, only the Messy GA found optimal matches in all 54 test cases. Additional refinements to the Messy GA are certainly possible, and perhaps the most interesting would be to bias the selection phase to favor recombination of parents which imply similar object pose estimates.

Acknowledgments

work was sponsored by the Defense Advanced Research Projects Agency (DARPA) Image Understanding Program under contract 96-14-112 monitored by the Army Topographic Engineering Laboratory (TEC), contracts DAAH04-93-G-422 and DAAH04-95-1-0447, monitored by the U. S. Army Research Office as well as by the National Science Foundation under grant IRI-9503366.

References

Ballard, D. H. 1981. Generalizing the hough transform to detect arbitrary shapes. *Pattern Recognition* 13(2):111 – 122.

Beveridge, J. R. 1993. *Local Search Algorithms for Geometric Object Recognition: Optimal Correspondence and Pose.* Ph.D. Dissertation, University of Massachusetts at Amherst.

Burns, J. B.; Hanson, A. R.; and Riseman, E. M. 1986. Extracting straight lines. *IEEE Trans. on Pattern Analysis and Machine Intelligence* PAMI-8(4):425 – 456.

Cass, T. A. 1992. Polynomial-time object recognition in the presence of clutter, occlusion, and uncertainty. In *Proceedings: Image Understanding Workshop*, 693 – 704. San Mateo, CA: DARPA.

D. Whitley, J. Ross Beveridge, C. Graves and K. Mathias. 1996. Test Driving Three 1995 Genetic Algorithms: New Test Functions and Geometric Matching. *Journal of Heuristics* 1:77 – 104.

Davis, L. S., and Yam, S. 1980. A generalized Hough-like transformation for shape recognition. Technical Report TR-134, University of Texas, Computer Science.

Firschein, O., and Strat, T. 1997. *Reconnaissance, Surveilance, and Target Acquisition for the Unmanned Ground Vehicle.* Morgan Kaufmann.

Goldberg, D. E.; Korb, B.; and Deb, K. 1989. Messy genetic algorithms: Motivation, analysis, and first results. Technical report, University of Alabama.

Grimson, W. E. L. 1990. *Object Recognition by Computer: The Role of Geometric Constraints.* Cambridge, MA: MIT Press.

Huttenlocher, D. P., and Ullman, S. 1990. Recognizing Solid Objects by Alignment with an Image. *International Journal of Computer Vision* 5(2):195 – 212.

J. Mundy and A. Zisserman (editors). 1992. *Geometric Invariance in Computer Vision.* Cambridge: MIT Press.

J. Ross Beveridge, E. M. R., and Graves, C. R. 1997. How Easy is Matching 2D Line Models Using Local Search? *IEEE Trans. on Pattern Analysis and Machine Intelligence* 19(6):564 – 579.

J. Ross Beveridge, C. R. G., and Steinborn, J. 1997. Comparing Random-Starts Local Search with Key-Feature matching. In *Proc. 1997 International Joint Conference on Artificial Intelligence*, 1476 – 1481.

Lamdan, Y.; Schwartz, J. T.; and Wolfson, H. J. 1990. Affine invariant model-based object recognition. *IEEE Transactions on Robotics and Automation* 6(5):578 – 589.

Lowe, D. G. 1985. *Perceptual Organization and Visual Recognition.* Kluwer Academic Publishers.

Olson, C. 1994. Time and space efficient pose clustering. In *CVPR94*, 251–258.

Ray Rimey. 1995. RSTA Sept94 Data Collection Final Report. Technical report, Martin Marietta Astronautics, Denver, CO.

Roberts, L. G. 1965. Machine perception of three-dimensional solids. In Tippett, J. T., ed., *Optical and Electro-Optical Information Processing.* Cambridge, MA: MIT Press. chapter 9, 159 – 197.

Stockman, G. 1987. Object recognition and localization via pose clustering. *CVGIP* 40(3):361–387.

Whitley, D., and Starkweather, T. 1990. Genitor ii: A distributed genetic algorithm. *Journal of Experimental and Theoretical Artificial Intelligence* 2(3):189 – 214.

Learning Cooperative Lane Selection Strategies for Highways

David E. Moriarty
Information Sciences Institute
University of Southern California
4676 Admiralty Way
Marina Del Rey, CA 90292
moriarty@isi.edu

Pat Langley
Adaptive Systems Group
Daimler-Benz Research & Technology Center
1510 Page Mill Road
Palo Alto, CA 94304
langley@rtna.daimlerbenz.com

Abstract

This paper presents a novel approach to traffic management by coordinating driver behaviors. Current traffic management systems do not consider lane organization of the cars and only affect traffic flows by controlling traffic signals or ramp meters. However, drivers should be able to increase traffic throughput and more consistently maintain desired speeds by selecting lanes intelligently. We pose the problem of intelligent lane selection as a challenging and potentially rewarding problem for artificial intelligence, and we propose a methodology that uses supervised and reinforcement learning to form distributed control strategies. Initial results are promising and demonstrate that intelligent lane selection can better approximate desired speeds and reduce the total number of lane changes.

Introduction

A large effort is under way by government and industry in America, Europe, and Japan to develop intelligent vehicle and highway systems. These systems incorporate ideas from artificial intelligence, intelligent control, and decision theory, among others, to automate many aspects of driving and traffic control. The goals of this effort are quite broad and include increased traffic throughput, fewer accidents, reduced fuel consumption, and a better driving experience.

The work in this paper targets one component of the overall task: the problem of managing traffic. Advanced traffic management systems are designed to reduce congestion and increase overall traffic throughput. Almost all such systems maintain efficient traffic flows by controlling traffic signals or highway ramp meters, treating traffic as a single mass and normally ignoring the behavior of individual cars (Gilmore, Elibiary, & Forbes, 1994; Kagolanu, Fink, Smartt, Powell, & Larson, 1995; Pooran, Tarnoff, & Kalaputapu, 1996). This view, however, misses an important component of traffic management: coordination of the cars themselves.

Surprisingly, very little research has addressed how the cars themselves can sense and intelligently affect traffic flows. Drivers generate local behaviors such as lane changes and speed selections. These behaviors could be coordinated to better maintain desired speeds and achieve greater traffic throughput. Such strategies should complement existing efforts in traffic management by providing better throughput in between traffic signals and better-defined driver behaviors for traffic-flow prediction.

A challenging problem for artificial intelligence lies in the development of cooperative driving strategies for traffic management. This paper explores one form of this problem: intelligent lane selection. Each car receives local input of the surrounding traffic patterns and the desired speed of the driver, then outputs the lane in which to drive. A car's lane selections should consider not only the maintenance of its own desired speed, but also how the selection will affect the speeds of other cars. In this way, the cars should organize themselves into a cooperative system that lets the fast drivers pass through, while still letting the slow drivers maintain their speeds.

The work in this paper is exploratory in nature, and follows Dietterich's (1990) model for exploratory machine learning research. We formulate the problem of traffic management from a car-centered, machine learning perspective and present initial results of cooperative lane selection.

Problem Definition

We recast the traffic management problem as a problem in distributed artificial intelligence, where each car represents an individual agent in a multi-agent system. Cars act on their world (highway) by selecting appropriate lanes to drive in. They interact with other cars by competing for resources (spaces on the highway). Each action is local in nature, and may not produce any noticeable benefit to the car. Collectively, however, the local actions can improve the global performance of the traffic. For example, yielding a lane to a faster car does not produce any local benefit to the slower car, but does increase the overall traffic throughput and let the passing car maintain its desired speed.

Figure 1(a) illustrates a situation where lane coordination is beneficial. The figure illustrates five cars along with their speeds, which will be used as identifiers. Car

Copyright 1998, American Association for Artificial Intelligence (www.aaai.org). All rights reserved.

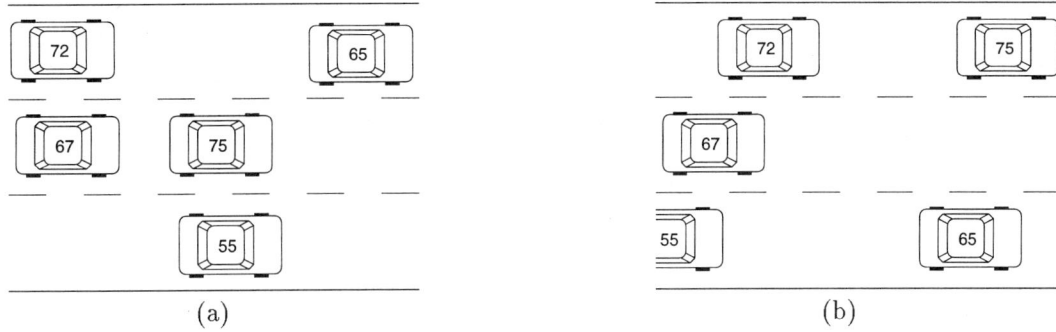

Figure 1: (a) An example traffic situation in which the traffic flows from left to right and the number on each car shows the car's speed, and (b) traffic after reorganization in which car 75 and 65 swap lanes.

72 is approaching car 65 and is unable to pass because of the position of car 67. Without reorganization, car 65 forces car 72 to reduce its speed and wait for car 67 to pass car 65, which will decrease traffic throughput and car 72's satisfaction. A solution is for car 75 and car 65 to swap lanes, followed by car 65 moving into the bottom lane. This maneuver ensures that no speeds are reduced and no throughput is lost.

Global traffic performance could be defined in many different ways. Governments want high traffic throughput, whereas drivers want to maintain desired speeds with few lane changes. We selected the driver-oriented metric, since drivers are likely to be the harshest critics of cooperative driving. The performance function P we devised for a set of cars C is given by the equation:

$$P(C) = \frac{\sum_{t=1}^{T} \sum_{i=1}^{N} (S_{it}^a - S_{it}^d)^2}{TN} - \frac{60 \sum_{i=1}^{N} L_i}{TN}, \quad (1)$$

where T is the total time steps (in seconds), N is the number of cars, S_{it}^d is the desired speed of car i at time t, S_{it}^a is the actual speed of car i at time t, and L_i is the total number of lane changes for car i over T time steps. The goal is to minimize the difference between actual speeds and desired speeds averaged over several time steps and over all cars. Each speed difference is squared to penalize extreme behavior. For example, driving 60 m/h 90% of the time and 10 m/h 10% of the time gives an average of 55 m/h but is clearly less desirable than driving 56 m/h 50% and 54 m/h 50% of the time, which also gives an average of 55 m/h. To discourage excessive lane changes, the performance function is adjusted by subtracting the number of lane changes per minute averaged over all cars.

The problem is thus to find a strategy or a set of strategies to maximize equation 1. A naive strategy for each car, which most traffic management systems assume, is to select the lane that lets it most consistently achieve its desired speed and only change lanes if a slower car is encountered. The disadvantage of such a strategy is that it does not take into account the global criteria of traffic performance. A slow car should not drive in the "fast" lane simply because it can maintain its desired speed. We will refer to cars that employ the naive strategy as *selfish cars*, since they maximize the local performance of their respective car. We are interested in strategies that maximize the aggregate performance of traffic. Cars that employ cooperative selection strategies will be termed *smart cars*.

Ideally, the smart cars should coexist with current drivers on the highways. This situation poses interesting research questions. How many smart drivers are necessary to make cooperation worthwhile? How quickly does the system break down when selfish drivers are introduced in the system? The experimental evaluation section presents some evidence that, even in distributions as high as 95% selfish cars, cooperative lane selection can improve traffic performance.

Communication and Coordination

The previous section defined the problem of car-centered traffic management, but left open some important issues in designing a distributed artificial intelligence system for this task. Specifically, we left open the level of communication between the cars and the amount of knowledge available on other cars' state. The multi-agent literature is often divided on these matters, and we feel that it is not central to the problem definition. Here we describe our assumptions about communication and state information.

We assume that cars have access to information on their own state, including knowledge of their current driving speed and the driver's desired speed. One could imagine a driver specifying desired speeds at the start of a trip, or the system could infer this information from the driver's historical behavior. We also assume that cars can perceive limited state information of surrounding cars, such as their relative speeds. The system could sense this information using radar or receive it directly from other cars via radio waves or the Internet. Cars should also sense which surrounding cars are cooperative and which are selfish.

Figure 2 illustrates the input for a car in a specific traffic situation. The middle car receives as input its current speed, its desired speed, the relative speeds of surrounding traffic, and whether surrounding cars are

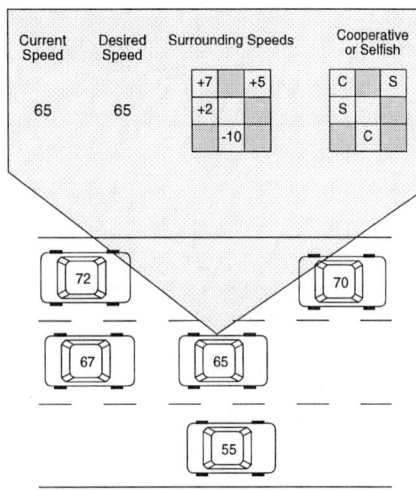

Figure 2: An illustration of the input to each car.

cooperative or selfish. The range and granularity of the relative speed inputs could be adjusted to take into account both local traffic and upcoming traffic.

Note that the cars only receive a partial view of the overall traffic situation. Another design option is to give all of the cars complete information of all other cars and treat the problem as a global optimization problem. We selected the local input representation for two reasons. First, we believe that it is more realistic to assume that only local traffic information is available. Second, we believe that a local policy will provide more effective generalization across different highways.

We assume that the controller's output consists of three options: (1) stay in the current lane, (2) change lanes to the left, or (3) change lanes to the right. The output does not specify the best lane to drive in, but rather whether the lanes immediately left or immediately right are better than the current lane. This control provides flexibility, since it does not depend on the number of lanes on the roadway or knowledge of the current driving lane.

We assume that the controller's output represents a ranking of the three possible choices, with the highest ranked choice that is both valid and safe selected as the car's next action. For a choice to be valid, there must be a lane available in the specified direction. For a choice to be safe, there must not be a car in the same longitudinal position in the new lane. We assume that it is always safe to remain in the current lane.

Another important issue concerns the representation of the different types of lane-selection strategies. Clearly, different types of drivers should select lanes differently. Slower drivers will normally change lanes to create openings for faster traffic. Faster drivers change lanes to pass through slower traffic. Maintaining explicit control policies for each type of driver, however, requires *a priori* knowledge of the number of driver types and the boundaries that separate them. We chose instead to maintain a single control policy which takes as input the type of driver (desired speed input). Each car thus contains the same control policy, but since it receives driving style as input, it behaves differently for different drivers.

Learning Distributed Control Strategies

Creating distributed lane-changing controllers by hand appears quite difficult. It is unclear whether experts exist in this domain and, even if they do, experts often find it difficult to verbalize complex control skills, which creates a *knowledge acquisition bottleneck*. Also, the innumerable traffic patterns and varying driving styles create a very large problem space. Even with significant expert domain knowledge, hand crafting a controller that operates effectively in all areas of the problem space may not be feasible.

Our solution is to apply machine learning to develop controllers through experience with the domain. Unfortunately, the lane-selection problem appears out of reach of the more standard, *supervised* machine learning methods. Supervised learning would require examples of correct lane decisions, which are difficult to obtain without expert domain knowledge. We also do not want to mimic real drivers, since we believe that drivers do not currently select lanes cooperatively.

We chose a multi-level learning approach that capitalizes on the available domain knowledge, but is also flexible enough to learn under sparse reinforcements. The learning system consists of three main components: reinforcement learning using SANE, supervised learning from pre-existing domain knowledge, and a local learning strategy that is similar in spirit to temporal difference methods. Figure 3 illustrates the interaction of the different learning methods, which we describe in the next three sections.

Reinforcement Learning using SANE

The backbone of the learning system is the SANE reinforcement learning method (Moriarty & Miikkulainen, 1996; Moriarty, 1997). Here we give a brief outline of SANE and its advantages; the aforementioned references provide more detailed information.

SANE (Symbiotic, Adaptive Neuro-Evolution) was designed as an efficient method for forming decision strategies in domains where it is not possible to generate training data for normal supervised learning. SANE maintains a population of possible strategies, evaluates the goodness of each from its performance in the domain, and uses an evolutionary algorithm to generate new strategies. The evolutionary algorithm modifies the strategies through genetic operators like selection, crossover, and mutation (Goldberg, 1989).

SANE represents its decision strategies as artificial neural networks that form a direct mapping from sensors to decisions and provide effective generalization over the state space. The evolutionary algorithm searches the space of hidden neuron definitions, where

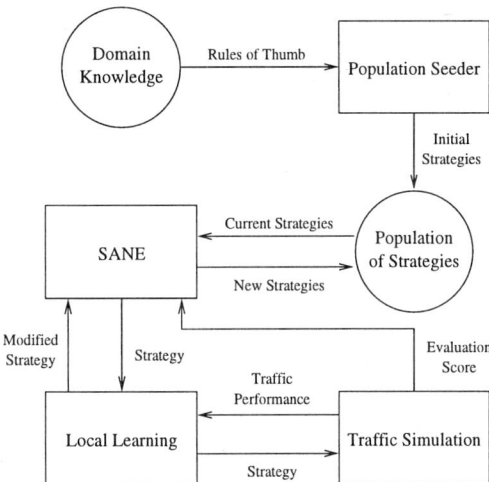

Figure 3: The organization and interaction of the different learning modules.

each hidden neuron defines a set of weighted connections between a fixed input and fixed output layer. In other words, SANE evolves all of the connections and weights between the hidden layer and the input and output layers in a three-layer network.

SANE offers two important advantages for reinforcement learning that are normally not present in other implementations of neuro-evolution. First, it decomposes the search for complete solutions into a search for partial solutions. Instead of searching for complete neural networks all at once, solutions to smaller problems (good neurons) are evolved, which can be combined to form effective full solutions (neural networks). In other words, SANE effectively performs a problem reduction search on the space of neural networks.

Second, the system maintains diverse populations. Unlike the canonical evolutionary algorithm that converges the population on a single solution, SANE forms solutions in an *unconverged* population. Because different types of neurons are necessary to build an effective neural network, there is inherent evolutionary pressure to develop neurons that perform different functions and thus maintain different types of individuals within the population. Diversity lets recombination operators such as crossover continue to generate new neural structures even in prolonged evolution. This feature helps ensure that the solution space will be explored efficiently throughout the learning process.

SANE represents each lane-selection strategy as a neural network that maps a car's sensory input into a specific lane-selection decision. Each network consists of 18 input units, 12 hidden units, and 3 output units. A network receives input on the car's current and desired speeds and the speeds of surrounding traffic, and it outputs a ranking of the three possible choices.

A strategy is evaluated by placing it in a traffic simulator and letting it make lane changes in a certain percentage of the cars. Each strategy is evaluated independently of other strategies in the population. The fitness of a strategy is measured using equation 1 after some number of simulated seconds. SANE uses these evaluations to bias its genetic selection and recombination operations towards the more profitable lane-selection strategies.

Incorporating Domain Knowledge

The second learning component capitalizes on pre-existing domain knowledge and gives SANE a good set of initial strategies. Although expert information is difficult to obtain in this problem, general rules of thumb are not. For example, one good heuristic specifies that a very slow driver should in general not drive in the far left lane. Supervised learning from these general rules will not generate optimal lane selection strategies, but it can give the learning system a good head start towards intelligent behavior.

The population seeder applies such heuristics in the traffic simulator and generates a series of input and output pairs, which represent decisions made from the rules of thumb based on specific sensory input. These pairs denote examples of good behavior that can be fed to a supervised learning method to form initial strategies. Since SANE's strategies are represented as neural networks, the population seeder employs the backpropagation algorithm (Rumelhart, Hinton, & Williams, 1986) to train the networks over the training examples. To maintain diversity within the initial population of neural networks and not overly bias SANE toward the rules of thumb, only a subset of the networks are seeded using the default knowledge. In practice, we seed 25% of the initial population.

We used four rules to seed SANE's population of strategies:

- If your desired speed is 55 m/h or less and the right lane is open, then change lanes right.
- If you are in the left lane, a car behind you has a higher speed, and the right lane is open, then change lanes right.
- If a car in front of you has a slower current speed than your desired speed and the left lane is open, then change lanes left.
- In the previous situation, if the left lane was not open but the right lane is, then change lanes right.

These rules are based on our interpretation of the "slower traffic yield to the right" signs posted on the highways. We will refer to this strategy hereafter as the *polite strategy*. The selfish strategy described earlier in the paper operates using only the last two rules.

Local Learning

We also implemented a local learning module that, like the population seeder, was included to increase learning efficiency and thereby reduce the amount of simulation time necessary to form good strategies. Local learning occurs during the evaluation of a lane-selection strategy and makes small refinements to the strategy based on immediate rewards or penalties. A reward or positive training signal is given if there is a significant increase in traffic performance and a penalty or negative training signal is given if there is a significant decrease. In practice, traffic performance is sampled every 10 simulated seconds and a reward or penalty is generated if the difference in performance from equation 1 is larger than 10.

If a training signal is generated, all actions performed in the sampling interval are considered responsible. If the signal is positive, each of those actions is reinforced; if it is negative, they are punished. Reinforcement and punishment are achieved by backpropagating error signals associated with the network's activation in that situation and a training example derived from the training signal. For example, reinforcement on a *change left* decision would create a training example of the previous input paired with the target output (0.0, 1.0, 0.0). The targets of *stay center* and *change right* are 0.0 and change left is 1.0. Using the standard backpropagation procedure, the weights are updated based on this training example and the resulting network is more likely to choose *change left* in a similar situation. A negative training signal in the previous example would generate a target output of (1.0, 0.0, 1.0), and the resulting network would be less likely to choose *change left* in similar situations.

The learning strategy is somewhat similar to the temporal difference methods for reinforcement learning (Sutton, 1988), in that updates are based on the performance differences over successive time periods. However, temporal difference methods treat performance differences as prediction errors from which they can learn to predict future rewards. Our local learning component uses the differences to determine whether to reinforce or penalize specific decisions. A temporal difference method could also be used as a local learning component in our framework, and we expect to evaluate this approach in the near future.

Experimental Evaluation

Intelligent lane selection appears to offer important advantages for traffic control and our learning approach appears to be a plausible methodology to generate the selection strategies. In this section, we test these hypotheses in a simulated traffic environment.

A Simulated Traffic Environment

To evaluate intelligent lane selection, we developed a simulator to model traffic on a highway. For each car, the simulator updates the continuous values of position, velocity, and acceleration at one second intervals. The acceleration and deceleration functions were set by visualizing traffic performance under different conditions and represent our best estimate of the behavior of actual drivers. Acceleration (A) is adjusted based on the equation $A(s) = 10s^{-0.5}$, where s represents the current speed in miles per hour (m/h).

Deceleration occurs at the rate of -2.0 m/h per second if the difference in speed from the immediate preceding car is greater than twice the number of seconds separating the two cars. In other words, if a car approaches a slower car, the deceleration point is proportional to the difference in speed and the distance between the cars. If there is a large difference in speed, cars will decelerate sooner than if the speed differences are small. If the gap closes to two seconds, the speed is matched instantaneously. Lane changes are only allowed if the change maintains a two-second gap between preceding and following cars.

The simulated roadway is 3.3 miles long, but the top of each lane "wraps around" to the bottom, creating an infinite stretch of roadway. The simulator was designed as a tool to efficiently evaluate different lane-selection strategies and thus makes several simplifying assumptions about traffic dynamics. The primary assumptions in the current model are that:

- cars are the same size;
- cars use the same acceleration rules;
- cars accelerate to and maintain their desired speed if there are no slower, preceding cars;

Although these assumptions do not hold for real traffic, they are also not crucial to evaluate the merits of intelligent lane selection. Removing these assumptions unnecessarily complicates the model, which creates unacceptable run times for exploratory research. In future work, we will expand our experiments to a more realistic simulator such as SmartPATH (Eskafi, 1996).

During training, the learning system uses the traffic simulator to evaluate candidate lane-selection strategies. Each evaluation or *trial* lasts 400 simulated seconds and begins with a random dispersement of 200 cars over three lanes on the 3.3 mile roadway. Desired speeds are selected randomly from a normal distribution with mean 60 m/h and standard deviation 8 m/h. In each trial, the percentage of smart cars is random with a minimum percentage of 5%. All other cars follow the selfish lane selection strategy.

Each training run begins with a population of 75 random lane selection strategies and 25 seeded strategies, which are modified by SANE and the local learning module over 30 simulated driving hours. SANE keeps track of the best strategy found so far based on its performance over a trial. When a better strategy is found, it is saved to a file for later testing. The saved strategies are each tested over ten 2000-second trials and the best is considered the final strategy of the training run.

Experiment 1: Traffic Densities

Our first study compared the performance of traffic under different traffic densities using three different lane-selection schemes: a selfish strategy, a polite strategy, and the learned strategy. The selfish and polite

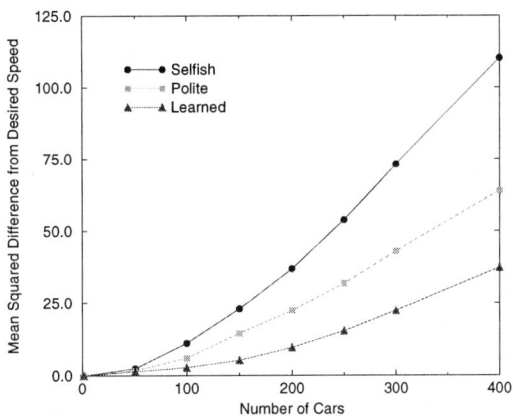

Figure 4: Average speed error using different lane selection strategies under different densities.

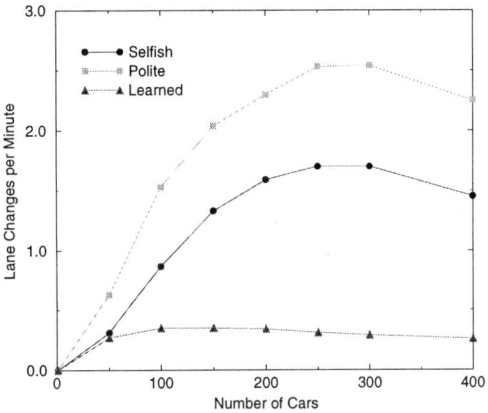

Figure 5: Average number of lane changes using different lane selection strategies under different traffic densities.

strategies operate as described previously in this paper. The learned strategy is the best strategy from the five training runs. Here we are not interested in the aggregate performance over several learning runs, but rather in the performance of a single learned strategy that could be used in traffic. Experiments that more thoroughly evaluate the learning system and present learning curves averaged over all training runs can be found in Moriarty and Langley (1997).

Strategies were tested over car densities of 50 to 400 cars per 3.3 miles and performance was measured over 20 simulations at each density. In this experiment, all cars on the highway in a given condition employed the same strategy.

Figure 4 shows the error in driving speed for the selfish, polite, and learned strategy under different traffic densities. The error is computed from the first term in equation 1 and represents the average squared difference between actual speeds and desired speeds in m/h. The figure shows the clear advantage of the learned strategy. In sparse traffic (50–100 cars), the performance of the three strategies is comparable; however, in more dense traffic, the learned strategy produces significantly lower divergence from desired speeds. At a density of 200 cars, the learned strategy incurs only a quarter of the error of the selfish strategy and less than half the error of the polite strategy. The selfish strategy error grows faster in dense traffic than the polite and learned strategies, because of the many bottlenecks generated by the unyielding, slow drivers. The polite strategy solves many of these bottlenecks by moving slower drivers to the right, but still maintains a error of at least 20 m/h^2 over the learned strategy.

Figure 5 plots the average number of lane changes per car under each strategy. There is a large contrast in behavior between the polite and learned strategy. Even in very sparse traffic, the polite strategy produces over twice as many lane changes as the learned strategies. In heavy traffic, the polite strategy calls for almost nine times as many lane changes. The learned strategies reach a maximum lane change rate of 0.35 changes per minute, whereas the polite strategy reaches 1.53 lane changes per minute. The selfish strategy generates fewer lane changes than the polite strategy, since it does not have a yielding component; however, it still generates over five times as many lane changes as the learned strategy in denser traffic. Thus, compared to both the selfish and polite strategy, the learned strategy makes far fewer lane maneuvers, which should increase driver acceptance of intelligent lane selection and hopefully reduce accident rates.

Figure 6 provides a visualization of lane utilization under the different selection strategies for a density of 200 cars. Each graph represents an average over 20 simulations of the percentage of time a driver with a given desired speed spends in each lane. The selfish strategy, shown in Figure 6(a), assigns no lane bias to faster or slower drivers, and thus drivers at different speeds are spread across all three lanes fairly evenly. The polite strategy, in Figure 6(b), does bias slow drivers towards the right lane and fast drivers towards the left lane, but does so with a rigid partition at 55 m/h. Thus, a car with a desired speed of 54 m/h behaves quite differently from a car with a desired speed of 56 m/h. This partition comes from the polite rule that moves cars traveling slower than 55 m/h to the right lane. The learned strategy, in Figure 6(c), produces a much smoother lane utilization bias.

Another contrast between the three strategies lies in the overall utilization of the three lanes across all speeds. Table 1 shows the overall lane distribution for all cars. The learned strategy has a significant bias towards the right lane and places almost half of the cars there. This organization seems reasonable and quite effective since slower cars encounter fewer slower preceding cars and should operate more efficiently in higher traffic density than faster cars. The learned lane-selection strategy essentially moves half of the traffic to the right lane and uses the middle and left lanes to or-

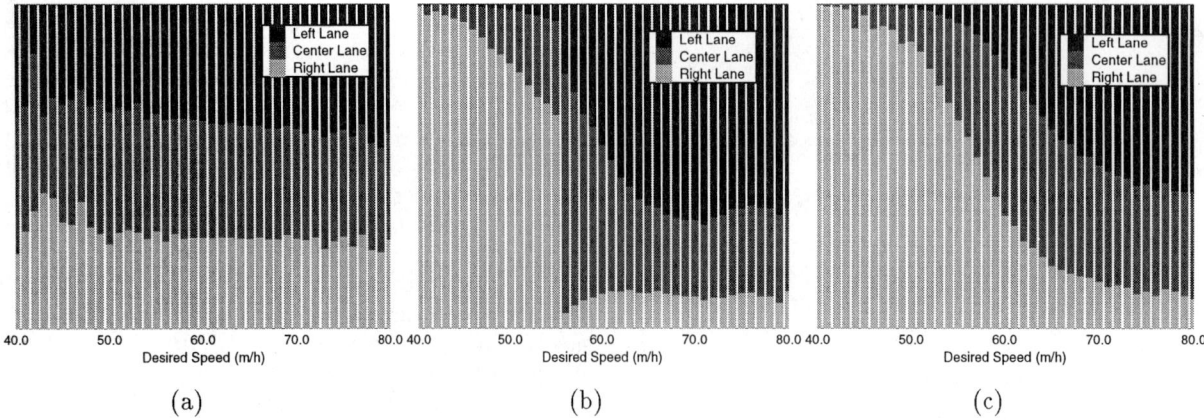

Figure 6: Utility of lanes with respect to desired speeds for the (a) selfish, (b) polite, and (c) learned strategies. The graph shows the percentage of time that cars drive in the left, center, and middle lanes as a function of desired speeds. These tests used a traffic density of 200 cars per 3.3 miles.

	Left Lane	Center Lane	Right Lane
Selfish	0.35	0.35	0.30
Polite	0.35	0.26	0.39
Learned	0.25	0.27	0.48

Table 1: The distribution of traffic for the three lane selection strategies.

ganize the faster traffic. It is also important to note from Figure 6 that the faster cars do appear in the right lane, but the slower cars never appear in the left lane. The likely reason is that a slow car in the left lane causes large disruptions to traffic flow, whereas a fast car in the right lane will normally only disrupt its own performance.

Experiment 2: Mixing Strategies

The second experiment evaluated the learned strategy in the presence of selfish cars. The aim was to examine the robustness of the smart car's group behavior to cars that do not follow the same rules. We were interested in how quickly the learned strategy degrades as selfish drivers are added and how many smart cars are necessary to make cooperative behavior worthwhile.

Figure 7 shows the error in driving speeds under different smart car distributions. The figure plots the speed error for both the smart cars and the selfish cars, and illustrates how the performance of both increases with the introduction of more smart cars. The figure shows that, even at distributions as low as 5% smart cars, there is incentive to cooperate. At 100% selfish traffic, cars average a 36.80 m/h^2 driving error, while at 95% selfish traffic the error drops to 34.40 m/h^2. While this is not a substantial improvement it demonstrates that very few smart cars are necessary to generate an increase in traffic performance. Moreover, performance

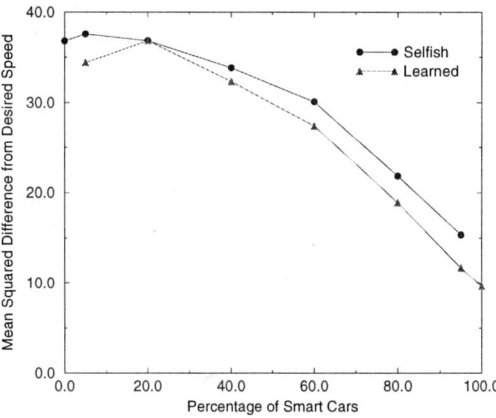

Figure 7: The average squared error of smart and selfish cars under different smart car distributions. These tests used 200 cars.

improves steadily as more cars cooperate, which provides further motivation to drive cooperatively. Finally, at 100% smart cars the average speed error drops to 9.66 m/h^2, which is approximately one fourth of the error when all traffic is selfish.

Related Work

Intelligent lane selection appears to be a novel approach to traffic management that has received almost no attention in the traffic management literature. After a lengthy literature search and several email inquiries, we have found only one project with similar goals. Carrara and Morello have proposed a system called DOMINC that employs cooperative driving techniques to increase traffic efficiency.[1] The main objective of the DOMINC project is to explore the benefits in traffic effi-

---
[1] The paper that we have does not include a reference.

ciency, comfort, and safety of cooperative driving. The project's vision is thus very close to our formulation of car-centered traffic management. However, the paper that we have only describes the potential benefits and does not propose a specific methodology for cooperative driving.

There are a number of systems designed to learn lane selection for a single-agent, non-cooperative system. McCallum (1996) used reinforcement learning to train a driving agent to weave around traffic, a task that he calls "New York driving". Sukthankar, Baluja, and Hancock (1997) used an approach similar to evolutionary algorithms to form a voting scheme that determines the appropriate driving lane and speed for a single car. Finally, the Bayesian Automated Taxi (BAT) project, an attempt to build a fully automated vehicle that can drive in normal traffic (Forbes, Huang, Kanazawa, & Russell, 1995), will eventually contain a module for lane selection. Each of these systems were designed to maximize the performance of a single vehicle and do not form cooperative controllers. Our approach is directed at the global traffic management problem, where cooperation is important.

Summary and Conclusions

Coordination of local car behaviors is a novel approach to traffic management that poses a challenging problem to both artificial intelligence and machine learning. In this paper, we proposed one formulation of this problem: intelligent lane selection to maintain desired driving speeds and reduce lane changes. Given only information on the local traffic patterns and the desired speed, cars can coordinate local lane changes to let faster traffic pass through while still allowing slower traffic to maintain desired speeds.

We described and evaluated an approach that uses supervised and reinforcement learning to generate the lane-selection strategies through trial and error interactions with the traffic environment. Compared to both a selfish strategy and the standard "yield to the right" strategy, the smart cars maintained speeds closer to the desired speeds of their drivers while making fewer lane changes. Additionally, intelligent lane selection was robust in the presence of selfish drivers. Traffic performance improves even when as few as five percent of the cars cooperate. Future work will explore more realistic traffic and driver models, as well as variations on the coordination task.

References

Carrara, M., & Morello, E. Advanced control strategies and methods for motorway of the future. In *The Drive Project DOMINC: New Concepts and Research Under Way*.

Dietterich, T. G. (1990). Exploratory research in machine learning. *Machine Learning*, *5*, 5–9.

Eskafi, F. (1996). *Modeling and Simulation of the Automated Highway System*. Ph.D. thesis, Department of EECS, University of California, Berkeley.

Forbes, J., Huang, T., Kanazawa, K., & Russell, S. (1995). The BATmobile: Towards a Bayesian automated taxi. In *Proceedings of the 14th International Joint Conference on Artificial Intelligence* Montreal, CA.

Gilmore, J. F., Elibiary, K. J., & Forbes, H. C. (1994). Knowledge-based advanced traffic management system. In *Proceedings of IVHS America* Atlanta, GA.

Goldberg, D. E. (1989). *Genetic Algorithms in Search, Optimization and Machine Learning*. Addison-Wesley, Reading, MA.

Kagolanu, K., Fink, R., Smartt, H., Powell, R., & Larson, E. (1995). An intelligent traffic controller. In *Proceedings of the Second World Congress on Intelligent Transport Systems*, pp. 259–264 Yokohama, Japan.

McCallum, A. K. (1996). Learning to use selective attention and short-term memory in sequential tasks. In *Proceedings of Fourth International Conference on Simulation of Adaptive Behavior*, pp. 315–324 Cape Cod, MA.

Moriarty, D. E. (1997). *Symbiotic Evolution of Neural Networks in Sequential Decision Tasks*. Ph.D. thesis, Department of Computer Sciences, The University of Texas at Austin.

Moriarty, D. E., & Langley, P. (1997). Automobile traffic management through intelligent lane selection: A distributed, machine learning approach. Tech. rep. 98-2, Daimler-Benz Research & Technology Center, Palo Alto, CA.

Moriarty, D. E., & Miikkulainen, R. (1996). Efficient reinforcement learning through symbiotic evolution. *Machine Learning*, *22*, 11–32.

Pooran, F. J., Tarnoff, P. J., & Kalaputapu, R. (1996). RT-TRACS: Development of the real-time control logic. In *Proceedings of the 1996 Annual Meeting of ITS America*, pp. 422–430 Houston, TX.

Rumelhart, D. E., Hinton, G. E., & Williams, R. J. (1986). Learning internal representations by error propagation. In Rumelhart, D. E., & McClelland, J. L. (Eds.), *Parallel Distributed Processing: Explorations in the Microstructure of Cognition, Volume 1: Foundations*, pp. 318–362. MIT Press, Cambridge, MA.

Sukthankar, R., Baluja, S., & Hancock, J. (1997). Evolving an intelligent vehicle for tactical reasoning in traffic. In *Proceedings of the IEEE International Conference on Robotics and Automation*.

Sutton, R. S. (1988). Learning to predict by the methods of temporal differences. *Machine Learning*, *3*, 9–44.

Boosting in the limit: Maximizing the margin of learned ensembles

Adam J. Grove and **Dale Schuurmans**[*]
NEC Research Institute
4 Independence Way
Princeton NJ 08540, USA
{grove,dale}@research.nj.nec.com

Abstract

The "minimum margin" of an ensemble classifier on a given training set is, roughly speaking, the smallest vote it gives to any correct training label. Recent work has shown that the Adaboost algorithm is particularly effective at producing ensembles with large minimum margins, and theory suggests that this may account for its success at reducing generalization error. We note, however, that the problem of finding good margins is closely related to linear programming, and we use this connection to derive and test new "LPboosting" algorithms that achieve better minimum margins than Adaboost.

However, these algorithms do *not* always yield better generalization performance. In fact, more often the opposite is true. We report on a series of controlled experiments which show that no simple version of the minimum-margin story can be complete. We conclude that the crucial question as to *why* boosting works so well in practice, and how to further improve upon it, remains mostly open.

Some of our experiments are interesting for another reason: we show that Adaboost sometimes does overfit—eventually. This may take a very long time to occur, however, which is perhaps why this phenomenon has gone largely unnoticed.

1 Introduction

Recently, there has been great interest in ensemble methods for learning classifiers, and in particular in *boosting* [FS97] (or *arcing* [Bre96a]) algorithms. These methods take a given "base" learning algorithm and repeatedly apply it to reweighted versions of the original training data, producing a collection of hypotheses $h_1, ..., h_b$ which are then combined in a final aggregate classifier via a weighted linear vote. Despite their "black box" construction—one typically does not need to modify the base learner at all—these techniques have proven surprisingly effective at improving generalization performance in a wide variety of domains, and for diverse base learners.

For these procedures there are several conceivable ways to determine the example reweightings at each step, as well as the final hypothesis weights. The best known boosting

[*]Primary affiliation: Institute for Research in Cognitive Science, University of Pennsylvania.
Copyright ©1998, American Association for Artificial Intelligence (www.aaai.org). All rights reserved.

Adaboost.M1(t training instances **x** and labels **y**,
base learner H,
max boosting rounds b)
$\mathbf{u} := (1/t, ..., 1/t)$;(example weights)
for $j = 1...b$
　　$h_j := H(\mathbf{x}, \mathbf{y}, \mathbf{u})$;(base hypothesis)
　　$\epsilon_j := \sum_{i: h_j(x_i) \neq y_i} u_i$;(weighted error)
　　if $\epsilon_j > 1/2$, $b := j - 1$, break
　　$w_j := \log \frac{\epsilon_j}{1 - \epsilon_j}$;(hypothesis weight)
　　for each u_i
　　　　if $h_j(x_i) \neq y_i$, $u_i := u_i/(2\epsilon_j)$
　　　　else, $u_i := u_i/(2(1 - \epsilon_j))$
　　end
end
return $\mathbf{h} = (h_1, ..., h_b)$, $\mathbf{w} = (w_1, ..., w_b)$, b

---

Figure 1: Procedure Adaboost

procedure, **Adaboost** [FS97], computes them in a particular way: at each round j, the example weights for the next round $j + 1$ are adjusted so that the most recent base hypothesis only obtains error rate $1/2$ on the reweighted training set (Figure 1). The intuition behind this is to force the learner to focus on the "difficult" training examples and pay less attention to those that the most recent hypothesis got right. Adaboost then uses a specific formula for hypothesis weights that yields a nice theoretical guarantee about training performance: if the base learner can always find a hypothesis with error bounded strictly below $1/2$ for any reweighting of the training data, then Adaboost is guaranteed to produce a final aggregate hypothesis with zero training set error after a finite number of boosting rounds [FS97].

Of course, this only addresses training error, and there is no real reason from this to believe that Adaboost should *generalize* well to unseen test examples. In fact, one would naively expect the opposite: since Adaboost produces increasingly complex hypotheses from a larger space, one would think that Adaboost should quickly "overfit" the training data and produce a final hypothesis with worse test error than the single original hypothesis returned by the base learner. However, there is a growing body of empirical evidence that suggests Adaboost is remarkably effective at reducing the test set error of several well-known learning algorithms, often significantly and across a variety of domains (more or less robustly, but with occasional exceptions) [FS96a, Qui96, MO97, BK97].

This raises a central question of the field: why is boosting so successful at improving the generalization performance of already carefully designed learning algorithms? One thing that is clear is that boosting's success cannot be directly attributed to a notion of variance reduction [Bre96b, BK97]. This mystery is further compounded by the observation that Adaboost's generalization error often continues to decrease even after it has achieved perfect accuracy on the training set. What more information could it possibly be obtaining from the training data? If we could "explain" boosting's real-world success satisfactorily, we might hope to construct better procedures based upon that explanation.

Recent progress in understanding this issue has been made by [SFBL97] who appeal to the notion of *margins*. Rather than focus exclusively on classification error, Schapire *et al.* consider the *strength* of the votes given to the correct class labels. They observe that even after zero training error has been achieved, Adaboost tends to increase the vote it gives to the correct class label (relative to the next strongest label vote), and they posit this as an explanation for why Adaboost's test set error continues to decrease.

[SFBL97] examines the effect of Adaboost on the distribution of margins as a whole. However, one of their experimental observations is that Adaboost seems to be particularly effective at increasing the margins of "difficult" examples (those with small margins), perhaps even at the price of reducing the margins of other examples. This suggests the more concrete hypothesis that the size of the *minimum* (worst) margin is the key to generalization performance, and that Adaboost's success is due to its ability to increase this minimum. Supporting this conjecture are two theoretical results, also from [SFBL97]: (1) in the limit, Adaboost is guaranteed to achieve a minimum margin that is at least half the best possible, and (2) given that a minimum margin of $\theta > 0$ can be achieved, then there is a $O(1/\theta)$ bound on generalization error that holds *independently* of the size of the ensemble. (See Section 2 for more about this theory.)

This, then, is the background for our work. As we observe in Sections 3 and 4 it is often quite easy to improve upon the minimum margins found by Adaboost by using Linear Programming (LP) techniques in a variety of ways. So *if* minimum margins really are the principle determiner of learning-success, this should lead to even more effective ensemble methods. The truth, though, seems to be more complex. We run a series of controlled experiments to test the significance of margins, using various real world data-sets from the UCI repository. As we discuss in Section 5 the results are at times mixed, but overall it seems clear that the single-minded pursuit of good minimum margins is detrimental.[1]

A different set of experiments, in Section 6, considers the long run behavior of Adaboost. When we boost well beyond the range of previously reported experiments, margins may improve for a long time—but beyond some point, generalization error often deteriorates simultaneously. This is additional evidence against any simple version of the minimum margin story. It also demonstrates that (in the limit) Adaboost is vulnerable to overfitting, which is just as one would expect *a priori*, but perhaps contrary to the lessons one might take from most of the short-run experiments reported in the literature.

We would have been happier to report that the minimum margin story was unambiguously complete and correct—we would then truly "understand" boosting's success *and* be able to improve upon it substantially. Our more negative results, though, are still important. It is always necessary to test theoretical proposals of this type with rigorous experimentation. We conclude that the key problem of discovering properties of training set performance that are predictive of generalization error in real-world practice still demands significant research effort.

2 The minimum margin

We begin by defining the *margin* and other relevant terminology more carefully. An *ensemble* $\mathbf{h} = (h_1, ..., h_b)$ is a finite vector of hypotheses. Given an ensemble, together with a matching set of *weights* $\mathbf{w} = (w_1, ..., w_b)$, where $w_j \geq 0$ and $\sum w_j = 1$, one classifies examples by taking a weighted vote among the individual hypotheses and choosing the label that receives the largest vote.

Let the training set be a collection of labeled examples $(x_1, y_1), ..., (x_t, y_t)$, where the labels come from $L = \{1, ..., l\}$. Each individual hypothesis maps an example to a single label[2] in L. Let $v_{i,y}$ be the total vote that the weighted ensemble casts for label y on example x_i; that is $v_{i,y} = \sum_{h_j : h_j(x_i) = y} w_j$. Note that $\sum_{y \in L} v_{i,y} = 1$.

For a given example x_i, we would like more votes to go to the true label y_i than to any other label, because then the ensemble would classify x_i correctly. This suggests defining the margin m_i as $v_{i,y_i} - \max_{y \neq y_i} v_{i,y}$; that is, the total vote for the true label minus the vote for the most popular wrong label. This quantity is in the range $[-1, 1]$ and is positive iff the weighted ensemble classifies x_i correctly. It is 1 when there is a unanimous vote for the correct label. The definition just given can be found in [SFBL97] and [Bre97b].

However, we instead concentrate on a different, but similar, quantity defined by $m_i = v_{i,y_i} - \sum_{y \neq y_i} v_{i,y} (= 2v_{i,y_i} - 1)$. When $|L| = 2$ this is identical to the previous definition; but it is only a lower bound in general (and thus, it can be negative even when the correct label gets the most votes—*i.e.*, when there is a plurality but not a majority).[3] This alternative definition is much easier to work with, since it involves a sum rather than a max. In fact, most of the theoretical work in the literature uses the second notion (or else considers the 2-class case where there is no distinction).[4] For this reason, we will dispense with the first definition entirely, and from this point use the term *margin* always to

---
[1] We note that [Bre97a] reports a single experiment that corroborates this point, but as noted in [Bre97b], there is some question as to whether this controlled for all relevant factors.

[2] We note that it easy to generalize our results to handle the case where hypotheses map examples to *distributions* over L.

[3] Breiman has sometimes called this second quantity the *edge*.

[4] However, see the extended version of [SFBL97], available at www.research.att.com/~schapire.

refer to $m_i = v_{i,y_i} - \sum_{y \neq y_i} v_{i,y}$. The reader should remain aware of this subtle terminological distinction.

As discussed in the introduction, there is some recent and important theory involving the margin. [SFBL97] show a result bounding generalization error in terms of the margin distribution achieved on the training set. More precisely, if the distribution of margins has at most a fraction $f(\theta)$ below θ, the we get a bound on the test error of $f(\theta) + O\left(1/\sqrt{t}(\frac{\log t \log H}{\theta^2} + \log(1/\delta))^{1/2}\right)$, where t is the size of the training sample, H is the size of the base hypothesis class, and δ is the confidence.[5] This theorem applies if we know the $(100 f(\theta))$ %-ile margin θ for any $\theta > 0$. However, the only *a priori* theoretical connection to Adaboost we know of involves the minimum margin (*i.e.*, $\theta^* = \sup\{\theta : f(\theta) = 0\}$): [SFBL97] show that Adaboost achieves at least half of the best possible minimum (see Section 6 for more discussion). Recently Breiman has proven a similar generalization theorem [Bre97b], which speaks *only* about the minimum margin—and thereby obtains even stronger bounds. Of course, neither of these results is likely to be accurate in predicting the actual errors achieved in particular real-world problems (among other reasons, because of the $O(\cdot)$ formulation in [SFBL97]); perhaps their real importance is in suggesting the *qualitative effect* of the minimum margin achieved all else being equal.

3 Maximizing margins: A Linear Program

The recent theoretical results just discussed suggest that, beyond minimizing training-set error, we should attempt to make the minimum margin as large as possible. It has already been observed [Bre97a] that this maximization problem can be formulated as a linear program.[6] Here we quickly re-demonstrate this formulation, because it is the starting point and basis to our work.

For a fixed ensemble $\mathbf{h}$ and training set $(\mathbf{x}, \mathbf{y})$, define an *error* matrix Z which contains entries z_{ij} such that $z_{ij} = 1$ if $h_j(x_i) = y_i$ and $z_{ij} = -1$ if $h_j(x_i) \neq y_i$. In terms of Z, the margin obtained on example i corresponds to the simple dot product $m_i = \sum_j w_j z_{ij} = \mathbf{w} \cdot \mathbf{z}_i$.

$$
\begin{array}{c|ccc|c}
x_1 & z_{11} & \cdots & z_{1b} & m_1 \\
\vdots & \vdots & & \vdots & \vdots \\
x_t & z_{t1} & \cdots & z_{tb} & m_t \\
& h_1 & \cdots & h_b & \\
& w_1 & \cdots & w_b &
\end{array}
$$

Our goal is to find a weight vector $\mathbf{w}$ that obtains the largest possible margin subject to the constraints $w_j \geq 0$ and $\sum w_j = 1$. This is a maxi-min problem where we choose $\mathbf{w}$ to maximize $\min_i \mathbf{w} \cdot \mathbf{z}_i$ subject to $w_j \geq 0$ and $\sum w_j = 1$. We turn this into a linear programming problem simply by conjecturing a lower bound, m, on the minimum value and choosing $(m, \mathbf{w})$ to maximize m subject to $\mathbf{w} \cdot \mathbf{z}_i \geq m$,

---
[5]These results can be extended to infinite base hypothesis spaces to appealing to the standard VC dimension bounds.

[6]See also [FS96b], which predates the "margin" terminology and also casts the definitions in terms of game theory rather than linear programming, but otherwise makes the same point.

LP-Adaboost($\mathbf{x}, \mathbf{y}, H, b$)
  $(\mathbf{h}, \mathbf{w}, b) := $ Adaboost($\mathbf{x}, \mathbf{y}, H, b$)
  Construct error matrix Z (of dimension $t \times b$)
  $(m, \mathbf{w}) := $ solve linear program: minimize m
        subject to $\sum_{j=1}^{b} w_j z_{ij} \geq m$,
                $w_j \geq 0, \sum w_j = 1$
  return $\mathbf{h}, \mathbf{w}$

Figure 2: Procedure LP-Adaboost

$i = 1, ..., t$, and $w_j \geq 0$, $\sum w_j = 1$. (Note that m is not constrained to be nonnegative.)

Although straightforward, this suggests a simple test of how important "minimum margins" are for real learning problems. Consider the ensemble produced by Adaboost on a given problem. Although Adaboost also provides a weighting over this ensemble, we could simply ignore this and instead re-solve for the weights using the LP just formulated. We call this procedure **LP-Adaboost**; see Figure 2. Clearly this will achieve a minimum margin at least as good as the Adaboost weighting does. In fact, as we see in Section 5, it generally does significantly better. Importantly, this uses the same ensemble as Adaboost and so completely controls for expressive power (which otherwise can be a problem; see [Bre97b]). To the extent to which minimum margins really determine generalization error, we should expect this to improve generalization performance. But as we see in Section 5, this expectation is not realized empirically.

As an aside, we note that LP-Adaboost is clearly more computationally expensive than Adaboost, since it has to construct the Z matrix and then solve the resulting LP. However, this is still feasible for few thousands of examples and hundreds of hypotheses using the better LP packages known today; this range covers many (although definitely not all) experiments being reported in the literature. The deeper question is, of course, whether one would want to use LP-Adaboost at all (even ignoring computational costs).

4 The Dual Linear Program

Before investigating the empirical performance of LP-Adaboost, we first show that the *dual* of the linear program formulated in Section 3 leads to another boosting procedure which uses an alternative technique for computing the *example* reweightings. This procedure can provably achieve the optimal margin over the entire base hypothesis space.

From the work of [Bre97a, FS96b] it is known that the dual of the previous linear program has a very natural interpretation in our setting. (For a review of the standard concepts of primality and duality in LP see [Van96, Lue84].) In the dual problem we maintain a weight u_i for each training example, and a constraint $\sum_i u_i z_{ij} \leq s$ for each hypothesis (*i.e.*, column in Z). Here, s is the conjectured bound on the dual objective. The dual linear program then is to choose $(s, \mathbf{u})$ to *minimize* s subject to $\sum_i u_i z_{ij} \leq s$, $j = 1, ..., b$, and $\sum_i u_i = 1$, $u_i \geq 0$ [Van96, p70].

Notice that these constraints have a natural interpretation. The vector $\mathbf{u}$ is constrained to be (formally) a probability distribution over the *examples*, and the j'th column of Z corresponds to the sequence of predictions (1 if correct, -1

DualLPboost(x, y, H, tolerance ϵ, max iterations $b_{\max}$)
  $\mathbf{u} := (1/t, ..., 1/t), b := 0, m := -1, s := 1$
  repeat
    $b := b + 1$
    $h_b := H(\mathbf{x}, \mathbf{y}, \mathbf{u})$
    $s := \sum_{i=1}^{t} u_i z_{ib}$;(score of h_b on $\mathbf{u}$)
    if $s - m < \epsilon$ or $b > b_{\max}$, $b := b - 1$, break
    $(m, \mathbf{w}, s, \mathbf{u}) :=$ solve primal/dual linear program:
      maximize m s.t. $\sum_{j=1}^{b} w_j z_{ij} \geq m$,
                        $w_j \geq 0, \sum w_j = 1$
      minimize s s.t. $\sum_{i=1}^{t} u_i z_{ij} \leq s$,
                        $u_i \geq 0, \sum u_i = 1$
  end
  return $\mathbf{h}, \mathbf{w}, b$

Figure 3: Procedure DualLPboost

if wrong) made by hypothesis h_j on these examples. Thus, $\sum_i u_i z_{ij}$ is simply the (weighted) *score* achieved by h_j on the reweighting of the training set given by $\mathbf{u}$. (*I.e.*, score on a scale where -1 means it gets all the examples incorrect and $+1$ means all were correct.) Thus, for each h_j, we have a constraint that h_j achieves score of at most s. Minimizing s means to find the worst possible best score. We can therefore rephrase the dual problem as follows: Find a reweighting of (*i.e.*, probability distribution over) the training set, such that the score s of the best hypothesis in the ensemble is as small as possible. Basically, we are looking for a *hard* distribution.

By duality theory, there is a correspondence between the primal and dual problems; it is enough to solve just one of them, and a solution to the other is easily recovered. Moreover, the optimal objective value is the *same* in both the primal and the dual. For us, this implies: *The largest minimum margin achievable for given Z (by choosing the best weight vector over the ensemble) is exactly the same as the smallest best score achievable* (by choosing the "hardest" reweighting of the training set). This remarkable fact, an immediate consequence of duality theory, also appears in [Bre97a, Bre97b] and [FS96b].

This notion of duality can extend to the entire base hypothesis space: if we implicitly consider an ensemble that contains every base hypothesis and yet somehow manage to identify the hardest example reweighting that yields the lowest maximum score over all base hypotheses, then this will correspond to a (hopefully sparse) weight vector over the entire base hypothesis space that yields the best possible margin. One way of attempting to do this leads to our next boosting strategy, **DualLPboost** (Figure 3).

This procedure follows a completely different approach to identifying hard example reweightings than Adaboost. The idea is to take a current ensemble $h_1, ..., h_{b-1}$, solve the resulting LP problem, and take the dual solution vector $\mathbf{u}$ as the next example reweighting. It then calls the base learner to add another base hypothesis to the ensemble.

By construction, $\mathbf{u}$ is maximally hard for the given ensemble, so either a new hypothesis can be found that obtains a better score on this reweighting, or we have converged to an optimal solution. This gives us a convergence test—if we cannot find a good enough base hypothesis, then we know that we have obtained the best achievable margin for the entire space, even if we have only seen a small fraction of the base hypotheses.[7] Contrast this with Adaboost, which only stops if it cannot find a hypothesis that does better than chance (*i.e.*, score of exactly 0). In practice, Adaboost may never terminate.

Proposition 1 *Suppose we have a base learner H that can always find the best base hypothesis for any given reweighting. Then, if the base hypothesis space is finite, DualLPboost is guaranteed to achieve optimal weight vector $\mathbf{w}$ after a finite number of boosting rounds.*

The key point to realize is that DualLPboost shares the most important characteristic of boosting algorithms: it only accesses a base learner by repeatedly sending it reweighted versions of the given training sample, and incrementally builds its ensemble. The only difference is that DualLPboost keeps much more state between calls to the base learner: it needs to maintain the entire Z matrix, whereas Adaboost only needs to keep track of the current reweighting. How much of a problem this causes depends on the computational effort of LP solving vs. the time taken by the base learner.

5 Generalization performance

We tested these procedures on several of the data sets from the UCI repository ([MM, KSD96]). Generally, we trained on a randomly drawn subset of 90% of the examples in a data set, and tested on the other 10%; we repeated this 100 times for each set and averaged the results.[8] For all procedures we set $b_{\max} = 50$, although they could terminate with a smaller ensemble if any of the various stopping conditions were triggered. By construction, LP-Adaboost uses the same ensemble as Adaboost.

We report average error rates for each method. We omit confidence intervals in the tables, but instead report winning percentages for each method against Adaboost as the baseline; this allows for a statistically weaker but distribution-free comparison. This number is the percentage of the 100 runs in which each method had higher accuracy than Adaboost (allocating half credit for a tie). In general, these winning percentages correlate well with test error.

We tested two base learners. The first, [FS96a]'s FindAttrTest, searches a very simple hypothesis space. Each classifier is defined by a single attribute A, a value V for that attribute, and three labels $l_{yes}, l_{no}, l_?$. For discrete attributes A, one tests an example's value of A against V; if the example has no value for A predict $l_?$, if the example's value for A equals V then predict l_{yes}, otherwise predict l_{no}. For continuous attributes V functions as a threshold—we predict l_{yes} if an example's value for A is $\leq V$; otherwise we predict l_{no} or $l_?$ as appropriate. This simple hypothesis class has some nice properties for our experiments: First, it is fast to learn,

---
[7]Note that this depends crucially on the base learner always being able to find a sufficiently good hypothesis if one exists; see Section 5 for further discussion of this issue.

[8]However, for some large data sets, *chess* and *splice*, we inverted the train/test proportions.

| | FindAttrTest | | Adaboost | | LP-Adaboost | | | DualLPboost | | |
Data set	error%	win%	error%	margin	error%	win%	margin	error%	win%	margin
Audiology	52.30	50.0	52.30	-1.0	52.30	50.0	-1.0	54.70	47.0	-0.804
Banding	27.00	19.5	18.88	-0.080	22.37	31.0	0.021	23.88	25.0	0.032
Chess	32.60	0.0	5.24	-0.099	6.49	14.0	0.0	6.59	17.5	0.010
Colic	18.68	44.5	17.95	-0.179	23.08	22.5	-0.005	23.59	19.5	0.002
Glass	47.80	50.0	47.80	-1.0	47.80	50.0	-1.0	45.80	55.5	-0.427
Hepatitis	18.38	49.0	18.19	-0.026	21.44	36.0	0.063	21.44	34.0	0.071
Labor	24.00	14.0	6.50	0.255	7.00	48.0	0.295	6.83	49.5	0.298
Promoter	28.09	4.5	8.82	0.165	9.45	47.5	0.212	9.36	46.5	0.223
Sonar	27.29	12.0	16.76	0.052	17.81	42.5	0.113	19.76	37.0	0.099
Soybean	69.50	50.0	69.50	-1.0	69.50	50.0	-1.0	71.70	37.0	-0.733
Splice	37.70	0.0	10.56	-0.695	17.10	7.5	-0.415	12.34	25.0	-0.170
Vote	4.16	40.0	3.43	-0.056	4.00	41.5	0.002	5.50	24.5	0.019
Wine	34.40	0.5	4.00	0.011	3.06	55.5	0.073	5.00	41.5	0.081

Figure 4: FindAttrTest Results

| | C4.5 | | Adaboost | | LP-Adaboost | | | DualLPboost | | |
Data set	error%	win%	error%	margin	error%	win%	margin	error%	win%	margin
Audiology	22.70	17.0	16.39	0.446	16.48	49.0	0.501	18.09	38.5	0.370
Banding	25.58	12.5	15.00	0.528	15.42	45.5	0.565	22.50	20.0	0.430
Chess	4.18	12.5	2.70	0.657	2.74	46.5	0.730	2.97	37.0	0.560
Colic	14.46	67.5	17.03	0.051	18.97	31.5	0.182	18.16	44.0	0.108
Glass	30.91	22.0	23.95	0.513	23.91	49.5	0.624	26.86	38.0	0.386
Hepatitis	21.06	38.0	18.94	0.329	17.56	59.0	0.596	20.00	45.5	0.385
Labor	15.33	43.0	12.83	0.535	13.83	47.0	0.684	15.17	42.0	0.599
Promoter	21.09	10.5	7.55	0.599	8.00	47.0	0.694	13.55	29.5	0.378
Sonar	28.81	16.0	18.10	0.628	18.62	48.0	0.685	25.00	23.0	0.478
Soybean	8.86	28.5	6.97	-0.005	6.55	62.0	0.017	8.41	33.5	0.003
Splice	16.18	0.0	6.83	0.535	7.00	25.0	0.569	11.01	0.0	0.393
Vote	4.95	51.0	5.02	0.723	5.30	44.5	0.795	5.27	44.5	0.756
Wine	9.11	27.0	4.61	0.869	4.89	47.5	0.912	4.50	50.5	0.814

Figure 5: C4.5 Results

so we can easily boost for hundreds of thousands of iterations (see Section 6). We can also explicitly solve the LP for this space to determine the optimal ensemble (according to the minimum margin criterion). But most importantly, [FS96a] have shown that the benefits of Adaboost are particularly decisive for FindAttrTest.

The second learning method we considered is a version of Quinlan's decision tree learning algorithm C4.5 [Qui93].[9] This is at the other end of the spectrum of base learners in that it produces hypotheses from a very expressive space. Adaboost is generally effective for C4.5 but, as [FS96a] point out, the gains are not as dramatic and in fact there is sometimes significant deterioration [Qui96].

In Tables 4 and 5 we present the statistics discussed, along with the average minimum margins obtained over 100 runs. (Note that the base learners invariably obtain margins of -1.) First, consider the behavior of LP-Adaboost vs. Adaboost. When C4.5 is used as the base learner, LP-Adaboost always improves Adaboost's margins, by an average of about 0.1. Similarly, there is a fairly consistent increase in the margins with FindAttrTest; generally around 0.05 with greater relative increase. And yet we do not see any consistent improvement in generalization error! For FindAttrTest, LP-Adaboost is almost always worse, sometimes much so. For C4.5, the typical case shows only slight deterioration—we are not being hurt so much here, but there is definitely no gain on average. Since all else is controlled for in this experiment, this seems to decisively refute any simple version of the minimum margin story. (Of course, this immediately raises the question of whether there is some other property of the margin distribution which is more predictive of generalization performance; see [SFBL97].)

Next, consider the behavior of DualLPboost with FindAttrTest. With one exception (explained below) this yields even better margins. And yet, in comparison with Adaboost, we are frequently hurt even more. (Note however, that DualLPboost constructs a different ensemble, so this comparison is not as tightly controlled.)

The behavior of DualLPboost with C4.5 is also curious. There is a seeming anomaly here: why are the margins sometimes *worse*? There are two reasons. First, even un-

---
[9]We hedge by saying "a version of C4.5" because it is in fact a re-implementation of this program, based closely on the presentation in [Qui93]. However, it produces identical output in direct comparisons. Our program corresponds to all C4.5's default settings *including pruning*.

der ideal conditions DualLPboost can take many rounds to achieve the best minimum margin, and we stopped it after only 50. So here at least, its convergence rate seems slower. Second, DualLPboost relies crucially on the assumption that the base learner finds a good hypothesis whenever one exists. If the base learner is unable (or unwilling) to find such a hypothesis, then DualLPboost can easily become stuck with no way of continuing. For a classifier like C4.5, which may not even *try* to find the best hypothesis (because of pruning), it is not surprising that DualLPboost can show inferior performance at finding large minimum margins.

Returning to the generalization comparisons, *why* is all our extra effort to optimize margins hurting us? In many cases the answer seems to be the intuitive one; namely we are sometimes increasing the minimum margin at the expense of all the other margins. Essentially, the margin distribution becomes more concentrated near its lower end, which counteracts the fact that the lower margin is higher. Table 6 shows the (average) difference between the 10'th lower-percentile margin and the minimum margin for a few of the data sets; note how these are much closer together these are for LP-Adaboost. Quite frequently 10% of the points (or more) all have margins within 0.001 of the minimum. This table also shows the *median* margin: note that even as the minimum margin is always improved by LP-Adaboost, the median never improves by as much and (especially for FindAttrTest) often *decreases*.

The final illustration of the effect of our optimization on the overall margin distribution is given in Figure 7. Here we plot the cumulative margin distributions obtained by the three procedures on a few data sets. These plots show the distribution obtained from a single run, along with the "mean" distribution obtained over 100 runs (formed by sorting the margins for each of the 100 runs and averaging corresponding values). These plots graphically show the concentration effect discussed above. (The location of the minimum margins are highlighted by the short vertical lines.)

Our observations about the effects of margin distributions on test error emphasize the central open question raised by this work: precisely *what* characteristic of the margin distribution should we be trying to optimize in order to obtain the best possible generalization performance? The minimum margin is not the answer.

6 Boosting in the limit

Our second set of experiments investigates what happens when one runs Adaboost far beyond the 10's to 100's of iterations normally considered. Here we focus on the FindAttrTest base learner, because of its greater tractability, and also because we are able to exactly solve the corresponding LP over the entire hypothesis space. In fact, we do this by running DualLPboost to completion, which generally takes a few hundred rounds at most. (This always works because, for FindAttrTest, we can certainly find the best hypothesis for each reweighting.)

The results show several interesting phenomena. First, we often continue to see significant changes in performance even after 10^5–10^6 boosting rounds. We observe that the minimum margin increases more or less monoton-

Data/Learner	Adaboost $\Delta_{\min,10\%}$	median	LP-Adaboost $\Delta_{\min,10\%}$	median
Band–C4.5	0.022	0.584	0.000	0.606
Chess–C4.5	0.025	0.752	0.000	0.859
Colic–C4.5	0.185	0.353	0.021	0.382
Hep–C4.5	0.130	0.626	0.000	0.760
Labor–C4.5	0.018	0.064	0.000	0.749
Splice–C4.5	0.025	0.599	0.000	0.607
Vote–C4.5	0.049	0.890	0.002	0.933
Wine–C4.5	0.018	0.933	0.000	0.968
Band–FindAtt	0.044	0.165	0.000	0.171
Chess–FindAtt	0.110	0.187	0.008	0.142
Colic–FindAtt	0.178	0.173	0.000	0.029
Hep–C4.5	0.031	0.247	0.000	0.171
Labor–FindAtt	0.008	0.368	0.000	0.339
Splice–FindAtt	0.594	0.074	0.104	0.171
Vote–FindAtt	0.198	0.402	0.098	0.350
Wine–C4.5	0.083	0.257	0.000	0.228

Figure 6: Properties of the margin distributions

ically (excluding fluctuations near the beginning). Furthermore, in our experiments Adaboost's minimum margin always asymptotes at the optimal value found by LP.[10] The theory we are aware of only guarantees half the value—so are we seeing an artifact of FindAttrTest, or does Adaboost always have this property? If the latter, Adaboost can presumably turned into a general, albeit very slow, LP solver.[11] Moreover, if this is the case, then Adaboost would be expected to do exactly as well as DualLPboost (or other exact LP solvers) in the limit, and thus its empirical superiority would have to be explained (somehow) using the fact that it is typically *not* run to anywhere near its asymptotic limit. We believe that this theoretical question is one of the most significant issues raised by our work.

Another important aspect of our results is the correlation of minimum margin with generalization error. The minimum margin always increases, but the test error often deteriorates with large numbers of boosting rounds (although this can sometimes take tens of thousands of rounds before it becomes apparent). One implication is that these experiments give another, independent, refutation of the straightforward minimum-margin story—because, again, we see errors sometimes increase even as the margin gets better. But this phenomenon is also interesting because it counters what seems to be very common "folklore" that boosting is strongly resistant to overfitting. To a certain extent this may be true, but our experiments suggest that this is perhaps only the case in certain regimes (which presumably differ with the problem and the base learner being considered), and should not be relied on in general.

Figures 8, 9, and 10 illustrate three typical asymptotic

---

[10]But note that there are typically many different solutions that achieve the same best minimum margin. Thus, even though the asymptotic margins coincide, there is no guarantee that Adaboost and our particular LP solver will find the same weighted ensembles.

[11]I.e., an LP solver that does not require any tuning based on prior knowledge of the LP's solution value. It is in this sense that such a result, if true, would strengthen [FS96b].

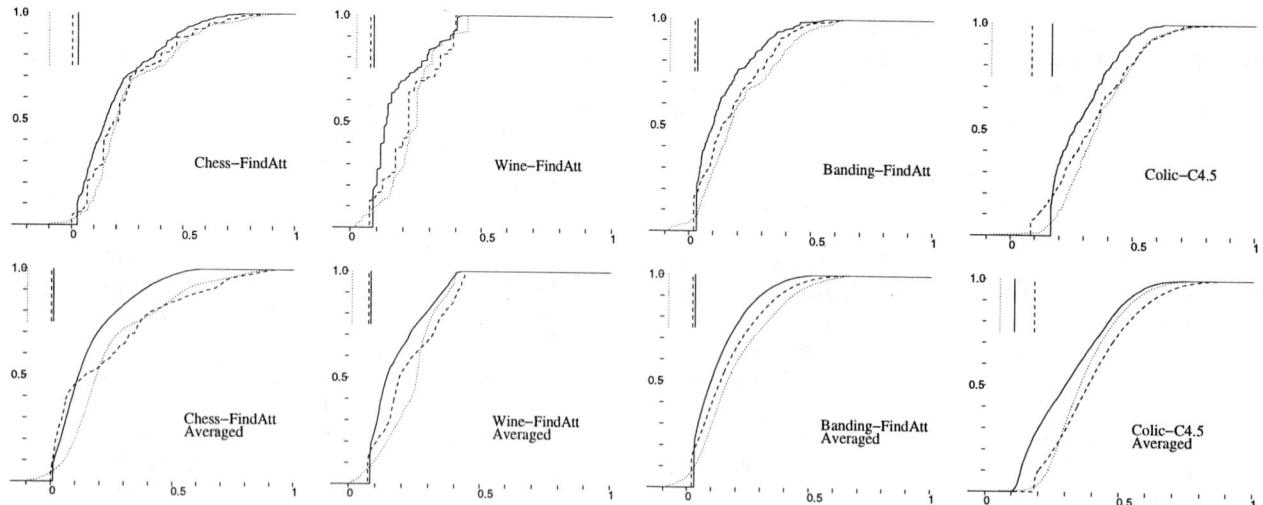

Figure 7: Cumulative margin distributions for (·····) Adaboost, (– – – –) LP-Adaboost, (———) DualLPboost

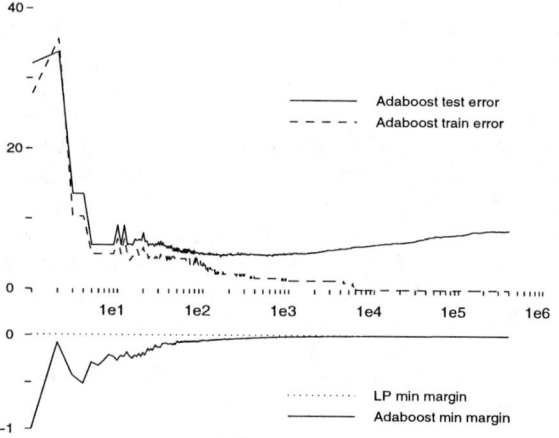

Figure 8: Adaboost with FindAttrTest on "chess"

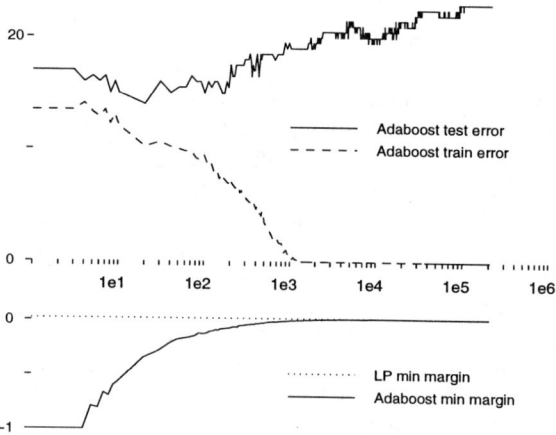

Figure 9: Adaboost with FindAttrTest on "crx"

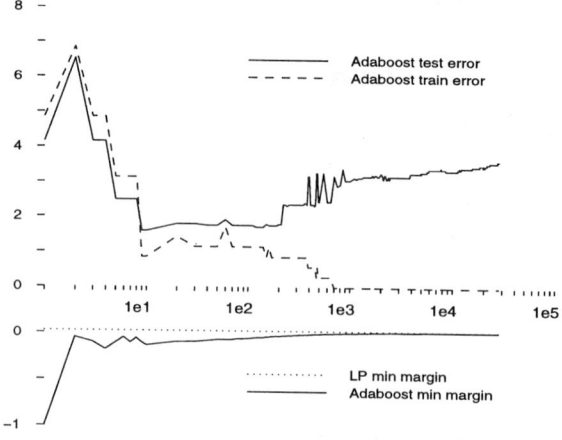

Figure 10: Adaboost with FindAttrTest on "allhypo"

runs. Here we consider a single train/test split for each problem. The horizontal axis measures boosting rounds on a logarithmic scale. At the top we show training and test error, and below we plot the corresponding minimum margin over the training set. The dotted reference line shows the minimum margin obtained by the exact LP solution.

7 Conclusions

Recent work in the theory of ensemble methods has given us new insight as to why boosting, and related methods, are as successful as they are. But only careful experimentation can tell us how correct or comprehensive this theory is in explaining the "real world" behavior of these methods. The principal contribution of this paper is that we have carried out some of the experiments needed to test the significance of the "minimum margin" in ensemble learning. In the process, we have further elaborated on the deep connection between boosting and linear programming techniques, suggesting new algorithms more directly motivated by LP.

Our experiments prove that increasing the minimum margin is *not* the final, or even the dominant, explanation of Adaboost's success. The question of why Adaboost performs so well on real problems, and whether there are yet better techniques to be found, is still more open than closed.

Finally, our experiments have brought to light other intriguing phenomenon, particularly concerning the very long run behavior of Adaboost. *Eventually*, it seems, Adaboost can overfit (as one would naively expect, but contrary to what one gets by extrapolating most short-run experiments).

8 Further Directions

We close with a few miscellaneous observations about the connection between minimum margins and linear programming which, while interesting, do not directly relate to the main concern of this work. All suggest additional experimental research.

The first concerns the duality result mentioned in Section 4. This suggests a new stopping criteria for boosting algorithms in general, including Adaboost. At each step of a boosting algorithm, we can compute the margin actually achieved by the current weighted ensemble. We can also keep track of the lowest (*i.e.*, worst) score the base learner has been able to achieve (on any reweighting of the training set that it has been presented with). But duality theory, *the optimal achievable margin lies between these values*. Once the gap between these is sufficiently small, one knows that little additional improvement is possible and so can stop. As observed in Section 6, the question of when a procedure like Adaboost has really "converged" can be a difficult one in practice.

Second, and also related to the dual LP formulation, we note the existence of the *ellipsoid algorithm* for solving linear programs, famous because it was the first guaranteed polynomial time algorithm for LP [Kha79, Chv83]. But it has another interesting property that it does not need to see the explicit constraint matrix. Instead, one only needs an "oracle" which—given any proposed assignment to the variables—will produce a violated constraint if one exists. Given such an oracle, the algorithm can find a solution (to some given precision) in polynomial number of calls to the oracle (independent of how many constraints there actually are). It is intriguing that in the dual formulation of our LP *the base learner is such an oracle*: violated constraints correspond to base hypotheses that do better on the current example reweighting than any member of the current weighted ensemble. It therefore seems possible that this idea could lead to another "boosting" algorithm in the style of DualLPboost, but with perhaps different convergence properties and (at each step) vastly superior computational complexity.

Finally, the idea of minimizing margins is reminiscent of the idea of support vector machines [CV95]. There, however, one tries to find a linear combination that achieves the best worst separation in the sense of Euclidean (*i.e.*, L_2) distance, as opposed to the L_1 notion used to define margins (in a straightforward way but one which we do not formalize here). It turns out that SVMs maximize L_2 margins using quadratic rather than linear programs. But a benefit of maximizing L_1 rather than L_2 margins is that L_1 has a much stronger tendency to produce *sparse* weight vectors. This can yield smaller representations of the learned ensemble, which can be an important consideration in practice [MD97]. In fact our experiments support this. We often find that LP-Adaboost, for instance, ends up giving zero (or negligible) weight to many of the hypothesis in the ensemble and so the *effective* ensemble size is smaller.

Acknowledgments

We would like to thank Leo Breiman, Yoav Freund and Llew Mason for very useful discussions and comments.

References

[BK97] E. Bauer and R. Kohavi. An empirical comparison of voting classification algorithms: bagging, boosting, and variants. http:// robotics. stanford. edu/ users/ ronnyk, 1997.

[Bre96a] L. Breiman. Arcing classifiers. Technical report, Statistics Department, U. C. Berkeley, 1996. http:// www. stat. berkeley. edu/ users/ breiman.

[Bre96b] L. Breiman. Bias, variance, and arcing classifiers. Technical report, Statistics Department, U. C. Berkeley, 1996.

[Bre97a] L. Breiman. Arcing the edge. Technical report, Statistics Department, U. C. Berkeley, 1997.

[Bre97b] L. Breiman. Prediction games and arcing algorithms. Technical report, Statistics Department, U. C. Berkeley, 1997.

[Chv83] V. Chvátal. *Linear Programming*. W. H. Freeman, New York, 1983.

[CV95] C. Cortes and V. Vapnik. Support-vector networks. *Machine Learning*, 20:273–97, 1995.

[FS96a] Y. Freund and R. Schapire. Experiments with a new boosting algorithm. In *ICML-96*, pages 148–156, 1996.

[FS96b] Y. Freund and R. Schapire. Game theory, on-line prediction and boosting. In *COLT-96*, pages 325–332, 1996.

[FS97] Y. Freund and R. Schapire. A decision-theoretic generalization of on-line learning and an application to boosting. *Journal of Computer and Systems Sciences*, 55(1), 1997.

[Kha79] L. Khachian. A polynomial algorithm in linear programming. *Doklady Adademiia Nauk SSSR*, 244:1093–96, 1979. (In Russian) Cited by [Chv83].

[KSD96] R. Kohavi, D. Sommerfield, and J. Dougherty. Data mining using MLC++: A machine learning library in C++. In *Tools with Artificial Intelligence*. IEEE Computer Society, 1996. http:// www. sgi. com/ technology /mlc.

[Lue84] D. Luenberger. *Linear and Nonlinear Programming*. Addison-Wesley, Reading, MA, 1984.

[MD97] D. Margineantu and T. Dietterich. Pruning adaptive boosting. In *ICML-97*, pages 211–218, 1997.

[MM] C. Merz and P. Murphy. UCI repository of machine learning databases. http:// www. ics. uci. edu/ ~mlearn/ MLRepository. html.

[MO97] R. Maclin and D. Opitz. An empirical evaluation of bagging and boosting. In *AAAI-97*, pages 546–551, 1997.

[Qui93] J. Quinlan. *C4.5: Programs for Machine Learning*. Morgan Kaufmann, San Mateo, CA, 1993.

[Qui96] J. Quinlan. Bagging, boosting, and C4.5. In *AAAI-96*, pages 725–730, 1996.

[SFBL97] R. Schapire, Y. Freund, P. Bartlett, and W. Lee. Boosting the margin: a new explanation for the effectiveness of voting methods. In *ICML-97*, pages 322–330, 1997.

[Van96] R. Vanderbei. *Linear Programming: Foundations and Extensions*. Kluwer, Boston, 1996.

Boosting Classifiers Regionally

Richard Maclin
Computer Science Department
University of Minnesota-Duluth
Duluth, MN 55812
email: rmaclin@d.umn.edu

Abstract

This paper presents a new algorithm for Boosting the performance of an ensemble of classifiers. In Boosting, a series of classifiers is used to predict the class of data where later members of the series concentrate on training data that is incorrectly predicted by earlier members. To make a prediction about a new pattern, each classifier predicts the class of the pattern and these predictions are then combined. In standard Boosting, the predictions are combined by weighting the predictions by a term related to the accuracy of the classifier on the training data. This approach ignores the fact that later classifiers focus on small subsets of the patterns and thus may only be good at classifying similar patterns. In RegionBoost, this problem is addressed by weighting each classifier's predictions by a factor measuring how well that classifier performs on similar patterns. In this paper we examine several methods for determining how well a classifier performs on similar patterns. Empirical tests indicate RegionBoost produces gains in performance for some data sets and has little effect on others.

Introduction

Boosting (Breiman 1996b; Drucker & Cortes 1996; Freund & Schapire 1996) is a technique for creating *ensemble* classifiers, classifiers that combine the predictions of multiple component classifiers. It has proven extremely effective over a number of different domains (Breiman 1996b; Freund & Schapire 1996; Maclin & Opitz 1997; Quinlan 1996). This paper presents RegionBoost, a modification of existing Boosting techniques. The focus of RegionBoost is to do a better job of combining the predictions of the classifiers in the ensemble by considering the performance of each of these classifiers in different regions of problem space. Boosting techniques generally either average the predictions of the classifiers or produce a weighted average of the classifiers where the weight is a single value for each classifier. The advantage of RegionBoost is that a classifier that performs well in only one portion of problem space will be weighted more highly on data points from that portion of problem space (and low on other points). Quinlan (1996) and Woods et al. (1997) present approaches similar to RegionBoost, but Quinlan's technique is specific to decision trees and Woods et al.'s technique selects a single classifier rather than combining the predictions of the classifiers.

To test the effect of RegionBoost, I present experiments using ensembles of neural networks on 19 data sets from the UCI repository. These experiments show that RegionBoost often significantly outperforms standard Boosting, though it has little effect on performance for some problems. These results are especially interesting in that Boosting often produces the most accurate classifiers for many domains.

Background: Ensembles

An ensemble classifier consists of a set of individual classifiers (components) and a mechanism for combining the predictions of the components (see Figure 1). To classify a point using an ensemble, the input vector is passed to the component classifiers, each of which predicts the class of the point. These predictions are then merged by the combiner mechanism into a single prediction for the classifier. For example, the combiner could take a majority vote of the components. Research on ensembles generally focuses on: (1) which component classifiers to combine; and (2) how to com-

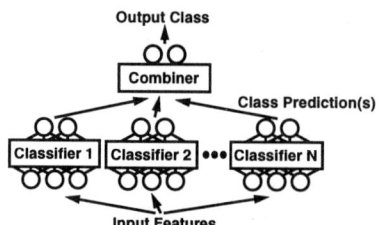

Figure 1: A classifier ensemble made up of N component classifiers and a combiner mechanism.

Copyright ©1998, American Association for Artificial Intelligence (www.aaai.org). All rights reserved.

bine the predictions of the classifiers.

Empirical evidence suggests that an ensemble classifier almost always outperforms an average classifier from the ensemble (Maclin & Opitz 1997; Quinlan 1996). Often the ensemble outperforms *all* of its component classifiers. Theoretical work (Hansen & Salamon 1990; Krogh & Vedelsby 1995) on ensemble methods indicates that ensembles are effective when the components are accurate and differ in their predictions. Krogh and Vedelsby (1995) demonstrated that the performance of an ensemble is mathematically based on the average error rate of its components minus a term that measures the differences between the components.

Research on selecting classifiers to use as components generally focuses (if only indirectly) on the selection of component classifiers that are accurate and differ in their predictions. Examples of mechanisms that have been used to create component classifiers include using different training parameters with a single learning method (Alpaydin 1993; Maclin & Shavlik 1995), using different subsets of the training data with a single learning method (Breiman 1996a; Freund & Schapire 1996), using different learning methods (Zhang, Mesirov, & Waltz 1992), and explicitly searching for a set of classifiers that is both accurate and diverse (Opitz & Shavlik 1996). Boosting is a method that creates component classifiers by using different subsets of the training data.

Numerous methods have been suggested for combining the predictions of classifiers. Sample combination functions include voting (Hansen & Salamon 1990), simple averages (Lincoln & Skrzypek 1989), weighted averages (Freund & Schapire 1996; Rogova 1994), using a voting sequence of combiners (Asker & Maclin 1997), and *learning* a combiner function (Wolpert 1992). Wolpert's (1992) Stacking mechanism is a powerful general mechanism for producing an effective combining function by training a learner to predict the corrections needed for each of the individual components, though it is limited in that for it to be effective it needs a set of held-out training data that was not used in creating the component classifiers. But Clemen (1989) suggests that simple mechanisms are often as effective as any complex combining method.

Background: Boosting

Boosting (Freund & Schapire 1996) encompasses a family of methods. The focus of these methods is to produce a *series* of classifiers. The training set used for each member of the series is chosen based on the performance of the earlier classifier(s) in the series. In Boosting, examples that are incorrectly predicted by previous classifiers in the series are chosen more often than examples that were correctly predicted. Thus Boosting attempts to produce new classifiers that are better able to predict examples for which the current ensemble's performance is poor.

In this work we will be building on a powerful form of Boosting called Ada-Boosting (Freund & Schapire 1996). In Ada-Boosting, a training set of size N is selected for classifier $K + 1$ by probabilistically selecting (with replacement) N examples from the original N training examples (since there is replacement and the probabilities differ, some examples may be selected more than once and some not at all). For classifier $K + 1$, the probability depends on how often that example was misclassified by the previous K classifiers. Initially the probability of picking each example is set to $1/N$. After a classifier is added to the ensemble, the probabilities of selecting examples are adjusted by a factor based on ϵ_k, the sum of the probabilities for those examples that are incorrectly classified by classifier K. The probability of selecting each of the misclassified examples is multiplied by the value $(1 - \epsilon_k)/\epsilon_k$. The probabilities of selecting each of the examples are then renormalized so that they sum to 1. This process has the effect of increasing the probability of misclassified examples and reducing (through the normalization) the probability of the correctly classified examples. In this work we use Breiman's (1996b) variation where the probabilities are all reset to $1/N$ if ϵ_k equals 0 or becomes greater than 0.5. In the latter case, multiplying by $(1 - \epsilon_k)/\epsilon_k$ would *decrease* the probability of misclassified examples, while in the former case the value $(1 - \epsilon_k)/\epsilon_k$ is undefined.

A critical factor in Ada-Boosting is that the predictions of the component classifiers are not simply averaged. In later classifiers the training set may focus heavily on certain examples and ignore others, producing a classifier that is very good at classifying a small subset of the points but is not effective at classifying all points. For example, Figure 2 shows the average *training* error of the different classifiers in the Boosting ensembles used in the experiments later in this paper. Even with Breiman's resetting variation, the accuracy of later classifiers in the ensemble drops off quickly. To address this problem, Ada-Boosting weights the pre-

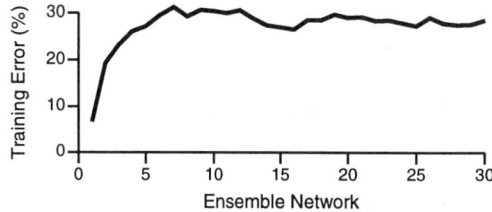

Figure 2: Composite *training* error from the classifiers in the Boosting experiments from the Results section.

dictions of classifiers by $log((1-\epsilon_k)/\epsilon_k)$. Classifiers with small values of ϵ_k are weighted higher than classifiers with large values. Although this strategy is effective, it does not make full use of the data available, a limitation addressed by RegionBoost.

RegionBoost

Ada-Boosting (Freund & Schapire 1996) addresses the problem of combining classifiers by weighting the classifiers with respect to their accuracy. But by weighting each of the classifiers by a single value, Ada-Boosting loses some of the value of the Boosting approach. In Boosting, later classifiers concentrate on correctly classifying examples that were not correctly classified by previous classifiers. Thus it is reasonable to assume that the later classifiers will be better at some types of examples and worse at other types. To address this limitation using only a single weight *undervalues* a later classifier's ability to classify examples similar to the ones it was trained with and *overvalues* its ability to classify other examples. A better approach is to weight the predictions of each classifier by how well it predicted examples similar to the one being examined.

Intuitively, the idea behind RegionBoost's approach to weighting is to use the training data to estimate the accuracy of the classifier. Although this estimate is likely to suffer from overfitting, it does have an advantage in that Boosting leave some of the data out (and in the case of later classifiers, possibly significant portions may not be included in the training set for that classifier). Rather than using a single measure of the accuracy on the training data, in RegionBoost we take advantage of the idea that some classifiers perform well only for certain regions of problem space by estimating the likely accuracy of the classifier for each new point. In this work we will examine two approaches to estimating the accuracy of the classifier.

One approach to estimating accuracy will use a simple k-Nearest-Neighbor (Cover & Hart 1967) approach to find the k points in the training set nearest to the new point we are trying to classify and assessing how well each classifier performed for each of those points. The weighting for that classifier's prediction is the sum of how well the classifier predicted each of these k training data points divided by k. In the limit, if we choose $k = N$, this method approximates the standard Ada-Boosting approach to weighting predictions. A second approach will be to train a second classifier for each classifier in the ensemble, in this work a separate neural network, to predict the accuracy for new points. For both approaches we will need to estimate the accuracy of a classifier for each training data point.

One estimate of the accuracy for a training data

Table 1: Summary of the data sets used in this paper. Shown are the number of examples and output classes, plus the number of inputs, outputs, hidden units and training epochs used for each network.

Data Set	Case	Out	In	Hid	Epch
breast-cancer-w	699	2	9	5	20
credit-a	690	2	47	10	35
credit-g	1000	2	63	10	30
diabetes	768	2	8	5	30
glass	214	6	9	10	80
heart-cleveland	303	2	13	5	40
hepatitis	155	2	32	10	60
house-votes-84	435	2	16	5	40
hypo	3772	5	55	15	40
ionosphere	351	2	34	10	40
iris	159	3	4	5	80
kr-vs-kp	3196	2	74	15	20
labor	57	2	29	10	80
promoters-936	936	2	228	20	30
segmentation	2310	7	19	15	20
sick	3772	2	55	10	40
sonar	208	2	60	10	60
soybean	683	19	134	25	40
vehicle	846	4	18	10	40

point (the *Discrete* method) will simply assign the value of one if the pattern is correctly predicted and zero otherwise. A second method (*Continuous*) will estimate accuracy based on the output produced by the classifier. In this approach the accuracy estimate will be based on the average distance between the actual and expected output for a pattern. For example, in a three-class problem where the expected prediction is {0,1,0} (i.e., in class 2) and the actual prediction is {0.1,0.8,0.1}, the accuracy would be 0.867 (1 - 0.133) where 0.133 is the average of the distances between 0 and 0.1, 1 and 0.8, and 0 and 0.1 divided by 3.

Results

This section presents experiments to evaluate the effect of the RegionBoost approach on classification accuracy. The tests use 19[1] of the 23 data sets from the UCI data set repository (Murphy & Aha 1994) used in a previous study of Boosting (Maclin & Opitz 1997). Table 1 gives details for these data sets. For each data set we report error rates for Ada-Boosting and RegionBoost.

Methodology

All results are averaged over ten standard 10-fold cross validation experiments. For each 10-fold cross validation, the data set is first partitioned into 10 equal-sized sets, and each set is in turn used as the test set while the classifier trains on the other nine sets. For each fold an ensemble of 30 networks are created

---
[1] The 4 data sets excluded require more computational resources than were available.

Table 2: Results of experiments shown to test the effects of RegionBoost on the data sets listed in Table 1. The second, eleventh and thirteenth columns (Ada, Perceptron-Ada and NearN) show error rates using these methods. The results in the other columns represent percentage point reductions in error rate (or increases for negative numbers). For example, in the third column next to breast-cancer-w, the number is 0.3 which indicates that the error rate using this method was 3.7%. See the text for descriptions of the experiments producing these numbers.

| Data Set | Ada | RegionBoost | | | | | | Net Accuracy | | Perceptron | | NearN |
| | | NearN:Discrete | | | NearN:Continuous | | | | | | | |
		k-7	k-11	k-15	k-7	k-11	k-15	Disc	Cont	Ada	RB Disc k-15	k-15
breast-cancer-w	4.0	*0.3*	*0.3*	*0.3*	0.2	0.3	0.2	0.7	*0.4*	4.0	0.1	3.8
credit-a	15.9	*1.1*	*0.8*	*0.7*	0.8	0.9	0.7	*1.9*	*1.3*	14.9	0.4	16.2
credit-g	25.5	0.0	*0.3*	*0.3*	0.2	0.3	0.3	*0.4*	0.8	25.6	*0.6*	27.0
diabetes	22.9	-0.3	-0.2	-0.1	0.0	0.4	0.2	0.0	0.3	23.0	*-0.6*	25.1
glass	32.4	*1.2*	*1.0*	*1.3*	1.0	1.0	1.3	1.0	1.0	36.7	*1.8*	38.2
heart-cleveland	19.8	0.4	*0.6*	*0.7*	0.1	0.1	0.2	0.3	0.0	19.4	0.0	20.6
hepatitis	18.7	*0.8*	*0.8*	*0.8*	0.8	1.3	0.7	0.5	0.6	18.3	0.4	19.4
house-votes-84	5.1	0.2	0.2	0.2	0.2	*0.3*	*0.3*	0.2	0.2	5.6	0.0	6.5
hypo	6.2	0.1	0.0	0.0	0.1	0.0	0.0	0.0	0.0	6.2	0.1	7.0
ionosphere	7.9	-0.4	-0.4	-0.3	0.0	0.0	0.0	*0.8*	*0.8*	12.8	*1.2*	16.3
iris	3.8	-0.1	-0.1	0.0	0.0	0.1	0.0	-0.1	-0.1	3.5	0.2	3.4
kr-vs-kp	0.4	0.0	0.0	0.0	0.0	0.0	0.0	0.0	0.0	0.9	*0.2*	7.6
labor	4.2	0.2	0.2	0.2	0.3	0.3	0.2	*1.7*	*1.7*	3.3	0.1	24.2
promoters-936	4.4	0.0	0.0	0.1	0.0	0.1	0.0	-0.1	-0.1	5.5	0.1	8.5
segmentation	3.5	*0.2*	*0.2*	*0.2*	0.1	0.2	0.2	0.0	0.0	7.1	*2.8*	5.6
sick	4.3	0.2	0.1	0.1	*0.2*	*0.2*	*0.4*	*0.2*	0.2	4.5	0.0	4.3
sonar	12.7	0.1	0.2	0.1	*0.4*	*0.5*	*0.4*	0.2	*0.4*	18.3	*0.5*	31.2
soybean	7.0	0.1	0.0	0.0	0.0	0.0	0.1	0.1	-0.1	6.9	-0.1	12.6
vehicle	19.7	-0.2	-0.1	-0.1	*0.6*	*0.6*	*0.7*	*0.7*	*0.7*	22.6	*1.1*	31.0

(for a total of 300 networks for each 10-fold cross validation). Parameter settings for the neural networks include a learning rate of 0.15, a momentum term of 0.9, and weights are initialized randomly to be between -0.5 and 0.5. The parameters used in training were the same as used by Maclin and Opitz (1997).

Experimental Results

Table 2 incorporates the results for several of the experiments discussed in this section. The second column of this table shows the baseline Ada-Boosting results produced for each of these data sets. The next three columns show the results for the RegionBoost approach with the k-Nearest-Neighbor method (for k=7,11,15) and the Discrete method for estimating training data accuracy. The following three columns show similar results using the Continuous method for estimating accuracy. These results show reductions (or increases) in error rate for each of the data sets by percentage point (e.g., 1.1 in the third column for credit-a indicates the error rate goes from 15.9% to 14.8%). Statistically significant changes in error are shown in *italics*.

Several interesting results can be observed from these experiments. First, RegionBoost significantly decreases the error for a number of the data sets (six to ten of the 19), and it produces little or no change for the other data sets. RegionBoost only significantly increases the error for one case. There also seems to be a relation between the performance of the different methods. Several data sets always see reductions in error rate. One difference between the two methods for weighting the confidence of predictions is that the Continuous method produces significant gains for two data sets, sonar and vehicle, for which the Discrete method does not perform well.

In a second set of experiments we tested the idea of using RegionBoost where the estimated accuracy for a new point is predicted by a neural network. A network is trained after each component is created and is used to predict the estimated accuracy of the training data points for that component. This network is trained using the training data in which the expected output signal is either the Discrete (correct or incorrect) value associated with each training point (see ninth column) or the Continuous estimate of the accuracy of the training point (tenth column). The number of hidden units in these networks is the same as the number of hidden units in the component network. The results of these experiments are similar to those obtained using the nearest neighbor methods, and produce significant gains for two other data sets (labor and ionosphere).

Together, these experiments indicate that the overall RegionBoost approach can produce significant gains for many (though not all) data sets. One question which might be raised is how RegionBoost affects Boosting's performance on different learning approaches. To answer this question, we apply Boosting and RegionBoost to a much simpler form of neu-

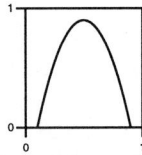

Figure 3: The "arch" problem. Two dimensional data points are randomly generated with points above the line being labeled as positive examples and points below negative examples.

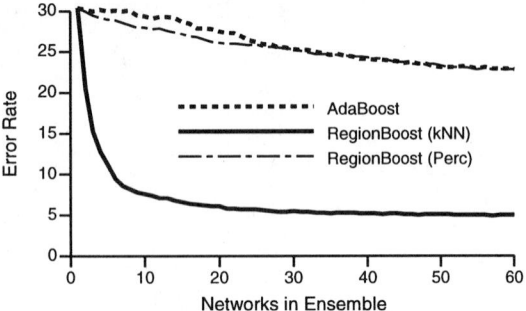

Figure 4: Error rates for Ada-Boosting and two RegionBoost approaches to the "arch" problem. One RegionBoost approach uses a Nearest Neighbor measure of accuracy; the other a perceptron.

ral networks, perceptrons. The two columns labeled Perceptron show Ada-Boosting and RegionBoost using the Discrete, Nearest Neighbor approach results for these data sets. For many of these data sets, RegionBoost again produces significant gains in performance, often on the same data sets where it previously worked well. This result holds even though the performance of the perceptron approach is often significantly different from the performance of the other neural networks.

An interesting question now arises, namely how is RegionBoost affected by the different methods used for estimating the classifiers' accuracy for a new data point? Since the two different approaches (nearest neighbor and network) often work well on the same data sets this might suggest that RegionBoost's effects are entirely dependent on aspects of the data set. To test this notion we looked at a standard Boosting problem, the "arch" problem shown in Figure 3. This problem is interesting since it has been shown that a Boosting approach can combine a sequence of classifiers that use only linear decision surfaces to solve this problem. But approaches that are not restricted to linear decision surfaces (such as a Nearest Neighbor approach) can perform extremely well on this problem (a simple Nearest Neighbor approach with k=15 has a 3.1% error rate on this problem). Figure 4 shows results for a standard Boosting approach on perceptron component classifiers, a RegionBoost approach using the Discrete, Nearest Neighbor (k=15) accuracy estimate and a RegionBoost approach using a perceptron (linear) accuracy estimate. These results indicate that

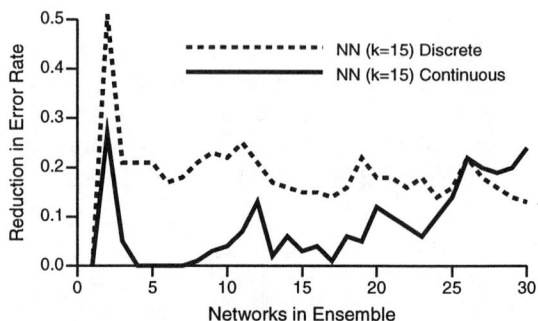

Figure 5: Reductions in error rate (versus Ada-Boosting) plotted as a function of number of classifiers combined using two Nearest Neighbor (k=15) RegionBoost approaches, one using Discrete and the other using a Continuous measure of error.

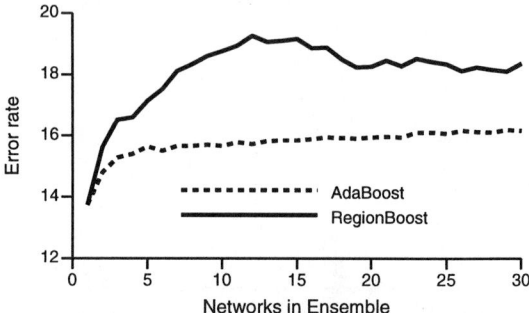

Figure 6: Error rate for a problem with "one-sided noise" using Ada-Boosting and RegionBoost.

for this problem, RegionBoost achieves much better performance when using Nearest Neighbor estimation. This suggests the effect of RegionBoost is not entirely dependent on the data set but also on the method used for estimating the accuracy of the classifier.

Which approach for assessing the accuracy of an example is more appropriate? Figure 5 plots the reduction in error over all of the data sets for two approaches: the Nearest Neighbor (k=15) method of measuring accuracy with (1) Discrete and (2) Continuous measures. These results indicate that the effect of the Discrete method is strongest for the first few classifiers but tails off, whereas the Continuous method shows an early gain which quickly disappears and only after a large number of classifiers again does significantly better.

Finally, we consider the question of whether RegionBoost is subject to overfitting as described in Opitz and Maclin (1998). They constructed artificial data sets with "one-sided noise." These data sets have two relevant features and four irrelevant features where the concept consisted of a simple hyperplane based on the two relevant features. The data consists of a set of randomly generated points from each side of the hyperplane. Then a certain percentage of the points on one side of the hyperplane are mislabeled (creating "one-sided" noise). Results from experiments with this type of data set indicate Boosting often produces significant increases in error. Figure 6 shows the performance of Ada-Boosting and RegionBoost on one of these domains. These results indicate that RegionBoost is even more susceptible to overfitting than Ada-Boosting (this is not surprising given that RegionBoost depends on the training data to estimate classifier accuracy).

Future Work

The experiments presented indicate a significant effect for RegionBoost in many cases. Further experiments will evaluate the effect of RegionBoost on other learning methods (e.g., decision trees). It would also be useful to examine the value of using RegionBoost to combine different types of classifiers (e.g., decision trees and neural networks). Comparisons will also be made between RegionBoost and Boosting with Stacking (Wolpert 1992) combining.

One major advantage of RegionBoost is its ability to produce effective ensembles using components that are only effective for small regions of problem space. This advantage makes it possible to look at Boosting approaches that focus much more strongly on incorrectly labeled points. For examples, Breiman's (1996b) method includes a parameter that can be used to increase the likelihood that incorrectly labeled patterns are focused on in later classifiers. With RegionBoost it is possible to use much larger values of this parameter since the resulting classifiers (which may focus on small numbers of patterns) will be highly weighted only for problems on which they appear to be effective.

Conclusions

This paper presents RegionBoost, a new algorithm for producing a Boosting ensemble of classifiers. RegionBoost differs from standard Boosting in how it combines the predictions of the classifiers making up the ensemble. Other Boosting methods usually weight the predictions of the components by a single value, whereas RegionBoost attempts to estimate the accuracy of each of the classifiers based on the accuracy of the classifiers for similar data points in the training set. Two approaches for estimating the accuracy of each classifier are explored, a k-Nearest-Neighbor and a neural network method. Empirical results on several data sets indicate both RegionBoost approaches often produce statistically significant gains in accuracy. Detailed experiments investigating various aspects of RegionBoost seem to indicate that the effects of RegionBoost are based partially on the data set being examined and partially on the method used for estimating classifier accuracy. Experiments also show that while RegionBoost is often effective, it can suffer from overfitting problems just like Boosting.

References

Alpaydin, E. 1993. Multiple networks for function learning. In *Proc IEEE Int Conf Neur Nets*, 27–32.

Asker, L., and Maclin, R. 1997. Ensembles as a sequence of classifiers. In *IJCAI-97*.

Breiman, L. 1996a. Bagging predictors. *Machine Learning* 24(2):123–140.

Breiman, L. 1996b. Bias, variance, and arcing classifiers. Technical Report TR 460, UC-Berkeley, Berkeley, CA.

Clemen, R. 1989. Combining forecasts: A review and annotated bibliography. *Journal of Forecasting* 5:559–583.

Cover, T., and Hart, P. 1967. Nearest neighbor pattern classification. *IEEE Trans on Info The* 13:21–27.

Drucker, H., and Cortes, C. 1996. Boosting decision trees. In Touretsky, D.; Mozer, M.; and Hasselmo, M., eds., *NIPS-8*, volume 8, 479–485. Cambridge, MA: MIT Press.

Freund, Y., and Schapire, R. 1996. Experiments with a new boosting algorithm. In *ICML-96*, 148–156.

Hansen, L., and Salamon, P. 1990. Neural network ensembles. *IEEE Trans on Pat Ana and Mach Int* 12:993–1001.

Krogh, A., and Vedelsby, J. 1995. Neural network ensembles, cross validation, and active learning. In Tesauro, G.; Touretzky, D.; and Leen, T., eds., *NIPS-7*, 231–238. Cambridge, MA: MIT Press.

Lincoln, W., and Skrzypek, J. 1989. Synergy of clustering multiple back propagation networks. In Touretzky, D., ed., *NIPS-2*, 650–659. San Mateo, CA: Morg. Kauf.

Maclin, R., and Opitz, D. 1997. An empirical evaluation of bagging and boosting. In *AAAI-97*.

Maclin, R., and Shavlik, J. 1995. Combining the predictions of multiple classifiers: Using competitive learning to initialize neural networks. In *IJCAI-95*, 524–530.

Murphy, P., and Aha, D. 1994. UCI repository of machine learning databases (machine-readable data repository). UCI, Dept of Info and Comp Sci.

Opitz, D., and Maclin, R. 1998. Popular ensemble methods: An empirical study. *Machine Learning (submitted)*. (Also appears as UMD CS TR 98-1).

Opitz, D., and Shavlik, J. 1996. Generating accurate and diverse members of a neural-network ensemble. In Touretsky, D.; Mozer, M.; and Hasselmo, M., eds., *NIPS-8*, 535–541. Cambridge, MA: MIT Press.

Quinlan, J. R. 1996. Bagging, boosting, and c4.5. In *AAAI-96*, 725–730.

Rogova, G. 1994. Combining the results of several neural-network classifiers. *Neural Networks* 7:777–781.

Wolpert, D. 1992. Stacked generalization. *Neural Networks* 5:241–259.

Woods, K.; Kegelmeyer, W.; and Bowyer, K. 1997. Combination of multiple classifiers using local accuracy estimates. *IEEE Trans on Pat Ana Mach Int* 19:405–410.

Zhang, X.; Mesirov, J.; and Waltz, D. 1992. Hybrid system for protein secondary structure prediction. *Journal of Molecular Biology* 225:1049–1063.

Robust classification systems for imprecise environments

Foster Provost
Bell Atlantic Science and Technology
400 Westchester Avenue
White Plains, New York 10604
foster@basit.com

Tom Fawcett
Bell Atlantic Science and Technology
400 Westchester Avenue
White Plains, New York 10604
fawcett@basit.com

Abstract

In real-world environments it is usually difficult to specify target operating conditions precisely. This uncertainty makes building robust classification systems problematic. We show that it is possible to build a hybrid classifier that will perform at least as well as the best available classifier for any target conditions. This robust performance extends across a wide variety of comparison frameworks, including the optimization of metrics such as accuracy, expected cost, lift, precision, recall, and workforce utilization. In some cases, the performance of the hybrid can actually surpass that of the best known classifier. The hybrid is also efficient to build, to store, and to update. Finally, we provide empirical evidence that a robust hybrid classifier is needed for many real-world problems.

Introduction

Traditionally, classification systems have been built by experimenting with many different classifiers, comparing their performance and choosing the classifier that performs best. Unfortunately, this experimental comparison is often difficult in real-world environments because key parameters are not known. For example, the optimal cost/benefit tradeoffs and the target class distribution are seldom known precisely. This information is crucial to the choice of an optimal classifier.

We argue that it is possible and desirable to avoid committing to a single best classifier during system construction. Instead, a hybrid classification system can be built from the best available classifiers, and this hybrid will perform best under any target cost/benefit and class distributions. Target conditions can then be specified at run time. Moreover, in cases where precise information is still unavailable when the system is run (or if the conditions change dynamically during operation), the hybrid system can be tuned easily based on feedback from its actual performance.

The argument is structured as follows. First we sketch briefly the traditional approach to building such systems, in order to demonstrate that it is brittle under the types of imprecision common in real-world problems. In the subsequent sections we prove that the ROC Convex Hull, which is a method for comparing and visualizing classifier behavior in imprecise environments (Provost & Fawcett 1997), is also an elegant solution to the problem of building a robust classification system. The solution is elegant because the resulting hybrid classifier is robust for a wide variety of problem formulations, and it is efficient to build, to store, and to update. We then show that the hybrid can actually do better than the best known classifier in some situations. Finally, we provide empirical evidence that this type of system is needed for real-world problems.

Brittle and robust classifiers

Consider a generic example. A systems-building team wants to create a system that will take a large number of instances and identify those for which an action should be taken. The instances could be potential cases of fraudulent account behavior, of faulty equipment, of responsive customers, of interesting science, etc. We consider problems for which the best method for classifying or ranking instances is not well-defined, so the system builders may consider AI methods such as expert systems, neural networks, learned decision trees and case-based systems as potential classification models. Ignoring for the moment issues of efficiency, the foremost question facing the system builders is: which of the available models performs "best" at classification?

Traditionally, an experimental approach has been taken to answer this question, because the distribution of instances is not known a priori, but usually can be sampled. The standard approach is to estimate the error rate of each model statistically and then to choose the model with the lowest error rate. This strategy is common in machine learning, pattern recognition, data mining, expert systems and medical diagnosis. In some cases, other measures such as cost or benefit are used as well. Applied statistics provides methods such as cross-validation

Copyright ©1998, American Association for Artificial Intelligence (www.aaai.org). All rights reserved.

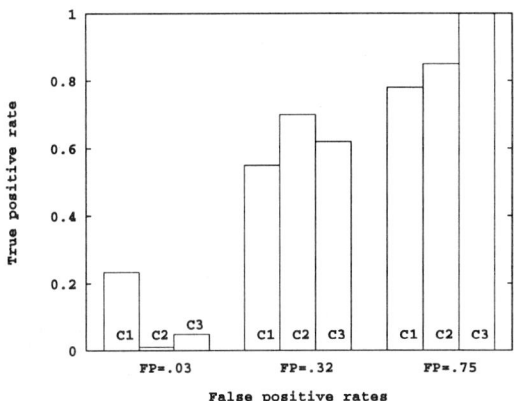

Figure 1: Three classifiers under three different Neyman-Pearson decision criteria

and the bootstrap for estimating model error rates and recent studies have compared the effectiveness of these different statistical methods (Salzberg 1997; Dietterich 1998).

Unfortunately, this experimental approach is brittle under two types of imprecision that are common in real-world environments. Specifically, costs and benefits usually are not known precisely, and class distributions often are known only approximately as well. This fact has been pointed out by many authors (Bradley 1997; Catlett 1995), and is in fact the concern of a large subfield of decision analysis (Weinstein & Fineberg 1980). Imprecision also arises because the environment may change between the time the system is conceived and the time it is used, and even as it is used. For example, levels of fraud and levels of customer responsiveness change continually over time and from place to place.

In this paper we address two-class problems. Formally, each instance I is mapped to one element of the set $\{\mathbf{p}, \mathbf{n}\}$ of (correct) positive and negative classes. A *classification model* (or *classifier*) is a mapping from instances to predicted classes. To distinguish between the actual class and the predicted class of an instance, we will use the labels $\{\mathbf{Y}, \mathbf{N}\}$ for the classifications produced by a model. For our discussion, let $c(classification, class)$ be a two-place error cost function where $c(\mathbf{Y}, \mathbf{n})$ is the cost of a false positive error and $c(\mathbf{N}, \mathbf{p})$ is the cost of a false negative error. We represent class distributions by the classes' prior probabilities $p(\mathbf{p})$ and $p(\mathbf{n}) = 1 - p(\mathbf{p})$.

The traditional experimental approach is brittle because it chooses one model as "best" with respect to a specific set of cost functions and class distribution. If the target conditions change, this system may no longer perform optimally, or even acceptably. As an example, assume that we have a maximum false positive rate, $FP = p(\mathbf{Y}|\mathbf{n})$, that must not be exceeded. We want to find the classifier with the highest possible true positive rate, $TP = p(\mathbf{Y}|\mathbf{p})$, that does not exceed the FP limit. This is the Neyman-Pearson decision criterion (Egan 1975). Three classifiers, under three such FP limits, are shown in Figure 1. A different classifier is best for each FP limit; any system built with a single "best" classifier is brittle if the FP requirement can change.

We address this brittleness by extending the traditional comparison/selection framework to produce **robust classifiers**, defined as satisfying the following. *Under any target cost and class distributions, a robust classifier will perform at least as well as the best classifier for those conditions.* For this paper, statements about optimality are practical: the "best" classifier may not be the Bayes-optimal classifier, but it is better than all other known classifiers. Stating that a classifier is robust is stronger than stating that it is optimal. A robust classifier is optimal under all possible conditions.

Classification brittleness could be overcome by saving all possible classifiers (neural nets, decision trees, expert systems, probabilistic models, etc.) and then performing an automated run-time comparison under the desired target conditions. However, such a system is not feasible because of time and space limitations—there are myriad possible classification models, arising from the different data mining methods available under their many different parameter settings. Storing all the classifiers is not practical, and tuning the system by comparing classifiers on the fly under different conditions is not practical. Moreover, we will show that it is sometimes possible to do better than any of these classifiers.

Hybrid classifiers using the ROC convex hull

We will show that robust hybrid classifiers can be built using the ROC Convex Hull (ROCCH).

Definition 1 *Let $\mathbf{I}$ be the space of possible instances and let $\mathbf{C}$ be the space of sets of classification models. Let a μ-hybrid classifier comprise a set of classification models $C \in \mathbf{C}$ and a function*

$$\mu : \mathbf{I} \times \Re \times \mathbf{C} \to \{\mathbf{Y}, \mathbf{N}\}.$$

A μ-hybrid classifier takes as input an instance $I \in \mathbf{I}$ for classification and a number $x \in \Re$. As output, it produces the classification produced by $\mu(I, x, C)$.

Things will get more involved later, but for the time being consider that each set of cost and class distributions defines a value for x, which is used to select the (predetermined) best classifier for those conditions. To build a μ-hybrid classifier, we must define μ and the set C. We would like C to include only those models that perform optimally under some conditions (class and cost distributions), since these will be stored by the system, and we would like μ to be general enough to apply to a variety of problem formulations.

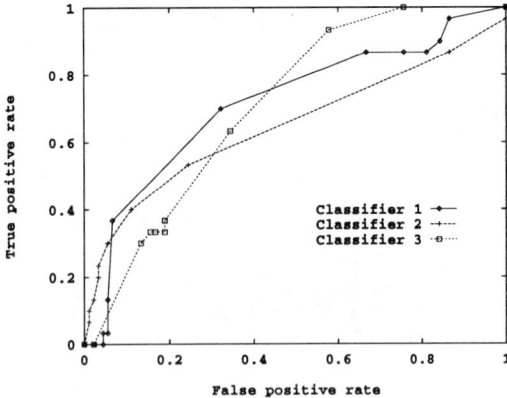

Figure 2: ROC graph of three classifiers

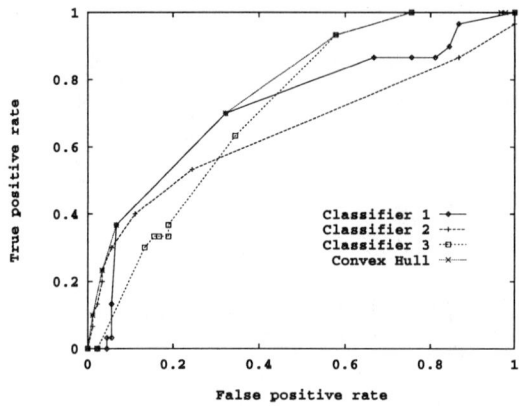

Figure 3: ROC curves with convex hull

At this point, it is necessary to review briefly some of the basics of Receiver Operating Characteristic (ROC) analysis, a classic methodology from signal detection theory that is now common in medical diagnosis and has recently begun to be used more generally in AI classifier work (Swets 1988). *ROC space* denotes the coordinate system used for visualizing classifier performance. In ROC space, TP is represented on the Y axis and FP is represented on the X axis. Each classifier is represented by the point in ROC space corresponding to its (FP, TP) pair. For models that produce a continuous output, e.g., an estimate of the posterior probability of an instance's class membership, these statistics vary together as a threshold on the output is varied between its extremes (each threshold value defines a classifier); the resulting curve is called the ROC curve. An ROC curve illustrates the error tradeoffs available with a given probabilistic model. Figure 2 shows a graph of three typical ROC curves; in fact, these are the complete ROC curves of the classifiers shown in Figure 1. ROC graphs illustrate the predictive behavior of a classifier *without regard to class distribution or error cost*, so they decouple classification performance from these factors.

As described in detail by Provost and Fawcett (1997) the ROCCH method takes as input a set of classifiers, along with their classification performance statistics, and plots them in ROC space. Then it finds the convex hull (Barber, Dobkin, & Huhdanpaa 1993) of the set of points in ROC space (the ROCCH). The convex hull of a set of points is the smallest convex set that contains the points. The ROCCH is the "northwest boundary" of the points in ROC space. The classifiers corresponding to the points comprising the ROCCH are the potentially optimal classifiers, because (roughly) points in ROC space that are more northwest are better. Figure 3 shows the three ROC curves with the convex hull drawn.

We claim that the models comprising the ROCCH can be combined to form an μ-hybrid classifier that is an elegant, robust classifier.

Definition 2 *The* ROCCH*-hybrid is a μ-hybrid classifier where C is the set of classifiers that comprise the* ROCCH *and μ makes classifications using the classifier on the* ROCCH *with $FP = x$.*

Note that for the moment the ROCCH-hybrid is defined only for FP values corresponding to ROCCH vertices.

Robust classification

Our definition of robust classifiers was intentionally vague about what it means for one classifier to be better than another, because different situations call for different comparison frameworks. We now show that the ROCCH-hybrid is robust for a wide variety of comparison frameworks. We begin with minimizing expected cost, because the process of proving that the ROCCH-hybrid minimizes expected cost for any cost and class distributions provides a deep understanding of why the ROCCH-hybrid works. We then show that it is also robust for a variety of other practical metrics. After that we discuss how the ROCCH can be used in imprecise environments. Finally, we show that for some problems the ROCCH-hybrid can actually do better than all known classifiers.

Minimizing expected cost

Decision analysis (Weinstein & Fineberg 1980) provides us with a method for determining when one classification model is better than another. Specifically, the expected cost of applying a classifier is:

$$p(\mathbf{p}) \cdot (1 - TP) \cdot c(\mathbf{N}, \mathbf{p}) \; + \\ p(\mathbf{n}) \cdot FP \cdot c(\mathbf{Y}, \mathbf{n}) \qquad (1)$$

We now can show that the ROCCH-hybrid is robust for problems where the "best" classifier is the classifier with the minimum expected cost.

Definition 3 *For minimizing expected cost, environmental conditions, viz., cost and class distributions,* are translated to a single real value as follows:

$$m_{mec} = \frac{c(\mathbf{Y},\mathbf{n})p(\mathbf{n})}{c(\mathbf{N},\mathbf{p})p(\mathbf{p})} \quad (2)$$

This is the product of the cost ratio and the reciprocal of the class ratio. Every set of conditions will define an $m_{mec} \geq 0$.

The slope of the ROCCH is an important tool in our argument. The ROCCH is a piecewise-linear, convex-down "curve." Therefore, as x increases, the slope of the ROCCH is monotonically non-increasing with $k-1$ discrete values, where k is the number of ROCCH component classifiers, including the degenerate classifiers that define the ROCCH endpoints. Where there will be no confusion, we use phrases such as "points in ROC space" as a shorthand for the more cumbersome "classifiers corresponding to points in ROC space." For this subsection, "points on the ROCCH" refer to vertices of the ROCCH.

Definition 4 *For any real number $m \geq 0$, **the point where the slope of the** ROCCH **is** m is one of the (arbitrarily chosen) endpoints of the segment of the ROCCH with slope m, if such a segment exists. Otherwise, it is the vertex for which the left adjacent segment has slope greater than m and the right adjacent segment has slope less than m.*

For completeness, the leftmost endpoint of the ROCCH is considered to be attached to a segment with infinite slope and the rightmost endpoint of the ROCCH is considered to be attached to a segment with zero slope. Note that every $m \geq 0$ defines at least one point on the ROCCH.

Lemma 1 *For any set of cost and class distributions, there is a point on the ROCCH with minimum expected cost.*
Proof: *(by contradiction) Assume that for some conditions there exists a point C with smaller expected cost than any point on the ROCCH. By equations (1) and (2), a point (FP_2, TP_2) has the same expected cost as a point (FP_1, TP_1), if*

$$\frac{TP_2 - TP_1}{FP_2 - FP_1} = m_{mec}$$

*Therefore, for conditions corresponding to m_{mec}, all points with equal expected cost form a line, an **iso-performance line**, in ROC space with slope m_{mec}. Also by (1) and (2), points on lines with larger y-intercept have lower expected cost. Now, point C is not on the ROCCH, so it is either above the curve or below the curve. If it is above the curve, then the ROCCH is not a convex set enclosing all points, which is a contradiction. If it is below the curve, then the iso-performance line through C also contains a point P that is on the ROCCH. Since all points on an iso-performance line have the same expected cost, point C does not have smaller expected cost than all points on the ROCCH, which is also a contradiction.* □

Although it is not necessary for our purposes here, it can be shown that *all* of the minimum expected cost classifiers are *on* the ROCCH.

Definition 5 *An iso-performance line with slope m is an **m-iso-performance line**.*

Lemma 2 *For any cost and class distributions that translate to m_{mec}, a point on the ROCCH has minimum expected cost only if the slope of the ROCCH at that point is m_{mec}.*
Proof: *(by contradiction) Suppose that there is a point D on the ROCCH where the slope is not m_{mec}, but the point does have minimum expected cost. By Definition 4, either (a) the segment to the left of D has slope less than m_{mec}, or (b) the segment to the right of D has slope greater than m_{mec}. For case (a), consider point N, the vertex of the ROCCH that neighbors D to the left, and consider the (parallel) m_{mec}-iso-performance lines l_D and l_N through D and N. Because N is to the left of D and the line connecting them has slope less than m_{mec}, the y-intercept of l_N will be greater than the y-intercept of l_D. By the construction in the proof to Lemma 1, this means that N will have lower expected cost than D, which is a contradiction. The argument for (b) is analogous (symmetric).* □

Lemma 3 *If the slope of the ROCCH at a point is m_{mec}, then the point has minimum expected cost.*
Proof: *If this point is the only point where the slope of the ROCCH is m_{mec}, then the proof follows directly from Lemma 1 and Lemma 2. If there are multiple such points, then by definition they are connected by an m_{mec}-iso-performance line, so they have the same expected cost, and once again the proof follows directly from Lemma 1 and Lemma 2.* □

It is straightforward now to show that the ROCCH-hybrid is robust for the problem of minimizing expected cost.

Theorem 4 *The ROCCH-hybrid minimizes expected cost for any cost distribution and any class distribution.*
Proof: *Because the ROCCH-hybrid is composed of the classifiers corresponding to the points on the ROCCH, this follows directly from Lemmas 1, 2, and 3.* □

Optimizing other common metrics

The previous section showed that the ROCCH-hybrid is robust when the goal is to provide the minimum expected cost classification. The ROCCH-hybrid is robust for other common metrics as well. For example, even for accuracy maximization the preferred classifier may be different for different target class distributions. This is rarely taken into account in experimental comparisons of classifiers.

Corollary 5 *The ROCCH-hybrid minimizes error rate (maximizes accuracy) for any target class distribution.*
Proof: *Error rate minimization is cost minimization with uniform error costs.* □

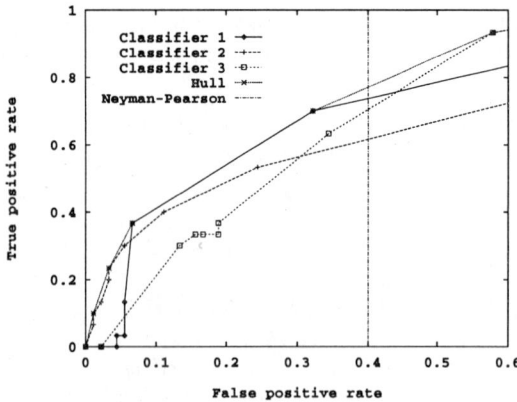

Figure 4: The ROC Convex Hull used to select a classifier under the Neyman-Pearson criterion

An alternative metric, used often in ROC analysis to compare models, is the area under the ROC curve (AUC) (Bradley 1997). It is especially useful for situations where either the target cost distribution or class distribution is *completely* unknown. The AUC represents the probability that a randomly chosen positive instance will be rated higher than a negative instance, and thereby is also estimated by the Wilcoxon test of ranks (Hanley & McNeil 1982). A criticism of the use of AUC for model choice is that for specific target conditions, the classifier with the maximum AUC may be suboptimal (as we will see below). Fortunately, not only is the ROCCH-hybrid optimal for any specific target conditions, it has the maximum AUC.

Theorem 6 *There is no classifier with AUC larger than that of the ROCCH-hybrid.*
Proof: *(by contradiction) Assume the ROC curve for another classifier had larger area. This curve would have to have at least one point in ROC-space that falls outside the area enclosed by the ROCCH. This means that the convex hull does not enclose all points, which is a contradiction.* □

Recall that the Neyman-Pearson decision criterion specifies a maximum acceptable FP rate. In standard ROC analysis, selecting the best classifier for the Neyman-Pearson criterion is easy: plot ROC curves, draw a vertical line at the desired maximum FP, pick ROC curve with the largest TP at the intersection with this line.

For minimizing expected cost it was sufficient for the ROCCH-hybrid to choose a *vertex* from the ROCCH for any m_{mec} value. For problem formulations such as the Neyman-Pearson criterion, the performance statistics at a non-vertex point on the ROCCH may be preferable (see Figure 4). Fortunately, with a slight extension, the ROCCH-hybrid can yield a classifier with these performance statistics.

Theorem 7 *A ROCCH-hybrid can achieve the TP:FP tradeoff represented by any point on the ROCCH, not just the vertices.*
Proof: *(by construction) Extend $\mu(I, x, C)$ to non-vertex points as follows. Pick the point P on the ROCCH with $FP = x$ (there is exactly one). Let TP_x be the TP value of this point. If (x, TP_x) is a ROCCH vertex, use the corresponding classifier. If it is not a vertex, call the left endpoint of the hull segment C_l and the right endpoint C_r. Let d be the distance between C_l and C_r, and let p be the distance between C_l and P. Make classifications as follows. For each input instance flip a weighted coin and choose the answer given by classifier C_l with probability $\frac{p}{d}$ and that given by classifier C_r with probability $1 - \frac{p}{d}$. It is straightforward to show that FP and TP for this classifier will be x and TP_x.* □

Corollary 8 *For the Neyman-Pearson criterion, the performance of the ROCCH-hybrid is at least as good as that of any known classifier.*
Proof: *Similar to minimum expected cost proofs—no classifier can be above the ROCCH.* □

There are still other realistic problem formulations. For example, consider the decision support problem of optimizing *workforce utilization*, in which a workforce is available to process a fixed number of cases. Too few cases will under-utilize the workforce, but too many cases will leave some cases unattended (expanding the workforce usually is not a short-term solution). If the workforce can handle C cases, the system should present the best possible set of C cases. This is similar to the Neyman-Pearson criterion, but with an absolute cutoff (C) instead of a percentage cutoff (FP).

Theorem 9 *For workforce utilization, the ROCCH-hybrid will provide the best set of C cases, for any choice of C.*
Proof: *(by construction) The decision criterion is: maximize TP subject to the constraint:*

$$TP \cdot P + FP \cdot N \leq C$$

The optimal point is found by intersecting the constraint line with the ROCCH, because, similarly to the previous arguments, no classifier can be above the ROCCH. The rest follows from Theorem 7. □

Similar arguments hold for many other comparison metrics. It can be shown that for maximizing lift (Berry & Linoff 1997), precision or recall, subject to absolute or percentage cutoffs on case presentation, the ROCCH-hybrid will provide the best set of cases.

As with minimizing expected cost, imprecision in the environment forces us to favor a robust solution for these other comparison frameworks. For many real-world problems, the precise desired cutoff will be unknown or will change (*e.g.*, because of fundamental uncertainty, variability in case difficulty or competing responsibiliities). The ROCCH-hybrid provides a robust solution because it is the optimal solution for any cutoff. For example, for document retrieval the ROCCH-hybrid will yield the best N documents for any N.

An apparent solution to the problem of robust classification is to use a system that ranks cases, rather than one that provides classifications, and just work down the ranked list of cases (the cutoff is implicit). However, for most practical situations, choosing the best ranking model is equivalent to choosing which classifier is best *for the cutoff that will be used*. Remember that ROC curves are formed from case rankings by moving the cutoff from one extreme to the other. For different cutoffs, implicit or explicit, different ranking functions perform better. This is exactly the problem of robust classification, and is solved elegantly by the ROCCH-hybrid—the ROCCH-hybrid comprises the set rankers that are best for all possible cutoffs. Formal arguments are beyond the scope of this paper, but as an example, consider two ranking functions R_a and R_b. R_a is perfect for the first 10 cases, and picks randomly thereafter. R_b randomly chooses the first 10 cases, and ranks perfectly thereafter. R_a is preferable for a cutoff of 10 cases and R_b is preferable for much larger cutoffs.

Using the ROCCH-hybrid

To use the ROCCH-hybrid for classification, we need to translate environmental conditions to x values to plug into $\mu(I, x, \mathcal{C})$. For minimizing expected cost, equation 2 shows how to translate conditions to m_{mec}. For any m_{mec}, by Lemma 3 we want the FP value of the point where the slope of the ROCCH is m_{mec}, which is straightforward to calculate. For the Neyman-Pearson criterion the conditions are defined as FP values. For workforce utilization with conditions corresponding to a cutoff C, the FP value is found by intersecting the line $TP \cdot P + FP \cdot N = C$ with the ROCCH.

We have argued that target conditions (misclassification costs and class distribution) are rarely known. It may be confusing that we now seem to require exact knowledge of these conditions. The ROCCH-hybrid gives us two important capabilities. First, the need for precise knowledge of target conditions is deferred until runtime. Second, in the absence of precise knowledge even at run-time, the system can be optimized easily with minimal feedback.

By using the ROCCH-hybrid, information on target conditions is not needed to train and compare classifiers. This is important because of temporal (or geographic) differences that may exist between training and use. Building a system for a real-world problem introduces a non-trivial delay between the time data are gathered and the time the learned models will be used. The problem is exacerbated in domains where error costs or class distributions change over time; even with slow drift, a brittle model may become suboptimal quickly. In these scenarios, costs and class distributions can be specified (or respecified) at run time with reasonable precision by sampling from the current population, and used to ensure that the ROCCH-hybrid always performs optimally.

In some cases, even at run time these quantities are not known exactly. A further benefit of the ROCCH-hybrid is that it can be tuned easily to yield optimal performance with only minimal feedback from the environment. Conceptually, the ROCCH-hybrid has one "knob" that varies x in $\mu(I, x, \mathcal{C})$ from one extreme to the other. For any knob setting, the ROCCH-hybrid will give the optimal $TP{:}FP$ tradeoff for the target conditions corresponding to that setting. Turning the knob to the right increases TP; turning the knob to the left decreases FP. Because of the monotonicity of the ROCCH-hybrid, simple hill-climbing can guarantee optimal performance. For example, if the system produces too many false alarms, turn the knob to the left; if the system is presenting too few cases, turn the knob to the right.

Beating the component classifiers

Perhaps surprisingly, in many realistic situations a ROCCH-hybrid system can do *better* than any of its component classifiers. Consider the Neyman-Pearson decision criterion. The ROCCH may intersect the FP-line *above* the highest component ROC curve. This occurs when the FP-line intersects the ROCCH between vertices; therefore, there is no component classifier that actually produces these particular (FP,TP) statistics (as in Figure 4).

Theorem 10 *The ROCCH-hybrid can surpass the performance of its component classifiers for some Neyman-Pearson problems.*
Proof: *For any non-vertex hull point (x, TP_x), TP_x is larger than the TP for any other point with $FP = x$. By Theorem 7, the ROCCH-hybrid can achieve any TP on the hull. Only a small number of FP values correspond to hull vertices.* □

The same holds for other problem formulations, such as workforce utilization, lift maximization, precision maximization, and recall maximization.

Time and space efficiency

We have argued that the ROCCH-hybrid is robust for a wide variety of problem formulations. It is also efficient to build, to store, and to update.

The time efficiency of building the ROCCH-hybrid depends first on the efficiency of building the component models, which varies widely by model type. Some models built by machine learning methods can be built in seconds (once data are available). Hand-built models can take years to build. However, we presume that this is work that would be done anyway. The ROCCH-hybrid can be built with whatever methods are available, be there two or two thousand; as described below, as new classifiers become available, the ROCCH-hybrid can be updated incrementally. The time efficiency depends also on the efficiency of the experimental evaluation of the classifiers. Once again, we presume that this is work that would be done anyway (more on this in

Limitations). Finally, the time efficiency of the ROCCH-hybrid depends on the efficiency of building the ROCCH, which can be done in $O(N \log N)$ time using the Quick-Hull algorithm (Barber, Dobkin, & Huhdanpaa 1993) where N is the number of classifiers.

The ROCCH is space efficient, too, because it comprises only classifiers that might be optimal under some target conditions.

Theorem 11 *For minimizing expected cost, the ROCCH-hybrid comprises only classifiers that are optimal under some cost and class distributions.*
Proof: *Follows directly from Lemmas 1–3 and Definitions 3 and 4.* □

The number of classifiers that must be stored can be reduced if bounds can be placed on the potential target conditions. As described by Provost and Fawcett (1997), ranges of conditions define segments of the ROCCH. Thus, the ROCCH-hybrid may need only a subset of C.

Adding new classifiers to the ROCCH-hybrid is also efficient. Adding a classifier to the ROCCH will either (i) extend the hull, adding to (and possibly subtracting from) the ROCCH-hybrid, or (ii) conclude that the new classifiers are not superior to the existing classifiers in any portion of ROC space and can be discarded.

The run-time (classification) complexity of the ROCCH-hybrid is never worse than that of the component classifiers. In situations where run-time complexity is crucial, the ROCCH should be constructed without prohibitively expensive classification models. It will then find the best subset of the computationally efficient models.

Empirical demonstration of need

Robust classification is of theoretical interest because it concentrates on weakening two very strong assumptions. We have argued that the assumptions of precise knowledge of cost and class distributions are too strong, citing evidence from AI work as well as a subfield of decision analysis dedicated to quantifying costs and benefits. However, might it not be that existing classifiers are already robust? For example, if a given classifier is optimal under one set of conditions, might it not be optimal under all?

It is beyond the scope of this paper to offer an in-depth experimental study of this question, but we can still provide solid evidence that the answer is "no." To this end, we refer to a comprehensive ROC analysis of medical domains recently conducted by Bradley (1997). His purpose was not to answer this question; fortunately his published results do anyway.

A classifier *dominates* if its ROC curve completely defines the ROCCH (which means dominating classifiers are robust and vice versa). If there exist more than a trivially few domains where no classifier dominates, then techniques like the ROCCH-hybrid are essential.

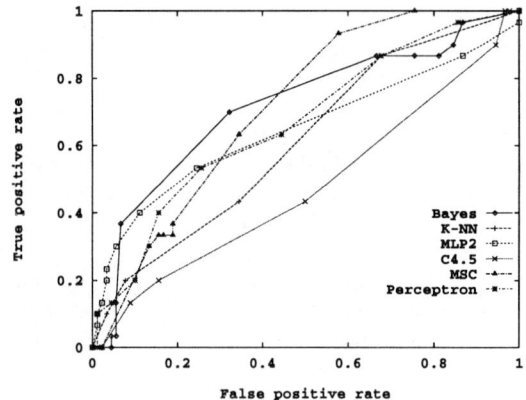

Figure 5: Bradley's classifier results for the heart bleeding data.

Bradley studied six medical data sets, noting that "unfortunately, we rarely know what the individual misclassification costs are." He plotted the ROC curves of six classifier learning algorithms (two neural nets, two decision trees and two statistical techniques).

On *not one* of these data sets was there a dominating classifier. This means that for each domain, there exist different sets of conditions for which different classifiers are preferable. In fact, the three example classifiers used in this paper are the three best classifiers from Bradley's results on the heart bleeding data; his results for the full set of six classifiers can be found in Figure 5. Classifiers constructed for the Cleveland heart disease data, are shown in Figure 6.

Bradley's results show clearly that for many domains the classifier that maximizes any single metric—be it accuracy, cost, or the area under the ROC curve—will be the best for some cost and class distributions and will not be the best for others.[1] We have shown that the ROCCH-hybrid will be the best for all.

Limitations

There are limitations to the ROCCH-hybrid as we have presented it here. We have defined it only for two-class problems. We believe that it can be extended to multi-class problems, but have not done so. It should be noted that the dimensionality of the "ROC-hyperspace" grows quadratically in the number of classes. We have also assumed constant error costs for a given *type* of error, e.g., all false positives cost the same. For some problems, different errors of the same type have different costs. In many cases, such a problem can be transformed into an equivalent problem with uniform intra-type error costs by duplicating instances in proportion to their costs for evaluation.

---

[1] More recently, an independent study showed a dominating classifier for only one of ten standard machine learning benchmarks (Provost, Fawcett, & Kohavi 1998).

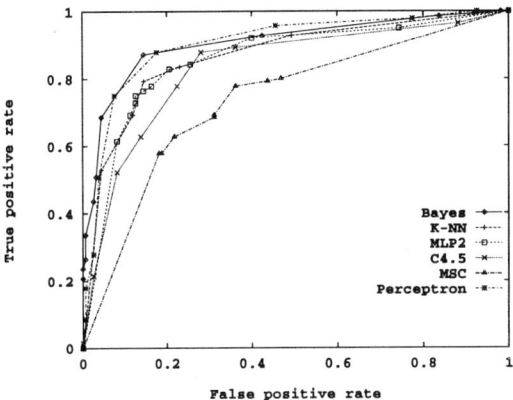

Figure 6: Bradley's classifier results for the Cleveland heart disease data

We have also assumed for this paper that the estimates of the classifiers' performance statistics (FP and TP) are very good. As mentioned above, much work has addressed the production of good estimates for simple performance statistics such as error rate. Much less work has addressed the production of good ROC curve estimates. It should be noted that, as with simpler statistics, care should be taken to avoid overfitting the training data and to ensure that differences between ROC curves are meaningful. Cross-validation with averaging of ROC curves is one possible solution (Provost, Fawcett, & Kohavi 1998).

Finally, we have addressed predictive performance and computational performance. These are not the only concerns in choosing a classification model. What if comprehensibility is important? The easy answer is that for any particular setting, the ROCCH-hybrid is as comprehensible as the underlying model it is using. However, this answer falls short if the ROCCH-hybrid is interpolating between two models or if one wants to understand the "multiple-model" system as a whole.

Conclusion

The ROCCH-hybrid performs optimally under any target conditions for many realistic problem formulations. It is efficient to build in terms of time and space, and can be updated incrementally. Therefore, we conclude that it is an elegant, robust classification system.

The motivation for this work is fundamentally different from recent machine learning work on combining multiple models (Ali & Pazzani 1996). That work combines models in order to boost performance for a fixed cost and class distribution. The ROCCH-hybrid combines models for robustness across different cost and class distributions. These methods should be independent—multiple-model classifiers are candidates for extending the ROCCH. However, it may be that some multiple-model classifiers achieve increased performance for a specific set of conditions by (effectively) interpolating along edges of the ROCCH.

Acknowledgements

We thank the many with whom we have discussed ROC analysis and classifier comparison, especially Rob Holte, George John, Ron Kohavi, Ron Rymon, and Peter Turney. We thank Andrew Bradley for supplying data from his analysis.

References

Ali, K. M., and Pazzani, M. J. 1996. Error reduction through learning multiple descriptions. *Machine Learning* 24(3):173–202.

Barber, C.; Dobkin, D.; and Huhdanpaa, H. 1993. The quickhull algorithm for convex hull. Technical Report GCG53, University of Minnesota. Available from ftp://geom.umn.edu/pub/software/qhull.tar.Z.

Berry, M. J. A., and Linoff, G. 1997. *Data Mining Techniques: For Marketing, Sales, and Customer Support*. John Wiley & Sons.

Bradley, A. P. 1997. The use of the area under the ROC curve in the evaluation of machine learning algorithms. *Pattern Recognition* 30(7):1145–1159.

Catlett, J. 1995. Tailoring rulesets to misclassificatioin costs. In *Proceedings of the 1995 Conference on AI and Statistics*, 88–94.

Dietterich, T. G. 1998. Approximate statistical tests for comparing supervised classification learning algorithms. *Neural Computation*. to appear.

Egan, J. P. 1975. *Signal Detection Theory and ROC Analysis*. Series in Cognitition and Perception. New York: Academic Press.

Hanley, J. A., and McNeil, B. J. 1982. The meaning and use of the area under a receiver operating characteristic (roc) curve. *Radiology* 143:29–36.

Provost, F., and Fawcett, T. 1997. Analysis and visualization of classifier performance: Comparison under imprecise class and cost distributions. In *Proceedings of the Third International Conference on Knowledge Discovery and Data Mining (KDD-97)*, 43–48. AAAI Press.

Provost, F.; Fawcett, T.; and Kohavi, R. 1998. Building the case against accuracy estimation for comparing induction algorithms. Submitted to IMLC-98. AAAI Press. Available from http://www.croftj.net/~fawcett/papers/ICML98-submitted.ps.gz.

Salzberg, S. L. 1997. On comparing classifiers: Pitfalls to avoid and a recommended approach. *Data Mining and Knowledge Discovery* 1:317–328.

Swets, J. 1988. Measuring the accuracy of diagnostic systems. *Science* 240:1285–1293.

Weinstein, M. C., and Fineberg, H. V. 1980. *Clinical Decision Analysis*. Philadelphia, PA: W. B. Saunders Company.

Recommendation as Classification: Using Social and Content-Based Information in Recommendation

Chumki Basu*
Bell Communications Research
445 South Street
Morristown, NJ 07960-6438
cbasu@bellcore.com

Haym Hirsh
Department of Computer Science
Rutgers University
Piscataway, NJ 08855
hirsh@cs.rutgers.edu

William Cohen
AT&T Laboratories
180 Park Ave, Room A207
Florham Park, NJ 07932
wcohen@research.att.com

Abstract

Recommendation systems make suggestions about artifacts to a user. For instance, they may predict whether a user would be interested in seeing a particular movie. Social recomendation methods collect ratings of artifacts from many individuals, and use nearest-neighbor techniques to make recommendations to a user concerning new artifacts. However, these methods do not use the significant amount of other information that is often available about the nature of each artifact — such as cast lists or movie reviews, for example. This paper presents an inductive learning approach to recommendation that is able to use both ratings information and other forms of information about each artifact in predicting user preferences. We show that our method outperforms an existing social-filtering method in the domain of movie recommendations on a dataset of more than 45,000 movie ratings collected from a community of over 250 users.

Introduction

Recommendations are a part of everyday life. We usually rely on some external knowledge to make informed decisions about an artifact of interest or a course of action, for instance when we are going to see a movie or going to see a doctor. This knowledge can be derived from social processes. When we are buying a CD, we can rely on the judgment of a person who shares similar tastes in music. At other times, our judgments may be based on available information about the artifact itself and our known preferences. There are many factors which may influence a person in making these choices, and ideally one would like to model as many of these factors as possible in a recommendation system.

There are some general approaches to this problem. In one approach, the user of the system provides ratings of some artifacts or items and the system makes informed guesses about what other items the user may like. It bases these decisions on the ratings other users have provided. This is the framework for *social-filtering* methods (Hill, Stead, Rosenstein & Furnas 1995; Shardanand & Maes 1995). In a second approach, the system accepts information describing the nature of an item, and based on a sample of the user's preferences, learns to predict which items the user will like (Lang 1995; Pazzani, Muramatsu, & Billsus 1996). We will call this approach *content-based filtering*, as it does not rely on social information (in the form of other user's ratings). Both social and content-based filtering can be cast as learning problems: in both cases, the objective is to learn a function that can take a description of a user and an artifact and predict the user's preferences concerning the artifact.

Well-known recommendation systems like *Recommender* (Hill, Stead, Rosenstein & Furnas 1995) and *Firefly* (http://www.firefly.net) (Shardanand & Maes 1995) are based on social-filtering principles. *Recommender*, the baseline system used in the work reported here, recommends as yet unseen movies to a user based on his prior ratings of movies and their similarity to the ratings of other users. Social-filtering systems perform well using only numeric assessments of worth, i.e., ratings. However, there is often readily available information concerning the content of each artifact. Social-filtering methods leave open the question of what role content can play in the recommendation process.

For many types of artifacts, there is already a substantial store of information that is becoming more and more readily accessible while at the same time growing at a healthy rate. Let's take, for instance, a sample of the information a person can obtain about a favorite movie on the Web alone: a complete breakdown of cast/crew, plot, movie production details, reviews, trailer, film and audio clips, (and ratings too) and the list goes on. When users decide on a movie to see, they are likely to be influenced by data provided by one or more of these sources. Social-filtering may be characterized as a generic approach, unbiased by the regularities exhibited by properties associated with the items of interest (Hill, Stead, Rosenstein & Furnas 1995). (Indeed, a significant motivation for some of the work on such systems is to explore the utility of recognizing communities of users based solely on similarities in their preferences.) However, the fact that

---

*Department of Computer Science, Rutgers University, Piscataway, NJ 08855
We would like to thank Susan Dumais for useful discussions during the early stages of this work.
Copyright ©1998, American Association for Artificial Intelligence (www.aaai.org). All rights reserved.

content-based properties can be identified at low cost (with no additional user effort and that people are influenced by these regularities make a compelling reason to investigate how best to use them.

In what situations are ratings alone insufficient? Social-filtering makes sense when there are enough other users known to the system with overlapping characteristics. Typically, the requirement for overlap in most of these systems is that the users of the system rate the same items in order to be judged similar/dissimilar to each other. It is dependent upon the current state of the system — the number of users and the number and selection of movies that have been rated.

As an example of the limitations of using ratings alone, consider the case of an artifact for which no ratings are available, such as when a new movie comes out. Since there will be a period of time when a recommendation system will have little ratings data for this movie, the recommendation system will initially not be able to recommend this movie reliably. However, a system which makes use of content might be able to make predictions for this movie even in the absence of ratings.

In this paper, we present a new, inductive learning approach to recommendation. We show how pure social-filtering can be accomplished using this approach, how the naive introduction of content-based information does not help — and indeed harms — the recommendation process, and finally, how the use of hybrid features that combine elements of social and content-based information makes it possible to achieve more accurate recommendations. We use the problem of movie recommendation as our exploratory domain for this work since it provides a domain with a large amount of data (over 45,000 movie evaluations across more than 250 people), as well as a baseline social-filtering method to which we can compare our results (Hill, Stead, Rosenstein & Furnas 1995).

The Movie Recommendation Problem

As noted above, in the social filtering approach, a recommendation system is given as input a set of ratings of specific artifacts for a particular user. In recommending movies, for instance, this input would be a set of movies that the user had seen, with some numerical rating associated with each of these movies. The output of the recommendation system is another set of artifacts, not yet rated by the user, which the recommendation system predicts the user will rate highly.

Social-filtering systems would solve this problem by focusing solely on the movie ratings for each user, and by computing from these ratings a function that can give a rating to a user for a movie that others have rated but the user has not. These systems have traditionally output ratings for movies, rather than a binary label. They compute ratings for unseen objects by finding similarities between peoples' preferences about the rated items. Similarity assessments are made amongst individual users of a system and are computed using a variety of statistical techniques. For example, *Recommender* computes for a user a smaller group of reference users known as recommenders. These recommenders are other members of the community most similar to the user. Using regression techniques, these recommenders' ratings are then used to predict ratings for new movies. In this social recommendation approach recommended movies are usually presented to the user as a rank-ordered list.

Content-based recommendation systems, on the other hand, would reflect solely the non-ratings information. For each user they would take a description of each liked and disliked movie, and learn a procedure that would take the description of a new movie and predict whether it will be liked or disliked by the user. For each user a separate recommendation procedure would be used.

Our Approach

The goal of our work is to develop an approach to recommendation that can exploit both ratings and content information. We depart from the traditional social-filtering approach to recommendation by framing the problem as one of classification, rather than artifact rating. On the other hand, we differ from content-based filtering methods in that social information, in the form of other users' ratings, will be used in the inductive learning process.

In particular, we will formalize the movie recommendation problem as a learning problem—specifically, the problem of learning a function that takes as its input a user and a movie and produces as output a label indicating whether the movie would be liked (and therefore recommended) or disliked:

$$f(\langle user, movie \rangle) \rightarrow \{liked, disliked\}$$

As a problem in classification, we also are interested in predicting whether a movie is liked or disliked, not an exact rating. Our output is also not an ordered list of movies, but a set of movies which we predict will be liked by the user. Most importantly, we are now able to generalize our inputs to the problem to other information describing both users and movies.

The information we have available for this process is a collection of user/movie ratings (on a scale of 1-10), and certain additional information concerning each movie.[1] To present the results as sets of movies predicted to be liked or disliked by a user we compute a ratings threshold for each user such that 1/4 of all the user's ratings exceed and the remaining 3/4 do not, and we return as recommended any movie whose predicted rating is above the training-data-based threshold on movies.

---

[1] It would be desirable to make the recommendation process a function of user attributes such as age or gender, but since that information is not available in the data we are using in this paper, we are forced to neglect it here.

Below we will outline a number of alternative ways that a user/movie rating might be represented for the learning system. We will first describe how we represent social recommendation information, which we call "collaborative" features, then how we represent "content" features, and finally describe the hybrid features that form the basis for our most successful recommendation system.

Collaborative Features

As an initial representation we use a set of features that take into account, separately, user characteristics and movie characteristics. For instance, perhaps a group of users were identified as liking a specific movie:

Mary, Bob, and Jill liked *Titanic*.

We defined an attribute called *users who liked movie X* to group users like these into a single feature, the value of which is a set. (*E.g.*, { Mary, Bob, Jill} would be the value of the feature *users who liked movie X* for the movie *Titanic*). Since our ground ratings data contain numerical ratings, we say a user likes a movie if it is rated in the top-quartile of all movies rated by that user.[2]

We also found it important to note that a particular user was interested in a set of movies, namely the ones which appeared in his top-quartile:

Tim liked the movies, *Twister*, *Eraser*, and *Face/Off*.

This led us to develop an attribute, *movies liked by user*, which encoded a user's favorite movies as another set-valued feature. We called these attributes *collaborative features* because they made use of the data known to social-filtering systems: users, movies, and ratings.

The result of this is that every user/movie rating gets converted into a tuple of two set-valued features. The first attribute is a set containing the movies the given user liked, and can be thought of as a single attribute describing the user. The second attribute is a set containing the users who like the given movie, and can be thought of as a single attribute describing the movie. Each such tuple is labeled by whether it was liked or disliked by the user, according to whether it was in the top-quartile for the user.

The use of set-valued features led naturally to use of *Ripper*, an inductive learning system that is able to learn from data with set-valued attributes (Cohen 1995; 1996). *Ripper* learns a set of rules, each rule containing a conjunction of several tests. In the case of a set-valued feature f, a test may be of the form "$e_i \in f$" where e_i is some constant that is an element of f in some example. As an example, *Ripper* might learn a rule containing the test $Jaws \in movies\text{-}liked\text{-}by\text{-}user$.

---

[2]The value of 1/4 was chosen rather arbitrarily, and our results are similar when this value was changed to 20% or 30%.

Content Features

Content features are more naturally available in a form suitable for learning, since much of the information concerning a movie are available from (semi-) structured online repositories of information. An example of such a resource which we found very useful for movie recommendation is the Internet Movie Database (IMDb) (http://www.imdb.com). The IMDb contains an extensive collection of movies and factual information relating to movies. All of our content features were extracted from this resource. In particular, the features we used in our experiments using "naive" content features were: Actors, Actresses, Directors, Writers, Producers, Production Designers, Production Companies, Editors, Cinematographers, Composers, Costume Designers, Genres, Genre Keywords, User-submitted Keywords, Words in Title, Aka (also-known-as) Titles, Taglines, MPAA rating, MPAA reason for rating, Language, Country, Locations, Color, Soundmix, Running Times, and Special Effects Companies.

Hybrid Features

Our final set of features reflect the common human-engineering effort that involves inventing good features to enable successful learning. Here this resulted in *hybrid features*, arising from our attempts to merge data that was not purely content-based nor collaborative. We looked for content that was frequently associated with the movies in our data and that is often used when choosing a movie. One such content feature turned out to be a movie's *genre*. However, to make effective use of the *genre* feature, it turned out to be necessary to relax an apparently natural assumption: that a $\langle user, movie \rangle$ pair would be encoded as a set of collaborative features, plus a set of content features describing the movie. Instead, it turned out to be more effective to define new collaborative features that are influenced by content. We call these features *hybrid* features.

We isolated three of the most frequently occurring genres in our data — comedy, drama, and action. We then introduced features that isolated groups of users who liked movies of the same genre, such as *users who liked dramas*. Similar features were defined for comedy and action movies. These hybrid features combine knowledge about users who liked a set of movies with knowledge of a particular content feature associated with the movies in a set. Definitions concerning what it means for a user to like a movie remain the same (top-quartile) as in the earlier parts of this paper.

Experiments and Results

We conducted a number of experiments using different sets of features. Below we will report on some of the significant results.

Training and Test Data

Our data set consists of more than 45,000 movie ratings collected from approximately 260 users. This data originated from a data set that was used to evaluate *Recommender*. However, over the course of our work we discovered that the training and test distributions in this data were distributed very differently. We therefore generated a new partition of data into a training set which contained 90% of the data and a testing set which contained the remaining 10%, for which the two distributions would be be more similar. Unfortunately, for some of the users *Recommender* failed to run correctly, and those few users were dropped from this study. Note that this was the only reason for dropping users. No users were dropped due to the performance of our own methods.

We generated a testing set by taking a *stratified random sample* of the data, in the following way:

- For every user, separate and group his movie/rating pairs into intervals defined by the ratings. Movies are rated on a scale from 1 to 10.

- For each interval, take a random sample of 10% of the data and combine the results.

Among the advantages of using stratified random sampling (Moore 1985), the primary one for us is that we have clearly defined intervals where all the units in an interval share a common property, the rating. Therefore, the holdout set we computed is more representative of the distribution of ratings for the entire data set than it would have been if we had used simple random sampling.

Evaluation Criteria

As mentioned earlier, we differ from other approaches in the output that we desire. This stems from how we compare ratings of different movies to deal with similarity. Rather than getting the exact rating right, we are interested in predicting whether a movie would be amongst the user's favorites. This has the nice effect of dealing with the fact that the intervals on the ratings scale are *not equidistant*. For instance, given a scale of 1 to 10 where 1 indicates low preference and 10, high preference, the "qualitative" difference between a rating of 1 and a rating of 2 is less when compared to the difference between 6 and 7, for any user whose ratings are mostly 7 and above. Our evaluating a movie as being liked if it is in the top-quartile reflects our belief that knowing the actual rating of a movie is not as important as knowing where the rating was relative to other ratings for a given user.

Both (Hill, Stead, Rosenstein & Furnas 1995) and (Karunanithi & Alspector 1996) evaluate the recommendations returned by their respective systems using *correlation* of ratings. For instance, they compared how well their results correlated with actual user ratings and the ratings of movie critics. Strong positive correlations are indicative of good recommendations. However, since we are not predicting exact ratings, we cannot use this method of evaluation.

We instead use two metrics commonly used in information retrieval — *precision* and *recall*. Precision gives us an estimate of how many of the movies predicted to be in the top-quartile for a user really belong to that group. Recall estimates how many of all the movies in the user's top-quartile were predicted correctly. A system that returns all movies as liked can achieve high recall. On the other hand, if we are more generous and consider all movies except those in the lowest quartile as liked, then we would expect precision estimates to increase. Therefore, we cannot consider any one measure in isolation.

However, we feel that when recommending movies, the user is more interested in examining a small set of recommended movies rather than a long list of candidates. Unlike document retrieval, where the user can narrow a list of retrieved items by actually reading some of the documents, here, the user is really interested in seeing just one movie. Therefore, our objective for movie recommendation is to maximize precision without letting recall drop below a specified limit. Precision represents the fact that a movie selected from the returned set will be liked, and the recall cutoff reflects the fact that there should be a non-trivial number of movies returned (for example, in case a video store is out of some of the recommended titles).

Baseline Results

In our initial experiment, we use *Recommender*'s social-filtering methods to compute predictions for $\langle user, movie \rangle$ pairs on the holdout data set. To do this, for every user, we separate his data from the holdout set. The rest of the data is made available to *Recommender*'s analysis routines, which means that every other user's test data serves as part of the training data for a given hold-out-user's test data. Then, for every movie in the user's holdout data, we apply *Recommender*'s evaluation routines to compute a rating. These routines look for a set of recommenders correlated with the user and compute a rating for a movie using a prediction equation with the recommenders as variables.

For every rating computed by *Recommender*, we need to determine whether it is in the top-quartile. To do this, we precompute *thresholds* for every user corresponding to the ratings which separate the top from the lower quartiles. To convert a rating, we use this rule:

- If a *predicted rating* $>=$ *user's threshold*, set the rating to "+".

- Otherwise, set the rating to "−".

These thresholds are set individually for each user, using only the training data ratings for the training data threshold, but the full set of data for a user is used to set the testing data threshold.

Our precision estimates are *microaveraged* (Lewis 1991). Microaveraging meant that our prediction decisions were made from a single group and an overall precision estimate was computed. This is preferable to *macroaveraging*, in which one computes results on a per individual basis and averages them at the end, giving equal weight to each user. Unfortunately, in some cases (due to the small amount of data for some users) no movies were recommended, leaving precision ill-defined in these cases. Microaveraging does not suffer this problem (unless no movies are returned for any users). As shown in Table 1, the *Recommender* achieved microaveraged values of 78% for precision and 33% for recall.

Inductive Learning Results

In the first of our inductive learning recommendation experiments using *Ripper*, we use the same training and holdout sets described above. However, now every data point is represented by a collaborative feature vector. The collaborative features we used were:

- Users who liked the movie
- Users who disliked the movie
- Movies liked by the user

The ratings are converted to the appropriate binary classification as described earlier. The entire training set and holdout set are made available to *Ripper* in two separate files. We then ran *Ripper* on this data and generated a classification for each example in the holdout set. *Ripper* produces a set of rules that it learns for this data which it uses to make predictions about the class of an example.

When running *Ripper*, we have the choice of setting a number of parameters. The parameters we found most useful in adjusting from the default settings allow *negative tests in set-valued attributes* and varying the *loss ratio*. The first parameter allows the tests in rules to check for non-containment of attribute values within a set-valued feature. (*E.g.*, tests like *Jaws $\notin$ movies-liked-by-user* are allowed.) The *loss ratio* is the ratio of the perceived cost of a false positive to the cost of a false negative; increasing this parameter encourages *Ripper* to improve precision, generally at the expense of recall. In most of the experiments, we varied the loss ratio until we achieved a high value of precision with a a reasonable recall. At a loss ratio of 1.9, we achieved a microaveraged precision of 77% and a recall of 27% (see Table 1). This level of precision is comparable to *Recommender*, but at a lower level of recall.

In the second set of experiments, we replaced the collaborative feature vector with a new set of features. In our studies, we extracted 26 different features from the IMDb. The features we chose ranged from common attributes such as *actors* and *actresses* to lesser known features such as *taglines*. We also chose a few features which were assigned to movies by users, such as *keyword* descriptors.

We began by adding the 26 content features to the collaborative features. With these new features, we were not able to improve precision and recall at the same time (see Table 1). Recalling that high precision was more important to us than high recall, we find these results generally inferior to that of *Recommender*. Furthermore, examining the rules that *Ripper* generated, we found that content features were seldom used.

Two points should be noted from this experiment. First, the collaborative data appear to be better predictors of user preferences than our initial encoding of content; as a result, *Ripper* learned rules which ignored all but a few of the content features. Secondly, given the high dimensionality of our feature space, it appears to be difficult to make reasonable associations amongst the examples in our problem.

In our next attempt, we created features that combined collaborative with content information relating to the genre of a movie. These hybrid features were:

- Comedies liked by user
- Dramas liked by user
- Action movies liked by user

Although the movies in our data set are not limited to these three genres, we took a conservative approach to adding new features and began with the most popular genres as determined by the data.

To introduce the next set of collaborative features, we face a new issue. For example, we want a feature to represent the set of users who liked comedies. Although we have defined what it means to like a movie, we have not defined what it means to like movies of a particular genre. How many of the movies in the user's top-quartile need to be of a particular genre in order for the user to like movies of that genre?

Surveying the data, we found that the proportion of movies of any particular genre appearing in a user's top-quartile usually fall into some broad clusters. As a first cut, we divided the proportions of movies of different genres into four groups and created features to reflect the degree to which the user liked a particular genre. For each of the popular genres, *comedy*, *drama*, and *action*, we defined the following features:

- Users who liked many movies of genre X
- Users who liked some movies of genre X
- Users who liked few movies of genre X
- Users who disliked movies of genre X

We also add features including, for example, the genre of a particular movie. Running *Ripper* on this data with a loss ratio of 1.5, we achieved a microaveraged precision of 83% with a recall of 34%. These results are summarized in Table 1.

Using the standard test for a difference in proportions (Mendenhall, Scheaffer, & Wackerly 1981, pages 311-315) it can be determined that *Ripper* with hybrid features attains a statistically significant improvement

Method	Precision	Recall
Recommender	78%	33%
Ripper (no content)	77%	27%
Ripper (simple content)	73%	33%
Ripper (hybrid features)	83%	34%

Table 1: Results of the different recommendation approaches.

over the baseline *Recommender* system with respect to precision ($z = 2.25, p > 0.97$), while maintaining a statistically indistinguishable level of recall.[3] *Ripper* with hybrid features also attains a statistically significant improvement over *Ripper* without content features with respect to both precision ($z = 2.61, p > 0.99$) and recall ($z = 2.61, p > 0.998$).

Observations

Our results indicate that an inductive approach to learning how to recommend can perform reasonably well when compared to social-filtering methods, evaluated on the same data. We have also shown that by formulating recommendation as a problem in classification, we are able to combine meaningfully information from multiple sources, from ratings to content.

At equal levels of recall, our evaluation criteria would favor results with higher precision. Our results using hybrid features show that even with high precision, we also have a slight edge over recall as well.

We can comment on our features in terms of their effects on recall and precision. When we try to improve recall we are trying to be more inclusive — to add more items in our pot at the expense of unwanted items. On the flip side, when we improve precision, we are being more selective about those items we add. Features like *users who like comedies* help to increase recall. They are a generalization of simple collaborative features like *users who liked movie X*. Features like *comedies liked by user* have the reverse effect. They are a specialization of the collaborative feature, *movies liked by user*, and thereby focus our attention on a subset of a larger space of examples and increase precision.

Related Work

We have already described previous work on recommendation in our discussion of the *Recommender* system. There has also been work which explored the use of content features in selecting movies, in the context of another system designed on social-filtering principles. This previous study compared *clique-based* and *feature-based* models for movie selection (Karunanithi & Alspector 1996). A clique is a set of users whose movie ratings are similar, comparable to the set of recommenders in (Hill, Stead, Rosenstein & Furnas 1995). Those members of the clique who have rated a movie that the user has not seen predict a rating for that movie. Clique formation is dependent upon two parameters. The first is a correlation threshold which is the minimum correlation necessary to become a member of another user's clique. The second is a size threshold which defines a lower limit on the number of movies that a user must see and rate to become a of that clique. In their implementation, the authors set the size parameter to a constant value of 10 and set the correlation threshold such that the number of users in the clique is held at a constant 40. After a clique is formed, a movie rating is estimated by calculating the arithmetic mean of the ratings of the members of the clique. This mean serves as the predicted rating for the user. The authors also outline a general algorithm for a feature-based approach to recommendation:

1. Given a collection of rated movies, extract features for those movies.
2. Build a model for the user where the features serve as input and the ratings as output.
3. For every new movie not seen by the user, estimate the rating based on the features of the movie.

They used a neural-network model which associated these features (inputs to the model) with movie ratings (outputs of the model).

In this study, the authors isolated six features describing movies (not necessarily gathered from the IMDb): MPAA ratings, Category (genre), Maltin (critic's) rating, Academy Award, Length of movie, and Origin (related to the country of origin). They justified their choice of features on the grounds that they wanted to start with as small a set of features as possible, and that they found these features easiest to encode for their model.

The category and MPAA ratings were first fed into hidden units. Unlike the other features, which were nominal valued, these two features had a 1-of-N unary encoding. In other words, the feature is encoded as a N-bit vector where each bit represents one of the feature's possible values. (Only one bit corresponding to the feature's value in the example is set.) Although this representation is suited for their model and allows the feature to take multiple values, it is limited to the extent that all the values need to be enumerated at the outset.

In our case, the majority of features, content as well as collaborative, turned out to be set-valued. Set-valued features are more flexible than the 1-of-N unary features. These values can grow over time and need not be predetermined. Computationally, set-valued features are also much more efficient to work with than the corresponding 1-of-N encoding, particularly in cases for which N is large.

In the feature-based study, the authors found that by using features, in most cases, they outperformed a

---

[3] More precisely, one can be highly confident that there is no practically important loss in recall relative to the baseline; with confidence 95%, the recall rate for *Ripper* with hybrid features is at least 32.8%.

human critic but almost consistently did worse than the clique method. Our initial results with content features supported these findings. However, we also demonstrated that content information can lead to improved recommendations, if encoded in an appropriate manner.

Fab (Balabanovic & Shoham 1997) is a system which tackles both issues of content-based filtering and social-filtering. In the *Fab* system, content information is maintained by two types of agents: *user agents* associated with individuals and *collection agents* associated with sets of documents. Each collection agent represents a different topic of interest. Each of these agent-types maintains its own profiles, consisting of terms extracted from documents, and uses these profiles to filter new documents. These profiles are reinforced over time with user feedback, in the form of ratings, for new documents. In so doing, the goal is to evolve the agents to better serve the interests of the user and the larger community of users (who receive documents from the collection agents). There are some key differences in our approach. Ours is not an agent-based framework. We do not have access to topics of interest information, which in Fab, were collected from the users. We also do not use ratings as relevance feedback for updating profile information. Since we are not dealing with documents, we do not employ IR techniques for feature extraction.

Another well known social-filtering system is *Firefly*. *Firefly*, which has since expanded beyond the domain of music recommendation, is a descendant of *Ringo* (Shardanand & Maes 1995), a music recommendation system. *Ringo* presents the user with a list of artists and albums to rate. This system maintains this information on behalf of every user, in the form of a user profile. The profile is a record of the user's likes and dislikes and is updated over time as the user submits new ratings. The profile is used to compare an individual user with others who share similar tastes. During similarity assessment, the system selects profiles of other users with the highest correlation with an individual user. In the *Ringo* system, two of the metrics used to determine similarity are *mean-squared difference* and the *Pearson-R measure*. In the first case, *Ringo* makes predictions by thresholding with respect to how dissimilar two profiles are based on their mean-squared difference. Then, it computes a weighted average of the ratings provided by the most similar users. In the second case, *Ringo* makes predictions by using Pearson-R coefficients as weights in a weighted-average of other users' ratings.

Final Remarks

In this paper, we have presented an inductive approach to recommendation. This approach has been evaluated via experiments on a large, realistic set of ratings. One advantage of the inductive approach, relative to other social-filtering methods, is that it is far more flexible; in particular it is possible encode collaborative and content information as part of the problem representation, without making any algorithmic modifications. Exploiting this flexibility, we have evaluated a number of representations for recommendation, including two types of representations that make use of content features. One of these representations, based on hybrid features, significantly improves performance over the purely collaborative approach. We have thus begun to realize the impact of multiple information sources, including sources that exploit a limited amount of content. We believe that this work provides a basis for further work in this area, particularly in harnessing other types of information content.

References

Balabanovic, M.; and Shoham Y. 1997. Content-Based, Collaborative Recommendation. *Communications of the ACM* Vol. 40, No. 3. March, 1997.

Cohen, W. 1995. Fast Effective Rule Induction. In *Proceedings of the Twelfth Conference on Machine Learning*. Lake Taho, California.

Cohen, W. 1996. Learning Trees and Rules with Set-valued Features. In *Proceedings of the Thirteenth National Conference on Artificial Intelligence*.

Hill, W.;Stead, L.;Rosenstein, M.; and Furnas, G. 1995. Recommending and Evaluating Choices in a Virtual Community of Use. In *Proceedings of the CHI-95 Conference*. Denver, CO.

Karunanithi, N.; and Alspector, J. 1996. Feature-Based and Clique-Based User Models for Movie Selection. In *Proceedings of the Fifth International Conference on User Modeling*. Kailua-Kona, HI.

Lang, K. 1995. NewsWeeder: Learning to filter netnews. In *Machine Learning: Proceedings of the Twelfth International Conference*. Lake Taho, California: Morgan Kaufmann.

Lewis, D. 1991. Evaluating Text Categorization. In *Proceedings of the Speech and Natural Language Workshop*. Asilomar, CA.

Mendenhall, W.; Scheaffer, R.; and Wackerly, D., eds. 1981. *Mathematical Statistics with Applications*. Duxbury Press, second edition.

Moore, D. 1985. *Statistics: concepts and controversies*. W. H. Freeman.

Pazzani, M.; Muramatsu, J.; and Billsus, D. 1996. Syskill & Webert: identifying interesting web sites. In *Proceedings of the Thirteenth National Conference on Artificial Intelligence*.

Shardanand, U.; and Maes, P. 1995. Social Information Filtering: Algorithms for Automating "Word of Mouth". In *Proceedings of the CHI-95 Conference*. Denver, CO.

Learning to Predict User Operations for Adaptive Scheduling

Melinda T. Gervasio and Wayne Iba and Pat Langley
Institute for the Study of Learning and Expertise
2164 Staunton Court, Palo Alto, California 94306
{gervasio,iba,langley}@isle.org

Abstract

Mixed-initiative systems present the challenge of finding an effective level of interaction between humans and computers. Machine learning presents a promising approach to this problem in the form of systems that automatically adapt their behavior to accommodate different users. In this paper, we present an empirical study of learning user models in an adaptive assistant for crisis scheduling. We describe the problem domain and the scheduling assistant, then present an initial formulation of the adaptive assistant's learning task and the results of a baseline study. After this, we report the results of three subsequent experiments that investigate the effects of problem reformulation and representation augmentation. The results suggest that problem reformulation leads to significantly better accuracy without sacrificing the usefulness of the learned behavior. The studies also raise several interesting issues in adaptive assistance for scheduling.

Introduction

In recent years, there has been a surging interest in the mixed-initiative paradigm where multiple agents—specifically humans and software systems—share control by partitioning the responsibilities in problem solving. This trend holds not only for the ubiquitous applications on the Web, but also in domains such as planning and scheduling where the traditional AI approach has involved autonomous systems. Ideally, a mixed-initiative system benefits from the individual strengths of its constituents—the expertise of the human user and the computational power of the computer. For this synergy to occur, however, the division of responsibilities must be mutually beneficial and the two participants must be able to work together effectively. Meeting these requirements with a single, static system will be difficult because different users will have different abilities and preferences. In addition, as software systems become more powerful, they may outgrow the user's ability to communicate tasks or requests that best take advantage of those abilities. Machine learning can help address these problems by providing adaptive systems that automatically tailor their behavior to different users.

In this paper, we present an empirical study of learning user models in an adaptive scheduling assistant. We begin by describing our application, a synthetic domain that involves responding to hazardous materials incidents. We also describe INCA, the interactive assistant we are developing for this domain. Traces of user interactions with INCA provided the data for our learning experiments. We formulate the scheduling assistant's task of predicting user operations as a classification problem, and we discuss the results of a baseline study, which showed some benefit from learning but also left room for improvement. The three subsequent experiments investigate the effects of problem representation and formulation on performance. Their results show that problem reformulation can lead to much better adaptation without sacrificing the usefulness of the learned concepts. The experiments raised a number of issues, which we consider in our closing discussion of related and future work.

Scheduling for Crisis Response

A dominant theme in crisis response is *urgency*—an agent is compelled to act to avert an undesirable situation in a limited amount of time. Finding an efficient level of interaction between the human user and the computer is thus particularly important. Our response to urgency relies on machine learning to acquire user models to facilitate this interaction. To illustrate our ideas and to lay the groundwork for the experiments in this paper, we will discuss them in the context of a synthetic hazardous materials domain (HAZMAT) and the INteractive Crisis Assistant (INCA) that we developed for this domain. INCA provides assistance for both planning and scheduling, but we will focus on the scheduling task here.

HAZMAT Response Using INCA

In developing the synthetic HAZMAT domain, we consulted the 1996 North American Emergency Response Guidebook (Transport Canada et al., 1996), a handbook for first responders to hazardous materials inci-

Copyright © 1998, American Association for Artificial Intelligence (www.aaai.org). All rights reserved.

dents. A HAZMAT problem consists of a spill and possibly a fire involving one of 50 types of hazardous material. There are 4000 classes of HAZMAT incidents, varying in the type and amount of material involved, the location of the incident, and the characteristics of the spill and any fire. Incidents also have associated fire and health hazards that, respectively, characterize the probability of a fire and the danger to people's health.

There are 49 types of actions and 25 types of resources available for responding to a HAZMAT incident. In any given problem, only a subset of the actions will be applicable, as indicated in the Guidebook. Each action addresses particular aspects of a HAZMAT problem and requires some minimum set of resources. The specific resources available, and their associated capacity and quantity constraints, vary with every problem.

INCA is an interactive system that provides planning and scheduling assistance for HAZMAT response. In the planning phase, the user interacts with INCA to choose the *schedulable* actions, a subset of the applicable actions to the problem. The input to the scheduling phase is this set of schedulable actions, the set of available resources, and an initial (possibly empty) candidate schedule provided by INCA.

In a departure from traditional scheduling, the task is to choose some *subset* of the schedulable actions and to assign them to resources. Moreover, actions may be allocated a variable number of resources and arbitrary duration. Consider the action of extinguishing a fire with a hose. Allocating more resources (firefighters, hoses, hydrants, etc.) to the action, as well as simultaneously scheduling other extinguishment actions (e.g., extinguish with dry sand), will put out the fire more quickly. This interdependence among actions, resources, and effects makes it difficult to completely determine resource requirements and action durations prior to scheduling. With effective heuristics being difficult to engineer for the resulting underconstrained problem, machine learning becomes even more attractive.

Scheduling an action involves four decisions: the number of resources to allocate to the action, the specific resources to allocate, the start time, and the duration. Scheduling in INCA takes place in a repair space, where the operators include adding and removing actions from the schedule as well as modifying parameters of scheduled actions. Specifically, the user interacts with INCA through a graphical interface that provides the user with five scheduling operators: add a new action, remove an action, shift the start time of an action, change the duration of an action, and switch an action from one resource to another.

The final schedule must be *feasible*—that is, it must not violate any capacity or quantity constraints. A resource is *oversubscribed* if there is any time at which the number of simultaneously scheduled actions on that resource exceeds its capacity. Similarly, a resource is *overallocated* if the actions scheduled on it consume more than the available resource quantity. An *infeasibly scheduled* action is one that participates in the oversubscription or overallocation of any resource. Using the five available operators, the user modifies the schedule until it is feasible and he considers it acceptable.

INCA currently assists the user in scheduling by providing an initial candidate schedule retrieved from a case library, by suggesting heuristically determined default values for resources, durations and start times, and by checking the feasibility of schedules. By integrating learning into INCA, we hope to improve its assistant capabilities by letting it adapt its behavior to individual users.

Acquiring and Applying User Models

A user will have personal beliefs about what actions are appropriate for a problem, what actions are more important than others, and what actions should be performed first. These preferences are reflected by the operators that the user selects and their results—what actions are included and how they are ordered in the schedule, how resources are allocated to different actions, and how different conflicts are resolved. The goal of learning in INCA is to extract such information from traces of its interactions with the user and to use this information to adapt its behavior accordingly. For example, INCA might use this preference information to suggest resources, durations, and start times that are similar to the user's previous choices when adding the action. Or it might apply scheduling operators based on this information to specifically tailor initial candidate schedules. By making suggestions that the user is more likely to accept, INCA can make the HAZMAT response process more efficient, thereby directly addressing the urgency aspect of crisis response.

As our first step in integrating learning into INCA, we focused on the prediction of scheduling operations. Specifically, INCA's user modeling task was: Given a particular scheduling state—as characterized by the problem, available resources, schedulable actions, and current schedule—predict the user's next scheduling operation. This can be translated into a standard classification task, with the class being the scheduling operation and the instance being the scheduling state for which the prediction is being made.

Baseline Study: Effects of Learning

We extracted the data for our learning experiments from the individual traces of two users, each interacting with INCA over 140 HAZMAT problems. Each scheduling operation performed while solving a problem corresponds to a training or test instance. From traces of the first and second users, we extracted 935 examples (data set A) and 1049 examples (data set B) respectively.

Nearly all fielded applications of machine learning (Langley & Simon, 1995) rely on attribute-value representations and standard supervised induction methods, so we decided to investigate the feasibility of such an approach here. This has the advantage of either avoiding the cost of engineering a special-purpose approach

Table 1: Percentage accuracy in predicting user operations during scheduling.

	A	B
test on same user	22.15 ± 2.22	26.87 ± 2.03
test on other user	18.70 ± 0.58	18.67 ± 0.58

Table 2: Percentage accuracy in predicting user operations after various problem reformulations.

	A	B
temporal attributes	18.81 ± 1.73	26.18 ± 1.68
abstracted	42.30 ± 3.15	36.63 ± 2.06
alternative classes	59.33 ± 2.39	64.30 ± 2.53
no illegal predictions	78.24 ± 1.66	76.61 ± 1.73

or justifying the need for more complex representations and algorithms.

For the baseline study, we used 86 attributes to describe the scheduling state. We represented the problem using 12 nominal attributes directly corresponding to the material, spill, fire, and hazard features of the HAZ-MAT problem. We represented the resources with 25 Boolean features, one for each resource type, with the value denoting whether there is at least one resource of that type available. Finally, we represented the schedulable set of actions and the schedule with 49 attributes corresponding to the 49 possible actions. These attributes had four possible values: not schedulable, unscheduled, feasibly scheduled, or infeasibly scheduled.

There are several levels at which the prediction task can be formulated. At the highest level is the prediction of a general scheduling operator such as ADD *any* action. At the lowest level is the prediction of a specific instantiation of a scheduling operator such as ADD the absorb-with-dry-sand action on crew members #1 and #4 and dry sand #2 starting at time 21 for a duration of 10 time units. For the baseline study, we chose an intermediate level, requiring the specification of a particular action but not specific resources or amounts. We also combined the remove action, change duration, shift action, and switch resource operators into a single REPAIR operator. This resulted in ADD and REPAIR operations for each of the 49 actions, for a total of 98 different classes.

We can thus state the learning task as: Given a set of training examples, learn a classifier that makes correct predictions on new examples. Preliminary studies with supervised learning algorithms from the repository maintained by the Machine Learning Group at the University of Texas at Austin revealed ID3 (Quinlan, 1986) to be the most promising, so we chose to use this in our formal experiments.[1]

We had two hypotheses for the baseline experiment. The first was that learning would improve accuracy, and the second was that greater gains would result if we trained and tested on data from the same user than if we trained on data from one user and tested on data from another. The aim of learning is to model a specific user, so we expected some benefit from learning on another user but not as much as learning from the same user.

We tested these hypotheses by first running ten trials on each user's data set, with each trial using 800 randomly chosen examples for training and the rest for testing. We then ran another ten trials, this time using the entire other user's data set for testing. Table 1 shows the results for each data set, averaged over the ten runs for each condition (95% confidence intervals). The results suppport both our hypotheses: under each condition, the resulting accuracies were notably better than guessing randomly (1.02%) and guessing the most frequent class (8.57%), with the performance from training and testing on data from the same user being significantly better than that from training on one user and testing on another (paired t test, $p < 0.01$).

Improving Accuracy Through Problem Reformulation

The baseline study showed that learning improved performance but, even in the best case (26.87% for data set B, within-user test), there were more than twice as many misclassifications as correct classifications. This calls into question the utility of the predictions in the context of a scheduling assistant. Our analysis of the results suggested our formulation of the problem as a prime suspect for this poor performance. We identified three ways to reformulate the problem: adding contextual temporal information, abstracting the class labels, and modifying the prediction task. We now describe the three experimental studies we conducted to test whether these problem reformulations would increase predictive accuracy. We also propose a modification to the prediction element that promises substantial performance improvement.

Adding Temporal Information

In the first experiment, we wanted to determine the effects of augmenting the problem representation with information about the other operators used in solving the problem. Our statement of the performance task requires INCA to predict the user's *immediate* next operation. This is likely to depend on the other operators the user selects within the same problem, particularly the most recent operators selected, but the base problem representation included no such explicit contextual information.

Our hypothesis in this experiment was that adding contextual temporal information would improve accuracy. To test this hypothesis, we extended the instance representation with five attributes to represent the five most recent operations the user performed prior to the

---
[1] The repository resides at www.cs.utexas.edu/users/ml. We obtained similar results with the C4.5 system.

Table 3: Total percentage of prediction errors and percentage due to illegal predictions.

	A		B	
	total	illegal	total	illegal
base condition	77.85	19.78	73.13	14.94
temporal attributes	81.18	41.11	73.82	36.95

operation associated with that instance.[2] We then ran ten trials on each data set using the same training and test splits as in the baseline study.

Table 2 and Figure 1 present the results (95% confidence intervals) from the problem reformulation experiments. The results from the first experiment (Table 2, temporal attributes) did not support our hypothesis: temporal information did not affect accuracy. One explanation lies in the number of errors that involved predicting an illegal operation. Incorrect predictions may be divided into two types: *legal* predictions that correspond to operations that can be performed in the scheduling state and *illegal* operations that cannot. Specifically, an ADD-*action* operation is illegal if the *action* is already in the schedule or it is not in the schedulable set; a REPAIR-*action* operation is illegal if the *action* is not in the schedule. Table 3 shows that the percentage of examples that were misclassified into illegal operations increased with the introduction of the temporal attributes to account for over half of all the misclassifications. These results reveal that the problem representation is not sufficiently balancing the necessary contextual and legality information to let the system make good, legal predictions. They also suggest additional analysis and experimentation on problem representation to shed light on this issue.

Class Abstraction

In the second experiment, we wanted to investigate the utility of simplifying the problem via class abstraction. As stated earlier, the prediction task can be formulated at different levels, and for the baseline study we chose an intermediate level requiring the specification of an ADD or REPAIR on a particular action but not the specification of particular resources or amounts.

Our hypothesis in the second experiment was that performance would improve on a more abstract prediction task. To test this hypothesis, we chose to abstract one level to require predicting an ADD/REPAIR operation on a class of actions rather than on individual actions. For example, the abstract ADD "extinguish with hose" replaces the set of specific ADDs on actions such as "extinguish with hose using water from a hydrant" and "extinguish with hose using foam and a pumper". We felt this was a reasonable abstraction in that it makes few additional demands on the user,

---

[2] We tried adding one to five previous operations and found no significant differences.

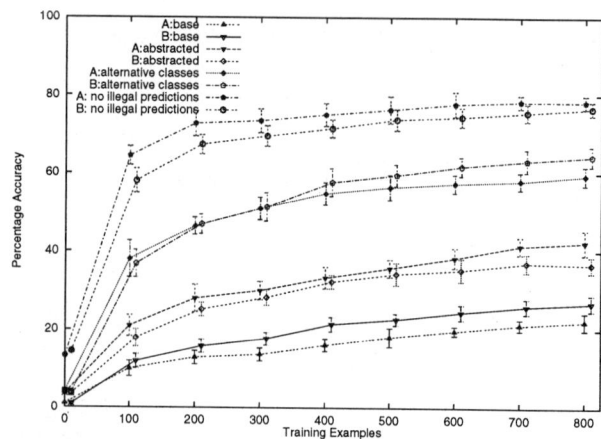

Figure 1: Learning curves for the various experimental conditions, showing the improvement due to successive problem reformulations.

who must only choose from a small set of corresponding more specific actions. Abstracting the problem in this manner reduced the original 98 classes into 28 abstract classes, and also increased the proportion of the most frequent class from 8.57% to 11.19%. We ran ten trials on each data set, using the same training and test splits as in the baseline study.

The results support our hypothesis: accuracy increased significantly (paired t test, $p < 0.001$) for both data sets with class abstraction (Table 2 and Figure 1, abstracted). This result may not be surprising since the abstraction results in a simpler prediction task. However, it raises the issue of determining an appropriate task level in mixed-initiative settings such as interactive scheduling. Formulating the prediction task at higher levels transfers more decision-making responsibility to the human user, but this is not undesirable if it leads to more effective interaction overall.

Redefining Correctness

In the third experiment, we wanted to investigate the effects of modifying the prediction task by allowing alternative class labels. The formulation of the learning problem as the problem of predicting the user's next operation was a natural fit to the data provided by the user traces. However, it is an unnecessarily difficult learning task in that it requires the system to predict a user's immediate next action. A user may arrive at the same schedule through different sequences of operations, many of which may be equally acceptable to the user. Thus, a more appropriate learning task might be to predict any one of the user's subsequent operations, subject to legality given the current state.

Our hypothesis in this experiment was that accuracy would improve under the redefined correctness criterion. To test this hypothesis, we first modified the original examples to include a set of alternative classes, consisting of all the subsequent operations the user invoked to solve the HAZMAT incident minus those that were illegal in the current state. We ran ten trials on each data set, again using the same training and test splits. Training proceeded as before but, during testing, we judged a prediction to be correct if it matched the instance's label or one of its alternative classes.

The results support our hypothesis: significantly greater accuracy (paired t test, $p < 0.001$) was achieved on the reformulated task (Table 2 and Figure 1, alternative classes). Again, the results might seem obvious since allowing alternative classes simplifies the prediction task. However, as stated earlier, this may in fact be a more appropriate task in that it may better capture what concerns users in the scheduling process.

Correcting for Illegal Operations

The observation that many errors involved illegal operations (Table 3) suggests another change to the prediction element. The revised system would check to determine if a given prediction is illegal and, if so, would move on to the next most likely prediction, continuing in this manner until it predicts a legal operation. Implementing this scheme is straightforward for some classifiers, like naive Bayes and nearest neighbor, which rank their predictions, but it is more complicated for decision trees.

We are still in the process of considering various approaches to implementing this filtering scheme. However, we can estimate the new accuracy by factoring out the existing illegal predictions. Let us assume that the learned predictor's accuracy will be the same on the illegal classifications as on the legal ones. Let a be the accuracy with abstraction, s be the gain from alternative classes, and i be the misclassifications that were illegal. The accuracy under this new scheme would be $a + s + \frac{a+s}{100}i$. This results in accuracies in the 75 to 80% range (Table 2 and Figure 1, no illegal predictions), which are much more promising than the baseline results.[3]

Related and Future Work

Previous work on learning for scheduling has focused on autonomous systems, with the aim of improving scheduling efficiency or schedule quality. For example, Gratch and Chien (1993) increased efficiency in a deep space network scheduler by acquiring effective domain-specific heuristics. Similarly, Eskey and Zweben (1990) increased scheduling efficiency in payload processing for the NASA space shuttle by acquiring rules to avoid chronic resource contention. Zhang and Dietterich (1995) used reinforcement learning on the same task, but to acquire heuristics that resulted in shorter schedules. Our framework for learning differs in its emphasis on acquiring user-specific performance criteria and, as a result, in its reliance on detailed traces of user decisions.

---

[3]For naive Bayes, we have obtained actual results that were as good or better than these estimates.

Some recent AI scheduling systems (e.g., Smith et al., 1996; Fukunaga et al., 1997) have mixed-initiative modes, but few incorporate learning or adaptation to different users. The same holds for AI crisis response systems such as O-Plan2 (Tate et al., 1994) and SOCAP (Bienkowski, 1996). An exception is CABINS (Miyashita & Sycara, 1995), an assistant for job-shop scheduling that learns user preferences on repair heuristics. Like INCA, CABINS acquires preferences from user traces and uses these to direct a repair-space search for a solution. CABINS differs in that it invokes a heuristic scheduler to generate an initial schedule and a case-based method to learn user preferences, whereas INCA uses a case-based method to retrieve an initial schedule and other learning techniques to acquire user preferences. We believe this approach provides a better fit to crisis domains, where case libraries can be built from standard operating procedures or the results of planning exercises.

Much work on personalization, particularly for computer-aided instruction, has focused on methods for constructing models of user behaviors that can then be used to classify users and modify system interaction accordingly (e.g., Sleeman & Smith, 1981; Clancey, 1979; Anderson & Reiser, 1985). Langley (1997) uses the term *adaptive user interfaces* to refer to systems like INCA that instead use machine learning to construct user models from interaction traces. Previous work in this area include Schlimmer and Hermens' (1993) interface for repetitive form filling; Dent et al.'s (1992) CAP, a calendar apprentice for scheduling appointments; and Pazzani et al.'s (1996) SYSKILL & WEBERT, a Web page recommendation service. Like INCA, these systems use their learned user models to tailor their behavior to individual users. The work described in this paper differs in its focus on an explicit evaluation of the factors affecting success.

A priority for future work involves fully integrating the learned predictors into INCA, which would let us directly evaluate our hypothesis that learning user preferences will produce more rapid HAZMAT response. This will also let us test our hypotheses about appropriate task formulations. Initially, we plan to use an offline setting, in which we train INCA on user traces, incorporate the learned model into the system, and then let the same user interact with INCA while measuring performance. Eventually, we plan to integrate learning in an online setting, where the system updates its user model during the course of its interactions. In such settings, it becomes particularly important that the system avoid making suggestions that are so unacceptable and distracting that the user would have been better off without assistance. One response, which we plan to explore in future work, is to incorporate confidence measures into system predictions to prevent it from making suggestions until they exceed some minimum threshold.

Another important area for future work is task reformulation. The results on abstraction suggest that we look for simple learning problems that would benefit from standard induction algorithms. One approach would be to divide the prediction task into a set of smaller tasks—for example, predicting specific resources, durations, and start times once an action has already been selected for scheduling; or proceeding with prediction hierarchically through more and more specific operations. The results on alternative classes suggest that we reevaluate our task definition in light of the kinds of suggestions (i.e., system predictions) the user will find helpful. We are currently exploring alternative formulations of the learning task along these lines. We also expect to see greater benefits from combinations of successful reformulations.

We also need to revisit our representational options. The results on adding temporal attributes indicate that there may be important information that is currently not being captured. The attribute-value scheme is simple but it does not let us easily represent specific schedules (i.e., what actions use what resources over what time intervals) or the relationship between what actions address what problem features. This information, which may play a role in user preferences, can be more easily captured in a relational representation, which we plan to investigate in future versions of INCA.

Concluding Remarks

In this paper, we reviewed INCA, an adaptive assistant for crisis scheduling, and presented empirical studies of learning user models aimed at improving the system's behavior. We formulated the task of the scheduling assistant as predicting the user's action in response to a particular problem, set of resources, and current schedule. We set out to explore the limits of simple problem representations and established learning algorithms, and our initial study revealed some benefits from learning, but also left room for improvement.

Subsequent experiments demonstrated that abstractions of the learning task, as well as reformulations of the prediction task, result in substantially better performance without sacrificing, and possibly even improving, the usefulness of the learned behavior. These findings suggest that adaptive interfaces like INCA, which learn models of user preferences, constitute a promising approach to mixed-initiative scheduling that deserves fuller exploration in future research.

Acknowledgments. This research was supported by the Office of Naval Research under Grant N000014-96-1-1221. We would also like to thank Mark Maloof for his helpful comments on the paper, and the Organizational Dynamics Center group at Stanford University for many interesting discussions on crisis response.

References

Anderson, J. R. and Reiser, B. J. 1985. The LISP Tutor. *Byte* 10:159–175.

Bienkowski, M. 1996. SOCAP: System for Operations Crisis Action Planning. In *Advanced Planning Technology*, Tate, A., ed., 70–76. Menlo Park: AAAI Press.

Clancey, W. J. 1979. Dialogue Management for Rule-Based Tutorials. In *Proceedings of the Sixth International Joint Conference on Artificial Intelligence*.

Dent, L.; Boticario, J.; McDermott, J.; Mitchell, T.; and Zaborowski, D. 1992. A Personal Learning Apprentice. In *Proceedings of the Tenth National Conference on Artificial Intelligence*, 96–103.

Eskey, M., and Zweben, M. 1990. Learning Search Control for Constraint-Based Scheduling In *Proceedings of the Eighth National Conference on Artificial Intelligence*, 908–915.

Fukunaga, A.; Rabideau, G.; Chien, S.; and Yan, D. 1997 Toward an Application Framework for Automated Planning and Scheduling. In *Proceedings of the 1997 International Symposium on Artificial Intelligence, Robotics and Automation for Space*. Tokyo, Japan.

Gratch, J., and Chien, S. 1993. Learning Effective Control Strategies for Deep-Space Network Scheduling. In *Proceedings of the Tenth International Conference on Machine Learning*, 135–142.

Langley, P., and Simon, H. A. 1995. Applications of Machine Learning and Rule Induction. *Communications of the ACM* 38:55–64.

Langley, P. 1997. Machine Learning for Adaptive User Interfaces. In *Proceedings of the Twenty-First German Annual Conference on Artificial Intelligence*, 53–62.

Miyashita, K. and Sycara, K. 1995. CABINS: A Framework of Knowledge Acquisition and Iterative Revision for Schedule Improvement and Reactive Repair. *Artificial Intelligence* 76: 337–426.

Pazzani, M.; Muramatsu, J.; and Billsus, D. 1996. SYSKILL & WEBERT: Identifying Interesting Web Sites. In *Proceedings of the Thirteenth National Conference on Artificial Intelligence*, 54–61.

Quinlan, R. 1986. Induction of Decision Trees. *Machine Learning* 1:81–106.

Sleeman, D. H. and Smith, M. J. 1981. Modelling Pupil's Problem Solving. *Artificial Intelligence* 16:171–187.

Smith, S.; Lassila, O.; and Becker, M. 1996. Configurable, Mixed-Initiative Systems for Planning and Scheduling. In *Advanced Planning Technology*, Tate, A., ed., 235–241. Menlo Park: AAAI Press.

Tate, A., Drabble, B., and Kirby, R. B. 1994. O-Plan2: an Open Architecture for Command Planning and Control. In *Intelligent Scheduling*, Zweben, M. and Fox, M. S., eds. San Francisco: Morgan Kaufmann.

Transport Canada, the U.S. Department of Transportation, and the Secretariat of Communications and Transportation of Mexico. *1996 North American Emergency Response Guidebook*.

Zhang, W. and Dietterich, T. 1995. A Reinforcement Learning Approach to Job-shop Scheduling. In *Proceedings of the Fourteenth International Conference on Artificial Intelligence*.

Adaptive Web Sites: Automatically Synthesizing Web Pages

Mike Perkowitz   Oren Etzioni[*]

Department of Computer Science and Engineering, Box 352350
University of Washington, Seattle, WA 98195
{map, etzioni}@cs.washington.edu
(206) 616-1845   Fax: (206) 543-2969
Content Areas: data mining, machine learning, applications, user interfaces

Abstract

The creation of a complex web site is a thorny problem in user interface design. In IJCAI '97, we challenged the AI community to address this problem by creating *adaptive web sites*: sites that automatically improve their organization and presentation by mining visitor access data collected in Web server logs. In this paper we introduce our own approach to this broad challenge. Specifically, we investigate the problem of *index page synthesis* — the automatic creation of pages that facilitate a visitor's navigation of a Web site.

First, we formalize this problem as a clustering problem and introduce a novel approach to clustering, which we call *cluster mining*: Instead of attempting to partition the entire data space into disjoint clusters, we search for a small number of cohesive (and possibly overlapping) clusters. Next, we present PageGather, a cluster mining algorithm that takes Web server logs as input and outputs the contents of candidate index pages. Finally, we show experimentally that PageGather is both faster (by a factor of three) and more effective than traditional clustering algorithms on this task. Our experiment relies on access logs collected over a month from an actual web site.

Adaptive Web Sites

Designing a rich web site so that it readily yields its information can be tricky. The problem of good web design is compounded by several factors. First, different visitors have distinct goals. Second, the same visitor may seek different information at different times. Third, many sites outgrow their original design, accumulating links and pages in unlikely places. Fourth, a site may be designed for a particular kind of use, but be used in many different ways in practice; the designer's *a priori* expectations may be violated. Too often web site designs are fossils cast in HTML, while web navigation is dynamic, time-dependent, and idiosyncratic. In (Perkowitz & Etzioni 1997a), we challenged the AI community to address this problem by creating **adaptive web sites:** *web sites that automatically improve their organization and presentation by learning from visitor access patterns*. In this paper we report on our own progress.

Sites may be adaptive in two basic ways. *Customization* is adapting the site's presentation to the needs of individual visitors, based on information about those individuals. In order to specialize itself to individual users, the site must maintain multiple copies of itself and gather quite a bit of information from users. Providing such information to the site can be time-consuming and may be an invasion of privacy. *Optimization* is improving the site's structure based on interactions with all visitors. Instead of making changes for each individual, the site learns from numerous past visitors to make the site easier to use for all, including those who have never used it before.

While previous work has focused on customizing web sites, we chose to investigate web site optimization through the automatic synthesis of index pages. In the next section, we discuss our general approach and present the *index page synthesis problem*. We then present our technique, which we call cluster mining, and its instantiation in the PageGather algorithm; PageGather solves the subproblem of automatically synthesizing the set of links that comprises an index page. Following, we present the results of experiments run using our implemented system. Finally, we discuss related work and future directions.

The Index Page Synthesis Problem

Our approach to adaptive web sites is motivated by four goals: (1) avoiding additional work for visitors (e.g. filling out questionnaires); (2) making the web site easier to use for everyone, not just specific individuals; (3) using web sites as they are, without relying on meta-information not currently available (e.g., XML annotations); and (4) protecting the site's original design from destructive changes. When creating a web site, a human meticulously designs the look and feel of the site, the structure of the information, and the kinds of interactions available. When making automatic changes to such a site, we wish to avoid damaging the site.

Our approach, therefore, is to apply only *nondestructive transformations*: changes to the site that leave ex-

---

[*]Copyright (c) 1998, American Association for Artificial Intelligence (www.aaai.org). All rights reserved.

isting structure intact. We may add links but not remove them, create pages but not destroy them, add new structures but not scramble existing ones. Such transformations may include highlighting links, *promoting* links to the front page, cross-linking related pages, and creating new pages of related links. Based on the access log, the site decides when and where to perform these transformations. In (Perkowitz & Etzioni 1997b), we sketched several such transformations. In this paper, we focus on a single, novel transformation: the creation of new index pages – pages consisting of links to pages at the site relating to a particular topic. We illustrate this transformation with a simple real-world example.

The *Music Machines* web site contains information about various kinds of electronic musical equipment (see http://www.hyperreal.org/music/machines/). The information is primarily grouped by manufacturer. For each manufacturer, there may be multiple entries for the different instrument models available — keyboards, electric guitars, amplifiers, etc. For each model, there may be pictures, reviews, user manuals, and audio samples of how the instrument sounds. We might notice that, when exploring the site, visitors comparing electric guitars from many different manufacturers tend to download the audio samples of each guitar. A comprehensive page of "Electric Guitar Audio Samples" would facilitate this comparison; this is the kind of page we would like our system to generate automatically.

Page synthesis is the automatic creation of web pages. An *index page* is a page consisting of links to a set of pages that cover a particular topic (e.g., electric guitars). Given this terminology we define the **index page synthesis problem**: given a web site and a visitor access log, create new index pages containing collections of links to related but currently unlinked pages. A web site is restricted to a collection of HTML documents residing at a single server — we are not yet able to handle dynamically-generated pages or multiple servers. An access log is a document containing one entry for each request answered by the web server. Each request lists at least the origin (IP address) of the request, the URL requested, and the time of the request. *Related but unlinked* pages are pages that share a common topic but are not currently linked at the site; two pages are considered linked if there exists a link from one to the other or if there exists a page that links to both of them.

In synthesizing a new index page, we must solve several subproblems.

1. **What are the contents of the index page?**
2. How are the contents ordered?
3. What is the title of the page?
4. How are the hyperlinks on the page labeled?
5. Is the page consistent with the site's overall graphical style?
6. Is it appropriate to add the page the site? If so, where?

In this paper, we focus on the first subproblem—generating the *contents* of the new web page. The remaining subproblems are topics for future work. We note that some subproblems, particularly the last one, are quite difficult and may be solved in collaboration with the human webmaster.

Rather than attempting to understand the content of every page at our site and to figure out which are related, our approach is based on the analysis of each "visit". We define a *visit* to be an ordered sequence of pages accessed by a single visitor in a single session. We make the **visit-coherence assumption**: *the pages a user visits during one interaction with the site tend to be conceptually related.* We do not assume that *all* pages in a single visit are related. After all, the information we glean from individual visits is noisy; for example, a visitor may pursue multiple distinct tasks in a single visit. To overcome noise, we accumulate statistics over many visits by numerous users and search for overall trends.

The PageGather Algorithm

In this section, we present a novel approach to clustering, called *cluster mining*, that was motivated by our task; in addition, we introduce *PageGather* — the first index page-contents synthesis algorithm. Given a large access log, our task is to find collections of pages that tend to co-occur in visits. Clustering (see (Voorhees 1986; Rasmussen 1992; Willet 1988)) is a natural technique for this task. In clustering, documents are represented in an N-dimensional space (for example, as word vectors). Roughly, a cluster is a collection of documents close to each other and relatively distant from other clusters. Standard clustering algorithms *partition* the documents into a set of mutually exclusive clusters.

Cluster *mining* is a variation on traditional clustering that is well suited for our task. Instead of attempting to partition the entire space of documents, we try to find a small number of high quality clusters. Furthermore, whereas traditional clustering is concerned with placing each document in exactly one cluster, cluster mining may place a single document in multiple overlapping clusters. The relationship between traditional clustering and cluster mining is parallel to that between classification and data mining as described in (Segal 1996). Segal contrasts mining "nuggets" — finding high-accuracy rules that capture patterns in the data — with traditional classification — classifying *all* examples as positive or negative — and shows that traditional classification algorithms do not make the best mining algorithms.

The *PageGather algorithm* uses cluster mining to find collections of related pages at a web site, relying on the visit-coherence assumption. In essence, PageGather takes a web server access log as input and maps it into a form ready for clustering; it then applies cluster mining to the data and produces candidate index-page contents as output. The algorithm has four basic steps:

1. Process the access log into visits.
2. Compute the co-occurrence frequencies between pages and create a similarity matrix.
3. Create the graph corresponding to the matrix, and find cliques (or connected components) in the graph.
4. For each cluster found, create a web page consisting of links to the documents in the cluster.

We discuss each step in turn.

1. Process the access log into visits. As defined above, a visit is an ordered sequence of pages accessed by a single user in a single session. An access log, however, is a sequence of *hits*, or requests made to the web server. Each request typically includes the time of the request, the URL requested, and the machine from which the request originated. For our purposes, however, we need to be able to view the log as containing a number of discrete visits. We first assume that each originating machine corresponds to a single visitor.[1] A series of hits in a day's log from one visitor, ordered by their time-stamps, corresponds to a single session for that visitor. Furthermore, we make sure that we log every access to every page by disabling caching — every page contains a header saying that it expires immediately; browsers will therefore load a new copy every time a user views that page.

2. Compute the co-occurrence frequencies between pages and create a similarity matrix. For each pair of pages P_1 and P_2, we compute $P(P_1|P_2)$, the probability of a visitor visiting P_1 if she has already visited P_2 and $P(P_2|P_1)$, the probability of a visitor visiting P_2 if she has already visited P_1. The co-occurrence frequency between P_1 and P_2 is the minimum of these values.

We use the minimum of the two conditional probabilities to avoid mistaking an asymmetrical relationship for a true case of similarity. For example, a popular page P_1 might be on the most common path to a more obscure page P_2. In such a case $P(P_1|P_2)$ will be high, perhaps leading us to think the pages similar. However, $P(P_2|P_1)$ could be quite low, as P_1 is on the path to many pages and P_2 is relatively obscure.

As stated above, our goal is to find clusters of related *but currently unlinked* pages. Therefore, we wish to avoid finding clusters of pages that are already linked together. We prevent this by setting the matrix cell for two pages to zero if they are already linked in the site. Essentially, we create a matrix corresponding to existing connections and subtract it from the similarity matrix created from the log.

A graph corresponding to the similarity matrix would be completely (or almost completely) connected. In order to reduce noise, we apply a threshold and remove edges corresponding to low co-occurrence frequency. We treat all remaining arcs as being of equivalent strength.[2] By creating a sparse graph, we can use graph algorithms to find clusters, which turn out to be faster than traditional clustering methods.

3. Create the graph corresponding to the matrix, and find cliques (or connected components) in the graph. We create a graph in which each page is a node and each nonzero cell in the matrix is an arc. In this graph, a cluster corresponds to a set of nodes whose members are directly connected with arcs. A clique – a subgraph in which every pair of nodes has an edge between them – is a cluster in which every pair of pages co-occurs often. A connected component – a subgraph in which every pair of nodes has a path of edges between them – is a cluster in which every node is similar to at least one other node in the cluster. While cliques form more coherent clusters, connected components are larger, faster to compute, and easier to find.

4. For each cluster found, create a web page consisting of links to the documents in the cluster. Our research so far has focused on generating the content of index pages — the set of links — rather than the other aspects of the problem. We therefore use simple solutions which will be improved in future work. Page titles are generated by the human webmaster. Pages are linked into the site at one particular location as part of a "helpful tour guide" metaphor. Links on pages are ordered alphabetically by their titles. Page layouts are based on a template defined for all pages at the site.

What is the running time of the PageGather algorithm? Let L be the number of hits in the log, N the number of pages at the site, E be the number of edges in our graph, and C be the largest cluster we wish to find.[3] In step (1), we must group the hits by their originating machine. We do this by sorting hits by origin and time, so step (1) requires $O(L \log L)$ time. In step (2), we must create a matrix of size $O(N^2)$ and examine each cell in the matrix. Step (2) is therefore $O(N^2)$. In step (3) we may look for either cliques or connected components. In general, finding maximal cliques in a graph is NP-complete. However, since we search for cliques whose size is bounded by a constant C, this step is a polynomial of order C. Finding a connected component requires a depth-first search in the graph. The complexity of depth-first search is $O(E)$, where E

---

[1] In fact, this is not necessarily the case. Many Internet service providers channel their users' HTTP requests through a small number of gateway machines, and two users might simultaneously visit the site from the same machine. Fortunately, such coincidences are too uncommon to affect the data significantly; if necessary, however, more accurate logs can be generated with visitor-tracking software such as WebThreads.

[2] While we consider all arcs equivalent for the purpose of finding clusters, we use the arc strengths for ranking clusters later.

[3] Note that we place a maximum size on discovered clusters not only in the interest of performance but because large clusters are not useful output — we cannot, practically speaking, create a new web page containing hundreds of links.

may be $O(N^2)$ in the worst case but is less in our sparse graphs. Note that the asymptotically most expensive part of PageGather is the creation of the similarity matrix; even a version that did not use our cluster mining technique would have at least this cost.

Experimental Validation

In this Section, we report on experiments designed to test the effectiveness of our approach by comparing it with traditional clustering methods; we also experiment with several PageGather variants to assess the impact of key facets of the algorithm on its performance. Our experiments draw on data collected from http://www.hyperreal.org/music/machines/. The site is composed of about 2500 distinct documents and receives approximately 10,000 hits per day from 1200 different visitors. We have been accumulating access logs for over a year.

In our experiment, each algorithm chooses a small number k of high-quality clusters. We then compare the running time and performance of each algorithm's top k clusters. We modified traditional clustering algorithms to return a small number of clusters (not necessarily a partition of the space), converting them into cluster mining algorithms as needed for our task. In all cases, clusters are ranked by their *average pairwise similarity* — calculated by averaging the similarity between all pairs of documents in the cluster — and the top k clusters are chosen. In our experiment, the training data is a collection of access logs for an entire month; each algorithm creates ten clusters based on these logs. The test data is a set of logs from a subsequent ten-day period.

There are literally hundreds of clustering algorithms and variations thereof. To compare PageGather with traditional methods, we picked two widely used document clustering algorithms: hierarchical agglomerative clustering (HAC)(Voorhees 1986), and K-Means clustering (Rocchio 1966). HAC is probably the most popular document clustering algorithm, but it proved to be quite slow. Subsequently, we chose K-Means because it is a linear time algorithm known for its speed. Of course, additional experiments are required to compare PageGather with other clustering algorithms before general conclusions can be drawn. We also compared two versions of PageGather — one using connected components and one using cliques.

Our first experiment compared the speed of the different algorithms as shown in Figure 1. Because all algorithms share the cost of creating the similarity matrix, we compare only the clustering portion of PageGather. We implemented two of HAC's many variations: complete link clustering, in which the distance between two clusters is the distance between their *farthest* points, and single link, in which the distance between two clusters is the distance between their *nearest* points. To generate k clusters, we had HAC iterate until it created a small number of clusters (about $2k$)

	Run time (min:sec)	Average cluster size
PageGather		
Connected Component	1:05	14.9
Clique	1:12	7.0
K-Means	48:38	231.9
K-Means (modified)	3:35	30.0
HAC	48+ hours	—

Figure 1: Running time and average cluster size of PageGather and standard clustering algorithms.

and then chose the best k by average pairwise similarity. We found HAC to be very slow compared to our algorithm; the algorithm ran for over 48 hours without completing (three orders of magnitude slower than PageGather).[4] HAC algorithms, in this domain, are asymptotically (and practically!) quite slow. We therefore decided to investigate a faster clustering algorithm.

In K-Means clustering, a target number of clusters (the "K") is chosen. The clusters are seeded with randomly chosen documents and then each document is placed in the closest cluster. The process is restarted by seeding new clusters with the centroids of the old ones. This process is iterated a set number of times, converging on better clusters. To generate k clusters for our experiment, we set K-Means to generate $2k$ clusters and then chose the top k by average pairwise similarity. As with the HAC algorithm, the costly similarity measure in our domain makes K-Means quite slow — the algorithm takes approximately 48 minutes in our experiment. However, just as we make our clique algorithm tractable by limiting the size of clusters to 30, we limited cluster size in the K-Means algorithm to 30 as well. We compared this modified version to PageGather and still found it to be slower by a factor of three.

We also compared PageGather using cliques in step 3 with PageGather using connected components. We found relatively little difference in speed. Finding connected components in a graph is a very fast operation. Although finding maximal cliques is generally intractable, it too is extremely fast when we limit the maximum clique size and the graph is sparse; in our experiment, the graph contained approximately 2500 nodes and only 13,000 edges after applying the threshold.

Next, we compared the algorithms in terms of the quality of candidate index pages they produce. Measuring cluster quality is a notoriously difficult problem.

---

[4]We chose simple implementations of two popular HAC algorithms; more efficient algorithms exist which may run faster. Our domain, however, differs from more standard domains such as document clustering. Documents can be represented as word vectors; word vectors can be compared or even averaged to create new centroid vectors. We, however, have no vectors, but only a similarity matrix. This limitation makes certain kinds of algorithmic optimizations impossible.

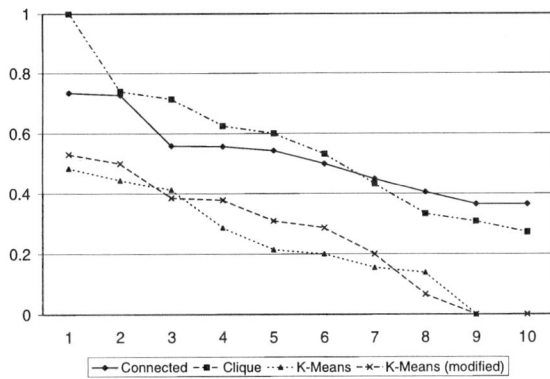

Figure 2: Predictive performance of PageGather (using both connected components and cliques) and K-Means clustering on access data from a web site.

To measure the quality of a cluster as an index page candidate, we need some measure of whether the cluster captures a set of pages that are viewed by users in the same visit. If so, then grouping them together on an index page will save the user the trouble of traversing the site to find them. Thus, as an approximate measure we ask: if a user visits any one page in the cluster, how likely is she to visit more? More formally, if $n(i)$ is the number of pages in cluster i that a person examines during one visit to the site, then the quality $Q(i)$ of a cluster is $P(n(i) \geq 2|n(i) \geq 1)$. The higher this conditional probability, the more valuable the candidate index page represented by the cluster. Of course, this measure is imperfect for a several reasons. Most seriously, the measure is biased toward larger clusters. We do not penalize a cluster for being overly inclusive or measure how much of a cluster a user visits. Figure 1 shows average cluster size for each algorithm. Note that the K-Means algorithm consistently generates larger clusters than PageGather. Thus, the bias in the metric works against PageGather. Although the K-means algorithm found, on average, larger clusters, it did not find significantly *fewer* than PageGather. PageGather, therefore had no advantage in being able to select the best from among a larger number of clusters.

Figure 2 shows the performance of four different algorithms. For each algorithm, we show the quality Q of its chosen ten best clusters. We graph each algorithm's top ten ordered by performance. As both K-Means variants produce significantly larger clusters than PageGather, we might expect better performance from K-means, but we see immediately that the PageGather variants perform better than either of the K-Means variants. PageGather is both faster and more accurate.

Comparing the two variants of PageGather, we find that neither is obviously superior. The connected component version, however, creates clusters that are, on average, about twice as large as those found with the clique approach. The best clique clusters are also somewhat better. The clique approach, we conclude, finds smaller, more coherent clusters.

To test our hypothesis that creating overlapping clusters is beneficial in this domain, we created a variant of PageGather that creates mutually exclusive clusters by forcing each page into exactly one cluster. We compared the performance of PageGather with and without overlapping. For readability, we omit the non-overlapping version of the clique algorithm in Figure 2, but the performance of the non-overlapping version drops substantially, though it is still better than either K-Means variant. The removal of overlapping did not substantially change the performance of PageGather using connected components.

Having applied this performance measure, we might also ask: qualitatively, how good are the clusters we find? Do they seem to correspond to concepts people would understand? We have not yet performed the kind of user testing necessary to answer this question in a fully satisfying way. However, a number of the clusters output by PageGather are convincingly coherent. For example, PageGather created one cluster containing most of the audio samples found at the site. Other clusters grouped similar keyboards from various manufacturers and downloadable software from across the site. Most clusters appear highly coherent — most of the less useful ones are composed entirely of pages from a single section of the site and hence do not represent an interesting "discovery". However, if PageGather makes one or two interesting discoveries out of every ten suggestions to the webmaster, it may still be quite useful.

Related Work

Automatic customization has been investigated in a variety of guises. (see (Joachims, Freitag, & Mitchell 1997; Fink, Kobsa, & Nill 1996)). These approaches tend to share certain characteristics. First, the web site or agent dynamically presents information – typically an enhancement of the currently viewed web page – to the visitor. Second, that information is customized to that visitor or a class of visitors based on some model the system has of that individual or class. Third, that model is based on information gleaned from the visitor and on the actions of previous visitors. In contrast, our approach makes offline changes to the entire site, makes those changes visible to all visitors, and need not request (or gather) information from a particular visitor in order to help her.

(Perkowitz & Etzioni 1997b) presented the web site optimization problem in terms of *transformations* to the web site which improve its structure. We sketched several kinds of transformations and discussed when to automatically apply them. Index page synthesis may be viewed as a novel transformation of this sort. Whereas that work broadly described a range of possible transformations, we have now implemented and tested one in depth.

Footprints (Wexelblat & Maes 1997) also takes an optimizing approach. Their motivating metaphor is that of travelers creating footpaths in the grass over time. Visitors to a web site leave their "footprints" behind; over time, "paths" accumulate in the most heavily traveled areas. New visitors to the site can use these well-worn paths as indicators of the most interesting pages to visit. Footprints are left automatically (and anonymously), and any visitor to the site may see them; visitors need not provide any information about themselves in order to take advantage of the system. Footprints is similar to our approach in that it makes changes to the site, based on user interactions, that are available to all visitors. However, Footprints provides essentially *localized* information; the user sees only how often links between adjacent pages are traveled. We allow the site to create new pages that may link together pages from across the site.

Future Work and Conclusions

This work is part of an our ongoing research effort; it is both an example of our approach and a step toward our long-term goal of creating adaptive web sites. We list our main contributions toward this goal below.

1. We formulated the novel task of automatic index page synthesis and decomposed the task into five subproblems, defining an agenda for future work on adaptive web sites. We focused on the subproblem of page-contents synthesis and formalized it as a clustering problem. In the process, we introduced key ideas including the distinction between optimization and customization, the visit-coherence assumption, and the principle of "nondestructive transformations".

2. We introduced PageGather, the first page-contents synthesis algorithm, and demonstrated its feasibility; PageGather takes Web site access logs as input and appears to produce coherent page contents as output. This is a proof of concept; in future work we will investigate its generality and seek to extend it to cover the full index page synthesis problem.

3. PageGather is based on *cluster mining*, a novel approach to clustering that, instead of partitioning the entire space into a set of mutually exclusive clusters, attempts to efficiently identify a small set of maximally coherent (and possibly overlapping) clusters. We demonstrated the benefits of cluster mining over traditional clustering experimentally in our domain. We believe that cluster mining will also prove beneficial in other domains, but this is a topic for future work.

Although the PageGather algorithm finds promising clusters in access logs, it is far from a complete solution to index page synthesis. Cluster mining is good for finding clumps of related pages — for example, several audio samples of guitars — but it has trouble finding the *complete* set of pages on a topic — e.g., *all* the guitar samples at the site. Yet visitors expect complete listings — a page titled "Audio Samples" had better list all of them. One way to create complete clusters is to use cluster mining to generate the original clusters, but then use the elements of the cluster as training data for learning a simple, general rule that defines membership in the cluster. The index page generated will contain links to *all* pages that match the rule.

PageGather could also potentially *flatten* the site's structure by grouping pages from across the web site onto a single page; important structural and hierarchical information may be lost, or fundamentally different kinds of pages might be grouped together. If we have *meta-information* about how the site is structured — for example, a simple ontology of the types of pages available — we should be able to find more homogeneous clusters. The use of meta-information to customize or optimize web sites has been explored in a number of projects (see, for example, (Khare & Rifkin 1997; Fernandez *et al.* 1997; Luke *et al.* 1997) and Apple's Meta-Content Format).

References

Fernandez, M., Florescu, D., Kang, J., Levy, A., and Suciu, D. 1997. System Demonstration - Strudel: A Web-site Management System. In *ACM SIGMOD Conference on Management of Data*.

Fink, J., Kobsa, A., and Nill, A. 1996. User-oriented Adaptivity and Adaptability in the AVANTI Project. In *Designing for the Web: Empirical Studies*.

Joachims, T., Freitag, D., and Mitchell, T. 1997. Webwatcher: A tour guide for the world wide web. In *Proc. 15th Int. Joint Conf. AI*, 770–775.

Khare, R., and Rifkin, A. 1997. XML: A Door to Automated Web Applications. *IEEE Internet Computing* 1(4):78–87.

Luke, S., Spector, L., Rager, D., and Hendler, J. 1997. Ontology-based web agents. In *Proc. First Int. Conf. Autonomous Agents*.

Perkowitz, M., and Etzioni, O. 1997a. Adaptive web sites: an AI challenge. In *Proc. 15th Int. Joint Conf. AI*.

Perkowitz, M., and Etzioni, O. 1997b. Adaptive web sites: Automatically learning from user access patterns. In *Proceedings of the Sixth Int. WWW Conference*.

Rasmussen, E. 1992. Clustering algorithms. In Frakes, W., and Baeza-Yates, R., eds., *Information Retrieval*. Prentice Hall, Eaglewood Cliffs, N.J. 419–442.

Rocchio, J. 1966. *Document Retrieval Systems — Optimization and Evaluation*. Ph.D. Dissertation, Harvard University.

Segal, R. 1996. *Data Mining as Massive Search*. Ph.D. Dissertation, University of Washington. http://www.cs.washington.edu/homes/segal/brute.html.

Voorhees, E. 1986. Implementing agglomerative hierarchical clustering algorithms for use in document retrieval. *Information Processing & Management* 22:465–476.

Wexelblat, A., and Maes, P. 1997. Footprints: History-rich web browsing. In *Proc. Conf. Computer-Assisted Information Retrieval (RIAO)*, 75–84.

Willet, P. 1988. Recent trends in hierarchical document clustering: a critical review. *Information Processing and Management* 24:577–97.

Feature Generation for Sequence Categorization

Daniel Kudenko and Haym Hirsh
lastname@cs.rutgers.edu
Department of Computer Science
Rutgers University
Piscataway, NJ 08855

Abstract

The problem of sequence categorization is to generalize from a corpus of labeled sequences procedures for accurately labeling future unlabeled sequences. The choice of representation of sequences can have a major impact on this task, and in the absence of background knowledge a good representation is often not known and straightforward representations are often far from optimal. We propose a feature generation method (called FGEN) that creates Boolean features that check for the presence or absence of heuristically selected collections of subsequences. We show empirically that the representation computed by FGEN improves the accuracy of two commonly used learning systems (C4.5 and Ripper) when the new features are added to existing representations of sequence data. We show the superiority of FGEN across a range of tasks selected from three domains: DNA sequences, Unix command sequences, and English text.

Introduction

The *sequence categorization problem* is to take a collection of labeled sequences of variable length and form a procedure for accurately assigning labels in the future to otherwise unlabeled sequences. For example, in biological sequence recognition, when given a collection of nucleotide (or amino acid) sequences that are marked with class labels based on a structural or functional property, the goal is to find a hypothesis that enables a computer to classify future unlabeled sequences. Another common sequence categorization problem is e-mail filtering. Given a collection of e-mail texts with topic labels, the inductive learner has to generate a classifier which is able to assign a topic label to future incoming e-mail automatically.

Our goal is to develop a general method for sequence categorization tasks that works across many domains and does not need specialized knowledge for each domain. In particular, we focus on the class of inductive learning methods that apply when data can be described as *feature vectors*, i.e., as values assigned to a fixed set of attributes describing each object. Doing so requires representing sequences as feature vectors, and there are numerous ways to do this. For example, attributes could take the form of "The item in position i in the sequence", i.e., each position in the sequence gives a new attribute, whose value is the item (e.g., character) at that position. Or attributes could take the form of "The subsequence S occurs somewhere in the sequence", i.e., each such attribute tests for the presence or absence of a particular subsequence in the given sequence. This, of course, requires deciding what subsequences should be used in such features. For example, one could choose to create a feature for *every* possible subsequence up to a certain length k (i.e., make a feature for all n-grams for n ranging from 1 to k).

Unfortunately, such straightforward, albeit general, representations need not perform well. For example, Hirsh and Noordewier (Hirsh & Noordewier 1994) have shown that the choice of features for DNA sequence categorization problems can have a substantial impact on the accuracy of feature-based learners. Their features, based on domain knowledge, performed dramatically better than a straightforward positional encoding of data commonly used on this problem.

This paper proposes a method, called FGEN, to generate new feature-based sequence representations automatically from a collection of training data sequences. Each new feature is a kind of macro-feature that tests for the number of occurrences of each of a collection of subsequences within a sequence of interest. Since many learning methods involve forms of greedy search, such multi-sequence features may be selected for the hypothesis by such methods even when the individual sequences within them might not be selected by the learner when used in isolation, thereby leading to improved results in learning.

We evaluated FGEN representations on a wide range of sequence categorization tasks: English text, DNA sequences, and Unix command sequences. The evaluation was done by comparing the accuracy of C4.5 (Quinlan 1994) and Ripper (Cohen 1995) using straightforward sequence representations to the ac-

---

We thank William Cohen and our colleagues at Rutgers for many helpful discussions. The first author was partially supported by DIMACS, a cooperative project of Rutgers University, Princeton University, AT&T Labs, Bellcore, and Bell Labs.
Copyright ©1998, American Association for Artificial Intelligence (www.aaai.org). All rights reserved.

curacy of those learners using FGEN's features appended to these representations. Our results show that FGEN's features often improved the accuracy of the respective learning algorithms, and in those cases when they didn't, had only modest impact.

In the next section we describe straightforward approaches to representing sequences as feature vectors and the internal cross-validation approach to optimize the choice of representation. Afterwards we present the feature language of FGEN and the feature generation algorithm. Finally, test domains and the test strategy are described and the test results are shown.

Baseline Sequence Representations

There are many ways to formulate a sequence classification problem as one to which feature-based learners can be applied. This section presents the two general approaches to representing sequences as feature vectors that we use as baselines in this work. Note that although in some domains, notably text, the sequences can be broken up into well-defined tokens (e.g., words), each of which can serve as a feature, we do not consider such representations here due to our interest in more general approaches to sequence categorization that apply even when there are no a priori well-defined (and domain-specific!) tokenizations of sequences. Similarly, we do not consider numerical features that measure, for example, the proportion of sequence location occupied by a particular item (e.g., letter), out of a belief that, although general, the range of problems to which such representations would be relevant are fairly limited.

For notation, we write a vector of n features as an n-tuple, where each element is of the form (*feature-name feature-value*). A vector representation with 3 features F1, F2, and F3 having values V1, V2, and V3 respectively would therefore be described as ((F1 V1) (F2 V2) (F3 V3)).

Positional Representations

In the positional representation of sequences each feature denotes a certain position of the sequence. For example, if feature Pi denotes the feature corresponding to position i in a sequence, the sequence ABBB would be represented ((P1 A) (P2 B) (P3 B) (P4 B)), i.e., that there is an A in position 1, a B in position 2, etc. This is the simple positional representation for sequences that we will be using in the experiments that we discuss later in this paper.

To represent a collection of sequences, each sequence would be re-encoded as a vector of position/value pairs. However, although this is a fairly general way to represent sequences, it only works as described when all the data sequences are of the same length, since feature-based learners require all data to be described using identical sets of attributes. In cases where sequences can vary in length, this representation can still be used, although less elegantly, by "padding" all shorter sequences with repetitions of some "filler" character so that the same-vector-length requirement of this representation is satisfied.

Subsequence Representations

The preceding positional representation has the limitation that information concerning the adjacency of elements of a sequence are much more difficult to identify and represent. Consider, for example, what it would take to say that there is an A immediately adjacent to a B in the above positional representation when sequences are of length 1000.

An alternative approach to representing sequences considers the presence or number of occurrences of various subsequences in a sequence. For example, a simple representation would be to generate a feature for each n-gram that can occur in a sequence. Thus, if using a 2-gram representation and sequences are over the three-letter alphabet {A, B, C}, the sequence ABBB would represented as: ((AA 0) (AB 1) (AC 0) (BA 0) (BB 2) (BC 0) (CA 0) (CB 0) (CC 0)). This representation says that the 2-gram AB occurs once and BB occurs twice in the sequence ABBB while all other 2-grams do not. We also consider a closely related representation, in which each potential subsequence is a Boolean variable rather than a count — the feature is true if the subsequences it represents are present in a given sequence. We call the above two representations the subsequence frequency and presence representations, respectively.

In the results to be described shortly, we use as features the set of all n-grams that occur in any sequence in the data (there is no need to enumerate all n-grams, since only those occurring somewhere in the data would ever be used), for n ranging from 1 to some value k. Although in some cases this is a general approach to representing sequences, one of its major limits is precisely when positional representations would excel — when the exact location of some sequence element is crucial for the classification task.

The FGEN Representation Formalism

FGEN takes a collection of sequence data and creates a set of new Boolean features out of the data. The idea is that each such feature tests that, for each of a set of subsequences, the number of times it occurs in a sequence is at least some minimum count. For instance, an FGEN feature could specify that it is true for a sequence if and only if it has at least two occurrences of the subsequence AC and at least three occurrences of the subsequence CB. One intuition behind considering such features is that they are *macro*-features, i.e., they represent information concerning more than a single subsequence. This combination can contain information that stays hidden from a learning algorithm that works in a greedy fashion.

More formally, each FGEN feature can be written as a function from the set of all sequences to $\{T, F\}$. The function denoted by a feature F can be

```
/* main function that computes the set of FGEN features.
   Ti union Pi are training examples of class i.
   Pi is used as a holdout set for evaluation purposes
   (usually 1/3 of the training set).  */
GenerateFeatures(T1,T2,P1,P2) {
  Seeds = T1;   /* set of potential seeds */
  Features = {};
  while (Seeds not empty) {
    Let s be the sequence in Seeds which starts the generation of
      the feature that subsumes most sequences in T1;
    F = ComputeFeature(s,T1,T2,P1,P2);   /* let F be such a feature */
    Features = Features union {F};
    C = set of sequences in T1 that are subsumed by F;
    Seeds = Seeds - C;   /* remove all elements of C from Seeds */
  }
  return Features;
}

/* compute a feature corresponding to a cluster built around seed s */
ComputeFeature(s,T1,T2,P1,P2) {
  F = feature denoting the minimum frequency restrictions on all
      subsequences up to length 8 of s;
  OldValue = GetValue(F,P1,P2); /* compute heuristic that evaluates F */
  repeat
    Let s' be the sequence that is ``most similar'' to F;
    Remove s' from T1;
    FG = least generalization of F that subsumes s';
    NewValue = GetValue(FG,P1,P2);
    if (NewValue >= OldValue) then F = FG;
  until NewValue < OldValue;  /* Hillclimbing on heuristic evaluation of F */
  return F;
}


/* heuristic evaluation function for features:
     proportional classification accuracy on the holdout set*/
GetValue(F,P1,P2) {
  p = number of sequences in P1 that are subsumed by F;
  n = number of sequences in P2 that are subsumed by F;
  P = number of sequences in P1;
  N = number of sequences in P2;
  return ((p*N/P)+(N-n))/(2*N);
}
```

Figure 1: FGEN feature building algorithm

The FGEN algorithm

The input to FGEN are pre-classified training examples. The output is a set of features as described above, which can be used to map each training and test example into a Boolean feature vector. FGEN generates a set of features for each class separately, and returns the union of the sets. Although the current implementation of FGEN only works on two-class learning problems, it can be easily extended for multi-class settings.

The basic idea behind the FGEN feature generation algorithm is that a representation which focuses on combinations of subsequences that occur mostly in training examples of one class and not in the examples of the other class will improve classification accuracy.

The FGEN algorithm consists out of two main parts: feature building (shown in Figure 1) and generalization (Figure 2).

written as: $F(S) = s_1^{n_1}(S) \wedge s_2^{n_2}(S) \wedge \ldots \wedge s_k^{n_k}(S)$ where $s_i^{n_i}$ is a boolean function and $s_i^{n_i}(S) = True$ for a sequence S if the sequence s_i occurs at least n_i times in S. ($s_i^{n_i}$ is called a minimum frequency restriction of F.) For example, if $F = AC^2 \wedge CB^3$ then $F(ACBBACBCB) = T$ and $F(ACBAC) = F$.

We say that a feature F subsumes a sequence S, if $F(S) = T$, i.e. S is compatible with all subsequence frequency restrictions of F. Furthermore, a feature F_1 is more general than a feature F_2, if the set of sequences subsumed by F_1 is a superset of the set of sequences subsumed by F_2. In other words, F_1 contains less restrictions than F_2.

FGEN features can be efficiently implemented using a data structure based on suffix trees, which has been described in detail in (Hirsh & Kudenko 1997).

```
prune(F,P1,P2) {
  OldValue = GetValue(F,P1,P2);
  repeat
    Decrement a frequency restriction in F;
    Let FP be the feature resulting from the
      above operation for which GetValue(FP,P1,P2)
      is maximized;
    NewValue = GetValue(FP,P1,P2);
    if (NewValue >= OldValue) then F = FP;
  until NewValue < OldValue;
  return F;
}
```

Figure 2: Feature Generalization Algorithm

Features are built incrementally, starting with a feature that corresponds to just a single example of the target class (the seed around which a feature is generated). This seed feature denotes the minimum frequency restrictions on all subsequences of the seed sequence.[1] For example, if the seed sequence s is equal to ABB, then the corresponding seed feature is defined as follows: $F_s = A^1 \wedge B^2 \wedge AB^1 \wedge BB^1 \wedge ABB^1$.

A feature is built step by step by making it more general to subsume at least one additional sequence from the target class in each iteration. The additional sequence is one that requires the fewest changes to the current feature to subsume the additional sequence. In other words, the additional sequence is "most similar" to the feature.

After each iteration the new feature is heuristically evaluated. As a heuristic we use classification accuracy of the feature on a holdout set, which is one third of the training set (since FGEN features are Boolean they can be interpreted as two-class classifiers). The generalization steps are continued, until the resulting feature has a lower heuristic value than the feature in the previous step.

This feature generation algorithm creates features that tend to over-fit the training data. In order to solve this problem each computed feature is subsequently generalized after it is created. The algorithm is shown in Figure 2. FGEN's generalization step removes subsequence restrictions one by one from a feature. This is done by decrementing a minimum frequency restriction on some subsequence. Once a minimum frequency restriction has reached 0, it can be removed completely, since it does not contain any information.[2]

---

[1] In order to limit the complexity we arbitrarily chose to restrict the length of such subsequences to 8. This choice seems reasonable, because we never encountered a domain where subsequences of length greater than 5 had a considerable impact on classification accuracy. Furthermore, a high value of n implies a sparse distribution of n-grams.

[2] In the actual implementation of FGEN we restrict the decrementing of frequency restrictions to single characters for efficiency reasons. The changes in frequency restrictions are propagated to all subsequences that start with the given character. Furthermore, we allow the frequency restriction of certain subsequences to be set to 0 in one

The generalization is performed in a greedy hill-climbing fashion by trying to increase the heuristic value of the pruned feature as much as possible and stopping the generalization as soon as a local maximum is reached (i.e. the heuristic value of the current feature is lower than the value of the feature of the last iteration).

Evaluation

This section describes the empirical tests we performed to show that the FGEN feature representation improves accuracy of feature-based learners. We chose C4.5 and Ripper as two common and representative systems. C4.5 is a widely used decision-tree learning algorithm, in which trees are built in a divide-and-conquer fashion using an information-gain heuristic. Ripper, on the other hand, forms rules in a method similar to that used in inductive logic programming, and has been successfully used in many applications, showing a comparably high accuracy.

There are certain complexity limits to the straightforward baseline representations that were described previously in this paper. When the alphabet is large, the representations based on the presence or frequency of subsequences can result in a very large number of features.[3] In such cases C4.5 required a reduction in the number of features. For representations based on the presence of subsequences we chose to retain the 1000 most frequent features (i.e., subsequences), and did not use representations based on subsequence frequencies for datasets with large alphabets (English texts and Unix command sequences).

On the other hand, Ripper allows features to be set-valued, which can be exploited to simplify the baseline representation based on the presence of subsequences. In Ripper a sequence S can be represented as a single set-valued feature F that contains all subsequences of S of length less than or equal to some n. The sequence ABBB can therefore be represented in the form ((F {A,B,AB,BB})) for n = 2. This made it possible to use the full set of features.

In our empirical tests we use as a baseline whatever representation appeared to be best on the training data. The representations that were tried were the pure positional representation and subsequence presence and frequency representations for subsequences up a certain length n for $n \in \{2, 3, 4, 5\}$.[4] For each run the learner used 10-fold cross-validation on the training set to find the "best" baseline representation amongst those described above (i.e., the one yielding the lowest cross-validation error rate on the training set). Although this method will not always choose the optimal

---

step. These feature simplification operations can be computed efficiently on the data structure for FGEN features, which is based on suffix trees (Hirsh & Kudenko 1997).

[3] The number of features is in the order of $|\Sigma|^n$, where Σ is the alphabet and n is the length of the subsequences underlying the representation.

[4] For tractability reasons we restricted n to 5 or less.

representation, it will yield the better performance on average, as has been shown in (Schaffer 1993). Afterwards, the training and test data is represented in the winning format and the error rate with this representation is reported.

The second strategy works like the first with the exception that FGEN features are appended to the winning representation and the error rate for this extended representation is reported. Since FGEN's features are created independently of which representation is selected by the internal representation-selecting cross-validation runs, it is computed separately, and then added on once the baseline representation selection is made.

Datasets

In order to show the applicability of FGEN across a wide range of sequence categorization tasks we tested it on three domains: English text (3 sub-domains), DNA sequences (3 sub-domains), and Unix Command sequences (1 sub-domain). We describe each domain in more detail.

DNA Sequences

Promoter: This dataset contains 600 DNA sequences of length 100; 300 of them classified as Promoters and 300 as Non-Promoters. All DNA sequences are over a four letter alphabet.

A/B-DNA: This dataset contains three types of DNA: sequences in A, B, and Z confirmation. Since there were only a small number of Z-DNA sequences, the two learning tasks were to learn to distinguish A-DNA from the union of B-DNA and Z-DNA data, and B-DNA from the union of A-DNA and Z-DNA data. This dataset contains 138 relatively short sequences (between 4 and 12 characters per sequence), most of which are A-DNA and B-DNA in equal proportions.

Human/Phage DNA: We generated this dataset by extracting 300 Human and 300 Phage DNA sequences of length 100 from GenBank.[5] The goal is to learn to distinguish Human from Phage DNA.

Unix command sequences

The goal of these datasets is to identify a user through Unix command sequences. The datasets contain 225 non-overlapping Unix command sequences of length 20 from three users (75 sequences from user 1, 101 from user 2, and 49 from user 3). The alphabet size (i.e., the number of different commands used in the sequences) varied from 40 to 90.[6] One of the users forms the target class (a different one for each dataset) while the other two form the background class.

English Text

Newsgroup topic spotting: We generated three datasets by extracting postings from three different newsgroups: comp.os.ms-windows, rec.games.backgammon, and sci.classics. Each dataset has one of the three topics as the target class and the other two as the background class. The size of the datasets ranges from 350 to 550, with 30% to 50% of the data being texts from the target class. For complexity reasons the length of individual postings has been restricted to the first 500 characters.

Email topic spotting: These four datasets are extracted from four different personal mail folders. The target class are talk announcement messages.[7] The datasets contain between 150 and 600 examples, 10-50% of which are from the target class. For complexity reasons the length of individual postings has been restricted to the first 500 characters.

Book passage categorization: This dataset contains 600 character sequences of length 100 from two books (300 from each).[8] The goal of this dataset is to learn to identify the book given the character sequence.

Test Results

Table 1 shows the error rates on each single dataset of the three domains. The winning error rate is shown in bold. All error rates have been obtained by performing 10-fold cross-validation. (Note that this is separate from the cross-validation being performed to select the best representation for learning — each of the 10-fold cross-validation runs itself involves a 10-fold cross-validation run on the respective training set to select that run's representation.)

As can be seen in the table FGEN features help in many cases and hurt only in very few (11 wins, 2 ties, 2 losses with Ripper, and 8 wins, 2 ties, 5 losses with C4.5). Overall, the wins outweigh the losses considerably. Furthermore, the losses are relatively small in most cases, while some of the wins are dramatic. The results reflect our intuition that the learning systems will not use FGEN features in their hypothesis when they would increase the error rate considerably.

Note that the number of features generated by FGEN never exceeded 20 on any dataset. This is remarkable, given the large size of the space of potential features.

Related Work

Previous work in sequence categorization includes Hidden Markov Models (Rabiner 1989), learning of finite automata, and entropy-based induction (LLLAMA)

---

[5] The choice of sequence length 100 was arbitrary, as is the case for the book sequence dataset and the Unix command sequence dataset.

[6] The superset of this data has been collected for experiments in Unix command prediction (Davison & Hirsh 1997).

[7] This data was previously used in a previous study on e-mail filtering (Cohen 1996; Cohen & Kudenko 1997).

[8] The book texts have been taken from the Calgary Corpus, a collection of files for compression benchmarks.

Table 1: Error Rates on Test Domains

Dataset	Ripper	Ripper+FGEN	C4.5	C4.5+FGEN
Promoter	18.9	**16.0**	20.8	**16.7**
A-DNA	20.0	**16.7**	13.3	**11.1**
B-DNA	**7.1**	**7.1**	**3.8**	**3.8**
Hum/Pha DNA	11.2	**5.8**	8.3	**6.0**
Unix User 1	13.3	**7.1**	**6.7**	9.5
Unix User 2	6.3	**5.5**	9.7	**7.4**
Unix User 3	4.7	1.7	3.4	**0.9**
News 1	13.8	**9.4**	13.4	**9.6**
News 2	**8.8**	10.3	9.7	**9.1**
News 3	17.8	14.4	**12.4**	13.5
Talks 1	**10.1**	10.2	15.4	15.7
Talks 2	5.3	**5.1**	**4.1**	4.2
Talks 3	**4.0**	**4.0**	**4.7**	**4.7**
Talks 4	7.8	**3.9**	5.1	5.5
Books	23.8	20.3	16.2	**12.7**

(Loewenstern, Berman, & Hirsh 1998). Hidden Markov Models require an initial model, which is usually based on domain knowledge. LLLAMA has been designed mainly with biological sequences in mind. This is contrary to the philosophy of FGEN which has been designed to be independent of domain knowledge and to be applied across a wide range of domains. Learning of finite automata has been mainly applied to datasets that have been generated by finite automata in the first place.

Feature-based learners have been applied to sequence categorization using either one of the baseline representations presented in this paper, or using features that have been suggested by domain experts (Hirsh & Noordewier 1994; Salzberg 1995; Norton 1994).

An overview of the area of constructive induction, which deals with the automatic generation of representations for learning, is presented in (Saitta 1996). We are not aware of any constructive induction research for sequence categorization.

Final Remarks

We presented a feature generation method for sequence categorization that creates boolean features based on minimum subsequence frequencies. We have shown empirically that the representation computed by this method improves learning accuracy across a wide range of domains, compared to straightforward representations.

It is interesting to note that FGEN follows a bottom-up approach, starting with a specific feature and then generalizing it to compute the result. This is in contrast to C4.5 and Ripper, which both use a top-down approach. They start with an empty hypothesis and make it more specific. Using the FGEN representation results in a hybrid approach, which might be one of the reasons for the success of FGEN. It would be interesting to further investigate the reasons for this success. We plan to examine the properties of datasets in which the FGEN representation succeeds and in which it fails.

References

Cohen, W., and Kudenko, D. 1997. Transferring and retraining learned information filters. In *Proceedings of the Fourteenth National Conference on Artificial Intelligence*.

Cohen, W. 1995. Fast effective rule induction. In *Proceedings of the Twelfth International Conference on Machine Learning*.

Cohen, W. 1996. Learning rules that classify e-mail. In *Proceedings of the 1996 AAAI Spring Symposium on Machine Learning in Information Access*.

Davison, B., and Hirsh, H. 1997. Toward an adaptive command line interface. In *Seventh International Conference on Human-Computer Interaction*.

Hirsh, H., and Kudenko, D. 1997. Representing sequences in description logics. In *Proceedings of the Fourteenth National Conference on Artificial Intelligence*.

Hirsh, H., and Noordewier, M. 1994. Using background knowledge to improve inductive learning of DNA sequences. In *Proceedings IEEE Conference on AI for Applications*.

Loewenstern, D.; Berman, H.; and Hirsh, H. 1998. Maximum a posteriori classification of DNA structure from sequence information. In *Proceedings of PSB-98*.

Norton, S. W. 1994. Learning to recognize promoter sequences in E.coli. In *Proceedings of the Eleventh National Conference on Artificial Intelligence*.

Quinlan, J. R. 1994. *C4.5: programs for machine learning*. San Mateo, CA: Morgan Kaufmann.

Rabiner, L. 1989. A tutorial on hidden Markov models and selected applications in speech recognition. In *Proceedings IEEE*.

Saitta, L. 1996. Representation change in machine learning. *AI Communications* 9:14–20.

Salzberg, S. 1995. Locating protein coding regions in human DNA using a decision tree algorithm. *Journal of Computational Biology* 2(3).

Schaffer, C. 1993. Selecting a classifier method by cross-validation. *Machine Learning* 13.

Concepts From Time Series

Michael T. Rosenstein and Paul R. Cohen

Computer Science Department, LGRC
University of Massachusetts
Box 34610
Amherst, MA 01003-4610
{mtr, cohen}@cs.umass.edu

Abstract

This paper describes a way of extracting concepts from streams of sensor readings. In particular, we demonstrate the value of attractor reconstruction techniques for transforming time series into clusters of points. These clusters, in turn, represent perceptual categories with predictive value to the agent/environment system. We also discuss the relationship between categories and concepts, with particular emphasis on class membership and predictive inference.

Introduction

This research is part of an effort to explain how sensorimotor agents develop symbolic, conceptual thought, as every human child does. As in (Cohen et al. 1996) we are trying to "grow" an intelligent agent from minimal beginnings by having it interact with a complex environment. One problem with such projects is the transformation of streams of sensor data into symbolic concepts, cf. the symbol grounding problem (Harnad 1990). Hence, the focus of this paper is an unsupervised learning mechanism for extracting concepts from time series of sensor readings.

Concepts are abstractions of experience that confer a predictive ability for new situations. Moreover, for this project we assume a *predictive semantics* where the meaning of a concept is the predictions it makes. This working definition applies equally well to both objects and activities and depends upon a notion of *category*. For instance, just as one can form the category TOY for objects BALL and TOP, one can also create the category PLAY for activities BOUNCE and SPIN. From the *interactionist* perspective (Lakoff 1984; Johnson 1987), this correspondence is a natural one. Indeed, objects and activities seem to be duals — linked by sensorimotor experience — with a category of one connected to a category of the other.

Epistemically, a category is simply a collection of instances (of objects or activities) and a concept is a category plus its *entailments* (or consequences of category membership). A similar definition follows from the influential work of Rosch involving categories and their abstractions, called *prototypes* (Rosch & Lloyd 1978). A prototype is best understood as a representative category member that may or may not correspond to any observed instance. (In fact, the latter case is true for the results in this paper.) Thus, whenever such abstractions can take the place of a category, one can think of a concept as a category prototype plus its *meaning* or predictive inferences.

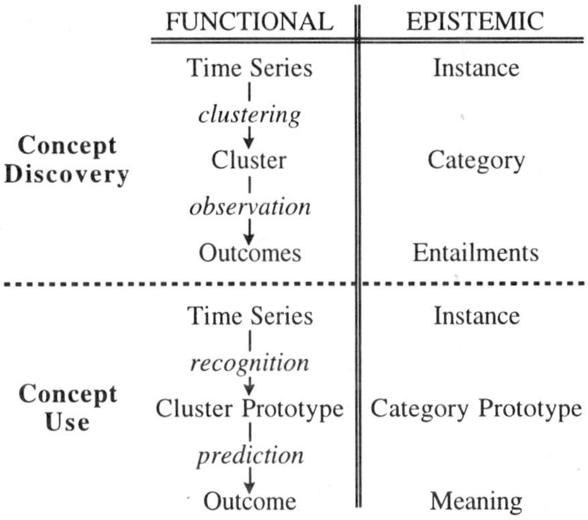

	FUNCTIONAL	EPISTEMIC
Concept Discovery	Time Series ↓ *clustering* Cluster ↓ *observation* Outcomes	Instance Category Entailments
Concept Use	Time Series ↓ *recognition* Cluster Prototype ↓ *prediction* Outcome	Instance Category Prototype Meaning

Figure 1: Functional view of concepts and the corresponding epistemic terms.

Figure 1 illustrates the way we realize these definitions of concepts. In particular, we begin with time series data and form clusters of points that have something in common. We then observe the subsequent outcomes, i.e., the future properties of the cluster members. Since we equate clusters with categories and outcomes with entailments, we also equate the corresponding acts of *clustering* and *observation* with the *discovery* of concepts. Concept *use* then follows a similar two-step procedure: (1) *Recognition*. Given a new time series, find the cluster prototype most like the new instance. (2) *Prediction*. Report the most likely outcome for the

Copyright © 1998, American Association for Artificial Intelligence (www.aaai.org). All rights reserved.

cluster referred to by the matching prototype.

Experimental Environment

To demonstrate concept discovery and use, a simple experimental environment was created where two agents interact based on their predetermined movement strategies. These agents are entirely reactive and pursue or avoid one another using one of four basic behaviors:

1. NONE. The agent follows a line determined by its initial velocity. No attention is paid to the opponent's position.
2. AVOID. The agent attempts to move away from its opponent and avoid contact.
3. CRASH. The agent attempts to move toward its opponent and initiate contact.
4. KISS. The agent slows down before making contact (implemented as a combination of AVOID and CRASH).

Figure 2 shows two examples from the pursuit/avoidance simulator. During each trial, the agents interact only when they are close enough to detect one another, as represented by the inner circle in Figure 2. A trial ends when the agents make contact, when they get too far apart, or when the trial exceeds a time limit which is large compared to the duration of a typical interaction. The simulator implements a movement strategy by varying the agent's acceleration in response to the relative position of its opponent. (See (Rosenstein et al. 1997) for details.) In particular, movement strategies are equations of the form

$$a = i \cdot f(d, \dot{d}), \qquad (1)$$

where a is acceleration, d is distance between agents, f is a function that gives one of the basic movement strategies, and i is a scale factor that represents the agent's strength or *intensity*.

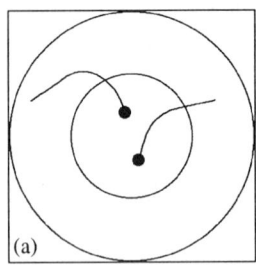 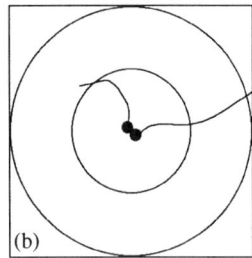

Figure 2: Simulator screen dump showing a representative trial of: (a) AVOID vs. CRASH; (b) KISS vs. KISS.

Activity Maps

Our previous approach to concept discovery was based on representations of dynamics called *activity maps* (Rosenstein et al. 1997). In keeping with the functional view of concepts in Figure 1, we also made the distinction between two types of activity maps: *behavior maps* for recognizing agent behaviors such as CRASH or KISS, and *interaction maps* for predicting outcomes such as CONTACT or NO-CONTACT. These representations, in turn, were based on *phase portraits* and *basins of attraction* — common tools used by dynamicists for understanding system behavior.

During a learning phase, a library of activity maps was constructed by running thousands of trials in the simulator while recording the movement patterns of each agent as well as the outcome of every trial. In a supervised manner, one behavior map was built for each of eight agent types (four basic movement strategies with three levels of intensity for AVOID and CRASH), and one interaction map was built for each of the 36 distinct pairs of behaviors (64 possible pairs minus 28 symmetrically equivalent pairs). With the pursuit/avoidance simulator, this library of activity maps proved sufficient for recognizing the participants of a new trial and for predicting a CONTACT or NO-CONTACT outcome.

Table 1 illustrates the performance of the recognition algorithm in (Rosenstein et al. 1997). Interestingly, this *confusion table* demonstrates the misinterpretation of the various behaviors. For example, 66% of the time the algorithm confused KISS with one of the CRASH movement strategies, yet rarely mistook KISS for one of the AVOID types. The reason for this sort of confusion is that *apparent* behavior is dependent upon not only the agent's predetermined movement strategy, but also the circumstances, i.e., initial velocity and opponent behavior. Actually, in some situations, a KISS agent reacts just like a CRASH type, and vice versa. These results suggest that another way to categorize interactions is by the nature of the interaction itself. In fact, the explicit step of behavior recognition is no longer necessary with the clustering approach described shortly.

Actual	||	N	A-	A	A+	C-	C	C+	K
					Recognizer Response				
N	||	**40**	21	7	3	26	3	0	0
A-	||	18	**53**	19	5	5	0	0	0
A	||	2	16	**74**	8	0	0	0	0
A+	||	0	2	8	**90**	0	0	0	0
C-	||	26	6	3	1	**35**	23	0	6
C	||	2	2	0	1	21	**25**	21	28
C+	||	0	0	0	0	1	9	**77**	13
K	||	8	1	0	0	21	20	25	**25**

Table 1: Confusion table illustrating recognition performance with agent behaviors chosen randomly. Shown are response percentages, where behavior names are shortened to first letters only, and - and + indicate weak and strong forms, respectively.

Despite the success of activity maps at recognizing behaviors and predicting outcomes, the approach has two drawbacks worth mentioning. First, even for a simple simulator with just two agents, the size of the map library scales as $O(n^2)$, where n is the number of movement strategies. Preferably, the concept library should have size proportional to the number of needed concepts. Second, thousands of trials are necessary to build just one map and the associated learning algorithm must operate in a supervised fashion. Instead, an agent should find the relevant categories for itself, without the imposed biases of an external teacher. For these reasons, we developed the current approach to concept discovery based on clustering techniques. Below, we show that few clusters and few experiences are needed to recognize situations and predict outcomes — without a supervisor — and to do so quite accurately.

The Method of Delays

The formation of clusters requires a metric and so one must first devise a suitable metric space for the data. In this work we make use of an *attractor reconstruction* technique called the *method of delays* or *delay-space embedding*. Takens proved that the method of delays provides a means for mapping a time series to a topologically equivalent spatial representation (an *embedding*) of an underlying dynamical system (Takens 1981). This mapping is accomplished by forming an m-dimensional vector of *delay coordinates*,

$$\mathbf{X}_i^T = [x_i \; x_{i-J} \; x_{i-2J} \; ... \; x_{i-(m-1)J}], \quad (2)$$

where $\{x_1, x_2, ..., x_n\}$ is the n-point time series, m is called the *embedding dimension*, and J is the *embedding delay*. As described in (Rosenstein, Collins, & De Luca 1994), and references therein, the practical application of Takens theorem requires some care on the experimenter's part when choosing the delay value. In any case, the theoretical basis of attractor reconstruction is geared toward dynamical systems, although the techniques often prove useful for uncovering patterns in time series data, regardless of their source.

For instance, Figure 3 shows a *delay portrait* with representative trajectories leading to three different outcomes in the pursuit/avoidance simulator. Each curve is based on the distance time series recorded during one interaction. We chose `object-distance` as the agent's only sensor because we want to demonstrate concept discovery while supplying as little innate knowledge or structure as possible. Additionally, the ability to measure object distance is a reasonable assumption since most mobile robots are equipped with sonar or video-based position sensors.

The method of delays is important for this research, not because we have attractors to reconstruct, but because we need some basis for discovering concepts without detailed knowledge of the agent/environment system. In all but the simplest applications, an agent is unable to measure all relevant quantities in the world, and so the intuition behind delay-space embeddings is

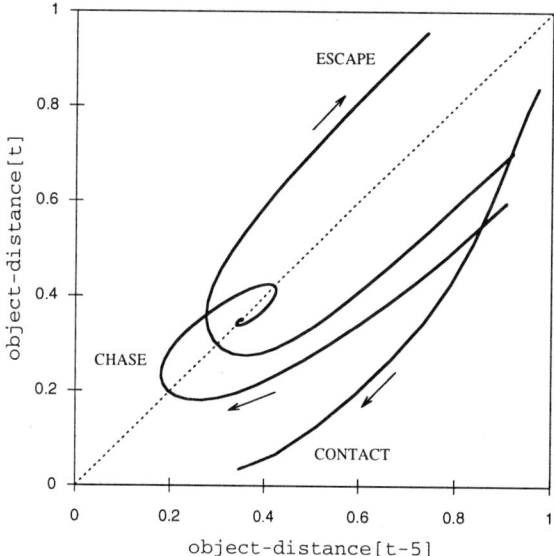

Figure 3: Two-dimensional delay portrait with $J = 5$ and trajectories illustrating CONTACT, ESCAPE, and CHASE.

this: if the state of the environment at time t is uncertain because the agent has, say, one sensor, then examination of sensor readings prior to time t will reduce the ambiguity.

Concepts and Clusters

As shown earlier in Figure 1, there is a close relationship between concepts and categories. Indeed, "there is nothing more basic than categorization to our thought, perception, action, and speech" (Lakoff 1984). But before any agent can make use of concepts, it must first discover the pertinent categories.

One general technique for discovering categories is to form clusters of points in a suitable space. This was the basis of Elman's work on learning lexical classes from word co-occurrence statistics (Elman 1990). Elman first trained a recurrent neural network to predict successive words in a long input string. This then set the stage for hierarchical clustering of the hidden-unit activation space, where the result was groups of words that coincide with classes like NOUN-FOOD or VERB-PERCEPT. Similarly, Omlin and Giles described a way to identify clusters in a network's hidden-unit space, with each cluster representing a node in an associated finite-state machine (Omlin & Giles 1996).

Our approach to clustering works directly from delay coordinates and proceeds with no prior training. For the pursuit/avoidance simulator, we begin with the first observed interaction and immediately create a cluster consisting of this lone experience. A cluster itself is simply a data structure that stores the number of members, the frequency of each outcome, and a prototype for the class. Whenever a new experience arrives, the algorithm creates a new cluster from the data and then attempts to merge existing clusters based on a measure of similarity. Specifically, two clusters are replaced by one formed from their constituent information whenever the Euclidean distance between them (in delay-coordinate space) is less than a threshold parameter, θ_s. Hence, the algorithm continually updates its list of categories to reflect new experiences. Central to this updating procedure is the use of cluster prototypes.

Figure 4 shows the six cluster prototypes derived from 100 agent interactions, where the movement strategies were chosen randomly and the similarity threshold was set to 20% of the range in the distance data. Each prototype is simply the average `object-distance` time series formed from all interactions that make up a given cluster. (Strictly speaking, a prototype consists of m delay coordinates, although we show the entire time series to illustrate distinctive patterns.) This implementation is entirely consistent with Rosch's work on prototypes (Rosch & Lloyd 1978), and also serves two practical purposes: as a way for testing cluster similarity, and as a way for understanding the meaning of a cluster.

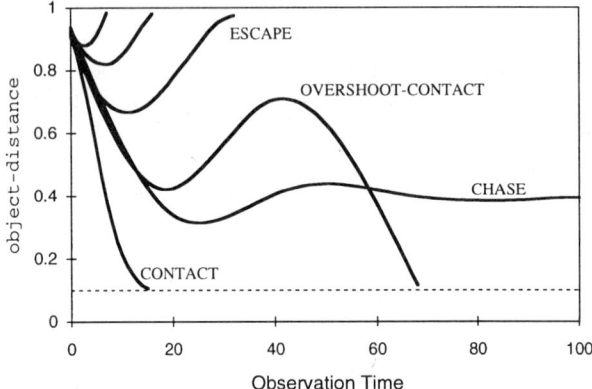

Figure 4: Cluster prototypes formed at observation time $t = 50$, with similarity threshold $\theta_s = 0.2$, embedding dimension $m = 5$, and embedding delay $J = 1$.

The prototypes in Figure 4 correspond to six different categories of agent interactions, with each category possessing its own entailments. Thus, the clustering algorithm discovered six concepts about the experimental domain. Moreover, these prototypes reflect actual differences in the simulated environment. In particular, the algorithm found concepts that one could describe as "chase," "contact," contact after the agents first "overshoot" one another, and "escape" with short, medium, and long escape times. But are these clusters any good for recognition and prediction?

The agents in the pursuit/avoidance simulator have implicit goals of CONTACT and ESCAPE. These goals correspond to two possible outcomes, and the experimental domain affords a third, emergent outcome of CHASE. To evaluate the usefulness of a set of clusters, we generated 1000 additional interactions, predicted one of these outcomes for each trial, and recorded the percentage of correct responses. The prediction scheme was a straightforward voting algorithm that followed the two-step procedure for concept use: (1) *Recognition*. Find the cluster prototype nearest the time series in delay-coordinate space. (2) *Prediction*. Report the majority outcome for the corresponding cluster. Figure 5 illustrates the prediction performance as a function of observation time (the time when clusters are formed). The graph shows that the algorithm's response improves as the interaction unfolds and more data become available. For example at observation time $t = 10$ the prediction is correct only 64% of the time, but by $t = 35$ prediction performance exceeds 90%.

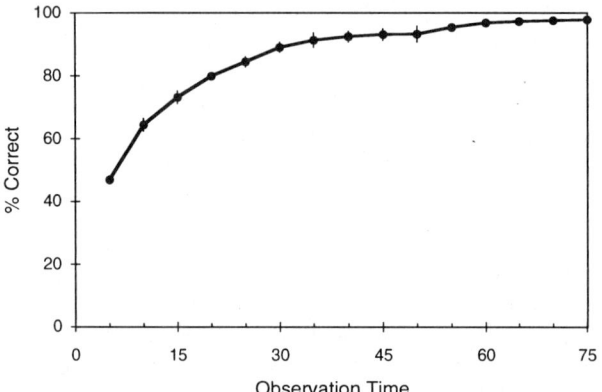

Figure 5: Prediction performance versus observation time for 1000 test interactions and the clusters shown in Figure 4. Clustering was based on 100 trials with $\theta_s = 0.2$, and error bars show the standard deviation for five replications.

How Many Concepts?

Our previous work using three intensity levels, $i = \{0.5, 1.0, 2.0\}$, required 36 interaction maps and, therefore, 36 concepts. With our present effort, we made things more difficult and selected i randomly from the interval $[0.5, 2.0]$. Nevertheless, clustering in delay-coordinate space resulted in far fewer concepts with no substantial differences in prediction performance. Even when we increased the number of trials to 10,000, we observed little change in the number of clusters formed. (See Figure 6.) In fact, very few trials — and, therefore, very few clusters — were needed to achieve a reasonable level of performance, after which the algorithm improved prediction performance by fine-tuning the existing clusters rather than creating new ones. Our explanation is that the algorithm discovered all the concepts that were available for discovering in the first place.

One caveat about clustering is that the results can become skewed by making a poor choice for the similarity threshold. For example, Figure 7a shows the number of clusters formed for several values of θ_s. When the similarity threshold is too small, trials seem to have little in common with one another and the number of clus-

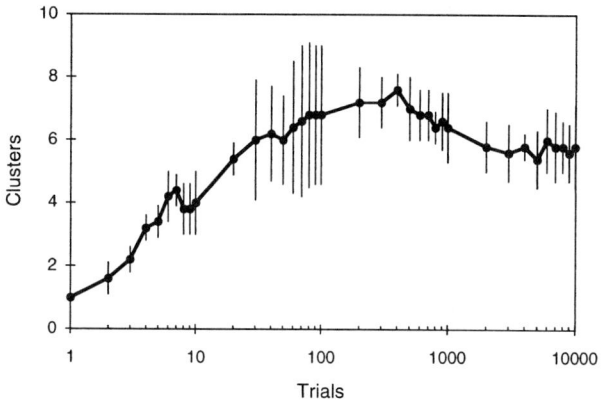

Figure 6: Semi-log plot of the number of clusters formed versus number of trials, where $\theta_s = 0.2$. Error bars show the standard deviation for five replications.

ters is roughly the same as the number of trials. As expected, an increase in θ_s yields a shorter cluster list, with the total number approaching the limiting value of 1. Figure 7b illustrates the other half of the story. When θ_s is too large, too few concepts are discovered and prediction performance is poor. But once the number of clusters exceeds a value of about five, prediction performance saturates and there is no benefit to learning a more detailed breakdown of "concept space." Put differently, plots such as Figure 7 offer a way to determine the number of concepts worth learning in the given domain.

Delay Coordinates

In this section we demonstrate the benefits of delay coordinates for reducing ambiguity in sensor readings. Our results thus far rely on the choice of observation time, not the dynamics, to tease apart different interactions. In particular, Figure 4 suggests that by time $t = 20$ we could classify most interactions correctly from a single sensor reading. To make the task more difficult (and more realistic) we now show clustering at a given value for object-distance. In other words, we fix the first delay coordinate so all trials appear the same to a naive algorithm that performs clustering without accounting for the dynamics. Moreover, we make use of delay coordinates *forward* in time, with Eq. (2) replaced by

$$\mathbf{X}_i^T = [x_i \; x_{i+J} \; x_{i+2J} \; ... \; x_{i+(m-1)J}]. \quad (3)$$

In practice, delay coordinates — both forward and backward in time — require the agent to wait until the data become available. The difference is simply a matter of perspective. For the forward view, the agent buffers its sensor readings when triggered by an event, such as the proximity of an opponent. For delay coordinates backward in time, the agent updates its sensor buffer continuously and associates an event with the most recent delay coordinate, rather than the oldest one.

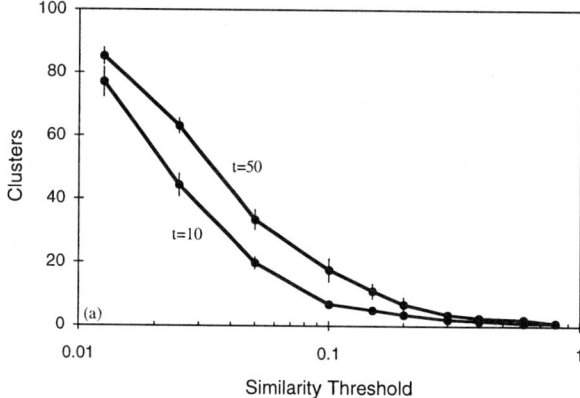

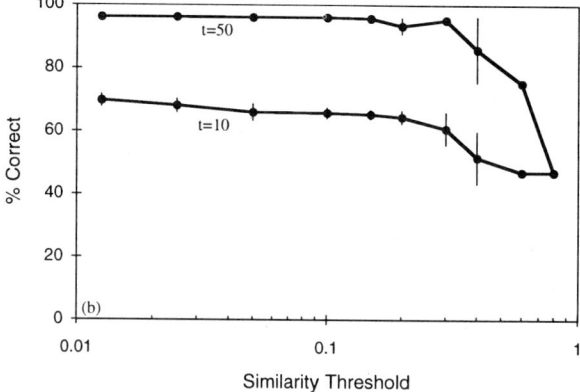

Figure 7: Effects of similarity threshold on (a) number of clusters and (b) prediction performance, for observation times $t = 10, 50$. Clustering was based on 100 trials and error bars show the standard deviation for five replications.

Figure 8a shows the result of clustering in a five-dimensional delay-coordinate space with delay $J = 1$. One prototype is similar to the category for CONTACT in Figure 4, whereas the other is an amalgam of all three basic outcomes. For Figure 8b, we increased the embedding delay to $J = 3$ so the delay-coordinate vector described by Eq. (3) spans a larger portion of the sensor stream (for the same fixed dimension). The effect is clusters of greater homogeneity since the algorithm is able to capture many of the subtle distinctions between two interactions.

Figure 9 illustrates more clearly the role of the embedding dimension. When m is too small, there is little time to observe a change between the first and last delay coordinates, and so many interactions fall near one another in delay-coordinate space. This situation yields relatively few clusters and poor prediction performance, much like Figure 7 for large values of θ_s. As m increases, points spread apart in embedding space since the additional coordinates reveal latent differences in the corresponding time series.

Learning 743

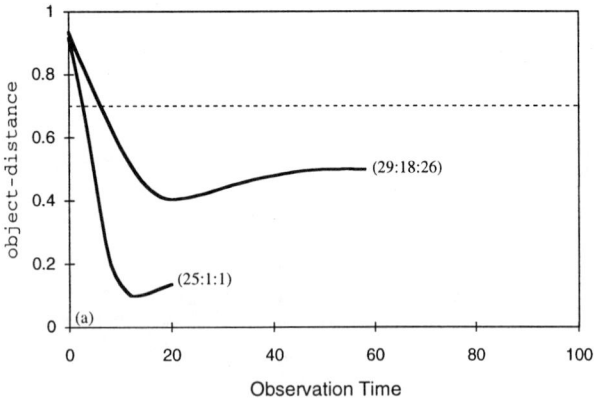

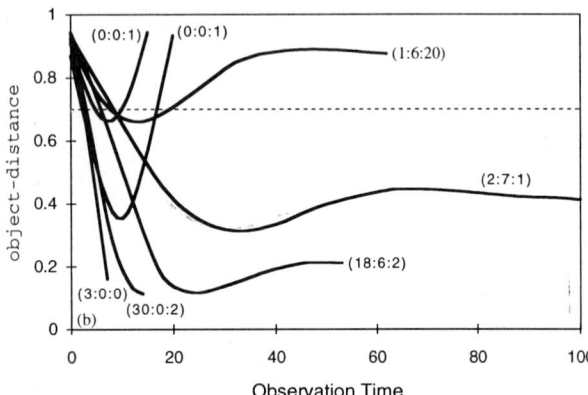

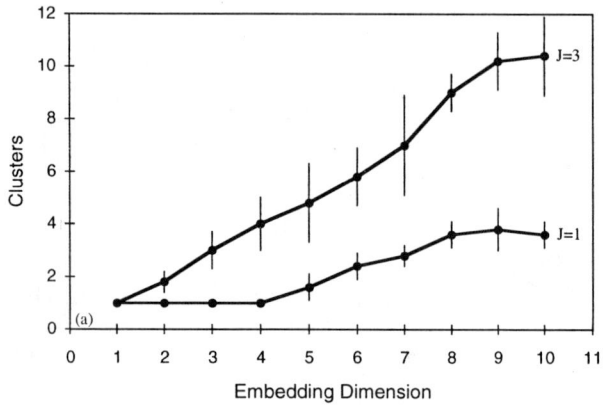

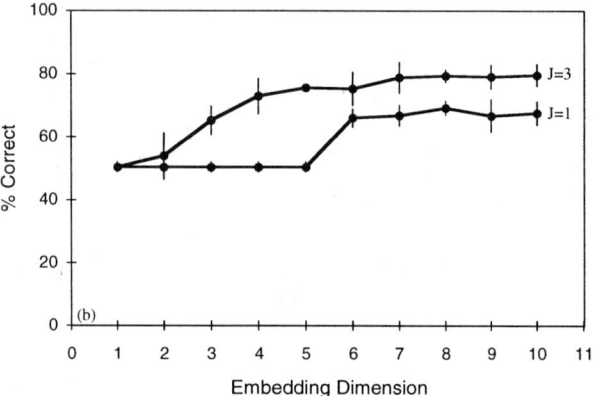

Figure 8: Cluster prototypes for object-distance=0.7, with $\theta_s = 0.1$, embedding dimension $m = 5$, and embedding delay (a) $J = 1$ and (b) $J = 3$. Labels show the makeup of each cluster. For instance, (29:18:26) indicates that the prototype was formed from 29 interactions ending in CONTACT, 18 ending in CHASE, and 26 ending in ESCAPE.

Figure 9: Effects of embedding dimension on (a) number of clusters and (b) prediction performance, for embedding delays $J = 1, 3$. Clustering was based on 100 trials, where $\theta_s = 0.1$ and object-distance=0.7. Error bars show the standard deviation for five replications.

Interaction Maps

With the pursuit/avoidance simulator, the clustering approach to concept acquisition afforded a prediction performance exceeding 95%. However, in more complicated, possibly noisy, environments it may not be possible to achieve this level of success with a prediction algorithm based solely on outcome frequencies. Our solution is to exploit the dynamics in the environment and store more detailed information about entailments in the form of interaction maps. We avoid the combinatorial drawbacks of map libraries by creating just one interaction map per cluster.

Interaction maps are similar to diagrams that show *basins of attraction*, or sets of initial conditions that lead to different *limit sets* (long-term outcomes). One way to build an interaction map involves the partitioning of delay-coordinate space into cells, where every cell contains a counter for each interesting outcome. As two agents interact, they generate a trajectory in this space, and once the outcome is known, the corresponding counter is incremented in each cell visited by the trajectory. The map is then colored as a function of the counter values in each cell.

Figure 10 shows the interaction map for the extreme case where all trials are placed into just one cluster. (For graphical purposes, we split the map into three grayscale images, one for each outcome, although one color diagram is often more informative.) Whenever a trajectory enters a dark region of a map, one can confidently predict the corresponding outcome. With interaction maps we saw a boost in prediction performance from 48% to 78% at $t = 10$ and to 88% at $t = 50$. Notice that these results compare favorably to those for six clusters as in Figure 5.

Conclusions

Perhaps the most promising aspect of this work is the possibility of an agent discovering concepts for itself. An emphasis on the agent not only aids our understanding of human cognitive development, but also influences the design of autonomous agents for more pragmatic purposes. In practical applications, someone, either agent or designer, must carve up the world in some

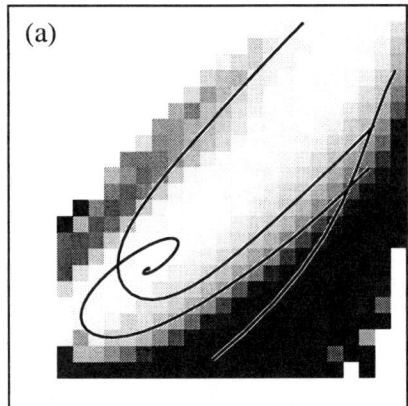 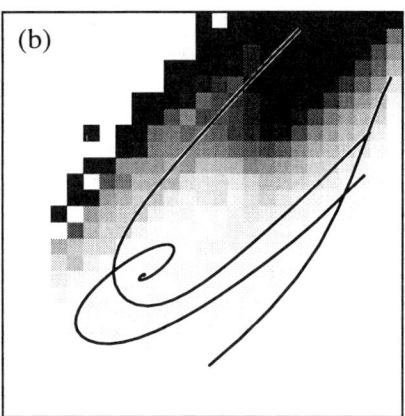 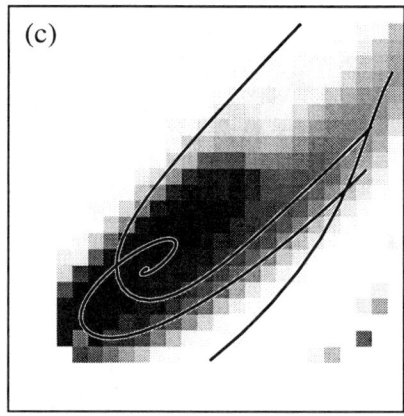

Figure 10: Interaction maps from one cluster with outcomes (a) CONTACT, (b) ESCAPE, and (c) CHASE. Darker shades of gray indicate a greater likelihood of the associated outcome. Also shown is an overlay of the delay portrait in Figure 3.

appropriate way, but what one deems relevant is quite dependent on one's perceptions of the world and one's ability to affect those percepts through action. For instance, as part of another project in our lab (Schmill *et al.* 1998), a mobile robot discovered an unexpected solution to the problem of being jammed between two objects. Whereas a programmer might instruct the robot to rock back-and-forth — as an automobile driver caught in mud or snow — the robot found on its own that opening its gripper could push itself far enough away from one of the objects. The point of this example is that a solution was found through interaction with the world. Indeed, Lakoff (Lakoff 1984) and Johnson (Johnson 1987) provide cogent arguments that more advanced symbolic thought is founded upon this very sort of sensorimotor interaction.

Although it may be a bit of a stretch to say that our pursuit/avoidance agents perform "sensorimotor" interaction, the results in this paper provide a beginning for future work with mobile robots. At the heart of the approach is the discovery of sensor reading patterns, and the specific contribution of this paper is a technique for deducing such patterns, i.e., clusters, from time series data. These clusters, together with their entailments, then provide a means for recognizing situations and predicting outcomes in the agent's world.

Acknowledgments

This research is supported by the National Defense Science and Engineering Graduate Fellowship and by DARPA under contract No. N66001-96-C-8504. The U.S. Government is authorized to reproduce and distribute reprints for governmental purposes notwithstanding any copyright notation hereon. The views and conclusions contained herein are those of the authors and should not be interpreted as the official policies or endorsements, either expressed or implied, of DARPA or the U.S. Government.

References

Cohen, P. R.; Oates, T.; Atkin, M. S.; and Beal, C. R. 1996. Building a baby. In *Proceedings of the Eighteenth Annual Conference of the Cognitive Science Society*, 518–522.

Elman, J. L. 1990. Finding structure in time. *Cognitive Science* 14:179–211.

Harnad, S. 1990. The symbol grounding problem. *Physica D* 42:335–346.

Johnson, M. 1987. *The Body in the Mind*. University of Chicago Press.

Lakoff, G. 1984. *Women, Fire, and Dangerous Things*. University of Chicago Press.

Omlin, C. W., and Giles, C. L. 1996. Extraction of rules from discrete-time recurrent neural networks. *Neural Networks* 9(1):41–52.

Rosch, E., and Lloyd, B. B. 1978. *Cognition and Categorization*. Hillsdale, NJ: Lawrence Erlbaum Associates.

Rosenstein, M.; Cohen, P. R.; Schmill, M. D.; and Atkin, M. S. 1997. Action representation, prediction and concepts. University of Massachusetts Computer Science Department Technical Report 97-31, also presented at the 1997 AAAI Workshop on Robots, Softbots, Immobots: Theories of Action, Planning and Control.

Rosenstein, M. T.; Collins, J. J.; and De Luca, C. J. 1994. Reconstruction expansion as a geometry-based framework for choosing proper delay times. *Physica D* 73:82–98.

Schmill, M. D.; Rosenstein, M. T.; Cohen, P. R.; and Utgoff, P. 1998. Learning what is relevant to the effects of actions for a mobile robot. To appear in *Proceedings of the Second International Conference on Autonomous Agents*.

Takens, F. 1981. Detecting strange attractors in turbulence. *Lecture Notes in Mathematics* 898:366–381.

The Dynamics of Reinforcement Learning in Cooperative Multiagent Systems

Caroline Claus and Craig Boutilier
Department of Computer Science
University of British Columbia
Vancouver, B.C., Canada V6T 1Z4
{cclaus,cebly}@cs.ubc.ca

Abstract

Reinforcement learning can provide a robust and natural means for agents to learn how to coordinate their action choices in multiagent systems. We examine some of the factors that can influence the dynamics of the learning process in such a setting. We first distinguish reinforcement learners that are unaware of (or ignore) the presence of other agents from those that explicitly attempt to learn the value of joint actions and the strategies of their counterparts. We study (a simple form of) Q-learning in cooperative multiagent systems under these two perspectives, focusing on the influence of that game structure and exploration strategies on convergence to (optimal and suboptimal) Nash equilibria. We then propose alternative *optimistic* exploration strategies that increase the likelihood of convergence to an optimal equilibrium.

1 Introduction

The application of learning to the problem of coordination in multiagent systems (MASs) has become increasingly popular in AI and game theory. The use of reinforcement learning (RL), in particular, has attracted recent attention [22, 20, 16, 11, 7, 15]. As noted in [16], using RL as a means of achieving coordinated behavior is attractive because of its generality and robustness.

Standard techniques for RL, for example, Q-learning [21], have been applied directly to MASs with some success. However, a general understanding of the conditions under which RL can be usefully applied, and exactly what form RL might take in MASs, are problems that have not yet been tackled in depth. We might ask the following questions:

- Are there differences between agents that learn as if there are no other agents (i.e., use single agent RL algorithms) and agents that attempt to learn both the values of specific *joint* actions and the strategies employed by other agents?

- Are RL algorithms guaranteed to converge in multiagent settings? If so, do they converge to (optimal) equilibria?

- How are rates of convergence and limit points influenced by the system structure and action selection strategies?

In this paper, we begin to address some of these questions in a specific context, namely, repeated games in which agents have common interests (i.e., cooperative MASs). We focus our attention on a simplified form of Q-learning, due to its relative simplicity (certainly not for its general efficacy), consider some of the factors that influence the dynamics of multiagent Q-learning, and provide partial answers to these questions. Though we focus on an simple setting, we expect many of our conclusions to apply more broadly.

We first distinguish and compare two forms of multiagent RL (MARL). *Independent learners* (ILs) apply Q-learning in the classic sense, ignoring the existence of other agents. *Joint action learners* (JALs), in contrast, learn the value of their own actions in conjunction with those of other agents via integration of RL with equilibrium (or coordination) learning methods [24, 5, 6, 9]. We then briefly consider the importance of exploitive exploration strategies and examine, through a series of examples, how game structure and exploration strategies influence the dynamics of the learning process and the convergence to equilibrium. We show that both JALs and ILs will converge to an equilibrium in this specific setting of fully cooperative, repeated games. In fact, even though JALs have much more information at their disposal, they do not perform much differently from ILs in the straightforward application of Q-learning to MASs. We also observe that in games with multiple equilibria, optimality of the "agreed upon" equilibrium is not assured. We then describe several *optimistic* exploration strategies, designed to increase the likelihood of reaching an optimal equilibrium. This provides one way of having JALs exploit the additional information that they possess. We conclude with a discussion of related work and mention several issues that promise to make the integration of RL with coordination learning an exciting area of research for the foreseeable future.

2 Preliminary Concepts and Notation
2.1 Single Stage Games

Our interest is in the application of RL algorithms to sequential decision problems in which the system is being controlled by multiple agents. However, in the interests of simplicity, our investigations in this paper are focussed on *n-player cooperative (or common interest) repeated games*. Sequential optimality will not be of primary interest, though we will discuss this issue in Sections 5 and 6.[1] We can view the prob-

---

Copyright © 1998, American Association for Artificial Intelligence (www.aaai.org). All rights reserved.

[1] Many of our conclusions hold *mutatis mutandis* for sequential, *multiagent Markov decision processes* [2] with multiple states; but

lem at hand, then, as a *distributed bandit problem*.

More formally, we assume a collection α of n (heterogeneous) agents, each agent $i \in \alpha$ having available to it a finite set of *individual actions* A_i. Agents repeatedly play a *stage game* in which they each independently select an individual action to perform. The chosen actions at any point constitute a *joint action*, the set of which is denoted $\mathcal{A} = \times_{i \in \alpha} A_i$. With each $a \in \mathcal{A}$ is associated a distribution over possible rewards; though the rewards are stochastic, for simplicity, we often simply refer to the expected reward $R(a)$. The decision problem is *cooperative* since each agent's reward is drawn from the same distribution, reflecting the utility assessment of all agents. The agents wish to choose actions that maximize (expected) reward.

We adopt some standard game theoretic terminology [13]. A *randomized strategy* for agent i is a distribution $\pi \in \Delta(A_i)$ (where $\Delta(A_i)$ is the set of distributions over the agent's action set A_i). Intuitively, $\pi(a^i)$ denotes the probability of agent i selecting the individual action a^i. A strategy π is *deterministic* if $\pi(a^i) = 1$ for some $a^i \in A_i$. A *strategy profile* is a collection $\Pi = \{\pi_i : i \in \alpha\}$ of strategies for each agent i. The expected value of acting according to a fixed profile can easily be determined. If each $\pi_i \in \Pi$ is deterministic, we can think of Π as a joint action. A *reduced profile for agent i* is a strategy profile for all agents but i (denoted Π_{-i}). Given a profile Π_{-i}, a strategy π_i is a *best response* for agent i if the expected value of the strategy profile $\Pi_{-i} \cup \{\pi_i\}$ is maximal for agent i; that is, agent i could not do better using any other strategy π_i'. Finally, we say that the strategy profile Π is a *Nash equilibrium* iff $\Pi[i]$ (i's component of Π) is a best response to Π_{-i}, for every agent i. Note that in cooperative games, deterministic equilibria are easy to find. An equilibrium (or joint action) is *optimal* if no other has greater value.

As an example, consider the simple two-agent stage game:

	a0	a1
b0	x	0
b1	0	y

Agents A and B each have two actions at their disposal, $a0, a1$ and $b0, b1$, respectively. If $x > y > 0$, $\langle a0, b0 \rangle$ and $\langle a1, b1 \rangle$ are both equilibria, but only the first is optimal: we would expect the agents to play $\langle a0, b0 \rangle$.

2.2 Learning in Coordination Games

Action selection is more difficult if there are multiple optimal joint actions. If, for instance, $x = y > 0$ in the example above, neither agent has a reason to prefer one or the other of its actions. If they choose them randomly, or in some way reflecting personal biases, then they risk choosing a suboptimal, or *uncoordinated* joint action. The general problem of *equilibrium selection* [13] can be addressed in several ways. For instance, communication between agents might be admitted [22] or one could impose conventions or rules that restrict behavior so as to ensure coordination [18]. Here we entertain the suggestion that coordinated action choice might be learned through repeated play of the game with the same agents [5, 6, 9, 11]. (Repeated play with a random selection of similar agents from a large population has also been the object of considerable study [17, 10, 24].)

One especially simple, yet often effective, learning model for achieving coordination is *fictitious play* [3, 5]. Each agent i keeps a count $C_{a^j}^j$, for each $j \in \alpha$ and $a^j \in A_j$, of the number of times agent j has used action a^j in the past. When the game is encountered, i treats the relative frequencies of each of j's moves as indicative of j's current (randomized) strategy. That is, for each agent j, i assumes j plays action $a^j \in A_j$ with probability $\Pr_{a^j}^i = C_{a^j}^j / (\sum_{b^j \in A_j} C_{b^j}^j)$. This set of strategies forms a reduced profile Π_{-i}, for which agent i adopts a best response. After the play, i updates its counts appropriately, given the actions used by the other agents. We think of these counts as reflecting the beliefs an agent has regarding the play of the other agents (initial counts can also be weighted to reflect priors).

This simple adaptive strategy will converge to an equilibrium in our simple cooperative games assuming that agents randomize when multiple best responses exist [12], and can be made to converge to an optimal equilibrium if appropriate mechanisms are adopted [1]; that is, the probability of coordinated equilibrium after k interactions can be made arbitrarily high by increasing k sufficiently. It is also not hard to see that once the agents reach an equilibrium, they will remain there—each best response reinforces the beliefs of the other agents that the coordinated equilibrium remains in force.

We note that most game theoretic models assume that each agent can observe the actions executed by its counterparts with certainty. As pointed out and addressed in [1, 7], this assumption is often unrealistic. A more general model allows each agent to obtain an *observation* which is related stochastically to the actual joint action selected, where $\Pr_a(o)$ denotes the probability of observation o being obtained by all agents when joint action a is performed. We will not investigate this model further, but mention it here since it subsumes the two special cases we describe below.

2.3 Reinforcement Learning

Action selection is more difficult still if agents are unaware of the rewards associated with various joint actions. In such a case, *reinforcement learning* can be used by the agents to estimate, based on past experience, the expected reward associated with individual or joint actions. We refer to [8] for a survey of RL techniques.

A simple, well-understood algorithm for single agent learning is *Q-learning* [21]. The formulation of Q-learning for general sequential decision processes is more sophisticated than we need here. In our stateless setting, we assume a *Q-value*, $Q(a)$, that provides an estimate of the value of performing (individual or joint) action a. An agent updates its estimate $Q(a)$ based on sample $\langle a, r \rangle$ as follows:

$$Q(a) \leftarrow Q(a) + \lambda(r - Q(a)) \quad (1)$$

The sample $\langle a, r \rangle$ is the "experience" obtained by the agent: action a was performed resulting in reward r. Here λ is the learning rate ($0 \leq \lambda \leq 1$), governing to what extent the new sample replaces the current estimate. If λ is decreased "slowly" during learning and all actions are sampled infinitely, Q-learning will converge to true Q-values for all actions in the single agent setting [21].[2]

---

[2] Generally, $Q(a, s)$ is taken to denote the long-term value of per-

Convergence of Q-learning does not depend on the *exploration strategy* used. An agent can try its actions at any time—there is no requirement to perform actions that are currently estimated to be best. Of course, if we hope to enhance overall performance during learning, it makes sense (at least intuitively) to bias selection toward better actions. We can distinguish two forms of exploration. In *nonexploitive exploration*, an agent randomly chooses its actions with uniform probability. There is no attempt to use what was learned to improve performance—the aim is simply to learn Q-values. In *exploitive exploration* an agent chooses its best estimated action with probability p_x, and chooses some other action with probability $1 - p_x$. Often the exploitation probability p_x is increased slowly over time. We call a nonoptimal action choice an *exploration step* and $1 - p_x$ the exploration probability. Nonoptimal action selection can be uniform during exploration, or can be biased by the magnitudes of Q-values. A popular biased strategy is *Boltzmann exploration*: action a is chosen with probability

$$\frac{e^{Q(a)/T}}{\sum_{a'} e^{Q(a')/T}} \quad (2)$$

The temperature parameter T can be decreased over time so that the exploitation probability increases (and can be done in such a way that convergence is assured [19]).

The existence of multiple agents, each simultaneously learning, is a potential impediment to the successful employment of Q-learning (or RL generally) in multiagent settings. When agent i is learning the value of its actions in the presence of other agents, it is learning in a nonstationary environment. Thus, the convergence of Q-values is not guaranteed. Naive application of Q-learning to MASs can be successful if we can ensure that each agent's strategy will eventually "settle." This is one of the questions we explore below. Application of Q-learning and other RL methods have met with some success in the past [22, 16, 17, 15].

There are two distinct ways in which Q-learning could be applied to a multiagent system. We say a MARL algorithm is an *independent learner* (IL) algorithm if the agents learn Q-values for their individual actions based on Equation (1). In other words, they perform their actions, obtain a reward and update their Q-values without regard to the actions performed by other agents. Experiences for agent i take the form $\langle a^i, r \rangle$ where a^i is the action performed by i and r is a reward. If an agent is unaware of the existence of other agents, cannot identify their actions, or has no reason to believe that other agents are acting strategically, then this is an appropriate method of learning. Of course, even if these conditions do not hold, an agent may choose to ignore information about the other agents' actions.

A *joint action learner* (JAL) is an agent that learns Q-values for joint actions as opposed to individual actions. The experiences for such an agent are of the form $\langle a, r \rangle$ where a is a joint action. This implies that each agent can observe the actions of other agents. The contrast between ILs and JALs can be illustrated in our example above: if A is an IL, then it will learn Q-values for actions $a0$ and $a1$; if A is a JAL, it will learn Q-values for all four joint actions, $\langle a0, b0 \rangle$, etc.

For JALs, exploration strategies require some care. In the example above, if A currently has Q-values for all four joint actions, the expected value of performing $a0$ or $a1$ depends crucially on the strategy adopted by B. To determine the relative values of their *individual* actions, each agent in a JAL algorithm maintains beliefs about the strategies of other agents. Here we will use empirical distributions, possibly with initial weights as in fictitious play. Agent A, for instance, assumes that each other agent B will choose actions in accordance with A's current beliefs about B (i.e., A's empirical distribution over B's action choices). In general, agent i assesses the expected value of its individual action a^i to be

$$EV(a^i) = \sum_{a^{-i} \in A_{-i}} Q(a^{-i} \cup \{a^i\}) \prod_{j \neq i} \{\Pr^i_{a^{-i}[j]}\}$$

Agent i can use these values just as it would Q-values in implementing an exploration strategy.[3]

We note that both JALs and ILs can be viewed as special cases of the partially observable model mentioned above, by allowing experiences of the form $\langle a^i, o, r \rangle$ where a^i is the action performed by i, and o is its (joint action) observation. A preliminary version of this paper [4] studies the methods below within this model.

3 Comparing Independent and Joint-Action Learners

We first compare the relative performance of independent and joint-action learners on a simple coordination game of the form described above:

	a0	a1
b0	10	0
b1	0	10

The first thing to note is that ILs using nonexploitive exploration will not deem either of their choices (on average) to be better than the other. For instance, A's Q-values for both action $a0$ and $a1$ will converge to 5, since whenever, say, $a0$ is executed, there is a 0.5 probability of $b0$ and $b1$ being executed. Of course, at any point, due to the stochastic nature of the strategies and the decay in learning rate, we would expect that the learned Q-values will not be identical; thus the agents, once they converge, might each have a reason to prefer one action to the other. Unfortunately, these biases need not be coordinated.

Rather than pursuing this direction, we consider the case where both the ILs and JALs use Boltzmann exploration (other exploitive strategies could be used). Exploitation of the known values allows the agents to "coordinate" in their choices for the same reasons that equilibrium learning methods work when agents know the reward structure. Figure 1 shows the probability of two ILs and JALs selecting an op-

---

forming action a in state s, and incorporates consideration of the values of possible states s' to which action a leads. This learning method is, in fact, a basic stochastic approximation technique [14]. We use (perhaps, misuse) the Q notation and terminology to emphasize the connection with action selection.

[3] The expression for $EV(a^i)$ makes the justifiable assumption that the other agents are selecting their actions independently. Less reasonable is the assumption that these choices are uncorrelated, or even correlated with i's choices. Such correlations can often emerge due to the dynamics of belief updating without agents being aware

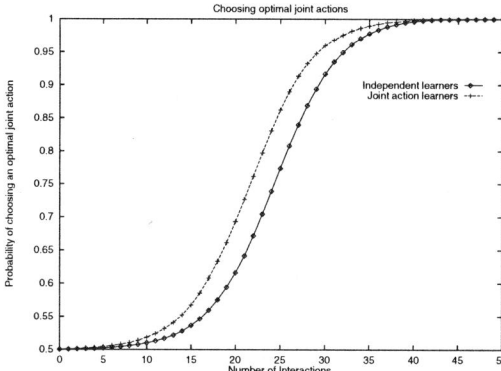

Figure 1: Convergence of coordination for ILs and JALs (averaged over 100 trials).

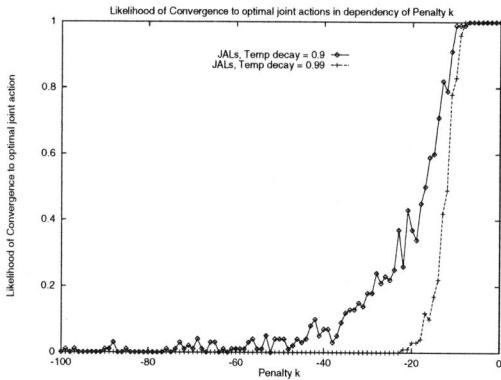

Figure 2: Likelihood of convergence to opt. equilibrium as a function of penalty k (averaged over 100 trials).

timal joint action as a function of the number of interactions they have. The temperature parameter is $T = 16$ initially and decayed by a factor of 0.9^t at the $t + 1$st interaction. We see that ILs coordinate quite quickly. There is no preference for either equilibrium point: each of the two equilibria was attained in about half of the trials. We do not show convergence of Q-values, but note that the Q-values for the actions of the equilibria attained (e.g., $\langle a0, b0 \rangle$) tended to 10 while the other actions tended to 0. Probability of optimal action selection does not increase smoothly within individual trials; the averaged probabilities reflect the likelihood of having reached an equilibrium by time t, as well as exploration probabilities. We also point out that much faster convergence can be had for different parameter settings (e.g., decaying temperature T more rapidly). We defer general remarks on convergence to Section 4.

The figure also shows convergence for JALs under the same circumstances. JALs do perform somewhat better after a fixed number of interactions, as shown in the graph. While the JALs have more information at their disposal, convergence is not enhanced dramatically. In retrospect, this should not be too surprising. While JALs are able to distinguish Q-values of different joint actions, their ability to use this information is circumscribed by the action selection mechanism. An agent maintains beliefs about the strategy being played by the other agents and "exploits" actions according to expected value based on these beliefs. In other words, the value of individual actions "plugged in" to the exploration strategy is more or less the same as the Q-values learned by ILs—the only distinction is that JALs *compute* them using explicit belief distributions and joint Q-values instead of updating them directly. Thus, even though the agents may be fairly sure of the relative Q-values of joint actions, Boltzmann exploration does not let them exploit this.[4]

___

of this correlation, especially if frequencies of particular joint actions are ignored.

[4] The key reason for the difference in ILs and JALs is the larger difference in Q-values for JALs, which bias Boltzmann exploration slightly more toward the estimated optimal action. Note that other exploitive strategies alleviate this problem to a certain degree.

4 Convergence and Game Structure

In the simple game considered above, it isn't difficult to see that both independent Q-learners and joint action Q-learners will converge on equilibria, as long as an exploitive exploration strategy with decreasing exploration is used. However, convergence is not always so smooth as illustrated in Figure 1. We know consider the ways in which the game structure can influence the dynamics of the learning process.

Consider the following class of games, with a variable (expected) *penalty* $k \leq 0$.

	a0	a1	a2
b0	10	0	k
b1	0	2	0
b2	k	0	10

This game (for any penalty) has three deterministic equilibria, of which two ($\langle a0, b0 \rangle$, $\langle a2, b2 \rangle$) are preferred. If, say, $k = -100$, during initial exploration agent A will find its first and third actions to be unattractive because of B's random exploration. If A is an IL, the average rewards (and hence Q-values) for $a0, a2$ will be quite low; and if A is a JAL, its beliefs about B's strategy will afford these actions low expected value. Similar remarks apply to B, and the self-confirming nature of equilibria virtually assure convergence to $\langle a1, b1 \rangle$. However, the closer k is to 0, the lower the likelihood the agents will find their first and third actions unattractive—the stochastic nature of exploration means that, occasionally, these actions will have high estimated utility and convergence to one of the optimal equilibria will occur. Figure 2 shows how the probability of convergence to one of the optimal equilibria is influenced by the magnitude of the "penalty" k. Not surprisingly, different equilibria can be attained with different likelihoods.[5]

Thus far, our examples show agents proceeding on a direct route to equilibria (albeit at various rates, and with destinations "chosen" stochastically). Unfortunately, convergence is not so straightforward in general. Consider the following *climbing* game:

___

[5] These results are shown for JALs; but the general pattern holds true for ILs as well.

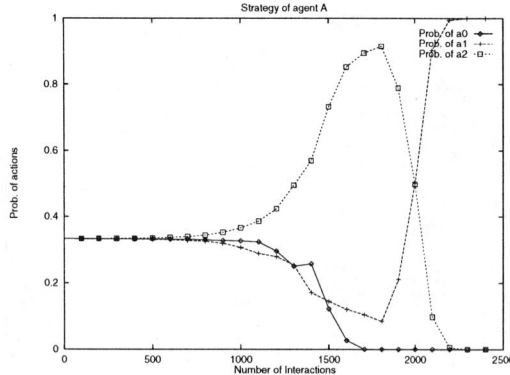

Figure 3: A's strategy in climbing game

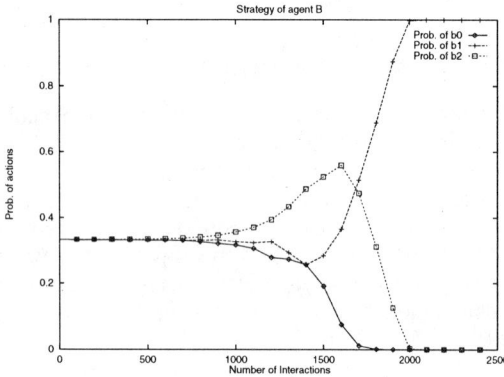

Figure 4: B's strategy in climbing game

	$a0$	$a1$	$a2$
$b0$	11	-30	0
$b1$	-30	7	6
$b2$	0	0	5

Initially, the two learners are almost certainly going to begin to play the nonequilibrium strategy profile $\langle a2, b2 \rangle$. This is seen clearly in Figures 3, 4 and 5.[6] However, once they "settle" at this point, as long as exploration continues, agent B will soon find $b1$ to be more attractive—so long as A continues to primarily choose $a2$. Once the nonequilibrium point $\langle a2, b1 \rangle$ is attained, agent A tracks B's move and begins to perform action $a1$. Once this equilibrium is reached, the agents remain there.

This phenomenon will obtain in general, allowing one to conclude that the multiagent Q-learning schemes we have proposed will converge to equilibria almost surely. The conditions that are required in both cases are:

- The learning rate λ decreases over time such that $\sum_{\lambda=0}^{t} \lambda = \infty$ and $\sum_{\lambda=0}^{t} \lambda^2 < \infty$.

- Each agent samples each of its actions infinitely often.

---
[6] Parameter settings for these figures: initial temperature 10000 is decayed at rate 0.995^t.

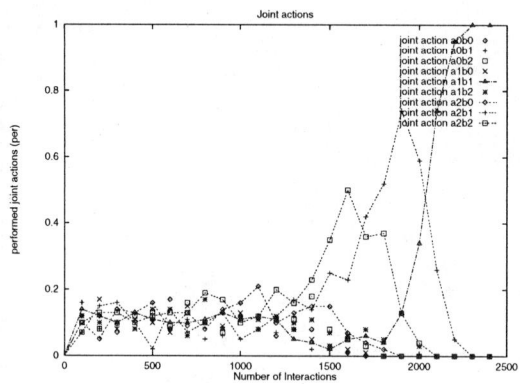

Figure 5: Joint actions in climbing game

- The probability $P_t^i(a)$ of agent i choosing action a is nonzero.

- Each agent's exploration strategy is exploitive. That is, $\lim_{t \to \infty} P_t^i(X_t) = 0$, where X_t is a random variable denoting the event that some nonoptimal action was taken based on i's estimated values at time t.

The first two conditions are required of Q-learning, and the third, if implemented appropriately (e.g., with appropriately decayed temperature), will ensure the second. Furthermore, it ensures that agents cannot adopt deterministic exploration strategies and become strictly correlated. Finally, the last condition ensures that agents exploit their knowledge. In the context of ficticious play and its variants, this exploration strategy would be *asymptotically myopic* [5]. This is necessary to ensure that an equilibrium will be reached. Under these conditions we have:

Theorem 1 *Let E_t be a random variable denoting the probability of a (deterministic) equilibrium strategy profile being played at time t. Then for both ILs and JALs, for any $\delta, \varepsilon > 0$, there is an $T(\delta, \varepsilon)$ such that*

$$\Pr(|E_t - 1| < \varepsilon) > 1 - \delta$$

for all $t > T(\delta, \varepsilon)$.

Intuitively (and somewhat informally), the dynamics of the learning process behaves as follows. If the agents are in equilibrium, there is a nonzero probability of moving out of equilibrium; but this generally requires a (rather dense) series of exploratory moves by one or more agents. The probability of this occurring decreases over time, making the likelihood of leaving an equilibrium just obtained vanish over time (both for JALs and ILs). If at some point the agents' estimated Q-values are such that a nonequilibrium is most likely, the likelihood of this state of affairs remaining also vanishes over time. As an example, consider the climbing game above. Once agents begin to play $\langle a2, b2 \rangle$ regularly, agent B is still required to explore. After a sufficient sampling of action $b1$—without agent A *simultaneously* exploring and moving away from $a2$—$b1$ will look more attractive than $b2$ and this best reply will be adopted. Decreasing exploration ensures that the odds of simultaneous exploration decrease fast enough to assure that this happens with high probability. Similar reasoning shows that a best reply path will eventually be followed to a point of equilibrium.

This theoretical guarantee of convergence may be of limited practical value for sufficiently complicated games. The key difficulty is that convergence relies on the use of decaying exploration: this is necessary to "approximate" the best-response condition of fictitious play. This gradual decay, however, makes the time required to shift from the current entrenched strategy profile to a better profile rather long. If the agents initially settle on a profile that is a large distance (in terms of a best reply path) from an equilibrium, each shift required can take longer to occur because of the decay in exploration. Furthermore, as pointed out above, the probability of concurrent exploration may have to be sufficiently small to ensure that the expected value of a shift along the best reply path is greater than no shift, which can introduce further delays in the process. The longer these delays are, the lower the learning rate λ becomes, requiring more experience to overcome the initially biased estimated Q-values.

Finally, the key drawback for JALs (which know the joint Q-values) is the fact that beliefs based on a lot of experience require a considerable amount of contrary experience to be overcome. For example, once B has made the shift from $b2$ to $b1$ above, a significant amount of time is needed for A to switch from $a2$ to $a1$: it has to observe B performing $b1$ enough to overcome the rather large degree of belief it had that B would continue doing $b2$. Although we don't report on this here, our initial experiments using *windows* or finite histories upon which to base beliefs has shown considerable practical value.[7]

5 Biasing Exploration Strategies for Optimality

One thing we notice about the MARL strategies described above is that they do not ensure convergence to an optimal equilibrium. Little can be done about this is the case of ILs.[8] However, JALs have considerably more information at there disposal in the form of joint Q-values. For example, in the penalty game, agents A and B might converge to the suboptimal equilibrium $\langle a1, b1 \rangle$; but both agents have learned the game structure and realize their coordinated strategy profile is suboptimal. Once attained, the usual exploration strategies permit escape from this equilibrium only with small, diminishing probability.

Intuitively, we can imagine both agents trying to break out of this equilibrium in an attempt to reach a more desirable point (say, $\langle a2, b2 \rangle$). For instance, agent B might sample $b2$ a number of times in order to induce A to switch its strategy to $a2$. In fact, this can be worthwhile if the "penalties" received in the attempt are compensated for by the long run sequence of high rewards obtained once the optimal equilibrium is achieved. Note that this type of action selection runs counter to the requirement that a best response be cho-

---

[7]Fictitious play based on histories of an appropriately chosen length is shown to converge in [24].

[8]One could imagine that an IL might bias its action selection toward those whose Q-values have high variance, or adhere to a multimodal distribution, perhaps indicative of another agent acting simultaneously; but this seems to run contrary to the "spirit" of ILs.

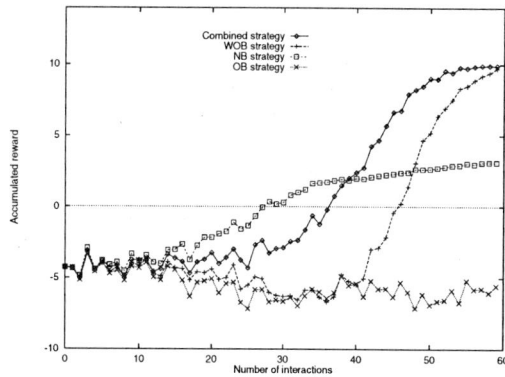

Figure 6: Sliding avg. reward in the penalty game

sen except for "random" exploration. This type of switch requires that agents intentionally choose (immediately) suboptimal actions.

Ultimately, the decision to attain a long run optimal equilibrium at the expense of a finite sequence of penalties can be cast as a sequential decision problem. For instance, if future rewards are highly discounted, agents may not risk deviating from a suboptimal equilibrium. However, such a decision problem (especially when we move to more complex settings) can be intractable. Instead, we consider augmented exploration strategies that will encourage long run optimality. What we propose below are *myopic heuristics*, based only on the current state, that tend to induce long run optimal behavior. Three such heuristics are:

Optimistic Boltzmann (OB): For agent i, action $a_i \in A_i$, let $MaxQ(a_i) = \max_{\Pi_{-i}} Q(\Pi_{-i}, a_i)$. Choose actions with Boltzmann exploration (another exploitive strategy would suffice) using $MaxQ(a_i)$ as the value of a_i.

Weighted OB (WOB): Explore using Boltzmann using factors $MaxQ(a_i) \cdot \Pr_i(\text{optimal match } \Pi_{-i} \text{ for } a_i)$.

Combined: Let $C(a_i) = \rho \, MaxQ(a_i) + (1 - \rho)EV(a_i)$, for some $0 \leq \rho \leq 1$. Choose actions using Boltzmann exploration with $C(a_i)$ as value of a_i.

OB is optimistic in the sense that an agent assesses each of its actions as though the agents around it will act in order to "match" its choice of an action. WOB is a more realistic version of OB: the assessment of an action is tempered by the likelihood that a matching will be made (according to its current beliefs). Finally the combined strategy is more flexible: it uses a normal exploration strategy but introduces the *MaxQ* factor to bias exploration toward actions that have "potential." The coefficient ρ allows one to tune this bias. The experiment below uses $\rho = 0.5$.

We have performed some preliminary experimentation with these heuristics. Figure 6 illustrates the results of these three heuristics, as well as normal Boltzmann (NB) exploration, for the penalty game ($k = -10$). It shows (sliding) average reward obtained over the last ten interactions for each strategy. Thus it shows not only the convergence behavior, but the penalties incurred in attempting to reach an optimal equilibrium. NB behaves as above, sometimes converging to the optimal (10) and suboptimal (2) equilibrium. Not surprisingly, OB fares poorly: the presence of multiple equilibria make it impossible to do well (although it behaves reasonably well in simpler games). The two agents cannot coordinate because the are not permitted to account for the strategy of the other agent. WOB circumvents the difficulty with OB by using beliefs to ensure coordination; it converges to an optimal equilibrium each time. The Combined strategy also guarantees long run optimality, but it has better performance along the way.

We can draw few formal conclusions at this time; but we think the use of myopic heuristics for exploration deserves considerably more study. Methods like the Combined strategy that allow problem dependent tuning of the exploration strategy seem especially promising. By focusing on particular sequential optimality criteria, intelligent parameter tuning should be possible.

6 Concluding Remarks

We have seen described two basic ways in which Q-learning can be applied in multiagent cooperative settings, and examined the impact of various features on the success of the interaction between equilibrium selection learning techniques with RL techniques. We have demonstrated that the integration requires some care, and that Q-learning is not nearly as robust as in single-agent settings. Convergence guarantees are not especially practical for complex games, but new exploration heuristics may help in this regard.

Several proposals have been put forth that are closely related to ours. Tan [20] and Sen, Sekaran and Hale [16] apply RL to *independent* agents and demonstrate empirical convergence. These results are consistent with ours, but properties of the convergence points (whether they are optimal or even in equilibrium are not considered). Wheeler and Narendra [23] develop a learning automata (LA) model for fully cooperative games. They show that using this model agents will converge to equilibrium if there is a *unique* pure strategy equilibrium; thus the coordination problem that interests us here is not addressed directly. Furthermore, the LA model is different from the Q-learning model we address. However, the connections between the two models deserve further exploration.

A number of important directions remain to be pursued. The most obvious is the generalization of these ideas to general, multistate, sequential problems for which Q-learning is designed (for instance, as addressed in [20, 16]. An interesting issue that emerges when one tries to directly apply fictitious play models to such a setting is estimating the value of actions using the Q-values of future states when the actual future value obtained can hinge on coordination (or lack thereof) at these future states. The application of generalization techniques to deal with large state and action spaces is also of great importance, especially in multiagent domains where the size of joint action spaces can grow exponentially with the number of agents. Finally, we expect these ideas to generalize to other settings (such as zero-sum games) where fictitious play is also known to converge.

Acknowledgements: Thanks to Leslie Kaelbling and Michael Littman for their helpful discussions in the early stages of this work and Daniel Koditschek for helpful pointers. This work was supported by NSERC Grant OGP0121843 and IRIS-II Project IC-7.

References

[1] C. Boutilier. Learning conventions in multiagent stochastic domains using likelihood estimates. *Proc. 12th Intl. Conf. Uncertainty in AI*, pp.106–114, Portland, OR, 1996.

[2] C. Boutilier. Planning, learning and coordination in multiagent decision processes. *Proc. 6th Conf. Theor. Aspects of Rationality and Knowledge*, pp.195–210, Amsterdam, 1996.

[3] G. W. Brown. Iterative solution of games by fictitious play. In T. C. Koopmans, editor, *Activity Analysis of Production and Allocation*. Wiley, New York, 1951.

[4] C. Claus and C. Boutilier. The Dynamics of Reinforcement Learning in Cooperative Multiagent Systems. *AAAI-97 Work. Multiagent Learning*, pp.13–18, Providence, 1997.

[5] D. Fudenberg and D. M. Kreps. *Lectures on Learning and Equilibrium in Strategic Form Games*. CORE Foundation, Louvain-La-Neuve, Belgium, 1992.

[6] D. Fudenberg and D. K. Levine. Steady state learning and Nash equilibrium. *Econometrica*, 61(3):547–573, 1993.

[7] J. Hu and M. P. Wellman. Self-fulfilling bias in multiagent learning. *Proc. ICMAS-96*, pp.118–125, Kyoto, 1996.

[8] L. P. Kaelbling, M. L. Littman, A. W. Moore. Reinforcement learning: A survey. *J. Art. Intel. Res.*, 4:237–285, 1996.

[9] E. Kalai and E. Lehrer. Rational learning leads to Nash equilibrium. *Econometrica*, 61(5):1019–1045, 1993.

[10] M. Kandori, G. Mailath, R. Rob. Learning, mutation and long run equilibria in games. *Econometrica*, 61:29–56, 1993.

[11] M. L. Littman. Markov games as a framework for multi-agent reinforcement learning. In *Proc. 11th Intl. Conf. on Machine Learning*, pp.157–163, New Brunswick, NJ, 1994.

[12] D. Monderer, L. S. Shapley. Fictitious play property for games with identical interests. *J. Econ. Th.*, 68:258–265, 1996.

[13] R. B. Myerson. *Game Theory: Analysis of Conflict*. Harvard University Press, Cambridge, 1991.

[14] H. Robbins and S. Munro. A stochastic approximation method. *Annals Math. Stat.*, 22:400–407, 1951.

[15] T. Sandholm and R. Crites. Learning in the iterated prisoner's dilemma. *Biosystems*, 37:147–166, 1995.

[16] S. Sen, M. Sekaran, J. Hale. Learning to coordinate without sharing information. *AAAI-94*, pp.426–431, Seattle, 1994.

[17] Y. Shoham and M. Tennenholtz. Emergent conventions in multi-agent systems: Initial experimental results and observations. *KR-92*, pp.225–231, Cambridge, 1992.

[18] Y. Shoham and M. Tennenholtz. On the synthesis of useful social laws for artificial agent societies. *Proc. AAAI-92*, pp.276–281, San Jose, 1992.

[19] S. Singh, T. Jaakkola, M. L. Littman, and C. Szepesvári. Convergence results for single-step on-policy reinforcement learning algorithms. *Machine Learning*, 1998. To appear.

[20] M. Tan. Multi-agent Reinforcement Learning: Independent vs. Cooperative Agents. *Proc. 10th Intl. Conf. on Machine Learning*, pp.330–337, Amherst, MA, 1993.

[21] C. J. C. H. Watkins and P. Dayan. Q-learning. *Machine Learning*, 8:279–292, 1992.

[22] G. Weiß. Learning to coordinate actions in multi-agent systems. *Proc. IJCAI-93*, pp.311–316, Chambery, FR, 1993.

[23] R. M. Wheeler and K. S. Narendra. Decentralized learning in Markov chains. *IEEE Trans. Aut. Control*, 31:519–526, 1951.

[24] H. Peyton Young. The evolution of conventions. *Econometrica*, 61(1):57–84, 1993.

Applying Online Search Techniques to Continuous-State Reinforcement Learning

Scott Davies*   **Andrew Y. Ng[†]**   **Andrew Moore***

* School of Computer Science
Carnegie-Mellon University
Pittsburgh, PA 15213

† Artificial Intelligence Lab
Massachusetts Institute of Technology
Cambridge, MA 02139

Abstract

In this paper, we describe methods for efficiently computing better solutions to control problems in continuous state spaces. We provide algorithms that exploit online search to boost the power of very approximate value functions discovered by traditional reinforcement learning techniques. We examine local searches, where the agent performs a finite-depth lookahead search, and global searches, where the agent performs a search for a trajectory all the way from the current state to a goal state.

The key to the success of the local methods lies in taking a value function, which gives a rough solution to the hard problem of finding good trajectories from every single state, and combining that with online search, which then gives an accurate solution to the easier problem of finding a good trajectory *specifically* from the current state.

The key to the success of the global methods lies in using aggressive state-space search techniques such as uniform-cost search and A^*, tamed into a tractable form by exploiting neighborhood relations and trajectory constraints that arise from continuous-space dynamic control.

Introduction

A common approach to Reinforcement Learning involves approximating the value function, and then executing the greedy policy with respect to the learned value function.

However, particularly in high-dimensional continuous state spaces, it can often be computationally expensive to fit a highly accurate value function, even when our agent is given a perfect model of the world. This problem is even worse when the agent is learning a model of the world and is repeatedly updating its dynamic programming solution online. What's to be done?

In this paper, we investigate the idea that rather than executing greedy policies with respect to approximated value functions in continuous-state domains, we can use online search techniques to find better trajectories. We restrict our attention to deterministic domains. The

Copyright ©1998, American Association for Artificial Intelligence (www.aaai.org). All rights reserved.

paper consists of a progression of improvements to conventional action-selection from value functions, along the way using techniques from value function approximation (Davies, 1997), real-time search (Korf, 1990), constrained trajectories (Burghes and Graham 1980), and robot motion planning (Latombe 1991, Boyan et al. 1995, Boone 1997). All of the algorithms perform search online to find a good trajectory from some current state. Briefly, the progression is as follows:

- **LS: Local Search.** Takes a forward-dynamics model and an approximate value function, and performs a limited-depth lookahead search of possible trajectories from the current state before suggesting an action.

- **CLS: Constrained Local Search.** Does a similar job as LS, but considers only trajectories in which the action is changed infrequently. This results in substantial computational savings that allow it to search much deeper or faster.

- **UGS: Uninformed Global Search.** For least-cost-to-goal problems, takes a forward-dynamics model and plans an approximately-least-cost path from the current state all the way to the goal, using LS or CLS along with a neighborhood-based pruning technique to permit tractable searches even when they cover large areas of the continuous state space.

- **IGS: Informed Global Search.** Does a similar job as UGS, but uses an approximate value function to guide the search in a manner very similar to A^* (Nilsson 1971), thereby vastly reducing the search time and (somewhat surprisingly) often dramatically improving the solution quality as well.

- **LLS: Learning Local Search.** *Learns* a forward-dynamics model, and uses it to generate approximate value functions for the LS and CLS approaches.

- **LGS: Learning Global Search.** *Learns* a forward-dynamics model, and uses it to generate approximate value functions for the LS and CLS approaches.

In this paper, the approximate value functions are obtained by k-dimensional simplex interpolation combined with value iteration (Davies 1997), but the approaches are applicable for accelerating any model-based reinforcement learning algorithm that produces approximate value functions, such as an LQR solution to a linearized problem or a neural net value function computed with TD.

With such searches, we perform online computation that is directed towards finding a good trajectory *from the current state*; this is in contrast to, say, offline learning of a value function, which tries to solve the much harder problem of learning a good policy for every point in the state space. However, the global search algorithms go beyond shallow lookahead methods and instead use a pruned "bush" of search trajectories to find continuous trajectories all the way to the goal.

We apply these search techniques to several continuous-state problems, and demonstrate that they often dramatically improve the quality of solutions at relatively little computational expense.

MOUNTAIN-PARKING: An example of a continuous-space dynamic control task

Figure 1 depicts a car (idealized as a frictionless puck) on a very steep hill. The car can accelerate forward or backward with a limited maximum thrust. The goal is to park the car in a space near the top of the hill (that is, occupy the space while having a near-zero velocity). Because of gravity, there is a region near the center of the hill at which the maximum forward thrust is not strong enough to accelerate up the slope. This is depicted on the two-dimensional diagram in Figure 2. Thus if the goal is at the top of the slope, a strategy that proceeded by greedily choosing actions to thrust towards the goal would get stuck. Figure 3 shows a sample minimum-time path for one possible initial state. This task, although trivial to solve by dynamic programming on a very fine grid, will be used as an illustration during the exposition because its state space can be drawn as a two-dimensional diagram. In the Experiments section we will see empirical results for problems that would be intractably expensive for dynamic programming on a fine grid.

LS: Local Search

Given a value function, agents typically execute a greedy policy using a one-step lookahead search, possibly using a learned model for the lookahead. The computational cost per step of this is $O(|A|)$ where A is the set of actions. This can be thought of as performing a depth 1 search for the 1-step trajectory T that gives the highest $R_T + \gamma V(s_T)$, where R_T is the reinforcement, s_T is the state (possibly according to a learned world model) reached upon executing T, and γ is the discount factor. A natural extension is then to perform a search of depth d, to find the trajectory that maximizes $R_T + \gamma^d V(s_T)$, where discounting is incorporated in the natural way into R_T. The computational expense is $O(d|A|^d)$.

During execution, the LS algorithm iteratively finds the best trajectory T of length d with the search algo-

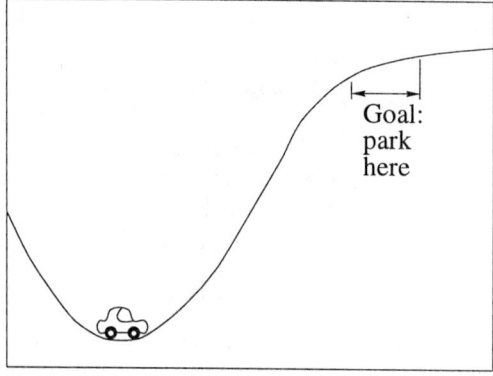

Figure 1: A car acted on by gravity and limited forward/backward thrust. The car must park in the goal area as quickly as possible.

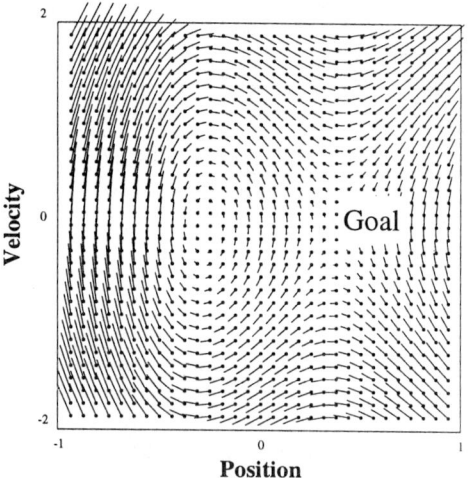

Figure 2: The state transition function for a car constantly thrusting to the right with maximum thrust. A point on the diagram represents a state of the car. Horizontal position denotes the physical car position. Vertical diagram position denote the car's velocity.

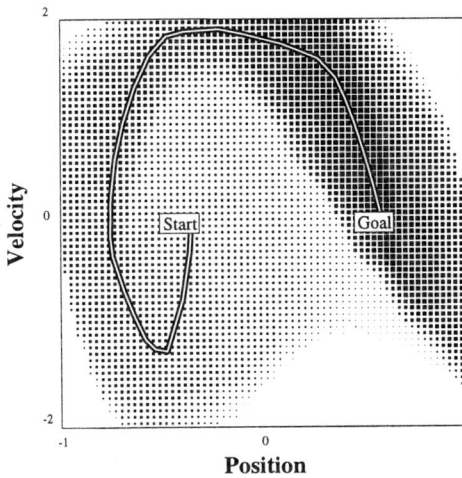

Figure 3: A minimum-time path for the car on the hill. The optimal value function is shown by dots. The shorter the time to goal, the larger the black dot.

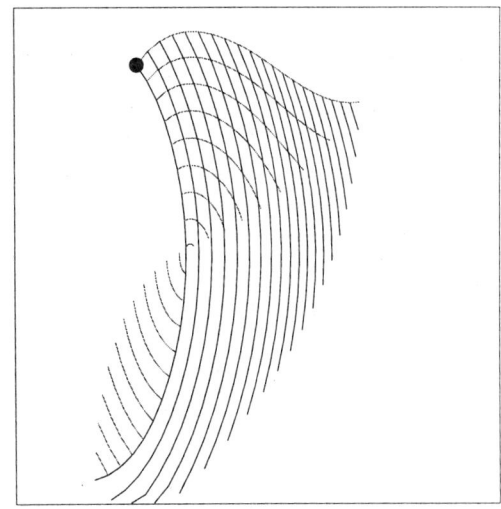

Figure 4: Constrained Local Search (CLS) example: a twenty-step search with at most one switch in actions

rithm above, executes the first action on that trajectory, and then does a new search from the resulting state. If B is the "parallel backup operator" (Bertsekas 1995) so that $BV(s) = max_{a \in A} R(s,a) + \gamma V(\delta(s,a))$, then executing the full $|A|^d$ search is formally equivalent to executing the greedy policy with respect to the value function $B^{d-1}V$. Noting that, under mild regularity assumptions, as $k \to \infty$, $B^k V$ becomes the optimal value function, we can generally expect $B^{d-1}V$ to be a better value function than V. For example, in discounted problems, if the largest absolute error in V is ε, the largest absolute error in $B^{d-1}V$ is $\gamma^{d-1}\varepsilon$.

This approach, a form of receding horizon control, has most famously been applied to minimax game playing programs (Russell and Norvig 1995) and has also been used in single-agent systems on discrete domains (e.g. (Korf 1990)). In game-playing scenarios it has also been used in conjunction with automatically learned value functions, such as in Samuel's celebrated checkers program (Samuel 1959) and Tesauro's backgammon player (Tesauro and Galperin, 1997).

CLS: Constrained Local Search

To make deeper searches computationally cheaper, we might consider only a subset of all possible trajectories of depth d. Especially for dynamic control, often an optimal trajectory repeatedly selects and then *holds* a certain action for some time, such as suggested by (Boone 1997). Therefore, a natural subset of the $|A|^d$ possible trajectories are trajectories that switch their actions rarely. When we constrain the number of switches between actions to be s, the time for such a search is then $O(d\binom{d}{s}|A|^{s+1})$—considerably cheaper than a full search if $s \ll d$. We also suggest that s is easily chosen for a particular domain by an expert, by asking how often action switches can reasonably be expected in an optimal trajectory, and then picking s accordingly to allow an appropriate number of switches in a trajectory of length d. Figure 4 shows CLS performed in the MOUNTAIN-PARKING task using $d = 20$ and $s = 1$.

Since LS is the same as CLS with the maximum-number-of-switches parameter s set to $d - 1$, we may use "LS" or "local search" to refer generically to both CLS and LS at certain points throughout the rest of the paper.

UGS: Uninformed Global Search

Local searches (LS and CLS) are not the only way to more effectively use an approximated value function. Here, we describe global search for solving least-cost-to-goal problems in continuous state spaces with non-negative costs. We assume the set of goal states is known.

Why not continue growing a search tree until it finds a goal state? The answer is clear—the combinatorial explosion would be devastating. In order to deal with this problem, we borrow a technique from robot motion planning (Latombe 1991). We first divide the state space up into a fine uniform grid. A sparse representation is used so that only grid cells that are visited take up memory[1].

A local search procedure (LS or CLS) is then used to find paths from one grid element to another. Multiple trajectories entering the same grid element are pruned, keeping only the least-cost trajectory into that grid element (breaking ties arbitrarily). The point at which this least-cost trajectory first enters a grid element is used as the grid element's "representative state," and

---

[1]This has a flavor not dissimilar to the hashed sparse coarse encodings of (Sutton 1996).

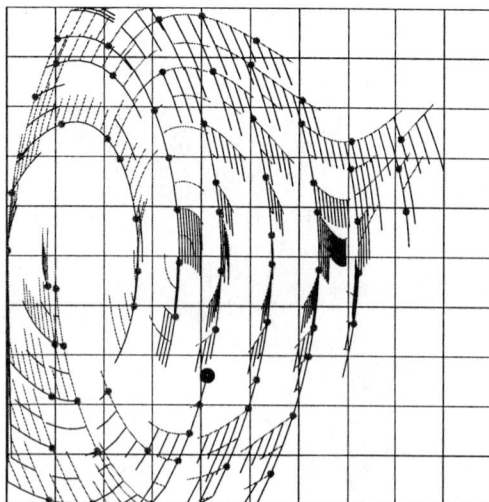

Figure 5: Uninformed Global Search (UGS) example. Velocity on x-axis, car position on y axis. Large black dot is starting state; the small dots are grid elements' "representative states."

acts as the starting point for the local search. The rationale for the pruning is an assumed similarity among points in the same grid element. In this manner, the algorithm attempts to builds a complete trajectory to the goal using the learned or provided world model. When the planner finds a trajectory to the goal, it is executed in its entirety.

The overall procedure is essentially a lowest-cost-first search over a graph structure in which the graph nodes correspond to grid elements, and in which the edges between graph nodes correspond to trajectories between grid elements as found by the CLS procedure. A graph showing such a search for the MOUNTAIN-PARKING domain is depicted in Figure 5.

IGS: Informed Global Search

We can modify Uninformed Global Search (UGS) by using an approximated value function to *guide* the search expansions in the style of A^* search (Nilsson 1971), as written out in detail below. The search proceeds from the most promising-looking states first, where the "promise" of a state is the cost to get to the state (along previously searched trajectories) plus the remaining-cost-to-go as estimated with the value function. With the perfect value function, this causes the search to traverse exactly the optimal path to the goal; with only an approximation to the value function, it can still dramatically reduce the fraction of the state space that is searched.

As in UGS, the grid is represented sparsely. Notice also that like LS and CLS, we are performing on-line computation in the sense that we are performing a search only when we know the "current state," and to find a trajectory specifically from the current state; this is in contrast to offline computation for finding a value function, which tries to solve the much more difficult problem of finding a good trajectory to the goal from every single point in the state space.

Written out in full, the search algorithm is:

1. Suppose $g(s_0)$ is the grid element containing the current state s_0. Set $g(s_0)$'s "representative state" to be s_0, and add $g(s_0)$ to a priority queue P with priority $V(s_0)$, where V is an approximated value function.

2. Until a goal state has been found, or P is empty:
   - Remove a grid element g from the top of P. Suppose s is g's "representative state."
   - Starting from s, perform LS or CLS as described in the Local Search section, except search trajectories are pruned once they reach a state in a different grid element g'. If g' has not been visited before, add g' to P with a priority $p(g') = R_T(s_0, \ldots, s') + \gamma^{|T|}V(s')$, where R_T is the reward accumulated along the recorded trajectory T from s_0 to s', and set g''s "representative state" to s'. Similarly, if g' has been visited before, but $p(g') \le R_T(s_0, \ldots, s') + \gamma^{|T|}V(s')$, then update $p(g')$ to the latter quantity and set g''s "representative state" to s'. Either way, if g''s "representative state" was set to s', record the sequence of actions required to get from s to s', and set s''s predecessor to s.

3. If a goal state has been found, execute the trajectory. Otherwise, the search has failed, because our grid was too coarse, our state transition model inaccurate, or the problem insoluble.

The above procedure is very similar to a standard A^* search, with two important differences. First, the heuristic function used here is an automatically generated approximate value function rather than a hand-coded heuristic. This has the advantage of being a more autonomous approach requiring relatively little hand-encoding of domain-specific knowledge. On the other hand, it also typically means that the heuristic function used here may sometimes overestimate the cost required to get from some points to the goal, which can sometimes lead to suboptimal solutions – that is, the approximated value function is not necessarily an *optimistic* or *admissible* heuristic (Russell and Norvig 1995). *However, within the context of the search procedure used above, inadmissible but relatively accurate value functions can lead to much better solutions than those found with optimistic but inaccurate heuristics.* (Note that UGS is essentially IGS with an optimistic but inaccurate heuristic "value function" of 0 everywhere.) This is due to the second important difference between our search procedure above and a standard A^* search in a discrete-state domain: IGS uses the approximated value function not only to decide what grid element to search from next, but also from what particular point in that grid element it will search for local trajectories to neighboring grid elements.

The above algorithm is also similar in spirit to algorithms presented in (Atkeson, 1994). Atkeson's algorithms also found continuous trajectories from start states to goals. The search for such trajectories was

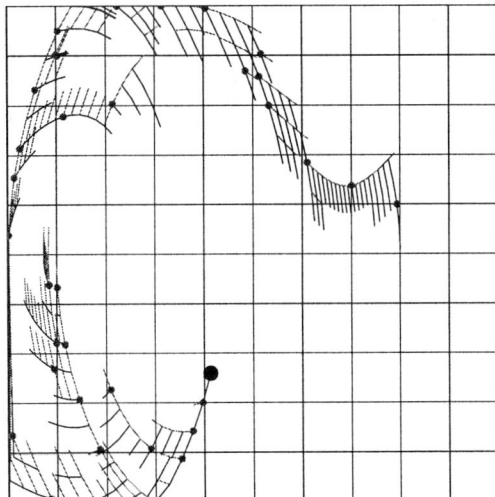

Figure 6: Informed Global Search (IGS) example on MOUNTAIN-PARKING, with a crudely approximated value function.

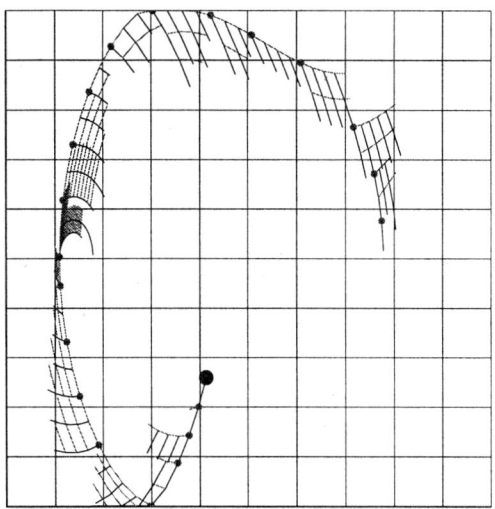

Figure 7: Informed Global Search (IGS) example on MOUNTAIN-PARKING, with a more accurately approximated value function.

performed either within the context of a regular grid (as in the algorithm above) or a pair of constant-cost contours gradually grown out from the start and goal states. Our algorithms differ from Atkeson's in that our algorithm works with a small set of discrete actions and can handle some discontinuities in the dynamics, whereas Atkeson's algorithm requires smooth dynamics (continuous first and second derivatives) with continuous actions. Unlike Atkeson's work, our algorithm does not yet locally optimize the trajectories found by our search algorithms. However, also unlike Atkeson's work, we first compute a crude but quick approximation to the value function (except in the case of uninformed global search), and using this approximate value function speeds up the search considerably.

An example of IGS on the MOUNTAIN-PARKING domain is shown in Figure 6. The value function was approximated with a simplex-based interpolation (Davies 1997) on a coarse 7 by 7 grid, with all other parameters the same as in Figure 5. Much less of state space is searched than by UGS.

In Figure 7, the value function was approximated more accurately with a simplex-based interpolation on a 21 by 21 grid. With this accurate a value function, the search goes straight down a near-optimal path to the goal. Naturally, in such a situation the search is actually unnecessary, since merely greedily following the approximated value function would have produced the same solution. However, when we move to higher-dimensional problems, such as problems examined in the next section, high-resolution approximated value functions become prohibitively expensive to calculate, and IGS can be a very cost-effective way of improving performance.

Experiments

We tested our algorithms on the following domains[2]:

- MOUNTAIN-PARKING (2 dimensional): As described in the Introduction. This is slightly more difficult than the normal mountain-car problem, as we require a velocity near 0 at the top of the hill (Moore and Atkeson 1995). State consists of x-position and velocity. Actions are accelerate forward or backward.

- ACROBOT (4 dimensional): An acrobot is a two-link planar robot acting in the vertical plane under gravity with only one weak actuator at its elbow joint. The goal is to raise the hand at least one link's height above the shoulder (Sutton 1997). State consists of joint angles and angular velocities at the shoulder and elbow. Actions are positive or negative torque.

- MOVE-CART-POLE (4 dimensional): A cart-and-pole system (Barto et al. 1983) starting with the pole upright is to be moved some distance to a goal state, keeping the pole upright (harder than the stabilization problem). It terminates with a huge penalty (-10^6) if the pole falls over. State consists of the cart position and velocity, and the pole angle and angular velocity. Actions are accelerate left or right.

- SLIDER (4 dimensional): Like a two-dimensional mountain car, where a "slider" has to reach a goal region in a two-dimensional terrain. The terrain's contours are shown in Figure 8. State is two-dimensional position and two-dimensional velocity. Actions are acceleration in the NE, NW, SW, or SE directions.

All four are undiscounted tasks. MOVE-CART-POLE's cost on each step is quadratic in distance to goal. The

---

[2]C code for all 4 domains (implemented with numerical integration and smooth dynamics) will shortly be made available on the Web.

d	1	2	3	4	5	6	7	8	9	10
cost	49994	42696	31666	14386	10339	27766	11679	8037	9268	10169
time	0.66	0.64	1.24	1.02	1.13	2.07	3.32	3.84	7.30	15.50

Table 1: Local search (LS) on MOVE-CART-POLE

d	1	2	3	4	6	8	12	16	24
cost	187	180	188	161	140	133	133	134	112
time	0.02	0.05	0.10	0.16	0.36	0.70	2.08	4.62	12.44

Table 2: Constrained Local search (CLS) on MOUNTAIN-PARKING

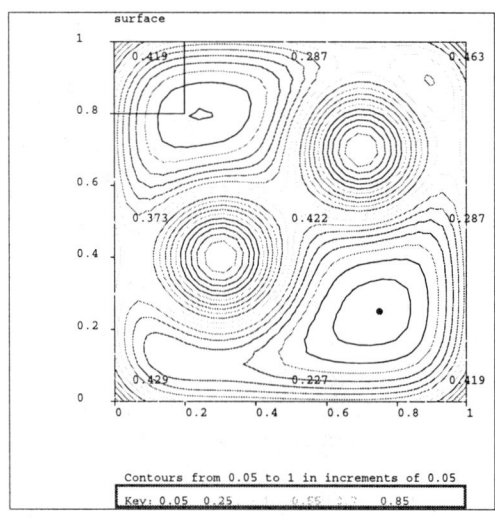

Figure 8: SLIDER's terrain. Goal at upper left.

other three domains cost a constant -1 per step. All results are averages of 1000 trials with a start state chosen uniformly at random in the state space, with the exception of the MOVE-CART-POLE, in which only the pole's initial distance from its goal configuration is varied.

For now, we consider only the case where we are given a model of the world, and leave the model-learning case to the next section. In this case, the value functions used during search (except by the Uniformed Global Search) are calculated using the simplex-interpolation algorithm described in (Davies 1997); once generated, they need not be updated during the search process.

Local Search

Here, we look at the effects of different parameter settings for Local Search. We first consider MOVE-CART-POLE. Empirically, good trajectories in this domain "switch" actions very often; therefore, we chose not to assume much "action-holding," and set $s = d - 1$. The approximate value function was found using a four-dimension simplex-interpolation grid with quantization 13^4, which is about the finest resolution simplex-grid that we could reasonably afford to use. (Calculating the approximate value function even with this seemingly low resolution can take minutes of CPU time and most of the system's memory.) See Table 1; as we increase the depth of the search from 1 (greedy policy with respect to V) up to 10 (greedy policy with respect to B^9V), we see that performance is significantly improved, but with CPU time per trial (on a 100MHz HP C300 9000, given in seconds) increasing exponentially.

The next experiment we consider here is MOUNTAIN-PARKING on a coarse (7^2) grid. Empirically, entire trajectories (of > 100 steps) to the goal can often be executed with 2 or 3 action switches, and the optimal trajectory to the goal from the bottom of the hill at rest requires only about 3 switches. Thus, for the depth of searches we performed, we very conservatively chose $s = 2$. In Table 2, our experimental results again show solution quality significantly increased by Local Search, but with running times growing much more slowly with d than before.

Comparative Experiments

Table 3 summarizes our experimental results[3]. *cost* is average cost per trial, *time* is average CPU seconds per trial, and *#LS* is the average number of local searches performed by the global search algorithms (which indicates the amount of state space considered).

Trends we draw attention to are: Local Search consistently beat No Search, but at the cost of increased computational time. Informed Global Search (IGS) significantly beats No Search; and it also searches *much* less of state space than Uninformed Global Search (UGS), resulting in correspondingly faster running times. In fact, because the solutions found by IGS are often of much shorter length than when using no search at all, the computational time per trial is sometimes essentially *the same* for IGS and No Search, while the quality of the solution found by IGS is many times better — for example, a factor of 4 in the SLIDER domain. (It performs a factor of 10 better in the MOVE-CART-POLE

---
[3]The parameters for the 4 domains were, in order: value function simplex interpolation grid resolution: $7^2, 13^4, 13^4, 13^4$; Local Search: $d = 6, s = 2, d = 5, s = 4, d = 5, s = 4, d = 10, s = 1$; Global Search Grid resolution: $50^2, 50^4, 50^4, 20^4$; Local search within Global search: $d = 20, s = 1$ for all 4.

	No Search		Local Search		Uninformed Global			Informed Global		
	cost	time	**cost**	time	**cost**	#LS	time	**cost**	#LS	time
MOUNTAIN-PARKING	**187**	0.02	**140**	0.36	**FAIL**	–	–	**151**	259	0.14
ACROBOT	**454**	0.10	**305**	1.2	**407**	14250	5.8	**198**	914	0.47
MOVE-CART-POLE	**49993**	0.66	**10339**	1.13	**3164**	7605	3.45	**5073**	1072	0.64
SLIDER	**212**	1.9	**197**	51.72	**104**	23690	94	**54**	533	2.0

Table 3: Summary of comparative experimental results

domain, but that is largely a function of the particular penalty associated with the pole falling over.) Also note that because of the sparse representation of Global Search grids, we can comfortably use grid resolutions as high as 50^4 without running out of memory.

While relatively simple, MOUNTAIN-PARKING demonstrates interesting phenomena. Despite the use of a 50^2 grid for the global search, UGS often surprisingly fails to find a path to the goal, where IGS, despite searching much less of the state space, succeeds. This is because IGS uses a value function to guide its pruning of multiple trajectories entering the same grid cell, and therefore makes better selection of "representative states" for grid elements. This also helps explain IGS finding better solutions than UGS on 2 of the 3 four-dimensional domains.

When the Global Search grid resolution is increased to 100^2 for MOUNTAIN-PARKING, both UGS and IGS consistently succeed. But, UGS (mean cost 109) now finds better solutions than IGS (mean cost 138). The finer search grid causes good selection of representative states to be less important; meanwhile, inaccuracies in the value function guiding Informed Global Search causes it to miss certain good trajectories. This is a phenomenon that often occurs in A^*-like searches when one's heuristic evaluation function is not strictly optimistic (Russell and Norvig 1995). This is not a problem for UGS, which is effectively using the maximally optimistic "constant 0" evaluation function. It is interesting to note that in the MOVE-CART-POLE domain, in which UGS found better solutions than IGS, the step size was large enough and the dynamics nonlinear enough that single steps often crossed multiple grid elements, and each grid element was typically reached no more than once during the search. Thus, this was a case in which IGS's ability to discriminate between good and bad states within the same grid element was not relevant.

LLS and LGS: Learning a Model Online

Occasionally, the state transition function is not known but rather must be learned online. This does not preclude the use of online search techniques; as a toy example, Figure 9 shows cumulative reward learning curves for MOUNTAIN-PARKING. For each action, a kd-tree implementation of 1-nearest-neighbor (Friedman et al. 1977) is used to learn the state transitions, and to encourage exploration, states sufficiently far from points stored in both trees are optimistically assumed to be

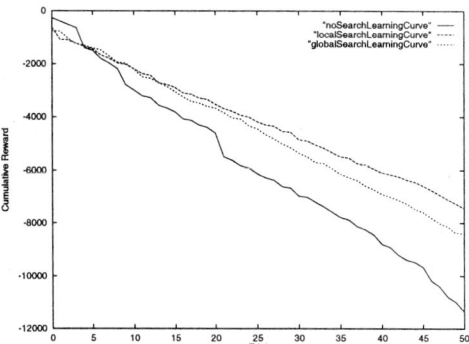

Figure 9: Cumulative reward curves on MOUNTAIN-PARKING with model learning. (Shallow gradients are good.)

zero-cost absorbing states. A 7-by-7 simplex interpolation grid used for the value function approximator is updated online with the changing state transition model. Without search, the learner eventually attains an average cost per trial of about 212; with Learning Global Search (LGS) (search grid resolution 50^2), it quickly (after about 5 trials) achieves an average cost of 155; with Learning Local Search (LLS) ($d = 20, s = 1$), it achieves an average cost of 127 (also after about 5 trials).

As before, when the planner finds a trajectory to the goal, it is executed in its entirety in an open-loop fashion. But in the case where we are learning a model of the world, it is possible to successfully plan a continuous trajectory using the learned world model, but for the agent to fail to reach the goal when it tries to follow the planned trajectory. In this case, failure to follow the successfully planned trajectory can directly be attributed to inaccuracies in the agent's model; and in executing the path anyway, the agent will naturally reach the area where the actual trajectory diverges from the predicted/planned trajectory and thereby improve its model of the world in that area.

However, several interesting issues do arise when the state transition function is being approximated online. Inaccuracies in the model may cause the Global Searches to fail in cases where more accurate models would have let them find paths to the goal. Optimistic exploration policies can be used to help the system gather enough data to reduce these inaccuracies, but in even moderately high-dimensional spaces such exploration would become very expensive. Furthermore, trajectories supposedly found during search will certainly not be followed exactly by an open-loop controller; adaptive closed-loop controllers may help alleviate this problem to some extent. Finally, using the models to predict state transitions should be computationally cheap, since we will be using them to update the approximated value function with the changing model, as well as to perform searches.

Future Research

How well will these techniques extend to non-deterministic systems? They may work for problems in which certain regularity assumptions are reasonable, but more sophisticated state transition function approximators may be required when learning a model online.

How useful is Local Search in comparison with building a local linear controller for trajectories? During execution some combination of the two may be best. Local Search also plays an important role in the inner loop of global search; it is unclear how local linear control could do the same.

The experiments presented here are low-dimensional. It is encouraging that informed search permits us to survive 50^4 grids, but to properly thwart the curse of dimensionality we can conclude that

1. Informed Global Search (IGS) is often much more tractable than Uninformed Global Search (UGS), even with relatively crudely approximated value functions.

2. However, more accurate (yet computationally tractable) value function approximators may be needed than the simplex-grid-based approximators used here.

3. Variable resolution methods (e.g. extensions to (Moore and Atkeson 1995)) would probably be needed for the Global Search's state-space partitions rather than the uniform grids used here.

The algorithms tested in this paper calculated the approximate value functions used by their search procedures independently of any particular trajectories that were subsequently searched or executed. However, it might be better to use points along such trajectories to further update the value function in order to concentrate computational time and value function approximator accuracy on the most relevant parts of the state space. The resulting algorithm would be reminiscent of Korf's *RTA** (Korf 1990) and Barto's *RTDP* (Barto et al. 1995).

The trajectories found by the algorithms described in this paper use a small discrete set of actions, and do not always switch between these actions in a completely locally optimal manner. In domains where the action space is actually continuous, it would be useful to use a local trajectory optimization routine such as that used in (Atkeson, 1994) in order to fine-tune the discovered trajectories.

Lastly, algorithms to learn reasonably accurate yet consistently "optimistic" (Russell and Norvig 1995) value functions might be helpful for Informed Global Search.

References

Atkeson, C. G. 1989. Using Local Models to Control Movement. In *Proceedings of Neural Information Processing Systems Conference*.

Barto, A. G.; Bradtke, S. J.; and Singh, S. P. 1994. Realtime Learning and Control using Asynchronous Dynamic Programming. *AI Journal, to appear (also published as UMass Amherst Technical Report 91-57 in 1991)*.

Barto, A. G.; Sutton, R. S.; and Anderson, C. W. 1983. Neuronlike Adaptive elements that that can learn difficult Control Problems. *IEEE Trans. on Systems Man and Cybernetics* 13(5):835–846.

Bertsekas, D. P. 1995. *Dynamic Programming and optimal control*, volume 1. Athena Scientific.

Boone, G. 1997. Minimum-Time Control of the Acrobot. In *International Conference on Robotics and Automation*.

Boyan, J. A.; Moore, A. W.; and Sutton, R. S., eds. 1995. *Proceedings of the Workshop on Value Function Approximation*. Machine Learning Conference: CMU-CS-95-206. Web: http://www.cs.cmu.edu/~reinf/ml95/.

Burghes, D., and Graham, A. 1980. *Introduction to Control Theory including Optimal Control*. Ellis Horwood.

Davies, S. 1997. Multidimensional Triangulation and Interpolation for Reinforcement Learning. In *Neural Information Processing Systems 9, 1996*. Morgan Kaufmann.

Friedman, J. H.; Bentley, J. L.; and Finkel, R. A. 1977. An Algorithm for Finding Best Matches in Logarithmic Expected Time. *ACM Trans. on Mathematical Software* 3(3):209–226.

Korf, R. E. 1990. Real-Time Heuristic Search. *Artifical Intelligence* 42.

Latombe, J. 1991. *Robot Motion Planning*. Kluwer.

Moore, A. W., and Atkeson, C. G. 1995. The Parti-game Algorithm for Variable Resolution Reinforcement Learning in Multidimensional State-spaces. *Machine Learning* 21.

Nilsson, N. J. 1971. *Problem-solving Methods in Artificial Intelligence*. McGraw Hill.

Russell, S., and Norvig, P. 1995. *Artificial Intelligence A Modern Approach*. Prentice Hall.

Samuel, A. L. 1959. Some Studies in Machine Learning using the Game of Checkers. *IBM Journal on Research and Development* 3. Reprinted in E. A. Feigenbaum and J. Feldman, editors, *Computers and Thought*, McGraw-Hill, 1963.

Sutton, R. S. 1996. Generalization in Reinforcement Learning: Successful Examples Using Sparse Coarse Coding. In Touretzky, D.; Mozer, M.; and Hasselmo, M., eds., *Neural Information Processing Systems 8*.

Tesauro, G., and Galperin, G. R. 1997. On-line Policy Improvement using Monte-Carlo Search. In Mozer, M. C.; Jordan, M. I.; and Petsche, T., eds., *Advances in Neural Information Processing Systems 9*. Morgan Kaufmann.

Bayesian Q-learning

Richard Dearden
Department of Computer Science
University of British Columbia
Vancouver, BC V6T 1Z4, Canada
dearden@cs.ubc.ca

Nir Friedman [*]
Computer Science Division
387 Soda Hall
University of California
Berkeley, CA 94720
nir@cs.berkeley.edu

Stuart Russell
Computer Science Division
387 Soda Hall
University of California
Berkeley, CA 94720
russell@cs.berkeley.edu

Abstract

A central problem in learning in complex environments is balancing *exploration* of untested actions against *exploitation* of actions that are known to be good. The benefit of exploration can be estimated using the classical notion of *Value of Information*—the expected improvement in future decision quality that might arise from the information acquired by exploration. Estimating this quantity requires an assessment of the agent's uncertainty about its current value estimates for states. In this paper, we adopt a Bayesian approach to maintaining this uncertain information. We extend Watkins' Q-learning by maintaining and propagating probability distributions over the Q-values. These distributions are used to compute a myopic approximation to the value of information for each action and hence to select the action that best balances exploration and exploitation. We establish the convergence properties of our algorithm and show experimentally that it can exhibit substantial improvements over other well-known model-free exploration strategies.

1 Introduction

Reinforcement learning is a rapidly growing area of interest in AI and control theory. In principle, reinforcement learning techniques allow an agent to become competent simply by exploring its environment and observing the resulting percepts and rewards, gradually converging on estimates of the value of actions or states that allow it to behave optimally. Particularly in control problems, reinforcement learning may have significant advantages over supervised learning: first, there is no requirement for a skilled human to provide training examples; second, the exploration process allows the agent to become competent in areas of the state space that are seldom visited by human experts and for which no training examples may be available.

In addition to ensuring more robust behavior across the state space, exploration is crucial in allowing the agent to discover the reward structure of the environment and to determine the optimal policy. Without sufficient incentive to explore, the agent may quickly settle on a policy of low utility simply because it looks better than leaping into the unknown. On the other hand, the agent should not keep exploring options that it already has good reason to believe are suboptimal. Thus, a good exploration method should balance the expected gains from exploration against the cost of trying possibly suboptimal actions when better ones are available to be exploited.

Optimal solution of the exploration/exploitation tradeoff requires solving a Markov decision problem over *information states*—that is, the set of all possible probability distributions over environment models that can be arrived at by executing all possible action sequences and receiving any possible percept sequence and reward sequence. The aim is to find a policy for the agent that maximizes its expected reward. Although this problem is well-defined, given a prior distribution over possible environments, it is not easy to solve exactly. Solutions are known only for very restricted cases—mostly the so-called *bandit problems* in which the environment has a single state, several actions, and unknown rewards [3].

Section 2 discusses several existing approaches to exploration, as well as the model-free Q-learning algorithm we use as our underlying learning method. This paper presents two new approaches to exploration:

Q-value sampling: Wyatt [17] proposed Q-value sampling as a method for solving bandit problems. The idea is to represent explicitly the agent's knowledge of the available rewards as probability distributions; then, an action is selected stochastically according to the current probability that it is optimal. This probability depends monotonically not only on the current expected reward (exploitation) but also on the current level of uncertainty about the actual reward (exploration). In this work, we extend this approach to multi-state reinforcement learning problems. The primary contribution here is a Bayesian method for representing, updating, and propagating probability distributions over rewards.

Myopic-VPI: Myopic value of perfect information [8] provides an approximation to the utility of an information-gathering action in terms of the expected improvement in decision quality resulting from the new information. This provides a direct way of evaluating the exploration/exploitation tradeoff. Like Q-value sampling, myopic-VPI uses the current probability distributions over rewards to control exploratory behavior.

Section 3 describes these two algorithms in detail, along with the Bayesian approach to computing reward distributions. In Section 4 we prove convergence results for the algorithms, and in Section 5 we describe the results of a

---

[*]Current address: Institute of Computer Science, The Hebrew University, Givat Ram, Jerusalem 91904, Israel, nir@cs.huji.ac.il.

Copyright 1998, American Association for Artificial Intelligence (www.aaai.org). All rights reserved.

> 1. Let the current state be s.
> 2. Select an action a to perform.
> 3. Let the reward received for performing a be r, and the resulting state be t.
> 4. Update $Q(s,a)$ to reflect the observation $<s,a,r,t>$ as follows:
> $Q(s,a) = (1-\alpha)Q(s,a) + \alpha(r + \gamma \max_{a'} Q(t,a'))$
>   where α is the current learning rate.
> 5. Go to step 1.

Figure 1: The Q-learning algorithm.

number of experiments comparing them against other exploration strategies. In our experiments, myopic-VPI was uniformly the best approach.

2 Q-Learning

We assume the reader is familiar with the basic concepts of MDPs (see, e.g., Kaelbling et al. [9]). We will use the following notation: An MDP is a 4-tuple, $(\mathcal{S}, \mathcal{A}, p_t, p_r)$ where $\mathcal{S}$ is a set of *states*, $\mathcal{A}$ is a set of *actions*, $p_t(s \xrightarrow{a} t)$ is a *transition model* that captures the probability of reaching state t after we execute action a at state s, and $p_r(r|s,a)$ is a *reward model* that captures the probability of getting reward r when executing action a at state s.

In this paper, we focus on infinite-horizon MDPs with a discount factor $0 < \gamma < 1$. The agent's aim is to maximize the *expected discounted total reward* $E[\sum_i \gamma^i r_i]$, where r_i denotes the reward received at step i. Letting $V^*(s)$ denote the optimal expected discounted reward achievable from state s and $Q^*(s,a)$ denote the value of executing a at s, we have the standard Bellman equations [2]:

$$V^*(s) = \max_a Q^*(s,a)$$
$$Q^*(s,a) = \sum_r r \cdot p_r(r|s,a) + \gamma \sum_t p_t(s \xrightarrow{a} t) V^*(t),$$

Reinforcement learning procedures attempt to maximize the agent's expected reward when the agent *does not* know p_t and p_r. In this paper we focus on *Q-learning* [14], a simple and elegant *model-free* method that learns Q-values without learning the model p_t. In Section 6, we discuss how our results carry over to model-based learning procedures.

A Q-learning agent works by estimating the values of $Q^*(s,a)$ from its experiences. It then select actions based on their Q-values. The algorithm is shown in Figure 1. If every action is performed in every state infinitely often, and α is decayed appropriately, $Q(s,a)$ will eventually converge to $Q^*(s,a)$ for all s and a [15].

The strategy used to select an action to perform at each step is crucial to the performance of the algorithm. As with any reinforcement learning algorithm, some balance between exploration and exploitation must be found. Two commonly used methods are *semi-uniform random exploration* and *Boltzmann exploration*. In semi-uniform random exploration [16], the best action is selected with some probability p, and with probability $1-p$, an action is chosen at random. In some cases, p is initially set quite low to encourage exploration, and is slowly increased. Boltzmann exploration [14] is a more sophisticated approach in which the probability of executing action a in state s is:

$$Pr(a) = \frac{e^{Q(s,a)/T}}{\sum_{a'} e^{Q(s,a')/T}}$$

where T is a temperature parameter that can be decreased slowly over time to decrease exploration. In this approach, the probability of an action being selected increases with the current estimate of its Q-value. This means that sub-optimal but good actions tend to be selected more often than clearly poor actions.

Both these exploration methods are *undirected*, meaning that no exploration-specific knowledge is used. A number of *directed* methods have also been proposed, of which the best known is *interval estimation* [10]. Most of the directed techniques can be thought of as selecting an action to perform based on the expected value of the action plus some *exploration bonus* [11]. In the case of interval estimation, we assume a normal distribution for the observed future values of each action in each state, and select an action by maximizing the upper bound of a $100(1-\alpha)\%$ confidence interval (for some confidence coefficient α) over this distribution. The exploration bonus for interval estimation is half the width of the confidence interval. Other exploration bonuses have been proposed, based on the frequency or recency with which each action has been performed, or on the difference between predicted and observed Q-values.

The exploration-specific information in the Interval Estimation algorithm is strictly local in nature. The exploration bonus is calculated only from the future values observed from the current state. Exploration can also be done globally, selecting actions now that we believe will lead us to less-explored parts of the state space in the future. We can do this by backing up exploration specific information along with the Q-values. Meuleau and Bourgine [11], propose IEQL+, which is closely related to interval estimation in that it backs up Q-values and uses them to compute a local exploration bonus. Unlike interval estimation, IEQL+ also backs up an exploration bonus and combines the two to compute the new exploration value of the action.

For a survey of directed and undirected exploration techniques, see [13].

3 Bayesian Q-learning

In this work, we consider a Bayesian approach to Q-learning in which we use probability distributions to represent the uncertainty the agent has about its estimate of the Q-value of each state. As is the case with undirected exploration techniques, we select actions to perform solely on the basis of local Q-value information. However, by keeping and propagating distributions over the Q-values, rather than point estimates, we can make more informed decisions. As we shall see, this results in global exploration, but without the use of an explicit exploration bonus.

3.1 Q-Value Distributions

In the Bayesian framework, we need to consider prior distributions over Q-values, and then update these priors based on the agent's experiences. Formally, let $R_{s,a}$ be a random variable that denotes the *total* discounted reward received when action a is executed in state s and an optimal policy is followed thereafter. What we are initially uncertain about is how $R_{s,a}$ is distributed; in particular, we want to learn the value $Q^*(s,a) = E[R_{s,a}]$.

We start by making the following simplifying assumption:

Assumption 1: $R_{s,a}$ has a normal distribution.

We claim that this assumption is fairly reasonable. The accumulated reward is the (discounted) sum of immediate rewards, each of which is a random event. Thus, appealing to the central limit theorem, if γ is close to 1 and the underlying MDP is ergodic when the optimal policy is applied, then $R_{s,a}$ is approximately normally distributed.

This assumption implies that to model our uncertainty about the distribution of $R_{s,a}$, it suffices to model a distribution over the *mean* $\mu_{s,a}$ and the *precision* $\tau_{s,a}$ of $R_{s,a}$. (The precision of a normal variable is the inverse of its variance, that is, $\tau_{s,a} = 1/\sigma_{s,a}^2$. As it turns out, it is simpler to represent uncertainty over the precision than over the variance.) Of course, the mean, $\mu_{s,a}$, corresponds to the Q-value of (s,a).

Our next assumption is that the *prior* beliefs about $R_{s,a}$ are independent of those about $R_{s',a'}$.

Assumption 2: The prior distribution over $\mu_{s,a}$ and $\tau_{s,a}$ is independent of the prior distribution over $\mu_{s',a'}$ and $\tau_{s',a'}$ for $s \neq s'$ or $a' \neq a$.

This assumption is fairly innocuous, in that it restricts only the form of prior knowledge about the system. Note that this assumption does *not* imply that the *posterior* distribution satisfy such independencies. (We return to this issue below.)

Next we assume that the prior distributions over the parameters of each $R_{s,a}$ are from a particular family:

Assumption 3: The prior $p(\mu_{s,a}, \tau_{s,a})$, is a *normal-gamma* distribution.

We will now define and motivate the choice of the normal-gamma distribution. See [7] for more details.

A normal-gamma distribution over the mean μ and the precision τ of an unknown normally distributed variable R is determined by a tuple of *hyperparameters* $\rho = \langle \mu_0, \lambda, \alpha, \beta \rangle$. We say that $p(\mu, \tau) \sim NG(\mu_0, \lambda, \alpha, \beta)$ if

$$p(\mu, \tau) \propto \tau^{\frac{1}{2}} e^{-\frac{1}{2}\lambda\tau(\mu-\mu_0)^2} \tau^{\alpha-1} e^{\beta\tau}$$

Standard results show how to update such a prior distribution when we receive independent samples of values of R:

Theorem 3.1: [7] *Let $p(\mu, \tau) \sim NG(\mu_0, \lambda, \alpha, \beta)$ be a prior distribution over the unknown parameters for a normally distributed variable R, and let $r_1, \ldots, r_n$ be n independent samples of R with $M_1 = \frac{1}{n}\sum_i r_i$ and $M_2 = \frac{1}{n}\sum_i r_i^2$. Then $p(\mu, \tau \mid r_1, \ldots, r_n) \sim NG(\mu_0', \lambda', \alpha', \beta')$ where $\mu_0' = \frac{\lambda\mu_0 + nM_1}{\lambda+n}$, $\lambda' = \lambda + n$, $\alpha' = \alpha + \frac{1}{2}n$, and $\beta' = \beta + \frac{1}{2}n(M_2 - M_1^2) + \frac{n\lambda(M_1-\mu_0)^2}{2(\lambda+n)}$.*

That is, given a single normal-gamma prior, the posterior after any sequence of independent observations is also a normal-gamma distribution.

Assumption 3 implies that to represent the agent's prior over the distribution of $R_{s,a}$, we only need to maintain a tuple of hyperparameters $\rho_{s,a} = \langle \mu_0^{s,a}, \lambda^{s,a}, \alpha^{s,a}, \beta^{s,a} \rangle$. Given Assumptions 2 and 3, we can represent our prior by a collection of hyperparameters for each state s and action a. Theorem 3.1 implies that, had we had independent samples of each $R_{s,a}$, the same compact representation could have been used for the joint posterior. We now assume that the posterior has this form

Assumption 4: At any stage, the agent's posterior over $\mu_{s,a}$ and $\tau_{s,a}$ is independent of the posterior over $\mu_{s',a'}$ and $\tau_{s',a'}$ for $s \neq s'$ or $a' \neq a$.

In an MDP setting, this assumption is likely to be violated; the agent's observations about the reward-to-go at different states and actions can be strongly correlated—in fact, they are related by the Bellman equations. Nonetheless, we shall assume that we can represent the posterior as though the observations were independent, i.e., we use a collection of hyperparameters $\rho_{s,a}$ for the normal-gamma posterior for the mean and precision parameters of each $R_{s,a}$.

We exploit this compact representation in the Bayesian Q-learning algorithm, which is similar to the standard Q-learning algorithm, except that instead of storing the Q-value $Q_{s,a}$, we now store the hyperparameters $\rho_{s,a}$. In the following sections, we address the two remaining issues: how to select an action based on the current belief state about the MDP, and how to update these beliefs after a transition.

3.2 Action Selection

In every iteration of the Q-learning algorithm we need to select an action to execute. Assuming that we have a probability distribution over $Q(s,a) = \mu_{s,a}$ for all states s and actions a, how do we select an action to perform in the current state? We consider three different approaches, which we call *greedy*, *Q-value sampling*, and *myopic-VPI*.

Greedy selection One possible approach is the *greedy* approach. In this approach, we select the action a that maximizes the expected value $E[\mu_{s,a}]$. Unfortunately, it is easy to show that $E[\mu_{s,a}]$ is simply our estimate of the mean of $R_{s,a}$. Thus, the greedy approach would select the action with the greatest mean, and would not attempt to perform exploration. In particular, it does not take into account any uncertainty about the Q-value.

Q-value sampling Q-value sampling was first described by Wyatt [17] for exploration in multi-armed bandit problems. The idea is to select actions stochastically, based on our current subjective belief that they are optimal. That is, action a is performed with probability given by

$$Pr(a = \arg\max_{a'} \mu_{s,a'}) = Pr(\forall a' \neq a, \mu_{s,a} > \mu_{s,a'})$$
$$= \int_{-\infty}^{\infty} Pr(\mu_{s,a} = q_a) \prod_{a' \neq a} Pr(\mu_{s,a'} < q_a) \, dq_a \quad (1)$$

The last step in this derivation is justified by Assumption 4 that states that our posterior distribution over the values of separate actions is independent.

To evaluate this expression, we use the marginal density of μ given a normal-gamma distribution.

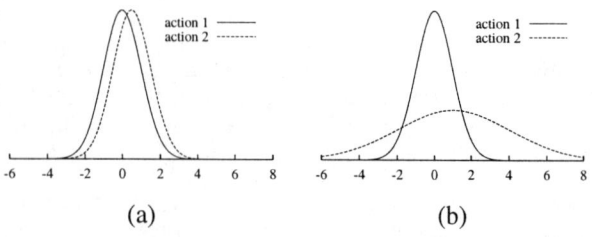

(a)   (b)

Figure 2: Examples of Q-value distributions of two actions for which Q-value sampling has the same exploration policy even though the payoff of exploration in (b) is higher than in (a).

Lemma 3.2: [7] *If* $p(\mu, \tau) \sim NG(\mu_0, \lambda, \alpha, \beta)$, *then*

$$p(\mu) = \left(\frac{\lambda}{2\pi}\right)^{\frac{1}{2}} \beta^{\alpha} \frac{\Gamma(\alpha+\frac{1}{2})}{\Gamma(\alpha)} \left(\beta + \frac{1}{2}\lambda(\mu-\mu_0)^2\right)^{-(\alpha+\frac{1}{2})}, \quad (2)$$

and

$$Pr(\mu < x) = T((x - \mu_0)\left(\frac{\lambda\alpha}{\beta}\right)^{\frac{1}{2}} : 2\alpha)$$

where $T(x : d)$ *is the cumulative t-distribution with d degrees of freedom. Moreover,* $E[\mu] = \mu_0$, *and* $\text{Var}[\mu] = \frac{\beta}{\lambda(\alpha-1)}$.

In practice, we can avoid the computation of (1). Instead, we sample a value from each $p(\mu_{s,a})$, and execute the action with the highest sampled value. It is straightforward to show that this procedure selects a with probability given by (1). Of course, sampling from a distribution of the form of (2) is non-trivial and requires evaluation of the cumulative distribution $P(\mu < x)$. Fortunately, $T(x : d)$ can be evaluated efficiently using standard statistical packages. In our experiments, we used the library routines of Brown et al. [5].

Q-value sampling resembles, to some extent, Boltzmann exploration. It is a stochastic exploration policy, where the probability of performing an action is related to the distribution of the associated Q-values. One drawback of Q-value sampling is that it only considers the *probability* that a is best action, and does not consider the *amount* by which choosing a might improve over the current policy. Figure 2 show examples of two cases where Q-value sampling would generate the same exploration policy. In both cases, $Pr(\mu_{a_2} > \mu_{a_1}) = 0.6$. However, in case (b) exploration seems more useful than in case (a), since the potential for larger rewards is higher for the second action in this case.

Myopic-VPI selection This method considers quantitatively the question of policy improvement through exploration. It is based on *value of information* [8]. Its application in this context is reminiscent of its use in tree search [12], which can also be seen as a form of exploration. The idea is to balance the expected gains from exploration—in the form of improved policies—against the expected cost of doing a potentially suboptimal action.

We start by considering what can be gained by learning the true value $\mu_{s,a}^*$ of $\mu_{s,a}$. How would this knowledge change the agent's future rewards? Clearly, if this knowledge does not change the agent's policy, then rewards would not change.

Thus, the only interesting scenarios are those where the new knowledge does change the agent's policy. This can happen in two cases: (a) when the new knowledge shows that an action previously considered sub-optimal is revealed as the best choice (given the agent's beliefs about other actions), and (b) when the new knowledge indicates that an action that was previously considered best is actually inferior to other actions. We now derive the value of the new information in both cases.

For case (a), suppose that a_1 is the best action; that is, $E[\mu_{s,a_1}] \geq E[\mu_{s,a'}]$ for all other actions a'. Moreover suppose that the new knowledge indicates that a is a better action; that is, $\mu_{s,a}^* > E[\mu_{s,a_1}]$. Thus, we expect the agent to gain $\mu_{s,a}^* - E[\mu_{s,a_1}]$ by virtue of performing a instead of a^*.

For case (b), suppose that a_1 is the action with the highest expected value and a_2 is the second-best action. If the new knowledge indicates that $\mu_{s,a_1} < E[\mu_{s,a_2}]$, then the agent should perform a_2 instead of a_1 and we expect it to gain $E[\mu_{s,a_2}] - \mu_{s,a_1}^*$.

To summarize this discussion, we define the gain from learning the value of $\mu_{s,a}^*$ of $\mu_{s,a}$ as:

$$\text{Gain}_{s,a}(\mu_{s,a}^*) = \begin{cases} E[\mu_{s,a_2}] - \mu_{s,a}^* & \text{if } a = a_1 \\ & \text{and } \mu_{s,a}^* < E[\mu_{s,a_2}] \\ \mu_{s,a}^* - E[\mu_{s,a_1}] & \text{if } a \neq a_1 \\ & \text{and } \mu_{s,a}^* > E[\mu_{s,a_1}] \\ 0 & \text{otherwise} \end{cases}$$

where, again, a_1 and a_2 are the actions with the best and second best expected values respectively. Since the agent does not know in advance what value will be revealed for $\mu_{s,a}^*$, we need to compute the *expected* gain given our prior beliefs. Hence the expected value of perfect information about $\mu_{s,a}$ is:

$$VPI(s,a) = \int_{-\infty}^{\infty} \text{Gain}_{s,a}(x) Pr(\mu_{s,a} = x) dx$$

Using simple manipulations we can reduce $VPI(s,a)$ to a closed form equation involving the cumulative distribution of $\mu_{s,a}$ (which can be computed efficiently).

Proposition 3.3: $VPI(s,a)$ *is equal to* $c + (E[\mu_{s,a_2}] - E[\mu_{s,a_1}])Pr(\mu_{s,a_1} < E[\mu_{s,a_2}])$ *when* $a = a_1$, *and it is equal to* $c + (E[\mu_{s,a}] - E[\mu_{s,a_1}])Pr(\mu_{s,a} > E[\mu_{s,a_1}])$ *when* $a \neq a_1$, *where*

$$c = \frac{\alpha_{s,a}\Gamma(\alpha_{s,a}+\frac{1}{2})\sqrt{\beta_{s,a}}}{(\alpha_{s,a}-\frac{1}{2})\Gamma(\alpha_{s,a})\Gamma(\frac{1}{2})\alpha_{s,a}\sqrt{2\lambda_{s,a}}} \left(1 + \frac{E^2[\mu_{s,a}]}{2\alpha_{s,a}}\right)^{-\alpha_{s,a}+\frac{1}{2}}.$$

The value of perfect information gives an upper bound on the myopic value of information for exploring action a. The expected *cost* incurred for this exploration is given by the difference between the value of a and the value of the current best action, i.e., $\max_{a'} E[Q(s,a')] - E[Q(s,a)]$. This suggests we choose the action that maximizes

$$VPI(s,a) - (\max_{a'} E[Q(s,a')] - E[Q(s,a)]).$$

Clearly, this strategy is equivalent to choosing the action that maximizes:

$$E[Q(s,a)] + VPI(s,a).$$

We see that the value of exploration estimate is used as a way of boosting the desirability of different actions. When the agent is confident of the estimated Q-values, the VPI of each action is close to 0, and the agent will always choose the action with the highest expected value.[1]

3.3 Updating Q-values

Finally, we turn to the question of how to update the estimate of the distribution over Q-values after executing a transition. The analysis of the updating step is complicated by the fact that a distribution over Q-values is a distribution over *expected, total* rewards, whereas the available observations are instances of *actual, local* rewards. Thus, we cannot use the Bayesian updating results in Theorem 3.1 directly.

Suppose that the agent is in state s, executes action a, receives reward r, and lands up in state t. We would like to know the complete sequence of rewards received from t onwards, but this is not available. Let R_t be a random variable denoting the discounted sum of rewards from t. If we assume that the agent will follow the apparently optimal policy, then R_t is distributed as R_{t,a_t}, where a_t is the action with the highest expected value at t.

We might hope to use this distribution to substitute in some way for the unknown future experiences. We now discuss two ways of going about this.

Moment updating The idea of moment updating is, notionally, to randomly sample values $R_t^1, \ldots, R_t^n$ from our distribution, and then update $P(R_{s,a})$ with the sample $r + \gamma R_t^1, \ldots, r + \gamma R_t^n$, where we take each sample to have weight $\frac{1}{n}$. Theorem 3.1 implies that we only need the first two moments of this sample to update our distribution. Assuming that n tends to infinity, these two moments are:

$$\begin{aligned} M_1 &= E[r + \gamma R_t] = r + \gamma E[R_t] \\ M_2 &= E[(r + \gamma R_t)^2] = E[r^2 + 2\gamma r R_t + \gamma^2 R_t^2] \\ &= r^2 + 2\gamma r E[R_t] + \gamma^2 E[R_t^2] \end{aligned}$$

Now, since our estimate of the distribution of R_t is a normal-gamma distribution over the mean and variance of R_t, we can use standard properties of normal-gamma distributions to compute the first two moments of R_t.

Lemma 3.4: *Let R be a normally distributed variable with unknown mean μ and unknown precision τ, and let $p(\mu, \tau) \sim NG(\mu_0, \lambda, \alpha, \beta)$. Then $E[R] = \mu_0$, and $E[R^2] = \frac{\lambda+1}{\lambda} \cdot \frac{\beta}{\alpha-1} + \mu_0^2$.*

Now we can update the hyperparameters $\rho_{s,a}$ as though we had seen a collection of examples with total weight 1, mean M_1, and second moment M_2.

This approach results in a simple closed-form equation for updating the hyperparameters for $R_{s,a}$. Unfortunately, it quickly becomes too confident of the value of the mean $\mu_{s,a}$. To see this, note that we can roughly interpret the parameter λ as the confidence in our estimate of the unknown mean. The

---

[1] It is clear that the value of perfect information is an optimistic assessment of the value of performing a; by performing a once, we do not get perfect information about it, but only one more training instance. Thus, we might consider weighting the VPI estimate by some constant. We leave this for future work.

method we just described updates μ_0 and λ with the mean of the unknown reward, which is just $r + \gamma E[R_t]$, as if we were confident of this being a true sample. Our uncertainty about the value of R_t is represented by the second moment M_2, which mainly affects the estimate of the variance of $R_{s,a}$. Thus, our uncertainty about R_t is not directly translated to uncertainty about the mean of $R_{s,a}$. Instead, it leads to higher estimate of the variance of $R_{s,a}$. The upshot of all this is that the precision of the mean increases too fast, leading to low exploration values and hence to premature convergence on sub-optimal strategies.

One ad-hoc way of dealing with this problem is to use *exponential forgetting*. This method reduces the impact of previously seen examples on the priors by a constant (which is usually close to 1) at each update. Due to space considerations, we do not review the details of this forgetting operation.

Mixture updating The problem described in the preceding section can be avoided by using the distribution over R_t in a slightly different way. Let $p(\mu_{s,a}, \tau_{s,a} \mid R)$ be the posterior distribution over $\mu_{s,a}, \tau_{s,a}$ after observing discounted reward R. If we observed the value $R_t = x$, then the updated distribution over $R_{s,a}$ is $p(\mu_{s,a}, \tau_{s,a} \mid r + \gamma x)$. We can capture our uncertainty about the value x by weighting these distribution by the probability that $R_t = x$. This results in the following *mixture* posterior:

$$p_{r,t}^{mix}(\mu_{s,a}, \tau_{s,a}) = \int_{-\infty}^{\infty} p(\mu_{s,a}, \tau_{s,a} \mid r + \gamma x) p(R_t = x) dx$$

Unfortunately, the posterior $p_{r,t}^{mix}(\mu_{s,a}, \tau_{s,a})$ does not have a simple representation, and so updating this posterior would lead to a more complex one, and so on. We can avoid this complexity by approximating $p_{r,t}^{mix}(\mu_{s,a}, \tau_{s,a})$ with a normal-gamma distribution after each update.

We compute the best normal-gamma approximation by minimizing the KL-divergence [6] from the true distribution.

Theorem 3.5: *Let $q(\mu, \tau)$ be some density measure over μ and τ and let $\epsilon > 0$. If we constrain α to be greater than $1 + \epsilon$, the distribution $p(\mu, \tau) \sim NG(\mu_0, \lambda, \alpha, \beta)$ that minimizes the divergence $KL(q, p)$ is defined by the following equations:*

$$\begin{aligned} \mu_0 &= E_q[\mu\tau]/E_q[\tau] \\ \lambda &= \left(E_q[\mu^2\tau] - E_q[\tau]\mu_0^2\right)^{-1} \\ \alpha &= \max(1 + \epsilon, f(\log E_q[\tau] - E_q[\log \tau])) \\ \beta &= \alpha/E_q[\tau] \end{aligned}$$

where $f(x)$ is the inverse of $g(y) = \log y - \psi(y)$, and $\psi(x) = \frac{\Gamma'(x)}{\Gamma(x)}$ is the digamma function.

The requirement that $\alpha \geq 1 + \epsilon$ is to ensure that $\alpha > 1$ so that the normal-gamma distribution is well defined. Although this theorem does not give a closed-form solution for α, we can find a numerical solution easily since $g(y)$ is a monotonically decreasing function [1].

Another complication with this approach is that it requires us to compute $E[\tau_{s,a}]$, $E[\tau_{s,a}\mu_{s,a}]$, $E[\tau_{s,a}\mu_{s,a}^2]$ and

$E[\log \tau_{s,a}]$ with respect to $p_{r,t}^{mix}(\mu_{s,a}, \tau_{s,a})$. These expectations do not have closed-form solutions, but can be approximated by numerical integration, using formulas derived fairly straightforwardly from Theorem 3.5.

To summarize, in this section we discussed two possible ways of updating the estimate of the values. The first, *moment update* leads to an easy closed form update, but might become overly confident. The second, *mixture update*, is more cautious, but requires numerical integration.

4 Convergence

We are interested in knowing whether our algorithms converge to optimal policies in the limit. It suffices to show that the means $\mu_{s,a}$ converge to the true Q-values, and that the variance of the means converges to 0. If this is the case, then both the Q-value sampling and the myopic-VPI strategies will, eventually, execute an optimal policy.

Without going into details, the standard convergence proof [15] for Q-learning requires that each action is tried infinitely often in each state in an infinite run, and that $\sum_{n=0}^{\infty} \alpha(n) = \infty$ and $\sum_{n=0}^{\infty} \alpha(n)^2 < \infty$ where α is the learning rate. If these conditions are met, then the theorem shows that the approximate Q-values converge to the real Q-values.

Using this theorem, we can show that when we use moment updating, our algorithm converges to the correct mean.

Theorem 4.1: *If each action a is tried infinitely often in every state, and the algorithm uses moment updating, then the mean $\mu_{s,a}$ converges to the true Q-value for every state s and action a.*

Moreover, for moment updating we can also prove that the variance will eventually vanish:

Theorem 4.2: *If each action a is tried infinitely often in every state, and the algorithm uses the moment method to update the posterior estimates, then the variance $\text{Var}[\mu_{s,a}]$ converges to 0 for every state s and action a.*

Combining these two results, we see that with moment updating, the procedure will converge on an optimal policy if all actions are tried eventually often. This is the case when we select actions by Q-value sampling.

If we select actions using myopic-VPI, then we can no longer guarantee that each action is tried infinitely often. More precisely, myopic VPI might starve certain actions and hence we cannot apply the results from [15]. Of course, we can define a "noisy" version of this action selection strategy (e.g., use a Boltzmann distribution over the adjusted expected values), and this will guarantee convergence.

At this stage, we do not yet have counterparts to Theorems 4.1 and 4.2 for mixture updating. Our conjecture is that the estimated mean does converge to the true mean, and therefore similar theorems holds.

5 Experimental Results

We have examined the performance of our approach on several different domains and compared it with a number of different exploration techniques. The parameters of each algorithm were tuned as well as possible for each domain. The algorithms we have used are as follows:

Semi-Uniform Q-learning with semi-uniform random exploration.

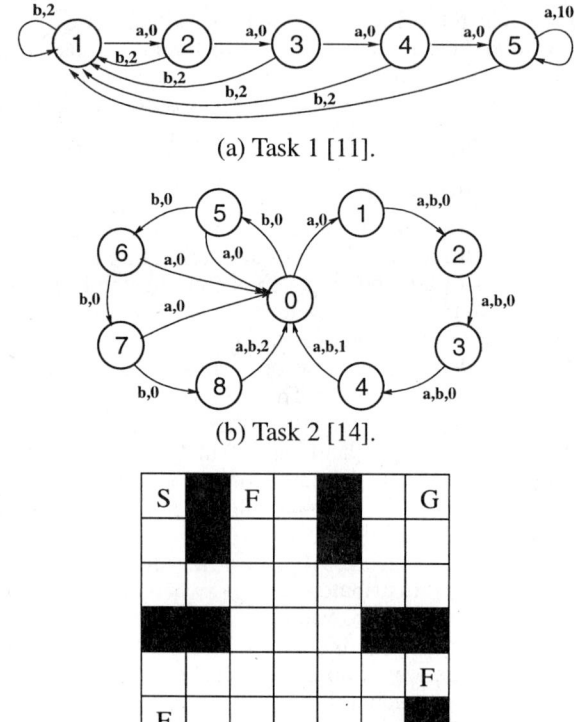

(a) Task 1 [11].

(b) Task 2 [14].

(c) Task 3. A navigation problem. S is the start state. The agent receives a reward upon reaching G based on the number of flags collected.

Figure 3: The three domains used in our experiments.

Boltzmann Q-learning with Boltzmann exploration.

Interval Q-learning using Kaelbling's interval-estimation algorithm [10].

IEQL+ Meuleau's IEQL+ algorithm [11].

Bayes Bayesian Q-learning as presented above, using either Q-value sampling or myopic-VPI to select actions, and either Moment updating or Mixture updating for value updates. These variants are denoted QS, VPI, Mom, Mix, respectively. Thus, there are four possible variants of the Bayesian Q-Learning algorithm, denoted, for example, as VPI+Mix.

We tested these learning algorithms on three domains:

Chain This domain consists of the chain of states shown in Figure 3(a). It consists of six states and two actions a and b. With probability 0.2, the agent "slips" and actually performs the opposite action. The optimal policy for this domain (assuming a discount factor of 0.99) is to do action a everywhere. However, learning algorithms can get trapped at the initial state, preferring to follow the b–loop to obtain a series of smaller rewards.

Loop This domain consists of two loops, as shown in Figure 3(b). Actions are deterministic. The problem here is that a learning algorithm may have already converged on action a for state 0 before the larger reward available in state 8 has been backed up. Here the optimal policy is to do action b everywhere.

Domain	Method	1st Phase Avg.	1st Phase Dev.	2nd Phase Avg.	2nd Phase Dev.
chain	Uniform	1519.0	37.2	1611.4	34.7
	Boltzmann	1605.8	78.1	1623.4	67.1
	Interval	1522.8	180.2	1542.6	197.5
	IEQL+	2343.6	234.4	2557.4	271.3
	Bayes QS+Mom	1480.8	206.3	1894.2	364.7
	Bayes QS+Mix	1210.0	86.1	1306.6	102.0
	Bayes VPI+Mom	1875.4	478.7	2234.0	443.9
	Bayes VPI+Mix	1697.4	336.2	2417.2	650.1
loop	Uniform	185.6	3.7	198.3	1.4
	Boltzmann	186.0	2.8	200.0	0.0
	Interval	198.1	1.4	200.0	0.0
	IEQL+	264.3	1.6	292.8	1.3
	Bayes QS+Mom	190.0	19.6	262.9	51.4
	Bayes QS+Mix	203.9	72.2	236.5	84.1
	Bayes VPI+Mom	316.8	74.2	340.0	91.7
	Bayes VPI+Mix	326.4	85.2	340.0	91.7
maze	Uniform	105.3	10.3	161.2	8.6
	Boltzmann	195.2	61.4	1024.3	87.9
	Interval	246.0	122.5	506.1	315.1
	IEQL+	269.4	3.0	253.1	7.3
	Bayes QS+Mom	132.9	10.7	176.1	12.2
	Bayes QS+Mix	128.1	11.0	121.9	9.9
	Bayes VPI+Mom	403.2	248.9	660.0	487.5
	Bayes VPI+Mix	817.6	101.8	1099.5	134.9

Table 1: Average and standard deviation of accumulated rewards over 10 runs. A phase consists of 1,000 steps in chain and loop, and of 20,000 steps in maze.

Maze This is a maze domain where the agent attempts to "collect" flags and get them to the goal. In the experiments we used the maze shown in Figure 3(c). In this figure, S marks the start state, G marks the goal state, and F marks locations of flags that can be collected. The reward received on reaching G is based on the number of flags collected. Once the agent reaches the goal, the problem is reset. There are a total of 264 states in this MDP. The agent has four actions—up, down, left, and right. There is a small probability, 0.1, that the agent will slip and actually perform an action that goes in a perpendicular direction. If the agent attempts to move into a wall, its position does not change. The challenge is to do sufficient exploration to collect all three flags before reaching the goal.

The first two domains are designed so that there are sub-optimal strategies that can be exploited. Thus, if the learning algorithm converges too fast, then it will not discover the higher-scoring alternatives. The third domain is larger and less "tricky" although it also admits inferior policies. We use it to evaluate how the various exploration stratgies scale up.

There are several ways of measuring the performance of learning algorithms. For example, we might want to measure the quality of the policy they "recommend" after some number of steps. Unfortunately, this might be misleading, since the algorithm might recommend a good exploiting policy, but might still continue to explore, and thus receive much smaller rewards. We measured the performance of the learning algorithms by the total reward collected during a fixed number of time steps (Table 1). Additionally, we measured the discounted total reward-to-go at each point in the run. More precisely, suppose the agent receives rewards $r_1, r_2, \ldots, r_N$ in a run of length N. Then we define the reward-to-go at time t to be $\sum_{t' \geq t} r_{t'} \gamma^{t'-t}$. Of course, this estimate is reliable only for points that are far enough from the end of the run. In Figure 4, we plot the average reward-to-go as a function of t by averaging these values over 10 runs with different random

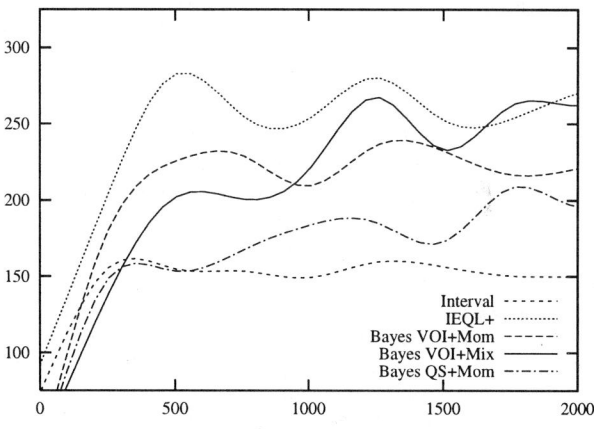

(a) Results for the chain domain.

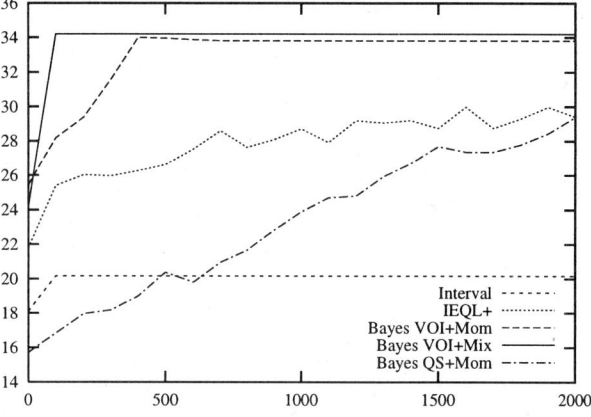

(b) Results for the loop domain.

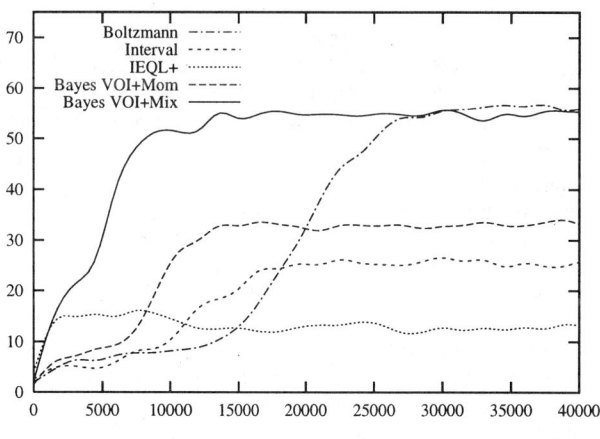

(c) Results for the maze domain.

Figure 4: Plots of actual discounted reward (y-axis) as a function of number of steps (x-axis) for several methods in three domains. The curves are avarege of 10 runs for each method. The curves for chain and maze were smoothed.

seeds.[2]

Our results show that in all but the smallest of domains our methods are competitive with or superior to state of the art exploration techniques such as IEQL+. Our analysis suggests that this is due to our methods' more effective use of small numbers of data points. Results from the maze domain in particular show that our VPI-based methods begin directing the search towards promising states after making significantly fewer observations than IEQL+ and interval estimation. Overall, we have found that using mixture updating combined with VPI for action selection gives the best performance, and expect these to be the most valuable techniques as we expand this work to model-based learning.

One weakness of our algorithms is that they have significantly more parameters than IEQL+ or interval estimation. In the full version of the paper we analyze the dependence of these results on various parameters. The main parameters that seem to effect the performance of our method is the variance of the initial prior, that is, the ratio $\frac{\beta}{\lambda(\alpha-1)}$. Priors with larger variances usually lead to better performance.

6 Conclusion

We have described a Bayesian approach to Q-learning in which exploration and exploitation are directly combined by representing Q-values as probability distributions and using these distributions to select actions. We proposed two methods for action selection — Q-value sampling and myopic-VPI. Experimental evidence has shown that (at least for some fairly simple problems) these approaches explore the state space more effectively than conventional model-free learning algorithms, and that their performance advantage appears to increase as the problems become larger. This is due to an action selection mechanism that takes advantage of much more information than previous approaches.

A major issue for this work is that the computational requirements are greater than for conventional Q-learning, both for action selection and for updating the Q-values. However, we note that in most applications of reinforcement learning, performing actions is more expensive tha computation time.

We are currently investigating ways to use a Bayesian approach such as this with model-based reinforcement algorithms. In this case, we explicitly represent our uncertainty about the dynamics of the system to estimate the usefulness of exploration. We are also investigating alternative action selection schemes, and approximations that could be used to reduce the computational requirements of this algorithm. Finally, it should be possible to use function approximators to extend this work to problems with large and/or continuous state spaces. There is a well-understood theory of Bayesian neural network learning [4, Ch. 10] that allows posterior means and variances to be computed for each point in the input space; these can be fed directly into our algorithm.

---

[2] We performed parameter adjustment to find the best-performing parameters for each method. Thus the results reported for each algorithm are probably somewhat optimistic. In the full version of the paper we intend to also show the sensitivity of each method to changes in the parameters.

Acknowledgments

We are grateful for useful comments from David Andre, Craig Boutilier, Daphne Koller and Ron Parr. We thank Nicolas Meuleau for help in implementing the IEQL+ algorithm. Nir Friedman and Stuart Russell were supported in part by ARO under the MURI program "Integrated Approach to Intelligent Systems", grant number DAAH04-96-1-0341, and by ONR under grant number N00014-97-1-0941.

References

[1] M. Abramowitz and I. A. Stegun, editors. *Handbook of Mathematical Functions.* Dover, 1964.

[2] R. E. Bellman. *Dynamic Programming.* Princeton Univ. Press, 1957.

[3] D. A. Berry and B. Fristedt. *Bandit Problems: Sequential Allocation of Experiments.* Chapman and Hall, 1985.

[4] C. M. Bishop. *Neural Networks for Pattern Recognition.* Oxford Univ. Press, 1995.

[5] B. W. Brown, J. Lovato, and K. Russell. Library of routines for cumulative distribution functions, inverses, and other parameters, 1997. ftp://odin.mdacc.tmc.edu/pub/source/dcdflib.c-1.1.tar.gz.

[6] T. M. Cover and J. A. Thomas. *Elements of Information Theory.* Wiley, 1991.

[7] M. H. Degroot. *Proability and Statistics.* Addison-Wesley, 1986.

[8] R. A. Howard. Information value theory. *IEEE Trans. Systems Science and Cybernetics*, SSC-2:22–26, 1966.

[9] L. P. Kaelbling, M. L. Littman, and A. W. Moore. Reinforcement learning: A survey. *J. Artificial Intelligence Research*, 4:237–285, 1996.

[10] L. P. Kaelbling. *Learning in Embedded Systems.* MIT Press, 1993.

[11] N. Meuleau and P. Bourgine. Exploration of multi-states environments: Local measures and back-propogation of uncertainty. *Machine Learning*, 1998. To appear.

[12] S. J. Russell and E. H. Wefald. *Do the Right Thing: Studies in Limited Rationality.* MIT Press, 1991.

[13] S. B. Thrun. The role of exploration in learning control. In D. A. White and D. A. Sofge, eds., *Handbook of Intelligent Control: Neural, Fuzzy and Adaptive Approaches.* Van Nostrand Reinhold, 1992.

[14] C. J. Watkins. *Models of Delayed Reinforcement Learning.* PhD thesis, Psychology Department, Cambridge University, 1989.

[15] C. J. Watkins and P. Dayan. Q-learning. *Machine Learning*, 8(3):279–292, 1992.

[16] S. D. Whitehead and D. H. Ballard. Learning to percieve and act by trial and error. *Machine Learning*, 7:45–83, 1991.

[17] J. Wyatt. *Exploration and Inference in Learning from Reinforcement.* PhD thesis, Department of Artificial Intelligence, University of Edinburgh, 1997.

Tree Based Discretization for Continuous State Space Reinforcement Learning

William T. B. Uther and **Manuela M. Veloso**
Computer Science Department
Carnegie Mellon University
Pittsburgh, PA 15213
{uther,veloso}@cs.cmu.edu

Abstract

Reinforcement learning is an effective technique for learning action policies in discrete stochastic environments, but its efficiency can decay exponentially with the size of the state space. In many situations significant portions of a large state space may be irrelevant to a specific goal and can be aggregated into a few, relevant, states. The U Tree algorithm generates a tree based state discretization that efficiently finds the relevant state chunks of large propositional domains. In this paper, we extend the U Tree algorithm to challenging domains with a continuous state space for which there is no initial discretization. This Continuous U Tree algorithm transfers traditional regression tree techniques to reinforcement learning. We have performed experiments in a variety of domains that show that Continuous U Tree effectively handles large continuous state spaces. In this paper, we report on results in two domains, one gives a clear visualization of the algorithm and another empirically demonstrates an effective state discretization in a simple multi-agent environment.

Introduction

Reinforcement learning is a technique for learning a control policy for an agent as it moves through a world and receives a series of rewards for its actions (Kaelbling, Littman, & Moore 1996).

The number of states that need to be considered by a traditional reinforcement learning algorithm increases exponentially with the dimensionality of the state space. The dimensionality of the state space in turn increases linearly with, for example, the number of agents in the world.

However, there are parts of the state space where the exact position in state space is irrelevant to the agent. All the states in a region where this is true are equivalent and can be replaced by a single state, reducing the state space explosion. In many environments this reduction is significant. The concept of starting with many states and joining them is known as state aggregation. Techniques using a non-uniform discretization are referred to as variable resolution techniques (Moore 1991).

The Parti-game algorithm (Moore 1994) is an algorithm for automatically generating a variable resolution discretization of a continuous, deterministic domain based on observed data. This algorithm uses a greedy local controller to move within a state or between adjacent states in the discretization. When the greedy controller fails the resolution of the discretization is increased in that state.

Copyright © 1998, American Association for Artificial Intelligence (www.aaai.org). All rights reserved.

The G algorithm (Chapman & Kaelbling 1991) and the U Tree algorithm (McCallum 1995) are similar algorithms that automatically generate a variable resolution discretization by re-discretizing propositional state spaces. A policy can then be found for the new discretization using traditional techniques. Like Parti-game, they both start with the world as a single state and recursively split it where necessary. The Continuous U Tree algorithm described in this paper extends these algorithms to work with continuous state spaces rather than propositional state spaces.

To scale up reinforcement learning techniques, the standard approach is to substitute a function approximator for the table of states in a standard algorithm. If done naively this can lead to convergence problems (Boyan & Moore 1995). Gordon (1995) showed how to use an averaging system to sub-sample the state space. This system could only interpolate between sub-sampled points, not extrapolate outside its sampled range. Baird (1995) describes a technique for using any gradient descent function approximator instead of a table of values.

The Continuous U Tree algorithm described below can be viewed as using a regression tree (Breiman et al. 1984; Quinlan 1986) to store the state values. Markov Decision Problems (MDPs) are similar to reinforcement learning problems except that they assume a complete and correct prior model of the world. MDPs can also be solved using state aggregation techniques (Dean & Lin 1995).

In this paper we describe Continuous U Tree, a generalizing, variable-resolution, reinforcement learning algorithm that works with continuous state spaces. To evaluate Continuous U Tree we used two domains, a small two dimensional domain and a larger seven dimensional domain. The small domain, a robot travelling down a corridor, shows some of the main features of the algorithm. The larger domain, hexagonal grid soccer, is similar to the one used by Littman (1994) to investigate Markov games. It is ordered discrete rather than strictly continuous. We increased the size of this domain, both in number of states and number of actions per state, to test the generalization capabilities of our algorithm.

In the machine learning formulation of reinforcement learning there are a discrete set of states, s, and actions, a. The agent can detect its current state, and in each state can choose to perform an action which will in turn move it to its next state. For each state/action/resulting state triple, (s, a, s'), there is a reinforcement signal, $R(s, a, s')$.

The world is assumed to be Markovian. For each state/action pair, (s, a), there is a probability distribution,

$P_{(s,a)}(s')$, giving the probability of reaching a particular successor state, s'.

The foundations of reinforcement learning are the Bellman Equations (Bellman 1957):

$$Q(s,a) = \sum_{s'} P_{(s,a)}(s') \left(R(s,a,s') + \gamma V(s') \right) \quad (1)$$
$$V(s) = \max_{a} Q(s,a) \quad (2)$$

These equations define a Q function, $Q(s,a)$, and a value function, $V(s)$. The Q function is a function from state/action pairs to an expected sum of discounted reward (Watkins & Dayan 1992).

Continuous U Tree

U Tree (McCallum 1995) includes a method to apply propositional decision tree techniques to reinforcement learning. We introduce an extension to U Tree that is capable of directly handling both propositional and continuous-valued domains. Our resulting algorithm, "Continuous U Tree", uses decision tree learning techniques (Breiman et al. 1984; Quinlan 1986) to find a discretization of the continuous state space.

Continuous U Tree is different from U Tree and traditional reinforcement learning algorithms in that it does not require a prior discretization of the world into separate states. The algorithm takes a continuous, or ordered discrete, state space and automatically splits it to form a discretization. Any discrete, state-based, reinforcement learning algorithm can then be used on this discretization.

In both U Tree and Continuous U Tree there are two distinct concepts of state. In Continuous U Tree the first type of state is the fully continuous state of the world that the agent is moving through. We term this *sensory input*. The second type of state is the position in the discretization being formed by the algorithm. We will use the term *state* in this second sense. Each state is an area in the sensory input space, and each sensory input falls within a state. In many previous algorithms these two concepts were identical. Sensory input was discrete and each different sensory input corresponded to a state.

The translation between these two concepts of state is in terms of a *state tree* that describes the discretization. Each node in this binary tree corresponds to an area of sensory input space. Each internal node has a *decision* attached to it that describes a way to divide its area of sensor space in two. These decisions are described in terms of an attribute of the sensory input to split on, and a value of that attribute. Any sensory input where the relevant attribute falls above or below the stored value is passed down the left or right side of the tree respectively. Leaf nodes in the tree correspond to states. A state tree enables generalization – states become areas of sensory input space.

We refer to each step the agent takes in the world as a *transition*. Each saved transition is a vector of the starting sensory input I, the action performed a, the resulting sensory input I' and the reward obtained for that transition r, (I, a, I', r). The sensory input is itself a vector of values. These values can be fully continuous.

As the agent is forming its own discretization, there is no prior discretization that can be used to aggregate the data. (If a partial prior discretization exists, this can be utilized by the algorithm by initializing the state tree with that discretization but this is not required.) Only a subset of the transitions need to be saved, but they need to be saved with full sensor accuracy. Deciding which subset of the transitions is saved will be discussed later.

Each transition (I, a, I', r) gives one *datapoint* $(I, a, q(I, a))$ – a triple of the sensory input I, the action a, and a value $q(I,a)$. The value of a datapoint is its expected reward for performing that transition and behaving optimally from then on, $q(I,a)$ (defined below).

Continuous U Tree forms a discretization by recursively growing the state tree. Table 1 summarizes the algorithm. In a nutshell, the algorithm is as follows: Initially the world is considered to be a single state with an expected reward, $V(s) = 0$. The state tree is a single leaf node describing the entire sensory input space. The algorithm then loops through a two phase process: Datapoints are accumulated for learning in a data gathering phase, then a processing phase updates the discretization. During the data gathering phase the algorithm behaves as a standard reinforcement learning algorithm, with the added step of using the state tree to translate sensory input to a state. It also remembers the transitions it sees. During the processing phase, the values of all the datapoints, $q(I,a)$, are re-calculated. If a "significant" difference (defined below) in the distribution of datapoint values is found within a state, then that state is split in two. A split adds two new leaves to the state tree representing the two new states formed from the old state. The MDP defined over the new discretization is solved to find the state values. Initializing the state values to the values in the previous discretization and using an incremental algorithm makes updating these values relatively fast. Deciding when to execute a pass through the processing phase is a parameter to the algorithm.

This is similar to the recursive partitioning of a decision or regression tree, except that the values of the datapoints can change when more data is gathered and the MDP is re-solved after each processing phase. Splitting is also breadth-first rather than depth-first.

The value of a datapoint $q(I,a)$ is calculated using a modification of the Bellman equations. Using the value for the resulting state of a transition $V(s')$ and the recorded reward for the transition r, we can assign a value to the corresponding datapoint: $q(I,a) = r + \gamma V(s')$.

Having calculated these datapoint values, Continuous U Tree then tests if they vary systematically within any state, and, if so, finds the best single decision to use to divide that state in two. This is done using decision tree techniques. Each attribute in the sensory input is considered in turn. The datapoints are sorted according to that attribute. The algorithm loops through this sorted list and a trial split is added between each consecutive pair of datapoints. This split divides the datapoints into two sets. These two sets

- Data Gathering Phase:
  - Pass the current sensory input I, down the state tree to find the current state s in the discretization.
  - Use Q values for the state s to choose an action $a = \arg\max_{a'} Q(s, a')$
  - Store transition datapoint (I, a, I', r).
  - (optional) Update the value function using a standard, discrete Reinforcement Learning technique.
- Processing Phase:
  - For each leaf:
    * Update the values of datapoints in that leaf: $q(I, a) = r + \gamma V(s')$.
    * Find the best split point using the splitting criterion.
    * If the split point satisfies the stopping criterion, then split the leaf into two states.
  - Calculate the transition probabilities $P_{(s,a)}(s')$, and expected rewards $R(s, a, s')$, using the recorded transitions (I, a, I', r).
  - Solve the MDP so specified to find $V(s)$ and $Q(s, a)$.

Table 1: The Continuous U Tree algorithm

are compared using a *splitting criterion* (see below) which returns a single number describing how different the two distributions are. The trial split that leads to the largest difference between the two distributions is remembered. The "best" split is then evaluated by a fixed *stopping criterion* (see below) to check whether the difference is significant.

Having found a discretization, the problem has been reduced to a standard, discrete, reinforcement learning problem: finding Q values for the new states, $Q(s, a)$. This is done by calculating state transition probabilities, $P_{(s,a)}(s')$, and expected rewards, $R(s, a, s')$, from the recorded transitions and then solving the MDP so specified. We have used both Prioritized Sweeping (Moore & Atkeson 1993) and conjugate gradient descent on the sum-squared Bellman residuals (Baird 1995) to solve the MDP defined over this new discretization.

Splitting Criteria: Testing for a difference between data distributions

We tried two different splitting criteria. The first is a non-parametric statistical test – the Kolmogorov-Smirnov test. The second is based on sum-squared error.

The first splitting criterion is that used by McCallum (1995) in the original U Tree algorithm, which looked for violations of the Markov assumption. If the distribution of datapoint values in each of the two new states was different, then there was a violation of the Markov assumption – more information about the world is available by knowing where the agent is within the old state. The splitting criterion was then a test of the statistical similarity of the distributions of the datapoints on either side of the split. We used the Kolmogorov-Smirnov non-parametric test. This test is based on the difference in the cumulative distributions of the two datasets.

Figure 1 illustrates the cumulative distributions of two datasets. The arrow between the two lines marks the maximum difference D between the cumulative probability distributions, C_1 and C_2. This distance has a distribution that can be approximately calculated for two independent, but identically distributed, sets of datapoints regardless of what distribution the sets are drawn from. Assuming the cumulative distributions are C_1 and C_2, with dataset sizes of N_1 and N_2 respectively, the probability that the observed difference could be generated by noise is calculated using the equations in Table 2 (Press *et al.* 1992). The smaller this probability, the more evidence there is of a true difference. If it is small enough to pass the stopping criterion, then a split is introduced.

$$D = \max_{-\infty < x < \infty} |C_1(x) - C_2(x)| \quad (3)$$

$$N_e = \frac{N_1 N_2}{N_1 + N_2} \quad (4)$$

$$\lambda = \left[\sqrt{N_e} + 0.12 + 0.11/\sqrt{N_e}\right] D \quad (5)$$

$$P_{Noise} = 2 \sum_{j=1}^{\infty} (-1)^{j-1} e^{-2j^2 \lambda^2} \quad (6)$$

Table 2: The Kolmogorov-Smirnov test equations

We investigated a second squared-error based splitting criterion (Breiman *et al.* 1984). The aim is to approximate the Q values of the transitions, $q(I, a)$, using only the Q values of the states, $Q(s, a)$. The error measure for this fit is the sum-squared error.

Assuming the other Q values do not change, the Q values of the two new states will equal the mean of the datapoints in those states. The mean-squared error equals to the expected squared deviation from the mean, i.e. the variance. The splitting criterion is the weighted sum of the variances of the Q values of the transitions on either side of the split. A second justification for this splitting criterion is the finding of Williams & Baird (1993) that reducing the Bellman residual of a value function increases performance.

Both these splitting criteria can be made more sensitive by performing the tests separately for each action and then combining the results. For the mean-squared error test a

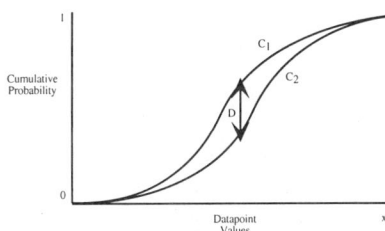

Figure 1: Two cumulative probability distributions

weighted sum was used. For the Kolmogorov-Smirnov test we multiply the probabilities calculated.

Importantly from an efficiency viewpoint, both of these tests can be done at least partly incrementally. For the sum-squared error, we can keep track of $\sum_n x$ and $\sum_n x^2$ and use these to estimate the variance, $V = \frac{\sum_n x^2 - \frac{(\sum_n x)^2}{n}}{n-1}$. The time complexity of a series of tests on the data in a leaf is then $O(n)$.

For the Kolmogorov-Smirnov test, the datasets need to be sorted to find the cumulative probability distributions. This sorting can be performed once by trading $O(n)$ space, but we still need to loop over the distributions to find D for each test making the total time $O(n^2)$.

Stopping Criteria: Should we split?

When learning a regression tree from data, the standard technique is to grow the tree by recursively splitting the data until a stopping criterion is met. Obviously, if all the datapoints in a leaf have the same value, the algorithm can stop. Similarly, it can stop if there is no way to separate the data – for example all datapoints fall at the same point in the sensory input space.

More generally, the algorithm should stop when it cannot detect a "significant" difference between the datasets on either side of the best split in a leaf. Here the word significant can have different meanings. For the Kolmogorov-Smirnov test we use significant to mean statistically significant at the $P = 0.05$ level.

The stopping criterion for the squared-error based test is the reduction in mean squared-error. If the difference between the variance of the entire dataset and the weighted mean variance of the datasets induced by the split is below a threshold, then there is not a significant difference. This test is less theoretically based than the other test, but with careful adjustment of the threshold produced reasonable results.

In the tree based learning literature, it is well known that stopping criteria often have to be weak to find good splits hidden low in the tree. To stop overly large trees being produced, the trees are often pruned before being used. We are assuming that little error is introduced by over-discretizing.

Datapoint sampling: What do we save?

In the description of the algorithm above, we simply noted that transitions are saved. Notably, Continuous U Tree does not need to save all of the transitions. Its generalization capabilities allow it to learn from non-continuous trajectories through state space. Recording all of the transitions is expensive, both in terms of memory to record the data and in processing time when testing for splits. However, the fewer transitions recorded the harder it is to detect differences within a leaf.

When limiting the number of saved datapoints, we simply recorded a fixed number of datapoints per state. Even once the number of transitions to store is set, it is still unclear which transitions to store. In the experiments reported we remembered all transitions until the preset per-state limit was reached. We then made room for new transitions by discarding a random transition from that state. This has the advantage that no bias, which might mislead our splitting or stopping criterion, is introduced.

A Corridor Domain

To qualitatively test our algorithm we introduce a simple 2-D domain simulating a robot moving in a corridor. The domain has two state dimensions: location and temperature. Location is an ordered, discrete attribute where the agent needs to distinguish every value to represent the correct value function. Temperature is continuous, but can be divided into three qualitatively different regions - cold, normal and hot. The robot is not given this division. As we will see, Continuous U Tree correctly and autonomously finds the three qualitatively different temperature regions. It also finds that the distance down the corridor is needed at full accuracy.

In this domain the length of the corridor is divided into three sections: sections A, B and C. These three sections of corridor each have a different base temperature. A is cooled, B is normal temperature and C is heated. The robot starts at a random position in the corridor and is rewarded when it reaches the right-hand end of the corridor. The robot is temperature sensitive, but also has limited temperature control on board. The robot must learn to move towards the correct end of the corridor, to turn its heater on in section A and to turn its cooler on in section C.

The robot's actions make it move and change its temperature control settings. The robot has 6 actions it can perform: move forward or backward 1 unit, each with either heater on, cooler on, or neither on. The robot moves nondeterministically as a function of its temperature. While the robot's temperature is in the $(30°, 70°)$ range, it successfully moves with 90% probability, otherwise it only moves with a 10% probability.

The robot's temperature is the base temperature of that section of corridor adjusted by the robot's temperature control unit. In our experiments, the corridor was 10 units long. Sections A, B and C were 3, 4 and 3 units in length respectively, with base temperature ranges of $(5°, 35°)$, $(25°, 75°)$ and $(65°, 95°)$ respectively. The robot's temperature control unit changed the temperature of the robot to differ from the corridor section base temperature by $(25°, 45°)$ if the heater was on, and by $(-25°, -45°)$ when the cooler was on. All temperatures and temperature adjustments were independently sampled from a uniform distribution in the range given for each time-step. Figure 2 illustrates some of the state transitions for this domain.

Figure 3 shows the discretization and policy for this task after 3000 steps in the world. The y axis is the temperature of the robot on a scale of $0 - 100$. The x axis is the location of the robot in the corridor, on a scale of $1 - 10$.

In the tests run in the corridor domain, both splitting criterion behaved similarly. The sum-squared error testing is significantly faster however.

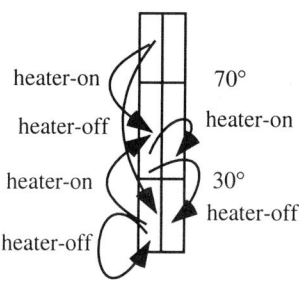

The y axis is the robot's temperature. The x axis represents two consecutive locations in the cool section of the corridor. High probability transitions moving right are shown.

Figure 2: Sample transitions for part of the corridor domain

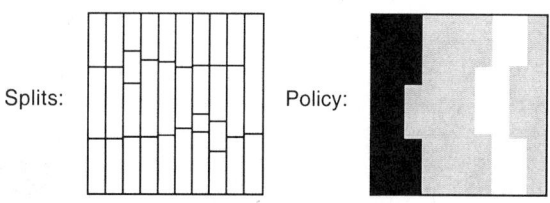

The y axis is the robot's temperature. The x axis is the location along the corridor. The goal is on the right hand edge. The policy was to move right at every point. Black areas indicate the heater was to be active. White areas indicate the cooler was to be active.

Figure 3: The learnt discretization and policy for the corridor task after 3000 steps

A Hexagonal Soccer Domain

As a more complex domain for empirical evaluation of Continuous U Tree we introduce a hexagonal grid based soccer (Hexcer) simulation. Hexcer is similar to, but larger than, the game framework used by Littman (1994) to test Minimax Q Learning. We test Continuous U Tree by having it learn to play Hexcer against another reinforcement learning algorithm. Uther & Veloso (1997) compare a number of reinforcement learning algorithms in the Hexcer domain. They found Prioritized Sweeping to be the best of the tradition reinforcement learning algorithms. We compare Continuous U Tree against Prioritized Sweeping here.

Hexcer consists of a field with a hexagonal grid of 53 cells, two players and a ball. Each player can be in any cell not already occupied by the other player. The ball is either in the center of the board, or is controlled by (in the same cell as) one of the players. This gives a total of 8268 distinct states in the game.

The two players start in fixed positions on the board, as shown. The game then proceeds in rounds. During each round the players make simultaneous moves to a neighboring cell in any of the six possible directions. Players must specify a direction in which to move, but if a player attempts to move off the edge of the grid, it remains in the same cell. Once one player moves onto the ball, the ball stays with that player until stolen by the other player. When a cell is contested the winner is decided nondeterministically with the winner getting the ball.

Players score by taking the ball into their opponent's goal. When the ball arrives in a goal the game ends. The player guarding the goal loses the game and gets a negative reward. The opponent receives an equal magnitude, but positive, reward. It is possible to score an own goal.

We performed empirical comparisons along two different dimensions – how fast does each algorithm learn to play, and to what level of expertise does the algorithm learn to play, discounting a "reasonable" initial learning period? Essentially we have two points on a learning curve.

In this experiment the pair of algorithms played each other at Hexcer for 1000 games. Wins were recorded for the first 500 games and the second 500 games. The first 500 games allowed us to measure learning speed as the agents started out with no knowledge of the game. The second 500 games gave an indication of the level of ability of the algorithm after the initial learning period.

This 1000 game test was then repeated 20 times. The results shown in table 3 are the number of games (mean ± standard deviation) won by each algorithm. The percentage at the end of each row is the level of statistical significance of the difference.

Table 3 shows that Continuous U Tree performs better than Prioritized Sweeping. Interestingly, looking at the (often quite large) trees generated by Continuous U Tree we can see that it has managed to learn the concept of "opponent behind."

Discussion

Continuous U Tree learns to play Hexcer with much less world experience than Prioritized Sweeping. Despite requiring less data, the Continuous U Tree algorithm is slower in real-time than the prioritized sweeping algorithm for the domains tested. For domains where data can be expensive or time-consuming to gather, trading algorithm speed for efficient use of data is important. In this area Continuous U Tree has an advantage over traditional reinforcement learning algorithms.

The corridor domain makes clear a number of details about the algorithm. Firstly, our algorithm successfully reduced a continuous space down to a discrete space with only 32 states (see figure 3). The algorithm has managed to find the 30° and 70° cutoff points with reasonable accuracy - it does not try to represent the entire temperature range. Continuous U Tree does not make perfect splits initially, but introduces further splits to refine its discretization. A possible enhancement would be to have old splits reconsidered in the light of new data and optimize them directly.

Secondly, the algorithm has divided the length of the corridor up as much as possible. Unlike the temperature axis, where large numbers of different datapoints values are grouped in one state, every different corridor location is in a different state.

The location of the agent in the corridor is directly relevant to achieving the goal. The state values in a fully discretized world change along this axis. By comparison,

	Prioritized Sweeping		Continuous U Tree		Significance
First 500 games	175 ± 93	$35\% \pm 19\%$	325 ± 93	$65\% \pm 19\%$	1%
Second 500 games	197 ± 99	$39\% \pm 20\%$	303 ± 99	$61\% \pm 20\%$	5%
Total	372 ± 183	$37\% \pm 18\%$	628 ± 183	$63\% \pm 18\%$	1%

Table 3: Hexcer results: Prioritized Sweeping vs. Continuous U Tree

the values of different points below 30° in the temperature range, but with the same corridor location, are equal. Once the agent is below 30° it will only move 10% of the time – no further information is needed. In ongoing work we are attempting to generalize over the cost to move between states in addition to the value of states.

The simple form of decision recorded by Continuous U Tree in the state tree can only divide the space parallel to the axes of the input space. Other more complex types of decision exist in regression tree literature (Utgoff & Brodley 1991), but simple decisions have been shown to be remarkably effective, and much faster to find than more complex decisions. By adding redundant attributes that are linear combinations of the primary attributes we can allow the algorithm to find diagonal splits.

Like U Tree, Continuous U Tree inherits from its decision tree background the ability to handle moderately high dimensional state spaces. The original U Tree work used this capability to partially remove the Markov assumption. As we were playing a Markov game we did not implement this part of the U Tree algorithm in Continuous U Tree although there is no reason why this could not be done.

Conclusion

Large state spaces affect learning speed, but often the exact location in that space is not relevant to achieving the goal. We have described an effective generalizing reinforcement learning algorithm, Continuous U Tree, that can discretize a continuous state space while leaving equivalent areas as single states. Our generalizing algorithm performs significantly better than non-generalizing algorithms.

Acknowledgements: This research is sponsored by the Defense Advanced Research Projects Agency (DARPA) and the Air Force Research Laboratory (AFRL) under agreement number F30602-97-2-0250. The views and conclusions contained herein are those of the authors only.

References

Baird, L. C. 1995. Residual algorithms: Reinforcement learning with function approximation. In Prieditis, A., and Russell, S., eds., *Machine Learning: Proceedings of the Twelfth International Conference (ICML95)*, 30–37. San Mateo: Morgan Kaufmann.

Bellman, R. E. 1957. *Dynamic Programming*. Princeton, NJ: Princeton University Press.

Boyan, J. A., and Moore, A. W. 1995. Generalization in reinforcement learning: Safely approximating the value function. In Tesauro, G.; Touretzky, D. S.; and Leen, T. K., eds., *Advances in Neural Information Processing Systems*, volume 7. Cambridge, MA: The MIT Press.

Breiman, L.; Friedman, J. H.; Olshen, R. A.; and Stone, C. J. 1984. *Classification And Regression Trees*. Monterey, CA: Wadsworth and Brooks/Cole Advanced Books and Software.

Chapman, D., and Kaelbling, L. P. 1991. Input generalization in delayed reinforcement learning: An algorithm and performance comparisons. In *Proceedings of the Twelfth International Joint Conference on Artificial Intelligence (IJCAI-91)*, 726–731.

Dean, T., and Lin, S.-H. 1995. Decomposition techniques for planning in stochastic domains. In *Proceedings of the Fourteenth International Joint Conference on Artificial Intelligence*.

Gordon, G. J. 1995. Online fitted reinforcement learning. In *Value Function Approximation workshop at ML95*.

Kaelbling, L. P.; Littman, M. L.; and Moore, A. W. 1996. Reinforcement learning: A survey. *Journal of Artificial Intelligence Research* 4:237–285.

Littman, M. L. 1994. Markov games as a framework for multi-agent reinforcement learning. In *Machine Learning: Proceedings of the Eleventh International Conference (ICML94)*, 157–163. San Mateo: Morgan Kaufmann.

McCallum, A. K. 1995. *Reinforcement Learning with Selective Perception and Hidden State*. Phd. thesis, Department of Computer Science, University of Rochester.

Moore, A., and Atkeson, C. G. 1993. Prioritized sweeping: Reinforcement learning with less data and less real time. *Machine Learning* 13.

Moore, A. W. 1991. Variable resolution dynamic programming: Efficiently learning action maps in multivariate real-values state-spaces. In Birnbaum, L., and Collins, G., eds., *Machine Learning: Proceedings on the Eighth International Workshop*. Morgan Kaufmann.

Moore, A. W. 1994. The parti-game algorithm for variable resolution reinforcement learning in multidimensional state-spaces. In Cowan, J. D.; Tesauro, G.; and Alspector, J., eds., *Advances in Neural Information Processing Systems 6*, 711–718. Morgan Kaufmann.

Press, W. H.; Teukolsky, S. A.; Vetterling, W. T.; and Flannery, B. P. 1992. *Numerical Recipes in C: the art of scientific computing*. Cambridge University Press.

Quinlan, J. R. 1986. Induction of decision trees. *Machine Learning* 1:81–106.

Sutton, R. S. 1984. *Temporal Credit Assignment in Reinforcement Learning*. Ph.D. Dissertation, University of Massachusetts, Amherst.

Utgoff, P. E., and Brodley, C. E. 1991. Linear machine decision trees. Tech. Report 91-10, University of Massachusetts.

Uther, W. T. B., and Veloso, M. M. 1997. Adversarial reinforcement learning. *Journal of Artificial Intelligence Research*. To be submitted.

Watkins, C. J. C. H., and Dayan, P. 1992. Q-learning. *Machine Learning* 8(3):279–292.

Williams, R. J., and Baird, L. C. I. 1993. Tight performance bounds on greedy policies based on imperfect value functions. Tech. report, College of Computer Science, Northeastern University.

Natural Language

A Sampling-Based Heuristic for Tree Search Applied to Grammar Induction

Hugues Juillé and Jordan B. Pollack
Computer Science Department
Brandeis University
Waltham, Massachusetts 02254-9110
{hugues, pollack}@cs.brandeis.edu

Abstract

In the field of Operation Research and Artificial Intelligence, several stochastic search algorithms have been designed based on the theory of global random search (Zhigljavsky 1991). Basically, those techniques iteratively sample the search space with respect to a probability distribution which is updated according to the result of previous samples and some predefined strategy. Genetic Algorithms (GAs) (Goldberg 1989) or Greedy Randomized Adaptive Search Procedures (GRASP) (Feo & Resende 1995) are two particular instances of this paradigm. In this paper, we present SAGE, a search algorithm based on the same fundamental mechanisms as those techniques. However, it addresses a class of problems for which it is difficult to design transformation operators to perform local search because of intrinsic constraints in the definition of the problem itself. For those problems, a procedural approach is the natural way to construct solutions, resulting in a state space represented as a tree or a DAG. The aim of this paper is to describe the underlying heuristics used by SAGE to address problems belonging to that class. The performance of SAGE is analyzed on the problem of grammar induction and its successful application to problems from the recent Abbadingo DFA learning competition is presented.

Introduction

The design of massively parallel search algorithms requires the use of new strategies to take advantage of highly distributed architectures. Some examples of such algorithms are Genetic Algorithms (GAs) (Goldberg 1989), Genetic Programming (GP) (Koza 1992), Evolutionary Programming (EP) (Fogel 1962) or Evolutionary Strategies (ES) (Bäck, Hoffmeister, & Schwefel 1991) that have shown very good performance on large scale problems (Hillis 1992; Koza et al. 1996). Those algorithms admit an efficient parallel implementation and, basically, sample the search space in order to gather information about the regularities in the distribution of solutions. Then, the search is focused by keeping for the next stage the most promising states according to an objective function. Those algorithms are exploring the state space by applying search operators on a representation for states. Those operators can perform a "recombination" for which a new state is constructed by taking elements from two or more selected states or a "mutation" which alters randomly some elements of a selected state. As a consequence, those search algorithms rely heavily on a local search operator. They require the design of a representation for the state space and the definition of a neighborhood structure over this representation that presents regularities that can be exploited. Problems for which solutions are constructed using an imperative procedure, i.e. each step of the construction depending strongly on the previous steps, make difficult to design a representation and operators which capture the constraints that apply for the construction of valid solutions while at the same time exhibiting an appropriate neighborhood structure with respect to the search procedure. If the representation and the operators can't capture the construction constraints or if the neighborhood structure doesn't present some regularities that can be exploited by the search operators, the search becomes trapped in poor local optima. Such undesirable property of a representation is sometimes referred to as *epistasis*, meaning that the degree of interdependency between the components of the representation is very high and makes the problem very deceptive with respect to the search operators.

On the other hand, traditional artificial intelligence backtracking search algorithms which are designed to explore problem spaces would be appropriate to tackle such problems. However, to face the problem of combinatorial explosion, some heuristics have to be used to control the search. Such heuristics use problem-specific knowledge that has been identified for the problem at hand. However, those heuristics don't use any information about the distribution of solutions in the state space unless this information has been provided explicitly in the definition of the evaluation function (Baum 1992). So far, very little work has been done to explore

Copyright © 1998, American Association for Artificial Intelligence (www.aaai.org). All rights reserved.

the idea of using the distribution of solutions when such an evaluation function is not known or difficult to design.

Our goal was to design an algorithm for tree search that would be able to extract and exploit information about the distribution of solutions and would admit an efficient parallel implementation in order to address large scale problems. The main idea for that algorithm is to collect information about the distribution for the value of the leaves of the search tree corresponding to the alternatives under consideration by performing a series of random sampling. Then, this information is used to focus the search on the most promising alternatives. This result is achieved by using a model of local competition between the elements of the distributed model which allows the algorithm to allocate more "resources" (i.e., processing elements) to the most promising alternatives in a self-adaptive manner. As described later in this paper, such a model provides this algorithm with the advantage of allowing a highly distributed implementation because of a loose central control. Because of this architecture, we named this algorithm *Self-Adaptive Greedy Estimate* (SAGE) search procedure. So far, random sampling techniques on search trees have been used essentially to predict the complexity of search algorithms (Knuth 1975; Chen 1992), but never as a heuristic to control the search. We believe our algorithm to be the first to exploit that knowledge.

This paper presents the application of this search algorithm to the *grammar induction* problem. This application originated from the Abbadingo DFA learning competition (Lang & Pearlmutter 1997) which took place between March and November 1997. This competition proposed a set of difficult instances for the problem of DFA learning as a challenge to the machine learning community and to encourage the development of new algorithms for grammar induction. The SAGE search algorithm ended up as one of the two winners of this competition. The second winner was an algorithm that exploits a new evidence-driven heuristic first discovered by Rod Price during the competition.

The paper is organized as follows: Section 2 presents in details the SAGE search algorithm. Section 3 describes the work performed for the Abbadingo competition. In the following section, an analysis compares the performance of SAGE to the Trakhtenbrot-Barzdin algorithm and to our own implementation of the evidence-driven heuristic.

Presentation of SAGE

Principle

We consider the class of problems for which any feasible solution can be generated by a construction procedure. Hence, a search algorithm will proceed by making an ordered sequence of decisions, each decision being selected among a list of choices with respect to a particular strategy. At each iteration, the construction procedure determines this list of choices from the current state of the partial solution. So, the construction procedure defines the search space as a tree. A solution is a path from the root of that tree to a leaf and internal nodes represent partial solutions. Eventually, the search space can be a directed acyclic graph (DAG) if there are equivalent nodes in the tree.

There is a well-known AI algorithm for search in DAGs and trees called *Beam search*. Beam search examines in parallel a number of nearly optimal alternatives (the *beam*). This search algorithm progresses level by level in the tree of states and it moves downward only from the best w nodes at each level. Consequently, the number of nodes explored remains manageable: if the branching factor in the tree is at most b then there will be at most wb nodes under consideration at any depth. SAGE is similar to this algorithm in the sense that it is a distributed model that implements multi-threaded search. That is, SAGE is composed of a population of *processing elements*. Each of them is playing the role of an elementary search algorithm and is seen as one alternative in the beam. In tree search algorithms, a *fitness* (or score) is assigned to internal nodes in order to determine which nodes will be explored further and which nodes will be ignored. In the case of beam search, heuristics are used to score the different alternatives. However, this approach assumes the existence of such an evaluation function to score nodes. The new idea proposed by SAGE is to estimate the score of internal nodes by performing a random sampling from this node. That is, a path is constructed incrementally and randomly until a leaf (or valid solution) is reached. Then, the score of this solution is directly computed with respect to the problem objective function and it is assigned to the initial node.

More precisely, SAGE is an iterative search procedure for which each iteration is composed of two phases, a *construction* phase and a *competition* phase. SAGE implements a population of elementary randomized search algorithms and a *meta-level heuristic* which controls the search procedure by distributing the alternatives under consideration among this population of processing elements. For any iteration, all the alternatives represented in the population have the same depth in the search tree. At the beginning of the search, this depth is null and it increases with the number of iterations according to a strategy implemented by the meta-level heuristic. During each iteration, the following operations are performed:

- *construction phase*: each processing element calls the construction procedure designed for the current problem. This procedure starts the construction from the internal node which represents the alternative assigned to the calling processing element and thereafter makes each decision by randomly selecting one choice from the list of choices available at each step. Each random selection is performed with respect to a uniform probability distribution.

- *competition phase*: the purpose of this phase is to focus the search on most promising alternatives by assigning more representatives to them. The details of that phase are described below.

In summary, SAGE is a population-based model in which each processing element is the representative of one alternative for the current level of search in the tree. Then, the search space is explored according to the following strategy:

1. Initially, the search is restricted to the first level of the tree and each processing element in the population randomly selects one of the first-level nodes.
2. Each processing element scores its associated alternative by performing a random sampling. This is the construction phase.
3. The competition phase is operated. It results in the search focusing on most promising alternatives.
4. The meta-level heuristic determines whether the level of search is increased by one or not. In the affirmative, each processing element selects uniformly randomly one of the children of its associated node and this node becomes the new alternative assigned to the processing element.
5. The search stops if no new node can be explored (because the search reached the leaves of the tree); otherwise it continues with step 2.

In the SAGE model, the level of search in the tree is called the *commitment degree* since it corresponds to a commitment to the first choices of the incremental construction of the current best solution. The next three sections describe the construction phase, the competition phase and the management of the commitment degree.

Construction Phase

The construction procedure used during this phase plays a very important role since it determines the distribution of solutions when sampling the search tree. The design of this procedure allows some flexibility. In particular, some problem-specific heuristics can be introduced to drive the search in a particular direction, the search space can be reduced by introducing some constraints or the distribution of solutions can be modified by using some strategies. The *multiple-sampling* technique is an example of such a strategy. This technique simply evaluates the score of an alternative by taking the best out of n samples. In practice, n cannot be too large since the computational resource required increases linearly with its value. However, increasing n can be an interesting alternative to a larger population size since the amount of memory required to store the members of the population can quickly become overwhelming for complex problems.

Competition Phase

The SAGE search algorithm uses a population of geographically distributed processing elements. This architecture makes it amenable to an easy implementation on several models of computer networks and parallel machines. For the sake of simplicity, we will consider a model in which the population of processing elements is mapped on a wrap-around mesh (i.e. a torus). A processing element is assigned to each node of the mesh. In such a setup, the competition phase can be performed by implementing a local competition among the processing elements. Each processing element compares the score of the alternative it represents to those in its neighborhood. This neighborhood is composed of the nodes in the mesh whose Manhattan distance from the current node is lesser than a given value. If there is a node with a higher score then the processing element becomes a representative of the same alternative as that neighbor. In case of a tie, one alternative is selected randomly. So, if a given alternative for the current level of search in the tree is more likely to lead to a high score solution then more copies of that alternative will be represented in the population of processing elements as a result of this competition phase (therefore focusing the beam).

Management of the Commitment Degree

Successive competition phases result in most promising alternatives being represented by a larger and larger number of processing elements. Ultimately, if one waits until all the population agrees on the same alternative before continuing the search on the next level, the beam would be reduced to the exploration of a single alternative. On the contrary, if the level of search is increased too frequently, the beam would become very wide, making the search unreliable. Clearly, for the search to be efficient, a balance must be maintained between those two extremes.

We experimented two different strategies to control the commitment degree. The first one simply increases the commitment degree every n iterations. The drawback of this strategy is that n has to be chosen astutely in order to maintain the right balance between exploration and exploitation. This makes this strategy very brittle. The second strategy performs a measure of the state of the population called *diversity measure* which is an estimate of the width of the beam. To compute this measure, each processing element in the population counts the number of neighbors that correspond to a different alternative than itself. Then, this number is summed over all the members of the population and the result is the diversity measure. This measure reflects the degree of convergence of the population. If only a few alternatives are represented in the population then this measure is small because most of the processing elements represent the same alternative as their neighbors. On the other hand, if many alternatives are explored the diversity measure is large. As the population focus on most promising alternatives because of the competition phase, the diversity measure decreases. When this measure reaches an arbitrarily fixed threshold (which is a parameter of the model), the meta-level strategy considers that the width of the beam is small enough and the search can continue on the next level of the tree. The drawback of this strategy is that it can take a long time for the diversity measure to reach the given threshold if several alternatives lead to equivalent solutions. In that case, a combination of the two strategies offers a good compromise, the first strategy preventing such deadlocks.

Discussion

As discussed previously, the performance of SAGE relies heavily on the construction procedure. Indeed, the construction procedure determines the distribution of solutions when the search space is sampled. The underlying heuristic exploited by SAGE at each iteration is to focus the search on domains of the state space for which sampled solutions are of better quality. Thus, the assumption is that reliable information is collected by the sampling procedure to control the search. If the construction procedure is not compatible with this assumption, the performance of the search is very poor. In practice, a few tries are often required to discover an appropriate procedure which results in a good performance. As a rule of thumb, the construction procedure should be designed so that early choices result in a reliable discrimination between poor domains of the search space and domains that are worth being explored.

Induction of DFAs

Presentation

The aim of inductive inference is to discover an abstract model which captures the underlying rules of a system from the observation of its behavior and thus to become able to give some prediction for the future behavior of that system. In the field of grammar induction, observations are strings that are labeled "accepted" or "rejected" and the goal is to determine the language that generates those strings. (Angluin & Smith 1983) present an excellent survey of the field, covering in particular the issue of computational complexity and describing some inference methods for inductive learning.

The application of the SAGE search algorithm to this problem has been motivated by the Abbadingo competition organized by (Lang & Pearlmutter 1997). It is a challenge proposed to the machine learning community in which a set of increasingly difficult DFA induction problems have been designed. Those problems are supposed to be just beyond the current state of the art for today's DFA learning algorithms and their difficulty increases along two dimensions: the size of the underlying DFA and the sparsity of the training data. (Gold 1978) has shown that inferring a minimum finite state automaton compatible with given data consisting of a finite number of labeled strings is NP-complete. However, (Lang 1992) empirically found out that the average case is tractable. That is, randomly generated target DFAs are approximately learnable even from sparse data when this training data is also generated at random. One of the aims of the Abbadingo competition is to estimate an empirical lower bound for the sparsity of the training data for which DFA learning is still tractable. The competition has been setup as follows. A set of DFAs of various size have been randomly generated. Then, a training set and a test set have been generated from each of those DFAs. Only the labeling for the training sets have been released. Training sets are composed of a number of strings which varies with the size of the target DFA and the level of sparsity desired. The goal of the competition is to discover a model for the training data that has a predictive error rate smaller than one percent on the test set. Since the labeling for the test sets has not been released, the validity of a model can be tested only by submitting a candidate labeling to an "Oracle" implemented on a server at the University of New Mexico (Lang & Pearlmutter 1997) which returns a "pass/fail" answer. Table 1 presents the different problems that compose this competition. The size and the depth of the target DFA are provided as a piece of information to estimate how close a DFA hypothesis is from the target. The rule of the competition is that the first person to solve a problem owns it. Because of the two dimensions for the evaluation of the difficulty of problems (namely sparsity of training data and size of target DFA), a partial order is defined over problems resulting in the possibility of multiple winners. This partial order is represented in table 2. In this table, a given problem dominates all those that are in the top-left square whose bottom-right corner corresponds to the position of that problem. For instance, problem 6 dominates problems 1, 2, 3, 4 and 5. At the end, a winner is somebody who owns a problem which is not dominated by any other solved problem. The different naming conventions for problems come from the fact that problems R, S and T were added later in the competition. Table 2 also describes which algorithm was the first to solve each problem. In the competition, SAGE first took the lead by solving problems 1, 2, 4 and 5. Then, the evidence-driven heuristic (EDH) was discovered and defeated SAGE by solving problems 3, R, 6 and S. However, SAGE later solved problem 7, hereby becoming a co-winner. Problems 8, 9 and T were not solved by the end of the competition.

In the next sections, two algorithms are presented to address this grammar induction problem. First, the construction procedure to be used in the SAGE search algorithm is described. Then, our own implementation of an algorithm exploiting the evidence-driven heuristic is presented.

Implementation for SAGE

The construction procedure makes use of the state merging method described in (Trakhtenbrot & Barzdin 1973). It takes as input the prefix tree acceptor constructed from the training data. Then, a finite state automaton is iteratively constructed, one transition at a time. This method allows the design of a construction

Problem name	Target DFA states	Target DFA depth	Strings in training set
1	63	10	3478
2	138	12	10723
3	260	14	28413
R	499	16	87500
4	68	10	2499
5	130	12	7553
6	262	14	19834
S	506	16	60000
7	65	10	1521
8	125	12	4382
9	267	14	11255
T	519	16	32500

Table 1: Abbadingo data sets.

		Training set density		
		dense		sparse
Target DFA size	small	1: SAGE	4: SAGE	7: SAGE
		2: SAGE	5: SAGE	8: unsolved
		3: EDH	6: EDH	9: unsolved
	large	R: EDH	S: EDH	T: unsolved

Table 2: Partial order over problems and status of each problem.

Begin with a single state mapped to the root of the prefix tree
The list $\mathcal{L}$ of unprocessed states consists of that state
do
   Pick randomly a state S from $\mathcal{L}$
   Compute the set $\mathcal{T}_0$ of valid transitions on "0" from state S
   Pick randomly a transition t_0 from $\mathcal{T}_0$
   if (t_0 goes to an existing state) **then**
      Merge corresponding nodes in the prefix tree
   else
      Create a new state, map it to the corresponding node in the prefix tree and add it to $\mathcal{L}$
   endif

   Compute the set $\mathcal{T}_1$ of valid transitions on "1" from state S
   Pick randomly a transition t_1 from $\mathcal{T}_1$
   if (t_1 goes to an existing state) **then**
      Merge corresponding nodes in the prefix tree
   else
      Create a new state, map it to the corresponding node in the prefix tree and add it to $\mathcal{L}$
   endif
until ($\mathcal{L}$ is empty)
/* The output is a DFA consistent with the training data */

Figure 1: Randomized construction procedure for DFA learning used by SAGE.

procedure which satisfies the rule of thumb discussed in the description of SAGE. Indeed, an incorrect merge performed early in the construction of a DFA results in the propagation of several incorrect constraints and has much more effect on the following steps of the search compared to an incorrect merge performed a few iterations later. Therefore, the sampling technique gives a good idea about which merges are more likely to be correct, provided the training data is not too sparse.

The construction procedure begins with a single state (the initial state of the DFA) which is attached to the root of the prefix tree. Then, at each step of the construction, one of the states that has no outgoing transition is selected at random and the "0" and "1" transitions are created for that state. Two cases are possible when considering a new transition: either it goes to an existing state or it goes to a newly created state. As the hypothesis DFA is constructed, states are mapped with nodes in the prefix tree and transitions between states are mapped with edges. When a new transition is created going to an existing state, corresponding nodes in the prefix tree are merged. When two nodes in the prefix tree are merged, the labels in the tree are updated accordingly and the merging of more nodes can be recursively triggered so that the prefix tree reflects the union of the labeled string suffixes that are attached to those nodes. Thus, as the DFA is constructed, the prefix tree is collapsed into a graph which is an image of the final DFA when the construction procedure is finished. This merging procedure provides the mechanism to test whether a transition between two existing states is consistent with the labeling and should be considered as a potential choice in the construction procedure. Indeed, if there is an inconsistency in the labeling when trying to merge two nodes, this means that the corresponding transition is not valid. The merging is then undone in order to restore the state of the prefix tree before the operation was performed. The pseudo-code describing this construction procedure is given in Figure 1.

The Evidence-Driven Heuristic

The state merging method implemented in (Trakhtenbrot & Barzdin 1973) considers a breadth-first order for merging nodes, with the idea that a valid merge involving the largest sub-trees in the prefix tree has a higher probability of being correct than other merges. The evidence-driven heuristic doesn't follow that intuition and considers instead the number of labeled nodes that are mapped over each other and match when merging sub-trees in the prefix tree. Different control strategies can be designed to explore the space of DFA constructions exploiting this heuristic. Our implementation maintains a list of valid destinations for each undecided transition for the current partial DFA and, as a policy, always gives priority to "forced" creation of new states over merge operations. The pseudo-code for this algorithm is presented in figure 2.

Begin with a single state mapped to the root of the
    prefix tree
The list $\mathcal{S}$ of states in the DFA consists of that state
The list $\mathcal{T}$ of unprocessed transitions consists of the
    outgoing transitions from that state
For each $t \in \mathcal{T}$, compute:
    . the subset $\mathcal{S}_{dest}(t)$ from $\mathcal{S}$ of valid destinations
    . the merge count for each destination in $\mathcal{S}_{dest}(t)$
do
    Construct $\mathcal{T}_0 = \{t \in \mathcal{T} \ s.t. \ \mathcal{S}_{dest}(t) = \emptyset\}$
    /* A new state is created if $\mathcal{T}_0$ is not empty */
    if $(\mathcal{T}_0 \neq \emptyset)$ **then**
        Select $t_0 \in \mathcal{T}_0$ outgoing from the shallowest node
            (break ties at random)
        Remove t_0 from $\mathcal{T}$
        Create a new state S_0 mapped to the destination
            node for t_0 in the prefix tree
        $\mathcal{S} \leftarrow \mathcal{S} \bigcup S_0$
        $\mathcal{T} \leftarrow \mathcal{T} \bigcup \{\text{outgoing transitions from } S_0\}$
        For each outgoing transition t' from S_0:
           . compute $\mathcal{S}_{dest}(t')$
           . evaluate merge count for each destination
                in $\mathcal{S}_{dest}(t')$
        For each transition $t \in \mathcal{T}$, add S_0 to $\mathcal{S}_{dest}(t)$ if
            S_0 is a valid destination for t and compute
            its merge count
    else
        /* Operate a merge */
        Select $t_0 \in \mathcal{T}$ with the highest merge count
            (break ties at random)
        Merge the destination node for t_0 in the prefix
            tree with the destination node corresponding to this highest merge count
        Remove t_0 from $\mathcal{T}$
        For each $t \in \mathcal{T}$, update $\mathcal{S}_{dest}(t)$ and the merge
            counts
    endif
until $(\mathcal{T} = \emptyset)$

Figure 2: Pseudo-code of our DFA construction algorithm exploiting the evidence-driven heuristic.

Experimental Results
Results for Problems in the Competition.

In a first stage, we have been using a sequential implementation of SAGE since small populations were enough to solve the smallest instances of the Abbadingo competition. Later, a network of workstations was used to scale the population size and address the most difficult problem instances in the competition. In particular, the solution to problems 5 and 7 involved around 16 workstations on average. This parallel implementation uses a server that manages the population of partial solutions and distributes the work load among several clients. This architecture presents the advantage that clients can be added or removed at any time.

SAGE has been able to solve problems 1, 2, 4, 5 and 7 from table 1. To solve problem 7, we proceeded in two steps. First, the construction procedure described previously has been extended with the evidence-driven heuristic in order to prune the search tree. The construction procedure switches to this heuristic when the number of states in the current DFA has reached a given size. Before that threshold size is reached, the construction procedure remains unchanged. After about 10 runs, a DFA with 103 states has been discovered very early. Then, in a second step, more experiments were performed using the original construction procedure but starting with the same first few choices as those that had been made for the 103-state DFA. This resulted in a DFA of size 65. This second step uses SAGE for local search, starting from a good prefix for the DFA construction. The appropriate size for the prefix has been determined experimentally. It is clear from those experiments that the density for the training data available for problem 7 is at the edge of what SAGE can manage. This observation is confirmed by the analysis presented in the following section.

Table 3 presents the experimental setup along with the results for some of the DFAs that passed the "Oracle" test. We decided to report in this table the value for parameters that had been used when each problem was solved for the first time. Experiments for problems 1, 2 and 4 have been performed on a Pentium PC 200MHz. For problems 5 and 7, a network of Pentium PCs and SGI workstations has been used. Our implementation of the evidence-driven heuristic can solve all the problems in the first and the second column in Table 2 except problem 5. Since this algorithm implements a greedy strategy, the time performance is much better than for SAGE. In particular, it takes a few seconds to solve problems 1 and 4 and about 8 minutes to solve problem S on a Pentium PC 200MHz.

Procedure for Generation of Problems.

For the experimental analysis of our algorithms, we constructed a set of problem instances, using the same procedure as for the generation of Abbadingo challenges.

- *Generation of target DFAs*: To construct a random DFA of nominal size n, a random digraph with $\frac{5}{4}n$ nodes is constructed, each vertex having two outgoing edges. Then, each node is labeled "accept" or "reject" with equal probability, a starting node is picked, nodes that can't be reached from that starting node are discarded and, finally, the Moore minimization algorithm is run. If the resulting DFA's depth isn't $\lfloor(2\log_2 n)-2\rfloor$, the procedure is repeated. This condition for the depth of DFAs corresponds to the average case of the distribution. It is a design constraint which allows the generation of a set of problems whose relative complexity remains consistent along the dimension of target size.

- *Generation of training and testing sets*: A training set for a n-state target DFA is a set drawn without replacement from a uniform distribution over the set of all strings of length at most $\lfloor(2\log_2 n)+3\rfloor$. The

Problem name	1	2	4
Population size	64	64	256 (+ best of 2 samples)
Neighborhood radius for competition phase	1	1	1
Value of the threshold for commitment degree increase (radius neighborhood = 1)	200	200	800
Number of generations	200	1600	100
Results (size of DFA model)	63 states	150 states	71 states
Execution time	1 hour (sequential)	40 hours (sequential)	4 hours (sequential)

Problem name	5	7 (step 1)	7 (step 2)
Population size	576 (+ best of 8 samples)	1024	4096
Neighborhood radius for competition phase	1	1	1
Value of the threshold for commitment degree increase (radius neighborhood = 1)	2400	2000	10000
Number of generations	250	20	100
Results (size of DFA model)	131 states	103 states	65 states
Execution time	40 hours (parallel)	2 hours (parallel)	4 hours (parallel)

Table 3: Experimental results for the SAGE search algorithm applied to problems 1, 2, 4, 5 and 7 of the Abbadingo competition.

same procedure is used to construct the testing set but strings already in the training set are excluded.

Comparative Performance Analysis.

In a comparative study, the performance of the three approaches: Trakhtenbrot-Barzdin (T-B) algorithm, evidence-driven heuristic and SAGE has been evaluated against a set of random problem instances generated using the procedure described in the previous section. For each target DFA, the three algorithms were evaluated across a range of density for the training data in order to observe the evolution of each approach when working with sparser data. For the first two algorithms, 1000 problems were used while only 100 problems were used to evaluate SAGE because of the requirement in computational resources. This comparison has been performed for three values of the population size for SAGE: 64, 256 and 1024 and for two values of the targets nominal size: 32 and 64 states (Figures 3 and 4 respectively).

In those experiments, the performance is the ratio of problems for which the predictive ability of the model constructed by the algorithm is at least 99% accurate. This threshold is the same as the success criterion for solving problems in the Abbadingo competition. Figures 3 and 4 show the dependence of SAGE on the population size for its performance. Indeed, a larger population results in a better reliability for the control of the focus of the search because of a larger sample.

For the set of problems generated for the purpose of this analysis, SAGE and the evidence-driven heuristic clearly outperform the T-B algorithm. With a population size large enough, SAGE also exhibits a performance consistently better than the evidence-driven heuristic. However, it is difficult to compare those two approaches since SAGE is a general purpose search algorithm while the other is a greedy algorithm using a problem-specific heuristic. For this reason, SAGE doesn't scale up as well as the evidence-driven heuristic (or the T-B algorithm) for larger target DFAs. The introduction of problem-specific heuristics in the construction procedure becomes necessary for SAGE to address this scaling issue.

Conclusion

This paper presents SAGE, a new algorithm for search in trees and directed graphs based on a random sampling strategy to evaluate the score of internal nodes and on the management of a population to adaptively focus the search on most promising alternatives. This stochastic algorithm admits a parallel implementation on both fine-grained and coarse grained distributed systems because of the loose central control.

The performance of SAGE has been analyzed on the problem of DFA learning, inspired from the recent Abbadingo competition. Those experiments have shown that for average size target DFAs (on the order of 64 to 128 states) SAGE compares favorably to the well-known

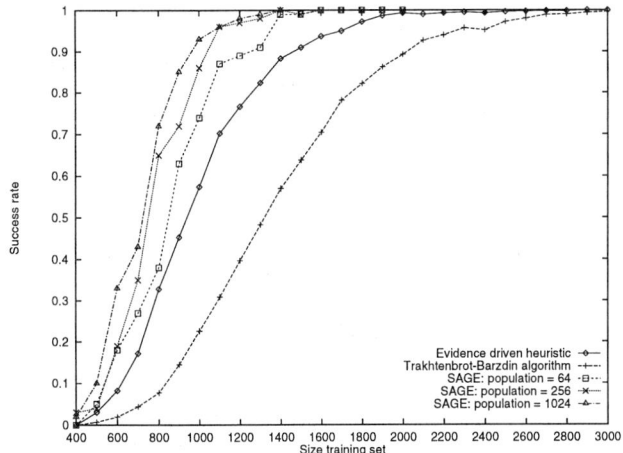

Figure 3: Comparison of performance for target DFAs of nominal size 32.

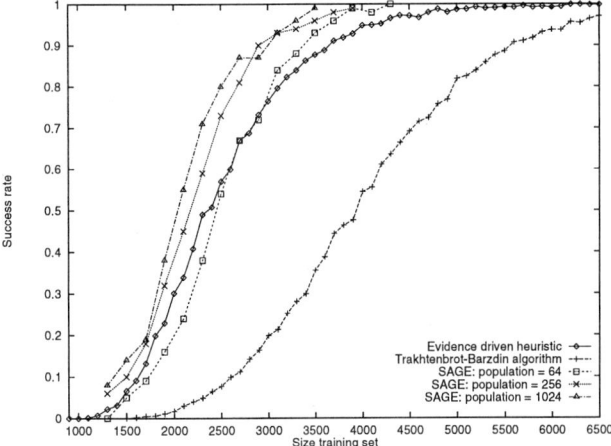

Figure 4: Comparison of performance for target DFAs of nominal size 64.

Trakhtenbrot-Barzdin algorithm and to a new evidence-driven heuristic. However, as the size of the target DFA increases, SAGE doesn't scale up and requires a prohibitive amount of computer resource. To search such a large state space, the introduction of problem-specific heuristics becomes necessary.

One important contribution of this paper is to provide some insights concerning the domain of stochastic search algorithms. The general idea for search algorithms is to exploit some information about the state space. This information can be provided either explicitly (hand-coded knowledge) or extracted by performing some form of statistical analysis. Then, this knowledge is exploited to decide how to focus the search. However, the actual distribution of solutions in the search space is a source of information that has rarely been exploited in the context of tree exploration. We believe that SAGE is a first example of a tree search algorithm able to exploit this information efficiently.

References

Angluin, D., and Smith, C. H. 1983. Inductive inference: Theory and methods. *Computing Surveys* 15:237–269.

Bäck, T.; Hoffmeister, F.; and Schwefel, H.-P. 1991. A survey of evolution strategies. In Belew, R. K., and Booker, L. B., eds., *Proceedings of the Fourth International Conference on Genetic Algorithms*, 2–9. San Mateo, California: Morgan Kaufmann.

Baum, E. B. 1992. On optimal game tree propagation for imperfect players. In *Proceedings of the Tenth National Conference on Artificial Intelligence*, 507–512.

Chen, P. C. 1992. Heuristic sampling: a method for predicting the performance of tree searching programs. *SIAM Journal on Computing* 21:295–315.

Feo, T. A., and Resende, M. G. 1995. Greedy randomized adaptive search procedures. *Journal of Global Optimization* 6:109–133.

Fogel, L. J. 1962. Autonomous automata. *Industrial Research* 4:14–19.

Gold, E. M. 1978. Complexity of automaton identification from given data. *Information and Control* 37:302–320.

Goldberg, D. E. 1989. *Genetic Algorithms in Search, Optimization and Machine Learning*. Addison-Wesley.

Hillis, W. D. 1992. Co-evolving parasites improve simulated evolution as an optimization procedure. In Langton, C., et al., eds., *Artificial Life II*, 313–324. Addison Wesley.

Knuth, D. E. 1975. Estimating the efficiency of backtracking programs. *Math. Comp.* 29:121–136.

Koza, J. R.; Bennett, F. H.; Andre, D.; and Keane, M. A. 1996. Four problems for which a computer program evolved by genetic programming is competitive with human performance. In *Proceedings of the Third IEEE International Conference on Evolutionary Computation*, 1–10. IEEE Press.

Koza, J. R. 1992. *Genetic Programming: On the Programming of Computers by Means of Natural Selection*. MIT Press.

Lang, K. J., and Pearlmutter, B. A. 1997. Abbadingo one: Dfa learning competition. http://abbadingo.cs.unm.edu.

Lang, K. J. 1992. Random dfa's can be approximately learned from sparse uniform examples. In *Proceedings of the Fifth Annual ACM Workshop on Computational Learning Theory*, 45–52.

Trakhtenbrot, B. A., and Barzdin, Y. M. 1973. *Finite Automata: Behavior and Synthesis*. North Holland Publishing Company.

Zhigljavsky, A. A. 1991. *Theory of Global Random Search*. Kluwer academic. volume 65 of Mathematics and Its Applications (Soviet Series).

Ambiguity and Constraint in Mathematical Expression Recognition

Erik G. Miller and **Paul A. Viola**
Massachusetts Institute of Technology
Artificial Intelligence Laboratory
545 Technology Square, Office 707
Cambridge, MA 02139
emiller@ai.mit.edu   viola@ai.mit.edu

Abstract

The problem of recognizing mathematical expressions differs significantly from the recognition of standard prose. While in prose significant constraints can be put on the interpretation of a character by the characters immediately preceding and following it, few such simple constraints are present in a mathematical expression. In order to make the problem tractable, effective methods of recognizing mathematical expressions will need to put intelligent constraints on the possible interpretations. The authors present preliminary results on a system for the recognition of both handwritten and typeset mathematical expressions. While previous systems perform character recognition out of context, the current system maintains ambiguity of the characters until context can be used to disambiguate the interpretation. In addition, the system limits the number of potentially valid interpretations by decomposing the expressions into a sequence of compatible convex regions. The system uses A-star to search for the best possible interpretation of an expression. We provide a new lower bound estimate on the cost to goal that improves performance significantly.

Introduction

Handwriting recognition has greatly improved in recent years, in both the handprinting and cursive domains, yielding commercial systems for a wide variety of applications (for example (Yaeger, Lyon, & Webb 1995)). It may appear that the problem of mathematical expression recognition is essentially equivalent to the recognition of standard prose, but there are critical differences which distinguish the two problems and preclude us from applying the standard solutions of handwriting recognition to mathematical expressions.

Mathematical Expression Recognition

A mathematical expression is a binary image in which collections of black pixels represent symbols which are at different scales and positions:

$$\boxed{5e^x} \; -\text{OR}- \; \boxed{5e^x}$$

Copyright ©1998, American Association for Artificial Intelligence (www.aaai.org). All rights reserved.

Our goal is to take a mathematical expression and return a semantic interpretation:

$$\boxed{\texttt{5 * (e \^{} x)}}$$

This representation can be used for document retrieval or an interactive algebraic manipulation system(Fateman & Tokuyasu 1996; Okamoto & Miyazawa 1992; Lee & Wang 1997; Lee & Lee 1994; Lavirotte & Pottier 1997; Martin 1967).

We adopt a generative model approach for the recognition of mathematical expressions. Several authors (Winkler, Fahrner, & Lang 1995; Hull 1996; Chou 1989) have noted that *stochastic context-free grammars* (SCFG's) represent a good generative model for most types of mathematical expressions[1]. SCFG's enable modeling of many types of relationships such as the pairing of parentheses, braces, and brackets, and the association of an integral sign ($\int$) with its differential such as dx. In order to model the spatial layout of symbols in a mathematical expression, the spatial layout rules for various productions (like exponentiation) must be also specified, as in (Hull 1996). Recognition inverts the generative process and produce the appropriate semantics[2].

Context-free grammars have proven to be very useful in the parsing of programming languages (Hopcroft & Ullman 1979). Recently stochastic context free grammars have also been applied successfully to the parsing of natural languages (Charniak 1993). In a programming language the symbols are perfectly unambiguous and linearly ordered. But in an image of a mathematical expression each symbol is ambiguous and there is no natural ordering. As we will see, both ambiguity and ordering are critical issues which, if not handled effectively, will lead to algorithms which are intractable.

In this paper we present a new approach for limiting the number of possible parses. We also present a new method for dealing with character ambiguity so that characters can be interpreted in context rather than

---

[1]A stochastic context free grammar associates a probability with each production and as a result every valid expression can be assigned a non-zero probability.

[2]Others have used stochastic grammars as models of generic problems in visual recognition (Mjolsness 1990).

in isolation, and so that no probability threshold must be applied in the character recognition process. The search for the most likely interpretation is performed using A-star search (following the work of (Hull 1996)). We propose a new underestimate to the goal that significantly reduces computation time.

Polynomial Time Parsing

The parsing of programming languages is a solved problem. The Cocke-Younger-Kasami (CYK) algorithm (Hopcroft & Ullman 1979), a dynamic programming algorithm, is cubic in the number of characters. The first step of CYK is to build a table (or "chart") with one entry for every sub-sequence of symbols. Each sub-sequence can be indexed by its starting symbol, a number between 1 and N, and its ending symbol, also between 1 and N. There are approximately $\frac{N^2}{2}$ such entries. The algorithm then attempts to find the most likely interpretation for each sub-sequence, an inherently recursive process in which the interpretation of a long sequence is dependent on the interpretation of shorter constituent sub-sequences. The key to computational efficiency is the observation that a particular sub-sequence will be the constituent of many larger sub-sequences, yet the computation need only be done once.

The computational efficiency afforded by the CYK algorithm depends on the existence of a decomposition of the problem into a polynomial number of unique sub-problems. This polynomial nature is a direct result of the linear ordering of text. If such a linear sequence exists we can with impunity limit the set of sub-problems to the set of all consecutive sub-sequences of characters. Mathematical expressions, which are collections of symbols arranged in two dimensions, do not have a straightforward decomposition into a polynomial number of subsets.

Take for example the expression shown in Figure 1. Written out in Matlab syntax, which relies on a linear ordering of symbols, it would be "e ^ x * (A / B)". In the linear form we can conclude that 'x' is part of the exponential because it is separated from the fraction by a parenthesis. In the graphical form 'x' is equally close to the 'A' and the 'e'. There is almost no local information from which we can conclude attachment. In this case we must rely on contextual information, in the form of a graphical SCFG, to make the attachment. Like CYK parsing, in order to find the best possible parse of a mathematical expression we must enumerate all possible subsets of symbols. Since there is no simple linear constraint we must find some other constraints on the number of allowable subsets. Other authors have dealt with this issue in several ways.

Rectilinear mathematical expressions

Chou (Chou 1989) presents a system in which expressions are represented as rectangular arrays of terminal symbols. He limits the number of potential parses dramatically by requiring that the baselines of characters

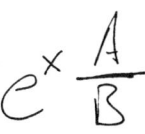

Figure 1: A simple expression which is difficult to decompose into a small number of subsets.

be within one pixel of their expected location. While this works well for the simulated data presented, it cannot be expected to extend to handwritten input, since the variation in handwritten input is frequently more than a pixel.

A recognizer with moderate positional flexibility

Winkler et al. (Winkler, Fahrner, & Lang 1995) describe a more flexible system in which two subexpressions can be considered as part of a larger expression as long as the second expression is within certain predefined regions relative to the first expression. However, this system imposes severe limits on the distance which a symbol can be from another symbol while still being part of a common subexpression. We wish to avoid this type of limit, as we believe it will rule out the true answer in some situations. This system also decides on characters out of context, which has problems that are discussed below.

Modeling positions of characters as Gaussian variables

Hull (Hull 1996) comes closer to our desired goal, by allowing more general positioning of terminals and subexpressions relative to each other. The probability that two subexpressions are in a particular relationship relative to each other (e.g. one is the subscript of the other) is defined by a two dimensional Gaussian distribution around the expected position of the second expression. Hence, the further the second expression is from the center of the Gaussian defining that relationship, the lower the probability of that particular operation.

With this more flexible model of character positions, there are no rigid geometric constraints which can be used to automatically prune away the exponential number of symbol subsets. Instead Hull's algorithm attempts to enumerate all possible subsets, and prunes away those that are very unlikely. Because of the potentially exponential number of subsets, Hull uses A-star search to order the enumeration of subsets. Our implementation also uses an implementation of A-star search, explained below.

A-Star Search A-star search is similar to best-first search, but in addition requires that one produce an underestimate of the "distance" to the goal (a full parse) from a given sub-parse. To apply A-star in a proba-

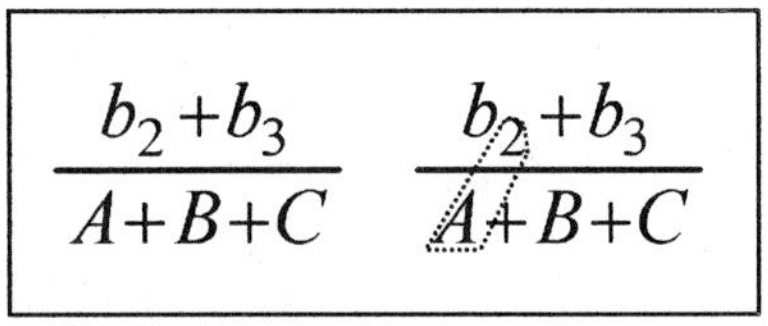

$$\boxed{\dfrac{b_2+b_3}{A+B+C} \qquad \dfrac{b_2+b_3}{A+B+C}}$$

Figure 2: An expression where convex hulls are useful for pruning interpretations. Note that the probability that the enclosed characters are in fact the expression A^2 is reasonable. But this subset is eliminated because their convex hull intersects the fraction symbol.

bilistic setting, one conventionally uses the negative log likelihood as the notion of distance. The probability of an interpretation of an image is the product of the unconditional terminal probabilities multiplied by the probabilities which stem from the geometry rules. The unconditional terminal probabilities are an underestimate of the cost to achieve the final goal – an interpretation of the entire image. This underestimate is added to the negative log likelihood of a sub-parse in order to evaluate whether the sub-parse is a good candidate for expansion.

We compute the A-star estimate by accumulating maximum likelihood estimates of the terminals. Hence, the A-star penalty is computed as:

$$\sum_{c \in \mathcal{C}} \min_{t \in \mathcal{T}} (-\ln Pr(c=t))$$

where $\mathcal{C}$ is the set of uninterpreted connected components (terminals) and $\mathcal{T}$ represents all possible characters in the grammar.

Convex Hulls: A new pruning criterion

As a second method for pruning the search space of parses, we attempt to prune away possible subsets based on a simple geometric test: a subset of characters is *not allowed* if the convex hull of the subset contains a character that is not part of the subset[3]. We define the convex hull of the character to be the smallest convex polygon that contains all of the pixels which define the character (for handwritten text the convex hull is the smallest convex polygon which contains all of the strokes defining the character). The convex hull of a set of characters is the convex hull of the union of the convex hulls of each character in the set (see Figure 2).

There are several justifications for this criterion:

- It is consistent with the layout rules for typeset expressions and is not violated for any of our test data. In fact, we are unaware of a typeset expression for which the constraint is violated.

- For linear text this criteria is identical to the constraint that subsets must contain consecutive symbols. Any non-consecutive subset will have a convex hull that contains a character which is not in the set.

---

[3]This rigid rule could be converted to a soft constraint in our probabilistic framework.

- The algorithms necessary for computing with convex hulls are very efficient. A convex hull of a point set can be computed in $O(n \log n)$, where n is the number of points (Cormen, Leiserson, & Rivest 1991). Computing the convex hull union of two convex hulls is $O(m+l)$, where l and m are the number of vertices in the convex hulls. The intersection of two convex hulls can be found in $O(m+l)$ also.

Unfortunately it is possible to construct an artificial arrangement of two dimensional symbols for which this criterion yields no pruning[4]. But, for many two dimensional mathematical expressions there are roughly N^3 allowable subsets.

Furthermore, some valid expressions violate the convex hull rule described above. This could be at least partially remedied by eroding characters a small amount before the convex hull test is performed. The preliminary convex hull results are encouraging (See Figure 8).

Maintaining ambiguity of character identification

In addition to dealing with all of the possible arrangements of symbols and deducing the operations based on relative positions, we must tackle the problem of disambiguating individual characters. As already suggested, ambiguity makes recognition of the whole expression difficult. We categorize the problems caused by ambiguity into three groups.

The first we call the "q-9" problem, and it is illustrated in Figure 3. There are pairs of characters which are, without context, impossible to distinguish. Accurate recognition requires that multiple character hypotheses be maintained until the ambiguity can be resolved from context. There are many examples of confusable characters, even when the characters are written quite carefully. For sloppily handwritten text the overlap among character classes becomes quite large.

The second type of problem caused by ambiguity we call the "threshold problem". This is illustrated in Figure 4. It shows an example of a situation in which the constraints provided by the grammar could allow us to successfully interpret the '+', even though out of context, it would appear extremely unlikely to be a '+'. Any system which discards hypotheses based on a probability threshold runs the risk of missing a correct recognition in such cases.

The third type of problem arising from ambiguity is "interpretation explosion". When multiple hypotheses are maintained for a single character the number of possible parses grows rapidly. For example, the geometric measures of grammar classes such as "exponentiation expression" depend upon the baseline of the base of the exponent. When we maintain ambiguity in the individual characters we must also maintain ambiguity in these

---

[4]Take a set of very small symbols arranged uniformly on the circumference of a very large circle. The convex hull of every possible subset of symbols is allowable.

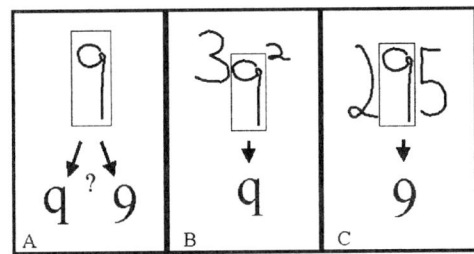

Figure 3: **A.** *The isolated analysis of a character has inherent ambiguities which cannot be resolved without context.* **B.** *Clearly the context here suggests that the character is the letter '9'.* **C.** *The context in this figure suggests the character is the digit '9'.*

dependent higher level classes. This causes the size of the grammar to grow by a factor which is roughly equal to the number of character classes for which we maintain ambiguity. This can make the grammar impractically large. Below, we discuss a compromise between committing to a character *out of context* (to be avoided) and maintaining all possible character hypotheses during the parsing process (too complex).

Returning for a moment to previous work, we note that Hull performs a pre-processing step that recognizes each of the characters in the expression. Because this recognition takes place before parsing, it does not make use of available contextual information. He is thus vulnerable to the "q-9" problem discussed above.

The following simple analysis demonstrates the necessity of maintaining multiple character hypotheses in developing a robust system. Suppose we have a system for which isolated character recognition is correct with probability R. If an expression consists of t characters, we have probability R^t of correctly recognizing all of the characters without contextual information. With $R = 0.95$ and $t = 20$, we obtain a surprisingly low probability, $0.95^{20} \approx 0.36$, of getting every character right. This is an *upper bound* on the probability we will correctly parse the entire expression (it is possible that the parse might fail for other reasons). Obviously, this upper bound will only shrink if we recognize larger expressions or allow a more varied set of characters.

The system described in (Chou 1989) maintains ambiguity, but in a limited sense. For each character it retains only those interpretations which are above a certain likelihood. His character models are Gaussian; he proposes a threshold at three standard deviations from the mean. While this may seem like a conservative threshold, a similar analysis shows that in a 20 character expression, on average one correct character will be eliminated for more than 5 percent of expressions, since $1 - 99.74^{20} \approx 0.0507$. Also, this scheme may lead to keeping around large number of character hypotheses in handwriting recognition, where the characters have large variations.

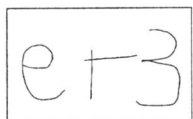

Figure 4: An example of an expression with a very noisy character. The '+' is very difficult to interpret correctly without the context, but with constraints provided by the grammar could potentially be correctly identified.

A Compromise: Maintaining a Hypothesis for Each Character Class Many of the terminals in our grammar are in the same syntactic class. As a result a grammatical analysis can never resolve ambiguity between them. So for example if a character is slightly more likely to be a 'b' than an 'h' there is no syntactic information that can resolve this ambiguity[5]. We can save a lot of effort by simply deciding at the outset that the terminal is a 'b'. On the other hand, as we saw in Figure 4 the ambiguity in the central symbol can be resolved through syntactical analysis. In this case it is important that multiple hypotheses be maintained.

As a middle ground, between maintaining hypotheses for all possible terminal symbols and committing to the single most likely character, we define classes of characters which play the same syntactic role in the grammar. Since the characters in these classes are grammatically equivalent, no constraint from the SCFG can ever be used to disambiguate members of the class. Only the single most likely interpretation for each syntactic class need be maintained.

The concept of syntactic class must be expanded to account for the fact that characters which are traditionally considered syntactically equivalent (like 'p' and 'P') may behave differently with respect to the geometric aspects of the grammar. An example is shown in Figure 5, where the most likely *out of context* interpretation of the leftmost character is *lowercase* 'p'. There is no advantage in maintaining the hypothesis that the character is a 'q'; it has low probability and all of the important spatial properties of the glyph as a 'p' (its baseline, for example) are the same as if it were a 'q'. This is not true for the interpretation as a 'P' however, since the baseline under this interpretation would be higher. And in this case, it turns out that the most likely *context-dependent* interpretation is as a 'P', not as a 'p'.

This leads to *four* terminal classes of *letters* (a single class traditionally) for which we maintain hypotheses throughout the interpretation process. These classes are ascending letters, descending letters, small letters (neither ascending nor descending), and large letters (both ascending and descending). "P", "p", "e", and "Q" represent examples from each respective class. Other authors have used similar classes but not to

---

[5]Other forms of contextual information might be useful for this sort of problem. We are currently exploring this possibility.

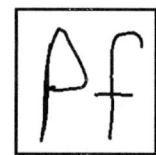

Figure 5: The first character (a "p" or a "P"?) can only be resolved by considering its relationship to the subsequent character.

maintain different classification hypotheses (Winkler, Fahrner, & Lang 1995).

In addition to these separate letter classes which are based strictly on their geometric properties, other classes were defined based on their non-spatial role in the grammar. For example, other syntactic terminal classes include: "zero", non-zero digits, left parentheses, right parentheses, and fractions. Each of these plays a distinctively different role in the grammar of a mathematical expression. In all, a separate hypothesis for each of the 14 different terminal classes is maintained.

A New Approach

Hence, our approach contains three innovations. The first is the geometric convex hull constraint, which limits the growth of the number of possible parses of the expression. The second is a new (but still conservative) A-star completion estimate. The third is the bookkeeping necessary to maintain an hypothesis for each character class, which allows us to interpret individual characters using greater contextual information. We now describe some implementation details of a preliminary system.

Implementation

Certain assumptions were made in order to get a preliminary system working. In the typeset version of the system, it is assumed that all characters are distinct and do not overlap. We make no attempt to deal with scanner distortion. In fact, all of the typeset examples in this paper were generated on-line and are essentially distortion-free.

Overview

The typeset system takes a binary image as input. A simple connected components algorithm is run on the image, generating a list of terminals. A character recognizer based on the Hausdorff distance (Huttenlocher, Klanderman, & Rucklidge 1993) is used to generate probabilities that each connected component or pair of connected components is a particular character. The set of terminals for the initial system is, according to class:

- ascender letters: $b, d, h, i, k, l, t, \delta, A\text{-}Z$ (except Q),
- descender letters: g, p, q, y, γ,
- small letters: $a, c, e, m, n, o, r, s, u, v, w, x, z, \alpha$,
- ascender/descenders: f, j, Q, β,
- binary operators: $+, -, =$,
- zero: 0,
- non-zero digits: 1-9,
- other symbols (each its own class): $(,), [,], \{, \}$, fraction symbol.

While the grammar is much too large to include here (80 classes, 200 productions), it is worth mentioning the following:

- It is represented in Chomsky Normal Form. This facilitates the coding of the grammar.
- It contains productions supporting exponentiation, subscripting, fractions, "loose" concatenation (multiplication), and "tight" concatenation (the appending of digits in a number).
- The *a priori* probability of each operation is the same. Probabilities of operations are assigned only according to the geometry of the layout and the probability of their sub-parses.

After the program has calculated the probability of each character being in each class, the program starts the dynamic programming process which is closely related to the CYK algorithm mentioned before. The first step in this process is to build the previously mentioned "table" in which there is one entry for every subsequence of characters. This can be done in order from the shorter sequences to the longer sequences, by first computing the probability of each sequence of length 1, then from these computing the probability of each sequence of length 2, and so on.

In our implementation, we limit the size of the parse table using a very conservative restriction on the distance between sub-sequences as an initial filter and the convex hull criterion described previously as a second filter. When we finish building the table, the entry which has the full number of characters and the highest probability represents the best legal parse of the given mathematical expression.

Building the Table

Figure 6 shows how the parse table is generated for a sample mathematical expression show in Figure 7. The table contains one column for each subset of terminals, and one row for each possible interpretation for that subset. The input to the parsing algorithm is a set of connected components. Associated with each component is a probability vector, containing the conditional probability for each possible terminal symbol. As a first step only the most likely terminal from each syntactic class is retained. For example, the most likely interpretation for the leftmost component is as an 'a'. Nevertheless several other hypotheses are maintained: as an ascender it is most likely to be an 'O'; as a descender it is most likely to be a 'q'; as an ascender/descender

	Trmnl 1	Trmnl 2	Trmnl 3	Trmnls 1,2	Trmnls 2,3	Trmnls 1-3
Global properties of the connected component set	Min x, max x, min y, max y, centroid	Min x, max x, min y, max y, centroid	Min x, max x, min y, max y, centroid	Min x, max x, min y, max y, centroid	Min x, max x, min y, max y, centroid	Min x, max x, min y, max y, centroid
As a small letter	Prob: 0.1 Baseline: 47 Pt-size: 12	Prob: 0.05 Baseline: 55 Pt-size: 13	Prob: 0.05 Baseline: 52 Pt-size: 10	Prob: 0.0 Baseline: 0.0 Pt-size: 0.0	Prob: 0.0 Baseline: 0.0 Pt-size: 0.0	Prob: 0.0 Baseline: 0.0 Pt-size: 0.0
As a large letter	Prob: 0.01 Baseline: 45 Pt-size: 8	Prob: 0.02 Baseline: 53 Pt-size: 9	Prob: 0.01 Baseline: 50 Pt-size: 9	Prob: 0.0 Baseline: 0.0 Pt-size: 0.0	Prob: 0.0 Baseline: 0.0 Pt-size: 0.0	Prob: 0.0 Baseline: 0.0 Pt-size: 0.0
As a digit	Prob: 0.03 Baseline: 47 Pt-size: 9	Prob: 0.02 Baseline: 55 Pt-size: 11	Prob: 0.01 Baseline: 52 Pt-size: 11	Prob: 0.0 Baseline: 0.0 Pt-size: 0.0	Prob: 0.0 Baseline: 0.0 Pt-size: 0.0	Prob: 0.0 Baseline: 0.0 Pt-size: 0.0
As an exponentiation	Prob: 0.0 Baseline: 0.0 Pt-size: 0.0	Prob: 0.0 Baseline: 0.0 Pt-size: 0.0	Prob: 0.0 Baseline: 0.0 Pt-size: 0.0	Prob: 0.001 Baseline: 47 Pt-size: 12	Prob: 0.00007 Baseline: 55 Pt-size: 13	Prob: 0.0003 Baseline: 47 Pt-size: 12
As subscript	Prob: 0.0 Baseline: 0.0 Pt-size: 0.0	Prob: 0.0 Baseline: 0.0 Pt-size: 0.0	Prob: 0.0 Baseline: 0.0 Pt-size: 0.0	Prob: 0.00005 Baseline: 47 Pt-size: 12	Prob: 0.002 Baseline: 55 Pt-size: 13	Prob: 0.00000043 Baseline: 47 Pt-size: 12

Figure 6: Part of a parse table used to do dynamic programming.

it is most likely to be a 'Q'[6], and so on. In addition to computing these probabilities, we compute certain interpretation-dependent quantities of the characters such as the baseline and the point size. They are interpretation-dependent since they are different for different rows of the table. Finally, we also compute global properties of the current connected component group. These properties include the minimum and maximum coordinates, the centroid, the convex hull, and so forth. These global properties only need to be computed once per connected component group, since they are invariant to the interpretation of the group.

In addition to the terminal classes there are rows in the table for compound expressions made up of multiple terminals (e.g. exponentiation, fractions, binary operations, etc.) There is zero probability that these expressions can generate an output with a single component.

The initial state of the system is shown in the first three columns of the table. There is one entry for each distinct component in the image. Parsing is a process by which new columns are added to the table, each describing a valid subset of components from the original image. The table is expanded toward the right, as large collections of components are enumerated and evaluated.

There are three possible two-character combinations

---

[6]This is a very unlikely hypothesis, but it is the best in that class.

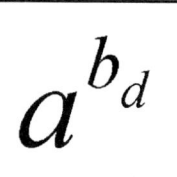

Figure 7: The sample mathematical expression used in the description of table building. Notice that no entry was made in the table for the two-character combination of characters "a" and "d". This is because the a-d pair do not fit the convex hull criterion.

of the three characters. However, if the two characters fail the convex hull test described above, as with the "a" and the "d" in our example, then an entry in the table will not be made. Since the two component groups cannot be interpreted as a single terminal, these rows are flagged as impossible. As new columns are added to the table, the interpretation-dependent and global properties of the group are computed.

The final column in the table shows probabilities of interpretations of the entire expression. Column 6 shows that the correct interpretation (as an exponentiation at the highest level) has the highest probability, so in this case the procedure worked properly.

Experiments

To verify the basic functionality of the system, we performed a simple series of tests. For each letter x in the system, the following expressions were used as inputs to the system: x_x, x^x, x^{x_x}, $\frac{x}{x}$. Where allowed by the grammar, the digits were also used in these tests. All of these test images were evaluated correctly by the system.

We attempted to evaluate the effectiveness both of the the convex hull pruning constraint and A-star search using our underestimate of the distance to goal. Without using either type of heuristic, parse times were very long – on the order of minutes. Using both criteria parse times are in the seconds. In order to quantify this we created a series of expressions of varying complexity from 3 terminals to 20 terminals. On the left of Figure 8 is the performance of the A-star system with and without the convex hull constraint. On the right is the performance using the convex hull constraint with and without the A-star heuristic[7]. There is significant improvement in performance using either of these heuristics, and even greater improvement when both are used. We collected data from the system running without either heuristic, but this curve quickly exists the top of the graph.

It is interesting to note how the system performed on "illegal" images, for example the expression 0^{0_0}. This input is considered illegal since our grammar provided no mechanism for subscripting a number. As a result the system recognized the input as the expression "600". This can be understood as follows: since the system could not generate 0_0, it apparently concluded that the last two zeroes were effectively the same size. However, the output 0^{00} would also be illegal since a two digit number cannot begin with a 0. The system's fix was to consider all three digits as being approximately the same size, and then using a much less likely, but legal interpretation of the first digit, it settled on "600" as the best interpretation. This example illustrates a good deal about the system's flexibility in generating reasonable answers in tough situations.

Anecdotal examples of expressions which the system successfully parsed are given in Figure 9. The actual time spent parsing these expressions on a 266MHz Pentium Pro was approximately 4, 0.2, 16, and 25 seconds. This does not include the time to generate character hypotheses for the connected components. These examples are not difficult, but they validate the basic method and show that it is feasible to do the extra bookkeeping which we have incorporated in this system. The only failures in the current typeset system were due to mis-recognition of characters.

---

[7] The points on the two graphs are the same set of expressions, the graph on the left contains fewer points because the computation time for A-star without convex hull pruning grows far too rapidly for us to measure. We simply gave up after many minutes of run time.

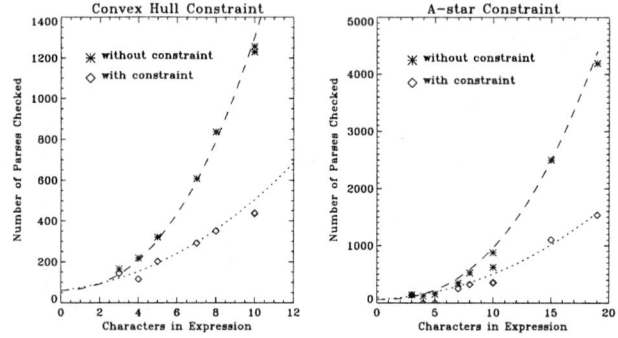

Figure 8: The left graph shows the pruning of the search space by the convex hull criterion. The right graph shows the performance gained by adding the A-star constraint. The algorithm reduces to best-first search without the A-star constraint.

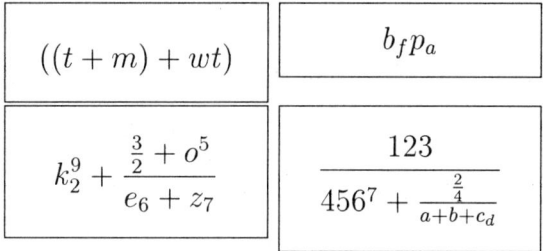

Figure 9: Some of the expressions successfully recognized by the system.

Future Work

A major focus in developing this system was to prepare for the migration to handwritten mathematical expressions. Our preliminary work with handwritten expressions is illustrated in Figure 10. We show three examples, the first of which was parsed correctly, the second of which contains a geometry-based error, and the third of which contains a character-identification error. We hope that by improving the character recognizer and learning the parameters of our geometry models that we can significantly improve the performance of the system in the future. While the accuracy of the current system needs great improvement, we feel we have laid the groundwork for a practical system's implementation.

Acknowledgments

We would like to thank Tom Rikert and Nicholas Matsakis for contributions and discussions related to this work.

References

Charniak, E. 1993. *Statistical Language Learning*. Cambridge, MA: MIT Press.

Chou, P. A. 1989. Recognition of equations using a two-dimensional stochastic context-free grammar. In

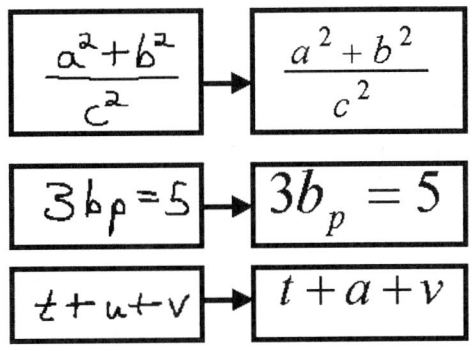

Figure 10: Some examples of handwriting and their parses.

SPIE Vol. 1199 Visual Communications and Image Processing, SPIE, 852–863. Murray Hill, NJ: SPIE.

Cormen, T. H.; Leiserson, C. E.; and Rivest, R. L. 1991. *Introduction to Algorithms*. Cambridge, Mass.: MIT Press.

Fateman, R. J., and Tokuyasu, T. 1996. Progress in recognizing typeset mathematics. In *Document Recognition III, SPIE Volume 2660*, 37–50. Murray Hill, NJ: SPIE.

Hopcroft, J. E., and Ullman, J. D. 1979. *Introduction to Automata Theory, Languages, and Computation*. Reading, Mass.: Addison-Wesley.

Hull, J. F. 1996. Recognition of mathematics using a two-dimensional trainable context-free grammar. Master's thesis, Massachusetts Institute of Technology, Department of Electrical Engineering and Computer Science.

Huttenlocher, D. P.; Klanderman, G. A.; and Rucklidge, W. J. 1993. Comparing images using the hausdorff distance. *IEEE Transactions on Pattern Analysis and Machine Intelligence* 15(9):850–863.

Lavirotte, S., and Pottier, L. 1997. Optical formula recognition. In *Fourth International Conference on Document Analysis and Recognition*, ICDAR, 357–361. Ulm, Germany: IEEE.

Lee, H.-J., and Lee, M.-C. 1994. Understanding mathematical expressions using procedure-oriented transformation. *Pattern Recognition* 27(3):447–457.

Lee, H.-J., and Wang, J.-S. 1997. Design of a mathematical expression understanding system. *Pattern Recognition Letters* 18:289–298.

Martin, W. A. 1967. A fast parsing scheme for hand-printed mathematical expressions. MIT AI Project Memo 145, Massachusetts Institute of Technology, Computer Science Department, MIT, Cambridge, MA.

Mjolsness, E. 1990. Bayesian inference on visual grammars by neural nets that optimize. Technical Report 854, Yale University, Department of Computer Science, Computer Science Department, Yale University, New Haven, CT.

Okamoto, M., and Miyazawa, A. 1992. An experimental implementation of a document recognition system for papers containing mathematical expressions. In Baird, H. S.; Bunke, H.; and Yamamoto, K., eds., *Structured Document Image Analysis*. Berlin: Springer-Verlag. 36–63.

Winkler, H. J.; Fahrner, H.; and Lang, M. 1995. A soft-decision approach for structural analysis of handwritten mathematical expressions. In *International Conference on Acoustics, Speech, and Signal Processing*.

Yaeger, L.; Lyon, R.; and Webb, B. 1995. Effective training of a neural network character classifier for word recognition. In Mozer, M.; Jordan, M.; and Petsche, T., eds., *Advances in Neural Information Processing*, volume 9. Denver 1996: MIT Press, Cambridge.

Learning to Classify Text from Labeled and Unlabeled Documents

Kamal Nigam[†]
knigam@cs.cmu.edu

Andrew McCallum[‡†]
mccallum@cs.cmu.edu

Sebastian Thrun[†]
thrun@cs.cmu.edu

Tom Mitchell[†]
mitchell+@cs.cmu.edu

[†]School of Computer Science
Carnegie Mellon University
Pittsburgh, PA 15213

[‡]Just Research
4616 Henry Street
Pittsburgh, PA 15213

Abstract

In many important text classification problems, acquiring class labels for training documents is costly, while gathering large quantities of unlabeled data is cheap. This paper shows that the accuracy of text classifiers trained with a small number of labeled documents can be improved by augmenting this small training set with a large pool of unlabeled documents. We present a theoretical argument showing that, under common assumptions, unlabeled data contain information about the target function. We then introduce an algorithm for learning from labeled and unlabeled text based on the combination of Expectation-Maximization with a naive Bayes classifier. The algorithm first trains a classifier using the available labeled documents, and probabilistically labels the unlabeled documents; it then trains a new classifier using the labels for all the documents, and iterates to convergence. Experimental results, obtained using text from three different real-world tasks, show that the use of unlabeled data reduces classification error by up to 33%.

Introduction

Consider the problem of training a computer to automatically classify text documents. Given the growing volume of online text available through the World Wide Web, Internet news feeds, electronic mail, and digital libraries, this problem is of great practical significance. There are statistical text learning algorithms that can be trained to approximately classify documents, given a sufficient set of labeled training examples. These text classification algorithms have been used to automatically catalog news articles (Lewis & Ringuette 1994; Joachims 1998) and web pages (Craven *et al.* 1998), automatically learn the reading interests of users (Pazzani, Muramatsu, & Billsus 1996; Lang 1995), and automatically sort electronic mail (Lewis & Knowles 1997).

One key difficulty with these current algorithms, and the issue addressed by this paper, is that they require a large, often prohibitive, number of labeled training examples to learn accurately. Take, for example, the task of learning which newsgroup postings are of interest to a person reading UseNet news, as examined by Lang (1995). After reading and classifying about 1000

Copyright 1998, American Association for Artificial Intelligence (www.aaai.org). All rights reserved.

postings, precision of the learned classifier was about 50% for the top 10% of documents ranked by the classifier. As a practical user of such a filtering system, one would obviously prefer learning algorithms that can provide accurate classifications after hand-labeling only a dozen postings, rather than a thousand.

In this paper we describe an algorithm that learns to classify text documents more accurately by using *unlabeled* documents to augment the available *labeled* training examples. In our example, the labeled documents might be just 10 postings that have been read and judged by the user as interesting or not. Our learning algorithm can make use of the vast multitude of unlabeled postings available on UseNet to augment these 10 labeled examples. In many text domains, especially those involving online sources, collecting unlabeled examples is trivial; it is the labeling that is difficult.

We present experimental results showing that this unlabeled data can boost learning accuracy in three text classification domains: newsgroup postings, web pages, and newswire articles. For example, to identify the source newsgroup for a UseNet posting with 70% classification accuracy, our algorithm takes advantage of 10,000 unlabeled examples and requires only 300 labeled examples; on the other hand, a traditional learner requires 1000 labeled examples to achieve the same accuracy. So, in this case, the technique reduces the need for labeled training examples by a factor of three.

Why do unlabeled examples boost learning accuracy? In brief, they provide information about the joint probability distribution over words within the documents. Suppose, for example, that using only the labeled data we determine that documents containing the word "lecture" tend to belong to the class of academic **course** web pages. If we use this fact to estimate the classification of the many unlabeled documents, we might find that the word "homework" occurs frequently in the unlabeled examples that are now believed to belong to the **course** class. Thus the co-occurrence of the words "lecture" and "homework" over the large set of unlabeled training data can provide useful information to construct a more accurate classifier that considers both "lecture" and "homework" as indicators of **course** web pages.

The specific approach we describe here is based on a combination of two well-known learning algorithms: the naive Bayes classifier (Lewis & Ringuette

1994; McCallum & Nigam 1998) and the Expectation-Maximization (EM) algorithm (Dempster, Laird, & Rubin 1977). The naive Bayes algorithm is one of a class of statistical text classifiers that uses word frequencies as features. Other examples include TFIDF/Rocchio (Salton 1991), Support Vector Machines (Joachims 1998), k-nearest-neighbor (Yang & Pederson 1997), exponentiated-gradient and regression models (Lewis *et al.* 1996). EM is a class of iterative algorithms for maximum likelihood estimation in problems with incomplete data. The result of combining these two is an algorithm that extends conventional text learning algorithms by using EM to dynamically derive pseudo-labels for unlabeled documents during learning, thereby providing a way to incorporate unlabeled data into supervised learning. Previous supervised algorithms for learning to classify from text do not incorporate unlabeled data.

A similar approach was used by Miller and Uyar (1997) for non-text data sources. We adapt this approach for the naive Bayes text classifier and conduct a thorough empirical analysis. Furthermore, we show theoretically that, under certain conditions, unlabeled data carry information useful for improving parameter estimation and classification accuracy. We also introduce a method for balancing the contributions of the labeled and unlabeled data that avoids degradation in classification accuracy when these conditions are violated. A more detailed version of this paper is available (Nigam *et al.* 1998).

The Probabilistic Framework

To ground the theoretical aspects of our work, and to provide a setting for our algorithm, this section presents a probabilistic framework for characterizing the nature of documents and classifiers. The framework follows commonly used assumptions (Lewis & Ringuette 1994; Domingos & Pazzani 1997) about the data: (1) that our data is produced by a mixture model, and (2) that there is a one-to-one correspondence between generative mixture components and classes.

In this setting, every document d_i is generated according to a probability distribution given by a mixture model, which is parameterized by θ. The mixture model consists of generative components $c_j \in \mathcal{C} = \{c_1, ..., c_{|\mathcal{C}|}\}$, each component being parameterized by a disjoint subset of θ. Thus a document is created by (1) selecting a component according to the prior probabilities, $P(c_j|\theta)$, then (2) having that component generate a document according to its own parameters, with distribution $P(d_i|c_j;\theta)$. We can characterize the likelihood of a document with a sum of total probability over all generative components:

$$P(d_i|\theta) = \sum_{j=1}^{|\mathcal{C}|} P(c_j|\theta) P(d_i|c_j;\theta). \quad (1)$$

Each document has a class label. We assume that there is a one-to-one correspondence between classes and mixture model components, and thus use c_j to indicate both the jth mixture component and the jth class. The class label of document d_i is written y_i, and if document d_i was generated by component c_j we say $c_j = c_{y_i}$. This class label may or may not be known for a given document.

Proof of the Value of Unlabeled Data

In this section we show that, given this setting, documents with unknown class labels are useful for learning concept classes. 'Learning concept classes' in this setting is equivalent to estimating parameters of an unknown mixture model that produced the given training documents. For unlabeled data to carry information about the parameters θ, it is sufficient that the learning task is not *degenerate*, that is,

$$\exists d_i, c_j, \theta', \theta''. \quad P(d_i|c_j;\theta') \neq P(d_i|c_j;\theta'') \\ \wedge \quad P(c_j|\theta') \neq P(c_j|\theta''). \quad (2)$$

This assumption excludes tasks where learning is impossible, for the reason that all parameterizations θ' yield equivalent results. High-dimensional mixture models meet this condition.

To show that knowledge about unlabeled documents carries information about the parameters θ, we need to demonstrate the conditional dependence of θ on D, a random variable over the unlabeled document distribution. That is, show $P(\theta|D) \neq P(\theta)$. If this conjecture holds, a direct implication is that unlabeled data contain information about the parameters of θ. We provide a proof by contradiction. For this, we temporarily assume that θ and D are independent, that is, $\forall \theta'. P(\theta'|D) = P(\theta')$. One direct conclusion of this assumption is that any two parameterizations, θ' and θ'', provide the same class probabilities for any sample. By applying Bayes' rule to our assumption, and substituting using Equation 1 this gives:

$$\sum_{j=1}^{|\mathcal{C}|} P(d_i|c_j;\theta') P(c_j|\theta') = \sum_{j=1}^{|\mathcal{C}|} P(d_i|c_j;\theta'') P(c_j|\theta''). \quad (3)$$

From here, it is a straightforward exercise to construct a document d_i and two parameterizations to generate a contradiction, making use of the non-degeneracy assumption above. Our assumption of non-degeneracy requires that for some document the individual terms in Equation 3 must differ for some θ' and θ''; we can construct one for which the total probability of the document also differs for θ' and θ''. Thus, our assumption of conditional independence is contradicted, and parameterizations must be conditionally dependent on the documents. This signifies that unlabeled data indeed contain information about parameters of the generative model.

However, this does not show that unlabeled data aids the reduction of classification error. For example, unlabeled data does not help if there is already an infinite amount of labeled data; all parameters can be recovered from just the labeled data and the resulting classifier is Bayes-optimal (McLachlan & Basford 1988). With an infinite amount of unlabeled data and no labeled data, the parameters can be estimated except classes cannot be matched with components, so classification error remains unimproved. But, with infinite unlabeled data and finite labeled data, there is classification improvement. With infinite unlabeled data, the classification error approaches the Bayes optimal solution at an exponential rate in the number of labeled examples given (Castelli & Cover 1995). Thus, infinite amounts of unlabeled data are shown to help classification when there is some, but not infinite, amounts of labeled data. Unfortunately, little is known for the case in which there are finite amounts of each.

Naive Bayes for Text Classification

In this section, we present the naive Bayes classifier—a well-known, probabilistic algorithm for classifying text that is one instantiation of a mixture model. This algorithm forms the foundation upon which we will later incorporate unlabeled data. The learning task for the naive Bayes classifier is to use a set of training documents to estimate the mixture model parameters, then use the estimated model to classify new documents.

Document d_i is considered to be an ordered list of word events. We write $w_{d_{ik}}$ for the word in position k of document d_i, where the subscript of w indicates an index into the vocabulary $V = \langle w_1, w_2, \ldots, w_{|V|} \rangle$. In order to generate a document, after a mixture component is selected, a document length is chosen independently of the component and the words in the document. Then, the selected mixture component generates a sequence words of the specified length. Thus, we can expand the second term from Equation 1, and correctly express the probability of a document given its class using the general multiplication rule over the sequence of individual word events:

$$P(d_i|c_j;\theta) = P(|d_i|) \prod_{k=1}^{|d_i|} P(w_{d_{ik}}|c_j;\theta;w_{d_{iq}},\forall q < k).$$
(4)

Next we make the standard naive Bayes assumption: that the words of a document are generated independently of context, that is, independently of the other words in the same document given the class. We further assume that the probability of a word is independent of its position within the document. Thus, we can rewrite Equation 4 more simply as:

$$P(d_i|c_j;\theta) = P(|d_i|) \prod_{k=1}^{|d_i|} P(w_{d_{ik}}|c_j;\theta).$$
(5)

The parameters of an individual mixture component are the collection of word probabilities, such that $\theta_{w_t|c_j} = P(w_t|c_j;\theta)$, where $t = \{1,\ldots,|V|\}$ and $\sum_t P(w_t|c_j;\theta) = 1$. The other parameters of the model are the class prior probabilities $\theta_{c_j} = P(c_j|\theta)$, which indicate the probabilities of selecting the different mixture components. Document length is not parameterized because we assume it is independent of classification.

Given these underlying assumptions of how the data is produced, the task of learning a text classifier consists of forming an estimate of θ, written $\hat{\theta}$, based on a set of training data. With labeled training documents, $\mathcal{D} = \{d_1,\ldots,d_{|\mathcal{D}|}\}$, we can calculate Bayes-optimal estimates for the parameters of the model that generated these documents (Vapnik 1982). To calculate the probability of a word given a class, $\theta_{w_t|c_j}$, simply count the fraction of times the word occurs in the data for that class, augmented with a Laplacean prior. This smoothing prevents zero probabilities for infrequently occurring words. These word probability estimates $\hat{\theta}_{w_t|c_j}$ are:

$$\hat{\theta}_{w_t|c_j} = \frac{1 + \sum_{i=1}^{|\mathcal{D}|} N(w_t, d_i) P(c_j|d_i)}{|V| + \sum_{s=1}^{|V|} \sum_{i=1}^{|\mathcal{D}|} N(w_s, d_i) P(c_j|d_i)},$$
(6)

where $N(w_t, d_i)$ is the count of the number of times word w_t occurs in document d_i and where $P(c_j|d_i) = \{0,1\}$, given by the class label. The class prior probabilities, $\hat{\theta}_{c_j}$, are estimated in the same fashion of counting, but without smoothing:

$$\hat{\theta}_{c_j} = \frac{\sum_{i=1}^{|\mathcal{D}|} P(c_j|d_i)}{|\mathcal{D}|}.$$
(7)

Given estimates of these parameters calculated from the training documents, it is possible to turn the generative model around and calculate the probability that a particular component generated a given document. We formulate this by an application of Bayes' rule, and then substitutions using Equations 1 and 5:

$$\begin{aligned}P(c_j|d_i;\hat{\theta}) &= \frac{P(c_j|\hat{\theta})P(d_i|c_j;\hat{\theta})}{P(d_i|\hat{\theta})} \\ &= \frac{P(c_j|\hat{\theta}) \prod_{k=1}^{|d_i|} P(w_{d_{ik}}|c_j;\hat{\theta})}{\sum_{r=1}^{|\mathcal{C}|} P(c_r|\hat{\theta}) \prod_{k=1}^{|d_i|} P(w_{d_{ik}}|c_r;\hat{\theta})}.\end{aligned}$$
(8)

If the task is to classify a test document d_i into a single class, simply select the class with the highest posterior probability, $\arg\max_j P(c_j|d_i;\hat{\theta})$.

Note that our assumptions about the generation of text documents are all violated in practice, and yet empirically, naive Bayes does a good job of classifying text documents (Lewis & Ringuette 1994; Craven et al. 1998; Yang & Pederson 1997; Joachims 1997). This paradox is explained by the fact that classification estimation is only a function of the sign (in binary cases) of the function estimation (Domingos & Pazzani 1997; Friedman 1997). Also note that our formulation of naive Bayes assumes a multinomial event model for documents; this generally produces better text classification accuracy than another formulation that assumes a multi-variate Bernoulli (McCallum & Nigam 1998).

Incorporating Unlabeled Data with EM

When naive Bayes is given just a small set of labeled training data, classification accuracy will suffer because variance in the parameter estimates of the generative model will be high. However, by augmenting this small set with a large set of unlabeled data and combining the two sets with EM, we can improve our parameter estimates. As described in Table 1, EM alternately generates probabilistically-weighted labels for the unlabeled documents, and a more probable model with smaller parameter variance. EM finds a local maximum likelihood parameterization using more data—both the labeled and the unlabeled. This section describes how to use EM within the probabilistic framework of the previous section. This is a special case of the more general missing values formulation, as presented by Ghahramani and Jordan (1994).

We are given a set of training documents $\mathcal{D}$ and the task is to build a classifier of the form in the previous section. However, unlike previously, in this section we assume that only some of the documents $d_i \in \mathcal{D}^l$ come with class labels $y_i \in \{1, \ldots, |\mathcal{C}|\}$, and for the rest of the documents, in subset $\mathcal{D}^u$, the class labels are unknown. Thus there is a disjoint partitioning of $\mathcal{D}$, such that $\mathcal{D} = \mathcal{D}^l \cup \mathcal{D}^u$.

Consider the probability of *all* the training data, $\mathcal{D}$. The probability of all the data is simply the product over all the documents, because each document is independent of the others given the model. Using Equation 1, this is:

$$P(\mathcal{D}|\theta) = \prod_{d_i \in \mathcal{D}^u} \sum_{j=1}^{|\mathcal{C}|} P(c_j|\theta) P(d_i|c_j;\theta)$$
$$\times \prod_{d_i \in \mathcal{D}^l} P(c_{y_i}|\theta) P(d_i|c_{y_i};\theta). \quad (9)$$

For the unlabeled documents, we use a direct application of Equation 1. For the labeled documents, we are given the generative component by the label y_i and thus do not need to sum over all class components.

Again, learning a classifier in our context corresponds to calculating a maximum likelihood estimate of θ—finding the parameterization that is most likely given our training data: $\arg\max P(\theta|\mathcal{D})$. By Bayes' rule, $P(\theta|\mathcal{D}) = P(\mathcal{D}|\theta)P(\theta)/P(\mathcal{D})$. $P(\mathcal{D})$ is a constant; maximum likelihood estimation assumes that $P(\theta)$ is a constant, so taking the log, we define the constant $\eta = \log(P(\theta)/P(\mathcal{D}))$. Maximizing the log likelihood is the same as maximizing the likelihood. Using Equation 9 and Bayes rule, we write the log likelihood, $l(\theta|\mathcal{D}) \equiv \log(P(\theta|\mathcal{D}))$, as:

- Build an initial classifier by calculating $\hat{\theta}$ from the labeled documents only (Equations 6 and 7).
- Loop while classifier parameters change:
  - Use the current classifier to calculate probabilistically-weighted labels for the unlabeled documents (Equation 8).
  - Recalculate the classifier parameters $\hat{\theta}$ given the probabilistically assigned labels (Equations 6 and 7).

Table 1: The Algorithm.

$$l(\theta|\mathcal{D}) = \eta + \sum_{d_i \in \mathcal{D}^u} \log \sum_{j=1}^{|\mathcal{C}|} P(c_j|\theta) P(d_i|c_j;\theta)$$
$$+ \sum_{d_i \in \mathcal{D}^l} \log \left(P(c_{y_i}|\theta) P(d_i|c_{y_i};\theta) \right). \quad (10)$$

Because the first line of this equation has a log of sums, it is not computable in closed-form. However, if we knew all the class labels, as in $\mathcal{D}^l$, then we could avoid this log of sums. Representing this potential knowledge about the class labels as the matrix of binary indicator variables $\mathbf{z}$, $\mathbf{z}_i = \langle z_{i1}, \ldots, z_{i|\mathcal{C}|} \rangle$, where $z_{ij} = 1$ iff $y_i = j$ else $z_{ij} = 0$, we can express the complete log likelihood of the parameters, $l_c(\theta|\mathcal{D}, \mathbf{z})$:

$$l_c(\theta|\mathcal{D}, \mathbf{z}) = \eta + \sum_{i=1}^{|\mathcal{D}|} \sum_{j=1}^{|\mathcal{C}|} z_{ij} \log \left(P(c_j|\theta) P(d_i|c_j;\theta_j) \right).$$
$$(11)$$

This formulation of the log likelihood would be readily computable in closed-form. Dempster, Laird and Rubin (1977) use this insight in the formulation of the Expectation-Maximization algorithm, which finds a *local* maximum likelihood $\hat{\theta}$ by an iterative procedure that recomputes the expected value of $\mathbf{z}$ and the maximum likelihood parameterization given $\mathbf{z}$. Note that for the labeled documents $\mathbf{z}_i$ is already known. It must be estimated for the unlabeled documents. If we denote the expected value of $\mathbf{z}$ at iteration k, by $Q^{(k)}$, we can find a local maximum for $l(\theta|\mathcal{D})$ by iterating the following two steps:

- E-step: Set $Q^{(k)} = E[\mathbf{z}|\mathcal{D}; \hat{\theta}^{(k)}]$.
- M-step: Set $\hat{\theta}^{(k+1)} = \arg\max_\theta P(\theta|\mathcal{D}; Q^{(k)})$.

In practice, the E-step corresponds to calculating probabilistic labels $P(c_j|d_i; \hat{\theta})$ for every document by using the current estimate $\hat{\theta}$ and Equation 8. The M-step corresponds to calculating a new maximum likelihood estimate for θ given the current estimates for document labels, $P(c_j|d_i; \hat{\theta})$ using Equations 6 and 7. See Table 1 for an outline of our algorithm. In summary, EM finds the $\hat{\theta}$ that locally maximizes the probability of all the data, both the labeled and the unlabeled.

Experimental Results

In this section, we give empirical evidence that using the algorithm in Table 1 outperforms traditional naive Bayes. We present experimental results with three different text corpora.[1]

Datasets and Protocol

The 20 Newsgroups data set (Joachims 1997), collected by Ken Lang, consists of 20,017 articles divided almost evenly among 20 different UseNet discussion groups. We remove words from a stoplist of common short words and words that occur only once. When tokenizing this data, we skip the UseNet headers (thereby discarding the subject line); tokens are formed from contiguous alphabetic characters, which are left unstemmed. Best performance was obtained with no feature selection, and by normalizing word counts by document length. Accuracy results are reported as averages of ten test/train splits, with 20% of the documents randomly selected for placement in the test set.

The WebKB data set (Craven et al. 1998) contains web pages gathered from university computer science departments. In this paper, we use the four most populous entity-representing categories: student, faculty, course and project, all together containing 4199 pages. We did not use stemming or a stoplist; we found that using a stoplist actually hurt performance because, for example, "my" is the fourth-ranked word by information gain, and is an excellent indicator of a student homepage. As done previously (Craven et al. 1998), we use only the 2000 most informative words, as measured by average mutual information with the class variable (Yang & Pederson 1997; Joachims 1997). Accuracy results presented below are an average of twenty test/train splits, again randomly holding out 20% of the documents for testing.

The 'ModApte' test/train split of the Reuters 21578 Distribution 1.0 data set consists of 12902 articles and 135 topic categories from the Reuters newswire. Following other studies (Joachims 1998) we present results on the 10 most populous classes, building binary classifiers for each class that include all 134 other classes in the negative category. We use a stoplist, but do not stem. Vocabulary selection, when used, is again performed with average mutual information with the class variable. Results are reported as averages of ten randomly selected subsets of ModApte's training set. The complete ModApte test set is used to calculate precision-recall breakeven points, a standard information retrieval measure for binary classification.

All experiments were performed with eight EM iterations; significant changes occur in the first few iterations. We never found classification accuracy to improve beyond the eighth iteration.

[1] All three of these data sets are available on the Internet. See http://www.cs.cmu.edu/~textlearning and http://www.research.att.com/~lewis.

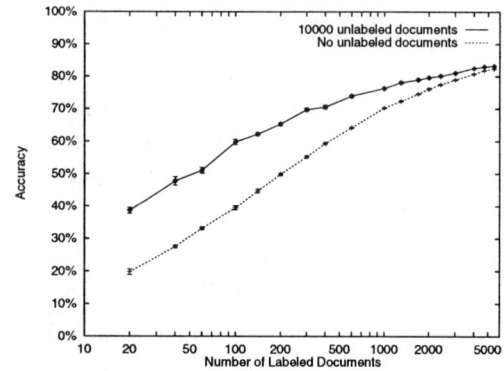

Figure 1: Classification accuracy on the 20 Newsgroups data set. The narrow error bars on each data point are twice the standard error.

Results

Figure 1 shows the effect of using EM with unlabeled data in the 20 Newsgroups data set. We vary the amount of labeled training data, and compare the classification accuracy of traditional naive Bayes (no unlabeled data) with an EM learner that has access to 10000 unlabeled documents. EM performs significantly better. For example, with 300 labeled documents (15 documents per class), naive Bayes reaches 55% accuracy, while EM achieves 70%—providing a 33% reduction in error. Note here that EM performs well even with a very small number of labeled documents; with only 20 documents (a single labeled document per class), naive Bayes gets 19%, EM 39%. As expected, when there is a lot of labeled data, and the naive Bayes learning curve has flattened, having unlabeled data does not help.

These results demonstrate that EM finds a model with more probable parameter estimates, and that these improved estimates reduce classification accuracy and the need for labeled training examples. For example, to get 70% classification accuracy, EM requires 300 labeled examples, while naive Bayes requires 1000 labeled examples to achieve the same accuracy.

To gain some intuition about why EM works, we present a detailed trace of one example. Table 2 provides a window into the evolution of the classifier over the course of EM iterations for this example. Based on the WebKB data set, each column shows the ordered list of words that the model believes are most "predictive" of the course class. Words are judged to be "predictive" using a weighted log likelihood ratio. At Iteration 0, the parameters were estimated from a randomly-chosen single labeled document per class. Notice that the course document seems to be about a specific Artificial Intelligence course at Dartmouth. After two EM iterations with 2500 unlabeled documents, we see that EM has used the unlabeled data to find words that are more generally indicative of courses. The classifier corresponding to the first column gets 50% accuracy; by the eighth (final) iteration, the classifier achieves 71% accuracy.

Iteration 0	Iteration 1	Iteration 2
intelligence	*DD*	*D*
DD	*D*	*DD*
artificial	lecture	lecture
understanding	cc	cc
*DD*w	*D*⋆	*DD:DD*
dist	*DD:DD*	due
identical	handout	*D*⋆
rus	due	homework
arrange	problem	assignment
games	set	handout
dartmouth	tay	set
natural	*DD*am	hw
cognitive	yurttas	exam
logic	homework	problem
proving	kfoury	*DD*am
prolog	sec	postscript
knowledge	postscript	solution
human	exam	quiz
representation	solution	chapter
field	assaf	ascii

Table 2: Lists of the words most predictive of the course class in the WebKB data set, as they change over iterations of EM for a specific example. The symbol *D* indicates an arbitrary digit.

The graph in Figure 2 shows the benefits of 2500 unlabeled documents on the WebKB data set. Again, EM improves accuracy significantly, especially when the amount of labeled data is small. When there are 12 labeled documents (three per class), traditional naive Bayes attains 50% accuracy, while EM reaches 64%. When there is a lot of labeled data, however, EM hurts performance slightly.

Varying the Weight of the Unlabeled Data

We hypothesize that the reason EM hurts performance here is that the data does not fit the assumptions of our model as well as 20 Newsgroups does—that is, the generative components that best explain the unlabeled data are not in good correspondence with the class labels. As seen in Figure 2, EM can still help in spite of somewhat violated assumptions when EM has very little labeled training data, because parameter estimation is so desperate for guidance. However, when there is enough labeled training data that the labeled data alone is already sufficient for good parameter estimation, the estimates can be modestly thrown off by EM's incorporation of the unlabeled data. It is not surprising that the unlabeled data can throw off parameter estimation when one considers that the number of unlabeled documents is always much greater than the number of labeled documents (*e.g.* 2500 versus 280). Thus, the great majority of the probability mass used in the M-step actually comes from the unlabeled data.

This insight suggests a simple fix. We can add a learning parameter that varies the relative contributions of the labeled and unlabeled data in the M-step. In our implementation this parameter is embodied by a

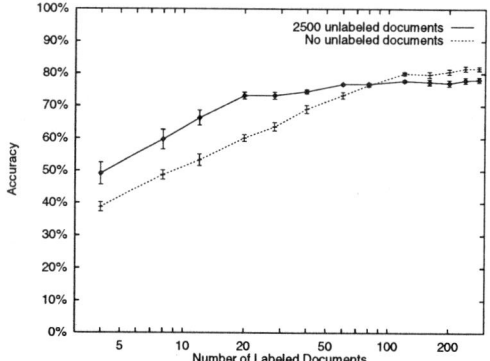

Figure 2: Classification accuracy on the WebKB data set, both with and without 2500 unlabeled documents, averaged over 20 trials per data point.

factor, $0 \leq \alpha \leq 1$, that reduces the weight of unlabeled documents in the estimation of $\theta_{w_t|c_j}$ in Equation 6. In essence, we can make each unlabeled document count as only a fraction, α, of a document, thus correctly balancing the "mass" of the labeled and unlabeled documents to optimize performance. We can build models for varying values of α and choose the best value using leave-one-out cross-validation on the training data after EM has iterated to convergence.

Re-running the WebKB experiment in Figure 2 with α selected by cross-validation provides two results of note: (1) Cross-validation picks the optimal value most of the time, and a near-optimal value otherwise. These optimal values for α do not fall at the 0/1 extremes, and are smaller when there is a lot of labeled data, and larger when there is little. (2) The accuracy of this classifier is equal to or slightly higher than the maximum of naive Bayes and EM without α-tuning. This result indicates that, even when our assumptions about the correspondence between generative components and classes are violated, we can automatically avoid any degradation in accuracy when using EM, and can still preserve the performance improvements seen when the labeled data is scarce.

Multiple Generative Components per Class

Faced with data that does not fit the assumptions of our model, the α-tuning approach described above addresses this problem by allowing the model to incrementally ignore the unlabeled data. Another, more direct approach is to change the model so that it more naturally fits the data. Flexibility can be added to the mapping between generative components and class labels by allowing *multiple* components per class—relaxing our assumption about a one-to-one correspondence between generative components and classes into a model with a many-to-one correspondence. We expect this to improve performance when data for each class is actually multi-modal.

With an eye towards testing this hypothesis, we apply EM to the Reuters corpus. Since the documents in this

Category	NB 1	EM 1	EM 20	EM 40	Diff
acq	75.9	39.5	88.4	**88.9**	+13.0
corn	40.5	21.1	**39.8**	39.1	-0.7
crude	60.7	27.8	63.9	**66.6**	+5.9
earn	92.6	90.2	**95.3**	95.2	+2.7
grain	51.7	21.0	54.6	**55.8**	+4.1
interest	52.0	25.9	48.6	**50.3**	-1.7
money-fx	57.7	28.8	54.7	**59.7**	+2.0
ship	58.1	9.3	46.5	**55.0**	-3.1
trade	56.8	34.7	54.3	**57.0**	+0.2
wheat	48.9	13.0	42.1	**44.2**	-4.7

Table 3: Precision-Recall breakeven points showing performance of binary classifiers on Reuters with traditional naive Bayes, EM with one generative component per class, and EM with varying multi-component models for the **negative** class. The best multi-component model is noted in bold, and the difference in performance between it and naive Bayes is noted in the rightmost column.

data set can have multiple class labels, each category is traditionally evaluated with a binary classifier. Thus, the **negative** class covers 134 distinct categories, and we expect that this task strongly violates the assumption that all the data for the **negative** class is generated by a single component. For these experiments, we randomly selected 10 positively labeled documents, 40 negatively labeled documents, and 7000 unlabeled documents.

The left column of Table 3 shows average precision-recall breakeven points for naive Bayes. These numbers are presented at the best vocabulary size for each task. The second column of Table 3 shows the results of performing EM on the data with a single **negative** generative component, as in previous experiments, without α-tuning. As expected, EM's results are dramatically worse than traditional naive Bayes because fitting a single naive Bayes component with EM to multi-modal **negative** data does not accurately capture its distribution. However, by running EM on an appropriate model with multiple components per class, we obtain results that improve upon naive Bayes. The remainder of Table 3 shows the effects of modeling the **negative** class with 20 or 40 generative components. These components are each initialized for EM with randomly assigned **negative** documents. A paired t-test on each trial over all categories shows that the improvement in average breakeven point from 59.5% to 61.3% is statistically significant ($p < 0.0001$).

These results indicate that correct model selection is crucial for EM when there is not a simple one-to-one correspondence between generative components and classes. When the data is accurately modeled, EM provides significant gains in performance. One obvious question is how to select the best model. AutoClass (Cheeseman & Stutz 1996) does this for unsupervised clustering tasks by selecting the most probable model given the data and a prior that prefers smaller models. For classification tasks, it may be more beneficial to use classification accuracy with leave-one-out cross-validation, as was successful for α-tuning.

Related Work

Two other studies use EM to combine labeled and unlabeled data for classification (Miller & Uyar 1997; Shahshahani & Landgrebe 1994). Instead of naive Bayes, Shahshahani and Landgrebe use a mixture of Gaussians; Miller and Uyar use Mixtures of Experts. They demonstrate experimental results on non-text data sets with up to 40 features. In contrast, our textual data sets have three orders of magnitude more features. Shahshahani and Landgrebe present a proof that unlabeled data reduce variance in parameter estimation. Their proof does not apply in our case, however, because our target concept can not be learned without some labeled data. (There is no efficient estimator for *all* parameters.)

Our work is an example of applying EM to fill in missing values—the missing values are the class labels of the unlabeled training examples. Ghahramani and Jordan (1994) use EM with mixture models to fill in missing values. The emphasis of their work is on missing feature values, where we focus on augmenting a very small but complete set of labeled data.

The AutoClass project (Cheeseman & Stutz 1996) investigates the combination of the EM algorithm with an underlying model of a naive Bayes classifier. The emphasis of their research is the discovery of novel clusterings for unsupervised learning over unlabeled data. AutoClass has not been applied to text or classification.

Several other text classifiers have been used by others in a variety of domains (Yang & Pederson 1997; Joachims 1998; Cohen & Singer 1997). Naive Bayes has a strong probabilistic foundation for EM, and is more efficient for large data sets. The thrust of this paper is to straightforwardly demonstrate the value of unlabeled data; a similar approach could apply unlabeled data to more complex classifiers.

Summary and Conclusions

This paper has explored the question of when and how unlabeled data may be used to supplement scarce labeled data in machine learning problems, especially when learning to classify text documents. This is an important question in text learning, because of the high cost of hand-labeling data and because of the availability of huge volumes of unlabeled data. In this paper we have presented a theoretical model, an algorithm, and experimental results that show significant improvements from using unlabeled documents for training classifiers in three real-world text classification tasks.

Our theoretical model characterizes a setting in which unlabeled data can be used to boost the accuracy of learned classifiers: when the probability distribution that generates documents can be described as a mixture distribution, and where the mixture components correspond to the class labels. These conditions fit exactly the model used by the naive Bayes classifier.

Since the complexity of natural language text will not soon be completely captured by statistical models, it is interesting to consider the sensitivity of a classifier's model to data that is inconsistent with that model. We believe that our algorithm and others using unlabeled data require a closer match between the data and the model than those using only labeled data. When the data is inconsistent with the assumptions of the model, our method for adjusting the weight of the contribution of unlabeled data, (as presented in our results on WebKB), prevents the unlabeled data from hurting classification accuracy. With our results on Reuters, we study ways to improve the model so that it better matches the assumptions about the correspondence between generative components and classes. The results show improved classification accuracy, and suggest exploring the use of even more complex mixture models that better correspond to textual data distributions.

We see several interesting directions for future work using EM and unlabeled data. Work in progress suggests that active learning can benefit from explicitly modeling the unlabeled data by incorporating EM iterations at every stage; this allows better selection of examples for which to request class labels from a labeler. Also, an incremental learning algorithm that re-trains throughout the testing phase could use the unlabeled test data received early in the testing phase in order to improve performance on later test data.

Other problem domains share some similarities with text domains, and also have abundant unlabeled data with limited, expensive labeled data. Robotics, vision, and information extraction are three such domains. Applying the techniques in this paper could improve classification in these areas as well.

Acknowledgments

We thank Larry Wasserman for his extensive help on some of the theoretical aspects of this work. We thank Doug Baker for help formatting the Reuters data set. This research was supported in part by the Darpa HPKB program under contract F30602-97-1-0215.

References

Castelli, V., and Cover, T. 1995. On the exponential value of labeled samples. *Pattern Recognition Letters* 16:105–111.

Cheeseman, P., and Stutz, J. 1996. Bayesian classification (AutoClass): Theory and results. In Fayyad, U.; Piatetski-Shapiro, G.; Smyth, P.; and Uthurusamy, R., eds., *Advances in Knowledge Discovery and Data Mining*. Cambridge: MIT Press.

Cohen, W., and Singer, Y. 1997. Context-sensitive learning methods for text categorization. In *Proceedings of ACM SIGIR Conference*.

Craven, M.; DiPasquo, D.; Freitag, D.; McCallum, A.; Mitchell, T.; Nigam, K.; and Slattery, S. 1998. Learning to extract symbolic knowledge from the World Wide Web. In *Proceedings of AAAI-98*.

Dempster, A. P.; Laird, N. M.; and Rubin, D. B. 1977. Maximum likelihood from incomplete data via the EM algorithm. *Journal of the Royal Statistical Society, Series B* 39:1–38.

Domingos, P., and Pazzani, M. 1997. Beyond independence: Conditions for the optimality of the simple Bayesian classifier. *Machine Learning* 29:103–130.

Friedman, J. H. 1997. On bias, variance, 0/1 - loss, and the curse-of-dimensionality. *Data Mining and Knowledge Discovery* 1:55–77.

Ghahramani, Z., and Jordan, M. 1994. Supervised learning from incomplete data via an EM approach. In *Advances in Neural Information Processing Systems (NIPS 6)*.

Joachims, T. 1997. A probabilistic analysis of the Rocchio algorithm with TFIDF for text categorization. In *Intl. Conference on Machine Learning (ICML-97)*.

Joachims, T. 1998. Text categorization with Support Vector Machines: Learning with many relevant features. In *European Conference on Machine Learning (ECML-98)*.

Lang, K. 1995. Newsweeder: Learning to filter netnews. In *Intl. Conference on Machine Learning (ICML-95)*.

Lewis, D. D., and Knowles, K. A. 1997. Threading electronic mail: A preliminary study. *Information Processing and Management* 33(2):209–217.

Lewis, D., and Ringuette, M. 1994. A comparison of two learning algorithms for text categorization. In *Third Annual Symposium on Document Analysis and IR*.

Lewis, D.; Schapire, R.; Callan, J.; and Papka, R. 1996. Training algorithms for linear text classifiers. In *Proceedings of ACM SIGIR Conference*.

McCallum, A., and Nigam, K. 1998. A comparison of event models for naive Bayes text classification. In *AAAI-98 Workshop on Learning for Text Categorization*. http://www.cs.cmu.edu/~mccallum.

McLachlan, G., and Basford, K. 1988. *Mixture Models*. New York: Marcel Dekker.

Miller, D. J., and Uyar, H. S. 1997. A mixture of experts classifier with learning based on both labelled and unlabelled data. In *Advances in Neural Information Processing Systems (NIPS 9)*.

Nigam, K.; McCallum, A.; Thrun, S.; and Mitchell, T. 1998. Learning to classify text from labeled and unlabeled documents. Technical Report CMU-CS-98-120, Carnegie Mellon University.

Pazzani, M. J.; Muramatsu, J.; and Billsus, D. 1996. Syskill & Webert: Identifying interesting Web sites. In *Proceedings of AAAI-96*.

Salton, G. 1991. Developments in automatic text retrieval. *Science* 253:974–979.

Shahshahani, B., and Landgrebe, D. 1994. The effect of unlabeled samples in reducing the small sample size problem and mitigating the Hughes phenomenon. *IEEE Trans. on Geoscience and Remote Sensing* 32(5):1087–1095.

Vapnik, V. 1982. *Estimation of dependences based on empirical data*. Springer.

Yang, Y., and Pederson, J. 1997. Feature selection in statistical learning of text categorization. In *Intl Conference on Machine Learning (ICML-97)*, 412–420.

Knowledge Lean Word–Sense Disambiguation[*]

Ted Pedersen
Department of Computer Science and Engineering
Southern Methodist University
Dallas, TX 75275-0112
pedersen@seas.smu.edu

Rebecca Bruce
Department of Computer Science
University of North Carolina at Asheville
Asheville, NC 28804
bruce@cs.unca.edu

Abstract

We present a corpus–based approach to word–sense disambiguation that only requires information that can be automatically extracted from untagged text. We use unsupervised techniques to estimate the parameters of a model describing the conditional distribution of the sense group given the known contextual features. Both the EM algorithm and Gibbs Sampling are evaluated to determine which is most appropriate for our data. We compare their disambiguation accuracy in an experiment with thirteen different words and three feature sets. Gibbs Sampling results in small but consistent improvement in disambiguation accuracy over the EM algorithm.

Introduction

Resolving the ambiguity of words is a central problem in natural language processing. A wide range of approaches have been applied to word–sense disambiguation. However, most require manually crafted knowledge such as annotated text, machine readable dictionaries or thesari, semantic networks, or aligned bilingual corpora. We present a corpus–based approach to disambiguation that relies strictly on knowledge that is automatically identifiable within the text being processed. This avoids dependence on external knowledge sources and is therefore a *knowledge lean* approach.

We are given N sentences that each contain a particular ambiguous word. Each is converted into a feature vector $(F_1, F_2, \ldots, F_n, S)$ where $(F_1, \ldots, F_n)$ represent selected properties of the context in which the ambiguous word occurs and S represents the sense of the ambiguous word. Our objective is to divide these N instances of an ambiguous word into a specified number of sense groups. These sense groups must be mapped to sense tags in order to evaluate system performance. We use the mapping that results in the highest classification accuracy.

There are a wide range of unsupervised learning techniques that could be applied to this problem. We use a parametric model to assign a sense group to each ambiguous word. In each case, we assign the most probable group given the context as defined by the Naive Bayes model where the parameter estimates are formulated via unsupervised techniques. The advantage of this approach is two-fold: (1) there is a large body of evidence recommending the use of the Naive Bayes model in word–sense disambiguation (e.g., (Leacock, Towell, & Voorhees 1993), (Mooney 1996), (Ng 1997)) and (2) unsupervised techniques for parameter estimation, once developed, could be easily applied to other parametric forms in the class of decomposable models.

We employ the Expectation Maximization (EM) algorithm (Dempster, Laird, & Rubin 1977) and Gibbs Sampling (Geman & Geman 1984) to estimate model parameters from untagged data. Both are well known and widely used iterative algorithms for estimating model parameters in the presence of missing data; in our case, the missing data are the senses of the ambiguous words. The EM algorithm formulates a maximum likelihood estimate of each model parameter, while Gibbs Sampling is a simulation technique for estimating the mode of the posterior distribution of each model parameter. When the likelihood function is not well approximated by a normal distribution, simulation techniques often provide better estimates of the model parameters. Our data, as is typical of Natural Language Processing data, is sparse and skewed and therefore not necessarily well characterized by large sample approximations. In this study, we compare maximum likelihood estimates to those produced using a more expensive simulation technique.

First, we describe the application of the Naive Bayes model to word–sense disambiguation. The following sections introduce the EM algorithm and Gibbs Sampling, respectively. We present the results of an extensive evaluation of three different feature sets applied to each of thirteen ambiguous words. We close with a discussion of related work and our future directions.

Naive Bayes Model

In the Naive Bayes model, all features are assumed to be conditionally independent given the value of the

---

[*]Copyright ©1998, American Association for Artificial Intelligence (www.aaai.org). All rights reserved.

classification variable. When applied to word–sense disambiguation, the model specifies that all contextual features are conditionally independent given the sense of the ambiguous word. The joint probability of observing a certain combination of contextual features with a particular sense is expressed as:

$$p(F_1, F_2, \ldots, F_n, S) = p(S) \prod_{i=1}^{n} p(F_i|S) \qquad (1)$$

The parameters of this model are $p(S)$ and $p(F_i|S)$. The sufficient statistics, i.e., the summaries of the data needed for parameter estimation, are the frequency counts of events described by the interdependent variables (F_i, S). Given these marginal counts, parameter estimates follow directly. However, when the sense tags are missing, direct estimates are not possible; instead we use the EM algorithm and Gibbs Sampling to impute a sense group for the missing data and estimate the parameters.

EM Algorithm

There are two steps in the EM algorithm, expectation (E–step) and maximization (M–step). The E–step calculates the expected values of the sufficient statistics given the current parameter estimates. The M–step makes maximum likelihood estimates of the parameters given the imputed values of the sufficient statistics. These steps alternate until the parameter estimates in iteration $k-1$ and k differ by less than ϵ.

The EM algorithm for the exponential family of probabilistic models is introduced in (Dempster, Laird, & Rubin 1977). The Naive Bayes model is a decomposable model which is a member of the exponential family with special properties that simplify the formulation of the E–step (Lauritzen 1995).

The EM algorithm for Naive Bayes proceeds as follows:

1. randomly initialize $p(F_i|S)$, set $k = 1$
2. E–step: $count(F_i, S) = p(S|F_i) \times count(F_i)$
3. M–step: re-estimate $p(F_i|S) = \frac{count(F_i, S)}{count(S)}$
4. $k = k + 1$
5. go to step 2 if parameter estimates from iteration k and $k-1$ differ by more than ϵ.

Gibbs Sampling

Gibbs Sampling is a Markov Chain method of generating random samples from a distribution when sampling directly from that distribution is difficult. We use Gibbs Sampling to impute the missing values for S and then sample values for the parameters.

Gibbs Sampling is often cast as a stochastic version of the EM algorithm (e.g., (Meng & van Dyk 1997)). However, in general Gibbs Sampling is applicable to a wider class of problems than the EM algorithm.

A Gibbs Sampler generates chains of values for the missing senses S and the parameters $p(F_i|S)$ via iterative sampling. These chains will eventually converge to a stationary distribution. The early iterations of the sampler produce values that vary quite a bit. It is suggested that some portion of the early iterations be discarded. This process is commonly known as a "burn–in". We use a 500 iteration burn–in and monitor the following 1000 iterations for convergence using the measure proposed in (Geweke 1992). If the chains have not converged, then additional iterations are performed until they do. Below we show the general procedure for Gibbs Sampling with the Naive Bayes model. *burn_in* represents the number of initial iterations that are discarded and *chain_size* is the number of iterations that are monitored.

1. randomly initialize $p(F_i|S)$, set $k = 1$
2. sample value for S from
$$p(S|F_1, \ldots, F_n) = \frac{p(S)\prod_i^n p(F_i|S)}{p(F1, F2, \ldots, F_n)}$$
3. sample from parameters $p(F_i|S)$
4. $k = k + 1$
5. if $k <$ *chain_size* goto 2
6. does chain from (*burn_in* to *chain_size*) converge?
7. if not, increase *chain_size* and go to step 2

Prior knowledge can be conveniently incorporated using the conjugate prior for a multinomial distribution, a Dirichlet prior. The resulting posterior Dirichlet distribution is the distribution sampled from in steps 2 and 3. However, in these experiments, we do not assume any prior knowledge and therefore use uninformative priors.

Methodology

A series of experiments were conducted to disambiguate all occurrences of thirteen different words. Three different feature sets were defined for each word and used to formulate a Naive Bayes model describing the distribution of sense groups of that word. The parameters of each model were estimated using both the EM algorithm and Gibbs Sampling. In total, this amounts to 78 different disambiguation experiments. In addition, each experiment was repeated 25 times in order to measure the variance introduced by randomly selecting the initial parameter estimates. The disambiguation accuracy figures reported for these experiments measure how well the automatically defined sense groups map to the sense groups established by a human judge.

Data

The words used in these experiments and their sense distributions, as determined by a human judge, are shown in Figures 1, 2, and 3. *Total count* is the number of occurrences of each word. Each word was limited

chief: (total count: 1048)	
highest in rank:	86%
most important; main:	14%
common: (total count: 1060)	
as in the phrase 'common stock':	84%
belonging to or shared by 2 or more:	8%
happening often; usual:	8%
last: (total count: 3004)	
on the occasion nearest in the past:	94%
after all others:	6%
public: (total count: 715)	
concerning people in general:	68%
concerning the government and people:	19%
not secret or private:	13%

Figure 1: Adjective Senses

bill: (total count: 1341)	
a proposed law under consideration:	68%
a piece of paper money or treasury bill:	22%
a list of things bought and their price:	10%
concern: (total count: 1235)	
a business; firm:	64%
worry; anxiety:	36%
drug: (total count: 1127)	
a medicine; used to make medicine:	57%
a habit-forming substance:	43%
interest: (total count: 2113)	
money paid for the use of money:	59%
a share in a company or business:	24%
readiness to give attention:	17%
line: (total count: 1149)	
a wire connecting telephones:	37%
a cord; cable:	32%
an orderly series:	30%

Figure 2: Noun Senses

agree: (total count: 1109)	
to concede after disagreement:	74%
to share the same opinion:	26%
close: (total count: 1354)	
to (cause to) end:	77%
to (cause to) stop operation:	23%
help: (total count: 1267)	
to enhance - inanimate object:	78%
to assist - human object:	22%
include: (total count: 1526)	
to contain in addition to other parts:	91%
to be a part of - human subject:	9%

Figure 3: Verb Senses

to the 2 or 3 most frequent senses. The frequency-based features employed here do not lend themselves to distinguishing among very small minority senses. In addition, the *line* data was reduced from 6 to 3 senses despite having a fairly uniform distribution. Initially this was done to maintain a similar total count and number of senses with the other words. However, preliminary experiments with 6 senses show that accuracy degrades considerably, to approximately 25 to 30 percent, depending on the feature set. This indicates that different features may be needed to accommodate larger numbers of senses.

The *line* data (Leacock, Towell, & Voorhees 1993) is taken from the ACL/DCI Wall Street Journal corpus and the American Printing House for the Blind corpus and tagged with WordNet senses. The remaining twelve words (Bruce, Wiebe, & Pedersen 1996) were taken from the ACL/DCI Wall Street Journal corpus and tagged with senses from the Longman Dictionary of Contemporary English.[1]

Feature Sets

We defined three different feature sets for use in these experiments. Our objective in doing so is two-fold: (1) to study the impact of the dimensionality of the event space on unsupervised parameter estimation, and (2) to study the informativeness of different feature types in word–sense disambiguation. Our feature sets are composed of various combinations of the following five types of features.

Morphology The feature M represents the morphology of the ambiguous word. For nouns, M is binary indicating singular or plural. For verbs, the value of M indicates the tense of the verb and can have up to seven possible values.[2] This feature is not used for adjectives.

Part–of–Speech The features PL_i and PR_i represent the part–of–speech (POS) of the word i positions to the left or right, respectively, of the ambiguous word. In these experiments, $i = 1$ or 2. Each POS feature can have one of five possible values: noun, verb, adjective, adverb or other. These tags were assigned automatically using the Unix command *style -P*.

Co–occurrences The features C_i are binary variables representing whether the ith most frequent content word in all sentences containing the ambiguous word occurs anywhere in the sentence being processed. In these experiments, $i = 1, 2$ and 3.

Unrestricted Collocations The features UL_i and UR_i indicate the word occurring in the position i places to the left or right, respectively, of the ambiguous word.

---

[1] In these experiments, sense tags are used only in the evaluation of the sense groups found by the unsupervised learning procedures. If sense–tagged text were not available, the evaluation process would require manually mapping the sense groups to sense tags.

[2] All morphologically equivalent verb tenses were grouped as one; ambiguous morphology was not addressed.

event	Full Joint			Naive Bayes		
count	A	B	C	A	B	C
0	98.7	99.9	99.9	6.9	22.5	33.3
1–5	1.1	0.1	0.1	8.0	25.7	5.2
6–10	0.1	0.0	0.0	4.6	11.6	3.0
11–100	0.1	0.0	0.0	33.3	31.7	31.1
100+	0.0	0.0	0.0	47.1	8.4	27.4

Figure 4: Event Distribution for Noun *interest*

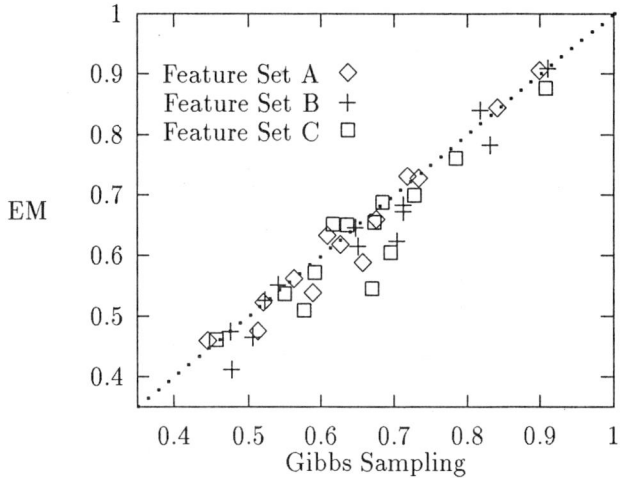

Figure 6: Accuracy of EM versus Gibbs

In these experiments $i = 1$ or 2. All features of this form have twenty-one possible values. Nineteen correspond to the most frequent words that occur in that fixed position in all sentences that contain the particular ambiguous word.[3] There is also a value (*none*) that indicates when the position i to the left or right is occupied by a word that is not among the nineteen most frequent, and a value (*null*) indicating that the position i to the left or right falls outside of the sentence boundary.

Content Collocations The features CL_1 and CR_1 indicate the content word occurring in the position 1 place to the left or right, respectively, of the ambiguous word. The values of these features correspond to the nineteen most frequent content words in that position plus *none* and *null*.

The features described above are defined over a small contextual window (local–context) and are selected to produce low dimensional event spaces. Local–context features have been used successfully in a variety of supervised approaches to disambiguation (e.g., (Bruce & Wiebe 1994), (Ng & Lee 1996)).

Feature Sets A, B and C The 3 feature sets used in these experiments are designated A, B and C pand are formulated as shown below. The particular feature combinations chosen were found to yield reasonable results in a preliminary evaluation.

- A: $M, PL_2, PL_1, PR_1, PR_2, C_1, C_2, C_3$
  Joint Events: 10,000 – 105,000
  Marginal Events: 78 – 99
- B: $M, UL_2, UL_1, UR_1, UR_2$
  Joint Events: 388,962 – 4,084,101
  Marginal Events: 168 – 273
- C: $M, PL_2, PL_1, PR_1, PR_2, CL_1, CR_1$
  Joint Events: 551,250 – 5,788,125
  Marginal Events: 160 – 207

"Joint Events" shows the range of the number of possible combinations of feature values in the full joint distribution of each feature set. We contrast this with "Marginal Events", the range of the possible combinations of feature values in the marginal distributions of the Naive Bayes model. Figure 4 shows an example of how the event count distribution of *interest* is smoothed by reducing the number of possible events though the use of the Naive Bayes model.

Discussion of Results

Figure 5 shows the average accuracy and standard deviation of disambiguation over 25 random trials for each combination of word, feature set and learning algorithm. Also included is the percentage of each sample that is composed of the majority sense. Figure 6 shows the correlation between the accuracy of disambiguation when using the EM algorithm versus Gibbs Sampling for all combinations of words and feature sets. Points that fall on or near the line $x = y$ are associated with words that were disambiguated with similar accuracy by both methods.

Method There are only a few cases where the use of Gibbs Sampling resulted in significantly more accurate disambiguation than the EM algorithm; this was judged by a two–tailed t-test with $p = .01$. The significant differences are shown in bold face. While the number of significant differences is small, Figure 6 shows a consistent increase in the accuracy of the Gibbs Sampler relative to the EM algorithm.

The EM algorithm found much the same parameter estimates as Gibbs Sampling. This is somewhat surprising given that the EM algorithm can converge to local maxima when the distribution of the likelihood function is not well approximated by the normal distribution. However, in our experiments the EM algorithm often converged quite quickly, usually within 20 iterations, to a global maximum. These results suggest that a combination of the EM algorithm and Gibbs Sampling might be appropriate. (Meng & van Dyk 1997) propose that the Gibbs Sampler start at the point the

---

[3] Nineteen distinct word forms were recognized to control the dimensionality of the feature set while still allowing the recognition of relevant correlations. This value was arrived at empirically; other values considered were 5, 11, and 31.

	Maj.	Feature Set A		Feature Set B		Feature Set C	
		Gibbs	EM	Gibbs	EM	Gibbs	EM
chief	.861	.719±.01	.729±.06	.648±.00	.646±.01	.728±.04	.697±.06
common	.842	.522±.00	.521±.00	.507±.07	.464±.06	**.670±.11**	.543±.09
last	.940	.900±.00	.903±.00	.912±.00	.909±.00	.908±.00	.874±.07
public	.683	**.514±.00**	.473±.03	**.478±.04**	.411±.03	**.578±.00**	.507±.03
adjectives	.832	.663	.657	.636	.608	**.721**	.655
bill	.681	.590±.04	.537±.05	.705±.10	.624±.08	.592±.04	.569±.04
concern	.638	.842±.00	.842±.00	.819±.01	.840±.02	.785±.01	.758±.09
drug	.567	.676±.00	.658±.03	.543±.04	.551±.05	.674±.06	.652±.04
interest	.593	.627±.08	.616±.06	.652±.04	.615±.05	.617±.05	.649±.09
line	.373	.446±.02	.457±.01	.477±.03	.474±.03	.457±.01	.458±.01
nouns	.570	.636	.622	.639	.621	.625	.617
agree	.740	.609±.07	.631±.08	.714±.14	.683±.14	.685±.14	.685±.14
close	.771	.564±.09	.560±.08	.714±.05	.672±.06	.636±.05	.648±.05
help	.780	**.658±.04**	.586±.05	.524±.00	.526±.00	**.696±.05**	.602±.03
include	.910	.734±.08	.725±.02	**.833±.03**	.783±.07	.551±.06	.535±.00
verbs	.800	.641	.626	.696	.666	.632	.618
overall	.734	.646	.634	.657	.631	.659	.629

Figure 5: Experimental Results - accuracy ± standard deviation

EM algorithm converges rather than being randomly initialized. If the EM algorithm has found a local maximum then the Gibbs Sampler would be able to escape it and find the global maximum. However, if the EM algorithm has already found the global maximum then the Gibbs Sampler will converge quickly and confirm this result.

Feature Set The accuracy of disambiguation for nouns is fairly consistent across the feature sets. However, there are exceptions. The accuracy achieved for *bill* is much higher with feature set B than with A or C. The accuracy for *drug*, on the other hand, is much lower with feature set B than with A or C. This variation across feature sets may indicate that certain features are more or less appropriate for certain words.

The accuracy for verbs was highest with feature set B although *help* is a glaring exception. Feature set B is made up of local-context collocations.

The highest average accuracy achieved for adjectives occurs when Gibbs Sampling is used in combination with feature set C. This is a high dimensional feature set, additionally, the sense distributions of the adjectives are the most skewed. Under these circumstances, it seems unlikely that the EM algorithm would reliably find a global maximum, and, indeed, it appears that the EM algorithm found local maxima when processing *common* and *public*.

While frequency-based features, such as those used in this work, reduce sparsity, they are less likely to be useful in distinguishing among minority senses. Indeed, the more skewed the distribution of senses in the data sample, the more likely it is that frequency-based features will be indicative of only the majority sense.

Related Work

There is an abundance of literature on word-sense disambiguation. Our knowledge-lean approach differs from most in that it does not require any knowledge resources beyond raw text. Corpus-based approaches often use supervised learning algorithms with sense-tagged text (e.g., (Leacock, Towell, & Voorhees 1993), (Bruce & Wiebe 1994), (Mooney 1996)) or multi-lingual parallel corpora (e.g., (Gale, Church, & Yarowsky 1992)).

An approach that significantly reduces the amount of sense-tagged data required is described in (Yarowsky 1995). Yarowsky suggests a variety of options for automatically seeding a supervised disambiguation algorithm; one is to identify collocations that uniquely distinguish between senses. Yarowsky achieves an accuracy of more than 90% when disambiguating between two senses for twelve different words. This result demonstrates the effectiveness of a small number of representative collocations as seeds in an iterative bootstrapping approach.

A comparison of the EM algorithm and two agglomerative clustering algorithms as applied to unsupervised word-sense disambiguation is discussed in (Pedersen & Bruce 1997). Using the same data used in this study, (Pedersen & Bruce 1997) found that McQuitty's agglomerative algorithm is significantly more accurate for adjectives and verbs while the EM algorithm is significantly more accurate for nouns. These results indicate that McQuitty's analysis, which is based on counts of dissimilar features, is most appropriate for highly skewed data sets. The performance of Gibbs Sampling in the current study also falls short of that of McQuitty's for adjectives and verbs which supports the previous conclusion.

The EM algorithm is used with a Naive Bayes classifier in (Gale, Church, & Yarowsky 1995) to distinguish city names from people's names. A narrow window of context, one or two words to either side, was found to perform better than wider windows. They report an accuracy percentage in the mid-nineties when applied to *Dixon*, a name found to be quite ambiguous.

A recent knowledge–lean approach to sense discrimination is discussed in (Schütze in press 1998). Ambiguous words are clustered into sense groups based on *second-order co-occurrences*: two instances of an ambiguous word are assigned to the same sense if the words that they co–occur with likewise co–occur with similar words in the training data. Schütze evaluates sense groupings based on their effectiveness in several information retrieval problems.[4]

Future Work

There are several issues to address in future work. First, the possibility of using the EM algorithm as a starting point for Gibbs Sampling seems particularly intriguing in that it addresses the limitations of both approaches. Second, we would like to use models other than Naive Bayes in these knowledge–lean approaches. More complicated models, while potentially resulting in distributions that are inappropriate for the EM algorithm, could provide stronger disambiguation results when used in combination with Gibbs Sampling. We would also like to investigate the use of informative priors in Gibbs Sampling. Finally, we will continue investigating local–context features in the hopes of increasing our accuracy with minority senses without substantially increasing the dimensionality of the problem.

Acknowledgments

This research was supported by the Office of Naval Research under grant number N00014-95-1-0776.

References

Bruce, R., and Wiebe, J. 1994. Word-sense disambiguation using decomposable models. In *Proceedings of the 32nd Annual Meeting of the Association for Computational Linguistics*, 139–146.

Bruce, R.; Wiebe, J.; and Pedersen, T. 1996. The measure of a model. In *Proceedings of the Conference on Empirical Methods in Natural Language Processing*, 101–112.

Dempster, A.; Laird, N.; and Rubin, D. 1977. Maximum likelihood from incomplete data via the EM algorithm. *Journal of the Royal Statistical Society B* 39:1–38.

Gale, W.; Church, K.; and Yarowsky, D. 1992. A method for disambiguating word senses in a large corpus. *Computers and the Humanities* 26:415–439.

Gale, W.; Church, K.; and Yarowsky, D. 1995. Discrimination decisions for 100,000 dimensional spaces. *Journal of Operations Research* 55:323–344.

Geman, S., and Geman, D. 1984. Stochastic relaxation, Gibbs distributions and the Bayesian restoration of images. *IEEE Transactions on Pattern Analysis and Machine Intelligence* 6:721–741.

Geweke, J. 1992. Evaluating the accuracy of sampling–based approaches to calculating posterior moments. In Bernardo, J.; Berger, J.; Dawid, A.; and Smith, A., eds., *Bayesian Statistics 4*. Oxford: Oxford University Press.

Lauritzen, S. 1995. The EM algorithm for graphical association models with missing data. *Computational Statistics and Data Analysis* 19:191–201.

Leacock, C.; Towell, G.; and Voorhees, E. 1993. Corpus-based statistical sense resolution. In *Proceedings of the ARPA Workshop on Human Language Technology*, 260–265.

Meng, X., and van Dyk, D. 1997. The EM algorithm – an old folk–song sung to a new fast tune (with discussion). *Journal of Royal Statistics Society, Series B* 59(3):511—567.

Mooney, R. 1996. Comparative experiments on disambiguating word senses: An illustration of the role of bias in machine learning. In *Proceedings of the Conference on Empirical Methods in Natural Language Processing*, 82–91.

Ng, H., and Lee, H. 1996. Integrating multiple knowledge sources to disambiguate word sense: An exemplar-based approach. In *Proceedings of the 34th Annual Meeting of the Society for Computational Linguistics*, 40–47.

Ng, H. 1997. Exemplar–based word sense disambiguation: Some recent improvements. In *Proceedings of the Second Conference on Empirical Methods in Natural Language Processing*, 208–213.

Pedersen, T., and Bruce, R. 1997. Distinguishing word senses in untagged text. In *Proceedings of the Second Conference on Empirical Methods in Natural Language Processing*, 197–207.

Schütze, H. (in press) 1998. Automatic word sense discrimination. *Computational Linguistics*.

Yarowsky, D. 1995. Unsupervised word sense disambiguation rivaling supervised methods. In *Proceedings of the 33rd Annual Meeting of the Association for Computational Linguistics*, 189–196.

---

[4] In Schütze's evaluation, tagged text is not required to label the sense groupings and establish the accuracy of the disambiguation experiment. Thus the experiment is fully automatic and free from dependence on any external knowledge source.

Learning to Resolve Natural Language Ambiguities: A Unified Approach

Dan Roth
Department of Computer Science
University of Illinois at Urbana-Champaign
Urbana 61801
danr@cs.uiuc.edu

Abstract

We analyze a few of the commonly used statistics based and machine learning algorithms for natural language disambiguation tasks and observe that they can be re-cast as learning linear separators in the feature space. Each of the methods makes a priori assumptions, which it employs, given the data, when searching for its hypothesis. Nevertheless, as we show, it searches a space that is as rich as the space of *all* linear separators. We use this to build an argument for a data driven approach which merely searches for a *good* linear separator in the feature space, without further assumptions on the domain or a specific problem.

We present such an approach - a sparse network of linear separators, utilizing the Winnow learning algorithm - and show how to use it in a variety of ambiguity resolution problems. The learning approach presented is attribute-efficient and, therefore, appropriate for domains having very large number of attributes.

In particular, we present an extensive experimental comparison of our approach with other methods on several well studied lexical disambiguation tasks such as context-sensitive spelling correction, prepositional phrase attachment and part of speech tagging. In all cases we show that our approach either outperforms other methods tried for these tasks or performs comparably to the best.

Introduction

Many important natural language inferences can be viewed as problems of resolving ambiguity, either semantic or syntactic, based on properties of the surrounding context. Examples include part-of speech tagging, word-sense disambiguation, accent restoration, word choice selection in machine translation, context-sensitive spelling correction, word selection in speech recognition and identifying discourse markers. In each of these problems it is necessary to disambiguate two or more [semantically, syntactically or structurally]-distinct forms which have been fused together into the same representation in some medium. In a prototypical instance of this problem, word sense disambiguation, distinct semantic concepts such as `interest rate` and `has interest in Math` are conflated in ordinary text. The surrounding context - word associations and syntactic patterns in this case - are sufficient to identify the correct form.

Many of these are important stand-alone problems but even more important is their role in many applications including speech recognition, machine translation, information extraction and intelligent human-machine interaction. Most of the ambiguity resolution problems are at the lower level of the natural language inferences chain; a wide range and a large number of ambiguities are to be resolved simultaneously in performing any higher level natural language inference.

Developing learning techniques for language disambiguation has been an active field in recent years and a number of statistics based and machine learning techniques have been proposed. A partial list consists of Bayesian classifiers (Gale, Church, & Yarowsky 1993), decision lists (Yarowsky 1994), Bayesian hybrids (Golding 1995), HMMs (Charniak 1993), inductive logic methods (Zelle & Mooney 1996), memory-based methods (Zavrel, Daelemans, & Veenstra 1997) and transformation-based learning (Brill 1995). Most of these have been developed in the context of a specific task although claims have been made as to their applicativity to others.

In this paper we cast the disambiguation problem as a learning problem and use tools from computational learning theory to gain some understanding of the assumptions and restrictions made by different learning methods in shaping their search space.

The learning theory setting helps in making a few interesting observations. We observe that many algorithms, including naive Bayes, Brill's transformation based method, Decision Lists and the Back-off estimation method can be re-cast as learning linear separators in their feature space. As learning techniques for linear separators these techniques are limited in that, in general, they cannot learn *all* linearly separable functions. Nevertheless, we find, they still search a space that is as complex, in terms of its VC dimension, as the space of all linear separators. This has implications to the generalization ability of their hypotheses. Together with

[0]Copyright © 1998, American Association for Artificial Intelligence (www.aaai.org). All rights reserved.

the fact that different methods seem to use different a priori assumptions in guiding their search for the linear separator, it raises the question of whether there is an alternative - search for the best linear separator in the feature space, without resorting to assumptions about the domain or any specific problem.

Partly motivated by these insights, we present a new algorithm, and show how to use it in a variety of disambiguation tasks. The architecture proposed, *SNOW*, is a Sparse Network Of linear separators which utilizes the Winnow learning algorithm. A target node in the network corresponds to a candidate in the disambiguation task; all subnetworks learn autonomously from the same data, in an on line fashion, and at run time, they compete for assigning the correct meaning. The architecture is data-driven (in that its nodes are allocated as part of the learning process and depend on the observed data) and supports efficient on-line learning. Moreover, The learning approach presented is attribute-efficient and, therefore, appropriate for domains having very large number of attributes. All together, We believe that this approach has the potential to support, within a single architecture, a large number of simultaneously occurring and interacting language related tasks.

To start validating these claims we present experimental results on three disambiguation tasks. *Prepositional phrase attachment (PPA)* is the task of deciding whether the Prepositional Phrase (PP) attaches to the noun phrase (NP), as in Buy the car with the steering wheel or to the verb phrase (VP), as in Buy the car with his money. *Context-sensitive Spelling correction (Spell)* is the task of fixing spelling errors that result in valid words, such as It's not to late, where too was mistakenly typed as to. *Part of speech tagging (POS)* is the task of assigning each word in a given sentence the part of speech it assumes in this sentence. For example, assign N or V to talk in the following pair of sentences: Have you listened to his (him) talk ?. In all cases we show that our approach either outperforms other methods tried for these tasks or performs comparably to the best.

This paper focuses on analyzing the learning problem and on motivating and developing the learning approach; therefore we can only present the bottom line of the experimental studies and the details are deferred to companion reports.

The Learning Problem

Disambiguation tasks can be viewed as general classification problems. Given an input sentence we would like to assign it a single property out of a set of potential properties. Formally, given a sentence s and a predicate p defined on the sentence, we let $C = \{c_1, c_2, \ldots c_m\}$ be the collection of possible values this predicate can assume in s. It is assumed that one of the elements in C is the *correct* assignment, $c(s,p)$. c_i can take values from $\{site, cite, sight\}$ if the predicate p is the correct spelling of any occurrence of a word from this set in the sentence; it can take values from $\{v, n\}$ if the predicate p is the attachment of the PP to the preceding VP (v) or the preceding NP (n), or it can take values from $\{industrial, living\ organism\}$ if the predicate is the meaning of the word plant in the sentence. In some cases, such as part of speech tagging, we may apply a collection P of different predicates to the same sentence, when tagging the first, second, kth word in the sentence, respectively. Thus, we may perform a classification operation on the sentence multiple times. However, in the following definitions it would suffice to assume that there is a single pre-defined predicate operating on the sentence s; moreover, since the predicate studied will be clear from the context we omit it and denote the correct classification simply by $c(s)$.

A *classifier* h is a function that maps the set S of all sentences[1], given the task defined by the predicate p, to a single value in C, $h : S \to C$.

In the setting considered here the classifier h is selected by a training procedure. That is, we assume[2] a class of functions $\mathcal{H}$, and use the training data to select a member of this class. Specifically, given a *training corpus* S_{tr} consisting of *labeled example* $(s, c(s))$, a learning algorithm selects a hypothesis $h \in \mathcal{H}$, the classifier.

The performance of the classifier is measured empirically, as the fraction of correct classifications it performs on a set S_{ts} of test examples. Formally,

$$Perf(f) = |\{s \in S_{ts} | h(s) = c(s)\}| / |\{s \in S_{ts}\}|. \quad (1)$$

A sentence s is represented as a collection of *features*, and various kinds of feature representation can be used. For example, typical features used in correcting context-sensitive spelling are *context words* – which test for the presence of a particular word within $\pm k$ words of the target word, and *collocations* – which test for a pattern of up to ℓ contiguous words and/or part-of-speech tags around the target word.

It is useful to consider features as sequences of *tokens* (e.g., words in the sentence, or pos tags of the words). In many applications (e.g., n-gram language models), there is a clear ordering on the features. We define here a natural partial order $\prec$ as follows: for features f, g define $f \prec g \equiv f \subseteq g$, where on the right end side features are viewed simply as sets of tokens[3]. A feature f is of *order* k if it consists of k tokens.

A definition of a disambiguation problem consists of the task predicate p, the set $\mathcal{C}$ of possible classifications and the set $\mathcal{F}$ of features. $\mathcal{F}^{(k)}$ denotes the features of order k. Let $|\mathcal{F}| = n$, and x_i be the ith feature. x_i can either be present (*active*) in a sentence s (we then say that $x_i = 1$), or absent from it ($x_i = 0$). Given that,

---

[1]The basic unit studied can be a paragraph or any other unit, but for simplicity we will always call it a sentence.

[2]This is usually not made explicit in statistical learning procedures, but is assumed there too.

[3]There are many ways to define features and order relations among them (e.g., restricting the number of tokens in a feature, enforcing sequential order among them, etc.). The following discussion does not depend on the details; one option is presented to make the discussion more concrete.

a sentence s can be represented as the set of all *active* features in it $s = (x_{i_1}, x_{i_2}, \ldots x_{i_m})$.

From the stand point of the general framework the exact mapping of a sentence to a feature set will not matter, although it is crucially important in the specific applications studied later in the paper. At this point it is sufficient to notice that the a sentence can be mapped into a binary feature vector. Moreover, w.l.o.g we assume that $|C| = 2$; moving to the general case is straight forward. From now on we will therefore treat classifiers as Boolean functions, $h : \{0,1\}^n \rightarrow \{0,1\}$.

Approaches to Disambiguation

Learning approaches are usually categorized as statistical (or probabilistic) methods and symbolic methods. However, all learning methods are statistical in the sense that they attempt to make inductive generalization from observed data and use it to make inferences with respect to previously unseen data; as such, the statistical based theories of learning (Vapnik 1995) apply equally to both. The difference may be that symbolic methods do not explicitly use probabilities in the hypothesis. To stress the equivalence of the approaches further in the following discussion we will analyze two "statistical" and two "symbolic" approaches.

In this section we present four widely used disambiguation methods. Each method is first presented as known and is then re-cast as a problem of learning a linear separator. That is, we show that, there is a linear condition $\sum_{x_i \in \mathcal{F}} w_i x_i > \theta$ such that, given a sentence $s = (x_{i_1}, x_{i_2}, \ldots x_{i_m})$, the method predicts $c = 1$ if the condition holds for it, and $c = 0$ otherwise.

Given an example $s = (x_1, x_2 \ldots x_m)$ a probabilistic classifier h works by choosing the element of C that is most probable, that is $h(s) = argmax_{c_i \in C} Pr(c_i | x_1, x_2, \ldots x_m)^4$, where the probability is the empirical probability estimated from the labeled training data. In general, it is unlikely that one can estimate the probability of the event of interest $(c_i | x_1, x_2, \ldots x_m)$ directly from the training data. There is a need to make some probabilistic assumptions in order to evaluate the probability of this event indirectly, as a function of "more frequent" events whose probabilities can be estimated more robustly. Different probabilistic assumptions give rise to difference learning methods and we describe two popular methods below.

The naive Bayes estimation (NB) The naive Bayes estimation (e.g., (Duda & Hart 1973)) assumes that given the class value $c \in C$ the features values are statistically independent. With this assumption and using Bayes rule the Bayes optimal prediction is given by: $h(s) = argmax_{c_i \in C} \Pi_{i=1}^m Pr(x_j | c_i) P(c_i)$.

The prior probabilities $p(c_i)$ (i.e., the fraction of training examples labeled with c_i) and the conditional probabilities $Pr(x_j | c_i)$ (the fraction of the training examples labeled c_i in which the jth feature has value x_j) can be estimated from the training data fairly robustly[5], giving rise to the naive Bayes predictor. According to it, the optimal decision is $c = 1$ when

$$P(c=1)\Pi_i P(x_i|c=1)/P(c=0)\Pi_i P(x_i|c=0) > 1.$$

Denoting $p_i \equiv P(x_i = 1|c = 1)$, $q_i \equiv P(x_i = 1|c = 0)$, $P(c = r) \equiv P(r)$, we can write this condition as

$$\frac{P(1)\Pi_i p_i^{x_i}(1-p_i)^{1-x_i}}{P(0)\Pi_i q_i^{x_i}(1-q_i)^{1-x_i}} = \frac{P(1)\Pi_i (1-p_i)(\frac{p_i}{1-p_i})^{x_i}}{P(0)\Pi_i (1-q_i)(\frac{q_i}{1-q_i})^{x_i}} > 1,$$

and by taking log we get that using naive Bayes estimation we predict $c = 1$ if and only if

$$\log \frac{P(1)}{P(0)} + \sum_i \log \frac{1-p_i}{1-q_i} + \sum_i (\log \frac{p_i}{1-p_i} \frac{1-q_i}{q_i}) x_i > 0.$$

We conclude that the decision surface of the naive Bayes algorithm is given by a linear function in the feature space. Points which reside on one side of the hyperplane are more likely to be labeled 1 and points on the other side are more likely to be labeled 0.

This representation immediately implies that this predictor is optimal also in situations in which the conditional independence assumption does no hold. However, a more important consequence to our discussion here is the fact that not all linearly separable functions can be represented using this predictor (Roth 1998).

The back-off estimation (BO) Back-off estimation is another method for estimating the conditional probabilities $Pr(c_i|s)$. It has been used in many disambiguation tasks and in learning models for speech recognition (Katz 1987; Chen & Goodman 1996; Collins & Brooks 1995). The back-off method suggests to estimate $Pr(c_i|x_1, x_2, \ldots, x_m)$ by interpolating the more robust estimates that can be attained for the conditional probabilities of more general events. Many variation of the method exist; we describe a fairly general one and then present the version used in (Collins & Brooks 1995), which we compare with experimentally.

When applied to a disambiguation task, BO assumes that the sentence itself (the basic unit processed) is a feature[6] of maximal order $f = f^{(k)} \in \mathcal{F}$. We estimate

$$Pr(c_i|s) = Pr(c_i|f^{(k)}) = \sum_{\{f \in \mathcal{F} | f \prec f^{(k)}\}} \lambda_f Pr(c_i|f).$$

---

[4] As usual, we use the notation $Pr(c_i|x_1, x_2, \ldots x_m)$ as a shortcut for $Pr(c = c_i|x_1 = a_1, x_2 = a_2, \ldots x_m = a_m)$.

[5] Problems of sparse data may arise, though, when a specific value of x_i observed in testing has occurred infrequently in the training, in conjunction with c_j. Various *smoothing* techniques can be employed to get more robust estimations but these considerations will not affect our discussion and we disregard them.

[6] The assumption that the maximal order feature is the classified sentence is made, for example, in (Collins & Brooks 1995). In general, the method deals with multiple features of the maximal order by assuming their conditional independence, and superimposing the NB approach.

The sum is over all features f which are more general (and thus occur more frequently) than $f^{(k)}$. The conditional probabilities on the right are empirical estimates measured on the training data, and the coefficients λ_f are also estimated given the training data. (Usually, these are maximum likelihood estimates evaluated using iterative methods, e.g. (Samuelsson 1996)).

Thus, given an example $s = (x_1, x_2 \ldots x_m)$ the BO method predicts $c = 1$ if and only if

$$\sum_{i=1}^{|\mathcal{F}|} \lambda_i (Pr(c=1|x_i) - Pr(c=0|x_i)) x_i > 0,$$

a linear function over the feature space.

For computational reasons, various simplifying assumptions are made in order to estimate the coefficients λ_f; we describe here the method used in (Collins & Brooks 1995)[7]. We denote by $\mathcal{N}(f^{(j)})$ the number of occurrences of the jth order feature $f^{(j)}$ in the training data. Then BO estimates $P = Pr(c_i|f^{(k)})$ as follows:

If $\mathcal{N}(f^{(k)}) > 0$, $\quad P = Pr(c_i|f^{(k)})$
Else if $\sum_{f \in \mathcal{F}^{(k-1)}} \mathcal{N}(f) > 0$, $P = \frac{1}{|\mathcal{F}^{(k-1)}|} \sum Pr(c_i|f^{(k-1)})$
Else if ...
Else if $\sum_{f \in \mathcal{F}^{(1)}} \mathcal{N}(f) > 0$, $\quad P = \frac{1}{|\mathcal{F}^{(1)}|} \sum Pr(c_i|f^{(1)})$

In this case, it is easy to write down the linear separator defining the estimate in an explicit way. Notice that with this estimation, given a sentence s, only the highest order features active in it are considered. Therefore, one can define the weights of the jth order feature in an inductive way, making sure that it is larger than the sum of the weights of the smaller order features. Leaving out details, it is clear that we get a simple representation of a linear separator over the feature space, that coincides with the BO algorithm.

It is important to notice that the assumptions made in the BO estimation method result in a linear decision surface that is, in general, *different* from the one derived in the NB method.

Transformation Based Learning (TBL) Transformation based learning (Brill 1995) is a machine learning approach for rule learning. It has been applied to a number of natural language disambiguation tasks, often achieving state-of-the-art accuracy.

The learning procedure is a mistake-driven algorithm that produces a set of rules. Irrespective of the learning procedure used to derive the TBL representation, we focus here on the final hypothesis used by TBL and how it is evaluated, given an input sentence, to produce a prediction. We assume, w.l.o.g, $|C| = 2$.

The hypothesis of TBL is an ordered list of transformations. A *transformation* is a rule with an antecedent t and a consequent[8] $c \in C$. The antecedent t is a condition on the input sentence. For example, in Spell, a condition might be word W occurs within $\pm k$ of the target word. That is, applying the condition to a sentence s defines a feature $t(s) \in \mathcal{F}$. Phrased differently, the application of the condition to a given sentence s, checks whether the corresponding feature is active in this sentence. The condition holds if and only if the feature is active in the sentence.

An ordered list of transformations (the TBL hypothesis), is evaluated as follows: given a sentence s, an initial label $c \in C$ is assigned to it. Then, each rule is applied, in order, to the sentence. If the feature defined by the condition of the rule applies, the current label is replaced by the label in the consequent. This process goes on until the last rule in the list is evaluated. The last label is the output of the hypothesis.

In its most general setting, the TBL hypothesis is not a classifier (Brill 1995). The reason is that the truth value of the condition of the ith rule may change while evaluating one of the preceding rules. However, in many applications and, in particular, in Spell (Mangu & Brill 1997) and PPA (Brill & Resnik 1994) which we discuss later, this is not the case. There, the conditions do not depend on the labels, and therefore the output hypothesis of the TBL method can be viewed as a classifier. The following analysis applies only for this case.

Using the terminology introduced above, let $(x_{i_1}, c_{i_1}), (x_{i_2}, c_{i_2}), \ldots (x_{i_k}, c_{i_k})$ be the ordered sequence of rules defining the output hypothesis of TBL. (Notice that it is quite possible, and happens often in practice, for a feature to appear more than once in this sequence, even with different consequents). While the above description calls for evaluating the hypothesis by sequentially evaluating the conditions, it is easy to see that the following simpler procedure is sufficient:

Search the ordered sequence in a reversed order. Let x_{i_j} be the first active feature in the list (i.e., the largest j). Then the hypothesis predicts c_{i_j}.

Alternatively, the TBL hypothesis can be represented as a (positive) 1-Decision-List (p1-DL) (Rivest 1987), over the set $\mathcal{F}$ of features[9]. Given the p1-DL representation

If	x_{i_k} is active then predict c_k.
Else	If $x_{i_{k-1}}$ is active then predict c_{k-1}.
Else	...
Else	If x_1 is active then predict c_1.
Else	Predict the initial value

Figure 1: TBL as a p1-Decision List

---

[7]There, the empirical ratios are smoothed; experimentally, however, this yield only a slight improvement, going from 83.7% to 84.1% so we present it here in the pure form.

[8]The consequent is sometimes described as a *transformation* $c_i \to c_j$, with the semantics – if the current label is c_i, relabel it c_j. When $|C| = 2$ it is equivalent to simply using c_j as the consequent.

[9]Notice, the order of the features is reversed. Also, multiple occurrences of features can be discarded, leaving only the last rule in which this feature occurs. By "positive" we mean that we never condition on the absence of a feature, only on its presence.

tation (Fig 1), we can now represent the hypothesis as a linear separator over the set $\mathcal{F}$ of features. For simplicity, we now name the class labels $\{-1, +1\}$ rather than $\{0, 1\}$. Then, the hypothesis predicts $c = 1$ if and only if $\sum_{j=1}^{k} 2^j \cdot c_{i_j} \cdot x_{i_j} > 0$. Clearly, with this representation the active feature with the highest index dominates the prediction, and the representations are equivalent[10].

Decision Lists (p1-DL) It is easy to see (details omitted), that the above analysis applies to p1-DL, a method used, for example, in (Yarowsky 1995). The BO and p1-DL differ only in that they keep the rules in reversed order, due to different evaluation methods.

The Linear Separator Representation

To summarize, we have shown:
claim: *All the methods discussed – NB, BO, TBL and p1-DL search for a decision surface which is a linear function in the feature space.*

This is not to say that these methods assume that the data is linearly separable. Rather, all the methods assume that the feature space is divided by a linear condition (i.e., a function of the form $\sum_{x_i \in \mathcal{F}} w_i x_i > \theta$) into two regions, with the property that in one of the defined regions the more likely prediction is 0 and in the other, the more likely prediction is 1.

As pointed out, it is also instructive to see that these methods yield *different* decision surfaces and that they cannot represent every linearly separable function.

Theoretical Support for the Linear Separator Framework

In this section we discuss the implications these observations have from the learning theory point of view.

In order to do that we need to resort to some of the basic ideas that justify inductive learning. Why do we hope that a classifier learned from the training corpus will perform well (on the test data) ? Informally, the basic theorem of learning theory (Valiant 1984; Vapnik 1995) guarantees that, if the training data and the test data are sampled from the same distribution[11], good performance on the training corpus guarantees good performance on the test corpus.

If one knows something about the model that generates the data, then estimating this model may yield good performance on future examples. However, in the problems considered here, no reasonable model is known, or is likely to exist. (The fact that the assumptions discussed above disagree with each other, in general, may be viewed as a support for this claim.)

In the absence of this knowledge a learning method merely attempts to make correct predictions. Under these conditions, it can be shown that the error of a classifier selected from class $\mathcal{H}$ on (previously unseen) test data, is bounded by the sum of its training error and a function that depends linearly on the complexity of $\mathcal{H}$. This complexity is measured in terms of a combinatorial parameter - the VC-dimension of the class $\mathcal{H}$ (Vapnik 1982) - which measures the richness of the function class. (See (Vapnik 1995; Kearns & Vazirani 1992)) for details).

We have shown that all the methods considered here look for a linear decision surface. However, they do make further assumptions which seem to restrict the function space they search in. To quantify this line of argument we ask whether the assumptions made by the different algorithms significantly reduce the complexity of the hypothesis space. The following claims show that this is not the case; the VC dimension of the function classes considered by all methods are as large as that of the full class of linear separators.

Fact 1: *The VC dimension of the class of linear separators over n variables is $n + 1$.*
Fact 2: *The VC dimension of the class of p1-DL over n variables*[12] *is $n + 1$.*
Fact 3: *The VC dimension of the class of linear separators derived by either NB or BO over n variables is bounded below by n.*

Fact 1 is well known; 2 and 3 can be derived directly from the definition (Roth 1998).

The implication is that a method that merely searches for the optimal linear decision surface given the training data may, in general, outperform all these methods also on the test data. This argument can be made formal by appealing to a result of (Kearns & Schapire 1994), which shows that even when there is no perfect classifier, the optimal linear separator on a polynomial size set of training examples is optimal (in a precise sense) also on the test data.

The optimality criterion we seek is described in Eq. 1. A linear classifier that minimizes the number of disagreements (the sum of the false positives and false negatives classifications). This task, however, is known to be NP-hard (Höffgen & Simon 1992), so we need to resort to heuristics. In searching for good heuristics we are guided by computational issues that are relevant to the natural language domain. An essential property of an algorithm is being feature-efficient. Consequently, the approach describe in the next section makes use of the *Winnow* algorithm which is known to produce good results when a linear separator exists, as well as under certain more relaxed assumptions (Littlestone 1991).

---

[10] In practice, there is no need to use this representation, given the efficient way suggested above to evaluate the classifier. In addition, very few of the features in $\mathcal{F}$ are active in every example, yielding more efficient evaluation techniques (e.g., (Valiant 1998))

[11] This is hard to define in the context of natural language; typically, this is understood as texts of similar nature; see a discussion of this issue in (Golding & Roth 1996).

[12] In practice, when using p1-DL as the hypothesis class (i.e., in TBL) an effort is made to discard many of the features and by that reduce the complexity of the space; however, this process, which is data driven and does not a-priori restrict the function class can be employed by other methods as well (e.g., (Blum 1995)) and is therefore orthogonal to these arguments.

The *SNOW* Approach

The *SNOW* architecture is a network of threshold gates. Nodes in the first layer of the network are allocated to input features in a data-driven way, given the input sentences. Target nodes (i.e., the element $c \in C$) are represented by nodes in the second layer. Links from the first to the second layer have weights; each target node is thus defined as a (linear) function of the lower level nodes. (A similar architecture which consists of an additional layer is described in (Golding & Roth 1996). Here we do not use the "cloud" level described there.)

For example, in Spell, target nodes represent members of the confusion sets; in POS, target nodes correspond to different pos tags. Each target node can be thought of as an autonomous network, although they all feed from the same input. The network is *sparse* in that a target node need not be connected to all nodes in the input layer. For example, it is not connected to input nodes (features) that were never active with it in the same sentence, or it may decide, during training to disconnect itself from some of the irrelevant inputs.

Learning in *SNOW* proceeds in an on-line fashion[13]. Every example is treated autonomously by each target subnetworks. Every labeled example is treated as positive for the target node corresponding to its label, and as negative to all others. Thus, every example is used once by all the nodes to refine their definition in terms of the others and is then discarded. At prediction time, given an input sentence which activates a subset of the input nodes, the information propagates through all the subnetworks; the one which produces the highest activity gets to determine the prediction.

A local learning algorithm, Winnow (Littlestone 1988), is used at each target node to learn its dependence on other nodes. Winnow is a mistake driven on-line algorithm, which updates its weights in a multiplicative fashion. Its key feature is that the number of examples it requires to learn the target function grows linearly with the number of *relevant* attributes and only logarithmically with the total number of attributes. Winnow was shown to learn efficiently any linear threshold function and to be robust in the presence of various kinds of noise, and in cases where no linear-threshold function can make perfect classifications and still maintain its abovementioned dependence on the number of total and relevant attributes (Littlestone 1991; Kivinen & Warmuth 1995).

Notice that even when there are only two target nodes and the cloud size (Golding & Roth 1996) is 1 *SNOW* behaves differently than pure Winnow. While each of the target nodes is learned using a positive Winnow algorithm, a winner-take-all policy is used to determine the prediction. Thus, we do not use the learning algorithm here simply as a discriminator. One reason is that the *SNOW* architecture, influenced by the Neuroidal system (Valiant 1994), is being used in a system

---

[13] Although for the purpose of the experimental study we do not update the network while testing.

Table 1: **Spell System comparison.** The second column gives the number of test cases. All algorithms were trained on 80% of Brown and tested on the other 20%; Baseline simply identifies the most common member of the confusion set during training, and guesses it every time during testing.

Sets	Cases	Baseline	NB	TBL	*SNOW*
14	1503	71.1	89.9	88.5	93.5
21	4336	74.8	93.8		96.4

developed for the purpose of learning knowledge representations for natural language understanding tasks, and is being evaluated on a variety of tasks for which the node allocation process is of importance.

Experimental Evidence

In this section we present experimental results for three of the most well studied disambiguation problems, Spell, PPA and POS. We present here only the bottom-line results of an extensive study that appears in companion reports (Golding & Roth 1998; Krymolovsky & Roth 1998; Roth & Zelenko 1998).

Context Sensitive Spelling Correction Context-sensitive spelling correction is the task of fixing spelling errors that result in valid words, such as *It's not to late*, where *too* was mistakenly typed as *to*.

We model the ambiguity among words by *confusion sets*. A confusion set $C = \{c_1, \ldots, c_n\}$ means that each word c_i in the set is ambiguous with each other word. All the results reported here use the same pre-defined set of confusion sets (Golding & Roth 1996).

We compare *SNOW* against TBL (Mangu & Brill 1997) and a naive-Bayes based system (NB). The latter system presents a few augmentations over the simple naive Bayes (but still shares the same basic assumptions) and is among the most successful methods tried for the problem (Golding 1995). An indication that a Winnow-based algorithm performs well on this problem was presented in (Golding & Roth 1996). However, the system presented there was more involved than *SNOW* and allows more expressive output representation than we allow here. The output representation of all the approaches compared is a linear separator.

The results presented in Table 1 for NB and *SNOW* are the (weighted) average results of 21 confusion sets, 19 of them are of size 2, and two of size 3. The results presented for the TBL[14] method are taken from (Mangu & Brill 1997) and represent an average on a subset of 14 of these, all of size 2.

Prepositional Phrase Attachment The problem is to decide whether the Prepositional Phrase (PP) attaches to the noun phrase, as in Buy the car with

---

[14] Systems are compared on the same feature set. TBL was also used with an enhanced feature set (Mangu & Brill 1997) with improved results of 93.3% but we have not run the other systems with this set of features.

Table 2: **PPA System comparison.** All algorithms were trained on 20801 training examples from the WSJ corpus tested 3097 previously unseen examples from this corpus; all the system use the same feature set.

Test cases	Baseline	NB	TBL	BO	*SNOW*
3097	59.0	83.0	81.9	84.1	83.9

the steering wheel or the verb phrase, as in Buy the car with his money. Earlier works on this problem (Ratnaparkhi, Reynar, & Roukos 1994; Brill & Resnik 1994; Collins & Brooks 1995) consider as input the four head words involved in the attachment - the VP head, the first NP head, the preposition and the second NP head (in this case, buy, car, with and steering wheel, respectively). These four-tuples, along with the attachment decision constitute the labeled input sentence and are used to generate the feature set. The features recorded are all sub-sequences of the 4-tuple, total of 15 for every input sentence. The data set used by all the systems in this in this comparison was extracted from the Penn Treebank WSJ corpus by (Ratnaparkhi, Reynar, & Roukos 1994). It consists of 20801 training examples and 3097 separate test examples. In a companion paper we describe an extensive set of experiments with this and other data sets, under various conditions. Here we present only the bottom line results that provide direct comparison with those available in the literature[15]. The results presented in Table 2 for NB and *SNOW* are the results of our system on the 3097 test examples. The results presented for the TBL and BO are on the same data set, taken from (Collins & Brooks 1995).

Part of Speech Tagging A part of speech tagger assigns each word in a sentence the part of speech that it assumes in that sentence. See (Brill 1995) for a survey of much of the work that has been done on POS in the past few years. Typically, in English there will be between 30 and 150 different parts of speech depending on the tagging scheme. In the study presented here, following (Brill 1995) and many other studies there are 47 different tags. Part-of-speech tagging suggests a special challenge to our approach, as the problem is a multi-class prediction problem (Roth & Zelenko 1998). In the *SNOW* architecture, we devote one linear separator to each pos tag and each sub network learns to separate its corresponding pos tag from all others. At run time, all class nodes process the given sentence, applying many classifiers simultaneously. The classifiers then compete for deciding the pos of this word, and the node that records the highest activity for a given word in a sentence determines its pos. The methods compared use

---

[15] *SNOW* was evaluated with an enhanced feature set (Krymolovsky & Roth 1998) with improved results of 84.8%. (Collins & Brooks 1995) reports results of 84.4% on a different enhanced set of features, but other systems were not evaluated on these sets.

Table 3: **POS System comparison.** The first column gives the number of test cases. All algorithms were trained on 550,000 words of the tagged WSJ corpus. Baseline simply predicts according to the most common pos tag for the word in the training corpus.

Test cases	Baseline	TBL	*SNOW*
250,000	94.4	96.9	96.8

context and collocation features as in (Brill 1995).

Given a sentence, each word in the sentence is assigned an initial tag, based on the most common part of speech in the training corpus. Then, for each word in the sentence, the network processes the sentence, and makes a suggestion for the pos of this word. Thus, the input for the predictor is noisy, since the initial assignment is not accurate for many of the words. This process can repeat a few times, where after predicting the pos of a word in the sentence we re-compute the new feature-based representation of the sentence and predict again. Each time the input to the predictors is expected to be slightly less noisy. In the results presented here, however, we present the performance without the recycling process, so that we maintain the linear function expressivity (see (Roth & Zelenko 1998) for details).

The results presented in Table 3 are based on experiments using 800,000 words of the Penn Treebank Tagged WSJ corpus. About 550,000 words were used for training and 250,000 for testing. *SNOW* and TBL were trained and tested on the same data.

Conclusion

We presented an analysis of a few of the commonly used statistics based and machine learning algorithms for ambiguity resolution tasks. We showed that all the algorithms investigated can be re-cast as learning linear separators in the feature space. We analyzed the complexity of the function space in which each of these method searches, and show that they all search a space that is as complex as the space of all linear separators. We used these to argue motivate our approach of learning a sparse network of linear separators (*SNOW*), which learns a network of linear separator by utilizing the Winnow learning algorithm. We then presented an extensive experimental study comparing the *SNOW* based algorithms to other methods studied in the literature on several well studied disambiguation tasks. We present experimental results on Spell, PPA and POS. In all cases we show that our approach either outperformed other methods tried for these tasks or performs comparably to the best. We view this as a strong evidence to that this approach provides a unified framework for the study of natural language disambiguation tasks.

The importance of providing a unified framework stems from the fact the essentially all ambiguity resolution problems that are addressed here are at the lower level of the natural language inferences chain. A large number of different kinds of ambiguities are to be resolved simultaneously in performing any higher level natural language inference (Cardie 1996). Naturally, these processes, acting on the same input and using the same "memory", will interact. A unified view of ambiguity resolution within a single architecture, is valuable if one wants understand how to put together a large number of these inferences, study interactions among them and make progress towards using these in performing higher level inferences.

References

Blum, A. 1995. Empirical support for Winnow and weighted-majority based algorithms: results on a calendar scheduling domain. In *Proc. 12th International Conference on Machine Learning*, 64–72. Morgan Kaufmann.

Brill, E., and Resnik, P. 1994. A rule-based approach to prepositional phrase attachment disambiguation. In *Proc. of COLING*.

Brill, E. 1995. Transformation-based error-driven learning and natural language processing: A case study in part of speech tagging. *Computational Linguistics* 21(4):543–565.

Cardie, C. 1996. *Embedded Machine Learning Systems for natural language processing: A general framework.* Springer. 315–328.

Charniak, E. 1993. *Statistical Language Learning.* MIT Press.

Chen, S., and Goodman, J. 1996. An empirical study of smoothing techniques for language modeling. In *Proc. of the Annual Meeting of the ACL*.

Collins, M., and Brooks, J. 1995. Prepositional phrase attachment through a backed-off model. In *Proceedings of Third the Workshop on Very Large Corpora*.

Duda, R. O., and Hart, P. E. 1973. *Pattern Classification and Scene Analysis.* Wiley.

Gale, W. A.; Church, K. W.; and Yarowsky, D. 1993. A method for disambiguating word senses in a large corpus. *Computers and the Humanities* 26:415–439.

Golding, A. R., and Roth, D. 1996. Applying winnow to context-sensitive spelling correction. In *Proc. of the International Conference on Machine Learning*, 182–190.

Golding, A. R., and Roth, D. 1998. A winnow-based approach to word correction. *Machine Learning.* Special issue on Machine Learning and Natural Language; to appear.

Golding, A. R. 1995. A bayesian hybrid method for context-sensitive spelling correction. In *Proceedings of the 3rd workshop on very large corpora, ACL-95*.

Höffgen, K., and Simon, H. 1992. Robust trainability of single neurons. In *Proc. 5th Annu. Workshop on Comput. Learning Theory*, 428–439. New York, New York: ACM Press.

Katz, S. M. 1987. Estimation of probabilities from sparse data for the language model component of a speech recognizer. *IEEE Transactions on Acoustics, speech, and Signal Processing* 35(3):400–401.

Kearns, M., and Schapire, R. 1994. Efficient distribution-free learning of probabilistic concepts. *Journal of Computer and System Sciences* 48:464–497.

Kearns, M., and Vazirani, U. 1992. *Introduction to computational Learning Theory.* MIT Press.

Kivinen, J., and Warmuth, M. K. 1995. Exponentiated gradient versus gradient descent for linear predictors. In *Proceedings of the Annual ACM Symp. on the Theory of Computing*.

Krymolovsky, Y., and Roth, D. 1998. Prepositional phrase attachment. In Preparation.

Littlestone, N. 1988. Learning quickly when irrelevant attributes abound: A new linear-threshold algorithm. *Machine Learning* 2:285–318.

Littlestone, N. 1991. Redundant noisy attributes, attribute errors, and linear threshold learning using Winnow. In *Proc. 4th Annu. Workshop on Comput. Learning Theory*, 147–156. San Mateo, CA: Morgan Kaufmann.

Mangu, L., and Brill, E. 1997. Automatic rule acquisition for spelling correction. In *Proc. of the International Conference on Machine Learning*, 734–741.

Ratnaparkhi, A.; Reynar, J.; and Roukos, S. 1994. A maximum entropy model for prepositional phrase attachment. In *ARPA*.

Rivest, R. L. 1987. Learning decision lists. *Machine Learning* 2(3):229–246.

Roth, D., and Zelenko, D. 1998. Part of speech tagging using a network of linear separators. Submitted.

Roth, D. 1998. Learning to resolve natural language ambiguities:a unified approach. Long Version, in Preparation.

Samuelsson, C. 1996. Handling sparse data by successive abstraction. In *Proc. of COLING*.

Valiant, L. G. 1984. A theory of the learnable. *Communications of the ACM* 27(11):1134–1142.

Valiant, L. G. 1994. *Circuits of the Mind.* Oxford University Press.

Valiant, L. G. 1998. Projection learning. In *Proc. of the Annual ACM Workshop on Computational Learning Theory*, xxx–xxx.

Vapnik, V. N. 1982. *Estimation of Dependences Based on Empirical Data.* New York: Springer-Verlag.

Vapnik, V. N. 1995. *The Nature of Statistical Learning Theory.* New York: Springer-Verlag.

Yarowsky, D. 1994. Decision lists for lexical ambiguity resolution: application to accent restoration in Spanish and French. In *Proc. of the Annual Meeting of the ACL*, 88–95.

Yarowsky, D. 1995. Unsupervised word sense disambiguation rivaling supervised methods. In *Proceedings of ACL-95*.

Zavrel, J.; Daelemans, W.; and Veenstra, J. 1997. Resolving pp attachment ambiguities with memory based learning.

Zelle, J. M., and Mooney, R. J. 1996. Learning to parse database queries using inductive logic proramming. In *Proc. National Conference on Artificial Intelligence*, 1050–1055.

Generating Inference-Rich Discourse Through Revisions of RST-Trees

Helmut Horacek

Universität des Saarlandes, FB 14 Informatik
Postfach 1150
D-66041 Saarbrücken, Germany
horacek@cs.uni-sb.de

Abstract

The majority of generation systems to date are able to communicate information only by uttering it explicitly. Rhetorical Structure Theory (RST), one of the most frequently used discourse theories for text planning in natural language generation, does not support more flexibility either, because it ignores implicit rhetorical relations and accepts only one prominent relation between clauses. In formal systems, however, the underlying information is represented in a very detailed way, which requires easily inferable parts to be left implicit for producing natural and comprehensible discourse. In order to improve the quality of texts generated from fine-grained semantic specifications, we present an approach that successively revises an explicit text plan by introducing addressee dependent short-cuts and communicatively justified reorganizations. Text plan revisions include the compactification of state-action and reasoning sequences, the omission of redundant conditions, and the reorganization of arguments for presentation purposes. Our techniques enable us to generate shorter and better understandable texts from detailed representations, as in formal systems, especially in deduction systems.

Introduction

The majority of generation systems to date are able to communicate information intended to be conveyed only by uttering it explicitly. Especially Rhetorical Structure Theory (RST) (Mann and Thompson 1987a), one of the most frequently used discourse theories for text planning, does not support more flexibility either. It ignores implicit rhetorical relations and accepts only one prominent relation between clauses. In contrast to that, the underlying information is typically represented in a semantically fine-grained way in formal systems, especially in deduction systems, which requires easily inferable parts to be left implicit for producing natural and comprehensible discourse. In such applications, RST provides an insufficient basis for generating fluent texts from facts underlying a situation.

In order to improve the quality of texts generated from semantically fine-grained background information, as available in formal systems, we present an approach that successively revises an explicit and detailed text plan by introducing addressee dependent short-cuts and communicatively justified reorganizations. Text plan revisions include the compactification of state-action and reasoning sequences, the omission of redundant conditions, and the reorganization of arguments for purposes of presentation.

This paper is organized as follows. We first review approaches that attempt to convey information in discourse indirectly, especially extensions to RST. Then we present the functionality of our method, realized by a small set of presentation rules that initiate revisions of RST trees. Finally, we demonstrate the improvements obtained for presenting mathematical proofs in natural language.

Planning Inference-Rich Discourse

Even at an early stage of NL generation research, (Mann and Moore 1981) have stated that information stemming from any reasonably complete body of knowledge needs to be condensed and generated selectively. Their knowledge filter is extremely simple in marking pieces of knowledge known to the addressee for omission in the output, coherence permitting. (Mellish and Evans 1989) apply algebraic simplification rules to reduce plan constructs, such as consequences of actions, and (McDonald 1992) exploits domain-specific conditions to reduce the information conveyed explicitly. In contrast to these early systems, recent methods are better motivated in linguistic or in cognitive terms. In TECH-DOC (Stede 1993), state-action transitions are modeled for multi-lingual instruction generation so that compactly expressing them becomes a matter of lexical choice. In WISHFUL-II (Zukerman and McConachy 1993), concise explanations are produced by using a constraint-based optimization mechanism addressing the user's inferences. (Green and Carberry 1994) consult coherence rules for the generation of indirect answers to accomplish complementary discourse goals by modeling potential obstacles that prevent intended achievements.

Within the framework of RST, (Moore and Pollack 1992) have shown that relations on the informational as well as on the intentional level may be relevant for understanding and for producing discourse in a principled way. However, their work does not provide an operational model. (Maier 1995) has developed a text planner that can handle some co-occurrence patterns between ideational and textual relations, even with divergent semantics.

Copyright © 1998, American Association for Artificial Intelligence (www.aaai.org). All rights reserved.

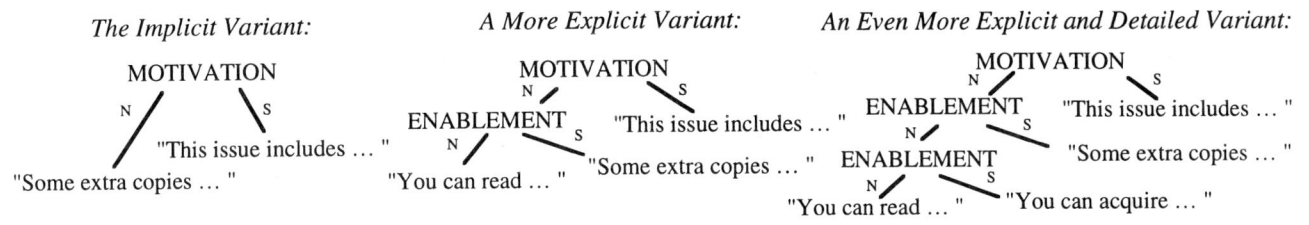

Figure 1: A MOTIVATION relation in RST, in varying degrees of explicitness and detail

(Horacek 1997) aims at capturing inference relations between generic and referential pieces of knowledge through rules expressing aspects of conversational implicature. The rules operate on an RST tree and annotate contextually inferable parts that can be left out when a text is generated.

While there is no doubt that these approaches advance generation capabilities, the kinds of implicitness they can cope with are still too limited – especially when presenting or explaining results obtained by formal systems.

Implicit Relations behind RST Trees

In this section, we examine implicit relations underlying RST representations, and we categorize them. We illustrate this discussion by examples from everyday knowledge and by text portions from the domain of mathematical proofs. For the former, we assume underlying relations in a knowledge base; for the latter, we refer to proof graphs of theorem provers. Let us start with the following text. In

(1) "Some extra copies of the Spring 1984 issue of AI Magazine are available in the library. This issue includes a "Research in Progress" report on AI research at ISI." (Matthiessen and Thompson 1987)

a MOTIVATION relation is conveyed (see Figure 1, left side). However, the action the MOTIVATION refers to, is not the mere availability of copies, but the potentiality to acquire and read such a copy. This justifies the extended relations (see the middle and right parts of Figure 1), which we assume to be present in an underlying knowledge base. Given such a representation, a good text planner should be able to produce concise and natural texts from it rather than mechanically expressing all relations explicitly.

In the domain of mathematical proofs, a similar case is the occurrence of nested causality: for example, if '0 < a' is a direct cause for some proposition p, '1 < a' as an assumption in the underlying proof is usually preferred for justifying proposition p, because the truth of '0 < a' easily follows from '1 < a'. Because avoiding a redundancy here leads to omission of intermediate reasoning or action sequence steps, we call this case *Compactification*.

Sentence (2) (Mann and Thompson 1983) relies on background knowledge to be understood correctly. However, adding a clause to it as in (2)' would lead to an apparent redundancy or somewhat bizarre markedness (Mann and Thompson 1985), see the left and middle parts of Figure 2.

(2) "I'm hungry. Let's go to the Fuji Gardens."
(2)' "I'm hungry. Let's go to the Fuji Gardens. My going to the Fuji Gardens would contribute significantly to solving the problem of my hunger."

While explicitly expressing some of the intermediate steps in a *Compactification* case is not uncommon and may even be preferable in knowledge-intensive domains, this is unacceptable in (2)'. In theorem proving systems, this sort of redundancy is a central part of their reasoning mechanism: the pattern in the right part of Figure 2 (only one relation name is different) is the classical modus ponens inference. Because avoiding a redundancy here leads to omission of an implication (a rule), we call this case *Rule-Cutting*.

Besides these omissions, there may be structural changes (see (Maier 1995)). They prominently occur in the context of sequences or enumerations, which are best represented without expansions. Further details precede or follow the entire sequence or enumeration in the text, although they are in fact related to one of the elements of that construct.

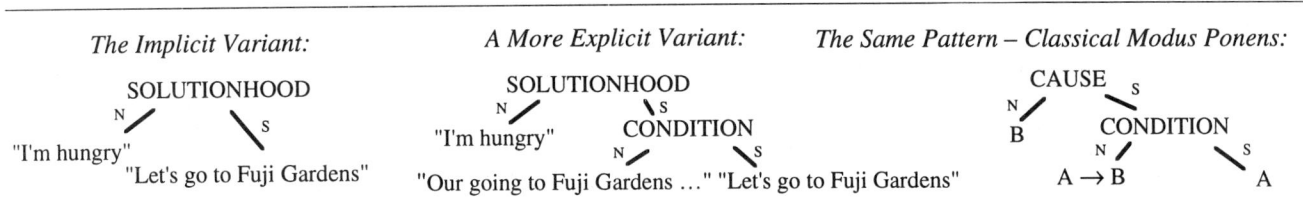

Figure 2: RST relation in varying degrees of redundancy for texts from different domains

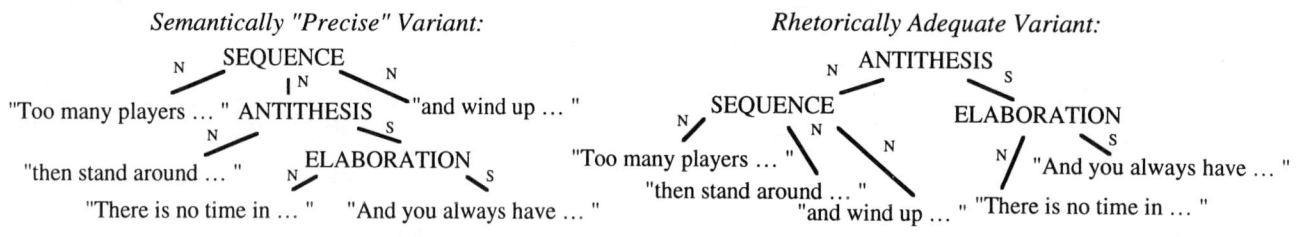

Figure 3: RST relation in varying degrees of argumentative organization

In text (3) (Mann and Thompson 1987b), the antithesis semantically relates to the second clause of the sequence (see Figure 3). Moreover, if the same text span appears in multiple places, lifting it may help in improving the text.

(3) "Too many players hit an acceptable shot, then stand around admiring it and wind up losing the point. There is no time in an action game like tennis to applaud yourself and still get in position for the next shot. And you always have to assume there will be a next shot."

In the domain of mathematical proofs, this situation occurs frequently, motivated by special presentation modes (series of inequations (Fehrer and Horacek 1997b)), or by multiply used assumptions. Because reorganizing argumentation involves structural changes, we call this case *Restructuring*.

Formalizing the Revision Model

In this section, we illustrate how RST trees that express relations implicitly as discussed in the previous section can be generated from underlying detailed representations. This is achieved by the aid of *presentation* rules that capture the cases identified above: *Rule-Cutting*, *Compactification*, and *Restructuring* rules. These rules operate on an RST tree and revise it by adding more direct or lifted relations. These additions are beneficially kept as alternatives for a number of reasons (the first one is specific to our application domain): (1) special presentation modes such as building chains of inequations may not work for some short-cuts, (2) the cognitive accessibility of antecedents is unpredictable at the local level where the *Restructuring*-rule operates, so that resulting changes may not be realizable globally, (3) simultaneously available alternatives prove valuable for presentations to addressees with divergent knowledge and in interactive environments. In the following, we first illustrate the model of the addressee's knowledge and inferential capabilities which constrain the application of the presentation rules. Then we give formalizations of these rules, and we describe their application.

For the model of mental capabilities, we distinguish the following categories of knowledge and communicative competence attributed to the audience:

- *knowledge per se*, taxonomic and referential knowledge,
- the *attentional state* of the addressee,
- *taxonomic* inferences,
- *logical* inferences, and
- *communicatively motivated* inferences.

Communicatively motivated inferences concern the capability to augment logically incomplete pieces of information in a given context, which is expressed by the presentation rules themselves. Assumptions about the addressee's taxonomic and referential knowledge are represented by simple stereotypes (see (Fehrer and Horacek 1997a)), and the dialog memory and focus mechanisms of our proof presentation system PROVERB (Huang and Fiedler 1997), respectively. The remaining categories need more explanation.

The attentional state is modeled by attributing the user with *awareness* concerning the facts needed to mentally reconstruct implicit information, which is more than just being acquainted with these facts. For generic knowledge, that is, domain regularities, the user is considered to be aware of those parts of his/her knowledge that belong to 'basic' world knowledge or to special knowledge about the issue presented – this criterion expresses coherence and expectation of some sort. For referential knowledge, the user is credited with being aware of all facts mentioned or implied so far within the current discourse segment – this criterion expresses human memory limitations, as intensively examined in (Walker 1996). For the domain of mathematical proofs, the underlying categorization of knowledge is oriented on relevant mathematical theories: basic axioms and axioms within the particular subarea of the proof presented are considered to be part of the user's awareness, and discourse segments essentially follow the structure of the proof (e.g., subproof, case analysis).

The remaining inference categories, taxonomic and logical inferences, are understood here as elementary clues, either relying on purely taxonomic knowledge, or following a standard logical inference pattern such as podus ponens. The mechansim that computes these inferences operates on pieces of domain knowledge and takes into account memory limitations. To assess these skills in our domain, we have categorized the reasoning steps in the derivation of machine-generated proofs, and we have examined the complexity of the substitutions involved, in a number of text book examples and in machine-found proofs. Typical reasoning steps are generalizations of terms and relations, and abstractions from individuals, embedded in modus ponens derivarions, with substitutions intro-

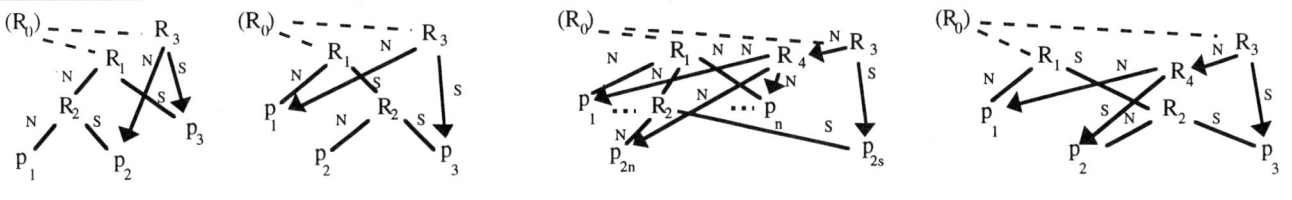

Figure 4: Patterns for tree condensation additions

Figure 5: Patterns for tree restructuring additions

ducing one additional operator, at most. Hence, if a reasoning step concluding p from q remains within certain complexity limits, we say that '$q \vdash p$' holds ('$\vdash$' denotes the 'human' calculus), and the addressee is assumed to be able to make that inference on his/her own, so that it can be left out in a presentation.

A further issue involved is the composition of inference steps. According to psychological experiments, leaving out intermediate steps in a chain of argumentation should still be understood as a 'direct' cause, while 'indirect' causes negatively affect the reasoning effort (Thüring and Wender 1985) – this criterion needs also be modeled for the domain at hand. In a previous approach to expert system explanations, this aspect has been modeled by requiring purposes of domain rules involved to be identical (Horacek 1997). For proofs, we try to capture it by a structural similarity between intermediate and final conclusions.

Details about these categories of knowledge and inferential skills are formalized by the following predicates:

AWARE-OF (User, p) – the user's attentional state,
which subsumes that the user knows p.
GENERIC (p) – replaces all variables in p by their categories (according to the definitions in the proof).
ABLE-INFER (User, φ_1, φ_2) – inferential skill: $\varphi_1 \vdash \varphi_2$.
SIMILAR(p_1, p_2) holds in our domain, if the propositions p_1 and p_2 are structurally identical.
MISFIT(p_1, p_2, R) holds between propositions p_1 and p_2 when being connected by relation R, that is, some of the conditions associated with R are violated.
PREFER((p, E), (p, F)) means that p is better presentable with expansion E than with expansion F, such as (<equation>, {}) and (<equation>, F) for $F \neq \{\}$.
MULT(E,{T}) – text span E is an element of set {T}.
TREE(T) yields the set of nodes rooting in node T.

The rules' funcionality in terms of changes made in the text structure tree is illustrated by the diagrams in Figures 4 and 5, whose applicability is restricted by the conditions listed in Figure 6. These figures can essentially be seen as overlays of the explicit and implicit tree representation variants, as exemplified in Figures 1 to 3. In Figures 4 and 5, full lines represent tree portions that need to be matched against subtrees of the text structure tree under consideration, and lines with an arrow represent the additions to be made, applicability conditions permitting. The dashed lines in these Figures indicate that, unless the top level relation of a pattern matches the root node of the text structure tree,

the top relations of the nodes added and of the existing nodes have the same predecessor node (R_0). All nodes are associated with variables, distinguishing relations (R) from propositions (p), which may or may not be expanded further in the text structure tree examined. These variables are referred to from the application conditions in Figure 6.

The application conditions as shown in Figure 6 verify the applicability of these rules by matching them against the model of the mental capabilities of the addressee. As the formalizations demonstrate, the presentation rules are expressed in a widely domain-independent way; domain-specific aspects can and to some extent must be integrated through, e.g., operationalizations of the calculus '$\vdash$', and interpretations of the predicates SIMILAR and PREFER.

For the *Compactification* rule, there are variants for nucleus expansion and for satellite expansion, which refer to tree patterns on the left and right side of Figure 4, correspondingly. Compactification is licensed if the user is credited with the ability to infer the original relation pattern from the communicated relation and its associated facts ($R_1(R_2(p_1,p_2),p_3)$ from $R_3(p_2,p_3)$ or $R_1(p_1,R_2(p_2,p_3))$ from $R_3(p_1,p_3)$, respectively). Whether this ability can be ascribed to the user depends on the expansion direction. For satellite expansions, we are confronted with chains of arguments. In this case, the proposition left implicit and the 'remaining' proposition must be 'similar' – to a certain extent, this criterion is tailored to our domain. For nucleus extensions, a certain mismatch between the facts explicitly conveyed and the relation linking them on the surface must be present in order to motivate the hearer to mentally search for the information left implicit (see the left pattern in Figure 1 – a MOTIVATION relation between these two facts cannot be taken as a motivation proper, which suggests the insertion of an ENABLEMENT relation).

The *Rule-Cutting* rule – the right side in Figure 4 shows the underlying pattern – applies to a CONDITION relation (R_2) within the context of some other relation (R_1). If R_1 is a CAUSE relation, the added relation (R_3) is always a REASON relation because some argument is left out in the precise and logically complete CAUSE relation; otherwise, R_1 and R_3 are identical. In order for this rule to be licensed, the user must be acquainted with the principle underlying the condition (the generic form of the rule, GENERIC(p_2)), and he/she must be 'aware' of that rule in the sense that the rule coherently 'fits' in the context of the CONDITION relation. In addition, the user must be able to infer that

---

Compactification rule (nucleus expansion)

MISFIT $(p_2, p_3, R_3) \wedge$
ABLE-INFER(User, $(p_2 \wedge p_3 \wedge R_3(p_2,p_3))$,
$\quad\quad\quad \varphi \wedge R_1(R_2(\varphi,p_2),p_3) \wedge (\varphi \Rightarrow p_1))$

The underlying pattern appears in Figure 4, left side, with $R_1 = R_3$, e.g., MOTIVATION, and R_2 mostly ENABLEMENT.

Compactification rule (satellite expansion)

SIMILAR $(p_1, p_2) \wedge$
ABLE-INFER(User, $(p_1 \wedge p_3 \wedge R_3(p_1,p_3))$,
$\quad\quad\quad (\varphi \wedge R_1(p_1,R_2(\varphi,p_3)) \wedge (\varphi \Rightarrow p_2)))$

The underlying pattern appears in Figure 4, right side, mostly for a chain of arguments, with $R_1 = R_3$. R_1 is typically a REASON, as is R_2 in case of chained arguments.

Rule-Cutting rule

AWARE-OF(User,GENERIC $(p_2)) \wedge$
ABLE-INFER(User, $(p_1 \wedge p_3 \wedge R_3(p_1,p_3))$,
$\quad\quad\quad (R_1(p_1,R_2(\varphi,p_3)) \wedge (\varphi \Rightarrow p_2)))$

The underlying pattern appears in Figure 4, right side, with $R_1 = R_3$, unless R_1 is a CAUSE - then R_3 is a REASON, while R_2 is always a CONDITION.

Restructuring rule (multi-nucleus expansion)

AWARE-OF(User,$p_{2s}) \wedge$
$\quad$ (PREFER$((p_{2n},\{\}),(p_{2n}, R_2(p_{2n},p_{2s}))) \vee$
$\quad$ MULT$(p_{2s}$, TREE(ROOT)))

The underlying pattern appears in Figure 5, left side, with $R_1 = R_4$ and $R_2 = R_3$, R_1 is typically SEQUENCE or JOINT.

Restructuring rule (satellite expansion)

AWARE-OF(User,$p_3) \wedge$
$\quad$ (PREFER$((p_2,\{\}),(p_2, R_2(p_2,p_3))) \vee$
$\quad$ MULT$(p_3$, TREE(ROOT)))

The underlying pattern appears in Figure 5, right side, with
$\quad\quad\quad R_1 = R_4$ and $R_2 = R_3$

Figure 6: Application conditions for presentation rules

some regularity (φ) is needed to fully explain the relation R_3 between p_1 and p_3, and that φ entails p_2.

For the *Restructuring* rule, finally, there are also two variants, one for multi-nucleus and one for nucleus-satellite relations (for the underlying patterns, see the left and the right parts of Figure 5, correspondingly). The proposition p_3 (or p_{2s} for the multi-nucleus case) expanding R_2 is lifted according to the underlying patterns if the user is aware of this proposition (that is, it is in the current focus of attention), and if there are presentation preferences in favor of the lifting operation (expressed by the predicate PREFER), or if p_3 has co-references in the entire text structure tree (expressed by the predicate MULT).

The application of the presentation rules in context is organized by building an initial RST tree, invoking the rules in the specific order described below, and expressing the resulting tree in natural language. The initial RST tree is built on the basis of the proof graph obtained by a theorem prover: logical derivation steps are transduced into modus ponens constructs, conjoined preconditions are linked by a JOINT relation, and multiple references are resolved by copying the head node and attaching expansions to the first occurrence in the tree.

Presentation rules are applied to yield all feasible short-cuts by traversing the RST tree from its leaf nodes to the root node, without returning to direct or indirect ancestor nodes. This strategy assures that the application conditions of a rule once it has been applied successfully remain unchanged throughout further processing. This procedure is carried out in two cycles. In the first one, the *Rule-Cutting* rule and then the *Compactification* rule are applied to each node; in the second cycle, the *Restructuring* rule is applied.

For communicating the RST tree in natural language, propositions associated with the nodes are handed over to the surface generator, by starting from the root node down to all reachable leaf nodes. Due to the alternative routes available via short-cuts, a number of nodes and even some leaf nodes may be left out in this path construction process. In our application, alternatives among the available relations are chosen according to the following preferences: (1) hypotheses and lemmas are expressed at the earliest opportunity, (2) the number of REASON relations to be verbalized is minimized (by following short-cuts whenever possible), and (3) compact notations forms, such as chains of inequations, are applied wherever possible (criterion (3) may overrule the other two criteria).

An Example from Proof Presentation

In order to illustrate the combined functionality of our presentation rules, we demonstrate the proof of theorem 1.11:

<u>Theorem 1.11</u> (Lüneburg 1981): Let K be an ordered field. If $a \in K$, then $1 < a$ implies $0 < a^{-1} < 1$, and vice-versa.

<u>Lemma 1.10</u> (Lüneburg 1981): Let K be an ordered field. If $a \neq 0 \in K$, then $0 < a$ implies $0 < a^{-1}$, and vice-versa.

<u>Proof</u> (for $1 < a \Rightarrow 0 < a^{-1} < 1$): Let $1 < a$. According to Lemma 1.10 we then have $a^{-1} > 0$. Therefore $a^{-1} = 1a^{-1} < aa^{-1} = 1$.

Proof presentation is invoked with the RST tree shown in Figure 7 which originates from a proof graph on the assertion level (Huang 1994) that is obtained by transforming the result produced by the theorem prover OTTER (McCune 1994). Individual nodes are labeled by numbers to ease references in the text. The audience is assumed to know basic axioms for ordered fields, such as unit and inverse elements, and other axioms such as transitivity, monotony, etc. Awareness about these axioms is assumed, too. In this environment, revisions are invoked as follows:

First, the *Rule-Cutting* rule is applied to the subtree rooted in node *27*, adding a REASON node *27'* as satellite

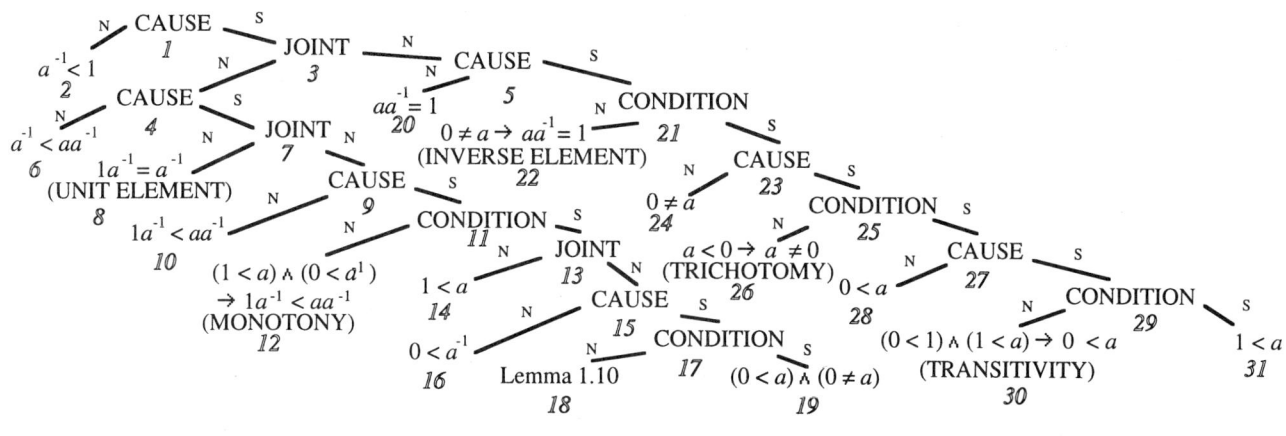

Figure 7: Initial RST tree for the proof of theorem 1.11 in (Lüneburg 1981)

of node *25*, with node *28* as nucleus and node *31* as satellite. Then the *Compactification* rule is applied, which introduces a direct connection from node *25* to node *31*, so that the new REASON node *27'* is not needed for the final presentation. This operation sequence is identically repeated with the nodes *23*, *23'*, *21*, *24*, and *31*, correspondingly. Moreover, the *Rule-Cutting* rule is applied to the subtree rooted in node *5*, adding a REASON node *5'* with node *20* as nucleus and node *31* as satellite. Unlike in previous cases, the *Compactification* rule is not applicable to the resulting subtree, because the predicate SIMILAR fails for $aa^{-1} = 1$ and $1 < a$. Altogether, the right branch of the JOINT relation (node *3*) can be fully expressed by the short-cut via the REASON relation in node *5'* (see Figure 8, left side; newly created relations are printed in italics, and links as dashed lines with arrows). In the left branch of the RST tree, coreference is exploited for the satellite of the CONDITION of lemma 1.10 by adding a link from node *17* to a copy of node *31*, node *31'* as its satellite. From there, the *Rule-Cutting* rule is applied to the subtree rooted in node *9*, yielding a REASON node *9'*, making node *10* its nucleus and *13* its satellite (see the left side of Figure 8).

Applications of the *Restructuring* rule concern the nodes *14*, *31*, *31'*, and *17*, that is, the assumption $1 < a$ (three times), and the proposition $0 < a^{-1}$, together with its extension, Lemma 1.10. $1 < a$ is lifted to the top of the RST tree because it is referred to from several relations, even from both main branches of the RST tree. $0 < a^{-1}$ is also lifted near the top of that tree because it expands a node that is presented in the special form within a series of inequations, together with the other nodes below node *4*. The right part of Figure 8 shows the relevant parts of the final result. A most concise text expressing it is:

Let $1 < a$. $0 < a^{-1}$ follows from $1 < a$ and Lemma 1.10. Therefore $a^{-1} = 1a^{-1} < aa^{-1} = 1$ holds.

which pretty much resembles the book proof, and is much better than the verbalization *without* presentation rules:

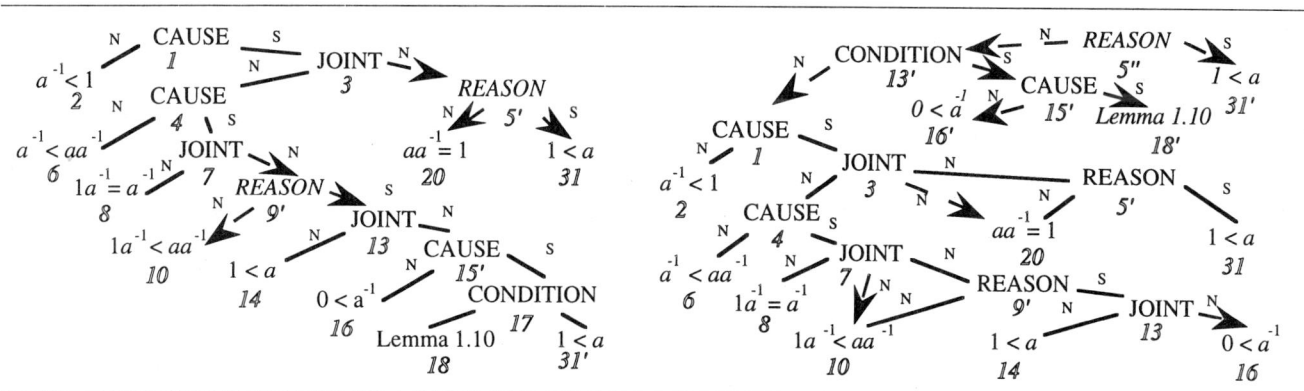

Figure 8: Fragments of the revised RST tree – parts of an intermediate state (left side) and parts of the final state (right side)

Proof (PROVERB): Let $1 < a$. Then $0 < a$, because '<' is transitive and $0 < 1$. $0 \neq a$ follows from the trichotomy of '<'. Lemma 1.10 implies $0 < a^{-1}$. Since '<' is monotone and $1 < a$, $1 a^{-1} < a a^{-1}$. $a^{-1} < a a^{-1}$ because of the definition of the unit element of K. $a a^{-1} = 1$ because of the definition of the inverse element of K for $a \neq 0$. Hence $a^{-1} < 1$.

Conclusion

In this paper, we have presented an approach to generate natural and concise argumentations from semantically fine-grained representations typically available in formal systems. We achieve this result by revising RST trees, through compactifying state-action and reasoning sequences, omitting redundant conditions, and reorganizing arguments for purposes of presentation. In comparison to previous approaches, we can deal with significantly more structural differences between an underlying knowledge representation and RST trees representing text structures – these differences lead to the introduction of new relations, additions of links, and regrouping of subtrees. We have motivated our approach by texts from everyday discourse.

We have elaborated the application conditions of these operations for the domain of mathematical proofs and integrated them into a dedicated presentation system. Since the associated modeling is and must be domain-specific to a certain degree, we have also made clear which parts in the formalization need to be adapted. Our method constitutes an important step in making the results obtained by reasoning systems better accessible to its users. In addition to the quality improvements in generating inference-rich discourse in general, our method enhances also the contribution of RST for generating these kinds of texts.

References

Fehrer, D.; and Horacek, H. 1997a. Exploiting the Addressee's Inferential Capabilities in Presenting Mathematical Proofs. In Proceedings of the Fifteenth International Joint Conference on Artificial Intelligence, 556-560. Menlo Park, Calif.: International Joint Conferences on Artificial Intelligence, Inc.

Fehrer, D.; and Horacek, H. 1997b. Presenting Inequations in Mathematical Proofs. In Proceedings of JCIS'97, Special Section on Logical Methods for Computational Intelligence, North Carolina.

Green, N.; and Carberry, S. 1994. A Hybrid Reasoning Model for Indirect Answers. In Proceedings of ACL-94, Las Cruces, New Mexico.

Horacek, H. 1997. A Model for Adapting Explanations to the User's Likely Inferences. *User Modeling and User Adapted Interaction* 7:1-55.

Huang, X. 1994. Reconstructing Proofs at the Assertional Level. In Proceedings of the 12th International Conference on Automated Deduction, 738-752, Springer-Verlag.

Huang, X.; and Fiedler, A. 1997. Proof Verbalization as an Application of NLG. In Proceedings of the 15th International Joint Conference on Artificial Intelligence, 965-971, Menlo Park, Calif.: International Joint Conferences on Artificial Intelligence, Inc.

Lüneburg, H. 1981. *Vorlesungen über Analysis*. BI Wissenschaftsverlag.

Maier, E. 1995. Textual Relations as Parts of Multiple Links Between Text Segments. In Trends in Natural Language Generation – An Artificial Intelligence Perspective, 68-87, Springer-Verlag.

Mann, W.; and Moore, J. 1981. Computer Generation of Multiparagraph English Text. *Computational Linguistics* 7(1):17-29.

Mann, W.; and Thompson, S. 1983. Rhetorical Structure Theory: A Theory of Text Organization. Technical Report, ISI/RR-83-115, ISI at University of Southern California.

Mann, W.; and Thompson, S. 1985. Assertions from Discourse Structure. Technical Report, ISI/RR-85-155, ISI at University of Southern California.

Mann, W.; and Thompson, S. 1987a. Rhetorical Propositions in Discourse. The Structure of Discourse. Polanyi L. ed., Norwood, Ablex.

Mann, W.; and Thompson, S. 1987b. Antithesis: A Study in Clause Combining and Discourse Structure. Technical Report, ISI/RR-87-171, ISI at University of Southern California.

Matthiessen, C.; and Thompson, S. 1987. The Structure of Discourse and Subordination. Technical Report, ISI/RR-87-183, ISI at University of Southern California.

McCune, W. 1994. Otter 3.0 Reference Manual and Guide, Technical Report, ANL-94/6, Argonne National Lab.

McDonald, D. 1992. Type-Driven Suppression of Redundancy in the Generation of Inference-Rich Reports. In Aspects of Automated Natural Language Generation, 72-88, Springer-Verlag.

Mellish, C.; and Evans, R. 1989. Natural Language Generation from Plans. *Computational Linguistics* 15(4):233-249.

Moore, J., and Pollack, M. 1992. A Problem for RST. The Need for Multi-Level Discourse Analysis. *Computational Linguistics* 18(4):537-544.

Stede, M. 1993. Lexical Choice Criteria in Language Generation. In Proceedings of the 6th Conference of the European Chapter of the Association for Computational Linguistics, 454–459.

Thüring, M., and Wender, K. 1985. Über kausale Inferenzen beim Lesen. *Sprache und Kognition* 2:76-86.

Walker, M. 1996. The Effect of Resource Limits and Task Complexity on Collaborative Planning in Dialogue. *Artificial Intelligence* 85:181-243.

Zukerman, I.; and McConachy, R. 1993. Generating Concise Discourse that Addresses a User's Inferences. In Proceedings of the 13th International Joint Conference on Artificial Intelligence, 1202-1207, Menlo Park, Calif.: International Joint Conferences on Artificial Intelligence, Inc.

Machine Learning of Generic and User-Focused Summarization

Inderjeet Mani and Eric Bloedorn
The MITRE Corporation,
11493 Sunset Hills Road, W640, Reston, VA 22090, USA
{imani,bloedorn}@mitre.org

Abstract

A key problem in text summarization is finding a salience function which determines what information in the source should be included in the summary. This paper describes the use of machine learning on a training corpus of documents and their abstracts to discover salience functions which describe what combination of features is optimal for a given summarization task. The method addresses both "generic" and user-focused summaries.

Introduction[1]

With the mushrooming of the quantity of on-line text information, triggered in part by the growth of the World Wide Web, it is especially useful to have tools which can help users digest information content. Text summarization attempts to address this need by taking a partially-structured source text, extracting information content from it, and presenting the most important content to the user in a manner sensitive to the user's or application's needs. The end result is a condensed version of the original. A key problem in summarization is determining what information in the source should be included in the summary. This determination of the salience of information in the source (i.e., a salience function for the text) depends on a number of interacting factors, including the nature and genre of the source text, the desired compression (summary length as a percentage of source length), and the application's information needs. These information needs include the reader's interests and expertise (suggesting a distinction between "user-focused" versus "generic" summaries), and the use to which the summary is being put, for example, whether it is intended to alert the user as to the source content (the "indicative" function), or to stand in place of the source (the "informative" function), or even to offer a critique of the source (the "evaluative" function (Sparck-Jones 1997)).

A considerable body of research over the last forty years has explored different levels of analysis of text to help determine what information in the text is salient for a given summarization task. The salience functions are usually sentence filters, i.e. methods for scoring sentences in the source text based on the contribution of different features. These features have included, for example, location (Edmundson 1969), (Paice and Jones 1993), statistical measures of term prominence (Luhn 1958), (Brandow, Mitze, and Rau 1995), rhetorical structure (Miike et al. 1994), (Marcu 1997a), similarity between sentences (Skorokhodko 1972), presence or absence of certain syntactic features (Pollock and Zamora 1975), presence of proper names (Kupiec, Pedersen, and Chen 1995), and measures of prominence of certain semantic concepts and relationships (Paice and Jones 1993), (Maybury 95), (Fum, Guida, and Tasso 85). In general, it appears that a number of features drawn from different levels of analysis may combine together to contribute to salience. Further, the importance of a particular feature can of course vary with the genre of text.

Consider, for example, the feature of text location. In newswire texts, the most common narrative style involves lead-in text which offers a summary of the main news item. As a result, for most varieties of newswire, summarization methods which use leading text alone tend to outperform other methods (Brandow, Mitze, and Rau 1995). However, even within these varieties of newswire, more anecdotal lead-ins, or multi-topic articles, do not fare well with a leading text approach (Brandow, Mitze, and Rau 1995). In other genres, other locations are salient: for scientific and technical articles, both introduction and conclusion sections might contain pre-summarized material; in TV news broadcasts, one finds segments which contain trailing information summarizing a forthcoming segment. Obviously, if we wish to develop a summarization system that could adapt to different genres, it is important to have an automatic way of finding out what location values are useful for that genre, and how it should be combined with other features. Instead of selecting and combining these features in an adhoc manner,

---

[1] Copyright ©1998, American Association for Artificial Intelligence (www.aaai.org). All rights reserved.

which would require re-adjustment for each new genre of text, a natural suggestion would be to use machine learning on a training corpus of documents and their abstracts to discover salience functions which describe what combination of features is optimal for a given summarization task. This is the basis for the trainable approach to summarization.

Now, if the training corpus contains "generic" abstracts (i.e., abstracts written by their authors or by professional abstractors with the goal of dissemination to a particular - usually broad - readership community), the salience function discovered would be one which describes a feature combination for generic summaries. Likewise, if the training corpus contains "user-focused" abstracts, i.e., abstracts relating information in the document to a particular user interest, which could change over time, then then we learn a function for user-focused summaries. While "generic" abstracts have traditionally served as surrogates for full-text, as our computing environments continue to accommodate increased full-text searching, browsing, and personalized information filtering, user-focused abstracts have assumed increased importance. Thus, algorithms which can learn both kinds of summaries are highly relevant to current information needs. Of course, it would be of interest to find out what sort of overlap exists between the features learnt in the two cases.

In this paper we describe a machine learning approach which learns both generic summaries and user-focused ones. Our focus is on machine learning aspects, in particular, performance-level comparison between different learning methods, stability of the learning under different compression rates, and relationships between rules learnt in the generic and the user-focused case.

Overall Approach

In our approach, a summary is treated as a representation of the user's information need, in other words, as a query. The training procedure assumes we are provided with training data consisting of a collection of texts and their abstracts. The training procedure first assigns each source sentence a relevance score indicating how relevant it is to the query. In the basic "boolean-labeling" form of this procedure, all source sentences above a particular relevance threshold are treated as "summary" sentences. The source sentences are represented in terms of their feature descriptions, with "summary" sentences being labeled as positive examples. The training sentences (positive and negative examples) are fed to machine learning algorithms, which construct a rule or function which labels any new sentence's feature vector as a summary vector or not. In the generic summary case, the training abstracts are generic: in our corpus they are author-written abstracts of the articles. In the user-focused case, the training abstract for each document is generated automatically from a specification of a user information need.

It is worth distinguishing this approach from other previous work in trainable summarization, in particular, that of (Kupiec, Pedersen, and Chen 1995) at Xerox-Parc (referred to henceforth as Parc), an approach which has since been followed by (Teufel and Moens 97). First, our goal is to learn rules which can be easily edited by humans. Second, our approach is aimed at both generic summaries as well as user-focused summaries, thereby extending the generic summary orientation of the Parc work. Third, by treating the abstract as a query, we match the entire abstract to each sentence in the source, instead of matching individual sentences in the abstract to one or more sentences in the source. This tactic seems sensible, since the distribution of the ideas in the abstract across sentences of the abstract is not of intrinsic interest. Further, it completely avoids the rather tricky problem of sentence alignment (including consideration of cases where more than one sentence in the source may match a sentence in the abstract), which the Parc approach has to deal with. Also, we do not make strong assumptions of independence of features, which the Parc based work which uses Bayes' Rule does assume. Other trainable approaches include (Lin and Hovy 1997); in that approach, what is learnt from training is a series of sentence positions. In our case, we learn rules defined over a variety of features, allowing for a more abstract characterization of summarization. Finally, the learning process does not require any manual tagging of text; for "generic" summaries it requires that "generic" abstracts be available, and for user-focused abstracts, we require only that the user select documents that match her interests.

Features

The set of features studied here are encoded as in Table 1, where they are grouped into three classes. *Location* features exploit the structure of the text at different (shallow) levels of analysis. Consider the *Thematic* features[2]. The feature based on proper names is extracted using SRA's NameTag (Krupka 1995), a MUC6-fielded system. We also use a feature based on the standard tf.idf metric : the weight $dw(i,k,l)$ of term k in document i given corpus l is given by:

$$dw(i,k,l) = tf_{ik}.(\ln(n) - \ln(df_k) + 1)$$

where tf_{ik} = frequency of term k in document i divided by the maximum frequency of any term in document i, df_k = number of documents in l in which term k occurs, n = total number of documents in l. While

---

[2]Filter 1 sorts all the sentences in the document by the feature in question. It assigns 1 to the current sentence iff it belongs in top c of the scored sentences, where c = compression rate. As it turns out, removing this discretization filter completely, to use raw scores for each feature, merely increases the complexity of learnt rules without improving performance

Location Features		
Feature	Values	Description
sent-loc-para	{1, 2, 3}	sentence occurs in first, middle or last third of para
para-loc-section	{1, 2, 3}	sentence occurs in first, middle or last third of section
sent-special-section	{1, 2, 3}	1 if sentence occurs in introduction, 2 if in conclusion, 3 if in other
depth-sent-section	{1, 2, 3, 4}	1 if sentence is a top-level section, 4 if sentence is a subsubsubsection
Thematic Features		
sent-in-highest-tf	{1, 0}	average tf score (Filter 1)
sent-in-highest-tf.idf	{1, 0}	average tf.idf score (Filter 1)
sent-in-highest-G^2	{1, 0}	average G^2 score (Filter 1)
sent-in-highest-title	{1, 0}	number of section heading or title term mentions (and Filter 1)
sent-in-highest-pname	{1, 0}	number of name mentions (Filter 1)
Cohesion Features		
sent-in-highest-syn	{1, 0}	number of unique sentences with a synonym link to sentence (Filter 1)
sent-in-highest-co-occ	{1, 0}	number of unique sentences with a co-occurrence link to sentence (Filter 1)

Table 1: Text Features

the tf.idf metric is standard, there are some statistics that are perhaps better suited for small data sets (Dunning 1993). The G^2 statistic indicates the likelihood that the frequency of a term in a document is greater than what would be expected from its frequency in the corpus, given the relative sizes of the document and the corpus. The version we use here (based on (Cohen 1995)) uses the raw frequency of a term in a document, its frequency in the corpus, the number of terms in the document, and the sum of all term counts in the corpus.

We now turn to features based on *Cohesion*. Text cohesion (Halliday and Hasan 1996) involves relations between words or referring expressions, which determine how tightly connected the text is. Cohesion is brought about by linguistic devices such as repetition, synonymy, anaphora, and ellipsis. Models of text cohesion have been explored in application to information retrieval (Salton et al., 1994), where paragraphs which are similar above some threshold to many other paragraphs, i.e., "bushy" nodes, are considered likely to be salient. Text cohesion has also been applied to the explication of discourse structure (Morris and Hirst 1991), (Hearst 97), and has been the focus of renewed interest in text summarization (Boguraev and Kennedy 1997), (Mani and Bloedorn 1997),(Barzilay and Elhadad 1997). In our work, we use two cohesion-based features: synonymy, and co-occurrence based on bigram statistics. To compute synonyms the algorithm uses WordNet (Miller 1995), comparing contentful nouns (their contentfulness determined by a "function-word" stoplist) as to whether they have a synset in common (nouns are extracted by the Alembic part-of-speech tagger (Aberdeen et al. 1995)). Co-occurrence scores between contentful words up to 40 words apart are computed using a standard mutual information metric (Fano 1961), (Church and Hanks 1989): the mutual information between terms j and k in document i is:

$$mutinfo(j,k,i) = \ln(\frac{n_i tf_{ji,ki}}{tf_{ji} tf_{ki}})$$

where $tf_{ji,ki}$ = maximum frequency of bigram jk in document i, tf_{ji} = frequency of term j in document i, n_i = total number of terms in document i. The document in question is the entire cmp-lg corpus. The co-occurrence table only stores scores for tf counts greater than 10 and mutinfo scores greater than 10.

Training Data

We use a training corpus of computational linguistics texts. These are 198 full-text articles and (for the generic summarizer) their author-supplied abstracts, all from the Computation and Language E-Print Archive (cmp-lg), provided in SGML form by the University of Edinburgh. The articles are between 4 and 10 pages in length and have figures, captions, references, and cross-references replaced by place-holders. The average compression rate for abstracts in this corpus is 5%.

Once the sentences in each text (extracted using a sentence tagger (Aberdeen et al. 1995)) are coded as feature vectors, they are labeled with respect to relevance to the text's abstract. The labeling function uses the following similarity metric:

$$N1 + \frac{\sum_{i=1}^{N2} i_{s1} \cdot i_{s2}}{\sqrt{\sum_{i=1}^{N2} i_{s1}^2 \cdot \sum_{i=1}^{N2} i_{s2}^2}}$$

where i_{s1} is the tf.idf weight of word i in sentence s1, N1 is the number of words in common between s1 and s2, and N2 is the total number of words in s1 and s2.

In labeling, the top $c\%$ (where c is the compression rate) of the relevance-ranked sentences for a document are then picked as positive examples for that document. This resulted in 27,803 training vectors, with considerably redundancy among them, which when removed yielded 900 unique vectors (since the learning implementations we used ignore duplicate vectors), of which 182 were positive and the others negative. The 182 positive vectors along with a random subset of

Metric	Definition
Predictive Accuracy	Number of testing examples classified correctly / total number of test examples.
Precision	Number of positive examples classified correctly / number of examples classified positive, during testing
Recall	Number of positive examples classified correctly / Number known positive, during testing
(Balanced) F-score	$2(Precision \cdot Recall)/(Precision + Recall)$

Table 2: Metrics used to measure learning performance

214 negative were collected together to form balanced training data of 396 examples. The labeled vectors are then input to the learning methods.

Some preliminary data analysis on the "generic" training data indicates that except for the two cohesion features, there is a significant difference between the summary and non-summary counts for some feature value of each feature (χ^2 test, $\rho < 0.001$). This suggests that this is a reasonable set of features for the problem, even though different learning methods may disagree on importance of individual features.

Generating user-focused training abstracts

The overall information need for a user is defined by a set of documents. Here a subject was told to pick a sample of 10 documents from the cmp-lg corpus which matched his interests. The top content words were extracted from each document, scored by the G^2 score (with the cmp-lg corpus as the background corpus). Then, a centroid vector for the 10 user-interest documents was generated as follows. Words for all the 10 documents were sorted by their scores (scores were averaged for words occurring in multiple documents). All words more than 2.5 standard deviations above the mean of these words' scores were treated as a representation of the user's interest, or topic (there were 72 such words). Next, the topic was used in a spreading activation algorithm based on (Mani and Bloedorn 1997) to discover, in each document in the cmp-lg corpus, words related to the topic.

Once the words in each of the corpus documents have been reweighted by spreading activation, each sentence is weighted based on the average of its word weights. The top $c\%$ (where c is the compression rate) of these sentences are then picked as positive examples for each document, together constituting a user-focused abstract (or extract) for that document. Further, to allow for user-focused features to be learnt, each sentence's vector is extended with two additional user-interest-specific features: the number of reweighted words (called *keywords*) in the sentence as well as the number of keywords per contentful word in the sentence[3]. Note that the *keywords*, while including terms in the user-focused abstract, include many other related terms as well.

Learning Methods

We use three different learning algorithms: Standardized Canonical Discriminant Function (SCDF) analysis (SPSS 97), C4.5-Rules (Quinlan 1992), and AQ15c (Wnek et al. 1995). SCDF is a multiple regression technique which creates a linear function that maximally discriminates between summary and non-summary examples. While this method, unlike the other two, doesn't have the advantage of generating logical rules that can easily be edited by a user, it offers a relatively simple method of telling us to what extent the data is linearly separable.

Results

The metrics for the learning algorithms used are shown in Table 2. In Table 3, we show results averaged over ten runs of 90% training and 10% test, where the test data across runs is disjoint[4].

Interestingly, in the C4.5 learning of generic summaries on this corpus, the thematic and cohesion features are referenced mostly in rules for the negative class, while the location and tf features are referenced mostly in rules for the positive class. In the user-focused summary learning, the number of *keywords* in the sentence is the single feature responsible for the dramatic improvement in learning performance compared to generic summary learning; here the rules have this feature alone or in combination with tests on locational features. User-focused interests tend to use a subset of the locational features found in generic interests, along with user-specific keyword features.

Now, SCDF does almost as well as C4.5 Rules for the user-focused case. This is because the *keywords* feature is most influential in rules learnt by either algorithm. However, not all the positive user-focused examples which have significant values for the *keywords* feature are linearly separable from the negative ones; in cases where they aren't, the other algorithms yield useful rules which include *keywords* along with other features. In the generic case, the positive examples are linearly separable to a much lesser extent.

Overall, although our figures are higher the 42% reported by Parc, their performance metric is based on

---

[3] We don't use specific keywords as features, as we would prefer to learn rules which could transfer across interests.

[4] SCDF uses a holdout of 1 document.

Method	Predictive Accuracy	Precision	Recall	F-score
SCDF (Generic)	.64	.66	.58	.62
SCDF (User-Focused)	.88	.88	.89	.88
AQ (Generic)	.56	.49	.56	.52
AQ (User-Focused)	.81	.78	.88	.82
C4.5 Rules (Generic, pruned)	.69	.71	.67	.69
C4.5 Rules (User-Focused, pruned)	.89	.88	.91	.89

Table 3: Accuracy of learning algorithms (at 20% compression)

overlap between positively labeled sentences and individual sentences in the abstract, whereas ours is based on overlap with the abstract as a whole, making it difficult to compare. It is worth noting that the most effective features in our generic learning are a subset of the Parc features, with the cohesion features contributing little to overall performance. However, note that unlike the Parc work, we do not avail of "indicator" phrases, which are known to be genre-dependent. In recent work using a similar overlap metric, (Teufel and Moens 97) reports that the indicator phrase feature is the single most important feature for accurate learning performance in a sentence extraction task using this corpus; it is striking that we get good learning performance without exploiting this feature.

Analysis of C4.5-Rules learning curves generated at 20% compression reveal some learning improvement in the generic case - (.65-.69) Predictive Accuracy, and (.64-.69) F-Score, whereas the user-focused case reaches a plateau very early - (.88-.89) Predictive Accuracy and F-Score. This again may be attributed to the relative dominance of the *keyword* feature. We also found surprisingly little change in learning performance as we move from 5% to 30% compression. These latter results suggests that this approach maintains high performance over a certain spectrum of summary sizes. Inspection of the rules shows that the learning system is learning similar rather than different rules across compression rates.

Some example rules are as follows:

```
If the sentence is in the conclusion
and it is a high tf.idf sentence,
then it is a summary sentence.
(C4.5 Generic Rule 20, run 1, 20% compression.)

If the sentence is in a section of depth 2
and the number of keywords is between 5 and 7
and the keyword to content-word ratio is
between 0.43 and 0.58 (inclusive),
then it is a summary sentence.
(AQ User-Focused Rule 7, run 4, 5% compression.)
```

As can be seen, the learnt rules are highly intelligible, and thus are easily edited by humans if desired, in contrast with approaches (such as SCDF or naive Bayes) which learn a mathematical function. In practice, this becomes useful because a human may use the learning methods to generate an initial set of rules, whose performance may then be evaluated on the data as well as against intuition, leading to improved performance.

Conclusion

We have described a corpus-based machine learning approach to produce generic and user-specific summaries. This approach shows encouraging learning performance. The rules learnt for user-focused interests tend to use a subset of the locational features found in rules for generic interests, along with user-specific keyword features. The rules are intelligible, making them suitable for human use. The approach is widely applicable, as it does not require manual tagging or sentence-level text alignment. In the future, we expect to also investigate the use of regression techniques based on a continuous rather than boolean labeling function. Of course, since learning the labeling function doesn't tell us anything about how useful the summaries themselves are, we plan to carry out a (task-based) evaluation of the summaries. Finally, we intend to apply this approach to other genres of text, as well as languages such as Thai and Chinese.

Acknowledgments

We are indebted to Simone Teufel, Marc Moens and Byron Georgantopoulos (University of Edinburgh) for providing us with the cmp-lg corpus, and to Barbara Gates (MITRE) for helping with the co-occurrence data.

References

Aberdeen, J., Burger, J., Day, D., Hirschman, L., Robinson, P., and Vilain, M. MITRE: Description of the Alembic System Used for MUC-6. In *Proceedings of the Sixth Message Understanding Conference (MUC-6)*, Columbia, Maryland, November 1995.

Barzilay, R., and Elhadad, M. "Using Lexical Chains for Text Summarization", in Mani, I., and Maybury, M., eds., Proceedings of the ACL/EACL'97 Workshop on Intelligent Scalable Text Summarization, Madrid, Spain, pp. 10-17, 1997.

Boguraev, B., and Kennedy, C. "Salience-based Content Characterization of Text Documents", in Mani, I., and Maybury, M., eds., Proceedings of the ACL/EACL'97 Workshop on Intelligent Scalable Text Summarization, Madrid, Spain, pp. 2-9, 1997.

Brandow, R., Mitze, K., and Rau, L. "Automatic condensation of electronic publications by sentence selection." Information Processing and Management, 31, 5, 675-685, 1994.

Computation and Language E-Print Archive, http://xxx.lanl.gov/cmp-lg/.

Kenneth Church and Patrick Hanks. Word Association Norms, Mutual Information, and Lexicography. In *Proceedings of ACL-89*, Vancouver, British Columbia, June, 1989.

Cohen, J.D., "Hilights: Language- and Domain-Independent Automatic Indexing Terms for Abstracting", Journal of the American Society for Information Science, 46, 3, 162-174, 1995. See also vol. 47, 3, 260 for a very important erratum.

Dunning, T., "Accurate Methods for the Statistics of Surprise and Coincidence", Computational Linguistics, 19, 1, 1993.

Edmundson, H.P., "New methods in automatic abstracting", Journal of the Association for Computing Machinery, 16, 2, pp. 264-285, 1969.

Fano, R., "Transmission of Information", MIT Press, 1961.

Fum, D., Guida, G., and Tasso, C. "Evaluating importance: A step towards text summarization", Proceedings of IJCAI 85, pp.840-844.

Halliday, M. and Hasan, R. "Cohesion in Text", London, Longmans, 1996.

Hearst, M., "TextTiling: Segmenting Text into Multi-Paragraph Subtopic passages", Computational Linguistics, 23, 1, 33-64, 1997.

George Krupka. SRA: Description of the SRA System as Used for MUC-6. In *Proceedings of the Sixth Message Understanding Conference (MUC-6)*, Columbia, Maryland, November 1995.

Julian Kupiec, Jan Pedersen, and Francine Chen. A Trainable Document Summarizer. In *Proceedings of ACM-SIGIR'95*, Seattle, WA.

Lin, C.Y., and Hovy, E.H. "Identifying Topics by Position", Proceedings of the Applied Natural Language Processing Conference, 1997.

Luhn, H.P. "The automatic creation of literature abstracts", IBM Journal of Research and Development, 2, 159-165, 1959.

Mani, I., and Bloedorn, E. "Multi-document Summarization by Graph Search and Merging", Proceedings of the Fourteenth National Conference on Artificial Intelligence (AAAI-97), Providence, RI, pp. 622-628.

Marcu, D. "From discourse structures to text summaries", in Mani, I., and Maybury, M., eds., Proceedings of the ACL/EACL'97 Workshop on Intelligent Scalable Text Summarization, Madrid, Spain, pp. 82-88, 1997.

Maybury, M. "Generating Summaries from Event Data", Information Processing and Management, 31, 5, 735-751, 1995.

Miike, S., Itoh, E., Ono, K., and Sumita, K. "A Full-Text Retrieval System with a Dynamic Abstract Generation Function", Proceedings of ACM-SIGIR'94, Dublin, Ireland.

Miller, G. WordNet: A Lexical Database for English. In *Communications of the ACM*, 38, 11, 39-41, 1995.

Morris, J., and Hirst, G. "Lexical Cohesion Computed by Thesaural Relations as an Indicator of the Structure of Text", Computational Linguistics, 17, 1, pp. 21-43, 1991.

Paice, C. and Jones, P. "The Identification of Important Concepts in Highly Structured Technical Papers", Proceedings of ACM-SIGIR'93, Pittsburgh, PA.

Pollock, J., and Zamora, A. "Automatic Abstracting Research at Chemical Abstracts Service, Journal of Chemical Information and Computer Sciences, 15, 4, 1975.

Quinlan, J. "C4.5: Programs for Machine Learning", Morgan Kaufmann, San Mateo, CA, 1992.

Salton, G., Allan J., Buckley C., and Singhal A., "Automatic Analysis, Theme Generation, and Summarization of Machine-Readable Texts", Science, 264, June 1994, pp. 1421-1426.

Skorokhodko, E.F. "Adaptive method of automatic abstracting and indexing", IFIP Congress, Ljubljana, Yugoslavia 71, pp. 1179-1182,1972.

Sparck-Jones, K., "Summarizing: Where are we now? Where should we go?", in Mani, I., and Maybury, M., eds., Proceedings of the ACL/EACL'97 Workshop on Intelligent Scalable Text Summarization, Madrid, Spain, 1997.

SPSS Base 7.5 Applications Guide, SPSS Inc., Chicago, 1997.

Wnek, K., Bloedorn, E., and Michalski, R., "Selective Inductive Learning Method AQ15C: The Method and User's Guide.", Machine Learning and Inference Laboratory Report ML95-4, George Mason Unviersity, Fairfax, Virginia, 1995.

Teufel, S. and Moens, M, "Sentence extraction and Rhetorical Classification for Flexible Abstracts", in Working Notes of the AAAI Spring Symposium on Intelligent Text Summarization, Spring 1998, Technical Report, AAAI, 1998.

Hermes: Supporting Argumentative Discourse in Multi-Agent Decision Making

Nikos Karacapilidis
Department of Computer Science
Swiss Federal Institute of Technology
IN Ecublens, 1015 Lausanne, Switzerland
karacapi@di.epfl.ch

Dimitris Papadias
Department of Computer Science
Hong Kong Univ. of Science & Technology
Clearwater Bay, Hong Kong
dimitris@cs.ust.hk

Abstract

This paper describes HERMES, a system that enhances group decision making by providing an argumentation framework to the agents involved. The system organizes the existing knowledge in a discussion graph, which consists of *issues*, *alternatives*, *positions* and *preference relations*. Argumentation is performed through a set of *discourse acts* which trigger appropriate procedures for the propagation of information in the graph. HERMES is able to handle incomplete, qualitative and inconsistent information, and provides mechanisms for weighing arguments.

Introduction

Group Decision Support Systems (GDSSs) have been defined as interactive computer-based systems which facilitate the solution of ill-structured problems by a set of decision makers, working together as a team (Kreamer and King 1988). The main objective of a GDSS is to augment the effectiveness of decision groups through the interactive sharing of information between group members and the computer. This can be achieved by (i) removing communication impediments, and (ii) providing techniques for structuring the decision analysis and systematically directing the pattern, timing, or content of the discussion. Among the major issues arising during the development of such a system are the effective work organization in order to improve coordination, and the use of communication technology to make decision making more efficient. Provision of rules and procedures for achieving consistency and automation of data processing, especially in data intensive decision making situations, are also of high importance.

This paper presents HERMES, an advanced GDSS that addresses the above issues by supporting argumentative discourse among decision makers. It is implemented in Java applets and runs on the Web, thus

Copyright © 1998, American Association for Artificial Intelligence (www.aaai.org). All rights reserved.

provides relatively inexpensive access to a broad public. HERMES can be used for distributed, asynchronous or synchronous collaboration, allowing agents to surpass the requirements of being in the same place and working at the same time.

Numerous *web-based conferencing systems* have already been deployed, such as *AltaVista Forum Center, Open Meeting, NetForum,* and *UK Web's Focus,* to mention some. They usually provide means for discussion structuring and user administration tools, while the more sophisticated ones allow for sharing of documents, on-line calendars, embedded e-mail and chat tools, etc. Discussion is structured via a variety of links, such as simple *responses* or different *comment types* (e.g., *qualify, agree, example* in *Open Meeting*) to a previous message. However, the above systems merely provide threaded discussion forums, where messages are linked "passively", which usually leads to an unsorted collection of vaguely associated comments. As pointed out by the developers of *Open Meeting*, there is a lack of consensus seeking abilities and decision making methods (Hurwitz and Mallery 1995). On the contrary, HERMES focuses on aiding decision makers reach a decision, not only by efficiently structuring the discussion, but also by providing reasoning mechanisms for it. It is an *active* system, that constantly checks for inconsistencies and updates the discourse status.

Increasing interest also develops in implementing *argumentation support systems* for different types of groups and application areas. As opposed to the above category, such systems follow an argumentative perspective to address the needs of a user to *interpret* knowledge during a discourse. For instance, *gIBIS* (Conklin and Begeman 1987) is a workstation-based hypertext groupware tool that aims at capturing the rationale of design processes; *Euclid* (Smolensky et al. 1987) provides a graphical representation language for generic argumentation; *JANUS* (Fischer, McCall, and Morch 1989) is based on acts of critiquing existing knowledge in order to foster the understanding of design knowledge. Finally, *Belvedere* (Suthers et al. 1995) uses a rich graphical language to represent different logical and rhetorical relations within a debate. It was originally designed to support students engaged in critical discussion of science issues. Although this second category of systems provides a cognitive argumentation environment that stimulates discussion among participants, it also lacks decision making capabilities.

Argumentation and Decision Making

Most approaches to argumentative discourse follow two main methodologies, namely, formal and informal logic. According to the *formal perspective*, arguments are de-contextualized sets of sentences or symbols viewed in terms of their syntactic or semantic relationships. On the other hand, *informal logic* views arguments as pragmatic, i.e., their meaning is a function of their purposive context. Most AI researchers have focused on formal models of argumentation based on various logics. For instance, Brewka (Brewka 1994) reconstructed Rescher's theory of formal disputation (Rescher 1977), while Gordon's work (Gordon 1995), was based on Geffner and Pearl's concepts of conditional entailment (Geffner and Pearl 1992).

Argumentation elements

The argumentation framework of HERMES is a variant of the informal IBIS model of argumentation (Rittel and Webber 1973) and has its roots in the ZENO framework (Gordon and Karacapilidis 1997), (Karacapilidis et al. 1997). HERMES supports as argumentation elements *issues, alternatives, positions*, and *constraints* representing *preference relations*. Throughout this paper, we use a real example about the planning of cyclepaths in the city of Bonn. The agents involved in the discussion, namely the representatives from the Cyclists Union and the related City Hall department, bring up the necessary argumentation in order to express their interests and perspectives. Figure 1 illustrates an instance of the corresponding HERMES *discussion forum*. As shown, our approach maps a multi-agent decision making process to a discussion graph with a hierarchical structure.

Issues correspond to decisions to be made, or goals to be achieved (e.g., issue-188: "selection of a cyclepath for the city"). They are brought up by agents and are open to dispute. Issues consist of a set of *alternatives* that correspond to potential choices (e.g., alternative-190: "select the already planned cyclepath", and alternative-191: "Build a ring around the city center" belong to issue-188, and have been proposed by the City of Bonn and the Cyclists Union, respectively).

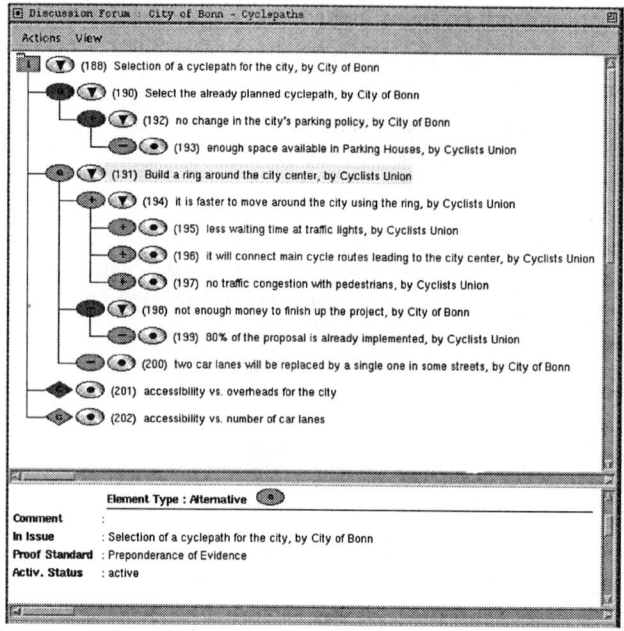

Figure 1: The system's basic user interface.

Issues can be inside other issues in cases where some alternatives need to be grouped together. For instance, assume that there were two potential ring plans, say "Build a ring around the city center, according to the x plan" and "Build a ring around the city center, according to the y plan". In this case, the last two alternatives should have been grouped in an internal issue (say, the *subissue* "select the most appropriate plan for a city ring") and, after the related discourse, the selected (best) one would have been compared to alternative-190. Only one alternative in each issue is finally proposed by the system.

Positions are asserted in order to support the selection of a specific course of action (alternative), or avert the agents' interest from it by expressing some objection. For instance, position-192 "no change in the city's parking policy" has been asserted to support alternative-190, while position-198 "not enough money to finish up the project" to express the City's objection to alternative-191. Positions may also refer to some other position in order to provide additional information about it, e.g., position-193 "enough space available in Parking Houses" (arguing *against* position-192), and position-195 "less waiting time at traffic lights" (arguing *in favor* of position-194). A position always *refers to* a single other position or alternative, while an alternative is always *in* a single issue.

In decision making environments, one has usually to define priorities among actions and weigh different criteria. Unfortunately, well defined utility and probability functions regarding properties or attributes of alternatives (used in traditional approaches), as well as complete ordering of these properties are usually absent.

In HERMES, *constraints* provide a qualitative way to weigh reasons for and against the selection of a certain course of action. A constraint is a tuple of the form [position, preference_relation, position], where the preference relation can be *more (less) important than* or *of equal importance to*. Constraints may give various levels of importance to alternatives. Like the other argumentation elements, they are subject to discussion; therefore, they may be "linked" with positions supporting or challenging them. In Figure 1, constraint-201: "accessibility vs. overheads for the city" expresses the preference relation "position-194 is more important than position-192", while constraint-202: "accessibility vs. number of car lanes" the relation "position-194 is more important than position-200".

Two types of preferences can be expressed by the system: (i) *Local*, when a constraint refers to a position, or another constraint. In this case, the positions compared through the constraint (called consistuent positions hereafter) must refer to the same element (i.e., have the same father). In the example shown in Figure 1, a preference of this type can be expressed by the constraint "position-195 is less important than position-197". A constraint of the form "position-195 is less important than position-194" is not permitted. (ii) *Non-local*, when a constraint refers to an issue. In this case, its consistuent positions must refer to alternatives (not necessarily the same one) of this very issue (e.g., constraint-201 and constraint-202).

Proof Standards

Alternatives, positions and constraints have an *activation label* indicating their current status (it can be *active* or *inactive*). This label is calculated according to the argumentation underneath and the *type of evidence* specified for them. In general, different elements of the argumentation, even in the same debate, do not necessarily need the same type of evidence. Quoting the well-used legal domain example, the arguments required to indict someone need not be as convincing as those needed to convict him (Farley and Freeman 1995). Therefore, a generic argumentation system requires different *proof standards* (work on AI and Law uses the term *burdens of proof*). In the sequel, we describe the ones implemented in our system (the names have the same interpretation as in the legal domain). We do not claim that the list is exhaustive; other standards, that match specific application needs, can be easily incorporated to the system.

Scintilla of Evidence (SoE): according to this proof standard, a position p_i is active, if at least one active position argues in favor of it: $active(p_i) \Leftrightarrow \exists p_j \, (active(p_j) \land in\_favor(p_j, p_i))$.

Beyond Reasonable Doubt (BRD): according to BRD, a position p_i is active if there are not any active positions that speak against it: $active(p_i) \Leftrightarrow \neg \exists p_j \, (active(p_j) \land against(p_j, p_i))$.

Activation in our system is a recursive procedure; a change of the activation label of an element (alternative, position or constraint) is propagated upwards. When an alternative is affected during the discussion, the issue it belongs to should be updated since a new choice may be made. This brings us to the last proof standard, namely *Preponderance of Evidence* (PoE), used for the selection of the best alternative (however, it can also be used for activation/inactivation of positions). In the case of PoE, each position has a $weight = (max\_weight + min\_weight)/2$, while an alternative has $weight = min\_weight$. Max_weight and min_weight are initialized to some pre-defined values (in the following, we assume that initially $min\_weight = 0$ and $max\_weight = 10$; this may be changed by preference constraints). The *score* of an element e_i is used to compute its *activation label* (score is calculated on-the-fly). If an element does not have any arguments, its score is equal to its weight; otherwise, the score is calculated from the weights of the active positions that refer to it:

$$score(e_i) = \sum_{\substack{in\_favor(p_j, e_i) \land \\ active(p_j)}} weight(p_j) - \sum_{\substack{against(p_k, e_i) \land \\ active(p_k)}} weight(p_k)$$

Preponderance of Evidence (PoE): According to this standard, a position is *active* when the active positions that support it outweigh those that speak against it: $active(p_i) \Leftrightarrow score(p_i) \geq 0$. Concerning alternatives, PoE will produce positive activation label for a_i when there are no alternatives with larger score in the same issue: $active(a_i) \Leftrightarrow \forall a_j \, in\_issue(a_i), (score(a_j) \leq score(a_i))$.

In the discussion instance of Figure 1, the proof standard is SoE for all positions and PoE for alternatives. Position-192 and position-198 are inactive (their accompanying icons are shown in dark grey color) since position-193 and position-199, respectively, are active and speak against them. On the contrary, position-194 is active (the accompanying icon appears in light grey color) since there is at least one active position that speaks in favor of it (actually, there are three such positions; even if two of them become inactive at a future instance of the discussion, position-194 will remain active). Active positions are considered "accepted" due to discussion underneath (e.g., strong supporting arguments, no counter-arguments), while inactive positions are (temporarily) "rejected".

Similarly, active alternatives correspond to "recommended" choices, i.e., choices that are the strongest among the alternatives in their issue. Note that alternative-190 is not actually supported or objected by any position (only the inactive position-192 is underneath), while alternative-191 is actually supported by position-194 and objected by position-200 (position-198 is inactive). The mechanisms for the calculation of activation labels of alternatives depend on the related constraints.

The activation label of constraints is decided by two factors: the discussion underneath (similarly to what happens with positions) and the activation label of their consistuent positions. In Figure 1, constraint-201 is currently inactive because position-192 is also inactive. According to the evolution of the discussion, the insertion of position-193 inactivated position-192, which in turn inactivated constraint-201. Both constraints have BRD as proof standard, therefore constraint-202 is active (no active positions speak against it). If in the sequel of the discussion, a new position inactivates position-193, this will result in a new activation of both position-192 and constraint-201 (assuming that nothing else related to them changes).

Consistency checking

Apart from an activation label, each constraint has a *consistency label* which can be *consistent* or *inconsistent*. Every time a constraint is inserted in the discussion graph, the system checks if both positions of the new constraint exist in another, previously inserted, constraint. If yes, the new constraint is considered either *redundant*, if it also has the same preference relation, or *conflicting*, otherwise. A redundant constraint is ignored, while a conflicting one is grouped together with the previously inserted constraint in an issue automatically created by the system, the rationale being to gather together conflicting constraints and stimulate further argumentation on them until only one becomes active.

If both positions of the new constraint do not exist in a previously inserted constraint, its consistency is checked against previous active and consistent constraints referring to the same element (or belonging to the same issue). This process is based on a polynomial ($O(N^3)$, where N the number of the associated positions) *path consistency* algorithm (Mackworth and Freuder 1985). Although path consistency, as most discourse acts described in the sequel, interacts with the database where the discussion graph is stored (*Oracle 7* is used), the algorithm is very efficient. Even for non-local preferences involving issues with numerous alternatives and positions linked to them, execution time is negligible compared to communication delay.

Active and consistent constraints participate in the weighting scheme (only constraint-202 in the example of Figure 1). In order to demonstrate how the algorithm for altering weights works, we use the example of Figure 2. There exist five positions and four constraints that relate them as illustrated in Figure 2a. The arrowed lines correspond to the *"more important than ($>$)"* relation (e.g., $p_1 > p_2$) and the dotted line to the *"equally important to ($=$)"* relation (e.g., $p_3 = p_4$). *Topological sort* is applied twice to compute the possible maximum and minimum weights for each position (Figure 2b). The *weight* is the average of the new *max_weight* and *min_weight*: $weight(p_1) = 6$, $weight(p_2) = 4.5$, $weight(p_3) = 5$, $weight(p_4) = 5$ and $weight(p_5) = 4$.

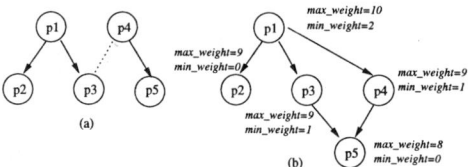

Figure 2: The weighting scheme.

The basic idea behind the above scheme is that the weight of a position is increased every time the position is more important than another one (and decreased when is less important), the aim being to extract a total order of alternatives. Since only partial information may be given, the choice of the initial maximum and minimum weights may affect the system's recommendation. Furthermore, this weighting scheme is not the only solution; alternative schemes, based on different algorithms, are under implementation.

The scores of alternative-190 and alternative-191 in Figure 1 are 0 and 1, respectively, since the former has no active positions "linked" to it, while for the latter, position-194 and position-200 have scores 5.5 and 4.5, respectively, and position-198 is inactive. Therefore, alternative-191 is active and recommended by the system. If position-192 were active, the scores of alternative-190 and alternative-191 would be 4.5 and 1, respectively. In this case, alternative-190 would be the recommended one.

Discourse Acts

Argumentation in our framework is performed through a variety of *discourse acts*. These acts may have different functions and roles in the argumentative discourse. We classify them in two major categories: *agent acts* and *internal (system) acts*. Agent acts concern user actions and correspond to functions directly supported by the user interface. Such functions include the opening of an issue, submission of an alternative, etc.

Figure 3: Adding a new alternative.

The applet window for adding a new alternative to an existing issue is shown in Figure 3. When an alternative alt_i is added to another alt_j (and not directly to the issue iss_j where alt_j belongs), a new issue iss_i is automatically created inside iss_j (a similar applet window is used in such a case). Both alt_i and alt_j are now put inside the new issue and compared through update(iss_i). Update(iss_j) will be called from update(iss_i) and the recommended choice between alt_i and alt_j will be compared against the other alternatives of the external (initial) issue. Note that in Figure 3, users can give a *subject* (title) of the new alternative, but also provide more details about their entry through the URL pane. In such a way they can "attach" to their elements pieces of text, images, etc.

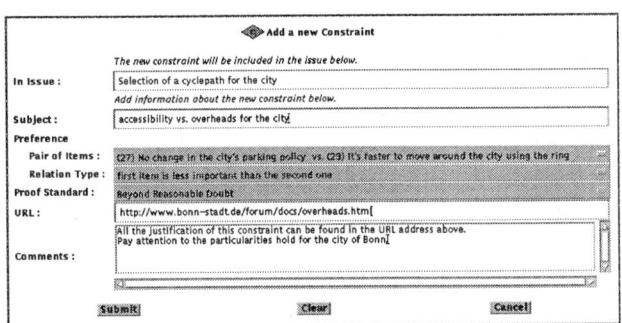

Figure 4: Adding a new constraint.

Figure 4 illustrates the applet window for adding a new constraint to an issue. Depending on the argumentation element selected for its insertion, the *pair of items* pane provides users a menu with all valid pairs, preventing users from making errors in expressing a preference. The *relation type* menu includes the preference relations *more (less) important than* and *equally important to*. The pseudo-code for adding a constraint to a position is as follows:

add_Constr._to_Posit.(*constraint con, position pos*) {
   if (redundant(*con*)) return; /* ignore */
   refersTo(*con*)=*pos*;
   for all *constraints* con_j that refer to *pos*
     if (conflicting(con_j, *con*))
     {   create new issue *iss*;
         In(*iss*)=con_j; In(*iss*)=*con*;
         update(*iss*); return; }
   if (contains_inactive(*con*)) ¬active(*con*);
   else { active(*con*);
      if (¬consistent_with_previous(*con*))
         ¬consistent(*con*);
      else { consistent(*con*); update(*pos*); }}}

Redundant and conflicting constraints were discussed earlier. Contains_inactive(*con*) checks whether one or both positions that *con* consists of are *inactive*, in which case *con* becomes *inactive*. The justification is that it does not make sense to argue about the relevant importance of positions that are rejected (*con* will be activated automatically when the compared positions get activated - see activate(*position pos*)). If *con* does not contain_inactive, then it is checked for consistency. Only if it is found consistent, the position that it refers to is updated, since inconsistent constraints do not participate in the weighting scheme.

Internal acts are functions performed by the system in order to check consistency, update the discussion status and recommend solutions. These functions are called by the agent acts and are hidden from the end user. For instance, consistent_with_previous(*con*), called by add_Constr._to_Posit., constructs a graph similar to Figure 2 and applies path consistency. Other representative internal acts are:

boolean compute_activation(*position pos*) {
boolean ¬ status_changed, old_activation=activation(*pos*);
switch Proof_Standard(*pos*) {
   case *Scintilla of Evidence* {
     ¬activation(*pos*);
     for all *positions* pos_j that refer to *pos*
       if (active(pos_j) ∧ in_favor(pos_j, *pos*))
         { activation(*pos*); break; }}
   case *Beyond Reasonable Doubt* {
     activation(*pos*);
     for all *positions* pos_j that refer to *pos*
       if (active(pos_j) ∧ against(pos_j, *pos*))
         { ¬activation(*pos*); break; }}
   case *Preponderance of Evidence* {
     score(*pos*)=0;
     calculate_weights(*pos*);
     for all *positions* pos_j that refer to *pos*
       if (active(pos_j) ∧ in_favor(pos_j, *pos*))
         score(*pos*) += weight(pos_j);
       else if (active(pos_j) ∧ against(pos_j, *pos*))
         score(*pos*) -= weight(pos_j);
     if (score(*pos*) ≥ 0) activation(*pos*);
      else ¬activation(*pos*) }}
if (old_activation != activation(*pos*)) status_changed;
return status_changed; }

Compute_activation returns *status_changed*, which is *true* if the activation label of the position changed. Activation is calculated according to the proof standard used. Proof standards are a straightforward implementation of the previously given definitions. In case of PoE, calculate_weights(pos) calls topological sort to compute the weights of the positions in favor and against pos.

```
update(position pos) {
if (compute_activation(pos)) {
    if (active(pos)) activate(pos);
        else inactivate(pos);
    update(RefersTo(pos)); }}    /*propagate upwards */
```

Update calls compute_activation to check whether activation label has changed. If this is the case, activate (see below) or inactivate are called and the change is propagated upwards.

```
activate(position pos) {
posⱼ=refersTo(pos);
for all constraints conⱼ that refer to posⱼ
    if (¬active(conⱼ) ∧ conⱼ has a prefer. relation on pos)
        if (compute_activation(conⱼ)) {
            if (consistent_with_previous(conⱼ))
                consistent(conⱼ);
            else ¬consistent(conⱼ); }}
```

Activation of a position pos involves the retrieval of the constraints where pos appears (these constraints must refer to the same position as pos) and a check as to whether they can now become *active* and *consistent*. Inactivation of positions is similar, in the sense that when a position becomes inactive, the system searches for the constraints where the position appears and inactivates them as well. This may cause some other inconsistent constraints to become consistent, so consistency check is performed again for the related constraints. A number of additional internal acts were implemented for the activation/inactivation of constraints, update of issues, etc. The procedures described in this section, although only a subset of the whole set of functions performed by the system, give an indication of its dynamic structure. A single insertion in the discussion graph may update a large portion of the tree. Every time there is a change, the status of the argumentation elements is recorded in the database.

Conclusion

In general, it is very difficult to completely automate the processes involved in argumentative discourse. Rather, HERMES acts as an *assistant* and *advisor*, by facilitating communication and recommending solutions, but leaving the final enforcement of decisions to the agents. The use of information technology may assist in various ways. One important goal is to provide easy access to the current knowledge, at any time. Another, and this is the primary goal of the project, is to provide direct computer support for argumentation in a decision making environment, where the quality and acceptability of decisions depends not only on the availability of accurate information, but also on the fairness and openness of the procedure.

References

Brewka, G. 1994. A Reconstruction of Rescher's Theory of Formal Disputation Based on Default Logic. In Working Notes of the AAAI'94 Workshop on Computational Dialectics, 15–27.

Conklin, J., and Begeman, M.L. 1987. gIBIS: A Hypertext Tool for Team Design Deliberation. In Proc. of Hypertext'89 Conference, 247–252. New York:ACM.

Farley, A.M., and Freeman, K. 1995. Burden of Proof in Legal Argumentation. In Proc. of the ICAIL'95 Conference, 156–164. New York:ACM Press.

Fischer, G., McCall, R., and Morch, A. 1989. JANUS: Integrating Hypertext with a Knowledge-based Design Environment. In Proc. of the Hypertext'89 Conference, 105–117. New York: ACM.

Geffner, H., and Pearl, J. 1992. Conditional Entailment: Bridging two Approaches to Default Reasoning. *Artificial Intelligence* 53(2-3):209–244.

Gordon, T. 1995. *The Pleadings Game: An Artificial Intelligence Model of Procedural Justice*. Kluwer.

Gordon, T., and Karacapilidis, N. 1997. The Zeno Argumentation Framework. In Proc. of the ICAIL'97 Conference, 10–18. New York: ACM Press.

Hurwitz, R., and Mallery, J.C. 1995. The Open Meeting: A Web-Based System for Conferencing and Collaboration. In Proc. of 4th Int. WWW Conference.

Karacapilidis, N., Papadias, D., Gordon, T., and Voss, H. 1997. Collaborative Environmental Planning with GeoMed. *European Journal of Operational Research* 102(2): 335–346.

Kreamer, K.L., and King, J.L. 1988. Computer-based systems for cooperative work and group decision making. *ACM Computing surveys* 20(2): 115–146.

Mackworth, A., and Freuder, E. 1985. The Complexity of some Polynomial Network Consistency Algorithms for Constraint Satisfaction Problems. *Artificial Intelligence* 25: 65–74.

Rescher, N. 1977. *Dialectics: A Controversy-Oriented Approach to the Theory of Knowledge*. Albany: State University of New York Press.

Rittel, H., and Webber, M. 1973. Dilemmas in a General Theory of Planning. *Policy Sciences* 155–169.

Smolensky, P., Fox, B., King, R., and Lewis, C. 1987. Computer-aided Reasoned Discourse, or How to Argue with a Computer. In Guindon, R. (ed.) *Cognitive Science and its Applications for Human-Computer Interaction*, 109–162. Hillsdale, NJ: Erlbaum.

Suthers, D., Weiner, A., Connelly, J., and Paolucci, M. 1995. Belvedere: Engaging Students in Critical Discussion of Science and Public Policy Issues. In Proc. of the 7th World Conf. on AI in Education, 266–273.

Acknowledgements: Nikos Karacapilidis is supported by the Commission of the European Communities through the ERCIM Fellowship Programme. Dimitris Papadias by the DAG96/97.EG36 grant from Hong Kong RGC.

Bayesian Reasoning in an Abductive Mechanism for Argument Generation and Analysis

Ingrid Zukerman, Richard McConachy and **Kevin B. Korb**
School of Computer Science and Software Engineering, Monash University
Clayton, Victoria 3168, AUSTRALIA
email: {ingrid,ricky,korb}@csse.monash.edu.au

Abstract

Our argumentation system, NAG, uses Bayesian networks in a user model and in a normative model to assemble and assess arguments which balance persuasiveness with normative correctness. Attentional focus is simulated in both models to select relevant subnetworks for Bayesian propagation. The subnetworks are expanded in an iterative abductive process until argumentative goals are achieved in both models, when the argument is presented to the user.

Introduction

In this paper, we describe the operation of our argument generation-analysis system, NAG (*Nice Argument Generator*). Given a goal proposition, NAG generates *nice* arguments, i.e., arguments that are normatively strong while also being persuasive for the target audience. NAG also analyzes users' arguments, and prepares rebuttals if appropriate. The focus of this paper is on the generation aspect of our work.

Figure 1 shows the main modules of NAG. The Strategist may receive as input a goal proposition or a user-generated argument. During argument generation, it activates a generation-analysis cycle as follows (§ *Generation-Analysis Cycle*). Firstly, it uses semantic activation to quickly form an initial *Argument Graph* for an argument, or to quickly extend an already existing Argument Graph. An Argument Graph is a network with nodes that represent propositions, and links that represent the inferences that connect these propositions. The Strategist then calls the Generator to continue the argument building process (§ *Extending the Argument Graph*). The Generator fleshes out the Argument Graph by activating *Reasoning Agents* to consult several sources of information, and incorporating the inferences and propositions returned by these agents into the Argument Graph. This Argument Graph is returned to the Strategist, which passes it to the Analyzer (§ *Argument Analysis*) to evaluate its niceness.

To estimate the persuasive power of an argument represented by an Argument Graph, the Analyzer consults a revisable user model that reflects the beliefs of the target audience; a normative model is used to gauge the normative strength of an argument. Belief updating in both the user and

Copyright ©1998, American Association for Artificial Intelligence (www.aaai.org). All rights reserved.

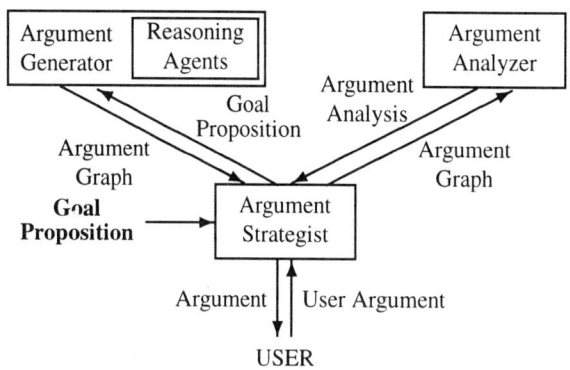

Figure 1: System Architecture

the normative model is done by a constrained Bayesian propagation scheme. If the Analyzer reports that the Argument Graph is nice enough, the Strategist presents an argument based upon this graph to the user (§ *Argument Presentation*). Otherwise, the Analyzer highlights the weaknesses to be fixed in the argument, and the Argument Graph is returned to the Strategist for another cycle of argument extension and analysis. This process is typically performed more than once before the argument is presented to the user. It iterates until a successful Argument Graph is built, or NAG is unable to continue, e.g., due to time running out or failing to find further evidence.

Knowledge Representation

When constructing an argument, NAG relies on a normative model composed of different types of *Knowledge Bases* (KBs) and a user model also composed of different types of KBs which represent the user's presumed beliefs and inferences. A single KB represents information in one form, e.g., a semantic network (SN), Bayesian network (BN), rule-based system or database. During argument generation, relevant material from several KBs may need to be combined into a common representation. We have chosen BNs for this purpose because of their ability to represent normatively correct reasoning under uncertainty.

When constructing an Argument Graph, NAG develops two BNs: the BN forming one of the KBs in the user model, and the BN forming one of the KBs in the normative model. As arguments are built up, material obtained from other KBs may be converted to BN form and added to the appropriate BN, e.g., material from a rule-based system in the user model may be added to the user model BN (§ *Extending the Argument Graph*). To reduce the amount of information NAG must deal with, we apply a focusing mechanism which highlights the portion of the complete BN in each model that is needed for the current argument (§ *Focusing the Argument*). Hence, each of the user model and the normative model contains a single Bayesian subnetwork that is in focus. The structural intersection of these Bayesian subnetworks forms the Argument Graph. When analyzing this graph, propagation is performed twice, once over the Bayesian subnetwork in the user model and once over the Bayesian subnetwork in the normative model, each time using probabilistic information sourced from within the model being propagated (§ *Argument Analysis*). Thus, we measure the strength of the same argument in the user model and the normative model.

Generation-Analysis Cycle

NAG receives the following inputs: (1) a proposition to be argued for; (2) an initial argument context; and (3) two target ranges of degrees of belief to be achieved (one each for the normative model and the user model). The initial argument context, denoted $context_0$, is composed of the propositions and concepts mentioned in a preamble to the argument plus the argument's goal; this context is expanded as the Argument Graph grows. The degrees of belief to be achieved are expressed as ranges of probabilities, e.g., [0.5, 0.6], in order to be able to represent a variety of goals, e.g., inducing doubt when a strong belief is inappropriate.

Upon completion of the argumentation process, the Strategist produces an Argument Graph which starts from *admissible premises* and ends in the goal proposition. Admissible premises are propositions that start out being believed by NAG and the user (sufficiently for the argument to work).

The Strategist executes the following algorithm during argument generation. In principle, this procedure is applicable to any proposition, and hence also to special forms such as promises and modal propositions. However, it does not currently have facilities to treat these forms in any special way.

Generation-Analysis Algorithm
1. $i \leftarrow 0$.
2. Clamp any items in the current context, $context_i$, and perform spreading activation. This yields an Argument Graph containing: the clamped nodes, the activated nodes (whose activation exceeds a threshold), plus the links connecting these nodes (§ *Focusing the Argument*).
3. Identify new subgoals in the current Argument Graph (§ *Choosing Argument Subgoals*).
4. Pass the argument subgoals identified in Step 3 to the Generator, which adds the new information returned by its Reasoning Agents to the current Argument Graph (§ *Extending the Argument Graph*).
5. Pass the Argument Graph generated in Step 4 to the Analyzer for evaluation (§ *Argument Analysis*).
6. If the Analyzer reports that the current Argument Graph is sufficiently nice, then present an argument based on this

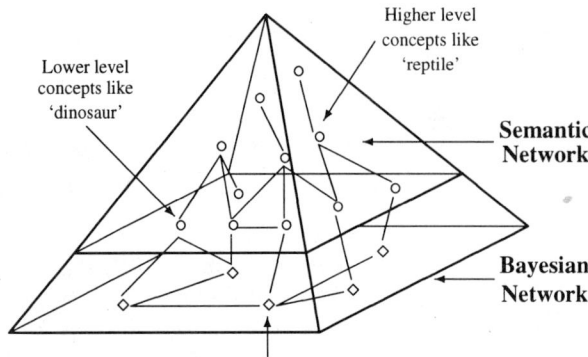

Figure 2: Sample Semantic-Bayesian Network

graph to the user, and wait for a response (§ *Argument Presentation*). Otherwise, continue.
7. $i \leftarrow i + 1$.
8. $context_i \leftarrow context_{i-1}$ + new nodes connected to the goal during cycle $i-1$.
9. Go to Step 2.

When receiving a user's argument, an analysis-generation cycle is activated. This cycle begins in Step 5, which results in the acceptance of the user's argument if no flaws are detected. Otherwise, the cycle is completed, and the generation part of the cycle is performed (Steps 2, 3 and 4) to try to bridge small inferential gaps in the user's argument. This cycle is repeated only a few times, since large gaps in a user's argument make it more likely that NAG and the user are using different lines of reasoning.

Focusing the Argument

Bayesian network propagation (Pearl 1988) is an NP-hard problem in the general case (Cooper 1990). NAG is designed to be an interactive system, potentially drawing upon very large knowledge bases, so complete propagation over large BNs is not feasible. In addition, NAG's user model is designed to model human cognitive abilities, and humans normally cannot absorb and analyze all data relevant to a complex problem. To cope with both of these limits on complexity we emulate the principal means available to humans for applying limited cognitive capacity to problem solving, namely attention (see, for example, Baars 1987).

NAG uses two hierarchical SNs, one built on top of the user model BN and one built on top of the normative model BN, to capture associative connections between information items (Figure 2 illustrates a semantic-Bayesian network). The initial semantic-Bayesian networks are currently built manually, but they may be automatically extended during argument generation (§ *Extending the Argument Graph*). Both the SN and the BN are used by NAG to simulate attentional focus in each model. However, the resulting Argument Graph contains only propositions and links from the BN.

NAG takes the context in which the argument occurs as providing an initial set of salient objects. For example, if the user presents an argument to NAG, the concepts occurring in the propositions within the argument or in the preceding

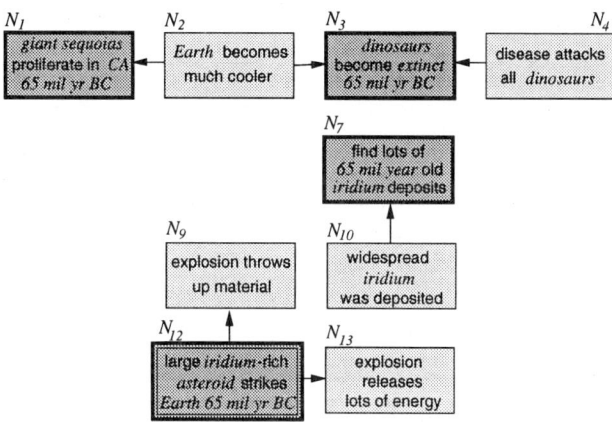

Figure 3: Initial Argument Graph for the Asteroid Example

discussion will be marked as salient. We use activation with decay (Anderson 1983), spreading from the salient objects (which are clamped) to determine the focus of attention. All items in the semantic-Bayesian networks which achieve a threshold activation level during the spreading activation process are brought into the span of attention. This process passes activation through the semantic-Bayesian networks, each node being activated to the degree implied by the activation levels of its neighbors, the strength of association to those neighbors, and its immediately prior activation level (vitiated by a time-decay factor). By these means we have a direct implementation of attention which we use to zero-in upon the more relevant portions of the semantic-Bayesian networks. This iterative process ceases when an activation cycle fails to activate a new node.

Determining the more relevant portions of the semantic-Bayesian networks in this way allows NAG to save processing time in two ways: NAG restricts itself to searching for information connected with the propositions in focus (§ *Choosing Argument Subgoals*), rather than all of the propositions known to it; and NAG analyzes its arguments with respect to just the same propositions in focus, saving time during Bayesian propagation (§ *Argument Analysis*).

Focusing – Example. Consider the generation of an argument for the proposition "A large *iridium*-rich *asteroid* struck *Earth* about *65-million-years BC*," preceded by the preamble "Approximately *65-million-years BC* the *dinosaurs*, large *reptiles* that dominated the *Earth* for many millions of years, became *extinct*. At about the same time, the number of *giant sequoias* in *California* greatly increased." Initially, the goal proposition and the preamble activate any propositions containing two or more of the italicized concepts, i.e., nodes N_1, N_3, N_7 and N_{12} in Figure 3 (shown in dark grey boxes).

After clamping the nodes that correspond to this discourse context and performing spreading activation, additional nodes become activated in the SNs and BNs. All the nodes whose activation level exceeds a threshold are retained and added to the Argument Graph. For this example, this yields an Argument Graph composed of nodes N_2, N_4, N_9, N_{10} and N_{13} (shown in light grey boxes in Figure 3) in addition to the clamped nodes. The links between the nodes in Figure 3 were obtained from the BNs. However, the activation of these nodes involved spreading activation through the BNs and the SNs. Additional nodes, such as [California has fault-lines] (not shown in Figure 3), were activated via the SNs. However, if no causal or evidential links are found between such nodes and the goal, they are eventually excluded from the Argument Graph.

Choosing Argument Subgoals
Having used semantic priming to add items of likely interest to the current Argument Graph, NAG must now decide which of these newly added items should be set as argument subgoals requiring further inspection. At present, nodes which have a path to the goal in the Argument Graph or whose activation level is high (exceeds a subgoaling threshold) are tagged as subgoals to be investigated, provided they have not been previously passed to the Reasoning Agents (§ *Extending the Argument Graph*).

Choosing Subgoals – Example Continued. At this stage in the argument planning process, none of the nodes in the current Argument Graph (Figure 3) have been passed to the Reasoning Agents. Thus, the following nodes are passed to the Reasoning Agents in order to obtain additional information (§ *Extending the Argument Graph*): those in the subgraph containing the goal node (N_9, N_{12} and N_{13}), plus the three clamped (highly active) nodes in the graph fragments not connected to the goal node (N_1, N_3 and N_7).

Extending the Argument Graph

The initial Argument Graph consists of the subset of the BNs which was activated by the attentional mechanism. The Generator then activates the Reasoning Agents to collect information relevant to each subgoal in the current Argument Graph. Upon their return, the Generator must determine: (1) which newly returned inferences should be integrated into the Argument Graph; (2) the structure of the additions to the Argument Graph representing the new inferences; and (3) the parameters of the new inferences and propositions.

Which propositions and inferences to integrate. New propositions returned by the Reasoning Agents are added to the current Argument Graph as new nodes. NAG decides whether to introduce new inferences returned by the Reasoning Agents into the Argument Graph (or to replace existing inferences with new ones) by applying the following rules, which ensure that each relationship between propositions in the Argument Graph is represented only once:

1. *At most one inference may directly connect any two propositions in the Bayesian subnetwork in each of the user model and the normative model.*

2. *When selecting from multiple candidate inferences, prefer inferences sourced from more expressive representations, where expressiveness means how much probabilistic information can be expressed by the representation.*

For example, assume NAG's qualitative rule-based system agent finds a rule stating "If D then E is possible". If the agent responsible for quantitative rule-based systems also finds the rule "If D then E with prob = x", which NAG translates into $D \stackrel{evidence}{\longrightarrow} E$ with $P(E|D) = x$ (assuming independence from other links incident upon node E), then which of these inference rules, if any, should be added to the Argument Graph? The first rule above states that at most one of these two inferences will be incorporated into the current Argument Graph.[1] NAG selects which one of the two inferences it will incorporate by applying the second rule. This is done via the following preference ordering for expressiveness: BNs, quantitative rule-based systems, qualitative rule-based systems and database lookups.

Structure of the new propositions and inferences. The various Reasoning Agents return argument fragments which take the form of propositions linked by inferences. After the above mentioned rules have been applied to determine which of these fragments should be incorporated in the Argument Graph, the selected fragments are added to the Bayesian subnetwork in the appropriate model, e.g., fragments sourced from KBs in the normative model are added to the subnetwork in the normative model.

Adding parameters for the propositions and inferences. Normally, the prior probability of a proposition returned by a Reasoning Agent is copied directly into the Argument Graph. This works so long as the new values fill gaps in the Argument Graph. However, if the current Argument Graph already contains a prior probability for the proposition under consideration, then that previous probability will be retained and the new information ignored.[2]

Adding information to the Argument Graph about joint conditional probabilities associated with new inferences is done as follows. If a Reasoning Agent can provide complete conditional probability information for a new inference which takes into account other inferences that impinge upon the proposition targeted by this inference, then this information replaces the corresponding conditional probability matrix. However, if complete probabilistic information is unavailable, the new information (often a simple conditional probability) is assumed to be conditionally independent of the other inferences impinging upon the node in question. Since assuming conditional independence is dangerous, NAG records this assumption in a log file, so that a human operator can diagnose where NAG went wrong should one of its arguments be incorrect. The operator can then edit NAG's KBs to remove the offending inference or to add extra information about the joint conditional probabilities.

Extending the Graph – Example Continued

In this step, the information returned by the Reasoning Agents is incorporated into the Argument Graph (Figure 4). Some of the nodes found by these agents have already been activated through spreading activation (those in light grey in Figure 4), while others are new to the Argument Graph (those in white) (node N_{15} and the links $N_{11} \rightarrow N_{15}$ and

---
[1]NAG does not try to merge information gleaned from more than one available source since it is unclear how to do so.

[2]Since we are not modeling the reliability of the various KBs, there is no reason to prefer the prior probabilities obtained from one KB to conflicting priors obtained from another. Thus, we retain whatever information is already in the BN.

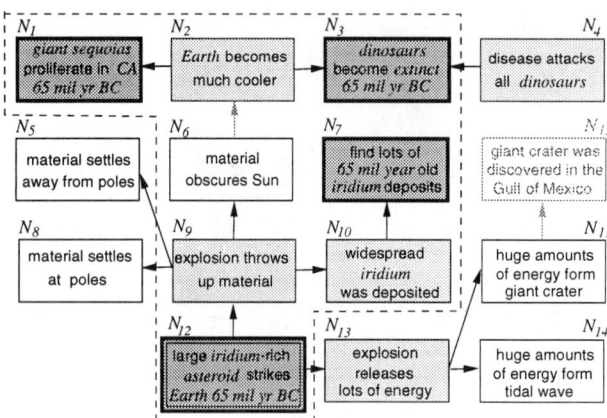

Figure 4: Argument Graph for the Asteroid Example

$N_6 \rightarrow N_2$ have not been discovered yet). All the links returned by the Reasoning Agents are causal or evidential, as these are the only types of relations incorporated at present in the arguments generated by NAG. Some of this information will be included in the final Argument Graph presented to the user, e.g., the newly found node N_6 and the link connecting $N_9 \rightarrow N_6$, while other information, e.g., node N_5, will be eventually excluded (§ *Argument Presentation*). Upon completion of this step, the Argument Graph consists of two separate subgraphs: one containing nodes N_5–N_{14} and another containing nodes N_1–N_4.

Argument Analysis

The process of computing the anticipated belief in a goal proposition as a result of presenting an argument starts with the belief in the premises of the Argument Graph and ends with a new degree of belief in the goal proposition. The Analyzer computes the new belief in a proposition by combining the previous belief in it with the result of applying the inferences which precede this proposition in the Argument Graph. This belief computation process is performed by applying propagation procedures to the Bayesian subnetwork corresponding to the current Argument Graph in the user model and separately to the subnetwork corresponding to the current Argument Graph in the normative model.

In propagating only over the subnetworks initially seeded by the focusing mechanism (§ *Focusing the Argument*) and extended with information returned by the Reasoning Agents (§ *Extending the Argument Graph*), NAG ignores those parts of the complete BNs in the user and normative models not deemed relevant to the current argument. Propagating over the subnetwork corresponding to the current Argument Graph in the user and normative models is much faster than having to perform propagation over the complete BN in each model, but the trade off is a less accurate estimate of the final belief in the goal proposition. Still, in a system designed to be interactive, some such trade off is necessary in view of the complexity of Bayesian propagation.

After propagation, the Analyzer returns the following measures for an argument: its *normative strength*, which is its effect on the belief in the goal proposition in the normative model, and its *persuasiveness*, which is its effect on the user's belief in the goal proposition (estimated according to the user model). Of course, an argument's persuasiveness may be quite different from its normative strength.

After the Analyzer has evaluated the normative strength and persuasiveness of the Argument Graph it returns an assessment, which points out any propositions within the Argument Graph that are not sufficiently supported.[3] The generation of support for such propositions is automatically handled by the Generation-Analysis algorithm as follows. Propositions that became connected to the goal during the current cycle are automatically added to the context (Step 8 of the Generation-Analysis algorithm). These propositions are clamped in Step 2 of the next cycle, and those which have not been previously passed to the Reasoning Agents are identified as subgoals (Step 3). It is possible that some propositions will remain insufficiently supported after being investigated by the Reasoning Agents. Often, these propositions are eventually removed from the Argument Graph after alternative, stronger subarguments have been found (§ *Argument Presentation*).

After integrating the new subarguments into the Argument Graph, the now enlarged Argument Graph is again sent to the Analyzer for inspection. Thus, by completing additional focusing-generation-analysis cycles, NAG can often improve Argument Graphs that are initially unsatisfactory.

Analyzing the Graph – Example Continued

The argument that can be built at this stage has three main branches: (1) from nodes N_5, N_6 and N_8 to N_9 and then N_{12}, (2) from N_7 to N_{10}, then N_9 and then N_{12}, and (3) from N_{11} and N_{14} to N_{13} and then N_{12}. However, only N_7 is currently believed by the user, hence it is the only admissible premise among the potential premise nodes. Thus, the anticipated final belief in the goal node in both the normative and the user model falls short of the desired ranges. This is reported by the Analyzer to the Strategist. Nodes N_5, N_6, N_8–N_{11}, N_{13} and N_{14} are now added to the context (which initially consisted of N_1, N_3, N_7 and N_{12}), and the next cycle of the Generation-Analysis algorithm is activated. After spreading activation (Step 2), several nodes become active. However, the main node of interest in this example is N_2, which is activated by N_1, N_3 and N_6. The activation from N_6 results in the argument fragment composed of nodes N_1–N_4 being linked to the goal. The subgoal selection step (Step 3) now identifies nodes N_2, N_4, N_5, N_6, N_8, N_{10}, N_{11} and N_{14} as subgoals to be passed to the Generator, since these nodes now have a path to the goal node and have not been previously passed to the Reasoning Agents. These agents can find the following new information only: node N_{15} and links $N_6 \rightarrow N_2$ and $N_{11} \rightarrow N_{15}$. The resulting Argument Graph is returned to the Analyzer again (Step 5), which determines that the anticipated belief in the goal is now within the target ranges in both models. Thus, the Argument Graph can be passed to the presentation step.

---

[3]Argument flaws such as reasoning cycles and weak inferences are also detected by the Analyzer, and are corrected by the Strategist and the Generator if possible. However, discussion of the correction procedures is beyond the scope of this paper.

Argument Presentation

During argument presentation, NAG attempts to minimize the size of the Argument Graph by searching for the subgraph with the fewest nodes which still yields a sufficiently nice argument. During this process, it tries to make the argument more concise by iteratively deleting nodes and invoking the Analyzer to determine whether the belief in the goal proposition in the now smaller Argument Graph still suffices. This process is desirable since, upon completion of the generation-analysis cycles, some of the propositions in the Argument Graph may be supported more strongly than is necessary for the argument to work.

The subgraph corresponding to an argument generated for the asteroid example is outlined with a dashed box in Figure 4. Premise nodes N_4, N_5, N_8 and N_{14} are omitted because of their weak contribution to the goal. The subgraph composed of $N_{15} \rightarrow N_{11} \rightarrow N_{13}$ is omitted because the desired belief ranges can be achieved without it.

At present, the resulting Argument Graph can be rendered graphically through a graphical interface which allows users to build and receive arguments in an annotated network form. Methods for rendering NAG's output in English, such as those described in (Huang & Fiedler 1997; Reed & Long 1997), are also being considered.

Evaluation

A preliminary Web-based evaluation of NAG's output was conducted by a pre-test elicitation of subjects' beliefs regarding the following key propositions in the argument in Figure 4: (N_{12}) a large asteroid struck the Earth about 65 million years ago, (N_2) there was a sudden cooling of the Earth's climate about 65 million years ago, ($N_{7.1}$) iridium is abundant in the Earth's crust, ($N_{7.2}$) iridium is abundant in asteroids (the last two factors are related to node N_7). According to the replies, an argument was selected among several options previously generated by NAG. For instance, if a respondent indicated belief in N_2, then a subargument supporting this proposition was omitted. After presenting an argument to a respondent, a post-test was administered to assess changes in belief in the pre-test propositions.

Among the 32 respondents, there was a clear tendency to shift belief towards the (final and intermediate) targets in response to NAG's argument. The following percentages of the respondents who had no opinion or a previous incorrect belief shifted to a correct belief: 58% for N_{12}, 36% for N_2, 83% for $N_{7.1}$, and 92.5% for $N_{7.2}$ (which was sourced from the Encyclopedia Britannica). These shifts represent 50%, 32%, 84% and 181% of a standard deviation unit respectively, indicating that NAG's arguments were reasonably persuasive.[4] In future, we shall undertake more rigorous testing in order to compare NAG's arguments against human-generated arguments.

NAG was tested on five sample scenarios in order to assess the effect of using spreading activation to simulate attention.

---

[4]Technically, due to the high variation in the responses, only the largest of these shifts is statistically significant with $p = 0.035$ (when a normal distribution is assumed).

Table 1: Test scenarios for NAG

Name	# nodes in SN	# nodes in BN	average connect.	ave. time with SA	ave. time w/o SA
asteroid	100	50	~3.25	12.5(4)	25(4)
finance	100	120	~4	32.8(5)	131.4(5)
alphabet	50	50	~4	8.5(4)	25.8(4)
phobos	20	30	~3	3.5(2)	6.0(2)
papers	20	20	~3	3.3(2)	6.5(2)

Table 1 shows the number of nodes and average connectivity in these scenarios, and the average time (in cpu seconds) required for generating arguments with and without spreading activation (columns 5 and 6 respectively; the number of runs performed appears in parenthesis). These results were obtained using mid-range (spreading activation) parameter values for a variety of goals (one goal per run). In all but one run the same arguments were generated with and without spreading activation. A slower decay and a lower activation threshold (§ *Focusing the Argument*) resulted in the incorporation of more nodes into the Argument Graph. In extreme cases this yielded longer argument generation times than without spreading activation due to the need to inspect nodes that were only marginally related to the goal. A quick decay and a high activation threshold resulted in the incorporation of fewer nodes into the Argument Graph. In extreme cases this also extended argument generation times, since the search for an argument became mainly goal based.

Related Research

The mechanism presented in this paper uses Bayesian reasoning to perform abduction during argument generation, and performs spreading activation to focus the argument. This use of spreading activation resembles Charniak and Goldman's (1993) use of a marker passing mechanism to focus attention in a Bayesian plan recognition system.

The approach of "interpretation as abduction" used in (Hobbs *et al.* 1993) aims to recover the premises and inferential links which lead to the conclusion of some given argument. This is similar to NAG's analysis-generation cycle. However, NAG is a system that reasons under uncertainty and can generate as well as analyze its own arguments. A generative system based on the work of Hobbs *et al.* is described in (Thomason, Hobbs, & Moore 1996). That system deals with what can be readily inferred, and so deleted, during communication, but the generated discourse does not present an argument in support of a proposition. Horacek (1997) and Mehl (1994) describe systems that turn an explicit argument into one where easily inferred information is left implicit. However, both of these systems require a complete argument as input, while NAG constructs its own arguments.

NAG's generation-analysis cycle resembles the propose-evaluate-modify cycle in (Chu-Carroll & Carberry 1995). However, NAG uses Bayesian reasoning to determine the impact of an argument on an addressee's beliefs, and it may combine several lines of reasoning to achieve its goal, rather than selecting a single proposition.

Conclusion

We have offered a mechanism for argument generation and analysis which uses a series of focusing-generation-analysis cycles to build two BNs (one in the normative model and another in the user model) that contain the information required to construct a nice argument. This use of two models enables us to distinguish between normatively correct and persuasive arguments. An attentional mechanism is used to focus the search during argument generation, and partial propagation, performed over the Bayesian subnetworks in focus (the current Argument Graph), is used to estimate the impact of the resultant argument on an addressee's beliefs. A preliminary evaluation of NAG's arguments yielded encouraging results; an evaluation of NAG's attentional mechanism shows that it substantially reduces argument generation times without appreciable effects on argument quality.

Acknowledgments

This research was supported in part by Australian Research Council grant A49531227.

References

Anderson, J. 1983. *The Architecture of Cognition*. Harvard University Press.

Baars, B. 1987. *A Cognitive Theory of Consciousness*. Cambridge University Press.

Charniak, E., and Goldman, R. P. 1993. A Bayesian model of plan recognition. *Artificial Intelligence* 64(1):50–56.

Chu-Carroll, J., and Carberry, S. 1995. Response generation in collaborative negotiation. In *Proceedings of the Thirty-Third Annual Meeting of the Association for Computational Linguistics*, 136–143.

Cooper, G. 1990. The computational complexity of probabilistic inference using belief networks. *Artificial Intelligence* 42:393–405.

Hobbs, J.; Stickel, M.; Appelt, D.; and Martin, P. 1993. Interpretation as abduction. *Artificial Intelligence* 63(1-2):69–142.

Horacek, H. 1997. A model for adapting explanations to the user's likely inferences. *User Modeling and User-Adapted Interaction* 7(1):1–55.

Huang, X., and Fiedler, A. 1997. Proof verbalization as an application of NLG. In Proceedings of the Fifteenth International Joint Conference on Artificial Intelligence, 965–970. Int. Joint Conferences on AI, Inc.

Mehl, S. 1994. Forward inferences in text generation. In *Proceedings of the Eleventh European Conference on Artificial Intelligence*, 525–529. John Wiley & Sons.

Pearl, J. 1988. *Probabilistic Reasoning in Intelligent Systems*. Morgan Kaufmann Publishers.

Reed, C., and Long, D. 1997. Content ordering in the generation of persuasive discourse. In Proceedings of the Fifteenth International Joint Conference on Artificial Intelligence, 1022–1027. Int. Joint Conferences on AI, Inc.

Thomason, R.; Hobbs, J.; and Moore, J. 1996. Communicative goals. In *ECAI-96 Workshop Proceedings – Gaps and Bridges: New Directions in Planning and NLG*, 7–12.

Nonmonotonic Reasoning

Fixpoint 3-valued semantics for autoepistemic logic

Marc Denecker
Department of Computer Science
K.U.Leuven
Celestijnenlaan 200A, B-3001 Heverlee, Belgium
marcd@cs.kuleuven.ac.be

Victor Marek and Mirosław Truszczyński
Computer Science Department
University of Kentucky
Lexington, KY 40506-0046
marek|mirek@cs.engr.uky.edu

Abstract

The paper presents a constructive 3-valued semantics for autoepistemic logic (AEL). We introduce a derivation operator and define the semantics as its least fixpoint. The semantics is 3-valued in the sense that, for some formulas, the least fixpoint does not specify whether they are believed or not. We show that complete fixpoints of the derivation operator correspond to Moore's stable expansions. In the case of modal representations of logic programs our least fixpoint semantics expresses well-founded semantics or 3-valued Fitting-Kunen semantics (depending on the embedding used). We show that, computationally, our semantics is simpler than the semantics proposed by Moore (assuming that the polynomial hierarchy does not collapse).

Introduction

We describe a 3-valued semantics for modal theories that approximates skeptical mode of reasoning in the autoepistemic logic introduced in (Moore 1990; 1985). We present results demonstrating that our approach is, indeed, appropriate for modeling autoepistemic reasoning. We discuss computational properties of our semantics and connections to logic programming.

Autoepistemic logic is among the most extensively studied nonmonotonic formal systems. It is closely related to default logic (Reiter 1980). It can handle default reasonings under a simple and modular translation in the case of prerequisite-free defaults (Marek & Truszczyński 1993). In the case of arbitrary default theories, a somewhat more complex non-modular translation provides a one-to-one correspondence between default extensions and stable (autoepistemic) expansions (Gottlob 1995). Further, under the so called Gelfond translation, autoepistemic logic captures the semantics of stable models for logic programs (Gelfond 1987). Under the Konolige encoding of logic programs as modal theories, stable expansions generalize the concept of the supported model semantics (Marek & Truszczyński 1993). Autoepistemic logic is also known to be equivalent to several other modal nonmonotonic reasoning systems.

The semantics for autoepistemic logic (Moore 1985) assigns to a modal theory T a collection of its *stable expansions*. This collection may be empty, may consist of exactly one expansion or may consist of several different expansions. Intuitively, expansions are designed to model belief states of agents with *perfect* introspection powers: for every formula F, either the formula KF (expressing a belief in F) or the formula $\neg KF$ (expressing that F is not believed) belongs to an expansion. We will say that expansions contain no *meta-ignorance*.

In many applications, the phenomenon of multiple expansions is desirable. There are situations where we are not interested in answers to queries concerning a single atom or formula, but in a *collection* of atoms or formulas that satisfy some constraints. Planning and diagnosis in artificial intelligence, and a range of combinatorial optimization problems, such as computing hamilton cycles or k-colorings in graphs, are of this type. These problems may be solved by means of autoepistemic logic precisely due to the fact that multiple expansions are possible. The idea is to represent a problem as an autoepistemic theory so that solutions to the problem are in one-to-one correspondence with stable expansions. While conceptually elegant, this approach has its problems. Determining whether expansions exist is a Σ_2^P-complete problem (Niemelä 1992; Gottlob 1992), and all known algorithms for computing expansions are highly inefficient.

In a more standard setting of knowledge representation, the goal is to model the knowledge about a domain as a theory in some formal system and, then, to use some inference mechanism to resolve queries against the theory or, in other words, establish whether

Copyright ©1998, American Association for Artificial Intelligence (www.aaai.org). All rights reserved.

particular formulas are entailed by this theory. Autoepistemic logic (as well as other nonmonotonic systems) can be used in this mode, too. Namely, under the so called *skeptical* model, a formula is entailed by a modal theory, if it belongs to all stable expansions of this theory. The problem is, again, with the computational complexity of determining whether a formula belongs to all expansions.

We propose an alternative semantics for autoepistemic reasoning that allows us to *approximate* the skeptical approach described above. Our semantics has the property that if it assigns to a formula the truth value **t**, then this formula belongs to all stable expansions and, dually, if it assigns to a formula the truth value **f**, then this formula does not belong to any expansion. Our semantics is 3-valued and some formulas are assigned the truth value **u** (unknown). While only approximating the skeptical mode of reasoning, it has one important advantage. Its computational complexity is lower (assuming that the polynomial hierarchy does not collapse on some low level). Namely, the problem to determine the truth value of a formula is in the class Δ_2^P.

Clearly, the semantics we propose can be applied whenever the situation requires that autoepistemic logic be used in the skeptical mode. However, it has also another important application. It can be used as a pruning mechanism in algorithms that compute expansions. The idea is to first compute our 3-valued interpretation for an autoepistemic theory (which is computationally simpler than the task of computing an expansion) and, in this way, find some formulas which are in all expansions and some that are in none. This restricts the search space for expansions and may yield significant speedups.

Conceptually, our semantics plays the role similar to that played by the well-founded semantics in logic programming. Deciding whether an atom is in all stable models is a co-NP-complete problem. However, the well-founded semantics, which approximates the stable model semantics can be computed in polynomial time. Furthermore, well-founded semantics is used both as the basis for top-down query answering implementations of logic programming (Chen, Swift, & Warren 1995), and as a search space pruning mechanism by some implementations to compute stable model semantics (Niemelä & Simons 1995).

Our 3-valued semantics for autoepistemic logic is based on the notion of a *belief pair*. These are pairs (P, S), where P and S are sets of 2-valued interpretations of the underlying first-order language, and $S \subseteq P$. The motivation to consider belief pairs comes from Moore's possible-world characterization of stable expansions (Moore 1990). Moore characterized consistent expansions in terms of *possible-world structures*, that is, non-empty sets of 2-valued interpretations. A belief pair (P, S) can be viewed as an approximation to a possible-world structure W such that $S \subseteq W \subseteq P$: interpretations not in P are known not to be in W, and those in S are known to be in W. Observe that while expansions (or the corresponding possible-world structures) do not contain meta-ignorance, belief pairs, in general, do.

Our semantics is defined in terms of fixpoints of a monotone operator defined on the set of belief pairs. This operator, $\mathcal{D}_T$, is determined by an initial theory T. Given a belief pair $B = (P, S)$, $\mathcal{D}_T$ establishes that some interpretations that are in P must, in fact, belong to S. In addition, some other interpretations in P are eliminated altogether, as inappropriate for describing a possible state of the world (given the agent's initial knowledge). The operator attempts to simulate a constructive process rational agents might use to produce an "elementary" improvement on their current set of beliefs and disbeliefs.

We say that (P_1, S_1) "better approximates" the agent's beliefs and disbeliefs entailed by the agent's initial assumptions than (P, S) if $S \subseteq S_1 \subseteq P_1 \subseteq P$. The operator $\mathcal{D}_T$ is monotone with respect to this ordering and, thus, it has the least fixpoint. We propose this fixpoint as a *constructive* approximation to the semantics of stable expansions.

A fundamental property that makes the above construction meaningful is that *complete* belief pairs (those with P equal to S) that are fixpoints of $\mathcal{D}$ are precisely Moore's S5-models characterizing expansions. Thus, by the general properties of fixpoints of monotone operators over partially ordered sets, the least fixpoint described above indeed approximates the skeptical reasoning based on expansions. Moreover, as mentioned above, the problem of computing the least fixpoint of the operator D requires only polynomially many calls to the satisfiability testing engine, that is, it is in Δ_2^P. Another property substantiating our approach is that under some natural encodings of logic programs as modal theories, our semantics yields both well-founded semantics (Van Gelder, Ross, & Schlipf 1991) and the 3-valued Fitting-Kunen semantics (Fitting 1985; Kunen 1987).

Autoepistemic logic — preliminaries

The language of autoepistemic logic is the standard language of propositional modal logic over a set of atoms Σ and with a single modal operator K. We will refer to this language as $\mathcal{L}_K$. The propositional fragment of $\mathcal{L}_K$ will be denoted by $\mathcal{L}$.

The notion of a 2-*valued interpretation* of the alphabet Σ is defined as usual: it is a mapping from Σ to $\{\mathbf{t},\mathbf{f}\}$. The set of all interpretations of Σ is denoted $\mathcal{A}_\Sigma$ (or $\mathcal{A}$, if Σ is clear from the context).

A possible-world semantics for autoepistemic logic was introduced by Moore (Moore 1990) and proven equivalent with the semantics of stable expansions. A possible-world structure W (over Σ) is a set of 2-valued interpretations of Σ. Alternatively, it can be seen as a Kripke structure with a total accessibility relation. Given a pair (W, I), where W is a set of interpretations and I is an interpretation (not necessarily from W), one defines a truth assignment function $\mathcal{H}_{W,I}$ inductively as follows:
(1) For an atom A, we define $\mathcal{H}_{W,I}(A) = I(A)$;
(2) The boolean connectives are handled in the usual way;
(3) For every formula F, we define $\mathcal{H}_{W,I}(KF) = \mathbf{t}$ if for every $J \in W, \mathcal{H}_{W,J}(F) = \mathbf{t}$, and $\mathcal{H}_{W,I}(KF) = \mathbf{f}$, otherwise.

We write $(W,I) \models F$ to denote that $\mathcal{H}_{W,I}(F) = \mathbf{t}$. Further, for a modal theory T, we will write $(W,I) \models T$ if $\mathcal{H}_{W,I}(F) = \mathbf{t}$ for any $F \in T$. Finally, for a possible world structure W we define the *theory* of W, $Th(W)$, by: $Th(W) = \{F : (W,I) \models F, \text{ for all } I \in W\}$.

It is well known that for every formula F, either $KF \in Th(W)$ or $\neg KF \in Th(W)$ ($\mathcal{H}_{W,I}(KF)$ is the same for all interpretations $I \in W$). Thus, possible-world structures have no meta-ignorance and, as such, are suitable for modeling belief sets of agents with *perfect* introspection capabilities. It is precisely this property that made possible-world structures fundamental objects in the study of modal nonmonotonic logics (Moore 1990; Marek & Truszczyński 1993).

Definition 1 *An* autoepistemic model *of a modal theory T is a possible-world (S5) structure W which satisfies the following fixpoint equation:*

$$W = \{I : (W,I) \models T\}.$$

The following theorem, relating stable expansions of (Moore 1985) and autoepistemic models, was proved in (Levesque 1990) and was discussed in detail in (Schwarz 1992).

Theorem 1 *For any two modal theories T and E, E is a consistent stable expansion of T if and only if $E = Th(W)$ for some nonempty autoepistemic model W of T.*

A fixpoint 3-valued semantics for autoepistemic logic

Our semantics for autoepistemic logic is defined in terms of possible-world structures and fixpoint conditions. The key difference with the semantics proposed by Moore is that we consider *approximations* of possible-world structures by *pairs* of possible-world structures. Recall from the previous section, that $\mathcal{A}$ denotes the set of all interpretations of a fixed propositional language $\mathcal{L}$.

Definition 2 *A* belief pair *is a pair (P, S) of sets of interpretations P and S such that $P \supseteq S$. When $B = (P,S)$, $S(B)$ denotes S and $P(B)$ denotes P. The belief pair $(\mathcal{A}, \emptyset)$ is denoted $\bot$. The set $\{(P,S) : P, S \in \mathcal{A} \text{ and } P \supseteq S\}$ of all belief pairs is denoted by $\mathcal{B}$.*

The interpretations in $S(B)$ can be viewed as states of the world which are known to be possible (belong to W). They form a lower approximation to W. The interpretations in $P(B)$ can be viewed as an upper approximation to W. In other words, interpretations not in $P(B)$ are known not to be in W.

We will extend now the concept of an interpretation to the case of belief pairs and consider the question of meta-ignorance and meta-knowledge of belief pairs. We will show that, being only approximations to possible-world structures, belief pairs may contain meta-ignorance. We will use three logical values, $\mathbf{f}$, $\mathbf{u}$ and $\mathbf{t}$. In the definition, we will use the *truth* ordering: $\mathbf{f} \leq_{tr} \mathbf{u} \leq_{tr} \mathbf{t}$ and define $\mathbf{f}^{-1} = \mathbf{t}, \mathbf{t}^{-1} = \mathbf{f}, \mathbf{u}^{-1} = \mathbf{u}$.

Definition 3 *Let $B = (P,S)$ be a belief pair and let I be an interpretation. The truth function $\mathcal{H}_{B,I}$ is defined inductively:*

$$\begin{aligned}
\mathcal{H}_{B,I}(A) &= I(A) \quad (A \text{ is an atom}) \\
\mathcal{H}_{B,I}(\neg F) &= \mathcal{H}_{B,I}(F)^{-1} \\
\mathcal{H}_{B,I}(F_1 \vee F_2) &= max\{\mathcal{H}_{B,I}(F_1), \mathcal{H}_{B,I}(F_2)\} \\
\mathcal{H}_{B,I}(F_1 \wedge F_2) &= min\{\mathcal{H}_{B,I}(F_1), \mathcal{H}_{B,I}(F_2)\} \\
\mathcal{H}_{B,I}(F_2 \supset F_1) &= max\{\mathcal{H}_{B,I}(F_1), \mathcal{H}_{B,I}(F_2)^{-1}\}
\end{aligned}$$

The formula $K(F)$ is evaluated as follows:

$$\mathcal{H}_{B,I}(K(F)) = \begin{cases} \mathbf{t} & \text{if } \forall_{J \in P} \mathcal{H}_{B,J}(F) = \mathbf{t} \\ \mathbf{f} & \text{if } \exists_{J \in S} \mathcal{H}_{B,J}(F) = \mathbf{f} \\ \mathbf{u} & \text{otherwise} \end{cases}$$

The truth value of a modal atom KF, $\mathcal{H}_{B,I}(KF)$, does not depend on the choice of I. Consequently, for a modal atom KF we will write $\mathcal{H}_B(KF)$ to denote this, common to all interpretations from $\mathcal{A}$, truth value of KF.

Let us define the *meta-knowledge* of a belief pair B as the set of formulas $F \in \mathcal{L}_K$ such that $\mathcal{H}_B(KF) = \mathbf{t}$ or $\mathcal{H}_B(KF) = \mathbf{f}$. The *meta-ignorance* is formed by all other formulas, that is, those formulas $F \in \mathcal{L}_K$ for which $\mathcal{H}_B(KF) = \mathbf{u}$.

Clearly, a belief pair $B = (W,W)$ naturally corresponds to a possible-world structure W. Such a belief pair is called *complete*. We will denote it by (W). The following straightforward result indicates that $\mathcal{H}_{B,I}$ is a generalization of $\mathcal{H}_{W,I}$ to the case of belief pairs. It also states that a complete belief pair contains no meta-ignorance.

Proposition 1 *If B is a complete belief pair (W), then $\mathcal{H}_{B,I}$ is 2-valued. Moreover, for every formula F, $\mathcal{H}_{B,I}(F) = \mathcal{H}_{W,I}(F)$.*

In our approach to autoepistemic reasoning we will model the agent who, given an initial theory T, starts with the belief pair $\perp$ (with the smallest meta-knowledge content) and, then, iteratively constructs a sequence of belief pairs with increasing meta-knowledge (decreasing meta-ignorance) until no more improvement is possible. To this end, we will introduce now a partial ordering on the set $\mathcal{B}$ of belief pairs. Given two belief pairs B_1 and B_2, we define $B_1 \leq_p B_2$ if $P(B_1) \supseteq P(B_2)$ and $S(B_1) \subseteq S(B_2)$. This ordering is consistent with the ordering defined by the "amount" of meta-knowledge contained in a belief pair: the "higher" a belief pair in the ordering $\leq_p$, the more meta-knowledge it contains (and the less meta-ignorance). It is also consistent with the concept of the *information ordering* of the truth values: $\mathbf{u} \leq_{kn} \mathbf{f}, \mathbf{u} \leq_{kn} \mathbf{t}, \mathbf{f} \not\leq_{kn} \mathbf{t}$ and $\mathbf{t} \not\leq_{kn} \mathbf{f}$.

Proposition 2 *Let B_1 and B_2 be belief pairs. If $B_1 \leq_p B_2$ then for every $F \in \mathcal{L}_K$ and for every interpretation I, $\mathcal{H}_{B_1,I}(F) \leq_{kn} \mathcal{H}_{B_2,I}(F)$.*

The ordered set $(\mathcal{B}, \leq_p)$ is not a lattice. In fact, for every $W \subseteq \mathcal{A}$, (W) is a maximal element in $(\mathcal{B}, \leq_p)$. If $W_1 \neq W_2$, then (W_1) and (W_2) have no least upper bound (l.u.b.) in $(\mathcal{B}, \leq_p)$. The pair $\perp = (\mathcal{A}, \emptyset)$ is the least element of $(\mathcal{B}, \leq_p)$.

The ordered set $(\mathcal{B}, \leq_p)$ is *chain-complete*. That is, every set of pairwise comparable elements has the l.u.b. A monotone operator defined on a chain-complete ordered set with a least element has a least fixpoint, which is the limit of the iterations of the operator starting at the least element $\perp$ (Markowsky 1976).

We will now define a monotone operator on the ordered set $(\mathcal{B}, \leq_p)$ and will use it to define a stepwise process of constructing belief pairs with increasing meta-knowledge. To this end, we will define two satisfaction relations: *weak* (denoted by $\models_w$) and *strong* (denoted by $\models$):

$(B,I) \models_w F$ if $\mathcal{H}_{B,I}(F) \neq \mathbf{f}$ (i.e. $\mathcal{H}_{B,I}(F) \geq_{tr} \mathbf{u}$)
$(B,I) \models F$ if $\mathcal{H}_{B,I}(F) = \mathbf{t}$

Definition 4 *Given $B \in \mathcal{B}$, the value of the derivation operator $\mathcal{D}_T$ is defined as follows:*

$$\mathcal{D}_T(B) = (\{I \mid B,I \models_w T\}, \{I \mid B,I \models T\}).$$

Thus, $P(\mathcal{D}_T(B))$ consists of the states which weakly satisfy T, according to B, while $S(\mathcal{D}_T(B))$ are the states which strongly satisfy T according to B. The subscript T is omitted when T is clear from the context.

Example 1 Consider $T = \{K(p) \supset q\}$. Then $\mathcal{D}(\perp) = (\mathcal{A}, \{pq, \bar{p}q\})$. Indeed, $\mathcal{H}_\perp(Kp) = \mathbf{u}$. Consequently, for every I, $\mathcal{H}_{\perp,I}(Kp \supset q) \neq \mathbf{f}$, that is, $(\perp, I) \models_w Kp \supset q$. For the same reason, $\mathcal{H}_{\perp,I}(Kp \supset q) = \mathbf{t}$ if and only if $I(q) = \mathbf{t}$. To compute $\mathcal{D}^2(\perp)$, observe that $\mathcal{H}_{\mathcal{D}(\perp)}(Kp) = \mathbf{f}$. Consequently, for every I, $\mathcal{H}_{\mathcal{D}(\perp),I}(Kp \supset q) = \mathbf{t}$. It follows that $\mathcal{D}^2(\perp) = (\mathcal{A}, \mathcal{A})$. It is also easy to see now that $(\mathcal{A}, \mathcal{A})$ is the fixpoint of $\mathcal{D}$. Notice that the belief pair $(\mathcal{A})$, obtained by iterating $\mathcal{D}$, corresponds to the possible-world structure $\mathcal{A}$ that defines the unique stable expansion of T.

Basic properties of the operator $\mathcal{D}$ are gathered in the following proposition.

Proposition 3 *Let T be a propositionally consistent modal theory. Then, for every belief pair B:*
(1) $\mathcal{D}_T(B)$ is a belief pair.
(2) $\mathcal{D}_T$ is monotone on $\mathcal{B}$.
(3) If B is complete, then $\mathcal{D}_T(B)$ is complete.

Since $(\mathcal{B}, \leq_p)$ is a chain-complete ordered set with least element $\perp$ and $\mathcal{D}$ is monotonic, $\mathcal{D}$ has a least fixpoint. We will denote it by $\mathcal{D} \uparrow$. We propose this fixpoint as the semantics of modal theories. This semantics reflects the reasoning process of an agent who gradually constructs belief pairs with increasing information content. In the remainder of the paper, we will study properties of this semantics and, more generally, of fixpoints of the operator $\mathcal{D}$. The next three results relate fixpoints of $\mathcal{D}$ to Moore's semantics.

Theorem 2 *Let $T \subseteq \mathcal{L}_K$. A possible-world structure W is an autoepistemic model of T if and only if (W) is a fixpoint of $\mathcal{D}_T$. If $\mathcal{D}_T \uparrow$ is complete then it is the unique autoepistemic model of T.*

Using Propositions 1 and 2, we can extract a relationship between stable expansions and fixpoints of the derivation operator $\mathcal{D}_T$.

Corollary 1 *For any pair T, E of modal theories, E is a consistent stable expansion of T if and only if $E = Th(S)$ for some complete fixpoint (S) of $\mathcal{D}_T$. If $\mathcal{H}_{\mathcal{D}_T \uparrow}(F) = \mathbf{t}$ then F belongs to all expansions of T. If $\mathcal{H}_{\mathcal{D}_T \uparrow}(F) = \mathbf{f}$ then F does not belong to any expansion of T.*

Consistent stratified autoepistemic theories (Gelfond 1987) have a unique autoepistemic model (stable expansion). Our semantics coincides with the Moore's semantics on stratified theories.

Theorem 3 *If T is a consistent stratified autoepistemic theory, then $\mathcal{D} \uparrow$ is complete. Hence, it is the unique autoepistemic model of T.*

Thus, the semantics defined by the least fixpoint of the operator $\mathcal{D}$ has several attractive features. It is defined for every consistent modal theory T. It coincides with the semantics of autoepistemic logic on stratified theories and, in the general case, provides an approximation to all stable expansions (or, in other words, to skeptical autoepistemic reasoning).

An effective implementation of $\mathcal{D}$

The approach proposed and discussed in the previous section does not directly yield itself to fast implementations. The definition of the operator $\mathcal{D}$ refers to all interpretations of the language $\mathcal{L}$. Thus, computing $\mathcal{D}(B)$ by following the definition is exponential, even for modal theories of a very simple syntactic form. Moreover, representing belief pairs is costly. Each of the sets $P(B)$ and $S(B)$ may contain exponentially many elements.

In this section, we describe a characterization of the operator $\mathcal{D}$ that is much more suitable for investigations of algorithmic issues associated with our semantics. The strategy is to represent a belief set B as a theory $Rep(B)$. Since the theory $Rep(B)$ needs to represent *two* sets of valuations, $Rep(B)$ will be a theory in the propositional language extended by three constants $\mathbf{t}$, $\mathbf{f}$ and $\mathbf{u}$. These constants will always be interpreted by the logical values $\mathbf{t}$, $\mathbf{f}$ and $\mathbf{u}$, respectively. We will call such theories 3-FOL theories.

Let F be a 3-FOL formula. By $(F)^{wk}$ we denote the formula obtained by substituting $\mathbf{t}$ for all positive occurrences of $\mathbf{u}$ and $\mathbf{f}$ for all negative occurrences of $\mathbf{u}$. Similarly, by $(F)^{str}$ we denote the formula obtained by substituting $\mathbf{t}$ for all negative occurrences of $\mathbf{u}$ and $\mathbf{f}$ for all positive occurrences of $\mathbf{u}$. Given a 3-FOL theory Y, we define $(Y)^{str}$ and $(Y)^{wk}$ by standard setwise extension.

Clearly, $(F)^{str}$ and $(F)^{wk}$ do not contain $\mathbf{u}$. Consequently, they can be regarded as formulas in the propositional language extended by two constants $\mathbf{t}$ and $\mathbf{f}$ with standard interpretations as truth and falsity, respectively. We will call this language 2-FOL. We will write $\vdash$ and $\models$ to denote provability and entailment relations in 2-FOL. An important observation here is that if an interpretation satisfies the formula $(F)^{str}$ then it also satisfies $(F)^{wk}$. That is $(F)^{str} \supset (F)^{wk}$ is a tautology of 2-FOL. For a 2-FOL theory U, we define: $Mod(U) = \{I : \text{for all } F \in U, I \models F\}$. It follows that for a 3-FOL theory Y, $Mod((Y)^{str}) \subseteq Mod((Y)^{wk})$. Thus, $(Mod((Y)^{wk}), Mod((Y)^{str}))$ is a belief pair and Y can be viewed as its representation.

We show now how, similarly to belief pairs, 3-FOL theories can be used to assign truth values to *modal* atoms (and, hence, to all modal formulas). Let Y be a 3-FOL theory, and let F be a modal formula. Define $\mathcal{H}_Y(K(F))$ by induction of depth of formula F as follows:

(1) If F is objective, then define:
$$\mathcal{H}_Y(K(F)) = \begin{cases} \mathbf{t} & \text{if } (Y)^{wk} \vdash (F)^{str} \\ \mathbf{f} & \text{if } (Y)^{str} \nvdash (F)^{wk} \\ \mathbf{u} & \text{otherwise.} \end{cases}$$

(2) If F is not objective, then replace all modal atoms $K(G)$ in F by $\mathcal{H}_Y(K(G))$. This yields an objective formula F'. Define $\mathcal{H}_Y(K(F)) = \mathcal{H}_Y(K(F'))$.

Let T be a modal theory and let Y be a 3-FOL theory. By the Y-instance of T, T_Y, we mean a 3-FOL theory obtained by substituting all modal literals $K(F)$ (not appearing under the scope of any other occurrence of K) by $\mathcal{H}_Y(K(F))$. Observe that for a finite modal theory T and a finite 3-FOL theory Y, T_Y can be computed by means of polynomially many calls to the propositional provability procedure.

Let T be a modal theory. We will now define a counterpart to the operator $\mathcal{D}_T$. Let Y be a 3-FOL theory. Define $\mathcal{SD}_T(Y) = T_Y$.

The key property of the operator $\mathcal{SD}_T$ is that, for a finite modal theory T and for a finite 3-FOL theory Y, $\mathcal{SD}_T(Y)$ can be computed by means of polynomially many calls to the propositional provability procedure.

We will show that $\mathcal{SD}_T$ can be used to compute $\mathcal{D}_T$. In particular, we will show that the least fixpoint of $\mathcal{D}_T$ can be computed by iterating the operator $\mathcal{SD}_T$. To this end, for every 3-FOL theory Y, define $\mathcal{B}el(Y) = (Mod((T)^{wk}), Mod((T)^{str}))$.

First, the following theorem shows that the truth values of modal atoms evaluated according to a 3-FOL theory T and according to the corresponding belief pair $\mathcal{B}el(T)$ coincide.

Theorem 4 *Let Y be a 3-FOL theory. Then, for every modal formula F,*
$$\mathcal{H}_{\mathcal{B}el(Y)}(K(F)) = \mathcal{H}_Y(K(F)).$$

Next, let us observe that the operator $\mathcal{D}$ can be described in terms of the operator $\mathcal{B}el$. Let T be a modal theory and let B be a belief pair. By the B-instance of T, T_B, we mean a 3-FOL theory obtained by substituting all modal literals $K(F)$ (not appearing under the scope of any other occurrence of K) by $\mathcal{H}_B(K(F))$.

Theorem 5 *Let T be a modal theory and let B be a belief pair. Then, $\mathcal{D}_T(B) = \mathcal{B}el(T_B)$*

This theorem indicates that, given a modal theory T, belief pairs that are in the range of the operator $\mathcal{D}_T$ can be represented by objects of size polynomial in the size of T. Namely, every belief pair of the form $\mathcal{D}_T(B)$ can be represented by a 3-FOL theory T_B.

Theorems 4 and 5 imply the main result of this section.

Theorem 6 *Let T be a modal theory and let Y be a 3-FOL theory.*
(1) $Bel(\mathcal{SD}_T(Y)) = \mathcal{D}_T(Bel(Y))$.
(2) If a belief pair B is a fixpoint of $\mathcal{D}_T$, then T_B is a fixpoint of $\mathcal{SD}_T$.
(3) If Y is a fixpoint of $\mathcal{SD}_T$ then $Bel(Y)$ is a fixpoint of $\mathcal{D}_T$.

Observe that $Bel(\{\mathbf{u}\}) = \bot$. It follows directly from Theorem 6 (by induction) that for every ordinal number α, $\mathcal{D}_T^\alpha(\bot) = Bel(\mathcal{SD}_T^\alpha(\{\mathbf{u}\}))$.

Clearly, if $\mathcal{SD}_T^\alpha(\bot) = \mathcal{SD}_T^{\alpha+1}(\bot)$ then $\mathcal{D}_T^\alpha(\bot) = \mathcal{D}_T^{\alpha+1}(\bot)$. Moreover, by Theorems 4, 5 and 6, and by induction, it is easy to show that if $\mathcal{D}_T^\alpha(\bot) = \mathcal{D}_T^{\alpha+1}(\bot)$ then $\mathcal{SD}_T^{\alpha+1}(\bot) = \mathcal{SD}_T^{\alpha+2}(\bot)$.

Consequently, the least fixpoint of $\mathcal{D}_T$ (its polynomial-size representation) can be computed by iterating the operator $\mathcal{SD}_T$. In the case when T is finite, the number of iterations is limited by the number of top level (unnested) modal literals in T. Originally, they may all be evaluated to $\mathbf{u}$. However, at each step, at least one $\mathbf{u}$ changes to either $\mathbf{t}$ or $\mathbf{f}$ and this value is preserved in the subsequent evaluations. Thus, the problem of computing a polynomial size representation of the least fixpoint of the operator $\mathcal{D}$, the corresponding 3-FOL theory, is in the class Δ_2^P.

Relationship to Logic Programming

Autoepistemic logic is closely related to several semantics for logic programs with negation. It is well-known that both stable and supported models of logic programs can be described as expansions of appropriate translations of programs into modal theories (see, for instance, (Marek & Truszczyński 1993)). In this section, we briefly discuss connections of the semantics defined by the least point of the operator $\mathcal{D}$ to some 3-valued semantics of logic programs. The details will be provided in a forthcoming work.

Given a logic programming clause

$$r = a \leftarrow b_1, \ldots, b_k, \mathbf{not}(c_1), \ldots, \mathbf{not}(c_m),$$

define:

$$ael_1(r) = b_1 \wedge \ldots \wedge b_k \wedge \neg Kc_1 \wedge \ldots \wedge \neg Kc_m \supset a$$

and

$$ael_2(r) = Kb_1 \wedge \ldots \wedge Kb_k \wedge \neg Kc_1 \wedge \ldots \wedge \neg Kc_m \supset a$$

Embeddings $ael_1()$ and $ael_2()$ can be extended to logic programs P.

Let B be a belief pair. Define the *projection*, $Proj(B)$, as the 3-valued interpretation I such that $I(p) = \mathcal{H}_B(K(p))$.

It turns out that fixpoints of the operator $\mathcal{D}_{ael_1(P)}$ ($\mathcal{D}_{ael_2(P)}$, respectively) precisely correspond to 3-valued stable (supported, respectively) models of P (the projection function $Proj(\cdot)$ establishes the correspondence). Moreover, complete fixpoints of $\mathcal{D}_{ael_1(P)}$ describe 2-valued stable (supported, respectively) models of P. Finally, the least fixpoint of $\mathcal{D}_{ael_2(P)}$ captures the Fitting-Kunen 3-valued semantics of a program P, and the least fixpoint of $\mathcal{D}_{ael_1(P)}$ captures the well-founded semantics of P.

Acknowledgments

This work was partially supported by the NSF grants IRI-9400568 and IRI-9619233

References

Chen, W.; Swift, T.; and Warren, D. 1995. Efficient top-down computation of queries under the well-founded semantics. *Journal of Logic Programming* 24:161–199.

Fitting, M. C. 1985. Kripke-Kleene semantics for logic programs. *Journal of Logic Programming* 2:295–312.

Gelfond, M. 1987. On stratified autoepistemic theories. In *Proceedings of AAAI-87*, 207–211. Morgan Kaufmann.

Gottlob, G. 1992. Complexity results for nonmonotonic logics. *Journal of Logic and Computation* 2:397–425.

Gottlob, G. 1995. Translating default logic into standard autoepistemic logic. *Journal of the ACM* 42:711–740.

Kunen, K. 1987. Negation in Logic Programming. *Journal of Logic Programming* 4(3):289–308.

Levesque, H. J. 1990. All I know: a study in autoepistemic logic. *Artificial Intelligence* 42:263–309.

Marek, W., and Truszczyński, M. 1993. *Nonmonotonic logics; context-dependent reasoning.* Springer-Verlag.

Markowsky, G. 1976. Chain-complete posets and directed sets with applications. *Algebra Universalis* 6:53–68.

Moore, R. 1985. Semantical considerations on nonmonotonic logic. *Artificial Intelligence* 25:75–94.

Moore, R. 1990. Possible-world semantics for autoepistemic logic. In Ginsberg, M., ed., *Readings on nonmonotonic reasoning*, 137–142.

Niemelä, I., and Simons, P. 1995. Evaluating an algorithm for default reasoning. In *Proceedings of the IJCAI-95 Workshop on Applications and Implementations of Nonmonotomic Reasoning Systems*.

Niemelä, I. 1992. On the decidability and complexity of autoepistemic reasoning. *Fundamenta Informaticae* 17:117–155.

Reiter, R. 1980. A logic for default reasoning. *Artificial Intelligence* 13:81–132.

Schwarz, G. 1992. Minimal model semantics for nonmonotonic modal logics. In *Proceedings of LICS-92*, 34–43.

Van Gelder, A.; Ross, K.; and Schlipf, J. 1991. Unfounded sets and well-founded semantics for general logic programs. *Journal of the ACM* 38:620–650.

Experimenting with Power Default Reasoning

Eric Klavins and William C. Rounds
Artificial Intelligence Laboratory
University of Michigan
Ann Arbor, Michigan 48109
klavins@umich.edu, rounds@umich.edu

Guo-Qiang Zhang
Dept. of Computer Science
University of Georgia
Athens, Georgia 30602
gqz@cs.uga.edu

Abstract

In this paper we explore the computational aspects of Propositional Power Default Reasoning (PDR), a form of non-monotonic reasoning in which the underlying logic is Kleene's 3-valued propositional logic. PDR leads to a concise meaning of the problem of skeptical entailment which has better complexity characteristics than the usual formalisms (co-NP(3)-Complete instead of Π_2^P-Complete). We take advantage of this in an implementation called powdef to encode and solve hard graph problems and explore randomly generated instances of skeptical entailment.

Introduction [1]

Many forms of propositional default reasoning have unexpectedly intractable complexity problems. For example, deciding skeptical entailment in normal propositional default logic (Reiter 1980) is Π_2^P-complete, a result due to Gottlob (Gottlob 1992). Even special cases stay this way – they tend to be NP-hard when we might expect them to be polynomial (Kautz and Selman 1989). This somewhat paradoxical situation has tended to inhibit full-scale use of such reasoning systems.

Recently, however, experimental tests of default reasoning systems have been carried out even in the face of these discouraging complexity results. Perhaps most notably, work with the system DeReS at the University of Kentucky (Cholewiński, Marek and Truszczyński 1994) has shown that it is possible to encode heuristics for graph search problems in a default formalism, and to employ non-monotonic theorem provers to find solutions to these problems (from the Stanford Graph Base (Knuth 1993)) in a relatively efficient manner. (See also (Niemelä and Simons 1997)).

Even more recently, Rounds and Zhang (Zhang and Rounds 1997) introduced a version of Reiter's default logic which they called Power Default Reasoning (PDR). The fundamental difference between PDR and standard default logic is that instead of working with a syntactic representation of knowledge, it uses a *semantic* one based on the tools of *domain theory*, introduced by Dana Scott (Scott 1982) in 1970 as a theory of computation in the semantics of programming languages and developed extensively since then. Rounds and Zhang use default rules to build up partial models instead of using them to "prove" theorems. They can build up *disjunctive* models using a standard construction known as the *Smyth powerdomain*. The concept of *extension*, central to Reiter's logic, is retained in PDR, but it is represented directly as a set of partial models instead of as a theory.

Working this way with models instead of theories improves dramatically on the complexity of non-monotonic reasoning. For example, while deciding skeptical entailment in standard propositional default logic is Π_2^P-complete, the corresponding problem in PDR is co-NP(3)-complete[2]. This means essentially that a non-deterministic algorithm can decide entailment using at most three calls to an oracle for the satisfiability problem. This result, however, is only theoretical. It provides little information about how such an algorithm could be efficiently implemented, and it leaves open the question as to the distribution of positive and negative instances of entailment – it is perfectly conceivable that almost no instances of the problem would be positive.

In this paper we explore the computational aspects of PDR using a new implementation called powdef. We consider propositional logic, and take partial models to be partial truth assignments to the variables of propositional formulae. We use Kleene's strong 3-valued tables to evaluate propositional formulae. Since the co-NP(3) complexity result mentioned above suggests the use of three "oracle" calls to a SAT checker, we give reductions for transforming aspects of power default systems into instances of (2-valued) SAT. Our system has a slot for a SAT checker (we tested several) to find truth assignments. Sets of such assignments are the non-monotonic extensions of a default system; we can use these to check non-monotonic entailment.

We use powdef to solve hard graph problems from the Stanford Graph Base. This enables a compari-

---

[1] Copyright © 1998, American Association for Artificial Intelligence (www.aaai.org). All rights reserved.

[2] A Co-NP(3) problem of the Boolean Hierarchy can be expressed as $(L_1 \cap L_2) \cup L_3$, where L_1 and L_3 are in co-NP, and L_2 is in NP (Cai et al. 1988).

son with DeReS, although we are not really comparing implementations of the same theoretical model, but rather, trying to see if overall run-times are nearly the same on similar instances of graph search problems. We also use different encodings of these search problems. PDR allows us to state instances of a search problem (e.g., Hamiltonian cycle) using disjunctive defaults. This is a natural way to express such problems, but is not straightforward to do in a theory-based system like DeReS. Our running times depend on the kind of SAT checker used, and the class of problem solved. In several cases they are much faster than DeReS, and in a few cases very much slower.

We feel that a simple comparison of our system with DeReS, however, is only part of the experimental story. Since entailment in PDR is co-NP(3)-complete, we decided to check entailment in randomly generated instances of the problem. (This is, in fact, the first general attempt to provide a map of instances of a complete problem in this complexity class.) Our preliminary results show that the entailment problem is remarkably similar to the satisfiability problem, in that hard instances of the problem congregate in special regions, and in that "phase-transition" phenomena can be observed.

In Section 2, we give an overview of PDR. We keep most of this exposition to the finite case (propositional formulae over a finite set of variables), and note that the results hold for the infinite case as well (e.g. first order logic). In Section 3, we describe the translation to SAT. Finally, in Section 4, we present our experimental results.

Power Defaults

In this section we give an overview of PDR. This involves some definitions from domain theory and an introduction to Kleene's 3-valued logic. Domains –in particular, the Scott domains – arise in denotational semantics for programming languages (Scott 1982). In keeping with the idea that a Scott domain provides a semantics for a program, we think of default logic as a kind of logic programming and we will find a natural domain for default rules and extensions. In the rest of this paper we will encounter two Scott domains: the domain of partial truth assignments, which we describe next, and the Smyth powerdomain of a finite domain.

The Domain of Partial Truth Assignments

In our system, the meaning of a propositional formula ϕ will be the set of all partial truth assignments that satisfy it. A partial truth assignment of a formula over a set of variables V is a partial function from V into $\{0,1\}$. For convenience we will use the following definition:

Definition 1 *Given a set of propositional variables V, a truth assignment over V is a function $e : V \to \{0, 1, \bot\}$.*

Here, 0 means false, 1 means true and $\bot$ means undefined. It is customary to denote truth assignments as products or implicants. For example, suppose e is the truth assignment over $\{a, b, c\}$ that maps a to 1, b to $\bot$ and c to 0. Then we write $e = ac'$.

Definition 2 *A satisfier e of a propositional formula ϕ is a truth assignment such that ϕ evaluates to 1 under e. We write $e \models \phi$.*

To evaluate a formula under a partial truth assignment we use Kleene's strong 3-valued logic, specified by the following truth tables:

$\wedge$	1	0	$\bot$	$\vee$	1	0	$\bot$	p	$\neg p$
1	1	0	$\bot$	1	1	1	1	1	0
0	0	0	0	0	1	0	$\bot$	0	1
$\bot$	$\bot$	0	$\bot$	$\bot$	1	$\bot$	$\bot$	$\bot$	$\bot$

Let D be the set of truth assignments over a set of variables V. This is isomorphic to the set of partial functions from V to $\{0, 1\}$. We can define a partial order $(D, \sqsubseteq)$ as follows. First, $\{0, 1, \bot\}$, the *flat domain*, is ordered $\bot \sqsubseteq 0, \bot \sqsubseteq 1$ and reflexively. Then, if d and e are truth assignments in D, $d \sqsubseteq e$ if $d(v) \sqsubseteq e(v) \; \forall v \in V$. (e.g. $ac' \sqsubseteq ab'c'd$ while ac and ac' are incomparable). Thus, if $d \sqsubseteq e$, then e defines at least all the variables d does and in the same way. We can say that e contains at least as much information as d does and is furthermore in agreement with the information that d gives. In fact, the partial order $(D, \sqsubseteq)$ of partial truth assignments is a Scott domain.

Next, we mention some properties of $(D, \sqsubseteq)$. First, if S is a subset of D, then the *upward closure* $\uparrow S$ of S is the set $\{y \in P | \exists x \in S \text{ such that } x \sqsubseteq y\}$. If $S = \uparrow S$ then S is *upward closed*. $\uparrow \{e\}$ is written $\uparrow e$. An important upward closed subset of the Scott domain of partial truth assignments $(D, \sqsubseteq)$ is the set of all satisfiers of a formula ϕ, written $[\![\phi]\!]$ (this follows from the fact that if $d \sqsubseteq e$ and $d \models \phi$ then $e \models \phi$).

The Smyth Powerdomain

The Smyth powerdomain[3] $P^\sharp(D)$ of a finite Scott domain D is defined to be the set of all nonempty upward closed subsets of D, ordered by reverse subset inclusion. In $P^\sharp(D)$, the ordering $\supseteq$, is commonly denoted by $\sqsubseteq^\sharp$. A disjunction of literals gives rise to an upward-closed set of satisfiers, so the Smyth powerdomain is a natural way to model disjunctive default conclusions. It turns out that the Smyth powerdomain of any Scott domain is again a Scott domain.

Power Defaults

A propositional default system[4] is a triple, $S = (\phi, \Sigma, \psi)$, where ϕ and ψ are propositional formulas called the *initial information* and the *query* respectively, and Σ is a set of *syntactic constraints*. The

---

[3] For the general case of the Smyth powerdomain and Power Defaults see (Zhang and Rounds 1997).

constraints in Σ have the form $\tau \leadsto \theta$ where τ and θ are propositional formulas with the approximate meaning: "if τ is known and it is consistent to believe θ, then believe θ". We note for purposes of comparison that in Reiter's notation (Reiter 1980), this rule might be written $\frac{\tau : \theta}{\theta}$. We may sometimes refer to a system $S = (\phi, \Sigma)$ when the query is not important.

Extensions

In default logic an extension is a minimal theory that contains the initial information about the world and which is closed under applications of default rules. The insight of Rounds and Zhang is that the fixed-point definition of Reiter carries over almost word for word to elements of a Scott domain. Since the set of partial models of a formula in Kleene logic lives in the Smyth powerdomain, we may use Reiter's definition on the space of partial models, of a set of formulas, rather than on the space of theories.

It is not necessary here to go into the details of how Rounds and Zhang define extensions in the Smyth powerdomain. They show how to "compile" a set Σ of syntactic default rules into a set Δ of semantic (normal) defaults, so that Reiter's definition of extension may be applied. It is, however, important to define non-monotonic entailment, or *skeptical entailment* for a default system:

Definition 3 *Given a system $S = (\phi, \Sigma, \psi)$ we say that ψ is a **non-monotonic consequence** of ϕ with respect to the set of power defaults Δ constructed from Σ if $[\![\psi]\!] \sqsubseteq^\sharp E$ for every extension E of $[\![\phi]\!]$. We write $\phi \hspace{1pt}|\hspace{-3pt}\sim \psi$.*

Notice how sets of partial models, ordered by reverse inclusion, here replace theories, ordered by inclusion.

We now turn to the concept of *safe* and *unsafe* elements and extensions.

Definition 4 *We say that a truth assignment e over variables in $S = (\phi, \Sigma)$ is safe if and only if $e \models \phi$ and for every $\tau \leadsto \theta \in \Sigma$, if $e \models \tau$ then $e \models \theta$. If a system has a safe extension, it is said to be safe.*

The key to the Rounds-Zhang co-NP(3) complexity result, which also enables our implementation, is the following theorem.

Theorem 1 *(Dichotomy Theorem) For a system $S = (\phi, \Sigma, \psi)$, either the set of partial models of ϕ has a unique safe extension, or else all extensions of this set are unsafe, and are sets containing a single, total truth assignment g (one that doesn't assign $\bot$ to any variable) such that $g \models \phi$.*

---

[4] Although we are only concerned with propositional default systems in this paper, first order logic or any other logic may be used as long as there is a way to express the semantics of the logic as a Scott domain.

Remarkably, we then have that for a system $S = (\phi, \Sigma, \psi)$ that $\phi \hspace{1pt}|\hspace{-3pt}\sim \psi$ if there is a safe element and $e \models \psi$ for all safe elements (we call this *safe entailment*), or if the system is not safe and $\phi \to \psi$ is a (classical) tautology. This implies that only 3 NP "oracle" calls are needed to decide full skeptical entailment for a propositional system. See (Zhang and Rounds 1997) for the details of this complexity result.

Computing Skeptical Entailment
Translation to 2-Valued SAT

We would like to be able to compute the safe extensions of a system since doing so would solve the safe entailment problem and safe extensions may be interesting in their own right. One might be tempted to construct a new formula for the system by considering the defaults as implications, conjoining the initial formula and finding 2-valued satisfiers for it. That is, consider $\phi \wedge (\tau_1 \to \theta_1) \wedge \ldots \wedge (\tau_n \to \theta_n)$. But in 3-valued logic, $e \not\models \tau$ is not the same as $e \models \neg \tau$ so this simple construction fails. Nevertheless, given $S = (\phi, \Sigma)$ we can construct a 2-valued formula Φ such that there is a one-to-one correspondence between the satisfiers of Φ and the safe elements of S. To do this we first assume that our formulas are in Negation Normal Form (NNF), where negations appear only on atoms. The NNF of a formula can be found in polynomial time by Demorgan's laws. It is necessary for the proof of Proposition 1, which is by induction on the structure of the formula. We then introduce, for each of the n variables i occurring in S, two new variables P_i and N_i with the intended meaning that P_i is 1 only when variable i is 1 and N_i is 1 when variable i is 0 and P_i and N_i are both 0 only when variable i is $\bot$. Next we construct a sub-formula Ψ of Φ as follows:

$$\Psi = \bigwedge_{i=1}^{n} (\neg P_i \vee \neg N_i).$$

This formula limits the range of the 2-valued satisfiers we will consider by mimicking the 3-valued world of S. Clearly, any satisfier of Ψ will not assign 1 to both P_i and N_i.

Next, for an arbitrary 3-valued NNF formula α, let $R(\alpha)$ be the formula that results from replacing positive occurrences of variable i in α with P_i and negative occurrences of variable i in α with N_i for all i.

Proposition 1 *Let d be a 3-valued truth assignment for a NNF formula α and let $f(d)$ be the satisfying 2-valued truth assignment of Ψ constructed for variables in α that assigns P_i 1 if variable i is 1 in d, N_i 1 if variable i is 0 in d, and N_i and P_i both 0 if variable i is $\bot$ in d. Then $d \models \alpha$ if and only if $f(d) \models \Psi \wedge R(\alpha)$.*

Note that f is one-to-one. This implies that whenever we have a 2-valued satisfier for $\Psi \wedge R(\alpha)$ we may always reconstruct a 3-valued satisfier for α. Also note that R preserves connectives. Finally, our desired two-valued formula Φ is

$$\Psi \wedge R(\phi) \wedge \bigwedge_{\tau \leadsto \theta \in \Sigma} R(\tau) \rightarrow R(\theta).$$

Proposition 2 *Let e be a truth assignment over the variables in $S = (\phi, \Sigma)$, Φ be the 2-valued formula constructed from S as above, and $f(e)$ be a satisfier of Ψ constructed as in Proposition 1. Then e is a safe element of S if and only if $f(e) \models \Phi$.*

Notice that by these two propositions, "$e \models \psi$ for all safe elements" is equivalent to "$\Phi \rightarrow R(\psi)$ is a tautology".

Experiments

The Implementation

Our implementation of safety checking and safe entailment is a program written in C called `powdef`. Given a system S as input, `powdef` constructs a CNF formula equivalent to Φ as above and then uses a complete SAT checker to check whether or not Φ is satisfiable (SAT checkers usually prefer their input to be in CNF). If Φ is satisfiable (so that S is safe), `powdef` checks that $\Phi \rightarrow R(\psi)$ is a tautology. Otherwise, `powdef` checks that $\phi \rightarrow \psi$ is a tautology. If the tautology check succeeds `powdef` returns "yes", otherwise it returns "no". Note that with a SAT checker we can check that a formula $\alpha \rightarrow \beta$ is a tautology by checking that $\alpha \wedge \neg \beta$ is *not* satisfiable.

If the action specified to `powdef` is not to check entailment but to find minimal safe elements, a list of safe elements found so far is kept. When a new one is found, old safe elements that are greater than the new one, in the Scott domain ordering, are thrown out. If a new satisfier is found to be greater than one already found, it is not added to the list. In practice, this method has proved the most efficient of those we tried, which included conjoining expressions to Φ to limit satisfiers to those that corresponded to minimal safe elements. The addition of such formulas usually resulted in prohibitively many CNF clauses.

The SAT checker we use in most of our experiments uses the simple Davis-Putnam procedure for CNF-SAT (Davis and Putnam 1960), modified to return all satisfiers. We compared several SAT checkers including Selman's randomized SAT checker WalkSAT (Selman, Kautz and Cohen 1993).

A Comparison with an Existing Implementation

In this section we try to compare `powdef` to DeReS (Cholewiński, Marek and Truszczyński 1994). DeReS uses Reiter's default theories, so this comparison is tenuous at best.

Expressing Hard Graph Problems The DeReS implementation uses a subsystem TheoryBase which converts instances of graph problems, such as COLORABILITY, HAMILTON CIRCUIT or KERNELS into instances of default theories, the extensions of which are solutions to the problems. The graphs are generated using the Stanford Graph Base (Knuth 1993). Since we do not use theories, we do not use TheoryBase. We do, however, use the Stanford Base to generate instances. It is easy to represent instances of such problems as power default systems.

Example 1 *Finding Kernels* Let $G = (V, E)$ be a directed graph with n vertices. A *kernel* in G is a subset K of V such that no two vertices in K are joined by an edge in E and such that for every $v \in V \setminus K$ there is a $u \in K$ such that $(u, v) \in E$. A default system $S(G)$ is constructed such that G has a kernel if and only if $S(G)$ has a safe element. The minimal safe elements of the system will correspond exactly to the kernels of the graph. Let $K(i)$ represent the fact that node i is in the kernel for $1 \leq i \leq n$. We use ϕ to seed the kernel by saying each node is either in or not in the kernel:

$$\phi = \bigwedge_{1 \leq i \leq n} K(i) \vee \neg K(i)$$

To specify the conditions under which a node is in a kernel we use default rules. For each $1 \leq i \leq n$ we have the two default rules

$$K(i) \leadsto \bigwedge_{(i,j) \in E} \neg K(j) \quad and \quad \neg K(i) \leadsto \bigvee_{(i,j) \in E} K(j).$$

The first states that, normally, if a node is in a kernel then none of its neighbors are. The second states that, normally, if a node is not in a kernel then at least one of its neighbors is.

Note that a kernel is only completely specified if each $K(i)$ is defined as either 1 or 0. Thus, all safe elements are total truth assignments over the n variables and we need only find the 2-valued satisfiers of the system considered as the 2-valued formula

$$\phi \wedge \bigwedge_{\tau \leadsto \theta \in \Sigma} (\tau \rightarrow \theta).$$

This means that kernels are not an adequate test of our three-valued model, so we turn to another example.

Example 2 *k-Coloring* Let $G = (V, E)$ be an undirected graph with n vertices. A *coloring* of G with k colors is an assignment of one of k colors to each node of G such that no two adjacent nodes have the same color. We construct default system $S(G)$ such that G is k-colorable iff $S(G)$ has at least one safe element. The minimal safe elements, if there are any, are truth assignments that represent possible k colorings of G. The construction of $S(G)$ is as follows. We choose propositional variables $C(i, c)$ for $1 \leq i \leq n$ and $1 \leq c \leq k$ to represent the fact that node i is colored with color c.

				1 solution				all solutions	
m	vars	clauses	sols	DP	POSIT	WalkSAT	DeReS	DP	DeReS
2	16	81	2	0.01	0.001	0.001	0.01	0.01	0.02
4	32	161	6	0.02	0.001	0.001	0.07	0.03	0.32
6	48	241	5	0.02	0.03	0.002	0.57	0.08	1.90
8	64	321	134	0.03	0.002	0.016	1.45	1.16	18.97
10	80	401	267	0.04	0.003	0.017	9.14	3.69	141.74

Figure 1: finding kernels in 8xm knight's wrapped chess boards

n	DP	POSIT	WalkSAT	DeReS
200	10.73	0.541	0.147	0.18
400	40.78	2.235	0.291	0.34
600	-	5.181	0.441	0.50
800	-	9.156	0.664	0.68
1000	-	14.666	0.182	0.84

Figure 2: coloring on a 2xn ladder, one solution — a "-" indicates a CPU time greater than two minutes

The initial formula ϕ states that each node must have a color,

$$\phi = \bigwedge_{i=1}^{n} \bigvee_{c=1}^{k} C(i,c)$$

and each default rule states roughly that, normally, if a node is colored with a color c then none of its neighbors are colored with color c. Note that if a node has more than one color then it can be assigned any of those possible colors. Thus, the defaults are

$$C(i,c) \rightsquigarrow \bigwedge_{\{i,j\} \in E} \neg C(j,c)$$

for each $1 \leq i \leq n$ and $1 \leq c \leq k$.

Here, since the defaults allow for a node to be colored with any color that is consistent with a coloring, the minimal safe elements are not complete truth assignments and we must use the reduction described in the previous section.

Experimental Results For this experiment, we used the Stanford Graph Base to give us instances of KERNELS and 3-COLORING. In general, the problems were generated and encoded as CNF-SAT and then solved in turn with the various SAT checkers discussed above to compare performance. None of the SAT checkers is necessarily optimized for finding all solutions, as SAT checkers are usually optimized for decision problems. Our tables report CPU times in seconds on a Sun Ultra. Times for DeReS on the same problems are quoted from (Cholewiński, Marek and Truszczyński 1994); keep in mind that we are not comparing implementations of the same model here, although we are solving the same graph problems.

Figure 1 shows results for the kernel problem applied to the class of graphs generated by 8xm knight's wrapped chess boards for $m = 2, 4, 6, 8, 10$. Since the solutions are total, this example was simply coded as the conjunction of ϕ and all the default rules considered as implications, and solved for minimal three-valued satisfiers. The time for one solution (safe element) using our simple implementation of the Davis-Putnam method (Davis and Putnam 1960), Jon Freeman's POSIT (Freeman 1995), and Bart Selman's random hill-climbing WalkSAT (Selman, Kautz and Cohen 1993) are shown. Only the Davis-Putnam procedure was used in finding all safe elements. In this example we see the most dramatic improvement since the translation to 2-valued SAT is not needed.

Figure 2 shows results for the 3-coloring problem applied to 2xn ladders (graphs that can be laid out to look like ladders). Since there are a large number of colorings for a ladder we only report the time to find one safe element. Note that DP and POSIT perform poorly on this problem because of the large number of variables. Because it is randomized, WalkSAT consistently performs better on problems of this type.

The results of this section are promising, but we feel that graph problems do not capture the essence of nonmonotonicity. In the colorability problem, for example, we say that normally, a node can't be colored the same way as any of its neighbors. In fact, though, a node can *never* be colored the same way as one of its neighbors. For general graph problems, solutions correspond to minimal safe elements, and there are no exceptions. That is, if e is safe and $e \sqsubseteq f$, then f is also safe. This is not generally the case: a system with exceptions will have *rogue* elements – unsafe elements f with a safe element e with $e \sqsubseteq f$. For example, consider the simple system:

$$S = (tweety, \{bird \rightsquigarrow fly, tweety \wedge bird \rightsquigarrow \neg fly\}).$$

The minimal safe element of S is the assignment e that only defines *tweety* to 1. The assignment f that assigns

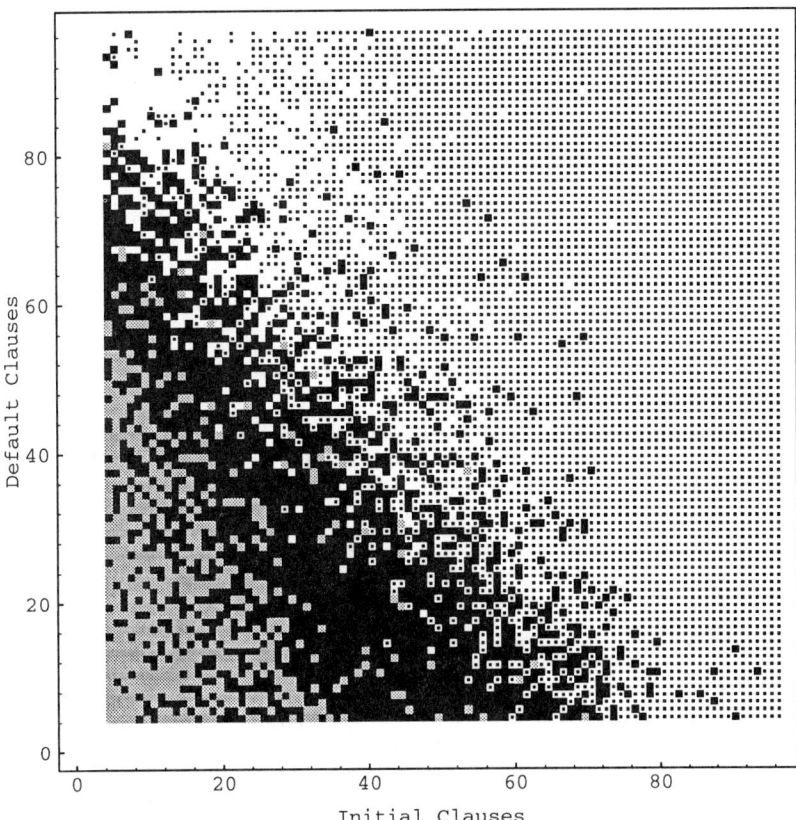

Figure 3: $v = 20, q = 5, i$ and d varied. For each coordinate, (i, j) a random instance with i initial clauses and j defaults was checked. Gray squares are safely not entailed, black are safely entailed, white are unsafe instances and sqaures with a dot are unsafe but entailed.

tweety to 1 and *bird* to 1 is not safe but is such that $e \sqsubseteq f$, so f is a rogue.

Given these observations, we experimented with random instances of default systems, to see the general layout of the skeptical entailment problem.

Randomly Generated Instances

Our experiment in this section is inspired by the SAT community's exploration of randomly generated 3-SAT problems. The following parameters determine the nature of a randomly generated default system:

- v = Number of variables
- i = Number of 3 literal clauses in ϕ
- d = Number of defaults in Σ of the form $a \leadsto b \vee c$
- q = Number of literals in ψ

where ϕ is a CNF formula with i clauses and ψ is a disjunction of q (positive or negative) literals.

The experiment consisted of fixing v at 20 variables, the number of literals in the query at $q = v/4 = 5$ and varying i and d from 4 to 120 to get an idea of the dependence of safety and safe entailment on i and d. Thus, 116×116 random instances were generated and checked for skeptical entailment. Figure 3 shows the results of this experiment. Note that for i and d small, the system is under-specified, and thus, there are many safe elements. In these cases, the probability that ψ will be satisfied by all of them is low. As i and d increase, there are fewer safe elements and ψ is more likely to be entailed. As $i + d$ exceeds about 70 to 75, the systems become over-specified and are more often unsafe. Remarkably, systems seem to become unsafe approximately when $i + d = 4.3v = 68.8$. The number 4.3 is the well-known phase transition point for the 2-valued SAT problem (Mitchell, Selman and Levesque 1992). This intriguing similarity with random 3-SAT problems deserves more exploration.

We omit details of CPU times for this experiment and simply note that in the large majority of instances the CPU time required to decide skeptical entailment was small (under a second). The times were the greatest when i and d were small and the system was under-specified. As the number of safe elements decreased, so did the CPU time needed. It seems likely that in an application of power defaults, it would not be difficult to keep the system from being under-specified. That CPU times for i and d small tend to be large is probably due to the fact that with under-specified systems there are (many) more safe elements to check. Experimentation with a more direct algorithm (not given here) also suggests that CPU times for i and d small may not be subject to much improvement.

Whether or not a query is entailed in a system depends on the "liberalness" of the query. The number of entailed instances in a large sample of random instances grows with the number of literals in the query (a disjunction of literals). The query size also affects the liklihood that $\phi \rightarrow \psi$ will be a tautology. Notice in Figure 3 that unsafe, entailed instance (small dots) become less abundant after a certain point. Where this happens corresponds to the query size. A less liberal query would move this point to the right. Also notice that whether or not these instances are entailed is independent of the defaults.

The results of this section tell us that safety is not a completely elusive property, which is exciting. If it is likely that a system is safe, then checking for safety is not a wasted exercise because we can find safe elements and then check entailment. Our results do show that a fair number of systems actually have only one extension (the safe one, by the Dichotomy Theorem).

Conclusion

We conclude by noting some areas of the work that seem worthy of further exploration. We described an indirect method of computing extensions based on a translation to SAT. We are currently testing a more direct algorithm – a three-valued generalization of the Davis-Putnam procedure. We hope that such an algorithm may be extended to the case of first-order logic.

PDR can express graph problems very naturally. However, we noted that these problems, while good for testing non-monotonic systems, are not essentially non-monotonic themselves. It is difficult to say what a real-life large-scale non-monotonic problem is; likely candidates might be found in the areas of planning, diagnosis and synthesis. It may be that a formal distinction based on the presence or absence of rogue elements can be made.

Ginsberg (Ginsberg 1991) suggests that default rules can be used as computational aids by providing soft rules (islands) that limit the search space of a problem — even though the problem may be solvable without the rules. This seems to be a good general strategy, according with Dichotomy Theorem. That is, if the default rules tell you something consistent and usable, then use it; otherwise, decide entailment without the default rules. This direction may also lead to algorithms for *learning* default rules from examples.

Finally, some theoretical questions; (1) Can we treat non-normal defaults? (2) Can we consider defaults in CPO's besides Scott domains? (3) How expressive is the non-disjunctive case of PDR? For this case entailment is a low-order polynomial-time problem (Zhang and Rounds 1997).

References

J. Cai, T. Gundermann, J. Hartmanis, L. Hemachandra, V. Sewelson, K. Wagner, and G. Wechsung, "The Boolean Hierarchy I: Structural Properties", *SIAM Journal of Computing*, 17, 1232-1252, 1988.

P. Cholewiński, V. W. Marek and M. Truszczyński, "Default Reasoning System DeReS", in *Proceedings of KR-96*, 1996.

M. Davis and H. Putnam, "A computing procedure for quantification", *J. Assoc. Computing Mach.*, 7, 201-215, 1960.

J.W. Freeman, "Improvements to Propositional Satisfiability Search Algorithms", Ph.D. Dissertation, Department of Computer and Information Science, University of Pennsylvania, May 1995.

M.L. Ginsberg, "The Computational Value of Nonmonotonic Reasoning", *Proceedings of KR-91*, 1991.

G. Gottlob, "Complexity results for non-monotonic logics", *J. Logic and Computation*, 2(3):397-425, 1992.

H. Kautz and B. Selman, "Hard Problems for Simple Default Logics", in *Proceedings of KR-89*, 1989.

D.E Knuth, *The Stanford Graph Base: a platform for combinatorial computing*, Addison-Wesley, 1993.

D. Mitchel, B. Selman, H.J. Levesque, "Hard and easy distributions of SAT problems", in *Proceedings of AAAI-92*, San Jose, CA, 459-465, 1992.

I. Niemelä and Patrik Simons, "Smodels – and Implementation of the Stable Model and Well-Founded Semantics for Normal Logic Programs", in *Proceedings of LPNMR-97*, 1997.

B. Selman, H.A. Kautz, B. Cohen, "Local Search Strategies for Satisfiability Testing", Presented at the *Second DIMACS Challenge on Cliques, Coloring, and Satisfiability*, Oct. 1993.

R. Reiter, "A logic for default reasoning", *Artificial Intelligence*, 13:81-132, 1980.

G.-Q. Zhang and W. Rounds, "Complexity of power default reasoning", *Proceedings of the 12th Annual IEEE Symposium on Logic in Computer Science*, 328-339, 1997.

D.S. Scott, "Domains for denotational semantics", In *Lecture Notes in Computer Science 140*, 577-613, 1982.

Reducing query answering to satisfiability in nonmonotonic logics

Riccardo Rosati
Dipartimento di Informatica e Sistemistica
Università di Roma "La Sapienza"
Via Salaria 113, 00198 Roma, Italy
rosati@dis.uniroma1.it

Abstract

We propose a unifying view of negation as failure, integrity constraints, and epistemic queries in nonmonotonic reasoning. Specifically, we study the relationship between satisfiability and logical implication in nonmonotonic logics, showing that, in many nonmonotonic formalisms, it is possible and easy to reduce logical implication to satisfiability. This result not only allows for establishing new complexity results for the satisfiability problem in nonmonotonic logics, but also establishes a clear relationship between the studies on epistemic queries and integrity constraints in monotonic knowledge bases with the work on negation by default in nonmonotonic reasoning and logic programming. From the perspective of the design of knowledge representation systems, such a reduction allows for defining both a simple method for answering epistemic queries in knowledge bases with nonmonotonic abilities, and a procedure for identifying integrity constraints in the knowledge base, which can be employed for optimizing reasoning in such systems.

Introduction

Research in logical formalization of nonmonotonic reasoning has come up with a variety of proposals, which try to overcome the limitations of classical logic with respect to the representation of forms of commonsense reasoning by identifying suitable ways for completing the knowledge of a rational agent. This corresponds to making assumptions and drawing conclusions on the basis of information not specified to the agent, which is not possible in a monotonic, first-order logic setting.

On the one hand, nonmonotonicity allows for representing forms of commonsense reasoning in terms of a logical theory; on the other hand, some interesting properties of classical logic are generally missing in a nonmonotonic framework. In particular, the deduction theorem, namely the property

$$\Sigma \models \varphi \text{ iff } \models \Sigma \supset \varphi$$

does not hold in nonmonotonic logics, with the major exception of Levesque's logic of only-knowing[1] (Levesque

---

Copyright ©1998, American Association for Artificial Intelligence (www.aaai.org). All rights reserved.

[1] Actually, such a logic is monotonic, although it allows for representing knowledge closure.

1990). This property is important not only from a theoretical viewpoint, but also for the design of deductive methods for such logics. In fact, the deduction theorem implies that it is possible to turn logical implication (and hence all the basic reasoning tasks) into satisfiability.

In this paper we analyze in detail the relationship between epistemic queries and knowledge bases in nonmonotonic logics. The results of this study provide a unifying view of the notions of negation as failure, integrity constraints, and epistemic queries in nonmonotonic reasoning.

Specifically, we first study the relationship between logical implication and satisfiability in several nonmonotonic formalisms: Lifschitz's logic of minimal knowledge and negation as failure MKNF (Lifschitz 1991), McDermott and Doyle's modal logics (McDermott and Doyle 1980; McDermott 1982), Moore's autoepistemic logic (Moore 1985), Halpern and Moses' modal logic of minimal knowledge (Halpern and Moses 1985), and Reiter's default logic (Reiter 1980). We show the existence of easy reductions in all these formalisms: in particular, we provide a reduction of query answering to unsatisfiability in MKNF, which highlights the relationship between the notion of epistemic query (Levesque 1984; Levesque 1990; Reiter 1990) and the notion of negation as failure (Gelfond and Lifschitz 1991). Such a reduction also allows for establishing the computational complexity of the satisfiability problem in MKNF.

Notably, the existence of such reductions allows for defining simple methods for answering epistemic queries in knowledge representation systems with nonmonotonic abilities. Such methods rely on usual non-epistemic query answering abilities of the system, reducing the problem of computing answers to epistemic queries to the problem of checking satisfiability of a knowledge base. In particular, we show that it is possible to reduce epistemic query answering to satisfiability in any knowledge representation system which allows for expressing default rules.

Based on the above result, we then provide a generalization of the notion of epistemic integrity constraint introduced by Reiter (Reiter 1990; Demolombe and Jones 1996), which in turn highlights the deep relationship between the notions of integrity constraint and negation as failure. A clear connection is thus established between the studies on epistemic queries and integrity constraints in first-order, monotonic knowledge bases with the work on negation by default in nonmonotonic reasoning and logic programming. In particular, we prove that this generalized, epistemic view of integrity constraints corresponds to a form of nonmonotonic reasoning which is nicely captured by the notion of negation as failure.

Finally, the above characterization of integrity constraints can be exploited in order to speed up the deduction process in nonmonotonic knowledge bases. Specifically, we define an algorithm for establishing whether a formula is an integrity constraint in the setting of MKNF.

The paper is organized as follows. First, we recall nonmonotonic modal logics, in particular Lifschitz's MKNF and McDermott and Doyle's logics. Then, we deal with the problem of reducing query answering to unsatisfiability in nonmonotonic logics. Finally, we study the relationship between negation as failure and Reiter's epistemic interpretation of integrity constraints.

Preliminaries

In this section we briefly recall Lifschitz's logic MKNF (Lifschitz 1991) and McDermott and Doyle's (MDD) logics (McDermott 1982; Marek and Truszczyński 1993).

MKNF is a modal logic with two epistemic operators: a "minimal knowledge" modality K and a "negation as failure" (also called "negation by default") modality not; however, for ease of notation, in the following we will use the symbol A (introduced in (Lin and Shoham 1992)), which stands for $\neg not$. We use $\mathcal{L}$ to denote a fixed propositional language built in the usual way from an alphabet $\mathcal{A}$ of propositional symbols (atoms), the symbols true, false, and the propositional connectives $\wedge, \neg$ ($\vee, \supset$ are defined as usual in terms of $\wedge, \neg$). Formulas from $\mathcal{L}$ are called *objective*. We denote with $\mathcal{L}_M$ the modal extension of $\mathcal{L}$ with the modalities K and A (and call *MKNF formula* a formula from $\mathcal{L}_M$), with $\mathcal{L}_K$ the set of formulas from $\mathcal{L}_M$ in which the modality A does not occur (called *K-formulas*), and with $\mathcal{L}_A$ the set of formulas from $\mathcal{L}_M$ in which K does not occur (called *A-formulas*). We call φ a *subjective* formula if each propositional symbol in φ appears in the scope of at least one modality. Moreover, we call *modal atom* any formula of the form $K\psi$ or $A\psi$; the set $MA(\varphi)$ of modal atoms of $\varphi \in \mathcal{L}_M$ is the set of modal atoms which are subformulas of φ, and $MA(\Sigma)$, when $\Sigma \subseteq \mathcal{L}_M$, is the union of the modal atoms of all formulas from Σ.

We now recall the notion of MKNF model. An *interpretation* I is a subset of propositional symbols from $\mathcal{A}$ ($p \in \mathcal{A}$ is true in I iff $p \in I$). Satisfiability of a formula $\varphi \in \mathcal{L}$ in I (which we denote as $I \models \varphi$) is defined in the usual way. A set of interpretations M is called *cluster*, since modal formulas are evaluated in M as in the Kripke model in which each world corresponds to an interpretation in M and the accessibility relation between worlds is universal. We denote with $Th(M)$ the set of modal formulas from $\mathcal{L}_K$ which are satisfied in M. An MKNF structure is a triple (I, M_k, M_a), where I is an interpretation and M_k, M_a are clusters, which are denoted respectively as the K-cluster and the A-cluster of (I, M_k, M_a). Satisfiability of a formula in an MKNF structure is inductively defined as follows:

1. if φ is an atom, φ is true in (I, M_k, M_a) iff $\varphi \in I$;
2. $\neg\varphi$ is true in (I, M_k, M_a) iff φ is not true in (I, M_k, M_a);
3. $\varphi_1 \wedge \varphi_2$ is true in (I, M_k, M_a) iff φ_1 is true in (I, M_k, M_a) and φ_2 is true in (I, M_k, M_a);
4. $K\varphi$ is true in (I, M_k, M_a) iff, for every $J \in M_k$, φ is true in (J, M_k, M_a);
5. $A\varphi$ is true in (I, M_k, M_a) iff, for every $J \in M_a$, φ is true in (J, M_k, M_a).

Given a pair (M_k, M_a) of clusters, and a formula $\varphi \in \mathcal{L}_M$, we write $(M_k, M_a) \models \varphi$ (and say that φ is satisfied in (M_k, M_a)) iff for each $I \in M_k$, φ is true in (I, M_k, M_a). When $\varphi \in \mathcal{L}_K$ sometimes we abbreviate $(M_k, M_a) \models \varphi$ with $M_k \models \varphi$, since the A-cluster M_a is not considered in the evaluation of K-formulas. If $\Sigma \subseteq \mathcal{L}_M$, we write $(I, M_k, M_a) \models \Sigma$ iff $(I, M_k, M_a) \models \varphi$ for each $\varphi \in \Sigma$.

Definition 1 *A cluster M is a MKNF model (or simply model) for $\Sigma \subseteq \mathcal{L}_M$ iff $(M, M) \models \Sigma$ and, for each cluster M', if $(M', M) \models \Sigma$ then $M' \not\supset M$.*

We say that a formula $\varphi \in \mathcal{L}_K$ is logically implied by $\Sigma \in \mathcal{L}_M$ in MKNF (and write $\Sigma \models \varphi$) iff φ is true in every MKNF model for Σ. We say that $\Sigma \subseteq \mathcal{L}_M$ is MKNF-satisfiable if Σ has an MKNF model (MKNF-unsatisfiable otherwise). When dealing with the entailment problem $\Sigma \models \varphi$, we call *knowledge base* the formula Σ, and *query* the formula φ. Notice that only K-formulas are allowed as queries, since each MKNF model corresponds to a structure where the A-cluster coincides with the K-cluster, therefore A would be interpreted in the same way as K in the query.

It has been proved (Lifschitz 1991) that MKNF is able to embed many of the best known formalisms for nonmonotonic reasoning, e.g. default logic, autoepistemic logic, circumscription, and extended disjunctive logic programs. Such a logic has therefore been considered as a unifying framework for nonmonotonic reasoning.

Example 2 Let $\Sigma = \{Kp\}$. The only MKNF model for Σ is $M = \{I : I \models p\}$. Hence, $\Sigma \models Kp$, and $\Sigma \models \neg K\psi$ for each $\psi \in \mathcal{L}$ such that $p \supset \psi$ is not a propositional tautology. Therefore, the agent modeled by Σ has minimal knowledge, in the sense that she only knows p and the objective facts logically implied by p. Also, let $\Sigma = \{\neg Ap \supset Kq\}$. It is easy to see that the only MKNF model for Σ is $M = \{I : I \models q\}$, since p can be assumed not to hold by the agent modeled by Σ, which is then able to conclude q.

It turns out that, when restricting to K-formulas, MKNF corresponds to the modal logic of minimal knowledge due to Halpern and Moses (Halpern and Moses 1985), also known as ground nonmonotonic modal logic $\mathsf{S5}_G$. The semantics of K-formulas can be given by simplifying Definition 1 as follows (Shoham 1987): M is a model for $\Sigma \in \mathcal{L}_K$ iff $M \models \Sigma$ and, for each M', if $M' \models \Sigma$ then $M' \not\supset M$.

In other words, when $\Sigma \in \mathcal{L}_K$, a cluster M satisfying Σ is compared with all other clusters satisfying Σ, while in the case $\Sigma \in \mathcal{L}_M$ the cluster M is only compared with those clusters M' such that (M', M) satisfies Σ. Hence, the main difference between MKNF and S5$_G$ lies in the fact that in S5$_G$ all models are maximal wrt set containment (or minimal wrt the objective knowledge which holds in the model), while in MKNF this property is not generally true. E.g., the theory $\Sigma = \{Aq \supset Kq\}$ has two models: M_1, corresponding to the set of all interpretations (which represents the case in which Aq is not assumed to hold); and $M_2 = \{I : I \models q\}$. Namely, if Aq is assumed to hold, then Kq must be assumed to hold in order to satisfy Σ: that is, the initial assumption is *justified* by the knowledge derived on the basis of such assumption (Lin and Shoham 1992).

Finally, we briefly recall MDD logics, a family of unimodal nonmonotonic modal formalisms which are among the most studied logics for nonmonotonic reasoning (McDermott and Doyle 1980; McDermott 1982; Marek and Truszczyński 1993). Here we report a characterization of MDD logics in terms of a preference semantics on Kripke models (Schwarz 1992), which is better suited to our purposes than the original, equivalent characterization in terms of expansions (i.e. sets of modal formulas).

Definition 3 *Given a modal logic $\mathcal{S}$, a cluster M is an $\mathcal{S}_{MDD}$ model for $\Sigma \subseteq \mathcal{L}_K$ if: (i) $M \models \Sigma$; (ii) for each Kripke model $\mathcal{N}$ for the logic $\mathcal{S}$, if $\mathcal{N} \models \Sigma \cup \{\neg K\psi : \psi \in \mathcal{L}_K - Th(M)\}$, then $Th(\mathcal{N}) = Th(M)$.*

We write $\Sigma \models_{\mathcal{S}_{MDD}} \varphi$ iff φ is satisfied in all $\mathcal{S}_{MDD}$ models for Σ. We say that Σ is $\mathcal{S}_{MDD}$-satisfiable if it has an $\mathcal{S}_{MDD}$ model. We remark that the logic KD45$_{MDD}$ corresponds to well-known Moore's autoepistemic logic (AEL) (Moore 1985). It can also be shown that AEL in turn corresponds to the K-free fragment of MKNF (Lin and Shoham 1992; Rosati 1997b). We denote with Σ^K the theory obtained by replacing in Σ all occurrences of the modality A with K in all formulas from Σ.

Proposition 4 *Let $\Sigma \subseteq \mathcal{L}_A$. Then, M is an MKNF model for Σ iff M is a KD45$_{MDD}$ model for Σ^K.*

The previous property implies that the modality A has in MKNF exactly the *same* interpretation of the modal operator of autoepistemic logic.

From query answering to satisfiability

In this section we study the problem of reducing logical implication (or query answering) to unsatisfiability in nonmonotonic logics. In particular, we analyze this problem in the following settings: MKNF, MDD logics, AEL, S5$_G$, and default logic.

Generally speaking, it is not immediate to perform such a reduction in nonmonotonic logics, since the deduction theorem does not hold in these formalisms. In order to reduce query answering to unsatisfiability, we look for a translation $\mathcal{E}(\varphi)$ of the query φ such that, for each knowledge base Σ, $\Sigma \cup \{\mathcal{E}(\varphi)\}$ is unsatisfiable iff φ is satisfied in all models for Σ. The basic idea is to obtain a formula $\mathcal{E}(\varphi)$ from φ such that the effect of adding $\mathcal{E}(\varphi)$ to Σ is to rule out all those models for Σ satisfying φ, while preserving all other models for Σ. It turns out that such a translation is extremely easy to define for many nonmonotonic logics.

We start by analyzing the case of MDD logics.

Theorem 5 *Let $K \subseteq \mathcal{S} \subseteq S5, \Sigma \subseteq \mathcal{L}_K, \varphi \in \mathcal{L}_K$. Then, $\Sigma \models_{\mathcal{S}_{MDD}} \varphi$ iff the theory $\Sigma \cup \{\neg K\varphi\}$ is $\mathcal{S}_{MDD}$-unsatisfiable.*

The proof of this theorem can be obtained by showing that adding a formula of the form $\neg K\varphi$ to Σ not only rules out all $\mathcal{S}_{MDD}$ models for Σ satisfying φ, but also cannot give rise to any model for $\Sigma \cup \{\varphi\}$ different from a model for Σ. In fact, suppose M is a cluster satisfying both Σ and $\neg K\varphi$. It is easy to see that if M is an $\mathcal{S}_{MDD}$ model for Σ, then M is an $\mathcal{S}_{MDD}$ model for $\Sigma \cup \{\neg K\varphi\}$. Now suppose M is not an $\mathcal{S}_{MDD}$ model for Σ. Then, by Definition 3 there exists a Kripke model $\mathcal{N}$ such that $\mathcal{N} \models \Sigma \cup \{\neg K\psi : \psi \in \mathcal{L}_K - Th(M)\}$, and since $M \not\models \varphi$, it follows that $\neg K\varphi \in \{\neg K\psi : \psi \in \mathcal{L}_K - Th(M)\}$. Consequently, the properties of model $\mathcal{N}$ imply that Condition 2. in Definition 3 is false, hence M is not an $\mathcal{S}_{MDD}$ model for $\Sigma \cup \{\neg K\varphi\}$.

An analogous result can be obtained in the case of MKNF, through the translation function $\mathcal{E}_{MKNF}(\cdot)$.

Definition 6 *Let $\varphi \in \mathcal{L}_K$. Then, $\mathcal{E}_{MKNF}(\varphi) \in \mathcal{L}_M$ is the formula obtained from φ by substituting each occurrence of the modality K in φ with A.*

The proof of the following property follows from the semantic definition of MKNF, in a way similar to the proof of Theorem 5.

Theorem 7 *Let $\Sigma \subseteq \mathcal{L}_M, \varphi \in \mathcal{L}_K$. Then, $\Sigma \models_{MKNF} \varphi$ iff the theory $\Sigma \cup \{\mathcal{E}_{MKNF}(\neg K\varphi)\}$ is MKNF-unsatisfiable.*

The above theorem establishes a precise relationship between the notions of epistemic query and negation as failure: more precisely, it implies a duality between the epistemic modality used in query expressions and the negation as failure (or autoepistemic) operator of MKNF. Informally, a formula can pass from the right-hand side to the left-hand side of the logical implication symbol in MKNF by negating it and replacing all its modalities with the A operator.

Notice that both Theorem 5 and Theorem 7 imply the same translation for autoepistemic logic (corresponding to the case $\mathcal{S} =$ KD45 in Theorem 5 and to the use of the only modality A in MKNF).

On the other hand, it is easy to show that it is impossible to easily reduce query answering to unsatisfiability in S5$_G$, the A-free fragment of MKNF. In fact, the following computational result holds: the problem $\Sigma \models_{S5_G} \varphi$ is Π_3^p-complete,[2] while S5$_G$-unsatisfiability is coNP-complete. Hence, unless the polynomial hierarchy collapses, it is not possible to find a polynomial-time translation of φ for turning query answering into unsatisfiability in S5$_G$.

---

[2] We refer to (Johnson 1990) for the definition of the complexity classes mentioned in the paper.

Finally, we deal with the problem of reducing query answering to unsatisfiability in Reiter's default logic. First, we briefly recall Reiter's default logic (DL in the following). A default theory is a pair (D, W) such that $W \in \mathcal{L}$ and D is a set of default rules, each one of the form

$$d = \frac{\alpha : \beta_1, \ldots, \beta_n}{\gamma} \quad (1)$$

where $n \geq 0$ and $\alpha, \beta_1, \ldots, \beta_n, \gamma \in \mathcal{L}$. We recall that a default extension is a deductively closed set of propositional formulas, which can be constructed starting from $\{W\}$ and increasing such a set by applying the special inference rules in D. In order to apply a default rule of the form (1) (i.e. adding the conclusion γ to the extension), the prerequisite α must be implied by the set of formulas representing the part of the extension constructed so far, while each negated justification $\neg \beta_i$ must not be implied set of formulas obtained after applying all defaults. We refer to (Reiter 1980) for a detailed definition of the semantics of DL.

In order to define epistemic queries over default theories, we establish a natural correspondence between extensions and clusters: we say that $\varphi \in \mathcal{L}_K$ is logically implied by a default theory (D, W) iff, for each extension E of (D, W), $M(E) \models \varphi$, where $M(E)$ is the cluster $\{I : I \models E\}$.

We now define a translation $\mathcal{E}_{DL}(\cdot)$ of epistemic queries into default rules. Let $\varphi \in \mathcal{L}_K$. We denote with $DNF(\varphi)$ the formula corresponding to a modal disjunctive normal form of φ, precisely the following formula (which is equivalent to $K\varphi$ in modal logic S5):

$$DNF(\varphi) = \bigwedge_i \neg K\alpha^i \vee K\beta_1^i \vee \ldots \vee K\beta_{n_i}^i \quad (2)$$

where all $\alpha^i, \beta_j^i \in \mathcal{L}$. Any formula $\varphi \in \mathcal{L}_K$ can be put in such a normal form (e.g. through the transformation reported in (Hughes and Cresswell 1968)).

Given a formula φ such that $DNF(\varphi)$ has the form (2), $\mathcal{E}_{DL}(\varphi)$ is the set of default rules

$$\bigcup_i \left\{ \frac{\alpha^i : \neg \beta_1^i, \ldots, \neg \beta_{n_i}^i}{\text{false}} \right\}$$

In the following, we call *conclusion-free* default a default rule whose conclusion is the formula false. Observe that the translation $\mathcal{E}_{DL}(\cdot)$ is polynomial if φ is in modal conjunctive normal form, i.e.:

$$\varphi = \bigvee_i K\alpha^i \wedge \neg K\beta_1^i \wedge \ldots \wedge \neg K\beta_{n_i}^i$$

Theorem 8 *Let (D, W) be a default theory, and let $\varphi \in \mathcal{L}_K$. Then, φ is logically implied by (D, W) iff the default theory $(D \cup \mathcal{E}_{DL}(\neg K\varphi), W)$ has no extensions.*

The above results show that in general it is quite easy to reduce query answering to unsatisfiability in nonmonotonic logics. Moreover, the reductions presented can be employed in the realization of epistemic query answering in nonmonotonic knowledge representation systems: in fact, a simple method for adding epistemic queries to a system with the ability of expressing negation as failure consists of first adding the translation of the epistemic query to the knowledge base, and then checking unsatisfiability of the knowledge base thus obtained through the non-epistemic query false. E.g., such a method can be employed in those knowledge representation systems which provide the ability of expressing defaults for answering epistemic queries (in modal conjunctive normal form) in such systems, by first translating each epistemic query in terms of a set of conclusion-free defaults, then adding such defaults to the knowledge base, and finally checking whether the new knowledge base implies the query false.

Finally, the above results can be used, together with known computational analyses of query answering in nonmonotonic logics, for establishing the computational characterizations of the satisfiability problem in such formalisms. The following theorem characterizes the computational complexity of satisfiablity in MKNF.

Theorem 9 *Let $\Sigma \subseteq \mathcal{L}_M$. Then, the problem of establishing whether Σ is MKNF-unsatisfiable is Π_3^p-complete.*

The proof of the above property directly follows from the following facts: (i) query answering in MKNF is Π_3^p-complete (Rosati 1997); (ii) $\mathcal{E}_{MKNF}(\varphi)$ can be computed in time linear wrt the size of φ; (iii) validity of Theorem 7.

Integrity constraints in nonmonotonic logics

In this section we deal with the representation of integrity constraints (ICs) in nonmonotonic logics. We start by recalling Reiter's epistemic interpretation of ICs in first-order knowledge bases (Reiter 1990): an IC is not a statement about the world, it is a statement about what the knowledge base is said to know. Under this interpretation, an IC φ is not analogous to a usual piece of information in the knowledge base Σ, which causes inconsistency of $\Sigma \cup \{\varphi\}$ iff φ contradicts other information in Σ: it is a property which *must hold* in Σ in order to preserve consistency of Σ.

Reiter pointed out that this kind of ICs could be formalized in terms of epistemic queries to first-order knowledge bases, if the knowledge base is interpreted according to a minimal knowledge semantics (what is not logically implied by Σ is assumed as *not known* by Σ). Under this semantics, any consistent first-order knowledge base Σ has one (epistemic) model, which consists of the set of all first-order interpretations satisfying Σ. An integrity constraint ψ can be checked by verifying whether the property ψ (which is in general an epistemic formula) is satisfied in this model: if it is not the case, then Σ is inconsistent wrt ψ.

Example 10 *Let φ, ψ be propositional formulas, and let $\mathcal{I}$ be the IC: "If φ is known to hold, then ψ must be known to hold", which expresses the fact that those models for Σ in which φ holds and ψ does not hold should be ruled out. $\mathcal{I}$ can be expressed as an epistemic query by the formula $\mathcal{I}' = K\varphi \supset K\psi$, which can be used for discarding such models* during the evaluation of another query ξ against Σ, since it can be shown that $\Sigma \models_{MKNF} \xi$ iff $\Sigma \models_{MKNF} (\mathcal{I}' \supset \xi)$.

In a nonmonotonic logic setting, a knowledge base has in general many epistemic models. The natural generalization of Reiter's interpretation of integrity constraints to this case is to consider a formula as an IC iff the effect of adding it to a knowledge base reduces the set of models of the knowledge base, without producing any new model. That is, φ is an IC iff for each knowledge base Σ, $MOD(\Sigma) \supseteq MOD(\Sigma \cup \{\varphi\})$, where $MOD(\Sigma)$ represents the set of models of Σ. In other words, the effect of φ is just to rule out those models for Σ which do not satisfy φ.

We formally generalize the above notion of integrity constraint to the case of MKNF through the following definition (in which $MOD(\Sigma)$ denotes the set of MKNF models for Σ), which can be easily instantiated to the case of all other nonmonotonic logics dealt with by the paper.

Definition 11 *A formula $\varphi \in \mathcal{L}_M$ is an integrity constraint iff for each $\Sigma \subseteq \mathcal{L}_M$, $MOD(\Sigma) \supseteq MOD(\Sigma \cup \{\varphi\})$.*

Let us now go back to the reduction of query answering to satisfiability in MKNF. It is not hard to see that, given any query $\psi \in \mathcal{L}_K$, the formula $\mathcal{E}_{MKNF}(\psi)$ is an IC. This shows the perfect duality between the above notion of integrity constraint and the notion of epistemic query: not only any IC can be checked through an epistemic query (as shown by Reiter), but also any epistemic query has a corresponding IC. This property, together with the relationship between negation as failure and epistemic queries previously illustrated, establishes a tight connection between integrity constraints and negation as failure: any IC in MKNF is equivalent to a subjective A-formula. That is, the negation as failure (or autoepistemic) modality is *the* epistemic operator for expressing ICs.

The above results show that epistemic queries and integrity constraints are dual notions, and both can be naturally expressed by the negation as failure modality.

Example 12 (10 cont'd) We now show that $\mathcal{I}$ can directly be expressed as a formula inside the MKNF knowledge base, by simply substituting in $\mathcal{I}'$ all occurrences of K with A: $\mathcal{I}'' = A\varphi \supset A\psi$. Indeed, the models for $\Sigma \cup \{\mathcal{I}''\}$ are exactly those models for Σ verifying $\mathcal{I}$ (and $\mathcal{I}'$). Adding $\mathcal{I}'$ to Σ does *not* correctly formalize $\mathcal{I}$: informally, $\mathcal{I}'$ rules out only those models for Σ which satisfy φ and are inconsistent with ψ (e.g. which satisfy $\neg\psi$), while it *forces* knowledge of ψ in those models for Σ satisfying φ and consistent with ψ, which is not the intended meaning of the IC.

As for reasoning in nonmonotonic knowledge bases, recognizing ICs may help to speed up the deduction process in such systems. For example, it would be very useful to establish that a piece of information that has to be added to a knowledge base is an IC, since in this case the knowledge base shows a "monotonic" behaviour. Suppose e.g. that Σ has to be updated with a formula φ. Now, if φ is an IC, then (i) it could be processed by an ad-hoc procedure for ICs: if e.g. the models of Σ have been stored, then it is sufficient to evaluate φ against such models in order to find the set of models of $\Sigma \cup \{\varphi\}$ (those models of Σ satisfying φ); (ii) all queries true in Σ are also true in $\Sigma \cup \{\varphi\}$, which can be helpful for reusing previously computed answers to queries.

A first and straightforward way to identify ICs is by looking at their syntactic form. E.g. in MKNF, the fact that φ is a subjective A-formula implies that φ is an IC; in DL, any conclusion-free default is an IC. However, these are just sufficient conditions for establishing whether a piece of information is an IC: e.g., it can be shown that the formula $K\varphi \supset A\psi$ with $\varphi, \psi \in \mathcal{L}$ is an IC in MKNF, while in DL any default rule whose conclusion is propositionally equivalent to false is an IC. Such examples show that, in general, it is not immediate to check a formula against the necessary and sufficient condition reported in Definition 11.

In the following we study the problem of establishing whether a formula is an IC in the setting of MKNF. We remark that in principle the techniques employed in this case can also be used for other nonmonotonic modal logics. First, we provide an alternative characterization of *non*-ICs in MKNF, which is easily derived from the definition of MKNF model.

Theorem 13 *A formula $\varphi \in \mathcal{L}_M$ is not an integrity constraint iff there exist two clusters M, M' such that the following conditions hold: (i) $(M, M) \models \varphi$; (ii) $M' \supset M$; (iii) $(M', M) \not\models \varphi$.*

In fact, it can be shown that the existence of two clusters M, M' verifying the conditions in the above theorem imply the existence of a $\Sigma \subseteq \mathcal{L}_M$, which is both satisfied in (M, M) and in (M', M) (and hence M is not an MKNF model for Σ), while M is an MKNF model for $\Sigma \cup \{\varphi\}$.

Based on the above theorem, it is possible to define an algorithm for checking whether a formula $\varphi \in \mathcal{L}_M$ is an IC. The technique used in the algorithm for verifying the conditions reported in Theorem 13 is based on a finite characterization of clusters which is widely used in deduction methods for nonmonotonic modal logics (see e.g. (Niemelä 1988; Marek and Truszczyński 1993)). Specifically, it is possible to reason about the infinite set of all possible clusters by analyzing the finite set of all possible partitions of modal atoms of φ, and to represent a single cluster through a propositional formula, called *objective knowledge* of the cluster, such that all interpretations in the cluster satisfy such a formula.

In order to define the algorithm, we need some auxiliary definitions. Let P, N be disjoint subsets of modal atoms from $\mathcal{L}_M$. Then, $\varphi(P, N)$ is the formula obtained by replacing in φ each occurrence of a modal atom from P with true and each occurrence of a modal atom from N with false. We also give the following definitions:

$$Obj^-(P, N) = \bigwedge_{K\psi \in P} \psi(P, N)$$

$$Obj_A(P, N) = \bigwedge_{A\psi \in P} \psi(P, N)$$

$$Obj(\varphi, P, N) = Obj^-(P, N) \wedge \varphi(P, N)$$

Let $\varphi \in \mathcal{L}_M$, and let (P, N) be a partition of $MA(\varphi)$. Then, (P, N) is *consistent* with $\varphi \in \mathcal{L}_M$ iff:
(i) the propositional formula $Obj(\varphi, P, N)$ is consistent;
(ii) the propositional formula $Obj_A(P, N)$ is consistent;
(iii) for each $K\psi \in N$, $Obj(\varphi, P, N) \not\vdash \psi(P, N)$;
(iv) for each $A\psi \in N$, $Obj_A(P, N) \not\vdash \psi(P, N)$.

In the following, φ^K denotes the formula obtained from φ by replacing all modalities A with K, and $\vdash$ denotes logical implication in propositional logic. The algorithm is reported below.

Algorithm Not-IC(φ)
Input: formula $\varphi \in \mathcal{L}_M$;
Output: true if φ is not an IC, false otherwise.
  if there exist partition (P, N) of $MA(\varphi^K)$
  and partition (P', N') of $MA(\varphi)$
  such that
    (a) (P, N) is consistent with φ^K **and**
    (b) (P', N') is consistent with true **and**
    (c) $Obj(\varphi, P, N) \vdash Obj^-(P', N')$ **and**
    (d) $Obj^-(P', N') \not\vdash Obj(\varphi, P, N)$ **and**
    (e) $Obj^-(P', N') \not\vdash \varphi(P', N')$ **and**
    (f) **for each** $A\psi \in MA(\varphi)$,
      $A\psi \in P'$ iff $Obj(\varphi, P, N) \vdash \psi(P', N')$
  then return true
  else return false

Correctness of the above algorithm can be proved by exploiting previous results on finite characterizations of clusters (Marek and Truszczyński 1993; Rosati 1997). An intuitive explanation of the algorithm can be given as follows. Roughly speaking, partition (P, N) represents the MKNF structure (M, M), while (P', N') represents (M', M). $Obj(\varphi, P, N)$ represents the objective knowledge of M, while $Obj^-(P', N')$ represents the objective knowledge of M'. The three conditions reported in Theorem 13 are checked by the algorithm as follows. (i) $(M, M) \models \varphi$ is verified through condition (a); (ii) $M' \supset M$ is verified through conditions (c) and (d); (iii) $(M', M) \not\models \varphi$ is verified through condition (e). Finally, condition (b) is necessary in order to detect when (P', N') is a self-contradictory guess on modal formulas, while condition (f) guarantees that the two structures identified by (P, N) and (P', N') have the same A-cluster.

Theorem 14 *Let $\varphi \in \mathcal{L}_M$. Then, φ is an IC iff Not-IC(φ) returns* false.

It can be shown that the above algorithm, when considered as a non-deterministic procedure, has a cost of Σ_2^p. Hence, the problem of establishing whether an MKNF formula is an IC is in Π_2^p.

Conclusions

The main contributions of this paper can be summarized as follows. First, logical implication can be easily reduced to satisfiability in many nonmonotonic logics. Second, there exists a tight relationship between the notions of epistemic query, integrity constraints, and negation as failure. Third, it is possible to exploit the above results for improving automated nonmonotonic reasoning methods. In particular, the relationship between negation as failure and epistemic queries suggests a new reading of the computational and epistemological properties of logic programs with negation as failure. We are currently addressing this research topic.

Acknowledgments

This resarch has been partially supported by EC Esprit LTR project DWQ, "Foundations of Data Warehouse Quality". The author is thankful to Joeri Engelfriet, Daniele Nardi, and Francesco M. Donini for stimulating discussions on the subject of the paper.

References

R. Demolombe and A. Jones. Integrity constraints revisited. *Journal of the IGPL*, 4(3):369–383, 1996.

M. Gelfond and V. Lifschitz. Classical negation in logic programs and deductive databases. *New generation computing*, 9:365–385, 1991.

J. Y. Halpern and Y. Moses. Towards a theory of knowledge and ignorance: Preliminary report. Technical Report CD-TR 92/34, IBM, 1985.

G. E. Hughes and M. J. Cresswell. An introduction to modal logic. Methuen, London, 1968.

D. S. Johnson. A catalog of complexity classes. In J. van Leeuwen, editor, *Handbook of Theoretical Computer Science*, volume A, chapter 2. Elsevier, 1990.

H.J. Levesque. Foundations of a functional approach to knowledge representation. *AI Journal*, 23:155–212, 1984.

H.J. Levesque. All I know: a study in autoepistemic logic. *AI Journal*, 42:263–310, 1990.

V. Lifschitz. Nonmonotonic databases and epistemic queries. In *Proc. of IJCAI-91*, 381–386, 1991.

V. Lifschitz. Minimal belief and negation as failure. *AI Journal*, 70:53–72, 1994.

F. Lin and Y. Shoham. A logic of knowledge and justified assumptions. *AI Journal*, 57:271–289, 1992

W. Marek and M. Truszczyński. *Nonmonotonic Logics – Context-Dependent Reasoning*. Springer-Verlag, 1993.

D. McDermott and J. Doyle. Non-monotonic logic I. *AI Journal*, 13:41–72, 1980.

D. McDermott. Non-monotonic logic II: Non-monotonic modal theories. *Journal of the ACM*, 29:33–57, 1982.

R. C. Moore. Semantical considerations on nonmonotonic logic. *AI Journal*, 25:75–94, 1985.

I. Niemelä. Decision procedure for autoepistemic logic. In *Proc. of CADE-88*, 675–684, 1988.

R. Reiter. A logic for default reasoning. *AI Journal*, 13:81–132, 1980.

R. Reiter. What should a database know? *Journal of Logic Programming*, 14:127–153, 1990.

R. Rosati. Reasoning with minimal belief and negation as failure: algorithms and complexity. In *Proc. of AAAI-97*, 430–435, 1997.

R. Rosati. Embedding minimal knowledge into autoepistemic logic. *Proc. of the 6th Conf. of the Italian Association for AI (AI*IA-97)*, 231–241, LNAI 1321. Springer-Verlag, 1997.

G. Schwarz. Minimal model semantics for nonmonotonic modal logics. In *Proc. of LICS-92*, 34–43. IEEE Press, 1992.

G. Schwarz and M. Truszczyński. Minimal knowledge problem: a new approach. *AI Journal*, 67:113–141, 1994.

Y. Shoham. Nonmonotonic logics: Meaning and utility. In *Proc. of IJCAI-87*, pp. 388–392, 1987.

Planning

Improving Big Plans

Neal Lesh, Nathaniel Martin, James Allen*
Computer Science Department
University of Rochester
Rochester NY 14627
{lesh,martin,james}@cs.rochester.edu

Abstract

Past research on assessing and improving plans in domains that contain uncertainty has focused on analytic techniques that are exponential in the length of the plan. Little work has been done on choosing from among the many ways in which a plan can be improved. We present the IMPROVE algorithm which simulates the execution of large, probabilistic plans. IMPROVE runs a data mining algorithm on the execution traces to pinpoint defects in the plan that most often lead to plan failure. Finally, IMPROVE applies qualitative reasoning and plan adaptation algorithms to modify the plan to correct these defects. We have tested IMPROVE on plans containing over 250 steps in an evacuation domain, produced by a domain-specific scheduling routine. In these experiments, the modified plans have over a 15% higher probability of achieving their goal than the original plan.

Introduction

Large, complex domains call for large, robust plans. However, today's state-of-the-art planning algorithms cannot efficiently generate large or robust plans from first principles. We have combined work on data mining (Agrawal & Srikant 1995), qualitative reasoning (Wellman 1990), planning (Nebel & Koehler 1995), and simulation to construct the IMPROVE algorithm which modifies a given plan so that it has a higher probability of achieving its goal.

An algorithm for improving big plans is useful only if big, but not especially robust, plans can be generated to begin with. We believe domain specific and collaborative planning algorithms (e.g. (Ferguson, Allen, & Miller 1996)) will produce such plans. In our experiments, we use a greedy, domain specific algorithm to produce plans with 250 to 300 steps in an evacuation domain. This algorithm, however, ignores projected weather patterns and undesirable outcomes of actions such as buses overheating or helicopters crashing.

The IMPROVE algorithm repeatedly simulates the input plan, analyzes the execution traces to identify what went wrong when the plan failed, and then generates a set of modifications that might avoid these problems. Finally, the algorithm re-simulates to determine which, if any, of the modifications best improves the robustness of the plan. This whole process is repeated until the modifications cease to improve the plan.

In the first step, we use a discrete event simulator to generate execution traces based on a probabilistic model of the domain. We show that simulation is an attractive alternative to analytic techniques for determining the probability of a plan achieving its goal. Simulation is linear in the length of the plan and fast in practice. Further, the estimate produced by simulation converges, as more simulations are performed, to the true probability that a plan will achieve its goal.

In the second step, we use SPADE (Zaki 1997), a sequential discovery data mining algorithm to extract patterns of events that are common in traces of plan failures but uncommon in traces of plan successes. The patterns are used to determine what to fix in the plan. For example, if the plan often fails when Bus1 gets a flat tire *and* overheats, then IMPROVE attempts to prevent at least one of those problems from occurring.

In the third step, we apply qualitative reasoning techniques (Wellman 1990) to modify the plan to avoid the problems that arose in simulation. For example, if the problem is that a bus is getting a flat tire then this step might suggest changing its tires.

Finally, plan modifications can necessitate further planning. For example, adding an action to a plan requires that the preconditions of the action be satisfied, perhaps by adding more actions. We show how this problem is closely related to the problem of plan re-use or adaptation (Nebel & Koehler 1995).

---

*Many thanks to George Ferguson, Mitsu Ogihara, and Mohammed Zaki as well as the AAAI reviewers for comments and discussion. This material is based upon work supported by ARPA under Grant number F30602-95-1-0025.
Copyright ©1998, American Association for Artificial Intelligence (www.aaai.org). All rights reserved.

Below, we first formulate the plan improvement problem. We then describe our four components: simulation, data mining, qualitative reasoning, planning. We then present our improvement algorithm, describe our experiments, and then conclude.

Formulation

In this section, we define our terms and specify the input and output of the plan improvement problem.

The problem of planning under uncertainty has recently been addressed by a variety of researchers. See (Goldman & Boddy 1996) and (Boutilier, Dean, & Hanks 1995) for comparisons of various approaches. We use the representation of actions used by the Buridan planner (Kushmerick, Hanks, & Weld 1995), which allows for probabilistic and conditional effects, but not for exogenous events or for actions to be executed in parallel or have varying durations. In our actual system, we allow for limited forms of all of these factors.

An *action* is a set of *consequences* $\{ \langle t_1, e_1, p_1 \rangle, ..., \langle t_n, e_n, p_n \rangle \}$, where for every i, t_i is an expression called the consequence's *trigger*, e_i is a set of literals called the consequence's *effects*, and $0 \leq p_i \leq 1$ indicates the probability that the action will have effect e_i if executed in a state in which t_i holds. The triggers must be mutually exclusive and exhaustive. For our purposes, each action a_i is associated with a set of *outcomes*, such that there is a unique outcome label $o_{i,k}$ for every possible effect e_k of action a_i.

Let $P[G \mid \mathcal{I}, \mathcal{A}]$ be the probability of goal G holding in the state resulting from executing action sequence $\mathcal{A}$ from state $\mathcal{I}$. See (Kushmerick, Hanks, & Weld 1995) for an exact description of how to compute the probability of a plan achieving a goal, as well as the probability of a state resulting from executing a given action from a given state.

A *plan improvement* problem is a tuple $\langle \mathcal{A}, G, \mathcal{I}, \mathcal{O} \rangle$ where $\mathcal{A}$ is a sequence of actions, G is a goal, $\mathcal{I}$ is the initial state, and $\mathcal{O}$ is a set of possible actions. A solution to a plan improvement problem is a sequence of actions $\mathcal{A}'$ such that every member of $\mathcal{A}'$ is also a member of $\mathcal{O}$ and $P[G \mid \mathcal{I}, \mathcal{A}'] > P[G \mid \mathcal{I}, \mathcal{A}]$.

The intent is that $\mathcal{A}'$ will resemble $\mathcal{A}$ and could be produced by applying a small number of simple operations (deleting, adding, or re-ordering actions) to $\mathcal{A}$.

Components

We now describe the four components of our system.

Simulation

In this section, we briefly describe how we simulate probabilistic plans. Our simulator maps from an initial state and an action sequence to an execution trace randomly chosen from the distribution of possible executions of the action sequence. To simulate a plan, we start with the initial state and for each action we "roll the dice" to determine the action's effects and, consequently, the next state. We repeat the process for every action in the plan, to produce an execution trace. For each simulation, we record which of the possible outcomes of each action occurred, as well as the sequence of states that arose.

Since simulation explores only one possible execution path at a time, the complexity of simulation is linear in the length of the plan. Previous analytic techniques for assessing plans are exponential in the length of the plan (e.g. (Kushmerick, Hanks, & Weld 1995)).

We now briefly discuss the advantages of using simulation in probabilistic planning. Standard statistical arguments (McClave & II 1982) show that simulation converges in the sense that one can guarantee there is a high probability that the estimate returned by simulation is within some ϵ of the true probability. What's more, the probability that the true probability, p, is more than ϵ away from our estimate is approximately $z_{\alpha/2}\sqrt{(p(1-p))}$.[1] For example, even making the most pessimistic assumptions about p, 10,000 simulations yields about a 95% confidence that the estimate is within 0.01 of the correct answer. This is a lot of simulations. But note that it is independent of plan length! In contrast, adding a single action can double the work required by an analytic technique.

Furthermore, a small number of simulations can be used to reject a bad plan. Suppose a plan succeeds in 20 of 100 simulations and we need a plan that succeeds with at least .6 probability. Reasoning about sample size indicates that there is well over 99% confidence that a plan that fails in 100 randomly chosen simulation has lower than a .6 probability of succeeding.

Data mining for significant flaws

In this section, we describe how we use data mining to determine what went wrong in the plans that failed during simulation. The objective is a function which outputs expressions of the form Prevent($a_i, o_{i,k}$) which translates to "Try to prevent action a_i from having outcome $o_{i,k}$." This process is more completely described in (Zaki, Lesh, & Ogihara 1997).

Sequential discovery (Agrawal & Srikant 1995) is the problem of mining patterns from sequences of unordered sets of items, such as

$$ABC \mapsto DE \mapsto EF \mapsto GHI$$
$$CD \mapsto AB \mapsto CIJ \mapsto BG$$

---

[1] Values for z can be found in any statistics textbook. For example, $z_{.05} = 1.645$, $z_{.025} = 1.96$ and $z_{.005} = 2.575$.

$$AB \mapsto E \mapsto IJ$$

where $A, B, C..J$ are items. The algorithms find patterns that occur with high frequency. For example, the sequence $A \mapsto I$ occurs in all three of the above sequences, and $AB \mapsto E \mapsto I$ occurs in two of them.

We have applied the SPADE algorithm (Zaki 1997) to the execution traces produced by the simulator. We convert the ith trace into a sequence of actions $(A_1^i, ..., A_{m_i}^i)$, where each action is represented as a set composed of the action's id, the action's name, the parameters of the action, and the outcome of the action. This is a simple transformation, in that we know that action a_i was executed at time i in every trace, and so what varies from trace to trace is what outcome the action had. For example, suppose that action a_8 is a Move action on Bus1 from Delta to Abyss, and that in the 12th simulation the outcome of a_8 was Flat, then A_8^{12} would be:

(id8 Move Veh=Bus1 Frm=Delta To=Abyss Flat)

We then apply the SPADE algorithm to extract patterns that occur with high frequency in the failed plans but low frequency in the successful plans. An example pattern the data mining algorithm might return is:

(Move Bus1 Flat) $\rightarrow$ (Move Bus1 Overheat)

which indicates that Bus1 gets a flat tire in one Move action and overheats in a subsequent Move action.

We can be reasonably confident that significant trends will emerge from our data mining, if we have sufficient numbers of both successful and failed plan traces. Let seq be some sequential pattern of events. In order to correctly assess whether seq predicts failure, we need an accurate estimate of its frequency in $both$ the successful and failed plans. Let C_s be the probability that the frequency of seq in the successful traces will be within some ϵ of the true probability of seq occurring in a successful plan. Similarly, let C_f be the probability that the frequency of seq in the failed plan traces will be within some ϵ of the true probability of seq occurring in a failed plan. The probability that seq will be represented accurately in both successful and failed plans is $C_s \times C_f$, which will be high iff both C_s and C_f are high. Thus, a significant trend is likely to emerge if our simulations include a sufficient number of both successful and failed plans.

If a pattern is common in failed plan traces but uncommon in successful traces then we speculate that preventing this sequence from occurring might increase the plan's success rate. The sequence represents a chain of events that causes failure and thus can be broken by preventing any part of the chain from occurring. For example, if data mining extracts the pattern (id8 Flat) $\mapsto$ (id17 Overheat) then we assert Prevent(a_8,Flat) and Prevent(a_{17}, Overheat). But the patterns might not include specific actions. Given the pattern Flat $\mapsto$ Overheat, we re-examine the simulation traces to find actions that often resulted in a Flat or Overheat.

More formally, we generate Prevent statements as follows. Let $\mathcal{P} = (p_{1,1} \mapsto p_{1,2} ... \mapsto p_{1,m_1}), ..., (p_{n,1} \mapsto p_{n,2} ... \mapsto p_{n,m_n})$ be the patterns returned by the data mining routine. For every action a_i and outcome $o_{i,k}$, let $\mathcal{A}$ be all occurrences of action a_i in the simulations where the outcome was $o_{i,k}$. For every $p_{o,l} \in \mathcal{P}$, we count the number of actions in $\mathcal{A}$ that $p_{o,l}$ matches (i.e. $p_{o,l}$ is a subset of the action in the trace). If this number is above a user-defined threshold, normally about .1 of the total number of traces, then we assert Prevent($a_i, o_{i,k}$). The Prevent statements can be calculated in a single pass through the execution traces by keeping a separate counter for each action-outcome pair for every $p_{o,l} \in \mathcal{P}$.

The highly structured nature of the database of plan traces makes it difficult to mine rules that predict failure. A compuational problem is that there are a staggering number of highly frequent, but unpredictive, rules such as (Move) $\mapsto$ (Load) $\mapsto$ (Move) which appears in every plan trace. The typical strategy of mining all highly frequent rules and then removing all unpredictive ones is not efficient in this case. A second problem is that the existence of one rule that predicts failure, say (Bus1 Flat) $\mapsto$ (Bus1 Overheat), implies the existence of many related, equally predictive rules, such as (Move Bus1) $\mapsto$ (Move Bus1) $\mapsto$ (Bus1 Flat) $\mapsto$ (Bus1 Overheat), since the Move action is so common. (Zaki, Lesh, & Ogihara 1997) discusses these problems and describes pruning stratagies for addressing them.

Qualitative reasoner

In this section, we describe a function for mapping from a statement of the form Prevent($a_i, o_{i,k}$) to a set of suggestions for changing the plan to decrease the likelihood that action a_i will have outcome $o_{i,k}$.

The function SUGGESTCHANGES takes in the Prevent statement, the original plan, the set of possible actions $\mathcal{O}$, and also a set of $qualitative\ rules\ \mathcal{QR}$. The qualitative rules indicate positive and negative influences among state variables, actions, and action-outcome pairs. Informally,

- An action a_i positively influences a boolean state variable v_j iff $P[v_j|a_i] > P[v_j]$, i.e. if v_j is more likely to hold in the current state if action a_i was just executed than otherwise.[2]

---

[2]Currently, we assert a positive influence only if there

- A state variable v_j negatively influences an action outcome pair $\langle a_i, o_{i,k}\rangle$ iff $P[\langle a_i, o_{i,k}\rangle|v_j] > P[\langle a_i, o_{i,k}\rangle]$, i.e. if action a_i is more likely to have outcome $o_{i,k}$ if v_j is true in the state in which a_i is executed than if v_j is false.

For example, if a_i is the Change-Tire action then a_i might positively influence $v_j =$ TireConditionGood which would negatively influence $\langle a_k,$ Flat$\rangle$.

Positive and negative influences can be combined and chained in the obvious way: if a positively influences b and b positively influences c then a positively influences c. If a negatively influences b and b positively influences c then a negatively influences c. And, finally, if a negatively influences b and b negatively influences c then a positively influences c.

Currently, we employ the following simple strategy for inserting actions:

Func:SUGGESTCHANGES $(\langle a_i, o_{i,k}\rangle, \{a_1, .., a_n\}, \mathcal{QR}, \mathcal{O})$

- If action $a' \in \mathcal{O}$ is not in $a_1, ..., a_n$ and action a' negatively influences $\langle a_i, o_k\rangle$ given the rules in $\mathcal{QR}$ then assert Insert(a', a_i) which indicates that a' should be inserted into $a_1, ..., a_n$ prior to a_i.

Currently, we hand code a set of qualitative rules $\mathcal{QR}$ for the domain.

Our approach can be described as a simple case of a qualitative probabilistic network (QPN) (Wellman 1990). QPNs are used to perform inference over qualitative influences. The complexity of determining if one node positively or negatively influences another is $O(|\mathcal{V}|^2)$ where $\mathcal{V}$ is the number of nodes. These techniques are thus suitable for large domains. We intend to extend our use of qualitative networks to take more advantage of their power including the ability to add more than one action to the plan.

Recall that data mining focused our improvement efforts on preventing some actions from having certain outcomes. There are, however, many ways of making it less likely that a given action will have a given outcome. For example, one might add any action which could make any aspect of the trigger of that effect false. We believe that qualitative reasoning is a promising technique for further focusing an improvement algorithm on a subset of the possible ways of preventing the sequences detected by data mining.

Plan adaptation

We have shown how analysis of simulated execution traces can suggest modifications to improve the plan,

---

does not exist any state in which executing a_i decreases the probability that v_j will be true.

such as inserting an action. However, these modifications might result in an unexecutable plan. For example, the new action may have unsatisfied preconditions. We now address the problem of further modifying the plan to accommodate the new changes.

Variations of this problem arise in case-based planning (Hammond 1989; 1990), transformational planning (Simmons 1988), or plan re-use or plan adaptation (Nebel & Koehler 1995). In each case, a plan that almost solves a given goal is modified, or repaired, to solve the goal. In particular our problem, can be mapped into a plan-reuse or plan adaptation problem (Nebel & Koehler 1995), for which there are several domain-independent algorithms including SPA (Hanks & Weld 1995), PRIAR (Kambhampati & Hendler 1992), and NOLIMIT (Veloso 1994).

We focus on SPA, which is based on the SNLP partial-order planner (McAllester & Rosenblitt 1991). Planning by adaptation is similar to planning from first principles. The primary difference is that search begins from the plan to be adapted rather than from a null plan. As a consequence, plans can be refined by retracting elements from, as well as adding elements to, the plan.

Plan adaptation is suitable for large plans in that the complexity of plan adaptation is *not* exponential in the length of the given plan. The complexity is, however, exponential in the number of adaptations needed to repair the plan. In the worst case, of course, the entire given plan will be dismantled and a new plan built up. We do not expect our system to find such repairs. Rather, we are encouraged by the fact that small repairs to large plans are feasible even though large repairs to large plans are not. Our hope is that as new techniques are developed for generating plans more efficiently, these same techniques will extend the extent to which large plans can be repaired.

In the previous section, we showed how to generate suggestions of the form Insert(a', a_i). We now describe the INSERTACTION function which inserts action a' before action a_i in the given plan $a_1, ..., a_n$. We can map a call to INSERTACTION directly into a call to the SPA plan adaptation algorithm. The basic idea is to generate two unique predicates q_1 and q_2, and then add q_1 as an effect of a' and as a precondition of a_i. This will force SPA to add a' in order to keep a_i in the plan. Additionally, we add q_2 as an effect of a_i and as a precondition of the goal so that SPA cannot remove a_i from the plan, since no other action can achieve q_2. We set q_1 and q_2 to be false in the initial state.

However, the SPA function is only defined for deterministic STRIPS operators, as opposed to the probabilistic actions used in our formulation. To bridge this gap, formally, we would have to extend SPA or instead rely on abstract models of our probabilistic actions.[3]

For our system, we have implemented a domain-specific version of INSERTACTION. The input and output of our domain-specific program satisfy the SPA input/output specification, but the internals of the program resemble a scheduling routine more than a planning routine. It is very fast, but does not perform any general purpose reasoning. We describe the domain-specific INSERTACTION below, in the section describing the domain.

Plan improvement algorithm

In this section, we put together the pieces described above to form the IMPROVE algorithm.

As shown in figure 1, the first step of IMPROVE is to simulate the input plan many (typically 1000) times. We then feed the traces into the data mining algorithm, which produces a set of statements of the form Prevent$(a_i, o_{i,k})$ which translates to "Try to prevent action a_i from having outcome $o_{i,k}$." We then use the qualitative reasoning function, SUGGESTCHANGES to convert each Prevent statement into a set of suggested changes, of the form Insert(a', a_i) which translates to "Insert action a' before action a_i in the plan.

We then call INSERTACTION on each Insert statement which returns a new plan or nil, if it couldn't produce a plan with a' before a_i. If INSERTACTION does return a plan, for the statement Insert(a', a_i), then the plan will contain a' but other actions may have been added, removed, or re-arranged as well.

At this point we have a new set of plans. IMPROVE calls the simulator on each new plan to estimate the probability the plan has of achieving the goal. If any new plan has a better chance that the original plan, then the plan with the highest probability is chosen and the process is repeated on it. Otherwise, the original plan is returned.

Experimental validation

We now describe experiments that measure IMPROVE's ability to increase the probability of goal satisfaction.

Domain

We tested our system in an evacuation domain consisting of 35 cities, 45 roads, 100 people, 2 buses, a helicopter and a variety of bus maintenance equipment. Buses and helicopter can move between cities (only by road for buses), pick up and drop off people and equipment and also apply a variety of bus maintenance actions. Buses can carry 25 people and helicopters can

---

[3]We are not claiming that either option is straightforward.

Func. IMPROVE($\langle \{a_1, ..., a_n\}, G, \mathcal{I}, \mathcal{O} \rangle$, $\mathcal{QR}, k$)
- Set $\mathcal{A}' = \{a_1, ..., a_n\}$
- Repeat
  1. Simulate plan $\mathcal{A}'$ k times from state $\mathcal{I}$.
  2. Set $base$ to be the number of simulations in which G holds in the final state in the trace.
  3. Call the data mining routines on the simulated traces to produce a set of statements of the form Prevent(a_i, o_i, k).
  4. For each statement Prevent(a_i, o_i, k) call SUGGESTCHANGES$(\langle a_i, o_{i,k} \rangle, \mathcal{A}', \mathcal{QR}, \mathcal{O})$, and collect all the results into a set of statements of the form Insert(a', a_j).
  5. Set $\mathcal{TEST} = \emptyset$.
     For each statement Insert(a', a_j) call INSERTACTION$(a', a_j, \{a_1, ..., a_n\}, \mathcal{I}, G, \mathcal{O})$. If INSERTACTION returns a plan, then add it to $\mathcal{TEST}$.
  6. For each plan $\mathcal{A}_i$ in $\mathcal{TEST}$, simulate the plan k times from state $\mathcal{I}$ and count the number of times that G is true in the final state.
  7. IF no plan $\mathcal{A}_i$ scored better than $base$ in step 6, then RETURN($\mathcal{A}'$),
     ELSE set $\mathcal{A}'$ to the plan that scored the highest in step 6.

Figure 1: The IMPROVE algorithm

carry 1 person at a time. The goal is for all people to be in one specified city by a specified time.

The plan fails if a bus gets stuck or breaks down or a helicopter crashes. Buses can also malfunction in a variety of other ways, such as getting flat tires or overheating, that do not cause the plan to fail but can cause delays and make other malfunctions more likely. Each road has properties, such as being steep or bumpy, which make certain malfunctions more likely. For every malfunction, there is a maintenance action, such as adding coolant to prevent overheating, that will drastically reduce the probability that the malfunction will happen for a fixed amount of future driving. The maintenance actions, however, have preconditions of having one or two tools. The tools are at various cities on the map, and so adding a maintenance action can require a side trip to pick up the tool.

Finally, there is also a storm which makes certain malfunctions more likely. In each experiment, we randomly choose when and where the storm will hit and how fast it will move. Additionally, we vary the number and location of the people and tools, as well as the probability with which various combinations of bus malfunctions will cause the bus to break down.

We wrote a greedy scheduling algorithm that produces a plan to get all the people to the evacuation point. This algorithm ignores all the stochastic factors of the domain, such as weather and road conditions.

We also wrote a domain specific version of INSERTACTION. The primary use of it is to add bus maintenance actions, which require various tools. First, the algorithm adds the maintenance action to the plan at the specified point. The algorithm then finds the city with a required tool that is closest to the bus's route prior to the maintenance action. The algorithm then adds a side trip to pick up the tool from that city. The algorithm repeats the process until the bus has all the tools required for the maintenance action.

Results

In each experiment, we generate a new random problem, which defines an initial state $\mathcal{I}$ and then call our scheduling routine to produce a sequence of move, load, and unload actions $a_1, ..., a_n$ to solve this problem. In all our trials, the sequence contained at least 250 actions. We then call IMPROVE with $a_1, ..., a_n$, which returns a new sequence of actions, typically with several additional move, pickup, and maintenance operations.

To evaluate IMPROVE, we use the simulator to compare the performance of original plan against the plan that IMPROVE returns. We use the simulator because the plans were too big to manage analytically.

As shown in table 1, our algorithm significantly improved the given plan. The initial plans achieved their goal about 82% of the time, and the improved plans achieved their goal about 98% of the time. On average, 11.7 alternative plans were simulated per invocation of IMPROVE.

Note that without the possibility of malfunctions, the plans produced by the greedy algorithm would succeed 100% of the time. The IMPROVE algorithm does not result in a more efficient schedule for evacuating people, which we consider the "easy" part of the domain in these experiments. The "hard" part of the domain is to deciding which maintenance actions to perform, and when to perform them. While the greedy algorithm can quickly generate a reasonable plan, it does not have any mechanism for reasoning about which maintenance actions to add.

To show that is not trivial to add maintenance actions to make the plan more robust against failure, we compared IMPROVE against two "straw men" algorithms. First, we tested the RANDOM algorithm which repeatedly chooses five random maintenance actions, uses the INSERTACTION algorithm to add them to the plan, simulates the five new plans, and selects the one with the best performance. RANDOM repeats the process until no change improves the performance of the plan. As shown, RANDOM only improved the plan slightly. Adding a maintenance action can make the plan worse because the side trips required to get the

	initial plan length	final plan length	initial success rate	final success rate	number plans tested
IMPROVE	272.3	278.9	0.82	0.98	11.7
Random	272.3	287.4	0.82	0.85	23.4
High	272.6	287.0	0.82	0.83	23.0

Table 1: Performance of IMPROVE, compared against two simple. Results averaged over 70 trials.

iteration	number of plans tested	improvement per plan	improvement of best plan
1	4.2	.073	.123
2	7.9	.016	.042
3	9.3	.013	.028
4	16	.012	.024

Table 2: Details of IMPROVE's performance.

necessarily tools can lead to other malfunctions and also delay the plan so that the weather is worse.

We also evaluated an algorithm we called HIGH which works just like IMPROVE except that instead of data mining, it simply tries to prevent the five malfunctions that occurred most often, in each iteration. As shown, this algorithm also performed very badly demonstrating the need to focus repair efforts on the defects in the plan that are most responsible for failure.

Many of the actions IMPROVE added were in service of actions directly suggested by the data mining and qualitative reasoning components. There were at most four iterations of the simulation-mining-reasoning-adapting cycle. In each iteration, one maintenance operation is inserted into the plan, and then more actions are inserted to obtain the necessary tools for that action. Table 2 shows how many plans were considered per iteration of IMPROVE and the average and best improvement, on average, of those plans.

The data mining routine was written in C++ and run on an SGI with a 100MHz processor. The other functions were written in LISP and run on a variety of SPARC stations. Each test of IMPROVE took on average, based on the ten runs we measured, 75 minutes. About 34 minutes was spent in data mining, at a rate of 0.9 plans mined per CPU second. About 25 minutes was spent, on average, in simulation, at a rate of 3.2 plans simulated per CPU second. Much of the remaining time was spent generating the plan, doing bookkeeping, and file-based I/O between the processes.

Discussion

We now discuss some limitations of our current approach. Although the repairs considered by our algorithm can include many steps, they are all in service of a single action added to prevent some outcome from occurring. Many improvements, however, might require several actions such as adding but later removing snow chains from a bus, or adding coolant several times to top off the radiator. Furthermore, we only mine the execution traces for reasons that cause failure, instead of also looking for patterns that predict success.

Furthermore, there may be a variety of opportunities for improving the plan that never arise in the executions of that plan, such as substituting one action for another, or using a helicopter rather than a bus to evacuate some city. Again, our approach will not currently improve the plan in this way because we only focus on preventing sequences that were common in the failed simulated traces and uncommon in the successful ones.

Finally, there are ways of improving a plan besides adding actions to it. For example, although we have not described it, we have explored techniques for improving a plan by re-ordering its actions. For example, in our domain, we might first evacuate the cities that the storm is going to hit first.

Related work

We now discuses several areas of related work.

Analyzing execution traces

Much work has been done on analyzing planning episodes, i.e. invocations of the planner, to improve future planning performance in terms of efficiency or quality. (e.g. (Minton 1990)). In contrast, we analyze execution traces to improve the quality of the plan at hand, not the planning process. Both types of techniques can be used in conjunction. But note that our approach is relevant only in domains with uncertainty, in which multiple executions of the same plan might differ from each other.

(McDermott 1994) describes a system in which a robot repeatedly simulates the execution of a plan while executing the plan, with hopes of finding a more robust alternative. Each error in the simulations is considered a bug and categorized into an extensive taxonomy of plan failure modes. This contrasts to our work, in which each simulation contains a great number of undesirable effects, such as buses getting flat tires or overheating, and our analysis attempts to discover important trends that distinguish successful from unsuccessful executions.

Plan repair

CHEF (Hammond 1990) is a case-based planning system addresses many issues. We focus on those most related to our work. CHEF composes a plan from plans in its memory, simulates it, and then analyzes the execution trace to improve the plan. CHEF employs a variety of repair strategies, including modifying the plan to avoid a side-effect of an action. Much of the similarities between CHEF and our IMPROVE algorithm are superficial, however, in that CHEF was motivated primarily by the idea of using episodic memory to perform planning. CHEF simulates a plan once and performs an analysis of the result using a deep causal model, and then applies repair-strategies that have worked previously. In contrast we simulate our plans hundreds of times and apply shallow, statistical methods to pinpoint defects and apply general plan adaptation techniques to repair plans.

The GORDIUS system (Simmons 1992) also applies repair strategies to a plan, by replacing an incorrect assumption which gave rise to the flaw. While our notion of plan repair is certainly no more rich than GORDIUS's, we focus on flaws that arise not from a defective assumption about the world but instead on probabilistic trends that arise frequently in the execution of the plan. One limitation of GORDIUS is that it can only resolve flaws that arise from a single mistaken assumption. We find problems that arise from sequences of defects that cause the problem.

The overall spirit of our approach resembles *robustification* in (Drummond & Bresina 1990). Here, a reactive plan is incrementally refined by detecting the state in which it is most likely to fail and then producing new instructions for that state. We use very different techniques than theirs. We use data mining to detect defects in the plan, rather than a set of heuristics to identify bad states. Furthermore, we focus on repairing a large, non-reactive plan to *avoid* the trouble, whereas Drummond and Bresnia enhance a reactive plan to get itself out of trouble once it has occurred.

(Alterman 1988) describes *run-time* repair of plans by, for example, replacing a step that just failed with a similar action. This is rather different that our approach of repairing plans in advance. We believe both techniques are necessary. In our domain, for example, there are maintenance actions which must be performed *before* the error occurs and require advanced planning to obtain the necessary tools.

Probabilistic planning

Classical planners have been extended to probabilistic domains (e.g. (Kushmerick, Hanks, & Weld 1995; Draper, Hanks, & Weld 1994; Goldman & Boddy 1994)). If this work scaled to the point where it could produce as large plans as anyone needed, then there would not be much need for our research on improving plans. However, both the complexity and the branching factor of probabilistic planning is much worse than classical planning, which itself has not produced very large plans. We believe domain-specific and collaborative techniques will yield large plans, which can be used as the starting point for our IMPROVE algorithm.

Furthermore, this work addresses a crucial problem that probabilistic planners also face: deciding how to improve a plan that is not sufficiently reliable. In traditional planning, a plan has easily detectable flaws (i.e. unsatisfied or threatened preconditions). A planner needs to address each flaw and if there are no flaws, then the plan is sufficiently good. And it is these conditions that enable backchaining to work so effectively. In probabilistic planning, a plan might have no critical flaws, but still not be sufficiently good. In this case, there are many ways of improving the plan: for example, the planner can add an action that will increase the support of *any* of the preconditions in the plan. To our knowledge, no system uses analysis of the plan to guide the choice of what to work on next. In this paper, we have explored the use of data mining and qualitative reasoning techniques to focus attention of a planner on how to improve a plan.

Conclusions

This work was motivated by the desire to work with large plans. Our long term objective is to combine work on simulation, data mining, qualitative reasoning, and planning to produce tools for developing large, robust plans for complex domains. This paper has, hopefully, shown that such a system is possible and sketched out some of the key ideas.

We have shown that simulation, qualitative reasoning, and data mining are all well suited for working with large plans. Plan adaptation is not as well suited, but the complexity of improving plans is, at least, not exponential in the length of the plan to be improved.

We have described and implemented the IMPROVE algorithm which takes in a large plan, containing over 250 steps, and modifies it to improve the probability of goal satisfaction by over 15% in our experiments.

References

Agrawal, R., and Srikant, R. 1995. Mining sequential patterns. In *Intl. Conf. on Data Engg.*

Alterman, R. 1988. Adaptive planning. *Cognitive Science* 12:393–421.

Boutilier, C.; Dean, T.; and Hanks, S. 1995. Planning under uncertainty: Structural assumptions and computational leverage. In *Proc. 2nd European Planning Workshop*.

Draper, D.; Hanks, S.; and Weld, D. 1994. Probabilistic planning with information gathering and contingent execution. In *Proc. 2nd Intl. Conf. AI Planning Systems*.

Drummond, M., and Bresina, J. 1990. Anytime Synthetic Projection: Maximizing the Probability of Goal Satisfaction. In *Proc. 8th Nat. Conf. AI*, 138–144.

Ferguson, G.; Allen, J. F.; and Miller, B. 1996. TRAINS-95: Towards a mixed-initiative planning assistant. In *Proceedings of the Third International Conference on AI Planning Systems (AIPS-96)*.

Goldman, R. P., and Boddy, M. S. 1994. Epsilon-safe planning. In *Proc. 10th Conf. Uncertainty in Artifical Intelligence*.

Goldman, R. P., and Boddy, M. S. 1996. Expressive Planning And Explicit Knowledge. In *Proc. 3rd Intl. Conf. AI Planning Systems*.

Hammond, K. 1989. *Case-Based Planning: Viewing Planning as a Memory Task*. Academic Press.

Hammond, K. 1990. Explaining and repairing plans that fail. *J. Artificial Intelligence* 45:173–228.

Hanks, S., and Weld, D. S. 1995. A domain-independent algorithm for plan adaptation. *J. Artificial Intelligence Research* 319–360.

Kambhampati, S., and Hendler, J. 1992. A validation structure based theory of plan modification and reuse. *J. Artificial Intelligence* 55:193–258.

Kushmerick, N.; Hanks, S.; and Weld, D. 1995. An Algorithm for Probabilistic Planning. *J. Artificial Intelligence* 76:239–286.

McAllester, D., and Rosenblitt, D. 1991. Systematic nonlinear planning. In *Proc. 9th Nat. Conf. AI*, 634–639.

McClave, J. T., and II, F. H. D. 1982. *Statistics*. San Francisco: Dellen Publishing Company.

McDermott, D. 1994. Improving robot plans during execution. In *Proc. 2nd Intl. Conf. AI Planning Systems*, 7–12.

Minton, S. 1990. Quantitative results concerning the utility of explanation-based learning. *Artificial Intelligence* 42(2–3).

Nebel, B., and Koehler, J. 1995. Plan reuse versus plan generation: a theoretical and emperical analysis. *J. Artificial Intelligence* 76:427–454.

Simmons, R. 1988. A theory of debugging plans and interpretations. In *Proc. 7th Nat. Conf. AI*, 94–99.

Simmons, R. 1992. The roles of associational and causal reasoning in problem solving. *J. Artificial Intelligence* 159–208.

Veloso, M. 1994. Flexible strategy learning: Analogical replay of problem solving episodes. In *Proc. 12th Nat. Conf. AI*, 595–600.

Wellman, M. P. 1990. Fundamental concepts of qualitative probabilistic networks. *AI Magazine* 44:257–303.

Zaki, M. J.; Lesh, N.; and Ogihara, M. 1997. Sequence mining for plan failuresk. Technical Report URCS TR 671, University of Rochester.

Zaki, M. J. 1997. Fast mining of sequential patterns in very large databases. Technical Report URCS TR 668, University of Rochester.

Controlling Communication in Distributed Planning Using Irrelevance Reasoning

Michael Wolverton   **Marie desJardins**

SRI International
333 Ravenswood Ave
Menlo Park, CA 94025
{mjw|marie}@erg.sri.com

Abstract

Efficient and effective distributed planning requires careful control over how much information the planning agents broadcast to one another. Sending too little information could result in incorrect plans, while sending too much information could overtax the distributed planning system's resources (bandwidth and computational power). Ideally, distributed planning systems would have an efficient technique for filtering a large amount of irrelevant information from the message stream while retaining all the relevant messages. This paper describes an approach to controlling information distribution among planning agents using *irrelevance reasoning* (Levy & Sagiv 1993). In this approach, each planning agent maintains a data structure encoding the planning effects that could potentially be relevant to each of the other agents, and uses this structure to decide which of the planning effects that it generates will be sent to other agents. We describe an implementation of this approach within a distributed version of the SIPE-2 planner. Our experiments with this implementation show two important benefits of the approach: first, a noticeable speedup of the distributed planners; second—and, we argue, more importantly—a substantial reduction in message traffic.

The Problem

Real-world plans in modern organizations are often developed by committee, with multiple planners who are each responsible for a particular part of the plan or a specific activity within the planning process, and who cooperate to combine their results into a final integrated plan. There is a growing need for technology that supports this decentralized planning activity by providing the functionality of AI planning systems in a distributed environment. In this model, multiple planning agents are distributed across different processes and locations, perhaps each supporting a user in a mixed-initiative planning session. They cooperate to develop a single integrated plan for a joint planning problem. Each agent is assigned a collection of subgoals from the high-level goal to work on. To plan effectively, the agents

[0]Copyright ©1998, American Association for Artificial Intelligence (www.aaai.org). All rights reserved.

must communicate with one another during the planning process. This means that a given agent must send messages to some or all of the other agents about the current state of its subplan development: what conditions are being made true or false in its current partial plan, what resources are being used, what constraints have been generated, and so forth. This communication is necessary so that the planning agents can detect and avoid potential conflicts and potential duplications of work early in the process, instead of having to replan major portions of the joint plan if the conflicts are discovered at the end of the process when the completed subplans are merged.

This need for communication introduces a new problem: what exactly should the agents send to one another? More specifically, how does a planning agent, A, determine whether a given planning decision it has made is important to the problem solving of another agent, B? It cannot answer this last question precisely without actually solving B's subplan, so it must rely on a heuristic answer to a slightly different question: is the planning decision *likely* to be important to B's planning? The consequences for having either an overly permissive or an overly strict answer to that question are serious. If the heuristic allows too many messages to be sent—for example, by broadcasting every planning decision made by every agent to every other agent—it can quickly overburden the resources of the distributed planning system in several ways:

- By overloading the communication links between planners, especially in situations where bandwidth is limited
- By bogging down the planning algorithms with numerous irrelevant predicates and constraints to add to the agents' partial plans
- By overwhelming the human operators at each of the planning nodes with a flood of messages they do not need to see.

On the other hand, a heuristic that sends too little information will suppress messages that reveal conflicts and other interactions between agents' subplans. If even one such message goes unsent, an undetected conflict can lead to extensive replanning when the subplans are merged, or, depending on the planning algorithm, the inability of the system to find a correct plan at all. One possible approach would be to bypass the heuristic entirely, and instead have a user or set of users select the information that gets passed from agent to agent. This, however, is clearly an impossibly large task in complex, real-world planning domains.

Example Figure 1 shows a simple transportation example demonstrating the problem. In this example, there are two Hierarchical Transition Network (HTN) planning agents cooperating to transfer a payload from TRUCK-A to TRAIN-A. The truck agent is responsible for moving the truck from LOC-A to LOC-C and unloading the payload there. The train agent is responsible for moving the train to LOC-C and loading the payload there. The agents' current partial plans are shown in Figures 1(a) and 1(b). In those displays, rounded rectangles represent primitive actions, and they are shown with all the planning effects they produce. Hexagons represent unexpanded goals. The lighter-shaded goals are the responsibility of the plan's owner, while the darker-shaded goals are the responsibility of the other agent.

At this point in the distributed planning process, the truck agent has completed its part of the joint plan—the only two unexpanded goals in its display are the responsibility of the other agent—and is ready to broadcast the relevant effects of its actions to the train agent. It could broadcast all the effects its actions produced, including all of the effects having to do with the location of TRUCK-A. However, a cursory glance at the planning operators that the train agent will use to solve its goals reveals that the location of TRUCK-A cannot possibly be relevant to the train agent's planning. For example, LOAD-OP, the operator that the train agent will use to solve its (LOADED ...) goal, is shown (Figure 1(c)). TRUCK-A will not unify with the variable PAYLOAD1, so none of the truck agent's (AT-LOC TRUCK-A ...) effects can possibly threaten or satisfy LOAD-OP's first precondition. Also, if LOAD-OP is to be used to solve the train agent's (LOADED ...) goal, the variable VEHICLE1 will be instantiated to TRAIN-A; since TRUCK-A will not unify with TRAIN-A, the truck-agent's (AT-LOC TRUCK-A ...) effects also will not be relevant to LOAD-OP's second precondition. Those effects are similarly irrelevant to the train agent's other goal.

The only effect that could be relevant is in the last action—(AT-LOC PAYLOAD-A LOC-C)—which unifies with LOAD-OP's first precondition. The truck agent must inform the train agent of that effect only. It can avoid sending all the other effects, if it can get a description of the predicates that might be relevant to the train agent's problem solving (via the train agent or by its own analysis of the train agent's goals and planning operators).

This paper describes an approach to reducing message traffic among distributed HTN planning agents by using *irrelevance reasoning* (Levy & Sagiv 1993). In this approach, agents identify relevant planning effects by constructing a set of *query trees* based on an analysis of their planning operators and assigned goals. These query trees are then used to generate a list of predicates that could possibly be relevant to each agent's planning, and each other agent uses that list to select which of its own planning effects it will send to the agent in question. We have implemented this approach within a distributed version of the SIPE-2[1] planner (Wilkins 1988), called Distributed SIPE. Our experiments with Distributed SIPE show two important benefits of the approach: first, a noticeable speedup of the distributed planners; second—and, we argue, more importantly—a substantial reduction in message traffic.

In the remainder of this paper we first introduce irrelevance reasoning and then describe our application of it to distributed planning. Next, we discuss our implementation of the approach and present experimental results. Last, we discuss some of the issues raised by our project and some of the open research problems in this area.

The Approach
Irrelevance Reasoning

This section presents a very brief introduction to Levy and Sagiv's approach to irrelevance reasoning. For a more thorough explanation, see (Levy & Sagiv 1993) or (Levy 1993).

Irrelevance reasoning is a term describing a class of techniques for identifying those parts of a knowledge base (KB) that are irrelevant to a given query. Levy and Sagiv identify several distinctions that can be made between different definitions of "irrelevant." In this paper we are concerned with what they term *strong irrelevance*: a closed formula ϕ in a KB is strongly irrelevant to a query ψ if ϕ does not appear in any possible derivation of ψ.[2]

To determine which formulas are irrelevant to a given query, Levy and Sagiv construct a *query tree*, an AND-OR tree consisting of goal nodes and rule nodes. The root of the tree is a goal node labeled with the query. Each goal node labeled g is an OR node, and has as its children rule nodes for all the rules whose consequent unifies with g. Each rule node labeled r is an AND node, and has as its children goal nodes for each conjunct in the precedent of r. There are special procedures for handling recursive rules. Query trees provide an efficient means for deriving various types of irrelevance claims about the KB. The result of most concern

---

[1] System for Interactive Planning and Execution.
[2] This is actually a specialization of Levy and Sagiv's more general definition of strong irrelevance.

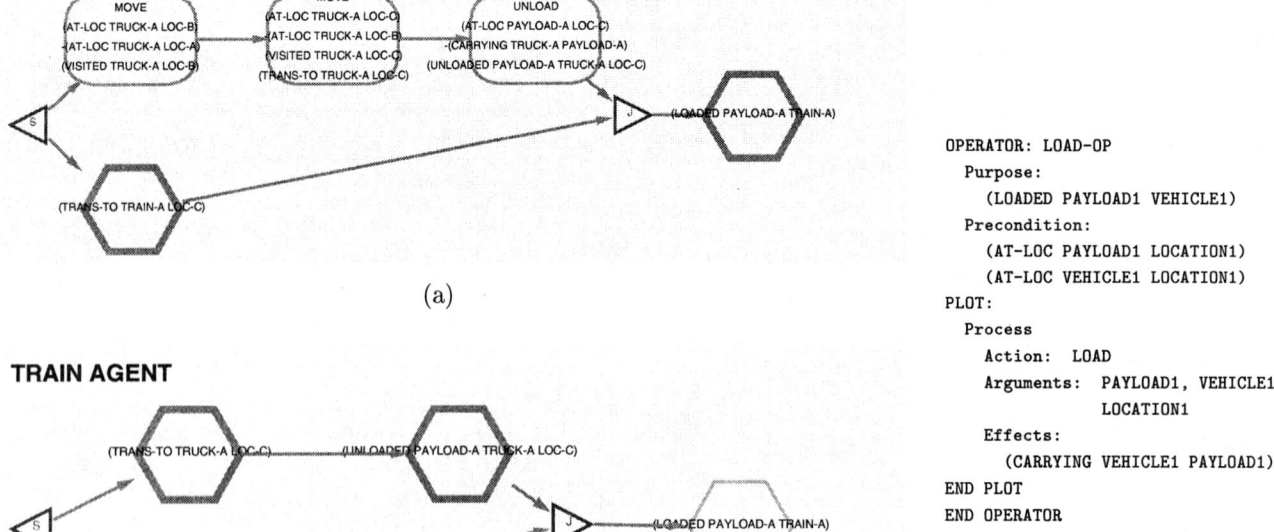

Figure 1: Time slice of a distributed planning session: (a) TRUCK AGENT's completed partial plan; (b) TRAIN AGENT's incomplete partial plan; and (c) planning operator for solving TRAIN AGENT's (LOADED ...) goal.

to us is the following: a ground fact $p(a_1, \ldots, a_n)$ is strongly irrelevant to ψ if and only if $a_1, \ldots, a_n$ does not satisfy the label of any goal node of p in the query tree for ψ.

By removing from the KB formulas that are strongly irrelevant to a query before searching the KB for an answer to the query, irrelevance reasoning can substantially reduce problem solving time. Levy and Sagiv tested their query tree technique on various databases and queries. They found that removing strongly irrelevant facts from the KB produced speedups in problem solving of between 23% and 97%. In most test cases, the time taken to construct the query tree and use it to filter irrelevant facts was insignificant compared to the time needed to find an answer to the query.

Selective Communication

Irrelevance reasoning speeds up problem solving by shrinking the knowledge base—that is, by preventing the problem solver from seeing facts and rules that could not possibly be useful in its problem solving. This technique can also be used to limit messages in distributed planning, provided we can construct a query tree from a planning knowledge base. Fortunately, while the problem solved by HTN planners is not equivalent to that solved by deductive database search engines, HTN operators do provide the same information that is used to construct query trees—knowledge about which rules (operators) can be used to solve a given goal, knowledge about the subgoals that must be solved when a rule (operator) is applied, and knowledge about how variables are constrained when a rule (operator) is unified with a goal.

An HTN operator typically contains four components:

- a *purpose*—a predicate representing the higher-level goal that the operator solves.

- *preconditions*—a collection of predicates representing conditions that must be true in the world state before the operator can be applied.

- a *plot*—a plan fragment that is inserted into the plan in place of the higher-level goal matched by the purpose. The plot consists of a partial ordering of goals and primitive actions.

- *constraints* on the variables that are used as arguments of the other three components. Our present implementation propagates only class constraints, but in principle the approach supports other types of constraints as well.

The construction of a query tree using these kinds of planning operators is similar to the method described in the previous section. The root of the tree is a goal node labeled with an agent's planning goal. Each goal node labeled g is an OR node, and has as its children rule nodes for all the operators whose purpose unifies with *g*. The contents of the rule node are the predicates that result in unifying the operator's purpose and its preconditions with *g*. The label of the rule node is the result of unifying the operator with *g*. Each rule node labeled *Op* is an AND node, and has as its children goal nodes for each subgoal contained in the plot of *Op*.

The use of the query tree for controlling communication in distributed planning works in three steps:

(1) When a planning agent is assigned new goals to solve, it constructs a query tree for *each* goal.

(2) The agent generates a list of relevant predicates for itself by walking the query trees and collecting all the contents of rule nodes.

(3) The agent sends the collected list of relevant predicates to each of the other planning agents.

During the course of distributed planning, whenever an agent, A, is considering sending a planning effect to another agent, B, A checks the effect against B's list of relevant predicates. If a predicate on the list unifies with the effect, it is sent to B. Otherwise, it is not.

A variant on steps (1) and (2) above is to have each agent compute the query trees for each other agent, instead of computing the tree only for itself and broadcasting the results to all other planners. This variant is possible when all planning agents share the same planning knowledge base and when each agent knows the other agents' goals, as is the case in Distributed SIPE. It is desirable when communication bandwidth is at a premium, since it requires no extra communication between agents.

The query tree for the (LOADED ...) goal of the example in Figure 1 is a simple one, with the goal node root and a single child rule node. The rule node represents the operator LOAD-OP unified with the goal, which is already fully instantiated. As a result, only three ground predicates are relevant for that goal:

```
(LOADED PAYLOAD-A TRAIN-A)
(AT-LOC PAYLOAD-A LOC-C)
(AT-LOC TRAIN-A LOC-C)
```

Experimental Results

We have implemented the irrelevance reasoning communication filtering method described above in Distributed SIPE (desJardins & Wolverton 1998), a distributed planning system built on the SIPE-2 planner. In Distributed SIPE, multiple planning agents, running as different processes and usually on different platforms, cooperate to produce a joint plan. Each agent is a running instance of SIPE-2, with the following additional capabilities:

- An agent can assign one or more of its subgoals to another agent.
- An agent can send some or all of the planning effects contained in its current partial plan (i.e., effects created by the actions and goals in its partial plan)

Domain/Problem			*Unfiltered*	*Filtered*
Name	# ops	# acts	# Effects	# Effects
JMCAP	30	41	45	16
Trans	5	24	37	1

Table 1: Message Traffic Reduction

to another agent. It can send effects manually, in which case a user selects the effects to be sent, or automatically, in which case the irrelevance reasoning procedure selects the relevant effects from the complete set of effects in the current plan. Along with an effect, the sending agent sends information that allows the receiving agent to know where to place the effect in its plan.

- An agent can submit its completed subplan to a coordinating agent.
- A coordinating agent can merge the subplans that have been submitted to it.

Our experiments were designed to measure the utility of irrelevance reasoning in distributed planning along two dimensions: how effectively the approach reduces message traffic, and to what extent the reduced message traffic speeds up the planners. We measured these effects in two domains: (1) a real-world maritime planning domain, JMCAP,[3] in which U.S. Navy and Marine Corps planners cooperate to produce a plan for a Noncombatant Evacuation Operation (NEO); and (2) a simple transportation domain from which the example in Figure 1 is drawn.[4] Table 1 gives some details about the two domains and problems used in the experiments, specifically the number of planning operators in the domain ("# ops"), and the number of actions in the bottom level of the final joint plan ("# acts"). In each domain, we partition the top-level subgoals between two agents, and then allow one agent to plan its assigned subgoals to completion. That agent then sends some or all of its planning effects to the other agent, which in turn completes its subplan, resolving any conflicts and capitalizing on any opportunities presented by the effects of first agent's plan. We took measurements in two different modes: using irrelevance reasoning to filter irrelevant effects, and using no filtering (i.e., sending all the agent's effects). We measured the number of messages that were sent in these two modes, along with the CPU time used by query tree construction, filtering effects, sending the effects across a network, and the second agent's planning of its subproblem.

Table 1 shows the reduction in message traffic from applying irrelevance reasoning. Both domains showed substantial reductions in the number of effects broadcast. In the JMCAP domain, where there is significant overlap and interaction between the goals assigned

---

[3]Joint Maritime Crisis Action Planning.

[4]For the experiments, we solved a larger problem in this domain than the one in Figure 1.

to the two agents, the filtered message passing sent 16 of the total 45 effects. In the transportation domain, which was specifically designed to have very little overlap between the responsibilities of the two agents, irrelevance reasoning reduced the message traffic from 37 effects down to only one.

Table 2 shows the results of the planning time experiments. The "Sending" columns represent the time it takes for an agent to walk through the plan and collect possible effects, filter out the irrelevant ones (if in filtering mode), and send the messages to the other agents.[5] The "Planning" columns represent the time it takes for the second agent to complete its planning after it has received all the effects sent by the first agent. The "QT Gen." column represents the time it takes to generate a query tree in filtered mode. Each "Total" column represents the sum of the previous numbers; it adds the times of all activities in a distributed planning session that are part of or are effected by message filtering. Each number represents an average over 20 runs of the system. The results show mild speedup in the maritime domain, and substantial speedup in the transportation domain. In JMCAP, sending and planning combined were 5% faster in the filtered mode, even when query tree construction time was added. In the transportation domain, the speedup was much more significant: combined sending and planning (and QT construction) was 35% faster in filtered mode. The result is better for the transportation domain primarily because the effects sent by the first agent represent a relatively small part of the total planning problem of the second agent in JMCAP—that is, the second agent in JMCAP has a larger problem to solve than the first. The total time difference between the filtered and unfiltered approaches is statistically significant for $t > 0.99$ in both domains.

It is important to note that, for many real-world domains, reducing message traffic can be a much higher priority than reducing planning time at the agent nodes. Our application runs on a cluster of Sun SPARC Ultra workstations linked by high-bandwidth connections, but for many of the domains that drive this work—for example, the maritime planning domain of JMCAP—it is unreasonable to assume such high-bandwidth connections between agents. It is more likely that agents will be communicating over low-bandwidth, wireless channels, and in these situations, the indiscriminate broadcasting of all planning decisions made by all agents is unacceptable. A second factor motivating the importance of controlling message traffic is the need for avoiding information overload of the human operator(s)

---

[5]Observant readers may put Table 1 and Table 2 together and notice that it takes less than twice as much time to send 16 effects in the JMCAP domain as it takes to send one in the transportation domain, and that it takes less than three times as much time to send 37 effects as it takes to send one in the transportation domain. This is because walking through the plan collecting the effects represents a large portion of the time reported in the "Sending" column.

at each agent. In many real-world domains, the distributed planning agents described here will not be operating autonomously, but will each be serving as a tool for a human planner or planning team. In these situations, even if the automated planning software may be able to handle many irrelevant effects with a tolerable increase in planning time, the human operator can more easily be overloaded by being sent numerous facts irrelevant to his own tasks. Irrelevance reasoning can help avoid overloading human planners as well as computer planning systems.

Related Work

COLLAGE (Lansky 1994; Lansky & Getoor 1995) uses a technique called *localization* to decompose a planning problem into subproblems called *regions*. An agenda-based mechanism generates a subplan for each region (corresponding to the distributed agents in Distributed SIPE), and a consistency agenda is used to propagate changes between regions (corresponding to message passing in Distributed SIPE). This approach improves overall planning efficiency by permitting COLLAGE to solve the subproblems in each region (relatively) independently.

Localizations in COLLAGE can be automatically generated based on abstraction levels or scope. COLLAGE uses a set of heuristics to find regions that minimize the number of interactions that can occur between regions. This approach focuses on the problem of assigning parts of the planning problem to regions or agents, in contrast to our work, which uses the notion of irrelevance (similar to COLLAGE's notion of scope) to manage the information flow among the distributed agents. The specification of the regions, and of which constraints need to be propagated between regions, is based on a set of action and constraint types rather than a reachability analysis of the planning operators as described in this paper. However, a modified version of COLLAGE's techniques could be applied to Distributed SIPE to distribute the planning problem in such a way that the interaction among the agents is minimized.

Corkill (1979) describes a distributed version of NOAH, a nonlinear hierarchical planner from which SIPE is conceptually descended. Corkill's distributed NOAH allocates subgoals to distributed planners, and applies distributed versions of NOAH's plan critics to identify interactions among the subplans. Corkill's implementation does interplanner constraint management at a very fine grain, and communicates all constraints that are possibly related to another planner without doing any relevance filtering, so the system entails heavy message traffic between the planners.

DIPART (Pollack 1996) is a distributed, real-time planning system that focuses on issues arising in higher-level control of distributed planning (such as the load balancing of tasks). Communication among agents is primarily at this higher, task-based, level, with some support for incrementally merging subplans. However,

Domain	Unfiltered			Filtered			
	Sending	Planning	Total	QT Gen.	Sending	Planning	Total
JMCAP	459	15237	15696	994	231	13631	14856
Transportation	406	877	1283	18	175	646	839

Table 2: Effect on Planning Time (in miliseconds)

to our knowledge, DIPART does not include a method for automatically controlling message passing between distributed planning agents.

STEAM (Tambe 1997) is a distributed agent architecture that builds on joint intentions theory (Levesque, Cohen, & Nunes 1990) to enable coordinating agents to maintain a coherent view of the team's goals and plans. STEAM uses *team operators* to represent shared goals and to identify achieved, unachievable, or irrelevant goals; these in turn determine which information is potentially relevant to other agents. This approach is extended with a decision-theoretic framework that incorporates the costs and benefits of communication, as well as the probability that other agents already have the information in question. STEAM's notion of relevance is rather different from Distributed SIPE's—rather than determining whether a piece of information is (ir)relevant to another agent's subgoals, the team operators are used to determine whether a piece of information directly contributes to the success or failure of a joint goal. However, the decision-theoretic approach, which is also used in (Gmytrasiewicz, Durfee, & Wehe 1991), represents an interesting extension that could be layered on top of Distributed SIPE's irrelevance computation to incorporate additional decision-making factors in deciding whether and when to communicate information between planning agents.

Huber and Hadley (1997) describe a multiagent system in which reactive agents coordinate as teammates in playing an internet game called Netrek. They have applied plan-recognition techniques for agents to implicitly coordinate (by understanding each others' activities), and developed a limited communication scheme for the agents to inform each other about their activities. The key to the success of this approach is that it uses an a priori analysis of the domain (performed manually by the designers) to identify what information would be useful to communicate.

Discussion

We have described a technique for using irrelevance reasoning to reduce message traffic in a distributed planning system. The current implementation controls the sending of effects generated by agents' subplans. The technique is general, and could be applied to other types of message traffic in distributed planning systems, or to other types of distributed problem solving system. For example, irrelevance reasoning could be used to determine whether to send requests for other agents to solve subgoals, or to achieve or maintain preconditions. Another application of irrelevance reasoning would be to use the query trees to allocate subgoals among agents, based on some notion of locality, to minimize interactions among subplans (similar to the localization process in COLLAGE).

The irrelevance reasoning approach could also be extended by incorporating notions of probability and utility: how *likely* is it that an agent will in fact need to know a piece of information, and how *useful* will it be to the agent to know it? Also, at some cost in bandwidth, query trees could be dynamically pruned as subplans are generated (e.g., when an alternative planning strategy has been ruled out, the associated preconditions would no longer be relevant).

This paper addresses only the problem of managing information flow by selecting which messages agents should send each other. There are many other significant challenges in developing distributed planning systems, including how to synchronize the activities of the planning agents (who should do what, and when), how to resolve conflicts when they arise, and how to merge multiple subplans. Although we do not discuss these issues in this paper, many of them are being addressed in our ongoing research (desJardins & Wolverton 1998).

In summary, we have developed a novel method for using irrelevance reasoning to control information flow in a distributed planning system. We have implemented the method in Distributed SIPE, and have demonstrated its usefulness in a real domain. Irrelevance reasoning has previously been used successfully in deduction; this work extends the evaluation of this technique into a new application area. In addition, this work represents an investigation of irrelevance reasoning in a fundamentally different context, one in which irrelevant facts have costs beyond simply increasing KB size—for example, consuming valuable bandwidth. Limiting information flow has not been addressed by most previous work in distributed planning and problem solving, and the irrelevance reasoning approach will reduce the message traffic in such systems substantially.

Acknowledgments

This research was funded by the Office of Naval Research and the Space and Naval Warfare Systems Command (SPAWAR) under contract N66001-97-C-8515. The JMCAP domain was constructed based on expertise provided by Mr. Bob Rubin of Program Advancement Group, Inc. The authors would like to thank

Mr. Dave Swanson, JMCAP Project Manager, for valuable guidance on our work. Thanks also to Karen Myers, David Wilkins, and the anonymous AAAI reviewers for insightful comments on an earlier version of this paper.

References

Corkill, D. D. 1979. Hierarchical planning in a distributed environment. In *IJCAI-79*.

desJardins, M., and Wolverton, M. J. 1998. Coordinating planning activity and information flow in a distributed planning system. In desJardins, M., ed., *AAAI Fall Symposium on Distributed Continual Planning*. AAAI Press Technical Report (forthcoming).

Gmytrasiewicz, P. J.; Durfee, E. H.; and Wehe, D. K. 1991. The utility of communication in coordinating intelligent agents. In *AAAI-91*, 166–172.

Huber, M. J., and Hadley, T. 1997. Multiple roles, multiple teams, dynamic environment: Autonomous Netrek agents. In *Autonomous Agents '97*.

Lansky, A. L., and Getoor, L. C. 1995. Scope and abstraction: Two criteria for localized planning. In *IJCAI-95*.

Lansky, A. L. 1994. Located planning with diverse plan construction methods. Technical Report FIA-TR-9405, NASA Ames Research Center.

Levesque, H. J.; Cohen, P. R.; and Nunes, J. 1990. On acting together. In *AAAI-90*.

Levy, A. Y., and Sagiv, Y. 1993. Exploiting irrelevance reasoning to guide problem solving. In *IJCAI-93*.

Levy, A. Y. 1993. *Irrelevance Reasoning in Knowledge Based Systems*. Ph.D. Dissertation, Computer Science Department, Stanford University.

Pollack, M. E. 1996. Planning in dynamic environments: The "DIPART" system. In Tate, A., ed., *Advanced Planning Technology: Technology Achievements of the ARPA/Rome Laboratory Planning Initiative*. Morgan Kaufmann.

Tambe, M. 1997. Agent architectures for flexible, practical teamwork. In *AAAI-97*.

Wilkins, D. E. 1988. *Practical Planning: Extending the Classical AI Planning Paradigm*. Morgan Kaufmann.

Automatic OBDD-based Generation of Universal Plans in Non-Deterministic Domains

Alessandro Cimatti, Marco Roveri, Paolo Traverso
IRST, Povo, 38050 Trento, Italy
{cimatti,roveri,leaf}@irst.itc.it

Abstract

Most real world environments are non-deterministic. Automatic plan formation in non-deterministic domains is, however, still an open problem. In this paper we present a practical algorithm for the automatic generation of solutions to planning problems in non-deterministic domains. Our approach has the following main features. First, the planner generates Universal Plans. Second, it generates plans which are guaranteed to achieve the goal in spite of non-determinism, if such plans exist. Otherwise, the planner generates plans which encode iterative trial-and-error strategies (e.g. try to pick up a block until succeed), which are guaranteed to achieve the goal under the assumption that if there is a non-deterministic possibility for the iteration to terminate, this will not be ignored forever. Third, the implementation of the planner is based on symbolic model checking techniques which have been designed to explore efficiently large state spaces. The implementation exploits the compactness of OBDDs (Ordered Binary Decision Diagrams) to express in a practical way universal plans of extremely large size.[*]

Introduction

Several planning domains (e.g. robotics, navigation and control) are non-deterministic. The external environment can be highly dynamic, incompletely known and unpredictable, and the execution of an action in the same state may have - non-deterministically - possibly many different effects. For instance, a robot may fail to pick up an object, or while a mobile robot is navigating, doors might be closed/opened, e.g. by external agents. Moreover, the initial state of a planning problem may be partially specified. For this reason, the fundamental assumption underlying classical planning (see e.g. (Fikes & Nilsson 1971; Penberthy & Weld 1992)) to consider only deterministic domains appears to be too restrictive in many practical cases. There are several reactive planners (see e.g. (Georgeff & Lansky 1986)) which relax this assumption, and deal with non-determinism at execution time, i.e. are able to test the different possible outcomes of the executed action and are able to execute iterative plans implementing trial-and-error strategies.

[*]Copyright 1998, American Association for Artificial Intelligence (www.aaai.org). All rights reserved.

However, the ability of generating automatically such plans is still an open problem. The automatic generation of plans in non-deterministic domains presents indeed some peculiar difficulties, related to the fact that the execution of a given plan depends on the nondeterminism of the domain and may result, in general, in more than one state. In several applications, a planner should be able, whenever possible, to generate "safe" plans, i.e. plans which are *guaranteed* to achieve the goal despite of non-determinism, for all possible outcomes of execution due to non-determinism. We call such plans *strong solutions*, to stress the difference with *weak solutions*, i.e. plans which might achieve the goal but are not guaranteed to do so. A key problem to plan generation in non-deterministic domains is that an iterative plan (e.g. "pick up block A until succeed") might in principle loop forever, under an infinite sequence of failures. However, this could be an acceptable solution, considering that the probability of success increases with the number of iterations. More than acceptable, in certain domains a trial-and-error strategy might be the *only* acceptable solution, because a certain effect might never be guaranteed.

In this paper we address the problem of the automatic generation of plans in non-deterministic domains. We present a planning algorithm which generates iterative and conditional plans which repeatedly sense the world, select an appropriate action, execute it, and iterate until the goal is reached. These plans are similar to universal plans (Schoppers 1987) in the sense that they map a set of states to an action to be executed. This allows the planner to decide at execution time what to do next in order to achieve the goal, depending on the actual outcomes of non-deterministic actions and the actual state of the environment. To tackle the known problem of the large amount of space required for universal plans, we encode them as OBDDs (Ordered Binary Decision Diagrams) (Bryant 1986). OBDDs allow for a very concise representation of universal plans, since the dimension, i.e. the number of nodes, of an OBDD does not necessarily depend on the actual number of states and corresponding actions. The planning algorithm generates universal plans by incrementally building the OBDDs representing universal plans using symbolic model checking techniques (see, e.g., (Clarke, Grumberg, & Long 1994; Burch et al. 1992)).

The planning algorithm returns strong solutions, i.e. plans which are guaranteed to achieve the goal in spite of non-determinism, if such plans exist. Otherwise, the planning algorithm generates iterative trial-and-error strategies which are guaranteed to achieve the goal under the assumption that, if there is a possibility for the iteration to terminate, this will not be ignored forever. We call such solutions, *strong cyclic solutions*. Intuitively, they are "strong" since they still assure that, under the given assumption, there are no executions of the plan which do not achieve the goal. This extends significantly the applicability of the planning algorithm to the domains where trial and error strategies are acceptable or the only possible solutions. If no strong cyclic solution exists, a failure is returned. The planning procedure always terminates. Moreover, the returned solutions are optimal in the following sense: strong solutions have the "worst" execution of minimal length among the possible non-deterministic plan executions.

A remark is in order. In some practical domains, a reasonable plan may not be strong, e.g. lead to failures in very limited cases, i.e. some forms of weak solutions might be acceptable. In this paper we focus on strong and strong cyclic solutions since they are open problems at the current state of the art for plan generation. In general, the "right" kind of solution to be searched for may be in a continuum from weak to strong solutions and highly depend on the integration of planning with execution and control. Nevertheless, planning for strong solutions and strong cyclic solutions allows us to explore new building blocks for planning (and also for integrating planning with execution) which can be combined in different ways.

This paper builds on the framework of "planning via model checking", first presented in (Cimatti et al. 1997), which proposes a planning procedure limited to weak solutions as sequences of basic actions. The planning procedure presented in (Cimatti, Roveri, & Traverso 1998) extends the work in (Cimatti et al. 1997), but it cannot deal with trial-and-error strategies.

This paper is structured as follows. We first review the language that we use for describing non-deterministic domains. We define formally the universal plans generated by the planner and discuss their representation in terms of OBDDs. Then, we describe the planning procedure which generates strong and strong cyclic plans and discuss its properties. Finally, we describe some experimental results, discuss related works and draw some conclusions.

Non-Deterministic Domains

We describe non-deterministic domains through the $\mathcal{AR}$ language (Giunchiglia, Kartha, & Lifschitz 1997). There are three main reasons for this choice. First, $\mathcal{AR}$ is one of the most powerful formalisms solving the

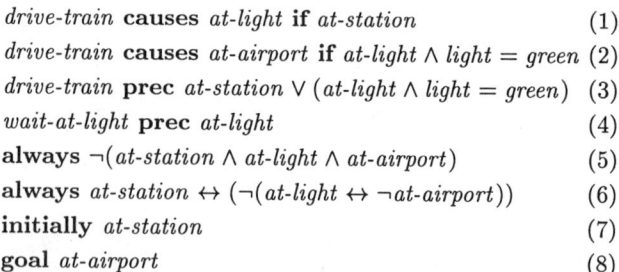

$$\text{drive-train } \textbf{causes } \text{at-light } \textbf{if } \text{at-station} \quad (1)$$
$$\text{drive-train } \textbf{causes } \text{at-airport } \textbf{if } \text{at-light} \wedge \text{light} = \text{green} \quad (2)$$
$$\text{drive-train } \textbf{prec } \text{at-station} \vee (\text{at-light} \wedge \text{light} = \text{green}) \quad (3)$$
$$\text{wait-at-light } \textbf{prec } \text{at-light} \quad (4)$$
$$\textbf{always } \neg(\text{at-station} \wedge \text{at-light} \wedge \text{at-airport}) \quad (5)$$
$$\textbf{always } \text{at-station} \leftrightarrow (\neg(\text{at-light} \leftrightarrow \neg \text{at-airport})) \quad (6)$$
$$\textbf{initially } \text{at-station} \quad (7)$$
$$\textbf{goal } \text{at-airport} \quad (8)$$

Figure 1: An example of $\mathcal{AR}$ description

"frame problem" and the "ramification problem". Second, it provides a natural and simple way to describe non-deterministic actions and environmental changes. Third, its semantics is given in terms of finite state automata. This allows us to apply symbolic model checking to generate plans by searching for a solution through the automata. Rather than reviewing the formal syntax and semantics of $\mathcal{AR}$ (the reader is referred to (Giunchiglia, Kartha, & Lifschitz 1997) for a detailed formal account), we describe the language through the simple example in figure 1. The planning problem is to move a pack from the train station to the airport. Sentence (1) states that the pack is at the traffic light after we drive the train from the train station, i.e. *at-light* holds after we execute the action *drive-train* in a state in which *at-station* holds. *at-light* and *at-station* (as well as *at-airport*) are propositional inertial fluents, i.e. fluents which obey to the law of inertia. Propositional fluents are atomic formulas. In sentence (2), *light* is a non-propositional fluent whose value is *green* or *red*, $light = green$ is an atomic formula and $at\text{-}light \wedge light = green$ is a formula. A formula is a propositional combination of atomic formulae. *light* is a non-inertial fluent, i.e. its value may non-deterministically change independently of action executions and thus not obey to the law of inertia. This allows us to describe non-deterministic environmental changes. Sentence (3) states that *drive-train* can be executed only in states where the formula following **prec** holds (A **prec** P is an abbreviation for A **causes** $\perp$ **if** $\neg P$, where $\perp$ stands for falsity). *wait-at-light* can be executed only at the traffic light (sentence (4)). For the law of inertia, it does not affect the position of the pack. Only non-inertial fluents (*light*), may change their value when it is executed. Sentences (5) and (6) are ramification constraints: they state that the pack is in exactly one of the three possible locations. Sentences (7) and (8) define the initial states and the goal of the planning problem, respectively.

This example shows how $\mathcal{AR}$ allows for describing non-deterministic actions (*drive-truck*) and non-deterministic environmental changes (non-inertial fluent *light*). It is also possible to express conditional effects, i.e. the fact that an action may have different effects depending on the state in which it is executed (e.g., see action *drive-train*). All of this makes the language

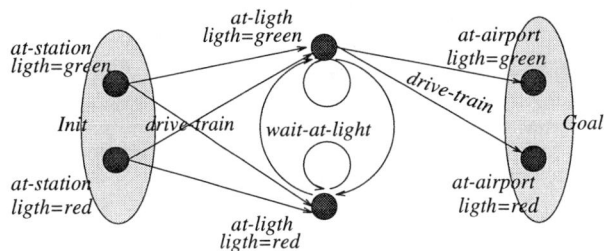

Figure 2: The automaton of the example of figure 1

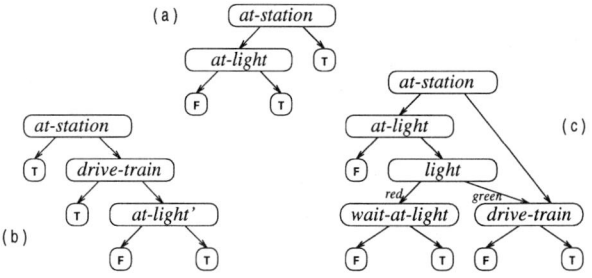

Figure 3: Some examples of OBDDs

far more expressive than STRIPS-like (Fikes & Nilsson 1971) or ADL-like (Penberthy & Weld 1992) languages.

An $\mathcal{AR}$ domain description is given semantics in terms of automata. The states of the automaton are the valuations to fluents, a *valuation* being a function that associates to each fluent one of its values. The transitions from state to state in the automaton represent execution of actions. The resulting automaton takes into account the law of inertia. It is thus possible to give semantics to a planning problem description in terms of a triple, $<Res, Init, Goal>$. Res defines the transitions from states to states, i.e. $Res(s, \alpha, s')$ holds for all actions α and states s, s' such that α leads from s to s' in the automaton. $Init$ and $Goal$ are the sets of initial states and goal states, respectively. Figure 2 shows the automaton corresponding to the example in figure 1.

In the rest of this paper we call $\mathcal{D}$ a given planning problem description, $\mathcal{F}$ the finite set of its fluents, and $\mathcal{A}$ the finite set of its actions, and we assume a given (non-deterministic) planning problem $<Res, Init, Goal>$, where $Init$ is non-empty.

We represent automata symbolically by means of OBDDs (Ordered Binary Decision Diagrams) (Bryant 1986). OBDDs are a compact representation of the assignment satisfying (and falsifying) a given propositional formula[1]. Graph (a) in figure 3 is the OBDD for the formula $at\text{-}station \vee at\text{-}light$. Each box is a node. The reading (from top to bottom) is "If $at\text{-}station$ is true (right arc) then the formula is true, else (left arc) if $at\text{-}light$ is true the formula is true, else it is false". The above OBDD represents the set of states of the automaton where either $at\text{-}station$ or $at\text{-}light$ hold. These are the four leftmost states in figure 2. Notice that this includes all the possible combinations of values of $light$.

The transitions of the automaton are also represented by OBDDs. The idea is to have variables to store the action labeling the transition, and the value of fluents *after* the execution of the action. OBDD (b) in figure 3 represents the four transitions corresponding to the execution of action $drive\text{-}train$ in $at\text{-}station$. The informal reading is that if $at\text{-}station$ holds, and the action $drive\text{-}train$ is executed, then the primed variable $at\text{-}light'$, representing the value of the fluent $at\text{-}light$ af-

ter the execution, must have value true. The variables $light$ and $light'$ do not occur in the OBDD, as all the combinations of assignments are possible.

A basic advantage of OBDDs is that their size (i.e. the number of nodes) does not necessarily depend on the actual number of assignments (each representing, e.g., a state or a transition). Furthermore, OBDDs provide for an efficient implementation of the operations needed for manipulating sets of states and transitions, e.g. union, projection and intersection.

Universal Plans

Our goal is to find strong solutions for non-deterministic planning problems, i.e. establish course of actions which are guaranteed to achieve a given goal regardless of non-determinism. However, searching for strong solutions in the space of classical plans, i.e. sequences of basic actions, is bound to failure. Even for a simple problem as the example in figure 1, there is no sequence of actions which is a strong solution to the goal. Non-determinism must be tackled by planning conditional behaviors, which depend on the (sensing) information which can be gathered at execution time. For instance, we would expect to decide what to do when we get at the traffic light according to the status of the traffic light. Furthermore, it must be possible to represent trial-and-error strategies, which are important when an action can not guarantee to achieve an effect. To this extent we use universal plans (Schoppers 1987), which associate to each possibly reachable state an action, and implement a reactive loop, where the status of the world is sensed, the corresponding action is chosen, and the process is iterated until actions are no longer available. Intuitively, a universal plan can be seen as a set of pairs state-action that we call state-action table (SA).

In order to make this notion precise, we extend the (classical) notion of plan (i.e. sequence of actions) to include non-deterministic choice, conditional branching, and iterative plans.

Definition 0.1 ((Extended) Plan) *Let Φ be the set of formulae constructed from fluents in $\mathcal{F}$. The set of (Extended) Plans $\mathcal{P}$ for $\mathcal{D}$ is the least set such that*

if $\alpha \in \mathcal{A}$, then $\alpha \in \mathcal{P}$;
if $\alpha, \beta \in \mathcal{P}$, then $\alpha; \beta \in \mathcal{P}$;
if $\alpha, \beta \in \mathcal{P}$, then $\alpha \cup \beta \in \mathcal{P}$;

---
[1] For non-propositional variables, we use a boolean encoding similarly to (Ernst, Millstein, & Weld 1997).

if $\alpha, \beta \in \mathcal{P}$ and $p \in \Phi$, then if p then α else $\beta \in \mathcal{P}$;
if $\alpha \in \mathcal{P}$ and $p \in \Phi$, then if p then $\alpha \in \mathcal{P}$;
if $\alpha \in \mathcal{P}$ and $p \in \Phi$, then while p do $\alpha \in \mathcal{P}$.

Extended plans are a subset of program terms in Dynamic Logic (DL) (Harel 1984) modeling constructs for SDL and non-deterministic choice. (See (Cimatti, Roveri, & Traverso 1998) for a semantic account of extended plans.) In the following we call $Exec[\alpha](S)$ the set of states resulting from the execution of action α in any state in the set S.

$$Exec[\alpha](S) = \{s' | s \in S, Res(s, \alpha, s')\}$$

In this framework, the universal plan corresponding to a given state-action table SA can be thought of as an extended plan of the form

$$UP_{SA} \doteq \text{while } Domain_{SA} \text{ do } IfThen_{SA}$$

where $Domain_{SA} \doteq \bigvee_{\exists \alpha. <\alpha, s> \in SA} s$ and

$IfThen_{SA} \doteq \bigcup_{\langle s, \alpha \rangle \in SA}$ if s then α.

Intuitively, $Domain_{SA}$ is a formula expressing the states in the state-action table SA, and $IfThen_{SA}$ is the plan which, given a state s, executes the corresponding action α such that $\langle s, \alpha \rangle \in SA$. The universal plan for the example in figure 2 is the following.

```
while (at-light ∨ at-station) do
  if  (at-light ∧ light = green) then drive-train   ∪
  if  (at-light ∧ light = red)   then wait-at-light ∪
  if       (at-station)           then drive-train   ∪
```

Universal plans can be efficiently executed in practice. However, reasoning about universal plans may require the manipulation of data structures of extremely large size. In order to tackle this problem, we represent universal plans symbolically using OBDDs. OBDD (c) in figure 3 represents the universal plan of the example. A universal plan is encoded as (an OBDD representing) a propositional formula in fluent variables (representing the state of affairs) and action variables (representing the actions to be executed). The models of this formula represent the associations of actions to states. This approach allows for a very concise representation of state-action maps. Notice for instance that, in OBDD (c) in figure 3, the right lowest subgraph has multiple pointers, thus resulting in sharing.

The Planning Algorithm

In this section we describe the planning procedure STRONGCYCLICPLAN, which looks for a universal plan solving the non-deterministic planning problem given in input. The underlying intuition is that *sets* of states (instead of single states) are manipulated during search. The implementation of the algorithm is based on manipulation of OBDDs, which allow for compact representation and efficient manipulation of sets of states

```
1. procedure STRONGCYCLICPLAN(Init, Goal)
2.   OldAcc := ∅; Acc := Goal; SA := ∅;
3.   while (Acc ≠ OldAcc)
4.     if Init ⊆ Acc
5.       then return SA;
6.     PreImage := STRONGPREIMAGE(Acc);
7.     PrunedPreImage := PRUNESTATES(PreImage, Acc);
8.     if PrunedPreImage ≠ ∅
9.       then  SA := SA ∪ PrunedPreImage;
10.            OldAcc := Acc;
11.            Acc := Acc ∪ PROJACT(PrunedPreImage);
12.     else STRONGCYCLES;
13.  return Fail;
```

Figure 4: The Strong Cyclic Planning Algorithm

and state-action tables. In the following we will present the routines by using standard set operators (e.g. $\subseteq, \backslash$), hiding the fact that the actual implementation is performed in terms of OBDD manipulation routines.

STRONGCYCLICPLAN, shown in figure 4, is given the set of states satisfying the goal $Goal$, and the set of initial states $Init$. It returns a state-action table SA representing a universal plan solving the problem, if a solution exists, otherwise it returns $Fail$. In order to construct SA, the algorithm loops backwards, from the goal towards the initial states. At each step, an extension to SA is computed, until the set of states Acc, for which a solution has been found, includes the set of initial states $Init$ (step 4). If no extension to SA was possible, i.e. Acc is the same as at previous cycle ($OldAcc$), then there is no solution to the problem, the loop is exited (step 3), and $Fail$ is returned (step 13).

At each step, two attempts are made to extend SA. The first, based on the STRONGPREIMAGE function, finds the state-action pairs which necessarily lead to previously visited states, regardless of non determinism (steps 6-11). If the first attempt fails, the STRONGCYCLES procedure looks for an extension to SA implementing a cyclic trial-and-error strategy.

The basic step STRONGPREIMAGE is defined as

$$\text{STRONGPREIMAGE}(S) = \{<s, \alpha> : s \in State, \alpha \in \mathcal{A}, \emptyset \neq Exec[\alpha](s) \subseteq S\} \quad (9)$$

where $State$ is the set of the states of the automaton. STRONGPREIMAGE(S) returns the set of pairs state-action $<s, \alpha>$ such that action α is applicable in state s ($\emptyset \neq Exec[\alpha](s)$) and the (possibly non-deterministic) execution of α in s necessarily leads inside S ($Exec[\alpha](s) \subseteq S$). Intuitively, STRONGPREIMAGE(S) contains all the states from which S can be reached with a one-step plan regardless of non-determinism. PRUNESTATES($PreImage, Acc$) (step 7) eliminates from $PreImage$ the state-action pairs whose states are already in Acc, and thus have already been visited.

If $PreImage$ contains new states (step 8), we have a one-step plan leading necessarily to Acc, $PrunedPreImage$ is added to SA (step 9) and Acc is

```
1. procedure STRONGCYCLES
2.   WpiAcc := ∅; OldWpiAcc := ⊤; CSA := ∅;
3.   while (CSA = ∅ and OldWpiAcc ≠ WpiAcc)
4.     IWpi := WPREIMAGE(PROJACT(WpiAcc) ∪ Acc)
5.     CSA:= Outgoing:= PRUNESTATES(IWpi, Acc);
6.     while (CSA ≠ ∅ and Outgoing ≠ ∅)
7.       Outgoing := OSA(CSA, PROJACT(CSA) ∪ Acc);
8.       CSA:= CSA \ Outgoing;
9.     if (CSA ≠ ∅)
10.    then  SA := SA ∪ CSA; OldAcc := Acc;
11.          Acc := Acc ∪ PROJACT(CSA);
12.    else  OldWpiAcc := WpiAcc;
13.          WpiAcc := WpiAcc ∪ IWpi;
```

Figure 5: The Strong Cycles Algorithm

updated with the new states in *PreImage* (step 11). PROJACT, given a set of state-action pairs, returns the corresponding set of states.

If *PreImage* does not contain new states, then the STRONGCYCLES procedure is called (step 12). STRONGCYCLES (figure 5) operates on the variables *SA*, *Acc* and *OldAcc* of STRONGCYCLICPLAN. The basic step of STRONGCYCLES is the WPREIMAGE function (which stands for "weak-pre-image"), defined as

$$\text{WPREIMAGE}(S) = \{<s,\alpha> : s \in State, \alpha \in \mathcal{A}, Exec[\alpha](s) \cap S \neq \emptyset\} \quad (10)$$

WPREIMAGE(S) returns the set of pairs state-action $<s,\alpha>$ such that there exists at least one execution of α in s which leads inside S. At each cycle, STRONGCYCLES applies the WPREIMAGE routine to the set of states visited so far. At the j-th iteration, *IWpi* contains potential cycles which can lead to *Acc* in j steps. The inner loop (steps 6-8) detects cycles necessarily leading to *Acc*, and stores them in *CSA* (Connected *SA*). The basic step of the iteration is the OSA (Outgoing *SA*) routine which, given a set of state-action pairs *CSA* and a set of states S, computes the state-action pairs which may lead out of S:

$$\text{OSA}(CSA,S) = \{<s,\alpha> \in CSA \,.\, Exec[\alpha](s) \not\subseteq S\} \quad (11)$$

The state-action pairs which may lead out of *Acc* and *CSA* are stored in *Outgoing* (step 7) and eliminated from *CSA* (step 8). The process loops until all the *Outgoing* state-action pairs have been eliminated, or *CSA* is empty. In the former case, the state-action pairs stored in *CSA* are added to *SA* and STRONGCYCLES returns control to STRONGCYCLICPLAN. In the latter case, STRONGCYCLES performs the $j+1$ iteration, i.e. looks for cycles which can lead to *Acc* in $j+1$ steps. This is done by accumulating in *WpiAcc* the states visited so far. This process is iterated till either a cycle is found (the inner loop exits with a non empty *CSA*) or a fix point is reached, i.e. there are no new state-action pairs to be visited, i.e. *WpiAcc* is the same as at previous cycle (*OldWpiAcc*).

STRONGCYCLICPLAN is guaranteed to terminate. The construction of the sets *Acc* and *WpiAcc* is monotonic and has a least fix point (see (Clarke, Grumberg, & Long 1994) for a similar proof). Moreover, if STRONGCYCLICPLAN returns a state-action table *SA*, then the corresponding universal plan UP_{SA} is a strong cyclic solution. If STRONGCYCLICPLAN returns a solution without invoking STRONGCYCLES then the corresponding universal plan UP_{SA} is a (non-cyclic) strong solution. If STRONGCYCLICPLAN returns *Fail* then there exists no strong cyclic solution. Finally, STRONGCYCLICPLAN avoids cycles whenever possible.

Experimental Results

The algorithm described in previous section is the core of MBP, a planner built on top of NUSMV, an OBDD-based symbolic model checker (Cimatti et al. 1998). MBP allows for generating the automaton starting from the action description language, finding strong (cyclic) solutions to planning problems, and directly executing universal plans encoded as OBDDs. At each execution step, the planner encodes in terms of OBDDs the information acquired from the environment, retrieves the action corresponding to the current state by accessing the state-action table of the universal plan, and activates its execution.

We performed an experimental analysis of the automatic generation of universal plans. Though very preliminary, the experiments define some basic test cases for non-deterministic planning, show that MBP is able to deal in practice with cases of significant complexity, and settle the basis for future comparisons.

One of the very few examples of a non-deterministic domain that we have found in the literature is the "hunter-prey" moving target search problem, presented in (Koenig & Simmons 1995) as an explanatory case study, where a hunter must reach the same position of a moving prey. We have parameterized the problem in the number of possible locations of the hunter and the prey (in (Koenig & Simmons 1995) 6 locations are used), and we have developed an automatic problem generator. We have run the planner on problems of different size, from 6 to 4000 locations. The results are depicted in figure 6 (all tests were performed on a 200MHz Pentium PRO with 64Mb RAM.) The search time needed for the 4000 locations case is less than 8 minutes. The size of the OBDD representing the state-action table is about 10000 nodes.

We have also experimented with the "universal" version of the problem, where the initial situation is completely unspecified. This version of the problem is much harder, as it requires to traverse the whole state space. However, we obtain search times of the same order of magnitude. Even more interestingly, the number of nodes of the OBDD representing the state action table is about 8000 nodes, *lower* than in the original problem. This contrasts with the fact that the state-action table covers a higher number of states (16 millions states against 4 millions in the original case). This is a clear

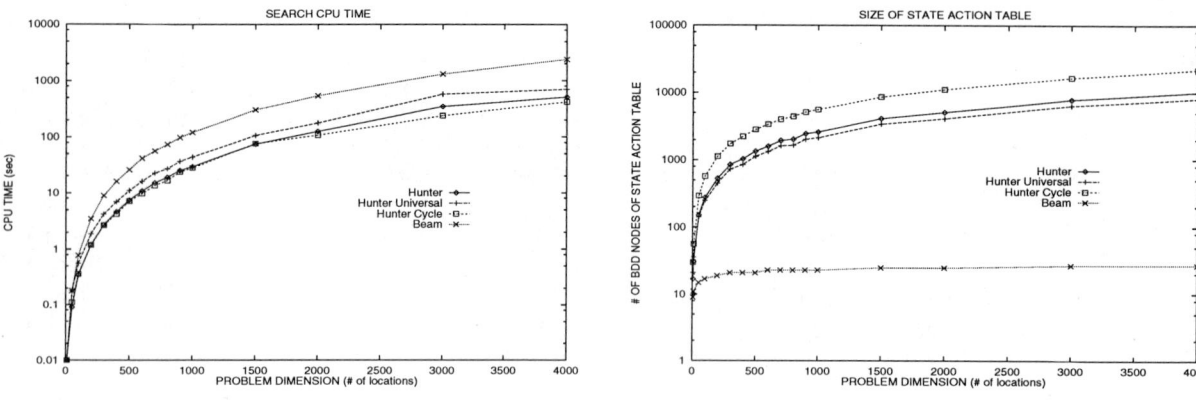

Figure 6: Search times (sec.) and size of the SA (number of nodes) for the different tests

example of the advantage of OBDDs: the size of an OBDD in terms of nodes is not, in general, related to the information "extensionally" encoded in it.

The above problems allow for strong solutions without cycles. We have then modified the problem by requiring that the hunter must "grab" the prey once they are in the same location. The prey may nondeterministically escape from a grab attempt, and this results in cycles. Again, we have experimented with different configurations of this domain, from 6 to 4000. As shown in figure 6, the search times are again of the same order of magnitude, while the size of the state action tables grows to about 22000 nodes.

Finally, in order to stress the strong cycle algorithm, we have experimented with a further example where the distance of the cycles in the solution is proportional to the dimension of the configuration. The problem consists of an agent whose purpose is to walk to the end of a beam. At each position on the beam, the walk action moves non-deterministically from position UPi-1 to UPi or to position DOWNi. If the agent falls down, it has to go back to the starting position (DOWN1) and retry from the beginning.

The results show that the regularity of the domain contains the computation load, and greatly reduces the size of the OBDDs of the resulting state-action table.

Conclusion and related work

In this paper we have presented an approach to automatic plan generation in non-deterministic domains. In order to tackle non-determinism, we construct universal plans which encode conditional iterative course of actions. We present a planning algorithm which automatically generates universal plans which are guaranteed to achieve a goal regardless of the non-determinism and are able to encode iterative trial-and-error strategies. The planning procedure always terminates, even in the case no solution exists. In case the solution does not involve cycles, it is optimal, in the sense that the worst-case length of the plan (in terms of number of actions) is minimal with respect to other possible solution plans. In principle, the algorithm is general, and its implementation could make use of different techniques. We have chosen OBDDs, which allow for an efficient encoding and construction of universal plans. We have tested the planning algorithm on some examples and the performance are promising.

Our work relies heavily on the work on symbolic model checking: we search the state space by manipulating sets of states and re-use the basic building blocks implemented in state of the art model checkers, e.g. those for computing pre-images and fix-point and for manipulating OBDDs. Nevertheless, (symbolic) model checking has been designed for verification, i.e. checking whether an automaton satisfies a given property. Its application to a synthesis problem like plan generation is a major conceptual shift which has required novel technical solutions. This has required the design of a novel algorithm which constructs and accumulates state-action pairs which are guaranteed to lead to a set of states for any action outcome.

The work described in this paper is limited in the following respects. First, compared to the previous research in planning, we restrict to a finite number of states. This hypothesis, though quite strong, allows us to treat many significant planning problems. Second, the algorithm presented in this paper can be significantly optimized. For instance, when looking for cycles which can lead to a set of states in n steps, it does not make use of the previous computations searching for loops which can lead to the set of states in $n-1$ steps. Moreover, it does not fully exploit several existing model checking optimization techniques, e.g. variable reordering, cone of influence reduction, frontier simplification, partitioning (Clarke, Grumberg, & Long 1994; Burch et al. 1992). Third, the current search strategy is committed to one particular notion of optimality, i.e.

it looks first for strong solutions. This might not be the most natural strategy for all the application domains. Finally, we do not have the complete assurance that the approach can scale up to very complex problems. Even if the preliminary results are promising, and even if symbolic model checking has been shown to do well in complex industrial verification tasks, we still need to experiment with extensive tests and with real-world large-scale applications.

Only few previous works address the automatic generation of (universal) plans in domains which are not deterministic. In (Kabanza, Barbeau, & St-Denis 1997), a planning algorithm searches the non-deterministic automaton representing the domain in order to solve complex goals specified as temporal logic formulae. The approach is based on explicit state search, and heuristics are required to contain the state explosion problem. Koenig and Simmons (Koenig & Simmons 1995) describe an extension of real-time search (called min-max LRTA*) to deal with non-deterministic domains. As any real-time search algorithm, min-max LRTA* does not plan ahead (it selects actions at-run time depending on a heuristic function) and, in some domains, it is not guaranteed to find a solution.

The approach to planning based on Markov Decision Processes (MDP) (see, e.g. (Dean et al. 1995; Cassandra, Kaelbling, & Littman 1994)) shares some similarities with our approach: it deals with actions with possible multiple outcomes, it generates a policy which encodes a universal plan, and it uses a representation based on automata. There are several differences, both technical and in focus. The MDP approach deals with stochastic domains, while we deal only with non-deterministic domains. We do not deal with probabilistic information and rewards, which can provide a greater expressivity for describing planning problems. On the other hand, the fact that we are limited to non-deterministic domains allows us to generate automatically the automata starting from a high level description in $\mathcal{AR}$. $\mathcal{AR}$ provides a natural way of describing ramifications and non-deterministic environmental changes (through the use of non-inertial fluents) and releases the user from the task of describing the effects of the law of inertia. Problem descriptions in $\mathcal{AR}$ are very concise and simple, compared with the corresponding automata (see for instance the simple example in figures 1 and 2). (Dean et al. 1995) describes an algorithm which can be used for anytime planning, by finding the solution for a restricted state space and then increasing iteratively the state space which is considered. Our algorithm searches for a solution backward from the goal to the initial states. It would be interesting to apply the same kind of strategy used in (Dean et al. 1995) within our approach, for instance by searching first for a weak solution, and then extending it step-by-step with state-action pairs returned by the STRONGPREIMAGE.

Acknowledgments
We thank Marco Daniele for finding a bug in an early version of the planning algorithm.

References

Bryant, R. E. 1986. Graph-Based Algorithms for Boolean Function Manipulation. *IEEE Transactions on Computers* C-35(8):677–691.

Burch, J.; Clarke, E.; McMillan, K.; Dill, D.; and Hwang, L. 1992. Symbolic model checking: 10^{20} states and beyond. *Information and Computation* 98(2):142–170.

Cassandra, A.; Kaelbling, L.; and Littman, M. 1994. Acting optimally in partially observable stochastic domains. In *Proc. of AAAI-94*. AAAI-Press.

Cimatti, A.; Clarke, E.; Giunchiglia, F.; and Roveri, M. 1998. NUSMV: a reimplementation of SMV. Technical Report 9801-06, IRST, Trento, Italy.

Cimatti, A.; Giunchiglia, E.; Giunchiglia, F.; and Traverso, P. 1997. Planning via Model Checking: A Decision Procedure for $\mathcal{AR}$. In *Proc. of ECP-97*.

Cimatti, A.; Roveri, M.; and Traverso, P. 1998. Strong Planning in Non-Deterministic Domains via Model Checking. In *Proc. of AIPS-98*. AAAI-Press.

Clarke, E.; Grumberg, O.; and Long, D. 1994. Model checking. In *Proc. of the International Summer School on Deductive Program Design, Marktoberdorf*.

Dean, T.; Kaelbling, L.; Kirman, J.; and Nicholson, A. 1995. Planning Under Time Constraints in Stochastic Domains. *Artificial Intelligence* 76(1-2):35–74.

Ernst, M.; Millstein, T.; and Weld, D. 1997. Automatic SAT-compilation of planning problems. In *Proc. IJCAI-97*.

Fikes, R. E., and Nilsson, N. J. 1971. STRIPS: A new approach to the application of Theorem Proving to Problem Solving. *Artificial Intelligence* 2(3-4):189–208.

Georgeff, M., and Lansky, A. L. 1986. Procedural knowledge. *Proc. of IEEE* 74(10):1383–1398.

Giunchiglia, E.; Kartha, G. N.; and Lifschitz, V. 1997. Representing action: Indeterminacy and ramifications. *Artificial Intelligence* 95(2):409–438.

Harel, D. 1984. Dynamic Logic. In Gabbay, D., and Guenthner, F., eds., *Handbook of Philosophical Logic*, volume II. D. Reidel Publishing Company. 497–604.

Kabanza, F.; Barbeau, M.; and St-Denis, R. 1997. Planning control rules for reactive agents. *Artificial Intelligence* 95(1):67–113.

Koenig, S., and Simmons, R. 1995. Real-Time Search in Non-Deterministic Domains. In *Proc. of IJCAI-95*, 1660–1667.

Penberthy, J., and Weld, D. 1992. UCPOP: A sound, complete, partial order planner for ADL. In *Proc. of KR-92*.

Schoppers, M. J. 1987. Universal plans for Reactive Robots in Unpredictable Environments. In *Proc. of IJCAI-87*, 1039–1046.

Hybrid Planning for Partially Hierarchical Domains

Subbarao Kambhampati*, Amol Mali & Biplav Srivastava
Department of Computer Science and Engineering
Arizona State University, Tempe AZ 85287-5406
email: {rao,amol.mali,biplav}@asu.edu
WWW: http://rakaposhi.eas.asu.edu/yochan.html

Abstract

Hierarchical task network and action-based planning approaches have traditionally been studied separately. In many domains, human expertise in the form of hierarchical reduction schemas exists, but is incomplete. In such domains, hybrid approaches that use both HTN and action-based planning techniques are needed. In this paper, we extend our previous work on refinement planning to include hierarchical planning. Specifically, we provide a generalized plan-space refinement that is capable of handling non-primitive actions. The generalization provides a principled way of handling partially hierarchical domains, while preserving systematicity, and respecting the user-intent inherent in the reduction schemas. Our general account also puts into perspective the many surface differences between the HTN and action-based planners, and could support the transfer of progress between HTN and action-based planning approaches.

1 Introduction

Traditionally, classical planning problem is posed as one of finding an action sequence that will take an agent from a specified initial state of the world to a desired goal state, given only the description of the executable actions in the domain. In many realistic domains, there exist human experts, who are ready to share their significant planning experience with automated planners. Efficiency of a planner, as well as the acceptability of solutions produced by it, may depend crucially on the ability to effectively use this expertise. Ever since Sacerdoti's work on NOAH [19], the conventional wisdom in the planning community has held that non-primitive (abstract) actions, and action reduction schemas provide a flexible way of capturing the human expertise, as well as using it to control planning. Planners that use such action reduction (also called "task reduction") schemas have come to be known as "hierarchical task network (HTN) planners."

HTN planners, such as SIPE [22], O-Plan [7] and VICAR [5] have been used in several industrial applications. However, much of the formalization of planning algorithms has been confined to traditional action-based planning approaches such as plan-space and state-space planning. The few existing formalizations of HTN planning, such as [8; 2], tend to start from scratch instead of building on top of the well-understood action-based formalizations. These suffer from two inherent disadvantages: First, they make it harder to transfer the progress being made in scaling-up traditional planners (e.g [3; 15; 14]) to hierarchical planning. Second, perhaps more important, most real-world domains tend to be "partially hierarchical" in that human expertise, in the form of task reduction knowledge, exists for only some parts of the domain. In such domains, the planner is forced to employ a hybrid approach of using the reduction knowledge where available, and defaulting to primitive actions for the otherwise.

Providing a principled framework for hybrid HTN and action-based planning is the main objective of this paper. To show how HTN planning can co-exist with action-based planning, we extend the unified refinement planning framework that we had developed earlier for action-based planning [11; 12; 13] to cover HTN planning. Our existing framework covers the full spectrum of action-based planning approaches by characterizing plan-space and state-space planners as independent refinements operating on a uniform plan representation [12]. In order to include HTN planning in this framework, we need to consider non-primitive actions and their reduction schemas as part of the domain specification, and generalize the plan-space and state-space refinements to handle plans containing non-primitive actions. We shall illustrate the issues involved in refining such plans by generalizing the plan-space refinement to handle non-primitive actions. Specifically, the plan-space refinement will be modified to introduce non-primitive actions in addition to primitive actions during precondition establishment, and handle them during

---

*This research is supported in part by an NSF young investigator award (NYI) IRI-9457634, and ARPA/Rome Laboratory planning initiative grants F30602-93-C-0039 and F30602-95-C-0247. We thank Tony Barrett, Reiko Tsuneto, Austin Tate and David Wilkins for critical comments on a previous draft. Copyright(c) 1998, American Association for Artificial Intelligence (www.aaai.org). All rights reserved.

conflict resolution. The non-primitive actions thus introduced can be replaced with the help of action reduction schemas at later stages.

We will see that the technical challenges in this hybridization include understanding and ensuring properties such as systematicity, completeness, preservation of user-intent, and parsimony of solutions. Developing HTN planning on top of the existing formalization of action-based planning allows us to put into perspective the many surface differences between HTN and action-based planners (including the differing notions of completeness, the need for phantom establishments, and the difficulties in conflict resolution). Such a development could also support transfer of progress between action-based planning and HTN planning.

The rest of this paper is organized as follows: In the next section, we review the refinement planning framework developed for action-based planning approaches. Section 3 introduces HTN planning, and shows how the action-based refinement planning framework is enriched to allow non-primitive actions and their reduction. Section 4 shows how plan-space refinement can be extended to handle non-primitive actions. In Section 5, we discuss the strengths of our hybrid approach, and relate it to previous work. Section 6 presents the conclusions.

2 Preliminaries of Action-based Refinement planning

A planning problem is a 3-tuple $\langle I, G, \mathcal{A} \rangle$, where I is the complete description of an initial state, G is the (partial) description of the goal state, and $\mathcal{A}$ is a set of actions (also called "operators"). An action sequence S is said to be a solution for the planning problem, if S can be executed from I, and the resulting state of the world implies G.

A partial plan $\mathcal{P}$ is a 5-tuple $\langle T, O, \mathcal{B}, \mathcal{ST}, \mathcal{L} \rangle$ where: T is the set of steps in the plan; T contains two distinguished step names t_0 and t_∞ corresponding to the beginning and ending points of the plan. $\mathcal{ST}$ maps step names to actions. Actions are modeled in the familiar STRIPS/ADL representation [18] with precondition and effect lists. O is a set of ordering constraints among the steps in T, which includes: "precedence constraints" of the form "$t_i \prec t_j$" that require t_i to precede t_j with other steps possibly intervening between them, and "contiguity constraints" of the form "$t_i * t_j$" that require t_i to come *immediately* before t_j. $\mathcal{B}$ is a set of binding constraints on the variables appearing in the preconditions and post-conditions of the actions. $\mathcal{L}$ is a set of auxiliary constraints that involve statements about truth of specific conditions over particular time intervals. Two important types of auxiliary constraints are: (1) *Interval Preservation Constraints (IPCs)* of the form "$(t \stackrel{p}{-} t')$" which demand that a condition p be preserved between steps t and t', and (2) *Point Truth Constraints (PTCs)* of the form "$\stackrel{p}{\rightarrow} t$" which demand that a condition p be necessarily true [4] in the situation before the step t.

Algorithm UCP($\mathcal{P}$) /*Returns refinements of $\mathcal{P}$ */

0. Termination Check: If a minimal candidate of $\mathcal{P}$ is a solution to the problem, return it and terminate.

1. Progressive Refinement: Select and apply a (progressive) refinement. Examples include forward state space, backward state space or plan space refinement. (*To include HTN planning, the existing refinements need to be generalized to handle non-primitive actions; see Figure 4 and Section 4.1.*)

2. Non-progressive (Tractability Refinements) (optional) Select and apply one or more tractability refinements. These include pre-satisfaction (also called conflict resolution), pre-ordering and pre-positioning refinements. (*To include HTN planning, we need to add a new tractability refinement called Pre-reduction, shown in Figure 3, and generalize the existing ones to handle non-primitive actions; see Secion 4.2.*)

3. Consistency Check: (Optional) If the partial plan is inconsistent (i.e., has empty candidate set).

4. Recursive Invocation: Call UCP on the the refined partial plan (if it is not pruned).

Figure 1: UCP: A generalized algorithm template for classical planning

The semantics of partial plans are given in terms of "candidate sets." A candidate of a partial plan is an action sequence that is consistent with the action, ordering, binding and auxiliary constraints in the plan. For example, if a partial plan contains a single action a, then any action sequence that does not contain at least one instance of a can not belong to the candidate set of that plan (see [11; 13] for more details). The shortest length candidates of a plan are called its minimal candidates, and these correspond to the ground linearizations of the plan that satisfy all auxiliary constraints.

Figure 1 describes a generic refinement planning template. Each recursive invocation of the planner checks to see if one of the minimal candidates of the supplied plan is a solution to the problem. If it is, then the planning process terminates. If not, the current plan needs to be refined further. This involves selecting one of the state-space or plan-space refinements and applying them to the plan. Optionally, a set of tractability refinements are also applied [13]. Finally, the algorithm is invoked recursively on the resulting plans (after an optional consistency check to prune out inconsistent plans).

3 Extending the model to include HTN Planning

3.1 Introduction to HTN Planning

HTN planning problem can be seen as a generalization of the classical planning problem, where, in addition to the primitive actions in the domain, the domain writer also specifies a set of non-primitive actions, and provides a set of schemas for reducing the non-primitive actions into other primitive and non-primitive actions. As an example, consider the travel domain example shown in Figure 2. Here, in addition to the

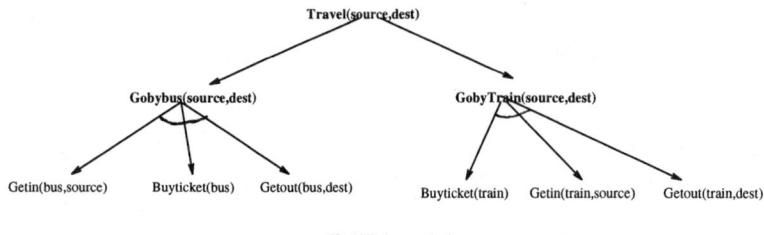

Figure 2: Schematic description of the actions and their relations in a travel domain. See the text for formal description of reduction schemas.

primitive actions, *Getin, Buyticket, Getout,* and *Hitch-hike,* we also have non-primitive actions *Gobybus, Gobytrain,* and *Travel*. Moreover, the action *Travel* can be reduced to either *Gobybus* or *Gobytrain,* and the action *Gobybus* in turn can be reduced (see below) to a plan fragment containing actions *Getin, Buyticket* and *Getout*.

We can view the reduction schemas as encoding a user's (domain-writer's) prescriptions about what constitute good plans. Informally, the only acceptable solutions are those that not only achieve the top-level goals upon execution, but can also be parsed in terms of the non-primitive actions that are provided to support those top-level goals [2]. We also say that such solutions "respect (preserve) user-intent." As an example, in the travel domain, although hitch-hiking or traveling without tickets are possible ways of achieving an $At(x)$ goal, they can not be parsed in terms of the *Gobybus* or *Gobytrain* non-primitive actions that are provided as ways to support the $At(x)$ goal, and are thus not acceptable. The preceding also implies that the completeness of HTN planners cannot be judged with respect to the set of all action sequences, but rather only with respect to those sequences that can be parsed by the schemas. In particular, in travel domain, an HTN planner's failure to find a plan based on hitch-hiking cannot be seen as an indication of its lack of completeness.

Indeed, there are two distinct notions of completeness that are relevant for HTN planners: The first, that we shall call "**schema completeness**" ensures that the non-primitive actions and task reduction schemas cover all desirable solutions for all problems of interest. The second, which we call "**planner completeness**," ensures that the planner is able to return every solution that can be parsed in terms of the non-primitive actions provided for the corresponding top-level goals. While the planning algorithm can guarantee planner completeness, it is not responsible in any way for schema completeness (just as it is not responsible for the correctness of the action specifications given to it). In practice, schema completeness needs to be analyzed through interactive validation techniques, and can be quite tedious. Surprisingly, there is very little acknowledgement of the importance of this validation in the literature on applications of HTN planning; Chien's work on applying HTN planning to a NASA image processing domain is a refreshing exception [6].

3.2 Modeling schemas and action reduction

The only extension required to the partial plan representation described in Section 2 to handle HTN planning is to allow non-primitive actions into the plan. Specifically, the steps T in the partial plan $\langle T, O, \mathcal{B}, \mathcal{ST}, \mathcal{L} \rangle$, will now be mapped to two types of actions: *primitive actions* which correspond to the usual executable actions, and *non-primitive (abstract) actions*. The non-primitive actions have similar precondition/effect structure as the primitive actions. A subset of the effects of a non-primitive action may be distinguished by the domain writer as its "**primary effects**," with the implicit intention that the action may only be used to support its primary effects (see the discussion of non-minimality in Section 4.1). Candidates of the plan, as well as the solutions of the planning problem will still be primitive action sequences.

Reduction Schemas: The domain specification links each non-primitive action o to a set of reduction schemas. Each reduction schema $\mathcal{S}_i$ can be seen as a 2-tuple: $\langle \mathcal{P}_i, \mathcal{M}_i^{\mathcal{L}} \rangle$ where $\mathcal{P}_i$ is the partial plan fragment which can replace o, and $\mathcal{M}_i^{\mathcal{L}}$ maps (redirects) the auxiliary constraints involving o into new auxiliary constraints involving steps of $\mathcal{P}_i$.

Consider, for example, the reduction schema for reducing the non-primitive action $Gobybus(Src, Dest)$ (referred to in Figure 2)

$$\left\langle \mathcal{P}_i : \left\langle \begin{array}{c} T, \mathcal{ST} : \{t_1 : Getin(bus, Src), t_2 : Buyticket(bus) \\ t_3 : Getout(bus, Dest)\} \\ O : \{(t_1 \prec t_2)(t_2 \prec t_3)\} \\ \mathcal{L} : \{(t_1 \stackrel{In(bus)}{-} t_3), (t_2 \stackrel{have(busticket)}{-} t_3)\} \end{array} \right\rangle \right. \\ \left. \mathcal{M}^{\mathcal{L}} : \{(? \stackrel{have(money)}{-} t_2), (t_3 \stackrel{At(Dest)}{-} ?)\} \right\rangle$$

This schema specifies that $Gobybus(Src, Dest)$ action can be replaced by the plan fragment containing three actions of getting into the bus, buying the ticket, and getting out of the bus at the destination. The plan fragment also contains IPCs specifying that the ticket should be kept throughout the journey and that the agent should stay in the bus throughout the journey. Finally, the mapping part of the schema states that any IPC incident on the $Gobybus(Src, Dest)$ action which preserves the condition $have(money)$ should be redirected to the $Buyticket(bus)$ action of the new plan fragment (since the identity of the source of the IPC is not known until reduction time, it is denoted by "?").

Reduction of non-primitive actions: The procedure in Figure 3 describes the process of replacing a non-primitive action using a reduction schema. Consider a plan $\mathcal{P}$: $\langle T, O, \mathcal{B}, \mathcal{ST}, \mathcal{L} \rangle$ containing an abstract action t. Let $\mathcal{S}$: $\langle \mathcal{P}' : \langle T', O', \mathcal{B}', \mathcal{ST}', \mathcal{L}' \rangle, \mathcal{M}^{\mathcal{L}} \rangle$ be a reduction schema for t.

The partial plan that results from the reduction of the action t in $\mathcal{P}$ with the reduction schema $\mathcal{S}$ is denoted by $Reduce(\mathcal{P}, t, \mathcal{S})$, and is computed as follows:

$$Reduce(\mathcal{P}, t, \mathcal{S}) = \mathcal{P}_R : \left\langle \begin{array}{l} \{(T-t) \cup T'\}, \\ \{(O - O_t) \cup O' \cup O_m\}, \\ \{\mathcal{B} \cup \mathcal{B}' \cup \mathcal{B}'_m\}, \\ \{\mathcal{ST} \cup \mathcal{ST}'\}, \\ \{(\mathcal{L} - \mathcal{L}_t) \cup \mathcal{L}' \cup \mathcal{M}(\mathcal{L}_t)\} \end{array} \right\rangle$$

Where O_t and $\mathcal{L}_t$ are the ordering and auxiliary constraints involving t. These are replaced by the redirected constraints O_m and $\mathcal{M}(\mathcal{L}_t)$ during reduction. Note that in replacing t with its reduction, we need to redirect any constraints that explicitly name t, to steps in its reduction. The redirection of IPCs is done by the mapping $\mathcal{M}$ specified by the reduction schema. For the ordering constraints, the redirection is done automatically as follows. When t is reduced, the last step(s) of $\mathcal{P}'$ (i.e., those steps that do not precede any other steps in $\mathcal{P}'$) are forced to precede all the steps t' such that $t \prec t'$ before the reduction. Similarly, the first step(s) of $\mathcal{P}'$ are forced to follow all steps t'' such that $t'' \prec t$ before the reduction. Contiguity constraints are redirected in a similar manner.

Candidate set Semantics: We now explain how non-primitive actions constrain the candidate set of a plan. Let o be a non-primitive action, and let C_o be the set of all partial plans containing only primitive actions (called concretizations) that are obtained by starting with o and repeatedly reducing non-primitive actions using the user-supplied reduction schemas. If o is present in a partial plan $\mathcal{P}$, then the candidate set of $\mathcal{P}$ cannot contain any action sequence that does not satisfy the constraints corresponding to at least one concretization in C_o. Non-primitive actions can thus be seen as *"disjunctive constraints"* on the partial plan. The process of reducing non-primitive actions, described below, can be seen as making the implicit disjunction explicit, and pushing it into the search space. Consequently, reduction can be seen as a "tractability refinement" in the refinement planning terminology [13; 12].

Keeping track of partial hierarchicalization: Non-primitive actions and their associated reduction schemas are the only additions needed to the problem specification if the domain is fully hierarchicalized. If on the other hand, the domain is only partially hierarchicalized, then the domain writer needs a way of informing the planner as to which aspects of the domain are hierarchicalized. Although there are potentially many ways in which the hierarchicalization may be incomplete, we shall assume in this paper that the incompleteness is characterized with respect to specific conditions, using assertions of type "$hierarchicalized(condition)$." In par-

---

Algorithm Pre-reduce($\mathcal{P}$)

1. **Action Selection:** Pick an unreduced action $t \in T$ from $\mathcal{P}$ to work on. *Not a backtrack point.*
2. **Action Reduction:** Non-deterministically select a reduction schema $\mathcal{S}: \mathcal{P}'$ for reducing t. Replace t in $\mathcal{P}$ with $\mathcal{P}'$ (This involves removing t from $\mathcal{P}$, merging the step, binding, ordering, symbol table and auxiliary constraints fields of $\mathcal{P}'$ with those of $\mathcal{P}$, and redirecting the ordering and auxiliary constraints in $\mathcal{P}$ which refer to t so that they refer to elements of $\mathcal{P}'$).
Backtrack point; all reduction possibilities must be considered

---

Figure 3: Pre-reduction Refinement. Can be called as a tractability refinement at step 2 in Figure 2

ticular, the fact that a condition c is fully hierarchicalized is denoted by $hierarchicalized(c)$. It means that all desirable plans for achieving the condition c can be parsed in terms of a non-primitive action whose primary effects include c. A fully hierarchicalized domain is denoted in shorthand by $hierarchicalized(-)$.[1] This approach of keeping track of hierarchicalization of a domain in terms of individual conditions is akin to keeping track of completeness of a knowledge base with localized closed world assumptions [10].

Extending the refinement planning template: To extend the refinement planning template in Figure 1 to handle HTN planning, we need to add the pre-reduction refinement (see Figure 3) as one of the tractability refinements in step 2, and need to generalize the action-based progressive and tractability refinements in steps 1 and 2 to handle non-primitive actions.[2]

In the next section, we will illustrate the issues involved in this generalization by considering plan space and pre-satisfaction (conflict resolution) refinements. Our choice of plan-space refinement for illustration purposes is motivated by the fact that most implemented HTN planners can be seen as using such generalized plan-space refinements.

4 Generalizing refinements to consider non-primitive actions

4.1 Generalizing Plan Space Refinement

Traditional plan-space (PS) refinement involves adding constraints to support a pre-requisite $c@t$ (where c is required to be true at step t) with the help of the effects of a new or exist-

---

[1] It is possible to have a finer characterization of the hierarchicalization of a condition, by allowing the domain writer to specify a context in which the hierarchicalization of c is complete. The context may include information about sibling goals of c, as well as properties of the initial state.

[2] Another way of including HTN planning into the template in Figure 1 would be to leave all refinements as they are, and add an extra filter to the consistency check to prune partial plans that cannot be parsed in terms of the non-primitive actions. This approach, that we can call "bottom-up" HTN planning, has been advocated by Barrett and Weld [2].

ing step t'. As part of the establishment, t' is constrained to precede t, and is forced to give c (if c is a conditional effect, this involves adding the causation precondition of c as a precondition to t' [18]). Optionally, IPCs of the form $(t' \stackrel{c}{-} t)$ are posted to preserve the condition c between t' and t. The HPS refinement, which is a generalized version of the PS refinement to handle non-primitive actions, is shown in Figure 4.[3] We shall explain its development from the PS refinement in the following.

Consider the travel domain of Figure 2. Suppose our top-level goal is $At(SF)$, and we have $At(Phx)$ in the initial state. Six of the ten actions in the domain – *Travel(Phx,SF)*, *Gobybus(Phx,SF)*, *GobyTrain(Phx,SF)*, *Getout(bus,SF)*, *Getout(train,SF)*, and *Hitchhike(car,SF)* – are all capable of achieving this condition. Which of these actions should HPS refinement consider in its different establishment branches?

We note that if HPS refinement considers only the primitive actions, it will correspond to the traditional plan-space refinement. Such a version may however violate the user-intent inherent in the schema specification (as it will for example, permit plans that involve ticket-less travel, which does not respect the intent of the schemas in Figure 2). If we generate branches corresponding to non-primitive actions along side branches for all primitive actions (as is done for example in DPOCL [24]), we will have a redundant search space. As an example, if HPS refinement considered all six actions as establishment possibilities in our example, then two of its refinements would be $\mathcal{P}_1 : t_0 \prec Gobybus(Phx, SF) \prec t_\infty$ and $\mathcal{P}_2 : t_0 \prec Getout(bus, SF) \prec t_\infty$. Since the non-primitive action $Gobybus(Phx, SF)$ ultimately gets reduced into a plan containing the primitive action $Getout(bus, SF)$, the plans have overlapping candidate sets, thus making HPS refinements non-systematic.

To avoid redundancy in the search space, and to respect user-intent, we use the convention that a goal should be established by considering the dominance relations between actions. We consider an action t to be **dominated** by another action t', if there exists a reduction of t' that contains t. Dominance relation is asymmetric except in those cases where the reduction schemas contain recursion. Such dominance relations can be computed easily from an action hierarchy graph such as the one shown in Figure 2. In the travel domain, the action $Gobybus(Phx, SF)$ dominates $Getout(Phx, SF)$ and is dominated by $Travel(Phx, SF)$.

Considering undominated actions to ensure systematicity: Assuming that we are using a systematic plan-space refine-

---
[3]Although the algorithm in the figure enforces a precedence relation between t' and t, if either one or both of them are non-primitive, then such an ordering could be too conservative. We really only need to add an ordering between the eventual action in the concretization of t' that gives c and the corresponding action in the concretization of t that requires c. Such an ordering will need to be re-directed incrementally as t' and t are being reduced. However, most implementations and formalizations of HTN planning retain the conservative orderings to avoid having to deal with redirection of ordering constraints.

Algorithm Refine-plan-hybrid-plan-space ($\mathcal{P}$) /*Returns refinements of $\mathcal{P}$ */

1. **Goal Selection:** Pick an open prerequisite $c@t$ from $\mathcal{P}$ to work on. *Not a backtrack point.*

2. **Goal Establishment:** Non-deterministically select a new or existing establisher step t' for $c@t$ which is capable of giving c. If t' is a *new step*, make sure that it is *maximally abstract* with respect to c (i.e., there is no non-primitive action t'' which can also give c and which dominates t'). If t' is also non-primitive, make sure that c is a primary effect of t'. Introduce enough constraints into the plan such that (i) t' will precede t (ii) t' will have an effect c, and (iii) c will persist until t. Backtrack point; all establishers need to be considered.

3. **Bookkeeping:** (Optional) Add interval preservation constraints of the form $(t' \stackrel{c}{-} t)$ and $(t' \stackrel{\neg c}{-} t)$ noting the establishment decisions, to ensure that these decisions are not violated or duplicated by the latter refinements.

4. **Phantom Establishment:** If $\mathcal{P}$ contains non-primitive actions, then in addition to the plans generated above, consider also $\mathcal{P}'$ which is $\mathcal{P}+ \stackrel{c}{\to} t$. (The PTC $\stackrel{c}{\to} t$ in $\mathcal{P}'$ will never be considered for establishment explicitly. However, any solution derived from $\mathcal{P}'$ must satisfy it [12]).

Figure 4: Plan Space Refinement Modified to work in the presence of non-primitive actions. This can be called as a progressive refinement at step 1 of the procedure in Figure 2.

ment as the basis for HPS, we can ensure that the plans generated by HPS will have non-overlapping candidate sets by requiring that none of the actions considered for the establishment of a given goal are dominated by the other actions being considered for the same goal. Thus we cannot consider $Travel(Phx, SF)$ and $Gobybus(Phx, SF)$ together as sibling choices in establishment *if* we want systematicity.

Considering maximally abstract actions to respect user-intent: An action t is said to be *maximally abstract* with respect to a condition, if it is not dominated by any other action giving that condition. We will respect user intent if we ensure that all the actions considered for establishment of a condition are maximally abstract with respect to that condition. Thus, we will select $Travel(Phx, SF)$ action rather than the $Gobybus(Phx, SF)$ or $Gobytrain(Phx, SF)$ actions to establish $At(SF)$ condition.

The maximal abstractness restriction applies only to step-addition and not to simple establishment, since once a primitive action capable of giving the condition is already in the plan, we may as well use it.

Handling primitive actions during establishment: In satisfying the "maximal abstractness" restriction, there is a question as to whether or not the HPS refinement should consider primitive actions which can establish some condition c, but are not dominated by any other actions (e.g. the $Hitchhike$ action in the travel domain example). If the domain specification contains $hierarchicalized(c)$ (see Section 3), then no primitive actions need to be considered for any goals that are also fulfilled by non-primitive actions. Otherwise, we will allow un-dominated primitive actions along side non-primitive actions. To prefer solutions that can be parsed by existing schemas where possible, we would want to bias the search such that establishment branches corresponding to non-primitive actions are preferred over the branches corresponding to primitive ones.

Use of primary effects to avoid non-minimal plans: Another potential concern is that selecting maximally abstract actions to establish a goal may lead us into scenarios where a complex plan is being executed only because the agent is interested in a secondary side effect of some non-primitive action in that plan. For example, suppose the planner has a single top-level goal "$have(trainticket)$" (presumably because the agent is an avid ticket collector). The action $Buytrainticket()$ will give the condition, and so presumably does the more abstract action $Gobytrain(x,y)$. Since the latter dominates the former, maximal abstract step restriction would require us to select the $Gobytrain()$ action to achieve $have(trainticket)$, which leads to a non-minimal plan for the agent.

We punt this problem by using only primary effects (see Section 3.2) during establishment with non-primitive actions, and assuming that the domain writer has specified the primary effects of non-primitive actions with appropriate care. Thus, if the domain writer listed on $At(x)$ as a primary effect of $Gobytrain()$ action, then we would not consider it to establish $have(Trainticket)$ goal. Our use of primary effects here is similar to (and explains the motivation behind) the "to-do" and "use-only-for" slots in the Nonlin [21] and O-Plan [7] reduction schemas, and the "purpose" slots in SIPE's [22] reduction schemas.

Phantom Establishments: Since non-primitive actions do not advertise all the possible effects of the actions involved in their eventual reductions, their presence necessitates a change to the "simple-establishment" phase (wherein the prerequisite is established by the effects of steps currently existing in the plan) of the action-based plan-space refinement. Specifically, even if none of the explicit effects of the existing steps support a pre-requisite $c@t$, if one of the steps t' in the plan corresponds to a non-primitive action, then one of the primitive actions resulting from the eventual reduction of t' may very well have an effect c (and can thus support $c@t$). If we do not account for this possibility, we can lose completeness (since plan-space refinement considers each pre-requisite only once, i.e., does not backtrack on the goal order).

In order to handle this scenario, we provide an additional way of establishing the $c@t$ pre-requisite, viz., converting it into a point truth constraint "$\xrightarrow{c} t$." This process, called "phantomization," essentially leaves open a back door for supporting $c@t$ with the effects of actions that come into the plan through reduction (since the only way this PTC can be satisfied eventually is if c becomes necessarily true at t because of the effects of the actions present in the plan at that time).[4]

4.2 Conflict resolution with non-primitive actions

In normal action-based planning, the need for conflict resolution arises if the plan has an IPC ($t_1 \xrightarrow{p} t_2$) and a step t_3 which has a potential effect $\neg p$. The conflict is resolved by posting the constraints to ensure that either t_3 precedes t_1, or it follows t_2, or t_3 will not give $\neg p$. Generalizing conflict resolution with non-primitive actions presents some problems. Suppose t_1, t_2 and t_3 in the above example are all non-primitive. To avoid this conflict, we need to only ensure that the specific primitive step t_3^p, which actually deletes p in the eventual reduction of t_3 should come outside the interval between t_1^p and t_2^p, where the latter two are the primitive steps resulting from reduction of t_1 and t_2 that add and need p respectively. Since the identity of t_3^p, t_1^p and t_2^p will not be known until the three non-primitive actions are completely reduced, one cannot post simple ordering relations between these non-primitive actions to resolve the threat. Furthermore, even if the introduced ordering relations are found to be inconsistent with the existing constraints of the plan, it still doesn't mean that the conflict cannot be eventually resolved after further reduction [23].

In order to handle these problems, we require that conflict resolution be applied only with respect to IPCs and threats where the producer and consumer steps of the IPC as well as the threatening step are all primitive.

5 Discussion and related work

We have presented a hybrid planning approach that has the ability to consistently handle partially hierarchical domains. This ability supports incremental hierarchicalization of a domain: the domain-writer (or an autonomous learner) acting in concert with the planner may continue to provide additional reduction schemas making the domain fully hierarchicalized with respect to more conditions. Reduction schemas will be used for the parts of the problem for which they are present; and normal action-based planning will be used for the other parts in a seamless fashion. As the experience of the domain-writer/learner increases, more and more schemas may be written, tightening the control over the planner's search space.

The ability to handle partially hierarchicalized domains also removes one of the main criticisms of HTN planning from the reactive planning community (c.f. [20; 16])–viz., HTN planning reduces the flexibility of an agent to respond to situations that are not anticipated by the writer of the task-reduction schemas. It may thus increase the acceptance of HTN approaches in that community.

---

[4]It is possible to reduce the number of phantom establishment branches, if we keep track of the "possible" effects of non-primitive actions. A condition c is a possible effect of a non-primitive action a, if c is an effect of a or any action that is dominated by a. We can avoid generating phantom establishment branches for condition c if none of the non-primitive actions in the plan have c as a possible effect.

Developing HTN planning on top of the existing formalization of action-based planning confers us two advantages. First, it allows us us to put into perspective the many surface differences between HTN and action-based planners, such as the need for phantomization, and the differing notions of completeness. Second and perhaps more important, our work also helps us exploit recent progress on action-based planners, including SATPLAN [15] and Graphplan [3], in the context of HTN planners [14]. Indeed, some of our ongoing work involves adapting the planning as satisfiability approach to HTN planning [17]. As in this paper, our HTN encodings are obtained by generalizing the encodings for action-based planning.

In theory, it is also possible to represent partially hierarchical domains in existing HTN planners such as SIPE [22] and O-Plan [7], as well as in the existing HTN formalizations [8; 2]. For every undominated primitive action, we simply introduce a non-primitive action and a degenerate reduction schema that reduces it to the primitive action. What is novel about our framework is that we explicitly consider the issues involved in ensuring systematicity, and preserving user-intent in such partially hierarchical domains.

Some previous systems, including IPEM [1] and DPOCL [24], attempted to explicitly combine task reduction and plan-space planning. Neither of these approaches however guarantees an integration that ensures systematicity and preservation of user-intent. For example, DPOCL allows for the establishment of a precondition both with a non-primitive action and a primitive action which it dominates. As we argued earlier, this can lead to a loss of systematicity as well as violation of user-intent. Our approach also provides clear semantics of plans containing non-primitive actions, and thus explains the essential differences between the completeness results of plan-space and HPS refinements.

Another research effort that allows combination of HTN and plan-space planning approaches is that of Chien and his co-workers [5]. They argue that the HTN and plan-space techniques should be kept separate, with the former working on "activity" goals while the latter work on "state" goals. Domain information pertaining to these techniques is also kept separate. While our approach allows for such a separation, it also allows for HTN and plan-space approaches to work together on the same class of goals in a principled way.

6 Conclusion

In this paper, we have argued for hybrid planning approaches that combine HTN and action-based planning algorithms. Such approaches facilitate planning in partially hierarchical domains. We presented such a hybrid planning framework by extending our existing refinement planning framework for action-based planning [11; 13; 12]. The extensions involve considering non-primitive actions and their reduction schemas as part of the domain specification, and generalizing the traditional refinements to handle plans containing non-primitive actions. We illustrated the issues involved in such generalization in the context of plan-space and conflict resolution refinements. We discussed what it takes for such a hybrid approach to respect user-intent, while guaranteeing systematicity and completeness. We have also discussed the relation between our hybrid framework and previous attempts to formalize HTN planning. Developing HTN planning on top of the existing formalization of action-based planning allows us to put into perspective the many surface differences between HTN and action-based planners, and could help in transferring progress between HTN and action-based planning approaches. As an example of the latter, we recently extended the SATPLAN [15] approach to HTN planning [17].

References

[1] J.A. Ambros-Ingerson and S. Steel. Integrating Planning, Execution and Monitoring. In *Proc. 7th AAAI*, 1988.

[2] A. Barrett and D. Weld. Task Decomposition via Plan Parsing. In *Proc. AAAI-94*.

[3] A. Blum and M. Furst, Fast planning through planning graph analysis, Proc. of IJCAI-95, 1636-1642.

[4] D. Chapman. Planning for conjunctive goals. *Artificial Intelligence*, 32:333–377, 1987.

[5] S. Chien, T. Estlin and X. Wang. An argument for hybrid HTN/Operator Planning. In Proc. 4th European Conference on Planning. 1997.

[6] S. Chien. Static and Completion analysis for planning knowledge base development and verification. In *Proc. AIPS-96*, 1996.

[7] K. Currie and A. Tate. O-Plan: The Open Planning Architecture. *Artificial Intelligence*, 51(1), 1991.

[8] K. Erol. Hierarchical task network planning: Formalization, Analysis and Implementation, Ph.D thesis, Dept. of computer science, Univ. of Maryland, College Park, 1995.

[9] K. Erol, J. Hendler, D.S. Nau and R. Tsuneto. A critical look at critics in HTN planning. In *Proc. IJCAI-95*, 1995.

[10] O. Etzioni, K. Golden and D. Weld. Sound and efficient closed-world reasoning for planning. *Artificial Intelligence*, 89(1-2), 113–148.

[11] S. Kambhampati, C. Knoblock and Q. Yang. Planning as Refinement Search: A Unified framework for evaluating design tradeoffs in partial order planning. *Artificial Intelligence* special issue on Planning and Scheduling. Vol. 76. 1995. and

[12] S. Kambhampati and B. Srivastava. Universal Classical Planner: An algorithm for unifying state space and plan space approaches. In New Trends in AI Planning: EWSP 95, IOS Press, 1995. (Extended version available as technical report ASU CSE 96-006 at http://rakaposhi.eas.asu.edu/ucp-tr.ps).

[13] S. Kambhampati, Refinement search as a unifying framework for plan synthesis, AI magazine, Summer 1997.

[14] S. Kambhampati. Challenges in bridging plan synthesis paradigms, Proc. IJCAI-97, 1997.

[15] H. Kautz and B. Selman, Pushing the envelope: Planning, Propositional logic and Stochastic search, Proc. of AAAI-96.

[16] P. Maes, Situated agents can have goals, Robotics and autonomous systems 6, 1990, 49-70.

[17] A. Mali and S. Kambhampati. Encoding HTN planning in propositional logic. Proc. 4th AI Planning Systems Conf., 1998.

[18] E.P.D. Pednault. Synthesizing Plans that contain actions with Context-Dependent Effects. *Computational Intelligence*, Vol. 4, 356-372 (1988).

[19] E. Sacerdoti. The nonlinear nature of plans. In *Proc. IJCAI-75*, 1975.

[20] R. Simmons, Structured control for autonomous robots, IEEE transactions on robotics and automation, Feb. 1994.

[21] A. Tate. Generating Project Networks. In *Proceedings of IJCAI-77*, pages 888–893, Boston, MA, 1977.

[22] D. Wilkins. *Practical Planning*. Morgan Kaufmann (1988).

[23] Q. Yang. Formalizing planning knowledge for hierarchical planning. *Computational Intelligence Journal*, 6:12–24, 1990.

[24] R.M. Young, M.E. Pollack and J.D. Moore. Decomposition and Causality in Partial-Order Planning. In *Proc. 2nd Intl. Conf. on AI Planning Systems*, 1994.

Conformant Graphplan

David E. Smith

NASA Ames Research Center
Mail stop 269–2
Moffett Field, CA 94035
de2smith@ptolemy.arc.nasa.gov

Daniel S. Weld

Department of Computer Science and Engineering
University of Washington
Seattle, WA 98195
weld@cs.washington.edu

Abstract

Planning under uncertainty is a difficult task. If sensory information is available, it is possible to do *contingency planning* – that is, develop plans where certain branches are executed conditionally, based on the outcome of sensory actions. However, even without sensory information, it is often possible to develop useful plans that succeed no matter which of the allowed states the world is actually in. We refer to this type of planning as *conformant planning*.

Few conformant planners have been built, partly because conformant planning requires the ability to reason about disjunction. In this paper we describe Conformant Graphplan (CGP), a Graphplan-based planner that develops sound (non-contingent) plans when faced with uncertainty in the initial conditions and in the outcome of actions. The basic idea is to develop separate plan graphs for each possible world. This requires some subtle changes to both the graph expansion and solution extraction phases of Graphplan. In particular, the solution extraction phase must consider the unexpected side effects of actions in other possible worlds, and must confront any undesirable effects.

We show that CGP performs significantly better than two previous (probabilistic) conformant planners.

Introduction

There are two basic approaches to planning when uncertainty is present in the world:

1. *Contingency planning* – develop plans where some branches are executed conditionally, based on the outcome of sensory actions.

2. *Conformant planning* – develop non-conditional plans that do not rely on sensory information, but still succeed no matter which of the allowed states the world is actually in.

When sensory actions are cheap, but effectory actions are expensive or dangerous, contingency planning makes a great deal of sense. However, both of these options have their place. In situations where sensing is difficult or impossible, conformant planning may be the best (or only) alternative. As an example, it might be difficult to determine if a particular work surface is clean, or if an instrument is sterile. Yet it may be a simple matter to clean the work surface or sterilize the instrument, thus resolving the uncertainty.

In these two examples, conformant planning involves removing some of the uncertainty in the world by forcing propositions into known states. More generally, conformant planning involves case analysis to make sure the goals are achieved in any of several situations. For example, suppose a patient has one of several diseases, but it cannot be determined precisely which one. Finding a drug therapy plan that covers all the cases (without bad drug interactions) is a conformant planning problem.

There are a number of planning systems that do contingency planning, including: Warplan-C (Warren 1976), CNLP (Peot and Smith 1992), SENSP (Etzioni, et al. 1992), Plinth (Goldman and Boddy 1994), XII (Golden, Etzioni and Weld 1994), Cassandra (Pryor and Collins 1996), C-Buridan (Draper, Hanks and Weld 1994), and DTPOP (Peot 1998). However, only Buridan (Kushmerick, Hanks and Weld 1995), C-Buridan and UDTPOP (Peot 1998) do conformant planning. All three of these systems are probabilistic planners and are limited to propositional actions. Furthermore, these planners are incredibly slow – so slow that they make planners like UCPOP (Penberthy and Weld 1992) and Prodigy (Veloso et al. 1995) look positively zippy.

Recently, there has been a great deal of interest in Graphplan (Blum and Furst 1995, 1997), which seems to have a significant performance advantage over planners like UCPOP and Prodigy. As originally described, Graphplan is limited to simple STRIPS operators. In this paper we describe Conformant Graphplan (CGP) – a modification of Graphplan that deals with uncertainty by constructing conformant plans. Unlike Buridan, C-Buridan and UDTPOP, CGP is not probabilistic – the initial conditions may contain disjunction and actions may have uncertain outcomes, but the system has no notion of the likelihood of different propositions.

The basic idea in CGP is to create a different plan graph for each possible world. Unfortunately, this doesn't quite work, because, in the absence of sensing actions, an action cannot be confined to one possible world. This complicates the solution extraction phase of Graphplan. In particular, when CGP selects an action in one possible world, it must consider what might happen if it is in another possible world. If the consequences of the action are undesirable in that other possible world, CGP must *confront* the action in that other possible world. In some cases it is possible to recognize problematic interactions between worlds and derive mutual exclusion relationships between propositions in the different possible worlds. This results in a considerable efficiency improvement but complicates the mutual exclusion rules for CGP.

In the next section we briefly review the Graphplan algorithm. In Section 3 we describe the modifications necessary to make this algorithm handle uncertainty in the initial conditions. In Section 4 we extend the algorithm to handle actions with uncertain outcomes. Finally, we show that CGP dramatically outperforms previous conformant planners.

Graphplan background

Graphplan (Blum and Furst 1995, 1997) accepts action schemata in the STRIPS representation – preconditions are conjunctions of positive literals and effects are a conjunction of positive or negative literals (i.e., composing the add and delete lists). Graphplan alternates between two phases: *graph expansion* and *solution extraction*. The graph expansion phase extends a *planning graph* until it has achieved a necessary (but insufficient) condition for plan existence. The solution extraction phase performs a backward-chaining search for an actual solution; if no solution is found, the cycle repeats.

The planning graph contains two types of nodes, proposition nodes and action nodes, arranged into levels. Even numbered levels contain proposition nodes, and the zeroth level consists precisely of the propositions that are true in the initial state of the planning problem. Nodes in odd-numbered levels correspond to action instances; there is an odd-numbered node for each action instance whose preconditions are present (and are mutually consistent) at the previous level. Directed edges connect proposition nodes to the action instances (at the next level) whose preconditions mention those propositions. Directed edges connect action nodes to subsequent propositions made true by the action's effects.

The most interesting aspect of Graphplan is its use of local consistency methods during graph creation – this appears to yield a dramatic speedup during solution extraction. Graphplan defines a binary mutual exclusion relation ("mutex") between nodes in the same level as follows:

1. Two action instances at level i are mutex if either
   - *Interference / Inconsistent Effects*: one action deletes a precondition or effect of another, or
   - *Competing needs*: the actions have preconditions that are mutually exclusive at level i-1.
2. Two propositions at level i are mutex if all ways of achieving the propositions (i.e. actions at level i-1) are mutex.

Suppose that Graphplan is trying to generate a plan for a goal with n conjuncts, and it has finally extended the planning graph to an even level, i, in which all goal propositions are present and none are pairwise mutex. Graphplan now searches for a solution plan by considering each of the n goals in turn. For each such proposition at level i, Graphplan chooses an action a at level i-1 that achieves the goal. This is a backtracking choice – all possible actions must be considered to guarantee completeness. If a is consistent (non-mutex) with all actions that have been chosen so far at this level, then Graphplan proceeds to the next goal, otherwise if no such choice is available, Graphplan backtracks. After Graphplan has found a consistent set of actions at level i-1 it recursively tries to find a plan for the set of all the preconditions of those actions at level i-2. The base case for the recursion is level zero – if the propositions are present there, then Graphplan has found a solution. If, on the other hand, Graphplan fails to find a consistent set of actions at some level and backtracking is unsuccessful, then it continues to alternate between growing the planning graph and searching for a solution (until it reaches a set limit or the graph levels off).

Negated Preconditions

Although methods for handling negated preconditions were not presented in (Blum and Furst 1995, 1997), they are both straightforward and essential prerequisites for handling conditional effects. Clearly proposition p and ¬p are mutually exclusive in any given level. Whenever an action instance deletes a proposition (i.e. has a negated literal as an effect), one must add that negative literal to the subsequent proposition level in the planning graph.

Conditional effects

As originally described, Graphplan supports only simple STRIPS operators. Recently, several authors have described methods that allow Graphplan to handle operators with conditional effects (Gazen and Knoblock 1997, Koehler et al. 1997, Anderson, Smith and Weld 1998). For pedagogical reasons we adopt the simple approach used by Gazen and Knoblock, which breaks operators with conditional effects up into a number of separate operators (by considering all minimal consistent combinations of antecedents in the conditional effects). To illustrate, consider the ADL operator:

```
OP    pre:   P
      eff:   (and E (when C_1 F)
                    (when C_2 G))
```

This operator would be expanded into the following four STRIPS operators:

```
OP1   pre:   (and P ¬C_1 ¬C_2)
      eff:   E

OP2   pre:   (and P ¬C_1 C_2)
      eff:   (and E G)

OP3   pre:   (and P C_1 ¬C_2)
      eff:   (and E F)

OP4   pre:   (and P C_1 C_2)
      eff:   (and E F G)
```

We will refer to these four operators as *aspects* of the original ADL operator.

Conformant Graphplan

To begin, we limit consideration to cases where uncertainty occurs only in the initial conditions (i.e. action effects are certain), but we relax this restriction in the following section. With Graphplan, the initial conditions are specified as a conjunction of positive and negative literals. We augment this language to allow the use of disjunction (or) and exclusive or (xor).

Plan graph expansion

The basic idea behind conformant Graphplan is to express the uncertainty in the initial conditions as a set of completely specified *possible worlds*, and run the Graphplan expansion procedure on each of these possible worlds in parallel. To do this, we first initialize a separate plan graph for each possible world. The expansion phase of Graphplan is then the same as for a normal plan graph; we just have to do it for each of the possible worlds.

To illustrate, consider the simple "bomb in the toilet" problem from (Mcdermott 1987). There are two packages, one of which contains a bomb. Dunking the package with the bomb in it renders the bomb disarmed. We formalize the initial conditions as (and armed (xor In(P1) In(P2))). The goal is ¬Armed and the single operator

Dunk (?pkg)   pre:
              eff: (when In(?pkg) ¬Armed)

has only one aspect with non-empty effects:

Dunk* (?pkg) pre: In(?pkg)
              eff: ¬Armed

Figure 1 shows the first level of the possible world plan graphs (PWPGs) for this example. In world w_1, Dunk*(P1) can be used to achieve ¬Armed, while in world w_2, Dunk*(P2) can be used to achieve ¬Armed. In each of the two graphs there is a mutex relationship between the Dunk* action and the persistence of Armed, because a proposition and its negation cannot both be true. Note that the two plan graphs in Figure 1 are separate – there are no links that cross from one world to the other. In the solution extraction phase, we have to consider interactions between aspects in different worlds but the graphs will remain separate. Later on, we introduce explicit mutual exclusion relationships between propositions in different PWPGs.

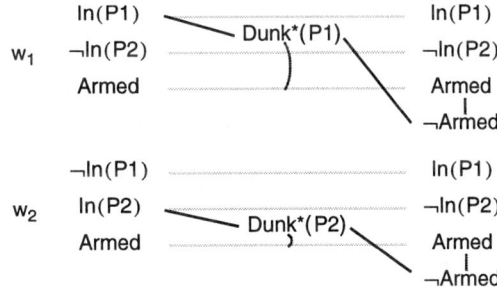

Figure 1: Possible world plan graphs for the basic bomb in toilet problem. Gray arcs indicate no-op steps for persistence of propositions from one level to the next. Arcs between steps and arcs between propositions are mutex relationships.

For convenience we use the notation p:w to refer to the proposition p in world w. Similarly, we use a:w to refer to aspect a in world w.

Solution extraction

Graphplan searches backwards for a plan whenever all the goal literals occur at the current level of the plan graph, and none of those literals are mutex with each other. With uncertainty present, we need to guarantee that the goal is satisfied in all possible worlds. This requires several changes to the solution extraction phase of Graphplan. First, CGP searches for a plan at an even level only when the goal literals appear at that level in each of the possible world plan graphs (and none of those literals are mutex with each other). Second, the search proceeds backwards one level at a time, simultaneously through all of the possible world plan graphs[1]. Third, as is shown later, the search needs to consider interactions across different possible worlds.

Consider the possible world plan graphs in Figure 1 and recall that the goal is ¬Armed. At level 1, ¬Armed is present in both PWPGs, so CGP should search backwards for a plan. The goal ¬Armed in world 1 can only be achieved using the aspect Dunk*(P1):w_1. Likewise, ¬Armed in world 2 can only be achieved using the aspect Dunk*(P2):w_2. These two aspects are not mutex, and their subgoals at level 0 are achieved by the initial conditions. Thus, it appears that the plan of dunking both packages achieves the goal (and in this case it actually works to dunk both packages).

Unfortunately, there is a problem with this simple-minded approach. If we choose to perform an action, we must consider its effects in all worlds, not just the specific world in which the action was added. This is because (without sensing) the planner doesn't know which of the worlds it is really in and therefore cannot confine the effects of an action to just one possible world. To compound matters, each world is different, so performing an action may lead to one aspect of the action in one possible world and a completely different aspect in another possible world.

To illustrate this problem, we augment the bomb in the toilet problem by adding both a precondition (that the toilet is not clogged) and an unconditional effect (that the toilet is clogged afterwards) to the Dunk operation:

Dunk (?pkg)   pre: ¬Clogged
              eff: (and Clogged
                       (when In(?pkg) ¬Armed))

This action has two aspects:

Dunk– (?pkg) pre: (and ¬Clogged ¬In(?pkg))
              eff: Clogged

Dunk+ (?pkg) pre: (and ¬Clogged In(?pkg))
              eff: (and Clogged ¬Armed)

We also augment the initial conditions to include the fact that the toilet is not initially clogged. With these additions the problem cannot be solved for all possible worlds, because we will not be able to dunk both packages. Figure 2 shows the first level of the plan graph for this new problem.

---

1. This is not strictly necessary. Other search strategies (like searching the worlds sequentially) could also be used, but interactions between aspects in different possible worlds would not be recognized as early.

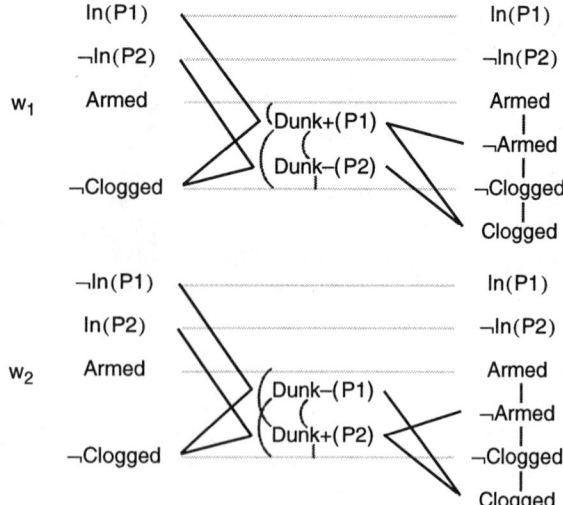

Figure 2: A Possible worlds plan graph when the dunk operation clogs the toilet.

At level 1, ¬Armed is present in both PWPGs, so CGP would search backwards for a plan. The goal ¬Armed:w_1 can only be achieved using the aspect Dunk+(P1):w_1. Likewise, the goal ¬Armed:w_2 can only be achieved using the aspect Dunk+(P2):w_2.

Next we must consider the consequences of these two aspects in the opposite possible world. Consider the aspect Dunk+(P1):w_1. To guarantee that aspect in world 1, we must perform the action Dunk(P1), which results in the aspect Dunk+(P1):w_1 as well as the aspect Dunk–(P1):w_2. Since Dunk–(P1):w_2 is mutex with Dunk+(P2):w_2, the plan of dunking both packages fails. We formalize these intuitions as:

Definition 1: Suppose aspect a:w is present at level i in a PWPG and a':v ($v \neq w$) is another aspect of the *same* action at level i in the PWPG. We say that a:w *possibly induces* a':v, and vice versa.

In the example above, Dunk+(P1):w_1 possibly induces Dunk–(P1):w_2 and vice versa. Likewise for Dunk–(P2):w_1 and Dunk+(P2):w_2.

Sometimes it is possible to prevent an undesirable possibly induced aspect using *confrontation*[2]. To prevent or confront aspect a':v, the planner needs to assure that its precondition is false at level i-1 and remains false during the execution of the other aspects at level i. (Otherwise, a':v might fire if a is executed after its precondition becomes established.) Thus if a':v has preconditions $p_1, p_2, ..., p_n$ the planner must find a precondition p_j:v that can be made false at level i-1 and can be held false until level i+1. One easy way

---

2. In UCPOP, confrontation is used to prevent undesirable conditional effects of a chosen action within a single world (no uncertainty). Here we do not need to do this within a given possible world because we expanded conditional effects out into aspects that are mutually exclusive. However, even with this expansion into aspects, we still need to prevent possibly induced aspects from occurring in other possible worlds.

to implement this is to check that the no-op operation persisting ¬p_j:v

1. exists at level i, and
2. is not mutex with any other aspect in the plan at level i.

If so, this no-op is added to the plan, and its precondition ¬p_j:v is added to the subgoals at level i-1. Note that when doing confrontation, there may be a choice of which precondition p_j:v to confront. This provides an additional backtrack point during the solution extraction process.

With the notions of possibly induced aspects and confrontation, we can now describe the solution extraction phase of CGP more precisely. Let i+1 be the newest proposition level in the graph and let S_{i+1} (the set of subgoals to be achieved at level i+1) be initialized to the set of goals G tagged with each possible world: $\{g:w \mid g \in G, w \in W\}$.

1. Initialize A_i (the set of aspect-world pairs chosen at level i) to the empty set.
2. For each subgoal g:w ∈ S_{i+1} choose (backtrack point) an aspect a:w at level i that achieves g:w, and is consistent (not mutex) with every other aspect in A_i. Unless a:w is already in A_i:
   - Add a:w to the set A_i.
   - For each precondition p:w of a:w, unless p:w is already in S_{i-1}, add p:w to S_{i-1}.
3. Let D_i refer to the set of all aspects possibly induced by aspects in A_i. For each aspect a:w in A_i, confront (backtrack point) each possibly induced aspect in D_i that is mutex with a:w.
4. If i=1, return the completed plan $A_1, A_3, ..., A_{n-1}$, otherwise reduce i by 2 and repeat.

Note that in doing the confrontation in step 3, a new no-op may get added to the set A_i. This no-op must also be made safe from all aspects in D_i. As a result, step 3 continues as long as A_i keeps growing. (D_i does not grow during this process because no-ops don't induce other aspects.)

Induced mutex

In the example in Figure 2, we had to commit to the aspect Dunk+(P1):w_1 during solution extraction before we discovered that the possibly induced aspect Dunk–(P1):w_2 could not be prevented. Since Dunk–(P1):w_2 was mutex with the desired aspect Dunk+(P2):w_2, the plan failed. In fact, we can discover this problem much earlier. The key is to recognize that Dunk+(P1):w_1 always induces the aspect Dunk–(P1):w_2 at that level. Since Dunk–(P1):w_2 is mutex with Dunk+(P2):w_2 this means that Dunk+(P1):w_1 should also be labelled as mutex with Dunk+(P2):w_2. We formalize this notion with the following definition:

Definition 2: Suppose aspect a:w is present at level i of a PWPG, and a':v ($v \neq w$) is another aspect of the *same* action at level i in the PWPG. We say that a:w *necessarily induces* a':v at level i if for every precondition p_j of a':v either:

¬p_j:v is not present at level i-1, or

¬p_j:v is mutex with some precondition of a:w at level i-1.

These conditions guarantee that a':v cannot be confronted at level i.

In the example above, we note that Dunk–(P1):w_2 cannot be confronted at level 1, because none of the negations of its preconditions are present at level 0. As a result, Dunk+(P1):w_1 necessarily induces Dunk–(P1):w_2. (The converse also holds in this case, as do similar relationships for the aspects of Dunk(P2).)

Given the definition for necessarily induces, we can now state the induced mutex rule:

Induced mutex: If aspect a:w necessarily induces a':v at level i and a':v is mutex with another aspect b:u at level i, then a:w is also mutex with b:u.

This rule is illustrated in Figure 3. Figure 4 illustrates just a few of the resulting induced mutex relationships for the example of Figure 2. The most important of these is that Dunk+(P1):w_1 and Dunk+(P2):w_2 are mutex. This means that, according to the usual mutex rules, ¬Armed:w_1 and ¬Armed:w_2 are mutex. As a result, no backward search will take place for this problem at level 2.

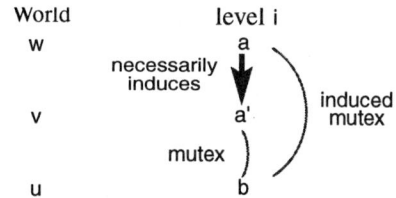

Figure 3: Induced mutex relationships.

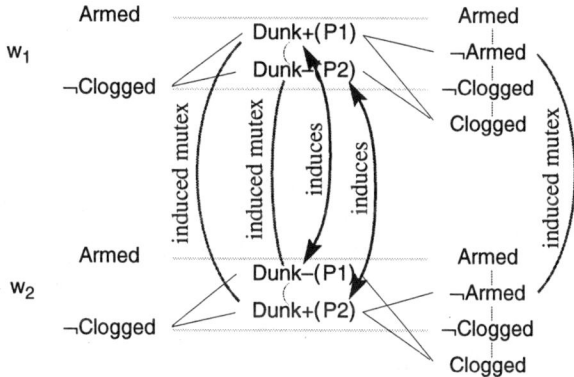

Figure 4: Two of the induced mutex relationships for the bomb in the toilet problem. For clarity, the static preconditions In(P1) and In(P2), and some of the other mutex relationships have been omitted from the PWPG. For this problem, there are many more induced mutex relationships between the dunk operations and persistence actions. For example, Dunk+(P1):w_1 is mutex with the persistence of Armed in w_1, so Dunk–(P1):w_2 will be mutex with the persistence of Armed in w_1.

Note that deriving induced mutex relationships is strictly an efficiency measure. Without it CGP still discovers conflicts due to induced aspects by virtue of the confrontation mechanism (during solution extraction). However, as we will illustrate in the results section, deriving induced mutex relationships substantially improves the performance of CGP.

Conversely, deriving induced mutex relationships, does not eliminate the need for confrontation during solution extraction. Induced mutex relationships only eliminate conflicts do to necessarily induced aspects. They do not eliminate potential conflicts due to possibly induced aspects.

Actions with uncertain outcomes

So far we have assumed that all uncertainty results from uncertainty in the initial conditions. We now expand our treatment to include actions with uncertain outcomes. In keeping with the representation used in Buridan (Kushmerick, Hanks and Weld 1995), we specify uncertain outcomes for an action by replacing the effects by a list of disjoint outcomes, each element of which is a traditional effects list. (An ordinary STRIPS action would therefore have only a single element in its outcomes list.)

For example, suppose that after performing a Dunk operation it is uncertain whether the toilet will be clogged or not. Thus, the Dunk operator becomes:

Dunk (?pkg)   pre: ¬Clogged
              outcomes: (when In(?pkg) ¬Armed)
                         (and Clogged
                              (when In(?pkg) ¬Armed))

As before, we break this action into two aspects:

Dunk– (?pkg) pre: (and ¬Clogged ¬In(?pkg))
              outcomes: ∅
                         Clogged

Dunk+ (?pkg) pre: (and ¬Clogged In(?pkg))
              outcomes: ¬Armed
                         (and Clogged ¬Armed)

where ∅ signifies the empty effect. (Note that we need to include the empty outcome for aspect Dunk–, to indicate that the aspect may have no effect.)

Plan graph expansion

When uncertainty is confined to the initial conditions, expansion of each PWPG was essentially the same as for an ordinary plan graph. For actions with uncertain outcomes, this is no longer the case – each time such an action occurs in the plan graph, the number of possible worlds is multiplied by the number of possible outcomes of the action. Consider the aspect Dunk+(P1) in the plan graph shown in Figure 5. The

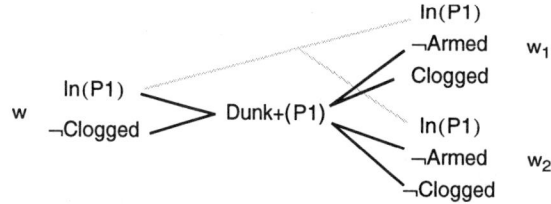

Figure 5: World splitting from an uncertain outcome.

world w is split into two possibilities, w_1 and w_2 corresponding to the two outcomes of Dunk+(P1). When a world is split, the outcomes of other actions must be split as well. For example, the persistence action for In(P1) supports the proposition In(P1) in both of the new possible worlds.

In our example, suppose that the aspect Dunk–(P2) also occurs at this level of the plan graph. It too has an uncertain outcome, so world w really must be split into four possibilities, as shown in Figure 6.

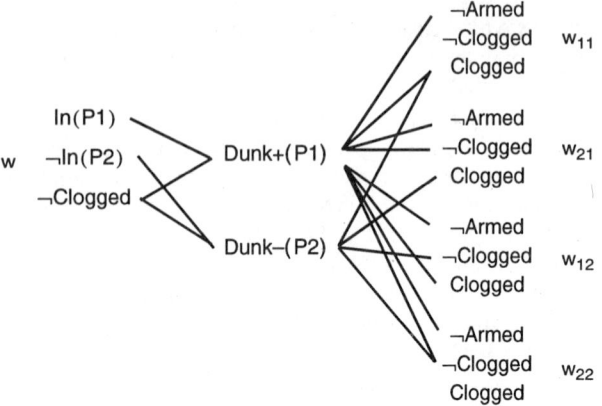

Figure 6: World splitting from two uncertain outcomes.

The splitting operation requires changes to the expansion phase of CGP. As before we add each of the new aspects to the plan graph for a possible world. However, we delay adding the propositions to the next proposition level until all the aspects are added (so that we know how many ways the possible world must be split.)

Consider one particular world w at the current level of the plan graph. Let $U=\{u_1,...,u_n\}$ be the aspects in that world with uncertain outcomes and let o_j be the number of different outcomes for aspect u_j. World w will be split into

$$\prod_{j=1}^{n} o_j$$

new worlds. We label these new possible worlds with a sequence of subscripts, $s_1...s_n$, one subscript for each of the n aspects with uncertain outcomes. The total set of possible worlds derived from w will be:

$$\{w_{s_1,...,s_n} \mid s_j = 1,...,o_j\}$$

If a is an aspect with no uncertainty, then its effects get added to each of the above possible worlds, and links are added from a to those effects. However, if a is an uncertain aspect u_m, the effects of outcome k of a will only get added to the subset of the worlds corresponding to outcome k, namely, the subset where $s_m=k$:

$$\{w_{s_1,...,s_{m-1},k,s_{m+1},...,s_n} \mid s_j = 1,...,o_j, j \neq m\}$$

As before, these effects get linked to the aspect a.

If aspects with uncertain outcomes appear frequently in the plan graph, this can lead to an explosion in the number of possible worlds. One trick for cutting down the number of possible worlds is to take advantage of mutex relationships between aspects. In particular, if two mutex aspects have uncertain outcomes, they can share possible worlds, so the number of possible worlds required is the maximum (rather than the product) of the number of outcomes for the two aspects. In general, sharing worlds between three or more aspects requires that they all be pairwise mutually exclusive. This leads to the interesting side problem of partitioning the uncertain aspects into mutex cliques in order to minimize the total number of worlds created.

Mutual exclusion

Remarkably enough, world splitting does not require any changes to the solution extraction algorithm we gave in the previous section. However, actions with uncertain outcomes do mandate a slight change in the definition of mutex relationships. Since we cannot predict which outcome of an uncertain aspect will actually occur, we must be conservative and allow for the worst. In particular, if *any* outcome of an aspect deletes a precondition or *possible* effect of another aspect, the two aspects are mutex. To fix this, we modify one of Graphplan's basic mutex rules as follows:

- *Interference / Inconsistent Effects*: Two aspects at level i are mutex if one action can *possibly* delete a precondition or *possible* effect of another.

Results

CGP is implemented in Common Lisp and accepts domains in the PDDL format, augmented to allow disjunction in the initial conditions and operators with uncertain outcomes. The implementation generates a single plan graph in which each proposition at each level is labelled with the possible world that it is in.

Table 1 shows the performance of Buridan (Kushmerick, Hanks and Weld 1995), UDTPOP (Peot 1998), CGP, and CGPx (CGP without induced mutex relationships) on a series of increasingly complicated "bomb in the toilet" problems. The domain contains two operator schemas, Dunk and Flush. Dunk clogs the toilet unconditionally and disarms the bomb if it is present in the dunked package. Flush clears a clogged toilet. The problems vary the number of toilets available (from 1 to 3) and the number of packages that the bomb can be in (from 2 to 6).

Both Buridan and UDTPOP are propositional, so we created propositional versions of the domains and problems for these systems. These planners are also probabilistic; so for the initial conditions, we divided the probability mass equally among each one of the initial possible worlds. As with CGP, the operators for these test problems all had certain (probability 1) outcomes.

As can be seen in the table, Buridan's performance was abysmal; it was only able to solve the three tiniest (two package) problems. On all other problems, progress was halted after the generation of 100,000 nodes (which corresponded to somewhere between 5 and 7 minutes of CPU time). UDT-

Toilets	Pkgs	Steps	Buridan	UDTPOP	CGPx	CGP
1	2	3	.44	.072	.010	.009
	3	5	*	.70	.073	.021
	4	7	*	8.4	3.24	.057
	5	9	*	149	119	.21
	6	11	*	*	*	.94
2	2	2	.57	.15	.007	.006
	3	4	*	3.0	.024	.022
	4	6	*	99	.071	.04
	5	8	*	*	156	1.2
	6	10	*	*	*	2.7
3	2	2	1.0	.26	.008	.007
	3	3	*	5.2	.011	.011
	4	5	*	*	.15	.070
	5	7	*	*	.92	.15
	6	9	*	*	6.4	.27

Table 1: Mean CPU times for various instances of the bomb clogs toilet example. All times are in seconds on a Macintosh 8600/300 using MCL 4.2. A * indicates that no solution was found in 5 CPU minutes. All tests were run 10 times. The largest variation ($\sigma = 7\%$) was on the smallest (first) problem.

POP performed much better, but still had difficulty with larger numbers of packages.

CGPx (CGP without induced mutex) outperformed UDTPOP slightly on the single toilet problems. However, as the number of toilets was increased, the gulf widened considerably. In fact, for three toilets and four or more packages CGPx is more than two orders of magnitude faster than UDTPOP. We speculate that this advantage is due to Graphplan's ability to deal with actions in parallel. For example, in the three toilet problems, three dunk operations can be done in parallel at level 1, three flush operations can be done in parallel at level three, and so on. As a result, the depth of search required to find a plan is significantly lower than for more traditional partial-order planners.

Although CGPx performs better than UDTPOP, full CGP with induced mutex relationships is far superior. In fact CGP is one to two orders of magnitude faster than CGPx on the hardest problems. CGP is two to three orders of magnitude faster than UDTPOP on the harder problems.

Despite this impressive improvement, even CGP slows down significantly as the number of packages grows beyond seven. The reason is that, although this problem is conceptually trivial, it is combinatorially quite hard. As the number of packages grows, the solutions consist of progressively longer sequences of dunking and flushing operations. For example, with one toilet and seven packages, 13 steps are required. The trouble is, the packages can be dunked in any of 7! possible orders. So CGP spends all of its time generating and investigating these different possible orderings.

One obvious concern is how CGP performs as the amount of uncertainty increases. If there are k independent uncertain propositions in the initial conditions, there will be 2^k possible worlds. To see what effect this has on CGP, we added between one and five irrelevant uncertain propositions to the initial conditions for the single toilet problems. The results are shown in Table 2. The additional uncertainty significantly degrades performance, more so for the problems that require a deeper plan graph. It is certainly possible to use preprocessing to eliminate irrelevant propositions, and hence control the growth in number of possible worlds, but this will not be enough to allow CGP to solve real problems with many real sources of uncertainty.

Pkgs	Irrelevant uncertain propositions					
	0	1	2	3	4	5
2	.009	.018	.065	.46	3.4	29
3	.021	.070	.53	13.3	*	*
4	.057	.33	9.1	*	*	*
5	.21	3.2	*	*	*	*
6	.94	38	*	*	*	*

Table 2: Mean CPU times for varying number of packages (one toilet) with additional irrelevant uncertain propositions in the initial conditions. Note that five additional irrelevant propositions corresponds to multiplying the number of possible worlds by 2^5.

Conclusions

CGP is a Graphplan-based planner that does conformant planning; it attempts to construct non-contingent plans that succeed no matter which of the allowed states the world is actually in. The central idea behind CGP is to create separate plan graphs for each possible world. The expansion phase of Graphplan is changed so that it 1) adds aspects to the plan graph for each possible world separately, and 2) further splits the possible worlds when aspects with uncertain outcomes are added to a graph.

The solution extraction phase of Graphplan tries to achieve the goal in all possible worlds. To preserve soundness, it must consider interactions between aspects chosen in the different possible worlds. More precisely, it must use confrontation whenever an aspect chosen in one world induces an undesirable aspect in another.

Finally, additional mutex relationships can sometimes be inferred between aspects in different possible worlds (which leads to mutex relationships between propositions in different possible worlds). As shown in the results section, these induced mutex relationships significantly improve the performance of the solution extraction process.

Our objective in developing CGP was to see if the impressive performance of Graphplan on STRIPS planning problems would extend to planning problems involving uncertainty. Our experiments indicate that the answer is yes. CGP performs significantly better than previous conformant planners. However, there are some drawbacks and limitations to our approach.

First of all, although the possible worlds mechanism is conceptually clear, it is also cumbersome. As the amount of uncertainty grows, the number of possible worlds grows exponentially and performance deteriorates. To fix this, we would like to confine the representation of uncertainty to only those propositions that we are uncertain about. In the bomb in the toilet problem, if Dunk clogs the toilet unconditionally, there should never be any uncertainty about whether the toilet is clogged or not. We would therefore like to avoid duplicating clogged and ¬clogged in all the possible worlds. Second, we would like to be able to treat independent sources of uncertainty independently, without generating the cross product of the possible worlds. Although we have experimented with some ways of doing this, we have not yet found a completely satisfactory solution. There appear to be difficult trade-offs here; if we use a more compact representation, we loose the ability to capture some of the mutual exclusion relationships, which degrades performance of the solution extraction phase.

A second limitation of CGP is that it does not take probability information into account. We believe that this is not an inherent limitation. Optimistic probabilities could be calculated and stored with each proposition at a level during the expansion phase. Solution extraction should not be attempted at a level unless all the goal propositions appear at that level with probabilities above the desired thresholds. The actual probabilities for a plan could be computed during the solution extraction phase. The Graphplan framework also seems natural for multiple support (Kushmerick, Hanks and Weld 1995), since all ways of achieving a proposition are represented at a level.

Finally, the possible worlds approach taken here can also be used to do sensory and contingent planning. We have done this, and the technique and results are described in (Weld, Anderson and Smith, 1998).

Acknowledgments

Thanks to Mark Peot for providing an initial Lisp implementation of Graphplan, and for providing and assisting with UDTPOP. Thanks to Keith Golden, Mark Friedman, Pandu Nayak, and anonymous reviewers for comments on earlier versions of this paper. This research was supported by Office of Naval Research Grants N00014-94-1-0060 and N00014-98-1-0147, by National Science Foundation Grant IRI-9303461, by ARPA / Rome Labs grant F30602-95-1-0024, by a gift from Rockwell Palo Alto Research Lab, and by NASA Ames Research Center. This work was initiated while the first author was a visiting scholar at University of Washington.

References

Anderson, C., Smith, D. and Weld, D. 1998. Conditional effects in Graphplan. In *Proc. 4th Int. Conf. AI Planning Systems*.

Blum, A., and Furst, M. 1995. Fast planning through planning graph analysis. In *Proc. Int. Joint Conf. AI*, 1636–1642.

Blum, A., and Furst, M. 1997. Fast planning through planning graph analysis. *Artificial Intelligence* 90(1–2):281–300.

Draper, D. Hanks, S., and Weld, D. 1994. Probabilistic planning with information gathering and contingent execution. In *Proc. 2nd Int. Conf. AI Planning Systems*, 31–36.

Etzioni, O., Hanks, S., Weld, D, Draper, D., Lesh, N. and Williamson, M. 1992. An approach to planning with incomplete information. In *Proc. 3rd Int. Conf. Principles of Knowledge Representation and Reasoning*, 115–125.

Gazen, B., and Knoblock, C. 1997. Combining the expressivity of UCPOP with the efficiency of Graphplan. In *Proc. 4th European Conf. on Planning*, 223–235.

Golden, K. and Weld, D. 1996. Representing sensing actions: the middle ground revisited. In *Proc. 5th Int. Conf. Principles of Knowledge Representation and Reasoning*, 174–185.

Golden, K., Etzioni, O., and Weld, D. 1994. Omnipotence without omniscience: efficient sensor management for planning. In *Proc. 12th National Conf. on AI*. 1048–1054.

Goldman, R. and Boddy, M. 1994. Conditional linear planning. In *Proc. 2nd Int. Conf. AI Planning Systems*, 80–85.

Goldman, R. and Boddy, M. 1996. Expressive planning and explicit knowledge, In *Proc. 3rd Int. Conf. AI Planning Systems*, 110-117.

Koehler, J., Nebel, B., Hoffmann, J. and Dimopoulos, Y. 1997. Extending planning graphs to an ADL subset. In *Proc. 4th European Conf. on Planning*, 275–287.

Kushmerick, N., Hanks, S., and Weld, D. 1995. An algorithm for probabilistic planning. *Artificial Intelligence* 76(1–2):239–286.

McDermott, D. 1987. A critique of pure reason. *Computational Intelligence* 3:151–160.

Penberthy, J. and Weld, D. 1992. UCPOP: A sound, complete, partial order planner for ADL. In *Proc. 3rd Int. Conf. Principles of Knowledge Representation and Reasoning*, 103–114.

Peot, M. 1998. Decision-Theoretic Planning. Ph.D. Dissertation, Dept. of Engineering-Economic Systems, Stanford University.

Peot, M., and Smith, D. 1992. Conditional Nonlinear Planning, In *Proc. 1st Int. Conf. AI Planning Systems*, 189-197.

Pryor, L. and Collins, G. 1996. Planning for contingencies: a decision-based approach. *J. Artificial Intelligence Research* 4:287–339.

Veloso, M., Carbonell, J., Perez, A., Borrajo, D., Fink, E. and Blythe, J. 1995. Integrating planning and learning: the prodigy architecture. *J. Experimental and Theoretical AI* 7:81–120.

Warren, D. 1976. Generating Conditional Plans and Programs. In *Proc. Summer Conf. on AI and Simulation of Behavior*.

Weld, D., Anderson, C. and Smith, D. 1998. Extending Graphplan to handle uncertainty & sensing actions. In *Proc. 15th National Conf. on AI*.

Extending Graphplan to Handle Uncertainty & Sensing Actions*

Daniel S. Weld **Corin R. Anderson**
Department of Computer Science & Engineering
University of Washington, Box 352350
Seattle, WA 98195-2350 USA
{weld, corin}@cs.washington.edu

David E. Smith
Nasa Ames Research Center
Mail Stop 269-2
Moffett Field, CA 94035 USA
de2smith@ptolemy.arc.nasa.gov

Abstract

If an agent does not have complete information about the world-state, it must reason about alternative possible states of the world and consider whether any of its actions can reduce the uncertainty. Agents controlled by a contingent planner seek to generate a robust plan, that accounts for and handles all eventualities, in advance of execution. Thus a contingent plan may include sensing actions which gather information that is later used to select between different plan branches. Unfortunately, previous contingent planners suffered defects such as confused semantics, incompleteness, and inefficiency. In this paper we describe SGP, a descendant of Graphplan that solves contingent planning problems. SGP distinguishes between actions that sense the value of an unknown proposition from those that change its value. SGP does not suffer from the forms of incompleteness displayed by CNLP and Cassandra. Furthermore, SGP is relatively fast.

1 Introduction

Classical planners make the unrealistic assumption that the agent has complete information about the initial state of the world. Reactive systems and agents that interleave planning and execution, on the other hand, have imperfect look-ahead and can get caught by irreversible actions. Contingent planning — the generation of a plan whose course of action varies based on the information gained from executing sensing actions — has the potential to yield robust plans even in the face of uncertainty. The prospect of contingent planning is especially desirable in high stakes domains where even an improbable mistake could prove costly. Unfortunately, previous contingent planners have failed to attract widespread adoption due to serious liabilities:

- They often fail to distinguish between sensory and causal effects of actions, or treat sensing explicitly.
- They are often unable to generate a successful plan if sensory actions are unavailable — even if such a plan exists.
- Previous contingent planners are slow.

This paper presents the SGP contingent planning algorithm, an extension of Graphplan [Blum & Furst, 1997] that handles planning problems with uncertainty in the initial conditions[1] and with actions that combine causal and sensory effects. Although we have not completed a formal proof, we believe SGP is complete; certainly, it finds plans missed by CNLP [Peot & Smith, 1992] and Cassandra [Pryor & Collins, 1996]. While contingent planning will always be harder than corresponding problems graced with complete information, SGP solves small problems quickly — a dramatic improvement over previous contingent planners, whose performance was so abysmal that execution times were always omitted from publications.

2 Background: Conformant Graphplan

Since SGP is based on previous planners, we briefly summarize the Graphplan algorithm [Blum & Furst, 1997] as extended to handle conditional effects [Gazen & Knoblock, 1997] and conformant planning, i.e., uncertainty but no sensing actions [Smith & Weld, 1998].

---

*We thank Mark Peot who provided an initial Lisp implementation of basic Graphplan. Our paper was improved by discussions with Marc Friedman, Keith Golden, Rao Kambhampati, Alon Levy, and Mike Perkowitz. This research was funded by Office of Naval Research Grant N00014-98-1-0147, by National Science Foundation Grant IRI-9303461, and by ARPA / Rome Labs grant F30602-95-1-0024.
Copyright © 1998, American Association for Artificial Intelligence (www.aaai.org). All rights reserved.

[1]Space precludes description of a direct method of handling actions with uncertain effects (see [Smith & Weld, 1998]), but they can be modeled as actions whose deterministic effects are conditional on hidden state variables defined in the initial state.

Graphplan, in its original form, solves STRIPS planning problems in a deterministic, fully-specified world. Both the preconditions and effects of its action schemata are conjunctions of literals (*i.e.*, denoting the add and delete lists). Graphplan alternates between two phases: *graph expansion* and *solution extraction*. The graph expansion phase extends a *planning graph* until it has achieved a necessary (but insufficient) condition for plan existence. The solution extraction phase then performs a backward-chaining search for an actual solution; if no solution is found, the cycle repeats.

2.1 Graph Expansion

The planning graph contains two types of nodes, proposition nodes and action nodes, arranged into levels. Even-numbered levels contain proposition nodes (*i.e.*, ground literals), and the zeroth level consists precisely of the propositions that are true in the initial state of the planning problem. Nodes in odd-numbered levels correspond to action instances; there is one such node for each action instance whose preconditions are present (and are mutually consistent) at the previous level. Directed edges connect proposition nodes to the action instances (at the next level) whose preconditions mention those propositions, and directed edges connect action nodes to subsequent propositions made true by the action's effects. Graphplan defines a binary mutual exclusion relation ("mutex") between nodes in the same level as follows:

- Two action instances at level i are mutex if either
  - *Interference / Inconsistent Effects:* one action deletes a precondition or effect of another, or
  - *Competing Needs:* the actions have preconditions that are mutually exclusive at level $i - 1$.
- Two propositions at level i are mutex if all ways of achieving the propositions (*i.e.*, actions at level $i - 1$) are mutex.

2.2 Solution Extraction

Suppose that Graphplan is trying to generate a plan for a goal with n conjuncts, and it has finally extended the planning graph to an even level, i, in which all goal propositions are present and none are pairwise mutex. Graphplan now searches for a solution plan by considering each of the n goals in turn. For each such proposition at level i, Graphplan chooses (backtrack point) an action a at level $i - 1$ that achieves the goal. If a is consistent (non-mutex) with all actions that have been chosen so far at this level, then Graphplan proceeds to the next goal, otherwise if no such choice is available Graphplan backtracks. After Graphplan has found a consistent set of actions at level $i - 1$ it recursively tries to find a plan for the set of all the preconditions of those actions at level $i - 2$. The base case for the recursion is level zero — if the propositions are present there, then Graphplan has found a solution. Otherwise, if backtracking fails, then Graphplan extends the planning graph and tries again.

2.3 Conditional Effects

Recently, several authors have described methods that allow Graphplan to handle operators with conditional effects. The simplest approach breaks operators with conditional effects into a number of separate operators (by considering all minimal consistent combinations of antecedents in the conditional effects) [Gazen & Knoblock, 1997]. To illustrate, consider the following simple model of the action of taking medication:

Medicate: pre: eff: (when I ¬I)
                                          (when ¬H D)

in which I means the patient is Infected, H means he is Hydrated, and D means he is Dead. If the patient is Infected before the action then he will no longer be Infected afterwards: ¬I. But if the patient takes medication when he is not Hydrated (*i.e.*, ¬H), then the result is Death. This ADL operator is expanded into the following 4 disjoint[2] STRIPS operators, called *aspects* of the ADL original:

Med$_1$:   pre: (and I H)   eff: ¬I
Med$_2$:   pre: (and I ¬H)   eff: (and ¬I D)
Med$_3$:   pre: (and ¬I H)   eff:
Med$_4$:   pre: (and ¬I ¬H)   eff: D

Note that Med$_3$ has no effects; we count it as an aspect to facilitate subsequent bookkeeping.

2.4 Conformant Planning

For simplicity, we only describe the Graphplan extensions required to handle uncertainty in the initial conditions; [Smith & Weld, 1998] explains how to handle actions whose effects are uncertain as well. In classical Graphplan, the initial conditions are specified as a complete conjunction of positive and negative literals. To model uncertain initial conditions, one provides a set of w possible worlds, each modeled as a conjunction of literals. The basic idea behind conformant Graphplan (CGP) is to extend a separate planning graph for each possible world (PW), keeping track of mutual exclusion relations across worlds, and then search backwards for a plan that works in all possible worlds.

To illustrate the algorithm, suppose that there is a Drink action with a single effect that makes the patient Hydrated unconditionally. Drink has one aspect:

Drink$_1$:   pre: eff: H

---

[2] Although the different aspects of an action are mutually exclusive, multiple aspects may appear at levels ≥ 3 because proposition levels (except the initial state) can contain both a proposition and its negation.

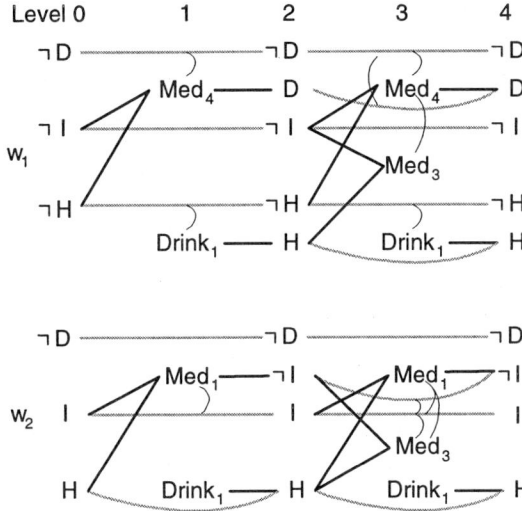

Figure 1: Planning graph for two possible worlds. Gray arcs indicate No-op actions for persistence of propositions from one level to the next. Arcs between two actions denote mutex relationships (to avoid clutter, not all mutexes are shown).

Suppose that initially there are two PWs: $w_1 = \{\neg I, \neg H, \neg D\}$, and $w_2 = \{I, H, \neg D\}$; the goal is to get the patient uninfected and not dead: $\neg I \wedge \neg D$. As we shall see, the best plan in this example is to first Drink (eliminating the interaction between dehydration and subsequent medication in w_1) and then to Medicate. Figure 1 shows the planning graph expanded to level four.

Since both of the goal propositions occur (nonmutex[3]) at level 2 in *each* of the possible worlds, there is the potential of a solution and conformant Graphplan must try to extract a solution.

CGP considers each PW in turn. In w_1 both goals are initially true and hence are carried through by No-op actions. In w_2 $\neg D$ is also made true by a No-op while $\neg I$ can only be achieved by Med_1. Since there are no mutex relations between any of these actions one might think that we have found a solution, but an additional check is necessary. If we choose to perform an action, we must consider its effects in *all* worlds, not just the specific PW in which the action was added. This is because (without sensing) CGP doesn't know which of the worlds it is really in and therefore cannot confine the effects of an action to a single PW. To compound matters, each world is different, so performing an action may lead to one aspect of the action in one possible world and a completely different aspect in another PW. Our example

---
[3] Actually it is possible to derive cross-world "induced mutexes" in this example, but while this optimization speeds planning (*e.g.*, it would eliminate the need for searching backwards at level 2), space precludes its presentation; see [Smith & Weld, 1998] for the details.

illustrates these complications. The decision to execute Medicate in w_2 (which manifests as Med_1) means that some aspect of Medicate will execute in w_1 as well: Med_4, in fact. Thus, CGP must consider the effect of Med_4 in w_1— which unfortunately includes death, D, in violation of the goal. Since no backtracking alternative remains, CGP concludes that no solution exists at level 2.

Before proceeding, we augment our terminology. We write A:u to refer to aspect A in world w_u. Similarly, we use P:u to refer to proposition P in world w_u. Suppose aspect A:u is present at level i in a PW planning graph and A':v is another aspect of the *same* action at level i in the graph, and $v \neq u$. We say that A:u *possibly induces* A'v, and vice versa. In the example above Med_1:2 possibly induces Med_4:1 at level 1.

Sometimes it is possible to prevent an undesirable, possibly-induced aspect using *confrontation*. To prevent or confront aspect A':v at level i, the planner needs to assure that its precondition is false at level $i-1$ and *remains false* during the execution of the other aspects at level i. (Otherwise, A':v might fire if some other parallel action happened to be executed first, and this parallel action established the precondition of A':v.) Thus if A':v has preconditions $P_1, P_2, \ldots, P_k$ CGP must choose (backtrack point) a precondition P_i:v that can be made false at level $i-1$ and can be held false until level $i+1$. One easy way to implement this is to check that the No-op operation persisting $\neg P_j$:v

1. Exists at level i, and
2. Is not mutex with any other aspect added during solution extraction at level i.

If so, this No-op is added to the plan, and its precondition $\neg P_j$:v is added to the subgoals at level $i-1$. Note that when doing confrontation, the choice of precondition to confront provides an additional backtrack point.

For an example of confrontation, consider what happens when CGP tries to extract a solution from level 4 of the medication example. At first glance, level 4 appears identical to level 2. In w_1 both goals are present at level 4 solely due to No-op actions, so these are added to the plan. In w_2 there is also no choice: $\neg D$ is made true by a No-op alone, while $\neg I$ can only be achieved by Med_1:2. Again, CGP must consider the effects of the aspects that are possibly induced by Med_1:2, but this time there are two such aspects: harmless Med_3:1 and deadly Med_4:1. As before CGP discovers that Med_4:1 is mutex with the $\neg D$-No-op:1 already in the plan, so Med_4:1 must be confronted, and this decision leads to a choice: which of Med_4:1's preconditions should be negated? Suppose CGP chooses to negate $\neg H$, then CGP adds an H-No-op action to the plan. H-No-op causes H:1 to be a subgoal at level 2 which eventually leads CGP to add $Drink_1$:1 to the plan at level 1. Thus the final, successful plan is: Drink; Medicate — it achieves the goals in both PWs.

3 Representing Sensory Actions

For SGP we define a simple but expressive sensor model called SSM. In addition to traditional causal effects, actions have zero or more observational effects, each of which is specified using the syntax (sense *wff*) where *wff* denotes an arbitrary logical expression composed of Graphplan propositions. Thus each sense effect corresponds to a primitive observation that returns one bit of information when executed: T if the logical expression is true in the world immediately prior to execution, and F otherwise.

In order to simplify SGP's handling of sensory actions, we make the following restrictions: sense terms may not be placed in the consequent of conditional effects, and actions with sense effects may not have preconditions. To understand why banning sense terms from the consequents of conditional effects does not limit expressiveness, consider a hypothetical action which does exactly that: (when P (sense Q)). Presumably, the intent behind this statement is for the agent to observe *nothing* if P is false, and to gain information about Q otherwise. Thus, by executing this action, the agent is distinguishing between worlds in which the following mutually exclusive conditions hold: $\neg P$, $P \land Q$, and $P \land \neg Q$. In SSM we simply require that this information gain be made explicit with the use of multiple unconditional sense effects. For example, one could achieve the same result with the pair of effects: (sense P) and (sense (and P Q)). The other restriction was that no sensory action could have preconditions; this is of no consequence since every action with preconditions can be rewritten to use conditional effects with the addition of a special *error* proposition.

SSM is capable of representing any noise-free sensor that returns a bounded amount of information. To see this, note that if a sensor returns a bounded amount of information, then its information gain can be encoded in k bits and k sense effects will suffice.

4 Representing an Agent's Knowledge

After executing an action with effect (sense P) the agent knows whether P is true or false, but this form of knowledge is difficult for the planner to exploit. As we shall see, it is much easier to generate a contingent plan if we explicitly represent the agent's ability to discriminate between its PW and the other possibilities. To this end, we define the proposition $K\neg u{:}v$ to mean that if the agent is in w_v then it will know that it is not in w_u.[4]

---

[4] For readers familiar with possible world semantics, the following translation may help. If the planning domain contains k propositions, then in theory there are 2^k possible worlds. But the planning problem's initial conditions rules out all but w of these. The Kripke structure for the initial state of our planning problem has every remaining PW accessible from all $w-1$ other worlds, because the planner has no additional knowledge of which of the w worlds the agent is in.

Consider a domain described in terms of two propositions, P and Q; suppose that we have no knowledge about the initial state, so there are four PWs covering all possible combinations of T and F values. Suppose further that there are two actions: A senses $P \land Q$ and B senses $P \lor Q$. The table below shows the knowledge propositions that result from executing A, B, or both sensory actions.

	Init	After A	After B	After A,B
w_1	$P \land Q$	$K\neg 2{:}1$ $K\neg 3{:}1$ $K\neg 4{:}1$	$K\neg 4{:}1$	$K\neg 2{:}1$ $K\neg 3{:}1$ $K\neg 4{:}1$
w_2	$P \land \neg Q$	$K\neg 1{:}2$	$K\neg 4{:}2$	$K\neg 1{:}2$ $K\neg 4{:}2$
w_3	$\neg P \land Q$	$K\neg 1{:}3$	$K\neg 4{:}3$	$K\neg 1{:}3$ $K\neg 4{:}3$
w_4	$\neg P \land \neg Q$	$K\neg 1{:}4$	$K\neg 1{:}4$ $K\neg 2{:}4$ $K\neg 3{:}4$	$K\neg 1{:}4$ $K\neg 2{:}4$ $K\neg 3{:}4$

Note that each sensor defines a different partition on the possible worlds. If the agent is in w_1 and executes A then it will know that it is not in *any* of the other worlds, but if the agent is in w_2, A will only tell it that it is *not* in w_1.

5 SGP Graph Expansion

Like its ancestor Graphplan, SGP is composed of graph expansion and solution extraction phases. SGP's expansion phase is based on that of CGP, with one major difference: SGP calculates the set of possible knowledge propositions for level $i+1$ from each action's logical sensor definitions and the state of the planning graph at proposition level $i-1$. This calculation is especially tricky when $i \geq 3$ because both proposition P and its negation $\neg P$ might coexist in any given world at proposition levels past the initial state.

For example, suppose that there are two worlds: $w_1 = \{\neg I, \neg B\}$ and $w_2 = \{I, \neg B\}$ where I means that the patient is Infected, and B means that the culture is Blue. There are two actions. Inspect senses B, while Stain has a conditional effect that makes the culture blue exactly when the patient is infected. We show the aspects of Stain below, and Figure 2 shows the planning graph after SGP has extended it to level 4.

Stain$_1$: pre: I   eff: B
Stain$_2$: pre: $\neg$I eff:

Note that executing the sensing action Inspect has no effects at level 1. Since $\neg B$ is true in both w_1 and w_2, the agent receives no useful information when told that B is false. The situation is different, however, when Stain is executed at level 1 and Inspect is executed at level 3. Stain's conditional effect changes the world in a way that allows Inspect to discriminate. As a result level

---

$K\neg u{:}v$ means that the agent has received information such that w_u is no longer accessible from w_v in the new Kripke structure [Fagin *et al.*, 1995].

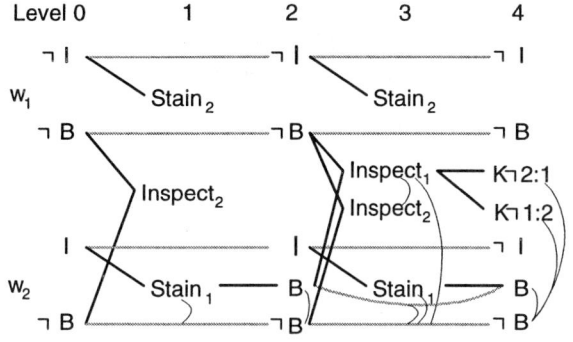

Figure 2: Planning graph showing interaction between causal (Stain) and sensing (Inspect) actions.

4 contains K¬2:1 and K¬1:2; note that these special propositions are supported by a single action instance which links to preconditions in two separate worlds. This type of structure is quite unique to SGP.

Intuitively, the SGP planning graph expansion algorithm considers the set of possible sensor values obtainable in each PW, then takes the cross product to determine the set of partitions which could be induced by the sensor (typically there will be more than one possible partition if causal actions can affect a sensed proposition). These partitions lead to the introduction of K¬u:v propositions at subsequent levels.

Before making this procedure precise, we introduce more terminology. We say a proposition P is *certain in possible world* w_u *at level* i if either P or ¬P is *missing* from the planning graph for w_u at level i. Note that all propositions are certain in all PWs at level 0. In general, a proposition will be certain in a world unless a causal action can change its value. For example, B is certain in w_1 at level 2, but not in w_2 at level 2.

Figure 3 presents the SGP planning graph expansion procedure. Suppose we call it to expand the graph of Figure 2 from level 2 to 4. After SGP adds the purely causal aspects $Stain_2:1$ and $Stain_1:2$ to level 3, SGP considers Inspect and iterates over PWs to compute $C = \{\langle\langle F\rangle,\langle T\rangle\rangle,\langle\langle F\rangle,\langle F\rangle\rangle\}$. Mapping the sensor function (which in this case is the identity function) on the first element of C yields $D = \langle F, T\rangle$ shows that the sensor can distinguish the two worlds. Thus SGP adds K¬2:1 and[5] K¬1:2. Note that mapping the sensor func-

---

[5] If sensors are noiseless, then these knowledge propositions will always be symmetric. To see how asymmetric knowledge could be deduced from a noisy sensor, suppose the patient is uninfected in w_1 and infected in w_2, and consider a blood test that might give false positives but never false negatives. One value of D will return F for w_1 and T for w_2, and since the agent knows that the F can't be a false negative it can conclude K¬2:1. The view from w_2 is different, however; the agent can't rule out the possibility of a false positive and hence gains no information.

ExpandGraph from prop level $i - 1$ to $i + 1$
Foreach possible world w_u
    Foreach aspect A of a nonsensory action
        If A's preconditions occur non-mutex at level $i - 1$,
        Then instantiate A at level i, its effects at $i + 1$, and
        link the instance to its preconditions and effects.
Foreach sensory action, S, with effect (sense ϕ)
    Suppose ϕ mentions k atomic propositions $\{P_1, \ldots, P_k\}$.
    Foreach possible world w_u
        Let V_j denote the set of values of P_j:u at level $i - 1$
        ;; I.e. V_j is either $\{T\}$, $\{F\}$, or $\{T, F\}$
        Let C_u be a subset of $V_1 \times \ldots \times V_k$
        by filtering out all mutex combos
        ;; If each prop is certain in w_u at $i - 1$ then $|C_u| = 1$
        ;; But in the worst case $|C_u| = 2^k$ for each PW w_u
    Let C be a subset of $C_i \times \ldots \times C_w$, by
    filtering out cross-world mutexes
    ;; If each P_j is certain in all worlds, then $|C| = 1$
    ;; Worst case: $|C| = (2^k)^w$
    Foreach element, $c \in C$
        ;; c is a w-tuple of k-tuples of boolean values for P_j
        ;; Each k-tuple, thus leads to a value for ϕ
        Let SA be a new instance of S at level i
        Link the elements of c at $i - 1$ as preconds of SA
        Add any causal effects of SA to level $i + 1$
        Map ϕ on c getting a boolean w-vector, D
        ;; D = the possibly sensed vals in all w worlds
        For $u = 1$ to the number of possible worlds w
            For $v = u + 1$ to w
                If $D(u) \neq D(v)$
                Then add K¬u:v and K¬v:u to level $i + 1$, and
                link them to SA
Add all mutex relations for action level i
Add all mutex relations for prop level $i + 1$
;; There are no changes to the mutex rules!

Figure 3: Pseudocode for SGP Graph Expansion

tion on the other element of C yields $D = \langle F, F\rangle$ which shows that the sensor's ability to distinguish is not assured. In particular, the agent must stain the culture before inspecting. Note how the precondition arcs for $Inspect_1$ in Figure 3 store this information for exploitation during solution extraction.

6 SGP Solution Extraction

Classical plans, *e.g.* those produced by UCPOP, Graphplan, and CGP, correspond to straight-line programs; each action is executed in sequence. Contingent plans, on the other hand, correspond to programs with if-then-else statements; they can be modeled as an execution tree whose branches refer to information gained by previous sensory actions [Etzioni *et al.*, 1992]. An alternative model, used in C-Buridan [Draper, Hanks, & Weld, 1994] corresponds to a DAG and hence allows plans that rejoin after branches. In this representation each action in the plan is associated with a *context* that specifies the conditions (based on previous observations) under which to execute the action. When an action is first added to the plan, its context is T; conditions get conjoined in response to threats via *conditioning*, the decision not to execute an action in certain worlds [Peot & Smith, 1992].

SGP's solution extraction procedure is a logical generalization of CGP's algorithm [Smith & Weld, 1998]. When SGP adds aspect A:u into the plan in service of goal P:u, it considers all possibly-induced aspects A':v to see if they are mutex with previously added aspects. If A':v does conflict, then there are three choices:

1. SGP can confront A':v, which amounts to forcing a different aspect, A":v, of the action to execute instead, or

2. SGP can condition A':v on a sensor, by finding some sensor that discriminates between w_u and w_v so the agent can execute A in w_u but not in w_v, or

3. SGP can backtrack, *i.e.* retract its decision to support P:u with A:u (or retract an even earlier decision).

6.1 Representing Contingent Plans

From an implementation point of view, however, SGP's solution extraction procedure is very different from CGP's, because SGP represents each level of the partially-specified plan as a dynamic constraint satisfaction problem (CSP) [Mittal & Falkenhainer, 1990], *i.e.* a dynamically-varying set of variables and values with associated constraints. When an aspect of action A is added to level i of a plan with w possible worlds, SGP creates w new CSP variables: $A_1, \ldots, A_w$. The set of possible values of A_u equals the set of aspects of A that are present in the planning graph in w_u at level i *plus* the special value No-exec. Suppose SGP assigns A_1 and A_2 both to equal the value No-exec, and for all $u > 2$ A_u denotes an aspect of A. This assignment of values represents the decision to execute A in all PWs except w_1 and w_2.

Of course, the only way that an agent *could* execute A in all PWs except w_1 and w_2 is if the agent is capable of *distinguishing* between w_1 or w_2 and all other worlds. Hence, the assignment above will lead to knowledge subgoals at level $i - 1$. Specifically, the agent must know both K¬u:v and K¬v:u for $v \in \{1,2\}$ and forall $u > 2$. Note that the agent *need not know which world it is in* (*e.g.*, it need not distinguish between w_1 and w_2); it simply must be able to *rule out* those worlds when in some other world w_u.

6.2 Example

Consider a domain with the Medicate, Stain and Inspect actions defined earlier (but not Drink). Suppose there are two initial worlds: $w_1=\{¬I, ¬H, ¬B, ¬D\}$ and $w_2=\{I, H, ¬B, ¬D\}$. In other words, the culture is definitely not Blue, the patient is not Dead, it is unknown if the patient is Infected and if he is Hydrated, but these last two propositions are correlated. The goal is to have the patient uninfected and alive: ¬I ∧ ¬D. As we shall see, the best plan is to stain the culture, inspect it, and medicate only if the culture is blue.

<u>ExtractSoln</u>(goals $G = \{\ldots, P:x, \ldots\}$ at level i)
  If $i = 0$ and all goals in G are in the appropriate initial PW
  Then return success
  Elseif $i = 0$ or G contains P:x and Q:y which are mutex
  Then backtrack.
  Let $V = \{\}$; *V will be the CSP variables to be solved*
  Foreach P:x $\in G$ do
    Choose aspect A_j:x (from level $i - 1$) that produces P:x
    Backtrack if there is no such A_j:x, or
    If $\exists v \in V$ such that A_j:x is mutex with all of v's values
    Let A be the action from which aspect A_j:x was derived
    For each PW w_y create the new CSP variable A_y
      If A_y is not already in V, then add it
      ;; *The domain of values for A_y is the set of aspects*
      ;; *of A in w_y, plus the special value* No-exec
    Restrict the domain of A_x to A_j
  Foreach pair of variables $A_y, B_z \in V$
    Let the consistency constraints between A_y and B_z
    be the set of non-mutex pairs of aspects A_j:y, B_k:z
    where A_y and B_z derive from actions A and B
  Foreach action A
    Forall distinct pairs of worlds w_y, w_z
      If K¬y:z in the planning graph at level i
      Then A_y = No-exec is consistent with all values for A_z
      Else A_y = No-exec is only consistent with A_z = No-exec
  Use any CSP method to choose an assignment $\forall v \in V$
  Backtrack if no assignment exists.
  Let $G_{i-2} = \{\}$; *This will hold the set of next goals*
  Foreach $A_x \in V$
    If $A_x \neq$ No-exec
    Then let $G_{i-2} = G_{i-2} \cup$ the preconds of the *value* of A_x
    Else foreach $A_y \in V$ whose value $\neq$ No-exec
      Let $G_{i-2} = G_{i-2} \cup \{$K¬x:y, K¬y:x$\}$
  Recursively call ExtractSoln($G_{i-2}, i - 2$)

Figure 4: Pseudocode for SGP solution extraction

We now explain how the solution extraction algorithm (Figure 4) derives this plan from the planning graph shown in Figure 5, starting at level 6. In w_1, both goals can only be supported by No-ops, so SGP commits to them. In w_2 SGP has a choice between No-op and Med$_1$; suppose it chooses Med$_1$. This spurs the creation of two CSP variables: M_1 and M_2. The domain of M_2 is simply Med$_1$, but the domain of $M_1 = \{$Med$_4$, No-exec$\}$. Since Med$_4$ is mutex with ¬D-No-op, constraint propagation demands that Medicate not be executed in w_1. Note that confrontation is ruled out by the absence of alternative aspects in the domain of M_1 — the only consistent choice is No-exec. This leads SGP to subgoal on K¬2:1 and K¬1:2 at level 4 which eventually causes Inspect$_1$ to be added from level 3 and Stain$_1$ to be added from level 1.

7 Experimental Results

SGP is implemented in Allegro Common Lisp 4.3 and accepts variablized action schemata as input. Table 6

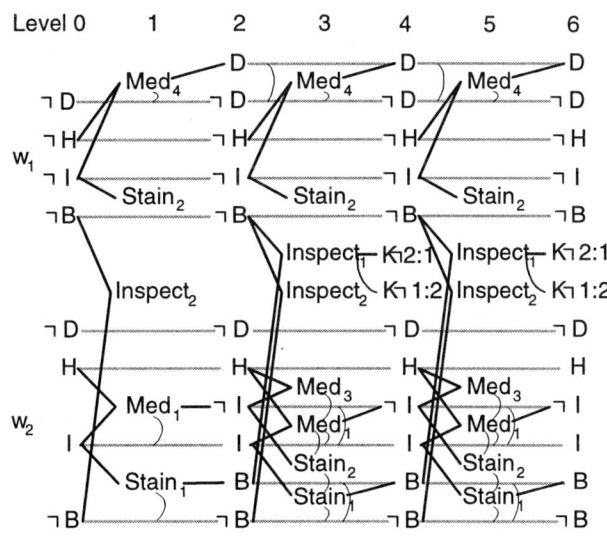

Figure 5: Planning graph for Medical-1 problem.

Name	# PWs	CPU	Plan graph size (a, p)
Medical-1	2	20	(11,6) (18,8) (20,8)
Medical-2	3	40	(30,12) (50,14) (52,14)
Medical-3	4	230	(45,15) (94,18) (100,18)
Medical-4	5	2600	(60,17) (156,21) (168,21)
Ski	3	2152	(57,13) (210,18) (224,19) (227,19) (227,19)
Evanston	2	26	(30, 12) (46, 16) (51, 16) (52, 16)
Fetch-2	4	48	(36, 13) (80, 14) (84, 14)
Coin-1	2	12	(14, 8) (25, 10) (28, 10)

Figure 6: Performance of SGP on sample problems. CPU times are in msec on a 300Mhz Pentium II. For each pair of levels in the planning graph, we show (a, p) — the number of actions and the number of propositions.

shows SGP's performance on a variety of domains, as measured on a 300 MHz Pentium II running Linux. The Medical-1 problem was described in the previous section. In the other medical problems the patient is either healthy or has one of n diseases; there are n separate medicate actions that provide specific cures, but all medications are deadly unless the patient has the corresponding infection. Ski refers to the navigation problem (uncertain road closure) of [Peot & Smith, 1992]. Evanston, Fetch-2, and Coin-1 are from [Pryor & Collins, 1996].

Next, we examined the effect of additional sensory actions on SGP's performance. We chose the "Bomb in the toilet" domain [McDermott, 1987] with five packages and a single toilet. Exactly one of the packages contains a bomb. To defuse the bomb, the offending package must be dunked in an unclogged toilet. Dunking any package will clog the plumbing, so the agent must be careful to dunk correctly. Each sensory action sensed a propo-

Number of sensory actions	1	2	3	4
CPU time (msec)	400	420	460	500

Figure 7: Performance of SGP on "Bomb in the toilet" domain problems with five packages and one toilet.

# PWs	CPU time (msec)	Plan graph size (a,p)
4	10	(18,8) (34,8)
8	40	(36,12) (84,12)
12	120	(54,16) (150,16)
16	400	(72,20) (232,20)
20	1590	(90,24) (330,24)
24	7450	(108,28) (444,28)

Figure 8: Performance of SGP as a function of uncertainty in the initial state.

sition (e.g., metal-present) that was perfectly correlated with the existence of the bomb in the particular package. As shown in Figure 7, the performance of SGP degrades roughly linearly with the number of sensory actions.

In the next experiment (Figure 8), we held the number of sensory actions fixed while we varied the uncertainty of the initial state. We used an artificial domain for this experiment; the goal was to achieve proposition P. As we varied the number of PWs, P was made initially true in half of them. To increase the number of possible worlds, we introduced a number of other unused propositions, exactly one of which was ever allowed to be true.

During our experimentation, we found domains which caused SGP difficulty. The factor limiting SGP seems to be the large number of sensory actions that can be instantiated — worst case 2^{kw} where w is the number of PWs and k denotes the number of atoms in the formula being sensed. In domains where actions sense a single proposition that is certain in most worlds, SGP runs quite quickly. However, when the sensed proposition is not certain in many of the PWs or a complicated formula is being sensed, then SGP creates an exponential number of sensory actions, which slows both graph expansion and solution extraction. Fortunately, most domains can be engineered (i.e., by thinking carefully about the ontology) to avoid these problems.

8 Conclusions

This paper described SGP, an extension of Graphplan that handles uncertain initial conditions and actions with a mixture of causal and sensory effects (as expressed in the SSM sensor language). The central innovations in the SGP algorithm are:

1. An extension to the forward-chaining, graph-expansion phase that derives knowledge propositions from SSM sensor definitions and the previous planning-graph proposition layer.

2. The incorporation of the *conditioning* threat-resolution method into the backward-chaining,

solution-extraction phase.

In addition, SGP generates contingent plans with branches that can rejoin (*i.e.*, a plan is a DAG not a tree). Furthermore, SGP's formulation of solution extraction as a dynamic CSP problem is novel.

Since there might be an exponential number of PWs, contingent planning can be exponentially slower than planning with complete information; however, in domains where mistakes are devastating, the cost may be worth it. Previous papers on contingent planners have neglected to provide quantitative measures of planner speed, instead admitting "less than practical" performance. In contrast, we demonstrate that SGP handles small to medium-sized problems quite quickly.

8.1 Related Work

Space precludes a discussion of work on interleaved planning and execution or the representation of uncertainty; we focus on previous contingent planners. Warplan-C [Warren, 1976] is the patriarch. Universal plans [Schoppers, 1987] and Gapps [Kaelbling, 1988] provide methods for constructing exhaustive contingent plans, but they did not allow explicit description of sensing actions; instead they assumed that complete sensory information would be available at every point during the execution. CNLP [Peot & Smith, 1992] extended SNLP to construct contingent plans. CNLP is notable for its introduction of conditioning, but it assumed free sensing (*i.e.*, it assumed the agent always knew the result of nondeterministic actions once they were performed). UWL [Etzioni *et al.*, 1992] formalized the notion of observational actions using runtime variables, and provided an algorithm for generating contingent plans. [Genesereth & Nourbakhsh, 1993] described techniques for speeding world-space search given incomplete information. Cassandra [Pryor & Collins, 1996] was a fully-implemented contingent planner that distinguished between sensing actions and actions that have uncertain outcomes; in addition Cassandra allowed operators with conditional effects. PLINTH [Goldman & Boddy, 1994] is a total-order planner akin to CNLP. None of these systems could cope with uncertainty if sensing actions were unavailable — even if a working (conformant) plan existed. The probabilistic C-Buridan planner [Draper, Hanks, & Weld, 1994] overcame this limitation and in addition incorporated an elegant sensor model which accounted for noisy sensors. Unfortunately, C-Buridan was so slow that it could not solve the problems listed in this paper.

8.2 Future Work

In the future we hope to augment the SGP sensor model to handle probabilities associated with initial PWs. We would also like to model noisy sensors ala C-Buridan. A different thread would be to extend SGP to handle sensory actions that use runtime variables [Etzioni *et al.*, 1992]. There are many optimizations to be explored, and we seek to run more experiments.

References

[Blum & Furst, 1997] Blum, A., and Furst, M. 1997. Fast planning through planning graph analysis. *J. Artificial Intelligence* 90(1–2):281–300.

[Draper, Hanks, & Weld, 1994] Draper, D., Hanks, S., and Weld, D. 1994. Probabilistic planning with information gathering and contingent execution. In *Proc. 2nd Intl. Conf. AI Planning Systems*.

[Etzioni *et al.*, 1992] Etzioni, O., Hanks, S., Weld, D., Draper, D., Lesh, N., and Williamson, M. 1992. An approach to planning with incomplete information. In *Proc. 3rd Int. Conf. on Principles of Knowledge Representation and Reasoning*, 115–125.

[Fagin *et al.*, 1995] Fagin, R., Halpern, J., Moses, Y., and Vardi, M. 1995. *Reasoning about Knowledge*. Cambridge, Mass.: MIT Press.

[Gazen & Knoblock, 1997] Gazen, B., and Knoblock, C. 1997. Combining the expressivity of UCPOP with the efficiency of Graphplan. In *Proc. 4th European Conference on Planning*.

[Genesereth & Nourbakhsh, 1993] Genesereth, M., and Nourbakhsh, I. 1993. Time-saving tips for problem solving with incomplete information. In *Proc. 11th Nat. Conf. AI*, 724–730.

[Goldman & Boddy, 1994] Goldman, R. P., and Boddy, M. S. 1994. Conditional Linear Planning. In *Proc. 2nd Intl. Conf. AI Planning Systems*, 80–85.

[Kaelbling, 1988] Kaelbling, L. P. 1988. Goals as parallel program specifications. In *Proc. 7th Nat. Conf. AI*. Morgan Kaufmann.

[Koehler *et al.*, 1997] Koehler, J., Nebel, B., Hoffmann, J., and Dimopoulos, Y. 1997. Extending planning graphs to an ADL subset. In *Proc. 4th European Conference on Planning*.

[McDermott, 1987] McDermott, D. 1987. A critique of pure reason. *Computational Intelligence* 3:151–160.

[Mittal & Falkenhainer, 1990] Mittal, S., and Falkenhainer, B. 1990. Dynamic constraint satisfaction problems. In *Proc. 8th Nat. Conf. AI*, 25–32.

[Peot & Smith, 1992] Peot, M., and Smith, D. 1992. Conditional Nonlinear Planning. In *Proc. 1st Intl. Conf. AI Planning Systems*, 189–197.

[Pryor & Collins, 1996] Pryor, L., and Collins, G. 1996. Planning for contingencies: A decision-based approach. *J. Artificial Intelligence Research*.

[Schoppers, 1987] Schoppers, M. 1987. Universal plans for reactive robots in unpredictable environments. In *Proc. 10th Int. Joint Conf. AI*, 1039–1046.

[Smith & Weld, 1998] Smith, D., and Weld, D. 1998. Conformant Graphplan. In *Proc. 15th Nat. Conf. AI*.

[Warren, 1976] Warren, D. 1976. Generating Conditional Plans and Programs. In *Proceedings of AISB Summer Conference*, 344–354.

Inferring State Constraints for Domain-Independent Planning*

Alfonso Gerevini
Dipartimento di Elettronica per l'Automazione
Università di Brescia
Via Branze 38, 25123 Brescia, Italy
E-mail: gerevini@bsing.ing.unibs.it

Lenhart Schubert
Department of Computer Science
University of Rochester
Rochester, NY 14627-0226
E-mail: schubert@cs.rochester.edu

Abstract

We describe some new preprocessing techniques that enable faster domain-independent planning. The first set of techniques is aimed at inferring state constraints from the structure of planning operators and the initial state. Our methods consist of generating hypothetical state constraints by inspection of operator effects and preconditions, and checking each hypothesis against all operators and the initial conditions. Another technique extracts (supersets of) predicate domains from sets of ground literals obtained by Graphplan-like forward propagation from the initial state. Our various techniques are implemented in a package called DISCOPLAN. We show preliminary results on the effectiveness of adding computed state constraints and predicate domains to the specification of problems for SAT-based planners such as SATPLAN or MEDIC. The results suggest that large speedups in planning can be obtained by such automated methods, potentially obviating the need for adding hand-coded state constraints.

Introduction

State constraints in a planning domain are laws that hold in every state that can be reached from the initial state. For instance in blocks world problems any object y other than the TABLE is necessarily NOT CLEAR in a state where another object x is ON y. State constraints are important in planning for two reasons. In planning formalisms that specify only the direct (or "primary") effects of actions, state constraints are needed to infer indirect effects (i.e., the ramifications of the direct effects). In all types of formalisms, state constraints can also be a powerful means of restricting the search space within which a plan is sought.

It is this latter role of state constraints that concerns us here. We are particularly interested in recent planners that use propositional satisfiability testing to discover plans. These are currently among the most powerful domain-independent planners, but their performance appears to depend strongly on whether or not state constraints are included in the propositional formulation of a planning problem (even when these

*Copyright 1998 ©, American Association for Artificial Intelligence (www.aaai.org). All rights reserved.

constraints are logically unnecessary for the solution of the problem). This is true, for instance, of Kautz et al.'s SATPLAN system, and, as we shall see, of Ernst et al.'s method of compiling UCPOP domain specifications and a particular problem into SAT clauses and then applying a solver such as Tableau (Crawford & Auton 1993), Walksat (Selman, Kautz, & Cohen 1994) or Relsat (Bayardo & Schrag 1997) to obtain a plan.

To make effective use of state constraints and predicate domain constraints in the above types of planners, we need to know what these constraints are. But many planning formalisms leave some or all such constraints implicit in the structure of the operators and the initial state. In the following we describe several ways of inferring state constraints from the structure of STRIPS-like operators. In addition to the kinds of state constraints traditionally discussed in planning, we also consider constraints on predicate domains, in the form of sets of possible tuples of arguments. We infer such sets by forward propagation of ground atoms from the initial state in the manner of Graphplan (Blum & Furst, 1995) but without exclusion calculations. These methods have been implemented in our DISCOPLAN package (DIScovering COnstraints for PLANning), and we propose some additional, provably correct techniques to be added in the future.

We then report preliminary results in the use of both types of constraints to accelerate SAT-based planners (without recourse to any hand-coded constraints). These results suggest that automated methods for inferring constraints in domain-independent planning should be able to largely supplant hand-coding of such constraints, providing comparable speedups in planning.

Inferring State Constraints from Domain Descriptions

Let us treat state (or situation or time) variables as implicit, as is done in planners such as STRIPS or UCPOP. Syntactically speaking, a state constraint in a particular planning domain, for particular initial conditions, could then be any closed logical formula involving the predicates and individual constants occurring in the domain. (Some planners allow functions as well, but we shall neglect these.) As a state constraint, such a formula is regarded as holding in all states; we could make this quantification over states (or times) explicit by adding a state (or time) variable s to each fluent predicate, and prefixing a wide-scope universal quantifer ($\forall s$) to the formula. Examples of such state constraints in a blocks world, with implicit universal quantification of free variables, are

$ON(x,y) \wedge NEQ(y,TABLE) \Rightarrow \neg CLEAR(y),$
$ON(x,y) \wedge NEQ(y,z) \Rightarrow \neg ON(x,z).$

Note that in the first constraint, all variables occurring anywhere also occur in one of the antecedent literals, namely $ON(x,y)$. We will refer to such state constraints as *implicative constraints*. The second constraint (though also formulated as an implication here) contains no literal with an all-inclusive set of variables. It is a *single-valuedness constraint* (*sv-constraint*), i.e., it asserts that no object x can be ON more than one object y. It is our impression from examining various domains such as those in the UCPOP test suite that the most prevalent constraints – at least among those expressible as simple logical formulas – are implicative and sv-constraints. We will abbreviate sv-constraints by writing "*" or a variable prefixed by "*" for the value that must be unique (if it exists at all), for any given values of the remaining arguments. So the second formula above becomes $ON(x,*)$.

Frequently there are also constraints on cooccurrence of predicate arguments. For instance, in a blocks world with just two blocks A, B, the possible ON-relationships might be ON(A,TABLE), ON(A,B), ON(B,TABLE), and ON(B,A). Although we use an entirely separate technique for inferring such predicate domains, note that they *do* comprise state constraints. For instance, the constraint above can be written as

$ON(x,y) \Rightarrow (x=A \wedge y=TABLE) \vee (x=A \wedge y=B) \vee$
$(x=B \wedge y=TABLE) \vee (x=B \wedge y=A).$

We now describe our specific techniques for inferring implicative and sv-constraints, and then our techniques for inferring predicate domains. While many useful implicative constraints can be inferred in isolation, others can only be inferred jointly with certain sv-constraints. This is true, for example, in the case of the constraint $ON(x,y) \Rightarrow \neg CLEAR(y)$ (possibly with supplementary constraints) in the blocks world. Thus we first discuss "dedicated" methods for implicative and sv-constraints, and then methods for inferring combinations of the two types of constraints. We have formal proofs of correctness for all of our methods, but will have to restrict ourselves herein to some sketchy indications why the inferred constraints are correct.

Implicative Constraints

We first consider implicative constraints of the form
$(\phi \Rightarrow \psi)\sigma_1...\sigma_k),$
where ϕ, ψ, and $\sigma_1,...,\sigma_k$ are simple *literals*, i.e., negated or unnegated atomic formulas whose arguments are constants or variables. Such constraints are to be interpreted as saying "In every state, for all values of the variables, if ϕ then ψ, provided that σ_1, ..., and σ_k. We assume that the predicate in ϕ is a fluent predicate, while that in ψ may be fluent or static, and those in $\sigma_1,...,\sigma_k$ are static. $\sigma_1,...,\sigma_k$ are *supplementary conditions*; they could of course be conjoined to ϕ, but we keep them separate because of the way they are determined algorithmically. Writing $V(\chi)$ for the variables occurring in a literal χ, we also assume (in accord with the earlier remarks) that $V(\psi) \subseteq V(\phi)$ and $V(\sigma) \subseteq V(\phi)$ for all $\sigma \in \{\sigma_1...\sigma_k\}$.

We restrict ourselves here to STRIPS-like operators as used, for example, in POP (Weld 1994) or Graphplan (Blum & Furst 1995), allowing for a list of (possibly typed) parameters, a set of precondition literals and a set of effect literals. We define *persistent preconditions* as those precondition literals of an operator (including any type constraints on parameters) that do not resolve against any effect literals of the operator. Here resolution is understood as constrained by NEQ preconditions: a variable x is considered unifiable with a constant or variable τ *unless* there is a precondition $NEQ(x,\tau)$.[1]

For example, if an operator $STACKUP(x,y)$ has preconditions

$CLEAR(x), CLEAR(y), ON(x,TABLE), NEQ(x,y),$
$NEQ(y,TABLE)$

and effects

$\neg ON(x,TABLE), ON(x,y), \neg CLEAR(y),$

then $CLEAR(x)$ is persistent, since it doesn't resolve against the effect $\neg CLEAR(y)$, in view of the precondition $NEQ(x,y)$. $NEQ(x,y)$ and $NEQ(y,TABLE)$ are also persistent, since no EQ condition appears among the effects of this (or indeed any) operator.

The number of syntactically legal implicative constraints can be very large.[2] However, at least in the relatively simple worlds that have so far served as test domains for domain-independent planners, the majority of useful implicative constraints seem to involve no more than two fluent literals, possibly along with some static literals (such as type constraints or EQ/NEQ-constraints on predicate arguments). Here fluent literals are literals whose predicates occur in operator effects, while static literals are ones whose predicates occur only in the initial conditions or in operator preconditions (including EQ/NEQ conditions, and type constraints on operator parameters). Even with an upper bound of two fluent literals, we cannot afford to consider all syntactically possible constraints, so we focus on those for which we have *a priori* evidence in the form of co-occurring literals in an operator.

The idea behind our basic algorithm for inferring implicative state constraints of the form $\phi \Rightarrow \psi$ (for the moment ignoring supplementary conditions) is the

---

[1] We assume here that there are no EQ-preconditions, so we needn't worry about preconditions $NEQ(x,\tau')$ where τ' is equated directly or indirectly to τ.

[2] In particular, in a domain containing m constants and n_i predicates of arity i, $i \leq k$, there are more than $\Sigma_{i=0}^{k} 2n_i m^i$ literals (there are more than that because arguments may be variables as well as constants). Thus there are more than N^l formulas with l literals, where N is the previous sum.

following. We hypothesize constraints by choosing ϕ to be an effect of an operator and choosing ψ to be an effect or persistent precondition of that operator, where $V(\psi) \subseteq V(\phi)$. Restricting ϕ to operator effects ensures that it will be a fluent literal. We then attempt to verify the constraints.

To arrive at verification conditions, we observe that $\phi \Rightarrow \psi$ will hold in all reachable states if

1. It is true initially, for all substitutions of constants in the planning domain for the variables $V(\phi)$; and
2. Whenever some instance of ϕ becomes true as a result of applying an operator, the corresponding instance of ψ will also be true in the resultant state; and
3. Whenever some instance of ψ becomes false as a result of applying an operator, all corresponding instances of ϕ will also be false in the resultant state. (Since ϕ may have more variables than ψ, there may be many possible instances of ϕ corresponding to an instance of ψ.)

Concerning (1), suppose that we write the hypothetical implicative constraint as a clause $\lambda_1 \vee \lambda_2$. To verify this in the initial state, we must be able to verify at least one of the two literals for each way of substituting domain constants for the free variables. A substitution instance of a positive literal is verified if and only if it appears explicitly in the initial conditions or is of the form $EQ(\kappa, \kappa)$, where κ is a constant. (We count NEQ-literals as negative, and assume that $\neg$NEQ is transformed to EQ in the clausal form of a constraint.) A substitution instance $\neg \alpha$ of a negative literal (where α is not an EQ-atom) is verified if and only if α does *not* appear in the initial conditions; $NEQ(\kappa, \kappa')$ (or $\neg EQ(\kappa, \kappa')$) is verified if and only if κ and κ' are distinct constants. Note that we have used a closed world assumption (CWA) and a unique names assumption in the initial conditions.

We can easily translate these observations into an algorithm for verifying a hypothetical state constraint (in clause form) in the initial state. We iterate through substitutions for the free variables of the constraint, trying to verify the first literal, and if that fails, the second literal for each substitution. If for some substitution, the verification fails for both literals, the hypothesis is refuted and we can cut short the iteration. The generalization to the case where there are k supplementary conditions is obvious: we will have a clause $\lambda_1 \vee ... \vee \lambda_{k+2}$ instead of a binary clause, and for each substitution we will try to verify one of the $k+2$ literals.

Concerning (2), suppose that an operator has a declared effect ϕ' which unifies with ϕ (subject to NEQ-preconditions), with unifier u. (Besides substituting constants for variables and operator parameters, the unification is allowed to substitute operator parameters for variables of ϕ, never *vice versa*.) Then a sufficient (and easily confirmed) condition for (2) to hold is that ψ_u is an effect or a persistent precondition of the operator, where ψ_u is the result of applying substitution u to ψ.[3]

Finally, (3) is trivially true if no operator has an effect matching $\overline{\psi}$ (complement of ψ). In addition, in cases where $V(\phi) = V(\psi)$, (3) can be verified just like (2) except that it applies to operators with a declared effect matching $\overline{\psi}$ with unifier u, and we look for persistent precondition or effect $\overline{\phi}_u$. If neither case applies, we need a different technique altogether (described later). For both (2) and the special cases of (3), the verification algorithm consists of scanning operator effects for effects that unify with ϕ or $\overline{\psi}$, and checking whether the corresponding persistent preconditions or effects ψ_u or $\overline{\phi}_u$ are present.

When we hypothesize a state constraint $\phi \Rightarrow \psi$ based on an operator, the static preconditions of the operator (not involved in ψ) are good candidates as supplementary conditions. For instance, the law may only hold when the specified type constraints on the parameters hold, or a specified NEQ-precondition holds. Thus when hypothesizing a state constraint based on an operator we initially include the static preconditions of that operator as candidate supplementary conditions.

In testing a state constraint augmented with candidate supplementary conditions, we need to do some extra book-keeping if condition (2) or (3) is found to be violated. In particular, if condition (2) is violated, we keep track of (a) the name of the operator and name of the effect ϕ' for which we did not find a matching instance of ψ, and (b) the names of the candidate supplementary conditions which are *denied* in the preconditions of the operator, under substitution u. Note that any false supplementary condition can "rescue" the seemingly violated state constraint, since a conditional formula with a false condition is automatically true. If condition (3) is violated, we save analogous (a)-data and (b)-data.

After collecting all such (a)-data and (b)-data by going through all the operators, we try to select a minimal set of supplementary conditions sufficient to "rescue" the hypothetical state constraint relative to all the apparent violations that were encountered. The problem of finding a true minimal set turns out to be a variant of the (NP-hard) set-cover problem, so we do not insist on finding a true minimal set. Rather, we use a kind of greedy algorithm to find a small set of supplementary conditions sufficient to "excuse" all apparent violations. (The user can provide an upper bound on the permissible number of supplementary conditions.) If no such set of conditions is found, the hypothetical state constraint is discarded.

We have proved the computation of implicative constraints according to the above scheme to be

---

[3]Note that this sufficient condition is not necessary. It turns out that in order to obtain a necessary and sufficient condition we would have to generate the entire state space of the problem, to determine the exact set of possible parameter settings of each operator. This is in general impractical.

polynomial-time, in terms of the total number of preconditions and effects on the operators, and the number of atoms and constants in the initial conditions (assuming a fixed bound on predicate arity).

Single-Valuedness Constraints

Next we describe a simple, "dedicated" method for finding sv-constraints. In the next section we will see how to infer implicative and sv-constraints in combination.

The idea of the dedicated method is to scan operators for effect literals that occur in pairs of the form $P(\tau_1, ..., \tau_k)$, $\neg P(\tau_1, ..., \tau_{i-1}, \tau', \tau_{i+1}, ..., \tau_k)$ (with $\tau_i \neq \tau'$). For such pairs, we conjecture single-valuedness of P in its ith argument.

We then check (a) whether positive P-occurrences in effects *always* occur paired in this way with negative P-occurrences, and in all cases we also have $P(\tau_1, ..., \tau_{i-1}, \tau', \tau_{i+1}, ..., \tau_k)$ among the preconditions; and (b) whether the single-valuedness property under consideration holds for the positive P-occurrences in the initial state; i.e., there are no pairs of instances of the form $P(\tau_1, ..., \tau_k)$, $P(\tau_1, ..., \tau_{i-1}, \tau', \tau_{i+1}, ..., \tau_k)$, (with $\tau_i \neq \tau'$) in the initial state.

Note that condition (a) ensures that the "old" P-instance, with τ' instead of τ_i as ith argument, goes from true to false. We need to check the truth of the old P-instance in the preconditions, since otherwise that instance may have been false already. In that case it is not *made* false by the action, i.e., the action only *adds* a new P-instance, and this may destroy single-valuedness.

The suggested method of hypothesizing sv-constraints misses predicates that occur in the initial conditions but not in effects. However, we can easily identify such predicates, and see if they are single-valued initially (and hence throughout the state space).

So under these conditions we conclude that
$P(x_1, ..., x_{i-1}, *, x_{i+1}, ..., x_k)$.

Once again the techniques described are polynomial time-bounded, in the previous sense. Also it is possible to allow for supplementary conditions as in the case of implicative constraints, but in this case we have not pursued the matter.

Inferring Combinations of Constraints

Blocks-world encodings often employ an operator MOVE(x, y, z), meaning "move x from y to z". In such a setting, the constraint ON$(x, y) \Rightarrow \neg$CLEAR(y) cannot be verified by the methods outlined earlier (even with a suitable supplementary condition on y). The reason is that there will be an effect CLEAR(y) (the previous support block becomes clear), and condition (3) for the validity of implicative constraints then requires $\neg$ON(x, y) to hold for *all* x, i.e., *nothing* is on y. But this universal is not explicitly asserted in the usual formulation of MOVE-effects; rather, the effects merely assert $\neg$ON(x, y) for the *particular* x that was moved.

We can overcome this difficulty by simultaneously inferring ON$(*, y)$, i.e., at most one thing can be on y. For in that case, if just one particular x is moved off y, y will indeed become clear. This observation leads to a general method of dealing with cases that our previous verification conditions for (3) couldn't handle: if for the hypothesized implicative constraint $\phi \Rightarrow \psi$, $V(\psi) \subset V(\phi)$ and $\overline{\psi}$ matches some operator effect, then try to establish simultaneously that the predicate in ϕ is single-valued in its "extra" arguments, $V(\phi) - V(\psi)$. (This means that for each assignment of values to $V(\phi) \cup V(\psi)$, there is at most one satisfying assignment of values to $V(\phi) - V(\psi)$.)

We have formulated the following verification conditions for such simultaneous constraints, and proved them correct (we set aside supplementary conditions):
1. Suppose that an operator has a declared effect ϕ' that matches ϕ (subject to NEQ-preconditions), with unifier u. Then $\overline{\psi_u}$ is a precondition and, ψ_u is an effect; and if there is another declared effect ϕ'' that matches ϕ, with unifier u', then if u and u' make distinct substitutions for the "extra" variables of ϕ, they also make distinct substitutions for the shared variables of ϕ and ψ.
2. Suppose that an operator has a declared effect $\overline{\psi'}$ that matches $\overline{\psi}$, with unifier u (subject to NEQ-preconditions). Then for some substitution v for the extra variables of ϕ, ϕ_{uv} is a precondition and $\overline{\phi_{uv}}$ is an effect of the operator.

In addition, we have formulated, and proved correct, verification conditions for simultaneous implicative and sv-constraints, for implicative constraints $\phi \Rightarrow \psi$ where both ϕ and ψ may contain variables not shared between them. An example of such a combination of constraints from the Logistics domain (referred to in our experiments below) is the following:
((IN$(x, *y) \Rightarrow \neg$AT$(x, *z)$) OBJECT(x)),
i.e., if an object x is in (a vehicle) y then x is at no (external) location; and an object can be in at most one vehicle, and in at most one location. However, we have only implemented the first of the above methods of inferring combined constraints.

Predicate Domain Constraints

Constraints on the predicate domains can be computed by first constructing a *forward action graph* which is a simplified planning graph in the sense of Graphplan (Blum & Furst 1995). The main difference between a forward action graph and a planning graph is that the latter contains mutual exclusion relations between action nodes and fact nodes, which are not present in the former. Since the number of such exclusion relations at any level of the graph can be quadratic in the number of the nodes at that level, it follows that the forward action graph of a given planning problem can be computed much more efficiently than the corresponding planning graph, in both time and space.

Our program for constructing the forward action graph of a given planning problem is based on a simple modification of IPP's C-code for building a planning graph (Koehler *et al.* 1997),[4] in which we avoid computing and propagating mutual exclusion relations. The depth of the action graph can be determined either by explicitly setting a parameter before running the program, or by letting the graph construction run until the graph "levels off" at some time step i (the facts of level $i-1$ are the same as those of level i, and further extension of the graph cannot introduce any new fact (Blum & Furst 1995)).

The computation of the forward action graph using this simple method was considerably faster than the computation of the corresponding planning graph. For example, for the bw-large.c problem in the blocks world domain, which is examined in the next sections, it was about twenty times faster.

From the nodes of the fact levels of a forward action graph, we can extract information about the possible domains and codomains of the predicates appearing in the operator preconditions and effects. In fact, for any positive operator precondition or effect ϕ, the only possible ground instances of ϕ that can hold at any reachable state in t time steps are a subset of the facts appearing as nodes of the action graph at level t. Therefore if a ground predication $\hat{\phi}$ does not appear at level t of the action graph, then under the CWA and the action closure assumption (Schubert 1994) (which are commonly used in most current planning systems) $\hat{\phi}$ is false at time t.

So, the *absence* of ground predications in the forward action graph can be used to formulate explicit constraints on the domains and codomains of the predicate arguments. Similarly, it is possible to use the action nodes of the forward action graph to derive constraints on the possible instantiations of the operators in the planning domain. However, in our preliminary experiments, which will be described in the next section, we have not yet tested the use of action variable constraints.

Using State Constraints in SAT-based Planning

We have implemented our basic techniques for inferring implicative, single-valuedness and predicate domain constraints in the DISCOPLAN system.

Table I gives the implicative and sv-constraints computed by DISCOPLAN when applied to the blocks world problems used by Kautz and Selman (1996) to test their SATPLAN system. The domain formalization consists of two "move" operators, each of which contains two conditional effects, which we translated into four equivalent operators without conditional effects. Each object (including the table) is modeled as a block, and each object can be either "fixed" (the table) or "non-fixed" (an ordinary block). Moved objects must be non-fixed blocks, while source and destination objects can be either fixed or non-fixed.[5] The

---
[4]IPP is of public domain and is available at www.informatik.uni-freiburg.de/~koehler/ipp.html.

[5]Note that the conjunction of the 1st and 3rd impli-

```
(((IMPLIES (CLEAR ?X) (BLOCK ?X)))
 ((IMPLIES (CLEAR ?X) (NOT (FIXED ?X))))
 ((IMPLIES (NOT (BLOCK ?X)) (CLEAR ?X)))
 ((IMPLIES (ON ?*X ?Y) (NOT (CLEAR ?Y)))
          (NOT (FIXED ?Y)))
 ((IMPLIES (ON ?X ?Y) (BLOCK ?X)))
 ((IMPLIES (ON ?X ?Y) (BLOCK ?Y)))
 ((IMPLIES (ON ?X ?Y) (NOT (FIXED ?X))))
 ((IMPLIES (ON ?X ?Y) (NEQ ?X ?Y)))
 ((IMPLIES (NOT (ON ?X ?Y)) (BLOCK ?Y)))
 ((IMPLIES (NOT (ON ?X ?Y)) (BLOCK ?X))))
```

Table I: Implicative and sv-constraints discovered by DISCOPLAN for Kautz & Selman's formalization of the blocks world. Kautz & Selman's hand-coded constraints included the 4th, 7th and 8th implications, and the sv-constraint (ON ?*X ?Y); they also posited that ON is non-commutative and that non-fixed blocks are ON just one thing, which DISCOPLAN currently does not infer.

CPU-time required to compute implicative and sv-constraints was 420 milliseconds on a SUN SPARCstation 4.

For the other domains that we tested the computation of these constraints required between 30 and 80 milliseconds, except for the Logistics domain. The state constraints inferable for this domain include implicative constraints $\phi \Rightarrow \psi$ where both ϕ and ψ contain variables not shared between them. We did the computation of these constraints by hand, since the implementation of the corresponding method is still in progress. (We expect, however, that the computational time will not be significantly different from the cpu-times that we have given for the other domains).

Also the computation of the forward action graph was very efficient, and we believe it can be made even more efficient by omitting some data structures used by IPP that are not necessary for the construction of a forward action graph.[6]

In the rest of this section we describe the application of discovered constraints to SAT-based planning, and give preliminary empirical results illustrating their utility for this style of planning.

Compiling discovered constraints into SATPLAN and MEDIC

In order to use the constraints discovered by DISCOPLAN in the context of SAT-based planning, we have extended two recent systems for compiling a planning problem specification into a set of propositional clauses: SATPLAN (Kautz & Selman 1996) and MEDIC (Ernst, Millstein, & Weld 1997).

While SATPLAN has its own planning language based on logical axiom schemas, MEDIC accepts

---
cation in Table I is consistent since every object of the domain, including the table, is predicated to be a block.

[6]The required cpu-time is dominated by the solution time in all 29 cases presented in the next section, except for Relsat applied to the easiest of the blocks worlds we considered. In this particular case Relsat solved the problem in 0.35 seconds, while the construction of the forward action graph required 1.91 seconds.

| Planning | Walksat | | | |
problems	With constr.	Without constr.	Speedup factors	Failure reduction
bw-large.b	17.7	95.5	5.4	0%
bw-large.c	261	3,128-100%	> 59.2	100%
bw-large.d	504	4,211-100%	> 41.7	100%
Hanoi4	1,238-100%	1,200-100%	0.97	0%
Ferry2-3	7.46	26.51-80%	> 3.5	80%
Ferry3-3	16.05	163.15-100%	> 50.8	100%
Ferry4-4	503.8-20%	848.6-100%	> 1.6	80%
Monkey-test2	0.32	34.4	107	0%

Table II: Average CPU-time (seconds) required by Walksat for solving encodings with and without the clauses derived from the discovered constraints (five runs for each problem). -n% indicates an n% failure rate in finding a solution. The last two columns indicate the improvements due to use of inferred constraints, in terms of cpu-time speedup and reduction in failure rates. Monkey-test3 is not included because it is unsolvable, and Walksat cannot detect this.

| Planning | Relsat | | | |
problems	With constr.	Without constr.	Speedup factors	Failure reduction
bw-large.b	0.35	7.85	22.42	0%
bw-large.c	18.55	600-100%	> 33.3	100%
bw-large.d	287.02	600-100%	> 2	100%
Hanoi4	79.69	600-100%	> 7.5	100%
Ferry2-3	0.17	1.65	9.7	0%
Ferry3-3	0.42	11.40	27.1	0%
ferry4-4	18.07	600-100%	> 33.2	100%
Monkey-test2	0.07	7.5	107.1	0%
Monkey-test3	0.29	600-100%	> 2,068	100%
Logistics.a	3.63	4.35	1.19	0%
Logistics.b	2.90	437.03-50%	> 150	50%
Logistics.c	16.64	382.96-30%	> 23	30%

Table III: Average CPU-time required by Relsat for solving encodings with and without the clauses derived from the discovered constraints (20 runs for each problem; each run had a search limit of 10 minutes). Times are in seconds. -n% indicates an n% failure rate (either no solution was found, though there was one, or the solver failed to establish unsolvability, though the problem was unsolvable). The last two columns indicate the improvements due to use of inferred constraints in terms of cpu-time speedup and failure rate reduction.

UCPOP-like specifications as input(Penberthy & Weld 1992), and offers the possibility of automatically compiling them using several representational settings (for details see (Ernst, Millstein, & Weld 1997)).[7] Our extended versions of SATPLAN and MEDIC expand the *un*simplified CNF files generated by SATPLAN and MEDIC respectively, by adding to them a set of clauses. These extra clauses are automatically computed by instantiating the discovered constraints. Each implicative and sv-constraint is instantiated to a set of ground clauses formed by literals appearing in the CNF file, and corresponding to initial conditions, action preconditions, action effects, and final goals (literals representing actions are not considered).

Predicate domain constraints can be extracted from a forward action graph in the following way. For each positive literal in the SAT encoding representing a *fluent*, we check whether the corresponding symbolic predication P is a node of the action graph at the appropriate level. (Note that we automatically detect which predicates are static, and which are fluents during the computation of the implicative state con-

| Planning | Tableau | | |
problems	With	Without	Speedup factors
bw-large.b	5	65	13
bw-large.c	8	> 26h	> 11,700
bw-large.d	5,260	> 26h	> 18
Hanoi4	26	13,371	514
Ferry2-3	0.45	35	77
Ferry3-3	0.74	> 10h	> 48,640
Ferry4-4	13	> 8,400	> 646
Monkey-test2	0.53	0.57	1.07
Monkey-test3	3	> 10,800	> 3,600

Table IV: CPU-time required by Tableau for solving encodings with and without the clauses derived from the discovered constraints. Times are in seconds, unless differently indicated ("h" means hours). > t means that the process was stopped after time t without reaching a solution, or without proving that the problem was unsolvable.

straints.) If this is not the case, then we generate the unit clause $\neg P$. The resulting set of unit clauses is then added to the SAT encoding together with the clauses derived from the implicative and sv-constraints.

The expanded SAT encodings can then be simplified by using a CNF simplifier such as SATPLAN's *Simplify* program or MEDIC's *Compact-cnf* program. In our tests we used Simplify version 2.1.

---

[7]In our tests we used the following settings, which in (Ernst, Millstein, & Weld 1997) were empirically shown to produce relatively small, easily solved encodings: regular action representation, explanatory frame axioms, parallel exclusion axioms, types elimination.

Problems	Tableau	Walksat	Relsat	Vars	Clauses
bw-large.b	2	23.8	0.53	1,087	13,772
bw-large.c	7	296	31.21	3,016	50,457
bw-large.d	4,503	2,047	395.99	6,325	131,973

Table V: CPU-time (seconds) and size of the encoding for the AT&T's blocks world problems as originally formulated, i.e., including hand-written domain axioms. The CPU-times for Walksat and Relsat are averages over 5 runs.

Preliminary Empirical Results

Tables II, III, IV, V, VI give preliminary empirical results on the use of inferred constraints for improving SAT-based planning. For AT&T's blocks world (ATT-BW), we ran the following experiment.[8] First we removed from SATPLAN's specification of ATT-BW all the hand-written domain-specific axioms, and we tested the performance of several SAT solvers on encodings of the ATT-BW problems generated by SATPLAN for the revised specification. The revised encodings were very hard to solve not only for the stochastic solver Walksat (as already observed in (Ernst, Millstein, & Weld 1997)), but also for the systematic solver Tableau and for the more recent Relsat (Bayardo & Schrag 1997), which was tested using "relevance-bounded learning" of order 4. These results are given in the 3rd columns of Tables II, III and IV.

We then augmented the SAT encodings of these revised specifications with the clauses derived from the instantiation of our discovered constraints.[9] Finally, the resulting expanded encodings were first simplified and then solved using the three solvers mentioned above (for Tableau see the 2nd column of Table IV; for Walksat see the 2nd column of Table II; for Relsat see 2nd column of III). The results show that the use of the inferred constraints dramatically boosted speed and success in finding solutions regardless the kind of solver used. This is surprising since Kautz and Selman's experiments in (Kautz & Selman 1992) suggest that systematic SAT solvers based on the Davis-Putnam procedure such as Tableau could not be expected to benefit from addition of "axioms that explicitly rule out various impossible states" (Kautz & Selman 1992). The performance of Tableau for these encodings was very close to its performance for the original formalization of ATT-BW including hand-written domain-specific axioms (compare the 2nd columns of Table IV and V). The performance of Walksat and Relsat for these encodings was even better than the performance for the original ones (compare the 2nd columns of Tables II and III with the 3rd and the 4th of Table V respectively).

---

[8] All our tests were conducted on a SUN Ultra 1 with 128 Mbytes of RAM. The tests for Walksat were conducted with the following "cutoff" and "noise" settings. For the ATT-BW problems we used the settings suggested by Kautz and Selman; while for the other problems we used noise 30–100 and cutoff 2,000,000 for Hanoi4 and Ferry4-4, cutoff 500,000 for Ferry3-3 and cutoff 100,000 for Ferry2-3 (i.e., we used smaller cutoffs for easier problems).

[9] The constraints were inferred using a set of four STRIPS operators that we derived from SATPLAN's axiomatic formalization of the blocks world.

DISCOPLAN constr.	CPU-time	Vars	Clauses
Implicative	7	3,016	20,717
All the constraints	8	3,016	36,949
Implicative and SV	9	3,016	33,704
Predicate Domain	1,302	3,016	18,603
Single-valuedness (SV)	> 8,000	3,526	38,340
No constraints	> 93,600	3,526	21,957

Table VI: Average CPU-time (seconds) required by Tableau and size of the encodings for bw-large.c using each kind of discovered constraints.

In order to test the individual impact of each of the discovered constraints, we separately tested each of them on the ATT-BW problem bw-large.c (involving 15 blocks on a table). For each kind of constraint we generated a different SAT encoding formed by the unsimplified set of the clauses generated by SATPLAN (excluding those corresponding to all the hand-written domain specific axioms) and by the clauses derived from the discovered constraints of the kind under consideration. Similarly we tested the impact of the implicative constraints combined with single-valuedness. The solution times required by Tableau for solving these SAT instances are given in Table VI. They show that in ATT-BW the most useful discovered constraints are the implicative constraints. Interestingly, in this domain sv-constraints do not help when used alone, or in combination with implicative constraints. On the other hand, predicate domain constraints do help to guide the solver towards a solution, though not as effectively as implicative constraints.

It addition to the ATT-BW problems we tested the use of our techniques in four other well-known domains taken from the test suites of UCPOP, MEDIC or SATPLAN: Tower of Hanoi, Ferry, Monkey and ATT-logistics. The SAT encodings for these domains where automatically obtained using MEDIC. Hanoi4 is the Tower of Hanoi problem with four disks. Ferry-2-3 is a Ferry problem with two "autos" to be transported and three locations (analogously for Ferry-3-3 and Ferry-4-4). Monkey-test2 and Monkey-test3 are problems in the Monkey domain; the first is solvable, while the second is unsolvable. Finally, Logistics.a, Logistics.b and Logistics.c are the problems in the ATT-logistics domain that were used by Kautz and Selman to test their SATPLAN system, and which, like the ATT-BW problems, are very hard to solve for planners based on planning graphs (Kautz & Selman 1996; Koehler et al. 1997).

The results for these problems are given in Tables III and IV. They show that inferred state constraints can be extremely useful in these domains as well. In the tests for the Ferry and the Monkey problems we used the sv-constraints that are discovered both in combination with implicative laws, and by using the dedicated method that we discussed in the previous sections. The constraints derivable using the dedicated method are {(at-ferry *)}, for the Ferry domain, and {(AT monkey *)} for the Monkey domain. They represent the intuitive constraint that in any legal state the ferry and the monkey can be at most one location. Without these sv-constraints the performance of Tableau was significantly worse. For example, Ferry-3-3 was solved in 119 seconds, instead of 0.74. In contrast with the blocks world, this is an example of a domain where sv-constraints are important. The same is true for monkey-test3, in which we found that the sv-constraint for the location of the monkey is crucial in enabling Tableau to prove that the problem has no solution.

Concerning the ATT-Logistics problems, the use of state constraints considerably improved the performance of Relsat. However, for Tableau and Walksat these problems were hard to solve even with the addition of state constraints.

Finally, the fourth and fifth columns of Tables II and III give the speedup factors and the improvement in failure rate that we obtained for all the problems we tested. In almost all cases we obtained either a drastic speedup or a considerable reduction in failure rate, regardless the CNF solver used.

Conclusions and Further Work

We have provided provably correct, polynomial-time methods for inferring a variety of state constraints in STRIPS-like planning domains. Our preliminary experiments show that automatically inferred constraints can be very effective in speeding up SAT-based planners.

Current and future work includes

- Generalization of our implemented methods to allow for UCPOP-like conditional effects; much of our code already allows for this, but the selection of supplementary constraints becomes more complicated;
- Implementation of additional methods in DISCOPLAN; some were already mentioned, and some not, such as exclusion and subsumption relations among static predicates, non-commutativity laws, and strict sv-laws;
- Further experiments to test the usefulness of automatically inferred constraints; and
- "bootstrapping" the discovery of constraints by feeding confirmed constraints back into the hypothesize-and-test process.

We also expect that inferred constraints will prove useful in other types of planners; for instance, they could be used for "unachievability pruning" in deductive or regression planners (Genesereth & Nilsson 1987). Past experience in AI attests that any search process can benefit from the imposition of local constraints on the search space.

Acknowledgments

This research was supported in part by NATO grant CRG951285, by CNR project SCI*SIA (first author), and by ARPA/SSTO grant F30602-95-1-0025 (second author). We thank the anonymous referees for their helpful comments.

References

Bayardo Jr., R., and Schrag, R.C. 1997. Using CSP look-back techniques to solve real-world SAT instances. In *Proc. of the 14th Nat. Conf. of the American Assoc. for Artificial Intelligence (AAAI-97)*, 203–208. Morgan Kaufmann.

Blum, A., and Furst, M. 1995. Fast planning through planning graph analysis. In *Proc. of the 14th Int. Joint Conf. on Artificial Intelligence (IJCAI-95)*, 1636–1642. Morgan Kaufmann.

Crawford, J., and Auton, L. 1993. Experimental results on the cross-over point in satisfiability problems. In *Proc. of the 11th Nat. Conf. of the American Assoc. for Artificial Intelligence (AAAI-93)*, 21–27.

Ernst, M.; Millstein, T.; and Weld, D. 1997. Automatic SAT-compilation of planning problems. In *Proc. of the 15th Int. Joint Conf. on Artificial Intelligence (IJCAI-97)*, 1169–1176. Morgan Kaufmann.

Genesereth, M.; Nilsson, N. 1987. *Logical Foundations of Artificial Intelligence*. Morgan Kaufmann.

Gerevini, A.; Schubert, L.K. 1996. Accelerating partial-order planners: Some techniques for effective search control and pruning, *J. of Artificial Intelligence Research (JAIR)* 5, 95–137.

Kautz, H., and Selman, B. 1992. Planning as satisfiability. In *Proc. of the 10th European Conf. on Artif. Intell. (ECAI-92)*, 359–363. John Wiley and Sons.

Kautz, H., and Selman, B. 1996. Pushing the envelope: Planning, propositional logic, and stochastic search. In *Proc. of the 13th Nat. Conf. of the American Assoc. for Artificial Intelligence (AAAI-96)*.

Koehler, J.; Nebel, B.; J., H.; and Dimopoulos, Y. 1997. Extending planning graphs to an ADL subset. In *Proc. of the 4th European Conf. on Planning (ECP'97)*. Springer Verlag.

Penberthy, J., and Weld, D. 1992. UCPOP: A sound, complete, partial order planner for ADL. In Nebel, B.; Rich, C.; and Swartout, W., eds., *Proc. of the 3rd Int. Conf. on Princ. of Knowledge Representation and Reasoning (KR'92)*, 103–114. Morgan Kaufmann.

Schubert, L. 1994. Explanation closure, action closure, and the Sandewall test suite for reasoning about change. *J. of Logic and Computation* 4(5):679–700.

Selman, B.; Kautz, H.; and Cohen, B. 1994. Noise strategies for local search. In *Proc. of the 12th Nat. Conf. of the American Assoc. for Artificial Intelligence (AAAI-94)*, 337–343. Morgan Kaufmann.

Weld, D. An introduction to least commitment planning. *AI Magazine*, 15(4), 27–62.

Analyzing External Conditions to Improve the Efficiency of HTN Planning

Reiko Tsuneto, James Hendler and Dana Nau

Department of Computer Science
and Institute of Systems Research
University of Maryland, College Park, MD 20705
{reiko, hendler, nau}@cs.umd.edu

Abstract

One difficulty with existing theoretical work on HTN planning is that it does not address some of the planning constructs that are commonly used in HTN planners for practical applications. Although such constructs can make it difficult to ensure the soundness and completeness of HTN planning, they are important because they can greatly improve the efficiency of planning in practice. In this paper, we describe a way to achieve some of the advantages of such constructs while preserving soundness and completeness, through the use of what we will call *external conditions*. We describe how to detect some kinds of external conditions automatically by preprocessing the planner's knowledge base, and how to use this knowledge to improve the efficiency of the planner's refinement strategy. We present experimental results showing that by making use of external conditions as described here, an HTN planner can be significantly more efficient and scale better to large problems.

Introduction

Problem Description

Applied work in AI planning has typically favored approaches based on hierarchical decomposition rather than causal chaining. In particular, most successful planners for practical applications have used *hierarchical task network* (HTN) planning (Sacerdoti 1977; Tate 1977; Currie and Tate 1991; Wilkins 1990), an AI planning methodology that creates plans by *task decomposition*. This is a process in which the planning system decomposes tasks into smaller and smaller subtasks, until primitive tasks are found that can be performed directly. HTN planning systems have knowledge bases containing *methods* (also called *schemas* by some researchers). Each method includes (1) a prescription for how to decompose some task into a set of subtasks, (2) various restrictions that must be satisfied in order for the method to be applicable, and (3) various constraints on the subtasks and the relationships among them. Given a task to accomplish, the planner chooses an applicable method, instantiates it to decompose the task into subtasks, and then chooses and instantiates other methods to decompose the subtasks even further. If the constraints on the subtasks or the interactions among them prevent the plan from being feasible, the planner will backtrack and try other methods.

Although HTN-style planners have been the ones most used in practical applications (Aarup *et al.* 1994; Wilkins and Desimone 1994; Agosta 1995; Smith *et al.* 1996; Estlin *et al.*[1] 1997), most theoretical work to date is in the area of partial-order refinement planners such as UCPOP (Penberthy and Weld 1992) and more recently in graph- and circuit-based planners (Blum and Furst 1997; Kautz and Selman 1992).

One exception has been theoretical work on HTN planning at the University of Maryland. This work has shown HTN planning to be strictly more expressive than planning with STRIPS-style operators (Erol *et al.* 1994b), has established the soundness and completeness of HTN planning algorithms (Erol *et al.* 1994a), and has explored the complexity of HTN planning problems (Erol *et al.* 1996) and the efficiency of various search strategies (Tsuneto *et al.* 1996; Tsuneto *et al.* 1997). The code for the UMCP domain-independent planner (which we used for the experiments reported in this paper) is available at <http://www.cs.umd.edu/projects/plus/umcp>.

Unfortunately, the above work did not incorporate several of the planning constructs used in previous HTN planning systems, such as unsupervised conditions and high-level effects (Tate 1977). Such constructs are often used in practical applications of HTN planning because they can be very useful for improving the efficiency of planning—but the UMCP planner does not incorporate them because they can make it difficult to guarantee the planner's soundness and completeness.

As an example, consider high-level effects. Some HTN-style planners allow the user to state in the planner's

---

Copyright © 1998, American Association for Artificial Intelligence (www.aaai.org). All rights reserved.

[1] Their DPLAN and MVP planners are not completely HTN planners, but they employ a combination of HTN planning and operator-based planning.

knowledge base that various non-primitive tasks will achieve various effects. Such planners can use these high-level effects to establish applicability conditions, and can prune the partial plan if a high-level effect threatens an applicability condition. This can interfere with the planner's soundness. For example, if a non-primitive task t has a high-level effect o, but one of the sub-plans that t can be decomposed into does not have the effect o, then this may cause the planner to produce an inconsistent plan. Also, even when there is a high-level effect to establish a condition, there may be a threat to that establishment that can only be found by looking at primitive tasks. This problem can be overcome, but only by imposing restrictions on how high-level effects are used (Bacchus and Yang 1991, Young *et al.* 1994).

Despite these problems, the ability to recognize important effects early is critical to the good performance of a planner. By examining those actions most likely to effect others, pruning of the search space can occur and much backtracking can be avoided. Ways are needed to provide the sort of information needed for this pruning without sacrificing soundness or completeness.

Approach

In this paper, we describe one way to address the problem discussed above, through the use of what we call *external conditions*. We also show that if an HTN planner recognizes and makes use of external conditions in an appropriate fashion, this can greatly improve the efficiency of HTN planning, while preserving soundness and completeness.

External conditions can be described intuitively as follows. Suppose that to accomplish some task in a plan P, we decide to use some method M. Furthermore, suppose that there is some condition C that must be satisfied in order for M to be successful, but that there is no way to decompose M into a sub-plan that achieves C. Then the plan P may still be successful, but only if some other portion of P achieves C. In this case, we say that the condition C is *external* to the method M.

External conditions do not really have a good analog in STRIPS-style planning, but they are somewhat analogous to the unsupervised conditions used in the Nonlin planner (Tate 1977) and external-condition goals used in the SIPE-2 planner (Wilkins 1990). The main difference is that instead of being specified explicitly as unsupervised conditions or external-condition goals are, external conditions occur as a result of the structure of the planner's knowledge base, and can be detected by examining the knowledge base. We also believe that external conditions may be a good way to capture many of the benefits found in some planners via the use of high-level effects.

Background

How Constraints Are Handled in HTN Planning

Just as a STRIPS-style planning operator specifies preconditions that must be satisfied before the operator can be executed, an HTN method M may include specifications of several different kinds of conditions that must be satisfied in order for M to be used successfully. We describe the most important ones here, using the notation that is used for them in the UMCP HTN planner.

- A *predicate task*, which is sometimes called a GOAL node (Tate 1977) or an achievement task, is analogous to a precondition in a STRIPS-style planning operator: it is a condition that must be true at the time that the method M begins executing.

- An *initial state constraint* specifies a condition that must be true in the initial state in order for M to be used. For example, if M contains the constraint (initially (~ Q ?x)), this constraint can be satisfied only if it is possible to bind the variable ?x to some value C such that (Q C) is false in the initial state. Normally, one would use an initial state constraint only to refer to a condition that will never change throughout the plan.

- A *'before' state constraint* such as (before (P ?x) n) specifies a condition that must be true just before some subtask n of the method M. This state constraint can be *established* by a task T if T has the effect (P ?y), T precedes the task n in the plan, and the variables ?x and ?y are instantiated to the same value. Similarly, (before (P ?x) n) can be *threatened* by a task T if T has the effect (~P ?z), T precedes the task n, no establisher of the constraint occurs after T and before n, and the variables ?x and ?z are instantiated to the same value.

- A *'between' state constraint* specifies a condition that needs to be true during a specific time interval. For example, the 'between' state constraint (between (P ?x) n1 n2) is satisfied if the condition (P ?x) is true from the end of the task n1 to the beginning of the task n2. A 'between' state constraint can be established or threatened in a manner similar to a 'before' constraint.

Task Selection and FAF

One characteristic of partial-order planners—regardless of whether they use HTN decomposition or STRIPS-style operators—is that they search a space in which the nodes are partially developed plans. The planner refines the plans into more and more specific plans, until either a completely developed solution is found or every plan is found incapable of solving the problem.

During this process, a planner may often have many different options for what kind of refinement to perform next. A planner that uses STRIPS-style operators may need to choose which unachieved goal to work on next, which operator to use to achieve a goal, or which technique to use (promotion, demotion, or variable separation) to resolve a goal conflict. An HTN planner usually has an even larger array of options: it may need to choose which unachieved task to work on next, which method to use to accomplish the task, or which constraint (from among a number of different possibilities) to impose on the plan. The planner's efficiency depends greatly on its *plan refinement strategy*, which is the way it goes about choosing among these options.

Of the various plan refinement strategies that have been explored by AI planning researchers, one of the best that has been found so far is a strategy that we call the "fewest alternatives first" (FAF) strategy, which chooses the refinement that has the fewest immediate child nodes in the search. The first use of FAF by planning researchers seems to have occurred relatively recently (Currie and Tate 1991), but a similar heuristic has been known in the constraint satisfaction literature for more than 20 years (Bitner and Reingold 1975; Purdom 1983). In recent experimental studies comparing various versions of FAF with other well known plan refinement strategies (Joslin and Pollack 1994; Tsuneto *et al.* 1996), FAF outperformed the other refinement strategies on many planning problems and planning domains. Furthermore, theoretical analyses of FAF (Tsuneto *et al.* 1997) have shown that FAF can produce exponential savings in the size of the planner's search space. Since FAF is a general search heuristic,. however, it does not always do as well as other strategies that use domain-specific planning knowledge.

When there are two or more goal tasks in a problem, the tasks can often be interleaved; i.e., an effect of one goal task can be used to satisfy the state constraints of another goal task. By interleaving goal tasks, the planner can create plans that have fewer redundant actions—and in some cases, interleaving may be the only way to generate a plan at all.

While interleaving tasks is essential in HTN planning, it is often hard for the planner to know which tasks can be interleaved successfully. The planner does not know exactly what effects a non-primitive task has until the task is decomposed into primitive tasks; and the decomposition process can introduce more state constraints to the plan that may not already be established. The failure to interleave tasks successfully often leads to a large backtracking cost.

Although FAF does generally better than other strategies, its performance is still ragged for many multiple-goal problems. If the planner is trying to establish more than one constraint, often it will do so by trying to interleave tasks; and if it tries to interleave several tasks at once, then the number of possible ways to interleave them can be combinatorially large. Thus, if the interleaving doesn't work, the planner can waste large amounts of time exploring a large search space. In order to avoid such difficulties, the planner needs to know which state constraints should be established early by interleaving

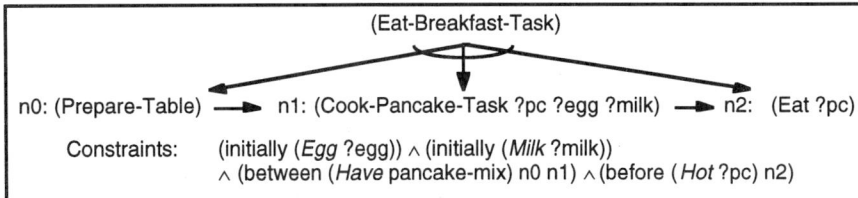

Figure 2: The pancake method for (Eat-Breakfast-Task). The downward-pointing arrows represent task decomposition, and the right-pointing arrows represent precedence. The tasks in the decomposition are labeled as n0, n1, and n2 so that they can be referred to in the constraint formula.[3]

tasks, and the task selection should use such knowledge to arrange the search.

External Conditions

An external condition of a method is a state constraint that cannot be established by any task that may result from the method. Thus, if the method is to be used successfully in a plan, the plan must establish this state constraint by something *external* to the method (such as the initial state or some other task in the planning problem).

More formally, let $M = <T, \phi>$ be a method, where T is the set of subtasks created by the method and ϕ is the set of constraints for the method. Then a condition c is an *external condition* of M if:

1. c is a state constraint but not an initial state constraint;
2. c must be necessarily true to satisfy ϕ; and
3. no primitive descendants[2] of tasks in T can establish c.

As an example, suppose you want to eat a breakfast of either pancakes (made from pancake mix) or cereal. We can encode this situation as an HTN planning problem in which there is a task called Eat-Breakfast-Task that has two decomposition methods: one to eat pancakes (as shown in Figure 2) and one to eat cereal. As shown in Figure 2, the pancake method decomposes Eat-Breakfast-Task into three subtasks: Prepare-Table, Cook-Pancake-Task, and Eat. Let us assume that the methods for these tasks involve (1) putting the syrup, fork and knife on the table, (2) cooking the pancakes, and (3) serving and eating the pancakes, respectively.

The pancake method has four state constraints. The following analysis shows that the only external condition for this method is (between (*Have* pancake-mix) n0 n1):

- (initially (*Egg* ?egg)) and (initially (*Milk* ?milk)) are not external conditions, because they are initial state constraints.
- (between (*Have* pancake-mix) n0 n1) is an external condition, because preparing the table does not cause a

---

[2] A descendent of a task t is a task that appears as a result of recursively decomposing t.
[3] To distinguish between task names and predicate names (both here and throughout this paper), we put the latter in italics.

pancake mix to be there and no subtasks can occur before n0.

- (before (*Hot* ?pc) n2) is not an external condition, because the condition "the pancake ?pc is hot" is caused by the task n1.

The ExCon Strategy

After some method *M* is instantiated as part of some partial plan, every external condition of *M* becomes one of the *applicability conditions* in the partial plan; i.e., it is a condition that must be established *somewhere* in any completion of the partial plan if the completion is to be successful for the current problem. If the applicability condition cannot be satisfied, the planner may not be able to tell this until long after it has instantiated the method *M*, in which case the planner will incur large backtracking costs. In many situations, the planner has to backtrack over more than one applicability condition, which multiplies the backtracking costs.

Consider the breakfast example again. Suppose we have a planning problem with two goal tasks, Shopping-Task and Eat-Breakfast-Task (see Figure 3). Suppose that the initial state does not contain (Have pancake-mix), but that depending on what is on sale at the store, one possible outcome of Shopping-Task is to buy a pancake mix. Given the goal, a task-selection strategy such as FAF may choose Eat-Breakfast to work on first. This will generate two partial plans, one using the pancake method (Plan1 in the figure) and the other using the cereal method. The planner has to choose a non-primitive task such as Cook-Pancake-Task or Shopping-Task in Plan1 to work on next.

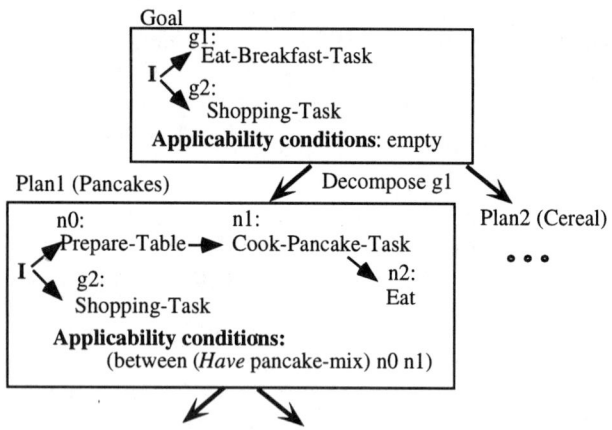

Figure 3: A part of the search tree for the breakfast problem. 'I' represents the initial state.

If sometime later the planner finds that the Shopping-Task does not actually buy a pancake mix, then the entire search branch derived from Plan1 fails. The cost of such backtracking can be significantly large if the planner worked on the task Cook-Pancake-Task down to the detailed level and then finds the failure while working on the Shopping-Task.

The idea of the ExCon strategy is to shift the attention of the planner to concentrate on establishing applicability conditions in the partial plan. This requires the following:

1. When it loads its knowledge base, the planner must pre-compute external conditions for every decomposition method in the domain and store the information.
2. The data structure of a partial plan keeps the stack of applicability conditions. Initially, the partial plan has no applicability conditions. During a method instantiation, the external conditions of the method are pushed onto the top of this stack. The condition on top is the current priority to the planner.
3. When selecting a task to decompose, the priorities are given to (1) tasks which can possibly establish the current top condition, or (2) tasks which can possibly threaten the current top condition, based on the presence of a primitive establisher.

The algorithm for the third step (selecting a task to decompose) is shown in Figure 4. For selecting tasks in Steps 1, 4, and 5, the algorithm uses whatever task-selection strategy the user wishes (we use FAF for this purpose in the experiments described in the next section). We now describe the details of the algorithm.

Algorithm select-task-ExCon(*PartialPlan*)
1. If the applicability condition stack of *PartialPlan* is empty, then select a task from *PartialPlan* and return the result.
2. Else, set *c* to the first element of the applicability condition stack in *PartialPlan*.
3. If *c* is true in *PartialPlan*, then remove *c* from the applicability condition stack and go back to Step 1.
4. If there is no primitive task that establishes *c*, then compute possible establishers for *c*. Select a task among them and return the result.
5. Else, compute possible threats for *c*. Select a task among them and return the result.
6. If there are no possible establishers or possible threats, remove *c* from the applicability condition stack of *PartialPlan* and go back to Step 1.

Figure 4: The task selection algorithm for ExCon.

In Step 1, if there are no applicability conditions to achieve, then the planner selects and returns a task. When there are applicability conditions, Step 2 picks the one on top of the stack. If the current condition is already established without threats in the partial plan, then Step 3 removes the condition from the stack and goes back to select something else. Otherwise, Step 4 computes the non-primitive tasks in the plan that can possibly establish the condition, provided the condition is not established by any primitive task currently in the plan. If it is established by a primitive task, then possible threats are computed and one is selected in Step 5. Otherwise, there are only primitive tasks that might affect this condition, so Step 6 will remove it from the stack and go back to select another one.

Note that since ExCon's task-selection strategy merely

specifies the order in which a planner will prefer to expand tasks, it has no effect on the planner's soundness and completeness: a planner that is sound and complete without it will also be sound and complete with it.

Experiments

We implemented FAF and ExCon in UMCP version 1.0, using Allegro Common Lisp version 4.3 on SUN workstations. We ran two sets of experiments: one on a small artificial domain and one on the Translog domain. We incorporated each task selection strategy into UMCP's default commitment strategy, and used depth-first search for all the experiments. Although we do not show CPU-time results for the experiments described below, the CPU times in our experiments were basically proportional to the node counts.

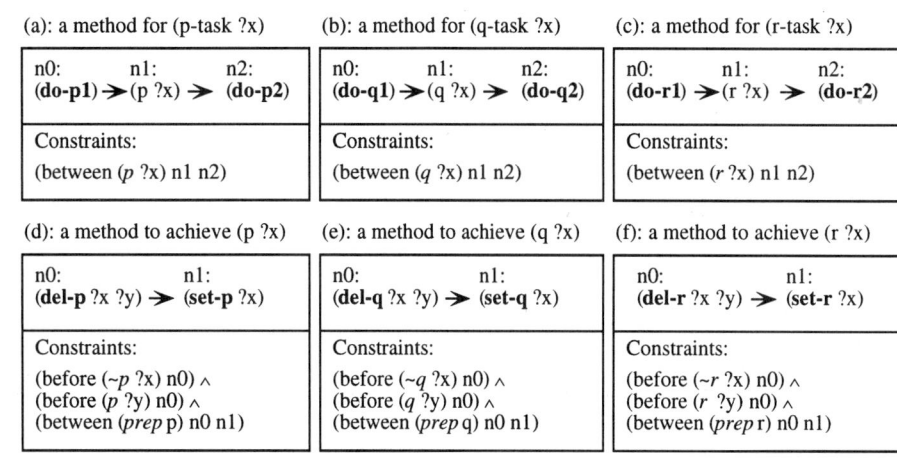

Figure 5: The decomposition methods for the test domain. Each non-primitive task has exactly one method specified. The tasks shown in boldface are primitive tasks.

Implementation of ExCon in UMCP

Automatically extracting external conditions. Computing precisely which state constraints are external conditions is not a trivial matter since it requires the planner to know the exact variable bindings that can occur during the planning. To see which tasks affect which constraints, UMCP uses a *possible-effects table* to store information about which non-primitive tasks are capable of causing various kinds of effects. Since the exact effect of each non-primitive task depends on which decomposition methods are used and how the variables are bound, the table only specifies which non-primitive task can possibly affect each predicate. The table is a table of pairs $\langle p, t \rangle$ where p is a positive or a negative predicate symbol and t is a non-primitive task. A pair $\langle p, t \rangle$ is in the table if one of the possible decompositions of the task t contains a primitive task s such that one of s's effects is the literal (p arguments).

The possible effects table can be constructed by a planner by preprocessing the domain. During the planning, the planner can look up the table to see which non-primitive task in the current partial plan can possibly establish or threaten certain constraints in order to prune partial plans that have no way of satisfying necessary state constraints.

To extract the external conditions of each method in the domain, we modified UMCP to look at each non-initial state constraint and find all the subtasks that are not explicitly ordered after the point where the condition needs to be true. If none of those subtasks can possibly establish the condition, the state constraint is marked as an external condition. This method will not necessarily extract all external conditions. We are currently trying to find a better way to extract them.

Computing possible establishers and possible threats. As shown in Figure 4, Steps 4 and 5 of ExCon's task-selection compute the possible establishers and the possible threats of the applicability condition. In our implementation, the planner uses the possible effects table to compute them. First the planner finds all non-primitive tasks in the partial plan that are not ordered after the point where the condition needs to be true. It then looks up the possible effects table to see if any of them can possibly establish or threaten the condition, and returns the result. Although this method returns (as possible establishers or possible threats) some tasks that can never establish nor threaten the condition, it finds every possible establisher and possible threat to the condition.

Experiments on an artificial domain

We hypothesized that in comparison with FAF, ExCon should perform best in problems that contain lots of interleaved tasks, and also in problems where there are many possible ways to interleave the same tasks. To test these hypotheses, we experimented with ExCon on the test domain described below.

The test domain contains methods for accomplishing compound tasks called p-task, q-task, and r-task. As shown in Figure 5, these methods decompose the compound tasks into other tasks. Most of the other tasks are primitive tasks, but a few of them (p, q, and r) are predicate tasks. Most of the primitive tasks (do-p1, do-p2, do-q1, do-q2, do-r1 and do-r2) have no preconditions and effects. Each predicate task has two methods that are capable of achieving it: one of the methods shown in Figure 5(d)–5(f), and a Do-Nothing method.[4]

---

[4] If a predicate task has already been established, it is said to be *phantomized* because the planner will not need or want to

The primitive task (del-p ?x ?y) has the effects (~p ?y) and (prep p). The task (set-p ?x) has the effects (p ?x) and (~prep p). The predicate task (p W) for some value W can be achieved in two ways: by phantomizing it if the literal (p W) is true at the beginning of the task (p W); or by doing (del-p W Z) followed by (set-p W) if at the beginning of the task (p W), the literal (p W) is false and the literal (p Z) is true for some value Z. The tasks del-q and del-r are defined similarly to the task del-p, and the tasks set-q and set-r are defined similarly to the task set-p. An initial state for this domain consists of three ground atoms $(p\ w_p)\ (q\ w_q)$ and $(r\ w_r)$, where w_p, w_q and w_r are constant values randomly chosen from the set {C1, C2, C3, C4, C5, C6}.

In this test domain, the amount of interleaving can be altered by varying the arguments of the goal tasks: a problem is highly interleaved if the arguments of most p-task goal tasks are the same, and it is less interleaved if the arguments of most p-task goal tasks are different.

Figure 6: A sample problem with 2 goals, 3 predicates and 50% overlap. I represents the initial state which consists of (p C6), (q C4) and (r C4).

We generated test problems as follows. Goals were random sequences of one (p-task only), two (p-task and q-task) or three (p-task, q-task and r-task) different tasks that need to be done. How many different tasks were in the goals decided the number of predicates in the problems. A problem consisted of two or three goals, with no ordering constraints between them. We randomly assigned arguments to the tasks based on an "overlap rate" of 10%, 50% or 90%. For example, if the overlap rate were 100%, all the arguments of the p-task tasks would be identical to the p value in the initial state. If the overlap rate were 0%, the arguments for p-task's and the p value in the initial state would all be unique. If the overlap rate were 30%, there would be a 30% probability that the argument of a p-task is used in another p-task or the atom p in the initial state. We varied the overlap rate to create problems with various degrees of interleaving. We also varied the number of predicates appearing in the problems to change the chances that the planner tries to interleave multiple predicate tasks. A sample problem is shown in Figure 6.

We created and tested 100 problems of 1, 2 or 3 predicates used, 10%, 50% or 90% overlap, and 2 or 3 goals, totaling 1800 problems tested. We counted the number of search nodes, i.e. partial plans, created during the planning and computed the average for each type of problem. The results are shown in Table 1.

The ExCon strategy first extracts the external conditions of each of the methods. The methods in Figure 5(a)–(c)

establish it yet again. There are several well known ways to handle phantomization. UMCP handles it by inserting a Do-Nothing method (basically a no-op) into the plan.

have no external conditions while the methods in Figure 5(d)–(f) have two external conditions each (the first two 'before' state constraints). Also, the Do-Nothing method for each predicate task has one external condition. (ex. the constraint (before (p ?x) n) is the external condition for the Do-Nothing method of the task (p ?x).)

Table 1: The average numbers of search nodes created over the 100 randomly generated problems in the artificial test domain.

2 goals	FAF	ExCon	FAF	ExCon	FAF	ExCon
	1 predicate		2 predicates		3 predicates	
90%	10.5	10.5	22.5	21.9	35.8	32.6
50%	12.3	12.3	30.2	26.2	56.2	38.3
10%	14.2	14.2	36.1	29.7	68.7	43.8
3 goals	1 predicate		2 predicates		3 predicates	
90%	16.5	16.2	40.2	38.8	79.1	52.5
50%	34.5	34.8	176	64.4	1414	105
10%	53.6	53.5	473	101	3302	141

Table 1 shows our experimental results. At 90% overlap, most predicate tasks can be phantomized and the amount of backtracking is minimal. Thus, the performances of the two strategies are almost the same. As the overlap rate decreases to 50% and 10%, less and less predicate tasks can be phantomized. The planner has a harder time trying to order tasks consistently in such a way that phantomization will work between the goals. For example, consider the problem shown in Figure 6. If the planner orders the task g3 before the task g4, the subtask (p C6) of g3 can be phantomized by the initial state. On the other hand, if the planner orders the task g6 before the task g2, then the subtask (r C4) of g6 can be phantomized. However, the planner cannot phantomize both (p C6) and (r C4) because of the ordering constraints.

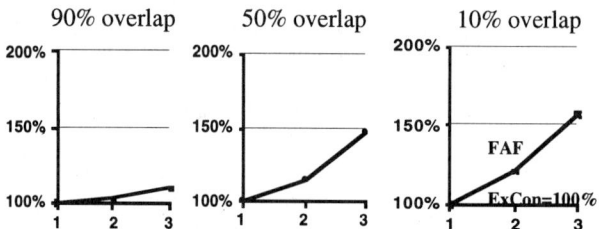

Figure 7: The relative performance of FAF and ExCon on 2-goal problems. The x-axis gives the number of predicates in the goals, and the y-axis gives the ratio (# search nodes by FAF) / (# search nodes by ExCon).

Figures 7 and 8 are graphs of the data in Table 1, that show how the relative performance of FAF and ExCon depends on number of predicates in the goal. Note that as the number of predicates increases, FAF's performance degrades much more quickly than ExCon's. This is because FAF creates many more search nodes in order to phantomize predicate tasks. Since ExCon works on one predicate at a time until it is established or fails, the planner does not have to backtrack over multiple predicates as it does with FAF.

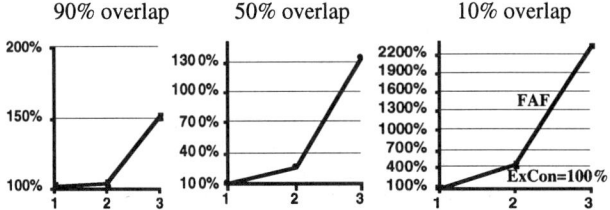

Figure 8: The relative performances of FAF and ExCon for 3-goal problems. The x-axis gives the number of predicates in the goals, and the y-axis gives the ratio (# search nodes by FAF) / (# search nodes by ExCon).

The graphs in Figure 9 show how the relative performance of FAF and ExCon depends on the overlap rate. For the problems with 1 predicate, the difference between FAF and ExCon is insignificant. For the problems with 2 or 3 predicates in the goals, FAF is clearly spending more time backtracking than ExCon.

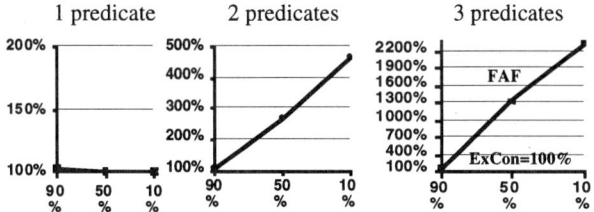

Figure 9: The relative performance of FAF and ExCon on 3-goal problems. The x-axis gives the overlap rate, and the y-axis gives the ratio (# search nodes by FAF) / (# search nodes by ExCon).

ExCon does slightly worse than FAF on average for the problems with 3 goals, 1 predicate, and 50% overlap. For other types of problems, ExCon may perform worse than FAF on certain problems but on average, ExCon performs better. ExCon may not do well if search branches fail for reasons such as the failure of variable bindings, or state constraints except external conditions. We need to study commitment strategies as a whole to improve such situations. in the future

Experiments with the Translog Domain

We now describe our experiments with FAF and ExCon in the Translog domain (Andrews, *et al.* 1995). Translog is a transportation logistics domain specifying various delivery methods for various types of packages. For example, it specifies granular packages such as grain must be delivered by hopper trucks. If the packages are the same type and the itineraries are the same, then two delivery tasks can be interleaved by using the same truck and carrying the packages at the same time. Even if the itineraries are different, if the destination of a package A is the initial location of the other package B, then the task of moving the truck to the initial location of B can be interleaved by carrying and delivering package A first.

We tested (a) one-package delivery problems, (b) two package delivery problems where the packages are of the same package type and have the same initial location and destination, (c) two package delivery problems where the packages are of the same package type and the destination of one of the packages is the same as the initial location of the other package, (d) two package delivery problems where the packages are of the same type but none of the initial locations or the destinations are the same, and (e) two package delivery problems where the packages are of the different types. We randomly created 50 problems, 10 problems for each type of problems, with various package types (regular, bulky, liquid, livestock or granular) and locations (among 15 locations). The results are shown in Table 2.

Table 2: Average number of nodes generated by FAF and ExCon on Translog problems. For two-package delivery problems, "Package types" shows whether the packages have the same type and so can be carried by the same delivery truck.

Problem	Package types	FAF	ExCon	FAF/ExCon
1pack (a)	—	67.9	67.9	1.00
2pack (b)	same	932.6	1331.4	0.70
2pack (c)	same	799.9	721.7	1.11
2pack (d)	same	1415.9	731.9	1.93
2pack (e)	different	1366.3	518.2	2.64

For one-package delivery problems, there is almost no interleaving in the problem, so the performances of FAF and ExCon are similar. For two-package delivery problems, the performances of the two strategies depends on how much tasks can be successfully interleaved between two goal tasks. For the problems of type (b), the task of moving trucks to the necessary locations can be completely interleaved between the two goals. So FAF can perform well on these problems. On our ten test problems, FAF produced fewer search nodes on average than ExCon although ExCon outperformed FAF on 7 out of 10 problems. For the problems of type (c), the task of moving a truck to the initial location of the second package can be interleaved by delivering the first package first. ExCon does this more efficiently than FAF. For the problems of type (d), although the two packages are of the same type, and same trucks can be used, no interleaving can actually work, since the locations are all different. Both ExCon and FAF make attempts to interleave tasks, but ExCon realizes the failure faster than FAF does. The similar occurrence takes place for the problems of type (e) where the two package types are different.

Conclusions

In this paper, we have shown how an HTN planner can

avoid many situations that cause complexity in multiple-goal and interleaved problems, by identifying and handling *external conditions*. We have presented ExCon, a task selection strategy that makes use of these conditions. ExCon causes the planner to explore tasks that are likely to affect the applicability conditions of other tasks first, significantly reducing backtracking. In our empirical studies, ExCon consistently outperformed FAF on complex problems, doing increasingly well on the problems where the task interactions occurred recursively and where multiple goals were involved.

Since ExCon enables the planner to establish conditions in the plan at less detailed levels, it produces some of the same improvements in planning efficiency that one might try to get using planning constructs such as unsupervised preconditions or high-level effects. In addition, it has the following advantages:

- External conditions do not have to be specified explicitly by the user, but instead are found automatically by the planning system when it pre-compiles its knowledge base. This will make it much easier for users to maintain the knowledge base.

- ExCon is a task-selection strategy, not a search-space pruning heuristic: it simply specifies the order in which a planner will prefer to expand tasks. Thus, it has no effect on the planner's soundness and completeness: a planner that is sound and complete without it will also be sound and complete with it.

Acknowledgments

This research was supported in part by grants from ONR (N00014-J-91-1451), ARPA (N00014-94-1090, DABT-95-C0037, F30602-93-C-0039), ARL (DAAH049610297) and NSF (NSF EEC 94-02384, IRI-9306580).

References

Aarup, M.; Arentoft, M. M.; Parrod, Y.; Stader, J.; and Stokes, I. 1994. OPTIMUM-AIV: A knowledge-based planning and scheduling system for spacecraft AIV. In Fox, M. and Zweben, M., editors, *Intelligent Scheduling*, 451–469. Calif: Morgan Kaufmann,.

Agosta, J. M. 1995. Formulation and Implementation of an Equipment Configuration Problem with the SIPE-2 Generative Planner. In *Proc. AAAI-95 Spring Symposium on Integrated Planning Applications*, 1–10.

Andrews, S.; Kettler, B.; Erol, K.; and Hendler, J. 1995. UM Translog: A planning domain for the development and benchmarking of planning systems, Technical Report, CS-TR-3487, University of Maryland.

Bacchus, F. and Yang, Q. 1991. The downward refinement property. In *Proc. IJCAI-91*.

Bitner, J. and Reingold, E. 1975. Backtrack Programming Techniques. *CACM* 18(11).

Blum, A. L. and Furst, M. L. 1997. Fast Planning Through Planning Graph Analysis. *Artificial Intelligence*, 90(1-2):281–300.

Currie, K. and Tate, A. 1991. O-Plan: The Open Planning Architecture. *Artificial Intelligence*, 52:49–86.

Erol. K; Hendler, J.; and Nau, D. 1994a. UMCP: A Sound and Complete Procedure for Hierarchical Task-network Planning. In *Proc. Second Conference on AI Planning Systems (AIPS-94)*.

Erol. K.; Hendler, J.; and Nau, D. 1994b. HTN Planning: Complexity and Expressivity. In *Proc. AAAI-94*.

Estlin, T. A.; Chien, S. A.; and Wang, X. 1997. An Argument for Hybrid HTN/Operator-Based Approach to Planning. In *Proc. Fourth European Conference on Planning (ECP-97)*, 184–196.

Joslin, D. and Pollack, M. E. 1994. Least-Cost Flaw Repair: A Plan Refinement Strategy for Partial-Order Planning. In *Proc. AAAI-94*, 1004–1009.

Kautz, H. and Selman, B. 1992. Planning as Satisfiability. In *Proc. Tenth European Conference on Artificial Intelligence*, 359–363.

Penberthy, J. S. and Weld, D. 1992. UCPOP: A Sound, Complete, Partial Order Planner for ADL. In *Proc. KR-92*.

Pollack, M. E.; Joslin, D.; and Paolucci, M. 1997. Flaw Selection Strategies for Partial-Order Planning. *Journal of Artificial Intelligence Research* 6, 223-262.

Purdom, P. W. 1983. Search Rearrangement Backtracking and Polynomial Average Time. *Artificial Intelligence* 21: 117–133.

Sacerdoti, E. 1977. *A Structure for Plans and Behavior.* American Elsevier Publishing Company.

Smith, S. J.; Nau, D.; and Throop, T. 1996. Total-Order Multi-Agent Task-Network Planning for Contract Bridge. In *Proc. AAAI-96*.

Tate, A. 1977. Generating Project Networks. In *Proc. IJCAI-77*, 888–893.

Tsuneto, R.; Erol, K.; Hendler, J.; and Nau, D. 1996. Commitment Strategies in HTN Planning. In *Proc. AAAI-96*, 536-542.

Tsuneto, R.; Hendler, J.; and Nau, D. 1997. Space-Size Minimization in Refinement Planning. In *Proc. Fourth European Conference on Planning(ECP-97)*.

Wilkins, D. 1990. Can AI planners solve practical problems?. *Computational Intelligence* 6 (4): 232–246.

Wilkins, D. E. and Desimone, R. V. 1994. *Applying an AI planner to military operations planning*. In Fox, M. and Zweben, M., editors, Intelligent Scheduling, 685—709. Calif.: Morgan Kaufmann.

Young, R. M.; Pollack, M. E.; and Moore, J. D. 1994. Decomposition and Causality in Partial-Order Planning. In *Proc. Second Conference on AI Planning Systems.*

Managing Multiple Tasks in Complex, Dynamic Environments

Michael Freed
NASA Ames Research Center
mfreed@mail.arc.nasa.gov

Abstract

Sketchy planners are designed to achieve goals in realistically complex, time-pressured, and uncertain task environments. However, the ability to manage multiple, potentially interacting tasks in such environments requires extensions to the functionality these systems typically provide. This paper identifies a number of factors affecting how interacting tasks should be prioritized, interrupted, and resumed, and then describes a sketchy planner called APEX that takes account of these factors when managing multiple tasks.

Introduction

To perform effectively in many environments, an agent must be able to manage multiple tasks in a complex, time-pressured, and partially uncertain world. For example, the APEX agent architecture described below has been used to simulate human air traffic controllers in a simulated aerospace environment (Freed and Remington, 1997). Air traffic control consists almost entirely of routine activity; complexity arises largely from the need to manage multiple tasks. For example, the task of guiding a plane to landing at a destination airport typically involves issuing a series of standard turn and descent authorizations to each plane. Since such routines must be carried out over minutes or tens of minutes, the task of handling any individual plane must be periodically interrupted to handle new arrivals or resume a previously interrupted plane-handling task.

Plan execution systems (e.g. Georgoff and Lansky, 1988; Firby, 1989; Cohen et al., 1989; Gat, 1992; Simmons, 1994; Hayes-Roth, 1995; Pell, et al., 1997), also called *sketchy planners*, have been designed specifically to cope with the time-pressure and uncertainty inherent in these kinds of environments. This paper discusses a sketchy planner called APEX which incorporates and builds on multitask management capabilities found in previous systems.

© 1998, American Association for Artificial Intelligence (www.aaai.org). All rights reserved.

Multitask Resource Conflicts

The problem of coordinating the execution of multiple tasks differs from that of executing a single task because tasks can interact. For example, two task interact benignly when one reduces the execution time, likelihood of failure, or risk of some undesirable side effect from the other. Perhaps the most common interaction between routine tasks results from competition for resources.

An agent's cognitive, perceptual, and motor resources are typically limited in the sense that each can normally be used for only one task at a time. For example, a task that requires the *gaze* resource to examine a visual location cannot be carried out at the same time as a task that requires gaze to examine a different location. When separate tasks make incompatible demands for a resource, a *resource conflict* between them exists. To manage multiple tasks effectively, an agent must be able to detect and resolve such conflicts.

To resolve a resource conflict, an agent needs to determine the relative priority of competing tasks, assign control of the resource to the winner, and decide what to do with the loser. The latter issue differentiates strategies for resolving the conflict. There are at least three basic strategies (cf. (Schneider and Detweiler, 1988)).

> **Shedding**: eliminate low importance tasks
> **Delaying/Interrupting**: force temporal separation between conflicting tasks
> **Circumventing**: select methods for carrying out tasks that use different resources

Shedding involves neglecting or explicitly foregoing a task. This strategy is appropriate when demand for a resource exceeds availability. For the class of resources we are presently concerned with, those which become blocked when assigned to a task but are not depleted by use, demand is a function of task duration and task temporal constraints. For example, a task can be characterized as requiring the gaze resource for 15 seconds and having a completion deadline 20 seconds hence.

Excessive demand occurs when the combined demands of two or more tasks cannot be satisfied. For example, completion deadlines for two tasks with the above profile cannot both be satisfied. In such cases, it makes sense to abandon the less important task.

A second way to handle a resource conflict is to *delay or interrupt* one task in order to execute (or continue executing) another. Causing tasks to impose demands at different times avoids the need to shed a task, but introduces numerous complications. For example, deferring execution can increase the risk of task failure, increase the likelihood of some undesirable side-effect, and reduce the expected benefit of a successful outcome. Mechanisms for resolving a resource conflict should take these effects into account in deciding whether to delay a task and which should be delayed.

Interrupting an ongoing task not only delays its completion, but may also require specialized activities to make the task robust against interruption. In particular, handling an interruption may involve carrying out actions to stabilize progress, safely wind down the interrupted activity, determine when the task should be resumed, and then restore task preconditions violated during the interruption interval. Mechanisms for deciding whether to interrupt a task should take the cost of these added activities into account.

The third basic strategy for resolving a conflict is to *circumvent* it by choosing non-conflicting (compatible) methods for carrying out tasks. For example, two tasks A and B might each require the gaze resource to acquire important and urgently needed information from spatially distant sources. Because both tasks are important, shedding one is very undesirable; and because both are urgent, delaying one is not possible. In this case, the best option is to find compatible methods for the tasks and thereby enable their concurrent execution. For instance, task A may also be achievable by retrieving the information from memory (perhaps with some risk that the information has become obsolete); switching to the memory-based method for A resolves the conflict. To resolve (or prevent) a task conflict by circumvention, mechanisms for selecting between alternative methods for achieving a task should be sensitive to potential resource conflicts (Freed and Remington, 1997).

In addition to these basic strategies, conflicts can also be resolved by incorporating the tasks into an explicit, overarching procedure, effectively making them subtasks of a new, higher level task. For example, an agent can decide to timeshare, alternating control of a resource between tasks at specified intervals. Or instead, conflicting tasks may be treated as conjunctive goals to be planned for by classical planning mechanisms. The process of determining an explicit coordinating procedure for conflicting tasks requires deliberative capabilities beyond those present in a sketchy planner. The present work focuses on simpler heuristic techniques needed to detect resource conflicts and carry out the basic resolution strategies described above.

APEX

Our approach to multitask management has been incorporated into the APEX architecture (Freed, 1998) which consists primarily of two parts. The *action selection component*, a sketchy planner, interacts with the world through a set of cognitive, perceptual, and motor resources which together constitute *a resource architecture*. Resources represent agent limitations. In a human resource architecture, for example, the visual resource provides action selection with detailed information about visual objects in the direction of gaze but less detail with increasing angular distance. Cognitive and motor resources such as hands, voice, memory retrieval, and gaze are limited in that they can only be used to carry out one task a time

To control resources and thereby generate behavior, action selection mechanisms apply procedural knowledge represented in a RAP-like (Firby, 1989) notation called PDL (Procedure Definition Language) . The central construct in PDL is a **procedure** (see figure 1), which includes at least an **index** clause and one or more **step** clauses. The index identifies the procedure and describes the goal it serves. Each step clause describes a subgoal or auxiliary activity related to the main goal.

The planner's current goals are stored as task structures on the planner's *agenda*. When a task becomes enabled (eligible for immediate execution), two outcomes are possible. If the task corresponds to a primitive action, a description of the intended action is sent to a resource in the resource architecture which will try to carry it out. If instead, the task is a non-primitive, the planner retrieves a procedure from the procedure library whose index clause matches the task's description. Step clauses in the selected procedure are then used as templates to generate new tasks, which are themselves added to the agenda. For example, an enabled non-primitive task {turn-on-headlights}[1] would retrieve a procedure such as that represented in figure 1.

---

[1] APEX has only been tested in a simulated air traffic control environment. The everyday examples used to describe its behavior are for illustration and have not actually been implemented.

In APEX, steps are assumed to be concurrently executable unless otherwise specified. The **waitfor** clause is used to indicate ordering constraints. The general form of a waitfor clause is *(waitfor <eventform>*)* where eventforms can be either a procedure step-identifier or any parenthesized expression. Tasks created with waitfor conditions start in a pending state and become enabled only when all the events specified in the waitfor clause have occurred. Thus, tasks created by steps s1 and s2 begin enabled and may be carried out concurrently. Tasks arising from the remaining steps begin in a pending state.

```
(procedure
    (index (turn-on-headlights)
    (step s1 (clear-hand left-hand))
    (step s2 (determine-loc headlight-ctl => ?loc)
    (step s3 (grasp knob left-hand ?loc)
        (waitfor ?s1 ?s2))
    (step s4 (pull knob left-hand 0.4) (waitfor ?s3))
    (step s5 (ungrasp left-hand) (waitfor ?s4))
    (step s6 (terminate) (waitfor ?s5)))
```

Figure 1 Example PDL procedure

Events arise primarily from two sources. First, perceptual resources (e.g. vision) produce events such as *(color object-17 green)* to represent new or updated observations. Second, the sketchy planner produces events in certain cases, such as when a task is interrupted or following execution of an enabled **terminate** task (e.g. step s6 above). A terminate task ends execution of a specified task and generates an event of the form *(terminated <task> <outcome>)*; by default, <task> is the terminate task's parent and <outcome> is 'success.' Since termination events are often used as the basis of task ordering, waitfor clauses can specify such events using the task's step identifier as an abbreviation – for example, *(waitfor (terminated ?s4 success)) = (waitfor ?s4)*.

Detecting Conflicts

The problem of detecting conflicts can be considered in two parts: (1) determining which tasks should be checked for conflict and when; and (2) determining whether a conflict exist between specified tasks. APEX handles the former question by checking for conflict between task pairs in two cases. First, when a task's non-resource preconditions (waitfor conditions) become satisfied, it is checked against ongoing tasks. If no conflict exists, its state is set to *ongoing* and the task is executed. Second, when a task has been delayed or interrupted to make resources available to a higher priority task, it is given a new opportunity to execute once the needed resource(s) become available – i.e. when the currently controlling task terminates or becomes suspended. The delayed task is then checked for conflicts against all other pending tasks.

Determining whether two tasks conflict requires only knowing which resources each requires. However, it is important to distinguish between two senses in which a task may require a resource. A task requires *direct control* in order to elicit primitive actions from the resource. For example, checking the fuel gauge in an automobile requires direct control of gaze. Relatively long-lasting and abstract tasks require *indirect control*, meaning that they are likely to be decomposed into subtasks that need direct control. For example, the task of driving an automobile requires gaze in the sense that many of driving's constituent subtasks involve directing visual attention.

Indirect control requirements are an important predictor of direct task conflicts. For example, driving and visually searching for a fallen object both require indirect control over the gaze resource, making it likely that their respective subtasks will conflict directly. Anticipated conflicts of this sort should be resolved just like direct conflicts – i.e. by shedding, delaying, or circumventing.

Resources requirements for a task are undetermined until a procedure is selected to carry it out. For instance, the task of searching for a fallen object will require gaze if performed visually, or a hand resource if carried out by grope-and-feel. PDL denotes resource requirements for a procedure using the PROFILE clause. For instance, the following clause should be added to the turn-on-headlights procedure described above:

(profile (left-hand 8 10))

The general form of a profile clause is
(profile (<resource> <duration> <continuity>)*). The <resource> parameter specifies a resource defined in the resource architecture – e.g. gaze, left-hand, memory-retrieval; <duration> denotes how long the task is likely to need the resource; and <continuity> specifies how long an interrupting task has to be before it constitutes a *significant interruption*. Tasks requiring the resource for an interval less than the specified continuity requirement are not considered significant in the sense that they do not create a resource conflict and do not invoke interruption-handling activities (as described further on).

For example, the task of driving a car should not be interrupted in order to look for restaurant signs near the side of the road, even though both tasks need to control gaze. In contrast, the task of finding a good route on a road map typically requires the gaze resource for a much longer interval and thus conflicts with driving. Note that an interruption considered insignificant for a task may be significant for its subtasks. For instance, even though searching the roadside might not interrupt driving per se, subtasks such as tracking nearby traffic and maintaining a minimum distance from the car ahead may have to be briefly interrupted to allow the search to proceed.

Prioritization

Prioritization determines the value of assigning control of resources to a specified task. The prioritization process is automatically invoked to resolve a newly detected resource conflict. It may also be invoked in response to evidence that a previous prioritization decision has become obsolete – i.e. when an event occurs that signifies a likely increase in the desirability of assigning resources to a deferred task, or a decrease in desirability of allowing an ongoing task to maintain resource control. Which particular events have such significance depends on the task domain.

In PDL, the prioritization process may be procedurally reinvoked for a specified task using a primitive **reprioritize** step; eventforms in the step's waitfor clause(s) specify conditions in which priority should be recomputed. For example, a procedure describing how to drive an automobile would include steps for periodically monitoring numerous visual locations such as dashboard instruments, other lanes of traffic, the road ahead, and the road behind. Task priorities vary dynamically, in this case to reflect differences in the frequency with which each should be carried out. The task of monitoring behind, in particular, is likely to have a low priority at most times. However, if a driver detects a sufficiently loud car horn in that direction, the monitor-behind task becomes more important. The need to reassess its priority can be represented as follows:

```
(procedure
  (index (drive-car))
  ...
  (step s8 (monitor-behind))
  (step s9 (reprioritize ?s8)
    (waitfor (sound-type ?sound car-horn)
             (loudness ?sound ?db (?if (> ?db 30))))))
```

The relative priority of two tasks determines which gets control of a contested resource, and which gets shed, deferred, or changed to circumvent the conflict. In PDL, task priority is computed from a PRIORITY clause associated with the step from which the task was derived.

Step priority may be specified as a constant or arithmetic expression as in the following examples:

```
(step s5 (monitor-fuel-gauge) (priority 3))
(step s6 (monitor-left-traffic) (priority ?x))
(step s7 (monitor-ahead) (priority (+ ?x ?y)))
```

In the present approach, priority derives from the possibility that specific, undesirable consequences will result if a task is deferred too long. For example, waiting too long to monitor the fuel gauge may result in running out of gas while driving. Such an event is a *basis* for setting priority. Each basis condition can be associated with an importance value and an urgency value. *Urgency* refers to the expected time available to complete the task before the basis event occurs. *Importance* quantifies the undesirability of the basis event. Running out of fuel, for example, will usually be associated with a relatively low urgency and fairly high importance. The general form used to denote priority is:

```
(priority <basis> (importance <expression>)
                  (urgency <expression>))
```

In many cases, a procedure step will be associated with multiple bases, reflecting a multiplicity of reasons to execute the task in a timely fashion. For instance, monitoring the fuel gauge is desirable not only to avoid running out of fuel, but also to avoid having to refuel at inconvenient times (e.g. while driving to an appointment for which one is already late) or in inconvenient places (e.g. in rural areas where finding fuel may be difficult). Multiple bases are represented using multiple priority clauses.

```
(step s5 (monitor-fuel-gauge)
  (priority (run-empty) (importance 6) (urgency 2))
  (priority (delay-to-other-task) (importance ?x)
            (urgency 3))
  (priority (excess-time-cost refuel) (importance ?x)
            (urgency ?y)))
```

The priority value derived from a priority clause depends on how busy the agent is when the task needs the contested resource. If an agent has a lot to do (workload is high), tasks will have to be deferred, on average, for a relatively long interval. There may not be time to do all desired tasks – or more generally – to avoid all basis events. In such conditions, the importance associated with avoiding a basis event should be treated as more relevant than urgency in computing a priority, thus ensuring that those basis events which do occur will be the least damaging.

In low workload, the situation is reversed. With enough time to do all current tasks, importance may be irrelevant. The agent must only ensure that deadlines associated with each task are met. In these conditions, urgency should dominate the computation of task priority. The tradeoff between urgency and importance can be represented by the following equation:

$$priority_b = S*I_b + (S_{max}-S)U_b$$

S is subjective workload (a heuristic approximation of actual workload); I_b and U_b represent importance and urgency for a specified basis (b). To determine a task's priority, APEX first computes a priority value for each basis, and then selects the maximum of these values.

Interruption Issues

A task acquires control of a resource in either of two ways. First, the resource becomes freely available when its current controller terminates. In this case, all tasks whose execution awaits control of the freed up resource are given current priority values; control is assigned to whichever task has the highest priority. Second, a higher priority task can seize a resource from its current controller, interrupting it and forcing it into a suspended state.

A suspended task recovers control of needed resources when it once again becomes the highest priority competitor for those resources. In this respect, such tasks are equivalent to pending tasks which have not yet begun. However, a suspended task may have ongoing subtasks which may be affected by the interruption. Two effects occur automatically: (1) subtasks no longer inherit priority from the suspended ancestor and (2) each subtask is reprioritized, possibly causing it to become interrupted. Other effects are procedure-specific and must be specified explicitly. PDL includes several primitives steps useful for this purpose, including RESET and TERMINATE.

(step s4 (turn-on-headlights))
(step s5 (reset) (waitfor (suspended ?s4))

For example, step s5 causes a turn-on-headlight task to terminate and restart if it ever becomes suspended. This behavior makes sense because interrupting the task is likely to undo progress made towards successful completion. For example, the driver may have gotten as far as moving the left hand towards the control knob at the time of suspension, after which the hand will likely be moved to some other location before the task is resumed.

Robustness against interruption

Discussions of planning and plan execution often consider the need to make tasks robust against failure. For example, the task of starting an automobile ignition might fail. A robust procedure for this task would incorporate knowledge that, in certain situations, repeating the turn-key step is a useful response following initial failure. The possibility that a task might be interrupted raises issues similar to those associated with task failure, and similarly requires specialized knowledge to make a task robust. The problem of coping with interruption can be divided into three parts: wind-down activities to be carried out as interruption occurs, suspension-time activities, and wind-up activities that take place when a task resumes.

It is not always safe or desirable to immediately transfer control of a resource from its current controller to the task that caused the interruption. For example, a task to read information off a map competes for resources with and may interrupt a driving task. To avoid a likely accident following abrupt interruption of the driving task, the agent should carry out a wind-down procedure (Gat, 1992) that includes steps to, e.g., pull over to the side of the road. The following step within the driving procedure achieves this behavior.

(step s15 (pull-over)
  (waitfor (suspended ?self))
  (priority (avoid-accident) (importance 10)
     (urgency 10)))

Procedures may prescribe additional wind-down behaviors meant to (1) facilitate timely, cheap, and successful resumption, and (2) stabilize task preconditions and progress – i.e. make it more likely that portions of the task that have already been accomplished will remain in their current state until the task is resumed. All such actions can be made to trigger at suspension-time using the waitfor eventform *(suspended ?self)*.

In some cases, suspending one task should enable others meant to be carried out during the interruption interval. Typically, these will be either monitoring and maintenance tasks meant, like wind-down tasks, to insure timely resumption and maintain the stability of the suspended task preconditions and progress. Windup activities are carried out before a task regains control of resources and are used primarily to facilitate resuming after interruption. Typically, windup procedures will include steps for assessing and "repairing" the situation at resume-time – especially including progress reversals and violated preconditions. For example, a windup activity following a driving interruption and subsequent pull-over behavior might involve moving safely moving back on to the road and merging with traffic.

Continuity and intermittency

Interruption raises issues relating to the continuity of task execution. Three issues seem especially important. The first, discussed in section 4, is that not all tasks requiring control of a given resource constitute significant interruptions of one another's continuity. The PROFILE clause allows one to specify how long a competing task must require the resource in order to be considered a source of conflict.

Second, to the extent that handling an interruption requires otherwise unnecessary effort to wind-down, manage suspension, and wind-up, interrupting an ongoing task imposes opportunity costs, separate from and in addition to the cost of deferring task completion. These costs should be taken account of in computing a task's priority. In particular, an ongoing task should have its priority increased (over what it would be if not yet begun) in proportion to the costs imposed by interruption. In PDL, this value is specified using the INTERRUPT-COST clause. For example, the clause

(interrupt-cost 5)

within the driving procedure indicates that a driving interruption should cause 5 to be added to a driving task's priority if it is currently ongoing.

The third major issue associated with continuity concerns *slack time* in a task's control of a given resource. For example, when stopped behind a red light, a driver's need for hands and gaze is temporarily reduced, making it possible to use those resources for other tasks. In driving, as in many other routine behaviors, such intermittent resource control requirements are normal; slack time arises at predictable times and with predictable frequency. A capable multitasking agent should be able to take advantage of these intervals to make full use of resources. In PDL, procedures denote the start and end of slack-time using the SUSPEND and REPRIORITIZE primitives.

```
(step s17 (suspend ?self)
   (waitfor (shape ?object traffic-signal)
      (color ?object red)))
(step s18 (monitor-object ?object) (waitfor ?s17))
(step s19 (reprioritize ?self)
   (waitfor (color ?object green)))
```

Thus, in this example, the driving task will be suspended upon detection of a red light, making resources available for other tasks. It also enables a suspension-time task to monitor the traffic light, allowing timely reprioritization (and thus resumption) once the light turns green.

Computing Priority

To compute priority, APEX uses a version of the previously described priority equation that takes into account two additional factors. First, an interrupt cost value is added to priority if an interrupt-cost has been specified and the task is currently ongoing. Second, the computation should recognize limited interaction between the urgency and importance terms. For example, it is never worth wasting effort on a zero-importance task, even it has become highly urgent. Similarly, a highly important task with negligible urgency should be delayed to avoid the opportunity cost of execution. Such interactions are represented by the discount term $1/(1+x)$. Thus the priority function[2]:

$$priority_b = IC + S(1 - \frac{1}{U+1})I_b + (S_{max} - S)(1 - \frac{1}{I_b+1})U_b$$

where IC represents interrupt cost and other parameters are as previously described.

Future Work

APEX development has been driven primarily by the need to perform capably in a simulated air traffic control world (Freed and Remington, 1997), a task environment that is especially demanding on an agent's ability to manage multiple tasks. Applying the model to ever more diverse air traffic control scenarios has helped to characterize numerous factors affecting how multiple tasks should be managed. Many of these factors have been accounted for in the current version of APEX; many others have yet to be handled.

For example, the current approach sets a task's priority equals the maximum of its basis priorities. This is appropriate when all bases refer to the same underlying factor (e.g. being late to a meeting vs. being very late). However, when bases represent distinct factors, overall priority should derive from their sum. Although APEX does not presently include mechanisms for determining basis distinctness, PDL anticipates this development by requiring a basis description in each priority clause.

---

[2] Prioritization mechanisms also incorporate a factor designated *task refractory-state* representing reduced priority for a repeating task immediately following execution. The problem of managing repetition is not considered here.

Other prospective refinements to current mechanisms include allowing a basis to be suppressed if its associated factor is irrelevant in the current context, and allowing prioritization decisions to be made between compatible task groups rather than between pairs of tasks. The latter ability is important because the relative priority of two tasks is not always sufficient to determine which should be executed. For example: tasks A and B compete for resource X while A and C compete for Y. Since A blocks both B and C, their combined priority should be considered in deciding whether to give resources to A.

Perhaps the greatest challenge in extending the present approach will be to incorporate deliberative mechanisms needed to optimize multitasking performance and handle complex task interactions. The current approach manages multiple tasks using a heuristic method that, consistent with the sketchy planning framework in which it is embedded, assumes that little time will be available to reason carefully about task schedules. Deliberative mechanisms would complement this approach by allowing the agent to manage tasks more effectively when more time is available.

Acknowledgements

Thanks to Jim Johnston, Roger Remington, and Michael Shafto for their interest and support, and to Barney Pell for comments on a previous draft of this paper.

References

Cohen, P.R., Greenberg, M.L., Hart, D., and Howe, A.E. 1989. An Introduction to Phoenix, the EKSL Fire-Fighting System. EKSL Technical Report,. Department of Computer and Informational Science. University of Massachusetts, Amherst.

Firby, R.J. 1989. Adaptive Execution in Complex Dynamic worlds. Ph.D. thesis, Yale University.

Freed, M. & Remington, R.W. 1997. Managing Decision Resources in Plan Execution. In Proceedings of the Fifteenth Joint Conference on Artificial Intelligence, Nagoya, Japan.

Freed, M. 1998. Simulating human performance in complex, dynamic environments. Ph.D. thesis, Northwestern University.

Gat, Erann. 1992. Integrating planning and reacting in heterogeneous asynchronous architecture for controlling real-world mobile robots. In *Proceedings of 1992 National Conference on Artificial Intelligence.*

Georgeff, M and Lansky, A. 1987. Reactive Resoning and Planning: An Experiment with a Mobile Robot. *Proceedings of 1997 National Conference on Artificial Intelligence.*

Hayes-Roth, B. 1995. An architecture for adaptive intelligent systems. Artificial Intelligence, 72, 329-365.

Pell, B., Bernard, D.E., Chien, S.A.., Gat, E., Muscettola, N., Nayak, P.P., Wagner, M., and Williuams, B.C. 1997. An autonomous agent spacecraft prototype. *Proceedings of the First International Conference on Autonomous Agents*, ACM Press.

Schneider, W. and Detweiler, M. 1988. The Role of Practice in Dual-Task Performance: Toward Workload Modeling in a Connectionist/Control Architecture. *Human Factors*, 30(5): 539-566.

Simmons, R. 1994. Structured control for autonomous robots. *IEEE Transactions on Robotics and Automation.* 10(1).

Maintaining Consistency in Hierarchical Reasoning

Robert E. Wray, III and John Laird
Artificial Intelligence Laboratory
The University of Michigan
1101 Beal Ave.
Ann Arbor, MI 48109-2110
{robert.wray,laird}@umich.edu

Abstract

We explore techniques for maintaining consistency in reasoning when employing dynamic hierarchical task decompositions. In particular, we consider the difficulty of maintaining consistency when an agent non-monotonically modifies an assumption in one level of the task hierarchy and that assumption depends upon potentially dynamic assertions higher in the hierarchy. The hypothesis of our work is that reasoning maintenance can be extended to hierarchical systems such that consistency is maintained across all levels of the hierarchy. We introduce two novel extensions to standard reason maintenance approaches, *assumption justification* and *dynamic hierarchical justification*, both of which provide the necessary capabilities. The key difference between the two methods is whether a particular assumption (assumption justification) or an entire level of the hierarchy (dynamic hierarchical justification) is disabled when an inconsistency is found. Our investigations suggest that dynamic hierarchical justification has advantages over assumption justification, especially when the task decomposition is well-constructed. Agents using dynamic hierarchical justification also compare favorably to agents using less complete methods for reasoning consistency, improving the reactivity of hierarchical architectures while eliminating the need for knowledge that otherwise would be required to maintain reasoning consistency.

Introduction

A rational agent makes decisions to select actions that lead to the achievement of its goals given the current situation. For many tasks, these decisions can be simplified by dynamically decomposing the task into subtasks. Subtasks are further decomposed until the agent selects among primitive operators that perform actions in the world. The decomposition localizes knowledge and supports the sharing of subtasks, greatly simplifying the construction of the intelligent agent. Such *hierarchical decomposition* has been used in many agent architectures (Firby 1987; Georgeff & Lansky 1987; Laird, Newell, & Rosenbloom 1987) for execution tasks in complex, dynamic environments.

For example, TacAir-Soar (Tambe *et al.* 1995), which has been successfully used to simulate human pilots in large-scale distributed simulations, has over 450 tasks and subtasks in hierarchies that can grow to over 10 levels. Figure 1 shows how the task of intercepting an enemy plane is decomposed until a relatively simple decision can be made to turn the aircraft. Without the task decomposition, significantly more knowledge would be required for selecting each primitive operator in a vast number of particular task situations because the knowledge could not be localized to the subtasks and thus shared across many tasks.

In this work, we investigate the effect dynamic hierarchical task decompositions have upon the ability of an agent to maintain consistency in reasoning across hierarchy levels. In particular, we consider the inconsistency that can result when an agent needs to assert and possibly change a hypothetical assumption in one level of the hierarchy and that assumption also depends upon previously asserted knowledge higher in the hierarchy. If consistency is not maintained, reasoning in the subtasks can become unsituated, so that a subtask attempts to solve a problem that is no longer relevant to the current situation. Current hierarchical architectures do not automatically support fully dynamic "cross-level" reason maintenance and thus must rely upon programmer-developed consistency maintenance knowledge. This additional knowledge increases the effort to build the agent and the computation required to perform its reasoning.

We begin by reviewing reason maintenance methods in non-hierarchical systems and the challenges of ex-

---

Escort friendly planes
Intercept enemy plane(s)
Attack (defensive)
Achieve proximity
Turn to heading

Figure 1: Decomposition of behavior into subtasks.

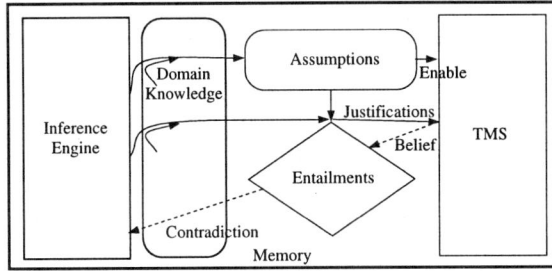

Figure 2: An simple, non-hierarchical agent.

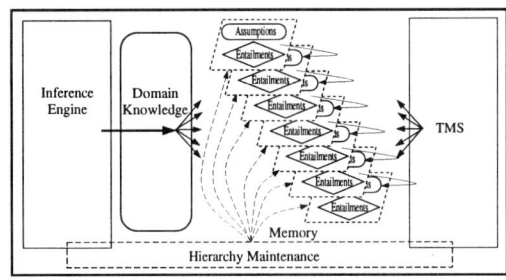

Figure 3: A hierarchical agent.

tending them to hierarchical systems. After examining a number of previous approaches and their limitations, we introduce two novel extensions to standard reason maintenance approaches: *assumption justification* and *dynamic hierarchical justification*. We analyze these methods and argue that dynamic hierarchical justification provides a better solution for dynamic tasks when good task decompositions are available. Using a research version of TacAir-Soar, we empirically compare the performance and knowledge requirements of an agent with dynamic hierarchical justification to agents with more limited reason maintenance techniques.

Reasoning Consistency in Non-Hierarchical Systems

In non-hierarchical agents, illustrated in Figure 2, an inference engine and truth maintenance system (TMS) (Doyle 1979; Forbus & deKleer 1993) work together to ensure reasoning consistency. Using domain (task) knowledge, the inference engine creates *assumptions*. An assumption is simply a fact that the inference engine wants to treat as being true in the world, even though such a belief is not necessarily entailed by the current state. The agent then *enables* the assumption, informing the TMS that it should treat the assumption as held belief. In order to maintain reasoning consistency, domain knowledge must be formulated such that no enabled assumptions are contradictory.

The inference engine also uses its domain knowledge and assumptions to make additional, monotonic inferences, or *entailments*. Entailments differ from assumptions because they are justified by prior assertions (assumptions and entailments). The inference engine communicates justifications to the TMS. The agent continues making inferences and may non-monotonically change its assumptions. The TMS recognizes when an entailment is no longer justified, and the entailment is removed from the set of currently believed facts. Thus, the agent relies on the truth maintenance system to maintain the consistency of entailments[1] while the inference system uses task knowledge to ensure consistency among unjustified assumptions.

---

[1]This capability is only one of several for which truth maintenance systems are employed.

Reasoning Consistency in Hierarchical Systems

This basic reason maintenance scheme can present difficulty in a hierarchical system, such as the one illustrated in Figure 3. In such an agent, the inference engine and TMS are chiefly identical to the non-hierarchical agent. For convenience, the specific actions of the inference engine and TMS are represented only with the arcs of solid, arrowed lines, although the functions are the same as in Figure 2.

When a subtask is attempted, a new level is created that will contain assumptions and entailments local to the subtask. Figure 3 includes a new component, "hierarchy maintenance," that is responsible for creating and retracting levels when subtasks are invoked and terminated. Hierarchy maintenance is represented in the diagram by the fan of dotted, arrowed lines. Implementations differ as to whether the maintenance is mediated by domain knowledge, TMS-like mechanisms, or other agent processes.

Within a specific level, reason maintenance can go on as before. However, the hierarchical structure adds a significant complication to the creation of assumptions. Assumptions in a flat system are not dependent on other assertions. However, in a hierarchical system, the assumptions at one level can be dependent on higher levels of the hierarchy. This dependence is shown in Figure 3 by the solid, arrowed lines extending from one level to the assumptions of the next level.

Changes in higher levels may invalidate the assumptions of lower levels. Further, for agents embedded in dynamic, exogenous domains, one expects the context to be changing almost continuously. The changing context is not problematic for entailments because TMS will retract any entailment not justified in the new context. However, the assumptions of one level must be managed to ensure that they are consistent with the current situation as defined by the assumptions, entailments, and sensor data of higher levels. If they are allowed to persist independent of context changes, the reasoning in a subtask can become irrelevant to the actual tasks being pursued.

```
        Escort friendly planes
          Intercept enemy plane(s)
            Count enemy planes
            Count friendly planes
            Attack (defensive)
              Achieve proximity
                ....
```

Figure 4: Trace of behavior leading to intercept tactic.

For example, consider a TacAir-Soar agent that is intercepting a group of enemy planes. For interception, we assume that there are three tactics, one of which the agent will pursue. The first tactic (scare) is to engage and attempt to scare away the enemy planes without using deadly force. This tactic is selected independent of the number of planes when the rules of engagement specify that deadly force should not be used. The second tactic (offensive attack) can be used when deadly force is allowed. It is appropriate when friendly planes outnumber or equal enemy planes. The third tactic (defensive attack) is used when enemy planes outnumber friendly planes and deadly force is permitted.

Now assume a specific scenario in which deadly force is permitted and the agent has decided to intercept. Figure 4 shows the resulting subtasks.[2] The agent must count the relevant enemy and friendly planes. We assume that determining a plane's "side" and its relevance to the count is sufficiently complex that entailment of the count is not possible. Thus, counting is necessarily non-monotonic, because a count must be replaced when incremented. We assume the agent determines that enemy planes outnumber friendly ones and the agent then selects `defensive attack`, leading to further decomposition.

Given this scenario, what happens if an enemy plane suddenly turns to flee, thus reducing the actual count of relevant enemy planes by one? The count maintained by the agent is now invalid but standard TMS reasoning is insufficient to retract the count, because it is an assumption, not an entailment. If the actual number of enemy and friendly planes is now equal, then the agent should switch its tactic to offensive attack. Continuing the defensive attack is not consistent with the agent's knowledge. Thus the agent needs to recognize the inconsistency and remove the existing count.

Previous Solutions

How can an agent accommodate unjustified assumptions while also ensuring consistent behavior with respect to its environment? We review three approaches.

---

[2]This task could be decomposed many different ways. We chose this specific decomposition to illustrate issues in reasoning maintenance.

Knowledge-based Assumption Consistency

An agent with a flat representation requires domain knowledge to ensure that its assumptions remain consistent. The same approach can be used to ensure reasoning consistency in a hierarchical agent by formulating explicit domain knowledge that recognizes potential inconsistencies and responds by removing assumptions. We call this approach *knowledge-based assumption consistency* (KBAC). With KBAC, a knowledge engineer must not only specify the conditions under which an assumption is asserted but also *all* the conditions under which it must be removed. In the interception example, the agent requires knowledge that disables all assumptions that depend upon the number of enemy airplanes when the enemy plane flees. To be complete, an agent must have knowledge of the potential dependencies between assumptions in a local level and any higher levels in the hierarchy. Thus, this knowledge must "cross" levels. As a result, the complexity necessary to represent all the dependencies explicitly in the domain knowledge can greatly lessen the advantages of hierarchical task decompositions

Limiting Assumptions

Another possibility is to limit the use of assumptions such that only monotonic assumptions are created in subtasks. In this case, regular truth maintenance can provide reasoning consistency in hierarchical architectures. Theo (Mitchell *et al.* 1991) is an extreme example of this approach where all reasoning is derived from the entailments of sensors. The drawback of this approach is that assumptions cannot be deliberately modified within subtasks. An assumption (e.g., one of the counts in the TacAir-Soar example) can be dependent on an earlier assumption within the level that was deliberately removed (the prior count). The new count should not be removed just because the earlier count was removed to make way for it. Non-monotonic assumptions are still possible in the initial level of the hierarchy. However, assumption consistency knowledge is necessary to maintain consistency among these assumptions, as in KBAC.

Fixed Hierarchical Justification

An alternative approach is to concentrate on ensuring that the reasons for initiating a level are still valid throughout the execution of the subtask, as illustrated in Figure 5. When each new level of the hierarchy is created, the architecture identifies assertions at each of the higher levels in the hierarchy that led to the creation of the new level. These assertions together form what we will call a "subtask support set" (or just "support set"). In Figure 5, assertions a_{14}, a_{15}, e_{14}, and e_{19} are the support set for $Level_2$ while a_{12}, a_{22}, e_{22} "support" $Level_3$. These support sets, in effect, form justifications for levels in the hierarchy. When an assertion in a support set is removed (e.g., a_{22}),

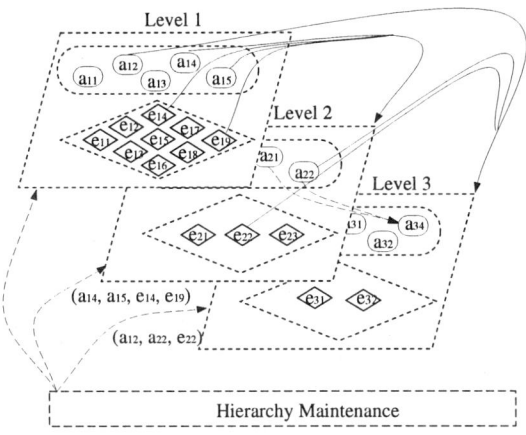

Figure 5: Fixed Hierarchical Justification

the agent responds by removing the level. Architectures such as PRS (Georgeff & Lansky 1987) and Soar (Laird, Newell, & Rosenbloom 1987) use architectural mechanisms to retract complete levels of the hierarchy when the support set no longer holds.

A significant disadvantage of the support set is that it is *fixed*, computed when the subtask is initiated but not updated as problem solving progresses. In Figure 5, suppose that assumption a_{34} depends upon assumptions a_{22} and a_{21} (represented in the figure by the dotted, arrowed lines). The support set does not include a_{21} (a_{21} may not have even been present when $Level_3$ was created.) Thus, approaches using *fixed hierarchical justification* (FHJ) either limit the subtask to testing only those aspects of the world used to initiate the subtask, or they require knowledge-based assumption consistency for assumptions in the subtask. The first method is insufficient in the TacAir-Soar example when there is a change in the number of enemy planes, which was not a precondition of deciding to intercept. Unfortunately, when a local assumption depends upon an assertion not in the support set, then a change in that assertion will not directly lead to the retraction of the assumption or the level. Fixed hierarchical justification does require less explicit reasoning consistency knowledge than the previous solutions but still requires it if access to the whole task hierarchy is possible (as it is in Soar). In either case, the agent's ability to make subtask-specific reactions to unexpected changes in the environment is limited by the knowledge designer's ability to anticipate and explicitly encode the consequences of those changes.

New Approaches for Reasoning Consistency in Hierarchical Systems

All the previous solutions required additional cross-level assumption consistency knowledge, provided by a programmer. We now present two new solutions for reasoning maintenance in hierarchical systems that will require no additional cross-level assumption consistency knowledge, allow locally unjustified, non-monotonic assumptions, and architecturally resolve potential inconsistencies. Both solutions assume that the agent can compute the higher level dependencies of every assumption in a subtask, requiring that the inference engine record every variable test made during the course of processing. In Soar, these calculations are available from its production rule matcher. However, these calculations may not be supported in other architectures, requiring modifications to the underlying inference engine.

Although we will explore these solutions in some depth, they represent only two points in the space of all possible solutions. Other approaches (including combinations of the new approaches) could be investigated as well. We were led to the first approach, assumption justification, by a desire for fine-grain reasoning maintenance where each assumption could be individually maintained or retracted as appropriate. We were led to the second approach when empirical (and belated theoretical) analysis suggested that fine-grain maintenance came at a significant computational overhead, and when we observed the structure of problem solving for well-decomposed tasks.

Assumption Justification

Assumption justification treats each assumption in the hierarchy as if it were an entailment with respect to assertions higher in the hierarchy. Locally, the assumption is handled exactly like an assumption in a flat system. However, each assumption is justified with respect to dependent assertions in higher levels. When this justification is no longer supported, the architecture retracts the assumption. For example, assumption a_{34} in Figure 5 depends upon a_{22} and a_{21}. We assume that a_{22} remains a member of the fixed support set of $Level_3$. Thus, if a_{22} is retracted, $Level_3$ (and thus a_{34}) is removed, as in fixed hierarchical justification. However, now when a_{34} is created, a justification for the assumption is built containing a_{22} and a_{21}. If a_{21} is retracted, the justification for a_{34} is no longer supported and a_{34} is retracted. Reasoning consistency is maintained across hierarchy levels because the assumption never persists longer than any higher level assertion used in its creation.

Creating assumption justifications requires computing dependencies for each assumption. The justification procedure must examine all the local assertions that contributed to the situation in which the assumption was created because assumption dependencies can be indirect. For example, the count in the TacAir-Soar example is dependent upon the previous count, so the dependencies of the prior count must be included in the dependency of the new count.

A complication arises when an assumption non-monotonically replaces another assumption. The ini-

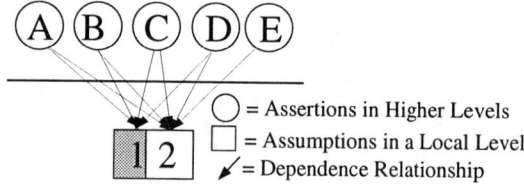

Figure 6: A non-monotonic assumption.

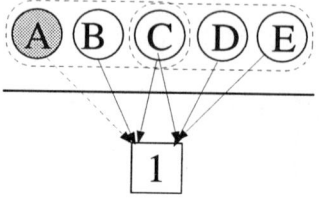

Figure 7: Multiple assumption justifications.

tial assumption must be disabled, rather than permanently deleted from memory, because this assumption must be restored if the second assumption is retracted. In Soar, this requires that an assumption be removed from the agent's primary or "working" memory but retained in a secondary memory. For example, in Figure 6, when **E** is asserted, **2** is asserted in the local level, replacing **1**. If **E** is removed, assumption justification will retract **2**, as desired, but it must also re-enable **1**, adding it back to the agent's working memory. Thus assumption **1** must remain in memory, although disabled. More concretely, consider again the TacAir-Soar example. When the enemy plane departs, the current count is retracted. However, the previous count must be re-enabled, because each iteration of the count non-monotonically replaced the previous one. For the prior count to be immediately available, the agent must store this prior assumption in memory. Assumption justification thus requires the storage of every subtask assumption during the subtask.

Figure 7 illustrates a second difficult problem. An assumption can have multiple dependency sets and these sets can change as problem solving progresses. Assumption **1** is initially dependent upon assertions **A**, **B**, and **C** in higher levels. Now assume that later in the processing, **A** is removed, which normally would result in the retraction of **1**. However, in the meantime, the context has changed such that **1** is now also justified by {**C, D, E**}. Now when **A** is removed, the architecture cannot immediate retract **1** but must determine if **1** is justified from other sources. Thus, as problem solving progresses within a level, new justifications of the local assumptions must be recognized and created as they occur.

The worst case complexity of creating a single assumption justification is $O(n)$, or linear in the number of assertions, n, in the level. Due to the issue we illustrated in Figure 6, n is bound not by the number of "active" assertions but by the total number of assertions made while the subtask is asserted. The worst case cost for building all the justifications in a particular level is $O(n^2)$, because the number of assumptions in a level is bounded by the number of assertions. Thus, the longer a particular subtask is active, the more likely assumption justification will begin to severely impact overall performance due to its complexity.

Further, when we added assumption justification to Soar, and tested it in Air-Soar (Pearson *et al.* 1993), a flight simulator domain, the overhead of maintaining all prior assumptions in a level negatively impacted agent performance. In this domain, assumption justification had significant computational cost, requiring 50% more time than the original for the same task. In addition, the number of assumption justifications maintained within a level continued to grow during execution. In Air-Soar, some levels could persist for many minutes as the plane performed a maneuver, leading to a continual increase in the amount of memory required. This experience, along with tests on simpler tasks, led us to consider other alternatives that had the potential of being computationally more efficient, in both time and memory.

Dynamic Hierarchical Justification

Our second solution provides a coarser-grain maintenance of assumptions in a level, finessing some of the complexities of assumption justification. Instead of maintaining support information for each individual assumption, our second solution maintains support information for the complete level. This decreases the complexity and memory requirements for the support calculations, but means that the complete level is retracted when any dependent assertion is removed, just as with fixed hierarchical justification. We call this solution dynamic hierarchical justification (DHJ), because the support set grows dynamically as assumptions are made for the subtask. When a_{34} in Figure 5 is created in a DHJ agent, the support set for $Level_3$ is updated to include a_{21}. Assumption a_{22} is already a member of the support set and does not need to be added again. When any member of the support set for $Level_3$ changes, the entire level will be retracted. Thus reasoning consistency under DHJ is enforced because a level in the hierarchy persists only as long as all higher-level dependent assertions.

Whenever a new assumption is created, the dependencies are determined as for assumption justification but are added now to the support set for the local level. As before, the worst case complexity to compute the dependencies is linear in the number of assertions already in the level. However, unlike assumption justification, DHJ requires at most one inspection of any individual assertion, because the dependencies of previously-inspected assertions already have been

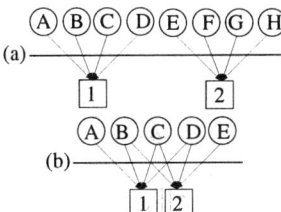

Figure 8: Examples of (a) independent dependencies and (b) intersecting assumption dependencies.

added to the subtask's support set. Thus, the worst case cost of computing the dependencies over all the assumptions in a level with DHJ remains $O(n)$.

DHJ is not impacted by the two technical problems we outlined for assumption justification. DHJ never needs to restore a previous assumption because when a dependency changes, the entire level is retracted. Thus, DHJ can immediately delete from memory nonmonotonically replaced assumptions. Secondly, DHJ collects all dependencies for assumptions, so there is no need to switch from one justification to another. In Figure 7, dependencies **A**, **B**, **C**, **D**, and **E** are all added to the support set. These simplifications can make the support set overly specific but reduce the memory and computation overhead incurred by assumption justification.

In DHJ, significant parts of a previous subtask will sometimes need to be re-derived if the retraction affected only a small part of the subtask assertions. In the TacAir-Soar agent, for example, if the enemy plane fled as we described, DHJ would retract the entire level associated with the counting subtask. The count would then need to be re-started from the beginning. Assumption justification, on the other hand, would retract only those assumptions that depended upon the presence of the departed plane. In the best case, if this plane was counted last, only the final count would need to be retracted, and no new counting would be necessary. The cost incurred through the *regeneration* of previously-derived assertions is the primary drawback of dynamic hierarchical justification. An initial implementation in Soar of DHJ in a blocks world domain suggested that DHJ cost little in performance or memory overhead, and did not suffer severe regenerations. We will present the results of applying DHJ to a more complex domain later in the discussion.

Influence of the Task Decomposition

Given the individual drawbacks of each of our solutions, can we chose one over another? Consider the examples in Figure 8. In (a), assumptions **1** and **2** each depend upon orthogonal sets of assertions. With assumption justification, removal of any assertion in **1**'s justification will result in the retraction of **1**; **2** is unchanged. Thus, assumption justification supports dependency-directed backtracking (Stallman & Sussman 1977) at the level of individual assumptions. On the other hand, with DHJ, the entire level is removed in this situation because all the dependent assertions are collected in the support set for the level. Further, if the same level is reinstated, assumption **2** may need to be regenerated as we described above. Thus, DHJ leads to a much coarser dependency-directed backtracking, with the grain size of a subtask.

In Figure 8 (b), the dependencies of assumptions **1** and **2** have a large intersection. If assertions **B**, **C**, or **D** change, then all the local assertions will be retracted, if we assume that everything in the local level is derived from **1** or **2**. In this situation, assumption justification pays the high overhead cost to track individual assumptions, when (most) everything in the local level is removed simultaneously. Because DHJ incurs no such overhead, DHJ is a better choice when the intersection between assumption dependencies is high.

In arbitrary domains, of course, we expect both intersecting and independent dependencies among different assumptions. However, among assumptions *in a particular subtask*, we can argue that (b) represents a better task decomposition than (a). The goal of a hierarchical decomposition is to separate, independent subtasks from one another. A consequence of this separation is that the the dependency between a subtask and higher levels in the hierarchy is minimized. In (a), two independent assumptions are being pursued, resulting in a more complex relationship between the two levels. In (b), on the other hand, the assumptions in the subtask are closely tied together in terms of their dependencies and represent more tightly focused problem solving. Thus, (b) represents a better decomposition than (a) because the total number of dependent assertions does not necessarily grow as a function of the assumptions in the local level, while in (a) it does.

To summarize, assumption justification excels when there are many orthogonal dependencies in a subtask, which represents a poor decomposition. DHJ compares favorably to assumption justification when the decomposition is a good one. In this situation, DHJ suffers from few unnecessary regenerations while avoiding the overhead costs of assumption justification. Another benefit of DHJ is that it can point out problem areas in the decomposition, acting as an aid for the development of better decompositions. We will return to this aspect of DHJ as we explore its impact in a representative task domain.

Empirical Analysis using TacAir-Soar

Based on our analysis and preliminary implementations, we decided to further investigate DHJ by testing it in a complex, dynamic agent domain, a research version of TacAir-Soar, called "micro-TacAir-Soar" (μTAS for short). μTAS agents use the TacAir-Soar simulator and interface but cannot fly the complete range of missions available in the full system.

	Lead Agent				Wing Agent			
	FHJ	DHJ_1	DHJ_2	FHJ_{dhj_2}	FHJ	DHJ_1	DHJ_2	FHJ_{dhj_2}
Rules	596	550	546	551	596	550	546	551
CPU Time (ms)	4358	19505	4453	4164	9840	23868	4562	6826
Rule Firings	1919	7312	1729	1891	11518	18711	4275	4955

Table 1: μTAS run data for lead and wing agents under different run-time architectures and knowledge bases.

However, μTAS uses the same tactics and doctrine as TacAir-Soar. In the restricted domain, a team of two agents ("lead" and "wing") fly a patrol mission and engage any hostile aircraft that meet their commit criteria (are headed toward them, and are within a specific range). Because there is no clearly-defined termination for this task, we ran each agent for a total of five minutes of simulator time. During this time, each agent had time to take off, fly in formation with its partner on patrol, intercept one enemy agent, and return to patrol after the intercept.

In comparing the performance of DHJ agents to agents originally developed for this domain under Soar's fixed hierarchical justification, we concentrate on three metrics. First, we measure the total number of rules required to generate comparable behavior. We expect the number of rules to decrease because no assumption consistency knowledge is necessary in the DHJ agents. Second, we look at the CPU time used in each agent. Differences in CPU time accurately reflect differences in agent computation because we used a fixed-time cycle in the simulator that guarantees the same number of execution opportunities for each agent in each run. Third, we looked at the total knowledge used during the task, easily measured in Soar as rule firings. If regeneration is high, we expect the knowledge used to increase.

Table 1 shows the results of running FHJ (the original Soar) and two different versions of DHJ agents. The columns labeled "DHJ_1" show the results of running DHJ agents with few changes to the agent's original (FHJ) knowledge. The DHJ_2 columns exhibit the results of running the simulation following a partial re-formulation of the agents' knowledge, which we describe below. The FHJ_{dhj_2} columns exhibit the results of running agents in the original FHJ architecture, but using the knowledge of the DHJ_2 agents.

As the table suggests, the initial DHJ_1 agents suffered from severe regeneration in the TacAir-Soar domain. This regeneration resulted in significant increases in the number of rule firings and similar increases in CPU time. The extra cost negatively impacted behavior when run with variable-time cycles: DHJ_1 agents more frequently missed their missile shots, took longer to perform the intercept, and thus exposed themselves to more risk than the FHJ agents.

Creating Better Decompositions

We examined the knowledge in these agents and found that the original decomposition violated a number of the assumptions we had made about "good" decompositions. We now provide two examples of poor decomposition and relate how DHJ, through regeneration, led us to improve the task decomposition, and, in turn, overall task performance.

The first example involves the way in which the agent generates motor commands for the plane. For example, the agent generates commands to turn to a new heading, as in Figure 1. This calculation usually depends upon the current heading. When the agent generates the command to turn, the heading changes soon thereafter. In DHJ, because this desired heading depends upon the current heading, the subtask that generated the command will be retracted when the heading changes, leading to many (unnecessary) regenerations for the same motor command.

The agent's knowledge is treating a global value (the motor command) as a local value. The motor command is not local to the subtask because it can (and often will) lead to changes throughout the context. For instance, the wing agent, whose job is to follow the lead agent in a particular formation, may initiate a turn when it realizes that the lead has begun to turn. Once the wing begins to turn, it will want to use the motor command (desired heading) to determine if further course changes are necessary. If the course correction is local, however, the wing cannot utilize this knowledge at higher levels.

In order to address this limitation, we made motor commands global rather than local in the agents. Because assumptions in the highest level of the hierarchy are unjustified (there can be no assertions in higher levels on which they depend), we returned all motor commands to this global level. The agent now has access to motor commands throughout the hierarchy and can make use of them in specific subtasks. No unnecessary regeneration occurs because the agent always has access to the current motor command and thus generates a new one only when the motor command would be different. The solution, of course, requires consistency knowledge because the motor commands are unjustified and thus must be explicitly removed. However, in this specific case, the agents always replaced old motor commands when generating new ones, so no additional consistency knowledge was necessary. In general, however, making a value global necessitates consistency knowledge to manage it.

The second example involves instances in which several serial tasks had been grouped as a single subtask, resulting in dependencies like those in Figure 8 (a). For example, pushing a button to launch a missile and waiting for a missile to clear the aircraft were combined into a single subtask. However, these tasks have different and mutually exclusive dependencies. `Push-fire-button` requires that no missile is already in the air. However, the subsequent waiting requires counting while the newly launched missile is in the air. In the FHJ agent, these activities could be combined because the absence of a missile in flight was not part of the local subtask's fixed support set. However, DHJ always removed the local level as soon as the missile was fired, leading to regeneration. We made the subtasks independent by creating a new subtask, `wait-for-missile-to-clear`, which depends only on having a newly launched missile in the air.

The knowledge changes made for DHJ_2 affected only a fraction of the agent's total knowledge (about 30% of the rules required some change), and they were easy to locate via regenerations. The DHJ_2 columns of Table 1 show that the rule firings decrease in the DHJ_2 agents in comparison to the FHJ agents, while CPU time increases only slightly (in the lead) and even decreases (in the wing). The significance of these results is: 1) The total number of rules required to encode the task is less than both the original FHJ and DHJ_1 agents. This demonstrates that DHJ is eliminating maintenance-specific knowledge, and that a good decomposition further decreases domain-specific knowledge. 2) The overhead for adding DHJ to the architecture is mostly offset by the decrease in knowledge utilization (rule firings). Further, when the amount of accessed knowledge can be decreased substantially, as it is in the wing agent, the overall computational cost, measured here as CPU time, actually decreases.

The rightmost column of data for each agent allows us to separate the costs and contributions of DHJ vs. the task decomposition. FHJ_{dhj_2} takes the reformulated task decomposition, and then adds the domain-specific reasoning maintenance knowledge required to run with FHJ (the original Soar architecture). There is no guarantee that the added knowledge is sufficient to handle all cross-level consistency maintenance issues, although it was sufficient for the scenarios we ran. Our results show that the task reformulation did contribute to the speed up in DHJ_2, but that the architectural mechanisms in DHJ_2 do not add significant overhead compared to the decrease in knowledge use they provide. An additional advantage of DHJ_2 over FHJ_{dhj_2} is that it is guaranteed to do the reasoning maintenance in subtasks correctly, while in FHJ_{dhj_2} it is done by knowledge added by hand.

Conclusions

Our empirical results demonstrate that DHJ can improve overall task performance while eliminating the need for cross-level assumption consistency knowledge. These results assume the availability of good task decompositions. The generality of these results is unclear, although we have found similar improvements with tasks other than μTAS. μTAS is a worthwhile example because it was not written by the authors of this paper, and it is representative of a larger, fielded AI system. However, the tradeoffs between regeneration and architectural calculation of finer-grain justifications across a much wider variety of tasks, with varying quality of task decompositions, is an open question and may lead to other variants of hierarchical support. However, for the tasks which we have examined thus far, DHJ is a sufficient solution, decreasing the demand for task specific knowledge, improving in efficiency, and guaranteeing consistency in hierarchical reasoning.

Should hierarchical reasoning maintenance be considered for other architectures that support hierarchical task decomposition? It depends on the details of the architecture. In Soar, the dependency calculations are easily computed because each assertion is generated by a rule. In other architectures, dependency calculations may be impossible or expensive. If dependencies can be calculated efficiently, DHJ has significant advantages: a guarantee of correct hierarchical reasoning maintenance and a decrease in knowledge specification and use.

References

Doyle, J. 1979. A truth maintenance system. *Artificial Intelligence* 12:231–272.

Firby, R. J. 1987. An investigation into reactive planning in complex domains. In *Proceedings of the National Conference on Artificial Intelligence*, 202–206.

Forbus, K. D., and deKleer, J. 1993. *Building Problem Solvers*. Cambridge, MA: MIT Press.

Georgeff, M., and Lansky, A. L. 1987. Reactive reasoning and planning. In *Proceedings of the National Conference on Artificial Intelligence*, 677–682.

Laird, J. E.; Newell, A.; and Rosenbloom, P. S. 1987. Soar: An architecture for general intelligence. *Artificial Intelligence* 33:1–64.

Mitchell, T. M.; Allen, J.; Chalasani, P.; Cheng, J.; Etzioni, O.; Ringuette, M.; and Schlimmer, J. C. 1991. Theo: A framework for self-improving systems. In VanLehn, K., ed., *Architectures for Intelligence*. Lawrence Erlbaum Associates. chapter 12, 323–355.

Pearson, D. J.; Huffman, S. B.; Willis, M. B.; Laird, J. E.; and Jones, R. M. 1993. A symbolic solution to intelligent real-time control. *Robotics and Autonomous Systems* 11:279–291.

Stallman, R. M., and Sussman, G. J. 1977. Forward reasoning and dependency-directed backtracking in a system for computer aided circuit analysis. *Artificial Intelligence* 9(2):135–196.

Tambe, M.; Johnson, W. L.; Jones, R. M.; Koss, F.; Laird, J. E.; Rosenbloom, P. S.; and Schwamb, K. 1995. Intelligent agents for interactive simulation environments. *AI Magazine* 16(1):15–39.

Acquisition of Abstract Plan Descriptions for Plan Recognition

Mathias Bauer
German Research Center for Artificial Intelligence (DFKI)
Stuhlsatzenhausweg 3
66123 Saarbrücken, Germany
bauer@dfki.de

Abstract

While most plan recognition systems make use of a plan library that contains the set of available plan hypotheses, little effort has been devoted to the question of how to create such a library. This problem is particularly difficult to deal with when only little domain knowledge is available—a common situation when e.g. developing a help system for an already existing software system. This paper describes how operational decompositions of plans can be extracted from a set of sample action sequences, thus providing the basis for automating the acquisition of plan libraries. Efficient algorithms for the approximation of optimal decompositions and experimental results supporting their feasibility are presented.

Introduction

Most plan recognition systems use a predefined set of plans to delimit the search space of potential plan hypotheses. In these cases plan recognition mainly amounts to determining a plan entry that covers the currently observed action sequence as one of its concrete instances. So far, relatively little work has been devoted to the question of how to actually *construct* such a plan library (Mooney 1988; Lesh & Etzioni 1996).

Creating an adequate representation of the plans in a given domain is a nontrivial task. Even when leaving aside completeness and optimality considerations, the knowledge engineer still has to find a concise plan representation supporting the recognition process. This is particularly difficult when sufficient domain knowledge about the actions and objects to be manipulated is not readily available, e.g. when a help system is to be developed for an already existing software system and the semantics of the various commands has to be determined a posteriori. This paper presents an approach to the automatic acquisition of abstract plan descriptions from logged action traces. The algorithms presented even work in the complete absence of domain knowledge, but can also make use of such information if provided. Based on the assumption that an element

Copyright ©1998, American Association for Artificial Intelligence (www.aaai.org). All rights reserved.

of a plan—i.e. an action or a constraint describing its internal structure—is *necessary* for its correct execution just in case it occurs in *all* possible action sequences forming an instance of this plan, the system tries to detect the common aspects of a number of sample logs at some level of abstraction, thereby incrementally establishing an intensional representation of a class of action sequences containing all the samples provided.

The rest of this paper is organized as follows. The next section characterizes a simple representation formalism for plans. Then the basic algorithms are introduced and empirical results supporting their feasibility are presented. Finally, related work is reviewed before the results are summarized and future work is discussed.

Plan Representation

The most basic step in plan recognition is the mapping of observed actions onto the available plan hypotheses. The important information on which actions form the elementary steps of a plan—that is, the "recipe" of how to achieve the associated goal—is contained in the so-called *plan decompositions*.[1] Obviously, a *good* plan representation covers all the essential conditions that have to be met by an observed action sequence in order to be recognized as belonging to a particular class of activities leading to some specific domain goal. Examples of such conditions include the actions involved, their temporal ordering, and structural relationships among the objects being manipulated. However, the description of a plan should not be excessively restrictive by containing conditions that are not crucial to the successful achievement of its associated goal. To summarize, an ideal plan decomposition is restrictive enough to discriminate competing hypotheses without limiting the whole bandwidth of possible behaviors subsumed.

Plans or *plan decompositions* are represented as tuples $\langle p, A_p, C_p \rangle$, where p is the name of a plan, A_p is a set of actions—either primitive or abstract—and C_p is a set of

---
[1] In the following, the notions of "plan" and "plan decomposition" will often be used as synonyms.

constraints regarding these actions such as conditions about temporal relationships among elements of A_p or restrictions regarding the objects manipulated by these actions. So, the complete information on how a given plan can be executed is represented without restricting it to one possible action sequence: p might, for example, describe a *non-linear plan* where the temporal ordering of the actions is only partial and thus allows for a number of concrete execution instances. Further types of abstraction contained in a plan decomposition include abstract actions and variable action arguments instead of domain constants.

Remark: This notion of a plan does not include preconditions or effects. One the one hand, these cannot be inferred without detailed knowledge about the semantics of actions. On the other hand, they are not absolutely required for plan recognition purposes—as is the case here—where the focus is on representing features that support the identification of user goals on the basis of observed user actions only.

Acquisition of Plan Decompositions

For the following discussion the existence of three kinds of domain knowledge is assumed. D is a logical theory describing general aspects of the given domain like information about structure and types of domain objects. Additionally D_t and D_a represent an *object type* and *action type hierarchy*, resp., containing information about abstraction relations between the types of domain objects and actions.[2]

The operation msa yielding the most specific *non-trivial* common abstraction of a set of concepts (either object types or action types) is defined on D_t and D_a. Let $t_1, ..., t_n$ be object types. Then $msa(\{t_1, ..., t_n\}) =$

$$\begin{cases} t', \text{if } mss(\{t_1, ..., t_n\}) = \{t'\} \text{ and } t' \neq root(D_t) \\ msa(\{t'_1, ..., t'_m\}), \text{if } mss(\{t_1, ..., t_n\}) = \{t'_1, ..., t'_m\} \\ \qquad \text{and } m > 1 \\ \text{undefined, otherwise} \end{cases}$$

where mss is the *most specific subsumer* operation (Woods & Schmolze 1991) computing the set of least general concepts subsuming the disjunction of concepts contained in its argument (the same applies to D_a). If no hierarchical information is available (i.e. if D_t or $D_a = \emptyset$), then $msa(\{x_1, ..., x_n\}) = x_1$ if $x_i = x_1$ for all $1 \leq i \leq n$. Otherwise its value is undefined.

As will become clear from the following discussion, any component of the potentially available domain knowledge may be empty, that is, the mechanism to be presented will also work without additional information.

---

[2]It is important to distinguish between the notions of an *action* or *action instance* and an *action type*. In the UNIX domain, for example, "cp paper.tex /tmp" is a concrete, observable instance of the action type cp. In this case the file paper.tex is copied to another directory.

Input Data

Assume a number of test subjects (e.g. software testers, students) are given a set of goals $g_1, ..., g_m$ to be achieved. Their attempts in doing so are recorded and grouped according to common goals. Let $AS_1, ..., AS_N$ be the set of action sequences belonging to some goal g. Each of these sequences consists of a set of temporally ordered actions $\hat{a}_1, ..., \hat{a}_{l_j}$ where $\hat{a}_i = a_i(o_{i1}, ..., o_{in_i})$. Here a_i is the *action type* this particular observed instance belongs to (e.g. ls or cd in a UNIX context), and the various o_{ij} are constants representing the domain objects being manipulated (the action parameters). In the current version, the actions are assumed to be represented in a canonical way, i.e. with a fixed number of parameters for each action type.

In a first step, these action sequences are transformed into labeled graphs G_{AS_i} making the interrelationships among the constituents of AS_i explicit. While the action instances contained in AS_i form the nodes, there are two types of edges. An edge $\hat{a}_i \stackrel{<}{\rightarrow} \hat{a}_j$ represents the temporal order between both actions (in this case $\hat{a}_i$ occurs before $\hat{a}_j$), while an edge $a_i(o_{i1}, ..., o_{in_i}) \stackrel{\langle p,k,l \rangle}{\longrightarrow} a_j(o_{j1}, ..., o_{jn_j})$ represents the fact that relation p holds between the action arguments o_{ik} and o_{jl}. The resulting *action graph* then has the form $G_{AS_i} = \langle AS_i, T_i \cup S_i \rangle$ with a set of *temporal edges* $T_i = \{\hat{a}_i \stackrel{<}{\rightarrow} \hat{a}_j \mid i < j\}$ and a set of *structural edges* $S_i = \{\hat{a}_i \stackrel{\langle p,k,l \rangle}{\longrightarrow} \hat{a}_j \mid D \models p(o_{ik}, o_{jl})\}$. If $D = \emptyset$, i.e. if no domain knowledge is provided, only the equality of two objects can be recognized and made explicit within S_i.

Example: If $\hat{a}_1 = ls(/opt)$[3] and $\hat{a}_2 = cd(/opt/bin)$ then—assuming availability of the corresponding domain knowledge—an edge between $\hat{a}_2$ and $\hat{a}_1$ labeled $\langle subdir\_of, 1, 1 \rangle$ indicating that the first argument of $\hat{a}_2$ is a subdirectory of the first argument of $\hat{a}_1$ can be established.

The Abstraction Mechanism

As already mentioned, a good plan representation is limited to those elements that are absolutely necessary in order to reach some specific goal and thus have to be contained in *each* concrete execution of this plan. Given only a finite set of sample action sequences, the necessity of an element can only be approximately determined; if it occurs in all sequences *available*, it *might* be necessary. As a consequence, an approximation of the "ideal" plan decomposition can be created by determining those aspects—actions, temporal and structural relations—that are common to all samples and representing them at some level of abstraction. To this end, the components of two action graphs are compared pairwise and—provided they satisfy some compatibility condition—are included in the result in an abstract

---

[3]This is the internal representation of the UNIX shell command "ls /opt" displaying the contents of directory /opt.

form. The *join* operator defined in the following performs the required tests.

Let $G_1 = \langle A_1, T_1 \cup S_1 \rangle$ and $G_2 = \langle A_2, T_2 \cup S_2 \rangle$ be two action graphs. Let $\hat{a}_i = a_i(o_{i1}, ..., o_{in}) \in A_i, i = 1, 2$. Then $join(\hat{a}_1, \hat{a}_2) = a(o_1, ..., o_n)$ where $a = msa(\{a_1, a_2\})$ and for all $1 \leq i \leq n$:

- $o_{1i} = o_{2i} = o_i$ is a constant or
- o_i is a variable of type $msa(\{type(o_{1i}), type(o_{2i})\})$.

That is, the abstract representation of the common information contained in two action instances $\hat{a}_1$ and $\hat{a}_2$ is a new action instance the type of which is the msa of both action types—if defined—and the arguments of which are either a concrete domain object represented by a constant o_i (if both actions had the same object as a parameter in the same place) or a newly introduced variable the type of which is determined from the types of the originally occurring domain action arguments.

A temporal or structural edge is considered to be common to both G_1 and G_2 iff the corresponding action nodes to which the edge is incident could be joined using the above criterion. That is,

$$join(\hat{a}_{11} \xrightarrow{\leq} \hat{a}_{12}, \hat{a}_{21} \xrightarrow{\leq} \hat{a}_{22}) = \hat{a}_1 \xrightarrow{\leq} \hat{a}_2$$

if $join(\hat{a}_{11}, \hat{a}_{21}) = \hat{a}_1$ and $join(\hat{a}_{12}, \hat{a}_{22}) = \hat{a}_2$ and undefined otherwise. The join of two structural edges with identical labels is defined analogously.

Summarizing, the abstraction of two action sequences represented as action graphs G_1 and G_2 is $join(G_1, G_2) = \langle A, T \cup S \rangle$ where

$$A = \{join(\hat{a}_{1i}, \hat{a}_{2j}) \mid \hat{a}_{1i} \in A_1, \hat{a}_{2j} \in A_2\}$$
$$T = \{join(e_{t1}, e_{t2}) \mid e_{t1} \in T_1, e_{t2} \in T_2\}$$
$$S = \{join(e_{s1}, e_{s2}) \mid e_{s1} \in S_1, e_{s2} \in S_2\}$$

Remarks: 1. The *join* operator is associative and commutative. This is important for the definition of an incremental procedure to the acquisition of plan decompositions. Its complexity is $O(|A_1| \cdot |A_2| + |T_1| \cdot |T_2| + |S_1| \cdot |S_2|)$.
2. It is straightforward to transform $join(G_1, G_2)$ into a plan decomposition by simply reversing the preprocessing step described above.

Example: Assume the action sequences AS_1 and AS_2 as depicted in Figure 1 are given. For sake of simplicity, only structural and direct temporal edges connecting subsequent actions are shown. That is, temporal edges like the one between a1 and a3 are left out. Action arguments like "spag_1" refer to particular domain objects. The domain knowledge available is limited to an action hierarchy containing the relation tuples $\langle$make_spaghetti,make_pasta$\rangle$, $\langle$make_fettucini,make_pasta$\rangle$, $\langle$make_pesto,make_sauce$\rangle$, and $\langle$make_marinara,make_sauce$\rangle$ which introduce the abstract actions make_pasta and make_sauce each of which

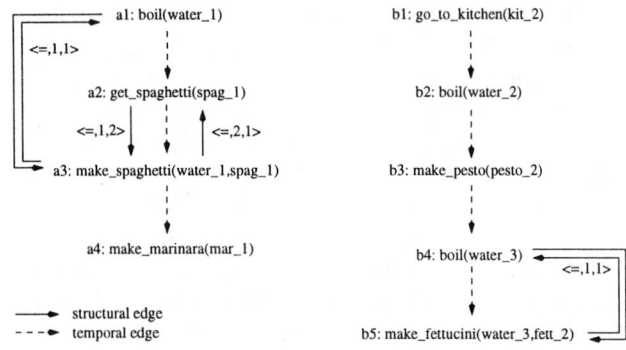

Figure 1: Two action sequences from the "cooking world".

subsumes two of the actions contained in the sample sequences. The following action joins can be computed using the above operator.[4]

α_1: $join$(a1,b2) = $boil(x_1)$
α_2: $join$(a1,b4) = $boil(x_2)$
α_3: $join$(a3,b5) = $make\_pasta(x_3, x_4)$
α_4: $join$(a4,b3) = $make\_sauce(x_5)$

Additionally the following temporal and structural edges are contained in the join of G_{AS_1} and G_{AS_2}.

$$\alpha_1 \xrightarrow{\leq} \alpha_4 \quad \alpha_1 \xrightarrow{\leq} \alpha_3 \quad \alpha_2 \xrightarrow{\leq} \alpha_3$$
$$\alpha_2 \xrightarrow{\langle =,1,1 \rangle} \alpha_3 \quad \alpha_3 \xrightarrow{\langle =,1,1 \rangle} \alpha_2$$

Let's have a closer look at the last temporal edge. Action a1 occurred before a3 in AS_1 and b4 was before b5 in AS_2. Joining a1 with b4 and a3 with b5 yielded α_2 and α_3, resp. As a consequence, the temporal relationship between the boiling of water and the respective making of pasta—the water must be boiled *before* the noodles can be cooked—could be recognized as common to both action sequences.

As obviously at most one boil action is necessary—otherwise AS_1 would have contained more than one occurrence—it is not desirable to include both α_1 and α_2 in the plan decomposition. Generally speaking, each action may be joined with at most one action from the other sequence.

Definition 1: A *valid join* of two action graphs $G_1 = \langle A_1, T_1 \cup S_1 \rangle$ and $G_2 = \langle A_2, T_2 \cup S_2 \rangle$ is a maximum subgraph $\langle A_v, T_v \cup S_v \rangle$ of $join(G_1, G_2)$ such that $\forall a_1 \in A_1, a_2 \in A_2$: if $join(a_1, a_2) \in A_v$ then $\forall a'_1 \in A_1, a'_2 \in A_2 : join(a'_1, a_2) \notin A_v$ and $join(a_1, a'_2) \notin A_v$. □

Example (contd.): Two valid joins exist in the above example:

$$G_{v1} = \langle \{\alpha_1, \alpha_3, \alpha_4\}, \{\alpha_1 \xrightarrow{\leq} \alpha_4, \alpha_1 \xrightarrow{\leq} \alpha_3\} \rangle$$
$$G_{v2} = \langle \{\alpha_2, \alpha_3, \alpha_4\},$$
$$\{\alpha_2 \xrightarrow{\leq} \alpha_3, \alpha_2 \xrightarrow{\langle =,1,1 \rangle} \alpha_3, \alpha_3 \xrightarrow{\langle =,1,1 \rangle} \alpha_2\} \rangle$$

---
[4]The various x_i denote variables that are untyped due to missing type information.

While G_{v1} represents more temporal information than G_{v2}, the latter additionally reflects the structural interdependencies between the boil and the make_pasta actions by making explicit the fact that the previously boiled water is exactly the one used for cooking the noodles.

Remarks: 1. Each valid join of a given pair of action sequences has the same number of actions.

2. Plan libraries of existing plan recognition systems often contain alternative decompositions for single plans when the associated goals can be achieved in a number of ways differing significantly from each other. As a consequence action sequences observed during the execution of these alternatives will have little in common, that is, applying the join operator is likely to produce trivial results containing only a small number of common concepts. To deal with this problem, a similarity test between the action graphs currently under consideration is performed. The join will be computed just in case the percentage of actions that can be joined exceeds a certain threshold for both sequences.

3. As each valid join is an action graph itself, the join operator can also be used to form a common abstraction of the results of two or more previous steps. This way, to use the well-known "cooking world" example from (Kautz 1991), joining the abstract plan descriptions for making pasta and meat dishes, resp., the even more abstract plan of preparing a meal can be derived without having to restart the whole process beginning with the sample action sequences.

Abstraction Heuristics

In realistic applications like command traces from the UNIX domain with 20 or more steps, the number of valid joins quickly becomes intractable. So a criterion is needed to characterize the various alternatives and efficiently compute the desired variant without enumerating all possibilities. Depending on the application context in which the plan recognition system will work, at least two interesting alternatives exist. If, for example, the system is to monitor an agent's activity in order to recognize suboptimal behavior, it is important to detect deviations from the intended way at an early stage. To this end, it is important for the plan decompositions to be as restrictive as possible. In a help system context, however, it may be desirable to be more lenient towards spurious actions of the user as long as his/her acting is somehow related to the hypothesized plan. In this case the plan decompositions should contain as few constraints as possible in order to cover a wide spectrum of possible user behaviors.

The *degree of restrictiveness* of a candidate plan description can be quantified using the function

$$deg_r(\langle A, T \cup S \rangle) = w_a \cdot |A| + w_p \cdot |PA| + w_t \cdot |T| + w_s \cdot |S|.$$

$PA \subseteq A$ is the set of *primitive actions* contained in A, i.e. those that do not abstract another domain action in the abstraction hierarchy D_a. If $D_a = \emptyset$, PA and A are obviously identical. The *non-negative* numerical weights w_a, w_p, w_t, and w_s assess the relative influence of the various components of a plan description. The degree of restrictiveness deg_r monotonically decreases with each join operation.

Example (contd.): Assuming the values $w_a = 1$, $w_p = 1$, $w_t = 1$, and $w_s = 2$, the resulting values for the valid joins G_{v1} and G_{v2} as computed above are

$$deg_r(G_{v1}) = 6, \quad deg_r(G_{v2}) = 9.$$

Here structural constraints are considered more important than temporal ones when comparing the restrictiveness of various decompositions. So the most restrictive plan decomposition is G_{v2} which represents the partially ordered abstract plan with the actions boil(x), make_pasta(x,y), and make_sauce(z) and the additional conditions that the first occurs before the second and both share their first action parameter.

The optimal choice according to maximum/minimum value of deg_r can be reliably approximated using two heuristics. After computing the join of the action graphs G_1 and G_2, the resulting nodes are numerically assessed using the same parameters as in deg_r:

$$deg_n(a) = w_a + w_p \cdot \delta_a + w_t \cdot |T_a| + w_s \cdot |S_a|. \quad (1)$$

Here δ_a is 1 if a contains a primitive action and 0 otherwise. T_a (S_a) is the subset of temporal (structural) edges of $join(G_1, G_2)$ incident to a. For the first heuristic, APL$^+$, approximating the selection of the most restrictive valid join, all action nodes of $join(G_1, G_2)$ are sorted according to *decreasing* value of (1). Then action nodes are taken from this ordered list starting with the highest deg_n values and added to the result without violating the condition of unique action joins from Definition 1. Eventually, the corresponding temporal and structural edges are added.

For the second heuristic, APL$^-$, approximating the selection of the least restrictive valid join the action nodes are sorted according to *increasing* values of (1), that is, those with the smallest deg_n values are added first.

Experimental Results

The performance of both heuristics can be read from Figures 2 and 3. In the first case the test data were UNIX command sequences mainly collected at the University of Washington containing up to 24 steps. For these tests, 8 collections each containing 11 sequences with identical associated goals were joined. This was repeated 10 times with randomly permuted input sets. The average degree of restrictiveness after each join is depicted relative to the maximum value that could be reached after 10 joins (this value is depicted as 100%). The "max" and "min" curves represent the respective deg_r values of the actually most and least restrictive valid joins (that is, the final value of "max" corresponds to 100%). Obviously both APL$^+$ and APL$^-$

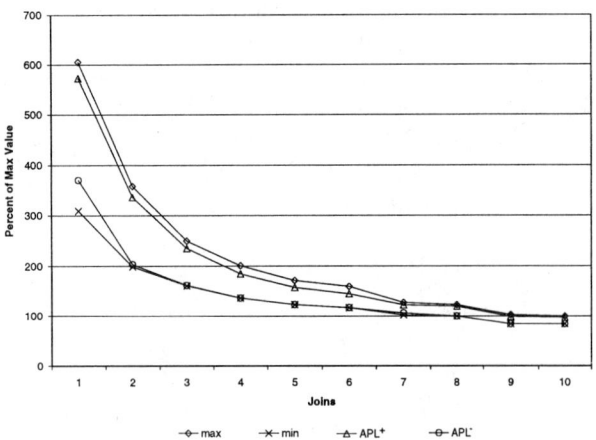

Figure 2: Performance of APL$^+$ and APL$^-$ in the UNIX domain.

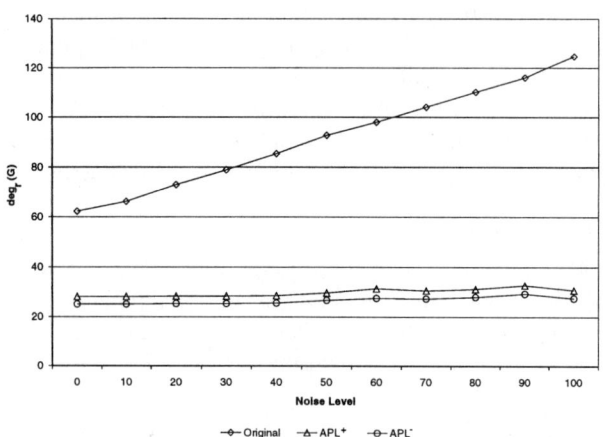

Figure 4: Impact of noise on APL$^+$ and APL$^-$.

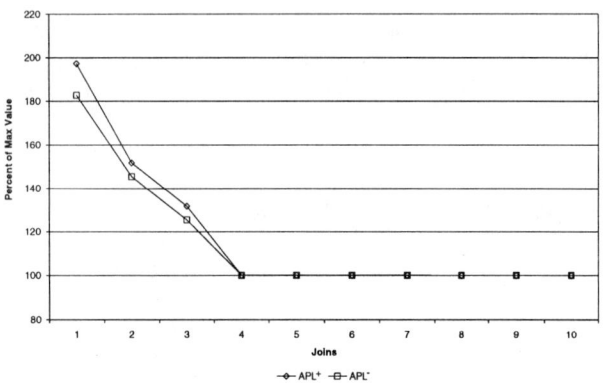

Figure 3: Performance of APL$^+$ and APL$^-$ in the cooking world.

yield almost optimal results. Additionally, this figure shows that the observed action sequences contained a huge number of spurious commands (in this case mostly "sensory" commands like `ls`) that could be "abstracted away".[5]

In the second case, identical tests as above were performed using artificially generated action sequences for the 5 basic and 4 abstract goals contained in the "cooking-world" library (Kautz 1991, Section 2.2.2) including spurious actions like leaving the kitchen to answer the phone. These sequences contained about 7 actions on average. The number of valid joins turned out to be much smaller than in the UNIX domain.[6] As a consequence, both APL$^+$ and APL$^-$ produce optimal results, i.e. their curves in Figure 3 are identical to the max and min curves, resp. Additionally, the optimum value (corresponding to the 100% line) is reached after only 4 joins.

Figure 4 depicts the impact of noise on the performance of both heuristics in the UNIX case. The same data as above were enhanced by a certain percentage—ranging from 0 to 100—of spurious actions and corresponding temporal and structural constraints.[7] This is reflected in the upper-most curve representing the average deg_r values of the modified sample sequences. The other curves depict the average deg_r values after 10 joins as in the experiment described above. As could be expected, both heuristics are only minimally affected as elements not occurring in *all* input sequences are filtered out.

Besides these quantitative aspects, the *quality* of plan decompositions produced may not be neglected. Applying APL$^+$ to the cooking world sequences yielded results that in most cases were equivalent to the decompositions presented in (Kautz 1991). The number of samples required to reach this level of precision was between 4 and 10. First experiments in both domains suggest that the acquired plans can indeed be successfully used by a plan recognition system (Bauer 1996).

Remark: An additional speedup can be reached by sorting the input sequences according to their lengths—the number of actions occurring—and first joining the shortest sequences.

Related Work

There has been a number of approaches devoted to generalizing problem solutions to create plans to be reused for efficient planning from second principles (e.g. (Minton 1985)). As a consequence an exact characterization of their preconditions and effects is required that has to be extracted from the semantics of the domain actions. In the context of the approach discussed in this paper—acquisition of discriminating schemata for plan recognition in scarcely modeled

---

[5] The average maximum degree of restrictiveness after 10 joins is only about one sixth of the value after the first join.

[6] This is mostly due to the fact that activities in the kitchen domain were more goal-directed as they did not involve a lengthy "navigation phase" as was the case in the first test.

[7] That is, in the highest noise level, each action sequence contained the double number of actions and constraints compared to the original.

domains—this knowledge is usually not available.

(Yoshida & Motoda 1995) describes how a graph representing a UNIX user's typical behavior can be learned from sample action sequences. *Graph-based induction* identifies common patterns in these traces. Using transition probabilities between the various nodes (actions), the user's next command can be predicted. However, only the use of deep domain knowledge guarantees a high prediction accuracy. While the notion of *plans* plays no role, these might be extracted by following the most probable paths through the graph.

(Bauer 1996) describes how both qualitative and quantitative information about a user's typical reaction to certain situations can be gained from an interaction history. The resulting model of the user's *preferences* is used to improve focusing during the plan recognition process. One drawback is that, as usual, the existence of a fixed plan library is assumed without indicating how it might be constructed.

In (Albrecht *et al.* 1997) dynamic Bayesian networks are used to map the behaviors of players in a multi-user dungeon to the goals ("quests") currently being pursued. While the set of possible goals can be completely enumerated, the enormous number of actions and places renders any attempt to create a complete domain model futile. As a consequence, there is no such thing as an operational description of the various possible ways to achieve a particular goal. Instead, given a set of sample action sequences, the current quest is predicted on the basis of statistical correlations between the previous quest and the current location and action. This method demonstrates its feasibility in a scenario where there is no standard way to reach a particular goal state. In a help system context, however, it is of little use to merely recognize the intended plan/goal if the system cannot give hints on what has to be done next.

(Mooney 1988) uses explanation-based learning (EBL) to generalize the plans underlying short narratives. As EBL is a knowledge-intensive technique, its feasibility is limited to well-formalized domains.

In (Lesh & Etzioni 1996) the goal and plan libraries are only *implicitly* defined by a set of goal predicates and actions and a corresponding goal and plan *bias* that allow the search space to be enumerated. While this enables the application of efficient search algorithms in the version space so constructed, doing so has at least two drawbacks. First, the system is not able to handle plans for *arbitrary* domain goals. Second, complete planning knowledge is required in order to determine the consistency of an observed action with the hypothesized goals. That is, a perfect description of all the preconditions and effects of each action to be observed has to be provided.

Conclusion and Future Work

This paper presented an approach towards the acquisition of plan decompositions from logged action sequences. The necessity of an action (or condition) that is manifested by its occurrence in *all* possible action sequences instantiating an abstract plan description is approximated by is presence in all sample data.

The mechanism presented can make use of various kinds of domain knowledge without being dependent on their availability. That is, minimum input data are sufficient to come up with approximated plan decompositions the quality of which can be improved by exploiting information about the elements occurring in a given domain. In case no domain knowledge is provided, the plan decompositions will exclusively contain basic actions. In this case the abstraction is limited to removing unnecessary temporal and structural relations among actions and replacement of domain constants by variables. Empirical tests demonstrated that the optimal choice of a most or least restrictive plan decomposition can be efficiently approximated within given bounds.

Future work will be devoted to handling a richer set of temporal relations and control structures like loops within plan decompositions. Additionally, the acquisition of abstraction relations among plans—an important component of plan *hierarchies*—will be a central topic.

Acknowledgments

I would like to thank Hiroshi Motoda and Neal Lesh for providing rich test data from the UNIX domain and Dietmar Dengler and the anonymous reviewers for their valuable comments.

References

Albrecht, D.; Zukerman, I.; Nicholson, A.; and Bud, A. 1997. Towards a Bayesian Model for Keyhole Plan Recognition in Large Domains. *User Modeling 97*, 365–376.

Bauer, M. 1996. Acquisition of User Preferences for Plan Recognition. *User Modeling 96*, 105–112.

Kautz, H. 1991. A Formal Theory of Plan Recognition and its Implementation. In *Reasoning About Plans*. Morgan Kaufmann. chapter 2.

Lesh, N., and Etzioni, O. 1996. Scaling up goal recognition. *KR96*, 178–189.

Minton, S. 1985. Selectively Generalizing Plans for Problem-Solving. *IJCAI 85*, 596–599.

Mooney, R. 1988. *A General Explanation-Based Learning Mechanism and its Application to Narrative Understanding*. Ph.D. Diss., Univ. of Illinois, Urbana.

Woods, W., and Schmolze, J. 1991. The KL-ONE family. *Computers and Mathematics with Applications* 23(2-5):133–177.

Yoshida, K., and Motoda, H. 1995. CLIP: concept learning from inference patterns. *Artificial Intelligence* 75:63–92.

Needles in a Haystack : Plan Recognition in Large Spatial Domains Involving Multiple Agents

Mark Devaney and Ashwin Ram

College of Computing
Georgia Institute of Technology
Atlanta, GA 30332-0280
markd@cc.gatech.edu
ashwin@cc.gatech.edu

Abstract

While plan recognition research has been applied to a wide variety of problems, it has largely made identical assumptions about the number of agents participating in the plan, the observability of the plan execution process, and the scale of the domain. We describe a method for plan recognition in a real-world domain involving large numbers of agents performing spatial maneuvers in concert under conditions of limited observability. These assumptions differ radically from those traditionally made in plan recognition and produce a problem which combines aspects of the fields of plan recognition, pattern recognition, and object tracking. We describe our initial solution which borrows and builds upon research from each of these areas, employing a pattern-directed approach to recognize individual movements and generalizing these to produce inferences of large-scale behavior.

Introduction

Plan recognition, the problem of inferring goals, intentions, or future actions given observations of ongoing behavior, has been widely studied in Artificial Intelligence in the context of a number of different applications. Some of these applications include the inference of a user's beliefs in natural language or story understanding (e.g., Di Eugenio 1995), inference of a user's intents in intelligent user interfaces (e.g., Wærn 1996), identification of an autonomous agent's goal in order to coordinate activity (e.g., Huber and Durfee 1995), and for program understanding in the field of software engineering (e.g., Woods and Yang 1998).

However, even in these diverse application contexts, three major assumptions are typically made:

Single agent The plan is being carried out by a single agent acting alone. Work in "multi-agent" plan recognition shares this assumption as well, the distinction being that an agent is considering the possible *individual* plans of several agents (e.g., Huber and Durfee 1995; Tambe 1995) or that there are other agents active in the world which may be causing changes (e.g., Traum and Allen 1991).

Complete and correct information The observations available are correct, i.e., they correspond to the actual behavior of the observed agent, and they are complete, i.e., no actions were performed which were not noticed. This assumption generally follows from the assumption that the watched agent is either actively facilitating observation ("intended plan recognition") or is at least not actively obstructing it ("keyhole plan recognition").

Small-scale data The input to the recognition process comes from a fairly limited set of potential actions and occurs over relatively short time periods. This assumption, particularly when combined with the single agent assumption, allows use of computationally intensive methods such as exhaustive search, probabilistic methods, and reasoning from first principles.

In contrast, we are researching the problem of plan recognition in a very complex real-world domain in which these assumptions do not hold. Specifically, we are concerned with methods which may be used to identify and predict behaviors in a domain involving hundreds of agents moving together over large distances and long time scales and in which the observer receives noisy and incomplete observational data.

The problem presents an interesting combination of issues from plan and pattern recognition, agent and object tracking, qualitative representation, and geographical information system (GIS) theory. We are interested in investigating how the task of plan recognition can be accomplished when traditional assumptions do not hold, a situation we expect to become increasingly prevalent as domains of research are expanded to more real-world scenarios.

Problem description

The domain in which we are conducting our research consists of data obtained from training battles conducted by actual troops at the US Army's National Training Center (NTC). These battles involve hundreds of participants, last several days, and take place over a very large geographical area. The problem is constrained such that the only input available to the recognition system is limited to low-level telemetry information – positions of participants (with identifiers) over time, as would be the case with human observation of the same battles. In particular, we make no assumptions about the availability of information such as terrain, weather conditions, etc., which could be useful but cannot be assumed to exist in many real world situations.

Copyright ©1998, American Association for Artificial Intelligence (www.aaai.org). All rights reserved.

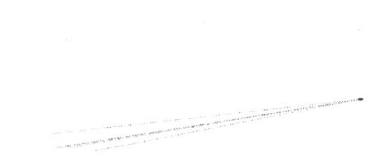

Figure 1: The needle : a gathering maneuver

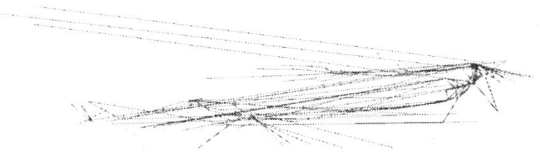

Figure 2: The haystack : all movements

The task of our research is to identify from this data repeated patterns of movement which correspond to planned "maneuvers" being executed by the participants. This is possible because military doctrine, much like plays in football, largely consists of prescribed sets of tactical maneuvers which are executed in fairly stereotypical ways. The observed battles are not random melees but are the (largely) purposeful actions of intelligent agents acting in pursuit of high level goals or plans. The execution of these plans requires coordinated activities which generate identifiable patterns of movement that can be employed by a recognition process to both identify these plans and predict future movements.

To illustrate the nature of the problem, figure 1 is an example of a short-term maneuver corresponding to a meeting in which a significant number of agents collect at a point, most likely in preparation for some future coordinated activity. The lines indicate the paths traveled by the participating units and the (small) circle spatially bounds their ending points.

The difficulty of performing this recognition is shown by figure 2 which depicts all of the input data up to the time at which the gathering occurred, the space of information from which the maneuver must be "picked out". This corresponds to the paths of each unit from the beginning of the battle to the time the meeting occurs.

Working with domain experts, we have identified several such strategic patterns which our system needs to isolate and recognize during the course of actual battles. Both the inherent qualities of the domain and the realities of collecting data from the real world require assumptions fundamentally different from those usually made in plan recognition research:

Multiple agents The step-by-step actions of individual agents are significantly less important than the coordinated activities of *groups* of agents. In complex multi-agent domains, "interesting" maneuvers require the simultaneous participation of multiple agents, and furthermore, these maneuvers are very often only representable as relationships between agents and not as agglomerations of identical actions performed by single agents. For example, "meeting at a location" is an inherently multi-agent maneuver and one which is independent of the specific details of the movements of any of the individual agents involved. Moreover, the agents participating in the meeting maneuver will have a wide variety of patterns of movement and it is only when considered in relation to the other participants do they have "meaning". The degree of noise in the input can also be a factor in the choice to disregard the actions of individual agents as much more confidence can be ascribed to hypotheses which are supported by information acquired from multiple agents.

Incomplete and incorrect information Data collection from the real world is inherently noisy, and this fact is compounded in large-scale domains. For example, in the domain of training battles described here, telemetry information is obtained from GPS sensors physically attached to participants and it is still highly incomplete and incorrect. Ideally, for each agent, the sensors would supply a position report for each time step of the battle. In reality, agents are "lost" during the course of a battle and no positions are reported for those time intervals. Additionally, there is a great deal of noise in the form of incorrectly-reported positions, making it appear that an agent is traveling in a highly erratic path. In an actual battle or surveillance task, telemetry information would have to be obtained from satellite and other intelligence gathering sources and would exhibit an even greater degree of noise and incompleteness.

Large-scale data Domains involving multiple agents acting over long time intervals or requiring high rates of sampling can generate enormous quantities of information. The number of agents can range from the order of tens in sporting events, for example, to hundreds, as is the case in the domain described here. Depending on the length of activity in the domain and the rate at which information is sampled, there can be anywhere from tens to thousands of state descriptions generated *per agent*. A further distinguishing characteristic of a real-world domain is that the data not only arrives in real time, but more importantly, must be processed in real time (Barès, et. al. 1994). A final assumption resulting from the scale of the data is that much of the input does not correspond to any meaningful pattern of activity. It is not noise *per se* in that it is correct information, it represents random or unplanned movements rather than purposeful action.

While the combination of these assumptions presents a relatively novel problem, previous research in a number of fields has addressed some of the issues raised here. Work by Mohnhaupt and Neumann (1991) examines the task of generating movement events such as "park" and "turn-off" from telemetry information in the domain of moving vehicles. However, they employ rather complex data structures and algorithms which do not scale efficiently to the type of domain in which we are working. A similar problem, referred to as spatio-temporal surveillance, is addressed by Howarth and Buxton (1992), also in the domain of vehicle movements, but which relies on the ability to identify "regions" in the geographic space, which we are unable to do. The goals of their research, though, are very similar to ours, with the exception that we are primarily interested in longer-term events which are composed from more primitive actions, rather than the primitive actions themselves.

Huber and Durfee (1992) address the problem of predicting movements in a real-world task involving autonomous robots. However, this approach assumes that an agent will move directly to its destination without avoiding obstacles or "feinting", and is further limited to the actions of a single agent, two assumptions which do not hold in our domain. However, their use of probabilistic methods has proven useful in overcoming noise and is something which we intend to investigate further. Tambe (1995) also describes research in tracking the behavior of agents in a real-world task, but like Huber and Durfee, focuses on the behavior of individual agents or groups of agents acting identically.

Another very closely related problem is the identification of stereotypical groupings of military forces or "templates". Woods (1993) addresses this problem for static positions and employs a constraint satisfaction framework along with a technique for abstracting the representation to overcome noise and complexity in the domain. While our research is focused on dynamic patterns of movement rather than position, we plan to investigate the potential usefulness of a similar approach, particularly for representation and recognition of more complex patterns of activity.

Solution

A solution to the problem of plan recognition in a domain such as the one described here must be capable of identifying changing relationships between agents but not have high computational or storage requirements nor be sensitive to noise in the data. Our solution has required both computations of parsimonious yet robust representations as well as an efficient pattern matching algorithm.

Constructing representations

Given that the only input directly available to the plan recognition process is the position of agents in a global coordinate system over large time periods, there is a need to both augment the amount of information that can be provided to the recognition process and a competing need to condense the amount of information to prevent computational intractability. Our approach has been a layered one in which successively higher levels of representation are computed from the raw data, generating decreasing amounts of data which convey more focused information. The lowest level of representation is information about individual agents such as position and velocity, followed by representations of relationships between pairs of agents, and finally, representations of patterns of agent-pair relationships.

Individual agents The first level of representation identifies important characteristics of individual agents. A subset of the features identified as useful by Mohnhaupt and Neumann (1991) is used at this level to describe agents at each time step : velocity, heading (orientation), and position (absolute). Velocity is computed as distance traveled during the prior temporal interval. Heading, or direction of travel, is computed from the path of travel which is first smoothed using a non-lookahead smoothing function and then converted to a relative compass orientation, an approach often used in the field of qualitative reasoning (e.g., Hernández 1994). These are the only features used at this time, although there are additional features which can be constructed such as relative positions (e.g., behind) or qualitative descriptions of movement such as "starting" or "stopping". Whether additional features will be required to represent more complex plans remains to be seen, however our general approach does not preclude the use of finer or more complex representations as long as they are computable within the constraints of the problem. It is also possible to construct higher-level attributes from raw data using domain-specific knowledge (e.g., Devaney and Ram, 1997), but this, of course, incurs additional computational overhead. Currently we are most interested in what type of success can be achieved using the minimum amount of knowledge, but the processes described here are independent of which attributes are employed. Ultimately, the decision of what properties to compute is a tradeoff between the cost of computing those properties and the degree to which they influence the quality of solutions obtainable.

Agent-pair relationships One of our primary assumptions of plan recognition involving multiple agents is the necessity of representing interactions among groups of units. To initially identify potential groups, the next stage of representation describes the relationships between all *pairs* of agents. These representations are comparisons of the primary attributes of individual units, and again, because of the potential for computational complexity in domains of this scale, we seek to represent the least amount of information possible which can still be of use. For this reason, the differences are represented qualitatively, with only important distinctions being preserved. Relative distances are computed as a percentage of the maximum possible distance given the bounding rectangle of all units, a representation that has proven useful for spatial reasoning (Gahegan 1995). Heading is stored simply as a binary comparison (same/not-same), although it may prove necessary to employ a slightly finer-grained range representation in the future (such as that described by Clementini, Di Felice, and Hernanández 1997). Finally, relative velocity is stored as a three-attribute feature (both moving, neither moving, different).

These properties of agent-pairs are referred to as the "primitive" relationships because they are obtained directly from the low-level data. Again, these relationships may need to be augmented or refined in order to capture more complex patterns in the data, but these have proven useful in our initial research.

There are eighteen possible combinations of the three attributes, described in table 1.

The number of primitive relationships depends, of course, on the number of primary attributes and their possible values and can get fairly large if more detailed representations are employed. In our domain we have

Table 1: Taxonomy of primitive relationships

Heading	Velocity	Distance	name
not same	not same	same	[uninteresting]
not same	not same	decreasing	s-approach
not same	not same	increasing	s-move away
not same	neither moving	same	not moving
not same	neither moving	decreasing	(impossible)
not same	neither moving	increasing	(impossible)
not same	both moving	same	[uninteresting]
not same	both moving	decreasing	approach
not same	both moving	increasing	move away
same	not same	same	[uninteresting]
same	not same	decreasing	s-approach
same	not same	increasing	s-move away
same	neither moving	same	not moving
same	neither moving	decreasing	(impossible)
same	neither moving	increasing	(impossible)
same	both moving	same	move together
same	both moving	decreasing	approach
same	both moving	increasing	move away

found these attributes sufficient for capturing interesting patterns of movements, and the number of potential primitives in a more robust representation is actually not as large as may first seem. This is due to the fact that many combinations are physically impossible (e.g., it is not possible for two units to have no velocity yet the distance between them change), and many are "uninteresting" in the sense that they do not capture a significant change in the relationship between units. Finally, many of the relationships are symmetrical and can thus be converted into a single equivalence class. For example, out of the eighteen possible combinations of the primitive attributes used in the training battle domain, four are impossible, three are inherently uninteresting, and six of the relationships form three equivalence classes, leaving only six types of primitive relationship which need to be represented and maintained.

Even this relatively simple representation of agent pair relationships is $O(n^2)$, which precludes storing these values over time intervals of any significant length given that n can be on the order of hundreds. Therefore, it is essential to retain these relationships only as long as necessary. This is performed by the plan recognition process, which identifies and retains only those relationships which combine to form interesting patterns in the data.

Plan recognition

The agent-pair relationships described above are best viewed as *events*, actions which can be described by a verb (Neumann 1991), essentially changes in the relationships between primitive attributes of agents (Howarth 1994). Research in object tracking has been primarily concerned with movements at this level, however we are interested in more complex patterns of action as produced by the execution of plans as well as patterns involving groups rather than single agents.

In our approach, the primitive relationships are the building blocks of more complex patterns which are formed from temporal combinations of events, such as the gather maneuver described in figure 1 in which an event of units moving together is followed by an event of them waiting in position. This representation is recursive in nature, in that higher-level patterns are formed from combinations of other patterns. For example, a "gather-disperse" maneuver is a combination of the gather and the dispersal patterns which are themselves combinations of lower-level patterns, etc.

The other unique aspect of our research is that we are ultimately concerned with identification of *groups* of agents engaged in common patterns of behavior and that these group behaviors are formed from the different behaviors of individual agents occurring together. The fact that diverse individual behaviors combine to form group behaviors together with the fact that there is no one distance metric which could capture groupings for all possible patterns, precludes an approach which relies on clustering of the data prior to the recognition of patterns and plans. Rather, the key to our solution has been to reverse the usual approach and detect patterns first among agent-pairs and then leverage this knowledge to form groups based on co-occurring actions.

Since we are operating under constraints of real time and large-scale data, it is crucial that any algorithms be sensitive to potential computational complexity and the amount of space needed to hold computed information. Since there are $(n^2)/2$ groups of unit pair relationships, a large number given that n is on the order of hundreds in this domain, it is computationally infeasible to attempt to compute all possible groupings or even to maintain all unit pair relationships for more than a limited number of time steps. Instead, we employ a pattern-directed approach (Hayes-Roth and Waterman 1978) whereby the retention of information is governed by its potential "interestingness". In other words, the only information retained about agent-pair relationships is that which has the potential to instantiate a known pattern.

Briefly, the algorithm consists of computing all possible agent-pair relationships at each time step, then comparing these with a library of pattern templates. Relationships which match any of these templates are retained in a list of potentially satisfiable patterns indexed by the agents participating in the relationship. Once an agent-pair has been identified as potentially instantiating a pattern or patterns, its events are retained for succeeding time intervals by linking them into the pattern(s) which it partially instantiates. These partial instantiations are examined at each time step as well, and one of three conditions occurs:

complete instantiation The new event completely instantiates a pattern template and the event sequence is replaced by that higher-level representation.

decay The new event does not match the template and the pattern has remained uninstantiated for too long, at which point it is discarded.

chaining The new event neither fully instantiates the pattern nor causes it to decay completely, so it is just added to the event chain.

Table 2: Plan recognition algorithm

At each time step t
1) For each agent i, compute state of $agent_i$ at $time_t$
2) For each agent i and j ($i\ !=\ j$)
   A) Compute agent-pair relationships for $agent_i$, $agent_j$ at $time_t$
   B) If $relationship_{ij}$ matches beginning of new pattern template, instantiate a new potential $pattern_{ij}$
   C) For each existing $pattern_{ij}$
      i) add $relationship_{ij}$ to event chain of $pattern_{ij}$
      ii) mark $pattern_{ij}$ as fully instantiated if $relationship_{ij}$ matches next event in $pattern_{ij}$ and that event is the last in the chain.
      iii) increment decay value of $pattern_{ij}$ if $relationship_{ij}$ does not match next event in $pattern_{ij}$
      iv) discard potential $pattern_{ij}$ if decay threshold exceeded
3) For each fully instantiated $pattern_{ij}$, combine all patterns involving i or j which occur co-temporally.

Event sequences correspond to a temporal ordering, and we employ a temporal representation based on Allen's (1991) temporal calculus which has proven sufficient to capture the maneuvers identified by our domain experts as interesting. Essentially, a pattern consists of a series of events, some of which are co-occurring and others which occur in succession. In our implementation, an event is considered co-occurring with another if there is any amount of temporal overlap between the two states. We employ a similarly generous definition of succession – two events are considered to occur in succession if one begins after the other one has ended. The co-occurrence relation is relatively unproblematic, however, our notion of succession raises the issue of how much time can elapse between state changes for a pattern to still be counted as such. There is a conflicting need to allow intermediate states which may be caused by noise or deliberate deception but also to require that patterns have some temporal "cohesiveness". The solution to this problem involves associating a decay value with partially instantiated patterns which is increased as unmatched states accrue. The partial patterns are discarded when this decay exceeds a threshold.

The identification of group behaviors occurs when an agent-pair fully instantiates a known pattern. At the end of processing all agent-pair relationships, the algorithm combines all newly instantiated full patterns based on spatial and temporal co-occurrence by examining patterns which have common participants. This results in a set of high-level behaviors involving multiple units and these behaviors can be ranked based on the number of participants, indicating a relative "interestingness".

The algorithm is described in more detail in table 2.

Evaluation

In contexts where the researcher knows what the right answer should be, evaluation is more or less a matter of running a system and measuring its success at finding that right answer under a number of conditions. This, however, requires that sufficient domain knowledge exists for a solution to be calculated and that someone with that domain knowledge exists and is available for evaluation of the system. In other contexts, evaluation is more subjective because there is no one "right" answer and the output must be judged by some criteria determined by the researcher as to its interestingness.

Our evaluation thus far has employed the use of several domain experts (US Army officers) to identify patterns of movement in actual battle data which they deem relevant or interesting. These patterns occur with moderate frequency within battles and among different battles, further indicating their usefulness as sources of prediction. The patterns currently are at the level of the "gather" maneuver depicted in figure 1, involving event chains of several time steps in length. Our system is able to isolate and identify these patterns in real battle data which exhibits high degrees of complexity and noise.

A formal and comprehensive evaluation will be required to more fully examine the claims made, but should follow the general pattern of the informal evaluations already made. We have made plans for further consultation with domain experts who should be able to augment the library with interesting and useful patterns. Once the library has been become sufficiently complex a systematic evaluation can be made, running the pattern recognition system on the entire corpus and annotating the battles with the patterns identified. This output can then be judged by both experts and non-experts as "sensible", i.e., were all patterns identified as specific maneuvers reasonably indicative of those maneuvers.

Finally, while our current evaluation has focused on the ability of the system to represent and identify patterns having significance in the military domain in which we are working, our research claims are made at a higher level, that of spatio-temporal patterns as produced by the movements of multiple agents. Therefore, future evaluation will also be concerned with the ability of the system to represent and recognize patterns which occur with high frequency without consideration of domain-specific importance.

Conclusions and future work

Research in plan recognition has traditionally focused on domains in which the task is to identify the goals and future behavior of a single agent acting from a relatively small space of potential activities in a context of perfect or near-perfect observability. In contrast, we describe the problem of plan recognition in complex multi-agent domains in which these assumptions do not hold. These domains require an approach which focuses on the interactions *among* agents, is sensitive to the potential for computational complexity, and does not require complete observability.

Our solution has been to employ fairly simple representations which capture successively higher levels of description of input data and to retain only that data which has the potential to be part of a known plan. The motivation for a parsimonious representation has been due to computational considerations and also due to the desire for the development of a system which is able to autonomously *learn* or *discover* patterns directly from the raw data. While the choice of primitives used in the representation will ultimately depend on the particular application domain, the general approach has proven both computationally tractable and effective.

Future work will focus on exploring the scalability of

the approach in order to identify limitations on the size of the plan library and the complexity of its plans while remaining within the real-time constraints of the problem. The issue of real-time response is critical in many applications, and ideally a recognition system in a real-world domain such as the one described here should be able to rapidly generate hypotheses while input data streams in. This requires the ability to generate multiple candidate matches using partial information and to rank them by some confidence metric, and is particularly important when the plan library becomes larger and more complex. Currently we have not had the need to address these issues because of the fairly small size of our plan library, but as the number and complexity of the pattern templates increases these issues will become increasingly important.

While we suspect that relatively minor modifications and enhancements will need to be made in our basic representations, we are confident that the general approach will prove successful as the size and complexity of the patterns is increased. The ability to reason about interactions among agents in competitive or cooperative situations is becoming increasingly useful as more and more attention is devoted to multi-agent research. The trend toward applying AI techniques to real-world problems is also placing demands on these techniques that they be scalable as well as effective.

Acknowledgements

This research was funded by the US Army Research Laboratory under grant DAKF11-97-D-0001-0007. The authors wish to thank Sven Koenig and the anonymous AAAI reviewers for their helpful comments and suggestions.

References

Allen, J.F. 1991. Temporal reasoning and planning. In J.F. Allen, et. al. *Reasoning About Plans*, 1-67. San Mateo, CA : Morgan Kaufmann.

Barès, M., et. al. 1994. XPLANS: Case-based reasoning for plan recognition. *Applied Artificial Intelligence* 8:617-643.

Clementini, E., Di Felice, P., and Hernández, D. 1997. Qualitative representation of positional information. *Artificial Intelligence* 95:317-356.

Devaney, M. and Ram, A. 1997. Situation development in a complex real-world domain. In *Proceedings ICML '97 Workshop on Applications of ML to the Real World*.

Di Eugenio, B. 1995. Plan Recognition and Natural Language Understanding. In *Proceedings IJCAI '95 Workshop : The Next Generation of Plan Recognition Systems : Challenges for and Insight from Related Areas of AI*.

Gahegan, M. 1995. Proximity operators for qualitative spatial reasoning. In A. U. Frank & W. Kuhn (Eds.), *Spatial Information Theory. A Theoretical Basis for GIS, International Conference (COSIT '95)*, Lecture Notes in Computer Science 988, 31 - 43, Springer-Verlag.

Hernández, D. 1994. *Qualitative Representation of Spatial Knowledge*, Lecture Notes in Computer Science 804, Springer Verlag.

Howarth, R.J. 1994. Spatial Representation, Reasoning and Control for a Surveillance System. Ph.D. diss., Queen Mary and Westfield College.

Howarth, R.J. and Buxton, H. 1992. Analogical representation of spatial events for understanding traffic behaviour. In *Proceedings European Conference on Artificial Intelligence (ECAI)*, 785 - 789.

Huber, M. J. and Durfee, E. H. 1992. Plan recognition for real-world autonomous robots: Work in progress. In *Working Notes AAAI Symposium : Applications of AI to Real-World Autonomous Robots*.

Huber, M. J. and Durfee, E. H. 1995. Deciding when to commit to action during observation-based coordination. *Proceedings of the First International Conference on Multi-Agent Systems (ICMAS)*, 163 - 170.

Mohnhaupt, M. and Neumann, B. 1991. Understanding object motion: Recognition, learning, and spatiotemporal reasoning. *Robotics and Autonomous Systems* 8:65 - 91.

Neumann, B. 1989. Natural language description of time-varying scenes. In D. Waltz (Ed.), *Semantic Structures : Advances in Natural Language Processing*, 167 - 204. Lawrence Erlbaum Associates.

Tambe, M. 1995. Recursive agent and agent-group tracking in a real-time, dynamic environment. In *Proceedings of International Conference on Multi-Agent Systems (ICMAS)*, 368-375.

Traum, D. R. and Allen, J.F. 1991. Causative forces in multi-agent planning. In Y. Demazeau & J-P. Müller (Eds.), *Decentralized AI*, 89 - 105. Elsevier.

Wærn, A. 1996. Recognising human plans: Plan recognition in human-computer interaction. Ph.D. diss., Swedish Institute of Computer Science.

Waterman, D.A. and Hayes-Roth, F. eds. 1978. *Pattern-directed Inference Systems*. Academic Press.

Woods, S. 1993. A method of interactive recognition of spatially defined model deployment templates using abstraction. In H. Merklinger et al. (Eds.), *Proceedings of the Knowledge-based Systems and Robotics Workshop*, 665-675. Department of National Defence, Government of Canada.

Woods, S. and Yang, Q. 1998. Program understanding as constraint satisfaction. *Journal of Automated Software Engineering* 5(2). Kluwer Academic Publishers.

Act, and the Rest Will Follow: Exploiting Determinism in Planning as Satisfiability

Enrico Giunchiglia
DIST — Università di Genova
Viale Causa 13
16145 Genova, Italy

Alessandro Massarotto
DIST — Università di Genova
Viale Causa 13
16145 Genova, Italy

Roberto Sebastiani
IRST, 38050 Povo,
Trento, Italy

Abstract

In this paper we focus on Planning as Satisfiability (SAT). We build from the simple consideration that the values of fluents at a certain time point *derive deterministically* from the initial situation and the sequence of actions performed till that point. Thus, the choice of actions to perform is the only source of nondeterminism. This is a rather trivial consideration, but which has important positive consequences if implemented in current planners via SAT. In fact, it produces a dramatic size reduction of the space of the truth assignments searched in by the SAT decider used to solve the final SAT problem. To justify this claim, we repeat many of the experiments reported in (Ernst, Millstein, & Weld 1997), and show that the CPU time requested to solve a problem can go down up to 4 orders of magnitude.

Introduction

Historically, planning has been dealt with as a problem of deduction in first order logic (Green 1969; McCarthy & Hayes 1969) or later through the definition of special purpose algorithms (see e.g. (Blum & Furst 1995)). Kautz and Selman (1992) proposed a different approach, where any planning problem is first limited in size (by looking for plans whose length is $\leq n$ for some fixed n), and then reduced to a satisfiability problem in propositional logic. Several reductions are possible, each having a different asymptotic size and number of variables (see (Kautz & Selman 1992; 1996; Kautz, McAllester, & Selman 1997; Ernst, Millstein, & Weld 1997)).

In this paper we build from the following simple consideration:

> The values of fluents at a certain time point *derive deterministically* from the initial situation and the sequence of actions performed till that point. Thus, the choice of actions to perform is the only source of nondeterminism.

This is a rather trivial consideration, but which has important positive consequences if implemented in current planners via SAT. In fact, it produces a dramatic size reduction of the space of the truth assignments searched in by the SAT decider used to solve the final SAT problem. To experimentally support this claim we consider many of the problems reported in (Ernst, Millstein, & Weld 1997) and distributed with the MEDIC planner.[1] We generate various SAT encodings with MEDIC and solve each of them using both the TABLEAU system[2] –as done in (Ernst, Millstein, & Weld 1997)– and TABLEAU*, a version of TABLEAU modified in order to incorporate the above idea. Finally, we compare the results and show that:

- The search space effectively searched by TABLEAU* (i.e. the number of nodes in the search tree) is up to 4 orders of magnitude less than the search space analyzed by TABLEAU.

- The CPU time requested by TABLEAU* to solve a problem is up to 4 orders of magnitude less than the CPU time requested by TABLEAU on the same problem.

Planning as Satisfiability

In the following, we will restrict our attention to six of the eight automatic encodings which have been studied and comparatively experimentally evaluated in (Ernst, Millstein, & Weld 1997). More in detail, we consider the

- explanatory-regular-parallel-eliminate (erpe),
- classical-regular-sequential-eliminate (crse),
- explanatory-simple split-sequential-eliminate (ecse),
- classical-simple split-sequential-eliminate (ccse),
- explanatory-bitwise-sequential-eliminate (ebse),
- classical-bitwise-sequential-eliminate (cbse).

It is not our goal to describe these six encodings in detail. This has been already done in (Ernst, Millstein,

---

Copyright 1998, American Association for Artificial Intelligence (www.aaai.org). All rights reserved.

[1] The MEDIC system is available at http://www.cs.washington.edu/research/projects/ai/-www/planning.html.
[2] The TABLEAU system is available at http://www.cirl.uoregon.edu/crawford/crawford.html.

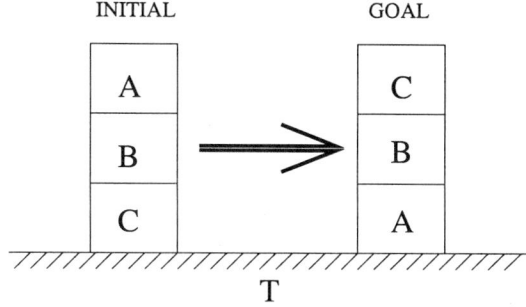

$Move(b, s, d)$
PRECOND : $Block(b) \wedge Clear(b) \wedge On(b,s) \wedge$
$(Clear(d) \vee Table(d)) \wedge$
$b \neq s \wedge b \neq d \wedge s \neq d$
EFFECT : $Clear(s) \wedge \neg On(b,s) \wedge$
$On(b,d) \wedge \neg Clear(d)$

Figure 1: A Blocks World, Initial and Goal States

& Weld 1997). We will recall the underlying ideas and illustrate them through the simple blocks reverse problem in Figure 1. This planning problem is characterized by the single operator *Move*, 4 individuals (the 3 blocks A, B, C and the table T), initial and goal states as in the Figure.

We will use the same notation and terminology employed in (Ernst, Millstein, & Weld 1997). Thus, time takes nonnegative integer values, fluents occur at even time points, and actions occur at odd time points. We represent the fluent e.g. $On(A, B)$ at time t by $On_t(A, B)$, and the action e.g. $Move(A, B, C)$ at time t by $Move_t^r(A, B, C)$. Notice the index r to actions: it indicates it is a representation which varies according to the particular encoding used.

Before illustrating the various encodings, we recall that, for any given planning problem and plan length $n \geq 0$, the clauses corresponding to the following facts always belong to the final SAT problem:

- For any action, if it is executed at time $0 < t < 2n$ then its preconditions and its effects must be satisfied at time $t-1$ and at time $t+1$ respectively. For example, for the action $Move_t^r(A, B, C)$ we will have (*action axioms*)

  $Move_t^r(A, B, C) \supset$
  $Clear_{t-1}(A) \wedge On_{t-1}(A, B) \wedge Clear_{t-1}(C) \wedge$
  $Clear_{t+1}(B) \wedge \neg On_{t+1}(A, B) \wedge$
  $On_{t+1}(A, C) \wedge \neg Clear_{t+1}(C)$.

- At time 0 the formula specifying the initial state must be satisfied. In our example, all the fluents are assumed to be false at time 0 except for

  $On_0(A, B), On_0(B, C), On_0(C, T), Clear_0(A)$.

- At time $2n$ the formula specifying the goal states must be satisfied:

  $On_{2n}(C, B) \wedge On_{2n}(B, A) \wedge On_{2n}(A, T)$.

Finally, we always employ the optimizations described in (Ernst, Millstein, & Weld 1997) and implemented in the MEDIC planner, such as factoring and type optimizations. These allow to reduce the number of actions (e.g. the actions in which b is not a block, or in which $b = s$ or $b = d$ or $s = d$ are not generated), the number of fluents (e.g. fluents like $Table(A)$ are automatically considered to be false at each even time step), and the size of the encodings.

The encodings differ for the "Frame axioms representation" (Classical/Explanatory), "Action representation" (Regular/Simple-split/Bitwise), "Planning strategy" (Sequential/Parallel).

Frame axioms representation

Classical (McCarthy & Hayes 1969): any action specifies that the non affected fluents keep their values. For example, moving A from B to T does not affect whether block C is clear or not:

$Move_t^r(A, B, T) \wedge Clear_{t-1}(C) \supset Clear_{t+1}(C)$,
$Move_t^r(A, B, T) \wedge \neg Clear_{t-1}(C) \supset \neg Clear_{t+1}(C)$.

"At-least-one-action" axioms guarantee that at each odd time step some action occurs, thus preventing fluents from changing freely due to non-action:

$$\bigvee_{\substack{b,s,d \in \{A,B,C,T\} \\ b \neq s, b \neq d, s \neq d, b \neq T}} Move_t^r(b, s, d).$$

Explanatory (Haas 1987): If a fluent changes its value, some action affecting it must have occurred. For example, if block C becomes unclear, then either we have moved A or B on top of C:

$\neg Clear_{t+1}(C) \wedge Clear_{t-1}(C) \supset$
$Move_t^r(A, B, C) \vee Move_t^r(A, T, C) \vee$
$Move_t^r(B, A, C) \vee Move_t^r(B, T, C)$.

Action representation

Regular : each action is represented by a distinct variable, e.g. $Move_t^r(A, B, C)$ is $Move_t(A, B, C)$. In our example there are 18 actions and thus we will have 18 variables per odd time step.

Simple-split : each n-ary action is replaced by the conjunction of n distinct variables, e.g. $Move_t^r(A, B, C)$ is

$MoveArg1_t(A) \wedge MoveArg2_t(B) \wedge MoveArg3_t(C)$.

In our example we will have 11 variables per odd time step.

Bitwise : each action corresponds to a conjunction of $\lceil log_2 \mathcal{A} \rceil$ literals, where $\mathcal{A}$ is the number of actions. The conjunction corresponds to a sequence of bits numbering the set of action. In our example 5 bits are sufficient. If we number the set of actions according to the lexicographic order, $Move_t^r(A, B, C)$ is

$\neg Bit1_t \wedge \neg Bit2_t \wedge \neg Bit3_t \wedge \neg Bit4_t \wedge \neg Bit5_t$.

Planning Strategy

Sequential: for each pair of actions α and β, add axioms of the form $\neg \alpha_t^r \vee \neg \beta_t^r$ for each odd time step. For example, we will have:

$$\neg Move_t^r(A,B,C) \vee \neg Move_t^r(A,B,T).$$

These axioms ensure that at each time step at most one action is executed. They are not included (since not necessary) for encodings using a bitwise action representation (i.e. ebse and cbse) or the classical frame axioms (i.e. crse, ccse and cbse).

Parallel: for each pair of actions α and β, add axioms of the form $\neg \alpha_t^r \vee \neg \beta_t^r$ for each odd time step if α effects contradict β preconditions. For example, we will have

$$\neg Move_t^r(B,T,A) \vee \neg Move_t^r(A,B,C).$$

These axioms do not prohibit to execute more than one action at some time step, and the result is a plan whose actions form a partial order. However, imposing any total order compatible with the partial order constitutes a valid plan.

Act, and the rest will follow

In the next two sections, we will use the symbol L to denote a literal; the symbol A_t^i to denote the i-th action variable at time t; the symbol F_t^j to denote the j-th fluent variable at time t; the symbols $\mathbf{A}_t$ and $\mathbf{F}_t$ to denote respectively the sets of action variables $\{A_t^1, A_t^2, \ldots\}$ and fluent variables $\{F_t^1, F_t^2, \ldots\}$ at time t; the expressions $preconds(A_t^i)$ and $effects(A_t^i)$ to denote the sets of precondition and effect variables respectively of action A_t^i. We denote with $\mathcal{A}$ and $\mathcal{F}$ the cardinality of $\mathbf{A}_t$ and $\mathbf{F}_t$ respectively (which do not depend on t), and with n the length of the searched plan.

The work underlying this paper starts from observing that, independently from the encoding used, the following simple facts hold:

1. for each t, the truth values of the fluent variables in $\mathbf{F}_t$ derive deterministically from the initial values $\mathbf{F}_0$ and from the truth values of the action variables in $\mathbf{A}_1, \ldots, \mathbf{A}_{t-1}$, representing all the actions performed before t. Thus:

2. the choice of the truth values for the action variables A_t^i's is the only source of non-determinism in SAT-encoded planning.

These facts translate into SAT-encoded planning the consideration about determinism in the introductory section.

Consider, for instance, the regular representation of actions and the classical frame axioms. For each odd time t, if all the fluent variables F_{t-1}^j have been assigned a truth value and one action variable A_t^i has been assigned true, then all the fluent variables F_{t+1}^j which are in $effects(A_t^i)$ can be deterministically assigned as a consequence of the action axioms, while

```
DP(Γ, U)
    if ∅ ∈ Γ then return;
    if Γ = ∅ then exit with a model of U;
    UNIT-PROPAGATE(Γ, U);
    L := a literal such that L or ¬L occurs in Γ;
    DP(Γ ∪ {L}, U);
    DP(Γ ∪ {¬L}, U);

UNIT-PROPAGATE(Γ, U)
    while there is a unit clause {L} in Γ
        U := U ∪ {L};
        for every clause C ∈ Γ
            if L ∈ C then Γ := Γ \ {C}
            else if ¬L ∈ C then
                Γ := Γ \ {C} ∪ {C \ {¬L}}
        end for
    end while
```

Figure 2: The Davis-Putnam procedure

all the other fluent variables F_{t+1}^k can be assigned as a consequence of the frame axioms. Notice that the reverse is not true, that is, the values of actions A_t^i's are not a deterministic consequence of the values of the variables in $\mathbf{F}_{t-1}$ and in $\mathbf{F}_{t+1}$.

Current SAT-based planners do not take advantage of these issues. In fact, the SAT decider run over the SAT-encoded problem – typically a local search engine like WalkSAT (Kautz & Selman 1996) or a Davis-Putnam implementation like TABLEAU (Ernst, Millstein, & Weld 1997) – performs a search on the whole spectrum of encoded variables, branching on both action and fluent variables, without distinction. As a consequence, it searches in a space of truth assignments of size $2^{(\mathcal{A}+\mathcal{F}) \cdot n}$, while Fact 2. suggests a size bound of $2^{\mathcal{A} \cdot n}$.

Exploiting determinism on fluent values

Consider the standard Davis-Putnam procedure described in Figure 2. Intuitively, at each step DP performs first all the deterministic assignments by invoking UNIT-PROPAGATE; then it performs a non-deterministic step by choosing a literal L, and recurses sequentially with $L = true$ and $L = false$. L can be both an action or a fluent literal.

Fact 2. in the previous section suggests that in SAT-based Planning the search should be restricted to find values to action variables only, as the values for fluent variables can be eventually obtained for free. To this extent, we introduce DP*, which is obtained from DP by substituting the literal choice step with the following:

$L :=$ an <u>action</u> literal such that L or $\neg L$ occurs in Γ;

that is, we force DP* to select only action literals like A_t^i or $\neg A_t^i$ in the non-deterministic step.

DP* terminates for every encoding used, as all fluent variables are assigned deterministically by UNIT-PROPAGATE. The idea is that all encodings create clauses with at most two fluent variables, of the form F_{t-1}^j, F_{t+1}^j. If no more action variables occur in Γ, then only unit clauses like (F_{t-1}^j) and $(\neg F_{t-1}^j)$ and binary clauses like $(\neg F_{t-1}^j \vee F_{t+1}^j)$ and $(F_{t-1}^j \vee \neg F_{t+1}^j)$ are left over, which are all solved by UNIT-PROPAGATE, from (F_0^j)'s and $(\neg F_0^j)$'s onward.

For example, assume that the regular representation of actions and the classical frame axioms have been used. For each action variable A_t^i, the SAT encoding contains the following clauses:

Regular action representation:

$$\bigwedge_{L \in preconds(A_t^i)} (\neg A_t^i \vee L) \quad (1)$$

$$\bigwedge_{L \in effects(A_t^i)} (\neg A_t^i \vee L) \quad (2)$$

Classical frame axioms:

$$\bigwedge_{F_{t+1}^j \in \mathbf{F}_{t+1}/|effects(A_t^i)|} (\neg A_t^i \vee \neg F_{t-1}^j \vee F_{t+1}^j) \quad (3)$$

$$\bigwedge_{F_{t+1}^j \in \mathbf{F}_{t+1}/|effects(A_t^i)|} (\neg A_t^i \vee F_{t-1}^j \vee \neg F_{t+1}^j) \quad (4)$$

where $|effects(A_t^i)|$ denotes the set of F_{t+1}^j's s.t. either $F_{t+1}^j \in effects(A_t^i)$ or $\neg F_{t+1}^j \in effects(A_t^i)$.

At-least-one axiom:

$$\bigvee_{A_t^i \in \mathbf{A}_t} A_t^i \quad (5)$$

First, we notice that, if all fluent variables $F_{t-1}^j \in \mathbf{F}_{t-1}$ are assigned and one action variable A_t^i is assigned true, then UNIT-PROPAGATE assigns deterministically all $F_{t+1}^j \in \mathbf{F}_{t+1}$ by resolving A_t^i with the action clauses (2) if $F_{t-1}^j \in effects(A_t^i)$, and with the frame axiom clauses (3),(4) if $F_{t-1}^j \notin effects(A_t^i)$. Then we notice that, if it is reached a situation where no more action variables occur in Γ and no unit propagations can be performed, then all fluent variables have already been assigned, and thus it is reached either a solution or a backtrack condition. In fact, the at-least-one axiom clauses (5) ensure that at least one A_t^i has been assigned true, for all t. Thus all fluent variables have been assigned, from those in $\mathbf{F}_0$ onward.

On the whole, DP* searches in a space of truth assignments of size $2^{\mathcal{A} \cdot n}$, allowing a reduction of a $2^{\mathcal{F} \cdot n}$ factor, as predicted in the previous section.

Experimental Results

In this Section we report on some comparative analysis we have performed using the MEDIC system for the SAT problem generation, and TABLEAU and TABLEAU* as propositional solvers.[3] TABLEAU is an efficient implementation of the Davis-Putnam procedure (Crawford & Auton 1996). TABLEAU* is exactly the same as TABLEAU except that is has been modified –as described in the previous section– in order to split only over action variables.[4]

More in detail, we considered a suite of planning problems as encoded and distributed in the MEDIC system. Most of these problems are the same analyzed in (Ernst, Millstein, & Weld 1997). For each problem, we generated with MEDIC the corresponding SAT-problem for each of the six encodings we have considered. Finally, we ran TABLEAU and TABLEAU* on these encodings. Table 1 summarizes the results. For each run, Table 1 reports both the CPU time (top line) and the number of nodes of the search trees of the two systems (bottom line) on the first of the satisfiable instances generated by MEDIC. (Notice that we do not take into consideration the time that MEDIC took to generate the SAT problems.) A "–" means that the system has been stopped after 2700s of CPU time. For convenience, we plot the CPU time for the erpe and ecse encodings (i.e. the two encodings using the regular action representation) in Figure 3. In this figure

- TABLEAU's and TABLEAU*'s values are represented by the dashed and the black bar respectively.

- An apparently missing line (like TABLEAU* CPU time for FIXA-2 in Figure 3, left) corresponds to a value too small to appear on the plot.

Notice the logarithmic scale on the horizontal axis of the figure.

As it can be seen, TABLEAU* (when it terminates within the time limit) performs better than TABLEAU on any problem of a certain size. Notice that the cases where TABLEAU performs better than TABLEAU* are very few, and the corresponding gaps are minor. If we limit our attention to the CPU times, we see that:

- For the erpe encodings (Figure 3, left and Table 1, second column), TABLEAU* always performs better than TABLEAU. The gap between the two can go up till 2 orders of magnitude (for BIG-BW1 and HANOI-STRIPS3).

---

[3]TABLEAU* and detailed instructions about how to reproduce all our experiments can be found at ftp://ftp.mrg.dist.unige.it/ in pub/mrg-systems. All the experiments have been performed on a Pentium II 266MHz, 96MBRam.

[4]This has been accomplished by dividing the set of variables in the SAT problem into the two separate sets of fluent variables and action variables. TABLEAU* chooses the variables to split among those in this last set.

- For the crse encodings (Figure 3, right and Table 1, third column), TABLEAU* always performs better on problems that take more than one second to be solved. The gap between TABLEAU* and TABLEAU can go up to more than three orders of magnitude (TABLEAU was not able to solve both MONKEY-TEST1 and HANOI-STRIPS3 within the time limit, while TABLEAU* solved these problems in 2.93s and 1.28s respectively).

- For the ecse encodings (Table 1, fourth column), TABLEAU* always performs better on problems that take more than one second to be solved. The gap between TABLEAU* and TABLEAU can go up to more than three orders of magnitude (TABLEAU was not able to solve MONKEY-TEST2 within the time limit, while TABLEAU* solved this problem in 0.50s).

- For the ccse encodings (Table 1, fifth column), TABLEAU* always performs better on problems that take more than one second to be solved. The gap between TABLEAU* and TABLEAU can go up to more than four orders of magnitude (TABLEAU was not able to solve SMALL-BW1 within the time limit, while TABLEAU* solved this problem in 0.08s).

- For the ebse encodings (Table 1, sixth column), the two systems perform in roughly the same way.

- For the cbse encodings (Table 1, seventh column), TABLEAU* always performs better than TABLEAU. The gap between the two can go up till 4 orders of magnitude (TABLEAU was not able to solve FIX2-STRIPS within the time limit, while TABLEAU* solved this problem in 0.41s).

Considering the values reporting the number of nodes in the search trees traversed by the two systems, we see that they reflect the values of the corresponding CPU times. The biggest gap between the two systems is obtained with the crse encoding on SMALL-BW1: TABLEAU has traversed 100,689 nodes, while TABLEAU* traversed 17 nodes.

We also see that our experiments using TABLEAU* confirm the observations in (Ernst, Millstein, & Weld 1997). Namely:

- The erpe encodings result to be the smallest and the ones which can be solved fastest.
- The explanatory encodings perform better than the corresponding classical.
- The bitwise (ebse and cbse) encodings take more time to be solved than the respective regular (erpe and crse) and simple split (ecse and ccse) encodings.

This last fact might sound surprising since the bitwise encodings greatly reduce the number of action variables. The worse behavior than the other encodings might be due to the fact that the resulting SAT problems do not contain (or contain only few) binary clauses. This last fact makes TABLEAU and TABLEAU* splitting heuristics ineffective (see (Crawford & Auton 1996)).

Conclusion

In this paper we build from a very simple idea: given an initial state, the actions to be performed are the only sources of nondeterminism in STRIPS planning problems. This is very simple, but implementing this idea in current planners via SAT has important consequences, since it greatly reduces the size of the search space searched in by the SAT decider used to solve the final SAT problem. To justify the claim, we conducted a serie of experiments, showing that we can obtain an up to 4 orders of magnitude speed up.

Of course, we do not claim that these almost always positive results are indipendent from (a) the particular problems considered, or (b) the particular STRIPS formulations, or (c) the particular method used to generate the SAT problem, or (d) the particular SAT decider used. We do not expect this to be the case. Changing any of the above four elements may lead to very different results.

Finally, it is clear that this work opens an interesting line of research. Namely, how to build efficient SAT deciders tailored for STRIPS planning problems. TABLEAU* is a first attempt to build this decider. Future work will be to explore other directions.

References

Blum, A., and Furst, M. 1995. Fast planning through planning graph analysis. In *Proc. of IJCAI-95*, 1636–1642.

Crawford, J., and Auton, L. 1996. Experimental results on the crossover point in satisfiability problems. *Artificial Intelligence* 81(1-2):31–58.

Ernst, M.; Millstein, T.; and Weld, D. 1997. Automatic SAT-compilation of planning problems. In *Proc. IJCAI-97*.

Green, C. 1969. Application of theorem proving to problem solving. In *Proc. IJCAI*, 219–240.

Haas, A. 1987. The case for domain-specific frame axioms. In Brown, F. M., ed., *The Frame Problem in Artificial Intelligence, Proc. 1987 Workshop*.

Kautz, H., and Selman, B. 1992. Planning as satisfiability. In *Proc. ECAI-92*, 359–363.

Kautz, H., and Selman, B. 1996. Pushing the envelope: planning, propositional logic and stochastic search. In *Proc. AAAI-96*, 1194–1201.

Kautz, H.; McAllester, D.; and Selman, B. 1997. Encoding plans in propositional logic. In *Proc. KR-97*, 374–384.

McCarthy, J., and Hayes, P. 1969. Some philosophical problems from the standpoint of artificial intelligence. In Meltzer, B., and Michie, D., eds., *Machine Intelligence*, volume 4. Edinburgh: Edinburgh University Press. 463–502. Reproduced in (McCarthy 1990).

McCarthy, J. 1990. *Formalizing Common Sense: Papers by John McCarthy*. Norwood, NJ: Ablex.

DOMAIN	ERPE		CRSE		ECSE		CCSE		EBSE		CBSE	
	TAB	TAB*	TAB	TAB*	TAB	TAB*	TAB	TAB*	TAB	TAB*	TAB	TAB*
BIG-BW1	33.55	0.44	–	–	–	61.26	–	–	–	–	–	–
	12580	82	–	–	–	5738	–	–	–	–	–	–
MED-BW1	0.07	0.06	–	–	0.33	0.17	–	1.13	11	10.69	–	–
	9	1	–	–	84	22	–	112	1334	1335	–	–
SMALL-BW1	0.04	0.03	532.24	0.52	0.05	0.05	–	0.08	0.15	0.12	–	606
	3	0	100689	17	6	4	–	6	33	23	–	232431
FIXA-2	0.02	0.01	0.15	0.21	0.2	0.17	1.09	1.15	0.02	0.06	3.18	3.21
	4	4	111	146	48	39	344	347	8	59	4019	4351
FIXA-1	0.02	0.01	0.25	0.09	0.18	0.18	1.83	0.68	0.03	0.03	10.95	5.81
	4	4	191	58	43	39	648	207	8	7	21764	10746
FERRY3	0.02	0.02	0.03	0.01	0.02	0.02	0.02	0.01	0.01	0.01	0.02	0.01
	1	1	0	1	0	0	1	1	1	1	3	2
FIX2-STRIPS	0.02	0.02	0.11	0.08	0.06	0.07	0.12	0.12	0.04	0.03	2700	0.41
	11	7	2	6	2	2	5	4	3	3	–	192
FIX1-STRIPS	0.03	0.03	0.14	0.14	0.11	0.1	0.17	0.25	0.09	0.08	2700	268.47
	16	11	7	2	2	3	8	20	23	19	–	121532
MONKEY-TEST2	39.39	1.28	–	–	–	0.5	–	478.86	–	–	–	–
	46035	976	–	–	–	13	–	45646	–	–	–	–
MONKEY-TEST1	0.95	0.05	–	2.93	0.4	0.16	–	0.57	0.74	0.59	–	2.21
	1291	3	–	200	119	11	–	95	463	269	–	178
HANOI-STRIPS3	16.82	0.13	–	1.28	22.42	0.21	–	0.95	1.22	2.97	–	–
	14674	27	–	90	7047	38	–	260	364	904	–	–
HANOI-STRIPS2	0.02	0.02	0.03	0.04	0.04	0.03	0.04	0.03	0.04	0.04	43.12	0.94
	3	2	9	4	5	4	11	2	14	13	124423	2207
PRODIGY-SUSSMAN-3	0.03	0.03	0.42	0.74	0.06	0.04	5.31	0.12	1.52	0.07	–	144.01
	8	4	155	209	16	2	2863	24	928	11	–	132803
PRODIGY-SUSSMAN-2	0.03	0.02	0.06	0.05	0.03	0.03	0.18	0.04	0.05	0.04	–	1.68
	2	1	8	4	3	2	125	2	5	6	–	1992
PRODIGY-SUSSMAN-1	0.02	0.01	0.03	0.02	0.02	0.02	0.03	0.02	0.03	0.02	87.29	0.06
	0	0	0	0	0	0	0	1	1	1	285701	53
ATT-LOGISTICS3	–	–	–	–	–	–	–	–	–	–	–	–
	–	–	–	–	–	–	–	–	–	–	–	–
ATT-LOGISTICS2	0.08	0.03	2606.47	23.07	1.45	0.93	–	91.81	11.85	5.73	–	–
	91	12	944295	4900	214	115	–	20968	9922	4533	–	–
ATT-LOGISTICS1	0.02	0.02	1.69	0.84	0.21	0.21	5.68	0.66	0.23	0.04	–	326.31
	14	9	929	196	17	17	1755	176	227	9	–	404976
ATT-LOGISTICS0	0.02	0.02	0.04	0.03	0.08	0.08	0.09	0.08	0.02	0.02	259.55	0.33
	6	6	5	2	2	1	10	7	8	8	627061	773

Table 1: CPU time (top line) and nodes in the search tree (bottom line) for the six encodings

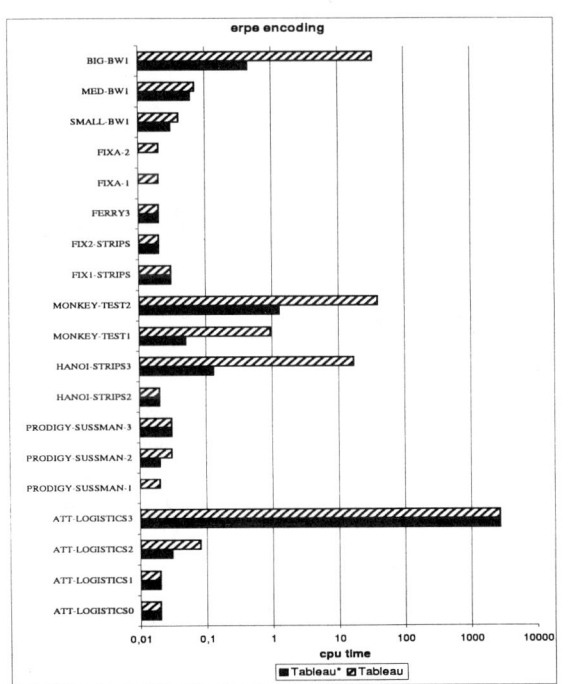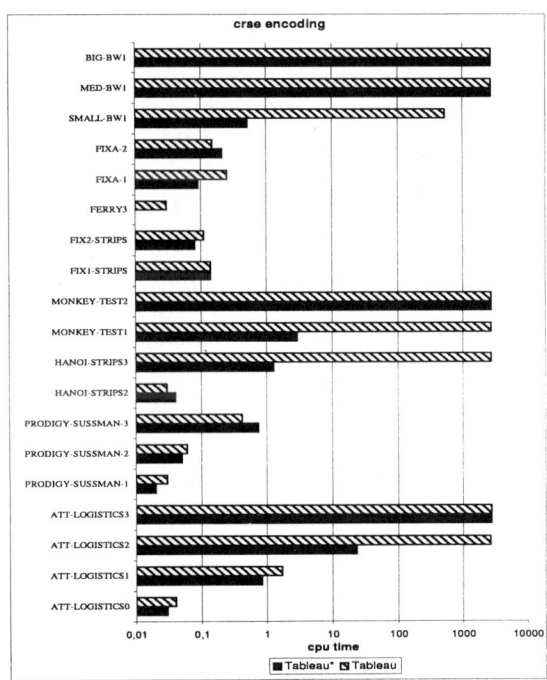

Figure 3: CPU time for erpe (left) and crse (right) encodings

Using Caching to Solve Larger Probabilistic Planning Problems

Stephen M. Majercik and Michael L. Littman

Department of Computer Science
Duke University
Durham, NC 27708-0129
{majercik,mlittman}@cs.duke.edu

Abstract

Probabilistic planning algorithms seek effective plans for large, stochastic domains. MAXPLAN is a recently developed algorithm that converts a planning problem into an E-MAJSAT problem, an NP^{PP}-complete problem that is essentially a probabilistic version of SAT, and draws on techniques from Boolean satisfiability and dynamic programming to solve the E-MAJSAT problem. This solution method is able to solve planning problems at state-of-the-art speeds, but it depends on the ability to store a value for each CNF subformula encountered in the solution process and is therefore quite memory intensive; searching for moderate-size plans even on simple problems can exhaust memory. This paper presents two techniques, based on caching, that overcome this problem without significant performance degradation. The first technique uses an LRU cache to store a fixed number of subformula values. The second technique uses a heuristic based on a measure of subformula difficulty to selectively save the values of only those subformulas whose values are sufficiently difficult to compute and are likely to be reused later in the solution process. We report results for both techniques on a stochastic test problem.

INTRODUCTION

Classical artificial intelligence planning techniques can operate in large domains but, traditionally, assume a deterministic universe. Planning as practiced in operations research can operate in probabilistic domains, but classical algorithms for solving Markov decision processes (MDPs) and partially observable MDPs are capable of solving problems only in relatively small domains. Research in probabilistic planning aims to explore a middle ground between these two well-studied extremes with the hope of developing systems that can reason efficiently about plans in large, uncertain domains.

In this paper we describe MAXPLAN, a new approach to probabilistic planning. MAXPLAN converts a planning problem into an E-MAJSAT problem, an NP^{PP}-complete problem that is essentially a probabilistic version of SAT, and draws on techniques from Boolean satisfiability and dynamic programming to solve the resulting E-MAJSAT problem. In the first section, we discuss complexity results that motivated our research strategy, and compare MAXPLAN to SATPLAN, a similar planning technique for deterministic domains. The next three sections summarize our earlier work on MAXPLAN and describe the details of its operation: the planning domain representation, the conversion of problems to E-MAJSAT form and the algorithm for solving these E-MAJSAT problems, and some comparative results. The next section introduces a framework for using caching in our solver and shows how good caching strategies can greatly increase the size of problems the solver can handle without substantially altering the scaling properties of the time it takes to solve them. The final sections discuss future work and conclusions.

COMPLEXITY RESULTS

A probabilistic planning domain is specified by a set of states, a set of actions, an initial state, and a set of goal states. The output of a planning algorithm is a controller for the planning domain whose objective is to reach a goal state with sufficiently high probability. In its most general form, a plan is a *program* that takes as input observable aspects of the environment and produces actions as output. We classify plans by their *size* (the number of internal states) and *horizon* (the number of actions produced *en route* to a goal state). In a *propositional* planning domain, states are specified as assignments to a set of propositional variables.

If we place reasonable bounds—polynomial in the size of the planning problem—on both plan size and plan horizon, the planning problem is NP^{PP}-complete (Littman, Goldsmith, & Mundhenk 1998) (perhaps easier than PSPACE-complete) and may be amenable to heuristics. Littman, Goldsmith, & Mundhenk (1998) provide a survey of relevant results. Membership in this complexity class suggests a solution strategy analogous to that of SATPLAN (Kautz & Selman 1996), a successful deterministic planner that converts a planning problem into a satisfiability (SAT) problem and solves the SAT problem instead. In the same way that deterministic planning can be expressed as the NP-complete problem SAT, probabilistic plan-

---

Copyright ©1998, American Association for Artificial Intelligence (www.aaai.org). All rights reserved.

ning can be expressed as the NP^PP-complete problem E-MAJSAT (Littman, Goldsmith, & Mundhenk 1998):

> Given a Boolean formula with *choice variables* (variables whose truth status can be arbitrarily set) and *chance variables* (variables whose truth status is determined by a set of independent probabilities), find the setting of the choice variables that maximizes the probability of a satisfying assignment with respect to the chance variables.

As we will discuss below, the choice variables can be made to correspond to a possible plan, while the chance variables can be made to correspond to the uncertainty in the planning domain. Thus, our research strategy is to show that we can efficiently turn planning problems into E-MAJSAT problems, and then focus our efforts on finding algorithms to solve the E-MAJSAT problems.

PROBLEM REPRESENTATION

A planning domain $M = \langle \mathcal{S}, s_0, \mathcal{A}, \mathcal{G} \rangle$ is characterized by a finite set of states $\mathcal{S}$, an initial state $s_0 \in \mathcal{S}$, a finite set of actions $\mathcal{A}$, and a set of goal states $\mathcal{G} \subseteq \mathcal{S}$. Executing action a in a state s results in a probabilistic transition to a new state. The objective is to choose a sequence of actions to move from the initial state s_0 to one of the goal states with probability above some threshold θ. In this work, we assume a completely unobservable domain—the effects of previous actions cannot be used in selecting the current action; thus, optimal plans are sequences of actions.

MAXPLAN represents planning domains in the sequential-effects-tree (ST) representation (Littman 1997). For each action, there is an ordered set of decision trees, one for each proposition, describing how the propositions change as a function of the state and action, perhaps probabilistically. A formal description of ST is available (Littman 1997); a brief example follows.

SAND-CASTLE-67 is a simple probabilistic planning domain concerned with building a sand castle at the beach (Figure 1). The domain has four states, described by combinations of two Boolean propositions, **moat** and **castle** (propositions appear in boldface). The proposition **moat** signifies that a moat has been dug; **castle** signifies that the castle has been built. In the initial state, both **moat** and **castle** are False, and the goal set is {**castle**} (a goal state is any state in which all the propositions in the goal set are True).

There are two actions: dig-moat and erect-castle (actions appear in sans serif). For brevity, we describe only the second decision tree (effect on **moat**) of the erect-castle action. There is no effect when **moat** is False (right branch) since erect-castle cannot dig a moat. But trying to erect a castle may destroy an existing moat (left branch). If the castle existed when erect-castle was selected, the moat remains intact with probability 0.75. If the castle did not exist, but erect-castle creates a new castle (**castle:new** refers to the value of **castle** *after* the first decision tree is evaluated), **moat** remains True.

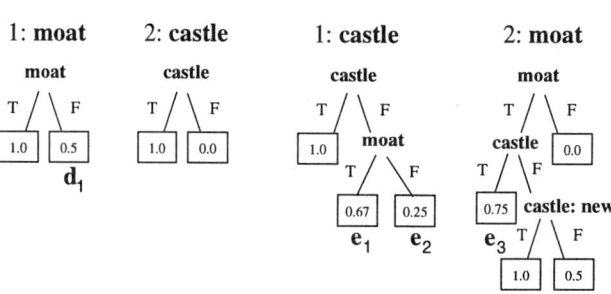

Figure 1: Sequential-Effects-Tree Representation For SAND-CASTLE-67

If erect-castle fails to build a castle, **moat** remains True with probability 0.5.

CONVERSION AND SOLUTION

MAXPLAN's conversion unit is a LISP program that takes a planning problem in ST form and a plan horizon N and produces an E-MAJSAT CNF formula. This formula has the property that, given an assignment to the choice variables (an N-step plan), the probability of a satisfying assignment with respect to the chance variables is the probability of success for that plan. The converter operates by time indexing each proposition and action, and making satisfaction equivalent to the enforcement of the following conditions:

- the initial conditions hold at time 0 and the goal conditions at time N,
- actions at time t are mutually exclusive ($1 \leq t \leq N$),
- proposition p is True at time t if it was True at time $t-1$ and the action taken at t does not make it False, or the action at t makes p True ($1 \leq t \leq N$).

The first two conditions are not probabilistic and can be encoded in a straightforward manner (Kautz & Selman 1996), but the third condition is complicated by the fact that chance variables sometimes intervene between actions and their effects on propositions.

The conversion process is detailed elsewhere (Majercik & Littman 1998); here we summarize some key facts. The total number of variables in the formula is $V = (A+P+R)N+P$, where A, P, and R are the number of actions, propositions, and random propositions, respectively. The total number of clauses is bounded by a low-order polynomial in the size of the problem: $2P + \left(\binom{A}{2}+1\right)N + 2N\sum_{i=1}^{A} L_i$, where L_i is the number of leaves in the decision trees of action i. The average clause size is dominated by the average path length of all the decision trees.

Note that fixing a plan horizon does not prevent MAXPLAN from solving planning problems where the horizon is unknown. By using *iterative lengthening*, a process in which successive instances of the planning problem with increasing horizons are solved, the optimal plan horizon can be discovered dynamically. This, in fact, was the process used in the MAXPLAN/BURIDAN comparison described later. We have not yet determined the feasibility of *incremental iterative lengthening*, a more sophisticated approach, in which the current instance of the planning problem with horizon N is incrementally extended to the instance with horizon $N+1$ and earlier results are reused to help solve the extended problem.

Solver

An algorithm for solving the E-MAJSAT problem produced by the conversion described above needs to find the assignment to the choice variables that maximizes the probability of a satisfying assignment; for plan-generated formulas, such an assignment is directly interpretable as an optimal straight-line plan. Our algorithm is based on an extension of the Davis-Putnam-Logemann-Loveland (DPLL) procedure for determining satisfiability. Essentially, we use DPLL to determine all possible satisfying assignments, sum the probabilities of the satisfying assignments for each possible choice-variable assignment, and then return the choice-variable assignment (plan) with the highest probability of producing a satisfying assignment (goal satisfaction).

Determining all the satisfying assignments can be envisioned as constructing a binary tree in which each node represents a choice (chance) variable, and the two subtrees represent the two possible remaining subformulas given the two possible assignments (outcomes) to the parent choice (chance) variable. At any leaf of this tree, the chain of variable bindings leading to the root is sufficient to evaluate the Boolean formula—at least one literal in each clause is True or all literals in one clause are False. It is critical to construct an efficient tree to avoid evaluating an exponential number of assignments. In the process of constructing this tree:

- an *active variable* is one that has not yet been assigned a truth value,
- an *active clause* is one that has not yet been satisfied by assigned variables,
- the *current CNF subformula* is uniquely specified by the current sets of active clauses and variables, and
- the *value* of a CNF subformula is

$$\max_{\mathbf{D}} \sum_{\mathbf{S}} \left(\prod_{v_i \in \mathbf{CH}} \pi_i^{tr(v_i)} (1-\pi_i)^{1-tr(v_i)} \right),$$

where $\mathbf{D}$ is the set of all possible assignments to the active choice variables, $\mathbf{S}$ is the set of all satisfying assignments to the active chance variables, $\mathbf{CH}$ is the set of all active chance variables, $tr(v_i) \in \{0,1\}$ is the truth value of v_i (0 = False, 1 = True), and π_i is the probability that v_i is True.

In general, a brute-force computation of a CNF subformula value is not feasible. To prune the number of assignments that must be considered, full DPLL uses several variable selection heuristics (Majercik & Littman

1998). Our modified DPLL uses only one of these; we select, whenever possible, a variable that appears alone in an active clause and assign the appropriate value (unit propagation, **UNIT**). For chance variable i, this decreases the success probability by a factor of π_i or $1-\pi_i$. This can be shown to leave the value of the current CNF formula unchanged.

When there are no more unit clauses, we must split on an active variable (always preferring choice variables). If we split on a choice (chance) variable, we return the maximum (probability weighted average) of assigning True to the variable and recurring or assigning False and recurring. The splitting heuristic used is critical to the algorithm's efficiency; experiments (Majercik & Littman 1998) indicate that splitting on the variable that would appear earliest in the plan—time-ordered splitting (**TIME**)—is a very successful heuristic.

The solver still scaled exponentially with plan horizon, however, even on some simple plan-evaluation computations. The fact that a simple dynamic-programming plan evaluation algorithm can be created that scales linearly with plan horizon (see the following section) led us to incorporate dynamic programming into the solver in the form of memoization: the algorithm stores the values of solved subformulas for possible reuse. This greatly extends the size of the plan we can feasibly evaluate (Majercik & Littman 1998).

We tested modified DPLL (**UNIT/TIME**) on the full plan-generation problem in SAND-CASTLE-67 for plan horizons ranging from 1 to 10. Optimal plans found by MAXPLAN exhibit a rich structure: beyond a horizon of 3, the horizon i plan is not a subplan of the horizon $i+1$ plan. The optimal 10-step plan is D-E-D-E-E-D-E-D-E-E (D = dig-moat, E = erect-castle). This plan succeeds with near certainty (probability 0.9669) and MAXPLAN finds it in approximately 8 seconds on a Sun Ultra-1 Model 140 with 128 Mbytes of memory.

COMPARISONS

We compared MAXPLAN to three other planning techniques (Majercik & Littman 1998):

- BURIDAN (Kushmerick, Hanks, & Weld 1995), a classical AI planning technique that extends partial-order planning to probabilistic domains,
- Plan enumeration with dynamic programming for plan evaluation (ENUM), and
- Dynamic programming (incremental pruning) to solve the corresponding finite-horizon partially observable MDP (POMDP).

There are other important comparisons that should be made; belief networks and influence diagrams (Pearl 1988) are closely related to our work and there are efficient techniques for evaluating them, but their performance relative to MAXPLAN is unknown.

Table 1 summarizes the performance of MAXPLAN on two probabilistic planning problems described by Kushmerick, Hanks, & Weld (1995). Also shown are the running times reported for the two versions of BURIDAN

	Planning time in CPU secs		
	MAXPLAN	BURIDAN	
	Modified DPLL	Forward	Forward-Max
SLIPPERY GRIPPER	0.4	4.5	0.5
BOMB/TOILET	0.3	6.9	7.0

Table 1: Comparison of running times for two probabilistic planning domains

that performed best on these two problems. MAXPLAN does as well as BURIDAN on SLIPPERY GRIPPER and has an order of magnitude advantage on BOMB/TOILET.

We also compared the scaling behavior of MAXPLAN to that of ENUM and POMDP on two problems: SAND-CASTLE-67 and DISARMING-MULTIPLE-BOMBS (Majercik & Littman 1998). MAXPLAN scales exponentially ($O(2.24^N)$) as the horizon increases in SAND-CASTLE-67. ENUM, as expected, also scales exponentially ($O(2.05^N)$). But POMDP, remarkably, scales linearly as the horizon increases. We see much different behavior in DISARMING-MULTIPLE-BOMBS, a problem that allows us to enlarge the state space without increasing the optimal plan horizon. As the state space increases, both ENUM and POMDP scale exponentially ($O(7.50^N)$ and $O(3.50^N)$ respectively), while MAXPLAN's solution time remains constant (less than 0.1 second) over the same range.

CACHING IN THE SOLVER

Further tests of MAXPLAN, however, uncovered a significant problem. Because it stores the value of all subformulas encountered in the solution process, the algorithm is very memory intensive and, in fact, is unable to find the best plan with horizon greater than 15 due to insufficient memory. The situation is illustrated in Figure 2, which compares the performance of full DPLL without memoization to that of modified DPLL (**UNIT/TIME**) with memoization. Note that this is a log plot and that we show the results starting with a plan horizon of 4 since the asymptotic behavior of the algorithm does not become clear until this point.

The top plot shows the performance of full DPLL without memoization. We can extrapolate to estimate performance on larger problems (dotted line), but solution times become prohibitively long. The lower plot ending with an "X" shows the performance of modified DPLL with memoization. The much lower slope of this line (2.24 compared to 3.82 for full DPLL without memoization) indicates the superior performance of this algorithm, but the "X" indicates that no extrapolation is possible beyond horizon 15 due to insufficient memory. In fact, performance data for the horizon 15 plan already indicate memory problems. The wall-clock time is more than three times the CPU time, indicating that the computation is I/O-bound. Memoization allows the algorithm to run orders of magnitude faster but ultimately limits the size of problems that can be solved.

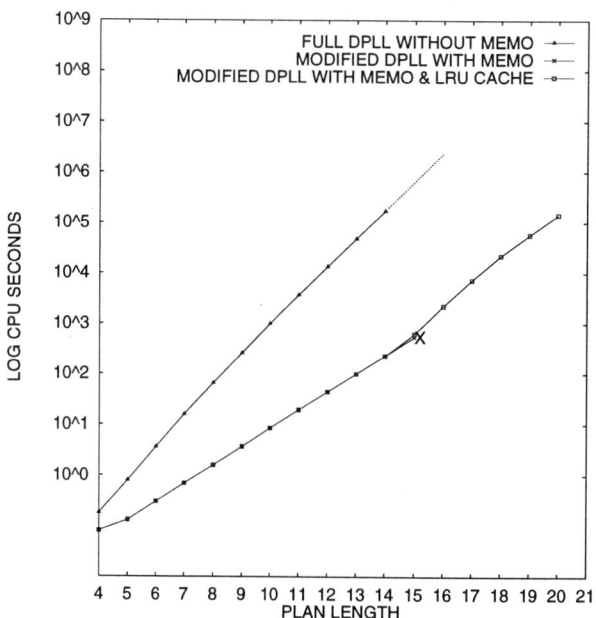

Figure 2: Full DPLL without memoization v. modified DPLL with memoization v. modified DPLL with memoization and LRU caching for SAND-CASTLE-67

LRU Caching

Our solution is to treat the fixed amount of memory available as a *cache* for subformulas and their values. Given a cache size appropriate for the amount of memory on the machine running the algorithm, the problem becomes one of finding the best replacement policy for this cache. We compared two well-known cache replacement policies: first-in-first-out (FIFO) and least-recently-used (LRU). Both were implemented through a linked list of subformulas maintained in the order they were saved. When the cache is full we merely remove the subformula at the head of the list. Under an LRU policy, however, whenever we use a subformula we move it to the end of the linked list. As shown in Figure 3, the LRU cache outperforms the FIFO cache by an average of approximately 18% across the entire range of cache sizes for the 10-step SAND-CASTLE-67 plan.

We tested the LRU caching technique for generating SAND-CASTLE-67 plans with horizons ranging from 1 to 20. For plan horizons from 1 to 15, the cache was made as large as possible without producing significant I/O problems. For larger problems—with larger subformulas to be saved—we calculated cache size so as to

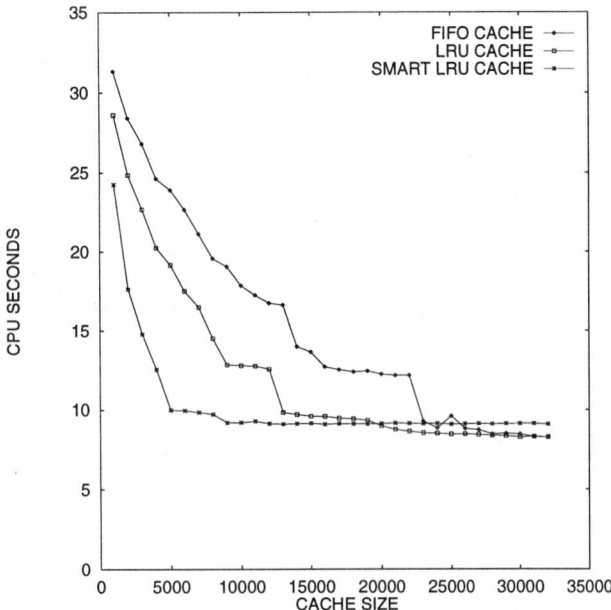

Figure 3: FIFO v. LRU v. Smart LRU for the 10-step plan for SAND-CASTLE-67

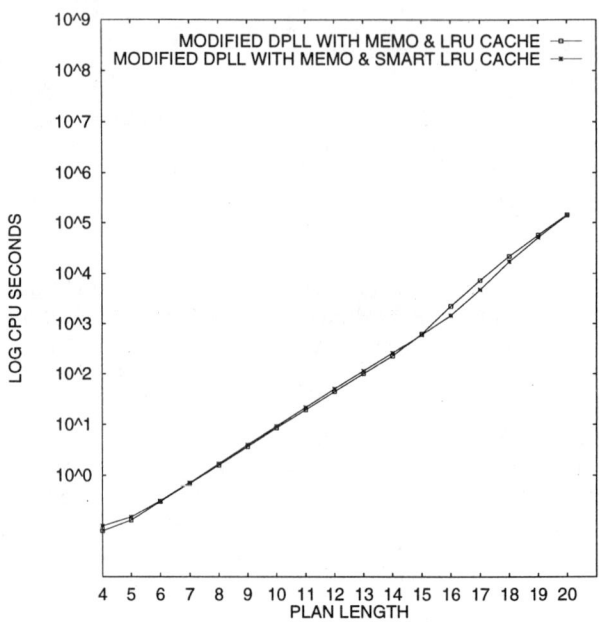

Figure 4: Modified DPLL with memoization and LRU caching v. modified DPLL with memoization and smart LRU caching for SAND-CASTLE-67

keep total cache bytes approximately constant. These results are shown in Figure 2; the performance plot for LRU caching is essentially coincident with the modified DPLL plot up to a plan horizon of 15. For longer plan horizons, LRU caching allows us to break through the memory insufficiency that blocked us before (the "X") yet retain a significant degree of the improved performance that memoization gave us. Solution times for full DPLL without memoization grow as $O(3.82^N)$, where N is the plan horizon. In contrast, modified DPLL with memoization scales as only $O(2.24^N)$, but can only solve problems of a bounded size. Modified DPLL with memoization and caching behaves like modified DPLL with memoization for small N, and then appears to grow as $O(2.96^N)$ once N is large enough for the cache replacement policy to kick in. Thus, the rate of increase for the variant with caching exhibits a growth rate comparable to that of modified DPLL with memoization while eliminating that algorithm's limitation on problem size—it trades away some performance for the ability to solve larger problems. As reported above, ENUM scales as $O(2.05^N)$ without any memory problems.

Smart LRU Caching

We can sometimes improve performance by being selective about the subformulas we cache. The hierarchical relationship among subformulas makes it redundant to save every subformula, but which ones do we save? Large subformulas are unlikely to be reused, and small subformulas, whose value we could quickly recompute, yield little time advantage. This suggests a strategy of saving mid-size subformulas, but experiments indicate that this approach fails for the SAND-CASTLE-67 problem. Another approach is to save subformulas based on difficulty, defined as the number of recursive function calls required to solve that subformula. We experimentally determined that the optimal difficulty range for the SAND-CASTLE-67 problem was 5 to 14. Saving only those subformulas with a difficulty in this range allowed us to find the best 10-step plan for the SAND-CASTLE-67 problem with only an approximate 10% increase in CPU time, and this performance was nearly constant over a broad range of cache sizes (10,000 up to the maximum usable cache of 32,000); see Figure 3.

Applying this "smart" LRU caching technique to plan generation in the SAND-CASTLE-67 domain, we obtained as much as a 37% decrease in CPU seconds compared to straight LRU caching (Figure 4). Unfortunately, the advantages of smart caching seem to disappear as plan horizon increases. Also, it is not obvious how this technique could be exploited in a practical algorithm since we performed extensive tests to determine the optimal difficulty range—tests with other domains indicate that this range is problem dependent.

FUTURE WORK

In addition to the problems described above, we have tested MAXPLAN on several variants of BOMB/TOILET (with clogging and asymmetric actions). But the scaling behavior of MAXPLAN with respect to the size of the state space and the number of actions in the planning domain is largely unexplored. DISARMING-MULTIPLE-BOMBS shows that MAXPLAN can find *simple* solutions efficiently as the state space grows, but we need to test our planner on more complicated domains.

Although our improvements have increased the efficiency of MAXPLAN by orders of magnitude over our initial implementation, more work needs to be done before MAXPLAN can be successfully applied to large-scale probabilistic planning problems. Efficiency could probably be improved by using a better CNF encoding of the planning problem and by using more sophisticated data structures for storing the CNF formulas.

Another promising area is splitting heuristics. Our time-ordered splitting heuristic does not specify an ordering for variables associated with the same time step. A heuristic that addresses this issue could provide a significant performance gain in real-world problems that have a large number of variables at each time step.

When we convert a planning problem to an E-MAJSAT problem, the structure of the planning problem becomes obscured, making it difficult to use our intuition to develop search control heuristics or to prune plans. Although the current E-MAJSAT solver uses heuristics to prune the number of *assignments* that must be considered, this does not directly translate into pruned *plans*. We would like to be able to use our knowledge and intuition about the planning process to develop search control heuristics and plan-pruning criteria. Kautz & Selman (1998), for example, report impressive performance gains resulting from the incorporation of domain-specific heuristic axioms in the CNF formula for deterministic planning problems.

Our experiments with caching yielded promising results, but there are three areas where further work needs to be done. First, although smart LRU caching yielded significant performance improvements, it is not practical unless we can determine the optimal difficulty range for subformulas to be cached without extensive testing. Second, it appears that we could do even better than smart caching. Performance on the 10-step SAND-CASTLE-67 problem deteriorates significantly if the cache size is less than approximately 5000 (Figure 3), yet we know that there are only 1786 distinct subformulas that are reused in the solution process. A better heuristic for selecting subformulas to save could improve the benefits of this technique. Finally, a more sophisticated cache replacement policy could yield additional performance gains.

Approximation techniques need to be explored. Perhaps we can solve an approximate version of the problem quickly and then explore plan improvements in the remaining available time, sacrificing optimality for "anytime" planning and performance bounds. This does not improve worst-case complexity, but is likely to help for typical problems.

Finally, the current planner assumes complete unobservability and produces an optimal straight-line plan; a practical planner must be able to represent and reason about *conditional plans*, which can take advantage of circumstances as they evolve, and *looping plans*, which can express repeated actions compactly (Littman, Goldsmith, & Mundhenk 1998).

CONCLUSIONS

We have described an approach to probabilistic planning that converts the planning problem to an equivalent E-MAJSAT problem—a type of Boolean satisfiability problem—and then solves that problem. The solution method we have devised uses an adaptation of a standard systematic satisfiability algorithm to find all possible satisfying assignments, along with memoization to accelerate the search process. This solution method solves some standard probabilistic planning problems at state-of-the-art speeds, but is extremely memory intensive and exhausts memory searching for moderate-size plans on simple problems.

We described two techniques, based on caching, for reducing memory requirements while still preserving performance to a significant degree. The first technique, using an LRU cache to store subformula values, is generally applicable, regardless of the specific planning problem being solved. The second technique, selectively saving subformula values in an LRU cache based on their computational difficulty, is, at present, problem dependent. But this technique demonstrates the significant performance benefits that can be obtained with smarter LRU caching.

Acknowledgments

This work was supported in part by grant NSF-IRI-97-02576-CAREER.

References

Kautz, H., and Selman, B. 1996. Pushing the envelope: Planning, propositional logic, and stochastic search. In *Proceedings of the Thirteenth National Conference on Artificial Intelligence*, 1194–1201. AAAI Press/The MIT Press.

Kautz, H., and Selman, B. 1998. The role of domain-specific knowledge in the planning as satisfiability framework. To appear in *Proceedings of the Fourth International Conference on Artificial Intelligence Planning*.

Kushmerick, N.; Hanks, S.; and Weld, D. S. 1995. An algorithm for probabilistic planning. *Artificial Intelligence* 76(1-2):239–286.

Littman, M. L.; Goldsmith, J.; and Mundhenk, M. 1998. The computational complexity of probabilistic plan existence and evaluation. Submitted.

Littman, M. L. 1997. Probabilistic propositional planning: Representations and complexity. In *Proceedings of the Fourteenth National Conference on Artificial Intelligence*, 748–754. AAAI Press/The MIT Press.

Majercik, S. M., and Littman, M. L. 1998. MAXPLAN: A new approach to probabilistic planning. To appear in *Proceedings of the Fourth International Conference on Artificial Intelligence Planning*.

Pearl, J. 1988. *Probabilistic Reasoning in Intelligent Systems*. San Mateo, CA: Morgan Kaufmann.

Robotics

Alternative Essences of Intelligence

Rodney A. Brooks, Cynthia Breazeal (Ferrell), Robert Irie, Charles C. Kemp,
Matthew Marjanović, Brian Scassellati, Matthew M. Williamson

MIT Artificial Intelligence Lab, Cambridge, MA, 02139, USA
{brooks,ferrell,irie,cckemp,maddog,scaz,matt}@ai.mit.edu

Abstract

We present a novel methodology for building human-like artificially intelligent systems. We take as a model the only existing systems which are universally accepted as intelligent: humans. We emphasize building intelligent systems which are not masters of a single domain, but, like humans, are adept at performing a variety of complex tasks in the real world. Using evidence from cognitive science and neuroscience, we suggest four alternative essences of intelligence to those held by classical AI. These are the parallel themes of development, social interaction, embodiment, and integration. Following a methodology based on these themes, we have built a physical humanoid robot. In this paper we present our methodology and the insights it affords for facilitating learning, simplifying the computation underlying rich behavior, and building systems that can scale to more complex tasks in more challenging environments.

Introduction

An early development in the history of AI was the claim of Newell & Simon (1961) that humans use physical symbol systems to "think". Over time, this has become adopted into Artificial Intelligence as an implicit and dominant hypothesis (see (Brooks 1991a) for a review). Although this assumption has begun to soften in recent years, a typical AI system still relies on uniform, explicit, internal representations of capabilities of the system, the state of the outside world, and the desired goals. These systems are dominated by search problems to both access the relevant facts, and determine how to apply them. Neo-classical AI adds Bayesian or other probabilistic ideas to this basic framework (Pearl 1988).

The underlying assumption of these approaches is that because a description of reasoning/behavior/learning is possible at some level, then that description must be made explicit and internal to any mechanism that carries out the reasoning/behavior/learning. The realization that descriptions and mechanisms could be separated was one of the great breakthroughs of Rosenschein & Kaelbling (1986), but unfortunately that realization has been largely ignored. This introspective confusion between surface observations and deep structure has led AI away from its original goals of building complex, versatile, intelligent systems and towards the construction of systems capable of performing only within limited problem domains and in extremely constrained environmental conditions.

In this paper we present a methodology based on a different set of basis assumptions. We believe that human intelligence is a direct result of four intertwined attributes: developmental organization, social interaction, embodiment and physical coupling, and multimodal integration. Development forms the framework by which humans successfully acquire increasingly more complex skills and competencies. Social interaction allows humans to exploit other humans for assistance, teaching, and knowledge. Embodiment and physical coupling allow humans to use the world itself as a tool for organizing and manipulating knowledge. Integration allows humans to maximize the efficacy and accuracy of complementary sensory and motor systems.

We have followed this methodology to construct physical humanoid robots (see Figure 1). We design these robots to follow the same sorts of developmental paths that humans follow, building new skills upon earlier competencies. People interact with these robots through behavioral coupling and direct physical contact. The variety of sensory and motor systems on the robots provide ample opportunity to confront integration issues.

Using evidence from human behavior, and early results from our own work, we argue that building systems in this manner affords key insights into how to simplify the computation underlying rich behavior, how to facilitate learning, and how to create mechanisms that can scale to more complex tasks in more challenging environments.

The next section of this paper explores the assumptions about human intelligence which are deeply embedded within classical AI. The following sections explain how our methodology yields a plausible approach to creating robustly functioning intelligent systems, draw-

---

Copyright 1998, American Association for Artificial Intelligence (www.aaai.org). All rights reserved.

Figure 1: Our humanoid robot has undergone many transformations over the last few years. This is how it currently appears.

ing on examples from our research. The final section presents an outline of the key challenges to be faced along this new road in AI.

Assumptions about Intelligence

In recent years, AI research has begun to move away from the assumptions of classical AI: monolithic internal models, monolithic control, and general purpose processing. However, these concepts are still prevalent in much current work, and are deeply ingrained in many architectures for intelligent systems. For example, in the recent AAAI-97 Proceedings, one sees a continuing interest in planning ((Littman 1997, Hauskrecht 1997, Boutilier & Brafman 1997, Blythe & Veloso 1997, Brafman 1997)) and representation ((McCain & Turner 1997, Costello 1997, Lobo, Mendez & Taylor 1997)), which build on these assumptions.

The motivation for our alternative methodology comes from a modern understanding of cognitive science and neuroscience, which counterposes the assumptions of classical AI, as described in the following sections.

Humans have no full monolithic internal models. There is evidence that in normal tasks humans tend to minimize their internal representation of the world. Ballard, Hayhoe & Pelz (1995) have shown that in performing a complex task, like building a copy of a display of blocks, humans do not build an internal model of the entire visible scene. By changing the display while subjects were looking away, Ballard found that subjects noticed only the most drastic of changes; rather than keeping a complete model of the scene, they instead left that information in the world and continued to refer back to the scene while performing the copying task.

There is also evidence that there are multiple internal representations, which are not mutually consistent. For example, in the phenomena of blindsight, cortically blind patients can discriminate different visual stimuli, but actually report seeing nothing (Weiskrantz 1986). This inconsistency would not be a feature of a single central model of visual space.

These experiments and many others like it (e.g. (Rensink, O'Regan & Clark 1997, Gazzaniga & LeDoux 1978)) convincingly demonstrate that humans do not construct a full, monolithic model of the environment. Instead humans tend to only represent what is immediately relevant from the environment, and those representations do not have full access to one another.

Humans have no monolithic control. Naive introspection and observation can lead one to believe in a neurological equivalent of the central processing unit – something that makes the decisions and controls the other functions of the organism. While there are undoubtedly control structures, this model of a single, unitary control system is not supported by evidence from cognitive science.

One example comes from studies of split brain patients by Gazzaniga & LeDoux (1978). These are patients where the corpus callosum (the main structure connecting the two hemispheres of the brain) has been cut. The patients are surprisingly normal after the operation, but with deficits that are revealed by presenting different information to either side of the (now unconnected) brain. Since each hemisphere controls one side of the body, the experimenters can probe the behavior of each hemisphere independently (for example, by observing the subject picking up an object appropriate to the scene that they had viewed). In one example, a snow scene was presented to the right hemisphere and the leg of a chicken to the left. The subject selected a chicken head to match the chicken leg, explaining with the verbally dominant left hemisphere that "I saw the claw and picked the chicken". When the right hemisphere then picked a shovel to correctly match the snow, the left hemisphere explained that you need a shovel to "clean out the chicken shed" (Gazzaniga & LeDoux 1978, p.148). The separate halves of the subject independently acted appropriately, but one side falsely explained the choice of the other. This suggests that there are multiple independent control systems, rather than a single monolithic one.

Humans are not general purpose. The brain is conventionally thought to be a general purpose machine, acting with equal skill on any type of operation that it performs by invoking a set of powerful rules. However, humans seem to be proficient only in particular sets of skills, at the expense of other skills, often in non-obvious ways. A good example of this is the Stroop effect (Stroop 1935). When presented with a list of words written in a variety of colors, performance in a color recognition and articulation task is actually dependent on the semantic content of the words; the task is very difficult if names of colors are printed in non-corresponding colors. This experiment demonstrates the specialized nature of human computational processes and interactions.

Even in the areas of deductive logic, humans often perform extremely poorly in different contexts. Wason (1966) found that subjects were unable to apply the negative rule of if-then inference when four cards were labeled with single letters and digits. However, with additional context—labeling the cards such that they were understandable as names and ages—subjects could easily solve exactly the same problem.

Further, humans often do not use subroutine-like rules for making decisions. They are often more emotional than rational, and there is evidence that this emotional content is an important aspect of decision making (Damasio 1994).

Essences of Human Intelligence

Since humans are vastly complex systems, we do not expect to duplicate every facet of their operation. However, we must be very careful not to ignore aspects of human intelligence solely because they appear complex. Classical and neo-classical AI tends to ignore or avoid these complexities, in an attempt to simplify the problem (Minsky & Papert 1970). We believe that many of these discarded elements are essential to human intelligence and that they actually simplify the problem of creating human-like intelligence.

Development Humans are not born with complete reasoning systems, complete motor systems, or even complete sensory systems. Instead, they undergo a process of development where they are able to perform more difficult tasks in more complex environments en route to the adult state. This is a gradual process, in which earlier forms of behavior disappear or are modified into more complex types of behavior. The adaptive advantage of the earlier forms appears to be that they prepare and enable more advanced forms of behavior to develop within the situated context they provide. The developmental psychology literature abounds with examples of this phenomenon. For instance, the work of Diamond (1990) shows that infants between five and twelve months of age progress through a number of distinct phases in the development of visually guided reaching. In one reaching task, the infant must retrieve a toy from inside a transparent box with only one open side. In this progression, infants in later phases consistently demonstrate more sophisticated reaching strategies to retrieve the toy in more challenging scenarios. As the infant's reaching competency develops, later stages incrementally improve upon the competency afforded by the previous stage.

Social Interaction Human infants are extremely dependent on their caregivers, relying upon them not only for basic necessities but also as a guide to their development. The presence of a caregiver to nurture the child as it grows is essential. This reliance on social contact is so integrated into our species that it is hard to imagine a completely asocial human. However, severe developmental disorders sometimes give us a glimpse of the importance of social contact. One example is autism. Autistic children often appear completely normal on first examination; they look normal, have good motor control, and seem to have normal perceptual abilities. However, their behavior is completely strange to us, in part because they do not recognize or respond to normal social cues (Baron-Cohen 1995). They do not maintain eye contact, recognize pointing gestures, or understand simple social conventions. Even the most highly functioning autistics are severely disabled in our society.

Embodiment Perhaps the most obvious, and most overlooked, aspect of human intelligence is that it is embodied. Humans are embedded in a complex, noisy, constantly changing environment. There is a direct physical coupling between action and perception, without the need for an intermediary representation. This coupling makes some tasks simple and other tasks more complex. By exploiting the properties of the complete system, certain seemingly complex tasks can be made computationally simple. For example, when putting a jug of milk in the refrigerator, you can exploit the pendulum action of your arm to move the milk (Greene 1982). The swing of the jug does not need to be explicitly planned or controlled, since it is the natural behavior of the system. Instead of having to plan the whole motion, the system only has to modulate, guide and correct the natural dynamics. For an embodied system, internal representations can be ultimately grounded in sensory-motor interactions with the world (Lakoff 1987).

Integration Humans have the capability to receive an enormous amount of information from the world. Visual, auditory, somatosensory, and olfactory cues are all processed simultaneously to provide us with our view of the world. However, there is evidence that the sensory modalities are not independent; stimuli from one modality can and do influence the perception of stimuli in another modality. Churchland, Ramachandran & Sejnowski (1994) describe an experiment illustrating how audition can cause illusory visual motion. A fixed square and a dot located to its left are presented to the observer. Without any sound stimuli, the blinking of the dot does not result in any perception of motion. If a tone is alternately played in the left and right ears, with the left ear tone coinciding with the dot pre-

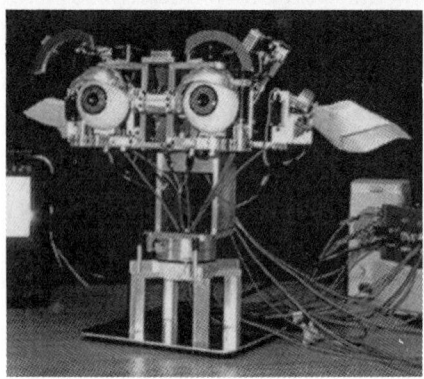

Figure 2: We have built two active vision heads, similar in design to Cog's head. On top is a desktop version with a 1 DOF neck, and below a head with actuators to include facial expressions.

sentation, there is an illusory perception of back and forth motion of the dot, with the square acting as a visual occluder. Vision can cause auditory illusions too, such as the McGurk effect (Cohen & Massaro 1990). These studies demonstrate that humans' perception of their senses cannot be treated as completely independent processes.

Methodology

Our methodology—exploring themes of development, social interaction, physical interaction and integration while building real robots—is motivated by two ideas. First, we believe that these themes are important aspects of human intelligence. Second, from an engineering perspective, these themes make the problems of building human intelligence easier.

Embodiment

A principle tenet of our methodology is to build and test real robotic systems. We believe that building human-like intelligence requires human-like interaction with the world (Brooks & Stein 1994). Humanoid form is important to allow humans to interact with the robot in a natural way. In addition we believe that building a real system is computationally less complex than simulating such a system. The effects of gravity, friction, and natural human interaction are obtained for free, without any computation.

Our humanoid robot, named Cog and shown in Figure 1, approximates a human being from the waist up with twenty-one degrees-of-freedom (DOF) and a variety of sensory systems. The physical structure of the robot, with movable torso, arms, neck and eyes gives it human-like motion, while the sensory systems (visual, auditory, vestibular, and proprioceptive) provide rich information about the robot and its immediate environment. These together present many opportunities for interaction between the robot and humans.

In addition to the full humanoid, we have also developed active head platforms, of similar design to Cog's head, as shown in Figure 2 (Scassellati 1998a). These self-contained systems allow us to concentrate on various issues in close human-machine interaction, including face detection, imitation, emotional display and communication, etc. (Scassellati 1998b, Ferrell 1998c).

Development

Building systems developmentally facilitates learning both by providing a structured decomposition of skills and by gradually increasing the complexity of the task to match the competency of the system.

Bootstrapping Development is an *incremental* process. As it proceeds, prior structures and their behavioral manifestations place important constraints on the later structures and proficiencies. The earlier forms bootstrap the later structures by providing subskills and knowledge that can be re-used. By following the developmental progression, the learning difficulties at each stage are minimized. Within our group, Scassellati (1996) discusses how a humanoid robot might acquire basic social competencies through this sort of developmental methodology.

The work of Marjanović, Scassellati & Williamson (1996) applied bootstrapping techniques to our robot, coordinating visual and motor systems by learning to point toward a visual target. A map used for a saccading behavior (visual/eye-movement map), was reused to learn a reaching behavior (visual/arm-movement map). The learned saccadic behavior bootstrapped the reaching behavior, reducing the complexity of the overall learning task. Other examples of developmental learning that we have explored can be found in (Ferrell 1996).

Gradual increase in complexity The developmental process, starting with a simple system that gradually becomes more complex allows efficient learning throughout the whole process. For example, infants are born with low acuity vision which simplifies the visual input they must process. The infant's visual performance develops in step with their ability to process the influx of stimulation (Johnson 1993). The same is true for the motor system. Newborn infants do not have independent control over each degree of freedom of their limbs, but through a gradual increase in the granularity of their motor control they learn to coordinate the full complexity of their bodies. A process where the acuity of both sensory and motor systems are gradually increased significantly reduces the difficulty of the learning problem (Thelen & Smith 1994).

To further facilitate learning, the gradual increase in internal complexity associated with development should be accompanied by a gradual increase in the complexity of the external world. For an infant, the caregiver biases how learning proceeds by carefully structuring and controlling the complexity of the environment. This approach is in stark contrast to most machine learning methods, where the robot learns in a usually hostile environment, and the bias, instead of coming from the robots' interaction with the world, is included by the designer. We believe that gradually increasing the complexity of the environment makes learning easier and more robust.

By exploiting a gradual increase in complexity both internal and external, while reusing structures and information gained from previously learned behaviors, we hope to be able to learn increasingly sophisticated behaviors. We believe that these methods will allow us to construct systems which do scale autonomously (Ferrell & Kemp 1996).

Social Interaction

Building social skills into an artificial intelligence provides not only a natural means of human-machine interaction but also a mechanism for bootstrapping more complex behavior. Our research program has investigated social interaction both as a means for bootstrapping and as an instance of developmental progression.

Bootstrapping Social interaction can be a means to facilitate learning. New skills may be socially transferred from caregiver to infant through mimicry or imitation, through direct tutelage, or by means of scaffolding, in which a more able adult manipulates the infant's interactions with the environment to foster novel abilities. Commonly scaffolding involves reducing distractions, marking the task's critical attributes, reducing the number of degrees of freedom in the target task, and enabling the subject to experience the end or outcome before the infant is cognitively or physically able of seeking and attaining it for herself (Wood, Bruner & Ross 1976).

We are currently engaged in work studying bootstrapping new behaviors from social interactions. One research project focuses on building a robotic system capable of learning communication behaviors in a social context where the human provides various forms of scaffolding to facilitate the robot's learning task (Ferrell 1998b). The system uses expressive facial gestures (see Figure 2) as feedback to the caregiver (Ferrell 1998a). The caregiver can then regulate the complexity of the social interaction to optimize the robot's learning rate.

Development of social interaction The social skills required to make use of scaffolding are complex. Infants acquire these social skills through a developmental progression (Hobson 1993). One of the earliest precursors is the ability to share attention with the caregiver. This ability can take many forms, from the recognition of a pointing gesture to maintaining eye contact.

In our work, we have also examined social interaction from this developmental perspective. One research program focuses on a developmental implementation of shared attention mechanisms based upon normal child development, developmental models of autism[1], and on models of the evolutionary development of social skills (Scassellati 1996). The first step in this developmental progression is recognition of eye contact. Human infants are predisposed to attend to socially relevant stimuli, such as faces and objects that have humanlike motion. The system is currently capable of detecting faces in its peripheral vision, saccading to the faces, and finding eyes within its foveal vision (Scassellati 1998b). This developmental chain has also produced a simple imitation behavior; the head will mimic yes/no head nods of the caregiver (Scassellati 1998c).

Physical Coupling

Another aspect of our methodology is to exploit interaction and tight coupling between the robot and its environment to give complex behavior, to facilitate learning, and to avoid the use of explicit models. Our systems are physically coupled with the world and operate directly in that world without any explicit representations of it (Brooks 1986, Brooks 1991b). There are representations, or accumulations of state, but these only refer to the internal workings of the system; they are meaningless without interaction with the outside world. The embedding of the system within the world enables the internal accumulations of state to provide useful behavior (this was the fundamental approach taken by Ashby (1960) contemporaneously with the development of early AI).

One example of such a scheme is implemented to control our robot's arms. As detailed in (Williamson 1998a, Williamson 1998b), a set of self-adaptive oscillators are used to drive the joints of the arm. Each joint is actuated by a single oscillator, using proprioceptive information at that joint to alter the frequency and phase of the joint motion. There are no connections between the oscillators, except indirectly through

---

[1] Some researchers believe that the missing mechanisms of shared attention may be central to autism disorders (Baron-Cohen 1995). In comparison to other mental retardation and developmental disorders (like Williams and Downs Syndromes), the deficiencies of autism in this area are quite specific (Karmiloff-Smith, Klima, Bellugi, Grant & Baron-Cohen 1995).

the physical structure of the arm. Without using any kinematic or dynamical models, this simple scheme has been used for a variety of different coordinated tasks, including turning a crank and playing with a slinky toy. The interaction between the arm and the environment enables the oscillators to generate useful behavior. For example, without the slinky to connect the two arms, they are uncoordinated, but when the arms are coupled through the slinky, the oscillators tune into the dynamics of the motion and coordinated behavior is achieved. In all cases, there is no central controller, and no modeling of the arms or the environment; the behavior of the whole system comes from the coupling of the arm and controller dynamics. Other researchers have built similar systems which exhibit complex behavior with either simple or no control (McGeer 1990, Schaal & Atkeson 1993) by exploiting the system dynamics.

Sensory Integration

Sensory Integration Simplifies Computation
Some tasks are best suited for particular sensory modalities. Attempting to perform the task using only one modality is sometimes awkward and computationally intensive. Utilizing the complementary nature of separate modalities results in a reduction of overall computation. We have implemented several mechanisms on Cog that use multimodal integration to aid in increasing performance or developing competencies.

For example, Peskin & Scassellati (1997) implemented a system that stabilized images from a moving camera using vestibular feedback. Rather than attempting to model the camera motion, or to predict motion effects based on efference copy, the system mimics the human vestibular-ocular reflex (VOR) by compensating for camera motion through learned feedback from a set of rate gyroscopes. By integrating two sensory systems, we can achieve better performance than traditional image processing methods, while using less computation.

Sensory Integration Facilitates Learning By integrating different sensory modalities we can exploit the complex nature of stimuli to facilitate learning. For example, objects that make noise often move. This correlation can be exploited to facilitate perception. In our work, we have investigated primarily the relationship between vision and audition in learning to orient toward stimuli.

We can characterize this relationship by examining developmental evidence. Wertheimer (1961) has shown that vision and audition interact from birth; even ten-minute-old children will turn their eyes toward an auditory cue. This interaction between the senses continues to develop, indeed related investigations with young owls have determined that visual stimuli greatly affect the development of sound localization. With a constant visual bias from prisms, owls adjusted their sound localization to match the induced visual errors (Knudsen & Knudsen 1985).

Irie (1997) built an auditory system for our robot that utilizes visual information to train auditory localization; the visually-determined location of a sound source with a corresponding motion is used to train an auditory spatial map. This map is then used to orient the head toward the object. This work highlights not only the development of sensory integration, but also the simplification of computational requirements that can be obtained through integration.

Challenges for Intelligent Systems

This new approach to designing and studying intelligent systems leaves us with a new set of challenges to overcome. Here are the key questions which we must now answer.

- Scaling and Development: What learning structures and organizational principles will allow us to design successful developmental systems?
- Social Interaction:
  - How can the system learn to communicate with humans?
  - What attributes of an infant must the machine emulate in order to elicit caregiver behavior from humans?
  - What drives, motivations and emotions are necessary for the system to communicate effectively with humans?
- Physical Coupling:
  - How can a system scale the complexity of its coordinated motion while still exploiting the dynamics?
  - How can the system combine newly learned spatial skills with previously learned spatial skills? How is that memory to be organized?
  - How can the system use previously learned skills in new contexts and configurations?
- Integration:
  - How can a conglomerate of subsystems, each with different or conflicting goals and behaviors, act with coherence and stability?
  - At what scale should we emulate the biological organism, keeping in mind engineering constraints?
  - What are good measures of performance for integrated systems which develop, interact socially and are physically coupled with the world?

Conclusion

We have reported on a work in progress which incorporates a new methodology for achieving Artificial Intelligence. We have built a humanoid robot that operates and develops in the world in ways that are similar to the ways in which human infants operate and develop. We have demonstrated learning to saccade, learning to correlate auditory and occular coordinate systems, self adapting vestibular-ocular systems, coordinated neck and ocular systems, learning of hand-eye coordination, localization of multiple sounds streams, variable stiffness arms that interact safely with people, arm control based on biological models of invertebrate spinal circuits, adaptive arm control that tunes into to subtle physical cues from the environment, face detection, eye detection to find gaze direction, coupled human robot interaction that is a precursor to caregiver scaffolding for learning, large scale touch sensitive body skin, and multi-fingered hands that learn to grasp objects based on self-categorized stiffness properties. These are components for higher level behaviors that we are beginning to put together using models of shared attention, emotional coupling between robot and caregiver, and developmental models of human infants.

We have thus chosen to approach AI from a different perspective, in the questions we ask, the problems we try to solve, and the methodology and inspiration we use to achieve our goals. Our approach has led us not only to formulate the problem in the context of general human-level intelligence, but to redefine the essences of that intelligence. Traditional AI work has sought to narrowly define a problem and apply abstract rules to its solution. We claim that our goal of creating a learning, scalable, intelligent system, with competencies similar to human beings, is altogether relevant in trying to solve a broad class of real-world situated problems. We further believe that the principles of development, social interaction, physical coupling to the environment, and integration are essential to guide us towards our goal.

Acknowledgments

This project is partially funded by an ONR/ARPA Vision MURI Grant (No. N00014-95-1-0600).

References

Ashby, W. R. (1960), *Design for a Brain*, second edn, Chapman and Hall.

Ballard, D., Hayhoe, M. & Pelz, J. (1995), 'Memory representations in natural tasks', *Journal of Cognitive Neuroscience* pp. 66–80.

Baron-Cohen, S. (1995), *Mindblindness*, MIT Press.

Blythe, J. & Veloso, M. (1997), Analogical Replay for Efficient Conditional Planning, in 'Proceedings of American Association of Artificial Intelligence (AAAI-97)', pp. 668–673.

Boutilier, C. & Brafman, R. I. (1997), Planning with Concurrent Interacting Actions, in 'Proceedings of American Association of Artificial Intelligence (AAAI-97)', pp. 720–726.

Brafman, R. I. (1997), A Heuristic Variable Grid Solution Method for POMDPs, in 'Proceedings of American Association of Artificial Intelligence (AAAI-97)', pp. 727–733.

Brooks, R. A. (1986), 'A Robust Layered Control System for a Mobile Robot', *IEEE Journal of Robotics and Automation* **RA-2**, 14–23.

Brooks, R. A. (1991a), Intelligence Without Reason, in 'Proceedings of the 1991 International Joint Conference on Artificial Intelligence', pp. 569–595.

Brooks, R. A. (1991b), 'Intelligence Without Representation', *Artificial Intelligence Journal* **47**, 139–160. originally appeared as MIT AI Memo 899 in May 1986.

Brooks, R. A. & Stein, L. A. (1994), 'Building brains for bodies', *Autonomous Robots* **1**(1), 7–25.

Churchland, P., Ramachandran, V. & Sejnowski, T. (1994), A Critique of Pure Vision, in C. Koch & J. Davis, eds, 'Large-Scale Neuronal Theories of the Brain', MIT Press.

Cohen, M. & Massaro, D. (1990), 'Synthesis of visible speech', *Behaviour Research Methods, Intruments and Computers* **22**(2), pp. 260–263.

Costello, T. (1997), Beyond Minimizing Change, in 'Proceedings of American Association of Artificial Intelligence (AAAI-97)', pp. 448–453.

Damasio, A. R. (1994), *Descartes' Error*, G.P. Putnam's Sons.

Diamond, A. (1990), Developmental Time Course in Human Infants and Infant Monkeys, and the Neural Bases of Inhibitory Control in Reaching, in 'The Development and Neural Bases of Higher Cognitive Functions', Vol. 608, New York Academy of Sciences, pp. 637–676.

Feigenbaum, E. A. & Feldman, J., eds (1963), *Computers and Thought*, McGraw-Hill, New York.

Ferrell, C. (1996), Orientation Behavior using Registered Topographic Maps, in 'From Animals to Animats: Proc 1996 Society of Adaptive Behavior', Cape Cod, Massachusetts, pp. 94–103.

Ferrell, C. (1998a), Emotional Robots and Learning During Social Exchanges. Submitted to Autonomous Agents-98.

Ferrell, C. (1998b), 'Learning by Scaffolding'. MIT Ph.D. Thesis Proposal.

Ferrell, C. (1998c), A Motivational System for Regulating Human-Robot Interaction. Submitted to AAAI-98.

Ferrell, C. & Kemp, C. (1996), An Ontogenetic Perspective to Scaling Sensorimotor Intelligence, in 'Embodied Cognition and Action: Papers from the 1996 AAAI Fall Symposium', AAAI Press.

Gazzaniga, M. S. & LeDoux, J. E. (1978), *The Integrated Mind*, Plenum Press, New York.

Greene, P. H. (1982), 'Why is it easy to control your arms?', *Journal of Motor Behavior* **14**(4), 260–286.

Hauskrecht, M. (1997), Incremental Methods for computing bounds in partially observable Markov decision processes, in 'Proceedings of American Association of Artificial Intelligence (AAAI-97)', pp. 734–739.

Hobson, R. P. (1993), *Autism and the Development of Mind*, Erlbaum.

Irie, R. E. (1997), Multimodal Sensory Integration for Localization in a Humanoid Robot, *in* 'Proceedings of Second IJCAI Workshop on Computational Auditory Scene Analysis (CASA'97)', IJCAI-97.

Johnson, M. H. (1993), Constraints on Cortical Plasticity, *in* M. H. Johnson, ed., 'Brain Development and Cognition: A Reader', Blackwell, Oxford, pp. 703–721.

Karmiloff-Smith, A., Klima, E., Bellugi, U., Grant, J. & Baron-Cohen, S. (1995), 'Is there a social module? Language, face processing, and theory of mind in individuals with Williams Syndrome', *Journal of Cognitive Neuroscience* **7:2**, 196–208.

Knudsen, E. I. & Knudsen, P. F. (1985), 'Vision Guides the Adjustment of Auditory Localization in Young Barn Owls', *Science* **230**, 545–548.

Lakoff, G. (1987), *Women, Fire, and Dangerous Things: What Categories Reveal about the Mind*, University of Chicago Press, Chicago, Illinois.

Littman, M. L. (1997), Probabilistic Propositional Planning: Representations and Complexity, *in* 'Proceedings of American Association of Artificial Intelligence (AAAI-97)', pp. 748–754.

Lobo, J., Mendez, G. & Taylor, S. R. (1997), Adding Knowledge to the Action Description Language $\mathcal{A}$, *in* 'Proceedings of American Association of Artificial Intelligence (AAAI-97)', pp. 454–459.

Marjanović, M. J., Scassellati, B. & Williamson, M. M. (1996), Self-Taught Visually-Guided Pointing for a Humanoid Robot, *in* 'From Animals to Animats: Proceedings of 1996 Society of Adaptive Behavior', Cape Cod, Massachusetts, pp. 35–44.

McCain, N. & Turner, H. (1997), Causal Theories of Action and Change, *in* 'Proceedings of American Association of Artificial Intelligence (AAAI-97)', pp. 460–465.

McGeer, T. (1990), Passive Walking with Knees, *in* 'Proc 1990 IEEE Intl Conf on Robotics and Automation'.

Minsky, M. & Papert, S. (1970), 'Draft of a proposal to ARPA for research on artificial intelligence at MIT, 1970-71'.

Newell, A. & Simon, H. (1961), GPS, a program that simulates thought, *in* H. Billing, ed., 'Lernende Automaten', R. Oldenbourg, Munich, Germany, pp. 109–124. Reprinted in (Feigenbaum and Feldman, 1963, pp.279–293).

Pearl, J. (1988), *Probabilistic Reasoning in Intelligent Systems*, Morgan Kaufmann, San Mateo, CA.

Peskin, J. & Scassellati, B. (1997), Image Stabilization through Vestibular and Retinal Feedback, *in* R. Brooks, ed., 'Research Abstracts', MIT Artificial Intelligence Laboratory.

Rensink, R., O'Regan, J. & Clark, J. (1997), 'To See or Not to See: The Need for Attention to Perceive Changes in Scenes', *Psychological Science* **8**, 368–373.

Rosenschein, S. J. & Kaelbling, L. P. (1986), The Synthesis of Machines with Provable Epistemic Properties, *in* J. Halpern, ed., 'Proc. Conf. on Theoretical Aspects of Reasoning about Knowledge', Morgan Kaufmann Publishers, Los Altos, California, pp. 83–98.

Scassellati, B. (1996), Mechanisms of Shared Attention for a Humanoid Robot, *in* 'Embodied Cognition and Action: Papers from the 1996 AAAI Fall Symposium', AAAI Press.

Scassellati, B. (1998*a*), A Binocular, Foveated Active Vision System, Technical report, MIT Artificial Intelligence Lab. In submission.

Scassellati, B. (1998*b*), Finding Eyes and Faces with a Foveated Vision System, *in* 'Proceedings of the American Association of Artificial Intelligence'. Submitted to AAAI-98.

Scassellati, B. (1998*c*), Imitation and Mechanisms of Shared Attention: A Developmental Structure for Building Social Skills, *in* 'Agents in Interaction - Acquiring Competence through Imitation: Papers from a Workshop at the Second International Conference on Autonomous Agents'.

Schaal, S. & Atkeson, C. G. (1993), Open loop Stable Control Strategies for Robot Juggling, *in* 'Proceedings 1993 IEEE International Conference on Robotics and Automation', Vol. 3, pp. 913–918.

Stroop, J. (1935), 'Studies of interference in serial verbal reactions', *Journal of Experimental Psychology* **18**, 643–62.

Thelen, E. & Smith, L. (1994), *A Dynamic Systems Approach to the Development of Cognition and Action*, MIT Press, Cambridge, MA.

Wason, P. C. (1966), *New Horizons in Psychology*, Vol. 1, Penguin Books, Harmondsworth, England, pp. 135–51.

Weiskrantz, L. (1986), *Blindsight: A Case Study and Implications*, Clarendon Press, Oxford.

Wertheimer, M. (1961), 'Psychomotor coordination of auditory and visual space at birth', *Science* **134**, 1692.

Williamson, M. M. (1998*a*), Exploiting natural dynamics in robot control, *in* 'Fourteenth European Meeting on Cybernetics and Systems Research (EMCSR '98)', Vienna, Austria.

Williamson, M. M. (1998*b*), Rhythmic robot control using oscillators. Submitted to IROS '98.

Wood, D., Bruner, J. S. & Ross, G. (1976), 'The role of tutoring in problem-solving', *Journal of Child Psychology and Psychiatry* **17**, 89–100.

Eye Finding via Face Detection for a Foveated, Active Vision System

Brian Scassellati
545 Technology Square
MIT Artificial Intelligence Lab
Cambridge, MA, 02139, USA
scaz@ai.mit.edu

Abstract

Eye finding is the first step toward building a machine that can recognize social cues, like eye contact and gaze direction, in a natural context. In this paper, we present a real-time implementation of an eye finding algorithm for a foveated active vision system. The system uses a motion-based prefilter to identify potential face locations. These locations are analyzed for faces with a template-based algorithm developed by Sinha (1996). Detected faces are tracked in real time, and the active vision system saccades to the face using a learned sensorimotor mapping. Once gaze has been centered on the face, a high-resolution image of the eye can be captured from the foveal camera using a self-calibrated peripheral-to-foveal mapping.

We also present a performance analysis of Sinha's ratio template algorithm on a standard set of static face images. Although this algorithm performs relatively poorly on static images, this result is a poor indicator of real-time performance of the behaving system. We find that our system finds eyes in 94% of a set of behavioral trials. We suggest that alternate means of evaluating behavioral systems are necessary.

Introduction

The ability to detect another creature looking at you is critical for many species. Many vertebrates, from snakes (Burghardt 1990), to chickens (Ristau 1991), to primates (Povinelli & Preuss 1995), have been observed to change their behavior based on whether or not eyes are gazing at them. In humans, eye contact serves a variety of social functions, from indicating interest to displaying aggression (Nummenmaa 1964).

Eye direction can also be a critical element of social learning. Eye direction, like a pointing gesture, serves to indicate what object an individual is currently considering. While infants initially lack many social conventions (understanding pointing gestures may not occur until the end of the first year), recognition of eye contact is present from as early as the first month (Frith 1990; Thayer 1977). Detection of eye direction is believed to be a critical precursor of linguistic development (Scaife & Bruner 1975), theory of mind (Baron-Cohen 1995), and social learning and scaffolding (Wood, Bruner, & Ross 1976).

This paper presents the first steps on a developmental progression for building robotic systems that can utilize eye direction as a social signal (Scassellati 1996). The initial goal of our system is to obtain a high resolution image that contains an eye for further processing. We present an algorithm for finding faces and eyes in a cluttered environment. The algorithm that we present has been implemented on a binocular, foveated active vision system (Scassellati 1998), which is part of a humanoid robot project (Brooks & Stein 1994; Brooks et al. 1998).

Overview

The nature of the active vision system constrains our implementation (Ballard 1989). Three copies of this hardware system are currently in use, one on a humanoid robot (see Figure 1) and two as desktop development platforms (see Figure 2). Each has an identical computational environment and very similar mechanical and optical properties (Scassellati 1998). Similar to other active vision systems (Sharkey et al. 1993; Coombs 1992), there are three degrees of freedom; each eye has an independent vertical axis of rotation (pan) and the eyes share a joint horizontal axis of rotation (tilt). We use a foveated vision system to gain both a wide field of view while retaining a high acuity central area, which is a rough approximation of the unequal distribution of photoreceptors on the human retina (Tsotsos 1988). Unlike other foveated systems (Kuniyoshi et al. 1995; van der Spiegel et al. 1989), there are two cameras per eye, one which captures a wide-angle view of the periphery and one which captures a narrow-angle view of the central (foveal) area.[1]

The active vision platform is attached to a parallel network of digital signal processors (Texas Instruments TMS320C40). Each node in the network contains one processor with the option for more specialized hardware

---
[1] The peripheral camera has an approximate field of view of 120°, while the foveal camera has an approximate field of view of 20°.

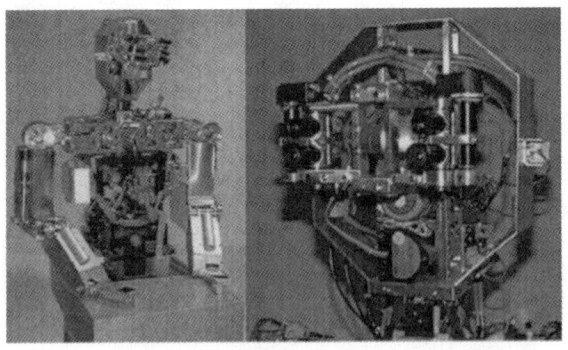

Figure 1: At left, Cog, an upper-torso humanoid robot. At right, a close-up of Cog's active vision system.

Figure 2: One of the desktop active vision development platforms used in this work.

for capturing images, performing convolution quickly, or displaying images to a VGA display. Nodes may be connected with arbitrary bi-directional hardware connections, and distant nodes may communicate through virtual connections. Each camera is attached to its own frame grabber, which can transmit captured images to connected nodes.

The initial goal of our system is to obtain high resolution images of the eyes of a person anywhere in the robot's environment. Because the peripheral camera has a very wide field of view (see Figure 5), we cannot extract eye features from this image. Just as humans must foveate an object to discriminate fine detail, our foveal cameras must be pointed in the direction of a given object in order to provide sufficient resolution. Other research has focused on the tracking of eyes and facial features for video conferencing (Graf *et al.* 1996; Maurer & von der Malsburg 1996), as a user interface (Baluja & Pomerleau 1994; Heinzmann & Zelinsky 1997), or in animation (Terzopoulous & Waters 1991), however, these techniques generally begin with calibrated high resolution images where the face dominates the visual field. Our behavioral goal also provides a constraint on the speed and accuracy of the processing; we are not as concerned with missing a face in a single image since we will have another opportunity to detect in the next frame. Highly accurate (and computationally expensive) techniques for face and eye detection (Rowley, Baluja, & Kanade 1995; Turk & Pentland 1991; Sung & Poggio 1994) may not be necessary. Finally, to better fit with the goals of building social skills developmentally (Scassellati 1996), we prefer an implementation that is biologically plausible.

Our strategy for finding eyes decomposes into the following five steps:

1. The incoming wide-field image is filtered using motion and past history to find potential face locations.
2. For each potential face location, a face detection algorithm based on ratio templates (Sinha 1996) is used to verify the presence of a face.
3. The face location with the highest score is selected and the active vision system saccades to that face using a learned sensorimotor mapping.
4. With the template estimate of the eye locations, and a self-calibrated peripheral-to-foveal mapping, the location of the eye in the foveal image is computed.
5. A high-resolution foveal image of the eye is captured for further processing.

We begin with a detailed discussion of the ratio template face detection algorithm, and then discuss the pre-filtering technique that we use to enable the algorithm to run in real time.

Finding Faces

Our choice of a face detection algorithm was based on three criteria. First, it must be a relatively simple computation that can be performed in real time. Second, the technique must perform well under social conditions, that is, in an unstructured environment where people are most likely to be looking directly at the robot. Third, it should be a biologically plausible technique. Based on these criteria, we selected the ratio template approach described by Sinha (1994).

The ratio template algorithm was designed to detect frontal views of faces under varying lighting conditions, and is an extension of classical template approaches (Sinha 1996). While other techniques handle rotational invariants more accurately (Sung & Poggio 1994), the simplicity of the ratio template algorithm allows us to operate in real time while detecting faces that are most likely to be engaged in social interactions. Ratio templates also offer multiple levels of biological plausibility; templates can be either hand-coded or learned adaptively from qualitative image invariants (Sinha 1994).

A ratio template is composed of a number of regions and a number of relations, as shown in Figure 3. For each target location in the grayscale peripheral image, a template comparison is performed using a special set of comparison rules. Overlaying the template with a 14 pixel by 16 pixel grayscale image patch at a potential face location, each region is convolved with the grayscale image to give the average grayscale value for that region. Relations are comparisons between region values, for example, between the "left forehead" region and the "left temple" region. The relation is satisfied if the ratio of the first region to the second region exceeds a constant value (in our case, 1.1). This ratio allows us to compare the intensities of regions without relying on the absolute intensity of an area. In Figure 3, each arrow indicates a relation, with the head of the arrow denoting the second region (the denominator of the ratio). This template capitalizes on illumination-invariant observations. For example, the eyes tend to be darker than the surrounding face, and the nose is generally brighter than its surround. We have adapted the ratio template algorithm to process video streams. In doing so, we require the absolute difference between the regions to exceed a noise threshold, in order to eliminate false positive responses for small, noisy grayscale values.

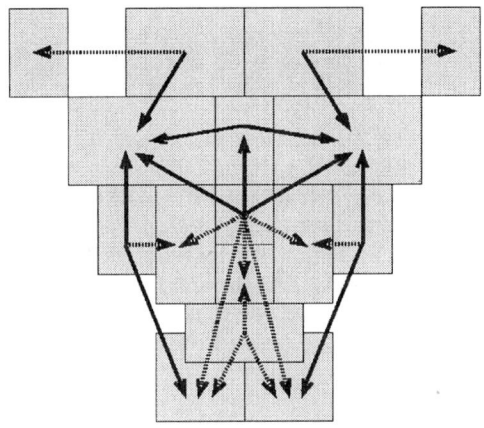

Figure 3: A 14 pixel by 16 pixel ratio template for face detection. The template is composed of 16 regions (the gray boxes) and 23 relations (shown by arrows). Adapted from Sinha (1996).

The ratio template algorithm can easily be modified to detect faces at multiple scales. Multiple nodes of the parallel network run the same algorithm on different sized input images, but without changing the size of the template. This allows the system to respond more quickly to faces that are closer to the robot, since closer faces are detected in smaller images which require less computation. With this hardware platform, a 64×64 image and a 14×16 template can be used to detect faces within approximately three to four feet of the robot. The same size template can be used on a 128×128 image to find faces within approximately ten feet of the robot.

Improving the Speed of Ratio Templates

To improve the speed of the ratio template algorithm, we have implemented two optimizations: an early-abort scheme and a motion-based prefilter.

At the suggestion of Sinha (1997), we further classified the relations of our ratio-template into two categories: eleven essential relations, shown as solid arrows in Figure 3, and twelve confirming relations, shown as dashed arrows. We performed a post-hoc analysis of this division upon approximately ten minutes of video feed in which one of three subjects was always in view. For this post-hoc analysis, an arbitrary threshold of eighteen of the twenty-three relations was required to be classified as a face. This threshold eliminated virtually all false positive detections while retaining at least one detected face in each image. An analysis of the detected faces indicated that at least ten of the eleven essential relations were always satisfied. None of the confirming relations achieved that level of specificity. Based on this analysis, we established a new set of thresholds for face detection: ten of the eleven essential relations and eight of the twelve confirming relations must be satisfied. As soon as two or more of the essential relations have failed, we can reject the location as a face. This increases the speed of our computation by a factor of 4, as shown in Table 1, without any observable decrease in performance.

To further increase the speed of our computation, we use a pre-filtering technique based on motion. The prefilter allows us to search only locations that are likely to contain a face. Consecutive images are differenced, thresholded, and then convolved with a 14×16 kernel of unitary value (the same size as the ratio template) in order to generate the average amount of super-threshold movement for each potential face location. If that average motion value for a location exceeds threshold, then that location is a candidate for face detection. For each incoming frame, a location is a potential target for the face detection routine if it has had motion within the last five frames, if the ratio template routine verified a face in that location within the last five frames, or if that location had not been checked for faces within the last three seconds. In this way, we capture faces that have just entered the field of view (through the motion clause) and faces that have stopped moving (through the past history clause). The prefilter also resets every three seconds, allowing the system to re-acquire faces that have dropped below the noise threshold. The prefilter automatically resets any time the active system moves, since this generates induced motion of the visual field. This filtering technique increased the speed of the face detection routines by a factor of five for 64×64 images and a factor of eight for 128×128 images (see Table 1). The smaller image size appeared to saturate at 20 Hz due to constant computational loads in the rest of the system, primarily from drawing display images to a VGA display. The filtering technique greatly reduced the number of background locations to be searched without any observable loss of accuracy.

Static Evaluation of Ratio Templates

To evaluate the static performance of the ratio template algorithm, we ran the algorithm on a test set of static

| Image | Detection Method | | |
Size	Template	+ Early-Reject	+ Prefilter
64 × 64	1 Hz	4 Hz	20 Hz
128 × 128	.25 Hz	1 Hz	8 Hz

Table 1: Processing speed for two image sizes with various optimizations. The original ratio template method is enhanced by a factor of four with the addition of the early-reject optimization, and by an additional factor of five to eight by the prefilter optimization. The system saturated near 20 Hz due to constant computational loads in other parts of the network. All statistics are for a single TMS320C40 node with no other processes.

face images first used by Turk and Pentland (1991). The database contains images for 16 subjects, each photographed under three different lighting conditions and three different head rotations.

To test lighting invariance, we considered only the images with an upright head position at a single scale, giving a test set of 48 images under lighting conditions with the primary light source at 90 degrees, 45 degrees, and head-on. Figure 4 shows the images from two of the subjects under each lighting condition. The ratio template algorithm detected 34 of the 48 test faces. Of the 14 faces that were missed, nine were the result of three subjects that failed to be detected under any lighting conditions. One of these subjects had a full beard, while another had very dark rimmed glasses, both of which seem to be handled poorly by the static detection algorithm. Of the remaining five misses, two were from the 90 degree lighting condition, two from the 45 degree lighting condition, and one from the head-on condition. While this detection rate (71%) is considerably lower than other face detection schemes (Rowley, Baluja, & Kanade 1995; Turk & Pentland 1991; Sung & Poggio 1994), this result is a poor indicator of the performance of the algorithm in a complete, behaving system, as we will see below.

Using the real-time system, we determined approximate rotational ranges of the ratio template algorithm. Subjects began looking directly at the camera and then rotated their head until the system failed to detect a face. Across three subjects, the average ranges were ±30 degrees pitch, ±30 degrees yaw, and ±20 degrees roll.

Finding Eyes

Once a face has been detected, the active vision system must accurately saccade to that location, bringing the foveal camera into position to capture a high-resolution image of the eye. To solve this sensorimotor problem, we could build an accurate kinematic and dynamic model of the robotic system and use that model to compute saccade motions. However, the kinematic solution is difficult to characterize accurately, taking into account the misalignments of the cameras, the op-

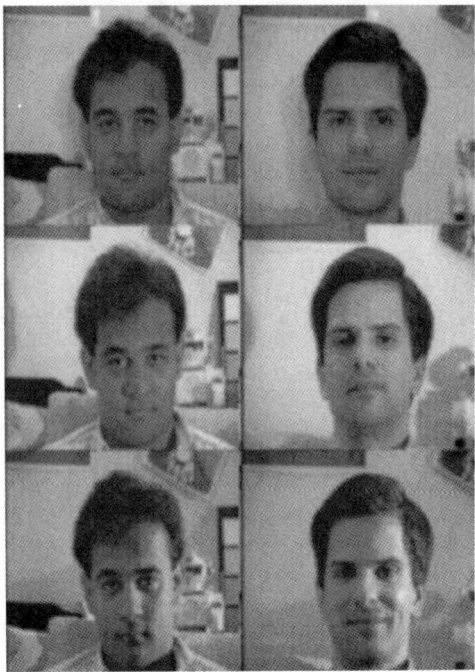

Figure 4: Six of the static test images from Turk and Pentland (1991) used to evaluate the ratio template face detector. Each face appears in the test set with three lighting conditions, head-on (top), from 45 degrees (middle), and from 90 degrees (bottom). The ratio template correctly detected 71% of the faces in the database, including each of these faces except for the middle image from the first column.

tical imperfections, and the imperfect construction of any real system (Ballard 1989). An accurate kinematic solution is also extremely hardware dependent; the kinematic solution for one of the development platforms would differ significantly from the solution for the active vision system of the humanoid robot.

An alternative is to learn the functional mapping between the position of the target on the image plane and the motor commands necessary to foveate that object. A learned solution can be adapted not only for each instance of a hardware platform, but also each time a specific hardware platform undergoes some kind of change. We desire the system to be completely self-supervised and on-line so that learning can proceed continuously and without any human intervention.

Because the ratio template algorithm gives us an implicit location for the eyes within a verified face, we need to solve only two problems: how to learn to saccade to the target face, and how to map the locations in the peripheral image to locations in the foveal image. We choose to saccade to the target face, and then to relocate the position of the face in the peripheral image, not only to resist noise in the saccade mapping but also to allow for slight movements of the subject during the saccade.

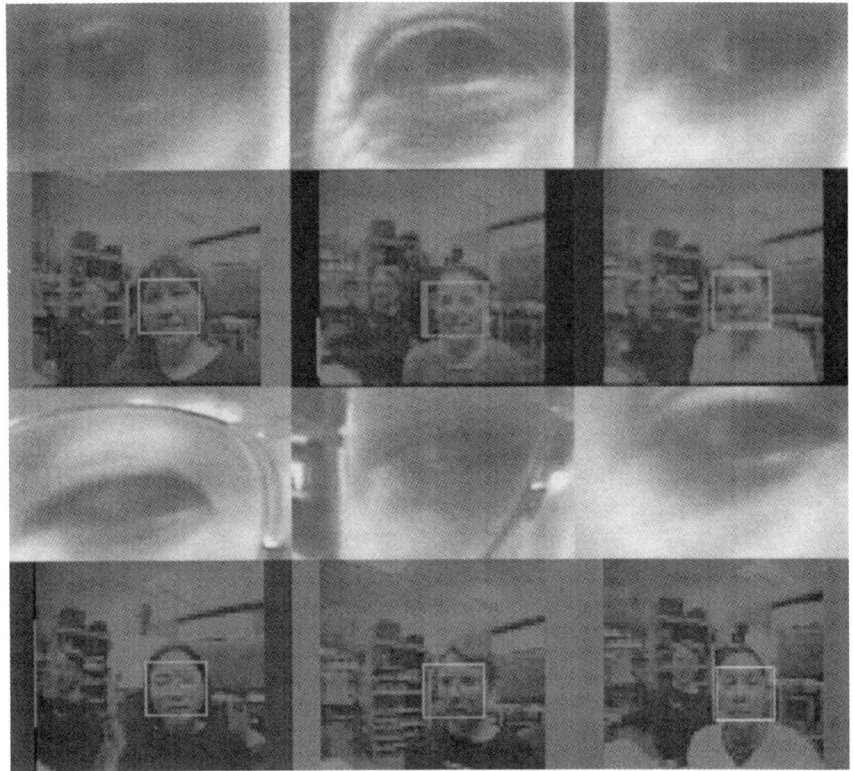

Figure 6: Six detected faces and eyes. The lower image of each pair shows the post-saccade location of the detected face. The upper image of each pair shows the section of the foveal image obtained from mapping the peripheral template location to the foveal coordinates. Only faces of a single scale (roughly within four feet of the robot) are shown here.

Figure 5: An example face in a cluttered environment. The 128x128 grayscale image was captured by the active vision system, and then processed by the pre-filtering and ratio template detection routines. One face was found within the image, and is shown outlined.

Saccading to a Face

The problem of saccading to a visual target can be viewed as a function approximation problem, where the equation

$$\vec{S}(\vec{e}, \vec{x}) \mapsto \Delta\vec{e} \qquad (1)$$

defines the saccade function $\vec{S}$ which transforms the current motor positions $\vec{e}$ and the location of a target stimulus in the image plane $\vec{x}$ to the change in motor position necessary to move that target to the center of the visual field.

Marjanović, Scassellati, and Williamson (1996) learned a saccade function for this hardware platform using a 17×17 interpolated lookup table. The map was initialized with a linear set of values obtained from self-calibration. For each learning trial, a visual target was randomly selected. The robot attempted to saccade to that location using the current map estimates. The target was located in the post-saccade image using correlation, and the L_2 offset of the target was used as an error signal to train the map. The system learned to center pixel patches in the peripheral field of view. The system converged to an average of < 1 pixel of error in a 128×128 image per saccade after 2000 trials (1.5 hours). With this map implementation, a face could be centered in the peripheral field of view. However, this does not necessarily place the eye in a known location in the foveal field of view. We must still convert an image location in the peripheral image to a location in the foveal image.

Mapping Peripheral to Foveal Images

After the active vision system has saccaded to a face, the face and eye locations from the template in the peripheral camera are mapped into the foveal camera using a second mapping. This mapping matches a rectangular region of pixels in the peripheral image with a (larger) rectangular region of pixels in the foveal image. To estimate this function, four parameters must be determined: the scale factor in each dimension between the peripheral and foveal images (to determine the size of the foveal rectangle), and the offset between the peripheral rectangle and the foveal rectangle in each dimension.

To estimate the difference in scale between the two cameras, we exploit the active nature of the system. We can estimate the difference in scale factors by moving the eyes at a constant velocity and observing the rates of optical flow of a background patch. The ratio of the flow rates is the ratio of the scale between the cameras. To accomplish this, the system first verifies that there is no motion within the field of view, using the motion detection routines established for the prefilter. The system then selects a patch of background pixels from the center of the field of view. Once the eye begins moving, a simple correlation-based tracking algorithm monitors the rate that the peripheral and foveal patches move. While it is possible to estimate both the horizontal and vertical scale factors in one movement, the initial implementation of this system used separate horizontal and vertical motions to estimate the scale parameters. For both the development platform and the active vision head of the humanoid robot, the scale factors in both the horizontal and vertical dimensions was 4.0. The scale factor is a function of the differences in the cameras and lenses, not in the alignment of the cameras. This value is thus stable between the eyes and throughout the lifetime of the system.

Once we have an estimation of the scale factors, we can find the differences in offset position using image correlation. The foveal image is scaled down by the computed ratios. The scaled-down image can then be correlated with the peripheral image to find the best match location. Because the foveal and peripheral cameras are aligned vertically, the depth of the patch being considered can affect the row position of the best match. For our initial estimates of this function, we record the correlation when the ratio template algorithm, running at a specific scale, has detected a face. This gives us an estimate of where the face occurs in the foveal image for faces of this size. This method is imprecise, but obtains results that are sufficient for the overall behavior of the complete system. For one ratio template scale running on the development platform, the best match for the left eye was located at an offset of 168 rows and 248 columns, and at an offset of 184 rows and 250 columns for the right eye (based on 512 × 512 images). We expect slightly different values for each eye, since the offset values are affected by misalignments in the individual camera mountings.

Once this mapping has been obtained, whenever a face is foveated we can extract the image of the eye from the foveal image. This extracted image is then ready for further processing. Figure 5 shows the result of the face detection routines on a typical grayscale image before the saccade. After the face was detected, the system saccaded to that position, converted the template-specified eye location in the peripheral image to a foveal bounding box, and extracted the portion of the foveal image. Examples of this process are shown in Figure 6. While the peripheral image has barely enough information to detect the face, the foveal image contains a great deal of detail.

Evaluation

The evaluation of this system must be based on the behavior that it produces, which can often be difficult to quantify. The system succeeds when it eventually finds a face and is able to extract a high resolution image of an eye. However, to compare the performance of the entire system with the performance of the ratio template algorithm on static images, a strawman quantitative analysis of a single behavior was studied. To simplify the analysis, we considered only a single scale of face detection, requiring the subjects to sit within 4 feet of one of the active vision platforms. The subject was to remain stationary during each trial, but was encouraged to move to different locations between trials. These tests were conducted in the complex, cluttered background of our laboratory workspace (identical to Figure 5).

For each behavioral trial, the system began with the eyes in a fixed position, roughly centered in the visual field. The system was allowed one saccade to foveate the subject's right eye (an arbitrary choice). The system used the prefiltering and ratio template face detection routines to generate a stream of potential face locations. Once a face was detected, and remained stable (within an error threshold) for six cycles (indicating the person had remained stationary), the system attempted to saccade to that location. In a total of 140 trials distributed between 7 subjects, the system extracted a foveal image that contained an eye on 131 trials (94% accuracy). Of the missed trials, two resulted from an incorrect face identification (a face was falsely detected in the background clutter), and seven resulted from either an inaccurate saccade or motion of the subject.

This quantitative analysis of the system is extremely promising. However, the true test of the behavioral system is in eventually obtaining the goal. Even in this simple analysis, we can begin to see that the total behavior of the system may be able to correct for errors in individual components of the system. For example, one incorrect face identification was a temporary effect between part of the subject's clothing and the background. Once the system had shifted its gaze to the (false) face location, the location no longer appeared face-like. Without the arbitrary imposition of behavioral trials, the natural behavior of the system would then have been to saccade to what it did consider a face, achieving the original goal. Also, in some failures that resulted from incorrect saccades, the system correctly identified a face location but failed to center that location due to an incompletely trained saccade map. The system extracted only a portion of the eye in these cases. The saccade map is extremely non-linear in the far reaches of the visual field due to the extremely wide field of view of the peripheral cameras (as described in Scassellati (1998)). If the system had been allowed to continue behaving, rather than being forced into the next trial, it would again have detected a face, this time very close to the center of the field of view and within the well-trained region of the saccade map, and corrected for its slight error.

If our behavioral test had allowed for a second chance to obtain the goal, the failure rate can be estimated as the product of the failure rates for each individual trial. If we assume that these are independent saccades, the probability of failure for a two-attempt behavior becomes $0.06 \times 0.06 = .0036$. As we allow for more and more corrective behavior, the stability of the system increases. While individual trials are probably not completely statistically independent, we can see from this example how the behavior of the system can be self-stabilizing without requiring extremely accurate perceptual tools.

Issues like these make quantitative analysis of behaving systems difficult, and often misleading (Brooks 1991). Our system does not require a completely general-purpose face recognition engine. In a real-world environment, the humans to whom the robot must attend in order to gain the benefits of social interaction are generally cooperative. They are attempting to be seen by the robot, keeping their own attention focused on the robot, facing toward it, and often unconsciously moving to try to attract its attention. Further, the system need not be completely accurate on every timestep; its behavior need only converge to the correct solution. If the system can adequately recognize these situations, then it has fulfilled its purpose.

Future Work

The eye detection system presented here performs the localization task reasonably well. However, there are still many open research questions, and many implementation details that require additional support, including:

- A better arbitration scheme for multiple faces at multiple scales.
- Additional tolerance to face rotation.
- Depth-based prefiltering.
- A richer characterization of the peripheral to foveal map to include depth discrepancies.
- Continuous smooth-pursuit tracking for acquired faces.

These additions will enhance the richness of the overall behavior of the system.

This paper has presented the first step toward building social skills for a humanoid robot. With the ability to obtain high resolution images of eyes, it is possible for the system to detect eye contact and to identify where a person is looking. Building a general system that can recognize direction of gaze requires the following additional competencies:

- The ability to detect head and eye orientation.
- The ability to integrate head and eye orientation to produce a visual gaze angle.
- The ability to extrapolate a gaze angle toward an object in the world (perhaps utilizing a rough depth map).

These research areas in turn lead to more interesting social behaviors, allowing a human-like robot to interact with humans in a natural, social context and providing a mechanism for social learning.

Conclusions

This paper has presented an eye and face finding system for a foveated active vision system. The basic face detection algorithm was based on the ratio template design developed by Sinha (1996) and adapted for the recognition of frontal views of faces under varying lighting conditions. We have further developed this algorithm to increase the processing speed by a factor of twenty by using a combination of early-abort detection and a motion-based prefilter. While this algorithm performed relatively poorly on a standard test set of static face images, this measurement was a poor indicator of how the algorithm would perform on live video streams. By utilizing a pair of learned sensorimotor mappings, our system was capable of saccading to faces and extracting high resolution images of the eye on 94% of trials. However, even this statistic was misleading, since the behavior of the overall system eventually corrected for trials where the first saccade missed the target. To further evaluate behaving systems in complex environments, more refined observation techniques are necessary.

Acknowledgments

The author receives support from a National Defense Science and Engineering Graduate Fellowship. Support for this project is provided in part by an ONR/ARPA Vision MURI Grant (No. N00014-95-1-0600). The author wishes to thank Rod Brooks, Pawan Sinha, and the members of the Cog group for their continued support.

References

Ballard, D. 1989. Behavioral constraints on animate vision. *Image and Vision Computing* 7:1:3–9.

Baluja, S., and Pomerleau, D. 1994. Non-intrusive gaze tracking using artificial neural networks. Technical Report CMU-CS-94-102, Carnegie Mellon University.

Baron-Cohen, S. 1995. *Mindblindness*. MIT Press.

Brooks, R., and Stein, L. A. 1994. Building brains for bodies. *Autonomous Robots* 1:1:7–25.

Brooks, R. A.; Ferrell, C.; Irie, R.; Kemp, C. C.; Marjanovic, M.; Scassellati, B.; and Williamson, M. 1998. Alternative essences of intelligence. In *Proceedings of the Fifteenth National Conference on Artificial Intelligence (AAAI-98)*. AAAI Press.

Brooks, R. A. 1991. Intelligence without reason. In *Proceedings of the 1991 International Joint Conference on Artificial Intelligence*, 569–595.

Burghardt, G. 1990. Cognitive ethology and critical anthropomorphism: A snake with two heads and hog-nosed snakes that play dead. In Ristau, C., ed., *Cognitive Ethology: The Minds of Other Animals*. Erlbaum.

Coombs, D. J. 1992. Real-time gaze holding in binocular robot vision. Technical Report TR415, U. Rochester.

Frith, U. 1990. *Autism : Explaining the Enigma*. Basil Blackwell.

Graf, H. P.; Chen, T.; Petajan, E.; and Cosatto, E. 1996. Locating faces and facial parts. Technical Report TR-96.4.1, AT&T Bell Laboratories.

Heinzmann, J., and Zelinsky, A. 1997. Robust real-time face tracking and gesture recognition. In *Proceedings of IJCAI-97*, volume 2, 1525–1530.

Kuniyoshi, Y.; Kita, N.; Sugimoto, K.; Nakamura, S.; and Suehiro, T. 1995. A foveated wide angle lens for active vision. In *Proc. IEEE Int. Conf. Robotics and Automation*.

Marjanović, M.; Scassellati, B.; and Williamson, M. 1996. Self-taught visually-guided pointing for a humanoid robot. In *From Animals to Animats 4: Proceedings of the Fourth International Conference on Simulation of Adaptive Behavior (SAB-96)*, 35–44. Bradford Books.

Maurer, T., and von der Malsburg, C. 1996. Tracking and learning graphs and pose on image sequences of faces. In *Proc. 2nd Int. Conf. on Automatic Face- and Gesture-Recognition*, 176–181. IEEE Press.

Nummenmaa, T. 1964. *The Language of the Face*, volume 9 of *University of Jyvaskyla Studies in Education, Psychology and Social Research*. Reported in Baron-Cohen (1995).

Povinelli, D. J., and Preuss, T. M. 1995. Theory of mind: evolutionary history of a cognitive specialization. *Trends in Neuroscience* 18(9):418–424.

Ristau, C. 1991. Attention, purposes, and deception in birds. In Whiten, A., ed., *Natural Theories of Mind*. Blackwell.

Rowley, H.; Baluja, S.; and Kanade, T. 1995. Human face detection in visual scenes. Technical Report CMU-CS-95-158, Carnegie Mellon University.

Scaife, M., and Bruner, J. 1975. The capacity for joint visual attention in the infant. *Nature* 253:265–266.

Scassellati, B. 1996. Mechanisms of shared attention for a humanoid robot. In *Embodied Cognition and Action: Papers from the 1996 AAAI Fall Symposium*. AAAI Press.

Scassellati, B. 1998. A binocular, foveated active vision system. Technical Report 1628, MIT Artificial Intelligence Lab Memo.

Sharkey, P. M.; Murray, D. W.; Vandevelde, S.; Reid, I. D.; and McLauchlan, P. F. 1993. A modular head/eye platform for real-time reactive vision. *Mechatronics Journal* 3(4):517–535.

Sinha, P. 1994. Object recognition via image invariants: A case study. *Investigative Ophthalmology and Visual Science* 35:1735–1740.

Sinha, P. 1996. *Perceiving and recognizing three-dimensional forms*. Ph.D. Dissertation, Massachusetts Institute of Technology.

Sinha, P. 1997. Personal communication. August, 1997.

Sung, K.-K., and Poggio, T. 1994. Example-based learning for view-based human face detection. Technical Report 1521, MIT Artificial Intelligence Lab Memo.

Terzopoulous, D., and Waters, K. 1991. Techniques for realistic facial modeling and animation. In Magnenat-Thalmann, M., and Thalmann, D., eds., *Computer Animation '91*. Springer-Verlag.

Thayer, S. 1977. Children's detection of on-face and off-face gazes. *Developmental Psychology* 13:673–674.

Tsotsos, J. K. 1988. A "complexity level" analysis of vision. *International Journal of Computer Vision* 1(4).

Turk, M., and Pentland, A. 1991. Eigenfaces for recognition. *Journal of Cognitive Neuroscience* 3(1).

van der Spiegel, J.; Kreider, G.; Claeys, C.; Debusschere, I.; Sandini, G.; Dario, P.; Fantini, F.; Belluti, P.; and Soncini, G. 1989. A foveated retina-like sensor using ccd technology. In Mead, C., and Ismail, M., eds., *Analog VLSI implementation of neural systems*. Kluwer Academic Publishers. pp. 189–212.

Wood, D.; Bruner, J. S.; and Ross, G. 1976. The role of tutoring in problem-solving. *Journal of Child Psychology and Psychiatry* 17:89–100.

Template-Based Recognition of Pose and Motion Gestures On a Mobile Robot

Stefan Waldherr Sebastian Thrun Roseli Romero Dimitris Margaritis

Computer Science Department
Carnegie Mellon University
Pittsburgh, PA

Abstract

For mobile robots to assist people in everyday life, they must be easy to instruct. This paper describes a gesture-based interface for human robot interaction, which enables people to instruct robots through easy-to-perform arm gestures. Such gestures might be static *pose gestures*, which involve only a specific configuration of the person's arm, or they might be dynamic *motion gestures* (such as waving). Gestures are recognized in real-time at approximate frame rate, using a hybrid approach that integrates neural networks and template matching. A fast, color-based tracking algorithm enables the robot to track and follow a person reliably through office environments with drastically changing lighting conditions. Results are reported in the context of an interactive clean-up task, where a person guides the robot to specific locations that need to be cleaned, and the robot picks up trash which it then delivers to the nearest trash-bin.

Introduction

The field of robotics is currently undergoing a change. While in the past, robots where predominately used in factories for purposes such as manufacturing and transportation, a new generation of "service robots" has recently begun to emerge. Service robots cooperate with people and assist them in their everyday tasks. A landmark service robot is Helpmate Robotics's Helpmate robot, which has already been deployed at numerous hospitals worldwide (King & Weiman 1990). In the near future, similar robots are expected to appear in various branches of entertainment, recreation, health-care, nursing, etc., and we expect them to interact closely with people.

This upcoming generation of service robots opens up new research opportunities. While the issue of *mobile robot navigation* has been researched quite extensively (see e.g., (Kortenkamp, Bonassi, & Murphy 1998; Borenstein, Everett, & Feng 1996)), considerably little attention has been paid to issues of *human-robot interaction*. However, many service robots will be operated by non-expert users, who might not even be capable of operating a computer keyboard. It is therefore essential that these robots be equipped with "natural" human robot interfaces that facilitate the interaction of robots and people.

Copyright 1998, American Association for Artificial Intelligence (www.aaai.org). All rights reserved.

The need for more effective human robot interfaces has been recognized. For example, in his M.Sc. thesis, Torrance developed a natural language interface for teaching mobile robots names of places in an indoor environment (Torrance 1994). Due to the lack of a speech recognition system, his interface still required the user to operate a keyboard; however, the natural language component made instructing the robot significantly easier. More recently, Asoh and colleagues (Asoh *et al.* 1997) developed an interface that integrates a speech recognition system into a phrase-based natural language interface. They successfully instructed their "office-conversant" robot to navigate to office doors and other significant places in their environment, using verbal commands. Other researchers have proposed vision-based interfaces that allow people to instruct mobile robots via arm gestures. For example, Kortenkamp and colleagues (Kortenkamp, Huber, & Bonassi 1996) recently developed a gesture-based interface, which is capable of recognizing arm poses such as pointing towards a location on the ground. In a similar effort, Kahn and colleagues (Kahn *et al.* 1996) developed a gesture-based interface which has been demonstrated to reliably recognize static arm poses (pose gestures) such as pointing. This interface was successfully integrated into Firby's reactive plan-execution system RAP (Firby *et al.* 1995), where it enabled people to instruct a robot to pick up free-standing objects. Both of these approaches, however, recognize only static pose gestures. They cannot recognize gestures that are defined through specific temporal patterns of arm movements, such as waving. Motion gestures, which are commonly used for communication among people, provide additional freedom in the design of gestures. In addition, they reduce the chances of accidentally classifying arm poses as gestures that were not intended as such. Thus, they appear better suited for human robot interaction than static pose gestures.

This paper presents a vision-based human robot interface that has been designed to instruct a mobile robot through both pose and motion gestures. An adaptive dual-color tracking algorithm enables the robot to find, track, and follow a person around at speeds of up to one foot per second. This tracking algorithm can quickly adapt to different lighting conditions. Gestures are recognized by a real-time template-matching algorithm. This algorithm works in two phases: one that recognizes static arm poses, and one that recognizes gestures.

Figure 1: AMELIA, the robot used in our research, is a RWI B21 robot equipped with a color camera mounted on a pan-tilt unit, 24 sonar sensors, and a 180° SICK laser range finder.

The algorithm can recognize both pose and motion gestures.

This approach has been integrated into our existing robot navigation and control software (Thrun *et al.* 1998; Burgard *et al.* 1998), where it enables human operators

- to provide direct motion commands (e.g., stopping),
- to guide the robot to places which it can memorize
- to indicate the location of objects (e.g., trash on the floor)
- and to initiate clean-up tasks, where the robot searches for trash, picks it up, and delivers it to the nearest trash-bin.

In a pilot study, we have successfully instructed our robot to pick up trash scattered in an office building, and to deposit it into a trash-bin. This task was motivated by the "clean-up an office" task, which was designed for the AAAI-94 mobile robot competition (Simmons 1995). Our scenario differs from the competition task in that a human interacts with the robot and initiates the clean-up task, which is then performed autonomously by the robot.

In our experiments, we found the interface to be reliable and relatively easy to use. While this is only an example application designed to test the utility of motion gestures in human robot interaction, we believe that our interface is applicable to a larger range of upcoming service robots.

Visual Tracking and Servoing

The lowest-level component of our approach is a color-based tracking algorithm, which enables the robot to find, track, and follow people in real-time. Visual tracking of people has been studied extensively (Darrel, Moghaddam, & Pentland 1996; Crowley 1997; Wren *et al.* 1997). Many existing approaches assume that the camera is mounted at a fixed location. Such approaches typically rely on a static background, so that human motion can be detected through image differencing. Some approaches (e.g., (Yang & Waibel 1995)) can track people if the camera is mounted on a pan-tilt unit, which can impose mild changes in illumination. Recognizing gestures with a robot-mounted camera is more difficult due to the occasional occurrence of drastic changes in background and lighting conditions that are caused by robot motion. This problem has previously been addressed by (Wong, Kortenkamp, & Speich 1995; Huber & Kortenkamp 1995), who successfully devised algorithms for tracking people visually similar to the one proposed here.

Since our algorithm for finding people is a specialization of our tracking algorithm, let us first describe the tracking algorithm. This algorithm tracks people based on a combi-

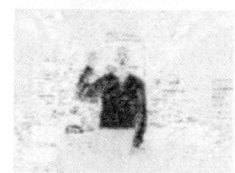 
 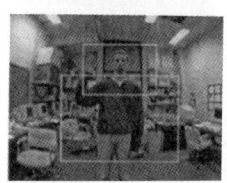

Figure 2: Tracking a person: (a) Raw camera image, (b) face-color filtered image, and (c) body-color filtered image. The darker a pixel in the filtered images, the smaller the Mahalanobis distance to the mean color. (d) Projection of the filtered image onto the horizontal axis (within a search window). (e) Face and body center, as used for tracking and adaptation of the filters. (f) Search window, in which the person is expected to be found in the next image.

nation of two colors, namely face color and body color (i.e., shirt color). It iterates four steps:

Step 1: Color Filtering. Two Gaussian color filters are applied to each pixel in the image. Each filter is of the form

$$c_i = \begin{pmatrix} e^{(X_i - \hat{X}_{\text{face}})^T \Sigma_{\text{face}}^{-1} (X_i - \hat{X}_{\text{face}})} \\ e^{(X_i - \hat{X}_{\text{body}})^T \Sigma_{\text{body}}^{-1} (X_i - \hat{X}_{\text{body}})} \end{pmatrix} \quad (1)$$

where X_i is the color vector of the i-th image pixel, $\hat{X}_{\text{face}}$ and Σ_{face} are the mean and covariance matrix of a face color model, and $\hat{X}_{\text{body}}$ and Σ_{body} are the mean and covariance matrix of a body (shirt) color model. The result of this operation are two filtered images, example of which are shown in Figures 2b&c. These images are then smoothed locally using a pseudo-Gaussian kernel with width 5, in order to reduce the effects of noise.

Step 2: Alignment. Next, the filtered image pair is searched for co-occurrences of vertically aligned face and body color. This step rests on the assumption that a person's face is above his/her shirt in the camera image. First, the image is mapped into a horizontal vector, where each value corresponds to the combined face- and body-color integrated vertically. Figure 2d illustrates the results of this alignment step. The gray-level in the two center regions indicate graphically the horizontal density of face and body color. The darker a region, the better the match. Both responses are then multiplied, to determine the estimated horizontal coordinates of the person. Finally, the filtered image regions are searched vertically for the largest occurrence of the respective color, to determine the vertical coordinates of face and body. Figure 2e shows the results of this search. We found this scheme to be highly reliable, even for people that moved hastily in

Figure 3: Example gestures: (a) stop gesture and (b) follow gesture. While the stop gesture is a pose gesture, the follow gesture involves motion, as indicated by the arrows.

front of the robot.

Step 3: Servoing. If the robot is in visual servoing mode (meaning that it is following a person), it issues a motion command that makes the robot turn and move towards this person. The command is passed on to a collision avoidance method (Fox, Burgard, & Thrun 1997) that sets the actual velocity and motion direction of the robot in response to proximity sensor data.

Step 4: Adaptation. Finally, the means and covariances $\hat{X}_{\text{face}}, \Sigma_{\text{face}}, \hat{X}_{\text{body}}, \Sigma_{\text{body}}$ are adapted, to compensate changes in illumination. The robot computes new means and covariances from small rectangular regions around the center of the face and the body (shown in Figure 2e). Let $\hat{X}^*_{\text{face}}, \Sigma^*_{\text{face}}, \hat{X}^*_{\text{body}}, \Sigma^*_{\text{body}}$ denote these new values, obtained from the most recent image. The means and covariances are updated according to the following rule, which is a temporal estimator with exponential delay:

$$\begin{aligned}
\hat{X}_{\text{face}} &\longleftarrow \alpha \hat{X}^*_{\text{face}} + (1-\alpha)\hat{X}_{\text{face}} \\
\sigma_{\text{face}} &\longleftarrow \alpha \sigma^*_{\text{face}} + (1-\alpha)\sigma_{\text{face}} \\
\hat{X}_{\text{body}} &\longleftarrow \alpha \hat{X}^*_{\text{body}} + (1-\alpha)\hat{X}_{\text{body}} \\
\sigma_{\text{body}} &\longleftarrow \alpha \sigma^*_{\text{body}} + (1-\alpha)\sigma_{\text{body}}
\end{aligned} \quad (2)$$

Here α is a decay factor, which we set to 0.1 in all our experiments.

Finding a person. To find a person and acquire an initial color model, the robot scans the image for face color only, ignoring its body color filter. Once a color blurb larger than a specific threshold is found, the robot acquires its initial body color model based on a region below the face. Thus, the robot can track people with arbitrary shirt colors, as long as they are sufficiently coherent.

Our tracking algorithm, which can be viewed of a two-color extension of basic color-based tracking algorithms such as those described in (Yang & Waibel 1995; Swain 1991), was found to work reliably when tracking people and following them around through buildings with rapidly changing lighting conditions. The tracking routine is executed at a rate of 20 Hertz on a 200 Mhz Pentium PC. This speed is achieved by focusing the computation (Steps 1 and 2) on a small window around the location where the person was previously seen. Thus far, we tested the tracker only for various types of single-color shirts with long sleeves; experiments for multi-colored shirts were not yet conducted.

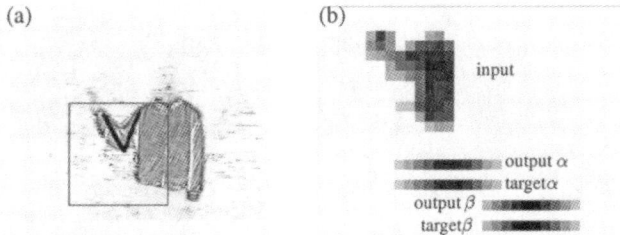

Figure 4: Neural network pose analysis: (a) Camera image, with the two arm angles as estimated by the neural network superimposed. The box indicates the regions which is used as network input. (b) The input to the neural network, a down-sampled, color-filtered image of size 10 by 10, and the outputs and targets of the networks for the two angle.

Template-Based Recognition of Pose and Motion Gestures

A primary goal of this work has been to devise a vision-based interface that is capable of recognizing both pose and motion gestures. Pose gestures involve a static configuration of a person's arm, such as the "stop" gesture shown in Figure 3a, whereas motion gestures are defined through specific motion patterns of an arm, such as the "follow me" gesture shown in Figure 3b.

Our approach employs two phases, one for recognizing poses from a single image (pose analysis), and one for recognizing sequences of poses from a stream of images (temporal template matching).

Pose Analysis

In the first phase, a probability distribution over all poses is computed from a camera image. Our approach integrates two alternative methods for image interpretation: a neural-network based method and a graphical template matcher (called: pose template matcher). Both approaches operate on a color-filtered sub-region of the image which contains the person's right side, as determined by the tracking module. They output a probability distribution over arm poses.

The *neural network-based approach* predicts the angles of the two arm segments relative to the person's body from the image segment. The input to the network is a down-sampled image segment, and the output are the angles, encoded using multi-unit Gaussian representations (Pomerleau 1993). In our implementation, we used 60 output units, 30 for each of the two arm angles. The network was trained with Back-propagation, using a database of 758 hand-labeled training images. After training, the average error was 4.91° for the angle of the upper arm segment and 5.54° for the angle of the lower arm segment. These numbers were obtained using an independent set of 252 testing images. Figure 4a shows an example image. Superimposed here are the two angle estimates, as generated by the neural network. Figure 4b shows the input, output, and target values for the network. The input is a down-sampled, color-filtered image of size 10 by 10. The output is Gauss-encoded. The nearness of the outputs (first and third row) and the targets (second and forth row) suggests that in this example, the network predicts the angle with high accuracy.

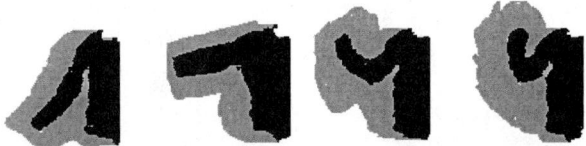

Figure 5: Examples of pose templates. The excitatory region is shown in black and the inhibitory in gray. White regions are not considered in the matching process.

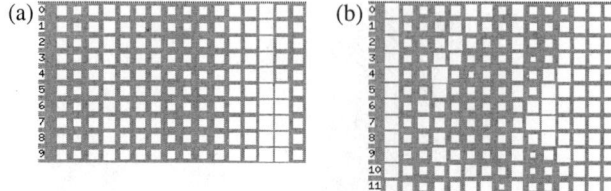

Figure 6: Examples of gesture templates. Gesture templates are sequences of prototype feature vectors. Shown here are gesture templates for (a) stop gesture (does not involve motion), (b) follow gesture (involves motion, as indicated by the change over time).

Our approach also employs a template-based algorithm for analyzing poses, which compares poses to a set of pre-recorded *pose templates*. More specifically, the color-filtered image is correlated with a set of 16 pre-recorded templates of arm poses. Each pose template consist of three regions: an *excitatory region*, which specifies where the arm is to be expected for a specific pose, an *inhibitory region*, where the arm should *not* be for this pose, and a *don't-know region*, which is not considered when computing the correlation. Figure 5 shows examples of pose templates. Here excitatory regions are shown in black, whereas inhibitory regions are shown in gray. The templates are constructed from labeled examples of human arm poses (one per template), where the excitatory region is extracted from the largest coherent region in the filtered image segment, and a straightforward geometric routine is employed to determine a nearby inhibitory region. In a experiment involving 122 example images, we recorded that in 85.8% of all cases, the correct pose was identified; in 9.68% a nearby pose was recognized, and in only 4.52% the pose template matcher produced an answer that was clearly wrong. While the choice of 16 as the number of templates is somewhat ad hoc, we found that it covered the space of possible arm poses in sufficient density for the tasks at hand.

Both methods, the neural network-based method and the pose template matcher, generate multi-dimensional *feature vectors*, one for each image. The integration of two different methods for pose analysis was originally driven by the goal of understanding the different strengths and weaknesses of the approaches. While neural networks generate information at much higher accuracy (floating-point accuracy vs. 1-out-of-16), in preliminary evaluations we observed that they are less robust to occlusions of body parts. These results, however, are preliminary, and a systematic experimental comparison is currently underway.

Temporal Template Matching

In the second phase, a temporal template matcher compares the temporal stream of feature vectors with a set of pre-recorded prototypes (gesture templates) of individual gestures.

Figure 6 shows examples of gesture templates, for the gestures "stop" (Figure 6a) and "follow" (Figure 6b). Each of these templates is a sequence of prototype feature vectors, where time is arranged vertically. The size of the white boxes indicates the magnitude of the corresponding numerical value. Gesture templates are composed of a sequence of feature vectors, constructed from a small number (e.g., 5) of training examples. For graphical clarity, only feature vectors with 16 components obtained with the pose template matchers are shown here. As can be seen in this figure, the stop gesture is a pose gesture (hence all feature vectors look alike), whereas the follow gesture involves motion. Both types of gestures—pose gestures and motion gestures—are encoded through such gesture templates.

The temporal template matcher continuously analyzes the stream of incoming feature vectors for the presence of gestures. It does this by matching the gesture template to the most recent n feature vectors, for varying numbers of n (in our implementation, $n = 40, 50, \ldots, 80$); notice that the gesture templates are much shorter than n. To compensate differences in the exact timing when performing gestures, our approach uses the Viterbi algorithm (Rabiner & Juang 1986) for time alignment. The Viterbi alignment employs dynamic programming to find the best temporal alignment between the feature vector sequence and the gesture template, thereby compensating for variations in the exact timing of a gesture. Figure 7 shows an actual sequence, during which a person performs the follow gesture. The reader should notice that this example exhibits a similar pattern as shown in Figure 6b. The arrow marks the point in time at which the follow gesture is complete and recognized as such by the Viterbi algorithm.

Learning

Both sets of templates, the pose templates and the gesture templates, are learned from examples, just like the neural network. To teach the robot a new gesture, the person presents itself in front of the robot and executes this gesture several times, in pre-specified time intervals. Our approach then segments these examples into pieces of equal length, and uses the average feature vector in each time segment as a prototype segment. We found the current training scheme to be robust to variations of various sorts, as long as the person exercises reasonable care when training the robot. In most cases, a single training gesture suffices to build a reliable template.

Integration and Results

The gesture-based approach has been integrated into our previously developed mobile robot navigation system, thereby building a robot that can be instructed by natural means (Thrun *et al.* 1998; Burgard *et al.* 1998). In a nutshell, our navigation methods enable robots to navigate safely while acquiring maps of unknown environments. A fast motion planner allows robots to move from point to point or, alternatively, to explore unknown terrain. Collisions with obsta-

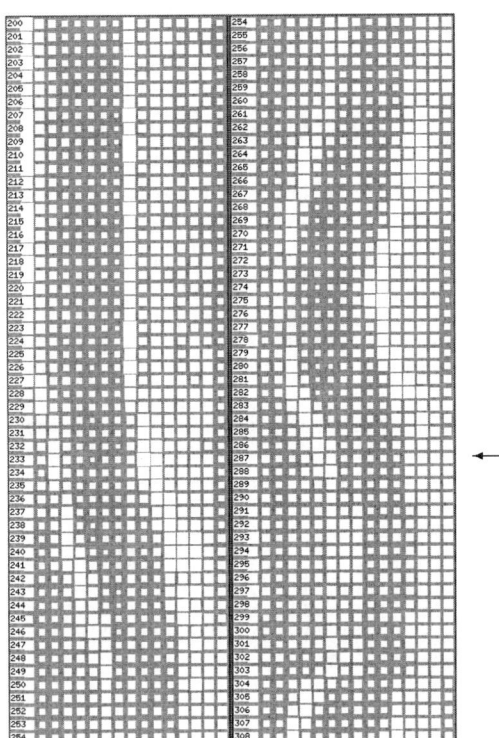

Figure 7: Example of a feature vector stream that contains a *follow* gesture. The arrow indicates the point in time when *follow* is recognized.

	recognition result					
	follow	stop	point-1	point-2	abort	no gesture
follow	59	-	-	-	-	-
stop	-	39	1	-	-	-
point-1	-	-	44	-	-	6
point-2	-	-	-	42	-	-
abort	1	2	-	-	16	1
no gesture	-	-	-	-	-	50

Table 1: Recognition results. Each row shows the recognition result for examples of a specific gesture (including 50 tests where the human subject did not perform any gesture).

cles are avoided by a fast, reactive routine, which sets the velocity and travel direction of the robot according to periodic measurements of the robot's various proximity sensors (laser, sonar, infrared, tactile). While the robot is in motion, a concurrent localization method continuously tracks the robot's position, by comparing sensor readings with the learned map of the environment. Permanent blockages lead to modifications of the map, and thus to new motion plans.

We tested the effectiveness of the gesture-based interface in the context of a clean-up task that involved human user interaction and mobile manipulation. The specific choice of the task was motivated by past AAAI mobile robot competitions, in which robots were asked to find and remove all sorts of objects (trash, tennis balls, etc.).

- **Follow**: If the robot is shown a follow gesture, it follows a person around. The follow gesture involves waving the arm, as indicated in Figure 3a.
- **Stop**: If the robot is shown a stop gesture, it immediately stops. The stop gesture is a pose gesture, as shown in Figure 3b.
- **Pointing**: If the person points towards an object on the ground, the robot starts searching for an object within its visual field. If it succeeds, it moves towards the object, picks it up, and then returns to the nearest trash-bin. The location of trash-bins is known to the robot. In our implementation, the pointing gesture is actually a motion gesture, which involves moving the arm from the body towards the pointing direction and back. We found this version of the pointing gesture to lead to fewer false-positives.
- **Abort**: If the person shows an abortion gesture, the robot moves back to its initial position and waits for a new person.

Table 1 surveys experimental results for the recognition accuracy of the gesture-based interface. Each row corresponds to a number of experiments, in which a human subject presented a specific gesture. Because of the diversity of possible pointing gestures, this specific gesture was realized by two different gesture templates, one for pointing towards the floor (labeled "point-1" in Table 1) and one for pointing horizontally (labeled "point-2"). In some experiments, no gesture was shown, to test the robot's ability to detect gestures only if the person actually performed one.

As can be seen in Table 1, our approach recognizes gestures fairly accurately. In 211 experiments in which a human showed a gesture and an additional 50 experiments where the human did not show a gesture, the robot classified 95.8% of the examples correctly. With 95% confidence, the overall accuracy is in the range $[93.3\%; 98.3\%]$. Some gestures had a 100% recognition rate (follow and point-2), whereas the point-1 gesture was only recognized with 88% accuracy.

Figure 8 shows an example run, in which our robot AMELIA is instructed to pick up a piece of trash. Shown there is a map of the the robot's environment, constructed using an occupancy grid technique (Moravec 1988; Thrun et al. 1998), along with the actual path of the robot and the (known) location of a trash-bin. Initially, the robot waited in the corridor for a person. The person instructed the robot to follow him into the lab (using the follow gesture), where it first stopped the robot (using the stop gesture), then pointed at a piece of trash (a can). The robot picked up the can, and returned to the corridor where it deposited the trash in a bin. We found that operating the robot at low speed (0.7 feet per second) made it easier to instruct the robot. Tests at higher speeds (1.5 feet per second) made it difficult to position the robot reliably close to a trash can, even though our software can manage much higher speeds. In the future, we plan to extend the interface so that the person can select the speed, and in addition give direct commands to the robot (such as "rotate left" or "move 2 feet back").

Discussion

This paper described a gesture-based interface for human-robot interaction. A hybrid approach, consisting of an adap-

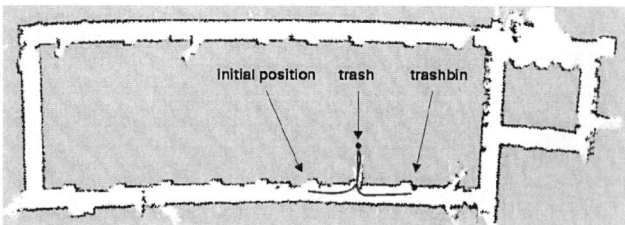

Figure 8: Map of the robot's operational range (80 by 25 meters) with trace of a specific example of a successful clean-up operation. The robot waited in the corridor, was then guided by a human into a lab, where it picked up a can and later deposited it into a trash-bin.

tive color-filter, two template matchers and an artificial neural network, were described for recognizing human arm gestures from streams of camera images. Our approach is capable of recognizing both static pose gestures and dynamic motion gestures. The paper demonstrated the usefulness of the interface in the context of a clean-up task, where a person cooperated with the robot in cleaning up trash.

We believe that finding "natural" ways of communication between humans and robots is of importance for the field of robotics, as a variety of recent changes in both robotic hardware and software suggests that service robots will soon become possible, and commercially viable. This research is intended to be a step towards this goal.

There are several open questions and limitations that warrant further research. For example, the tracking module is currently unable to deal with multi-colored shirts, or to follow people who do not face the robot. We believe, however, that the robustness can be increased by considering other cues, such as shape and texture, when tracking people. Secondly, our approach currently lacks a method for teaching robots new gestures. This is not really a limitation of the basic gesture-based interface, as it is a limitation of the robot's finite state machine that controls its operation. Future work will include providing the robot with the ability to learn new gestures, and to associate those with specific actions and/or locations. Together with our existing mapping and navigation software, this should lead to a robot that can be taught a collection of tasks in novel indoor environments. Thus, by providing the robot with the ability to learn new things, we seek to explore further the practical utility of gesture-based instruction in the context of mobile service robotics. Finally, we believe it is worthwhile to augment the interface by a speech-based interface, so that both gestures and speech can be combined when instructing a mobile robot.

Acknowledgment

Partial financial support by Daimler-Benz Research, the Defense Advanced Research Projects Agency (DARPA) via the Airforce Missile System Command under contract number F04701-97-C-0022, and FAPESP (Brazil) under grant number 96/4515-8 is gratefully acknowledged.

References

Asoh, H.; Hayamizu, S.; Hara, I.; Motomura, Y.; Akaho, S.; and Matsui, T. 1997. Socially embedded learning of office-conversant robot jijo-2. In *Proceedings of IJCAI-97*. IJCAI, Inc.

Borenstein, J.; Everett, B.; and Feng, L. 1996. *Navigating Mobile Robots: Systems and Techniques*. Wellesley, MA: A. K. Peters, Ltd.

Burgard, W.; Cremers, A.; Fox, D.; Hähnel, D.; Lakemeyer, G.; Schulz, D.; Steiner, W.; and Thrun, S. 1998. The interactive museum tour-guide robot. In *Proceedings of AAAI-98*.

Crowley, J. 1997. Vision for man-machine interaction. *Robotics and Autonomous Systems* 19:347–358.

Darrel, T.; Moghaddam, B.; and Pentland, A. 1996. Active face tracking and pose estimation in an interactive room. In *Proceedings of ICCV-96*, 67–72.

Firby, R.; Kahn, R.; Prokopowicz, P.; and Swain, M. 1995. An architecture for active vision and action. In *Proceedings of IJCAI-95*, 72–79.

Fox, D.; Burgard, W.; and Thrun, S. 1997. The dynamic window approach to collision avoidance. *IEEE Robotics and Automation* 4(1).

Huber, E., and Kortenkamp, D. 1995. Using stereo vision to pursue moving agents with a mobile robot. In *Proceedings of IEEE ICRA-95*.

Kahn, R.; Swain, M.; Prokopowicz, P.; and Firby, R. 1996. Gesture recognition using the perseus architecture. In *Proceedings of the IEEE CVPR-96*, 734–741.

King, S., and Weiman, C. 1990. Helpmate autonomous mobile robot navigation system. In *Proceedings of the SPIE Conference on Mobile Robots*, 190–198. Volume 2352.

Kortenkamp, D.; Bonassi, R.; and Murphy, R., eds. 1998. *AI-based Mobile Robots: Case studies of successful robot systems*. Cambridge, MA: MIT Press.

Kortenkamp, D.; Huber, E.; and Bonassi, P. 1996. Recognizing and interpreting gestures on a mobile robot. In *Proceedings of AAAI-96*, 915–921.

Moravec, H. P. 1988. Sensor fusion in certainty grids for mobile robots. *AI Magazine* 61–74.

Pomerleau, D. 1993. *Neural Network Perception for Mobile Robot Guidance*. Boston, MA: Kluwer Academic Publishers.

Rabiner, L., and Juang, B. 1986. An introduction to hidden markov models. In *IEEE ASSP Magazine*.

Simmons, R. 1995. The 1994 AAAI robot competition and exhibition. *AI Magazine* 16(1).

Swain, M. 1991. Color indexing. *International Journal of Computer Vision* 7.

Thrun, S. et al. 1998. Map learning and high-speed navigation in RHINO. In Kortenkamp, D.; Bonassi, R.; and Murphy, R., eds., *AI-based Mobile Robots: Case studies of successful robot systems*. Cambridge, MA: MIT Press.

Torrance, M. C. 1994. Natural communication with robots. Master's thesis, MIT Department of EECS, Cambridge, MA.

Wong, C.; Kortenkamp, D.; and Speich, M. 1995. A mobile robot that recognizes people. In *Proceedings of ICTAI-95*.

Wren, C.; Azarbayejani, A.; Darrell, T.; and Pentland, A. 1997. Pfinder: Real-time tracking of the human body. *IEEE Transactions on Pattern Analysis and Machine Learning* 19(7):780–785.

Yang, J., and Waibel, A. 1995. Tracking human faces in real-time. Technical Report CMU-CS-95-210, School of Computer Science, Carnegie Mellon University, Pittsburgh, PA.

Position Estimation for Mobile Robots in Dynamic Environments

Dieter Fox, Wolfram Burgard, Sebastian Thrun[‡], Armin B. Cremers

Computer Science Department III
University of Bonn
Bonn, Germany

[‡]School of Computer Science
Carnegie Mellon University
Pittsburgh, PA

Abstract

For mobile robots to be successful, they have to navigate safely in populated and dynamic environments. While recent research has led to a variety of localization methods that can track robots well in *static* environments, we still lack methods that can robustly localize mobile robots in dynamic environments, in which people block the robot's sensors for extensive periods of time or the position of furniture may change. This paper proposes extensions to Markov localization algorithms enabling them to localize mobile robots even in densely populated environments. Two different filters for determining the "believability" of sensor readings are employed. These filters are designed to detect sensor readings that are corrupted by humans or unexpected changes in the environment. The technique was recently implemented and applied as part of an installation, in which a mobile robot gave interactive tours to visitors of the "Deutsches Museum Bonn." Extensive empirical tests involving datasets recorded during peak traffic hours in the museum demonstrate that this approach is able to accurately estimate the robot's position in more than 98% of the cases even in such highly dynamic environments.

Introduction

To operate autonomously, mobile robots must know where they are. *Mobile robot localization*, that is the process of determining and tracking the position (location) of a mobile robot relative to its environment, has received considerable attention over the past few years. Accurate localization is a key prerequisite for successful navigation in large-scale environments, particularly when global models are used, such as maps, drawings, topological descriptions, and CAD models (Kortenkamp, Bonasso, & Murphy 1998). As demonstrated by a recent survey of localization methods (Borenstein, Everett, & Feng 1996), the number of existing approaches is diverse. Mobile robot localization techniques can be categorized at least along the following two dimensions: local vs. global approaches, and approaches for static vs. dynamic environments:

1. Local vs. global localization Local approaches to localization are designed to compensate odometric error based on sensor data. They usually require that the initial location of the robot is known, and are only capable of *tracking* the location of a robot. The majority of existing localization approaches falls into this category. Global approaches are more general. They can localize a robot globally, that is, they can determine its location without knowledge of the initial location and thus can handle the "kidnaped robot problem" (Engelson 1994). Recently, several researchers proposed a new localization paradigm, called *Markov localization*, which enables robots to localize themselves under global uncertainty. Global approaches have two important advantages over local ones: First, the initial location of the robot does not have to be specified and, second, they provide an additional level of robustness, due to their ability to recover from localization failures.

2. Static vs. dynamic environments A second dimension along which localization methods can be grouped is concerned with the nature of the environment which they can master. The majority of approaches can only cope with *static* environments, that is, environments where, according to the robot's sensors, the only aspect that may change over time is the robot's own location. However, these approaches are typically brittle in environments where the dynamics are perceived through the robot's sensors. The approach of (King & Weiman 1990) uses cameras pointed towards the ceiling and thus cannot perceive most of the changes that occur in typical office environments. Unfortunately, such an approach is only applicable if the ceiling contains enough structure for accurate position estimation. Thus, the development of methods that can localize a robot in dynamic environments is still an important goal of research on mobile robot navigation.

This paper proposes a localization algorithm that can localize robots in the most difficult of all situations, namely localization under global uncertainty and in highly dynamic environments. The approach is based on Markov localization. Like Markov localization, it localizes robots *probabilistically*, that is, it maintains multiple hypotheses as to where the robot might be, weighted by a numerical probability factor. As a consequence, our approach inherits from Markov localization the ability to localize a robot under global uncertainty (see (Burgard *et al.* 1996)). Markov localization is based on the assumption that the position of the robot is the only state in the world. Unfortunately, this assumption

Copyright ©1998, American Association for Artificial Intelligence (www.aaai.org). All rights reserved.

is violated if not all aspects of the environment are covered by the world model, which is the case for most dynamic environments. Thus, although Markov localization has been found to be robust to occasional dynamical effects (such as people walking by or doors being closed), it typically fails to localize a robot in densely crowded environments. Unlike Markov localization, however, our approach actively filters sensor data to eliminate the damaging effect of sensor data corrupted by external (unmodeled) dynamics. In this paper, we propose and compare two such filters, one that filters sensor data based on entropy change, and one that incorporates additional knowledge concerning the nature of possible corruptions.

In an experimental study, our extended Markov localization is compared to the original Markov localization without filtering. These experiments are conducted using data gathered during a six-day deployment of our mobile robot RHINO in the "Deutsches Museum Bonn" shown in Figure 1(a) (see also (Burgard et al. 1998)). Our comparisons show that in such situations, conventional Markov localization fails to track the robot's location. Our filter techniques, in contrast, successfully accommodate the environment's dynamics. Additionally, our approach can reliably recover from localization errors.

 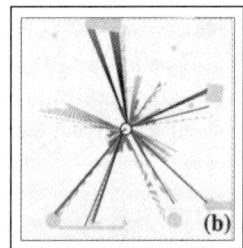

Fig. 1. (a) RHINO surrounded by visitors and (b) a highly corrupted sensor scan.

The remainder of this paper is organized as follows. After introducing Markov localization in the following section, we will describe our extension, followed by experimental comparisons and a discussion section.

Markov localization

This section briefly outlines the basic Markov localization algorithm upon which our approach is based. The key idea of Markov localization which has recently been applied with great success at various sites (Nourbakhsh, Powers, & Birchfield 1995; Simmons & Koenig 1995; Kaelbling, Cassandra, & Kurien 1996; Burgard et al. 1996) is to compute a probability distribution over all possible locations in the environment. Let $l = \langle x, y, \theta \rangle$ denote a location in the state space of the robot, where x and y are the robot's coordinates in a world-centered Cartesian reference frame, and θ is the robot's orientation. The distribution $Bel(l)$ over all locations l expresses the robot's subjective belief for being at position l. Initially, $Bel(l)$ reflects the initial state of knowledge: if the robot knows its initial position, $Bel(l)$ is centered on the correct location; if the robot does not know its initial location, $Bel(l)$ is uniformly distributed to reflect the global uncertainty of the robot. As the robot operates, $Bel(l)$ is incrementally refined.

Markov localization applies two different probabilistic models to update $Bel(l)$, an action model to incorporate movements of the robot into $Bel(l)$ and a perception model to update the belief upon sensory input.

Robot motion is modeled by a conditional probability $p(l \mid l', a)$ specifying the probability that a measured movement action a, when executed at l', carries the robot to l. $Bel(l)$ is then updated according to the following general formula coming from the domain of Markov chains (Chung 1960):

$$Bel(l) \longleftarrow \sum_{l'} P(l \mid l', a) \cdot Bel(l') \qquad (1)$$

The term $p(l \mid l', a)$ represents a model of the robot's kinematics. In our implementation we assume the errors of the odometry to be normally distributed.

Sensor readings are integrated according to the well-known Bayesian update formula. Let s denote a sensor reading and $p(s \mid l)$ the likelihood of perceiving s given that the robot is at position l, then $Bel(l)$ is updated according to the following rule:

$$Bel(l) \longleftarrow \alpha \, p(s \mid l) \, Bel(l) \qquad (2)$$

Here α is a normalizer ensuring that $Bel(l)$ sums up to 1 over all l.

Strictly speaking, both update steps are only applicable if the problem is *Markovian*, that is, if past sensor readings are conditionally independent of future readings given the location of the robot. The Markov assumption thus assumes that the world is static. While in practice, the approach has been applied even in environments that contained people and hence violate the Markov assumption, the experiments reported here indicate that it does not scale to densely populated environments.

In this paper we use a fine-grained grid-based representation of the state space, just like the approach described in (Burgard et al. 1996). In all our experiments, the resolution of robot orientation was $2°$, and the spatial resolution was 15cm. Different optimization techniques described in (Fox, Burgard, & Thrun to appear) allow the robot to efficiently update such large state spaces in real-time, without restricting the power of the approach in any noticeable way. The primary advantage of the high resolution are the resulting accuracy of position estimates and the ability to incorporate raw data of proximity sensors, which were required in the specific application domain described below.

Localization in Highly Dynamic Environments

The standard Markov localization approach has been found to be robust in static environments. However, as argued in the introduction to this paper (and demonstrated in the results section), it is prone to fail in densely populated environments which violate the underlying Markov assumption. In the museum, where the robot is naturally accompanied by crowds of people, this assumption is clearly violated. To illustrate this point, Figure 1(b) shows a typical example situation where RHINO has been projected into the map at its correct position. The lines indicate the current proximity measurements and the different shading of the measurements indicates the two classes they belong to: the black values correspond to static obstacles that are part of the map, whereas others are caused by humans and thus violate the Markov assumption (max-range measurements are not shown).

The proximity of people usually increases the robot's belief of being close to modeled obstacles, which has the effect that the robot frequently loses track of its position when relying on *all* sensor measurements. Approaches for concurrent estimation of the state of the world and of the position of the robot as proposed in (Gutmann & Schlegel 1996; Lu & Milios 1997; Thrun, Fox, & Burgard to appear), unfortunately, require too many computational resources to be applied on-line or even in real-time. Our approach to solve this problem is to develop filters which select those readings of a complete scan which with high likelihood are not due to static obstacles in the map thus making the system more robust against such kind of noise.

In the following two sections we will describe two different filters aiming at detecting corrupted readings and thus allowing the robot to keep track of its location even in considerably difficult situations, in which more than 50% of all readings are misleading. The first filter is a general method for filtering sensor data in dynamic environments. It selects only those readings that increase the robot's certainty, which is measured by the entropy of the belief $Bel(l)$. The second filter is especially designed for proximity sensors, as it attempts to filter such readings which with high probability are shorter than expected according to the model of the environment and the current belief state $Bel(l)$ of the robot.

Entropy filter

The first filter used in our implementation is called *entropy filter*. The *entropy* $H(l)$ of a distribution over l is defined by

$$H(l) = -\sum_{l} Bel(l) \log Bel(l). \tag{3}$$

Entropy is a measure of uncertainty: The larger the entropy, the higher the robot's uncertainty as to where it is. The *entropy filter* measures the relative change of entropy upon incorporating a sensor reading into the belief $Bel(l)$. More specifically, let s denote the measurement of a sensor (in our case a single range measurement). The change of the *entropy* of $Bel(l)$ given s is defined as:

$$\Delta H(l \mid s) := H(l) - H(l \mid s). \tag{4}$$

While a positive change of entropy indicates that after incorporating s, the robot is less certain about its position, a negative change indicates an increase in certainty.

RHINO's *entropy filter* uses only such sensor measurements s for which $\Delta H(l \mid s) \geq 0$. Thus, the entropy filter makes robot perception highly selective, in that it considers only sensor readings confirming the robot's current belief.

Novelty filter

While the entropy filter makes no assumptions about the nature of the sensor data and the kind of disturbances to expect in dynamic environments, the second filter is especially designed for proximity sensors and detects additional obstacles in the environment. This filter is called *novelty filter*, since it selects sensor readings based on the degree of their "novelty." To be more specific, a measurement s is assumed to be "novel" to the robot, if it is reflected by an obstacle not represented in the map. Obviously, for proximity measurements such a case can only be detected if the measurement is *shorter* than expected.

The novelty filter removes those proximity measurements which with probability higher than θ (this threshold is set to 0.99 in all experiments) are shorter than expected. Suppose $d_1, \ldots, d_n$ is a discrete set of possible distances measured by a proximity sensor. Let $p(d_j \mid l)$ denote the probability of measuring distance d_j if the sensor detects the next obstacle in the map. This distribution describes the *expected* measurement, and a distribution for laser-range finder given the distance o_l to the next obstacle is shown by the dashed line in Figure 2 (see (Fox, Burgard, & Thrun to appear) for further discussion of the proximity sensor models we use). Now we can derive $p_n(d_i \mid l)$, namely the probability of d_i being shorter than expected, by the following equation (c.f. 2):

$$p_n(d_i \mid l) = 1.0 - \sum_{j \leq i} p(d_j \mid l). \tag{5}$$

In order to deal with situations in which the position of the robot is not known with absolute certainty, we average over all possible locations of the robot to obtain the probability that d_i is shorter than expected:

$$p_n(d_i) = \sum_{l} p_n(d_i \mid l) Bel(l). \tag{6}$$

The selection scheme of the novelty filter is to exclude all measurements d with $p_n(d) > \theta$.

The difference between both filters can be characterized as follows: the entropy filter always tries to confirm the current belief of the robot (whether this is right or wrong) while the novelty filter also forces the incorporation of very unlikely sensor measurements (especially too long readings).

Experimental Results

Localization using the entropy filter was a central component of the tour-guide robot in the Deutsches Museum Bonn. Accurate position estimation was a crucial component, as many

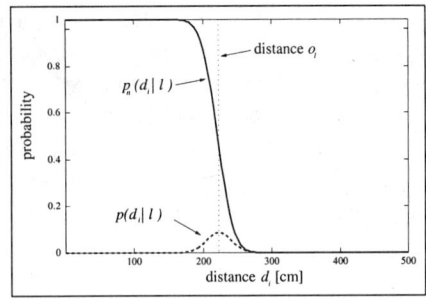
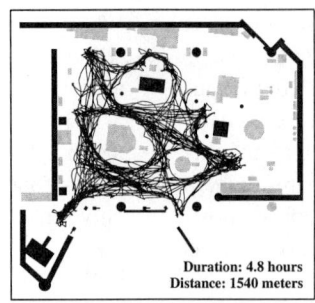
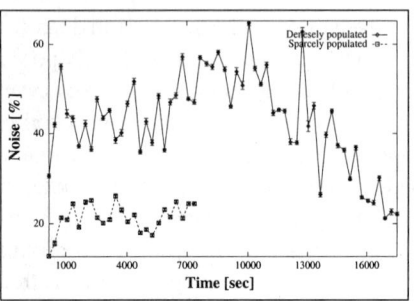

Fig. 2. Probability $p_n(d_i \mid l)$ that the sensing s_i is shorter than the expected sensing.

Fig. 3. Path of the robot in the second dataset.

Fig. 4. Percentage of noisy sensor measurements.

of the obstacles were "invisible" to the robot's sensors (such as glass cages, metal bars, staircases, and the alike). Only through accurate localization could collisions with those obstacles be avoided (Fox et al. 1998). Using Markov localization with entropy filters, our approach led only to a single software-related collision, which involved an "invisible" obstacle and which was caused by a localization error that was slightly larger than a 30cm safety margin. During six days of operation, RHINO traversed approximately 18.5 km at an average speed of approximately 36.6 cm/sec. In this application, the entropy filter was used and the novelty filter was developed post the fact, based on an analysis of the collision reported above, in an attempt to prevent similar effects in future installations.

The evidence from the museum is purely anecdotal. We also investigated the merit of the approaches proposed here more systematically, and under even more extreme conditions. In particular, we were interested in the localization results (1) when the environment is densely populated and (2) when the robot suffers from extreme dead-reckoning errors.

Datasets

Two datasets were used in our comparison, which both were recorded in the museum, and which mainly differed by the amount of disturbances.

1. The first dataset was collected during 2.0 hours of robot motion, during which the robot traversed as much as 1,000 meters. This data was collected when the museum was closed, and the robot guided only remote internet-visitors through the museum. The robot's top speed was limited to 50cm/sec. Thus, this dataset was "ideal" in that the environment was only extremely sparsely populated, and the robot moved slowly.

2. Figure 3 shows the second dataset, which represents 1,540 meters of robot motion through dense crowds over a period of 4.8 hours. This dataset was collected during peak traffic hours on the most crowded day during the entire exhibition. When collecting this data, the robot was frequently faced with situations as illustrated in Figure 1(a) and (b). The top speed in this dataset was 80cm/sec.

Both datasets consist of logs of odometry and laser-range finder scans collected while the robot moved through the museum. Using the time stamps in the logs, all tests have been conducted in real-time simulation on a SUN-Ultra-Sparc 1 (177-MHz). The first dataset contained more than 32,000, and the second dataset more than 73,000 laser scans. The reader may notice that only the obstacles shown in black in Figure 3 were actually used for localization; the others were either invisible, or could not be detected reliably.

Figure 4 shows the estimated percentage of corrupted sensor readings over time for both datasets. The dashed line corresponds to the first dataset while the solid line illustrates the corruption of the second (longer) dataset. In the second dataset, more than half of all measurements were corrupted for extended durations of time. These numbers are estimates only; they were obtained by analyzing each laser reading as to whether it could be "explained" by the obstacles represented in the map.

To evaluate the different localization methods, we generated two *reference paths* through nine independent runs for each filter on the datasets (with small random disturbances) to determine the location of *all* sensor scans. Visual inspection made us believe that the resulting reference locations were indeed correct and accurate enough. In order to estimate the *accuracy* of the methods on the second dataset, we selected 118 representative reference positions, for which we manually determined the robot's location as closely as possible through careful comparison of sensor scans, the robot's path, and the environment.

Localization in densely populated environments

In our first series of experiments, we were interested in comparing the localization performance of all three approaches — plain Markov localization, localization with entropy filters, and localization with novelty filters — under normal working conditions.

Table 1 summarizes the results obtained for the different approaches. The first row provides the percentage of *failures* (including 95% confidence intervals) for the different filters on the first dataset. Position estimates were considered as a "failure," if the estimated location deviated from the reference path by more than 45cm. All three approaches worked nicely for tracking the robot's position in the empty museum (first dataset), exhibiting only negligible errors in localiza-

Filter	None	Entropy	Novelty
Tracking Ability			
failures$_I$ [%]	1.6 ±0.4	0.9 ±0.4	0.0 ±0.0
failures$_{II}$ [%]	26.8 ±2.4	1.1 ±0.3	1.2 ±0.7
Accuracy in Dataset II			
$\bar{d}$ [cm]	188.9 ±26.9	9.2 ±0.5	11.4 ±3.4
Recovery			
$\bar{t}_{rec_I}$ [sec]	237 ±27	1779 ±548	188 ±30
$\bar{t}_{rec_{II}}$ [sec]	269 ±60	1310 ±904	235 ±46

Table 1: Experimental results.

tion. The results obtained for the second, more challenging dataset, however, were quite different. While plain Markov localization failed in 27% of all cases, both filter techniques showed a failure rate well below 2% (see second row). The third row, labeled $\bar{d}$, gives the average Euclidean error between the estimated position and the 118 reference positions. Here as well, the gap between conventional Markov localization and our approaches is large. The reader may notice that the accuracy of the filter techniques is higher than the grid resolution of 15cm.

To shed light onto the question as to why Markov localization performs so poorly when compared to the algorithms proposed in this paper, we analyzed the sensor readings that each method considered during localization. Figure 5 shows, for a small fraction of the data, the endpoints of the measurements that were incorporated into the robot's belief. The figures illustrate that both approaches proposed here manage to focus their attention on the "right" sensor measurements, whereas conventional Markov localization incorporates massive amounts of corrupted (misleading) measurements. Moreover, both filters show similar behavior. As also can be seen in Figure 5, both filter-based approaches produce more accurate results for this example. These results demonstrate that our approach scales much better to populated and dynamic environments than Markov localization.

Recovery from extreme localization failures

One of the key advantage of the original Markov localization technique lies in its ability to *recover* from extreme localization failures. Re-localization after a failure is often more difficult than global localization from scratch, since the robot has to (1) detect that its current belief is wrong and (2) globally re-localize itself afterwards. Since the filter-based approaches incorporate sensor data selectively, it is not clear that they still maintain the ability to recover from global localization failures.

Our experiments under normal operation conditions did not lead to such failures for the two methods proposed in this paper; thus, we manually introduced such failures into the data to test the robustness of these methods in the extreme. More specifically, in our experiments we "tele-ported" the robot at random points in time to other locations. Techni-

cally, this was done by changing the robot's orientation by 180±90 degree and shifting it by 0±100 cm, without letting the robot know. These perturbations were introduced randomly, with a probability of 0.005 per meter of robot motion. Obviously, such incidents make the robot lose its position. Each method was tested on 23 differently corrupted datasets. This resulted in an overall of 133 position failures. For each of these failures we measured the time until the methods re-localized the robot correctly. Re-localization was assumed to have succeeded if the distance between the estimated position and the reference position was smaller than 45cm for more than 10 seconds.

The two bottom rows in Table 1 summarize the results for the two datasets. $\bar{t}_{rec}$ represents the average time in seconds needed to recover from a situation when the position was lost. Both conventional Markov localization and the extension using novelty filters are relatively efficient in recovering from extreme positioning errors, whereas the entropy filter-based approach is an order of magnitude less efficient. The results illustrate that despite the fact that sensor readings are processed selectively, the novelty filter-based approach recovers as efficiently from extreme localization errors as the conventional Markov approach. These findings are specifically interesting in the light of the fact that in the Deutsches Museum Bonn the entropy-based filter was used, which, according to these results, would have led to poor recovery from extreme failures.

In summary, these experiments suggest that only the localization algorithm with the novelty filter is able to localize robots in densely crowded environments, while retaining the ability to efficiently recover from extreme localization errors.

Conclusions

This paper proposed an approach for global robot localization that has been demonstrated to reliably localize mobile robots even in extremely challenging dynamic environments. These environments are characterized by the presence of various dynamic effects, such as crowds of people that frequently block the robot's sensors. Our approach is based on Markov localization, a popular method for mobile robot localization, which provides the ability to recover from arbitrary failures in localization. It extends Markov localization by an approach that filters sensor data, so that the damaging effect of corrupted data is reduced. Two specific filters were proposed and evaluated, one which considers conditional entropy for selecting sensor readings, and one which takes into account additional knowledge about the effects of possible environment dynamics.

Our approach was essential for operating a robot successfully in a crowded museum. Experimental comparisons using data collected there demonstrated that the technique proposed in this paper is superior to state-of-the-art localization methods. These results also demonstrated that by processing sensor readings selectively, one of the proposed approaches

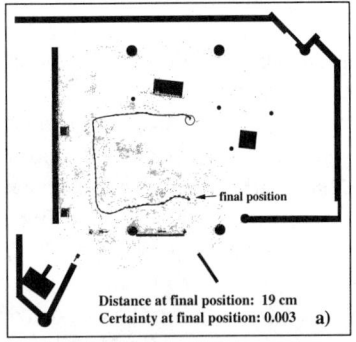 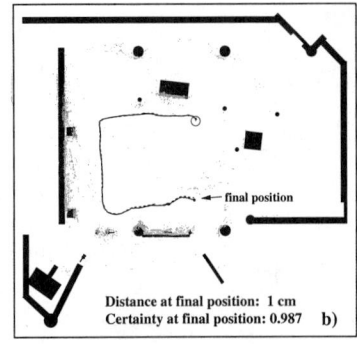 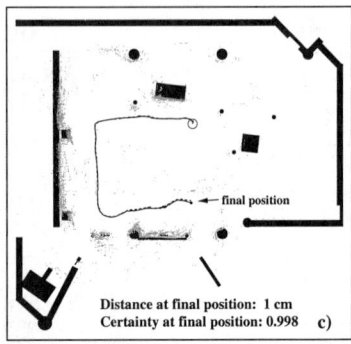

Fig. 5. Estimated and real paths of the robot along with endpoints of integrated sensor measurements using (a) no filter, (b) entropy filter, and (c) novelty filter.

still retains the ability to recover from global failures in localization. Additional tests in our office environment have shown that our technique can deal with situations in which only an outline of the environment is used as a world model (c.f. 6(a)). In this case sensor readings reflected by the furniture (c.f. 6(b)) are successfully filtered out. We believe that these results are essential for operating mobile robots in highly dynamic and densely populated environments.

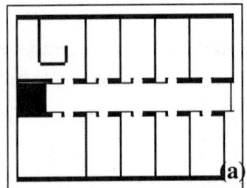 

Fig. 6. (a) Outline used for localization and (b) environment including furniture.

How specific are these results to the problem of mobile robot localization? We believe that the first filter proposed here, the entropy filter, is applicable to a much wider variety of state estimation (and learning) problems in dynamic environments. Loosely speaking, this filter makes robot perception highly selective, in that only sensor readings are considered that confirm the robot's current belief. This filter rests only on two assumptions: First, that the variable to be estimated is represented probabilistically, and second, that sensor readings can be sorted into two bins, one which only contains corrupted readings, and one that contains authentic (non-corrupted) measurements. A promising application of this filter is the compensation of hard-ware failures of sensors, a problem addressed in (Murphy & Hershberger 1996). Future work will aim at analyzing quantitatively, to what extent this filter can make robots more robust to sensor failures.

References

Borenstein, J.; Everett, B.; and Feng, L. 1996. *Navigating Mobile Robots: Systems and Techniques*. A. K. Peters, Ltd.

Burgard, W.; Fox, D.; Hennig, D.; and Schmidt, T. 1996. Estimating the absolute position of a mobile robot using position probability grids. In *Proc. of the 13th National Conference on Artificial Intelligence*.

Burgard, W.; Cremers, A.; Fox, D.; Hähnel, D.; Lakemeyer, G.; Schulz, D.; Steiner, W.; and Thrun, S. 1998. The interactive museum tour-guide robot. In *Proc. of the 15th National Conference on Artificial Intelligence*.

Chung, K. 1960. *Markov chains with stationary transition probabilities*. Berlin: Springer Publisher.

Engelson, S. 1994. *Passive Map Learning and Visual Place Recognition*. Ph.D. Dissertation, Department of Computer Science, Yale University.

Fox, D.; Burgard, W.; Thrun, S.; and Cremers, A. B. 1998. A hybrid collision avoidance method for mobile robots. In *Proc. of the IEEE International Conference on Robotics and Automation*. to appear.

Fox, D.; Burgard, W.; and Thrun, S. Active markov localization for mobile robots. *Robotics and Autonomous Systems*. accepted for publication.

Gutmann, J.-S., and Schlegel, C. 1996. Amos: Comparison of scan matching approaches for self-localizati on in indoor environments. In *Proc. of the 1st Euromicro Workshop on Advanced Mobile Robots*. IEEE Computer Society Press.

Kaelbling, L.; Cassandra, A.; and Kurien, J. 1996. Acting under uncertainty: Discrete bayesian models for mobile-robot navigation. In *Proc. of the IEEE/RSJ International Conference on Intelligent Robots and Systems*.

King, S., and Weiman, C. 1990. Helpmate autonomous mobile robot navigation system. In *Proc. of the SPIE Conference on Mobile Robots*, 190–198. Volume 2352.

Kortenkamp, D.; Bonasso, R.; and Murphy, R., eds. 1998. *Artificial intelligence and mobile robots*. Cambridge, MA: MIT Press.

Lu, F., and Milios, E. 1997. Globally consistent range scan alignment for environment mapping. *Autonomous Robots* 4:333–349.

Murphy, R. R., and Hershberger, D. 1996. Classifying and recovering from sensing failures in autonomous mobile robots. In *Proc. of the 13th National Conference on Artificial Intelligence*.

Nourbakhsh, I.; Powers, R.; and Birchfield, S. 1995. DERVISH an office-navigating robot. *AI Magazine* 16(2).

Simmons, R., and Koenig, S. 1995. Probabilistic robot navigation in partially observable environments. In *Proc. of the International Joint Conference on Artificial Intelligence*.

Thrun, S.; Fox, D.; and Burgard, W. to appear. A probabilistic approach for concurrent map acquisition and localization for mobile robots. *Machine Learning / Autonomous Robots*.

Integrating Topological and Metric Maps for Mobile Robot Navigation: A Statistical Approach

Sebastian Thrun[1] **Jens-Steffen Gutmann[2]** **Dieter Fox[3]** **Wolfram Burgard[3]** **Benjamin J. Kuipers[4]**

[1]Computer Science Department
Carnegie Mellon University
Pittsburgh, PA 15213

[2]Institut für Informatik
Universität Freiburg
D-79110 Freiburg, Germany

[3]Institut für Informatik III
University of Bonn
D-53117 Bonn, Germany

[4]Computer Science Department
University of Texas at Austin
Austin, TX 78712

Abstract

The problem of concurrent mapping and localization has received considerable attention in the mobile robotics community. Existing approaches can largely be grouped into two distinct paradigms: topological and metric. This paper proposes a method that integrates both. It poses the mapping problem as a statistical maximum likelihood problem, and devises an efficient algorithm for search in likelihood space. It presents an novel mapping algorithm that integrates two phases: a topological and a metric mapping phase. The topological mapping phase solves a global position alignment problem between potentially indistinguishable, significant places. The subsequent metric mapping phase produces a fine-grained metric map of the environment in floating-point resolution. The approach is demonstrated empirically to scale up to large, cyclic, and highly ambiguous environments.

Introduction

Over the past two decades, the problem of building maps in indoor environments has received significant attention in the mobile robotics community. The problem of building maps is the problem determining the location of certain entities, such as landmarks or obstacles, in a global frame of reference. To build a map of its environment, a robot must know where it is. Since robot motion is inaccurate, constructing maps of large indoor environments requires a robot to solve an inherent concurrent localization problem.

As of to date, there exist two major paradigms for mobile robot mapping: *Metric and topological*. Approaches in the *metric paradigm* generate fine-grained, metric descriptions of a robot's environment (Moravec 1988; Lu & Milios 1997). Approaches in the *topological paradigm*, on the other hand, generate coarse, graph-like descriptions of environments, where nodes correspond to significant, easy-to-distinguish places or landmarks, and arcs correspond to actions or action-sequences that connect neighboring places (Mataric 1990; Dudek et al. 1991). Examples of metric and topological methods are provided towards the end of this paper.

It has long been recognized (Chatila & Laumond 1985; Kuipers & Byun 1991) that either paradigm alone, metric or topological, has significant drawbacks. In principle, topological maps should scale better than metric maps to large-scale environments, because a coarse-grained, graph-structured representation is much more compact than a dense array, and more directly suited to problem-solving algorithms (Kuipers & Byun 1991; Dudek et al. 1991). However, purely topological maps have difficulty distinguishing adequately among different places, and have not, in practice, been applied successfully to large environments. Recent progress in metric mapping (Lu & Milios 1997; Thrun 1998) has made it possible to build useful and accurate metric maps of reasonably large-scale environments, but memory and time complexity pose serious problems.

In this paper, we propose and evaluate a new algorithm that integrates the topological and metric approach. We show that both the topological and the metric mapping problems can be solved as different instances of a class of statistical estimation problems, in which a robot seeks to find the most likely map from a set of observations and motion commands. These estimation problems are solved by a variant of the EM algorithm, which is an efficient hill-climbing method for maximum likelihood estimation in high-dimensional spaces. In the context of mapping, EM iterates two alternating steps: a *localization step*, in which the robot is localized using a previously computed map, and a *mapping step*, which computes the most likely map based on the previously pose estimates.

The statistical framework is the foundation for two algorithmic phases, one that builds topological maps and one that builds metric maps. Both components possess orthogonal strengths and weaknesses. The topological map builder is capable of solving global alignment problems that occur in datasets with unbounded odometric error and perceptual ambiguity. Its result, however, is only approximate, partially because it ignores much of the sensor data. The metric approach, on the other hand, builds fine-grained metric maps in floating-point resolution. However, it can only compensate small odometric errors. By integrating both, topological and metric mapping, the algorithm can build high-resolution maps in large and highly ambiguous indoor environments.

Statistical Foundations

This paper poses the problem of mapping as a statistical *maximum likelihood estimation problem* (Thrun, Fox, & Burgard 1998). To generate a map, we assume that a robot is given a stream of data, denoted

$$d = \{o^{(1)}, u^{(1)}, o^{(2)}, u^{(2)}, \ldots o^{(T-1)}, u^{(T)}, o^{(T)}\}, \quad (1)$$

Copyright 1998, American Association for Artificial Intelligence (www.aaai.org). All rights reserved.

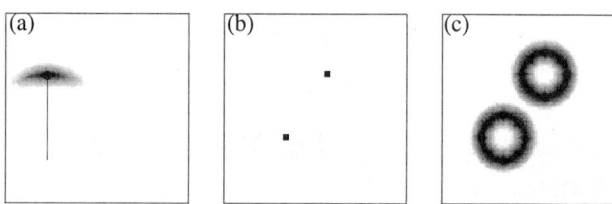

Figure 1: Basic probabilistic models: (a) Robot motion model. Shown here is the accumulated uncertainty after moving 40 meter, starting at a known pose. (b-c) Perceptual model. (b) shows a map with two indistinguishable landmarks, and (c) displays the uncertainty after sensing a landmark in 5 meter distance.

where $o^{(t)}$ stands for an *observation* that the robot made at time t, and $u^{(t)}$ for an action command that the robot executed between time t to time $t + 1$. T denotes the total number of time steps in the data. Without loss of generality, we assume that the data is an alternated sequence of actions and observations.

In statistical terms, the problem of mapping is the problem of finding the most likely map given the data. *Maps* will be denoted by $m = \{m_{x,y}\}_{x,y}$. A map is an assignment of "properties" $m_{x,y}$ to each x-y-locations in the world. In topological approaches to mapping, the properties-of-interest are usually locations of landmarks (Chown, Kaplan, & Kortenkamp 1995) or, alternatively, location of significant places (Kuipers & Byun 1991; Choset 1996). Metric approaches, on the other hand, usually use the location of obstacles as properties-of-interest (Chatila & Laumond 1985; Moravec 1988; Lu & Milios 1997).

Our approach assumes that the robot is given two basic, probabilistic models, one that describes robot motion, and one that models robot perception.

- **The motion model**, denoted $P(\xi'|u, \xi)$, describes the probability that the robot's pose is ξ', if it previously executed action u at pose ξ. Here ξ is used to refer to a pose, that is the x-y-location of a robot together with its heading direction. Figure 1a illustrates the motion model, by showing the probability distribution for ξ' upon executing the action *"go forward 40 meters."* Notice that in these and other diagrams, poses are projected into x-y-space (the heading direction is omitted).

- **The perceptual model**, denoted $P(o|m, \xi)$, models the likelihood of observing o in situations where both the world m and the robot's pose ξ are known. For low-dimensional sensors such as proximity sensors, perceptual models can readily be found in the literature (Burgard *et al.* 1996; Moravec 1988). Figure 1b&c illustrates a perceptual model for a robot that can detect landmarks and that can measure, with some uncertainty, their relative orientations and distances. Figure 1b shows an example map m, in which the dark spots indicate the locations of two indistinguishable landmarks. Figure 1c plots $P(o|m, \xi)$ for different poses ξ, for the specific observation that the robot observed a landmark ahead in five meters distance. The darker a pose, the more likely it is under this observation.

These three quantities—the data d, the motion model $P(\xi'|u, \xi)$, and the perceptual model $P(o|m, \xi)$—form the statistical basis of our approach.

The Map Likelihood Function

In statistical terms, the problem of mapping is the problem of finding the most likely map given the data

$$m^* = \underset{m}{\operatorname{argmax}} P(m|d). \quad (2)$$

The probability $P(m|d)$ can be written as

$$P(m|d) = \int P(m|\xi, d)\, P(\xi|d)\, d\xi. \quad (3)$$

Here the variable ξ denotes the *set of all poses* at times $1, 2, \ldots, T$, that is, $\xi := \{\xi^{(1)}, \ldots, \xi^{(T)}\}$, where $\xi^{(t)}$ denotes the robot's pose at time t. By virtue of Bayes rule, the probability $P(m|\xi, d)$ on the right hand side of Equation (3) can be re-written as

$$P(m|\xi, d) = \frac{P(d|m, \xi)\, P(m|\xi)}{P(d|\xi)} \quad (4)$$

Based on the observation that $o^{(t)}$ at time t depends only on the map m and the corresponding location $\xi^{(t)}$, the first term on the right hand side of Equation (4) can be transformed into

$$P(d|m, \xi) = \prod_{t=1}^{T} P(o^{(t)}|m, \xi^{(t)}) \quad (5)$$

Furthermore, $P(m|\xi) = P(m)$ in Equation (4), since in the absence of any data, m does not depend on ξ. $P(m)$ is the Bayesian *prior* over all maps, which henceforth will be assumed to be uniformly distributed. Finally, the term $P(\xi|d)$ in Equation (3) can be re-written as

$$P(\xi|d) = \prod_{t=1}^{T-1} P(\xi^{(t+1)}|u^{(t)}, \xi^{(t)}) \quad (6)$$

The latter transformation is based on the observation that the robot's pose $\xi^{(t+1)}$ depends only on the robot's pose $\xi^{(t)}$ one time step earlier and the action $u^{(t)}$ executed there. Putting all this together leads to the likelihood function

$$P(m|d) = \int \frac{\prod_{t=1}^{T} P(o^{(t)}|m, \xi^{(t)})\, P(m)}{P(d|\xi)} \\ \prod_{t=1}^{T-1} P(\xi^{(t+1)}|u^{(t)}, \xi^{(t)})\, d\xi. \quad (7)$$

Since we are only interested in maximizing $P(m|d)$, not in computing an exact value, we can safely drop the constants $P(m)$ and $P(d|\xi)$. The resulting expression,

$$\underset{m}{\operatorname{argmax}} \int \prod_{t=1}^{T} P(o^{(t)}|m, \xi^{(t)}) \prod_{t=1}^{T-1} P(\xi^{(t+1)}|u^{(t)}, \xi^{(t)})\, d\xi, \quad (8)$$

is a function of the data d, the perceptual model $P(o|m, \xi)$, and the motion model $P(\xi'|u, \xi)$. Maximizing this expression is equivalent to finding the most likely map.

Efficient Estimation

Unfortunately, computing (8) is computationally challenging. This is because finding the most likely map involves search in the space of all maps. For the size environments considered here, this space often has 10^6 dimensions or more if crude approximations are used. To make matters worse, the evaluation of a single map would require integrating over all possible poses at all points in time, which for the datasets considered in this paper would require integration over more than 10^5 independent pose variables, each of which can take 10^8 values or so.

Fortunately, there exists an efficient and well-understood technique for hill-climbing in likelihood space: the *EM algorithm* (Dempster, Laird, & Rubin 1977), which in the context of Hidden Markov Models is often referred to as *Baum-Welch* or *alpha-beta algorithm* (Rabiner & Juang 1986). EM is a hill-climbing routine in likelihood space, which alternates two steps, an *expectation step* (E-step) and a *maximization step* (M-step). In the context of robot mapping, these steps correspond roughly to a localization step and a mapping step (see also (Koenig & Simmons 1996; Shatkay & Kaelbling 1997)):

1. In the E-step, the robot computes probabilities $P(\xi|m, d)$ for the robot's poses ξ at the various points in times, based on the currently best available map m (in the first iteration, there will be no map).

2. In the M-step, the robot determines the most likely map by maximizing $\text{argmax}_m P(m|\xi, d)$, using the location estimates computed in the E-step.

The E-step corresponds to a localization step with a fixed map, whereas the M-step implements a mapping step which operates under the assumption that the robot's locations (or, more precisely, probabilistic estimates thereof) are known. Iterative application of both rules leads to a refinement of both, the location estimates and the map. Our approach is, thus, a hill-climbing procedure that does not provide a guarantee of global optimality; given the complexity of the problem, however, it is unclear whether a globally optimal routine exists that is computationally tractable.

The E-Step

The E-step uses the current-best map m along with the data to compute probabilities $P(\xi^{(t)}|d, m)$ for the robot's poses at times $t = 1, \ldots, T$. With appropriate assumptions, $P(\xi^{(t)}|d, m)$ can be expressed as the normalized product of two terms

$$P(\xi^{(t)}|d, m) = \eta \underbrace{P(\xi^{(t)}|o^{(1)}, \ldots, o^{(t)}, m)}_{:= \alpha^{(t)}} \underbrace{P(\xi^{(t)}|u^{(t+1)}, \ldots, o^{(T)}, m)}_{:= \beta^{(t)}} \quad (9)$$

Here η is a normalizers that ensure that the left-hand side of Equation (9) sums up to one (see (Thrun, Fox, & Burgard 1998) for a mathematical derivation). Both terms, $\alpha^{(t)}$ and $\beta^{(t)}$, as defined in (9), are computed separately, where the former is computed forward in time and the latter is computed backwards in time. Notice that $\alpha^{(t)}$ and $\beta^{(t)}$ are analogous to those in the alpha-beta algorithm (Rabiner & Juang 1986).

The computation of the α-values is a version of *Markov localization*, which has recently been used with great success for robot localization in *known* environments by various researchers (Burgard *et al.* 1996; Kaelbling, Cassandra, & Kurien 1996; Koenig & Simmons 1996; Nourbakhsh, Powers, & Birchfield 1995; Simmons & Koenig 1995). The β-values add additional knowledge to the robot's pose, typically not captured in Markov-localization. They are, however, essential for revising past belief based on sensor data that was received later in time, which is a necessary prerequisite of building large-scale maps.

Computing the α-Values: Initially, the robot is assumed to be at the center of the global reference frame and $\alpha^{(1)}$ is given by a Dirac distribution centered at $(0, 0, 0)$:

$$\alpha^{(1)} = P(\xi^{(1)}|o^{(1)}, m) = \begin{cases} 1, & \text{if } \xi^{(1)} = (0,0,0) \\ 0, & \text{if } \xi^{(1)} \neq (0,0,0) \end{cases} \quad (10)$$

All other $\alpha^{(t)}$ are computed recursively:

$$\alpha^{(t)} = \eta \, P(o^{(t)}|\xi^{(t)}, m) \, P(\xi^{(t)}|o^{(1)}, \ldots, u^{(t-1)}, m) \quad (11)$$

where η is again a probabilistic normalizer. The rightmost term of (11) can be transformed to

$$P(\xi^{(t)}|o^{(1)}, \ldots, u^{(t-1)}, m)$$
$$= \int P(\xi^{(t)}|u^{(t-1)}, \xi^{(t-1)}) \, \alpha^{(t-1)} \, d\xi^{(t-1)} \quad (12)$$

Substituting (12) into (11) yields a recursive rule for the computation of all $\alpha^{(t)}$ with boundary condition (10). See (Thrun, Fox, & Burgard 1998) for a more detailed derivation.

Computing the β-Values: The computation of $\beta^{(t)}$ is completely analogous but takes place backwards in time. The initial $\beta^{(T)}$, which expresses the probability that the robot's final pose is ξ, is uniformly distributed, since $\beta^{(T)}$ does not depend on data. All other β-values are computed in the following way:

$$\beta^{(t)} = \eta \int P(\xi^{(t+1)}|u^{(t)}, \xi^{(t)})$$
$$P(o^{(t+1)}|\xi^{(t+1)}, m) \, \beta^{(t+1)} \, d\xi^{(t+1)} \quad (13)$$

The derivation of the equations are analogous to that of the computation rule for α-values and can be found in (Thrun, Fox, & Burgard 1998). The result of the E-step, the products $\alpha^{(t)} \beta^{(t)}$, are estimates of the robot's locations at the various points in time t.

The M-Step

The M-step maximizes $P(m|\xi, d)$, that is, in the M-step the robot computes the most likely map based on the pose probabilities computed in the E-step. Generating maps with *known* robot poses, which is basically what the M-step amounts to, has been studied extensively in the literature on mobile robot mapping (see e.g., (Borenstein & Koren. 1991; Elfes 1989; Moravec 1988)).

By applying Bayes rule and with the appropriate assumptions, the estimation problem can be temporally decomposed into

$$P(m|\xi, d) = \alpha \prod_{t=1}^{T} P(o^{(t)}|\xi^{(t)}, m) \quad (14)$$

where α is a normalizer that can safely be ignored in the maximization. It is common practice to decompose the problem spatially, by solving the optimization problem independently for different x-y-locations:

$$\operatorname*{argmax}_{m} P(m|\xi, d) = \left\{ \operatorname*{argmax}_{m_{x,y}} \prod_{t=1}^{T} P(o^{(t)}|\xi^{(t)}, m_{x,y}) \right\}_{x,y} \quad (15)$$

While technically speaking, this independence assumption is not warranted for sensors that cover many x-y-locations (such as sonar sensors), it is typically made in the literature to make the estimation problem tractable. The resulting local maximum likelihood estimations problems are highly tractable, since each of them involves only a single, discrete random variable.

The Mapping Algorithm

A key feature of the statistical approach is that it can equally be applied to both topological and metric maps. The mapping algorithm proposed in this paper first constructs coarse-grained topological maps, based on which it then builds detailed metric maps. Both of mapping steps are specialized versions of the same statistical approach described above.

Both mapping steps exhibit orthogonal strengths and weaknesses, arising from differences in representations and the ways sensor data is processed. The topological step is specialized to solve a *global alignment problem*. It can deal with arbitrarily large errors in the robot's odometry; yet it only produces maps with low spatial resolution. The metric step addresses a *local alignment problem*. It assumes that the odometric error is already small, and generates metric maps of the robot's environment with floating-point resolution.

Topological Maps

Following (Kuipers & Byun 1991; Choset 1996; Matarić 1990; Shatkay & Kaelbling 1997), the topological component of our algorithm seeks to determine the location of *significant places* in the environment, along with an order in which these places were visited by the robot.

In the topological mapping step, the robot can only observe whether or not it is at a *significant place*. Our definition of significant places follows closely the notion of "distinctive places" in Kuipers's Spatial Semantic Hierarchy (Kuipers & Byun 1991), and the notion of "meetpoints" in Choset's Generalized Voronoi Graphs (Choset 1996). In our experiments, we simulated these methods by manually pressing a button whenever the robot crossed a significant place. To test the most general (and difficult) case, our approach assumes that the significant places are *indistinguishable*. Thus, the robot observes only a single bit of information, namely whether or not it is at a significant place. This deviates from Kuipers and Byun's work, in which places are assumed to be locally

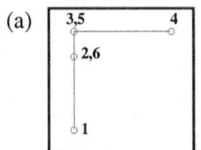 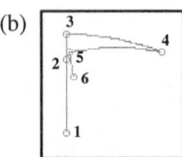

Figure 2: Illustrative example. (a) A path taken by the robot, along which it observed six indistinguishable landmarks (in the order of the numbers). (b) The robot's odometry yields erroneous readings between the third and the fifth landmark observation.

distinctive. Nodes in the topological map correspond to *significant places*. Arcs between nodes are created if nodes are adjacent in the data set d. The robot is not told how many significant places exist in its environment; neither does it know whether or not it visited a significant place more than once. Instead, it guesses the number of nodes as a side-effect of maximizing the map likelihood function.

The topological mapper represents all probabilities (poses, maps, ...) with evenly-spaced, piecewise constant functions (also called: grids). In all our experimental results, the spatial resolution was 1 meter and the angular resolution was 5°.

Figures 2 and 3 illustrate the topological mapper for an artificial example. Figure 2a shows a path of a robot, in a world that possesses four significant places. The numbers indicate the order in which the robot traverses these places. Figure 2b shows the odometry information. In our example, the robot suffers significant odometric error between its third and its fifth place observation. Based on the odometry information alone, the fifth place appears to be closest to the second, although the robot really went back to the third.

To illustrate the algorithm, let us first consider the situation after the robot made its fifth place observation. Figure 3a shows $\alpha^{(t)}$, $\beta^{(t)}$, and $\alpha^{(t)}\beta^{(t)} \propto P(\xi^{(t)}|d, m)$ after the *first* iteration of EM, for the time steps $t = 2, \ldots, 5$ ($t = 1$ is omitted since the pose $\xi^{(1)}$ is known by definition). Since in the first iteration, there is no map available, the α-values are directly obtained by iteratively "chaining together" the motion model, and the β-values are fairly unspecific. Figure 3b shows the same values two EM iterations later, along with the "corrected" odometry information. The most important density is the one in the upper right corner of Figure 3b, labeled $\alpha^{(5)}$, $\beta^{(5)}$. As can be seen there, the maximum likelihood estimate is incorrect in that it assumes the fifth landmark observation corresponds to the second one (and not the third, which would be correct). This comes at no surprise, as the robot's odometry suggested that the fifth place is much closer to the second, than it is to the third. It is interesting to notice, however, that the algorithm assigns non-zero likelihood to both possibilities, as indicated by the bimodal distribution in the upper right corner-diagram in Figure 3b.

As the robot moves on to the next (=sixth) place observation, the picture changes. The final densities are shown in Figure 3c. Now the robot assigns higher likelihood to the correct topological assignment, and the resulting path (and map) is topologically correct.

This example illustrates two important aspects: First, our algorithm uses future data to revise beliefs backwards in time.

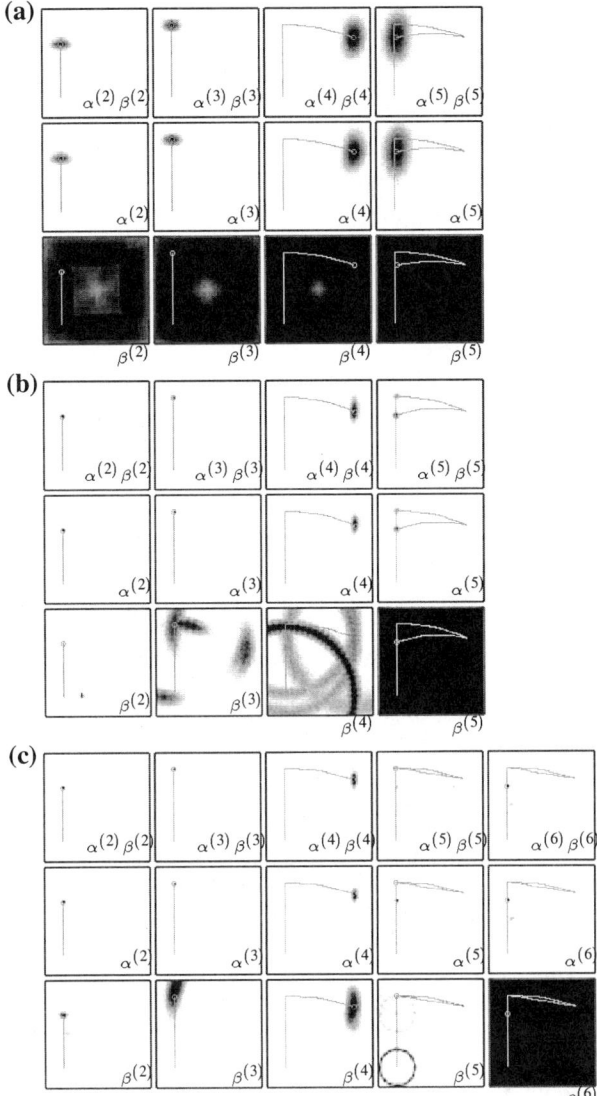

Figure 3: The pose probabilities $P(\xi)$ and their factors α, β for the example. (a) Five-step dataset, first iteration of EM, (b) Five-step dataset, third iteration, (c) Six-step dataset, third iteration.

Second, it considers multiple hypotheses, not just a single one. Both aspects differ from the vast majority of work in the field. We conjecture that both are essential for scaling up mapping to larger environments.

Metric Maps

The metric mapper, which is based on the same statistical framework as the topological mapper, is a modified version of an approach previously proposed in (Gutmann & Schlegel 1996; Lu & Milios 1997).

The metric mapper uses proximity measurements (range scans) obtained with a laser range finder for building the metric map. Its perceptual model is defined through a geometric map matching method, which determines the likelihood of laser scan based on the proximity of perceived obstacles in x-y-coordinates. The metric mapper represents all densities (poses, maps, motion model, and perceptual model) by Gaussian distributions (Kalman filters). Gaussians have a dual advantage: First they permit determining robot poses and location of obstacles with floating-point resolution, yielding high-resolution maps. Second, they make possible to apply highly efficient linear programming methods when maximizing the likelihood function (Lu & Milios 1997). However, Gaussians are uni-modal; Thus, the metric mapper cannot represent two distinct hypothesis, as can the topological mapper. As a direct consequence, the metric mapper can only be applied if the initial odometric error is small (e.g., smaller than 2 meters), so that the correct solution lies in the vicinity of the initial guess. Fortunately, the topological mapper, if successful, generates maps that meet this criterion.

Technically, the metric mapper builds a *network of spatial relations* among all poses where range scans have been taken. Spatial probabilistic constraints between poses are derived from matching pairs of range scans and from odometry measurements. In the E-step, the metric mapper estimates all poses. In the M-step, it remaps the scans based on the previously estimated poses. Both steps are iterated. In our experiments, we found that the metric mapper consistently converged to the limit of machine accuracy after four or five iterations of EM.

The metric mapper is computationally highly efficient. As noticed above, our approach employs linear programming for efficient likelihood maximization. To do so, it approximates the likelihood function linearly, which leads to a closed form solution for all pose variables. Each iteration of the procedure involves solving a linear equation with a $3T \times 3T$ matrix, which can be computationally challenging for large datasets. This matrix, however, is usually sparse (unless the robot moves only on the spot). Our implementation employs a highly efficient linear programming package that exploits this sparseness. It also employs an efficient grouping mechanisms for reducing the effective number of range scans, prior to constructing the map.

Experimental Results

The mapping algorithm was applied to various datasets obtained in indoor environments, using the RWI B21 robot equipped with 24 sonar sensors and a SICK laser range finder. Figures 4a&b show a dataset collected in our university building, in which circles indicate significant place observations. Here the final odometric error is approximately 24.9 meter.

What makes this dataset challenging is the large circular hallway (60 by 25 meter). When traversing the circle for the first time, the robot cannot exploit landmarks to improve its pose estimates; thus, it accumulates odometric error. Since significant places are indistinguishable, it is difficult to determine the robot's position when the circle is closed for the first time (here the odometric error is larger than 14 meter). Only as the robot proceeds through known territory can it use its perceptual clues to estimate where it is (and was), in order to build a consistent map.

Figure 4c shows the result of topological mapping, including the "corrected" path taken by the robot. While this map is topologically correct, the position estimates are only ap-

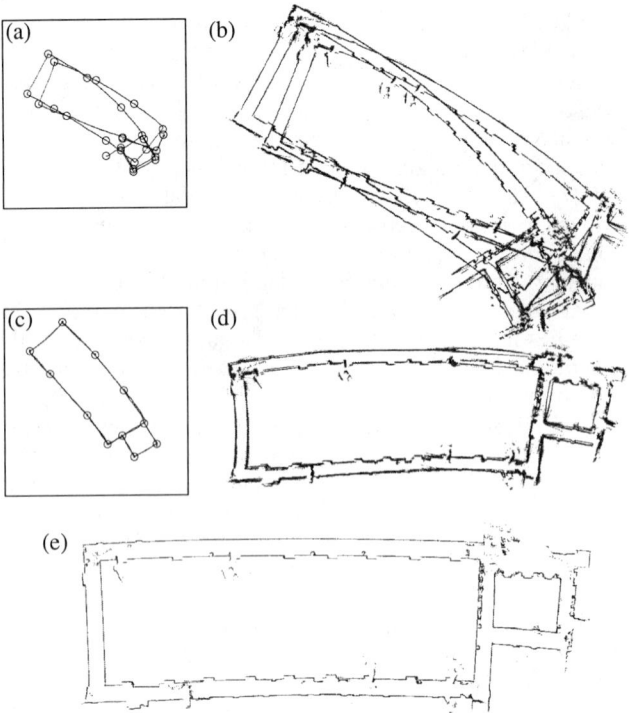

Figure 4: (a) Raw data, obtained in an environment of size 80 by 25 meters. Circles indicate (indistinguishable) places. (b) Sensor map generated from laser range finder data using the raw odometric data. (c) The topological mapper generates a map that correctly describes the topology of the environment. (d) The initial metric map, generated using the pose estimates derived in the topological mapping phase, is still imperfect, although the errors are small. (e) The metric mapper finally generates a highly detailed map.

proximately correct, as demonstrated by Figure 4d. Figure 4e shows the map subsequently generated by the metric mapper. Although the final metric map is slightly bent (which, in fact, appears more plausible given the original data), it is sufficient for our current navigation routines (Gutmann & Nebel 1997; Thrun *et al.* 1998).

Other examples are shown in Figure 5. As can be seen there, our approach produces high-accuracy topological-metric maps in all cases. So far, we did not observe a single failure of the mapping routines. All maps displayed in this paper were generated in less than one hour of computational time, using a 200Mhz Pentium PC for topological mapping and a Sparc Ultra-30 for metric mapping. In all cases, the data collection required less than 20 minutes.

Related Work

Probably the most successful metric approach to date are occupancy grids, which were originally proposed in (Elfes 1989; Moravec 1988; Borenstein & Koren. 1991) and which since have been employed in numerous systems. Other metric approaches, such as those described in (Chatila & Laumond 1985; Cox 1994; Lu & Milios 1997), describe the environment by geometric atoms such as straight lines (walls) or points (range scans). Approaches that fall strictly into the topological paradigm can be found in (Chown, Kaplan, & Kortenkamp 1995;

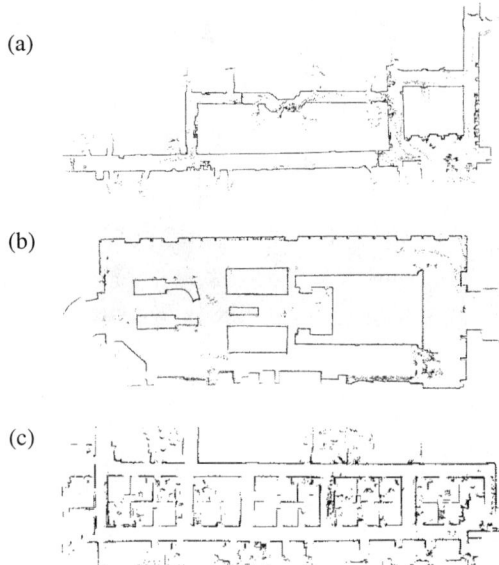

Figure 5: Maps generated in other large-scale environments of sizes (a) 75m, (b) 45m, and (c) 50m. In some of these runs, the cumulative odometric error exceeds 30 meters and 90 degrees.

Kortenkamp & Weymouth 1994; Kuipers & Byun 1991; Mataric 1990; Shatkay & Kaelbling 1997). Some of these approaches do not annotate topological maps with metric information at all; instead, they rely on procedural knowledge for moving from one topological entity to another.

Topological approaches often face severe problems of disambiguating places that look alike. The need to integrate both metric and topological representations has been long recognized (Chatila & Laumond 1985; Kuipers 1978; Thrun 1998), with the current approach just being one example. Other related work is reviewed in (Thrun, Fox, & Burgard 1998).

Our approach differs from most work in the field (see also the surveys in (Thrun 1998; Lu & Milios 1997)) in two important technical aspects. First, robot poses are revised forward *and* backwards in time—as pointed out by Lu and Milios (Lu & Milios 1997), most existing approach do not revise pose estimations backwards in time. Second, by using probabilistic representations, the approach considers multiple hypotheses as to where a robot might have been, which facilitates the recovery from errors. The approaches in (Lu & Milios 1997) and (Shatkay & Kaelbling 1997) are similar in this respect to the one proposed here. Shatkay/Kaelbling proposed to use the alpha-beta algorithm for learning topological maps, based on (Koenig & Simmons 1996), who used the same algorithm for a restricted version of the mapping problem. However, both methods face severe scaling limitations. The approach by Lu/Milios, which in essence constitutes the metric phase of our algorithm, is only able to compensate small odometric error; thus, it alone is insufficient for the problems investigated here. The method by Shatkay/Kaelbling does not represent poses in Cartesian coordinates. It is unclear whether the approach can produce topologically correct maps for the data used in this paper. To the best of our knowledge, no other method has been demonstrated to generate maps of similar size and accuracy.

Conclusion

This paper proposes a statistical approach to building large scale maps in indoor environments. This approach integrates topological and metric representations: It first constructs a coarse-grained topological map, based on which it generates a detailed metric map. The topological approach tackles the global alignment problem, thereby correcting large odometric errors. The metric approach fine-tunes the estimations locally, resulting in maps with floating-point resolution.

Both the topological and the metric approaches are based on the same statistical framework, which treats the problem of concurrent mapping and localization as a maximum likelihood estimation problem. An efficient hill-climbing algorithm was devised to maximize the likelihood function. The algorithm has empirically been validated in cyclic environments of size up to 80 by 25 meters. While strictly speaking, EM is not guaranteed to converge to the global optimum, visual inspection of the results suggest that the most likely map is indeed found in all experiments. In fact, in every single experiment that we ran so far, the approach successfully identified maps that were topologically correct and sufficiently accurate for navigation.

We believe that the results reported here shed new light onto the problem as to how to achieve scalability in mobile robot mapping. First, they demonstrate that both paradigms, metric and topological, can be expressed in the same statistical framework. Under this model, the difference between topological and metric mapping appears to be rather minor. Second, this work illustrates that topological approaches indeed scale up to large and highly ambiguous environments. The environments tested here are difficult in that they possess large cycles, and in that local sensor information is insufficient to disambiguate locations. Our approach managed to produce larger maps than, to the best of our knowledge, any other approach ever has. Third, this paper demonstrates that relatively basic statistical methods are well-suited to solve large-scale mapping problems, suggesting that they might be fit for other high-dimensional state estimation problems in robotics.

Acknowledgment

Partial financial support by Daimler-Benz Research and the Defense Advanced Research Projects Agency (DARPA) via the Airforce Missile System Command under contract number F04701-97-C-0022 is gratefully acknowledged.

References

Borenstein, J., and Koren., Y. 1991. The vector field histogram–fast obstacle avoidance for mobile robots. *IEEE Journal of Robotics and Automation* 7(3):278–288.

Burgard, W.; Fox, D.; Hennig, D.; and Schmidt, T. 1996. Estimating the absolute position of a mobile robot using position probability grids. In *Proceedings of AAAI-96*.

Chatila, R., and Laumond, J.-P. 1985. Position referencing and consistent world modeling for mobile robots. In *Proceedings of ICRA-85*.

Choset, H. 1996. *Sensor Based Motion Planning: The Hierarchical Generalized Voronoi Graph*. Ph.D. Dissertation, Caltech.

Chown, E.; Kaplan, S.; and Kortenkamp, D. 1995. Prototypes, location, and associative networks (plan): Towards a unified theory of cognitive mapping. *Cognitive Science* 19:1–51.

Cox, I. 1994. Modeling a dynamic environment using a bayesian multiple hypothesis approach. *Artificial Intelligence* 66:311–344.

Dempster, A.; Laird, A.; and Rubin, D. 1977. Maximum likelihood from incomplete data via the em algorithm. *Journal of the Royal Statistical Society, Series B* 39(1):1–38.

Dudek, G.; Jenkin, M.; Milios, E.; and Wilkes, D. 1991. Robotic exploration as graph construction. *IEEE Transactions on Robotics and Automation* 7(6):859–865.

Elfes, A. 1989. *Occupancy Grids: A Probabilistic Framework for Robot Perception and Navigation*. Ph.D. Dissertation, CMU.

Gutmann, J.-S., and Nebel, B. 1997. Navigation mobiler roboter mit laserscans. In *Autonome Mobile Systeme*. Springer Verlag.

Gutmann, J.-S., and Schlegel, C. 1996. Amos: Comparison of scan matching approaches for self-localization in indoor environments. In *Proceedings of the 1st Euromicro Workshop on Advanced Mobile Robots*.

Kaelbling, L.; Cassandra, A.; and Kurien, J. 1996. Acting under uncertainty: Discrete Bayesian models for mobile-robot navigation. In *Proceedings of IROS-96*.

Koenig, S., and Simmons, R. 1996. Passive distance learning for robot navigation. In *Proceedings ICML-96*.

Kortenkamp, D., and Weymouth, T. 1994. Topological mapping for mobile robots using a combination of sonar and vision sensing. In *Proceedings of AAI-96*.

Kuipers, B., and Byun, Y.-T. 1991. A robot exploration and mapping strategy based on a semantic hierarchy of spatial representations. *Journal of Robotics and Autonomous Systems* 8:47–63.

Kuipers, B. J. 1978. Modeling spatial knowledge. *Cognitive Science* 2:129–153.

Lu, F., and Milios, E. 1997. Globally consistent range scan alignment for environment mapping. *Autonomous Robots* 4:333–349.

Matarić, M. J. 1990. A distributed model for mobile robot environment-learning and navigation. Master's thesis, MIT.

Moravec, H. P. 1988. Sensor fusion in certainty grids for mobile robots. *AI Magazine* 61–74.

Nourbakhsh, I.; Powers, R.; and Birchfield, S. 1995. DERVISH an office-navigating robot. *AI Magazine* 16(2):53–60.

Rabiner, L., and Juang, B. 1986. An introduction to hidden markov models. In *IEEE ASSP Magazine*.

Shatkay, H., and Kaelbling, L. 1997. Learning topological maps with weak local odometric information. In *Proceedings of IJCAI-97*.

Simmons, R., and Koenig, S. 1995. Probabilistic robot navigation in partially observable environments. In *Proceedings of IJCAI-95*.

Thrun, S. et al. 1998. Map learning and high-speed navigation in RHINO. In Kortenkamp, D.; Bonassi, R.; and Murphy, R., eds., *AI-based Mobile Robots: Case studies of successful robot systems*. Cambridge, MA: MIT Press.

Thrun, S.; Fox, D.; and Burgard, W. 1998. A probabilistic approach to concurrent mapping and localization for mobile robots. *Machine Learning* and *Autonomous Robots* (joint issue). To appear.

Thrun, S. 1998. Learning maps for indoor mobile robot navigation. *Artificial Intelligence*. To appear.

Sound Understanding

The Role of Data Reprocessing in Complex Acoustic Environments

Frank Klassner

Computing Sciences Department
Villanova University
Villanova, PA 19085
klassner@monet.csc.vill.edu

Victor Lesser

Computer Science Department
University of Massachusetts
Amherst, MA 01003
lesser@cs.umass.edu

Hamid Nawab

ECE Department
Boston University
Boston, MA 02215
hamid@bu.edu

Abstract

The *Integrated Processing and Understanding of Signals* (IPUS) architecture is a general blackboard framework for structuring bidirectional interaction between front-end signal processing algorithms (SPAs) and signal understanding processes. To date, reported work on the architecture has focused on proof-of-concept demonstrations of how well a sound-understanding testbed (SUT) based on IPUS could use small libraries of sound models and small sets of SPAs to analyze acoustic scenarios. In this paper we evaluate how well the architecture scales up to more complex environments. We describe knowledge-representation and control-strategy issues involved in scaling up an IPUS-based SUT for use with a library of 40 sound models, and present empirical evaluation that shows (a) the IPUS data reprocessing paradigm can increase interpretation accuracy by 25% – 50% in complex scenarios, and (b) the benefit increases with increasing complexity of the environment.

Introduction[1]

The *Integrated Processing and Understanding of Signals* (IPUS) architecture (Lesser et al., 1995) is a general blackboard framework for structuring bidirectional interaction between front-end signal processing algorithms (SPAs) and signal interpretation processes. It is designed for complex environments, which are characterized by variable signal to noise ratios, unpredictable source behaviors, and the simultaneous occurrence of objects whose signal signatures can interact with each other. It has been shown that in these environments, the choice of numeric signal processing algorithms (SPAs) and their control parameter values is crucial; parameter values inappropriate to the current scenario can render an interpretation system unable to recognize entire classes of signals (Dorken et al., 1992). IPUS provides an interpretation system with the ability to dynamically modify its front-end SPAs to handle scenario changes and to reprocess ambiguous or distorted data. This adaptation is organized as two concurrent search processes: one for correct interpretations of SPAs' outputs and another for SPAs and control parameters appropriate for the environment. Interaction between these search processes is structured by a formal theory of how inappropriate SPA usage can distort SPA output.

Much of the work associated with IPUS has focused on applying the architecture to the domain of auditory scene analysis (Bregman 1990), which involves the decomposition of an acoustic signal into the sound sources that could have generated the original signal. Because auditory scene analysis in even moderately complex environments raises many issues concerning the relationship between SPA-appropriateness and multi-sound interactions, it is an appropriate domain for studying IPUS' effectiveness.

To date, reported work on IPUS has been oriented toward proof-of-concept demonstrations of how a sound-understanding testbed (SUT) based on IPUS could use small libraries of sound models (≤ 5) and small sets of SPAs to analyze acoustic scenarios. In this paper we empirically evaluate how well the architecture scales up to a more complex environment which has an order of magnitude more sounds (40), a variety of time-frequency behaviors (e.g. impulsive, harmonic, chirping, periodic). and scenarios with three or more simultaneous sounds. In particular, we (1) review the basic IPUS architecture, (2) present the SUT and new knowledge representations and control strategies we added to accomplish the scale-up, (3) describe experimental evaluation of the new SUT in a more complex acoustic environment, and (4) conclude with analysis which shows that (a) the IPUS data reprocessing paradigm can improve recognition accuracy in complex scenarios by 25 – 50% over that obtained from non-reprocessing systems, and (b) the improvement increases with environmental complexity.

IPUS Overview

The following discussion summarizes the IPUS blackboard architecture's basic control loop shown in Figure 1 (Klassner, 1996; Lesser et al., 1995). For each block of data, the loop starts by processing the signal with an initial configuration of SPAs (i.e. a front end Short Time Fourier Transform (STFT) (Nawab and Quatieri, 1988) with analysis window length N and window overlap D) selected both to identify the signals most likely to occur in the environment, and to provide indications of when less likely or unknown signals have occurred. In the next part of the loop, a *discrepancy detection* process tests for discrepancies between the output

---

[1] Copyright 1998, American Association for Artificial Intelligence (www.aaai.org). All rights reserved.

of each SPA in the current configuration and (1) the output of other SPAs in the configuration, (2) application-domain constraints, and (3) the outputs' anticipated form based on high-level expectations. Architectural control permits this process to execute both after SPA output is generated and after interpretation problem solving hypotheses are generated. If discrepancies are detected, a *diagnosis* process attempts to explain them by mapping them to a sequence of qualitative distortion hypotheses (e.g. the discrepancy of an expected frequency track not being found in a section of a spectrogram could be explained as being caused by inadequate frequency resolution provided by an STFT's control parameters). The loop ends with a *signal reprocessing* stage [2] that proposes and executes a search plan to find a new front end to eliminate or reduce the hypothesized distortions. After the loop's completion for a given data block, if there are any similarly-rated competing top-level interpretations, a *differential diagnosis* process selects and executes a reprocessing plan to find outputs for features that discriminate among alternatives.

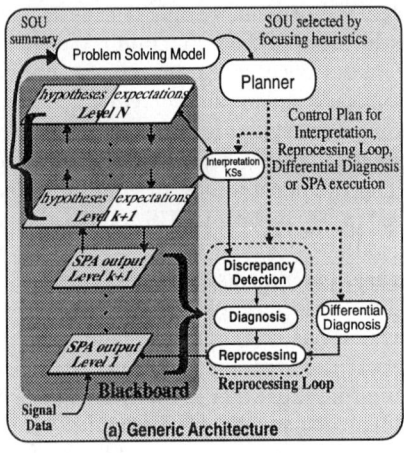

Figure 1: *The abstract IPUS architecture.*

Although the architecture requires the initial processing of data one block at a time, the loop's diagnosis, reprocessing, and differential diagnosis components are not restricted to examining only the current block's processing results. If the current block's processing results imply the possibility that earlier blocks were misinterpreted or inappropriately reprocessed, those components can be applied to the earlier blocks as well as the current blocks. Additionally, the reprocessing strategies and discrepancy-detection tests can specify the postponement of reprocessing or discrepancy determination until specified conditions are met in some later data block (e.g. wait until a frequency track in a spectrogram extends more than 2 seconds in length). The reader

---

[2] Related in concept, though not degree of formal structure, to work in various perceptual domains on reapplying SPAs to recover expectation-driven features. (Ellis, 1996; Nakatani *et al.*, 1995; Bobick and Bolles, 1992; Kohl *et al.*, 1987)

is referred to (Klassner, 1996) for greater detail concerning the implementation of the architecture and its control loop.

IPUS implements perception as the integration of search in a front-end-SPA space with search in an interpretation space. This dual search becomes apparent in IPUS with the following two observations. First, each time signal data is reprocessed, a new state in a front-end-SPA search space is examined and tested for how well it eliminates or reduces distortions. Second, failure to remove a hypothesized distortion after a bounded search in the front-end-SPA space leads to more search in the interpretation space because it indicates a stronger likelihood that the current interpretation is not correct. In general, the search process whose current state produces the lower uncertainty serves as the standard against which progress toward a complete interpretation or adequate front end is measured in the other. Within the interpretation search process "uncertainty" refers to the portion of the signal not accounted for by the current interpretation state and the strength of the negative (i.e. missing or incomplete) evidence against each hypothesis in the interpretation. Within the front-end search process "uncertainty" refers to the degree of inconsistency found among the results from SPAs whose outputs are supposed to be related according to their domain signal processing theory.

Each time an SPA is executed within IPUS, the hypotheses representing the execution's results are annotated with the name of the SPA and the control parameter values used in the execution. This annotation is the outputs' *parameter context*. Each SPA output is also annotated with a *processing context*, or a data structure listing the SPA sequence that generated the hypothesis from the input signal.

Three categories of signal processing knowledge are stored as part of the definition of SPAs in IPUS. They are used along with the processing context mechanism to support SPA (re)application and efficient reuse of results from earlier reprocessings. The first is a set of rules defining how individual SPA control parameters should be modified to eliminate or reduce various classes of distortions that could be manifested in the algorithm's outputs and identified by discrepancy diagnosis. The second information category is a mapping function that takes two parameter contexts and the output hypotheses produced from the first context (i.e. execution of an SPA), and returns a list of the hypotheses modified to reflect how they would appear had they been produced by the second context. The third information category is a list of "supercontext methods" that take as input a parameter context and an "information category." They return context patterns indicating the range of values for each control-parameter in an SPA parameter-context that would permit the SPA to produce outputs having the same or greater detail in the category as found in the specified parameter context. This information allows an IPUS system to identify results from earlier detailed reprocessings that could be reused to verify interpretations without incurring the cost of actual SPA reapplication.

SUT Design and Scale-Up Issues

Our goal in this paper is to determine whether and how well IPUS scales up in handling acoustic environments much more complex than previously reported. To this end we constructed a sound understanding testbed (SUT) using the architecture, with the intent to interpret acoustic scenarios from an environmental library with 40 sounds. The library's models were developed from at least 5 instances of each sound, and were specifically selected to provide a complex subset of the acoustic behaviors (e.g. impulsive, harmonic, periodic, chirping) and sound interactions (e.g. masking, start/end time blurring, overlapping frequency content) that can arise in random real-world auditory scenarios. The sounds' durations range from 0.2 to 30.0 seconds, and, with the exception of one sound, the expected frequency range of every narrowband component (e.g. ≤ 100 Hz wide) of each library sound overlaps a component of at least one other sound. Figure 2 shows the library's distribution of frequency content. The average number of narrowband tracks per sound is 4. For each narrowband component of a given sound, on average another 5.3 sounds have potential overlapping frequency content. This is significantly more spectral overlap than in reported work (0.4). Note that the greater the number of overlapping tracks there can be in a spectral region, the greater the amount of interpretation search that must be done to determine (1) whether in fact overlapping tracks are present, and (2) which subset of the tracks that could be in the region of overlap are actually present.

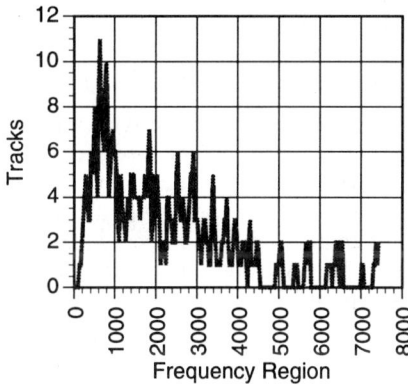

Figure 2: *Histogram of SUT Library Narrowband Components.*

After preliminary tests of the basic design, we found it necessary to extend the SUT's evidential hierarchy and control strategy beyond reported work in order to handle the greater complexity of this test environment. We first describe the evidential extension. Our SUT uses thirteen partially-ordered evidence representations to construct an interpretation of incoming signals. Figure 3 illustrates the support relationships among the representations. These include three new levels (envelope, event, and noisebed), that provide additional information for use in disambiguating among different sounds, a new "script" level that allows us to include more complex sounds in our library, and, as will be discussed later in the section, a spectral-band level to support a knowledge approximation strategy that avoids reliance on strict narrowband descriptions (contours) of signals' frequency content.

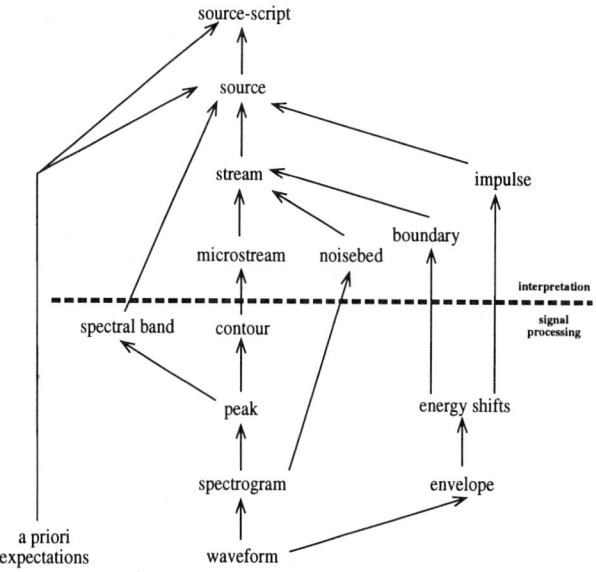

Figure 3: *SUT Acoustic Abstraction Hierarchy. "A priori expectations" refers to hypotheses from the previous block of data.*

The following descriptions highlight the representations' content and importance in interpretation:

- *WAVEFORM:* the raw waveform data;

- *ENVELOPE:* the shape of the time-domain signal;

- *SPECTROGRAM:* time-frequency representation derived with SPAs such as the Short-Time Fourier Transform (STFT);

- *PEAK:* local maximum spectral energy regions in each time-slice in a spectrogram, indicating narrow-band features in a signal's spectral representation;

- *SHIFT:* sudden energy changes in the envelope;

- *EVENT:* time-domain events, grouping shifts into boundaries (i.e. a "step" in time domain energy indicating possible end or start of a sound) and impulses (i.e. sudden spikes in the signal);

- *CONTOUR:* groups of peaks whose time indices, frequencies, and amplitudes show uniform frequency and energy behavior in time-frequency;

- *SPECTRAL BAND:* spectrogram-peak clusters;

- *MICROSTREAM:* contour sequences (tracks) that exhibit changes in energy that follow an onset-steady-decay pattern (e.g. increasing energy followed by steady energy levels followed by decreasing energy levels);

- *NOISEBED:* the wideband spectral component of short-time impulsive events;

- *STREAM:* a set of microstreams and noisebeds grouped as a perceptual unit on the basis of streaming criteria developed in the psychoacoustic community (Bregman 1990) (e.g. harmonic sets);
- *SOURCE:* stream hypotheses, with their durations supported by boundaries, are interpreted as sound-source hypotheses according to how closely they match source-models available in the testbed library;[3]
- *SCRIPT:* temporal grouping of a sequence of sources into a single unit (e.g. "footsteps" being composed of a sequence of footfalls).

The control strategy we adopted for our SUT differs in two significant ways from reported work. The first is that contouring (i.e. tracking of energy trends in a spectrogram without any interpretation context) is not performed as part of the initial default front-end processing for each data block, but rather through expectation-driven processing guided by initial source hypotheses based on mappings from the rough frequency regions covered by spectral bands to the possible frequency ranges of library models. This change was made to address the library sounds' greater amount of shared frequency content (Figure 2), as well as the increased instance-variability of each sound. We found that these two factors, combined with the possibility of sounds' simultaneous occurence, made the results of data-driven contouring too unreliable for use in hypothesizing new sources' occurrences. Accumulated evidence from spectral-band time-frequency region coverage and time-domain events were found to serve better as the basis for hypothesizing new sources and confirming termination of previously-active sources.

The second important control strategy enhancement is that before analyzing the next data block, our SUT examines the current interpretation for gobal consistency with respect to how well members of sets of competing source hypotheses, taken as a whole, explain the observed signal energy. This extension was necessary to address (1) a problem in which arbitrary hypothesis rating cutoffs caused (correct) long-term source hypotheses with initially low amounts of support evidence to be disbelieved in favor of (incorrect) shorter-term sources with locally superior support before enough data blocks of evidence could be accumulated, and (2) a problem in which system execution time was impacted by the large number of competing sources arising from spectral bands that overlapped the lower frequency regions shared by tracks of many of the library sounds, as shown in Figure 2.

To explain this extension, we first consider interpretation evaluation before the end of a data block's processing. During the interpretation of a given data block, source hypotheses are considered to be in competition with all other hypothesized sounds whose frequency components (microstreams or noisebeds) overlap in time, and their individual belief ratings are modified by the pooled strength of their common support. As evidence is gathered for each competitor, their belief ratings change relative to each other. If a source hypothesis' rating drops below an arbitrary threshold, it is dropped from further consideration, leaving its competitors with one less competitor to dilute their support's strength.

This local comparison process works well when all possible sources have similar length and behaviors, but increasingly penalizes sources as their durations (and concomitant minimum required support duration) increase beyond the average duration of sounds in the library. It also precludes the possibility of deciding that two competitors are actually present together. What is needed is an interpretation control strategy that considers not only the local goodness of a hypothesis with respect to its overlapping competitors, but also the global goodness of a hypothesis in regard to how much overall signal energy it and its noncompetitors can account for. We use the following five-stage strategy at the end of each data block's processing to address this.

1. All source hypotheses are grouped as *viable*, *dropped*, or *suspended*. Viable sources are those that are currently believed because of their evidential rating, while dropped sources are those that have been disbelieved, or "pruned" from the interpretation, in favor of a higher-rated competing source. Suspended sources are those hypotheses that were disbelieved or eliminated from further consideration before all possible evidence for them had been sought because of some interpretation-search pruning heuristic.

2. Sources whose competitors (source hypotheses with overlapping frequency content) have higher belief are iteratively disbelieved, or dropped from the interpretation (i.e. the set of viable sources), until only the highest-rated source of each set of competitors is left.

3. An energy sufficiency heuristic is applied to determine the current interpretation's adequacy: does the total narrowband time-frequency energy of the viable sources account for some threshold percent of the signal energy? If it does, the control strategy proceeds to analyze the next data block. If it does not, however, one or both of the next two steps are performed.

4. Dropped sources are reconsidered in order of rating to determine through differential diagnosis and reprocessing whether in fact *both* the dropped source and its higher-ranked competitor are present. The energy sufficiency heuristic is applied again. If it indicates sufficient signal energy is accounted for in the interpretation, the control strategy proceeds to analyze the next data block, otherwise, stage 5 is executed.

5. Suspended sources are reconsidered in order of rating to determine through discrepancy diagnosis and reprocessing whether in fact a suspended hypothesis had been discarded from viability too soon. At the end of this stage, regardless of the outcome of the energy sufficiency criterion, the control strategy proceeds to the next data block's analysis.

This extension allows our SUT to correctly process situations such as the following. Assume for a scenario with two

---

[3] Partial matches (e.g. a stream missing a microstream, or a stream with duration shorter than expected) are accepted, but these matches will later cause the SUT to attempt to account for the missing or ill-formed evidence as artifacts of inappropriate front-end processing.

overlapping sounds A and C that there are three competing sound hypotheses **A**, **B** and **C**, where **A** competes with **B**, **B** competes with **C**, and **B** has a temporarily higher rating than **C**. The new strategy can permit the recognition that because **C** and **A**, taken together, provide a more complete explanation of the signal energy, **B**'s locally higher rating should be discounted and **B** should be dropped from the current interpretation.

Experimental Evaluation

The IPUS framework is designed around its reprocessing loop. It is important, therefore, to evaluate what effect the reprocessing loop has on the quality of scenario interpretations, and to observe what relationships exist between scenario complexity and reprocessing frequency. The experiment suite in this section uses two versions of the SUT to examine these questions. The first version is the one described earlier in this paper, and the second version is identical to the first except that it performs no discrepancy diagnosis or reprocessing, and assumes that missing or incomplete spectrogram evidence is never caused by inappropriate SPAs or parameter settings. These versions are each tested on two sets of acoustic scenarios. The first set, called *SIMPLE*, has 40 single-sound scenarios. The second set, called *COMPLEX*, has 15 scenarios that contain a number of simultaneous sounds. In the remainder of this section we describe (1) how these scenario sets were generated, (2) how the front-ends of the SUT versions were configured, and (3) what experiment data were collected.

Scenario Generation Protocols

Each SIMPLE scenario contains a "single" sound from the SUT library. The term "single" is qualified because in some cases, such as clock ticks or footsteps, the scenario will contain a sequence of sound instances. The scenarios were generated by randomly choosing an instance of the sound used to generate the acoustic models. At least 5 instances (sampled at 16 KHz) were available for each SUT library sound's model. Regardless of content, each scenario signal was amplified so that all scenarios have the same average power. SIMPLE scenarios could range in length from 1 to 5 seconds, and were always an integer number of seconds long. If a library sound could last more than 5 seconds, the scenario for it was limited to 5 seconds, consisting entirely of that sound. If a library sound instance was less than 5 seconds long, its scenario was set as the minimum integer number of seconds spanning the instance's duration. In the SIMPLE set, the total number of sound instances is 71, and the total time duration of all instances is 110.45 seconds.

The following 5-step method was used to generate the COMPLEX set's 15 scenarios with a bias toward simultaneous sounds. First, four sounds were randomly selected from the SUT library. Second, a random instance of each sound was selected from those used in the SIMPLE scenario set. Third, start-times for each instance were randomly selected with uniform distribution within a 7-second base timeframe. Fourth, a 5-second window was randomly chosen within the base timeframe such that all four sounds were included for at least their length or 1 second, whichever was shorter. When start times precluded such a window, steps 3 and 4 were repeated until this criterion was met. Fifth, each scenario was scaled so that all had the same average power. Since some sound-creation events, such as footsteps and phone ring sequences, are really composed of several instances, the average number of instances in each scenario is 7.3 rather than 4, as might have been expected. There are a total of 110 sound instances in the 15 scenarios, and the total time duration of all instances is 114 seconds.

Experiment Design

The default, first-pass front-end for both SUTs was chosen so that the no-reprocessing SUT could (1) pick enough peaks from a spectrogram to identify the maximum possible number of tracks for any single sound, (2) resolve the nonoverlapping narrowband tracks of sounds that were closest in frequency to each other, and (3) resolve the short-term time-domain features of noisebeds. Since no sound in the SUT library has more than 7 narrowband tracks, the first criterion required that the front-end by default pick the 7 highest-energy peaks over a background-noise threshold per spectrogram time-slice. The last two criteria required that the front end use a time-frequency SPA that balanced their time and frequency constraints: a Short-Time Fourier Transform SPA with 1024-pt rectangular analysis window and 128-pt decimation interval was selected. From preliminary tests we selected an energy-sufficiency threshold value of 70%. That is, an interpretation is considered sufficient if it accounts for 70% of a signal's energy. The reprocessing-enabled SUT modelled STFT-induced time- and frequency-resolution distortions, as well as distortions introduced by the peak-picking SPA when insufficient peaks are picked for the number of sounds present.

Results

Table 1 reports statistics for the SUT versions' performance in three evaluation categories:

System Performance: "hit rate" refers to the number of sound-instances (e.g. individual footsteps in a sequence) in the scenario which overlapped with a correct interpretation hypothesis and "false-alarm rate" refers to the number of incorrectly-believed hypotheses that were hypothesized for the final interpretation at the end of the 5 seconds of data. Note that the reported values are relative to the total number of sound instances over all scenarios. "Track+" refers to the duration for which "hit" sound instances were tracked relative to the total amount of time for which all sound instances lasted and "Track-" refers to the duration covered by all false alarm answer hypotheses relative to all answer hypotheses' total time.

SPA-search cost: "Param Cntxt" refers to the number of time-frequency-SPA reprocessing parameter contexts per scenario, averaged over all scenarios, and "Total Ops" refers to the total number (first-pass + reprocessing) of spectrogram-based mathematical operations (additions and multiplications) per scenario, averaged over all scenarios.

		Simple Environment		Complex Environment	
	REPROCESSING?:	no	yes	no	yes
System Perform.	Hit Rate	0.63	0.79	0.47	0.60
	FAlarm Rate	0.32	0.38	0.40	0.39
	Track+ Rate	0.54	0.65	0.44	0.67
	Track- Rate	0.15	0.18	0.27	0.19
SPA Search Cost	Param Cntxt	1.00	1.95	1.00	4.20
	Total Ops	2.7e7	2.8e7	4.0e7	5.5e7
Interp. Search Cost	Total Hyps	8.18	7.32	8.53	8.14
	Answers	0.93	1.26	0.79	0.86
	Nonanswers	7.25	6.06	7.74	7.28
	DD Rate	0.00	5.82	0.00	12.63

Table 1: *Experiment Results. SPA-search cost is averaged per scenario, while interpretation-search cost and system performance are averaged per total sound instances (hit and false-alarm rates, number of hyps, diagnosis rate) or total sound instance duration (tracking). "Total Ops" includes additions and multiplications performed during both initial front-end analysis and reprocessing.*

Interpretation-search cost: "Answers" refers to the number of hypotheses (*both* false alarm and hits) reported in the final interpretation, averaged over all scenarios, and "Nonanswers" refers to the average number of sound-source hypotheses that were considered but rejected by the end of processing for a scenario. "Total Hyps" refers to the average total number of sound hypotheses considered (Answers + Nonanswers) during a scenario's processing. "DD rate" shows the number of invocations of the discrepancy diagnosis component per scenario, as a measure of how often the SUT encountered missing or inconclusive evidence and needed to explain the situation as a SPA-tuning issue.

Analysis and Conclusions

Table 1 is divided to show the performance of each SUT version (i.e. Reprocessing?=no or yes) in each environment (i.e. SIMPLE or COMPLEX). In both environments, the table shows that the presence of the reprocessing loop significantly improves both the hit rate and the tracking rate. Although the false-alarm rate remains stable though all runs, in the COMPLEX environment the reprocessing loop significantly reduces the amount of time for which the SUT tracks false alarms. In the SIMPLE environment the *Track-* results seem to indicate that reprocessing is not useful in simple environments.

Since the COMPLEX scenarios were designed to have a higher incidence of sound interactions that could violate SPA parameter-setting assumptions than SIMPLE scenarios, one might expect that the interpretation of complex scenarios would benefit from reprocessing more than would the interpretation of single-source scenarios. Indeed, the rate at which discrepancy diagnosis occurs (*DD rate*) doubles between the two environments, indicating that more discrepanies and/or missed expectations occurred in the COMPLEX environment. In the SIMPLE portion of Table 1, though, the reprocessing loop improves the hit rate by $(.79 - .63)/.63 \approx 25\%$ whereas in the table's COMPLEX portion the improvement is also $(.60 - .47)/.47 \approx 28\%$. This is only an apparent contradiction to the expectation, however, once tracking rate improvements are taken into consideration. In the SIMPLE experiments the reprocessing loop improved the tracking rate by $(.65 - .54)/.54 \approx 20\%$ while in the COMPLEX experiments the reprocessing loop improved tracking by $(.67 - .44)/.44 \approx 52\%$. The justification for using tracking rate improvement instead of hit rate improvement to verify the expectation is that a hit only requires that *some* time-region of the sound be identified correctly. Thus, the no-reprocessing SUT can attain a somewhat higher hit rate when sounds that might otherwise interfere with each other's spectral signatures do not completely overlap each other in time. The tracking rate, on the other hand, indicates more reliably how much of each sound was correctly tracked *and* identified, and therefore ought to be used to verify the expectation that reprocessing should show greater benefit in complex scenarios.

In connection with environmental complexity effects, we note that the cost of reprocessing increases with environmental complexity. In the SIMPLE environment reprocessing cost an additional 1.0×10^6 mathematical operations (*Total Ops*), (3% increase) to improve the system performance, while in the COMPLEX environment it cost an additional 1.5×10^7 operations (37% increase) to improve system performance. The total interpretation search space (*total hyps*) examined in the COMPLEX environment is marginally larger than that examined in the SIMPLE environment, as might be expected. It is significant to note that in both environments the reprocessing component *reduced* the interpretation state space by preventing the verification of fewer hypotheses that would become *nonanswer* hypotheses (i.e. dropped sources).

At first glance one might have expected the hit rates for the SIMPLE runs to be closer to 1.00 than 0.63 and 0.79, with allowance for misses due to the similar frequency content and temporal behaviors of several sounds in the library. However, as mentioned earlier, several of the "single-source" scenarios actually contained more than one sound, and not all of these instances in a sound-sequence were correctly matched to the sound models. If one measures hit rate on the basis of whether at least one instance in a sound-sequence was identified, the reprocessing SUT's hit rate under SIMPLE conditions becomes 0.85, and the no-reprocessing SUT's hit rate becomes 0.65. In both hit-rate measures, we see that reprocessing can be beneficial even in straightforward scenarios, by handling evidence missed because of variations within individual sounds.

Analysis of the experiment runs false-alarm rates, however, indicates that (1) the high false-alarm rates of both SUTs are due to an interaction between the energy-sufficiency heuristic for limiting interpretation search and SUT sound models' shortcomings, and (2) reprocessing exacerbates this problem in SIMPLE scenarios. Some of the sounds in the library have long-term wideband spectral energy not well modelled by the narrowband, microstream-oriented models. Occasionally this wideband energy manifests itself as isolated clusters of spectrogram peaks that ordinarily would be ignored by the SUTs, but in situations where interpretations based on narrowband spectral energy do not account for enough of the total signal energy, the energy-sufficiency heuristic forces the SUTs to consider sounds overlapping the small unexplained spectral bands from the wideband energy. The reprocessing component exacerbates the problem by tracking these "hallucinations" for longer time periods.

These experiments lend support for two claims about the IPUS architecture's data reprocessing component: (1) it has potential for scaling to handle moderately complex environments and, more significantly, (2) it can provide increasing interpretation improvement with increasing environment complexity. Additionally, these results provide support for the growing school of thought within the nascent computational auditory scene analysis community (Ellis, 1996) that argues for the utility of high-level expectation-driven analysis in acoustic environments.

Future work will focus in two areas. The first involves creating a more flexible energy-sufficiency heuristic to address the simple-scenario shortcoming mentioned earlier. The second involves determining new strategies for reducing reprocessing costs, such as applying reprocessing SPAs to *portions* of the regions in which sources have missing or ambiguous evidence, rather than to the entire problematic region, as is currently done.

Acknowledgment

This research was sponsored by the Department of the Navy, Office of the Chief of Naval Research, under contract number ONR #N00014-95-1-1198. The content of this paper does not necessarily reflect the position or policy of the government, and no official endorsement should be inferred.

References

Bobick, A. F. and Bolles, R. C., "The representation space paradigm of concurrent evolving object descriptions," *IEEE Trans. on Pattern Analysis and Machine Intelligence*, vol. 14, no. 2, pp. 146–156, Feb. 1992.

Bregman, A., *Auditory Scene Analysis: The Perceptual Organization of Sound*. MIT Press. 1990.

Dorken, E., Nawab, S. H., and Lesser, V., "Extended model variety analysis for integrated processing and understanding of signals," *1992 IEEE Conf. on Acoust., Speech and Signal Proc.*, vol. V, pp. 73-76, San Francisco, CA, 1992.

Ellis, D., "Prediction-driven computational auditory scene analysis," Ph.D. thesis, Electrical Engineering and Computer Science Dept., MIT, 1996.

Klassner, F., Lesser, V., Nawab, H., "Combining approximate front end signal processing with selective reprocessing in auditory perception," *AAAI-97*, pp. 661–666, Providence, RI, July 1997.

Klassner, F., "Data reprocessing in signal understanding systems," Ph.D. thesis, Computer Science Dept., Univ. of Massachusetts, Amherst, MA, 1996.

Kohl, C., Hanson, A., and Reisman, E., "A goal-directed intermediate level executive for image interpretation," *IJCAI-87*, pp. 811–814, Milan, Aug. 1987.

Lesser, V., Nawab, H., and Klassner, F., "IPUS: an architecture for the integrated processing and understanding of signals," *Artificial Intelligence*, vol. 77, no. 1, pp. 129–171, Aug. 1995.

Nakatani, T., Okuno, H. G., and Kawabata, T., "Residue-driven architecture for computational auditory scene analysis," *IJCAI-95*, vol. 1, pp. 165–172, Montreal, 1995.

Nawab, H. and Quatieri, T., "Short-time fourier transform," *Advanced Topics in Signal Processing*, Prentice Hall, NJ, 1988.

Sound Ontology for Computational Auditory Scene Analysis

Tomohiro Nakatani[†] and Hiroshi G. Okuno

NTT Basic Research Laboratories
Nippon Telegraph and Telephone Corporation
3-1 Morinosato-Wakamiya, Atsugi, Kanagawa 243-0198, JAPAN
okuno@nue.org

Abstract

This paper proposes that sound ontology should be used both as a common vocabulary for sound representation and as a common terminology for integrating various sound stream segregation systems. Since research on computational auditory scene analysis (CASA) focuses on recognizing and understanding various kinds of sounds, sound stream segregation which extracts each sound stream from a mixture of sounds is essential for CASA. Even if sound stream segregation systems use a harmonic structure of sound as a cue of segregation, it is not easy to integrate such systems because the definition of a harmonic structure differs or the precision of extracted harmonic structures differs. Therefore, sound ontology is needed as a common knowledge representation of sounds.

Another problem is to interface sound stream segregation systems with applications such as automatic speech recognition systems. Since the requirement of the quality of segregated sound streams depends on applications, sound stream segregation systems must provide a flexible interface. Therefore, sound ontology is needed to fulfill the requirements imposed by them. In addition, the hierarchical structure of sound ontology provides a means of controlling top-down and bottom-up processing of sound stream segregation.

Introduction

Sound is gathering attention as important media for multi-medal communications, but is less utilized as input media than characters or images. One reason is the lack of a general approach to recognize auditory events from a mixture of sounds. Usually, people hear a mixture of sounds, and people with normal hearing can segregate sounds from the mixture and focus on a particular voice or sound in a noisy environment. This capability is known as the *cocktail party effect* (Cherry 1953). Perceptual segregation of sounds, called *auditory scene analysis*, has been studied by psychoacoustic and psychophysical researchers for more than forty years. Although many observations have been analyzed and reported (Bregman 1990), it is only recently that researchers have begun to use computer modeling of auditory scene analysis.

This emerging research area is called *computational auditory scene analysis (CASA)* (Brown and Cooke 1992; Cooke et al. 1993; Nakatani, Okuno, and Kawabata 1994a; Rosenthal and Okuno 1998), and its goal is the understanding of an arbitrary sound mixture including non-speech sounds and music. Computers need to be able to decide which parts of a mixed acoustic signal are relevant to a particular purpose – which part should be interpreted as speech, for example, and which should be interpreted as a door closing, an air conditioner humming, or another person interrupting. CASA focuses on the computer modeling and implementation for the understanding of acoustic events

One of its main research topics of CASA is sound stream segregation. In particular, CASA focuses on a general model and mechanism of segregating various kinds of sounds, not limited to specific kinds of sounds, from a mixture of sounds.

Sound stream segregation can be used as a front-end for automatic speech recognition in real-world environments (Okuno, Nakatani, and Kawabata 1996). As seen in the cocktail-party effect, humans have the ability to selectively attend to a sound from a particular source, even when it is mixed with other sounds. Current automatic speech recognition systems can understand *clean* speech well in relatively noiseless laboratory environments, but break down in more realistic, noisier environments.

Speech enhancement is essential to enable automatic speech recognition to work in such environments. Conventional approaches to speech enhancement are classified as noise reduction, speaker adaptation, and other robustness techniques (Minami and Furui 1995). Speech stream segregation is a novel approach to speech enhancement, and works as the front-end system for automatic speech recognition just as hearing aids for hearing impaired people.

Of course, speech stream segregation as a front-end for ASR is the first step toward more robust ASR. The

---

[†]Current address: NTT Multimedia Business Department, *nak@mbd.mbc.ntt.co.jp*
Copyright ©1998, American Association for Artificial Intelligence (www.aaai.org). All rights reserved.

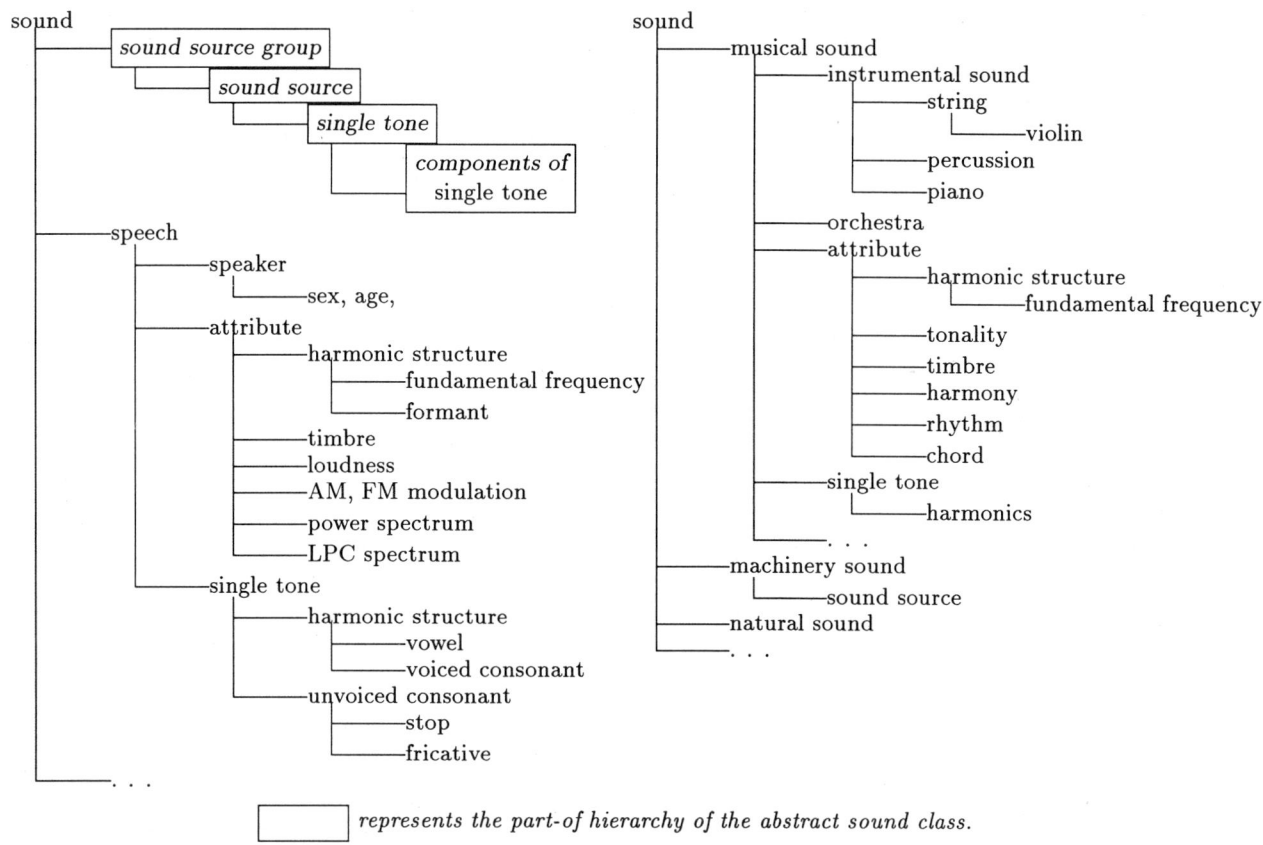

Figure 1: Example of sound ontology.

next step may be to integrate speech stream segregation and ASR by exploiting top-down and bottom-up processings.

Sound ontology is important in musical and speech stream segregation on the following aspects:

1. integrating sound stream segregation systems,
2. interfacing sound stream segregation systems with applications, and
3. integrating bottom-up and top-down processings in sound stream segregation.

For example, speech stream segregation system and musical stream segregation system are combined to develop a system that can recognize both speeches and music from a mixture of voiced announcements and background music. Although the both systems use a harmonic structure of sounds as a cue of segregation, harmonic structures extracted by one system can not be utilized by the other system because the definition of a harmonic structure and the precision of extracted harmonic structure differ. Therefore, sound ontology is needed to share the similar information by the both systems. In addition, sound ontology is expected to play an important role in making the system expandable and scalable.

The second example is one of AI challenges, that is, the problem of listening to three simultaneous speeches which is proposed as a challenging problem for AI and CASA (Okuno, Nakatani, and Kawabata 1997). This *CASA challenge* requires sound stream segregation systems to be interfaced with automatic speech recognition systems. In order to attain better performance of speech recognition, extracted speech streams should fulfill the requirements on the input of automatic speech recognition systems. Some automatic speech recognition systems use power spectrum as a cue of recognition, while others use LPC spectrum. Therefore, speech stream segregation systems should improve the property of extracted speech streams that is required by a particular automatic speech recognition system. If one sound stream segregation system is designed to be interfaced with these two kinds of automatic speech recognition systems, sound ontology may be used as a design model for such a system.

The third example is that speech stream segregation should incorporate two kinds of processings, primitive segregation of speech stream and schema-based segregation of speech streams. Primitive segregation may be considered as bottom-up processing by means of lower level properties of sound such harmonic structures, timbre, loudness, AM or FM modulation. Schema-based segregation may be considered as top-down processing by means of learned constraints. It includes a memory based segregation that uses a memory of specific speaker's voices, and a semantic based segregation that uses contents of speeches. The important issue is how to integrate the both processing and sound ontology may be used as a driving power of integration.

The rest of the paper is organized as follows. Section 2 presents a sound ontology and Section 3 discusses its usage with respect to the above-mentioned three issues. Section 4 presents the ontology-based integration of speech stream and musical stream segregation systems. Section 5 and 6 discuss related work and concluding remarks.

Sound Ontology

Sound ontology is composed of *sound classes*, *definitions of individual sound attributes*, and *their relationships*. It is defined hierarchically by using the following two attributes:

- **Part-of hierarchy** — a hierarchy based on the inclusion relation in sound

- **Is-a hierarchy** — a hierarchy based on the abstraction level in sound

Some part of sound ontology concerning speech and music is shown in Fig. 1. Other parts may be defined on demand of segregating corresponding sounds. In this paper, we focus on speech and musical stream segregation.

A box depicts a Part-of hierarchy of basic sound classes for speech and music, which is composed of four layers of sound classes. A *sound source* in the figure is a temporal sequence of sounds generated by a single sound source. A *sound source group* is a set of sound sources that share some common characteristics as music. A *single tone* is a sound that continues without any durations of silence, and it has some low-level attributes such as harmonic structure. In each layer, an upper class is composed of lower classes which are components that share some common characteristics. For example, a harmonic stream is composed of frequency components that have harmonic relationships.

The Is-a hierarchy can be constructed using any abstraction level. For example, voice, female voice, the voice of a particular woman, and the woman's nasal voice form an Is-a hierarchy. (Not specified in Fig. 1.)

With sound ontology, each class has some attributes, such as fundamental frequency, rhythm, and timbre. A lower class in the Is-a hierarchy inherits the attributes of its upper classes by default unless another special specification is given. In other words, an abstract sound class has attributes that are common to more concrete sound classes. In addition, an actually generated sound, such as uttered speech, is treated as an instance of a sound class. In this representation, segregating a sound stream means generating an instance of a sound class and extracting its attributes from an input sound mixture.

Proposed Usage of Sound Ontology
Ontology-Based Integration

Sound stream segregation should run incrementally, not in batch, because it is usually combined with applications and is not a stand-alone system. For incremental processing, we exploit not only sharing of information but also sharing of processing. Therefore, for integration of existing segregation systems they are first decomposed into processing modules by using the sound ontology as a common specification.

In this paper, we take an example of integrating speech and musical stream segregation. The rough procedure of modularization is as follows. First, existing segregation systems are divided into processing modules, each of which segregates a class of sound in sound ontology, such as, harmonic structure, voiced segment, and musical note. Then, these modules are combined to segregating streams according to their identified sound types.

Obviously, such an integration requires the procedure of interaction between different kinds of modules. To specify the relationships between sounds, a *relation class* is defined between two sound classes. It is represented by a pair of sound classes, such as "[speech, musical note]". A relation class has the same two hierarchical structures as sound classes defined as follows: if and only if both classes of a relation class are at a level higher than those of another relation class in the Is-a hierarchy (or in the Part-of hierarchy), the former is at a higher level. In the Is-a hierarchy, processing modules and interaction modules are inherited from a upper level to a lower level unless other modules are specified at some lower class.

Ontology-based sound stream segregation is executed by generating instances of sound classes and extracting their attributes. This process can be divided into four tasks:

1. find new sound streams in a sound mixture,
2. identify classes of individual sound streams,
3. extract attributes of streams according to their sound classes, and
4. extract interaction between streams according to their relation classes.

Since classes of sound streams are usually not given in advance, sound streams are treated initially as instances of abstract classes. These streams are refined to more concrete classes as more detailed attributes are extracted. At the same time, these streams are identified as components of stream groups at a higher level of the Part-of hierarchy, such as the musical stream. As a result, the attributes of these streams are extracted more precisely by using operations specific to concrete classes and by using attributes extracted for group streams.

Sound Ontology Based Interfacing

The CASA challenge requires speech stream segregation systems to interface with automatic speech recognition systems. First, speech stream segregation system that extracts each speech stream from a mixture of sounds. Then each extracted speech stream is recognized by a conventional automatic speech recognition system.

As such an approach, Binaural Harmonic Stream Segregation (Bi-HBSS) was used as a speech stream segregation (Okuno, Nakatani, and Kawabata 1996). By taking the structure of "Vowel (V) + Consonant (C) + Vowel (V)" of speech into consideration, a speech stream was extracted by the following three successive subprocesses:

1. Harmonic stream fragment extraction,
2. Harmonic grouping, and
3. Residue substitution.

The first two subprocesses reconstruct the harmonic parts of speech and calculates the residue by subtracting all extracted harmonic parts for the input. Since any major attributes for extracting non-harmonic parts have not been known yet, it is reasonable to substitute the residue for non-harmonic parts. Since Bi-HBSS takes binaural sounds (a pair of sounds recorded by a dummy head microphone) as inputs, it uses the direction of the sound source for segregation. They reported that the recognition performance with the Hidden Markov Model based automatic speech recognition system called HMM-LR (Kita, Kawabata, and Shikano 1990) is better when the residue of all directions is substituted than when the residue of the sound source direction (Okuno, Nakatani, and Kawabata 1996).

This interface is not, however, valid for another automatic speech recognition system. Our experiment with one of the popular commercial automatic speech recognition systems, HTK (Young et al. 1996), shows that the interface won't work well and that if the residue of the sound source direction is used by residue substitution the recognition performance is improved. That is, the reason why Bi-HBSS does not work well with HTM is that the cues of recognition used by HMM-LR and HTK differs. HMM-LR uses only power spectrum and ignores input signals of weak power, while HTK uses LPC spectrum and the power of input is automatically normalized. Therefore, weak harmonic structures included in the residue that are usually ignored by HMM-LR causes HTK's poor recognition performance.

Thus, speech stream segregation systems should generate an output appropriate to successive processing. Since the system architecture of sound stream segregation is constructed on the basis of sound ontology, adaptive output generation is also realized by the same architecture.

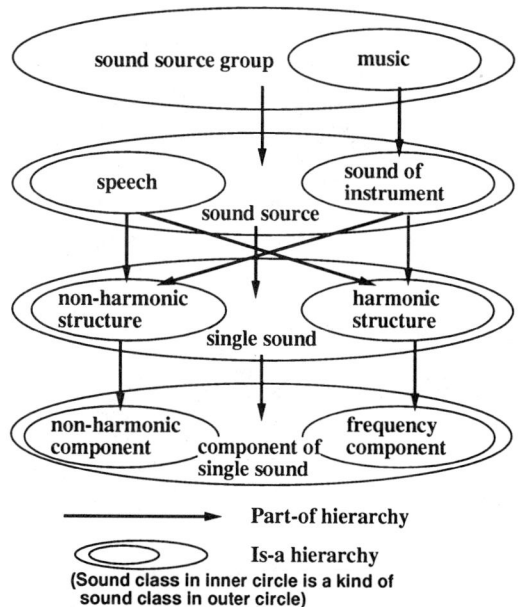

Figure 2: Hierarchical structure of sound ontology.

Integration of Bottom-up and Top-down Processing

The representation of single tone components also has analysis conditions under which the system extracts the attributes of individual components. This is because the quantitative meaning of sound attributes may differ by analysis means, such as FFT, auditory filter bank, LPC analysis, and by analysis parameters.

For example, interface agents use a common abstract terminology "harmonic structure" in exchanging information on voiced segments and on musical notes because voiced segments and musical notes both are a kind of harmonic structure based on sound ontology. Of course, voiced segments and musical notes do not entirely have the same attributes. In fact, the time patterns of voiced segments are much more complex than those of musical notes, so that some harmonic components appear and/or disappear according to their phoneme transitions, while the piano exhibits quite marked deviations from harmonicity during its attack period. Moreover, many frequency components of a musical note are often impossible to discriminate from those of other notes and thus are treated as a set of harmonic sounds, because they continuously overlap each other in a chord. These attributes should be handled somewhat differently in each system. Therefore, the specific sound classes of a harmonic structure (i.e., a voiced segment or a musical note) also have attributes specific to the classes.

Thus, sound ontology enables segregation systems to share information on extracted sound streams by providing common representation of sounds and correspondence between different analysis conditions.

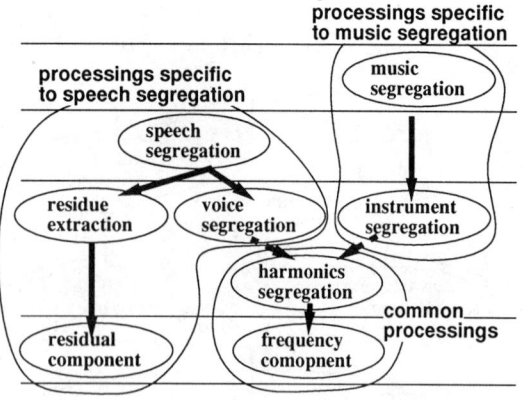

Figure 3: Common and specific processing modules for speech and musical stream segregation.

Ontology-Based Speech and Musical Stream Segregation

Sound segregation processing modules

Speech and musical stream segregation systems are integrated on the basis of sound ontology. As mentioned before, two systems, Bi-HBSS and OPTIMA (Kashino et al. 1995) are decomposed into primitive processing modules as follows:

- Processing modules for speech stream segregation:
  1. voice segregation,
  2. unvoiced consonants (residual signal after all harmonic sounds are subtracted from input signal) extraction,
  3. sequential grouping of voice, and
  4. unvoiced consonant interpolation.

- Processing modules for musical stream segregation:
  1. note extraction,
  2. identification of sound sources (instruments),
  3. rhythm extraction,
  4. code extraction, and
  5. knowledge sources that store musical information statistics.

The relationship between processing modules are shown in Fig. 3. Some are common, while others are specific to speech or musical stream segregation.

Three interfacing modules are designed to integrate the modules; discriminator of voice and musical notes, primitive fundamental frequency tracer, and mediator of single tone tracers.

Discriminator of voice and musical note

Many signal processing algorithms have been presented to distinguish sound classes, such as discriminant analysis and the subspace method (Kashino et al. 1995). For simplicity, we adopt a heuristics on the fundamental frequency pattern of a harmonic stream. A Harmonic sound is recognized as a musical note if the standard deviation of the fundamental frequency, denoted σ_{f_0}, for n millisecond from the beginning of the stream satisfies the following inequality:

$$\sigma_{f_0}/\bar{f}_0 < c,$$

where n and c are constants, and $\bar{f}_0$ is the average fundamental frequency. Otherwise, the sound is treated as a part of speech.

Primitive fundamental frequency tracer

A primitive fundamental frequency tracer is redesigned, although such a tracer is implicitly embedded in Bi-HBSS or Optima. The primitive fundamental frequency tracer extracts a harmonic structure at each time frame as follows:

1. the fundamental frequency at the next time frame is predicted by linearly extending its transition pattern, and
2. a harmonic structure whose fundamental frequency is in the region neighboring the predicted one in the next frame is tracked as the fundamental frequency.

Since musical notes have a specific fundamental frequency pattern, that is, musical scale, it can be used as a constraint on musical stream. If a sound being traced is identified as a musical stream, the primitive fundamental frequency tracer is replaced by musical fundamental frequency tracer. First, fundamental frequency is predicted by calculating its average fundamental frequency, and the search region for the fundamental frequency is restricted to a narrower region than the default. As a result of using stricter constraints, more precise and less ambiguous fundamental frequencies of musical notes can be extracted.

Mediator of single sound tracers

Two types of interaction modules between single sound tracers are designed in order to assign individual harmonic components to a musical or speech stream segregation system: one module in the relation class "[harmonic structure, harmonic structure]", and another in the relation class "[musical note, musical note]".

The interaction module in the relation class "[harmonic structure, harmonic structure]" defines default interaction, because "[harmonic structure, harmonic structure]" is the parent relation class of "[musical note, musical note]" and so on. This interaction module decompses overlapping frequency components into streams in the same way as Bi-HBSS (Nakatani, Okuno, and Kawabata 1995b).

The other module in the relation class "[musical note, musical note]" leaves overlapping frequency components shared between sinle sound tracers, because such decomposing is quite difficult (Kashino et al. 1995).

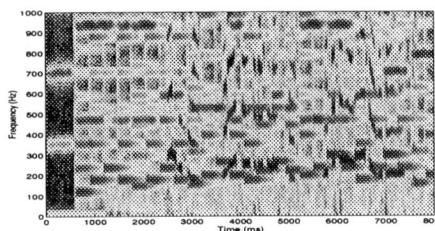

(a) Input mixture of music (Auld Lang Syne) and narration (female voice)

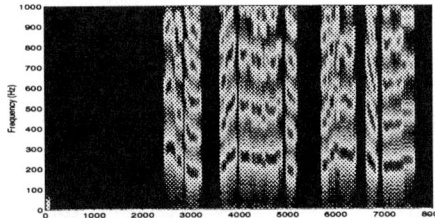

(b) Segregated harmonic stream corresponding to narration (female voice)

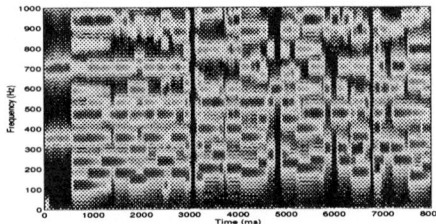

(c) Segregated harmonic stream corresponding to music (Auld Lang Syne)

Figure 4: Spectrograms of input mixture and segregated harmonic streams.

The other relation classes such as "[speech, speech]" are not explicitly specified, but inherit the interaction modules of the default relation class "[harmonic structure, harmonic structure]".

Results of speech and musical segregation

Evaluation is performed with a mixture of the musical piece "Auld Lang Syne" played on flute and piano (sound synthesized by a sampler) and a narration by a woman uttering a Japanese sentence. The spectrograms of the input and extracted two harmonic streams are shown in Fig. 4. Although the prototype system takes monaural sounds as input instead of binaural sounds, its performance of segregation is better in terms of pitch errors and spectral distortion than that of Bi-HBSS. Of course, when fundamental frequencies of voice and music cross each other, two sounds are not segregated well. This problem is unavoidable if harmonics is the only clue for segregation. As mentioned before, Bi-HBSS overcomes the problem by using directional information.

Some additional modules such as an unvoiced consonant interpolation module and rhythm and chord extraction modules are under development to improve the performance of segregation of all parts of voice and music.

Related work

Nawab *et al.* proposed "unified terminology" as universal representation of speech and sporadic environmental sounds, and developed a spoken digit recognition system using the IPUS architecture, a variant of blackboard architecture (Nawab *et al* 1995). The idea of combining processing modules based on unified terminology is quite similar to our ontology-based sound stream segregation. Since a module is implemented as a separate knowledge source, the processing is performed in batch and incremental processing is difficult. We think that HEARSAY-II like usage of blackboard architecture which each knowledge source has a limited capability would require a sound ontology

Minsky suggested a *musical CYC project*, a musical common sense database, to promote researches on understanding music (Minsky and Laske 1992). However, a collection of various musical common sense databases may be more easily to construt than a monolith huge database, and we expect that a music ontology will play an important role in combining musical common sense databases.

Conclusion

Sound ontology is presented as a new framework for integrating existing sound stream segregation systems, interfacing sound stream segregation systems with applications, and integration of top-down and bottom-up processings. That is, sound ontology specifies a common representation of sounds and a common specification of sound processing to combine individual sound stream segregation systems. We believe that sound ontology is a key to an expansible CASA system because it provides a systematic and comprehensive principle of integrating segregation technologies.

Future work includes design of more universal sound ontology, full-scale implementation of speech and musical segregation systems, and attacking of the CASA challenge. Last but not least, controling bottom-up processing with top-down processing along with a sound ontology is an important and exciting future work.

Acknowledgments

We thank Drs. Kunio Kashino, Takeshi Kawabata, Hiroshi Murase, and Ken'ichiro Ishii of NTT Basic Research Labs, Dr. Masataka Goto of Electro Technology Lab, and Dr. Hiroaki Kitano of Sony CSL for their valuable discussions.

References

Bregman, A.S. 1990. *Auditory Scene Analysis – the Perceptual Organization of Sound*. MIT Press.

Brown, G.J., and Cooke, M.P. 1992. A computational model of auditory scene analysis. In *Proceedings of Intern'l Conf. on Spoken Language Processing*, 523–526.

Cherry, E.C. 1953. Some experiments on the recognition of speech, with one and with two ears. *Journal of Acoustic Society of America* 25:975–979.

Cooke, M.P., Brown, G.J., Crawford, M., and Green, P. 1993. Computational Auditory Scene Analysis: listening to several things at once. *Endeavour*, 17(4):186–190.

Kashino, K., Nakadai, K., Kinoshita, T., and Tanaka, H. 1995. Organization of Hierarchical Perceptual Sounds: Music Scene Analysis with Autonomous Processing Modules and a Quantitative Information Integration Mechanism, In *Proceedings of 14th International Joint Conference on Artificial Intelligence (IJCAI-95)*, vol.1:173–178, IJCAI.

Kita, K., Kawabata, T., and Shikano, K. 1990. HMM continuous speech recognition using generalized LR parsing. *Transactions of Information Processing Society of Japan*, 31(3):472–480.

Lesser, V., Nawab, S.H., Gallastegi, I., and Klassner, F. 1993. IPUS: An Architecture for Integrated Signal Processing and Signal Interpretation in Complex Environments. In *Proceedings of Eleventh National Conference on Artificial Intelligence (AAAI-93)*, 249–255, AAAI.

Minami, Y., and Furui, S. 1995. A Maximum Likelihood Procedure for A Universal Adaptation Method based on HMM Composition. In *Proceedings of 1995 International Conference on Acoustics, Speech and Signal Processing*, vol.1:129–132, IEEE.

Minsky, M., and Laske, O. 1992. Forward: Conversation with Marvin Minsky, In Balaban, M., Ebcioğlu, K., and Laske, O. eds. *Understanding Music with AI: Perspectives on Music Cognition*, ix–xxx, AAAI Press/MIT Press.

Nakatani, T., Okuno, H.G., and Kawabata, T. 1994a. Auditory Stream Segregation in Auditory Scene Analysis with a Multi-Agent System. In *Proceedings of 12th National Conference on Artificial Intelligence (AAAI-94)*, 100–107, AAAI.

Nakatani, T., Okuno, H.G., and Kawabata, T. 1995b. Residue-driven architecture for Computational Auditory Scene Analysis. In *Proceedings of 14th International Joint Conference on Artificial Intelligence (IJCAI-95)*, vol.1:165–172, IJCAI.

Nawab, S.H., Espy-Wilson, C.Y., Mani, R., and Bitar, N.N. 1995. Knowledge-Based analysis of speech mixed with sporadic environmental sounds. In Rosenthal and Okuno, eds. *Working Notes of IJCAI-95 Workshop on Computational Auditory Scene Analysis*, 76–83.

Okuno, H.G., Nakatani, T., and Kawabata, T. 1996. Interfacing Sound Stream Segregation to Speech Recognition Systems — Preliminary Results of Listening to Several Things at the Same Time. In *Proceedings of 13th National Conference on Artificial Intelligence (AAAI-96)*, 1082–1089.

Okuno, H.G., Nakatani, T., and Kawabata, T. 1997. Understanding Three Simultaneous Speakers. In *Proceedings of 15th International Joint Conference on Artificial Intelligence (IJCAI-97)*, Vol.1:30–35.

Ramalingam, C.S., and Kumaresan, R. 1994. Voiced-speech analysis based on the residual interfering signal canceler (RISC) algorithm. In *Proceedings of 1994 International Conference on Acoustics, Speech, and Signal Processing*, 473–476, IEEE.

Rosenthal, D., and Okuno, H.G. eds. 1998. *Computational Auditory Scene Analysis*, NJ.:Lawrence Erlbaum Associates, (*in print*).

Young, S., Jansen, J., Odell, J., Ollanson, D., and Woodland, P. 1996. *the HTK Book for HTK V2.0*. Entropic Combridge Reseach Lab. Inc.

Innovative Applications of Artificial Intelligence Papers

Deployed Applications

Multi Machine Scheduling: An Agent-based Approach

Rama Akkiraju
Sesh Murthy

Pinar Keskinocak
Frederick Wu

IBM T.J. Watson Research Center
Route 134 and Taconic
Yorktown Heights, NY 10598
{ *akkiraju|pinar|murthy|fwu*}@watson.ibm.com

Abstract

Scheduling of multiple parallel machines in the face of sequence dependent setups and downstream considerations is a hard problem. No single efficient algorithm is guaranteed to produce optimal results. We describe a solution for an instance of this problem, in the domain of paper manufacturing. The problem has additional job machine restrictions and fixed costs of assigning jobs to machines. We consider multiple objectives such as minimizing (weighted) tardiness, minimizing job-machine assignment costs. We solve the problem using a simple agent architecture called the Asynchronous team (A-team), in which agents cooperate by exchanging results. We have built agents each of which encapsulates a different problem solving strategy for solving the multi-machine scheduling problem. The A-team framework enables the agents to cooperate to produce better results than those of any individual agent. In this paper we define the problem, describe the individual agents, and show with experimental results that the A-team produces very good results compared to schedulers alone.

Introduction

Effective production scheduling is at the heart of an efficient manufacturing process, and can result in improved on-time delivery of products, reduced inventory costs, increased productivity, and fewer setups. However, scheduling is a very complex task due to the need to optimize multiple competing objectives such as customer satisfaction, production efficiency, and profitability. In this paper, we present an effective way of addressing the multi-machine scheduling problem for non-identical, parallel machines subject to sequence dependent setups, job-machine restrictions, batch size preferences, and downstream scheduling consequences, considering multiple objectives simultaneously. To the best of our knowledge, this problem (especially with multiple objectives) has not been considered earlier. We developed a novel application of an agent-based architecture, called *A-Teams*, to solve this complex multi-criteria optimization problem.

We consider a set of jobs that must be run and there is a set of machines available to execute the jobs. Jobs may be classified into groups of similar job types. Each machine can run only one job type at a time, and each machine may have some unique characteristics, such as production rate. Each job has a due date, on which production should have been completed, and certain jobs may be restricted to a subset of the available machines. When a machine changes from one job type to another, there may be some setup time which depends on the similarity of the job types. To avoid frequent setups, schedulers[1] form batches of jobs of the same type to be run on a machine in sequence. Machine characteristics may also dictate batch size preferences if, for example, very small batches result in higher defect rates. When the machines are not located in the same facility, the cost of transporting the product to its destination is machine-dependent, which implies a job-machine assignment cost. In many applications, there are downstream consequences of scheduling that strongly influence the goodness of a schedule. In such complex scheduling problems, performance measures to be minimized include: tardiness, setup cost and time, inventory cost, job-machine assignment cost, batch size violations, and downstream bottlenecks or inefficiencies.

Armed with an understanding of the realities of manufacturing scheduling, one can see that a solution that deals only with a subset of the objectives and constraints is of limited usefulness. On the other hand, a monolithic solution that considers all the aspects of scheduling for a given domain would be impractical and unwieldy. What is needed is a modular architecture in which each component can be concerned with a subset of the objectives and constraints, and a framework that allows the components to work together to solve the entire problem. In our work, we use an agent architecture called Asynchronous Teams (A-Teams) to address this multi-criteria optimization problem of multi-machine scheduling. A-Teams is a simple framework wherein multiple problem solving methods

---

[1] In this paper, we use the term 'scheduler' to refer to the human scheduler.

(agents) cooperate with each other by exchanging results. In the next section, we briefly discuss this agent architecture and our solution approach in detail.

Several related problems have been extensively studied in the literature (Pinedo 1995). Scheduling jobs on a single machine to minimize (weighted) tardiness is studied in (Abdul-Razaq et. al. 1990), (Koulamas 1994), (Panwalkar and Iskander 1977), (Panwalkar, Smith and Koulmas 1993), (Potts and Van Vassenhove 1991), (Russell and Holsenback 1997). The extension to multiple machines is considered in (Arkin and Roundy 1989), (Barnes and Brennan 1977), (Ho and Chang 1991). Scheduling subject to sequence dependent setup times is considered in (Lee, Bhaskaran and Pinedo 1997) for single machine; in (Lee and Pinedo 1997) and (Clements et.al. 1997) for parallel identical machines. Du and Leung (1990) proved that minimizing the total tardiness on one machine is NP-hard. Further complexity results on machine scheduling problems can be found in (Lenstra and Rinnoy Kan 1997). Most of these papers consider only one scheduling objective, e.g. minimizing total tardiness. To the best of our knowledge, there are no models that address the complex problem of job scheduling on parallel non-identical machines with sequence dependent setup times and job-machine restrictions, considering multiple objectives (such as the total weighted tardiness and job-machine assignment cost). In many manufacturing environments these types of restrictions and different objectives are important and are part of the scheduling problem the planners and schedulers face every day.

Recently it has been shown that agent-based architectures hold promise for solving complex multi-objective optimization problems. Liu and Sycara (1996) have shown the benefits of a tightly-coupled agent architecture in solving the job shop scheduling problem. Beck and Fox (1994) presented a mediated approach to multi-agent coordination in the context of a supply chain management system. A model of the supply chain in which each of the key players in the chain is encapsulated in an autonomous agent is described in (Swaminathan, Smith and Sadeh 1996). A blackboard-style architecture is used in Smith et.al. (1990) for generating and revising factory schedules, wherein a set of distinct methods are selectively employed to generate, revise or analyze specific components of the overall schedule.

As an example of the problem studied in this paper, we consider the enterprise wide scheduling problem in paper manufacturing, which was one of the prime motivations for this study. A typical large paper manufacturing enterprise has a number of paper mills in various locations and one or more paper machines in each mill. Each paper machine is capable of producing some subset of the company's products (job-machine restrictions) at different production rates. Paper production is a continuous process in which a machine can make only one type, or "grade" of paper at a time (Bierman 1993). When the grade being made on a machine is changed, the machine continues to operate, but the paper it produces is of poor quality for some time after the change is initiated. The length of this "transition time" depends on the composition of the grades before and after the transition; transitions between similar grades are shorter than transitions between very different grades (sequence-dependent setup times). The transition times between grades can also be machine dependent. Often there is a manufacturing policy that bounds the length of a production batch, or "run." A lower bound on run length is typically set because very short runs are likely to produce paper with quality problems.

Each customer of the paper company orders a number of rolls of a grade of paper of specified dimensions to be delivered on the due date to a specified location. The paper manufacturer is responsible for the freight cost from its mill to the customer's location, which can constitute as much as 15% of its total costs. Minimizing tardiness and transportation costs (job-machine assignment cost) are important objectives in scheduling paper production.

Scheduling of production on paper machines has major downstream implications that must be taken into account. One of the key downstream processes is known as "trimming." The output of a paper machine is large rolls of paper of fixed width (on modern machines this may be as large as 10 meters). Trimming is the process of cutting the large rolls into smaller rolls having widths ordered by the customers. A production run usually consists of many orders for different widths. Since it is important to utilize the full width of the reel efficiently, this is an example of the cutting stock problem. The best achievable trim efficiency is strongly dependent on the mix of order widths and quantities in the production run. Maximizing trim efficiency is an important scheduling objective that is determined by a downstream process.

Solution Approach

A-Team Agent Architecture

An Asynchronous Team or A-Team (Talukdar, Souza, Murthy 1993), (Murthy 1992) is an agent based architecture that is well suited for multi-objective optimization problems (Souza 1993). In this architecture, multiple problem solving methods (agents) cooperate with each other in evolving a population of solutions towards what is called a Pareto-optimal frontier. The outcome is the non-dominated set of solutions from the population.

Agents communicate through a population of candidate solutions. There are three types of agents which create and modify this population. They are:

1. *Constructors* that create initial solutions.
2. *Improvers* that take existing solutions, and modify them to produce a new solution. Some of the solutions they create may not be better than existing solutions, but are valuable because they serve to explore the solution space and may discover a path to a good solution.
3. *Destroyers* that keep the size of the population of solutions in check by deleting bad or redundant schedules.

Figure 1 shows the essential features of the A-Team architecture. The A-Team architecture does not define the content of the agents, but only their possible roles. This gives us complete freedom to use a broad range of algorithms encapsulated as agents. Each agent is independent and can make its own decisions of *when* to work, *how* often to work, and *what* to work on.

In an A-Team, agents can cooperate since one agent can work on the output of another. In general, agents may take as input any number of existing solutions and produce as output any number of solutions. For example, in the job allocation and sequencing problem, a solution may consist of a set of machine schedules, each schedule containing a particular sequence of jobs. Imagine two agents A and B. Agent A moves a job from one machine to another in order to balance the load on the machines but might have delayed the production of the job, while agent B moves a job ahead of the time on to another machine to reduce it tardiness. It is thus possible to achieve cooperation between agents in a way that reveals potential tradeoffs between cost and on-time delivery.

In order for an A-Team to achieve a balanced population of solutions that approach the Pareto-optimal frontier, it is important that the agents be well balanced as a collection. No single agent need have the ability to optimize or even improve a solution with regard to *all* the objectives. However, the collection should have at least one agent which can address each of the objectives. This provides assurance that any damage done to a solution by an agent with regard to one objective can be repaired or more than overcome by another, possibly on the path toward a solution that is improved in all respects.

In addition to enhanced optimization performance, A-Teams also provide an intrinsically modular, scalable and fault-tolerant computing environment. If a new algorithm is discovered for solving a particular problem, its capability can be readily assimilated without requiring fundamental changes to the underlying software.

Decision Support Using A-Teams

In any complex scheduling problem, there may be considerations and constraints that are not known to the scheduling system. The system may not know of them because they are highly dynamic, or because they exist only in the minds of the schedulers. For example, a customer may have expressed some willingness to take part of an order late as long as one truckload is ready on time. Because such contingencies arise very often, a scheduling system should be designed to allow the schedulers to interact with the system and to modify schedules easily. If the system meets these criteria, then it is truly a decision-support system, and not a decision-making system.

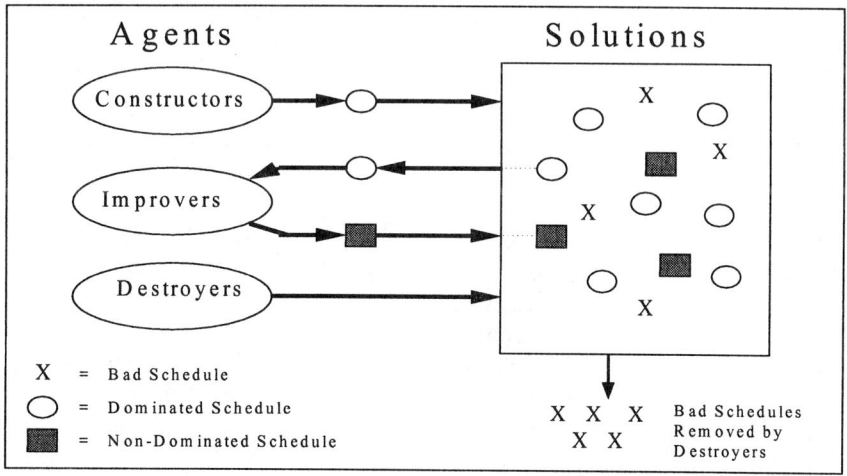

Figure 1. The Essential Features of the A-Team architecture employed by our scheduling system

The A-Team architecture is a natural choice for a decision support system, because it creates multiple solutions that approach optimality. An A-Team based scheduling system displays the non-dominated set of solutions to the scheduler, who can select any of the solutions and modify it if necessary. The scheduler can also insert a modified solution back into the A-Team population, allowing the agents to try to improve it further. In this way the scheduler takes on the role of another agent (possibly with greater or more current knowledge) and cooperates with the other agents in the A-Team. After acceptable solutions have been obtained, the scheduler makes the final decision from among the alternatives (Murthy et al. 1997).

Overview of Algorithms

In this section we briefly describe some of the algorithms that we have used in our scheduling system. Our algorithms are mainly of 2 kinds. Construction heuristics and Improvement heuristics.

Construction Heuristics: There are mainly two types of construction agents, namely: 1) Allocation of jobs to machines and initial sequencing, 2) Sequencing of jobs on a given machine.

The goal of the allocation algorithms is to optimize the allocation of jobs to machines based on transportation cost considerations (machines could be distributed geographically), due dates of the orders, and balance of the load on the machines. The algorithm framework we use for job-machine allocation and initial sequencing is called Allocate_and_Sequence. The idea is to sort all the jobs according to some criteria, such as due date and processing time, and then allocate the next job in the list to a machine based on the INDEX of the job-machine pair.

Allocate_and_Sequence:
Step 1: Sort the jobs according to specified sort criteria.
Step 2: Pick the next job in the list. Compute the job-machine INDEX for this job and for all the machines, which can process this job. Assign the job to the machine with the lowest job-machine INDEX.

Sort criteria can be based on any combination of job properties, such as due date, processing time tardiness penalty and so on. For example we may sort the orders in increasing order of their due dates (due date is the primary sort criterion), and then we may sort the orders with the same due date based on their grades (grade is the secondary sort criterion). In our implementation, we use several such combinations for the initial sorting of the orders.

Let i be the last job processed on machine k. The INDEX for job j and machine k is computed by considering several combinations of job and machine properties (assuming job j will be processed immediately after job i on machine k). Here are some examples of the INDEX we used in our implementation:
1. Processing time of job j on machine k, and the transition time from job i to job j.
2. Completion time of job j.
3. The (weighted) tardiness of job j.
4. The absolute difference between the due date of job j and its completion time on machine k.
5. A measure of downstream implications of this allocation. For instance, in paper mill scheduling, orders with certain width specifications can be trimmed very well on machines with certain physical characteristics.
6. The transportation cost.
7. The weighted combination of any of the items above.

These allocation heuristics do not violate the job-machine assignment constraints.

At the sequencing stage, the goal is to sequence the jobs based on their due dates and group the ones of the same kind (in the case of paper mill scheduling, this is analogous to orders of the same grade) into
batches to minimize setups. The algorithm framework we use for sequencing jobs on a given machine is called Single_Dispatch. Once a job-machine allocation is given, we use this framework to obtain an alternative sequence for the jobs on any given machine. The idea is to select one job at a time from the set of remaining jobs, and schedule it as the next job on that machine. Suppose that we are given machine k and the set of jobs allocated to it.

Single_Dispatch:
Step 0: Let the set of unscheduled jobs be U_k, initially equal to the set of jobs allocated to machine k.
Step 1: For each job in U_k, compute the INDEX of scheduling this job as the next job on machine k. *Step 2*: Schedule the job with the smallest INDEX as the next job and remove from U_k. If U_k is not empty, repeat *Step 1*.

INDEX for a job j in U_k is computed by considering several combinations of job properties. Some of the INDEX computations use the *slack* concept. The slack of a job is defined as the difference between the due date of the job and the earliest possible completion time of the job (based on the jobs scheduled so far). Again, let i be the last job scheduled so far on machine k. Consider scheduling job j immediately after job i. Here are some examples of the INDEX we used in our implementation within the Single_Dispatch framework: processing time of job j on machine k and the transition time from job i to job j;

completion time of job j; tardiness of job j; the absolute difference between the due date of job j and its completion time on machine k; slack of job j; the weighted combination of any of these items with the transition time.

Improvement Heuristics: Improvement agents take the existing schedules from the population and improve them in several different dimensions. For example they move
- a single job in order to improve tardiness,
- batches in order to decrease the number of small batches (if we move a batch next to a batch of the same type, i.e. if no setup is required in between, those two batches can be combined into a single larger batch),
- a subset of jobs in a batch to improve the solution of a downstream problem (e.g. moving a set of jobs to a different run to improve trim efficiency),
- jobs/batches to improve transportation cost or machine load balance,
- jobs/batches to improve any combination of the measures above.

The jobs can be moved to a new position on the same machine, or on a different machine. The goal of any exchange may be to improve a single objective only, such as tardiness, or a combination of objectives such as minimizing transportation cost and load balancing on the machines. Each agent selectively picks a solution to work on based on certain criteria. For instance, a tardiness improvement agent picks a schedule from the population that needs improvement in tardiness. A load balancing agent picks a schedule whose load is unevenly balanced and attempts to fix it and so on.

Since multiple agents work on each others' results, these agents together attain results that may not be achieved by any single agent on its own. These iterative refinements to the set of schedules in the population drive them towards the optimal frontier in the search space.

Experimental Results

We have applied our model to a real-world scheduling problem in paper industry, with multiple mills and machines. The problem consists of more than 5000 orders (jobs) to be scheduled on the 9 machines which are part of 4 different mills. The given set of orders constitute about 8 weeks of production. Each order is for one of the 15 grades of paper that the company produces. Each of these machines has a different production capacity and can only produce certain grades of paper. The geographical location of a particular machine plays a significant role in allocating a job to a machine as it has significant impact on the transportation cost of the schedule. There is a setup time to switch from one grade of paper to another on each paper machine and smooth cycles of grades is desired to reduce the setup times. The goal is to allocate the orders to the machines and sequence them for production such that:
1) The overall transportation cost is minimized.
2) The tardiness and earliness of the orders is minimized.
3) The total setup time is minimized.
4) The number of batches (grade runs) that violate the minimum batch size requirements is minimized.
5) The composition of the orders within each batch does not negatively affect the downstream processes. (Each grade run should be able to trim well with minimum possible waste of paper.)
6) The load is evenly balanced on all the machines.

In this implementation, the measures we used for evaluating the solutions are the following: tardiness and earliness (in ton-days), number of orders late and early, transportation cost (in dollars), number of run size violations (runs longer or shorter than the desired bounds) and the trim efficiency (paper lost due to trimming as a percentage of total production). (It is to be noted that these evaluation metrics are customer dependent and can change from one customer to another. We obtain this information during the design study and incorporate them into the system during the benchmarking process.) These measures are presented in the first 6 columns of Table 1 for each of the 10 non-dominated solutions generated by the system.

We used the A-Team framework to enable the cooperation among various problem solving methods to address this multi-machine scheduling problem. Our A-Team consisted of 15 constructors and 5 improvers. Each agent (constructor or an improver) is an embodiment of the algorithms described in the earlier sections (run with various parameter settings). For an A-Team invocation of 1 1/2 hours of CPU time on a single processor IBM RS/6000 Model 43P (64M of memory), the scheduling system generated 10 non-dominated solutions. (The termination criterion is set by the user by specifying the amount of time to run the A-Team.) As the A-Team approach aims toward monotonic improvement of the solutions, the longer we run the system, the better the results would be. However, within the system we provide several configuration settings for the users to choose to from. Table 1, given below, is a summary of the solutions.

Schedule	Tardiness (ton-days)	Earliness (ton-days)	# of Orders Late	# of Orders Early	Transp. Cost ($)	# of Run Size Violations	Trim Efficiency %	Total Production Tons	Trim Loss Tons
01	464,516	216,810	621	537	$6,503,788	11	97.682	239,892	5,693
02	464,131	159,592	644	436	$6,503,890	9	97.751	240,002	5,522
03	659,086	1,231,163	882	1863	$6,500,465	2	98.523	240,094	3,600
04	460,285	223,339	616	571	$6,500,465	13	97.682	239,911	5,693
05	465,734	903,938	793	1487	$6,507,095	5	98.26	243,433	4,310
06	674,495	1,079,403	909	1737	$6,505,312	2	98.511	239,975	3,628
07	465,780	200,199	587	548	$6,505,511	10	97.741	243,260	5,623
08	649,871	1,162,401	851	1859	$6,505,511	2	98.535	243,220	3,617
09	656,482	1,094,900	856	1770	$6,510,074	2	98.556	243,277	3,565
10	560,422	251,897	717	650	$6,511,978	9	98.862	243,204	2,801
100	613,015	176,012	Not given	Not given	$6,565,750	Not given	98.84	243,405	2,967

Table 1. A summary of the experimental results obtained by the application of A-Teams to an instance of multi-machine scheduling problem in paper domain.

Analysis of Results

Table 1 shows the evaluation of each solution according to the above mentioned set of objectives. For comparison, we also show the evaluation of the actual schedule used by our client paper company (solution # 100). The client's schedule was created manually, based on the experience and intelligence of the scheduling team. The schedulers have numerous rules of thumb and guidelines which they apply to all aspects of scheduling, from allocation of orders to mills and machines through run formation and sequencing. However, the process of scheduling by hand is so time consuming that it is not practical for the schedulers to explore a large number of alternate ways to schedule the orders; consequently they may not be considering some significantly better scheduling decisions.

As can be seen from the table, the solutions created by the scheduling system reveal tradeoffs among the multiple objectives such as transportation cost vs. order tardiness and trim efficiency vs. order tardiness. For example, solutions 03 and 04 have the same transportation cost, which suggests that they have almost the same allocation of orders to the mills. However, they differ significantly in their tardiness and trim efficiencies. Solution 03 sacrificed order tardiness for better trim while solution 04 sacrificed trim for better on-time order delivery. Comparison of a solution, such as solution 10, with the client's actual schedule showed that the scheduling system could provide significant reductions in costs (e.g. 6% savings in annual transportation costs) and improvements in customer satisfaction (reduced tardiness). Since our scheduling system is designed as *a decision support* system, the schedulers can modify the solutions provided by the system and improve them further by using their domain expertise.

Conclusions

In this paper we described an effective solution approach for scheduling jobs on multiple non-identical machines subject to sequence-dependent setups and job-machine restrictions with multiple objectives. The problem is of interest both to the academic community (it generalizes the problems studied earlier) and to scheduling practitioners (it captures additional constraints and objectives that exist in manufacturing environments). To the best of our knowledge, this is the first attempt to solve this general problem.

We used the A-Team solution architecture, encapsulating multiple solution strategies as agents that cooperate with each other and the schedulers. Experimental results on a large sample of data from a paper manufacturer demonstrate the excellent performance of our approach.

References

Abdul-Razaq T. S., Potts C. N., and Van Wassenhove L. N., 1990. A Survey of Algorithms for the Single Machine Total Weighted Tardiness Scheduling Problem. *Discrete Applied Mathematics*, 26, 235-253.

Arkin E.M., Roundy R.O. 1989. Weighted-tardiness Scheduling on Parallel Machines with Proportional Weights. *Operations Research*, 39, 64-81.

Barnes J.W., Brennan J.J. 1977. An Improved Algorithm for Scheduling Jobs on Identical Machines. *AIIE Transactions*, 9, 23-31.

Beck J. C. and Fox M. S. 1994. Supply Chain Coordination via Mediated Constraint Relaxation. Proceedings of the First Canadian Workshop on Distributed Artificial Intelligence, Banff, AB, May 15, 1994.

Biermann C. 1993. *Essentials of Pulping and Papermaking*, San Diego Academic Press.

Clements D.P., Crawford J.M., Joslin D.E., Nemhauser G.L., Puttlitz M.E., Savelsbergh M.W.P. 1997. Heuristic Optimization: A hybrid AI/OR approach. Workshop on Industrial Constraint-Directed Scheduling.

Du J., and Leung J. Y. 1990. Minimizing Total Tardiness on One Machine is NP-hard. *Mathematics of Operations Research*, 15, 483-494.

Ho J.C., Chang Y. 1991. Heuristics for Minimizing Mean Tardiness for *m* Parallel Machines. *Naval Research Logistics*, 38, 367-381.

Koulamas C. 1994. The Total Tardiness problem: Review and Extensions. *Operations Research*, 42, 1025-1041.

Lee Y. H., Bhaskaran K., and Pinedo M. 1997. A Heuristic to Minimize the Total Weighted Tardiness With Sequence Dependent Setups. *IIE Transactions*, 29, 45-52.

Lee Y.H., Bhaskaran K., Pinedo M. 1997. A Heuristic to Minimize the Total Weighted Tardiness with Sequence-dependent Setups. *IIE Transactions*, 29, 45-52.

Lee Y. H., and Pinedo M. 1997. Scheduling Jobs on Parallel Machines With Sequence Dependent Setup Times. *European Journal of Operational Research*, 100, 464-474.

Lenstra J. K., Rinnoy Kan, A. H. G, and Brucker P. 1977. Complexity of Machine Scheduling Problems. *Annals of Discrete Mathematics*, 1, 343-362.

Liu J.-S. and Sycara K. P. 1996. Multiagent Coordination in Tightly Coupled Task Scheduling. Second International Conference on Multiagent Systems (ICMAS '96), Kyoto, Japan, December 1996.

Murthy S. 1992. Synergy in Cooperating Agents: Designing Manipulators from Task Specifications, Ph. D. Dissertation, Dept. of Computer Science, Carnegie Mellon University.

Murthy S., Rachlin J., Akkiraju R., and Wu F. 1997. Agent-based Cooperative Scheduling. Submitted to the Fifteenth National Conference on Artificial Intelligence (AAAI-98), Madison WI, July 1998.

Panwalkar S. S., Iskander Wafik 1977. A Survey of Scheduling Rules. *Operations Research*, Vol25, No1, 45-62.

Panwalkar S. S., Smith M. L., and Koulamas C. P., 1993. A Heuristic for the Single Machine Tardiness Problem. *European Journal of Operational Research*, 70, 304-310.

Pinedo M. 1995. Scheduling : Theory, Algorithms and Systems, Prentice Hall

Potts C.N., Van Wassenhove L.N. 1991. Single Machine Tardiness Sequencing Heuristics. *IIE Transactions*, 23, 346-354.

Russell R.M., Holsenback J.E. 1997. Evaluation of Leading Heuristics for the Single Machine Tardiness Problem. *European Journal of Operational Research*, 96, 538-545.

Smith F.S., Ow P.S., Potwin J., Muscettola N., Matthys D.C. 1990. An Integrated Framework for Generating and Revising Factory Schedules. *Journal of the Operational Research Society*, 41, 539-552.

Souza P de. 1993. Asynchronous Organizations for Multi-Algorithm Problems, Ph. D. Dissertation, Dept. of Computer Science, Carnegie Mellon University.

Swaminathan J. M., Smith S. F. and Sadeh N. M. 1996. A Multi-Agent Framework for Modeling Supply Chain Dynamics. Proceedings NSF Research Planning Workshop on Artificial Intelligence and Manufacturing, Albuqerque, NM, June 1996.

Talukdar S. N., Souza P.de, and Murthy S. 1993. Organization for Computer-Based Agents, *Engineering Intelligent Systems*, 1:2

Producing BT's Yellow Pages with Formation

Gail Anderson, Andrew Casson-du Mont, Ann Macintosh and Robert Rae
AIAI, University of Edinburgh
80 South Bridge
Edinburgh EH1 1HN, Scotland UK
email:aiai@aiai.ed.ac.uk
tel: +44 31 650 2732 fax: +44 31 650 6513

Barry Gleeson
Pindar Set Ltd.
Newlands Park Drive
Scarborough, North Yorkshire YO12 6DT
email:barry@pindar.com
tel: +44 1723 500455 fax: +44 1723 367852

Abstract

This case study illustrates how the adoption of AI technology can benefit smaller companies as well as major corporations.

Pindar Set is a small UK company which has originated the Yellow Pages directories for British Telecommunications plc since 1979. AIAI is a technology transfer organisation which has delivered innovative solutions to industrial clients since 1984. Together, AIAI and Pindar have developed a next-generation layout system, **Formation**.

Formation is fast, easy to use and flexible, and had already delivered benefits through marketing trials before being successfully deployed in production of the Yellow Pages in December 1997.

The heart of **Formation** is a 2D layout engine which formats input data according to styles written in LSSL, a domain-specific language developed at AIAI.

Through representing the layout knowledge in **Formation** explicitly in LSSL styles, and ensuring that it can easily be modified, Pindar has enabled itself to respond far better to its customer's present and future needs.

Background

Pindar's print works in Scarborough, NE England, were founded in 1836. In the 1960s, Pindar introduced photo typesetting to widen its market, and in the 1970s it became an early investor in computer technology. Pindar won the contract to originate the British Telecommunications Yellow Pages (BTYP) directories

in 1979. Although a small company employing only 200 people, Pindar Set, the company within the Pindar group of companies which services BTYP, has invested in new technology which can provide faster, better services for its client.

AIAI at Edinburgh University was established in 1984 to promote the application of AI techniques. Since then, it has delivered solutions to many industrial and commercial clients. With its record of producing innovative solutions for industry – and, importantly, carrying out technology transfer to ensure that they work – AIAI was a natural choice to partner Pindar in producing a next-generation layout solution for BTYP, **Formation**.

Task Description

BTYP publishes 74 different regionally-based classified directories annually. Print runs vary from about 25,000 copies for the Isle of Man to over half a million for Glasgow South. A typical 1,500 page directory may contain 30,000 businesses under 3,000 classification headings, and 5,000 display advertisements. Pindar has used computers to lay out BTYP from the beginning, and today's tight timescales and large directory sizes make computer-based layout essential. However, Pindar had found the layout programs difficult to maintain in the face of changing requirements.

By the beginning of the 1990's, advertisers were becoming more demanding, and BTYP wanted to introduce new features which required extensive market testing. Pindar needed to be able to respond to changes such as the introduction of new advertisement

Copyright © 1998, American Association for Artificial Intelligence (www.aaai.org). All rights reserved.

types, and be able to try out different layout scenarios quickly and reliably.

Pindar's increasing presence in worldwide classified telephone directory (CTD) production, and Pindar's future requirement to be able to use the new system to lay out other types of publication (such as newspapers or catalogues) meant that the system had to be flexible and configurable enough to produce publications with many different layout requirements. Layout requirements for CTDs are usually expressed in terms of page appearance, usability, and aesthetics. Increasingly, publishers also need to able to provide more specialised and customised services for their advertisers, who may want their entries to appear in particular positions on the page, and so on.

Pindar needed a knowledge-based system which allowed publishers to specify their requirements both naturally and precisely. The layout knowledge used by the system needed to be explicit rather than implicit, so that it could easily be modified. For commercial reasons, it was important that the system could run on standard PC hardware. Although knowledge-based layout systems did exist (Camara, Martins, & Jácome 1990; Chew & Liang 1994; Graf 1995), none of them met all Pindar's requirements for flexibility, speed, predictability, maintainability and price, so work began on **Formation** in 1994. Formation went into full production use at Pindar in December 1997; the first directory produced by the new system was for the Shrewsbury area – the same directory first produced by Pindar in 1980.

Application Description

Each BTYP directory covers a single geographical area. Sales representatives visit businesses throughout the area selling display advertising, and telephone sales representatives sell smaller, cheaper advertisements. Most display advertisements are produced by Pindar's and BTYP's graphics studios: once each has been approved by the advertiser, it is sent to Pindar's production site in Scarborough.

When the directory is "closed" (that is, when no more orders will be accepted from advertisers), BTYP produces compiled data containing classification headings, display and semi-display advertisements, and listings. This data is presented in sequence, with advertisers appearing alphabetically within their class. The task of the layout system is to place all the entries within the directory in as close a sequence as possible to the original alphabetical sequence, while minimising the number of pages used and hence the amount of "filler" material generated. Maintaining a good visual balance is also increasingly important.

Formation lays out input data according to particular layout styles, and a BTYP style has been implemented. This specifies things like where particular types of item can be placed on the page, and what changes to the input sequence are allowed. Layout styles are implemented in the Layout Style Specification Language (LSSL), an object-oriented domain-specific language designed by AIAI. It is intended to enable the LSSL programmer to describe the layout process in a natural manner, while remaining precise.

Once layout is complete, Pindar carries out post-processing of the data, and combines the layout produced using **Formation** with the graphics produced by the studio to produce film ready for printing.

Formation Overview

The diagram in figure 1 shows how the **Formation** system can be delivered to a particular publisher. At its core is the general 2D layout engine, the LSSL interpreter. In addition to this, there is a library of generic style elements, implemented in LSSL.

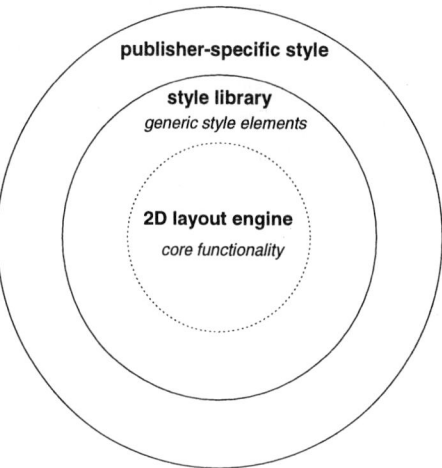

Figure 1: Formation design

At present, the style library contains elements which deal with layout in general and elements which are useful specifically for layout of classified telephone directories. As our experience with using **Formation** to lay out different documents grows, we are adding to the style library.

Using these generic elements and LSSL primitives, a style is implemented to specify the publisher's in-house requirements. Usually, the style will provide parameters through which the user can control the finished layout. For example, one of the parameters in the BTYP style specifies how groups of line entries can be split, and the CTD style described in an earlier paper (Anderson et al. 1996), which was produced for use in production of certain US telephone directories, has a parameter which specifies whether or not a display advertisement has to appear amongst the line entries of its own classification.

The publisher can use the **Formation** graphical user interface to configure the house style, setting the parameters to specify exactly how each publication should be laid out, with no programming required.

Once the publisher is happy, the same interface can be used in production to control and monitor layout. Figure 2 shows the **Formation** user interface laying out some pages from a BTYP directory.

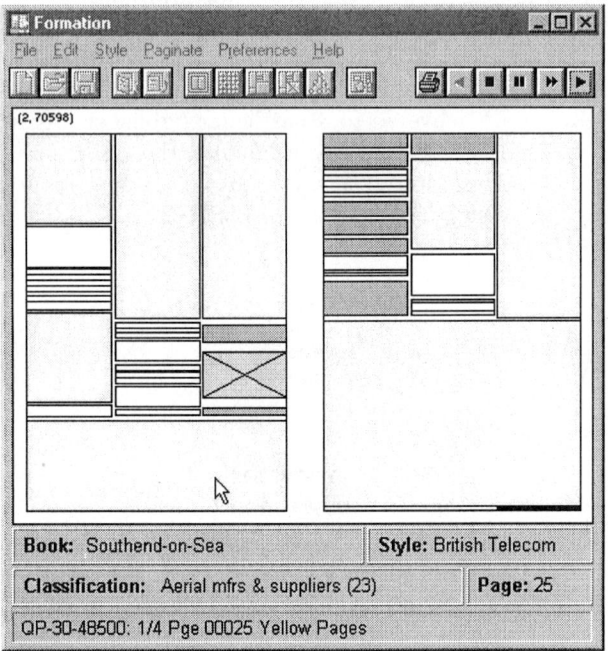

Figure 2: The **Formation** GUI under Windows95

Through the judicious provision of style parameters, the publisher can therefore be offered a great deal of flexibility in choosing the layout of his documents. At Pindar, the **Formation** user interface also provides a natural and accessible way of demonstrating the power of the layout engine to Pindar's clients.

However, should the customer want greater flexibility than is offered through configuring an existing style, he can have it, because the full power of LSSL is available to the style programmer.

There are inevitably practical difficulties in fully and unambiguously describing how to handle every interaction that can result from every possible combination of input data, so very occasionally the operators need to make manual changes to the finished layout. More commonly, the publisher has to make late changes – such as the inclusion of new advertisers, or corrections to the text of line entries – so support for human intervention is a continuing requirement. When it is used to produce the BTYP directories at Pindar, the LSSL interpreter is harnessed to a page editor developed by Pindar.

LSSL and the Layout Engine

The 2D layout engine is a LSSL interpreter. It is implemented in Allegro Common Lisp, and runs on a Pentium-based Windows PC in production at Pindar. Because it is in Common Lisp, it is portable, and it also runs under Macintosh and UNIX operating systems.

LSSL is a small, object-oriented language for describing general 2D layout requirements. It has dynamic typing, simple object semantics, and provides mechanisms for event-driven programming which support precise specification of the layout process.

The representation of a LSSL document is based on the concepts of *block* and *grid*. A block is a rectangle; blocks are sub-typed into *regions*, which are rectangles which can be filled by the layout process, and *items*, which represent the data to be laid out. Regions can be divided into smaller regions by *divider* grids, enabling the style programmer to specify different logical parts of the page, while *page* grids are used to specify the positions in which items can be placed.

Using these concepts, then, the geometry of the page is described. The document is represented as a queue of *spread* regions. A spread is usually – but not necessarily – two facing pages (see figure 3).

LSSL provides primitives for defining styles and documents, and for controlling pagination. Layout is usually carried out through calling the built-in `paginate` procedure, as follows. First, there is some pre-layout preparation: input and output files are opened, and various objects needed for layout are initialised. Then the document is laid out in a well-defined process. At the end, things are tidied up, and `paginate` compiles and writes out a layout report.

The Style Library

The style library provides generic and reusable style elements, implemented in LSSL, which can be customised by a style programmer. Through the use of the inheritance mechanisms provided by LSSL the style programmer can define ever more specific requirements. At present, the style library contains completely generic elements for 2D layout, plus elements which are of use within the more specialised domain of CTD layout.

For example, we said that a spread is usually *but not necessarily* two facing pages. The concept of a spread is built in to the style library, and by default, a spread will contain a 2 by 1 divider grid. This type of grid is

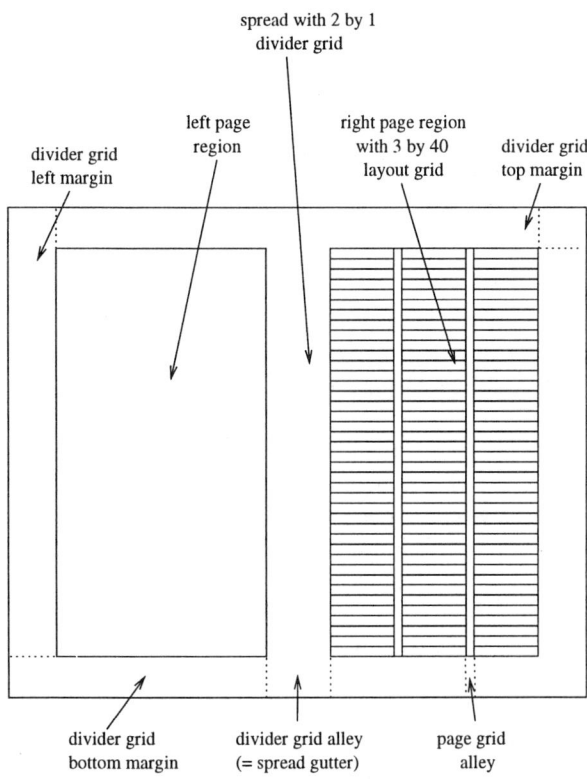

Figure 3: Spread structure with regions and grids

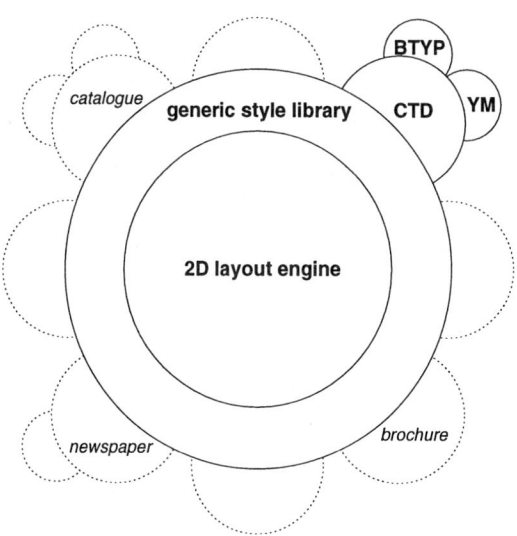

Figure 4: Development of the style library

the norm for CTDs in general, and BTYP directories are no exception. However, if we wanted to write a style for laying out a single-page flier, we could do so by defining a single-spread page, overriding the default. Figure 4 shows how the style library is developing.

The Formation User Interface and the Page Editor

The Formation user interface (see figure 2) is written using the Allegro Common Lisp GUI Builder, and runs only on a PC under Windows. The Page Editor, however, is implemented in C++ using Microsoft Foundation Classes. This gives Pindar portability across the PC, Apple and Sun platforms, as well as allowing easy access to PC dependent facilities such as OLE.

As well as allowing the user to configure a style through changing and specifying its parameters (and in particular, changing the parameters of the strategy and methods), the user interface provides facilities for describing the page geometry and the types of item which can appear in the book.

The Contents of a Style

A layout style comprises: the page geometry (regions and grids); the different types of item which can appear on a page (a hierarchy of types, usually specifiying sizes, and required spacing); a specification of the required layout process, or *strategy* (e.g. lay out a spread at a time, or consider a whole classification at once); and detailed knowledge about how to position items on a page, in the form of layout *methods* and *rules*.

Note that in LSSL a layout method is simply an object which encapsulates knowledge about a particular aspect of page layout. For example, in the BTYP style, there is a particular method which specifies how to keep entries in sequence, and another which specifies how to position multi-column display advertisements. Each layout method is implemented as a package of event-driven layout rules; a rule defines a set of actions which is to be carried out when a particular event happens.

Layout Rules

LSSL provides the programmer with the ability to control the layout of a page through rules which are defined for certain objects and are executed when particular events occur. LSSL layout rules are therefore not production rules. While production rules encode their conditions explicitly, LSSL layout rules do not. Instead, the conditions under which LSSL rules are fired are defined in terms of LSSL events. Built-in LSSL procedures – such as *get-space*, which finds a space in which an item can fit, and *align*, which tests to see whether the item can be positioned in that space given the layout requirements – signal events, but the LSSL programmer can also signal his own events.

Since every rule defined for an item at a particular event is executed when that event occurs, it is important that rules do not conflict. Some care is necessary to package rules together in discrete methods which can be enabled or disabled on demand.

For example, the method for keeping entries in sequence in BTYP contains a rule to check that an entry is aligned following the last one already placed on a page:

```
;;; Keep entries in sequence

(a method eis "Entries in sequence"
   ("Sequenced entry type" entry))

;;; Align a sequenced entry following the
;;; last one on the page

(a rule eis.follows-last? (for eis.entry)
                          (at align)
                          :(it gd _ _) ->
   (or (not gd.last-entry)
       (eis.follows? it gd.last-entry)))
```

The rule is part of the `eis` method, and is stored in a slot in that method. Note that the type of item for which it is defined can be configured through the method parameter `eis.entry`. `eis.follows-last?` will be executed when any item of this type is aligned. It carries out a simple test to see whether there are any entries on `gd`, the page grid on which this item is being aligned, and, if there are, it runs a method-specific procedure `eis.follows?` to check whether this entry is aligned following the last. Of course, the definition of `eis.follows?` could be changed to accommodate the requirements of a different publisher.

Through encapsulating the knowledge about the look of a finished page in methods and rules, then, we are able build up a library of configurable, reusable components.

Design Criteria

Formation was designed to satisfy two important requirements: flexibility in describing or modifying the details of a particular style of layout, and high throughput. It was required to produce CTDs for BTYP, but was always intended to be more general. It therefore has a modular design, and is based on the general-purpose framework provided by LSSL. Unlike other systems (Camara, Martins, & Jácome 1990; Graf 1995), the emphasis was on carrying out correctly and predictably what has been specified, rather than selecting an optimal solution from several candidates.

Uses of AI Technology

Since Pindar required a system which would run reliably in production, AIAI chose to use mature technology. Common Lisp was chosen as the development language because it is particularly well-suited for manipulating symbolic data, and because features such as automatic storage management improve programmer productivity. AIAI staff already had Lisp expertise. Franz Inc's Allegro Common Lisp was used because it provides a high-quality, well-supported development environment.

In developing **Formation**, AIAI's skills and experience in knowledge acquisition, knowledge representation and symbolic computation were particularly useful. A disciplined knowledge-engineering approach was taken from the beginning, and in the early stages of development AIAI carried out structured interviews with Pindar staff. Through these we were able to capture: BTYP's current requirements; expertise resulting from the continuing need to edit pages after layout is complete; and previous experience of laying out CTDs by hand before computerised layout was possible. The results were used to produce a layout ontology from which LSSL and the style library have developed.

It was important to Pindar that the delivered system be maintainable by Pindar staff, so modularity has been important to the design and development of **Formation**. We decided early on that given Pindar's requirements, including tight timescales and the requirement for mature technology, the available constraint-based technologies would not suit. However, we originally expected to use a very simple representation of layout constraints in the layout engine.

Early experiments with these proved that in order to meet BTYP's requirement to be able to specify (and monitor) layout very precisely, we needed a much more deterministic approach. The event-driven rules in LSSL were the result, and we found it easy to incorporate them into the general and modular framework we had developed. Should there be a requirement for a more constraint-based alternative approach in the future, **Formation**'s design, and the object-oriented nature of LSSL, will accommodate this.

Pindar chose to implement the page editor in C++ for business reasons, including the ability to take advantage of in-house skills in C++. The choice of Microsoft Foundation Classes provided portability, and delivery on a PC made it easy and cheap to deliver hardware for production as well as permitting off-site demonstration on laptop computers.

Application Use and Payoff

Formation is used in production at Pindar in batch mode. The text listings to be included in a book – such as the classification headers and plain text listings – are typeset; when typesetting is complete, the space needed on the printed page for each text entry is known. LSSL object definitions for these entries are then combined with definitions for the graphical entries – such as the display advertisements – to produce a single input stream. Pindar production staff then run Formation in batch mode. When layout is complete, the output stream of LSSL object definitions is combined with the typesetting information and graphics to produce printed pages for proof-reading. On the occasions when editing is necessary, perhaps because of last-minute changes from the publisher, these are made using the page editor developed by Pindar. The whole process, from the point when the compiled data arrives at Pindar till the finished film is sent to the printers, typically takes only 3 days.

Long before Formation went into full production use for laying out BTYP at Pindar in December 1997, its high throughput and great flexibility had already brought Pindar clear business benefits.

The ability to describe layout knowledge in a concise and modular way has enabled us to make changes requested by BTYP very quickly, and Pindar has been very pleased with the speed at which styles can be updated. Changes can be made to the layout produced by Formation in hours or days; with previous systems, even apparently minor changes might take weeks. The introduction of new advertisement types has proved painless.

Using Formation, Pindar has been able to produce special sections such as Eating-Out Guides which were previously compiled manually by the operators. The ability to trial different layouts has helped Pindar to produce samples which BTYP have used for market research, with the confidence that should BTYP decide to produce directories with these new features, Pindar can deliver quickly and easily.

The ability to collect statistics such as the total percentage of filler space in the book, or the number of full-page display advertisements, and to control through LSSL styles which of these are reported to the operator or user, is an additional benefit. It provides Pindar with a mechanism for measuring the impact of changes to layout quantitatively, and for identifying those which will have a direct impact on costs.

Although the ability to program styles in LSSL makes Formation extremely flexible, the provision of the Formation GUI makes the system very easy for a non-programmer to use and understand. Apart from reducing training costs, this ease of use means that Pindar can readily demonstrate Formation to existing and prospective customers. Furthermore, since Pindar has the ability to reconfigure a style's parameters and lay its example document out again and again in front of a customer, it is easy for the customer to see and to understand the impact of changes and the potential benefits they will bring him.

As the detailed knowledge which controls the 'look and feel' of the finished document is readily identifiable, it can also be used to inform advertisers about the rules that are applied to determine the positioning of their advertisements. This is important to BTYP, as their staff have to be in a position to explain to advertisers why their entries appear where they do; the ability to give precise answers could eventually reduce costs incurred by BTYP through customer complaints.

Speed of layout is an important aspect of the system due to both the number of directories that have to be processed and the relatively short timescales involved in their production and printing. Formation can lay out a typical directory of 1500 pages at a speed of well over 1,000 pages per hour on a 100 MHz Pentium-based PC.

Although Formation was intended specifically to produce classified telephone directories, it is a much more general system and can be used for the two-dimensional layout of general shapes based on rectangles. Because of this general framework, Pindar can see enormous potential for marketing Formation in Europe, the USA and the Far East.

Application Development and Deployment

Formation was developed at AIAI by a project team of five. The skills of the individuals in the team complemented each other, and covered requirements capture, knowledge elicitation and modelling, AI software design and implementation, and project management. The initial development of the LSSL interpreter and the BTYP style took approximately 1 man year, and was carried out over a period of 10 months; during which regular review meetings were held with Pindar staff. The system was delivered on time and to specification.

In order to ensure that the system met operational requirements, Pindar's Production Operations Manager was involved, from specifying the requirements through to accepting the delivered system. His input was essential, as he has overall responsibility for the typesetting and formatting process by which the BTYP directories are produced.

Throughout its development, a high priority has been to ensure that Pindar is able to maintain and modify **Formation** in the future. As a technology transfer organisation, AIAI aimed not to deliver a 'black box' product, but to provide its client with a long-term solution. Pindar's technical staff visited AIAI regularly to work with the project team, and they were involved in discussion and comment at all stages of design and implementation. Following project delivery, members of Pindar's support staff spent further time at AIAI learning about the system.

Since January 1996 **Formation** has been used by Pindar in development and for market research, and it has proved very flexible. During this time it was also used in production trials, and we gained a great deal of expertise about layout specification. It became clear early on that page layout systems are very liable to incomplete and inaccurate specification. Some of AIAI's efforts in technology transfer, therefore, have centred on providing tutorial material which will help Pindar to write clear and concise style specifications. A great deal of effort has gone into ensuring that the BTYP style is very well documented and that Pindar technical staff can modify it.

By contrast, since **Formation** is used in production in batch mode, very little training in its use has been necessary for production staff.

Formation successfully replaced the previous system in production use in December 1997, together with the Page Editor. The first book produced with it was the 1998 directory for the Shrewsbury area.

Maintenance

It is very important to Pindar that maintenance of the layout system is not dependent on the developers; AIAI delivers tutorials to ensure that Pindar staff understand new developments, as well as producing reference and tutorial documentation.

The strategic partnership between AIAI and Pindar enables continuing development, and current efforts are concentrated on further development of the style library.

The provision of style parameters which can be modified though the user interface has enabled even beginners to change **Formation**'s behaviour. The additional facilities in the interface for specifying page geometry and item types allow the user to make changes to the declarative knowledge defined by the style without ever needing to program.

These facilities, together with the growing style library and the ability to program entirely new features in a modular and natural fashion, are particularly useful in this time of rapid change in publishing and advertising. BTYP's layout requirements have changed several times since work on **Formation** began in 1994,
but it has proved easy to accommodate those changes. Pindar expects to make even greater use of **Formation**'s flexibility in future, as new features currently under discussion start to appear in BTYP directories.

Conclusion

The successful development and deployment of **Formation** illustrates how a relatively small, privately owned company can benefit from using applied AI technology. Through working with AIAI to ensure that its layout knowledge is understandable and easily modified, Pindar Set has enabled itself to respond far better to its customer's needs, both present and future.

References

Anderson, G.; Casson, A.; Macintosh, A.; Rae, R.; Gleeson, B.; and Carter, S. 1996. Formation: Knowledge-based layout of classified telephone directories. In *Applications and Innovations in Expert Systems IV: Proceedings of Expert Systems 96*. British Computer Society.

Camara, J. A.; Martins, J. F.; and Jácome, M. S. 1990. ATENA: A knowledge based system for automatic pagination of Yellow Directories. In *Research and development in expert systems VII: Expert Systems 90, Proceedings of the Tenth Annual Technical Conference of the British Computer Society specialist group on Expert Systems*.

Chew, H.-G., and Liang, M. 1994. ALEXIS: An Intelligent Layout Tool for Publishing. In *Proceedings of the 6th Innovative Applications of Artificial Intelligence Conference*. Seattle, Washington: AAAI.

Graf, W. H. 1995. The Constraint-Based Layout Framework LayLab and its Applications. In *Proceedings of the Workshop on Effective Abstractions in Multimedia Layout, Presentations, and Interaction*. San Francisco: ACM.

Using Artificial Intelligence Planning to Automate SAR Image Processing for Scientific Data Analysis

Forest Fisher, Steve Chien
Jet Propulsion Laboratory
California Institute of Technology
4800 Oak Grove Drive, M/S 525-3660
Pasadena, CA 91109-8099
forest.fisher@jpl.nasa.gov

Edisanter Lo, Ronald Greeley
Department of Geology
Arizona State University
P.O. Box 871404,
Tempe, AZ 85287-1404

Abstract

In recent times, improvements in imaging technology have made available an incredible array of information in image format. While powerful and sophisticated image processing software tools are available to prepare and analyze the data, these tools are complex and cumbersome, requiring significant expertise to properly operate. Thus, in order to extract (e.g., mine or analyze) useful information from the data, a user (in our case a scientist) often must possess both significant science and image processing expertise.

This paper describes the use of AI planning techniques to represent scientific, image processing, and software tool knowledge to automate elements of science data preparation and analysis of *synthetic aperture radar (SAR)* imagery for planetary geology. In particular, we describe the Automated SAR Image Processing system (ASIP) which is currently in use by the Dept. of Geology at ASU supporting aeolian science analysis of synthetic aperture radar images. ASIP reduces the number of manual inputs in science product generation by 10-fold, decreases the CPU time to produce images by 30%, and allows scientists to directly produce certain science products.

Introduction

Recent breakthroughs in imaging technology have led to an explosion of available data in image format. However, these advances in imaging technology have brought with them a commensurate increase in the complexity of image processing and analysis technology. When analyzing newly available image data to discover patterns or to confirm scientific theories, a complex set of operations is often required. First, before the data can be used it must often be reformatted, cleaned, and many correction steps must be applied. Then, in order to perform the actual data analysis, the user must manage all of the analysis software packages and their requirements on format, required information, etc.

Furthermore, this data analysis process is not a one-shot process. Typically a scientist will set up some sort of analysis, study the results, and then use the results of this analysis to modify the analysis to improve it. This analysis and refinement cycle may occur many times - thus any reduction in the scientist effort or cycle time can dramatically improve scientist productivity. Consider the goal of studying the soil sediment transport (wind erosion patterns). In order to do this the scientist uses a z0map (described later) to analyze the surface wind velocities using SAR data. In order to generate the z0map the scientist must go through a number of processes:

- data acquisition: getting the data from a proprietary tape format using the CEOS reader software package

- data conversion: the data must be decompressed using yet another software package

- pre-processing: header and label files must be added to the date files

- processing: using the z0map software package a z0 map image is created and

- post processing: depending on the desired data format the z0 map image files may need to be converted to VICAR format (yet another proprietary format).

Unfortunately, this data preparation and analysis process is both knowledge and labor intensive.

In order to correctly be able to produce this science product for analysis, requires knowledge of a wide range of sources including:

- the particular science discipline of interest (e.g., atmospheric science, planetary geology),

- image processing and the image processing libraries available,

- where and how the images and associated information are stored (e.g., calibration files), and

- the overall image processing environment to know how to link together libraries and pass information from one program to another.

It takes many years of training and experience to acquire the knowledge necessary to perform these analyses. Needless to say, these experts are in high demand. One factor which exacerbates this shortage of experts is the extreme breadth of knowledge required. Many users might be knowledgable in one or more of the above areas but not in all the areas. In addition, the status quo requires that users possess considerable knowledge about software infrastructure. Users must know how to specify input parameters (format, type, and options) for each software package that they are using and must often expend considerable effort in translating information from one package to another.

Using automated planning technology to represent and automate many of these data analysis functions (Fayyad96) p. 50 (Chien96) and enables novice users to utilize the software libraries to prepare and analyze data. It also allows users who may be expert in some areas but less knowledgable in other to use the software tools.

The remainder of this article is organized as follows. First, we provide a brief overview of the key elements of AI planning. We then describe the ASIP system - which automates elements of image processing for science data analysis of synthetic aperture radar (SAR) images.

Artificial Intelligence Planning Techniques

We have applied and extended techniques from Artificial Intelligence Planning to address the knowledge-based software reconfiguration problem in general, and science data analysis in specific. In order to describe this work, we first provide a brief overview of the key concepts from planning technology [1].

Planning technology relies on an encoding of possible actions in the domain. In this encoding, one specifies for each action in the domain: *preconditions*, *postconditions*, and *subactivities*. Preconditions are requirements which must be met before the action can be taken. These may be pieces of information which are required to correctly apply a software package (such as the image format, availability of calibration data, etc.) Postconditions are things that are made true by the execution of the actions, such as the fact that the data has been photometrically corrected (corrected for the relative location of the lighting source) or that

3-dimensional topography information has been extracted from an image. Subactivities are lower level activities which comprise the higher level activity. For instance, returning to our previous example of analyzing soil sediment transport using SAR data. The different tasks (e.g., data acquisition, data conversion, etc.) are considered subtasks of the overall product generation process. The planner begins with the process of "determining parameters". This in turn is driven by the type of data format or mode of the SAR during data collection. Through this decomposition process parameters to be used in the z0map calculation are initialized. Given this encoding of actions, a planner is able to solve individual problems, where each problem is a current state and a set of goals. The planner uses its action models to synthesize a plan (a set of actions) to achieve the goals from the current state.

Planning consists of three main mechanisms: subgoaling, task decomposition, and conflict analysis. In subgoaling, a planner ensures that all of the preconditions of actions in the plan are met. This can be done by ensuring that they are true in the initial state or by adding appropriate actions to the plan. In task decomposition, the planner ensures that all high level (abstract) activities are expanded so that the lower level (subactivities) are present in the plan. This ensures that the plan consists of executable activities. Conflict analysis ensures that different portions of the plan do not interfere with each other.

The Automated SAR Image Processing (ASIP) System

ASIP automates synthetic aperture radar (SAR) image processing based on user request and a knowledge-base model of SAR image processing using AI automated planning techniques (Fisher97). SAR operates simultaneously in multipolarizations[2] and multifrequencies to produce different images consisting of radar backscatter coefficients (s0) through different polarizations at different frequencies. ASIP enables construction of an aerodynamic roughness image/map (z0 map) from raw SAR data - thus enabling studies of Aeolian processes.

Studies of Aeolian Processes

The aerodynamic roughness length (z0) is the height above a surface at which a wind profile assumes zero velocity. z0 is an important parameter in studies of atmospheric circulation and aeolian sediment transport (in layman's terms: wind patterns, wind erosion patterns, and sand/soil drift caused by wind) (Greeley87;

---

[1] For Further details on planning the user is referred to (Pemberthy92; Erol94).

[2] There are four combinations of polarization: HH, HV, VH, and VV, where H = Horizontal and V = Vertical.

Greeley87; Greeley91). Estimating z0 with radar is important because it enables large areas to be mapped quickly to study aeolian processes, as opposed to the slow painstaking process of manually taking field measurements (Blumberg95). The final science product is a VICAR image called a z0 map that the scientists use to study the aeolian processes.

Planning to Generate Aerodynamic Roughness Maps

ASIP is an end-to-end image processing system automating data abstraction, decompression, and (radar) image processing sub-systems, that integrates a number of SAR and z0 image processing sub-systems. Using a knowledge base of SAR processing actions and a general-purpose planning engine, ASIP reasons about the parameter and sub-system constraints and requirements: extracting needed parameters from image format and header files as appropriate (freeing the user from these issues). These parameters, in conjunction with the knowledge-base of SAR processing steps(see Figure 1), and a minimal set of required user inputs (entered through a graphical user interface (GUI)), are then used to determine the processing plan. ASIP represents a number of processing constraints (e.g., that only some subset of all possible combinations of polarizations are legal as dependent on the input data). ASIP also represents image processing knowledge about how to use polarization and frequency band information to compute parameters used for later processing of backscatter to aerodynamic roughness length conversions - thus freeing the user from having to understand these processes (see Figure 1).

The design of ASIP focuses on automation to make a variety of software tools function together. In the process of accomplishing this goal, many of the interfaces of the individual tools where modified to provide automated interfaces. Through these new automated interfaces, considerable information, previously entered into each tool through an interactive shell, is passed from one tool to another. In many cases the same information must be provided to many of the tools. In some cases the information is the same but the required format may differ from one tool to another. Many of the parameters provided to the tools are interdependent on as many as five other parameters. As the parameters become more interdependent it becomes more difficult to understand the process. Through these new automated interfaces many of these parameters are passed to the planning system and the knowledge base i sused by the planner to reason about the interdependencies to set the resulting parameters appropriately. Going back to the ASIP design, ASIP actually calls the planner twice. In the first call the planner determines the steps (tools) necessary to accomplish the processing task (goals); and determines how to set parameters needed in generating the header files. Once the data has been extracted and more data has been gathered the planner is called a second time further reason about the parameter settings needed to complete the remainder of the processing goals. The two knowledge bases combined contain 29 rules.

```
(decomprule get_z0map_coef_l-hv
    lhs
      (initialgoals ( (get_z0map_coef l-hv)
                    )
      )
    rhs
      (newgoals ( (m0  -6.419)
                  (m1   9.957)
                  (r_chit  0)
                  (r_psit 90)
                  (r_chir  0)
                  (r_psir  0)
                  (i_polcode 2)
                  (polar l-hv)
                )
      )
    doc [ ]
)
```

Figure 1: Sample Decomposition Rule from ASIP SAR Domain

Figure 1 shows an example of a task decomposition rule. In the rule *get_z0map_coef_l-hv*, we see that if the *preconditions* spelled out in the *lhs* (left-hand side) are meet then the parameters and coefficients of the *rhs* (right-hand side) are set for later use. Although not shown, the *lhs* of the *get_z0map_coef_l-hv* rule is satisfied by the application of other planning operators and rules.

Figure 2 shows an aerodynamic roughness length map of a site near Death Valley, California generated using the ASIP system (the map uses the L band (24 cm) SAR with HV polarization). Each of the greyscale bands indicated signifies a different approximate aerodynamic roughness length. This map is then used to study aeolian processes at the Death Valley site.

Application Use and Payoffs

Since the ASIP system was fielded in January 1997, it has proven to be very useful in the use of generating aerodynamic roughness maps with three major benefits.

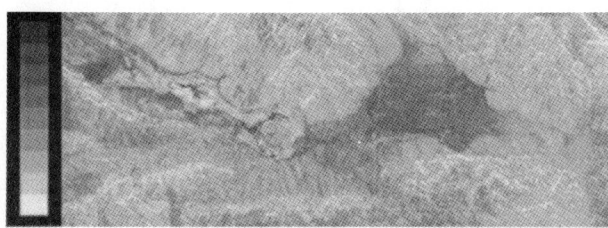

Figure 2: Aerodynamic Roughness Length Map Produced Using ASIP

- First, ASIP has enabled a 10 fold reduction in the number of manual inputs required to produce an aerodynamic roughness map.

- Second, ASIP has enabled a 30% reduction in CPU processing time to produce such a map (by producing more efficient plans).

- Third, and most significantly ASIP has enabled scientists to process their own data (previously programming staff were required).

By enabling scientists to directly manipulate that data and reducing processing overhead and turnaround, science is directly enhanced.

Application Development, Deployment and Maintenance

The development of the ASIP system took approximately six months. During that time period the system was developed and deployed using an iterative waterfall development cycle containing three incremental deployments. The development team consisted of one AI Planning researcher from JPL and one SAR domain expert from ASU, who later became one of the users of the system after deployment to the ASU Planetary Geology Department. The system was both developed and deployed on a Sun UNIX workstation using a combination of C, FORTRAN, and TCL/TK.

The maintenance of the ASIP system, is done by the users of the system at ASU. Because of the nature of the SAR domain modifications to the knowledge-base are not expected to be frequent, but in the event that through greater understanding of SAR data the values of the coefficients change this an easy modification to make.

Related Work

Related work can be broadly classified into: related image processing languages, related automated image processing work, and related AI planning work. In terms of related image processing languages, there are many commercial and academic image processing packages - such as IDL, Aoips, and Merlyn. Generally, these packages have only limited ability to automatically determine how to use different image processing programs or algorithms based on the problem context (e.g., other image processing goals and initial image state). These packages only support such context sensitivity for a few pre-anticipated cases.

However, there are several previous systems for automatic image processing that use a domain independent mechanism. The work at the Canadian Centre for Remote Sensing (CCRS) (Charlebois91) differs from ASIP in that they use a case-based reasoning approach in which a problem is solved by searching for a previous problem and solution. Grimm and Bunke (Grimm93) developed an expert system to assist in image processing within the SPIDER library of image processing routines. This system uses many similar approaches in that: 1. it classifies problem types similar to the fashion in which ASIP performs skeletal planning; and 2. it also decomposes larger problems into subproblems which ASIP performs in decomposition planning. This system is implemented in a combination of an expert system shell called TWAICE (which includes both rules and frames) and Prolog. Previous work on automating the use of the SPIDER library includes (Sakaue85) which performs constraint checking and step ordering for a set of conceptual image processing steps and generation of executable code. This work differs from ASIP in that: 1. they do not infer missing steps from step requirements; 2. they do not map from a single abstract step to a context-dependent sequence of image processing operations; and 3. they do not reason about negative interactions between subproblems. ASIP has the capability to represent and reason about all 3 of these cases. Other work by Jiang and Bunke (Jian94) involves generation of image processing procedures for robotics. This system performs subgoaling to construct image processing plans. However their algorithm does not appear to have a general way of representing and dealing with negative interactions between different subparts of the plans. In contrast, the general Artificial Intelligence Planning techniques used by ASIP use conflict resolution methods to guarantee correct handling of subproblem interactions.

Another piece of related work is the SATI system (Capdevielle94) which uses an interactive dialogue with the user to drive an automated programming approach to generating code to satisfy the user request. OCAPI (Clement93), a semantically integrated automated image processing system, while being very general provides no clear way to represent the large number of logical constraints associated with the problems ASIP was designed to solve. Another image processing system (Matsuyama89) provides a means for representing knowledge of image analysis strategies in an expert system but does not use the more declarative AI planning representation. Perhaps the most similar planning and image processing system is COLLAGE (Lansky95). The COLLAGE planning differs from ASIP in that COLLAGE uses solely the decomposition approach to planning.

Finally, the most closely related system to ASIP is MVP (Chien96). The greatest similarity being MVP and ASIP use the same AI Planning techniques to capture and reason about the knowledge of image processing. The primary differences lie in the domains and in the packaging. MVP produces VICAR procedure definition files (PDFs) for VICAR image processing (LaVoie89), while ASIP performs end-to-end closed loop integration of all the tools for SAR image processing.

Conclusions

This paper has described knowledge-based reconfiguration of data analysis software using AI planning techniques. In particular, we have described the ASIP system which automates production of aerodynamic roughness maps to support geological science analysis. ASIP reduces the number of manual inputs in science product generation by 10-fold, has reduced the CPU processing time by 30%, and has enabled scientists to directly produce certain science products.

Acknowledgements

Portions of this work were performed by the Jet Propulsion Laboratory, California Institute of Technology, under contract with the National Aeronautics and Space Administration. Other portions of this work were performed at the Department of Geology, Arizona State University under JPL Contract 960559. The authors would also like to acknowledge other contributors to the ASIP project including: Dan Blumberg (ASU), Anita Govindjee (JPL), John McHone (ASU), Keld Rasmussen (ASU), and Todd Turco (JPL).

References

D. Blumberg and R. Greeley, "Field Studies of Aerodynamic Roughness Length," Jnl. Arid Environ. (1993) 25:39-48.

O. Capdevielle, P. Dalle, "Image Processing Chain Construction by Interactive Goal Specification," Proceedings of the First IEEE Int. Conf. on Image Processing, Austin, TX, Nov 1994, Vol. 3, pp. 816-819.

D. Charlebois, J. DeGuise, G. Goodenough, S. Matwin, and M. Robson, "A Case-based Planner to Automate Reuse of ES Software for Analysis of Remote Sensing Data," Internation Geoscience and Remote Sensing Symposium (IGARSS), Vol 3, pp. 1851-1854, 1991.

S. A. Chien and H. B. Mortensen, "Automating Image Processing for Scientific Data Analysis of a Large Image Database," IEEE Transactions on Pattern Analysis and Machine Intelligence 18 (8): pp. 854-859, August 1996.

V. Clement and M. Thonnat, "A Knowledge-based Approach to Integration of Image Processing Procedures," Image Understanding, 57:166-184, March 1993.

K. Erol, J. Hendler, and D. Nau, "UMCP: A Sound and Complete Procedure for Hierarchical Task Network Planning," Proceedings of the 2nd International Conference on AI Planning Systems, Chicago, IL, June 1994, pp. 249-254.

U. Fayyad, G. Piatetsky-Shapiro, P. Smyth, "From Data Mining to Knowledge Discovery in Databases," AI Magazine, Vol 17 No. 3, Fall 1996, pp. 37-54.

F. Fisher, E. Lo, S. Chien, R. Greeley, "Using Artificial Intelligence Planning to Automate SAR Processing for Planetary Geoplogy", NASA Science Information Systems, March/April 1997, Issue 42

R. Greeley and J.D. Iversen, "Measurements of Wind Friction Speeds over Lava Surfaces and Assessment of Sediment Transport," G.R.L. 14 (1987):925-928.

R. Greeley, P.R. Christensen, and J.F. McHone, "Radar Characteristics of Small Craters: Implications for Venus," EMP 37 (1987):89-111.

R. Greeley, L. Gaddis, A. Dobrovolskis, J. Iversen, K. Rasmussen, S. Saunders, J. vanZyl, S. Wall, H. Zebker, and B. White, "Assessment of Aerodynamic Roughness Via Airborne Radar Observations," 1991, Acta Mechanica Suppl.2, 77-88.

F. Grimm and H. Bunke, "An Expert System for the Selection and Application of Image Processing Subroutines, " Expert Systems, May 1993, Vol. 10, No. 2, pp. 61-74.

X. Jian and H. Bunke, "Vision Planner for an Intelligence Multisensory Vision System," Technical Report, University of Bern (extended version of a paper appearing in ICPR 1994).

A. Lansky, M. Friedman, L. Getoor, S. Schmidler, and N. Short Jr., "The Collage/Khoros Link: Planning for Image Processing Tasks," Proceedings of the 1995 AAAI Spring Symposium on Integrated Planning Applications, March 1995, pp. 67-76.

S. LaVoie, D. Alexander, C. Avis, H. Mortensen, C. Stanley, and L. Wainio, "VICAR User's Guide, Version 2," JPL Internal Document D-4186, Jet Propulsion Lab., California Institute of Tech., Pasadena, CA, 1989.

T. Matsuyama, "Expert Systems for Image Processing: Knowledge-Based Composition of Image Analysis Processes," Computer Vision, Graphics, and Image Processing 48, (1989), pp. 22-49.

J. S. Pemberthy and D. S. Weld, "UCPOP: A Sound Complete, Partial Order Planner for ADL," Proceedings of the 3rd International Conference on Knowledge Representation and Reasoning, Oct 1992.

K. Sakaue and H. Tamura, "Automatic Generation of Image Processing Programs by Knowledge-based Verification," IEEE Conference on Computer Vision and Pattern Recognition, pp. 189-192, 1985.

Turbine Engine Diagnostics (TED): An Expert Diagnostic System for the M1 Abrams Turbine Engine

Richard Helfman, Ed Baur, John Dumer, Tim Hanratty, and Holly Ingham

U.S. Army Research Laboratory
AMSRL-IS-CI
Aberdeen Proving Ground, MD 21005

helfman@arl.mil, baur@arl.mil, dumer@arl.mil, hanratty@arl.mil, hollyo@arl.mil

Abstract

Turbine Engine Diagnostics (TED) is a diagnostic expert system to aid the M1 Abrams tank mechanic find and fix problems in the AGT-1500 turbine engine. TED was designed to provide the apprentice mechanic the ability to diagnose and repair the turbine engine like an expert mechanic. The expert system was designed and built by the U.S. Army Research Laboratory (ARL) and the U.S. Army Ordnance Center and School (OC&S). This paper discusses the relevant background, development issues, reasoning method, system overview, test results, return on investment, and fielding history of the project. Limited fielding began in 1994 to select Army National Guard units, and complete fielding to all M1 Abrams tank maintenance units started in 1997 and will finish by the end of 1998. The Army estimates that TED will save roughly $10 million per year through improved diagnostic accuracy and reduced waste. The development and fielding of the TED program represents the Army's first successful fielded maintenance system in the area of AI. There are several reasons associated with the success of the TED program: an appropriate domain with proper scope, a close relationship with the expert, extensive user involvement, plus others that are discussed in this paper.

Problem description

The U. S. Army holds title to one of the most envied weapon systems developed— the M1 Abrams tank. The Gulf War confirmed that the Abrams tank epitomizes lethality and survivability on today's battlefield. Logistically, on the other hand, the negative corollary is that the Abrams is expensive to operate, support, and maintain. Central to these costs is the maintenance for its turbine engine.

Maintenance on the Abrams engine is accomplished at three levels: organizational, direct support (DS), and depot. Depot is usually in the United States. Items that cannot be fixed at one level are sent to the next higher level. See Figure 1.

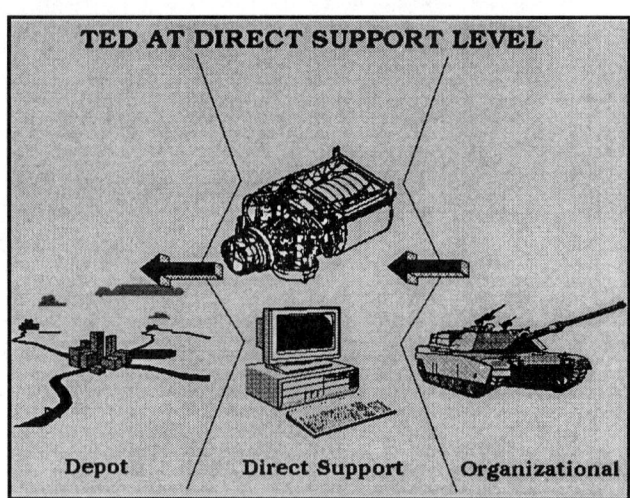

Figure 1: Maintenance-Level Military Structure

For the TED program, Abrams tank maintenance was quickly identified as the proper domain with special focus on the engine. Several factors contributed to the selection of tank maintenance as an appropriate domain for expert system development. First and foremost, the cost associated with maintaining the engine of the Abrams tank represented the largest portion of its operation and support costs. An engine that cannot be fixed at DS is shipped back to depot for repair and rebuild. One study determined that in one year, out of 360 turbine engines returned to depot for repair, 40 percent were reported as "no evidence of failure" (NEOF). This means 40 percent of the engines returned for repair were actually in running condition and should not have been removed from the tank (Textron 1988, 1989). The unnecessary cost related to NEOF conditions was estimated at $18 million per year for the fleet of M1 turbine engines before TED. One of the main goals of the TED program was to substantially reduce the $18 million NEOF waste per year (Johnson 1997)].

The Army had tried for years to reduce the high incidence of NEOF. By 1991, there had been three failed attempts at building a diagnostic expert system for the M1 engine.

Application description

System overview

Early into the project, the turbine subject matter experts (SMEs) and the knowledge engineers at ARL established several design goals. These goals were based primarily on the SMEs' extensive experience as mechanics and instructors for engine maintenance classes. The SMEs had extensive experience with soldier mechanics--their likes and their dislikes. The following lists the main design goals for the TED software. The software should:
- be accurate,
- be easy to use,
- be flexible,
- be task oriented,
- be able to support multiple levels of expertise.

First, the software should be accurate. It need not be perfect, but it should be significantly better at diagnosing faults than the system it is replacing. Otherwise, it will lose soldier respect and will not be used. Second, it must be easy to use; otherwise, it will sit on the shelf. Mechanics have favorite stories of diagnostic equipment that does nothing but occupy lots of storage space. Third, it must be flexible enough to support a variety of diagnostic styles. For example, some mechanics are thorough and methodical, and a structured step-by-step approach is best for them. A few have a sixth sense and "know" what is wrong with an engine. They have only limited need for the information in TED and will only use it as an occasional reference. Other soldiers have a mixture of styles. They may know a lot about some parts of the engine but need guidance in other areas. Fourth, TED must be task structured in a way that is natural for the soldier. The current technical manuals (TMs) have a structure that is difficult to use and to follow. Experts can navigate the TMs, but others find the structure confusing. Finally, the last goal recognizes that mechanics come with different skill levels. Experts need little or no help from TED. Beginners need extensive step-by-step instructions. A system aimed at just one level of expertise would bore the expert or baffle the beginner.

System organization

TED is organized into five functional areas that represent the various actions performed by M1 mechanics:

- Diagnostics,
- Repair parts,
- Maintenance,
- Bookkeeping,
- Training.

The software allows multimode access, either menu-driven or data-driven. The choice is made by the soldier.

Diagnostics. This functional area represents the major share of the code in TED. It contains 14 modules that find out what is wrong with the engine. The modules organize DS diagnostic logic by terms easily recognized by mechanics, regardless of experience. Troubleshooting areas include: No Start, Low Power, High Oil Consumption, Engine Smokes, Metal Contamination, Quick Coast Down, Idle Faults, Engine Shutdown, Fault Finder, and Protective Modes. Each of the submodules contains diagnostic logic to first determine the cause of the faulty symptom and, once the cause has been detected, to link the appropriate maintenance and repair parts modules.

Repair Parts. After a fault has been diagnosed, parts often need to be ordered. The second main module of TED is the repair parts and special tools list (RSPTL) module. This module greatly enhances the mechanics ability to interrogate the parts-ordering information for every aspect of the Abrams engine and transmission. Provided to the mechanic is the ability to search for items of interest in a variety of ways. In addition to being automatically linked from a diagnostic procedure, the mechanic can peruse the system from a general table of contents or choose to search on specific part number, national stock number, or nomenclature.

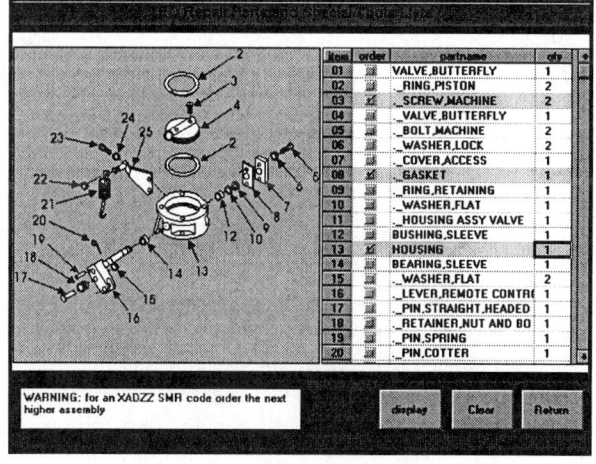

Figure 2: Typical Parts Ordering Screen

Displayed in Figure 2 is a typical ordering selection form. For each figure, its associated parts list is displayed on the right side while its drawing is detailed on the left. Items are selected from the parts list by buttoning the particular order box. When necessary, portions of a drawing may be magnified to highlight areas of interest. Information from the RPSTL is automatically associated with its corresponding work order.

Maintenance. Maintenance actions for any component include adjust, repair, remove, and replace. The procedures can be invoked in either browse mode or data-driven mode. When in browse mode, maintenance procedures are manually selected through menus and submenus. This provides experienced mechanics the flexibility of viewing only the procedures that they need, while bypassing familiar or routine tasks. When in the data- driven mode, TED automatically establishes the correct links to all pertinent maintenance procedures and to sections of the repair parts manual.

Bookkeeping. All work done on an engine must be documented, and this is done automatically in TED. Found under the System Administration module are the report writing and database maintenance functions. In addition to allowing the mechanic the ability to print the necessary DA 2404 Technical Inspection Form, the system provides numerous work order and statistical summaries. For the database maintenance, routines to update and delete information are also available.

Training. The first of the special applications is the Diagnostic Intelligent Tutoring System (DITS). DITS is an embedded tutorial system that covers basic maintenance procedures, theory of engine operations, and guidance on such tasks as hooking up the Ground Hop Support Set and using a multimeter. Using interactive review and troubleshooting modules, mechanics can hone their skills in a field environment. DITS, a diagnostic trainer, complements TED, a diagnostic tool, by providing mechanics a complete system.

Hardware

An invariable factor associated with every software system developed is its hardware constraints. From the onset, careful consideration must be given to the delivery platform (i.e. on what machine or machines will the system reside). Where possible, the identification should occur immediately. The earlier a target machine is identified the sooner the program can capitalize on its strengths and minimize its weaknesses. For many applications, selection of the delivery platform is a moot point. Where selection is possible, dialog with the user is paramount, giving special consideration to cost, the user's environment, available software, and connectivity.

For the TED program, hardware constraints were predetermined. The delivery platform selected was a 80486 PC which was part of the Army common computer hardware. The computer has now been upgraded to a Pentium laptop.

Software

In the past, computer systems were typically characterized by the proprietary coupling of unique software to a specific hardware platform. Today, contemporary computer systems are breaking the sole-source syndrome and emphasizing greater interoperability and portability. Increasing is the number of systems adopting the "collection of components" approach; better known as commercial off-the-shelf (COTS).

In general terms, COTS software supports a large commercial following, is readily available, and easily meets or extends a system's capability requirements. Systems developed using a COTS approach are generally less costly, quicker to be fielded, and more flexible than products developed with non-COTS methods. Limiting the COTS approach is the careful examination that is required to correctly match system requirements with the COTS model, the potential for run-time fees, and the need for specialized wrapper programs that could exist. While the true efficacy of COTS products is not without bounds, the benefits outweigh the costs.

For the TED program, the adoption of COTS software was considered beneficial. Time was judged better spent on knowledge acquisition and testing than on pure code development. Chosen as the primary subsystem was the commercially available procedural-based expert system shell, Visual Expert, by Softsell. Additional features to the TED program are provided by the COTS products from Visual Basic, Access, Toolbook, and HyperWriter. In-house code was developed with Microsoft C++ and Borland's Delphi.

AI Technology

The main diagnostic software in TED is a Windows-based shell called Visual Expert from SoftSell. Visual Expert is based on a reasoning paradigm called **Procedural Reasoning System** (PRS) (Georgeff and Lansky, 1983, 1986). PRS is a visual method of encoding reasoning strategies used by expert problem solvers. The knowledge is represented graphically with semantics suited to the procedural, goal oriented style of problem solving, and PRS is best suited for problems that are both procedural and goal-oriented. A procedural approach uses an ordered step-by-step prescription to obtain a desired result, possibly including alternate paths in case of failure. Such an approach is also goal oriented if some steps are goals to be achieved rather than specific actions to be performed (ADS 1988). Army TMs closely follow this paradigm. They are often graphical in nature with decision trees displayed on the page. Some nodes represent goals to be achieved; others represent specific tasks to be performed. These tasks can themselves become goals whose solution is to be given on another page (or in another manual) (Ingham et al. 1997).

PRS is endowed with the attitudes of belief, desire, and intention. (See Figure 3). The generalized system is composed of a system database, a set of procedures or plans, an interpreter or inference engine, and a process stack. The database contains the current beliefs of the system. These beliefs could be static properties of the domain or beliefs derived by the system itself as it executes its plans. The plans are descriptions of how to accomplish given goals or to react to certain situations and are represented by declarative procedure specifications. The body of these procedures is represented as a graphical network with sequences of subgoals to be achieved as well as primitive actions to be accomplished. The interpreter runs the entire system, executing active goals and deciding what course of action to take based on the beliefs the system has at a point in time (Klock et al. 1994).

PRS combines features from several programming paradigms. Like PROLOG, it has goal-directed inferencing and depth-first search. Like expert system shells, it provides a frame system for global objects. Like LISP, it is well suited for rapid prototyping. SMEs quickly learned how to read Visual Expert's visual code, and some began writing their own code or modifying code written by the knowledge engineers.

Application use and payoff

Formal testing

During the week of 15 to 21 August 1993, an initial field test of the TED program was conducted at Fort Stewart, GA. Participating in the test were 30 soldiers from the Tennessee Army National Guard. Keeping in mind the target audience (DS mechanics), the test had two objectives: First, measure how accurately and quickly mechanics could identify randomly assigned faults on the engine using TED versus using TMs; second, decide if the program was soldier-friendly. For the test, the 30 mechanics were divided into 3 levels of 10 mechanics each based on their enlisted rank: E1-E4, E5, and E6-E7.

Each mechanic inspected two engines, one with TED and one with the TMs. The engines had a random number of faults

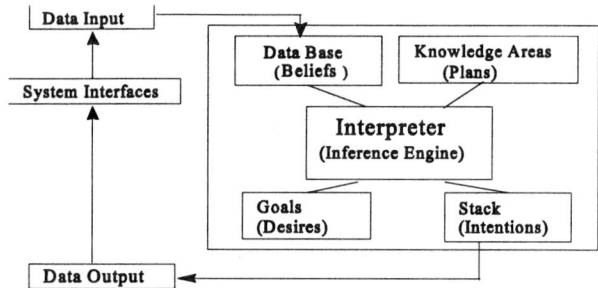

Figure 3: PRS Architecture

installed from a randomized list of possible faults. There was a 1-hour time limit for each inspection. An observer, with a score card, was present with each mechanic to log faults and the times that each fault was located. The conditions of the test approximated the actual working environment of the mechanics. There were three types of data collected during the field test: first, the observer's score card (mentioned previously), which served as the basis for the statistical analysis; second, a questionnaire completed by each mechanic, which allowed him to express his impressions of TED; third, each observer recorded personal comments, which served as an additional source of information for further revisions.

Rank	Manual Faults Detected	TED Faults Detected
E1 - E4	26%	52%
E5	11%	42%
E6 - E7	42%	56%
Overall	26%	52%

Table 1: Field Test Results

At each level, TED outperformed the current TM procedures (see Table 1). TED assisted the junior enlisted (E1 - E4) and the junior noncommissioned officers (E5) in finding at least **twice as many faults** as compared to the TMs. Note that even though TED is designed for junior mechanics, senior mechanics (E6 - E7) were able to increase their efficiency by using TED. Overall, the mechanics demonstrated a 96% increase in their ability to efficiently diagnose the engine (Taylor and Monyak 1994).

The ease of use became readily apparent to the observers during the initial training session. Because many of the mechanics had never used a computer, the observers allocated a 1-hour training block for each mechanic. In less than 10 minutes, mechanics who had never used a computer were effectively maneuvering through the software and hardware. Soldier acceptance was also unanimously positive. Both computer- and non-computer-literate mechanics readily accepted TED as the preferred tool for maintaining the engine (Baur et al. 1996).

Beta testing

Based on the success of the 1993 tests, the National Guard agreed to become beta testers for TED. In 1994, two states, Tennessee and Georgia, were given early copies of 2 TED software modules for testing. During 1995 and 1996, ARL delivered TED software and training to a total of 66 National Guard units in 29 states as follows:

Date:	State (# units within state)
Jan 1995	TX(9), TN(3), MO(1)
Mar 1995	ID(4), CA(2), CO(1), OR(1), WA(1)
May 1995	MS(7), LA(1), KS(1), KY(2)
Jun 1995	GA(4), AL(2), FL(1), SC(1), NJ(2), NY(4), PA(3), VT(1)
Sep 1995	IA(2), OH(2), MI(2), MN(1), MT(2), NC(2), VA(2), WV(1), WI(1)

Totals: 29 states 66 units

In early 1997, TED was sufficiently developed and tested to be released to units in the active Army. By the end of 1998, there will be a total of 200 copies of TED in use by the National Guard, the Marines, and the active Army.

Payoff

The goal of the TED program is to save money by reducing the diagnostic error rate. An 80% error reduction will save roughly $10 million each year by avoiding unneeded repair. The TED program is on its way to achieving this goal.

> In 1993, the University of Delaware conducted a formal user test using 30 soldiers from the Tennessee National Guard. The results showed that **TED cut the error rate by 50%**.
>
> In the summer of 1994, units from two different state National Guards received early versions of the TED software. Each state had three broken engines slated for turn-in. Each state had diagnosed the bad engines before TED arrived. On Saturday, 9 July, TED was used on the three engines from one state, and on Sunday, 10 July, on the three engines from the other state. On all six engines, the pre-TED diagnosis was wrong, and the TED diagnosis was right. Thus, **in the first two days of fielding, TED saved the Guard six incorrect engine repairs at a cost savings of over $50K.**
>
> By the summer of 1996, TED diagnostics had **error rates well below 5%**.

Application development and deployment

History

The TED program started in 1991 at the OC&S as an effort to seek solutions to some of the maintenance problems the Army was having with its equipment. ARL joined the program in the summer of 1991 as knowledge engineers and technical advisors, with the OC&S supplying the SMEs to provide the expert diagnostic knowledge and to guide the development direction of the system. The OC&S also supplied engines and soldiers as needed to test the new software being developed.

The first TED prototype was ready by January 1992. For the next 18 months, existing modules were expanded and new modules were begun. In March of 1993, the TED program was nominated and received the American Defense Preparedness Association's award for outstanding logistics and AI application. By August of the same year, the program was sufficiently developed to warrant formal field testing. Preliminary results showed TED improved fault identification by 96 % over the older manual methods.

In January 1994, Program Manager-Abrams (PM-Abrams), the primary proponent for the Abrams tank, decided to field TED to all active DS units with Abrams tanks. In addition, further production of paper manuals for the AGT1500 engine was halted. By March of the same year, the National Guard Bureau asked to have TED for its National Guard units as soon as possible. Fielding to the first two National Guard units (Georgia and Tennessee) began in July 1994. The National Guard Bureau continued to incrementally field TED until 65 units in 29 states with Abrams tanks had the TED software.

Development guidelines

The TED software engineers quickly established some important guidelines that remain in effect today.

Establish and Maintain Communication. Software engineers and SMEs do not generally speak the same language. Software engineers talk of frames and objects. The SMEs for the TED program are M1 tank mechanics. M1 tank mechanics talk of inlet guide vane (IGV) angles and of rotational variable differential transformers (RVDTs). Each needs to learn some of the other's language, but the main effort is on the software engineer to learn the language of the mechanic.

The best way to learn what the user does is to observe the user in his environment. The TED team attended and videotaped classes for M1 mechanics. This produced three important benefits. First, it quickly immersed the software engineers into the language of the mechanic. The IGV is located in front of the engine, and the angle determines how much air gets through to the turbine blades. Second, it gave an accurate picture of how a mechanic performs his job and how software might improve that job. The TED team noticed during that first session that the original scope of work was too narrow. There was a whole suite of software that could help the mechanic better perform his job. Third, it established a bond between the software engineer and the soldier. Soldiers could sense that the team was serious and that soldier's needs would be given serious attention. They were thus eager to cooperate.

When the aim is to produce software that not only works as planned, but also gets used by the mechanic, then user participation in the development process is critical. The TED team heard many stories from soldiers about equipment that never gets used, and about equipment that is difficult to use, but with a small change would have made the item soldier-friendly. The TED SMEs were assigned full-time to the project.

New technology is often met with resistance when it is thrown at an unaware and/or ill-prepared user. Rarely can a user, at the start of a project, envision how technology can improve his job. A system based on initial user expectations will at best be shallow, and may even be useless. The software engineer and the SME are each constantly learning about the other. The software engineer is continually learning about the needs and duties of the mechanic, and the mechanic is learning about the potential impact of new software on his future.

Rapid Prototyping. A prototype is essential for two-way communication. It allows the user to see and touch what the software engineer envisions for the user. It gives the user the earliest opportunity to comment on his system, and it gives him some clue as to the potential of the project. The user does not always know what technology is available, and the hands-on experience of the prototype is often the best way to educate the user. A prototype serves as a common reference point. Without a prototype, not much useful feedback can occur. It also shows how well the software engineer understands the user's needs.

Spiral Model. Boehm's spiral model (Boehm 1986) incorporates an incremental development schema. Successive prototypes are produced that expand upon user requirements. In addition, the software engineer is able to break down complex tasks into smaller components. As each component is developed, it is evaluated against user requirements. The user requirements are re-evaluated as each successive module is developed. Consequently, the user is an integral part of the development team. His input is essential. There are two reasons behind selecting the spiral method for the TED program: rapid changes in PC hardware and software and the need to keep the user in the loop. In 1991, it was obvious that hardware and software for the PC would continue to improve and become more affordable. Computer memory continues to expand and deflate in price. Hard drives continue to get bigger and cheaper. Screen resolution expands, and video cards improve. The price of a Pentium system today rivals the price of a 386 system in 1991.

Software follows the same pattern outlined for hardware. Every year, software improves, new products are announced, and existing products offer upgrades at an astounding pace and price. Goals that were impossible or difficult in the past may now be relatively easy tasks. The TED team continues to meet formally once a month to decide on the direction and scope of the project. Unsatisfied goals are re-evaluated, and some may be dropped from the list, while new goals may be added.

Software Maintenance

The incremental design used for TED incorporates software maintenance into the process. Early software modules have been in use since 1994, and the last software was delivered in September 1996. ARL continues to receive bug reports and wish lists from the field, although these have diminished significantly. ARL is now training other Army personnel to take over the maintenance for the TED program.

TED WEB Site

For more information, visit the TED WEB site at HTTP://RPSTL.ARL.MIL/TED.HTML

References

Advanced Decision Systems. 1988. Procedural Reasoning Systems. Working Paper, TR-ADS-0015.

Baur, Dumer, Hanratty, Helfman, and Ingham. 1996. Technology and Tank Maintenance. *Expert Systems with Applications*, 11(2): 99-107, Pergamon Press.

Boehm, B.W.. 1986. A Spiral Model of Software Development and Enhancement. ACM Software Engineering Notes.

Georgeff, M.P, and Lansky, A.L. 1983. Procedural Expert Systems. In Proceedings of the Eighth International Joint Conference on AI.

Georgeff, M.P, and Lansky, A.L. 1986. A System of Reasoning in Dynamic Domains: Fault Diagnostics on the Space Shuttle. Technical Notes # 375, SRI International.

Ingham, Helfman, Hanratty, Dumer, and Baur. 1997. TED - A Practical Application of a Diagnostic Expert System. In IEEE Proceedings of the Ninth International Conference on Tools With Artificial Intelligence pp 438-445, Nov.

Johnson, C.J. 1997. Meet TED, The Army's Computerized Tank Mechanic. *Program Manager Magazine*, May/June: Cover and pp 2-13.

Klock, M.; Rauch, B.; Sperry, S.; and Himes, A. 1994. Visual Expert Guide. Visual Expert Manual, Version 2.21.

Taylor, M.S., and Monyak, J.T. 1994. Statistical Analysis of Turbine Engine Diagnostic (TED) Field Test Data. ARL Technical Report ARL-TR-614.

Textron Lycoming. 1988. Internal Memo.

Textron Lycoming. 1989. Internal Memo.

Countrywide Automated Property Evaluation System - CAPES

Ingemar A.E. Hulthage and Iain Stobie

Countrywide Home Loans, Artificial Intelligence Division, 55 S. Lake Avenue, Pasadena, California 91109
Email: <firstname>_<lastname>@Countrywide.com

Abstract

The purpose of CAPES is to estimate the market value of residential properties in order to assess the collateral on Countrywide mortgage loans. CAPES estimates market value by comparison of the subject property to other similar nearby properties, for which recent sales information is available. In some cases price indices describing the change in property values over time are also used. In addition to the estimated market value, CAPES produces a measure of the uncertainty in the result. It uses several models, including heuristics derived from company-specific business rules, and accesses both commercial and proprietary property databases. Its accuracy has been validated extensively on batches of properties by comparing its results to known sales prices. It is integrated with Countrywide's underwriting expert system and is currently being used by over thirty departments on a daily basis.

Problem Description

Countrywide is the nation's leading independent residential mortgage lender, currently funding over 50 thousand new loans a month and servicing mortgages for more than 1.7 million homes. Mortgage banking consists of three major activities: originating mortgages from borrowers or brokers, or purchasing mortgages from banks or credit unions; selling mortgages (usually as part of a large pool of loans) to secondary market investors; and servicing mortgages on behalf of the investors (collecting monthly mortgage payments, addressing requests to refinance or cancel mortgage insurance, and handling problems such as late payments and foreclosures).

At many stages in these processes an assessment of the market value of the property associated with a mortgage is of major importance. Market value is defined by federal financial institutions as:

> "... the most probable price a property should bring in a competitive and open market under all conditions requisite to a fair sale, the buyer and seller each acting prudently, knowledgeably, and assuming the price is not affected by undue stimulus."

Appraisals are the primary means for estimating the market value of properties. Traditionally conducted by certified appraisers using the market comparable approach, a few similar neighboring properties (comparables or "comps" for short) that have sold recently are used to estimate a property's market value. (The current discussion only concerns the valuation of residential single-unit homes; different appraisal techniques apply to investment, commercial and industrial properties.) Ideally the selected comparables should be identical to the subject property (model matches). However, such comparables are rarely available and therefore the appraiser adjusts for the differences, guided by accepted principles of appraising. In addition, the subject property is physically inspected and neighborhood trends evaluated. An appraisal thus formalizes the process knowledgeable homebuyers use when purchasing a home.

Accurate property valuation is difficult because no truly "objective value" exists. The purchase of a home is not a purely rational process. Both buyer and seller have limited information and are subject to personal taste and needs. For example, the number of bedrooms is of greater importance to homebuyers with children than to those without children. The price is also dependent on the negotiation skills of the parties involved. These and other factors cause the value of a property to have an inherent spread, in that repeated sales of the property under identical conditions would yield a distribution of prices. The standard deviation of this distribution has been estimated to be 5%-7% of the average value (Case & Shiller 1987).

The impact of property characteristics on value is also hard to quantify. Although values can be calculated by estimating construction costs plus land value (the "cost approach"), this method is unreliable and not often used. The most important characteristics of a transaction – the time frame of the sale and location of the property -- are so hard to quantify that they are factored out of the process entirely by considering only "recent neighboring" comps.

Appraisals can create a bottleneck in originating a mortgage and their manual nature makes them inappropriate for bulk transactions such as estimating the total market value of a portfolio of loans and data mining (e.g., to market products to borrowers with equity in their home).

Objectives of Automated Property Valuation

Although statisticians have studied the problem of automated property valuation for decades, only in the last few years has the advent of commercial property databases made implementation feasible.

The major goal is price reduction and improved speed, thereby creating a more efficient origination process for both borrower and lender. Automation also offers objectivity (by minimizing the individual taste of a particular

---

Copyright © 1998, American Association for Artificial Intelligence (www.aaai.org). All rights reserved.

buyer/seller or pressures on the appraiser) and consistency (by minimizing individual differences between appraisers).

However, there are issues and aspects of the appraisal process that automated systems will probably never be able to adequately address. Specifically:

- Property databases, usually derived from public records, cover only about half the country and can be incomplete and inaccurate.
- Available databases have no reliable information about the condition of properties. The fact that a property has been constructed, improved, or even destroyed may not be reflected in available databases.
- Other data (e.g., view) may be subjective or imprecise.
- Heterogeneous neighborhoods and unusual properties pose additional problems.

For these and other reasons it is neither appropriate nor desirable to eliminate human involvement from appraisals. Instead, the CAPES project provides an alternative property valuation method that can be used to complement manual appraisals or in situations where the advantage of a human appraisal is less significant (Eckert et al. 1993). Countrywide has a variety of property valuation needs and requires a system that supports a wide range of uses, from an interactive appraiser's assistant that can be tailored using expert knowledge of the neighborhood or subject property, to a fully automated expert system that can be used by novices or by a batch process. Depending on the other risk factors on the loan, a physical property inspection may still be required to double-check the accuracy of the data.

Approaches to Automated Property Valuation

All approaches follow the same basic strategy.

- Define a set of significant residential property features
- Collect information on these features for the subject and nearby properties
- Develop a model to estimate the expected sales price of the subject property based on the selected features
- Apply the model to the subject to compute a value, and preferably an estimate of confidence in the value

The approaches differ in the features defined as significant and the type of model used. At one extreme are "Home Price Index" models, using only sales prices and dates to calculate what amounts to the "average" price change in an area (zip code or county) over time (Case et al. 1991, Shiller 1991). Although this provides a useful "macro" model, it does not take into account improvement or deterioration of the subject over time and its accuracy decreases the older the previous sales date. Most models use additional property features, including: physical characteristics such as living and lot area, number of bedrooms and bathrooms, age, and presence of pool, garage, etc.; location identification such as street address, latitude and longitude, and census tract; and qualitative information such as view. Models that are based on property features are sometimes called hedonic. The property information usually comes from county assessors and recorders offices, cleaned up and repackaged by commercial vendors in electronically accessible databases. Another source is proprietary property and appraisal databases maintained by large lenders such as Countrywide.

Dimensions and volume of information distinguish human from automated valuation. Human appraisers (and homebuyers) perceive broad and detailed information, including such hard to quantify features as view, condition, "flow" and "appeal," from the visual inspection of only a few comparables. In contrast, automated systems can review hundreds of comparables but have access to only specific, limited information on each.

Linear Regression has long been applied to this problem, modeling price as a linear function of the property features and thereby automatically determining what adjustments should be made for differences in features. However, straightforward regression fails to consistently yield accurate results, as has been repeatedly reported in the literature (Murphy 1988). The set of properties that are available for the regression analysis often is too heterogeneous (Newsome & Zietz 1992) and the technique too sensitive to correlation between variables (for example, the numbers of bedrooms and bathrooms).

Non-Linear Regression and other variations on basic linear regression have been proposed (Do & Grudnitski 1992; Knight et al. 1993), but they involve additional assumptions or may require more input (Weirick & Ingram 1990).

Neural Networks are used by some systems (Jost et al. 1994). However, the unfeasibility of learning in real-time necessitates off-line learning, resulting in a macro model of neighborhoods, not individual properties.

Rules-based methods are a natural choice for this problem, because human appraisals are based on established principles and professional guidelines, such as the "Uniform Standards of Professional Appraisal Practice" (USPAP). Although an element of judgment is often involved, these rules can be applied in a principled manner that is well described in several texts (Betts & Ely 1994). Additional expertise can be drawn from interviewing professional appraisers. A final advantage of these methods over "black box" regression and Neural Network techniques, is that the declarative representation of rules can be used to explain why the result was obtained.

Application Description

Countrywide's overall computing infrastructure is a decentralized collection of personal computers and servers connected by local area and wide area networks.

CAPES is a client / server application implemented in MS Visual C++ and based on the Distributed Common Object Model (DCOM) (Grimes 1997). DCOM simplifies the implementation of client / server applications by allowing the creation of COM objects remotely on another machine. This architecture makes it possible to create a variety of clients served by the same server. In addition to the client

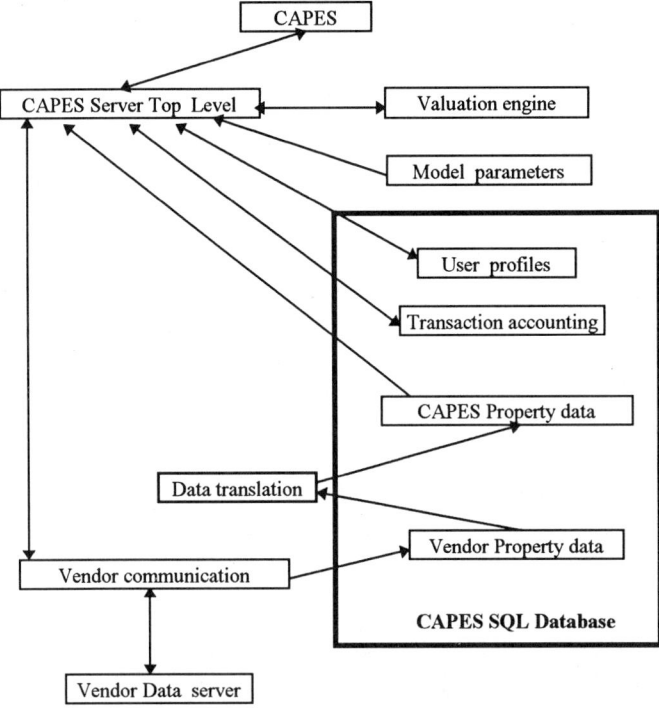

Figure 1: CAPES is a client/server system, where the server handles all communication with internal and external data sources.

described in this paper, there is a client that interfaces with CLUES (Talebzadeh et al. 1995) and another that makes CAPES available on the Internet/Intranet.

The CAPES server application runs as a service on a Windows NT 4.0 server and handles all users. The client application runs on the user machine, which may be running Windows NT 4.0 or Windows 95 (with a MS patch to support DCOM). The connection is normally made over a WAN, but can also be made via RAS.

The server application is connected via a telnet connection over a leased phone line to DataQuick, our main present property data supplier. All property data and most results from CAPES runs (including usage statistics, error logs, etc.) are permanently stored in an SQL database. The client applications have no direct connection to the database or to the data suppliers.

In general CAPES is designed from the ground up in an object oriented style, using derived and template classes, virtual functions, etc. The data representations are defined by classes. Much of the computation is performed by creating objects of specific classes, which encapsulate the input data, the computation or reasoning, and the result.

CAPES also uses the C++ Standard Template Library (STL) (Stepanov & Lee 1995), a general-purpose library of generic data structures (such as lists and maps) and operations (such as insertion of elements and sorting). STL makes programming more productive by handling memory management and providing a framework for decomposing many programming problems.

CAPES client

The client application receives and displays all information on the subject property, control information from the user, and qualitative and quantitative information, including the estimated value with uncertainty and status information.

The client user interface is implemented using MS Foundation Classes (MFC) and third party OCX controls. The client is a Multi Document Interface (MDI), where each subject property is assigned a separate window (Figure 2) consisting of five tabbed child windows (Subject, Results, Comp Selection, Market Analyses, and Messages). Each tab provides specific user interface features.

CAPES allows a large degree of flexibility in the level of control and expertise required from the user. It begins by performing an automatic evaluation that requires minimal input and direction from the user. This mode is convenient and suitable for users without in-depth knowledge of appraisal methodology. Then, depending on the estimated uncertainty of the results, or for other reasons, users can:

- Edit the information on the subject property and control the selection of comps in detail
- Evaluate the result based on detailed quantitative and qualitative output
- Iteratively repeat this process and compare the results

To start an evaluation, users must uniquely identify the subject property, usually by specifying the street number, name, and zip code, as shown in the upper part of Figure 2. When the Find Subject button is selected CAPES searches the data source for matching property data and, if found, displays it on two lines, as seen in the middle of Figure 2. The lower line is the data retrieved from the data source while the upper line is the data actually used in the evaluation. The data used by CAPES is, by default, equal to the data retrieved, but the user can edit any incorrect information on the upper line. In the figure the user has changed the number of bathrooms from 1.70 (i.e. 1¾) to 2.00. These lines scroll horizontally and contain additional characteristics.

When satisfied that the right property has been found and that its characteristics are as accurate as possible, the user starts the evaluation by selecting the Compute button. CAPES attempts to find comparable properties and performs the steps of the automated evaluation (described below). The result is displayed on the bottom line and includes: the estimated value; a measure of uncertainty, expressed as a percentage of the value; the number of comps

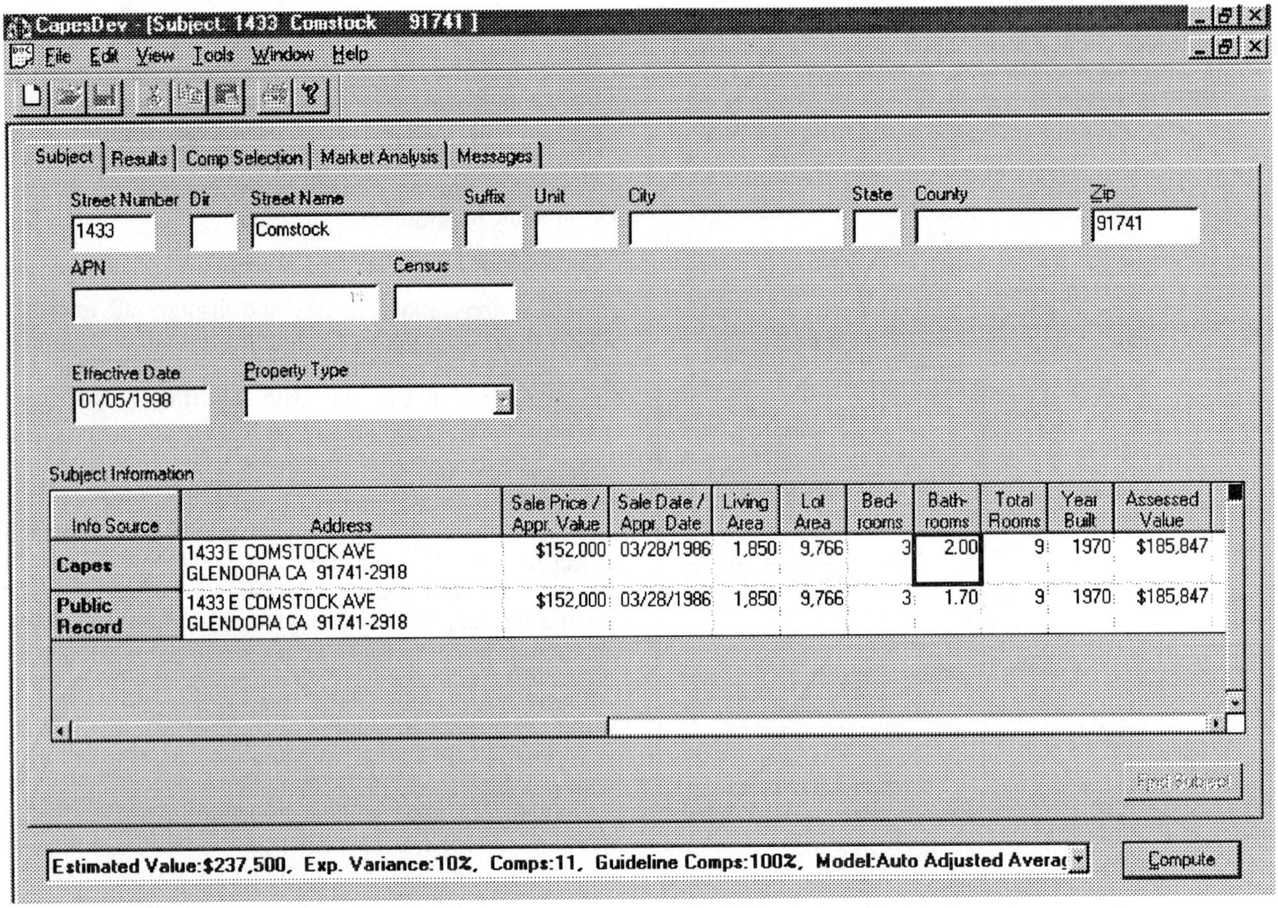

Figure 2: An automatic CAPES appraisal only requires minimal property identification input

used; the percentage of the comps that meet guidelines defined by the major funding agencies; and the model used to make the estimate. (The guidelines for comps apply to traditional appraisals, which may include as few as two comps. When CAPES uses many more comps, they are not all required to meet these guidelines.)

Expert users with detailed knowledge of the appraising process, or perhaps of the subject property or area, may further customize the evaluation using the functionality implemented on the remaining tabs.

- The Comp Selection tab initially displays the filters selected by CAPES and a collection of statistics on the current comp set. A filter is a parameterized operator to subset collections of properties. Many simply choose an interval for a feature, e.g. 2-3 bedrooms.

  Using the selected filters and statistics as a guide, users may modify (completely or in part) the set of filters that determine the selection of comps. This is the most important control action available to users.

- The Market Analysis tab displays the comp set in a tabular format similar to the display of subject characteristics shown in Figure 2. Expert users may eliminate any comp from the comp set.

- The Results tab displays the results of all applied valuation models. It also contains other qualitative and quantitative information to help expert users judge the reliability of the estimated value. For example, if the comp set is biased because most comps are either more or less valuable than the subject, a warning message displays on the Results tab. In most such cases no value is displayed on the bottom line.

- The Messages tab displays error and other miscellaneous messages that may be of interest to expert users. All users are alerted to serious failures, such as the failure to find subject or comp data, through pop-up windows.

A batch facility utilizing the automatic mode is also available. Users insert property identification data in a template table stored in a file. The file is read by CAPES and the properties evaluated one by one. When the evaluation is complete, results are reported in a file merging the original input with a number of columns holding the corresponding results. Once started this batch mode runs unattended, making it easy to evaluate portfolios of properties.

CAPES server

The server top level provides the methods available to clients and controls the interaction with clients. It also coordinates finding subject and comp information and invoking the valuation engine.

CAPES Valuation Engine

The valuation engine uses available information on the subject property and a relatively large set of property sales. If possible, more than 150 comparable sales are retrieved from a commercial data vendor. The only restrictions on this initial set are that they must be fairly recent full value sales within a reasonable distance of the subject property.

To achieve a valuation with a low uncertainty it is usually necessary to reduce the set of comps by applying one or more filters. CAPES automatically selects a set of filters.

Given a set of comps, the value of the subject is estimated by several models. These models include regression and other models based on statistical analysis, as well as an adjustment model which seeks to follow the practices of appraisers. Regional home price indices are also used when historic sales price and date information is available. These models are described in some detail in the next section.

An important issue is that information is often missing for the subject or one or more comps. Missing information is treated as a special value, rather than as zero or some other default value, and the models are designed to accommodate this.

The result of each model is checked against a set of constraints to ensure that a lack of information (or some other reason) does not produce an invalid value. The uncertainty in each model result is estimated as the standard deviation in the subject property value. The model with the lowest estimated uncertainty that also satisfies the checks is returned as the estimated value. If no model satisfies the constraints, no value is returned to the user.

Model parameters

Some details of the valuation models are controlled by model parameters defined in the code or the database. The most important model parameters are adjustments for property features. An adjustment parameter assigns a dollar value to a feature (e.g., a bathroom might be worth $1,000) based on expert knowledge. Adjustments are collected in tables and are differentiated by criteria such as price tiers and property types.

User profiles

Access to CAPES is controlled by the user's network logon. A user table in the database grants privileges ranging from no access to full access, and also contains contact and cost accounting information.

Transaction accounting

To monitor the use of CAPES and any errors that may occur, and to allow CAPES results to be reconstructed, each transaction, along with all data and results, is logged in the database.

CAPES property data and translation

CAPES stores the raw property data from vendors and internal sources verbatim and translates from these formats into a single internal format that is used by the valuation engine A translation module implements the semantics required to interpret the various representations and conventions of these data sources.

Vendor communication

Communication with the data vendor is via a telnet connection over a leased phone line.

Reasoning about property evaluation

The main inference techniques used in CAPES are described in this section.

Statistical models

The median or average value of the filtered comp set is sometimes the best model of value. Statistics based on other sets, such as the neighborhood or the nearest neighbors, are also of interest.

Regression model

The regression model performs a linear regression of the sales prices in the set of comparable properties. Property characteristics are used as independent parameters and the regression function is used to model the value of the subject property. It is implemented with the singular value decomposition method, which is robust against missing and redundant data. (Press et al. 1992, Jefferys 1980,1981; Lybanon 1984)

Adjustment model

The adjustment model seeks to follow the practices of appraisers. The known sales prices of a set of comparables are adjusted based on differences in the characteristics of the subject and each comparable property. The average of the adjusted sales prices is the value estimated by the adjustment model.

Home price indices

Price indices are constructed by reviewing repeated sales of properties and calculating an index value for a point in time. Given the sales price of a property at a specific time, the value at any other time (within the period for which the index is valid) can be computed by multiplying the original sales price by the ratio of the index values. To improve the accuracy a collection of indices is used, with different indices for different property types, price tiers, and areas.

Best first search

CAPES differs from other property valuation systems by using heuristic search as the core of the evaluation engine.

The main principle of appraising is to select a set of

"comparable" properties that have recently sold in so-called "arms length" transactions. If the concept of comparable property was well defined, and if sufficient information to identify comparable properties was always available, there would be no need to search. The only thing needed would be a set of rules, or constraints, to classify comps as suitable or unsuitable for a specific appraisal.

However, experience shows that when a fixed set of criteria are applied, in many cases either a too small or an unnecessarily large set of comparables is selected. (A comp set can be too large in the sense that a more accurate evaluation can be obtained from a smaller, more carefully selected set of comps.) Further reducing the usefulness of fixed criteria is the uncertainty of the information on the subject and comparable properties. Several characteristics, such as the condition of the property, are not captured in the public records, while other information (on the subject or one or more comps) may be missing or simply wrong.

This situation suggests searching for a set of comparables that optimizes the accuracy of an appraisal based on that set. If an initial set of N recent transactions in the subject neighborhood is chosen, the search space of all subsets is of the order of 2^N. For example, recent transactions in the neighborhood could mean all transactions in the last 12 months within a radius of one half mile from the subject. In a typical suburban area this would often include more than 100 potential comparables. The corresponding search space of subsets is too large to search exhaustively; fortunately, as explained below, an exhaustive search is not necessary or desirable.

The goal of the search is to minimize the error in the estimated value of the subject property. Because the true error is not known, the search must be guided by an estimate of the error, such as the standard deviation of the sales prices of the comp set. However, this evaluation function tends toward over-fitting. That is, the search finds a set of properties that happen to have a small range of sales prices (and therefore generate a low error estimate) but aren't otherwise particularly suitable as comps.

The operators in the search select a subset of a given set and are therefore called filters. By using filters that systematically generate all the subsets of the initial set, an exhaustive search has an overwhelming risk of over-fitting. To reduce the complexity and minimize the problem of over-fitting we only use search operators that are heuristically well motivated.

A heuristic property filter excludes properties from the comp set based on rules known by appraisers to be useful. Such rules generally focus on property characteristics. For example, assume the subject has three bedrooms and the comp set contains properties with either three or four bedrooms. Heuristic filtering based on the number of bedrooms would yield only two nodes: the original set and the subset with exactly three bedrooms. Other filters (based on the number of bathrooms, living area, etc.) typically generate additional nodes. However, the number of nodes is reduced by dependencies among the operators. For example, applying a filter limiting the living area to ± 10% difference from the subject frequently yields a subset with all remaining comparables having the same number of bedrooms. In this case, applying the bedroom filter doesn't produce a new node.

Heuristic filtering reduces the search space dramatically. If there are 10 commuting filters, the search space is now at most on the order of 2^{10} nodes. The number of nodes generated is also limited by the Best-First search, which is well described elsewhere (Rich 1983). Furthermore, because of the inherent spread in a property's value, nothing is gained by continuing the search when a node with an error estimate below some level (e.g. 5%) is found. Finally, experimentation shows that the search can be limited to a fairly small number of nodes (e.g., 100) without increasing the average real error. As explained above, the risk of over-fitting out weighs the advantage of generating more nodes.

Outlier detection and removal

The inherent spread of property prices, and the fact that the properties in a comp set are not identical, implies that the prices in a comp set is a statistical distribution. It's reasonable to assume that this is approximately a normal distribution. However, one frequently observes sales prices that are many standard deviations away from the average. There are many possible reasons for anomalous sales prices, such as a distressed sale, a sale within a family, or extraordinary features that reduce or increase the property's value. Such data points are often called outliers (Barnett & Lewis 1995). CAPES uses statistical criteria to remove comps that are outliers in price and other selected characteristics.

Uncertainty model

An important part of CAPES is the attempt to estimate the standard deviation in the estimated value. This modeling of uncertainty is based on statistical principles and including contributions from different sources of uncertainty, such as differences between subject and comps or missing information.

Incomplete information

The information on the subject and comparable properties is frequently incomplete. Almost any attribute can be randomly or systematically missing. Examples of systematically missing information are the availability of total number of rooms and number of bedrooms. In some areas both attributes are provided, while in other areas only one or neither are provided. CAPES doesn't presently utilize knowledge about such systematic differences; instead, all missing values are represented as special values (distinct from valid values) and treated appropriately. For example if the number of bedrooms is missing for the subject, no adjustments are made for the comps based on number of bedrooms. This approach has the advantage of being robust against randomly missing information while avoiding the overhead of maintaining a knowledge base of regional differences in data availability.

Constraint reasoning

A critical part of the valuation process is critique of the model results. There are many rules that can be applied to a model's results to determine weather the result is reliable or if it is more or less accurate than the results of other models. These rules are either heuristic or statistical, and are expressed in CAPES as constraints, using a simple constraint propagation system (Tsang 1993) which finds the subset of model valuations satisfying all constraints. If more than one model remains, the one with the lowest uncertainty estimate is chosen. If no model remain, a failure is reported.

Application Development and Deployment

Since its creation in late 1991 the Countrywide AI department has developed a number of applications (Stobie 1996). A study of selected automated property valuation systems was done in 1995. No system allowed the degree of control that our expert users require or allowed us to use company-specific expertise, rules of business, and proprietary appraisal databases. After deciding that no commercial system met Countrywide's broader needs the CAPES project was initiated in February 1996. By July 1996 a prototype demonstrating the feasibility of the project had been developed and received the support of senior management. It focused on the core AI problem of computing a property's value from a set of comps, using a simple user interface and commercially available data.

A full-scale development effort took place to implement a client / server architecture, access remote and internal databases, and create a user-interface powerful enough to support the functions required of an appraiser's assistant. In parallel, the AI and statistical models were continually refined based on ongoing knowledge acquisition and experience of using the system. In May 1997 the roll out of CAPES began and has since been deployed to a growing number of departments. A User's Manual and periodic training sessions adequately prepare users for CAPES, while the developers themselves support the product via telephone and e-mail. In October 1997 CAPES was formally demonstrated at the Mortgage Banking Association conference in New York city.

Object-oriented design and analysis together with rapid prototyping was used to develop CAPES. Each time a change to the core valuation engine is proposed, it is implemented as quickly as possible and a batch test run to determine the effect of the change on the accuracy and coverage of the system.

- Accuracy is measured by how closely the estimated values compare to the known sales prices, according to average error, average absolute error, maximum error, and distribution of errors. Comparison to the subject sales price is not a perfect benchmark (because of the occasional forced sale or other non-arms-length transaction), but we believe it is the best available.
- Coverage is measured by how often a subject property is found and a final result produced.

The fact that all CAPES runs are archived in a database allows re-running batch tests of thousands of properties in minutes, generating statistics on the results, and judging whether the changes have been implemented correctly and have improved performance. We are also benchmarking CAPES against other valuation systems, as opportunities arise.

Application Use and Payoff

CAPES is used by over 30 departments at Countrywide, many on a daily basis. The marginal cost of a CAPES valuation (costing only a few dollars and taking only a few minutes) makes it practical for a wide variety of applications.

- CAPES is used to analyze the collateral value of a portfolio of loans purchased from a smaller bank as part of the "due diligence" process. Because CAPES is statistically nearly unbiased, its average signed error is close to zero—the over-estimates cancel out the under-estimates. By randomly sampling a subset of the portfolio of loans in regions covered by our property databases and running the properties through CAPES, a quick and reliable total value of the portfolio can be obtained. Since these properties have already been appraised, this also facilitates a focused quality control procedure: loans where the appraised value differs greatly from the CAPES value are carefully reviewed.
- This use of CAPES to review appraisals is also applied by the Quality Control, Internal Audit, and other departments.
- The Foreclosure department uses CAPES to estimate the potential loss (the difference between the estimated property value and the balance of the loan) incurred when a loan defaults.
- Once a loan has been foreclosed and the property belongs to Countrywide, the Real Estate Management department uses CAPES as an aid to determine a reasonable sales price.

The challenge to using CAPES for loan origination is that most investors (to whom we deliver the loans) have not yet approved automated valuation as an acceptable appraisal method.

Integrating CAPES (automated property valuations) and CLUES (automated credit underwriting) potentially increases the accuracy of both systems. For example, CLUES verifies that the comparables used by the appraiser are within a reasonable distance of the subject, that they are not all more or less expensive than the subject, and that the adjustments are not excessively high. CAPES enhances CLUES by verifying the accuracy of the subject and comps used in the appraisal, and providing a second, independent estimate of value.

Speed is of the essence in today's competitive mortgage lending business and automation is a major success factor. With CLUES analyzing the credit history and financial ability of the borrowers to repay the mortgage and CAPES evaluating the collateral, AI at Countrywide provides a quick, inexpensive, and increasingly accurate "streamlined" approval of low-risk loans. Countrywide is considering offering this capability directly to customers, for example over the Internet.

Maintenance and Planned Enhancements

The CAPES development team continues to maintain and enhance the system. Weekly meetings with experts address issues based on feedback from the large user base and new industry directions. The near monthly release of enhanced versions of the software is greatly facilitated by the use of object-oriented design, cleanly separated modules, and declarative rules.

Several enhancements are planned, including more sophisticated spatial reasoning using location of the subject and maps. For example, it is currently quite possible that nearby properties are chosen as comps when in fact they are from an adjacent, but very different neighborhood.

Additional data sources are required to achieve higher coverage and more detailed and accurate data. To permit valuations in less than a second, it is imperative to install these databases locally at Countrywide, rather than accessing them remotely via a leased line. This opens the door to using CAPES for data mining applications, such as identifying candidates from Countrywide's portfolio of 1.7 million loans that may benefit from refinance or are in danger of foreclosure. Data mining techniques could also automate some of the knowledge acquisition, such as empirically determining the value for adjustments. For example, the value of a swimming pool in a specific neighborhood (perhaps as a function of other features) can probably be derived by comparing a number of properties in that neighborhood

References

Barnett, V. and Lewis, T. 1995, *Outliers in statistical Data*, John Wiley & Sons.

Betts, R.M. and Ely, S.J. 1994. *Basic Real Estate Appraisal*. 3rd edition, Prentice-Hall.

Case, K.E., Bradford, Pollakowski, H., and Wacter, S., 1991. On choosing among house price index methodologies. *AREUEA Journal*, 1991:19, 286-307.

Case, K.E., and Shiller, R..J. 1987, Prices of Single Family Homes since 1970: New indexes for Four Cities. *New England Economic Review*, 1987, 45-56.

Do, H and Grudnitski. 1992. A Neural Network Approach to Residential Property Appraisal. *The Real Estate Appraiser* December 1992:38-45.

Eckert, J.K., O'Connor, P.M. and Chamberlain, C. Computer-Assisted Real Estate Appraisal: A California Savings and Loan Case Study. *The Appraisal Journal*, October 1993:524-532.

Grimes, R., 1997. *Professional DCOM programming*, Wrox Press Ltd.

Jefferys, W.H. 1980. On the method of least squares. 1980,1981 *The Astronomical Journal* 85(2):177-181 and 86(1):149-155. Errata 95(4).

Jost, A., Nelson J., Gophinatan, K., Smith C., Real estate appraisal using predictive modeling. U.S. Patent 5,361,201, Nov 1, 1994.

Knight, J.R., Hill R.C. and Sirmans, C.F. 1993. Stein Rule Estimation in Real Estate Appraisal. *The Appraisal Journal*, October 1993:539-544.

Lybanon. M. 1984. A better least-square method when both variables have uncertainties. *Am. Journal of Phys.* 52(1):22-26.

Murphy L.T. III. 1989. Determining the Appropriate Equation in Multiple Regression Analysis. *The Appraisal Journal*, October 1989:498-517.

Newsome, B. A. and Zietz, J. 1992. Adjusting Comparable Sales Using Multiple Regression Analysis – The Need for Segmentation. *The Appraisal J.*, January 1992: 129-135.

Press W.H. Teukolsky S.A., Vetterling W.T. and Flannery, B.P. 1992. *Numerical Recipes in FORTRAN*. 2nd edition, Cambridge University Press.

Rich, E., 1983. *Artificial Intelligence*, pp. 78, McGraw-Hill.

Shiller, R..J. 1991. Arithmetic repeat sales price estimators. *Journal of Housing Economics*, 1991:1, 110-126.

Stepanov, A.A. and Lee, M., 1995. The Standard Template Library, Hewlett-Packard Technical Report, HPL-94-34, revised 1995.

Stobie, I., Artificial Intelligence at Countrywide, Proceedings of Wescon/96:468-472.

Talebzadeh, H., Mandutianu, S., Winner, C. F., Countrywide Loan Underwriting Expert System, AI Magazine, Volume 16, No. 1, 51-64, Spring 1995

Tsang, E., 1993. *Foundations of Constraint Satisfaction*, Academic Press.

Weirick W.N. and Ingram F.J. 1990. Functional Form Choice in Applied Real Estate Analysis. *The Appraisal Journal*, January 1990:57-73.

Automated Intelligent Pilots for Combat Flight Simulation

Randolph M. Jones, John E. Laird, and Paul E. Nielsen

Artificial Intelligence Laboratory
University of Michigan
1101 Beal Avenue
Ann Arbor, MI 48109-2110
{rjones, laird, nielsen}@umich.edu

Abstract

TacAir-Soar is an intelligent, rule-based system that generates believable "human-like" behavior for military simulations. The innovation of the application is primarily a matter of scale and integration. The system is capable of executing most of the airborne missions that the United States military flies in fixed-wing aircraft. It accomplishes this by integrating a wide variety of intelligent capabilities, including reasoning about interacting goals, reacting to rapid changes in real time (or faster), communicating and coordinating with other agents (including humans), maintaining situational awareness, and accepting new orders while in flight. The system is currently deployed at the Oceana Naval Air Station WISSARD, and its most dramatic use to date was in the Synthetic Theater Of War 1997, an operational training exercise consisting of 48 straight hours and approximately 700 fixed-wing aircraft flights, all flown by instances of the TacAir-Soar system.

In 1992 we began development of a software system that emulates the behavior of military personnel performing missions in fixed-wing aircraft (Tambe et al, 1995). The general goal is to generate behavior that "looks human", when viewed by a training audience participating in operational military exercises. The resulting rule-based system, called TacAir-Soar, is currently deployed at the WISSARD training facility in the Oceana Naval Air Station, which is administered by BMH Associates, a collection of active and retired military aviators who also served as our primary sources of subject-matter expertise. As the system has developed, it has taken part in a number of tests, technology demonstrations, and operational training exercises. Its most dramatic use to date was in the Synthetic Theater Of War 1997 (STOW '97)/United Endeavor Advanced Concept Technology Demonstration, held at the end of October, 1997. STOW '97 was an operational training exercise consisting of 48 straight hours and approximately 700 fixed-wing aircraft flights, all flown by instances of the TacAir-Soar system.

TacAir-Soar relies on mature intelligent systems technology, including a rule-based, hierarchical representation of goals and situation descriptions. The innovation of the system lies in the large-scale integration of a number of intelligent capabilities in a complex domain. The system does not just model a small set of tasks pertinent to military fixed-wing missions; it generates appropriate behavior for *every* such mission routinely used by the the US Navy, Air Force, and Marines; the UK Royal Air Force; and "opponent forces" in full-scale exercises. In addition to reasoning about complex sets of goals, the system coördinates and communicates with humans and other automated entities. The system must generate its behavior in real time (and sometimes faster). It must also integrate seamlessly into current military training exercises, and be able to cover unanticipated situations, so it does not interrupt the flow of training. Finally, all of the task requirements are set by existing military needs, and we were thus not able to tailor or simplify the domain to suit our purposes.

Simulated Tactical Air Combat

The application domain for TacAir-Soar is military training simulations. The United States military uses a wide range of tools to create simulated training environments. These include networked manned simulators for various vehicles (such as tanks, fighters, and bombers); digitized maps of world-wide terrain; software systems to simulate the dynamics of vehicles, weapons, and sensors; technology to link real soldiers and vehicles into a virtual environment; and software systems to simulate the results of interactions between various participants (human and automated) in the simulation.

The military uses simulation environments because they are cheaper, more flexible, and safer than live training maneuvers. Such training is particularly important in the post-cold war era, with general reductions in the defense budget. The tradeoff is that the military wants to "train as they fight". The concern is that some aspects of current simulation environments are not realistic enough to provide effective training.

Our task was to improve the behavior of individual, automated entities participating in simulation ex-

---

[0]Copyright (c) 1998, American Association for Artificial Intelligence (www.aaai.org). All rights reserved.

ercises. Before TacAir-Soar was developed, the state of the art for entity-level behavior used software systems called Semi-Automated Forces (SAFORs). SAFORs consist of high-fidelity models of vehicle dynamics (for example, using differential equations to model the control surfaces of an aircraft) together with relatively simple automated behaviors for controlling the vehicle, using finite-state machines. For example, a SAFOR aircraft can be told to circle a particular point at a certain altitude. Similarly, it can be told to shoot its air-to-air missiles at any airborne target that is detected within a specific "commit" range by its simulated radar. However, a human controller makes tactical decisions and uses a graphical tool to give the SAFOR new orders. The number of SAFORs that a single human can control depends on the type of platform being simulated, the expertise of the controller, the desired fidelity of the simulation, and other factors. In any event, a number of highly trained humans are required to oversee and adjust the runtime behavior of such entities. Aside from the expense of having humans in the loop, realism of the simulation suffers when these controllers must devote close attention to more than one entity at a time. There is a desire to increase the quality and autonomy of force behavior in order to increase realism and decrease the cost of training. To complicate matters further, there are additional goals to run as many forces on a single machine as possible, and to be able to run the simulation faster than real time for some applications.

In response, DARPA funded a project to create Intelligent Forces (IFORs), to use intelligent systems technology to develop autonomous systems that generate "human-like" behavior. Our group at the University of Michigan (plus researchers at the University of Southern California Information Sciences Institute, and Carnegie Mellon University) created a prototype system to generate behaviors for a small number of air-to-air missions (Tambe et al., 1995). The initial work combined the efforts of two university professors, two research scientists, and two programmers, with the research scientists working full time on the implementation of intelligent behaviors, and the programmers working full time on maintaining the software architecture, infrastructure, and interfaces. Two years into the project the groups divided, with the ISI group focusing on behaviors for missions flown by rotary-wing aircraft (Hill et al., 1997). Our group at UM hired an additional research scientist and programmer, and continued the work on fixed-wing aircraft with a team of five. This effort led to the development and deployment of TacAir-Soar. The currently deployed version of the system was completed in October, 1997.

The Simulation Environment

Before describing the details of the system that implements behavior for tactical combat simulations, it is worth discussing the details of the environment in which the system operates. We have already presented a general overview of military simulations. This section focuses on the details of the simulation structure with which TacAir-Soar currently interacts.

The core of the simulation environment is a network attached to a number of simulation systems (see Figure 1). Some systems are manned vehicle simulators (for tanks, aircraft, etc.). Some are real vehicles, equipped with hardware and software to interface with the simulation network. Finally, some are workstations running software to simulate various types of vehicles and human forces. STOW '97 did not include the participation of real vehicles or manned simulators, but they have been part of other tests and exercises in which TacAir-Soar was used.

In this simulation environment, each workstation maintains its own copy of fixed aspects of the environment (such as a detailed terrain database). Individual machines simulate the entities and changeable environmental features. In addition, each station predicts position information for other entities, reckoning from the last known entity state vector. Each workstation broadcasts new information on the network when it is simulating an entity that undergoes a change in state that cannot be predicted by the other machines (like a change in heading or velocity). Any other station on the network can use the new information to change its local knowledge of the entity, and then detect possible interactions between entities or with environmental features. Some of the distributed machines are devoted to special-purpose needs. For example, ordnance servers exclusively simulate the dynamics of guided weapons. Weather servers simulate meteorological features, sometimes using information from live feeds in the area of the world in which the simulation takes place.

TacAir-Soar runs within a simulation system called ModSAF (Calder et al., 1993). The ModSAF program provides realistic simulation of a large variety of military vehicles (including fixed-wing aircraft), weapons systems, and sensors. The system also provides a graphical interface for creating and controlling SAFORs, but this portion of ModSAF was not used by TacAir-Soar. Rather, we used additional code, called the Soar-ModSAF Interface (SMI; Schwamb, Koss, & Keirsey, 1994), to translate simulated sensor and vehicle information into the symbolic representation used by Soar and to translate Soar's action representation into ModSAF function calls (e.g., to control the vehicle and to manipulate weapons, sensors, and radios). We designed the SMI to provide a realistic interface to TacAir-Soar agents. That is, the SMI only passes to TacAir-Soar information that a real pilot would normally receive in a similar situation via cockpit readouts, the radar screen, visually, etc. Likewise, TacAir-Soar can only send commands to the interface that map onto the types of controls that real pilots have to fly the aircraft, employ weapons, manipulate sensors, and communicate. Each "instance" of TacAir-Soar controls a single entity.

We maintain a strong distinction between the code that generates intelligent behavior and the code that simulates physical systems. This distinction is not al-

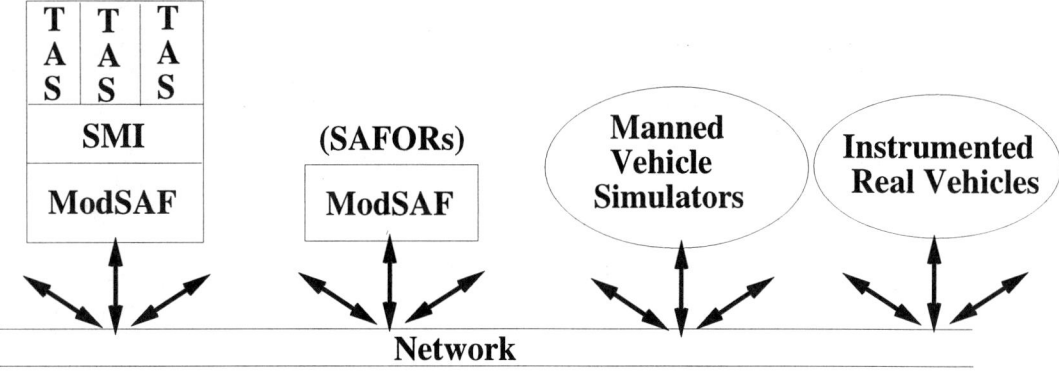

Figure 1: TacAir-Soar's niche in the simulation environment.

ways made in the development of SAFORs, but we found that it eased development, knowledge acquisition, and verification. This design will also ease the transition of TacAir-Soar to other simulation platforms. In the current deployment, ModSAF performs the simulation of the physical world; TacAir-Soar represents the mind that senses, reasons, and creates intentions; and the SMI represents an idealization of the perceptual-motor processes that allow the mind to interact with the world. We have also developed additional tools to translate orders from existing military tools into mission specifications for TacAir-Soar (Coulter & Laird, 1996; Kenny et al., 1998), and for commanders to update an entity's orders dynamically during execution (Jones, 1998). These tools allow us to present TacAir-Soar to the training audience as a "seamless" participant in the overall exercise. Laird et al. (1998) provide a more thorough discussion of this integration.

The TacAir-Soar System

TacAir-Soar is a rule-based system, built within the Soar architecture for cognition (Laird, Newell, & Rosenbloom, 1991). Soar uses production rules as the basic unit of long-term knowledge (or the "program"). Soar also provides architectural support for objects called "operators" and "goals". Each operator and goal can be viewed as a grouping of one or more production rules. TacAir-Soar currently contains approximately 5200 production rules, organized into about 450 operators and 130 goals. The rules represent the sum total of the system's knowledge about all of the missions it can fly. Each agent loads all of the rules, but does not usually use them all over the course of a single mission. There are significant numbers of general rules that are used in many different missions, and some rules that only apply in very specific situations.

Operators in Soar generally represent discrete, relatively fine-grained steps in a chain of reasoning. In the tactical air domain, some example operators are "Determine the identity of a radar blip", "Select a missile to fire", "Push the fire button", and "Set the aircraft to fly a particular heading". Unlike many other production system architectures, Soar requires a uniform representation for both selecting which operator to execute and implementing its functions. All production systems use the conditions of rules to determine candidate operators, but when there are multiple candidates many architectures use a fixed, implicit algorithm for selecting between the candidates, and then explicitly execute a list of operator actions. In contrast, Soar systems use rules to suggest choices between the candidate operators, and then use more rules to execute the set of actions for each operator. Thus, individual rules comprise a set of fairly simple conjunctive conditions (that are efficient to match) plus a set of discrete actions. However, these rules can fire in parallel and in sequence in order to implement complex conditional or iterative actions for each operator.

In our representation, explicit goals are a proper subset of operators. The Soar architecture generates a new goal structure when an operator takes more than a small, discrete unit of time (one *decision cycle*, in Soar parlance) to execute. The new goal provides a context for the system to apply more operators. For example, one of TacAir-Soar's operators is "Intercept an aircraft". This is not a discrete action that the system can "just do", so Soar creates a new goal structure. In the context of the new goal, the system proposes additional operators, such as "Achieve proximity to the aircraft", "Lock my radar on the aircraft", or "Employ weapons against the aircraft". The Soar architecture strongly supports hierarchical reasoning and execution, which is one of the reasons we used it. This support turned out to be important for a number of reasons. Hierarchical reasoning and execution directly address the requirements of the task.

The Advantages of Execution Hierarchies

One obvious advantage to a hierarchical knowledge representation is that the military structures nearly everything it does hierarchically. In particular, command and control hierarchies delegate different tasks to different levels of forces. Even small groups of 2 or 4 aircraft use a hierarchical command structure. One of TacAir-Soar's requirements is to interact with other forces within the command structure, so it is clear that the system must reason about and with hierarchies for at least part of its behavior. In the interests of a uniform integration, we extended the hierarchy into all of the reasoning that the system performs. In addition to interacting with others, this includes breaking personal goals into further decomposable subgoals and actions. Additionally, a hierarchical representation enhances the extendibility and maintainability of the system, by allowing us to compartmentalize knowledge, so it can be reused across appropriate contexts.

The hierarchical representation is also important to flexibly using default behaviors. When we began the TacAir-Soar project, our attitude was that we would not (initially) build a "complete" agent. The entire domain of tactical air combat is certainly huge, so we expected to spell out clearly which subset our system would address, and engineer the knowledge necessary to support those behaviors. While this initial assumption has held to some extent, it eventually became clear that we needed much broader coverage of behavior. The training audience (the military commanders and soldiers interacting with the simulation) found it unacceptable for a simulated entity not to do *something* in response to any situation, even if the behavior was not 100% correct, and even if our subject-matter experts had decided those situations were not worth our effort. This suggested a need for TacAir-Soar to include default behaviors, in order to perform reasonably in those situations for which we had not specifically engineered knowledge. The hierarchical representation of knowledge made it possible to create default actions for different levels of goals. Thus, rather than having only one or two brittle default behaviors, the defaults are sensitive to different types of situations and goals, so the system will generally do something reasonable.

As an example, when the system is trying to employ weapons against a target, there are many different tactics and flight patterns to use, based on the current situation. However, a generally good default action is to fly a collision course to the target, in order to approach it as rapidly as possible. In contrast, once the system has maneuvered the target into weapons range, its next action (a subgoal of employing weapons) is to fire a missile at the target. Once again, there are certain good actions to take in order to get off the best shot possible. But if something goes wrong, in this case a good default action is to point straight at the target (rather than flying a collision course). Thus, the appropriate default behaviors are dependent on the current reasoning context imposed by the knowledge hierarchy.

Opportunistic Operators

At execution time, the goal hierarchy generates top down. Most of the time every TacAir-Soar agent has one general active goal, called Execute-Mission. Depending on the mission type and the current situation, the agent will select one of a number of subgoals, including Fly-Route, Intercept-Target, or Follow-Leader. These in turn will have subgoals. Depending on the situation, the system creates more specific goals until it reaches a level where it can manipulate the environment directly, such as to issue a command to fly the aircraft to a new heading or altitude.

There are also a number of important actions that do not fit nicely into a strict goal hierarchy. These include relatively context-insensitive actions, such as "Determine threat of unknown contacts", and actions in the service of sweeping, general goals, such as "Evade a missile", which serves the general goal of survival. Operators for these actions are not part of the explicit goal hierarchy. Rather, they are represented as *opportunistic* operators, which can be selected independently of the currently active, explicit goals. This mixture of goal-driven and opportunistic behaviors is crucial to capturing the ways in which humans interleave complex sequences of actions in the service of multiple goals (Jones et al., 1994).

Situation-Representation Hierarchy

These two classes of operators play key roles in generating the rich variety of behaviors required by the task. In each case, operators and goals activate at execution time based on the current *situation*. This raises the question of how that situation is represented. Certainly, one important part of the agent's situation is the current set of active goals. A great deal of the situation is also provided by symbols describing the current state of the external environment, as seen through the vehicle's sensors. This is where a second representational hierarchy comes into play.

There are usually a number of different ways to describe an air combat situation, based on the different types of decisions that need to be made. Consider the case where an aircraft has a potential target contact on its radar screen. In some cases, it is important to reason about the heading or bearing of the contact. In others, it is important to notice whether the target is flying to the left or the right (which can be computed from a combination of the target's heading and the agent's heading). It is also often important to reason about the target's position relative to other contacts that may be flying with the target. In general, it is difficult to restrict the agent to reasoning about the primitive attributes that describe the situation. It is preferable to combine these attributes based on the current context, in order to make different types of decisions.

Thus, many of TacAir-Soar's rules are not associated directly with an operator. They are instead part of a data-driven, situation-interpretation hierarchy, which generates descriptions of the situation from the bottom up. The benefits of the interaction between the top-down and bottom-up hierarchies are illustrated by the example shown in Figures 2 and 3. Assume Figure 2 describes an agent's current "mental state" at some point in time. The boxes represent a subset of the agent's active goals, and the other items are a subset of the

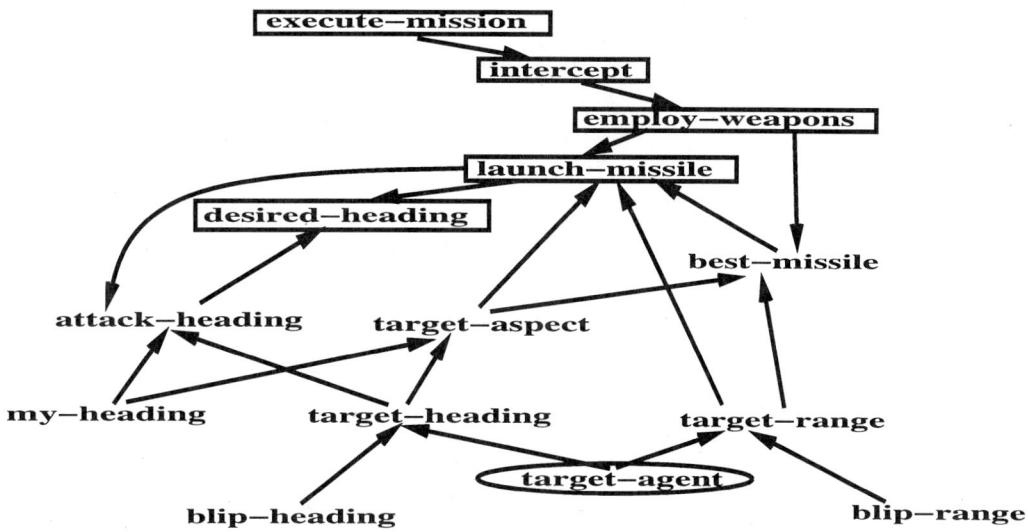

Figure 2: A sample active goal hierarchy for TacAir-Soar.

current situation description. The generation of these goals and features is fairly rapid, but it does take some time. Thus, it is undesirable for the agent routinely to expend significant effort maintaining the hierarchies, because it may run out of time to react.

However, because of the hierarchical representation, the system can make incremental adjustments to its current mental state as the situation warrants. In Figure 2, the agent has chosen a missile to employ against a target, and is using the target's position information to aim the aircraft for the best shot. If the target turns a small amount, it may not lead to any change in the active hierarchies at all. Rather, the change in target heading will cause a rule to fire that computes a new attack heading, and the agent will adjust the aircraft heading in response. If the target turns by a larger amount, the new geometry of the situation may take the target out of the envelope of the currently selected missile. This could cause the agent to delete its current Launch-Missile goal, select a new missile to use, and then create a new Launch-Missile goal. Finally, if the target turns by an even larger amount (for example, to run away), the agent may have to make significant adjustments, leading to the situation in Figure 3. In this case, the agent determines that the target may be running away, so there is no longer a need to shoot it. Therefore, the agent deactivates the goal to launch a missile against the target, and instead pursue's the target, to observe its behavior for some time.

This example illustrates TacAir-Soar's solution to the combined constraints of generating complex behavior in an efficient manner. The system's internal representation is extremely intricate at any point in time (the figures are highly simplified). However, the interaction of top-down and bottom-up hierarchies, together with opportunistic operators, allows a smooth and efficient implementation of reactive, yet goal-driven, behavior.

The Problem of Efficiency

The representations above provide a framework for creating complex reactive behavior, but we needed further work to address the real-time constraints on TacAir-Soar. The system needs enough time to make appropriate, human-like decisions, even when the environment is changing quickly. Additionally, simulation must be as inexpensive as possible, while meeting the training goals. One way to keeps costs down is to execute as many automated forces on a single computer as possible. Thus, there are multiple reasons for TacAir-Soar to be efficient. We increased the efficiency of the system in a number of ways, which can be categorized as enhancing the rule-based architecture, moving non-symbolic computation into the SMI, improving the context sensitivity of processing, and using fast but cheap hardware.

The first point to mention is the reïmplementation of the Soar architecture. In the Summer of 1992, just prior to the start of this project, Doorenbos (1993) completed a new version of Soar, which is written in C (previous versions were in Lisp) and contains a very efficient implementation of the RETE rule-matching algorithm (Forgy, 1982). The new version of Soar was approximately 15-20 times faster than the previous version. This system provided the required infrastructure for us to even hope to build systems for intelligent, real-time control. It also gave us the speed to run our agents faster than real time in some situations, and to run multiple agents on a single machine.

As the project progressed, we discovered other architectural adjustments that address efficiency. One adjustment arose from the fact that TacAir-Soar does not currently make any use of the Soar architecture's built-in learning mechanism. This is because the current system models expert behavior, not the acquisition of expert behavior. The learning mechanism has some over-

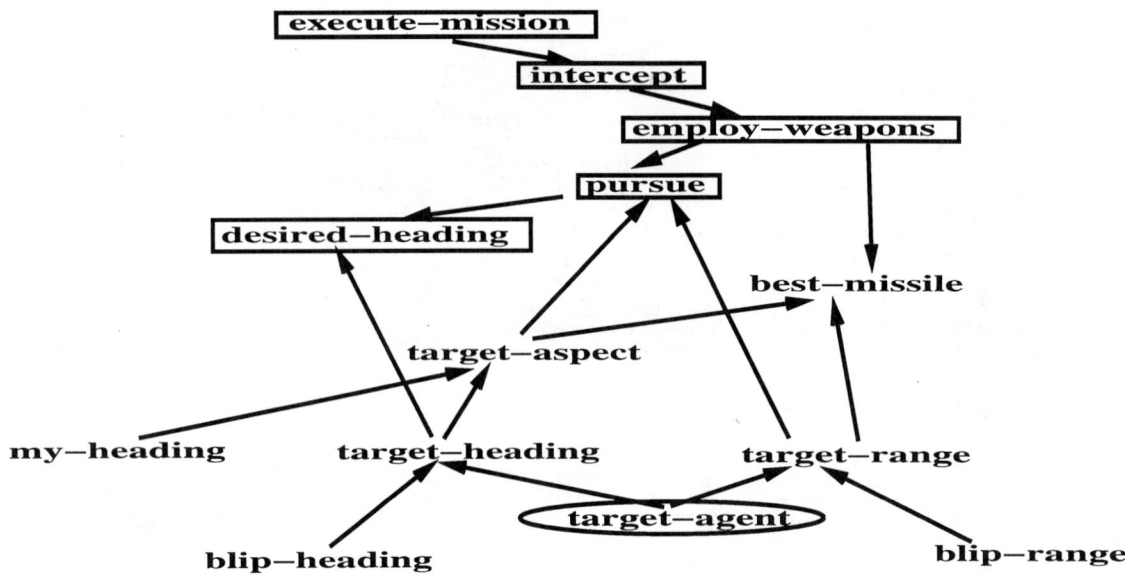

Figure 3: TacAir-Soar changes the goal hierarchy in response to changes in the situation-representation hierarchy (and vice versa).

head associated with it, so we selectively disabled the support for learning. We should stress that this does not represent a change in the "Soar unified theory of cognition" (Newell, 1990), but is a departure based on the pragmatic goal of increasing efficiency when learning is not important. However, it is worth noting that our experiences with TacAir-Soar have suggested some *potential* adjustments to the theory, which are being explored (Wray, Laird, & Jones, 1996).

Another technique to increase efficiency was to migrate processing from rule-based behaviors into the SMI. Initial implementations restricted the agent's sensory input from the SMI to sparse representations. For example, for an active radar contact, the SMI would pass only those numbers that are accessible on a real radar display. To perform intercepts, however, a pilot uses geometric and spatial reasoning, such as to compute a collision course. Early versions of TacAir-Soar contained rules to compute such values. The rules fired for a new computation every time one of the relevant input values changed. Combat aircraft often fly near the speed of sound, and they maneuver against each other, so these situation-interpretation rules can fire very often. However, such fixed, goal-independent processing is much more efficiently implemented in C code than in the match-and-fire interpretation cycle inherent in rules. We recovered significant processing time by moving such expensive, "non-intelligent" computations into the SMI. The new version of the SMI passes a contact's geometric information (such as the collision course) along with the normal numeric information. TacAir-Soar uses this information as before, without the inefficient computational overhead.

Another rather naïve (in hindsight) early design decision allowed the system to process more information than is strictly necessary for decision making. For example, early versions of the situation-interpretation hierarchy processed primitive input information from the SMI into as many different representations as it could. Also, the SMI would compute many different geometric quantities for every active radar contact. The motivation behind this approach was to make the system more easily extendible. The "right" set of features would be available any time we added new behaviors, because the system would represent the situation in so many different ways. As a simple example, based on numeric sensor information for a radar contact, we would compute whether the contact is to our left or right, in front of us or in back of us, pointing at us, turning, descending or climbing, and so on.

This approach *did* make it easier to expand the capabilities of the system. However, we soon disovered that TacAir-Soar was doing so much processing, it was sometimes running out of time to make appropriate decisions. Thus, we tempered our goals of software extendibility in the service of a more efficient knowledge representation. To this end, we only use situation-interpretation rules to compute new features if those features are relevant to the agent's current context. Similarly, the SMI does not need to compute *all* the possible geometric information for most contacts. If the agent knows that a radar contact on its scope is friendly, there is no reason to compute relational position features, because friendly forces can often be ignored. Similarly, there may be no reason to compute whether an enemy aircraft is pointing at the agent's aircraft if the enemy aircraft is known not to carry air-to-air missiles. In response, we equipped the system with methods to focus attention and interpret the situation based on the current context. These changes were sometimes tedious, but the purely functional concern of efficiency forced us to create a more plausible representation of human reasoning.

As a final point on efficiency, we should not ignore the power of brute-force solutions. Over the five years that TacAir-Soar has been developed, computer system speeds have continued their familiar dramatic improvements. For STOW '97, we did not try to find the fastest computers available, because low cost was also a goal. We did try to find the best ratio of cycle time to system cost, and ended up using Intel-based machines running the Linux operating system. With these machines, and our attention to efficiency within TacAir-Soar's design, we were able to run up to around 6 instances of TacAir-Soar simultaneously on a single machine, without significant degradation in the quality of behavior.

Details of Deployment

TacAir-Soar has taken part in a number of tests, technology demonstrations, and operational exercises (involving real training of military personnel). The system is fulfilling its role, providing an important part of the environment for simulation training. TacAir-Soar's is primarily used at the WISSARD Laboratory on the Oceana Naval Air Station, in Virginia Beach. In early tests, the system participated in simple engagements (e.g., 1 vs. 1 air-to-air combat), fighting against humans who were "flying" various types of flight simulators. This type of test fit into the original role we had envisioned for TacAir-Soar: providing intelligent automated opponents to train small groups of combat pilots in offensive and defensive tactics. However, there are many different potential applications of this technology, and the particular requirements for this system changed as the project progressed.

In STOW '97, TacAir-Soar was used for commander training, where the trainees receive reports from the battlefield, and task combat units to perform various functions. The simulation runs concurrently, leading to new battlefield reports and an assessment of the effectiveness of the orders. Various types of simulators play out these training scenarios, including entity-level SAFOR simulations and aggregate-level "war game" simulations. The military uses TacAir-Soar to increase the realism of such simulations. In addition to generating more realistic general behavior, TacAir-Soar communicates (in simplified English) and coördinates with humans. Commanders actually observe and interact with the forces as the simulation plays out, leading to a much more realistic training scenario. TacAir-Soar is primarily used for this type of theater-level command-and-control training. However, there are plans to make more frequent use of TacAir-Soar to train small groups of pilots in adversarial and cooperative situations. A number of active and retired military personnel have expressed surprise and enthusiasm at the difference between TacAir-Soar's behavior and other simulations.

As might be expected, expanded training requirements greatly increased the demands on the project. The ultimate requirements were for the system to include appropriate behaviors for every mission that is performed on a fixed-wing aircraft in the United States military, as well as to provide behaviors for "opponent force" (OPFOR) aircraft and aircraft from the United Kingdom's Royal Air Force. The missions that TacAir-Soar flies include offensive and defensive counter-air, close-air support, suppression of enemy air defense (SEAD), strategic attack, escort, reconnaissance/intelligence, airborne early warning, mid-air tanking, and forward air control. In addition, the system had to be resistant to generating anomalous behavior or software failures, so that it would not interrupt the continuity of the training exercise. Finally, the system had to integrate seamlessly with existing military structure for exercises. Standard procedure in the United States military is to generate an Air Tasking Order (ATO) every 24 hours. This order specifies airborne mission information for the next day, created and distributed with a database tool. For live exercises, the ATO is sent to wing commanders, who then create specific orders for the details of each aircraft flight. We developed additional tools for scenario management (Coulter & Laird, 1996; Kenny et al., 1998), in order to automate this process. These tools translate the ATO into mission specifications for TacAir-Soar, so the interactions between commanders and our system are as similar as possible to their interactions with real wing commanders and combatants.

TacAir-Soar's participation in STOW '97 took place over 48 straight hours. In that time, the system generated behavior for 722 scheduled flights, including every type of mission that TacAir-Soar is capable of flying. There were up to 4000 total entities in the simulation environment at a time, with TacAir-Soar controlling between 30 and 100 at a time on 28 different machines. Missions varied in length from 90 minutes to 8 hours. After the missions had been entered into the computer, the behaviors generated by TacAir-Soar were entirely autonomous. The entities were sometimes re-tasked by active-duty personnel, but this occurred within acceptably realistic interactions, using a speech recognition system or a graphical tool to send the entities simulated radio messages in semi-natural language. There were generally one or two people monitoring all of the entities to keep an eye out for incorrect behavior. Unfortunately, we do not have cost-estimate comparisons, but this is significantly less manpower than is required to run a similar number of SAFOR aircraft.

Future Plans

STOW '97 was a complete technical success. Based on this success, the system continues to be used for technology demonstrations at the Oceana Naval Air Station, and there are plans to use the system in additional operational training exercises in the coming year. Under the auspices of a new company, Soar Technology, we have installed the system at additional military training sites, and we are continuing its development in a number of ways. One obvious area of development is to expand and broaden the general behaviors and missions that TacAir-Soar performs, to increase its participation and realism in theater-level simulations like STOW '97. To address other types of training, we are also putting significant effort into engineering TacAir-Soar for specific, individual training roles. Some example roles are synthetic wingmen to provide partners to individual lead fighter pilots, synthetic fighters to interact closely with human AWACS controllers, and high-fidelity enemy aircraft to train fighter pilots in air-to-air engagements. These focused behavior areas require us to emphasize the development of TacAir-Soar's ability to communicate using natural language and speech, and to engineer deeper knowledge of the targeted mission areas. Additional development involves parameterizing the behavior model so it more realistically emulates the differences in behavior between different types of pilots, and pilots in different branches of the military (each with their own standard operating procedures).

In the academic arena, we are using TacAir-Soar as the basis for a variety of research projects in intelligent systems and cognitive science. These projects includes studies of how intelligent systems can use explanation-based learning in situated domains (Wray, Laird, & Jones, 1996), how systems can acquire expert-level combat pilot knowledge through training (van Lent & Laird, 1998), and how we can use TacAir-Soar to make predictions about the effects of fatigue on pilot behavior (Jones, Neville, & Laird, 1998).

Acknowledgements

Milind Tambe and Paul Rosenbloom participated in the design and implementation of early versions of TacAir-Soar, before breaking off to work on the system for rotary-wing vehicles. Karl Schwamb, Frank Koss, Karen Coulter, and Patrick Kenny provided programming support in the form of the SMI and other software tools. Randall Hill, Jonathan Gratch, and Johnny Chen also aided in the development of the rotary-wing system, and their work provided us with valuable insights. The version of TacAir-Soar described in this paper was developed under the auspices of the University of Michigan and the Information Sciences Institute of the University of Southern California, under contract N00014-92-K-2015 from the Advanced Systems Technology Office of DARPA and ONR, and contract N66001-95-C-6013 from the Advanced Systems Technology Office of DARPA and the RDT&E division of NOSC.

References

Calder, R., Smith, J., Courtenmanche, A., Mar, J., & Ceranowicz, A. 1993. ModSAF Behavior Simulation and Control. *Proc. of the 3rd Conf. on Computer Generated Forces and Beh. Representation*. Orlando, FL.

Coulter, K. J., & Laird, J. E. 1996. A Briefing-Based Graphical Interface for Exercise Specification. In *Proc. of the 6th Conf. on Computer Generated Forces and Beh. Representation*, 113–117. Orlando, FL.

Doorenbos, R. 1993. Matching 100,000 Learned Rules. In *Proc. of the 11th Nat. Conf. on Artificial Intelligence*, 290–296. Menlo Park, CA: AAAI Press.

Forgy, C. L. 1982. Rete: A Fast Algorithm for the Many Pattern / Many Object Pattern Match Problem. *Artificial Intelligence*, 19:17–38.

Hill, R. W., Chen, J., Gratch, J., Rosenbloom, P., & Tambe, M. 1997. Intelligent Agents for the Synthetic Battlefield: A Company of Rotary Wing Aircraft. In *Proc. of 9th Conf. on Inn. App. of Artificial Intelligence*, 1006–1012. Menlo Park, CA: AAAI Press.

Jones, R. M. 1998. A Graphical User Interface for Human Control of Intelligent Synthetic Forces. In *Proc. of the 7th Conf. on Computer Generated Forces and Beh. Representation*. Orlando, FL.

Jones, R. M., Neville, K., & Laird, J. E. 1998. Modeling Pilot Fatigue with a Synthetic Behavior Model. In *Proc. of the 7th Conf. on Computer Generated Forces and Beh. Representation*. Orlando, FL.

Jones, R. M., Laird, J. E., Tambe, M., & Rosenbloom, P. S. 1994. Generating Behavior in Response to Interacting Goals. In *Proc. of the 4th Conf. on Computer Generated Forces and Beh. Representation*, 317–324. Orlando, FL.

Kenny, P. G., Coulter, K. J, Laird, J. E., & Bixler, S. 1998. *Integrating Real-World Mission Specification and Reporting Activities with Computer Generated Forces at STOW-97*. In *Proc. of the 7th Conf. on Computer Generated Forces and Beh. Rep.* Orlando, FL.

Laird, J. E., Coulter, K. J., Jones, R. M., Kenny, P. G., Koss, F. V., & Nielsen, P. E. 1998. Integrating Intelligent Computer Generated Forces in Distributed Simulation: TacAir-Soar in STOW-97. In *Proc. of the 1998 Simulaton Interop. Workshop*. Orlando, FL.

Laird, J. E., Newell, A., & Rosenbloom, P. S. 1991. Soar: An Architecture for General Intelligence. *Artificial Intelligence*, 47:289–325.

Newell, A. 1990. *Unified Theories of Cognition*. Cambridge, MA: Harvard University Press.

Schwamb, K. B., Koss, F. V., & Keirsey, D. 1994. Working with ModSAF: Interfaces for Programs and Users. In *Proc. of the 4th Conf. on Computer Generated Forces and Beh. Representation*. Orlando, FL.

Tambe, M., Johnson, W. L., Jones, R. M., Koss, F., Laird, J. E., Rosenbloom, P. S., & Schwamb, K. B. 1995. Intelligent Agents for Interactive Simulation Environments. *AI Magazine*, 16(1):15–39.

van Lent, M., & Laird, J. E. 1998. Learning by Observation in a Complex Domain. In *Proc. of the Workshop on Knowledge Acquisition, Modeling, and Management*. Banff, Alberta.

Wray, R. E., III, Laird, J. E., & Jones, R. M. 1996. Compilation of Non-Contemporaneous Constraints. In *Proc. of the Thirteenth Nat. Conf. on Artificial Intelligence*, 771–778. Menlo Park, CA: AAAI Press.

The NASD Regulation Advanced Detection System (ADS)[*]

J. Dale Kirkland, Ted E. Senator, James J. Hayden[+],
Tom Dybala, Henry G. Goldberg, Ping Shyr

National Association of Securities Dealers (NASD) Regulation, Inc., 9513 Key West Avenue, Rockville, MD 20850
[+]SRA International Inc., 2000 15th Street North Arlington, VA 22201
kirkland@nasd.com, senatort@nasd.com, jim_hayden@sra.com

Abstract

The NASD Regulation Advanced Detection System (ADS) monitors trades and quotations in the Nasdaq stock market to identify patterns and practices of behavior of potential regulatory interest. ADS has been in operational use at NASD Regulation since summer 1997 by several groups of analysts, processing approximately 2 million transactions per day, generating over 7000 breaks. More important, it has greatly expanded surveillance coverage to new areas of the market and to many new types of behavior of regulatory concern. ADS combines detection and discovery components in a single system which supports multiple regulatory domains and which share the same market data. ADS makes use of a variety of AI techniques, including visualization, pattern recognition, and data mining, in support of the activities of regulatory analysis, alert and pattern detection, and knowledge discovery.

Introduction

The National Association of Securities Dealers, Inc. (NASD®) has been regulating the securities industry since its founding in 1939. Regulation of securities markets and firms is undertaken by its NASD Regulation, Inc. subsidiary. Our mission of investor protection includes monitoring trading and quotation activities on the Nasdaq Stock Market, the Over the Counter (OTC) Market, and the Third Market, to identify and correct any potential violative activities by over 5500 member firms. Central to this job is the Advanced Detection System, or ADS.

We have been using ADS since the summer of 1997 to provide analysts in the Market Regulation Department with significant leads to potential patterns or practices of regulatory concern, or **breaks**. ADS generates these breaks by integrating and then reviewing all quotation and trade records, almost 2 million on a typical day, for patterns which indicate the occurrence of targeted scenarios.

Since beginning production operations, the system has detected over 7000 breaks, of which more than 10% have merited follow-up actions of various types, a threefold increase in effectiveness compared to previous techniques. More important, it has greatly expanded our surveillance coverage to new areas of the market and to many new types of behavior of regulatory concern.

ADS relies on a rule pattern matcher and a time-sequence pattern matcher. Two- and three-dimensional visualizations allow analysts to see the market context of breaks and temporal relationships of events in large amounts of data. Data mining tools permit discovery of new patterns of potential regulatory interest.

ADS' development is continuing, to remain current with changes in market behavior, to increase its effectiveness, to add additional features, to incorporate additional market data, to cover additional types of potential violations and to keep up with improvements in market structure.

Task Description

Nasdaq is a screen-based dealer market consisting of competing market makers who risk their own capital to provide liquidity. A **market maker** provides quotations for issues in which he makes a market. A **quotation** consists of both a **price** and a **size** (number of shares) at which he is willing to buy or sell, respectively, a particular security, or **issue**. The price at which he is willing to buy is known as a **bid** and at which he is willing to sell as an **ask** or **offer**. The highest bid and lowest ask at a particular time is known as the **inside quote**. Quotations are available to other market makers, to other brokers, and to investors through the distributed computing system that forms the heart of the Nasdaq Stock Market. Trades are executed between market makers (acting as principals for their own account or as agents for customers) and dealers (acting as agents for customers) using one of several automated systems. All trades are reported, shortly after they occur, to a common system, resulting in the well-known stock ticker.

Nasdaq currently has more than 6000 issues on the Nasdaq National Market and the Small Cap Market. There are an average of about 10 market makers per issue. A typical day consists of over 900,00 quote updates, 400,000 inside quote updates, and 800,000 trades on both tiers of the Nasdaq Stock Market and on the OTC Market.

Individual trades or quotes, can often be justified before disciplinary committees. Broad patterns and practices,

---

[*]The authors of this paper are employees of the National Association of Securities Dealers (NASD) Regulation, Inc. or its contractors. The views expressed herein are those of the authors and do not represent an official policy statement of NASD Regulation, Inc.

however, cannot. A key goal of ADS is to detect patterns and practices of violative activity. Another goal of ADS was to raise the level of surveillance from issue-based to firm-based patterns and practices.

Our data problem is in part statistical. Statistical techniques are effective at identifying outliers. However, outliers often occur in the context of unusual market activity, while potential violations occur during normal market conditions. Even after a potential concern is identified, an analyst needs to review large amounts of market information to determine if there is a potential explanation for the apparent violation. Prior to ADS, analysts reviewed this information in tabular formats, from which it was difficult to discern relationships. We needed the right mix of statistics, data classification, data visualization, and pattern recognition on a huge database of activity structured in time sequence.

ADS currently covers three areas, or domains, of potential violations, each with its own user team having a distinct set of business procedures, and needing unique data, knowledge, and tools to perform their function. However, because of the large overlap between necessary and available data and tools, a single system was customized to meet the needs of each team. This approach is allowing us to cost-effectively extend ADS to additional domains as requirements demand and resources permit.

Late Trade Reporting. In order to provide accurate information to the marketplace, trades must be reported within 90 seconds of execution. However, for various reasons, sometimes trades are not reported within this window. The Market Regulation Department is responsible for surveillance of all late reported trades to determine the reason and determine whether or not to initiate regulatory action. Examples which could initiate regulatory action are: A trader delays reporting a large customer trade so the customer doesn't see that there was another trade at a better price at the same time. A market maker has a much higher incidence than his peer firms of reporting trades late.

Market Integrity. The integrity of the Nasdaq Stock Market depends upon free and open price competition between market makers. Some market makers may be dissuaded from competitive pricing by others through a variety of methods of harassment. These methods have been used to "enforce" improper pricing conventions which can result in unfair profits to the market makers at the expense of the customer. Additionally, market makers may coordinate their pricing and trading activity to hide information from other participants and customers, who

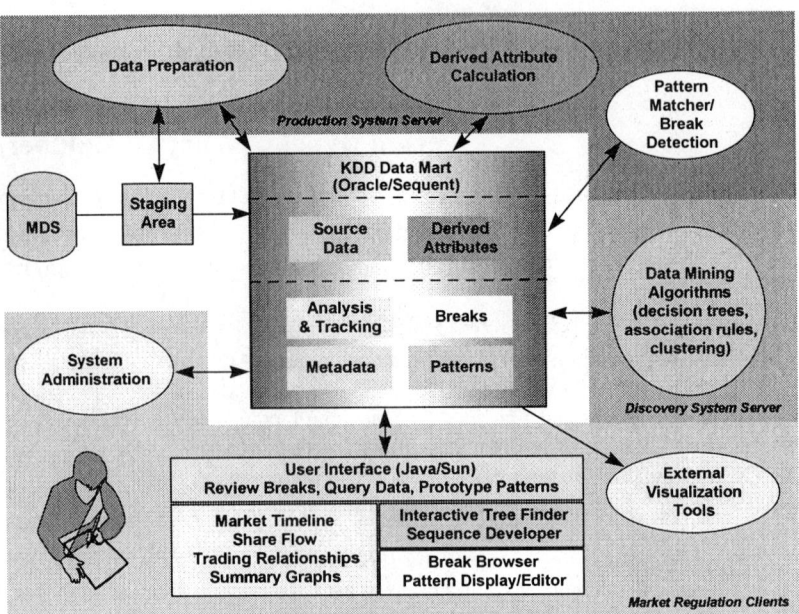

Figure 1 -- ADS Architecture

have a right to it, as a means of influencing prices. The Market Regulation Department is responsible for surveillance of the market with respect to these and any other schemes involving unfair coordination or anti-competitive behavior. Some examples for which the system provides surveillance: After receiving a large customer order to purchase a particular security, a market maker buys the stock from a second market maker, then resells it to the customer at a higher price; the customer could have purchased the stock from the second market maker at the lower price. A market maker stops receiving orders after he narrows his quotes in a security; the orders return when he returns his quotes to a more typical level.

Best Execution. The Best Execution (BE) rule states that the price received by an investor should be as favorable as possible under prevailing market conditions. Such a favorable price is usually achieved when executing a trade within the inside quote. The regulatory enforcement of the BE rule is greatly complicated by market conditions such as relative volatility and liquidity, the size and type of transaction, available communications, accessibility to the primary markets, and quotation sources which may grant exceptions to the rule.

Application Description

This section describes ADS: how it works and what it is. The ADS Architecture is illustrated in figure 1. The key functional modules of ADS are:
- ADS Data Warehouse
- Detection Programs
- Discovery Programs
- User Interface

Data Warehouse

The ADS data warehouse is the heart of the system. It is currently about 240GB. It consists of two sets of tables, referred to as **source** tables and **metadata** tables. The source tables contain market data about trades, quotes, and insides. These tables consist of attributes from systems from which ADS receives information as well as additional attributes and indices that are calculated for use by other components of ADS, as well as summary and profile information about issues and firms. Metadata tables hold set-up and execution control parameters for the break detection and discovery jobs, the rule and sequence patterns that are matched by the detection jobs, the results of the break detection and discovery jobs (breaks and rules), and data necessary for various user interface components.

Data load and preparation programs update the data warehouse daily. They combine information from the source tables and calculate additional attributes deemed useful for detection and discovery. The data sources for ADS present a view of the market as a series of transactions with separate trades and price updates. Matching these transactions to produce a more coherent market state is a major computational effort, but is essential to provide the derived attributes which capture market context.

Detection Programs

ADS Detection programs consist of two pattern matchers: a Rule Matcher and a Time Sequence Matcher, which are run weekly to generate breaks. Breaks are assigned to analysts through distinct automated break assignment modules which reflect each user team's work process.

Sequence Matcher The sequence matcher is a program for finding instances of temporal patterns in databases. It seeks triggering events that, in turn, seek other events in either forward or reverse time sequence and order that could indicate deliberate behavior of concern. The algorithm was independently developed at SRA, drawing upon work in discovery of temporal associations. (see Mannila 1995)

The sequence matcher algorithm works by querying the metadata tables to load a pattern into memory. The sequence matcher algorithm is similar to a regular expression matcher. It maintains a list of potential match states. At each step, a row is fetched and a new state is started for each pattern. Existing states are advanced if they match the constraints on the pattern location they are currently at. When a state reaches the end of a pattern, it is a match. The sequence matcher may be run in forward or reverse mode, fetching rows in increasing or decreasing time order depending on whether the triggering event for the sequence occurs before or after the other necessary conditions. In a single pass, multiple tables may be scanned for several patterns concurrently. The sequence pattern language uses a syntax and precedence similar to the C programming language.

There are three types of inputs to the sequence matcher: target configurations, patterns, and callback functions. A target configuration details the database columns to be processed, along with any row-ordering conditions. Patterns are specified either from the metadata tables or a text file. Callback functions are C++ functions compiled into a dynamically loadable object. They may be time filters or actions. A time filter is a way of coordinating the ordering of rows from heterogeneous tables. Output of the sequence matcher is determined by the action functions that are called. The break generation action function populates the metadata tables with breaks. The break generation callback inserts a new row into a table for every match found. Each matching state has some number of rows that are the instantiation of the pattern.

Rule Matcher The rule matcher fetches trade data and produces breaks based on the detection of repeated instances of pre-defined behaviors, represented formally as rules with an antecedent and an optional consequent. Each rule has two measures of strength, called confidence (fraction of rows satisfying the antecedent where the consequent is also true) and support (fraction of rows in the entire table that this rule holds on), which are used as parameters to ensure that breaks which are generated by the rule correspond to significant patterns of activity. An example pattern would be one that looked for firms showing a high percentage of trades involving more than 10000 shares that are designated late.

The Rule Matcher internally represents each attribute that is mentioned in at least one pattern and uses the attribute names to build the query that will retrieve the targeted trade data. The patterns are represented as conjunctions tests on attributes. Trees are created that contain the pattern conjunctions and counts corresponding to the number of times the conjunction is detected.

Each record retrieved is given an internal representation that facilitates tree traversal based on attribute tests passed. If an attribute has a bind test defined for it a new test is added whenever a new value for the attribute is encountered in the data. The record representation is given to the tree structures and all necessary conjunction counts are updated. The output of Rule Matching results in storing breaks and break-related data in the database.

Discovery Programs

ADS includes parallel and scaleable decision tree and association rule implementations which can be used to discover new rules reflecting changing behaviors in the marketplace.

Association Rules The association rule algorithm is a procedure for generating rules from a table. (see Agrawal, et. al. 1993) Our implementation of the association rules algorithm is written in C++ and performs direct access to an Oracle8 RDBMS through a database class library invoking the Oracle Call Interface (OCI) API. Parallelism is achieved using an implementation of the Message Passing Interface (MPI). The algorithm uses parallelism in several places to divide up tasks. Each process is CPU-intensive and allocates its own memory.

Attribute filters are used to reduce the number of association rules reported by the algorithm. They provide guidelines about how certain attributes make a rule interesting or not interesting. There are four types of attribute filters that add the capability to include or exclude attributes, group attributes in rules, and specify functional dependencies. These filters are instrumental in reducing the number of redundant and definitional rules generated.

Decision Trees The decision tree algorithm is a data mining tool designed to find patterns with respect to a single specified data column called the "dependent attribute." (See Quinlan 1993) The input data consists of a number of "examples" each of which is a vector of attribute/value pairs. The algorithm outputs a set of rules that use the independent attributes to predict or characterize values of the dependent attribute. These rules have a conjunction of independent attributes on the left-hand-side and contain only the dependent attribute on the right-hand-side.

Rules are extracted from a decision tree by tracing the path from a leaf up to the root of the tree. The dependent attribute value assigned to that node become the right-hand-side of the rule, and the independent attributes and values in the nodes on the path to the root become the conditions on the left-hand-side of the rule.

Rules are pruned by dropping conditions from the left-hand-side and seeing if a better rule is produced. If a rule has N conditions in the left-hand-side, then dropping each condition can produce N possible alternative rules. Each of these rules is evaluated, and if any are better than the original rule, then the best alternative is chosen and the process is repeated. A rule's quality is determined by calculated using its normalized estimated net worth. Once each rule is pruned, duplicates are removed.

Rule Management. A run of decision trees or association rules against a data sample of one firm or one security

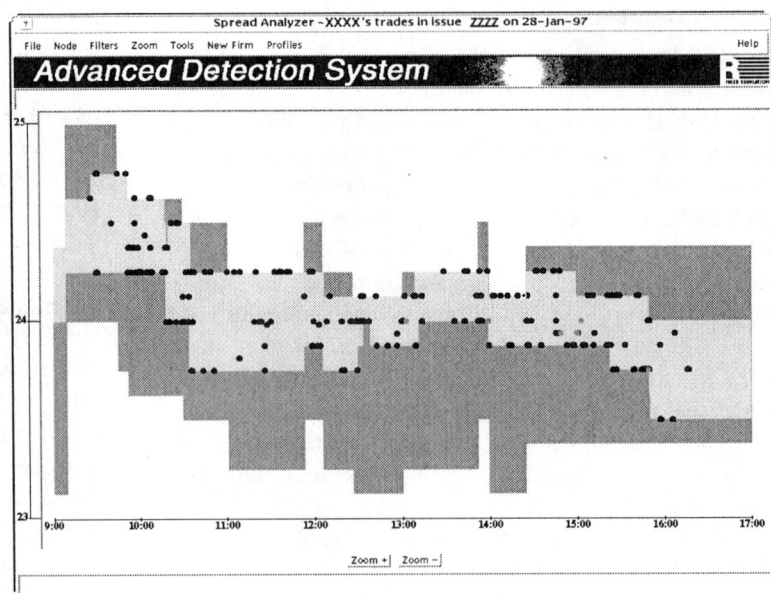

Figure 2 – Market Spread Timeline

usually produces several rules; thousands of rules may result from runs against all securities and firms, necessitating automated rule management capabilities. Moreover, to follow dynamic behavior of the market the pattern base must be highly adaptive, allowing additions refinements, and deletions. The Rule Management module supports transformations of discovered rules to break detection patterns, similar to the approach described in [Fawcett and Provost 1997]. Rule management comprises three operations: filtering, refinement, and deletion.

During filtering, discovered rules are pruned to a subset which are unique (not repeated among themselves), new (different from existing patterns and rules), have high confidence, and good support in data. Filtering compares the generality of two rules by examining similarity of the rules' conditions and conclusion (Michalski 1983, Tecuci & Duff 1994). The comparison algorithm uses domain specific and domain independent heuristics to capture the meaning of various rule attributes. The filtering process decreases the number of rules from thousands to hundreds, which are still firm or security specific.

During refinement, rules obtained from the filtering process are refined by generalizing their conditions and ranking them against random data samples, to generalize rules by dropping market participant or security specific information, to perform generalization according to the specified refinement heuristics (Dybala at el. 1995), and to rank the obtained rules by testing them against various data sets to refine their support and confidence thresholds. Finally, the best performing rules are selected. Rules which pass the refinement process are unique, general, and different. The result of the refinement process are several or possibly tens of new rules which are presented to the analysts for a review, for a final selection for promotion to active break detection patterns.

User Interface

The ADS user interface consists of screens for break processing and management, tabular displays for viewing detailed trade and quotation information associated with a particular break, two-dimensional graphical displays that allow an analyst to easily visualize market activity at the time of a break, and three-dimensional displays that are useful for viewing large aggregates of information.

The market context around the time of a suspected violation in a security is determined by three things: the trades in that security, the bids and asks of the market makers in that security, and the inside bid and ask. The difference between a bid and an ask price is called the spread. This context is captured visually in the market spread timeline (see Figure 2). A market maker's bid and ask in an issue are plotted against time in one color and the inside bid prices and ask prices in another. Trades are displayed as dots. Details of trades and quotes are available through a drill-down capability. The visual display allows analysts to quickly identify important events such as the inside spread being narrowed, multiple small trades being executed against a market maker, or a market maker buying up a lot of shares in an issue.

The share flow display (Figure 3) shows a group of trades in order by execution time. Each trade is represented as an arrow from the buyer to the seller marked with the number of shares and price. When a group of trades is displayed by time, patterns of share flow are visible. A firm may collect shares through multiple medium-sized buys, and sell them in one large sale. Shares may pass through multiple firms before reaching their final destination. These patterns of share flows are crucial for analyzing potential violations.

Detecting any potential conventions or regularities in market behavior which might indicate improper coordination by market participants requires the ability to rapidly review large amounts of market data for patterns

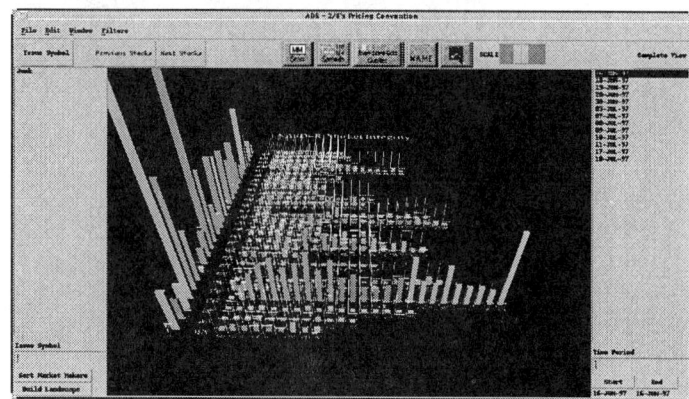

Figure 4 -- Pricing Landscape

and anomalies. To provide this ability, Visible Decisions Inc. Discovery software was selected for three-dimensional displays. (See Martin96) Two three-dimensional "landscapes" have been developed. The Pricing landscape (see Figure 4) displays a large amount of summary data regarding quotation activity by multiple market makers in many issues. It highlights the possible pricing conventions in portions of the market. These may be agreements among market makers to quote only in specific price intervals. If these agreements are enforced by peer pressure or harassment, they become anti-competitive and are violative practices. A visual examination of this display permits an analyst to rapidly determine patterns of quotations in an issue and similarities between the quotation behavior of different market makers. Situations where the pricing conventions hold for all but a few market makers are those most likely to result in anti-competitive behavior and warrant the closest review. In addition, new conventions are more easily visible, since the display may be adjusted by various thresholds and filters.

The second display, called a Spread landscape (see figure 5), allows an analyst to view the quotation and trading behavior of a set of market makers in a particular issue over a specified time period. This display may be viewed as a generalization of the two-dimensional spread display described above.

Hardware and System Software Environment.

ADS system hardware currently consists of a 12-processor Sequent NUMA-Q host computer acting as the production database server. Scaleability and growth were significant factors in the choice of a server platform. Sun SparcStations serve as user workstations running the ADS client as well as other applications. A second, smaller Sequent NUMA-Q is used as a development and knowledge discovery platform, and a variety of file servers are installed on Sun SparcStations. The operating systems are varieties of Unix. Oracle v.8.0.4 is the RDBMS. The ADS client is written in Java, which has

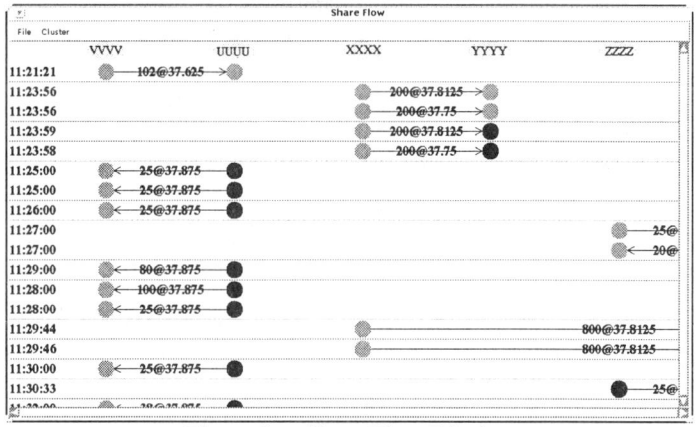

Figure 3 -- Share Flow Display

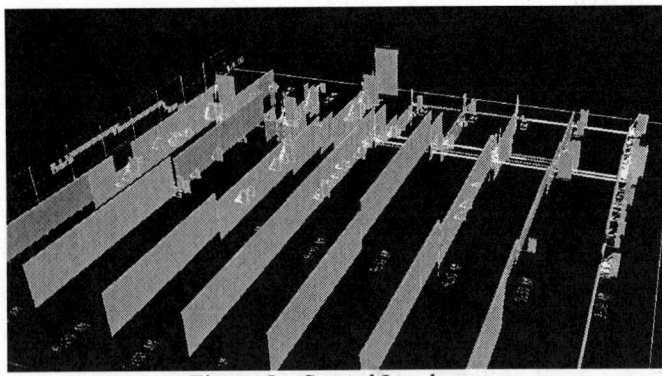

Figure 5 – Spread Landscape

proven to be an effective language for both prototyping and final implementation.

Uses of Artificial Intelligence Technology

ADS integrates data mining (decision trees and association rules), pattern matching (rules and time sequences) and visualization techniques in a single large-scale application, as detailed in previous sections. It represents an advance over previously reported applications because of the large scale of the application, the combination of discovery and detection components with the ability to discover new rules and promote them into the detection system, the explicit representation of rules in the database for use in detection and as a result of discovery, the development of the time sequence pattern matcher, and the direct database access parallel implementations of the detection and discovery components.

Commercial Tool Evaluation

We evaluated off-the-shelf knowledge discovery/data mining tools during the proof-of-concept phase of ADS development. We surveyed more than 20 off-the-shelf KDD products and conducted a detailed evaluation of two of them. But none of them appeared to meet our needs for a system that would do the following, so we developed the components as part of a custom application[1]:
- function in NASD's hardware and software environment
- have an open architecture for integration with other necessary system components, especially the database management system and the to-be-developed workflow management components
- function in a highly dynamic environment
- integrate a comprehensive variety of methods

---

[1] SRA has taken the custom application developed for NASD and converted it into a generic KDD toolkit that meets all these requirements and can be applied to other application domains. Details of this product are available at www.knowledgediscovery.com on the web.

- provide intermediate results to all components
- scale to handle production volumes of over one million trades and quotes per day; and, most important
- provide an integrated structure for ongoing detection of improper activity combined with analysis to identify new patterns of potential regulatory interest.

Related Applications

The FinCEN AI System (FAIS), described in [Senator, Goldberg et. al. 1995] motivated some of the basic ideas of ADS, although the specific requirements differ. Both are instances of a type of fraud detection system called Break Detection Systems described in [Goldberg and Senator 1997], which also contrasts the two domains along several characteristics. ADS advances over FAIS along several dimensions, in particular, its much larger data volume, its incorporation of automated discovery techniques for identification of new patterns of potential regulatory interest, its explicit representation of multiple domains and user groups, and its use of a time sequence pattern matcher for detection.

[Fawcett and Provost 1997] describe an approach to cellular telephone fraud detection that automatically learns indicators of potential fraud from a large database of transactions. It uses the indicators to create monitors which profile legitimate and anomalous behavior; and combines the output of the monitors to generate alarms. This system employs more automated learning techniques than ADS and it focuses on identification of fraudulent transactions, while ADS looks for multiple types of violations and for patterns and practices of these violations in the context of an integrated application.

Application Use and Payoff

The development of ADS has taken the Market Regulation Department to a new level in monitoring the markets we are charged to monitor and regulate. For a number of years the Department has had systems that point to potential instances of regulatory concern on market data. And we have a history of taking disciplinary or enforcement action on those in which action warranted. But prior to ADS, we have not had a system to help us detect potential violative patterns and practices in quotation and trade data. We depended upon human analysts to recognize patterns and practices as a series of activities became known to them. Now we search proactively through all of our quote and trade data for those pattern or practices of regulatory concern. Individual instances of violative activity can be explained away by a perpetrator, but strong evidence of a pattern or practice is more difficult for a perpetrator to defend.

What is the payback? First, we have seen notable success in the area of late trades, the first of the areas of concern targeted by ADS. We have increased the hit ratio of good breaks, or leads, to overall breaks by a factor of three over the best of our prior approaches. This permits the analysts to spend less time on efforts that expose no regulatory concern. It permits all the analysts, those with much experience and skill and those with less experience and skill, to be effective at a higher level. It enables new analysts to develop a level of sophistication much more quickly -- about half the time. We have been able to bring many more actions in this area than previously. Second, we have been able to establish a new team to monitor concerns in market integrity. We have been able to point to potential anti-competitive, harassment, or collaborative activity in a way not possible previously. This team is now able to proactively surveil the market instead of reacting to customer complaints. Third, we have started a pilot in a third area to monitor firm responsibilities for best execution. We have had this kind of monitoring in the past, but not in the form of detecting patterns and practices. Fourth, we have the visualization tools that permit the analysts to "see" things that our processing may miss. Fifth, we have a system that can be adapted quickly to new market realities, or changes in activity. Sixth, we monitor the data thoroughly. We do not sample. We run tests exhaustively over all data. This has required quick algorithms and quick machines to handle a truly large amount of data.

From June 1997 through February 1998 ADS has generated over 7000 breaks that have resulted in more than 800 follow-up actions of various types (such as requesting records from the securities traders involved or referral to other units of NASD Regulation). This rate, over 10%, is a factor of three increase over previous break detection systems. Another 80% have been closed, yielding valuable experience which has been re-applied to the detection process. The apparently high "false alarm" rate is acceptable because breaks can be closed quickly when no action is warranted, and because the trade-off cost of missing a real violation is extremely high, corresponding to a "zero-tolerance" for major violations. Further, the process of investigating a break, even a false alarm, is a significant deterrent to violative behavior and typically results in market improvements.

A key payback for a surveillance system is the degree of coverage – in terms of the number, type, and detail of potential violations we can monitor and in terms of the amount of market data we can review. Our initial estimates of improved surveillance coverage with ADS compared to manual surveillance is a factor of about 225. We have also seen 75% reductions in the complexity of some surveillance protocols (corresponding to 300% productivity improvements), as well as significant reductions in potential violations in the areas of both late trade reporting and market integrity, corresponding to an improved market for all investors.

Application Development and Deployment

The ADS project team consisted of staff from NASD Regulation, Inc. (Office of Technology Services and Market Regulation Department), NASD Production Services Department, and SRA International, Inc. At its peak, the team consisted of approximately 22 people.

Table 1 lists key ADS development milestones.

ADS began as a proof-of-concept in the area of late trade reporting. The project was initiated and a team assembled in April 1996. Scenarios and corresponding patterns were identified and rule matching and discovery algorithms were developed, resulting in a demonstration that this approach could be effective in improving late trade surveillance and a July 1996 project Steering Committee decision to proceed with a pilot on live data. This pilot was deployed in October 1996. During the summer of 1996, the market integrity area was determined to be of key importance, and the decision made to expand the Late Trade Pilot into ADS during 1997. The time sequence matcher was developed during 1997 for the needs of MI and for some LT scenarios that could not be adequately represented by rules. ADS went into full production on 31 July 1997.

ADS was one of the first production implementations of Oracle 8, undergoing conversion within a month of becoming operational. Because of the success of late trade reporting and market integrity, it was decided to add the best execution domain and work begin in late 1997 to develop patterns and scenarios. Continued improvements in functionality based on feedback from the users and in meeting NASD Production Services standards for a well documented and predictable system was a major emphasis in late 1997 and early 1998. Release 2.0 in spring 1998 formally recognizes the distinction between the ADS application and SRA's KDD Explorer Toolkit which serves as the underlying discovery and detection engines.

The separate domains came on line at different times. Each domain began as an operational pilot, with live data generating experimental breaks, so the patterns could be tuned appropriately and analyst feedback could be incorporated into the development. The Late Trade domain analysts have been evaluating breaks since October, 1996, as a pilot project. The Market Integrity team began work in July, 1997, with the entire system beginning full accountability in August, 1997. An application of ADS to the enforcement of the Best Execution rule is currently in a pilot stage. The system generates experimental breaks for some types of trades. The breaks are reviewed by analysts who recommend

April 1996	Late Trade Pilot: project initiation
July 1996	LTP Proof-of-Concept
October 1996	Late Trade Pilot (release 1.0)
January 1997	Market Integrity project initiation
June 1997	Late Trade Production / Market Integrity Pilot (release 1.1)
July 31, 1997	Market Integrity Production (release 1.2)
September 1997	Oracle 8 Conversion
January 1998	Best Execution Pilot
January 1998	ADS Release 1.3
April 1998	ADS Release 2.0

Table 1: ADS Development Milestones

further tuning of patterns. The first production application of ADS to enforcement of the Best Execution rule is expected in early Spring 1998.

Knowledge Maintenance

Because ADS applies to multiple dynamic domains, knowledge maintenance is a key issue. Knowledge maintenance is enabled by processes and tools. Weekly meetings are held with key users in each domain area to review current breaks and pattern performance. At these meetings, new scenarios are discussed and prototype patterns are evaluated for inclusion in the system. Tuning of operational parameters is done at these reviews, so that the quantity of breaks is consistent with the analysts' ability to evaluate them. As break quality improves, thresholds can be adjusted to allow more, marginal breaks, as well as allowing new patterns to be detected.

A combination of manual and automated discovery was anticipated, with the emphasis early in the project on manual specification of detection patterns in order to "jump start" the project and make use of the Market Regulation department's expertise. As ADS matures and we reach the limits of what analysts already know, we expect automated discovery to play an increasing role in shaping the system's knowledge component.

The application includes tools to introduce new and modify existing rule and sequence patterns. The sequence editor provides a graphical structure for modifying the more complex specifications of multi-input, non-deterministic, temporal patterns.

The ADS user interface provides features for managing "experimental" patterns, which are run in production but are not yet validated as producing breaks of regulatory value. The use of experimental patterns allows us to evaluate newly proposed or modified patterns on current data, ensuring they stay current with market conditions.

Finally, we anticipate the regular addition of new domains to ADS, requiring new sets of patterns corresponding to the types of potentially violative behavior of interest.

Acknowledgments

We thank all our colleagues at NASD and SRA who aided in the development of ADS or contributed to its knowledge bases, especially our Executive Sponsors and our Steering Committee. Most important, we thank Mr. Jim Cangiano, Senior Vice President of Market Regulation, whose vision and support made the project possible.

References

Agrawal, R., Imielinski, T., and Swami, A., "Mining Association Rules Between Sets of Items in Large Databases", In *Proc. ACM SIGMOD Conf. On Management of Data*, pp. 207-216, 1993

Dybala T. 1996. Shared Expertise Model for Building Interactive Learning Agents. Ph.D. Dissertation, George Mason University, Fairfax, Virginia.

Fawcett, Tom And Provost, Foster, "Adaptive Fraud Detection" Data Mining and Knowledge Discovery 1, 291-316 (1997).

Goldberg, Henry G. And Senator, Ted E., "Break Detection Systems" in AI Approaches to Fraud Detection and Risk Management: Collected Papers from the 1997 Workshop, Technical Report WS-97-07, AAAI Press.

Mannila, Heikki, Toivonen, Hannu, and Verkamo, A. Inkeri, "Discovering Frequent Episodes in Sequences," *Proc. of the First International Conference on Knowledge Discovery and Data Mining*, Montreal, August, 1995.

Martin, James, Beyond pie charts and spreadsheets, *Computerworld*, May 27, 1996.

Michalski R.S. 1983. A Theory and Methodology of Inductive Learning. In Michalski R.S., Carbonell J.G. and Mitchell T.M. (editors) Machine Learning: An Artificial Intelligence Approach, vol. 1 Tioga Publishing Co.

Quinlan, J. Ross, *C4.5 Programs for Machine Learning*, Morgan Kaufamn, San Mateo, CA, 1993.

Senator, Ted E., Goldberg, Henry G., et. al., "The FinCEN Artificial Intelligence System: Identifying Potential Money Laundering from Reports of Large Cash Transactions," *Proc. of the Seventh Innovative Applications of Artificial Intelligence Conference*, Montreal, Canada, August 1995.

Tecuci G. and Duff D. 1994. A Framework for Knowledge Refinement through Multistrategy Learning and Knowledge Acquisition. Knowledge Acquisition Journal, vol. 6 No. 2. pp. 137-162.

A New Technique Enables Dynamic Replanning and Rescheduling of Aeromedical Evacuation

Alexander Kott, Victor Saks, Albert Mercer

Carnegie Group, Inc.
5 PPG Place
Pittsburgh, PA 15222
akott@cgi.com, saks@cgi.com, mercer@cgi.com

Abstract

We describe an application of a dynamic replanning technique in a highly dynamic and complex domain: the military aeromedical evacuation of patients to medical treatment facilities. U.S. Transportation Command (USTRANSCOM) is the DoD agency responsible for evacuating patients during wartime and peace. Doctrinally, patients requiring extended treatment must be evacuated by air to a suitable Medical Treatment Facility (MTF). The Persian Gulf war was the first significant armed conflict in which this concept has been put to a serious test. The results were far from satisfactory -- about 60% of the patients ended up at the wrong destinations. In early 1993, the Department of Defense tasked USTRANSCOM to consolidate the command and control of medical regulation and aeromedical evacuation operations. The ensuing analysis led to TRAC2ES (TRANSCOM Regulating and Command and Control Evacuation System), a decision support system for planning and scheduling medical evacuation operations. Probably the most challenging aspect of the problem has to do with the dynamics of a domain in which requirements and constraints continuously change over time. Continuous dynamic replanning is a key capability of TRAC2ES. This paper describes the application and the AI approach we took in providing this capability.

Problem Description

U.S. Transportation Command (USTRANSCOM) is the DoD agency responsible for evacuating patients during wartime and peace. Doctrinally, patients requiring extended treatment must be evacuated by air to a suitable Medical Treatment Facility (MTF). The process of identifying an MTF that constitutes a suitable destination for a given patient (based on matching the patient's medical condition and MTF's capability, and on economics and transportation availability) is called regulating. The process of routing and scheduling the required aeromedical evacuation flights (missions) and assigning patients to suitable missions is evacuation planning and execution.

Copyright © 1998, American Association for Artificial Intelligence (www.aaai.org). All rights reserved.

There has been very limited experience with this approach to handling patients other than in peace time. The Persian Gulf war was the first significant armed conflict in which this concept has been put to a serious test. The results were far from satisfactory -- about 60% of the patients ended up at the wrong destinations and half in the wrong country (Endoso1994).

In early 1993, the Department of Defense tasked USTRANSCOM to consolidate the command and control of medical regulation and aeromedical evacuation operations during peace, war and projected contingencies. The ensuing analysis led to the development of a decision-support system -- TRAC2ES (TRANSCOM Regulating and Command and Control Evacuation System).

The integrated medical regulation/evacuation problem requires the dynamic identification of appropriate Medical Treatment Facilities (MTFs) for new patients and the planning/scheduling of aeromedical evacuation operations to transport these patients from current locations to selected MTFs. This is a large-scale, highly dynamic planning and scheduling problem that can involve hundreds or even thousands of simultaneous patient movement requests. Each patient has one or several medical requirements that constrain the type of MTF to which he or she can be evacuated and a ready-time prior to which evacuation cannot start. Additional constraints can include a maximum altitude above which the evacuation aircraft cannot take the patient, a maximum number of hours that a patient can spend in a flight before requiring an overnight rest, etc. Planning/scheduling operations in this domain require the dynamic coordination and (re)allocation of a large number of resources subject to a wide variety of constraints. Key assets/resources and associated constraints include aircrafts and their different characteristics (e.g. capacity, refueling requirements, etc.), air and medical crews and restrictions on the number of hours they can work in any given day, airports and their characteristics (e.g. capacity, types of aircraft they can accommodate, etc.), hospital beds at MTFs located all around the globe and the types of patients each MTF can accommodate, etc.

Probably the most challenging aspect in planning and scheduling medical evacuation operations has to do with the dynamics of a domain in which requirements and constraints continuously change over time. New patient requests come in, others get canceled. Patient conditions change over time possibly requiring the delay, acceleration or cancellation of a patient's evacuation or a change in the patient's destination. Availability of key assets is also subject to unpredictable events (e.g., aircraft maintenance problems, hospital beds not getting freed on time, airfield attrition, etc.). Weather conditions can affect evacuation, requiring that a mission be delayed, rerouted or canceled.

In building and revising evacuation plans a number of objectives and preferences need to be taken into account. The number of patients evacuated to adequate MTFs has to be maximized, with urgent patients given priority over routine ones. The time to pickup and deliver patients to their MTFs, especially urgent ones, should be as short as possible. The time each patient spends in a flight and the number of stops during his/her evacuation also have to be minimized. Other important considerations include minimizing the number of missions, maximizing aircraft capacity utilization, etc.

Features of the Aeromedical Regulation and Evacuation Problem

From the computational point of view, the problem of military Aeromedical Regulation and Evacuation (ARE) of patients to medical treatment facilities is a complex extension of the well-known Dial-A-Ride-Problem (DARP) (Sadeh and Kott 1996). The ARE problem exhibits a number of features commonly found in dynamic transportation problems that require dynamic replanning and rescheduling:

- Multiple demands to transport commodities or entities (in our example -- patients) from/to origin or destination points (e.g., airports and hospitals);
- Multiple resources (e.g., planes, hospitals) are to be routed and scheduled to meet the demands;
- Time window constraints, e.g., in our example a patient cannot be picked up at the origin point until he/she is prepared for departure and delivered to the airport;
- Capacity constraints, e.g., an aeromedical evacuation mission has a limited number of seats available;
- Multiple other constraints of varied nature, such as constraints on duration of tours associated with vehicles and/or with particular requests;
- Demands can change dynamically while the schedule is executing, e.g., new patients may need to be evacuated, or medical condition of a patient may change;
- Resources may also change dynamically, e.g., a mission can be delayed or canceled, or an airport may be closed due to the weather.
- Destination and/or origin points may have to be determined dynamically, e.g., patient's destination may be determined based on the available missions or available hospital beds.

Planning and Scheduling - Reactive and Predictive

Now a few words about some of the terminology we use in this paper, particularly the meaning of "reactive." In a planning problem the solver is given a description of the current state of the problem world and a set of goals to achieve. The task is to find a plan -- a sequence (or more generally -- a network) of activities that will lead to the desired goals. In a scheduling problem the solver is given a plan of activities and a set of available resources. The task is to find a schedule -- an assignment of the activities to the appropriate resources in suitable time windows.

In both problems, the solution must satisfy a given set of constraints, such as precedence constraints on activities or capacities and capabilities of resources. Usually, the solution should also attempt to minimize some "cost" or "value" measure, such as the cost of the resources employed to accomplish the activities. In real-world problems, these two problems are often closely coupled; we treat these two problems as a combined planning and scheduling problem. We use the terms plan and planning to include also schedule and scheduling.

The predictive (also called static) formulation of this problem assumes that all activities are to take place in the future. In the reactive (dynamic or real-time) problem, some of the activities are occurring at the same time that the planning problem is being solved. The reactive problem normally occurs when the current plan has been disrupted either by unexpected events in the world or by changes in goals (Fig. 1). This paper is concerned with the more difficult reactive problem.

At first glance, the reactive problem can be reduced to a predictive problem by determining what the current state of the world is and then formulating a new predictive problem, where all activities are to take place in the future. Although this is indeed possible, the difficulty with this approach is that a new "clean sheet" plan is likely to introduce major destabilizing disruptions into the plan execution and control process.

The key concern in reactive replanning is plan continuity -- the new plan should not introduce unnecessary disruptions.

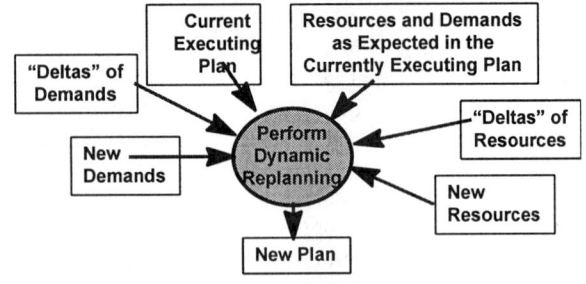

Figure 1. The context of dynamic replanning.

Continuity - The Key Issue of Reactive Replanning and Rescheduling

It is useful to note that the ARE problem can be seen as a constrained optimization problem. The example problem formulation can be briefly outlined as follows:
- Given: current data of patients, missions, MTFs, airfields, ASFs (Airport Staging Facility for patients in transit) ...
- Find: mission schedules and patient itineraries
- Subject to constraint: mission capacity, MTF capacity...
- Optimize or Prefer: minimum time to delivery, minimum use of resources, minimum deviation from the already existing plan/schedule.

The last preference - minimum deviation from the existing plans – deserves a special attention and presents a particularly difficult challenge. When searching for a solution to a dynamic rescheduling problem, one must attempt to minimize the extent of disruptions that the new plan introduces into current execution activities. Dynamic changes to a current plan violate some commitments and waste some investments made into preparing or executing the activities scheduled in the current plan.

For example, significant efforts are expended to prepare for a particular mission: flight and medical crew are assembled and briefed, paper work is issued, flight controllers insert this mission into their plans, maintenance and refueling resources are allocated, etc. By changing a mission, we negate some of these investments and force expenditure of additional resources to undo the effects of some of the activities.

Increased risk is another harmful effect. A plan change increases the risk of mishaps, miscommunications, erroneous data entries and erroneous decision-making. Thus, a mandatory feature of a dynamic replanning process is the ability to minimize the number of changes -- violations of commitments made by the earlier plan.

Sliding Scale of Commitment

It is important to note that the less time is left between the current moment and the time when the activity is planned to happen, the costlier is the change. For example, it is much more expensive to make a change to a mission that takes off in 20 minutes than to a mission that is scheduled to take off in 20 hours.

Other factors in addition to time increase the cost of disruption. One such factor is the extent to which the decision has been communicated to the world. E.g., if the MTF has already begun preparations to receive the patient, then the cost goes up even more.

These observations led to Sliding Scale of Commitment (SSC) - a concept proposed by Dr. V. Saks and W. Elm at Carnegie Group, Inc., circa 1993. The observation is that the key to dynamic rescheduling is to minimize violations of commitment made in the current executing schedule.

Specific components of the SSC concept include:

- there is a cost (the commitment cost) to be paid for rescheduling, even for actions yet to be executed;
- the cost is a function of time, the closer -- the costlier (Fig. 2);
- the cost may also be dependent on domain-specific details of commitment, e.g., who has been notified, what preparations are necessary, etc.

In summary, we argue that the issue of continuity/stability is key to effective dynamic replanning. In fact, it is the dimension that distinguishes reactive replanning from repetitive application of predictive planning. The sliding scale of commitment adds yet another dimension of complexity to the issue of plan continuity. Prior research has not addressed this issue in a systematic and explicit manner.

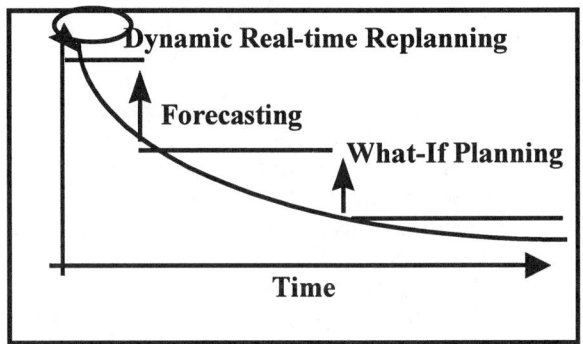

Figure 2. The degree of commitment to plan decisions, and the associated cost of changing these decisions, is a function of time.

Application Description

TRAC2ES Roots and Motivation

According to (Endoso 1994), during the Persian Gulf war medical regulating and evacuation process produced less than satisfactory results - about 60% of the patients ended up at the wrong destination. In early 1993, the Department of Defense (DOD), via DOD Directive 5154.6 and DOD Instruction 6000.11, tasked USTRANSCOM to develop a global command and control (C2) system to remedy deficiencies in medical regulating and evacuation. USTRANSCOM undertook a business re-engineering study and identified two important concepts.

First, separate regulating and evacuation activities were combined into a single, "one-stop shopping" process for patient movement. Merging separate responsibilities of the medical regulator and evacuation coordinator creates a single "evacuation broker" responsible for both regulating and evacuation. The second major concept was that of the "lift bed" which relates medical capability to transportation capability. The study pointed to the need for automated support to implement these two major concepts and provide a global C2 system.

USTRANSCOM decided to explore possible automated information system solutions. This led to the development of TRAC2ES, a large-scale system that involved in excess of 140 person-years of development and deployment effort.

TRAC2ES Functions

TRAC2ES is a Command and Control (C2) application that provides USTRANSCOM with enhanced computer-aided capabilities to forecast, plan, coordinate, and execute the global process of regulating and evacuation of military patients. Although a very large and multi-functional system in itself, TRAC2ES is seen as a part of even broader framework - Global Transportation Network (GTN) which combines a number of databases and Decision Support Systems such as TRAC2ES and encompasses all aspects of U.S. military transportation. Within the GTN, TRAC2ES focuses on the medical transportation aspects, and shares will GTN many functions that also apply to non-medical transportation:

- provide entry and communication mechanisms that enable personnel of MTFs (e.g., field hospitals) request evacuation of a patient and define the medical requirements for the evacuation process;
- perform automated or semi-automated planning of such new requests: match the patient with appropriate hospital, aeromedical evacuation flights, intermediate rest facilities, etc.; this may require dynamic revision of prior plans;
- request additional resources, e.g., additional evacuation flights along suitable routes or hospital beds in bottleneck locations, when current capacity is insufficient to meet the demands;
- coordinate evacuation plans between different regional planning centers (TPMRC's) and assure that there is no conflicts between their intended uses of shared resources;
- store all plans in the databases that are globally accessible to all authorized parties (medical and transportation personnel), and issue notifications to hospitals (when and whom to prepare for evacuation or for arrival and treatment), to transportation organizations (when, where and whom to pickup and deliver), etc.;
- collect and provide near-real-time data regarding the current in-transit status (location, condition, future plans) of all patients and critical assets (medical transportation, equipment, crews);
- continuously monitor the execution of the plans, alert about disruptions of the plan, and provide dynamic replanning to accommodate the disruptions.

TRAC2ES Users

TRAC2ES users include (Fig. 3):
- personnel at the origination hospitals (e.g., military field hospitals): they use TRAC2ES to enter requests for evacuation of a patient and to receive notification of when and how this request will be satisfied;
- personnel at the destination hospitals (e.g., large hospitals in U.S.): they use TRAC2ES to notify of their available bed capacity, to receive notifications about arrival of new patients;
- staff of the regional patient movement centers (TPMRCs or JPMRCs): they use TRAC2ES to monitor all new requests or disruptions in the current plan (Fig. 4), to generate a modified plan and to issue orders to the performing organizations;
- staff of the global patient movement center (GPMRC, part of the USTRANSCOM staff): they monitor the overall global process of evacuation, resolve conflicts over the use of shared resources, procure and allocate additional resources;
- personnel of the transportation organizations (both dedicated aeromedical transporters, as well as military cargo transporters and civilian airlines who are also frequently pressed into aeromedical evacuation service): they use TRAC2ES to receive orders to transport a patient, and to report actual success of executing the order and any disruptions;
- all authorized personnel of the U.S. Government - they can use TRAC2ES to find the location and status of any TRAC2ES-monitored patient while in-transit.

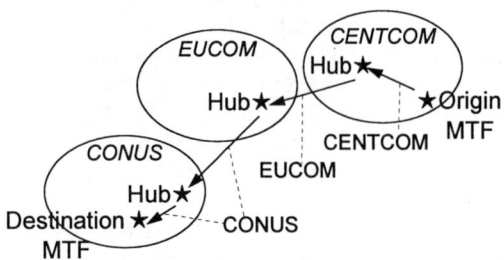

Figure 3. The evacuation planning and execution process involves originating MTF, destination MTF, one or several theater patient movement centers, aeromedical transport organizations, and global patient movement center.

TRAC2ES Operation

Let us consider an example (Braidic 1996). Suppose an American soldier is injured in Europe and receives initial care at a Medical Treatment Facility (MTF) in Germany. Data about the injured soldier is entered at the MTF and sent to the European Theater Patient Movement Requirements Center (TPMRC) workstation. A few days later, the soldier is ready to be moved to an MTF near the soldier's home in the U.S. Information about all flights of the military aircraft is located on a workstation at the Global Patient Movement Requirements Center (GPMRC) in the United States. Available beds and medical care capabilities at hospitals in the United States are stored on a TPMRC workstation located in Illinois. TRAC2ES component at European TPMRC will analyze mission data and bed data and assist planners in providing the soldier with a safe, speedy, and cost effective trip home to a hospital having the appropriate personnel, equipment and facilities. The journey may involve multiple connecting flights, and may require use of overnight rest facilities, available at some airports. This planning process may, if necessary, involve replanning of movements of some other patients, to open the bottlenecks in transportation or medical assets. TRAC2ES will monitor the movement of this soldier from the beginning of the soldier's journey in Europe to the destination hospital in the U.S. The system will react along the way, if necessary, to problems such as airport closings, missed flights, and changes in hospital bed availability.

Even an example of a single patient involves a degree of complexity. TRAC2ES however, is designed to handle simultaneously many thousands of patients. This leads to a combinatorial puzzle of missions, hospitals, airports and other resources of astronomical size and complexity.

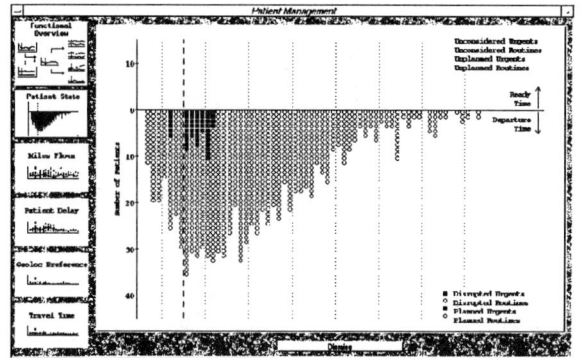

Figure 4: Advanced GUI for monitoring the dynamic changes in the evacuation process were designed using Cognitive Systems Engineering (Potter et al. 1996).

TRAC2ES Components

MTF component: multiple MTFs access TRAC2ES via the World Wide Web (WWW) using commercially available web browsers. TRAC2ES server provides a site which the MTF personnel can access to enter a request for evacuating a patient, the condition of the patient, and any preferences for the evacuation. The same site allows them to find out about the status of the request, i.e., if the patient has been scheduled for evacuation. MTFs also receive e-mail notification of the evacuation schedule automatically generated via the TRAC2ES server. Hardware: PC's running Windows. Technologies used: web server, web browser, HTML, JavaScript.

TMPRC component: each theater (military region) of operations includes an organization responsible for movement of patients to, from, and within the theater. This organization - TPMRC - uses a TPMRC-specific component of TRAC2ES, which receives requests for patient movements, plans/replans them, and issues orders to appropriate transportation and medical organizations to execute the planned movements. In particular, the dynamic replanning capability resides within the TPMRC component. Hardware: Sun workstations under Solaris. Technologies: Versant distributed object-oriented DBMS, C++, Motif.

Fly Away component: a version of the TPMRC component in a self-contained configuration, used to set up a movement planning center rapidly in any new region.

GPMRC component: global patient movement center at USTRANSCOM uses this component (a modification of the TPMRC component) to monitor the movements of patients world-wide, and to perform what-if planning.

Use of AI Technology - Continuity-Guided Regeneration

A very large, distributed application with multiple types of users and functions, TRAC2ES encompasses a number of novel technological aspects. In this paper we focus on one of these technological aspects, but it is worthwhile to mention others at least briefly and to point the reader to the corresponding references:

- broad use of world-wide distributed Object-Oriented Databases and rigorous object-oriented design and development methodology (Braidic 1996);
- novel user interfaces developed using the methodology of Cognitive System Engineering (Potter et al. 1996);
- multi-agent problem solving process (Saks et al. 1997).

In the following discussion we focus on one key function of TRAC2ES that is particularly relevant to the AI perspective of this conference – the planning and scheduling function – and the corresponding AI technologies – Continuity-Guided Regeneration (Kott and Saks 1996).

Continuity-Guided Regeneration in Planning and Scheduling

We saw the issue of continuity as the key challenge in the dynamic replanning and scheduling function of TRAC2ES. In response to this challenge we developed the technique of Continuity-Guided Regeneration (CGR). CGR is an extension of the ideas originally developed at CGI for solving re-design problems, circa 1990, within the SPEx design and configuration shell (Berry and Kott 1992). The key idea is to regenerate the plan while using the currently executing plan as a constraint on the solution. One significance of this idea is that it assures plan continuity without having to answer the difficult question of how much of the current plan to undo. We extended the Continuity-Guided Regeneration idea of SPEx to make it capable of accounting for the sliding scale of commitment.

In TRAC2ES, we applied it to modify a particular scheduling approach, micro-opportunistic search, an instantiation of Constrained Heuristic Search (Sadeh 1991). The main steps of the micro-opportunistic search procedure can be summarized as follows:

1. A set of candidate plans is created for each requirement;
2. "Reliance" (dependencies) of the requirement on each of the available resources are computed;
3. Each requirement distributes its demand to the resources and time line;

4. Overall contention for each resource is computed by time bucket;
5. The most contended for resource is selected;
6. The requirement that is most reliant (dependent) on the selected resource is assigned to the resource.
7. Go to 2.

We modified this approach using the idea of commitment constraint. We elected to use the reliance computation as the area of the search procedure where the commitment constraints enter the picture. For each requirement (in our specific case - a patient movement request):

1. retrieve the resource which has been committed to this requirement in the existing Plan;
2. compute a measure of Importance of Preserving the same Commitment (IPC) based on how far in the future the use of this resource is to take place and taking into account other domain-dependent commitment measures;
3. increase reliance measure associated with this requirement-resource pair using the IPC;
4. use the assignment mechanism to assign a resource to the requirement. The higher reliance value leads to a better chance that the requirement will be assigned to the same resource as in the existing Plan, if such an assignment is feasible.

We believe that the Continuity-Guided Regeneration paradigm can be used not only as an add-on to the micro-opportunistic search but also with other planning and scheduling approaches. A key advantage of the Continuity-Guided Regeneration approach is that it eliminates the key dilemma of the re-scheduling problem: how much of the prior schedule to undo.

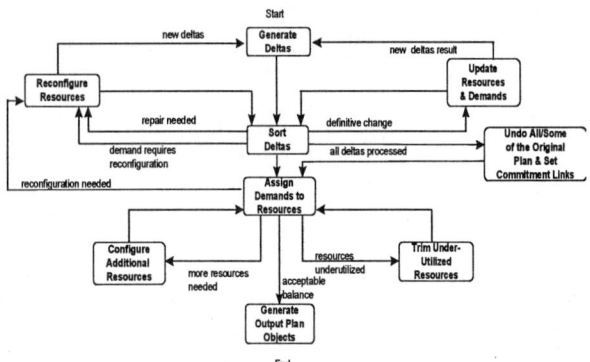

Figure 5: Overall flow of the dynamic replanning process using the Continuity-Guided Regeneration approach.

Applying the CGR Approach to the TRAC2ES Dynamic Replanning Problem

The solution process (Fig. 5) begins with the arrival of disruptive events, such as closure of an airport. Each event is decomposed into one or more of so called "world deltas." Each world delta is a description of a difference between the expected state of an entity (e.g., airport is open) and its actual state (e.g., airport is closed).

The deltas are sorted, using domain-specific heuristics, in the order of significance and downstream impact. Depending on the nature of each delta, the algorithm then may create new deltas, update attributes and associations of existing resources and demands, or reconfigure existing resources (missions). For example, the following operations can be performed on missions:

- update modified missions with a complete route/schedule given;
- "repair" missions which have been diverted for some reason and for which continuation of the mission is not given;
- re-route missions, if necessary, to provide suitable route for new urgent patients.

All patient itineraries that have been in any way affected by any of the deltas are marked as invalid. This "undoing" of itineraries in the original plan is done liberally, i.e., we prefer to err on side of undoing more itineraries than necessary given that the Continuity-Guided Regeneration provides continuity.

At this point, the process of assigning patients to resources (e.g., missions and hospitals) is performed. It involves re-assigning Patients to resources (missions, hospitals, etc.) using the Continuity-Guided Regeneration approach. An assignment of a patient to the same resources as in the original plan is given a higher score. The increase in score is computed in inverse proportion to how far in the future the use of the resources begin (to account for the Sliding Scale of Commitment).

Finally, the system generates a recommendation that describes the impact of the world deltas and the set of suggested modifications to the plan

Current Use of TRAC2ES

The most significant use of TRAC2ES to date has been at military exercises – most demanding tests of military capabilities short of real war. It should be pointed out that benefits of TRAC2ES capabilities are more difficult to demonstrate in peace time - the flow rate of patients is fairly low, resources are not overconstrained, and a handful of human planners can do a good job planning, executing and monitoring the evacuation process in an essentially manual process. However, the situation is entirely different at the time of war, or its closest possible approximation -- military exercise. The flow of patients is large, resources are overconstrained, disruptions are unrelenting, and human planners are unable to cope with the volume of information and complexity of the problem. That's where TRAC2ES delivers a capability that simply cannot be delivered by any other means.

Consider one of the exercises - Unified Endeavor 98-1 -- where TRAC2ES has been actively used and where it demonstrated its benefits. Unified Endeavor 98-1 was conducted in October/November 1997. It was a computer-assisted exercise that involved components from U.S. Army, Marine, Navy, Air Force, and military of United

Kingdom. In the scenario, the operation responded to an aggressive northern nation in the Middle East that threatened a smaller southern nation's sovereignty. US Central Command (USCENTCOM) tasked USACOM to provide a Combined Joint Task Force (CJTF) to deter the aggressor while USCENTCOM deployed additional forces to the region. United Kingdom forces participated in UE 98-1 through a collateral exercise, UK PURPLE LINK 97; their Joint Rapid Deployment Forces (JRDF) consisted of a reinforced brigade with maritime, air, special forces, and logistics elements in coalition with US forces.

The exercise was supported by the TRAC2ES FlyAway 1.3.1 version which supported a single theater patient movement capability consistent with the UE 98-1 concept of operation. Wounded-in-action casualties were generated from several sources, including Master Scenario Event List and a battle simulation model. The exercise controllers periodically injected additional casualty situations into exercise play. There were several MTF nodes distributed over the U.S. Each MTF was submitting patient movement requests the JPMRC component of TRAC2ES. Users and observers stated that the exercises demonstrated a number of "value added" capabilities provided by TRAC2ES (as compared to conventional near-manual operation), including:

- much more robust method of communicating patients movement requests from MTFs to the JPMRC; the ability of MTF to see if patient has been scheduled for movement and how; the ability of MTF personnel to view the entire planned itinerary of the patient;
- users at a variety of locations (including UK components) were able to obtain information about patient's information; planned movements, etc.,
- dynamic replanning capability deserved particular mention. Numerous extremely disruptive events were injected into the exercise: closure or movement of various facilities; cancellation or rescheduling of flights; changes in requested patient movements. It was common for nearly all patients previously scheduled to be disrupted due to a single event injection; many occurred while patients were already enroute. It was clear to the observers, that without TRAC2ES JPMRC officers would be unable to deal with the resulting chaos and to remedy disrupted movement schedules. The dynamic replanning capability of TRAC2ES helped users to quickly and easily create solutions to problems caused by disruptive events. Helping the JPMRC staff to solve the hardest, most time-consuming parts of the patient movement scheduling process, TRAC2ES freed them up for other tasks.

Development and Deployment Process

TRAC2ES automated information system development started with a Proof of Concept (POC) prototype, followed by two Operational Prototype releases that tested key functionality and deployment to TRAC2ES owners issues.

The POC, successfully completed in early 1994, featured tests of preliminary algorithms that used constraint-based reasoning for development of "lift beds" and rudimentary airlift schedules.

OP1 (Operational Prototype 1), delivered in October 1994, began prototyping TRAC2ES hardware with network communications. OP1 software, while introducing some limited features, was primarily a demonstration capability used to illustrate future directions and applications capabilities TRAC2ES may contain. OP2, delivered in June 1995, was based on a newly designed prototype architecture which includes a distributed, object-oriented database. The OP2 GUI and algorithm provided enhanced functionality including coordinated planning by one global and several theater-based centers. In fall of 1995, the next operational prototype OP3 was released, featuring a number of enhancements to the GUI (Graphic User Interface) and the planning algorithm. In 1996 and 1997, the work focused on extending the OP3 system into a self-contained, readily deployable TPMRC system that could be used for rapid installation in exercises and real-life contingencies. This resulting system was named TRAC2ES FlyAway. It is this version of TRAC2ES that was used in the exercise Unified Endeavor 98-1 we discussed in section 4 above.

From its inception, $TRAC^2ES$ has involved users in shaping its "to be" vision via national award winning business process re-engineering and the incorporation of multi-disciplinary user feedback. USTRANSCOM sponsored numerous Corporate Information Management (CIM) workshops, each of which focused on re-engineering a portion of the patient regulating and evacuation process into a seamless whole. One of the key challenges in the TRAC2ES development and deployment process was the fact that both the system and the business process were evolving in parallel and heavily influenced each other: on one hand, the user community continued to work on modifying and optimizing the business process as they learnt more about feasibility and capabilities of TRAC2ES; on the other hand, TRAC2ES was redesigned and modified to meet the evolution of the business process. From the software methodology perspective, TRAC2ES development has two particularly salient features: a very prominent role played by the object-oriented CASE tool with automated code generation capability, and the extensive use of Object-Oriented DBMS (Braidic 1996).

Maintenance

Developers of applications involving AI techniques and domain-specific knowledge-bases often envision that the maintenance of the knowledge base will be eventually undertaken by the knowledge engineers who are part of the end-user organization, or possibly by the end-users themselves. Other common visions of application maintenance involve self-learning of the system.

We did not feel that these concepts are practical in the context of TRAC2ES. Although several key techniques utilized in TRAC2ES belong to the field of AI, TRAC2ES does not have a large and prominent knowledge base. TRAC2ES relies in its problem-solving approach on a relatively small collection of constraints and preferences, which are fairly stable and do not change frequently. The life-critical nature of the application also indicates against any maintenance process that is not extremely rigorously controlled.

The maintenance process of TRAC2ES is structured around a rigorous tracking, analysis and prioritization of request for bug fixes and enhancements; continuous development process involving rigorous and formal cycles of requirements maintenance, design modifications via a object-oriented CASE tool, extensive reviews, implementation that involves large percentage of automatically generated code, verification and validation, quality assurance and extensive testing.

Conclusion

TRAC2ES is a very large system that serves a broad range of users worldwide, and involved several hundred person-years of development effort. While providing a range of functions and benefits, and relying on a number of advanced technology, TRAC2ES is critically dependent on a particular capability - continuous dynamic replanning. One might argue that the entire doctrine of large-scale aeromedical evacuation (and the associated business process) could be considered infeasible without such a capability.

We found that plan continuity is a key concern in devising a dynamic replanning technique. It is the key differentiator between predictive and dynamic planning.

Our prior work in design and redesign led to the novel technique of Continuity-Guided Regeneration. The key idea is to regenerate the plan while using the currently executing plan as a constraint on the solution. One significance of this idea is that it assures the plan continuity without having to answer the difficult question of how much of the current plan to undo.

Our implementation of this approach in application to aeromedical evacuation demonstrated that this approach fully addresses the continuity issue, enables sliding scale of commitment, eliminates the "extent of undoing" question, and provides an effective mechanism to control the balance between the demands of continuity and optimality.

TRAC2ES has demonstrated capabilities of dynamic replanning, not feasible via current near-manual methods, in the demanding environment of modern military exercises.

Acknowledgements

This work was supported by the United States Transportation Command. Leadership was provided by W. Elm and A. Mercer (Carnegie Group, Inc.), R. Simpson (MITRE), J. Simpson and C. Kirschner (USTRANSCOM).

References

Berry, F. and Kott, A. The SPEx Shell: an Approach to Automating Application and Sales Engineering Processes. In *Proceedings of the 1992 ASME Computers In Engineering Conference*. ASME.

Braidic, G. 1996. Mission-critical Patient Care. *Object Magazine,* February.

Endoso, J. 1994. TRANSCOM Wants Casualties To Get Where They Belong. *Government Computer News*, May 2.

Kott, A. and Saks, V. 1996. Continuity-Guided Regeneration: An Approach to Reactive Replanning and Rescheduling, In *Proceedings of the Florida Artificial Intelligence Research Symposium*, Key West, FL

Potter, S., Ball, R. and Elm, W. 1996. Supporting Aeromedical Evacuation Planning Through Information Visualization, In *Proceedings of the 3rd Annual Symposium on Human Interactions with Complex Systems.*

Sadeh, N. 1991. Look-ahead Techniques for Micro-opportunistic Job Shop Scheduling. Doctoral dissertation, School of Computer Science, Carnegie Mellon University.

Sadeh, N.M. and Kott, A. 1996. Models and Techniques of Dynamic Demand-Responsive Transportation Planning. Technical Report CMU-RI-TR-96-09, The Robotics Institute, Carnegie Mellon University, Pittsburgh, PA.

Saks, V., Braidic, G., Kott, A. and Kirschner, C. 1997. Distributed Medical Evacuation Planning: Which Problem Should Each Agent Solve. 14th National Conference on Artificial Intelligence, Workshop on Constraints and Agents.

Saks, V., Kepner, A. and Johnson, I. 1992. Knowledge Based Distribution Planning. In American Defense Preparedness Association Conference.

Knowledge-based Avoidance of Drug-Resistant HIV Mutants

Richard H. Lathrop, Nicholas R. Steffen, Miriam P. Raphael, Sophia Deeds-Rubin, Michael J. Pazzani

Department of Information and Computer Science,
University of California, Irvine, CA 92717 USA
{ rickl | nsteffen | mraphael | sophiadr | pazzani }@uci.edu

Paul J. Cimoch

Director, Center for Special Immunology
100 Pacifica #100, Irvine, CA 92718 USA
gr82bpnc@msn.com

Darryl M. See, Jeremiah G. Tilles

Department of Medicine,
University of California, Irvine, CA 92717 USA
{ dmsee | jgtilles }@uci.edu

Abstract

We describe an artificial intelligence (AI) system (CTSHIV) that connects the scientific AIDS literature describing specific HIV drug resistances directly to the Customized Treatment Strategy of a specific HIV patient. Rules in the CTSHIV knowledge base encode knowledge about sequence mutations in the HIV genome that have been found to result in drug resistance in the HIV virus. Rules are applied to the actual HIV sequences of the virus strains infecting the specific patient undergoing clinical treatment in order to infer current drug resistance. A search through mutation sequence space identifies nearby drug resistant mutant strains that might arise. The possible drug treatment regimens currently approved by the US Food and Drug Administration (FDA) are considered and ranked by their estimated ability to avoid identified current and nearby drug resistant mutants. The highest-ranked treatments are recommended to the attending physician. The result is more precise treatment of individual HIV patients, and a decreased tendency to select for drug resistant genes in the global HIV gene pool. The application is currently in use in human clinical trials on HIV patients. Initial results from a small clinical trial are encouraging and further clinical trials are planned. From an AI viewpoint the case study demonstrates the extensibility of knowledge-based systems because it illustrates how existing encoded knowledge can be used to support new applications that were unanticipated when the original knowledge was encoded.

Copyright ©1998, American Association of Artificial Intelligence (www.aaai.org). All rights reserved.

Problem Description

Human immunodeficiency virus (HIV) causes progressive deterioration of the immune system leading almost invariably to AIDS and death from opportunistic cancers and infections. Currently in the USA it is estimated to infect 3–5 million persons, is the leading cause of death in adults from age 14 to 35, and is the nation's leading cause of productive years of life lost aggregated over all age groups. HIV is estimated to infect 40–50 million persons worldwide (CDC 1997).

The high rate of HIV viral mutation both makes development of a vaccine difficult and results in rapid positive selection for drug resistant mutant strains. Recent multi-drug combination therapies are encouraging, but in most cases ultimately fail due to the development of drug resistance (O'Brian et al. 1996). A general theory of HIV drug resistance still is not in hand, but a number of specific sequence mutations in the HIV genome have been described in the scientific literature and associated with increased resistance to certain drugs.

In this paper we describe an AI system intended to improve the clinical treatment of individual HIV patients by identifying drug resistance in advance and avoiding it in treatment. This is done by first identifying drug resistant HIV mutant strains that already exist in the patient or are likely to be positively selected for by certain treatments, and then recommending a customized treatment designed to avoid selection of such mutants. The result is more precise treatment of individual HIV patients, and a decreased tendency to select for drug resistant genes in the global HIV gene pool.

Project Goals

The project goals are:

1. Connect knowledge contained in the scientific literature about HIV drug resistance directly to the treatment of individual HIV patients;
2. Enable customized treatment strategies to be based on the HIV genotype that currently infects an individual HIV patient;
3. Identify the nature and extent of drug resistance currently present in an individual HIV patient;
4. Identify nearby drug resistant mutant strains that could be positively selected for by some treatments;
5. Rank the possible FDA-approved treatments by an estimate of their ability to avoid both current and nearby drug resistant mutants;
6. Estimate the costs of the higest-ranked treatments;
7. Recommend treatments that are estimated to be most likely to avoid known HIV drug resistance.

Related Work

An expert system based on experimental data from HIV patients (immunologic markers) has been used to diagnose the opportunistic non-Hodgkin's lymphomas which often develop (Diamond *et al.* 1994). Knowledge-based systems have been applied to HIV patient medical record systems (Musen *et al.* 1995; Safran *et al.* 1996), monitoring ongoing HIV patient protocols (Musen *et al.* 1996; Tu *et al.* 1995; Sonnenberg, Hagerty, & Kulikowski 1994; Sobesky *et al.* 1994), and HIV patient assessment (Xu 1996; Ohno-Machado *et al.* 1993). Less closely related are knowledge-based systems that apply qualitative modeling and process simulation to HIV laboratory systems (Sieburg 1994; Ruggiero *et al.* 1994). To our knowledge CTSHIV is the first system to use HIV sequence data from HIV patients to estimate current and nearby drug resistant mutants and recommend treatment combinations to avoid both.

Domain Background

The information content of an HIV virus is contained in a set of genes encoded in its genome. Each gene is a sequence of bases or nucleotides of four varieties. A gene can be represented as a string over an alphabet of four characters, one character representing each nucleotide. The HIV genome ultimately causes the production of gene products, often proteins, important in the virus life cycle. A protein is a sequence of amino acids of twenty varieties, and can be represented as a string over an alphabet of twenty characters. Each amino acid in the protein is encoded by a block of three adjacent nucleotides in the genome, called a codon. The two proteins targeted by current FDA-approved drugs are called "reverse transcriptase" (RT) and "protease" (PRO). An example RT protein structure (Hsiou *et al.* to be published) is shown in Figure 1.

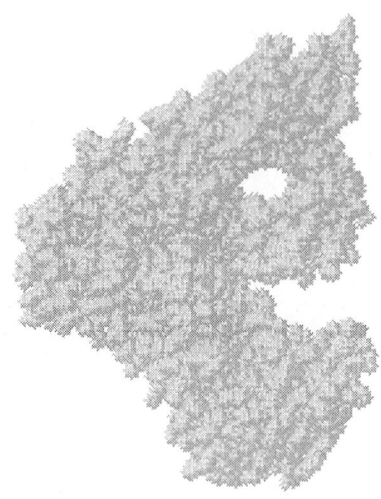

Figure 1: The 3D structure of the HIV reverse transcriptase protein (PDB code 1DLO). Each sphere represents an atom. The structure is encoded in the HIV reverse transcriptase sequence (see Figure 3). Mutations in the sequence cause changes in the number, type, or spatial arrangement of atoms in the structure.

The genome string must be copied from one generation to the next during the virus life cycle. Copying errors occur frequently, and are called mutations. Mutations can change the structure or function of the virus, and thus alter how it interacts with its environment. Mutant strains with genome sequences very similar to the patient's current strain (close in Hamming or edit distance) appear spontaneously and continuously. In a full-blown case of AIDS, it is estimated that every single point mutation appears every day, every coordinated pair of point mutations appears once or more during the course of the infection, and even coordinated triples of point mutations may appear (Condra *et al.* 1995).

A drug typically works by blocking a key part of the virus life cycle. A drug resistant mutation occurs when a copying error in the viral genome so alters the virus that it can perform the targeted step of its life cycle even in the presence of the drug. In the continued presence of the drug the mutant strain may out-compete the dominant strain, and thereby may itself become the dominant stain in the patient. This is often called selective drug resistance, because the resistant mutant is selected for by the drug's presence. If unrecognized, the current treatment may lose its effect and the patient's condition may deteriorate. The resulting strain is more challenging to treat because the treatment options have been reduced. If the drug treatment is changed in response, the potential for a new drug resistant mutation to develop is present. The use of an increasing variety of drugs has led to virus strains increasingly resistant to multiple drugs simultaneously. Sadly, increasing prevalence of drug resistant strains in the HIV global gene pool means that new patients may be infected by mutant strains that already have accrued resistance from previous hosts (Gu et al. 1994). Consequently it is important to avoid selecting for drug resistant mutants.

Combination treatments involving multiple drugs are one approach to avoiding drug resistance (Lange 1995). If the virus mutates to resist one drug but still is inhibited by another, it may be suppressed or unviable. In this case the mutation may not be positively selected for. Combinations may contain up to four simultaneous drugs, but usually do not exceed three due to the potential for intolerable side-effects and toxicity. Severe side-effects often induce a patient to stop one or more drugs without knowledge of their physician, called non-adherence (formerly non-compliance). Non-adherence negates combination therapy and increases the likelihood of selecting for drug resistant mutants.

Combinations containing at least one protease inhibitor are referred to as Highly Active Anti-Retroviral Therapy (HAART). HAART typically results in a dramatic drop in viral load within two weeks, often sustained for long periods of time. Enthusiasm for the potential of HAART to eradicate HIV has been tempered by the inevitable failure of these regimens due to the eventual development of drug resistance (Carpenter et al. 1996). The virus appears to remain in a proviral state in resting memory T-cells, where it is inaccessible to antiretroviral drugs (Wong et al. 1997; Finzi et al. 1997). Mutations still can occur under HAART, though the mutation rate is greatly decreased (Jacobsen et al. 1996).

There are important limitations of the approach below. Sequence-based rules capture only part of the domain knowledge about drug resistance, albeit a clinically useful part. Drug resistance may arise for other domain-specific reasons that cannot be represented easily as rules. Current sequencing techniques may provide only partial or no information about minority strains. The rule set is only as complete as current scientific knowledge allows. Currently it may be possible to infer when resistance is likely to occur, based on genome sequences actually seen in the patient that correspond to resistance-conferring mutations described in the scientific literature. However, it is impossible to guarantee the non-existence of an unsuspected resistant mutant.

Nonetheless, knowledge of current or nearby mutants putatively resistant to one or more drugs is valuable to a physician treating an HIV patient. In conjunction with HAART, such knowledge may help select a combination of drugs less likely to be resisted. Currently there are 11 drugs approved by the FDA for HIV, plus one available for compassionate use. These 12 result in 407 different combination treatments of four or fewer drugs, as some drugs should not be used together. A physician may find it tedious to scan many sequences, be unfamiliar with the latest HIV drug resistant mutations reported, or have difficulty ranking the hundreds of treatment choices for each patient. CTSHIV mediates between the scientific literature and the patient's current infection to help a physician avoid HIV drug resistance.

Application Description

The application (1) accepts as input experimentally determined HIV sequences extracted from the patient; (2) extracts the relevant codons and constructs virtual genomes; (3) estimates current resistance by applying knowledge base rules; (4) searches nearby mutation sequence space to identify nearby putatively resistant mutants; (5) ranks the possible FDA-approved treatment regimens according to their ability to avoid selective drug resistance; and (6) recommends the highest-ranked treatment regimens to the attending physician. See the application overview flowchart in Figure 2.

Patient's Experimental Data

The reverse transcriptase and protease portions of the POL gene are amplified from each patient. Clones are produced, plasmid DNA is extracted, and the sequence is determined using a commercially available ABI sequencer. The reverse transcriptase sequence contains 1,299 letters (433 codons) and the protease sequence contains 297 letters (99 codons). Figure 3 shows an example HIV sequence from an HIV patient.

The sequences are pre-aligned to a standard reference HIV sequence (HXB2) using standard sequence alignment algorithms. Deviations from the reference sequence correspond to mutations in the virus infecting the patient. Typically five reverse transcriptase sequences and five protease sequences, a total of 7,980 letters of HIV genomic information, are the input experimental data on the patient's current infection.

Extract Features, Objects

Processing in this step is routine. The features extracted are exactly those codons in positions referred to by the antecedent of some rule. Other positions are not yet associated with known drug resistance. Currently 55 rules mention 31 different codon positions, 20 in RT and 11 in PRO. HIV sequences are replaced by abstract objects consisting of only those codon positions. All possible virtual genomes are formed consistent with the experimental sequences.

Identify Current Resistance

Current drug resistance is identified by applying the 55 rules in the knowledge base to the HIV sequences from the patient. The rules represent knowledge about HIV drug resistance as a set of if-then rules of the form:

IF ⟨ antecedent ⟩ THEN ⟨ consequent ⟩ [weight].

For example, one such rule in CTSHIV is:

IF Methionine is encoded by RT codon 151, THEN do not use AZT, ddI, d4T, or ddC. [weight= 1.0]
(Iversen et al. 1996)

The weight associated with a rule is not a confidence as in many expert systems. Rather, it reflects the estimated level of resistance to a particular drug, and is part of the consequent. Weights range from 0.1 (low)

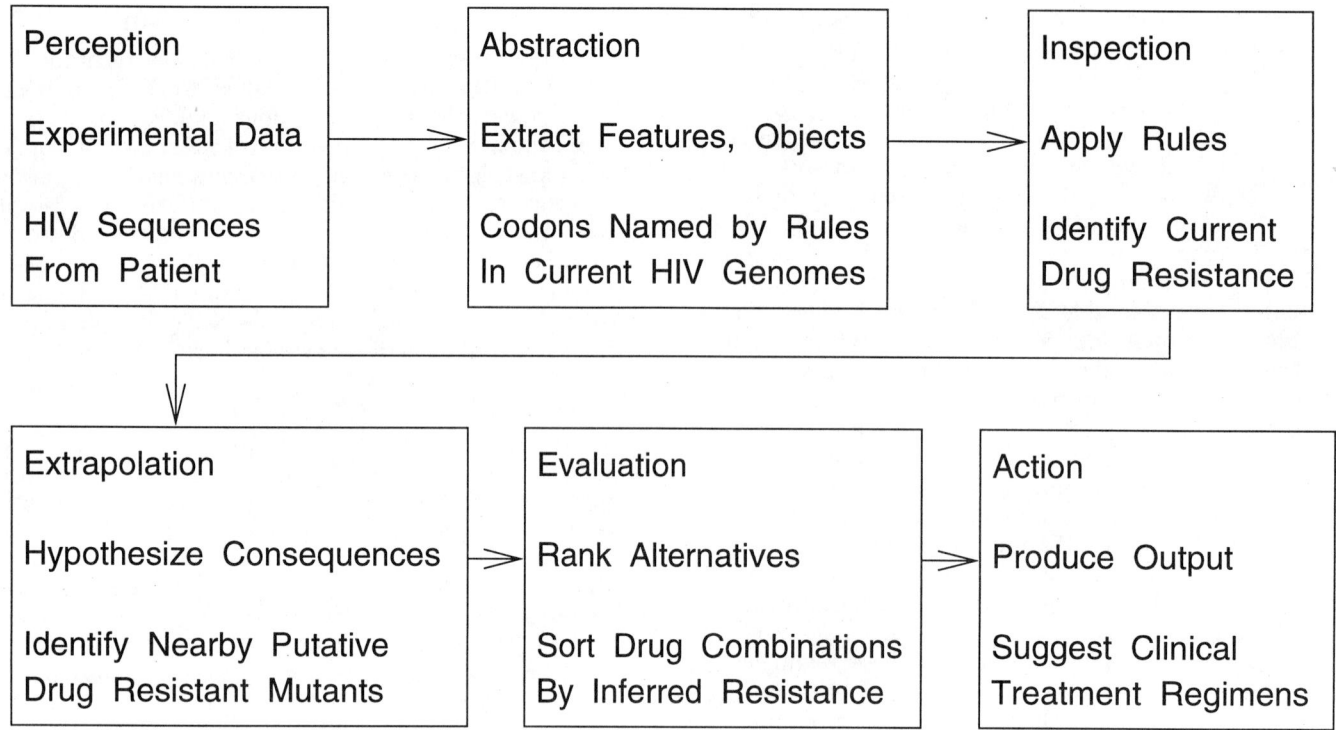

Figure 2: Application overview flowchart.

to 1.0 (high) based upon expert advice and the level of resistance reported in the literature.

To estimate current resistance, rule weight is multiplied by the fraction of viral sequences that trigger the rule, and combined additively. As a summary metric we use

$$CurrWt(D) = \sum_{r \in \text{Rules}(D)} \sum_{s \in S} \text{Apply}(r,s)/|S|$$

where D is a set of drugs comprising a combination therapy, Rules(D) are the rules that confer resistance to a drug in D, S is the set of the HIV sequences extracted from the patient, and Apply(r, s) yields the rule weight of r if r fires on s and 0 if not. $CurrWt$ is comparable only between combinations with the same number of drugs because any superset of a drug combination has equal or greater current weight.

Under this model, the total current level of resistance to a multi-drug combination is the sum of the current resistances to each drug. The effect of this is to identify drug combinations that have little or no current resistance and therefore attack the virus strongly.

Predict Nearby Resistant Mutants

Nearby resistant mutants are predicted by a backward-chaining search through mutation sequence space, beginning with the patient's current HIV sequences. At each step, a sequence that does not fire a rule is used to generate several new sequences that do. The new sequences are identical except that codon positions mentioned by the rule are modified so that the rule does fire. They represent mutants that are close in Hamming distance but resist the drugs mentioned by the rule. Conceptually, every virtual mutant within a pre-determined Hamming distance cut-off is examined. Currently all mutants up to and including Hamming distance three are considered. Branch-and-bound techniques speed the search by pruning unnecessary examinations. Currently CTSHIV runs in about a minute per patient, which is acceptable for now.

To predict nearby mutants, rule weights are combined by taking the maximum across all mutants of the minimum across all drugs in the combination. As a summary metric we use

$\mathbf{m\_dist}(D)$
$$= \min\{h | \exists x \in M(S,h), \forall d \in D, 0 < \sum_{r \in \text{Rules}(d)} \text{Apply}(r,x)\}$$

$\mathbf{m\_wt}(D)$
$$= \max_{x \in M(S,\mathbf{m\_dist}(D))} \min_{d \in D} \sum_{r \in \text{Rules}(d)} \text{Apply}(r,x)$$

$MutScore(D)$
$$= \max\{0, h_{max} - \mathbf{m\_dist}(D) + \mathbf{m\_wt}(D)\}$$

where h_{max} bounds the maximum Hamming distance

```
CCC/ATT/AGC/CCT/ATT/GAG/ACT/GTA/CCA/GTA/AAA/TTA/AAG/CCA/GGA/ATG/GAT/GGC/CCA/AAA/GTT/AAA/CAA/TGG/CCA/TTG/
ACA/GAA/GAA/AAA/ATA/AAA/GCA/TTA/GTA/GAA/ATT/TGT/ACA/GAG/ATG/GAA/AAG/GAA/GGG/*AA/ATT/TCA/AAA/ATT/GGG/CCT/
GAA/AAT/CCA/TAC/AAT/ACT/CCA/GTA/TTT/GCC/ATA/AAG/AAA/AAA/GAC/AGT/ACT/AAA/TGG/AGA/AAA/TTA/GTA/GAT/TTC/AGA/
GAA/CTT/AAT/AAG/AGA/ACT/CAA/GAC/TTC/TGG/GAA/GTT/CAA/TTA/GGA/ATA/CCA/CAT/CCC/GCA/GGG/TAA/AAA/AAG/AAA/AAA/
TCA/GTA/ACA/GTA/CTG/GAT/GTG/GGT/GAT/GCA/TAT/TTT/TCA/GTT/CCC/TTA/GAT/GAA/GAC/TTC/AGG/AAG/TAT/ACT/GCA/TTT/
ACC/ATA/CCT/AGT/ATA/AAC/AAT/GAG/ACA/CCA/GGG/ATT/AGA/TAT/CAG/TAC/AAT/GTG/CTT/CCA/CAG/GGA/TGG/AAA/GGA/TCA/
CCA/GCA/ATA/TTC/CAA/AGT/AGC/ATG/ACA/AAA/ATC/TTA/GAG/CCT/TTT/AGA/AAA/CAA/AAT/CCA/GAC/ATA/GTT/ATC/TAT/CAA/
TAC/ATG/GAT/GAT/TTG/TAT/GTA/GGA/TCT/GAC/TTA/GAA/ATA/GGG/GAG/CAT/AGA/ACA/AAA/ATA/GAG/GAG/CTG/AGA/CAA/CAT/
CTG/TTG/AGG/TGG/GGA/CTT/ACC/ACA/CCA/GAC/AAA/AAA/CAT/CAG/AAA/GAA/CCT/CCA/TTC/CTT/TGG/ATG/GGT/TAT/GAA/CTC/
CAT/CCT/GAT/AAA/TGG/ACA/GTA/CAG/CCT/ATA/GTG/CTG/CCA/GAA/AAA/GAC/AGC/TGG/ACT/GTC/AAT/GAC/ATA/CAG/AAG/TTA/
GTG/GGG/AAA/TTG/AAT/TGG/GCA/AGT/CAG/ATT/TAC/CCA/GGG/ATT/AAA/GTA/AGG/CAA/TTA/TGT/AAA/CTC/CTT/AGA/GGA/ACC/
AAA/GCA/CTA/ACA/GAA/GTA/ATA/CCA/CTA/ACA/GAA/GAA/GCA/GAG/CTA/GAA/CTG/GCA/GAA/AAC/AGA/GAG/ATT/CTA/TAA/GAA/
CAA/GTA/CAT/GGA/GTG/TAT/TAT/GAC/CCA/TCA/AAA/GAC/TTA/ATA/GCA/GAA/ATA/CAG/AAG/CAG/GGG/CAA/GGC/CAA/TGG/ACA/
TAT/CAA/ATT/TAT/CAA/GAG/CCA/TTT/AAA/AAT/CTG/AAA/ACA/GGA/AAA/TAT/GCA/AGA/ATG/AGG/GGT/GCC/CAC/ACT/AAT/GAT/
GTA/AAA/CAA/ATA/ACA/GAG/GCA/GTG/CAA/AAA/ATA/ACC/ACA/GAA/AGC/ATA/GTA/ATA/TGG/TGA/AAG/ACT/CCT/AAA/TTT/AAA/
CTG/CCC/ATA/CAA/AAG/GAA/ACA/TGG/GAA/ACA/TGG/TGG/ACA/GAG/TAT/TGG/CAA/GCC/ACC/TGG/ATT/CCT/GAG/TGG/GAG/TTT/
GTT/AAT/ACC/CCT/CCC/ATA/GTG/AAA/TTA/TGG/TAC/CAG/TTA/GAG/AAA/GAA/CCC
```

Figure 3: The genomic sequence of HIV reverse transcriptase extracted from HIV patient "AA." Each letter (A, C, G, T) represents a nucleotide; * represents any nucleotide. Each group of three letters represents a codon, set apart by slashes. This sequence encodes a 3D protein structure similar to that shown in Figure 1, but differing from it to some extent as specified by mutations in the sequence.

considered and $M(S, h)$ is the set of mutants of S at Hamming distance h. $\mathbf{m\_dist}(D)$ is the minimum Hamming distance at which a mutant occurs that resists every drug in D, and $\mathbf{m\_wt}(D)$ is the rule weight of the least resisted drug in D by the most resistant such mutant. *MutScore* is comparable between drug combinations with different numbers of drugs. $MutScore(D)$ is zero if no mutant within Hamming distance h_{max} of S resists every drug in D. Otherwise, its integer part is h_{max} minus the Hamming distance to such a mutant, and its fractional part is the maximum minimum rule weight of such mutants.

Under this model, a mutant resists a drug combination only as strongly as it resists the least-resisted drug in the combination, and a drug combination suppresses a virus population only as strongly as it suppresses the most-resistant member of the population. The effect of this is to identify nearby mutants that resist every drug in a combination, and drug combinations such that no nearby mutant resists every drug.

Rank Alternatives

CTSHIV ranks alternative drug combinations using the current resistance weight (*CurrWt*) and the nearby mutant resistances (*MutScore*). The best ranked combinations of 1, 2, 3, and 4 drugs are generated independently. This is done by sorting the combinations by any monotonic function of *CurrWt* and *MutScore*. Currently we use Euclidean distance, $\sqrt{CurrWt^2(D) + MutScore^2(D)}$, to rank drug combination D. Values near or at zero indicate little or no resistance, and increasing positive values indicate increasing resistance. The best ranked combinations represent a satisficing compromise along both metrics simultaneously.

Suggest Clinical Treatment Protocols

The final result of application processing is to recommend the five highest-ranked combinations of 1, 2, 3, and 4 drugs. The next highest-ranked RT-only combination is shown for comparison. Figure 4 shows 3-drug combinations recommended for an HIV patient. Figure 5 shows an example nearby resistant mutant.

It is hoped that the CTSHIV output will increase patient adherence, by clearly showing the deleterious effects of failing to take all medication. Figure 6 shows the projected consequences of non-adherence to the highest-ranked 3-drug combination of Figure 4.

Uses of AI Technology

The key enabling AI technology is knowledge representation of the relevant scientific literature about HIV drug resistance as a set of sequence pattern rules on the HIV genome. Rule-based expert systems declaratively represent knowledge of a specialized problem and facts about a specific case, and from these draw inferences about the case. Here, the rules encode information on drug resistant mutations of HIV, the facts are the sequences of HIV genome obtained from a specific individual, and the inference to be drawn is a set of drug combinations to be recommended for the patient.

Rule forward chaining from the patient's current HIV sequences yields currently resistant HIV mutants. Rule backward chaining through sequence space yields the nearby putatively resistant mutants. Together, they allow CTSHIV to avoid both sets of mutants.

The intelligent agent paradigm proved useful as an organizing principle. Except for the lowest level (domain-specific), Figure 2 could represent any intelligent agent connecting perception to action. Also, AI heuristic search methods are used to search sequence space.

```
These protocols with 3 drugs are recommended:  CurrWt  MutScor  0 Mut  1 Mut  2 Mut  3 Mut
    A5 SAQUINAVIR NELFINAVIR D4T:                 0.06    0.1     0.0    0.0    0.0    0.1
    B3 SAQUINAVIR DELAVIRDINE D4T:                0.00    0.2     0.0    0.0    0.0    0.2
    C3 SAQUINAVIR NEVIRAPINE D4T:                 0.00    0.4     0.0    0.0    0.0    0.4
    D4 SAQUINAVIR DELAVIRDINE AZT:                0.00    0.6     0.0    0.0    0.0    0.6
    E4 SAQUINAVIR NEVIRAPINE AZT:                 0.00    0.6     0.0    0.0    0.0    0.6
    RF3 DELAVIRDINE DDI AZT:                      0.08    1.2     0.0    0.0    0.2    0.9
```

Figure 4: Example 3-drug output from HIV patient "AA," showing a favorable resistance profile. For the highest-ranked treatment, current resistance (CurrWt) and nearby mutation score (MutScor) are small, and only a weakly-resistant mutant appears even out to Hamming distance three (3 Mut). The letters A–F identify treatments. Treatment F is the best RT-only treatment (indicated by the prefixed letter R). Digits after the letters indicate cost codes (0 = \$0 to \$200, ..., 3 = \$600 to \$800, 4 = \$800 to \$1000, 5 = \$1000 to \$1200, ..., per month estimated average wholesale cost).

```
                                         CurrWt  MutScor  0 Mut  1 Mut  2 Mut  3 Mut
A5 D4T NELFINAVIR SAQUINAVIR:              0.06    0.1     0.0    0.0    0.0    0.1
   Current: (NELFINAVIR)    RT 151:CAG->ATG by R11 (D4T)    PRO 90:TTG->ATG by R28 (SAQUINAVIR)
```

Figure 5: Example output for HIV patient "AA" showing one example of the closest mutants inferred to most resist every drug in the top-ranked 3 drug combination of Figure 4. Three letters must change simutaneously. Currently Nelfinavir is resisted; changing two letters at RT 151 resists D4T and changing one at PRO 90 resists Saquinavir.

```
                                         CurrWt  MutScor  0 Mut  1 Mut  2 Mut  3 Mut
A5 SAQUINAVIR NELFINAVIR D4T:              0.06    0.1     0.0    0.0    0.0    0.1
   If stop NELFINAVIR:                              0.6     0.0    0.0    0.0    0.6
   If stop SAQUINAVIR:                              1.1     0.0    0.0    0.1    1.0
   If stop D4T:                                     2.1     0.0    0.1    0.6    1.1
```

Figure 6: Example output for HIV patient "AA" showing the projected result from stopping any single drug in the top-ranked 3 drug combination of Figure 4 (Saquinavir, Nelfinavir, D4T). Mutants are closer or worse or both. Stopping Nelfinavir is bad, stopping Saquinavir is worse, and stopping D4T is worst of all.

Application Use and Payoff

The first HIV patient data was run through the CTSHIV system in June, 1996. In February, 1997, the application began its first round of human clinical trials on 15 HIV patients at the University of California, Irvine, and at the Center for Special Immunology as a satellite site. Informed consent was obtained using a form approved by the UC Irvine Institutional Review Board. All patients had detectable viral load at baseline (mean $\log_{10}$ load of 4.67 ± 2.16), weakened immune system (CD4 counts < 500 cells/mm^3), and failure of at least one previous antiviral treatment regimen.

While these trials are still ongoing, initial results are encouraging (See et al. 1998). At three months, 10 of 15 patients who had failed at least one prior treatment regimen had an undetectable viral load (67% success). This compares to about 20% in everyday practice in the same patient population. Currently, at the midway point of the study, 12 of 15 patients have undetectable viral loads at six or nine months (80% success). The other three subjects all have at least a 2-log reduction in viral load compared to baseline. Note that in usual clinical trials, the percentage of viral-load undetectable patients diminishes over time. We expect and are seeing *improvement* over time based upon CTSHIV suggested treatment regimens. Further detailed results will be presented in the domain literature.

Currently a total of 58 HIV patients have been run through the CTSHIV system. A new round of phase II clinical trials of CTSHIV involving 30 HIV patients who previously failed multiple antiretroviral regimens has been initiated at the University of California, Irvine, and Stanford University, Santa Clara campus. The control group will use plasma HIV RNA and CD4 cell counts as in conventional therapy, while the test group will be identical but also provide CTSHIV recommendations to the primary care physician. Collaborations with several other groups involved in the treatment of HIV patients have begun and are expanding. An Affymetrix gene chip machine has been purchased and sequencing throughput will increase dramatically when it comes online. Because of the early encouraging results of the clinical trials, wide-spread recognition of the drug resistance problem, and the high rate of HIV infection in the general population, we expect use of the application to increase sharply in the near future.

Application Development, Deployment

Three domain experts (Darryl See, Douglas Richman, Edison Schroeder) began extracting rules from the scientific literature in September, 1995. The first rule set was completed in May, 1996.

The first rule-based system prototype was developed to identify current resistance already present in the patient's HIV infection (Pazzani *et al.* 1997b). It was coded in FOCL-1-2-3 (Pazzani & Kibler 1992), a LISP based expert shell. It was begun in March, 1996, and completed in June, 1996. It was re-coded in JAVA between April and June of 1997 (Pazzani *et al.* 1997a).

The ability to use the rules to search mutation sequence space for nearby drug resistant mutants was unanticipated when the original knowledge was encoded and the first prototype developed, and so demonstrates the robustness and extensibility of knowledge-based systems. A LISP based mutation space search engine was begun in November, 1996, and completed in May, 1997. The two subsystems were integrated and re-coded in LISP between October and December, 1997.

The application is deployed primarily by the email exchange of input clinical data and output recommended treatments. We have developed an automatic email server, as well as a WWW-based graphical interface to the email server. The server extracts patient data from the body of an email message, automatically enqueues the application to process it, and emails the results back to the sender.

Deployment has been smooth largely because the application end-users so far have been enthusiastic domain experts who are currently treating HIV patients. For cases where a treatment regimen has failed due to the development of drug resistance, the application enables them to base their next choice of treatment regimen on scientific principles and experimental data. This replaces the blind intuition and guess-work that formerly guided treatment switches after treatment failure. They are glad to see their patients improve, anxious to see the application succeed, and tolerant of the few glitches.

Maintenance

It is doubtful that the knowledge base will be complete until HIV is eradicated. Maintenance of CTSHIV is equivalent to adding new rules from the scientific AIDS literature. The rules are revised by three domain experts every three months by extracting new rules that have appeared in the literature in the interim. Relevant articles are retrieved by keyword-based literature search, old rules revised as needed, and new rules composed manually.

In the future we anticipate that the challenge of extending the knowledge base will provide fruitful opportunities for intelligent applications. An intelligent information retrieval system could monitor the literature, retrieve papers that mention HIV drug resistant mutations, extract candidate rules, and automatically enqueue review by domain experts. Other AI approaches could suggest when to test a patient strain for possible resistance to a specific drug. Predicting when a putative mutant is unviable, and coping with resistance that occurs outside the rule set, are further challenges for intelligent systems. Machine learning and data mining techniques could learn new rules, infer trends and recognize regularities in resistance patterns.

Summary

We have described an AI application (CTSHIV) that connects the scientific literature describing specific HIV drug resistances directly to the HIV virus strain infecting a specific HIV patient. The application identifies current and nearby drug resistant mutant strains, ranks the current FDA-approved treatment regimens according to their estimated ability to avoid the resistant mutants, and recommends a Customized Treatment Strategy for the individual patient involved. Thus the significance of the application is (1) a method for addressing HIV drug resistance in the clinic, especially treatment switches after treatment failure, based on scientific principles and experimental data, (2) a decreased tendency to select for drug resistance in the global HIV gene pool, and (3) a possible model for the use of knowledge-based systems in other drug resistant viruses.

This paper also illustrated the robustness and extensibility of knowledge-based systems. It showed how knowledge originally encoded to perform one knowledge-based task easily may be re-directed to perform another, even one not anticipated when the original knowledge was encoded. This result supports knowledge-base efforts to encode knowledge in societally important areas.

Acknowledgments

Douglas Richman and Edison Schroeder helped extract the original knowledge base from the AIDS scientific literature, and help revise the knowledge base every 3 months. Doug Cable and Winnie Huang co-supervised the first CTSHIV clinical trials. Data entry and analysis was done by Richard Haubrich and Allen McCutchan at the University of California at San Diego. Carol Kemper is co-supervising the next round of clinical trials. Tom Gingeras contributed useful practical insights and advice. We gratefully acknowledge the technical assistance of Tonya Clark and Marikel Chatard in cloning, PCR, and RNA/DNA extraction.

Funding has been provided by Roche Molecular Systems, the California University-wide AIDS Research Program through the California Collaborative Treatment Group (CCTG), and the National Science Foundation under grant IRI-9624739.

CTSHIV is available from University/Industry Research and Technology, 380 University Tower, University of California, Irvine, 92717 USA.

References

Carpenter, C.; Fischl, M.; Hammer, S.; Hirsch, M.; Jacobsen, D.; Katzenstein, D.; Montaner, J.; Richman, D.; Saag, M.; Schooley, R.; Thompson, M.; et al. 1996. Antiretroviral therapy for HIV infection in 1996. *J. American Medical Assoc.* 276:146–154.

CDC. 1997. *HIV/AIDS Surveillance Report*. Centers for Disease Control and Prevention, Atlanta, Georgia, USA, 9(1) edition.

Condra, J.; Schlief, W.; Blahy, O.; Gabryelski, L.; Graham, D.; Quintero, J.; Rhodes, A.; Robbins, H.; Roth, E.; Shivaprakash, M.; Titus, D.; et al. 1995. In vivo emergence of HIV-1 variants resistant to multiple protease inhibitors. *Nature* 374:569–571.

Diamond, L.; Nguyen, D.; Jouault, H.; Imbert, M.; and Sultan, C. 1994. An expert system for the interpretation of flow cytometric immunophenotyping data. *J. of Clinical Computing* 22:50–58.

Finzi, D.; Hermankova, M.; Pierson, T.; Carruth, L.; Buck, C.; Chaisson, R.; Quinn, T.; Chadwick, K.; Margolick, J.; Brookmeyer, R.; Gallant, J.; et al. 1997. Identification of a reservoir for HIV-1 in patients on highly active antiretroviral therapy. *Science* 278:1295–1300.

Gu, Z.; Gao, Q.; Fang, H.; Parniak, M.; Brenner, B.; and Wainberg, M. 1994. Identification on novel mutations that confer drug resistance in the human immunodeficiency virus polymerase gene. *Leukemia* 8S1:5166–5169.

Hsiou, Y.; Ding, J.; Das, K.; Hughes, S.; and Arnold, E. to be published. Structure of unliganded human immunodeficiency virus type 1 reverse transcriptase at 2.7 Angstroms resolution.

Iversen, A.; Shafer, R.; Wearly, K.; Winters, M.; Mullins, J.; Chesebro, B.; and Morgan, T. 1996. Multidrug-resistant human immunodeficiency virus type 1 strains resulting from combination antiretroviral therapy. *J. Virology* 70:1086–1090.

Jacobsen, H.; Hanggi, M.; Ott, M.; Duncan, I.; Owen, S.; Andreoni, M.; Vella, S.; and Mous, J. 1996. In vivo resistance to a human immunoeficiency type-1 proteinase inhibitor. *J. Infect. Diseases* 173:1379–1387.

Lange, J. 1995. Triple combinations: present and future. *J. of AIDS and Human Retrovirology* 10 Suppl 1:S77–82.

Musen, M.; Wieckert, K.; Miller, E.; Campbell, K.; and Fagan, L. 1995. Development of a controlled medical terminology: knowledge acquisition and knowledge representation. *Methods of Information in Medicine* 34:85–95.

Musen, M.; Tu, S.; Das, A.; and Shahar, Y. 1996. EON: a component-based approach to automation of protocol-directed therapy. *J. Amer. Medical Informatics Assoc.* 3:367–388.

O'Brian, W.; Hartigan, P.; Martin, D.; Esinhart, J.; Hill, A.; Benoit, S.; Rubin, M.; Simberkoff, M.; and Hamilton, J. 1996. Changes in plasma HIV-1 and CD4+ lymphocyte counts and the risk of progression to AIDS. *New England J. Medicine* 334:426–431.

Ohno-Machado, L.; Parra, E.; Henry, S.; Tu, S.; and Musen, M. 1993. AIDS 2: A decision-support tool for decreasing physician's uncertainty regarding patient eligibility for HIV treatment protocols. In *Proc. of the 17th Annual Symp. on Computer Applications in Medical Care*, 429–433.

Pazzani, M., and Kibler, D. 1992. The utility of prior knowledge in inductive learning. *Machine Learning* 9:54–97. FOCL-1-2-3 is available from http://www.ics.uci.edu/~mlearn/FOCL.html.

Pazzani, M.; Iyer, R.; See, D.; Shroeder, E.; and Tilles, J. 1997a. CTSHIV: A knowledge-based system in the management of HIV-infected patients. In *Proc. of the Intl. Conf. on Intelligent Information Systems*.

Pazzani, M.; See, D.; Shroeder, E.; and Tilles, J. 1997b. Application of an expert system in the management of HIV-infected patients. *J. of AIDS and Human Retrovirology* 15:356–362.

Ruggiero, C.; Giacomini, M.; Varnier, O. E.; and Gaglio, S. 1994. A qualitative process theory based model of the HIV-1 virus-cell interaction. *Computer Methods and Programs in Biomedicine* 43:255–259.

Safran, C.; Rind, D.; Sands, D.; Davis, R.; Wald, J.; and Slack, W. 1996. Development of a knowledge-based electronic patient record. *M.D. Computing* 13:46–54.

See, D.; Cimoch, P.; Lathrop, R.; Pazzani, M.; and Reiter, W. 1998. Succesful use of an expert program in managing antiretroviral use in patients that have failed haart therapy. In *Proc. of the 9th Intl. AIDS Conf.*, to appear.

Sieburg, H. 1994. Methods in the Virtual Wetlab I: rule-based reasoning driven by nearest-neighbor lattice dynamics. *AI in Medicine* 6:301–319.

Sobesky, M.; Michelet, C.; Thomas, R.; and LeBeux, P. 1994. Decision making system. *J. Clinical Computing* 22:20–26.

Sonnenberg, F.; Hagerty, C.; and Kulikowski, C. 1994. An architecture for knowledge-based construction of decision models. *Medical Decision Making* 14:27–39.

Tu, S.; Eriksson, H.; Gennari, J.; Shahar, Y.; and Musen, M. 1995. Ontology-based configuration of problem-solving methods and generation of knowledge-acquisition tools. *AI in Medicine* 7:257–289.

Wong, J.; Hezareh, M.; Günthard, H.; Havlir, D.; Ignacio, C.; Spina, C.; and Richman, D. 1997. Recovery of replication-competent HIV despite prolonged suppression of plasma viremia. *Science* 278:1291–1295.

Xu, L. 1996. An integrated rule- and case-based approach to AIDS initial assessment. *Intl. J. of Bio-Medical Computing* 40:197–207.

Success in Spades: Using AI Planning Techniques to Win the World Championship of Computer Bridge

Stephen J. J. Smith

Department of Mathematics
and Computer Science
Hood College
Frederick, MD, USA
sjsmith@nimue.hood.edu

Dana S. Nau

Department of Computer Science,
and Institute for Systems Research
University of Maryland
College Park, MD, USA
nau@cs.umd.edu

Thomas A. Throop

Great Game Products
8804 Chalon Drive
Bethesda, MD, USA
brbaron@erols.com

Abstract

The latest world-championship competition for computer bridge programs was the *Baron Barclay World Bridge Computer Challenge*, hosted in July 1997 by the American Contract Bridge League. As reported in *The New York Times* and *The Washington Post*, the competition's winner was a new version of Great Game Products' *Bridge Baron* program. This version, Bridge Baron 8, has since gone on the market; and during the last three months of 1997 it was purchased by more than 1000 customers.

The Bridge Baron's success also represents a significant success for research on AI planning systems, because Bridge Baron 8 uses Hierarchical Task-Network (HTN) planning techniques to plan its declarer play. This paper gives an overview of those techniques and how they are used.

Problem Description

To be successful both in bridge competitions and as a commercial product, a computer program for the game of bridge must perform as well as possible in all aspects of the game. Customers want as challenging an opponent as possible, and of course the strongest program has the best chance of winning a competition. However, although researchers have had great success in developing high-performance programs for games such as chess and checkers, they have not had as much success in the game of contract bridge. Even the best bridge programs can be beaten by the best players at many local bridge clubs.

One important reason why it is difficult to develop good computer programs for bridge is that bridge is an imperfect information game. Bridge players don't know what cards are in the other players' hands (except for, after the opening lead, what cards are in the dummy's hand); thus each player has only partial knowledge of the state of the world, the possible actions, and their effects. If we were to use a naive adaptation of the classical game-tree search techniques used in computer programs for games such as chess and checkers, the game tree would need to include

---

Copyright © 1998, American Association for Artificial Intelligence (www.aaai.org). All rights reserved.

all of the moves a player *might* be able to make. The size of this tree would vary depending on the particular bridge deal—but it would include about 5.6×10^{44} leaf nodes in the worst case (Smith 1997, p. 226), and about 2.3×10^{24} leaf nodes in the average case (Lopatin 1992, p. 8). Since a bridge hand is normally played in just a few minutes, there is not enough time for a game-tree search to search enough of this tree to make good decisions.

Until recently, the approach that was most successful in computer programs for the game of bridge was to use domain-dependent pattern-matching techniques that do not involve a lot of look-ahead. Most commercially available bridge programs use this approach, including the previous version of Great Game Products' *Bridge Baron* (Throop 1983, Great Game Products 1997). The Bridge Baron is generally acknowledged to be the best available commercial program for the game of contract bridge. Before the incorporation of AI techniques (described later in this paper), it had won four international computer bridge championships. In their review of seven commercially available bridge-playing programs (Manley 1993), the American Contract Bridge League rated the Bridge Baron to be the best of the seven, and rated the skill of the Bridge Baron to be the best of the five that do declarer play without "peeking" at the opponents' cards.

Despite the success of the Bridge Baron, improving its performance became more and more difficult as its relatively simple pattern-matching techniques revealed their limitations. Without more sophisticated techniques, the Bridge Baron would risk becoming less competitive with other bridge programs. Thus, we needed to develop more sophisticated AI techniques to improve the performance of the Bridge Baron.

Application Description

Overview of Bridge

Bridge is a game played by four players, using a standard deck of 52 playing cards, divided into four *suits* (spades ♠, hearts ♥, diamonds ♦, and clubs ♣), each containing 13

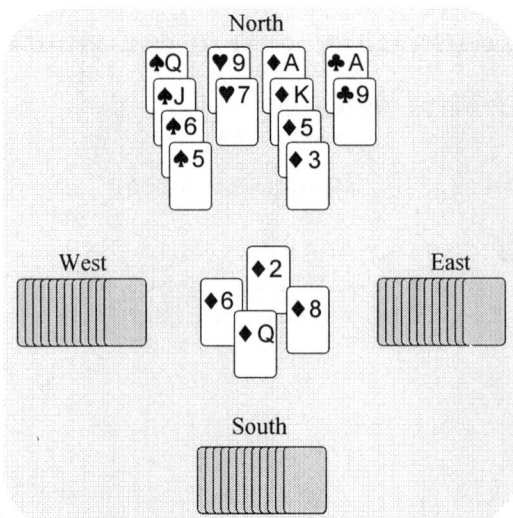

Figure 1. An example of a bridge hand during the play of the first trick. Here, South is declarer, North is dummy, and West and East are defenders.

cards. The players (who are normally referred to as North, South, East, and West), play as two opposing teams, with North and South playing as partners against East and West. A bridge deal consists of two phases, *bidding* and *play*:

Bidding. The cards are dealt equally among the four players. The players make *bids* for the privilege of determining which suit is trump and what the *level* of the contract is. Nominally, each bid consists of two parts: some number of *tricks* (see below) that the bidder promises to take, and which suit the bidder is proposing as the trump suit. However, various bidding conventions have been developed in which these bids are also used to convey information to the bidder's partner about how strong the bidder's hand is.

The bidding proceeds until no player wishes to make a higher bid. At that point, the highest bid becomes the *contract* for the hand. In the highest bidder's team, the player who bid this suit first becomes *declarer*, and declarer's partner becomes *dummy*. The other two players become the *defenders*.

Play. The first time that it is dummy's turn to play a card (see below), dummy lays her or his cards on the table, face-up so that everyone can see them; and during the card play, declarer plays both declarer's cards and dummy's cards.

The basic unit of card play is the *trick*, in which each player in turn *plays* a card by placing it face-up on the table as shown in Figure 1. The first card played is that card that was *led*; and whenever possible, the players must *follow suit*, that is, play cards in the suit of the card that was led. The trick is taken by whoever played the highest card in the suit led, unless some player plays a card in the trump suit, in which case whoever played the highest trump card wins the trick.

The card play proceeds, one trick at a time, until no player has any cards left. At that point, the bridge hand is scored according to how many tricks each team took, and whether declarer's team took as many tricks as they promised to take during the bidding.

The Bridge Baron

The Bridge Baron consists of tens of thousands of lines of C code. Separate Bridge Baron executables run as a Windows application, an MS-DOS application, and a Macintosh application; the Windows application accounts for the overwhelming majority of sales.

In the Bridge Baron, over fifty thousand lines of code are devoted solely to the *bridge engine*, which calculates what bids to make and what cards to play. The bridge engine can be roughly divided into three parts, based on functionality: declarer play, defensive play, and bidding. The bridge engine represents knowledge largely through ad-hoc pieces of code developed to address particular bridge situations.

Other tens of thousands of lines of code handle the user interface. The user interface allows customers to play matches against the computer, to generate deals that conform to particular specifications, to see how the Bridge Baron determines its bids, and the like.

The user interface interacts with the bridge engine by calling C functions that recommend a particular bid or play in the current situation. The user interface also updates the data structures that provide the bridge engine with the details of the current situation.

Most commonly, a customer sits down with the Bridge Baron to play some number of deals. The customer takes the role of one of the four players, and the Bridge Baron takes the role of the customer's partner. The Bridge Baron also takes the roles of the customer's two opponents. Each role is separate: for example, one opponent does not know what cards the other opponent has, nor what cards the customer's partner has. (The customer can allow all of the Bridge Baron players to have complete knowledge of all of the cards by changing an option.)

For declarer play, previous versions of the Bridge Baron used ad-hoc pattern-matching techniques. However, Bridge Baron 8 (the latest version) makes use of the new AI planning techniques described later in this paper. Users may select whether they want to use the new AI planning techniques or the old ad-hoc techniques, which we did not remove from the Bridge Baron. We added options to limit the time that the new AI planning techniques spend on a particular play to 30 seconds, 60 seconds, or 120 seconds. This new version of the Bridge Baron became commercially available in October 1997.

Uses of AI Technology

To improve the play of the Bridge Baron, we supplemented its previously existing routines for declarer play with routines based on HTN (Hierarchical Task-Network) planning techniques. Our approach (Smith et al. 1996a; Smith et al. 1996c; Smith et al. 1996e; Smith 1997) grew out of the observation that bridge is a game of planning. In playing the cards, there are a number of standard tactical ploys that may be used by the various players to try to win tricks. These have standard names (such as ruffing, cross-ruffing, finessing, cashing out, and discovery plays); and the ability of a bridge player depends partly on how skillfully that player can plan and execute these ploys. This is especially true for declarer, who is responsible for playing both declarer's cards and dummy's cards. In most bridge hands, declarer will spend some time at the beginning of the game formulating a rough plan for how to play declarer's cards and dummy's cards. This plan will normally be some combination of various tactical ploys. Because of declarer's uncertainty about what cards are in the opponents' hands and how the opponents may choose to play those cards, the plan will usually need to contain contingencies for various possible card plays by the opponents.

We have taken advantage of the planning nature of bridge, by adapting and extending some ideas from HTN planning. We use planning techniques to develop game trees in which the number of branches at each node correspond to the different *strategies* that a player might pursue rather than the different cards the player might be able to play. Since the number of sensible strategies is usually much less than the number of possible card plays, this lets us develop game trees that are small enough to be searched completely, as shown in Table 1. Below we give an overview of HTN planning, and describe how we adapted it for use in the Bridge Baron.

Table 1. Game-tree size produced in bridge by a full game-tree search and by our HTN planning approach.

	Brute-force search	Our approach
Worst case	$\approx 5.6 \times 10^{44}$ leaves	$\approx 305{,}000$ leaves
Avg. case	$\approx 2.3 \times 10^{24}$ leaves	$\approx 26{,}000$ leaves

Overview of HTN Planning

HTN planning was originally developed more than 20 years ago (Sacerdoti 1974; Tate 1977), and has long been thought to have good potential for use in real-world planning problems (Currie and Tate 1985; Wilkins 1988), but it has only been recently that researchers have developed a coherent theoretical basis for HTN planning. Recent mathematical analyses of HTN planning have shown that it is strictly more expressive than planning with STRIPS-style operators (Erol *et al.* 1994b), and have established a number of properties such as soundness and completeness of planning algorithms (Erol *et al.* 1994a), complexity (Erol *et al.* 1996), and the relative efficiency of various control strategies (Tsuneto *et al.* 1996; Tsuneto *et al.* 1997). A domain-independent HTN planner is available at <http://www.cs.umd.edu/projects/plus/umcp/manual> for use in experimental studies, and domain-specific HTN planners are being developed for several industrial problems (Aarup *et at.* 1994; Hebbar *et al.* 1996; Smith *et al.* 1996b; Smith *et al.* 1996d; Wilkins & Desimone 1994).

To create plans, HTN planning uses *task decomposition*, in which the planning system decomposes tasks into smaller and smaller subtasks until primitive tasks are found that can be performed directly. HTN planning systems have knowledge bases containing *methods*. Each method includes a prescription for how to decompose some task into a set of subtasks, with various restrictions that must be satisfied in order for the method to be applicable, and various constraints on the subtasks and the relationships among them. Given a task to accomplish, the planner chooses an applicable method, instantiates it to decompose the task into subtasks, and then chooses and instantiates other methods to decompose the subtasks even further. If the constraints on the subtasks or the interactions among them prevent the plan from being feasible, the planning system will backtrack and try other methods.

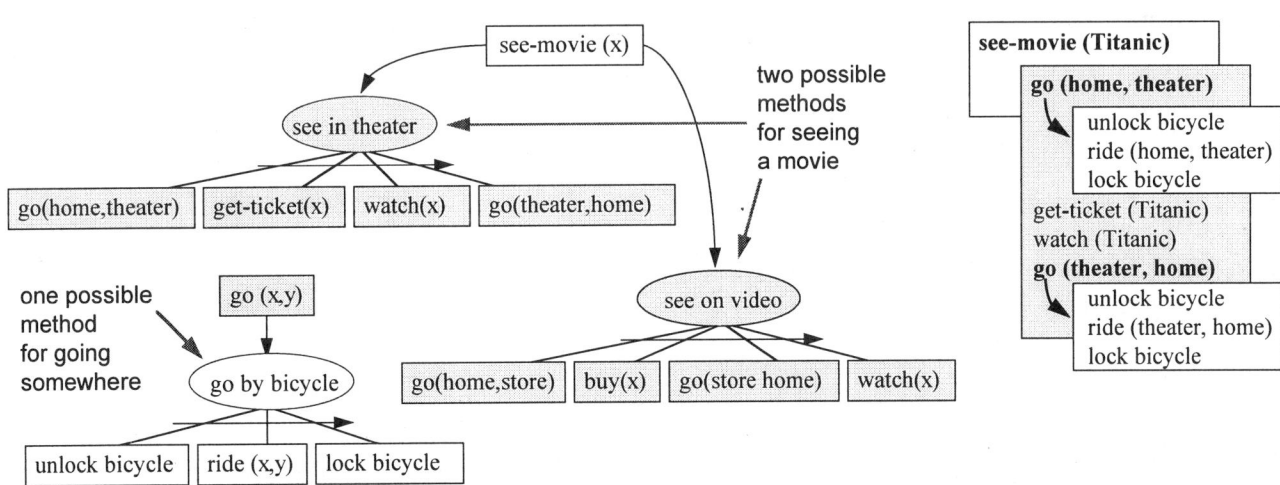

Figure 2. A very simple example illustrating how HTN planning might be used to plan to see a movie.

As a very simple example, Figure 2 shows two methods for seeing a movie: seeing it in a theater, and seeing it at home on videotape. Seeing it in a theater involves going to the theater, getting a ticket to the movie, watching the movie, and going home. Seeing it at home involves going to the store, buying the videotape, going home, and watching the movie. Figure 2 also shows one method for going places: riding a bicycle.

Now, consider the task of seeing the movie *Titanic*. Figure 2 shows how a planner might instantiate the "see in theater" method for this task, and how it might instantiate the "ride bicycle" method twice to handle the subtasks of getting to the theater and getting home.

Solving a planning problem using HTN planning is generally much more complicated than in this simple example. For example, the planner may need to recognize and resolve interactions among the subtasks (such as the necessity of getting to the theater before the movie begins). If such interactions cannot be worked out, then the planner may need to backtrack and try another method instead.

HTN Planning for Declarer Play

The *Tignum 2* portion of Bridge Baron 8 uses an adaptation of HTN planning techniques to plan declarer play in contract bridge. To represent the various tactical schemes of card-playing in bridge, Tignum 2 uses structures similar to HTN methods, but modified to represent multi-agency and uncertainty. Tignum 2 uses *state information sets* to represent the locations of cards about which declarer is certain, and *belief functions* to represent the probabilities associated with the locations of cards about which declarer is not certain.

Some methods refer to actions performed by the opponents. In Tignum 2, we allow these methods to make assumptions about the cards in the opponents' hands, and design our methods so that most of the likely states of the world are each covered by at least one method. In any of our methods, the subtasks are totally ordered; that is, the order in which the subtasks are listed for a method is the order in which these subtasks must be completed.

For example, Figure 3 shows how our algorithm would instantiate some of its methods on a specific bridge hand. Here, South (declarer) is trying a *finesse*, a tactical ploy in which a player tries to win a trick with a high card, by playing it after an opponent who has a higher card. If West (a defender) has the ♥K, but does not play it when hearts are led, then North (dummy) will be able to win a trick with the ♥Q, because North plays after West. (West wouldn't play the ♥K if she or he had any alternative, because then North would win the trick with the ♥A and win a later trick with the ♥Q.) However, if East (the other defender) has the ♥K, East will play it after North plays the ♥Q, and North will not win the trick. Note that the methods refer to actions performed by each of the players in the game.

To generate game trees, our planning algorithm uses a procedure similar to task decomposition to build up a game tree whose branches represent moves generated by these methods. It applies all methods applicable to a given state of the world to produce new states of the world, and continues recursively until there are no applicable methods that have not already been applied to the appropriate state of the world. For example, Figure 4 illustrates the evaluation of the game tree resulting from the instantiation of the finessing method. This game tree is produced by taking the plays shown in Figure 3 and listing them in the order in which they will occur. In Figure 4, declarer has a choice between the finessing method and the *cashing-out* method, in which declarer simply plays all of the high cards that are guaranteed to win tricks.

For a game tree generated in this manner, the number of branches from each state is not the number of moves that an agent can make (as in conventional game-tree search procedures), but instead is the number of different tactical schemes the agent can employ. As shown in Table 1, this game tree is small enough that it can be searched all the way to the end, to predict the likely results of the various

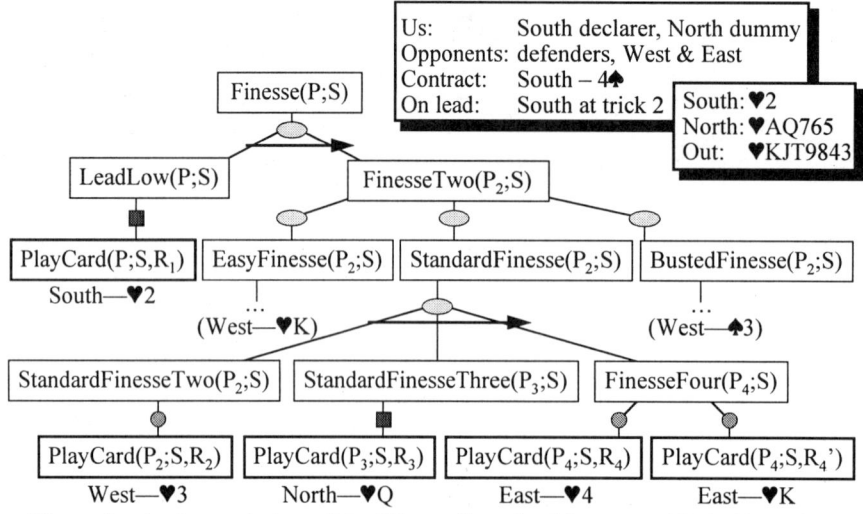

Figure 3: An instantiation of the "finesse" method for a specific bridge hand.

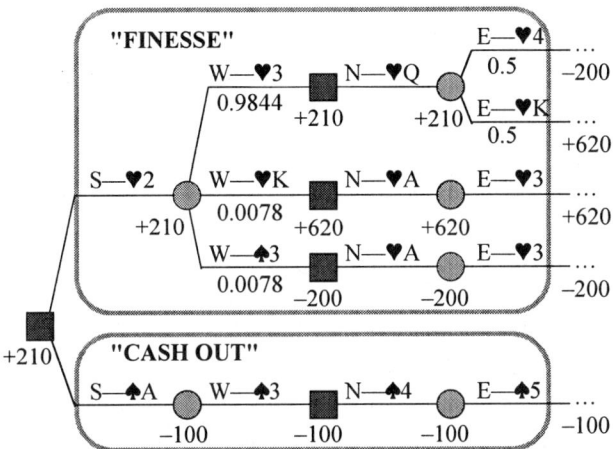

Figure 4: Evaluating the game tree produced from the instantiated "finesse" method of Figure 3.

sequences of cards that the players might play.

To evaluate the game tree at nodes where it is declarer's turn to play a card, our algorithm chooses the play that results in the highest expected score. For example, in Figure 4, South chooses to play the ♥2 that resulted from the "finesse" method, which results in an expected score of +210, rather than the ♠A that resulted from the "cash out" method, which results in a score of -100.

To evaluate the game tree at nodes where it is an opponent's turn to play a card, our algorithm takes a weighted average of the node's children, based on probabilities generated by our belief function. For example, because the probability is 0.9844 that North holds at least one "low" heart—that is, at least one heart other than the ♥K—and because North is sure to play a low heart if North has one, our belief function generates the probability of 0.9844 for North's play of a low heart. North's other two possible plays are much less likely and receive much lower probabilities.

Application Use and Payoff

We brought a pre-release version of Bridge Baron 8 to the most recent world-championship competition for computer bridge programs: the *Baron Barclay World Bridge Computer Challenge*, which was hosted by the American Contract Bridge League (ACBL). The five-day competition was held in Albuquerque, New Mexico, from 28 July 1997 to 1 August 1997. As reported in *The New York Times* (Truscott 1997) and *The Washington Post* (Chandrasekaran 1997), the winner of the competition was the Bridge Baron—more specifically, the winner was the pre-release version of Bridge Baron 8, incorporating our Tignum 2 code. The contenders included five computer programs; the final place of each program in the competition is shown in Table 2.

Table 2: The contenders in the *Baron Barclay World Bridge Computer Challenge*, and their final places.

Program	Country	Performance
Bridge Baron	USA	1st place
Q-Plus	Germany	2nd place
MicroBridge 8	Japan	3rd place
Meadowlark	USA	4th place
GIB	USA	5th place

The official release of Bridge Baron 8 went on sale in October 1997; and during the last three months of 1997, more than 1000 customers purchased it. In his review of bridge programs, Jim Loy (1997) said of this new version of the Bridge Baron: "The card play is noticeably stronger, making it the strongest program on the market."

Application Development and Deployment

Chronology

A single graduate student did all of the programming of our HTN planning techniques for bridge, reusing a few hundred lines of code from the Bridge Baron. Other people—primarily two of them, with occasional assistance from at least two others—helped by discussing what knowledge to incorporate and how to perform the implementation. We did not use any formal development methods.

We began our work on adapting HTN planning techniques to bridge with a program called *Tignum*. We began working on some routines for reasoning about the probable locations of cards in 1989, most of which were eventually abandoned because they required too much execution time. We began work in earnest on Tignum in 1991, and after writing nine thousand lines of code, abandoned almost all of it in 1993.

We abandoned Tignum because it was poorly implemented. It did not allow us to consider alternative plays; it required every piece of bridge knowledge to be coded by hand with very little possibility of code reuse; it ran slowly; and it was difficult to maintain.

After abandoning Tignum in 1993, we began work immediately on Tignum 2, a much better implementation of the ideas used in Tignum. Tignum 2 allowed us to consider alternative plays. While bridge knowledge still had to be coded by hand, judiciously chosen macros and well-designed components made code reuse easy. Tignum 2 ran more quickly and was much easier to maintain.

Tignum 2 became ultimately successful in February 1997. To test our implementation of it, we played it against an older version of the Bridge Baron. In (Smith 1997) we reported the results of our comparison of Tignum 2 against this version of the Bridge Baron on 1,000 randomly generated bridge deals (including both suit and no-trump contracts). Each deal was played twice, once with Tignum 2 as declarer and once with Bridge Baron as declarer; the winner of the deal was defined to be whichever declarer did better. On declarer play, Tignum 2 defeated Bridge Baron by 250 to 191, with 559 ties. These results are statistically significant at the $a = 0.025$ level. We had never run Tignum 2 on any of these deals before this test, so these results are free from any training-set biases.

These results allowed us to move forward with the incorporation of Tignum 2 into a new version of the Bridge Baron, *Bridge Baron 8*. In Bridge Baron 8, we added an option to allow customers to select whether they wanted to use the new AI planning techniques or the old ad-hoc techniques, which we did not remove from the Bridge Baron. We added options to limit the length of Tignum 2's planning time on a particular play to 30 seconds, 60 seconds, or 120 seconds. This new version of the Bridge Baron became commercially available in October 1997.

Lessons Learned

We learned several lessons from the development of this product. We wish we had thought out the implementation more carefully before beginning to write code for it. Having Tignum as an unintended prototype before the full implementation in Tignum 2 worked out surprisingly well; in the future, we intend to plan our development to include both a prototype and a full implementation.

To develop Tignum 2, we needed to extend HTN planning to include ways to represent and reason about possible actions by other agents (such as the opponents in a bridge game), as well as uncertainty about the capabilities of those agents (for example, lack of knowledge about what cards they have). However, to accomplish this, we needed to restrict how Tignum 2 goes about constructing its plans. Most HTN planners develop plans in which the actions are partially ordered, postponing some of the decisions about the order in which the actions will be performed. In contrast, Tignum 2 is a total-order planner that expands tasks in left-to-right order.

Tignum 2 expands tasks in the same order that they will be performed when the plan executes, and so when it plans for each task, Tignum 2 already knows the state of the world (or as much as can be known about it in an imperfect-information game) at the time that the task will be performed. Consequently, we can write each method's preconditions as arbitrary computer code, rather than using the stylized logical expressions found in most AI planning systems. For example, by knowing the current state, Tignum 2 can decide which of 26 finesse situations are applicable: with partial-order planning, it would be much harder to decide which of them *can be made* applicable. The arbitrary computer code also enables us to encode the complex numeric computations needed for reasoning about the probable locations of the opponents' cards.

Maintenance

To date, only the original programmer has maintained the HTN planning routines in Bridge Baron 8, though we hope to have another programmer begin modifying these routines soon. In the past, the Bridge Baron has been improved on a daily basis, to make its performance of bidding and play better; in the future, we expect this to continue. Domain knowledge about bridge changes relatively infrequently, but plenty of domain knowledge about bridge has simply not been implemented yet in our HTN planning techniques.

The HTN planning routines in Bridge Baron 8 explicitly handle many bridge techniques: cashing out, ruffing out, crossing, finesses, free finesses, automatic finesses, marked finesses, proven finesses, sequence winners, length winners, winners that depend on splits, opponents on lead, opponents finessing against declarer and dummy, dangerous opponents, ducking, hold-up plays, discarding worthless cards, drawing trumps, ruffing, and setting up ruffs. Some obvious domain knowledge missing from these routines include endplays and squeezes; we have not handled these techniques because they are relatively rare. As well, the existing techniques certainly need to be improved.

HTN planning techniques are based on tasks. The HTN planning routines in Bridge Baron 8 have a separate C function for each task that it can perform in declarer play during a bridge deal. These separate functions are very important for ease of maintenance; if Bridge Baron 8 is not performing well in particular types of situations, we can often rapidly improve its performance in many similar situations by changing the way it performs a single task, and these changes are often restricted to a single C function.

Conclusions

For games such as chess and checkers, the best computer programs are based on the use of game-tree search techniques that "think" about the game quite differently from how human players do (Biermann 1978, IBM 1997). For bridge, our new version of the Bridge Baron bases its declarer play on the use of HTN planning techniques that more closely approximate how a human might plan the play of a bridge hand.

Since computer programs still have far to go before they can compete at the level of expert human bridge players, it is difficult to say what approach will ultimately prove best for computer bridge. However, the Bridge Baron's championship performance in the *Baron Barclay World Bridge Computer Challenge* suggests that bridge may be a game in which HTN planning techniques can be very successful.

Furthermore, we believe that our work illustrates how AI planning is finally "coming of age" as a tool for practical planning problems. Other AI planning researchers have begun to develop practical applications of AI planning techniques in several other domains, such as marine oil spills (Agosta 1996), spacecraft assembly (Aarup et al. 1994), and military air campaigns (Wilkins and Desimone 1994). Furthermore, the same adaptation of HTN planning that we used for computer bridge is also proving useful for the generation and evaluation of manufacturing plans for microwave transmit/receive modules, as part of a project that some of us have with Northrop Grumman Corporation (Hebbar et al. 1996; Smith et al. 1996b; Smith et al. 1996d; Smith 1997). Since the same approach works well in domains that are as different as these, we are optimistic that it will be useful for a wide range of practical planning problems.

Acknowledgments

This work was supported in part by an AT&T PhD scholarship to Stephen J. J. Smith, by Maryland Industrial Partnerships (MIPS) Grant 501.15, by ARPA grant DABT 63-95-C-0037, and by National Science Foundation Grants NSF EEC 94-02384 and IRI-9306580. Any opinions, findings, and conclusions or recommendations expressed in this material are those of the authors and do not necessarily reflect the view of the funders.

References

Aarup, M.; Arentoft, M. M.; Parrod, Y.; Stader, J.; and Stokes, I. 1994. OPTIMUM-AIV: A knowledge-based planning and scheduling system for spacecraft AIV. In Fox, M. and Zweben, M., editors, *Intelligent Scheduling*, 451–469. Morgan Kaufmann, San Mateo, California.

Agosta, J. M. 1996. Constraining influence diagram structure by generative planning: an application to the optimization of oil spill response. *Proceedings of the 12th Conference on Uncertainty in Artificial Intelligence*, 11–19. AAAI Press, Menlo Park, California.

Biermann, A. 1978. Theoretical issues related to computer game playing programs. *Personal Computing*, Sept. 1978, 86–88.

Chandrasekaran, R. 1997. Program for a better bridge game: A college partnership aids industry research. *The Washington Post*, Sept. 15, 1997. Washington Business section, pp. 1, 15, 19.

Currie, K. and Tate, A. 1985. O-Plan—control in the open planner architecture. BCS Expert Systems Conference, Cambridge University Press, UK.

Erol, K.; Hendler, J.; and Nau, D. 1994. UMCP: a sound and complete procedure for Hierarchical Task-Network planning," *Proc. 2nd Int'l Conf. on AI Planning Systems*, 249-254.

Erol, K.; Nau, D.; Hendler, J. 1994. HTN planning: complexity and expressivity." *Proc. AAAI-94*.

Erol, K.; Hendler, J.; and Nau, D. Complexity results for hierarchical task-network planning. *Annals of Mathematics and Artificial Intelligence* 18:69–93, 1996.

Great Game Products. 1997. *Bridge Baron*. <http://www.bridgebaron.com>.

Hebbar, K.; Smith, S. J. J.; Minis, I.; and Nau, D. S. 1996. Plan-based evaluation of design for microwave modules. In *ASME Design for Manufacturing Conference*, p. 262 (abstract; full paper on CD-ROM).

IBM. 1997. How Deep Blue works. <http://www.chess.ibm.com/meet/html/d.3.2.html>.

Korf, R. 1994. Presentation of "Best-First Minimax Search: Othello results" at *Twelfth National Conference on Artificial Intelligence*.

Lopatin, A. 1992. Two combinatorial problems in programming bridge game. *Computer Olympiad*, unpublished.

Loy, J. 1997. Review of bridge programs for PC compatibles. Usenet newsgroup *rec.games.bridge*, 9 October 1997, Message-Id: <343CAB0B.C6E7D2B1@pop.mcn.net>.

Manley, B. 1993. Software "judges" rate bridge-playing products. *The Bulletin* (published monthly by the American Contract Bridge League), **59:11**, November 1993, 51—54.

Sacerdoti, E. D. 1974. Planning in a hierarchy of abstraction spaces. *Artificial Intelligence* 5:115-135.

Schaeffer, J. 1993. Presentation at plenary session, *AAAI Fall Symposium*.

Smith, S. J. J.; Nau, D. S.; and Throop, T. 1996a. A planning approach to declarer play in contract bridge. *Computational Intelligence* **12:1**, February 1996, 106–130. An earlier version is at <http://www.cs.umd.edu/TR/UMCP-CSD:CS-TR-3513>.

Smith, S. J. J.; Nau, D. S.; Hebbar, K.; and Minis, I. 1996b. Hierarchical task-network planning for process planning for manufacturing of microwave modules. *Proceedings: Artificial Intelligence and Manufacturing Research Planning Workshop*, 189—194. AAAI Press, Menlo Park, CA.

Smith, S. J. J.; Nau, D. S.; and Throop, T. 1996c. Total-order multi-agent task-network planning for contract bridge. *AAAI-96*, 108–113.

Smith, S. J. J.; Hebbar, K.; Nau, D. S.; and Minis, I. 1996d. Integrated electrical and mechanical design and process planning. *IFIP Knowledge Intensive CAD Workshop*, CMU, 16-18 September 1996.

Smith, S. J. J.; Nau, D. S.; and Throop, T. 1996e. AI planning's strong suit. *IEEE Expert*, **11:6**, December 1996, 4–5.

Smith, S. J. J. 1997. *Task-Network Planning Using Total-Order Forward Search, and Applications to Bridge and to Microwave Module Manufacture*. Ph.D. Dissertation, University of Maryland at College Park. <http://www.cs.umd.edu/users/sjsmith/phd>.

Tate, A. 1977. Generating project networks. *IJCAI-77*.

Throop, T. 1983. *Computer Bridge*. Hayden Book Company, Rochelle Park, NJ.

Truscott, A. 1997. Bridge. *New York Times*, 16 August 1997, p. A19.

Tsuneto, R.; Erol, K.; Hendler, J.; and Nau, D. 1996. Commitment strategies in hierarchical task network planning. In *Proc. Thirteenth National Conference on Artificial Intelligence*, pp. 536-542.

Tsuneto, R.; Nau, D.; and Hendler, J. 1997. Plan-refinement strategies and search-space size. In *Proc. European Conference on AI Planning*.

Wilkins, D. E. 1988. *Practical Planning*. Morgan Kaufmann, San Mateo, California.

Wilkins, D. E. and Desimone, R. V. 1994. Applying an AI planner to military operations planning. In Fox, M. and Zweben, M., editors, *Intelligent Scheduling*, 685—709. Morgan Kaufmann, San Mateo, California.

ANSWER: Network Monitoring Using Object-Oriented Rules

Gary M. Weiss[†], Johannes P. Ros and Anoop Singhal

AT&T Labs
480 Red Hill Road
Middletown, NJ 07748
{gmweiss, hros, anoopsinghal}@att.com

Abstract

This paper describes ANSWER, the expert system responsible for monitoring AT&T's 4ESS switches. These switches are extremely important, since they handle virtually all of AT&T's long distance traffic. ANSWER is implemented in R++, a rule-based extension to the C++ object-oriented programming language, and is *innovative* because it employs both rule-based *and* object-oriented programming paradigms. The use of object technology in ANSWER has provided a principled way of modeling the 4ESS and of reasoning about failures within the 4ESS. This has resulted in an expert system that is more clearly organized, easily understood and maintainable than its predecessor, which was implemented using the rule-based paradigm alone. ANSWER has been deployed for more than a year and handles all 140 of AT&T's 4ESS switches and processes over 100,000 4ESS alarms per week.

Introduction

Network reliability is of critical concern to AT&T, since its reputation for network reliability has taken many years to establish and is one of its most valuable resources. Nonetheless, in today's fiercely competitive environment, high levels of reliability must be achieved in a cost-effective manner. This paper will focus on the problem of efficiently monitoring the 140 4ESS switches in the AT&T network, which collectively handle virtually all of AT&T's long distance traffic.

Problem Description

Upon detecting a problem or experiencing an anomalous event, a 4ESS switch will generate an alarm and send it to one of AT&T's two technical control centers for further processing. At these sites, an expert human "analyst" examines the alarm, possibly runs diagnostics on the switch and then determines if human intervention is required. If intervention is required, the analyst creates a "trouble ticket" and electronically dispatches it to a technician at the site housing the switch. This maintenance process requires the analysts at the technical control centers to monitor over 100,000 alarms per week. Many of these alarms indicate a transient problem—a problem that requires further monitoring but does not require immediate human intervention. Thus, a maintenance process that requires each alarm to be handled by an analyst will be extremely time-consuming, costly and wasteful. Nonetheless, for many years the maintenance process operated in such a manner.

The *problem* is to provide a monitoring system that partially assumes the role of the analyst, so that only those problems that require further analysis are brought to the analysts' attention. Such a system will reduce staffing costs and allow the analysts to focus their attention on the more difficult problems. Specifically, such a monitoring application should correlate alarms coming from different components, ignore transient problems, identify chronic problems, and run diagnostics when appropriate. If a problem is isolated that can only be fixed by a technician, then a trouble ticket should be autonomously generated and electronically dispatched to a field technician. Only when further analysis of problem is required will an "alert" be generated and sent to an analyst at one of the technical control centers. Thus, the monitoring system must provide *filtering* of the 4ESS alarms and intelligent work delivery. In addition, the monitoring application must operate in a manner that allows for changes and updates to be handled easily and quickly as the AT&T network continues to evolve. This objective became a priority due to deficiencies in previous solutions, and is a key focus of this paper. Finally, one overriding requirement on any solution is that it must be capable of processing the alarm messages in real-time.

Why Use AI?

The decision to use an expert system to perform network monitoring and alarm filtering was a very natural one, given the need to automate a task performed by human a expert within a limited domain. Furthermore, the fact that the task to be automated is essentially a diagnosis task lends even more support to this decision, since diagnosis is amenable to AI techniques and such problems have been widely solved using AI methods. In fact, there are many examples within the telecommunication industry of such systems. NYNEX uses the MAX expert system (Rabinowitz, Flamholz, Wolin & Euchner 1991) to locate

---

[†]Also Rutgers University

Copyright © 1998, American Association for Artificial Intelligence (www.aaai.org). All rights reserved.

problems in the local loop (the segment connecting each subscriber to the central office), Pacific Bell uses the trouble locator system (Chen, Hollidge, & Sharma 1996) to locate troubles in a local cable network and AT&T uses the Scout system (Sasisekharan, Seshadri, & Weiss 1996) to identify recurring transient network faults.

A variety of AI techniques could be used by an expert system to perform network monitoring and alarm filtering. Machine learning methods are of particular relevance for diagnosis and are the basis of the trouble locator system, which employs a causal network and the Scout system, which employs data mining techniques. However, a rule-based expert system was deemed most appropriate since it was believed that in some cases our problem required highly specific domain knowledge—knowledge available from the 4ESS analysts in the form of "rules". It should be noted, however, that there have been several recent efforts to supplement the knowledge in the rule-based system with knowledge induced via machine learning methods (Weiss & Hirsh 1998; Weiss, Eddy, Weiss, & Dube 1998).

Previous Approaches

Originally, no alarm filtering was provided and the analysts had to operate on the raw alarms directly. A system to help monitor the 4ESS switch was first implemented in C. Due to software maintenance problems with this approach, in 1990 this system was redesigned and reimplemented using C5, a C version of the popular OPS5 rule-based programming language (Cooper & Wogrin 1988). However, as additional rules were added to this new 4ESS-ES (4ESS expert system) in response to changes in the network, this system became less maintainable. We believe this resulted due to the lack of a clearly defined domain model and the widespread use of fairly shallow, ad-hoc, rules. Similar problems have been observed in other "first-generation" expert systems. Thus, this system did not satisfy our ease of maintainability criterion.

Application Description

ANSWER (Automated Network Surveillance with Expert Rules) is a complete operation support system (OSS) for maintaining the 4ESS switches in the AT&T network. In this paper we focus on the expert system component, which is the central and most important part of the application. The remaining part of the application is primarily concerned with allowing the expert system to interface with its environment (e.g., collect messages from the 4ESS switches). For the purposes of this paper, ANSWER will refer to the 4ESS expert system component. Each 4ESS switch is handled by its own instance of ANSWER; thus, since there are 140 4ESS switches, there are 140 instances of ANSWER. These instances of ANSWER run on a single HP T520 server with 4 GB of RAM.

Functional Overview

ANSWER is responsible for the operation support system's intelligent behavior. The basic input/output functionality of ANSWER is shown in Figure 1.

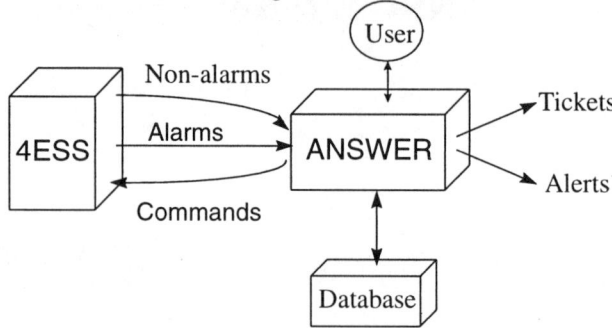

Figure 1: Functional View of ANSWER

The key inputs to ANSWER are alarm and non-alarm messages from the 4ESS switches. The alarm messages provide information about problems detected by a specific device within the 4ESS while non-alarm messages provide status information or the results of diagnostics previously requested by ANSWER. The key outputs of ANSWER are alerts to the analysts at the technical control centers and tickets to the on-site technicians. ANSWER can also send commands to the 4ESS to run diagnostics. Users can interact with ANSWER to retrieve information, such as the status of a 4ESS component, and to customize the behavior of ANSWER. A database provides long-term persistent information storage, so that users can examine the past history of the 4ESS switch. The database is also used to store information required by ANSWER, including information specific to each 4ESS. The rules in the expert system are responsible for determining ANSWER's behavior when receiving a new alarm.

The Object Model

One of the key advantages and distinguishing characteristics of ANSWER is that, in addition to using rule-based programming, it also uses object-oriented technology—a technology now in widespread use in industrial applications. For object oriented technology to be useful in this context, there must be a way for ANSWER to model the 4ESS as a collection of objects. A simplified version of the object model is shown in Figure 2, using Rumbaugh's Object Modeling Technique (Rumbaugh, Blaha, Premerlani & Eddy 1991).

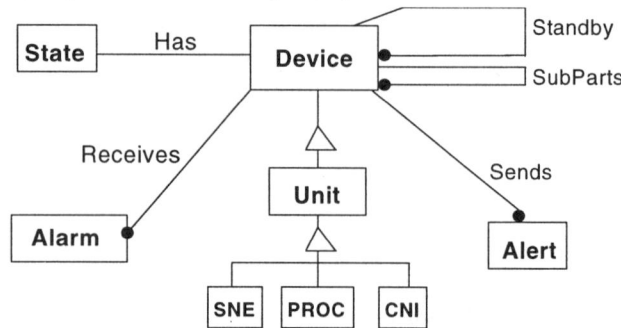

Figure 2: The 4ESS Object Model

The 4ESS is readily viewed as a collection of devices and consequently *device* is the central object in the 4ESS object model. The object model is described by the following:

- *subparts*: an aggregation relation on device that allows any device (including the 4ESS itself) to be viewed as a hierarchical collection of devices
- *standby*: a one to many relation on device that specifies the devices able to take over for a device if it fails
- *state*: the state of a device (e.g., in-service) and the time it entered that state
- *alarm*: each device has an ordered list of alarms, which contains the alarms generated by the 4ESS on behalf of the device
- *alert*: alerts are associated with a device and are created when ANSWER decides the device requires further analysis, by a human

In addition, Figure 2 specifies an inheritance hierarchy for the device class. Device is intended to represent a relatively abstract object. The device class has a subclass named Unit which represents a generic 4ESS device. Finally, the unit class has many subclasses, of which only three are shown. These subclasses represent either a very specific 4ESS hardware component (e.g., PROC represents the main processor) or a specific class of equipment that shares many common characteristics. Inheritance allows us to share and/or specialize device behavior, as appropriate. By having an object-oriented language integrated with a rule-based language, we inherit not only methods and data members (i.e., functions and variables), but also rule-driven behavior. For example, ANSWER's PROC class contains only rules which specify behavior unique to processor devices—generic device behavior is inherited from the unit and device classes.

The Device Model and Model Instantiation

Devices are the key object in our model and therefore it is important to understand how these objects are used, and in particular, how they are created. A key requirement for our model is that it be *dynamically* built from the information sent to it from the 4ESS. There are two reasons for this requirement: flexibility and efficiency. The flexibility of a dynamic model arises from the fact that no up-front configuration information is required—which is essential since each 4ESS switch is unique and components are continually added and removed. The second advantage of a dynamic model is that it permits us to model only the components which have abnormal activity, thereby reducing the size of the model and thus realizing time and space savings.

The expert system is primarily driven by two types of events: 4ESS (alarm and non-alarm) messages and one-second timer ticks. Each 4ESS message refers to a device by specifying up to three levels of device information (i.e., the 4ESS device hierarchy is at most 3 levels deep, excluding the 4ESS itself). At each level in the hierarchy, a device type is specified, along with an integer-valued device identifier, to ensure that each device within a 4ESS switch is unique. The timer ticks update the expert system's internal clock and drives all of its time-based behavior. A device model, which is a "snapshot" of the devices in the object model, is shown in Figure 3. This figure will be used to describe the device creation process.

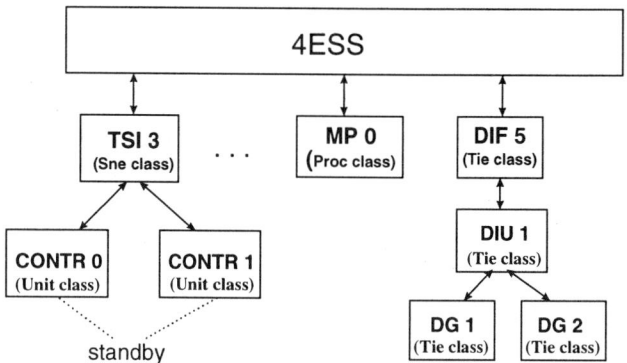

Figure 3: A Device Model

When the expert system receives an alarm and the device specified in the alarm doesn't already exist in the model, then it is created. The class of the device object is determined by a table lookup. For example, when a TSI:3 device is created, an object of class SNE is created. The model requires that all "ancestors" of this device (i.e., devices that contain this device) be present in the model, so if they do not already exist in the model, they are created. For example, when ANSWER receives an alarm for the device "DIF:5 DIU:1 DG:2" it will first attempt to create the DG:2 object. However, if the DIU:1 or DIF:5 of which this DG:2 is a part do not already exist in the model, then they will be created first. When devices are created, data driven rules check for "invariant" relations and create them in the model. For example, if "TSI:3 CONTR:1" is created and "TSI:3 CONTR:0" already exists in the model, then a *standby* relation will be formed between these two objects (controllers for the same device can take over for one another). Device deletion is driven by timer events; a device is deleted if it is in the "in-service" state and has remained in that state, without experiencing any problems, for a specified period of time.

Alternative Solutions

By 1992 it became clear that object-oriented technology would improve the maintainability of our rule-based expert systems. In 1993 a formal process was defined for evaluating existing object-oriented languages that provided data-driven rules. This process involved defining required and desired language features[1] and then creating a "representational benchmark", a set of mini-problems

---

[1] Required features included the ability to represent a taxonomy of objects and to have typed slots; desired features included the ability to put procedural code in the left-hand side of a rule.

similar to those we encounter when constructing systems that must represent large, physical models (like a model of a telecommunication network element). The evaluation process involved requesting vendors of 10 object-oriented languages with data-driven rules to implement these benchmarks. These 10 languages could be classified into three categories: "rules in C++" (Ilog rules, CLIPS++, Rete++, RAL), other "rules + objects" languages (Kappa, ART Enterprise, G2, Nexpert Object) and AT&T internal languages (C5, MCL). The vendor's returned the implementations and the languages were evaluated based on the implementations and the language features. Subsequently, however, the importance of integration with C++ was raised in priority and the focus then became limited to the "rules in C++" languages. Only one language came close to satisfying all requirements, but this rule language lacked the required ability to handle inter-object pointers. The vendor of the language was requested to enhance the language, but stated that the language could not be easily extended to add this capability. As a consequence, a decision was made to develop a rule-based extension to C++.

R++: A Rule-Based Extension to C++

R++ is a relatively small extension to the C++ language which adds object-oriented rules. R++ rules are simply another type of C++ member function and share the object-oriented properties of C++ member functions: inheritance, polymorphism and dynamic binding. R++ is implemented as a preprocessor which runs before the C++ compiler is invoked. Figure 4 shows a partial declaration of ANSWER's Device class. Note that each device's *sub_parts* and *standby* devices are represented as a set. The optional *monitored* keyword in the class declaration identifies data members which may trigger rule evaluation. The declaration also includes the declaration of the *link_standbys* rule, which ensures that the standby relation is always kept up-to-date (a standby relation exists between two devices if one is capable of taking over for the other).

```
class Device {
protected:
  String              type;         // type of device(e.g., TSI)
  int                 number;       // uniquely identifies device
  monitored State     *state;       // ptr. to device's state info.
  monitored Alarm     *new_alarm;   // ptr. to newest alarm
  monitored Device    *part_of;     // ptr. to containing device
  monitored Set<Device> sub_parts;  // set of sub-parts devices
  monitored Set<Device> standby;    // set of standby devices
  rule link_standbys;
};
```

Figure 4: Declaration of Class "Device"

Rules have a special *if-then* syntax, where the if (antecedent) and then (consequent) parts are separated by an arrow (⇒). The rule in figure 5 can be translated as: *if, for this device, there is a new alarm and the state of a standby of this device is out-of-service, then send an alert.*

```
// alert if get alarm and standby out of service
rule Device::alert_if_standby_out_service
{
  new_alarm &&
  Device *stby = standby &&
  State *st = stby→state &&
  st→name == "out-of-service"
⇒
  send_alert("standby_oos, this, stby);
};
```

Figure 5: Alert if Standby Out of Service R++ Rule

R++ also provides the ability to write rules which operate on container classes, like sets and lists. Using an R++ feature called "branch binding", a rule can be applied to each element of the container (the at-sign "@" is the branch-binding operator). The rule in Figure 6 relies on the fact that the list called *Devices* contains all of the devices in the model. For those not familiar with C++, the variable *this* always refers to the object itself—in the case of the rule in Figure 6, the device on whom *link_standbys* is being performed. The antecedent of the rule in Figure 6 can be translated as: *for each device dev in the set Devices, check if dev is the standby of this device*. The consequent then updates the standby field of each device to reflect the new standby relationship.

```
// link standby devices together
rule Device::link_standbys
{
  Device *dev @ Devices &&
  is_standby(dev)
⇒
  this→add-standby(dev);
  dev→add-standby(this);
};
```

Figure 6: Link Standby R++ Rule

The key difference between rules and ordinary C++ member functions is that changes to data members in the antecedent of the rule automatically causes the rule to be evaluated and, if the antecedent evaluates to TRUE, then the consequent is executed. Thus, rules are *data-driven*. In the example in Figure 5, whenever a new alarm is received on a device or the state of one of its standby devices changes, the rule will be automatically reevaluated. The key difference between R++ rules and rules in other rule-based languages is that R++ rules are *path-based*. This means that the antecedent of an R++ rule can only include data members which the class has access to—typically through a pointer reference. Even though R++ rules are therefore less expressive than rules in other languages (because they cannot reference arbitrary objects), we consider this an *advantage* because it ensures that R++ rules *respect the object model*. Finally, R++ is very efficient and in most cases is far more efficient that other rule-based systems, due to the path-based nature of its rules. For those interested in a more in-depth understanding of R++ or in receiving a copy of R++, see the R++ home page (Patel-Schneider, 1998).

Uses of AI Technology

AI technology plays a central role in ANSWER. R++ rules declaratively encode domain knowledge and C++'s object-oriented language features allow the 4ESS switch to be modeled as a hierarchical collection of devices. Although object technology is not commonly associated with AI, it nonetheless can be considered an AI technology. In fact, most of the key ideas behind object-oriented languages have come from AI (e.g., frame-based languages). R++ integrates these two complementary technologies and thus allowed us to get the benefits of each.

AI has always been interested in problem solving. In our case, the problem is related to diagnosing 4ESS faults. The AI problem solving techniques we use include abstraction and a primitive form of model-based reasoning.

Use of AI Techniques for Diagnostic Reasoning

The 4ESS object model provides an abstract model of the 4ESS and thus provides a framework for our diagnostic reasoning. This model implicitly contains information about the structure and behavior of the 4ESS. For example, if a standby relationship exists between two device objects, A and B, then device A's standby field will point to device B, and vice-versa. Much of the *reasoning* in ANSWER is accomplished by using *affective relations*. Affective relations define a highly abstract, non-behavioral, representation for modeling devices and are named for the fact that one component affects another in a diagnostically important way (Crawford et al. 1995; Singhal, Weiss & Ros 1996; Mishra et al. 1996). These relations are too weak to *simulate* device behavior, but serve to organize the domain knowledge in a coherent way; ad-hoc heuristics are replaced by a smaller set of general principles based on affective relations. Affective relations express aspects of the design at a level of abstraction that expert troubleshooters use to link symptoms to faults, and hence are easily acquired.

Two important affective relations used by ANSWER are the standby and sub-part relations. These relations are very general and can potentially apply to any device. Rules which maintain and use the standby relation were shown earlier in Figures 5 and 6. The sub-part relation is very important for diagnosis, since it can be used to isolate faults. For example, ANSWER has a rule that states that if many of device A's sub-parts fail, then the fault is most likely located in device A (*not* in its sub-parts).

It is worthwhile to compare the reasoning in ANSWER with that of its C5-based predecessor, the 4ESS-ES. In the 4ESS-ES, the reasoning was not based on affective relations, due to the lack of a general model of the 4ESS; instead, the reasoning in that system was based on many (overly) specialized ad-hoc rules. There were many cases where a single general rule was not quite adequate due to small differences in device behavior. The solution to this problem in the 4ESS-ES was to have a completely separate, nearly identical, rule for each device; the solution in ANSWER is to have a single general rule and specialize it using inheritance, as necessary.

Application Development, Use and Payoff

Application Development

The requirements for the expert system were available, having been written by system engineers for the 4ESS-ES. The design and implementation of ANSWER began with an object-oriented analysis of the 4ESS. Next, the design phase led to an object model, similar to what was shown earlier in Figure 2. Then, R++ code was written to implement some very basic functionality, to show the viability of combining rules and objects. Three developers then worked full-time over a one year period to complete the design, implementation and testing of the ANSWER expert system. The expert system contains 218 rules distributed over 23 object classes. Much of the basic functionality, or "building blocks" of the expert system (e.g., the code to query the database for information) are written as procedural functions using C++. These functions are then used within the declarative R++ rules that define ANSWER's intelligent behavior. Thus, for each programming task we were able to use the programming paradigm we felt was most appropriate. The expert system contains 3000 lines of R++ source code and 8000 lines of hand-written C++ source code. The 3000 lines of R++ source code were subsequently translated by the R++ preprocessor into 17,000 lines of C++ code, yielding a total of 25,000 lines of C++ source code.

The construction of the expert system progressed smoothly, with the majority of the problems resulting from outdated documentation. Several bugs were found with the implementation of the R++ language, but this was expected since we were the first serious application to use R++. However, these bugs were fixed quickly and they actually affected our productivity less than problems in our commercial development tools. Overall, our experiences with R++ were very favorable.

Application Deployment

Deployment of ANSWER began toward the end of 1996 and the system has been fully deployed since July of 1997. ANSWER handles 140 4ESS switches and approximately 100,000 alarms per week. The system executes 24 hours a day, 7 days a week (a disaster recovery machine ensures availability). Although initially there were a few problems with the overall operation support system, very few problems have been found with the expert system component.

Payoff and Benefits

We begin this section by describing the most *visible* benefits of ANSWER. ANSWER is able to intelligently filter the 4ESS alarms so that a much smaller number of alerts is generated. Experience has shown that the number of alerts is typically one-tenth the number of alarms. It is also important to note that these alerts are more meaningful than the alarms. The deployment of the expert systems (4ESS-ES and then ANSWER) have enabled the total number of analysts in the technical control centers to be reduced from 48 to 18 (this includes all 3 work shifts). Furthermore, ANSWER also saves a great deal of human effort by autonomously generating tickets, propagated with detailed relevant information, for those problems it can isolate—it takes on average one hour for an analyst to manually create a ticket containing the same information. ANSWER is also able to fix certain problems simply by sending a "restore" command to the 4ESS switch[2]. This use of ANSWER's "auto-ticketing" and "auto-restore" capabilities are expected to further reduce the number of analysts from 18 to 12.

We will now focus on the benefits of ANSWER over the previous C5-based expert system—that is, on the benefits derived from using object-oriented technology and object-oriented rules. The main benefits derived from using R++ and our object-oriented modeling approach are:

- *increased comprehensibility*: the object model provides an organizing framework for the expert system. Rules associated with each object class are located in a separate file. In the 4ESS-ES no such organizing principle existed and the rules were located in a few large files. Furthermore, in ANSWER the scope and impact of rules are easily determined, since R++'s path-based rules cannot reference arbitrary objects—*they must obey the object model*.

- *improved maintainability*: the use of an abstract object model, encapsulation as provided for by C++ objects, the use of an inheritance hierarchy to organize and share behavior, and the increased comprehensibility of the code lead to a highly maintainable system.

- *speed and reduced hardware costs*: our R++ based expert system was much faster than the 4ESS-ES, which was implemented in C5 (C5 is in turn faster than most commercial rule-based languages). Partly as a consequence of this, all 140 instances of ANSWER are able to execute on a single server, greatly reducing hardware costs.

- *reduced learning curve*: since we were already familiar with C++, learning R++ was quite simple. Learning a new rule-based language would have taken significantly more time.

- *easier integration with the rest of the OSS*: Since R++ is a superset of C++, the expert system was trivially able to interface to other parts of the operational support system. The 4ESS-ES, on the other hand, required a separate, hand-coded interface layer so that information could flow between the C5-based expert system and the remainder of the system, which was coded in C++.

- *use of procedural code within the expert system*: for some tasks, C++ code is clearly more effective than rules; R++ allows the developer to choose the most appropriate programming paradigm.

In addition to these benefits, the use of R++ and an abstract object model have led to reusable groups of rules. In fact, some of the rules from ANSWER have been adapted to model and monitor the behavior of other network elements. Another key insight is that we were able to use rules not only to encode domain knowledge, but to facilitate inter-object communication. For example, we were able to use rules to trigger activity based on a value in one object being greater than the value in another object; implementing this without rules requires the programmer to distribute code throughout both of the involved objects. This is an awkward, time-consuming and error prone process, which essentially requires the programmer to hand-generate the code that would automatically be generated by the R++ preprocessor. During the course of the project it became clear that some of the more complicated communication patterns (e.g., publish-subscribe) we were using could also be implemented using rules. Using the terminology of the object-oriented programming community, we focused on *behavioral design patterns*—pieces of reusable code that control how cooperating objects interact and distribute responsibility (Gamma, Helm, Johnson & Vlissides 1995). A description of how we used R++'s object-oriented rules to implement behavioral design patterns in ANSWER is provided by Weiss & Ros (1999).

Maintenance

Given the fact that maintainability was a key factor in the design of our expert system, many maintenance issues have already been discussed. To summarize, our use of an abstract object model and general relations using that model, along with certain features of object-oriented languages (inheritance, encapsulation) have made ANSWER easy to maintain. The expert system is being maintained by one of the three original developers. Based on his experience, we estimate that adding new functionality to ANSWER takes only about one-half the development time that would be required to add the same functionality to the 4ESS-ES. In particular, based on our use of a fairly generic device model, he frequently finds that much of the code necessary to implement the new functionality is already present in the system. Finally, we believe that this reuse has led to higher quality code, with fewer bugs.

---

[2] Please note that while the 4ESS-ES did perform alarm filtering, the auto-ticketing and auto-restore capabilities are new to ANSWER.

Conclusion

The use of both rule-based and object-oriented technologies in ANSWER has proven to be highly effective. By providing an abstract device object with diagnostically motivated affective relations, a simple form of model-based reasoning was able to be applied to a domain normally too complex for such methods. Thus, this approach has led to a middle-ground between model-based reasoning and heuristic (ad-hoc) first generation expert systems. The use of object technology has also provided a principled approach for designing, implementing and organizing the expert system and is responsible for ANSWER being a more comprehensible and maintainable system than its predecessor, the 4ESS-ES.

Our experience with R++ and the modeling approach described in this paper has been very positive. In fact, we have been surprised at how few problems we have seen since the application has been deployed. We attribute this success to the benefits of our approach, which we have already described in detail, as well as to the up-front work in developing a good, comprehensive, object model.

ANSWER is fully deployed and is monitoring and maintaining all of AT&T's 4ESS switches. Additional operation support systems are now being implemented using R++ and the approach described in this paper—using some design principles we have identified. Active development is continuing on R++, in order to enhance its capabilities. As mentioned earlier, R++ is now publicly available.

The approach described in this paper is very important for one additional reason—we believe it provides a way for data-driven programming to enter the mainstream. Currently, rule-based languages are considered "AI languages" and are not used by the large number of "mainstream" developers. As we showed earlier, in addition to representing knowledge, rules can facilitate inter-object communication. By adding rules to an existing, popular language, these and other benefits of data-driven programming, long known to AI programmers, can be shared by a much larger population of developers.

References

Chen, C., Hollidge, T., and Sharma, D. 1996. Localization of Troubles in Telephone Cable Networks, *Innovative Applications of Artificial Intelligence*, Vol. 2, AAAI Press, Menlo Park, CA., pp. 1461-1470.

Cooper T., and Wogrin, N. 1988. *Rule-Based Programming with OPS5*, Morgan Kaufmann, San Mateo, CA.

Crawford, J., Dvorak, D., Litman, D., Mishra, A., and Patel-Schneider, P. 1995. Device Representation and Reasoning with Affective Relations, *Proceedings of the Fourteenth International Conference on Artificial Intelligence* (IJCAI-95), pp. 1814-1820, Montreal, Quebec, Canada.

Gamma, E., Helm, R., Johnson, R., Vlissides, J., *Design Patterns: Elements of Reusable Object-Oriented Software*, Addison-Wesley.

Mishra, A., Ros, J., Singhal, A., Weiss, G., Litman, D., Patel-Schneider, P., Dvorak, and D., Crawford, J. 1996. R++: Using Rules in Object-Oriented Designs, *Addendum Object-Oriented Programming Systems, Languages, and Applications* (OOPSLA).

Patel-Schneider, P. 1998. The R++ home page: http://www.research.att.com/sw/tools/r++.

Rabinowitz, H., Flamholz, J., Wolin, E., and Euchner, J. 1991. NYNEX MAX: A Telephone Trouble Screening Expert, *Innovative Applications of Artificial Intelligence 3*, Smith, R. & Scott, C., eds., AAAI Press, Menlo Park, CA., pp. 213-230.

Rumbaugh, J., Blaha, M., Premerlani, W., and Eddy, F. 1991. *Object-Modeling and Design*, Prentice Hall.

Sasisekharan, R., Seshadri, V., and Weiss, S. 1996. Data Mining and Forecasting in Large-Scale Telecommunication Networks, *IEEE Expert*, 11(1): 37-43.

Singhal, A., Weiss, G. M., and Ros, J. P. 1996. A Model Based Reasoning Approach to Network Monitoring, *Proceedings of the ACM Workshop on Databases for Active and Real Time Systems* (DART '96), Rockville, Maryland, pp. 41-44.

Weiss, G. M., and Ros, J. P. 1999. Implementing Design Patterns with Object-Oriented Rules, *Journal of Object Oriented Programming*. To be published January, 1999.

Weiss, G. M., and Hirsh, H. 1998. Learning to Predict Rare Events in Categorical Time-Series Data, *Proceedings of the 1998 AAAI/ICML Workshop on Time-Series Analysis*, Madison, Wisconsin.

Weiss, G., Eddy, J., Weiss, S., and Dube, R. 1998. Intelligent Telecommunication Technologies, *Knowledge-Based Intelligent Techniques in Industry (chapter 8)*, L.C. Jain, ed., CRC press.

Emerging Applications

Warfighter's Information Packager

Yigal Arens
Weixiong Zhang
USC/Information Sciences Institute
4676 Admiralty Way
Marina del Rey, CA 90292

{arens,zhang}@isi.edu

Yongwon Lee
Jon Dukes-Schlossberg
Lockheed Martin
Intelligent Systems Center
3251 Hanover St. H1-43
Palo Alto, CA 94304
{ylee,slosh}@ict.atc.lmco.com

Marc Zev

ISX Corporation
4353 Park Terrace Dr.
Westlake Village, CA 91361

mzev@isx.com

Abstract

The Warfighter's Information Packager (WIP) is a suite of distributed components that allows users to easily obtain information from diverse heterogeneous data sources and to display the results in a user-defined predictable manner.

WIP is based on research performed under DARPA's Intelligent Integration of Information program. WIP uses a combination of AI and non-AI technologies to take advantage of the information push technology being developed for DARPA's Battlefield Awareness and Data Dissemination (BADD) program, and being deployed during the Fall of 1998.

Together, the WIP components create a distributed system that serves as a valuable tool for information analysis by: 1) allowing the user to define high-level information products, *information packages,* which are parameterized by user interests and specific tasks and roles; 2) providing a web-based package viewer that dynamically constructs packages for the user on demand and performs value-added information *linking*; 3) allowing users to make high-value complex information requests that can span multiple data sources without a priori knowledge of the schema of the sources,; and 4) monitoring data sources and *anticipating* useful modifications to a user's information package.

1 Problem Description

The Warfighter's Information Packager (WIP) system addresses the problem of how to support the needs of users to view and manipulate required data in an information push environment. In such an environment, traditional query-based data retrieval is replaced by asynchronous information delivery based on information profiles registered with sources.

Information push is intended to address the following

Copyright © 1998, American Association for Artificial Intelligence (www.aaai.org). All rights reserved.

problem: When information is generated in many sources and on a continual basis, it is onerous and inefficient to require users to issue multiple repeated queries for their information. It would be far more efficient if responsibility for disseminating the information were transferred to the sources. The sources contain the actual information and can more readily detect changes. In such an architecture, the consumer registers an *information profile* with the source, or with a system overseeing the source, that describes the kind of information they need.

There are many ways in which such a scheme may be implemented. The BADD program was established to deal with the issue of information push in a battlefield environment. BADD has chosen an architecture wherein profiles are registered with a central Information Dissemination Manager (IDM), and the IDM ensures that data matching the profiles is transferred to the deployed sources. This still leaves open the questions of how to construct and use applications that require the pushed data, and how to determine which profiles must be registered in order to support these applications. The WIP system addresses these issues.

WIP provides end-users with a facility for producing an *information package.* WIP, using IDM, ensures that necessary data is pushed to deployed sources when it is available. An *Information Integrator* satisfies information package queries by retrieving data from the deployed sources. Throughout both the specification and utilization of the product, an *Anticipator* component observes user and world events and may trigger the modification of existing packages. This capability allows profiles to be updated dynamically, in response to changing circumstances.

The specific problems that WIP addresses are:

1. The warfighter has a task to perform and has specific information needs. Information needs in BADD are specified as profiles that do not necessarily match up conveniently with actual source queries. This is due to the profile registration facility of the IDM having a language far less powerful than familiar database query languages. Furthermore, the context in which the task ends up being performed may require variation of the profile—something that is hard for the end-user to anticipate.

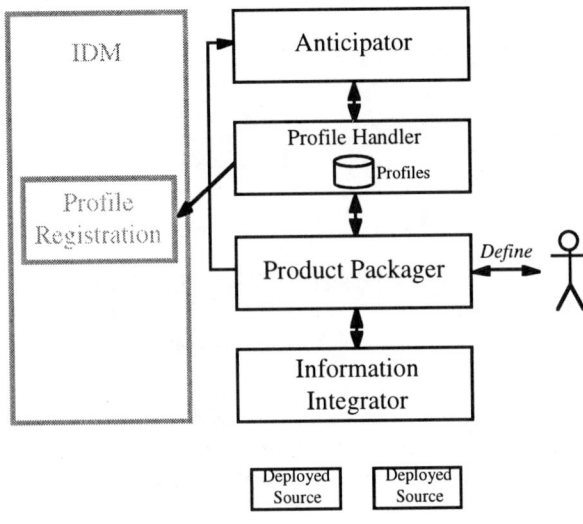

Figure 1: Information Package Specification

2. The data is delivered to the end-user's computer environment in formats that may differ from one environment to the next due to variations in data management facilities. For example, one warfighter may have a database facility available for a certain type of data, while another may not. In such a situation the IDM will deposit the information in a file. For similar reasons, data storage formats used in the deployed sources may differ from those used in original sources against which the profiles are registered. In addition, data needed for a single task may end up being distributed over different deployed sources. The end result is that any processing of deployed information will necessarily involve an information integration and/or translation task. Making WIP packages portable requires that this integration be done in a general manner and that queries to the information integrator be at a semantic level, independent of precise sources used and their organization.

We have chosen to use selected AI technologies, some developed as part of DARPA's Intelligent Integration of Information (I3) program, to address this problem.

2 Application Description

This section describes WIP's *product specification phase* and *product utilization phase*. Both phases complement each other, and the IDM, to provide an end-to-end information push system.

2.1 Information Package Specification

Figure 1 presents the architecture of the product specification phase. During this phase, the user interacts with the Product Packager to define the information package and the information profiles ultimately required for its successful utilization. It consults the Information Integrator in order to determine which sources are to be monitored. Since the local, deployed sources are mirrors of the original sources accessible through the IDM, (even if their organization and DBMS may differ) the Information Integrator can provide the Product Packager with necessary information to locate the appropriate sources. Defined profiles are handed to the Package Handler for local storage and for IDM registration. They are also handed to the Anticipator to infer user and world events that would necessitate modification of the information package.

The following sections describe the operations and capabilities of each of the modules in Figure 1 in more detail.

2.1.1 Product Packager

The Product Packager: 1) allows the user to define high-level information products, *information packages*, which are parameterized by user information needs and specific tasks and roles; 2) describes how the information should be formatted when presented to the user; 3) provides a web-based viewer that dynamically constructs packages for the user on demand and performs value-added information linking.

The Product Packager module, developed at ISX, is composed of two main components: the Package Editor and the Product Viewer. The Package Editor provides an environment for creating information package templates. These templates include parameterized queries and display formatting information. WIP's query description methodology allows users to easily describe their information needs based on a descriptive domain ontology. WIP's parameterization allows the dynamic modification of the precise semantics of queries without revising queries. This is accomplished by providing late-time binding of variables within the query expressions, enabling information requirements such as: "Get the target information for all targets on today's target list" to be expressed.

The Package Editor also performs the registration of necessary data profiles so that data can be deployed to the user's system. The Product Viewer, discussed more thoroughly in Section 2.2.1, collects the information results from the information integrator module, formats them based on the format defined in the package template, and displays the packaged product to the user.

2.1.2 Information Integrator

The Information Integrator module is an application of SIMS AI technology, developed at USC/ISI. SIMS serves as a single access point for information distributed over a collection of heterogeneous data sources. The underlying technology is described in Section 3.2. During the specification phase, the Information Integrator uses its knowledge of the distribution of data over sources accessible to the IDM (also mirrored, as noted earlier, by the distribution of potential data over local deployed

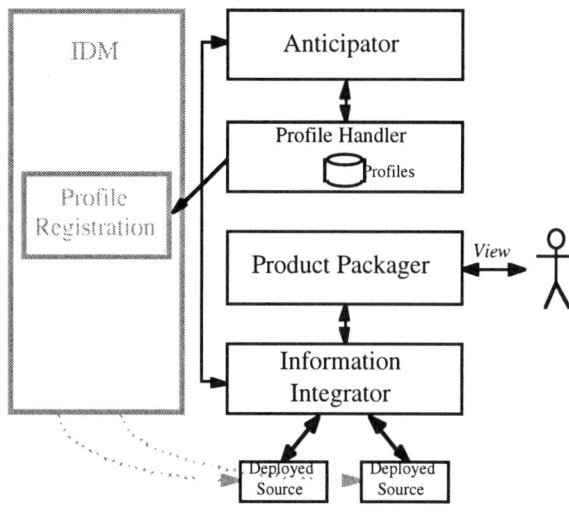

Figure 2: Information Package Utilization

sources) to provide the Product Packager with the identity of sources against which profiles must be registered. This enables the package being defined to have the information required for its operation at utilization time. Furthermore, SIMS' capability to determine which queries will have to be asked of each component source to satisfy the package's needs is used by the Product Packager. The package defines the profiles that will eventually be handed to the Package Handler for processing and registration.

2.1.3 Profile Anticipator

The Profile Anticipator dynamically updates user information needs in response to circumstances that have changed since the original information profile was defined. It handles conditional and unexpected information needs of users, once their basic information needs are registered. "Basic" information refers to required information to be delivered at all times, while "conditional" information refers to data to be delivered only when a certain condition is met (e.g., only when the mission is completed, send me the video image of the target). The Anticipator is an integral part of the WIP system not only to achieve dynamic intelligent information packaging but also to simplify the complexity of package entry.

Upon notification of an information profile registration, the Anticipator examines its contents and generates an anticipator profile for that user. An anticipator profile specifies the conditions under which the user's profile needs to be modified. For example, as a user moves from one location to another, the Anticipator monitors the user's current location to update information needs that may change. The anticipator profile is registered through the Product Packager just as the user's information profile is registered. The Anticipator then generates a package monitor that continuously and periodically requests the data for this package from the Product Packager to check the occurrence of "significant" and "interesting" events. When such events are detected, the monitor notifies the Anticipator that then carries out appropriate actions, i.e., the user's information profile is updated. When a user's information profile is deactivated, the associated anticipator profile and its package monitor are also deactivated.

The Anticipator maintains a rule base to provide domain-specific knowledge necessary for generating the anticipator profiles and to specify definitions of "interesting" events and associated appropriate actions. The Anticipator rules are represented in OEM (Object Exchange Model [Goldman et al. 96]), and implemented in Java.

2.1.4 Package Handler

The Package Handler maintains a local store of profiles defined specifically by WIP, handles communications, and registers and de-registers these profiles with the IDM.

2.2 Information Package Utilization

In the package utilization phase, packages are run and their information can be viewed and manipulated by the end-user. The package typically needs specific information—it requests data from the Information Integrator, which queries the deployed sources. The Profile Anticipator will monitor those same deployed sources via the Information Integrator in order to update users' information profiles, if and when necessary.

Figure 2 presents the architecture for the information package utilization phase. The following sections describe the operations and capabilities of each of the modules in more detail.

2.2.1 Product Packager

During the package specification phase, the Package Editor was responsible for user interactions. However, during the package utilization phase the Product Viewer is the focus of the system's operation. During the package specification phase the Product Packager enhances a user's ability to analyze information by allowing the creation of query expressions based on a high-level domain model, and by defining the formats of results both on a query by query basis and the package as a whole. In this phase, the Product Packager manages the returned information in order to provide the user with additional semantic insight to the data.

Using the Product Viewer, the user requests that a package be displayed. The Product Packager retrieves the requested package from the Package Handler and submits the package's queries to the Information Integrator. Upon receipt of the queried information, the Product Packager aids the user by identifying semantic links among the user's requested information and that requested by others, including information gathered on behalf of the Anticipator. The Product Packager then formats the information as specified in the package and renders the package, dynamically, based on the user's currently available bandwidth and display options, using the Product Viewer.

While formatting and rendering the package, the Product Packager adds hyperlinks to the value-added linked information.

2.2.2 Information Integrator

In this phase the Information Integrator performs its "standard" function of query answering. It receives queries from the Product Packager and the Anticipator for data in the local sources, and provides it. The queries are in a high-level language using terms from the domain model (see Section 3.2 for details), hiding from the other WIP modules the details of source distribution, organization and language. The same package will work in different environments as long as the Information Integrator's description of the available sources is revised to reflect the specifics of the local situation.

2.2.3 Profile Anticipator

Because the Anticipator can add and update a user's information needs, information packages can contain new information the user does not specify in his/her profile. The operation of the Profile Anticipator is not modified during the package utilization stage, and it performed its monitoring of data sources regardless of user interactions with the Product Viewer.

2.2.4 Package Handler

During the utilization phase, the Package Handler acts the same as during the specification phase.

3 Use of AI Technology

3.1 Product Packager and Profile Editor

3.1.1 Information Package Template Selection

In military situations, such as the one WIP is designed for, it is typical that many users have the same or a similar data capacity. For this reason and for the efficiency of use, having pre-staged information package templates (IPTs) would be advantageous. However, because it is impossible to predetermine the information needs of every user, a better way is to establish IPTs that reflect the information needs based on an encapsulation of a particular user role. For instance, it would be far easier to determine the general information needs of someone in the Bosnian theater and store that as a specific IPT, store the information needs of a tank commander in a separate IPT, etc. Then, when the user needs to register an information package he needs only describe himself by his roles (e.g. tank commander in the Bosnian theater) and a specialized IPT can be constructed based on the aggregation of smaller, specific information package templates.

The ability to perform the aggregation of IPTs relies on the definition of roles for both the users and the IPTs. The purpose of a role is to provide a meaningful way of recognizing an IPT by the type of information requests contained within it. An IPT's role does not necessarily identify it uniquely, but it serves as a way to measure the commonality between that IPT and others. The idea is to define a role as some set of attributes common to all IPTs. Once a role is established for an IPT it is used as the index to find it again.

Collecting the appropriate IPTs for a user is not as simple as performing a *find* in a relational database. The determination of which IPTs are suitable can be based on a data-driven, rule-based methodology. Within military operations there are very specific rules about how information can flow, typically this means up through the chain of command. An example how this might work is as follows: a tank company commander in the Bosnian theater is interested in creating an appropriate IPT. An appropriate set of IPT might be: one for tank commanders, one for the Bosnian theater, one for the army. However, an IPT for a battalion would not be appropriate. The battalion commander in the same theater might get the tank commander's IPT plus IPTs for artillery companies. But if no IPT exists for the battalion level for Bosnia, a battalion level IPT for Europe might be appropriate. The IPT selection process is defined within an expert system, using a rule-based domain ontology.

3.1.2 Semantic Linking of Information

The Product Packager manages the information that is returned from the information integrator for all users of the WIP system at a given deployed site. As the Package Products are requested and viewed via the Product Viewer, a request is made to the Information Integrator to gather the data. Using a rule-based domain ontology as a guide, the Product Packager reviews all the data gathered from all users and makes a determination whether the data is relevant to the information requested in the original package. For instance, if the package has been registered to a tank unit and weather data has been collected and it is raining, the Product Packager would determine that road conditions would be a useful piece of information to include. If road conditions for the appropriate geographical area are available, then the Product Packager will add a hyper-inked connection to the original package pointing to the value added data.

3.2 Information Integrator

The Information Integrator module is an application of SIMS technology in the battlefield data dissemination domain. The overall goal of the SIMS project at USC/ISI is to provide integrated access to information distributed over multiple, heterogeneous sources: databases, knowledge bases, flat files, Web pages, programs, etc. In providing such access, SIMS insulates human users and application programs from the need to be aware of the location of sources and distribution of queried data over them, individual source query languages, their organization, data model, size, and so forth. The processing of user requests should be robust, capable of recovery from execution-time failures and able to handle and/or report inconsistency and incompleteness of data sources. At the same time SIMS has the goal of making the process of incorporating new sources as simple and automated as possible.

The SIMS approach to this integration problem has been based largely on research in Artificial Intelligence, primarily in the areas of knowledge representation, planning, and machine learning. A model of the application domain is created, using a knowledge representation system to establish a fixed vocabulary for describing objects in the domain, their attributes and relationships among them. Using this vocabulary, a description is created for each information source. Each description indicates the data model used by the source, the query language, network location, size estimates, etc., and describes the contents of its fields in relation to the domain model. SIMS' descriptions of different information sources are independent of each other, greatly easing the process of extending the system. Some of the modeling is aided by source analysis software developed as part of the SIMS effort.

Queries to SIMS are written in a high-level language (a subset of SQL or Loom) using the terminology of the domain model – independent of the specifics of the information sources. Queries need not contain information indicating which sources are relevant to their execution or where they are located. Queries do not need to state how information present in different sources should be joined or otherwise combined or manipulated.

SIMS uses a planner to determine how to identify and combine the data necessary to process a query. In a pre-processing stage, all data sources possibly relevant to the query are identified. The planner then selects a set of sources that contain the queried information and generates an initial plan for the query. This plan is repeatedly refined and optimized until it meets given performance criteria. The plan itself includes, naturally, sub-queries to appropriate information sources, specification of locations for processing intermediate data, and parallel branches when appropriate. The SIMS system then executes the plan. The plan's execution is monitored and replanning is initiated if its performance meets with difficulties such as unexpectedly unavailable sources. It is also possible for the plan to include explicit replanning steps, after reaching a state where more is known about the circumstances of plan execution.

Changes to information sources are handled by changing source descriptions only. The changes will automatically be considered by the SIMS planner in producing future plans that utilize information from the modified sources. This greatly facilitates extensibility.

A variety of detailed publications describing SIMS is available (e.g., [Arens et al 96], [Arens et al 93], [Knoblock 95], [Knoblock 94]).

3.3 Profile Anticipator

The current prototype Anticipator module, developed at LM/ISC, implements data-driven, rule-based anticipation of information needs: data sources are continuously monitored for occurrences of interesting events. When such events occur, one or more anticipation rules are fired to update user's information needs. Researchers in both database (source subscription) and AI (knowledge engineering and representation) have enabled the current approach.

The anticipator uses domain-specific rules to determine data sources to be monitored, conditions (interesting events) to be checked, and actions to be executed when conditions are met. The anticipator rules are obtained through standard knowledge engineering techniques with military experts. All rules are deterministic, i.e., there is no probabilistic inference. The rules are described using high-level domain terms and the translation of these terms to source specific terms is performed by the Information Integrator module. A key feature of anticipator rules is their expressive event descriptions. Currently, a limited set of event descriptions is possible including comparisons of values of multiple attributes in two information packages.

The rules are represented in OEM, taking advantage of its flexibility (less structural constraints) and self-declarative and self-describing features. It is worth noting that anticipator rules contain neither data source nor implementation specific information. For example, to generate source monitors, rules specify sources and possibly attribute names, but not database queries in some query language (e.g., SQL).

The WIP anticipator module along with the Package Handler is an extension of Profile and Event Manager components of Intelligent Information Dissemination Server (IIDS) [Dukes-Schlossberg et al., 97], and is an implementation of an ongoing effort toward a fully automated information profiling system. We are currently designing an advanced information profiling system, which uses both Bayesian networks and anticipation rules to predict user's information needs from their identity information such as user type, location, status, and mission. That is, rather than explicitly asking what information is needed, users' information needs are predicted and their information profiles automatically constructed from what and where they are, and what mission they are engaged in.

4 Application Innovation

The design of the BADD system, as envisioned by DARPA and executed under its guidance, does not involve any technology that could be classified as part of Artificial Intelligence. The participants in the effort described in this paper found that the incorporation of additional technology based on AI research and techniques could relatively easily (e.g., using an order of magnitude smaller funding) provide a very substantial added value. The information integration functionality provided by the Information Integrator, which uses AI planning technology, enables WIP to be operational on different information sources in multiple existences, including databases, legacy information systems and the World Wide Web. The semantic information linking function of Product Packager and anticipating function provided by the Anticipator, both of which use domain ontology and rule-based AI technologies, significantly extend WIP's usability to the end users. Combined, these two functions not only provide information that directly meets users' needs, but also supply and present context and other related information that makes the required information meaningful.

We would also like to point out that although WIP is developed for the BADD system in a military domain, the concept and WIP system itself can be easily applied to other applications. Specifically, WIP can be adapted to a personal digital assistant in an information rich environment to help a user collect information based on particular information needs. The information can then be presented in a format compliant with the user's preferences.

5 Evaluation

The WIP system is the integration of three distinct technologies: information integration, product packaging and information anticipation. The development of each of these technologies has been pursued independently, and the integration of components has taken place in the past between some of the contributors. Prototype systems with limited functionality exist for the components of the Product Packager. The Information Integrator (SIMS), responsible for satisfying information requests, is currently supporting several projects in extended prototype form. The Anticipator, which is responsible for anticipating users' information needs, is currently in development. The development schedule currently places the integration of WIP with the rest of the BADD system during the Summer of 1998. BADD will then be deployed as a working system in the Fall of 1998.

References

[Arens et al. 96] Yigal Arens, Craig A. Knoblock, and Wei-Min Shen. *Query Reformulation for Dynamic Information Integration.* Journal of Intelligent Information Systems, Vol. 6, No. 2/3, 1996.

[Arens et al. 93] Yigal Arens, Chin Y. Chee, Chun-Nan Hsu, and Craig A. Knoblock. *Retrieving and Integrating Data from Multiple Information Sources.* International Journal of Intelligent and Cooperative Information Systems. Vol. 2, No. 2. Pp. 127-158, 1993.

[Dukes-Schlossberg et al. 97] Jon Dukes-Schlossberg, Yongwon Lee, and Nancy Lehrer. *IIDS: Intelligent Information Dissemination Server.* Proceedings of MILCOM 1997.

[Goldman et al 96] Roy Goldman, Sudarshan Chawathe, Auturo Crespo, Jason McHugh. *A Standard Textual Interchange Format for the Object Exchange Model (OEM).* Technical Report, Stanford University, 1996.

[Knoblock 95] Craig A. Knoblock. *Planning, Executing, Sensing, and Replanning for Information Gathering.* Proceedings of the Fourteenth International Joint Conference on Artificial Intelligence, Montreal, Canada, 1995.

[Knoblock 94] Craig A. Knoblock. *Applying a General-Purpose Planner to the Problem of Query Access Planning.* Proceedings of the AAAI Fall Symposium on Planning and Learning: On to Real Applications, 1994.

Realtime Constraint-Based Cinematography for Complex Interactive 3D Worlds*

William H. Bares and **Joël P. Grégoire** and **James C. Lester**

Multimedia Laboratory
Department of Computer Science
North Carolina State University
Raleigh, NC 27695-7534
{whbares, jgregoi, lester}@eos.ncsu.edu

Abstract

In 3D interactive fiction systems, a virtual camera must "film" the behaviors of multiple autonomous characters as they unpredictably interact with one another, are modified by the viewer, and manipulate artifacts in 3D worlds with complex scene geometries. It must continuously plan camera movements to clearly shoot the salient visual features of each relevant character. To address these issues, we have developed a 3D interactive fiction system with a narrative planner that, together with a bank of autonomous character directors, creates cinematic goals for a constraint-based realtime 3D virtual cinematography planner. As interactive narratives unfold, a cinematic goal selector creates view constraints to film the most salient activities performed by the characters. These constraints are then passed to a camera planner, which employs a partial constraint-based approach to compute the position and orientation of the virtual camera. This framework has been implemented in a prototype 3D interactive fiction system, COPS&ROBBERS, a testbed with multiple characters interacting in an intricate cityscape.

Introduction

One of the most promising unexplored fields of AI applications lies in the entertainment industry, and perhaps no family of applications offers more potential than interactive fiction systems. While natural language story generation has been a goal of AI for more than two decades (Meehan 1976) and text-based interactive fiction systems have been the subject of increasing attention (Murray 1997), it is the prospect of coupling sophisticated inference with believable characters (Bates 1994) that offers the potential of realizing the long-held goal of fiction generation in a visually compelling environment.

---

*Support for this work was provided by a grant from the NSF (Faculty Early Career Development Award IRI-9701503), the IntelliMedia Initiative of North Carolina State University and an industrial gift from Novell, Inc. Copyright ©1998, American Association of Artificial Intelligence (www.aaai.org). All rights reserved.

A key problem in bringing 3D interactive fiction systems to fruition is accommodating the viewing demands of an interactive, and therefore unpredictable, narrative. Intelligent realtime camera planning is critical for the dynamic worlds of 3D interactive fiction in which multiple autonomous characters inhabit complex environments. As narratives dynamically unfold, characters unpredictably interact with one another and with artifacts in the environment as they meander through sprawling landscapes and intricate cityscapes. From moment to moment, the virtual camera must "film" all of these interactions in realtime as they play out in the surrounding physical context, regardless of how visually complicated it may be. This entails continuously planning camera movements so that it clearly shoots the salient visual features of each relevant character, artifact, and structure. To do so, it must plan vantage angles and distances that allow the viewer to immediately comprehend the actions as they occur in the scene while continuously avoiding intervening occluding obstacles.

Previous work on automated camera planning does not provide a general-purpose solution that addresses these requirements. One family of systems employs camera positions that are pre-specified relative to the subject(s) being viewed (Bares & Lester 1997; Butz 1997; Feiner 1985; Karp & Feiner 1990). The IBIS system (Seligmann & Feiner 1991) takes a similar approach but also supplements it with limited ability to overcome viewing failures by using cutaways of occluding objects and creating multi-view illustrations. A second family of systems encodes idiom-based knowledge of cinematography as sequences of shots to depict commonly occurring actions (Karp & Feiner 1993; Christianson *et al.* 1996; He, Cohen, & Salesin 1996). Each shot of an idiom is encoded as a camera position pre-specified relative to the subject(s). Consequently, they work well for filming subjects performing stereotypical actions in a predictable fashion in simple surroundings, e.g., filming a conversation between two actors. However, both of these approaches fail when the camera must simultaneously film arbitrary combinations of subject objects with arbitrary constraints on vantage and/or distance, or when unexpected structures in the surroundings occlude the subjects of in-

Figure 1: Example scene from COPS&ROBBERS

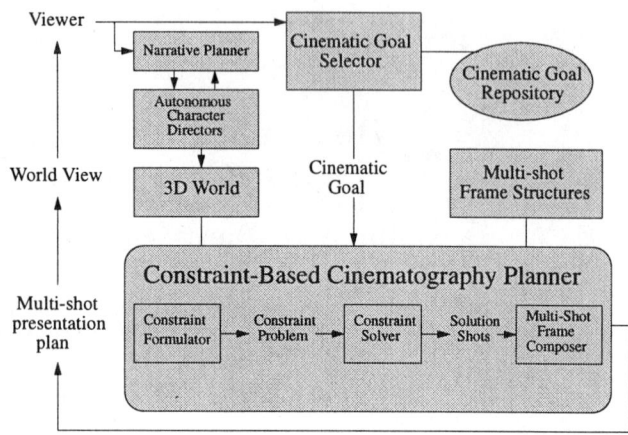

Figure 2: The 3D Interactive Fiction Architecture

terest. Lacking methodologies for reasoning about the viewing problem in the context of the surrounding environment, they can only respond by selecting one of the pre-specified relative camera positions, e.g., placing the camera at a point displaced by a given vector from the subject(s).

In contrast, the constraint satisfaction approach to automated cinematography casts camera planning as a constraint satisfaction problem (Drucker & Zeltzer 1995). Given a request to view particular subjects of interest and a specification of how each should be viewed, the CAMDROID constraint solver attempts to find a solution. In general, the constraint-based approach offers significantly greater flexibility than alternate approaches. However, this initial constraint-based effort does not offer a systematic solution for handling constraint failures that can occur frequently in dynamic environments with complex scene geometries.

To address these issues, we have developed a general-purpose, constraint-based framework for intelligent realtime 3D cinematography. By reasoning from a kind of "cinematic first principles" of scene geometries, camera planners can clearly present the behaviors of multiple autonomous characters as they unpredictably interact with one another and manipulate artifacts in complex 3D worlds. By employing partial constraint satisfaction, they can provide alternate solutions when constraints cannot be completely satisfied. When constraints fail, they relax weak constraints and, if necessary, decompose a single shot to create a set of camera placements, which they then present with either a temporal sequence of shots or composite shots with simultaneous multiple viewports.

This framework has been implemented in an CONSTRAINTCAM, a realtime camera planner for complex dynamic 3D virtual worlds. To investigate its performance, CONSTRAINTCAM's behavior has been studied in COPS&ROBBERS (Figure 1) a 3D interactive fiction testbed in which a policeman and two robbers compete with one another to capture a money bag lost in a cityscape populated by a multitude of potentially oc-

cluding buildings. CONSTRAINTCAM films the characters in realtime as they exhibit goal-directed stochastic behaviors such as searching for the money bag, pursuing each other, grabbing the money bag from another, and attempting to return it to the bank or their hideouts. The camera planner can monitor the autonomous action, and automatically shift the camera's focus to interesting events as the plot progresses. To further stress test the camera, the viewer may at any time modify the course of the narrative by changing any of characters' attributes of eyesight range and speed. CONSTRAINTCAM's realtime performance and the results of a focus group study with the COPS&ROBBERS testbed have yielded encouraging results.

3D Interactive Fiction Cinematography

In the 3D interactive fiction architecture, the narrative planner invokes autonomous character directors to initiate the behaviors of each of the characters. It directs them to accomplish their tasks by navigating the world defined by the scene layouts and 3D models in the environment. At any time, viewers can modify the characters' behaviors, which will affect the activities of the narrative planner and update its directives to the cinematic goal selector. During the narrative, the cinematography planner will receive cinematic goals which specify which characters or objects the camera should film. As the action in the world unfolds, the cinematic goal selector triggers cinematic goals to reflect new developments in the action. For example, when one character begins pursuing another character, a new cinematic goal to view the pursuit is automatically selected and passed to the constraint-based cinematography planner. In addition, viewers can post a new cinematic goal to see the behaviors or relative locations of particular sets of characters.

When the cinematography planner receives a goal, it formulates a cinematic constraint problem consisting of a set of subjects and, for each subject, a set of subject inclusion, vantage angle, shot distance, and occlusion avoidance constraints. The constraint solver analyzes the constraints and attempts to find a single camera placement that will satisfy all of the constraints with respect to the scene geometry of the surrounding environment. If a solution in the form of a single shot cannot be found, then the constraint solver builds an incompatible constraints pair graph to guide the relaxation of weak constraints or the decomposition of the constraint problem to form a multi-shot solution. The multi-shot frame composer exploits a repository of multi-shot frame structures to create sequential or composite presentations of the multiple shot solution. The entire process repeats continuously in realtime to reflect new developments in the world.

3D Narrative Planning

The *3D narrative planner* begins by initializing the goals of each of the characters in the interactive story. For example, in the COPS&ROBBERS testbed, three characters, a cop and two robbers, are all given the initial goal of seeking a lost money bag. The bank of *autonomous character directors* then determines the behaviors appropriate for accomplishing each character's current goal. Characters navigate through the 3D world and interact, both with one another and with world artifacts, e.g., the money bag. Characters navigate by examining a grid, each cell of which represents either an obstacle or a navigable passageway. They sight each other by scanning grid cells for their objective until reaching either their eyesight range or an obstacle cell. Characters walk about at random until they have sighted their objective, at which point a shortest-path algorithm is used to direct them efficiently towards their objective. When a character achieves a goal, the narrative planner dictates the successor goal. For example, in the COPS&ROBBERS testbed, when the cop spots a robber stealing the money bag, he is instructed by the narrative planner to give pursuit. At any point, the viewer can modify the ongoing narrative by changing characters' attributes, e.g., eyesight range, which affects how he/she interacts with all of the other characters.

In addition to incrementally posting goals for the characters, the narrative planner tracks *epochs* of the story, each of which is defined by significant turning points in the narrative's events. Types of epochs include:

- *Visual Identification:* For example, a character sights the money bag and heads towards it.

- *Transportation:* For example, a character carries the money bag to his destination.

- *Pursuit:* For example, the cop sights a robber with the money bag and gives chase.

The *cinematic goal selector* monitors the progress of the current epoch and posts cinematic viewing goals that call for the camera to depict the most salient activities in the current epoch. To illustrate, in the COPS&ROBBERS interactive fiction testbed, suppose a policeman has just sighted a money bag and begins to head towards it. The camera planner should compute a view that indicates the policeman's progress towards the money bag. Informally, this *cinematic goal* specifies that we want a camera view that clearly shows him, the terrain ahead, and the money bag free of occlusions so that the viewer can determine their relative locations.

Constraint-Based Camera Planning

Once a cinematic goal indicating the characters of interest has been passed to the cinematography planner, the constraint formulator creates a constraint problem by specifying the set of characters of interest and the preferred way in which each character is to be viewed. The cinematography planner accommodates four types of constraints, each of which can be applied to any character, includes a relative strength, and a marker indicating whether that constraint can be relaxed. *Subject inclusion* constraints specify which characters to include in the camera's field of view. *Vantage angle* constraints indicate the permissible and optimal relative orientations between the camera and the character. *Shot distance* constraints specify the minimum, maximum, and optimal distances between the camera and a character. Finally, *occlusion avoidance* constraints indicate whether the camera position should be displaced from the optimal vantage angle when necessary to prevent the character from being occluded by obstacles.

The cinematic constraint solver must identify a region of space that is satisfactory to all constraints within which it can position the camera. The cinematic constraint algorithm (Figure 3) begins by determining the consistent region of 3D space in which the camera can be placed to satisfy each of the constraints (Step 1). The critical step converts the consistent regions, which are expressed as spatial relations relative to individual subjects, into a corresponding representation in terms of a common "global" composite spherical coordinate system with origin at the midpoint of all subjects.

If the intersection of the consistent regions I (Step 2) is non-empty, then the cinematographer searches for the spherical coordinates point within I that is nearest the optimal vantage for viewing the subject(s) (Step 3). The camera distance from the aim point (central to the subject objects) is computed via intersecting distance intervals corresponding to the consistent regions for the viewing distance constraints. The solution point is then converted from spherical coordinates to Cartesian coordinates to determine the camera position. However, if the intersection I is empty, then constraint relaxation and possibly shot decomposition methods (discussed below) are employed to compute an alternate solution.

If no solution can be found for the given constraint problem, then the cinematography planner attempts to find an alternative (Steps 4, 5, and 6). The cinematography planner first identifies the combinations of constraints that are incompatible, then tries to find a maximal solution which satisfies as many of the higher priority constraints as possible. Combinations of in-

1. Compute consistent region of space $R_{s,i}$ that satisfies constraint $C_{s,i}$, for all $1 \leq s \leq NumSubjects$, and $1 \leq i \leq NumConstraints_s$.

2. Compute the intersection I of all consistent regions.
$$I = \bigcap_{\substack{1 \leq s \leq NumSubjects \\ 1 \leq i \leq NumConstraints_s}} R_{s,i}$$

3. If the intersection I is non-empty, then compute and return shot solution.

4. If relaxation or decomposition is desired, then identify incompatible constraint pairs of the form $C_{s1,i1}$, $C_{s2,i2}$ such that $R_{s1,i1} \not\cap R_{s2,i2}$ where $1 \leq s1, s2 \leq NumSubjects$, $1 \leq i1 \leq NumConstraints_{s1}$, $1 \leq i2 \leq NumConstraints_{s2}$ and $s1 \neq s2$.

5. Perform relaxation by considering each constraint of an incompatible constraint pair $C_{s1,i1}$, $C_{s2,i2}$ in order of weakest to strongest. If a constraint $C_{s1,i1}$ can be relaxed, then mark it relaxed and delete all incompatible constraint pairs $C_{s1,i1}$, $C_{x,y}$ that conflicted with relaxed constraint $C_{s1,i1}$. Continue until either all constraints are considered or no incompatible constraint pairs remain. If no incompatible pairs remain, then return the solution for the relaxed constraint problem.

6. Perform decomposition by placing $C_{s1,i1}$ and $C_{s2,i2}$ in separate constraint sub-problems P_1 and P_2 if there exists an incompatible constraint pair arc between $C_{s1,i1}$, $C_{s2,i2}$. Into each resulting sub-problem P_i, insert all constraints $C_{x,y}$ that are compatible with the constraints in sub-problem P_i. Return a solution for each sub-problem.

7. Given the camera solution of $NumShots$, select a graphical shot decomposition strategy to present the resulting shots in either sequence, or multiple viewport layout.

Figure 3: The Cinematic Constraint Algorithm

compatible constraints are identified by constructing an *incompatible constraints pair graph*. The cinematographer first creates a node for each constraint $C_{s,i}$. Next, it adds an arc connecting a pair of nodes $C_{s1,i1}$, $C_{s2,i2}$ if their consistent regions $R_{s1,i1}$ and $R_{s2,i2}$ fail to intersect (Step 4).

The cinematography planner then repeatedly relaxes weak constraints until no incompatible constraint pairs remain (Step 5). Relaxation is accomplished by scanning over the constraints $C_{s,i}$ that are involved in at least one arc of the incompatible constraint pairs graph. Constraints are considered for relaxation in order of lowest priority. If the constraint $C_{s,i}$ being considered is deemed "weak," then it marks that constraint as being relaxed and deletes all incompatible constraint graph arcs that involve this constraint. It continues until either no more constraints remain to be considered or no more arcs remain in the graph. If no incompatible constraint pairs arcs remain, then it submits the resulting relaxed constraint problem to the constraint solver. If relaxation was successful, it returns a single shot camera solution.

If relaxation is not possible, then the cinematography planner considers decomposing the original viewing constraint problem into several sub-problems (Step 6). It attempts to satisfy as many constraints as possible in each sub-problem to avoid needless camera shots. It therefore places each constraint of an incompatible constraint pair $C_{s1,i1}$, $C_{s2,i2}$ in a distinct sub-problem P_i (unless that constraint has already been placed in a new sub-problem) and then inserts all possible compatible constraints into each sub-problem. Thus, for sub-problem P_i including constraint $C_{s1,i1}$, it adds constraint $C_{s2,i2}$ if no arc in the incompatible constraint pairs graph connects them.

If the cinematography planner has decomposed a constraint problem into a multi-shot solution, it must then determine how to present the set of multiple camera shots (Step 7). In some cases, it may be important to display several shots in the solution set simultaneously using composite shots. Composited shots use both a main viewport and an inset viewport so that the viewer can compare the subjects in the shots or gauge some relationship between their attributes such as relative location or size. In other cases, it may be preferable to focus on the details in each shot individually, in which case a sequence of shots is shown.

Implementation

The constraint-based cinematography framework has been implemented in CONSTRAINTCAM, a realtime 3D camera planner.[1] CONSTRAINTCAM's shot composition behaviors are driven by the partial constraint satisfaction and relaxation methods presented above. For physically complex environments and the up to 16 simultaneously active constraints in the testbed interactive fiction world discussed below, CONSTRAINTCAM's full implementation of the the constraint-based cinematography algorithm (Figure 4) executes in approximately 25 milliseconds for worst case four shot solutions on a 233 MHz Pentium II with 64 MB with a Permedia2 3D accelerator running Windows NT 4.0. Depending on the number of viewports to draw per frame, it achieves frame rates of between 7 and 15 frames/second.

The 3D Interactive Fiction Testbed

To investigate CONSTRAINTCAM's behavior, it has been studied in COPS&ROBBERS, a 3D interactive fiction testbed with multiple characters interacting with each other in an intricate cityscape. Three autonomous characters, Murphy the policeman and two robbers, Sam and Jake, try to capture the lost money bag dropped by a careless bank teller. If the policeman finds the money bag, he dutifully returns it to the bank. But if either of the two miscreants find the unclaimed money, they will scurry off to Joe's Place to spend their new

---

[1] CONSTRAINTCAM, which together with the 3D interactive fiction world testbed consist of approximately 55,000 lines of C++, employs the OpenGL 3D graphics library for realtime 3D rendering.

found loot. If the cop catches either robber carrying the money, he will immobilize him and return the money bag to the bank. When the narrative begins, the initial locations of the three characters are randomly assigned, and then they begin to meander randomly through the town searching for the lost money bag.

To challenge CONSTRAINTCAM's ability to handle large sets of cinematography constraints that emerge in an unpredictable fashion, at any time viewers can (1) affect the plot's outcome by specifying the speed and eyesight range of each of the three characters, (2) specify preferences for the optimal vantage angle for viewing each character, and (3) post cinematic goals by indicating which of the three characters, the money bag, the bank, and/or Joe's Place to view. To challenge CONSTRAINTCAM's occlusion performance, the interactive fiction testbed was populated with a number of buildings including a bank, Joe's Place, five other buildings, two city parks, and a surrounding mountain range. In the most challenging case, the viewer can request that the camera track all four principals (the policeman, the two robbers, and the money bag), each with four constraints. The viewer can also indicate preferences for one of three varying amounts of information content per screen, which influences the degree to which multi-shot decompositions employ simultaneous inset viewports.

3D Interactive Fiction Example

This example illustrates how the cinematographer films events in the dynamic interactive fiction testbed in response to cinematic goals. The viewer begins with a preference for the cinematographer to present a low information content per screen (no insets), and specifies a cinematic goal to show the whereabouts of the three characters. Due to their separation the camera cannot find a shot that satisfies all constraints. The low information content per screen preference results in only one shot displayed per screen. The multiple shot solution is presented using a sequential multi-shot frame structure that opens with a relaxed constraint overview shot of all characters to be followed by detail shots of each character (Figure 4 a).

After about one minute of wandering the first robber Sam spots the money bag and begins moving in to claim the prize. The Cinematic Goal Selector automatically triggers a new cinematic goal to show the location of Sam relative to the money bag in response to the escalating world actions. In this case, the camera constraint solver was able to find a single shot that clearly showed both Sam and the money bag (Figure 4 b).

The viewer decides to stir things up by increasing the police officer's speed and eye sight range to improve his odds of spotting Sam with the money and catching him. He then executes his search more aggressively, and soon rounds the corner and spots Sam carrying the money bag. A hot pursuit ensues as the officer tries to catch Sam and reclaim the money for its rightful owner. The Cinematic Goal Selector enacts a cinematic goal to show the locations of the policeman and Sam. In this case the result is a single shot of both characters with a viewing angle setup to favor the optimal viewing angle (behind-the-back) for the policeman, the highest priority subject in this pursuit goal (Figure 4 c).

After immobilizing the robber, the policeman, reclaims the money bag to return it to the bank. A cinematic goal is triggered to depict the his progress towards the bank. With the bank located several blocks away and behind another building, the cinematography planner computes a multiple shot solution. The newly specified medium information content per screen permits a multi-shot frame structure that includes a relaxed constraint overview shot to establish the relative locations of the bank and the officer, and uses the inset viewport to present the shots of the decomposition, the first of which gives a detail shot of the bank (Figure 4 d).

Focus Group Study

To assess the performance of CONSTRAINTCAM with real users, an informal focus group study was conducted with 8 subjects interacting with the COPS&ROBBERS testbed. The study was conducted to (1) investigate how effective CONSTRAINTCAM is at communicating key events of dynamic narrative structures in unpredictable, complex environments and (2) to determine how well it responds to user's possibly idiosyncratic view requests. The findings suggest that CONSTRAINTCAM can consistently track multiple subjects interacting with each other and moving between obstacles (buildings of the city) in realtime. CONSTRAINTCAM's ability to depict complex scenes by relaxing constraints to create bird's-eye overview shots composited with inset shots from constraint decomposition were particularly well received. Some subjects suggested improving shot continuity and transitions, and also avoiding inset shots that present information that is redundant with respect to other viewports.

Conclusions and Future Work

As interactive 3D worlds appear in an expanding range of entertainment systems, they place an increasingly greater demand on intelligent virtual cinematographers that can film their activities. We have proposed a narrative generation *cum* camera planning framework for filming the worlds of interactive fiction. By coupling a narrative planner that includes a bank of autonomous character directors with a cinematic goal selector that formulates viewing constraints, a constraint-based camera planner can compose moment-by-moment shots of the most salient actions in the scene. While this work addresses many of the core issues in cinematography for interactive 3D fiction systems, much remains to be done. A particularly intriguing line of investigation is that of complementing the visual impact of virtual 3D narrative cinematography with natural language generation for running commentary. We will be exploring these issues in future research.

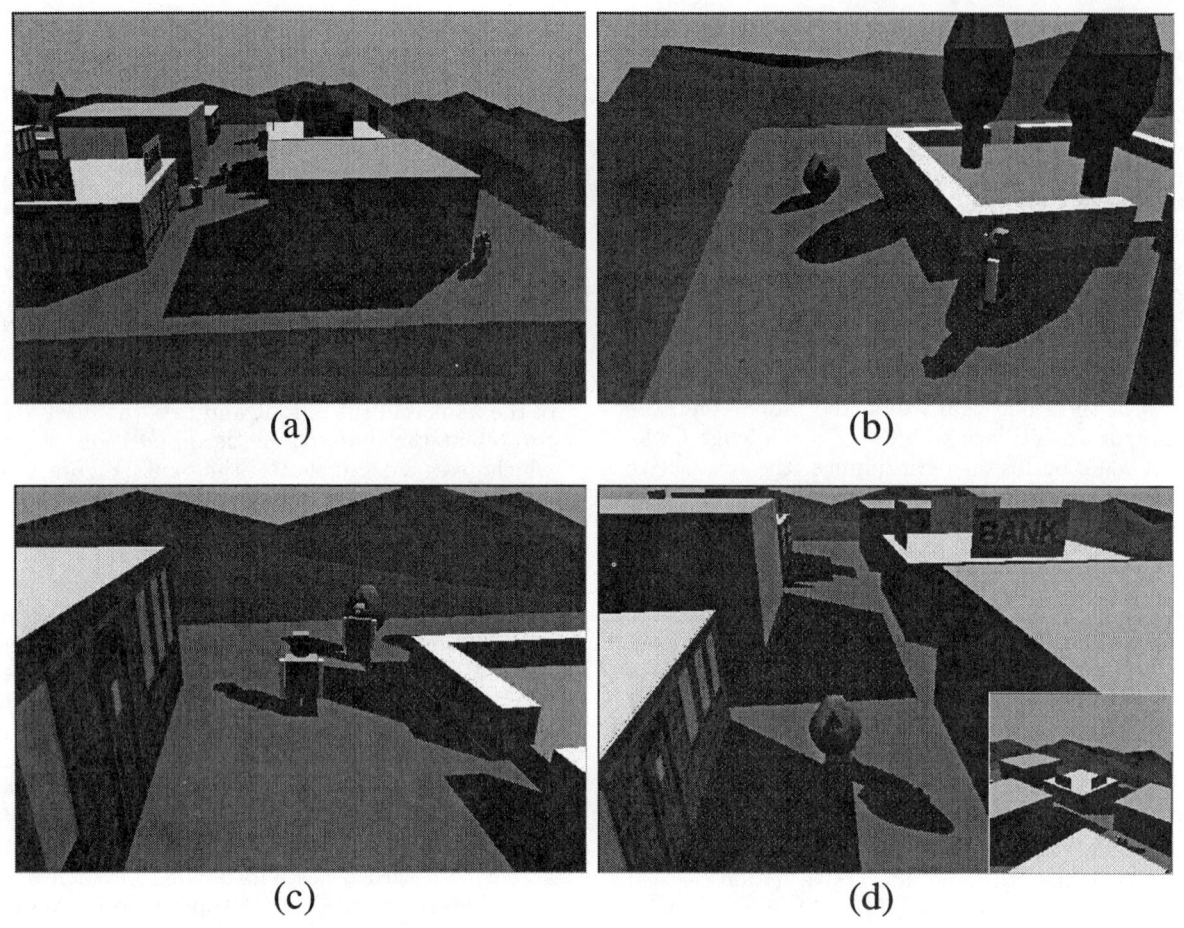

Figure 4: Example COPS&ROBBERS narrative sequence

References

Bares, W. H., and Lester, J. C. 1997. Realtime generation of customized 3D animated explanations for knowledge-based learning environments. In *AAAI-97: Proceedings of the Fourteenth National Conference on Artificial Intelligence*, 347–354.

Bates, J. 1994. The role of emotion in believable agents. *Communications of the ACM* 37(7):122–125.

Butz, A. 1997. Anymation with CATHI. In *Proceedings of the Ninth Innovative Applications of Artificial Intelligence Conference*, 957–62.

Christianson, D. B.; Anderson, S. E.; He, L.-W.; Salesin, D. H.; Weld, D. S.; and Cohen, M. F. 1996. Declarative camera control for automatic cinematography. In *Proceedings of the Thirteenth National Conference on Artificial Intelligence*, 148–155.

Drucker, S., and Zeltzer, D. 1995. CamDroid: A system for implementing intelligent camera control. In *Proceedings of the 1995 Symposium on Interactive 3D Graphics*, 139–144.

Feiner, S. 1985. APEX: An experiment in the automated creation of pictorial explanations. *IEEE Computer Graphics and Applications* 29–37.

He, L.; Cohen, M.; and Salesin, D. 1996. The virtual cinematographer: A paradigm for automatic real-time camera control and directing. In *Proceedings of ACM SIGGRAPH '96*, 217–224.

Karp, P., and Feiner, S. 1990. Issues in the automated generation of animated presentations. In *Proceedings of Graphics Interface '90*, 39–48.

Karp, P., and Feiner, S. 1993. Automated presentation planning of animation using task decomposition with heuristic reasoning. In *Proceedings of Graphics Interface '93*, 118–127.

Meehan, J. 1976. *The Metanovel: Writing Stories by Computer*. Ph.D. Dissertation, Yale University, New Haven, Connecticutt.

Murray, J. H. 1997. *Hamlet on the Holodeck: The Future of Narrative in Cyberspace*. The Free Press.

Seligmann, D. D., and Feiner, S. K. 1991. Automated generation of intent-based 3D illustrations. *Computer Graphics* 25(4):123–132.

Expert System Technology for Nondestructive Waste Assay

J.C. Determan, G.K. Becker

Idaho National Engineering and Environmental Laboratory
P.O. Box 1625
Idaho Falls, Idaho 83415
jcd@inel.gov

Abstract

A system combining genetic algorithms and a fuzzy-rule induction routine has been developed. Two prototype expert systems, one derived analytically, and one derived empirically by the fuzzy-rule induction system, were developed to evaluate the utility of expert system technology relative to waste nondestructive assay (NDA) data review. Technical review of waste NDA measurement data, though warranted with respect to present day waste NDA system capabilities, is labor intensive. Hence it is desirable to have an automated system to perform technical review. It has been shown that both the analytically and empirically derived expert systems produce reasonable results, but that the automatic system can produce fuzzy rules more efficiently and accurately than the analytical method. A visual explanation facility for fuzzy expert systems has also been developed.

Copyright © 1998, American Association for Artificial Intelligence (www.aaai.org). All rights reserved.

Content areas: AI systems, expert systems, fuzzy reasoning, inductive learning, applications.

Tracking number: I-34

Introduction

Management of U. S. Department of Energy (DOE) defense generated containerized transuranic (TRU) waste requires determination of the entrained TRU material quantity and associated parameters. Nondestructive assay (NDA) techniques are the most common and efficient means to determine the TRU material quantity. Quality assurance objectives (QAOs) for NDA techniques used to characterize TRU waste destined for the Waste Isolation Pilot Plant are delineated in the National TRU Program Transuranic Waste Characterization Quality Assurance Program Plan (QAPP) (DOE 1996).

Technically justifying compliance with applicable requirements and QAOs for the variety of TRU waste forms in the DOE inventory can be a complex process. Some waste form configurations manifest NDA system response complexities that diminish the ability to clearly establish compliance. Such complexities require that a technical review be performed at the data generation level for each assay to ensure operational boundaries are maintained relative to QAPP requirements.

Technical review of waste NDA measurement data, though warranted with respect to present day waste NDA system capabilities, is labor intensive. Hence it is desirable to have an automated system to perform the technical review. Therefore, an evaluation of methods to represent knowledge, reason, and make decisions was undertaken. The automated system must be capable of providing a comprehensive waste assay data assessment, and must be reproducible, auditable and compatible with the overall throughput requirements of the waste characterization process. Expert system technology is under consideration to perform this task.

Analytically Derived Expert System

The prototype analytically derived expert system consists of a module of fuzzy rules characterizing the quality of waste assay TRU mass estimates, as measured by the Stored Waste Examination Pilot Plant (SWEPP) passive-active neutron assay system (SAS). The expert system was built using the package FuzzyCLIPS (Orchard 1995), a fuzzy variant of the expert system shell CLIPS (Giarratano 1994). The input to the expert system consists of various SAS neutron measures for a given waste assay. These are processed into figures of merit and passed to the expert system module. The expert system operates on these inputs to arrive at a set of confidence values for the particular assay. The expert system output is comparable to the confidence a domain expert would assign to mass estimates resulting from the assay in terms of compliance with the National TRU Program QAOs.

SAS Fundamentals

The analytically derived expert system design is predicated on the operating principles of the neutron detection, acquisition and data reduction technique implemented in the SAS. The means by which the SAS detects the presence of TRU materials, processes detected signals and reduces the information to a mass estimate defines the attainable functional performance and resulting assay validity. Waste form configuration also influences the mass estimation routine. Hence, the SAS neutron measures input to the expert system must embed base

The SAS has two primary modes of operation: passive neutron detection and active neutron interrogation. The SAS is currently calibrated to assay the quantity of ^{240}Pu in the passive measurement mode, and ^{239}Pu in the active mode. Selection of either the ^{240}Pu or ^{239}Pu mass as the most appropriate measure to apply to the waste container assay is based on criteria coded in the SAS algorithm.

Physically, the SAS neutron detection system consists of an aluminum structure supporting a top, bottom and four side walls, which contain neutron detection assemblies. The SAS chamber accommodates a 55 gal waste drum.

All six sides of the chamber contain two types of detection assemblies: bare and shielded. The shielded assemblies are preferentially sensitive to fast neutrons, while the bare detection assemblies are sensitive to both slow and fast neutrons. This dual response system allows a degree of neutron energy discrimination. The combined response of the bare and shielded assemblies is termed the system response.

Neutrons detected in the passive mode are the result of TRU spontaneous fission and (α,n) neutron processes. The spontaneous fission neutrons are time-correlated and distinguished from the (α,n) neutrons, which are not time-correlated, through a data acquisition technique known as coincidence event counting. In this type of counting, a coincident event is recorded when two or more neutrons are detected by the system within a specified time window. The coincidence signal is converted to the desired Pu mass using appropriate conversion factors.

In the SAS active mode, the shielded detector assemblies are used to detect neutrons produced by stimulated fission resulting from thermal neutron interrogation. The interrogation neutron source is a Zetatron 14 MeV neutron generator located inside the cavity. The signal of interest is taken from a time gated count of the shielded detectors from 700 μsec to 2700 μsec following each interrogating neutron burst. To account for the neutron background that may be included in this measure, another count window is opened from 5.7 to 15.7 msec after each neutron burst. The net induced fission neutron signal used for quantifying the Pu mass is arrived at by taking the difference of these signals. The active mode also employs the response of two additional neutron counters: the cavity flux monitor and the barrel flux monitor. These monitors are used to acquire information regarding neutron moderation and absorption processes occurring in the waste matrix.

Analytically Derived System Input Variables

A number of signals from the SAS signal processing modules provide output carrying the response of the passive and active detection assemblies and active flux monitors. These signals are combined into figures of merit that characterize the system response, and become the expert system input variables. Table 1 tabulates the input variables for each of the three SAS mass estimation modes. The selected variables are not all inclusive, but contain sufficient SAS neutron response information to assess expert system utility for assay data review.

Input Variable	Derivation
Passive System Mode	
Passive System Total Rate	System Total Counts/ (10 kHz clock ticks/10000)
System Total/ Gated Event Ratio	System Total Counts/ Long Gate System Events
Early Barrel/ Cavity Count Ratio	Barrel Flux Monitor/ Flux Monitor
Passive Shielded Mode	
Passive Shielded Total Rate	Shielded Total Counts/ (10 kHz clock ticks/10000)
Shielded Total/ Gated Event Ratio	Shielded Total Counts/ Short Gate Shielded Events
Early Barrel/ Cavity Count Ratio	Barrel Flux Monitor/ Flux Monitor
Active Mode	
Active/Passive Shielded Rate Ratio	(Shielded Counts/4)/ Passive Shielded Total Rate
Early/ Late Count Ratio	Shielded Counts/ Shielded Background Counts
Early Barrel/ Cavity Count Ratio	Barrel Flux Monitor/ Flux Monitor

Table 1. Expert system input variables.

Input Variable Membership Function Definitions

The figures of merit discussed in the previous section comprise the input variables to the expert system. The fuzzy variables *Low*, *Medium* and *High* are assigned by the domain expert to span the range of possible values for each input variable by defining appropriate membership functions. The membership function definitions are based on known SAS responses associated with the inventory of waste forms to which the SAS will be applied. Figure 1 illustrates a typical set of membership functions.

Active/Passive Shielded Rate Ratio

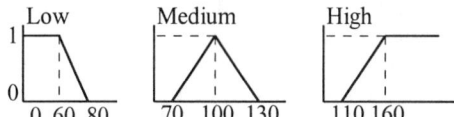

Figure 1. Typical membership function definitions.

Analytically Derived System Fuzzy Rules

To form the set of fuzzy rules, a table is constructed listing all possible combinations of the three input variables (i.e., *Low*, *Medium* and *High*) for each SAS measurement mode. The domain expert then makes a judgment for each indicator combination for each measurement mode as to the level of confidence that should be attributed to the assay estimate for a particular combination. Examples of some active mode confidence rules are provided in

Table 2. Similar rule sets exist for the passive system and passive shielded SAS response modes.

Each of the confidence consequents is also defined by membership function specifications. The confidence membership functions required calibration and are discussed in the Test Results section.

Rule ID	Antecedents			Consequent
	Active/ Passive Shielded Rate Ratio	Early/ Late Count Ratio	Early Barrel/ Cavity Count Ratio	Active Mode Confidence
A3	High	High	High	High
A4	High	Medium	Low	Low
A12	Medium	High	High	Medium
A22	Low	Medium	Low	Low

Table 2. Active mode confidence rules.

Explanation Facility

Decisions in a fuzzy expert system are not arrived at via a simple causal chain: Producing an explanation for a given decision is more difficult in a fuzzy expert system than in a crisp expert system. In a fuzzy expert system, every fact that supports a given conclusion contributes in some degree to the final decision, and an explanation becomes an attempt to represent the influence of each fact on the final decision. Thus, an inverted tree structure was chosen to represent the decision process. Individual facts are shown in the top level of the structure (i.e., input variable names and their associated values). The next level displays the names of the rules that were fired to arrive at a given decision, with lines of varying thickness connecting the facts to the rules. The match strength between an individual fact and its associated rule antecedent is proportional to the interconnecting line thickness. The bottom level of the structure is a single node representing the decision, in this case an assay confidence value. The line thickness for the line connecting a rule to the final decision represents the overall match strength of the rule. The rule match strength is the minimum match strength of the facts that support the rule, hence the rule strength line thickness is the minimum line thickness of the lines connecting facts to the given rule.

Empirically Derived Expert System

Eliciting expert knowledge through the formulation of fuzzy rules was resource-intensive; therefore, methods of automatic fuzzy rule generation from data were examined (Yager and Filev 1994) (Chiu 1994). One method of fuzzy rule generation consists of rule estimation by subtractive clustering, followed by gradient descent optimization. This process is repeated many times under the control of a genetic algorithm in order to find an optimal rule set. The rule set derived in this manner is referred to as the empirically derived expert system.

The automatic rule generation process is an instance of supervised learning; therefore, correctly classified training and test data must be provided. The input data is some set of figures of merit that a domain expert has deemed significant. In this instance, the same figures of merit used in the analytically derived expert system were used in the empirically derived expert system. The training and test data was classified by a panel of domain experts.

Automatic Rule Generation Procedure

In subtractive clustering, the data are viewed as input/output vectors in a hyperspace, the dimension of which is the sum of the number of input and output elements. A cluster of data points in this hyperspace represents an approximate relationship from input to output, a relationship that can be represented as a fuzzy rule. The number of clusters to be found is not directly specified; instead, a parameter between zero and one called the cluster radius is specified. The number of clusters found increases as the cluster radius decreases.

In general, for n input and m output elements in each datum, the generated fuzzy rules take the following form:

if $(x_1$ matches $A_1)$ and ... $(x_n$ matches $A_n)$
then $(y_1$ is $B_1)$ and ... $(y_m$ is $B_m)$, where

$x_1 ... x_n$ are normalized rule input values,
$y_1 ... y_m$ are rule output values,
$A_1 ... A_n$ are exponential membership functions, and
$B_1 ... B_m$ are symmetric membership functions.

The use of symmetric output functions allows for a simpler solution, in that only the centroids of the output membership functions need be determined. The input membership functions are expressed as follows:

$A_j(x_j) = \exp(-.5((x_j-x_j^*)/\sigma_j)^2)$, $j=1..n$, where

x_j^* and σ_j are derived as discussed below.

For simplicity, the remainder of the discussion will focus on the more specific case of one output element in each rule, or m = 1. This simplification is employed because the assay confidence assignment is the only output element.

The result of the calculation $A_j(x_j)$ is referred to as the match strength of the input x_j with the associated membership function A_j. The match strength of a rule with multiple inputs is the product of the component match strengths. This differs from the analytically derived expert system, in which the rule match strength is the minimum of the input match strengths. The rule strength is given the symbol μ and is expressed as:

$\mu(x_j) = \exp(-.5 \Sigma ((x_j-x_j^*)/\sigma_j)^2)$, $j=1...n$.

Using a standard method of defuzzification (the center of

gravity algorithm), the output of the system is found from:

$y = \Sigma_{i=1}(\mu_i y_i^*)/\Sigma_{i=1}\mu_i$, i=1...l, where
y_i^* is a vector of output membership function centroids.

The membership function parameters x_j^* and y_i^* are initialized from the cluster center coordinates, and the parameters σ_j are initially derived from the cluster radius, where there is one vector x_j^* and σ_j, for each rule in the system, resulting in the matrices x_{ij}^* and σ_{ij}. The y_i^* are centroids of the symmetric output membership functions B. The rules as initialized with data found in the clustering phase are a first approximation.

Gradient descent optimization is performed on the parameters x_{ij}^*, y_i^*, and σ_{ij} to fit them to the training data. This process is analogous to back-propagation training of neural networks. The following equation is the basic equation for back-propagation in neural networks and gradient descent optimization of fuzzy rule parameters:

$z_{new} = z_{old} - \alpha\, \delta E/\delta z$,
$E = 0.5\, e_k^2$

where z could be an interconnection weight in a neural network, or any of the parameters σ_{ij}, x_{ij}^* or y_i^*. The term, e_k, is the error between the predicted and assigned confidence value of a given assay, and α is the learning rate. The learning rate is a value between zero and one, where low values accelerate convergence. Convergence is achieved when the root-mean-square (RMS) error of the system with respect to the training data becomes relatively constant (i.e., the difference in successive iteration-averaged RMS values is below a specified criterion).

The back-propagation method described in (Yager and Filev 1994) employed incremental back-propagation. Other enhancements to back-propagation commonly used in the training of neural networks (Hassoun 1995) were employed in the current application, including a variable learning rate and the inclusion of a momentum term. The learning rate was initialized to a user specified value, and decreased in finite steps as the convergence criteria was approached, resulting in an initially elevated learning rate, to accelerate convergence, and a reduced learning rate as convergence progressed, improving the effectiveness of the training process. The momentum term is intended to accelerate convergence, and involves a user specified factor between zero and one. Higher values of this factor increase the rate of convergence, but may induce numerical instabilities. A momentum factor set to 0.1 resulted in stable calculations that quickly converged.

Genetic Algorithm Search for Rule Generation Parameters

The clustering and optimization procedures just discussed require the specification of a cluster radius, a learning rate, and a convergence criteria. The performance of the generated system is highly dependent on the values of these rule generation parameters. System generation, given a set of rule generation parameters, can take anywhere from several seconds to several minutes, depending on the number of rule inputs and the values of these rule generation parameters. Because more than one hundred trials were typically required to achieve optimal performance, finding an optimal set of rule generation parameters was labor-intensive and the decision was made to automate the search. Genetic algorithms (Goldberg 1989) were selected to control the procedure. The C++ genetic algorithm class library developed at the Massachusetts Institute of Technology called GAlib, version 2.4.2, was acquired and employed in this effort. The application of genetic algorithms in fuzzy-system design has been studied by a number of authors (Heider and Drabe 1997) (Takagi and Lee 1993) (Karr 1991).

To use GAlib, an initializer is defined to create a population of potential solutions over the space of valid rule generation parameters. Methods for performing genetic crossover and mutation are either selected from a set of standard methods, or defined for a particular problem. For example, the standard one-point crossover method was employed in the current application. A specialized mutator was defined that varied the value of a gene by a small delta. The set of three rule generation parameters was encoded as three real-valued genes in a chromosome. Finally, an objective function was defined that scored a particular chromosome based on performance of the system with respect to a specified test set. The objective function first trained a set of rules using the rule generation parameters within the current chromosome, and then scored the derived set of rules with respect to the test data. To accelerate the search, if a particular chromosome recurred, training and testing were not repeated, rather, the score for that chromosome was retrieved from memory.

The genetic algorithm employed in the current application assumed a constant population. The children replaced the parents in succeeding generations, except that elitism was employed. Selection of individuals for mating was performed by the standard roulette-wheel method, in which the most fit individuals have the highest probability of being selected for reproduction.

A few parameters were required by the genetic algorithm. The population size was chosen to be six individuals, as this supplied a reasonable initial diversity in the population. The calculation was terminated by specifying a maximum number of generations. Two hundred generations was typically ample to provide thorough coverage of the search space. Two probabilities were also required: the probability of cross-over, and the probability of mutation. Crossover was given a probability of 0.9, as crossover is the primary means of expanding the search space. Mutation was given a probability of 0.1, as some mutation was needed to thoroughly explore the search space, but too much mutation could result in the loss of a good solution from the population. A mutation probability of 0.1 may appear high, but it is appropriate to the number of unique individuals generated during the search. Six individuals per generation multiplied by

200 generations yields a maximum of 1200 individuals. But many duplications occurred, resulting in at most a few hundred unique individuals in the search space. Were the mutation probability to be much lower than 0.1, so few mutations would occur as to be insignificant.

Test Results

The results of testing both systems are presented in this section. To test the performance of the prototype expert systems, a set of SAS generated waste container assays with known validity confidence ratings was generated. Calibration of the analytically derived expert confidence membership functions was also required.

Test Set Normalization

A panel of three waste NDA experts was assembled and given a set of SAS generated waste assays to assign validity confidence ratings, on a scale from zero to ten. They rated their confidence in each of the three measurement modes of the system, for each assay. The set contained 99 assays evenly selected from the waste types, graphite, combustibles, and glass. Disagreement existed between the experts as to the proper classification of each assay, due partly to differing internal scales of judgment used by each expert, and partly to the considerable uncertainty inherent in the interpretation of NDA results. A normalization procedure was adopted to reduce the scaling bias of each expert. Assays with normalized scores that still did not agree between the experts were removed from the test set.

The score sets for each confidence value were normalized as follows. The mean and standard deviation for each expert's set of scores, and for all the scores combined were calculated. Each expert's set of scores was adjusted via calculated scaling factors to have the mean and standard deviation of the total population.

Where there was good agreement for each confidence value between all three experts the normalized confidence scores were considered reliable. Assays for which disagreement occurred were removed, yielding a total of 67 assays in the test set. These assays were used for calibration of the analytically derived expert system, for training of the automated rule generation system, and for testing the performance of both systems. Sixteen assays were used for calibration and training, and 51 were used for testing. The calibration and training sets were selected to thoroughly represent the spectrum of confidence values.

Analytically Derived Expert System Calibration

During initial design of the expert system, the confidence membership functions were arbitrarily set to triangular functions of width 0.33 and centered on 0.17, 0.5, and 0.83. These arbitrary definitions did not produce results consistent with the test data, hence some of the data were segregated and used to calibrate the confidence scale. Table 3 compares the calibrated and uncalibrated system responses, indicating an initial poor level of agreement to test data.

Calibration was performed as follows: the equations used by FuzzyCLIPS to obtain a defuzzified output were set equal to the normalized and averaged test scores for a selected set of 16 assays. The confidence level outputs produced by FuzzyCLIPS are determined by the center of gravity defuzzification algorithm. One equation of the following form was derived for each of the 16 calibration data points:

$$\Sigma C_i x_i^* = \text{scored confidence value,}$$

where each x_i^* is the centroid coordinate of a confidence membership function (*Low*, *Medium* or *High*), and C_i is the area of the same membership function, normalized by the sum of the areas of all contributing membership functions. Multiple linear regression was used to find values for the three confidence membership function centroids that best fit the calibration data points.

% Correct Classifications	Active Mode Confidence	Pass. System Confidence	Pass. Shd. Confidence
Uncalibrated	57%	22%	66%
Calibrated	78%	61%	76%

Table 3. Comparison of uncalibrated and calibrated analytically derived expert system performances.

Table 4 lists the centroid values found for each measurement mode confidence value. The *Medium* centroid value for passive confidence were not reasonable (the centroid of *Medium* exceeded the centroid of *High*). This is due to the fact that few data points among the training and test data employed either the passive system or passive shielded *Medium* membership functions. Thus, reasonable calibration data was not available. By the same token, the current results are not greatly affected.

Confidence Value	Low	Medium	High
Active	.28	.53	.76
Passive System	.36	.80	.75
Passive Shielded	.26	.69	.87

Table 4. Calibrated centroid values.

System Performance Comparison

Table 5 compares results of the prototype expert systems. The table indicates that the empirically derived expert system performed as well as or better than the analytically derived expert system for all modes of operation.

% Correct Classifications	Active Mode Confidence	Pass. System Confidence	Pass. Shd. Confidence
Analytical	78%	61%	76%
Empirical	78%	90%	88%

Table 5. Prototype expert system performances.

The design of both expert systems is at a prototype stage, intended to demonstrate the utility of the expert system approach to waste NDA data review. Only neutron measurement data was initially available to develop and assess the performance of the expert systems. Gamma spectroscopy data is also required to arrive at the final assay. Therefore, expert system development was limited by not having all the data used to determine an assay value. Despite this limitation, the results obtained indicate that even prototypes can achieve a high rate of correct classification when applied to actual waste assay data.

The analytically derived expert system required 123 rules, as implemented. The empirically derived expert system partitioned the input space into a total of 18 rules. Hence the empirically derived expert system was simpler in structure than the analytically derived expert system.

With respect to performance of the genetic algorithm a few comments should be made. Initial attempts to find an optimal rule set with a manual search required one day's effort for each confidence value, and produced rule sets that performed at about the 60% correct level. Initial application of the genetic algorithm located rule sets that performed at about the 70% correct level, and required no more than four hours execution time for each confidence value. Improvements in the genetic algorithm search procedure resulted in the performance levels reported in Table 5, such that it can be confidently stated that the application of genetic algorithms resulted in the more efficient location of higher accuracy rule sets.

Acknowledgments

This document was prepared for the U.S. Department of Energy Assistant Secretary for Environmental Management Under DOE Idaho Operations Office Contract DE-AC07-94ID13223.

Conclusions

Two expert systems were developed to operate on neutron assay data acquired using the SAS waste NDA system. Both systems performed well, especially considering that only partial waste NDA data was available for expert system processing (i.e. neutron data only). System performance was benchmarked against domain expert assessments of the compliance quality of the test and training data. The empirically derived expert system was more accurate than the analytically derived expert system for the passive system and passive shielded confidence assessments, and as good as the analytically derived expert system for the active mode confidence assessment.

An important lesson learned during development is that an empirically derived expert system is less labor intensive to develop than an analytically derived expert system. This was due to time consuming work required to define analytically derived expert system fuzzy rules, fuzzy membership functions for the input variables and calibration of the analytically derived expert system output. Therefore, where knowledge is available in the form of data, future development will employ the empirical method of rule formation. As it is expected that analytical rule formation will be required in some instances, methods for integrating empirically and analytically derived rules into a common expert system architecture will be developed.

Initial requirements on the function of the expert system have for the most part been demonstrated. These requirements include representation of domain expert NDA knowledge, and reasoning with supplied data and represented knowledge. A technique to interpret the empirically derived rules is planned as part of the future expert system development activities. At the present time there is ample indication that the expert system technique can be refined to accommodate the balance of NDA data (i.e., gamma measurements), needed to make a comprehensive assessment of waste NDA data quality in accordance with the National TRU Program requirements.

References

U. S. Department of Energy Carlsbad Area Office 1996. Transuranic Waste Characterization Quality Assurance Program Plan, Interim Change Version, Technical Report, CAO-94-1010, U. S. DOE Carlsbad Area Office 1996.

Orchard, R. A. 1995. FuzzyCLIPS Version 6.04 User's Guide, Technical Report, ERB-1045, National Research Council Canada.

Giarratano, J. C. 1994. CLIPS User's Guide, Technical Report, JSC-25013, Lyndon B. Johnson Space Center, National Aeronautics and Space Administration.

Yager, R. R.; Filev, D. P. 1994. Generation of Fuzzy Rules by Mountain Clustering, *Journal of Intelligent and Fuzzy Systems*, 2: 209 - 219.

Chiu, S. L. 1994. Fuzzy Model Identification based on Cluster Estimation, *Journal of Intelligent and Fuzzy Systems*, 2: 267 - 278.

Hassoun, M. H. 1995. *Fundamentals of Artificial Neural Networks*, Cambridge, Massachusetts: The M.I.T. Press.

Heider, H.; Drabe, T. 1997, A Cascaded Genetic Algorithm for Improving Fuzzy-System Design, *International Journal of Approximate Reasoning*, 17:351 - 368.

Takagi, H.; Lee, M. A. 1993, "Neural Networks and Genetic Algorithm Approaches for Auto-Design of Fuzzy Systems," In *Artificial Intelligence Conference -- Fuzzy Logic in Artificial Intelligence*, 68-79. Linz, Austria: Springer Verlag .

Karr, C. L. 1991. Applying genetics to fuzzy logic. *AI Expert*, 6:3, 38-43.

Bayesian Network Models for Generation of Crisis Management Training Scenarios

Eugene Grois, William H. Hsu, Mikhail Voloshin, David C. Wilkins

Beckman Institute
University of Illinois at Urbana-Champaign
{e-grois | w-hsu | voloshin | dcw}@uiuc.edu

Abstract

We present a noisy-OR Bayesian network model for simulation-based training, and an efficient search-based algorithm for automatic synthesis of plausible training scenarios from constraint specifications. This randomized algorithm for approximate causal inference is shown to outperform other randomized methods, such as those based on perturbation of the maximally plausible scenario. It has the added advantage of being able to generate acceptable scenarios (based on a maximum penalized likelihood criterion) faster than human subject matter experts, and with greater diversity than deterministic inference. We describe a field-tested interactive training system for crisis management and show how our model can be applied offline to produce scenario specifications. We then evaluate the performance of our automatic scenario generator and compare its results to those achieved by human instructors, stochastic simulation, and maximum likelihood inference. Finally, we discuss the applicability of our system and framework to a broader range of modeling problems for computer-assisted instruction.

1 Introduction

Probabilistic networks are used extensively in diagnostic applications where a causal model can be learned from data or elicited from experts [He90, HW95]. In this paper, we first present a formulation of *scenario generation* in computer-assisted instruction as a Bayesian inference problem. Previous approaches to synthesis of training scenarios have predominantly been dependent on the expertise of a human instructor [GD88, GFH94]. The inferential model alleviates this problem by mapping constraints specified by an instructor to a causal explanation in the network model. These constraints are events in the causal model (such as a firemain rupture in training systems for damage control and fire fighting, or a medical complication in training for surgical anesthesiologists) [GD88, De94]. Constraints are literals in a formal specification language for training objectives to be met by a scenario. Explanations, the specification language, and objectives are defined in Section 2.

We then give an efficient randomized algorithm for finding plausible scenarios that meet training objectives,

have well-differentiated explanations, are unique, and are diverse. We define a penalized likelihood function (based upon precision and accuracy in meeting training criteria as well as pure likelihood). The output of the algorithm is a set of explanations that maximize this function subject to the specification. These explanations, which we call *proposed scenarios*, determine the fixed parameters for interactive training scenarios (including the initial conditions for dynamic simulation).

Finally, we show that, subject to quantitative metrics for the above criteria, both the acceptance rate of our algorithm is high and the efficiency (number of acceptable scenarios divided by the computational cost of generating all proposed scenarios) is high. We evaluate the system using the penalized likelihood function, relative to naive and perturbation-based stochastic scenario generators. We also study the empirical performance of the system — that is, how its relatively high acceptance rate and asymptotic efficiency allow it to compete effectively with human instructors in designing scenarios. We report on a deployed training system and quantitatively compare the scenarios produced by our system to those applied and tested in the classroom setting.

1.1 Role of Scenario Generation in Crisis Management Training

Immersive Training Systems. It is well known that effective human performance on complex tasks requires deliberate practice under realistic conditions [EKT93]. To provide realistic practice scenarios in an interactive setting, *immersive training systems* are often used [GD88, WFH+96]. In military and medical professions, these systems have evolved in recent years from ad-hoc physical mock-ups to virtual environments with a high degree of automation and standardization [De94, GFH94, WFH+96]. A common aspect of many crisis management tasks is time-critical decision making, requiring a model of problem-solving actions on the environment [HB95, WFH+96]. In this project, we concentrate on specification of simulation parameters by instructors, rather than the later stage of interaction with the trainee.

The effectiveness of computer simulation for training and critiquing has been demonstrated by deployed systems in many high-risk domains, such as surgical anesthesia and ship damage control [HGYS92, WFH+96]. Similar diagnostic models have been designed to support intelligent displays for space shuttle flight control, and for medical monitoring [HB95, HLB+96]. To assess and improve the decision-making skills of future practitioners in time-critical situations, an interactive simulation is typically used to produce a dynamic model of the crisis. A graphical user interface and a visualization or multimedia system (or a physical mock-up with appropriate sensors and actuators) are used to deliver the scenario. Intelligent control of the multimedia components of this system is required throughout the life cycle of a training scenario, from design through deployment to the critiquing and feedback stage of professional education [WFH+96]. Such an ensemble provides an adequate simulation of genuine crisis conditions to evoke realistic stress levels during problem solving [BDS96].

The purpose of scenario generation in this framework, therefore, is to provide collaborative assistance with human instructors to design useful models for dynamic simulation.

Computer-Assisted Instruction (CAI) Issues. We now explain our notion of useful models for dynamic simulation. Much of the research and development effort in computer-assisted instruction (CAI) for crisis management has gone into easing the design burden for simulations of time-critical decision making under stress [BDS96]. This design task can be isolated into the offline *specification* phase (where training objectives are mapped into fixed simulation parameters and initial conditions) and the online *delivery* phase (where interactive simulation occurs). Our research has shown that uncertain reasoning is useful not only in the second phase (where the trainee may interact with intelligent agent models and receive critiquing from an expert system), but in the first (where instructor objectives are used to stochastically generate scenarios) [MW96].

For example, training objectives in medical applications (e.g., complications to be handled by the specialist-in-training) may be achieved by various causes (preexisting conditions, surgical incidents, *etc.*) [GFH94]. In our deployed application (training for shipboard damage control), the objective is to train officers in responding to loss of critical ship functions (maintaining combat readiness and "ship survivability" while minimizing casualties from the damage control process). The specification tool is a graphical probabilistic model of functional dependencies in the ship. Search-based inference is used to determine which causes (damage-initiating events, such as a mine detonation, missile impact, or ignition of a shipboard fire) best explain the *specified* deactivations. For CAI purposes, the entire explanation (not just the "diagnosis") is useful to instructors, because it aids in plan recognition and the generation of critiques during and after the online simulation phase [De94, BDS96, WFH+96].

1.2 The DCTrain System

In the naval domain, typical damage control scenarios involve explosions, mass conflagrations, flooding, vital system failure, and other types of disaster. A special officer, called the Damage Control Assistant (DCA) is responsible for coordinating all crisis response and recovery efforts. Because real-life major crises on US Naval vessels are extremely rare, DCAs seldom get exposure to serious crisis situations, and as a result find it difficult to obtain the expertise to deal with them if they ever do occur. Training runs on actual ships are extremely expensive, time-consuming, fatiguing, not to mention dangerous – and so are kept to a minimum. As a result, the Navy has identified an acute need for an inexpensive, but effective computerized damage control training system.

In response to this need, the Knowledge-based Systems Group at the University of Illinois has developed the Illinois DCA Training System (DCTrain), a framework of four essentially independent modules that interact with the user to provide an immersive environment for damage control training. Figure 1 shows a diagram of the complete DCTrain system. The Ship Crisis Simulator module comprises a comprehensive numerical/rule-based simulation of ship processes, system functions, and crew actions. The Multimedia/Visualization module implements a powerful interface for user-system interaction. The Critiquing module provides performance feedback to the user. The proposed scenario generation module, utilizing the ScenGen algorithm, is designed to fit into the existing framework. Its task is to design a training scenario in accordance with prescribed training objectives, and guide the simulator through that scenario configuration. As a whole, the system constitutes a comprehensive training tool.

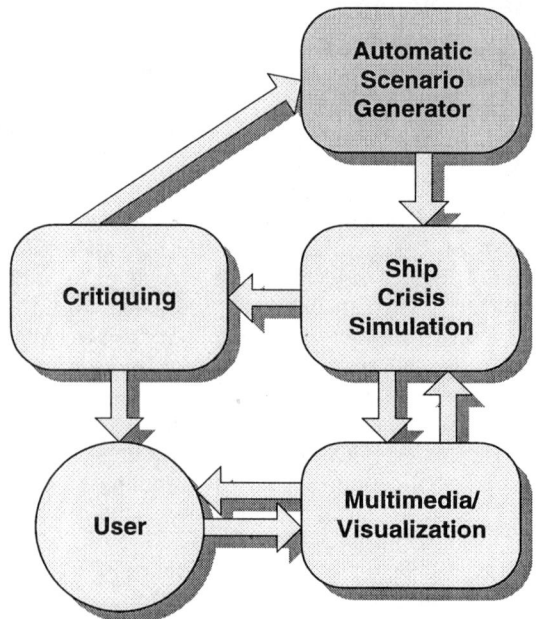

Figure 1. Overview of the Illinois DCA Training System (DCTrain)

Due to its dynamic simulation engine [WFH+96], DCTrain boasts the capability to produce numerous distinct scenarios on demand. A powerful critiquing module, combined with a state-of-the-art multimedia interface provide real-time, and post-mortem context-specific feedback to the user.

In May 1997, DCTrain was tested at the Navy's Surface Warfare Officers' School (*SWOS*) against an existing system called IDCTT [De94]. IDCTT relies on a set of pre-programmed scenario scripts, and as a result offers only one damage control scenario. It also has very limited critiquing capability.

Performance results collected from the May '97 graduating class of DCAs at SWOS clearly indicate the superiority of DCTrain over IDCTT. Exposure to multiple scenarios, and the benefit of expanded critiquing led to significant performance gains in crisis management.

We believe that the addition of an automated scenario generation module to the DCTrain system will improve its training effectiveness yet further. The ability to not only produce scenarios on demand, but to quickly and easily tailor them to specific training requirements, or even to the needs of individual students will provide users with an unprecedented degree of flexibility.

In the following section we give a formal model for scenario representation, and in section 3 we present the ScenGen algorithm for automated scenario generation.

2 A Bayesian Network Model of Training Scenarios

Given that a probabilistic model is needed to map from training objectives to explanations (including placement of both initial and timed events), we seek a diagrammatic representation of the scenario that permits efficient inference. We exploit the property that crisis training scenarios are similar to diagnostic models, and can be *constructed* in a simplified Bayesian network form.

Formal Model: Noisy-OR Bayesian Networks (NOBNs) *Noisy-OR Bayesian networks* (NOBNs) are Bayesian networks which observe the properties of *accountability* and *exception independence*, as defined by Pearl [Pe88]. Accountability is simply a negation-as-failure property for probabilistic models. Specifically, for Bayesian networks with boolean variables, an event is presumed false (i.e., has zero probability) if all its stated causes are. In NOBNs, accountability is achieved using a "leak node" (or "miscellaneous cause") to circumscribe every non-root event [Pe88, RN95]. This is expressed for vertices x with parents $\pi(x)$ as:

$$P(x) = 0 \text{ if for all } i, P(\pi_i(x)) = 0 \quad (1)$$

Define an *inhibitor* as a mechanism that mediates the conditional probability of an event given a particular cause (i.e., prevents the effect given the cause). *Exception independence* requires every inhibitor of an event under one cause to be independent of the inhibitors of the event under all other causes. Inhibitors are explicitly represented as events in some graphical models [Pe88, HW95], but it suffices to express them as *noise parameters*, q_i [RN95]:

$$q_i = P(\neg x \mid \pi_i(x) \wedge \forall j \neq i, \neg \pi_j(x)) \quad (2)$$

$$P\left(x \mid \pi'_1(x),...,\pi'_t(x), \neg \pi''_1(x),...,\neg \pi''_f(x)\right) = 1 - \prod_{i=1}^{f}\left(1 - P(x \mid \neg \pi''_i(x))\right) \quad (3)$$

The benefits of NOBNs are as follows:

1. Converting from a general Bayesian network to an NOBN achieves a best-case exponential reduction in the number of interactions. This reduction yields a commensurate increase in inferential efficiency and is due to linearization of conditional probability tables, which require 2^k entries in a general form Bayesian network for a vertex with k parents).
2. NOBNs can be factored for an empirical speedup of 3-4 times [HH97].

The exponential speedup has been realized in real-world diagnostic Bayesian networks – most famously the *CPCS-BN* knowledge base for liver and gall bladder diseases, which is still among the largest Bayesian networks in use [PPMH94, HH97].

2.2 Construction of NOBN Models

The NOBN models used for scenario generation in the ship damage control domain are constructed from diagrams called *damage control plates*, for U.S. Navy ships (e.g., the DDG-51 and DDG-53). Subjective probability assessments were elicited from subject matter experts such as former damage control assistants and instructors at *SWOS*. These instructors were also consulted for compilation of the benchmarking scenarios produced by human experts. Some low-level assessments of probabilistic dependencies (generic events such as water main ruptures, combustion, and electrical deactivation) were contributed by the authors after consultation with domain experts.

Language of Training Objectives. A training objective is a task or skill at which the student is to become proficient (e.g., managing limited water resources for fire fighting in shipboard damage control). In accordance with established training methodology, an instructor selects desired training objectives, and then designs a scenario composed of a series of crisis events requiring application of the desired skills.

An automated scenario generation system can mimic this approach. Training objectives may either be provided by a human instructor, or suggested by an intelligent critiquing module. The system can then choose applicable keyed events from a knowledgebase, and use them to dynamically construct a scenario. Because of the causal nature of event interactions, we prefer to represent such a knowledgebase as a belief network, and due to the efficiency arguments given above, specifically as a NOBN.

In our framework, *constraints* are literals in a monotone disjunctive normal form (DNF) specification language. Each primitive training objective, O_i, denotes one conjunct of constraints c_{ij}. A scenario specification S is the top-level disjunction of all training objectives:

$$S = \vee_{i=1}^{k}(O_i) = \vee_{i=1}^{k}\left(\wedge_{j=1}^{n_i}(c_{ij})\right)$$

This representation allows composite training objectives simply because the disjunction is implicit. When multiple primitive objectives are specified, candidate scenarios can be generated one objective at a time. The results are filtered to obtain acceptable components, then composed by set union.

This achieves three benefits:

- The scenario generation problem is reduced to an offline computation requiring much less interaction with a human designer (i.e., many alternative scenarios can be generated and a criterion applied to reject implausible, unsound, incomplete, and duplicate scenarios).
- Using NOBNs as the probabilistic model for scenario generation reduces empirical complexity. Furthermore, there exists an efficient approximate inference algorithm that produces plausible yet diverse explanations, as is shown in section 3.
- The NOBN model makes stochastic search with a *penalized* likelihood function simple and efficient. For such an approximate inference algorithm, plausibility need not be the sole criterion: precision and accuracy can be assigned quantitative credit as appropriate.

In our implementation, we exploit the first two points using our search algorithm and apply a rejection test as the penalty function. This helps to standardize our evaluation metric, because calibration of a penalty function is somewhat subjective.

3 The ScenGen Algorithm

We have demonstrated how the problem of generating a scenario can be formulated as search-based inference in an NOBN. The deterministic algorithms we discuss in this section produce most probable explanations, which correspond to maximally plausible scenarios. To generate *non-trivially* diverse scenarios (those that are not effectively redundant for training purposes), however, we must relax our maximum likelihood requirement. To meet instructor objectives through inference, we must also *sample from the posterior distribution* of scenarios, given specifications. We now describe our stochastic search-based algorithm.

In order to guide its search through the Bayesian network, our algorithm employs a heuristic which computes the *combined most probable path* (CMPP) from the given set of constraint vertices to a root vertex. For such a set of constraint vertices and a root vertex in a network, the CMPP is composed of the set of *most probable paths* (MPPs), one for each constrain-root pair. This is an admissible heuristic because the CMPP is an overestimate of the actual probability from the constraints to the root. In other words, it is an *underestimate* of the *cost* of any such path. Combining stochastic branch-and-bound with our CMPP heuristic produces a search based-inference algorithm for our NOBN encoding of a scenario design space.

Figure 2 shows a generalized noisy-OR Bayesian network. In this figure, the vertices X and Y are constraints, and vertices R_1 through R_4 are initial events (roots). A parent set consists of one parent for X and one for Y (e.g., {P1(X), P3(Y)}, {P3(X), P3(Y)}). The first part of the search iteration begins by computing the CMPPs for each parent set of the current constraints. Those parent sets resulting in a CMPP probability of 0 are immediately discarded, since they are guaranteed to lead to a dead end. Parent sets resulting in a CMPP probability falling below some predetermined threshold (e.g., one standard deviation from the maximum) are discarded as well, since they will not lead to very likely (realistic) scenarios. The remaining parent sets result in CMPPs with high enough probabilities as to be considered "plausible".

The second part of each iteration involves stochastically selecting from among the "plausible" parent sets. Which ever parent set is thus chosen becomes the new constraint set.

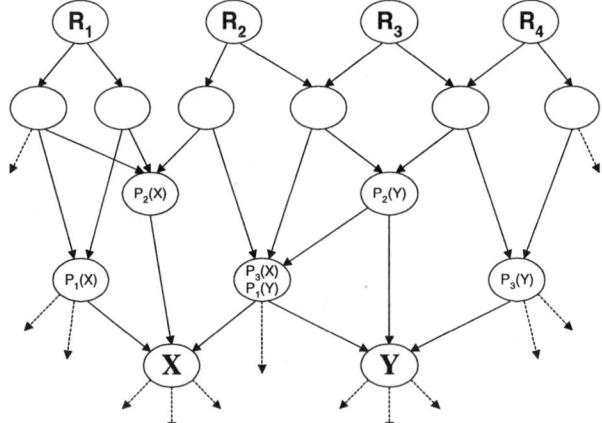

Figure 2. Generalized noisy-Or Bayesian network.

4 Evaluation

In this section we present experimental results from evaluating ScenGen against three competing algorithms.

4.1 Competing Scenario Generation Algorithms

We evaluate the ScenGen algorithm by direct comparison to three alternative scenario generation techniques:

1. Manual design by human subject matter experts (*MDHE*).
2. Naïve random generation (*NRG*).
3. Case-based stochastic perturbation (*CBSP*).

We take scenarios designed by human subject matter experts as our point of reference for scenario quality (i.e., completeness, soundness, and plausibility). Since, in the final analysis, a human expert is the best judge of a given scenario's quality it seems logical to assume that this expert will produce the best possible scenarios. Efficiency, however, will not be very high since the time a human subject matter expert takes to design such a scenario will be orders of magnitude higher than that of even the most expensive computer-based method.

Randomly instantiated scenarios are created by selecting a random initial event (which corresponds to a root node in the NOBN), and then evaluating the NOBN by propagating forward in the graph. This technique is cheap, but in general the quality of most scenarios produced will be poor. Also, efficiency will be low due to the large number of useless scenarios.

Case-based stochastic perturbation is a hybrid of the first two methods. It involves using scenarios designed by human subject matter experts as seeds, and perturbing them so as to obtain variability. This technique has the capability of producing a large number of admissible scenarios by derivation from the human-designed seeds, and can be expected to have reasonably good scenario space coverage due to the stochastic perturbation with respect to the seed. Furthermore, because once the seeds are obtained, the entire process is automated, efficiency should be better than for human experts. However, the downside is that the stochastic nature of the approach is likely to result in at least some unacceptable scenarios, which will lead to a lowering of efficiency.

4.2 Evaluation Criteria

We evaluate the ScenGen algorithm by comparing its performance to that of three other scenario generation techniques. The performance of an algorithm is considered to be the *efficiency* with which it generates *quality* scenarios. There are four metrics that are used to evaluate the quality of a scenario:

1. Empirical Accuracy (*EA*)
2. Empirical Precision (*EP*)
3. Plausibility (*P*)
4. Variability (*V*)

Empirical Accuracy measures the degree to which *all* specified learning objectives are satisfied. The inability of a scenario generation technique to guarantee the satisfaction of all requested learning objectives greatly diminishes its usefulness.

Empirical Precision measures the degree to which *only* specified objectives are satisfied. It has been shown that learning takes place most efficiently when training material is presented in a planned and controlled [GFH94]. For this reason, the generation of "sloppy" training scenarios (i.e., those addressing extraneous learning objectives) is likely to confuse the student, and complicate the learning process.

The Plausibility criterion evaluates the realism of the scenario. The ScenGen algorithm is intended for complex, real-world domains, which generally result in a vast scenario space. Because we define a learning objective simply as a disjunction of event sets, numerous collections of events may satisfy a given learning objective or set of learning objectives. However, not necessarily all of these collections of events are probable or even possible. Thus, we require that a "quality" scenario be *plausible*.

Variability measures how well a given technique can generate *distinct* scenarios. Two scenarios are distinct if they differ in at least one event. Variability is an important criterion because the generation of duplicate scenarios is wasteful of resources, and thus undesirable. We prefer techniques that minimize or even avoid duplication.

The Quality criterion is composed of these four metrics. Formally, the Quality criterion is defines as follows:

Definition Quality criterion. A quality scenario satisfies all specified objectives, and only the specified objectives. It is plausible, and distinct from any other scenario previously generated.

Each time a scenario is generated, it is checked for consistency with the Quality criterion by a series of four rejection tests, corresponding to the four metrics outlined above. Any scenario not passing all four of the rejection tests is deemed unacceptable, and discarded. Those scenarios found to be consistent with the Quality criterion are considered to be "quality" or acceptable scenarios.

Definition Performance. The performance of a scenario generation algorithm is the efficiency with which it generates quality scenarios.

We evaluate the performance of ScenGen by comparing its efficiency in generating quality scenarios with those of competing algorithms. We calculate Efficiency as follows:

Let
n_a = number of admissible scenarios
n_t = total number of scenarios generated
P_{acc} = acceptance probability
C_a = average cost of generating one admissible scenario
C_t = total cost of generating all scenarios

P_{acc} can be defined as

$$P_{acc} = \frac{n_a}{n_t} \quad (4)$$

We now calculate C_a as follows:

$$C_a = \frac{C_t}{n_t} \times \frac{1}{P_{acc}} \qquad (5)$$

$$C_a = \frac{C_t}{n_t} \times \frac{n_t}{n_a} \qquad (6)$$

$$C_a = \frac{C_t}{n_a} \qquad (7)$$

Since Efficiency is defined to be

$$E = \frac{1}{C_a}, \qquad (8)$$

given equation (4), we can express it as

$$E = \frac{n_a}{C_t}. \qquad (9)$$

4.3 Methodology

Figure 1 shows the a portion of the NOBN used by ScenGen, RSI, and CBSP[1] to generate scenarios. The full network consists of approximately 150 vertices, and roughly 400 edges. A representative learning objective, which involved dealing with loss of electrical power and chill water was selected for the evaluation.

One trial of the experiment consists of asking one of the algorithms to generate one "quality" scenario. Each algorithm is run for approximately 200 trials. Importantly, as the experiment proceeds, the effects of each trial are accumulated. In accordance with equation (4), the acceptance probability is determined by dividing the number of admissible scenarios found in trial run so far by the total number of scenarios requested. The scenarios are found to be acceptable if and only if they are consistent with the Quality criterion, as described in section 4.2. In each trial, the Efficiency is calculated by dividing the number of admissible scenarios found by the total cost of generating all scenarios, as given by equation (9).

5 Results

Plots 1 and 2 show, in graphical form, the results of comparative evaluation experiments run on ScenGen, RSI, and CBSP. Plot 1 shows the incremental cost (in terms of time) of generating increasing numbers of admissible scenarios. Plot 2 compares the three algorithms on their efficiency of generating acceptable scenarios.

Looking at Plot 1, we see that all three algorithms appear to exhibit an asymptotically increasing incremental cost behavior. This is explained by the fact that the algorithms are operating in a finite domain. The more acceptable scenarios that are found, the more difficult it becomes to find additional acceptable, yet distinct scenarios.

In terms of absolute cost per acceptable scenario, we see that NRG performs by far the worst. This is due to the fact that the vast majority of scenarios it generates are rejected by the Quality criterion, and thus discarded. This results in a large, steadily growing average cost per acceptable scenario. Interestingly, CBSP does slightly better than ScenGen for the first few acceptable scenarios it finds. This is explained by the fact that given a "good" scenario as a seed, it is not difficult to obtain several more "good" scenarios by small, inexpensive random perturbations. However, as additional distinct scenarios are requested, the random perturbations degenerate into a random search, much like NRG. ScenGen, on the other hand, has a very low rejection rate, which outweighs the rather high cost it incurs in generating individual scenarios, since it needs to generate approximately an order of magnitude fewer scenarios total than its competitors.

Unfortunately, the very selection bias that gives ScenGen its power, also significantly limits its accessibility of many portions of the search space. We see that of the three algorithms it is the first to exhaust its space of accessible scenarios. For the given domain model, it is unable to find more than about 230 distinct acceptable scenarios. For NRG and CBSP we do not actually see a vertical asymptote in the plot, but there is certain to be one because there exists only a finite number of event combinations in the model.

In light of such a comparison, ScenGen's selection bias may appear as a disadvantage. However, when all trade-offs are taken into account, it is seen that this is by no means the case. As can be seen from Plot 2, ScenGen finds those scenarios which are accessible to it far more efficiently that either of the other two algorithms. In addition, the actual location of ScenGen's vertical asymptote (as those of NRG and CBSP) is determined to a large extent by the size and complexity of the domain. Thus, in large and complex domain ScenGen's performance relative to the other two algorithms will actually improve.

We have succeeded, thus, in demonstrating that ScenGen outperforms both CBSP and RSI, its two main competitors. Because it generates only admissible scenarios, and in spite of the high cost associated with the required search heuristics, ScenGen achieves the best efficiency of the three algorithms. We believe that given a

---

[1] Since only a small number of human expert-designed scenarios were available, MDHE could not be included in any statistical comparison. It was used for qualitative comparison only.

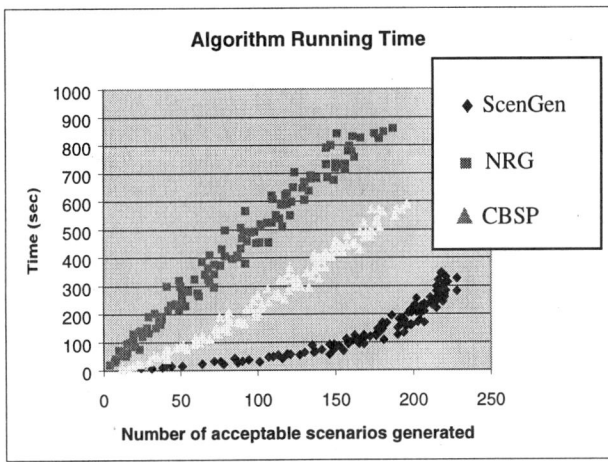

Plot 1. Algorithm Running Time

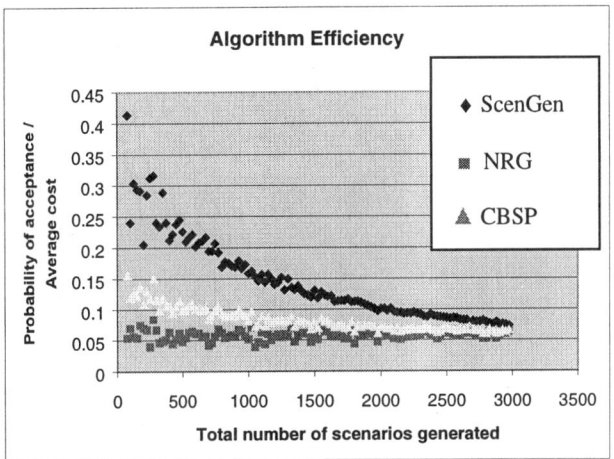

Plot 2. Algorithm Efficiency

larger search space (with a correspondingly larger number of admissible scenarios), the gap between ScenGen and CBSP will be seen to widen dramatically. ScenGen will not be hampered by a rapidly diminishing number of admissible scenarios, and will be able to maintain a high acceptability rate even when many quality scenarios are requested. This will most likely cause its efficiency to shoot up, while those of the other two algorithms will remain the more or less constant, or perhaps even drop (which will be due to the drawback of the random nature of these algorithms becoming more pronounced in a large search space).

6 Conclusion and Future Work

We have presented a Noisy-OR Bayesian network model for simulation-based training, and ScenGen, an efficient search-based algorithm for automatic synthesis of plausible training scenarios from constraint specification. ScenGen is shown to outperform other randomized methods, such as those based on naïve random instantiation of scenarios, and stochastic perturbation of known "good" scenarios. ScenGen's strength lies in its ability to guarantee the "quality" of each and every scenario it generates through a carefully designed selection bias. While other algorithms are far less costly on a per scenario basis, the multitude of low-accuracy scenarios they produce (or their inability to find a sufficiently large number of "good" scenarios") drastically reduces their respective efficiencies, and results in poor overall performance.

One of our goals for the near future is to integrate ScenGen into DCTrain, the Illinois immersive damage control training environment. DCTrain combines the state-of-the-art in immersive multimedia environments with an accurate numerical/rule-based simulation of ship processes and crew behavior. The system has been extensively field-tested at the Surface Warfare Officer's School (*SWOS*), and found to be an effective and highly useful training tool [BDS96]. At the present time, all scenarios used with DCTrain must be manually constructed by domain experts. The integration of ScenGen would tremendously simplify the problem of scenario generation, thus making the system far more versatile, and greatly increasing its effectiveness.

7 Acknowledgements

The authors would like to thank Pavel Yusim for his significant contributions to the first implementation of the ScenGen algorithm. We gratefully acknowledge the support of ONR grant N00014-95-1-0749.

8 References

[BJM83] L. R. Bahl, F. Jelinek, R. L. Mercer. A Maximum Likelihood Approach to Continuous Speech Recognition. *IEEE Transactions on Pattern Analysis and Machine Intelligence*, 5(2):179-190, 1983.

[BDS96] M. R. Baumann, M. A. Donovan, and J. A. Sniezek. *Evaluation of the Integrated Damage Control Training Technology (IDCTT)*. University of Illinois, Knowledge Based Systems Group, Technical Report UIUC-BI-KBS-96005, 1996.

[De94] P. Derosier. *Integrated Damage Control Training Technology (IDCTT)*. Center for Interactive Media in Medicine (CIMM), Bethesda, MD, 1994.

[EKT93] K. A. Ericsson, R. T. Krampe, and C. Tesch-Romer. The Role of Deliberate Practice in the Acquisition of Expert Performance. *Psychological Review*, 100(3): 363-407, 1993.

[Fo73] G. D. Forney. The Viterbi Algorithm. *Proceedings of the IEEE*, 61(3):268-278, 1973.

[GD88] D. M. Gaba and A. DeAnda. A Comprehensive Anesthesia Simulation Environment: Re-creating the Operating Room for Research and Training. *Anesthesia*, 69:387-394, 1988.

[GFH94] D. M. Gaba, K. J. Fish, and S. K. Howard. *Crisis Management In Anesthesiology*. Churchill Livingstone, New York, NY, 1994.

[HLB+96] B. Hayes-Roth, J. E. Larsson, L. Brownston, D. Gaba, and B. Flanagan. *Guardian Project Home Page*, URL: http://www-ksl.stanford.edu/projects/guardian/index.html, 1996.

[HW95] D. A. Heckerman and M. P. Wellman. Bayesian Networks. *Communications of the ACM*, 38(3):27-30, March, 1995.

[He90] M. Henrion. Towards Efficient Probabilistic Diagnosis in Multiply Connected Belief Networks. In R. M. Oliver and J. Q. Smith (eds.), *Influence Diagrams, Belief Nets, and Decision Analysis*, p. 385-410. John Wiley and Sons, New York, NY.

[HB95] E. Horvitz and M Barry. Display of Information for Time-Critical Decision Making. In *Proceedings of UAI-95*, URL: http://research.microsoft.com/research/dtg/horvitz/VISTA.HTM, 1995.

[HGYS92] S. K. Howard, D. M. Gaba, G. S. Yang, and F. H. Sarnquist. Anesthesia Crisis Resource Management Training: Teaching Anesthesiologists to Handle Critical Incidents. *Aviation, Space, and Environmental Medicine*, 63:763-770, 1992.

[HH97] K. Huang and M. Henrion. Efficient Search-Based Inference for Noisy-OR Belief Networks: TopEpsilon. In *Proceedings of the 13th Conference on Uncertainty in Artificial Intelligence*, p. 325-331, 1997.

[Le89] K.-F. Lee. *Automatic Speech Recognition: The Development of the SPHINX System*. Kluwer Academic Publishers, Boston, MA, 1989.

[MW96] O. J. Mengshoel and D. C. Wilkins. Recognition and Critiquing of Erroneous Agent Actions. In *AAAI-96 Workshop on Agent Modeling*, p. 61-68. AAAI Press, Portland, OR, 1996.

[Ne93] R. M. Neal. *Probabilistic Inference Using Markov Chain Monte Carlo Methods*. Technical Report CRG-TR-93-1, Department of Computer Science, University of Toronto, 1993.

[Ni80] N. J. Nilsson. *Principles of Artificial Intelligence*. Morgan Kaufmann, San Mateo, CA.

[Pe84] J. Pearl. *Heuristics: Intelligent Search Strategies for Computer Problem Solving*. Addison-Wesley, Reading, MA, 1984.

[Pe88] J. Pearl. *Probabilistic Reasoning in Intelligent System: Networks of Plausible Inference*. Morgan-Kaufmann, San Mateo, CA, 1988.

[PPMH94] M. Pradhan, G. Provan, G. Middleton, and M. Henrion. Knowledge Engineering for Large Belief Networks. In *Proceedings of UAI-94*, p. 484-490. Morgan-Kaufmann, Seattle, WA, 1994.

[RN95] S. Russell and P. Norvig. *Artificial Intelligence: A Modern Approach*. Prentice Hall, Englewood Cliffs, NJ, 1995.

[WFH+96] D. C. Wilkins, C. Fagerlin, W. H. Hsu, D. Kruse, and E. T. Lin. *Design of a Damage-Control Simulator*. Technical Report UIUC-BI-KBS-96005, UIUC, Knowledge Based Systems Group, 1996.

Hybrid knowledge based system for automatic classification of B-scan images from ultrasonic rail inspection

J. Jarmulak[1,2], E.J.H. Kerckhoffs[1], P.P. van't Veen[2]

[1] Delft University of Technology, Faculty of Information Technology and Systems,
Department of Technical Informatics, P.O. Box 356, 2600 AJ Delft, The Netherlands.
[2] TNO - Institute of Applied Physics, P.O. Box 155, 2600 AD Delft, The Netherlands.
jacek@kgs.twi.tudelft.nl

Abstract

Dutch Railways use a special train for the ultrasonic inspection of rails. The output of the ultrasonic scanning system installed on the train consists of echo images – so-called B-scans. The B-scans contain images of rail constructions, noise artifacts, and/or defects. Originally, all the images were interpreted and classified by an operator. Later, a simple rule-based classifier was build which could classify some of the images automatically. Recently, a new version of the train has been built capable of faster and more detailed rail inspection. This necessitated improvement of the automatic classification software. A prototype system has been developed which uses both a rule-based expert system and case-based reasoning (CBR) for the image classification. A hybrid architecture has been chosen because it satisfies the requirements better than systems based on one technique only. The paper describes the overall system design and presents the results of tests on real data. The future work necessary for the deployment of the system on the inspection train is outlined.

Introduction

To guarantee safe operation of the railway net periodical inspection has to be carried out in order to detect damage before it leads to disruption of the normal operation. One type of damage that can occur are cracks usually found in the head of the rail, at the bolt holes, or at the welded joints. These cracks can be detected using ultrasonic inspection techniques. Special transducers are used to send ultrasonic pulses into the rails and the returning echoes are recorded. The echoes can come from the bottom of the rail, the bolt holes (or other construction elements), or the cracks.

Dutch Railways use a special train to perform ultrasonic inspection of the rail net in the Netherlands as well as abroad (Roos 1990). Inspection (data acquisition) is done at speeds up to 50km/h (75km/h using the new train) by a set of ultrasonic transducers (each placed at a different angle) gliding over the rails on a water film. On a clean rail only an echo from the bottom of the rail is present and it is ignored. On sections where other echoes are present they are assembled to form an image (so-called B-scan), see e.g. Figure 1. Any cracks present in the rails will be visible in these images. However, most of the images show the constructions present in the rails and/or noise (see Figure 2). There is no simple method of defect detection available and all images have to be analyzed to determine if they contain any echoes from defects or not.

When the ultrasonic rail-inspection system was first introduced the B-scan image analysis was performed entirely by an operator. Later, automatic classification was added to the system, first using SQL queries on Oracle database, and later using a rule-based expert system (Clips (Giarratano and Riley 1989)). With the help of the automatic classification it was possible to deliver a full inspection report at the end of each work day.

Recently, a new inspection train has been build with more transducers per rail (8 instead of 4) and a higher inspection speed. To keep up with the larger amount of data a better automatic classification system (achieving higher recognition ratio) had to be developed.

This paper describes the results of the research in better methods of automatic B-scan image interpretation. First, a description of the problem is given and the choice for the use of a hybrid rule-based/CBR system is motivated. Then, the design of the prototype system is described. The results of the tests on real data are presented. The chosen way of deployment of the system on the inspection train is discussed before the conclusions are presented.

Problem Description

The problem that has to be solved concerns classification of images, in which pixels correspond to echoes from various channels, into two main classes: defects or non-defects.

Types of Images

There are various types of images showing rail constructions, noise, defects, or combinations of these. The most common image type is the loss of the bottom echo constituting approx. 60% of all images. These are trivial to recognize. The research

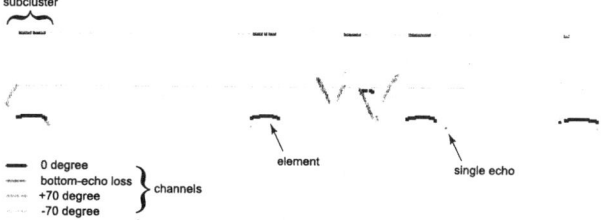

Figure 1. Ultrasonic B-scan of a fish-plated joint. (Vertical placement of the bottom-echo-loss indications is arbitrary.)

Copyright © 1998, American Association for Artificial Intelligence (www.aaai.org). All rights reserved.

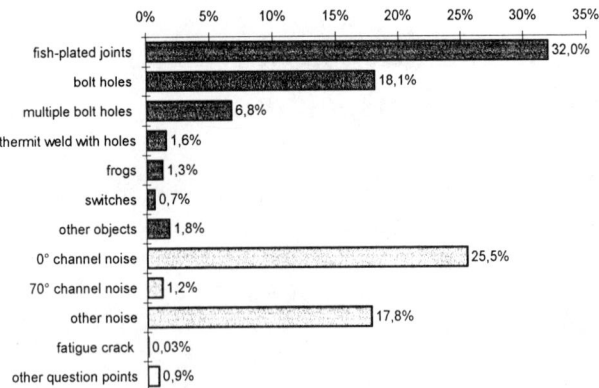

Figure 2. Objects present in the rails (percentages add up to more than 100% because some categories may overlap).

Table 1. Possible combinations of real and found classifications.

real	classified as	shown to operator	remarks
non-defect	non-defect	no	desired behavior
non-defect	defect	yes	acceptable, but reduces confidence in the system
non-defect	unknown	yes	acceptable if not too often
defect	defect	yes	desired behavior
defect	non-defect	no	**should not occur**
defect	unknown	yes	almost the desired behavior

concentrated on the recognition of the remaining images and whenever recognition percentages are presented in this paper they do not include the bottom-echo-loss images.

The classes recognized among the non-bottom-echo-loss images are listed in Figure 2. As one can see the defects are rare. The so-called question points (images with possibly defects) constitute only about 1% of the non-bottom-echo-loss images. The low percentage of defects is common in NDT (non-destructive testing) problems.

Classification Goals

As already stated, the goal of the system is to automatically classify the B-scan images. First of all, we want to distinguish between defect and non-defect images. Additionally, in the process of recognizing non-defect images, the image type (e.g. bolt hole) is determined. The possible combinations of real and automatic classifications are shown in Table 1.

The two main parameters which describe the performance of the system are: the percentage of the images automatically classified (not shown to the operator) and the percentage of the defects classified as non-defects. Obviously, we want the first percentage to be as high as possible and the second one as low as possible. For an inspection company it is especially important that the percentage of missed defects is as very low. To keep it low one is ready to sacrifice the overall automatic recognition ratio.

A system destined for field use should be able to do the classification fast enough. In practice it means that it should be at least as fast as the human inspector. As far as the speed is concerned, one can distinguish between average processing speed (e.g. calculated over the hole data set) and a worst-case speed (e.g. for a very complex image) – important when the system has to work interactively with an operator.

Methodology Choice

There exist only a few rail inspection systems similar to the one owned by Dutch Railways. The articles published about these systems contain few details about the techniques used. For example system described in (Havira & Chen 95) uses syntactic pattern recognition for classification, but the article does not describe the recognition algorithm at all. Lesiak (92) also gives no details of the classification algorithms, but the low resolution of the system (128x24 cells) suggests that a technique like template matching could be used.

A system for interpretation of ultrasonic B-scans, however not of rails but of welds, is described in (Hopgood et al. 93). It is build around a blackboard rule-based system and uses neural networks for local defect classification. Though this problem is in many aspects similar to ours the differences in the images and the difficulties in knowledge formalization (described further) did not let us use the same techniques.

A common method of data classification used in NDT problems is the use of statistical classifiers (or neural networks), e.g. (Chien-Ping et al. 93). This usually requires being able to describe the data with a fixed length feature vector and the availability of a training set.

In our problem the images are combinations of constructions, acquisition system disturbances, noise, and defects. As a result the images are very inhomogenous and impossible to describe with a fixed length feature vector. The number of all possible image types is very high thus obtaining an exhaustive set of data examples is practically impossible. Related to this is the fact that there is always a chance of occurrence of unexpected data (significantly different from the training set) and most statistical classifiers are not good at handling such data. Also, obtaining a good classifier is difficult when one class is only a small fraction of the possible classes (as are the defects). Moreover, statistical classifiers are difficult to maintain by the end users. Making changes to the system requires good insight into the working of the classifier otherwise the reliability may be compromised. Altogether, statistical classifiers were found unsuitable for the task.

As there was already a working rule-based classification system, one way of improving the classification ratio would be to add extra rules to the rule base. After initial study, it became clear that describing the images using rules was not feasible. Apart from the images already described by rules, the knowledge about the images was not well formalized, the record kept from past inspections was incomplete because not all images were fully classified, and the knowledge acquired from the operator in a few acquisition sessions was either limited to very typical (ideal) images or anecdotal of character. There was a large variety of images, thus apart from a few simple image types, any particular image description would apply to only a small fraction of all possible images. Additionally, because of the workload at the inspection company, it was difficult to arrange knowledge acquisition sessions.

Even if a rule-based system could be successfully constructed the problem of rule maintenance would still be un-

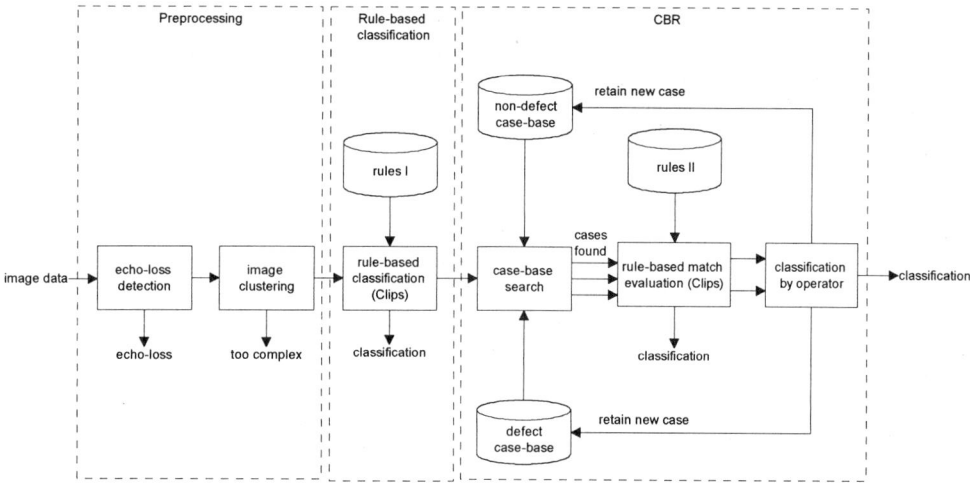

Figure 3. Schema of the prototype hybrid classification system.

solved. Already in the old system there was an example of reduced recognition ratio after changes were made to the acquisition system and the rules not updated accordingly. Besides, during the project the data from the new 8-channel system was not available, which meant that any rule-base designed using data from the 4-channel system would require serious adaptation to the new data.

Because the knowledge acquisition and maintenance were such a big problem, our attention turned to learning systems. Because statistical classifiers and neural networks were already dismissed, and the various types of decision trees suffered form similar problems as these two, a choice was made in favor of case-based reasoning, which let us develop an adaptable, reliable, and easy to maintain system.

However, because the existing rule-base performed quite well we decided to keep it. If one knows how to describe the images then they can be recognized quicker by the rule-base. Besides, large noise images are very difficult for the case-based reasoner because per definition they are not repeatable.

The Prototype

The overall design of the prototype is shown Figure 3. The system consists of three main stages: preprocessing, rule-based classification, and case-based classification.

Preprocessing
In the preprocessing stage the B-scan image consisting of pixels corresponding to echoes from various channels is segmented into meaningful elements like lines, parabolas and regions of noise. The segmentation algorithm begins with constructing a minimum-spanning tree through all the echo points in a channel. The tree is then split on the longer edges and lines and parabolas are fitted through the branches. More details of the segmenting algorithm are described in (Jarmulak 1996).

Apart from segmenting into elements each image can be divided into subclusters. The subclustering thresholds have been chosen so that, e.g. multiple-bolt-hole objects are divided into single bolt holes (see Figure 1).

Rule-Based Classification
Information about image elements is represented as fact strings and sent to the Clips shell. Twenty six rules process the facts in two stages: first the image subclusters are classified, and then the subcluster classifications are combined into the final classification.

After processing by the inference engine the resulting classification facts (both for the subclusters and the whole image) are retrieved from Clips. If the image was recognized the processing stops here.

Case-Based Reasoning
The case-based classifier maintains two case-bases: one with defect images and one with non-defect images. For each new image a search is done in both case-bases for similar images. The image to be classified and the retrieved images together with the match results are processed by a set of rules which either arrive at the final classification or decide that the image has to be classified by the operator. The images classified by the operator are stored in the appropriate case-base for future use.

Case. A case contains first of all the information about the image elements and the correct image classification. For each element its type, location, and equation of the fitted parabola or line are stored. Each case also contains pointers to the whole image data (all echoes) stored in a separate file. The subcluster classifications assigned by the rule-based classifier are also stored. For the purpose of case-base maintenance the date of entry, the number of all matches and the number of better matches are stored with each case.

Case matching. Matching is done in stages corresponding to the image hierarchy: whole image, subclusters, channels, elements.

For each corresponding pair of image elements their location, size, and orientation are compared. For each parameter an absolute and/or relative difference is calculated and then mapped via a fuzzy membership function into the [0..1] range. Because a channel in a subcluster may contain more than one element and the number of elements in the channels being matched may differ, the channels are matched using inexact graph matching. Within the subclusters the channel locations and within the whole image the subcluster locations are compared. Subresults are combined using a *min* operator. The matching procedure is broken off when it becomes clear that the current match would be worse than the best match so far.

Case-base. In the prototype the case-base has a two level organization. The top level has a simple hierarchical organization with divisions based on the number of subclusters, channels present and the length of an image. The leaves of the hierarchy are collections of clusters of similar cases. For each cluster of cases a representative case is found which has the smallest distance to the remaining cases in the cluster. When a new case is added to the case-base it is inserted into the cluster which contains the best matching case. A cluster has a certain size limit and if after adding a new case the limit is exceeded then the cluster is split into two new clusters.

Case retrieval. Looking for the best match in the case-base proceeds fastest if a good match is found at the very beginning of the search, this way matching with many remaining less similar cases does not have to be carried out in full. To increase the probability of finding a good match at the beginning of the search the following is done:
- the top level of the case-base guides the search to a collection of clusters of cases with characteristics similar to the current case,
- a collection of clusters of cases is sorted on the good match ratio for the cluster representatives, so that clusters usually giving high matches are searched first,
- within a collection the matching is first done with the cluster representatives and the further search is done beginning with the clusters with higher representative matches.

The system can retrieve several best matching cases – in the current system three.

Match evaluation. For each of the retrieved cases the match evaluation is done by Clips using a set of 25 rules. The simpler rules look at the values of the overall matches with defect and non-defect cases. The more complex rules look at the differences between the images and decide if for a given image type the differences are significant or not.

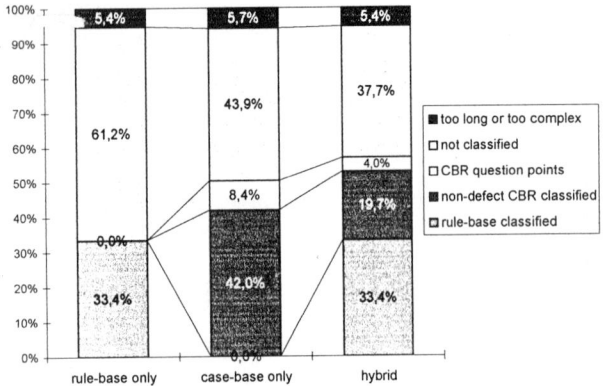

Figure 4. Comparison of classification results for rule-based, case-based, and hybrid classifiers.

Implementation

The software has been written entirely using Visual C++. As an expert system shell Clips from NASA was used. A possibility of using an existing CBR shell has been considered but they seem not well suited to processing cases consisting of images (Watson and Marir 1994).

The Clips code has been encapsulated in a separate program – a Clips server. The main application communicates with it by sending and receiving messages via the socket interface. Because rule processing is done twice by two different sets of rules there are two Clips servers running, each listening to a different port number.

Tests, Results, and Observations

Because the processing speed is an important factor in evaluating the system it is important to note here that all the tests described in this section have been done on a single CPU 300MHz Pentium II computer with 64MB RAM. Because the data files correspond to a certain length of track inspected the system performance is expressed in kilometers of track-data processed per hour (km/h).

Test Data Set

All the data ever acquired with the ultrasonic rail-inspection system is available on optical disks. It would seem that it would be easy to obtain a training set, however, it turns out that only the computer classified images have the detailed classification (e.g. 0° noise, bolt hole), all the remaining images were given classification only when a possible defect was present. This means that the available data had practically only defect/non-defect classification. Several test runs were done on this data, however, the results did not provide the required detail on information about what type of images are recognized and what not.

For the purpose of the test a set of data files had to be fully classified. After a period of working on the project we had enough experience to be able to do classification without the help of the inspector. It took more than a week to fully classify a set of 128 normal data files and 12 files containing defect images (extracted from a large number of normal data files). The test data sequence consisted of 6 randomly ordered defect files (to fill the defect case-base), 128 randomly ordered normal data files, and again 6 defect files (to test the system reliability). Altogether, the test set contained approx. 38000 non-bottom-echo-loss images from approx. 1000 km of track.

Rule-Based vs. Case-Based vs. Hybrid Classifier.

Three test runs were done to compare the performance of the rule-based, the case-based, and the hybrid classifiers. The overall classification results are shown in Figure 4. The rule based classifier has the lowest recognition ratio, however, it was approx. 14 times faster than the other two classifiers (the avg. processing speed was 401 km/h, 23 km/h and 28 km/h respectively). Important things that can be noticed are:
- rule-base is capable of recognizing some complex noise images which are unrecognized by the case-based classifier (5.7% vs. 5.4%),

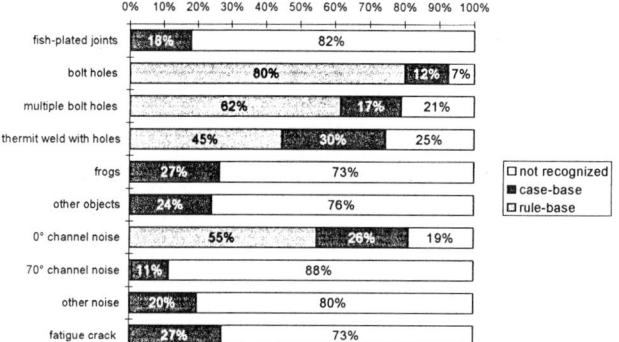

Figure 5. Average recognition ratios for various image types for the hybrid system.

- CBR question points are these images which had a close match to a defect case – rule base recognizes some of them correctly as noise, while the case-based classifier shows them to the operator.
- in the hybrid system the case-based classifier uses some information from the rule-based classification during matching and match evaluation – this information is not available in a case-based only system.

It is clear that the results of the hybrid classifier, as far as the recognition ratio is concerned, are the best. It has certainly advantages over the case-based-only classifier especially as the rule-based part is already being used and can easily be incorporated into the new system. In spite of a much lower processing speed than the rule-based classifier, the adaptability and maintainability of the CBR system is considered as a big enough advantage to outweigh the longer processing time.

Results for the Hybrid System

The recognition percentages for the various categories of images are shown in Figure 5. Only 27% recognized fatigue cracks does not mean that some of these defects were missed by the system – the remaining 73% were classified as belonging to the question point class and shown to the operator.

For a CBR system one can expect an increasing recognition ratio with an increasing size of a case base. This trend is visible especially at the beginning of the scan where the CBR system quickly (after approx. 30 data files) learns to recognize simpler images like bolt holes and 0° noise. It takes much longer to improve recognition ratio of the more complex images like fish-plated joints (see Figure 6).

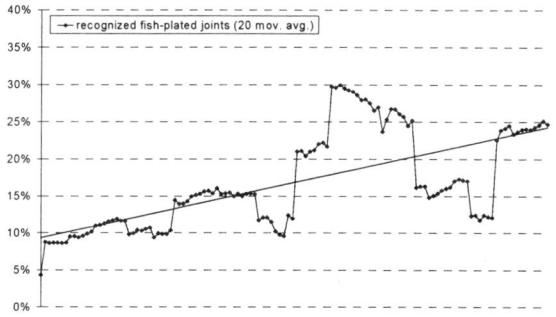

Figure 6. Increasing fish-plated-joint recognition ratio with an increasing size of the case-base (20-file moving average).

At the end of the scan the non-defect case-base contained approx. 13000 cases (15.5MB) and the defect case-base 1700 cases (1.7MB).

The system has turned out to be very reliable. The discrepancies between the classifications done by an expert and by the system were analyzed and it has turned out that, except for two cases, they concerned ambiguities in possible interpretation or inconsistent use of some classifications in the pre-classified files.

Future Work

The results of the tests have been found satisfactory enough to continue the work and make the system suitable for deployment on the train. The work goes mainly towards improving the recognition ratio and the speed. Because larger and more case-bases will be used, methods for case-base maintenance will also have to be developed.

Improving Recognition Ratio

Obviously the recognition ratio will improve with the increased number of cases in the case-base. However, the larger the case-base the slower the whole system becomes.

Another way to increase the recognition ratio is to optimize the image segmentation and matching algorithms. An optimal segmentation algorithm should return as small number of elements as possible without compromising the ability to detect defects.

The matching algorithms can be further optimized, mainly the membership functions used. Because of the amount and the variety of data the most useful method is by iteratively changing the parameters and testing the system on a large data set. Also, making use of the subcluster classifications (from the rule-based classifiers) during the case matching can improve the recognition ratio.

Extra rules can be added in the match evaluation rule-base to ignore certain types of noise or to make better use of the subcluster classifications.

Increasing Processing Speed

Increasing the speed of the system is a crucial factor for its success. Currently, the system reaches an average processing speed of approx. 25 km/h with a case-base of approx. 13000 cases. The goal is to reach a processing speed of approx. 75 km/h before the system will be deployed on the train.

Increase in the speed can be achieved by improving the algorithms, optimizing the code, and the use of faster hardware. For example, the top level case-base organization will be optimized using decision tree building algorithms.

The system will probably be implemented on a 2 CPU Pentium II hardware. The case-base search algorithm will be implemented so that it can search several clusters of cases in parallel (in multiple program threads), this way an optimal use of the two CPUs will be made.

Maintenance

Currently, the only case-base maintenance possibility is the ability to prune the cases with only bad matches. For the use in practice two types of tools will have to be made. First one will be used for keeping track of available case-bases. As the inspections are done on various types of rail track in various countries, therefore, it makes sense to have a set of case-bases from which the most appropriate can be used for a given type of track. Because the current system already uses an Oracle database for administration purposes, the case-base administration will probably be added to the existing administration system.

Another type of tool is needed for investigating and manipulating individual case-bases. One needs to be able to navigate the case-base hierarchy and see various statistics for the underlying branches. This tool would enable browsing the individual cases, e.g. allowing for selective case deletion.

Phased Deployment

Figure 7a shows schematically the current classification system used on the train. The classification is done in two stages. First the data is processed by the rule-based classifier. It writes the classifications to a classification file, marking every not recognized image as still-to-be-classified. The classification file is later read by the interactive classification program which allows the operator to step through the not classified images and do the final classification.

Figure 7b shows the outline of the new system as it will first be implemented on the train. The existing rule-based classifier will be used unchanged. As the new system will require entry of all the classifications, which was only optional in the old system, the interactive classification software will be adapted to simplify the entry of image classifications by providing good default values based on the best case-base matches.

The CBR system will work in batch mode, which means that it will not reach it full potential because it will not be able to learn directly from the classifications made by the user. Only afterwards, the case-base will be filled with batches of classified images.

This system will enable us to gather experience with the use of the CBR system in real-life conditions. If the results are satisfactory an integrated system will be developed which combines the rule-based, the case-based, and the interactive classifiers, see Figure 7c.

Conclusions

The project has shown that the use of a combination of a CBR and a rule-based system for the classification of complex images has many advantages. The CBR component is capable of adapting to a large variety of data by learning from the classifications made by the operator. The rule-based component makes it possible to use the a-priori knowledge about the images. Rules can also recognize large noise images which are difficult for a CBR system. Subclassifications made by the rule-based classifier can also improve the speed and recognition ratio of the CBR system. The rule-base size is kept small which should make the system maintenance easy.

The tested prototype has achieved satisfactory recognition ratio combined with very high reliability. The main disadvantage of the system is the low processing speed. However, the latest high-end PC hardware is fast enough to enable development of a system that can be used in practice. The system deployment will be done in phases so that minimum risk is taken and maximum experience can be gathered.

We think that presented approach can be useful for other problems where complex inhomogeneous data has to be classified and where the domain knowledge is difficult to formalize.

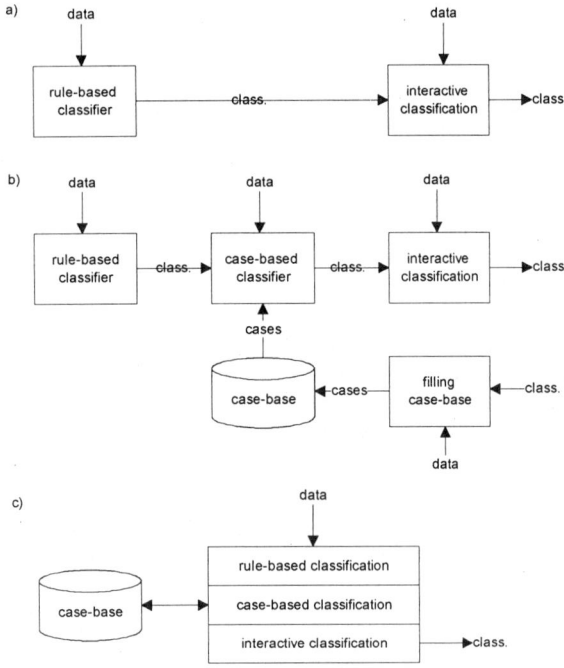

Figure 7. Phased deployment: a) current system, b) system extended with CBR capabilities (batch mode), c) goal system. (class. = classification file)

References

Chien-Ping, Ch., Shmerr, L.W., and Thompson, R.B. 1993. Ultrasonic flaw detection using neural network models and statistical analysis: Simulation studies. In *Review of Progress in QNDE*, Vol. 12, pp. 789-795.

Giarratano, R. and Riley, G. 1989. *Expert systems: Principles and Programming*, PWS-KENT Publishing Company.

Havira, R.M. and Chen J. 1995. "High Speed Rail Flaw Pattern Recognition and Classification", *Proc. SPIE* Vol. 2458, pp.64-73.

Hopgood, F.F., N. Woodcock, N.J. Hallam, and P.D. Picton, 1993. "Interpreting ultrasonic images using rules, algorithms and neural networks", *European Journal of NDT*, Vol. 2:4, April 1993, pp. 135-149.

Jarmulak, J. 1996. B-scan Image Clustering and Interpretation in Ultrasonic Rail-Inspection System. In *Proceedings of the second annual conference of the Advanced School for Computing and Imaging, Lommel, Belgium, June 5-7, 1996*, pp. 190-195.

Lesiak, P. 1992. "System for Automatic Ultrasonic Quality Control of Railroad Rails", *Russian Journal Of Nondestructive Testing*, Vol. 28:7, pp.383-388.

Roos, R. 1990. Het ultrasoon railinspectie systeem, *NAG Journal*, Nr. 105, november, pp. 21-34.

Watson, I. and Marir, F. 1994, Case-based reasoning: A review, *The Knowledge Engineering Review*, Vol. 9:4, pp. 327-354.

Control Strategies in HTN Planning: Theory Versus Practice

Dana S. Nau

Department of Computer Science,
and Institute for Systems Research
University of Maryland
College Park, MD, USA
nau@cs.umd.edu

Stephen J. J. Smith

Department of Mathematics
and Computer Science
Hood College
Frederick, MD, USA
sjsmith@nimue.hood.edu

Kutluhan Erol

Intelligent Automation Inc.
2 Research Place #202
Rockville, MD 20850
kutluhan@i-a-i.com

Abstract

AI planning techniques are beginning to find use in a number of practical planning domains. However, the backward-chaining and partial-order-planning control strategies traditionally used in AI planning systems are not necessarily the best ones to use for practical planning problems. In this paper, we discuss some of the difficulties that can result from the use of backward chaining and partial-order planning, and we describe how these difficulties can be overcome by adapting Hierarchical Task-Network (HTN) planning to use a total-order control strategy that generates the steps of a plan in the same order that those steps will be executed. We also examine how introducing the total-order restriction into HTN planning affects its expressive power, and propose a way to relax the total-order restriction to increase its expressive power and range of applicability.

Introduction

Although there has been much recent interest in exploring alternative control strategies for AI planning systems, one aspect of the control strategy that is usually taken for granted is the use of partial-order planning and backward chaining. However, a backward-chaining partial-order-planning strategy is not necessarily the best kind of strategy to use in practical planning problems. Two examples come from our recent use of HTN planning in two very different application domains:

- As reported in *The New York Times* and *The Washington Post*, a new version of Great Game Products' *Bridge Baron* program won the 1997 *Baron Barclay World Bridge Computer Challenge*. The competition, which was hosted by the American Contract Bridge League (ACBL) in July 1997, is effectively the world championship compeition for computer bridge programs. The first two authors helped develop this new version of the Bridge Baron (Smith *et al.*, 1996), incorporating HTN planning techniques into it to improve its declarer play.
- EDAPS (Hebbar *et al.*, 1996) is an integrated system for designing and planning the manufacture of microwave transmit/receive modules. EDAPS uses HTN planning to generate process plans for proposed designs, and evaluates these plans to provide feedback to the designer about the manufacturability of the design. The first author is currently working with Northrop Grumman to develop EDAPS into a product for use in their manufacturing facility in Baltimore.

These application domains were not amenable to the partial-order planning and backward chaining techniques used in most AI planning systems. Instead, we developed a total-order planning control strategy that expands tasks in the same order that they will be executed. This control strategy worked quite well in both application domains.

This experience has led us to question how well the reasons normally given for using partial-order planning and backward chaining apply to real-world planning domains—and in this paper, we try to answer that question. In particular, we do the following:

1. We examine some of the assumptions behind the use of backward chaining and partial-order planning, and conclude that these assumptions do not always apply to HTN planning in real-world domains.

2. We describe some of the difficulties that can be caused by backward chaining and partial-order planning, and explain how total-order HTN planning can overcome those difficulties.

3. While total-order HTN planning is strictly more expressive than planning with STRIPS-style operators, it is also strictly less expressive than unrestricted HTN planning. We propose a way to relax the "total-order" restriction, to produce a sound and complete forward-search approach to HTN planning that has the same expressive power as unrestricted HTN planning.

Overview of HTN Planning

The basic ideas used in HTN planning were originally developed more than 20 years ago (Sacerdoti 1977; Tate 1977). To create plans, HTN planning uses *task decomposition*, in which the planning system decomposes tasks into smaller and smaller subtasks until primitive tasks are found that can be performed directly. HTN planning systems have knowledge bases containing *methods*. As shown in Figure 1(a), each method includes a prescription for how to decompose some task into a set of subtasks,

Copyright © 1998, American Association for Artificial Intelligence (www.aaai.org). All rights reserved.

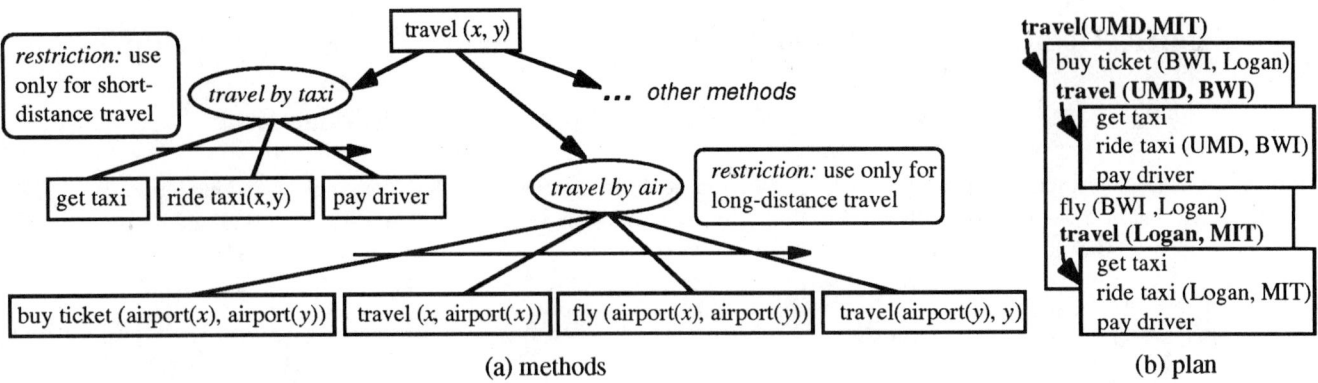

Figure 1: Methods for traveling, and their use in developing a plan for traveling from U. of Maryland to MIT.

with various restrictions that must be satisfied in order for the method to be applicable, and various constraints on the subtasks and the relationships among them. Given a task to accomplish, the planner chooses an applicable method, instantiates it to decompose the task into subtasks, and then chooses and instantiates other methods to decompose the subtasks even further, as illustrated in Figure 1(b). If the constraints on the subtasks or the interactions among them prevent the plan from being feasible, the planning system will backtrack and try other methods.

Formal analyses of HTN planning have shown that it is strictly more expressive than planning with STRIPS-style operators (Erol *et al.* 1994b), and have established properties such as soundness and completeness (Erol *et al.* 1994a), complexity (Erol *et al.* 1996), and the efficiency of various control strategies (Tsuneto *et al.* 1996, 1997). A domain-independent HTN planner is available at <http://www.cs.umd.edu/projects/plus/umcp/manual> for experimental use, and domain-specific HTN planners are being developed for several practical applications (Aarup *et at.* 1994; Hebbar *et al.* 1996; Smith *et al.* 1997; Smith *et al.* 1998; Wilkins & Desimone 1994).

Two Applications of HTN Planning

Contract Bridge

Although computer programs have done very well in games such as chess, checkers, and Othello (Schaeffer 1993; Korf 1994), human experts still outperform computers in the game of bridge. One reason for this is the difficulty of adapting traditional game-tree search techniques to imperfect-information games. Bridge players normally don't know what cards are in the other players' hands (except for what cards are in the dummy's hand)—and thus each player has only partial knowledge of the state of the world, the possible actions, and their effects. A game tree that represents all sequences of actions that *might* be possible would be much too large to be searched within the time available during a bridge game.

For declarer play in bridge, we have developed a different approach, that grows out of the observation that bridge is a game of planning. The bridge literature describes a number of tactical and strategic schemes (such as finessing, ruffing, and crossruffing) that people combine into plans for how to play their bridge hands. We have taken advantage of the planning nature of bridge, by adapting and extending some ideas from HTN planning.

To represent the tactical and strategic schemes of card-playing in bridge, we use structures similar to HTN methods—but modified to represent multi-agency and uncertainty. Each multi-agent method encodes a portion of some bridge tactic (such as finessing, ruffing, cross-ruffing, cashing out, etc.). To generate game trees, we apply HTN decomposition to these multi-agent methods. This produces a game tree in which each branch represents a move that fits into some coherent strategy. In comparison with a brute-force game-tree search, this gives us a smaller branching factor and a much smaller search tree: our approach generates game trees containing only about 305,000 nodes in the worst case and 26,000 nodes on the average, as compared to 5.55×10^{44} nodes in the worst case and 10^{24} nodes on the average if we had generated a conventional game tree. Thus, our algorithm can search the game tree all the way to the end, to predict the likely results of the various sequences of cards it might play.

We have incorporated our HTN planning techniques for declarer play into the latest version of Great Game Products' Bridge Baron program, *Bridge Baron 8*. As reported in *The New York Times* (Truscott 1997) and *The Washington Post* (Chandrasekaran 1997), a pre-release version of Bridge Baron 8 won the latest world-championship competition for computer bridge programs, the 1997 *Baron Barclay World Bridge Computer Challenge*. Table 1 shows how each of the contenders placed in the competition.

The official version of Bridge Baron 8 went on the

Table 1: The contenders in the *Baron Barclay World Bridge Computer Challenge*, and their final places.

Program	Country	Performance
Bridge Baron	USA	1st place
Q-Plus	Germany	2nd place
MicroBridge 8	Japan	3rd place
Meadowlark	USA	4th place
GIB	USA	5th place

market in October 1997. During the last three months of 1997, it was purchased by more than 1000 people. More information about Bridge Baron 8 appears elsewhere in this conference proceedings (Smith et al 1998).

Process Planning for Microwave Modules

Microwave transmit/receive modules are complex electronic devices that are used in such applications as radars and satellite communications. These modules include a number of analog and digital components mounted on a substrate. Since these modules operate in the 1-20 GHz range, the location and orientation of the components on the substrate—and the dimensions and location of the printed wiring—affect the electrical performance. Thus the design of these modules is a complex task.

As with many manufactured products, the cost of manufacturing microwave modules is largely determined by decisions made while the modules are being designed. Thus, while a designer is producing a design, it is important to consider how the design decisions will affect not only the design's performance but also its potential manufacturing cost.

EDAPS (Electro-Mechanical Design and Planning System) is a toolkit to aid in this task. It integrates electronic design with mechanical design by incorporating a commercial electronic CAD tool (Hewlett Packard's *EEsof*) and a mechanical CAD tool (Bentley Systems' *Microstation*). Furthermore, it uses an HTN planning system to generate manufacturing process plans from the CAD models. Manufacturing a microwave module involves both mechanical operations (to produce holes and pockets in the substrate) and electronic operations (such as artwork generation and soldering operations). Each of these is discussed briefly below:

- For complex machined parts it can be quite difficult to generate good process plans (Nau *et al.* 1995). In particular, if the part geometry is complicated, it can be very difficult to determine what machining operations to use in what order, and how best to clamp the part to hold it in place during machining. However, for microwave modules the geometry of the substrate is relatively simple, and thus the task is considerably easier. Since there are few interactions among the features to be machined on the substrate, it is possible to find a one-to-one correspondence between machined features in the substrate and the machining operations that will be used to make them. It is easy to encode the machining processes using HTNs, by representing each process with an HTN method, and easy to instantiate these methods to find process orderings that work.

- For electrical operations such as artwork generation and soldering, the process structure is more complicated than for the mechanical operations—but it decomposes naturally into tasks and subtasks that are performed in a fixed sequence. This decomposition

hierarchy can be represented quite naturally using HTNs, making it easy to develop plan details depending on the details of the design.

Once EDAPS has generated a process plan, it does calculations to estimate the plan's time, cost, and product quality. By generating and comparing several plans and displaying the pareto-optimal ones to the user, this allows the user to select the best plan and to make an informed decision about the manufacturability of the design.

Comparison with Conventional Planning

Both the Bridge Baron and EDAPS required some extensions to the usual formulation of HTN planning:

- The Bridge Baron needed ways to represent and reason about possible actions by other agents (such as the opponents in a bridge game), as well as uncertainty about their capabilities (for example, lack of knowledge about what cards they have).

- EDAPS needed a way for the planner to interact with CAD modelers to get information about the product to be manufactured.

In order to incorporate these extensions, we found it necessary to restrict the ways in which the Bridge Baron and EDAPS go about generating plans. Both the Bridge Baron and EDAPS use total-order planning, and both expand tasks in a "left-to-right" order, i.e., in the same order that the tasks will be executed later. For example, in Figure 1, this control strategy would plan the steps in exactly the order in which they appear in Figure 1(b).

In contrast, most planning systems described in the AI planning literature operate using partial-order planning and backward chaining. Below, we examine the assumptions that have led to this preference, and explain why those assumptions do not apply to the Bridge Baron and EDAPS.

Backward Chaining

Most AI planning systems use some form of goal-directed search to improve the efficiency of planning by reducing the branching factor of the search space. One of the most common kinds of goal-directed search is backward chaining, in which the planner chooses some condition that needs to be achieved (either because it is specified as a goal or is a precondition for an operator that is already in the plan) but has not yet been achieved, and looks for a way to achieve it.

For example, in the blocks-world problem shown in Figure 2, suppose the basic available planning operator is

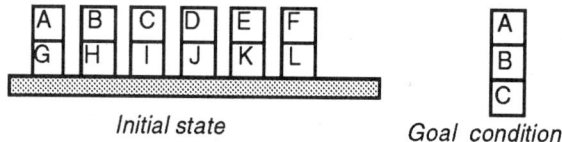

Initial state   *Goal condition*

Figure 2. A planning problem that illustrates the motivation for backward chaining.

the operator *move(X,Y)*, which can move *X* to *Y* if *X* is a clear block and *Y* is either the table or a clear block other than *X*. Then in the initial state there are 36 applicable instances of the "move" operation, but only one of them (namely *move(B,C)*) is of any use in achieving the goal. If a planner were to develop plans by searching forward from the initial state and considering all operator instances that are applicable at each point, it might easily search down lots of wrong paths before finding the right one. Instead, the planner focuses on achieving the goal conditions *on(A,B)* and *on(B,C)*; thus, it will immediately look at the only planning operations that can possibly be relevant: *move(A,B)* and *move(B,C)*. Some of the assumptions embodied in this example include the following:

- The number of operators that are applicable at each state of the world is generally higher than the number of operators capable of producing that state of the world. Thus, if we do forward chaining, the search space will have a higher branching factor than if we do backward chaining.
- Many of the paths in the search space can be much longer than the length of the plan we are trying to find. If we go down the wrong path, it may take a long time to discover this and backtrack to another path, so it is very important to minimize the number of paths we explore.

In contrast, the domains addressed by the Bridge Baron and EDAPS have the following characteristics:

- There may be many paths to goal states, and we want to find the optimal one. Most of the paths in the search space have length similar to the length of the plan we are trying to find, and many of these paths may actually lead to feasible plans. Although the problem can be very search-intensive, the search arises from examining many different feasible plans in order to try to find a *good* plan.
- HTN planners do not have to do backward chaining in order to do goal-directed search. In an HTN planning system, the goal is specified as a task or a task network. The planner will not consider every planning operator that is applicable to the current state, but only those that occur in HTN methods that apply to the task it is trying to accomplish. Often only one or two methods are applicable—the rest get pruned.

Partial-Order Planning

In a planning problem where there are several goals to achieve, a backward-chaining total-order planner such as STRIPS (Nilsson 1980) will plan for the individual goals one at a time, developing a complete plan for each one before going on to the next. This approach has difficulty with *deleted-condition interactions* such as the well known Sussman anomaly (Waldinger 1990).

The discovery of deleted-condition interactions has sometimes led researchers to conclude that unless a planning has explicit mechanisms for detecting and handling deleted-condition interactions, the planner is incomplete (i.e., it will sometimes fail to find a plan when in fact a plan exists). However, this conclusion is incorrect. Although STRIPS's total-order backward-chaining algorithm is incomplete, total-order forward chaining is complete: a breadth-first search that does total-order forward chaining will generate every possible plan for a problem. Thus, as shown by Gupta and Nau (1992), a simple total-order forward-chaining strategy has no difficulty with deleted-condition interactions, even though it has no explicit way of detecting and handling these interactions.

Another use of partial-order planning is to prevent excessive backtracking during the planning process, by avoiding premature commitments to the order of the steps in a plan. However, in the planning domains discussed in this paper, avoiding commitments to the order of the steps would not prevent much backtracking, primarily because there often is only one logical order in which to perform the steps.

Difficulty with Backward Chaining and Partial-Order Planning

The previous sections have shown that the reasons normally used to motivate the use of backward chaining and partial-order planning do not necessarily apply to HTN planning in real-world domains. In this section, we argue that in some real-world domains, backward chaining and partial-order planning can cause substantial difficulty. This derives primarily from that fact that if a planner is searching backward from the goal or is developing a partial-order plan, it often does not know the input state for each of its planning operators, which makes it difficult to reason about those planning operators. For example, in Figure 3, we cannot tell whether or not Step s_3 is executable unless we know whether Step s_2 comes before Step s_3, whether it comes before Step s_1, whether $z=y$, and whether $x=y$.

The standard way for AI planning systems to handle this problem is by requiring each planning operator to have its constraints and effects represented as lists of logical atoms, so that the planner can partially instantiate those atoms based on what things it *does* know. Such a representation makes planning possible, provided that the planning operators can represented in this fashion—but it makes it very difficult for the planner to do a number of things that may be important for realistic planning:

- doing complex numeric calculations (e.g., computing probabilities, kinematic calculations, or monetary calculations);
- interacting with external information sources (e.g., sensors, image analysis programs, or CAD modelers);

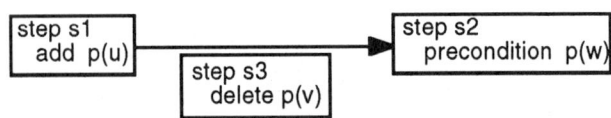

Figure 3. A partially-ordered plan.

- dealing with imperfect-information domains or multi-agent domains (such as contract bridge, negotiations, or military campaign planning).

Because the Bridge Baron and EDAPS expand tasks in the same order in which those tasks will be performed when the plan executes, this means that when they plan for each task, they already know as much as it is possible to know about what the state of the world will be at the time that the task will be performed. Consequently, the preconditions of each method could be written as arbitrary computer code, rather than as stylized logical expressions. This makes it feasible for EDAPS to make queries to a CAD modeler while developing a manufacturing plan, or for the Bridge Baron to do the complex numeric computations needed for reasoning about the probable locations of the opponents' cards in contract bridge.

For another example, consider finessing. This is a bridge tactic in which the declarer tries to win a trick with a high card, even though the opponents have a higher card. Depending on what cards the opponents have in their hands and how they choose to play them, the declarer may need to do different things as the finesse progresses; and to handle this, the Bridge Baron contains a table of *twenty-six* finesse situations. A partial-order planner might try using a finesse method while leaving some uninstantiated variables in the finesse method's preconditions, and then later in planning try to achieve these preconditions through the play of tricks earlier in the deal. Such a planner would have to decide which of the twenty-six situations to try to achieve—and it would not be immediately obvious which of them were even *possible* to achieve.

In contrast, because the Bridge Baron uses total-order planning to plan its declarer play, it would not try to apply any of the finesse methods until it had developed a partial plan resulting in a finesse situation. Furthermore, if it did generate a situation, it could easily check (using arbitrary computer code) whether the situation is an instance of one of the twenty-six different possible finesse situations—and then apply a finesse method, or not, as appropriate.

Theoretical Considerations

In STRIPS-style planning, total versus partial-order planning is an algorithmic issue; it does not affect the set of planning problems that can be represented or solved using STRIPS-style planning operators. However, the same is not true of HTN planning. As we explain below, only a proper subset of HTN planning problems can be represented if we force every method and the initial task network to be totally ordered. We also present a commitment strategy that will keep the task networks *mostly* totally-ordered without compromising the soundness or completeness of the planner.

Expressivity

Given a partially-ordered task network containing non-primitive tasks, in order to enforce the total-order restriction, one can consider enumerating all possible total orderings consistent with the partial order. However, this enumeration does not cover the whole set of candidate solutions for the original task network, because it precludes the possibility of interleaving subtasks of the non-primitive tasks in the task network. Below is an intuitive example:

Suppose you want to see a movie and have popcorn while you are doing so.

- The primitive tasks are Buy-Movie-Ticket, Buy-Popcorn, and Find-Seat; these tasks must be performed in this order (because you can only buy popcorn at the concession stand, which you can only get to if you have a ticket; and you certainly can't buy popcorn after you've found your seat.)
- The complex task is Watch-Movie, which decomposes into Buy-Movie-Ticket and Find-Seat.

An HTN planner starts out with the tasks Buy-Popcorn and Watch-Movie. A total-order planner must impose some ordering on these tasks, but neither ordering works: Buy-Popcorn before Watch-Movie leads to the primitive task sequence Buy-Popcorn, Buy-Movie-Ticket, and Find-Seat, but Buy-Movie-Ticket must be performed before Buy-Popcorn; and Watch-Movie before Buy-Popcorn leads to the primitive task sequence Buy-Movie-Ticket, Find-Seat, and Buy-Popcorn, but Buy-Popcorn must be performed before Find-Seat.

In contrast, a partial-order planner need not impose some ordering on Buy-Popcorn and Watch-Movie. It can start by decomposing Watch-Movie into Buy-Movie-Ticket and Find-Seat, and then interleaving Buy-Popcorn between Buy-Movie-Ticket and Find-Seat to produce a final plan. Thus, the expressivity of a partial-order HTN planning is stronger than the expressivity of a total-order HTN planning. This assertion can be proved using the definitions of complexity-based expressivity, model-theoretic expressivity, and operational expressivity developed by Erol *et al.* (1994b).

As reported in Erol *et al.* (1994b), the complexity of totally-ordered HTN planning is EXPSPACE-hard, and in DOUBLE-EXPTIME. In comparison, the complexity of HTN planning without this restriction is semi-decidable. Thus, from the computational-complexity perspective, totally-ordered HTN planning is significantly less expressive. Total-order HTN planning precludes the possibility of interleaving subtasks from different non-primitive tasks, thus eliminating inter-task interactions to a large extend. As a result, specialized algorithms that make use of this extra information can be developed. Note that the total-order restriction places HTN planning at the same complexity level as STRIPS-style planning, which is EXPSPACE-complete.

From the perspective of operational and model-theoretic expressivity, total-order HTN planning lies strictly between STRIPS-style planning and unrestricted HTN planning. Any problem represented in STRIPS language can be mapped to a total-order HTN planning problem. One such mapping is presented in (Erol et.al. 1994b). Obviously any total-order HTN planning problem can be represented by the unrestricted HTN language. On the other hand, total-order HTN planning is not as expressive as the unrestricted HTN language: The set of plans for any total-order HTN problem is a context-free set. The set of solutions to unrestricted HTN planning problems may form arbitrary intersections of context-free sets, which properly contain context-free sets. Total-order HTN planning is strictly more expressive (with respect to operational and model theoretic expressivity) than the STRIPS language because the set of plans to any STRIPS-style planning problem form a regular set, which is properly contained in the set of context-free sets.

Increasing Expressivity by Relaxing the Total-Order Restriction

Our experience in practical planning applications indicates that most planning problems have tight ordering constraints. This feature can be utilized to develop specialized, efficient planning algorithms. However, some parts of a planning problem may not be totally-ordered, and we need to be able to deal with those problems without compromising soundness or completeness. As explained in the previous section, simply enumerating all total orderings consistent with the constraints in the task network would sacrifice completeness. In this section, we present a commitment strategy that will address this issue.

A commitment strategy, in the context of HTN planning, refers to the selection of the refinement strategy to be applied to the current task network. Erol *et al.* (1994b) presented a sound and complete HTN planning system called UMCP. UMCP's basic planning algorithm, which is based on refinement search, is as follows:

1. Input a planning problem $P=<d,I,D>$
2. Initialize OPEN-LIST to contain only d
3. if OPEN-LIST is empty then return "no solution"
4. Remove a task network tn from the OPEN-LIST
5. if tn is primitive, tn's constraint formula is "TRUE" and all committed constraints have become true then return tn as a solution
6. Pick a refinement strategy R for tn
7. Apply R to tn. Insert the resulting set of task networks into OPEN-LIST
8. Goto Step 3.

The UMCP planner utilizes two refinement strategies (Step 6): Task decomposition refinement involves retrieving the set of methods associated with a non-primitive task in the task network, and then for each method generating a new task network by expanding the selected non-primitive task. Constraint enforcement refinement involves making the selected constraints necessarily true by restricting the possible values for variables and task orderings in the task network. Restrictions on possible values of variables and task orderings are stored in specialized data-structures, associated with each task network. Both of the refinement strategies are provably sound, complete, and systematic. As long as we give UMCP a sound and complete refinement strategy to use in Step 6, UMCP as a whole will be sound and complete. Below, we describe how to implement a sound and complete refinement strategy for UMCP that will explore earlier tasks first, while giving priority to ordering commitments, as well as variables that appear in earlier tasks.

Given a task network tn, let *tasks(tn)* denote the set of tasks in tn. Our modified refinement strategy for UMCP will construct a totally-ordered set of ground primitive tasks called *head(tn)*, such that these tasks are ordered to be before every other task in tn. Intuitively, *head(tn)* corresponds to a prefix of the final plan. In the initial task network input given to our modified version of UMCP, *head(tn)* is empty. Our refinement strategy will add ground primitive tasks to *head(tn)* as the planning proceeds. At the time that a solution is found, *head(tn)* will contain all the tasks in the final task network, and thus *head(tn)* will be the plan. Given a task network tn, here is how our refinement strategy will select what refinement to perform in Step 6 of UMCP:

1. If there are any constraints involving tasks in head(tn), then select constraint enforcement on them.
2. Let φ be the set of all tasks in *tasks(tn) − head(tn)* that are not necessarily ordered to come after any other tasks in *tasks(tn) − head(tn)*. If φ contains non-primitive tasks, then select task decomposition refinement on those tasks.
3. If φ consists of only primitive tasks, then for each ground linearization of those tasks in φ, generate a new task network where the ground linearization is appended to the *head(tn)*.

Refinement strategies 1 and 2 are from UMCP's original refinement strategies, and hence they are provably sound, complete, and systematic. These two refinement strategies are biased towards handling constraints and compound tasks that appear earlier in the task network.

Refinement strategy 3 enumerates all possible orderings and variable bindings for a set of primitive tasks in tn, which are already ordered before every other task in tn except for those in *tail(tn)*. Since those tasks are primitive, enumeration of their all possible ground linearizations preserves soundness, completeness, and systematicity. Note that this schema circumvents the problem with enumerating all possible orderings of the input task network tn right away: tn may contain non-primitive tasks, and ordering them would preclude the interleaving the subtasks of the non-primitive tasks.

Conclusions

AI planning is becoming increasing useful in practical planning problems—but the techniques that work well in practice are not always the ones that AI planning researchers might expect. For example, in developing successful HTN planning systems for two different practical problems, we found it better not to use the "traditional" techniques of backward chaining and partial-order planning, but instead to develop a total-order planning control strategy that expands tasks in the order that they will be executed.

In this paper we have examined the assumptions behind backward chaining and partial-order planning, and have explained why these assumptions do not always reflect the characteristics of real-world planning problems. We have further explained how backward chaining and partial-order planning can sometimes be very difficult to use in practice, and how total-order HTN planning can overcome those difficulties.

We have also examined the expressive power of total-order HTN planning, and concluded that while it is strictly more expressive than planning with STRIPS-style operators, it is strictly less expressive than unrestricted HTN planning. We have proposed a way to relax the "total-order" restriction, to produce a sound and complete forward-search approach that has the same expressive power as unrestricted HTN planning. A promising topic for future work will be to implement this control strategy and try it out on a variety of planning problems.

Acknowledgements

This work was supported in part by an AT&T PhD scholarship to Stephen J. J. Smith; Maryland Industrial Partnerships (MIPS) Grant 501.15; Great Game Products; by NSF grants NSF EEC 94-02384, IRI-9306580, and DDM-9201779; ARPA grant DABT63-95-C-0037; ONR grant N000149610888; and in-kind contributions from Spatial Technologies and Bentley Systems. Any opinions, findings, and conclusions or recommendations expressed in this material are those of the authors and do not necessarily reflect the views of the funders.

We also wish to thank James Hendler for many helpful discussions.

References

Chandrasekaran, R. 1997. Program for a better bridge game: A college partnership aids industry research. *The Washington Post*, Sept. 15, 1997. Washington Business section, pp. 1, 15, 19.

Erol, K.; Hendler, J.; and Nau, D. 1994. "UMCP: A Sound and Complete Procedure for Hierarchical Task-Network Planning," *Proc. 2nd Int'l Conf. on AI Planning Systems*, 249-254.

Erol, K.; Nau, D.; Hendler, J. 1994. "HTN Planning: Complexity and Expressivity." *Proc. AAAI-94*.

Erol, K.; Hendler, J.; and Nau, D. Complexity results for hierarchical task-network planning. *Annals of Mathematics and Artificial Intelligence* 18:69–93, 1996.

Great Game Products. 1997. *Bridge Baron*. <http://www.bridgebaron.com>.

Hebbar, K.; Smith, S.; Minis, I.; and Nau, D. 1996. "Plan-Based Evaluation of Designs for Microwave Modules," *ASME Computers in Engineering Conf.*

Korf, R. 1994. Best-first minimax search: Othello results. *AAAI-94*.

Gupta, N. and Nau, D. 1992. On the complexity of blocks-world planning. *Artificial Intelligence* 56(2-3), 223–254.

Nau, D.; Regli, W.; and Gupta, S. 1995. AI Planning Versus Manufacturing-Operation Planning: A Case Study. *IJCAI-95*.

Nilsson, N. 1980. *Principles of Artificial Intelligence*. Morgan Kaufmann.

Sacerdoti, E. D. 1977. *A Structure for Plans and Behavior*. American Elsevier Publishing Company.

Schaeffer, J. 1993. Presentation at plenary session, *AAAI Fall Symposium*.

Smith, S. J..; Nau, D. S.; and Throop, T. 1996. "A Planning Approach to Declarer Play in Contract Bridge", *Computational Intelligence*, 12(1), 106–130.

Smith, S. J.; Nau, D. S.; and Throop, T. 1996. "Total-Order Multi-Agent Task-Network Planning for Contract Bridge", *AAAI-96*, 108–113.

Smith, S. J.; Hebbar, K.; Nau, D.; and Minis, I. 1997. Integrating electrical and mechanical design and process planning. In Martti Mantyla, Susan Finger and Tetsuo Tomiyama (ed.), *Knowledge Intensive CAD, Volume 2*, pp. 269-288.

Smith, S. J.; Nau, D.; and Throop, T. 1998. Success in spades: using AI planning techniques to win the world championship of computer bridge. *IAAI-98*.

Tate, A. 1977. Generating project networks. *IJCAI-77*, 888–893.

Truscott, A. 1997. Bridge. *New York Times*, 16 August 1997, p. A19.

Tsuneto, R.; Erol, K.; Hendler, J.; and Nau, D. 1996. Commitment strategies in hierarchical task network planning. In *Proc. Thirteenth National Conference on Artificial Intelligence*, pp. 536-542.

Tsuneto, R.; Nau, D.; and Hendler, J. 1997. Plan-refinement strategies and search-space size. In *Proc. European Conference on AI Planning*.

Waldinger, R. 1990. Achieving several goals simultaneously. In J. Allen, J. Hendler, and A. Tate (ed.),*Readings in Planning*, Morgan Kaufmann, San Francisco, pp. 118-139.

A Prototype Application of Fuzzy Logic and Expert Systems in Education Assessment

James R. Nolan

Siena College
Departments of Quantitative Business Analysis and Computer Science
515 Loudon Road Loudonville, NY 12211 USA
jnolan@siena.edu

Abstract

This paper reports on the design and development of an expert fuzzy classification scoring system for grading student writing samples. The growing use of written response tests in the education sector provides fertile domain areas for new and innovative applications of soft computing and expert systems technology. The main function of the expert fuzzy classification scoring system is to support teachers in the evaluation of student writing samples by providing them with a uniform framework for generating ratings based on the consistent application of scoring rubrics. The system has been tested using actual student response data. A controlled experiment demonstrated that teachers using the expert fuzzy classification scoring system can make assessments in less time and with a level of accuracy comparable to the best teacher graders. The paper introduces fuzzy classification techniques that can encapsulate knowledge about imprecise qualities needed for constructing rule-based scoring models that provide consistent, uniform scoring results. This increased consistency in the application of the scoring rubrics allows for more valid individual and group assessment.

Introduction

A task central to all education programs is one of assessment. Assessment based on standardized tests is popular because it is thought that both individual and group comparisons will be possible if all participants take the same test and this test is graded the same way each time. The failure to perform *accurate* assessments in a timely manner may result in delays in providing student access to developmental activities needed to improve. In addition, students and school districts cannot be compared if the assessment process is not designed to be consistent and uniformly implemented.

Copyright © 1998, American Association for Artificial Intelligence (www.aaai.org). All rights reserved.

The last several years have seen an increased emphasis on assessment of student writing ability. Many school systems and state education departments have designed writing assessment instruments or have contracted with outside testing centers to develop and grade what are deemed to be standard evaluative tests for student writing. In 1995 alone, the Educational Testing Service, the world's largest provider and grader of exams that require narrative responses, rated by hand some nine million pieces of student writing (Page & Petersen, 1996).

The task of grading student writing on standardized tests is very repetitive and labor intensive. Typically a teacher must learn a scoring standard or "rubric" that he or she will consistently apply to all student writing samples. Applying the scoring rubric consistently generally takes a considerable amount of time. In addition, the scoring rubrics for writing assessment usually employ the use of linguistic categories and approximate reasoning. This makes it much more difficult to ensure uniform application of the scoring rubrics. Expert decision support help in making the grade decision could lead to quicker evaluation of writing samples and more valid individual and group assessment because the application of the scoring rubrics would be much more uniform.

Several researchers have designed rubrics for performance-based assessment of a student's writing ability (Brewer, 1996; Marzano, et al, 1993). To date, no one has reported on efforts to create an automated scoring system employing rubrics for grading student writing samples. Since any type of grading is a classification task, the use of a classification model based on the particular scoring rubrics will help to standardize the grading (Ebert, 1996). The rubrics developed for grading student writing generally use linguistic categories, e.g., "thorough" understanding. The problem with linguistic categories is that they are imprecise or "fuzzy". The purpose of this paper is to introduce an expert fuzzy classifier model for grading student writing samples. It will be shown that the expert fuzzy classifier model can encapsulate rules using linguistic categories and results in faster, more consistent grade assignments. An overview of the application, including the problems with human scoring, follows. The next section reviews the theory of fuzzy classification. We apply this theory and describe the development of an expert fuzzy classification scoring system for grading student writing on standardized tests. Finally, the expert fuzzy classifier system is validated and conclusions drawn. Areas for further research are highlighted.

Overview of the Application

The New York City School District has developed a program called Curriculum Frameworks which stresses language arts at all grade levels. They subsequently developed the Performance Assessment in Language Arts (PAL) test to measure both reading and writing, integral parts of the language arts curriculum effort. In the New York City Grade 4 PAL, fourth grade students are asked to read a story and a poem and to respond to essay response questions about each.

All items in the NYC Grade 4 PAL test require students to generate individual narrative responses, rather than select a response from a list of choices. The response is evaluated by teachers who have been trained to exercise their professional judgment in applying scoring rules called rubrics. The rubrics describe the kind of student work that corresponds to the various score points. By using rubrics with staff development training, it is hoped that grading standards will be applied consistently across the city-wide school system.

The scoring guide to be used by all teachers in grading the Grade 4 PAL test is divided into two sections. The first section describes how to score the test for reading comprehension. The second part details the scoring rules for writing in response to literature. The general reading comprehension rubric is designed to aid the teacher in making a holistic judgment as to which category the student's response fits into: *high* (insightful, thoughtful), *medium* (basic, no frills), or *low* (confused, missing pieces). The specific reading comprehension rubric, as opposed to the general or "holistic" reading comprehension rubric, gives the teacher examples of specific ideas directly related to the story and tells which score category they fit into (0 through 6, inclusive). Finally, the reading comprehension anchor papers are specific examples of responses to the questions. These responses are provided for each score category.

The writing in response to literature section of the test has two parts. The first part is designed to test for writing effectiveness. This involves two dimensions: content and style. Each dimension has its own rubric. After employing each rubric, the teacher adds the scores together. The second part of the writing in response to literature section of the NYC Grade 4 PAL test concerns writing mechanics, i.e., spelling, grammar, etc.

Problems with Human Scoring

As is evident from this brief overview of the NYC Grade 4 PAL test and its scoring rules or rubrics, the teachers are trained to follow a scoring rubric that asks them to group the student's response into one of three general categories - high, medium, or low. After that they are to assign a numerical score by using the specific guidelines and rules established for each score level. Because the results of this test are to be used as evaluative measures for both individuals and groups, it is imperative that the student papers are scored the same way every time. As mentioned earlier, ensuring this to be true is problematic. Although the New York City School District has done a good job of developing scoring rules and standards, there is no way of ensuring that they are being applied the same way by different raters. The literature shows that two raters will agree with each other only 65% of the time (Page & Petersen, 1996). Even more important than this statistic is the fact that their is no way to prove that a particular teacher grading the NYC Grade 4 PAL test is applying the scoring rubrics in the same exact way each time. Fatigue and a myriad of other personal factors may affect consistency.

The second problem is time itself. Dutifully applying these well thought-out scoring rubrics to thousands of student papers every year takes a considerable amount of teacher time. There would be significant benefits if an expert decision support system could be developed that would serve to help the teacher in applying these scoring rubrics for classifying student writing. The scoring rubrics would be applied the same way every time and the scoring of many writing samples could be done in a more efficient way, leaving valuable time for the teacher to spend on developmental tasks rather than evaluative tasks.

Since the NYC Grade 4 PAL scoring rubrics are composed of rules with imprecise categories for making grade classifications, fuzzy logic and fuzzy classification models were used to represent these rubrics in a rule-based expert system environment. The theory of fuzzy classification is described next.

Fuzzy Classification

Fuzzy logic refers to a mode of reasoning in the presence of imprecise or ambiguous information (Zadeh, 1997). Fuzzy logic technology enables one to perform approximate reasoning and improves performance of classification systems in three ways: through efficient numerical representation of vague terms and concepts, by increasing their range of operation in ill-defined environments, and by decreasing their sensitivity to noisy data.

Membership Functions

Contrary to its nomenclature, fuzzy logic-based systems operate based on the precise and rigorous mathematics of fuzzy sets. A fundamental concept of fuzzy sets is that an element **x** may be a member of set **A** with varying degrees, i.e., each member of the set is characterized by its *degree of membership* within the set. The degree of membership of element **x** in set **A** is denoted by $\mu_A(x)$. A mapping of the domain interval to its degree of membership defines the membership function μ.

For example, different teachers have different definitions of what is a *medium* level of understanding in reading comprehension. In fact, most teachers would agree that no single value defines the category perfectly. If the student's understanding of a reading was being measured by adding the number of reading comprehension questions answered correctly, *medium* could apply to a range of total correct answers, with each number in the interval being *more medium* or *less medium* relative to some "typical" or "ideal" value. Assuming that 5 questions answered correctly out of ten is a typical *medium* level of understanding, a membership function for understanding might appear as a bell-shaped curve centered around 5 questions answered correctly. To accelerate computations and/or to reduce computer memory requirements, membership function shapes are usually simplified to triangular or trapezoidal forms.

Each linguistic variable is usually associated with a complete set of membership functions that are defined over the entire operating range of that variable. In fact, in fuzzy logic systems, neighboring membership functions overlap to indicate that a value may belong to different sets at the same time, with different degrees of membership. The number of membership functions assigned to the features to be used for classification, and the shape of these membership functions, comprise an essential part of the knowledge embodied in a fuzzy logic system. This information is usually supplied by the domain expert and, when combined with the rulebase(s), a complete knowledge-base for a particular application is formed.

Fuzzification

Fuzzification refers to the process of determining the degree of membership of a crisp input data value among a feature variable's membership function set. The "fuzzified" values are determined by intersecting the input value to the fuzzy set associated with each linguistic label. For instance, an input value of 6 correct answers out of 10 reading comprehension questions might result in a degree of membership in the set labeled "medium" of 0.7 and a degree of membership in the set labeled "high" of 0.3.

Fuzzy Rulebase

Fuzzy logic classification systems are typically implemented in the form of an expert decision support system. These expert systems make decisions and generate output values (classifications) based on the knowledge provided by the designer in the form of IF<*condition*> THEN<*action*> rules. The rulebase contains a collection of rules and forms an integral part of the total knowledge embedded in the system.

Rules are generally specified by the domain expert. The <*condition*> and <*action*> parts of each rule are denoted as the antecedent and consequent parts, respectively. The antecedent part can be a simple or complex logical combination of conditions, and more than one action may be specified in the consequent part. Examples of some fuzzy logic rules are:

> IF understanding is *high* and character-recognition is *strong*
> THEN reading-comprehension is *high*
> IF understanding is *low* and character-recognition is *weak*
> THEN reading-comprehension is *low*

During each pass of the fuzzy logic system operation, the rulebase is evaluated and outputs generated. There are many ways of computing the output of individual rules and combining the results (and resolving conflicts). They are termed fuzzy inference methods.

Fuzzy Rule Evaluation (Inference)

Fuzzy or approximate reasoning involves decision making based on ambiguous or ill-defined assumptions and incomplete data (Kasabov, 1996; Zimmermann,

1991). A fuzzy logic-based classification system generates output categories by inferring cause-and-effect relationships provided in its knowledge-base (the collection of rules and membership functions). The goal is to generate the most logical (best possible) conclusions even for rules with multiple antecedent conditions and rulebases with conflicting rules. The process of "inferring" conclusions based on certain assumptions and premises that are satisfied in whole or in part, is termed the inference process. Fuzzy inference entails the evaluation of rules, resolution of conflicts, and aggregation of multiple recommendations.

Many different inference strategies exist, and each method varies in the combination of processing techniques for dealing with conjunctions/disjunctions in the rule antecedent, inferring the antecedent grade of membership to output fuzzy sets, resolving conflicts from multiple rules on the same output membership function, and merging the contribution of different rules to the same output variable. We will discuss what is arguably the most popular fuzzy inference strategy, max-min inference. In the max-min inference method, the min operation is used for the AND conjunction (set intersection) and the max operation is used for the OR disjunction (set union) in order to evaluate the grade of membership of the antecedent clause in each rule. For example, assume a student answers 6 out of 10 correct on the reading comprehension questions. Suppose fuzzification for the variable *understanding* produces a 0.7 degree of membership in the set "medium" and a 0.3 degree of membership in the set "high". Additionally, assume a student scores 3 out of 5 on the character recognition questions and fuzzification for the variable *character-recognition* produces a 0.6 degree of membership in the set "strong" and a 0.4 degree of membership in the set "weak", then:

>RULE 1: IF understanding is *medium* and
>character-recognition is *weak*
>THEN reading-comprehension is *medium*
>EVALUATION: min (0.7, 0.4) = 0.4 reading-comprehension is *medium*
>RULE 2: IF understanding is *high* and
>character-recognition is *strong*
>THEN reading-comprehension is *high*
>EVALUATION: min (0.6, 0.3) = 0.3 reading-comprehension is *high*

The value 0.4 is used to "clip" the *medium* reading-comprehension output membership function shape. Similarly, the value 0.3 is used to "clip" the reading-comprehension output membership function shape for *high*. If multiple rules have the same consequent label, the max operation is used to resolve conflicts. The clipped membership functions resulting from the application of many rules are then merged to produce one final fuzzy set. The max operation is used to merge overlapping regions.

Defuzzification

When the inference process is complete, the resulting data for each output of the fuzzy classification system is a collection of fuzzy sets or a single, aggregate fuzzy set. The process of computing a single number that best represents the outcome of the fuzzy set evaluations is called defuzzification. There are many methods that can be used for defuzzification. The centroid, also referred to as the "center-of-gravity method, produces "crisp" output data by computing the horizontal-axis component of the geometric centroid of the fuzzy set. Intuitively, the centroid method can be viewed as a "compromise" among the output actions recommended by different rules. For each output using this defuzzification method, the resultant fuzzy sets from all contributed rules are merged into a final aggregate shape. The centroid of the aggregate shape is then computed.

Applying Fuzzy Classification to Student Writing

This section describes the development of an expert fuzzy classification scoring system for scoring student writing samples. The scoring rubrics for the NYC Grade 4 PAL test have many of the characteristics of fuzzy logic that were described earlier. Classifying student writing samples from this test involves reasoning in the presence of imprecise or ambiguous information. For example, the NYC Grade 4 PAL test scoring rubric

>IF student demonstrates *high* level of
>understanding of the whole work
>AND exhibits a *strong* level of recognition of
>important characters
>AND recognizes *crucial* elements of the plot
>AND generates *new* ideas
>THEN rate reading comprehension *high*

involves the use of vague linguistic terms and concepts. Employing the fuzzy logic notion of degree of membership for each of the four underlined variables included in the antecedent (the IF portion) of the scoring rule cited above would allow us to "fuzzify" the data now used by the teachers to measure these terms. Identifying the possible categories for the variable in the consequent part of the scoring rubric will allow us to "defuzzify" the variable and obtain the final numeric score for reading comprehension. Doing this for all scoring rules will result in a knowledge-base similar to the one used by teachers who are trained to apply the scoring rubrics designed for the NYC Grade 4 PAL test.

Prototype Development

The development of the expert fuzzy classification system for scoring student writing samples proceeded in the following manner:

1. A group of expert teacher graders was selected and asked to develop ranges of scores corresponding to labels for each of the linguistic feature categories used in the scoring rubrics.
2. This "membership" data was used to develop membership function sets for each feature and classification variable.
3. A fuzzy rulebase was developed using the NYC Grade 4 PAL test scoring rubrics. This, along with the membership functions, comprised the knowledge-base of the expert fuzzy classification scoring system.
4. The expert fuzzy classification scoring system was validated by classifying test data sets.

The work resulted in the development of 21 membership function sets representing the feature and classification variables. The rulebase consists of over 200 rules. The teacher decides on the ratings to be given for each of the input feature variables, e.g., understanding, recognition of important characters, etc.. These ratings are automatically "fuzzified" and the appropriate rules from the rulebase are fired. The results are "defuzzified", resulting in numeric scores. The output from the classification component can be visualized and further explained by providing the underlying rules used to make the classification.

A commercially available software package called O'Inca Design Framework was used for developing the membership functions and rules. This fuzzy logic and expert system shell software package has additional facilities for simulation, on-line modification of rules and membership functions, and displaying output classifications and inference paths.

Testing and Validation

Two schools in New York City School District Six were selected as test sites. All grade 4 PAL tests completed by fourth grade students in these two schools were scored by teachers using the expert fuzzy classification scoring system. Over a one month period, 255 student writing samples were evaluated. At the end of the one month testing period, expert teacher graders from outside these schools reviewed the exams scored with the expert fuzzy classification scoring system and unanimously agreed the results of the scoring demonstrated consistent use of the rubrics designed for scoring the test. The teachers who used the system remarked about the speed with which they were able to evaluate the writing samples. They attributed this decrease in time needed to grade exams to relief of the burden of having to perform the mechanics of scoring them. They felt it enabled them to concentrate on evaluating the factors that are important in the holistic scoring method without having to worry about the actual manipulation of score categories.

A controlled experiment was set up to determine just how effective teachers evaluating student writing samples with the expert fuzzy classification scoring system were compared to domain experts (the expert teacher graders). Two hundred student writing samples were selected for the experiment. The three expert teacher graders reviewed each of the 200 writing samples and made an evaluation using the holistic scoring rubrics. The same 200 writing samples were independently reviewed and assessed by three different teachers using the expert fuzzy classification scoring system. The results indicated that the teachers using the expert fuzzy classification scoring system agreed with the three domain experts in 178 of the 200 cases for an agreement rate of 89%. Since it is not unusual for two teachers to disagree on the score to be assigned to the same sample of student writing, most standardized writing exams allow a difference of one point between the two graders before a compromise must be reached. If we use this criteria, 194 of the 200 cases would be considered in agreement (97%). There also was a significant difference in the time each group needed to do the scoring (see Tables 1 and 2).

Table 1
Comparison of Grade Classifications
Expert Teacher/Grader Assigned Scores

Scores Assigned By Teachers Using Expert Fuzzy Classification Scoring System	0	1	2	3	4	5	6
0	8						
1	1	23	2				
2	1	1	39	2	1		
3		1	1	38	1	1	
4			1	3	34	4	
5				1	2	18	1
6						6	10

Correct Classification Rate: 89%

Table 2
Average Evaluation Time

Grader:	Time (min.)
Expert Teacher/Graders	15
Grader 1 (with system)	11
Grader 2 (with system)	9
Grader 3 (with system)	9

Costs

The costs associated with the development and testing of the prototype expert fuzzy classification scoring system have totaled approximately $65,000 so far. This includes the cost of hardware, software, and teacher/staff time. The estimated cost for further development and implementation in New York City School District Six is $40,000. The District is committed to full implementation.

Conclusions and Further Research

The use of fuzzy classification in an expert system environment has proven to be of value in the domain of scoring student writing samples. The problems that arise in the management of uncertainty and vagueness in the scoring of student writing samples have been discussed. Fuzzy logic provided a natural conceptual framework for representation of the imprecise knowledge and inference processes associated with the scoring process. The benefits of the expert fuzzy classification system are:
1. A significant reduction in the time it takes to score the standardized New York City Grade 4 PAL exam.
2. Increased consistency in the application of the scoring rubrics.
3. The system enables less experienced teachers to become more familiar with the scoring rubrics.

The impact of the expert fuzzy classification scoring system on the time it takes teachers to score a student writing sample is important. As discussed previously, one of the problems with using standardized writing sample evaluations is that they are time consuming. By reducing the time for scoring a student writing sample by approximately one third, the writing sample evaluation process becomes more efficient.

This increase in efficiency would not be valuable if the accuracy of the evaluation suffered. The test results show that the accuracy and consistency of the evaluation performed by teachers using the expert fuzzy classification scoring system is equal to that of the expert teacher graders. Finally, the newer, less experienced teachers who took part in the testing have remarked about the usefulness of the system for both learning the scoring rubrics and providing explanations of the grading. They found the explanation of the grading useful for designing developmental work for the students.

Future Research

Rule-based fuzzy classification expert systems offer the potential for new and more powerful applications of AI in all areas of assessment. The direction for future research is to generalize this approach to other areas of assessment, e.g., portfolio assessment, evaluation of proposals by funding agencies, etc. A limitation of the current system is that teachers must still read and provide input on the student's written response to the standardized exam questions. A long range research goal is to develop a "front-end" to the expert fuzzy classification scoring system that will provide the inputs now given by the teacher.

REFERENCES

Brewer, R. (1996). *Exemplar's A Teacher's Solution.* Underhill, VT: Exemplar.

Ebert, C. (1996). Fuzzy classification for software criticality analysis. *Expert Systems with Applications*, 11(3), 323-342.

Kasabov, N. K. (1996). Foundations of neural networks, fuzzy systems, and knowledge engineering. Cambridge, MA: MIT Press.

Marzano, R., Pickering, D. & McTighe, J. (1993). *Assessing Student Outcomes: Performance Assessment Using the Dimensions of Learning Model.* Alexandria, VA: ASCD.

Page, E. B., & Petersen, N. S. (1996). The computer moves into essay grading: updating the ancient test. *Phi Delta Kappan*, March, 561-565.

Zadeh, L. (1997). In Jang, J. S., Sun, C. T., & Mizutani, E. (Eds.). *Neuro-fuzzy and soft computing: A conceptual approach to learning and machine intelligence*, Upper Saddle River, NJ: Prentice Hall.

Zimmermann, H. G. (1991). *Fuzzy set theory and its applications*, 2nd ed., Boston, MA: Kluwer.

Intelligent Control of Life Support Systems for Space Habitats

Debra Schreckenghost, Daniel Ryan, Carroll Thronesbery, Peter Bonasso, Daniel Poirot

Texas Robotics and Automation Center
NASA Johnson Space Center/ER
Houston, TX 77058
d.schreckenghost@jsc.nasa.gov

Abstract

The Interchamber Monitoring and Control (IMC) system is semi-autonomous, intelligent software that controls life support systems designed for recycling air in remote space habitats. The IMC system was developed using the 3T autonomous control architecture. This architecture integrates traditional control with reactive task sequencing and deliberative planning technology. The IMC system was used during the Phase III test of NASA's Lunar/Mars Life Support Test Program (LMLSTP). For this test, four crew members lived in a closed habitat for 91 days. The objective of using an intelligent control system was to reduce the need for crew involvement in nominal control of life support by automating control operations. Prior to this test, manually intensive traditional process control software had been used to control LMLSTP life support systems. It is impractical and inefficient for crew at a remote site to continuously monitor day-to-day operation of life support systems. Our intelligent control software autonomously handles nominal and expected anomalous situations. The crew only intervenes in exceptional or novel situations. During the Phase III test we demonstrated the viability of using intelligent control for such automation.

Description of Life Support Tasks

The Interchamber Monitoring and Control (IMC) system is semi-autonomous, intelligent software that controls life support systems designed for regenerating the air in remote space habitats. This software was used during the Phase III test of NASA's Lunar/Mars Life Support Test Program (LMLSTP). For this test, four crew members lived in a closed habitat for 91 days. Wheat for air recycling and food was grown in a separate closed chamber. The wheat was planted and harvested in stages, separated by 16-24 days. At any given time, there were four different stages in the plant chamber. This crop could provide enough oxygen (O2) for one of the four crew members. Crew solid waste was incinerated every four days; effluent from this incineration contained carbon dioxide (CO2) that the plants recycled into O2. Other sources of CO2 included gas removed from the air in the crew chamber and a pressurized bottle.

The IMC system managed the transfer of O2 and CO2 (called product gases) among gas reservoirs to ensure crew and crop health and to recycle gases produced by waste incineration (figure 1). These reservoirs included a crew habitat, a plant chamber, an airlock, and a number of pressurized tanks. The IMC system performed the following tasks autonomously during the 91 day test:

- Controlled the concentration of O2 in the plant chamber to maintain a setpoint
- Controlled the injection of CO2 into the plant chamber to maintain a setpoint needed for plant growth
- Managed the storage and transfer of O2 from the plant chamber to the crew habitat for use by the crew
- Managed the storage and transfer of O2 from the plant chamber for use during solid waste incineration
- Selected and configured for use the best available source of CO2 for the plants

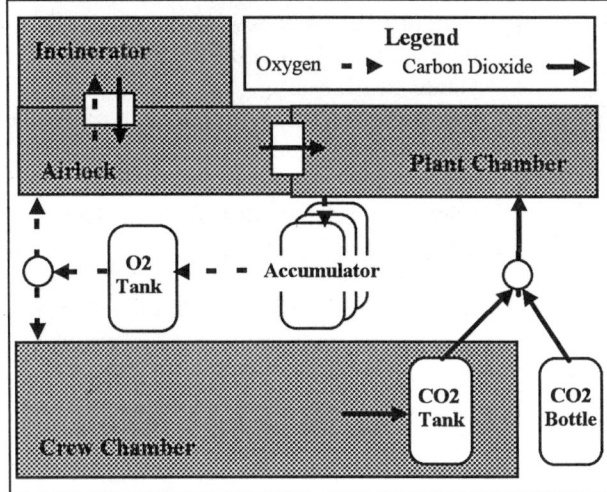

Figure 1. Product Gas Transfer for Phase III Test

The objective of building this intelligent control system was to reduce the need for human involvement in nominal control of life support systems by automating control

Copyright © 1998, American Association for Artificial Intelligence (www.aaai.org). All rights reserved.

operations. Prior to this test, traditional process control software had been used to control life support systems developed for LMLSTP. Operation of this software is manually intensive, requiring vigilance monitoring and frequent manual adjustment of control parameters. It is impractical and inefficient for crew at a remote space site to continuously monitor day-to-day operation of life support systems. Our intelligent control software autonomously handles nominal and expected anomalous situations. The crew only intervenes in exceptional situations. During the Phase III test we demonstrated the viability of using intelligent control for such automation.

Description of Control Application

The basis of the IMC system is the three tier (3T) autonomous agent control architecture (Bonasso, et. al.,1997a). 3T integrates traditional control with reactive task sequencing and deliberative planning technology. The lowest tier is the skill manager, which interfaces with the life support hardware controllers and sensors. The middle tier is the sequencer, which dynamically selects groups of skills to effect standard operating procedures and alarm handling. The top tier is the planner, which predicts product gas needs and availability and generates a plan based on these predictions that is implemented by the sequencer. All tiers of the 3T architecture continuously monitor data from sensors and reactively alter control at each level based on changes in the environment (figure 2).

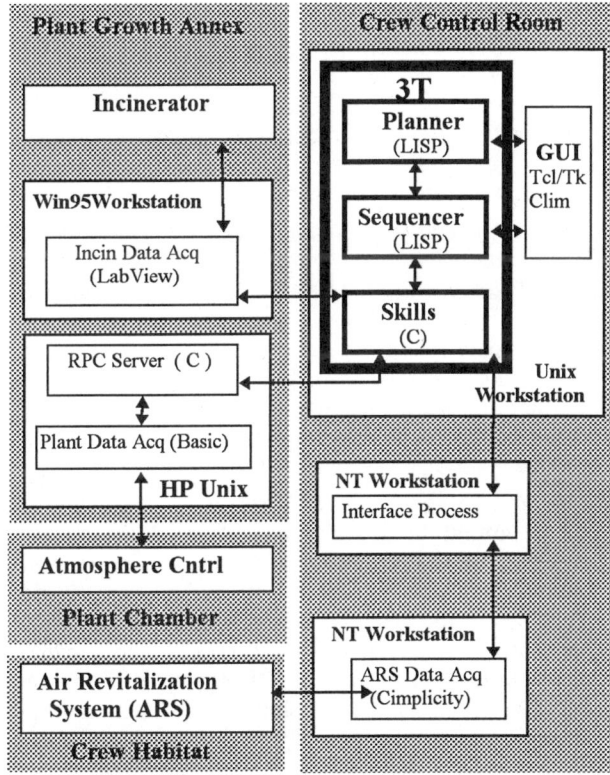

Figure 2. IMC Control Architecture

Each tier of 3T corresponds to a program. In the lowest tier, each skill manager is a C program. At the middle tier, the sequencer is the Reactive Action Package System (RAPS) (Firby, 1989). At the top tier, the planner is the Adversarial Planner (AP) (Elsaesser and MacMillan, 1991). Both the planner and sequencer are developed in LISP and are executed in separate LISP threads. All processes execute on a Sun Unix workstation.

Hierarchical Distributed Control

3T utilizes a different knowledge representation at each tier. The tiers usually are distributed as separate processes on different platforms. Thus, in addition to the usual communication between skill managers and the controlled system's effectors and sensors, 3T also defines protocols and a methodology for communication between the layers of the architecture. The sequencer tier acts as the locus of mediation between multiple skill manager processes, user interface processes, and the planning tier by employing a communication channel abstraction for integrating the various interprocess communication interactions.

The communication channel abstraction is implemented in object-oriented fashion with specialization for different types of channels possible on an abstract *link* class. These link specializations depend on the dimension of description including: (1) structure of the data being communicated (e.g., per-byte encoding, simple strings, nested structures), (2) lower level transmission mechanism (e.g., sockets, RPC, or CMU's IPC package), and (3) communications protocol shared with the connecting process (e.g., monitoring and control process such as a user interface). In addition to supporting the fundamental job of sending and receiving messages, every comm link responds to a standard set of messages for creating, destroying, starting, stopping, pausing, resuming, resetting, and clearing. Thus, the design for distributed communications makes possible dynamic and incremental reconfiguration of the architecture without affecting continuous operation of active processes.

The IMC system was distributed over four platforms:

- Sun Ultra Sparc running sequencer & planner (Lisp) and Tcl/Tk user interface with Solaris operating system
- Sun Sparc 5 running eight skill managers written in C and running under SunOS
- Pentium class PC running the user interface in the crew chamber under Windows 95
- Pentium class PC running one of the data servers described below under Windows NT

Beginning at 3T's lowest level with the skill interfaces to the existing life support hardware and software, there are 3 unique and custom interfaces to life support systems:

- Bi-directional data exchange with the data acquisition system for the crew chamber. IMC did not directly control crew chamber air regeneration hardware but it influenced this control by providing data about product gas transfer to the air regeneration control software.

- Data and command interface with the data acquisition system for the plant chamber
- Data monitoring interface with the control system for the solid waste incinerator

We used 8 skill managers to interface to these 3 systems.

In turn the sequencer interacts with each skill manager using an instantiation of a skill manager link class. These links utilize sockets for low-level transmission duties. The communications between sequencer and skill manager links are based on a protocol where the sequencer activates and deactivates control skills leading to contexts in which event occurrences are monitored. The sequencer may query the skill managers for local state information in addition to reconfiguring and resetting each skill manager individually. In the IMC application, 3T was operated in a number of skill configurations, depending upon ongoing operations. A skill manager was only executed when activities using its skills were in progress (e.g., incinerator skill manager was executed only during an incineration).

The interaction between planner and sequencer proceeds differently. Instead of the planner controlling the sequencer similar to the way the sequencer controls skill managers, the planner suggests modes of operation for the sequencer. In the IMC application the mechanics of this interaction were supported by having the planner and sequencer run in the same Lisp process but in different threads. The planner could then directly read from and write to sequencer memory. We describe this integration in more detail in the section on the uses of AI technology.

Interaction with the User

The 3T architecture was developed originally for control of autonomous systems. Practical demands of the IMC required user-initiated intervention in autonomous control. The integration of user initiative into the autonomous control architecture supports reactive manual control and reconfiguration in response to novel situations. Situations where such manual interaction was needed include:

- *Uncontrollable Events and Unanticipated Operations*: provide manual capability for responding to events the autonomous software cannot control (e.g., failure of external data source, such as rebooting data acquisition)
- *Unavailable Instrumentation*: accommodate events that could not be instrumented sufficiently to enable autonomous control (e.g., manual sensor calibration)
- *Safety*: permit a user to override the autonomous system for safety reasons (e.g. erroneous sensor measurement results in unsafe action by the autonomous system)
- *User Preferred Tactics*: permit a user to select which redundant sensor should be used for control or to specify control parameters (e.g., control setpoints)

Our application design has the following characteristics that enable such manual intervention:

- *Explicit specification of Level of Autonomy (LOA).* We parameterized the LOA for both O2 and CO2 control. The LOA specifies whether the autonomous system or the user isssues control commands (Bonasso, et al, 1997b). The LOA is specified at startup for each type of gas and can be changed during system execution.
- *Separation of monitoring and control.* The sequencer both changes controller states to handle nominal and expected anomalous situation (control) and detects caution and warning (C&W) situations (monitoring). Our sequencer design separates the modules performing monitoring from those performing control. This approach permits operating the system with only monitoring activated as well as with full monitoring and control. When LOA is manual, no changes to controllers are made by the autonomous system but the user is provided with C&W information useful in maintaining situation awareness while performing tasks manually. We also modularized separable control segments (O2 and CO2 control). This permits manual intervention in the control of one type of gas while remaining autonomous on the other type of gas.
- *Manual activation of each hardware controller.* For the 3T system, this corresponds to providing for user activation of skills to control life support hardware. We implemented this through the sequencing tier, which guarantees that the control system maintains accurate values for the current state of all manually controlled hardware (Kortenkamp, et al., 1997).
- *User-specified control preferences.* The product gas transfer system includes redundant and alternative sensors and controllers. IMC supports user in specifying preferred instrumentation when multiple are available. These preferences are used by the sequencer as context for selecting methods. Only data from a preferred sensor is monitored when determining control changes. Specifying a preferred controller reconfigures the gas flow network through the selected controller if possible.
- *Interlocks permitting manual override of autonomy.* For product gas transfer, interlocks are implemented to inhibit O2 concentration and CO2 injection in the plant growth chamber. These interlocks were needed to accommodate plant lighting profiles and to ensure human safety. Since these interlocks can be activated by either the user or the autonomous system, we provide a priority scheme where manually activated interlocks override autonomously activated interlocks.
- *Manual reconfiguration for hardware maintenance.* It was important to provide manual capability to take sensors out of the control loop (*offline*) temporarily with minimal effect on the control of product gas transfer. Every 2 days the gas analyzers needed to be calibrated. Occasionally a broken sensor needed to be repaired. The control tactics to take a sensor offline were implemented at the sequencing tier. When multiple sensors were available, we switched to a redundant sensor when one was offline. If all sensors were offline, we stopped all active control relying on that sensor until it became available. We also alerted the user.

- *Parameterized control setpoints and C&W thresholds.* The values of control setpoints and C&W thresholds could be changed during execution by either a user or the planning tier (e.g., planner lowered the O2 setpoint to accelerate CO2 consumption by the plants). These changes were interleaved with the execution of autonomous control to guarantee control was not executed with inconsistent settings.

This manual intervention capability in combination with modularity in control segments provides the flexibility to respond to situations that could not have been anticipated. For example, it was decided well after the Phase III test had started that we should change the control scheme for raising CO2 levels in the plant chamber after a crop harvest. Since there were few harvests remaining when this decision was made, we avoided major changes to the autonomous software by setting LOA manual for CO2 and manually activating the preferred method of CO2 injection until chamber concentrations were nominal. Throughout this operation, O2 control was autonomous.

The user interface supports supervisory monitoring as well as manual intervention. It provides test engineers with a summary of the current control situation. It can be scanned quickly for critical parameters, configurations, and anomalies. It logs control actions taken and alarms detected. Such a summary is useful when the control system is untended during round-the-clock operations. This user interface was developed using Tcl/Tk.

Uses of AI Technology

The IMC system combines a number of AI technologies with traditional control. The basis of the control system is an autonomous agent architecture. This architecture includes a deliberative planner, a reactive sequencer, and a set of tight sense/act processes that interface to control instrumentation. We use planning technology to predict gas needs and to specify activities that change control strategy to meet those needs. We use reactive task sequencing to automate standard operating procedures and alarm handling. The sequencer selects control tactics from a set of alternative approaches. This selection is based on matching a sensor-based assessment of situation to the method best suited for that situation. The sequencer also alters control tactics in response to anomalies in the environment or the control instrumentation.

This test was a 91 day experiment, so equipment and control schemes were changed and new data values obtained after analysis of previous activities. Thus, a 91 day plan would become infeasible after a few weeks. We made use of the fact that there are regular, repeated activities in the plan to partition the planning operators. Solid waste needed to be incinerated every 4 days and some portion of the plants were harvested and replanted every 16, 20 or 24 days. Lower level planning operators were developed to generate various types of four day plans (e.g., with planting and harvesting, with changes in setpoints), and higher level operators could compose these into longer plans based on plant crop rotations. Thus, plans of varying length could be generated, and new plans could be made at any time. This replanning was possible without stopping the sequencer since the planner draws its state conditions from the current sequencer memory.

To specify control strategy, the planner's primitive operators invoke top level sequences which change values in the sequencer memory that represent the desired strategy. The sequencer reacts to effect this control strategy as best as it can, given the current situation in the environment. This is an example of using plans as guides rather than as blueprints for execution (Agre and Chapman, 1990). This approach allows the sequencer to select an alternative to the preferred strategy, should there be a problem with implementing that strategy. For example, the planner may specify that the strategy for oxygen control is to accumulate O2 for an impending incineration. If the pressure in the O2 accumulator gets dangerously high because of an unexpectedly high output from the plants, the sequencer will ignore the preferred strategy to store O2 and will transfer gas out until the pressure is at a safe level. This approach also supports our phased integration approach described later by permitting the planning tier to be replaced by manual intervention.

Integration with User Interface

An important modification made to the 3T architecture was developing a principled approach for user-initiated interaction with the autonomous control software. We modified the sequencer for bi-directional communication with a user interface process and developed user interface capability that aided the user in communicating with the sequencer. The IMC supports a variety of modalities for the user to interact with the control system, including:

- User or the control system volunteers information
- User responds to information requests by the control system (e.g., the planner predicts a time region for incineration, but requests the user to confirm start time)
- User executes a function in the sequencer

There were several sequencer extensions required for human interaction. First, the approach whereby the sequencer monitors each skill manager for context-dependent events was generalized to allow for events received by *monitoring and control links*, such as a user interface. This enhancement included the ability for the sequencer to make arbitrary queries of monitoring and control links without blocking for answers. Second, a dynamically configurable facility for process and data subscription was created so that each user interface could subscribe to ongoing operational changes reflected in the sequencer memory or data store. Finally, a communication protocol message semantics for the monitoring and control links was defined to convey these new type of messages.

The graphical user interface (GUI) was an independent process which communicated with the control software by:

- *Data Updates* received periodically on a change-only basis. The GUI displayed this information on a continual basis, regardless of the level of autonomy.
- *Messages* from the sequencer containing information about caution and warning, observed states, and control states. The GUI logged this information in a file and optionally displayed messages as they were received.
- *Sequencer Function Execution Requests* from the GUI. User-initiated functions altered sequencer memory to accomplish changes in control strategy (e.g., change LOA) and tactics (e.g., change to a different controller).
- *Queries* from the sequencer to the user to obtain data not available from instrumentation. Queries could arrive in any order and could be answered in any order.
- *Hardware Control Commands* from the GUI. These commands were executed through the sequencer to avoid conflict with automatic controls by the sequencer.

Integration with Traditional Control Software

For the Phase III test, the IMC system was integrated with two legacy control systems (control for the plant chamber and for the crew habitat) and one new control system (for the incinerator). Intelligent control is integrated with these traditional control systems at the skill tier of 3T. Skills interface with the continuous control instrumentation, providing data which the sequencer translates into symbolic state information. The skills developed for the IMC ranged from simple binary switches to sophisticated adaptive controllers (e.g., feed forward & PID controllers).

IMC was not allowed to issue control commands through two of these legacy systems (crew habitat and solid waste incinerator). We integrated by monitoring data from these systems and making sure product gas transfer control actions that affected them were consistent with their control objectives and caused no harm. For example, IMC stopped providing oxygen to the crew habitat when O2 concentrations in that chamber were above normal. The O2 alert levels that we used to stop injection were well below the alert levels used by the legacy system so we would not reverse or impede its control actions to remedy the situation.

For the integration with the plant chamber control, no software could be changed in the legacy system. We were required to make all control inputs as if they were inputs from the user interface to the legacy system. This system only permitted one user input every data cycle (~15 seconds). Thus, we were unable to take advantage of parallelism inherent in the control problem because of the integration approach with the legacy system.

In all of these cases, however, our ability to devise strategies that integrated data transfer among these heterogeneous systems with minimal change to legacy software was pivotal in gaining the customer's cooperation and support. Another confidence-building integration strategy we implemented was the ability to hand over control to the legacy system in case of a serious alarm. During the test, we never exercised this capability because we never saw a serious alarm (i.e., IMC always recovered from anomalies before hand-over conditions occurred).

Application Development and Operation

The IMC system was developed at a 2 staff level in collaboration with a product gas engineer using an iterative development methodology. To demonstrate feasibility, we developed a subset of the control system that maintained gas concentrations for wheat grown in the plant chamber. This 5-month development included testing in the lab with an emulation of life support hardware and recorded data. Then we integrated this prototype with the life support hardware for the plant chamber and tested it during a wheat growth test (3.5 months). During this test, we demonstrated 2 modes of operation: monitoring only, and monitoring and control.

Once we had demonstrated feasibility, we began developing the operational system. The operational design was based on the feasibility prototype, with significant changes to address what we learned in the wheat test and to add full product gas transfer capability. Developing the operational system took 2 months. As with the feasibility prototype, we tested the operational system in the lab before integrating with the life support hardware. Integration took 2 months, and extended past the start of test because of delays in the installation of life support hardware, and network loading problems that required changing network hardware. Once these issues were resolved, the IMC operated round-the-clock for 73 days.

Phased Integration of Control

We integrated the 3T application in phases, starting with the lowest tier and moving to the top tier. As each tier was integrated, we provided a usable (though incomplete) capability. When the skills were integrated, we could manually control the life support system using a computer. When the sequencer was integrated, control tactics were automated but manual intervention was required for changes in control strategy. The full system capability was available only after the planner was integrated.

Product gas transfer was a new life support system with hardware installed just prior to using it in the Phase III test. The installation and checkout of this hardware did not always occur as planned, resulting in subsets of hardware becoming available for integration with the control software in an unpredictable order. The customer desired that we control "as much as possible as soon as possible". To achieve this objective, we modularized the control system into separable control segments, and provided the ability to control each segment either manually or autonomously. O2 control was a separate module from CO2 control. Since the CO2 gas transfer hardware was installed much sooner than the O2 gas transfer hardware, we were able to complete integration with CO2 control software and begin autonomous operation while still performing manual integration testing on O2 gas transfer hardware.

For phased integration of new capability into an operational system, the developer must be able to meet operational objectives and test new software at the same time. Software errors discovered while integrating new capability would bring down the operational system occasionally. It was important to provide a computer capability to monitor life support instrumentation for assessing system state and to take manual control actions for maintaining safety while the autonomous system was down. For the Phase III test, this capability was implemented below the skill tier. For future systems, it would be useful to include this capability at the skill tier.

Application Use

This application was developed to support the Phase III test of the LMLSTP. This test started on September 19, 1997. The control software was operational on October 6. It successfully managed the transfer of product gases round-the-clock until the end of test on December 19. Except when we were integrating new capability or responding to an anomaly, the system typically ran without human supervision or intervention. Three times a week a user would take gas analyzers offline for calibration. When waste was incinerated (every 4 days during portions of the test), we manually reconfigured skill interfaces to receive data from the incinerator control software. We also manually transferred data files logged by the IMC to a centralized computer 3 times a week.

The limited human role in operating the IMC contrasts significantly with the operation of the more traditional process control software used with the other life support systems developed for LMLSTP. Operation of other software was manually intensive, requiring vigilance monitoring and frequent manual adjustment of control parameters. One person was on shift for 16 hours daily to perform these tasks. Operating the IMC typically required 6-8 hours weekly of shift work, with an additional 6 hours for each incineration and 3 hours for each harvest.

An interesting aspect of the IMC application was the use of Lisp in a long duration operation. Lisp's use of garbage collection has been mentioned as a liability for its use in "real world" applications. We did not find this to be the case. We were able for the most part to perform garbage collection during times that did not affect system performance. Only when the Lisp process size increased significantly (above 30Mb) due to an as yet undiagnosed memory leak did garbage collection time become a factor.

Another benefit of using Lisp was the ease with which changes could be incorporated into the sequencer while executing. Using the Emacs to Franz Allegro Lisp interface, several Emacs Lisp buffers were used to interact with the running sequencer while receiving low-level status information from the Lisp process. This status information proved useful in determining possible sources of communications problems between the sequencer and the various interacting processes. One challenge we overcame was limiting the maximum size of the status buffer (i.e., ordinarily Emacs buffers retain a complete output history), and yet maintaining continuous output of status information to the buffer. An automated solution was implemented by which Emacs periodically checks the buffer size and deletes the oldest status information when the buffer history length reaches a specified size.

As described elsewhere, the IMC was integrated with a heterogeneous set of legacy software processes operating on different platforms. This diverse set of data connections resulted in a number of communications-related problems during operations, including loss of communication due to high bandwidth network traffic, failure to terminate another node on our network, and rebooting of legacy systems. Since most of these problems resulted in suspension or termination of communications among our processes, we could have recovered automatically from many of these problems if we had added software to monitor the health of process communication.

Future Work

The successful demonstration of autonomous control using AI technology during the Phase III test resulted in the selection of this architecture for controlling life support systems being developed for the Space Station. We are currently developing 3T control software for use in a 1999 ground-based demonstration of life support systems.

Acknowledgements. This work was funded by the National Aeronautics and Space Administration. We would like to thank M.Edeen/NASA for domain knowledge, R. Burridge/ Texas Robotics and Automation Center for CO2 injection skills, and D. Overland/NASA for an interface to a legacy control system.

References

Agre, P.E., and Chapman, D. 1990. What are Plans for? *Journal of Robotics and Autonomous Systems*. 6: 17-34.

Bonasso, P., Firby, J., Gat, E., Kortenkamp, D., Miller, D, and Slack, M. 1997a. Experiences with an Architecture for Intelligent, Reactive Agents. *Journal of Experimental Theory of Artificial Intelligence*. 9: 237-256.

Bonasso, P., Kortenkamp, D., and Whitney, T. 1997b. Using a Robot Control Architecture to Automate Shuttle Procedures. In *Proceedings of 9th Conference on Innovative Applications of Artificial Intelligence*, 949-956 Providence, R.I.

Elsaesser, C., & MacMillan, T.R. 1991. Representation and Algorithms for Multiagent Adversarial Planning. Technical Report MTR-91W000207. MITRE, Wash. D.C.

Firby, J. 1989. Adaptive Execution in Complex Dynamic Domains. Ph.D. diss., Yale University.

Kortenkamp, D., Bonasso, P., Ryan, D, Schreckenghost, D. 1997. Traded Control with Autonomous Robots as Mixed Initiative Interaction. *AAAI-97 Spring Symposium Workshop on Mixed Initiative Interaction*.

Split Up: The use of an argument based knowledge representation to meet expectations of different users for discretionary decision making

Andrew Stranieri and John Zeleznikow

School of Information Technology and Mathematical Sciences,
University of Ballarat, Ballarat, Victoria, Australia, 3353
E-mail: a.stranieri@ballarat.edu.au;
Phone (61) 3 53279440 ; Fax (61) 3 53279270

Database Research Laboratory,
Applied Computing Research Institute,
La Trobe University, Bundoora, Victoria, Australia, 3083
E-mail: johnz@latcs1.cs.latrobe.edu.au;
Phone: (61) 3 9479 1003; Fax: (61) 3 9479 3060

Abstract

Split Up is a rule / neural hybrid that represents knowledge using frames based on the argument structure proposed by the British philosopher, Toulmin. Split Up makes predictions about marital property following a divorce in Australia; a domain that is considered discretionary in that a judge has considerable flexibility. The end users of Split Up are judges and registrars of the Family Court of Australia, mediators and lawyers. Each end user has specific and divergent needs and thus uses the system in different ways however all users rely on effective explanations. The argument based representation of knowledge enables the system to have the flexibility required of different users, to generate effective explanations and also facilitates knowledge acquisition. The framework has been used to integrate rules with neural networks but can easily be used to integrate other inferencing methods.

1. Introduction

Discretionary fields of law are those in which a decision maker has a considerable degree of flexibility in determining an outcome. Family law in Australia is considered discretionary because a judge of the Family Court of Australia, in allocating property to couples following a divorce is required by statute to take various factors into account but has discretion in allocating a relative weighting to each factor. For example, the principle statute mandates that the health and age of both parties are relevant considerations yet is silent on their relative importance.

Modelling discretionary reasoning is difficult. Attempts to do so using heuristic rules has been found to be limited by (Edmunds and Huntley 1992) and also by (Stranieri and Zeleznikow 1992). The application of neural networks to modelling discretionary reasoning is suitable if sufficient past decisions can be collected from Courts to form a training set. Once trained, the network, exposed to a new case will output a result consistent with patterns of decisions in previous cases. However, neural networks have not often been used to model legal reasoning principally because explanations for neural network inferences are difficult to generate and because sufficiently large numbers of past cases often do not exist.

Split Up is a rule - neural hybrid system that integrates twenty neural networks with fifteen rules sets. The system predicts the percentage of marital property a Family Court of Australia judge will award litigants to a divorce. Consultations with domain experts from a state funded legal service identified a total of 94 relevant variables. Data reflecting values for these variables has been collected from over one hundred judgments made by decision makers in the Family Court. The data was used to train neural networks.

The system is currently being used by registrars (judicial assistants) and judges of the Family Court, mediators from a counselling service and four legal firms. The needs of each group of user is quite distinct and as a consequence the way the system is used and ensuing benefits differ. For example, registrars of the Family Court are required to attempt to mediate a settlement before a dispute is tried by a judge. This involves informing litigants about the basics of family law and judicial heuristics. Lawyers are less interested in educating their client but need to organise their arguments, validate their own predictions and be reminded of cases and statutes that would strengthen (or weaken) their arguments. Judges are required to arrive at an equitable outcome in the shortest amount of time possible.

The knowledge representation central to Split Up is a structure based on the argument structure proposed by

(Toulmin 1958). The argument based framework used in Split Up is not limited to rules and neural networks but can easily accommodate other forms of inferencing including fuzzy logic, inferential statistics and non-monotonic logic. The argument based structure we use has the following benefits:

- Explanations are generated independently from the reasoning method used to infer an outcome. Explanations are not traces of the inferencing and can be generated whether a neural network or a rule set produced the outcome.

- Knowledge acquisition from expert interview is facilitated because the argument structure enables domain experts to decompose the task of predicting a percentage split of marital assets into smaller sub-tasks. Each sub task can be modelled with a relatively small neural network that requires far fewer past cases to train than is the case for a large network.

2. The argument based frame in Split Up

(Toulmin 1958) suggested that reasoning that humans display in practice was distinct from the syllogistic reasoning that preoccupies logicians. Reasoning, in practice can be seen to conform to a simple structure now called a Toulmin argument structure (TAS). According to Toulmin an argument, regardless of the domain, makes a **claim** from **data**. The **claim** or assertion is made with a force called the **modality**. A **warrant** explains why the assertion follows from the datum and a **backing** provides evidential support for the validity of the warrant.

According to (Toulmin 1958), the warrant component of an argument is not the same as the universal premise (or rule) of syllogistic reasoning. Split Up presents a variation to the standard Toulmin Argument Structure in that a warrant represents a reason for why a data item is relevant to the argument. Furthermore, the Split Up structure differs from the Toulmin structure in its inclusion of an inference procedure used to infer a claim value from data variable values. In Split Up the inference procedure is a rule set for 15 arguments and a neural network for 20 others. Figure 1 represents the variant on the Toulmin structure used in the Split Up system.

Figure 1 illustrates three data items are directly relevant in determining a value on the claim variable. The inference procedure that is used to infer a claim value from data is a neural network. The reason that the data item "The husband has contributed more to the marriage" is relevant in the *percentage split* argument within Split Up is that a Statute makes this relevant. Section 79(4) of the Family Law Act obliges a decision maker to take past contributions into account. The reason the data item 'The marriage is of Z wealth' is relevant is that a precedent case has made it relevant. These reasons constitute a type of warrant we call the Relevance warrant. Figure 1 illustrates an additional type of warrant called the Inference warrant. This type of warrant represents reasons for why the inference procedure nominated is appropriate.

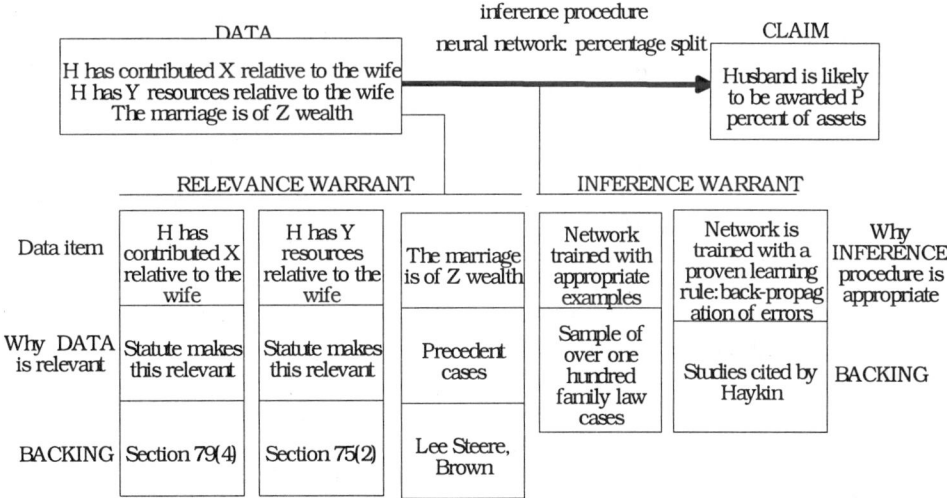

Figure 1. The culminating argument in Split Up: the percentage split argument

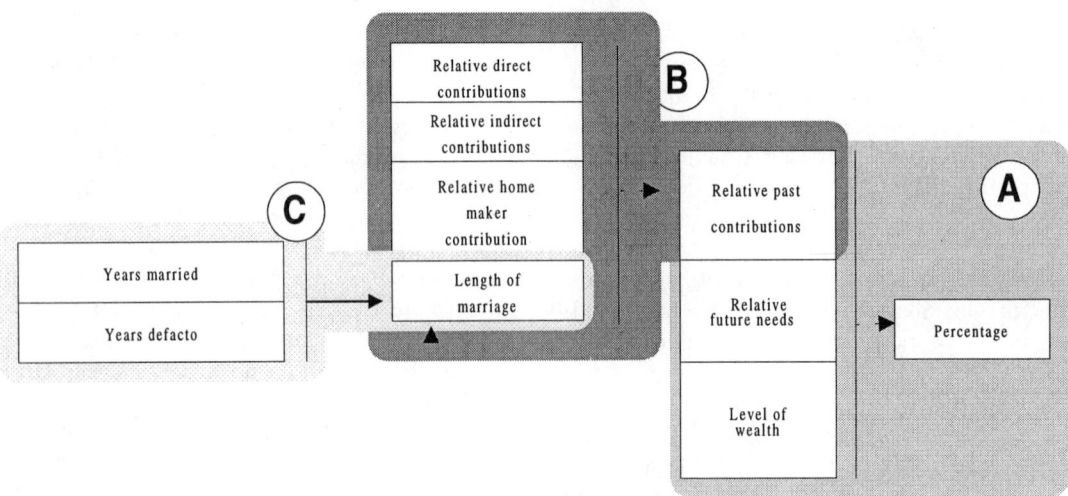

Figure 2. Data and Claim components of three arguments in Split Up

A chain (or tree) or reasoning emerges with the use of TAS because the claim of one argument is used as the data item of another as illustrated in Figure 2. This diagram represents only the data and claim components of three arguments. The data item *H has contributed X to the marriage* in Figure 1 is labelled the relative past contributions in Figure 2. This is the assertion of another argument (B) which has four data items. Knowledge is represented as a tree of arguments.

A central feature of the structure of each argument in Split Up is that the relevance warrant and the inference warrant in Split Up do not contribute to the generation of an outcome. A claim is inferred using the data items and inference procedure components. A claim is explained using the data and warrant components. The procedure used to generate an outcome is separated from the components used to explain the outcome.

The separation of reasoning and explanation advanced in Split Up relies very heavily on the concept of relevance. We adopt a pragmatic approach to the definition of relevance because a formal definition for relevance remains elusive. (van Dijk 1989) maintained that arguments can be made for the grounding of relevance in the pragmatics of natural language. He points out that well formedness is a concept central to syntax, truth or meaningfulness is a concept central to semantics, but the concept central to pragmatics is a appropriateness. Two propositions are relevant if a speaker considers their connection appropriate in a particular pragmatic context. A data item is relevant to an argument if a sentence expressing the reason for the relevance can be uttered and appear comprehensible. The hair colour of the judge was not considered relevant in any Split Up argument because domain experts could think of no reason that would make this feature relevant.

The structure used in Split Up omits the modality and rebuttal component of the original Toulmin structure. This was done for simplicity though future research is planned to develop the framework into a dialectical model that includes the rebuttal and modality.

The use of argumentation to represent knowledge and to model reasoning is a relatively recent phenomena in artificial intelligence. Researchers that use the original TAS as a knowledge representation framework include (Dick 1987), (Marshall 1989), (Bench-Capon, Lowes and McEnery 1991), (Clark 1991), (Johnson, Zualkernan and Tukey 1993) and (Ball 1994). Argumentation has also been used as the basis of a dialectical model with a non-monotonic logic by (Gordon 1993), (Farley and Freeman 1995), (Dung 1995) and with case based reasoning by (Ashley 1991).

3. Making and explaining inferences

Split Up is being used by judges, registrars, mediators and lawyers. Mediators in family law input a party's facts, peruse the resultant prediction and then explore the hierarchy of relevant data, warrant and backing factors with the party in order to inform and educate them. The facts of the other party are then input. Points of divergence between the two parties become obvious and the scale and loci of compromise are more easily identified. Split Up is currently being integrated into a general negotiation support system reported by (Bellucci and Zeleznikow 1997).

The Split Up system used data from commonplace and not landmark cases for neural network training. According to (Zeleznikow, Hunter and Stranieri 1997), commonplace cases are those which are not appealed and set no new or interesting precedent. Landmark cases are not useful for training networks because these cases change the way subsequent commonplace cases are decided.

Jurisprudential purists may object to the distinction between commonplace and landmark cases because a case that seems perfectly today may be used in the future to fundamentally alter a legal principal and thus be a landmark case. However, in practice the distinction between commonplace and landmark cases is used on a daily basis at least by the Family Court in order to decide which cases are to be published by Court reporting services. Over 95% of Australia's 48,000 annual divorces not considered interesting by the Family Court and are therefore not published.

The Split Up user is required to be sufficiently well versed with family law in order to identify a case as one which may potentially be significantly out of the ordinary and thus liable to incorrect predictions by Split Up. Thus the system is not recommended for use by users completely unfamiliar with family law.

Each group of users have a need different information is available to different users. This is accomplished in Split Up by placing the user in control of the explanation generation. The explanation facility is effective because it is tied closely to the argument frame but has limitations because it cannot engage the user in a dialogue.

The ability to explain reasoning is important for most tasks humans engage in. Explanations for predictions made by Split Up are under the guidance of the user. On presentation of a percentage output (or the claim of any argument) the user is presented with the data items that led to the prediction. She may:

- question the relevance of the data items in which case the relevance warrant and backing are retrieved from the argument frame. The warrant and backing elements often refer to precedent cases, or sections of a relevant statute. These references are implemented in Split Up as hypertext links to the full text.

- question the way in which the claim was inferred from the data in which case the inference procedure, warrant and backing are presented.

- question the data item value in which case the argument that produced that item as a claim is retrieved and the explanation proceeds with that argument.

Over fifty judges, lawyers, mediators and divorcees that have trialed Split Up report favourable comments regarding the predictions made and the explanations provided by the system. Furthermore, a comparison of Split Up outputs with a panel of eight family law specialists on the same cases demonstrated that Split Up predictions fell within the range of human prediction.

(Bench-Capon, Lowes and McEnery 1991) augment their logic programs with a Toulmin representation and report favourable user response from explanations generated in this way. The generation of an explanation directly from a TAS representation is an example of a types of explanatory system that (Moore 1995) labels the canned text approach. She notes the limitation of a canned text approach to explanation and advocates the generation of an explanatory dialogue that adapts to suit the needs and abilities of different users. We believe that the TAS representation will facilitate the generation of explanatory dialogue and aim to test this in future work. However, a critical component of any work with explanations involves their evaluation.

User satisfaction remains the most appealing criteria to assess an explanatory system. Current research aims to survey three groups of users; judges, registrars and mediators. The criteria for user satisfaction determination derive from (Buchanan *et al* 1995) and are information exchange, useability and attitude.

Another criteria for the evaluation of explanations involves a direct comparison of Split Up explanations with explanations offered in a judgement. This criteria is less appealing than user satisfaction because the explanatory content of judgements vary enormously. We believe this is largely because the explanation in a judgement is a monologue and confirms Moore's insistence on explanatory dialogues.

4. Knowledge acquisition

The argument based framework used in Split Up facilitated knowledge acquisition from experts. Domain experts are asked for factors most directly relevant to the claim in question; at the outset, to a percentage split judgement. The factor(s) elicited as relevant are entered as data components of the argument. The experts are then prompted for their reasons for the relevance of the factors and supporting evidence to justify their reasons. The inference procedure is not discussed during initial expert interviews. When an argument is complete with datum and relevance warrants, the knowledge engineer constructs new arguments for each of the datum components. Each new argument has, as claim, a data item of the completed argument.

In this way, complex knowledge is easily decomposed into conveniently sized frames. The expert is not necessarily burdened with the need to identify inference procedures at the same time as identifying relevant concepts. After the relevant factors for a claim are elicited, the knowledge engineer decides whether the manner in which factors combine are most plausibly captured by expert heuristics, or with a neural network trained with past data, a fuzzy rule, inferential statistics method or some other method.

As indicated above, 20 arguments were regarded as more suitable for a neural network inference method than a rule set. This was done on the basis of a classification scheme based on the extent to which experts believed an argument's data items combined in a structured way to infer a claim (the open textured dimension) and the extent to which experts believed the argument contained all items that could conceivably be regarded as relevant (we called this the boundedness dinmension in Stranieri *et al* 1998). For example according to experts there is a high liklihood that no additional data items will be found to be relevant for Argument C in Figure 2. Furthermore, experts could identify how the data items combined to yield a claim value. We call Argument C a narrow bounded argument and as such, conclude that a rule set derived from heuristics is adequate. Argument A is far more open textured because the way in which items are combined by judges seemed far more discretionary and opaque. Argument A was classified a Wide bounded argument and as a neural network was used as a consequence. We believe that tasks classified unbounded cannot be modelled using any techniques because experts suspect that data items important for an assertion are unknown at the present time.

The argument structure served as a template for the collection of data from actual cases. We had access to four hundred family law cases stored within the Melbourne registry of the Family Court of Australia. However, a large number of these cases involved custody issues in addition to property and could not be used because expert opinion indicated that property proceedings are certainly influenced by custody matters. One hundred and three cases involved only property. Two raters extracted data from these cases by reading the text of the judgment and recording values of ninety four template variables.

Each of the 20 networks were relatively small because of the task decomposition that the TAS enabled. We chose therefore to represent each data item as a bit string corresponding to value categories. For example, the claim of Argument C in Figure 2 had values 'very long', 'long', 'about average', 'short' and 'very short'. A long marriage was represented as bit string 01000.

Each network was trained using five fold cross validation on training/test set partitions of varying sizes using backpropagation of errors. We abandoned the number of test examples correctly classified as a performance criteria in order to avoid overfitting the data. Instead, we used a metric that measured the magnitude (but not the direction) of the error. A network output of 00001 erred by size 3 if the actual was output 01000. We ceased training when the average (over cross validation sets) proportion of errors of magnitude 3 (or more) was less than or equal to 3%.

Zeleznikow and Stranieri (1997) describe the process of collecting data to train networks within a TAS framework as one of few examples of knowledge discovery from databases (KDD) in the legal domain. Courts in the future may be enticed to collect data that reflects the reasoning processes used by judges in a computer friendly format so that KDD can be performed easily. Trend analysis can then become an automatic feature of any jurisdiction.

Split Up was written using the knowledgePro object-orientated, hypertext development environment for a PC/Windows platform. This environment was most convenient as each argument is implemented as an object and links within explanations were implemented as hypertext links. Neural networks were trained using public domain Unix based software tools but once trained a look-up table was created with each network. (Lewis, Stranieri and Zeleznikow 1997) describe a simple algorithm for the generation of, and retrieval from a look-up table. The look-up table stored the network output for every possible input and were transferred to the PC environment. This resulted in very fast inferences.

5. Conclusion

The TAS based knowledge representation structure used in Split Up represents a contribution to the conceptual modelling of any domain that is discretionary. Currently, the method used is being used for the integration of information retrieval with reasoning in a domain considerably more discretionary than family law; refugee law.

The Split Up system demonstrates a knowledge representation that facilitates the integration of rule based reasoning with neural networks. The flexibility inherent in this knowledge representation enables the generation of explanations that are useful to user's with different information needs. However, systems such as Split Up have to potential to make a significant impact on the practice of law.

7. References

Ashley, K. D. 1991. *Modelling legal argument: Reasoning with cases and hypotheticals.* Cambridge: MIT Press.

Ball, W.J. 1994. Using Virgil to analyse public policy arguments: a system based on Toulmin's informal logic. *Social Science Computer Review.* Vol: 12 Issue: 1 p. 26-37. Spring

Bellucci, E. and Zeleznikow, J. 1997. Family—Negotiator: an intelligent decision support system for negotiation in Australian Family Law. *Proceedings of the Fourth Conference of the International Society for Decision Support Systems,* Lausanne, International Society for Decision Support Systems:359-373.

Bench-Capon T.J.M, Lowes, D. and McEnery, A. M. 1991. Argument-based explanation of logic programs. Vol 4 No 3. Sept *Knowledge Based Systems* p177-183

Buchanan, B., Moore, J., Forsythe, D., Carenini, G., Ohlsson, S. and Banks, G., 1995. An Intelligent interactive system for delivering individualised information to patients. *Artificial Intelligence in Medicine.* 7 (1995) 117-154.

Clark, P . 1991. *A Model of Argumentation and Its Application in a Cooperative Expert System.* PhD thesis. Turing Institute. Department of Computer Science. University of Strathclyde. Glasgow.

Dick, J. P. 1991. *A conceptual, case-relation representation of text for intelligent retrieval.* Ph.D Thesis. University of Toronto. Canada.

Dung, Phan Minh. 1995. On the acceptability of arguments and its fundamental role in non-monotonic reasoning, logic programming and n-person games *Artificial Intelligence.* v. 7, issue 2., p. 321-357.

Edwards, L. and Huntley, A. J. K. 1992. Creating a Civil Jurisdiction Adviser. Law, *Computers and Artificial Intelligence*: 1(1), 5—40.

Farley, A. M and Freeman, K., 1995. Burden of Proof in Legal Argumentation. Proceedings of *Fifth International Conference on Artificial Intelligence and Law.* May 21-24. Boston. ACM Press, USA. p156-164.

Gordon , T. F. 1993. The Pleadings Game. *Proceedings of Fourth International Conference on Artificial Intelligence and Law.* Oxford. ACM Press. New York. pp10-17.

Johnson, P. E., Zualkernan, I. A. and Tukey, D. 1993. Types of expertise : an invariant of problem solving. *International Journal of Man Machine Studies*, v. 39, pp. 641.

Lewis, B., Stranieri, A and Zeleznikow, J. 1997. Scaling of neural network inferencing by efficient storage and retrieval of outputs *Applied computing 1997 : proceedings of the 1997 ACM Symposium on Applied Computing.* p. 10-14.

Marshall, C. C, 1989. Representing the structure of legal argument. *Proceedings of Second International Conference on Artificial Intelligence and Law.* ACM Press, USA. pp121-127.

Moore, J 1995. *Participating in Explanatory Dialogues. Interpreting and Responding to Questions in Context.* MIT Press. Cambridge MA.

Stranieri, A. and Zeleznikow, J. 1992. SPLIT-UP—Expert system to determine spousal property distribution on litigation in the Family Court of Australia. *Proceedings of Artificial Intelligence Conference (Australia)-92*, Hobart: World Scientific, 51-56.

Stranieri, A., Zeleznikow, J., Gawler, M. and Lewis, B. 1998. A hybrid—neural approach to the automation of legal reasoning in the discretionary domain of family law in Australia. To appear in *Artificial Intelligence and Law.*

Toulmin, S. 1958. *The uses of argument.* Cambridge: Cambridge University Press.

van Dijk, T. A. 1989. *Relevance in logic and grammar.* in *Directions in relevant logic* / J. Norman and R. Sylvan (Eds.). p. 25-57.

Zeleznikow, J. Hunter, D. and Stranieri, A. 1997. Using cases to build intelligent decision support systems. in Meersman, R. and Mark, L, *Database Applications Semantics.* Chapman Hall, pp443-460.

Zeleznikow, J. and Stranieri, A. 1997. Knowledge discovery in the Split-Up project. *Proceedings of Sixth International Conference on Artificial Intelligence and Law*, ACM: 89-97.

An Expert System for Alarm System Planning

Akira Tsurushima, Kenji Urushima, Daigo Sakata,
Hiroyuki Date, Masatomo Nakata, Yoshinobu Adachi, and Kazuhisa Takahashi
Artificial Intelligence Department SECOM Intelligent Systems Laboratory
Mitaka Tokyo 181, Japan
Email: akira@ai.isl.secom.co.jp

Abstract

This paper discusses the design and implementation of ESSPL, an expert system which generates security plans for alarm systems (Figure 1). Security planning is the task of determining an efficient layout of sensors, alarms, and the associated wiring for a building. ESSPL uses Rule Based System technology to generate a plan and Constraint Based technology to position the alarm equipment. A Constraint Logic Programming Language (CONTA) is developed to solve the positioning problem.

ESSPL proved to be an excellent tool in automatic planning in laboratory tests. Field tests were also carried out and examined whether there is a drawback to use ESSPL in the real world context. This is also discussed in this paper.

Problem Description

SECOM Co., Ltd. is the leading security service company in Japan, providing alarm system services to more than 400,000 subscribers over the country. When a sensor detects an abnormal situation, the alarm system sends a signal to the central monitoring station. A trained response officer is then dispatched to respond to the situation. To provide high quality alarm services, the remote sensors and equipment layout for a building is crucial. This design activity is called security planning. [1]

Security Planning

Security planning is the problem of determining an efficient arrangement of alarm equipment for a building based on an analysis of its potential risks. Poor planning results in an increase of false alarms and failures to alarm, decreasing the overall quality of security services.

Security planning is accomplished by solving three sub-problems; 1) alarm zoning, 2) sensor arrangement, and 3) system integration.

Alarm zoning is the process of dividing the building into several security zones depending on the building usage.

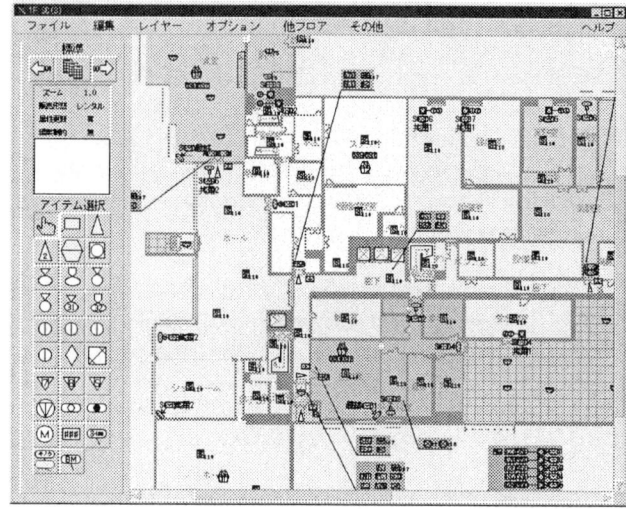

Figure 1: ESSPL: The Main Window

This allows customers to arm (unarm) all of the alarms in a given zones independently of other zones.

Sensor arrangement determines the best layout of sensors for a building. In this subproblem, there are two important decisions: 1) selection of the proper sensor for the situation and 2) positioning the sensor in the most appropriate location.

System integration connects all of the sensors which are distributed throughout the building and introduces all other necessary equipment to the security plan. This task involves determining security circuits by grouping sensors, selecting proper control equipment and peripherals, assigning addresses to the sensors and connecting all of the equipment.

Traditionally security planning has been undertaken by human engineers. However, security planning is a very complicated design task which requires experience and expertise especially for large scale buildings. Therefore there are only a few engineers who are able to design large security plans. This expert system was developed to overcome these limitations.

---

[1] In this paper, the term planning or plan is used in a somewhat different manner than is typically used in the AI community. The definition is close to that of design or configuration.

Copyright 1998, American Association for Artificial Intelligence (www.aaai.org). All right reserved.

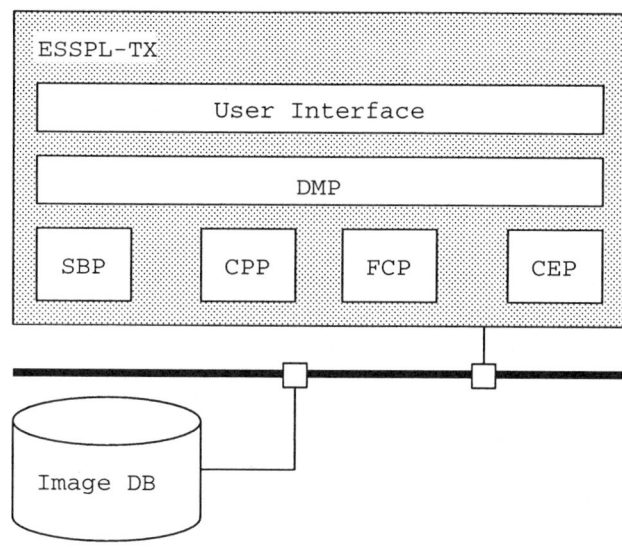

Figure 2: System Architecture

ESSPL : An Expert System for Security PLanning

There is relatively little work that has been published about the application of AI technology to the security field (Ward & Sena 1986; Lamont 1988) except in the field of computer security. Our work is an unique attempt to apply AI technology to the security service industry.

ESSPL (Expert System for Security PLanning) is an expert system which designs a security plan for SECOM ALARM SYSTEM, an alarm system specially designed for large scale office buildings and multi occupancy buildings.

Figure 2 shows the system architecture of ESSPL. First, ESSPL takes a raster image of a building floor plan from the image database. Using the user interface subsystem, the ESSPL user traces the basic architectural elements (e.g. rooms, doors, windows, etc.) of a building on the raster image. This template becomes the input to ESSPL and from this point on, the system creates a security plan without any user intervention. The completed security plan is then output as a printout.

ESSPL consists of the following six subsystems:
1. User Interface (UI)
2. Data Management (DMP)
3. Zone Planning (SBP[2])
4. Sensor Planning (CPP[3] & FCP[4])
5. Control Equipment Planning (CEP)

The knowledge base subsystems (SBP, CPP, FCP and CEP) and the data management subsystem (DMP) are implemented using a combination of CLIPS, SICStus Prolog, and CONTA, a constraint programming language developed for this project. The UI subsystem is implemented in Tcl/Tk.

---
[2]SBP—Security Block Planning
[3]CPP—Crime Prevention Planning
[4]FCP—Fire Containment Planning

User Interface

As shown in Figure 1 ESSPL has a CAD like user interface with the following functions:
1. Create building data by tracing a floor plan
2. Edit the resulting template
3. Display the result

Since the UI has almost all basic CAD capabilities, an user can design a plan manually without using the automatic planning function. These CAD capabilities are used to create building data and to modify the planning results.

In this project, one of the major design issues was system flexibility due to the following reasons:

- New products are frequently introduced, therefore ESSPL must be updated correspondingly.
- It is not possible to anticipate all necessary types of rooms since there are almost a limitless number of types.

For the first problem, the UI refers to a separate database of alarm system equipment which allows the program to be independent of equipment information. When new equipment is introduced, all the users need to do is to update the database, which does not require program modification.

For the second problem, the UI has a room type attribute table. In ESSPL, all room types are defined with respect to the following nine planning attributes:

1. appropriateness as a main final exit
2. appropriateness as a private zone
3. appropriateness as a entry route
4. appropriateness for general equipment placement
5. appropriateness for control equipment placement
6. appropriateness for monitoring equipment placement
7. level of intrusion risk in a lower floor
8. level of intrusion risk in a higher floor
9. type of fire detector

For example, room type 'office' is defined as 1. BAD, 2. EXCELLENT, 3. BAD, 4. GOOD, 5. FAIR, 6. FAIR, 7. LEVEL 3, 8. LEVEL 2, 9. SMOKE DETECTOR. Since ESSPL does not refer directly to the room types but rather these attributes, users can introduce new room types by setting these attributes. In this way ESSPL can handle new room types correctly.

Zone Planning (SBP)

Zone planning arranges the rooms in the building into several spatial units (zones) and determines each of their final exits. When a customer arms a zone (i.e., all sensors in the zone are switched on), they must leave the zone from the final exit, otherwise the alarms will activate. Zones are classified into three categories: private, public, and independent. Zones are determined by the following factors:

- room type attributes and door types
- building topology (how the rooms are connected by doors)
- customer request

Innovative Applications   1153

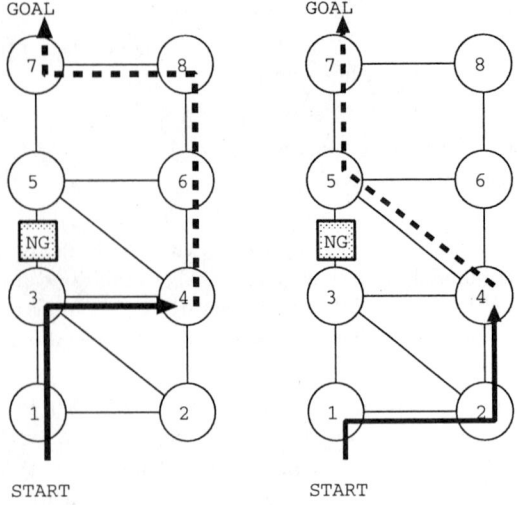

Figure 3: An example of the two paths through the same node (node 4)

The key element in zone planning is in determining the public zone. A public zone is a section of a building that anyone in the building is approved to enter. A public zone can only be armed after all other private zones are armed. Only one public zone is allowed per building owing to the system specification, and the final exit of this zone is called the main final exit of the building.

When determining a public zone, it is important to ensure that a customer can leave the building without entering any other private zones. Once a public zone is properly determined, arranging private zones may be trivial. The SBP subsystem searches for a route which connects the final exit of each private zone to the main final exit of the building. This is accomplished by a modified branch and bound algorithm with an evaluation function

$$f(n_i) = f(n_{i-1}) + C(n_i)$$

where n_i is the i-th room on the path. $C(n_i)$ is determined by the value of the 'appropriateness as a entry route' room type attribute of n_i as follows:

$$C(n_i) = \begin{cases} 20 & \text{if value} = \text{BAD} \\ 5 & \text{if value} = \text{FAIR} \\ 2 & \text{if value} = \text{GOOD} \\ 1 & \text{if value} = \text{EXCELLENT} \end{cases}$$

In ESSPL, an user can select any door as the final exit of a private zone. If a door is selected to be the final exit, the two rooms connected by the door cannot be members of the same zone. Therefore this condition must be treated as a constraint on the search procedure. This constraint is called **FE-constraint** and the set of nodes which are affected by FE-constraint the **prohibition node set** of the path.

For example, the graph in Figure 3 shows the room topology in a building, where the nodes and vertices represents rooms and doors, respectively. The box containing characters 'NG' represents the FE-constraint. In this example, nodes 3 and 5 are affected by this; therefore they both cannot be members of the same path. Suppose a search proceeds through nodes 1, 3 and 4. Node 5 is now a member of the prohibition node set because node 3 is on the path. Therefore, the path must proceed through nodes 6, 8 and 7 (as shown in the left hand side).

Suppose a search proceeds through nodes 1, 2 and 4. In this case, since node 3 is not on the path, the prohibition node set is empty, allowing node 5 to be placed on the path. Therefore the rest of the path can proceed through nodes 5 and 7 (as shown in the right hand side).

This example shows that the prohibited nodes are dynamically changes as the search proceeds. The whole search procedure is as follows.

Search (start goal)

1. Form a queue of partial paths. Let the initial queue consists of the zero-length path from the start node

2. While the queue is not empty repeat the following procedure

    (a) Remove the first path from the queue
    (b) Form new paths from the removed path by extending one step
    (c) Return the path if the goal is reached. Stop the procedure
    (d) Remove the paths that violate the FE-constraints
    (e) For each remaining path, do one of the following:
        i. Do nothing if there is a path which has the same last extended node, the same prohibition node set and a higher $f(n_i)$ value in the queue
        ii. Else, remove all the paths which have the same last extended node, the same prohibition node set and a lower $f(n_i)$ value from the queue. Insert the path into the queue and sort it by the evaluation function in ascending order

3. Report failure and stop the procedure

The FE-constraint is applied in step 2-(d). Since two paths having the same last extended node may results in two different solutions due to the FE-constraint, the queue must hold all paths rather than just the last extended nodes. Furthermore, the optimal path cannot be determined until the goal is reached. This makes the search procedure inefficient, especially for large graphs. Step 2-(e) handles this problem by pruning non-optimal paths from the queue.

Sensor Planning (CPP & FCP)

SECOM ALARM SYSTEM can detect two types of emergencies with its sensors: fire and intrusion. Security planning for both are carried out in a similar manner, therefore this section focuses on intrusion only. Sensors for detecting intrusion are classified into two categories:

Direct Detection Sensors Sensors in this category usually monitor a specific item, for example a door, shutter, window, etc. These sensors are mounted directly onto the target. This category includes magnetic reed switches, glass break sensors, etc.

Indirect Detection Sensors Sensors in this category detect intrusions by monitoring a predetermined area. This type of sensor is mounted away from the target. This category includes photoelectric beams, passive infrared sensors, etc.

These sensors are used in conjunction with the following detection methods:

Direct Outer Detection Intrusion detection at the boundaries of a building by a direct detection sensor

Indirect Outer Detection Intrusion detection just inside building boundaries by an indirect detection sensor

Inner Detection Intrusion detection inside of a building.

Target Detection Intrusion detection by monitoring specific items.

The sensor planning procedure consists of the following four steps: 1) Target Identification, 2) Threat Analysis, 3) Sensor Selection, and 4) Sensor Positioning.

Target Identification

Rooms and doors which are especially vulnerable from the viewpoint of intrusion risks are identified in this task. For example all entrances to the building are potentially high risk. All targets identified here are candidates for monitoring by alarm equipment.

Threat Analysis

Depending on the room and door type and the location of the room, security levels are assigned to each room; these levels designate which detection method is required, as follows:

Level 0 No detection is necessary

Level 1 Direct outer detection should be applied

Level 2 Indirect outer detection should be applied

Level 3 Direct or indirect outer detection should be applied

Level 4 Inner detection and either direct or indirect outer detection should be applied

Threat analysis determines detection methods for each target depending on the security level of the adjacent rooms.

Due to physical constraints, it may not be possible to install the proper sensors for the detection method which the threat analysis determines as necessary. In such a case, the detection method assigned to the target will be changed to another method or shifted to adjacent rooms depending on the situation.

On the basis of these detection methods, specific sensing techniques, e.g. closure-confirmation, shutter-control, etc., are assigned to each target.

Sensor Selection and Positioning

Sensor selection determines the type of sensor which can accomplish the designated sensing technique. The possible selections are:

- Direct Detection Sensors
- Indirect Detection Sensors
- A contact embedded in electric locks
- A contact embedded in elevator doors

The CPP subsystem has declarative knowledge about sensing techniques for different types of sensors. For example, to correlate the sensor 'SHTxxx' with targets which require closure confirmation and shutter control sensing techniques,

```
(selection-db DIRECT ENTRY-OBJECT ANY SHTxxx
 closure-confirmation shutter-control)
```

knowledge entry is declared.

The sensor positioning task determines the number of sensors required to monitor the targets and their coordinates within the building. The details are discussed in a later section.

Control Equipment Planning (CEP)

Equipment Selection

After sensor planning, the equipment required to integrate the sensors into an alarm system is introduced into the security plan, according to the following procedure:

1. Identify locations for equipment installation
2. Assign functional roles to each location to achieve desired system operation
3. Introduce system equipment which fulfills the functional role

Locations identified in the first step are as follows:

- inside and outside of the final exits of each zone
- building manager rooms
- rooms or spaces on each floor to keep the equipment out of view

Each location plays an important part in achieving alarm system operation. For example, a card reader is necessary near the exterior of a final exit to unarm the alarms in the zone and unlock the electric locking mechanism. The functional roles UNARMING and UNLOCKING can be assigned to the location. A device, in this case a card reader, can be placed at the location because it has the matching functional roles of UNARMING and UNLOCKING.

Equipment instances are created by the following procedures:

1. Determine the equipment model
2. Determine how much equipment is required for the situation
3. Determine installation location
4. Create equipment instances

Equipment Connections

System equipment introduced to the plan must be connected together for the system to function properly. SECOM ALARM SYSTEM incorporates a LAN for several devices, thus interconnections between those devices is relatively straightforward. However for other devices, the connections must be made in an arbitrary manner. In addition to the sensors, SECOM ALARM SYSTEM is able to control a portion of the building facilities (e.g. electric locks, automatic doors, shutters, elevators, etc.). For example, when a sensor detects a fire, all the electric locks in the building should be unlocked automatically to allow the occupants to evacuate. Since there are many variations in this kind of facility control, they are carried out through ad hoc connections. If all of these ad hoc connections are put into rules, the resulting program would be cumbersome. To avoid hard-coding the connection knowledge, simple case based reasoning (CBR) techniques are used to implement equipment connections. Therefore, we can maintain the connection knowledge separately from the program. The following is an example of a case.

```
(defcase case1
  "air-conditioning and light control"
  (deftype INTERLOCKING)

  (defcontext ZONE ANY-ZONE)
  (defcontext GOAL CONTROL-LIGHT)
  (defcontext GOAL CONTROL-AIR-CONDITIONING)

  (defactor *POT PO-T0210)
  (defactor *RLY RL-Y5700)
  (defactor *LIGHT MT-R0300)
  (defactor *AIR MT-R0310)

  (defrelation BLAN *POT)
  (imply (defrelation BINARY *POT *RLY)
         "set-signal")
  (defrelation BINARY *RLY *LIGHT)
  (defrelation BINARY *RLY *AIR)
)
```

In this example, equipment to be connected is represented by the *defactor* statements and the connections are represented by the *defrelation* statements. Cases are transformed to instances and stored in working memory prior to reasoning. For equipment connections, the closest case is selected by case retrieval rules and a similarity function. Then the connection rules compare the selected case with the equipment instances introduced by the equipment selection rules and then establish the necessary connections. The resulting connections are presented in the system diagram (Figure 4).

In ESSPL, CBR is not a major inference mechanism, using only the case retrieval feature in the CBR paradigm. Thus some advanced features such as learning, case adaptation or maintenance are not employed.

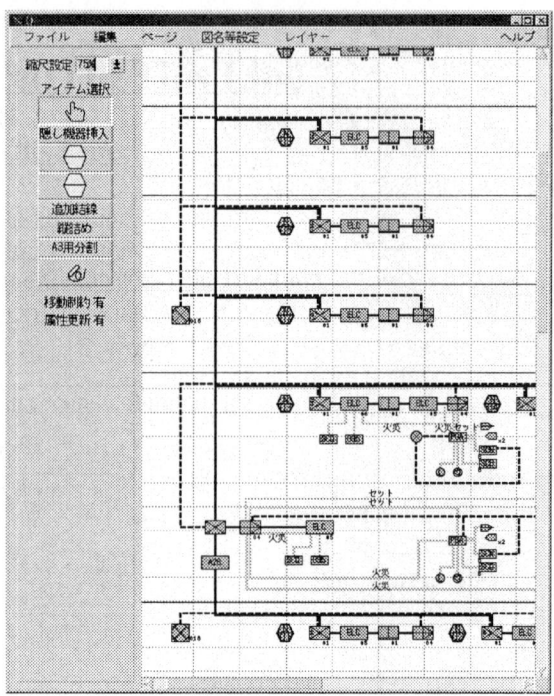

Figure 4: System Diagram Editor

Replanning Mechanism

Designing a building requires many changes, therefore security planning is a long term project. Whenever the design of a building is modified, the security plan must be updated to reflect the modification. Therefore, the replanning mechanism is an essential ESSPL feature. This mechanism must be invoked in the following three cases:

1. The building design is modified
2. Parts of a completed security plan is modified by the user
3. Part of a security plan is predefined by the user

For the first case, the plan must be updated as the building design changes. ESSPL deletes the portion of the plan which was affected by the modification and replans the location so that it is consistent with the rest of the plan.

In the second case, ESSPL removes the equipment which became unnecessary due to the user action. In this case, ESSPL does not introduce any new equipment to the plan, even if it is determined that it is required. This is sometimes required due to the terms of the customer contract. ESSPL is tolerant of some inconsistency arising from the user editing.

In the third case, ESSPL simply finishes the partially completed plan. The user input is considered as a constraint in this case.

In ESSPL, the replanning is handled by the DMP subsystem, shown in Figure 5. The user may stop the system during the execution, display and modify the partial solution, and resume the execution. Most likely the user intervention will conflicts with the partial plan that was being computed, therefore the DMP subsystem resolves the

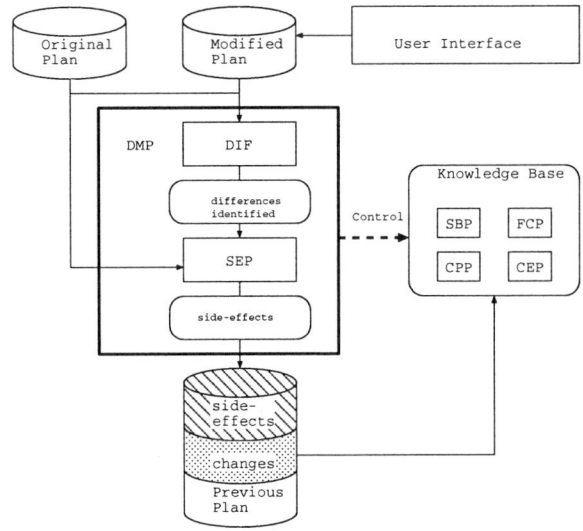

Figure 5: Replanning Mechanism

conflict automatically and attempts to keep the reasoning sound.

The DMP subsystem mediates between the user interface and the planning knowledge bases (SBP, CPP, FCP and CEP). It has two important roles:

1. Control the execution of planning knowledge bases
2. Prepare the proper input files for planning knowledge bases

The DMP subsystem consists of two parts, the DIF and SEP. The DIF compares the original plan to the user modified plan and identifies the changes which were made. These changes are translated into operators such as ADD, DELETE, CHANGE and HIDE.

The SEP identifies any side effects as a result of applying the operators to the original plan. The side effects are then translated into operators. This process is repeated until all side effects have been identified.

Finally, the DMP modifies and recreates the instances of the original plan on the basis of these changes and side effects. These new instances then become the input for the next execution of the knowledge bases.

Uses of AI Technology

Sensor Positioning by Geometric Constraints

In order to place the sensors, ESSPL must calculate the exact placement of the sensor in the security plan. In ESSPL, the Sensor Placement Subsystem (SPS) deals with this task. Since CLIPS does not have the capability to handle geometric or numeric constraints, a constraint logic programming language CONTA (Urushima 1993c; 1993a; 1993b) was developed to build the SPS.

In the case of indirect detection sensors, calculating their coordinates is difficult due to the number of geometric constraints to consider. For passive infrared sensors, we must consider the following constraints to find a suitable position:

1. Sensor must be placed inside of a room
2. All targets must be in its coverage area
3. Maintenance area is required
4. Coverage area should exclude windows
5. Placement near a corner of a room

To calculate the coordinates, all of these constraint must be considered and solved. The first and the second constraints are strong constraints, thus a solution must satisfy these two. On the other hand, the rest are weak constraints, thus a solution should satisfy them only if possible.

The SPS generates a spatial solution (coordinates) and checks whether the solution satisfies the above constraints. If the solution satisfies all of the constraints, it is adopted. Otherwise the geometric constraints are transformed to a set of numerical equations and solved by CONTA's constraint satisfaction capability.

CONTA : A Constraint Programming Language

CONTA is a general purpose constraint logic programming language designed to solve the sensor layout problem, developed on top of Prolog. CONTA can handle numeric equalities and inequalities as constraints like other Prolog clauses. A programmer needs only to state numerical equations with Prolog clauses in their program. Without giving the algorithm to solve these equations, CONTA automatically calculates a solution which satisfies the constraints by using the constraint solver (CS-Solver). CONTA has the following features:

- CONTA can handle linear equalities and inequalities
- CONTA has the capability to resolve conflicts between constraints
- CONTA looks for a solution which satisfies as many constraints as possible if no solution satisfies all constraints
- The programmer can set the strength of each constraint
- The programmer can state their preferences of feasible solutions with respect to the constraints.

These features allow CONTA to be useful for many engineering applications such as scheduling and layout problems. CONTA can handle the following three types of constraints.

1. **required constraint**

   All feasible solution must satisfy this constraint

2. **desired constraint**

   A feasible solution can may satisfy this constraint if possible. A solution which violates this constraints is still feasible.

3. **preferred constraint**

   If there is more than one feasible solution, the solutions are returned in the order preference as determined by this constraint.

These constraints are expressed in equalities and inequalities by using the following expressions:

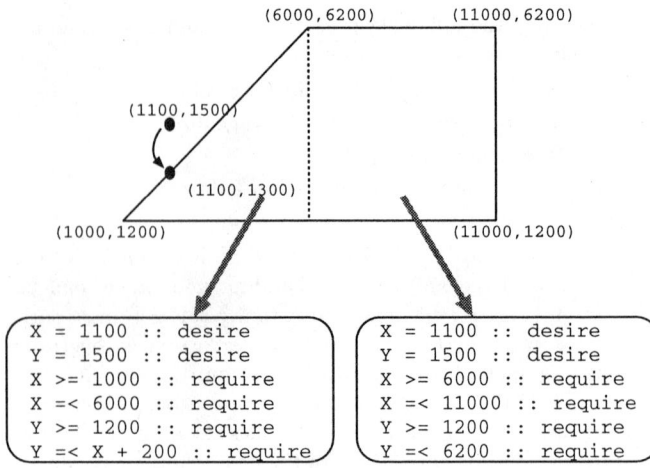
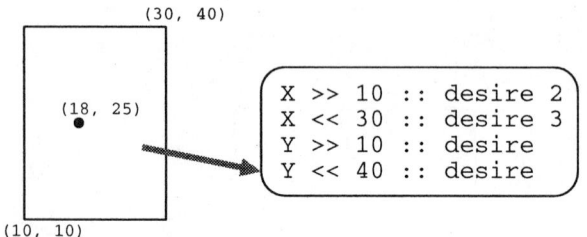

Figure 6: Positioning by CONTA

Figure 7: Example of diverging constraints

1. << : **diverging inequality sign**

   Inequality with preference for a larger difference between the right hand side and left hand side

2. ~< : **converging inequality sign**

   Inequality with preference for a smaller difference between the right hand side and left hand side

3. =< : **unrestricted inequality sign**

   Inequality with no preference

4. = : **equality sign**

   Equality

These constraints can also have weights. The programmer can declare the strength of the preference by setting a weight for each constraint. For example, if there are two conflicting constraints with the same weight, CONTA will generate a solution "in the middle" of the constraints. On the other hand, if one constraint has a higher weight than the other, the solution will be closer (in the case of converging inequality) to the constraint with the larger weight. The typical constraint

```
X >> 30 :: desire 5
```

implies that the variable X should be greater than 30 if possible. The greater it is, the better.

The CS-Solver transforms these numerical constraints into a linear programming standard form and solves them using the Simplex algorithm. (Urushima 1993b)

An example of positioning a passive infrared sensor in a room is shown in Figure 6. The polygon represents the desired area to position the sensor considering the required maintenance area. Supposing the spatial solution (1100, 1500) failed to satisfy the inside-of-a-room constraint, CONTA generates the positioning constraints by considering the following:

1. The solution should be inside of the polygon
2. The solution should be close to the spatial solution

The polygon is divided into two simpler polygons and procedure is applied to each. The above constraints are transformed into numeric constraints as shown in the boxes. The CS-Solver solves these constraints and returns the best solution (1100, 1200).

The following is an example of CONTA code to achieve this. The coordinates are found by proving the CONTA goal conta_inside_room.

```
conta_inside_room
    (Point, [[XAREA, YFOOT, YTOP]|T], [X,Y]) :-
    conta_near(Point, X, Y),
    conta_inside_x(XAREA, X),
    conta_larger_y(YFOOT, X, Y),
    conta_smaller_Y(YTOP, X, Y)
    ;
    conta_inside_room(Point, T, [X, Y]).
conta_near([Xp, Yp], X, Y) :-
    X = Xp :: desire,
    Y = Yp :: desire.
conta_inside_x([Xmin, Xmax], X) :-
    Xmin =< X :: require,
    X =< Xmax :: require.
conta_larger_y([X1, Y1, X2, Y2], X, Y) :-
    A is (Y1 - Y2)/(X1 - X2),
    Y >= A * (X - X1) + Y1 :: require.
conta_smaller_y([X1, Y1, X2, Y2], X, Y) :-
    A is (Y1 - Y2)/(X1 - X2),
    Y =< A * (X - X1) + Y1 :: require.
```

The use of diverging inequalities can be seen when placing a smoke detector. A smoke detector must be placed away from any walls. Figure 7 shows how the weights attached to the constraints affect the solution (18, 25).

Evaluation

Tests on Real Data

The ESSPL execution has been evaluated using customer data. ESSPL has shown to be of significant advantage when generating security plans from scratch. On average, for a small sized, 7 story office building, a human engineer took approximately 8 hours to complete the plan. A plan with equivalent quality was achieved in 1.5 hours with ESSPL. It is worth noting that 95% of the time was spent constructing the input data. The execution time to actually generate the plan was less than five minutes. In a large sized 15 story building, ESSPL took 2.5 hours while a human engineer took 2 days. The actual execution time was less than 15 minutes.

The Experiences of Field Tests

Field tests were carried out in a security planning department which deals with large-scale security plans. In field tests, ESSPL proved advantageous for automatic planning. However few drawbacks were found in using ESSPL in the real world context.

1. A large effort was required to construct the input data by tracing the floor plans. Most of the engineers in the department felt that it was difficult to use and cumbersome.

2. The side effects of the replanning mechanism when the user edited the plan were unpredictable, thus the user often found undesirable side effects at the end of the replanning process.

Even though few drawbacks are exist, we can conclude that ESSPL is very useful for security planning. We are expecting to utilize it in the department after a few modifications.

Future Directions

After examination of the field test results, the following policies were devised:

1. Automatic conflict resolution of the user input is not useful in most cases, since the users tend to be puzzled by the unpredictable side effects. Instead of one function which does everything, smaller functions, e.g. addressing, zone planning, etc., which give the users finer control over the planning process will be provided.

2. Currently, there is no way to reduce the effort required to construct the input data necessary for automatic zone and sensor planning. Although these two functions are the primary tasks in security planning, we have abandoned the use of these functions at this time.

Recently, the International Alliance for Interoperability (IAI) has proposed the Industrial Foundation Class (IFC), which is a high-level common language for building complexes. We are expecting to receive most building data in the IFC format in the near future, at which point, the problem of constructing the input data will become negligible and the automatic planning function of ESSPL will have full play of its ability.

Acknowledgements

The authors wish to express our appreciation to Yasuyuki Tauchi, Muneaki Saitoh and Dr. ShinIchiro Hashimoto of SECOM Intelligent Systems Laboratory, for their support and encouragement. In particular, we would like to thank Janelle Jurek Kozak, Joshua Hornik, Linda Chen and Dr. Taesik Jeong for their work and dedication to the project.

We are grateful to Yoshikazu Shinoda for reading the paper and providing many helpful suggestions.

References

Lamont, A. 1988. A computer model for identifying security system upgrades. In *Institute of Nuclear Materials Managment 29th Annual Meeting*.

Urushima, K. 1993a. A Constraint Logic Programming Language CONTA Ver 1.3 : Detailed Specification. Technical Report AI-93-014, SECOM Intelligent Systems Laboratory. in Japanese (unpublished).

Urushima, K. 1993b. A Constraint Logic Programming Language CONTA Ver 1.3 : Functional Specification. Technical Report AI-93-016, SECOM Intelligent Systems Laboratory. in Japanese (unpublished).

Urushima, K. 1993c. A Constraint Logic Programming Language CONTA Ver 1.3 : Outer Specification. Technical Report AI-93-013, SECOM Intelligent Systems Laboratory. in Japanese (unpublished).

Ward, J. D., and Sena, K. J. 1986. Senlex : Sensor Layout Expert System. In *Proceedings 1986 International Carnahan Conference on Security Technology: Electric Crime Countermeasures*.

Conversation Machines for Transaction Processing

Wlodek Zadrozny, Catherine Wolf, Nanda Kambhatla, Yiming Ye

IBM T.J Watson Research Center,
30 Saw Mill River Road,
Hawthorne, NY 10532
{wlodz, cwolf, nanda, yiming}@watson.ibm.com

Abstract

We have built a set of integrated AI systems (called conversation machines) to enable transaction processing over the telephone for limited domains like stock trading and banking. The conversation machines integrate the state-of-the-art technologies from computer telephony, continuous speech recognition, natural language processing and human-computer interaction. Users can interact with these systems using natural language to process simple transactions. We are currently installing a prototype conversation machine at a customer site (a large bank), while continuing research on each of the modules mentioned above and their integration.

In this paper, we describe the architecture of conversation machines and explain the design choices related to natural language dialog design, speech recognition errors, and human-computer interaction. We also discuss our experience with the new "market-driven research" methodology currently being tested at our company, of which the conversation machines project is an example. Our experience suggests that with this new methodology we can build integrated natural language dialog systems, even when working with error-prone recognition engines and imperfect grammars, by designing the dialog flow to reduce the likelihood of errors, and to enable quick error recovery. In this process, having a customer allows us to make more realistic design choices.

1. Introduction

In the past few years we have developed a set of integrated artificial intelligence (AI) systems, called conversation machines, that allow users to communicate with a computer using spoken language; for example, to make inquiries, pay bills or transfer money from a bank over the telephone. Other tasks we have dealt with include stock trading, fast food ordering, managing appointments in an on line calendar, and payroll processing. All of these tasks involve an integration of computer telephony interfaces, continuous speech recognition, spoken language understanding in small, but non-trivial, domains, and huma n computer interaction.

In a new model of research at our company, we are

Copyright © 1998, American Association for Artificial Intelligence (www.aaai.org). All rights reserved.

installing a prototype Conversation Machine for banking at one of the large American banks, while continuing research on each of the afore-mentioned modules and their integration. This system differs from other such systems in the market with respect to
- the quality and range of the human factors engineering in the system and
- the diversity of the number of sentences accepted by the system (for instance, the natural language grammar of our system accepts over 50 million natural language queries, as opposed to a few thousands for most such systems in the market).

We are planning to conduct trials with customers of the bank in 2-3 months to continue the research on human computer interaction issues and natural language dialog issues.

The Conversation Machine for banking allows customers to interact with their bank accounts by telephone, using spoken language dialog. The customers can speak requests in regular English, and the system performs the requested actions, asking for additional information if necessary. The customers can use any English phrase to request information or perform an action without having to remember a menu, as illustrated in the following three dialog fragments:

I'd like to transfer some money to my checking account.
To make sure I understand the amount of money to transfer, please enter the amount...
3 5 0 0 0 #
I am about to transfer $350.00 from your savings to your checking account. Do you want me to do it?
Yes.
Transfer completed. Your new savings balance is $1011.00. Your new checking balance is $1100.67.

Pay my phone, insurance and electricity bills.
I am about to pay $224.00 for your phone, insurance, and electricity bills. Do you want me to do it?
Yes.
I have paid your phone, insurance, and electricity bills. Your new checking balance is $507.00.

Mastercard and insurance bills please.
Your MasterCard balance is $125.00. Your insurance balance is $43.00. What else can I do for you?
Pay them.
...

In the next section, we describe the architecture and components of a Conversation Machine. In section 3, we discuss some of the tools we built to support research and development on the Conversation Machine. We then describe some of the lessons we learnt during the research, design and field trials of the conversation machine and present our conclusions.

2. Architecture of Conversation Machines

In this section, we describe the architecture of a Conversation Machine and briefly describe its component units.

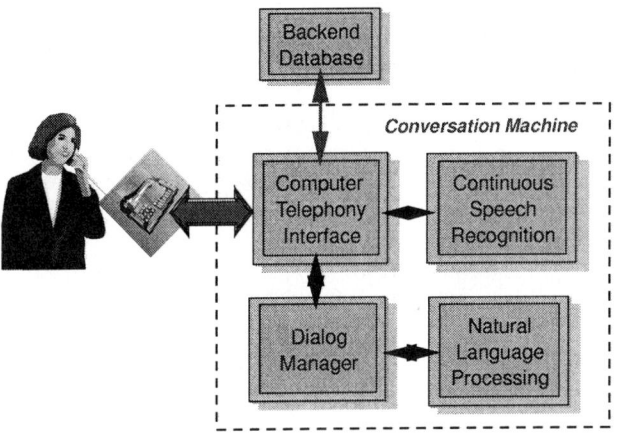

2.1 Architecture of a Conversation Machine

Figure 1 shows a schematic block diagram of a Conversation Machine (CM). A user interacts with the CM using a telephone. A computer telephony interface (CTI) unit answers the call and passes on the user's speech utterances to the continuous speech recognition engine. The speech recognition engine parses the speech utterances into sentences and passes them back to the CTI. The CTI then sends the recognized sentences to the dialog manager (DM) which, in turn sends the sentence to be analyzed by a natural language processing (NLP) unit. The NLP unit parses each sentence using either a *construction grammar* or a *semantic grammar* and returns an attribute value list called a *semantic signature* to the DM. (The details are given below). The dialog manager then determines the appropriate response to the user's speech utterance based on filled values of the semantic signature returned by the NLP unit. This action/response is communicated to the CTI unit which plays the corresponding prompts to the user along with (if necessary) some information obtained from a backend database (for instance, in response to a query asking for checking balance). The central role of CTI in the current system is due to the fact that it comes with all necessary communication devices.

2.2 System components

The Conversation Machine consists of four major modules: a Computer Telephony Interface, a Continuous Speech Recognition engine, a Natural Language Processing unit, and a Dialog Manager. The modules communicate through TCP/IP. The system is modular and runs on an RS/6000 model 390 under AIX.

Computer Telephony Interface: We used the IBM DT/6000, version 1.6 (to be replaced soon by version 2.1) system for providing a computer telephony interface (CTI). The CTI unit is responsible for
- answering a call by a user,
- sending the user's utterance to the continuous speech recognition engine,
- receiving a recognized sentence from the speech engine, and sending it to the dialog manager, and
- playing appropriate prompts to the user as directed by the dialog manager, by accessing the back-end database (if necessary).

Continuous Speech Recognition: Our system uses IBM Continuous Speech Recognition System for Telephony, VT-Tel, which supports large vocabulary speaker independent recognition. However, it works best if at any point of a conversation the active vocabulary does not exceed a few hundred words; therefore we have taken great care to design a dialog manager in a way that minimizes the active vocabulary at any point of conversation (by designing separate grammars with constrained vocabularies for nested subdialogs).

Natural Language Processing: We have built two versions of the natural language grammars. In the first version, the natural language grammars are represented as a collection of constructions (Goldberg, 1995), i.e. data structures where syntactic, semantic and pragmatic information are combined in one record. This representation has important computational advantages of being general, compact and object oriented. We also used semantic grammars designed to cover specific domains like telephony banking. These grammars are specific, compact, and easy to update and maintain. They can't be reused for new applications, but can be changed and updated by people with very limited computational linguistic skills. For space considerations, most of our discussion in this paper will focus on the version of conversation machines that use semantic grammars. For further information on construction grammars, see (Fillmore et al., 1988), (Goldberg, 1995), and (Jurafsky, 1992).

Dialog Manager: In our Conversation Machines, the Dialog Manager (DM) controls the flow of the conversation with a user. The DM is responsible for analyzing each sentence, deciding the next prompt(s) to be played, and the action to be taken, if any. Thus, the DM works in the conversation-for-action paradigm, i.e. it tries to find out which action to perform and what the parameters of the action are for each user sentence (after analysis by the NLP unit, in the form of a semantic signature). In other words, the DM is a finite collection of states and transitions plus a small number (<20) of global, contextual variables that help determine the next state and the utterance interpretation. If a whole utterance cannot be interpreted within a given context, the largest sub-part that makes sense is tried. Because of the possible ambiguities, there is a small set of rules (5 clauses) expressing the preferences in interpretation.

3. Building tools for the Conversation Machine

In this section, we briefly describe the tools we have developed for rapid development of conversation machines.

3.1 Speech grammar reviser

We have developed a speech grammar reviser- an interactive tool for constraining the sentences accepted by the speech recognition engine (Kambhatla and Zadrozny, 1998). Constraining the list of valid sentences reduces the likelihood of a sentence being mis-recognized. This is especially important for telephone based applications, where the recognition accuracy is not very high. Thus, the speech grammar needs to be both general enough to accept a large variety of sentences about the given application domain, and constrained enough to disallow all other sentences. Developing such tight grammars manually is a tedious and time consuming task. We have automated a large portion of this task through the grammar reviser tool.

Given an initial version of a speech grammar in Backus-Naur Form (BNF), the grammar reviser, in an interactive session with a grammar developer, identifies counter-examples, i.e. examples of sentences currently in the grammar but not appropriate for the given application domain. The grammar is then modified in such a fashion that the counter-examples are no longer accepted by the grammar. For each counter-example **c**, a parse tree is generated. For each non-terminal symbol **x** in the parse tree except for the TOP (or start) non-terminal, two new non-terminals are introduced which generate
- all the substrings generated by **x** except for substrings of **c** and
- the substring of **c** that **x** generates

respectively. The production rule that generated the sentence **c** from the TOP non-terminal is modified such that it no longer generates **c**. The above algorithm for grammar revision is described in detail in (Kambhatla and Zadrozny, 1998). Thus, a constrained version of the initial grammar is generated for use by the speech recognition engine.

3.2 Grammar Workbench

We used a grammar workbench developed at IBM TJ Watson Research Center to develop and maintain semantic grammars for our applications. The grammar workbench is a GUI tool designed to create and maintain grammars along with the corresponding dictionaries.

The dictionary is a list of all the words allowed by our dialog system along with a set of semantic categories that each word belongs to. For example, the following is an item in the dictionary for our stock trading system:
(cash *n_money ((tr (cash))) *n_accttype ((tr (cash)))).
Thus, the word "cash" belongs to the category *n-money (as in "I want to withdraw some cash") and also to the category *n-accttype (as in "charge it to my cash account"). The categories in the dictionary are carefully designed to reveal the hierarchical ontology structure of the application domain.

The grammar contains a set of production rules, each consisting of a syntactic rewrite rule followed by its corresponding compositional semantic translation rule. For example,
((teens -> (*numtens *numones)) (((tr 0) (+ (tr 1) (tr 2)))))
is a rule in our stock trading system that combines elements of two-word number names of category "*numtens" and "*numones" such as "fifty six" to create 2-digit number expressions of category "teens" such as "56" whose semantic translation "(tr 0)" is calculated by a Lisp function "(+ (tr 1) (tr 2))", where "(tr 1)" and "(tr 2)" refer to the semantic translations of "*numtens" and "*numones" respectively.

3.3 Chart Parser

We use a chart parser to parse recognized sentences into their semantic translations. For example, a sentence "what is my checking balance" generates a semantic translation "PROCESS = {[ACCTTYPE = {checking}, GETINFO = {balance}]}, SEM_TYPE = {info}, SYN_TYPE={np}]". Since chart parsing is a standard NLP tool (see e.g. (Gazdar and Mellish, 1989)), we will not discuss any of its internal characteristics in this paper.

3.4 Linguistic to domain translation using semantic signatures

We perform the mapping from the semantic translations returned by the chart parser to a set of (domain specific) actions for the dialog manager using *semantic signatures*.
The semantic translation of a sentence can be considered to be a template, some parts of which are useful for identifying the application domain topic, and other parts are not. The parts that can be used to identify a domain topic form a signature for this topic. For example, a semantic signature for the domain topic "query about account balance" is "PROCESS = {[ACCTTYPE = {*}, GETINFO = {balance}]}, SEM_TYPE = {info}, SYN_TYPE={np}]". Thus, using semantic signatures, the

process of mapping sentences into domain meanings can be divided into two stages. First, a semantic grammar maps a large number of sentences about a given topic onto a few semantic translations. Then, a specification of a few (perhaps a handful) appropriate semantic signatures maps these semantic translations onto domain topics. The semantic signatures for an application are in a separate file. Thus, whenever the grammar is changed to incorporate new sentences to cover an existing action, only the signature file needs to be changed. Also, the code for the dialog manager module is reduced in complexity.

3.5 Dialog Manager Workbench

We built a workbench with a graphical user interface, called the Dialog Management Workbench (DMW), for building dialog managers. The DMW provides a high level fourth generation language, specifically designed for writing dialog managers. Code written in this language is translated into Java by DMW. Thus, the DMW enables a dialog manager developer to focus mainly on the flow of the dialog without worrying about specific programming language constructs that have no relation with the dialog. For example, in our system, a developer need not know the insides of a module that is used to extract the semantic signatures and to map the signatures into the domain topic. Another objective of the DMW is to force the dialog developer to write the dialog manager in a modular fashion such that the code is both readable and easy to modify. The DMW facilitates three levels of module nesting. For example, one of the modules in our stock trading system ("Conversation Loop" module) consists of the following states:

"GetCustomerInputSentence",
"IdentifyDomainTopic",
"CheckAndHandleTopicParameters",
"ExecuteTopic".

Each state of the above corresponds to a lower level module that contains the flow of the dialogs for this topic. For example, the "IdentifyDomainTopic" state contains DMW codes that accepts an input sentence, sends the sentence to the semantic parser, and obtains a domain topic. Thus, the DMW enables a developer to rapidly write a portable, modular and easy to read dialog manager.

4. What we learned

4.1 Guiding the user

As we developed the Conversation Machine for banking, we were aware that the state of the art for both telephone speech recognition, and natural language understanding was inadequate to allow users to talk to the system in a completely unconstrained way. The dialogs and prompts we developed are intended to guide and gently constrain the user to produce utterances which the system can understand.

Guidance for the next step – The system provides guidance for the next step at every stage. At the top level, the prompt *"What else can I do for you?"* lets the user know that the system is ready for the next request. When the system has only partial information for a dialog, it prompts the user for the missing information. For example, if the system hears "Pay my bills" it will ask the user *"Which bills would you like me to pay?"*. This allows the user to proceed in small steps if desired, thus reducing the disfluencies and consequent speech recognition errors which often characterize long utterances (Oviatt, 1995). This feature is also useful in the case where a recognition failure has caused the Conversation Machine to miss some information included in the original utterance. For example, if a user says *"Pay my phone bill,"* and the speech recognizer fails to recognize *"phone"* the system will follow-up with *"Which bills would you like me to pay?"*. Thus, the user is guided to provide the missing information without repeating the entire request.

Our system also provides guidance which is helpful if a user is in a state inadvertently due to a mis-recognition. For example, if the prompt described above is unsuccessful in eliciting a valid response, the next prompt is *"Which bills? Please say electricity, phone, insurance, or MasterCard. To cancel, say cancel."* Reminding users how to get out of an unintended dialog can reduce frustration and help users get back on the right track.

Feedback for state –An important principle for the design of prompts in the Conversation Machine for banking was to always provide feedback for state in each prompt. For example, the prompt to enter the amount of money for a transfer is *"To make sure I understand the amount of money to transfer, please enter the amount…"*. The inclusion of the phrase *"to transfer"* lets the user know that he/she has entered the transfer sub-dialog. We were reminded of the importance of providing feedback for state when testing an earlier version of the system, which did not include this phrase for the transfer dialog. When users, who had asked to pay a bill, were in a transfer sub-dialog in error, they assumed they were being asked to enter an amount for bill payment. Only later in the dialog, did the mis-recognition error become apparent. Providing feedback for state in each prompt helps users detect errors and more quickly recover from them.

Progressive prompting –Another technique we use to help users recover from errors and avoid future errors is to give progressive prompting based on strategies that are likely to be successful and that users understand. As reported in (Wolf et al, 1997), some strategies that people spontaneously employed based on human-human communication are more likely to be successful with the Conversation Machine than others. Accordingly, our progressive prompting provides increasingly more direction with each consecutive error by suggesting generally successful strategies (see also Yankelovich et al., 1995).

For example, after the first recognition failure at the top level, the system simply suggests that the user "rephrase" the request. After a second failure, the system suggests using "short, simple requests." In usability studies with banking customers in the Fall of 1997, we found that this suggestion typically results in success. Finally, if the user is still unsuccessful, the system suggests the user try specific phrases "like transfer funds from checking to savings or…." The idea is to both suggest specific requests and give examples of the style of request that will likely be successful. In the near future, we plan to quasi-randomly select the example phrases so that the user may be exposed to a number of phrases in the course of a session or over a number of sessions. Progressive prompting is also used within sub-dialogs to guide the user to produce acceptable utterances.

4.2 Dialog manager issues

We designed our dialog managers to be robust with respect to ambiguous parses produced by the semantic grammars and both random and systematic errors made by the speech recognition engine.

For instance, to eliminate confusion resulting from random speech recognition errors, we disallowed nested conversations (e.g. asking for a checking balance in the middle of a money transfer transaction).

It is hard to write a semantic grammar that does not produce an ambiguous parse, even in a limited domain like banking. For example, a user might ask our stock trading system, "*Yes, what is the current volume of IBM?*". This sentence is unambiguous to a human operator. However, a parser might generate two parses: ``[PROCESS = { [ANSWER = {yes}] }, SEM_TYPE = {answer} , SYN_TYPE = {yesno} }], [PROCESS = {[GETINFO = { volume }, SECURITY = {IBM}] }, SEM_TYPE = {info}, SYN_TYPE = {np}]''. Here, each "PROCESS" corresponds to a separate semantic interpretation of the original sentence. The second parse tree is a representation of the volume request, while the first parse tree is a representation of a yes/no response to account for the "Yes" in the beginning of the sentence. We can disambiguate the sentence by mapping the duality of parses above to a volume request using a special semantic signature.

We can consider both ambiguous parse trees and systematic speech recognition errors (e.g. systematic substitution of plurals for singulars) to be special signatures. A dialog manager developer can write special semantic signatures to map these onto unique appropriate actions. Thus we can disambiguate from multiple parses and overcome speech recognition errors by specifically incorporating error conditions into the design of dialog managers.

4.3 Building the NLP component: a lesson in ease of maintenance

As mentioned in the introduction, the conversation machine system has two versions. The version based on construction grammars is currently being deployed, and the version based on semantic grammars, which was developed in parallel, is being tested and will replace the other version in the near future. There were two primary reasons for switching to semantic grammars: the problem of maintaining a construction grammar, and the issue of availability of tools for construction grammar development and maintenance. We realized that supporting and writing new construction grammars would require higher skills than the development group we are working with currently has, and that our research team cannot officially undertake customer support obligations. Therefore we were forced to move towards semantic grammars, where linguistic features are directly mapped onto domain meanings. It is also easier to develop semantic grammar templates for new domains (e.g. stock trading) because tools (e.g., a grammar workbench) are already available to work with semantic grammars.

The moral is that, though it is useful to employ the most advanced natural language understanding technology for a research prototype, the reality of providing system support can force a project towards a simpler, less general, and potentially more costly alternative, which allows the company to move to market faster.

Furthermore, switching to a different technology can open new engineering opportunities. We are currently contemplating the use of machine learning in maintaining and updating semantic grammars. If we are successful, the new ML techniques may also be applicable to similar problems facing construction grammars. This may eventually allow us to move back to using construction grammars for language understanding in commercially viable dialog systems.

4.4 Recovering from speech errors

During the course of building conversation machines for different domains, we used a multi-pronged strategy for handling errors made by the speech recognition module. The accuracy of speech recognition over the telephone at the phoneme, word or even the sentence level is far from perfect, even for the best engines. Thus, a good strategy for error recovery is paramount. Our approach was a multi-pronged one of constraining speech grammars, adding pronunciation models and designing the dialog prompts to enable quick and graceful recovery from errors.

We used the speech grammar reviser (described earlier) to constrain the speech grammar and thereby improve the recognition accuracy by limiting the number of possible sentences that an utterance is potentially interpreted as. For our banking domain, using an initial (over-generalizing) grammar as a baseform, we obtained about a 30-40% increase in recognition accuracy by constraining the grammar to accept only valid domain specific sentences. (Based on anecdotal evidence from 6 people who demonstrate the system to visitors. A more rigorous test is planned for this spring).

We added several pronunciation models for words and phrases to improve recognition accuracy for certain key words or phrases. For instance, for our banking application, it is more important to correctly recognize "checking balance" than "can you tell me" in a sentence "can you tell me my checking balance".

As mentioned earlier, we designed the dialog flow of our conversation machines in such a way that it is easy for a user to quit a transaction in progress, or to access help at any point in the conversation. Also, successive unsuccessful queries by a user result in the playing of more and more helpful messages and eventually after three successive unsuccessful queries, the user is automatically transferred to a service representative.

For transactions where all these techniques (Section 4.4) were used in tandem, we were able to obtain a first try successful transaction rate close to 90%. In a study with 16 participants, 9 women and 7 men, ages 21-50, conducted by an independent agency in fall of 1997. The participants were given a standard set of 15 common phone banking tasks. For different tasks, we obtained first try successful transaction rates ranging from 22% to 90%, proportional to the amount of tuning of the system using the techniques mentioned above (Section 4.4). The *methodology* of the trial is described in (Wolf et al, 1997). In addition, for a demonstration system where the system was tuned extensively using the above techniques, we obtained a first try successful transaction rate close to 90% for *all* tasks based on anecdotal evidence of 6 people who regularly demostrate our system.

Thus, an important lesson here is that even with poor to fair speech recognition accuracy, we can build a very useful and successful system by using techniques like the one described above.

5 Customer issues

Contributing to the challenge of creating a useable system of considerable scope and complexity was the fact that we did not have a complete specification of the functionality to be delivered to the customer. Late in the development cycle, a number of new requirements surfaced, with potentially pervasive effects on the design of the natural language processing and speech grammar components. To avoid the risk of making large changes late in the development cycle, we quickly evaluated several design alternatives with users and picked an acceptable alternative that minimized the need for changes to these components.

Another approach we are taking for managing the scope of the system is to try to anticipate a user's next request based on the current state, and present that anticipated request as an option to the user. This approach avoids resorting to the use of explicit modes, which unnaturally constrain a user's options. For instance, customers often call with the goal of verifying their checking balance. If the balance does not match their records, they frequently ask for checking transaction history in order to determine the cause of the mismatch. When a customer's initial request is for a checking balance, our system asks the user if she wants her checking transaction history, thus reducing the subsequent speech recognition task to a simple yes/no distinction. Similarly, in future systems, when users try to pay a bill but do not have enough money, they will be asked if they want to transfer money and pay the bill. This example is part of an overall strategy of moving towards a system based on user goals as opposed to banking transactions. This goal-based approach reduces recognition errors, and makes the system more efficient for users (see (Wolf and Zadrozny, 1998), for additional examples of design challenges based on customer issues).

Another issue when dealing with real customers and real systems, is the capability of the backend computers to handle complex transactions. For instance, we found that the backend computers of our bank partner were incapable of handling requests for all information relating to a user (as outlined in the above paragraph). Thus, the reality of dealing with primitive backend machines can also constrain an integrated transaction processing system to not being able to process more sophisticated transactions.

6. Conclusions

We have built an integrated AI system for speech enabled transaction processing over the telephone. Our system integrates state of the art technologies from the areas of computer telephony, continuous speech recognition, natural language processing and human computer interaction. Our system differs from other similar systems in the market with respect to both the variety of natural language sentences processed (e.g. the grammar can process around 50 million sentences for our banking system) and the complexity of transactions processed.

Based on the new methodology for research initiatives in our company, we are deploying a prototype "conversation machine" for banking at a customer site. We intend to conduct field trials with actual bank users to continue research on design issues related to dialog flow, computer human interaction, recovery from speech errors and overall integration.

In the process of designing and building conversation machines, the most important lesson we have learnt is that, to build a complete and working system, it is not necessary that each component is perfect. In fact, in most situations, it is impossible to guarantee this. This is true especially in integrated AI systems, where most of the building blocks are error prone. For example, both the continuous speech recognition unit, and, to a lesser extent, the natural language processing unit can produce errors. However, as described earlier, these errors can be overcome to a large extent by careful design and attention to the system modules, the dialog flow and human computer interaction issues, as illustrated by the following examples.

- Our system attempts to predict the user's next query/request and preemptively asks the user if she would like the system to process the query/request. This reduces the task of the speech recognition engine.
- The dialog and prompts in our system guide and gently constrain the user to produce utterances which the system can recognize and understand easily.
- Our system provides feedback about the current transaction at each step of the conversation, to enable users to detect errors, and quickly recover from them.
- Our system progressively prompts the user with increasingly more direction with each consecutive error by suggesting generally successful strategies.

We switched to using semantic grammars for our banking system to enable rapid development and easy maintenance of grammars.

- We add special semantic signatures for common mis-recognitions and ambiguously parsed sentences (for the given domain) to the dialog manager to make it more robust.
- We use a speech grammar reviser tool to constrain the speech grammar and improve recognition accuracy by limiting the number of possible sentences that an utterance is potentially interpreted as.
- We add several pronunciation models for words and phrases which are more important for a given domain topic than other words. For instance, recognition and parsing of the phrase "checking balance" is paramount to successfully handling any sentence which includes this phrase for our banking system.

For the transactions for which we used all the above techniques in tandem, we observed that users of our telephone banking system obtained a successful transaction rate close to 90%.

In future, we intend to work on developing machine learning algorithms for automatically mapping semantic signatures to domain topics, conduct research on allowing nested dialogs in applications and build Conversation Machines for larger domains.

We conclude that, with our new research methodology, it is possible to build a very robust and useful natural language dialog system, which integrates the AI technologies of telephone speech recognition, natural language processing and human computer interaction. We can overcome deficiencies in any of the component modules by paying careful attention to the dialog flow and mechanisms for error recovery as outlined in this paper. In the process, having a customer enables us to make more realistic design choices.

References

C.J. Fillmore, P. Kay, and M.C. O'Connor. (1988). Regularity and idiomaticity in grammatical constructions. *Language*, 64(3):501--538.

G. Gazdar and C.S. Mellish (1989). Natural language processing in Prolog: an introduction to computational linguistics. Addison Wesley.

A.E. Goldberg. (1995). *Constructions: a construction grammar approach to argument structure.* The University of Chicago Press, Chicago, IL.

D. Jurafsky. (1992). An On-line Computational Model of Sentence Interpretation. *PhD thesis, University of California, Berkeley*, Report No. UCB/CSD 92/676.

N. Kambhatla and W. Zadrozny (1998). Automated Grammar Revision Using Counter-Examples. *IBM T.J. Watson Research Center* Technical Report.

Oviatt, S. (1995). Predicting spoken disfluencies during human-computer interaction. *Computer Speech and Language, 9*, 19-35.

Wolf, C. G., Kassler, M., Zadrozny, W., Opyrchal, L. (1997). *Interact 97 Conference Proceedings,* 461-468.

Wolf, C. G. and Zadrozny, W. (1998). Evolution of the Conversation Machine: A case study of bringing advanced technology to the marketplace. *CHI'98 Conference Proceedings*, to appear.

Yankelovich, N. (1996). How do users know what to say? *Interactions*, 3.6, 32-43.

Yankelovich, N., Levow, G. A., and Marx, M. (1995). Designing SpeechActs: Issues in speech user interfaces. *CHI '95 Conference Proceedings*, 369-376.

SIGART / AAAI Doctoral Consortium

Optimizing Information Agents by Selectively Materializing Data *

Naveen Ashish

Information Sciences Institute, Integrated Media Systems Center and
Department of Computer Science
University of Southern California
4676 Admiralty Way, Marina del Rey, CA 90292
ashish@isi.edu

There is currently great interest in building information gathering agents that provide integrated access to data from a number of distributed Web sources. Some of the prominent research projects in this area include The Internet Softbot, Information Manifold, InfoMaster and InfoSleuth. A critical problem faced by such agents is a high query response time, due to the fact that a lot of data from Web sources has to be retrieved, extracted, and integrated to answer queries. The aim of this work is to develop an approach for improving query response time in information agents. The resulting system is being developed as part of the Ariadne project (Knoblock et al. 1998).

Our approach to optimizing an agent is to selectively materialize data from the different sources being integrated. In order to speed up query response time we materialize information that is frequently queried or used to construct answers to user queries. A key problem is to determine the classes of information that must be materialized. There are several factors that must be taken into account in order to determine such classes, including frequency of access by users, cost of getting the information from the actual Web sources, space required to store the data, and the frequency of updates at the original Web sources.

We have developed an algorithm that identifies classes of information to materialize by analyzing patterns in user queries. An important constraint is that the number of information classes materialized must be kept small. This is because each class materialized is defined as another information source that the agent can access. Having a large number of such sources will create performance problems for the query planner that must generate plans to retrieve information requested by the user from the various sources being integrated. Our strategy is to replace whenever possible, a number of fragmented information classes in which all the data is frequently accessed, by a single class that covers the data in all these classes and possibly some extra data not accessed at all. The advantage is that in this manner we are able to keep the number of materialized classes small. This algorithm thus attempts to cover frequently accessed data using the minimum number of information classes with the constraint that the extra data (data not frequently accessed by user queries but which is part of the classes identified by the algorithm) is within a certain threshold value. The algorithm utilizes the KR system LOOM to maintain a dynamically constructed ontology of subclasses of information frequently queried. The ontology guides the merging of a set of classes into a single class.

There are several other important issues that we will address as part of this dissertation. First, although the materialized data can be of great help in speeding up query processing time, we have to take into account the fact that the data in the original Web sources might change. Developing solutions to this problem requires considering several factors such as at what frequency the data in a Web source changes, is the time of change known, is the data stored affected by changes in the source, and also how critical it is for the users to have the absolute current data. Second, another important feature that must be present in an integration environment is to be able to materialize data in terms of classes that are an integrated or aggregated view over classes of information in individual sources. This is complicated because the integrated classes and the individual source classes cannot be analyzed independently for materialization.

Acknowledgments

I am grateful to my research advisor Craig Knoblock for guidance with this work. I also wish to thank Dennis McLeod and Cyrus Shahabi of USC, and Richard Hull and Gang Zhou of Bell Laboratories. This work has been supported by USC's Integrated Media Systems Center (IMSC), an NSF Engineering Research Center.

References

Knoblock, C.; Minton, S.; Ambite, J.-L.; Ashish, N.; Modi, P. J.; Muslea, I.; Philpot, A.; and Tejada, S. 1998. Modeling web sources for information integration. In *Proceedings of the Fifteenth National Conference on Artificial Intelligence*.

Generating Adequate Instructions: Knowing When to Stop

Juliet C. Bourne

Department of Computer and Information Science
University of Pennsylvania
200 South 33rd Street, Philadelphia PA 19104-6389
jcb@linc.cis.upenn.edu

Adequate instructions are essential to the correct performance of actions. An instruction is adequate if its action(s) and objects are identified sufficiently and unambiguously, given the instruction's context. For instance, the instruction *Turn the knob* would be inadequate if, in the context, more than one knob or one way of turning a knob were salient. However, even if the knob and the manner of turning were uniquely identifiable, the instruction could still be inadequate since it does not tell the reader when to stop turning the knob. What is missing here is the *termination information* for the action, or when the performance of the action is to end. Conveying such information in automated text generation is the focus of my research. I consider how to incorporate termination information into an action representation and how to generate adequate instructions from instances of the action representation, including how to choose appropriate expressions for conveying action termination.

To study termination information and how it is expressed in instructions, I have completed a preliminary corpus analysis of 3000 simple step-by-step instructions taken from several sources: *The Reader's Digest New Complete Do-It-Yourself Manual* (1991), a collection of *technical orders* (military instructions) for the maintenance of F-16 aircraft, and a small set of instructions for a mitre saw assembly line. I have coded the instructions for types of main verb phrases and types of additional phrases or subordinate clauses used with them. Rough analysis shows that nearly ninety percent of the termination condition clauses, such as *until* clauses, as well as nearly half of the clauses expressing purpose, co-occur with main verb phrases which do not themselves provide termination information. (Such verb phrases appear in about a quarter of the instructions.) This analysis has been the basis for my work on the representation of termination information and initial work on generating expressions of termination information.

One of the problems I face is that an action's termination often follows from other features of the action, either individually or together. An action's participants, path, purpose, and relationships with other actions can all provide termination information. Using knowledge about features of actions and their interconnections, as gleaned from the corpus analysis, I have begun to specify what an action representation needs to look like in order to generate adequate instructions. Given an action representation which contains all of the necessary slots for action information, including the plan which an action is part of, generating adequate instructions is then a matter of knowing how to express the information in the action representation and how to recognize when an instruction does not yet convey when to stop.

Since termination information appears throughout the representation of an action, realizing it involves different parts of an action's description. For example, possible ways to express termination for *Turn the knob* include: *...90 degrees, ...to the* OPEN *position, ...to open the door, ...until the door opens*. As such information is primarily expressed intra-sententially, albeit over multiple clauses, I have begun to use a generation system called SPUD (Stone & Doran 1997; Stone & Webber 1998) which plans sentences by forming descriptions of events, states, and objects. By matching the semantic and pragmatic information of its Lexicalized Tree-Adjoining Grammar entries against information it is told to convey, SPUD chooses those lexical items which serve its communicative goals best in describing an action. Encoding semantic and pragmatic information and associating it with realizations of termination information allows SPUD to generate appropriate action descriptions based on action information. SPUD's ability to check the semantic and pragmatic information provided by an instruction to see whether it contains termination information ensures the generation of adequate instructions.

Acknowledgments

Supported by a Patricia Harris Fellowship and partially funded by the Air Force through Hughes Aircraft (PO#8K-102190-7N) and BBN (Contract #501278). Many thanks to my advisor, Bonnie Webber.

References

Stone, M., and Doran, C. 1997. Sentence planning as description using tree-adjoining grammar. In *Proceedings of ACL/EACL'97*, 198–205.

Stone, M., and Webber, B. 1998. Textual economy through close coupling of syntax and semantics. International Workshop of Natural Language Generation.

HR - Automatic Concept Formation in Finite Algebras

Simon Colton

Department of Artificial Intelligence, University of Edinburgh,
80 South Bridge
Edinburgh. EH1 1HN. Scotland
simonco@dai.ed.ac.uk

We are investigating how and why mathematicians invent new concepts while developing a theory, and implementing our ideas into the HR system, which automatically produces, assesses and displays concepts in finite algebras, such as finite group theory. We first determined a reason for HR to produce concepts - to classify a given set of groups up to isomorphism. Doing so would involve inventing concepts which help describe groups, so a classification can occur, and inventing concepts which help generate new examples of groups, so that improvements to the classification are necessitated, perpetuating the process. Next, we developed measures to tell us how interesting the concepts produced were (see Colton 1997). This helped us determine the kinds of concepts HR should produce and with this in mind, we implemented production rules taking one (or two) concepts as input and outputting a new concept.

Computational Model

There are three levels of processing which allow HR to operate. In the interests of good methodology, we make clear distinctions between these levels. Firstly, HR uses production rules to transform an old concept (or two old concepts) into a new one. For example, given the group operation: $a*b = c$, then the 'match' production rule invents concepts such as $a*a = a$, where some or all of the parameters are equal.

A second layer of processing takes a newly invented concept and assesses its worth in terms of how well it classifies groups. To do this, we think of each concept as a function taking a single group as input, with the output describing the input group, eg. above, the function would be $f(G) = \{a \in G : a*a = a\}$. To determine the concept's value, HR compares how the concept describes pairs of group tables. If two group tables are isomorphic, then they should have the same description. If they are not isomorphic, then ideally they should have different descriptions. HR can count the number of pairs which are described correctly, and this is used to measure the classifying ability of the concept. If exploration, rather than classification, is the aim, an alternative measure is the novelty of a concept: by describing groups, a concept categorises them, and the novelty of this categorisation can be measured.

The top layer of processing keeps an agenda of which old concepts to base new concepts on, and which production rules to use to do this. This agenda is organised using the assessment of the concepts given by the measurements, and so relies on the heuristic that interesting concepts lead to further interesting concepts.

Initial Results and Future Work

Given two isomorphic group tables for the 8 groups of order less than seven, HR invents a concept in seconds which classifies them (ie. for the input group tables, it has different outputs for non-isomorphic tables, but the same output for isomorphic tables). It identifies this concept as being the most interesting so far, and writes and marks up a description of the concepts as a LATEX script which is displayed for the user. Initial findings suggest that the heuristic of building on the most interesting concepts first is effective.

At present, HR cannot generate new group tables. Using constraint satisfaction technology, future versions of HR will turn the descriptions of the groups into constraints on a search for more group tables. This will involve deriving different types of concepts, such as sequences of groups (eg. central series) and extensions (eg. central extensions), from the descriptive concepts (in this case, the centre of a group). A more detailed description of HR is due to appear in (Bundy 1998).

References

Colton, S; Cresswell, S; and Bundy, A; 1997. The Use of Classification in Automated Mathematical Concept Formation. In *Proceedings of SimCat 97*, Department of Artificial Intelligence, University of Edinburgh.

Bundy, A; Colton, S; and Walsh, T; 1998. HR - Automatic Concept Formation in Finite Group Theory. To appear in the *International Congress on Discovery and Creativity*, Gent, Belgium.

Acknowledgements[1]

This work is supported by EPSRC grant GR/L 11724.

---

[1] Copyright ©1998, American Association for Artificial Intelligence (www.aaai.org). All rights reserved.

Optimizing Initial Configurations of Neural Networks for the Task of Natural Language Learning

Jaime J. Dávila

Graduate School and University Center, City University Of New York
33 West 42nd Street
New York, NY 10031, USA
jdavila@broadway.gc.cuny.edu

One approach used to develop computer systems for natural language processing (NLP) is that of Artificial Neural Networks (NNs). Because of the large number of parameters a NN has (e.g. network topology, learning algorithm, transfer functions) and the way they interact, finding optimal parameter values for any particular task can be extremely difficult.

Topology can greatly affect the performance of a NN. Stolcke (1990) found that simple sentences could be processed by NNs with one hidden layer. Performance degraded, however, when the NN was presented with embedded sentences, for which more complex topologies were needed. What topology to use for any particular task is still an open question. Most decisions regarding NN topology are based on ideas of how the problem should be tackled. Jain (1991) used a NN that first decomposed a sentence into phrases and later defined relationships between the phrases. Miikkulainen (1996) divided a NN into a parser, a segmenter, and a stack. These NN vary in the number of layers, the number of nodes in each layer, and how these layers are connected to each other.

Another aspect affecting performance is the corpus used to train the NN. Nenov and Dyer (1994) found that training with individual words before showing sentences increased performance. Elman (1993) found that training a NN with simple sentences first and complex sentences later produced better results than presenting all sentences in one session.

Although researchers have been successful in using NN for NLP, choosing an initial configuration is quite complex. An automated process that can find an optimal set of parameters would be helpful in designing such a system.

In my research I use Genetic Algorithms (GAs) to find what NN parameter values produce better performance for a particular NL task. There is one input node for each word in the vocabulary. A sentence is presented to the NN one word at a time by activating the corresponding node at the input layer. The NN incrementally generates a description of the input by correctly identifying the parts of the sentence and how they relate to each other. For example, in the sentence <the boy runs> the NN should respond by (1) identifying each word in the sentence, e.g. <runs> is a movement verb; (2) identifying phrases, e.g.<the boy> is a noun phrase; and (3) identifying the relationships among phrases, e.g. <the boy> is the agent of <runs>. This is similar to Jain (1991).

The NN has 75 hidden nodes, divided into between 1 and 30 layers, as determined by the GA. The GA also determines how these layers are connected to each other, and which learning algorithm and transfer functions to use.

The NN is tested on a language of 508 sentences with three different complexity levels. The basic training set is 20% of the complete language. The GA makes three major decisions about training: (1) whether to train with sentences from all complexity levels at once, or with sentences from the simpler level first and more complex sentences later, (2) whether to train with sentences from all complexity levels in the same proportion, or with more sentences from one level or another; (3) whether the training set should be increased past the basic 20%. If it is, the NN's fitness is decreased by a factor equal to the increase in the training set.

By studying the configurations chosen by the GA, I hope to identify which parameters are critical for the NLP task and which values for these parameters produce the best performance. These results will provide a better understanding of NN behavior and point to improved NN configurations.

References

Elman, J. 1993. Learning and Development in Neural Networks: The Importance of Starting Small. *Cognition* 48:71-99.

Jain, A. 1991. Parsing Complex Sentences with Structured Connectionist Networks. *Neural Computation* 3:110-120.

Miikkulainen, R. 1996. Subsymbolic Case-Role Analysis of Sentences with Embedded Clauses. *Cognitive Science* 20:47-73.

Nenov, V.; and Dyer, M. 1994. Perceptually Grounded Language Learning. *Connection Science* 6.

Stolcke, A. 1990. Learning Featured-based Semantics with Simple Recurrent Networks, Technical Report, TR-90-015. International Computer Science Inst., Berkeley, CA.

Copyright © 1998, American Association for Artificial Intelligence (www.aaai.org). All rights reserved.

Pragmatic Multi-Agent Learning

Andrew Garland
Computer Science Department
Brandeis University
Waltham, MA 02254
aeg@cs.brandeis.edu

Early models of procedural learning assumed actors were isolated, model-based thinkers. More recently, learning techniques have become more sophisticated as this assumption has been replaced with more realistic ones. To date, however, there has been no thorough investigation of multiple, heterogeneous, situated agents who learn from the pragmatics of their domain rather than from a model. This research focuses on this important problem and develops learning techniques that allow agents to improve their performance in a dynamic environment by learning from past run-time behavior.

Humans provide a natural model of pragmatic agents situated in a multi-agent world. [1] argues that the development of distributed cooperative behavior in people is shaped by the accumulated cultural-historical knowledge of the community. Our learning techniques are motivated by this argument and use a structure called *collective memory* to store the accumulated procedural knowledge of a community of agents. Collective memory contains the breadth of knowledge the community acquires through interacting with each other and the world during the course of solving sequences of distinct problems. The cornerstone of collective memory is a cooperative procedures case-base that augments the agents' first-order planner [2]; in other words, this work follows in the tradition of second-order planners, extending them into multi-agent domains.

In our model of activity, each agent has her own point of view on how best to proceed, which often leads to uncoordinated and unproductive behavior. Furthermore, inefficient behavior would occur even if there was a consensus upon the best course of action to follow (perhaps legislated by a supervising agent or agreed to during community-wide communication) because of the community's initial lack of knowledge about their uncertain domain. Through the use of collective memory, however, agents behave more efficiently over the course of solving a problem sequence for two reasons. First, individual agents develop a point of view based upon shared experiences; second, they learn procedures that capture regularities both in the task environment and in the patterns of cooperation for solving problems in task domain. That is, an agent remembers successful cooperative behavior in which she was involved, and uses it as a basis for future interactions.

In addition to a case-base of cooperative procedures, collective memory currently contains a set of tree structures, called operator probabilities trees [3]. An agent uses these trees to construct higher quality plans by more accurately estimating the probability of success for operators she may attempt. More accurate estimates lead to plans that are more likely to succeed because the estimates are used to guide the first-order planner's search, including the selection of role bindings. Empirical results show that both cooperative procedures and operator probabilities trees lead to significant reductions in the amount of time a community takes to solve randomly generated problems. Furthermore, the two components of collective memory are more effective together than either alone, showing that they facilitate non-overlapping aspects of learning.

Presently, collective memory is implicitly represented as the (conceptual) union of the distributed, private memories of each of the agents in the community. We are developing alternate techniques that would store the procedural knowledge case-base in a central memory (one memory for all agents) or a guild memory (one memory for each group of homogeneous agents). We will conduct experiments to quantify the utility of both of these implementations, as well as of hybrid combinations that incorporate distributed memories.

We believe this research will clearly demonstrate that collective memory is an effective resource for pragmatic multi-agent learning. Hence, it will make a significant contribution to current literature on planning, memory, and group activity.

This work has been advised by Richard Alterman and supported in part by ONR grants N00014-96-1-0440 and N00014-97-1-0604.

References

[1] Michael Cole and Yrjö Engeström. A cultural-historical approach to distributed cognitition. In Gavriel Salomon, editor, *Distributed Cognitions*, pages 1–46. Cambridge University Press, 1993.

[2] Andrew Garland and Richard Alterman. Preparation of multi-agent knowledge for reuse. In *1995 AAAI Fall Symposium on Adaptation of Knowledge for Reuse*, pages 26–33, 1995.

[3] Andrew Garland and Richard Alterman. Multiagent learning through collective memory. In *1996 AAAI Spring Symposium on Adaptation, Coevolution and Learning in Multiagent Systems*, pages 33–38, 1996.

Perception, memory, and the field of view problem

William S. Gribble

Department of Electrical and Computer Engineering
University of Texas at Austin, Austin, Texas, 78712
grib@cs.utexas.edu

Robust control of a vision-based agent requires tight coupling between sensing and action. For mobile robots performing visually-guided navigation, this means closed-loop control of motion with respect to sensed features, landmarks, or other relevant parts of the visible environment. Real vision sensors have limited fields of view. This makes true closed-loop control with respect to an arbitrary set of landmarks impossible with practical vision systems, since only a fraction of the environment can be seen at any one time.

My dissertation describes a solution to the *field of view problem* for vision-based agents lacking omnidirectional sensors. I propose a unified object memory system which integrates short-term working memory of the local *visual space* with immediate object perceptions from the real-time image stream. Short-term memory includes a model of agent and object dynamics and a recursive position estimator. The significance of unification of short-term memory and direct perception is twofold. First, since the positions and properties of all relevant objects are either directly sensed or estimated from recent experience, navigation control laws can be written as closed-loop controllers operating without regard to the agent's current field of view. Second, given an estimator such as the Kalman filter which includes an estimate of state uncertainty, an independent *investigatory action* scheduler can dynamically optimize shifts of camera field of view.

In existing closed-loop visual control (or *visual servoing*) systems, the agent's plan contains explicit instructions for control of all actuators. The camera platform's degrees of freedom are used to maintain visual lock on a target, and locomotor degrees of freedom are used to cause the robot to follow a particular path or perform an action based on its sensory input. Envisioned as a closed-loop control system, this arrangement has a real-time stream of pixels as its input, a vector of motor controls as its output, and a set of vision and control algorithms – the plan, plus state and numerous transformation algorithms – in between. If camera field-of-view changes are required, they must be explicitly programmed as a part of the plan. This can be awkward or impossible when multiple goals must be pursued simultaneously.

Copyright 1998, American Association for Artificial Intelligence (www.aaai.org). All rights reserved.

The unified object memory allows us to split this loop into two parts:

- The camera controller and vision system, which has a stream of pixel arrays as its input, a pool of grounded symbolic descriptions of relevant objects (the unified working memory) as its output, and a *task-independent* controller and vision system in between. Field of view shifts are scheduled automatically to minimize uncertainty in estimates of object position and properties.

- The agent's planning and control system, which has grounded symbols representing relevant objects as its input and locomotor controls as its output. Feedback to the camera controller and vision system exists in the form of add and delete instructions to the working memory: when a new control algorithm is activated, it adds a list of relevant objects to the working memory. Likewise, objects are removed from working memory when they are no longer needed by any control laws.

There are significant benefits from this arrangement. Most importantly, the field of view problem is eliminated. Access to the properties of objects is not impeded when the physical field of view is directed elsewhere. Since the unified object memory has an estimate of the object's position and dynamics, the agent can reason sensibly about any set of objects regardless of their spatial separation. Direct observation is still of critical importance, since estimates are inherently uncertain and this uncertainty accumulates over time if no new observations are made. However, the agent is not required to directly observe an object in order to use it as a source of feedback for closed-loop locomotor control.

Also, plans can be written without explicit programming of sensing, tracking, and attention-shifting control. Rather than controlling sensors directly, the plan specifies a policy for identifying and tracking relevant objects and explicitly programs only those behaviors, such as locomotor control, that are directly related to task completion. This is a qualitative change in the nature of the agent's plan, a change which makes the plan appear more like an abstract algorithm for task completion and less like a series of open-loop procedural commands.

Exploiting Diversity for Natural Language Processing

John C. Henderson*
Department of Computer Science
Johns Hopkins University
Baltimore, MD 21218-2694
jhndrsn@cs.jhu.edu

The recent popularity of applying machine learning methods to computational linguistics problems has given rise to a large supply of trainable natural language processing systems. Most problems of interest have an array of off-the-shelf products or downloadable code implementing solutions of varying quality using varying techniques.

The task this thesis is concerned with is developing reasonable methods for combining the *outputs* of a diverse set of systems which all address the same task. The hope is that if the set has a high enough initial accuracy and independently assorted errors, we can produce a more accurate solution using an appropriate combining method. In addition, there are principles that initial system developers should keep in mind which will help them create a family of diverse systems. We are also interested in developing methods for increasing the diversity of a set of systems without sacrificing accuracy, for the sake of fruitful combination. Each task we approach will warrant a separate investigation into how to combine outputs, and hope lies in discovering the principles that are common among all tasks. We don't want to study just one learning method or task, instead we want to discover principles that can be applied universally, or to a broad class of problems.

Our proposed work can draw from a number of recent machine learning results involving combining outputs of systems. In the *bagging* technique, randomness is used as the basis of generating a diverse ensemble of classifiers, and results are combined using simple interpolation or majority voting depending on the type of predictor that is required (Breiman 1996). Bagging has been used in conjunction with a genetic algorithm that enforces diversity while it trains a collection of neural networks to boost accuracy (Opitz & Shavlik 1996). Given a set of classification systems, the *AdaBoost* system, in conjunction with certain types of classifier generators, can produce a new system that provably reduces the error of the ensemble (Freund & Schapire 1997). The principles these systems utilize can be applied to combining outputs of systems with more structure, such as those in the domain of natural language processing.

The overall plan is to start with computational linguistics problems that mesh well with current machine learning methods and progress toward problems with outputs that are full of rich structural dependencies. The lessons we learn and the techniques we perfect in coping with the simpler systems will be applied to the more complex systems.

The first step in pursuit of this thesis is to take off-the-shelf machine learning combining methods, such as majority voting, bagging, or boosting, and apply them to off-the-shelf natural language processing systems. The initial domains we are exploring in this way are text filtering and prepositional phrase attachment. These problems are well suited to this type of exploration because they are easily reformulated as standard classification problems.

We will then move toward more structured problems, those that do not lend themselves to classification-style output, such as part-of-speech (POS) tagging. The POS tagging problem is not simple classification because the input is a tape of words and the output is a tape of parts of speech. The identity of a single tag is highly dependent on tags assigned to nearby words.

Finally, we will attack the parsing problem. This problem is quite different from standard classification problems, as the output has a tree structure and the evaluation metric is highly sensitive to mistakes in the shape of that tree. For parsing we will most likely need to construct entirely new combining methods.

See `http://www.cs.jhu.edu/~jhndrsn/thesis.html` for an updated summary of progress toward this thesis.

References

Breiman, L. 1996. Bagging predictors. In *Machine Learning*, volume 24, 123.

Freund, Y., and Schapire, R. 1997. A decision-theoretic generalization of on-line learning and an application to boosting. *JCSS* 55(1):119–139.

Opitz, D. W., and Shavlik, J. W. 1996. Generating accurate and diverse members of a neural-network ensemble. In *NIPS8*.

Copyright © 1998, American Association for Artificial Intelligence (www.aaai.org). All rights reserved.
*The author was supported by NSF grant IRI-9502312.

Multimodal, Multilevel Selective Attention

Micheal Hewett
Department of Computer Sciences
University of Texas at Austin
Austin, Texas 78712-1188
hewett@cs.utexas.edu

Perception and Attention

Early knowledge based systems did not incorporate high-bandwidth I/O due to performance limitations of computers of that era. Today, intelligent agents and robots running on much more powerful computers can incorporate vision, sound, network, sonar and other modes of input. These additional inputs provide much more information about the environment, but bring additional problems related to control of perception.

Perceptual input streams (called *modes* in the psychology literature) can have greatly varying bandwidth. In people, the sense of touch has a low bandwidth, while the sense of vision has a very high bandwidth. The human brain can not completely process all of the information from one high bandwidth mode, much less simultaneously process all the information available from all modes. To control the amount of perceptual input processed, humans use *selective attention* (Treisman 1993).

Computer vision is a difficult problem which, if solved, could provide robots with a large amount of useful information. However, visual input can not be processed efficiently without using a top-down attention mechanism (Tsotsos 1987). Several computational models of visual selective attention have been developed (e.g. (Reece 1992)). [1]

Generalizing Selective Attention

Given the trends in computer hardware and robot technology, attention mechanisms are going to become even more important than they are now. Unfortunately, visual attention models can not be directly applied to other input modes. For example, (Ahmad 1991) utilizes a network containing three nodes for each of the pixels in a 256 by 256 visual array. This network would be useless for acoustic or textual input.

The goal of my thesis is to develop a generalized selective attention mechanism that handles all modes of input and ranges of bandwidths. Since it is doubtful that single attention mechanism can efficiently handle all types of input, the structure of the generalized mechanism is that of a programmable router. Attention control is routed from the cognitive component to relevant attention modules, each of which is specific to a mode. In return, data is routed from the attention modules to the cognitive component. All of the modules conform to a standard interface. The challenge is to make the interface general, yet transparent enough so that information is not lost as the data moves from its source to the cognitive component, and as attention commands move in the opposite direction.

Attention commands are routed to any applicable input mode. For example, a goal of finding a `wall` would send attention commands to the visual and sonar modes, while a goal of finding `people` would be routed to visual and acoustic modes. The relative priority of input modes would be governed by intermodal attention control.

Applying Multimodal Attention

We are applying multimodal, multilevel selective attention in an autonomous wheelchair The wheelchair contains infrared, sonar, visual and user interface sensors, each of which has a different bandwidth and data type. Since the primary goal of the project is assistance in navigation and movement, the sensor inputs are extremely important. We will use the generalized attention mechanism to control perception.

References

Ahmad, S. 1991. *VISIT: An Efficient Computational Model of Human Visual Attention*. Ph.D. Dissertation, University of Illinois at Urbana-Champaign, Urbana-Champaign, Illinois.

Reece, D. B. 1992. *Selective Perception for Robot Driving*. Ph.D. Dissertation, Carnegie-Mellon University, Pittsburgh, Pennsylvania.

Treisman, A. 1993. Features and objects. In Baddeley, A., and Weiskrantz, L., eds., *Attention: Selection, Awareness and Control*. Clarendon Press.

Tsotsos, J. K. 1987. A 'complexity level' analysis of immediate vision. *International Journal of Computer Vision* 1(4):303–320.

---

[1] Copyright © 1998, American Association for Artificial Intelligence (www.aaai.org). All rights reserved.

Learning in Markov Games with Incomplete Information

Junling Hu
Artificial Intelligence Laboratory
University of Michigan
Ann Arbor, MI 48109-2110, USA
junling@umich.edu
http://ai.eecs.umich.edu/people/junling

The Markov game (also called *stochastic game* (Filar & Vrieze 1997)) has been adopted as a theoretical framework for multiagent reinforcement learning (Littman 1994). In a Markov game, there are n agents, each facing a Markov decision process (MDP). All agents' MDPs are correlated through their reward functions and the state transition function. As Markov decision process provides a theoretical framework for single-agent reinforcement learning, Markov games provide such a framework for multiagent reinforcement learning.

In my thesis, I expand the framework of Littman of a 2-player zero-sum Markov game to a 2-player general-sum Markov game. In a zero-sum game, two players' rewards always sum to zero for any situation. That means one agent's gain is always the other agent's loss, thus agents have strictly opposite interests. In a general-sum game, agents' rewards can sum to any number. Agents may have incentive to cooperate if they all receive positive rewards in certain situations. Thus general-sum games include zero-sum games as a special case. The solution concept for general-sum games is Nash equilibrium, which requires every agent's strategy to be the best response to the other agents' strategies. In a Nash equilibrium, no agent can gain by unilateral deviation.

In Markov games with incomplete information, agents cannot observe the payoff functions of other agents. Thus they need to form certain beliefs about other agents by learning during the interactions with other agents. The learning must be online in dynamic systems (Hu & Wellman 1998). I aim to design a online Q-learning algorithm for Markov games, and prove that it converges to a Nash equilibrium.

Before designing an algorithm, I defined the equilibrium concept for Markov games under incomplete information. The definition has the following requirements: (1) Each agent's belief must be consistent with the actual outcome; (2) Each agent's strategy must be the best response to its belief about the other agent. When the system reaches equilibrium, there will be no more changes in agents' strategies and their beliefs. We

*Copyright 1998, American Association for Artificial Intelligence (www.aaai.org). All rights reserved.

call such equilibrium *conjectural equilibrium*. The study here follows our previous work on conjectural equilibrium in dynamic multiagent systems (Hu & Wellman 1996). Nash equilibrium is a special conjectural equilibrium in which agents' strategies are the same as in complete information case.

I have designed a multiagent Q-learning algorithm for 2-player Markov games. Each agent's Q-value function include both agents' actions and the state. A learning agent maintains two tables for every state, one for its own Q-values and one for the other agent's Q-values. The agent updates both Q tables for a given state after it observes the state, actions taken by both agents, and the rewards received by agents. The updating rule differs previous Q-learning algorithms in that it uses the one-period Nash equilibrium strategies of both agents to update their Q-value functions. I proved that this Q-learning algorithm converges to a Nash equilibrium of the whole game under certain assumptions of the game structure.

In the future work, I want to investigate the exploration and exploitation tradeoff in Markov games. I also want to reduce the large action space by using functional approximation.

Acknowledgments. Thanks to my advisor Michael Wellman for guidance and support. I also want to thank Craig Boutilier, Jun Zhang and Sridhar Mahadevan for helpful discussions.

References

Filar, J., and Vrieze, K. 1997. *Competitive Markov Decision Process*. Springer-Verlag.

Hu, J., and Wellman, M. P. 1996. Self-fulfilling bias in multiagent learning. In *Proceedings of the Second International Conference on Multiagent Systems*. AAAI Press.

Hu, J., and Wellman, M. P. 1998. Online learning about other agents in a dynamic multiagent system. To appear in the Proceedings of the second International Conference of Autonomous Agent.

Littman, M. L. 1994. Markov games as a framework for multi-agent reinforcement learning. In *ML-94*, 157–163. New Brunswick.

Extending the Classification Paradigm to Temporal Domains

Mohammed Waleed Kadous

School of Computer Science & Engineering
University of New South Wales
Sydney, NSW 2052, Australia
waleed@cse.unsw.edu.au

Introduction

One of the primary areas of machine learning research has been supervised concept learning – given some information about examples whose class is known, the goal is to produce a classifier which can classify examples whose class is not known. In general, research in this area has focused on situations where an object's attributes do not change in the short term. However, in many real-world domains, such as speech, sign language, robotics and medicine, many of the classification tasks involve dynamic attributes. Furthermore, temporal properties are critical to classification.

The current work involves developing a temporal classification learner that works in a variety of domains, does not require excessive amounts of data and is able to produce comprehensible descriptions of the concepts, while still having high predictive accuracy.

Model

Each domain has a specific set of channels, which are analogous to attributes in static classification. These channels are "sampled" at regular time intervals. The set of values of all channels at a particular instant is called a frame. A stream is a sequence of frames. The inputs to the learner are thus: a description of the channels; the set of classes; and a set of training streams labelled with their class. The output is a classifier that is capable of taking an unlabelled stream and predicting its class.

Testbed Applications

Currently work is progressing on three testbed applications:

Auslan Sign Recognition. Using instrumented gloves, isolated signs from Australian sign language are sampled. The goal is to produce a system which can recognise isolated signs from one of 95 classes.

ECG Analysis. Doctors can diagnose patients by examining their ECG's (electrocardiographs). It would also be possible to apply a temporal classification algorithm to the data. It might prove interesting to compare machine-generated rules to those used by doctors.

Robotics & Sensor Fusion. Much of what is interesting in a robot's domain may be the temporal variation and the correlation between sensors. A robot could be taught by example to deal with particular events, e.g. "door opening", "enemy robot firing weapon" etc.

Technique

Several techniques have been developed so far. There are three main families of techniques:

"Data-space" approaches. These deal with the channels directly. Techniques of this family so far have included treating each frame-channel pair as an attribute, then using instance-based learning; using entropy measures for each frame-channel pair as a bias to instance-based learning; extracting templates and using a χ^2 test to determine usefulness to classification.

"Segment-space" approaches. An algorithm for converting a channel to a sequence of line segments using a minimum description length heuristic has been developed. Once converted to a sequence of lines, the data is simpler to manipulate. For example, this information could be provided to an ILP system to extract rules from, or segments could be clustered, labelled and then a grammar induced.

A "hybrid" approach. Current research is based on the hypothesis that it is not important to recognise every part of the stream; but rather to isolate "markers" that are distinctive of a particular class. To the author's knowledge, this is a novel approach.

The approach being investigated uses an entropy-based data-space method to isolate markers, then applies a segment-space generalisation algorithm to generate a readable description. These are then used to build simple one-class classifiers which output confidence factors, which can then be combined to form a general classifier.

Acknowledgements

Thanks be to the Creator for giving me the ability to do this research. Thanks, secondarily, to Claude Sammut for many suggestions. This work is funded by an Australian Postgraduate Award.

Data mining for maintenance of complex systems

Sylvain Létourneau
School of Information Technology and Engineering
University of Ottawa, Canada
sletour@ai.iit.nrc.ca

The operation and maintenance of modern sensor-equipped systems such as aircraft generates vast amounts of complex data. Proper use of this data to predict or explain component failures may lead to saving of several thousands of dollars, reducing the number of delays, and increasing the overall level of safety. The field of Knowledge Discovery in Databases (KDD) has delivered a variety of techniques to discover patterns from vast amounts of data. However, none of these techniques are designed to handle the diverse forms of data typically generated during the operation and maintenance of such complex systems. In this research, we study the specific issues to consider during the analysis of commercial aircraft data and propose adequate enhancements of the data mining process to handle these difficulties. The anticipated contributions of this research are related to two fundamental problems in the field of knowledge discovery in databases: i) automatic preparation of the data prior to model development, and ii) use of diverse sources of information.

We aim at extracting useful information from large amounts of data collected from a fleet of 34 commercial aircraft over the last three years. Many issues with the analysis of this data have been identified (Létourneau, Famili, & Matwin 1997). First of all, diverse sources and formats of data are to be considered. Available data includes: i) various types of sensor measurement reports describing the status of the aircraft in different phases of operation, ii) warning and failure messages generated when particular conditions occur, and iii) descriptions of aircraft problems along with the maintenance actions taken for each of them. Various sources of background knowledge are also available such as troubleshooting guides, training manuals and empirical studies. A second difficulty comes from the complexity and the quality of the data. The number of parameters is high (i.e. often more than 100), several parameters are expected to have time-series relationships, and problems such as missing values, improper data types, and out-of-range data are frequently observed. Some sensor measurements must also be normalized due to the influence of variations in the environment.

We propose two major research directions to address these difficulties: i) development of a powerful data pre-processing approach to handle data complexity and data quality problems and ii) integration of the multiple sources of information described above to improve the quality of models learned from the data.

The data pre-processing approach proposed in this thesis should address the following tasks: i) normalization of the data according to the effects of contextual variations in the environment, ii) cleaning of the data, and iii) labeling of the instances so that supervised machine learning techniques can be used. We have developed the core of a novel domain independent normalization technique that makes use of the analysis of variance (Létourneau, Matwin, & Famili 1998). Results from experiments with a large dataset in the aircraft domain have shown that the proposed approach is powerful in reducing the number of false alarms caused by random fluctuations in the environment. The current focus is on cleaning of the data and labeling of the instances.

The second major aspect of this work will address the use of different sources of information available during the operation and maintenance of complex systems. We will study the use of these domain information regarding the following aspects: i) extraction of the most appropriate features, ii) analysis of meaningfulness of obtained models, and iii) improvement of the accuracy. This thesis is expected to enhance the process of knowledge discovery in databases so that it could be successfully applied to the maintenance and operation of complex systems.

Acknowledgments The author is grateful to Dr. Stan Matwin and Dr. A. Famili (from the National Research Council of Canada) for their help and guidance.

References

Létourneau, S.; Famili, A.; and Matwin, S. 1997. Discovering useful knowledge from aircraft operation/maintenance data. In *Proc. of the workshop on Machine Learning Applications, ICML*.

Létourneau, S.; Matwin, S.; and Famili, A. 1998. A normalization method for contextual data: Experience from a large-scale application. In *Proc. of the European Conference on Machine Learning*.

Empirical Acquisition of Word-Sense Distinctions

Tom O'Hara
Department of Computer Science
& Computing Research Laboratory
New Mexico State University
Las Cruces, NM 88003-0001
tomohara@nmsu.edu

Applications currently make use of many kinds of lexical information: categorial relations ("dog" *is-a* "canine"), synonymy ("pooch" *same-as* "dog") and word associations ("walk" *occurs-often-with* "dog"). However, an important type of information, *differentia*, is often omitted, especially in broad-coverage applications. Differentia are properties that distinguish a concept from others belonging to the same higher-level category. For instance, both beagles and wolfhounds are hounds, but the former are small, whereas the latter are quite large. Applications should incorporate differentia to provide finer word-sense distinctions and to facilitate inference of information not mentioned in the text.

Determining the differentia is a difficult task, since the available knowledge sources define these properties using natural language. For instance, WordNet (Miller 1990), a commonly used source of lexical knowledge, provides explicit information on categorial relationships but leaves the differentia implicit in the definitions. This work will investigate empirical approaches for extracting these properties from machine readable dictionaries (MRD's) and text corpora. The result will be lexical relations between the word being defined and words used in the definition. There has been some work on deriving differentia, but these have relied predominantly on manually developed heuristics. Here, corpus-derived associations will augment such heuristics for extracting information from MRD's. Furthermore, this work will investigate a novel use of Bayesian networks for representing the various types of lexical knowledge in order to model the uncertainty in the relations and support integration of statistical and analytical knowledge.

Dictionary definitions use certain fixed patterns, often with prepositional phrases, to indicate differentia. However, since prepositions are highly ambiguous, the same pattern can be used for different properties. To address this problem, syntactic pattern matching will be applied to each definition to identify potential properties. Then, statistical classification will be used to select the most plausible ones. To support this work, a representative sample of definitions will be annotated to indicate the properties that apply. This will serve as the primary training data for the classifier. To allow for a fallback mechanism, a separate classifier will be trained on the semantic role annotations in the second release of the Penn Treebank (Marcus *et al.* 1994).

Providing sufficient annotated training data for automated disambiguation of the definition text would require a large corpus of sense-tagged data for all content words, which is currently not available. Therefore, unsupervised corpus-based approaches will be used for disambiguation, such as extensions to Yarowsky's (1992) method. He uses co-occurrence statistics for the words listed under each Roget category to determine contextual support for that category. The extensions will include dynamic use of WordNet categories for defining the topics. In addition, training will be over definitions as well as over general text to allow for constraints on the potential topics.

To represent word-sense distinctions using Bayesian networks, lexical relations will be modeled by causal links among word sense nodes. We will use a representation with a clear probabilistic interpretation to enable us to take advantage of formal tools from the applied statistics literature. To support word-sense disambiguation, a Bayesian network used for modeling the interdependencies among word senses will be integrated with a statistical word-sense classifier that uses clues from the local syntactic context, following Bruce and Wiebe (1995). This work builds upon theirs by including the differentia, allowing for links between senses of words in different categories (augmenting the explicit WordNet links, which are mostly in the same category). Integrating differentia obtained from an MRD with information derived from a corpus should improve performance on word-sense disambiguation and other lexical applications as well.

References

Bruce, R., and Wiebe, J. 1995. Towards the acquisition and representation of a broad-coverage lexicon. In *Proc. AAAI Spring Symposium on Representation and Acquisition of Lexical Knowledge*, 174–179.

Marcus, M.; Kim, G.; Marcinkiewicz, M.; et al. 1994. The penn treebank: Annotating predicate argument structure. In *Human Language Technology Workshop*.

Miller, G. 1990. Wordnet: An on-line lexical database. *International Journal of Lexicography* 3(4).

Yarowsky, D. 1992. Word-sense disambiguation using statistical models of roget's categories trained on large corpora. In *Proc. COLING-92*, 454–460.

Neural approaches to blind separation and cumulant analysis and its application to diagnostics of nuclear power plants

Alexei Ourmanov

Institute of Physics and Power Engineering
Bondarenko sq. 1
Obninsk, Kaluga region, 249020, Russia
urmanov@ippe.obninsk.com

The problem concerned is to explore the possibility of using artificial intelligence techniques, namely neural networks, and design the appropriate neural network-based algorithm to detect signals of interest from multi-channel data recordings. The problem finds application in diagnostic systems of nuclear power plant with liquid-metal fast breeder. The idea of a whole approach is to make an adaptive diagnostic system of acoustic monitoring of a steam generator unit. The system is based on neural network feature extraction and pattern recognition of multi-channel acoustic signals generated by a steam generator unit. In the background noise environment the diagnostic system must detect water leaks in sodium which may occur in the steam generator unit under monitoring.

Unfortunately traditional linear techniques fail to solve the problem with extreme low signal to noise ratio that is the case in the application described above. The power spectra of acoustic background noise signal and leak signal are completely overlapped and there is no possibility to separate or extract signals used only second-order techniques which are based on auto- and cross-correlation.

Neural networks turn to be powerful tools in modeling underlying phenomena that are responsible for generation of real signals. Due to significantly nonlinear structure and adaptive learning behavior neural networks become very attractive and promising in solving such problems as described. Recently there appeared a new technique for multi-channel signal separation referred as Blind Source Separation (BSS) or Independent Component Analysis (ICA) treating original source signals as independent components which are then observed mixed in the multi-channel recordings. The aim is to combine the powerful of neural networks and the methods of blind separation to solve the problem of signal extraction with low signal to noise ratio and overlapped power spectra.

To apply BSS technique it is necessary to be sure that signals under consideration possess meaningful higher order statistics, namely cumulants of order higher than second, what leads to a problem of reliable estimation of cumulants from given data. The cumulant analysis of signals corresponds with the analysis of density distributions of the signals to make a decision whether signals have non-gaussian distribution density. Non-gaussianity of signals is the main feature signals must possess for one to apply ICA technique. In frequency domain ICA approach assumes to use higher-order spectra. Unfortunately classical approaches to BSS can not be applied to real data due to fairly simple mixture model and conditions imposed on signals. It is a task to explore new BSS techniques including delays in signals and possible convolutions with media.

An important aspect of problem to be considered is to extent the BSS technique on the case with a prior information available. In diagnostic systems for signal detection in noisy environment, as a rule, at least one source is known. The group of independent sources, which form the background noise component, is always known in such problems. More precisely there is information about all statistical characteristics of background noise signals, as there is a lot of background noise recordings provided to solve the problem of detection a signal of interest. In contrast to that there is no information about a signal to be detected before the "fault" appears. So the separation becomes not strictly blind. This circumstance makes the problem easier in some sense. The main difficult being arisen while working with real data is that due to unknown source signals it is difficult to interpret the obtained independent signals. Thus, forcing the known component to be as one of the output signals other outputs may be interpreted as signals being sought and further analyzed.

According to the problem stated, available to-date BSS techniques, and necessity of investigations and improvements of existing techniques a work plan had been drawn up and a certain progress in research has been achieved.

Copyright © 1998, American Association for Artificial Intelligence (www.aaai.org). All rights reserved.

Bayesian Reasoning for Tropical Cyclone Intensity Forecasting and Risk Analysis

Grace W Rumantir
School of Computer Science and Software Engineering
Monash University – Clayton Vic 3168 Australia
gwr@csse.monash.edu.au

Improved methods for tropical cyclone (TC) intensity forecasting and risk analysis are the end products of this project leading to the wider use in the mitigation of the devastating impacts of tropical cyclones. Single-disciplined approaches in TC intensity forecasting by meteorologists and in risk analysis by social scientists so far have not seen satisfactory results. This is because of the intrinsically high degree of complexity in both the modelling and the problem domain parts of the project.

The current techniques of TC intensity forecasting are limited to linear regression methods, which may not provide the maximum accuracy for the available information. Bayesian inductive inference using the Minimum Message Length (MML) principle (Wallace & Freeman 1987) is used to investigate the likelihood that various different models (linear and non-linear) can be applied to TC intensity data. The features of these models may well suggest new insights into the formation of TC, facilitating better explanation of the most probable underlying functions of TC intensity, with the aim of providing improved forecasting capacity. In the past, Rissanen's Minimum Description Length (MDL) (Rissanen 1987), a related form of Bayesian inference technique, has been successfully applied to time-series analysis in a different problem domain.

An MML regression algorithm has been implemented to build forecasting models using data for the Atlantic basin. The promising results have warranted further development and testing expansions to different TC basins with varying degrees of data quality. The next step will be to consider whether the forecasts can be improved by incorporating a wider range of meteorological data into the analysis.

Tropical cyclone risk analysis encompasses variables ranging from the cyclone threat through to vulnerability in the form of social factors and building standards. Much of the interactions amongst these variables have either not been investigated or only been done in a highly subjective manner. A naive approach to setting up a Bayesian causal network for risk factors would be to try to capture all the interactions and consequences for which available data would be inadequate to provide reliable estimates of all of the free parameters. Using MML principles, a restricted class of variable interaction models will be developed to reduce the number of free parameters to a feasible level. In principle, this is very similar to the use of factor models in explaining multivariate covariance structures amongst real valued variables. Here, a hierarchy of increasingly complex model covariance structures is defined. MML principles have already been successfully applied to this factor problem (Wallace & Freeman 1992). Although the mathematical details will be significantly different, the theoretical approach used there should be applicable to Bayesian networks involving discrete variables and non-linear interactions. The techniques to be developed should have applications in other problem domains.

Much work will initially be theoretical and programming to build general framework for Bayesian networks involving real and discrete variables and exploring restricted classes of models for inter-variable dependence, e.g. logistic regression and log-odds ratio function. Once sufficient data has been collected from the surveys conducted by the Tropical Cyclone Coastal Impacts Program (TCCIP), interaction parameters in model Bayesian networks or risk predictions can be estimated. Risk prediction models based on regression techniques will also be developed to compare the results of the two approaches.

Acknowledgments

This research is partially supported by grants from the Australian DEST and the US ONR under grant N-00014-94-I-0556. The author is a recipient of APA(I).

References

Rissanen, J. 1987. Stochastic complexity. *Journal of the Royal Statistical Society B* 49(1):223–239.

Wallace, C., and Freeman, P. 1987. Estimation and inference by compact coding. *Journal of the Royal Statistical Society B* 49(1):240–252.

Wallace, C., and Freeman, P. 1992. Single factor analysis by MML estimation. *Journal of the Royal Statistical Society B* 54(1):185–209.

Rational Multiagent Organization and Reorganization

Wayne A. Smith

Computer Science Department
University of South Carolina
Columbia, SC 29208
wasmith@cs.sc.edu

This research agenda has as its goal to apply principles from decision theory and organization theory to the problem of multiagent organization and reorganization. The result is a rational, dynamic multiagent architecture designed to address the following issues:
- Choosing the appropriate organizational structure (design from scratch);
- Choosing the appropriate reorganization (redesign);
- Adding, losing and moving agents within an organization; and
- Handling node and link failures that lead to agents becoming unavailable to the rest of the organization.

The architecture will be experimentally validated with different organization sizes ranging from four to fifty agents. These experiments will determine how well a dynamic organization fares versus a static one with respect to solution quality and response time.

The unique aspect of this approach to multiagent organization is the multi-stage, multi-tier representation of reorganization. Like the TAEMS approach (Decker and Lesser 1993), this architecture is designed to organize itself based on attributes of the task-environment. However the model of tasks, resources and environmental constraints includes more factors that predict the best organization. Like (So and Durfee 1994), this solution also considers multiple possible organizations before choosing the best for a given situation. This architecture will choose the best organization based on the maximum expected utility. Like the self-designing architecture of (Gasser and Ishida 1991), this design localizes reorganizations when appropriate based on constraints of resource allocations. However this approach will utilize more complex models of the resources and tasks at varying levels of granularity. Thus reorganization becomes an iterative problem in which high-level, approximate decisions are made concerning initial, coarse allocations of tasks and resources and each subset then organizes itself as an independent problem.

At this stage of the investigation, we have identified four core components of the architecture:

1. Organization Planner: A decision network used as a causal model whose input includes descriptions of the task and the resources and produces a list of organizational designs ranked based on how each maximizes expected utility.
2. Reorganization Assessment: A decision network designed to perform cost/benefit analysis of the proposed list of organizations. The marginal benefit of reorganizing is calculated as the maximum expected utility (MEU) of the target organization minus the sum of the MEU of the existing organization and the reorganization cost. Thus this component determines whether or not any of the reorganizations is worth pursuing given the current state of the organization.
3. Reorganization Decomposition: For relatively large organizations, reorganization across the entire community can be prohibitive with respect to cost of deliberation. This component chooses the appropriate level of detail to address allocation of resources and tasks. Therefore the system must have sufficient information to iteratively partition the task.
4. Organization Event Handler: This component must be able to handle the following events as variations of a reorganization problem: addition, loss or movement of an agent and reallocation of tasks and resources by higher levels in the organization.

References

Decker, E., and Lesser, V. 1993. Quantitative Modeling of Complex Computational Task Environments. In AAAI-93. Menlo Park, CA: AAAI.

Gasser, L., and Ishida, T. 1991. A Dynamic organizational architecture for adaptive problem solving. In AAAI-91. Menlo Park, CA: AAAI.

So, Y., and Durfee, E. 1994. Modeling and Designing Computational Organizations. In Working Notes of the AAAI Spring Symposium on Computational Organization Design. Menlo Park, CA: AAAI.

Copyright @ 1998, American Association for Artificial Intelligence (www.aaai.org). All rights reserved.

A Script-Based Approach to Modifying Knowledge-Based Systems

Marcelo Tallis
Department of Computer Science and Information Sciences Institute
University of Southern California
4676 Admiralty Way, Marina del Rey, CA 90292
tallis@isi.edu

Modifying knowledge-based systems (KBSs) is a complex activity that needs to be performed very often. The occurrence of changes in a KBSs environment, requests for extending the system's functionality, and the debugging of inadequate knowledge are some of the events that demand modifications to a KBSs. One of the difficulties of KBS modifications is that they might require the modification of several related portions of the system. Determining what portions have to be changed and how to change them requires a deep understanding of how the elements of the KBS interact. This requirement is especially hard for users when the rationale behind the design of a KBS or the details of its implementation are unknown.

Although current Knowledge Acquisition (KA) tools can lessen the burden of modifying KBSs, they do not directly address the issue of how to modify related portions of a KBS in coordination. Consequently, their support is limited. Some of these KA tools, like SALT (Marcus and McDermott 1989), support KBS modifications based on strong assumptions about the underlying problem-solving strategy used by the KBS. These tools can only support modifications to the domain-dependent knowledge manipulated by the system, which is a strong limitation of these tools. Other tools, like EXPECT (Gil 1994), support KBS modifications based on the understanding of how KBS components interact. These tools can support modifications to any aspect of the KBS. Unfortunately, the understanding of these interactions alone is insufficient to determine how related components have to be modified.

In this research, I aim to develop an approach for building KA tools that both, provide strong guidance to users and allow a wide range of modifications to a KBS. My proposed approach consists of providing a knowledge acquisition tools with *knowledge acquisition scripts* (or *KA scripts*) that represent prototypical procedures for modifying knowledge-based systems (KBSs). More specifically, a KA script describes a prototypical sequence of changes for following up the consequences of previous changes to the KBS. An example of a KA script is:

[1]Copyright ©1998, American Association for Artificial Intelligence (www.aaai.org). All rights reserved.

if a) a change to a KBS makes a goal more general and
  b) the modified goal cannot be achieved
then generalize method that achieved the original goal

KA scripts enable a KA tool to relate changes concerning different parts of the KBS.

We have implemented a Script-based KA tool called ETM that supports modifications of EXPECT KBSs. The role of ETM is to help a user to bring a KBS back to a coherent state after a user has performed some initial changes to the KBS using EXPECT conventional KA tool (the KBS is assumed to be coherent before starting its modification). ETM engages in a loop in which 1) it identifies unattended consequences of previous changes, 2) suggests KA Scripts that take care of those consequences, and 3) guides the user throughout the application of one of these KA Scripts (chosen by the user). A complete modification usually requires of the execution of several KA scripts. This is because some changes can have several consequences that have to be followed up by different KA scripts, and because the execution of some KA scripts have consequences that also need to be followed up.

In developing ETM we addressed several research issues that concerned the development of a KA script library, the coordination of the execution of KA scripts, and the model of interaction with the user. We have designed a KA script library that contains around 75 KA scripts (only a dozen were implemented).

We carried out a preliminary evaluation of ETM that compared the performance in modifying KBSs for subjects using ETM vs. subjects using EXPECT. The experiment showed that subjects using ETM outperformed the ones using EXPECT, especially in the more complex modification tasks. These results suggests that script-based knowledge-acquisition is a promising technology. In this first experiment we chose subjects that were already familiar with EXPECT but not with ETM. We expect that the difference in performance will be more significant in our future experiments involving subjects not familiar with EXPECT either.

References

Gil, Y. 1994. Knowledge Refinement in a Reflective Architecture. In AAAI-94, Seattle, WA, 1994.

Marcus, S. and McDermott, J. 1989. SALT: A Knowledge Acquisition Language for Propose-and-Revise Systems. *Artificial Intelligence*, 39(1):1-37.

Student Abstracts

Learning to Teach with a Reinforcement Learning Agent

Joseph E. Beck
Department of Computer Science
University of Massachusetts, Amherst
Amherst, MA 01003. U.S.A.
beck@cs.umass.edu

Intelligent tutoring systems (ITS) use artificial intelligence techniques to customize their instruction to fit the needs of each student. To do this, the system must have knowledge of the student being taught (commonly called a *student model*) and a set of pedagogical rules that enable the system to follow good teaching principles. Teaching rules are commonly represented as a set of "if-then" production rules, where the "if" side is dependent on the student model, and the "then" side is a teaching action. For example, a rule may be of the form "IF (the student has never been introduced to the current topic) THEN (teach the topic to the student)."

This approach is fairly straightforward from a knowledge engineering perspective, but has many drawbacks. First, there are many such rules, and it is very expensive to encode all of the rules the system will require to teach effectively. Second, it is difficult to incorporate knowledge that human tutors do not use themselves, since expert teachers cannot describe how the system should reason with such knowledge. Since machine tutors have a very different set of data available than human tutors (keystroke latencies, performance on a similar problem 3 weeks ago, etc.), knowledge that could dramatically improve the tutor's performance must be ignored.

We will use Reinforcement learning (RL) to train ITS to teach. RL is a mechanism that allows a machine learning (ML) agent to learn given only a description of the state and a reward for its performance. Thus RL supports unsupervised learning as it does not need to be told what the correct action is, but simply learns how to maximize its long term reward.

We will use the student model as a state description for the RL-agent. This saves considerable knowledge engineering work. Also, since the student model already accounts for student learning, the learning task becomes *stationary*. That is, for a given set of inputs the expected value will remain constant. The agent uses this state description as input to a function approximator, and uses this learned function to select a teaching action. After the selected action is performed, the system examines how the student performs on future problems to compute the effectiveness of the teaching action. If the teaching action was effective, student performance should improve, and the system will receive a positive reward. Less appropriate teaching actions will not be as effective at improving a student's performance, and will receive smaller rewards. We propose that a state-action learning algorithm such as SARSA(Sutton & Barto 1997), a on-line version of Q-learning, would be most applicable for this task. The system learns to map each student and his current knowledge to an optimal teaching action. For example, the system could learn when is the best time to present an example to the student, or when a topic should be taught, or when the student should be given a problem to solve.

It is unlikely the system will be able to learn this policy quickly enough from a single student. Therefore, the RL-agent will first be trained off-line using either empirical data, or simulations of students(VanLehn, Ohlsson, & Nason 1996). Once the system attains a reasonable level of teaching ability, it can be used by actual students. The learning mechanism will be left in place, so the system can fine-tune its performance to better fit with each student. This permits a level of customization that is impossible with precanned teaching rules.

Such a system would advance research in both ITS and ML. ITS would benefit from having more flexible teaching rules. These rules would be customized to each individual learner, and would be able to consider knowledge that is (at best) problematic to add when working with human experts. This represents a fundamental shift in system construction, and would potentially both reduce costs and provide great improvements in learning gains exhibited by the tutor's users.

This methodology explores how to train an ML system using a large quantity of poorer quality data (the empirical studies and simulations), and then fine-tune it with higher quality, but more scarce data (the interactions with the student using the system). This permits ML systems to be used in domains where they would normally be undeployable due to a scarcity of data.

References

Sutton, R., and Barto, A. 1997. *An Introduction to Reinforcement Learning.* MIT Press.

VanLehn, K.; Ohlsson, S.; and Nason, R. 1996. Applications of simulated students: An exploration. *Journal of Artificial Intelligence in Education* 5(2):135–175.

Genetic Search for Accurate Feature Sets

Brendan Burns
Williams College, 2127 Baxter Hall, Williamstown, Mass. 01267
98bdb@cs.williams.edu

This abstract describes a feature selection system, INDiGENT. INDiGENT has been to designed to enhance knowledge based neural networks by genetically searching the set of input features for an optimum subset. This search is designed to enable INDiGENT to make more accurate classifications. Significantly, INDiGENT has shown that it can obtain similar increases in accuracy as more complicated theory revision systems.

Expert systems have proven themselves effective decision makers for many types of problems. However, the accuracy of such systems is highly dependent upon the accuracy of the human expert's domain theory. To escape this dependency, many machine learning systems have been developed to automatically refine and correct an expert's domain theory.

Classification systems rely heavily upon having the best (i.e., most relevant) set of input data. Many domains have a variety of potential input features. Therefore, choosing the appropriate set of inputs is critical to the performance of any expert system, and specifically in this case, to the creation of accurate neural networks.

There are a number of systems which use neural network encodings to refine a variety of rule bases including finite state automata (Maclin & Shavlik 1993), certainty-factor rule bases (Mahoney 1996) and first-order horn clause logic (Towell, Shavlik, & Noordewier 1990). INDiGENT uses the KBANN method for encoding domain theories. There has also been work done on genetically refining neural network topologies (Opitz 1995), (Mahoney 1996). There are also a number of systems that utilize a variety of other search methods to find optimum feature sets (e.g. (Kira & Rendell 1992), (Asker & Maclin 1997)).

INDiGENT operates in the following manner. An initial set of input features is selected. These features are those which are explicitly referenced in the domain theory as well as those features which are not mentioned in the domain but have been identified by the inductive learner C4.5 as significant. This initial feature set is then mutated to create a population for the genetic search. All members of this population are then evaluated using ten-fold cross validation. Two parents are then selected proportional to their measured accuracy. The parents are crossed over and mutated to create a new child. This new child is then evaluated. If its accuracy is better than the worst member of the current population the child replaces the worst member. This process continues for an arbitrary number of generations.

Presently, experiments are complete for three domains. These domains involve the identification of signifigant locations in strands of DNA. INDiGENT's performance on these domains relative to several other existing systems is shown below.

All evaluations were reported using ten-fold cross validation to insure generalization. The results are signifigant because they show that simple feature set selection has the ability to perform on par with a more extensive theory revision system like REGENT. This result is important because it allows for the improvement of accuracy while maintaining the simplicity, and therefore legibility, of the initial domain information. TNT-INDiGENT (Total Neural Topology INDiGENT) has been designed to combine input feature set revision with the hidden layer theory revision performed by REGENT and is currently being evaluated to determine if even greater imrpvements in accuracy are possible.

System	Promoters	RBS	Splice Junctions
INDiGENT	95.56%	92.76%	94.96%
REGENT	95.83%	92.17%	95.92%
KBANN	93.70%	91.05%	94.75%
C4.5	88.0%	84.8%	

Table 1: INDiGENT's accuracy compared to several other systems

References

Asker, L., and Maclin, R. 1997. Feature engineering and classifier selection: A case study in venusian volcano detection. In *The Proceedings of ICML-1997*.

Kira, K., and Rendell, L. 1992. The feature selection problem: Traditional methods and a new algorithm. In *The Proceedings of AAAI-92*.

Maclin, R., and Shavlik, J. W. 1993. Using knowledge-based neural networks to improve algorithms: Refining the Chou-Fasman algorithm for protein folding. *Machine Learning* 11:195–215.

Mahoney, J. 1996. *Combining Symbolic and Connectionist Learning Methods to Refine Certaintty-Factor Rule-Bases*. Ph.D. Dissertation, University of Texas, Austin.

Opitz, D. W. 1995. *An Anytime Approach to Connectionist Theory Refinement: Refining the Topologies of Knowledge-Based Neural Networks*. Ph.D. Dissertation, Department of Computer Sciences, University of Wisconsin-Madison. (Also appears as UW Technical Report).

Towell, G. G.; Shavlik, J. W.; and Noordewier, M. O. 1990. Refinement of approximate domain theories by knowledge-based neural networks. In *Proceedings of AAAI-1990*, 861–866.

A First Analysis of Qualitative Influences and Synergies

Jesús Cerquides[1], Ramon López de Màntaras

Artificial Intelligence Research Institute, IIIA
Spanish Council for Scientific Research, CSIC
08193, Bellaterra, Barcelona, Spain
{cerquide,mantaras}@iiia.csic.es

Introduction[2]

Comprehensibility is a key characteristic for learning algorithms results to be useful in Knowledge Discovery in Databases tasks.

Bayesian reasoning has been usually criticized as hard to explain and understand, but achieves high performance rates with simple constructs, as happens for instance with the Naive-Bayes classifier.

Our approach can be viewed as a refinement of qualitative probabilistic networks in order to allow them to do the work probabilistic networks do, or as a way of showing that, slightly modified, Elsaesser's explanations can be used for reasoning and prediction, achieving results similar to Bayesian reasoning, while keeping intact their interpretability.

Influences and synergies revisited

Neufeld states a favours b if $Prob(b|a) > Prob(b)$ that is if $\frac{Prob(b|a)}{Prob(b)} > 1$. This quotient was also used by Elsaesser in his work trying to explain bayesian reasoning, to denote the shift in belief that a produces in b. We will define influence of a in b as:

$$Influence(a,b) = \frac{Prob(b|a)}{Prob(b)} \quad (1)$$

We note that:

$$Influence(a,b) = Influence(b,a) \quad (2)$$

We make use of the absolute order of magnitude model to discretize influences in order to gain in comprehensibility (Figure 1). Synergies can be seen as the difference in influence between two facts that happen together with respect to these two facts happening separately. We can give the following expression for synergies of two variables:

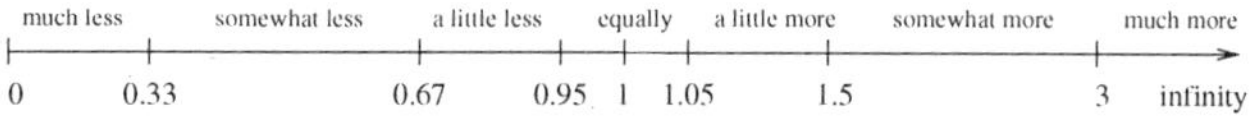

$$Synergy(\{a_1,a_2\},b) = \frac{Influence(a_1 \cap a_2, b)}{Influence(a_1,b) * Influence(a_2,b)} \quad (3)$$

We can discretize synergies as we do with influences.

Figure 1: Influence discretization scale

[1] Jesús Cerquides research is supported by a doctoral scholarship of the CIRIT (Generalitat de Catalunya).

[2] All the references can be found in (Cerquides & López de Màntaras 1998)

Copyright 1998, American Association for Artificial Intelligence (www.aaai.org). All rights reserved.

An application of qualitative influences and synergies: The Qualitative Bayesian Classifier

Qualitative influences and synergies can be used for reasoning and concretely for classification tasks, allowing high classification rates and having a good self-explanation hability. We have used them to get a qualitative version of a well known classification method, the Naive-Bayes classifier.

Assuming E_j's are independent, Naive-Bayes can be expressed as:

$$P(C=i|\mathbf{E}=\mathbf{e}) = P(C=i) * \prod_{j=1}^{N} Influence(E_j = e_j, C=i) \quad (4)$$

We can apply this rule with qualitative influences and analyze the difference between applying the Naive-Bayes classifier where shifts in belief grade continuously from 0 to 1 and our qualitative influences framework, where shifts only can have the seven values shown in Figure 1

Similarly we have created an approximation of the Second Order Bayesian classifier. In this case we have to avoid applying two synergy corrections over the same variable. Thus we apply the synergies in decreasing size order (from large ones to small ones).

Empirical results

We have tested the two classifiers against CN2, ID3, IBL and Naive-Bayes over 14 UCI datasets. The results of the first order classifier are slightly worse than the quantitative version (Naive-Bayes), but surprisingly 4 out of 14 times the qualitative version outperforms the quantitative one. The results of the second order one are as good as those from ID3, CN2 or IBL, and better than the Naive-Bayes ones.

Conclusions

We have introduced qualitative influences and synergies based on the absolute orders of magnitude model. We have shown that their accuracy results are good and they greatly improve the comprehensibility of probabilistic reasoning. These two facts make us believe that they can be useful within a KDD system.

References

Cerquides, J., and López de Màntaras, R. 1998. Qualitative Influences and Synergies: A Step Forward in Explaining Probabilistic Reasoning. Technical report, IIIA-98-04.

A New Approach to Rule Interest Measures

Jesús Cerquides[1], Ramon López de Màntaras

Artificial Intelligence Research Institute, IIIA
Spanish Council for Scientific Research, CSIC
08193, Bellaterra, Barcelona, Spain
{cerquide,mantaras}@iiia.csic.es

Introduction

Rule extraction is one of the main tasks in the Knowledge Discovery process. Our hypothesis is that the interestingness of rules is strongly related to statistical independence between facts. Human reasoning assumes by default statistical independence and when a rule breaks this assumption it is considered interesting. This fact has been noticed long ago and even proposed as a principle for rule-interest measures. However, to the best of our knowledge, nobody has correctly developed this principle. Until now, when facing the evaluation of a rule as $\mathcal{A} \to \mathcal{B}$, where $\mathcal{A}$ and $\mathcal{B}$ are complex conditions over a database universal relation, the way to evaluate the independence breaking principle was evaluating the fact that $\mathcal{A}$ and $\mathcal{B}$ were conditionally independent by using a function as

$$RI(\mathcal{A} \to \mathcal{B}) = Abs(|\mathcal{A} \wedge \mathcal{B}| - \frac{|\mathcal{A}||\mathcal{B}|}{N})$$

We claim that this result comes from an oversimplified analysis of the situation. Suppose we are looking for association rules. We have a database that contains a set of transactions. Suppose we can have only three items in each transaction and name them A, B and C. We do the rule search from the small to the large rules. Suppose that for rules with one condition you get:

$$Prob(C) = 10\%$$
$$A \to C \ [Conf. = 80\%, Support = 23500 \ registers]$$
$$B \to C \ [Conf. = 70\%, Support = 52700 \ registers]$$

Both rules are clearly interesting because they change the expected probability for item C, so we classify them as such and show them to the user. Imagine we know these two rules and we are told that for a concrete register A and B are both present. What will we think on the light of these rules about the presence of C? Common sense tells us that it is more plausible that C is present than absent. Suppose that for rules with two conditions you get:

$$A \wedge B \to C \ [Conf. = 10\%, Sup. = 3500 \ registers]$$

$RI(R)$ classifies the rule as extremely non-interesting. However we find this rule **very** interesting, because it allows us to know that the presence of A or B indicates the presence of C only when they happen separately, but not when they happen together. In other words, considering the rule as interesting prevents us

[1] Jesús Cerquides research is supported by a doctoral scholarship of the CIRIT (Generalitat de Catalunya).
Copyright 1998, American Association for Artificial Intelligence (www.aaai.org). All rights reserved.

from making the default conclusion that A and B together strongly influence C.

Instead of calculating interestingness as the difference between knowing that rule and knowing nothing we should calculate it as the difference between "knowing what we already know" and "knowing what we already know plus the rule we are trying to evaluate".

A necessary condition for interestingness

Let A, B, C be facts. A rule like $R = \{A \to B\}$ can only be interesting if $RI(R)$ is high.

A rule $A \wedge B \to C$ can only be interesting if $Prob(C|A \wedge B)$ is different of what we can predict with the knowledge at hand. What has been done until now is considering $A \wedge B$ as a single fact and calculating if

$$Prob(C|A \wedge B) \neq Prob(C)$$

where we can see $Prob(C)$ as an approximation to $Prob(C|A \wedge B)$ with the knowledge at hand. We claim that this approximation can be improved. What we propose is to consider that $A \wedge B$ is a composite fact, and we should take advantage of this fact to improve our approximation of $Prob(C|A \wedge B)$. If we have discovered all the rules with one condition previously, the real meaning of a rule as $A \wedge B \to C$ is that A and B together have a different effect than the *addition* of the effects of A and B over C separately. That is, when we say a rule like $A \wedge B \to C$ is interesting, what we are stating is that A and B are not conditionally independent given C. Approximating $Prob(C|A \wedge B)$ by assuming conditional independence of A and B given C we find that a rule like $A \wedge B \to C$ can only be interesting if:

$$Prob(C \wedge A \wedge B) \neq \frac{Prob(A \wedge C)Prob(B \wedge C)}{Prob(C)}$$

that is, if the conditional independence between A and B given C is not fulfilled.

For bigger rules the evaluation gets harder because different assumptions of conditional independence can be made that generate different approximations to the probability.

Conclusions

We have noticed a pitfall in the usual rule interest functions and proposed an alternative method based on the idea that human reasoning assumes independence between facts unless otherwise stated.

References

Cerquides, J., and López de Màntaras, R. 1998. A New Approach to Rule Interest Measures. Technical report, IIIA-98-08.

Classification Using an Online Genetic Algorithm

Brian D. Davison

Department of Computer Science
Rutgers, The State University of New Jersey
Piscataway, NJ 08855 USA
davison@cs.rutgers.edu

Genetic Algorithms (GAs) purport to mimic the behavior of natural selection. Many GAs, however, try to optimize their populations by means of a static fitness function — one that is derived from performance on a fixed set of examples. We propose an architecture for an *online genetic algorithm* (OLGA) for classification. An OLGA differs from standard genetic algorithms in that it does not repeatedly evaluate individuals against a fixed set of training examples. Instead, it is presented with a series of training examples, one at a time, and does not retain the entire set for training.

Being online and incremental, OLGAs, like evolution strategies (Dasgupta & Michalewicz 1997), are applicable to tasks that require continuous learning to handle *concept drift* such as in adaptive systems as well as tasks in which the dataset is too large to be kept on hand for repeated evaluation (as in many online and interactive problems). By evaluating individuals on recent examples, OLGAs also better mimic the behavior of natural selection, as real organisms live in environments that are not identical to that of their ancestors.

An OLGA is a GA, complete with a population of size p, fitness function, recombination operators, and mutation operators. However, unlike a traditional GA, the fitness of an individual changes over time, as it is exposed to more examples. In order to do so, we track the number of examples seen and the number of examples classified correctly for each individual and class. The fitness is calculated by summing over all classes the weight of the class times a function of *correctcount* and *totalseen*. The key idea in creating such a fitness function is to support newly created individuals so that they are not replaced before they have seen a reasonable number of examples (and thus have some estimate of their true fitness).

The individuals can represent entire solutions, or can form a solution as a group, as is done in most classifier systems (Goldberg 1989). When an individual is not a complete solution (such as rule that fires only when it applies), we track the number of times the rule was applied (instead of the number of examples seen). The overall classification is by majority vote of those individuals making a classification.

We have an implementation of an OLGA that we have applied to a set of related sample problems to test the feasibility of the architecture. The examples are a set of 6 boolean attributes, $a_1, a_2, ..., a_6$, (given the values 0 or 1), with the class set to true only when certain attributes are all 1. The value of a_i is set to 1 with a fixed probability.

The individuals in the GA for these problems represent the weights in weighted sum of attributes form, with a threshold of 0 to generate classifications ($\sum_i w_i a_i > 0$). Thus each individual has 7 genes (6 weights for the attributes, plus a bias weight). The possible values for each weight are -1, 0, and 1, with equal probability. The fitness function is as follows:
$$fitness_i = \sum_{c \in classes} \frac{1 + correctcount_{i,c}}{1 + totalseen_{i,c}}$$

The worst performing individual is replaced with a new individual created by a single operator that combines multi-point cross-over with mutation. Parents are randomly selected from the population but with fairly strong pressure toward the better scoring individuals. Each gene in the resulting child has a small chance (the mutation rate) of being set to one of the three values randomly. For speed of testing, we set $p = 20$, and we wait at startup until we've seen at least $1.5p$ before we start replacing individuals.

The system was tested on seven variations of this problem. Some classification functions were representable and easily learned, such as: $class(\overline{x}) = \cap(a_2, a_3)$. Others were not fully realizable by these individuals, such as $class(\overline{x}) = \cap(a_2, a_3, a_4)$. We also varied the attribute setting probability, which varied the overall class distribution (ranging from 22% to 64% positive examples). Throughout these variations, the system was able to achieve reasonable classification performance (86% to 98% accuracy). In addition, we attempted some more unusual tests, such as combining multiple conflicting classifiers and sharp changeovers from one distribution to another. Even on these problems, the OLGA was able to generate fairly high cumulative classification accuracies. While this is just one artificial domain, we take this success as initial, albeit weak, evidence for the applicability of the OLGA architecture. In future work we plan to apply this approach to non-artificial problems as well as compare it to other online algorithms.

References

Dasgupta, D., and Michalewicz, Z., eds. 1997. *Evolutionary algorithms in engineering applications*. New York, NY: Springer-Verlag.

Goldberg, D. E. 1989. *Genetic algorithms in search, optimization, and machine learning*. New York, NY: Addison-Wesley.

Plan Recognition in Complex Spatial Domains

Mark Devaney

College of Computing
Georgia Institute of Technology
Atlanta, GA 30332-0280
(404)894-5104
markd@cc.gatech.edu

Problem description

We are researching the problem of plan recognition in a complex real-world domain consisting of training battles conducted by actual troops at the US Army's National Training Center. These battles involve hundreds of participants, last several days, and take place over a very large geographical area. Our task is to identify from this data repeated patterns of movement which correspond to planned "maneuvers" — coordinated activities which generate identifiable patterns of movement that can be identified and used as a basis for prediction.

Figure 1 depicts the movements of agents in a training battle over a relatively short amount of time (approximately three hours).

Figure 1: Complex agent movements

Both the inherent qualities of the domain and the realities of collecting data from the real world require assumptions fundamentally different from those usually made in plan recognition research:

Multiple agents The step-by-step actions of individual agents are significantly less important than coordinated interactions among agents. This differs from other multi-agent research (e.g., Huber and Durfee 1995) which focuses on the plans of agents acting individually in the presence of others.

Incomplete and incorrect information Data collection from the real world is inherently noisy, and this fact is compounded in large-scale domains.

Large-scale data Depending on the length of activity in the domain and the rate at which information is sampled, there can be anywhere from tens to thousands of state descriptions generated *per agent*.

Approach

A solution to the problem of plan recognition as described here must be able to identify changing relationships between agents in the presence of noise but not have high computational or storage requirements. Our approach has been a layered one in which successively higher levels of qualitative representations are computed from the raw data, generating decreasing amounts of data which convey more focused information. Representations contain information about individual agents such as position and velocity (as in Mohnhaupt and Neumann 1991, for example), and are followed by relationships between pairs of agents, and finally, patterns of agent-pair relationships.

In our approach, the primitive patterns are the building blocks of more complex patterns which are formed from temporal combinations of events. This representation is recursive in nature, in that higher-level patterns are formed from combinations of other patterns or events. For example, a gathering maneuver consists of the event of units moving together followed by the event of them waiting at a location.

Another unique aspect of our research is that we are ultimately concerned with identification of *groups* of agents engaged in common patterns of behavior and that these group behaviors are formed from the different behaviors of individual agents occurring together. The key to our solution has been to detect patterns first among agent-pairs and then leverage this knowledge to form groups based on co-occurring actions.

Acknowledgements

This research was funded by the Army Research Laboratory under grant DAKF11-97-D-0001-0007. Thanks to the anonymous reviewers for their comments.

References

Huber, M. J. & Durfee, E. H. (1995). Deciding when to commit to action during observation-based coordination. *Proceedings of the First International Conference on Multi-Agent Systems (ICMAS)*, 163 - 170.

Mohnhaupt, M. & Neumann, B. (1991). Understanding object motion: Recognition, learning, and spatiotemporal reasoning. *Robotics and Autonomous Systems*, 8:65 - 91.

Nested Joint Probability Model for Morphological Analysis and its Grid Pruning

Koji FUJIMOTO, Nobuo INUI and Yoshiyuki KOTANI

Tokyo University of Agriculture and Technology, Department of Computer Science
2-24-16 Nakamachi, Koganei-city, Tokyo 184, Japan
{kfujim,nobu,kotani}@cc.tuat.ac.jp

Abstract

In recent work on morphological analysis based on statistical models, the conditional probability of the observed i-th word w_i with the i-th tag t_i after the $(i-1)$-th tag t_{i-1} is defined as the product of observation symbol probability and the state transition probability (i.e. $P(w_i | t_i) \cdot P(t_i | t_{i-1})$). In order to improve accuracy, we face the following problems: 1) if we build hidden state levels using stricter categories (e.g. lowest POS class, over 3-gram, or word themselves), the state transition probability matrix becomes much bigger and more sparse; 2) if we use rough categories, the reliability of statistical information becomes lower in some parts of speech; and 3) the best state level is not the same among POS category, and some heuristic knowledge is necessary to select the best state structure.

This paper presents a novel stochastic model based on a nested tag class structure (Nested Joint Probability Model) (Fujimoto,Inui, and Kotani 1998) and its grid pruning technique for data resource saving. This model estimates morpheme transition probability by frequency lattice which is a direct product of two nested tag hierarchies. After an important frequency subset on the lattice is selected by using statistical test criterion for every pair of morphemes, the most reliable transition probability is estimated automatically without heuristic knowledge. Consider a word sequence A B. Class A_i ($i=0,1,...m$; A_0 means all) is a category in the i-th layer of the previous morpheme $A(=A_m)$ in the word's hierarchy, and B_j ($j=0,1,...n$) is in the j-th layer of the target morpheme $B(=B_n)$. The nested joint probability model is formulated as a series of joint probabilities, $P(A_iB_j)=\{P(A_iB_{j-1}) \cdot P(A_{i-1}B_j)/P(A_{i-1}B_{j-1})\} \cdot I(A_iB_j)$ ($i=0,1,...m$; $j=0,1,...n$), where $I(A_iB_j)$ is the conditional interaction effect of A_i and B_j when both A_{i-1} and B_{j-1} are observed. The frequency lattice of A and B is defined as the set of lattice F_{ij} that is the joint frequency of A_i and B_j on a training dataset. An illustration of frequency lattice is shown in Figure 1. For example, if a set of two frequencies $\{F_{il}, F_{kj}\}$ is selected through statis-tical test against the null hypothesis of $I(A_iB_j)=1$ corresponding to F_{ij} on the lattice, the conditional probability $P(B|A)$ can be estimated by the optimized formula, $F_{0n}/F_{0l} \cdot F_{il}/F_{ij} \cdot F_{kj}/F_{k0}$.

The effectiveness of our model was tested, and compared with the established models: the Hidden Markov Model (HMM1 and HMM2), the bi-gram model (MM3) and the superposition model (SP) of a part of speech bi-gram and morpheme bi-gram[5], using Japanese RWC corpus. The results showed that the nested joint probability model (NEST) achieved the highest performance for open data condition: 95.8% precision rate against 94.5% of the superposition model and 94.0% of the established HMM2 model (Table 1). Also the model displayed only a small difference in performance between closed (training) data and open (variation) data condition, therefore we can claim that our model is more robust than the others.

Although the NEST model needs a large dataset of joint frequencies, we found that most of them are rejected by the statistical test and never used for the estimation. Therefore we also introduced a grid-pruning model of NEST that keeps only statistically significant interaction frequency data. This pruning model (DIET1) can save 94% of memory space for transition frequency data while maintaining almost the same accuracy as the NEST model (Table 1).

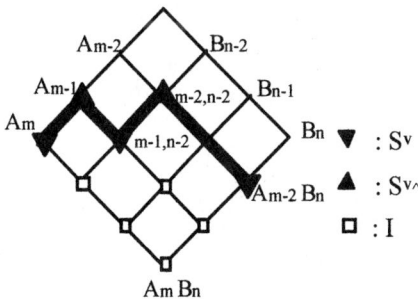

Figure 1 : Frequency Lattice

Table 1: Morphological Analysis Result of Nested Joint Probability Model (NEST) and the Grid Pruning Model (DIET1,2) Compared with HMMs and the Superposition Model

MODEL	Closed (Training) Data,N=6,916		Open (Validation) Data, N=9,015		Frequency Data Size**
	Recall Rate	Precision Rate	Recall Rate	Precision Rate	
HMM1	90.8	92.4	87.4	89.5	84
HMM2	94.9	96.3	92.0	94.0	737
MM3	97.2	97.4	68.2	75.0	31,656
SP	98.9	99.3	94.0	94.5	56,492
NEST	96.9	97.7	94.6	95.8	75,740
DIET1*	97.0	97.7	94.2	95.4	4,427
DIET2*	97.2	97.9	94.1	95.4	6,775

* DIET1 : Grid Puning based on the critical p=0.01% ; DIET2 : p=5%.
** # of Frequency cell in transition matrix excluding morphemes dictionary.

References

Fujimoto,K. ,Inui,N, and Kotani,Y. 1998. Nested Joint Probability Model for Morphological Analysis. In Proceedings of the IASTED International Conference Artificial Intelligence and Soft Computing , Forthcoming.

Generalized A* for Cyclic AND/OR Graphs *

Supriyo Ghose

SAP Center of Expertise
Price Waterhouse Associates Pvt. Ltd.
Plot Y14, Block EP, Sector V, Calcutta 700 091, INDIA.
email: supriyogh@hotmail.com

Abstract

The A* algorithm (Hart, Nilsson and Raphael 1968) has been the cornerstone of state-space search methods. Simultaneously, the vexing problem of cycles in AND/OR graphs has received considerable attention in recent times (Ghose 1998, Hvalica 1996, Chakrabarti 1994). We propose a generalization of A^* to search AND/OR graphs that may contain cycles. The basic idea is that, if each AND node in an AND/OR graph has exactly one child, then the graph is virtually an ordinary (OR) graph and can be searched by applying A^*-like steps. This idea is simulated in our algorithm, GA*, by making full expansion of OR nodes (as in A^*) but *partial expansion of AND nodes*. While expanding an AND node, GA* generates only the leftmost unsolved child, and adds to its cost the costs of all other children of the AND parent. This updated cost is maintained as the current cost provided the child has not been generated earlier in this iteration, or if the updated cost is less than the previously computed cost through some other path. This is done iteratively, using two lists OPEN and CLOSED. An iteration starts by putting s in OPEN, continues by selecting and expanding nodes like A*, and ends either (a) successfully by selecting a terminal leaf or a previously SOLVED node, or (b) unsuccessfully when it finds it has no more nodes to expand (in which case GA* terminates with FAILURE). At the end of an iteration, if s is SOLVED then GA* terminates with SUCCESS. Furthermore, in each iteration, backpointers are set from nodes to their parents, as in A*, to indicate the current minimum costly path to each node. When an iteration of GA* ends successfully, GA* traces these backpointers and updates the heuristic estimates of nodes "higher up" in the solution graph, and declares some of them SOLVED. Our conjecture is that, in each successful iteration of GA*, at least one distinct node is labeled SOLVED; this node has its heuristic estimate set to its minimum cost of solution. If N is the number of nodes lying on any path $\mathcal{P}$ from s such that cost of $\mathcal{P} \leq h^*(s)$, then GA* has a complexity of $O(N^2)$ node expansions with monotone heuristics; under admissible heuristics, its worst-case complexity of $O(N2^N)$ can be reduced to $O(N^3)$ by applying modifications similar to (Martelli 1977). The empirical performance of GA* is currently under investigation. A broad outline of GA* is given below.

While s is not SOLVED:
  (a) While a terminal or a SOLVED node, say n, is not selected from OPEN:
    Perform A*-like steps (expand AND nodes partially). If OPEN is empty, terminate with FAILURE.
  (b) Trace up backpointers from n, label nodes SOLVED, and update h-values.

Now we show the operation of GA* on an AND/OR graph G (s start node, t_1, t_2 terminal leaves.)

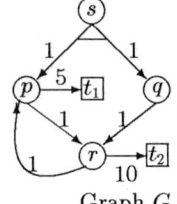
Graph G

Operation of GA* on G
Itn. 1: Generates s, p, t_1, r, t_2.
  Terminates by selecting t_1.
  t_1, p SOLVED. Costs 0, 5
Itn. 2: Generates s, q, r, p, t_2
  Terminates by selecting p
  (previously SOLVED node)
  r, q, s SOLVED. Costs 6, 7, 14

References

Ghose, S. 1998. Best First Search Algorithms for AND/OR Graphs with Cycles. Fellowship Diss., Indian Institute of Management Calcutta.

Ghose, S. and Mahanti, A. 1997. Search Algorithms for AND/OR Graphs with Cycles. Working Paper, WPS-295/97, Indian Institute of Management Calcutta.

Hvalica, D. 1996. Best-First Search Algorithm in AND/OR Graphs with Cycles. *Journal of Algorithms* 21:102-110.

Chakrabarti, P.P. 1994. Algorithms for Searching Explicit AND/OR Graphs and Their Applications to Problem Reduction Search. *Artificial Intelligence* 65:329-345.

Martelli, A. 1977. On the Complexity of Admissible Search Algorithms. *Artificial Intelligence* 8(1):1-13.

Hart, P.E., Nilsson, N.J. and Raphael, B. 1968. A formal basis for the heuristic determination of minimum cost paths. *IEEE Trans. Syst. Science and Cybernetics* SSC-4(2), 100-107.

---

*Copyright ©American Association for Artificial Intelligence (www.aaai.org). All rights reserved.

Selection of Conflict Resolution Strategies in Dynamically Organized Sensible Agent-based Systems

T.H. Liu and K.S. Barber

The Laboratory for Intelligent Processes and Systems
The University of Texas at Austin
Austin, TX 78712
thliu@lips.utexas.edu, barber@mail.utexas.edu

A Multi-Agent System can be seen as a group of entities interacting to achieve individual or collective goals. In the past two decades, researchers have developed various MAS architectures, one being the Sensible Agent (SA) model (Barber 1996). Because one specific level of autonomy is not suitable for all situations in dynamic environments, SAs are equipped with the capability to reason about and switch among levels of autonomy. Typical autonomy levels (which are assigned to goals instead of agents) include: command-driven, master, consensus, and locally autonomous.

The challenge of coordination and conflict resolution in SA-based systems arises from the dynamic organizational structures; when SAs switch their autonomy levels, they also modify their roles and organizational structures. No existing single coordination technique can satisfy such a variety of needs. Results of previous research on various Conflict Resolution (CR) strategies do provide a foundation to solve this problem, but there is limited research focusing on how agents can select proper one. In the work of Adler and his colleagues (Adler, et al. 1989), agents can select one of the following strategies: arbitration, self-modification (independence), centralization, negotiation, priority convention, and mutual accommodation. The criteria agents use to select CR strategies is the network performance. When network traffic is heavy, agents use arbitration for resolving conflicts; when the load is light agents may try negotiation as well as other CR strategies. For dynamically organized Sensible Agents systems, a more advanced decision process is necessary.

We propose that a SA should dynamically select a suitable conflict resolution strategy according to: 1) the nature of conflicts (e.g. goal conflict, plan conflict, or belief conflict), 2) the agent's social roles (represented by its autonomy levels), and 3) its solution preferences (based on an agent's local view). In addition to using utilities to evaluate potential solutions, agents also use certain indexes to evaluate available CR strategies, and finally agents conduct some trade-off reasoning between solutions and CR strategies. The following simplified formula (may not be linear) shows how an agent can estimate alternative combinations of specific solutions and CR strategies:

$$TotalValue = U_{weight} \times Utility - M_{weight} \times Cost_{modify} - CR_{weight} \times Cost_{CR\ strategy}$$

Utility is the total weighted utility value of a specific solution for its attributes. $Cost_{modify}$ is the estimated cost of modifying the agent's existing plans and $Cost_{CR\ strategy}$ is the estimated cost of applying CR strategies eliminating conflicts. U_{weight}, M_{weight}, and CR_{weight} are their associate weight factor functions. The indexes used to evaluate CR strategies include: 1) effectiveness, the complexity and uncertainty involved, 2) performance, the time/messages needed and the desired quality of solution, 3) agent properties, agents' preferences for CR strategies as well as capabilities/resources required to execute a CR strategy, 4) system properties, measure of the extent to which the system provides coordination mechanisms (e.g. available mediator/arbitrator, design convention, and priorities.) for helping agents to resolve conflicts.

Three kinds of decision making styles can be made by tuning the weight factors: CR strategies are selected before or after solutions, balanced consideration between solutions and CR strategies. In our preliminary experiments (Liu, et al. 1997) we designed a CR strategy selection algorithm for robot path planning. The results show that the system can endure highly dynamic and uncertain environments.

The decision making approach proposed here can also be applied to other conflict resolution problems in Multi-Agent Systems which require the flexibility of applying multiple CR strategies. Currently we are working on a series of experiments following the third decision style and results will be reported in the near future. We are also considering the use of cased based reasoning techniques (or other learning methods) for tuning weight factors and increasing agents' abilities to adapt to environment changes

References

Adler, M.R., Davis, A.B., Weihmayer, R. and Worrest, R. W. (1989). Conflict-resolution strategies for nonhierarchical distributed agents. *Distributed Artificial Intelligence II*. L. Gasser and M. N. Huhns. London, Pitman Pub., 139-161.

Barber, K.S. (1996). The Architecture for Sensible Agents. *International Multidisciplinary Conference, Intelligent Systems: A Semiotic Perspective*, Gaithersburg, MD., 49-54.

Liu, T.H., Chuter, C. and Barber, K. S. (1997). Virtual Environment Simulation for Visualizing Conflict Resolution Strategies in Multiple Robot Systems. *5th IASTED International Conference, Robotics and Manufacturing*, Cancun, Mexico, IASTED Press., 154-158.

---

* This research was supported in part by the Texas Higher Education Coordinating Board (#003658-415)

** Copyright © 1998, American Association for Artificial Intelligence (www.aaai.org). All rights reserved.

Refinement-based *Planning As Satisfiability*

Amol D. Mali
Department of Computer Science & Engineering,
Arizona State University, Tempe, AZ 85287-5406
amol.mali@asu.edu

A classical planning problem is the problem of computing a sequence of actions that transforms one state of the world into the desired. Traditional planners cast planning as a "split & prune" type search. These are called "refinement planners" since they start with a null plan and refine it by adding constraints. It has been shown recently that planning problems are far easier to solve when they are cast as model finding problems [2]. Some schemes for automated generation of the encodings of the planning problems in propositional logic have been designed [1]. However these schemes lack several of the refinements and pre-processing that traditional planners use. Since no single encoding has been shown to have the smallest size and the best performance, it is necessary to know what the space of the encodings is, to make a more flexible and efficient exploration of the encodings possible.

The plan refinements can proceed either in the forward direction (from initial state) or in the backward direction (from goal) or both. The steps of a plan can either be totally ordered (state space planning) or partially ordered (plan space or least commitment planning). The direction of refinement affects the branching factor in the search space and the nature of step ordering affects the completeness of the knowledge of the world state (complete world state is known in forward state space planning and causal planning is devoid of this knowledge). One can also do pre-processing to prune irrelevant information. These three dimensions show that many more novel plan encodings [4] exist.

We discuss some encodings from this space here. **1. State Space Encodings** - There are two categories of these encodings - linear and parallel. In linear encodings, only one action occurs at a time step. In parallel encodings, multiple actions can occur at the same time step, if they do not interfere. The state space encoding in [1] is not sensitive to the direction of refinement. Our encodings are sensitive to the direction of refinement (to enforce directional control in the declarative representation like a propositional encoding, we assign weights to the clauses). **a. Linear Forward Encoding** is based on forward state space refinement. We state that if the preconditions of an action are true at a time, that action or null action can occur at that time. We also say that if some precondition of an action is false at a time, the action cannot occur at that time. **b. Linear Backward Encoding** is based on backward state space refinement. **c. Linear Bidirectional Encoding** is formed for k step plans, where first k_1 steps are based on the linear forward refinement, and the remaining k_2 steps are based on the linear backward refinement. **2. Parallel Encodings** - These too can be forward, backward and bidirectional. **3. Hybrid Encoding** - This encoding is inspired by the idea that a planner can do both state space and plan space refinements. The first part for k_1 steps is based on state space refinement and the remaining k_2 step part is based on plan space refinement. **4. Pre-processing** - Not all actions in a domain are generally relevant to a given planning problem. Knowing this a priori does reduce the search space and allows the planner to focus on more relevant actions. Integrating the outcome of pre-processing yields smaller plan encodings (that contain fewer clauses and variables)[4]. Our work [3][4] bridges the gap between the previous research in planning (planning as refinement search) and the recent exciting developments (planning as model finding).

[1] **Henry Kautz, David McAllester and Bart Selman**, Encoding plans in propositional logic, Proc. of Knowledge Representation & Reasoning conference (KR), 1996.

[2] **Henry Kautz and Bart Selman**, Pushing the envelope: Planning, Propositional logic and Stochastic search, Proc. of the National Conference on Artificial Intelligence (AAAI), 1996.

[3] **Amol D. Mali**, Frugal propositional encodings of planning, Dept. of computer science, Arizona state university, TR-97-042.

[4] **Amol D. Mali**, Refinement-based planning as satisfiability, Dept. of computer science, Arizona state university, TR-97-043.

Goal and Responsibility Allocation in Sensible Agent-based Systems

Ryan McKay and K.S. Barber

The Laboratory for Intelligent Processes and Systems
The University of Texas at Austin
Austin, TX 78712
rmckay@lips.utexas.edu, barber@mail.utexas.edu

A Multi-Agent System(MAS) can be seen as a group of entities interacting to achieve individual or collective goals. Communication is a central issue in this interaction between agents. Protocols such as the Contract Net Protocol(CNP) (Smith, 1980) have been proposed to address the coordination level of communication in predefined organizational structures with predefined agent interaction mechanisms. The research presented here applies and extends this protocol to address issues in one particular MAS – Sensible Agents(SA) (Barber, 1996).

SAs carry out goals that have been allocated to them by another agent or by a user interacting with the system. Completion of a goal occurs in three phases: 1) planning – decomposing a goal into subgoals, 2) allocating the subgoals, and 3) executing the subgoals (which may themselves need to be further planned for). SAs are capable of dynamic agent organization based on dynamic adaptive autonomy where agents' roles in interactions can change.

SAs use the concept of an Autonomy Level(AL) to define their organizational roles with respect to goals. Autonomy level is a 4-tuple composed of values for the following autonomy constructs: responsibility, commitment, independence, and authority. A module in a SA assigns a distinct AL to each goal for which the agent bears some responsibility. Several typical autonomy levels are named: command-driven, consensus, locally autonomous, and master. The main difference between these ALs is the relationship between which agent owns the goal and which agent plans for the goal. A locally autonomous agent owns and plans its goal. A command-driven agent owns a goal, but has allocated responsibility for planning and subgoal allocation to a master agent. All agents in a Consensus Group(CG) share planning and allocation responsibility for some number of related goals owned by CG members.

Most ALs involve multiple agents, and so require an Autonomy Level Agreement(ALA) among them. In order to coordinate the agents' efforts of allocating goals to each other or allocating responsibility through an ALA, SAs need a communication protocol. The Goal and Responsibility Allocation Protocol and Language(GRAPL) based on the CNP (Smith, 1980) is proposed.

SAs immediately require GRAPL to extend CNP by the addition of two new ANNOUNCEMENT messages: GOAL ANNOUNCEMENT and ALA ANNOUNCEMENT. A SA uses the GOAL ANNOUNCEMENT message to inform other agents about a goal it wants to allocate. We can use the ALA ANNOUNCEMENT in much the same manner, by treating ALAs as responsibility allocations.

GRAPL, as outlined here, addresses the important issues of goal and responsibility allocation in SAs using extensions to the straightforward and effective CNP (Smith, 1980). However, much work remains. Current efforts focus on moving GRAPL beyond the ANNOUNCE-BID-AWARD model to incorporate other methods of coordination such as negotiation, voting, and arbitration. These alternatives provide increased flexibility both in obtaining a contract and within an agreed upon contract. The protocol will be implemented in a standard intentional language such as KQML (Finin et al., 1993). A battery of experiments on SA's communication capabilities is scheduled for June 1998, using the Sensible Agent Testbed (currently under development). The results of those experiments will be analyzed with the goal of developing algorithms that SAs will use to determine the appropriate coordination technique for given situations.

Acknowledgments

This research was supported in part by the Texas Higher Education Coordinating Board (#003658-415).

References

Barber, K. S. 1996. The Architecture for Sensible Agents. In Proceedings of the International Multidisciplinary Conference, Intelligent Systems: A Semiotic Perspective. Gaithersburg, MD.

Finin, T., Weber, J., Wiederhold, G., Genesereth, M., Fritzson, R., McKay, D., McGuire, J., Pelavin, R., Shapiro, S., and Beck, C. (1993) "Draft Specification of the KQML Agent-Communication Language." http://www.cs.umbc.edu/kqml/kqmlspec.ps, Current as of: 12-1-1997.

Smith, R. 1980. The Contract Net Protocol: High-level Communication and Control in a Distributed Problem-Solver. IEEE Transactions on Computers 29(12): 1104-1113.

Copyright © 1998, American Association for Artificial Intelligence (www.aaai.org). All rights reserved.

Tutorial Response Generation in a Writing Tool for Deaf Learners of English

Lisa N. Michaud
michaud@cis.udel.edu
http://www.eecis.udel.edu/~masterma
Computer and Information Sciences Department
214 Smith Hall
University of Delaware
Newark, DE 19716

ICICLE (Interactive Computer Identification and Correction of Language Errors) is a tutoring system under development that instructs deaf users of American Sign Language on written English skills[1]. (See (McCoy & Masterman (Michaud) 1997) for a discussion of overall system architecture.) The text generation module it will employ produces original text to instruct the user on errors found in his or her writing, tailored to the user's understanding and learning style. The model I propose for planning this text composes it according to a four-tier response anatomy. It combines bottom-up and top-down planning approaches and takes into account a detailed representation of user language proficiency and a history of interaction with a user in order to create text that is maximally understandable and informative to the individual.

The initial bottom-up part of the planning will employ a domain knowledge base containing information about the errors recognized by the system to cluster similar errors found in a piece of writing and to order those clusters according to guidelines directing the flow of a tutorial session. My work is concerned with the subsequent top-down phase which builds and fleshes out a hierarchical text plan to tutor on an error. This phase employs a response anatomy which is comprised of *content*, *method*, *form*, and *manner*. *Content* refers to the error(s) to be discussed; the *method* is the choice between possible pedagogical approaches to discussing the error; the *form* is the determination of how to structure the approach defined by the *method*; and the *manner* refers to cohesive factors involved in a contextually-aware explanation. The top-down planning begins with the posting of the goal of instructing the user on an error and the selection of plan operators that represent approaches toward realizing this goal. My plan operator design is based largely on the work in (Moore &

Paris 1992); operators are selected according to the *effect* they have on the user's knowledge and a list of *constraints* which state when an operator is applicable, referencing multiple sources of knowledge including the user proficiency model, the long-term history module, recent dialogue, and the domain knowledge base. When a selection is made from the first tier of operators representing *method* choices, subgoals are posted that help drive the further selection of *form* operators which contain schemata for structuring the text. A *manner* phase then applies operators to generate comparisons to established user knowledge and previous explanations. The contextually-aware final output is a theoretic text specification which can then be sent to a generator to be realized as English.

A longer discussion of my proposed planner can be found in (Michaud & McCoy 1998). Future tasks include refining the concept of the user model proposed in (McCoy, Pennington, & Suri 1996), developing a domain knowledge base, and further specifying our planning operators.

References

McCoy, K. F., and Masterman (Michaud), L. N. 1997. A tutor for teaching english as a second language for deaf users of american sign language. In *Proceedings of Natural Language Processing for Communication Aids, an ACL/EACL97 Workshop*, 160–164.

McCoy, K. F.; Pennington, C. A.; and Suri, L. Z. 1996. English error correction: A syntactic user model based on principled mal-rule scoring. In *Proceedings of User Modeling '96*.

Michaud, L. N., and McCoy, K. F. 1998. Planning text in a system for teaching english as a second language to deaf learners. In *Proceedings of Integrating Artificial Intelligence and Assistive Technology, an AAAI '98 Workshop*.

Moore, J. D., and Paris, C. L. 1992. Planning text for advisory dialogues: Capturing intentional and rhetorical information. *Computational Linguistics* 19(4):651–695.

---

[1] This work has been supported by NSF Grant # IRI-9416916, NSF Research Traineeship Grant #GER-9354869, and a Rehabilitation Engineering Research Center Grant from the National Institute on Disability and Rehabilitation Research of the U.S. Dept. of Education (#H133E30010).

Copyright 1998, American Association for Artificial Intelligence (www.aaai.org). All rights reserved.

Dependent Bigram Identification*

Ted Pedersen
Department of Computer Science & Engineering
Southern Methodist University
Dallas, TX 75275-0122
pedersen@seas.smu.edu

Dependent bigrams are two consecutive words that occur together in a text more often than would be expected purely by chance. Identifying such bigrams is an important issue since they provide valuable clues for machine translation, word sense disambiguation, and information retrieval. A variety of significance tests have been proposed (e.g., Church et. al., 1991, Dunning, 1993, Pedersen et. al, 1996) to identify these interesting lexical pairs. In this poster I present a new statistic, *minimum sensitivity*, that is simple to compute and is free from the underlying distributional assumptions commonly made by significance tests.

The challenge in identifying dependent bigrams is that most are relatively rare regardless of the amount of text being considered. This follows from the distributional tendencies of individual bigrams as described by Zipf's Law. If the frequencies of the bigrams in a text are ordered from most to least frequent, $(f_1, f_2, \ldots, f_m)$, these frequencies roughly obey $f_i \propto \frac{1}{i}$.

Consider the following example from a 1,300,000 word sample of the ACL/DCI Wall Street Journal Corpus. A contingency table containing the frequency counts of *oil* and *industry* is shown below. These counts show that *oil industry* occurs 17 times, *oil* occurs without *industry* 240 times, *industry* occurs without *oil* 1001 times, and bigrams other than *oil industry* occur 1,298,742 times. This distribution is sparse and skewed and thus violates a central assumption implicit in significance testing of contingency tables (Read & Cressie 1988).

		W_2 industry	¬industry	totals
W_1	oil	$n_{11}=$ 17	$n_{12}=$ 240	$n_{1+}=$ 257
	¬oil	$n_{21}=$ 1001	$n_{22}=$ 1298742	$n_{2+}=$ 1299743
	totals	$n_{+1}=$ 1018	$n_{+2}=$ 1298982	$n_{++}=$ 1300000

Sensitivity is classically defined as the proportion of true results that agree with the true state. For lexical relationships sensitivity is a conditional probability that is the ratio of how often a word occurs in a specific bigram $(w_1 w_2)$ to how often it occurs overall.

Sensitivity is computed as follows for each of the two words in a bigram:

$$S_{w_1} = \frac{n_{11}}{n_{+1}} = P(w_1|w_2) \quad S_{w_2} = \frac{n_{11}}{n_{1+}} = P(w_2|w_1)$$

These values range from 0 to 1 and their minimum serves as the measure of dependence between the two words. The minimum sensitivity is 1 when w_1 and w_2 always, and only, occur together. It is 0 when w_1 and w_2 never occur together. The greater the minimum sensitivity the higher the level of dependence between the two words in a bigram.

From the data in the contingency table, S_{w_1} indicates how sensitive *oil* is to *industry*. Given that *industry* occurs in a text, how often does *oil* precede it? $S_{w_1} = \frac{17}{1018} = .017$. S_{w_2} measures how sensitive *industry* is to *oil*. Given that *oil* occurs, how often does *industry* follow it? $S_{w_2} = \frac{17}{257} = .066$. The former is the minimum sensitivity value and is thus the measure of dependence between *oil* and *industry*.

Experimental results show that minimum sensitivity results in the identification of bigrams that are largely made up of content words. Significance tests frequently identify dependent bigrams where one of the words is a very high frequency non–content word such as *the* or *of*. For example, *the industry* is considered a dependent bigram by the significance tests but not by minimum sensitivity. The tendency of minimum sensitivity to filter out bigrams containing non–content words is an important quality in many practical language processing applications.

Acknowledgments

This research was supported by the Office of Naval Research under grant number N00014-95-1-0776.

References

Read, T., and Cressie, N. 1988. *Goodness of fit Statistics for Discrete Multivariate Data*. New York, NY: Springer-Verlag.

*Copyright ©1998, American Association for Artificial Intelligence (www.aaai.org). All rights reserved.

Raw Corpus Word Sense Disambiguation*

Ted Pedersen
Department of Computer Science & Engineering
Southern Methodist University
Dallas, TX 75275-0122
pedersen@seas.smu.edu

A wide range of approaches have been applied to word sense disambiguation. However, most require manually crafted knowledge such as annotated text, machine readable dictionaries or thesari, semantic networks, or aligned bilingual corpora. The reliance on these knowledge sources limits portability since they generally exist only for selected domains and languages. This poster presents a corpus–based approach where multiple usages of an ambiguous word are divided into a specified number of sense groups based strictly on features that are automatically obtained from the immediately surrounding raw text.

We are given N sentences, each of which contains a usage of a particular ambiguous word. Each sentence is converted into a feature vector $(F_1, F_2, \ldots, F_n, S)$ where $(F_1, \ldots, F_n)$ represent the observed contextual properties of the sentence and S represents the unobserved sense of the ambiguous word.

A probabilistic model is built from this data. First, a parametric form that describes the interactions among the observed contextual features and the unknown sense is specified. We use the form commonly known as Naive Bayes due to its favorable performance in previous studies of supervised disambiguation (e.g., Gale et. al., 1992, Mooney, 1996, Ng 1997).

The Naive Bayes model, when applied to disambiguation, implies that all contextual features are conditionally independent given the sense of the ambiguous word:

$$p(F_1, F_2, \ldots, F_n, S) = p(S) \prod_{i=1}^{n} p(F_i|S)$$

To complete the model the values of the parameters $p(F_i|S)$ must be estimated. However, since S is not observed in the text this can not be done directly. Instead, we use the Expectation Maximization (EM) algorithm and Gibbs Sampling, two popular methods for estimating parameters when data is missing.

Both algorithms iterate until convergence is detected. The EM algorithm imputes values for the missing data S and maximizes the parameter estimates $p(F_i|S)$ given those imputed values. While it is guaranteed to converge, the EM algorithm is susceptible to finding local maxima. We treat Gibbs Sampling as a stochastic version of the EM algorithm. It approximates the complete distribution of the parameters by repeatedly sampling from them rather than simply maximizing a point estimate. In so doing Gibbs Sampling finds the global maximum but also proves more difficult to monitor for convergence.

The evaluation of these methods is based on the degree to which the discovered sense groups agree with those created by a human judge. Both methods are used to disambiguate thirteen different words using three feature sets. Gibbs Sampling shows small but consistent improvments in accuracy over the EM algorithm. The comparable performance of these two methods is somewhat surprising given the tendency of the EM algorithm to converge at local maxima. However, in these experiments the EM algorithm often converges quite quickly, usually within 20 iterations, to a global maximum. These results suggest that some combination of the EM algorithm and Gibbs Sampling might be beneficial. A feature set using local context features, i.e., collocations that occur within ± 2 positions of the ambiguous word, generally results in higher disambiguation accuracy than a feature set based on co–occurrences from a wider window of context. A more detailed discussion of these experimental results is found in (Pedersen & Bruce, this volume).

There are three areas of future work. First, we will use the convergence points of the EM algorithm as initial values for Gibbs Sampling in the hopes of speeding the convergence of Gibbs Sampling. Second, we will experiment with parametric forms based on expert knowledge rather than simply relying on Naive Bayes. Finally, we will identify additional local context features that increase disambiguation accuracy without significantly increasing the dimensionality of the problem.

Acknowledgments

This research was supported by the Office of Naval Research under grant number N00014-95-1-0776.

---

*Copyright ©1998, American Association for Artificial Intelligence (www.aaai.org). All rights reserved.

DISCOURSE LEARNING:
Dialogue Act Tagging with Transformation-Based Learning[1]

Ken Samuel

Department of Computer and Information Sciences
The University of Delaware
Newark, DE 19716
samuel@cis.udel.edu
http://www.eecis.udel.edu/~samuel/

My central goal is to compute *dialogue acts* automatically. A dialogue act is a concise abstraction of a speaker's intention, such as SUGGEST and REQUEST. Recognizing dialogue acts is critical to understanding at the discourse level, and dialogue acts can also be useful for other applications, such as resolving ambiguity in speech recognition. But, often, a dialogue act cannot be directly inferred from a literal reading of an utterance.

Machine learning offers promise as a means of discovering patterns in corpora of data, since the computer can efficiently analyze large quantities of information. My research is the first to investigate using Brill's (1995) *Transformation-Based Learning* (TBL) algorithm to compute dialogue acts (Samuel, Carberry, & Vijay-Shanker 1998). There are several reasons that I selected this machine learning method over the alternatives for my task: TBL has been applied successfully to a similar problem, Part-of-Speech Tagging (Brill 1995); TBL produces an intuitive model; TBL can easily accommodate local context as well as distant context; TBL demonstrates resistance to overfitting; etc.

To address some limitations of the original TBL algorithm and to deal with the particular demands of discourse processing, I developed some extensions to my system, including a *Monte Carlo* approach that randomly samples from the space of available rules, rather than exhaustively generating all possible rules. This significantly improves efficiency without compromising accuracy (Samuel 1998). Also, to circumvent a sparse data problem, it is necessary to transform the input data by extracting values for a set of simple *features* of utterances, such as cue phrases and nearby dialogue acts. I am utilizing a very general set of *cue phrases* that includes patterns such as "but", "thanks", "what time", and "busy". To automatically collect those cue phrases that appear frequently in dialogue and provide useful clues to help determine the appropriate dialogue acts, I devised an *entropy approach* (selecting words so that the dialogue acts co-occurring with those words have low entropy) with a *filtering mechanism* (removing cue phrases that merely provide redundant information).

Other researchers have been investigating machine learning approaches for computing dialogue acts. Previously, the greatest experimental success was reported by Reithinger and Klesen (1997), whose system could correctly label 74.7% of the utterances with dialogue acts. As a direct comparison, I applied my system to exactly the same training and testing data that Reithinger and Klesen used, attaining an accuracy of 76.2%. Applying a Decision Trees implementation, C5.0 (Rulequest 1998), to this data produced an accuracy of 70.4%.

For the future, I have several plans to revise and extend this work. The main deficiency of TBL is that it doesn't offer any measure of confidence in its taggings, but I am working on a committee-based strategy to address this problem. In addition, I plan to examine the utility of other features, such as surface speech acts, subject type, and verb type. Also, as tagged dialogues are still difficult to acquire, I have proposed a weakly-supervised learning strategy, to learn from a small set of tagged data and a large set of untagged data.

I appreciate all of the help that my advisors, Sandra Carberry and K. Vijay-Shanker, have given me. I also wish to thank the members of the VERBMOBIL research group at DFKI in Germany, for providing me with the opportunity to work with them and generously granting me access to the VERBMOBIL corpora. This work was partially supported by the NSF Grant #GER-9354869.

References

Brill, E. 1995. Transformation-based error-driven learning and natural language processing: A case study in part-of-speech tagging. *Computational Linguistics* 21(4):543–566.

Reithinger, N., and Klesen, M. 1997. Dialogue act classification using language models. In *Proceedings of EuroSpeech-97*, 2235–2238.

Rulequest Research. 1998. Data mining tools see5 and c5.0. [http://www.rulequest.com/see5-info.html].

Samuel, K.; Carberry, S.; and Vijay-Shanker, K. 1998. Computing dialogue acts from features with transformation-based learning. In *Applying Machine Learning to Discourse Processing: Papers from the 1998 AAAI Spring Symposium*, 90–97. Technical Report SS-98-01.

Samuel, K. 1998. Lazy transformation-based learning. In *Proceedings of FLAIRS*.

---

[1] Copyright © 1998, American Association for Artificial Intelligence (www.aaai.org). All rights reserved.

Estimating the Expected Error of Empirical Minimizers for Model Selection

Tobias Scheffer
Technische Universität Berlin, FR 5-8,
Franklinstr. 28/29, 10587 Berlin, Germany
scheffer@cs.tu-berlin.de

Thorsten Joachims
Uni Dortmund, LS 8 Informatik
44221 Dortmund, Germany
thorsten@ls8.informatik.uni-dortmund.de

Abstract

Model selection [e.g., 1] is considered the problem of choosing a hypothesis language which provides an optimal balance between low empirical error and high structural complexity. In this Abstract, we discuss the intuition of a new, very efficient approach to model selection. Our approach is inherently Bayesian [e.g., 2], but instead of using priors on target functions or hypotheses, we talk about priors on *error values* – which leads us to a new mathematical characterization of the expected true error. In the setting of classification learning, a learner is given a sample, drawn according to an unknown distribution of labeled instances, and returns the empirical minimizer (the hypothesis with the least empirical error) which has a certain (unknown) true error. If this process is carried out repeatedly, the true error of the empirical minimizer will vary from run to run as the empirical minimizer depends on the (randomly drawn) sample. This induces a *distribution* of true errors of empirical minimizers, over the possible samples drawn according to the unknown distribution. If this distribution would be known, one could easily derive the *expected* true error of the empirical minimizer of a model by integrating over this distribution. This would immediately lead to an *optimal* model selection algorithm: Enumerate the models, calculate the expected error of each model by integrating over the error distribution, and select the model with the least expected error. PAC theory [3] and the VC framework provide worst-case *bounds* on the chance of drawing a sample such that the true error of the minimizer exceeds some ε – "worst-case" meaning that they hold for *any* distribution of instances and any concept in a given class. By contrast, we focus on how to *determine* this distribution for a *fixed, given learning problem* (under some specified assumptions). Unlike the worst-case bound (which depends only on the size, or VC-dimension of the hypothesis space) the actual error distribution depends on the hypothesis space and the unknown distribution of labeled instances itself. However, we can prove that, under a certain assumption of independence of hypotheses, the distribution of true errors – and hence the expected true error – can be expressed as a function of the distribution of empirical errors of uniformly drawn hypotheses (which can be thought of as a prior on error values). The latter distribution (which is *always* one-dimensional) can be *estimated* from a *fixed-sized* initial portion of the training data and a fixed-sized set of randomly drawn hypotheses. This estimate of the distribution now leads us to an *estimate* of the expected true error of the empirical minimizer of the model – which, in turn, leads to a highly efficient model selection algorithm. We study the behavior of this approach in several controlled experiments. Our results show that the accuracy of the error estimate is at least comparable to the accuracy of the estimate obtained by 10-fold cross-validation – provided the prior on error values can be estimated using at least 50 examples. But while 10-CV requires ten invocations of the learner per model, the time which our algorithm requires to assess each model is constant in the size of the model. We also study the robustness of our algorithm against violations of our independence assumptions. We can observe a bias in our predictions when the hypotheses space is of size four or less. When the hypothesis space is of size 40 or more, the dependencies are so diluted that the violations of our assumptions are negligible and do not incur a significant error. The full paper is available at **http://ki.cs.tu-berlin.de/~scheffer/papers/eed-report.ps**.

References

[1] M. Kearns, Y. Mansour, A. Ng, and D. Ron. An experimental and theoretical comparison of model selection methods. In *Machine Learning* 27: 7–50. 1997.

[2] J. Rissanen. Minimum-description-length principle. In *Ann. Statist.* 6: 461–464. 1985.

[3] L. G. Valiant. A Theory of the Learnable. In *Comm. ACM* 27. 1984.

Copyright ©1998, American Association for Artificial Intelligence (www.aaai.org). All rights reserved.

Pluto: Managing Multistrategy Learning Through Planning

Gordon T. Shippey   J. William Murdock   Ashwin Ram

Georgia Institute of Technology
College of Computing
Atlanta, Georgia 30322-0280
(shippey|murdock|ashwin)@cc.gatech.edu

Multistrategy learning systems are systems that employ multiple methods to solve learning problems. In many multistrategy systems, either the user or the system selects a single method to use on the current problem. At best, such a selection-type multistrategy learning system can solve the union of the problems solvable by the individual learning methods it contains. Another strategy is to have the user specify a sequence of methods to apply to a particular problem at compile time. Both of these strategies fails to tap the full potential of the learning methods under their control.

One way to overcome this limitation is to cast the learning task as a planning problem. By treating learning strategies as operators in a planning problem, several learning strategies can be linked together to form a network bridging the gap between the system's initial knowledge state, current inputs, and some knowledge goal. Coordinated networks of learning strategies can solve problems beyond the range of any individual learning strategy.

We are currently developing a computational model of the planning-to-learn process which we call PLUTO (Planning to Learn Using Transmutation Operators). The current version of PLUTO creates and executes learning plans in the domain of consumer decision making.

```
(defframe '(cheap-low-emis-vacuums
    (isa set)
    (members (?q
        (var-type knowledge-goal)))
    (restrictions (cheap-restriction
        (isa constraint)
        (constraint-type fuzzy-constraint)
        (slot-name :relation price)
        (goal minimize)
        (reference vacuum-cleaner))
      (low-emissions-restriction
        (isa constraint)
        (constraint-type fuzzy-constraint)
        (slot-name :relation emissions)
        (goal maximize)
        (reference vacuum-cleaner)))))
```
Figure 1. A knowledge goal in the PLUTO system.

PLUTO describes the knowledge it wishes to learn in the form of knowledge goals like the one shown in figure 1. PLUTO's knowledge goals are frames with variables holding the place of desired information. The knowledge goal in figure 1 could be interpreted as "find the set of vacuum cleaners which are inexpensive and low in emissions (i.e. vacuums that don't let dust inside the vacuum escape)". Note that this knowledge goal does not specify a specific price or a specific emissions level desired. The variable ? q is holding the place for the members of this set frame.

Given the knowledge goal in figure 1, a list of vacuum cleaner models with prices and emissions ratings, plus a library of knowledge operators, PLUTO can create several different plans to learn which of the vacuum cleaners in the knowledge base satisfy the requirements of the knowledge goal. Plans are generated by matching operators to open knowledge goals. Matching an operator to a knowledge goal produces an operator instance which may require new open knowledge goals to perform its task. For instance, an operator may break the goal to find vacuums that are cheap and low in emissions into two independent goals: find vacuums that are cheap, and find vacuums that are low in emissions. When a plan has no open knowledge goals, it is considered to be a finished plan and ready for execution.

During execution each operator instance in the plan takes its input from either the knowledge base or the output of other operators and then generates its own results, which will either be part of the final solution, or input for later operators to use as input.

There are several noteworthy properties of the planning and execution processes. First, PLUTO autonomously creates and executes learning plans. Second, PLUTO uses multiple knowledge operators in its plans. While none of the operators alone are sufficient to solve the problems, PLUTO can combine them into viable solutions, extending PLUTO's range beyond that of the select-and-apply multistrategy learning methods. Third, different instantiations of the same knowledge operator can be used in different contexts, even within the same plan. Fourth, PLUTO can generate several different plans to solve the same problem. Since plans sometimes fail, multiple plans give PLUTO multiple chances to succeed. For instance, there are multiple methods available to PLUTO to define "cheap". Fifth, a single plan may be valid over a space of knowledge goals, which makes plans a reusable resource for learning.

Copyright © 1998, American Association for Artificial Intelligence (www.aaai.org). All rights reserved.

A Framework for Reinforcement Learning on Real Robots

William D. Smart and **Leslie Pack Kaelbling**
Computer Science Department
Brown University
Providence, RI 02912
(401) 863-7667
{wds, lpk}@cs.brown.edu

Robots are now being used in complex, unstructured environments, performing ever more sophisticated tasks. As the task and environmental complexity increases, the need for effective learning on such systems is becoming more and more apparent. Robot programmers often find it difficult to articulate their knowledge of how to perform a given task in a form suitable for robots to use. Even when they can, the limitations of robot sensors and actuators might render their intuitions less effective. Also, it is often not possible to anticipate (and code for) all environments in which the robot might find itself having to perform a certain task. Therefore, it seems useful to have the robot be able to learn to act, in the hope of overcoming these two difficulties.

One promising approach to learning on real robots that is attracting considerable interest at the moment is *reinforcement learning*. The programmer must supply a *reward function* which maps states of the world onto a scalar reward, essentially saying how good or bad it is to be in a given state. Once given this function, the robot can, in theory, learn an appropriate action policy to maximize some measure of reward over time. Designing such a function seems more intuitive than writing code to perform the task, since we can do so in more general terms.

However, there are some significant problems when we attempt to use this strategy on a real, physical robot, including (but not limited to) the following.

Low data rate Since sensor data (and hence reward data) are being generated by physical processes, the rate at which we can gather such information is typically low, with rates of 10Hz or lower being common. Combining this with the often extreme size of the state space means that we have a very sparse coverage of this space, making learning much more difficult.

Exploration is dangerous To gather information about the utility of taking actions from a given state, a reinforcement learning system will typically take actions about which it knows little or nothing. In many applications, this is allowable, but on a physical system can be extremely dangerous. For example, the only way for the robot to find out the utility of falling down the stairs is to actually fall down them, something that we would hope to avoid. This is especially relevant in the early stages of learning, when little is known and most actions are exploratory.

In order to overcome these problems, we propose a new framework for reinforcement learning on real robots. The framework has three main components; a provided control policy and reward function, a policy learning process and a value learning process. Initially, the robot is under the control of the supplied policy. As it performs its task, the policy learner and value learner are both passively observing the sensor readings and effector commands issued by the supplied policy. The policy learner attempts to learn the mapping embodied in the supplied control policy, while the value learner attempts to learn a predictive version of the reward function.

Once the learned policy is performing as well as the supplied one, control passes over to it. From this point onwards, a reinforcement learning algorithm uses the learned value function in an attempt to improve the learned control policy. Eventually, the learned control policy will converge on one which is optimal with respect to the supplied reward function.

By supplying an initial control policy, we can bootstrap the reinforcement learning process and give is a useful bias. In the initial phase, we can gather information on the value function without performing exploratory actions and can also focus attention on the part of the state space that we will actually be using for the task at hand. Limiting ourselves to a part of the possible state space makes the learning tasks easier since, although we have a sparse data distribution over the whole space, it tends to be dense in the areas in which we are interested.

There are several questions that we hope to address in this work. What are the special requirements on the learning algorithms? How good does the initial policy have to be, and how much can we improve on it? How do we combine information from more than one initial policy? What sort of speed and performance benefits can be realized with this approach?

Copyright ©1998, American Association for Artificial Intelligence (www.aaai.org). All rights reserved.

Handling Inconsistency for Multi-Source Integration

Sheila Tejada   Craig A. Knoblock   Steven Minton

University of Southern California/ISI
4676 Admiralty Way, Marina del Rey, California 90292
{tejada,knoblock,minton}@isi.edu,
(310) 822-1511 x799

Abstract

The overwhelming amount of information sources now available through the internet has increased the need to combine or integrate the data retrieved from these sources in an intelligent and efficient manner. A desirable approach for information integration would be to have a single interface, like the SIMS information broker [1], which allows access to multiple information sources. An example application is to retrieve all the menus of restaurants from Joe's Favorite Restaurants site which have been rated highly by the Department of Health.

A special case for information integration is when data instances can exist in inconsistent formats across several sources, e.g. the restaurant "Art's Deli" can appear as "Art's Delicatessen" in another source. For the integration process each source can be seen as a relation; therefore, integrating the sources requires performing a join on the two relations by comparing the instances of the primary keys. Since the instances have inconsistent formats, some mapping information is needed to map one instance to another e.g. (Art's Deli, Art's Delicatessen). This information can be stored in the form of a mapping table, or as a mapping function, if a compact translation can be found to accurately convert data instances from one source into another. Once a mapping construct is created it can be modeled as a new information source. This integration technique allows SIMS to properly integrate data across several sources that contain inconsistent data instances.

Presently, mapping constructs are generated manually, but we are developing a semi-automate approach. The figure contains tuples from Joe's Restaurant source and the matching tuples from the Health Department:

Name	Address	Phone
1.(Art's Deli,	342 Beverly Blvd,	(310)302-5319)
(Art's Delicatessen,	342 Beverly Boulevard,	310-302-5319)
2. (CPK,	65 La Cienga Blvd,	310-987-8923)
(California Pizza Kitchen,	65 La Cienga Blvd,	310-987-8923)
3. (The Beverly,	302 MLK Blvd,	213-643-2154)
(Cafe Beverly,	302 Martin Luther King Jr. Boulevard,	645-4278)

The key idea behind our approach for generating mapping constructs is to compare all of the shared attributes of the sources in order to determine which tuples are matched, (**name** with **name**, **address** with **address**, and **phone** with **phone**). Since the data instances in the sources are represented in inconsistent formats they can not be compared using equality, but must be judged according to similarity. To determine the similarity between strings we developed general domain independent transformation rules to recognize transformations like substring, acronym, and abbreviation. For example, "Deli" is a substring transformation of "Delicatessen." A probabilistic similarity measure is calculated for each of the transformations between the strings of the two data instances; and then they each are combined to become the similarity measure of the data instances for that attribute. When comparing the data instance "Art's Deli" with "Art's Delicatessen," the probabilities are calculated for the string transformations of "Art's" to "Art's" and "Deli" to "Delicatessen." These probabilities are combined to be the similarity measure for the two instances. After the similarity measures are determined for each of the attributes, **name**, **address** and **phone**, then they are combined to measure the similarity for the two tuples. The most probable matching between the two sets of tuples is then determined. We are employing a statistical learning technique in order to iteratively refine the initial probability measures to increase the accuracy of the matches. Once the mapping is known then a mapping table can be created using the instances from the primary key attribute.

Related work by Cohen [3] determines the mappings by using the IR vector space model to perform similarity joins on the primary key. In this work stemming is used to measure similarity between strings; therfore, in the figure "CPK" would not match "California Pizza Kitchen." But, if the values from the other attributes were taken into consideration, the tuples would match. In experiments where an entire tuple is treated as one attribute accruracy was reduced. As illustrated by the third example, "The Beverly" from Joe's site would equally match the tuples for "Art's Delicatessen" and "Cafe Beverly." Our approach would be able to handle all of these examples, because it combines all of the measurements calculated individually for each shared attributes to determine the correct mapping.

References

[1] **Arens, et.al.** Query Processing in the SIMS Information Mediator. Advanced Planning Technology, editor, Austin Tate, AAAI Press, Menlo Park, CA, 1996.

[3] **William W. Cohen.** Knowledge integration for structured information sources containing text. The SIGIR-97 Workshop on Networked Information Retrieval, 1997.

Emotion-based Agents

Rodrigo M. M. Ventura and Carlos A. Pinto-Ferreira

Instituto de Sistemas e Robótica, Instituto Superior Técnico
Rua Rovisco Pais, 1
1096 Lisboa Codex, Portugal
{yoda,cpf}@isr.ist.utl.pt

To survive in a dynamic and rich environment, human beings have to process very complex stimuli in real time. Whatever artificial system satisfying the challenge of achieving a similar performance in complex data handling, ought to incorporate mechanisms specifically conceived to perform efficiently.

We hypothesize that such efficiency oriented systems process stimuli — simultaneously — under two different perspectives: a *cognitive*, elaborative — which allows them to understand what is happening and what they know about the world, and a *perceptual*, immediate — which permits them to react quickly and decide adequately in circumstances demanding urgent action. Hence, from the very same complex stimulus, two sets of facets are extracted: one, mostly directed to recognition and reasoning purposes, and another, aiming at assigning degrees of threat, danger, pleasure, and so on, to the current situation, constructing what we call a *vector of desirability*.

For instance, when faced with the image of a moving object, the cognitive processor provides elements to recognition (is it a lion or a rabbit?), whereas the perceptual processor delivers an assessment of the prevailing color, moving speed, dimension, and other relevant features found in the scene (is it a huge object with a particular color — a predator, or a little quick moving object — a prey?). These characteristics compose a "perceptual image" which serves two purposes: on the one hand, it allows a rough evaluation of the situation and the corresponding decision making. On the other, it helps the search which underlies the process of recognition: instead of comparing the "cognitive image" under processing with all the elements stored in memory, the search is bound to those objects sharing the same perceptual image. To reach this desideratum, "cognitive images" and "perceptual images" extracted from the same source stimulus should be associated and memorized in such a way that the latter indexes the former.

This kind of system should be bootstrapped by the incorporation of built-in associations. In fact, there should exist some stimuli which are *essential*, innate: for instance, animals faced with their preys or predators decide either to attack or run away as a function of the vector of desirability a perceptual image suggests. This assignment depends on the considered species.

When an unknown object appears in the scene, its perceptual image is extracted and a first estimate of the vector of desirability, as well as the corresponding decision making in the short term is performed. On the other hand, as the agent does not find the corresponding cognitive image in memory (because the object is unknown), a new cognitive-perceptual association is established. This seems to be the mechanism underlying the pavlovian reflex — as it lies on top of built-in associations. This also seems to be the basic mechanism responsible for the assignment of meaning to objects.

Systems incorporating this double processing and knowledge representation mechanism, indexing and storing two representations of the same object together with a vector of desirability, are here defined as emotion-based agents.

This model is corroborated by the work of several researchers in the field of neuroscience. Namely, in Papez circuit theory the functions performed by the hypothalamus and cingulate cortex (in the human brain) can be identified with the cognitive and perceptual processing discussed above (LeDoux 1996). And according to Damasio's ideas, emotions are essential to human decision making (Damasio 1994).

Several architectures have been proposed to deal with real time processing and decision making; in all of them it is possible to identify "cognitive" and "perceptual" levels. However these levels work independently and, in certain cases, one blocks the other. What makes this proposal different and appealing is the intertwining of both, and the consequent learning capabilities which it allows.

An architecture based on these concepts was implemented and the results are encouraging: not only does the agent learn new associations, but it also recognizes objects efficiently and decides correctly when faced with new, unknown situations. And interestingly, what can be considered as an emotional behavior, was observed.

We are afraid that, to reach intelligent behavior, we will end up implementing some of the (apparently) most stupid things human beings exhibit, including bad temper.

References

Damasio, A. R. 1994. *Descartes' Error: Emotion, Reason and the Human Brain*. Picador.

LeDoux, J. 1996. *The Emotional Brain*. Simon & Schuster.

---

*Copyright (c) 1998, American Association for Artificial Intelligence (www.aaai.org). All rights reserved.

DL-$elect: A Decision-List-Based Data-Mining System

Karl Weinmeister

Duke University
D101 Levine Science Research Center
Durham, NC 27708
karl.weinmeister@duke.edu

The application of machine-learning algorithms to the financial markets has been increasing in popularity in recent years. The majority of systems that have been created for the purpose of selecting stocks have utilized neural-network techniques. Our research has dealt with the feasibility of inductive logic approaches and the creation of a decision-list-based data-mining system, DL-$elect.

Neural networks can model a variety of data distributions and handle inconsistent data well. But for complex problems such as financial analysis, the structure of a neural network can be difficult to interpret. Decision lists (Rivest 1987), however, are represented in an easily understood form: an extended "if-then-elseif-...else-" rule.

Iterative algorithms for decision lists append rules into a list and remove examples from the data set that are covered by these rules. Effective future learning depends on early rule selection, which, if made poorly, can reduce the accuracy of the entire decision list. The algorithm described by Rivest (Rivest 1987) avoids this obstacle by assuming 100% accurate rules in the training data, but consequently leaves open the problem of noisy data. The learning algorithm used in DL-$elect, BruteDL (Segal and Etzioni 1994), addresses this and other issues by conducting a single search for homogenous rules—rules in which accuracy is independent of list position. Since homogenous rules need not be 100% accurate, BruteDL is better suited to handle the noise of financial-market data.

There has been significant discourse in the financial and academic community regarding the efficiency of financial markets. The efficient-markets hypothesis asserts that stock prices already reflect any available information, rendering forecasting attempts useless. DL-$elect is based on the notion that markets do in fact exhibit short-term inefficiencies—trends from the previous week of activity carry over to the next week. The portfolio gleaned from DL-$elect is not intended for a buy-and-hold strategy; rather, it is meant for weekly changes. By using fresh data each week, Dl-$elect avoids the issue of non-stationarity, in which statistical properties of the market change with time.

Two key data elements are needed by DL-$elect: a list of stock attributes such as price/earnings ratio, and a list of price changes acquired one week later, corresponding to the first list. DL-$elect assembles 11 attributes for 600 stocks into the attribute list, inserts the price-change data, and cleans any malformed data. Next, stocks from the resulting data file are labeled as excellent if they perform in the top α% (in our simulation α=20) since BruteDL is a classification algorithm that requires a category to predict (John and Miller 1996). The data file is then randomly partitioned into a 60% training, 30% testing, and 10% pruning blend and entered into BruteDL. The generated rules determine which variables make an "excellent" stock.

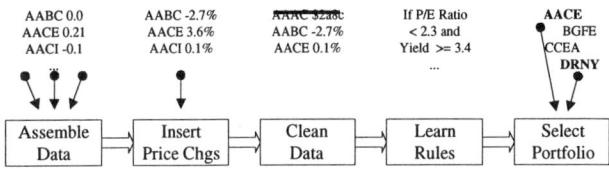

Figure 1: The DL-$elect process

BruteDL will return the most accurate set of rules based on testing, from which a portfolio is selected. In the simulation, the portfolio is a random subset of all stocks that conform to the given rules. The portfolio chosen November 29, 1997 showed a return of 4.83% over the Dow Jones Industrial Average and 4.10% over the S&P 500 index during the following week of December 1-5, 1997. The portfolio exhibits low risk, with an average $\beta=0.7$, a statistic that measures stocks' movement relative to the market. While the low risk of the portfolio is a fortuitous benefit, its high return confirms its potential.

The use of inductive logic and specifically decision lists are indeed useful for stock selection in the financial markets. We have developed a promising data-mining system, DL-$elect, which can aid in the determination of a short-term portfolio. Future work on DL-$elect includes further performance evaluations and the exploration of alternative knowledge-representation structures.

References

R. Rivest. Learning decision lists. *Machine Learning*, 2:229-246, 1987.

R. Segal and O. Etzioni. Learning decision lists using homogenous rules. In *Proceedings of the Twelfth National Conference on Artificial Intelligence*, July 1994.

G. John and P. Miller. Building long/short portfolios using rule induction. In *Computational Intelligence in Financial Engineering*, 134-140. Piscataway, NJ, 1996. IEEE Press.

Copyright © 1998, American Association for Artificial Intelligence (www.aaai.org). All rights reserved.

Ensuring Reasoning Consistency in Hierarchical Architectures

Robert E. Wray, III and John Laird
Artificial Intelligence Laboratory
The University of Michigan
1101 Beal Ave.
Ann Arbor, MI 48109-2110
{robert.wray,laird}@umich.edu

Ensuring reasoning consistency in agents employing hierarchical task decompositions can be difficult. We have identified two specific problems that result when hierarchical context changes during problem solving. First, the agent can be too responsive, taking an external act or making an internal derivation before higher context is fully elaborated. Second, the agent can fail to respond to a change in the context, leaving a local level "unsituated" with respect to the higher contexts. In both cases, an agent's assertions of knowledge in a local level can be inconsistent with the larger context, leading potentially to irrational behavior.

Previous methods for maintaining "cross-level" consistency have relied upon a combination of both architectural techniques and explicit knowledge. Architectural solutions preserve inexpensive knowledge design while knowledge-based methods compromise that advantage, requiring a knowledge engineer anticipate all situations in which inconsistency could arise. Thus, the goal of our work is to solve consistency problems *architecturally*, guaranteeing appropriate responsiveness within a level of the hierarchy to ensure reasoning consistency. Architectural solutions also solve a number of existing problems in run-time *compilation* (Goel 1991), thus enabling agents to learn execution knowledge that avoids decomposition overhead.

Our solution, hierarchical consistency (HC), consists of two parts which work together to ensure consistency. First, we have extended truth maintenance methods (Doyle 1979) to determine context dependencies for subtask processing. When a dependency is violated, the architecture responds by retracting dependent structure (Wray & Laird 1998). Second, we have synchronized activity among subtasks such that knowledge is asserted locally only when the higher context is stable. Together, these two methods allow locally non-monotonic, persistent and parallel assertions while ensuring that local problem solving is consistent with changes in the hierarchical context.

We have implemented the algorithms comprising HC in the Soar architecture (Laird, Newell, & Rosenbloom 1987) and applied HC to several domains, including a research version of TacAir-Soar (Tambe *et al.* 1995). We compared "HC agents" to previously-developed Soar agents in these domains. We summarize our experimental results as follows: 1) HC agents require less knowledge than the original agents, because no explicit across-level consistency knowledge is necessary; 2) knowledge access time in hierarchical consistency increases slightly, due to additional architecture processing; 3) total knowledge accesses decrease because less knowledge is needed; 4) overall task performance time often improves because fewer knowledge accesses offset the increase in cycle time; and 5) HC agents are more robust in situations unforeseen when they were designed. Additionally, hierarchical consistency solves the non-contemporaneous constraints problem (Wray, Laird, & Jones 1996), thus providing a structure for on-line compilation of dynamic, hierarchical execution knowledge. Based on these results, we believe hierarchical consistency provides efficient, general solutions for maintaining consistency in hierarchical architectures.

References

Doyle, J. 1979. A truth maintenance system. *Artificial Intelligence* 12:231–272.

Goel, A. K. 1991. Knowledge compilation: A symposium. *IEEE Expert* 6(2):71–93.

Laird, J. E.; Newell, A.; and Rosenbloom, P. S. 1987. Soar: An architecture for general intelligence. *Artificial Intelligence* 33:1–64.

Tambe, M.; Johnson, W. L.; Jones, R. M.; Koss, F.; Laird, J. E.; Rosenbloom, P. S.; and Schwamb, K. 1995. Intelligent agents for interactive simulation environments. *AI Magazine* 16(1):15–39.

Wray, R., and Laird, J. 1998. Maintaining consistency in hierarchical reasoning. In *Proceedings of the Fifteenth National Conference on Artificial Intelligence.*

Wray, R.; Laird, J.; and Jones, R. M. 1996. Compilation of non-contemporaneous constraints. In *Proceedings of the Thirteenth National Conference on Artificial Intelligence*, 771–778.

Copyright ©1998, American Association for Artificial Intelligence (www.aaai.org). All rights reserved.

Building agents from shared ontologies through apprenticeship multistrategy learning

Kathryn Wright, Mihai Boicu, Seok Won Lee and Gheorghe Tecuci

Learning Agents Laboratory, Department of Computer Science,
George Mason University, Fairfax, VA 22030, USA
{kwright mboicu swlee tecuci}@gmu.edu

The goal of this research is to create the Disciple Learning Agent Shell for efficient development of personal agents, that relies on importing ontologies from existing repositories using the Open Knowledge Base Connectivity (OKBC) protocol (Chaudhri et al, 1997) and on teaching the agents to perform various tasks through apprenticeship and multistrategy learning (Tecuci, 1998). We are performing significant developments of Disciple, and we are integrating it with OKBC into the following architecture of the Learning Agent Shell:

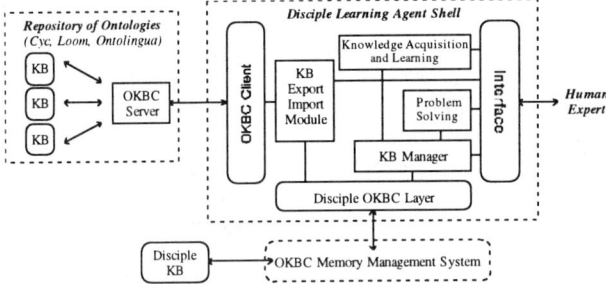

The knowledge base of a Disciple agent consists of an ontology that defines and organizes the concepts from the application domain, and a set of problem solving rules expressed in terms of these concepts. The process of building this knowledge base starts with creating a domain ontology by importing concepts from the shared ontologies of an OKBC server. Next the domain expert will teach the agent how to solve domain specific problems by providing a specific example of a problem and its solution, and by helping it to understand them. The explanations of the example will guide the agent to generalize the example to a general problem solving rule.

We are developing analogical reasoning methods that allow the Disciple agent to hypothesize the explanations of a problem solving episode by analogy with the explanations of a similar problem solving episode. For instance, if the agent "understands" why a company can build a floating bridge over a river then, by analogy, it can hypothesize many of the conditions required to use a floating bridge as a ferry, or to simply ford the river.

We are also developing methods that allow numbers to be generalized to intervals, functional and relational expressions, or symbolic concepts (such as "odd-number"). For instance, the explanation piece

floating-bridge-1 total-length 480m and river-segment-1 width 300m < 480m

is automatically generalized to

?f1 total-length ?t1, ?t1 is (* ?u1 ?n1), ?r1 width ?w1, ?w1 is-in [0, 2000], ?w1 < ?t1

Another development of Disciple is inspired by the Theory of Inductive Probability developed by the philosopher L. Jonathan Cohen (1989). As opposed to the Bayesian network approaches, Cohen's theory has the advantage that it does not require the assignment of numeric or traditional probabilistic measures to elements in the knowledge base. In this theory, probability is a generalization of the notion of provability. Following the inductive probability theory, the rules learned by Disciple are refined through a systematic process of experimentation which attempts to falsify the rule, using several heuristics as well as analogy with other rules and the conditions under which they fail. This results in a list of conditions under which rule failures occur and in a measure of inductive support of the rule.

We are also developing problem solving capabilities in Disciple which implement the use of inductive probabilities during rule evaluation and selection. The inductive probability of a rule instance is based upon the measure of the inductive support accorded to the rule and how much is known about the falsifying conditions.

To conclude, we investigate the claim that using existing ontologies, and a synergistic integration of symbolic multistrategy learning, knowledge acquisition and inductive probabilistic reasoning can form the basis of an efficient agent development environment.

References

Chaudhri, V. K., Farquhar, A., Fikes, R., Karp, P., and Rice, J. (1997). Open Knowledge Base Connectivity 2.0. *Technical Report*, SRI International and Stanford Univ.

Cohen, L. J., (1989). *An Introduction to the Philosophy of Induction and Probability.* Clarendon, Oxford.

Tecuci, G. (1998). *Building Intelligent Agents: An Apprenticeship Multistrategy Learning Theory, Methodology, Tool and Case Studies.* Academic Press, London.

Development of Outdoor Navigation for a Robotic Wheelchair System

Holly A. Yanco [*]
MIT Artificial Intelligence Laboratory
545 Technology Square, Room 705
Cambridge, MA 02139
holly@ai.mit.edu

The goal of this research is the creation of a complete robotic wheelchair system to be used by people unable to drive standard powered wheelchairs. A complete robotic wheelchair system must be able to navigate indoor and outdoor environments and should switch automatically between navigation modes. For the system to be useful, it must be easily customized for the specific access methods required for each user. This abstract focuses on the vision system being developed for outdoor navigation and the method for selecting whether to use the indoor navigation mode or the outdoor navigation mode. A report of the indoor navigation mode and user interface can be found in (Yanco In press).

Navigation is divided into two classes: indoor and outdoor. In both navigation modes, the user gives a high-level command ("forward," "left," "right," and "backward") through the graphical user interface which has been customized to accommodate the user's access method. The system carries out the user's command using common sense constraints such as obstacle avoidance. Since the user must be able to successfully navigate novel environments immediately, the system does not use maps or environment modification.

The navigation problem in an indoor environment is simplified by regularities such as level floors and walls. A vision system can be used in an indoor environment, but it is not necessary. Robots navigating indoors can use sonar and infrared sensors to avoid obstacles.

Outdoor navigation is not feasible using only sonar and infrared sensors. To facilitate navigation in outdoor environments, a vision system with one camera is being added to the wheelchair. Initial image processing is aimed at finding and navigating sidewalks, crosswalks, curb cuts and handicapped ramps. To stay on sidewalks and in crosswalks, the vision system will detect long straight lines that head towards the vanishing point. Ground-plane constraint or optical flow using successive frames will be used to approximate the distance of obstacles in the camera image from the wheelchair.

Outdoor navigation for a robotic wheelchair in a sidewalk domain differs from outdoor navigation for an automobile in a highway domain (see, for example, (Thorpe 1997)). Sidewalks are not as regular as roads; they may be made up of bricks, concrete segments, wooden boardwalks or tar and the materials may change as the user moves in front of a new building.

The robot must determine whether it is in an indoor or outdoor environment in order to select the proper navigation mode. Given the abilities and access methods of the system's users, it is not realistic to require the user to indicate a change of indoor/outdoor status. Researchers in the vision community have investigated ways to determine if an image is an indoor or outdoor scene. However, the user will not change between the environments with high frequency. For this reason, the vision system should not be devoting processing time to determining the current environment. Instead, this research includes the development of an indoor/outdoor detector which will determine the location of the chair by getting values for variables such as ultraviolet light, color characteristics of the light, polarization of the light, the characteristic frequency of electric lights, the presence or absence of a ceiling, and sudden temperature differences.

The indoor/outdoor detector and vision system for outdoor navigation under development will be added to the existing indoor navigation system and customizable user interface to form a complete robotic wheelchair system.

References

Mittal, V.; Yanco, H. A.; and Aronis, J., eds. In press. *Lecture Notes in Artificial Intelligence: Assistive Technology and Artificial Intelligence.* Springer-Verlag.

Thorpe, C. E., ed. 1997. *Intelligent Unmanned Ground Vehicles: Autonomous Navigation Research at CMU.* Kluwer Academic Publishers.

Yanco, H. A. In press. Wheelesley, a robotic wheelchair system: Indoor navigation and user interface. In Mittal et al. (In press).

---

[*]This research is supported by the Office of Naval Research under contract number N00014-95-1-0600 and the National Science Foundation under grant number CDA-9505200.
Copyright ©1998, American Association for Artificial Intelligence (www.aaai.org). All rights reserved.

Invited Talk

Structured Probabilistic Models: Bayesian Networks and Beyond

Daphne Koller
Stanford University
Stanford, CA 94305-9010
koller@cs.stanford.edu

Abstract

For many years, probabilistic models were largely neglected within the AI community. Now they play a fundamental role in many areas in AI, including diagnosis, planning, and learning. One of the crucial reasons for this transition is the use of structured model-based representations such as Bayesian networks. Building on this idea, we can extend the success of probabilistic modeling to much more complex domains, ones involving many components that interact and evolve over time. These domains are significantly beyond the scope of traditional Bayesian networks. I describe a broad class of structured probabilistic representations that extend Bayesian networks to deal with these new challenges. I argue that these representations can form the basis for agents that reason and act in complex uncertain environments.

1 Probabilistic Modeling

Over the last fifteen years, there has been a slow but steady revolution in the attitude of the AI community to probabilistic modeling. After being neglected for much of AI's history, probabilistic models are now playing an important role in many subfields of AI, including diagnosis, planning, and machine learning.

There are many factors contributing to this transition. One is the increase in range of AI applications, leading to the realization that, in many real-life domains, an explicit and coherent treatment of uncertainty is unavoidable. The other is the introduction of new probabilistic modeling languages, primarily Bayesian networks [12].

A Bayesian network (BN) is a graphical representation of a probability distribution over a large set of variables (domain attributes). A BN builds on qualitative intuitions regarding locality of influence to allow a compact and intuitive representation of a complex domain model. Informally, a BN is a directed acyclic graph, whose nodes represent the random variables and whose edges represent direct probabilistic influence. For example, in a medical diagnosis task we might have a node *Emphysema* representing a binary-valued variable whose value is *true* if the patient has emphysema. We might have an edge between *Smoking* and *Emphysema*, representing our domain knowledge that smoking causes emphysema. The absence of direct edges corresponds to *conditional independence* assumptions. For example, if there is no edge from *Smoking* to *Dyspnea*, we could conclude that although smoking may influence dyspnea, this influnece must be indirect (e.g., via *Emphysema*). Each node in the BN is associated with a local probabilistic model, which models the way in which a node's parents—its direct influences— probabilistically affect its value. By combining the local probabilistic models with the independence assumptions implicit in the BN structure, a BN completely specifies a full joint distribution over the possible assignments of values to the random variables.

Perhaps the most surprising aspect of the Bayesian network framework is the ease with which a single representation supports so many different tasks. The same BN model can be used both for prediction and for explanation. It can also be used to make optimal decisions regarding our actions; as actions include observation actions, we can also make optimal use of our information-gathering resources. Decision-support systems based on this technology have proven to be better decision makers than the experts from whom the knowledge was acquired [8]. Bayesian networks have been fielded in a wide variety of applications [1], making them one of the largest commercial successes of AI.

Bayesian networks have also demonstrated their utility for the inductive learning task [9]. Bayesian network learning algorithms easily integrate empirical data and prior knowledge acquired from experts. They have been used for tasks as simple as adapting the parameters of an existing Bayesian network to ones as complex as causal discovery.

2 Key lessons

The success of a modeling language rests on its ability to achieve three goals: compact and natural representation of domain knowledge, allowing effective knowledge acquisition; efficient versatile reasoning algorithms; and ability to learn from experience. Bayesian networks have demonstrated their success at all three tasks. What is the key to this success? What general lessons can we learn from Bayesian networks? In the talk, I discuss some of the factors contributing to the success of Bayesian networks and mention some general conclusions:

- **Realistic assumptions about the domain make life easier in the long run.** For example, by explicitly allowing for indeterminacy, we can fold myriad exceptions into a simple general purpose "noise" factor. The resulting models are simpler, easing knowledge acquisition, inference, and learning.

- **When possible, stand on the shoulders of giants.** Probabilistic methods come with a coherent semantics and an enormous array of useful techniques for inference, learning, and decision making. The ability to build on this

infrastructure was a major contributor to the rapid evolution of Bayesian networks.
- **Model your representation after the world.** Model-based representations are both cognitively satisfying and versatile, allowing the same representation to be used for many different purposes. Bayesian networks are simply model-based representations in the richer model class of probability distributions.
- **Capture and exploit domain structure.** Design your language around the structure in your domain. Explicit representations of structure are more natural and compact; they make it easier both for people and for reasoning algorithms to interact with the domain model.

The combination of these factors is what enables Bayesian networks to support representation, inference, and learning in a single framework.

This analysis is useful in several ways. Most immediately, we want to use these lessons as guidance in expanding the frontiers of the probabilistic modeling framework. More generally, we see that many of the conclusions are not specific to probabilistic models. Thus, we might hope that the insights we obtained will also apply to other approaches.

3 Beyond Bayesian networks

Despite their great success, Bayesian networks are not the complete solution to the many complex tasks that AI has to face. Consider, for example, the task of a robot working in a complex environment such as a large office building or a factory. In such domains, the world evolves over time, both endogenously and as a result of actions taken by the agent. The domain itself is complex, involving many entities of various types; for example, in the office building environment, there are entities corresponding to people, to rooms, to physical objects (e.g., printers or furniture), and even to events such as seminars. These entities interact, with the state of one affecting the state of another. The entities themselves often have structure, with complex entities being composed of simpler ones. For example, a room description might incorporate the description of the various objects it contains.

How do we extend the probabilistic modeling framework to these much more complex environments? It turns out that the same factors that played a key role in the success of Bayesian networks are even more crucial here. In the second part of the talk, I describe some of the important extensions to the probabilistic framework, and show how they share the same underlying themes.

Dynamic Bayesian Networks [6] extend the Bayesian network framework to models that evolve indefinitely over time. They exploit the regularity of temporal models, allowing a compact representation of complex stochastic processes.

Structured action models [5, 3] provide compact natural representations of the effects of an agent's actions on the world. New types of structure is introduced to make the preconditions and effects of actions more explicit. The explicit modeling of noise allows compact probabilistic solutions to both the frame problem and qualification problem.

Models with higher level structure [13, 10] allow us to model complex environments consisting of many entities. In such domains, it is important to model explicitly the notion of an entity (or object), thereby allowing an explicit declarative representation of the relationships between objects. For example, objects can be composed of other objects, e.g., in a model for a complex physical device or of different rooms in a building. Higher level structure allows building and reasoning about a domain at different levels of abstraction. It also allows the inference task to be effectively decomposed.

Explicit representations of structural uncertainty [8, 2, 11] allows us to express uncertainty about aspects of the model structure. Thus, for example, the probabilistic influences in the domain might be different in different circumstances, e.g., when the agent takes different actions. In more complex settings, we may even be uncertain about which entities are in the model. By making structures corresponding to entities and the relations between them first-class citizens in our representation, we provide the capability to represent uncertainty over them.

These extensions build on the lessons learned from the Bayesian network framework, utilizing model-based structured representations with explicit models for uncertainty. And, indeed, we are already starting to see evidence of similar benefits: modeling languages that allow effective knowledge representation, inference, and learning.

By combining these building blocks, we can model very complex domains: evolving systems composed of several interacting processes that are themselves structured. We can capture notions of sparse or weak interactions [7] and exploit this structure in inference [4]. These representations, with their ability to support effective inference and learning, allow us to deal with a new range of challenges. I argue that they can help us build agents that reason and act in complex uncertain environments.

References

[1] Deployed Bayesian-nets systems in routine use. http://www.auai.org/BN-Routine.html, 1996.

[2] C. Boutilier, N. Friedman, M. Goldszmidt, and D. Koller. Context-specific independence in Bayesian networks. In *Proc. UAI*, 1996.

[3] C.E. Boutilier and M. Goldszmidt. The frame problem and bayesian network action representations. In *Proc. CSCSI*, 1996.

[4] X. Boyen and D. Koller. Tractable inference for complex stochastic processes. Submitted to UAI, 1998.

[5] A. Darwiche and M. Goldszmidt. Action networks: A framework for reasoning about actions and change under uncertainty. In *Proc. UAI*, 1994.

[6] T. Dean and K. Kanazawa. A model for reasoning about persistence and causation. *Computational Intelligence*, 5(3), 1989.

[7] N. Friedman, D. Koller, and A. Pfeffer. Structured representation of complex stochastic systems. In *Proc. AAAI*, 1998. This proceedings.

[8] D. Heckerman. *Probabilistic Similarity Networks*. MIT Press, 1990.

[9] D. Heckerman. A tutorial on learning with Bayesian networks. Technical Report MSR-TR-95-06, Microsoft Research, 1995.

[10] D. Koller and A. Pfeffer. Object-oriented Bayesian networks. In *Proc. UAI*, 1997.

[11] D. Koller and A. Pfeffer. Probabilistic frame-based systems. In *Proc. AAAI*, 1998. This proceedings.

[12] J. Pearl. *Probabilistic Reasoning in Intelligent Systems*. Morgan Kaufmann, 1988.

[13] S. Srinivas. A probabilistic approach to hierarchical model-based diagnosis. In *Proc. UAI*, 1994.

Index

A* with Bounded Costs, 444
Abductive Planning with Sensing, 631
Acceleration Methods for Numeric CSPs, 19
Acquisition of Abstract Plan Descriptions for Plan Recognition, 936
Act, and the Rest Will Follow: Exploiting Determinism in Planning as Satisfiability, 948
Action Language Based on Causal Explanation: Preliminary Report, An, 623
Adachi, Yoshinobu, 1152
Adaptive Web Sites: Automatically Synthesizing Web Pages, 727
Agents, 25-104
Agents that Work in Harmony by Knowing and Fulfilling their Obligations, 89
AI and education, 105-119
Akkiraju, Rama, 1013
Alechina, Natasha, 444
Algebra for Cyclic Ordering of 2D Orientations, An, 643
Algorithm to Evaluate Quantified Boolean Formulae, An, 262
Algorithms for Propositional KB Approximation, 280
Allen, James F., 567, 860
Alternative Essences of Intelligence, 961
Ambiguity and Constraint in Mathematical Expression Recognition, 784
Ambite, Jose Luis, 211
Analyzing External Conditions to Improve the Efficiency of HTN Planning, 913
Anand, Sarabjot S., 574
Anderson, Corin R., 897
Anderson, Gail, 1020
Andersson, Martin R., 38, 46
ANSWER: Network Monitoring Using Object-Oriented Rules, 1087
Answering Questions for an Organization Online, 532

Anytime Approximate Modal Reasoning, 274
Anytime Coalition Structure Generation with Worst Case Guarantees, 46
Applying Online Search Techniques to Continuous-State Reinforcement Learning, 753
Architecture for Exploring Large Design Spaces, An, 143
Arens, Yigal, 1095
Ashish, Naveen, 211, 1168
Automated Intelligent Pilots for Combat Flight Simulation, 1047
Automated reasoning, 120-297
Automatic OBDD-Based Generation of Universal Plans in Non-Deterministic Domains, 875

Bacchus, Fahiem, 311
Backtracking Algorithms for Disjunctions of Temporal Constraints, 248
Bailey-Kellogg, Christopher, 232
Bailleux, Olivier, 386
Baluja, Shumeet, 469
Barber, K. S., 1193, 1195
Barbuceanu, Mihai, 89
Bares, William H., 1101
Basin, David, 500
Basu, Chumki, 714
Bauer, Mathias, 936
Baur, Ed, 1032
Bayesian Network Models for Generation of Crisis Management Training Scenarios, 1113
Bayesian Q-Learning, 761
Bayesian Reasoning for Tropical Cyclone Intensity Forecasting and Risk Analysis, 1181
Bayesian Reasoning in an Abductive Mechanism for Argument Generation and Analysis, 833
Beck, Joseph E., 1185
Becker, G. K., 1107

Belief Revision with Unreliable Observations, 127
Benferhat, S., 121
Beveridge, J. Ross, 677
Bienkowski, Marie A., 561
BIG: A Resource-Bounded Information Gathering Agent, 539
Billings, Darse, 493
Biswas, Gautam, 219
Bliek, Christian, 319
Bloedorn, Eric, 821
Boicu, Mihai, 1207
Bonasso, Peter, 1140
Boosting Classifiers Regionally, 700
Boosting Combinatorial Search through Randomization, 431
Boosting in the Limit: Maximizing the Margin of Learned Ensembles, 692
Boufkhad, Yacine, 280
Bourne, Juliet C., 1169
Boutilier, Craig, 127, 165, 746
Boyan, Justin A., 3
Bradley, Elizabeth, 181
Branch and Bound Algorithm Selection by Performance Prediction, 353
Branching Factor of Regular Search Spaces, The, 299
Breazeal, Cynthia (Ferrell), 54, 961
Brodie, Mark, 665
Brooks, Rodney A., 961
Bruce, Rebecca, 800
Building Agents from Shared Ontologies through Apprenticeship Multistrategy Learning, 1207
Burgard, Wolfram, 11, 983, 989
Burke, Robin D., 532
Burns, Brendan, 1186

Cadoli, Marco, 262
Callaway, Charles B., 112
Calvanese, Diego, 205

Carroll, Mark, 143
Casson-du Mont, Andrew, 1020
Cerquides, Jesús, 1187, 1188
Chandrasekaran, B., 143
Chaudhri, Vinay K., 600
Chien, Steve, 1027
Choueiry, Berthe Y., 326
Cimatti, Alessandro, 875
Cimoch, Paul J., 1071
Clancy, Daniel J., 240
Classification Using an Online Genetic Algorithm, 1189
Claus, Caroline, 746
Clements, David P., 340
Coen, Michael H., 547
Cohen, Paul R., 739
Cohen, William, 714
Cohn, Anthony G., 643
Colton, Simon, 1170
Complete Anytime Beam Search, 425
Complexity Analysis of Admissible Heuristic Search, 305
Computing Intersections of Horn Theories for Reasoning with Models, 292
Conati, Cristina, 106
Concepts from Time Series, 739
Conformant Graphplan, 889
Constrainedness Knife-Edge, The, 406
Constraint satisfaction and search, 19, 298-484
Constructing the Correct Diagnosis When Symptoms Disappear, 151
Control Strategies in HTN Planning: Theory Versus Practice, 1127
Controlling Communication in Distributed Planning Using Irrelevance Reasoning, 868
Conversation Machines for Transaction Processing, 1160
Cooperating with People: The Intelligent Classroom, 555
Countrywide Automated Property Evaluation System - CAPES, 1039
Craven, Mark, 509
Crawford, James M., 286
Cremers, Armin B., 11, 983

Dasgupta, Dipankar, 83

Data Mining for Maintenance of Complex Systems, 1178
Date, Hiroyuki, 1152
Davies, Scott, 469, 753
Dávila, Jaime J., 1171
Davison, Brian D., 477, 1189
De Giacomo, Giuseppe, 205
Dean, Thomas, 165
Dearden, Richard, 761
Decompositional, Model-Based Learning and its Analogy to Diagnosis, 197
Deeds-Rubin, Sophia, 1071
DeJong, Gerald, 665
Denecker, Marc, 840
Dependent Bigram Identification, 1197
Design Principles for Intelligent Environments, 547
desJardins, Marie, 868
Determan, J. C., 1107
Devaney, Mark, 942, 1190
Development of Outdoor Navigation for a Robotic Wheelchair System, 1208
DiPasquo, Dan, 509
Discourse Learning: Dialogue Act Tagging with Transformation-Based Learning, 1199
Discovering Admissible Simultaneous Equations of Large Scale Systems, 189
DL-$elect: A Decision-List-Based Data-Mining System, 1205
Dubois, D., 121
Dubois, Didier, 588
Dukes-Schlossberg, Jon, 1095
Dumer, John, 1032
Dung, Phan Minh, 637
Dybala, Tom, 1055
Dynamics of Reinforcement Learning in Cooperative Multiagent Systems, The, 746

Edelkamp, Stefan, 299
Eiter, Thomas, 292
Emotion Model for Life-Like Agent and Its Evaluation, 62
Emotion-Based Agents, 1204
Empirical Acquisition of Word-Sense Distinctions, 1179

Ensuring Reasoning Consistency in Hierarchical Architectures, 1206
Epstein, Susan L., 135
Erb, David A., 143
Erol, Kutluhan, 1127
Estimating the Expected Error of Empirical Minimizers for Model Selection, 1200
Etherington, David W., 286
Etzioni, Oren, 727
Evolvable hardware, 485-491
Evolvable Hardware Chip for High Precision Printer Image Compression, 486
Experimenting with Power Default Reasoning, 846
Expert System for Alarm System Planning, An, 1152
Expert System Technology for Nondestructive Waste Assay, 1107
Exploiting Diversity for Natural Language Processing, 1174
Extending GENET to Solve Fuzzy Constraint Satisfaction Problems, 380
Extending Graphplan to Handle Uncertainty & Sensing Actions, 897
Extending the Classification Paradigm to Temporal Domains, 1177
Eye Finding via Face Detection for a Foveated Active Vision System, 969

Farquhar, Adam, 600
Farwell, David, 76
Fast Algorithm for the Bound Consistency of Alldiff Constraints, A, 359
Fast Probabilistic Modeling for Combinatorial Optimization, 469
Fast Transformation of Temporal Plans for Efficient Execution, 254
Fawcett, Tom, 706
Feature Generation for Sequence Categorization, 733
Feature-Based Learning Method for Theorem Proving, A, 457
Ferguson, George, 567
Fikes, Richard, 600
Finding Optimal Strategies for Imperfect Information Games, 500
First Analysis of Qualitative Influences and Synergies, A, 1187

Fisher, Forest, 1027
Fitoussi, David, 26
Fixpoint 3-Valued Semantics for Autoepistemic Logic, 840
Formal Methodology for Verifying Situated Agents, A, 637
Fox, Dieter, 11, 983, 989
Framework for Reinforcement Learning on Real Robots, A, 1202
Frank, Ian, 500
Franklin, David, 555
Franklin, Stan, 83
Freed, Michael, 921
Freitag, Dayne, 509
Freitag, Dayne, 517
Friedman, Nir, 127, 157, 761
Fuchs, Matthias, 457
Fujimoto, Koji, 1191
Fuzzy Description Logic, A, 594

Game playing, 492-507
Garland, Andrew, 1172
Generalized A* for Cyclic AND/OR Graphs, 1192
Generalizing Partial Order and Dynamic Backtracking, 319
Generating Adequate Instructions: Knowing When to Stop, 1169
Generating Coordinated Natural Language and 3D Animations for Complex Spatial Explanations, 112
Generating Inference-Rich Discourse through Revisions of RST-Trees, 814
Genetic Search for Accurate Feature Sets, 1186
Gerevini, Alfonso, 905
Gertner, Abigail S., 106
Gervasio, Melinda T., 721
Ghose, Supriyo, 1192
Ginsberg, Matthew L., 334
Giovanardi, Andrea, 262
Giunchiglia, Enrico, 623, 948
Gleeson, Barry, 1020
Goal and Responsibility Allocation in Sensible Agent-Based Systems, 1195
Goldberg, Henry G., 1055
Gomes, Carla P., 431

Greeley, Ronald, 1027
Grégoire, Joël P., 1101
Gribble, William S., 1173
Grois, Eugene, 1113
Grove, Adam J., 692
Gupta, Gopal, 76
Gutmann, Jens-Steffen, 989

Hafner, Carole D., 615
Hahn, Udo, 524
Hähnel, Dirk, 11
Hall, J. Storrs, 477
Halpern, Joseph Y., 127
Hammond, Kristian J., 532
Handling Inconsistency for Multi-Source Integration, 1203
Hanratty, Tim, 1032
Hansen, Eric A., 412
Hard Problems for CSP Algorithms, 398
Hauskrecht, Milos, 165
Hayden, James J., 1055
Heckendorn, Robert B., 392
Helfman, Richard, 1032
Henderson, John C., 1174
Hendler, James, 913
Hermes: Supporting Argumentative Discourse in Multi-Agent Decision Making, 827
Heuristic Search in Cyclic AND / OR Graphs, 412
Hewett, Micheal, 1175
Highest Utility First Search Across Multiple Levels of Stochastic Design, 477
Higuchi, Tetsuya, 486
Hirayama, Yuji, 62
Hirsh, Haym, 714, 733
Hoebel, Louis J., 561
Hogg, Tad, 438
Horacek, Helmut, 814
Horling, Bryan, 539
HR—Automatic Concept Formation in Finite Algebras, 1170
Hsu, William H., 1113
Hu, Junling, 1176
Hughes, John G., 574
Hulthage, Ingemar A. E., 1039

Hybrid Knowledge Based System for Automatic Classificaton of B-scan Images from Ultrasonic Rail Inspection, 1121
Hybrid Planning for Partially Hierarchical Domains, 882

Iba, Wayne, 721
Ibaraki, Toshihide, 292
Improving Big Plans, 860
Inferring State Constraints for Domain-Independent Planning, 905
Information extraction, 508-537
Information Extraction from HTML: Application of a General Machine Learning Approach, 517
Ingham, Holly, 1032
Innovative applications, 1011-1166
Integer Local Search Method with Application to Capacitated Production Planning, An, 373
Integrated AI systems, 11, 538-572
Integrating AI Components for a Military Planning Application, 561
Integrating Topological and Metric Maps for Mobile Robot Navigation: A Statistical Approach, 989
Intelligent Control of Life Support Systems for Space Habitats, 1140
Interactive Museum Tour-Guide Robot, The, 11
Inui, Nobuo, 1191
Inuo, Takeshi, 486
Irie, Robert, 961
Ishida, Toru, 450
Isli, Amar, 643
Iterated Phantom Induction: A Little Knowledge Can Go a Long Way, 665
Iwata, Masaya, 486
Iyer, Naresh, 143
Iyer, Ramesh, 373

Jarmulak, J., 1121
Joachims, Thorsten, 1201
Jones, Randolph M., 1047
Josephson, John R., 143
Joslin, David E., 340
Juillé, Hugues, 776

Junghanns, Andreas, 419

Kadous, Mohammed Waleed, 1177
Kaelbling, Leslie Pack, 165, 1202
Kajihara, Nobuki, 486
Kambhampati, Subbarao, 882
Kambhatla, Nanda, 1160
Kaminka, Gal A., 97
Karacapilidis, Nikos, 827
Karp, Peter D., 600
Kautz, Henry, 431
Kemp, Charles C., 961
Kerckhoffs, E. J. H., 1121
Keskinocak, Pinar, 1013
Kim, Kee-Eung, 165
Kirkland, J. Dale, 1055
Klassner, Frank, 539, 997
Klavins, Eric, 846
Knoblock, Craig A., 211, 1203
Knowledge Intensive Exception Spaces, 574
Knowledge Lean Word—Sense Disambiguation, 800
Knowledge representation, 573-663
Knowledge-Based Avoidance of Drug-Resistant HIV Mutants, 1071
Koller, Daphne, 157, 580, 1210
Korb, Kevin B., 833
Korf, Richard E., 299, 305
Kotani, Yoshiyuki, 1191
Kott, Alexander, 1063
Koubarakis, Manolis, 248
Kudenko, Daniel, 733
Kuipers, Benjamin J., 240, 989
Kulyukin, Vladimir A., 532

Laird, John E., 928, 1047, 1206
Lakemeyer, Gerhard, 11
Lang, Jérôme, 121, 268
Langley, Pat, 684, 721
Larrosa, Javier, 347
Larson, Kate, 46
Lathrop, Richard H., 1071
Le Berre, Daniel, 588
Learning, 3, 664-774
Learning Cooperative Lane Selection Strategies for Highways, 684

Learning Evaluation Functions for Global Optimization and Boolean Satisfiability, 3
Learning in Markov Games with Incomplete Information, 1176
Learning Investment Functions for Controlling the Utility of Control Knowledge, 463
Learning to Classify Text from Labeled and Unlabeled Documents, 792
Learning to Extract Symbolic Knowledge from the World Wide Web, 509
Learning to Predict User Operations for Adaptive Scheduling, 721
Learning to Resolve Natural Language Ambiguities: A Unified Approach, 806
Learning to Teach with a Reinforcement Learning Agent, 1185
Lebbah, Yahia, 19
Ledeniov, Oleg, 463
Lee, Seok Won, 1207
Lee, Yongwon, 1095
Lemaître, Michel, 353
Lenzerini, Maurizio, 205
Lesh, Neal, 860
Lesser, Victor, 539, 997
Lester, James C., 112, 1101
Létourneau, Sylvain, 1178
Leung, Ho-fung, 380
Leuven, K. U., 840
Leveled Commitment Contracts with Myopic and Strategic Agents, 38
Lhomme, Olivier, 19
Li, Qingyuam, 143
Lifschitz, Vladimir, 623
Littman, Michael L., 954
Liu, T. H., 1193
Lo, Edisanter, 1027
Lobjois, Lionel, 353
Local Search for Statistical Counting, 386
Logan, Brian, 444
Logical Representation and Computation of Optimal Decisions in a Qualitative Setting, 588
López de Màntaras, Ramon, 1187, 1188
Love, Bradley C., 671

Machine Learning of Generic and User-Focused Summarization, 821
Macintosh, Ann, 1020
Maclin, Richard, 700
Maintaining Consistency in Hierarchical Reasoning, 928
Majercik, Stephen M., 954
Makino, Kazuhisa, 292
Mali, Amol D., 882, 1194
Managing Multiple Tasks in Complex, Dynamic Environments, 921
Mani, Inderjeet, 821
Marek, Victor, 840
Margaritis, Dimitris, 977
Marjanovic, Matthew, 961
Markovitch, Shaul, 463
Marquis, Pierre, 268
Martin, Nathaniel, 860
Massacci, Fabio, 274
Massarotto, Alessandro, 948
Matsubara, Hitoshi, 500
McCallum, Andrew, 509, 792
McConachy, Richard, 833
McGuinness, Deborah L., 608
McKay, Ryan, 1195
Medin, Douglas L., 671
Mercer, Albert, 1063
Meseguer, Pedro, 347
Metacognition in Software Agents Using Classifier Systems, 83
Meuleau, Nicolas, 165
Michaud, Lisa N., 1196
Millar, William, 197
Miller, Erik G., 784
Minimal Social Laws, 26
Minton, Steven, 211, 1203
Mitchell, David G., 398
Mitchell, Tom, 509, 792
Miura, Teruhisa, 450
Modeling Web Sources for Information Integration, 211
Modi, Pragnesh Jay, 211
Monderer, Dov, 32
Moore, Andrew W., 3, 753
Moriarty, David E., 684
Morris, Paul, 254
Mosterman, Pieter J., 219

Motivational System for Regulating Human-Robot Interaction, A, 54
Motoda, Hiroshi, 189
Multi Machine Scheduling: An Agent-Based Approach, 1013
Multimodal Reasoning for Automatic Model Construction, 181
Multimodal, Multilevel Selective Attention, 1175
Murdock, J. William, 1201
Murthy, Sesh, 1013
Muscettola, Nicola, 254
Muslea, Ion, 211

Nakajima, Hiroshi, 62
Nakata, Masatomo, 1152
Nakatani, Tomohiro, 1004
Nakaya, Shogo, 486
NASD Regulation Advanced Detection System (ADS), The, 1055
Natural language, 775-838
Natural Language Multiprocessing: A Case Study, 76
Nau, Dana S., 913, 1079, 1127
Nawab, Hamid, 997
Needles in a Haystack: Plan Recognition in Large Spatial Domains Involving Multiple Agents, 942
Nested Joint Probability Model for Morphological Analysis and Its Grid Pruning, 1191
Neural Approaches to Blind Separation and Cumulant Analysis and Its Application to Diagnostics of Nuclear Power Plants, 1180
New Approach to Rule Interest Measures, A, 1188
New Architecture for Automated Modelling, A, 225
New Technique Enables Dynamic Replanning and Rescheduling of Aeromedical Evacuation, A, 1063
Ng, Andrew Y., 753
Nielsen, Paul E., 1047
Nigam, Kamal, 509, 792
Nolan, James R., 1134
Nondeterministic Semantics for Tractable Inference, A, 286
Nonmonotonic reasoning, 839-858
Noubir, Guevara, 326

Noy, Natalya Fridman, 615

O'Hara, Tom, 1179
OKBC: A Programmatic Foundation for Knowledge Base Interoperability, 600
Okuno, Hiroshi G., 1004
On the Computation of Local Interchangeability in Discrete Constraint Satisfaction Problems, 326
On the Conversion between Nonbinary and Binary Constraint Satisfaction Problems, 311
Ontology for Transitions in Physical Dynamic Systems, An, 219
Opponent Modeling in Poker, 493
Optimal 2D Model Matching Using a Messy Genetic Algorithm, 677
Optimal Auctions Revisited, 32
Optimizing Information Agents by Selectively Materializing Data, 1168
Optimizing Initial Configurations of Neural Networks for the Task of Natural Language Learning, 1171
Ourmanov, Alexei, 1180
Outstanding papers, xxiv, 3-24

Papadias, Dimitris, 827
Papp, Denis, 493
Parkes, Andrew J., 334
Patel-Schneider, Peter F., 608
Patterson, David W., 574
Pazzani, Michael J., 1071
Pedersen, Ted, 800, 1197, 1198
Perception, Memory, and the Field of View Problem, 1173
Perkowitz, Mike, 727
Peshkin, Leonid, 165
Pfeffer, Avi, 157, 580
Philpot, Andrew G., 211
Pinto-Ferreira, Carlos A., 1204
Plan Recognition in Complex Spatial Domains, 1190
Planning, 859-959
PLUTO: Managing Multistrategy Learning through Planning, 1201
Poirot, Daniel, 1140
Pollack, Jordan B., 776
Pontelli, Enrico, 76

Position Estimation for Mobile Robots in Dynamic Environments, 983
Prade, Henri, 121, 588
Pragmatic Multi-Agent Learning, 1172
Preface, xix
Probabilistic Frame-Based Systems, 580
Procedural Help in Andes: Generating Hints Using a Bayesian Network Student Model, 106
Producing BT's Yellow Pages with Formation, 1020
Program committee, xxi
Prototype Application of Fuzzy Logic and Expert Systems in Education Assessment, A, 1134
Provost, Foster, 706
Puget, Jean-Francois, 359

Qualitative Analysis of Distributed Physical Systems with Applications to Control Synthesis, 232
Qualitative Simulation as a Temporally-Extended Constraint Satisfaction Problem, 240

Rae, Robert, 1020
Raja, Anita, 539
Ram, Ashwin, 942, 1201
Rana, Soraya, 392
Raphael, Miriam P., 1071
Rational Multiagent Organization and Reorganization, 1182
Raw Corpus Word Sense Disambiguation, 1198
Realtime Constraint-Based Cinematography for Complex Interactive 3D Worlds, 1101
Reasoning under Inconsistency Based on Implicitly-Specified Partial Qualitative Probability Relations: A Unified Framework, 121
Recommendation as Classification: Using Social and Content-Based Information in Recommendation, 714
Reducing Query Answering to Satisfiability in Nonmonotonic Logics, 853
Reed, Nancy E., 151
Refinement-Based Planning as Satisfiability, 1194
Reid, Michael, 305

Representing Scientific Experiments: Implications for Ontology Design and Knowledge Sharing, 615
Reversible DAC and Other Improvements for Solving Max-CSP, 347
Rice, James P., 600
Rizzoni, Giorgio, 143
Robotics, 960-995
Robust Classification Systems for Imprecise Environments, 706
Role of Data Reprocessing in Complex Acoustic Environments, The, 997
Romero, Roseli, 977
Ros, Johannes P., 1087
Rosati, Riccardo, 853
Rosenstein, Michael T., 739
Roth, Dan, 806
Rounds, William C., 846
Roveri, Marco, 875
Roy, Amitabha, 334
Rumantir, Grace W., 1181
Russell, Stuart, 173, 761
Ryan, Daniel, 1140

Sabbadin, Régis, 588
Saffiotti, A., 121
Sakanashi, Hidenori, 486
Sakata, Daigo, 1152
Saks, Victor, 1063
Salami, Mehrdad, 486
Sampling-Based Heuristic for Tree Search Applied to Grammar Induction, A, 776
Samuel, Ken, 1199
Sandholm, Tuomas W., 38, 46
Sattar, Abdul, 367, 656
Scassellati, Brian, 961, 969
Schaeffer, Jonathan, 419, 493
Schaerf, Marco, 262
Scheffer, Tobias, 1200
Schiex, Thomas, 347
Schnattinger, Klemens, 524
Schreckenghost, Debra, 1140
Schubert, Lenhart, 905
Schulz, Dirk, 11
Schuurmans, Dale, 692
Script-Based Approach to Modifying Knowledge-Based Systems, A, 1183

Sebastiani, Roberto, 948
See, Darryl M., 1071
Selection of Conflict Resolution Strategies in Dynamically Organized Sensible Agent-Based Systems, 1193
Selman, Bart, 431
Senator, Ted E., 1055
Shehory, Onn, 46
Shippey, Gordon T., 1201
Shyr, Ping, 1055
SIGART / AAAI Doctoral Consortium Abstracts, 1167-1183
Singhal, Anoop, 1087
Single-Agent Search in the Presence of Deadlocks, 419
Slattery, Seán, 509
Smart, William D., 1202
Smets, P., 121
Smith, David E., 889, 897
Smith, Neil, 225
Smith, Stephen J. J., 1079, 1127
Smith, Wayne A., 1182
Solving Very Large Weakly Coupled Markov Decision Processes, 165
Sound Ontology for Computational Auditory Scence Analysis, 1004
Sound understanding, 996-1010
Speech Recognition with Dynamic Bayesian Networks, 173
Split Up: The Use of an Argument Based Knowledge Representation to Meet Expectations of Different Users for Discretionary Decision Making, 1146
Sponsoring Organizations, xxiv
"Squeaky Wheel" Optimization, 340
Srivastava, Biplav, 882
Steffen, Nicholas R., 1071
Steinberg, Louis, 477
Steiner, Walter, 11
Stergiou, Kostas, 248
Stobie, Iain, 1039
Stochastic Node Caching for Memory-Bounded Search, 450
Stolle, Reinhard, 181
Stone, Matthew, 631
Straccia, Umberto, 594
Stranieri, Andrew, 1146

Structured Probabilistic Models: Bayesian Networks and Beyond, 1210
Structured Representation of Complex Stochastic Systems, 157
Student abstracts, 1184-1208
Success in Spades: Using AI Planning Techniques to Win the World Championship of Computer Bridge, 1079
Supermodels and Robustness, 334
SUSTAIN: A Model of Human Category Learning, 671
Szafron, Duane, 493

Takahashi, Kazuhisa, 1152
Tallis, Marcelo, 1183
Tambe, Milind, 97
Tan, Yao-Hua, 650
Tecuci, Gheorghe, 1207
Tejada, Sheila, 211, 1203
Template-Based Recognition of Pose and Motion Gestures on a Mobile Robot, 977
Temporal Analysis of Chisholm's Paradox, The, 650
Temporal Reasoning with Qualitative and Quantitative Information about Points and Durations, 656
Tennenholtz, Moshe, 26, 32
Thornton, John, 367
Thronesbery, Carroll, 1140
Throop, Thomas A., 1079
Thrun, Sebastian, 11, 792, 977, 983, 989
Tilles, Jeremiah G., 1071
Tohmé, Fernando, 46
Toward Design as Collaboration, 135
Towards Text Knowledge Engineering, 524
Towns, Stuart G., 112
Tractable Walsh Analysis of SAT and its Implications for Genetic Algorithms, A, 392
Traverso, Paolo, 875
Tree Based Discretization for Continuous State Space Reinforcement Learning, 769
TRIPS: An Integrated Intelligent Problem-Solving Assistant, 567

Truszczynski, Miroslaw, 840
Tsamardinos, Ioannis, 254
Tsuneto, Reiko, 913
Tsurushima, Akira, 1152
Turbine Engine Diagnostics (TED): An Expert Diagnostic System for the M1 Abrams Turbine Engine, 1032
Tutorial Response Generation in a Writing Tool for Deaf Learners of English, 1196
Two Forms of Dependence in Propositional Logic: Controllability and Definability, 268

Urushima, Kenji, 1152
Usability Issues in Knowledge Representation Systems, 608
Ushida, Hirohide, 62
Using Arc Weights to Improve Iterative Repair, 367
Using Artificial Intelligence Planning to Automate SAR Image Processing for Scientific Data Analysis, 1027
Using Caching to Solve Larger Probabilistic Planning Problems, 954
Uther, William R. B., 769

van Beek, Peter, 311
van der Torre, Leendert W. N., 650
VanLehn, Kurt, 106
van't Veen, P. P., 1121

Velásquez, Juan D., 70
Veloso, Manuela M., 769
Venkatasubramanyan, Narayan, 373
Ventura, Rodrigo M. M., 1204
Verfaillie, Gérard, 347
Viola, Paul A., 784
Voloshin, Mikhail, 1113

Wagner, Thomas, 539
Waldherr, Stefan, 977
Walser, Joachim P., 373
Walsh, Toby, 406
Warfighter's Information Packager, 1095
Wasacz, Bryon, 143
Washio, Takashi, 189
Weinmeister, Karl, 1205
Weiss, Gary M., 1087
Weld, Daniel S., 889, 897
Wetprasit, Rattana, 656
What Can Knowledge Representation Do for Semi-Structured Data?, 205
What Is Wrong With Us? Improving Robustness through Social Diagnosis, 97
When Robots Weep: Emotional Memories and Decision-Making, 70
Which Search Problems Are Random?, 438

Whitley, Darrell, 392
Wiebe, Janyce, 76
Wilkins, David C., 1113
Williams, Brian C., 197
Williamson, Matthew M., 961
Wolf, Catherine, 1160
Wolverton, Michael, 868
Wong, Jason H. Y., 380
Wray III, Robert E., 928, 1206
Wright, Kathryn, 1207
Wu, Frederick, 1013

Yamauchi, Tsukasa, 486
Yanco, Holly A., 1208
Ye, Yiming, 1160

Zadrozny, Wlodek, 1160
Zeleznikow, John, 1146
Zev, Marc, 1095
Zhang, Guo-Qiang, 846
Zhang, Shelley XQ., 539
Zhang, Weixiong, 425, 1095
Zhang, Zhaohua, 83
Zhao, Feng, 219, 232
Zilberstein, Shlomo, 412
Zukerman, Ingrid, 833
Zweig, Geoffrey, 173

DATE DUE

R80095
2597331

DEMCO, INC. 38-2971